Bill James presents. . .

STATS
Major League Handbook
2000

STATS, Inc. • Bill James

STATS
PUBLISHING

Published by STATS Publishing
A division of Sports Team Analysis & Tracking Systems, Inc.

Cover by Marc Elman, Ben Frobig and Chuck Miller

Cover photo by Scott Jordan Levy

First Edition: November, 1999

Printed in the United States of America

ISBN 1-884064-71-X

Acknowledgments

Numerous people contributed to the 2000 version of the *STATS Major League Handbook*. We'd like to thank everyone who had a hand in bringing you the best statistical annual in the business:

John Dewan, STATS' Chief Executive Officer, continues to make us the No. 1 source for sports statistics. Our President, Alan Leib, will help us grow in the years to come. John and Alan are assisted by Jennifer Manicki. Sue Dewan and Bob Meyerhoff are vice presidents involved in Research & Development/Special Projects. Sue's team includes Jim Osborne and Andy Tumpowsky. Bob's team includes Joe Sclafani.

Vice President of Publishing Products Don Zminda oversees the department that produces this and all of our other sports titles. Don's department includes Jim Callis, Thom Henninger, Jim Henzler, Chuck Miller and yours truly. Jim Henzler handled all of the programming assignments for this book, while Chuck was responsible for design and layout.

Spreading the word about this book and everything else in the world of STATS Publishing falls to Marc Elman and his team. Marc works with Ben Frobig (who created the cover), Mike Janosi, Antoinette Kelly and Mike Sarkis.

The wonderful statistics you hold in your hands were gathered by the Data Collection Department headed by Allan Spear. His staff consists of Jeremy Alpert, Michelle Blanco, Jeff Chernow, Ryan Ellis, Mike Hammer, Derek Kenar, Tony Largo, Jon Passman, Jeff Schinski, Matt Senter, Bill Stephens and Joe Stillwell. Together, they oversee a vast reporter network. Jeff Chernow oversaw our MLB data collection for the 1999 season, and he and Allan were invaluable in helping to resolve any questions we had along the way.

The efforts of the Commercial Products, Fantasy, Interactive Products and Sales departments help pay most of our bills at STATS. Alan Leib oversees our Commercial Products division, which includes Ethan D. Cooperson, Dan Matern and David Pinto. Steve Byrd is in charge of the Fantasy department, which consists of Bill Burke, Jim Corelis, Dan Ford, Stefan Kretschmann, Walter Lis, Marc Moeller, Mike Mooney, Oscar Palacios, Corey Roberts, Eric Robin, Jeff Smith, Yingmin Wang and Rick Wilton. Mike Canter heads the Interactive group and is assisted by Dave Carlson, Jake Costello, Will McCleskey, Tim Moriarty, Dean Peterson, Pat Quinn, John Sasman, Meghan Sheehan, Morris Srinivasan and Nick Stamm. Jim Capuano leads a Sales team comprised of Greg Kirkorsky and Jake Stein.

Our Financial/Administrative/Human Resources/Legal Department ensures that everything runs smoothly at our Morton Grove, Ill., headquarters. Howard Lanin overseas the financial details and is assisted by Kim Bartlett and Betty Moy. Susan Zamechek assists in finance and oversees the administrative aspects of the company with the help of Sherlinda Johnson, while Tracy Lickton is in charge of human resources. Carol Savier aids with legal matters. Art Ashley provides programming support to all four groups.

A curtain call for everyone.

—Tony Nistler

This book is dedicated to my family—
my beautiful wife, Ellyn,
and my fantastic children, Jacob and Sophie.
It is your love, support and encouragement
which give me strength and joy and the perspective
to know what is really important in life.

—Alan Leib

Table of Contents

Introduction

As the 1990s draw to a close, baseball also marks the closing of three ballparks with unique pasts. The Astrodome, labeled the Eighth Wonder of the World when it was the first domed stadium nearly 40 years ago, and the park formerly known as Candlestick, with its gusty winds and wintry, nighttime temperatures, closed their doors forever to baseball in October.

The saddest news is the closing of the grand old park at the corner of Michigan and Trumbull in Detroit, Tiger Stadium. I sojourned to Detroit in each of the last two seasons to enjoy the timeless feeling of watching baseball in one of the game's oldest parks. For one game I sat in the right-field upper deck, which has allowed fans to watch the game while peering over the shoulders of right fielders ranging from Babe Ruth to Al Kaline to Manny Ramirez.

Players complained about the crowded clubhouses and the dugouts built for shorter men. Fans stood in long lines because there weren't enough concession stands. Yet a game at Tiger Stadium was one of those ageless experiences. Fans sitting around the infield were close to the field. The upper deck in right field hung over the field of play. The all-blue decor of seats and facades were a trademark of the park, which opened in 1912. When I looked out toward left field, I still could see Willie Horton drifting back into the lights of the ground-level scoreboard. Thank goodness for memories like that, because the wooden seats, the dark, narrow walkways that housed the concessions, and the green field in that sea of blue are lost to baseball fans forever.

With Safeco Field's opening after the All-Star game last July, the Mariners join the Astros, Giants and Tigers in celebrating new homes for the 2000 season. STATS also opened new digs in the last year of the 1990s, leaving cramped quarters in Skokie for a spacious and visually-pleasing space in Morton Grove, Ill.

While I lament the fall of a classic ballpark, I can appreciate the benefits of better accommodations. And having new facilities doesn't mean that old traditions die.

You're holding the 11th edition of the *STATS Major League Handbook*. It's a tradition that will continue to summarize the most recent major league season, no matter what locale we call home. The *Handbook* is loaded with individual stats for every player who made a major league appearance in 1999, lefty-righty splits, leader boards, statistical analysis of the major league parks, and player projections for the 2000 season.

A game at Tiger Stadium on a lazy summer afternoon is something that no longer can be experienced, but the *Major League Handbook* documents another season passed that can be revisited again and again. Enjoy.

—Thom Henninger

What's Official and What's Not

The statistics in this book are technically unofficial. The official Major League Baseball averages are not released until December, but we can't wait that long. If you compare these stats with the official ones, you'll find few major differences. As always, we take extraordinary efforts to ensure accuracy.

Career Register

The Career Register includes the records of all players who saw major league action in 1999.

The abbreviations used in the register are defined below:

For all players, **Age** is seasonal age as of June 30, 2000; **Ht** = Height; **Wt** = Weight; **Lg** = Major League (**AL** = American League; **NL** = National League) or minor league classification. Class-A (A+, A, A-) and Rookie (R+, R) have separate classifications to distinguish the level of competition. **IND** = independent minor league.

For Batters, **R** = bats or throws right; **L** = bats or throws left; **B** = bats both right and left; **Pos** = number of games played at each position; **DH** = designated hitter; **PH** = pinch hitter; **PR** = pinch runner; **G** = games; **AB** = at-bats; **H** = hits; **2B** = doubles; **3B** = triples; **HR** = home runs; **Hm** = home runs at home; **Rd** = home runs on the road; **TB** = total bases; **R** = runs; **RBI** = runs batted in; **TBB** = total bases on balls; **IBB** = intentional bases on balls; **SO** = strikeouts; **HBP** = times hit by pitches; **SH** = sacrifice hits; **SF** = sacrifice flies; **SB** = stolen bases; **CS** = times caught stealing; **SB%** = stolen base percentage; **GDP** = times grounded into double plays; **Avg** = batting average; **OBP** = on-base percentage; **SLG** = slugging percentage.

For pitchers, **Pos** = number of games pitched as a starter and as a reliever; **SP** = starting pitcher; **RP** = relief pitcher; **G** = games pitched; **GS** = games started; **CG** = complete games; **GF** = games finished; **IP** = innings pitched; **BFP** = batters facing pitcher; **H** = hits allowed; **R** = runs allowed; **ER** = earned runs allowed; **HR** = home runs allowed; **SH** = sacrifice hits allowed; **SF** = sacrifice flies allowed; **HB** = hit batsmen; **TBB** = total bases on balls; **IBB** = intentional bases on balls; **SO** = strikeouts; **WP** = wild pitches; **Bk** = balks; **W** = wins; **L** = losses; **Pct.** = winning percentage; **ShO** = shutouts; **Sv** = saves; **Op** = save opportunities; **Hld** = holds; **ERA** = earned run average.

An asterisk (*) by a player's minor league stats indicates that these are his 1999 minor league numbers only; previous league experience is not included. Figures in **boldface** indicate the player led the league in that category.

For players who played for more than one major league team in a season, stats for each team are shown just above the bottom-line career totals.

Jeff Abbott

Bats: Right **Throws:** Left **Pos:** LF-17   **Ht:** 6'2" **Wt:** 200 **Born:** 8/17/72 **Age:** 27

Year Team	Lg	G	AB	H	2B	3B	HR	(Hm	Rd)	TB	R	RBI	TBB	IBB	SO	HBP	SH	SF	SB	CS	SB%	GDP	Avg	OBP	SLG
1999 Charlotte *	AAA	67	277	88	24	1	9	—	—	141	42	37	16	1	27	0	2	4	2	3	.40	6	.318	.350	.509
1997 Chicago	AL	19	38	10	1	0	1	(0	1)	14	8	2	0	0	6	0	0	0	0	0	.00	3	.263	.263	.368
1998 Chicago	AL	89	244	68	14	1	12	(5	7)	120	33	41	9	1	28	0	2	5	3	3	.50	2	.279	.298	.492
1999 Chicago	AL	17	57	9	0	0	2	(0	2)	15	5	6	5	0	12	0	1	1	1	1	.50	4	.158	.222	.263
3 ML YEARS		125	339	87	15	1	15	(5	10)	149	46	49	14	1	46	0	3	6	4	4	.50	9	.257	.281	.440

Jim Abbott

Pitches: Left **Bats:** Left **Pos:** SP-15; RP-5   **Ht:** 6'3" **Wt:** 210 **Born:** 9/19/67 **Age:** 32

Year Team	Lg	G	GS	CG	GF	IP	BFP	H	R	ER	HR	SH	SF	HB	TBB	IBB	SO	WP	Bk	W	L	Pct.	ShO	Sv-Op	Hld	ERA
1989 California	AL	29	29	4	0	181.1	788	190	95	79	13	11	5	4	74	3	115	8	2	12	12	.500	2	0-0	0	3.92
1990 California	AL	33	33	4	0	211.2	925	246	116	106	16	9	6	5	72	6	105	4	3	10	14	.417	1	0-0	0	4.51
1991 California	AL	34	34	5	0	243	1002	222	85	78	14	7	7	5	73	6	158	1	4	18	11	.621	1	0-0	0	2.89
1992 California	AL	29	29	7	0	211	874	208	73	65	12	8	4	4	68	3	130	2	0	7	15	.318	1	0-0	0	2.77
1993 New York	AL	32	32	4	0	214	906	221	115	104	22	12	4	3	73	4	95	9	0	11	14	.440	1	0-0	0	4.37
1994 New York	AL	24	24	2	0	160.1	692	167	88	81	24	9	5	2	64	1	90	8	1	9	8	.529	0	0-0	0	4.55
1995 CWS-Cal	AL	30	30	4	0	197	842	209	93	81	14	8	4	2	64	1	86	1	0	11	8	.579	1	0-0	0	3.70
1996 California	AL	27	23	1	2	142	654	171	128	118	23	4	10	4	78	3	58	13	1	2	18	.100	0	0-0	0	7.48
1998 Chicago	AL	5	5	0	0	31.2	134	35	16	16	2	0	1	1	12	0	14	0	0	5	0	1.000	0	0-0	0	4.55
1999 Milwaukee	NL	20	15	0	3	82	394	110	71	63	14	2	1	2	42	3	37	7	0	2	8	.200	0	0-0	0	6.91
1995 Chicago	AL	17	17	3	0	112.1	474	116	50	42	10	5	1	1	35	1	45	0	0	6	4	.600	0	0-0	0	3.36
California	AL	13	13	1	0	84.2	368	93	43	39	4	3	3	1	29	0	41	1	0	5	4	.556	1	0-0	0	4.15
10 ML YEARS		263	254	31	5	1674	7211	1779	880	791	154	70	47	32	620	30	888	53	11	87	108	.446	6	0-0	0	4.25

Kurt Abbott

Bats: R **Throws:** R **Pos:** 2B-66; PH/PR-18; 1B-8; SS-3; CF-2; RF-2   **Ht:** 6'0" **Wt:** 198 **Born:** 6/2/69 **Age:** 31

Year Team	Lg	G	AB	H	2B	3B	HR	(Hm	Rd)	TB	R	RBI	TBB	IBB	SO	HBP	SH	SF	SB	CS	SB%	GDP	Avg	OBP	SLG
1993 Oakland	AL	20	61	15	1	0	3	(0	3)	25	11	9	3	0	20	0	3	0	2	0	1.00	3	.246	.281	.410
1994 Florida	NL	101	345	86	17	3	9	(4	5)	136	41	33	16	1	98	5	3	2	3	0	1.00	5	.249	.291	.394
1995 Florida	NL	120	420	107	18	7	17	(12	5)	190	60	60	36	4	110	5	2	5	4	3	.57	6	.255	.318	.452
1996 Florida	NL	109	320	81	18	7	8	(6	2)	137	37	33	22	1	99	3	4	0	3	3	.50	7	.253	.307	.428
1997 Florida	NL	94	252	69	18	2	6	(1	5)	109	35	30	14	3	68	1	6	0	3	1	.75	5	.274	.315	.433
1998 Oak-Col		77	194	51	13	1	5	(3	2)	81	26	24	12	0	53	2	1	3	2	1	.67	5	.263	.308	.418
1999 Colorado	NL	96	286	78	17	2	8	(6	2)	123	41	41	16	0	69	0	2	1	3	2	.60	4	.273	.310	.430
1998 Oakland	AL	35	123	33	7	1	2	(1	1)	48	17	9	10	0	34	1	1	1	2	1	.67	3	.268	.326	.390
Colorado	NL	42	71	18	6	0	3	(2	1)	33	9	15	2	0	19	1	0	2	0	0	.00	2	.254	.276	.465
7 ML YEARS		617	1878	487	102	22	56	(32	24)	801	251	230	119	9	517	16	21	11	20	10	.67	35	.259	.307	.427

Paul Abbott

Pitches: Right **Bats:** Right **Pos:** RP-18; SP-7   **Ht:** 6'3" **Wt:** 195 **Born:** 9/15/67 **Age:** 32

Year Team	Lg	G	GS	CG	GF	IP	BFP	H	R	ER	HR	SH	SF	HB	TBB	IBB	SO	WP	Bk	W	L	Pct.	ShO	Sv-Op	Hld	ERA
1999 Tacoma *	AAA	2	2	0	0	14	63	21	11	10	1	1	1	1	4	0	10	0	0	1	1	.500	0	0--	—	6.43
1990 Minnesota	AL	7	7	0	0	34.2	162	37	24	23	0	1	1	1	28	0	25	1	0	0	5	.000	0	0-0	0	5.97
1991 Minnesota	AL	15	3	0	1	47.1	210	38	27	25	5	7	3	0	36	1	43	5	0	3	1	.750	0	0-0	0	4.75
1992 Minnesota	AL	6	0	0	5	11	50	12	4	4	1	0	1	1	5	0	13	1	0	0	0	.000	0	0-0	0	3.27
1993 Cleveland	AL	5	5	0	0	18.1	84	19	15	13	5	0	0	1	11	1	7	1	0	0	1	.000	0	0-0	0	6.38
1998 Seattle	AL	4	4	0	0	24.2	105	24	11	11	2	0	1	0	10	0	22	3	0	3	1	.750	0	0-0	0	4.01
1999 Seattle	AL	25	7	0	8	72.2	298	50	31	25	9	3	4	0	32	3	68	2	0	6	2	.750	0	0-2	3	3.10
6 ML YEARS		62	26	0	14	208.2	909	180	112	101	22	11	10	2	122	5	178	13	0	12	10	.545	0	0-2	3	4.36

Bobby Abreu

Bats: Left **Throws:** Right **Pos:** RF-146; DH-5; PH/PR-2   **Ht:** 6'0" **Wt:** 186 **Born:** 3/11/74 **Age:** 26

Year Team	Lg	G	AB	H	2B	3B	HR	(Hm	Rd)	TB	R	RBI	TBB	IBB	SO	HBP	SH	SF	SB	CS	SB%	GDP	Avg	OBP	SLG
1996 Houston	NL	15	22	5	1	0	0	(0	0)	6	1	1	2	0	3	0	0	0	0	0	.00	1	.227	.292	.273
1997 Houston	NL	59	188	47	10	2	3	(3	0)	70	22	26	21	0	48	1	0	0	7	2	.78	0	.250	.329	.372
1998 Philadelphia	NL	151	497	155	29	6	17	(10	7)	247	68	74	84	14	133	0	4	4	19	10	.66	6	.312	.409	.497
1999 Philadelphia	NL	152	546	183	35	11	20	(13	7)	300	118	93	109	8	113	3	0	4	27	9	.75	13	.335	.446	.549
4 ML YEARS		377	1253	390	75	19	40	(26	14)	623	209	194	216	22	297	4	4	8	53	21	.72	20	.311	.412	.497

Juan Acevedo

Pitches: Right **Bats:** Right **Pos:** RP-38; SP-12   **Ht:** 6'2" **Wt:** 228 **Born:** 5/5/70 **Age:** 30

Year Team	Lg	G	GS	CG	GF	IP	BFP	H	R	ER	HR	SH	SF	HB	TBB	IBB	SO	WP	Bk	W	L	Pct.	ShO	Sv-Op	Hld	ERA
1995 Colorado	NL	17	11	0	0	65.2	291	82	53	47	15	4	2	6	20	2	40	2	1	4	6	.400	0	0-0	1	6.44
1997 New York	NL	25	2	0	4	47.2	215	52	24	19	6	2	5	4	22	2	33	0	1	3	1	.750	0	0-4	3	3.59

		HOW MUCH HE PITCHED						WHAT HE GAVE UP												THE RESULTS					
Year Team	Lg	G	GS	CG	GF	IP	BFP	H	R	ER	HR	SH	SF	HB	TBB	IBB	SO	WP	Bk	W	L	Pct.	ShO	Sv-Op	Hld	ERA
1998 St. Louis	NL	50	9	0	29	98.1	394	83	30	28	7	8	1	4	29	2	56	3	0	8	3	.727	0	15-16	3	2.56
1999 St. Louis	NL	50	12	0	21	102.1	457	115	71	67	17	4	6	4	48	3	52	5	0	6	8	.429	0	4-6	4	5.89
4 ML YEARS		142	34	0	54	314	1357	332	178	161	45	18	14	18	119	9	181	10	2	21	18	.538	0	19-26	11	4.61

Terry Adams

Pitches: Right **Bats:** Right **Pos:** RP-52   **Ht:** 6'3" **Wt:** 205 **Born:** 3/6/73 **Age:** 27

		HOW MUCH HE PITCHED						WHAT HE GAVE UP												THE RESULTS					
Year Team	Lg	G	GS	CG	GF	IP	BFP	H	R	ER	HR	SH	SF	HB	TBB	IBB	SO	WP	Bk	W	L	Pct.	ShO	Sv-Op	Hld	ERA
1999 West Tenn *	AA	2	1	0	0	2.2	15	5	6	5	0	0	1	0	2	0	2	0	0	0	0	.000	0	0--	—	16.88
1995 Chicago	NL	18	0	0	7	18	86	22	15	13	0	0	0	0	10	1	15	1	0	1	1	.500	0	1-1	0	6.50
1996 Chicago	NL	69	0	0	22	101	423	84	36	33	6	7	3	1	49	6	78	5	1	3	6	.333	0	4-8	11	2.94
1997 Chicago	NL	74	0	0	39	74	341	91	43	38	3	1	2	1	40	6	64	6	0	2	9	.182	0	18-22	11	4.62
1998 Chicago	NL	63	0	0	15	72.2	330	72	39	35	7	3	3	1	41	3	73	4	3	7	7	.500	0	1-7	13	4.33
1999 Chicago	NL	52	0	0	38	65	277	60	33	29	9	1	3	0	28	2	57	6	0	6	3	.667	0	13-18	3	4.02
5 ML YEARS		276	0	0	121	330.2	1457	329	166	148	25	12	11	3	168	18	287	22	4	19	26	.422	0	37-56	38	4.03

Benny Agbayani

Bats: R **Throws:** R **Pos:** LF-47; RF-45; PH/PR-28; CF-4; DH-2   **Ht:** 6'0" **Wt:** 225 **Born:** 12/28/71 **Age:** 28

		BATTING														BASERUNNING				PERCENTAGES		
Year Team	Lg	G	AB	H	2B	3B	HR	(Hm	Rd)	TB	R	RBI	TBB	IBB	SO	HBP	SH	SF	SB	CS	SB%	GDP	Avg	OBP	SLG
1993 Pittsfield	A-	51	167	42	6	3	2	—	—	60	26	22	20	0	43	0	0	0	7	2	.78	4	.251	.332	.359
1994 St. Lucie	A+	119	411	115	13	5	5	—	—	153	72	63	58	2	67	10	1	5	8	6	.57	9	.280	.378	.372
1995 St. Lucie	A+	44	155	48	9	3	2	—	—	69	24	29	26	1	27	5	1	4	8	3	.73	4	.310	.416	.445
Binghamton	AA	88	295	81	11	2	1	—	—	99	38	26	39	0	51	5	1	1	12	3	.80	6	.275	.368	.336
1996 Binghamton	AA	21	53	9	1	0	2	—	—	16	7	8	11	0	13	1	1	1	1	0	1.00	2	.170	.318	.302
Norfolk	AAA	99	331	92	13	9	7	—	—	144	43	56	30	3	57	3	3	5	14	5	.74	5	.278	.339	.435
1997 Norfolk	AAA	127	468	145	24	2	11	—	—	206	90	51	67	0	106	6	0	3	29	14	.67	13	.310	.401	.440
1998 Norfolk	AAA	90	322	91	20	5	11	—	—	154	43	53	50	2	58	3	0	3	16	6	.73	9	.283	.381	.478
1999 Norfolk	AAA	28	101	36	8	1	8	—	—	70	21	32	16	1	19	2	0	2	5	3	.63	2	.356	.446	.693
1998 New York	NL	11	15	2	0	0	0	(0	0)	2	1	0	1	0	5	0	0	0	0	2	.00	1	.133	.188	.133
1999 New York	NL	101	276	79	18	3	14	(10	4)	145	42	42	32	4	60	3	0	3	6	4	.60	8	.286	.363	.525
2 ML YEARS		112	291	81	18	3	14	(10	4)	147	43	42	33	4	65	3	0	3	6	6	.50	9	.278	.355	.505

Rick Aguilera

Pitches: Right **Bats:** Right **Pos:** RP-61   **Ht:** 6'5" **Wt:** 208 **Born:** 12/31/61 **Age:** 38

		HOW MUCH HE PITCHED						WHAT HE GAVE UP												THE RESULTS					
Year Team	Lg	G	GS	CG	GF	IP	BFP	H	R	ER	HR	SH	SF	HB	TBB	IBB	SO	WP	Bk	W	L	Pct.	ShO	Sv-Op	Hld	ERA
1985 New York	NL	21	19	2	1	122.1	507	118	49	44	8	7	4	2	37	2	74	5	2	10	7	.588	0	0-0	0	3.24
1986 New York	NL	28	20	2	2	141.2	605	145	70	61	15	6	5	7	36	1	104	5	3	10	7	.588	0	0-1	0	3.88
1987 New York	NL	18	17	1	0	115	494	124	53	46	12	7	2	3	33	2	77	9	0	11	3	.786	0	0-0	1	3.60
1988 New York	NL	11	3	0	2	24.2	111	29	20	19	2	2	0	1	10	2	16	1	1	0	4	.000	0	0-0	1	6.93
1989 NYM-Min		47	11	3	19	145	594	130	51	45	8	7	1	3	38	4	137	4	3	9	11	.450	0	7-11	1	2.79
1990 Minnesota	AL	56	0	0	54	65.1	268	55	27	20	5	0	0	4	19	6	61	3	0	5	3	.625	0	32-39	0	2.76
1991 Minnesota	AL	63	0	0	60	69	275	44	20	18	3	1	3	1	30	6	61	3	0	4	5	.444	0	42-51	0	2.35
1992 Minnesota	AL	64	0	0	61	66.2	273	60	28	21	7	1	2	1	17	4	52	5	0	2	6	.250	0	41-48	0	2.84
1993 Minnesota	AL	65	0	0	61	72.1	287	60	25	25	9	2	1	1	14	3	59	1	0	4	3	.571	0	34-40	0	3.11
1994 Minnesota	AL	44	0	0	40	44.2	201	57	23	18	7	4	1	0	10	3	46	2	0	1	4	.200	0	23-29	0	3.63
1995 Min-Bos		52	0	0	51	55.1	223	46	16	16	6	1	4	1	13	1	52	0	0	3	3	.500	0	32-36	0	2.60
1996 Minnesota	AL	19	19	2	0	111.1	484	124	69	67	20	1	3	3	27	1	83	6	0	8	6	.571	0	0-0	0	5.42
1997 Minnesota	AL	61	0	0	57	68.1	285	65	29	29	9	5	3	2	22	3	68	3	0	5	4	.556	0	26-33	0	3.82
1998 Minnesota	AL	68	0	0	64	74.1	307	75	35	35	8	3	2	1	15	1	57	1	0	4	9	.308	0	38-49	0	4.24
1999 Min-ChC		61	0	0	41	67.2	267	54	25	22	8	4	2	2	12	1	45	4	1	9	4	.692	0	14-21	0	2.93
1989 New York	NL	36	0	0	19	69.1	284	59	19	18	3	5	1	2	21	3	80	3	3	6	6	.500	0	7-11	1	2.34
Minnesota	AL	11	11	3	0	75.2	310	71	32	27	5	2	0	1	17	1	57	1	0	3	5	.375	0	0-0	0	3.21
1995 Minnesota	AL	22	0	0	21	25	99	20	7	7	2	0	2	0	6	1	29	0	0	1	1	.500	0	12-15	0	2.52
Boston	AL	30	0	0	30	30.1	124	26	9	9	4	1	2	0	7	0	23	0	0	2	2	.500	0	20-21	0	2.67
1999 Minnesota	AL	17	0	0	16	21.1	76	10	3	3	2	0	0	0	2	0	13	1	1	3	1	.750	0	6-8	0	1.27
Chicago	NL	44	0	0	25	46.1	191	44	22	19	6	4	2	2	10	1	32	3	0	6	3	.667	0	8-13	4	3.69
15 ML YEARS		678	89	10	513	1243.2	5181	1186	540	486	127	51	33	32	333	40	992	52	10	85	79	.518	0	289-358	7	3.52

Scott Aldred

Pitches: Left **Bats:** Left **Pos:** RP-66   **Ht:** 6'4" **Wt:** 215 **Born:** 6/12/68 **Age:** 32

		HOW MUCH HE PITCHED						WHAT HE GAVE UP												THE RESULTS					
Year Team	Lg	G	GS	CG	GF	IP	BFP	H	R	ER	HR	SH	SF	HB	TBB	IBB	SO	WP	Bk	W	L	Pct.	ShO	Sv-Op	Hld	ERA
1990 Detroit	AL	4	3	0	0	14.1	63	13	6	6	0	2	1	0	10	1	7	0	0	1	2	.333	0	0-0	0	3.77
1991 Detroit	AL	11	11	1	0	57.1	253	58	37	33	9	3	2	0	30	2	35	3	1	2	4	.333	0	0-0	0	5.18
1992 Detroit	AL	16	13	0	0	65	304	80	51	49	12	4	3	3	33	4	34	1	0	3	8	.273	0	0-0	0	6.78
1993 Col-Mon	NL	8	0	0	2	12	65	19	14	12	2	2	0	1	10	1	9	2	0	1	0	1.000	0	0-1	0	9.00
1996 Det-Min	AL	36	25	0	0	165.1	748	194	125	114	29	7	7	6	68	4	111	10	1	6	9	.400	0	0-0	1	6.21
1997 Minnesota	AL	17	15	0	0	77.1	350	102	66	66	20	2	1	3	28	2	33	7	0	2	10	.167	0	0-0	0	7.68
1998 Tampa Bay	AL	48	0	0	8	31.1	135	33	13	13	1	3	0	2	12	3	21	2	0	0	0	.000	0	0-0	8	3.73
1999 TB-Phi		66	0	0	14	56.2	254	59	30	28	2	3	6	1	29	3	41	4	0	4	3	.571	0	1-4	6	4.45
1993 Colorado	NL	5	0	0	1	6.2	40	10	10	8	1	2	0	1	7	1	0	0	0	0	0	.000	0	0-0	0	10.80

4

		HOW MUCH HE PITCHED						WHAT HE GAVE UP												THE RESULTS						
Year Team	Lg	G	GS	CG	GF	IP	BFP	H	R	ER	HR	SH	SF	HB	TBB	IBB	SO	WP	Bk	W	L	Pct.	ShO	Sv-Op	Hld	ERA
Montreal	NL	3	0	0	1	5.1	25	9	4	4	1	0	0	0	1	0	4	1	0	1	0	1.000	0	0-1	0	6.75
1996 Detroit	AL	11	8	0	0	43.1	217	60	52	45	9	3	2	3	26	3	36	6	1	0	4	.000	0	0-0	0	9.35
Minnesota	AL	25	17	0	0	122	531	134	73	69	20	4	5	3	42	1	75	4	0	6	5	.545	0	0-0	1	5.09
1999 Tampa Bay	AL	37	0	0	9	24.1	114	26	15	14	1	2	1	2	14	0	22	1	0	3	2	.600	0	0-0	3	5.18
Philadelphia	NL	29	0	0	5	32.1	140	33	15	14	1	1	5	0	15	3	19	3	0	1	1	.500	0	1-4	3	3.90
8 ML YEARS		206	67	1	24	479.1	2172	558	342	321	75	26	20	18	220	20	291	29	2	19	36	.345	0	1-5	15	6.03

Manny Alexander

Bats: R **Throws:** R **Pos:** PH/PR-48; SS-30; 3B-22; 2B-17; RF-2   **Ht:** 5'10" **Wt:** 180 **Born:** 3/20/71 **Age:** 29

		BATTING																	BASERUNNING				PERCENTAGES		
Year Team	Lg	G	AB	H	2B	3B	HR	(Hm	Rd)	TB	R	RBI	TBB	IBB	SO	HBP	SH	SF	SB	CS	SB%	GDP	Avg	OBP	SLG
1992 Baltimore	AL	4	5	1	0	0	0	(0	0)	1	1	0	0	0	3	0	0	0	0	0	.00	0	.200	.200	.200
1993 Baltimore	AL	3	0	0	0	0	0	(0	0)	0	1	0	0	0	0	0	0	0	0	0	.00	0	.000	.000	.000
1995 Baltimore	AL	94	242	57	9	1	3	(2	1)	77	35	23	20	0	30	2	4	0	11	4	.73	2	.236	.299	.318
1996 Baltimore	AL	54	68	7	0	0	0	(0	0)	7	6	4	3	0	27	0	2	0	3	3	.50	2	.103	.141	.103
1997 NYM-ChC	NL	87	248	66	12	4	3	(0	3)	95	37	22	17	3	54	3	3	1	13	1	.93	6	.266	.320	.383
1998 Chicago	NL	108	264	60	10	1	5	(1	4)	87	34	25	18	1	66	1	5	1	4	1	.80	6	.227	.278	.330
1999 Chicago	NL	90	177	48	11	2	0	(0	0)	63	17	15	10	0	38	0	1	1	4	0	1.00	1	.271	.309	.356
1997 New York	NL	54	149	37	9	3	2	(0	2)	58	26	15	9	1	38	1	1	1	11	0	1.00	3	.248	.294	.389
Chicago	NL	33	99	29	3	1	1	(0	1)	37	11	7	8	2	16	2	2	0	2	1	.67	3	.293	.358	.374
7 ML YEARS		440	1004	239	42	8	11	(3	8)	330	131	89	68	4	218	6	15	3	35	9	.80	17	.238	.290	.329

Antonio Alfonseca

Pitches: Right **Bats:** Right **Pos:** RP-73   **Ht:** 6'5" **Wt:** 235 **Born:** 4/16/72 **Age:** 28

		HOW MUCH HE PITCHED						WHAT HE GAVE UP												THE RESULTS						
Year Team	Lg	G	GS	CG	GF	IP	BFP	H	R	ER	HR	SH	SF	HB	TBB	IBB	SO	WP	Bk	W	L	Pct.	ShO	Sv-Op	Hld	ERA
1997 Florida	NL	17	0	0	2	25.2	123	36	16	14	3	1	0	1	10	3	19	1	0	1	3	.250	0	0-2	0	4.91
1998 Florida	NL	58	0	0	27	70.2	316	75	36	32	10	7	6	3	33	9	46	1	0	4	6	.400	0	8-14	9	4.08
1999 Florida	NL	73	0	0	49	77.2	325	79	28	28	4	3	1	4	29	6	46	1	0	4	5	.444	0	21-25	5	3.24
3 ML YEARS		148	0	0	78	174	764	190	80	74	17	11	7	8	72	18	111	3	0	9	14	.391	0	29-41	14	3.83

Edgardo Alfonzo

Bats: Right **Throws:** Right **Pos:** 2B-158   **Ht:** 5'11" **Wt:** 187 **Born:** 11/8/73 **Age:** 26

		BATTING																	BASERUNNING				PERCENTAGES		
Year Team	Lg	G	AB	H	2B	3B	HR	(Hm	Rd)	TB	R	RBI	TBB	IBB	SO	HBP	SH	SF	SB	CS	SB%	GDP	Avg	OBP	SLG
1995 New York	NL	101	335	93	13	5	4	(0	4)	128	26	41	12	1	37	1	4	4	1	1	.50	7	.278	.301	.382
1996 New York	NL	123	368	96	15	2	4	(2	2)	127	36	40	25	2	56	0	9	5	2	0	1.00	8	.261	.304	.345
1997 New York	NL	151	518	163	27	2	10	(4	6)	224	84	72	63	0	56	5	8	5	11	6	.65	4	.315	.391	.432
1998 New York	NL	144	557	155	28	2	17	(8	9)	238	94	78	65	1	77	3	2	3	8	3	.73	11	.278	.355	.427
1999 New York	NL	158	628	191	41	1	27	(11	16)	315	123	108	85	2	85	3	1	9	9	2	.82	14	.304	.385	.502
5 ML YEARS		677	2406	698	124	12	62	(25	37)	1032	363	339	250	6	311	12	24	26	31	12	.72	44	.290	.356	.429

Luis Alicea

Bats: B **Throws:** R **Pos:** 2B-37; PH/PR-23; 3B-10; DH-7; LF-1   **Ht:** 5'9" **Wt:** 176 **Born:** 7/29/65 **Age:** 34

		BATTING																	BASERUNNING				PERCENTAGES		
Year Team	Lg	G	AB	H	2B	3B	HR	(Hm	Rd)	TB	R	RBI	TBB	IBB	SO	HBP	SH	SF	SB	CS	SB%	GDP	Avg	OBP	SLG
1988 St. Louis	NL	93	297	63	10	4	1	(1	0)	84	20	24	25	4	32	2	4	2	1	1	.50	12	.212	.276	.283
1991 St. Louis	NL	56	68	13	3	0	0	(0	0)	16	5	0	8	0	19	0	0	0	0	1	.00	0	.191	.276	.235
1992 St. Louis	NL	85	265	65	9	11	2	(2	0)	102	26	32	27	1	40	4	2	4	2	5	.29	5	.245	.320	.385
1993 St. Louis	NL	115	362	101	19	3	3	(2	1)	135	50	46	47	2	54	4	1	7	11	1	.92	9	.279	.362	.373
1994 St. Louis	NL	88	205	57	12	5	5	(3	2)	94	32	29	30	4	38	3	1	3	4	5	.44	1	.278	.373	.459
1995 Boston	AL	132	419	113	20	3	6	(0	6)	157	64	44	63	0	61	7	13	9	13	10	.57	10	.270	.367	.375
1996 St. Louis	NL	129	380	98	26	3	5	(4	1)	145	54	42	52	10	78	5	4	6	11	3	.79	4	.258	.350	.382
1997 Anaheim	AL	128	388	98	16	7	5	(2	3)	143	59	37	69	3	65	8	4	2	22	8	.73	4	.253	.375	.369
1998 Texas	AL	101	259	71	15	3	6	(1	5)	110	51	33	37	0	40	5	4	3	4	3	.57	1	.274	.372	.425
1999 Texas	AL	68	164	33	10	0	3	(0	3)	52	33	17	28	0	32	0	3	1	2	1	.67	4	.201	.316	.317
10 ML YEARS		995	2807	712	140	39	36	(15	21)	1038	394	304	386	24	459	38	36	37	70	38	.65	50	.254	.348	.370

Chad Allen

Bats: R **Throws:** R **Pos:** LF-133; PH/PR-7; DH-2; RF-1   **Ht:** 6'1" **Wt:** 195 **Born:** 2/6/75 **Age:** 25

		BATTING																	BASERUNNING				PERCENTAGES		
Year Team	Lg	G	AB	H	2B	3B	HR	(Hm	Rd)	TB	R	RBI	TBB	IBB	SO	HBP	SH	SF	SB	CS	SB%	GDP	Avg	OBP	SLG
1996 Fort Wayne	A	7	21	9	0	0	0	—	—	9	2	2	3	1	2	0	0	1	1	1	.50	0	.429	.480	.429
1997 Fort Myers	A+	105	401	124	18	4	3	—	—	159	66	45	40	2	51	2	2	2	27	15	.64	9	.309	.373	.397
New Britain	AA	30	115	29	9	1	4	—	—	52	20	18	9	0	21	0	1	1	2	0	1.00	3	.252	.304	.452
1998 New Britain	AA	137	504	132	31	7	8	—	—	201	70	82	51	0	78	6	1	5	21	9	.70	19	.262	.334	.399
1999 Minnesota	AL	137	481	133	21	3	10	(4	6)	190	69	46	37	1	89	2	1	2	14	7	.67	10	.277	.330	.395

Jermaine Allensworth

Bats: R **Throws:** R **Pos:** RF-15; CF-14; PH/PR-14; LF-10   **Ht:** 6'0" **Wt:** 190 **Born:** 1/11/72 **Age:** 28

								BATTING											BASERUNNING				PERCENTAGES		
Year Team	Lg	G	AB	H	2B	3B	HR	(Hm	Rd)	TB	R	RBI	TBB	IBB	SO	HBP	SH	SF	SB	CS	SB%	GDP	Avg	OBP	SLG
1999 Norfolk *	AAA	81	273	72	20	5	5	—	—	117	44	20	36	0	39	7	2	1	10	5	.67	3	.264	.363	.429
1996 Pittsburgh	NL	61	229	60	9	3	4	(4	0)	87	32	31	23	0	50	4	2	2	11	6	.65	2	.262	.337	.380
1997 Pittsburgh	NL	108	369	94	18	2	3	(1	2)	125	55	43	44	1	79	7	9	6	14	7	.67	5	.255	.340	.339
1998 Pit-KC-NYM		133	360	98	20	3	5	(2	3)	139	54	31	28	0	76	12	8	1	15	6	.71	1	.272	.344	.386
1999 New York	NL	40	73	16	2	0	3	(1	2)	27	14	9	9	0	23	1	2	1	2	1	.67	1	.219	.310	.370
1998 Pittsburgh	NL	69	233	72	13	3	3	(2	1)	100	30	24	17	0	43	7	3	1	8	4	.67	1	.309	.372	.429
Kansas City	AL	30	73	15	5	0	0	(0	0)	20	15	3	9	0	17	4	5	0	7	0	1.00	0	.205	.326	.274
New York	NL	34	54	11	2	0	2	(1	2)	19	9	4	2	0	16	1	0	0	0	2	.00	0	.204	.246	.352
4 ML YEARS		342	1031	268	49	8	15	(8	7)	378	155	114	104	1	228	24	21	10	42	20	.68	9	.260	.339	.367

Armando Almanza

Pitches: Left **Bats:** Left **Pos:** RP-14   **Ht:** 6'3" **Wt:** 205 **Born:** 10/26/72 **Age:** 27

		HOW MUCH HE PITCHED						WHAT HE GAVE UP											THE RESULTS					
Year Team	Lg	G	GS	CG	GF	IP	BFP	H	R	ER	HR	SH	SF	HB	TBB	IBB	SO	WP	Bk	W	L	Pct.	ShO	Sv-Op	Hld	ERA
1993 Cardinals	R	20	4	0	6	42	179	38	19	15	2	0	1	3	14	0	56	14	1	4	1	.800	0	0- -	—	3.21
Johnson Cy	R+	3	0	0	0	4.1	21	6	2	2	1	0	0	0	3	0	4	0	0	1	1	.500	0	0- -	—	4.15
1995 Savannah	A	20	20	0	0	108	476	108	62	47	13	5	4	3	40	1	72	6	1	3	9	.250	0	0- -	—	3.92
1996 Peoria	A	52	1	0	18	62	271	50	27	19	2	3	2	2	32	5	67	8	2	8	6	.571	0	0- -	—	2.76
1997 Pr William	A+	58	0	0	47	64.2	259	38	18	12	3	1	4	1	32	1	83	8	1	2	3	.400	0	36- -	—	1.67
1998 Arkansas	AA	28	0	0	16	32.2	140	27	13	12	2	0	0	2	18	0	46	4	0	4	1	.800	0	8- -	—	3.31
Memphis	AAA	31	0	0	9	35.2	163	35	18	12	1	1	1	0	19	1	45	6	2	3	1	.750	0	1- -	—	3.03
1999 Calgary	AAA	15	0	0	4	17.1	99	29	27	21	3	0	1	0	18	0	20	2	0	2	2	.500	0	0- -	—	10.90
Portland	AA	10	0	0	6	11.1	41	5	5	5	1	1	0	0	4	0	20	0	0	1	0	.000	0	3- -	—	3.97
1999 Florida	NL	14	0	0	2	15.2	64	8	4	3	1	1	1	1	9	1	20	0	1	0	1	.000	0	0-0	—	1.72

Carlos Almanzar

Pitches: Right **Bats:** Right **Pos:** RP-28   **Ht:** 6'2" **Wt:** 200 **Born:** 11/6/73 **Age:** 26

		HOW MUCH HE PITCHED						WHAT HE GAVE UP											THE RESULTS					
Year Team	Lg	G	GS	CG	GF	IP	BFP	H	R	ER	HR	SH	SF	HB	TBB	IBB	SO	WP	Bk	W	L	Pct.	ShO	Sv-Op	Hld	ERA
1994 Medcine Hat	R+	14	14	0	0	84.2	351	82	38	27	2	7	1	1	19	0	77	3	2	7	4	.636	0	0- -	—	2.87
1995 Knoxville	AA	35	19	0	7	126.1	546	144	77	56	10	3	6	3	32	1	93	4	1	3	12	.200	0	2- -	—	3.99
1996 Knoxville	AA	54	0	0	29	94.2	418	106	58	51	13	1	2	3	33	6	105	3	0	7	8	.467	0	9- -	—	4.85
1997 Knoxville	AA	21	0	0	19	25.2	109	30	14	14	2	2	2	0	5	1	25	0	0	1	1	.500	0	8- -	—	4.91
Syracuse	AAA	32	0	0	17	51	189	30	9	8	2	2	1	2	8	0	47	2	0	5	1	.833	0	3- -	—	1.41
1998 Syracuse	AAA	30	0	0	19	50.2	211	44	21	13	7	1	1	4	13	2	53	2	0	3	6	.333	0	10- -	—	2.31
1999 Las Vegas	AAA	11	3	0	5	22.2	107	32	25	24	11	0	2	2	8	1	18	1	0	1	3	.250	0	0- -	—	9.53
1997 Toronto	AL	4	0	0	2	3.1	12	1	1	1	1	0	0	0	1	0	4	0	0	0	1	.000	0	0-0	0	2.70
1998 Toronto	AL	25	0	0	8	28.2	129	34	18	17	4	1	0	1	8	2	20	0	0	2	2	.500	0	0-3	1	5.34
1999 San Diego	NL	28	0	0	11	37.1	173	48	32	31	6	2	1	3	15	2	30	2	0	0	0	.000	0	0-0	0	7.47
3 ML YEARS		57	0	0	21	69.1	314	83	51	49	11	3	1	4	24	4	54	2	0	2	3	.400	0	0-3	1	6.36

Hector Almonte

Pitches: Right **Bats:** Right **Pos:** RP-15   **Ht:** 6'2" **Wt:** 190 **Born:** 10/17/75 **Age:** 24

		HOW MUCH HE PITCHED						WHAT HE GAVE UP											THE RESULTS					
Year Team	Lg	G	GS	CG	GF	IP	BFP	H	R	ER	HR	SH	SF	HB	TBB	IBB	SO	WP	Bk	W	L	Pct.	ShO	Sv-Op	Hld	ERA
1997 Marlins	R	8	0	0	7	23.2	89	12	3	2	0	0	1	2	6	0	25	1	0	2	0	1.000	0	3- -	—	0.76
Kane County	A	8	1	0	3	14	59	11	6	6	1	1	2	1	6	0	10	2	0	0	1	.000	0	1- -	—	3.86
1998 Kane County	A	43	0	0	41	43.1	200	51	22	19	5	1	1	1	19	0	51	3	2	1	5	.167	0	21- -	—	3.95
1999 Portland	AA	47	0	0	41	44.1	202	42	14	14	1	8	1	2	26	3	42	4	0	1	4	.200	0	23- -	—	2.84
1999 Florida	NL	15	0	0	6	15	67	22	7	7	1	1	1	0	6	2	8	2	0	0	2	.000	0	0-0	2	4.20

Roberto Alomar

Bats: Both **Throws:** Right **Pos:** 2B-156; PH/PR-3; DH-2   **Ht:** 6'0" **Wt:** 185 **Born:** 2/5/68 **Age:** 32

								BATTING											BASERUNNING				PERCENTAGES		
Year Team	Lg	G	AB	H	2B	3B	HR	(Hm	Rd)	TB	R	RBI	TBB	IBB	SO	HBP	SH	SF	SB	CS	SB%	GDP	Avg	OBP	SLG
1988 San Diego	NL	143	545	145	24	6	9	(5	4)	208	84	41	47	5	83	3	16	0	24	6	.80	15	.266	.328	.382
1989 San Diego	NL	158	623	184	27	1	7	(3	4)	234	82	56	53	4	76	1	17	8	42	17	.71	10	.295	.347	.376
1990 San Diego	NL	147	586	168	27	5	6	(4	2)	223	80	60	48	1	72	2	5	5	24	7	.77	16	.287	.340	.381
1991 Toronto	AL	161	637	188	41	11	9	(6	3)	278	88	69	57	3	86	4	16	5	53	11	.83	5	.295	.354	.436
1992 Toronto	AL	152	571	177	27	8	8	(3	5)	244	105	76	87	5	52	5	6	2	49	9	.84	8	.310	.405	.427
1993 Toronto	AL	153	589	192	35	6	17	(8	9)	290	109	93	80	5	67	5	4	5	55	15	.79	13	.326	.408	.492
1994 Toronto	AL	107	392	120	25	4	8	(4	4)	177	78	38	51	2	41	2	7	3	19	8	.70	14	.306	.386	.452
1995 Toronto	AL	130	517	155	24	7	13	(7	6)	232	71	66	47	3	45	0	6	7	30	3	.91	16	.300	.354	.449
1996 Baltimore	AL	153	588	193	43	4	22	(14	8)	310	132	94	90	10	65	1	8	12	17	6	.74	14	.328	.411	.527
1997 Baltimore	AL	112	412	137	23	2	14	(7	7)	206	64	60	40	2	43	3	7	7	9	3	.75	10	.333	.390	.500
1998 Baltimore	AL	147	588	166	36	1	14	(7	7)	246	86	56	59	3	70	2	3	5	18	5	.78	11	.282	.347	.418
1999 Cleveland	AL	159	563	182	40	3	24	(12	12)	300	138	120	99	3	96	7	12	13	37	6	.86	13	.323	.422	.533
12 ML YEARS		1722	6611	2007	372	58	151	(85	66)	2948	1117	829	758	46	796	35	107	72	377	96	.80	145	.304	.375	.446

Sandy Alomar Jr.

Bats: Right **Throws:** Right **Pos:** C-35; DH-1; PH/PR-1 **Ht:** 6'5" **Wt:** 220 **Born:** 6/18/66 **Age:** 34

							BATTING											BASERUNNING				PERCENTAGES		
Year Team	Lg	G	AB	H	2B	3B	HR	(Hm | Rd)	TB	R	RBI	TBB	IBB	SO	HBP	SH	SF	SB	CS	SB%	GDP	Avg	OBP	SLG
1999 Buffalo *	AAA	10	33	9	2	1	2	—	—	19	9	10	6	0	3	1	0	0	0	0	.00	1	.273	.400	.576
Akron *	AA	10	29	9	0	0	1	—	—	12	8	6	3	0	2	0	0	2	1	0	1.00	1	.310	.353	.414
1988 San Diego	NL	1	1	0	0	0	0	(0 | 0)	0	0	0	0	0	1	0	0	0	0	0	.00	0	.000	.000	.000
1989 San Diego	NL	7	19	4	1	0	1	(1 | 0)	8	1	6	3	1	3	0	0	0	0	0	.00	1	.211	.318	.421
1990 Cleveland	AL	132	445	129	26	2	9	(5 | 4)	186	60	66	25	2	46	2	5	6	4	1	.80	10	.290	.326	.418
1991 Cleveland	AL	51	184	40	9	0	0	(0 | 0)	49	10	7	8	1	24	4	2	1	0	4	.00	4	.217	.264	.266
1992 Cleveland	AL	89	299	75	16	0	2	(1 | 1)	97	22	26	13	3	32	5	3	0	3	3	.50	7	.251	.293	.324
1993 Cleveland	AL	64	215	58	7	1	6	(3 | 3)	85	24	32	11	0	28	6	1	4	3	1	.75	3	.270	.318	.395
1994 Cleveland	AL	80	292	84	15	1	14	(4 | 10)	143	44	43	25	2	31	2	0	1	8	4	.67	7	.288	.347	.490
1995 Cleveland	AL	66	203	61	6	0	10	(4 | 6)	97	32	35	7	0	26	3	4	1	3	1	.75	8	.300	.332	.478
1996 Cleveland	AL	127	418	110	23	0	11	(3 | 8)	166	53	50	19	0	42	3	2	2	1	0	1.00	20	.263	.299	.397
1997 Cleveland	AL	125	451	146	37	0	21	(9 | 12)	246	63	83	19	2	48	3	6	1	0	2	.00	16	.324	.354	.545
1998 Cleveland	AL	117	409	96	26	2	6	(3 | 3)	144	45	44	18	0	45	3	5	3	0	3	.00	15	.235	.270	.352
1999 Cleveland	AL	37	137	42	13	0	6	(4 | 2)	73	19	25	4	0	23	0	1	2	0	1	.00	1	.307	.322	.533
12 ML YEARS		896	3073	845	179	6	86	(37 | 49)	1294	373	417	152	11	349	31	29	21	22	20	.52	92	.275	.314	.421

Moises Alou

Bats: Right **Throws:** Right **Pos:** LF/CF **Ht:** 6'3" **Wt:** 195 **Born:** 7/3/66 **Age:** 33

							BATTING											BASERUNNING				PERCENTAGES		
Year Team	Lg	G	AB	H	2B	3B	HR	(Hm	Rd)	TB	R	RBI	TBB	IBB	SO	HBP	SH	SF	SB	CS	SB%	GDP	Avg	OBP	SLG
1990 Pit-Mon	NL	16	20	4	0	1	0	(0	0)	6	4	0	0	0	3	0	1	0	0	0	.00	1	.200	.200	.300
1992 Montreal	NL	115	341	96	28	2	9	(6	3)	155	53	56	25	0	46	1	5	5	16	2	.89	5	.282	.328	.455
1993 Montreal	NL	136	482	138	29	6	18	(10	8)	233	70	85	38	9	53	5	3	7	17	6	.74	9	.286	.340	.483
1994 Montreal	NL	107	422	143	31	5	22	(9	13)	250	81	78	42	10	63	2	0	5	7	6	.54	7	.339	.397	.592
1995 Montreal	NL	93	344	94	22	0	14	(4	10)	158	48	58	29	6	56	9	0	4	4	3	.57	9	.273	.342	.459
1996 Montreal	NL	143	540	152	28	2	21	(14	7)	247	87	96	49	7	83	2	0	7	9	4	.69	15	.281	.339	.457
1997 Florida	NL	150	538	157	29	5	23	(12	11)	265	88	115	70	9	85	4	0	7	9	5	.64	13	.292	.373	.493
1998 Houston	NL	159	584	182	34	5	38	(19	19)	340	104	124	84	11	87	5	0	6	11	3	.79	14	.312	.399	.582
1990 Pittsburgh	NL	2	5	1	0	0	0	(0	0)	1	0	0	0	0	0	0	0	0	0	0	.00	1	.200	.200	.200
Montreal	NL	14	15	3	0	1	0	(0	0)	5	4	0	0	0	3	0	1	0	0	0	.00	0	.200	.200	.333
8 ML YEARS		919	3271	966	201	26	145	(74	71)	1654	535	612	337	52	476	28	9	41	73	29	.72	73	.295	.362	.506

Gabe Alvarez

Bats: R **Throws:** R **Pos:** DH-12; PH/PR-8; RF-5; 3B-2 **Ht:** 6'1" **Wt:** 205 **Born:** 3/6/74 **Age:** 26

							BATTING											BASERUNNING				PERCENTAGES		
Year Team	Lg	G	AB	H	2B	3B	HR	(Hm	Rd)	TB	R	RBI	TBB	IBB	SO	HBP	SH	SF	SB	CS	SB%	GDP	Avg	OBP	SLG
1995 Rancho Cuca	A+	59	212	73	17	2	6	—	—	112	41	36	29	0	30	5	0	2	1	0	1.00	3	.344	.431	.528
Memphis	AA	2	9	5	1	0	0	—	—	6	0	4	1	0	1	0	0	0	0	0	.00	0	.556	.600	.667
1996 Memphis	AA	104	368	91	23	1	8	—	—	140	58	40	64	1	87	3	0	3	2	3	.40	10	.247	.361	.380
1997 Mobile	AA	114	427	128	28	2	14	—	—	202	71	78	51	2	64	5	0	6	1	1	.50	21	.300	.376	.473
1998 Toledo	AAA	67	249	68	15	1	20	—	—	145	37	58	30	0	60	1	0	3	3	1	.75	7	.273	.350	.582
1999 Toledo	AAA	110	410	117	24	0	21	—	—	204	70	67	57	0	80	6	0	9	1	3	.25	8	.285	.373	.498
1998 Detroit	AL	58	199	46	11	0	5	(3	2)	72	16	29	18	1	65	2	0	2	1	3	.25	2	.231	.299	.362
1999 Detroit	AL	22	53	11	3	0	2	(2	0)	20	5	4	3	0	9	0	0	0	0	0	.00	0	.208	.250	.377
2 ML YEARS		80	252	57	14	0	7	(5	2)	92	21	33	21	1	74	2	0	2	1	3	.25	2	.226	.289	.365

Juan Alvarez

Pitches: Left **Bats:** Left **Pos:** RP-8 **Ht:** 6'1" **Wt:** 175 **Born:** 8/9/73 **Age:** 26

		HOW MUCH HE PITCHED					WHAT HE GAVE UP											THE RESULTS					
Year Team	Lg	G	GS	CG	GF	IP	BFP	H	R	ER	HR	SH	SF	HB	TBB	IBB	SO	WP	Bk	W	L	Pct.	ShO	Sv-Op	Hld	ERA
1995 Boise	A-	9	0	0	2	11.2	47	12	1	1	0	0	0	1	2	0	11	0	0	0	0	.000	0	0--	—	0.77
1996 Cedar Rapds	A	40	0	0	14	53	238	50	25	20	0	3	1	7	30	1	53	4	0	1	2	.333	0	3--	—	3.40
1997 Lk Elsinore	A+	27	0	0	10	51.1	196	33	9	8	2	2	1	4	13	2	46	2	2	4	2	.667	0	3--	—	1.40
Midland	AA	24	0	0	6	37	199	63	42	34	5	0	1	3	22	1	27	0	3	4	1	.800	0	0--	—	8.27
1998 Midland	AA	40	0	0	31	46	197	40	26	22	5	2	1	2	21	3	41	2	1	3	4	.429	0	12--	—	4.30
Vancouver	AAA	18	0	0	5	14.1	65	14	9	8	2	0	0	4	8	0	12	0	1	1	1	.500	0	0--	—	5.02
1999 Erie	AA	23	0	0	12	30.2	121	20	14	7	4	1	2	2	6	0	22	1	1	0	2	.333	0	4--	—	2.05
Edmonton	AAA	27	0	0	13	28.1	123	30	13	11	2	1	1	1	8	0	25	0	1	0	3	.000	0	0--	—	3.49
1999 Anaheim	AL	8	0	0	1	3	14	1	1	1	0	1	0	0	4	0	4	1	0	0	1	.000	0	0-0	1	3.00

Wilson Alvarez

Pitches: Left **Bats:** Left **Pos:** SP-28 **Ht:** 6'1" **Wt:** 245 **Born:** 3/24/70 **Age:** 30

		HOW MUCH HE PITCHED					WHAT HE GAVE UP											THE RESULTS					
Year Team	Lg	G	GS	CG	GF	IP	BFP	H	R	ER	HR	SH	SF	HB	TBB	IBB	SO	WP	Bk	W	L	Pct.	ShO	Sv-Op	Hld	ERA
1989 Texas	AL	1	1	0	0	0	5	3	3	3	2	0	0	0	2	0	0	0	0	0	1	.000	0	0-0	0	0.00
1991 Chicago	AL	10	9	2	0	56.1	237	47	26	22	9	3	1	0	29	0	32	2	0	3	2	.600	1	0-0	0	3.51
1992 Chicago	AL	34	9	0	4	100.1	455	103	64	58	12	3	4	4	65	2	66	2	0	5	3	.625	0	1-1	3	5.20
1993 Chicago	AL	31	31	1	0	207.2	877	168	78	68	14	13	6	7	122	8	155	2	1	15	8	.652	1	0-0	0	2.95
1994 Chicago	AL	24	24	2	0	161.2	682	147	72	62	16	6	3	0	62	1	108	3	0	12	8	.600	1	0-0	0	3.45
1995 Chicago	AL	29	29	3	0	175	769	171	95	84	21	6	5	2	93	4	118	1	2	8	11	.421	0	0-0	0	4.32

		HOW MUCH HE PITCHED				WHAT HE GAVE UP										THE RESULTS						
Year Team	Lg	G GS CG GF	IP	BFP	H	R	ER	HR SH SF HB	TBB IBB	SO WP Bk	W L	Pct	ShO	Sv-Op	Hld	ERA
1996 Chicago	AL	35 35 0 0	217.1	946	216	106	102	21 5 2 4	97 3	181 2 0	15 10	.600	0	0-0	0	4.22
1997 CWS-SF		33 33 2 0	212	896	180	97	82	18 10 6 4	91 4	179 5 1	13 11	.542	1	0-0	0	3.48
1998 Tampa Bay	AL	25 25 0 0	142.2	624	130	78	75	18 1 2 9	68 0	107 4 0	6 14	.300	0	0-0	0	4.73
1999 Tampa Bay	AL	28 28 1 0	160	703	159	92	75	22 3 3 6	79 1	128 3 0	9 9	.500	0	0-0	0	4.22
1997 Chicago	AL	22 22 2 0	145.2	613	126	61	49	9 6 5 3	55 1	110 4 0	9 8	.529	1	0-0	0	3.03
San Francisco	NL	11 11 0 0	66.1	283	54	36	33	9 4 1 1	36 3	69 1 1	4 3	.571	0	0-0	0	4.48
10 ML YEARS		250 224 11 4	1433	6194	1324	712	631	153 50 32 36	708 23	1074 24 4	86 77	.528	4	1-1	3	3.96

Rich Amaral

Bats: R **Throws:** R **Pos:** PH/PR-39; RF-19; DH-18; CF-18; LF-14; 1B-2; 2B-2; 3B-1   **Ht:** 6'0" **Wt:** 175 **Born:** 4/1/62 **Age:** 38

		BATTING															BASERUNNING			PERCENTAGES		
Year Team	Lg	G	AB	H	2B	3B	HR	(Hm Rd)	TB	R	RBI	TBB	IBB	SO	HBP	SH	SF	SB CS SB% GDP			Avg	OBP	SLG
1991 Seattle	AL	14	16	1	0	0	0	(0 0)	1	2	0	1	0	5	1	0	0	0 0 .00 1			.063	.167	.063
1992 Seattle	AL	35	100	24	3	0	1	(0 1)	30	9	7	5	0	16	0	4	0	4 2 .67 4			.240	.276	.300
1993 Seattle	AL	110	373	108	24	1	1	(0 1)	137	53	44	33	0	54	3	7	5	19 11 .63 5			.290	.348	.367
1994 Seattle	AL	77	228	60	10	2	4	(2 2)	86	37	18	24	1	28	1	7	2	5 1 .83 3			.263	.333	.377
1995 Seattle	AL	90	238	67	14	2	2	(1 1)	91	45	19	21	0	33	1	1	0	21 2 .91 5			.282	.342	.382
1996 Seattle	AL	118	312	91	11	3	1	(1 0)	111	69	29	47	0	55	5	4	1	25 6 .81 6			.292	.392	.356
1997 Seattle	AL	89	190	54	5	0	1	(0 1)	62	34	21	10	0	34	3	5	2	12 8 .60 7			.284	.327	.326
1998 Seattle	AL	73	134	37	6	0	1	(0 1)	46	25	4	13	0	24	1	0	1	11 1 .92 1			.276	.342	.343
1999 Baltimore	AL	91	137	38	8	1	0	(0 0)	48	21	11	15	0	20	1	1	2	9 6 .60 1			.277	.348	.350
9 ML YEARS		697	1728	480	81	9	11	(5 6)	612	295	153	169	1	269	16	29	13	106 37 .74 31			.278	.345	.354

Brady Anderson

Bats: L **Throws:** L **Pos:** CF-129; DH-10; LF-9; PH/PR-7   **Ht:** 6'1" **Wt:** 202 **Born:** 1/18/64 **Age:** 36

		BATTING															BASERUNNING			PERCENTAGES		
Year Team	Lg	G	AB	H	2B	3B	HR	(Hm Rd)	TB	R	RBI	TBB	IBB	SO	HBP	SH	SF	SB CS SB% GDP			Avg	OBP	SLG
1988 Bos-Bal	AL	94	325	69	13	4	1	(1 0)	93	31	21	23	0	75	4	11	1	10 6 .63 3			.212	.272	.286
1989 Baltimore	AL	94	266	55	12	2	4	(2 2)	83	44	16	43	6	45	3	6	2	16 4 .80 4			.207	.324	.312
1990 Baltimore	AL	89	234	54	5	2	3	(1 2)	72	24	24	31	2	46	5	4	5	15 2 .88 4			.231	.327	.308
1991 Baltimore	AL	113	256	59	12	3	2	(1 1)	83	40	27	38	0	44	5	11	3	12 5 .71 1			.230	.338	.324
1992 Baltimore	AL	159	623	169	28	10	21	(15 6)	280	100	80	98	14	98	9	10	9	53 16 .77 2			.271	.373	.449
1993 Baltimore	AL	142	560	147	36	8	13	(2 11)	238	87	66	82	4	99	10	6	6	24 12 .67 4			.263	.363	.425
1994 Baltimore	AL	111	453	119	25	5	12	(5 7)	190	78	48	57	3	75	10	3	2	31 1 .97 7			.263	.356	.419
1995 Baltimore	AL	143	554	145	33	10	16	(10 6)	246	108	64	87	4	111	10	4	2	26 7 .79 3			.262	.371	.444
1996 Baltimore	AL	149	579	172	37	5	50	(19 31)	369	117	110	76	1	106	22	6	4	21 8 .72 11			.297	.396	.637
1997 Baltimore	AL	151	590	170	39	7	18	(8 10)	277	97	73	84	6	105	19	2	1	18 12 .60 1			.288	.393	.469
1998 Baltimore	AL	133	479	113	28	3	18	(7 11)	201	84	51	75	1	78	15	4	1	21 7 .75 7			.236	.356	.420
1999 Baltimore	AL	150	564	159	28	5	24	(10 14)	269	109	81	96	7	105	24	1	1	36 7 .84 6			.282	.404	.477
1988 Boston	AL	41	148	34	5	3	0	(0 0)	45	14	12	15	0	35	4	4	1	4 2 .67 2			.230	.315	.304
Baltimore	AL	53	177	35	8	1	1	(1 0)	48	17	9	8	0	40	0	7	0	6 4 .60 1			.198	.232	.271
12 ML YEARS		1528	5483	1431	296	64	182	(83 99)	2401	919	661	790	48	987	136	67	41	283 87 .76 53			.261	.365	.438

Brian Anderson

Pitches: Left **Bats:** Both **Pos:** SP-19; RP-12   **Ht:** 6'1" **Wt:** 183 **Born:** 4/26/72 **Age:** 28

		HOW MUCH HE PITCHED				WHAT HE GAVE UP										THE RESULTS						
Year Team	Lg	G GS CG GF	IP	BFP	H	R	ER	HR SH SF HB	TBB IBB	SO WP Bk	W L	Pct	ShO	Sv-Op	Hld	ERA
1999 Tucson *	AAA	2 2 0 0	6.2	30	9	5	4	1 1 1 0	1 0	8 0 0	0 1	.000	0	0- --	—	5.40
1993 California	AL	4 1 0 3	11.1	45	11	5	5	1 0 0 0	2 0	4 0 0	0 0	.000	0	0-0	0	3.97
1994 California	AL	18 18 0 0	101.2	441	120	63	59	13 3 6 5	27 0	47 5 5	7 5	.583	0	0-0	0	5.22
1995 California	AL	18 17 1 0	99.2	433	110	66	65	24 5 5 3	30 2	45 1 3	6 8	.429	0	0-0	0	5.87
1996 Cleveland	AL	10 9 0 0	51.1	215	58	29	28	9 2 3 0	14 1	21 2 0	3 1	.750	0	0-0	1	4.91
1997 Cleveland	AL	8 8 0 0	48	199	55	28	25	7 0 5 0	11 0	22 1 0	4 2	.667	0	0-0	0	4.69
1998 Arizona	NL	32 32 2 0	208	845	221	109	100	39 8 3 4	24 2	95 3 6	12 13	.480	1	0-0	0	4.33
1999 Arizona	NL	31 19 2 4	130	549	144	69	66	18 4 0 1	28 3	75 0 2	8 2	.800	1	1-2	1	4.57
7 ML YEARS		121 104 5 7	650	2727	719	369	348	111 22 22 13	136 8	309 12 16	40 31	.563	2	1-2	2	4.82

Garret Anderson

Bats: L **Throws:** L **Pos:** CF-116; LF-32; RF-6; DH-4; PH/PR-1   **Ht:** 6'3" **Wt:** 215 **Born:** 6/30/72 **Age:** 28

		BATTING															BASERUNNING			PERCENTAGES		
Year Team	Lg	G	AB	H	2B	3B	HR	(Hm Rd)	TB	R	RBI	TBB	IBB	SO	HBP	SH	SF	SB CS SB% GDP			Avg	OBP	SLG
1994 California	AL	5	13	5	0	0	0	(0 0)	5	0	1	0	0	2	0	0	0	0 0 .00 0			.385	.385	.385
1995 California	AL	106	374	120	19	1	16	(7 9)	189	50	69	19	4	65	1	2	4	6 2 .75 8			.321	.352	.505
1996 California	AL	150	607	173	33	2	12	(7 5)	246	79	72	27	5	84	0	5	3	7 9 .44 22			.285	.314	.405
1997 Anaheim	AL	154	624	189	36	3	8	(3 5)	255	76	92	30	6	70	2	1	5	10 4 .71 20			.303	.334	.409
1998 Anaheim	AL	156	622	183	41	7	15	(4 11)	283	62	79	29	8	80	1	3	8	8 3 .73 13			.294	.325	.455
1999 Anaheim	AL	157	620	188	36	2	21	(10 11)	291	88	80	34	8	81	0	0	6	3 4 .43 15			.303	.336	.469
6 ML YEARS		728	2860	858	165	15	72	(33 39)	1269	355	393	139	31	382	4	11	21	34 22 .61 78			.300	.331	.444

8

Jimmy Anderson

Pitches: Left **Bats:** Left **Pos:** RP-9; SP-4   **Ht:** 6'1" **Wt:** 195 **Born:** 1/22/76 **Age:** 24

Year Team	Lg	HOW MUCH HE PITCHED						WHAT HE GAVE UP										THE RESULTS						
		G	GS	CG	GF	IP	BFP	H	R	ER	HR	SH	SF	HB	TBB	IBB	SO	WP	Bk	W	L	Pct.	ShO	Sv-Op	Hld	ERA
1994 Pirates	R	10	10	0	0	56.1	230	35	21	10	1	2	1	2	27	0	66	5	1	5	1	.833	0	0--	—	1.60
1995 Augusta	A	14	14	0	0	76.2	305	51	15	13	1	1	0	4	31	0	75	9	1	4	2	.667	0	0--	—	1.53
Lynchburg	A+	10	9	0	1	52.1	231	56	29	24	1	4	1	5	21	1	32	7	3	1	5	.167	0	0--	—	4.13
1996 Lynchburg	A+	11	11	1	0	65.1	267	51	25	14	2	2	0	2	21	0	56	1	0	5	3	.625	1	0--	—	1.93
Carolina	AA	17	16	0	0	97	411	92	40	36	3	1	0	3	44	3	79	13	5	8	3	.727	0	0--	—	3.34
1997 Carolina	AA	4	4	0	0	24.2	98	16	6	4	1	0	0	2	9	0	23	1	0	2	1	.667	0	0--	—	1.46
Calgary	AAA	21	21	0	0	103	486	124	78	65	9	6	5	5	64	3	71	9	4	7	6	.538	0	0--	—	5.68
1998 Nashville	AAA	35	17	0	8	123.2	570	144	87	69	8	11	5	4	72	6	63	13	1	9	10	.474	0	0--	—	5.02
1999 Nashville	AAA	21	21	1	0	133.2	579	153	67	57	5	6	0	3	41	0	93	8	0	11	2	.846	0	0--	—	3.84
1999 Pittsburgh	NL	13	4	0	2	29.1	127	25	15	13	2	2	1	1	16	2	13	4	0	2	1	.667	0	0-0	0	3.99

Marlon Anderson

Bats: Left **Throws:** Right **Pos:** 2B-121; PH/PR-8   **Ht:** 5'11" **Wt:** 200 **Born:** 1/6/74 **Age:** 26

Year Team	Lg	BATTING																BASERUNNING				PERCENTAGES		
		G	AB	H	2B	3B	HR	(Hm	Rd)	TB	R	RBI	TBB	IBB	SO	HBP	SH	SF	SB	CS	SB%	GDP	Avg	OBP	SLG
1995 Batavia	A-	74	312	92	13	4	3	—	—	122	52	40	15	2	20	4	2	4	22	8	.73	2	.295	.331	.391
1996 Clearwater	A+	60	257	70	10	3	2	—	—	92	37	22	14	1	18	2	4	0	26	1	.96	4	.272	.315	.358
Reading	AA	75	314	86	14	3	3	—	—	115	38	28	26	2	44	1	3	1	17	9	.65	5	.274	.330	.366
1997 Reading	AA	137	553	147	18	6	10	—	—	207	88	62	42	1	77	10	9	1	27	15	.64	8	.266	.328	.374
1998 Scranton-WB	AAA	136	575	176	32	4	16	—	—	284	104	86	28	1	77	7	5	5	24	12	.67	11	.306	.343	.494
1998 Philadelphia	NL	17	43	14	3	0	1	(1	0)	20	4	4	1	0	6	0	0	1	2	0	1.00	0	.326	.333	.465
1999 Philadelphia	NL	129	452	114	26	4	5	(4	1)	163	48	54	24	1	61	2	4	2	13	2	.87	6	.252	.292	.361
2 ML YEARS		146	495	128	29	4	6	(5	1)	183	52	58	25	1	67	2	4	3	15	2	.88	6	.259	.295	.370

Matt Anderson

Pitches: Right **Bats:** Right **Pos:** RP-37   **Ht:** 6'4" **Wt:** 200 **Born:** 8/17/76 **Age:** 23

Year Team	Lg	HOW MUCH HE PITCHED						WHAT HE GAVE UP										THE RESULTS						
		G	GS	CG	GF	IP	BFP	H	R	ER	HR	SH	SF	HB	TBB	IBB	SO	WP	Bk	W	L	Pct.	ShO	Sv-Op	Hld	ERA
1998 Lakeland	A+	17	0	0	13	26	108	18	4	2	0	2	1	0	8	0	34	2	0	1	0	1.000	0	3--	—	0.69
Jacksnville	AA	13	0	0	12	15	56	7	1	1	1	2	0	0	5	0	11	1	0	1	0	1.000	0	10--	—	0.60
1999 Toledo	AAA	24	4	0	18	38	173	32	27	27	9	0	1	1	31	0	35	4	1	0	4	.000	0	5--	—	6.39
1998 Detroit	AL	42	0	0	10	44	194	38	16	16	3	6	3	2	31	4	44	2	0	5	1	.833	0	0-4	6	3.27
1999 Detroit	AL	37	0	0	9	38	180	33	27	24	8	0	2	1	35	1	32	3	0	2	1	.667	0	0-2	3	5.68
2 ML YEARS		79	0	0	19	82	374	71	43	40	11	6	5	3	66	5	76	5	0	7	2	.778	0	0-6	9	4.39

Shane Andrews

Bats: R **Throws:** R **Pos:** 3B-101; 1B-19; PH/PR-10; DH-1   **Ht:** 6'0" **Wt:** 220 **Born:** 8/28/71 **Age:** 28

Year Team	Lg	BATTING																BASERUNNING				PERCENTAGES		
		G	AB	H	2B	3B	HR	(Hm	Rd)	TB	R	RBI	TBB	IBB	SO	HBP	SH	SF	SB	CS	SB%	GDP	Avg	OBP	SLG
1999 Ottawa *	AAA	2	8	2	0	0	1	—	—	5	1	4	0	0	2	0	0	0	0	0	.00	1	.250	.250	.625
1995 Montreal	NL	84	220	47	10	1	8	(2	6)	83	27	31	17	2	68	1	1	2	1	1	.50	4	.214	.271	.377
1996 Montreal	NL	127	375	85	15	2	19	(8	11)	161	43	64	35	8	119	2	0	2	3	1	.75	2	.227	.295	.429
1997 Montreal	NL	18	64	13	3	0	1	(2	2)	28	10	9	3	0	20	0	0	2	0	0	.00	0	.203	.232	.438
1998 Montreal	NL	150	492	117	30	1	25	(12	13)	224	48	69	58	3	137	0	2	7	1	6	.14	10	.238	.314	.455
1999 Mon-ChC	NL	117	348	68	12	0	16	(9	7)	128	41	51	50	3	109	1	0	5	1	1	.50	10	.195	.295	.368
1999 Montreal	NL	98	281	51	8	0	11	(5	6)	92	28	37	43	2	88	0	0	4	1	0	1.00	10	.181	.287	.327
Chicago	NL	19	67	17	4	0	5	(4	1)	36	13	14	7	1	21	1	0	1	0	1	.00	0	.254	.329	.537
5 ML YEARS		496	1499	330	70	4	72	(33	39)	624	169	224	163	16	453	4	3	18	6	9	.40	26	.220	.295	.416

Rick Ankiel

Pitches: Left **Bats:** Left **Pos:** SP-5; RP-4   **Ht:** 6'1" **Wt:** 210 **Born:** 7/19/79 **Age:** 20

Year Team	Lg	HOW MUCH HE PITCHED						WHAT HE GAVE UP										THE RESULTS						
		G	GS	CG	GF	IP	BFP	H	R	ER	HR	SH	SF	HB	TBB	IBB	SO	WP	Bk	W	L	Pct.	ShO	Sv-Op	Hld	ERA
1998 Peoria	A	7	7	0	0	35	128	15	8	8	0	1	1	2	12	0	41	1	0	3	0	1.000	0	0--	—	2.06
Pr William	A+	21	21	1	0	126	503	91	46	39	8	5	3	12	38	0	181	10	1	9	6	.600	0	0--	—	2.79
1999 Arkansas	AA	8	8	1	0	49.1	191	25	6	5	2	1	0	2	16	0	75	0	0	6	0	1.000	1	0--	—	0.91
Memphis	AAA	16	16	0	0	88.1	385	73	37	31	7	1	3	7	46	1	119	6	1	7	3	.700	0	0--	—	3.16
1999 St. Louis	NL	9	5	0	1	33	137	26	12	12	2	1	0	1	14	0	39	2	0	0	1	.000	0	1-1	0	3.27

Kevin Appier

Pitches: Right **Bats:** Right **Pos:** SP-34   **Ht:** 6'2" **Wt:** 200 **Born:** 12/6/67 **Age:** 32

Year Team	Lg	HOW MUCH HE PITCHED						WHAT HE GAVE UP										THE RESULTS						
		G	GS	CG	GF	IP	BFP	H	R	ER	HR	SH	SF	HB	TBB	IBB	SO	WP	Bk	W	L	Pct.	ShO	Sv-Op	Hld	ERA
1989 Kansas City	AL	6	5	0	0	21.2	106	34	22	22	3	0	3	0	12	1	10	0	0	1	4	.200	0	0-0	0	9.14
1990 Kansas City	AL	32	24	3	0	185.2	784	179	67	57	13	5	9	6	54	2	127	6	1	12	8	.600	3	0-0	0	2.76
1991 Kansas City	AL	34	31	6	1	207.2	881	205	97	79	13	8	6	2	61	3	158	7	1	13	10	.565	3	0-0	1	3.42
1992 Kansas City	AL	30	30	3	0	208.1	852	167	59	57	10	8	3	2	68	5	150	4	0	15	8	.652	1	0-0	0	2.46
1993 Kansas City	AL	34	34	5	0	238.2	953	183	74	68	8	3	5	1	81	3	186	5	0	18	8	.692	1	0-0	0	2.56

9

Year Team	Lg	HOW MUCH HE PITCHED						WHAT HE GAVE UP											THE RESULTS						
		G	GS	CG	GF	IP	BFP	H	R	ER	HR	SH	SF	HB	TBB	IBB	SO	WP	Bk	W	L	Pct.	ShO	Sv-Op	Hld	ERA
1994 Kansas City	AL	23	23	1	0	155	653	137	68	66	11	9	7	4	63	7	145	11	1	7	6	.538	1	0-0	0	3.83
1995 Kansas City	AL	31	31	4	0	201.1	832	163	90	87	14	3	3	8	80	1	185	5	0	15	10	.600	1	0-0	0	3.89
1996 Kansas City	AL	32	32	5	0	211.1	874	192	87	85	17	7	4	5	75	2	207	10	1	14	11	.560	1	0-0	0	3.62
1997 Kansas City	AL	34	34	4	0	235.2	972	215	96	89	24	4	4	4	74	2	196	14	1	9	13	.409	1	0-0	0	3.40
1998 Kansas City	AL	3	3	0	0	15	69	21	13	13	3	0	1	1	5	1	9	1	0	1	2	.333	0	0-0	0	7.80
1999 KC-Oak	AL	34	34	1	0	209	926	230	131	120	27	7	5	7	84	4	131	10	1	16	14	.533	0	0-0	0	5.17
1999 Kansas City	AL	22	22	1	0	140.1	613	153	81	76	18	5	3	6	51	3	78	5	0	9	9	.500	0	0-0	0	4.87
Oakland	AL	12	12	0	0	68.2	313	77	50	44	9	2	2	1	33	1	53	5	1	7	5	.583	0	0-0	0	5.77
11 ML YEARS		293	281	32	2	1889.1	7902	1726	804	743	143	54	50	40	657	31	1504	73	6	121	94	.563	10	0-0	1	3.54

Alex Arias

Bats: R **Throws:** R **Pos:** SS-95; PH/PR-23; 3B-2; 2B-1   **Ht:** 6'3" **Wt:** 197 **Born:** 11/20/67 **Age:** 32

Year Team	Lg	BATTING																	BASERUNNING				PERCENTAGES		
		G	AB	H	2B	3B	HR	(Hm	Rd)	TB	R	RBI	TBB	IBB	SO	HBP	SH	SF	SB	CS	SB%	GDP	Avg	OBP	SLG
1992 Chicago	NL	32	99	29	6	0	0	(0	0)	35	14	7	11	0	13	2	1	0	0	0	.00	4	.293	.375	.354
1993 Florida	NL	96	249	67	5	1	2	(1	1)	80	27	20	27	0	18	3	1	3	1	1	.50	5	.269	.344	.321
1994 Florida	NL	59	113	27	5	0	0	(0	0)	32	4	15	9	0	19	1	1	1	0	1	.00	5	.239	.298	.283
1995 Florida	NL	94	216	58	9	2	3	(2	1)	80	22	26	22	1	20	2	3	3	1	0	1.00	8	.269	.337	.370
1996 Florida	NL	100	224	62	11	2	3	(1	2)	86	27	26	17	1	28	3	1	1	2	0	1.00	2	.277	.335	.384
1997 Florida	NL	74	93	23	2	0	1	(0	1)	28	13	11	12	0	12	3	4	0	0	1	.00	6	.247	.352	.301
1998 Philadelphia	NL	56	133	39	8	0	1	(1	0)	50	17	16	13	3	18	1	1	1	2	0	1.00	3	.293	.358	.376
1999 Philadelphia	NL	118	347	105	20	1	4	(4	0)	139	43	48	36	6	31	4	1	2	2	2	.50	12	.303	.373	.401
8 ML YEARS		629	1474	410	66	6	14	(9	5)	530	167	169	147	11	159	19	13	11	8	5	.62	43	.278	.349	.360

George Arias

Bats: Right **Throws:** Right **Pos:** 3B-50; PH/PR-8   **Ht:** 5'11" **Wt:** 190 **Born:** 3/12/72 **Age:** 28

Year Team	Lg	BATTING																	BASERUNNING				PERCENTAGES		
		G	AB	H	2B	3B	HR	(Hm	Rd)	TB	R	RBI	TBB	IBB	SO	HBP	SH	SF	SB	CS	SB%	GDP	Avg	OBP	SLG
1999 Rancho Cuca *	A+	7	21	4	2	0	1	—	—	9	1	4	2	0	9	0	0	0	0	0	.00	1	.190	.261	.429
Las Vegas *	AAA	26	95	27	7	2	10	—	—	68	30	30	17	1	28	1	0	0	1	0	1.00	3	.284	.398	.716
1996 California	AL	84	252	60	8	1	6	(5	1)	88	19	28	16	2	50	0	0	6	2	0	1.00	6	.238	.284	.349
1997 Ana-SD		14	28	7	1	0	0	(0	0)	8	3	3	0	0	1	0	0	0	0	0	.00	2	.250	.250	.286
1998 San Diego	NL	20	36	7	1	1	1	(1	0)	13	4	4	3	0	16	2	0	0	0	0	.00	0	.194	.293	.361
1999 San Diego	NL	55	164	40	8	0	7	(2	5)	69	20	20	6	0	54	0	0	0	0	0	.00	6	.244	.271	.421
1997 Anaheim	AL	3	6	2	0	0	0	(0	0)	2	1	1	0	0	0	0	0	0	0	0	.00	0	.333	.333	.333
San Diego	NL	11	22	5	1	0	0	(0	0)	6	2	2	0	0	1	0	0	0	0	0	.00	2	.227	.227	.273
4 ML YEARS		173	480	114	18	2	14	(8	6)	178	46	55	25	2	121	2	6	0	2	0	1.00	14	.238	.278	.371

Tony Armas Jr.

Pitches: Right **Bats:** Right **Pos:** SP-1   **Ht:** 6'4" **Wt:** 205 **Born:** 4/29/78 **Age:** 22

Year Team	Lg	HOW MUCH HE PITCHED						WHAT HE GAVE UP											THE RESULTS						
		G	GS	CG	GF	IP	BFP	H	R	ER	HR	SH	SF	HB	TBB	IBB	SO	WP	Bk	W	L	Pct.	ShO	Sv-Op	Hld	ERA
1995 Yankees	R	5	4	0	0	14	61	12	9	1	1	1	0	1	6	0	13	3	1	0	1	.000	0	0--	—	0.64
1996 Oneonta	A-	3	3	0	0	15.2	73	14	12	10	1	0	1	0	11	0	14	4	0	1	1	.500	0	0--	—	5.74
Yankees	R	8	7	0	1	45.2	191	41	18	16	1	0	2	2	13	0	45	4	2	4	1	.800	0	1--	—	3.15
1997 Greensboro	A	9	9	2	0	51.2	207	36	13	6	3	1	1	3	13	0	64	1	1	5	2	.714	1	0--	—	1.05
Tampa	A+	9	9	0	0	46	191	43	23	17	1	3	4	1	16	3	26	2	0	3	1	.750	0	0--	—	3.33
Sarasota	A+	3	3	0	0	17.2	81	18	13	13	2	2	1	2	12	0	9	3	0	2	1	.667	0	0--	—	6.62
1998 Jupiter	A+	27	27	1	0	153.1	656	140	63	49	11	9	1	10	59	0	136	3	0	12	8	.600	1	0--	—	2.88
1999 Harrisburg	AA	24	24	2	0	149.2	611	123	62	48	10	8	1	3	55	0	106	5	1	9	7	.563	1	0--	—	2.89
1999 Montreal	NL	1	1	0	0	6	28	8	4	1	0	0	1	0	2	1	2	2	0	0	1	.000	0	0-0	0	1.50

Jamie Arnold

Pitches: Right **Bats:** Right **Pos:** RP-33; SP-3   **Ht:** 6'2" **Wt:** 188 **Born:** 3/24/74 **Age:** 26

Year Team	Lg	HOW MUCH HE PITCHED						WHAT HE GAVE UP											THE RESULTS						
		G	GS	CG	GF	IP	BFP	H	R	ER	HR	SH	SF	HB	TBB	IBB	SO	WP	Bk	W	L	Pct.	ShO	Sv-Op	Hld	ERA
1992 Braves	R	7	5	0	2	20	85	16	12	9	0	0	2	4	6	0	22	0	2	0	1	.000	0	0--	—	4.05
1993 Macon	A	27	27	1	0	164.1	692	142	67	57	5	3	4	16	56	0	124	13	2	8	9	.471	0	0--	—	3.12
1994 Durham	A+	25	25	0	0	145	656	144	96	75	26	3	1	14	79	4	91	8	4	7	7	.500	0	0--	—	4.66
1995 Durham	A+	15	14	1	0	80	347	86	42	35	5	4	1	9	21	0	44	4	0	4	8	.333	0	0--	—	3.94
Greenville	AA	10	10	0	0	56.2	266	76	42	40	8	0	2	7	25	1	19	6	0	1	5	.167	0	0--	—	6.35
1996 Greenville	AA	23	23	2	0	128	573	149	79	70	17	0	5	10	44	1	64	6	1	7	7	.500	0	0--	—	4.92
1997 Braves	R	5	5	0	0	19	74	13	6	6	1	0	0	0	6	0	21	0	0	1	0	1.000	0	0--	—	2.84
Durham	A+	5	5	0	0	24.1	115	25	21	16	2	2	0	1	13	0	21	2	0	2	2	.500	0	0--	—	5.92
Greenville	AA	1	1	0	0	4.2	27	10	6	6	3	0	0	1	2	0	3	1	0	0	1	.000	0	0--	—	11.57
1998 Greenville	AA	32	6	0	7	83.1	387	93	51	41	12	2	1	3	46	2	48	12	0	1	4	.200	0	1--	—	4.43
Richmond	AAA	9	2	0	0	20.2	102	30	22	22	1	1	3	1	17	1	10	3	0	1	0	1.000	0	1--	—	9.58
1999 Albuquerque	AAA	7	2	0	1	19.1	91	28	14	12	1	1	0	2	7	0	13	3	0	2	0	.000	0	0--	—	5.59
1999 Los Angeles	NL	36	3	0	18	69	313	81	50	42	6	3	0	6	34	2	26	3	0	2	4	.333	0	1-3	2	5.48

Rolando Arrojo

Pitches: Right **Bats:** Right **Pos:** SP-24   **Ht:** 6'4" **Wt:** 220 **Born:** 7/18/68 **Age:** 31

		HOW MUCH HE PITCHED						WHAT HE GAVE UP											THE RESULTS					
Year Team	Lg	G	GS	CG	GF	IP	BFP	H	R	ER	HR	SH	SF	HB	TBB	IBB	SO	WP	Bk	W	L	Pct.	ShO	Sv-Op	Hld	ERA
1997 St. Pete	A+	16	16	4	0	89.1	349	73	40	34	6	1	3	10	13	0	73	5	1	5	6	.455	1	0--	—	3.43
1999 St. Pete	A+	2	2	0	0	10	43	11	6	5	0	0	1	0	1	0	10	0	0	0	1	.000	0	0--	—	4.50
1998 Tampa Bay	AL	32	32	2	0	202	853	195	84	80	21	5	3	19	65	2	152	3	1	14	12	.538	2	0-0	0	3.56
1999 Tampa Bay	AL	24	24	2	0	140.2	630	162	84	81	23	5	3	14	60	2	107	2	0	7	12	.368	0	0-0	0	5.18
2 ML YEARS		56	56	4	0	342.2	1483	357	168	161	44	10	6	33	125	4	259	5	1	21	24	.467	2	0-0	0	4.23

Andy Ashby

Pitches: Right **Bats:** Right **Pos:** SP-31   **Ht:** 6'5" **Wt:** 202 **Born:** 7/11/67 **Age:** 32

		HOW MUCH HE PITCHED						WHAT HE GAVE UP											THE RESULTS					
Year Team	Lg	G	GS	CG	GF	IP	BFP	H	R	ER	HR	SH	SF	HB	TBB	IBB	SO	WP	Bk	W	L	Pct.	ShO	Sv-Op	Hld	ERA
1991 Philadelphia	NL	8	8	0	0	42	186	41	28	28	5	1	3	3	19	0	26	6	0	1	5	.167	0	0-0	0	6.00
1992 Philadelphia	NL	10	8	0	0	37	171	42	31	31	6	2	2	1	21	0	24	2	0	1	3	.250	0	0-0	0	7.54
1993 Col-SD	NL	32	21	0	3	123	577	168	100	93	19	6	7	4	56	5	77	6	3	3	10	.231	0	1-1	0	6.80
1994 San Diego	NL	24	24	4	0	164.1	682	145	75	62	16	11	3	3	43	12	121	5	0	6	11	.353	0	0-0	0	3.40
1995 San Diego	NL	31	31	2	0	192.2	800	180	79	63	17	10	4	11	62	3	150	7	0	12	10	.545	2	0-0	0	2.94
1996 San Diego	NL	24	24	1	0	150.2	612	147	60	54	17	6	2	3	34	1	85	3	0	9	5	.643	0	0-0	0	3.23
1997 San Diego	NL	30	30	2	0	200.2	851	207	108	92	17	13	6	5	49	2	144	3	0	9	11	.450	0	0-0	0	4.13
1998 San Diego	NL	33	33	5	0	226.2	939	223	90	84	23	8	5	7	58	8	151	7	0	17	9	.654	1	0-0	0	3.34
1999 San Diego	NL	31	31	4	0	206	862	204	95	87	26	10	1	7	54	4	132	6	0	14	10	.583	3	0-0	0	3.80
1993 Colorado	NL	20	9	0	3	54	277	89	54	51	5	3	3	3	32	4	33	2	3	0	4	.000	0	1-1	0	8.50
San Diego	NL	12	12	0	0	69	300	79	46	42	14	3	4	1	24	1	44	4	0	3	6	.333	0	0-0	0	5.48
9 ML YEARS		223	210	18	3	1343	5680	1357	666	594	146	67	33	44	396	35	910	45	3	72	74	.493	6	1-1	0	3.98

Paul Assenmacher

Pitches: Left **Bats:** Left **Pos:** RP-55   **Ht:** 6'3" **Wt:** 210 **Born:** 12/10/60 **Age:** 39

		HOW MUCH HE PITCHED						WHAT HE GAVE UP											THE RESULTS					
Year Team	Lg	G	GS	CG	GF	IP	BFP	H	R	ER	HR	SH	SF	HB	TBB	IBB	SO	WP	Bk	W	L	Pct.	ShO	Sv-Op	Hld	ERA
1986 Atlanta	NL	61	0	0	27	68.1	287	61	23	19	5	7	1	0	26	4	56	2	3	7	3	.700	0	7--	—	2.50
1987 Atlanta	NL	52	0	0	10	54.2	251	58	41	31	8	2	1	1	24	4	39	0	1	1	1	.500	0	2-6	10	5.10
1988 Atlanta	NL	64	0	0	32	79.1	329	72	28	27	4	8	1	1	32	11	71	7	0	8	7	.533	0	5-11	8	3.06
1989 Atl-ChC	NL	63	0	0	17	76.2	331	74	37	34	3	9	3	1	28	8	79	3	1	3	4	.429	0	0-3	13	3.99
1990 Chicago	NL	74	1	0	21	103	426	90	33	30	10	10	3	1	36	8	95	2	0	7	2	.778	0	10-20	10	2.80
1991 Chicago	NL	75	0	0	31	102.2	427	85	41	37	10	8	4	3	31	6	117	4	0	7	8	.467	0	15-24	14	3.24
1992 Chicago	NL	70	0	0	23	68	298	72	32	31	6	1	2	3	26	5	67	4	0	4	4	.500	0	8-13	20	4.10
1993 ChC-NYY		72	0	0	21	56	237	54	21	21	5	4	0	1	22	6	45	0	0	4	3	.571	0	0-5	17	3.38
1994 Chicago	AL	44	0	0	11	33	134	26	13	13	2	1	3	1	13	2	29	1	0	1	2	.333	0	1-3	14	3.55
1995 Cleveland	AL	47	0	0	12	38.1	160	32	13	12	3	1	2	3	12	3	40	1	0	6	2	.750	0	0-1	9	2.82
1996 Cleveland	AL	63	0	0	25	46.2	201	46	18	16	1	4	2	4	14	5	44	2	0	4	2	.667	0	1-3	13	3.09
1997 Cleveland	AL	75	0	0	20	49	205	43	17	16	5	1	2	1	15	5	53	4	0	5	0	1.000	0	4-5	20	2.94
1998 Cleveland	AL	69	0	0	17	47	213	54	22	17	5	2	2	1	19	6	43	0	0	2	5	.286	0	3-8	25	3.26
1999 Cleveland	AL	55	0	0	8	33	165	50	32	30	6	1	2	1	17	5	29	1	1	2	1	.667	0	0-2	7	8.18
1989 Atlanta	NL	49	0	0	14	57.2	247	55	26	23	2	7	2	1	16	7	64	3	1	1	3	.250	0	0-2	7	3.59
Chicago	NL	14	0	0	3	19	84	19	11	11	1	2	1	0	12	1	15	0	0	2	1	.667	0	0-1	6	5.21
1993 Chicago	NL	46	0	0	15	38.2	166	44	15	15	5	0	0	0	13	3	34	0	0	2	1	.667	0	0-4	12	3.49
New York	AL	26	0	0	6	17.1	71	10	6	6	0	4	0	1	9	3	11	0	0	2	2	.500	0	0-1	5	3.12
14 ML YEARS		884	1	0	275	855.2	3664	817	371	336	73	59	28	22	315	78	807	31	5	61	44	.581	0	56--	—	3.53

Pedro Astacio

Pitches: Right **Bats:** Right **Pos:** SP-34   **Ht:** 6'2" **Wt:** 210 **Born:** 11/28/69 **Age:** 30

		HOW MUCH HE PITCHED						WHAT HE GAVE UP											THE RESULTS					
Year Team	Lg	G	GS	CG	GF	IP	BFP	H	R	ER	HR	SH	SF	HB	TBB	IBB	SO	WP	Bk	W	L	Pct.	ShO	Sv-Op	Hld	ERA
1992 Los Angeles	NL	11	11	4	0	82	341	80	23	18	1	3	2	2	20	4	43	1	0	5	5	.500	4	0-0	0	1.98
1993 Los Angeles	NL	31	31	3	0	186.1	777	165	80	74	14	7	8	5	68	5	122	8	9	14	9	.609	2	0-0	0	3.57
1994 Los Angeles	NL	23	23	0	0	149	625	142	77	71	18	6	5	4	47	4	108	4	0	6	8	.429	1	0-0	0	4.29
1995 Los Angeles	NL	48	11	1	7	104	436	103	53	49	12	5	3	4	29	5	80	5	0	7	8	.467	1	0-1	2	4.24
1996 Los Angeles	NL	35	32	0	0	211.2	885	207	86	81	18	11	5	9	67	9	130	6	2	9	8	.529	0	0-0	0	3.44
1997 LA-Col	NL	33	31	2	2	202.1	862	200	98	93	24	9	7	9	61	0	166	6	3	12	10	.545	1	0-0	0	4.14
1998 Colorado	NL	35	34	0	0	209.1	938	245	160	145	39	12	3	17	74	0	170	2	0	13	14	.481	0	0-0	0	6.23
1999 Colorado	NL	34	34	7	0	232	1008	258	140	130	38	6	10	11	75	6	210	5	0	17	11	.607	0	0-0	0	5.04
1997 Los Angeles	NL	26	24	2	2	153.2	654	151	75	70	15	9	5	4	47	0	115	4	3	7	9	.438	1	0-0	0	4.10
Colorado	NL	7	7	0	0	48.2	208	49	23	23	9	0	2	5	14	0	51	2	0	5	1	.833	0	0-0	0	4.25
8 ML YEARS		250	207	20	9	1376.2	5872	1400	717	661	164	59	43	61	441	33	1029	37	14	83	73	.532	9	0-1	2	4.32

Rich Aurilia

Bats: Right **Throws:** Right **Pos:** SS-150; PH/PR-4   **Ht:** 6'1" **Wt:** 185 **Born:** 9/2/71 **Age:** 28

		BATTING															BASERUNNING			PERCENTAGES		
Year Team	Lg	G	AB	H	2B	3B	HR	(Hm | Rd)	TB	R	RBI	TBB	IBB	SO	HBP	SH	SF	SB	CS	SB%	GDP	Avg	OBP	SLG
1995 San Francisco	NL	9	19	9	3	0	2	(0 | 2)	18	4	4	1	0	2	0	1	1	1	0	1.00	0	.474	.476	.947
1996 San Francisco	NL	105	318	76	7	1	3	(1 | 2)	94	27	26	25	2	52	1	6	2	4	1	.80	1	.239	.295	.296
1997 San Francisco	NL	46	102	28	8	0	5	(1 | 4)	51	16	19	8	0	15	0	1	2	1	1	.50	3	.275	.321	.500

Year Team	Lg	G	AB	H	2B	3B	HR	(Hm	Rd)	TB	R	RBI	TBB	IBB	SO	HBP	SH	SF	SB	CS	SB%	GDP	Avg	OBP	SLG
1998 San Francisco	NL	122	413	110	27	2	9	(5	4)	168	54	49	31	3	62	2	5	2	3	3	.50	3	.266	.319	.407
1999 San Francisco	NL	152	558	157	23	1	22	(9	13)	248	68	80	43	3	71	5	3	5	2	3	.40	16	.281	.336	.444
5 ML YEARS		434	1410	380	68	4	41	(16	25)	579	169	178	108	8	202	8	16	12	11	8	.58	24	.270	.322	.411

Brad Ausmus

Bats: Right Throws: Right Pos: C-127; PH/PR-2 Ht: 5'11" Wt: 195 Born: 4/14/69 Age: 31

Year Team	Lg	G	AB	H	2B	3B	HR	(Hm	Rd)	TB	R	RBI	TBB	IBB	SO	HBP	SH	SF	SB	CS	SB%	GDP	Avg	OBP	SLG
1993 San Diego	NL	49	160	41	8	1	5	(4	1)	66	18	12	6	0	28	0	0	0	2	0	1.00	2	.256	.283	.413
1994 San Diego	NL	101	327	82	12	1	7	(6	1)	117	45	24	30	12	63	1	6	2	5	1	.83	8	.251	.314	.358
1995 San Diego	NL	103	328	84	16	4	5	(2	3)	135	44	34	31	3	56	2	4	4	16	5	.76	6	.293	.353	.412
1996 SD-Det		125	375	83	16	0	5	(2	3)	114	46	35	39	1	72	5	6	2	4	8	.33	8	.221	.302	.304
1997 Houston	NL	130	425	113	25	1	4	(1	3)	152	45	44	38	4	78	3	6	6	14	6	.70	8	.266	.326	.358
1998 Houston	NL	128	412	111	10	4	6	(2	4)	147	62	45	53	11	60	3	3	1	10	3	.77	18	.269	.356	.357
1999 Detroit	AL	127	458	126	25	6	9	(5	4)	190	62	54	51	0	71	14	3	1	12	9	.57	11	.275	.365	.415
1996 San Diego	NL	50	149	27	4	0	1	(0	1)	34	16	13	13	0	27	3	1	0	1	4	.20	4	.181	.261	.228
Detroit	AL	75	226	56	12	0	4	(2	2)	80	30	22	26	1	45	2	5	2	3	4	.43	4	.248	.328	.354
7 ML YEARS		763	2485	652	112	17	41	(22	19)	921	322	248	248	31	428	28	28	16	63	32	.66	61	.262	.334	.371

Bruce Aven

Bats: R Throws: R Pos: LF-78; PH/PR-34; RF-24; CF-9; DH-6 Ht: 5'9" Wt: 180 Born: 3/4/72 Age: 28

Year Team	Lg	G	AB	H	2B	3B	HR	(Hm	Rd)	TB	R	RBI	TBB	IBB	SO	HBP	SH	SF	SB	CS	SB%	GDP	Avg	OBP	SLG
1994 Watertown	A-	61	220	73	14	5	5	—	—	112	49	33	20	0	45	12	2	5	12	3	.80	1	.332	.409	.509
1995 Kinston	A+	130	479	125	23	5	23	—	—	227	70	69	41	3	109	13	0	1	15	9	.63	7	.261	.335	.474
1996 Canton-Akrn	AA	131	481	143	31	4	23	—	—	251	91	79	43	0	101	17	0	3	22	6	.79	9	.297	.373	.522
Buffalo	AAA	3	9	6	0	0	1	—	—	9	5	2	1	0	1	1	0	0	0	1	.00	0	.667	.727	1.000
1997 Buffalo	AAA	121	432	124	27	3	17	—	—	208	69	77	50	0	99	11	2	5	10	3	.77	10	.287	.371	.481
1998 Buffalo	AAA	5	15	3	1	0	1	—	—	7	4	1	6	0	5	0	0	0	3	0	1.00	0	.200	.429	.467
1997 Cleveland	AL	13	19	4	1	0	0	(0	0)	5	4	2	1	0	5	0	0	0	0	1	.00	0	.211	.250	.263
1999 Florida	NL	137	381	110	19	2	12	(3	9)	169	57	70	44	1	82	9	0	6	3	0	1.00	6	.289	.370	.444
2 ML YEARS		150	400	114	20	2	12	(3	9)	174	61	72	45	1	87	9	0	6	3	1	.75	6	.285	.365	.435

Steve Avery

Pitches: Left Bats: Left Pos: SP-19 Ht: 6'4" Wt: 205 Born: 4/14/70 Age: 30

Year Team	Lg	G	GS	CG	GF	IP	BFP	H	R	ER	HR	SH	SF	HB	TBB	IBB	SO	WP	Bk	W	L	Pct.	ShO	Sv-Op	Hld	ERA
1990 Atlanta	NL	21	20	1	1	99	466	121	79	62	7	14	4	2	45	2	75	5	1	3	11	.214	1	0-0	0	5.64
1991 Atlanta	NL	35	35	3	0	210.1	868	189	89	79	21	8	4	3	65	0	137	4	1	18	8	.692	1	0-0	0	3.38
1992 Atlanta	NL	35	35	2	0	233.2	969	216	95	83	14	12	8	0	71	3	129	7	3	11	11	.500	2	0-0	0	3.20
1993 Atlanta	NL	35	35	3	0	223.1	891	216	81	73	14	12	8	0	43	5	125	3	1	18	6	.750	1	0-0	0	2.94
1994 Atlanta	NL	24	24	1	0	151.2	628	127	71	68	15	4	6	4	55	4	122	5	2	8	3	.727	0	0-0	0	4.04
1995 Atlanta	NL	29	29	3	0	173.1	724	165	92	90	22	6	4	6	52	4	141	3	0	7	13	.350	1	0-0	0	4.67
1996 Atlanta	NL	24	23	1	0	131	567	146	70	65	10	7	3	4	40	8	86	5	0	7	10	.412	0	0-0	0	4.47
1997 Boston	AL	22	18	0	1	96.2	453	127	76	69	15	1	4	2	49	0	51	4	0	6	7	.462	0	0-0	1	6.42
1998 Boston	AL	34	23	0	4	123.2	546	128	74	69	14	3	0	4	64	0	57	7	0	10	7	.588	0	0-1	1	5.02
1999 Cincinnati	NL	19	19	0	0	96	426	75	62	55	11	3	6	1	78	0	51	4	1	6	7	.462	0	0-0	0	5.16
10 ML YEARS		278	261	14	6	1538.2	6538	1510	789	713	143	70	47	26	562	26	974	47	9	94	83	.531	6	0-1	2	4.17

Bobby Ayala

Pitches: Right Bats: Right Pos: RP-66 Ht: 6'3" Wt: 210 Born: 7/8/69 Age: 30

Year Team	Lg	G	GS	CG	GF	IP	BFP	H	R	ER	HR	SH	SF	HB	TBB	IBB	SO	WP	Bk	W	L	Pct.	ShO	Sv-Op	Hld	ERA
1992 Cincinnati	NL	5	5	0	0	29	127	33	15	14	1	2	0	1	13	2	23	0	0	2	1	.667	0	0-0	0	4.34
1993 Cincinnati	NL	43	9	0	8	98	450	106	72	61	16	9	2	7	45	4	65	5	0	7	10	.412	0	3-5	6	5.60
1994 Seattle	AL	46	0	0	40	56.2	236	42	25	18	2	1	2	0	26	0	76	2	0	4	3	.571	0	18-24	0	2.86
1995 Seattle	AL	63	0	0	50	71	320	73	42	35	9	2	3	6	30	4	77	3	0	6	5	.545	0	19-27	2	4.44
1996 Seattle	AL	50	0	0	26	67.1	285	65	45	44	10	2	2	2	25	3	61	2	0	6	3	.667	0	3-6	7	5.88
1997 Seattle	AL	71	0	0	33	96.2	403	91	45	41	14	3	6	3	41	3	92	6	0	10	5	.667	0	8-12	15	3.82
1998 Seattle	AL	62	0	0	36	75.1	351	100	66	61	9	8	6	1	26	4	68	4	0	1	10	.091	0	8-17	5	7.29
1999 Mon-ChC	NL	66	0	0	21	82	365	71	43	32	10	5	3	6	39	2	79	5	0	1	7	.125	0	0-1	10	3.51
1999 Montreal	NL	53	0	0	17	66	300	60	36	27	6	4	3	4	34	1	64	4	0	1	6	.143	0	0-1	7	3.68
Chicago	NL	13	0	0	4	16	65	11	7	5	4	1	0	2	5	1	15	1	0	0	1	.000	0	0-0	3	2.81
8 ML YEARS		406	14	0	214	576	2537	581	353	306	71	32	24	26	245	22	541	27	0	37	44	.457	0	59-92	45	4.78

Manny Aybar

Pitches: Right Bats: Right Pos: RP-64; SP-1 Ht: 6'1" Wt: 177 Born: 10/5/74 Age: 25

Year Team	Lg	G	GS	CG	GF	IP	BFP	H	R	ER	HR	SH	SF	HB	TBB	IBB	SO	WP	Bk	W	L	Pct.	ShO	Sv-Op	Hld	ERA
1997 St. Louis	NL	12	12	0	0	68	295	66	33	32	8	7	4	4	29	0	41	1	1	2	4	.333	0	0-0	0	4.24
1998 St. Louis	NL	20	14	0	1	81.1	369	90	58	54	6	4	1	2	42	1	57	2	0	6	6	.500	0	0-0	0	5.98

			HOW MUCH HE PITCHED						WHAT HE GAVE UP									THE RESULTS							
Year Team	Lg	G	GS	CG	GF	IP	BFP	H	R	ER	HR	SH	SF	HB	TBB	IBB	SO	WP	Bk	W	L	Pct.	ShO	Sv-Op	Hld	ERA
1999 St. Louis	NL	65	1	0	22	97	430	104	67	59	13	4	3	4	36	3	74	1	2	4	5	.444	0	3-5	12	5.47
3 ML YEARS		97	27	0	23	246.1	1094	260	158	145	27	15	8	10	107	4	172	4	3	12	15	.444	0	3-5	12	5.30

Carlos Baerga

Bats: B **Throws:** R **Pos:** 3B-28; 2B-19; PH/PR-17; DH-2; 1B-2   **Ht:** 5'11" **Wt:** 215 **Born:** 11/4/68 **Age:** 31

							BATTING												BASERUNNING				PERCENTAGES		
Year Team	Lg	G	AB	H	2B	3B	HR	(Hm	Rd)	TB	R	RBI	TBB	IBB	SO	HBP	SH	SF	SB	CS	SB%	GDP	Avg	OBP	SLG
1999 Indianapols *	AAA	52	221	64	10	0	3	—	—	83	32	27	10	3	18	1	2	2	2	1	.67	11	.290	.321	.376
Las Vegas *	AAA	21	91	26	7	0	2	—	—	39	15	9	9	0	5	1	0	0	0	0	.00	2	.286	.356	.429
1990 Cleveland	AL	108	312	81	17	2	7	(3	4)	123	46	47	16	2	57	4	1	5	0	2	.00	4	.260	.300	.394
1991 Cleveland	AL	158	593	171	28	2	11	(2	9)	236	80	69	48	5	74	6	4	3	3	2	.60	12	.288	.346	.398
1992 Cleveland	AL	161	657	205	32	1	20	(9	11)	299	92	105	35	10	76	13	2	9	10	2	.83	15	.312	.354	.455
1993 Cleveland	AL	154	624	200	28	6	21	(8	13)	303	105	114	34	7	68	6	3	13	15	4	.79	17	.321	.355	.486
1994 Cleveland	AL	103	442	139	32	2	19	(8	11)	232	81	80	10	1	45	6	3	8	8	2	.80	10	.314	.333	.525
1995 Cleveland	AL	135	557	175	28	2	15	(7	8)	252	87	90	35	6	31	3	0	5	11	2	.85	15	.314	.355	.452
1996 Cle-NYM		126	507	129	28	0	12	(5	7)	193	59	66	21	0	27	9	2	5	1	1	.50	23	.254	.293	.381
1997 New York	NL	133	467	131	25	1	9	(4	5)	185	53	52	20	1	54	3	3	5	2	6	.25	13	.281	.311	.396
1998 New York	NL	147	511	136	27	1	7	(3	4)	186	46	53	24	6	55	6	3	7	0	1	.00	21	.266	.303	.364
1999 SD-Cle		55	137	33	1	0	3	(2	1)	43	10	10	10	1	24	2	2	1	2	1	.67	5	.241	.300	.314
1996 Cleveland	AL	100	424	113	25	0	10	(5	5)	168	54	55	16	0	25	7	2	4	1	1	.50	15	.267	.302	.396
New York	NL	26	83	16	3	0	2	(0	2)	25	5	11	5	0	2	2	0	1	0	0	.00	8	.193	.253	.301
1999 San Diego	NL	33	80	20	1	0	2	(1	1)	27	6	5	6	0	14	2	1	0	1	0	1.00	2	.250	.318	.338
Cleveland	AL	22	57	13	0	0	1	(1	0)	16	4	5	4	1	10	0	1	1	1	1	.50	3	.228	.274	.281
10 ML YEARS		1280	4807	1400	246	17	124	(51	73)	2052	659	686	253	39	511	58	23	61	52	23	.69	135	.291	.330	.427

Jeff Bagwell

Bats: Right **Throws:** Right **Pos:** 1B-161; DH-2; PH/PR-2   **Ht:** 6'0" **Wt:** 195 **Born:** 5/27/68 **Age:** 32

							BATTING												BASERUNNING				PERCENTAGES		
Year Team	Lg	G	AB	H	2B	3B	HR	(Hm	Rd)	TB	R	RBI	TBB	IBB	SO	HBP	SH	SF	SB	CS	SB%	GDP	Avg	OBP	SLG
1991 Houston	NL	156	554	163	26	4	15	(6	9)	242	79	82	75	5	116	13	1	7	7	4	.64	12	.294	.387	.437
1992 Houston	NL	162	586	160	34	6	18	(8	10)	260	87	96	84	13	97	12	2	13	10	6	.63	17	.273	.368	.444
1993 Houston	NL	142	535	171	37	4	20	(9	11)	276	76	88	62	6	73	3	0	9	13	4	.76	20	.320	.388	.516
1994 Houston	NL	110	400	147	32	2	39	(23	16)	300	104	116	65	14	65	4	0	10	15	4	.79	12	.368	.451	.750
1995 Houston	NL	114	448	130	29	0	21	(10	11)	222	88	87	79	12	102	6	0	6	12	5	.71	9	.290	.399	.496
1996 Houston	NL	162	568	179	48	2	31	(16	15)	324	111	120	135	20	114	10	0	6	21	7	.75	15	.315	.451	.570
1997 Houston	NL	162	566	162	40	2	43	(22	21)	335	109	135	127	27	122	16	0	8	31	10	.76	14	.286	.425	.592
1998 Houston	NL	147	540	164	33	1	34	(20	14)	301	124	111	109	8	90	7	0	5	19	7	.73	14	.304	.424	.557
1999 Houston	NL	162	562	171	35	0	42	(12	30)	332	143	126	149	16	127	11	0	7	30	11	.73	18	.304	.454	.591
9 ML YEARS		1317	4759	1447	314	21	263	(126	137)	2592	921	961	885	121	906	82	3	71	158	58	.73	127	.304	.416	.545

Harold Baines

Bats: Left **Throws:** Left **Pos:** DH-121; PH/PR-18   **Ht:** 6'2" **Wt:** 195 **Born:** 3/15/59 **Age:** 41

							BATTING												BASERUNNING				PERCENTAGES		
Year Team	Lg	G	AB	H	2B	3B	HR	(Hm	Rd)	TB	R	RBI	TBB	IBB	SO	HBP	SH	SF	SB	CS	SB%	GDP	Avg	OBP	SLG
1980 Chicago	AL	141	491	125	23	6	13	(3	10)	199	55	49	19	7	65	1	2	5	2	4	.33	15	.255	.281	.405
1981 Chicago	AL	82	280	80	11	7	10	(3	7)	135	42	41	12	4	41	2	0	2	6	2	.75	6	.286	.318	.482
1982 Chicago	AL	161	608	165	29	8	25	(11	14)	285	89	105	49	10	95	0	2	9	10	3	.77	12	.271	.321	.469
1983 Chicago	AL	156	596	167	33	2	20	(12	8)	264	76	99	49	13	85	1	3	6	7	5	.58	15	.280	.333	.443
1984 Chicago	AL	147	569	173	28	10	29	(16	13)	308	72	94	54	9	75	0	1	5	1	2	.33	12	.304	.361	.541
1985 Chicago	AL	160	640	198	29	3	22	(13	9)	299	86	113	42	8	89	1	0	10	1	1	.50	23	.309	.348	.467
1986 Chicago	AL	145	570	169	29	2	21	(8	13)	265	72	88	38	9	89	2	0	8	2	1	.67	14	.296	.338	.465
1987 Chicago	AL	132	505	148	26	4	20	(12	8)	242	59	93	46	2	82	1	0	2	0	0	.00	12	.293	.352	.479
1988 Chicago	AL	158	599	166	39	1	13	(5	8)	246	55	81	67	14	109	1	0	7	0	0	.00	21	.277	.347	.411
1989 CWS-Tex		146	505	156	29	1	16	(5	11)	235	73	72	73	13	79	1	0	4	0	3	.00	15	.309	.395	.465
1990 Tex-Oak		135	415	118	15	1	16	(9	7)	183	52	65	67	10	80	0	0	7	0	3	.00	17	.284	.378	.441
1991 Oakland	AL	141	488	144	25	1	20	(11	9)	231	76	90	72	22	67	1	0	5	0	1	.00	12	.295	.383	.473
1992 Oakland	AL	140	478	121	18	0	16	(10	6)	187	58	76	59	6	61	0	0	6	1	3	.25	11	.253	.331	.391
1993 Baltimore	AL	118	416	130	22	0	20	(12	8)	212	64	78	57	9	52	0	1	6	0	0	.00	14	.313	.390	.510
1994 Baltimore	AL	94	326	96	12	1	16	(11	5)	158	44	54	30	6	49	1	0	0	0	0	.00	9	.294	.356	.485
1995 Baltimore	AL	127	385	115	19	1	24	(7	17)	208	60	63	70	13	45	0	0	4	0	2	.00	17	.299	.403	.540
1996 Chicago	AL	143	495	154	29	0	22	(9	13)	249	80	95	73	7	62	1	0	3	3	1	.75	20	.311	.399	.503
1997 CWS-Bal		137	452	136	23	0	16	(6	10)	207	55	67	55	11	62	0	0	3	0	1	.00	12	.301	.375	.458
1998 Baltimore	AL	104	293	88	17	0	9	(5	4)	132	40	57	32	4	40	1	0	2	0	0	.00	17	.300	.369	.451
1999 Bal-Cle		135	430	134	18	1	25	(13	12)	229	62	103	54	3	48	0	0	2	1	2	.33	16	.312	.387	.533
1989 Chicago	AL	96	333	107	20	1	13	(4	9)	168	55	56	60	13	52	1	0	3	0	1	.00	11	.321	.423	.505
Texas	AL	50	172	49	9	0	3	(1	2)	67	18	16	13	0	27	0	0	1	0	2	.00	4	.285	.333	.390
1990 Texas	AL	103	321	93	10	1	13	(6	7)	144	41	44	47	9	63	0	0	3	0	1	.00	13	.290	.377	.449
Oakland	AL	32	94	25	5	0	3	(3	0)	39	11	21	20	1	17	0	0	4	0	2	.00	4	.266	.381	.415
1997 Chicago	AL	93	318	97	18	0	12	(5	7)	151	40	52	41	10	47	0	0	2	0	1	.00	9	.305	.382	.475
Baltimore	AL	44	134	39	5	0	4	(1	3)	56	15	15	14	1	15	0	0	1	0	0	.00	3	.291	.356	.418
1999 Baltimore	AL	107	345	111	16	1	24	(12	12)	201	57	81	43	3	38	0	0	2	1	2	.33	14	.322	.395	.583
Cleveland	AL	28	85	23	2	0	1	(1	0)	28	5	22	11	0	10	0	0	0	0	0	.00	2	.271	.354	.329
20 ML YEARS		2702	9541	2783	474	49	373	(181	192)	4474	1270	1583	1018	180	1375	14	9	96	34	34	.50	290	.292	.358	.469

Paul Bako

Bats: Left **Throws:** Right **Pos:** C-71; PH/PR-3   **Ht:** 6'2" **Wt:** 205 **Born:** 6/20/72 **Age:** 28

							BATTING											BASERUNNING				PERCENTAGES		
Year Team	Lg	G	AB	H	2B	3B	HR	(Hm | Rd)	TB	R	RBI	TBB	IBB	SO	HBP	SH	SF	SB	CS	SB%	GDP	Avg	OBP	SLG
1993 Billings	R+	57	194	61	11	0	4	—	—	84	34	30	22	0	37	1	1	3	5	1	.83	5	.314	.382	.433
1994 Winston-Sal	A+	90	289	59	9	1	3	—	—	79	29	26	35	0	81	4	8	0	2	2	.50	6	.204	.299	.273
1995 Winston-Sal	A+	82	249	71	11	2	7	—	—	107	29	27	42	6	66	1	6	1	3	1	.75	6	.285	.389	.430
1996 Chattanooga	AA	110	360	106	27	0	8	—	—	157	53	48	48	5	93	5	2	4	1	0	1.00	5	.294	.381	.436
1997 Indianapols	AAA	104	321	78	14	1	8	—	—	118	34	43	34	3	81	2	1	4	0	5	.00	7	.243	.316	.368
1998 Toledo	AAA	13	48	14	3	1	1	—	—	22	5	6	1	0	13	0	0	1	0	0	.00	1	.292	.300	.458
1999 New Orleans	AAA	12	47	9	3	1	1	—	—	17	2	4	1	0	11	0	1	0	0	0	.00	1	.191	.208	.362
1998 Detroit	AL	96	305	83	12	1	3	(2 | 1)	106	23	30	23	4	82	0	1	4	1	1	.50	3	.272	.319	.348
1999 Houston	NL	73	215	55	14	1	2	(2 | 0)	77	16	17	26	3	57	0	3	3	1	1	.50	4	.256	.332	.358
2 ML YEARS		169	520	138	26	2	5	(4 | 1)	183	39	47	49	7	139	0	4	7	2	2	.50	7	.265	.325	.352

James Baldwin

Pitches: Right **Bats:** Right **Pos:** SP-33; RP-2   **Ht:** 6'3" **Wt:** 235 **Born:** 7/15/71 **Age:** 28

		HOW MUCH HE PITCHED						WHAT HE GAVE UP										THE RESULTS					
Year Team	Lg	G	GS	CG	GF	IP	BFP	H	R	ER	HR	SH	SF	HB	TBB	IBB	SO	WP	Bk	W	L	Pct.	ShO	Sv-Op	Hld	ERA
1995 Chicago	AL	6	4	0	0	14.2	81	32	22	21	6	0	0	0	9	1	10	1	0	0	1	.000	0	0-0	0	12.89
1996 Chicago	AL	28	28	0	0	169	719	168	88	83	24	2	2	4	57	3	127	12	1	11	6	.647	0	0-0	0	4.42
1997 Chicago	AL	32	32	1	0	200	879	205	128	117	19	3	6	5	83	3	140	14	3	12	15	.444	0	0-0	0	5.27
1998 Chicago	AL	37	24	1	3	159	712	176	103	94	18	3	5	10	60	2	108	5	1	13	6	.684	0	0-1	0	5.32
1999 Chicago	AL	35	33	1	1	199.1	886	219	119	113	34	4	7	7	81	1	123	11	1	12	13	.480	0	0-0	0	5.10
5 ML YEARS		138	121	3	4	742	3277	800	460	428	101	12	20	26	290	10	508	43	6	48	41	.539	0	0-1	0	5.19

John Bale

Pitches: Left **Bats:** Left **Pos:** RP-1   **Ht:** 6'4" **Wt:** 195 **Born:** 5/22/74 **Age:** 26

		HOW MUCH HE PITCHED						WHAT HE GAVE UP										THE RESULTS					
Year Team	Lg	G	GS	CG	GF	IP	BFP	H	R	ER	HR	SH	SF	HB	TBB	IBB	SO	WP	Bk	W	L	Pct.	ShO	Sv-Op	Hld	ERA
1996 St.Cathrnes	A-	8	8	0	0	33.1	148	39	21	18	2	0	1	0	11	0	35	4	2	3	2	.600	0	0--	—	4.86
1997 Hagerstown	A	25	25	0	0	140.1	603	130	83	67	11	4	3	1	63	1	155	11	0	7	7	.500	0	0--	—	4.30
1998 Dunedin	A+	24	9	0	5	66	290	68	39	34	5	3	5	4	23	1	78	6	1	4	5	.444	0	4--	—	4.64
Knoxville	AA	3	0	0	2	1.1	5	1	1	1	1	0	0	0	0	0	0	0	0	0	0	.000	0	0--	—	6.75
1999 Knoxville	AA	33	4	0	9	62.1	265	64	32	26	7	1	0	0	16	1	91	4	0	2	2	.500	0	1--	—	3.75
Syracuse	AAA	6	4	0	0	22.2	92	16	14	10	1	2	3	0	10	0	10	1	0	0	3	.000	0	0--	—	3.97
1999 Toronto	AL	1	0	0	0	2	10	2	3	3	1	0	0	0	2	0	4	0	0	0	0	.000	0	0-0	0	13.50

Brian Banks

Bats: B **Throws:** R **Pos:** 1B-44; C-40; PH/PR-33; LF-4; RF-1   **Ht:** 6'3" **Wt:** 208 **Born:** 9/28/70 **Age:** 29

							BATTING											BASERUNNING				PERCENTAGES		
Year Team	Lg	G	AB	H	2B	3B	HR	(Hm	Rd)	TB	R	RBI	TBB	IBB	SO	HBP	SH	SF	SB	CS	SB%	GDP	Avg	OBP	SLG
1999 Louisville *	AAA	6	24	5	2	1	1	—	—	12	3	6	2	1	5	0	0	1	0	0	.00	0	.208	.259	.500
1996 Milwaukee	AL	4	7	4	2	0	1	(0	1)	9	2	2	1	0	2	0	0	0	0	0	.00	0	.571	.625	1.286
1997 Milwaukee	AL	28	68	14	1	0	1	(0	1)	18	9	8	6	0	17	0	0	1	0	1	.00	1	.206	.267	.265
1998 Milwaukee	NL	24	24	7	2	0	1	(0	1)	12	3	5	4	0	7	0	0	0	0	0	.00	0	.292	.393	.500
1999 Milwaukee	NL	105	219	53	7	1	5	(4	1)	77	34	22	25	5	59	0	3	2	6	1	.86	2	.242	.317	.352
4 ML YEARS		161	318	78	12	1	8	(4	4)	116	48	37	36	5	85	0	3	3	6	2	.75	3	.245	.319	.365

Rod Barajas

Bats: Right **Throws:** Right **Pos:** C-5   **Ht:** 6'2" **Wt:** 220 **Born:** 9/5/75 **Age:** 24

							BATTING											BASERUNNING				PERCENTAGES		
Year Team	Lg	G	AB	H	2B	3B	HR	(Hm	Rd)	TB	R	RBI	TBB	IBB	SO	HBP	SH	SF	SB	CS	SB%	GDP	Avg	OBP	SLG
1996 Visalia	A+	27	74	12	3	0	0	—	—	15	6	8	7	0	21	1	0	0	0	0	.00	3	.162	.244	.203
Lethbridge	R+	51	175	59	9	3	10	—	—	104	47	50	12	0	24	2	0	4	2	1	.67	6	.337	.378	.594
1997 High Desert	A+	57	199	53	11	0	7	—	—	85	24	30	8	0	41	1	0	1	0	2	.00	7	.266	.297	.427
1998 High Desert	A+	113	442	134	26	0	23	—	—	229	67	81	25	2	81	7	0	7	1	1	.50	13	.303	.345	.518
1999 El Paso	AA	127	510	162	41	2	14	—	—	249	77	95	24	6	73	8	0	6	2	0	1.00	15	.318	.354	.488
1999 Arizona	NL	5	16	4	1	0	1	(1	0)	8	3	3	1	0	1	0	1	0	0	0	.00	0	.250	.294	.500

Brian Barber

Pitches: Right **Bats:** Right **Pos:** RP-5; SP-3   **Ht:** 6'1" **Wt:** 190 **Born:** 3/4/73 **Age:** 27

		HOW MUCH HE PITCHED						WHAT HE GAVE UP										THE RESULTS					
Year Team	Lg	G	GS	CG	GF	IP	BFP	H	R	ER	HR	SH	SF	HB	TBB	IBB	SO	WP	Bk	W	L	Pct.	ShO	Sv-Op	Hld	ERA
1999 Omaha *	AAA	19	19	2	0	120.1	520	128	68	61	21	4	1	5	29	1	75	6	0	9	5	.643	1	0--	—	4.56
1995 St. Louis	NL	9	4	0	2	29.1	130	31	17	17	4	0	3	0	16	0	27	3	0	2	1	.667	0	0-0	0	5.22
1996 St. Louis	NL	1	1	0	0	3	20	4	5	5	0	0	2	1	6	0	1	0	0	0	0	.000	0	0-0	0	15.00
1998 Kansas City	AL	8	8	0	0	42	180	45	28	28	5	0	3	1	13	1	24	4	0	2	4	.333	0	0-0	0	6.00
1999 Kansas City	AL	8	3	0	1	18.2	95	31	20	20	6	1	1	2	10	2	7	0	0	1	3	.250	0	1-1	1	9.64
4 ML YEARS		26	16	0	3	93	425	111	70	70	15	1	9	4	45	3	59	7	0	5	8	.385	0	1-1	1	6.77

Glen Barker

Bats: B **Throws:** R **Pos:** CF-46; PH/PR-43; RF-8; LF-4; DH-1 **Ht:** 5'10" **Wt:** 180 **Born:** 5/10/71 **Age:** 29

Year Team	Lg	G	AB	H	2B	3B	HR	(Hm	Rd)	TB	R	RBI	TBB	IBB	SO	HBP	SH	SF	SB	CS	SB%	GDP	Avg	OBP	SLG
1993 Niagara Fal	A-	72	253	55	11	4	5	—	—	89	49	23	24	0	71	4	2	3	37	12	.76	1	.217	.292	.352
1994 Fayettevlle	A	74	267	61	13	5	1	—	—	87	38	30	33	0	79	9	2	1	41	13	.76	5	.228	.332	.326
Lakeland	A+	28	104	19	5	1	2	—	—	32	10	6	4	0	34	2	0	0	5	3	.63	2	.183	.227	.308
1995 Jacksnville	AA	133	507	121	26	4	10	—	—	185	74	49	33	0	143	9	12	1	39	16	.71	1	.239	.296	.365
1996 Fayettevlle	A	37	132	38	1	0	1	—	—	42	23	9	16	1	34	3	3	0	20	6	.77	2	.288	.377	.318
Toledo	AAA	24	80	20	2	1	0	—	—	24	13	2	9	0	25	0	2	0	6	6	.50	1	.250	.326	.300
Jacksnville	AA	43	120	19	2	1	0	—	—	23	9	8	8	0	36	0	2	0	6	4	.60	2	.158	.211	.192
1997 Toledo	AAA	21	47	9	1	0	1	—	—	13	9	3	5	0	15	1	2	0	6	2	.75	0	.191	.283	.277
Lakeland	A+	13	57	18	4	0	1	—	—	25	9	11	4	0	17	0	3	0	7	1	.88	0	.316	.361	.439
Jacksnville	AA	69	257	72	8	4	6	—	—	106	47	29	29	0	72	5	8	3	17	8	.68	4	.280	.361	.412
1998 Jacksnville	AA	110	453	127	29	6	6	—	—	186	95	54	57	1	120	4	7	5	31	7	.82	1	.280	.362	.411
1999 Houston	NL	81	73	21	2	0	1	(0	1)	26	23	11	11	0	19	1	4	1	17	6	.74	0	.288	.384	.356

Kevin Barker

Bats: Left **Throws:** Left **Pos:** 1B-31; PH/PR-8 **Ht:** 6'3" **Wt:** 205 **Born:** 7/26/75 **Age:** 24

Year Team	Lg	G	AB	H	2B	3B	HR	(Hm	Rd)	TB	R	RBI	TBB	IBB	SO	HBP	SH	SF	SB	CS	SB%	GDP	Avg	OBP	SLG
1996 Ogden	R+	71	281	89	19	4	9	—	—	143	61	56	46	4	54	3	0	5	0	2	.00	4	.317	.412	.509
1997 Stockton	A+	70	267	81	20	5	13	—	—	150	47	45	25	4	60	0	0	1	4	3	.57	6	.303	.362	.562
El Paso	AA	65	238	66	15	6	10	—	—	123	37	63	28	0	40	2	0	5	3	3	.50	5	.277	.352	.517
1998 El Paso	AA	20	85	26	6	0	5	—	—	47	14	14	3	0	21	2	0	2	2	1	.67	2	.306	.337	.553
Louisville	AAA	124	463	128	26	4	23	—	—	231	59	96	36	1	97	3	0	4	2	5	.29	11	.276	.330	.499
1999 Louisville	AAA	121	442	123	27	5	23	—	—	229	89	87	59	5	94	4	0	7	2	2	.50	13	.278	.363	.518
1999 Milwaukee	NL	38	117	33	3	0	3	(1	2)	45	13	23	9	1	19	0	0	1	1	0	1.00	0	.282	.331	.385

Richie Barker

Pitches: Right **Bats:** Right **Pos:** RP-5 **Ht:** 6'2" **Wt:** 220 **Born:** 10/29/72 **Age:** 27

| | | HOW MUCH HE PITCHED | | | | | | WHAT HE GAVE UP | | | | | | | | | | | | THE RESULTS | | | | | | |
Year Team	Lg	G	GS	CG	GF	IP	BFP	H	R	ER	HR	SH	SF	HB	TBB	IBB	SO	WP	Bk	W	L	Pct.	ShO	Sv-Op	Hld	ERA
1994 Huntington	R+	17	0	0	6	39.1	187	36	35	26	3	2	2	7	25	0	22	2	3	2	4	.333	0	0--	—	5.95
1995 Rockford	A	32	0	0	15	43.2	196	45	20	18	2	1	0	2	20	1	23	5	0	2	0	1.000	0	1--	—	3.71
1996 Daytona	A+	17	0	0	7	27	135	34	23	17	0	2	1	2	18	0	14	10	0	4	0	1.000	0	0--	—	5.67
Rockford	A	19	0	0	9	33	156	42	24	19	2	1	4	0	15	0	23	3	0	1	1	.500	0	1--	—	5.18
1997 Daytona	A+	29	1	0	10	51	220	49	27	19	3	2	1	3	15	1	38	7	1	2	1	.667	0	1--	—	3.35
Orlando	AA	19	0	0	7	30	121	25	17	11	5	0	1	2	7	0	19	2	0	1	0	1.000	0	2--	—	3.30
1998 West Tenn	AA	51	0	0	42	53.2	227	51	22	16	3	4	0	2	17	0	23	1	1	2	5	.286	0	16--	—	2.68
Iowa	AAA	16	0	0	5	22.1	106	31	14	12	2	2	0	0	5	1	21	4	0	3	1	.750	0	0--	—	4.84
1999 Iowa	AAA	55	2	0	25	74	326	72	37	35	7	3	1	6	30	2	52	7	1	4	4	.500	0	7--	—	4.26
1999 Chicago	NL	5	0	0	1	5	25	6	4	4	0	0	1	0	4	1	3	1	0	0	0	.000	0	0-0	1	7.20

Michael Barrett

Bats: R **Throws:** R **Pos:** 3B-66; C-59; PH/PR-7; SS-2 **Ht:** 6'2" **Wt:** 195 **Born:** 10/22/76 **Age:** 23

Year Team	Lg	G	AB	H	2B	3B	HR	(Hm	Rd)	TB	R	RBI	TBB	IBB	SO	HBP	SH	SF	SB	CS	SB%	GDP	Avg	OBP	SLG
1995 Expos	R	50	183	57	13	4	0	—	—	78	22	19	15	1	19	0	0	1	7	6	.54	1	.311	.362	.426
Vermont	A-	3	10	1	0	0	0	—	—	1	0	1	1	0	1	0	0	0	0	0	.00	0	.100	.167	.100
1996 Delmarva	A	129	474	113	29	4	4	—	—	162	57	62	18	0	42	9	2	5	5	11	.31	9	.238	.277	.342
1997 Wst Plm Bch	A+	119	423	120	30	0	8	—	—	174	52	61	36	1	49	5	2	10	7	4	.64	11	.284	.340	.411
1998 Harrisburg	AA	120	453	145	32	2	19	—	—	238	78	87	27	5	43	2	2	4	7	6	.54	16	.320	.358	.525
1999 Ottawa	AAA	2	7	3	0	0	0	—	—	3	1	2	1	0	0	0	0	0	0	1	.00	0	.429	.500	.429
1998 Montreal	NL	8	23	7	2	0	1	(0	1)	12	3	2	3	0	6	1	0	0	0	0	.00	0	.304	.407	.522
1999 Montreal	NL	126	433	127	32	3	8	(5	3)	189	53	52	32	4	39	3	0	1	0	2	.00	18	.293	.345	.436
2 ML YEARS		134	456	134	34	3	9	(5	4)	201	56	54	35	4	45	4	0	1	0	2	.00	18	.294	.349	.441

Jeff Barry

Bats: B **Throws:** R **Pos:** CF-32; PH/PR-21; RF-15; LF-14 **Ht:** 6'1" **Wt:** 205 **Born:** 9/22/68 **Age:** 31

Year Team	Lg	G	AB	H	2B	3B	HR	(Hm	Rd)	TB	R	RBI	TBB	IBB	SO	HBP	SH	SF	SB	CS	SB%	GDP	Avg	OBP	SLG
1990 Jamestown	A-	51	197	62	6	1	4	—	—	82	30	23	17	2	25	0	2	0	25	5	.83	1	.315	.369	.416
1991 Wst Plm Bch	A+	116	437	92	16	3	4	—	—	126	47	31	34	4	67	4	2	2	20	14	.59	7	.211	.273	.288
1992 St. Lucie	A+	3	9	3	2	0	0	—	—	5	0	1	0	0	0	0	0	0	0	0	.00	0	.333	.333	.556
Mets	R	8	23	4	1	0	0	—	—	5	5	2	6	1	2	0	0	0	2	0	1.00	1	.174	.345	.217
1993 St. Lucie	A+	114	420	108	17	5	4	—	—	147	68	50	49	4	37	5	2	6	17	14	.55	7	.257	.338	.350
1994 Binghamton	AA	110	388	118	24	3	9	—	—	175	48	69	35	4	62	6	1	8	10	11	.48	10	.304	.364	.451
1995 Norfolk	AAA	12	41	9	2	0	0	—	—	11	3	6	3	0	6	1	0	2	0	0	.00	2	.220	.277	.268
Binghamton	AA	80	290	78	17	6	11	—	—	140	49	53	31	6	61	9	0	9	4	1	.80	4	.269	.348	.483
1996 Las Vegas	AAA	4	12	1	0	0	0	—	—	1	0	3	0	0	0	0	0	0	0	0	.00	0	.083	.267	.083
Memphis	AA	91	226	55	7	0	3	—	—	71	29	25	29	5	48	1	1	6	3	7	.30	6	.243	.324	.314
1997 New Haven	AA	40	146	32	4	0	5	—	—	51	21	12	4	0	34	3	1	1	3	2	.60	3	.219	.253	.349
Colo Sprngs	AAA	81	273	82	13	3	13	—	—	140	46	70	30	2	45	4	0	2	5	0	1.00	5	.300	.375	.513

Year Team	Lg	G	AB	H	2B	3B	HR	(Hm	Rd)	TB	R	RBI	TBB	IBB	SO	HBP	SH	SF	SB	CS	SB%	GDP	Avg	OBP	SLG
1998 Colo Sprngs	AAA	100	349	91	19	6	8	—	—	146	55	55	46	3	52	7	0	2	5	1	.83	6	.261	.356	.418
1999 Colo Sprngs	AAA	64	185	63	15	0	10	—	—	108	36	27	19	2	31	0	0	0	6	3	.67	6	.341	.402	.584
1995 New York	NL	15	15	2	1	0	0	(0	0)	3	2	0	1	0	8	0	0	0	0	0	.00	0	.133	.188	.200
1998 Colorado	NL	15	34	6	1	0	0	(0	0)	7	4	2	2	0	11	0	0	1	0	0	.00	0	.176	.216	.206
1999 Colorado	NL	74	168	45	16	0	5	(4	1)	76	19	26	19	1	29	2	0	3	0	4	.00	4	.268	.344	.452
3 ML YEARS		104	217	53	18	0	5	(4	1)	86	25	28	22	1	48	2	0	4	0	4	.00	4	.244	.314	.396

Kimera Bartee

Bats: Right **Throws:** Right **Pos:** CF-38; PH/PR-9; DH-1 **Ht:** 6'0" **Wt:** 200 **Born:** 7/21/72 **Age:** 27

Year Team	Lg	G	AB	H	2B	3B	HR	(Hm	Rd)	TB	R	RBI	TBB	IBB	SO	HBP	SH	SF	SB	CS	SB%	GDP	Avg	OBP	SLG
1999 Toledo *	AAA	104	416	119	13	8	12	—	—	184	64	43	38	0	76	0	5	3	21	9	.70	3	.286	.344	.442
1996 Detroit	AL	110	217	55	6	1	1	(0	1)	66	32	14	17	0	77	0	13	0	20	10	.67	1	.253	.308	.304
1997 Detroit	AL	12	5	1	0	0	0	(0	0)	1	4	0	2	0	2	1	0	0	3	1	.75	0	.200	.500	.200
1998 Detroit	AL	57	98	19	5	1	3	(3	0)	35	20	15	6	0	35	0	0	1	9	5	.64	1	.194	.238	.357
1999 Detroit	AL	41	77	15	1	3	0	(0	0)	22	11	3	9	0	20	0	3	0	3	3	.50	2	.195	.279	.286
4 ML YEARS		220	397	90	12	5	4	(3	1)	124	67	32	34	0	134	1	16	1	35	19	.65	4	.227	.289	.312

Miguel Batista

Pitches: Right **Bats:** Right **Pos:** RP-22; SP-17 **Ht:** 6'0" **Wt:** 190 **Born:** 2/19/71 **Age:** 29

		HOW MUCH HE PITCHED						WHAT HE GAVE UP												THE RESULTS					
Year Team	Lg	G	GS	CG	GF	IP	BFP	H	R	ER	HR	SH	SF	HB	TBB	IBB	SO	WP	Bk	W	L	Pct.	ShO	Sv-Op	Hld	ERA
1999 Ottawa *	AAA	3	3	0	0	8	30	3	2	2	1	0	0	0	4	0	7	0	0	0	1	.000	0	0--	—	2.25
1992 Pittsburgh	NL	1	0	0	1	2	13	4	2	2	1	0	0	0	3	0	1	0	0	0	0	.000	0	0-0	0	9.00
1996 Florida	NL	9	0	0	4	11.1	49	9	8	7	0	3	0	0	7	2	6	1	0	0	0	.000	0	0-0	0	5.56
1997 Chicago	NL	11	6	0	2	36.1	168	36	24	23	4	4	4	1	24	2	27	2	0	0	5	.000	0	0-0	0	5.70
1998 Montreal	NL	56	13	0	12	135	598	141	66	57	12	7	5	6	65	7	92	6	1	3	5	.375	0	0-0	3	3.80
1999 Montreal	NL	39	17	2	3	134.2	606	146	88	73	10	8	11	7	58	2	95	6	0	8	7	.533	1	1-1	0	4.88
5 ML YEARS		116	36	2	22	319.1	1434	336	188	162	27	22	20	14	157	13	221	15	1	11	17	.393	1	1-1	3	4.57

Tony Batista

Bats: Right **Throws:** Right **Pos:** SS-141; PH/PR-4 **Ht:** 6'0" **Wt:** 190 **Born:** 12/9/73 **Age:** 26

Year Team	Lg	G	AB	H	2B	3B	HR	(Hm	Rd)	TB	R	RBI	TBB	IBB	SO	HBP	SH	SF	SB	CS	SB%	GDP	Avg	OBP	SLG
1996 Oakland	AL	74	238	71	10	2	6	(1	5)	103	38	25	19	0	49	1	0	2	7	3	.70	2	.298	.350	.433
1997 Oakland	AL	68	188	38	10	1	4	(0	4)	62	22	18	14	0	31	2	3	0	2	2	.50	8	.202	.265	.330
1998 Arizona	NL	106	293	80	16	1	18	(9	9)	152	46	41	18	0	52	3	0	4	1	1	.50	7	.273	.318	.519
1999 Ari-Tor		142	519	144	30	1	31	(10	21)	269	77	100	38	4	96	6	3	7	4	0	1.00	12	.277	.330	.518
1999 Arizona	NL	44	144	37	5	0	5	(1	4)	57	16	21	16	3	17	2	0	2	2	0	1.00	1	.257	.335	.396
Toronto	AL	98	375	107	25	1	26	(9	17)	212	61	79	22	1	79	4	3	5	2	0	1.00	11	.285	.328	.565
4 ML YEARS		390	1238	333	66	5	59	(20	39)	586	183	184	89	4	228	12	6	13	14	6	.70	29	.269	.321	.473

Howard Battle

Bats: Right **Throws:** Right **Pos:** PH/PR-11; 3B-6 **Ht:** 6'0" **Wt:** 197 **Born:** 3/25/72 **Age:** 28

Year Team	Lg	G	AB	H	2B	3B	HR	(Hm	Rd)	TB	R	RBI	TBB	IBB	SO	HBP	SH	SF	SB	CS	SB%	GDP	Avg	OBP	SLG
1990 Medcine Hat	R+	61	233	62	17	1	5	—	—	96	25	32	15	2	38	2	0	0	5	2	.71	2	.266	.316	.412
1991 Myrtle Bch	A	138	520	147	33	4	20	—	—	248	82	86	49	2	88	3	0	4	15	7	.68	1	.283	.345	.477
1992 Dunedin	A+	136	520	132	27	3	17	—	—	216	76	85	49	3	89	5	1	5	6	8	.43	5	.254	.321	.415
1993 Knoxville	AA	141	521	145	21	5	7	—	—	197	66	70	45	3	94	7	1	3	12	9	.57	8	.278	.342	.378
1994 Syracuse	AAA	139	517	143	26	8	14	—	—	227	72	75	40	4	82	3	1	7	26	2	.93	15	.277	.328	.439
1995 Syracuse	AAA	118	443	111	17	4	8	—	—	160	43	48	39	2	73	3	1	2	10	11	.48	7	.251	.314	.361
1996 Scranton-WB	AAA	115	391	89	24	1	8	—	—	139	37	44	21	0	53	2	2	6	3	8	.27	15	.228	.267	.355
1997 San Antonio	AA	16	33	8	1	0	0	—	—	9	2	1	0	0	7	2	1	0	0	0	.00	0	.242	.286	.273
Albuquerque	AAA	50	139	33	3	2	3	—	—	49	14	16	6	0	23	0	0	2	1	2	.33	3	.237	.265	.353
1998 Birmingham	AA	12	39	7	4	0	1	—	—	14	6	5	4	0	7	0	0	2	0	0	.00	0	.179	.244	.359
Greenville	AA	79	291	96	27	2	10	—	—	157	41	50	35	2	51	2	0	3	3	2	.60	12	.330	.402	.540
1999 Richmond	AAA	121	454	129	29	1	24	—	—	232	80	74	33	2	66	3	0	5	2	3	.40	12	.284	.333	.511
1995 Toronto	AL	9	15	3	0	0	0	(0	0)	3	3	0	4	0	8	0	0	0	1	0	1.00	0	.200	.368	.200
1996 Philadelphia	NL	5	5	0	0	0	0	(0	0)	0	0	0	0	0	2	0	0	0	0	0	.00	0	.000	.000	.000
1999 Atlanta	NL	15	17	6	0	0	1	(1	0)	9	2	5	2	0	3	0	0	0	0	0	.00	0	.353	.421	.529
3 ML YEARS		29	37	9	0	0	1	(1	0)	12	5	5	6	0	13	0	0	0	1	0	1.00	0	.243	.349	.324

Justin Baughman

Bats: Right **Throws:** Right **Pos:** 2B/SS **Ht:** 5'11" **Wt:** 180 **Born:** 8/1/74 **Age:** 25

Year Team	Lg	G	AB	H	2B	3B	HR	(Hm	Rd)	TB	R	RBI	TBB	IBB	SO	HBP	SH	SF	SB	CS	SB%	GDP	Avg	OBP	SLG
1995 Boise	A-	58	215	50	4	3	1	—	—	63	26	20	18	0	38	2	4	1	19	4	.83	2	.233	.297	.293
1996 Cedar Rapds	A	127	464	115	17	8	5	—	—	163	78	48	45	2	78	6	15	1	50	17	.75	13	.248	.322	.351
1997 Lk Elsinore	A+	134	478	131	14	3	2	—	—	157	71	48	40	3	79	13	11	5	68	15	.82	5	.274	.343	.328
1998 Vancouver	AAA	54	222	66	10	4	0	—	—	84	35	15	13	0	28	4	5	2	26	8	.76	7	.297	.344	.378
1998 Anaheim	AL	63	196	50	9	1	1	(0	1)	64	24	20	6	0	36	1	5	3	10	4	.71	4	.255	.277	.327

Danny Bautista

Bats: R **Throws:** R **Pos:** RF-31; LF-22; CF-18; PH/PR-11 **Ht:** 5'11" **Wt:** 170 **Born:** 5/24/72 **Age:** 28

		BATTING																	BASERUNNING				PERCENTAGES		
Year Team	Lg	G	AB	H	2B	3B	HR	(Hm	Rd)	TB	R	RBI	TBB	IBB	SO	HBP	SH	SF	SB	CS	SB%	GDP	Avg	OBP	SLG
1999 Calgary *	AAA	38	135	43	8	1	8	—	—	77	25	28	11	2	18	1	0	0	3	3	.50	1	.319	.374	.570
1993 Detroit	AL	17	61	19	3	0	1	(0	1)	25	6	9	1	0	10	0	0	1	3	1	.75	1	.311	.317	.410
1994 Detroit	AL	31	99	23	4	1	4	(1	3)	41	12	15	3	0	18	0	0	0	1	2	.33	3	.232	.255	.414
1995 Detroit	AL	89	271	55	9	0	7	(3	4)	85	28	27	12	0	68	0	6	0	4	1	.80	6	.203	.237	.314
1996 Det-Atl		42	84	19	2	0	2	(1	1)	27	13	9	11	0	20	1	0	0	1	2	.33	4	.226	.323	.321
1997 Atlanta	NL	64	103	25	3	2	3	(1	2)	41	14	9	5	1	24	1	2	1	2	0	1.00	3	.243	.282	.398
1998 Atlanta	NL	82	144	36	11	0	3	(2	1)	56	17	17	7	0	21	0	3	2	1	0	1.00	4	.250	.281	.389
1999 Florida	NL	70	205	59	10	1	5	(2	3)	86	32	24	4	0	30	1	0	1	3	0	1.00	5	.288	.303	.420
1996 Detroit	AL	25	64	16	2	0	2	(1	1)	24	12	8	9	0	15	0	0	0	1	2	.33	1	.250	.342	.375
Atlanta	NL	17	20	3	0	0	0	(0	0)	3	1	1	2	0	5	1	0	0	0	0	.00	3	.150	.261	.150
7 ML YEARS		395	967	236	42	4	25	(10	15)	361	122	110	43	1	191	3	11	5	15	6	.71	26	.244	.277	.373

Rod Beck

Pitches: Right **Bats:** Right **Pos:** RP-43 **Ht:** 6'1" **Wt:** 235 **Born:** 8/3/68 **Age:** 31

		HOW MUCH HE PITCHED						WHAT HE GAVE UP												THE RESULTS						
Year Team	Lg	G	GS	CG	GF	IP	BFP	H	R	ER	HR	SH	SF	HB	TBB	IBB	SO	WP	Bk	W	L	Pct.	ShO	Sv-Op	Hld	ERA
1999 Iowa *	AAA	2	0	0	1	2	7	1	0	0	0	0	0	0	0	0	2	0	0	0	0	.000	0	0--	—	0.00
1991 San Francisco	NL	31	0	0	10	52.1	214	53	22	22	4	4	2	1	13	2	38	0	0	1	1	.500	0	1-1	1	3.78
1992 San Francisco	NL	65	0	0	42	92	352	62	20	18	4	6	2	2	15	2	87	5	2	3	3	.500	0	17-23	4	1.76
1993 San Francisco	NL	76	0	0	71	79.1	309	57	20	19	11	6	3	3	13	4	86	4	0	3	1	.750	0	48-52	0	2.16
1994 San Francisco	NL	48	0	0	47	48.2	207	49	17	15	10	3	3	0	13	2	39	0	0	2	4	.333	0	28-28	0	2.77
1995 San Francisco	NL	60	0	0	52	58.2	255	60	31	29	7	4	3	2	21	3	42	2	0	5	6	.455	0	33-43	0	4.45
1996 San Francisco	NL	63	0	0	58	62	248	56	23	23	9	0	2	1	10	2	48	1	0	0	9	.000	0	35-42	0	3.34
1997 San Francisco	NL	73	0	0	66	70	281	67	31	27	7	1	0	2	8	2	53	1	0	7	4	.636	0	37-45	1	3.47
1998 Chicago	NL	81	0	0	70	80.1	349	86	33	27	11	2	5	2	20	4	81	2	0	3	4	.429	0	51-58	1	3.02
1999 ChC-Bos		43	0	0	27	44	196	50	29	29	5	2	2	1	18	3	25	1	0	2	5	.286	0	10-15	3	5.93
1999 Chicago	NL	31	0	0	19	30	141	41	26	26	5	2	2	0	13	3	13	1	0	2	4	.333	0	7-11	1	7.80
Boston	AL	12	0	0	8	14	55	9	3	3	0	0	0	1	5	0	12	0	0	0	1	.000	0	3-4	2	1.93
9 ML YEARS		540	0	0	443	587.1	2411	540	226	209	68	28	22	14	131	24	499	16	2	26	37	.413	0	260-307	10	3.20

Rich Becker

Bats: L **Throws:** L **Pos:** PH/PR-53; CF-51; LF-33; RF-25; DH-3 **Ht:** 5'10" **Wt:** 193 **Born:** 2/1/72 **Age:** 28

		BATTING																	BASERUNNING				PERCENTAGES		
Year Team	Lg	G	AB	H	2B	3B	HR	(Hm	Rd)	TB	R	RBI	TBB	IBB	SO	HBP	SH	SF	SB	CS	SB%	GDP	Avg	OBP	SLG
1993 Minnesota	AL	3	7	2	2	0	0	(0	0)	4	3	0	5	0	4	0	0	0	1	1	.50	0	.286	.583	.571
1994 Minnesota	AL	28	98	26	3	0	1	(1	0)	32	12	8	13	0	25	0	1	0	6	1	.86	2	.265	.351	.327
1995 Minnesota	AL	106	392	93	15	1	2	(1	1)	116	45	33	34	0	95	4	6	2	8	9	.47	9	.237	.303	.296
1996 Minnesota	AL	148	525	152	31	4	12	(8	4)	228	92	71	68	1	118	2	5	4	19	5	.79	14	.291	.372	.434
1997 Minnesota	AL	132	443	117	22	3	10	(4	6)	175	61	45	62	1	130	1	2	2	17	5	.77	4	.264	.354	.395
1998 NYM-Bal		128	213	42	5	2	6	(4	2)	69	37	21	43	2	76	2	2	0	5	1	.83	7	.197	.337	.324
1999 Mil-Oak		129	264	68	8	2	6	(5	1)	98	36	26	58	0	81	4	2	3	8	2	.80	7	.258	.395	.371
1998 New York	NL	49	100	19	4	2	3	(3	0)	36	15	10	21	2	42	0	0	0	3	1	.75	1	.190	.331	.360
Baltimore	AL	79	113	23	1	0	3	(1	2)	33	22	11	22	0	34	2	2	0	2	0	1.00	6	.204	.343	.292
1999 Milwaukee	NL	89	139	35	5	2	5	(4	1)	59	15	16	33	0	38	0	2	0	5	0	1.00	4	.252	.395	.424
Oakland	AL	40	125	33	3	0	1	(1	0)	39	21	10	25	0	43	2	1	0	3	2	.60	3	.264	.395	.312
7 ML YEARS		674	1942	501	86	12	37	(23	14)	722	286	204	283	4	529	11	19	8	64	24	.73	43	.258	.354	.372

Tim Belcher

Pitches: Right **Bats:** Right **Pos:** SP-24 **Ht:** 6'3" **Wt:** 225 **Born:** 10/19/61 **Age:** 38

		HOW MUCH HE PITCHED						WHAT HE GAVE UP												THE RESULTS						
Year Team	Lg	G	GS	CG	GF	IP	BFP	H	R	ER	HR	SH	SF	HB	TBB	IBB	SO	WP	Bk	W	L	Pct.	ShO	Sv-Op	Hld	ERA
1987 Los Angeles	NL	6	5	0	1	34	135	30	11	9	2	2	1	0	7	0	23	0	1	4	2	.667	0	0-0	0	2.38
1988 Los Angeles	NL	36	27	4	5	179.2	719	143	65	58	8	6	1	2	51	7	152	4	0	12	6	.667	1	4-5	0	2.91
1989 Los Angeles	NL	39	30	10	6	230	937	182	81	72	20	6	6	7	80	5	200	7	2	15	12	.556	8	1-1	0	2.82
1990 Los Angeles	NL	24	24	5	0	153	627	136	76	68	17	5	6	2	48	0	102	6	1	9	9	.500	2	0-0	0	4.00
1991 Los Angeles	NL	33	33	2	0	209.1	880	189	76	61	10	11	3	2	75	3	156	7	0	10	9	.526	1	0-0	0	2.62
1992 Cincinnati	NL	35	34	2	1	227.2	949	201	104	99	17	12	11	3	80	2	149	3	1	15	14	.517	1	0-0	0	3.91
1993 Cin-CWS		34	33	5	0	208.2	886	198	108	103	19	8	4	8	74	4	135	6	0	12	11	.522	3	0-0	0	4.44
1994 Detroit	AL	25	25	3	0	162	750	192	124	106	21	3	3	4	78	10	76	6	1	7	15	.318	0	0-0	0	5.89
1995 Seattle	AL	28	28	1	0	179.1	802	188	101	90	19	4	5	5	88	5	96	6	0	10	12	.455	0	0-0	0	4.52
1996 Kansas City	AL	35	35	4	0	238.2	1021	262	117	104	28	6	10	6	68	4	113	7	0	15	11	.577	1	0-0	0	3.92
1997 Kansas City	AL	32	32	3	0	213.1	927	242	128	119	31	7	4	5	70	2	113	7	1	13	12	.520	1	0-0	0	5.02
1998 Kansas City	AL	34	34	2	0	234	1003	247	127	111	37	5	9	7	73	0	130	6	1	14	14	.500	0	0-0	0	4.27
1999 Anaheim	AL	24	24	0	0	132.1	600	168	104	99	27	6	3	5	46	0	52	7	1	6	8	.429	0	0-0	0	6.73
1993 Cincinnati	NL	22	22	4	0	137	590	134	72	68	11	6	3	7	47	4	101	6	0	9	6	.600	2	0-0	0	4.47
Chicago	AL	12	11	1	0	71.2	296	64	36	35	8	2	1	1	27	0	34	0	0	3	5	.375	1	0-0	0	4.40
13 ML YEARS		385	364	41	13	2402	10236	2378	1222	1099	256	81	72	56	838	42	1497	72	9	142	135	.513	18	5-6	0	4.12

Stan Belinda

Pitches: Right **Bats:** Right **Pos:** RP-29 **Ht:** 6'3" **Wt:** 215 **Born:** 8/6/66 **Age:** 33

		HOW MUCH HE PITCHED					WHAT HE GAVE UP											THE RESULTS					
Year Team	Lg	G	GS	CG	GF	IP	BFP	H	R	ER	HR	SH	SF	HB	TBB	IBB	SO	WP	Bk	W	L	Pct.	ShO	Sv-Op	Hld	ERA
1999 Indianapols *	AAA	10	0	0	2	11.1	47	7	3	3	1	0	0	2	6	0	10	0	0	2	0	1.000	0	0- –	—	2.38
1989 Pittsburgh	NL	8	0	0	2	10.1	46	13	8	7	0	0	0	0	2	0	10	1	0	0	1	.000	0	0-0	2	6.10
1990 Pittsburgh	NL	55	0	0	17	58.1	245	48	23	23	4	2	2	1	29	3	55	1	0	3	4	.429	0	8-13	9	3.55
1991 Pittsburgh	NL	60	0	0	37	78.1	318	50	30	30	10	4	3	4	35	4	71	2	0	7	5	.583	0	16-20	6	3.45
1992 Pittsburgh	NL	59	0	0	42	71.1	299	58	26	25	8	4	6	0	29	5	57	1	0	6	4	.600	0	18-24	0	3.15
1993 Pit-KC		63	0	0	44	69.2	287	65	31	30	6	3	2	2	17	4	55	2	0	4	2	.667	0	19-23	8	3.88
1994 Kansas City	AL	37	0	0	10	49	220	47	36	28	6	0	3	5	24	3	37	1	0	2	2	.500	0	1-2	5	5.14
1995 Boston	AL	63	0	0	30	69.2	285	51	25	24	5	0	4	4	28	3	57	2	0	8	1	.889	0	10-14	17	3.10
1996 Boston	AL	31	0	0	10	28.2	139	31	22	21	3	1	4	0	20	1	18	2	0	2	1	.667	0	2-4	7	6.59
1997 Cincinnati	NL	84	0	0	18	99.1	420	84	42	41	11	6	5	9	33	6	114	5	0	1	5	.167	0	1-5	28	3.71
1998 Cincinnati	NL	40	0	0	24	61.1	254	46	23	22	7	7	1	1	28	6	57	3	0	4	8	.333	0	1-2	4	3.23
1999 Cincinnati	NL	29	0	0	12	42.2	185	42	26	25	11	2	1	1	18	3	40	3	0	3	1	.750	0	2-2	2	5.27
1993 Pittsburgh	NL	40	0	0	37	42.1	171	35	18	17	4	1	2	1	11	4	30	0	0	3	1	.750	0	19-22	6	3.61
Kansas City	AL	23	0	0	7	27.1	116	30	13	13	2	2	0	1	6	0	25	2	0	1	1	.500	0	0-1	8	4.28
11 ML YEARS		529	0	0	246	638.2	2698	535	292	276	71	29	27	31	263	38	571	23	0	40	34	.541	0	78-109	88	3.89

David Bell

Bats: R **Throws:** R **Pos:** 2B-154; 1B-4; PH/PR-2; SS-1 **Ht:** 5'10" **Wt:** 175 **Born:** 9/14/72 **Age:** 27

		BATTING																BASERUNNING				PERCENTAGES		
Year Team	Lg	G	AB	H	2B	3B	HR	(Hm	Rd)	TB	R	RBI	TBB	IBB	SO	HBP	SH	SF	SB	CS	SB%	GDP	Avg	OBP	SLG
1995 Cle-StL		41	146	36	7	2	2	(1	1)	53	13	19	4	0	25	2	0	1	1	2	.33	0	.247	.275	.363
1996 St. Louis	NL	62	145	31	6	0	1	(1	0)	40	12	9	10	2	22	1	0	1	1	1	.50	3	.214	.268	.276
1997 St. Louis	NL	66	142	30	7	1	1	(1	0)	44	9	12	10	2	28	0	2	1	1	0	1.00	2	.211	.261	.310
1998 StL-Cle-Sea		132	429	117	30	2	10	(2	8)	181	48	49	27	4	65	2	1	5	0	4	.00	11	.273	.315	.422
1999 Seattle	AL	157	597	160	31	2	21	(11	10)	258	92	78	58	0	90	2	3	7	7	4	.64	7	.268	.331	.432
1995 Cleveland	AL	2	2	0	0	0	0	(0	0)	0	0	0	0	0	0	0	0	0	0	0	.00	0	.000	.000	.000
St. Louis	NL	39	144	36	7	2	2	(1	1)	53	13	19	4	0	25	2	0	1	1	2	.33	0	.250	.278	.368
1998 St. Louis	NL	4	9	2	1	0	0	(0	0)	3	0	0	0	0	3	0	0	0	0	0	.00	0	.222	.222	.333
Cleveland	AL	107	340	89	21	2	10	(2	8)	144	37	41	22	4	54	2	1	5	0	4	.00	8	.262	.306	.424
Seattle	AL	21	80	26	8	0	0	(0	0)	34	11	8	5	0	8	0	0	0	0	0	.00	3	.325	.365	.425
5 ML YEARS		458	1459	374	81	8	35	(16	19)	576	174	167	109	8	230	7	6	15	10	11	.48	23	.256	.308	.395

Derek Bell

Bats: Right **Throws:** Right **Pos:** RF-126; PH/PR-4 **Ht:** 6'2" **Wt:** 215 **Born:** 12/11/68 **Age:** 31

		BATTING																BASERUNNING				PERCENTAGES		
Year Team	Lg	G	AB	H	2B	3B	HR	(Hm	Rd)	TB	R	RBI	TBB	IBB	SO	HBP	SH	SF	SB	CS	SB%	GDP	Avg	OBP	SLG
1991 Toronto	AL	18	28	4	0	0	0	(0	0)	4	5	1	6	0	5	1	0	0	3	2	.60	0	.143	.314	.143
1992 Toronto	AL	61	161	39	6	3	2	(2	0)	57	23	15	15	1	34	5	2	1	7	2	.78	6	.242	.324	.354
1993 San Diego	NL	150	542	142	19	1	21	(12	9)	226	73	72	23	5	122	12	0	8	26	5	.84	7	.262	.303	.417
1994 San Diego	NL	108	434	135	20	0	14	(8	6)	197	54	54	29	5	88	1	0	2	24	8	.75	14	.311	.354	.454
1995 Houston	NL	112	452	151	21	2	8	(3	5)	200	63	86	33	2	71	8	0	6	27	9	.75	10	.334	.385	.442
1996 Houston	NL	158	627	165	40	3	17	(8	9)	262	84	113	40	8	123	8	0	9	29	3	.91	18	.263	.311	.418
1997 Houston	NL	129	463	136	29	3	15	(7	8)	216	67	71	40	3	94	12	0	2	15	7	.68	16	.276	.344	.438
1998 Houston	NL	156	630	198	41	2	22	(12	10)	309	111	108	51	0	126	4	0	10	13	3	.81	14	.314	.364	.490
1999 Houston	NL	128	509	120	22	0	12	(5	7)	178	61	66	50	1	129	4	0	5	18	6	.75	20	.236	.306	.350
9 ML YEARS		1020	3876	1090	198	14	111	(57	54)	1649	541	586	287	25	792	55	2	43	162	45	.78	105	.281	.336	.425

Jay Bell

Bats: R **Throws:** R **Pos:** 2B-148; PH/PR-4; DH-2; SS-1 **Ht:** 6'0" **Wt:** 184 **Born:** 12/11/65 **Age:** 34

		BATTING																BASERUNNING				PERCENTAGES		
Year Team	Lg	G	AB	H	2B	3B	HR	(Hm	Rd)	TB	R	RBI	TBB	IBB	SO	HBP	SH	SF	SB	CS	SB%	GDP	Avg	OBP	SLG
1986 Cleveland	AL	5	14	5	2	0	1	(0	1)	10	3	4	2	0	3	0	0	0	0	0	.00	0	.357	.438	.714
1987 Cleveland	AL	38	125	27	9	1	2	(1	1)	44	14	13	8	0	31	1	3	0	2	0	1.00	0	.216	.269	.352
1988 Cleveland	AL	73	211	46	5	1	2	(2	0)	59	23	21	21	0	53	1	1	2	4	2	.67	3	.218	.289	.280
1989 Pittsburgh	NL	78	271	70	13	3	2	(1	1)	95	33	27	19	0	47	1	10	2	5	3	.63	9	.258	.307	.351
1990 Pittsburgh	NL	159	583	148	28	7	7	(1	6)	211	93	52	65	0	109	3	39	6	10	6	.63	14	.254	.329	.362
1991 Pittsburgh	NL	157	608	164	32	8	16	(7	9)	260	96	67	52	1	99	4	30	3	10	6	.63	15	.270	.330	.428
1992 Pittsburgh	NL	159	632	167	36	6	9	(5	4)	242	87	55	55	0	103	4	19	2	7	5	.58	12	.264	.326	.383
1993 Pittsburgh	NL	154	604	187	32	9	9	(3	6)	264	102	51	77	6	122	6	13	1	16	10	.62	16	.310	.392	.437
1994 Pittsburgh	NL	110	424	117	35	4	9	(3	6)	187	68	45	49	1	82	3	8	3	2	0	1.00	15	.276	.353	.441
1995 Pittsburgh	NL	138	530	139	28	4	13	(8	5)	214	79	55	55	1	110	4	3	1	2	5	.29	13	.262	.336	.404
1996 Pittsburgh	NL	151	527	132	29	3	13	(7	6)	206	65	71	54	5	108	5	6	6	6	4	.60	10	.250	.323	.391
1997 Kansas City	AL	153	573	167	28	3	21	(10	11)	264	89	92	71	2	101	4	3	9	10	6	.63	13	.291	.368	.461
1998 Arizona	NL	155	549	138	29	5	20	(11	9)	237	79	67	81	3	129	7	5	3	3	5	.38	14	.251	.353	.432
1999 Arizona	NL	151	589	170	32	6	38	(21	17)	328	132	112	82	2	132	4	4	9	7	4	.64	9	.289	.374	.557
14 ML YEARS		1681	6240	1677	338	60	162	(80	82)	2621	963	732	691	21	1229	47	144	47	84	56	.60	143	.269	.344	.420

Albert Belle

Bats: Right **Throws:** Right **Pos:** RF-154; DH-7   **Ht:** 6'2" **Wt:** 225 **Born:** 8/25/66 **Age:** 33

Year Team	Lg	G	AB	H	2B	3B	HR	(Hm	Rd)	TB	R	RBI	TBB	IBB	SO	HBP	SH	SF	SB	CS	SB%	GDP	Avg	OBP	SLG
1989 Cleveland	AL	62	218	49	8	4	7	(3	4)	86	22	37	12	0	55	2	0	2	2	2	.50	4	.225	.269	.394
1990 Cleveland	AL	9	23	4	0	0	1	(1	0)	7	1	3	1	0	6	0	1	0	0	0	.00	1	.174	.208	.304
1991 Cleveland	AL	123	461	130	31	2	28	(8	20)	249	60	95	25	2	99	5	0	5	3	1	.75	24	.282	.323	.540
1992 Cleveland	AL	153	585	152	23	1	34	(15	19)	279	81	112	52	5	128	4	1	8	8	2	.80	18	.260	.320	.477
1993 Cleveland	AL	159	594	172	36	3	38	(20	18)	328	93	129	76	13	96	8	1	14	23	12	.66	18	.290	.370	.552
1994 Cleveland	AL	106	412	147	35	2	36	(21	15)	294	90	101	58	9	71	5	1	4	9	6	.60	5	.357	.438	.714
1995 Cleveland	AL	143	546	173	52	1	50	(25	25)	377	121	126	73	5	80	6	0	4	5	2	.71	24	.317	.401	.690
1996 Cleveland	AL	158	602	187	38	3	48	(22	26)	375	124	148	99	15	87	7	0	7	11	0	1.00	20	.311	.410	.623
1997 Chicago	AL	161	634	174	45	1	30	(14	16)	311	90	116	53	6	105	6	0	8	4	4	.50	26	.274	.332	.491
1998 Chicago	AL	163	609	200	48	2	49	(29	20)	399	113	152	81	10	84	1	0	15	6	4	.60	17	.328	.399	.655
1999 Baltimore	AL	161	610	181	36	1	37	(19	18)	330	108	117	101	15	82	7	0	4	17	3	.85	19	.297	.400	.541
11 ML YEARS		1398	5294	1569	352	20	358	(177	181)	3035	903	1136	631	80	893	51	4	71	88	36	.71	176	.296	.372	.573

Ron Belliard

Bats: R **Throws:** R **Pos:** 2B-119; PH/PR-6; 3B-1; SS-1   **Ht:** 5'8" **Wt:** 180 **Born:** 4/7/75 **Age:** 25

Year Team	Lg	G	AB	H	2B	3B	HR	(Hm	Rd)	TB	R	RBI	TBB	IBB	SO	HBP	SH	SF	SB	CS	SB%	GDP	Avg	OBP	SLG
1994 Brewers	R	39	143	42	7	3	0	—	—	55	32	27	14	1	25	3	2	1	7	0	1.00	3	.294	.366	.385
1995 Beloit	A	130	461	137	28	5	13	—	—	214	76	76	36	2	67	7	2	1	16	12	.57	10	.297	.356	.464
1996 El Paso	AA	109	416	116	20	8	3	—	—	161	73	57	60	1	51	4	4	3	26	10	.72	11	.279	.373	.387
1997 Tucson	AAA	118	443	125	35	4	4	—	—	180	80	55	61	1	69	11	3	5	10	7	.59	13	.282	.379	.406
1998 Louisville	AAA	133	507	163	36	7	14	—	—	255	114	73	69	2	77	8	1	4	33	12	.73	17	.321	.408	.503
1999 Louisville	AAA	29	108	26	4	0	1	—	—	33	14	8	14	0	13	1	0	1	12	3	.80	3	.241	.331	.306
1998 Milwaukee	NL	8	5	1	0	0	0	(0	0)	1	1	0	0	0	0	0	0	0	0	0	.00	0	.200	.200	.200
1999 Milwaukee	NL	124	457	135	29	4	8	(5	3)	196	60	58	64	0	59	0	6	4	4	5	.44	16	.295	.379	.429
2 ML YEARS		132	462	136	29	4	8	(5	3)	197	61	58	64	0	59	0	6	4	4	5	.44	16	.294	.377	.426

Clay Bellinger

Bats: R **Throws:** R **Pos:** 3B-16; PH/PR-14; 1B-8; DH-4; LF-2; 2B-1; SS-1   **Ht:** 6'3" **Wt:** 195 **Born:** 11/18/68 **Age:** 31

Year Team	Lg	G	AB	H	2B	3B	HR	(Hm	Rd)	TB	R	RBI	TBB	IBB	SO	HBP	SH	SF	SB	CS	SB%	GDP	Avg	OBP	SLG
1989 Everett	A-	51	185	37	8	1	4	—	—	59	29	16	19	0	47	1	1	0	3	2	.60	4	.200	.278	.319
1990 Clinton	A	109	382	83	17	4	10	—	—	138	52	48	28	0	102	7	5	3	13	6	.68	5	.217	.281	.361
1991 San Jose	A+	105	368	95	29	2	8	—	—	152	65	62	53	3	88	11	7	6	13	4	.76	3	.258	.363	.413
1992 Shreveport	AA	126	433	90	18	3	13	—	—	153	45	50	36	1	82	3	4	4	8	8	.47	15	.208	.271	.353
1993 Phoenix	AAA	122	407	104	20	3	6	—	—	148	50	49	38	4	81	4	7	5	7	7	.50	8	.256	.322	.364
1994 Phoenix	AAA	106	337	90	15	1	7	—	—	128	48	50	18	0	56	7	2	3	6	1	.86	8	.267	.315	.380
1995 Phoenix	AAA	97	277	76	16	1	2	—	—	100	34	32	27	1	52	2	2	3	3	2	.60	5	.274	.340	.361
1996 Rochester	AAA	125	459	138	34	4	15	—	—	225	68	78	33	0	90	6	1	11	8	4	.67	6	.301	.348	.490
1997 Columbus	AAA	111	416	114	31	3	12	—	—	187	55	59	34	2	74	7	2	1	10	4	.71	10	.274	.338	.450
1998 Columbus	AAA	115	397	89	20	2	9	—	—	140	35	40	35	2	79	5	1	4	6	3	.67	10	.224	.293	.353
1999 Columbus	AAA	40	141	33	10	1	2	—	—	51	19	14	11	0	32	2	0	4	6	0	1.00	1	.234	.300	.362
1999 New York	AL	32	45	9	2	0	1	(1	0)	14	12	2	1	0	10	0	0	0	1	0	1.00	1	.200	.217	.311

Carlos Beltran

Bats: Both **Throws:** Right **Pos:** CF-154; DH-2; PH/PR-1   **Ht:** 6'0" **Wt:** 175 **Born:** 4/24/77 **Age:** 23

Year Team	Lg	G	AB	H	2B	3B	HR	(Hm	Rd)	TB	R	RBI	TBB	IBB	SO	HBP	SH	SF	SB	CS	SB%	GDP	Avg	OBP	SLG
1995 Royals	R	52	180	50	9	0	0	—	—	59	29	23	13	0	30	3	1	3	5	3	.63	1	.278	.332	.328
1996 Lansing	A	11	42	6	2	0	0	—	—	8	3	0	1	0	11	0	0	0	1	0	1.00	1	.143	.163	.190
Spokane	A-	59	215	58	8	3	7	—	—	93	29	29	31	0	65	0	3	2	10	2	.83	4	.270	.359	.433
1997 Wilmington	A+	120	419	96	15	4	11	—	—	152	57	46	46	3	96	4	3	1	17	7	.71	10	.229	.311	.363
1998 Wilmington	A+	52	192	53	14	0	5	—	—	82	32	32	25	0	39	2	0	1	11	7	.61	2	.276	.364	.427
Wichita	AA	47	182	64	13	3	14	—	—	125	50	44	23	3	30	1	2	0	7	1	.88	4	.352	.427	.687
1998 Kansas City	AL	14	58	16	5	3	0	(0	0)	27	12	7	3	0	12	1	0	1	3	0	1.00	1	.276	.317	.466
1999 Kansas City	AL	156	663	194	27	7	22	(12	10)	301	112	108	46	2	123	4	0	10	27	8	.77	17	.293	.337	.454
2 ML YEARS		170	721	210	32	10	22	(12	10)	328	124	115	49	2	135	5	0	11	30	8	.79	19	.291	.336	.455

Rigo Beltran

Pitches: Left **Bats:** Left **Pos:** RP-33   **Ht:** 5'11" **Wt:** 185 **Born:** 11/13/69 **Age:** 30

	HOW MUCH HE PITCHED						WHAT HE GAVE UP											THE RESULTS					
Year Team	Lg	G	GS	CG	GF	IP	BFP	H	R	ER	HR	SH	SF	HB	TBB	IBB	SO	WP	Bk	W	L	Pct.	ShO	Sv-Op	Hld	ERA
1999 Norfolk *	AAA	21	0	0	4	22.1	93	16	5	4	1	1	0	1	12	1	27	1	0	2	1	.667	0	0- —	—	1.61
Colo Sprngs *	AAA	6	0	0	2	8	41	12	3	2	1	0	0	1	5	1	12	1	0	1	0	1.000	0	0- —	—	2.25
1997 St. Louis	NL	35	4	0	16	54.1	224	47	25	21	3	6	3	0	17	0	50	1	0	1	2	.333	0	1-1	2	3.48
1998 New York	NL	7	0	0	0	8	33	6	3	3	1	0	1	0	4	0	5	0	0	0	0	.000	0	0-0	1	3.38
1999 NYM-Col	NL	33	0	0	12	42	195	50	24	21	7	3	0	1	19	3	50	7	0	1	1	.500	0	0-0	1	4.50
1999 New York	NL	21	0	0	10	31	134	30	15	12	5	2	0	0	12	2	35	6	0	1	1	.500	0	0-0	1	3.48
Colorado	NL	12	0	0	2	11	61	20	9	9	2	1	0	1	7	1	15	1	0	0	0	.000	0	0-0	0	7.36
3 ML YEARS		75	4	0	28	104.1	452	103	52	45	11	9	4	1	40	3	105	8	0	2	3	.400	0	1-1	3	3.88

Adrian Beltre

Bats: Right **Throws:** Right **Pos:** 3B-152; PH/PR-1   **Ht:** 5'11" **Wt:** 165 **Born:** 4/7/78 **Age:** 22

								BATTING											BASERUNNING				PERCENTAGES		
Year Team	Lg	G	AB	H	2B	3B	HR	(Hm	Rd)	TB	R	RBI	TBB	IBB	SO	HBP	SH	SF	SB	CS	SB%	GDP	Avg	OBP	SLG
1996 Savannah	A	68	244	75	14	3	16	—	—	143	48	59	35	2	46	7	0	2	4	3	.57	7	.307	.406	.586
San Berndno	A+	63	238	62	13	1	10	—	—	107	40	40	19	0	44	5	1	5	3	4	.43	3	.261	.322	.450
1997 Vero Beach	A+	123	435	138	24	2	26	—	—	244	95	104	67	12	66	6	0	11	25	9	.74	9	.317	.407	.561
1998 San Antonio	AA	64	246	79	21	2	13	—	—	143	49	56	39	2	37	2	0	5	20	4	.83	3	.321	.411	.581
1998 Los Angeles	NL	77	195	42	9	0	7	(5	2)	72	18	22	14	0	37	3	2	0	3	1	.75	4	.215	.278	.369
1999 Los Angeles	NL	152	538	148	27	5	15	(6	9)	230	84	67	61	12	105	6	4	5	18	7	.72	4	.275	.352	.428
2 ML YEARS		229	733	190	36	5	22	(11	11)	302	102	89	75	12	142	9	6	5	21	8	.72	8	.259	.333	.412

Marvin Benard

Bats: L **Throws:** L **Pos:** CF-123; RF-20; PH/PR-11; LF-4   **Ht:** 5'9" **Wt:** 185 **Born:** 1/20/70 **Age:** 30

								BATTING											BASERUNNING				PERCENTAGES		
Year Team	Lg	G	AB	H	2B	3B	HR	(Hm	Rd)	TB	R	RBI	TBB	IBB	SO	HBP	SH	SF	SB	CS	SB%	GDP	Avg	OBP	SLG
1995 San Francisco	NL	13	34	13	2	0	1	(0	1)	18	5	4	1	0	7	0	0	0	1	0	1.00	1	.382	.400	.529
1996 San Francisco	NL	135	488	121	17	4	5	(2	3)	161	89	27	59	2	84	4	6	1	25	11	.69	8	.248	.333	.330
1997 San Francisco	NL	84	114	26	4	0	1	(0	1)	33	13	13	13	0	29	2	0	1	3	1	.75	2	.228	.315	.289
1998 San Francisco	NL	121	286	92	21	1	3	(2	1)	124	41	36	34	1	39	2	4	1	11	4	.73	3	.322	.396	.434
1999 San Francisco	NL	149	562	163	36	5	16	(9	7)	257	100	64	55	2	97	6	1	1	27	14	.66	5	.290	.359	.457
5 ML YEARS		502	1484	415	80	10	26	(13	13)	593	248	144	162	5	256	14	11	4	67	30	.69	19	.280	.355	.400

Alan Benes

Pitches: Right **Bats:** Right **Pos:** RP-2   **Ht:** 6'5" **Wt:** 215 **Born:** 1/21/72 **Age:** 28

		HOW MUCH HE PITCHED						WHAT HE GAVE UP											THE RESULTS					
Year Team	Lg	G	GS	CG	GF	IP	BFP	H	R	ER	HR	SH	SF	HB	TBB	IBB	SO	WP	Bk	W	L	Pct.	ShO	Sv-Op	Hld	ERA
1999 Arkansas *	AA	2	2	0	0	4.1	19	6	3	3	0	0	0	0	1	0	0	0	0	0	0	.000	0	0--	—	6.23
Potomac *	A+	2	2	0	0	5	18	1	1	1	0	0	1	0	4	0	2	0	0	0	0	.000	0	0--	—	1.80
Memphis *	AAA	3	3	0	0	5.2	25	8	3	2	0	0	0	0	2	0	3	0	0	0	0	.000	0	0--	—	3.18
1995 St. Louis	NL	3	3	0	0	16	76	24	15	15	2	1	0	1	4	0	20	3	0	1	2	.333	0	0-0	0	8.44
1996 St. Louis	NL	34	32	3	1	191	840	192	120	104	27	15	9	7	87	3	131	5	1	13	10	.565	1	0-0	0	4.90
1997 St. Louis	NL	23	23	2	0	161.2	666	128	60	52	13	5	4	4	68	3	160	9	2	9	9	.500	0	0-0	0	2.89
1999 St. Louis	NL	2	0	0	2	2	7	2	0	0	0	0	0	0	0	0	2	0	0	0	0	.000	0	0-0	0	0.00
4 ML YEARS		62	58	5	3	370.2	1589	346	195	171	42	21	13	12	159	6	313	17	3	23	21	.523	1	0-0	0	4.15

Andy Benes

Pitches: Right **Bats:** Right **Pos:** SP-32; RP-1   **Ht:** 6'6" **Wt:** 245 **Born:** 8/20/67 **Age:** 32

		HOW MUCH HE PITCHED						WHAT HE GAVE UP											THE RESULTS					
Year Team	Lg	G	GS	CG	GF	IP	BFP	H	R	ER	HR	SH	SF	HB	TBB	IBB	SO	WP	Bk	W	L	Pct.	ShO	Sv-Op	Hld	ERA
1989 San Diego	NL	10	10	0	0	66.2	280	51	28	26	7	6	2	1	31	0	66	0	3	6	3	.667	0	0-0	0	3.51
1990 San Diego	NL	32	31	2	1	192.1	811	177	87	77	18	5	6	1	69	5	140	2	5	10	11	.476	0	0-0	0	3.60
1991 San Diego	NL	33	33	4	0	223	908	194	76	75	23	5	4	4	59	7	167	3	4	15	11	.577	1	0-0	0	3.03
1992 San Diego	NL	34	34	2	0	231.1	961	230	94	86	14	19	6	5	61	6	169	1	1	13	14	.481	2	0-0	0	3.35
1993 San Diego	NL	34	34	4	0	230.2	968	200	111	97	23	10	6	4	86	7	179	14	2	15	15	.500	2	0-0	0	3.78
1994 San Diego	NL	25	25	2	0	172.1	717	155	82	74	20	11	1	1	51	2	189	4	0	6	14	.300	2	0-0	0	3.86
1995 SD-Sea		31	31	1	0	181.2	809	193	107	96	18	4	8	6	78	5	171	5	0	11	9	.550	1	0-0	0	4.76
1996 St. Louis	NL	36	34	3	1	230.1	963	215	107	107	28	2	6	6	77	7	160	6	0	18	10	.643	1	1-1	0	3.83
1997 St. Louis	NL	26	26	0	0	177	727	149	64	61	9	6	7	5	61	4	175	7	0	10	7	.588	0	0-0	0	3.10
1998 Arizona	NL	34	34	1	0	231.1	979	221	111	102	25	11	8	6	74	3	164	9	1	14	13	.519	0	0-0	0	3.97
1999 Arizona	NL	33	32	0	0	198.1	886	216	117	106	34	6	3	4	82	3	141	10	0	13	12	.520	0	0-0	0	4.81
1995 San Diego	NL	19	19	1	0	118.2	518	121	65	55	10	3	4	4	45	3	126	3	0	4	7	.364	1	0-0	0	4.17
Seattle	AL	12	12	0	0	63	291	72	42	41	8	1	4	2	33	2	45	2	0	7	2	.778	0	0-0	0	5.86
11 ML YEARS		328	324	19	2	2135	9009	2001	980	898	219	85	57	43	729	49	1721	61	16	131	119	.524	9	1-1	0	3.79

Armando Benitez

Pitches: Right **Bats:** Right **Pos:** RP-77   **Ht:** 6'4" **Wt:** 229 **Born:** 11/3/72 **Age:** 27

		HOW MUCH HE PITCHED						WHAT HE GAVE UP											THE RESULTS					
Year Team	Lg	G	GS	CG	GF	IP	BFP	H	R	ER	HR	SH	SF	HB	TBB	IBB	SO	WP	Bk	W	L	Pct.	ShO	Sv-Op	Hld	ERA
1994 Baltimore	AL	3	0	0	1	10	42	8	1	1	0	0	0	1	4	0	14	0	0	0	0	.000	0	0-0	0	0.90
1995 Baltimore	AL	44	0	0	18	47.2	221	37	33	30	8	2	3	5	37	2	56	3	1	1	5	.167	0	2-5	6	5.66
1996 Baltimore	AL	18	0	0	8	14.1	56	7	6	6	2	0	1	0	6	0	20	1	0	1	0	1.000	0	4-5	1	3.77
1997 Baltimore	AL	71	0	0	26	73.1	307	49	22	20	7	2	4	1	43	5	106	1	0	4	5	.444	0	9-10	20	2.45
1998 Baltimore	AL	71	0	0	54	68.1	289	48	29	29	10	3	2	4	39	2	87	0	0	5	6	.455	0	22-26	3	3.82
1999 New York	NL	77	0	0	42	78	312	40	17	16	4	0	0	0	41	4	128	2	0	4	3	.571	0	22-28	17	1.85
6 ML YEARS		284	0	0	149	291.2	1227	189	108	102	31	7	10	11	170	13	411	7	1	15	19	.441	0	59-74	47	3.15

Mike Benjamin

Bats: R **Throws:** R **Pos:** SS-93; 2B-12; PH/PR-8; 3B-6   **Ht:** 6'0" **Wt:** 169 **Born:** 11/22/65 **Age:** 34

								BATTING											BASERUNNING				PERCENTAGES		
Year Team	Lg	G	AB	H	2B	3B	HR	(Hm	Rd)	TB	R	RBI	TBB	IBB	SO	HBP	SH	SF	SB	CS	SB%	GDP	Avg	OBP	SLG
1989 San Francisco	NL	14	6	1	0	0	0	(0	0)	1	6	0	0	0	1	0	0	0	0	0	.00	0	.167	.167	.167

						BATTING															BASERUNNING				PERCENTAGES		
Year Team	Lg	G	AB	H	2B	3B	HR	(Hm	Rd)	TB	R	RBI	TBB	IBB	SO	HBP	SH	SF	SB	CS	SB%	GDP	Avg	OBP	SLG
1990 San Francisco	NL	22	56	12	3	1	2	(2	0)	23	7	3	3	1	10	0	0	0	1	0	1.00	2	.214	.254	.411
1991 San Francisco	NL	54	106	13	3	0	2	(0	2)	22	12	8	7	2	26	2	3	2	3	0	1.00	1	.123	.188	.208
1992 San Francisco	NL	40	75	13	2	1	1	(0	1)	20	4	3	4	1	15	0	3	0	1	0	1.00	1	.173	.215	.267
1993 San Francisco	NL	63	146	29	7	0	4	(3	1)	48	22	16	9	2	23	4	6	0	0	0	.00	3	.199	.264	.329
1994 San Francisco	NL	38	62	16	5	1	1	(1	0)	26	9	9	5	1	16	3	5	0	5	0	1.00	1	.258	.343	.419
1995 San Francisco	NL	68	186	41	6	0	3	(1	2)	56	19	12	8	3	51	1	7	0	11	1	.92	3	.220	.256	.301
1996 Philadelphia	NL	35	103	23	5	1	4	(0	4)	42	13	13	12	5	21	2	1	0	3	1	.75	2	.223	.316	.408
1997 Boston	AL	49	116	27	9	1	0	(0	0)	38	12	7	4	0	27	1	1	1	2	3	.40	2	.233	.262	.328
1998 Boston	AL	124	349	95	23	0	4	(2	2)	130	46	39	15	1	73	6	13	2	3	0	1.00	11	.272	.312	.372
1999 Pittsburgh	NL	110	368	91	26	7	1	(1	0)	134	42	37	20	3	90	2	11	3	10	1	.91	3	.247	.288	.364
11 ML YEARS		617	1573	361	89	12	22	(10	12)	540	192	147	87	19	353	21	50	8	39	6	.87	29	.229	.278	.343

Gary Bennett

Bats: Right **Throws:** Right **Pos:** C-32; PH/PR-8 **Ht:** 6'0" **Wt:** 210 **Born:** 4/17/72 **Age:** 28

						BATTING															BASERUNNING				PERCENTAGES		
Year Team	Lg	G	AB	H	2B	3B	HR	(Hm	Rd)	TB	R	RBI	TBB	IBB	SO	HBP	SH	SF	SB	CS	SB%	GDP	Avg	OBP	SLG
1990 Martinsvlle	R+	16	52	14	2	1	0	—	—	18	3	10	4	0	15	0	0	1	0	1	.00	—	.269	.316	.346
1991 Martinsvlle	R+	41	136	32	7	0	1	—	—	42	15	16	17	0	26	5	1	1	0	1	.00	5	.235	.340	.309
1992 Batavia	A-	47	146	30	2	0	0	—	—	32	22	12	15	0	27	2	3	0	2	1	.67	2	.205	.288	.219
1993 Spartanburg	A	42	126	32	4	1	0	—	—	38	18	15	12	0	22	1	2	1	0	2	.00	2	.254	.321	.302
Clearwater	A+	17	55	18	0	0	1	—	—	21	5	6	3	0	10	1	2	0	1	0	1.00	1	.327	.373	.382
1994 Clearwater	A+	19	55	13	3	0	0	—	—	16	6	10	8	0	6	0	1	0	0	0	.00	1	.236	.328	.291
Reading	AA	63	208	48	9	0	3	—	—	66	13	22	14	0	26	0	3	3	0	1	.00	6	.231	.276	.321
1995 Reading	AA	86	271	64	11	0	4	—	—	87	27	40	22	1	36	3	3	2	0	0	.00	12	.236	.299	.321
Scranton-WB	AAA	7	20	3	0	0	0	—	—	3	1	1	2	1	2	0	1	0	0	0	.00	1	.150	.227	.150
1996 Scranton-WB	AAA	91	286	71	15	1	8	—	—	112	37	37	24	2	43	3	3	3	1	0	1.00	10	.248	.310	.392
1997 Pawtucket	AAA	71	224	48	7	1	4	—	—	69	16	22	18	0	39	2	1	1	1	1	.50	10	.214	.278	.308
1998 Scranton-WB	AAA	86	282	72	18	0	10	—	—	120	33	40	25	0	41	2	2	4	0	0	.00	6	.255	.316	.426
1995 Philadelphia	NL	1	1	0	0	0	0	(0	0)	0	0	0	0	0	1	0	0	0	0	0	.00	0	.000	.000	.000
1996 Philadelphia	NL	6	16	4	0	0	0	(0	0)	4	0	1	2	1	6	0	0	0	0	0	.00	1	.250	.333	.250
1998 Philadelphia	NL	9	31	9	0	0	0	(0	0)	9	4	3	5	0	5	0	0	1	0	0	.00	1	.290	.378	.290
1999 Philadelphia	NL	36	88	24	4	0	1	(0	1)	31	7	21	4	0	11	0	0	2	0	0	.00	7	.273	.298	.352
4 ML YEARS		52	136	37	4	0	1	(0	1)	44	11	25	11	1	23	0	0	3	0	0	.00	8	.272	.320	.324

Joel Bennett

Pitches: Right **Bats:** Right **Pos:** SP-3; RP-2 **Ht:** 6'1" **Wt:** 171 **Born:** 1/31/70 **Age:** 30

		HOW MUCH HE PITCHED						WHAT HE GAVE UP												THE RESULTS						
Year Team	Lg	G	GS	CG	GF	IP	BFP	H	R	ER	HR	SH	SF	HB	TBB	IBB	SO	WP	Bk	W	L	Pct.	ShO	Sv-Op	Hld	ERA
1991 Red Sox	R	2	2	0	0	10	38	6	2	2	0	0	1	1	4	0	8	2	1	0	0	.000	0	0--	—	1.80
Elmira	A-	13	12	1	0	81	325	60	29	22	3	3	1	6	30	0	75	7	0	5	3	.625	1	0--	—	2.44
1992 Winter Havn	A+	26	26	4	0	161.2	690	161	86	76	7	7	5	7	55	2	154	7	3	7	11	.389	0	0--	—	4.23
1993 Lynchburg	A+	29	29	3	0	181	754	151	93	77	17	7	9	4	67	6	221	18	0	7	12	.368	0	0--	—	3.83
1994 New Britain	AA	23	23	1	0	130.2	560	119	65	59	9	2	2	4	56	0	130	10	0	11	7	.611	1	0--	—	4.06
Pawtucket	AAA	4	4	0	0	21	91	19	16	16	8	0	0	1	12	0	24	1	0	1	3	.250	0	0--	—	6.86
1995 Pawtucket	AAA	20	13	0	2	77	357	91	57	50	6	0	4	3	45	3	50	6	0	2	4	.333	0	0--	—	5.84
1996 Trenton	AA	3	0	0	1	4.1	18	3	4	4	2	0	0	0	2	0	8	0	0	1	0	1.000	0	0--	—	8.31
Newburgh	IND	9	9	2	0	57	211	18	8	5	2	0	1	2	16	0	82	3	0	6	0	1.000	2	0--	—	0.79
Bowie	AA	10	8	0	0	54.2	211	36	21	20	5	0	0	1	17	0	48	0	0	2	3	.400	0	0--	—	3.29
1997 Bowie	AA	44	10	0	12	113.1	461	89	45	40	12	6	3	4	40	6	146	2	1	6	8	.429	0	4--	—	3.18
1998 Rochester	AAA	18	15	1	0	101.1	425	99	46	41	9	2	3	2	37	1	99	3	0	10	0	1.000	0	0--	—	3.64
Scranton-WB	AAA	8	7	0	0	47.2	215	51	29	28	6	0	1	1	25	1	35	0	0	1	2	.333	0	0--	—	5.29
1999 Scranton-WB	AAA	20	20	1	0	127	550	134	71	65	10	2	6	6	47	2	125	5	0	10	4	.714	1	0--	—	4.61
1998 Baltimore	AL	2	0	0	2	2	11	2	1	1	0	0	0	0	3	0	0	0	0	0	0	.000	0	0-0	0	4.50
1999 Philadelphia	NL	5	3	0	0	17	83	26	17	17	10	2	0	0	7	0	13	0	0	2	1	.667	0	0-1	0	9.00
2 ML YEARS		7	3	0	2	19	94	28	18	18	10	2	0	0	10	0	13	0	0	2	1	.667	0	0-1	0	8.53

Shayne Bennett

Pitches: Right **Bats:** Right **Pos:** RP-4; SP-1 **Ht:** 6'5" **Wt:** 220 **Born:** 4/10/72 **Age:** 28

		HOW MUCH HE PITCHED						WHAT HE GAVE UP												THE RESULTS						
Year Team	Lg	G	GS	CG	GF	IP	BFP	H	R	ER	HR	SH	SF	HB	TBB	IBB	SO	WP	Bk	W	L	Pct.	ShO	Sv-Op	Hld	ERA
1999 Ottawa *	AAA	38	8	0	17	89.1	397	96	53	50	12	5	4	4	37	3	70	5	1	3	9	.250	0	8--	—	5.04
1997 Montreal	NL	16	0	0	3	22.2	98	21	9	8	2	1	3	0	9	3	8	0	0	0	1	.000	0	0-0	—	3.18
1998 Montreal	NL	62	0	0	11	91.2	417	97	61	56	8	9	6	6	45	3	59	3	1	5	5	.500	0	1-2	0	5.50
1999 Montreal	NL	5	1	0	1	11.1	59	24	18	18	4	0	1	1	3	0	4	0	0	0	1	.000	0	0-0	0	14.29
3 ML YEARS		83	1	0	15	125.2	574	142	88	82	14	10	10	7	57	6	71	3	1	5	7	.417	0	1-2	0	5.87

Kris Benson

Pitches: Right **Bats:** Right **Pos:** SP-31 **Ht:** 6'4" **Wt:** 190 **Born:** 11/7/74 **Age:** 25

		HOW MUCH HE PITCHED						WHAT HE GAVE UP												THE RESULTS						
Year Team	Lg	G	GS	CG	GF	IP	BFP	H	R	ER	HR	SH	SF	HB	TBB	IBB	SO	WP	Bk	W	L	Pct.	ShO	Sv-Op	Hld	ERA
1997 Lynchburg	A+	10	10	0	0	59.1	241	49	20	17	1	3	1	2	13	0	72	3	1	5	2	.714	0	0--	—	2.58
Carolina	AA	14	14	0	0	68.2	316	81	49	38	11	0	2	2	32	1	66	2	0	3	5	.375	0	0--	—	4.98
1998 Nashville	AAA	28	28	1	0	156	689	162	102	93	26	5	6	5	50	5	129	9	0	8	10	.444	1	0--	—	5.37
1999 Pittsburgh	NL	31	31	2	0	196.2	840	184	105	89	16	6	7	6	83	5	139	2	1	11	14	.440	0	0-0	0	4.07

Jason Bere

Pitches: Right Bats: Right Pos: SP-14; RP-3   Ht: 6'3" Wt: 215 Born: 5/26/71 Age: 29

| | | HOW MUCH HE PITCHED | | | | | | WHAT HE GAVE UP | | | | | | | | | | | | THE RESULTS | | | | | | |
Year Team	Lg	G	GS	CG	GF	IP	BFP	H	R	ER	HR	SH	SF	HB	TBB	IBB	SO	WP	Bk	W	L	Pct.	ShO	Sv-Op	Hld	ERA
1999 Indianapols *	AAA	5	4	0	1	17.2	94	25	20	20	3	0	1	0	19	0	8	0	0	0	2	.000	0	0--	—	10.19
Louisville *	AAA	5	5	0	0	26	102	21	8	6	0	2	2	0	8	0	27	1	0	2	1	.667	0	0--	—	2.08
1993 Chicago	AL	24	24	1	0	142.2	610	109	60	55	12	4	2	5	81	0	129	8	0	12	5	.706	0	0-0	0	3.47
1994 Chicago	AL	24	24	0	0	141.2	608	119	65	60	17	4	4	1	80	0	127	2	0	12	2	.857	0	0-0	0	3.81
1995 Chicago	AL	27	27	1	0	137.2	668	151	120	110	21	4	7	6	106	6	110	8	0	8	15	.348	0	0-0	0	7.19
1996 Chicago	AL	5	5	0	0	16.2	93	26	19	19	3	1	1	0	18	1	19	2	0	0	1	.000	0	0-0	0	10.26
1997 Chicago	AL	6	6	0	0	28.2	123	20	15	15	4	1	1	3	17	0	21	1	0	4	2	.667	0	0-0	0	4.71
1998 CWS-Cin		27	22	0	2	127.1	588	137	91	80	17	4	7	3	78	0	84	8	0	6	9	.400	0	0-0	0	5.65
1999 Cin-Mil	NL	17	14	0	0	66.2	322	79	52	45	9	6	2	2	50	3	47	6	0	5	0	1.000	0	0-0	0	6.08
1998 Chicago	AL	18	15	0	0	83.2	404	98	71	60	14	4	5	2	58	0	53	7	0	3	7	.300	0	0-0	0	6.45
Cincinnati	NL	9	7	0	2	43.2	184	39	20	20	3	0	2	1	20	0	31	1	0	3	2	.600	0	0-0	0	4.12
1999 Cincinnati	NL	12	10	0	0	43.1	220	56	37	33	6	5	1	2	40	3	28	2	0	3	0	1.000	0	0-0	0	6.85
Milwaukee	NL	5	4	0	0	23.1	102	23	15	12	3	1	1	0	10	0	19	4	0	2	0	1.000	0	0-0	0	4.63
7 ML YEARS		130	122	2	2	661.1	3012	641	422	384	83	24	24	20	430	10	537	35	0	47	34	.580	0	0-0	0	5.23

Dave Berg

Bats: R Throws: R Pos: SS-37; 2B-29; PH/PR-28; 3B-19; LF-3   Ht: 5'11" Wt: 185 Born: 9/3/70 Age: 29

| | | BATTING | | | | | | | | | | | | | | | | | BASERUNNING | | | | PERCENTAGES | | |
Year Team	Lg	G	AB	H	2B	3B	HR	(Hm	Rd)	TB	R	RBI	TBB	IBB	SO	HBP	SH	SF	SB	CS	SB%	GDP	Avg	OBP	SLG
1993 Elmira	A-	75	281	74	13	1	4	—	—	101	37	28	35	1	37	8	4	3	6	4	.60	8	.263	.358	.359
1994 Kane County	A	121	437	117	27	8	9	—	—	187	80	53	54	0	80	8	15	6	8	6	.57	10	.268	.354	.428
1995 Brevard Cty	A+	114	382	114	18	1	3	—	—	143	71	39	68	1	61	8	7	9	9	4	.69	5	.298	.407	.374
1996 Portland	AA	109	414	125	28	5	9	—	—	190	64	73	42	1	60	5	8	6	17	7	.71	10	.302	.368	.459
1997 Charlotte	AAA	117	424	125	26	6	9	—	—	190	76	47	55	1	71	3	10	3	16	7	.70	13	.295	.377	.448
1998 Florida	NL	81	182	57	11	0	2	(1	1)	74	18	21	26	1	46	0	4	3	3	0	1.00	1	.313	.393	.407
1999 Florida	NL	109	304	87	18	1	3	(1	2)	116	42	25	27	0	59	2	3	0	2	2	.50	7	.286	.348	.382
2 ML YEARS		190	486	144	29	1	5	(2	3)	190	60	46	53	1	105	2	7	3	5	2	.71	8	.296	.366	.391

Peter Bergeron

Bats: Left Throws: Right Pos: LF-13; CF-3; PH/PR-3   Ht: 6'1" Wt: 185 Born: 11/9/77 Age: 22

| | | BATTING | | | | | | | | | | | | | | | | | BASERUNNING | | | | PERCENTAGES | | |
Year Team	Lg	G	AB	H	2B	3B	HR	(Hm	Rd)	TB	R	RBI	TBB	IBB	SO	HBP	SH	SF	SB	CS	SB%	GDP	Avg	OBP	SLG
1996 Yakima	A-	61	232	59	5	3	5	—	—	85	36	21	28	0	59	0	3	0	13	9	.59	2	.254	.335	.366
1997 Savannah	A	131	492	138	18	5	5	—	—	181	89	36	67	3	110	2	5	3	32	21	.60	5	.280	.367	.368
San Berndno	A+	2	8	2	0	0	0	—	—	2	1	1	0	0	2	0	0	0	2	0	1.00	0	.250	.250	.250
1998 San Antonio	AA	109	416	132	17	8	8	—	—	189	81	54	61	1	69	2	9	1	33	9	.79	2	.317	.406	.454
Harrisburg	AA	34	134	33	8	4	0	—	—	49	22	9	17	0	26	0	2	0	8	3	.73	0	.246	.331	.366
1999 Harrisburg	AA	42	162	53	14	2	4	—	—	83	29	18	24	4	29	0	0	3	9	7	.56	0	.327	.407	.512
Ottawa	AAA	58	194	61	12	3	3	—	—	88	36	20	23	0	40	1	1	2	14	8	.64	1	.314	.386	.454
1999 Montreal	NL	16	45	11	2	0	0	(0	0)	13	12	1	9	0	5	0	1	0	0	0	.00	0	.244	.370	.289

Sean Bergman

Pitches: Right Bats: Right Pos: SP-16; RP-9   Ht: 6'4" Wt: 225 Born: 4/11/70 Age: 30

| | | HOW MUCH HE PITCHED | | | | | | WHAT HE GAVE UP | | | | | | | | | | | | THE RESULTS | | | | | | |
Year Team	Lg	G	GS	CG	GF	IP	BFP	H	R	ER	HR	SH	SF	HB	TBB	IBB	SO	WP	Bk	W	L	Pct.	ShO	Sv-Op	Hld	ERA
1999 New Orleans *	AAA	3	1	0	0	6.1	30	9	8	7	0	0	0	0	2	0	2	1	0	0	1	.000	0	0--	—	9.95
1993 Detroit	AL	9	6	1	1	39.2	189	47	29	25	6	3	2	1	23	3	19	3	1	1	4	.200	0	0-0	0	5.67
1994 Detroit	AL	3	3	0	0	17.2	82	22	11	11	2	0	1	1	7	0	12	1	0	2	1	.667	0	0-0	0	5.60
1995 Detroit	AL	28	28	1	0	135.1	630	169	95	77	19	5	3	4	67	8	86	13	0	7	10	.412	1	0-0	0	5.12
1996 San Diego	NL	41	14	0	11	113.1	482	119	63	55	14	8	4	2	33	3	85	7	2	6	8	.429	0	0-0	1	4.37
1997 San Diego	NL	44	9	0	13	99	451	126	72	67	11	7	4	3	38	4	74	6	0	2	4	.333	0	0-2	1	6.09
1998 Hou-Atl	NL	31	27	1	1	172	733	183	81	71	20	3	1	5	42	3	100	8	1	12	9	.571	0	0-0	0	3.72
1999 Houston	NL	25	16	2	2	105.1	455	135	62	61	9	4	4	3	29	1	44	3	0	5	6	.455	1	0-1	1	5.21
1999 Houston	NL	19	16	2	1	99	428	130	60	59	9	3	4	3	26	1	38	3	0	4	6	.400	1	0-0	1	5.36
Atlanta	NL	6	0	0	1	6.1	27	5	2	2	0	1	0	0	3	0	6	0	0	1	0	1.000	0	0-1	0	2.84
7 ML YEARS		181	103	5	28	682.1	3022	801	413	367	81	30	19	19	239	22	420	41	4	35	42	.455	2	0-3	3	4.84

Lance Berkman

Bats: B Throws: L Pos: LF-22; PH/PR-11; RF-8; 1B-1   Ht: 6'1" Wt: 210 Born: 2/10/76 Age: 24

| | | BATTING | | | | | | | | | | | | | | | | | BASERUNNING | | | | PERCENTAGES | | |
Year Team	Lg	G	AB	H	2B	3B	HR	(Hm	Rd)	TB	R	RBI	TBB	IBB	SO	HBP	SH	SF	SB	CS	SB%	GDP	Avg	OBP	SLG
1997 Kissimmee	A+	53	184	54	10	0	12	—	—	100	31	35	37	4	38	2	0	0	2	1	.67	2	.293	.417	.543
1998 Jackson	AA	122	425	130	34	0	24	—	—	236	82	89	85	10	82	4	0	3	6	4	.60	12	.306	.424	.555
New Orleans	AAA	17	59	16	4	0	6	—	—	38	14	13	12	1	16	2	0	0	0	0	.00	1	.271	.411	.644
1999 New Orleans	AAA	64	226	73	20	0	8	—	—	117	42	49	39	1	47	0	0	2	7	1	.88	10	.323	.419	.518
1999 Houston	NL	34	93	22	2	0	4	(2	2)	36	10	15	12	0	21	0	0	1	5	1	.83	2	.237	.321	.387

Geronimo Berroa

Bats: Right **Throws:** Right **Pos:** DH-17; PH/PR-4; LF-2   **Ht:** 6'0" **Wt:** 210 **Born:** 3/18/65 **Age:** 35

Year Team	Lg	G	AB	H	2B	3B	HR	(Hm	Rd)	TB	R	RBI	TBB	IBB	SO	HBP	SH	SF	SB	CS	SB%	GDP	Avg	OBP	SLG
1999 Syracuse *	AAA	10	33	9	0	0	3	—	—	18	7	8	8	1	5	0	0	0	0	0	.00	2	.273	.415	.545
Dunedin *	A+	4	5	1	1	0	0	—	—	2	1	2	2	0	1	1	0	0	0	0	.00	0	.200	.500	.400
1989 Atlanta	NL	81	136	36	4	0	2	(1	1)	46	7	9	7	1	32	0	0	0	0	1	.00	2	.265	.301	.338
1990 Atlanta	NL	7	4	0	0	0	0	(0	0)	0	0	0	1	1	1	0	0	0	0	0	.00	0	.000	.200	.000
1992 Cincinnati	NL	13	15	4	1	0	0	(0	0)	5	2	0	2	0	1	1	0	0	0	1	.00	1	.267	.389	.333
1993 Florida	NL	14	34	4	1	0	0	(0	0)	5	3	0	2	0	7	0	0	0	0	0	.00	2	.118	.167	.147
1994 Oakland	AL	96	340	104	18	2	13	(4	9)	165	55	65	41	0	62	3	0	7	7	2	.78	5	.306	.379	.485
1995 Oakland	AL	141	546	152	22	3	22	(10	12)	246	87	88	63	2	98	1	0	6	7	4	.64	12	.278	.351	.451
1996 Oakland	AL	153	586	170	32	1	36	(21	15)	312	101	106	47	0	122	4	0	6	0	3	.00	16	.290	.344	.532
1997 Oak-Bal	AL	156	561	159	25	0	26	(11	15)	262	88	90	76	4	120	4	0	7	4	4	.50	18	.283	.369	.467
1998 Cle-Det	AL	72	191	43	7	2	1	(1	0)	57	23	13	24	1	44	2	0	0	1	1	.50	5	.225	.318	.298
1999 Toronto	AL	22	62	12	3	0	1	(0	1)	18	11	6	9	0	15	2	0	0	0	0	.00	5	.194	.315	.290
1997 Oakland	AL	73	261	81	12	0	16	(6	10)	141	40	42	36	2	58	1	0	1	3	2	.60	12	.310	.395	.540
Baltimore	AL	83	300	78	13	0	10	(5	5)	121	48	48	40	2	62	3	0	6	1	2	.33	6	.260	.347	.403
1998 Cleveland	AL	20	65	13	3	1	0	(0	0)	18	6	3	7	0	17	0	0	0	1	0	1.00	2	.200	.278	.277
Detroit	AL	52	126	30	4	1	1	(1	0)	39	17	10	17	1	27	2	0	0	0	1	.00	3	.238	.338	.310
10 ML YEARS		755	2475	684	113	8	101	(48	53)	1116	377	377	272	9	502	17	0	26	19	16	.54	66	.276	.349	.451

Sean Berry

Bats: Right **Throws:** Right **Pos:** 1B-64; PH/PR-47   **Ht:** 5'11" **Wt:** 200 **Born:** 3/22/66 **Age:** 34

Year Team	Lg	G	AB	H	2B	3B	HR	(Hm	Rd)	TB	R	RBI	TBB	IBB	SO	HBP	SH	SF	SB	CS	SB%	GDP	Avg	OBP	SLG
1990 Kansas City	AL	8	23	5	1	1	0	(0	0)	8	2	4	2	0	5	0	0	0	0	0	.00	0	.217	.280	.348
1991 Kansas City	AL	31	60	8	3	0	0	(0	0)	11	5	1	5	0	23	1	0	0	0	0	.00	1	.133	.212	.183
1992 Montreal	NL	24	57	19	1	0	1	(0	1)	23	5	4	1	0	11	0	0	0	2	1	.67	1	.333	.345	.404
1993 Montreal	NL	122	299	78	15	2	14	(5	9)	139	50	49	41	6	70	2	3	6	12	2	.86	4	.261	.348	.465
1994 Montreal	NL	103	320	89	19	2	11	(4	7)	145	43	41	32	7	50	3	2	2	14	0	1.00	7	.278	.347	.453
1995 Montreal	NL	103	314	100	22	1	14	(5	9)	166	38	55	25	1	53	2	2	5	3	8	.27	5	.318	.367	.529
1996 Houston	NL	132	431	121	38	1	17	(4	13)	212	55	95	23	1	58	9	2	4	12	6	.67	11	.281	.328	.492
1997 Houston	NL	96	301	77	24	1	8	(4	4)	127	37	43	25	1	53	5	1	6	1	5	.17	8	.256	.318	.422
1998 Houston	NL	102	299	94	17	1	13	(6	7)	152	48	52	31	3	50	7	1	4	3	1	.75	8	.314	.387	.508
1999 Milwaukee	NL	106	259	59	11	1	2	(0	2)	78	26	23	17	0	50	3	0	2	0	0	.00	4	.228	.281	.301
10 ML YEARS		827	2363	650	151	10	80	(29	51)	1061	309	367	202	19	423	32	11	29	47	23	.67	49	.275	.337	.449

Dante Bichette

Bats: Right **Throws:** Right **Pos:** LF-144; PH/PR-5; DH-2   **Ht:** 6'3" **Wt:** 238 **Born:** 11/18/63 **Age:** 36

Year Team	Lg	G	AB	H	2B	3B	HR	(Hm	Rd)	TB	R	RBI	TBB	IBB	SO	HBP	SH	SF	SB	CS	SB%	GDP	Avg	OBP	SLG
1988 California	AL	21	46	12	2	0	0	(0	0)	14	1	8	0	0	7	0	0	4	0	0	.00	4	.261	.240	.304
1989 California	AL	48	138	29	7	0	3	(2	1)	45	13	15	6	0	24	0	0	2	3	0	1.00	3	.210	.240	.326
1990 California	AL	109	349	89	15	1	15	(8	7)	151	40	53	16	1	79	3	1	2	5	2	.71	9	.255	.292	.433
1991 Milwaukee	AL	134	445	106	18	3	15	(6	9)	175	53	59	22	4	107	1	1	6	14	8	.64	9	.238	.272	.393
1992 Milwaukee	AL	112	387	111	27	2	5	(3	2)	157	37	41	16	3	74	3	2	3	18	7	.72	13	.287	.318	.406
1993 Colorado	NL	141	538	167	43	5	21	(11	10)	283	93	89	28	2	99	7	0	8	14	8	.64	7	.310	.348	.526
1994 Colorado	NL	116	484	147	33	2	27	(15	12)	265	74	95	19	3	70	4	0	2	21	8	.72	17	.304	.334	.548
1995 Colorado	NL	139	579	197	38	2	40	(31	9)	359	102	128	22	5	96	4	0	7	13	9	.59	16	.340	.364	.620
1996 Colorado	NL	159	633	198	39	3	31	(22	9)	336	114	141	45	4	105	6	0	10	31	12	.72	18	.313	.359	.531
1997 Colorado	NL	151	561	173	31	2	26	(20	6)	286	81	118	30	1	90	3	0	7	6	5	.55	13	.308	.343	.510
1998 Colorado	NL	161	662	219	48	2	22	(17	5)	337	97	122	28	2	76	1	0	4	14	4	.78	22	.331	.357	.509
1999 Colorado	NL	151	593	177	38	2	34	(20	14)	321	104	133	54	3	84	2	0	10	6	6	.50	15	.298	.354	.541
12 ML YEARS		1442	5415	1625	339	24	239	(155	84)	2729	809	1002	286	28	911	34	4	65	145	69	.68	142	.300	.335	.504

Craig Biggio

Bats: R **Throws:** R **Pos:** 2B-155; LF-6; DH-2; PH/PR-2   **Ht:** 5'11" **Wt:** 180 **Born:** 12/14/65 **Age:** 34

Year Team	Lg	G	AB	H	2B	3B	HR	(Hm	Rd)	TB	R	RBI	TBB	IBB	SO	HBP	SH	SF	SB	CS	SB%	GDP	Avg	OBP	SLG
1988 Houston	NL	50	123	26	6	1	3	(1	2)	43	14	5	7	2	29	0	1	0	6	1	.86	1	.211	.254	.350
1989 Houston	NL	134	443	114	21	2	13	(6	7)	178	64	60	49	8	64	6	6	5	21	3	.88	7	.257	.336	.402
1990 Houston	NL	150	555	153	24	2	4	(2	2)	193	53	42	53	1	79	3	9	1	25	11	.69	11	.276	.342	.348
1991 Houston	NL	149	546	161	23	4	4	(0	4)	204	79	46	53	3	71	2	5	3	19	6	.76	2	.295	.358	.374
1992 Houston	NL	162	613	170	32	3	6	(3	3)	226	96	39	94	9	95	7	5	2	38	15	.72	5	.277	.378	.369
1993 Houston	NL	155	610	175	41	5	21	(8	13)	289	98	64	77	7	93	10	4	5	15	17	.47	10	.287	.373	.474
1994 Houston	NL	114	437	139	44	5	6	(4	2)	211	88	56	62	1	58	8	2	2	39	4	.91	5	.318	.411	.483
1995 Houston	NL	141	553	167	30	2	22	(6	16)	267	123	77	80	1	85	22	11	7	33	8	.80	6	.302	.406	.483
1996 Houston	NL	162	605	174	24	4	15	(7	8)	251	113	75	75	0	72	27	8	6	25	7	.78	10	.288	.386	.415
1997 Houston	NL	162	619	191	37	8	22	(7	15)	310	146	81	84	6	107	34	0	7	47	10	.82	0	.309	.415	.501
1998 Houston	NL	160	646	210	51	2	20	(10	10)	325	123	88	64	6	113	23	1	4	50	8	.86	10	.325	.403	.503
1999 Houston	NL	160	639	188	56	0	16	(10	6)	292	123	73	88	9	107	11	5	6	28	14	.67	5	.294	.386	.457
12 ML YEARS		1699	6389	1868	389	38	152	(64	88)	2789	1120	706	786	53	973	153	57	50	346	104	.77	72	.292	.380	.437

Brent Billingsley

Pitches: Left **Bats:** Left **Pos:** RP-8   **Ht:** 6'2" **Wt:** 200 **Born:** 4/19/75 **Age:** 25

			HOW MUCH HE PITCHED						WHAT HE GAVE UP											THE RESULTS						
Year Team	Lg	G	GS	CG	GF	IP	BFP	H	R	ER	HR	SH	SF	HB	TBB	IBB	SO	WP	Bk	W	L	Pct.	ShO	Sv-Op	Hld	ERA
1996 Utica	A-	15	15	0	0	89.2	373	83	46	40	6	0	4	3	28	0	82	5	1	4	5	.444	0	0--	—	4.01
1997 Kane County	A	26	26	3	0	170.2	697	146	67	57	9	7	1	11	50	0	175	13	1	14	7	.667	1	0--	—	3.01
1998 Portland	AA	28	28	0	0	171	741	172	90	71	24	5	2	6	70	2	183	17	1	6	13	.316	0	0--	—	3.74
1999 Calgary	AAA	21	21	0	0	116.2	522	133	81	72	15	9	3	1	48	0	79	8	0	2	9	.182	0	0--	—	5.55
1999 Florida	NL	8	0	0	3	7.2	42	11	14	14	3	0	1	2	10	0	3	1	0	0	0	.000	0	0-0	0	16.43

Willie Blair

Pitches: Right **Bats:** Right **Pos:** RP-23; SP-16   **Ht:** 6'1" **Wt:** 185 **Born:** 12/18/65 **Age:** 34

			HOW MUCH HE PITCHED						WHAT HE GAVE UP											THE RESULTS						
Year Team	Lg	G	GS	CG	GF	IP	BFP	H	R	ER	HR	SH	SF	HB	TBB	IBB	SO	WP	Bk	W	L	Pct.	ShO	Sv-Op	Hld	ERA
1990 Toronto	AL	27	6	0	8	68.2	297	66	33	31	4	0	4	1	28	4	43	3	0	3	5	.375	0	0-0	1	4.06
1991 Cleveland	AL	11	5	0	1	36	168	58	27	27	7	1	2	1	10	0	13	1	0	2	3	.400	0	0-1	0	6.75
1992 Houston	NL	29	8	0	1	78.2	331	74	47	35	5	4	3	2	25	2	48	2	0	5	7	.417	0	0-0	1	4.00
1993 Colorado	NL	46	18	1	5	146	664	184	90	77	20	10	8	3	42	4	84	6	1	6	10	.375	0	0-0	3	4.75
1994 Colorado	NL	47	1	0	13	77.2	365	98	57	50	9	3	1	4	39	3	68	4	0	0	5	.000	0	3-6	2	5.79
1995 San Diego	NL	40	12	0	11	114	485	112	60	55	11	8	2	2	45	3	83	4	0	7	5	.583	0	0-0	1	4.34
1996 San Diego	NL	60	0	0	17	88	377	80	52	45	13	4	3	7	29	5	67	2	0	2	6	.250	0	1-5	3	4.60
1997 Detroit	AL	29	27	2	0	175	739	186	85	81	18	3	6	3	46	2	90	6	1	16	8	.667	0	0-0	0	4.17
1998 Ari-NYM	NL	34	25	0	2	175.1	750	188	101	97	31	14	4	4	61	2	92	6	0	5	16	.238	0	0-0	0	4.98
1999 Detroit	AL	39	16	0	8	134	604	169	107	102	29	3	4	4	44	0	82	5	0	3	11	.214	0	0-0	0	6.85
1998 Arizona	NL	23	23	0	0	146.2	634	165	91	87	27	11	3	3	51	2	71	5	0	4	15	.211	0	0-0	0	5.34
New York	NL	11	2	0	2	28.2	116	23	10	10	4	3	1	1	10	0	21	1	0	1	1	.500	0	0-0	0	3.14
10 ML YEARS		362	118	3	66	1093.1	4780	1215	659	600	147	50	37	31	369	25	670	39	2	49	76	.392	0	4-12	13	4.94

Casey Blake

Bats: Right **Throws:** Right **Pos:** 3B-14   **Ht:** 6'2" **Wt:** 195 **Born:** 8/23/73 **Age:** 26

			BATTING													BASERUNNING				PERCENTAGES		
Year Team	Lg	G	AB	H	2B	3B	HR	(Hm	Rd)	TB	R	RBI	TBB	IBB	SO	HBP	SH	SF	SB	CS	SB%	GDP	Avg	OBP	SLG
1996 Hagerstown	A	48	172	43	13	1	2	—	—	64	29	18	11	1	40	7	0	2	5	3	.63	3	.250	.318	.372
1997 Dunedin	A+	129	449	107	21	0	7	—	—	149	56	39	48	2	91	6	2	2	19	9	.68	5	.238	.319	.332
1998 Dunedin	A+	88	340	119	28	3	11	—	—	186	62	65	30	1	81	9	3	7	9	6	.60	5	.350	.409	.547
Knoxville	AA	45	172	64	15	4	7	—	—	108	41	38	22	0	25	2	0	3	10	0	1.00	6	.372	.442	.628
1999 Syracuse	AAA	110	387	95	16	2	22	—	—	181	69	75	61	2	82	7	1	2	9	5	.64	10	.245	.357	.468
St.Cathrnes	A-	1	3	2	0	0	0	—	—	2	0	0	1	0	0	0	0	0	0	0	.00	0	.667	.750	.667
1999 Toronto	AL	14	39	10	2	0	1	(0	1)	15	6	1	2	0	7	0	0	0	0	0	.00	1	.256	.293	.385

Henry Blanco

Bats: Right **Throws:** Right **Pos:** C-86; PH/PR-5; LF-1   **Ht:** 5'11" **Wt:** 170 **Born:** 8/29/71 **Age:** 28

			BATTING													BASERUNNING				PERCENTAGES		
Year Team	Lg	G	AB	H	2B	3B	HR	(Hm	Rd)	TB	R	RBI	TBB	IBB	SO	HBP	SH	SF	SB	CS	SB%	GDP	Avg	OBP	SLG
1990 Dodgers	R	60	178	39	8	0	1	—	—	50	23	19	26	0	43	1	0	4	7	2	.78	6	.219	.316	.281
1991 Vero Beach	A+	5	7	1	0	0	0	—	—	1	0	0	2	0	0	0	0	0	0	0	.00	0	.143	.333	.143
Great Falls	R+	62	216	55	7	1	5	—	—	79	35	28	27	0	39	1	2	3	3	6	.33	5	.255	.336	.366
1992 Bakersfield	A+	124	401	94	21	2	5	—	—	134	42	52	51	3	91	9	10	9	10	6	.63	10	.234	.328	.334
1993 San Antonio	AA	117	374	73	19	1	10	—	—	124	33	42	29	0	80	4	2	1	3	3	.50	7	.195	.260	.332
1994 San Antonio	AA	132	405	93	23	2	6	—	—	138	36	38	53	2	67	2	5	3	6	6	.50	12	.230	.320	.341
1995 San Antonio	AA	88	302	77	18	4	12	—	—	139	37	48	29	2	52	4	0	0	1	1	.50	4	.255	.328	.460
Albuquerque	AAA	29	97	22	4	1	2	—	—	34	11	13	10	1	23	0	1	2	0	0	.00	3	.227	.294	.351
1996 San Antonio	AA	92	307	82	14	1	5	—	—	113	39	40	28	2	38	0	3	5	2	3	.40	8	.267	.324	.368
Albuquerque	AAA	2	6	1	0	0	0	—	—	1	1	0	0	0	3	0	0	0	0	0	.00	0	.167	.167	.167
1997 Albuquerque	AAA	91	294	92	20	1	6	—	—	132	38	47	37	2	63	1	1	3	7	4	.64	7	.313	.388	.449
1998 San Berndno	A+	7	19	6	1	0	2	—	—	13	5	3	4	0	6	0	0	0	1	0	1.00	1	.316	.435	.684
Albuquerque	AAA	48	134	36	11	0	4	—	—	59	19	23	22	1	27	0	0	2	2	0	1.00	5	.269	.367	.440
1999 Colo Sprngs	AAA	15	57	19	4	0	3	—	—	32	8	12	1	0	12	0	1	1	0	1	.00	1	.333	.339	.561
1997 Los Angeles	NL	3	5	2	0	0	1	(0	1)	5	1	1	0	0	1	0	0	0	0	0	.00	0	.400	.400	1.000
1999 Colorado	NL	88	263	61	12	3	6	(3	3)	97	30	28	34	1	38	1	3	2	1	1	.50	4	.232	.320	.369
2 ML YEARS		91	268	63	12	3	7	(3	4)	102	31	29	34	1	39	1	3	2	1	1	.50	4	.235	.321	.381

Jeff Blauser

Bats: R **Throws:** R **Pos:** PH/PR-53; 2B-25; SS-22; 3B-18; LF-1   **Ht:** 6'1" **Wt:** 190 **Born:** 11/8/65 **Age:** 34

			BATTING													BASERUNNING				PERCENTAGES		
Year Team	Lg	G	AB	H	2B	3B	HR	(Hm | Rd)	TB	R	RBI	TBB	IBB	SO	HBP	SH	SF	SB	CS	SB%	GDP	Avg	OBP	SLG
1987 Atlanta	NL	51	165	40	6	3	2	(1 | 1)	58	11	15	18	1	34	3	1	0	7	3	.70	4	.242	.328	.352
1988 Atlanta	NL	18	67	16	3	1	2	(2 | 0)	27	7	7	2	0	11	1	3	1	0	1	.00	1	.239	.268	.403
1989 Atlanta	NL	142	456	123	24	2	12	(5 | 7)	187	63	46	38	2	101	1	8	4	5	2	.71	7	.270	.325	.410
1990 Atlanta	NL	115	386	104	24	3	8	(3 | 5)	158	46	39	35	1	70	5	3	0	3	5	.38	4	.269	.338	.409
1991 Atlanta	NL	129	352	91	14	3	11	(7 | 4)	144	49	54	54	4	59	2	4	3	5	6	.45	4	.259	.358	.409
1992 Atlanta	NL	123	343	90	19	3	14	(7 | 7)	157	61	46	46	2	82	4	7	3	5	5	.50	2	.262	.354	.458
1993 Atlanta	NL	161	597	182	29	2	15	(4 | 11)	260	110	73	85	0	109	16	5	7	16	6	.73	13	.305	.401	.436
1994 Atlanta	NL	96	380	98	21	4	6	(3 | 3)	145	56	45	38	0	64	5	5	6	1	3	.25	11	.258	.329	.382

24

Year Team	Lg	G	AB	H	2B	3B	HR	(Hm	Rd)	TB	R	RBI	TBB	IBB	SO	HBP	SH	SF	SB	CS	SB%	GDP	Avg	OBP	SLG
1995 Atlanta	NL	115	431	91	16	2	12	(7	5)	147	60	31	57	2	107	12	2	2	8	5	.62	6	.211	.319	.341
1996 Atlanta	NL	83	265	65	14	1	10	(4	6)	111	48	35	40	3	54	6	0	1	6	0	1.00	7	.245	.356	.419
1997 Atlanta	NL	151	519	160	31	4	17	(9	8)	250	90	70	70	6	101	20	5	9	5	1	.83	13	.308	.405	.482
1998 Chicago	NL	119	361	79	11	3	4	(0	4)	108	49	26	60	1	93	8	3	3	2	2	.50	5	.219	.340	.299
1999 Chicago	NL	104	200	48	5	2	9	(7	2)	84	41	26	26	0	52	8	2	2	2	2	.50	0	.240	.347	.420
13 ML YEARS		1407	4522	1187	217	33	122	(57	65)	1836	691	513	569	22	937	91	48	41	65	41	.61	77	.262	.354	.406

Mike Blowers

Bats: R Throws: R Pos: 1B-14; PH/PR-5; 3B-4; DH-1   Ht: 6'2" Wt: 210 Born: 4/24/65 Age: 35

Year Team	Lg	G	AB	H	2B	3B	HR	(Hm	Rd)	TB	R	RBI	TBB	IBB	SO	HBP	SH	SF	SB	CS	SB%	GDP	Avg	OBP	SLG
1999 Tacoma *	AAA	3	13	3	1	0	0	—	—	4	1	2	0	0	4	0	0	0	0	0	.00	0	.231	.231	.308
1989 New York	AL	13	38	10	0	0	0	(0	0)	10	2	3	3	0	13	0	0	0	0	0	.00	1	.263	.317	.263
1990 New York	AL	48	144	27	4	0	5	(1	4)	46	16	21	12	1	50	1	0	0	1	0	1.00	4	.188	.255	.319
1991 New York	AL	15	35	7	0	0	1	(0	1)	10	3	1	4	0	3	0	1	0	0	0	.00	1	.200	.282	.286
1992 Seattle	AL	31	73	14	3	0	1	(0	1)	20	7	2	6	0	20	0	1	0	0	0	.00	3	.192	.253	.274
1993 Seattle	AL	127	379	106	23	3	15	(8	7)	180	55	57	44	3	98	2	3	1	1	5	.17	12	.280	.357	.475
1994 Seattle	AL	85	270	78	13	0	9	(3	6)	118	37	49	25	2	60	1	1	3	2	2	.50	12	.289	.348	.437
1995 Seattle	AL	134	439	113	24	1	23	(17	6)	208	59	96	53	0	128	0	3	3	2	1	.67	18	.257	.335	.474
1996 Los Angeles	NL	92	317	84	19	2	6	(4	2)	125	31	38	37	2	77	1	0	3	0	0	.00	11	.265	.341	.394
1997 Seattle	AL	68	150	44	5	0	5	(5	0)	64	22	20	21	1	33	0	4	2	0	0	.00	4	.293	.376	.427
1998 Oakland	AL	129	409	97	24	2	11	(2	9)	158	56	71	39	1	116	1	2	4	1	0	1.00	13	.237	.302	.386
1999 Seattle	AL	19	46	11	1	0	2	(1	1)	18	2	7	4	0	12	0	0	0	0	0	.00	2	.239	.300	.391
11 ML YEARS		761	2300	591	116	8	78	(41	37)	957	290	365	248	10	610	6	15	16	7	8	.47	80	.257	.329	.416

Geoff Blum

Bats: Both Throws: Right Pos: SS-42; PH/PR-3; 2B-2   Ht: 6'3" Wt: 195 Born: 4/26/73 Age: 27

Year Team	Lg	G	AB	H	2B	3B	HR	(Hm	Rd)	TB	R	RBI	TBB	IBB	SO	HBP	SH	SF	SB	CS	SB%	GDP	Avg	OBP	SLG
1994 Vermont	A-	63	241	83	15	1	3	—	—	109	48	38	33	0	21	3	1	1	5	5	.50	4	.344	.428	.452
1995 Wst Plm Bch	A+	125	457	120	20	2	1	—	—	147	54	62	34	1	61	3	1	7	6	5	.55	12	.263	.313	.322
1996 Harrisburg	AA	120	396	95	22	2	1	—	—	124	47	41	59	2	51	3	11	3	6	7	.46	11	.240	.341	.313
1997 Ottawa	AAA	118	407	101	21	2	3	—	—	135	59	35	52	1	73	3	12	6	14	6	.70	6	.248	.333	.332
1998 Ottawa	AAA	8	23	4	0	0	0	—	—	4	1	1	3	0	6	0	1	0	0	0	.00	0	.174	.269	.174
Expos	R	5	18	3	1	1	0	—	—	6	0	1	1	0	4	0	0	0	0	0	.00	0	.167	.211	.333
Jupiter	A+	5	29	8	6	0	0	—	—	22	13	5	13	1	14	1	2	1	1	0	1.00	0	.276	.411	.379
Harrisburg	AA	39	139	43	12	3	6	—	—	79	25	21	17	0	24	4	2	0	2	1	.67	3	.309	.400	.568
1999 Ottawa	AAA	77	268	71	14	1	10	—	—	117	43	37	37	1	39	2	3	7	6	1	.86	5	.265	.350	.437
1999 Montreal	NL	45	133	32	7	2	8	(0	8)	67	21	18	17	3	25	0	3	0	1	0	1.00	3	.241	.327	.504

Doug Bochtler

Pitches: Right Bats: Right Pos: RP-12   Ht: 6'3" Wt: 200 Born: 7/5/70 Age: 29

		HOW MUCH HE PITCHED						WHAT HE GAVE UP										THE RESULTS						
Year Team	Lg	G	GS	CG	GF	IP	BFP	H	R	ER	HR	SH	SF	HB	TBB	IBB	SO	WP	Bk	W	L	Pct.	ShO	Sv-Op	Hld	ERA
1999 Syracuse *	AAA	14	0	0	3	27.1	110	18	9	8	1	0	3	0	10	0	28	0	0	4	0	1.000	0	0--	—	2.63
Albuquerque *	AAA	18	0	0	9	22.2	93	16	9	8	3	0	0	0	11	1	25	5	0	3	4	.429	0	3--	—	3.18
1995 San Diego	NL	34	0	0	11	45.1	181	38	18	18	5	2	1	0	19	0	45	1	0	4	4	.500	0	1-4	8	3.57
1996 San Diego	NL	63	0	0	17	65.2	278	45	25	22	6	5	2	1	39	8	68	8	2	2	4	.333	0	3-7	20	3.02
1997 San Diego	NL	54	0	0	13	60.1	281	51	35	32	3	4	3	1	50	4	46	5	0	3	6	.333	0	2-3	9	4.77
1998 Detroit	AL	51	0	0	11	67.1	312	73	48	46	17	2	3	3	42	6	45	6	0	0	2	.000	0	0-2	2	6.15
1999 Los Angeles	NL	12	0	0	4	13	58	11	8	8	3	1	1	1	6	1	7	1	0	0	0	.000	0	0-0	—	5.54
5 ML YEARS		214	0	0	56	251.2	1110	218	134	126	34	14	10	6	156	19	211	21	2	9	16	.360	0	6-16	39	4.51

Brian Boehringer

Pitches: Right Bats: Both Pos: RP-22; SP-11   Ht: 6'2" Wt: 190 Born: 1/8/70 Age: 30

		HOW MUCH HE PITCHED						WHAT HE GAVE UP										THE RESULTS						
Year Team	Lg	G	GS	CG	GF	IP	BFP	H	R	ER	HR	SH	SF	HB	TBB	IBB	SO	WP	Bk	W	L	Pct.	ShO	Sv-Op	Hld	ERA
1995 New York	AL	7	3	0	0	17.2	99	24	27	27	5	0	1	1	22	1	10	3	0	0	3	.000	0	0-1	0	13.75
1996 New York	AL	15	3	0	0	46.1	205	46	28	28	6	3	3	1	21	2	37	1	0	2	4	.333	0	0-1	4	5.44
1997 New York	AL	34	0	0	11	48	210	39	16	14	4	3	2	0	32	6	53	2	0	3	2	.600	0	0-3	5	2.63
1998 San Diego	NL	56	1	0	18	76.1	347	75	38	37	10	5	1	4	45	4	67	1	0	5	2	.714	0	0-1	7	4.36
1999 San Diego	NL	33	11	0	8	94.1	409	97	38	34	10	6	4	1	35	4	64	2	0	6	5	.545	0	0-2	3	3.24
5 ML YEARS		145	18	0	38	282.2	1270	281	147	140	35	17	11	7	155	17	231	9	0	16	16	.500	0	0-8	19	4.46

Tim Bogar

Bats: R Throws: R Pos: SS-90; 3B-12; PH/PR-9; 2B-1   Ht: 6'2" Wt: 198 Born: 10/28/66 Age: 33

Year Team	Lg	G	AB	H	2B	3B	HR	(Hm	Rd)	TB	R	RBI	TBB	IBB	SO	HBP	SH	SF	SB	CS	SB%	GDP	Avg	OBP	SLG
1993 New York	NL	78	205	50	13	0	3	(1	2)	72	19	25	14	2	29	3	1	0	0	1	.00	2	.244	.300	.351
1994 New York	NL	50	52	8	0	0	2	(0	2)	14	5	5	4	1	11	0	2	1	1	0	1.00	0	.154	.211	.269
1995 New York	NL	78	145	42	7	0	1	(0	1)	52	17	21	9	0	25	0	2	1	1	0	1.00	2	.290	.329	.359

25

	BATTING																		BASERUNNING				PERCENTAGES		
Year Team	Lg	G	AB	H	2B	3B	HR	(Hm	Rd)	TB	R	RBI	TBB	IBB	SO	HBP	SH	SF	SB	CS	SB%	GDP	Avg	OBP	SLG
1996 New York	NL	91	89	19	4	0	0	(0	0)	23	17	6	8	0	20	2	3	2	1	3	.25	0	.213	.287	.258
1997 Houston	NL	97	241	60	14	4	4	(3	1)	94	30	30	24	1	42	3	3	4	4	1	.80	4	.249	.320	.390
1998 Houston	NL	79	156	24	4	1	1	(0	1)	33	12	8	9	2	36	2	1	1	2	1	.67	5	.154	.208	.212
1999 Houston	NL	106	309	74	16	2	4	(2	2)	106	44	31	38	5	52	4	0	3	5	5	.38	10	.239	.328	.343
7 ML YEARS		579	1197	277	58	7	15	(6	9)	394	144	126	106	11	215	14	12	13	12	11	.52	24	.231	.298	.329

Wade Boggs

Bats: L Throws: R Pos: 3B-74; DH-7; PH/PR-7; 1B-4; P-1   Ht: 6'2" Wt: 197 Born: 6/15/58 Age: 42

	BATTING																		BASERUNNING				PERCENTAGES		
Year Team	Lg	G	AB	H	2B	3B	HR	(Hm	Rd)	TB	R	RBI	TBB	IBB	SO	HBP	SH	SF	SB	CS	SB%	GDP	Avg	OBP	SLG
1982 Boston	AL	104	338	118	14	1	5	(4	1)	149	51	44	35	4	21	0	4	4	1	0	1.00	9	.349	.406	.441
1983 Boston	AL	153	582	210	44	7	5	(2	3)	283	100	74	92	2	36	1	3	7	3	3	.50	15	.361	.444	.486
1984 Boston	AL	158	625	203	31	4	6	(5	1)	260	109	55	89	6	44	0	8	4	3	2	.60	13	.325	.407	.416
1985 Boston	AL	161	653	240	42	3	8	(6	2)	312	107	78	96	5	61	4	3	2	2	1	.67	20	.368	.450	.478
1986 Boston	AL	149	580	207	47	2	8	(3	5)	282	107	71	105	14	44	0	4	4	0	4	.00	11	.357	.453	.486
1987 Boston	AL	147	551	200	40	6	24	(10	14)	324	108	89	105	19	48	2	1	8	1	3	.25	13	.363	.461	.588
1988 Boston	AL	155	584	214	45	6	5	(4	1)	286	128	58	125	18	34	3	0	7	2	3	.40	23	.366	.476	.490
1989 Boston	AL	156	621	205	51	7	3	(2	1)	279	113	54	107	19	51	7	0	7	2	6	.25	19	.330	.430	.449
1990 Boston	AL	155	619	187	44	5	6	(3	3)	259	89	63	87	19	68	1	0	6	0	0	.00	14	.302	.386	.418
1991 Boston	AL	144	546	181	42	2	8	(6	2)	251	93	51	89	25	32	0	0	6	1	2	.33	16	.332	.421	.460
1992 Boston	AL	143	514	133	22	4	7	(3	4)	184	62	50	74	19	31	4	0	6	1	3	.25	10	.259	.353	.358
1993 New York	AL	143	560	169	26	1	2	(1	1)	203	83	59	74	4	49	0	1	9	0	1	.00	10	.302	.378	.363
1994 New York	AL	97	366	125	19	1	11	(6	5)	179	61	55	61	3	29	1	2	4	2	1	.67	10	.342	.433	.489
1995 New York	AL	126	460	149	22	4	5	(4	1)	194	76	63	74	5	50	0	0	3	1	1	.50	13	.324	.412	.422
1996 New York	AL	132	501	156	29	2	2	(2	0)	195	80	41	67	7	32	0	1	5	1	2	.33	10	.311	.389	.389
1997 New York	AL	104	353	103	23	1	4	(0	4)	140	55	28	48	3	38	0	2	4	0	1	.00	3	.292	.373	.397
1998 Tampa Bay	AL	123	435	122	23	4	7	(7	0)	174	51	52	46	6	54	0	0	2	3	2	.60	13	.280	.348	.400
1999 Tampa Bay	AL	90	292	88	14	1	2	(1	1)	110	40	29	38	2	23	0	0	4	1	0	1.00	14	.301	.377	.377
18 ML YEARS		2440	9180	3010	578	61	118	(70	48)	4064	1513	1014	1412	180	745	23	29	96	24	35	.41	236	.328	.415	.443

Brian Bohanon

Pitches: Left Bats: Left Pos: SP-33   Ht: 6'2" Wt: 240 Born: 8/1/68 Age: 31

	HOW MUCH HE PITCHED						WHAT HE GAVE UP											THE RESULTS					
Year Team	Lg	G	GS	CG	GF	IP	BFP	H	R	ER	HR	SH	SF	HB	TBB	IBB	SO	WP	Bk	W	L	Pct.	ShO	Sv-Op	Hld	ERA
1990 Texas	AL	11	6	0	1	34	158	40	30	25	6	0	3	2	18	0	15	1	0	0	3	.000	0	0-0	0	6.62
1991 Texas	AL	11	11	1	0	61.1	273	66	35	33	4	2	5	2	23	0	34	3	1	4	3	.571	0	0-0	0	4.84
1992 Texas	AL	18	7	0	3	45.2	220	57	38	32	7	0	2	1	25	0	29	2	0	1	1	.500	0	0-0	0	6.31
1993 Texas	AL	36	8	0	4	92.2	418	107	54	49	8	2	5	4	46	3	45	10	0	4	4	.500	0	0-1	1	4.76
1994 Texas	AL	11	5	0	1	37.1	169	51	31	30	7	1	0	1	8	1	26	5	0	2	2	.500	0	0-0	0	7.23
1995 Detroit	AL	52	10	0	7	105.2	474	121	68	65	10	0	5	4	41	5	63	3	0	1	1	.500	0	1-1	10	5.54
1996 Toronto	AL	20	0	0	6	22	112	27	19	19	4	0	2	2	19	4	17	2	0	0	1	.000	0	1-1	2	7.77
1997 New York	NL	19	14	0	0	94.1	412	95	49	40	9	6	0	4	34	2	66	3	1	6	4	.600	0	0-0	0	3.82
1998 NYM-LA	NL	39	18	2	4	151.2	626	121	56	45	13	7	2	11	57	2	111	3	0	7	11	.389	0	0-1	1	2.67
1999 Colorado	NL	33	33	3	0	197.1	903	236	146	136	30	18	3	14	92	1	120	6	0	12	12	.500	1	0-0	0	6.20
1998 New York	NL	25	4	0	4	54.1	230	47	21	19	4	2	0	6	21	2	39	1	0	2	4	.333	0	0-1	1	3.15
Los Angeles	NL	14	14	2	0	97.1	396	74	35	26	9	5	2	5	36	0	72	2	0	5	7	.417	0	0-0	0	2.40
10 ML YEARS		250	112	6	26	842	3765	921	526	474	98	36	27	45	363	18	526	38	2	37	42	.468	1	2-4	14	5.07

Barry Bonds

Bats: Left Throws: Left Pos: LF-96; DH-4; PH/PR-3   Ht: 6'2" Wt: 210 Born: 7/24/64 Age: 35

	BATTING																		BASERUNNING				PERCENTAGES		
Year Team	Lg	G	AB	H	2B	3B	HR	(Hm	Rd)	TB	R	RBI	TBB	IBB	SO	HBP	SH	SF	SB	CS	SB%	GDP	Avg	OBP	SLG
1986 Pittsburgh	NL	113	413	92	26	3	16	(9	7)	172	72	48	65	2	102	2	2	2	36	7	.84	4	.223	.330	.416
1987 Pittsburgh	NL	150	551	144	34	9	25	(12	13)	271	99	59	54	3	88	3	0	3	32	10	.76	4	.261	.329	.492
1988 Pittsburgh	NL	144	538	152	30	5	24	(14	10)	264	97	58	72	14	82	2	0	2	17	11	.61	3	.283	.368	.491
1989 Pittsburgh	NL	159	580	144	34	6	19	(7	12)	247	96	58	93	22	93	1	1	4	32	10	.76	9	.248	.351	.426
1990 Pittsburgh	NL	151	519	156	32	3	33	(14	19)	293	104	114	93	15	83	3	0	6	52	13	.80	8	.301	.406	.565
1991 Pittsburgh	NL	153	510	149	28	5	25	(12	13)	262	95	116	107	25	73	4	0	13	43	13	.77	8	.292	.410	.514
1992 Pittsburgh	NL	140	473	147	36	5	34	(15	19)	295	109	103	127	32	69	5	0	7	39	8	.83	9	.311	.456	.624
1993 San Francisco	NL	159	539	181	38	4	46	(21	25)	365	129	123	126	43	79	2	0	7	29	12	.71	11	.336	.458	.677
1994 San Francisco	NL	112	391	122	18	1	37	(15	22)	253	89	81	74	18	43	6	0	3	29	9	.76	3	.312	.426	.647
1995 San Francisco	NL	144	506	149	30	7	33	(16	17)	292	109	104	120	22	83	5	0	4	31	10	.76	12	.294	.431	.577
1996 San Francisco	NL	158	517	159	27	3	42	(23	19)	318	122	129	151	30	76	1	0	6	40	7	.85	11	.308	.461	.615
1997 San Francisco	NL	159	532	155	26	5	40	(24	16)	311	123	101	145	34	87	8	0	5	37	8	.82	13	.291	.446	.585
1998 San Francisco	NL	156	552	167	44	7	37	(21	16)	336	120	122	130	29	92	8	1	6	28	12	.70	15	.303	.438	.609
1999 San Francisco	NL	102	355	93	20	2	34	(16	18)	219	91	83	73	9	62	3	0	3	15	2	.88	6	.262	.389	.617
14 ML YEARS		2000	6976	2010	423	65	445	(219	226)	3898	1455	1299	1430	298	1112	53	4	71	460	132	.78	116	.288	.409	.559

Ricky Bones

Pitches: Right Bats: Right Pos: RP-28; SP-2   Ht: 6'0" Wt: 200 Born: 4/7/69 Age: 31

	HOW MUCH HE PITCHED						WHAT HE GAVE UP											THE RESULTS					
Year Team	Lg	G	GS	CG	GF	IP	BFP	H	R	ER	HR	SH	SF	HB	TBB	IBB	SO	WP	Bk	W	L	Pct.	ShO	Sv-Op	Hld	ERA
1991 San Diego	NL	11	11	0	0	54	234	57	33	29	3	0	4	0	18	0	31	4	0	4	6	.400	0	0-0	0	4.83

Year Team	Lg	G	GS	CG	GF	IP	BFP	H	R	ER	HR	SH	SF	HB	TBB	IBB	SO	WP	Bk	W	L	Pct.	ShO	Sv-Op	Hld	ERA
		HOW MUCH HE PITCHED						WHAT HE GAVE UP												THE RESULTS						
1992 Milwaukee	AL	31	28	0	0	163.1	705	169	90	83	27	2	5	9	48	0	65	3		9	10	.474	0	0-0	0	4.57
1993 Milwaukee	AL	32	31	3	1	203.2	883	222	122	110	28	5	7	8	63	3	63	6	1	11	11	.500	0	0-0	0	4.86
1994 Milwaukee	AL	24	24	4	0	170.2	708	166	76	65	17	4	5	3	45	1	57	8	0	10	9	.526	1	0-0	0	3.43
1995 Milwaukee	AL	32	31	3	0	200.1	877	218	108	103	26	3	11	4	83	2	77	5	2	10	12	.455	0	0-0	0	4.63
1996 Milwaukee	AL	36	24	0	2	152	699	184	115	105	30	5	5	10	68	2	63	2	0	7	14	.333	0	0-0	3	6.22
1997 Cin-KC		30	13	1	4	96	450	133	81	72	12	3	8	7	36	4	44	1	0	4	8	.333	0	0-1	2	6.75
1998 Kansas City	AL	32	0	0	12	53.1	231	49	18	18	4	5	0	1	24	5	38	2	0	2	2	.500	0	1-2	3	3.04
1999 Baltimore	AL	30	2	0	7	43.2	207	59	29	29	7	2	1	2	19	0	26	3	0	0	3	.000	0	0-3	5	5.98
1996 Milwaukee	AL	32	23	0	2	145	658	170	104	94	28	4	4	9	62	2	59	2	0	7	14	.333	0	0-0	3	5.83
New York	AL	4	1	0	0	7	41	14	11	11	2	1	1	1	6	0	4	0	0	0	0	.000	0	0-0	0	14.14
1997 Cincinnati	NL	9	2	0	2	17.2	98	31	22	20	2	1	2	2	11	2	8	0	0	1	1	.000	0	0-0	0	10.19
Kansas City	AL	21	11	1	2	78.1	352	102	59	52	10	2	6	5	25	2	36	1	0	4	7	.364	0	0-1	2	5.97
9 ML YEARS		258	164	11	26	1137	4994	1257	672	614	154	29	46	44	404	17	464	34	5	57	75	.432	1	1-6	11	4.86

Bobby Bonilla

Bats: B **Throws:** R **Pos:** PH/PR-31; RF-23; 1B-4; DH-3; LF-2 **Ht:** 6'3" **Wt:** 240 **Born:** 2/23/63 **Age:** 37

Year Team	Lg	G	AB	H	2B	3B	HR	(Hm	Rd)	TB	R	RBI	TBB	IBB	SO	HBP	SH	SF	SB	CS	SB%	GDP	Avg	OBP	SLG
								BATTING											BASERUNNING				PERCENTAGES		
1999 Norfolk *	AAA	3	13	3	0	0	0	—	—	3	1	1	0	0	1	0	0	0	0	0	.00	0	.231	.231	.231
1986 CWS-Pit		138	426	109	16	4	3	(2	1)	142	55	43	62	3	88	2	5	1	8	5	.62	9	.256	.352	.333
1987 Pittsburgh	NL	141	466	140	33	3	15	(7	8)	224	58	77	39	4	64	2	0	8	3	5	.38	8	.300	.351	.481
1988 Pittsburgh	NL	159	584	160	32	7	24	(9	15)	278	87	100	85	19	82	4	0	8	3	5	.38	4	.274	.366	.476
1989 Pittsburgh	NL	163	616	173	37	10	24	(13	11)	302	96	86	76	20	93	1	0	5	8	8	.50	10	.281	.358	.490
1990 Pittsburgh	NL	160	625	175	39	7	32	(13	19)	324	112	120	45	9	103	1	0	15	4	3	.57	11	.280	.322	.518
1991 Pittsburgh	NL	157	577	174	44	6	18	(9	9)	284	102	100	90	8	67	2	0	11	2	4	.33	14	.302	.391	.492
1992 New York	NL	128	438	109	23	0	19	(5	14)	189	62	70	66	10	73	1	0	1	4	3	.57	11	.249	.348	.432
1993 New York	NL	139	502	133	21	3	34	(18	16)	262	81	87	72	11	96	0	0	8	3	3	.50	12	.265	.352	.522
1994 New York	NL	108	403	117	24	1	20	(8	12)	203	60	67	55	9	101	0	0	2	1	3	.25	10	.290	.374	.504
1995 NYM-Bal		141	554	182	37	8	28	(14	14)	319	96	99	54	10	79	2	0	4	0	5	.00	22	.329	.388	.576
1996 Baltimore	NL	159	595	171	27	5	28	(9	19)	292	107	116	75	7	85	5	0	17	1	3	.25	13	.287	.363	.491
1997 Florida	NL	153	562	167	39	3	17	(8	9)	263	77	96	73	8	94	5	0	8	6	6	.50	13	.297	.378	.468
1998 Fla-LA	NL	100	333	83	11	1	11	(8	3)	129	39	45	41	4	59	0	0	6	1	2	.33	16	.249	.326	.387
1999 New York	NL	60	119	19	5	0	4	(2	2)	36	12	18	19	1	16	1	0	2	0	1	.00	6	.160	.277	.303
1986 Chicago	AL	75	234	63	10	2	2	(2	0)	83	27	26	33	2	49	1	2	1	4	1	.80	4	.269	.361	.355
Pittsburgh		63	192	46	6	2	1	(0	1)	59	28	17	29	1	39	1	3	0	4	4	.50	5	.240	.342	.307
1995 New York	NL	80	317	103	25	4	18	(7	11)	190	49	53	31	10	48	1	0	2	0	3	.00	11	.325	.385	.599
Baltimore	AL	61	237	79	12	4	10	(7	3)	129	47	46	23	0	31	1	0	2	0	2	.00	11	.333	.392	.544
1998 Florida	NL	28	97	27	5	0	4	(3	1)	44	11	15	12	1	22	0	0	1	0	1	.00	6	.278	.355	.454
Los Angeles	NL	72	236	56	6	1	7	(5	2)	85	28	30	29	3	37	0	0	5	1	1	.50	10	.237	.315	.360
14 ML YEARS		1906	6800	1912	388	58	277	(125	152)	3247	1044	1124	852	123	1100	26	5	96	44	56	.44	162	.281	.359	.478

Aaron Boone

Bats: Right **Throws:** Right **Pos:** 3B-136; SS-6; PH/PR-3 **Ht:** 6'2" **Wt:** 200 **Born:** 3/9/73 **Age:** 27

Year Team	Lg	G	AB	H	2B	3B	HR	(Hm	Rd)	TB	R	RBI	TBB	IBB	SO	HBP	SH	SF	SB	CS	SB%	GDP	Avg	OBP	SLG
								BATTING											BASERUNNING				PERCENTAGES		
1999 Indianapols *	AAA	11	41	14	2	1	0	—	—	18	6	7	3	0	4	2	0	3	2	2	.50	1	.341	.388	.439
1997 Cincinnati	NL	16	49	12	1	0	0	(0	0)	13	5	5	2	0	5	0	1	0	1	0	1.00	1	.245	.275	.265
1998 Cincinnati	NL	58	181	51	13	2	2	(2	0)	74	24	28	15	1	36	5	3	2	6	1	.86	3	.282	.350	.409
1999 Cincinnati	NL	139	472	132	26	5	14	(7	7)	210	56	72	30	2	79	8	5	5	17	6	.74	5	.280	.330	.445
3 ML YEARS		213	702	195	40	7	16	(9	7)	297	85	105	47	3	120	13	9	7	24	7	.77	10	.278	.332	.423

Bret Boone

Bats: Right **Throws:** Right **Pos:** 2B-151; PH/PR-5 **Ht:** 5'10" **Wt:** 180 **Born:** 4/6/69 **Age:** 31

Year Team	Lg	G	AB	H	2B	3B	HR	(Hm	Rd)	TB	R	RBI	TBB	IBB	SO	HBP	SH	SF	SB	CS	SB%	GDP	Avg	OBP	SLG
								BATTING											BASERUNNING				PERCENTAGES		
1992 Seattle	AL	33	129	25	4	0	4	(2	2)	41	15	15	4	0	34	1	1	0	1	1	.50	4	.194	.224	.318
1993 Seattle	AL	76	271	68	12	2	12	(7	5)	120	31	38	17	1	52	4	6	4	2	3	.40	6	.251	.301	.443
1994 Cincinnati	NL	108	381	122	25	2	12	(5	7)	187	59	68	24	1	74	8	5	6	3	4	.43	10	.320	.368	.491
1995 Cincinnati	NL	138	513	137	34	2	15	(6	9)	220	63	68	41	0	84	6	5	1	5	1	.83	14	.267	.326	.429
1996 Cincinnati	NL	142	520	121	21	3	12	(7	5)	184	56	69	31	0	100	3	5	9	3	2	.60	9	.233	.275	.354
1997 Cincinnati	NL	139	443	99	25	1	7	(4	3)	147	40	46	45	4	101	4	4	5	5	5	.50	11	.223	.298	.332
1998 Cincinnati	NL	157	583	155	38	1	24	(13	11)	267	76	95	48	3	104	4	9	4	6	4	.60	23	.266	.324	.458
1999 Atlanta	NL	152	608	153	38	1	20	(9	11)	253	102	63	47	0	112	5	9	2	14	9	.61	11	.252	.310	.416
8 ML YEARS		945	3448	880	197	12	106	(53	53)	1419	442	462	257	9	661	35	44	35	39	29	.57	88	.255	.310	.412

Pedro Borbon

Pitches: Left **Bats:** Left **Pos:** RP-70 **Ht:** 6'1" **Wt:** 205 **Born:** 11/15/67 **Age:** 32

Year Team	Lg	G	GS	CG	GF	IP	BFP	H	R	ER	HR	SH	SF	HB	TBB	IBB	SO	WP	Bk	W	L	Pct.	ShO	Sv-Op	Hld	ERA
		HOW MUCH HE PITCHED						WHAT HE GAVE UP												THE RESULTS						
1992 Atlanta	NL	2	0	0	2	1.1	7	2	1	1	0	0	0	0	1	1	1	0	0	0	1	.000	0	0-0	0	6.75
1993 Atlanta	NL	3	0	0	0	1.2	11	3	4	4	0	1	0	0	3	0	2	0	0	0	0	.000	0	0-0	0	21.60
1995 Atlanta	NL	41	0	0	19	32	143	29	12	11	2	3	1	1	17	4	33	0	1	2	2	.500	0	2-4	6	3.09
1996 Atlanta	NL	43	0	0	19	36	140	26	12	11	1	4	0	1	7	0	31	0	0	3	0	1.000	0	1-1	4	2.75

			HOW MUCH HE PITCHED						WHAT HE GAVE UP											THE RESULTS					
Year Team	Lg	G	GS	CG	GF	IP	BFP	H	R	ER	HR	SH	SF	HB	TBB	IBB	SO	WP	Bk	W	L	Pct.	ShO	Sv-Op	Hld	ERA
1999 Los Angeles	NL	70	0	0	11	50.2	220	39	23	23	5	0	3	1	29	1	33	1	0	4	3	.571	0	1-2	15	4.09
5 ML YEARS		159	0	0	51	121.2	521	99	52	50	8	8	4	3	57	6	100	1	1	9	6	.600	0	4-7	25	3.70

Pat Borders

Bats: Right **Throws:** Right **Pos:** C-8; DH-3; 3B-1   **Ht:** 6'2" **Wt:** 200 **Born:** 5/14/63 **Age:** 37

					BATTING														BASERUNNING				PERCENTAGES		
Year Team	Lg	G	AB	H	2B	3B	HR	(Hm	Rd)	TB	R	RBI	TBB	IBB	SO	HBP	SH	SF	SB	CS	SB%	GDP	Avg	OBP	SLG
1999 Buffalo *	AAA	55	198	47	7	0	5	—	—	69	17	23	12	2	31	3	2	1	0	1	.00	5	.237	.290	.348
1988 Toronto	AL	56	154	42	6	3	5	(2	3)	69	15	21	3	0	24	0	2	1	0	0	.00	5	.273	.285	.448
1989 Toronto	AL	94	241	62	11	1	3	(1	2)	84	22	29	11	2	45	1	1	2	2	1	.67	7	.257	.290	.349
1990 Toronto	AL	125	346	99	24	2	15	(10	5)	172	36	49	18	2	57	0	1	3	0	1	.00	17	.286	.319	.497
1991 Toronto	AL	105	291	71	17	0	5	(2	3)	103	22	36	11	1	45	1	6	3	0	0	.00	8	.244	.271	.354
1992 Toronto	AL	138	480	116	26	2	13	(7	6)	185	47	53	33	3	75	2	1	5	1	1	.50	11	.242	.290	.385
1993 Toronto	AL	138	488	124	30	0	9	(6	3)	181	38	55	20	2	66	2	7	3	2	2	.50	18	.254	.285	.371
1994 Toronto	AL	85	295	73	13	1	3	(3	0)	97	24	26	15	0	50	0	1	0	1	1	.50	7	.247	.284	.329
1995 KC-Hou		63	178	37	8	1	4	(1	3)	59	15	13	9	2	29	0	0	0	0	0	.00	3	.208	.246	.331
1996 StL-Cal-CWS		76	220	61	7	0	5	(3	2)	83	15	18	9	0	43	0	5	0	0	2	.00	4	.277	.306	.377
1997 Cleveland	AL	55	159	47	7	1	4	(0	4)	68	17	15	9	0	27	2	0	0	0	2	.00	5	.296	.341	.428
1998 Cleveland	AL	54	160	38	6	0	0	(0	0)	44	12	6	10	0	40	2	2	1	0	2	.00	1	.238	.289	.275
1999 Cle-Tor	AL	12	34	9	0	1	1	(1	0)	14	3	6	1	0	5	0	0	0	0	1	.00	0	.265	.286	.412
1995 Kansas City	AL	52	143	33	8	1	4	(1	3)	55	14	13	7	1	22	0	0	0	0	0	.00	1	.231	.267	.385
Houston	NL	11	35	4	0	0	0	(0	0)	4	1	0	2	1	7	0	0	0	0	0	.00	2	.114	.162	.114
1996 St. Louis	NL	26	69	22	3	0	0	(0	0)	25	3	4	1	0	14	0	1	0	0	1	.00	1	.319	.329	.362
California	AL	19	57	13	3	0	2	(2	0)	22	6	8	3	0	11	0	1	0	0	0	.00	0	.228	.267	.386
Chicago	AL	31	94	26	1	0	3	(1	2)	36	6	6	5	0	18	0	3	0	0	1	.00	2	.277	.313	.383
1999 Cleveland	AL	6	20	6	0	1	0	(0	0)	8	2	3	0	0	3	0	0	0	0	1	.00	0	.300	.300	.400
Toronto	AL	6	14	3	0	0	1	(1	0)	6	1	3	1	0	2	0	0	0	0	0	.00	0	.214	.267	.429
12 ML YEARS		1001	3046	779	155	12	67	(36	31)	1159	266	327	149	12	506	10	26	18	6	13	.32	88	.256	.291	.380

Mike Bordick

Bats: Right **Throws:** Right **Pos:** SS-159; PH/PR-1   **Ht:** 5'11" **Wt:** 175 **Born:** 7/21/65 **Age:** 34

					BATTING														BASERUNNING				PERCENTAGES		
Year Team	Lg	G	AB	H	2B	3B	HR	(Hm	Rd)	TB	R	RBI	TBB	IBB	SO	HBP	SH	SF	SB	CS	SB%	GDP	Avg	OBP	SLG
1990 Oakland	AL	25	14	1	0	0	0	(0	0)	1	0	0	1	0	4	0	0	0	0	0	.00	0	.071	.133	.071
1991 Oakland	AL	90	235	56	5	1	0	(0	0)	63	21	21	14	0	37	3	12	1	3	4	.43	3	.238	.289	.268
1992 Oakland	AL	154	504	151	19	4	3	(3	0)	187	62	48	40	2	59	9	14	5	12	6	.67	10	.300	.358	.371
1993 Oakland	AL	159	546	136	21	2	3	(2	1)	170	60	48	60	2	58	11	10	6	10	10	.50	9	.249	.332	.311
1994 Oakland	AL	114	391	99	18	4	2	(1	1)	131	38	37	38	1	44	3	3	5	7	2	.78	9	.253	.320	.335
1995 Oakland	AL	126	428	113	13	0	8	(2	6)	150	46	44	35	2	48	5	7	3	11	3	.79	8	.264	.325	.350
1996 Oakland	AL	155	525	126	18	4	5	(2	3)	167	46	54	52	0	59	1	4	5	5	6	.45	8	.240	.307	.318
1997 Baltimore	AL	153	509	120	19	1	7	(5	2)	162	55	46	33	1	66	2	12	4	0	2	.00	23	.236	.283	.318
1998 Baltimore	AL	151	465	121	29	1	13	(10	3)	191	59	51	39	0	65	10	15	4	6	7	.46	13	.260	.328	.411
1999 Baltimore	AL	160	631	175	35	7	10	(3	7)	254	93	77	54	1	102	5	8	10	14	4	.78	25	.277	.334	.403
10 ML YEARS		1287	4248	1098	177	24	51	(28	23)	1476	480	426	366	9	542	49	85	43	68	44	.61	108	.258	.322	.347

Dave Borkowski

Pitches: Right **Bats:** Right **Pos:** SP-12; RP-5   **Ht:** 6'1" **Wt:** 200 **Born:** 2/7/77 **Age:** 23

					HOW MUCH HE PITCHED						WHAT HE GAVE UP										THE RESULTS					
Year Team	Lg	G	GS	CG	GF	IP	BFP	H	R	ER	HR	SH	SF	HB	TBB	IBB	SO	WP	Bk	W	L	Pct.	ShO	Sv-Op	Hld	ERA
1995 Tigers	R	10	10	1	0	51.2	212	45	24	17	2	1	0	5	8	0	36	1	2	3	2	.600	0	0- -	—	2.96
Lakeland	A+	1	1	0	0	5	17	2	0	0	0	0	0	0	1	0	3	0	0	1	0	1.000	0	0- -	—	0.00
1996 Fayettevlle	A	27	27	5	0	178.1	739	158	85	66	7	4	5	15	54	0	117	12	3	10	10	.500	0	0- -	—	3.33
1997 W Michigan	A	25	25	4	0	164	670	143	79	63	15	3	3	7	31	0	104	7	0	15	3	.833	2	0- -	—	3.46
1998 Jacksnville	AA	28	28	3	0	178.2	775	204	99	92	25	2	7	10	54	0	97	10	2	16	7	.696	1	0- -	—	4.63
1999 Toledo	AAA	19	19	3	0	126	530	119	59	49	16	0	3	10	43	0	94	10	0	6	8	.429	0	0- -	—	3.50
1999 Detroit	AL	17	12	0	2	76.2	351	86	58	52	10	1	2	4	40	0	50	3	0	2	6	.250	0	0-0	0	6.10

Ricky Bottalico

Pitches: Right **Bats:** Left **Pos:** RP-68   **Ht:** 6'1" **Wt:** 217 **Born:** 8/26/69 **Age:** 30

					HOW MUCH HE PITCHED						WHAT HE GAVE UP										THE RESULTS					
Year Team	Lg	G	GS	CG	GF	IP	BFP	H	R	ER	HR	SH	SF	HB	TBB	IBB	SO	WP	Bk	W	L	Pct.	ShO	Sv-Op	Hld	ERA
1994 Philadelphia	NL	3	0	0	3	3	13	3	0	0	0	0	0	0	1	0	3	0	0	0	0	.000	0	0-0	0	0.00
1995 Philadelphia	NL	62	0	0	20	87.2	350	50	25	24	7	3	1	4	42	3	87	1	0	5	3	.625	0	1-5	20	2.46
1996 Philadelphia	NL	61	0	0	56	67.2	269	47	24	24	6	4	2	2	23	2	74	3	0	4	5	.444	0	34-38	0	3.19
1997 Philadelphia	NL	69	0	0	61	74	324	68	31	30	7	1	2	2	42	4	89	5	0	2	5	.286	0	34-41	0	3.65
1998 Philadelphia	NL	39	0	0	28	43.1	206	54	31	31	7	1	2	1	25	5	27	2	0	1	5	.167	0	6-7	3	6.44
1999 St. Louis	NL	68	0	0	40	73.1	347	83	45	40	8	3	0	3	49	1	66	6	0	3	7	.300	0	20-28	8	4.91
6 ML YEARS		302	0	0	208	349	1509	305	156	149	35	12	7	12	182	15	346	15	0	15	25	.375	0	95-119	31	3.84

Kent Bottenfield

Pitches: Right **Bats:** Right **Pos:** SP-31   **Ht:** 6'3" **Wt:** 240 **Born:** 11/14/68 **Age:** 31

		HOW MUCH HE PITCHED						WHAT HE GAVE UP											THE RESULTS					
Year Team	Lg	G	GS	CG	GF	IP	BFP	H	R	ER	HR	SH	SF	HB	TBB	IBB	SO	WP	Bk	W	L	Pct.	ShO	Sv-Op	Hld	ERA
1992 Montreal	NL	10	4	0	2	32.1	135	26	9	8	1	1	2	1	11	1	14	0	0	1	2	.333	0	1-1	1	2.23
1993 Mon-Col	NL	37	25	1	2	159.2	710	179	102	90	24	21	4	6	71	3	63	4	1	5	10	.333	0	0-0	0	5.07
1994 Col-SF	NL	16	1	0	3	26.1	121	33	18	18	2	1	0	2	10	0	15	2	0	3	1	.750	0	1-1	0	6.15
1996 Chicago	NL	48	0	0	10	61.2	258	59	25	18	3	5	0	3	19	4	33	2	0	3	5	.375	0	1-3	4	2.63
1997 Chicago	NL	64	0	0	20	84	361	82	39	36	13	4	4	2	35	7	74	2	0	2	3	.400	0	2-4	8	3.86
1998 St. Louis	NL	44	17	0	11	133.2	578	128	72	66	13	11	3	4	57	3	98	3	2	4	6	.400	0	4-5	6	4.44
1999 St. Louis	NL	31	31	0	0	190.1	843	197	91	84	21	11	9	5	89	5	124	1	0	18	7	.720	0	0-0	0	3.97
1993 Montreal	NL	23	11	0	2	83	373	93	49	38	11	11	1	5	33	2	33	4	1	2	5	.286	0	0-0	0	4.12
Colorado	NL	14	14	1	0	76.2	337	86	53	52	13	10	3	1	38	1	30	0	0	3	5	.375	0	0-0	0	6.10
1994 Colorado	NL	15	1	0	3	24.2	112	28	16	16	1	1	0	2	10	0	15	2	0	3	1	.750	0	1-1	0	5.84
San Francisco	NL	1	0	0	0	1.2	9	5	2	2	1	0	0	0	0	0	0	0	0	0	0	.000	0	0-0	0	10.80
7 ML YEARS		250	78	1	48	688	3006	704	356	320	77	54	22	23	292	23	421	14	3	36	34	.514	0	9-14	19	4.19

Rafael Bournigal

Bats: R **Throws:** R **Pos:** SS-28; 2B-17; 3B-8; PH/PR-7; DH-1; LF-1   **Ht:** 5'11" **Wt:** 175 **Born:** 5/12/66 **Age:** 34

		BATTING																		BASERUNNING				PERCENTAGES		
Year Team	Lg	G	AB	H	2B	3B	HR	(Hm	Rd)	TB	R	RBI	TBB	IBB	SO	HBP	SH	SF	SB	CS	SB%	GDP	Avg	OBP	SLG
1999 Oklahoma *	AAA	17	56	21	6	0	3	—	—	36	16	14	12	0	5	0	0	1	1	1	.50	1	.375	.478	.643
1992 Los Angeles	NL	10	20	3	1	0	0	(0	0)	4	1	0	1	0	2	1	0	0	0	0	.00	0	.150	.227	.200
1993 Los Angeles	NL	8	18	9	1	0	0	(0	0)	10	0	3	0	0	2	0	0	0	0	0	.00	0	.500	.500	.556
1994 Los Angeles	NL	40	116	26	3	1	0	(0	0)	31	2	11	9	1	5	2	5	0	0	0	.00	4	.224	.291	.267
1996 Oakland	AL	88	252	61	14	2	0	(0	0)	79	33	18	16	0	19	1	8	0	4	3	.57	6	.242	.290	.313
1997 Oakland	AL	79	222	62	9	0	1	(0	1)	74	29	20	16	1	19	4	7	0	2	1	.67	11	.279	.339	.333
1998 Oakland	AL	85	209	47	11	0	1	(1	0)	61	23	19	10	1	11	2	6	2	6	1	.86	6	.225	.265	.292
1999 Seattle	AL	55	95	26	5	0	2	(2	0)	37	16	14	7	0	6	0	4	2	0	0	.00	5	.274	.317	.389
7 ML YEARS		365	932	234	44	3	4	(3	1)	296	104	85	59	3	64	10	30	4	12	5	.71	32	.251	.301	.318

Micah Bowie

Pitches: Left **Bats:** Left **Pos:** SP-11; RP-3   **Ht:** 6'4" **Wt:** 185 **Born:** 11/10/74 **Age:** 25

		HOW MUCH HE PITCHED						WHAT HE GAVE UP											THE RESULTS					
Year Team	Lg	G	GS	CG	GF	IP	BFP	H	R	ER	HR	SH	SF	HB	TBB	IBB	SO	WP	Bk	W	L	Pct.	ShO	Sv-Op	Hld	ERA
1994 Braves	R	6	5	0	1	29.2	124	27	14	10	1	0	2	1	5	0	35	1	0	0	3	.000	0	0--	—	3.03
Danville	R+	7	5	0	0	32.2	141	28	16	13	4	2	3	3	13	1	38	2	0	3	1	.750	0	0--	—	3.58
1995 Macon	A	5	5	0	0	27.2	104	9	8	7	1	0	0	3	11	0	36	1	0	4	1	.800	0	0--	—	2.28
Durham	A+	23	23	1	0	130.1	561	119	65	52	8	13	3	8	61	3	91	4	3	4	11	.267	0	0--	—	3.59
1996 Durham	A+	14	13	0	0	66.1	283	55	29	27	4	6	3	7	33	0	65	2	0	3	6	.333	0	0--	—	3.66
1997 Durham	A+	9	6	0	0	39.1	167	29	16	16	2	0	2	0	27	0	44	2	0	2	2	.500	0	0--	—	3.66
Greenville	AA	8	7	0	0	43.2	193	34	19	17	3	1	2	3	26	1	41	2	0	3	2	.600	0	0--	—	3.50
1998 Greenville	AA	30	29	1	0	163	676	132	73	63	12	7	2	6	64	0	160	7	3	11	6	.647	0	0--	—	3.48
1999 Richmond	AAA	13	13	0	0	73	288	65	24	24	4	2	2	0	14	0	82	2	0	4	4	.500	0	0--	—	2.96
1999 Atl-ChC	NL	14	11	0	2	51	265	81	60	58	9	3	3	2	34	2	41	4	2	2	7	.222	0	0-0	0	10.24
1999 Atlanta	NL	3	0	0	2	4	23	8	6	6	1	0	0	0	4	0	2	0	0	0	1	.000	0	0-0	0	13.50
Chicago	NL	11	11	0	0	47	242	73	54	52	8	3	3	2	30	2	39	4	2	2	6	.250	0	0-0	0	9.96

Jason Boyd

Pitches: Right **Bats:** Right **Pos:** RP-4   **Ht:** 6'3" **Wt:** 170 **Born:** 2/23/73 **Age:** 27

		HOW MUCH HE PITCHED						WHAT HE GAVE UP											THE RESULTS					
Year Team	Lg	G	GS	CG	GF	IP	BFP	H	R	ER	HR	SH	SF	HB	TBB	IBB	SO	WP	Bk	W	L	Pct.	ShO	Sv-Op	Hld	ERA
1994 Martinsvlle	R+	14	13	1	0	69	306	65	46	32	6	0	1	4	32	0	45	7	6	3	7	.300	0	0--	—	4.17
1995 Piedmont	A	26	24	1	1	151	638	151	77	60	8	5	3	4	44	0	129	18	2	6	8	.429	0	0--	—	3.58
1996 Clearwater	A+	26	26	2	0	161.2	674	160	75	70	12	3	6	3	49	1	120	7	1	11	8	.579	0	0--	—	3.90
1997 Reading	AA	48	7	0	9	115.2	509	113	65	62	16	2	3	3	64	7	98	1	2	10	6	.625	0	0--	—	4.82
1998 Tucson	AAA	15	0	3	0	21.2	109	28	22	15	4	0	0	1	14	1	13	0	1	2	2	.500	0	0--	—	6.23
1999 Tucson	AAA	44	0	0	17	75.2	325	76	42	38	6	2	4	3	27	2	60	6	2	6	5	.545	0	5--	—	4.52
Nashville	AAA	5	0	0	2	4.2	14	2	0	0	0	0	0	0	0	0	2	0	0	0	0	.000	0	0--	—	0.00
1999 Pittsburgh	NL	4	0	0	0	5.1	24	5	2	2	0	0	1	1	2	0	4	1	0	0	0	.000	0	0-0	0	3.38

Chad Bradford

Pitches: Right **Bats:** Right **Pos:** RP-3   **Ht:** 6'5" **Wt:** 205 **Born:** 9/14/74 **Age:** 25

		HOW MUCH HE PITCHED						WHAT HE GAVE UP											THE RESULTS					
Year Team	Lg	G	GS	CG	GF	IP	BFP	H	R	ER	HR	SH	SF	HB	TBB	IBB	SO	WP	Bk	W	L	Pct.	ShO	Sv-Op	Hld	ERA
1996 Hickory	A	28	0	0	27	30	121	21	7	3	1	2	1	3	7	1	27	0	0	0	2	.000	0	18--	—	0.90
1997 Winston-Sal	A+	46	0	0	41	54.2	247	51	30	24	2	4	0	5	25	5	43	2	0	3	7	.300	0	15--	—	3.95
1998 Birmingham	AA	10	0	0	7	17.1	72	13	6	5	2	0	0	0	8	0	14	2	0	1	1	.500	0	1--	—	2.60
Calgary	AAA	29	0	0	10	51	205	50	12	11	3	0	1	1	11	2	27	2	2	4	1	.800	0	0--	—	1.94
1999 Charlotte	AAA	47	0	0	19	74.1	293	63	19	16	2	3	0	2	15	0	56	0	0	9	3	.750	0	5--	—	1.94
1998 Chicago	AL	29	0	0	8	30.2	125	27	16	11	0	0	0	5	7	0	11	1	1	2	1	.667	0	1-3	9	3.23
1999 Chicago	AL	3	0	0	0	3.2	24	9	8	8	1	0	0	5	5	0	0	1	0	0	0	.000	0	0-0	0	19.64
2 ML YEARS		32	0	0	8	34.1	149	36	24	19	1	0	0	10	12	0	11	2	1	2	1	.667	0	1-3	9	4.98

Darren Bragg

Bats: L **Throws:** R **Pos:** CF-43; RF-33; LF-22; PH/PR-10   **Ht:** 5'9" **Wt:** 180 **Born:** 9/7/69 **Age:** 30

						BATTING												BASERUNNING				PERCENTAGES		
Year Team	Lg	G	AB	H	2B	3B	HR	(Hm | Rd)	TB	R	RBI	TBB	IBB	SO	HBP	SH	SF	SB	CS	SB%	GDP	Avg	OBP	SLG
1994 Seattle	AL	8	19	3	1	0	0	(0 | 0)	4	4	2	2	1	5	0	0	0	0	0	.00	0	.158	.238	.211
1995 Seattle	AL	52	145	34	5	1	3	(1 | 2)	50	20	12	18	1	37	4	1	2	9	0	1.00	2	.234	.331	.345
1996 Sea-Bos	AL	127	417	109	26	2	10	(7 | 3)	169	74	47	69	6	74	4	2	7	14	9	.61	5	.261	.366	.405
1997 Boston	AL	153	513	132	35	2	9	(3 | 6)	198	65	57	61	5	102	3	5	4	10	6	.63	16	.257	.337	.386
1998 Boston	AL	129	409	114	29	3	8	(3 | 5)	173	51	57	42	0	99	6	4	4	5	3	.63	16	.279	.351	.423
1999 St. Louis	NL	93	273	71	12	1	6	(4 | 2)	103	38	26	44	1	67	3	5	0	3	0	1.00	5	.260	.369	.377
1996 Seattle	AL	69	195	53	12	1	7	(4 | 3)	88	36	25	33	4	35	2	1	4	8	5	.62	2	.272	.376	.451
Boston		58	222	56	14	1	3	(3 | 0)	81	38	22	36	2	39	2	1	3	6	4	.60	3	.252	.357	.365
6 ML YEARS		562	1776	463	108	9	36	(18 | 18)	697	252	201	236	14	384	20	17	17	41	18	.69	44	.261	.351	.392

Jeff Brantley

Pitches: Right **Bats:** Right **Pos:** RP-10   **Ht:** 5'10" **Wt:** 190 **Born:** 9/5/63 **Age:** 36

		HOW MUCH HE PITCHED						WHAT HE GAVE UP										THE RESULTS						
Year Team	Lg	G	GS	CG	GF	IP	BFP	H	R	ER	HR	SH	SF	HB	TBB	IBB	SO	WP	Bk	W	L	Pct.	ShO	Sv-Op	Hld	ERA
1988 San Francisco	NL	9	1	0	2	20.2	88	22	13	13	2	1	0	1	6	1	11	0	1	0	1	.000	0	1-1	0	5.66
1989 San Francisco	NL	59	1	0	15	97.1	422	101	50	44	10	7	3	2	37	8	69	3	2	7	1	.875	0	0-1	11	4.07
1990 San Francisco	NL	55	0	0	32	86.2	361	77	18	15	3	2	2	3	33	6	61	0	3	5	3	.625	0	19-24	8	1.56
1991 San Francisco	NL	67	0	0	39	95.1	411	78	27	26	8	4	4	5	52	10	81	6	0	5	2	.714	0	15-19	12	2.45
1992 San Francisco	NL	56	4	0	32	91.2	381	67	32	30	8	7	3	3	45	5	86	3	1	7	7	.500	0	7-9	3	2.95
1993 San Francisco	NL	53	12	0	9	113.2	496	112	60	54	19	5	5	7	46	2	76	3	4	5	6	.455	0	0-3	10	4.28
1994 Cincinnati	NL	50	0	0	35	65.1	262	46	20	18	6	5	1	0	28	5	63	1	0	6	6	.500	0	15-21	1	2.48
1995 Cincinnati	NL	56	0	0	49	70.1	283	53	22	22	11	2	3	1	20	3	62	2	0	3	2	.600	0	28-32	0	2.82
1996 Cincinnati	NL	66	0	0	61	71	288	54	21	19	7	4	5	0	28	6	76	2	0	1	2	.333	0	44-49	0	2.41
1997 Cincinnati	NL	13	0	0	9	11.2	53	9	5	5	2	0	0	2	7	1	16	2	0	1	1	.500	0	1-3	0	3.86
1998 St. Louis	NL	48	0	0	33	50.2	209	40	26	25	12	5	3	1	18	3	48	1	0	0	5	.000	0	14-22	3	4.44
1999 Philadelphia	NL	10	0	0	9	8.2	40	5	6	5	0	0	1	0	8	0	11	0	0	1	2	.333	0	5-6	0	5.19
12 ML YEARS		542	18	0	325	783	3294	664	300	276	88	42	30	25	328	50	660	23	13	41	38	.519	0	149-190	48	3.17

Russ Branyan

Bats: Left **Throws:** Right **Pos:** 3B-8; DH-3   **Ht:** 6'3" **Wt:** 195 **Born:** 12/19/75 **Age:** 24

						BATTING												BASERUNNING				PERCENTAGES		
Year Team	Lg	G	AB	H	2B	3B	HR	(Hm	Rd)	TB	R	RBI	TBB	IBB	SO	HBP	SH	SF	SB	CS	SB%	GDP	Avg	OBP	SLG
1994 Burlington	R+	55	171	36	10	0	5	—	—	61	21	13	25	2	64	4	0	1	4	2	.67	3	.211	.323	.357
1995 Columbus	A	76	277	71	8	6	19	—	—	148	46	55	27	2	120	3	0	3	1	1	.50	6	.256	.326	.534
1996 Columbus	A	130	482	129	20	4	40	—	—	277	102	106	62	5	166	5	0	3	7	4	.64	4	.268	.355	.575
1997 Kinston	A+	83	297	86	26	2	27	—	—	197	59	75	52	4	94	5	0	5	3	1	.75	9	.290	.398	.663
Akron	AA	41	137	32	4	0	12	—	—	72	26	30	28	1	56	2	0	1	0	0	.00	1	.234	.369	.526
1998 Akron	AA	43	163	48	11	3	16	—	—	113	35	46	35	4	58	0	0	1	1	1	.50	2	.294	.417	.693
1999 Buffalo	AAA	109	395	82	11	1	30	—	—	185	51	67	52	2	187	4	0	2	8	3	.73	5	.208	.305	.468
1998 Cleveland	AL	1	4	0	0	0	0	(0	0)	0	0	0	0	0	2	0	0	0	0	0	.00	0	.000	.000	.000
1999 Cleveland	AL	11	38	8	2	0	1	(0	1)	13	4	6	3	0	19	1	0	0	0	0	.00	0	.211	.286	.342
2 ML YEARS		12	42	8	2	0	1	(0	1)	13	4	6	3	0	21	1	0	0	0	0	.00	0	.190	.261	.310

Billy Brewer

Pitches: Left **Bats:** Left **Pos:** RP-25   **Ht:** 6'1" **Wt:** 200 **Born:** 4/15/68 **Age:** 32

		HOW MUCH HE PITCHED						WHAT HE GAVE UP										THE RESULTS						
Year Team	Lg	G	GS	CG	GF	IP	BFP	H	R	ER	HR	SH	SF	HB	TBB	IBB	SO	WP	Bk	W	L	Pct.	ShO	Sv-Op	Hld	ERA
1999 Scranton-WB *	AAA	33	5	0	10	69	293	59	32	29	5	1	6	5	28	0	57	9	0	6	1	.857	0	2- -	—	3.78
1993 Kansas City	AL	46	0	0	14	39	157	31	16	15	6	1	1	0	20	4	28	2	1	2	2	.500	0	0-2	5	3.46
1994 Kansas City	AL	50	0	0	17	38.2	157	28	11	11	4	2	2	2	16	1	25	3	0	4	1	.800	0	3-7	12	2.56
1995 Kansas City	AL	48	0	0	13	45.1	200	54	28	28	9	1	0	2	20	1	31	5	1	2	4	.333	0	0-4	7	5.56
1996 New York	AL	4	0	0	1	5.2	32	7	6	6	0	0	0	0	8	0	8	0	0	1	0	1.000	0	0-0	1	9.53
1997 Oak-Phi		28	0	0	5	24	105	19	11	11	3	0	3	0	13	0	17	1	0	1	2	.333	0	0-2	5	4.13
1998 Philadelphia	NL	2	0	0	0	0.1	6	3	4	4	0	0	0	0	2	0	0	1	0	0	0	.000	0	0-0	0	108.00
1999 Philadelphia	NL	25	0	0	8	25.2	118	30	20	20	4	1	1	0	14	1	28	1	0	1	1	.500	0	2-2	1	7.01
1997 Oakland	AL	3	0	0	1	2	12	4	3	3	1	0	1	0	2	0	1	0	0	0	0	.000	0	0-0	0	13.50
Philadelphia	NL	25	0	0	4	22	93	15	8	8	2	0	2	0	11	0	16	1	0	1	2	.333	0	0-2	5	3.27
7 ML YEARS		203	0	0	58	178.2	784	172	96	95	26	5	7	4	93	7	137	12	2	11	11	.500	0	5-17	30	4.79

Doug Brocail

Pitches: Right **Bats:** Left **Pos:** RP-70   **Ht:** 6'5" **Wt:** 235 **Born:** 5/16/67 **Age:** 33

		HOW MUCH HE PITCHED						WHAT HE GAVE UP										THE RESULTS						
Year Team	Lg	G	GS	CG	GF	IP	BFP	H	R	ER	HR	SH	SF	HB	TBB	IBB	SO	WP	Bk	W	L	Pct.	ShO	Sv-Op	Hld	ERA
1992 San Diego	NL	3	3	0	0	14	64	17	10	10	2	2	0	0	5	0	15	0	0	0	0	.000	0	0-0	0	6.43
1993 San Diego	NL	24	24	0	0	128.1	571	143	75	65	16	10	8	4	42	4	70	4	1	4	13	.235	0	0-0	0	4.56
1994 San Diego	NL	12	0	0	4	17	78	21	13	11	1	1	1	2	5	3	11	1	1	0	0	.000	0	0-1	0	5.82
1995 Houston	NL	36	0	0	12	77.1	339	87	40	36	10	1	1	4	22	2	39	1	1	6	4	.600	0	1-1	0	4.19
1996 Houston	NL	23	4	0	4	53	231	58	31	27	7	3	2	2	23	1	34	0	0	1	5	.167	0	0-0	1	4.58
1997 Detroit	AL	61	4	0	20	78	332	74	31	28	10	1	3	3	36	4	60	6	0	3	4	.429	0	2-9	16	3.23
1998 Detroit	AL	60	0	0	24	62.2	247	47	23	19	8	3	3	1	18	0	55	6	0	5	2	.714	0	0-1	11	2.73

Year Team	Lg	G	GS	CG	GF	IP	BFP	H	R	ER	HR	SH	SF	HB	TBB	IBB	SO	WP	Bk	W	L	Pct.	ShO	Sv-Op	Hld	ERA
1999 Detroit	AL	70	0	0	22	70	82 326	60	23	23	7	4	2	4	25	1	78	4	1	4	4	.500	0	2-4	23	2.52
8 ML YEARS		289	42	0	86	512.1	2188	507	246	219	55	24	20	20	176	18	362	22	4	23	32	.418	0	5-16	51	3.85

Chris Brock

Pitches: Right **Bats:** Right **Pos:** SP-19   **Ht:** 6'0" **Wt:** 185 **Born:** 2/5/70 **Age:** 30

HOW MUCH HE PITCHED / **WHAT HE GAVE UP** / **THE RESULTS**

Year Team	Lg	G	GS	CG	GF	IP	BFP	H	R	ER	HR	SH	SF	HB	TBB	IBB	SO	WP	Bk	W	L	Pct.	ShO	Sv-Op	Hld	ERA
1997 Atlanta	NL	7	6	0	1	30.2	144	34	23	19	2	3	4	0	19	2	16	2	1	0	0	.000	0	0-0	0	5.58
1998 San Francisco	NL	13	0	0	4	27.2	120	31	13	12	3	2	0	0	7	1	19	0	0	0	0	.000	0	0-0	0	3.90
1999 San Francisco	NL	19	19	0	0	106.2	479	124	69	65	18	5	3	4	41	2	76	8	2	6	8	.429	0	0-0	0	5.48
3 ML YEARS		39	25	0	5	165	743	189	105	96	23	10	7	4	67	5	111	10	3	6	8	.429	0	0-0	0	5.24

Rico Brogna

Bats: Left **Throws:** Left **Pos:** 1B-157; PH/PR-2   **Ht:** 6'2" **Wt:** 205 **Born:** 4/18/70 **Age:** 30

BATTING / **BASERUNNING** / **PERCENTAGES**

Year Team	Lg	G	AB	H	2B	3B	HR	(Hm	Rd)	TB	R	RBI	TBB	IBB	SO	HBP	SH	SF	SB	CS	SB%	GDP	Avg	OBP	SLG
1992 Detroit	AL	9	26	5	1	0	1	(1	0)	9	3	3	3	0	5	0	0	0	0	0	.00	0	.192	.276	.346
1994 New York	NL	39	131	46	11	2	7	(2	5)	82	16	20	6	0	29	0	1	0	1	0	1.00	2	.351	.380	.626
1995 New York	NL	134	495	143	27	2	22	(13	9)	240	72	76	39	7	111	2	2	2	0	0	.00	10	.289	.342	.485
1996 New York	NL	55	188	48	10	1	7	(5	2)	81	18	30	19	1	50	0	0	4	0	0	.00	4	.255	.318	.431
1997 Philadelphia	NL	148	543	137	36	1	20	(9	11)	235	68	81	33	4	116	0	0	4	12	3	.80	12	.252	.293	.433
1998 Philadelphia	NL	153	565	150	36	3	20	(11	9)	252	77	104	49	8	125	0	0	10	7	7	.50	12	.265	.319	.446
1999 Philadelphia	NL	157	619	172	29	4	24	(14	10)	281	90	102	54	7	132	2	0	4	8	5	.62	19	.278	.336	.454
7 ML YEARS		695	2567	701	150	13	101	(55	46)	1180	344	416	203	27	568	4	3	24	28	15	.65	59	.273	.325	.460

Scott Brosius

Bats: Right **Throws:** Right **Pos:** 3B-132; PH/PR-2; DH-1   **Ht:** 6'1" **Wt:** 202 **Born:** 8/15/66 **Age:** 33

BATTING / **BASERUNNING** / **PERCENTAGES**

Year Team	Lg	G	AB	H	2B	3B	HR	(Hm	Rd)	TB	R	RBI	TBB	IBB	SO	HBP	SH	SF	SB	CS	SB%	GDP	Avg	OBP	SLG
1999 Tampa *	A+	3	1	1	0	0	0			1	0	0	0	0	0	0	0	0	0	0	.00	0	.333	.333	.333
1991 Oakland	AL	36	68	16	5	0	2	(1	1)	27	9	4	3	0	11	0	1	0	3	1	.75	2	.235	.268	.397
1992 Oakland	AL	38	87	19	2	0	4	(1	3)	33	13	13	3	1	13	2	0	1	3	0	1.00	0	.218	.258	.379
1993 Oakland	AL	70	213	53	10	1	6	(3	3)	83	26	25	14	0	37	1	3	2	6	0	1.00	6	.249	.296	.390
1994 Oakland	AL	96	324	77	14	1	14	(9	5)	135	31	49	24	0	57	2	4	6	2	6	.25	7	.238	.289	.417
1995 Oakland	AL	123	389	102	19	2	17	(12	5)	176	69	46	41	0	67	8	1	4	4	2	.67	5	.262	.342	.452
1996 Oakland	AL	114	428	130	25	0	22	(15	7)	221	73	71	59	4	85	7	1	5	7	2	.78	11	.304	.393	.516
1997 Oakland	AL	129	479	97	20	1	11	(7	4)	152	59	41	34	1	102	4	5	4	9	4	.69	9	.203	.259	.317
1998 New York	AL	152	530	159	34	0	19	(8	11)	250	86	98	52	1	97	10	8	3	11	8	.58	4	.300	.371	.472
1999 New York	AL	133	473	117	26	1	17	(4	13)	196	64	71	39	2	74	6	2	9	9	3	.75	13	.247	.307	.414
9 ML YEARS		891	2991	770	155	6	112	(60	52)	1273	430	418	269	9	543	40	25	34	54	26	.68	57	.257	.324	.426

Jim Brower

Pitches: Right **Bats:** Right **Pos:** RP-7; SP-2   **Ht:** 6'2" **Wt:** 205 **Born:** 12/29/72 **Age:** 27

HOW MUCH HE PITCHED / **WHAT HE GAVE UP** / **THE RESULTS**

Year Team	Lg	G	GS	CG	GF	IP	BFP	H	R	ER	HR	SH	SF	HB	TBB	IBB	SO	WP	Bk	W	L	Pct.	ShO	Sv-Op	Hld	ERA
1994 Hudson Val	A-	4	4	1	0	19.2	83	14	10	7	0	0	2	1	6	0	15	0	1	2	1	.667	0	0--	—	3.20
Chston-SC	A	12	12	3	0	78.2	312	52	18	15	2	1	1	5	26	1	84	6	0	7	3	.700	2	0--	—	1.72
1995 Charlotte	A+	27	27	2	0	173.2	740	170	93	75	16	3	3	8	62	1	110	11	0	7	10	.412	1	0--	—	3.89
1996 Charlotte	A+	23	21	2	2	145	607	148	67	61	11	5	4	4	40	0	86	7	2	9	8	.529	2	0--	—	3.79
Tulsa	AA	5	5	0	0	33.1	140	35	16	14	4	0	1	1	10	0	16	1	0	3	2	.600	1	0--	—	3.78
1997 Tulsa	AA	23	23	1	0	140	602	156	99	81	13	4	7	3	42	1	103	15	1	5	12	.294	0	0--	—	5.21
Okla City	AAA	4	3	0	0	18.2	92	30	17	15	3	0	2	1	8	0	7	3	0	2	1	.667	0	0--	—	7.23
1998 Akron	AA	23	23	2	0	155.2	630	142	60	52	9	4	3	7	38	0	91	5	0	9	4	.692	2	0--	—	3.01
1999 Buffalo	AAA	27	27	0	0	160	689	164	101	84	23	6	8	8	59	6	76	9	2	11	11	.500	0	0--	—	4.73
1999 Cleveland	AL	9	2	0	1	25.2	113	27	13	13	8	1	1	1	10	1	18	0	0	3	1	.750	0	0-0	0	4.56

Adrian Brown

Bats: B **Throws:** R **Pos:** RF-66; PH/PR-34; CF-29; LF-4   **Ht:** 6'0" **Wt:** 185 **Born:** 2/7/74 **Age:** 26

BATTING / **BASERUNNING** / **PERCENTAGES**

Year Team	Lg	G	AB	H	2B	3B	HR	(Hm	Rd)	TB	R	RBI	TBB	IBB	SO	HBP	SH	SF	SB	CS	SB%	GDP	Avg	OBP	SLG
1999 Nashville *	AAA	17	56	18	3	1	0	—	—	23	10	4	11	1	8	0	0	0	6	1	.86	0	.321	.433	.411
1997 Pittsburgh	NL	48	147	28	6	0	1	(0	1)	37	17	10	13	0	18	4	2	1	8	4	.67	3	.190	.273	.252
1998 Pittsburgh	NL	41	152	43	4	1	0	(0	0)	49	20	5	9	0	18	0	4	0	4	0	1.00	3	.283	.323	.322
1999 Pittsburgh	NL	116	226	61	5	2	4	(2	2)	82	34	17	33	2	39	1	6	1	5	3	.63	5	.270	.364	.363
3 ML YEARS		205	525	132	15	3	5	(2	3)	168	71	32	55	2	75	5	12	2	17	7	.71	11	.251	.327	.320

Brant Brown

Bats: L **Throws:** L **Pos:** RF-59; PH/PR-41; CF-23; 1B-7; DH-6 **Ht:** 6'3" **Wt:** 205 **Born:** 6/22/71 **Age:** 29

Year Team	Lg	G	AB	H	2B	3B	HR	(Hm	Rd)	TB	R	RBI	TBB	IBB	SO	HBP	SH	SF	SB	CS	SB%	GDP	Avg	OBP	SLG
1996 Chicago	NL	29	69	21	1	0	5	(3	2)	37	11	9	2	1	17	1	0	1	3	3	.50	1	.304	.329	.536
1997 Chicago	NL	46	137	32	7	1	5	(3	2)	56	15	15	7	0	28	3	1	0	2	1	.67	2	.234	.286	.409
1998 Chicago	NL	124	347	101	17	7	14	(10	4)	174	56	48	30	2	95	1	1	1	4	5	.44	1	.291	.348	.501
1999 Pittsburgh	NL	130	341	79	20	3	16	(4	12)	153	49	58	22	3	114	4	0	4	3	4	.43	4	.232	.283	.449
4 ML YEARS		329	894	233	45	11	40	(20	20)	420	131	130	61	6	254	9	2	6	12	13	.48	8	.261	.312	.470

Dee Brown

Bats: Left **Throws:** Right **Pos:** PH/PR-7; LF-3; DH-2 **Ht:** 6'0" **Wt:** 215 **Born:** 3/27/78 **Age:** 22

Year Team	Lg	G	AB	H	2B	3B	HR	(Hm	Rd)	TB	R	RBI	TBB	IBB	SO	HBP	SH	SF	SB	CS	SB%	GDP	Avg	OBP	SLG
1996 Royals	R	7	20	1	1	0	0	—	—	2	1	1	0	0	6	1	0	0	0	2	.00	0	.050	.095	.100
1997 Spokane	A-	73	298	97	20	6	13	—	—	168	67	73	38	5	65	2	0	1	17	4	.81	5	.326	.404	.564
1998 Wilmington	A+	128	442	114	30	2	10	—	—	178	64	58	53	5	115	7	1	0	26	10	.72	12	.258	.347	.403
1999 Wilmington	A+	61	221	68	10	2	13	—	—	121	49	46	44	6	56	4	0	0	20	8	.71	10	.308	.431	.548
Wichita	AA	65	235	83	14	3	12	—	—	139	58	56	35	1	41	3	1	2	10	8	.56	2	.353	.440	.591
1998 Kansas City	AL	5	3	0	0	0	0	(0	0)	0	2	0	0	0	1	0	0	0	0	0	.00	0	.000	.000	.000
1999 Kansas City	AL	12	25	2	0	0	0	(0	0)	2	1	0	2	0	7	0	0	0	0	0	.00	0	.080	.148	.080
2 ML YEARS		17	28	2	0	0	0	(0	0)	2	3	0	2	0	8	0	0	0	0	0	.00	0	.071	.133	.071

Emil Brown

Bats: Right **Throws:** Right **Pos:** LF-6; PH/PR-1 **Ht:** 6'2" **Wt:** 192 **Born:** 12/29/74 **Age:** 25

Year Team	Lg	G	AB	H	2B	3B	HR	(Hm	Rd)	TB	R	RBI	TBB	IBB	SO	HBP	SH	SF	SB	CS	SB%	GDP	Avg	OBP	SLG
1999 Nashville *	AAA	110	430	132	20	5	18	—	—	216	97	60	35	1	80	7	0	4	16	5	.76	7	.307	.366	.502
1997 Pittsburgh	NL	66	95	17	2	1	2	(1	1)	27	16	6	10	1	32	7	0	0	5	1	.83	1	.179	.304	.284
1998 Pittsburgh	NL	13	39	10	1	0	0	(0	0)	11	2	3	1	0	11	1	0	0	0	0	.00	0	.256	.293	.282
1999 Pittsburgh	NL	6	14	2	1	0	0	(0	0)	3	0	0	0	0	3	0	0	0	0	0	.00	0	.143	.143	.214
3 ML YEARS		85	148	29	4	1	2	(1	1)	41	18	9	11	1	46	8	0	0	5	1	.83	1	.196	.287	.277

Kevin Brown

Pitches: Right **Bats:** Right **Pos:** SP-35 **Ht:** 6'4" **Wt:** 200 **Born:** 3/14/65 **Age:** 35

| | | HOW MUCH HE PITCHED | | | | | | WHAT HE GAVE UP | | | | | | | | | | THE RESULTS | | | | | | |
Year Team	Lg	G	GS	CG	GF	IP	BFP	H	R	ER	HR	SH	SF	HB	TBB	IBB	SO	WP	Bk	W	L	Pct.	ShO	Sv-Op	Hld	ERA
1986 Texas	AL	1	1	0	0	5	19	6	2	2	0	0	0	0	0	0	4	0	0	1	0	1.000	0	0-0	0	3.60
1988 Texas	AL	4	4	1	0	23.1	110	33	15	11	2	1	0	1	8	0	12	1	0	1	1	.500	0	0-0	0	4.24
1989 Texas	AL	28	28	7	0	191	798	167	81	71	10	3	6	4	70	2	104	7	2	12	9	.571	0	0-0	0	3.35
1990 Texas	AL	26	26	6	0	180	757	175	84	72	13	2	7	3	60	3	88	9	2	12	10	.545	2	0-0	0	3.60
1991 Texas	AL	33	33	0	0	210.2	934	233	116	103	17	6	4	13	90	5	96	12	3	9	12	.429	0	0-0	0	4.40
1992 Texas	AL	35	35	11	0	265.2	1108	262	117	98	11	7	8	10	76	2	173	8	2	21	11	.656	1	0-0	0	3.32
1993 Texas	AL	34	34	12	0	233	1001	228	105	93	14	5	3	15	74	5	142	8	1	15	12	.556	3	0-0	0	3.59
1994 Texas	AL	26	25	3	1	170	760	218	109	91	18	2	7	6	50	3	123	7	0	7	9	.438	0	0-0	0	4.82
1995 Baltimore	AL	26	26	3	0	172.1	706	155	73	69	10	5	2	9	48	1	117	3	0	10	9	.526	1	0-0	0	3.60
1996 Florida	NL	32	32	5	0	233	906	187	60	49	8	4	4	16	33	2	159	6	1	17	11	.607	3	0-0	0	1.89
1997 Florida	NL	33	33	6	0	237.1	976	214	77	71	10	5	1	14	66	7	205	7	1	16	8	.667	2	0-0	0	2.69
1998 San Diego	NL	36	35	7	0	257	1032	225	77	68	8	13	3	10	49	4	257	10	0	18	7	.720	3	0-0	1	2.38
1999 Los Angeles	NL	35	35	5	0	252.1	1018	210	99	84	19	7	1	7	59	1	221	4	1	18	9	.667	1	0-0	0	3.00
13 ML YEARS		349	347	66	1	2430.2	10125	2313	1015	882	140	60	46	108	683	35	1701	82	13	157	108	.592	16	0-0	1	3.27

Kevin Brown

Bats: Right **Throws:** Right **Pos:** C-2 **Ht:** 6'2" **Wt:** 215 **Born:** 4/21/73 **Age:** 27

Year Team	Lg	G	AB	H	2B	3B	HR	(Hm	Rd)	TB	R	RBI	TBB	IBB	SO	HBP	SH	SF	SB	CS	SB%	GDP	Avg	OBP	SLG
1999 Syracuse *	AAA	88	295	76	18	2	13	—	—	137	39	51	21	1	79	2	0	2	0	1	.00	2	.258	.309	.464
1996 Texas	AL	3	4	0	0	0	0	(0	0)	0	1	1	2	0	2	1	0	1	0	0	.00	0	.000	.375	.000
1997 Texas	AL	4	5	2	0	0	1	(0	1)	5	1	1	0	0	0	0	0	0	0	0	.00	0	.400	.400	1.000
1998 Toronto	AL	52	110	29	7	1	2	(1	1)	44	17	15	9	0	31	2	3	4	0	0	.00	1	.264	.320	.400
1999 Toronto	AL	2	9	4	2	0	0	(0	0)	6	1	1	0	0	3	0	0	0	0	0	.00	0	.444	.444	.667
4 ML YEARS		61	128	35	9	1	3	(1	2)	55	20	18	11	0	36	3	3	5	0	0	.00	1	.273	.333	.430

Roosevelt Brown

Bats: L **Throws:** R **Pos:** PH/PR-17; LF-13; CF-5; RF-1 **Ht:** 5'11" **Wt:** 195 **Born:** 8/3/75 **Age:** 24

Year Team	Lg	G	AB	H	2B	3B	HR	(Hm	Rd)	TB	R	RBI	TBB	IBB	SO	HBP	SH	SF	SB	CS	SB%	GDP	Avg	OBP	SLG
1993 Braves	R	26	80	9	1	2	0	—	—	14	4	5	2	0	9	1	1	0	2	0	1.00	4	.113	.145	.175
1994 Idaho Falls	R+	48	160	53	8	1	3	—	—	72	28	22	17	0	15	1	0	1	8	6	.57	2	.331	.397	.450
1995 Eugene	A-	57	165	51	12	4	7	—	—	92	28	32	13	2	30	3	0	2	6	3	.67	1	.309	.366	.558
1996 Macon	A	113	413	115	27	0	19	—	—	199	61	64	33	4	60	3	0	3	21	11	.66	9	.278	.334	.482
Kane County	A	11	40	6	2	0	0	—	—	8	1	3	1	0	10	1	0	0	0	1	.00	0	.150	.190	.200

Year Team	Lg	G	AB	H	2B	3B	HR	(Hm	Rd)	TB	R	RBI	TBB	IBB	SO	HBP	SH	SF	SB	CS	SB%	GDP	Avg	OBP	SLG
						BATTING														BASERUNNING			PERCENTAGES		
1997 Kane County	A	61	211	50	7	1	4	—	—	71	29	30	22	2	52	1	0	0	5	4	.56	5	.237	.312	.336
Brevard Cty	A+	33	114	28	7	1	1	—	—	40	8	12	7	0	31	0	1	1	0	3	.00	4	.246	.287	.351
1998 Daytona	A+	68	244	84	15	5	9	—	—	136	49	43	23	3	46	2	0	2	3	2	.60	6	.344	.402	.557
West Tenn	AA	42	160	42	11	0	6	—	—	71	20	24	13	1	30	2	0	1	3	1	.75	6	.263	.324	.444
Iowa	AAA	1	3	1	1	0	0	—	—	2	0	2	0	0	0	0	0	0	0	0	.00	0	.333	.333	.667
1999 West Tenn	AA	34	125	37	12	0	3	—	—	58	12	12	14	1	29	2	0	0	6	1	.86	1	.296	.376	.464
Iowa	AAA	74	268	96	25	2	22	—	—	191	50	79	19	1	54	3	0	4	3	3	.50	8	.358	.401	.713
1999 Chicago	NL	33	64	14	6	1	1	(0	1)	25	6	10	2	0	14	0	3	1	1	0	1.00	2	.219	.239	.391

Mark Brownson

Pitches: Right Bats: Left Pos: SP-7   Ht: 6'2" Wt: 185 Born: 6/17/75 Age: 25

Year Team	Lg	G	GS	CG	GF	IP	BFP	H	R	ER	HR	SH	SF	HB	TBB	IBB	SO	WP	Bk	W	L	Pct.	ShO	Sv-Op	Hld	ERA
			HOW MUCH HE PITCHED								WHAT HE GAVE UP											THE RESULTS				
1994 Rockies	R	19	4	0	6	54.1	224	48	18	10	2	2	2	3	6	0	72	2	2	4	1	.800	0	3--	—	1.66
1995 Asheville	A	23	12	0	4	98.2	422	106	52	44	12	2	2	4	29	0	94	4	2	6	7	.462	0	1--	—	4.01
New Haven	AA	1	1	0	0	6	24	4	2	1	1	0	0	0	1	0	4	0	0	0	0	.000	0	0--	—	1.50
Salem	A+	9	1	0	5	15.2	71	16	8	7	0	0	0	1	4	0	9	4	0	2	1	.667	0	1--	—	4.02
1996 New Haven	AA	37	19	1	10	144	619	141	73	56	10	6	3	6	43	5	155	7	2	8	13	.381	0	3--	—	3.50
1997 New Haven	AA	29	29	2	0	184.2	779	172	101	86	24	8	5	14	55	1	170	5	2	10	9	.526	0	0--	—	4.19
1998 Colo Spngs	AAA	21	21	3	0	124.2	542	131	85	74	22	5	8	14	37	0	82	2	3	6	8	.429	0	0--	—	5.34
1999 Colo Spngs	AAA	17	16	2	0	103	446	120	75	71	24	2	6	7	24	0	81	6	2	6	6	.500	0	0--	—	6.20
1998 Colorado	NL	2	2	1	0	13.1	57	16	7	7	2	0	0	1	2	0	8	0	0	1	0	1.000	1	0-0	0	4.73
1999 Colorado	NL	7	7	0	0	29.2	139	42	26	26	8	4	0	1	8	0	21	2	0	0	2	.000	0	0-0	—	7.89
2 ML YEARS		9	9	1	0	43	196	58	33	33	10	4	0	2	10	0	29	2	0	1	2	.333	1	0-0	0	6.91

Jacob Brumfield

Bats: R Throws: R Pos: CF-40; PH/PR-21; LF-17; RF-8; DH-6   Ht: 6'0" Wt: 190 Born: 5/27/65 Age: 35

Year Team	Lg	G	AB	H	2B	3B	HR	(Hm	Rd)	TB	R	RBI	TBB	IBB	SO	HBP	SH	SF	SB	CS	SB%	GDP	Avg	OBP	SLG
						BATTING														BASERUNNING			PERCENTAGES		
1992 Cincinnati	NL	24	30	4	0	0	0	(0	0)	4	6	2	2	1	4	1	0	0	5	0	1.00	0	.133	.212	.133
1993 Cincinnati	NL	103	272	73	17	3	6	(1	5)	114	40	23	21	4	47	1	3	2	20	8	.71	1	.268	.321	.419
1994 Cincinnati	NL	68	122	38	10	2	4	(3	1)	64	36	11	15	0	18	0	2	2	6	3	.67	3	.311	.381	.525
1995 Pittsburgh	NL	116	402	109	23	2	4	(4	0)	148	64	26	37	0	71	5	0	1	22	12	.65	3	.271	.339	.368
1996 Pit-Tor		119	388	99	28	2	14	(8	6)	173	63	60	29	2	75	4	1	4	15	4	.79	14	.255	.311	.446
1997 Toronto	AL	58	174	36	5	1	2	(1	1)	49	22	20	14	0	31	1	1	1	4	4	.50	4	.207	.268	.282
1999 LA-Tor		80	187	45	8	4	2	(0	2)	67	29	20	19	0	44	0	3	3	1	2	.33	2	.241	.306	.358
1996 Pittsburgh	NL	29	80	20	9	0	2	(0	2)	35	11	8	5	1	17	0	0	1	3	1	.75	4	.250	.291	.438
Toronto	AL	90	308	79	19	2	12	(8	4)	138	52	52	24	1	58	4	1	3	12	3	.80	10	.256	.316	.448
1999 Los Angeles	NL	18	17	5	0	1	0	(0	0)	7	4	1	0	0	5	0	0	0	0	0	.00	0	.294	.294	.412
Toronto	AL	62	170	40	8	3	2	(0	2)	60	25	19	19	0	39	0	3	3	1	2	.33	2	.235	.307	.353
7 ML YEARS		568	1575	404	91	14	32	(17	15)	619	260	162	137	7	290	12	10	13	74	33	.69	27	.257	.318	.393

Will Brunson

Pitches: Left Bats: Left Pos: RP-17   Ht: 6'5" Wt: 185 Born: 3/20/70 Age: 30

Year Team	Lg	G	GS	CG	GF	IP	BFP	H	R	ER	HR	SH	SF	HB	TBB	IBB	SO	WP	Bk	W	L	Pct.	ShO	Sv-Op	Hld	ERA
			HOW MUCH HE PITCHED								WHAT HE GAVE UP											THE RESULTS				
1992 Princeton	R+	13	13	0	0	72.2	313	68	34	29	6	4	2	3	28	0	48	2	0	5	5	.500	0	0--	—	3.59
1993 Chstn-WV	A	37	15	0	4	123.2	545	119	68	54	10	4	4	11	50	1	103	7	2	5	6	.455	0	0--	—	3.93
1994 Winston-Sal	A+	30	22	3	3	165	711	161	83	73	22	5	7	12	58	2	129	6	4	12	7	.632	0	0--	—	3.98
1995 San Berndno	A+	13	13	0	0	83.1	334	68	24	19	4	3	5	5	21	0	70	3	0	10	0	1.000	0	0--	—	2.05
San Antonio	AA	14	14	0	0	80	356	105	46	44	4	3	1	4	22	0	44	5	1	4	5	.444	0	0--	—	4.95
1996 San Antonio	AA	11	5	0	1	42	166	32	13	10	2	2	0	1	15	0	38	2	1	3	1	.750	0	0--	—	2.14
Albuquerque	AAA	9	9	1	0	54.1	239	53	29	27	7	2	1	2	23	1	47	2	0	3	4	.429	0	0--	—	4.47
1997 Albuquerque	AAA	27	0	0	9	26.1	125	39	19	19	3	1	1	1	10	1	25	0	0	1	1	.500	0	0--	—	6.49
San Antonio	AA	17	11	2	4	72.2	299	68	30	28	8	3	1	6	13	0	71	2	0	5	5	.500	1	0--	—	3.47
1998 Albuquerque	AAA	34	15	1	5	120	520	135	69	62	11	5	3	4	40	1	100	3	1	5	8	.385	0	2--	—	4.65
1999 Toledo	AAA	38	1	0	15	47.2	201	45	28	24	5	3	0	2	17	1	41	2	1	3	1	.750	0	3--	—	4.53
1998 LA-Det		10	0	0	2	5.1	22	5	3	3	0	0	0	0	3	0	2	1	0	0	1	.000	0	0-0	2	5.06
1999 Detroit	AL	17	0	0	1	12	58	18	9	8	3	1	2	0	6	1	9	0	0	1	0	1.000	0	0-0	1	6.00
1998 Los Angeles	NL	2	0	0	1	2.1	11	3	3	3	0	0	0	0	2	0	1	0	0	0	1	.000	0	0-0	1	11.57
Detroit	AL	8	0	0	0	3	11	2	0	0	0	0	0	0	1	0	1	1	0	0	0	.000	0	0-0	0	0.00
2 ML YEARS		27	0	0	3	17.1	80	23	12	11	3	1	2	0	9	1	11	1	0	1	1	.500	0	0-0	3	5.71

Mike Buddie

Pitches: Right Bats: Right Pos: RP-2   Ht: 6'3" Wt: 210 Born: 12/12/70 Age: 29

Year Team	Lg	G	GS	CG	GF	IP	BFP	H	R	ER	HR	SH	SF	HB	TBB	IBB	SO	WP	Bk	W	L	Pct.	ShO	Sv-Op	Hld	ERA
			HOW MUCH HE PITCHED								WHAT HE GAVE UP											THE RESULTS				
1992 Oneonta	A-	13	13	1	0	67.1	301	69	36	29	3	0	1	3	34	0	87	7	5	1	4	.200	0	0--	—	3.88
1993 Greensboro	A	27	26	0	0	155.1	686	138	104	84	19	2	4	8	89	0	143	22	2	13	10	.565	0	0--	—	4.87
1994 Tampa	A+	25	24	0	0	150.1	643	143	75	67	7	6	8	5	66	2	113	9	4	12	5	.706	0	0--	—	4.01
1995 Norwich	AA	29	27	2	1	149.2	689	155	102	80	4	6	8	15	81	2	106	13	1	10	12	.455	0	1--	—	4.81
1996 Norwich	AA	29	26	4	0	159.2	708	176	101	79	10	8	5	8	71	5	103	16	0	7	12	.368	0	0--	—	4.45
1997 Norwich	AA	1	0	0	0	1	3	0	0	0	0	0	0	0	0	0	3	0	0	0	0	.000	0	0--	—	0.00

Year Team	Lg	HOW MUCH HE PITCHED						WHAT HE GAVE UP												THE RESULTS						
		G	GS	CG	GF	IP	BFP	H	R	ER	HR	SH	SF	HB	TBB	IBB	SO	WP	Bk	W	L	Pct.	ShO	Sv-Op	Hld	ERA
Columbus	AAA	53	0	0	13	75	319	85	24	22	4	4	3	2	25	0	67	5	0	6	6	.500	0	2- -	—	2.64
1998 Columbus	AAA	26	0	0	12	42.2	170	35	15	13	0	1	1	1	15	0	30	2	0	5	0	1.000	0	4- -	—	2.74
1999 Columbus	AAA	49	2	0	14	78.2	335	80	30	25	2	4	5	5	22	2	68	8	0	9	2	.818	0	0- -	—	2.86
1998 New York	AL	24	2	0	8	41.2	180	46	29	26	5	1	1	3	13	1	20	2	1	4	1	.800	0	0-0	0	5.62
1999 New York	AL	2	0	0	0	2	9	3	1	1	1	0	0	0	0	0	1	0	0	0	0	.000	0	0-0	0	4.50
2 ML YEARS		26	2	0	8	43.2	189	49	30	27	6	1		3	13	1	21	2	1	4	1	.800	0	0-0	0	5.56

Damon Buford

Bats: R Throws: R Pos: CF-82; PH/PR-12; DH-5; LF-5   **Ht: 5'10" Wt: 180 Born: 6/12/70 Age: 30**

Year Team	Lg	BATTING																	BASERUNNING				PERCENTAGES		
		G	AB	H	2B	3B	HR	(Hm	Rd)	TB	R	RBI	TBB	IBB	SO	HBP	SH	SF	SB	CS	SB%	GDP	Avg	OBP	SLG
1993 Baltimore	AL	53	79	18	5	0	2	(0	2)	29	18	9	9	0	19	1	1	0	2	2	.50	1	.228	.315	.367
1994 Baltimore	AL	4	2	1	0	0	0	(0	0)	1	2	0	0	0	1	0	0	0	0	0	.00	0	.500	.500	.500
1995 Bal-NYM		68	168	34	5	0	4	(2	2)	51	30	14	25	0	35	5	3	3	10	8	.56	3	.202	.318	.304
1996 Texas	AL	90	145	41	9	0	6	(3	3)	68	30	20	15	0	34	0	1	1	8	5	.62	3	.283	.348	.469
1997 Texas	AL	122	366	82	18	0	8	(4	4)	124	49	39	30	0	83	3	3	2	18	7	.72	8	.224	.287	.339
1998 Boston	AL	86	216	61	14	4	10	(4	6)	113	37	42	22	1	43	1	0	2	5	5	.50	5	.282	.349	.523
1999 Boston	AL	91	297	72	15	2	6	(3	3)	109	39	38	21	0	74	2	1	3	9	2	.82	5	.242	.294	.367
1995 Baltimore	AL	24	32	2	0	0	0	(0	0)	2	6	2	6	0	7	0	3	1	1	1	.75	0	.063	.205	.063
New York	NL	44	136	32	5	0	4	(2	2)	49	24	12	19	0	28	5	0	2	7	7	.50	3	.235	.346	.360
7 ML YEARS		514	1273	309	66	6	36	(16	20)	495	205	162	122	1	289	12	9	11	52	29	.64	25	.243	.312	.389

Jay Buhner

Bats: Right Throws: Right Pos: RF-85; PH/PR-3; 1B-1   **Ht: 6'3" Wt: 210 Born: 8/13/64 Age: 35**

Year Team	Lg	BATTING																	BASERUNNING				PERCENTAGES		
		G	AB	H	2B	3B	HR	(Hm	Rd)	TB	R	RBI	TBB	IBB	SO	HBP	SH	SF	SB	CS	SB%	GDP	Avg	OBP	SLG
1987 New York	AL	7	22	5	2	0	0	(0	0)	7	0	1	1	0	6	0	0	0	0	0	.00	1	.227	.261	.318
1988 NYY-Sea	AL	85	261	56	13	1	13	(8	5)	110	36	38	28	1	93	6	1	3	1	1	.50	5	.215	.302	.421
1989 Seattle	AL	58	204	56	15	1	9	(7	2)	100	27	33	19	0	55	2	0	1	1	4	.20	5	.275	.341	.490
1990 Seattle	AL	51	163	45	12	0	7	(2	5)	78	16	33	17	1	50	4	0	1	2	2	.50	6	.276	.357	.479
1991 Seattle	AL	137	406	99	14	4	27	(14	13)	202	64	77	53	5	117	6	2	4	0	1	.00	10	.244	.337	.498
1992 Seattle	AL	152	543	132	16	3	25	(9	16)	229	69	79	71	2	146	6	1	8	0	6	.00	12	.243	.333	.422
1993 Seattle	AL	158	563	153	28	3	27	(11	16)	268	91	98	100	11	144	2	2	8	2	5	.29	12	.272	.379	.476
1994 Seattle	AL	101	358	100	23	4	21	(8	13)	194	74	68	66	3	63	5	2	5	0	1	.00	7	.279	.394	.542
1995 Seattle	AL	126	470	123	23	0	40	(21	19)	266	86	121	60	7	120	1	2	6	0	1	.00	15	.262	.343	.566
1996 Seattle	AL	150	564	153	29	0	44	(21	23)	314	107	138	84	5	159	9	0	10	0	1	.00	11	.271	.369	.557
1997 Seattle	AL	157	540	131	18	2	40	(13	27)	273	104	109	119	3	175	5	0	1	0	0	.00	23	.243	.383	.506
1998 Seattle	AL	72	244	59	7	1	15	(6	9)	113	33	45	38	0	71	1	1	2	0	0	.00	2	.242	.344	.463
1999 Seattle	AL	87	266	59	11	0	14	(5	9)	112	37	38	69	0	100	0	3	3	0	0	.00	6	.222	.388	.421
1988 New York	AL	25	69	13	0	0	3	(1	2)	22	8	13	3	0	25	3	0	1	0	0	.00	1	.188	.250	.319
Seattle	AL	60	192	43	13	1	10	(7	3)	88	28	25	25	1	68	3	1	2	1	1	.50	4	.224	.320	.458
13 ML YEARS		1341	4604	1171	211	19	282	(129	153)	2266	744	878	725	38	1299	52	11	52	6	22	.21	110	.254	.359	.492

Kirk Bullinger

Pitches: Right Bats: Right Pos: RP-4   **Ht: 6'2" Wt: 170 Born: 10/28/69 Age: 30**

Year Team	Lg	HOW MUCH HE PITCHED						WHAT HE GAVE UP												THE RESULTS						
		G	GS	CG	GF	IP	BFP	H	R	ER	HR	SH	SF	HB	TBB	IBB	SO	WP	Bk	W	L	Pct.	ShO	Sv-Op	Hld	ERA
1992 Hamilton	A-	35	0	0	7	48.2	191	24	7	6	0	1	1	2	15	4	61	3	1	2	2	.500	0	2- -	—	1.11
1993 Springfield	A	50	0	0	46	51.1	208	26	19	13	5	3	2	2	21	1	72	6	0	1	3	.250	0	33- -	—	2.28
1994 St. Pete	A+	39	0	0	18	53.2	220	37	16	7	0	4	0	1	20	5	50	4	3	2	0	1.000	0	6- -	—	1.17
1995 Harrisburg	AA	56	0	0	39	67	282	61	22	18	4	4	1	0	25	5	42	2	2	5	3	.625	0	7- -	—	2.42
1996 Ottawa	AAA	10	0	0	4	15.1	62	10	6	6	3	0	0	0	9	1	9	1	0	2	1	.667	0	0- -	—	3.52
Harrisburg	AA	47	0	0	40	45.2	193	46	16	10	5	3	1	1	18	3	29	3	0	3	4	.429	0	22- -	—	1.97
1997 Wst Plm Bch	A+	2	0	0	0	3.2	15	3	0	0	0	0	0	0	0	0	7	1	0	2	0	1.000	0	0- -	—	0.00
Harrisburg	AA	21	0	0	12	27	106	22	9	8	4	1	0	1	6	0	21	0	0	3	0	1.000	0	6- -	—	2.67
Ottawa	AAA	22	0	0	14	31.2	119	17	7	6	0	2	1	0	10	0	15	1	0	3	4	.429	0	5- -	—	1.71
1998 Expos	R	2	2	0	0	4	14	2	0	0	0	0	0	0	0	0	7	0	0	0	0	.000	0	0- -	—	0.00
Jupiter	A+	8	0	0	1	10	42	9	7	6	1	0	0	0	2	0	12	2	0	0	0	.000	0	0- -	—	5.40
Ottawa	AAA	13	0	0	4	17	72	16	2	2	0	1	0	0	6	1	7	0	0	0	0	.000	0	3- -	—	1.06
1999 Trenton	AA	17	0	0	17	17	60	6	2	1	1	1	0	0	5	1	16	1	0	1	1	.500	0	10- -	—	0.53
Pawtucket	AAA	35	0	0	30	37.2	160	37	14	10	3	1	1	2	13	4	27	0	0	2	2	.000	0	15- -	—	2.39
1998 Montreal	NL	8	0	0	1	7	35	14	8	7	1	0	0	0	0	0	2	0	1	1	0	1.000	0	0-1	0	9.00
1999 Boston	AL	4	0	0	0	2	9	2	1	1	0	0	0	0	2	0	0	0	0	0	0	.000	0	0-0	2	4.50
2 ML YEARS		12	0	0	1	9	44	16	9	8	1	0	0	0	2	0	2	0	1	1	0	1.000	0	0-1	2	8.00

Mel Bunch

Pitches: Right Bats: Right Pos: RP-4; SP-1   **Ht: 6'1" Wt: 170 Born: 11/4/71 Age: 28**

Year Team	Lg	HOW MUCH HE PITCHED						WHAT HE GAVE UP												THE RESULTS						
		G	GS	CG	GF	IP	BFP	H	R	ER	HR	SH	SF	HB	TBB	IBB	SO	WP	Bk	W	L	Pct.	ShO	Sv-Op	Hld	ERA
1992 Royals	R	5	4	0	1	24	87	11	6	4	2	0	0	1	3	0	26	0	0	2	1	.667	0	0- -	—	1.50
Eugene	A-	10	10	0	0	64.2	265	62	23	20	5	2	2	1	13	0	69	2	1	5	3	.625	0	0- -	—	2.78
1993 Rockford	A	19	11	1	8	85	337	79	24	20	4	7	3	2	18	0	71	6	1	6	4	.600	0	4- -	—	2.12
Wilmington	A+	10	10	1	0	65.2	256	52	22	17	3	1	2	1	14	0	54	2	0	5	3	.625	0	0- -	—	2.33

Year Team	Lg	G	GS	CG	GF	IP	BFP	H	R	ER	HR	SH	SF	HB	TBB	IBB	SO	WP	Bk	W	L	Pct.	ShO	Sv-Op	Hld	ERA
		HOW MUCH HE PITCHED						**WHAT HE GAVE UP**												**THE RESULTS**						
1994 Wilmington	A+	15	12	0	0	61	252	52	30	23	8	1	1	0	15	0	62	2	0	5	3	.625	0	0--	—	3.39
1995 Omaha	AAA	12	11	1	0	65	272	63	37	33	10	3	4	0	20	2	50	8	1	1	7	.125	0	0--	—	4.57
1996 Omaha	AAA	33	27	0	2	146.2	663	181	106	99	32	1	4	7	59	1	94	8	1	8	9	.471	0	0--	—	6.08
1997 Harrisburg	AA	9	9	0	0	49.1	210	45	27	23	7	5	0	4	22	0	50	2	0	3	3	.500	0	0--	—	4.20
Ottawa	AAA	16	14	0	0	78	369	102	63	55	13	1	7	2	45	5	58	8	0	4	4	.500	0	0--	—	6.35
1998 Ottawa	AAA	25	19	0	2	104	456	101	58	53	17	3	3	11	48	0	99	7	2	6	6	.500	0	0--	—	4.59
1999 Tacoma	AAA	21	19	1	0	125	517	112	53	43	11	1	1	8	40	1	117	4	1	10	2	.833	1	0--	—	3.10
1995 Kansas City	AL	13	5	0	3	40	175	42	25	25	11	0	0	0	14	1	19	6	0	1	3	.250	0	0-0	0	5.63
1999 Seattle	AL	5	1	0	4	10	55	20	13	13	3	0	1	0	7	0	4	0	0	0	0	.000	0	0-0	0	11.70
2 ML YEARS		18	6	0	7	50	230	62	38	38	14	0	1	0	21	1	23	6	0	1	3	.250	0	0-0	0	6.84

Dave Burba

Ht: 6'4" Wt: 240 Born: 7/7/66 Age: 33

Pitches: Right **Bats:** Right **Pos:** SP-34

Year Team	Lg	G	GS	CG	GF	IP	BFP	H	R	ER	HR	SH	SF	HB	TBB	IBB	SO	WP	Bk	W	L	Pct.	ShO	Sv-Op	Hld	ERA
		HOW MUCH HE PITCHED						**WHAT HE GAVE UP**												**THE RESULTS**						
1990 Seattle	AL	6	0	0	2	8	35	8	6	4	0	2	0	1	2	0	4	0	0	0	0	.000	0	0-0	0	4.50
1991 Seattle	AL	22	2	0	11	36.2	153	34	16	15	6	0	0	0	14	3	16	1	0	2	2	.500	0	1-1	0	3.68
1992 San Francisco	NL	23	11	0	4	70.2	318	80	43	39	4	2	4	2	31	2	47	1	1	2	7	.222	0	0-0	0	4.97
1993 San Francisco	NL	54	5	0	9	95.1	408	95	49	45	14	6	3	3	37	5	88	4	0	10	3	.769	0	0-0	10	4.25
1994 San Francisco	NL	57	0	0	13	74	322	59	39	36	5	3	1	6	45	3	84	3	0	3	6	.333	0	0-3	11	4.38
1995 SF-Cin	NL	52	9	1	7	106.2	451	90	50	47	9	4	1	0	51	3	96	5	0	10	4	.714	1	0-1	5	3.97
1996 Cincinnati	NL	34	33	0	0	195	849	179	96	83	18	5	12	2	97	9	148	9	1	11	13	.458	0	0-0	0	3.83
1997 Cincinnati	NL	30	27	2	1	160	706	157	88	84	22	6	3	9	73	10	131	6	0	11	10	.524	0	0-0	0	4.73
1998 Cleveland	AL	32	31	0	0	203.2	870	210	100	93	30	3	10	7	69	4	132	6	0	15	10	.600	0	0-0	0	4.11
1999 Cleveland	AL	34	34	1	0	220	940	211	113	104	30	2	3	8	96	3	174	13	0	15	9	.625	0	0-0	0	4.25
1995 San Francisco	NL	37	0	0	7	43.1	191	38	26	24	5	3	1	0	25	2	46	2	0	4	2	.667	0	0-1	5	4.98
Cincinnati	NL	15	9	1	0	63.1	260	52	24	23	4	1	0	0	26	1	50	3	0	6	2	.750	1	0-0	0	3.27
10 ML YEARS		344	152	4	47	1170	5052	1123	600	550	138	33	37	38	515	42	920	48	2	79	64	.552	1	1-5	26	4.23

John Burkett

Ht: 6'3" Wt: 215 Born: 11/28/64 Age: 35

Pitches: Right **Bats:** Right **Pos:** SP-25; RP-5

Year Team	Lg	G	GS	CG	GF	IP	BFP	H	R	ER	HR	SH	SF	HB	TBB	IBB	SO	WP	Bk	W	L	Pct.	ShO	Sv-Op	Hld	ERA
		HOW MUCH HE PITCHED						**WHAT HE GAVE UP**												**THE RESULTS**						
1999 Tulsa *	AA	2	2	0	0	6.2	32	7	5	2	0	0	0	0	3	0	3	2	0	0	1	.000	0	0--	0	2.70
1987 San Francisco	NL	3	0	0	1	6	28	7	4	3	2	1	0	1	3	0	5	0	0	0	0	.000	0	0-0	0	4.50
1990 San Francisco	NL	33	32	2	1	204	857	201	92	86	18	6	5	4	61	7	118	3	0	14	7	.667	0	1-1	0	3.79
1991 San Francisco	NL	36	34	3	0	206.2	890	223	103	96	19	8	8	10	60	2	131	5	0	12	11	.522	1	0-0	0	4.18
1992 San Francisco	NL	32	32	3	0	189.2	799	194	96	81	13	11	4	4	45	6	107	0	0	13	9	.591	1	0-0	0	3.84
1993 San Francisco	NL	34	34	2	0	231.2	942	224	100	94	18	8	4	11	40	4	145	1	2	22	7	.759	1	0-0	0	3.65
1994 San Francisco	NL	25	25	0	0	159.1	676	176	72	64	14	12	5	7	36	7	85	2	0	6	8	.429	0	0-0	0	3.62
1995 Florida	NL	30	30	4	0	188.1	810	208	95	90	22	10	0	6	57	5	126	2	1	14	14	.500	0	0-0	0	4.30
1996 Fla-Tex	NL	34	34	2	0	222.2	934	229	117	105	19	12	6	5	58	4	155	0	0	11	12	.478	1	0-0	0	4.24
1997 Texas	AL	30	30	2	0	189.1	828	240	106	96	20	4	7	4	30	1	139	1	0	9	12	.429	0	0-0	0	4.56
1998 Texas	AL	32	32	0	0	195	854	230	131	123	19	7	5	8	46	1	131	3	0	9	13	.409	0	0-0	0	5.68
1999 Texas	AL	30	25	0	1	147.1	656	184	95	92	18	5	3	3	46	1	96	4	0	9	8	.529	0	0-0	0	5.62
1996 Florida	NL	24	24	1	0	154	645	154	84	74	15	11	4	3	42	2	108	0	0	6	10	.375	0	0-0	0	4.32
Texas	AL	10	10	1	0	68.2	289	75	33	31	4	1	2	2	16	2	47	0	0	5	2	.714	1	0-0	0	4.06
11 ML YEARS		319	308	18	3	1940	8274	2116	1011	930	182	84	47	63	482	38	1238	21	6	119	101	.541	4	1-1	1	4.31

Ellis Burks

Ht: 6'2" Wt: 205 Born: 9/11/64 Age: 35

Bats: Right **Throws:** Right **Pos:** RF-107; PH/PR-11; DH-3

Year Team	Lg	G	AB	H	2B	3B	HR	(Hm	Rd)	TB	R	RBI	TBB	IBB	SO	HBP	SH	SF	SB	CS	SB%	GDP	Avg	OBP	SLG
		BATTING																	**BASERUNNING**				**PERCENTAGES**		
1987 Boston	AL	133	558	152	30	2	20	(11	9)	246	94	59	41	0	98	2	4	1	27	6	.82	1	.272	.324	.441
1988 Boston	AL	144	540	159	37	5	18	(8	10)	260	93	92	62	1	89	3	4	6	25	9	.74	8	.294	.367	.481
1989 Boston	AL	97	399	121	19	6	12	(6	6)	188	73	61	36	2	52	5	2	4	21	5	.81	8	.303	.365	.471
1990 Boston	AL	152	588	174	33	8	21	(10	11)	286	89	89	48	4	82	1	2	2	9	11	.45	18	.296	.349	.486
1991 Boston	AL	130	474	119	33	3	14	(8	6)	200	56	56	39	2	81	6	2	3	6	11	.35	7	.251	.314	.422
1992 Boston	AL	66	235	60	8	3	8	(4	4)	98	35	30	25	2	48	1	0	2	5	2	.71	5	.255	.327	.417
1993 Chicago	AL	146	499	137	24	4	17	(7	10)	220	75	74	60	2	97	4	3	8	6	9	.40	11	.275	.352	.441
1994 Colorado	NL	42	149	48	8	3	13	(7	6)	101	33	24	16	3	39	0	0	1	3	1	.75	3	.322	.388	.678
1995 Colorado	NL	103	278	74	10	6	14	(8	6)	138	41	49	39	0	72	2	1	1	7	3	.70	7	.266	.359	.496
1996 Colorado	NL	156	613	211	45	8	40	(23	17)	392	142	128	61	2	114	6	3	2	32	6	.84	19	.344	.408	.639
1997 Colorado	NL	119	424	123	19	2	32	(17	15)	242	91	82	47	0	75	3	1	2	7	2	.78	17	.290	.363	.571
1998 Col-SF	NL	142	504	147	28	6	21	(10	11)	250	76	76	58	1	111	5	6	9	11	8	.58	12	.292	.365	.496
1999 San Francisco	NL	120	390	110	19	0	31	(16	15)	222	73	96	69	2	86	6	0	4	7	5	.58	11	.282	.394	.569
1998 Colorado	NL	100	357	102	22	5	16	(8	8)	182	54	54	39	0	80	2	2	5	3	7	.30	10	.286	.355	.510
San Francisco	NL	42	147	45	6	1	5	(2	3)	68	22	22	19	1	31	3	4	4	8	1	.89	2	.306	.387	.463
13 ML YEARS		1550	5651	1635	313	56	261	(135	126)	2843	971	916	601	21	1044	44	28	44	166	78	.68	127	.289	.360	.503

35

A.J. Burnett

Pitches: Right **Bats:** Right **Pos:** SP-7

Ht: 6'5" **Wt:** 205 **Born:** 1/3/77 **Age:** 23

Year Team	Lg	G	GS	CG	GF	IP	BFP	H	R	ER	HR	SH	SF	HB	TBB	IBB	SO	WP	Bk	W	L	Pct.	ShO	Sv-Op	Hld	ERA
1995 Mets	R	9	8	1	1	33.2	144	27	16	16	2	0	2	2	23	0	26	7	4	2	3	.400	0	0--	—	4.28
1996 Kingsport	R+	12	12	0	0	58	245	31	26	25	0	1	2	7	54	0	68	16	3	4	0	1.000	0	0--	—	3.88
1997 Mets	R	3	2	0	0	11.1	54	8	8	4	0	0	0	2	8	0	15	3	0	0	1	.000	0	0--	—	3.18
Pittsfield	A-	9	9	0	0	44	192	28	26	23	3	0	2	6	35	0	48	9	0	3	1	.750	0	0--	—	4.70
1998 Kane County	A	20	20	0	0	119	469	74	27	26	3	2	0	8	45	0	186	6	2	10	4	.714	0	0--	—	1.97
1999 Portland	AA	26	23	0	1	120.2	552	132	91	74	15	3	4	5	71	0	121	16	2	6	12	.333	0	0--	—	5.52
1999 Florida	NL	7	7	0	0	41.1	182	37	23	16	3	1	3	0	25	2	33	0	0	4	2	.667	0	0-0	0	3.48

Jeromy Burnitz

Bats: Left **Throws:** Right **Pos:** RF-127; DH-3

Ht: 6'0" **Wt:** 205 **Born:** 4/15/69 **Age:** 31

Year Team	Lg	G	AB	H	2B	3B	HR	(Hm	Rd)	TB	R	RBI	TBB	IBB	SO	HBP	SH	SF	SB	CS	SB%	GDP	Avg	OBP	SLG
1993 New York	NL	86	263	64	10	6	13	(6	7)	125	49	38	38	4	66	1	2	2	3	6	.33	2	.243	.339	.475
1994 New York	NL	45	143	34	4	0	3	(2	1)	47	26	15	23	0	45	1	1	0	1	1	.50	2	.238	.347	.329
1995 Cleveland	AL	9	7	4	1	0	0	(0	0)	5	4	0	0	0	0	0	0	0	0	0	.00	0	.571	.571	.714
1996 Cle-Mil	AL	94	200	53	14	0	9	(5	4)	94	38	40	33	2	47	4	0	2	4	1	.80	4	.265	.377	.470
1997 Milwaukee	AL	153	494	139	37	8	27	(18	9)	273	85	85	75	8	111	5	3	0	20	13	.61	8	.281	.382	.553
1998 Milwaukee	NL	161	609	160	28	1	38	(17	21)	304	92	125	70	7	158	4	1	7	7	4	.64	9	.263	.339	.499
1999 Milwaukee	NL	130	467	126	33	2	33	(12	21)	262	87	103	91	7	124	16	0	6	7	3	.70	11	.270	.402	.561
1996 Cleveland	AL	71	128	36	10	0	7	(4	3)	67	30	26	25	1	31	2	0	0	2	1	.67	3	.281	.406	.523
Milwaukee	AL	23	72	17	4	0	2	(1	1)	27	8	14	8	1	16	2	0	2	2	0	1.00	1	.236	.321	.375
7 ML YEARS		678	2183	580	127	17	123	(60	63)	1110	381	406	330	28	551	31	7	17	42	28	.60	36	.266	.367	.508

Mike Busby

Pitches: Right **Bats:** Right **Pos:** RP-15

Ht: 6'4" **Wt:** 225 **Born:** 12/27/72 **Age:** 27

Year Team	Lg	G	GS	CG	GF	IP	BFP	H	R	ER	HR	SH	SF	HB	TBB	IBB	SO	WP	Bk	W	L	Pct.	ShO	Sv-Op	Hld	ERA
1999 Memphis *	AAA	29	10	0	6	72.2	359	112	69	60	12	2	5	3	36	1	50	8	0	3	4	.429	0	0--	—	7.43
1996 St. Louis	NL	1	1	0	0	4	28	9	13	8	1	0	1	0	4	0	4	0	0	0	1	.000	0	0-0	0	18.00
1997 St. Louis	NL	3	3	0	0	14.1	67	24	14	14	2	1	1	0	4	0	6	0	0	0	2	.000	0	0-0	0	8.79
1998 St. Louis	NL	26	2	0	7	46	202	45	23	23	3	3	2	5	15	0	33	3	0	5	2	.714	0	0-2	5	4.50
1999 St. Louis	NL	15	0	0	3	17.2	86	21	15	14	2	0	0	2	14	0	7	1	0	0	1	.000	0	0-0	4	7.13
4 ML YEARS		45	6	0	10	82	383	99	65	59	11	5	3	8	37	0	50	4	0	5	6	.455	0	0-2	9	6.48

Homer Bush

Bats: Right **Throws:** Right **Pos:** 2B-109; SS-18; PH/PR-2

Ht: 5'10" **Wt:** 175 **Born:** 11/12/72 **Age:** 27

Year Team	Lg	G	AB	H	2B	3B	HR	(Hm	Rd)	TB	R	RBI	TBB	IBB	SO	HBP	SH	SF	SB	CS	SB%	GDP	Avg	OBP	SLG
1999 Dunedin *	A+	4	14	5	2	0	0	—	—	7	3	0	1	0	1	1	1	0	1	0	1.00	1	.357	.438	.500
1997 New York	AL	10	11	4	0	0	0	(0	0)	4	2	3	0	0	0	0	0	0	0	0	.00	0	.364	.364	.364
1998 New York	AL	45	71	27	3	0	1	(1	0)	33	17	5	5	0	19	0	2	0	6	3	.67	1	.380	.421	.465
1999 Toronto	AL	128	485	155	26	4	5	(2	3)	204	69	55	21	0	82	6	8	3	32	8	.80	9	.320	.353	.421
3 ML YEARS		183	567	186	29	4	6	(3	3)	241	88	63	26	0	101	6	10	3	38	11	.78	10	.328	.362	.425

Rich Butler

Bats: Left **Throws:** Right **Pos:** RF-4; LF-2; PH/PR-1

Ht: 6'1" **Wt:** 205 **Born:** 5/1/73 **Age:** 27

Year Team	Lg	G	AB	H	2B	3B	HR	(Hm	Rd)	TB	R	RBI	TBB	IBB	SO	HBP	SH	SF	SB	CS	SB%	GDP	Avg	OBP	SLG
1999 Durham *	AAA	90	332	96	28	2	10	—	—	158	52	63	41	4	70	3	3	3	2	5	.29	4	.289	.369	.476
1997 Toronto	AL	7	14	4	1	0	0	(0	0)	5	3	2	2	0	3	0	0	0	0	1	.00	0	.286	.375	.357
1998 Tampa Bay	AL	72	217	49	3	3	7	(6	1)	79	25	20	15	0	37	2	0	3	4	2	.67	4	.226	.278	.364
1999 Tampa Bay	AL	7	20	3	1	0	0	(0	0)	4	2	0	2	0	4	0	0	0	0	0	.00	0	.150	.227	.200
3 ML YEARS		86	251	56	5	3	7	(6	1)	88	30	22	19	0	44	2	0	3	4	3	.57	4	.223	.280	.351

Rob Butler

Bats: Left **Throws:** Left **Pos:** PH/PR-6; DH-3; LF-2

Ht: 5'11" **Wt:** 185 **Born:** 4/10/70 **Age:** 30

Year Team	Lg	G	AB	H	2B	3B	HR	(Hm	Rd)	TB	R	RBI	TBB	IBB	SO	HBP	SH	SF	SB	CS	SB%	GDP	Avg	OBP	SLG
1999 Knoxville *	AA	64	258	87	13	4	2	—	—	118	48	36	21	0	21	1	2	2	4	5	.44	6	.337	.384	.457
1993 Toronto	AL	17	48	13	4	0	0	(0	0)	17	8	2	7	0	12	1	0	0	2	2	.50	0	.271	.375	.354
1994 Toronto	AL	41	74	13	0	1	0	(0	0)	15	13	5	7	0	8	1	4	2	0	1	.00	3	.176	.250	.203
1997 Philadelphia	NL	43	89	26	9	1	0	(0	0)	37	10	13	5	0	8	0	0	1	1	0	1.00	0	.292	.326	.416
1999 Toronto	AL	8	7	1	0	0	0	(0	0)	1	1	1	0	0	0	1	0	0	0	0	.00	0	.143	.250	.143
4 ML YEARS		109	218	53	13	2	0	(0	0)	70	32	21	19	0	28	3	4	3	3	3	.50	5	.243	.309	.321

Paul Byrd

Pitches: Right Bats: Right Pos: SP-32 Ht: 6'1" Wt: 185 Born: 12/3/70 Age: 29

		HOW MUCH HE PITCHED					WHAT HE GAVE UP												THE RESULTS						
Year Team	Lg	G	GS	CG	GF	IP	BFP	H	R	ER	HR	SH	SF	HB	TBB	IBB	SO	WP	Bk	W	L	Pct.	ShO	Sv-Op	Hld	ERA
1995 New York	NL	17	0	0	6	22	91	18	6	5	1	0	2	1	7	1	26	1	2	2	0	1.000	0	0-0	3	2.05
1996 New York	NL	38	0	0	14	46.2	204	48	22	22	7	1	1	0	21	4	31	3	0	1	2	.333	0	0-2	3	4.24
1997 Atlanta	NL	31	4	0	9	53	236	47	34	31	6	2	2	4	28	4	37	3	1	4	4	.500	0	0-0	1	5.26
1998 Atl-Phi	NL	9	8	2	0	57	233	45	19	17	6	2	1	0	18	1	39	2	0	5	2	.714	1	0-0	0	2.68
1999 Philadelphia	NL	32	32	1	0	199.2	872	205	119	102	34	5	6	17	70	2	106	11	3	15	11	.577	0	0-0	0	4.60
1998 Atlanta	NL	1	0	0	0	2	11	4	3	3	0	0	0	0	1	0	1	0	0	0	0	.000	0	0-0	0	13.50
Philadelphia	NL	8	8	2	0	55	222	41	16	14	6	2	1	0	17	1	38	2	0	5	2	.714	1	0-0	0	2.29
5 ML YEARS		127	44	3	29	378.1	1636	363	200	177	54	10	12	22	144	12	239	20	6	27	19	.587	1	0-2	7	4.21

Tim Byrdak

Pitches: Left Bats: Left Pos: RP-33 Ht: 5'11" Wt: 160 Born: 10/31/73 Age: 26

		HOW MUCH HE PITCHED					WHAT HE GAVE UP												THE RESULTS						
Year Team	Lg	G	GS	CG	GF	IP	BFP	H	R	ER	HR	SH	SF	HB	TBB	IBB	SO	WP	Bk	W	L	Pct.	ShO	Sv-Op	Hld	ERA
1994 Eugene	A-	15	15	0	0	73.1	302	60	33	25	6	2	2	4	20	0	77	1	1	4	5	.444	0	0--	—	3.07
1995 Wilmington	A+	27	26	0	0	166.1	657	118	46	40	7	3	3	10	45	2	127	1	0	11	5	.688	0	0--	—	2.16
1996 Wichita	AA	15	15	0	0	84.2	388	112	73	65	15	5	1	0	44	0	47	8	0	5	7	.417	0	0--	—	6.91
1997 Wilmington	A+	22	2	0	15	41	169	34	17	16	3	5	1	2	12	4	47	4	0	4	3	.571	0	3--	—	3.51
1998 Wichita	AA	34	0	0	10	52	242	58	29	24	3	4	4	2	28	1	37	2	3	3	5	.375	0	2--	—	4.15
Omaha	AAA	26	0	0	8	36.2	161	31	13	10	3	4	0	2	20	0	32	2	0	2	1	.667	0	1--	—	2.45
1999 Omaha	AAA	33	0	0	17	49.2	216	39	19	10		2	2	6	28	2	51	2	0	3	1	.750	0	4--	—	1.81
1998 Kansas City	AL	3	0	0	0	1.2	9	5	1	1	1	0	0	0	0	0	1	0	0	0	0	.000	0	0-0	0	5.40
1999 Kansas City	AL	33	0	0	5	24.2	128	32	24	21	5	3	0	1	20	2	17	3	1	0	3	.000	0	1-4	10	7.66
2 ML YEARS		36	0	0	5	26.1	137	37	25	22	6	3	0	1	20	2	18	3	1	0	3	.000	0	1-4	10	7.52

Jolbert Cabrera

Bats: R Throws: R Pos: PH/PR-16; CF-12; 2B-6; DH-5; LF-4 Ht: 6'0" Wt: 177 Born: 12/8/72 Age: 27

		BATTING																		BASERUNNING				PERCENTAGES		
Year Team	Lg	G	AB	H	2B	3B	HR	(Hm	Rd)	TB	R	RBI	TBB	IBB	SO	HBP	SH	SF	SB	CS	SB%	GDP	Avg	OBP	SLG
1991 Sumter	A	101	324	66	4	0	1	—	—	73	33	20	19	0	62	4	4	2	10	11	.48	5	.204	.255	.225
1992 Albany	A	118	377	86	9	2	0	—	—	99	44	23	34	0	77	1	6	0	22	11	.67	8	.228	.294	.263
1993 Burlington	A	128	507	129	24	2	0	—	—	157	62	38	39	0	93	7	11	4	31	11	.74	13	.254	.314	.310
1994 Wst Plm Bch	A+	83	266	54	4	0	0	—	—	58	32	13	14	0	48	8	4	0	7	10	.41	4	.203	.264	.218
San Berndno	A+	30	109	27	5	1	0	—	—	34	14	11	14	0	24	0	4	2	2	2	.50	1	.248	.328	.312
Harrisburg	AA	3	2	0	0	0	0	—	—	0	0	0	0	0	1	0	0	0	0	0	.00	0	.000	.000	.000
1995 Wst Plm Bch	A+	103	357	102	23	2	1	—	—	132	62	25	38	0	61	8	6	4	19	12	.61	3	.286	.364	.370
Harrisburg	AA	9	35	10	2	0	0	—	—	12	4	1	1	0	3	0	2	0	3	1	.75	1	.286	.306	.343
1996 Harrisburg	AA	107	354	85	18	2	3	—	—	116	40	29	23	3	63	1	5	4	10	5	.67	9	.240	.285	.328
1997 Harrisburg	AA	48	171	43	9	0	2	—	—	58	28	11	28	0	28	1	3	0	5	4	.56	4	.251	.360	.339
Ottawa	AAA	68	191	54	10	4	0	—	—	72	28	12	11	0	31	0	4	1	15	5	.75	5	.283	.320	.377
1998 Buffalo	AAA	129	494	157	24	1	10	—	—	213	94	45	68	0	71	13	8	2	25	15	.63	10	.318	.412	.431
1999 Buffalo	AAA	71	279	74	13	4	0	—	—	95	44	27	26	0	43	2	7	5	20	4	.83	8	.265	.327	.341
1998 Cleveland	AL	1	2	0	0	0	0	(0	0)	0	0	0	0	0	1	0	0	0	0	0	.00	0	.000	.000	.000
1999 Cleveland	AL	30	37	7	1	0	0	(0	0)	8	6	0	1	0	8	1	0	0	3	0	1.00	1	.189	.231	.216
2 ML YEARS		31	39	7	1	0	0	(0	0)	8	6	0	1	0	9	1	0	0	3	0	1.00	1	.179	.220	.205

Jose Cabrera

Pitches: Right Bats: Right Pos: RP-26 Ht: 6'0" Wt: 160 Born: 3/24/72 Age: 28

		HOW MUCH HE PITCHED					WHAT HE GAVE UP												THE RESULTS						
Year Team	Lg	G	GS	CG	GF	IP	BFP	H	R	ER	HR	SH	SF	HB	TBB	IBB	SO	WP	Bk	W	L	Pct.	ShO	Sv-Op	Hld	ERA
1992 Burlington	R+	13	13	1	0	92.1	367	74	27	18	6	2	0	2	18	0	79	3	1	8	3	.727	0	0--	—	1.75
1993 Columbus	A	26	26	1	0	155.1	624	122	54	46	8	2	4	1	53	2	105	8	4	11	6	.647	0	0--	—	2.67
1994 Kinston	A+	24	24	0	0	133.2	575	134	84	66	15	6	3	5	43	0	110	5	5	4	13	.235	0	0--	—	4.44
1995 Canton-Akrn	AA	24	11	1	4	85	350	83	32	31	7	1	6	1	21	0	61	0	2	5	3	.625	1	0--	—	3.28
1996 Bakersfield	A+	7	7	0	0	41.1	183	40	25	18	7	2	2	1	21	0	52	5	0	2	2	.500	0	0--	—	3.92
Kinston	A+	4	3	0	0	17.2	68	7	2	2	0	1	1	1	8	0	19	3	0	1	1	.500	0	0--	—	1.02
Canton-Akrn	AA	15	9	1	4	62.1	278	78	45	39	10	2	3	1	17	2	40	4	0	4	3	.571	0	0--	—	5.63
1997 Buffalo	AAA	5	0	0	2	15	57	8	2	2	2	0	0	1	7	1	11	1	0	3	0	1.000	0	0--	—	1.20
New Orleans	AAA	31	0	0	5	46	181	31	13	13	2	1	0	2	13	3	48	0	1	2	2	.500	0	0--	—	2.54
1998 New Orleans	AAA	5	0	0	2	5	19	2	3	3	2	0	0	1	1	0	6	1	0	0	0	.000	0	1--	—	5.40
1999 New Orleans	AAA	31	0	0	19	51	201	34	18	16	3	2	2	2	12	3	41	2	0	3	1	.750	0	7--	—	2.82
1997 Houston	NL	12	0	0	6	15.1	57	6	2	2	1	0	3	0	6	0	18	0	0	0	0	.000	0	0-1	2	1.17
1998 Houston	NL	3	0	0	1	4.1	19	7	4	4	0	0	0	0	1	1	1	0	0	0	0	.000	0	0-0	0	8.31
1999 Houston	NL	26	0	0	11	29.1	119	21	7	7	3	0	3	0	9	2	28	4	0	4	0	1.000	0	0-1	6	2.15
3 ML YEARS		41	0	0	18	49	195	34	13	13	4	0	6	0	16	3	47	4	0	4	0	1.000	0	0-2	8	2.39

Orlando Cabrera

Bats: Right Throws: Right Pos: SS-102; PH/PR-2 Ht: 5'10" Wt: 175 Born: 11/2/74 Age: 25

		BATTING																		BASERUNNING				PERCENTAGES		
Year Team	Lg	G	AB	H	2B	3B	HR	(Hm	Rd)	TB	R	RBI	TBB	IBB	SO	HBP	SH	SF	SB	CS	SB%	GDP	Avg	OBP	SLG
1997 Montreal	NL	16	18	4	0	0	0	(0	0)	4	4	2	1	0	3	0	1	0	1	2	.33	1	.222	.263	.222

(continued)

Year Team	Lg	G	AB	H	2B	3B	HR	Hm	Rd	TB	R	RBI	TBB	IBB	SO	HBP	SH	SF	SB	CS	SB%	GDP	Avg	OBP	SLG
1998 Montreal	NL	79	261	73	16	5	3	(2	1)	108	44	22	18	1	27	0	5	1	6	2	.75	6	.280	.325	.414
1999 Montreal	NL	104	382	97	23	5	8	(6	2)	154	48	39	18	4	38	3	4	0	2	2	.50	9	.254	.293	.403
3 ML YEARS		199	661	174	39	10	11	(8	3)	266	96	63	37	5	68	3	10	1	9	6	.60	16	.263	.305	.402

Miguel Cairo

Bats: Right Throws: Right Pos: 2B-117; PH/PR-3; DH-2   Ht: 6'1" Wt: 200 Born: 5/4/74 Age: 26

Year Team	Lg	G	AB	H	2B	3B	HR	Hm	Rd	TB	R	RBI	TBB	IBB	SO	HBP	SH	SF	SB	CS	SB%	GDP	Avg	OBP	SLG
1999 Orlando *	AA	3	13	5	2	0	0	—	—	7	1	1	0	0	1	0	0	0	0	1	.00	0	.385	.385	.538
St. Pete *	A+	3	13	5	0	0	0	—	—	5	2	0	1	0	2	0	0	0	1	1	.50	0	.385	.429	.385
1996 Toronto	AL	9	27	6	2	0	0	(0	0)	8	5	1	2	0	1	0	0	0	0	0	.00	1	.222	.300	.296
1997 Chicago	NL	16	29	7	1	0	0	(0	0)	8	7	1	2	0	3	1	0	0	0	0	.00	0	.241	.313	.276
1998 Tampa Bay	AL	150	515	138	26	5	5	(3	2)	189	49	46	24	0	44	6	11	2	19	8	.70	9	.268	.307	.367
1999 Tampa Bay	AL	120	465	137	15	5	3	(1	2)	171	61	36	24	0	46	7	7	5	22	7	.76	13	.295	.335	.368
4 ML YEARS		295	1036	288	44	10	8	(4	4)	376	122	84	52	0	102	15	18	7	41	15	.73	23	.278	.320	.363

Mickey Callaway

Pitches: Right Bats: Right Pos: SP-4; RP-1   Ht: 6'2" Wt: 190 Born: 5/13/75 Age: 25

Year Team	Lg	G	GS	CG	GF	IP	BFP	H	R	ER	HR	SH	SF	HB	TBB	IBB	SO	WP	Bk	W	L	Pct.	ShO	Sv-Op	Hld	ERA
1996 Butte	R+	16	11	0	1	63	274	70	37	26	5	0	3	3	25	0	57	7	0	6	2	.750	0	0- --	—	3.71
1997 St. Pete	A+	28	28	3	0	170.2	696	162	74	61	9	2	3	5	39	0	109	7	7	11	7	.611	0	0- --	—	3.22
1998 Orlando	AA	18	17	0	0	89.2	407	103	56	44	8	1	1	4	44	0	57	7	2	5	6	.455	0	0- --	—	4.42
Durham	AAA	9	8	0	0	47.2	209	49	27	24	6	1	0	1	17	0	19	2	0	5	3	.625	0	0- --	—	4.53
1999 Orlando	AA	2	2	0	0	10	44	15	6	5	1	0	0	0	2	0	7	1	0	1	1	.500	0	0- --	—	4.50
Durham	AAA	15	15	0	0	81.1	350	86	45	38	5	0	3	8	28	0	56	6	1	7	1	.875	0	0- --	—	4.20
1999 Tampa Bay	AL	5	4	0	0	19.1	99	30	20	16	2	0	1	0	14	1	11	1	0	1	2	.333	0	0-0	0	7.45

Mike Cameron

Bats: Right Throws: Right Pos: CF-146; PH/PR-3   Ht: 6'2" Wt: 190 Born: 1/8/73 Age: 27

Year Team	Lg	G	AB	H	2B	3B	HR	Hm	Rd	TB	R	RBI	TBB	IBB	SO	HBP	SH	SF	SB	CS	SB%	GDP	Avg	OBP	SLG
1995 Chicago	AL	28	38	7	2	0	1	(0	1)	12	4	2	3	0	15	0	3	0	0	0	.00	0	.184	.244	.316
1996 Chicago	AL	11	11	1	0	0	0	(0	0)	1	1	0	1	0	3	0	0	0	0	1	.00	0	.091	.167	.091
1997 Chicago	AL	116	379	98	18	3	14	(10	4)	164	63	55	55	1	105	5	2	5	23	2	.92	6	.259	.356	.433
1998 Chicago	AL	141	396	83	16	5	8	(5	3)	133	53	43	37	0	101	6	1	3	27	11	.71	6	.210	.285	.336
1999 Cincinnati	NL	146	542	139	34	9	21	(12	9)	254	93	66	80	2	145	6	5	3	38	12	.76	4	.256	.357	.469
5 ML YEARS		442	1366	328	70	17	44	(27	17)	564	214	166	176	3	369	17	11	11	88	26	.77	18	.240	.332	.413

Ken Caminiti

Bats: Both Throws: Right Pos: 3B-75; PH/PR-4   Ht: 6'0" Wt: 200 Born: 4/21/63 Age: 37

Year Team	Lg	G	AB	H	2B	3B	HR	Hm	Rd	TB	R	RBI	TBB	IBB	SO	HBP	SH	SF	SB	CS	SB%	GDP	Avg	OBP	SLG
1999 New Orleans *	AAA	6	20	7	4	0	0	(Hm	—)	11	6	3	2	0	1	0	0	0	0	0	.00	0	.350	.409	.550
1987 Houston	NL	63	203	50	7	1	3	(2	1)	68	10	23	12	1	44	0	2	1	0	0	.00	6	.246	.287	.335
1988 Houston	NL	30	83	15	2	0	1	(0	1)	20	5	7	5	0	18	0	0	1	0	0	.00	3	.181	.225	.241
1989 Houston	NL	161	585	149	31	3	10	(3	7)	216	71	72	51	9	93	3	3	4	4	1	.80	8	.255	.316	.369
1990 Houston	NL	153	541	131	20	2	4	(2	2)	167	52	51	48	7	97	0	3	4	9	4	.69	15	.242	.302	.309
1991 Houston	NL	152	574	145	30	3	13	(9	4)	220	65	80	46	7	85	5	3	4	5	4	.44	18	.253	.312	.383
1992 Houston	NL	135	506	149	31	2	13	(7	6)	223	68	62	44	13	68	1	2	4	10	4	.71	14	.294	.350	.441
1993 Houston	NL	143	543	142	31	0	13	(6	7)	213	75	75	49	10	88	0	1	3	8	5	.62	15	.262	.321	.390
1994 Houston	NL	111	406	115	28	2	18	(6	12)	201	63	75	43	13	71	2	0	3	4	3	.57	8	.283	.352	.495
1995 San Diego	NL	143	526	159	33	0	26	(16	10)	270	74	94	69	8	94	1	0	6	12	5	.71	11	.302	.380	.513
1996 San Diego	NL	146	546	178	37	2	40	(20	20)	339	109	130	78	16	99	4	0	10	11	5	.69	15	.326	.408	.621
1997 San Diego	NL	137	486	141	28	0	26	(15	11)	247	92	90	80	7	118	3	0	7	11	2	.85	12	.290	.389	.508
1998 San Diego	NL	131	452	114	29	0	29	(14	15)	241	87	82	71	4	108	4	0	8	6	2	.75	6	.252	.353	.509
1999 Houston	NL	78	273	78	11	1	13	(4	9)	130	45	56	46	3	58	3	0	7	6	2	.75	7	.286	.386	.444
13 ML YEARS		1583	5724	1566	318	16	209	(103	106)	2543	816	897	642	100	1041	26	14	62	85	38	.69	138	.274	.346	.444

Robinson Cancel

Bats: Right Throws: Right Pos: C-15   Ht: 6'0" Wt: 195 Born: 5/4/76 Age: 24

Year Team	Lg	G	AB	H	2B	3B	HR	Hm	Rd	TB	R	RBI	TBB	IBB	SO	HBP	SH	SF	SB	CS	SB%	GDP	Avg	OBP	SLG
1994 Brewers	R	29	70	12	0	0	0	—	—	12	6	8	9	1	19	2	0	2	0	2	.00	2	.171	.277	.171
1995 Helena	R+	46	154	37	9	0	0	—	—	46	18	24	9	0	20	2	1	2	8	3	.73	5	.240	.287	.299
1996 Beloit	A	72	218	48	3	1	1	—	—	56	26	29	14	0	31	1	5	1	13	5	.72	7	.220	.269	.257
1997 Beloit	A	17	50	15	3	0	0	—	—	18	9	4	7	0	9	3	0	0	2	2	.00	1	.300	.417	.360
Stockton	A+	64	211	59	11	0	1	—	—	73	25	16	13	0	40	2	7	1	9	3	.75	6	.280	.326	.346
1998 Stockton	A+	11	32	6	1	0	0	—	—	7	3	2	4	0	8	0	0	0	2	1	.67	1	.188	.278	.219
El Paso	AA	58	158	51	10	0	1	—	—	64	17	30	22	1	32	0	4	1	2	2	.50	5	.323	.403	.405
1999 Huntsville	AA	66	223	56	10	1	5	—	—	83	35	32	23	0	38	3	0	1	8	5	.62	10	.251	.328	.372

Year Team	Lg	G	AB	H	2B	3B	HR	(Hm	Rd)	TB	R	RBI	TBB	IBB	SO	HBP	SH	SF	SB	CS	SB%	GDP	Avg	OBP	SLG
						BATTING													**BASERUNNING**				**PERCENTAGES**		
Louisville	AAA	39	117	43	8	0	5	—	—	66	22	28	14	0	28	1	1	1	6	2	.75	6	.368	.436	.564
1999 Milwaukee	NL	15	44	8	2	0	0	(0	0)	10	5	5	2	0	12	1	1	0	0	0	.00	0	.182	.234	.227

Tom Candiotti

Pitches: Right **Bats:** Right **Pos:** SP-13; RP-5 — **Ht:** 6'2" **Wt:** 230 **Born:** 8/31/57 **Age:** 42

Year Team	Lg	G	GS	CG	GF	IP	BFP	H	R	ER	HR	SH	SF	HB	TBB	IBB	SO	WP	Bk	W	L	Pct.	ShO	Sv-Op	Hld	ERA
				HOW MUCH HE PITCHED						**WHAT HE GAVE UP**											**THE RESULTS**				
1983 Milwaukee	AL	10	8	2	1	55.2	233	62	21	20	4	0	2	2	16	0	21	0	0	4	4	.500	1	0- –	—	3.23
1984 Milwaukee	AL	8	6	0	0	32.1	147	38	21	19	5	0	0	0	10	0	23	1	0	2	2	.500	0	0- –	—	5.29
1986 Cleveland	AL	36	34	17	1	252.1	1078	234	112	100	18	3	9	8	106	0	167	12	4	16	12	.571	3	0- –	—	3.57
1987 Cleveland	AL	32	32	7	0	201.2	888	193	132	107	28	8	10	4	93	2	111	13	2	7	18	.280	2	0-0	0	4.78
1988 Cleveland	AL	31	31	11	0	216.2	903	225	86	79	15	12	5	6	53	3	137	5	7	14	8	.636	1	0-0	0	3.28
1989 Cleveland	AL	31	31	4	0	206	847	188	80	71	10	6	4	4	55	5	124	4	8	13	10	.565	0	0-0	0	3.10
1990 Cleveland	AL	31	29	3	1	202	856	207	92	82	23	4	3	6	55	1	128	9	3	15	11	.577	1	0-0	0	3.65
1991 Cle-Tor	AL	34	34	6	0	238	981	202	82	70	12	4	11	6	73	1	167	11	0	13	13	.500	0	0-0	0	2.65
1992 Los Angeles	NL	32	30	6	1	203.2	839	177	78	68	13	20	6	3	63	5	152	9	2	11	15	.423	2	0-0	0	3.00
1993 Los Angeles	NL	33	32	2	0	213.2	898	192	86	74	12	15	9	6	71	1	155	6	0	8	10	.444	0	0-0	0	3.12
1994 Los Angeles	NL	23	22	5	0	153	652	149	77	70	9	9	8	5	54	2	102	9	0	7	7	.500	0	0-0	0	4.12
1995 Los Angeles	NL	30	30	1	0	190.1	812	187	93	74	18	7	5	9	58	2	141	7	0	7	14	.333	1	0-0	0	3.50
1996 Los Angeles	NL	28	27	1	0	152.1	657	172	91	76	18	8	5	3	43	3	79	3	1	9	11	.450	0	0-0	0	4.49
1997 Los Angeles	NL	41	18	0	6	135	573	128	60	54	21	3	2	11	40	4	89	4	0	10	7	.588	0	0-0	0	3.60
1998 Oakland	AL	33	33	3	0	201	878	222	124	108	30	7	8	9	63	2	98	14	0	11	16	.407	0	0-0	0	4.84
1999 Oak-Cle	AL	18	13	0	1	71.1	326	86	64	58	14	2	4	3	30	0	41	13	0	4	6	.400	0	0-0	0	7.32
1991 Cleveland	AL	15	15	3	0	108.1	442	88	35	27	6	1	7	2	28	0	86	6	0	7	6	.538	0	0-0	0	2.24
Toronto	AL	19	19	3	0	129.2	539	114	47	43	6	3	4	4	45	1	81	5	0	6	7	.462	0	0-0	0	2.98
1999 Oakland	AL	11	11	0	0	56.2	254	67	46	40	11	0	4	2	23	0	30	9	0	3	5	.375	0	0-0	0	6.35
Cleveland	AL	7	2	0	1	14.2	72	19	18	18	3	2	0	1	7	0	11	4	0	1	1	.500	0	0-0	0	11.05
16 ML YEARS		451	410	68	11	2725	11568	2662	1299	1130	250	108	91	85	883	31	1735	120	27	151	164	.479	11	0- –	—	3.73

John Cangelosi

Bats: Both **Throws:** Left **Pos:** PH/PR-7; LF-1 — **Ht:** 5'8" **Wt:** 160 **Born:** 3/10/63 **Age:** 37

Year Team	Lg	G	AB	H	2B	3B	HR	(Hm	Rd)	TB	R	RBI	TBB	IBB	SO	HBP	SH	SF	SB	CS	SB%	GDP	Avg	OBP	SLG
						BATTING													**BASERUNNING**				**PERCENTAGES**		
1999 Colo Sprngs *	AAA	29	109	36	7	0	1	—	—	46	22	13	24	0	16	1	1	1	4	3	.57	4	.330	.452	.422
1985 Chicago	AL	5	2	0	0	0	0	(0	0)	0	2	0	0	0	1	1	1	0	0	0	.00	0	.000	.333	.000
1986 Chicago	AL	137	438	103	16	3	2	(1	1)	131	65	32	71	0	61	7	6	3	50	17	.75	5	.235	.349	.299
1987 Pittsburgh	NL	104	182	50	8	3	4	(2	2)	76	44	18	46	1	33	3	1	1	21	6	.78	3	.275	.427	.418
1988 Pittsburgh	NL	75	118	30	4	1	0	(0	0)	36	18	8	17	0	16	1	3	0	9	4	.69	0	.254	.353	.305
1989 Pittsburgh	NL	112	160	35	4	2	0	(0	0)	43	18	9	35	2	20	3	1	2	11	8	.58	1	.219	.365	.269
1990 Pittsburgh	NL	58	76	15	2	0	0	(0	0)	17	13	1	11	0	12	1	2	0	7	2	.78	2	.197	.307	.224
1992 Texas	AL	73	85	16	2	0	1	(0	1)	21	12	6	18	0	16	0	3	0	6	5	.55	0	.188	.330	.247
1994 New York	NL	62	111	28	4	0	0	(0	0)	32	14	4	19	1	20	2	3	0	5	1	.83	1	.252	.371	.288
1995 Houston	NL	90	201	64	5	2	2	(2	0)	79	46	18	48	2	42	4	2	1	21	5	.81	3	.318	.457	.393
1996 Houston	NL	108	262	69	11	4	1	(1	0)	91	49	16	44	0	41	5	1	1	17	9	.65	4	.263	.373	.347
1997 Florida	NL	103	192	47	8	0	1	(1	0)	58	28	12	19	1	33	3	1	1	5	1	.83	3	.245	.321	.302
1998 Florida	NL	104	171	43	8	0	1	(1	0)	54	19	10	30	0	23	1	5	1	2	3	.40	5	.251	.365	.316
1999 Colorado	NL	7	6	1	1	0	0	(0	0)	2	0	0	0	0	4	0	0	0	1	0	1.00	0	.167	.167	.333
13 ML YEARS		1038	2004	501	73	15	12	(7	5)	640	328	134	358	7	322	31	29	10	154	61	.72	27	.250	.370	.319

Jay Canizaro

Bats: Right **Throws:** Right **Pos:** PH/PR-10; 2B-4 — **Ht:** 5'9" **Wt:** 170 **Born:** 7/4/73 **Age:** 26

Year Team	Lg	G	AB	H	2B	3B	HR	(Hm	Rd)	TB	R	RBI	TBB	IBB	SO	HBP	SH	SF	SB	CS	SB%	GDP	Avg	OBP	SLG
						BATTING													**BASERUNNING**				**PERCENTAGES**		
1993 Giants	R	49	180	47	10	6	3	—	—	78	34	41	22	1	40	0	0	3	12	3	.80	4	.261	.337	.433
1994 San Jose	A+	126	464	117	16	2	15	—	—	182	77	69	46	1	98	5	0	3	12	6	.67	7	.252	.324	.392
1995 Shreveport	AA	126	440	129	25	7	12	—	—	204	83	60	58	4	98	6	4	1	16	9	.64	9	.293	.379	.464
1996 Phoenix	AAA	102	363	95	21	2	7	—	—	141	50	64	46	2	77	4	1	5	14	4	.78	7	.262	.347	.388
1997 Shreveport	AAA	23	81	16	7	0	2	—	—	29	12	12	9	0	24	0	1	0	2	2	.50	2	.198	.278	.358
Shreveport	AA	50	176	45	9	0	11	—	—	87	36	38	26	0	44	2	0	2	2	2	.50	4	.256	.354	.494
1998 Shreveport	AA	83	281	63	7	1	12	—	—	108	47	32	53	1	46	4	1	3	5	2	.71	8	.224	.352	.384
Fresno	AAA	45	106	24	6	2	6	—	—	52	23	14	17	1	23	1	0	1	0	1	.00	3	.226	.336	.491
1999 Fresno	AAA	105	364	102	20	2	26	—	—	204	76	78	49	3	79	3	2	1	16	5	.76	9	.280	.364	.560
1996 San Francisco	NL	43	120	24	4	1	2	(1	1)	36	11	8	9	0	38	1	1	1	1	1	.50	0	.200	.260	.300
1999 San Francisco	NL	12	18	8	2	0	1	(0	1)	13	5	9	1	0	2	0	0	0	1	0	1.00	5	.444	.474	.722
2 ML YEARS		55	138	32	6	1	3	(1	2)	49	16	17	10	0	40	1	1	1	2	1	.33	5	.232	.287	.355

Jose Canseco

Bats: Right **Throws:** Right **Pos:** DH-106; LF-6; PH/PR-1 — **Ht:** 6'4" **Wt:** 240 **Born:** 7/2/64 **Age:** 35

Year Team	Lg	G	AB	H	2B	3B	HR	(Hm	Rd)	TB	R	RBI	TBB	IBB	SO	HBP	SH	SF	SB	CS	SB%	GDP	Avg	OBP	SLG
						BATTING													**BASERUNNING**				**PERCENTAGES**		
1985 Oakland	AL	29	96	29	3	0	5	(4	1)	47	16	13	4	0	31	0	0	0	1	1	.50	1	.302	.330	.490
1986 Oakland	AL	157	600	144	29	1	33	(14	19)	274	85	117	65	4	175	8	0	9	15	7	.68	12	.240	.318	.457
1987 Oakland	AL	159	630	162	35	3	31	(16	15)	296	81	113	50	2	157	2	0	9	15	3	.83	16	.257	.310	.470

39

		BATTING																	BASERUNNING				PERCENTAGES		
Year Team	Lg	G	AB	H	2B	3B	HR	(Hm	Rd)	TB	R	RBI	TBB	IBB	SO	HBP	SH	SF	SB	CS	SB%	GDP	Avg	OBP	SLG
1988 Oakland	AL	158	610	187	34	0	42	(16	26)	347	120	124	78	10	128	10	1	6	40	16	.71	15	.307	.391	.569
1989 Oakland	AL	65	227	61	9	1	17	(8	9)	123	40	57	23	4	69	2	0	6	6	3	.67	4	.269	.333	.542
1990 Oakland	AL	131	481	132	14	2	37	(18	19)	261	83	101	72	8	158	5	0	5	19	10	.66	9	.274	.371	.543
1991 Oakland	AL	154	572	152	32	1	44	(16	28)	318	115	122	78	8	152	9	0	6	26	6	.81	16	.266	.359	.556
1992 Oak-Tex	AL	119	439	107	15	0	26	(15	11)	200	74	87	63	2	128	6	0	4	6	7	.46	16	.244	.344	.456
1993 Texas	AL	60	231	59	14	1	10	(6	4)	105	30	46	16	2	62	3	0	3	6	6	.50	6	.255	.308	.455
1994 Texas	AL	111	429	121	19	2	31	(17	14)	237	88	90	69	8	114	5	0	2	15	8	.65	20	.282	.386	.552
1995 Boston	AL	102	396	121	25	1	24	(10	14)	220	64	81	42	4	93	7	0	5	4	0	1.00	9	.306	.378	.556
1996 Boston	AL	96	360	104	22	1	28	(17	11)	212	68	82	63	3	82	6	0	3	3	1	.75	7	.289	.400	.589
1997 Oakland	AL	108	388	91	19	0	23	(10	13)	179	56	74	51	1	122	3	0	4	8	2	.80	15	.235	.325	.461
1998 Toronto	AL	151	583	138	26	0	46	(25	21)	302	98	107	65	5	159	6	0	4	29	17	.63	7	.237	.318	.518
1999 Tampa Bay	AL	113	430	120	18	1	34	(12	22)	242	75	95	58	3	135	7	0	7	3	0	1.00	14	.279	.369	.563
1992 Oakland	AL	97	366	90	11	0	22	(12	10)	167	66	72	48	1	104	3	0	4	5	7	.42	15	.246	.356	.456
Texas	AL	22	73	17	4	0	4	(3	1)	33	8	15	15	1	24	3	0	0	1	0	1.00	1	.233	.385	.452
15 ML YEARS		1713	6472	1728	314	14	431	(204	227)	3363	1093	1309	797	61	1765	79	1	73	196	87	.69	167	.267	.351	.520

Dan Carlson

Pitches: Right **Bats:** Right **Pos:** RP-2   **Ht:** 6'0" **Wt:** 200 **Born:** 1/26/70 **Age:** 30

		HOW MUCH HE PITCHED						WHAT HE GAVE UP												THE RESULTS						
Year Team	Lg	G	GS	CG	GF	IP	BFP	H	R	ER	HR	SH	SF	HB	TBB	IBB	SO	WP	Bk	W	L	Pct.	ShO	Sv-Op	Hld	ERA
1990 Everett	A-	17	11	0	3	62.1	279	60	42	37	5	1	4	1	33	1	77	9	5	2	6	.250	0	0--	—	5.34
1991 Clinton	A	27	27	5	0	181.1	740	149	69	62	11	3	3	2	76	0	164	18	5	16	7	.696	3	0--	—	3.08
1992 Shreveport	AA	27	27	4	0	186	765	166	85	66	15	5	3	1	60	3	157	4	0	15	9	.625	1	0--	—	3.19
1993 Phoenix	AAA	13	12	0	0	70	320	79	54	51	12	2	1	5	32	1	48	4	0	5	6	.455	0	0--	—	6.56
Shreveport	AA	15	15	2	0	100.1	397	86	30	25	9	4	4	0	26	3	81	5	0	7	4	.636	1	0--	—	2.24
1994 Phoenix	AAA	31	22	0	2	151.1	665	173	80	78	21	3	9	1	55	1	117	10	0	13	6	.684	0	1--	—	4.64
1995 Phoenix	AAA	23	22	2	1	132.2	582	138	67	63	11	7	7	3	66	0	93	6	1	9	5	.643	0	0--	—	4.27
1996 Phoenix	AAA	33	15	2	3	146.2	604	135	61	56	18	5	5	2	46	0	123	3	0	13	6	.684	0	1--	—	3.44
1997 Bakersfield	A+	2	2	0	0	6	22	3	0	0	0	0	0	0	1	0	7	0	0	0	0	.000	0	0--	—	0.00
Phoenix	AAA	29	14	0	7	109	451	102	53	47	12	3	3	2	36	1	108	6	1	13	3	.813	0	3--	—	3.88
1998 Durham	AAA	19	11	0	3	68	316	87	52	48	8	1	1	3	28	0	59	4	1	3	5	.375	0	0--	—	6.35
1999 Tucson	AAA	32	18	0	5	117.2	527	130	82	71	19	3	1	6	52	6	118	4	2	4	9	.308	0	0--	—	5.43
1996 San Francisco	NL	5	0	0	3	10	46	13	6	3	2	0	2	0	2	0	4	0	0	1	0	1.000	0	0-0	0	2.70
1997 San Francisco	NL	6	0	0	2	15.1	72	20	14	13	5	0	1	0	8	1	14	0	0	0	0	.000	0	0-0	0	7.63
1998 Tampa Bay	AL	10	0	0	1	17.2	86	25	15	15	3	2	1	3	8	0	16	0	0	0	0	.000	0	0-0	0	7.64
1999 Arizona	NL	2	0	0	1	4	18	5	4	4	0	0	0	0	0	0	3	0	0	0	0	.000	0	0-0	0	9.00
4 ML YEARS		23	0	0	7	47	222	63	39	35	10	2	4	3	18	1	37	0	0	1	0	1.000	0	0-0	0	6.70

Buddy Carlyle

Pitches: Right **Bats:** Left **Pos:** SP-7   **Ht:** 6'3" **Wt:** 175 **Born:** 12/21/77 **Age:** 22

		HOW MUCH HE PITCHED						WHAT HE GAVE UP												THE RESULTS						
Year Team	Lg	G	GS	CG	GF	IP	BFP	H	R	ER	HR	SH	SF	HB	TBB	IBB	SO	WP	Bk	W	L	Pct.	ShO	Sv-Op	Hld	ERA
1996 Princeton	R+	10	9	1	1	46.1	204	47	33	24	4	2	1	1	16	0	42	8	0	2	4	.333	0	0--	—	4.66
1997 Chstn-WV	A	23	23	4	0	143	579	130	51	44	9	4	4	3	27	0	111	5	1	14	5	.737	1	0--	—	2.77
1998 Chattanooga	AA	1	1	0	0	5	20	6	3	3	0	0	0	0	0	0	3	0	0	1	0	1.000	0	0--	—	5.40
Mobile	AA	27	27	2	0	183.2	763	179	77	69	13	8	3	7	46	0	97	4	1	14	6	.700	1	0--	—	3.38
1999 Las Vegas	AAA	25	25	0	0	160	690	180	99	87	25	5	8	6	42	1	138	6	0	11	8	.579	0	0--	—	4.89
1999 San Diego	NL	7	7	0	0	37.2	162	36	28	25	7	1	2	2	17	0	29	1	0	1	3	.250	0	0-0	0	5.97

Rafael Carmona

Pitches: Right **Bats:** Left **Pos:** RP-9   **Ht:** 6'2" **Wt:** 185 **Born:** 10/2/72 **Age:** 27

		HOW MUCH HE PITCHED						WHAT HE GAVE UP												THE RESULTS						
Year Team	Lg	G	GS	CG	GF	IP	BFP	H	R	ER	HR	SH	SF	HB	TBB	IBB	SO	WP	Bk	W	L	Pct.	ShO	Sv-Op	Hld	ERA
1999 Tacoma *	AAA	27	0	0	9	43.1	185	39	18	17	6	1	0	1	20	0	38	2	0	1	3	.250	0	2--	—	3.53
1995 Seattle	AL	15	3	0	6	47.2	230	55	31	30	9	1	5	2	34	1	28	3	1	2	4	.333	0	1-2	0	5.66
1996 Seattle	AL	53	1	0	15	90.1	415	95	47	43	11	7	2	3	55	9	62	4	0	8	3	.727	0	1-5	8	4.28
1997 Seattle	AL	4	0	0	1	5.2	22	3	3	2	1	0	0	0	2	0	6	1	0	0	0	.000	0	0-0	0	3.18
1999 Seattle	AL	9	0	0	3	11.1	57	18	11	10	3	2	2	0	9	1	0	0	0	1	0	1.000	0	0-0	0	7.94
4 ML YEARS		81	4	0	25	155	724	171	92	85	24	10	9	5	100	11	96	8	1	11	7	.611	0	2-7	8	4.94

Chris Carpenter

Pitches: Right **Bats:** Right **Pos:** SP-24   **Ht:** 6'6" **Wt:** 215 **Born:** 4/27/75 **Age:** 25

		HOW MUCH HE PITCHED						WHAT HE GAVE UP												THE RESULTS						
Year Team	Lg	G	GS	CG	GF	IP	BFP	H	R	ER	HR	SH	SF	HB	TBB	IBB	SO	WP	Bk	W	L	Pct.	ShO	Sv-Op	Hld	ERA
1999 St.Cathrnes *	A-	1	1	0	0	4	18	5	2	2	0	0	0	0	1	0	6	1	0	0	0	.000	0	0--	—	4.50
1997 Toronto	AL	14	13	1	1	81.1	374	108	55	46	7	1	2	2	37	0	55	7	1	3	7	.300	1	0-0	0	5.09
1998 Toronto	AL	33	24	1	4	175	742	177	97	85	18	4	5	5	61	1	136	5	0	12	7	.632	0	0-0	0	4.37
1999 Toronto	AL	24	24	4	0	150	663	177	81	73	16	4	6	3	48	1	106	9	1	9	8	.529	1	0-0	0	4.38
3 ML YEARS		71	61	6	5	406.1	1779	462	233	204	41	9	13	10	146	2	297	21	2	24	22	.522	3	0-0	0	4.52

Hector Carrasco

Pitches: Right Bats: Right Pos: RP-39
Ht: 6'2" Wt: 220 Born: 10/22/69 Age: 30

		HOW MUCH HE PITCHED						WHAT HE GAVE UP										THE RESULTS					
Year Team	Lg	G	GS	CG	GF	IP	BFP	H	R	ER	HR	SH	SF	HB	TBB	IBB	SO	WP	Bk	W	L	Pct.	ShO	Sv-Op	Hld	ERA
1999 Fort Myers *	A+	1	1	0	0	2	8	2	1	1	0	0	0	0	1	0	1	0	0	1	0	1.000	0	0- -	—	4.50
Salt Lake *	AAA	3	0	0	3	4.1	18	3	0	0	1	0	0	0	1	0	3	0	0	1	0	1.000	0	1- -	—	0.00
1994 Cincinnati	NL	45	0	0	29	56.1	237	42	17	14	3	5	0	2	30	1	41	3	1	5	6	.455	0	6-8	3	2.24
1995 Cincinnati	NL	64	0	0	28	87.1	391	86	45	40	1	2	6	2	46	5	64	15	0	2	7	.222	0	5-9	11	4.12
1996 Cincinnati	NL	56	0	0	10	74.1	325	58	37	31	6	4	4	1	45	5	59	8	1	4	3	.571	0	0-2	15	3.75
1997 Cin-KC		66	0	0	22	86	388	80	46	42	7	4	3	8	41	5	76	11	2	4	2	.667	0	1-2	10	4.38
1998 Minnesota	AL	63	0	0	20	61.2	287	75	30	30	4	0	8	1	31	1	46	8	0	4	2	.400	0	1-2	7	4.96
1999 Minnesota	AL	39	0	0	10	49	204	48	29	27	3	0	1	1	18	0	35	4	0	2	3	.400	0	1-2	7	4.96
1997 Cincinnati	NL	38	0	0	11	51.1	237	51	25	21	3	3	1	4	25	2	46	3	2	1	2	.333	0	0-0	5	3.68
Kansas City	AL	28	0	0	11	34.2	151	29	21	21	4	1	2	4	16	3	30	8	0	1	6	.143	0	0-2	3	5.45
6 ML YEARS		333	0	0	119	414.2	1832	389	204	184	24	15	22	15	211	17	321	49	4	19	29	.396	0	13-25	54	3.99

Lance Carter

Pitches: Right Bats: Right Pos: RP-6
Ht: 6'1" Wt: 190 Born: 12/18/74 Age: 25

		HOW MUCH HE PITCHED						WHAT HE GAVE UP										THE RESULTS					
Year Team	Lg	G	GS	CG	GF	IP	BFP	H	R	ER	HR	SH	SF	HB	TBB	IBB	SO	WP	Bk	W	L	Pct.	ShO	Sv-Op	Hld	ERA
1994 Eugene	A-	8	7	0	1	26.1	118	28	17	16	2	1	3	1	15	0	23	4	3	0	1	1.000	0	0- -	—	5.47
Royals	R	5	5	0	0	31	110	19	1	1	1	1	0	0	3	0	36	1	0	3	0	1.000	0	0- -	—	0.29
1995 Springfield	A	27	24	1	0	137.2	584	151	77	61	14	2	4	8	22	0	118	11	1	9	5	.643	1	0- -	—	3.99
1996 Wilmington	A+	16	12	0	3	65.1	292	81	50	46	8	1	0	2	17	2	49	3	0	3	6	.333	0	0- -	—	6.34
1998 Lansing	A	15	2	0	10	40.1	158	34	6	3	0	1	1	0	9	1	37	0	0	3	1	.750	0	2- -	—	0.67
Wilmington	A+	28	1	0	11	52	217	50	21	19	5	5	3	4	14	1	61	4	0	1	4	.200	0	5- -	—	3.29
1999 Wichita	AA	44	0	0	33	69.2	282	49	10	6	1	1	1	2	27	5	77	3	0	5	2	.714	0	13- -	—	0.78
1999 Kansas City	AL	6	0	0	3	5.1	21	3	3	3	2	0	1	0	3	0	3	0	0	0	1	.000	0	0-0	0	5.06

Mike Caruso

Bats: Left Throws: Right Pos: SS-132; PH/PR-6; DH-2
Ht: 6'1" Wt: 172 Born: 5/27/77 Age: 23

		BATTING																	BASERUNNING				PERCENTAGES		
Year Team	Lg	G	AB	H	2B	3B	HR	(Hm	Rd)	TB	R	RBI	TBB	IBB	SO	HBP	SH	SF	SB	CS	SB%	GDP	Avg	OBP	SLG
1996 Bellingham	A-	73	312	91	13	1	2	—	—	112	48	24	16	2	23	2	3	6	24	10	.71	2	.292	.324	.359
1997 San Jose	A+	108	444	147	24	11	2	—	—	199	76	50	38	3	19	6	4	3	11	16	.41	3	.331	.391	.451
Winston-Sal	A+	28	119	27	3	2	0	—	—	34	12	14	4	0	8	2	0	0	3	0	1.00	0	.227	.264	.286
1998 Chicago	AL	133	523	160	17	6	5	(3	2)	204	81	55	14	0	38	7	8	3	22	6	.79	8	.306	.331	.390
1999 Chicago	AL	136	529	132	11	4	2	(0	2)	157	60	35	20	0	36	3	11	1	12	14	.46	6	.250	.280	.297
2 ML YEARS		269	1052	292	28	10	7	(3	4)	361	141	90	34	0	74	10	19	4	34	20	.63	14	.278	.305	.343

Sean Casey

Bats: Left Throws: Right Pos: 1B-148; PH/PR-3; DH-1
Ht: 6'4" Wt: 215 Born: 7/2/74 Age: 25

		BATTING																	BASERUNNING				PERCENTAGES		
Year Team	Lg	G	AB	H	2B	3B	HR	(Hm	Rd)	TB	R	RBI	TBB	IBB	SO	HBP	SH	SF	SB	CS	SB%	GDP	Avg	OBP	SLG
1997 Cleveland	AL	6	10	2	0	0	0	(0	0)	2	1	1	1	0	2	1	0	0	0	0	.00	0	.200	.333	.200
1998 Cincinnati	NL	96	302	82	21	1	7	(3	4)	126	44	52	43	3	45	3	0	3	1	1	.50	11	.272	.365	.417
1999 Cincinnati	NL	151	594	197	42	3	25	(11	14)	320	103	99	61	13	88	9	0	5	0	2	.00	15	.332	.399	.539
3 ML YEARS		253	906	281	63	4	32	(14	18)	448	148	152	105	16	135	13	0	8	1	3	.25	26	.310	.387	.494

Vinny Castilla

Bats: Right Throws: Right Pos: 3B-157; PH/PR-2
Ht: 6'1" Wt: 205 Born: 7/4/67 Age: 32

		BATTING																	BASERUNNING				PERCENTAGES		
Year Team	Lg	G	AB	H	2B	3B	HR	(Hm	Rd)	TB	R	RBI	TBB	IBB	SO	HBP	SH	SF	SB	CS	SB%	GDP	Avg	OBP	SLG
1991 Atlanta	NL	12	5	1	0	0	0	(0	0)	1	1	0	0	0	2	0	1	0	0	0	.00	0	.200	.200	.200
1992 Atlanta	NL	9	16	4	1	0	0	(0	0)	5	1	1	1	1	4	1	0	0	0	0	.00	0	.250	.333	.313
1993 Colorado	NL	105	337	86	9	7	9	(5	4)	136	36	30	13	4	45	2	0	5	2	5	.29	10	.255	.283	.404
1994 Colorado	NL	52	130	43	11	1	3	(1	2)	65	16	18	7	1	23	0	1	3	2	1	.67	3	.331	.357	.500
1995 Colorado	NL	139	527	163	34	2	32	(23	9)	297	82	90	30	2	87	4	4	6	2	8	.20	15	.309	.347	.564
1996 Colorado	NL	160	629	191	34	0	40	(27	13)	345	97	113	35	7	88	5	0	4	7	2	.78	20	.304	.343	.548
1997 Colorado	NL	159	612	186	25	2	40	(21	19)	335	94	113	44	9	108	8	0	4	2	4	.33	17	.304	.356	.547
1998 Colorado	NL	162	645	206	28	4	46	(26	20)	380	108	144	40	7	89	6	0	6	5	9	.36	14	.319	.362	.589
1999 Colorado	NL	158	615	169	24	1	33	(20	13)	294	83	102	53	7	75	1	0	5	2	3	.40	15	.275	.331	.478
9 ML YEARS		956	3516	1049	166	17	203	(123	80)	1858	518	611	223	38	521	27	6	33	22	32	.41	104	.298	.342	.528

Alberto Castillo

Bats: Right Throws: Right Pos: C-91; PH/PR-5
Ht: 6'0" Wt: 185 Born: 2/10/70 Age: 30

		BATTING																	BASERUNNING				PERCENTAGES		
Year Team	Lg	G	AB	H	2B	3B	HR	(Hm	Rd)	TB	R	RBI	TBB	IBB	SO	HBP	SH	SF	SB	CS	SB%	GDP	Avg	OBP	SLG
1995 New York	NL	13	29	3	0	0	0	(0	0)	3	2	0	3	0	9	1	0	0	1	0	1.00	0	.103	.212	.103
1996 New York	NL	6	11	4	0	0	0	(0	0)	4	1	0	0	0	4	0	0	0	0	0	.00	0	.364	.364	.364
1997 New York	NL	35	59	12	1	0	0	(0	0)	13	3	7	9	0	16	0	2	1	0	1	.00	3	.203	.304	.220
1998 New York	NL	38	83	17	4	0	2	(0	2)	27	13	7	9	0	17	1	6	0	0	2	.00	1	.205	.290	.325

Year Team	Lg	G	AB	H	2B	3B	HR	(Hm	Rd)	TB	R	RBI	TBB	IBB	SO	HBP	SH	SF	SB	CS	SB%	GDP	Avg	OBP	SLG
1999 St. Louis	NL	93	255	67	8	0	4	(2	2)	87	21	31	24	1	48	2	5	4	0	0	.00	6	.263	.326	.341
5 ML YEARS		185	437	103	13	0	6	(2	4)	134	40	45	45	1	94	4	13	5	1	3	.25	10	.236	.310	.307

Carlos Castillo

Pitches: Right Bats: Right Pos: RP-16; SP-2

Ht: 6'2" Wt: 250 Born: 4/21/75 Age: 25

Year Team	Lg	G	GS	CG	GF	IP	BFP	H	R	ER	HR	SH	SF	HB	TBB	IBB	SO	WP	Bk	W	L	Pct.	ShO	Sv-Op	Hld	ERA
1999 Charlotte *	AAA	20	20	5	0	136.1	583	150	88	78	28	3	4	3	30	1	105	5	3	9	6	.600	0	0--	--	5.15
1997 Chicago	AL	37	2	0	14	66.1	295	68	35	33	9	0	4	1	33	3	43	3	0	2	1	.667	0	1-1	3	4.48
1998 Chicago	AL	54	2	0	11	100.1	431	94	61	57	17	2	7	5	35	1	64	4	3	6	4	.600	0	0-2	3	5.11
1999 Chicago	AL	18	2	0	6	41	178	45	26	26	10	0	0	0	14	1	23	0	2	2	2	.500	0	0-0	1	5.71
3 ML YEARS		109	6	0	31	207.2	904	207	122	116	36	2	11	6	82	5	130	7	5	10	7	.588	0	1-3	7	5.03

Luis Castillo

Bats: Both Throws: Right Pos: 2B-126; PH/PR-5

Ht: 5'11" Wt: 175 Born: 9/12/75 Age: 24

Year Team	Lg	G	AB	H	2B	3B	HR	(Hm	Rd)	TB	R	RBI	TBB	IBB	SO	HBP	SH	SF	SB	CS	SB%	GDP	Avg	OBP	SLG
1996 Florida	NL	41	164	43	2	1	1	(0	1)	50	26	8	14	0	46	0	2	0	17	4	.81	0	.262	.320	.305
1997 Florida	NL	75	263	63	8	0	0	(0	0)	71	27	8	27	0	53	0	1	0	16	10	.62	6	.240	.310	.270
1998 Florida	NL	44	153	31	3	2	1	(0	1)	41	21	10	22	0	33	1	1	0	3	0	1.00	1	.203	.307	.268
1999 Florida	NL	128	487	147	23	4	0	(0	0)	178	76	28	67	0	85	0	6	3	50	17	.75	3	.302	.384	.366
4 ML YEARS		288	1067	284	36	7	2	(0	2)	340	150	54	130	0	217	1	10	3	86	31	.74	10	.266	.346	.319

Juan Castro

Bats: Right Throws: Right Pos: 2B-1; SS-1

Ht: 5'10" Wt: 187 Born: 6/20/72 Age: 28

Year Team	Lg	G	AB	H	2B	3B	HR	(Hm	Rd)	TB	R	RBI	TBB	IBB	SO	HBP	SH	SF	SB	CS	SB%	GDP	Avg	OBP	SLG
1999 Albuquerque *	AAA	116	423	116	25	4	7	--	--	170	52	51	34	2	70	0	6	4	2	3	.40	14	.274	.325	.402
1995 Los Angeles	NL	11	4	1	0	0	0	(0	0)	1	0	0	1	0	1	0	0	0	0	0	.00	0	.250	.400	.250
1996 Los Angeles	NL	70	132	26	5	3	0	(0	0)	37	16	5	10	0	27	0	4	0	1	0	1.00	3	.197	.254	.280
1997 Los Angeles	NL	40	75	11	3	1	0	(0	0)	16	3	4	7	1	20	0	2	0	0	0	.00	2	.147	.220	.213
1998 Los Angeles	NL	89	220	43	7	0	2	(0	2)	56	25	14	15	0	37	0	9	2	0	0	.00	5	.195	.245	.255
1999 Los Angeles	NL	2	1	0	0	0	0	(0	0)	0	0	0	0	0	1	0	0	0	0	0	.00	0	.000	.000	.000
5 ML YEARS		212	432	81	15	4	2	(0	2)	110	44	23	33	1	86	0	15	2	1	0	1.00	10	.188	.244	.255

Ramon Castro

Bats: Right Throws: Right Pos: C-24

Ht: 6'3" Wt: 225 Born: 3/1/76 Age: 24

Year Team	Lg	G	AB	H	2B	3B	HR	(Hm	Rd)	TB	R	RBI	TBB	IBB	SO	HBP	SH	SF	SB	CS	SB%	GDP	Avg	OBP	SLG
1994 Astros	R	37	123	34	7	0	3	--	--	50	17	14	17	1	14	2	0	0	5	5	.50	4	.276	.373	.407
1995 Kissimmee	A+	36	120	25	5	0	0	--	--	30	6	8	6	0	21	1	0	1	0	0	.00	0	.208	.250	.250
Auburn	A-	63	224	67	17	0	9	--	--	111	40	49	24	0	27	0	0	6	0	1	.00	1	.299	.358	.496
1996 Quad City	A	96	314	78	15	0	7	--	--	114	38	43	31	1	61	2	0	3	2	0	1.00	12	.248	.317	.363
1997 Kissimmee	A+	115	410	115	22	1	8	--	--	163	53	65	53	3	73	2	0	11	1	0	1.00	17	.280	.357	.398
1998 Jackson	AA	48	168	43	6	0	8	--	--	73	27	25	13	2	31	4	0	0	0	1	.00	3	.256	.324	.435
Portland	AA	31	88	22	3	0	3	--	--	34	9	11	8	0	21	0	0	2	0	0	.00	3	.250	.306	.386
1999 Calgary	AAA	97	349	90	22	0	15	--	--	157	43	61	24	3	64	2	0	3	0	0	.00	11	.258	.307	.450
1999 Florida	NL	24	67	12	4	0	2	(0	2)	22	4	4	10	3	14	0	0	1	0	0	.00	1	.179	.282	.328

Frank Catalanotto

Bats: L Throws: R Pos: 1B-32; 2B-32; PH/PR-28; 3B-21; DH-9

Ht: 6'0" Wt: 195 Born: 4/27/74 Age: 26

Year Team	Lg	G	AB	H	2B	3B	HR	(Hm	Rd)	TB	R	RBI	TBB	IBB	SO	HBP	SH	SF	SB	CS	SB%	GDP	Avg	OBP	SLG
1997 Detroit	AL	13	26	8	2	0	0	(0	0)	10	2	3	3	0	7	0	0	0	0	0	.00	0	.308	.379	.385
1998 Detroit	AL	89	213	60	13	2	6	(3	3)	95	23	25	12	1	39	4	0	5	3	2	.60	4	.282	.325	.446
1999 Detroit	AL	100	286	79	19	0	11	(6	5)	131	41	35	15	1	49	9	0	5	3	4	.43	5	.276	.327	.458
3 ML YEARS		202	525	147	34	2	17	(9	8)	236	66	63	30	2	95	13	0	10	6	6	.50	9	.280	.329	.450

Mike Cather

Pitches: Right Bats: Right Pos: RP-4

Ht: 6'2" Wt: 205 Born: 12/17/70 Age: 29

Year Team	Lg	G	GS	CG	GF	IP	BFP	H	R	ER	HR	SH	SF	HB	TBB	IBB	SO	WP	Bk	W	L	Pct.	ShO	Sv-Op	Hld	ERA
1999 Richmond *	AAA	45	0	0	20	67.2	308	71	57	51	4	8	5	1	34	2	60	5	3	2	7	.222	0	1--	--	6.78
1997 Atlanta	NL	35	0	0	10	37.2	155	23	12	10	1	2	0	2	19	4	29	0	0	2	4	.333	0	0-3	4	2.39
1998 Atlanta	NL	36	0	0	11	41.1	173	39	21	18	7	4	2	2	12	1	33	0	0	2	2	.500	0	0-3	1	3.92
1999 Atlanta	NL	4	0	0	0	2.2	13	5	3	3	2	0	0	1	0	0	0	0	1	0	1	1.000	0	0-1	0	10.13
3 ML YEARS		75	0	0	21	81.2	341	67	36	31	10	6	2	4	32	5	62	0	0	5	6	.455	0	0-7	5	3.42

Domingo Cedeno

Bats: B **Throws:** R **Pos:** SS-39; PH/PR-17; 2B-2; 3B-1   **Ht:** 6'0" **Wt:** 170 **Born:** 11/4/68 **Age:** 31

					BATTING															BASERUNNING				PERCENTAGES		
Year Team	Lg	G	AB	H	2B	3B	HR	(Hm	Rd)	TB	R	RBI	TBB	IBB	SO	HBP	SH	SF	SB	CS	SB%	GDP	Avg	OBP	SLG
1999 Tacoma *	AAA	33	112	30	8	1	1	—	—	43	17	13	7	1	36	2	0	0	1	2	.33	1	.268	.322	.384
1993 Toronto	AL	15	46	8	0	0	0	(0	0)	8	5	7	1	0	10	0	2	1	1	0	1.00	2	.174	.188	.174
1994 Toronto	AL	47	97	19	2	3	0	(0	0)	27	14	10	10	0	31	0	3	4	1	2	.33	1	.196	.261	.278
1995 Toronto	AL	51	161	38	6	1	4	(1	3)	58	18	14	10	0	35	2	1	0	1	0	1.00	3	.236	.289	.360
1996 Tor-CWS	AL	89	301	82	12	2	2	(0	2)	104	46	20	15	0	64	2	8	3	6	3	.67	7	.272	.308	.346
1997 Texas	AL	113	365	103	19	6	4	(2	2)	146	49	36	27	0	77	2	2	1	3	3	.50	5	.282	.334	.400
1998 Texas	AL	61	141	37	9	1	2	(1	1)	54	19	21	10	0	32	0	1	1	2	1	.67	4	.262	.309	.383
1999 Sea-Phi		53	108	19	6	0	3			34	9	13	10	0	31	1	1	0	1	2	.33	3	.176	.252	.315
1996 Toronto	AL	77	282	79	10	2	2	(0	2)	99	44	17	15	0	60	2	7	1	5	3	.63	6	.280	.320	.351
Chicago	AL	12	19	3	2	0	0	(0	0)	5	2	3	0	0	4	0	1	2	1	0	1.00	1	.158	.143	.263
1999 Seattle	AL	21	42	9	2	0	2	(1	1)	17	4	8	5	0	9	1	0	0	1	1	.50	1	.214	.313	.405
Philadelphia	NL	32	66	10	4	0	1	(1	0)	17	5	5	5	0	22	0	1	0	0	1	.00	2	.152	.211	.258
7 ML YEARS		429	1219	306	54	13	15	(6	9)	431	160	121	83	0	280	7	18	10	14	12	.54	25	.251	.300	.354

Roger Cedeno

Bats: B **Throws:** R **Pos:** RF-127; PH/PR-24; CF-21; LF-13; 2B-1   **Ht:** 6'1" **Wt:** 205 **Born:** 8/16/74 **Age:** 25

					BATTING															BASERUNNING				PERCENTAGES		
Year Team	Lg	G	AB	H	2B	3B	HR	(Hm	Rd)	TB	R	RBI	TBB	IBB	SO	HBP	SH	SF	SB	CS	SB%	GDP	Avg	OBP	SLG
1995 Los Angeles	NL	40	42	10	2	0	0	(0	0)	12	4	3	3	0	10	0	0	1	1	0	1.00	1	.238	.283	.286
1996 Los Angeles	NL	86	211	52	11	1	2	(0	2)	71	26	18	24	0	47	1	2	0	5	1	.83	0	.246	.326	.336
1997 Los Angeles	NL	80	194	53	10	2	3	(3	0)	76	31	17	25	2	44	3	3	2	9	1	.90	1	.273	.362	.392
1998 Los Angeles	NL	105	240	58	11	1	2	(2	0)	77	33	17	27	2	57	0	3	1	8	2	.80	1	.242	.317	.321
1999 New York	NL	155	453	142	23	4	4	(4	0)	185	90	36	60	3	100	3	7	2	66	17	.80	5	.313	.396	.408
5 ML YEARS		466	1140	315	57	8	11	(9	2)	421	184	91	139	7	258	7	15	6	89	21	.81	8	.276	.357	.369

Norm Charlton

Pitches: Left **Bats:** Both **Pos:** RP-42   **Ht:** 6'3" **Wt:** 205 **Born:** 1/6/63 **Age:** 37

		HOW MUCH HE PITCHED						WHAT HE GAVE UP												THE RESULTS					
Year Team	Lg	G	GS	CG	GF	IP	BFP	H	R	ER	HR	SH	SF	HB	TBB	IBB	SO	WP	Bk	W	L	Pct.	ShO	Sv-Op	Hld	ERA
1999 Durham *	AAA	18	0	0	9	31.2	132	27	13	13	7	1	0	3	10	1	29	1	0	3	2	.600	0	1--	—	3.69
1988 Cincinnati	NL	10	10	0	0	61.1	259	60	27	27	6	1	2	2	20	2	39	3	2	4	5	.444	0	0-0	0	3.96
1989 Cincinnati	NL	69	0	0	27	95.1	393	67	38	31	5	9	2	2	40	7	98	2	4	8	3	.727	0	0-1	8	2.93
1990 Cincinnati	NL	56	16	1	13	154.1	650	131	53	47	10	7	2	4	70	4	117	9	1	12	9	.571	1	2-3	9	2.74
1991 Cincinnati	NL	39	11	0	10	108.1	438	92	37	35	6	7	1	6	34	4	77	11	0	3	5	.375	0	1-4	3	2.91
1992 Cincinnati	NL	64	0	0	46	81.1	341	79	39	27	7	7	3	3	26	4	90	8	0	4	2	.667	0	26-34	7	2.99
1993 Seattle	AL	34	0	0	29	34.2	141	22	12	9	4	0	1	0	17	0	48	6	0	1	3	.250	0	18-21	1	2.34
1995 Phi-Sea		55	0	0	27	69.2	284	46	31	26	4	4	2	4	31	3	70	6	1	4	6	.400	0	14-16	12	3.36
1996 Seattle	AL	70	0	0	50	75.2	323	68	37	34	7	3	2	1	38	1	73	9	0	4	7	.364	0	20-27	8	4.04
1997 Seattle	AL	71	0	0	38	69.1	343	89	59	56	7	7	0	4	47	2	55	7	1	3	8	.273	0	14-25	9	7.27
1998 Bal-Atl		49	0	0	19	48	231	53	29	29	5	2	2	1	33	0	47	7	0	2	1	.667	0	1-2	5	5.44
1999 Tampa Bay	AL	42	0	0	9	50.2	233	49	29	25	4	2	3	1	36	0	45	4	0	2	3	.400	0	0-1	15	4.44
1995 Philadelphia	NL	25	0	0	5	22	102	23	19	18	2	1	1	3	15	3	12	1	0	2	5	.286	0	0-1	9	7.36
Seattle	AL	30	0	0	22	47.2	182	23	12	8	2	3	1	1	16	0	58	5	1	2	1	.667	0	14-15	3	1.51
1998 Baltimore	AL	36	0	0	11	35	178	46	27	27	5	1	1	0	25	0	41	5	0	2	1	.667	0	0-1	3	6.94
Atlanta	NL	13	0	0	8	13	53	7	2	2	0	1	1	1	8	0	6	2	0	0	0	.000	0	1-1	2	1.38
11 ML YEARS		559	37	1	268	848.2	3636	756	391	346	65	49	20	28	392	27	759	72	9	47	52	.475	1	96-134	77	3.67

Eric Chavez

Bats: L **Throws:** R **Pos:** 3B-105; PH/PR-16; DH-3; SS-2   **Ht:** 6'0" **Wt:** 204 **Born:** 12/7/77 **Age:** 22

					BATTING															BASERUNNING				PERCENTAGES		
Year Team	Lg	G	AB	H	2B	3B	HR	(Hm	Rd)	TB	R	RBI	TBB	IBB	SO	HBP	SH	SF	SB	CS	SB%	GDP	Avg	OBP	SLG
1997 Visalia	A+	134	520	141	30	3	18	—	—	231	67	100	37	1	91	2	3	2	13	7	.65	20	.271	.321	.444
1998 Huntsville	AA	88	335	110	27	1	22	—	—	205	66	86	42	4	61	1	3	3	12	4	.75	6	.328	.402	.612
Edmonton	AAA	47	194	63	18	0	11	—	—	114	38	40	12	0	32	1	0	2	2	3	.40	4	.325	.364	.588
1998 Oakland	AL	16	45	14	4	1	0	(0	0)	20	6	6	3	1	5	0	0	0	1	1	.50	1	.311	.354	.444
1999 Oakland	AL	115	356	88	21	2	13	(8	5)	152	47	50	46	4	56	0	0	0	1	1	.50	7	.247	.333	.427
2 ML YEARS		131	401	102	25	3	13	(8	5)	172	53	56	49	5	61	0	0	0	2	2	.50	8	.254	.336	.429

Robinson Checo

Pitches: Right **Bats:** Left **Pos:** RP-7; SP-2   **Ht:** 6'1" **Wt:** 185 **Born:** 9/9/71 **Age:** 28

		HOW MUCH HE PITCHED						WHAT HE GAVE UP												THE RESULTS					
Year Team	Lg	G	GS	CG	GF	IP	BFP	H	R	ER	HR	SH	SF	HB	TBB	IBB	SO	WP	Bk	W	L	Pct.	ShO	Sv-Op	Hld	ERA
1997 Sarasota	A+	11	11	0	0	56	250	54	37	33	9	3	5	1	27	0	63	4	5	1	4	.200	0	0--	—	5.30
Trenton	AA	1	1	0	0	7.2	29	6	3	2	0	1	0	0	1	0	9	0	0	1	0	1.000	0	0--	—	2.35
Pawtucket	AAA	9	9	2	0	55.1	220	41	22	21	8	1	0	0	16	0	56	3	0	4	2	.667	1	0--	—	3.42
1998 Red Sox	R	3	3	0	0	9	37	9	5	3	1	0	1	0	0	0	13	0	0	1	0	1.000	0	0--	—	3.00
Sarasota	A+	1	1	0	0	2	10	3	2	2	0	0	0	0	1	0	4	0	0	0	1	.000	0	0--	—	9.00
Pawtucket	AAA	11	10	0	0	53.1	233	48	30	27	9	0	2	5	26	1	46	4	0	6	2	.750	0	0--	—	4.56
1999 Toledo	AAA	2	1	0	0	5	19	2	0	0	0	0	0	0	1	0	6	0	0	0	0	.000	0	0--	—	0.00
San Berndno	A+	2	2	0	0	5	23	5	6	6	2	0	0	0	3	0	6	1	0	0	0	.000	0	0--	—	10.80

Year Team	Lg	G	GS	CG	GF	IP	BFP	H	R	ER	HR	SH	SF	HB	TBB	IBB	SO	WP	Bk	W	L	Pct.	ShO	Sv-Op	Hld	ERA
Albuquerque AAA		16	15	0	0	79	342	68	40	38	15	1	2	3	39	1	98	5	4	3	6	.333	0	0--	—	4.33
1997 Boston	AL	5	2	0	1	13.1	54	12	5	5	0	0	0	0	3	0	14	0	0	1	1	.500	0	0-0	1	3.38
1998 Boston	AL	2	2	0	0	7.2	34	11	8	8	3	0	0	0	5	0	5	1	0	0	2	.000	0	0-0	0	9.39
1999 Los Angeles	NL	9	2	0	1	15.2	85	24	20	18	5	0	0	0	13	1	11	2	0	2	2	.500	0	0-0	0	10.34
3 ML YEARS		16	6	0	2	36.2	173	47	33	31	8	0	0	0	21	1	30	3	0	3	5	.375	0	0-0	1	7.61

Bruce Chen

Pitches: Left **Bats:** Both **Pos:** RP-9; SP-7   **Ht:** 6'1" **Wt:** 180 **Born:** 6/19/77 **Age:** 23

Year Team	Lg	G	GS	CG	GF	IP	BFP	H	R	ER	HR	SH	SF	HB	TBB	IBB	SO	WP	Bk	W	L	Pct.	ShO	Sv-Op	Hld	ERA
1994 Braves	R	9	7	0	2	42.2	180	42	21	18	2	0	3	2	3	0	26	3	0	1	4	.200	0	1--	—	3.80
1995 Danville	R+	14	13	1	0	70.1	310	78	42	31	3	1	4	3	19	1	56	4	1	4	4	.500	0	0--	—	3.97
1996 Eugene	A-	11	8	0	0	35.2	151	23	13	9	1	1	0	3	14	0	55	2	1	4	1	.800	0	0--	—	2.27
1997 Macon	A	28	28	1	0	146.1	602	120	67	57	19	4	5	7	44	0	182	5	1	12	7	.632	1	0--	—	3.51
1998 Greenville	AA	24	23	1	0	139.1	572	106	57	51	12	8	5	5	48	0	164	6	0	13	7	.650	0	0--	—	3.29
Richmond	AAA	4	4	0	0	24	104	17	5	5	1	1	0	1	19	0	29	1	0	2	1	.667	0	0--	—	1.88
1999 Richmond	AAA	14	14	0	0	78	324	73	36	33	10	3	4	0	26	0	90	2	2	6	3	.667	0	0--	—	3.81
1998 Atlanta	NL	4	4	0	0	20.1	91	23	9	9	3	1	0	1	9	1	17	0	0	2	0	1.000	0	0-0	—	3.98
1999 Atlanta	NL	16	7	0	3	51	214	38	32	31	11	1	1	2	27	3	45	0	0	2	2	.500	0	0-0	0	5.47
2 ML YEARS		20	11	0	3	71.1	305	61	41	40	14	2	1	3	36	4	62	0	0	4	2	.667	0	0-0	0	5.05

Jin Ho Cho

Pitches: Right **Bats:** Right **Pos:** SP-7; RP-2   **Ht:** 6'3" **Wt:** 220 **Born:** 8/16/75 **Age:** 24

Year Team	Lg	G	GS	CG	GF	IP	BFP	H	R	ER	HR	SH	SF	HB	TBB	IBB	SO	WP	Bk	W	L	Pct.	ShO	Sv-Op	Hld	ERA
1998 Sarasota	A+	5	5	0	0	32	132	33	14	11	1	0	4	0	5	0	30	2	0	3	1	.750	0	0--	—	3.09
Trenton	AA	13	13	1	0	74	299	59	21	18	4	3	4	3	19	2	62	0	0	5	2	.714	1	0--	—	2.19
1999 Pawtucket	AAA	17	17	4	0	109.2	447	99	46	42	12	3	2	4	29	1	80	1	0	9	3	.750	0	0--	—	3.45
1998 Boston	AL	4	4	0	0	18.2	87	28	17	17	4	0	1	1	3	0	15	1	0	0	3	.000	0	0-0	0	8.20
1999 Boston	AL	9	7	0	1	39.1	171	45	26	25	7	1	3	2	8	0	16	0	0	2	3	.400	0	0-0	0	5.72
2 ML YEARS		13	11	0	1	58	258	73	43	42	11	1	4	3	11	0	31	1	0	2	6	.250	0	0-0	0	6.52

Bobby Chouinard

Pitches: Right **Bats:** Right **Pos:** RP-32   **Ht:** 6'1" **Wt:** 190 **Born:** 5/1/72 **Age:** 28

Year Team	Lg	G	GS	CG	GF	IP	BFP	H	R	ER	HR	SH	SF	HB	TBB	IBB	SO	WP	Bk	W	L	Pct.	ShO	Sv-Op	Hld	ERA
1999 Tucson *	AAA	12	9	0	1	62	259	70	33	28	8	5	1	2	13	0	63	0	0	4	1	.800	0	0--	—	4.06
1996 Oakland	AL	13	11	0	0	59	278	75	41	40	10	3	3	3	32	3	32	0	0	4	2	.666	0	0-0	0	6.10
1998 Mil-Ari	NL	27	2	0	9	41.1	181	46	24	19	5	4	2	0	11	2	27	5	0	0	2	.000	0	0-1	6	4.14
1999 Arizona	NL	32	0	0	9	40.1	161	31	16	12	3	4	4	0	12	2	23	1	0	5	2	.714	0	1-2	7	2.68
1998 Milwaukee	NL	1	0	0	0	3	12	5	1	1	0	0	1	0	0	0	1	0	0	0	0	.000	0	0-0	0	3.00
Arizona	NL	26	2	0	9	38.1	169	41	23	18	5	4	1	0	11	2	26	5	0	0	2	.000	0	0-1	6	4.23
3 ML YEARS		72	13	0	18	140.2	620	152	81	71	18	11	9	3	55	7	82	6	0	9	6	.600	0	1-3	13	4.54

McKay Christensen

Bats: Left **Throws:** Left **Pos:** CF-27; PH/PR-5   **Ht:** 5'11" **Wt:** 180 **Born:** 8/14/75 **Age:** 24

							BATTING									BASERUNNING				PERCENTAGES		
Year Team	Lg	G	AB	H	2B	3B	HR	(Hm	Rd)	TB	R	RBI	TBB	IBB	SO	HBP	SH	SF	SB	CS	SB%	GDP	Avg	OBP	SLG
1996 White Sox	R	35	133	35	7	5	1	—	—	55	17	16	10	0	23	3	0	1	10	3	.77	1	.263	.327	.414
Hickory	A	6	11	0	0	0	0	—	—	0	0	0	1	0	4	0	0	0	0	0	.00	0	.000	.083	.000
1997 Hickory	A	127	684	141	12	12	5	—	—	192	95	47	52	0	61	11	4	6	28	20	.58	2	.280	.357	.382
1998 Winston-Sal	A+	95	361	103	17	6	4	—	—	144	69	32	53	1	54	11	4	2	20	10	.67	3	.285	.391	.399
1999 Birmingham	AA	75	293	85	8	6	3	—	—	114	53	28	31	0	46	8	4	1	18	6	.75	6	.290	.372	.389
Charlotte	AAA	1	4	1	0	0	0	—	—	1	0	0	0	0	0	0	0	0	1	0	1.00	0	.250	.250	.250
1999 Chicago	AL	28	53	12	1	0	1	(1	0)	16	10	6	4	0	7	0	1	2	2	1	.67	1	.226	.271	.302

Ryan Christenson

Bats: Right **Throws:** Right **Pos:** CF-104; PH/PR-17; DH-1   **Ht:** 6'0" **Wt:** 191 **Born:** 3/28/74 **Age:** 26

							BATTING									BASERUNNING				PERCENTAGES		
Year Team	Lg	G	AB	H	2B	3B	HR	(Hm	Rd)	TB	R	RBI	TBB	IBB	SO	HBP	SH	SF	SB	CS	SB%	GDP	Avg	OBP	SLG
1995 Sou Oregon	A-	49	158	30	4	1	1	—	—	39	14	16	22	0	33	0	1	2	5	5	.50	3	.190	.286	.247
1996 Sou Oregon	A-	36	136	39	11	0	5	—	—	65	31	21	21	1	21	1	1	1	8	6	.57	3	.287	.376	.478
W Michigan	A	33	122	38	2	2	2	—	—	50	21	18	13	0	22	4	1	3	2	4	.33	2	.311	.387	.410
1997 Visalia	A+	83	308	90	18	8	13	—	—	163	69	54	70	1	72	2	3	1	20	11	.65	4	.292	.425	.529
Huntsville	AA	29	120	44	9	3	2	—	—	65	39	18	24	0	23	0	0	1	5	4	.56	3	.367	.469	.542
Edmonton	AAA	16	49	14	2	2	2	—	—	26	12	5	11	0	11	2	0	0	2	0	1.00	1	.286	.435	.531
1998 Edmonton	AAA	22	88	23	6	1	1	—	—	34	17	7	15	0	24	0	0	1	4	1	.80	1	.261	.365	.386
1999 Vancouver	AAA	33	128	44	8	1	1	—	—	57	30	16	22	2	21	0	0	0	7	2	.78	4	.344	.440	.445
1998 Oakland	AL	117	529	136	22	2	5	(2	3)	136	56	40	36	0	106	1	10	4	5	6	.45	4	.257	.321	.368
1999 Oakland	AL	106	268	56	12	1	4	(2	2)	82	41	24	38	0	58	1	8	4	7	5	.58	6	.209	.305	.306
2 ML YEARS		223	638	151	34	3	9	(4	5)	218	97	64	74	0	164	2	18	8	12	11	.52	7	.237	.314	.342

Jason Christiansen

Pitches: Left **Bats:** Right **Pos:** RP-39   **Ht:** 6'5" **Wt:** 242 **Born:** 9/21/69 **Age:** 30

		HOW MUCH HE PITCHED						WHAT HE GAVE UP											THE RESULTS					
Year Team	Lg	G	GS	CG	GF	IP	BFP	H	R	ER	HR	SH	SF	HB	TBB	IBB	SO	WP	Bk	W	L	Pct.	ShO	Sv-Op	Hld	ERA
1999 Altoona *	AA	2	1	0	0	3	11	1	0	0	0	0	0	0	1	0	2	0	0	0	0	.000	0	0--	—	0.00
Nashville *	AAA	2	0	0	0	2	6	0	0	0	0	0	0	0	0	0	1	0	0	0	0	.000	0	0--	—	0.00
1995 Pittsburgh	NL	63	0	0	13	56.1	255	49	28	26	5	6	3	3	34	9	53	4	1	1	3	.250	0	0-4	12	4.15
1996 Pittsburgh	NL	33	0	0	9	44.1	205	56	34	33	7	2	3	1	19	2	38	4	1	3	3	.500	0	0-2	2	6.70
1997 Pittsburgh	NL	39	0	0	9	33.2	154	37	11	11	2	0	0	2	17	3	37	4	0	3	0	1.000	0	0-2	8	2.94
1998 Pittsburgh	NL	60	0	0	19	64.2	269	51	22	18	2	5	1	0	27	7	71	3	0	3	3	.500	0	6-10	15	2.51
1999 Pittsburgh	NL	39	0	0	17	37.2	158	26	17	17	2	2	1	2	22	4	35	0	0	2	3	.400	0	3-5	7	4.06
5 ML YEARS		234	0	0	67	236.2	1041	219	112	105	18	15	8	8	119	25	234	15	2	12	12	.500	0	9-23	44	3.99

Jeff Cirillo

Bats: Right **Throws:** Right **Pos:** 3B-155; PH/PR-2   **Ht:** 6'1" **Wt:** 195 **Born:** 9/23/69 **Age:** 30

		BATTING																BASERUNNING				PERCENTAGES		
Year Team	Lg	G	AB	H	2B	3B	HR	(Hm	Rd)	TB	R	RBI	TBB	IBB	SO	HBP	SH	SF	SB	CS	SB%	GDP	Avg	OBP	SLG
1994 Milwaukee	AL	39	126	30	9	0	3	(1	2)	48	17	12	11	0	16	2	0	0	0	1	.00	4	.238	.309	.381
1995 Milwaukee	AL	125	328	91	19	4	9	(6	3)	145	57	39	47	0	42	4	1	4	7	2	.78	8	.277	.371	.442
1996 Milwaukee	AL	158	566	184	46	5	15	(6	9)	285	101	83	58	0	69	7	6	6	4	9	.31	14	.325	.391	.504
1997 Milwaukee	AL	154	580	167	46	2	10	(6	4)	247	74	82	60	0	74	14	4	3	4	3	.57	13	.288	.367	.426
1998 Milwaukee	NL	156	604	194	31	1	14	(6	8)	269	97	68	79	3	88	4	5	2	10	4	.71	26	.321	.402	.445
1999 Milwaukee	NL	157	607	198	35	1	15	(6	9)	280	98	88	75	4	83	5	3	7	7	4	.64	15	.326	.401	.461
6 ML YEARS		789	2811	864	186	13	66	(31	35)	1274	444	372	330	7	372	36	19	22	32	23	.58	80	.307	.384	.453

Chris Clapinski

Bats: B **Throws:** R **Pos:** PH/PR-19; 3B-9; SS-6; LF-3; 2B-2; DH-1   **Ht:** 6'0" **Wt:** 175 **Born:** 8/20/71 **Age:** 28

		BATTING																BASERUNNING				PERCENTAGES		
Year Team	Lg	G	AB	H	2B	3B	HR	(Hm	Rd)	TB	R	RBI	TBB	IBB	SO	HBP	SH	SF	SB	CS	SB%	GDP	Avg	OBP	SLG
1992 Marlins	R	59	212	51	8	1	1	—	—	64	36	15	49	2	42	4	3	2	5	6	.45	4	.241	.390	.302
1993 Kane County	A	82	214	45	12	1	0	—	—	59	22	27	31	0	55	1	8	4	3	8	.27	3	.210	.308	.276
1994 Brevard Cty	A+	65	157	45	12	3	1	—	—	66	33	13	23	2	28	3	7	1	3	2	.60	2	.287	.386	.420
1995 Portland	AA	87	208	49	9	3	4	—	—	76	32	30	28	2	44	2	5	5	5	2	.71	4	.236	.325	.365
1996 Portland	AA	23	73	19	7	0	3	—	—	35	15	11	13	1	13	2	1	1	3	1	.75	2	.260	.382	.479
Charlotte	AAA	105	362	103	20	1	10	—	—	155	74	39	47	0	54	3	8	5	13	6	.68	7	.285	.367	.428
1997 Charlotte	AAA	110	340	89	24	2	12	—	—	153	62	52	48	4	64	9	6	2	14	2	.88	9	.262	.366	.450
1998 Brevard Cty	A+	5	14	1	0	1	0	—	—	3	1	4	7	2	2	0	0	1	0	0	.00	1	.071	.364	.214
Charlotte	AAA	100	312	84	18	1	9	—	—	131	53	35	39	0	53	5	7	1	11	3	.79	7	.269	.359	.420
1999 Calgary	AAA	81	267	86	21	6	8	—	—	143	51	35	30	0	53	2	3	1	5	1	.83	6	.322	.393	.536
1999 Florida	NL	36	56	13	1	2	0	(0	0)	18	6	2	9	0	12	1	0	0	1	0	1.00	1	.232	.348	.321

Mark Clark

Pitches: Right **Bats:** Right **Pos:** SP-15   **Ht:** 6'5" **Wt:** 235 **Born:** 5/12/68 **Age:** 32

		HOW MUCH HE PITCHED						WHAT HE GAVE UP											THE RESULTS					
Year Team	Lg	G	GS	CG	GF	IP	BFP	H	R	ER	HR	SH	SF	HB	TBB	IBB	SO	WP	Bk	W	L	Pct.	ShO	Sv-Op	Hld	ERA
1999 Savannah *	A	1	1	0	0	4	14	2	0	0	0	0	0	0	1	0	1	0	0	0	0	.000	0	0--	—	0.00
Charlotte *	A+	2	2	0	0	7	26	5	1	1	0	0	1	0	1	0	2	0	0	0	0	.000	0	0--	—	1.29
1991 St. Louis	NL	7	2	0	1	22.1	93	17	10	10	3	0	3	0	11	0	13	2	0	1	1	.500	0	0-0	1	4.03
1992 St. Louis	NL	20	20	1	0	113.1	488	117	59	56	12	7	4	0	36	2	44	4	0	3	10	.231	1	0-0	0	4.45
1993 Cleveland	AL	26	15	1	1	109.1	454	119	55	52	18	1	1	1	25	1	57	1	0	7	5	.583	0	0-0	2	4.28
1994 Cleveland	AL	20	20	4	0	127.1	540	133	61	54	14	2	7	4	40	0	60	9	1	11	3	.786	0	0-0	0	3.82
1995 Cleveland	AL	22	21	2	0	124.2	552	143	77	73	13	3	6	4	42	0	68	8	0	9	7	.563	0	0-0	0	5.27
1996 New York	NL	32	32	2	0	212.1	883	217	98	81	20	8	4	3	48	8	142	6	2	14	11	.560	0	0-0	0	3.43
1997 NYM-ChC	NL	32	31	3	0	205	866	213	96	87	24	9	4	4	59	3	123	4	1	14	8	.636	0	0-0	0	3.82
1998 Chicago	NL	33	33	2	0	213.2	918	236	116	115	23	12	6	4	48	4	161	5	2	9	14	.391	1	0-0	0	4.84
1999 Texas	AL	15	15	0	0	74.1	353	103	73	71	17	1	4	1	34	1	44	7	0	3	7	.300	0	0-0	0	8.60
1997 New York	NL	23	22	1	0	142	608	158	74	67	18	9	2	3	47	2	72	4	0	8	7	.533	0	0-0	0	4.25
Chicago	NL	9	9	2	0	63	258	55	22	20	6	0	2	1	12	1	51	0	1	6	1	.857	0	0-0	0	2.86
9 ML YEARS		207	189	15	2	1202.1	5147	1298	645	599	144	43	39	21	343	19	712	46	6	71	66	.518	3	0-0	3	4.48

Tony Clark

Bats: Both **Throws:** Right **Pos:** 1B-132; DH-11; PH/PR-1   **Ht:** 6'7" **Wt:** 245 **Born:** 6/15/72 **Age:** 28

		BATTING																BASERUNNING				PERCENTAGES		
Year Team	Lg	G	AB	H	2B	3B	HR	(Hm	Rd)	TB	R	RBI	TBB	IBB	SO	HBP	SH	SF	SB	CS	SB%	GDP	Avg	OBP	SLG
1999 Toledo *	AAA	1	3	0	0	0	0	—	—	0	0	0	1	0	1	0	0	0	0	0	.00	0	.000	.250	.000
1995 Detroit	AL	27	101	24	5	1	3	(0	3)	40	10	11	8	0	30	0	0	0	0	0	.00	2	.238	.294	.396
1996 Detroit	AL	100	376	94	14	0	27	(17	10)	189	56	72	29	1	127	0	0	6	0	1	.00	7	.250	.299	.503
1997 Detroit	AL	159	580	160	28	3	32	(18	14)	290	105	117	93	13	144	3	0	5	1	3	.25	11	.276	.376	.500
1998 Detroit	AL	157	602	175	37	0	34	(18	16)	314	84	103	63	5	128	3	0	5	3	3	.50	16	.291	.358	.522
1999 Detroit	AL	143	536	150	29	0	31	(12	19)	272	74	99	64	7	133	6	0	3	2	1	.67	14	.280	.361	.507
5 ML YEARS		586	2195	603	113	4	127	(65	62)	1105	329	402	257	26	562	12	0	19	6	8	.43	50	.275	.351	.503

Will Clark

Bats: Left **Throws:** Left **Pos:** 1B-63; PH/PR-12; DH-3   **Ht:** 6'1" **Wt:** 200 **Born:** 3/13/64 **Age:** 36

Year Team	Lg	G	AB	H	2B	3B	HR	(Hm	Rd)	TB	R	RBI	TBB	IBB	SO	HBP	SH	SF	SB	CS	SB%	GDP	Avg	OBP	SLG
1986 San Francisco	NL	111	408	117	27	2	11	(7	4)	181	66	41	34	10	76	3	9	4	4	7	.36	3	.287	.343	.444
1987 San Francisco	NL	150	529	163	29	5	35	(22	13)	307	89	91	49	11	98	5	3	2	5	17	.23	2	.308	.371	.580
1988 San Francisco	NL	162	575	162	31	6	29	(14	15)	292	102	109	100	27	129	4	0	10	9	1	.90	9	.282	.386	.508
1989 San Francisco	NL	159	588	196	38	9	23	(9	14)	321	104	111	74	14	103	5	0	8	8	3	.73	6	.333	.407	.546
1990 San Francisco	NL	154	600	177	25	5	19	(8	11)	269	91	95	62	9	97	3	0	13	8	2	.80	7	.295	.357	.448
1991 San Francisco	NL	148	565	170	32	7	29	(17	12)	303	84	116	51	12	91	2	0	4	4	2	.67	5	.301	.359	.536
1992 San Francisco	NL	144	513	154	40	1	16	(11	5)	244	69	73	73	23	82	4	0	11	12	7	.63	5	.300	.384	.476
1993 San Francisco	NL	132	491	139	27	2	14	(5	9)	212	82	73	63	6	68	6	1	6	2	2	.50	10	.283	.367	.432
1994 Texas	AL	110	389	128	24	2	13	(9	4)	195	73	80	71	11	59	3	0	6	5	1	.83	5	.329	.431	.501
1995 Texas	AL	123	454	137	27	3	16	(10	6)	218	85	92	68	6	50	4	0	11	0	1	.00	7	.302	.389	.480
1996 Texas	AL	117	436	124	25	1	13	(9	4)	190	69	72	64	5	67	5	0	7	2	1	.67	10	.284	.377	.436
1997 Texas	AL	110	393	128	29	1	12	(6	6)	195	56	51	49	11	62	3	0	5	0	0	.00	4	.326	.400	.496
1998 Texas	AL	149	554	169	41	1	23	(10	13)	281	98	102	72	5	97	3	0	7	1	0	1.00	15	.305	.384	.507
1999 Baltimore	AL	77	251	76	15	0	10	(5	5)	121	40	29	38	2	42	2	0	3	2	2	.50	5	.303	.395	.482
14 ML YEARS		1846	6746	2040	410	45	263	(143	120)	3329	1108	1135	868	152	1121	52	13	97	62	46	.57	93	.302	.381	.493

Royce Clayton

Bats: Right **Throws:** Right **Pos:** SS-133   **Ht:** 6'0" **Wt:** 185 **Born:** 1/2/70 **Age:** 30

Year Team	Lg	G	AB	H	2B	3B	HR	(Hm	Rd)	TB	R	RBI	TBB	IBB	SO	HBP	SH	SF	SB	CS	SB%	GDP	Avg	OBP	SLG
1999 Oklahoma *	AAA	2	7	1	0	0	0	—	—	1	1	1	3	0	3	0	0	0	0	0	.00	0	.143	.400	.143
1991 San Francisco	NL	9	26	3	1	0	0	(0	0)	4	0	2	1	0	6	0	0	0	0	0	.00	1	.115	.148	.154
1992 San Francisco	NL	98	321	72	7	4	4	(3	1)	99	31	24	26	3	63	0	3	2	8	4	.67	11	.224	.281	.308
1993 San Francisco	NL	153	549	155	21	5	6	(5	1)	204	54	70	38	2	91	5	8	7	11	10	.52	16	.282	.331	.372
1994 San Francisco	NL	108	385	91	14	6	3	(1	2)	126	38	30	30	2	74	3	3	2	23	3	.88	7	.236	.295	.327
1995 San Francisco	NL	138	509	124	29	3	5	(2	3)	174	56	58	38	1	109	3	4	3	24	9	.73	7	.244	.298	.342
1996 St. Louis	NL	129	491	136	20	4	6	(6	0)	182	64	35	33	4	89	1	2	4	33	15	.69	13	.277	.321	.371
1997 St. Louis	NL	154	576	153	39	5	9	(5	4)	229	75	61	33	4	109	3	2	5	30	10	.75	19	.266	.306	.398
1998 StL-Tex		142	541	136	31	2	9	(2	7)	198	89	53	53	1	83	3	6	5	24	11	.69	16	.251	.319	.366
1999 Texas	AL	133	465	134	21	5	14	(6	8)	207	69	52	39	1	100	4	9	3	8	6	.57	6	.288	.346	.445
1998 St. Louis	NL	90	355	83	19	1	4	(1	3)	116	59	29	40	1	51	2	3	2	19	6	.76	10	.234	.313	.327
Texas	AL	52	186	53	12	1	5	(1	4)	82	30	24	13	0	32	1	3	3	5	5	.50	6	.285	.330	.441
9 ML YEARS		1064	3863	1004	183	34	56	(30	26)	1423	476	385	291	18	724	22	37	31	161	68	.70	96	.260	.313	.368

Roger Clemens

Pitches: Right **Bats:** Right **Pos:** SP-30   **Ht:** 6'4" **Wt:** 230 **Born:** 8/4/62 **Age:** 37

Year Team	Lg	G	GS	CG	GF	IP	BFP	H	R	ER	HR	SH	SF	HB	TBB	IBB	SO	WP	Bk	W	L	Pct.	ShO	Sv-Op	Hld	ERA
1984 Boston	AL	21	20	5	0	133.1	575	146	67	64	13	2	3	2	29	3	126	4	0	9	4	.692	1	0-0	0	4.32
1985 Boston	AL	15	15	3	0	98.1	407	83	38	36	5	1	2	3	37	0	74	1	3	7	5	.583	1	0-0	0	3.29
1986 Boston	AL	33	33	10	0	254	997	179	77	70	21	4	6	4	67	0	238	11	3	24	4	.857	1	0-0	0	2.48
1987 Boston	AL	36	36	18	0	281.2	1157	248	100	93	19	6	4	9	83	4	256	4	3	20	9	.690	7	0-0	0	2.97
1988 Boston	AL	35	35	14	0	264	1063	217	93	86	17	6	3	6	62	4	291	4	7	18	12	.600	8	0-0	0	2.93
1989 Boston	AL	35	35	8	0	253.1	1044	215	101	88	20	9	5	8	93	5	230	7	0	17	11	.607	3	0-0	0	3.13
1990 Boston	AL	31	31	7	0	228.1	920	193	59	49	7	7	5	7	54	3	209	8	0	21	6	.778	4	0-0	0	1.93
1991 Boston	AL	35	35	13	0	271.1	1077	219	93	79	15	6	8	5	65	12	241	6	0	18	10	.643	4	0-0	0	2.62
1992 Boston	AL	32	32	11	0	246.2	989	203	80	66	11	5	5	9	62	5	208	3	0	18	11	.621	5	0-0	0	2.41
1993 Boston	AL	29	29	2	0	191.2	808	175	99	95	17	5	7	11	67	4	160	3	1	11	14	.440	1	0-0	0	4.46
1994 Boston	AL	24	24	3	0	170.2	692	124	62	54	15	2	5	4	71	1	168	4	0	9	7	.563	1	0-0	0	2.85
1995 Boston	AL	23	23	0	0	140	623	141	70	65	15	2	3	14	60	0	132	9	0	10	5	.667	0	0-0	0	4.18
1996 Boston	AL	34	34	6	0	242.2	1032	216	106	98	19	4	7	4	106	2	257	8	1	10	13	.435	2	0-0	0	3.63
1997 Toronto	AL	34	34	9	0	264	1044	204	65	60	9	5	2	12	68	1	292	4	0	21	7	.750	3	0-0	0	2.05
1998 Toronto	AL	33	33	5	0	234.2	961	169	78	69	11	8	2	7	88	0	271	6	0	20	6	.769	3	0-0	0	2.65
1999 New York	AL	30	30	1	0	187.2	822	185	101	96	20	10	5	9	90	0	163	8	0	14	10	.583	1	0-0	0	4.60
16 ML YEARS		480	479	115	0	3462.1	14211	2917	1289	1168	234	82	72	114	1102	44	3316	90	18	247	134	.648	45	0-0	0	3.04

Matt Clement

Pitches: Right **Bats:** Right **Pos:** SP-31   **Ht:** 6'3" **Wt:** 195 **Born:** 8/12/74 **Age:** 25

Year Team	Lg	G	GS	CG	GF	IP	BFP	H	R	ER	HR	SH	SF	HB	TBB	IBB	SO	WP	Bk	W	L	Pct.	ShO	Sv-Op	Hld	ERA
1994 Spokane	A-	2	2	0	0	7.1	39	8	7	5	0	0	0	1	11	0	4	1	1	1	1	.500	0	0--	—	6.14
Padres	R	13	13	0	0	67	286	65	38	33	0	1	0	6	17	0	76	10	0	8	5	.615	0	0--	—	4.43
1995 Rancho Cuca	A+	12	12	0	0	57.1	267	61	37	27	1	2	4	5	49	0	33	12	0	3	4	.429	0	0--	—	4.24
Idaho Falls	R+	14	14	0	0	81	349	61	53	39	3	6	3	13	42	0	65	19	2	6	3	.667	0	0--	—	4.33
1996 Clinton	A	16	16	1	0	96.1	410	66	31	30	3	1	3	9	52	0	109	15	0	8	3	.727	1	0--	—	2.80
Rancho Cuca	A+	11	11	0	0	56.1	261	61	40	35	8	5	3	9	26	0	75	5	1	4	5	.444	0	0--	—	5.59
1997 Rancho Cuca	A+	14	14	2	0	101	410	74	30	18	3	2	1	9	31	1	109	6	0	6	3	.667	1	0--	—	1.60
Mobile	AA	13	13	1	0	88	382	83	37	25	4	4	1	12	32	0	92	12	0	6	5	.545	1	0--	—	2.56
1998 Las Vegas	AAA	27	27	1	0	171.2	763	157	94	76	12	4	4	30	85	2	160	18	2	10	9	.526	0	0--	—	3.98
1998 San Diego	NL	4	2	0	0	13.2	62	15	8	7	0	2	0	7	7	1	13	2	0	2	0	1.000	0	0-0	0	4.61
1999 San Diego	NL	31	31	0	0	180.2	803	190	106	90	18	7	6	9	86	2	135	11	0	10	12	.455	0	0-0	0	4.48
2 ML YEARS		35	33	0	0	194.1	865	205	114	97	18	9	6	9	93	3	148	13	0	12	12	.500	0	0-0	0	4.49

46

Edgard Clemente

Bats: R **Throws:** R **Pos:** CF-45; PH/PR-10; RF-4; LF-2   **Ht:** 5'11" **Wt:** 188 **Born:** 12/15/75 **Age:** 24

							BATTING											BASERUNNING				PERCENTAGES		
Year Team	Lg	G	AB	H	2B	3B	HR	(Hm | Rd)	TB	R	RBI	TBB	IBB	SO	HBP	SH	SF	SB	CS	SB%	GDP	Avg	OBP	SLG
1993 Rockies	R	39	147	36	4	2	2	—	—	50	20	20	16	0	35	0	2	2	7	5	.58	2	.245	.315	.340
1994 Asheville	A	119	447	106	22	3	11	—	—	167	50	39	23	0	120	3	3	2	9	9	.50	14	.237	.278	.374
1995 Salem	A+	131	497	149	25	6	13	—	—	225	74	69	40	4	102	4	3	7	7	10	.41	17	.300	.352	.453
1996 New Haven	AA	132	486	141	29	4	19	—	—	235	72	62	53	5	114	4	0	0	6	2	.75	7	.290	.365	.484
1997 Colo Sprngs	AAA	120	438	123	24	10	17	—	—	218	70	73	34	2	119	6	1	2	6	3	.67	8	.281	.340	.498
1998 Colo Sprngs	AAA	135	493	124	21	7	22	—	—	225	79	82	40	0	117	4	1	5	5	5	.50	6	.252	.310	.456
1999 Colo Sprngs	AAA	75	276	84	24	1	17	—	—	161	46	60	20	1	55	2	0	1	5	5	.50	7	.304	.355	.583
1998 Colorado	NL	11	17	6	0	1	0	(0 | 0)	8	2	2	2	0	8	0	0	0	0	0	.00	0	.353	.421	.471
1999 Colorado	NL	57	162	41	10	2	8	(7 | 1)	79	24	25	7	0	46	0	1	1	0	0	.00	4	.253	.282	.488
2 ML YEARS		68	179	47	10	3	8	(7 | 1)	87	26	27	9	0	54	0	1	1	0	0	.00	4	.263	.296	.486

Brad Clontz

Pitches: Right **Bats:** Right **Pos:** RP-56   **Ht:** 6'1" **Wt:** 195 **Born:** 4/25/71 **Age:** 29

		HOW MUCH HE PITCHED						WHAT HE GAVE UP											THE RESULTS					
Year Team	Lg	G	GS	CG	GF	IP	BFP	H	R	ER	HR	SH	SF	HB	TBB	IBB	SO	WP	Bk	W	L	Pct.	ShO	Sv-Op	Hld	ERA
1999 Nashville *	AAA	12	0	0	12	18	73	12	8	7	3	2	1	1	6	0	23	0	0	0	2	.000	0	7- —	—	3.50
1995 Atlanta	NL	59	0	0	14	69	295	71	29	28	5	3	2	4	22	4	55	0	0	8	1	.889	0	4-6	6	3.65
1996 Atlanta	NL	81	0	0	11	80.2	350	78	53	51	11	5	4	2	33	8	49	0	1	6	3	.667	0	1-6	17	5.69
1997 Atlanta	NL	51	0	0	16	48	203	52	24	20	3	0	2	1	18	3	42	1	0	5	1	.833	0	1-2	0	3.75
1998 LA-NYM	NL	20	0	0	6	23.2	101	19	16	16	4	0	0	2	12	4	16	0	0	2	0	1.000	0	0-1	3	6.08
1999 Pittsburgh	NL	56	0	0	16	49.1	223	49	21	15	6	2	1	3	24	5	40	2	0	1	3	.250	0	2-3	9	2.74
1998 Los Angeles	NL	18	0	0	6	20.2	87	15	13	13	3	0	0	2	10	4	14	0	0	2	0	1.000	0	0-1	3	5.66
New York	NL	2	0	0	0	3	14	4	3	3	1	0	0	0	2	0	2	0	0	0	0	.000	0	0-0	0	9.00
5 ML YEARS		267	0	0	63	270.2	1172	269	143	130	29	10	9	12	109	24	202	3	1	22	8	.733	0	8-18	35	4.32

Ken Cloude

Pitches: Right **Bats:** Right **Pos:** RP-25; SP-6   **Ht:** 6'1" **Wt:** 205 **Born:** 1/9/75 **Age:** 25

		HOW MUCH HE PITCHED						WHAT HE GAVE UP											THE RESULTS					
Year Team	Lg	G	GS	CG	GF	IP	BFP	H	R	ER	HR	SH	SF	HB	TBB	IBB	SO	WP	Bk	W	L	Pct.	ShO	Sv-Op	Hld	ERA
1999 Tacoma *	AAA	6	6	2	0	38.2	149	19	11	10	3	1	1	2	15	0	33	3	0	5	1	.833	0	0- —	—	2.33
1997 Seattle	AL	10	9	0	0	51	219	41	32	29	8	1	1	3	26	0	46	2	0	4	2	.667	0	0-0	0	5.12
1998 Seattle	AL	30	30	0	0	155.1	722	187	116	110	29	4	4	3	80	4	114	2	1	8	10	.444	0	0-0	0	6.37
1999 Seattle	AL	31	6	0	8	72.1	362	106	67	64	10	1	4	5	46	5	35	8	0	4	4	.500	0	1-3	0	7.96
3 ML YEARS		71	45	0	8	278.2	1303	334	215	203	47	6	9	11	152	9	195	12	1	16	16	.500	0	1-3	0	6.56

Danny Clyburn

Bats: R **Throws:** R **Pos:** LF-14; RF-10; PH/PR-5; DH-4   **Ht:** 6'4" **Wt:** 220 **Born:** 4/6/74 **Age:** 26

							BATTING											BASERUNNING				PERCENTAGES		
Year Team	Lg	G	AB	H	2B	3B	HR	(Hm	Rd)	TB	R	RBI	TBB	IBB	SO	HBP	SH	SF	SB	CS	SB%	GDP	Avg	OBP	SLG
1992 Pirates	R	39	149	51	9	0	4	—	—	72	26	25	5	0	20	1	0	2	7	3	.70	4	.342	.363	.483
1993 Augusta	A	127	457	121	21	4	9	—	—	177	55	66	37	1	97	5	0	0	5	5	.50	7	.265	.327	.387
1994 Salem	A+	118	461	126	19	0	22	—	—	211	57	90	20	2	96	0	0	5	4	5	.44	7	.273	.300	.458
1995 Winston-Sal	A+	59	227	59	10	2	11	—	—	106	27	41	13	1	59	4	0	2	2	4	.33	5	.260	.309	.467
Frederick	A+	15	45	9	4	0	0	—	—	13	4	4	4	0	18	2	0	0	1	1	.50	0	.200	.294	.289
High Desert	A+	45	160	45	3	1	12	—	—	86	20	37	17	1	41	4	0	3	2	1	.67	3	.281	.359	.538
1996 Bowie	AA	95	365	92	14	5	18	—	—	170	51	55	17	1	88	4	0	4	4	3	.57	5	.252	.290	.466
1997 Rochester	AAA	137	520	156	33	5	20	—	—	259	91	76	53	3	107	8	0	2	14	4	.78	7	.300	.372	.498
1998 Rochester	AAA	84	322	92	21	1	14	—	—	157	58	54	34	0	72	4	0	3	11	5	.69	4	.286	.358	.488
1999 Durham	AAA	82	303	71	11	1	9	—	—	111	38	33	19	2	74	6	0	6	2	0	1.00	7	.234	.287	.366
1997 Baltimore	AL	2	3	0	0	0	0	(0	0)	0	0	0	0	0	2	0	0	0	0	0	.00	0	.000	.000	.000
1998 Baltimore	AL	11	25	7	0	0	1	(0	1)	10	6	3	1	0	10	0	0	0	0	0	.00	0	.280	.308	.400
1999 Tampa Bay	AL	28	81	16	4	0	3	(1	2)	29	8	5	7	0	21	1	0	0	0	0	.00	5	.198	.270	.358
3 ML YEARS		41	109	23	4	0	4	(1	3)	39	14	8	8	0	33	1	0	0	0	0	.00	5	.211	.271	.358

Mike Colangelo

Bats: Right **Throws:** Right **Pos:** LF-1   **Ht:** 6'1" **Wt:** 185 **Born:** 10/22/76 **Age:** 23

							BATTING											BASERUNNING				PERCENTAGES		
Year Team	Lg	G	AB	H	2B	3B	HR	(Hm	Rd)	TB	R	RBI	TBB	IBB	SO	HBP	SH	SF	SB	CS	SB%	GDP	Avg	OBP	SLG
1998 Cedar Rapds	A	22	83	23	8	0	4	—	—	43	13	8	12	1	16	2	0	1	5	1	.83	0	.277	.378	.518
Lk Elsinore	A+	36	145	55	11	3	5	—	—	87	33	21	13	0	24	6	0	1	2	6	.25	2	.379	.448	.600
1999 Erie	AA	28	109	37	10	3	1	—	—	56	24	13	14	0	22	4	0	0	3	3	.50	5	.339	.433	.514
Edmonton	AAA	26	105	38	7	1	0	—	—	47	13	9	13	1	18	2	1	0	2	1	.67	5	.362	.442	.448
1999 Anaheim	AL	1	2	1	0	0	0	(0	0)	1	0	0	1	0	0	0	0	0	0	0	.00	0	.500	.667	.500

47

Greg Colbrunn

Bats: R **Throws:** R **Pos:** 1B-39; PH/PR-28; DH-2; 3B-2 **Ht:** 6'0" **Wt:** 205 **Born:** 7/29/69 **Age:** 30

Year Team	Lg	G	AB	H	2B	3B	HR	(Hm	Rd)	TB	R	RBI	TBB	IBB	SO	HBP	SH	SF	SB	CS	SB%	GDP	Avg	OBP	SLG
1992 Montreal	NL	52	168	45	8	0	2	(1	1)	59	12	18	6	1	34	2	0	4	3	2	.60	1	.268	.294	.351
1993 Montreal	NL	70	153	39	9	0	4	(2	2)	60	15	23	6	1	33	1	1	3	4	2	.67	1	.255	.282	.392
1994 Florida	NL	47	155	47	10	0	6	(3	3)	75	17	31	9	0	27	2	0	2	1	1	.50	3	.303	.345	.484
1995 Florida	NL	138	528	146	22	1	23	(12	11)	239	70	89	22	4	69	6	0	4	11	3	.79	15	.277	.311	.453
1996 Florida	NL	141	511	146	26	2	16	(7	9)	224	60	69	25	1	76	14	0	5	4	5	.44	22	.286	.333	.438
1997 Min-Atl		98	271	76	17	0	7	(3	4)	114	27	35	10	1	49	2	1	2	1	2	.33	8	.280	.309	.421
1998 Col-Atl	NL	90	166	51	11	2	3	(1	2)	75	18	23	10	0	34	4	0	0	4	3	.57	1	.307	.361	.452
1999 Arizona	NL	67	135	44	5	3	5	(2	3)	70	20	24	12	0	23	4	0	2	1	1	.50	3	.326	.392	.519
1997 Minnesota		70	217	61	14	0	5	(2	3)	90	24	26	8	1	38	1	0	2	1	2	.33	7	.281	.307	.415
Atlanta	NL	28	54	15	3	0	2	(1	1)	24	3	9	2	0	11	1	1	0	0	0	.00	1	.278	.316	.444
1998 Colorado	NL	62	122	38	8	2	2	(1	1)	56	12	13	8	0	23	1	0	0	3	3	.50	1	.311	.359	.459
Atlanta		28	44	13	3	0	1	(0	1)	19	6	10	2	0	11	3	0	0	1	0	1.00	0	.295	.367	.432
8 ML YEARS		703	2087	594	108	8	66	(31	35)	916	239	312	100	8	345	35	2	22	29	19	.60	54	.285	.325	.439

Michael Coleman

Bats: Right **Throws:** Right **Pos:** LF-1; CF-1; PH/PR-1 **Ht:** 5'11" **Wt:** 207 **Born:** 8/16/75 **Age:** 24

Year Team	Lg	G	AB	H	2B	3B	HR	(Hm	Rd)	TB	R	RBI	TBB	IBB	SO	HBP	SH	SF	SB	CS	SB%	GDP	Avg	OBP	SLG
1994 Red Sox	R	25	95	26	6	1	3	—	—	43	15	15	10	0	20	3	0	1	5	3	.63	3	.274	.358	.453
Utica	A-	23	65	11	2	0	1	—	—	16	16	3	14	0	21	0	3	0	11	1	.92	0	.169	.316	.246
1995 Michigan	A	112	422	113	16	2	11	—	—	166	70	61	40	1	93	6	6	3	29	5	.85	7	.268	.338	.393
1996 Sarasota	A+	110	407	100	20	5	1	—	—	133	54	36	38	1	86	8	7	3	24	5	.83	10	.246	.320	.327
1997 Trenton	AA	102	385	116	17	8	14	—	—	191	56	58	41	1	89	5	9	4	20	7	.74	5	.301	.372	.496
Pawtucket	AAA	28	113	36	9	2	7	—	—	70	27	19	12	0	27	2	0	1	4	2	.67	2	.319	.391	.619
1998 Pawtucket	AAA	93	340	86	13	0	14	—	—	141	47	37	27	0	92	8	3	1	12	9	.57	4	.253	.322	.415
1999 Pawtucket	AAA	115	467	125	29	2	30	—	—	248	95	74	51	1	128	3	4	4	14	6	.70	7	.268	.341	.531
1997 Boston	AL	8	24	4	1	0	0	(0	0)	5	2	2	0	0	11	0	1	0	1	0	1.00	0	.167	.167	.208
1999 Boston	AL	2	5	1	0	0	0	(0	0)	1	1	0	1	0	0	0	0	0	0	0	.00	0	.200	.333	.200
2 ML YEARS		10	29	5	1	0	0	(0	0)	6	3	2	1	0	11	0	1	0	1	0	1.00	0	.172	.200	.207

Lou Collier

Bats: R **Throws:** R **Pos:** PH/PR-35; SS-31; LF-9; 3B-7; 2B-4; RF-1 **Ht:** 5'10" **Wt:** 182 **Born:** 8/21/73 **Age:** 26

Year Team	Lg	G	AB	H	2B	3B	HR	(Hm	Rd)	TB	R	RBI	TBB	IBB	SO	HBP	SH	SF	SB	CS	SB%	GDP	Avg	OBP	SLG
1999 Louisville *	AAA	27	91	35	10	0	4	—	—	57	25	11	15	0	14	1	0	1	6	3	.67	2	.385	.472	.626
1997 Pittsburgh	NL	18	37	5	0	0	0	(0	0)	5	3	3	1	0	11	0	0	0	1	0	1.00	1	.135	.158	.135
1998 Pittsburgh	NL	110	334	82	13	6	2	(1	1)	113	30	34	31	6	70	6	3	5	2	2	.50	8	.246	.316	.338
1999 Milwaukee	NL	74	135	35	9	0	2	(2	0)	50	18	21	14	0	32	0	1	2	3	2	.60	2	.259	.325	.370
3 ML YEARS		202	506	122	22	6	4	(3	1)	168	51	58	46	6	113	6	4	7	6	4	.60	11	.241	.308	.332

Bartolo Colon

Pitches: Right **Bats:** Right **Pos:** SP-32 **Ht:** 6'0" **Wt:** 225 **Born:** 5/24/75 **Age:** 25

Year Team	Lg	G	GS	CG	GF	IP	BFP	H	R	ER	HR	SH	SF	HB	TBB	IBB	SO	WP	Bk	W	L	Pct.	ShO	Sv-Op	Hld	ERA
1997 Cleveland	AL	19	17	1	0	94	427	107	66	59	12	4	1	3	45	1	66	5	0	4	7	.364	0	0-0	0	5.65
1998 Cleveland	AL	31	31	6	0	204	883	205	91	84	15	10	2	3	79	5	158	4	0	14	9	.609	2	0-0	0	3.71
1999 Cleveland	AL	32	32	1	0	205	858	185	97	90	24	5	4	7	76	5	161	4	0	18	5	.783	1	0-0	0	3.95
3 ML YEARS		82	80	8	0	503	2168	497	254	233	51	19	7	13	200	11	385	13	0	36	21	.632	3	0-0	0	4.17

David Cone

Pitches: Right **Bats:** Left **Pos:** SP-31 **Ht:** 6'1" **Wt:** 190 **Born:** 1/2/63 **Age:** 37

Year Team	Lg	G	GS	CG	GF	IP	BFP	H	R	ER	HR	SH	SF	HB	TBB	IBB	SO	WP	Bk	W	L	Pct.	ShO	Sv-Op	Hld	ERA
1986 Kansas City	AL	11	0	0	5	22.2	108	29	14	14	2	0	0	1	13	1	21	3	0	0	0	.000	0	0--	0	5.56
1987 New York	NL	21	13	1	3	99.1	420	87	46	41	11	4	3	5	44	1	68	2	4	5	6	.455	0	1-1	2	3.71
1988 New York	NL	35	28	8	0	231.1	936	178	67	57	10	11	5	4	80	7	213	10	10	20	3	.870	4	0-0	1	2.22
1989 New York	NL	34	33	7	0	219.2	910	183	92	86	20	6	4	4	74	6	190	14	4	14	8	.636	2	0-0	0	3.52
1990 New York	NL	31	30	6	1	211.2	860	177	84	76	21	4	6	1	65	1	233	10	4	14	10	.583	2	0-0	0	3.23
1991 New York	NL	34	34	5	0	232.2	966	204	95	85	13	13	7	5	73	2	241	17	1	14	14	.500	2	0-0	0	3.29
1992 NYM-Tor		35	34	7	0	249.2	1055	201	91	78	15	6	9	12	111	7	261	12	1	17	10	.630	5	0-0	0	2.81
1993 Kansas City	AL	34	34	6	0	254	1060	205	102	94	20	7	9	10	114	2	191	14	2	11	14	.440	1	0-0	0	3.33
1994 Kansas City	AL	23	23	4	0	171.2	690	130	60	56	15	1	5	7	54	0	132	5	1	16	5	.762	3	0-0	0	2.94
1995 Tor-NYY		30	30	6	0	229.1	954	195	95	91	24	2	3	6	88	2	191	11	0	18	8	.692	2	0-0	0	3.57
1996 New York	AL	11	11	1	0	72	295	50	25	23	3	1	5	2	34	0	71	4	1	7	2	.778	0	0-0	0	2.88
1997 New York	AL	29	29	1	0	195	805	155	67	61	17	3	2	4	86	2	222	14	2	12	6	.667	0	0-0	0	2.82
1998 New York	AL	31	31	3	0	207.2	866	186	89	82	20	4	4	15	59	1	209	6	0	20	7	.741	0	0-0	0	3.55
1999 New York	AL	31	31	1	0	193.1	827	164	84	74	21	5	6	11	90	2	177	7	1	12	9	.571	1	0-0	0	3.44
1992 New York	NL	27	27	7	0	196.2	831	162	75	63	12	6	6	9	82	5	214	9	1	13	7	.650	5	0-0	0	2.88
Toronto	AL	8	7	0	0	53	224	39	16	15	3	0	3	3	29	2	47	3	0	4	3	.571	0	0-0	0	2.55
1995 Toronto	AL	17	17	5	0	130.1	537	113	53	49	12	2	2	5	41	2	102	6	1	9	6	.600	2	0-0	0	3.38

Year Team	Lg	HOW MUCH HE PITCHED						WHAT HE GAVE UP										THE RESULTS					
		G	GS	CG	GF	IP	BFP	H	R	ER	HR	SH	SF	HB	TBB	IBB	SO	WP	Bk	W	L	Pct.	ShO	Sv-Op	Hld	ERA
New York	AL	13	13	1	0	99	417	82	42	42	12	0	1	1	47	0	89	5	0	9	2	.818	0	0-0	0	3.82
14 ML YEARS		390	361	56	9	2590	10752	2144	1011	918	212	67	68	87	985	34	2420	129	32	180	102	.638	22	1-—	—	3.19

Jeff Conine

Bats: R **Throws:** R **Pos:** 1B-99; PH/PR-28; DH-19; LF-7; RF-6; 3B-4   **Ht:** 6'1" **Wt:** 220 **Born:** 6/27/66 **Age:** 34

Year Team	Lg	BATTING																		BASERUNNING				PERCENTAGES		
		G	AB	H	2B	3B	HR	(Hm	Rd)	TB	R	RBI	TBB	IBB	SO	HBP	SH	SF		SB	CS	SB%	GDP	Avg	OBP	SLG
1990 Kansas City	AL	9	20	5	2	0	0	(0	0)	7	3	2	2	0	5	0	0	0		0	0	.00	1	.250	.318	.350
1992 Kansas City	AL	28	91	23	5	2	0	(0	0)	32	10	9	8	1	23	0	0	0		0	0	.00	1	.253	.313	.352
1993 Florida	NL	162	595	174	24	3	12	(5	7)	240	75	79	52	2	135	5	0	6		2	2	.50	14	.292	.351	.403
1994 Florida	NL	115	451	144	27	6	18	(8	10)	237	60	82	40	4	92	1	0	4		1	2	.33	8	.319	.373	.525
1995 Florida	NL	133	483	146	26	2	25	(13	12)	251	72	105	66	5	94	1	0	12		2	0	1.00	13	.302	.379	.520
1996 Florida	NL	157	597	175	32	2	26	(15	11)	289	84	95	62	1	121	4	0	7		1	4	.20	17	.293	.360	.484
1997 Florida	NL	151	405	98	13	1	17	(7	10)	164	46	61	57	3	89	2	0	2		2	0	1.00	11	.242	.337	.405
1998 Kansas City	AL	93	309	79	26	0	8	(4	4)	129	30	43	26	1	68	2	0	6		3	0	1.00	8	.256	.312	.417
1999 Baltimore	AL	139	444	129	31	1	13	(7	6)	201	54	75	30	0	40	3	1	7		0	3	.00	12	.291	.335	.453
9 ML YEARS		987	3395	973	186	17	119	(59	60)	1550	434	551	343	17	667	18	1	44		11	11	.50	85	.287	.351	.457

Dennis Cook

Pitches: Left **Bats:** Left **Pos:** RP-71   **Ht:** 6'3" **Wt:** 190 **Born:** 10/4/62 **Age:** 37

Year Team	Lg	HOW MUCH HE PITCHED						WHAT HE GAVE UP										THE RESULTS					
		G	GS	CG	GF	IP	BFP	H	R	ER	HR	SH	SF	HB	TBB	IBB	SO	WP	Bk	W	L	Pct.	ShO	Sv-Op	Hld	ERA
1988 San Francisco	NL	4	4	1	0	22	86	9	8	7	1	0	3	0	11	1	13	1	0	2	1	.667	1	0-0	0	2.86
1989 SF-Phi	NL	23	18	2	1	121	499	110	59	50	18	5	2	2	38	6	67	4	2	7	8	.467	1	0-0	1	3.72
1990 Phi-LA	NL	47	16	2	4	156	663	155	74	68	20	7	7	2	56	9	64	6	3	9	4	.692	1	1-2	4	3.92
1991 Los Angeles	NL	20	1	0	5	17.2	69	12	3	1	0	1	2	0	7	1	8	0	0	1	0	1.000	0	0-1	1	0.51
1992 Cleveland	AL	32	25	1	1	158	669	156	79	67	29	3	3	2	50	2	96	4	5	5	7	.417	0	0-0	0	3.82
1993 Cleveland	AL	25	6	0	2	54	233	62	36	34	9	3	2	2	16	1	34	0	1	5	5	.500	0	0-2	2	5.67
1994 Chicago	AL	38	0	0	8	33	143	29	17	13	4	3	0	0	14	3	26	0	1	3	1	.750	0	0-1	3	3.55
1995 Cle-Tex	AL	46	1	0	10	57.2	255	63	32	29	9	4	5	2	26	3	53	1	0	0	2	.000	0	2-2	6	4.53
1996 Texas	AL	60	0	0	9	70.1	298	53	34	32	2	3	5	7	35	7	64	0	0	5	2	.714	0	0-2	11	4.09
1997 Florida	NL	59	0	0	12	62.1	272	64	28	27	4	1	1	2	28	4	63	0	0	1	2	.333	0	0-2	13	3.90
1998 New York	NL	73	0	0	18	68	286	60	21	18	5	3	3	3	27	4	79	1	1	8	4	.667	0	1-5	21	2.38
1999 New York	NL	71	0	0	12	63	262	50	27	27	11	1	2	1	27	1	68	0	0	10	5	.667	0	3-6	19	3.86
1989 San Francisco	NL	2	2	1	0	15	58	13	3	3	1	0	0	0	5	0	9	1	0	1	0	1.000	0	0-0	0	1.80
Philadelphia	NL	21	16	1	1	106	441	97	56	47	17	5	2	2	33	6	58	3	2	6	8	.429	1	0-0	1	3.99
1990 Philadelphia	NL	42	13	2	4	141.2	594	132	61	56	13	5	5	2	54	9	58	6	3	8	3	.727	1	1-2	3	3.56
Los Angeles	NL	5	3	0	0	14.1	69	23	13	12	7	2	2	0	2	0	6	0	0	1	1	.500	0	0-0	1	7.53
1995 Cleveland	AL	11	0	0	1	12.2	62	16	9	9	3	1	0	1	10	2	13	0	0	0	0	.000	0	0-0	1	6.39
Texas	AL	35	1	0	9	45	193	47	23	20	6	3	5	1	16	1	40	1	0	0	2	.000	0	2-2	5	4.00
12 ML YEARS		498	71	6	82	883	3735	823	418	373	112	34	35	23	335	42	635	17	13	56	41	.577	3	7-23	81	3.80

Brent Cookson

Bats: Right **Throws:** Right **Pos:** LF-2; RF-1   **Ht:** 6'0" **Wt:** 195 **Born:** 9/7/69 **Age:** 30

Year Team	Lg	BATTING																		BASERUNNING				PERCENTAGES		
		G	AB	H	2B	3B	HR	(Hm	Rd)	TB	R	RBI	TBB	IBB	SO	HBP	SH	SF		SB	CS	SB%	GDP	Avg	OBP	SLG
1991 Sou Oregon	A-	6	9	0	0	0	0	—	—	0	0	0	0	0	7	0	0	0		0	0	.00	1	.000	.000	.000
Athletics	R	1	1	0	0	0	0	—	—	0	0	0	0	0	0	0	0	0		0	0	.00	0	.000	.000	.000
1992 Clinton	A	46	145	31	5	1	8	—	—	62	30	20	22	0	48	3	1	1		9	3	.75	4	.214	.327	.428
San Jose	A+	68	255	74	8	4	12	—	—	126	44	49	25	0	69	3	0	2		9	5	.64	8	.290	.358	.494
1993 San Jose	A+	67	234	60	10	1	17	—	—	123	43	50	43	1	73	3	2	5		14	6	.70	5	.256	.372	.526
1994 Shreveport	AA	62	207	67	21	3	11	—	—	127	32	41	18	2	57	1	2	2		4	1	.80	4	.324	.377	.614
Phoenix	AAA	14	43	12	0	1	1	—	—	17	7	6	5	0	14	1	0	0		1	0	.00	1	.279	.367	.395
1995 Phoenix	AAA	68	210	63	9	3	15	—	—	123	38	46	25	2	36	1	1	2		3	3	.50	4	.300	.374	.586
Omaha	AAA	40	137	55	13	0	4	—	—	80	28	20	17	0	24	4	0	2		0	0	.00	3	.401	.475	.584
1996 Pawtucket	AAA	73	255	69	13	1	19	—	—	141	51	50	24	1	72	5	0	2		2	4	.33	9	.271	.343	.553
Rochester	AAA	30	113	30	7	0	6	—	—	55	22	21	9	0	20	2	0	1		2	1	.67	5	.265	.328	.487
1998 Tucson	AAA	36	100	36	12	0	6	—	—	66	24	19	18	0	26	2	0	1		0	0	.00	1	.360	.463	.660
1999 Albuquerque	AAA	85	277	89	18	1	28	—	—	193	57	70	38	2	56	2	1	4		7	1	.88	5	.321	.402	.697
1995 Kansas City	AL	22	35	5	1	0	0	(0	0)	6	2	5	2	0	7	0	1	0		1	0	1.00	1	.143	.189	.171
1999 Los Angeles	NL	3	5	1	0	0	0	(0	0)	1	0	0	0	0	1	0	0	0		0	0	.00	0	.200	.200	.200
2 ML YEARS		25	40	6	1	0	0	(0	0)	7	2	5	2	0	8	0	1	0		1	0	1.00	1	.150	.190	.175

Ron Coomer

Bats: R **Throws:** R **Pos:** 1B-71; 3B-57; PH/PR-10; DH-7; RF-1   **Ht:** 5'11" **Wt:** 206 **Born:** 11/18/66 **Age:** 33

Year Team	Lg	BATTING																		BASERUNNING				PERCENTAGES		
		G	AB	H	2B	3B	HR	(Hm	Rd)	TB	R	RBI	TBB	IBB	SO	HBP	SH	SF		SB	CS	SB%	GDP	Avg	OBP	SLG
1995 Minnesota	AL	37	101	26	3	1	5	(2	3)	46	15	19	9	0	11	1	0	0		0	1	.00	9	.257	.324	.455
1996 Minnesota	AL	95	233	69	12	1	12	(5	7)	119	34	41	17	1	24	0	0	3		3	0	1.00	10	.296	.340	.511
1997 Minnesota	AL	140	523	156	30	2	13	(4	9)	229	63	85	22	5	91	0	0	5		4	3	.57	11	.298	.324	.438
1998 Minnesota	AL	137	529	146	22	1	15	(6	9)	215	54	72	18	1	72	0	0	8		2	2	.50	22	.276	.295	.406
1999 Minnesota	AL	127	467	123	25	1	16	(6	10)	198	53	65	30	1	69	1	0	3		2	1	.67	16	.263	.307	.424
5 ML YEARS		536	1853	520	92	6	61	(23	38)	807	219	282	96	8	267	2	0	19		11	7	.61	68	.281	.314	.436

Brian Cooper

Pitches: Right   Bats: Right   Pos: SP-5   Ht: 6'1"   Wt: 185   Born: 8/19/74   Age: 25

Year Team	Lg	G	GS	CG	GF	IP	BFP	H	R	ER	HR	SH	SF	HB	TBB	IBB	SO	WP	Bk	W	L	Pct.	ShO	Sv-Op	Hld	ERA
1995 Boise	A-	13	11	0	1	62	264	60	31	27	5	4	1	6	22	1	66	4	1	3	2	.600	0	1--	—	3.92
1996 Lk Elsinore	A+	26	23	1	0	162.1	702	177	100	76	17	5	8	10	39	0	155	4	1	7	9	.438	1	0--	—	4.21
1997 Lk Elsinore	A+	17	17	1	0	117	497	111	56	46	7	6	2	10	27	0	104	6	0	7	3	.700	0	0--	—	3.54
1998 Midland	AA	32	24	5	4	161.2	750	215	138	128	35	5	6	9	59	1	141	7	0	8	10	.444	0	1--	—	7.13
1999 Erie	AA	22	22	6	0	158	640	146	61	58	17	3	1	13	29	0	143	5	1	10	5	.667	0	0--	—	3.30
Edmonton	AAA	5	5	0	0	31	130	30	17	13	0	0	2	1	10	0	32	1	0	2	1	.667	0	0--	—	3.77
1999 Anaheim	AL	5	5	0	0	27.2	124	23	15	15	3	0	1	4	18	0	15	0	0	1	1	.500	0	0-0	0	4.88

Rocky Coppinger

Pitches: Right   Bats: Right   Pos: RP-38; SP-2   Ht: 6'5"   Wt: 240   Born: 3/19/74   Age: 26

Year Team	Lg	G	GS	CG	GF	IP	BFP	H	R	ER	HR	SH	SF	HB	TBB	IBB	SO	WP	Bk	W	L	Pct.	ShO	Sv-Op	Hld	ERA
1999 Rochester *	AAA	5	5	0	0	32	133	28	13	13	3	0	1	0	12	0	37	1	0	2	2	.500	0	0--	—	3.66
1996 Baltimore	AL	23	22	0	1	125	548	126	76	72	25	2	5	2	60	1	104	4	0	10	6	.625	0	0-0	0	5.18
1997 Baltimore	AL	5	4	0	1	20	95	21	14	14	2	0	1	1	16	1	22	1	0	1	1	.500	0	0-0	0	6.30
1998 Baltimore	AL	6	1	0	3	15.2	72	16	9	9	3	0	0	0	7	1	13	0	0	0	0	.000	0	0-0	0	5.17
1999 Bal-Mil		40	2	0	17	58.1	269	60	37	35	13	0	2	0	42	3	56	1	0	5	4	.556	0	0-2	9	5.40
1999 Baltimore	AL	11	2	0	7	21.2	105	25	21	20	8	0	1	0	19	0	17	0	0	0	1	.000	0	0-0	0	8.31
Milwaukee	NL	29	0	0	10	36.2	164	35	16	15	5	0	1	0	23	3	39	1	0	5	3	.625	0	0-2	9	3.68
4 ML YEARS		74	29	0	22	219	984	223	136	130	43	2	8	3	125	6	195	6	0	16	11	.593	0	0-2	9	5.34

Trace Coquillette

Bats: Right   Throws: Right   Pos: 3B-11; 2B-6   Ht: 6'0"   Wt: 185   Born: 6/4/74   Age: 26

Year Team	Lg	G	AB	H	2B	3B	HR	(Hm	Rd)	TB	R	RBI	TBB	IBB	SO	HBP	SH	SF	SB	CS	SB%	GDP	Avg	OBP	SLG
1993 Wst Plm Bch	A+	6	18	5	3	0	0	—	—	8	2	3	2	0	5	0	1	0	0	0	.00	0	.278	.350	.444
Expos	R	44	159	40	4	3	2	—	—	56	27	11	37	0	28	7	1	3	16	3	.84	0	.252	.408	.352
1994 Burlington	A	5	17	3	1	0	0	—	—	4	2	0	1	0	4	0	0	1	1	0	1.00	0	.176	.222	.235
Vermont	A-	70	252	77	11	5	9	—	—	125	54	52	23	0	40	8	1	6	7	2	.78	5	.306	.374	.496
1995 Albany	A	128	458	123	27	4	3	—	—	167	67	57	64	2	91	9	4	6	17	16	.52	8	.269	.365	.365
1996 Expos	R	7	25	4	1	0	0	—	—	5	4	0	4	0	6	0	0	0	1	0	1.00	0	.160	.276	.200
Wst Plm Bch	A+	72	266	67	17	4	1	—	—	95	39	27	27	1	72	8	0	3	9	7	.56	5	.252	.336	.357
1997 Wst Plm Bch	A+	53	188	60	18	2	8	—	—	106	34	33	27	0	27	6	1	1	8	7	.53	1	.319	.419	.564
Harrisburg	AA	81	293	76	17	3	10	—	—	129	46	51	25	0	40	14	1	1	9	4	.69	5	.259	.345	.440
1998 Harrisburg	AA	49	187	62	10	0	9	—	—	99	40	23	15	0	41	6	0	1	10	3	.77	2	.332	.397	.529
Ottawa	AAA	74	252	64	14	0	7	—	—	99	30	40	17	1	38	7	2	3	3	3	.50	9	.254	.315	.393
1999 Ottawa	AAA	98	334	109	32	3	14	—	—	189	56	55	44	1	68	24	0	6	10	4	.71	6	.326	.434	.566
1999 Montreal	NL	17	49	13	3	0	0	(0	0)	16	2	4	4	0	7	1	1	0	1	0	1.00	3	.265	.333	.327

Alex Cora

Bats: Left   Throws: Right   Pos: SS-8; 2B-3; PH/PR-2   Ht: 6'0"   Wt: 180   Born: 10/18/75   Age: 24

Year Team	Lg	G	AB	H	2B	3B	HR	(Hm	Rd)	TB	R	RBI	TBB	IBB	SO	HBP	SH	SF	SB	CS	SB%	GDP	Avg	OBP	SLG
1996 Vero Beach	A+	61	214	55	5	4	0	—	—	68	26	26	12	0	36	3	4	0	5	5	.50	1	.257	.306	.318
1997 San Antonio	AA	127	448	105	20	4	3	—	—	142	52	48	25	4	60	3	7	1	12	9	.57	17	.234	.279	.317
1998 Albuquerque	AAA	81	299	79	16	6	5	—	—	122	42	45	15	1	38	3	6	3	10	7	.59	1	.264	.303	.408
1999 Albuquerque	AAA	80	302	93	11	7	4	—	—	130	51	37	12	0	37	8	9	3	9	5	.64	8	.308	.348	.430
1998 Los Angeles	NL	29	33	4	0	1	0	(0	0)	6	1	0	2	0	8	1	2	0	0	0	.00	0	.121	.194	.182
1999 Los Angeles	NL	11	30	5	1	0	0	(0	0)	6	2	3	0	0	4	1	0	0	0	0	.00	0	.167	.194	.200
2 ML YEARS		40	63	9	1	1	0	(0	0)	12	3	3	2	0	12	2	2	0	0	0	.00	1	.143	.194	.190

Archie Corbin

Pitches: Right   Bats: Right   Pos: RP-17   Ht: 6'4"   Wt: 230   Born: 12/30/67   Age: 32

Year Team	Lg	G	GS	CG	GF	IP	BFP	H	R	ER	HR	SH	SF	HB	TBB	IBB	SO	WP	Bk	W	L	Pct.	ShO	Sv-Op	Hld	ERA
1986 Kingsport	R+	18	1	0	9	30.1	149	31	23	16	3	0	1	0	28	0	30	8	1	1	1	.500	0	0--	—	4.75
1987 Kingsport	R+	6	6	0	0	25.2	128	24	21	18	3	0	0	2	26	0	17	6	0	2	3	.400	0	0--	—	6.31
1988 Kingsport	R+	11	10	4	0	69.1	277	47	23	12	5	2	0	3	17	0	47	1	1	7	2	.778	1	0--	—	1.56
1989 Columbia	A	27	23	4	3	153.2	664	149	86	77	16	4	4	5	72	0	130	2	0	9	9	.500	2	1--	—	4.51
1990 St. Lucie	A+	20	18	3	2	118	494	97	47	39	2	4	3	7	59	0	105	10	0	7	8	.467	0	0--	—	2.97
1991 Memphis	AA	28	25	1	0	156.1	692	139	90	81	7	4	6	8	90	1	166	13	0	8	8	.500	0	0--	—	4.66
1992 Memphis	AA	27	20	2	1	112.1	503	115	64	59	7	3	1	0	73	0	100	11	0	7	8	.467	0	0--	—	4.73
Harrisburg	AA	1	1	0	0	3	11	2	0	0	0	0	0	0	1	0	3	0	0	0	0	.000	0	0--	—	0.00
1993 Harrisburg	AA	42	2	0	21	73.1	314	43	31	30	0	1	5	2	59	1	91	5	1	5	3	.625	0	4--	—	3.68
1994 Buffalo	AAA	14	1	0	3	22.2	99	14	13	12	0	1	1	1	18	0	23	2	0	0	0	.000	0	0--	—	4.76
1995 Calgary	AAA	47	1	0	13	61	309	76	63	58	6	0	5	3	55	0	54	7	0	1	5	.167	0	1--	—	8.56
1996 Rochester	AAA	20	5	0	10	43.2	197	44	25	23	5	1	1	1	25	0	47	4	0	0	2	.000	0	1--	—	4.74
1997 Rochester	AAA	43	1	0	22	69.2	314	47	32	31	5	2	3	1	62	0	66	10	0	4	3	.571	0	5--	—	4.00
1998 Las Vegas	AAA	6	0	0	1	4.1	36	7	16	13	0	1	0	3	13	0	3	3	0	0	0	.000	0	0--	—	27.00
Charlotte	AAA	34	0	0	12	48.2	212	25	15	14	2	1	2	0	46	1	55	7	0	2	2	.500	0	3--	—	2.59

Year Team	Lg	G	GS	CG	GF	IP	BFP	H	R	ER	HR	SH	SF	HB	TBB	IBB	SO	WP	Bk	W	L	Pct.	ShO	Sv-Op	Hld	ERA
1999 Calgary	AAA	12	0	0	7	13.1	61	13	11	10	3	0	1	0	10	0	16	3	0	0	1	.000	0	0--	—	6.75
1991 Kansas City	AL	2	0	0	2	2.1	12	3	1	1	0	0	0	0	2	0	1	0	1	0	0	.000	0	0-0	—	3.86
1996 Baltimore	AL	18	0	0	5	27.1	123	22	7	7	2	0	1	0	22	0	20	2	0	2	0	1.000	0	0-0	3	2.30
1999 Florida	NL	17	0	0	4	21	104	25	20	17	2	1	1	1	15	0	30	3	0	0	1	.000	0	0-0	—	7.29
3 ML YEARS		37	0	0	11	50.2	239	50	28	25	4	1	2	2	39	0	51	5	1	2	1	.667	0	0-0	3	4.44

Francisco Cordero

Pitches: Right **Bats:** Right **Pos:** RP-20 **Ht:** 6'2" **Wt:** 200 **Born:** 8/11/77 **Age:** 22

Year Team	Lg	G	GS	CG	GF	IP	BFP	H	R	ER	HR	SH	SF	HB	TBB	IBB	SO	WP	Bk	W	L	Pct.	ShO	Sv-Op	Hld	ERA
1995 Fayettevlle	A	4	4	0	0	20	92	26	16	14	1	2	2	0	12	0	19	4	0	0	3	.000	0	0--	—	6.30
Jamestown	A-	15	14	0	0	88	392	96	62	51	3	3	3	8	37	0	54	11	0	4	7	.364	0	0--	—	5.22
1996 Fayettevlle	A	2	1	0	0	7	27	2	2	2	0	0	0	0	6	0	7	0	0	0	0	.000	0	0--	—	2.57
Jamestown	A-	2	2	0	0	11	39	5	1	1	0	0	0	0	2	0	10	0	0	0	0	.000	0	0--	—	0.82
1997 W Michigan	A	50	0	0	47	54.1	208	36	13	6	2	4	2	0	15	2	67	5	0	6	1	.857	0	35--	—	0.99
1998 Jacksnville	AA	17	0	0	15	16.2	79	19	12	9	1	1	1	1	9	0	18	0	0	1	1	.500	0	8--	—	4.86
Lakeland	A+	1	0	0	0	0.1	1	1	0	0	0	0	0	0	0	0	0	0	0	0	0	.000	0	0--	—	0.00
1999 Jacksnville	AA	47	0	0	43	52.1	218	35	9	8	3	2	0	3	22	0	58	3	0	4	1	.800	0	27--	—	1.38
1999 Detroit	AL	20	0	0	4	19	91	19	7	7	2	2	4	0	18	2	19	1	0	2	2	.500	0	0-0	6	3.32

Wil Cordero

Bats: Right **Throws:** Right **Pos:** LF-29; DH-23; PH/PR-6 **Ht:** 6'2" **Wt:** 200 **Born:** 10/3/71 **Age:** 28

Year Team	Lg	G	AB	H	2B	3B	HR	(Hm	Rd)	TB	R	RBI	TBB	IBB	SO	HBP	SH	SF	SB	CS	SB%	GDP	Avg	OBP	SLG
1999 Akron *	AA	3	11	4	2	0	0	(—	—)	6	2	0	0	0	3	1	0	0	0	0	.00	1	.364	.417	.545
1992 Montreal	NL	45	126	38	4	1	2	(1	1)	50	17	8	9	0	31	1	1	0	0	0	.00	3	.302	.353	.397
1993 Montreal	NL	138	475	118	32	2	10	(8	2)	184	56	58	34	8	60	7	4	1	12	3	.80	12	.248	.308	.387
1994 Montreal	NL	110	415	122	30	3	15	(5	10)	203	65	63	41	3	62	6	2	3	16	3	.84	8	.294	.363	.489
1995 Montreal	NL	131	514	147	35	2	10	(2	8)	216	64	49	36	4	88	9	1	4	9	5	.64	11	.286	.341	.420
1996 Boston	AL	59	198	57	14	0	3	(2	1)	80	29	37	11	4	31	2	1	1	2	1	.67	8	.288	.330	.404
1997 Boston	AL	140	570	160	26	3	18	(11	7)	246	82	72	31	7	122	4	0	4	1	3	.25	11	.281	.320	.432
1998 Chicago	AL	96	341	91	18	2	13	(5	8)	152	58	49	22	0	66	3	1	4	2	1	.67	7	.267	.314	.446
1999 Cleveland	AL	54	194	58	15	0	8	(3	5)	97	35	32	15	0	37	6	0	2	2	0	1.00	5	.299	.364	.500
8 ML YEARS		773	2833	791	174	13	79	(37	42)	1228	406	368	199	26	497	38	10	19	44	16	.73	67	.279	.333	.433

Francisco Cordova

Pitches: Right **Bats:** Right **Pos:** SP-27 **Ht:** 6'1" **Wt:** 191 **Born:** 4/26/72 **Age:** 28

Year Team	Lg	G	GS	CG	GF	IP	BFP	H	R	ER	HR	SH	SF	HB	TBB	IBB	SO	WP	Bk	W	L	Pct.	ShO	Sv-Op	Hld	ERA
1999 Altoona *	AA	2	2	0	0	9.2	48	13	8	5	0	0	0	0	4	0	12	1	1	1	1	.500	0	0--	—	4.66
Nashville *	AAA	2	2	0	0	12	47	10	2	1	1	0	0	0	1	0	7	0	0	2	0	1.000	0	0--	—	0.75
1996 Pittsburgh	NL	59	6	0	41	99	414	103	49	45	11	1	0	2	20	6	95	2	1	4	7	.364	0	12-18	1	4.09
1997 Pittsburgh	NL	29	29	2	0	178.2	744	175	80	72	14	3	7	9	49	4	121	4	0	11	8	.579	2	0-0	0	3.63
1998 Pittsburgh	NL	33	33	3	0	220.1	921	204	91	81	22	9	6	3	69	5	157	1	1	13	14	.481	2	0-0	0	3.31
1999 Pittsburgh	NL	27	27	2	0	160.2	682	166	83	79	16	7	4	4	59	6	98	5	0	8	10	.444	0	0-0	0	4.43
4 ML YEARS		148	95	7	41	658.2	2761	648	303	277	63	20	17	18	197	21	471	12	2	36	39	.480	4	12-18	3	3.78

Marty Cordova

Bats: R **Throws:** R **Pos:** DH-85; RF-25; PH/PR-16; LF-6 **Ht:** 6'0" **Wt:** 206 **Born:** 7/10/69 **Age:** 30

Year Team	Lg	G	AB	H	2B	3B	HR	(Hm	Rd)	TB	R	RBI	TBB	IBB	SO	HBP	SH	SF	SB	CS	SB%	GDP	Avg	OBP	SLG
1995 Minnesota	AL	137	512	142	27	4	24	(16	8)	249	81	84	52	1	111	10	0	5	20	7	.74	10	.277	.352	.486
1996 Minnesota	AL	145	569	176	46	1	16	(10	6)	272	97	111	53	4	96	8	0	9	11	5	.69	18	.309	.371	.478
1997 Minnesota	AL	103	378	93	18	4	10	(4	11)	164	44	51	30	2	92	3	0	2	5	3	.63	13	.246	.305	.434
1998 Minnesota	AL	119	438	111	20	2	10	(6	4)	165	52	69	50	3	103	5	0	6	3	6	.33	14	.253	.333	.377
1999 Minnesota	AL	124	425	121	28	3	14	(9	5)	197	62	70	48	2	96	9	0	6	13	4	.76	22	.285	.365	.464
5 ML YEARS		628	2322	643	139	14	79	(45	34)	1047	336	385	233	12	498	35	0	28	52	25	.68	77	.277	.348	.451

Rheal Cormier

Pitches: Left **Bats:** Left **Pos:** RP-60 **Ht:** 5'10" **Wt:** 187 **Born:** 4/23/67 **Age:** 33

Year Team	Lg	G	GS	CG	GF	IP	BFP	H	R	ER	HR	SH	SF	HB	TBB	IBB	SO	WP	Bk	W	L	Pct.	ShO	Sv-Op	Hld	ERA
1991 St. Louis	NL	11	10	2	1	67.2	281	74	35	31	5	1	3	2	8	1	38	2	1	4	5	.444	0	0-0	0	4.12
1992 St. Louis	NL	31	30	3	1	186	772	194	83	76	15	11	3	5	33	2	117	4	2	10	10	.500	0	0-0	0	3.68
1993 St. Louis	NL	38	21	1	4	145.1	619	163	80	70	18	10	4	4	27	3	75	6	0	7	6	.538	0	0-0	0	4.33
1994 St. Louis	NL	7	7	0	0	39.2	169	40	24	24	6	1	2	3	7	0	26	2	0	3	2	.600	0	0-0	0	5.45
1995 Boston	AL	48	12	0	3	115	488	131	60	52	12	6	2	3	31	2	69	4	0	7	5	.583	0	0-2	9	4.07
1996 Montreal	NL	33	27	1	1	159.2	674	165	80	74	16	4	8	9	41	3	100	8	0	7	10	.412	1	0-0	0	4.17
1997 Montreal	NL	1	1	0	0	1.1	9	4	5	5	1	0	0	0	1	0	0	0	0	0	1	.000	0	0-0	0	33.75
1999 Boston	AL	60	0	0	7	63.1	275	61	34	26	4	1	3	5	18	2	39	1	0	2	0	1.000	0	0-3	15	3.69
8 ML YEARS		229	108	7	17	778	3287	832	401	358	77	34	25	31	166	13	464	27	3	40	39	.506	1	0-5	24	4.14

Reid Cornelius

Pitches: Right **Bats:** Right **Pos:** RP-3; SP-2   **Ht:** 6'0" **Wt:** 200 **Born:** 6/2/70 **Age:** 30

Year Team	Lg	G	GS	CG	GF	IP	BFP	H	R	ER	HR	SH	SF	HB	TBB	IBB	SO	WP	Bk	W	L	Pct.	ShO	Sv-Op	Hld	ERA
1989 Rockford	A	17	17	0	0	84.1	391	71	58	40	6	3	3	11	63	0	66	13	3	5	6	.455	0	0--	—	4.27
1990 Wst Plm Bch	A+	11	11	0	0	56	245	54	25	21	1	0	4	5	25	0	47	3	3	2	3	.400	0	0--	—	3.38
1991 Wst Plm Bch	A+	17	17	0	0	109.1	449	79	31	29	3	9	4	7	43	1	81	3	6	8	3	.727	0	0--	—	2.39
Harrisburg	AA	3	3	1	0	18.2	76	15	6	6	3	0	0	2	7	0	12	0	0	2	1	.667	1	0--	—	2.89
1992 Harrisburg	AA	4	4	0	0	23	92	11	8	8	0	2	0	6	8	0	17	1	0	1	0	1.000	0	0--	—	3.13
1993 Harrisburg	AA	27	27	1	0	157.2	698	146	95	73	10	3	5	13	82	1	119	8	0	10	7	.588	0	0--	—	4.17
1994 Ottawa	AAA	25	24	1	1	148	661	149	89	72	18	1	4	8	75	2	87	10	0	9	8	.529	0	0--	—	4.38
1995 Ottawa	AAA	4	3	0	0	10.2	54	16	12	8	1	0	1	2	5	0	7	2	0	1	1	.500	0	0--	—	6.75
Norfolk	AAA	10	10	1	0	70.1	287	57	10	7	2	1	1	6	19	0	43	1	0	7	0	1.000	0	0--	—	0.90
1996 Buffalo	AAA	20	18	0	2	90	422	101	64	56	6	4	2	5	49	1	62	3	0	5	7	.417	0	0--	—	5.60
1997 Portland	AA	6	6	0	0	33	146	32	11	10	1	0	0	1	17	0	24	1	0	5	0	1.000	0	0--	—	2.73
Charlotte	AAA	22	22	1	0	130.2	555	134	82	74	19	5	8	4	43	1	80	5	1	12	5	.706	0	0--	—	5.10
1998 Tucson	AAA	19	16	0	2	94	412	108	70	62	16	2	2	3	26	1	65	3	2	4	7	.364	0	0--	—	5.94
Charlotte	AAA	8	8	1	0	49.1	215	50	25	22	5	2	0	2	13	2	31	0	0	3	2	.600	1	0--	—	4.01
1999 Calgary	AAA	27	27	2	0	172.1	750	184	96	86	9	4	8	7	68	3	135	12	2	10	6	.625	1	0--	—	4.49
1995 Mon-NYM	NL	18	10	0	1	66.2	301	75	44	41	11	4	3	3	30	5	39	2	1	3	7	.300	0	0-0	0	5.54
1999 Florida	NL	5	2	0	0	19.1	76	16	7	7	0	1	0	0	5	1	12	1	0	1	0	1.000	0	0-0	0	3.26
1995 Montreal	NL	8	0	0	1	9	43	11	8	8	3	0	0	2	5	0	4	1	0	0	0	.000	0	0-0	0	8.00
New York	NL	10	10	0	0	57.2	258	64	36	33	8	4	3	1	25	5	35	1	1	3	7	.300	0	0-0	0	5.15
2 ML YEARS		23	12	0	1	86	377	91	51	48	11	5	3	3	35	6	51	3	1	4	7	.364	0	0-0	0	5.02

Jim Corsi

Pitches: Right **Bats:** Right **Pos:** RP-36   **Ht:** 6'1" **Wt:** 230 **Born:** 9/9/61 **Age:** 38

Year Team	Lg	G	GS	CG	GF	IP	BFP	H	R	ER	HR	SH	SF	HB	TBB	IBB	SO	WP	Bk	W	L	Pct.	ShO	Sv-Op	Hld	ERA
1999 Rochester *	AAA	10	0	0	8	10.1	46	12	4	4	0	0	0	0	3	0	7	0	0	0	0	.000	0	2--	—	3.48
1988 Oakland	AL	11	1	0	7	21.1	89	20	10	9	1	3	3	0	6	1	10	1	1	0	1	.000	0	0-0	0	3.80
1989 Oakland	AL	22	0	0	14	38.1	149	26	8	8	2	2	2	1	10	0	21	0	0	1	2	.333	0	0-0	2	1.88
1991 Houston	NL	47	0	0	15	77.2	322	76	37	32	6	3	2	0	23	5	53	1	1	0	5	.000	0	0-3	4	3.71
1992 Oakland	AL	32	0	0	16	44	185	44	12	7	2	4	2	0	18	2	19	0	0	4	2	.667	0	0-0	4	1.43
1993 Florida	NL	15	0	0	6	20.1	97	28	15	15	1	3	1	0	10	3	7	0	0	0	2	.000	0	0-0	1	6.64
1995 Oakland	AL	38	0	0	7	45	187	31	14	11	2	5	1	2	26	1	26	0	0	2	4	.333	0	2-4	13	2.20
1996 Oakland	AL	56	0	0	19	73.2	312	71	33	33	6	9	2	3	34	4	43	1	0	6	0	1.000	0	3-6	10	4.03
1997 Boston	AL	52	0	0	14	57.2	251	56	26	22	1	3	3	4	21	7	40	2	0	5	3	.625	0	2-9	11	3.43
1998 Boston	AL	59	0	0	9	66	274	58	23	19	6	2	1	1	23	2	49	3	0	3	2	.600	0	0-3	18	2.59
1999 Bos-Bal	AL	36	0	0	8	37.1	166	40	19	18	6	4	1	2	20	3	22	0	0	1	3	.250	0	0-4	7	4.34
1999 Boston	AL	23	0	0	5	24	113	25	15	14	4	3	1	2	19	3	14	0	0	1	2	.333	0	0-3	6	5.25
Baltimore	AL	13	0	0	3	13.1	53	15	4	4	2	1	0	0	1	0	8	0	0	0	1	.000	0	0-1	1	2.70
10 ML YEARS		368	1	0	115	481.1	2032	450	197	174	33	38	18	13	191	28	290	8	2	22	24	.478	0	7-29	70	3.25

David Cortes

Pitches: Right **Bats:** Right **Pos:** RP-4   **Ht:** 5'11" **Wt:** 195 **Born:** 10/15/73 **Age:** 26

Year Team	Lg	G	GS	CG	GF	IP	BFP	H	R	ER	HR	SH	SF	HB	TBB	IBB	SO	WP	Bk	W	L	Pct.	ShO	Sv-Op	Hld	ERA
1996 Eugene	A-	15	0	0	11	24.2	95	13	2	2	0	1	0	0	6	0	33	0	0	2	1	.667	0	4--	—	0.73
1997 Macon	A	27	0	0	24	31.1	114	16	3	2	0	2	1	2	4	0	32	0	0	3	0	1.000	0	15--	—	0.57
Durham	A+	19	0	0	16	19.1	76	15	5	5	1	0	1	0	5	0	16	1	0	2	0	1.000	0	8--	—	2.33
Greenville	AA	3	0	0	1	5	20	4	1	1	1	0	0	0	1	0	7	0	0	1	0	1.000	0	0--	—	1.80
1998 Richmond	AAA	29	0	0	17	44.2	181	37	15	14	2	3	1	0	14	3	46	1	0	3	3	.500	0	4--	—	2.82
Colo Sprngs	AAA	6	0	0	0	7	37	14	6	6	0	0	0	0	2	0	5	0	0	1	0	1.000	0	0--	—	7.71
1999 Richmond	AAA	47	0	0	42	45.2	198	50	19	17	2	2	1	0	14	5	42	2	0	2	3	.400	0	22--	—	3.35
1999 Atlanta	NL	4	0	0	4	3.2	18	3	3	2	0	0	0	0	4	0	2	2	0	0	0	.000	0	0-0	0	4.91

Craig Counsell

Bats: Left **Throws:** Right **Pos:** 2B-50; PH/PR-44; SS-2   **Ht:** 6'0" **Wt:** 175 **Born:** 8/21/70 **Age:** 29

Year Team	Lg	G	AB	H	2B	3B	HR	(Hm	Rd)	TB	R	RBI	TBB	IBB	SO	HBP	SH	SF	SB	CS	SB%	GDP	Avg	OBP	SLG
1995 Colorado	NL	3	1	0	0	0	0	(0	0)	0	0	0	1	0	0	0	0	0	0	0	.00	0	.000	.500	.000
1997 Col-Fla	NL	52	164	49	9	2	1	(1	0)	65	20	16	18	2	17	3	3	1	1	1	.50	5	.299	.376	.396
1998 Florida	NL	107	335	84	19	5	4	(2	2)	125	43	40	51	7	47	4	8	1	3	1	0.100	5	.251	.355	.373
1999 Fla-LA	NL	87	174	38	7	0	0	(0	0)	45	24	11	14	0	24	0	5	2	1	0	1.00	2	.218	.274	.259
1997 Colorado	NL	1	0	0	0	0	0	(0	0)	0	0	0	0	0	0	0	0	0	0	0	.00	0	.000	.000	.000
Florida	NL	51	164	49	9	2	1	(1	0)	65	20	16	18	2	17	3	3	1	1	1	.50	5	.299	.376	.396
1999 Florida	NL	37	66	10	1	0	0	(0	0)	11	4	2	5	0	10	0	2	0	0	0	.00	1	.152	.211	.167
Los Angeles	NL	50	108	28	6	0	0	(0	0)	34	20	9	9	0	14	0	3	2	1	0	1.00	1	.259	.311	.315
4 ML YEARS		249	674	171	35	7	5	(3	2)	235	87	67	84	9	88	7	16	4	5	1	.83	12	.254	.341	.349

Darron Cox

Bats: Right **Throws:** Right **Pos:** C-14; PH/PR-3   **Ht:** 6'1" **Wt:** 205 **Born:** 11/21/67 **Age:** 32

Year Team	Lg	G	AB	H	2B	3B	HR	(Hm	Rd)	TB	R	RBI	TBB	IBB	SO	HBP	SH	SF	SB	CS	SB%	GDP	Avg	OBP	SLG
1989 Billings	R+	49	157	43	6	0	0	—	—	49	20	18	21	0	34	5	2	0	11	3	.79	1	.274	.377	.312
1990 Chstn-WV	A	103	367	93	11	3	1	—	—	113	53	44	40	2	75	7	4	3	14	3	.82	12	.253	.336	.308
1991 Cedar Rapds	A	21	60	16	4	0	0	—	—	20	12	4	8	0	11	4	1	0	7	1	.88	2	.267	.389	.333
Chattanooga	AA	13	38	7	1	0	0	—	—	8	2	3	2	0	9	0	1	1	0	0	.00	1	.184	.220	.211
Chstn-WV	A	79	294	71	14	1	2	—	—	93	37	28	24	0	40	2	1	7	8	4	.67	1	.241	.297	.316
1992 Chattanooga	AA	98	331	84	19	1	1	—	—	108	29	38	15	0	63	5	1	6	8	3	.73	7	.254	.291	.326
1993 Chattanooga	AA	89	300	65	9	5	3	—	—	93	35	26	38	2	63	3	7	1	7	4	.64	7	.217	.310	.310
1994 Iowa	AAA	99	301	80	15	1	3	—	—	106	35	26	28	4	47	4	3	0	5	2	.71	12	.266	.336	.352
1995 Orlando	AA	33	102	29	5	1	4	—	—	46	8	15	8	0	16	1	2	2	3	3	.50	3	.284	.336	.451
Iowa	AAA	33	94	22	6	0	1	—	—	31	7	14	8	0	21	2	2	4	0	0	.00	0	.234	.296	.330
1996 Richmond	AAA	55	168	40	9	0	3	—	—	58	19	20	5	0	22	3	2	2	1	0	1.00	5	.238	.270	.345
1997 Orlando	AA	3	9	2	1	0	1	—	—	6	2	4	1	0	1	0	0	1	0	0	.00	1	.222	.273	.667
1998 Durham	AAA	84	278	84	16	1	9	—	—	129	45	35	23	0	41	5	8	0	2	2	.50	6	.302	.366	.464
1999 Ottawa	AAA	3	9	0	0	0	0	—	—	0	0	0	1	0	2	0	0	0	0	0	.00	0	.000	.100	.000
1999 Montreal	NL	15	25	6	1	0	1	(1	0)	10	2	2	0	0	5	2	0	0	0	0	.00	0	.240	.296	.400

Steve Cox

Bats: Left **Throws:** Left **Pos:** 1B-4; LF-2; PH/PR-1   **Ht:** 6'4" **Wt:** 225 **Born:** 10/31/74 **Age:** 25

Year Team	Lg	G	AB	H	2B	3B	HR	(Hm	Rd)	TB	R	RBI	TBB	IBB	SO	HBP	SH	SF	SB	CS	SB%	GDP	Avg	OBP	SLG
1992 Athletics	R	52	184	43	4	1	1	—	—	52	30	35	27	1	51	3	0	2	2	1	.67	2	.234	.338	.283
1993 Sou Oregon	A-	15	57	18	4	1	2	—	—	30	10	16	5	0	15	0	0	0	0	0	.00	0	.316	.359	.526
1994 W Michigan	A	99	311	75	19	2	6	—	—	116	37	32	41	3	95	4	1	3	2	6	.25	5	.241	.334	.373
1995 Modesto	A+	132	483	144	29	3	30	—	—	269	95	110	84	6	88	14	0	10	5	4	.56	12	.298	.409	.557
1996 Huntsville	AA	104	381	107	21	1	12	—	—	166	59	61	51	6	65	6	2	3	2	2	.50	10	.281	.372	.436
1997 Edmonton	AAA	131	467	128	34	1	15	—	—	209	84	93	88	4	90	2	2	9	1	3	.25	16	.274	.385	.448
1998 Durham	AAA	119	430	109	23	2	13	—	—	175	64	67	56	6	100	2	2	5	3	4	.43	9	.253	.339	.407
1999 Durham	AAA	134	534	182	49	4	25	—	—	314	107	127	67	11	74	5	0	6	3	3	.50	12	.341	.415	.588
1999 Tampa Bay	AL	6	19	4	1	0	0	(0	0)	5	0	0	0	0	2	0	0	0	0	0	.00	2	.211	.211	.263

Tim Crabtree

Pitches: Right **Bats:** Right **Pos:** RP-68   **Ht:** 6'4" **Wt:** 220 **Born:** 10/13/69 **Age:** 30

Year Team	Lg	G	GS	CG	GF	IP	BFP	H	R	ER	HR	SH	SF	HB	TBB	IBB	SO	WP	Bk	W	L	Pct.	ShO	Sv-Op	Hld	ERA
1995 Toronto	AL	31	0	0	19	32	141	30	16	11	7	1	1	2	13	0	21	2	0	0	2	.000	0	0-2	1	3.09
1996 Toronto	AL	53	0	0	21	67.1	284	59	26	19	4	2	2	3	22	4	57	3	0	5	3	.625	0	1-5	17	2.54
1997 Toronto	AL	37	0	0	16	40.2	199	65	32	32	7	4	2	2	17	3	26	4	0	3	3	.500	0	2-5	8	7.08
1998 Texas	AL	64	0	0	14	85.1	371	86	40	34	3	1	6	3	35	2	60	6	0	6	1	.857	0	0-1	10	3.59
1999 Texas	AL	68	0	0	21	65	275	71	26	25	4	1	1	1	18	1	54	5	0	5	1	.833	0	0-3	14	3.46
5 ML YEARS		253	0	0	91	290.1	1270	311	140	121	19	8	12	11	105	10	218	20	0	19	10	.655	0	3-16	50	3.75

Doug Creek

Pitches: Left **Bats:** Left **Pos:** RP-3   **Ht:** 5'10" **Wt:** 205 **Born:** 3/1/69 **Age:** 31

Year Team	Lg	G	GS	CG	GF	IP	BFP	H	R	ER	HR	SH	SF	HB	TBB	IBB	SO	WP	Bk	W	L	Pct.	ShO	Sv-Op	Hld	ERA
1999 Iowa *	AAA	25	20	0	3	130.2	567	116	66	55	20	6	6	12	62	0	140	6	0	7	3	.700	0	1- —	0	3.79
1995 St. Louis	NL	6	0	0	1	6.2	24	2	0	0	0	0	0	0	3	0	10	0	0	0	0	.000	0	0-0	0	0.00
1996 San Francisco	NL	63	0	0	15	48.1	220	45	41	35	11	1	0	2	32	2	38	2	0	0	2	.000	0	0-1	7	6.52
1997 San Francisco	NL	3	3	0	0	13.1	64	12	12	10	1	0	0	0	14	0	14	0	0	1	2	.333	0	0-0	0	6.75
1999 Chicago	NL	3	0	0	2	6	32	6	7	7	1	0	1	0	8	1	6	1	0	0	0	.000	0	0-0	0	10.50
4 ML YEARS		75	3	0	18	74.1	340	65	60	52	13	1	1	2	57	3	68	3	0	1	4	.200	0	0-1	7	6.30

Tripp Cromer

Bats: R **Throws:** R **Pos:** PH/PR-16; 2B-9; SS-9; 3B-2; 1B-1; LF-1; RF-1   **Ht:** 6'2" **Wt:** 165 **Born:** 11/21/67 **Age:** 32

Year Team	Lg	G	AB	H	2B	3B	HR	(Hm	Rd)	TB	R	RBI	TBB	IBB	SO	HBP	SH	SF	SB	CS	SB%	GDP	Avg	OBP	SLG
1999 Albuquerque *	AAA	5	15	4	2	0	0	—	—	6	1	1	1	0	3	1	0	0	0	1	.00	0	.267	.353	.400
San Berndno *	A+	4	18	9	3	0	1	—	—	15	3	8	0	0	3	0	0	0	0	0	.00	0	.500	.500	.833
1993 St. Louis	NL	10	23	2	0	0	0	(0	0)	2	1	0	1	0	6	0	0	0	0	0	.00	0	.087	.125	.087
1994 St. Louis	NL	2	0	0	0	0	0	(0	0)	0	1	0	0	0	0	0	0	0	0	0	.00	0	.000	.000	.000
1995 St. Louis	NL	105	345	78	19	0	5	(2	3)	112	36	18	14	2	66	4	1	5	0	0	.00	14	.226	.261	.325
1997 Los Angeles	NL	28	86	25	3	0	4	(2	2)	40	8	20	6	3	16	0	2	1	0	0	.00	0	.291	.333	.465
1998 Los Angeles	NL	6	6	1	0	0	1	(0	1)	4	1	1	0	0	2	0	0	0	0	1	.00	0	.167	.167	.667
1999 Los Angeles	NL	33	52	10	0	0	2	(1	1)	16	5	8	5	0	10	0	0	0	0	0	.00	4	.192	.263	.308
6 ML YEARS		184	512	116	22	0	12	(5	7)	174	52	47	26	5	100	4	3	6	0	1	.00	20	.227	.266	.340

Rich Croushore

Pitches: Right **Bats:** Right **Pos:** RP-59 **Ht:** 6'4" **Wt:** 210 **Born:** 8/7/70 **Age:** 29

		HOW MUCH HE PITCHED						WHAT HE GAVE UP											THE RESULTS					
Year Team	Lg	G	GS	CG	GF	IP	BFP	H	R	ER	HR	SH	SF	HB	TBB	IBB	SO	WP	Bk	W	L	Pct.	ShO	Sv-Op	Hld	ERA
1993 Glens Falls	A-	31	0	0	11	41.1	184	38	16	14	1	4	1	2	22	4	36	6	0	4	1	.800	0	1--	—	3.05
1994 Madison	A	62	0	0	14	94.1	410	90	49	43	5	4	2	5	46	2	103	10	4	6	6	.500	0	0--	—	4.10
1995 St. Pete	A+	12	11	0	0	59	251	44	25	23	2	3	1	4	32	0	57	5	0	6	4	.600	0	0--	—	3.51
1996 Arkansas	AA	34	17	2	11	108	486	113	75	59	18	4	1	2	51	1	85	7	0	5	10	.333	0	3--	—	4.92
1997 Arkansas	AA	17	16	1	1	92.2	421	111	52	43	7	1	5	4	37	0	67	8	2	7	5	.583	0	0--	—	4.18
Louisville	AAA	14	6	0	3	43.2	173	37	14	12	3	0	0	0	13	0	41	4	0	1	2	.333	0	1--	—	2.47
1998 Memphis	AAA	23	0	0	9	28.2	115	21	16	15	3	1	0	1	9	0	40	2	0	0	3	.000	0	2--	—	4.71
1999 Memphis	AAA	7	0	0	5	6.2	34	8	5	5	1	1	0	6	0	11	1	0	1	0	1.000	0	4--	—	6.75
1998 St. Louis	NL	41	0	0	15	54.1	243	44	31	30	6	2	1	4	29	2	47	6	0	0	3	.000	0	8-11	6	4.97
1999 St. Louis	NL	59	0	0	12	71.2	329	68	42	33	9	7	1	3	43	4	88	9	0	3	7	.300	0	3-10	14	4.14
2 ML YEARS		100	0	0	27	126	572	112	73	63	15	9	2	7	72	6	135	15	0	3	10	.231	0	11-21	20	4.50

Deivi Cruz

Bats: Right **Throws:** Right **Pos:** SS-155 **Ht:** 6'0" **Wt:** 184 **Born:** 11/6/75 **Age:** 24

				BATTING															BASERUNNING				PERCENTAGES		
Year Team	Lg	G	AB	H	2B	3B	HR	(Hm	Rd)	TB	R	RBI	TBB	IBB	SO	HBP	SH	SF	SB	CS	SB%	GDP	Avg	OBP	SLG
1997 Detroit	AL	147	436	105	26	0	2	(0	2)	137	35	40	14	0	55	0	14	3	3	6	.33	9	.241	.263	.314
1998 Detroit	AL	135	454	118	22	3	5	(5	0)	161	52	45	13	0	55	3	5	2	3	4	.43	11	.260	.284	.355
1999 Detroit	AL	155	518	147	35	0	13	(9	4)	221	64	58	12	0	57	4	14	5	1	4	.20	10	.284	.302	.427
3 ML YEARS		437	1408	370	83	3	20	(14	6)	519	151	143	39	0	167	7	33	10	7	14	.33	30	.263	.284	.369

Ivan Cruz

Bats: Left **Throws:** Left **Pos:** PH/PR-4; 1B-1; RF-1 **Ht:** 6'3" **Wt:** 210 **Born:** 5/3/68 **Age:** 32

				BATTING															BASERUNNING				PERCENTAGES		
Year Team	Lg	G	AB	H	2B	3B	HR	(Hm	Rd)	TB	R	RBI	TBB	IBB	SO	HBP	SH	SF	SB	CS	SB%	GDP	Avg	OBP	SLG
1989 Niagara Fal	A-	64	226	62	11	2	7	—	—	98	43	40	27	4	29	3	0	1	2	0	1.00	2	.274	.358	.434
1990 Lakeland	A+	118	414	118	23	2	11	—	—	178	61	73	49	3	71	5	2	4	8	1	.89	8	.285	.364	.430
1991 Toledo	AAA	8	29	4	0	0	1	—	—	7	2	4	2	0	12	1	0	0	0	0	.00	0	.138	.219	.241
London	AA	121	443	110	21	0	9	—	—	158	45	47	36	5	74	4	1	2	3	3	.50	12	.248	.309	.357
1992 London	AA	134	524	143	25	1	14	—	—	212	71	104	37	1	102	4	0	6	1	1	.50	16	.273	.322	.405
1993 Toledo	AAA	115	402	91	18	4	13	—	—	156	44	50	30	2	85	3	0	2	1	1	.50	5	.226	.284	.388
1994 Toledo	AAA	97	303	75	11	2	15	—	—	135	36	43	28	0	83	2	0	3	1	0	1.00	7	.248	.313	.446
1995 Toledo	AAA	11	36	7	2	0	0	—	—	9	5	3	6	0	9	0	0	0	0	0	.00	1	.194	.302	.250
Jacksnville	AA	108	397	112	17	1	31	—	—	224	65	93	60	15	94	0	0	3	0	0	.00	7	.282	.374	.564
1996 Columbus	AAA	130	446	115	26	0	28	—	—	225	84	96	48	3	99	8	2	9	2	4	.33	9	.258	.335	.504
1997 Columbus	AAA	116	417	125	35	1	24	—	—	234	69	95	65	10	78	11	0	4	4	5	.44	8	.300	.404	.561
1998 Yankees	R	5	10	6	3	0	1	—	—	12	2	5	3	0	3	0	0	0	0	0	.00	6	.600	.692	1.200
Columbus	AAA	56	204	54	10	0	13	—	—	103	34	36	29	3	44	2	0	1	0	0	.00	6	.265	.360	.505
1999 Altoona	AA	3	13	2	1	0	0	—	—	3	1	3	1	0	8	0	0	0	0	0	.00	1	.154	.214	.231
Nashville	AAA	75	273	89	20	1	25	—	—	186	57	81	21	4	56	1	0	9	0	2	.00	7	.326	.365	.681
1997 New York	AL	11	20	5	1	0	0	(0	0)	6	0	3	2	0	4	0	0	0	0	0	.00	0	.250	.318	.300
1999 Pittsburgh	NL	5	10	4	0	0	1	(1	0)	7	3	2	0	0	2	0	0	0	0	0	.00	0	.400	.400	.700
2 ML YEARS		16	30	9	1	0	1	(1	0)	13	3	5	2	0	6	0	0	0	0	0	.00	0	.300	.344	.433

Jacob Cruz

Bats: L **Throws:** L **Pos:** CF-15; LF-11; PH/PR-11; DH-2; RF-2 **Ht:** 6'0" **Wt:** 179 **Born:** 1/28/73 **Age:** 27

				BATTING															BASERUNNING				PERCENTAGES		
Year Team	Lg	G	AB	H	2B	3B	HR	(Hm	Rd)	TB	R	RBI	TBB	IBB	SO	HBP	SH	SF	SB	CS	SB%	GDP	Avg	OBP	SLG
1994 San Jose	A+	31	118	29	7	0	0	—	—	36	14	12	9	0	22	2	2	2	0	2	.00	6	.246	.305	.305
1995 Shreveport	AA	127	458	136	33	1	13	—	—	210	88	77	57	6	72	8	4	2	9	8	.53	15	.297	.383	.459
1996 Phoenix	AAA	121	435	124	26	4	7	—	—	179	60	75	62	5	77	10	2	11	5	9	.36	16	.285	.378	.411
1997 Phoenix	AAA	127	493	178	45	3	12	—	—	265	97	95	64	9	64	3	0	5	18	3	.86	11	.361	.434	.538
1998 Fresno	AAA	89	342	102	17	3	18	—	—	179	60	62	46	2	57	8	2	1	12	5	.71	9	.298	.393	.523
Buffalo	AAA	43	169	56	8	2	13	—	—	107	32	36	13	0	26	1	0	1	3	3	.40	3	.331	.380	.633
1999 Buffalo	AAA	54	202	55	7	2	7	—	—	87	29	31	21	1	39	3	0	1	4	2	.67	7	.272	.348	.431
1996 San Francisco	NL	33	77	18	3	0	3	(3	0)	30	10	10	12	0	24	2	1	0	0	1	.00	2	.234	.352	.390
1997 San Francisco	NL	16	25	4	1	0	0	(0	0)	5	3	3	3	0	4	0	0	1	0	0	.00	0	.160	.241	.200
1998 SF-Cle		4	4	0	0	0	0	(0	0)	0	0	0	0	0	3	0	0	0	0	0	.00	0	.000	.000	.000
1999 Cleveland	AL	32	88	29	5	1	3	(3	0)	45	14	17	5	0	13	1	1	1	0	2	.00	4	.330	.368	.511
1998 San Francisco	NL	3	3	0	0	0	0	(0	0)	0	0	0	0	0	2	0	0	0	0	0	.00	0	.000	.000	.000
Cleveland	AL	1	1	0	0	0	0	(0	0)	0	0	0	0	0	1	0	0	0	0	0	.00	0	.000	.000	.000
4 ML YEARS		85	194	51	9	1	6	(6	0)	80	27	30	20	0	44	3	2	2	0	3	.00	6	.263	.338	.412

Jose Cruz

Bats: Both **Throws:** Right **Pos:** CF-97; LF-9; PH/PR-5 **Ht:** 6'0" **Wt:** 195 **Born:** 4/19/74 **Age:** 26

				BATTING															BASERUNNING				PERCENTAGES		
Year Team	Lg	G	AB	H	2B	3B	HR	(Hm	Rd)	TB	R	RBI	TBB	IBB	SO	HBP	SH	SF	SB	CS	SB%	GDP	Avg	OBP	SLG
1999 Syracuse *	AAA	31	103	19	3	1	3	—	—	33	17	14	28	3	20	0	0	1	5	0	1.00	3	.184	.356	.320
1997 Sea-Tor	AL	104	395	98	19	1	26	(11	15)	197	59	68	41	2	117	0	1	5	7	2	.78	5	.248	.315	.499
1998 Toronto	AL	105	352	89	14	3	11	(4	7)	142	55	42	57	3	99	0	0	4	11	4	.73	0	.253	.354	.403

BATTING

Year Team	Lg	G	AB	H	2B	3B	HR	(Hm	Rd)	TB	R	RBI	TBB	IBB	SO	HBP	SH	SF	SB	CS	SB%	GDP	Avg	OBP	SLG
1999 Toronto	AL	106	349	84	19	3	14	(8	6)	151	63	45	64	5	91	0	1	0	14	4	.78	6	.241	.358	.433
1997 Seattle	AL	49	183	49	12	1	12	(7	5)	99	28	34	13	0	45	0	1	1	1	0	1.00	3	.268	.315	.541
Toronto	AL	55	212	49	7	0	14	(4	10)	98	31	34	28	2	72	0	0	4	6	2	.75	2	.231	.316	.462
3 ML YEARS		315	1096	271	52	7	51	(23	28)	490	177	155	162	10	307	0	2	9	32	10	.76	11	.247	.342	.447

Nelson Cruz

Pitches: Right **Bats:** Right **Pos:** RP-23; SP-6   **Ht:** 6'1" **Wt:** 185 **Born:** 9/13/72 **Age:** 27

Year Team	Lg	G	GS	CG	GF	IP	BFP	H	R	ER	HR	SH	SF	HB	TBB	IBB	SO	WP	Bk	W	L	Pct.	ShO	Sv-Op	Hld	ERA
1991 Expos	R	12	8	1	0	48.1	207	40	18	13	1	3	1	2	19	0	34	2	3	2	4	.333	1	0--	—	2.42
1995 Bristol	R+	1	0	0	1	1	6	2	1	1	0	0	1	1	0	0	0	0	0	0	0	.000	0	0--	—	9.00
Hickory	A	44	0	0	29	66.2	285	65	31	20	6	3	1	4	15	2	68	5	0	2	7	.222	0	9--	—	2.70
Pr William	A+	9	0	0	7	19.1	75	12	1	1	1	0	0	2	6	0	18	0	0	2	1	.667	0	1--	—	0.47
1996 Birmingham	AA	37	18	2	8	149	627	150	65	53	10	7	6	8	41	2	142	3	1	6	6	.500	1	1--	—	3.20
1997 Nashville	AAA	21	20	1	0	123.1	533	139	75	70	20	1	4	9	31	0	93	1	2	11	7	.611	0	0--	—	5.11
1998 Calgary	AAA	35	18	2	4	126.2	571	159	85	75	18	2	5	11	40	1	101	5	1	10	6	.625	1	0--	—	5.33
1999 Toledo	AAA	10	10	4	0	62.2	247	47	20	19	5	0	0	4	21	0	41	1	0	7	1	.875	2	0--	—	2.73
1997 Chicago	AL	19	0	0	5	26.1	116	29	19	19	6	1	0	0	9	1	23	3	0	0	2	.000	0	0-0	6	6.49
1999 Detroit	AL	29	6	0	10	66.2	295	74	44	42	11	2	4	3	23	1	46	2	0	2	5	.286	0	0-0	4	5.67
2 ML YEARS		48	6	0	15	93	411	103	63	61	17	3	4	3	32	2	69	5	0	2	7	.222	0	0-0	10	5.90

Midre Cummings

Bats: L **Throws:** R **Pos:** PH/PR-7; DH-5; RF-5; LF-1   **Ht:** 6'0" **Wt:** 195 **Born:** 10/14/71 **Age:** 28

Year Team	Lg	G	AB	H	2B	3B	HR	(Hm	Rd)	TB	R	RBI	TBB	IBB	SO	HBP	SH	SF	SB	CS	SB%	GDP	Avg	OBP	SLG
1999 New Britain *	AA	24	93	35	7	0	2	—	—	48	28	15	17	1	14	2	0	2	3	1	.75	1	.376	.474	.516
Salt Lake *	AAA	69	261	84	19	4	13	—	—	150	50	68	23	0	43	3	0	1	4	4	.50	5	.322	.382	.575
1993 Pittsburgh	NL	13	36	4	1	0	0	(0	0)	5	5	3	4	0	9	0	0	1	0	0	.00	1	.111	.195	.139
1994 Pittsburgh	NL	24	86	21	4	0	1	(1	0)	28	11	12	4	0	18	1	0	1	0	0	.00	0	.244	.283	.326
1995 Pittsburgh	NL	59	152	37	7	1	2	(1	1)	52	13	15	13	3	30	0	0	1	0	0	1.00	1	.243	.303	.342
1996 Pittsburgh	NL	24	85	19	3	1	3	(2	1)	33	11	7	0	0	16	0	1	1	0	0	.00	0	.224	.221	.388
1997 Pit-Phi	NL	115	314	83	22	6	4	(3	1)	129	35	31	31	0	56	1	2	2	3	4	.43	0	.264	.330	.411
1998 Boston	AL	67	120	34	8	0	5	(4	1)	57	20	15	17	0	19	2	1	0	3	3	.50	2	.283	.381	.475
1999 Minnesota	AL	16	38	10	0	0	1	(1	0)	13	1	9	3	0	7	0	0	1	2	0	1.00	0	.263	.310	.342
1997 Chicago	NL	52	106	20	6	2	3	(2	1)	39	11	8	8	0	26	1	0	0	0	0	.00	1	.189	.252	.368
Philadelphia	NL	63	208	63	16	4	1	(1	0)	90	24	23	23	0	30	0	1	2	2	3	.40	2	.303	.369	.433
7 ML YEARS		318	831	208	45	8	16	(12	4)	317	96	92	72	3	155	4	4	6	6	6	.57	7	.250	.311	.381

Will Cunnane

Pitches: Right **Bats:** Right **Pos:** RP-24   **Ht:** 6'2" **Wt:** 175 **Born:** 4/24/74 **Age:** 26

Year Team	Lg	G	GS	CG	GF	IP	BFP	H	R	ER	HR	SH	SF	HB	TBB	IBB	SO	WP	Bk	W	L	Pct.	ShO	Sv-Op	Hld	ERA
1999 Las Vegas *	AAA	28	0	0	21	36.2	157	30	5	4	0	1	0	0	16	2	54	1	0	2	1	.667	0	11--	—	0.98
1997 San Diego	NL	54	8	0	16	91.1	430	114	69	59	11	1	1	5	49	1	79	3	0	6	3	.667	0	0-2	4	5.81
1998 San Diego	NL	3	0	0	1	3	14	4	2	2	1	0	0	0	1	1	1	0	0	0	0	.000	0	0-0	0	6.00
1999 San Diego	NL	24	0	0	2	31	130	34	19	18	8	2	0	0	12	3	22	3	0	2	1	.667	0	0-0	5	5.23
3 ML YEARS		81	8	0	19	125.1	574	152	90	79	20	3	1	5	62	7	102	6	0	8	4	.667	0	0-2	9	5.67

Chad Curtis

Bats: R **Throws:** R **Pos:** LF-72; PH/PR-39; DH-14; CF-6; RF-3   **Ht:** 5'10" **Wt:** 185 **Born:** 11/6/68 **Age:** 31

Year Team	Lg	G	AB	H	2B	3B	HR	(Hm	Rd)	TB	R	RBI	TBB	IBB	SO	HBP	SH	SF	SB	CS	SB%	GDP	Avg	OBP	SLG
1992 California	AL	139	441	114	16	2	10	(5	5)	164	59	46	51	2	71	6	5	4	43	18	.70	10	.259	.341	.372
1993 California	AL	152	583	166	25	3	6	(3	3)	215	94	59	70	2	89	4	7	7	48	24	.67	16	.285	.361	.369
1994 California	AL	114	453	116	23	4	11	(8	3)	180	67	50	37	0	69	5	4	7	25	11	.69	10	.256	.317	.397
1995 California	AL	144	586	157	29	3	21	(11	10)	255	96	67	70	3	93	7	0	7	27	15	.64	12	.268	.349	.435
1996 Det-LA		147	504	127	25	1	12	(9	3)	190	85	46	70	0	88	1	6	6	18	11	.62	15	.252	.341	.377
1997 Cle-NYY	AL	115	399	99	22	1	15	(4	11)	168	59	55	43	1	59	5	2	9	12	6	.67	7	.284	.362	.481
1998 New York	AL	151	456	111	21	1	10	(6	4)	164	79	56	75	3	80	7	1	6	21	5	.81	11	.243	.355	.360
1999 New York	AL	96	195	51	6	0	5	(0	5)	72	37	24	43	0	35	3	1	3	8	4	.67	6	.262	.398	.369
1996 Chicago	AL	104	400	105	20	1	10	(9	1)	157	65	37	53	0	73	1	6	6	16	10	.62	14	.263	.346	.393
Los Angeles	NL	43	104	22	5	0	2	(1	1)	33	20	9	17	0	15	0	0	0	2	1	.67	1	.212	.322	.317
1997 Cleveland	AL	22	29	6	1	0	3	(1	2)	16	8	5	7	0	10	0	0	0	0	0	.00	1	.207	.361	.552
New York	AL	93	320	93	21	1	12	(3	9)	152	51	50	36	1	49	5	2	9	12	6	.67	6	.291	.362	.475
8 ML YEARS		1058	3567	941	167	15	90	(40	50)	1408	576	403	459	11	584	38	29	46	202	94	.68	87	.264	.350	.395

Omar Daal

Pitches: Left **Bats:** Left **Pos:** SP-32   **Ht:** 6'3" **Wt:** 195 **Born:** 3/1/72 **Age:** 28

Year Team	Lg	G	GS	CG	GF	IP	BFP	H	R	ER	HR	SH	SF	HB	TBB	IBB	SO	WP	Bk	W	L	Pct.	ShO	Sv-Op	Hld	ERA
1993 Los Angeles	NL	47	0	0	12	35.1	155	36	20	20	5	2	2	0	21	3	19	1	2	2	3	.400	0	0-1	7	5.09

Year Team	Lg	G	GS	CG	GF	IP	BFP	H	R	ER	HR	SH	SF	HB	TBB	IBB	SO	WP	Bk	W	L	Pct.	ShO	Sv-Op	Hld	ERA
1994 Los Angeles	NL	24	0	0	5	13.2	55	12	5	5	1	1	0	0	5	0	9	1	1	0	0	.000	0	0-0	3	3.29
1995 Los Angeles	NL	28	0	0	0	20	100	29	16	16	1	1	1	1	15	4	11	0	1	4	0	1.000	0	0-1	4	7.20
1996 Montreal	NL	64	6	0	9	87.1	366	74	40	39	10	2	2	1	37	3	82	1	1	4	5	.444	0	0-4	9	4.02
1997 Mon-Tor		42	3	0	6	57.1	270	82	48	45	7	7	1	2	21	3	44	2	0	2	3	.400	0	1-3	3	7.06
1998 Arizona	NL	33	23	3	4	162.2	664	146	60	52	12	9	6	3	51	3	132	0	1	8	12	.400	1	0-0	1	2.88
1999 Arizona	NL	32	32	2	0	214.2	895	188	92	87	21	4	7	7	79	3	148	3	2	16	9	.640	1	0-0		3.65
1997 Montreal	NL	33	0	0	6	30.1	150	48	35	33	4	5	1	2	15	3	16	1	0	1	2	.333	0	1-3	3	9.79
Toronto	AL	9	3	0	0	27	120	34	13	12	3	2	0	0	6	0	28	1	0	1	1	.500	0	0-0	0	4.00
7 ML YEARS		270	64	5	36	591	2505	567	281	264	57	26	19	14	229	19	445	8	8	36	32	.529	2	1-9	27	4.02

Carl Dale

Pitches: Right **Bats:** Right **Pos:** RP-4   **Ht:** 6'2" **Wt:** 198 **Born:** 12/7/72 **Age:** 27

Year Team	Lg	G	GS	CG	GF	IP	BFP	H	R	ER	HR	SH	SF	HB	TBB	IBB	SO	WP	Bk	W	L	Pct.	ShO	Sv-Op	Hld	ERA
1994 New Jersey	A-	15	15	0	0	73	333	79	44	37	2	3	2	3	38	0	75	10	0	2	7	.222	0	0--		4.56
1995 Peoria	A	24	24	2	0	143.2	613	124	66	47	8	3	2	1	62	0	104	4	1	9	9	.500	1	0--		2.94
1996 Modesto	A+	26	24	0	0	128.1	565	124	79	61	11	2	5	5	72	0	102	12	0	8	2	.800	0	0--		4.28
1997 Huntsville	AA	20	16	0	2	85.1	389	95	61	51	10	1	3	8	43	0	57	4	0	6	4	.600	0	0--		5.38
1998 Huntsville	AA	3	3	0	0	13.2	60	13	7	7	2	0	2	0	8	0	10	0	0	1	1	.500	0	0--		4.61
Modesto	A+	3	3	0	0	19	74	15	6	5	1	0	0	3	2	0	14	0	0	1	2	.333	0	0--		2.37
Edmonton	AAA	11	11	1	0	64	276	64	31	29	12	1	2	6	26	0	41	3	0	5	3	.625	1	0--		4.08
1999 Vancouver	AAA	29	0	0	11	44	189	41	19	17	0	1	1	2	18	1	27	1	0	4	3	.571	0	4--		3.48
Louisville	AAA	7	0	0	2	11.2	48	8	6	6	2	0	1	0	5	0	8	0	0	0	1	.000	0	1--		4.63
1999 Milwaukee	NL	4	0	0	1	4	27	8	9	9	2	0	1	0	6	0	4	0	0	0	0	.000	0	0-0	0	20.25

Mark Dalesandro

Bats: R **Throws:** R **Pos:** C-8; PH/PR-7; DH-5; 3B-2   **Ht:** 6'0" **Wt:** 195 **Born:** 5/14/68 **Age:** 32

Year Team	Lg	G	AB	H	2B	3B	HR	(Hm	Rd)	TB	R	RBI	TBB	IBB	SO	HBP	SH	SF	SB	CS	SB%	GDP	Avg	OBP	SLG
1999 Syracuse *	AAA	20	71	16	2	0	0	(—	—)	18	3	5	1	0	7	2	0	2					.225	.250	.254
1994 California	AL	19	25	5	1	0	1	(1	0)	9	5	2	2	0	4	0	0	0	0	0	.00	2	.200	.259	.360
1995 California	AL	11	10	1	1	0	0	(0	0)	2	1	0	0	0	2	0	0	0	0	0	.00	0	.100	.100	.200
1998 Toronto	AL	32	67	20	5	0	2	(1	1)	31	8	14	1	0	6	0	0	0	0	0	.00	3	.299	.304	.463
1999 Toronto	AL	16	27	5	0	0	0	(0	0)	5	3	1	0	0	2	1	0	1	1	0	1.00	1	.185	.207	.185
4 ML YEARS		78	129	31	7	0	3	(2	1)	47	17	17	3	0	14	1	0	2	1	0	1.00	6	.240	.259	.364

Jeff D'Amico

Pitches: Right **Bats:** Right **Pos:** RP-1   **Ht:** 6'7" **Wt:** 250 **Born:** 12/27/75 **Age:** 24

Year Team	Lg	G	GS	CG	GF	IP	BFP	H	R	ER	HR	SH	SF	HB	TBB	IBB	SO	WP	Bk	W	L	Pct.	ShO	Sv-Op	Hld	ERA
1999 Beloit *	A	2	2	0	0	8	31	7	0	0	0	0	0	0	1	0	6	0	0	1	0	1.000	0	0--	—	0.00
Huntsville *	AA	1	1	0	0	2	15	6	8	8	3	0	0	1	2	0	2	0	0	0	1	.000	0	0--	—	36.00
Louisville *	AAA	1	1	0	0	3.1	15	6	5	5	0	0	0		2	0	1	0	0	0	0	.000	0	0--	—	13.50
1996 Milwaukee	AL	17	17	0	0	86	367	88	53	52	21	3	3	0	31	0	53	1	1	6	6	.500	0	0-0	0	5.44
1997 Milwaukee	AL	23	23	1	0	135.2	585	139	81	71	25	4	4	8	43	2	94	3	1	9	7	.563	1	0-0	0	4.71
1999 Milwaukee	NL	1	0	0	1	1	4	1	0	0	0	0	0	0	0	0	1	0	0	0	0	.000	0	0-0	0	0.00
3 ML YEARS		41	40	1	1	222.2	956	228	134	123	46	7	7	8	74	2	148	4	2	15	13	.536	1	0-0	0	4.97

Johnny Damon

Bats: L **Throws:** L **Pos:** LF-132; CF-8; DH-4; RF-3; PH/PR-1   **Ht:** 6'2" **Wt:** 190 **Born:** 11/5/73 **Age:** 26

Year Team	Lg	G	AB	H	2B	3B	HR	(Hm	Rd)	TB	R	RBI	TBB	IBB	SO	HBP	SH	SF	SB	CS	SB%	GDP	Avg	OBP	SLG
1995 Kansas City	AL	47	188	53	11	5	3	(1	2)	83	32	23	12	0	22	1	2	3	7	0	1.00	4	.282	.324	.441
1996 Kansas City	AL	145	517	140	22	5	6	(3	3)	190	61	50	31	3	64	3	10	5	25	5	.83	4	.271	.313	.368
1997 Kansas City	AL	146	472	130	12	8	8	(3	5)	182	70	48	42	0	70	3	6	1	16	10	.62	3	.275	.338	.386
1998 Kansas City	AL	161	642	178	30	10	18	(11	7)	282	104	66	58	4	84	4	3	3	26	12	.68	4	.277	.339	.439
1999 Kansas City	AL	145	583	179	39	9	14	(5	9)	278	101	77	67	5	50	3	3	4	36	6	.86	13	.307	.379	.477
5 ML YEARS		644	2402	680	114	37	49	(23	26)	1015	368	264	210	14	290	14	24	16	110	33	.77	26	.283	.342	.423

Pat Daneker

Pitches: Right **Bats:** Right **Pos:** SP-2; RP-1   **Ht:** 6'3" **Wt:** 195 **Born:** 1/14/76 **Age:** 24

Year Team	Lg	G	GS	CG	GF	IP	BFP	H	R	ER	HR	SH	SF	HB	TBB	IBB	SO	WP	Bk	W	L	Pct.	ShO	Sv-Op	Hld	ERA
1997 Bristol	R+	12	12	0	0	63.2	294	83	55	46	5	2	3	5	20	1	53	4	5	3	6	.333	0	0--	—	6.50
1998 Hickory	A	17	17	2	0	117	474	115	50	41	14	2	0	1	16	0	95	2	6	6	6	.500	0	0--	—	3.15
Winston-Sal	A+	7	7	2	0	53	210	51	13	12	3	2	0	2	5	1	43	1	4	5	0	1.000	0	0--	—	2.04
1999 Birmingham	AA	16	16	3	0	109	451	106	46	39	6	2	2	2	30	1	71	4	2	6	8	.429	0	0--	—	3.22
Charlotte	AAA	9	9	1	0	49.1	230	64	36	36	10	1	2	3	16	0	36	4	0	4	4	.500	0	0--	—	6.57
1999 Chicago	AL	3	2	0	1	15	64	14	8	7	1	2	1	0	6	0	5	0	0	0	0	.000	0	0-0	0	4.20

Vic Darensbourg

Pitches: Left **Bats:** Left **Pos:** RP-56   **Ht:** 5'10" **Wt:** 165 **Born:** 11/13/70 **Age:** 29

Year Team	Lg	G	GS	CG	GF	IP	BFP	H	R	ER	HR	SH	SF	HB	TBB	IBB	SO	WP	Bk	W	L	Pct.	ShO	Sv-Op	Hld	ERA
1992 Marlins	R	8	4	0	2	42	161	28	5	3	1	0	0	3	11	2	37	0	0	2	1	.667	0	2- -	—	0.64
1993 Kane County	A	46	0	0	31	71.1	300	58	17	17	3	3	3	4	28	3	89	2	0	9	1	.900	0	16- -	—	2.14
High Desert	A+	1	0	0	0	1	4	1	0	0	0	0	0	0	0	0	1	0	0	0	0	.000	0	0- -	—	0.00
1994 Portland	AA	34	21	1	9	149	631	146	76	63	18	7	4	6	60	3	103	4	2	10	7	.588	1	4- -	—	3.81
1996 Brevard Cty	A+	2	0	0	1	3	10	1	0	0	0	0	0	0	1	0	5	0	0	0	0	.000	0	0- -	—	0.00
Charlotte	AAA	47	0	0	25	63.1	280	61	30	26	7	3	2	2	32	3	66	3	1	1	5	.167	0	7- -	—	3.69
1997 Charlotte	AAA	27	0	0	6	24.2	110	22	12	12	4	2	0	2	15	3	21	1	0	4	2	.667	0	2- -	—	4.38
1999 Calgary	AAA	9	0	0	2	11.2	46	13	6	6	0	0	1	0	0	0	12	0	0	0	0	.000	0	1- -	—	4.63
1998 Florida	NL	59	0	0	10	71	287	52	29	29	5	3	3	0	30	6	74	4	0	0	7	.000	0	1-2	13	3.68
1999 Florida	NL	56	0	0	5	34.2	180	50	36	34	3	5	2	5	21	1	16	1	3	0	1	.000	0	0-1	10	8.83
2 ML YEARS		115	0	0	15	105.2	467	102	65	63	8	8	5	5	51	7	90	5	3	0	8	.000	0	1-3	23	5.37

Mike Darr

Bats: Left **Throws:** Right **Pos:** RF-21; PH/PR-6; CF-3   **Ht:** 6'3" **Wt:** 205 **Born:** 3/21/76 **Age:** 24

Year Team	Lg	G	AB	H	2B	3B	HR	(Hm	Rd)	TB	R	RBI	TBB	IBB	SO	HBP	SH	SF	SB	CS	SB%	GDP	Avg	OBP	SLG
1994 Bristol	R+	44	149	41	6	0	1	—	—	50	23	18	23	1	22	1	0	0	4	4	.50	3	.275	.376	.336
1995 Fayetteville	A	112	395	114	21	2	5	—	—	154	58	66	58	2	88	4	0	6	5	2	.71	5	.289	.380	.390
1996 Lakeland	A+	85	311	77	14	7	0	—	—	105	26	38	28	0	64	0	0	3	7	3	.70	7	.248	.307	.338
1997 Rancho Cuca	A+	134	521	179	32	11	15	—	—	278	104	94	57	1	90	4	0	5	23	7	.77	19	.344	.409	.534
1998 Mobile	AA	132	523	162	41	4	6	—	—	229	105	90	62	2	79	5	1	5	28	8	.78	18	.310	.385	.438
1999 Las Vegas	AAA	100	383	114	34	0	10	—	—	178	57	62	50	0	103	4	0	2	10	3	.77	11	.298	.384	.465
1999 San Diego	NL	25	48	13	1	0	2	(1	1)	20	6	3	5	0	18	0	0	0	2	1	.67	1	.271	.340	.417

Brian Daubach

Bats: L **Throws:** R **Pos:** 1B-61; DH-43; PH/PR-12; LF-2; 3B-1   **Ht:** 6'1" **Wt:** 201 **Born:** 2/11/72 **Age:** 28

Year Team	Lg	G	AB	H	2B	3B	HR	(Hm	Rd)	TB	R	RBI	TBB	IBB	SO	HBP	SH	SF	SB	CS	SB%	GDP	Avg	OBP	SLG
1990 Mets	R	45	152	41	8	4	1	—	—	60	26	19	22	0	41	2	0	3	2	1	.67	2	.270	.363	.395
1991 Kingsport	R+	65	217	52	9	1	7	—	—	84	30	42	33	5	64	6	1	2	1	3	.25	1	.240	.353	.387
1992 Pittsfield	A-	72	260	63	15	2	2	—	—	88	26	40	30	2	61	3	1	4	4	0	1.00	5	.242	.323	.338
1993 Capital Cty	A	102	379	106	19	3	7	—	—	152	50	72	52	5	84	5	1	7	6	1	.86	14	.280	.368	.401
1994 St. Lucie	A+	129	450	123	30	2	6	—	—	175	52	74	58	5	120	5	3	4	14	9	.61	3	.273	.360	.389
1995 Binghamton	AA	135	469	115	25	2	10	—	—	174	61	72	51	5	104	7	1	7	6	2	.75	5	.245	.324	.371
Norfolk	AAA	2	7	0	0	0	0	—	—	0	0	0	2	1	0	0	0	0	0	0	.00	0	.000	.222	.000
1996 Norfolk	AAA	17	54	11	2	0	0	—	—	13	7	6	6	0	14	0	0	1	1	1	.50	1	.204	.279	.241
Binghamton	AA	122	436	129	24	1	22	—	—	221	80	76	74	9	103	7	0	4	7	9	.44	8	.296	.403	.507
1997 Charlotte	AAA	136	461	128	40	2	21	—	—	235	66	93	65	4	126	6	1	10	1	8	.11	7	.278	.367	.510
1998 Charlotte	AAA	140	497	157	45	4	35	—	—	315	102	124	80	9	114	15	0	7	9	3	.75	15	.316	.421	.634
1999 Pawtucket	AAA	9	31	9	2	0	1	—	—	14	4	6	6	0	8	2	0	0	0	0	.00	0	.290	.436	.452
1998 Florida	NL	10	15	3	1	0	0	(0	0)	4	0	3	1	0	5	1	0	0	0	0	.00	0	.200	.294	.267
1999 Boston	AL	110	381	112	33	3	21	(11	10)	214	61	73	36	0	92	3	0	5	0	1	.00	5	.294	.360	.562
2 ML YEARS		120	396	115	34	3	21	(11	10)	218	61	76	37	0	97	4	0	5	0	1	.00	5	.290	.357	.551

Jeff DaVanon

Bats: B **Throws:** R **Pos:** LF-3; DH-2; RF-2; PH/PR-1   **Ht:** 6'0" **Wt:** 185 **Born:** 12/8/73 **Age:** 26

Year Team	Lg	G	AB	H	2B	3B	HR	(Hm	Rd)	TB	R	RBI	TBB	IBB	SO	HBP	SH	SF	SB	CS	SB%	GDP	Avg	OBP	SLG
1995 Sou Oregon	A-	57	167	42	6	2	1	—	—	55	29	17	34	0	49	0	5	1	6	5	.55	1	.251	.376	.329
1996 W Michigan	A	89	289	70	13	4	2	—	—	97	43	33	49	2	66	1	2	1	5	7	.42	6	.242	.353	.336
1997 Visalia	A+	119	408	104	17	3	6	—	—	145	70	38	81	1	101	0	10	2	23	14	.62	7	.255	.377	.355
1998 Modesto	A+	84	301	101	17	4	5	—	—	141	66	60	59	1	69	1	0	6	33	10	.77	4	.336	.439	.468
1999 Midland	AA	100	374	128	29	11	11	—	—	212	87	60	53	3	68	4	4	5	18	10	.64	6	.342	.424	.567
Edmonton	AAA	34	132	43	8	3	6	—	—	75	35	19	20	0	27	1	1	1	11	4	.73	1	.326	.416	.568
1999 Anaheim	AL	7	20	4	0	1	1	(1	0)	9	4	4	2	0	7	0	0	0	0	1	.00	0	.200	.273	.450

Joe Davenport

Pitches: Right **Bats:** Right **Pos:** RP-3   **Ht:** 6'5" **Wt:** 225 **Born:** 3/24/76 **Age:** 24

Year Team	Lg	G	GS	CG	GF	IP	BFP	H	R	ER	HR	SH	SF	HB	TBB	IBB	SO	WP	Bk	W	L	Pct.	ShO	Sv-Op	Hld	ERA
1994 Blue Jays	R	7	1	0	2	11	48	12	5	4	0	0	1	1	7	0	2	1	1	0	0	.000	0	0- -	—	3.27
1995 Hagerstown	A	13	0	0	2	17.2	91	22	19	12	3	0	0	1	13	0	13	6	0	0	1	.000	0	0- -	—	6.11
Blue Jays	R	15	10	1	1	55.2	267	67	47	35	2	3	2	3	30	0	29	9	3	2	3	.400	0	1- -	—	5.66
1996 St.Cathrnes	A-	20	8	0	3	66.2	295	71	44	38	5	4	3	5	23	0	43	8	0	2	4	.333	0	0- -	—	5.13
1997 Hagerstown	A	37	0	0	29	51.1	225	43	26	21	0	4	1	4	24	2	43	8	0	4	6	.400	0	10- -	—	3.68
1998 Winston-Sal	A+	20	0	0	15	26	106	25	9	4	0	0	1	2	4	0	26	3	0	2	0	1.000	0	2- -	—	1.38
Birmingham	AA	26	0	0	15	38.2	202	54	36	31	2	1	4	2	30	0	22	5	0	3	2	.600	0	1- -	—	7.22
1999 Charlotte	AAA	6	0	0	0	9	40	13	8	8	0	0	0	1	1	0	6	0	0	0	0	.000	0	0- -	—	8.00
Birmingham	AA	40	0	0	33	49.1	213	43	26	17	3	4	3	2	19	1	24	8	0	3	5	.375	0	10- -	—	3.10
1999 Chicago	AL	3	0	0	2	1.2	7	1	0	0	0	0	0	0	2	0	0	0	0	0	0	.000	0	0-0	0	0.00

Tom Davey

Pitches: Right **Bats:** Right **Pos:** RP-45 — **Ht:** 6'7" **Wt:** 230 **Born:** 9/11/73 **Age:** 26

		HOW MUCH HE PITCHED				WHAT HE GAVE UP					THE RESULTS			
Year Team	Lg	G GS CG GF	IP	BFP	H R ER HR SH SF HB	TBB IBB	SO WP Bk	W L Pct. ShO Sv-Op Hld	ERA
1994 Medcine Hat	R+	14 14 0 0	65	318	76 59 37 3 2 2 3	59 0	35 11 0	2 8 .200 0 0- —	5.12
1995 St.Cathrnes	A-	7 7 0 0	38	160	27 19 14 2 0 2 3	21 0	29 3 1	4 3 .571 0 0- —	3.32
Hagerstown	A	8 8 0 0	37.1	167	29 23 14 2 1 1 2	31 0	25 9 0	4 1 .800 0 0- —	3.38
1996 Hagerstown	A	26 26 2 0	155.2	675	132 76 67 7 5 5 15	91 0	98 15 1	10 9 .526 1 0- —	3.87
1997 Dunedin	A+	7 6 0 0	39.2	172	44 21 19 4 0 0 2	15 0	36 5 1	1 3 .250 0 0- —	4.31
Knoxville	AA	20 16 0 1	92.2	429	108 65 60 5 1 1 6	50 0	72 14 0	6 7 .462 0 0- —	5.83
1998 Knoxville	AA	48 9 0 32	76.2	348	70 35 33 2 3 2 3	52 3	78 9 1	5 3 .625 0 16-- —	3.87
1999 Syracuse	AAA	6 6 0 0	33.2	144	30 15 13 1 2 1 3	19 0	20 3 0	2 2 .333 0 0- —	3.48
1999 Tor-Sea	AL	45 0 0 15	65	298	62 41 34 5 1 2 7	40 1	59 6 0	2 1 .667 0 1-1 4	4.71
1999 Toronto	AL	29 0 0 10	44	198	40 28 23 5 1 2 3	26 0	42 6 0	1 1 .500 0 1-1 3	4.70
Seattle	AL	16 0 0 5	21	100	22 13 11 0 0 0 4	14 1	17 0 0	1 0 1.000 0 0-0 1	4.71

Cleatus Davidson

Bats: B **Throws:** R **Pos:** 2B-6; SS-4; PH/PR-4; DH-1 — **Ht:** 5'10" **Wt:** 170 **Born:** 11/1/76 **Age:** 23

		BATTING													BASERUNNING		PERCENTAGES	
Year Team	Lg	G AB H 2B 3B HR (Hm Rd) TB	R RBI TBB IBB SO HBP SH SF	SB CS SB% GDP	Avg OBP SLG
1994 Twins	R	24 85 15 1 0 0 — — 16	8 5 9 0 19 0 1 1	3 1 .75 0	.176 .253 .188
1995 Twins	R	21 75 15 2 1 0 — — 19	11 5 10 0 17 0 0 0	8 3 .73 0	.200 .294 .253
Elizabethtn	R+	39 152 45 6 2 3 — — 64	27 27 11 0 31 3 0 0	10 4 .71 2	.296 .355 .421
1996 Fort Wayne	A	59 203 36 8 3 0 — — 50	20 30 23 0 45 0 1 2	2 3 .40 4	.177 .259 .246
Elizabethtn	R+	65 248 71 10 6 6 — — 111	53 31 39 2 45 2 3 1	17 6 .74 5	.286 .386 .448
1997 Fort Wayne	A	124 478 122 16 8 6 — — 172	80 52 52 1 100 1 5 4	39 9 .81 7	.255 .327 .360
1998 Fort Myers	A+	130 527 127 12 7 2 — — 159	97 45 45 0 99 3 13 3	44 16 .73 6	.241 .303 .302
1999 New Britain	AA	127 491 120 16 10 2 — — 162	88 40 53 1 110 3 10 6	40 14 .74 8	.244 .318 .330
1999 Minnesota	AL	12 22 3 0 0 0 (0 0) 3	3 3 0 0 4 0 2 0	2 0 1.00 2	.136 .136 .136

Ben Davis

Bats: Both **Throws:** Right **Pos:** C-74; PH/PR-2 — **Ht:** 6'4" **Wt:** 215 **Born:** 3/10/77 **Age:** 23

		BATTING													BASERUNNING		PERCENTAGES	
Year Team	Lg	G AB H 2B 3B HR (Hm Rd) TB	R RBI TBB IBB SO HBP SH SF	SB CS SB% GDP	Avg OBP SLG
1995 Idaho Falls	R+	52 197 55 8 3 5 — — 84	36 46 17 1 36 1 3 1	0 0 .00 3	.279 .338 .426
1996 Rancho Cuca	A+	98 353 71 10 1 6 — — 101	35 41 31 0 89 0 4 2	1 1 .50 8	.201 .264 .286
1997 Rancho Cuca	A+	122 474 132 30 1 17 — — 215	67 76 28 2 107 2 2 3	3 1 .75 11	.278 .320 .454
1998 Mobile	AA	116 433 124 29 2 14 — — 199	65 75 42 3 60 6 1 7	4 2 .67 11	.286 .352 .460
1999 Las Vegas	AAA	58 201 62 18 1 7 — — 103	27 44 24 1 41 2 0 2	4 1 .80 5	.308 .384 .512
1998 San Diego	NL	1 1 0 0 0 0 (0 0) 0	0 0 0 0 0 0 0 0	0 0 .00 0	.000 .000 .000
1999 San Diego	NL	76 266 65 14 1 5 (1 4) 96	29 30 25 3 70 0 0 2	2 1 .67 9	.244 .307 .361
2 ML YEARS		77 267 65 14 1 5 (1 4) 96	29 30 25 3 70 0 0 2	2 1 .67 9	.243 .306 .360

Chili Davis

Bats: Both **Throws:** Right **Pos:** DH-132; PH/PR-19 — **Ht:** 6'3" **Wt:** 240 **Born:** 1/17/60 **Age:** 40

		BATTING													BASERUNNING		PERCENTAGES	
Year Team	Lg	G AB H 2B 3B HR (Hm Rd) TB	R RBI TBB IBB SO HBP SH SF	SB CS SB% GDP	Avg OBP SLG
1981 San Francisco	NL	8 15 2 0 0 0 (0 0) 2	1 0 1 0 2 0 0 0	2 0 1.00 1	.133 .188 .133
1982 San Francisco	NL	154 641 167 27 6 19 (6 13) 263	86 76 45 2 115 2 7 6	24 13 .65 13	.261 .308 .410
1983 San Francisco	NL	137 486 113 21 2 11 (7 4) 171	54 59 55 6 108 0 3 9	10 12 .45 9	.233 .305 .352
1984 San Francisco	NL	137 499 157 21 6 21 (7 14) 253	87 81 42 6 74 1 2 2	12 8 .60 13	.315 .368 .507
1985 San Francisco	NL	136 481 130 25 2 13 (7 6) 198	53 56 62 12 74 0 1 7	15 7 .68 16	.270 .349 .412
1986 San Francisco	NL	153 526 146 28 3 13 (7 6) 219	71 70 84 23 96 1 2 5	16 13 .55 11	.278 .375 .416
1987 San Francisco	NL	149 500 125 22 1 24 (9 15) 221	80 76 72 15 109 2 0 4	16 9 .64 8	.250 .344 .442
1988 California	AL	158 600 161 29 3 21 (11 10) 259	81 93 56 14 118 0 1 10	9 10 .47 13	.268 .326 .432
1989 California	AL	154 560 152 24 1 22 (6 16) 244	81 90 61 12 109 0 3 6	3 0 1.00 21	.271 .340 .436
1990 California	AL	113 412 109 17 1 12 (10 2) 164	58 58 61 4 89 0 0 3	1 2 .33 14	.265 .357 .398
1991 Minnesota	AL	153 534 148 34 1 29 (14 15) 271	84 93 95 13 117 1 0 4	5 6 .45 9	.277 .385 .507
1992 Minnesota	AL	138 444 128 27 2 12 (6 6) 195	63 66 73 11 76 3 0 9	4 5 .44 11	.288 .386 .439
1993 California	AL	153 573 139 32 0 27 (13 14) 252	74 112 71 12 135 1 0 0	4 1 .80 18	.243 .327 .440
1994 California	AL	108 392 122 18 1 26 (14 12) 220	72 84 69 11 84 1 0 6	3 2 .60 12	.311 .410 .561
1995 California	AL	119 424 135 23 0 20 (11 9) 218	81 86 89 12 79 0 0 9	3 3 .50 12	.318 .429 .514
1996 California	AL	145 530 155 24 0 28 (15 13) 263	73 95 86 11 99 0 1 6	5 2 .71 18	.292 .387 .496
1997 Kansas City	AL	140 477 133 20 0 30 (21 9) 243	71 90 85 16 96 1 0 4	6 3 .67 15	.279 .386 .509
1998 New York	AL	35 103 30 7 0 3 (1 2) 46	11 9 14 1 18 0 0 1	0 1 .00 6	.291 .373 .447
1999 New York	AL	146 476 128 25 1 19 (12 7) 212	59 78 73 7 100 2 0 3	4 1 .80 12	.269 .366 .445
19 ML YEARS		2436 8673 2380 424 30 350 (177 173) 3914	1240 1372 1194 188 1698 15 20 94	142 98 .59 232	.274 .360 .451

Doug Davis

Pitches: Left **Bats:** Right **Pos:** RP-2 — **Ht:** 6'3" **Wt:** 185 **Born:** 9/21/75 **Age:** 24

		HOW MUCH HE PITCHED				WHAT HE GAVE UP					THE RESULTS			
Year Team	Lg	G GS CG GF	IP	BFP	H R ER HR SH SF HB	TBB IBB	SO WP Bk	W L Pct. ShO Sv-Op Hld	ERA
1996 Rangers	R	8 7 0 0	42.2	174	28 13 9 0 1 2 0	26 1	49 2 2	3 1 .750 0 0-- —	1.90
1997 Rangers	R	4 4 0 0	21	88	14 5 4 0 0 1 2	15 0	27 1 1	3 1 .750 0 0-- —	1.71

Year Team	Lg	G	GS	CG	GF	IP	BFP	H	R	ER	HR	SH	SF	HB	TBB	IBB	SO	WP	Bk	W	L	Pct.	ShO	Sv-Op	Hld	ERA
Charlotte	A+	9	8	1	0	49.1	205	29	19	17	2	4	2	0	33	1	52	8	3	5	3	.625	0	0- -	—	3.10
1998 Charlotte	A+	27	27	1	0	155.1	665	129	69	56	8	1	3	13	74	0	173	8	0	11	7	.611	1	0- -	—	3.24
1999 Tulsa	AA	12	12	1	0	74.1	305	65	26	20	9	1	0	2	25	0	79	2	1	4	4	.500	0	0- -	—	2.42
Oklahoma	AAA	13	11	0	0	78	330	77	27	26	4	3	1	2	31	0	74	2	0	7	0	1.000	0	0- -	—	3.00
1999 Texas	AL	2	0	0	0	2.2	20	12	10	10	3	0	0	0	0	0	3	0	0	0	0	.000	0	0-0	0	33.75

Eric Davis

Bats: R **Throws:** R **Pos:** RF-50; PH/PR-7; CF-3; DH-2   **Ht:** 6'3" **Wt:** 200 **Born:** 5/29/62 **Age:** 38

								BATTING										BASERUNNING				PERCENTAGES		
Year Team	Lg	G	AB	H	2B	3B	HR	(Hm | Rd)	TB	R	RBI	TBB	IBB	SO	HBP	SH	SF	SB	CS	SB%	GDP	Avg	OBP	SLG
1984 Cincinnati	NL	57	174	39	10	1	10	(3 | 7)	81	33	30	24	0	48	1	0	1	10	2	.83	1	.224	.320	.466
1985 Cincinnati	NL	56	122	30	3	3	8	(1 | 7)	63	26	18	7	0	39	0	2	0	16	3	.84	1	.246	.287	.516
1986 Cincinnati	NL	132	415	115	15	3	27	(12 | 15)	217	97	71	68	5	100	1	0	3	80	11	.88	6	.277	.378	.523
1987 Cincinnati	NL	129	474	139	23	4	37	(17 | 20)	281	120	100	84	8	134	1	0	3	50	6	.89	6	.293	.399	.593
1988 Cincinnati	NL	135	472	129	18	3	26	(14 | 12)	231	81	93	65	10	124	3	0	3	35	3	.92	11	.273	.363	.489
1989 Cincinnati	NL	131	462	130	14	2	34	(15 | 19)	250	74	101	68	12	116	1	0	11	21	7	.75	16	.281	.367	.541
1990 Cincinnati	NL	127	453	118	26	2	24	(13 | 11)	220	84	86	60	6	100	2	0	3	21	3	.88	7	.260	.347	.486
1991 Cincinnati	NL	89	285	67	10	0	11	(5 | 6)	110	39	33	48	5	92	5	0	2	14	2	.88	4	.235	.353	.386
1992 Los Angeles	NL	76	267	61	8	1	5	(1 | 4)	86	21	32	36	2	71	3	0	2	19	1	.95	9	.228	.325	.322
1993 LA-Det		131	451	107	18	1	20	(10 | 10)	187	71	68	55	7	106	1	0	4	35	7	.83	12	.237	.319	.415
1994 Detroit	AL	37	120	22	4	0	3	(3 | 0)	35	19	13	18	0	45	0	0	0	5	0	1.00	4	.183	.290	.292
1996 Cincinnati	NL	129	415	119	20	0	26	(8 | 18)	217	81	83	70	3	121	6	1	4	23	9	.72	8	.287	.394	.523
1997 Baltimore	AL	42	158	48	11	0	8	(1 | 7)	83	29	25	14	0	47	1	0	3	6	0	1.00	1	.304	.358	.525
1998 Baltimore	AL	131	452	148	29	1	28	(16 | 12)	263	81	89	44	0	108	5	0	7	7	6	.54	13	.327	.388	.582
1999 St. Louis	NL	58	191	49	9	2	5	(2 | 3)	77	27	30	30	1	49	1	0	1	5	4	.56	1	.257	.359	.403
1993 Los Angeles	NL	108	376	88	17	0	14	(7 | 7)	147	57	53	41	6	88	1	0	4	33	5	.87	8	.234	.308	.391
Detroit	AL	23	75	19	1	1	6	(3 | 3)	40	14	15	14	1	18	0	0	0	2	2	.50	4	.253	.371	.533
15 ML YEARS		1460	4911	1321	218	23	272	(127 | 145)	2401	883	872	691	59	1300	31	3	47	347	64	.84	101	.269	.360	.489

Russ Davis

Bats: Right **Throws:** Right **Pos:** 3B-124; SS-2; PH/PR-1   **Ht:** 6'0" **Wt:** 195 **Born:** 9/13/69 **Age:** 30

								BATTING										BASERUNNING				PERCENTAGES		
Year Team	Lg	G	AB	H	2B	3B	HR	(Hm | Rd)	TB	R	RBI	TBB	IBB	SO	HBP	SH	SF	SB	CS	SB%	GDP	Avg	OBP	SLG
1994 New York	AL	4	14	2	0	0	0	(0 | 0)	2	0	1	0	0	4	0	0	0	0	0	.00	1	.143	.143	.143
1995 New York	AL	40	98	27	5	2	2	(2 | 0)	42	14	12	10	0	26	1	0	0	0	0	.00	0	.276	.349	.429
1996 Seattle	AL	51	167	39	9	0	5	(3 | 2)	63	24	18	17	1	50	2	4	0	2	0	1.00	1	.234	.312	.377
1997 Seattle	AL	119	420	114	29	1	20	(11 | 9)	205	57	63	27	2	100	2	3	2	6	2	.75	11	.271	.317	.488
1998 Seattle	AL	141	502	130	30	1	20	(7 | 13)	222	68	82	34	1	134	3	2	9	4	3	.57	10	.259	.305	.442
1999 Seattle	AL	124	432	106	17	1	21	(12 | 9)	188	55	59	32	1	111	5	7	2	3	3	.50	13	.245	.304	.435
6 ML YEARS		479	1633	418	90	5	68	(35 | 33)	722	218	235	120	5	425	13	16	13	15	8	.65	36	.256	.310	.442

Tommy Davis

Bats: Right **Throws:** Right **Pos:** C-4; 1B-1; PH/PR-1   **Ht:** 6'1" **Wt:** 195 **Born:** 5/21/73 **Age:** 27

								BATTING										BASERUNNING				PERCENTAGES		
Year Team	Lg	G	AB	H	2B	3B	HR	(Hm | Rd)	TB	R	RBI	TBB	IBB	SO	HBP	SH	SF	SB	CS	SB%	GDP	Avg	OBP	SLG
1994 Albany	A	61	216	59	10	1	5	—	—	86	35	35	18	0	52	2	0	3	2	4	.33	6	.273	.331	.398
1995 Frederick	A+	130	496	133	26	3	15	—	—	210	62	57	41	7	105	4	1	3	7	1	.88	14	.268	.327	.423
Bowie	AA	9	32	10	3	0	3	—	—	22	5	10	1	0	9	1	0	0	0	0	.00	1	.313	.353	.688
1996 Bowie	AA	137	524	137	32	2	14	—	—	215	75	54	41	4	113	10	3	3	5	8	.38	16	.261	.325	.410
1997 Rochester	AAA	119	438	133	22	2	15	—	—	204	74	62	43	2	90	2	3	1	6	1	.86	16	.304	.368	.466
1998 Bowie	AA	37	132	37	11	0	1	—	—	51	12	15	13	2	27	3	0	1	0	0	.00	1	.280	.356	.386
1999 Rochester	AAA	110	413	106	18	0	11	—	—	157	49	56	24	2	65	0	2	4	1	4	.20	11	.257	.295	.380
1999 Baltimore	AL	5	6	1	0	0	0	(0 | 0)	1	0	0	0	0	2	0	0	0	0	0	.00	1	.167	.167	.167

Travis Dawkins

Bats: Right **Throws:** Right **Pos:** SS-7; PH/PR-3   **Ht:** 6'1" **Wt:** 180 **Born:** 5/12/79 **Age:** 21

								BATTING										BASERUNNING				PERCENTAGES		
Year Team	Lg	G	AB	H	2B	3B	HR	(Hm | Rd)	TB	R	RBI	TBB	IBB	SO	HBP	SH	SF	SB	CS	SB%	GDP	Avg	OBP	SLG
1997 Billings	R+	70	253	61	5	0	4	—	—	78	47	37	30	0	38	0	3	6	16	6	.73	6	.241	.315	.308
1998 Burlington	A	102	367	97	7	6	1	—	—	119	52	30	37	0	60	1	2	2	37	10	.79	10	.264	.332	.324
1999 Rockford	A	76	305	83	10	6	8	—	—	129	56	32	35	2	38	0	1	1	38	13	.75	5	.272	.346	.423
Chattanooga	AA	32	129	47	7	0	2	—	—	60	24	13	14	0	17	0	2	0	15	5	.75	5	.364	.427	.465
1999 Cincinnati	NL	7	7	1	0	0	0	(0 | 0)	1	1	0	0	0	4	1	0	0	0	0	.00	0	.143	.250	.143

Steve Decker

Bats: R **Throws:** R **Pos:** C-17; 1B-6; DH-3; PH/PR-3   **Ht:** 6'3" **Wt:** 205 **Born:** 10/25/65 **Age:** 34

								BATTING										BASERUNNING				PERCENTAGES		
Year Team	Lg	G	AB	H	2B	3B	HR	(Hm | Rd)	TB	R	RBI	TBB	IBB	SO	HBP	SH	SF	SB	CS	SB%	GDP	Avg	OBP	SLG
1999 Edmonton *	AAA	64	225	64	19	2	15			132	51	51	46	3	38	3	0	7	0	0	.00	7	.284	.406	.587
1990 San Francisco	NL	15	54	16	2	0	3	(1 | 2)	27	5	8	1	0	10	0	1	0	0	0	.00	0	.296	.309	.500
1991 San Francisco	NL	79	233	48	7	1	5	(4 | 1)	72	11	24	16	1	44	3	2	4	0	1	.00	7	.206	.262	.309

Year Team	Lg	G	AB	H	2B	3B	HR	(Hm	Rd)	TB	R	RBI	TBB	IBB	SO	HBP	SH	SF	SB	CS	SB%	GDP	Avg	OBP	SLG
1992 San Francisco	NL	15	43	7	1	0	0	(0	0)	8	3	1	6	0	7	1	0	0	0	0	.00	0	.163	.280	.186
1993 Florida	NL	8	15	0	0	0	0	(0	0)	0	0	1	3	0	3	0	0	1	0	0	.00	0	.000	.158	.000
1995 Florida	NL	51	133	30	2	1	3	(2	1)	43	12	13	19	1	22	0	0	2	1	0	1.00	1	.226	.318	.323
1996 SF-Col	NL	67	147	36	3	0	2	(1	1)	45	24	20	18	4	29	0	4	2	1	0	1.00	3	.245	.323	.306
1999 Anaheim	AL	28	63	15	6	0	0	(0	0)	21	5	5	13	0	9	1	1	0	0	0	.00	4	.238	.372	.333
1996 San Francisco	NL	57	122	28	1	0	1	(0	0)	32	16	12	15	4	26	0	3	2	0	0	.00	3	.230	.309	.262
Colorado	NL	10	25	8	2	0	1	(1	0)	13	8	8	3	0	3	0	1	0	1	0	1.00	0	.320	.393	.520
7 ML YEARS		263	688	152	21	2	13	(8	5)	216	60	72	76	6	124	5	8	10	2	1	.67	18	.221	.299	.314

Rick DeHart

Pitches: Left Bats: Left Pos: RP-3

Ht: 6'1" Wt: 190 Born: 3/21/70 Age: 30

Year Team	Lg	G	GS	CG	GF	IP	BFP	H	R	ER	HR	SH	SF	HB	TBB	IBB	SO	WP	Bk	W	L	Pct.	ShO	Sv-Op	Hld	ERA
1999 Ottawa *	AAA	15	2	0	5	26.1	127	33	19	14	4	3	0	2	11	1	22	1	0	2	4	.333	0	0--	—	4.78
1997 Montreal	NL	23	0	0	7	29.1	130	33	21	18	7	1	2	0	14	4	29	2	0	2	1	.667	0	0-1	1	5.52
1998 Montreal	NL	26	0	0	6	28	134	34	22	15	3	3	1	0	13	1	14	1	1	0	0	.000	0	1-2	4	4.82
1999 Montreal	NL	3	0	0	0	1.2	14	6	4	4	2	0	0	1	3	1	1	0	0	0	0	.000	0	0-0	1	21.60
3 ML YEARS		52	0	0	13	59	278	73	47	37	12	4	3	0	30	6	44	3	1	2	1	.667	0	1-3	6	5.64

Mike DeJean

Pitches: Right Bats: Right Pos: RP-56

Ht: 6'2" Wt: 212 Born: 9/28/70 Age: 29

Year Team	Lg	G	GS	CG	GF	IP	BFP	H	R	ER	HR	SH	SF	HB	TBB	IBB	SO	WP	Bk	W	L	Pct.	ShO	Sv-Op	Hld	ERA
1999 Colo Spngs *	AAA	1	0	0	0	1	3	1	0	0	0	0	0	0	0	0	0	0	0	0	0	.000	0	0--	—	0.00
1997 Colorado	NL	55	0	0	15	67.2	295	74	34	30	4	3	1	3	24	2	38	2	0	5	0	1.000	0	2-4	13	3.99
1998 Colorado	NL	59	1	0	9	74.1	307	78	29	25	4	4	4	1	24	1	27	3	0	3	1	.750	0	2-3	11	3.03
1999 Colorado	NL	56	0	0	17	61	288	83	61	57	13	3	3	2	32	8	31	3	0	2	4	.333	0	0-4	9	8.41
3 ML YEARS		170	1	0	41	203	890	235	124	112	21	10	8	6	80	11	96	8	0	10	5	.667	0	4-11	33	4.97

Carlos Delgado

Bats: Left Throws: Right Pos: 1B-147; DH-5

Ht: 6'3" Wt: 225 Born: 6/25/72 Age: 28

Year Team	Lg	G	AB	H	2B	3B	HR	(Hm	Rd)	TB	R	RBI	TBB	IBB	SO	HBP	SH	SF	SB	CS	SB%	GDP	Avg	OBP	SLG
1993 Toronto	AL	2	1	0	0	0	0	(0	0)	0	0	0	1	0	0	0	0	0	0	0	.00	0	.000	.500	.000
1994 Toronto	AL	43	130	28	2	0	9	(5	4)	57	17	24	25	4	46	3	0	1	1	1	.50	5	.215	.352	.438
1995 Toronto	AL	37	91	15	3	0	3	(2	1)	27	7	11	6	0	26	0	0	2	0	0	.00	1	.165	.212	.297
1996 Toronto	AL	138	488	132	28	2	25	(12	13)	239	68	92	58	2	139	9	0	8	0	0	.00	13	.270	.353	.490
1997 Toronto	AL	153	519	136	42	3	30	(17	13)	274	79	91	64	9	133	8	0	4	0	3	.00	6	.262	.350	.528
1998 Toronto	AL	142	530	155	43	1	38	(20	18)	314	94	115	73	13	139	11	0	6	3	1	1.00	8	.292	.385	.592
1999 Toronto	AL	152	573	156	39	0	44	(17	27)	327	113	134	86	7	141	15	0	7	1	1	.50	11	.272	.377	.571
7 ML YEARS		667	2332	622	157	6	149	(73	76)	1238	378	467	313	35	624	46	0	28	5	5	.50	44	.267	.361	.531

Wilson Delgado

Bats: Both Throws: Right Pos: SS-20; 2B-15; PH/PR-7

Ht: 5'11" Wt: 165 Born: 7/15/75 Age: 24

Year Team	Lg	G	AB	H	2B	3B	HR	(Hm	Rd)	TB	R	RBI	TBB	IBB	SO	HBP	SH	SF	SB	CS	SB%	GDP	Avg	OBP	SLG
1994 Mariners	R	39	149	56	5	4	0	—	—	69	30	10	15	0	24	1	0	0	13	5	.72	2	.376	.436	.463
Appleton	A	9	31	6	0	0	0	—	—	6	2	0	0	0	8	0	0	0	0	0	.00	0	.194	.194	.194
1995 Port City	AA	13	41	8	4	0	0	—	—	12	3	1	6	0	8	0	0	0	0	0	.00	1	.195	.298	.293
Wisconsin	A	19	70	17	3	0	0	—	—	20	13	7	3	0	15	0	2	0	3	0	1.00	5	.243	.274	.286
Burlington	A	93	365	113	20	3	5	—	—	154	52	37	32	1	57	2	2	1	9	9	.50	7	.310	.368	.422
San Jose	A+	1	2	0	0	0	0	—	—	0	1	0	0	0	0	0	0	0	0	0	.00	0	.000	.000	.000
1996 San Jose	A+	121	462	124	19	6	2	—	—	161	59	54	48	0	89	2	4	4	8	2	.80	8	.268	.337	.348
Phoenix	AAA	12	43	6	0	1	0	—	—	8	1	1	3	1	7	0	0	0	0	1	.00	1	.140	.196	.186
1997 Phoenix	AAA	119	416	120	22	4	9	—	—	177	47	59	24	4	70	1	6	4	9	3	.75	9	.288	.326	.425
1998 Fresno	AAA	127	512	142	22	5	9	—	—	204	87	63	52	2	92	3	4	4	9	5	.64	6	.277	.345	.390
1999 Fresno	AAA	57	213	64	10	3	1	—	—	83	28	33	18	1	35	0	3	0	4	2	.67	8	.300	.355	.390
1996 San Francisco	NL	6	22	8	0	0	0	(0	0)	8	3	2	1	0	5	2	0	0	1	0	1.00	0	.364	.440	.364
1997 San Francisco	NL	8	7	1	1	0	0	(0	0)	2	1	0	0	0	2	0	1	0	0	0	.00	0	.143	.143	.286
1998 San Francisco	NL	10	12	2	1	0	0	(0	0)	3	1	1	1	0	3	0	0	0	0	0	.00	2	.167	.231	.250
1999 San Francisco	NL	35	71	18	2	1	0	(0	0)	22	7	3	5	1	9	1	1	0	1	0	1.00	2	.254	.312	.310
4 ML YEARS		59	112	29	4	1	0			35	12	6	7	1	19	3	2	0	2	0	1.00	2	.259	.320	.313

Jason Dellaero

Bats: Both Throws: Right Pos: SS-11

Ht: 6'2" Wt: 195 Born: 12/17/76 Age: 23

Year Team	Lg	G	AB	H	2B	3B	HR	(Hm	Rd)	TB	R	RBI	TBB	IBB	SO	HBP	SH	SF	SB	CS	SB%	GDP	Avg	OBP	SLG
1997 White Sox	R	5	15	3	2	0	0	—	—	5	1	1	1	0	2	0	0	1	0	0	.00	1	.200	.235	.333
Hickory	A	55	191	53	10	3	6	—	—	87	37	29	17	0	49	3	0	3	3	1	.75	4	.277	.341	.455
1998 Winston-Sal	A+	121	428	89	23	3	10	—	—	148	45	49	25	2	147	5	3	2	12	4	.75	5	.208	.259	.346
1999 Winston-Sal	A+	54	184	41	13	0	2	—	—	60	22	19	18	1	59	3	4	0	9	4	.69	2	.223	.302	.326

Year Team	Lg	G	AB	H	2B	3B	HR	(Hm	Rd)	TB	R	RBI	TBB	IBB	SO	HBP	SH	SF	SB	CS	SB%	GDP	Avg	OBP	SLG
Birmingham	AA	81	272	73	13	3	10	—	—	122	40	44	14	0	76	3	8	3	6	8	.43	5	.268	.308	.449
1999 Chicago	AL	11	33	3	0	0	0	(0	0)	3	1	2	1	0	13	0	0	1	0	0	.00	0	.091	.114	.091

David Dellucci

Bats: L **Throws:** L **Pos:** PH/PR-40; RF-19; LF-13; CF-4; DH-1   **Ht:** 5'10" **Wt:** 194 **Born:** 10/31/73 **Age:** 26

Year Team	Lg	G	AB	H	2B	3B	HR	(Hm	Rd)	TB	R	RBI	TBB	IBB	SO	HBP	SH	SF	SB	CS	SB%	GDP	Avg	OBP	SLG
1997 Baltimore	AL	17	27	6	1	0	1	(1	0)	10	3	3	4	1	7	1	0	0	0	0	.00	2	.222	.344	.370
1998 Arizona	NL	124	416	108	19	12	5	(1	4)	166	43	51	33	2	103	3	0	1	3	5	.38	6	.260	.318	.399
1999 Arizona	NL	63	109	43	7	1	1	(0	1)	55	27	15	11	0	24	3	0	0	2	0	1.00	3	.394	.463	.505
3 ML YEARS		204	552	157	27	13	7	(1	6)	231	73	69	48	3	134	7	0	1	5	5	.50	11	.284	.349	.418

Valerio de los Santos

Pitches: Left **Bats:** Left **Pos:** RP-7   **Ht:** 6'2" **Wt:** 180 **Born:** 10/6/75 **Age:** 24

Year Team	Lg	G	GS	CG	GF	IP	BFP	H	R	ER	HR	SH	SF	HB	TBB	IBB	SO	WP	Bk	W	L	Pct.	ShO	Sv-Op	Hld	ERA
1995 Brewers	R	14	12	0	1	82	341	81	34	20	3	5	4	6	12	2	57	6	2	4	6	.400	0	1--	—	2.20
1996 Beloit	A	33	23	5	10	164.2	715	164	83	65	11	8	5	3	59	4	137	8	3	10	8	.556	1	4--	—	3.55
1997 El Paso	AA	26	16	1	3	114.1	516	146	83	73	6	5	4	4	38	2	61	7	1	6	10	.375	0	2--	—	5.75
1998 El Paso	AA	42	4	0	32	66.2	305	81	34	29	2	5	3	1	25	1	62	5	1	6	2	.750	0	10--	—	3.92
Louisville	AAA	5	0	0	2	5	19	4	2	2	0	0	0	0	0	0	0	0	0	0	0	.000	0	0--	—	3.60
1998 Milwaukee	NL	13	0	0	3	21.2	75	11	7	7	4	0	0	0	2	0	18	1	0	0	0	.000	0	0-0	0	2.91
1999 Milwaukee	NL	7	0	0	3	8.1	43	12	6	6	1	0	0	1	7	0	5	1	0	0	1	.000	0	0-0	0	6.48
2 ML YEARS		20	0	0	6	30	118	23	13	13	5	0	0	1	9	0	23	2	0	0	1	.000	0	0-0	0	3.90

Miguel del Toro

Pitches: Right **Bats:** Right **Pos:** RP-14   **Ht:** 6'1" **Wt:** 160 **Born:** 6/22/72 **Age:** 28

Year Team	Lg	G	GS	CG	GF	IP	BFP	H	R	ER	HR	SH	SF	HB	TBB	IBB	SO	WP	Bk	W	L	Pct.	ShO	Sv-Op	Hld	ERA
1992 Pirates	R	11	10	1	1	60.1	266	64	30	23	0	0	3	4	21	0	42	5	5	2	5	.286	0	1--	—	3.43
1999 Fresno	AAA	40	0	0	12	71.1	323	76	41	35	11	5	2	6	29	0	71	5	1	4	2	.667	0	0--	—	4.42
1999 San Francisco	NL	14	0	0	2	23.2	102	24	11	11	5	0	0	0	11	0	20	0	0	0	0	.000	0	0-0	0	4.18

Rich DeLucia

Pitches: Right **Bats:** Right **Pos:** RP-6   **Ht:** 6'0" **Wt:** 190 **Born:** 10/7/64 **Age:** 35

Year Team	Lg	G	GS	CG	GF	IP	BFP	H	R	ER	HR	SH	SF	HB	TBB	IBB	SO	WP	Bk	W	L	Pct.	ShO	Sv-Op	Hld	ERA
1999 Buffalo *	AAA	44	0	0	33	47.1	210	39	24	22	6	1	1	2	29	3	46	4	0	2	3	.400	0	19--	—	4.18
1990 Seattle	AL	5	5	1	0	36	144	30	9	8	2	2	0	0	9	0	20	0	0	1	2	.333	0	0-0	0	2.00
1991 Seattle	AL	32	31	0	0	182	779	176	107	103	31	5	14	4	78	4	98	10	0	12	13	.480	0	0-0	0	5.09
1992 Seattle	AL	30	11	0	6	83.2	382	100	55	51	13	2	2	2	35	1	66	1	0	3	6	.333	0	1-3	3	5.49
1993 Seattle	AL	30	1	0	11	42.2	195	46	24	22	5	1	1	1	23	3	48	4	0	3	6	.333	0	0-4	6	4.64
1994 Cincinnati	NL	8	0	0	2	10.2	47	9	6	5	4	0	0	0	5	0	15	1	0	0	0	.000	0	0-0	0	4.22
1995 St. Louis	NL	56	0	0	8	82.1	342	63	38	31	9	5	2	3	36	2	76	5	0	8	7	.533	0	0-1	9	3.39
1996 San Francisco	NL	56	0	0	20	61.2	279	62	44	40	8	4	2	3	31	6	55	7	0	3	6	.333	0	0-2	11	5.84
1997 SF-Ana		36	0	0	13	44	186	35	21	19	5	2	2	2	27	2	44	2	0	6	4	.600	0	3-7	8	3.89
1998 Anaheim	AL	61	0	0	18	71.2	314	56	36	34	10	5	7	3	46	5	73	8	1	2	6	.250	0	3-6	12	4.27
1999 Cleveland	AL	6	0	0	2	9.1	50	13	7	7	4	0	0	0	9	2	7	1	0	0	1	.000	0	0-0	0	6.75
1997 San Francisco	NL	3	0	0	0	1.2	12	6	3	2	0	0	0	0	0	0	2	1	0	0	0	.000	0	0-0	1	10.80
Anaheim	AL	33	0	0	13	42.1	174	29	18	17	5	2	2	1	27	2	42	1	0	6	4	.600	0	3-7	7	3.61
10 ML YEARS		320	49	1	80	624	2718	590	347	320	91	26	30	17	299	25	502	39	1	38	51	.427	0	7-23	49	4.62

Ryan Dempster

Pitches: Right **Bats:** Right **Pos:** SP-25   **Ht:** 6'1" **Wt:** 201 **Born:** 5/3/77 **Age:** 23

Year Team	Lg	G	GS	CG	GF	IP	BFP	H	R	ER	HR	SH	SF	HB	TBB	IBB	SO	WP	Bk	W	L	Pct.	ShO	Sv-Op	Hld	ERA
1995 Rangers	R	8	6	1	0	34.1	154	34	21	9	1	0	1	2	17	0	37	2	1	3	1	.750	0	0--	—	2.36
Hudson Val	A-	1	1	0	0	5.2	24	7	2	2	0	1	0	0	1	0	6	0	0	1	0	1.000	0	0--	—	3.18
1996 Chston-SC	A	23	23	2	0	144.1	603	120	71	53	13	6	9	6	58	1	141	17	5	7	11	.389	0	0--	—	3.30
Kane County	A	4	4	1	0	26.1	109	18	10	8	0	1	0	1	18	0	16	2	0	2	1	.667	0	0--	—	2.73
1997 Brevard Cty	A+	28	26	2	0	165.1	721	190	100	90	19	3	4	13	46	1	131	8	1	10	9	.526	1	0--	—	4.90
1998 Portland	AA	7	7	0	0	44.2	180	34	20	16	8	3	0	3	15	0	33	1	0	4	3	.571	0	0--	—	3.22
Charlotte	AAA	5	5	1	0	33	137	33	14	12	4	0	2	1	12	1	24	2	0	3	1	.750	0	0--	—	3.27
1999 Calgary	AAA	5	5	0	0	30.2	132	30	17	17	6	1	2	0	10	1	29	4	0	1	1	.500	0	0--	—	4.99
1998 Florida	NL	14	11	0	1	54.2	272	72	47	43	6	5	6	9	38	1	35	5	0	1	5	.167	0	0-1	0	7.08
1999 Florida	NL	25	25	0	0	147	666	146	77	77	21	3	6	6	93	2	126	8	0	7	8	.467	0	0-0	0	4.71
2 ML YEARS		39	36	0	1	201.2	938	218	124	120	27	8	12	15	131	3	161	13	0	8	13	.381	0	0-1	0	5.36

Sean DePaula

Pitches: Right **Bats:** Right **Pos:** RP-11
Ht: 6'4" **Wt:** 215 **Born:** 11/7/73 **Age:** 26

		HOW MUCH HE PITCHED					WHAT HE GAVE UP											THE RESULTS					
Year Team	Lg	G	GS	CG	GF	IP	BFP	H	R	ER	HR	SH	SF	HB	TBB	IBB	SO	WP	Bk	W	L	Pct.	ShO	Sv-Op	Hld	ERA
1996 Burlington	R+	23	0	0	11	35.1	151	31	16	15	3	2	2	2	13	0	42	4	3	4	2	.667	0	1- -	—	3.82
Watertown	A-	1	0	0	0	2	6	0	0	0	0	0	0	0	0	0	5	0	0	0	0	.000	0	0- -	—	0.00
1997 Watertown	A-	9	0	0	2	19	86	21	6	6	1	1	1	1	8	0	17	0	0	1	1	.500	0	0- -	—	2.84
Columbus	A	29	1	0	7	71	336	71	56	41	4	3	7	4	43	3	75	9	0	4	5	.444	0	0- -	—	5.20
1998 Kinston	A+	28	1	0	14	49.2	226	50	20	13	0	2	1	3	18	3	59	6	0	3	2	.600	0	1- -	—	2.36
Akron	AA	8	1	0	1	17	81	16	10	9	0	1	1	0	15	0	17	3	0	1	1	.500	0	0- -	—	4.76
1999 Kinston	A+	23	0	0	14	51.1	208	36	17	13	6	0	0	3	17	0	75	4	0	4	2	.667	0	7- -	—	2.28
Akron	AA	14	0	0	6	28	122	20	11	11	2	2	0	2	17	0	31	2	0	1	0	1.000	0	1- -	—	3.54
Buffalo	AAA	5	0	0	5	5	19	0	0	0	0	0	0	1	3	0	7	1	0	0	0	.000	0	2- -	—	0.00
1999 Cleveland	AL	11	0	0	4	11.2	45	8	6	6	0	2	0	0	3	0	18	0	0	0	0	.000	0	0-0	3	4.63

Mark DeRosa

Bats: Right **Throws:** Right **Pos:** PH/PR-7; SS-2
Ht: 6'1" **Wt:** 195 **Born:** 2/2/75 **Age:** 25

		BATTING																BASERUNNING				PERCENTAGES		
Year Team	Lg	G	AB	H	2B	3B	HR	(Hm	Rd)	TB	R	RBI	TBB	IBB	SO	HBP	SH	SF	SB	CS	SB%	GDP	Avg	OBP	SLG
1996 Eugene	A-	70	255	66	13	1	2	—	—	87	43	28	38	1	48	5	0	2	3	4	.43	10	.259	.363	.341
1997 Durham	A+	92	346	93	11	3	8	—	—	134	51	37	25	2	73	10	2	4	6	8	.43	12	.269	.332	.387
1998 Greenville	AA	125	461	123	26	2	8	—	—	177	67	49	60	2	57	5	5	2	7	13	.35	18	.267	.356	.384
1999 Richmond	AAA	105	364	99	16	2	1	—	—	122	41	40	21	1	49	5	3	4	7	6	.54	5	.272	.317	.335
1998 Atlanta	NL	5	3	1	0	0	0	(0	0)	1	2	0	0	0	1	0	0	0	0	0	.00	0	.333	.333	.333
1999 Atlanta	NL	7	8	0	0	0	0	(0	0)	0	0	0	0	0	2	0	0	0	0	0	.00	0	.000	.000	.000
2 ML YEARS		12	11	1	0	0	0	(0	0)	1	2	0	0	0	3	0	0	0	0	0	.00	0	.091	.091	.091

Delino DeShields

Bats: Left **Throws:** Right **Pos:** 2B-93; PH/PR-9
Ht: 6'1" **Wt:** 175 **Born:** 1/15/69 **Age:** 31

		BATTING																BASERUNNING				PERCENTAGES		
Year Team	Lg	G	AB	H	2B	3B	HR	(Hm	Rd)	TB	R	RBI	TBB	IBB	SO	HBP	SH	SF	SB	CS	SB%	GDP	Avg	OBP	SLG
1999 Delmarva *	A	2	7	2	0	0	1	—	—	5	1	2	1	0	1	0	0	0	0	1	.00	0	.286	.375	.714
Frederick *	A+	2	8	1	0	0	1	—	—	4	1	2	0	0	1	0	0	0	0	0	.00	0	.125	.125	.500
Bowie *	AA	4	15	4	1	0	0	—	—	5	2	0	3	0	2	1	0	0	0	0	.00	0	.267	.421	.333
1990 Montreal	NL	129	499	144	28	6	4	(3	1)	196	69	45	66	3	96	4	1	2	42	22	.66	10	.289	.375	.393
1991 Montreal	NL	151	563	134	15	4	10	(3	7)	187	83	51	95	2	151	4	3	4	56	23	.71	6	.238	.347	.332
1992 Montreal	NL	135	530	155	19	8	7	(1	6)	211	82	56	54	4	108	3	9	3	46	15	.75	10	.292	.359	.398
1993 Montreal	NL	123	481	142	17	7	2	(2	0)	179	75	29	72	3	64	3	4	2	43	10	.81	6	.295	.389	.372
1994 Los Angeles	NL	89	320	80	11	3	2	(1	1)	103	51	33	54	0	53	0	1	1	27	7	.79	9	.250	.357	.322
1995 Los Angeles	NL	127	425	109	18	3	8	(2	6)	157	66	37	63	4	83	1	3	1	39	14	.74	6	.256	.353	.369
1996 Los Angeles	NL	154	581	130	12	8	5	(3	2)	173	75	41	53	7	124	1	2	5	48	11	.81	12	.224	.288	.298
1997 St. Louis	NL	150	572	169	26	14	11	(6	5)	256	92	58	55	1	72	3	7	6	55	14	.80	5	.295	.357	.448
1998 St. Louis	NL	117	420	122	21	8	7	(3	4)	180	74	44	56	2	61	0	4	4	26	10	.72	6	.290	.371	.429
1999 Baltimore	AL	96	330	87	11	2	6	(4	2)	120	46	34	37	0	52	1	5	1	11	8	.58	5	.264	.339	.364
10 ML YEARS		1271	4721	1272	178	63	62	(28	34)	1762	713	428	605	26	864	18	44	30	393	134	.75	75	.269	.353	.373

Alex Diaz

Bats: Both **Throws:** Right **Pos:** PH/PR-22; LF-7; RF-1
Ht: 5'11" **Wt:** 180 **Born:** 10/5/68 **Age:** 31

		BATTING																BASERUNNING				PERCENTAGES		
Year Team	Lg	G	AB	H	2B	3B	HR	(Hm	Rd)	TB	R	RBI	TBB	IBB	SO	HBP	SH	SF	SB	CS	SB%	GDP	Avg	OBP	SLG
1992 Milwaukee	AL	22	9	1	0	0	0	(0	0)	1	5	1	0	0	0	0	0	0	3	2	.60	0	.111	.111	.111
1993 Milwaukee	AL	32	69	22	2	0	0	(0	0)	24	9	1	0	0	12	0	3	0	5	3	.63	3	.319	.319	.348
1994 Milwaukee	AL	79	187	47	5	7	1	(0	1)	69	17	17	10	1	19	0	3	3	5	5	.50	5	.251	.285	.369
1995 Seattle	AL	103	270	67	14	0	3	(3	0)	90	44	27	13	2	27	2	5	2	18	8	.69	3	.248	.286	.333
1996 Seattle	AL	38	79	19	2	0	1	(1	0)	24	11	5	2	0	8	2	0	1	6	3	.67	2	.241	.274	.304
1997 Texas	AL	28	90	20	4	0	2	(0	2)	30	8	12	5	0	13	1	0	1	1	1	.50	3	.222	.268	.333
1998 San Francisco	NL	34	62	8	2	0	0	(0	0)	10	5	5	0	0	15	0	0	0	1	1	.50	0	.129	.129	.161
1999 Houston	NL	30	50	11	2	0	1	(1	0)	16	3	7	3	0	13	0	0	0	2	2	.50	0	.220	.264	.320
8 ML YEARS		366	816	195	31	7	8	(5	3)	264	102	75	33	3	107	5	11	7	41	25	.62	16	.239	.271	.324

Edwin Diaz

Bats: Right **Throws:** Right **Pos:** 2B-2; SS-2; PH/PR-2
Ht: 5'11" **Wt:** 170 **Born:** 1/15/75 **Age:** 25

		BATTING																BASERUNNING				PERCENTAGES		
Year Team	Lg	G	AB	H	2B	3B	HR	(Hm	Rd)	TB	R	RBI	TBB	IBB	SO	HBP	SH	SF	SB	CS	SB%	GDP	Avg	OBP	SLG
1993 Rangers	R	43	154	47	10	5	1	—	—	70	27	23	19	1	21	4	0	2	12	5	.71	4	.305	.391	.455
1994 Chston-SC	A	122	413	109	22	7	11	—	—	178	52	60	22	0	107	8	8	9	11	14	.44	7	.264	.308	.431
1995 Charlotte	A+	115	450	128	26	5	8	—	—	188	48	56	33	0	94	7	3	2	8	13	.38	10	.284	.341	.418
1996 Tulsa	AA	121	499	132	33	6	16	—	—	225	70	65	25	4	122	9	8	4	8	9	.47	9	.265	.309	.451
1997 Okla City	AAA	20	73	8	3	1	1	—	—	16	6	4	2	0	27	2	1	0	1	1	.50	1	.110	.156	.219
Tulsa	AA	105	440	121	31	1	15	—	—	199	65	46	33	0	102	8	2	2	6	9	.40	6	.275	.335	.452
1998 Tucson	AAA	131	510	134	31	12	2	—	—	195	61	49	27	0	105	4	2	5	6	4	.60	9	.263	.302	.382
1999 Tucson	AAA	107	415	129	24	1	11	—	—	188	72	50	17	3	77	7	3	4	6	7	.46	7	.311	.345	.453
1998 Arizona	NL	3	7	0	0	0	0	(0	0)	0	0	0	0	0	2	0	0	0	0	0	.00	0	.000	.000	.000
1999 Arizona	NL	4	5	2	2	0	0	(0	0)	4	2	0	3	1	1	0	0	0	0	0	.00	0	.400	.625	.800
2 ML YEARS		7	12	2	2	0	0	(0	0)	4	2	0	3	1	3	0	0	0	0	0	.00	0	.167	.333	.333

Einar Diaz

Bats: Right **Throws:** Right **Pos:** C-119; PH/PR-2   **Ht:** 5'10" **Wt:** 165 **Born:** 12/28/72 **Age:** 27

Year Team	Lg	G	AB	H	2B	3B	HR	(Hm	Rd)	TB	R	RBI	TBB	IBB	SO	HBP	SH	SF	SB	CS	SB%	GDP	Avg	OBP	SLG
1992 Burlington	R+	52	178	37	3	0	1	—	—	43	19	14	20	0	9	3	2	2	2	3	.40	4	.208	.296	.242
1993 Burlington	R+	60	231	69	15	3	5	—	—	105	40	33	8	0	7	4	2	4	7	3	.70	5	.299	.328	.455
Columbus	A	1	5	0	0	0	0	—	—	0	0	0	0	0	0	0	0	0	0	0	.00	0	.000	.000	.000
1994 Columbus	A	120	491	137	23	2	16	—	—	212	67	71	17	0	34	21	1	1	4	4	.50	18	.279	.330	.432
1995 Kinston	A+	104	373	98	21	0	6	—	—	137	46	43	12	2	29	8	1	4	3	6	.33	6	.263	.297	.367
1996 Canton-Akrn	AA	104	395	111	26	2	3	—	—	150	47	35	12	0	22	9	1	1	3	2	.60	11	.281	.317	.380
1997 Buffalo	AAA	109	336	86	18	2	3	—	—	117	40	31	18	1	34	5	4	2	2	6	.25	12	.256	.302	.348
1998 Buffalo	AAA	115	415	130	21	3	8	—	—	181	62	63	21	3	33	6	0	2	3	3	.50	8	.313	.354	.436
1996 Cleveland	AL	4	1	0	0	0	0	(0	0)	0	0	0	0	0	0	0	0	0	0	0	.00	0	.000	.000	.000
1997 Cleveland	AL	5	7	1	1	0	0	(0	0)	2	1	1	0	0	2	0	0	0	0	0	.00	0	.143	.143	.286
1998 Cleveland	AL	17	48	11	1	0	2	(1	1)	18	8	9	3	0	2	2	0	3	0	0	.00	1	.229	.286	.375
1999 Cleveland	AL	119	392	110	21	1	3	(2	1)	142	43	32	23	0	41	5	6	1	11	4	.73	10	.281	.328	.362
4 ML YEARS		145	448	122	23	1	5	(3	2)	162	52	42	26	0	45	7	6	4	11	4	.73	12	.272	.320	.362

Mike DiFelice

Bats: Right **Throws:** Right **Pos:** C-51   **Ht:** 6'2" **Wt:** 205 **Born:** 5/28/69 **Age:** 31

Year Team	Lg	G	AB	H	2B	3B	HR	(Hm	Rd)	TB	R	RBI	TBB	IBB	SO	HBP	SH	SF	SB	CS	SB%	GDP	Avg	OBP	SLG
1996 St. Louis	NL	4	7	2	1	0	0	(0	0)	3	0	2	0	0	1	0	0	0	0	0	.00	0	.286	.286	.429
1997 St. Louis	NL	93	260	62	10	1	4	(1	3)	86	16	30	19	0	61	3	6	1	1	1	.50	11	.238	.297	.331
1998 Tampa Bay	AL	84	248	57	12	3	3	(1	2)	84	17	23	15	0	56	1	3	2	0	0	.00	12	.230	.274	.339
1999 Tampa Bay	AL	51	179	55	11	0	6	(5	1)	84	21	27	8	0	23	3	0	1	0	0	.00	0	.307	.346	.469
4 ML YEARS		232	694	176	34	4	13	(7	6)	257	54	82	42	0	141	7	9	4	1	1	.50	24	.254	.301	.370

Jerry Dipoto

Pitches: Right **Bats:** Right **Pos:** RP-63   **Ht:** 6'2" **Wt:** 205 **Born:** 5/24/68 **Age:** 32

Year Team	Lg	G	GS	CG	GF	IP	BFP	H	R	ER	HR	SH	SF	HB	TBB	IBB	SO	WP	Bk	W	L	Pct.	ShO	Sv-Op	Hld	ERA
1993 Cleveland	AL	46	0	0	26	56.1	247	57	21	15	0	3	2	1	30	7	41	0	0	4	4	.500	0	11-17	6	2.40
1994 Cleveland	AL	7	0	0	1	15.2	79	26	14	14	1	0	4	1	10	0	9	0	0	0	0	.000	0	0-0	1	8.04
1995 New York	NL	58	0	0	26	78.2	330	77	41	33	2	6	3	4	29	8	49	3	1	4	6	.400	0	2-6	8	3.78
1996 New York	NL	57	0	0	21	77.1	364	91	44	36	5	7	4	3	45	8	52	3	3	7	2	.778	0	0-5	3	4.19
1997 Colorado	NL	74	0	0	33	95.2	422	108	56	50	6	3	7	4	33	5	74	4	1	5	3	.625	0	16-21	10	4.70
1998 Colorado	NL	68	0	0	51	71.1	295	61	31	28	8	2	2	3	25	3	49	7	0	3	4	.429	0	19-23	7	3.53
1999 Colorado	NL	63	0	0	18	86.2	379	91	44	41	10	1	5	3	44	4	69	6	0	5	4	.444	0	1-1	15	4.26
7 ML YEARS		373	0	0	176	481.2	2116	511	251	217	32	22	27	19	216	35	343	23	5	27	24	.529	0	49-73	50	4.05

Gary DiSarcina

Bats: Right **Throws:** Right **Pos:** SS-81   **Ht:** 6'2" **Wt:** 205 **Born:** 11/19/67 **Age:** 32

Year Team	Lg	G	AB	H	2B	3B	HR	(Hm	Rd)	TB	R	RBI	TBB	IBB	SO	HBP	SH	SF	SB	CS	SB%	GDP	Avg	OBP	SLG
1999 Lk Elsinore *	A+	4	12	1	0	0	0	—	—	1	0	0	1	0	0	0	1	0	0	0	.00	0	.083	.154	.083
Erie *	AA	5	20	6	0	0	0	—	—	6	1	2	0	0	4	0	0	0	0	2	.00	0	.300	.300	.300
1989 California	AL	2	0	0	0	0	0	(0	0)	0	0	0	0	0	0	0	0	0	0	0	.00	0	.000	.000	.000
1990 California	AL	18	57	8	1	1	0	(0	0)	11	8	0	3	0	10	0	1	0	1	0	1.00	3	.140	.183	.193
1991 California	AL	18	57	12	2	0	0	(0	0)	14	5	3	3	0	4	2	2	0	0	0	.00	0	.211	.274	.246
1992 California	AL	157	518	128	19	0	3	(2	1)	156	48	42	20	0	50	7	5	3	9	7	.56	15	.247	.283	.301
1993 California	AL	126	416	99	20	1	3	(2	1)	130	44	45	15	0	38	6	5	3	5	7	.42	13	.238	.273	.313
1994 California	AL	112	389	101	14	2	3	(2	1)	128	53	33	18	0	28	2	10	2	3	7	.30	10	.260	.294	.329
1995 California	AL	99	362	111	28	6	5	(1	4)	166	61	41	20	0	25	2	7	3	7	4	.64	10	.307	.344	.459
1996 California	AL	150	536	137	26	4	5	(2	3)	186	62	48	21	0	36	2	16	1	2	1	.67	18	.256	.286	.347
1997 Anaheim	AL	154	549	135	28	2	4	(2	2)	179	52	47	17	0	29	4	8	5	7	8	.47	18	.246	.271	.326
1998 Anaheim	AL	157	551	158	39	3	3	(0	3)	212	73	56	21	0	51	8	12	3	11	7	.61	11	.287	.321	.385
1999 Anaheim	AL	81	271	62	7	1	1	(1	0)	74	32	29	15	0	32	2	9	1	2	2	.50	8	.229	.273	.273
11 ML YEARS		1074	3706	951	184	20	27	(12	15)	1256	438	344	153	0	303	35	75	21	47	43	.52	104	.257	.291	.339

David Doster

Bats: R **Throws:** R **Pos:** 2B-77; PH/PR-24; 3B-6; SS-5   **Ht:** 5'10" **Wt:** 181 **Born:** 10/8/70 **Age:** 29

Year Team	Lg	G	AB	H	2B	3B	HR	(Hm	Rd)	TB	R	RBI	TBB	IBB	SO	HBP	SH	SF	SB	CS	SB%	GDP	Avg	OBP	SLG
1993 Spartanburg	A	60	223	61	15	0	3	—	—	85	34	20	25	1	36	3	6	1	1	0	1.00	5	.274	.353	.381
Clearwater	A+	9	28	10	3	1	0	—	—	15	4	2	2	0	2	0	0	0	0	0	.00	1	.357	.400	.536
1994 Clearwater	A+	131	480	135	42	4	13	—	—	224	76	74	54	3	71	11	3	8	12	7	.63	12	.281	.362	.467
1995 Reading	AA	139	551	146	39	3	21	—	—	254	84	79	51	2	61	7	8	4	11	7	.61	11	.265	.333	.461
1996 Scranton-WB	AAA	88	322	83	20	0	7	—	—	124	37	48	26	1	54	2	3	5	7	3	.70	8	.258	.313	.385
1997 Scranton-WB	AAA	108	410	129	32	2	16	—	—	213	70	79	30	1	60	8	2	3	5	5	.50	9	.315	.370	.520
1998 Scranton-WB	AAA	141	579	160	38	4	16	—	—	254	79	84	51	2	80	4	1	10	23	6	.79	14	.276	.334	.439
1996 Philadelphia	NL	39	105	28	8	0	1	(1	0)	39	14	8	7	0	21	0	1	0	0	0	.00	2	.267	.313	.371
1999 Philadelphia	NL	99	97	19	2	0	3	(2	1)	30	9	10	12	1	23	0	2	1	1	0	1.00	2	.196	.282	.309
2 ML YEARS		138	202	47	10	0	4	(3	1)	69	23	18	19	1	44	0	3	1	1	0	1.00	3	.233	.297	.342

Octavio Dotel

Pitches: Right **Bats:** Right **Pos:** SP-14; RP-5   **Ht:** 6'0" **Wt:** 175 **Born:** 11/25/75 **Age:** 24

Year Team	Lg	G	GS	CG	GF	IP	BFP	H	R	ER	HR	SH	SF	HB	TBB	IBB	SO	WP	Bk	W	L	Pct.	ShO	Sv-Op	Hld	ERA
1995 Mets	R	13	12	2	1	74.1	293	48	23	18	0	1	0	5	17	1	86	9	0	7	4	.636	0	0--	—	2.18
St. Lucie	A+	3	0	0	2	8	38	10	5	5	1	1	2	0	4	0	9	2	0	1	0	1.000	0	0--	—	5.63
1996 Capital Cty	A	22	19	0	3	115.1	480	89	49	46	7	1	4	7	49	0	142	12	4	11	3	.786	0	0--	—	3.59
1997 Mets	R	3	2	0	1	9.1	39	9	1	1	0	0	0	1	2	0	7	0	2	0	0	.000	0	1--	—	0.96
St. Lucie	A+	9	8	1	1	50	212	44	18	14	2	0	1	1	23	0	39	5	1	5	2	.714	1	0--	—	2.52
Binghamton	AA	12	12	0	0	55.2	266	66	50	37	5	1	0	0	38	1	40	2	1	3	4	.429	0	0--	—	5.98
1998 Binghamton	AA	10	10	2	0	68.2	261	41	19	15	4	1	1	0	24	1	82	0	1	4	2	.667	1	0--	—	1.97
Norfolk	AAA	17	16	1	0	99	424	82	47	38	9	6	2	2	43	1	118	9	1	8	6	.571	0	0--	—	3.45
1999 Norfolk	AAA	13	13	1	0	70.1	293	52	33	30	9	1	1	2	34	1	90	3	1	5	2	.714	0	0--	—	3.84
1999 New York	NL	19	14	0	1	85.1	368	69	52	51	12	3	5	6	49	1	85	3	2	8	3	.727	0	0-0	0	5.38

Jim Dougherty

Pitches: Right **Bats:** Right **Pos:** RP-2   **Ht:** 6'1" **Wt:** 225 **Born:** 3/8/68 **Age:** 32

Year Team	Lg	G	GS	CG	GF	IP	BFP	H	R	ER	HR	SH	SF	HB	TBB	IBB	SO	WP	Bk	W	L	Pct.	ShO	Sv-Op	Hld	ERA
1999 Nashville *	AAA	53	0	0	20	59.2	274	69	38	36	9	3	4	0	27	5	55	0	0	3	3	.500	0	10--	—	5.43
1995 Houston	NL	56	0	0	11	67.2	294	76	37	37	7	3	3	3	25	1	49	1	0	8	4	.667	0	0-2	5	4.92
1996 Houston	NL	12	0	0	2	13	64	14	14	13	2	1	1	1	11	1	6	0	0	0	2	.000	0	0-1	1	9.00
1998 Oakland	AL	9	0	0	4	12	59	17	11	11	2	1	0	1	9	0	3	0	0	0	2	.000	0	0-1	0	8.25
1999 Pittsburgh	NL	2	0	0	0	2	12	3	3	2	0	0	0	0	3	0	1	0	0	0	0	.000	0	0-0	0	9.00
4 ML YEARS		79	0	0	17	94.2	429	110	65	63	11	5	4	5	46	2	59	1	0	8	8	.500	0	0-4	6	5.99

Kelly Dransfeldt

Bats: Right **Throws:** Right **Pos:** SS-16   **Ht:** 6'2" **Wt:** 200 **Born:** 4/16/75 **Age:** 25

Year Team	Lg	G	AB	H	2B	3B	HR	(Hm	Rd)	TB	R	RBI	TBB	IBB	SO	HBP	SH	SF	SB	CS	SB%	GDP	Avg	OBP	SLG
1996 Hudson Val	A-	75	284	67	17	1	7	—	—	107	42	29	27	1	76	4	1	3	13	4	.76	2	.236	.308	.377
1997 Charlotte	A+	135	466	106	20	7	6	—	—	158	64	58	42	0	115	3	4	3	25	16	.61	8	.227	.294	.339
1998 Charlotte	A+	67	245	79	17	0	18	—	—	150	46	76	29	1	67	2	0	6	7	2	.78	4	.322	.390	.612
Tulsa	AA	58	226	57	15	4	9	—	—	107	43	36	18	0	79	2	0	3	8	1	.89	4	.252	.309	.473
1999 Oklahoma	AAA	102	359	85	21	2	10	—	—	140	55	44	24	0	108	3	3	3	6	3	.67	12	.237	.288	.390
1999 Texas	AL	16	53	10	1	0	1	(1	0)	14	3	5	3	0	12	0	1	0	0	0	.00	2	.189	.232	.264

Darren Dreifort

Pitches: Right **Bats:** Right **Pos:** SP-29; RP-1   **Ht:** 6'2" **Wt:** 211 **Born:** 5/3/72 **Age:** 28

Year Team	Lg	G	GS	CG	GF	IP	BFP	H	R	ER	HR	SH	SF	HB	TBB	IBB	SO	WP	Bk	W	L	Pct.	ShO	Sv-Op	Hld	ERA
1994 Los Angeles	NL	27	0	0	15	29	148	45	21	20	4	0	4	4	15	3	22	1	0	0	5	.000	0	6-9	3	6.21
1996 Los Angeles	NL	19	0	0	5	23.2	106	23	13	13	2	3	1	0	12	4	24	2	1	1	4	.200	0	0-2	1	4.94
1997 Los Angeles	NL	48	0	0	15	63	265	45	21	20	3	5	2	1	34	2	63	3	1	5	2	.714	0	4-7	9	2.86
1998 Los Angeles	NL	32	26	1	0	180	752	171	84	80	12	11	6	10	57	2	168	9	0	8	12	.400	1	0-0	4	4.00
1999 Los Angeles	NL	30	29	1	0	178.2	773	177	105	95	20	8	2	7	76	2	140	9	4	13	13	.500	1	0-0	0	4.79
5 ML YEARS		156	55	2	35	474.1	2044	461	244	228	37	30	11	22	194	13	417	24	6	27	36	.429	2	10-18	13	4.33

J.D. Drew

Bats: Left **Throws:** Right **Pos:** CF-97; PH/PR-8; LF-1   **Ht:** 6'1" **Wt:** 195 **Born:** 11/20/75 **Age:** 24

Year Team	Lg	G	AB	H	2B	3B	HR	(Hm	Rd)	TB	R	RBI	TBB	IBB	SO	HBP	SH	SF	SB	CS	SB%	GDP	Avg	OBP	SLG
1997 St. Paul	IND	44	170	58	6	1	18	—	—	120	51	50	30	0	40	2	0	1	5	3	.63	1	.341	.443	.706
1998 St. Paul	IND	30	114	44	11	2	9	—	—	86	27	33	21	5	32	6	0	0	8	1	.89	2	.386	.504	.754
Arkansas	AA	19	67	22	3	1	5	—	—	42	18	11	13	1	15	1	0	0	2	1	.67	0	.328	.444	.627
Memphis	AAA	26	79	25	8	1	2	—	—	41	15	13	22	0	18	1	0	0	1	3	.25	1	.316	.471	.519
1999 Memphis	AAA	25	87	26	5	1	2	—	—	39	11	15	8	0	20	2	0	0	6	1	.86	0	.299	.371	.448
1998 St. Louis	NL	14	36	15	3	1	5	(4	1)	35	9	13	4	0	10	0	0	1	0	0	.00	4	.417	.463	.972
1999 St. Louis	NL	104	368	89	16	6	13	(5	8)	156	72	39	50	0	77	6	3	3	19	3	.86	4	.242	.340	.424
2 ML YEARS		118	404	104	19	7	18	(9	9)	191	81	52	54	0	87	6	3	4	19	3	.86	8	.257	.350	.473

Rob Ducey

Bats: L **Throws:** R **Pos:** PH/PR-51; LF-39; RF-11; CF-9; DH-2   **Ht:** 6'2" **Wt:** 180 **Born:** 5/24/65 **Age:** 35

Year Team	Lg	G	AB	H	2B	3B	HR	(Hm	Rd)	TB	R	RBI	TBB	IBB	SO	HBP	SH	SF	SB	CS	SB%	GDP	Avg	OBP	SLG
1987 Toronto	AL	34	48	9	1	0	1	(1	0)	13	12	6	8	0	10	0	0	1	2	0	1.00	1	.188	.298	.271
1988 Toronto	AL	27	54	17	4	1	0	(0	0)	23	15	6	5	0	7	0	2	2	1	0	1.00	1	.315	.361	.426
1989 Toronto	AL	41	76	16	4	0	0	(0	0)	20	5	7	9	1	25	0	1	0	2	1	.67	2	.211	.294	.263
1990 Toronto	AL	19	53	16	5	0	0	(0	0)	21	7	7	7	0	15	1	0	1	1	1	.50	2	.302	.387	.396
1991 Toronto	AL	39	68	16	2	2	1	(0	1)	25	8	4	5	0	26	0	1	0	2	0	1.00	1	.235	.297	.368
1992 Tor-Cal	AL	54	80	15	4	0	0	(0	0)	19	7	2	5	0	22	0	0	1	2	4	.33	1	.188	.233	.238
1993 Texas	AL	27	85	24	6	3	2	(2	0)	42	15	9	11	2	17	0	2	2	2	3	.40	1	.282	.351	.494

Year Team	Lg	G	AB	H	2B	3B	HR	(Hm	Rd)	TB	R	RBI	TBB	IBB	SO	HBP	SH	SF	SB	CS	SB%	GDP	Avg	OBP	SLG
																			BASERUNNING				**PERCENTAGES**		
1994 Texas	AL	11	29	5	1	0	0	(0	0)	6	1	1	2	0	1	0	0	0	0	0	.00	1	.172	.226	.207
1997 Seattle	AL	76	143	41	15	2	5	(0	5)	75	25	10	6	0	31	0	0	2	3	3	.50	3	.287	.311	.524
1998 Seattle	AL	97	217	52	18	2	5	(2	3)	89	30	23	23	2	61	9	0	1	4	3	.57	4	.240	.336	.410
1999 Philadelphia	NL	104	188	49	10	2	8	(3	5)	87	29	33	38	1	57	0	0	1	2	1	.67	1	.261	.383	.463
1992 Toronto	AL	23	21	1	1	0	0	(0	0)	2	3	0	10	0	10	0	0	0	0	1	.00	0	.048	.048	.095
California	AL	31	59	14	3	0	0	(0	0)	17	4	2	5	0	12	0	0	1	2	3	.40	1	.237	.292	.288
11 ML YEARS		529	1041	260	70	12	22	(8	14)	420	154	108	119	6	272	10	6	11	21	16	.57	15	.250	.329	.403

Shawon Dunston

Bats: R **Throws:** R **Pos:** PH/PR-44; CF-27; LF-18; RF-9; 1B-8; SS-7; 3B-6; DH-2 **Ht:** 6'1" **Wt:** 180 **Born:** 3/21/63 **Age:** 37

Year Team	Lg	G	AB	H	2B	3B	HR	(Hm	Rd)	TB	R	RBI	TBB	IBB	SO	HBP	SH	SF	SB	CS	SB%	GDP	Avg	OBP	SLG
1985 Chicago	NL	74	250	65	12	4	4	(3	1)	97	40	18	19	3	42	0	1	2	11	3	.79	3	.260	.310	.388
1986 Chicago	NL	150	581	145	37	3	17	(10	7)	239	66	68	21	5	114	3	4	2	13	11	.54	5	.250	.278	.411
1987 Chicago	NL	95	346	85	18	3	5	(3	2)	124	40	22	10	1	68	1	0	2	12	3	.80	6	.246	.267	.358
1988 Chicago	NL	155	575	143	23	6	9	(5	4)	205	69	56	16	8	108	2	4	2	30	9	.77	6	.249	.271	.357
1989 Chicago	NL	138	471	131	20	6	9	(3	6)	190	52	60	30	15	86	1	6	4	19	11	.63	7	.278	.320	.403
1990 Chicago	NL	146	545	143	22	8	17	(7	10)	232	73	66	15	1	87	3	4	6	25	5	.83	9	.262	.283	.426
1991 Chicago	NL	142	492	128	22	7	12	(7	5)	200	59	50	23	5	64	4	4	11	21	6	.78	5	.260	.292	.407
1992 Chicago	NL	18	73	23	3	1	0	(0	0)	28	8	2	3	0	13	0	0	0	2	3	.40	0	.315	.342	.384
1993 Chicago	NL	7	10	4	2	0	0	(0	0)	6	3	2	0	0	1	0	0	0	0	0	.00	0	.400	.400	.600
1994 Chicago	NL	88	331	92	19	0	11	(2	9)	144	38	35	16	3	48	2	5	2	3	8	.27	4	.278	.313	.435
1995 Chicago	NL	127	477	141	30	6	14	(8	6)	225	58	69	10	3	75	6	7	3	10	5	.67	8	.296	.317	.472
1996 San Francisco	NL	82	287	86	12	2	5	(3	2)	117	27	25	13	0	40	1	5	1	8	0	1.00	8	.300	.331	.408
1997 ChC-Pit	NL	132	490	147	22	5	14	(10	4)	221	71	57	8	0	75	3	5	5	32	8	.80	9	.300	.312	.451
1998 Cle-SF	NL	98	207	46	13	3	6	(2	4)	83	36	20	6	0	28	4	1	3	9	4	.69	3	.222	.255	.401
1999 StL-NYM	NL	104	243	78	11	3	5	(4	1)	110	35	41	2	0	39	5	3	2	10	4	.71	6	.321	.337	.453
1997 Chicago	NL	114	419	119	18	4	9	(7	2)	172	57	41	8	0	64	3	3	4	29	7	.81	7	.284	.300	.411
Pittsburgh	NL	18	71	28	4	1	5	(3	2)	49	14	16	0	0	11	0	2	1	3	1	.75	2	.394	.389	.690
1998 Cleveland	AL	62	156	37	11	3	3	(1	2)	63	26	12	6	0	18	1	0	3	9	2	.82	2	.237	.265	.404
San Francisco	NL	36	51	9	2	0	3	(1	2)	20	10	8	0	0	10	3	1	0	0	2	.00	1	.176	.222	.392
1999 St. Louis	NL	62	150	46	5	2	5	(4	1)	70	23	25	2	0	23	3	2	1	6	3	.67	4	.307	.327	.467
New York	NL	42	93	32	6	1	0	(0	0)	40	12	16	0	0	16	2	1	1	4	1	.80	4	.344	.354	.430
15 ML YEARS		1556	5378	1457	266	57	128	(67	61)	2221	675	591	192	44	888	35	49	45	205	80	.72	85	.271	.298	.413

Todd Dunwoody

Bats: L **Throws:** L **Pos:** CF-44; PH/PR-9; LF-8; RF-5 **Ht:** 6'1" **Wt:** 195 **Born:** 4/11/75 **Age:** 25

Year Team	Lg	G	AB	H	2B	3B	HR	(Hm	Rd)	TB	R	RBI	TBB	IBB	SO	HBP	SH	SF	SB	CS	SB%	GDP	Avg	OBP	SLG
1999 Calgary *	AAA	65	246	67	16	7	9	—	—	124	35	36	10	1	56	2	0	2	7	8	.47	5	.272	.304	.504
1997 Florida	NL	19	50	13	2	2	2	(0	2)	25	7	7	7	0	21	1	0	0	2	0	1.00	1	.260	.362	.500
1998 Florida	NL	116	434	109	27	7	5	(2	3)	165	53	28	21	0	113	4	3	0	5	1	.83	6	.251	.292	.380
1999 Florida	NL	64	186	41	6	3	2	(1	1)	59	20	20	12	0	41	1	0	1	3	4	.43	1	.220	.270	.317
3 ML YEARS		199	670	163	35	12	9	(3	6)	249	80	55	40	0	175	6	3	1	10	5	.67	8	.243	.291	.372

Erubiel Durazo

Bats: Left **Throws:** Left **Pos:** 1B-44; PH/PR-10 **Ht:** 6'3" **Wt:** 225 **Born:** 1/23/74 **Age:** 26

Year Team	Lg	G	AB	H	2B	3B	HR	(Hm	Rd)	TB	R	RBI	TBB	IBB	SO	HBP	SH	SF	SB	CS	SB%	GDP	Avg	OBP	SLG
1999 El Paso	AA	64	226	91	18	3	14	—	—	157	53	55	44	6	37	2	0	3	2	1	.67	5	.403	.498	.695
Tucson	AAA	30	118	48	7	0	10	—	—	85	27	28	14	0	18	1	0	1	0	1	1.00	0	.407	.470	.720
1999 Arizona	NL	52	155	51	4	2	11	(4	7)	92	31	30	26	1	43	1	0	3	1	1	.50	1	.329	.422	.594

Chad Durbin

Pitches: Right **Bats:** Right **Pos:** RP-1 **Ht:** 6'1" **Wt:** 175 **Born:** 12/3/77 **Age:** 22

Year Team	Lg	G	GS	CG	GF	IP	BFP	H	R	ER	HR	SH	SF	HB	TBB	IBB	SO	WP	Bk	W	L	Pct.	ShO	Sv-Op	Hld	ERA
1996 Royals	R	11	8	1	1	44.1	187	34	22	21	3	0	1	4	25	0	43	6	3	3	2	.600	1	0- —	—	4.26
1997 Lansing	A	26	26	0	0	144.2	642	157	85	77	15	6	6	11	53	0	116	12	1	5	8	.385	0	0- —	—	4.79
1998 Wilmington	A+	26	26	0	0	147.2	624	126	57	48	10	5	7	8	59	3	162	13	1	10	7	.588	0	0- —	—	2.93
1999 Wichita	AA	28	27	1	0	157	664	154	88	81	20	1	10	6	49	1	122	12	1	8	10	.444	1	0- —	—	4.64
1999 Kansas City	AL	1	0	0	0	2.1	9	1	0	0	0	0	0	0	1	0	3	1	0	0	0	.000	0	0-0	0	0.00

Ray Durham

Bats: Both **Throws:** Right **Pos:** 2B-148; DH-4; PH/PR-2 **Ht:** 5'8" **Wt:** 180 **Born:** 11/30/71 **Age:** 28

Year Team	Lg	G	AB	H	2B	3B	HR	(Hm	Rd)	TB	R	RBI	TBB	IBB	SO	HBP	SH	SF	SB	CS	SB%	GDP	Avg	OBP	SLG
1995 Chicago	AL	125	471	121	27	6	7	(1	6)	181	68	51	31	2	83	6	5	4	18	5	.78	8	.257	.309	.384
1996 Chicago	AL	156	557	153	33	5	10	(3	7)	226	79	65	58	4	95	10	7	7	30	4	.88	6	.275	.350	.406
1997 Chicago	AL	155	634	172	27	5	11	(3	8)	242	106	53	61	0	96	6	2	8	33	16	.67	14	.271	.337	.382
1998 Chicago	AL	158	635	181	35	8	19	(10	9)	289	126	67	73	3	105	6	6	3	36	9	.80	5	.285	.363	.455

65

		BATTING																	BASERUNNING				PERCENTAGES		
Year Team	Lg	G	AB	H	2B	3B	HR	(Hm	Rd)	TB	R	RBI	TBB	IBB	SO	HBP	SH	SF	SB	CS	SB%	GDP	Avg	OBP	SLG
1999 Chicago	AL	153	612	181	30	8	13	(7	6)	266	109	60	73	1	105	4	3	2	34	11	.76	9	.296	.373	.435
5 ML YEARS		747	2909	808	152	32	60	(24	36)	1204	488	296	296	10	484	32	23	24	151	45	.77	42	.278	.348	.414

Trent Durrington

Bats: Right **Throws:** Right **Pos:** 2B-41; PH/PR-6; DH-1   **Ht:** 5'10" **Wt:** 172 **Born:** 8/27/75 **Age:** 24

		BATTING																	BASERUNNING				PERCENTAGES		
Year Team	Lg	G	AB	H	2B	3B	HR	(Hm	Rd)	TB	R	RBI	TBB	IBB	SO	HBP	SH	SF	SB	CS	SB%	GDP	Avg	OBP	SLG
1994 Angels	R	16	52	14	3	0	1	—	—	20	13	2	10	0	16	1	0	0	5	1	.83	1	.269	.406	.385
1995 Boise	A-	50	140	24	4	1	3	—	—	39	23	19	17	0	35	2	2	2	2	0	1.00	4	.171	.267	.279
1996 Boise	A-	40	154	43	7	2	0	—	—	54	38	14	31	1	32	13	0	0	24	5	.83	4	.279	.439	.351
Cedar Rapds	A	25	76	19	1	0	0	—	—	20	12	4	33	0	20	2	2	1	15	2	.88	2	.250	.482	.263
1997 Lk Elsinore	A+	123	409	101	21	3	3	—	—	137	60	36	51	1	90	11	17	3	52	18	.74	8	.247	.344	.335
1998 Midland	AA	112	351	79	10	1	1	—	—	94	62	30	50	0	74	17	7	4	24	12	.67	5	.225	.346	.268
1999 Erie	AA	107	396	114	26	1	3	—	—	151	84	34	52	1	66	9	12	5	59	16	.79	4	.288	.379	.381
1999 Anaheim	AL	43	122	22	2	0	0	(0	0)	24	14	2	9	0	28	0	5	0	4	3	.57	1	.180	.237	.197

Mike Duvall

Pitches: Left **Bats:** Right **Pos:** RP-40   **Ht:** 6'0" **Wt:** 200 **Born:** 10/11/74 **Age:** 25

		HOW MUCH HE PITCHED						WHAT HE GAVE UP												THE RESULTS					
Year Team	Lg	G	GS	CG	GF	IP	BFP	H	R	ER	HR	SH	SF	HB	TBB	IBB	SO	WP	Bk	W	L	Pct.	ShO	Sv-Op	Hld	ERA
1995 Marlins	R	16	1	0	10	28.1	120	15	8	7	1	0	0	2	12	1	34	4	2	5	0	1.000	0	1- -	—	2.22
1996 Kane County	A	41	0	0	28	48	210	43	20	11	0	2	0	0	21	2	46	3	0	4	1	.800	0	8- -	—	2.06
1997 Brevard Cty	A+	11	0	0	11	12.1	45	7	1	1	0	0	0	0	3	1	9	0	0	1	0	1.000	0	6- -	—	0.73
Portland	AA	45	0	0	25	68.1	291	63	20	14	4	9	1	2	20	2	49	2	0	4	6	.400	0	18- -	—	1.84
1998 St. Pete	A+	2	0	0	2	3.1	16	4	1	1	0	0	0	0	2	0	3	2	0	0	0	.000	0	0- -	—	2.70
Durham	AAA	32	9	1	5	72.2	314	74	31	26	3	0	1	2	32	3	55	5	0	5	3	.625	0	0- -	—	3.22
1999 Durham	AAA	19	1	0	4	30	131	32	20	18	4	0	0	0	12	1	27	0	0	2	2	.500	0	2- -	—	5.40
1998 Tampa Bay	AL	3	0	0	0	4	17	4	3	3	0	0	0	0	2	0	1	0	0	0	0	.000	0	0-0	0	6.75
1999 Tampa Bay	AL	40	0	0	7	40	188	46	21	18	5	1	1	2	27	1	18	4	1	1	1	.500	0	0-1	0	4.05
2 ML YEARS		43	0	0	7	44	205	50	24	21	5	1	1	2	29	1	19	4	1	1	1	.500	0	0-1	0	4.30

Jermaine Dye

Bats: Right **Throws:** Right **Pos:** RF-157; DH-1   **Ht:** 6'4" **Wt:** 220 **Born:** 1/28/74 **Age:** 26

		BATTING																	BASERUNNING				PERCENTAGES		
Year Team	Lg	G	AB	H	2B	3B	HR	(Hm	Rd)	TB	R	RBI	TBB	IBB	SO	HBP	SH	SF	SB	CS	SB%	GDP	Avg	OBP	SLG
1996 Atlanta	NL	98	292	82	16	0	12	(4	8)	134	32	37	8	0	67	3	0	3	1	4	.20	11	.281	.304	.459
1997 Kansas City	AL	75	263	62	14	0	7	(3	4)	97	26	22	17	0	51	1	1	1	2	1	.67	6	.236	.284	.369
1998 Kansas City	AL	60	214	50	5	1	5	(3	2)	72	24	23	11	2	46	1	0	4	2	2	.50	8	.234	.270	.336
1999 Kansas City	AL	158	608	179	44	8	27	(15	12)	320	96	119	58	4	119	1	0	6	2	3	.40	17	.294	.354	.526
4 ML YEARS		391	1377	373	79	9	51	(25	26)	623	178	201	94	6	283	6	1	14	7	10	.41	42	.271	.317	.452

Damion Easley

Bats: Right **Throws:** Right **Pos:** 2B-147; SS-19   **Ht:** 5'11" **Wt:** 185 **Born:** 11/11/69 **Age:** 30

		BATTING																	BASERUNNING				PERCENTAGES		
Year Team	Lg	G	AB	H	2B	3B	HR	(Hm	Rd)	TB	R	RBI	TBB	IBB	SO	HBP	SH	SF	SB	CS	SB%	GDP	Avg	OBP	SLG
1992 California	AL	47	151	39	5	0	1	(1	0)	47	14	12	8	0	26	3	2	1	9	5	.64	2	.258	.307	.311
1993 California	AL	73	230	72	13	2	2	(0	2)	95	33	22	28	2	35	3	1	2	6	6	.50	5	.313	.392	.413
1994 California	AL	88	316	68	16	1	6	(4	2)	104	41	30	29	0	48	4	4	2	4	5	.44	8	.215	.288	.329
1995 California	AL	114	357	77	14	2	4	(1	3)	107	35	35	32	1	47	6	6	4	5	2	.71	11	.216	.288	.300
1996 Cal-Det	AL	49	112	30	2	0	4	(1	3)	44	14	17	10	0	25	1	5	1	3	1	.75	0	.268	.331	.393
1997 Detroit	AL	151	549	139	37	3	22	(12	10)	248	97	72	68	3	102	16	4	5	28	13	.68	18	.264	.362	.471
1998 Detroit	AL	153	594	161	38	2	27	(19	8)	284	84	100	39	2	112	16	0	2	15	5	.75	8	.271	.332	.478
1999 Detroit	AL	151	549	146	30	1	20	(12	8)	238	83	65	51	2	124	19	2	6	11	3	.79	15	.266	.346	.434
1996 California	AL	28	45	7	1	0	2	(1	1)	14	4	7	6	0	12	0	3	0	0	0	.00	0	.156	.255	.311
Detroit	AL	21	67	23	1	0	2	(0	2)	30	10	10	4	0	13	1	2	1	3	1	.75	0	.343	.384	.448
8 ML YEARS		826	2836	732	155	11	86	(50	36)	1167	401	353	265	10	519	68	24	23	81	40	.67	67	.258	.334	.411

Derrin Ebert

Pitches: Left **Bats:** Right **Pos:** RP-5   **Ht:** 6'3" **Wt:** 200 **Born:** 8/21/76 **Age:** 23

		HOW MUCH HE PITCHED						WHAT HE GAVE UP												THE RESULTS					
Year Team	Lg	G	GS	CG	GF	IP	BFP	H	R	ER	HR	SH	SF	HB	TBB	IBB	SO	WP	Bk	W	L	Pct.	ShO	Sv-Op	Hld	ERA
1994 Braves	R	10	7	1	2	43	176	40	18	14	4	0	0	1	8	0	25	1	3	1	3	.250	1	0- -	—	2.93
1995 Macon	A	28	28	0	0	182	766	184	87	67	12	5	4	7	46	0	124	3	2	14	5	.737	0	0- -	—	3.31
1996 Durham	A+	27	27	2	0	166.1	711	189	102	74	13	8	4	4	37	1	99	5	0	12	9	.571	0	0- -	—	4.00
1997 Greenville	AA	27	25	0	0	175.2	743	191	95	80	24	9	6	4	48	1	101	10	0	11	8	.579	0	0- -	—	4.10
1998 Richmond	AAA	29	29	0	0	163.2	710	195	94	82	14	5	3	3	49	1	88	4	0	9	9	.500	0	0- -	—	4.51
1999 Richmond	AAA	25	24	2	0	150.2	646	173	79	72	13	5	6	2	44	0	82	7	0	8	7	.533	1	0- -	—	4.30
1999 Atlanta	NL	5	0	0	3	8	35	9	5	5	2	0	0	0	5	1	4	0	0	0	1	.000	0	1-1	0	5.63

Angel Echevarria

Bats: R **Throws:** R **Pos:** PH/PR-53; RF-31; LF-20; 1B-10   **Ht:** 6'3" **Wt:** 226 **Born:** 5/25/71 **Age:** 29

										BATTING								BASERUNNING				PERCENTAGES		
Year Team	Lg	G	AB	H	2B	3B	HR	(Hm | Rd)	TB	R	RBI	TBB	IBB	SO	HBP	SH	SF	SB	CS	SB%	GDP	Avg	OBP	SLG
1996 Colorado	NL	26	21	6	0	0	0	(0 | 0)	6	2	6	2	0	5	1	0	2	0	0	.00	0	.286	.346	.286
1997 Colorado	NL	15	20	5	2	0	0	(0 | 0)	7	4	0	2	0	5	0	0	0	0	0	.00	0	.250	.318	.350
1998 Colorado	NL	19	29	11	3	0	1	(1 | 0)	17	7	9	2	0	3	2	0	0	0	0	.00	4	.379	.455	.586
1999 Colorado	NL	102	191	56	7	0	11	(5 | 6)	96	28	35	17	0	34	3	0	0	1	3	.25	11	.293	.360	.503
4 ML YEARS		162	261	78	12	0	12	(6 | 6)	126	41	50	23	0	47	6	0	2	1	3	.25	15	.299	.366	.483

Jim Edmonds

Bats: L **Throws:** L **Pos:** CF-42; DH-9; 1B-2; PH/PR-2   **Ht:** 6'1" **Wt:** 218 **Born:** 6/27/70 **Age:** 30

										BATTING								BASERUNNING				PERCENTAGES		
Year Team	Lg	G	AB	H	2B	3B	HR	(Hm	Rd)	TB	R	RBI	TBB	IBB	SO	HBP	SH	SF	SB	CS	SB%	GDP	Avg	OBP	SLG
1999 Lk Elsinore *	A+	5	19	8	2	0	0	(—	—)	10	4	3	4	0	2	0	0	0	2	0	1.00	0	.421	.522	.526
1993 California	AL	18	61	15	4	1	0	(0	0)	21	5	4	2	1	16	0	0	0	0	2	.00	1	.246	.270	.344
1994 California	AL	94	289	79	13	1	5	(3	2)	109	35	37	30	3	72	1	1	1	4	2	.67	3	.273	.343	.377
1995 California	AL	141	558	162	30	4	33	(16	17)	299	120	107	51	4	130	5	1	5	1	4	.20	10	.290	.352	.536
1996 California	AL	114	431	131	28	3	27	(17	10)	246	73	66	46	2	101	4	0	2	4	0	1.00	8	.304	.375	.571
1997 Anaheim	AL	133	502	146	27	0	26	(14	12)	251	82	80	60	5	80	4	0	5	5	7	.42	8	.291	.368	.500
1998 Anaheim	AL	154	599	184	42	1	25	(9	16)	303	115	91	57	7	114	1	1	1	7	5	.58	16	.307	.368	.506
1999 Anaheim	AL	55	204	51	17	2	5	(3	2)	87	34	23	28	0	45	0	0	1	5	4	.56	3	.250	.339	.426
7 ML YEARS		709	2644	768	161	12	121	(62	59)	1316	464	408	274	22	558	15	3	15	26	24	.52	49	.290	.359	.498

Brian Edmondson

Pitches: Right **Bats:** Right **Pos:** RP-68   **Ht:** 6'2" **Wt:** 175 **Born:** 1/29/73 **Age:** 27

		HOW MUCH HE PITCHED						WHAT HE GAVE UP										THE RESULTS						
Year Team	Lg	G	GS	CG	GF	IP	BFP	H	R	ER	HR	SH	SF	HB	TBB	IBB	SO	WP	Bk	W	L	Pct.	ShO	Sv-Op	Hld	ERA
1991 Bristol	R+	12	12	1	0	69	289	72	38	35	7	1	2	3	23	1	42	5	2	4	4	.500	0	0--	—	4.57
1992 Fayettevlle	A	28	27	3	0	155.1	665	145	69	58	10	5	3	6	67	0	125	6	2	10	6	.625	1	0--	—	3.36
1993 Lakeland	A+	19	19	1	0	114.1	483	115	44	38	6	1	0	3	43	0	64	7	0	8	5	.615	0	0--	—	2.99
London	AA	5	5	1	0	23	109	30	23	16	2	1	0	0	13	0	17	1	0	0	4	.000	0	0--	—	6.26
1994 Trenton	AA	26	26	2	0	162	703	171	89	82	12	2	6	6	61	1	90	11	2	11	9	.550	0	0--	—	4.56
1995 Binghamton	AA	23	22	2	0	134.1	601	150	82	71	17	5	5	6	59	2	69	7	0	7	11	.389	1	0--	—	4.76
1996 Binghamton	AA	39	13	1	9	114.1	502	130	69	54	16	7	7	4	38	5	83	3	1	6	6	.500	0	0--	—	4.25
1997 Binghamton	AA	14	0	0	7	22	85	17	4	3	0	2	0	0	7	0	18	1	0	2	0	1.000	0	3--	—	1.23
Norfolk	AAA	31	4	0	8	68.1	296	62	27	22	5	3	4	4	37	2	65	4	1	4	3	.571	0	1--	—	2.90
1998 Atl-Fla	NL	53	0	0	13	76	334	76	38	33	10	5	3	3	37	5	40	5	0	4	4	.500	0	0-3	5	3.91
1999 Florida	NL	68	0	0	14	94	428	106	65	61	11	6	7	6	44	5	58	5	0	5	8	.385	0	1-6	9	5.84
1998 Atlanta	NL	10	0	0	3	16.2	73	14	10	8	2	0	0	0	8	1	8	4	0	0	1	.000	0	0-1	0	4.32
Florida	NL	43	0	0	10	59.1	261	62	28	25	8	5	3	3	29	4	32	1	0	4	3	.571	0	0-2	5	3.79
2 ML YEARS		121	0	0	27	170	762	182	103	94	21	11	10	9	81	10	98	10	0	9	12	.429	0	1-9	14	4.98

Dave Eiland

Pitches: Right **Bats:** Right **Pos:** SP-15; RP-6   **Ht:** 6'3" **Wt:** 208 **Born:** 7/5/66 **Age:** 33

		HOW MUCH HE PITCHED						WHAT HE GAVE UP										THE RESULTS						
Year Team	Lg	G	GS	CG	GF	IP	BFP	H	R	ER	HR	SH	SF	HB	TBB	IBB	SO	WP	Bk	W	L	Pct.	ShO	Sv-Op	Hld	ERA
1999 Durham *	AAA	10	10	0	0	59	242	60	26	22	7	1	3	1	9	0	46	0	0	5	3	.625	0	0--	—	3.36
1988 New York	AL	3	3	0	0	12.2	57	15	9	9	6	0	0	2	4	0	7	0	0	0	0	.000	0	0-0	0	6.39
1989 New York	AL	6	6	0	0	34.1	152	44	25	22	5	1	2	2	13	3	11	0	0	1	3	.250	0	0-0	0	5.77
1990 New York	AL	5	5	0	0	30.1	127	31	14	12	2	0	0	0	5	0	16	0	0	2	1	.667	0	0-0	0	3.56
1991 New York	AL	18	13	0	4	72.2	317	87	51	43	10	0	3	3	23	1	18	0	0	2	5	.286	0	0-0	0	5.33
1992 San Diego	NL	7	7	0	0	27	120	33	21	17	1	0	0	0	5	0	10	0	0	0	2	.000	0	0-0	0	5.67
1993 San Diego	NL	10	9	0	0	48.1	217	58	33	28	5	2	2	1	17	0	14	1	0	0	3	.000	0	0-0	0	5.21
1995 New York	AL	4	1	0	1	10	51	16	10	7	1	0	1	1	3	1	6	1	0	1	1	.500	0	0-0	0	6.30
1998 Tampa Bay	AL	1	1	0	0	2.2	17	6	6	6	0	0	0	0	3	0	1	0	0	0	1	.000	0	0-0	0	20.25
1999 Tampa Bay	AL	21	15	0	0	80.1	369	98	59	50	8	2	4	3	27	1	53	2	1	4	8	.333	0	0-1	0	5.60
9 ML YEARS		75	60	0	5	318.1	1427	388	228	194	38	5	12	12	100	7	136	4	2	10	24	.294	0	0-1	0	5.48

Scott Elarton

Pitches: Right **Bats:** Right **Pos:** RP-27; SP-15   **Ht:** 6'7" **Wt:** 240 **Born:** 2/23/76 **Age:** 24

		HOW MUCH HE PITCHED						WHAT HE GAVE UP										THE RESULTS						
Year Team	Lg	G	GS	CG	GF	IP	BFP	H	R	ER	HR	SH	SF	HB	TBB	IBB	SO	WP	Bk	W	L	Pct.	ShO	Sv-Op	Hld	ERA
1994 Astros	R	5	5	0	0	28	92	9	0	0	0	0	0	0	5	0	28	1	0	4	0	1.000	0	0--	—	0.00
Quad City	A	9	9	0	0	54.2	220	42	23	20	4	2	2	1	18	0	42	3	1	4	1	.800	0	0--	—	3.29
1995 Quad City	A	26	26	0	0	149.2	668	149	86	74	12	8	4	8	71	2	112	12	0	13	7	.650	0	0--	—	4.45
1996 Kissimmee	A+	27	27	3	0	172.1	715	154	67	56	13	7	6	8	54	0	130	5	0	12	7	.632	1	0--	—	2.92
1997 Jackson	AA	20	20	2	0	133.1	544	103	57	48	6	3	1	2	47	3	141	5	0	7	4	.636	0	0--	—	3.24
New Orleans	AAA	9	9	0	0	54	228	51	36	32	5	3	1	1	17	1	50	4	0	4	4	.500	0	0--	—	5.33
1998 New Orleans	AAA	14	14	2	0	92	383	71	42	41	6	0	3	4	41	3	100	3	0	9	4	.692	1	0--	—	4.01
1998 Houston	NL	28	2	0	7	57	227	40	21	21	5	1	1	1	20	0	56	1	0	2	1	.667	0	2-3	2	3.32
1999 Houston	NL	42	15	0	8	124	524	111	55	48	8	7	4	4	43	0	121	3	0	9	5	.643	0	1-4	5	3.48
2 ML YEARS		70	17	0	15	181	751	151	76	69	13	8	5	5	63	0	177	4	0	11	6	.647	0	3-7	7	3.43

Cal Eldred

Pitches: Right **Bats:** Right **Pos:** SP-15; RP-5   **Ht:** 6'4" **Wt:** 237 **Born:** 11/24/67 **Age:** 32

Year Team	Lg		HOW MUCH HE PITCHED							WHAT HE GAVE UP												THE RESULTS					
		G	GS	CG	GF	IP	BFP	H	R	ER	HR	SH	SF	HB	TBB	IBB	SO	WP	Bk	W	L	Pct.	ShO	Sv-Op	Hld	ERA
1999 Huntsville *	AA	2	2	1	0	12	55	13	10	10	2	0	0	2	3	0	10	0	0	0	1	.000	0	0- -	—	7.50
Louisville *	AAA	4	4	0	0	18.2	86	19	12	11	4	0	0	0	10	0	21	0	0	0	1	.000	0	0- -	—	5.30
1991 Milwaukee	AL	3	3	0	0	16	73	20	9	8	2	0	0	0	6	0	10	0	0	2	0	1.000	0	0-0	0	4.50
1992 Milwaukee	AL	14	14	2	0	100.1	394	76	21	20	4	1	0	2	23	0	62	3	0	11	2	.846	1	0-0	0	1.79
1993 Milwaukee	AL	36	36	8	0	258	1087	232	120	115	32	5	12	10	91	5	180	2	0	16	16	.500	1	0-0	0	4.01
1994 Milwaukee	AL	25	25	6	0	179	769	158	96	93	23	5	7	4	84	0	98	2	0	11	11	.500	0	0-0	0	4.68
1995 Milwaukee	AL	4	4	0	0	23.2	104	24	10	9	4	1	0	1	10	0	18	1	1	1	1	.500	0	0-0	0	3.42
1996 Milwaukee	AL	15	15	0	0	84.2	363	82	43	42	8	0	4	4	38	0	50	1	0	4	4	.500	0	0-0	0	4.46
1997 Milwaukee	AL	34	34	1	0	202	885	207	118	112	31	4	6	9	89	0	122	5	0	13	15	.464	1	0-0	0	4.99
1998 Milwaukee	NL	23	23	0	0	133	602	157	82	71	14	5	3	4	61	3	86	6	0	4	8	.333	0	0-0	0	4.80
1999 Milwaukee	NL	20	15	0	2	82	392	101	75	71	19	2	3	1	46	0	60	8	1	2	8	.200	0	0-0	0	7.79
9 ML YEARS		174	169	17	2	1078.2	4669	1057	574	541	137	23	35	35	448	8	686	28	2	64	65	.496	3	0-0	0	4.51

Alan Embree

Pitches: Left **Bats:** Left **Pos:** RP-68   **Ht:** 6'2" **Wt:** 190 **Born:** 1/23/70 **Age:** 30

Year Team	Lg		HOW MUCH HE PITCHED							WHAT HE GAVE UP												THE RESULTS					
		G	GS	CG	GF	IP	BFP	H	R	ER	HR	SH	SF	HB	TBB	IBB	SO	WP	Bk	W	L	Pct.	ShO	Sv-Op	Hld	ERA
1992 Cleveland	AL	4	4	0	0	18	81	19	14	14	3	0	2	1	8	0	12	1	1	0	2	.000	0	0-0	0	7.00
1995 Cleveland	AL	23	0	0	8	24.2	113	23	16	14	2	2	2	0	16	0	23	1	0	3	2	.600	0	1-1	6	5.11
1996 Cleveland	AL	24	0	0	2	31	141	30	26	22	10	1	3	0	21	3	33	3	0	1	1	.500	0	0-0	1	6.39
1997 Atlanta	NL	66	0	0	15	46	190	36	13	13	1	4	1	2	20	2	45	3	1	3	1	.750	0	0-0	16	2.54
1998 Atl-Ari	NL	55	0	0	16	53.2	237	56	32	25	7	4	1	1	23	0	43	3	0	4	2	.667	0	1-3	12	4.19
1999 San Francisco	NL	68	0	0	13	58.2	244	42	22	22	6	3	2	3	26	2	53	3	0	3	2	.600	0	0-3	22	3.38
1998 New York	NL	20	0	0	5	18.2	87	23	14	9	2	1	1	0	10	0	19	0	0	1	0	1.000	0	0-1	6	4.34
Arizona	NL	35	0	0	11	35	150	33	18	16	5	3	0	1	13	0	24	3	0	3	2	.600	0	1-2	6	4.11
6 ML YEARS		240	4	0	54	232	1004	206	123	110	29	14	11	7	114	7	209	14	2	14	10	.583	0	2-7	57	4.27

Juan Encarnacion

Bats: R **Throws:** R **Pos:** LF-118; CF-22; PH/PR-2; RF-1   **Ht:** 6'3" **Wt:** 187 **Born:** 3/8/76 **Age:** 24

Year Team	Lg				BATTING														BASERUNNING				PERCENTAGES		
		G	AB	H	2B	3B	HR	(Hm	Rd)	TB	R	RBI	TBB	IBB	SO	HBP	SH	SF	SB	CS	SB%	GDP	Avg	OBP	SLG
1997 Detroit	AL	11	33	7	1	1	1	(1	0)	12	3	5	3	0	12	2	0	0	1	1	.75	1	.212	.316	.394
1998 Detroit	AL	40	164	54	9	4	7	(4	3)	92	30	21	7	0	31	1	0	3	7	4	.64	2	.329	.354	.561
1999 Detroit	AL	132	509	130	30	6	19	(6	13)	229	62	74	14	1	113	9	4	2	33	12	.73	12	.255	.287	.450
3 ML YEARS		183	706	191	40	11	27	(11	16)	334	95	100	24	1	156	12	4	5	43	17	.72	15	.271	.304	.473

Todd Erdos

Pitches: Right **Bats:** Right **Pos:** RP-4   **Ht:** 6'1" **Wt:** 190 **Born:** 11/21/73 **Age:** 26

Year Team	Lg		HOW MUCH HE PITCHED							WHAT HE GAVE UP												THE RESULTS					
		G	GS	CG	GF	IP	BFP	H	R	ER	HR	SH	SF	HB	TBB	IBB	SO	WP	Bk	W	L	Pct.	ShO	Sv-Op	Hld	ERA
1992 Padres	R	12	9	1	2	57.2	233	36	28	17	1	3	1	3	18	0	61	8	3	3	4	.429	0	0- -	—	2.65
Spokane	A-	2	2	0	0	13	53	9	2	1	0	1	0	1	5	0	11	0	0	1	0	1.000	0	0- -	—	0.69
1993 Waterloo	A	11	11	0	0	47.2	235	64	51	44	9	2	3	4	31	2	27	8	1	1	9	.100	0	0- -	—	8.31
Spokane	A-	16	15	0	0	90.1	384	73	39	32	13	4	2	3	53	2	64	1	1	5	6	.455	0	0- -	—	3.19
1995 Rancho Cuca	A+	1	0	0	0	2.2	13	5	4	4	0	0	1	0	0	0	4	0	0	0	0	.000	0	0- -	—	13.50
Clinton	A	5	1	0	1	5	27	4	4	3	0	0	0	0	8	1	1	2	0	0	0	.000	0	0- -	—	5.40
Idaho Falls	R+	32	0	0	20	41.1	185	34	19	16	1	3	2	5	30	2	48	8	0	5	3	.625	0	1- -	—	3.48
1996 Rancho Cuca	A+	55	0	0	41	67.1	305	63	33	28	2	7	2	6	37	3	82	6	0	3	3	.500	0	17- -	—	3.74
1997 Mobile	AA	55	0	0	50	59	244	45	22	22	4	2	1	0	22	4	49	2	1	1	4	.200	0	27- -	—	3.36
1998 Columbus	AAA	39	0	0	33	48.2	216	52	27	25	4	1	3	2	20	0	50	2	0	3	2	.600	0	16- -	—	4.62
1999 Columbus	AAA	27	8	0	3	59	270	70	47	43	10	0	5	3	25	1	53	4	0	3	2	.600	0	0- -	—	6.56
1997 San Diego	NL	11	0	0	2	13.2	64	17	9	8	1	0	0	2	4	0	13	3	0	2	0	1.000	0	0-0	0	5.27
1998 New York	AL	2	0	0	1	2	11	5	2	2	0	0	0	0	1	1	0	0	0	0	0	.000	0	0-0	0	9.00
1999 New York	AL	4	0	0	1	7	31	5	4	3	2	0	1	0	4	0	4	1	0	0	0	.000	0	0-0	0	3.86
3 ML YEARS		17	0	0	4	22.2	106	27	15	13	3	0	1	2	9	1	17	4	0	2	0	1.000	0	0-0	0	5.16

Scott Erickson

Pitches: Right **Bats:** Right **Pos:** SP-34   **Ht:** 6'4" **Wt:** 230 **Born:** 2/2/68 **Age:** 32

Year Team	Lg		HOW MUCH HE PITCHED							WHAT HE GAVE UP												THE RESULTS					
		G	GS	CG	GF	IP	BFP	H	R	ER	HR	SH	SF	HB	TBB	IBB	SO	WP	Bk	W	L	Pct.	ShO	Sv-Op	Hld	ERA
1990 Minnesota	AL	19	17	1	1	113	485	108	49	36	9	5	2	5	51	4	53	3	0	8	4	.667	0	0-0	0	2.87
1991 Minnesota	AL	32	32	5	0	204	851	189	80	72	13	5	7	6	71	3	108	4	0	20	8	.714	3	0-0	0	3.18
1992 Minnesota	AL	32	32	5	0	212	888	197	86	80	18	9	7	8	83	3	101	6	1	13	12	.520	1	0-0	0	3.40
1993 Minnesota	AL	34	34	1	0	218.2	976	266	138	126	17	10	13	10	71	1	116	5	0	8	19	.296	0	0-0	0	5.19
1994 Minnesota	AL	23	23	2	0	144	654	173	95	87	15	3	4	9	59	0	104	10	0	8	11	.421	1	0-0	0	5.44
1995 Min-Bal	AL	32	31	7	1	196.1	836	213	108	105	18	3	3	5	67	0	106	3	2	13	10	.565	2	0-0	0	4.81
1996 Baltimore	AL	34	34	6	0	222.1	968	262	137	124	21	5	5	11	66	4	100	1	0	13	12	.520	0	0-0	0	5.02
1997 Baltimore	AL	34	33	3	0	221.2	922	218	100	91	16	3	4	5	61	5	131	11	0	16	7	.696	2	0-0	0	3.69
1998 Baltimore	AL	36	36	11	0	251.1	1102	284	125	112	23	7	2	13	69	4	186	4	0	16	13	.552	2	0-0	0	4.01
1999 Baltimore	AL	34	34	6	0	230.1	995	244	127	123	27	7	6	11	99	4	106	10	0	15	12	.556	3	0-0	0	4.81

68

Year Team	Lg	HOW MUCH HE PITCHED			WHAT HE GAVE UP				THE RESULTS		
		G GS CG GF	IP	BFP	H R ER HR SH SF HB	TBB IBB	SO WP Bk	W L	Pct.	ShO Sv-Op Hld	ERA
1995 Minnesota	AL	15 15 0 0	87.2	390	102 61 58 11 2 1 4	32 0	45 1 0	4 6	.400	2 0-0 0	5.95
Baltimore	AL	17 16 7 1	108.2	446	111 47 47 7 1 2 1	35 0	61 2 2	9 4	.692	2 0-0 0	3.89
10 ML YEARS		310 306 47 2	2013.2	8677	2154 1045 956 177 57 53 83	697 28	1111 57 3	130 108	.546	16 0-0 0	4.27

Darin Erstad

Bats: L **Throws:** L **Pos:** 1B-78; LF-67; DH-2; CF-2   **Ht:** 6'2" **Wt:** 210 **Born:** 6/4/74 **Age:** 26

Year Team	Lg	BATTING														BASERUNNING				PERCENTAGES		
		G	AB	H	2B	3B	HR	(Hm | Rd)	TB	R	RBI	TBB	IBB	SO	HBP SH SF	SB	CS	SB%	GDP	Avg	OBP	SLG
1996 California	AL	57	208	59	5	1	4	(1 | 3)	78	34	20	17	1	29	0 1 3	3	3	.50	3	.284	.333	.375
1997 Anaheim	AL	139	539	161	34	4	16	(8 | 8)	251	99	77	51	4	86	4 5 6	23	8	.74	5	.299	.360	.466
1998 Anaheim	AL	133	537	159	39	3	19	(9 | 10)	261	84	82	43	7	77	6 1 3	20	6	.77	2	.296	.353	.486
1999 Anaheim	AL	142	585	148	22	5	13	(7 | 6)	219	84	53	47	3	101	1 2 3	13	7	.65	16	.253	.308	.374
4 ML YEARS		471	1869	527	100	13	52	(25 | 27)	809	301	232	158	15	293	11 9 15	59	24	.71	26	.282	.339	.433

Kelvim Escobar

Pitches: Right **Bats:** Right **Pos:** SP-30; RP-3   **Ht:** 6'1" **Wt:** 195 **Born:** 4/11/76 **Age:** 24

Year Team	Lg	HOW MUCH HE PITCHED			WHAT HE GAVE UP				THE RESULTS		
		G GS CG GF	IP	BFP	H R ER HR SH SF HB	TBB IBB	SO WP Bk	W L	Pct.	ShO Sv-Op Hld	ERA
1997 Toronto	AL	27 0 0 23	31	139	28 12 10 1 2 0 0	19 2	36 0 0	3 2	.600	0 14-17 1	2.90
1998 Toronto	AL	22 10 0 2	79.2	342	72 37 33 5 0 3 0	35 0	72 0 0	7 3	.700	0 0-1 5	3.73
1999 Toronto	AL	33 30 1 2	174	795	203 118 110 19 2 8 10	81 2	129 6 1	14 11	.560	0 0-0 0	5.69
3 ML YEARS		82 40 1 27	284.2	1276	303 167 153 25 4 11 10	135 4	237 6 1	24 16	.600	0 14-18 6	4.84

Bobby Estalella

Bats: Right **Throws:** Right **Pos:** C-7; PH/PR-2   **Ht:** 6'1" **Wt:** 205 **Born:** 8/23/74 **Age:** 25

Year Team	Lg	BATTING														BASERUNNING				PERCENTAGES		
		G	AB	H	2B	3B	HR	(Hm | Rd)	TB	R	RBI	TBB	IBB	SO	HBP SH SF	SB	CS	SB%	GDP	Avg	OBP	SLG
1999 Clearwater *	A+	8	26	11	3	0	1	—	—	17	3	8	3	0	3	0 0 0	0	0	.00	0	.423	.483	.654
Scranton-WB *	AAA	110	386	89	23	2	15	—	—	161	58	62	55	1	100	5 0 6	4	1	.80	12	.231	.330	.417
1996 Philadelphia	NL	7	17	6	0	0	2	(0 | 2)	12	5	4	1	0	6	0 0 0	1	0	1.00	0	.353	.389	.706
1997 Philadelphia	NL	13	29	10	1	0	4	(1 | 3)	23	9	9	7	0	7	0 0 0	0	0	.00	2	.345	.472	.793
1998 Philadelphia	NL	47	165	31	6	1	8	(3 | 5)	63	16	20	13	0	49	1 0 3	0	0	.00	4	.188	.247	.382
1999 Philadelphia	NL	9	18	3	0	0	0	(0 | 0)	3	2	1	4	0	7	0 0 0	0	1	.00	0	.167	.318	.167
4 ML YEARS		76	229	50	7	1	14	(4 | 10)	101	32	34	25	0	69	1 0 3	1	1	.50	6	.218	.295	.441

Shawn Estes

Pitches: Left **Bats:** Right **Pos:** SP-32   **Ht:** 6'2" **Wt:** 195 **Born:** 2/18/73 **Age:** 27

Year Team	Lg	HOW MUCH HE PITCHED			WHAT HE GAVE UP				THE RESULTS		
		G GS CG GF	IP	BFP	H R ER HR SH SF HB	TBB IBB	SO WP Bk	W L	Pct.	ShO Sv-Op Hld	ERA
1995 San Francisco	NL	3 3 0 0	17.1	76	16 14 13 2 0 0 1	5 0	14 4 0	0 3	.000	0 0-0 0	6.75
1996 San Francisco	NL	11 11 0 0	70	305	63 30 28 3 5 0 2	39 3	60 4 0	3 5	.375	0 0-0 0	3.60
1997 San Francisco	NL	32 32 3 0	201	849	162 80 71 12 13 2 8	100 2	181 10 2	19 5	.792	2 0-0 0	3.18
1998 San Francisco	NL	25 25 1 0	149.1	661	150 89 84 14 15 4 5	80 6	136 6 1	7 12	.368	1 0-0 0	5.06
1999 San Francisco	NL	32 32 1 0	203	914	209 121 111 21 14 3 5	112 2	159 15 1	11 11	.500	1 0-0 0	4.92
5 ML YEARS		103 103 5 0	640.2	2805	600 334 307 52 47 9 21	336 13	550 39 4	40 36	.526	4 0-0 0	4.31

Horacio Estrada

Pitches: Left **Bats:** Left **Pos:** RP-4   **Ht:** 6'0" **Wt:** 160 **Born:** 10/19/75 **Age:** 24

Year Team	Lg	HOW MUCH HE PITCHED			WHAT HE GAVE UP				THE RESULTS		
		G GS CG GF	IP	BFP	H R ER HR SH SF HB	TBB IBB	SO WP Bk	W L	Pct.	ShO Sv-Op Hld	ERA
1992 Brewers	R	12 4 0 3	31	158	40 37 34 2 3 1 7	19 1	16 3 0	0 4	.000	0 0-- —	9.87
1995 Brewers	R	8 1 0 3	17	73	13 9 7 1 1 0 8	8 0	21 4 2	0 1	.000	0 2-- —	3.71
Helena	R+	13 0 0 1	30	144	27 21 18 3 5 0 3	24 0	30 2 0	1 2	.333	0 0-- —	5.40
1996 Beloit	A	17 0 0 9	29.1	136	21 8 4 2 2 0 0	11 1	34 5 1	2 1	.667	0 1-- —	1.23
Stockton	A+	29 0 0 11	51	214	43 29 26 7 1 1 2	21 2	62 3 0	1 3	.250	0 3-- —	4.59
1997 El Paso	AA	29 23 1 2	153.2	694	174 93 81 11 4 4 4	70 0	127 8 3	8 10	.444	0 1-- —	4.74
1998 El Paso	AA	8 8 0 0	49.2	206	50 27 25 3 6 2 2	21 0	37 4 1	5 0	1.000	0 0-- —	4.53
Louisville	AAA	2 2 0 0	12	50	10 4 4 1 0 0 0	5 0	4 0 0	0 0	.000	0 0-- —	3.00
1999 Louisville	AAA	25 24 1 0	131.2	575	128 87 83 21 3 8 9	65 1	112 8 1	6 6	.500	0 0-- —	5.67
1999 Milwaukee	NL	4 0 0 2	7.1	36	10 6 6 4 0 0 0	4 0	5 0 0	0 0	.000	0 0-0 0	7.36

Tony Eusebio

Bats: Right **Throws:** Right **Pos:** C-98; PH/PR-14   **Ht:** 6'2" **Wt:** 210 **Born:** 4/27/67 **Age:** 33

Year Team	Lg	BATTING														BASERUNNING				PERCENTAGES		
		G	AB	H	2B	3B	HR	(Hm | Rd)	TB	R	RBI	TBB	IBB	SO	HBP SH SF	SB	CS	SB%	GDP	Avg	OBP	SLG
1991 Houston	NL	10	19	2	1	0	0	(0 | 0)	3	4	0	6	0	8	0 0 0	0	0	.00	1	.105	.320	.158
1994 Houston	NL	55	159	47	9	1	5	(1 | 4)	73	18	30	8	0	33	0 2 5	0	1	.00	4	.296	.320	.459
1995 Houston	NL	113	368	110	21	1	6	(5 | 1)	151	46	58	31	1	59	3 1 5	0	2	.00	12	.299	.354	.410
1996 Houston	NL	58	152	41	7	2	1	(1 | 0)	55	15	19	18	2	20	0 0 2	0	0	.00	5	.270	.343	.362

69

BATTING																		BASERUNNING				PERCENTAGES		
Year Team	Lg	G	AB	H	2B	3B	HR	(Hm | Rd)	TB	R	RBI	TBB	IBB	SO	HBP	SH	SF	SB	CS	SB%	GDP	Avg	OBP	SLG
1997 Houston	NL	60	164	45	2	0	1	(0 | 1)	50	12	18	19	1	27	4	0	0	0	1	.00	4	.274	.364	.305
1998 Florida	NL	66	182	46	6	1	1	(1 | 0)	57	13	36	18	2	31	1	0	2	1	0	1.00	8	.253	.320	.313
1999 Houston	NL	103	323	88	15	0	4	(2 | 2)	115	31	33	40	4	67	0	0	0	0	0	.00	9	.272	.353	.356
7 ML YEARS		465	1367	379	61	5	18	(10 | 8)	504	139	194	140	10	245	8	3	14	1	5	.17	43	.277	.345	.369

Carl Everett

Bats: B **Throws:** R **Pos:** CF-118; RF-16; DH-2; LF-2; PH/PR-2   **Ht:** 6'0"   **Wt:** 190   **Born:** 6/3/70   **Age:** 30

BATTING																		BASERUNNING				PERCENTAGES		
Year Team	Lg	G	AB	H	2B	3B	HR	(Hm	Rd)	TB	R	RBI	TBB	IBB	SO	HBP	SH	SF	SB	CS	SB%	GDP	Avg	OBP	SLG
1993 Florida	NL	11	19	2	0	0	0	(0	0)	2	0	0	1	0	9	0	0	0	1	0	1.00	0	.105	.150	.105
1994 Florida	NL	16	51	11	1	0	2	(2	0)	18	7	6	3	0	15	0	0	0	4	0	1.00	0	.216	.259	.353
1995 New York	NL	79	289	75	13	1	12	(9	3)	126	48	54	39	2	67	2	1	0	2	5	.29	11	.260	.352	.436
1996 New York	NL	101	192	46	8	1	1	(1	0)	59	29	16	21	2	53	4	1	1	6	0	1.00	4	.240	.326	.307
1997 New York	NL	142	443	110	28	3	14	(11	3)	186	58	57	32	3	102	7	3	2	17	9	.65	3	.248	.308	.420
1998 Houston	NL	133	467	138	34	4	15	(5	10)	225	72	76	44	2	102	3	3	2	14	12	.54	11	.296	.359	.482
1999 Houston	NL	123	464	151	33	3	25	(11	14)	265	86	108	50	5	94	11	2	8	27	7	.79	5	.325	.398	.571
7 ML YEARS		605	1925	533	117	12	69	(39	30)	881	300	317	190	14	442	27	10	13	71	33	.68	34	.277	.348	.458

Scott Eyre

Pitches: Left   **Bats:** Left   **Pos:** RP-21   **Ht:** 6'1"   **Wt:** 200   **Born:** 5/30/72   **Age:** 28

HOW MUCH HE PITCHED						WHAT HE GAVE UP												THE RESULTS					
Year Team	Lg	G	GS	CG	GF	IP	BFP	H	R	ER	HR	SH	SF	HB	TBB	IBB	SO	WP	Bk	W	L	Pct.	ShO	Sv-Op	Hld	ERA
1999 Charlotte *	AAA	12	11	0	0	68.1	291	75	32	29	3	1	2	1	23	1	63	5	2	6	4	.600	0	0--	—	3.82
1997 Chicago	AL	11	11	0	0	60.2	267	62	36	34	11	1	2	1	31	1	36	2	0	4	4	.500	0	0-0	—	5.04
1998 Chicago	AL	33	17	0	10	107	491	114	78	64	24	2	3	2	64	0	73	7	0	3	8	.273	0	0-0	—	5.38
1999 Chicago	AL	21	0	0	8	25	129	38	22	21	6	0	1	1	15	2	17	1	0	1	1	.500	0	0-0	—	7.56
3 ML YEARS		65	28	0	18	192.2	887	214	136	119	41	3	6	4	110	3	126	10	0	8	13	.381	0	0-0	—	5.56

Jorge Fabregas

Bats: Left   **Throws:** Right   **Pos:** C-82; PH/PR-10; 1B-1   **Ht:** 6'3"   **Wt:** 215   **Born:** 3/13/70   **Age:** 30

BATTING																		BASERUNNING				PERCENTAGES		
Year Team	Lg	G	AB	H	2B	3B	HR	(Hm	Rd)	TB	R	RBI	TBB	IBB	SO	HBP	SH	SF	SB	CS	SB%	GDP	Avg	OBP	SLG
1994 California	AL	43	127	36	3	0	0	(0	0)	39	12	16	7	1	18	0	1	0	2	1	.67	5	.283	.321	.307
1995 California	AL	73	227	56	10	0	1	(1	0)	69	24	22	17	0	28	0	3	1	0	2	.00	9	.247	.298	.304
1996 California	AL	90	254	73	6	0	2	(1	1)	85	18	26	17	3	27	0	3	5	0	1	.00	7	.287	.326	.335
1997 Ana-CWS	AL	121	360	93	11	1	7	(1	6)	127	33	51	14	0	46	1	6	4	1	1	.50	16	.258	.285	.353
1998 Ari-NYM	NL	70	183	36	4	0	2	(0	2)	46	11	20	14	1	32	1	1	2	0	0	.00	4	.197	.255	.251
1999 Fla-Atl	NL	88	231	46	10	2	3	(1	2)	69	20	21	26	6	27	2	4	5	0	0	.00	9	.199	.280	.299
1997 Anaheim	AL	21	38	3	1	0	0	(0	0)	4	2	3	3	0	3	0	2	0	0	0	.00	2	.079	.146	.105
Chicago	AL	100	322	90	10	1	7	(1	6)	123	31	48	11	0	43	1	4	4	1	1	.50	14	.280	.302	.382
1998 Arizona	NL	50	151	30	4	0	1	(0	1)	37	8	15	13	1	26	1	0	2	0	0	.00	3	.199	.263	.245
New York	NL	20	32	6	0	0	1	(0	1)	9	3	5	1	0	6	0	1	0	0	0	.00	1	.188	.212	.281
1999 Florida	NL	82	223	46	10	2	3	(1	2)	69	20	21	26	6	27	2	4	5	0	0	.00	7	.206	.289	.309
Atlanta	NL	6	8	0	0	0	0	(0	0)	0	0	0	0	0	0	0	0	0	0	0	.00	2	.000	.000	.000
6 ML YEARS		485	1382	340	44	3	15	(4	11)	435	118	156	95	11	178	4	18	17	3	5	.38	50	.246	.293	.315

Brian Falkenborg

Pitches: Right   **Bats:** Right   **Pos:** RP-2   **Ht:** 6'6"   **Wt:** 195   **Born:** 1/18/78   **Age:** 22

HOW MUCH HE PITCHED						WHAT HE GAVE UP												THE RESULTS					
Year Team	Lg	G	GS	CG	GF	IP	BFP	H	R	ER	HR	SH	SF	HB	TBB	IBB	SO	WP	Bk	W	L	Pct.	ShO	Sv-Op	Hld	ERA
1996 Orioles	R	8	6	0	1	28	116	21	13	8	1	0	0	1	8	0	36	2	1	0	3	.000	0	0--	—	2.57
High Desert	A+	1	0	0	0	1	3	1	0	0	0	0	0	0	0	0	0	0	0	0	0	.000	0	0--	—	0.00
1997 Bowie	AA	1	1	0	0	1.2	11	3	3	3	0	0	0	0	3	0	0	0	0	0	1	.000	0	0--	—	16.20
Delmarva	A	25	25	0	0	127	547	122	73	63	6	3	2	13	46	2	107	17	0	7	9	.438	0	0--	—	4.46
1998 Frederick	A+	15	14	1	0	78	338	83	42	39	6	3	2	4	18	0	70	8	0	5	5	.500	1	0--	—	4.50
1999 Orioles	R	3	2	0	0	9	37	6	2	2	0	0	0	0	3	0	11	1	0	1	0	1.000	0	0--	—	2.00
Bowie	AA	16	16	0	0	83.1	361	77	40	35	11	2	0	5	36	0	77	1	0	3	6	.333	0	0--	—	3.78
1999 Baltimore	AL	2	0	0	0	3	12	2	0	0	0	0	0	0	2	0	1	0	0	0	0	.000	0	0-0	—	0.00

Steve Falteisek

Pitches: Right   **Bats:** Right   **Pos:** RP-10   **Ht:** 6'2"   **Wt:** 200   **Born:** 1/28/72   **Age:** 28

HOW MUCH HE PITCHED						WHAT HE GAVE UP												THE RESULTS					
Year Team	Lg	G	GS	CG	GF	IP	BFP	H	R	ER	HR	SH	SF	HB	TBB	IBB	SO	WP	Bk	W	L	Pct.	ShO	Sv-Op	Hld	ERA
1992 Jamestown	A-	15	15	2	0	96	407	84	47	38	3	4	1	5	31	2	82	9	10	3	8	.273	0	0--	—	3.56
1993 Burlington	A	14	14	0	0	76.1	345	86	59	50	4	4	1	2	35	0	63	4	1	3	5	.375	0	0--	—	5.90
1994 Wst Plm Bch	A+	27	24	1	0	159.2	658	144	72	45	3	0	6	3	49	0	91	11	4	9	4	.692	0	0--	—	2.54
1995 Harrisburg	AA	25	25	5	0	168	707	152	74	55	3	7	5	11	64	4	112	6	1	9	6	.600	0	0--	—	2.95
Ottawa	AAA	3	3	1	0	23	86	17	4	3	0	0	0	1	5	0	18	0	1	2	0	1.000	1	0--	—	1.17
1996 Ottawa	AAA	12	12	0	0	58	272	75	45	41	10	1	0	5	25	0	26	3	0	2	5	.286	0	0--	—	6.36
Harrisburg	AA	17	17	1	0	115.2	492	111	60	49	9	7	0	5	48	1	62	5	3	6	5	.545	0	0--	—	3.81
1997 Ottawa	AAA	22	22	1	0	125	555	135	67	55	10	7	7	5	54	1	56	12	1	6	9	.400	0	0--	—	3.96

Year Team	Lg	G	GS	CG	GF	IP	BFP	H	R	ER	HR	SH	SF	HB	TBB	IBB	SO	WP	Bk	W	L	Pct.	ShO	Sv-Op	Hld	ERA
1998 Ottawa	AAA	34	22	1	1	161.2	719	186	110	98	17	4	4	11	59	1	83	10	0	10	11	.476	0	0--	—	5.46
1999 Louisville	AAA	42	4	0	8	76.1	359	98	65	58	13	2	2	4	41	4	34	7	1	5	11	.313	0	0--	—	6.84
1997 Montreal	NL	5	0	0	2	8	34	8	4	3	0	0	2	1	3	0	2	0	0	0	0	.000	0	0-0	—	3.38
1999 Milwaukee	NL	10	0	0	3	12	52	18	10	10	3	0	1	0	3	0	5	0	0	0	0	.000	0	0-0	—	7.50
2 ML YEARS		15	0	0	5	20	86	26	14	13	3	0	3	1	6	0	7	0	0	0	0	.000	0	0-0	—	5.85

Kyle Farnsworth

Pitches: Right **Bats:** Right **Pos:** SP-21; RP-6   **Ht:** 6'4" **Wt:** 220 **Born:** 4/14/76 **Age:** 24

Year Team	Lg	G	GS	CG	GF	IP	BFP	H	R	ER	HR	SH	SF	HB	TBB	IBB	SO	WP	Bk	W	L	Pct.	ShO	Sv-Op	Hld	ERA
1995 Cubs	R	16	0	0	6	31	120	22	8	3	0	4	0	1	11	0	18	1	1	3	2	.600	0	1--	—	0.87
1996 Rockford	A	20	20	1	0	112	495	122	62	46	7	2	4	9	35	0	82	8	1	9	6	.600	0	0--	—	3.70
1997 Daytona	A+	27	27	2	0	156.1	684	178	91	71	13	6	2	6	47	1	105	5	1	10	10	.500	0	0--	—	4.09
1998 West Tenn	AA	13	13	0	0	81.1	330	70	32	25	6	2	3	1	21	0	73	2	2	8	2	.800	0	0--	—	2.77
Iowa	AAA	18	18	0	0	102.2	469	129	88	79	18	5	7	2	36	0	79	4	1	5	9	.357	0	0--	—	6.93
1999 Iowa	AAA	6	6	0	0	39.1	157	38	16	14	5	3	0	0	9	0	29	1	0	5	2	.500	0	0--	—	3.20
1999 Chicago	NL	27	21	1	1	130	579	140	80	73	28	6	2	3	52	1	70	7	1	5	9	.357	1	0-0	0	5.05

Sal Fasano

Bats: Right **Throws:** Right **Pos:** C-23   **Ht:** 6'2" **Wt:** 230 **Born:** 8/10/71 **Age:** 28

									BATTING										BASERUNNING				PERCENTAGES		
Year Team	Lg	G	AB	H	2B	3B	HR	(Hm Rd)	TB	R	RBI	TBB	IBB	SO	HBP	SH	SF	SB	CS	SB%	GDP	Avg	OBP	SLG
1999 Omaha *	AAA	88	280	77	15	0	21	— —	155	63	49	42	1	69	26	1	1	4	2	.67	7	.275	.415	.554
1996 Kansas City	AL	51	143	29	2	0	6	(1 5)	49	20	19	14	0	25	2	1	0	1	1	.50	3	.203	.283	.343
1997 Kansas City	AL	13	38	8	2	0	1	(0 1)	13	4	1	1	0	12	0	0	0	0	0	.00	1	.211	.231	.342
1998 Kansas City	AL	74	216	49	10	0	8	(4 4)	83	21	31	10	1	56	16	3	2	1	0	1.00	4	.227	.307	.384
1999 Kansas City	AL	23	60	14	2	0	5	(2 3)	31	11	16	7	0	17	7	0	1	1	0	1.00	1	.233	.373	.517
4 ML YEARS		161	457	100	16	0	20	(7 13)	176	56	67	32	1	110	25	4	3	2	2	.50	9	.219	.304	.385

Jeff Fassero

Pitches: Left **Bats:** Left **Pos:** SP-27; RP-10   **Ht:** 6'1" **Wt:** 195 **Born:** 1/5/63 **Age:** 37

Year Team	Lg	G	GS	CG	GF	IP	BFP	H	R	ER	HR	SH	SF	HB	TBB	IBB	SO	WP	Bk	W	L	Pct.	ShO	Sv-Op	Hld	ERA
1991 Montreal	NL	51	0	0	30	55.1	223	39	17	15	1	6	0	1	17	1	42	4	0	2	5	.286	0	8-11	7	2.44
1992 Montreal	NL	70	0	0	22	85.2	368	81	35	27	1	5	2	2	34	6	63	7	1	8	7	.533	0	1-7	12	2.84
1993 Montreal	NL	56	15	1	10	149.2	616	119	50	38	7	7	4	0	54	0	140	5	0	12	5	.706	0	1-3	6	2.29
1994 Montreal	NL	21	21	1	0	138.2	569	119	54	46	13	7	2	1	40	4	119	6	0	8	6	.571	0	0-0	0	2.99
1995 Montreal	NL	30	30	1	0	189	833	207	102	91	15	19	7	2	74	3	164	7	1	13	14	.481	0	0-0	0	4.33
1996 Montreal	NL	34	34	5	0	231.2	967	217	95	85	20	16	5	3	55	3	222	5	2	15	11	.577	1	0-0	0	3.30
1997 Seattle	AL	35	35	2	0	234.1	1010	226	108	94	21	7	10	3	84	6	189	13	2	16	9	.640	1	0-0	0	3.61
1998 Seattle	AL	32	32	7	0	224.2	954	223	115	99	33	8	8	10	66	2	176	12	0	13	12	.520	0	0-0	0	3.97
1999 Sea-Tex	AL	37	27	0	2	156.1	751	208	135	125	35	2	7	4	83	3	114	9	0	5	14	.263	0	0-0	2	7.20
1999 Seattle	AL	30	24	0	1	139	669	188	123	114	34	1	6	4	73	3	101	7	0	4	14	.222	0	0-0	2	7.38
Texas	AL	7	3	0	1	17.1	82	20	12	11	1	1	1	0	10	0	13	2	0	1	0	1.000	0	0-0	0	5.71
9 ML YEARS		366	194	17	64	1465.1	6291	1439	711	620	146	77	45	26	507	28	1229	68	6	92	83	.526	2	10-21	27	3.81

Carlos Febles

Bats: Right **Throws:** Right **Pos:** 2B-122; PH/PR-1   **Ht:** 5'11" **Wt:** 170 **Born:** 5/24/76 **Age:** 24

									BATTING										BASERUNNING				PERCENTAGES		
Year Team	Lg	G	AB	H	2B	3B	HR	(Hm Rd)	TB	R	RBI	TBB	IBB	SO	HBP	SH	SF	SB	CS	SB%	GDP	Avg	OBP	SLG
1995 Royals	R	54	188	53	13	5	3	— —	85	40	20	26	0	30	4	1	0	16	8	.67	5	.282	.381	.452
1996 Lansing	A	102	363	107	23	5	5	— —	155	84	43	66	0	64	11	7	4	30	14	.68	8	.295	.414	.427
1997 Wilmington	A+	122	438	104	27	6	3	— —	152	78	29	51	2	95	12	3	0	49	11	.82	13	.237	.333	.347
1998 Wichita	AA	126	432	141	28	9	14	— —	229	110	52	80	1	70	11	5	3	51	16	.76	6	.326	.441	.530
1998 Kansas City	AL	11	25	10	1	2	0	(0 0)	15	5	2	4	0	7	0	0	0	2	1	.67	0	.400	.483	.600
1999 Kansas City	AL	123	453	116	22	9	10	(5 5)	186	71	53	47	0	91	9	12	3	20	4	.83	16	.256	.336	.411
2 ML YEARS		134	478	126	23	11	10	(5 5)	201	76	55	51	0	98	9	12	3	22	5	.81	16	.264	.344	.421

Alex Fernandez

Pitches: Right **Bats:** Right **Pos:** SP-24   **Ht:** 6'1" **Wt:** 225 **Born:** 8/13/69 **Age:** 30

Year Team	Lg	G	GS	CG	GF	IP	BFP	H	R	ER	HR	SH	SF	HB	TBB	IBB	SO	WP	Bk	W	L	Pct.	ShO	Sv-Op	Hld	ERA
1990 Chicago	AL	13	13	3	0	87.2	378	89	40	37	6	5	0	3	34	0	61	1	0	5	5	.500	0	0-0	0	3.80
1991 Chicago	AL	34	32	2	1	191.2	827	186	100	96	16	7	11	2	88	2	145	4	1	9	13	.409	0	0-0	1	4.51
1992 Chicago	AL	29	29	4	0	187.2	804	199	100	89	21	6	4	8	50	3	95	3	0	8	11	.421	2	0-0	0	4.27
1993 Chicago	AL	34	34	3	0	247.1	1004	221	95	86	27	9	3	6	67	5	169	8	0	18	9	.667	3	0-0	0	3.13
1994 Chicago	AL	24	24	4	0	170.1	712	163	83	73	25	4	6	1	50	4	122	3	1	11	7	.611	3	0-0	0	3.86
1995 Chicago	AL	30	30	5	0	203.2	858	200	98	86	19	4	6	0	65	7	159	3	0	12	8	.600	2	0-0	0	3.80
1996 Chicago	AL	35	35	6	0	258	1071	248	110	99	34	5	7	7	72	4	200	5	0	16	10	.615	1	0-0	0	3.45
1997 Florida	NL	32	32	5	0	220.2	904	193	93	88	25	14	5	4	69	2	183	9	0	17	12	.586	1	0-0	0	3.59
1999 Florida	NL	24	24	1	0	141	590	135	60	53	10	3	6	4	41	1	91	2	0	7	8	.467	0	0-0	0	3.38
9 ML YEARS		255	253	33	1	1708	7148	1634	779	707	183	57	48	35	536	28	1225	38	2	103	83	.554	10	0-0	1	3.73

Jose Fernandez

Bats: Right Throws: Right Pos: 3B-6; PH/PR-2 Ht: 6'3" Wt: 220 Born: 11/2/74 Age: 25

Year Team	Lg	G	AB	H	2B	3B	HR	(Hm	Rd)	TB	R	RBI	TBB	IBB	SO	HBP	SH	SF	SB	CS	SB%	GDP	Avg	OBP	SLG
1994 Expos	R	44	168	39	8	0	5	—	—	62	27	23	13	0	33	2	0	1	11	1	.92	2	.232	.293	.369
1995 Vermont	A-	66	270	74	6	7	4	—	—	106	38	41	13	2	51	1	1	2	29	4	.88	2	.274	.308	.393
1996 Delmarva	A	126	421	115	23	6	12	—	—	186	72	70	50	5	76	7	0	3	23	13	.64	5	.273	.358	.442
1997 Wst Plm Bch	A+	97	350	108	21	3	9	—	—	162	49	58	37	3	76	7	0	0	22	14	.61	8	.309	.386	.463
Harrisburg	AA	29	96	22	3	1	4	—	—	39	10	11	11	0	28	1	0	0	2	0	1.00	4	.229	.315	.406
1998 Harrisburg	AA	104	369	109	27	1	17	—	—	189	59	58	36	3	73	9	1	5	16	6	.73	3	.295	.368	.512
Ottawa	AAA	21	60	16	4	1	0	—	—	22	8	4	5	0	14	0	1	1	3	1	.75	2	.267	.318	.367
1999 Ottawa	AAA	124	465	126	30	2	14	—	—	202	73	68	31	0	136	5	1	3	14	7	.67	11	.271	.321	.434
1999 Montreal	NL	8	24	5	2	0	0	(0	0)	7	0	1	1	0	7	0	0	0	0	0	.00	0	.208	.240	.292

Tony Fernandez

Bats: B Throws: R Pos: 3B-132; DH-9; PH/PR-5; 2B-1 Ht: 6'2" Wt: 195 Born: 6/30/62 Age: 38

Year Team	Lg	G	AB	H	2B	3B	HR	(Hm	Rd)	TB	R	RBI	TBB	IBB	SO	HBP	SH	SF	SB	CS	SB%	GDP	Avg	OBP	SLG
1983 Toronto	AL	15	34	9	1	1	0	(0	0)	12	5	2	2	0	2	1	1	0	0	1	.00	1	.265	.324	.353
1984 Toronto	AL	88	233	63	5	3	3	(1	2)	83	29	19	17	0	15	0	2	2	5	7	.42	3	.270	.317	.356
1985 Toronto	AL	161	564	163	31	10	2	(1	1)	220	71	51	43	2	41	2	7	2	13	6	.68	12	.289	.340	.390
1986 Toronto	AL	163	687	213	33	9	10	(4	6)	294	91	65	27	0	52	4	5	4	25	12	.68	8	.310	.338	.428
1987 Toronto	AL	146	578	186	29	8	5	(1	4)	246	90	67	51	3	48	5	4	4	32	12	.73	14	.322	.379	.426
1988 Toronto	AL	154	648	186	41	4	5	(3	2)	250	76	70	45	3	65	4	3	4	15	5	.75	9	.287	.335	.386
1989 Toronto	AL	140	573	147	25	9	11	(2	9)	223	64	64	29	1	51	3	2	10	22	6	.79	9	.257	.291	.389
1990 Toronto	AL	161	635	175	27	17	4	(2	2)	248	84	66	71	4	70	7	2	6	26	13	.67	17	.276	.352	.391
1991 San Diego	NL	145	558	152	27	5	4	(1	3)	201	81	38	55	0	74	0	7	1	23	9	.72	12	.272	.337	.360
1992 San Diego	NL	155	622	171	32	4	4	(3	1)	223	84	37	56	4	62	4	9	3	20	20	.50	6	.275	.337	.359
1993 NYM-Tor		142	526	147	23	11	5	(1	4)	207	65	64	56	3	45	1	8	3	21	10	.68	16	.279	.348	.394
1994 Cincinnati	NL	104	366	102	18	6	8	(3	5)	156	50	50	44	8	40	5	4	3	12	7	.63	5	.279	.361	.426
1995 New York	AL	108	384	94	20	2	5	(3	2)	133	57	45	42	4	40	4	3	5	6	6	.50	14	.245	.322	.346
1997 Cleveland	AL	120	409	117	21	1	11	(7	4)	173	55	44	22	0	47	2	6	3	6	6	.50	11	.286	.323	.423
1998 New York	AL	138	486	156	36	2	9	(3	6)	223	71	72	45	5	53	11	3	6	13	8	.62	11	.321	.387	.459
1999 Toronto	AL	142	485	159	41	0	6	(5	1)	218	73	75	77	11	62	10	0	4	6	7	.46	10	.328	.427	.449
1993 New York	NL	48	173	39	5	2	1	(0	1)	51	20	14	25	0	19	1	3	2	6	2	.75	3	.225	.323	.295
Toronto	AL	94	353	108	18	9	4	(1	3)	156	45	50	31	3	26	0	5	1	15	8	.65	13	.306	.361	.442
16 ML YEARS		2082	7788	2240	410	92	92	(41	51)	3110	1046	829	682	48	767	63	66	60	245	135	.64	158	.288	.347	.399

Mike Fetters

Pitches: Right Bats: Right Pos: RP-27 Ht: 6'4" Wt: 225 Born: 12/19/64 Age: 35

Year Team	Lg	G	GS	CG	GF	IP	BFP	H	R	ER	HR	SH	SF	HB	TBB	IBB	SO	WP	Bk	W	L	Pct.	ShO	Sv-Op	Hld	ERA
1999 Rochester *	AAA	4	0	0	0	3.2	14	0	0	0	0	0	0	0	2	0	6	0	0	0	0	.000	0	0- --	—	0.00
1989 California	AL	1	0	0	0	3.1	16	5	4	3	1	0	0	0	1	0	4	2	0	0	0	.000	0	0-0	0	8.10
1990 California	AL	26	2	0	10	67.2	291	77	33	31	9	1	0	2	20	1	35	3	0	1	1	.500	0	1-1	1	4.12
1991 California	AL	19	4	0	8	44.2	206	53	29	24	4	1	0	3	28	2	24	4	0	2	5	.286	0	0-1	0	4.84
1992 Milwaukee	AL	50	0	0	11	62.2	243	38	15	13	3	5	2	7	24	2	43	4	1	5	1	.833	0	2-5	8	1.87
1993 Milwaukee	AL	45	0	0	14	59.1	246	59	29	22	4	5	5	2	22	4	23	0	0	3	3	.500	0	0-0	8	3.34
1994 Milwaukee	AL	42	0	0	31	46	202	41	16	13	0	2	3	1	27	5	31	3	1	1	4	.200	0	17-20	3	2.54
1995 Milwaukee	AL	40	0	0	34	34.2	163	40	16	13	3	2	1	0	20	4	33	5	0	0	3	.000	0	22-27	2	3.38
1996 Milwaukee	AL	61	0	0	55	61.1	268	65	28	23	4	0	1	6	26	4	53	5	0	3	3	.500	0	32-38	1	3.38
1997 Milwaukee	AL	51	0	0	20	70.1	298	62	30	27	4	6	4	1	33	3	62	2	1	1	5	.167	0	6-11	11	3.45
1998 Oak-Ana	AL	60	0	0	28	58.2	264	62	34	28	5	4	2	1	25	2	43	6	0	2	8	.200	0	5-9	11	4.30
1999 Baltimore	AL	27	0	0	10	31	151	35	23	20	5	1	0	2	22	2	22	1	1	1	0	1.000	0	0-3	2	5.81
1998 Oakland	AL	48	0	0	22	47.1	214	48	26	21	3	4	2	1	21	2	34	3	0	1	6	.143	0	5-8	10	3.99
Anaheim	AL	12	0	0	6	11.1	50	14	8	7	2	0	0	0	4	0	9	3	0	1	2	.333	0	0-1	1	5.56
11 ML YEARS		422	6	0	221	539.2	2348	537	257	217	42	27	21	20	248	28	373	35	4	19	33	.365	0	85-115	47	3.62

Robert Fick

Bats: Left Throws: Right Pos: DH-8; C-4; PH/PR-3 Ht: 6'1" Wt: 189 Born: 3/15/74 Age: 26

Year Team	Lg	G	AB	H	2B	3B	HR	(Hm	Rd)	TB	R	RBI	TBB	IBB	SO	HBP	SH	SF	SB	CS	SB%	GDP	Avg	OBP	SLG
1996 Jamestown	A-	43	133	33	6	0	1	—	—	42	18	14	12	1	25	0	0	2	3	1	.75	4	.248	.306	.316
1997 W Michigan	A	122	463	158	50	3	16	—	—	262	100	90	75	11	74	1	0	7	13	4	.76	10	.341	.429	.566
1998 Jacksnville	AA	130	515	164	47	6	18	—	—	277	101	114	71	6	83	6	0	9	8	4	.67	8	.318	.401	.538
1999 Tigers	R	3	9	3	1	0	0	—	—	4	2	2	2	0	0	0	0	0	1	0	1.00	0	.333	.455	.444
W Michigan	A	3	11	3	0	0	0	—	—	3	2	0	2	0	0	0	0	0	1	0	1.00	0	.273	.385	.273
Toledo	AAA	14	48	15	0	1	2	—	—	23	11	8	8	0	5	1	0	1	1	0	1.00	1	.313	.414	.479
1998 Detroit	AL	7	22	8	1	0	3	(0	3)	18	6	7	2	0	7	0	0	0	1	0	1.00	1	.364	.417	.818
1999 Detroit	AL	15	41	9	0	0	3	(1	2)	18	6	10	7	0	6	0	0	1	1	0	1.00	1	.220	.327	.439
2 ML YEARS		22	63	17	1	0	6	(1	5)	36	12	17	9	0	13	0	0	1	2	0	1.00	2	.270	.356	.571

Mike Figga

Bats: Right **Throws:** Right **Pos:** C-43 **Ht:** 6'0" **Wt:** 200 **Born:** 7/31/70 **Age:** 29

Year Team	Lg	G	AB	H	2B	3B	HR	(Hm	Rd)	TB	R	RBI	TBB	IBB	SO	HBP	SH	SF	SB	CS	SB%	GDP	Avg	OBP	SLG
1990 Yankees	R	40	123	35	1	1	2	—	—	44	19	18	17	2	33	1	0	1	4	2	.67	2	.285	.373	.358
1991 Pr William	A+	55	174	34	6	0	3	—	—	49	15	17	19	0	51	0	2	1	2	1	.67	9	.195	.273	.282
1992 Pr William	A+	3	10	2	1	0	0	—	—	3	0	0	2	0	3	0	0	0	1	0	1.00	0	.200	.333	.300
Ft. Laud	A+	80	249	44	13	0	1	—	—	60	12	15	13	1	78	2	3	0	3	1	.75	7	.177	.223	.241
1993 San Berndno	A+	83	308	82	17	1	25	—	—	176	48	71	17	0	84	2	2	3	2	3	.40	7	.266	.306	.571
Albany-Colo	AA	6	22	5	0	0	0	—	—	5	3	2	2	0	9	0	0	0	1	0	1.00	0	.227	.292	.227
1994 Albany-Colo	AA	1	2	1	1	0	0	—	—	2	1	0	0	0	1	0	0	0	0	0	.00	0	.500	.500	1.000
Tampa	A+	111	420	116	17	5	15	—	—	188	48	75	22	1	94	2	1	5	3	0	1.00	12	.276	.312	.448
1995 Norwich	AA	109	399	108	22	4	13	—	—	177	59	61	43	3	90	1	2	6	0	1	.00	10	.271	.339	.444
Columbus	AAA	8	25	7	1	0	1	—	—	11	2	3	3	0	5	0	1	0	0	0	.00	0	.280	.357	.440
1996 Columbus	AAA	4	11	3	1	0	0	—	—	4	3	0	1	0	3	0	0	0	0	0	.00	0	.273	.333	.364
1997 Columbus	AAA	110	390	95	14	4	12	—	—	153	48	54	18	0	104	2	1	3	3	3	.50	9	.244	.278	.392
1998 Columbus	AAA	123	461	129	30	3	26	—	—	243	57	95	35	4	109	2	0	1	2	2	.50	15	.280	.333	.527
1997 New York	AL	2	4	0	0	0	0	(0	0)	0	0	0	0	0	3	0	0	0	0	0	.00	0	.000	.000	.000
1998 New York	AL	1	4	1	0	0	0	(0	0)	1	1	0	0	0	1	0	0	0	0	0	.00	0	.250	.250	.250
1999 NYY-Bal	AL	43	86	19	4	0	1	(0	1)	26	12	5	2	0	27	0	2	1	0	2	.00	1	.221	.236	.302
1999 New York	AL	2	0	0	0	0	0	(0	0)	0	0	0	0	0	0	0	0	0	0	0	.00	0	.000	.000	.000
Baltimore	AL	41	86	19	4	0	1	(0	1)	26	12	5	2	0	27	0	2	1	0	2	.00	1	.221	.236	.302
3 ML YEARS		46	94	20	4	0	1	(0	1)	27	13	5	2	0	31	0	2	1	0	2	.00	1	.213	.227	.287

Chuck Finley

Pitches: Left **Bats:** Left **Pos:** SP-33 **Ht:** 6'6" **Wt:** 226 **Born:** 11/26/62 **Age:** 37

Year Team	Lg	G	GS	CG	GF	IP	BFP	H	R	ER	HR	SH	SF	HB	TBB	IBB	SO	WP	Bk	W	L	Pct	ShO	Sv-Op	Hld	ERA
1986 California	AL	25	0	0	7	46.1	198	40	17	17	2	4	0	1	23	1	37	2	0	3	1	.750	0	0-0	1	3.30
1987 California	AL	35	3	0	17	90.2	405	102	54	47	7	2	2	3	43	3	63	4	3	2	7	.222	0	0-2	0	4.67
1988 California	AL	31	31	2	0	194.1	831	191	95	90	15	7	10	6	82	7	111	5	8	9	15	.375	0	0-0	0	4.17
1989 California	AL	29	29	9	0	199.2	827	171	64	57	13	7	3	2	82	0	156	6	2	16	9	.640	1	0-0	0	2.57
1990 California	AL	32	32	7	0	236	962	210	77	63	17	12	3	2	81	3	177	9	0	18	9	.667	2	0-0	0	2.40
1991 California	AL	34	34	4	0	227.1	955	205	102	96	23	4	3	8	101	1	171	6	3	18	9	.667	2	0-0	0	3.80
1992 California	AL	31	31	4	0	204.1	885	212	99	90	24	10	10	3	98	2	124	6	0	7	12	.368	1	0-0	0	3.96
1993 California	AL	35	35	13	0	251.1	1065	243	108	88	22	11	7	6	82	1	187	8	1	16	14	.533	2	0-0	0	3.15
1994 California	AL	25	25	7	0	183.1	774	178	96	88	21	9	6	3	71	0	148	10	0	10	10	.500	2	0-0	0	4.32
1995 California	AL	32	32	2	0	203	880	192	106	95	20	4	5	7	93	1	195	13	1	15	12	.556	1	0-0	0	4.21
1996 California	AL	35	35	4	0	238	1037	241	143	110	27	7	9	11	94	5	215	17	2	15	16	.484	1	0-0	0	4.16
1997 Anaheim	AL	25	25	3	0	164	690	152	79	77	20	3	4	5	65	0	155	10	2	13	6	.684	1	0-0	0	4.23
1998 Anaheim	AL	34	34	1	0	223.1	976	210	97	84	20	3	6	6	109	1	212	8	0	11	9	.550	1	0-0	0	3.39
1999 Anaheim	AL	33	33	1	0	213.1	913	197	117	105	23	7	3	8	94	2	200	15	0	12	11	.522	0	0-0	0	4.43
14 ML YEARS		436	379	57	24	2675	11398	2544	1234	1107	254	90	70	71	1118	27	2151	117	22	165	140	.541	14	0-2	1	3.72

Steve Finley

Bats: Left **Throws:** Left **Pos:** CF-155; PH/PR-3; DH-1 **Ht:** 6'2" **Wt:** 180 **Born:** 3/12/65 **Age:** 35

Year Team	Lg	G	AB	H	2B	3B	HR	(Hm	Rd)	TB	R	RBI	TBB	IBB	SO	HBP	SH	SF	SB	CS	SB%	GDP	Avg	OBP	SLG
1989 Baltimore	AL	81	217	54	5	2	2	(0	2)	69	35	25	15	1	30	1	6	2	17	3	.85	3	.249	.298	.318
1990 Baltimore	AL	142	464	119	16	4	3	(1	2)	152	46	37	32	3	53	2	10	5	22	9	.71	4	.256	.304	.328
1991 Houston	NL	159	596	170	28	10	8	(0	8)	242	84	54	42	5	65	2	10	6	34	18	.65	8	.285	.331	.406
1992 Houston	NL	162	607	177	29	13	5	(5	0)	247	84	55	58	6	63	3	16	2	44	9	.83	10	.292	.355	.407
1993 Houston	NL	142	545	145	15	13	8	(1	7)	210	69	44	28	1	65	3	6	3	19	6	.76	8	.266	.304	.385
1994 Houston	NL	94	373	103	16	5	11	(4	7)	162	64	33	28	0	52	2	13	1	13	7	.65	3	.276	.329	.434
1995 San Diego	NL	139	562	167	23	8	10	(4	6)	236	104	44	59	5	62	3	4	2	36	12	.75	8	.297	.366	.420
1996 San Diego	NL	161	655	195	45	9	30	(15	15)	348	126	95	56	5	87	4	1	5	22	8	.73	20	.298	.354	.531
1997 San Diego	NL	143	560	146	26	5	28	(5	23)	266	101	92	43	2	92	3	2	7	15	3	.83	10	.261	.313	.475
1998 San Diego	NL	159	619	154	40	6	14	(8	6)	248	92	67	45	0	103	3	3	4	12	3	.80	9	.249	.301	.401
1999 Arizona	NL	156	590	156	32	10	34	(17	17)	310	100	103	63	7	94	3	2	5	8	4	.67	4	.264	.336	.525
11 ML YEARS		1538	5788	1586	275	85	153	(60	93)	2490	905	649	469	35	766	29	73	42	242	82	.75	91	.274	.329	.430

John Flaherty

Bats: Right **Throws:** Right **Pos:** C-115; DH-1; PH/PR-1 **Ht:** 6'1" **Wt:** 200 **Born:** 10/21/67 **Age:** 32

Year Team	Lg	G	AB	H	2B	3B	HR	(Hm	Rd)	TB	R	RBI	TBB	IBB	SO	HBP	SH	SF	SB	CS	SB%	GDP	Avg	OBP	SLG
1992 Boston	AL	35	66	13	2	0	0	(0	0)	15	3	2	3	0	7	0	1	1	0	0	.00	0	.197	.229	.227
1993 Boston	AL	13	25	3	2	0	0	(0	0)	5	3	2	2	0	6	1	1	0	0	0	.00	0	.120	.214	.200
1994 Detroit	AL	34	40	6	1	0	0	(0	0)	7	2	4	1	0	11	0	2	1	0	1	.00	1	.150	.167	.175
1995 Detroit	AL	112	354	86	22	1	11	(6	5)	143	39	40	18	0	47	3	8	2	0	0	.00	8	.243	.284	.404
1996 Det-SD	AL	119	416	118	24	0	13	(8	5)	181	40	64	17	2	61	3	4	4	3	3	.50	13	.284	.314	.435
1997 San Diego	NL	129	439	120	21	1	9	(4	5)	170	38	46	33	7	62	0	2	4	4	4	.50	11	.273	.323	.387
1998 Tampa Bay	AL	91	304	63	11	0	3	(1	2)	83	21	24	22	0	46	1	4	3	0	5	.00	9	.207	.261	.273
1999 Tampa Bay	AL	117	446	124	19	0	14	(3	11)	185	53	71	19	0	64	6	1	10	1	2	.00	14	.278	.310	.415
1996 Detroit	AL	47	152	38	12	0	4	(2	2)	62	18	23	8	1	25	1	3	1	1	0	1.00	5	.250	.290	.408
San Diego	NL	72	264	80	12	0	9	(6	3)	119	22	41	9	1	36	2	1	3	2	3	.40	8	.303	.327	.451
8 ML YEARS		650	2090	533	102	2	50	(22	28)	789	199	253	115	9	304	14	23	23	7	15	.32	56	.255	.295	.378

Darrin Fletcher

Bats: Left   **Throws:** Right   **Pos:** C-113; PH/PR-4   **Ht:** 6'2"   **Wt:** 200   **Born:** 10/3/66   **Age:** 33

Year Team	Lg	G	AB	H	2B	3B	HR	(Hm	Rd)	TB	R	RBI	TBB	IBB	SO	HBP	SH	SF	SB	CS	SB%	GDP	Avg	OBP	SLG
1999 Syracuse *	AAA	4	15	4	0	0	0	—	—	4	0	0	1	0	1	0	0	0	0	0	.00	1	.267	.313	.267
1989 Los Angeles	NL	5	8	4	0	0	1	(1	0)	7	1	2	1	0	0	0	0	0	0	0	.00	0	.500	.556	.875
1990 LA-Phi	NL	11	23	3	1	0	0	(0	0)	4	3	1	1	0	6	0	0	0	0	0	.00	0	.130	.167	.174
1991 Philadelphia	NL	46	136	31	8	0	1	(1	0)	42	5	12	5	0	15	0	1	0	0	1	.00	2	.228	.255	.309
1992 Montreal	NL	83	222	54	10	2	2	(0	2)	74	13	26	14	3	28	2	2	4	0	2	.00	8	.243	.289	.333
1993 Montreal	NL	133	396	101	20	1	9	(5	4)	150	33	60	34	2	40	6	5	4	0	0	.00	7	.255	.320	.379
1994 Montreal	NL	94	285	74	18	1	10	(4	6)	124	28	57	25	4	23	3	0	12	0	0	.00	5	.260	.314	.435
1995 Montreal	NL	110	350	100	21	1	11	(3	8)	156	42	45	32	1	23	4	1	2	0	1	.00	15	.286	.351	.446
1996 Montreal	NL	127	394	105	22	0	12	(7	5)	163	41	57	27	4	42	6	1	3	0	0	.00	13	.266	.321	.414
1997 Montreal	NL	96	310	86	20	1	17	(10	7)	159	39	55	17	3	35	5	0	2	1	1	.50	6	.277	.323	.513
1998 Toronto	AL	124	407	115	23	1	9	(3	6)	167	37	52	25	7	39	6	1	7	0	0	.00	19	.283	.328	.410
1999 Toronto	AL	115	412	120	26	0	18	(10	8)	200	48	80	26	0	47	6	0	4	0	0	.00	16	.291	.339	.485
1990 Los Angeles	NL	2	1	0	0	0	0	(0	0)	0	0	0	0	0	1	0	0	0	0	0	.00	0	.000	.000	.000
Philadelphia	NL	9	22	3	1	0	0	(0	0)	4	3	1	1	0	5	0	0	0	0	0	.00	0	.136	.174	.182
11 ML YEARS		944	2943	793	169	7	90	(44	46)	1246	290	447	207	24	298	38	11	38	1	5	.17	92	.269	.322	.423

Bryce Florie

Pitches: Right   **Bats:** Right   **Pos:** RP-36; SP-5   **Ht:** 5'11"   **Wt:** 192   **Born:** 5/21/70   **Age:** 30

Year Team	Lg	G	GS	CG	GF	IP	BFP	H	R	ER	HR	SH	SF	HB	TBB	IBB	SO	WP	Bk	W	L	Pct.	ShO	Sv-Op	Hld	ERA
1999 Lakeland *	A+	1	1	0	0	3	9	0	0	0	0	0	1	0	0	0	7	0	0	0	0	.000	0	0--	—	0.00
1994 San Diego	NL	9	0	0	4	9.1	37	8	1	1	0	0	1	0	3	0	8	1	0	0	0	.000	0	0-0	0	0.96
1995 San Diego	NL	47	0	0	10	68.2	290	49	30	23	8	5	1	4	38	3	68	7	2	2	2	.500	0	1-4	9	3.01
1996 SD-Mil		54	0	0	16	68.1	312	65	40	36	4	1	3	6	40	5	63	6	1	2	3	.400	0	0-3	8	4.74
1997 Milwaukee	AL	32	8	0	6	75	332	74	43	36	4	1	4	3	42	2	53	4	1	4	4	.500	0	0-1	4	4.32
1998 Detroit	AL	42	16	0	6	133	580	141	80	71	16	3	2	4	59	6	97	9	0	8	9	.471	0	0-0	4	4.80
1999 Det-Bos	AL	41	5	0	10	81.1	368	94	50	42	8	3	2	2	35	5	65	8	0	4	1	.800	0	0-0	3	4.65
1996 San Diego	NL	39	0	0	11	49.1	222	45	24	22	1	0	1	6	27	3	51	3	1	2	2	.500	0	0-1	4	4.01
Milwaukee	AL	15	0	0	5	19	90	20	16	14	3	1	2	0	13	2	12	3	0	1	0	1.000	0	0-2	4	6.63
1999 Detroit	AL	27	3	0	6	51.1	234	61	31	26	6	3	1	1	20	2	40	4	0	2	1	.667	0	0-0	2	4.56
Boston	AL	14	2	0	4	30	134	33	19	16	2	0	1	1	15	3	25	4	0	2	0	1.000	0	0-0	1	4.80
6 ML YEARS		225	29	0	52	435.2	1919	431	244	209	40	13	13	19	217	21	354	35	4	20	19	.513	0	1-8	24	4.32

Cliff Floyd

Bats: Left   **Throws:** Right   **Pos:** LF-62; PH/PR-5; DH-3   **Ht:** 6'4"   **Wt:** 235   **Born:** 12/5/72   **Age:** 27

Year Team	Lg	G	AB	H	2B	3B	HR	(Hm	Rd)	TB	R	RBI	TBB	IBB	SO	HBP	SH	SF	SB	CS	SB%	GDP	Avg	OBP	SLG
1999 Calgary *	AAA	9	31	12	1	0	3	—	—	22	6	8	2	0	8	0	0	0	0	1	.00	0	.387	.424	.710
1993 Montreal	NL	10	31	7	0	0	1	(0	1)	10	3	2	0	0	9	0	0	0	0	0	.00	0	.226	.226	.323
1994 Montreal	NL	100	334	94	19	4	4	(2	2)	133	43	41	24	0	63	3	2	3	10	3	.77	3	.281	.332	.398
1995 Montreal	NL	29	69	9	1	0	1	(1	0)	13	6	8	7	0	22	1	0	0	3	0	1.00	1	.130	.221	.188
1996 Montreal	NL	117	227	55	15	4	6	(3	3)	96	29	26	30	1	52	5	1	3	7	1	.88	5	.242	.340	.423
1997 Florida	NL	61	137	32	9	1	6	(2	4)	61	23	19	24	0	33	2	1	1	6	2	.75	3	.234	.354	.445
1998 Florida	NL	153	588	166	45	3	22	(10	12)	283	85	90	47	7	112	3	0	3	27	14	.66	10	.282	.337	.481
1999 Florida	NL	69	251	76	19	1	11	(4	7)	130	37	49	30	5	47	2	0	2	5	6	.45	8	.303	.379	.518
7 ML YEARS		539	1637	439	108	13	51	(22	29)	726	226	235	162	13	338	16	4	12	58	26	.69	28	.268	.338	.443

Chad Fonville

Bats: Both   **Throws:** Right   **Pos:** 2B-2; PH/PR-2   **Ht:** 5'6"   **Wt:** 155   **Born:** 3/5/71   **Age:** 29

Year Team	Lg	G	AB	H	2B	3B	HR	(Hm	Rd)	TB	R	RBI	TBB	IBB	SO	HBP	SH	SF	SB	CS	SB%	GDP	Avg	OBP	SLG
1999 Pawtucket *	AAA	74	257	65	3	2	1	—	—	75	31	14	20	0	31	2	4	0	6	4	.60	4	.253	.312	.292
1995 Mon-LA	NL	102	320	89	6	1	0	(0	0)	97	43	16	23	1	42	1	6	0	20	7	.74	3	.278	.328	.303
1996 Los Angeles	NL	103	201	41	4	1	0	(0	0)	47	34	13	17	1	31	0	3	0	7	2	.78	1	.204	.266	.234
1997 LA-CWS	AL	18	23	3	0	0	0	(0	0)	3	2	2	3	0	4	0	1	0	2	1	.67	0	.130	.231	.130
1999 Boston	AL	3	2	0	0	0	0	(0	0)	0	1	0	2	0	0	0	0	0	1	0	1.00	0	.000	.500	.000
1995 Montreal	NL	14	12	4	0	0	0	(0	0)	4	2	0	0	0	3	0	0	0	0	0	.00	0	.333	.333	.333
Los Angeles	NL	88	308	85	6	1	0	(0	0)	93	41	16	23	1	39	1	6	0	20	5	.80	3	.276	.328	.302
1997 Los Angeles	NL	9	14	2	0	0	0	(0	0)	2	1	1	2	0	3	0	0	0	0	1	.00	0	.143	.250	.143
Chicago	AL	9	9	1	0	0	0	(0	0)	1	1	1	1	0	1	0	1	0	2	0	1.00	0	.111	.200	.111
4 ML YEARS		226	546	133	10	2	0	(0	0)	147	80	31	45	2	77	1	10	0	30	10	.75	4	.244	.302	.269

Brook Fordyce

Bats: Right   **Throws:** Right   **Pos:** C-103; PH/PR-11   **Ht:** 6'1"   **Wt:** 185   **Born:** 5/7/70   **Age:** 30

Year Team	Lg	G	AB	H	2B	3B	HR	(Hm	Rd)	TB	R	RBI	TBB	IBB	SO	HBP	SH	SF	SB	CS	SB%	GDP	Avg	OBP	SLG
1995 New York	NL	4	2	1	0	0	0	(0	0)	2	1	0	1	0	0	0	0	0	0	0	.00	0	.500	.667	1.000
1996 Cincinnati	NL	4	7	2	1	0	0	(0	0)	3	0	1	3	0	1	0	0	0	0	0	.00	0	.286	.500	.429
1997 Cincinnati	NL	47	96	20	5	0	1	(1	0)	28	7	8	8	1	15	0	0	1	2	0	1.00	0	.208	.267	.292
1998 Cincinnati	NL	57	146	37	9	0	3	(3	0)	55	8	14	11	3	28	1	0	1	0	1	.00	2	.253	.306	.377

Year Team	Lg	G	AB	H	2B	3B	HR	(Hm	Rd)	TB	R	RBI	TBB	IBB	SO	HBP	SH	SF	SB	CS	SB%	GDP	Avg	OBP	SLG
						BATTING													BASERUNNING				PERCENTAGES		
1999 Chicago	AL	105	333	99	25	1	9	(5	4)	153	36	49	21	0	48	3	3	2	2	0	1.00	5	.297	.343	.459
5 ML YEARS		217	584	159	41	1	13	(9	4)	241	52	72	44	4	92	3	4	3	4	1	.80	7	.272	.325	.413

Tony Fossas

Pitches: Left **Bats:** Left **Pos:** RP-5 **Ht:** 6'0" **Wt:** 198 **Born:** 9/23/57 **Age:** 42

Year Team	Lg	G	GS	CG	GF	IP	BFP	H	R	ER	HR	SH	SF	HB	TBB	IBB	SO	WP	Bk	W	L	Pct.	ShO	Sv-Op	Hld	ERA
				HOW MUCH HE PITCHED						WHAT HE GAVE UP												THE RESULTS				
1999 Columbus *	AAA	26	0	0	4	20	83	17	10	9	6	0	0	2	6	0	15	0	0	1	0	1.000	0	0- -	—	4.05
1988 Texas	AL	5	0	0	1	5.2	28	11	3	3	0	0	0	0	2	0	1	0	0	0	0	.000	0	0-0	0	4.76
1989 Milwaukee	AL	51	0	0	16	61	256	57	27	24	3	7	3	1	22	7	42	1	3	2	2	.500	0	1-3	13	3.54
1990 Milwaukee	AL	32	0	0	9	29.1	146	44	23	21	5	2	1	0	10	2	24	0	0	2	3	.400	0	0-2	8	6.44
1991 Boston	AL	64	0	0	18	57	244	49	27	22	3	5	0	3	28	9	29	2	0	3	2	.600	0	1-2	18	3.47
1992 Boston	AL	60	0	0	17	29.2	129	31	9	8	1	3	0	1	14	3	19	0	0	1	2	.333	0	2-3	14	2.43
1993 Boston	AL	71	0	0	19	40	175	38	28	23	4	0	1	2	15	4	39	1	1	1	1	.500	0	0-2	13	5.18
1994 Boston	AL	44	0	0	14	34	151	35	18	18	6	2	0	1	15	1	31	1	0	2	0	1.000	0	1-1	9	4.76
1995 St. Louis	NL	58	0	0	20	36.2	145	28	6	6	1	2	1	1	10	3	40	1	0	3	0	1.000	0	0-0	19	1.47
1996 St. Louis	NL	65	0	0	11	47	209	43	19	14	7	1	1	0	21	3	36	3	0	0	4	.000	0	2-7	15	2.68
1997 St. Louis	NL	71	0	0	14	51.2	239	62	32	22	7	3	1	1	26	3	41	0	0	2	7	.222	0	0-1	16	3.83
1998 Sea-ChC-Tex	AL	41	0	0	10	22.2	110	30	15	15	1	2	1	0	16	0	23	1	0	1	3	.250	0	0-1	4	5.96
1999 New York	AL	5	0	0	0	1	10	6	4	4	1	0	0	0	1	1	0	0	0	0	0	.000	0	0-0	0	36.00
1998 Seattle	AL	23	0	0	8	11.1	55	19	11	11	1	1	1	0	6	0	10	0	0	0	3	.000	0	0-1	3	8.74
Chicago	NL	8	0	0	1	4	26	8	4	4	0	1	0	0	6	0	6	0	0	0	0	.000	0	0-0	1	9.00
Texas	AL	10	0	0	1	7.1	29	3	0	0	0	0	0	0	4	0	7	1	0	1	0	1.000	0	0-0	0	0.00
12 ML YEARS		567	0	0	149	415.2	1842	434	211	180	39	27	9	10	180	36	324	11	4	17	24	.415	0	7-22	129	3.90

Keith Foulke

Pitches: Right **Bats:** Right **Pos:** RP-67 **Ht:** 6'0" **Wt:** 200 **Born:** 10/19/72 **Age:** 27

Year Team	Lg	G	GS	CG	GF	IP	BFP	H	R	ER	HR	SH	SF	HB	TBB	IBB	SO	WP	Bk	W	L	Pct.	ShO	Sv-Op	Hld	ERA
				HOW MUCH HE PITCHED						WHAT HE GAVE UP												THE RESULTS				
1997 SF-CWS		27	8	0	5	73.1	326	88	52	52	13	3	1	4	23	2	54	1	0	4	5	.444	0	3-6	5	6.38
1998 Chicago	AL	54	0	0	18	65.1	267	51	31	30	9	2	2	4	20	3	57	3	1	3	2	.600	0	1-2	13	4.13
1999 Chicago	AL	67	0	0	31	105.1	411	72	28	26	11	3	0	3	21	4	123	1	0	3	3	.500	0	9-13	22	2.22
1997 San Francisco	NL	11	8	0	0	44.2	209	60	41	41	9	2	0	4	18	1	33	1	0	1	5	.167	0	0-1	0	8.26
Chicago	AL	16	0	0	5	28.2	117	28	11	11	4	1	1	0	5	1	21	0	0	3	0	1.000	0	3-5	5	3.45
3 ML YEARS		148	8	0	54	244	1004	211	111	108	33	8	3	11	64	9	234	5	1	10	10	.500	0	13-21	40	3.98

Andy Fox

Bats: Left **Throws:** Right **Pos:** SS-82; PH/PR-14; 3B-12 **Ht:** 6'4" **Wt:** 202 **Born:** 1/12/71 **Age:** 29

Year Team	Lg	G	AB	H	2B	3B	HR	(Hm	Rd)	TB	R	RBI	TBB	IBB	SO	HBP	SH	SF	SB	CS	SB%	GDP	Avg	OBP	SLG
						BATTING													BASERUNNING				PERCENTAGES		
1996 New York	AL	113	189	37	4	0	3	(1	2)	50	26	13	20	0	28	1	9	0	11	3	.79	2	.196	.276	.265
1997 New York	AL	22	31	7	1	0	0	(0	0)	8	13	1	7	0	9	0	2	0	2	1	.67	1	.226	.368	.258
1998 Arizona	NL	139	502	139	21	6	9	(5	4)	199	67	44	43	0	97	18	0	1	14	7	.67	2	.277	.355	.396
1999 Arizona	NL	99	274	70	12	2	6	(2	4)	104	34	33	33	0	61	9	1	3	4	1	.80	4	.255	.351	.380
4 ML YEARS		373	996	253	38	8	18	(10	8)	361	140	91	103	0	195	28	12	4	31	12	.72	9	.254	.340	.362

Chad Fox

Pitches: Right **Bats:** Right **Pos:** RP-6 **Ht:** 6'3" **Wt:** 190 **Born:** 9/3/70 **Age:** 29

Year Team	Lg	G	GS	CG	GF	IP	BFP	H	R	ER	HR	SH	SF	HB	TBB	IBB	SO	WP	Bk	W	L	Pct.	ShO	Sv-Op	Hld	ERA
				HOW MUCH HE PITCHED						WHAT HE GAVE UP												THE RESULTS				
1997 Milwaukee	NL	30	0	0	8	27.1	120	24	12	10	4	0	0	0	16	0	28	4	0	0	1	.000	0	0-1	7	3.29
1998 Milwaukee	NL	49	0	0	12	57	242	56	27	25	4	6	0	1	20	0	64	5	0	1	4	.200	0	0-2	20	3.95
1999 Milwaukee	NL	6	0	0	2	6.2	36	11	8	8	1	0	0	1	4	0	12	1	1	0	0	.000	0	0-0	1	10.80
3 ML YEARS		85	0	0	22	91	398	91	47	43	9	6	0	2	40	0	104	10	1	1	5	.167	0	0-3	28	4.25

John Franco

Pitches: Left **Bats:** Left **Pos:** RP-46 **Ht:** 5'10" **Wt:** 185 **Born:** 9/17/60 **Age:** 39

Year Team	Lg	G	GS	CG	GF	IP	BFP	H	R	ER	HR	SH	SF	HB	TBB	IBB	SO	WP	Bk	W	L	Pct.	ShO	Sv-Op	Hld	ERA
				HOW MUCH HE PITCHED						WHAT HE GAVE UP												THE RESULTS				
1999 Binghamton *	AA	1	1	0	0	1.1	4	0	0	0	0	0	0	0	0	0	1	0	0	0	0	.000	0	0- -	—	0.00
1984 Cincinnati	NL	54	0	0	30	79.1	335	74	28	23	3	4	4	2	36	4	55	2	0	6	2	.750	0	4-8	2	2.61
1985 Cincinnati	NL	67	0	0	33	99	407	83	27	24	5	11	1	1	40	8	61	4	0	12	3	.800	0	12-14	11	2.18
1986 Cincinnati	NL	74	0	0	52	101	429	90	40	33	7	8	3	2	44	12	84	4	2	6	6	.500	0	29-38	2	2.94
1987 Cincinnati	NL	68	0	0	60	82	344	76	26	23	6	5	2	0	27	6	61	1	0	8	5	.615	0	32-41	0	2.52
1988 Cincinnati	NL	70	0	0	61	86	336	60	18	15	3	5	1	0	27	3	46	1	2	6	6	.500	0	39-42	1	1.57
1989 Cincinnati	NL	60	0	0	50	80.2	345	77	35	28	3	7	3	0	36	8	60	3	2	4	8	.333	0	32-39	1	3.12
1990 New York	NL	55	0	0	48	67.2	287	66	22	19	4	3	1	0	21	2	56	7	2	5	3	.625	0	33-39	0	2.53
1991 New York	NL	52	0	0	48	55.1	247	61	27	18	2	3	0	1	18	4	45	6	0	5	9	.357	0	30-35	0	2.93
1992 New York	NL	31	0	0	30	33	128	24	6	6	1	0	2	0	11	2	20	0	0	6	2	.750	0	15-17	1	1.64
1993 New York	NL	35	0	0	30	36.1	172	46	24	21	6	4	1	1	19	3	29	5	0	4	3	.571	0	10-17	1	5.20
1994 New York	NL	47	0	0	43	50	216	47	20	15	2	2	1	0	19	0	42	1	0	1	4	.200	0	30-36	1	2.70

Year Team	Lg	HOW MUCH HE PITCHED						WHAT HE GAVE UP												THE RESULTS						
		G	GS	CG	GF	IP	BFP	H	R	ER	HR	SH	SF	HB	TBB	IBB	SO	WP	Bk	W	L	Pct.	ShO	Sv-Op	Hld	ERA
1995 New York	NL	48	0	0	41	51.2	213	48	17	14	4	4	1	0	17	2	41	0	0	5	3	.625	0	29-36	0	2.44
1996 New York	NL	51	0	0	44	54	235	54	15	11	2	6	0	0	21	0	48	2	0	4	3	.571	0	28-36	0	1.83
1997 New York	NL	59	0	0	53	60	244	49	18	17	3	5	1	1	20	2	53	6	0	5	3	.625	0	36-42	0	2.55
1998 New York	NL	61	0	0	54	64.2	289	66	28	26	4	4	5	4	29	7	59	2	0	0	8	.000	0	38-46	0	3.62
1999 New York	NL	46	0	0	34	40.2	182	40	14	13	1	3	1	2	19	1	41	0	0	0	2	.000	0	19-21	0	2.88
16 ML YEARS		878	0	0	711	1041.1	4409	961	365	306	56	74	27	15	404	64	801	44	8	77	70	.524	0	416-507	19	2.64

Julio Franco

Bats: Right Throws: Right Pos: 1B-1; PH/PR-1   Ht: 6'1" Wt: 190 Born: 8/23/61 Age: 38

Year Team	Lg	BATTING																		BASERUNNING				PERCENTAGES		
		G	AB	H	2B	3B	HR	(Hm	Rd)	TB	R	RBI	TBB	IBB	SO	HBP	SH	SF	SB	CS	SB%	GDP	Avg	OBP	SLG
1982 Philadelphia	NL	16	29	8	1	0	0	(0	0)	9	3	3	2	1	4	0	1	0	0	2	.00	1	.276	.323	.310
1983 Cleveland	AL	149	560	153	24	8	8	(6	2)	217	68	80	27	1	50	2	3	6	32	12	.73	21	.273	.306	.388
1984 Cleveland	AL	160	658	188	22	5	3	(1	2)	229	82	79	43	1	68	6	1	10	19	10	.66	23	.286	.331	.348
1985 Cleveland	AL	160	636	183	33	4	6	(3	3)	242	97	90	54	2	74	4	0	5	13	9	.59	26	.288	.343	.381
1986 Cleveland	AL	149	599	183	30	5	10	(4	6)	253	80	74	32	1	66	0	0	5	10	7	.59	28	.306	.338	.422
1987 Cleveland	AL	128	495	158	24	3	8	(5	3)	212	86	52	57	2	56	3	0	5	32	9	.78	23	.319	.389	.428
1988 Cleveland	AL	152	613	186	23	6	10	(3	7)	251	88	54	56	4	72	2	1	4	25	11	.69	17	.303	.361	.409
1989 Texas	AL	150	548	173	31	5	13	(9	4)	253	80	92	66	11	69	1	0	6	21	3	.88	27	.316	.386	.462
1990 Texas	AL	157	582	172	27	1	11	(4	7)	234	96	69	82	3	83	2	2	2	31	10	.76	12	.296	.383	.402
1991 Texas	AL	146	589	201	27	3	15	(7	8)	279	108	78	65	8	78	3	0	2	36	9	.80	13	.341	.408	.474
1992 Texas	AL	35	107	25	7	0	2	(0	2)	38	19	8	15	2	17	0	1	0	1	1	.50	3	.234	.328	.355
1993 Texas	AL	144	532	154	31	3	14	(6	8)	233	85	84	62	4	95	1	5	7	9	3	.75	16	.289	.360	.438
1994 Chicago	AL	112	433	138	19	2	20	(10	10)	221	72	98	62	4	75	5	0	5	8	1	.89	14	.319	.406	.510
1996 Cleveland	AL	112	432	139	20	1	14	(7	7)	203	72	76	61	2	82	3	0	3	8	8	.50	14	.322	.407	.470
1997 Cle-Mil	AL	120	430	116	16	1	7	(5	2)	155	68	44	69	4	116	1	1	4	15	6	.71	17	.270	.369	.360
1999 Tampa Bay	AL	1	1	0	0	0	0	(0	0)	0	0	0	0	0	1	0	0	0	0	0	.00	0	.000	.000	.000
1997 Cleveland	AL	78	289	82	13	1	3	(2	1)	106	46	25	38	2	75	0	1	0	8	5	.62	13	.284	.367	.367
Milwaukee	AL	42	141	34	3	0	4	(3	1)	49	22	19	31	2	41	1	0	4	7	1	.88	4	.241	.373	.348
16 ML YEARS		1891	7244	2177	335	47	141	(72	69)	3029	1104	981	753	50	1006	33	15	68	260	101	.72	255	.301	.366	.418

Matt Franco

Bats: L Throws: R Pos: PH/PR-88; 1B-19; LF-15; 3B-12; DH-4; RF-3; P-2   Ht: 6'1" Wt: 210 Born: 8/19/69 Age: 30

Year Team	Lg	BATTING																		BASERUNNING				PERCENTAGES		
		G	AB	H	2B	3B	HR	(Hm	Rd)	TB	R	RBI	TBB	IBB	SO	HBP	SH	SF	SB	CS	SB%	GDP	Avg	OBP	SLG
1995 Chicago	NL	16	17	5	1	0	0	(0	0)	6	3	1	0	0	4	0	0	0	0	0	.00	0	.294	.294	.353
1996 New York	NL	14	31	6	1	0	1	(0	1)	10	3	2	1	0	5	1	0	1	0	0	.00	1	.194	.235	.323
1997 New York	NL	112	163	45	5	0	5	(3	2)	65	21	21	13	4	23	0	0	0	1	0	1.00	4	.276	.330	.399
1998 New York	NL	103	161	44	7	2	1	(1	0)	58	20	13	23	6	26	1	1	1	0	1	.00	8	.273	.366	.360
1999 New York	NL	122	132	31	5	0	4	(0	4)	48	18	21	28	3	21	0	0	1	0	0	.00	9	.235	.366	.364
5 ML YEARS		367	504	131	19	2	11	(4	7)	187	65	58	65	13	79	2	1	3	1	1	.50	22	.260	.345	.371

Ryan Franklin

Pitches: Right Bats: Right Pos: RP-6   Ht: 6'3" Wt: 165 Born: 3/5/73 Age: 27

Year Team	Lg	HOW MUCH HE PITCHED						WHAT HE GAVE UP												THE RESULTS						
		G	GS	CG	GF	IP	BFP	H	R	ER	HR	SH	SF	HB	TBB	IBB	SO	WP	Bk	W	L	Pct.	ShO	Sv-Op	Hld	ERA
1993 Bellingham	A-	15	14	1	0	74	321	72	38	24	2	2	1	3	27	0	55	7	3	5	3	.625	1	0--	--	2.92
1994 Appleton	A	18	18	5	0	118	493	105	60	41	6	3	1	17	23	0	102	6	3	9	6	.600	1	0--	--	3.13
Calgary	AAA	1	1	0	0	5.2	28	9	6	5	2	0	0	0	1	0	2	0	0	0	0	.000	0	0--	--	7.94
Riverside	A+	8	8	1	0	61.2	261	61	26	21	5	1	3	4	8	0	35	0	1	4	2	.667	1	0--	--	3.06
1995 Port City	AA	31	20	1	2	146	627	153	84	70	13	11	3	12	43	4	102	6	2	6	10	.375	1	0--	--	4.32
1996 Port City	AA	28	27	2	0	182	764	186	99	81	23	6	3	16	37	0	127	4	2	6	12	.333	0	0--	--	4.01
1997 Memphis	AA	11	8	2	2	59.1	234	45	22	20	4	0	3	1	14	1	49	1	0	4	2	.667	2	0--	--	3.03
Tacoma	AAA	14	14	0	0	90.1	386	97	48	42	11	7	2	8	24	1	59	1	1	5	5	.500	0	0--	--	4.18
1998 Tacoma	AAA	34	16	1	10	127.2	561	148	75	64	18	4	8	10	32	2	90	0	0	5	6	.455	0	1--	--	4.51
1999 Tacoma	AAA	29	19	2	4	135.2	574	142	81	71	17	2	4	9	33	1	94	1	1	6	9	.400	1	2--	--	4.71
1999 Seattle	AL	6	0	0	2	11.1	51	10	6	6	2	0	0	1	8	1	6	0	0	0	0	.000	0	0-0	1	4.76

John Frascatore

Pitches: Right Bats: Right Pos: RP-59   Ht: 6'1" Wt: 210 Born: 2/4/70 Age: 30

Year Team	Lg	HOW MUCH HE PITCHED						WHAT HE GAVE UP												THE RESULTS						
		G	GS	CG	GF	IP	BFP	H	R	ER	HR	SH	SF	HB	TBB	IBB	SO	WP	Bk	W	L	Pct.	ShO	Sv-Op	Hld	ERA
1994 St. Louis	NL	1	1	0	0	3.1	18	7	6	6	2	0	0	0	2	0	2	1	0	0	1	.000	0	0-0	0	16.20
1995 St. Louis	NL	14	4	0	3	32.2	151	39	19	16	3	1	1	2	18	1	21	0	0	1	1	.500	0	0-0	0	4.41
1997 St. Louis	NL	59	0	0	17	80	348	74	25	22	5	5	5	6	33	5	58	4	0	5	2	.714	0	0-4	3	2.48
1998 St. Louis	NL	69	0	0	15	95.2	415	95	48	44	11	4	1	3	36	3	49	2	0	3	4	.429	0	0-2	13	4.14
1999 Ari-Tor		59	0	0	24	70	297	73	32	29	11	6	3	2	21	8	37	5	0	8	5	.615	0	1-3	10	3.73
1999 Arizona	NL	26	0	0	10	33	136	31	16	15	6	1	1	1	12	4	15	0	0	1	4	.200	0	0-1	4	4.09
Toronto	AL	33	0	0	14	37	161	42	16	14	5	5	2	1	9	4	22	5	0	7	1	.875	0	1-2	6	3.41
5 ML YEARS		202	5	0	59	281.2	1229	288	130	117	32	16	10	13	108	17	167	12	0	17	13	.567	0	1-9	26	3.74

Hanley Frias

Bats: Both **Throws:** Right **Pos:** SS-53; PH/PR-17; 2B-8 **Ht:** 6'0" **Wt:** 173 **Born:** 12/5/73 **Age:** 26

Year Team	Lg	G	AB	H	2B	3B	HR	(Hm	Rd)	TB	R	RBI	TBB	IBB	SO	HBP	SH	SF	SB	CS	SB%	GDP	Avg	OBP	SLG
1992 Rangers	R	58	205	50	9	2	0	—	—	63	37	28	27	0	30	2	2	2	28	6	.82	1	.244	.335	.307
1993 Chston-SC	A	132	473	109	20	4	4	—	—	149	61	37	40	0	108	3	4	4	27	14	.66	8	.230	.292	.315
1994 High Desert	A+	124	452	115	17	6	3	—	—	153	70	59	41	1	74	2	5	3	37	12	.76	9	.254	.317	.338
1995 Charlotte	A+	33	120	40	6	3	0	—	—	52	23	14	15	0	11	1	3	1	8	6	.57	0	.333	.409	.433
Tulsa	AA	93	360	101	18	4	0	—	—	127	44	27	45	0	53	1	8	2	14	12	.54	6	.281	.360	.353
1996 Tulsa	AA	134	505	145	24	12	2	—	—	199	73	41	30	2	73	0	5	3	9	9	.50	19	.287	.325	.394
1997 Okla City	AAA	132	484	128	17	4	5	—	—	168	64	46	56	2	72	1	8	3	35	15	.70	8	.264	.340	.347
1998 Tucson	AAA	63	253	73	10	4	1	—	—	94	32	21	24	0	41	0	2	3	16	7	.70	4	.289	.346	.372
1999 Tucson	AAA	23	80	24	3	0	0	—	—	27	15	6	7	0	15	0	1	0	3	1	.75	2	.300	.356	.338
1997 Texas	AL	14	26	5	1	0	0	(0	0)	6	4	1	1	0	4	0	0	0	0	0	.00	1	.192	.222	.231
1998 Arizona	NL	15	23	3	0	1	1	(1	0)	8	4	2	0	0	5	0	0	0	0	0	.00	1	.130	.130	.348
1999 Arizona	NL	69	150	41	3	2	1	(1	0)	51	27	16	29	2	18	0	1	0	4	3	.57	2	.273	.391	.340
3 ML YEARS		98	199	49	4	3	2	(2	0)	65	35	19	30	2	27	0	1	0	4	3	.57	4	.246	.345	.327

Jeff Frye

Bats: R **Throws:** R **Pos:** 2B-26; 3B-7; PH/PR-7; DH-2; SS-2 **Ht:** 5'9" **Wt:** 170 **Born:** 8/31/66 **Age:** 33

Year Team	Lg	G	AB	H	2B	3B	HR	(Hm	Rd)	TB	R	RBI	TBB	IBB	SO	HBP	SH	SF	SB	CS	SB%	GDP	Avg	OBP	SLG
1999 Red Sox *	R	6	20	8	1	0	0	—	—	9	4	1	2	0	2	0	0	0	0	0	.00	0	.400	.455	.450
Pawtucket *	AAA	3	9	3	0	0	0	—	—	3	0	2	2	0	1	0	0	0	0	0	.00	0	.333	.455	.333
1992 Texas	AL	67	199	51	9	1	1	(0	1)	65	24	12	16	0	27	3	11	1	1	3	.25	2	.256	.320	.327
1994 Texas	AL	57	205	67	20	3	0	(0	0)	93	37	18	29	0	23	1	5	3	6	1	.86	1	.327	.408	.454
1995 Texas	AL	90	313	87	15	2	4	(2	2)	118	38	29	24	0	45	5	8	4	3	3	.50	7	.278	.335	.377
1996 Boston	AL	105	419	120	27	2	4	(3	1)	163	74	41	54	0	57	5	5	3	18	4	.82	6	.286	.372	.389
1997 Boston	AL	127	404	126	36	2	3	(2	1)	175	56	51	27	1	44	2	2	7	19	8	.70	12	.312	.352	.433
1999 Boston	AL	41	114	32	3	0	1	(1	0)	38	14	12	14	1	11	1	1	1	2	2	.50	2	.281	.362	.333
6 ML YEARS		487	1654	483	110	10	13	(8	5)	652	243	163	164	2	207	17	32	19	49	21	.70	30	.292	.358	.394

Travis Fryman

Bats: Right **Throws:** Right **Pos:** 3B-85 **Ht:** 6'1" **Wt:** 195 **Born:** 3/25/69 **Age:** 31

Year Team	Lg	G	AB	H	2B	3B	HR	(Hm	Rd)	TB	R	RBI	TBB	IBB	SO	HBP	SH	SF	SB	CS	SB%	GDP	Avg	OBP	SLG
1999 Akron *	AA	4	12	3	0	0	1	—	—	6	4	4	2	0	4	0	0	1	0	0	.00	1	.250	.333	.500
Buffalo *	AAA	3	11	2	0	0	1	—	—	5	1	2	0	0	3	0	0	0	0	0	.00	0	.182	.182	.455
1990 Detroit	AL	66	232	69	11	1	9	(5	4)	109	32	27	17	0	51	1	1	0	3	3	.50	3	.297	.348	.470
1991 Detroit	AL	149	557	144	36	3	21	(8	13)	249	65	91	40	0	149	3	6	6	12	5	.71	13	.259	.309	.447
1992 Detroit	AL	161	659	175	31	4	20	(9	11)	274	87	96	45	1	144	6	5	6	8	4	.67	13	.266	.316	.416
1993 Detroit	AL	151	607	182	37	5	22	(13	9)	295	98	97	77	1	128	4	1	6	9	4	.69	8	.300	.379	.486
1994 Detroit	AL	114	464	122	34	5	18	(10	8)	220	66	85	45	1	128	5	1	13	2	2	.50	6	.263	.326	.474
1995 Detroit	AL	144	567	156	21	5	15	(9	6)	232	79	81	63	4	100	3	0	7	4	2	.67	18	.275	.347	.409
1996 Detroit	AL	157	616	165	32	3	22	(10	12)	269	90	100	57	2	118	4	1	10	4	3	.57	18	.268	.329	.437
1997 Detroit	AL	154	595	163	27	3	22	(13	9)	262	90	102	46	5	113	5	0	11	16	3	.84	15	.274	.326	.440
1998 Cleveland	AL	146	557	160	33	2	28	(16	12)	281	74	96	44	0	125	3	0	4	10	8	.56	12	.287	.340	.504
1999 Cleveland	AL	85	322	82	16	2	10	(6	4)	132	45	48	25	1	57	1	0	2	2	1	.67	13	.255	.309	.410
10 ML YEARS		1327	5176	1418	278	33	187	(99	88)	2323	726	823	459	15	1113	35	15	65	70	35	.67	119	.274	.333	.449

Brad Fullmer

Bats: Left **Throws:** Right **Pos:** 1B-94; PH/PR-7 **Ht:** 6'1" **Wt:** 220 **Born:** 1/17/75 **Age:** 25

Year Team	Lg	G	AB	H	2B	3B	HR	(Hm	Rd)	TB	R	RBI	TBB	IBB	SO	HBP	SH	SF	SB	CS	SB%	GDP	Avg	OBP	SLG
1999 Ottawa *	AAA	39	142	45	9	0	11	—	—	87	31	32	12	1	16	3	0	1	2	2	.50	5	.317	.380	.613
1997 Montreal	NL	19	40	12	2	0	3	(1	2)	23	4	8	2	1	7	1	0	0	0	0	.00	0	.300	.349	.575
1998 Montreal	NL	140	505	138	44	2	13	(3	10)	225	58	73	39	4	70	2	0	1	6	6	.50	12	.273	.327	.446
1999 Montreal	NL	100	347	96	34	2	9	(4	5)	161	38	47	22	6	35	2	0	3	2	3	.40	14	.277	.321	.464
3 ML YEARS		259	892	246	80	4	25	(8	17)	409	100	128	63	11	112	5	0	4	8	9	.47	26	.276	.326	.459

Chris Fussell

Pitches: Right **Bats:** Right **Pos:** RP-9; SP-8 **Ht:** 6'2" **Wt:** 200 **Born:** 5/19/76 **Age:** 24

Year Team	Lg	G	GS	CG	GF	IP	BFP	H	R	ER	HR	SH	SF	HB	TBB	IBB	SO	WP	Bk	W	L	Pct.	ShO	Sv-Op	Hld	ERA
1994 Orioles	R	14	8	0	2	56.1	245	53	30	26	2	1	4	4	24	0	65	6	1	2	3	.400	1	0- -		4.15
1995 Bluefield	R+	12	12	1	0	65.2	265	37	18	16	4	1	1	7	32	0	98	3	1	9	1	.900	1	0- -		2.19
1996 Frederick	A+	15	14	1	0	86.1	369	71	36	27	8	1	1	6	44	0	94	5	0	5	2	.714	1	0- -		2.81
1997 Bowie	AA	19	18	0	0	82.1	398	102	71	65	12	1	5	10	58	3	71	7	0	1	8	.111	1	0- -		7.11
Frederick	A+	9	9	1	0	50	218	42	23	22	5	2	3	3	31	2	54	3	0	3	3	.500	1	0- -		3.96
1998 Bowie	AA	18	18	0	0	93	413	87	54	44	13	1	6	4	52	1	84	4	0	3	7	.300	0	0- -		4.26
Rochester	AAA	10	10	0	0	58.2	249	50	30	26	4	1	3	5	28	0	51	5	0	5	2	.714	0	0- -		3.99
1999 Omaha	AAA	14	13	1	1	81.1	332	66	35	32	11	0	2	2	27	0	80	4	0	10	3	.769	1	0- -		3.54
1998 Baltimore	AL	3	2	0	0	9.2	47	11	9	9	1	1	1	0	9	1	8	0	0	0	1	.000	0	0-0		8.38
1999 Kansas City	AL	17	8	0	3	56	265	72	51	46	9	1	4	5	36	3	37	6	0	0	5	.000	0	2-2	1	7.39
2 ML YEARS		20	10	0	3	65.2	312	83	60	55	10	2	5	5	45	4	45	6	0	0	6	.000	0	2-2	1	7.54

Mike Fyhrie

Pitches: Right Bats: Right Pos: RP-9; SP-7   Ht: 6'2" Wt: 190 Born: 12/9/69 Age: 30

Year Team	Lg	G	GS	CG	GF	IP	BFP	H	R	ER	HR	SH	SF	HB	TBB	IBB	SO	WP	Bk	W	L	Pct.	ShO	Sv-Op	Hld	ERA
1991 Eugene	A-	21	0	0	13	39.1	176	41	17	11	0	3	0	1	19	1	45	1	2	2	1	.667	0	5--	—	2.52
1992 Baseball Cy	A+	26	26	2	0	162	670	148	65	45	6	10	6	7	37	1	92	4	6	7	13	.350	0	0--	—	2.50
1993 Wilmington	A+	5	5	0	0	29.1	124	32	15	12	3	0	2	0	8	0	19	1	0	3	2	.600	0	0--	—	3.68
Memphis	AA	22	22	3	0	131.1	579	143	59	52	11	0	4	9	59	0	59	7	1	11	4	.733	0	0--	—	3.56
1994 Omaha	AAA	18	16	0	0	85	379	100	57	54	13	2	4	6	33	1	37	0	0	6	5	.545	0	0--	—	5.72
Memphis	AA	11	11	0	0	67	279	67	29	24	4	1	2	5	17	1	38	1	0	2	5	.286	0	0--	—	3.22
1995 Wichita	AA	17	9	0	3	74	312	76	31	25	4	1	1	1	23	0	41	3	1	3	2	.600	0	1--	—	3.04
Omaha	AAA	14	11	0	2	60.2	259	71	34	30	7	0	2	4	14	0	39	0	0	3	4	.429	0	0--	—	4.45
1996 Norfolk	AAA	27	27	2	0	169	678	150	61	57	16	2	2	5	33	1	103	8	2	15	6	.714	2	0--	—	3.04
1998 Norfolk	AAA	24	17	0	3	100.1	461	115	83	74	12	2	8	5	45	1	60	4	0	3	7	.300	0	0--	—	6.64
1999 Edmonton	AAA	19	18	0	0	114	460	90	47	44	8	1	3	3	40	0	113	0	0	9	5	.643	0	0--	—	3.47
1996 New York	NL	2	0	0	0	2.1	14	4	4	4	0	0	0	0	3	0	0	0	0	0	1	.000	0	0-0	0	15.43
1999 Anaheim	AL	16	7	0	5	51.2	235	61	36	29	8	0	1	0	21	1	26	0	0	0	4	.000	0	0-0	1	5.05
2 ML YEARS		18	7	0	5	54	249	65	36	33	8	0	1	0	24	1	26	0	0	0	5	.000	0	0-0	1	5.50

Gary Gaetti

Bats: R Throws: R Pos: 3B-81; PH/PR-32; 1B-8; P-1; SS-1   Ht: 6'0" Wt: 205 Born: 8/19/58 Age: 41

Year Team	Lg	G	AB	H	2B	3B	HR	(Hm	Rd)	TB	R	RBI	TBB	IBB	SO	HBP	SH	SF	SB	CS	SB%	GDP	Avg	OBP	SLG
1981 Minnesota	AL	9	26	5	0	0	2	(1	1)	11	4	3	0	0	6	0	0	0	0	0	.00	1	.192	.192	.423
1982 Minnesota	AL	145	508	117	25	4	25	(15	10)	225	59	84	37	2	107	3	4	13	0	4	.00	16	.230	.280	.443
1983 Minnesota	AL	157	584	143	30	3	21	(7	14)	242	81	78	54	2	121	4	0	8	7	1	.88	18	.245	.309	.414
1984 Minnesota	AL	162	588	154	29	4	5	(2	3)	206	55	65	44	1	81	4	3	5	11	5	.69	9	.262	.315	.350
1985 Minnesota	AL	160	560	138	31	0	20	(10	10)	229	71	63	37	3	89	7	1	4	13	5	.72	15	.246	.301	.409
1986 Minnesota	AL	157	596	171	34	1	34	(16	18)	309	91	108	52	4	108	6	1	6	14	15	.48	18	.287	.347	.518
1987 Minnesota	AL	154	584	150	36	2	31	(18	13)	283	95	109	37	7	92	3	1	3	10	7	.59	25	.257	.303	.485
1988 Minnesota	AL	133	468	141	29	2	28	(9	19)	258	66	88	36	5	85	5	1	6	7	4	.64	10	.301	.353	.551
1989 Minnesota	AL	130	498	125	11	4	19	(10	9)	201	63	75	25	5	87	3	1	9	6	2	.75	12	.251	.286	.404
1990 Minnesota	AL	154	577	132	27	5	16	(7	9)	217	61	85	36	1	101	3	1	8	6	1	.86	22	.229	.274	.376
1991 California	AL	152	586	144	22	1	18	(12	6)	222	58	66	33	3	104	8	2	5	5	5	.50	13	.246	.293	.379
1992 California	AL	130	456	103	13	2	12	(8	4)	156	41	48	21	4	79	6	0	3	3	1	.75	9	.226	.267	.342
1993 Cal-KC	AL	102	331	81	20	1	14	(6	8)	145	40	50	21	0	87	8	2	7	1	3	.25	5	.245	.300	.438
1994 Kansas City	AL	90	327	94	15	3	12	(5	7)	151	53	57	19	3	63	2	1	3	0	2	.00	9	.287	.328	.462
1995 Kansas City	AL	137	514	134	27	0	35	(16	19)	266	76	96	47	6	91	8	3	6	3	5	.50	7	.261	.329	.518
1996 St. Louis	NL	141	522	143	27	4	23	(13	10)	247	71	80	35	6	97	8	4	5	2	2	.50	10	.274	.326	.473
1997 St. Louis	NL	148	502	126	24	1	17	(7	10)	203	63	69	36	3	88	6	4	6	7	3	.70	20	.251	.305	.404
1998 StL-ChC	NL	128	434	122	34	1	19	(5	14)	215	60	70	43	2	62	10	1	4	1	1	.50	12	.281	.356	.495
1999 Chicago	NL	113	280	57	9	1	9	(6	3)	95	22	46	21	0	51	2	0	5	0	1	.00	3	.204	.260	.339
1993 California	AL	20	50	9	2	0	0	(0	0)	11	3	4	5	0	12	0	0	1	0	1	1.00	3	.180	.250	.220
Kansas City	AL	82	281	72	18	1	14	(6	8)	134	37	46	16	0	75	8	2	6	0	3	.00	2	.256	.309	.477
1998 St. Louis	NL	91	306	81	23	1	11	(1	10)	139	39	43	31	1	39	5	0	3	1	1	.50	10	.265	.339	.454
Chicago	NL	37	128	41	11	0	8	(4	4)	76	21	27	12	1	23	5	1	1	0	0	.00	2	.320	.397	.594
19 ML YEARS		2502	8941	2280	443	39	360	(173	187)	3881	1130	1340	634	57	1599	96	32	103	96	65	.60	236	.255	.308	.434

Eric Gagne

Pitches: Right Bats: Right Pos: SP-5   Ht: 6'2" Wt: 195 Born: 1/7/76 Age: 24

Year Team	Lg	G	GS	CG	GF	IP	BFP	H	R	ER	HR	SH	SF	HB	TBB	IBB	SO	WP	Bk	W	L	Pct.	ShO	Sv-Op	Hld	ERA
1996 Savannah	A	23	21	1	0	115.1	474	94	48	42	11	3	2	1	43	1	131	7	5	7	6	.538	1	0--	—	3.28
1998 Vero Beach	A+	25	25	3	0	139.2	584	118	69	58	16	2	4	4	48	0	144	5	3	9	7	.563	1	0--	—	3.74
1999 San Antonio	AA	26	26	0	0	167.2	683	122	55	49	17	2	2	8	64	0	185	6	0	12	4	.750	0	0--	—	2.63
1999 Los Angeles	NL	5	5	0	0	30	119	18	8	7	3	1	0	0	15	0	30	1	0	1	1	.500	0	0-0	0	2.10

Eddie Gaillard

Pitches: Right Bats: Right Pos: RP-8   Ht: 6'1" Wt: 200 Born: 8/13/70 Age: 29

Year Team	Lg	G	GS	CG	GF	IP	BFP	H	R	ER	HR	SH	SF	HB	TBB	IBB	SO	WP	Bk	W	L	Pct.	ShO	Sv-Op	Hld	ERA
1993 Niagara Fal	A-	3	3	0	0	14.2	63	15	6	6	0	0	0	0	4	0	12	0	0	1	2	.333	0	0--	—	3.68
Fayettevlle	A	11	11	0	0	61.2	261	64	30	28	8	2	0	4	20	0	41	1	1	5	2	.714	0	0--	—	4.09
1994 Lakeland	A+	30	9	0	8	92	389	82	37	29	3	1	2	10	29	0	51	3	1	6	1	.857	0	2--	—	2.84
1995 Jacksnville	AA	8	0	0	2	8	42	11	5	5	0	2	1	0	5	1	4	0	0	0	1	.000	0	0--	—	5.63
Lakeland	A+	43	0	0	38	55	227	48	13	8	1	1	3	0	18	2	51	2	1	2	4	.333	0	25--	—	1.31
1996 Jacksnville	AA	56	0	0	24	88	389	82	40	33	8	4	3	5	50	7	76	10	0	9	6	.600	0	0--	—	3.38
1997 Toledo	AAA	55	0	0	46	53	235	52	27	25	7	3	1	2	24	2	54	4	1	1	4	.200	0	28--	—	4.25
1998 St. Pete	A+	1	1	0	0	2	7	1	0	0	0	0	0	0	0	0	2	0	0	0	0	.000	0	0--	—	0.00
Devil Rays	R	2	2	0	0	4	13	0	0	0	0	0	0	1	1	0	5	0	0	0	0	.000	0	0--	—	0.00
Durham	AAA	18	0	0	1	20	98	27	18	17	5	0	1	3	11	0	21	3	0	2	0	1.000	0	0--	—	7.65
1999 Durham	AAA	59	0	0	52	67	283	67	30	20	6	3	1	4	23	3	67	2	0	3	6	.333	0	26--	—	2.89
1997 Detroit	AL	16	0	0	5	20.1	88	16	12	12	2	0	2	0	10	2	12	0	0	1	0	1.000	0	1-2	0	5.31
1998 Tampa Bay	AL	6	0	0	1	7.2	30	4	5	5	4	0	0	0	3	0	5	0	0	0	0	.000	0	0-0	0	5.87
1999 Tampa Bay	AL	8	0	0	1	8.2	43	12	9	2	1	0	1	0	4	0	7	0	0	1	0	1.000	0	0-0	0	2.08
3 ML YEARS		30	0	0	7	36.2	161	32	26	19	6	1	2	1	17	2	24	0	0	2	0	1.000	0	1-2	0	4.66

Andres Galarraga

Bats: Right **Throws:** Right **Pos:** 1B   **Ht:** 6'3" **Wt:** 235 **Born:** 6/18/61 **Age:** 39

Year Team	Lg	G	AB	H	2B	3B	HR	(Hm	Rd)	TB	R	RBI	TBB	IBB	SO	HBP	SH	SF	SB	CS	SB%	GDP	Avg	OBP	SLG
1985 Montreal	NL	24	75	14	1	0	2	(0	2)	21	9	4	3	0	18	1	0	0	1	2	.33	0	.187	.228	.280
1986 Montreal	NL	105	321	87	13	0	10	(4	6)	130	39	42	30	5	79	3	1	1	6	5	.55	8	.271	.338	.405
1987 Montreal	NL	147	551	168	40	3	13	(7	6)	253	72	90	41	13	127	10	0	4	7	10	.41	11	.305	.361	.459
1988 Montreal	NL	157	609	184	42	8	29	(14	15)	329	99	92	39	9	153	10	0	3	13	4	.76	12	.302	.352	.540
1989 Montreal	NL	152	572	147	30	1	23	(13	10)	248	76	85	48	10	158	13	0	3	12	5	.71	12	.257	.327	.434
1990 Montreal	NL	155	579	148	29	0	20	(6	14)	237	65	87	40	8	169	4	0	5	10	1	.91	14	.256	.306	.409
1991 Montreal	NL	107	375	82	13	2	9	(3	6)	126	34	33	23	5	86	2	0	0	5	6	.45	6	.219	.268	.336
1992 St. Louis	NL	95	325	79	14	2	10	(4	6)	127	38	39	11	0	69	8	0	3	5	4	.56	8	.243	.282	.391
1993 Colorado	NL	120	470	174	35	4	22	(13	9)	283	71	98	24	12	73	6	0	6	2	4	.33	9	.370	.403	.602
1994 Colorado	NL	103	417	133	21	0	31	(16	15)	247	77	85	19	8	93	4	0	5	8	3	.73	10	.319	.356	.592
1995 Colorado	NL	143	554	155	29	3	31	(18	13)	283	89	106	32	6	146	13	0	5	12	2	.86	14	.280	.331	.511
1996 Colorado	NL	159	626	190	39	3	47	(32	15)	376	119	150	40	3	157	17	0	8	18	8	.69	6	.304	.357	.601
1997 Colorado	NL	154	600	191	31	3	41	(21	20)	351	120	140	54	2	141	17	0	3	15	8	.65	16	.318	.389	.585
1998 Atlanta	NL	153	555	169	27	1	44	(16	28)	330	103	121	63	11	146	25	0	5	7	6	.54	8	.305	.397	.595
14 ML YEARS		1774	6629	1921	364	30	332	(167	165)	3341	1011	1172	467	92	1615	137	1	51	121	68	.64	134	.290	.347	.504

Ron Gant

Bats: Right **Throws:** Right **Pos:** LF-133; PH/PR-4; DH-2   **Ht:** 6'0" **Wt:** 200 **Born:** 3/2/65 **Age:** 35

Year Team	Lg	G	AB	H	2B	3B	HR	(Hm	Rd)	TB	R	RBI	TBB	IBB	SO	HBP	SH	SF	SB	CS	SB%	GDP	Avg	OBP	SLG
1987 Atlanta	NL	21	83	22	4	0	2	(1	1)	32	9	9	1	0	11	0	1	1	4	2	.67	3	.265	.271	.386
1988 Atlanta	NL	146	563	146	28	8	19	(7	12)	247	85	60	46	4	118	3	2	4	19	10	.66	7	.259	.317	.439
1989 Atlanta	NL	75	260	46	8	3	9	(5	4)	87	26	25	20	0	63	1	2	2	9	6	.60	0	.177	.237	.335
1990 Atlanta	NL	152	575	174	34	3	32	(18	14)	310	107	84	50	0	86	1	1	4	33	16	.67	8	.303	.357	.539
1991 Atlanta	NL	154	561	141	35	3	32	(18	14)	278	101	105	71	8	104	5	0	5	34	15	.69	6	.251	.338	.496
1992 Atlanta	NL	153	544	141	22	6	17	(10	7)	226	74	80	45	5	101	7	0	6	32	10	.76	10	.259	.321	.415
1993 Atlanta	NL	157	606	166	27	4	36	(17	19)	309	113	117	67	2	117	4	0	5	26	9	.74	14	.274	.345	.510
1995 Cincinnati	NL	119	410	113	19	4	29	(12	17)	227	79	88	74	5	108	3	1	5	23	8	.74	11	.276	.386	.554
1996 St. Louis	NL	122	419	103	14	2	30	(17	13)	211	74	82	73	5	98	3	1	4	13	4	.76	9	.246	.359	.504
1997 St. Louis	NL	139	502	115	21	4	17	(11	6)	195	68	62	58	3	162	1	0	1	14	6	.70	2	.229	.310	.388
1998 St. Louis	NL	121	383	92	17	1	26	(14	12)	189	60	67	51	2	92	2	0	2	8	0	1.00	6	.240	.331	.493
1999 Philadelphia	NL	138	516	134	27	5	17	(6	11)	222	107	77	85	0	112	1	0	3	13	3	.81	6	.260	.364	.430
12 ML YEARS		1497	5422	1393	256	43	266	(136	130)	2533	903	856	641	34	1172	29	8	44	228	89	.72	82	.257	.336	.467

Rich Garces

Pitches: Right **Bats:** Right **Pos:** RP-30   **Ht:** 6'0" **Wt:** 215 **Born:** 5/18/71 **Age:** 29

Year Team	Lg	G	GS	CG	GF	IP	BFP	H	R	ER	HR	SH	SF	HB	TBB	IBB	SO	WP	Bk	W	L	Pct.	ShO	Sv-Op	Hld	ERA
1999 Pawtucket *	AAA	21	0	0	15	27.2	117	24	11	10	5	1	1	0	10	0	24	1	0	1	0	1.000	0	7- –	—	3.25
1990 Minnesota	AL	5	0	0	3	5.2	24	4	2	1	0	0	0	0	4	0	1	0	0	0	0	.000	0	2-2	0	1.59
1993 Minnesota	AL	3	0	0	1	4	18	4	2	0	0	0	0	0	2	0	3	0	0	0	0	.000	0	0-0	0	0.00
1995 ChC-Fla	NL	18	0	0	7	24.1	108	25	15	12	1	1	0	0	11	2	22	0	0	0	2	.000	0	0-1	1	4.44
1996 Boston	AL	37	0	0	9	44	205	42	26	24	5	0	5	0	33	5	55	0	0	3	2	.600	0	0-2	4	4.91
1997 Boston	AL	12	0	0	4	13.2	66	14	9	7	2	0	1	1	9	0	12	0	0	0	1	.000	0	0-2	1	4.61
1998 Boston	AL	30	0	0	11	46	201	36	19	17	6	2	1	2	27	3	34	1	1	1	1	.500	0	1-3	6	3.33
1999 Boston	AL	30	0	0	4	40.2	164	25	9	7	1	0	0	0	18	1	33	0	0	5	1	.833	0	2-3	2	1.55
1995 Chicago	NL	7	0	0	4	11	46	11	6	4	0	0	0	0	3	0	6	0	0	0	0	.000	0	0-0	0	3.27
Florida	NL	11	0	0	3	13.1	62	14	9	8	1	1	0	0	8	2	16	0	0	0	2	.000	0	0-1	1	5.40
7 ML YEARS		135	0	0	39	178.1	786	150	82	68	15	3	7	3	104	11	160	1	1	9	7	.563	0	5-13	14	3.43

Amaury Garcia

Bats: Right **Throws:** Right **Pos:** 2B-8; PH/PR-2   **Ht:** 5'10" **Wt:** 160 **Born:** 5/20/75 **Age:** 25

Year Team	Lg	G	AB	H	2B	3B	HR	(Hm	Rd)	TB	R	RBI	TBB	IBB	SO	HBP	SH	SF	SB	CS	SB%	GDP	Avg	OBP	SLG
1994 Marlins	R	58	208	65	9	3	0	—	—	80	46	25	33	0	49	2	1	2	10	3	.77	4	.313	.408	.385
1995 Kane County	A	26	58	14	4	1	1	—	—	23	19	5	18	0	12	1	0	0	5	2	.71	1	.241	.429	.397
Elmira	A-	62	231	63	7	3	0	—	—	76	40	17	34	2	50	4	3	0	41	12	.77	1	.273	.375	.329
1996 Kane County	A	105	391	103	19	7	6	—	—	154	65	36	62	2	83	5	7	2	37	19	.66	8	.263	.370	.394
1997 Brevard Cty	A+	124	479	138	30	2	7	—	—	193	77	44	49	2	97	5	14	3	45	11	.80	4	.288	.358	.403
1998 Portland	AA	137	544	147	19	6	13	—	—	217	79	62	45	0	126	2	14	1	23	15	.61	7	.270	.328	.399
1999 Calgary	AAA	119	479	152	37	9	17	—	—	258	94	53	44	0	79	6	7	1	17	11	.61	9	.317	.381	.539
1999 Florida	NL	10	24	6	0	1	2	(0	2)	14	6	2	3	0	11	0	0	0	0	0	.00	0	.250	.333	.583

Carlos Garcia

Bats: Right **Throws:** Right **Pos:** 3B-4; 1B-1; PH/PR-1   **Ht:** 6'1" **Wt:** 197 **Born:** 10/15/67 **Age:** 32

Year Team	Lg	G	AB	H	2B	3B	HR	(Hm	Rd)	TB	R	RBI	TBB	IBB	SO	HBP	SH	SF	SB	CS	SB%	GDP	Avg	OBP	SLG
1999 Las Vegas *	AAA	78	274	77	19	0	3	—	—	105	36	28	17	1	61	3	0	0	5	0	1.00	10	.281	.330	.383
1990 Pittsburgh	NL	4	4	2	0	0	0	(0	0)	2	1	0	0	0	2	0	0	0	0	0	.00	0	.500	.500	.500
1991 Pittsburgh	NL	12	24	6	2	0	0	(0	0)	10	2	1	1	0	8	0	0	0	0	0	.00	1	.250	.280	.417

Year Team	Lg	G	AB	H	2B	3B	HR	(Hm	Rd)	TB	R	RBI	TBB	IBB	SO	HBP	SH	SF	SB	CS	SB%	GDP	Avg	OBP	SLG
1992 Pittsburgh	NL	22	39	8	1	0	0	(0	0)	9	4	4	0	0	9	0	1	2	0	0	.00	1	.205	.195	.231
1993 Pittsburgh	NL	141	546	147	25	5	12	(7	5)	218	77	47	31	2	67	9	6	5	18	11	.62	9	.269	.316	.399
1994 Pittsburgh	NL	98	412	114	15	2	6	(4	2)	151	49	28	16	2	67	4	1	1	18	9	.67	6	.277	.309	.367
1995 Pittsburgh	NL	104	367	108	24	2	6	(4	2)	154	41	50	25	5	55	2	5	3	8	4	.67	4	.294	.340	.420
1996 Pittsburgh	NL	101	390	111	18	4	6	(3	3)	155	66	44	23	3	58	4	3	2	16	6	.73	3	.285	.329	.397
1997 Toronto	AL	103	350	77	18	2	3	(0	3)	108	29	23	15	0	60	2	10	4	11	3	.79	7	.220	.253	.309
1998 Anaheim	NL	19	35	5	1	0	0	(0	0)	6	4	0	3	0	11	1	1	0	2	0	1.00	1	.143	.231	.171
1999 San Diego	NL	6	11	2	0	0	0	(0	0)	2	1	0	1	0	3	0	0	0	0	0	.00	2	.182	.250	.182
10 ML YEARS		610	2178	580	102	17	33	(18	15)	815	274	197	115	12	340	22	27	17	73	33	.69	33	.266	.307	.374

Freddy Garcia

Bats: R Throws: R Pos: PH/PR-21; LF-18; 3B-9; RF-7; DH-2; 1B-1 Ht: 6'2" Wt: 224 Born: 8/1/72 Age: 27

Year Team	Lg	G	AB	H	2B	3B	HR	(Hm	Rd)	TB	R	RBI	TBB	IBB	SO	HBP	SH	SF	SB	CS	SB%	GDP	Avg	OBP	SLG
1999 Nashville *	AAA	4	9	0	0	0	0	—	—	0	0	0	1	0	3	0	0	0	0	0	.00	0	.000	.100	.000
1995 Pittsburgh	NL	42	57	8	1	1	0	(0	0)	11	5	1	8	0	17	0	1	0	0	1	.00	0	.140	.246	.193
1997 Pittsburgh	NL	20	40	6	1	0	3	(0	3)	16	4	5	2	0	17	0	0	0	0	0	.00	0	.150	.190	.400
1998 Pittsburgh	NL	56	172	44	11	1	9	(2	7)	84	27	26	18	3	45	2	0	1	0	2	.00	3	.256	.332	.488
1999 Pit-Atl	NL	57	132	31	5	0	7	(6	1)	57	17	24	5	0	42	0	0	1	0	0	.00	3	.235	.261	.432
1999 Pittsburgh	NL	55	130	30	5	0	6	(5	1)	53	16	23	4	0	41	0	0	1	0	0	.00	3	.231	.252	.408
Atlanta	NL	2	2	1	0	0	1	(1	0)	4	1	1	1	0	1	0	0	0	0	0	.00	0	.500	.667	2.000
4 ML YEARS		175	401	89	18	2	19	(8	11)	168	53	56	33	3	121	2	1	2	0	3	.00	6	.222	.283	.419

Freddy Garcia

Pitches: Right Bats: Right Pos: SP-33 Ht: 6'4" Wt: 210 Born: 10/6/76 Age: 23

Year Team	Lg	G	GS	CG	GF	IP	BFP	H	R	ER	HR	SH	SF	HB	TBB	IBB	SO	WP	Bk	W	L	Pct.	ShO	Sv-Op	Hld	ERA
1995 Astros	R	11	11	0	0	58.1	256	60	32	29	2	3		6	14	0	58	5	0	6	3	.667	0	0--	—	4.47
1996 Quad City	A	13	13	0	0	60.2	265	57	27	21	3	1	1	4	27	0	50	5	5	5	4	.556	0	0--	—	3.12
1997 Kissimmee	A+	27	27	5	0	179	741	165	63	51	6	4	3	4	49	3	131	3	2	18	8	.556	2	0--	—	2.56
1998 Jackson	AA	19	19	2	0	119.1	505	94	48	43	8	4	0	6	58	0	115	8	0	6	7	.462	0	0--	—	3.24
New Orleans	AAA	2	2	0	0	14.1	56	14	5	5	2	0	0	1	10	0	13	2	0	1	0	1.000	0	0--	—	3.14
Tacoma	AAA	5	5	0	0	32.2	137	30	14	14	6	0	0	2	13	0	30	0	1	3	1	.750	0	0--	—	3.86
1999 Seattle	AL	33	33	2	0	201.1	888	205	96	91	18	3	6	10	90	4	170	12	3	17	8	.680	1	0-0	0	4.07

Guillermo Garcia

Bats: Right Throws: Right Pos: C-3; PH/PR-3 Ht: 6'3" Wt: 215 Born: 4/4/72 Age: 28

Year Team	Lg	G	AB	H	2B	3B	HR	(Hm	Rd)	TB	R	RBI	TBB	IBB	SO	HBP	SH	SF	SB	CS	SB%	GDP	Avg	OBP	SLG
1990 Mets	R	42	136	25	1	2	0	—	—	30	9	6	7	1	34	1	2	1	1	1	.50	2	.184	.228	.221
1991 Kingsport	R+	15	33	8	1	1	0	—	—	11	9	2	4	0	4	0	0	0	0	0	.00	1	.242	.324	.333
Pittsfield	A-	45	157	43	13	2	0	—	—	60	22	24	15	0	38	1	3	3	4	1	.80	5	.274	.335	.382
1992 Pittsfield	A-	73	272	54	11	1	2	—	—	73	36	26	20	0	52	2	0	3	3	4	.43	5	.199	.256	.268
1993 Capital Cty	A	119	429	124	28	2	3	—	—	165	64	72	49	1	60	10	1	3	10	8	.56	11	.289	.373	.385
1994 St. Lucie	A+	55	203	48	9	1	1	—	—	62	22	23	13	1	24	3	2	0	0	2	.00	6	.236	.292	.305
1995 Winston-Sal	A+	78	245	58	10	2	3	—	—	81	26	29	28	0	32	1	2	2	2	2	.50	7	.237	.315	.331
1996 Indianapols	AAA	16	47	12	2	0	0	—	—	14	4	0	2	2	6	0	0	0	0	0	.00	0	.255	.286	.298
Chattanooga	AA	60	203	64	12	0	6	—	—	94	25	36	12	2	32	1	2	1	3	3	.50	3	.315	.355	.463
1997 Chattanooga	AA	20	74	21	1	1	4	—	—	36	11	19	8	0	13	0	0	1	0	0	.00	1	.284	.349	.486
Indianapols	AAA	55	151	36	2	0	10	—	—	68	16	20	9	0	46	1	0	2	0	2	.00	9	.238	.282	.450
1998 Indianapols	AAA	93	334	85	20	0	19	—	—	162	48	60	22	1	81	0	1	0	0	2	.00	9	.254	.301	.485
1999 Chattanooga	AA	10	42	13	3	3	0	—	—	25	11	7	2	0	6	1	0	0	0	0	.00	3	.310	.356	.595
Indianapols	AAA	65	233	67	9	0	10	—	—	106	30	28	22	2	44	5	0	5	1	1	.50	12	.288	.355	.455
1998 Cincinnati	NL	12	36	7	2	0	2	(1	1)	15	3	4	2	0	13	0	0	0	0	0	.00	2	.194	.237	.417
1999 Florida	NL	4	4	1	0	0	0	(0	0)	1	0	0	0	0	2	0	0	0	0	0	.00	0	.250	.250	.250
2 ML YEARS		16	40	8	2	0	2	(1	1)	16	3	4	2	0	15	0	0	0	0	0	.00	2	.200	.238	.400

Jesse Garcia

Bats: R Throws: R Pos: SS-7; 2B-6; PH/PR-4; 3B-2; DH-1 Ht: 5'10" Wt: 171 Born: 9/24/73 Age: 26

Year Team	Lg	G	AB	H	2B	3B	HR	(Hm	Rd)	TB	R	RBI	TBB	IBB	SO	HBP	SH	SF	SB	CS	SB%	GDP	Avg	OBP	SLG
1993 Orioles	R	48	156	37	4	0	0	—	—	41	20	16	21	1	32	1	8	3	14	6	.70	1	.237	.326	.263
1995 Frederick	A+	124	365	82	11	3	3	—	—	108	52	27	49	0	75	9	7	2	5	10	.33	5	.225	.329	.296
1996 High Desert	A+	137	459	122	21	5	10	—	—	183	94	66	57	0	81	8	20	4	25	7	.78	7	.266	.354	.399
1997 Bowie	AA	141	437	103	18	1	5	—	—	138	52	42	38	0	71	6	24	2	7	7	.50	9	.236	.304	.316
1998 Bowie	AA	86	258	73	13	1	2	—	—	94	46	20	34	1	37	1	6	0	12	3	.80	3	.283	.369	.364
Rochester	AAA	44	160	47	4	0	1	—	—	61	20	18	7	0	22	3	2	3	7	5	.58	3	.294	.329	.381
1999 Rochester	AAA	62	220	56	10	2	2	—	—	76	25	23	11	0	21	0	11	1	9	6	.60	5	.255	.289	.345
1999 Baltimore	AL	17	29	6	0	0	2	(1	1)	12	6	2	2	0	3	0	3	0	0	0	.00	1	.207	.258	.414

Karim Garcia

Bats: L **Throws:** L **Pos:** RF-55; LF-35; PH/PR-16; DH-7 **Ht:** 6'0" **Wt:** 172 **Born:** 10/29/75 **Age:** 24

Year Team	Lg	G	AB	H	2B	3B	HR	(Hm	Rd)	TB	R	RBI	TBB	IBB	SO	HBP	SH	SF	SB	CS	SB%	GDP	Avg	OBP	SLG
1995 Los Angeles	NL	13	20	4	0	0	0	(0	0)	4	1	0	0	0	4	0	0	0	0	0	.00	0	.200	.200	.200
1996 Los Angeles	NL	1	1	0	0	0	0	(0	0)	0	0	0	0	0	1	0	0	0	0	0	.00	0	.000	.000	.000
1997 Los Angeles	NL	15	39	5	0	0	1	(0	1)	8	5	8	6	1	14	0	0	1	0	0	.00	0	.128	.239	.205
1998 Arizona	NL	113	333	74	10	8	9	(4	5)	127	39	43	18	1	78	0	0	3	5	4	.56	6	.222	.260	.381
1999 Detroit	AL	96	288	69	10	3	14	(4	10)	127	38	32	20	1	67	0	0	1	2	4	.33	2	.240	.288	.441
5 ML YEARS		238	681	152	20	11	24	(8	16)	266	83	83	44	3	164	0	0	5	7	8	.47	8	.223	.268	.391

Luis Garcia

Bats: Right **Throws:** Right **Pos:** SS-7; PH/PR-2; 2B-1 **Ht:** 6'0" **Wt:** 175 **Born:** 5/20/75 **Age:** 25

Year Team	Lg	G	AB	H	2B	3B	HR	(Hm	Rd)	TB	R	RBI	TBB	IBB	SO	HBP	SH	SF	SB	CS	SB%	GDP	Avg	OBP	SLG
1993 Bristol	R+	24	57	12	1	0	1	—	—	16	7	7	3	0	11	0	1	0	3	1	.75	1	.211	.250	.281
1994 Jamestown	A-	67	239	47	8	2	1	—	—	62	21	19	8	0	48	1	6	3	6	9	.40	4	.197	.223	.259
1995 Lakeland	A+	102	361	101	10	4	2	—	—	125	39	35	8	0	42	1	4	4	9	10	.47	6	.280	.294	.346
Jacksnville	AA	17	47	13	0	0	0	—	—	13	6	5	1	0	8	1	0	0	2	1	.67	0	.277	.306	.277
1996 Jacksnville	AA	131	522	128	22	4	9	—	—	185	68	46	12	1	90	2	7	2	15	12	.56	9	.245	.264	.354
1997 Jacksnville	AA	126	456	122	19	1	5	—	—	158	55	48	10	0	59	3	6	6	3	2	.60	15	.268	.284	.346
1998 Toledo	AAA	114	407	105	19	4	3	—	—	141	37	31	8	0	59	1	3	3	3	2	.60	11	.258	.272	.346
1999 Toledo	AAA	89	308	82	19	1	3	—	—	112	30	34	5	0	41	1	3	5	3	3	.50	12	.266	.276	.364
1999 Detroit	AL	8	9	1	1	0	0	(0	0)	2	0	0	0	0	2	0	0	0	0	0	.00	0	.111	.111	.222

Mike Garcia

Pitches: Right **Bats:** Right **Pos:** RP-7 **Ht:** 6'2" **Wt:** 220 **Born:** 5/11/68 **Age:** 32

Year Team	Lg	G	GS	CG	GF	IP	BFP	H	R	ER	HR	SH	SF	HB	TBB	IBB	SO	WP	Bk	W	L	Pct.	ShO	Sv-Op	Hld	ERA
1989 Bristol	R+	8	0	0	0	15.2	68	17	9	8	0	1	0	4	4	1	13	1	1	0	3	.000	0	0- -	—	4.60
Niagara Fal	A-	7	6	1	0	40.1	151	27	12	7	3	1	0	3	7	0	39	0	0	5	1	.833	0	0- -	—	1.56
1990 Fayettevlle	A	28	28	6	0	180.1	726	152	69	51	7	6	2	6	41	0	113	3	0	12	8	.600	2	0- -	—	2.55
1991 Lakeland	A+	25	24	0	0	144	596	130	63	50	5	4	2	6	41	2	109	3	2	6	8	.429	0	0- -	—	3.13
1992 London	AA	27	20	1	3	136.2	581	149	69	59	10	4	5	4	35	1	92	2	0	8	8	.500	1	0- -	—	3.89
1993 London	AA	6	0	0	2	11.1	55	12	8	7	0	1	0	0	6	0	12	1	0	1	0	1.000	0	0- -	—	5.56
Rochester	IND	16	16	1	0	94.2	396	89	36	31	8	1	4	1	27	0	100	5	0	9	2	.818	0	0- -	—	2.95
1999 Nashville	AAA	23	0	0	10	27.1	114	24	12	12	3	3	1	1	10	2	35	0	0	2	2	.000	0	2- -	—	3.95
1999 Pittsburgh	NL	7	0	0	2	7	25	2	1	1	1	0	0	0	3	0	9	0	0	1	0	1.000	0	0-0	1	1.29

Nomar Garciaparra

Bats: Right **Throws:** Right **Pos:** SS-134; PH/PR-1 **Ht:** 6'0" **Wt:** 180 **Born:** 7/23/73 **Age:** 26

Year Team	Lg	G	AB	H	2B	3B	HR	(Hm	Rd)	TB	R	RBI	TBB	IBB	SO	HBP	SH	SF	SB	CS	SB%	GDP	Avg	OBP	SLG
1996 Boston	AL	24	87	21	2	3	4	(3	1)	41	11	16	4	0	14	0	1	1	5	0	1.00	0	.241	.272	.471
1997 Boston	AL	153	684	209	44	11	30	(11	19)	365	122	98	35	2	92	6	2	7	22	9	.71	9	.306	.342	.534
1998 Boston	AL	143	604	195	37	8	35	(17	18)	353	111	122	33	1	62	8	0	4	12	6	.67	20	.323	.362	.584
1999 Boston	AL	135	532	190	42	4	27	(14	13)	321	103	104	51	7	39	8	0	4	14	3	.82	11	.357	.418	.603
4 ML YEARS		455	1907	615	125	26	96	(45	51)	1080	347	340	123	10	207	22	3	19	53	18	.75	40	.322	.367	.566

Mark Gardner

Pitches: Right **Bats:** Right **Pos:** SP-21; RP-8 **Ht:** 6'1" **Wt:** 220 **Born:** 3/1/62 **Age:** 38

Year Team	Lg	G	GS	CG	GF	IP	BFP	H	R	ER	HR	SH	SF	HB	TBB	IBB	SO	WP	Bk	W	L	Pct.	ShO	Sv-Op	Hld	ERA
1999 San Jose *	A+	2	2	0	0	10	44	10	5	5	0	0	0	1	3	0	13	0	1	1	0	1.000	0	0- -	—	4.50
1989 Montreal	NL	7	4	0	1	26.1	117	26	16	15	2	0	0	2	11	1	21	0	0	0	3	.000	0	0-0	—	5.13
1990 Montreal	NL	27	26	3	1	152.2	642	129	62	58	13	4	7	9	61	5	135	2	4	7	9	.438	3	0-0	0	3.42
1991 Montreal	NL	27	27	0	0	168.1	692	139	78	72	17	7	2	4	75	1	107	2	1	9	11	.450	0	0-0	0	3.85
1992 London	NL	33	30	0	1	179.2	778	179	94	87	15	12	7	9	60	2	132	2	0	12	10	.545	0	0-0	0	4.36
1993 Kansas City	AL	17	16	0	0	91.2	387	92	65	63	17	1	7	4	36	0	54	2	0	4	6	.400	0	0-0	0	6.19
1994 Florida	NL	20	14	0	3	92.1	391	97	53	50	14	4	5	1	30	2	57	3	1	4	4	.500	0	0-0	0	4.87
1995 Florida	NL	39	11	1	7	102.1	456	109	60	51	14	7	0	5	43	5	87	3	1	5	5	.500	1	1-1	4	4.49
1996 San Francisco	NL	30	28	4	0	179.1	782	200	105	88	28	6	5	8	57	3	145	2	0	12	7	.632	1	0-0	0	4.42
1997 San Francisco	NL	30	30	2	0	180.1	764	188	92	86	28	10	6	1	57	6	136	3	3	12	9	.571	1	0-0	0	4.29
1998 San Francisco	NL	33	33	4	0	212	886	203	106	102	29	6	7	6	65	5	151	6	1	13	6	.684	2	0-0	0	4.33
1999 San Francisco	NL	29	21	1	2	139	613	142	103	100	27	6	10	8	57	2	86	3	1	5	11	.313	0	0-1	1	6.47
11 ML YEARS		292	240	15	15	1524	6508	1504	831	772	204	63	56	57	552	32	1111	27	12	83	81	.506	8	1-2	6	4.56

Brent Gates

Bats: B **Throws:** R **Pos:** 3B-61; 2B-47; PH/PR-31; 1B-5; DH-1; SS-1 **Ht:** 6'1" **Wt:** 190 **Born:** 3/14/70 **Age:** 30

Year Team	Lg	G	AB	H	2B	3B	HR	(Hm	Rd)	TB	R	RBI	TBB	IBB	SO	HBP	SH	SF	SB	CS	SB%	GDP	Avg	OBP	SLG
1993 Oakland	AL	139	535	155	29	2	7	(4	3)	209	64	69	56	4	75	4	6	8	7	3	.70	17	.290	.357	.391

Year Team	Lg	G	AB	H	2B	3B	HR	(Hm	Rd)	TB	R	RBI	TBB	IBB	SO	HBP	SH	SF	SB	CS	SB%	GDP	Avg	OBP	SLG
1994 Oakland	AL	64	233	66	11	1	2	(0	2)	85	29	24	21	1	32	1	3	6	3	0	1.00	8	.283	.337	.365
1995 Oakland	AL	136	524	133	24	4	5	(3	2)	180	60	56	46	2	84	0	4	11	3	3	.50	15	.254	.308	.344
1996 Oakland	AL	64	247	65	19	2	2	(1	1)	94	26	30	18	0	35	2	5	2	1	1	.50	9	.263	.316	.381
1997 Seattle	AL	65	151	36	8	0	3	(1	2)	53	18	20	14	0	21	0	2	3	0	0	.00	6	.238	.298	.351
1998 Minnesota	AL	107	333	83	15	0	3	(1	1)	107	31	42	36	0	46	2	3	3	3	3	.50	6	.249	.324	.321
1999 Minnesota	AL	110	306	78	13	2	3	(2	1)	104	40	38	34	1	56	1	2	3	1	3	.25	11	.255	.328	.340
7 ML YEARS		685	2329	616	119	11	25	(12	13)	832	268	279	225	8	349	10	25	36	18	13	.58	72	.264	.327	.357

Jason Giambi

Bats: L **Throws:** R **Pos:** 1B-142; DH-15; PH/PR-2; 3B-1   **Ht:** 6'3" **Wt:** 235 **Born:** 1/8/71 **Age:** 29

Year Team	Lg	G	AB	H	2B	3B	HR	(Hm	Rd)	TB	R	RBI	TBB	IBB	SO	HBP	SH	SF	SB	CS	SB%	GDP	Avg	OBP	SLG
1995 Oakland	AL	54	176	45	7	0	6	(3	3)	70	27	25	28	0	31	3	1	2	2	1	.67	4	.256	.364	.398
1996 Oakland	AL	140	536	156	40	1	20	(6	14)	258	84	79	51	3	95	5	1	5	0	1	.00	15	.291	.355	.481
1997 Oakland	AL	142	519	152	41	2	20	(14	6)	257	66	81	55	3	89	6	0	11	0	1	.00	11	.293	.362	.495
1998 Oakland	AL	153	562	166	28	0	27	(12	15)	275	92	110	81	7	102	5	0	9	2	2	.50	16	.295	.384	.489
1999 Oakland	AL	158	575	181	36	1	33	(17	16)	318	115	123	105	6	106	7	0	8	1	1	.50	11	.315	.422	.553
5 ML YEARS		647	2368	700	152	4	106	(52	54)	1178	384	418	320	19	423	26	2	32	5	6	.45	57	.296	.381	.497

Jeremy Giambi

Bats: L **Throws:** L **Pos:** DH-48; 1B-26; PH/PR-11; LF-5   **Ht:** 6'0" **Wt:** 205 **Born:** 9/30/74 **Age:** 25

Year Team	Lg	G	AB	H	2B	3B	HR	(Hm	Rd)	TB	R	RBI	TBB	IBB	SO	HBP	SH	SF	SB	CS	SB%	GDP	Avg	OBP	SLG
1996 Spokane	A-	67	231	63	17	0	6	—	—	98	58	39	61	2	32	8	0	0	22	5	.81	5	.273	.440	.424
1997 Lansing	A	31	116	39	11	1	5	—	—	67	33	21	23	2	16	2	0	1	5	1	.83	1	.336	.451	.578
Wichita	AA	74	268	86	15	1	11	—	—	136	50	52	44	3	47	6	0	4	4	4	.50	7	.321	.422	.507
1998 Omaha	AAA	96	325	121	21	2	20	—	—	206	68	66	57	8	64	6	2	4	8	5	.62	4	.372	.469	.634
1999 Omaha	AAA	35	144	54	5	1	12	—	—	87	31	28	31	2	30	1	0	2	1	1	.50	2	.346	.472	.685
1998 Kansas City	AL	18	58	13	4	0	2	(0	2)	23	6	8	11	0	9	0	0	0	0	1	.00	3	.224	.343	.397
1999 Kansas City	AL	90	288	82	13	1	3	(2	1)	106	34	34	40	5	67	3	1	4	0	0	.00	7	.285	.373	.368
2 ML YEARS		108	346	95	17	1	5	(2	3)	129	40	42	51	5	76	3	1	5	0	1	.00	10	.275	.368	.373

Derrick Gibson

Bats: Right **Throws:** Right **Pos:** RF-10; PH/PR-2   **Ht:** 6'2" **Wt:** 244 **Born:** 2/5/75 **Age:** 25

Year Team	Lg	G	AB	H	2B	3B	HR	(Hm	Rd)	TB	R	RBI	TBB	IBB	SO	HBP	SH	SF	SB	CS	SB%	GDP	Avg	OBP	SLG
1993 Rockies	R	34	119	18	2	2	0	—	—	24	13	10	5	0	55	3	0	1	3	0	1.00	1	.151	.203	.202
1994 Bend	A-	73	284	75	19	5	12	—	—	140	47	57	29	5	102	9	0	1	14	4	.78	4	.264	.350	.493
1995 Asheville	A	135	506	148	16	10	32	—	—	280	91	115	29	5	136	19	1	6	31	13	.70	10	.292	.350	.553
1996 New Haven	AA	122	449	115	21	4	15	—	—	189	58	62	31	1	125	8	1	4	3	12	.20	15	.256	.313	.421
1997 New Haven	AA	119	461	146	24	2	23	—	—	243	91	75	36	7	100	10	0	2	20	13	.61	8	.317	.377	.527
Colo Sprngs	AAA	21	78	33	7	0	3	—	—	49	14	12	5	1	9	0	0	1	0	2	.00	1	.423	.458	.628
1998 Colo Sprngs	AAA	126	497	145	20	3	14	—	—	213	84	81	35	2	110	3	0	2	14	6	.70	17	.292	.341	.429
1999 Colo Sprngs	AAA	110	385	106	19	6	17	—	—	188	68	67	30	0	82	6	0	2	12	6	.67	5	.275	.336	.488
1998 Colorado	NL	7	21	9	1	0	0	(0	0)	10	4	2	1	0	4	1	0	0	0	0	.00	0	.429	.478	.476
1999 Colorado	NL	10	28	5	1	0	2	(2	0)	12	2	6	0	0	7	1	0	0	0	0	.00	2	.179	.207	.429
2 ML YEARS		17	49	14	2	0	2	(2	0)	22	6	8	1	0	11	2	0	0	0	0	.00	2	.286	.327	.449

Brian Giles

Bats: L **Throws:** L **Pos:** CF-108; RF-25; LF-8; DH-3   **Ht:** 5'10" **Wt:** 200 **Born:** 1/20/71 **Age:** 29

Year Team	Lg	G	AB	H	2B	3B	HR	(Hm	Rd)	TB	R	RBI	TBB	IBB	SO	HBP	SH	SF	SB	CS	SB%	GDP	Avg	OBP	SLG
1995 Cleveland	AL	6	9	5	0	0	1	(0	1)	8	6	3	0	0	1	0	0	0	0	0	.00	0	.556	.556	.889
1996 Cleveland	AL	51	121	43	14	1	5	(2	3)	74	26	27	19	4	13	0	0	3	3	0	1.00	6	.355	.434	.612
1997 Cleveland	AL	130	377	101	15	3	17	(7	10)	173	62	61	63	2	50	1	3	7	13	3	.81	10	.268	.368	.459
1998 Cleveland	AL	112	350	94	19	0	16	(10	6)	161	56	66	73	8	75	3	1	3	10	5	.67	7	.269	.396	.460
1999 Pittsburgh	NL	141	521	164	33	3	39	(24	15)	320	109	115	95	7	80	3	0	8	6	2	.75	14	.315	.418	.614
5 ML YEARS		440	1378	407	81	7	78	(43	35)	736	259	272	250	21	219	7	4	21	32	10	.76	37	.295	.401	.534

Bernard Gilkey

Bats: Right **Throws:** Right **Pos:** PH/PR-43; RF-40; LF-15   **Ht:** 6'0" **Wt:** 198 **Born:** 9/24/66 **Age:** 33

Year Team	Lg	G	AB	H	2B	3B	HR	(Hm	Rd)	TB	R	RBI	TBB	IBB	SO	HBP	SH	SF	SB	CS	SB%	GDP	Avg	OBP	SLG
1990 St. Louis	NL	18	64	19	5	2	1	(0	1)	31	11	3	8	0	5	0	0	0	6	1	.86	1	.297	.375	.484
1991 St. Louis	NL	81	268	58	7	2	5	(2	3)	84	28	20	39	0	33	1	1	2	14	8	.64	14	.216	.316	.313
1992 St. Louis	NL	131	384	116	19	4	7	(3	4)	164	56	43	39	1	52	1	3	4	18	12	.60	5	.302	.364	.427
1993 St. Louis	NL	137	557	170	40	5	16	(7	9)	268	99	70	56	2	66	4	0	5	15	10	.60	16	.305	.370	.481
1994 St. Louis	NL	105	380	96	22	1	6	(0	6)	138	52	45	39	2	65	10	0	2	15	8	.65	6	.253	.336	.363
1995 St. Louis	NL	121	480	143	33	4	17	(5	12)	235	73	69	42	3	70	5	1	3	12	6	.67	17	.298	.358	.490
1996 New York	NL	153	571	181	44	3	30	(14	16)	321	108	117	73	7	125	4	0	8	17	9	.65	18	.317	.393	.562
1997 New York	NL	145	518	129	31	1	18	(7	11)	216	85	78	70	1	111	6	0	12	7	11	.39	9	.249	.338	.417

Year Team	Lg	G	AB	H	2B	3B	HR	(Hm	Rd)	TB	R	RBI	TBB	IBB	SO	HBP	SH	SF	SB	CS	SB%	GDP	Avg	OBP	SLG
1998 NYM-Ari	NL	111	365	85	15	0	5	(2	3)	115	41	33	43	1	80	5	3	3	9	3	.75	11	.233	.320	.315
1999 Arizona	NL	94	204	60	16	1	8	(4	4)	102	28	39	29	2	42	2	1	5	2	2	.50	7	.294	.379	.500
1998 New York	NL	82	264	60	15	0	4	(1	3)	87	33	28	32	1	66	4	2	3	5	1	.83	6	.227	.317	.330
Arizona	NL	29	101	25	0	0	1	(1	0)	28	8	5	11	0	14	1	1	0	4	2	.67	5	.248	.327	.277
10 ML YEARS		1096	3791	1057	232	23	113	(44	69)	1674	581	517	438	19	649	38	9	44	115	70	.62	104	.279	.356	.442

Ed Giovanola

Bats: L Throws: R Pos: 3B-25; PH/PR-20; 2B-19; SS-7; P-1   Ht: 5'10" Wt: 188 Born: 3/4/69 Age: 31

Year Team	Lg	G	AB	H	2B	3B	HR	(Hm	Rd)	TB	R	RBI	TBB	IBB	SO	HBP	SH	SF	SB	CS	SB%	GDP	Avg	OBP	SLG
1999 Las Vegas *	AAA	36	106	30	6	1	2	—	—	44	23	10	16	1	23	0	0	0	2	0	1.00	3	.283	.377	.415
1995 Atlanta	NL	13	14	1	0	0	0	(0	0)	1	2	0	3	0	5	0	0	0	0	0	.00	1	.071	.235	.071
1996 Atlanta	NL	43	82	19	2	0	0	(0	0)	21	10	7	8	0	13	1	2	1	1	0	1.00	3	.232	.304	.256
1997 Atlanta	NL	14	8	2	0	0	0	(0	0)	2	0	0	2	1	1	0	0	0	0	0	.00	2	.250	.400	.250
1998 San Diego	NL	92	139	32	3	3	1	(1	0)	44	19	9	22	0	22	0	5	0	1	2	.33	2	.230	.335	.317
1999 San Diego	NL	56	58	11	0	0	0	(0	0)	13	10	3	9	0	8	0	1	1	2	0	1.00	1	.190	.294	.224
5 ML YEARS		218	301	65	5	4	1	(1	0)	81	41	19	44	1	49	1	8	2	4	2	.67	9	.216	.316	.269

Charles Gipson

Bats: R Throws: R Pos: 3B-17; RF-15; PH/PR-15; CF-9; LF-8; DH-4; 2B-3; SS-3   Ht: 6'2" Wt: 180 Born: 12/16/72 Age: 27

Year Team	Lg	G	AB	H	2B	3B	HR	(Hm	Rd)	TB	R	RBI	TBB	IBB	SO	HBP	SH	SF	SB	CS	SB%	GDP	Avg	OBP	SLG
1992 Mariners	R	39	124	39	2	0	0	—	—	41	30	14	13	1	19	6	2	1	11	5	.69	0	.315	.403	.331
1993 Appleton	A	109	348	89	13	1	0	—	—	104	63	20	61	0	76	27	9	1	21	15	.58	3	.256	.405	.299
1994 Riverside	A+	128	481	141	12	3	1	—	—	162	102	41	76	4	67	12	7	2	34	15	.69	8	.293	.401	.337
1995 Port City	AA	112	391	87	11	2	0	—	—	102	36	29	30	0	66	8	7	1	10	12	.45	13	.223	.291	.261
1996 Port City	AA	119	407	109	12	3	1	—	—	130	54	30	41	1	62	7	6	0	26	15	.63	9	.268	.345	.319
1997 Tacoma	AAA	11	35	11	2	0	0	—	—	13	5	5	4	0	3	1	0	0	0	1	.00	0	.314	.400	.371
Memphis	AA	88	320	79	9	4	1	—	—	99	56	28	34	2	71	13	2	1	31	6	.84	4	.247	.342	.309
1998 Tacoma	AAA	75	278	67	16	2	0	—	—	87	39	11	27	1	50	6	3	0	14	11	.56	17	.241	.322	.313
1999 New Haven	AA	5	18	0	0	0	0	—	—	0	2	0	3	0	2	0	1	0	1	0	1.00	0	.000	.143	.000
Tacoma	AAA	47	174	52	6	3	0	—	—	64	26	21	14	0	24	3	2	0	18	4	.82	5	.299	.361	.368
Everett	A-	1	2	1	0	1	0	—	—	3	0	1	2	0	0	0	0	0	1	0	1.00	0	.500	.750	1.500
1998 Seattle	AL	44	51	12	1	0	0	(0	0)	13	11	2	5	1	9	1	0	0	2	1	.67	1	.235	.316	.255
1999 Seattle	AL	55	80	18	5	2	0	(0	0)	27	16	9	6	0	13	1	2	0	3	4	.43	2	.225	.287	.338
2 ML YEARS		99	131	30	6	2	0	(0	0)	40	27	11	11	1	22	2	2	0	5	5	.50	3	.229	.299	.305

Joe Girardi

Bats: Right Throws: Right Pos: C-65; PH/PR-1   Ht: 5'11" Wt: 200 Born: 10/14/64 Age: 35

Year Team	Lg	G	AB	H	2B	3B	HR	(Hm	Rd)	TB	R	RBI	TBB	IBB	SO	HBP	SH	SF	SB	CS	SB%	GDP	Avg	OBP	SLG
1989 Chicago	NL	59	157	39	10	0	1	(0	1)	52	15	14	11	5	26	2	1	1	2	1	.67	4	.248	.304	.331
1990 Chicago	NL	133	419	113	24	2	1	(1	0)	144	36	38	17	11	50	3	4	4	8	3	.73	13	.270	.300	.344
1991 Chicago	NL	21	47	9	2	0	0	(0	0)	11	3	6	6	1	6	0	1	0	0	0	.00	0	.191	.283	.234
1992 Chicago	NL	91	270	73	3	1	1	(1	0)	81	19	12	19	3	38	1	0	1	0	2	.00	8	.270	.320	.300
1993 Colorado	NL	86	310	90	14	5	3	(2	1)	123	35	31	24	0	41	3	12	1	6	6	.50	6	.290	.346	.397
1994 Colorado	NL	93	330	91	9	4	4	(1	3)	120	47	34	21	1	48	2	6	2	3	3	.50	13	.276	.321	.364
1995 Colorado	NL	125	462	121	17	2	8	(6	2)	166	63	55	29	0	76	2	12	1	3	3	.50	15	.262	.308	.359
1996 New York	AL	124	422	124	22	3	2	(1	1)	158	55	45	30	1	55	5	11	3	13	4	.76	11	.294	.346	.374
1997 New York	AL	112	398	105	23	1	1	(1	0)	133	38	50	26	1	53	2	5	2	2	3	.40	15	.264	.311	.334
1998 New York	AL	78	254	70	11	4	3	(1	2)	98	31	31	14	1	38	2	8	1	2	4	.33	10	.276	.317	.386
1999 New York	AL	65	209	50	16	1	2	(1	1)	74	23	27	10	0	26	0	8	2	3	1	.75	16	.239	.271	.354
11 ML YEARS		987	3278	885	151	23	26	(15	11)	1160	365	343	207	24	457	22	68	18	42	30	.58	111	.270	.316	.354

Doug Glanville

Bats: Right Throws: Right Pos: CF-148; PH/PR-2   Ht: 6'2" Wt: 180 Born: 8/25/70 Age: 29

Year Team	Lg	G	AB	H	2B	3B	HR	(Hm	Rd)	TB	R	RBI	TBB	IBB	SO	HBP	SH	SF	SB	CS	SB%	GDP	Avg	OBP	SLG
1996 Chicago	NL	49	83	20	5	1	1	(1	0)	30	10	10	3	0	11	0	2	1	2	0	1.00	0	.241	.264	.361
1997 Chicago	NL	146	474	142	22	5	4	(2	2)	186	79	35	24	0	46	1	9	2	19	11	.63	9	.300	.333	.392
1998 Philadelphia	NL	158	678	189	28	7	8	(3	5)	255	106	49	42	1	89	6	5	4	23	6	.79	7	.279	.325	.376
1999 Philadelphia	NL	150	628	204	38	6	11	(5	6)	287	101	73	48	1	82	6	5	5	34	2	.94	9	.325	.376	.457
4 ML YEARS		503	1863	555	93	19	24	(11	13)	758	296	167	117	2	228	13	21	12	78	19	.80	25	.298	.342	.407

Troy Glaus

Bats: Right Throws: Right Pos: 3B-153; DH-1   Ht: 6'5" Wt: 225 Born: 8/3/76 Age: 23

Year Team	Lg	G	AB	H	2B	3B	HR	(Hm	Rd)	TB	R	RBI	TBB	IBB	SO	HBP	SH	SF	SB	CS	SB%	GDP	Avg	OBP	SLG
1998 Midland	AA	50	188	58	11	2	19	—	—	130	51	51	39	3	41	2	0	1	4	2	.67	4	.309	.430	.691
Vancouver	AAA	59	219	67	16	0	16	—	—	131	33	42	21	0	55	3	0	0	2	2	.60	1	.306	.374	.598
1998 Anaheim	AL	48	165	36	9	0	1	(0	1)	48	19	23	15	0	51	0	0	2	1	0	1.00	3	.218	.280	.291

			BATTING														BASERUNNING				PERCENTAGES		
Year Team	Lg	G	AB	H	2B	3B	HR	(Hm | Rd)	TB	R	RBI	TBB	IBB	SO	HBP	SH	SF	SB	CS	SB%	GDP	Avg	OBP	SLG
1999 Anaheim	AL	154	551	132	29	0	29	(12 | 17)	248	85	79	71	1	143	6	0	3	5	1	.83	9	.240	.331	.450
2 ML YEARS		202	716	168	38	0	30	(12 | 18)	296	104	102	86	1	194	6	0	5	6	1	.86	12	.235	.320	.413

Tom Glavine

Pitches: Left **Bats:** Left **Pos:** SP-35   **Ht:** 6'0" **Wt:** 185 **Born:** 3/25/66 **Age:** 34

		HOW MUCH HE PITCHED						WHAT HE GAVE UP											THE RESULTS					
Year Team	Lg	G	GS	CG	GF	IP	BFP	H	R	ER	HR	SH	SF	HB	TBB	IBB	SO	WP	Bk	W	L	Pct.	ShO	Sv-Op	Hld	ERA
1987 Atlanta	NL	9	9	0	0	50.1	238	55	34	31	5	2	3	3	33	4	20	1	1	2	4	.333	0	0-0	0	5.54
1988 Atlanta	NL	34	34	1	0	195.1	844	201	111	99	12	17	11	8	63	7	84	2	2	7	17	.292	0	0-0	0	4.56
1989 Atlanta	NL	29	29	6	0	186	766	172	88	76	20	11	4	2	40	3	90	2	0	14	8	.636	4	0-0	0	3.68
1990 Atlanta	NL	33	33	1	0	214.1	929	232	111	102	18	21	2	1	78	10	129	8	1	10	12	.455	0	0-0	0	4.28
1991 Atlanta	NL	34	34	9	0	246.2	989	201	83	70	17	7	6	2	69	6	192	10	2	20	11	.645	1	0-0	0	2.55
1992 Atlanta	NL	33	33	7	0	225	919	197	81	69	6	2	6	2	70	7	129	5	0	20	8	.714	5	0-0	0	2.76
1993 Atlanta	NL	36	36	4	0	239.1	1014	236	91	85	16	10	2	2	90	7	120	4	0	22	6	.786	2	0-0	0	3.20
1994 Atlanta	NL	25	25	2	0	165.1	731	173	76	73	10	9	6	1	70	10	140	8	1	13	9	.591	0	0-0	0	3.97
1995 Atlanta	NL	29	29	3	0	198.2	822	182	76	68	9	7	5	5	66	0	127	3	0	16	7	.696	1	0-0	0	3.08
1996 Atlanta	NL	36	36	1	0	235.1	994	222	91	78	14	15	2	0	85	7	181	4	0	15	10	.600	0	0-0	0	2.98
1997 Atlanta	NL	33	33	5	0	240	970	197	86	79	20	11	6	4	79	9	152	3	0	14	7	.667	2	0-0	0	2.96
1998 Atlanta	NL	33	33	4	0	229.1	934	202	67	63	13	6	2	2	74	2	157	3	0	20	6	.769	3	0-0	0	2.47
1999 Atlanta	NL	35	35	2	0	234	1023	259	115	107	18	22	10	4	83	14	138	2	0	14	11	.560	0	0-0	0	4.12
13 ML YEARS		399	399	45	0	2659.2	11173	2529	1110	1000	178	140	65	36	900	86	1659	55	7	187	116	.617	18	0-0	0	3.38

Gary Glover

Pitches: Right **Bats:** Right **Pos:** RP-1   **Ht:** 6'5" **Wt:** 200 **Born:** 12/3/76 **Age:** 23

		HOW MUCH HE PITCHED						WHAT HE GAVE UP											THE RESULTS					
Year Team	Lg	G	GS	CG	GF	IP	BFP	H	R	ER	HR	SH	SF	HB	TBB	IBB	SO	WP	Bk	W	L	Pct.	ShO	Sv-Op	Hld	ERA
1994 Blue Jays	R	2	0	0	0	1.1	13	4	8	7	1	0	0	1	4	0	2	1	1	0	0	.000	0	0--	—	47.25
1995 Blue Jays	R	12	10	2	0	62.1	279	62	48	34	4	4	3	11	26	0	46	8	0	3	7	.300	0	0--	—	4.91
1996 Medcine Hat	R+	15	15	2	0	83.2	410	119	94	72	14	2	4	6	29	1	54	8	1	3	12	.200	0	0--	—	7.75
1997 Hagerstown	A	28	28	3	0	173.2	751	165	94	72	9	3	5	10	58	1	155	20	4	6	17	.261	0	0--	—	3.73
1998 Knoxville	AA	8	8	0	0	37.1	183	41	36	28	2	1	3	4	28	0	14	2	0	0	5	.000	0	0--	—	6.75
Dunedin	A+	19	18	0	0	109.1	484	117	66	52	8	1	6	7	36	0	88	11	1	7	6	.538	0	0--	—	4.28
1999 Knoxville	AA	13	13	1	0	86	346	70	39	34	5	2	1	4	27	0	77	4	0	8	2	.800	0	0--	—	3.56
Syracuse	AAA	14	14	0	0	76.1	347	93	50	44	10	0	3	0	35	0	57	3	1	4	6	.400	0	0--	—	5.19
1999 Toronto	AL	1	0	0	1	1	3	0	0	0	0	0	0	0	1	0	0	0	0	0	0	.000	0	0-0	0	0.00

Ryan Glynn

Pitches: Right **Bats:** Right **Pos:** SP-10; RP-3   **Ht:** 6'3" **Wt:** 195 **Born:** 11/1/74 **Age:** 25

		HOW MUCH HE PITCHED						WHAT HE GAVE UP											THE RESULTS					
Year Team	Lg	G	GS	CG	GF	IP	BFP	H	R	ER	HR	SH	SF	HB	TBB	IBB	SO	WP	Bk	W	L	Pct.	ShO	Sv-Op	Hld	ERA
1995 Hudson Val	A-	9	8	0	0	44	192	56	27	23	0	0	1	3	16	1	21	10	3	3	3	.500	0	0--	—	4.70
1996 Chston-SC	A	19	19	2	0	121	526	118	70	61	10	6	6	8	59	2	72	12	0	8	7	.533	1	0--	—	4.54
1997 Charlotte	A+	23	22	5	1	134	579	148	81	74	13	2	7	4	44	0	96	9	1	8	7	.533	1	1--	—	4.97
Tulsa	AA	3	3	0	0	21.1	94	21	9	8	1	1	2	2	10	0	18	2	0	1	1	.500	0	0--	—	3.38
1998 Tulsa	AA	26	24	4	0	157	660	140	66	60	12	4	3	5	64	0	111	9	1	9	6	.600	1	0--	—	3.44
1999 Oklahoma	AAA	16	16	2	0	90.1	385	81	46	34	7	1	4	4	36	1	55	3	0	6	2	.750	1	0--	—	3.39
1999 Texas	AL	13	10	0	2	54.2	262	71	46	44	10	0	1	1	35	0	39	3	1	2	4	.333	0	0-0	0	7.24

Wayne Gomes

Pitches: Right **Bats:** Right **Pos:** RP-73   **Ht:** 6'2" **Wt:** 215 **Born:** 1/15/73 **Age:** 27

		HOW MUCH HE PITCHED						WHAT HE GAVE UP											THE RESULTS					
Year Team	Lg	G	GS	CG	GF	IP	BFP	H	R	ER	HR	SH	SF	HB	TBB	IBB	SO	WP	Bk	W	L	Pct.	ShO	Sv-Op	Hld	ERA
1997 Philadelphia	NL	37	0	0	13	42.2	191	45	26	25	4	2	0	1	24	0	24	2	0	5	1	.833	0	0-1	3	5.27
1998 Philadelphia	NL	71	0	0	16	93.1	408	94	48	44	9	5	1	3	35	4	86	6	0	9	6	.600	0	1-8	13	4.24
1999 Philadelphia	NL	73	0	0	58	74	341	70	38	35	5	5	3	2	56	2	58	3	1	5	5	.500	0	19-24	9	4.26
3 ML YEARS		181	0	0	87	210	940	209	112	104	18	12	4	6	115	6	168	11	1	19	12	.613	0	20-33	25	4.46

Chris Gomez

Bats: Right **Throws:** Right **Pos:** SS-75; PH/PR-1   **Ht:** 6'1" **Wt:** 195 **Born:** 6/16/71 **Age:** 29

			BATTING														BASERUNNING				PERCENTAGES		
Year Team	Lg	G	AB	H	2B	3B	HR	(Hm	Rd)	TB	R	RBI	TBB	IBB	SO	HBP	SH	SF	SB	CS	SB%	GDP	Avg	OBP	SLG
1999 Las Vegas *	AAA	10	27	9	1	0	0	—	—	10	3	4	2	0	6	1	0	0	0	0	.00	1	.333	.400	.370
1993 Detroit	AL	46	128	32	7	1	0	(0	0)	41	11	11	9	0	17	1	3	0	2	2	.50	2	.250	.304	.320
1994 Detroit	AL	84	296	76	19	0	8	(5	3)	119	32	53	33	0	64	3	3	1	5	3	.63	8	.257	.336	.402
1995 Detroit	AL	123	431	96	20	2	11	(5	6)	153	49	50	41	0	96	3	3	4	4	1	.80	13	.223	.292	.355
1996 Det-SD		137	456	117	21	1	4	(2	2)	152	53	45	57	1	84	7	6	2	3	3	.50	16	.257	.347	.333
1997 San Diego	NL	150	522	132	19	2	5	(2	3)	170	62	54	53	1	114	5	3	5	5	8	.38	16	.253	.326	.326
1998 San Diego	NL	145	449	120	32	3	4	(3	1)	170	55	39	51	7	87	5	7	3	1	3	.25	11	.267	.346	.379
1999 San Diego	NL	76	234	59	8	1	1			72	20	15	27	3	49	1	2	1	1	2	.33	6	.252	.331	.308
1996 Detroit	AL	48	128	31	5	0	1	(1	0)	39	21	16	18	0	20	1	3	0	1	1	.50	5	.242	.340	.305
San Diego	NL	89	328	86	16	1	3	(1	2)	113	32	29	39	1	64	6	3	2	2	2	.50	11	.262	.349	.345
7 ML YEARS		761	2516	632	126	10	33	(18	15)	877	282	267	271	12	511	25	27	14	21	22	.49	72	.251	.328	.349

Alex Gonzalez

Bats: Right **Throws:** Right **Pos:** SS-37; DH-1   **Ht:** 6'0" **Wt:** 200 **Born:** 4/8/73 **Age:** 27

Year Team	Lg	G	AB	H	2B	3B	HR	(Hm	Rd)	TB	R	RBI	TBB	IBB	SO	HBP	SH	SF	SB	CS	SB%	GDP	Avg	OBP	SLG
1994 Toronto	AL	15	53	8	3	1	0	(0	0)	13	7	1	4	0	17	1	1	0	3	0	1.00	2	.151	.224	.245
1995 Toronto	AL	111	367	89	19	4	10	(8	2)	146	51	42	44	1	114	1	9	4	4	4	.50	7	.243	.322	.398
1996 Toronto	AL	147	527	124	30	5	14	(3	11)	206	64	64	45	0	127	5	7	3	16	6	.73	12	.235	.300	.391
1997 Toronto	AL	126	426	102	23	2	12	(4	8)	165	46	35	34	1	94	5	11	2	15	6	.71	9	.239	.302	.387
1998 Toronto	AL	158	568	136	28	1	13	(7	6)	205	70	51	28	1	121	6	13	3	21	6	.78	13	.239	.281	.361
1999 Toronto	AL	38	154	45	13	0	2	(1	1)	64	22	12	16	0	23	3	0	0	4	2	.67	4	.292	.370	.416
6 ML YEARS		595	2095	504	116	13	51	(23	28)	799	260	205	171	3	496	21	41	12	63	24	.72	47	.241	.303	.381

Alex Gonzalez

Bats: Right **Throws:** Right **Pos:** SS-135; PH/PR-2   **Ht:** 6'0" **Wt:** 170 **Born:** 2/15/77 **Age:** 23

Year Team	Lg	G	AB	H	2B	3B	HR	(Hm	Rd)	TB	R	RBI	TBB	IBB	SO	HBP	SH	SF	SB	CS	SB%	GDP	Avg	OBP	SLG
1995 Brevard Cty	A+	17	59	12	2	1	0	—	—	16	6	8	1	0	14	1	0	0	1	1	.50	2	.203	.230	.271
Marlins	R	53	187	55	7	4	2	—	—	76	30	30	19	0	27	2	1	4	11	2	.85	2	.294	.358	.406
1996 Marlins	R	10	41	16	3	0	0	—	—	19	6	6	2	0	4	0	0	0	1	0	1.00	1	.390	.419	.463
Kane County	A	4	10	2	0	0	0	—	—	2	2	0	2	0	4	1	1	0	0	0	.00	1	.200	.385	.200
Portland	AA	11	34	8	0	1	0	—	—	10	4	1	2	2	10	1	0	0	0	0	.00	2	.235	.297	.294
1997 Portland	AA	133	449	114	16	4	19	—	—	195	69	65	27	5	83	7	3	3	4	7	.36	4	.254	.305	.434
1998 Charlotte	AAA	108	422	117	20	10	10	—	—	187	71	51	28	2	80	6	8	2	4	7	.36	6	.277	.330	.443
1998 Florida	NL	25	86	13	2	0	3	(1	2)	24	11	7	9	0	30	1	2	0	0	0	.00	2	.151	.240	.279
1999 Florida	NL	136	560	155	28	8	14	(7	7)	241	81	59	15	0	113	12	1	3	3	5	.38	13	.277	.308	.430
2 ML YEARS		161	646	168	30	8	17	(8	9)	265	92	66	24	0	143	13	3	3	3	5	.38	15	.260	.299	.410

Jeremi Gonzalez

Pitches: Right **Bats:** Right **Pos:** SP   **Ht:** 6'2" **Wt:** 205 **Born:** 1/8/75 **Age:** 25

Year Team	Lg	G	GS	CG	GF	IP	BFP	H	R	ER	HR	SH	SF	HB	TBB	IBB	SO	WP	Bk	W	L	Pct.	ShO	Sv-Op	Hld	ERA
1997 Chicago	NL	23	23	1	0	144	613	126	73	68	16	4	5	2	69	5	93	1	1	11	9	.550	1	0-0	0	4.25
1998 Chicago	NL	20	20	1	0	110	493	124	72	65	13	5	2	3	41	5	70	2	3	7	7	.500	1	0-0	0	5.32
2 ML YEARS		43	43	2	0	254	1106	250	145	133	29	9	7	5	110	10	163	3	4	18	16	.529	2	0-0	0	4.71

Juan Gonzalez

Bats: Right **Throws:** Right **Pos:** RF-131; DH-14   **Ht:** 6'3" **Wt:** 220 **Born:** 10/16/69 **Age:** 30

Year Team	Lg	G	AB	H	2B	3B	HR	(Hm	Rd)	TB	R	RBI	TBB	IBB	SO	HBP	SH	SF	SB	CS	SB%	GDP	Avg	OBP	SLG
1989 Texas	AL	24	60	9	3	0	1	(1	0)	15	6	7	6	0	17	0	2	0	0	0	.00	4	.150	.227	.250
1990 Texas	AL	25	90	26	7	1	4	(3	1)	47	11	12	2	0	18	2	0	1	0	1	.00	2	.289	.316	.522
1991 Texas	AL	142	545	144	34	1	27	(7	20)	261	78	102	42	7	118	5	0	3	4	4	.50	10	.264	.321	.479
1992 Texas	AL	155	584	152	24	2	43	(19	24)	309	77	109	35	1	143	5	0	8	0	1	.00	16	.260	.304	.529
1993 Texas	AL	140	536	166	33	1	46	(24	22)	339	105	118	37	7	99	13	0	1	4	1	.80	12	.310	.368	.632
1994 Texas	AL	107	422	116	18	4	19	(6	13)	199	57	85	30	10	66	7	0	4	6	4	.60	18	.275	.330	.472
1995 Texas	AL	90	352	104	20	2	27	(15	12)	209	57	82	17	3	66	0	0	5	0	0	.00	15	.295	.324	.594
1996 Texas	AL	134	541	170	33	2	47	(23	24)	348	89	144	45	12	82	3	0	3	2	0	1.00	16	.314	.368	.643
1997 Texas	AL	133	533	158	24	3	42	(18	24)	314	87	131	33	7	107	3	0	10	0	0	.00	12	.296	.335	.589
1998 Texas	AL	154	606	193	50	2	45	(21	24)	382	110	157	46	9	126	6	0	11	2	1	.67	20	.318	.366	.630
1999 Texas	AL	144	562	183	36	1	39	(14	25)	338	114	128	51	7	105	4	0	12	3	3	.50	10	.326	.378	.601
11 ML YEARS		1248	4831	1421	282	19	340	(151	189)	2761	791	1075	344	63	947	48	2	58	21	15	.58	129	.294	.343	.572

Luis Gonzalez

Bats: Left **Throws:** Right **Pos:** LF-148; DH-4; PH/PR-1   **Ht:** 6'2" **Wt:** 200 **Born:** 9/2/67 **Age:** 32

Year Team	Lg	G	AB	H	2B	3B	HR	(Hm	Rd)	TB	R	RBI	TBB	IBB	SO	HBP	SH	SF	SB	CS	SB%	GDP	Avg	OBP	SLG
1990 Houston	NL	12	21	4	2	0	0	(0	0)	6	1	0	2	1	5	0	0	0	0	0	.00	0	.190	.261	.286
1991 Houston	NL	137	473	120	28	9	13	(4	9)	205	51	69	40	4	101	8	1	4	10	7	.59	9	.254	.320	.433
1992 Houston	NL	122	387	94	19	3	10	(4	6)	149	40	55	24	3	52	2	1	2	7	7	.50	6	.243	.289	.385
1993 Houston	NL	154	540	162	34	3	15	(8	7)	247	82	72	47	7	83	10	3	10	20	9	.69	9	.300	.361	.457
1994 Houston	NL	112	392	107	29	4	8	(3	5)	168	57	67	49	6	57	3	0	6	15	13	.54	10	.273	.353	.429
1995 Hou-ChC	NL	133	471	130	29	8	13	(6	7)	214	69	69	57	8	63	6	1	6	6	8	.43	16	.276	.357	.454
1996 Chicago	NL	146	483	131	30	4	15	(6	9)	214	70	79	61	8	49	4	1	6	9	6	.60	13	.271	.354	.443
1997 Houston	NL	152	550	142	31	2	10	(4	6)	207	78	68	71	7	67	5	0	5	10	7	.59	12	.258	.345	.376
1998 Detroit	AL	154	541	146	35	5	23	(15	8)	260	84	71	57	7	62	8	0	8	12	7	.63	9	.267	.340	.475
1999 Arizona	NL	153	614	206	45	4	26	(10	16)	337	112	111	66	6	63	7	1	5	9	5	.64	13	.336	.403	.549
1995 Houston	NL	56	209	54	10	4	6	(1	5)	90	35	35	18	3	30	3	1	3	1	3	.25	8	.258	.322	.431
Chicago	NL	77	262	76	19	4	7	(5	2)	124	34	34	39	5	33	3	0	3	5	5	.50	8	.290	.384	.473
10 ML YEARS		1275	4478	1242	282	42	133	(60	73)	2007	644	661	474	57	602	53	8	52	98	69	.59	97	.277	.350	.448

Wiki Gonzalez

Bats: Right **Throws:** Right **Pos:** C-17; PH/PR-13   **Ht:** 5'11" **Wt:** 203 **Born:** 5/17/74 **Age:** 26

							BATTING											BASERUNNING				PERCENTAGES		
Year Team	Lg	G	AB	H	2B	3B	HR	(Hm | Rd)	TB	R	RBI	TBB	IBB	SO	HBP	SH	SF	SB	CS	SB%	GDP	Avg	OBP	SLG
1994 Pirates	R	41	143	48	8	2	4	—	—	72	25	26	13	1	13	3	1	1	2	4	.33	3	.336	.400	.503
1995 Augusta	A	84	278	67	17	0	3	—	—	93	41	36	26	0	32	2	2	5	5	4	.56	7	.241	.305	.335
1996 Augusta	A	118	419	106	21	3	4	—	—	145	52	62	58	1	41	7	2	5	4	6	.40	14	.253	.350	.346
1997 Rancho Cuca	A+	33	110	33	9	1	5	—	—	59	18	26	7	1	25	0	1	1	1	1	.50	1	.300	.339	.536
Mobile	AA	47	143	39	7	1	4	—	—	60	15	25	10	0	12	2	0	1	1	1	.50	5	.273	.327	.420
1998 Mobile	AA	22	67	26	9	0	4	—	—	47	20	26	14	0	4	2	0	2	0	0	.00	1	.388	.494	.701
Rancho Cuca	A+	75	292	84	24	2	10	—	—	142	51	59	26	1	54	2	0	4	0	0	.00	6	.288	.346	.486
1999 Mobile	AA	61	225	76	16	2	10	—	—	126	38	49	29	2	28	7	1	3	0	0	.00	8	.338	.424	.560
Las Vegas	AAA	24	92	25	6	0	6	—	—	49	13	12	5	0	10	3	0	0	0	0	.00	3	.272	.330	.533
1999 San Diego	NL	30	83	21	2	1	3	(1 | 2)	34	7	12	1	0	8	1	0	0	0	0	.00	5	.253	.271	.410

Dwight Gooden

Pitches: Right **Bats:** Right **Pos:** SP-22; RP-4   **Ht:** 6'3" **Wt:** 210 **Born:** 11/16/64 **Age:** 35

		HOW MUCH HE PITCHED						WHAT HE GAVE UP										THE RESULTS						
Year Team	Lg	G	GS	CG	GF	IP	BFP	H	R	ER	HR	SH	SF	HB	TBB	IBB	SO	WP	Bk	W	L	Pct.	ShO	Sv-Op	Hld	ERA
1999 Akron *	AA	1	1	0	0	3	12	3	2	1	0	0	0	0	1	0	2	0	0	0	0	.000	0	0--	—	3.00
Buffalo *	AAA	1	1	0	0	3.2	19	6	1	1	1	0	0	0	3	1	3	0	0	1	0	.000	0	0--	—	2.45
1984 New York	NL	31	31	7	0	218	879	161	72	63	7	3	2	2	73	2	276	3	7	17	9	.654	3	0-0	0	2.60
1985 New York	NL	35	35	16	0	276.2	1065	198	51	47	13	6	2	2	69	4	268	6	2	24	4	.857	8	0-0	0	1.53
1986 New York	NL	33	33	12	0	250	1020	197	92	79	17	10	8	4	80	3	200	4	4	17	6	.739	2	0-0	0	2.84
1987 New York	NL	25	25	7	0	179.2	730	162	68	64	11	5	5	2	53	2	148	1	1	15	7	.682	3	0-0	0	3.21
1988 New York	NL	34	34	10	0	248.1	1024	242	98	88	8	10	6	6	57	4	175	5	5	18	9	.667	3	0-0	0	3.19
1989 New York	NL	19	17	0	1	118.1	497	93	42	38	9	4	3	2	47	2	101	7	5	9	4	.692	0	1-1	1	2.89
1990 New York	NL	34	34	2	0	232.2	983	229	106	99	10	10	7	7	70	3	223	6	3	19	7	.731	1	0-0	0	3.83
1991 New York	NL	27	27	3	0	190	789	185	80	76	12	5	4	3	56	2	150	5	2	13	7	.650	1	0-0	0	3.60
1992 New York	NL	31	31	3	0	206	863	197	93	84	11	10	7	7	70	7	145	3	1	10	13	.435	0	0-0	0	3.67
1993 New York	NL	29	29	7	0	208.2	866	188	89	80	16	11	7	9	61	1	149	5	2	12	15	.444	2	0-0	0	3.45
1994 New York	NL	7	7	0	0	41.1	182	46	32	29	9	3	0	1	15	1	40	2	0	3	4	.429	0	0-0	0	6.31
1996 New York	AL	29	29	1	0	170.2	756	169	101	95	19	1	5	9	88	4	126	9	1	11	7	.611	1	0-0	0	5.01
1997 New York	AL	20	19	0	0	106.1	472	116	61	58	14	0	2	7	53	1	66	8	0	9	5	.643	0	0-0	0	4.91
1998 Cleveland	AL	23	23	0	0	134	580	135	59	56	13	1	4	9	51	0	83	3	0	8	6	.571	0	0-0	0	3.76
1999 Cleveland	AL	26	22	0	0	115	532	127	90	80	18	1	4	9	67	3	88	4	0	3	4	.429	0	0-0	0	6.26
15 ML YEARS		403	396	68	1	2695.2	11238	2445	1134	1036	187	80	66	75	910	39	2238	71	33	188	107	.637	24	1-1	1	3.46

Curtis Goodwin

Bats: Left **Throws:** Left **Pos:** CF-44; LF-36; PH/PR-23   **Ht:** 5'11" **Wt:** 180 **Born:** 9/30/72 **Age:** 27

							BATTING											BASERUNNING				PERCENTAGES		
Year Team	Lg	G	AB	H	2B	3B	HR	(Hm	Rd)	TB	R	RBI	TBB	IBB	SO	HBP	SH	SF	SB	CS	SB%	GDP	Avg	OBP	SLG
1995 Baltimore	AL	87	289	76	11	3	1	(0	1)	96	40	24	15	0	53	2	7	3	22	4	.85	5	.263	.301	.332
1996 Cincinnati	NL	49	136	31	3	0	0	(0	0)	34	20	5	19	0	34	0	1	0	15	6	.71	1	.228	.323	.250
1997 Cincinnati	NL	85	265	67	11	0	1	(1	0)	81	27	12	24	0	53	1	6	1	22	13	.63	6	.253	.316	.306
1998 Colorado	NL	119	159	39	7	0	1	(1	0)	49	27	6	16	0	40	0	10	1	5	1	.83	3	.245	.313	.308
1999 ChC-Tor		91	165	38	6	1	0	(0	0)	46	15	9	13	1	41	0	4	1	2	4	.33	7	.230	.285	.279
1999 Chicago	NL	89	157	38	6	1	0	(0	0)	46	15	9	13	1	38	0	4	1	2	4	.33	7	.242	.298	.293
Toronto	AL	2	8	0	0	0	0	(0	0)	0	0	0	0	0	3	0	0	0	0	0	.00	0	.000	.000	.000
5 ML YEARS		431	1014	251	38	4	3	(2	1)	306	129	56	87	1	221	3	28	6	66	28	.70	22	.248	.307	.302

Tom Goodwin

Bats: Left **Throws:** Right **Pos:** CF-107; PH/PR-4   **Ht:** 6'1" **Wt:** 175 **Born:** 7/27/68 **Age:** 31

							BATTING											BASERUNNING				PERCENTAGES		
Year Team	Lg	G	AB	H	2B	3B	HR	(Hm	Rd)	TB	R	RBI	TBB	IBB	SO	HBP	SH	SF	SB	CS	SB%	GDP	Avg	OBP	SLG
1999 Charlotte *	A+	3	11	4	1	0	0	—	—	5	2	0	1	0	4	0	0	0	1	1	.50	0	.364	.417	.455
1991 Los Angeles	NL	16	7	1	0	0	0	(0	0)	1	3	0	0	0	0	0	0	0	1	1	.50	0	.143	.143	.143
1992 Los Angeles	NL	57	73	17	1	1	0	(0	0)	20	15	3	6	0	10	0	0	0	7	3	.70	0	.233	.291	.274
1993 Los Angeles	NL	30	17	5	1	0	0	(0	0)	6	6	1	1	0	4	0	0	0	1	2	.33	1	.294	.333	.353
1994 Kansas City	AL	2	0	0	0	0	0	(0	0)	0	0	0	0	0	1	0	0	0	0	0	.00	0	.000	.000	.000
1995 Kansas City	AL	133	480	138	16	3	4	(2	2)	172	72	28	38	0	72	5	14	0	50	18	.74	7	.288	.346	.358
1996 Kansas City	AL	143	524	148	14	4	1	(0	1)	173	80	35	39	0	79	2	21	6	66	22	.75	3	.282	.334	.330
1997 KC-Tex	AL	150	574	149	26	6	2	(0	2)	193	90	39	44	1	88	3	11	3	50	16	.76	7	.260	.314	.336
1998 Texas	AL	154	520	151	13	3	2	(2	0)	176	102	33	73	0	90	2	10	3	38	20	.66	2	.290	.378	.338
1999 Texas	AL	109	405	105	12	6	3	(1	2)	138	63	33	40	0	61	0	7	3	39	11	.78	7	.259	.324	.341
1997 Kansas City	AL	97	367	100	13	4	2	(0	2)	127	51	22	19	0	51	2	11	1	34	10	.77	5	.272	.311	.346
Texas	AL	53	207	49	13	2	0	(0	0)	66	39	17	25	1	37	1	0	2	16	6	.73	2	.237	.319	.319
9 ML YEARS		794	2602	714	83	23	12	(5	7)	879	431	172	241	1	405	12	63	10	252	93	.73	27	.274	.338	.338

Tom Gordon

Pitches: Right **Bats:** Right **Pos:** RP-21   **Ht:** 5'9" **Wt:** 190 **Born:** 11/18/67 **Age:** 32

		HOW MUCH HE PITCHED						WHAT HE GAVE UP										THE RESULTS						
Year Team	Lg	G	GS	CG	GF	IP	BFP	H	R	ER	HR	SH	SF	HB	TBB	IBB	SO	WP	Bk	W	L	Pct.	ShO	Sv-Op	Hld	ERA
1988 Kansas City	AL	5	2	0	0	15.2	67	16	9	9	1	0	0	0	7	0	18	0	0	0	2	.000	0	0-0	2	5.17

Year Team	Lg	G	GS	CG	GF	IP	BFP	H	R	ER	HR	SH	SF	HB	TBB	IBB	SO	WP	Bk	W	L	Pct.	ShO	Sv-Op	Hld	ERA
		HOW MUCH HE PITCHED						**WHAT HE GAVE UP**												**THE RESULTS**						
1989 Kansas City	AL	49	16	1	16	163	677	122	67	66	10	4	4	1	86	4	153	12	0	17	9	.654	1	1-7	3	3.64
1990 Kansas City	AL	32	32	6	0	195.1	858	192	99	81	17	8	2	3	99	1	175	11	0	12	11	.522	1	0-0	0	3.73
1991 Kansas City	AL	45	14	1	11	158	684	129	76	68	16	5	3	4	87	6	167	5	0	9	14	.391	0	1-4	4	3.87
1992 Kansas City	AL	40	11	0	13	117.2	516	116	67	60	9	2	6	4	55	4	98	5	2	6	10	.375	0	0-2	0	4.59
1993 Kansas City	AL	48	14	2	18	155.2	651	125	65	62	11	6	6	1	77	5	143	17	0	12	6	.667	0	1-6	2	3.58
1994 Kansas City	AL	24	24	0	0	155.1	675	136	79	75	15	3	8	3	87	3	126	12	1	11	7	.611	0	0-0	0	4.35
1995 Kansas City	AL	31	31	2	0	189	843	204	110	93	12	7	11	4	89	4	119	9	0	12	12	.500	0	0-0	0	4.43
1996 Boston	AL	34	34	4	0	215.2	998	249	143	**134**	28	2	11	4	105	5	171	6	1	12	9	.571	1	0-0	0	5.59
1997 Boston	AL	42	25	2	16	182.2	774	155	85	76	10	3	4	3	78	1	159	5	0	6	10	.375	1	11-13	2	3.74
1998 Boston	AL	73	0	0	**69**	79.1	317	55	24	24	2	2	2	0	25	1	78	9	0	7	4	.636	0	46-47	0	2.72
1999 Boston	AL	21	0	0	15	17.2	82	17	11	11	2	0	0	1	12	2	24	0	0	0	2	.000	0	11-13	1	5.60
12 ML YEARS		444	203	18	158	1645	7142	1516	835	759	133	42	57	28	807	36	1431	91	4	104	96	.520	4	71-92	12	4.15

Mark Grace

Bats: Left **Throws:** Left **Pos:** 1B-160; PH/PR-2   **Ht:** 6'2" **Wt:** 200 **Born:** 6/28/64 **Age:** 36

Year Team	Lg	G	AB	H	2B	3B	HR	(Hm	Rd)	TB	R	RBI	TBB	IBB	SO	HBP	SH	SF	SB	CS	SB%	GDP	Avg	OBP	SLG
		BATTING																	**BASERUNNING**				**PERCENTAGES**		
1988 Chicago	NL	134	486	144	23	4	7	(0	7)	196	65	57	60	5	43	0	0	4	3	3	.50	12	.296	.371	.403
1989 Chicago	NL	142	510	160	28	3	13	(8	5)	233	74	79	80	13	42	0	3	3	14	7	.67	13	.314	.405	.457
1990 Chicago	NL	157	589	182	32	1	9	(4	5)	243	72	82	59	5	54	5	1	8	15	6	.71	10	.309	.372	.413
1991 Chicago	NL	160	**619**	169	28	5	8	(5	3)	231	87	58	70	7	53	3	4	7	3	4	.43	6	.273	.346	.373
1992 Chicago	NL	158	603	185	37	5	9	(4	5)	259	72	79	72	8	36	4	2	8	6	1	.86	14	.307	.380	.430
1993 Chicago	NL	155	594	193	39	4	14	(5	9)	282	86	98	71	14	32	1	1	9	8	4	.67	25	.325	.393	.475
1994 Chicago	NL	106	403	120	23	3	6	(5	1)	167	55	44	48	5	41	0	0	3	0	1	.00	10	.298	.370	.414
1995 Chicago	NL	143	552	180	**51**	3	16	(4	12)	285	97	92	65	9	46	2	1	7	6	2	.75	10	.326	.395	.516
1996 Chicago	NL	142	547	181	39	1	9	(4	5)	249	88	75	62	8	41	1	0	6	2	3	.40	18	.331	.396	.455
1997 Chicago	NL	151	555	177	32	5	13	(6	7)	258	87	78	88	3	45	2	1	8	2	4	.33	18	.319	.409	.465
1998 Chicago	NL	158	595	184	39	3	17	(7	10)	280	92	89	93	8	56	3	0	7	4	7	.36	17	.309	.401	.471
1999 Chicago	NL	161	593	183	44	5	16	(8	8)	285	107	91	83	4	44	2	0	10	3	4	.43	14	.309	.390	.481
12 ML YEARS		1767	6646	2058	415	42	137	(61	76)	2968	982	922	851	89	533	23	13	80	66	46	.59	167	.310	.386	.447

Mike Grace

Pitches: Right **Bats:** Right **Pos:** RP-22; SP-5   **Ht:** 6'4" **Wt:** 225 **Born:** 6/20/70 **Age:** 30

Year Team	Lg	G	GS	CG	GF	IP	BFP	H	R	ER	HR	SH	SF	HB	TBB	IBB	SO	WP	Bk	W	L	Pct.	ShO	Sv-Op	Hld	ERA
		HOW MUCH HE PITCHED						**WHAT HE GAVE UP**												**THE RESULTS**						
1999 Scranton-WB *	AAA	10	9	0	0	46.2	202	52	25	23	6	2	1	2	17	0	27	1	0	2	2	.500	0	0- --		4.44
1995 Philadelphia	NL	2	2	0	0	11.1	47	10	4	4	1	0	0	0	4	0	7	0	0	1	1	.500	0	0-0	0	3.18
1996 Philadelphia	NL	12	12	1	0	80	323	72	33	31	9	4	0	1	16	1	49	0	1	7	2	.778	1	0-0	0	3.49
1997 Philadelphia	NL	6	6	1	0	39	151	32	16	15	3	0	1	1	10	1	26	2	0	3	2	.600	1	0-0	0	3.46
1998 Philadelphia	NL	21	15	0	1	90.1	418	116	61	55	10	7	1	8	30	1	46	1	1	4	7	.364	0	0-0	0	5.48
1999 Philadelphia	NL	27	5	0	1	55	273	80	48	47	5	3	3	6	30	0	28	4	0	1	4	.200	0	0-0	1	7.69
5 ML YEARS		68	40	2	2	275.2	1212	310	162	152	27	15	5	16	90	3	156	7	2	16	16	.500	2	0-0	2	4.96

Tony Graffanino

Bats: R **Throws:** R **Pos:** 2B-17; SS-17; PH/PR-4; DH-1; 3B-1   **Ht:** 6'1" **Wt:** 195 **Born:** 6/6/72 **Age:** 28

Year Team	Lg	G	AB	H	2B	3B	HR	(Hm	Rd)	TB	R	RBI	TBB	IBB	SO	HBP	SH	SF	SB	CS	SB%	GDP	Avg	OBP	SLG
		BATTING																	**BASERUNNING**				**PERCENTAGES**		
1999 Durham *	AAA	87	345	108	25	6	9			172	66	58	37	0	46	3	3	5	16	9	.64	9	.313	.379	.499
1996 Atlanta	NL	22	46	8	1	1	0	(0	0)	11	7	2	4	0	13	1	0	1	0	0	.00	0	.174	.250	.239
1997 Atlanta	NL	104	186	48	9	1	8	(5	3)	83	33	20	26	1	46	1	3	5	4	6	.40	3	.258	.344	.446
1998 Atlanta	NL	105	289	61	14	1	5	(3	2)	92	32	22	24	0	68	2	1	1	4	6	.40	7	.211	.275	.318
1999 Tampa Bay	AL	39	130	41	9	4	2	(0	2)	64	20	19	9	0	22	1	2	0	3	2	.60	1	.315	.364	.492
4 ML YEARS		270	651	158	33	7	15	(8	7)	250	92	63	63	1	149	5	6	7	10	10	.50	11	.243	.311	.384

Joe Grahe

Pitches: Right **Bats:** Right **Pos:** RP-8; SP-5   **Ht:** 6'0" **Wt:** 200 **Born:** 8/14/67 **Age:** 32

Year Team	Lg	G	GS	CG	GF	IP	BFP	H	R	ER	HR	SH	SF	HB	TBB	IBB	SO	WP	Bk	W	L	Pct.	ShO	Sv-Op	Hld	ERA
		HOW MUCH HE PITCHED						**WHAT HE GAVE UP**												**THE RESULTS**						
1999 Reading *	AA	7	0	0	6	10	39	7	3	1	0	0	0	0	2	0	12	0	0	0	0	.000	0	4- --		0.90
Scranton-WB *	AAA	23	4	0	18	36	157	38	15	12	3	1	2	1	15	1	25	3	0	3	1	.750	0	10- --		3.00
1990 California	AL	8	8	0	0	43.1	200	51	30	24	3	0	0	3	23	1	25	1	0	3	4	.429	0	0-0	0	4.98
1991 California	AL	18	10	1	2	73	330	84	43	39	2	1	1	3	33	0	40	2	0	3	7	.300	0	0-0	1	4.81
1992 California	AL	46	7	0	31	94.2	399	85	37	37	5	4	4	6	39	2	39	3	0	5	6	.455	0	21-24	1	3.52
1993 California	AL	45	0	0	32	56.2	247	54	22	18	5	4	2	4	39	3	31	3	0	4	1	.800	0	11-13	3	2.86
1994 California	AL	40	0	0	32	43.1	218	68	33	32	5	3	3	6	18	4	26	4	1	2	5	.286	0	13-19	0	6.65
1995 Colorado	NL	17	9	0	0	56.2	265	69	42	32	6	3	3	2	27	2	27	3	2	4	3	.571	0	0-0	1	5.08
1999 Philadelphia	NL	13	5	0	4	32.2	153	40	16	14	1	0	3	3	17	0	16	2	1	1	4	.200	0	0-0	0	3.86
7 ML YEARS		187	39	1	101	400.1	1812	451	223	196	27	13	17	26	182	13	204	18	4	22	30	.423	0	45-56	6	4.41

Beiker Graterol

Pitches: Right Bats: Right Pos: SP-1 Ht: 6'2" Wt: 165 Born: 11/9/74 Age: 25

		HOW MUCH HE PITCHED						WHAT HE GAVE UP										THE RESULTS					
Year Team	Lg	G	GS	CG	GF	IP	BFP	H	R	ER	HR	SH	SF	HB	TBB	IBB	SO	WP	Bk	W	L	Pct.	ShO	Sv-Op	Hld	ERA
1996 St.Cathrnes	A-	14	13	1	0	84	330	59	24	14	6	3	3	4	21	0	66	2	1	9	1	.900	1	0- --	—	1.50
1997 Hagerstown	A	4	0	0	4	11	45	7	1	0	0	0	0	1	3	0	12	1	0	1	0	1.000	0	2- --	—	0.00
Dunedin	A+	17	10	1	1	81	352	86	46	38	9	5	2	5	26	1	54	0	1	4	7	.364	0	1- --	—	4.22
Knoxville	AA	3	3	0	0	16.2	81	24	12	10	1	0	0	1	9	0	11	0	0	2	1	.667	0	0- --	—	5.40
1998 Knoxville	AA	12	12	0	0	67	287	76	46	39	8	1	4	5	22	0	52	0	0	5	6	.455	0	0- --	—	5.24
Syracuse	AAA	16	16	0	0	96	422	103	55	49	10	1	1	12	32	1	62	3	1	9	2	.818	0	0- --	—	4.59
1999 Toledo	AAA	17	15	0	1	78.2	357	89	55	51	10	2	5	7	38	2	47	3	3	3	9	.250	0	0- --	—	5.83
1999 Detroit	AL	1	1	0	0	4	20	4	7	7	3	0	0	0	4	1	2	0	0	0	1	.000	0	0-0	0	15.75

Danny Graves

Pitches: Right Bats: Right Pos: RP-75 Ht: 5'11" Wt: 185 Born: 8/7/73 Age: 26

		HOW MUCH HE PITCHED						WHAT HE GAVE UP										THE RESULTS					
Year Team	Lg	G	GS	CG	GF	IP	BFP	H	R	ER	HR	SH	SF	HB	TBB	IBB	SO	WP	Bk	W	L	Pct.	ShO	Sv-Op	Hld	ERA
1996 Cleveland	AL	15	0	0	5	29.2	129	29	18	15	2	0	1	0	10	0	22	1	0	2	0	1.000	0	0-1	0	4.55
1997 Cle-Cin		15	0	0	3	26	134	41	22	16	2	3	2	0	20	1	11	1	0	0	0	.000	0	0-0	1	5.54
1998 Cincinnati	NL	62	0	0	35	81.1	340	76	31	30	6	2	2	0	28	4	44	4	0	2	1	.667	0	8-8	6	3.32
1999 Cincinnati	NL	75	0	0	56	111	454	90	42	38	10	5	2	2	49	4	69	3	0	8	7	.533	0	27-36	0	3.08
1997 Cleveland	AL	5	0	0	2	11.1	56	15	8	6	2	0	1	0	9	0	4	0	0	0	0	.000	0	0-0	0	4.76
Cincinnati	NL	10	0	0	1	14.2	78	26	14	10	0	3	1	0	11	1	7	1	0	0	0	.000	0	0-0	1	6.14
4 ML YEARS		167	0	0	99	248	1057	236	113	99	20	10	10	4	107	9	146	9	0	12	8	.600	0	35-45	7	3.59

Craig Grebeck

Bats: R Throws: R Pos: 2B-17; DH-10; PH/PR-5; SS-4; 3B-2 Ht: 5'7" Wt: 155 Born: 12/29/64 Age: 35

		BATTING																BASERUNNING				PERCENTAGES		
Year Team	Lg	G	AB	H	2B	3B	HR	(Hm	Rd)	TB	R	RBI	TBB	IBB	SO	HBP	SH	SF	SB	CS	SB%	GDP	Avg	OBP	SLG
1999 Syracuse *	AAA	4	16	4	1	0	1			8	3	2	1	0	1	0	0	0	0	0	.00	2	.250	.294	.500
1990 Chicago	AL	59	119	20	3	1	1	(1	0)	28	7	9	8	0	24	2	3	3	0	0	.00	2	.168	.227	.235
1991 Chicago	AL	107	224	63	16	3	6	(3	3)	103	37	31	38	0	40	1	4	1	1	3	.25	3	.281	.386	.460
1992 Chicago	AL	88	287	77	21	2	3	(2	1)	111	24	35	30	0	34	3	10	3	0	3	.00	5	.268	.341	.387
1993 Chicago	AL	72	190	43	5	0	1	(0	1)	51	25	12	26	0	26	0	7	0	1	2	.33	9	.226	.319	.268
1994 Chicago	AL	35	97	30	5	0	0	(0	0)	35	17	5	12	0	5	1	3	0	0	0	.00	1	.309	.391	.361
1995 Chicago	AL	53	154	40	12	0	1	(0	1)	55	19	18	21	0	23	1	4	0	0	0	.00	4	.260	.360	.357
1996 Florida	NL	50	95	20	1	0	1	(0	1)	24	9	4	14	1	14	1	1	2	0	0	.00	2	.211	.245	.253
1997 Anaheim	AL	63	126	34	9	0	1	(1	0)	46	12	6	18	1	11	0	5	1	0	1	.00	6	.270	.359	.365
1998 Toronto	AL	102	301	77	17	2	2	(2	0)	104	33	27	29	0	42	4	8	2	2	2	.50	8	.256	.327	.346
1999 Toronto	AL	34	113	41	7	0	0	(0	0)	48	18	10	15	0	13	2	3	1	0	0	.00	2	.363	.443	.425
10 ML YEARS		663	1706	445	96	8	16	(9	7)	605	200	162	201	2	232	17	48	13	4	11	.27	42	.261	.342	.355

Scarborough Green

Bats: R Throws: R Pos: PH/PR-14; DH-4; CF-4; LF-3; RF-3 Ht: 5'10" Wt: 170 Born: 6/9/74 Age: 26

		BATTING																BASERUNNING				PERCENTAGES		
Year Team	Lg	G	AB	H	2B	3B	HR	(Hm	Rd)	TB	R	RBI	TBB	IBB	SO	HBP	SH	SF	SB	CS	SB%	GDP	Avg	OBP	SLG
1993 Cardinals	R	33	95	21	3	1	0	—	—	26	16	11	7	0	17	3	1	0	3	2	.60	1	.221	.295	.274
1994 Johnson Cy	R+	54	199	48	5	0	0	—	—	53	32	11	25	1	61	0	4	2	22	7	.76	0	.241	.323	.266
1995 Savannah	A	132	429	98	7	6	1	—	—	120	48	25	55	0	101	3	9	1	26	9	.74	6	.228	.320	.280
1996 St. Pete	A+	36	140	41	4	1	1	—	—	50	26	11	21	1	22	2	2	0	13	9	.59	1	.293	.393	.357
Arkansas	AA	92	300	60	6	3	3	—	—	81	45	24	38	1	58	3	3	1	21	8	.72	3	.200	.295	.270
1997 Arkansas	AA	76	251	77	14	4	2	—	—	105	45	29	36	0	48	2	4	2	11	5	.69	2	.307	.397	.418
Louisville	AAA	52	209	53	11	2	3	—	—	77	26	13	22	0	55	0	1	0	10	7	.59	3	.254	.325	.368
1998 Memphis	AAA	26	81	16	5	0	0	—	—	21	11	2	8	1	22	0	1	0	1	4	.20	2	.198	.270	.259
Arkansas	AA	18	75	27	2	1	2	—	—	37	16	9	6	0	12	0	0	0	9	2	.82	0	.360	.407	.493
1999 Oklahoma	AAA	104	359	89	16	6	3	—	—	126	68	29	34	1	86	3	4	3	26	11	.70	3	.248	.316	.351
1997 St. Louis	NL	20	31	3	0	0	0	(0	0)	3	5	1	2	0	5	0	0	0	0	0	.00	0	.097	.152	.097
1999 Texas	AL	18	13	4	0	0	0	(0	0)	4	4	0	1	0	2	0	0	0	0	1	.00	0	.308	.357	.308
2 ML YEARS		38	44	7	0	0	0	(0	0)	7	9	1	3	0	7	0	0	0	0	1	.00	0	.159	.213	.159

Shawn Green

Bats: Left Throws: Left Pos: RF-152; PH/PR-1 Ht: 6'4" Wt: 200 Born: 11/10/72 Age: 27

		BATTING																BASERUNNING				PERCENTAGES		
Year Team	Lg	G	AB	H	2B	3B	HR	(Hm	Rd)	TB	R	RBI	TBB	IBB	SO	HBP	SH	SF	SB	CS	SB%	GDP	Avg	OBP	SLG
1993 Toronto	AL	3	6	0	0	0	0	(0	0)	0	0	0	0	0	1	0	0	0	0	0	.00	0	.000	.000	.000
1994 Toronto	AL	14	33	3	1	0	0	(0	0)	4	1	1	1	0	8	0	0	0	1	0	1.00	1	.091	.118	.121
1995 Toronto	AL	121	379	109	31	4	15	(5	10)	193	52	54	20	3	68	3	0	3	1	2	.33	4	.288	.326	.509
1996 Toronto	AL	132	422	118	32	3	11	(7	4)	189	52	45	33	3	75	8	0	2	5	1	.83	9	.280	.342	.448
1997 Toronto	AL	135	429	123	22	4	16	(10	6)	201	57	53	36	4	99	1	4	1	14	3	.82	4	.287	.340	.469
1998 Toronto	AL	158	630	175	33	4	35	(21	14)	321	106	100	50	2	142	5	1	3	35	12	.74	6	.278	.334	.510
1999 Toronto	AL	153	614	190	45	0	42	(20	22)	361	134	123	66	4	117	11	0	5	20	7	.74	13	.309	.384	.588
7 ML YEARS		716	2513	718	164	15	119	(63	56)	1269	402	376	206	16	510	28	2	17	76	25	.75	37	.286	.344	.505

Charlie Greene

Bats: Right **Throws:** Right **Pos:** C-31; PH/PR-2   **Ht:** 6'2" **Wt:** 190 **Born:** 1/23/71 **Age:** 29

Year Team	Lg	G	AB	H	2B	3B	HR	(Hm	Rd)	TB	R	RBI	TBB	IBB	SO	HBP	SH	SF	SB	CS	SB%	GDP	Avg	OBP	SLG
1991 Padres	R	49	183	52	15	1	5	—	—	84	27	39	16	0	23	3	2	6	6	1	.86	7	.284	.341	.459
1992 Chston-SC	A	98	298	55	9	1	1	—	—	69	22	24	11	0	60	5	3	2	1	2	.33	7	.185	.225	.232
1993 Waterloo	A	84	213	38	8	0	2	—	—	52	19	20	13	0	33	3	6	3	0	0	.00	5	.178	.233	.244
1994 Baltimore	AA	30	106	18	4	0	0	—	—	22	13	2	6	1	18	1	0	1	0	0	.00	3	.170	.219	.208
St. Lucie	A+	69	224	57	4	0	0	—	—	61	23	21	9	0	31	4	4	1	0	1	.00	3	.254	.294	.272
1995 Binghamton	AA	100	346	82	13	0	2	—	—	101	26	34	15	4	47	5	3	4	2	1	.67	10	.237	.276	.292
Norfolk	AAA	27	88	17	3	0	0	—	—	20	6	4	3	0	28	0	1	0	0	1	.00	1	.193	.220	.227
1996 Binghamton	AA	100	336	82	17	0	2	—	—	105	35	27	17	0	52	0	2	4	2	0	1.00	8	.244	.277	.313
1997 Norfolk	AAA	76	238	49	7	0	8	—	—	80	27	28	9	0	54	2	0	2	1	0	1.00	4	.206	.239	.336
1998 Rochester	AAA	77	250	53	10	0	4	—	—	75	23	28	9	0	54	3	5	0	1	1	.50	4	.212	.248	.300
1999 Louisville	AAA	56	161	34	8	0	4	—	—	54	16	15	7	1	26	0	0	0	0	0	.00	2	.211	.244	.335
1996 New York	NL	2	1	0	0	0	0	(0	0)	0	0	0	0	0	0	0	0	0	0	0	.00	0	.000	.000	.000
1997 Baltimore	AL	5	2	0	0	0	0	(0	0)	0	0	1	0	0	1	0	0	0	0	0	.00	0	.000	.000	.000
1998 Baltimore	AL	13	21	4	1	0	0	(0	0)	5	1	0	0	0	8	0	1	0	0	0	.00	1	.190	.190	.238
1999 Milwaukee	NL	32	42	8	1	0	0	(0	0)	9	4	1	5	0	11	0	1	1	0	0	.00	1	.190	.271	.214
4 ML YEARS		52	66	12	2	0	0	(0	0)	14	5	2	5	0	20	0	2	1	0	0	.00	1	.182	.236	.212

Rick Greene

Pitches: Right **Bats:** Right **Pos:** RP-1   **Ht:** 6'5" **Wt:** 200 **Born:** 1/2/71 **Age:** 29

Year Team	Lg	G	GS	CG	GF	IP	BFP	H	R	ER	HR	SH	SF	HB	TBB	IBB	SO	WP	Bk	W	L	Pct.	ShO	Sv-Op	Hld	ERA
1993 Lakeland	A+	26	0	0	11	40.2	184	57	28	28	1	6	0	1	16	1	32	5	2	2	3	.400	0	2--	—	6.20
London	AA	23	0	0	11	29	135	31	22	21	1	3	3	1	20	3	19	3	2	2	2	.500	0	0--	—	6.52
1994 Trenton	AA	20	0	0	14	19.1	92	17	17	17	0	3	2	0	21	2	5	2	0	1	1	.500	0	3--	—	7.91
Lakeland	A+	19	2	0	11	33.1	158	50	23	16	0	1	1	0	10	1	28	6	0	0	4	.000	0	4--	—	4.32
1995 Jacksnville	AA	32	0	0	6	38.2	177	45	19	15	3	1	0	3	15	2	29	0	0	6	2	.750	0	0--	—	3.49
1996 Jacksnville	AA	57	0	0	48	56	275	67	44	31	8	6	0	2	39	4	42	2	0	2	7	.222	0	30--	—	4.98
1997 Toledo	AAA	57	0	0	14	70	289	49	29	22	4	7	2	5	32	3	51	8	0	6	8	.429	0	1--	—	2.83
1998 Louisville	AAA	58	0	0	44	66.2	302	73	31	26	6	2	1	3	33	7	44	2	0	6	6	.500	0	18--	—	3.51
1999 Indianapolis	AAA	61	0	0	29	78	331	78	37	32	3	4	5	2	35	4	40	6	0	5	7	.417	0	9--	—	3.69
1999 Cincinnati	NL	1	0	0	0	5.2	25	7	4	3	2	0	0	0	1	0	3	0	0	0	0	.000	0	0-0	0	4.76

Todd Greene

Bats: R **Throws:** R **Pos:** DH-44; RF-25; PH/PR-14; C-12; LF-5   **Ht:** 5'10" **Wt:** 208 **Born:** 5/8/71 **Age:** 29

Year Team	Lg	G	AB	H	2B	3B	HR	(Hm	Rd)	TB	R	RBI	TBB	IBB	SO	HBP	SH	SF	SB	CS	SB%	GDP	Avg	OBP	SLG
1999 Edmonton *	AAA	19	74	18	6	0	5	—	—	39	10	14	0	0	12	1	0	0	0	0	.00	4	.243	.253	.527
1996 California	AL	29	79	15	1	0	2	(1	1)	22	9	9	4	0	11	1	0	0	2	0	1.00	4	.190	.238	.278
1997 Anaheim	AL	34	124	36	6	0	9	(5	4)	69	24	24	7	1	25	0	0	0	2	0	1.00	1	.290	.328	.556
1998 Anaheim	AL	29	71	18	4	0	1	(0	1)	25	3	7	2	0	20	0	0	0	0	0	.00	0	.254	.274	.352
1999 Anaheim	AL	97	321	78	20	0	14	(7	7)	140	36	42	12	0	63	3	0	2	1	4	.20	8	.243	.275	.436
4 ML YEARS		189	595	147	31	0	26	(13	13)	256	72	82	25	1	119	4	0	2	5	4	.56	13	.247	.281	.430

Willie Greene

Bats: L **Throws:** R **Pos:** DH-51; PH/PR-24; 3B-7; RF-3   **Ht:** 5'11" **Wt:** 192 **Born:** 9/23/71 **Age:** 28

Year Team	Lg	G	AB	H	2B	3B	HR	(Hm	Rd)	TB	R	RBI	TBB	IBB	SO	HBP	SH	SF	SB	CS	SB%	GDP	Avg	OBP	SLG
1999 Syracuse *	AAA	14	52	17	1	0	5	—	—	33	12	11	6	2	14	0	0	0	0	0	.00	1	.327	.397	.635
1992 Cincinnati	NL	29	93	25	5	2	2	(2	0)	40	10	13	10	0	23	0	0	1	0	2	.00	1	.269	.337	.430
1993 Cincinnati	NL	15	50	8	1	1	2	(2	0)	17	7	5	2	0	19	0	0	1	0	0	.00	1	.160	.189	.340
1994 Cincinnati	NL	16	37	8	2	0	0	(0	0)	10	5	3	6	1	14	0	0	1	0	0	.00	1	.216	.318	.270
1995 Cincinnati	NL	8	19	2	0	0	0	(0	0)	2	1	0	3	0	7	0	0	0	0	0	.00	0	.105	.227	.105
1996 Cincinnati	NL	115	287	70	5	5	19	(11	8)	142	48	63	36	6	88	0	1	1	0	1	.00	5	.244	.327	.495
1997 Cincinnati	NL	151	495	125	22	1	26	(13	13)	227	62	91	78	5	111	1	1	3	6	0	1.00	10	.253	.354	.459
1998 Cin-Bal		135	396	102	19	1	15	(9	6)	168	65	54	69	2	90	3	0	2	7	3	.70	9	.258	.370	.424
1999 Toronto	AL	81	226	46	7	0	12	(8	4)	89	22	41	20	0	56	0	0	0	0	0	.00	4	.204	.266	.394
1998 Cincinnati	NL	111	356	96	18	1	14	(8	6)	158	57	49	56	2	80	3	0	2	6	3	.67	7	.270	.372	.444
Baltimore	AL	24	40	6	1	0	1	(1	0)	10	8	5	13	0	10	0	0	0	1	0	1.00	2	.150	.358	.250
8 ML YEARS		550	1603	386	61	10	76	(45	31)	695	220	270	224	14	408	4	2	11	13	6	.68	32	.241	.333	.434

Rusty Greer

Bats: Left **Throws:** Left **Pos:** LF-145; PH/PR-2; DH-1   **Ht:** 6'0" **Wt:** 195 **Born:** 1/21/69 **Age:** 31

Year Team	Lg	G	AB	H	2B	3B	HR	(Hm	Rd)	TB	R	RBI	TBB	IBB	SO	HBP	SH	SF	SB	CS	SB%	GDP	Avg	OBP	SLG
1994 Texas	AL	80	277	87	16	1	10	(7	3)	135	36	46	46	2	46	2	2	4	0	0	.00	3	.314	.410	.487
1995 Texas	AL	131	417	113	21	2	13	(7	6)	177	58	61	55	1	66	1	2	3	3	1	.75	9	.271	.355	.424
1996 Texas	AL	139	542	180	41	6	18	(9	9)	287	96	100	62	4	86	3	0	10	9	0	1.00	9	.332	.397	.530
1997 Texas	AL	157	601	193	42	3	26	(18	8)	319	112	87	83	4	87	3	1	2	9	5	.64	11	.321	.405	.531
1998 Texas	AL	155	598	183	31	5	16	(8	8)	272	107	108	80	1	93	4	0	9	2	4	.33	18	.306	.386	.455
1999 Texas	AL	147	556	167	41	3	20	(10	10)	274	107	101	96	2	67	5	0	5	2	2	.50	17	.300	.405	.493
6 ML YEARS		809	2991	923	192	20	103	(55	48)	1464	516	503	422	14	445	18	5	33	25	12	.68	67	.309	.393	.489

Seth Greisinger

Pitches: Right Bats: Right Pos: SP   Ht: 6'3" Wt: 200 Born: 7/29/75 Age: 24

		HOW MUCH HE PITCHED						WHAT HE GAVE UP										THE RESULTS						
Year Team	Lg	G	GS	CG	GF	IP	BFP	H	R	ER	HR	SH	SF	HB	TBB	IBB	SO	WP	Bk	W	L	Pct.	ShO	Sv-Op	Hld	ERA
1997 Jacksnville	AA	28	28	1	0	159.1	710	194	103	92	29	3	6	3	53	0	105	12	2	10	6	.625	0	0--	—	5.20
1998 Toledo	AAA	10	10	0	0	58.2	247	50	21	19	5	1	1	5	22	0	37	3	2	3	4	.429	0	0--	—	2.91
1999 Lakeland	A+	1	1	0	0	4.2	17	2	2	2	1	0	0	0	1	0	2	0	0	0	0	.000	0	0--	—	3.86
Toledo	AAA	2	2	0	0	7.2	34	9	5	5	0	1	0	0	3	0	4	1	0	0	1	.000	0	0--	—	5.87
1998 Detroit	AL	21	21	0	0	130	562	142	79	74	17	2	5	4	48	2	66	3	0	6	9	.400	0	0-0	0	5.12

Ben Grieve

Bats: L Throws: R Pos: LF-131; PH/PR-10; RF-8; DH-4   Ht: 6'4" Wt: 230 Born: 5/4/76 Age: 24

		BATTING																	BASERUNNING				PERCENTAGES		
Year Team	Lg	G	AB	H	2B	3B	HR	(Hm	Rd)	TB	R	RBI	TBB	IBB	SO	HBP	SH	SF	SB	CS	SB%	GDP	Avg	OBP	SLG
1997 Oakland	AL	24	93	29	6	0	3	(3	0)	44	12	24	13	1	25	1	1	0	0	0	.00	1	.312	.402	.473
1998 Oakland	AL	155	583	168	41	2	18	(5	13)	267	94	89	85	3	123	9	0	1	2	2	.50	18	.288	.386	.458
1999 Oakland	AL	148	486	129	21	0	28	(13	15)	234	80	86	63	2	108	8	0	1	4	0	1.00	17	.265	.358	.481
3 ML YEARS		327	1162	326	68	2	49	(21	28)	545	186	199	161	6	256	18	1	2	6	2	.75	36	.281	.376	.469

Ken Griffey Jr.

Bats: Left Throws: Left Pos: CF-158; DH-6   Ht: 6'3" Wt: 205 Born: 11/21/69 Age: 30

		BATTING																	BASERUNNING				PERCENTAGES		
Year Team	Lg	G	AB	H	2B	3B	HR	(Hm	Rd)	TB	R	RBI	TBB	IBB	SO	HBP	SH	SF	SB	CS	SB%	GDP	Avg	OBP	SLG
1989 Seattle	AL	127	455	120	23	0	16	(10	6)	191	61	61	44	8	83	2	1	4	16	7	.70	4	.264	.329	.420
1990 Seattle	AL	155	597	179	28	7	22	(8	14)	287	91	80	63	12	81	2	0	4	16	11	.59	12	.300	.366	.481
1991 Seattle	AL	154	548	179	42	1	22	(16	6)	289	76	100	71	21	82	1	4	9	18	6	.75	10	.327	.399	.527
1992 Seattle	AL	142	565	174	39	4	27	(16	11)	302	83	103	44	15	67	5	0	3	10	5	.67	15	.308	.361	.535
1993 Seattle	AL	156	582	180	38	3	45	(21	24)	359	113	109	96	25	91	6	0	7	17	9	.65	14	.309	.408	.617
1994 Seattle	AL	111	433	140	24	4	40	(18	22)	292	94	90	56	19	73	2	0	2	11	3	.79	9	.323	.402	.674
1995 Seattle	AL	72	260	67	7	0	17	(13	4)	125	52	42	52	6	53	0	0	2	4	2	.67	4	.258	.379	.481
1996 Seattle	AL	140	545	165	26	2	49	(26	23)	342	125	140	78	13	104	7	1	7	16	1	.94	7	.303	.392	.628
1997 Seattle	AL	157	608	185	34	3	56	(27	29)	393	125	147	76	23	121	8	0	12	15	4	.79	12	.304	.382	.646
1998 Seattle	AL	161	633	180	33	3	56	(30	26)	387	120	146	76	11	121	7	0	4	20	5	.80	14	.284	.365	.611
1999 Seattle	AL	160	606	173	26	3	48	(27	21)	349	123	134	91	17	108	7	0	2	24	7	.77	8	.285	.384	.576
11 ML YEARS		1535	5832	1742	320	30	398	(212	186)	3316	1063	1152	747	170	984	47	6	56	167	60	.74	109	.299	.380	.569

Jason Grimsley

Pitches: Right Bats: Right Pos: RP-55   Ht: 6'3" Wt: 180 Born: 8/7/67 Age: 32

		HOW MUCH HE PITCHED						WHAT HE GAVE UP										THE RESULTS						
Year Team	Lg	G	GS	CG	GF	IP	BFP	H	R	ER	HR	SH	SF	HB	TBB	IBB	SO	WP	Bk	W	L	Pct.	ShO	Sv-Op	Hld	ERA
1989 Philadelphia	NL	4	4	0	0	18.1	91	19	13	12	2	1	0	0	19	1	7	2	0	1	3	.250	0	0-0	0	5.89
1990 Philadelphia	NL	11	11	0	0	57.1	255	47	21	21	1	2	1	2	43	0	41	6	1	3	2	.600	0	0-0	0	3.30
1991 Philadelphia	NL	12	12	0	0	61	272	54	34	33	4	3	2	3	41	3	42	14	0	1	7	.125	0	0-0	0	4.87
1993 Cleveland	AL	10	6	0	1	42.1	194	52	26	25	3	1	0	1	20	1	27	2	0	3	4	.429	0	0-0	1	5.31
1994 Cleveland	AL	14	13	1	0	82.2	368	91	47	42	7	4	2	6	34	1	59	6	1	5	2	.714	0	0-0	0	4.57
1995 Cleveland	AL	15	2	0	2	34	165	37	24	23	4	1	2	2	32	1	25	7	0	0	0	.000	0	1-1	0	6.09
1996 California	AL	35	20	2	4	130.1	620	150	110	99	14	4	5	13	74	5	82	11	0	5	7	.417	1	0-0	0	6.84
1999 New York	AL	55	0	0	25	75	336	66	39	30	7	3	3	4	40	5	49	8	0	7	2	.778	0	1-4	8	3.60
8 ML YEARS		156	68	3	32	501	2301	516	314	285	42	19	15	31	303	17	332	56	2	25	27	.481	1	2-5	9	5.12

Marquis Grissom

Bats: Right Throws: Right Pos: CF-149; PH/PR-9   Ht: 5'11" Wt: 188 Born: 4/17/67 Age: 33

		BATTING																	BASERUNNING				PERCENTAGES		
Year Team	Lg	G	AB	H	2B	3B	HR	(Hm	Rd)	TB	R	RBI	TBB	IBB	SO	HBP	SH	SF	SB	CS	SB%	GDP	Avg	OBP	SLG
1989 Montreal	NL	26	74	19	2	0	1	(0	1)	24	16	2	12	0	21	0	1	0	1	0	1.00	1	.257	.360	.324
1990 Montreal	NL	98	288	74	14	2	3	(2	1)	101	42	29	27	2	40	0	4	1	22	2	.92	3	.257	.320	.351
1991 Montreal	NL	148	558	149	23	9	6	(3	3)	208	73	39	34	0	89	1	4	0	76	17	.82	8	.267	.310	.373
1992 Montreal	NL	159	653	180	39	6	14	(8	6)	273	99	66	42	6	81	5	3	4	78	13	.86	12	.276	.322	.418
1993 Montreal	NL	157	630	188	27	2	19	(9	10)	276	104	95	52	6	76	3	0	8	53	10	.84	9	.298	.351	.438
1994 Montreal	NL	110	475	137	25	4	11	(4	7)	203	96	45	41	4	66	1	0	4	36	6	.86	10	.288	.344	.427
1995 Atlanta	NL	139	551	142	23	3	12	(5	7)	207	80	42	47	4	61	3	1	4	29	9	.76	8	.258	.317	.376
1996 Atlanta	NL	158	671	207	32	10	23	(11	12)	328	106	74	41	6	73	3	4	4	28	11	.72	12	.308	.349	.489
1997 Cleveland	AL	144	558	146	27	6	12	(5	7)	221	74	66	43	1	89	6	6	9	22	13	.63	12	.262	.317	.396
1998 Milwaukee	NL	142	542	147	28	1	10	(2	8)	207	57	60	24	2	78	2	2	8	13	8	.62	12	.271	.304	.382
1999 Milwaukee	NL	146	603	161	27	1	20	(9	11)	250	92	83	49	4	109	0	4	5	24	6	.80	12	.267	.320	.415
11 ML YEARS		1435	5603	1550	267	44	131	(58	73)	2298	839	601	412	35	783	24	29	41	382	95	.80	99	.277	.327	.410

Buddy Groom

Pitches: Left Bats: Left Pos: RP-76   Ht: 6'2" Wt: 207 Born: 7/10/65 Age: 34

		HOW MUCH HE PITCHED						WHAT HE GAVE UP										THE RESULTS						
Year Team	Lg	G	GS	CG	GF	IP	BFP	H	R	ER	HR	SH	SF	HB	TBB	IBB	SO	WP	Bk	W	L	Pct.	ShO	Sv-Op	Hld	ERA
1992 Detroit	AL	12	7	0	3	38.2	177	48	28	25	4	3	2	0	22	4	15	0	1	0	5	.000	0	1-2	0	5.82

Year Team	Lg	G	GS	CG	GF	IP	BFP	H	R	ER	HR	SH	SF	HB	TBB	IBB	SO	WP	Bk	W	L	Pct.	ShO	Sv-Op	Hld	ERA
1993 Detroit	AL	19	3	0	8	36.2	170	48	25	25	4	2	4	2	13	5	15	2	1	0	2	.000	0	0-0	1	6.14
1994 Detroit	AL	40	0	0	10	32	139	31	14	14	4	0	3	2	13	2	27	0	0	0	1	.000	0	1-1	11	3.94
1995 Det-Fla		37	4	0	11	55.2	274	81	47	46	8	2	2	2	32	4	35	3	0	2	5	.286	0	1-3	0	7.44
1996 Oakland	AL	72	1	0	16	77.1	341	85	37	33	8	2	0	3	34	3	57	5	0	5	0	1.000	0	2-4	10	3.84
1997 Oakland	AL	78	0	0	7	64.2	285	75	38	37	9	0	4	0	24	1	45	3	0	2	2	.500	0	3-5	12	5.15
1998 Oakland	AL	75	0	0	13	57.1	251	62	30	27	4	1	3	1	20	1	36	1	0	3	1	.750	0	0-6	16	4.24
1999 Oakland	AL	76	0	0	6	46	196	48	29	26	1	2	0	1	18	5	32	2	1	3	2	.600	0	0-3	27	5.09
1995 Detroit	AL	23	4	0	6	40.2	203	55	35	34	6	2	2	2	26	4	23	3	0	1	3	.250	0	1-3	0	7.52
Florida	NL	14	0	0	5	15	71	26	12	12	2	0	0	0	6	0	12	0	0	1	2	.333	0	0-0	0	7.20
8 ML YEARS		409	15	0	74	408.1	1833	478	248	233	42	12	18	11	176	25	262	16	3	15	18	.455	0	8-24	77	5.14

Kip Gross

Pitches: Right **Bats:** Right **Pos:** RP-10; SP-1 **Ht:** 6'2" **Wt:** 195 **Born:** 8/24/64 **Age:** 35

Year Team	Lg	G	GS	CG	GF	IP	BFP	H	R	ER	HR	SH	SF	HB	TBB	IBB	SO	WP	Bk	W	L	Pct.	ShO	Sv-Op	Hld	ERA
1999 Pawtucket *	AAA	10	2	0	2	21.2	98	24	14	13	3	0	1	2	12	0	16	2	0	1	0	1.000	0	0- -	—	5.40
1990 Cincinnati	NL	5	0	0	2	6.1	25	6	3	3	0	1	0	0	2	0	3	0	0	0	0	.000	0	0-0	0	4.26
1991 Cincinnati	NL	29	9	1	6	85.2	381	93	43	33	8	6	2	0	40	2	40	5	1	6	4	.600	0	0-0	1	3.47
1992 Los Angeles	NL	16	1	0	7	23.2	109	32	14	11	1	0	0	0	10	1	14	1	1	1	1	.500	0	0-0	2	4.18
1993 Los Angeles	NL	10	0	0	0	15	59	13	1	1	0	0	0	0	4	0	12	0	0	0	0	.000	0	0-0	0	0.60
1999 Boston	AL	11	1	0	7	12.2	64	15	11	11	3	1	1	3	8	2	9	1	0	0	2	.000	0	0-1	3	7.82
5 ML YEARS		71	11	1	22	143.1	638	159	72	59	12	7	4	3	64	5	78	7	2	7	7	.500	0	0-1	6	3.70

Mark Grudzielanek

Bats: Right **Throws:** Right **Pos:** SS-119; PH/PR-6 **Ht:** 6'1" **Wt:** 185 **Born:** 6/30/70 **Age:** 30

Year Team	Lg	G	AB	H	2B	3B	HR	(Hm	Rd)	TB	R	RBI	TBB	IBB	SO	HBP	SH	SF	SB	CS	SB%	GDP	Avg	OBP	SLG
1999 San Berndno *	A+	4	16	4	0	0	0	—	—	4	2	0	0	0	1	0	0	0	0	2	.00	1	.250	.250	.250
1995 Montreal	NL	78	269	66	12	2	1	(1	0)	85	27	20	14	4	47	7	3	0	8	3	.73	7	.245	.300	.316
1996 Montreal	NL	153	657	201	34	4	6	(5	1)	261	99	49	26	3	83	9	1	3	33	7	.83	10	.306	.340	.397
1997 Montreal	NL	156	649	177	54	3	4	(1	3)	249	76	51	23	0	76	10	3	3	25	9	.74	13	.273	.307	.384
1998 Mon-LA	NL	156	589	160	21	1	10	(5	5)	213	62	62	26	2	73	11	8	7	18	5	.78	18	.272	.311	.362
1999 Los Angeles	NL	123	488	159	23	5	7	(4	3)	213	72	46	31	1	65	10	2	3	6	6	.50	13	.326	.376	.436
1998 Montreal	NL	105	396	109	15	1	8	(3	5)	150	51	41	21	1	50	9	5	4	11	5	.69	11	.275	.323	.379
Los Angeles	NL	51	193	51	6	0	2	(2	0)	63	11	21	5	1	23	2	3	3	7	0	1.00	7	.264	.286	.326
5 ML YEARS		666	2652	763	144	15	28	(16	12)	1021	336	228	120	10	344	47	17	16	90	30	.75	61	.288	.328	.385

Eddie Guardado

Pitches: Left **Bats:** Right **Pos:** RP-63 **Ht:** 6'0" **Wt:** 194 **Born:** 10/2/70 **Age:** 29

Year Team	Lg	G	GS	CG	GF	IP	BFP	H	R	ER	HR	SH	SF	HB	TBB	IBB	SO	WP	Bk	W	L	Pct.	ShO	Sv-Op	Hld	ERA
1999 New Britain *	AA	3	0	0	0	4.2	17	3	1	1	0	0	0	0	0	0	5	0	0	0	0	.000	0	0- -	—	1.93
1993 Minnesota	AL	19	16	0	2	94.2	426	123	68	65	13	1	3	1	36	2	46	0	0	3	8	.273	0	0-0	0	6.18
1994 Minnesota	AL	4	4	0	0	17	81	26	16	16	3	1	2	0	4	0	8	0	0	2	0	.000	0	0-0	0	8.47
1995 Minnesota	AL	51	5	0	10	91.1	410	99	54	52	13	6	5	0	45	2	71	5	1	4	9	.308	0	2-5	5	5.12
1996 Minnesota	AL	83	0	0	17	73.2	313	61	45	43	12	6	4	3	33	4	74	3	0	6	5	.545	0	4-7	18	5.25
1997 Minnesota	AL	69	0	0	20	46	201	45	23	20	7	2	1	2	17	2	54	2	0	4	0	.000	0	1-1	13	3.91
1998 Minnesota	AL	79	0	0	12	65.2	286	66	34	33	10	3	6	0	28	6	53	2	0	3	1	.750	0	0-4	16	4.52
1999 Minnesota	AL	63	0	0	13	48	197	37	24	24	6	2	1	2	25	4	50	0	0	2	5	.286	0	2-4	15	4.50
7 ML YEARS		368	25	0	74	436.1	1914	457	264	253	64	21	22	8	188	20	356	12	1	18	34	.346	0	9-21	67	5.22

Creighton Gubanich

Bats: R **Throws:** R **Pos:** C-14; DH-2; 3B-1; PH/PR-1 **Ht:** 6'3" **Wt:** 200 **Born:** 3/27/72 **Age:** 28

Year Team	Lg	G	AB	H	2B	3B	HR	(Hm	Rd)	TB	R	RBI	TBB	IBB	SO	HBP	SH	SF	SB	CS	SB%	GDP	Avg	OBP	SLG
1991 Sou Oregon	A-	43	132	30	7	2	4	—	—	53	23	18	19	0	35	6	0	0	0	4	.00	2	.227	.350	.402
1992 Madison	A	121	404	100	19	3	9	—	—	152	46	55	41	1	102	16	8	1	0	7	.00	8	.248	.340	.376
1993 Madison	A	119	373	100	19	2	19	—	—	180	65	78	63	2	105	11	2	12	3	3	.50	7	.268	.379	.483
1994 Modesto	A+	108	375	88	20	3	15	—	—	159	53	55	54	0	102	7	5	2	5	4	.56	9	.235	.340	.424
1995 Huntsville	AA	94	274	60	7	1	13	—	—	108	37	43	48	0	82	7	2	5	1	0	1.00	5	.219	.344	.394
1996 Huntsville	AA	62	217	60	19	0	9	—	—	106	40	43	31	1	71	4	3	2	1	0	1.00	5	.276	.374	.488
Edmonton	AAA	34	117	29	7	1	4	—	—	50	14	19	6	0	33	1	0	1	3	0	1.00	5	.248	.288	.427
1997 Edmonton	AAA	43	145	48	13	0	7	—	—	82	23	34	14	0	42	2	1	1	0	2	.00	4	.331	.395	.566
Tucson	AAA	24	85	29	5	0	5	—	—	49	13	17	1	0	19	1	0	0	1	0	1.00	2	.341	.356	.576
Colo Spmgs	AAA	14	47	9	1	0	3	—	—	19	4	6	4	0	18	0	0	0	0	0	.00	2	.191	.255	.404
1998 Las Vegas	AAA	86	292	85	22	0	19	—	—	164	48	70	30	3	85	3	0	6	1	1	.50	4	.291	.356	.562
1999 Pawtucket	AAA	27	92	26	3	0	5	—	—	44	12	10	6	0	23	0	0	1	0	0	.00	4	.283	.323	.478
1999 Boston	AL	18	47	13	2	1	1	(0	1)	20	4	11	3	0	13	2	0	0	0	0	.00	3	.277	.346	.426

Vladimir Guerrero

Bats: Right **Throws:** Right **Pos:** RF-160; PH/PR-1   **Ht:** 6'3" **Wt:** 205 **Born:** 2/9/76 **Age:** 24

Year Team	Lg	G	AB	H	2B	3B	HR	(Hm	Rd)	TB	R	RBI	TBB	IBB	SO	HBP	SH	SF	SB	CS	SB%	GDP	Avg	OBP	SLG
1996 Montreal	NL	9	27	5	0	0	1	(0	1)	8	2	1	0	0	3	0	0	0	0	0	.00	1	.185	.185	.296
1997 Montreal	NL	90	325	98	22	2	11	(5	6)	157	44	40	19	2	39	7	0	3	3	4	.43	11	.302	.350	.483
1998 Montreal	NL	159	623	202	37	7	38	(19	19)	367	108	109	42	13	95	7	0	5	11	9	.55	15	.324	.371	.589
1999 Montreal	NL	160	610	193	37	5	42	(23	19)	366	102	131	55	14	62	7	0	2	14	7	.67	18	.316	.378	.600
4 ML YEARS		418	1585	498	96	14	92	(47	45)	898	256	281	116	29	199	21	0	10	28	20	.58	45	.314	.367	.567

Wilton Guerrero

Bats: B **Throws:** R **Pos:** PH/PR-58; 2B-54; LF-22; DH-5   **Ht:** 6'0" **Wt:** 175 **Born:** 10/24/74 **Age:** 25

Year Team	Lg	G	AB	H	2B	3B	HR	(Hm	Rd)	TB	R	RBI	TBB	IBB	SO	HBP	SH	SF	SB	CS	SB%	GDP	Avg	OBP	SLG
1996 Los Angeles	NL	5	2	0	0	0	0	(0	0)	0	1	0	0	0	2	0	0	0	0	0	.00	0	.000	.000	.000
1997 Los Angeles	NL	111	357	104	10	9	4	(2	2)	144	39	32	8	1	52	0	13	2	6	5	.55	7	.291	.305	.403
1998 LA-Mon	NL	116	402	114	14	9	2	(0	2)	152	50	27	14	0	63	1	6	3	8	2	.80	4	.284	.307	.378
1999 Montreal	NL	132	315	92	15	7	2	(0	2)	127	42	31	13	0	38	2	10	0	7	6	.54	4	.292	.324	.403
1998 Los Angeles	NL	64	180	51	4	3	0	(0	0)	61	21	7	4	0	33	1	3	2	5	2	.71	3	.283	.299	.339
Montreal	NL	52	222	63	10	6	2	(0	2)	91	29	20	10	0	30	0	3	1	3	0	1.00	1	.284	.313	.410
4 ML YEARS		364	1076	310	39	25	8	(2	6)	423	132	90	35	1	155	3	29	5	21	13	.62	15	.288	.311	.393

Giomar Guevara

Bats: Both **Throws:** Right **Pos:** SS-9; PH/PR-1   **Ht:** 5'8" **Wt:** 150 **Born:** 10/23/72 **Age:** 27

Year Team	Lg	G	AB	H	2B	3B	HR	(Hm	Rd)	TB	R	RBI	TBB	IBB	SO	HBP	SH	SF	SB	CS	SB%	GDP	Avg	OBP	SLG
1993 Bellingham	A-	62	211	48	8	3	1	—	—	65	31	23	34	2	46	2	4	0	4	7	.36	3	.227	.340	.308
1994 Appleton	A	110	385	116	23	3	8	—	—	169	57	46	42	1	77	2	5	1	9	16	.36	6	.301	.372	.439
Jacksnville	AA	7	20	4	2	0	1	—	—	9	2	3	2	0	9	0	1	0	0	0	.00	0	.200	.273	.450
1995 Riverside	A+	83	292	71	12	3	2	—	—	95	53	34	30	1	71	1	6	6	7	4	.64	4	.243	.310	.325
1996 Port City	AA	119	414	110	18	2	2	—	—	138	60	41	54	1	102	4	9	4	21	7	.75	12	.266	.353	.333
1997 Tacoma	AAA	54	176	43	5	1	2	—	—	56	29	13	5	0	39	1	5	0	3	7	.30	2	.244	.269	.318
Memphis	AA	65	228	60	10	4	4	—	—	90	30	28	20	0	42	0	0	1	5	5	.50	3	.263	.321	.395
1998 Lancaster	A+	19	61	15	4	0	0	—	—	19	15	3	14	0	20	1	0	0	1	1	.50	1	.246	.395	.311
Orlando	AA	14	45	15	5	1	0	—	—	22	13	6	8	0	11	0	1	0	0	0	.00	3	.333	.434	.489
1999 Tacoma	AAA	32	116	34	13	0	3	—	—	56	15	15	12	0	22	2	1	0	1	0	1.00	3	.293	.369	.483
1997 Seattle	AL	5	4	0	0	0	0	(0	0)	0	0	0	0	0	2	0	0	0	1	0	1.00	0	.000	.000	.000
1998 Seattle	AL	11	13	3	2	0	0	(0	0)	5	4	0	4	0	4	1	0	0	0	0	.00	1	.231	.444	.385
1999 Seattle	AL	10	12	3	2	0	0	(0	0)	5	2	2	0	0	2	0	0	0	0	0	.00	0	.250	.250	.417
3 ML YEARS		26	29	6	4	0	0	(0	0)	10	6	2	4	0	8	1	0	0	1	0	1.00	1	.207	.324	.345

Carlos Guillen

Bats: Both **Throws:** Right **Pos:** SS-3; 2B-2   **Ht:** 6'1" **Wt:** 180 **Born:** 9/30/75 **Age:** 24

Year Team	Lg	G	AB	H	2B	3B	HR	(Hm	Rd)	TB	R	RBI	TBB	IBB	SO	HBP	SH	SF	SB	CS	SB%	GDP	Avg	OBP	SLG
1995 Astros	R	30	105	31	4	2	2	—	—	45	17	15	9	1	17	1	1	2	17	1	.94	0	.295	.350	.429
1996 Quad City	A	29	112	37	7	1	3	—	—	55	23	17	16	2	25	0	0	3	13	6	.68	1	.330	.405	.491
1997 Jackson	AA	115	390	99	16	1	10	—	—	147	47	39	38	1	78	2	4	2	6	5	.55	9	.254	.322	.377
New Orleans	AAA	3	13	4	1	0	0	—	—	5	3	0	0	0	4	0	0	0	0	0	.00	0	.308	.308	.385
1998 New Orleans	AAA	100	374	109	18	4	12	—	—	171	67	51	31	1	61	5	6	4	3	4	.43	5	.291	.350	.457
Tacoma	AAA	24	92	21	1	1	1	—	—	27	8	4	9	0	17	0	1	0	1	2	.33	1	.228	.297	.293
1998 Seattle	AL	10	39	13	1	1	0	(0	0)	16	9	5	3	0	9	0	0	0	2	0	1.00	0	.333	.381	.410
1999 Seattle	AL	5	19	3	0	0	1	(1	0)	6	2	3	1	0	6	0	1	0	0	0	.00	1	.158	.200	.316
2 ML YEARS		15	58	16	1	1	1	(1	0)	22	11	8	4	0	15	0	1	0	2	0	1.00	1	.276	.323	.379

Jose Guillen

Bats: Right **Throws:** Right **Pos:** RF-84; PH/PR-4   **Ht:** 5'11" **Wt:** 195 **Born:** 5/17/76 **Age:** 24

Year Team	Lg	G	AB	H	2B	3B	HR	(Hm	Rd)	TB	R	RBI	TBB	IBB	SO	HBP	SH	SF	SB	CS	SB%	GDP	Avg	OBP	SLG
1999 Nashville *	AAA	35	132	44	10	0	5	—	—	69	28	22	8	0	21	2	0	1	0	1	.00	4	.333	.378	.523
Durham *	AAA	9	34	13	1	0	3	—	—	23	8	12	7	0	7	0	0	1	0	0	.00	2	.382	.476	.676
1997 Pittsburgh	NL	143	498	133	20	5	14	(5	9)	205	58	70	17	0	88	8	0	3	1	2	.33	16	.267	.300	.412
1998 Pittsburgh	NL	153	573	153	38	2	14	(10	4)	237	60	84	21	0	100	6	1	4	3	5	.38	7	.267	.298	.414
1999 Pit-TB		87	288	73	16	0	3	(1	2)	98	42	31	20	2	57	7	1	2	1	0	1.00	16	.253	.315	.340
1999 Pittsburgh	NL	40	120	32	6	0	1	(0	1)	41	18	18	10	1	21	0	1	1	1	0	1.00	7	.267	.321	.342
Tampa Bay	AL	47	168	41	10	0	2	(1	1)	57	24	13	10	1	36	7	0	1	0	0	.00	9	.244	.312	.339
3 ML YEARS		383	1359	359	74	7	31	(16	15)	540	160	185	58	2	245	21	2	9	5	7	.42	39	.264	.303	.397

92

Ozzie Guillen

Bats: L Throws: R Pos: SS-53; PH/PR-36; 3B-6; 2B-1 **Ht: 5'11" Wt: 165 Born: 1/20/64 Age: 36**

Year Team	Lg	G	AB	H	2B	3B	HR	(Hm	Rd)	TB	R	RBI	TBB	IBB	SO	HBP	SH	SF	SB	CS	SB%	GDP	Avg	OBP	SLG
1985 Chicago	AL	150	491	134	21	9	1	(1	0)	176	71	33	12	1	36	1	8	1	7	4	.64	5	.273	.291	.358
1986 Chicago	AL	159	547	137	19	4	2	(1	1)	170	58	47	12	1	52	1	12	5	8	4	.67	14	.250	.265	.311
1987 Chicago	AL	149	560	156	22	7	2	(2	0)	198	64	51	22	2	52	1	13	8	25	8	.76	10	.279	.303	.354
1988 Chicago	AL	156	566	148	16	7	0	(0	0)	178	58	39	25	3	40	2	10	3	25	13	.66	14	.261	.294	.314
1989 Chicago	AL	155	597	151	20	8	1	(0	1)	190	63	54	15	3	48	0	11	3	36	17	.68	8	.253	.270	.318
1990 Chicago	AL	160	516	144	21	4	1	(1	0)	176	61	58	26	8	37	1	15	5	13	17	.43	6	.279	.312	.341
1991 Chicago	AL	154	524	143	20	3	3	(1	2)	178	52	49	11	1	38	0	13	7	21	15	.58	7	.273	.284	.340
1992 Chicago	AL	12	40	8	4	0	0	(0	0)	12	5	7	1	0	5	0	1	1	1	0	1.00	1	.200	.214	.300
1993 Chicago	AL	134	457	128	23	4	4	(3	1)	171	44	50	10	0	41	0	13	6	5	4	.56	6	.280	.292	.374
1994 Chicago	AL	100	365	105	9	5	1	(1	0)	127	46	39	14	2	35	0	7	4	5	4	.56	5	.288	.311	.348
1995 Chicago	AL	122	415	103	20	3	1	(1	0)	132	50	41	13	1	25	0	4	1	6	7	.46	11	.248	.270	.318
1996 Chicago	AL	150	499	131	24	8	4	(0	4)	183	62	45	10	0	27	0	12	7	6	5	.55	10	.263	.273	.367
1997 Chicago	AL	142	490	120	21	6	4	(1	3)	165	59	52	22	1	24	0	11	4	5	3	.63	7	.245	.275	.337
1998 Bal-Atl		95	280	74	15	1	1	(1	0)	94	37	22	25	0	27	1	5	2	1	5	.17	3	.264	.325	.336
1999 Atlanta	NL	92	232	56	16	0	1	(0	1)	75	21	20	15	2	17	0	5	3	4	2	.67	6	.241	.284	.323
1998 Baltimore	AL	12	16	1	0	0	0	(0	0)	1	2	0	1	0	2	0	1	0	0	1	.00	1	.063	.118	.063
Atlanta	NL	83	264	73	15	1	1	(1	0)	93	35	22	24	0	25	1	4	2	1	4	.20	2	.277	.337	.352
15 ML YEARS		1930	6579	1738	271	69	26	(12	14)	2225	751	607	233	25	504	7	140	60	168	108	.61	113	.264	.288	.338

Eric Gunderson

Pitches: Left Bats: Right Pos: RP-11 **Ht: 6'0" Wt: 190 Born: 3/29/66 Age: 34**

Year Team	Lg	G	GS	CG	GF	IP	BFP	H	R	ER	HR	SH	SF	HB	TBB	IBB	SO	WP	Bk	W	L	Pct.	ShO	Sv-Op	Hld	ERA
1999 Oklahoma *	AAA	5	0	0	2	6.2	32	11	6	6	2	0	0	0	1	0	3	1	0	0	1	.000	0	1--	—	8.10
1990 San Francisco	NL	7	4	0	1	19.2	94	24	14	12	2	1	0	0	11	1	14	0	0	1	2	.333	0	0-0	0	5.49
1991 San Francisco	NL	2	0	0	1	3.1	18	6	4	2	0	0	0	0	1	0	2	0	0	0	0	.000	0	1-1	0	5.40
1992 Seattle	AL	9	0	0	4	9.1	45	12	12	9	1	0	2	1	5	3	2	0	2	2	1	.667	0	0-0	0	8.68
1994 New York	NL	14	0	0	3	9	31	5	0	0	0	0	0	0	4	0	4	0	0	0	0	.000	0	0-0	2	0.00
1995 NYM-Bos		49	0	0	8	36.2	161	38	17	17	2	2	2	3	17	4	28	1	0	3	2	.600	0	0-3	6	4.17
1996 Boston	AL	28	0	0	2	17.1	82	21	17	16	5	0	2	2	8	2	7	3	0	0	1	.000	0	0-0	3	8.31
1997 Texas	AL	60	0	0	11	49.2	209	45	19	18	5	2	3	2	15	3	31	2	1	2	1	.667	0	1-4	12	3.26
1998 Texas	AL	68	1	0	13	67.2	303	88	43	39	13	1	3	1	19	4	41	4	0	0	3	.000	0	0-2	9	5.19
1999 Texas	AL	11	0	0	3	10	51	20	8	8	1	0	1	0	2	0	6	3	0	0	0	.000	0	0-0	1	7.20
1995 New York	NL	30	0	0	7	24.1	103	25	10	10	2	0	1	1	8	3	19	1	0	1	1	.500	0	0-3	6	3.70
Boston	AL	19	0	0	1	12.1	58	13	7	7	0	2	1	2	9	1	9	0	0	2	1	.667	0	0-0	6	5.11
9 ML YEARS		248	5	0	46	222.2	994	259	134	121	29	6	13	9	82	17	135	13	3	8	10	.444	0	2-10	33	4.89

Mark Guthrie

Pitches: Left Bats: Right Pos: RP-57 **Ht: 6'4" Wt: 211 Born: 9/22/65 Age: 34**

Year Team	Lg	G	GS	CG	GF	IP	BFP	H	R	ER	HR	SH	SF	HB	TBB	IBB	SO	WP	Bk	W	L	Pct.	ShO	Sv-Op	Hld	ERA
1999 Pawtucket *	AAA	1	1	0	0	3	0	0	0	0	0	0	0	0	0	1	0	0	0	0	.000	0	0--	—	0.00
1989 Minnesota	AL	13	8	0	2	57.1	254	66	32	29	7	1	5	1	21	1	38	1	0	2	4	.333	0	0-0	0	4.55
1990 Minnesota	AL	24	21	3	0	144.2	603	154	65	61	8	6	0	1	39	3	101	9	0	7	9	.438	1	0-0	0	3.79
1991 Minnesota	AL	41	12	0	13	98	432	116	52	47	11	4	3	1	41	2	72	7	0	7	5	.583	0	2-2	5	4.32
1992 Minnesota	AL	54	0	0	15	75	303	59	27	24	7	4	2	0	23	7	76	2	0	2	3	.400	0	5-7	19	2.88
1993 Minnesota	AL	22	0	0	2	21	94	20	11	11	2	1	2	0	16	2	15	1	3	2	1	.667	0	0-0	4	4.71
1994 Minnesota	AL	50	2	0	13	51.1	234	65	43	35	8	2	6	2	18	2	38	7	0	4	2	.667	0	1-3	8	6.14
1995 Min-LA		60	0	0	14	62	272	66	33	29	6	4	0	2	25	5	67	5	1	5	5	.500	0	0-2	15	4.21
1996 Los Angeles	NL	66	0	0	16	73	302	65	21	18	3	4	4	1	22	2	56	1	0	2	3	.400	0	1-3	12	2.22
1997 Los Angeles	NL	62	0	0	18	69.1	305	71	44	41	12	10	3	0	30	6	42	2	1	1	4	.200	0	1-4	13	5.32
1998 Los Angeles	NL	53	0	0	11	54	241	56	26	21	3	5	0	2	24	1	45	2	0	2	1	.667	0	0-1	8	3.50
1999 Bos-ChC		57	0	0	15	58.2	254	57	38	35	10	2	3	2	24	5	45	3	0	1	3	.250	0	2-2	14	5.37
1995 Boston	AL	36	0	0	7	42.1	181	47	22	21	5	2	0	1	16	3	48	3	1	5	3	.625	0	0-2	10	4.46
Los Angeles	NL	24	0	0	7	19.2	91	19	11	8	1	2	0	1	9	2	19	2	0	0	2	.000	0	0-0	5	3.66
1999 Boston	AL	46	0	0	15	46.1	207	50	32	30	9	0	3	2	20	3	36	2	0	1	1	.500	0	2-2	12	5.83
Chicago	NL	11	0	0	0	12.1	47	7	6	5	1	2	0	0	4	2	9	1	0	0	2	.000	0	0-0	2	3.65
11 ML YEARS		502	43	3	119	764.1	3294	795	392	351	77	43	28	12	283	36	595	40	5	35	40	.467	1	12-25	106	4.13

Ricky Gutierrez

Bats: Right Throws: Right Pos: SS-80; PH/PR-5; 3B-1 **Ht: 6'1" Wt: 175 Born: 5/23/70 Age: 30**

Year Team	Lg	G	AB	H	2B	3B	HR	(Hm	Rd)	TB	R	RBI	TBB	IBB	SO	HBP	SH	SF	SB	CS	SB%	GDP	Avg	OBP	SLG
1999 Jackson *	AA	4	12	4	1	0	0	—	—	5	4	1	4	0	3	0	0	0	0	1	.00	0	.333	.500	.417
New Orleans *	AAA	4	14	3	0	0	0	—	—	3	0	1	2	0	3	0	0	0	0	0	.00	2	.214	.313	.214
1993 San Diego	NL	133	438	110	10	5	5	(5	0)	145	76	26	50	2	97	5	1	1	4	3	.57	7	.251	.334	.331
1994 San Diego	NL	90	275	66	11	2	1	(1	0)	84	27	28	32	1	54	2	2	3	2	6	.25	8	.240	.321	.305
1995 Houston	NL	52	156	43	6	0	0	(0	0)	49	22	12	10	3	33	1	1	1	5	0	1.00	6	.276	.321	.314
1996 Houston	NL	89	218	62	8	1	1	(0	1)	75	28	15	23	3	42	3	4	1	6	1	.86	4	.284	.359	.344
1997 Houston	NL	102	303	79	14	4	3	(0	3)	110	33	34	21	2	50	3	0	3	17	9	.65	4	.261	.315	.363
1998 Houston	NL	141	491	128	24	3	2	(1	1)	164	55	46	54	5	84	6	3	7	13	7	.65	20	.261	.337	.334
1999 Houston	NL	85	268	70	7	5	1	(1	0)	90	33	25	37	4	45	2	3	1	2	5	.29	9	.261	.354	.336
7 ML YEARS		692	2149	558	80	20	13	(9	4)	717	274	186	227	20	405	22	14	14	37	24	.61	69	.260	.335	.334

Cristian Guzman

Bats: Both **Throws:** Right **Pos:** SS-131; PH/PR-1
Ht: 6'0" **Wt:** 188 **Born:** 3/21/78 **Age:** 22

							BATTING											BASERUNNING				PERCENTAGES		
Year Team	Lg	G	AB	H	2B	3B	HR	(Hm | Rd)	TB	R	RBI	TBB	IBB	SO	HBP	SH	SF	SB	CS	SB%	GDP	Avg	OBP	SLG
1996 Yankees	R	42	170	50	8	2	1	—	—	65	37	21	10	0	31	3	2	2	7	6	.54	2	.294	.341	.382
1997 Tampa	A+	4	14	4	0	0	0	—	—	4	4	1	1	0	1	0	0	0	0	1	.00	0	.286	.333	.286
Greensboro	A	124	495	135	21	4	4	—	—	176	68	52	17	0	105	10	4	2	23	12	.66	3	.273	.309	.356
1998 New Britain	AA	140	566	157	29	5	1	—	—	199	68	40	21	1	111	1	17	1	23	14	.62	13	.277	.304	.352
1999 Minnesota	AL	131	420	95	12	3	1	(1 | 0)	116	47	26	22	0	90	3	7	4	9	7	.56	5	.226	.267	.276

Domingo Guzman

Pitches: Right **Bats:** Right **Pos:** RP-7
Ht: 6'0" **Wt:** 210 **Born:** 4/5/75 **Age:** 25

			HOW MUCH HE PITCHED						WHAT HE GAVE UP									THE RESULTS					
Year Team	Lg	G	GS	CG	GF	IP	BFP	H	R	ER	HR	SH	SF	HB	TBB	IBB	SO	WP	Bk	W	L	Pct.	ShO	Sv-Op	Hld	ERA
1994 Padres	R	13	13	0	0	70	309	65	39	32	1	1	2	11	25	0	55	5	2	8	4	.667	0	0- -	—	4.11
1995 Idaho Falls	R+	27	0	0	23	25.2	127	25	22	19	2	3	1	1	25	1	33	6	3	2	1	.667	0	11- -	—	6.66
1996 Clinton	A	6	5	0	1	20.2	112	32	33	29	2	0	1	2	19	0	18	5	0	0	5	.000	0	0- -	—	12.63
Idaho Falls	R+	15	10	1	1	65.1	278	52	41	30	7	2	1	7	29	0	75	13	0	4	2	.667	1	0- -	—	4.13
1997 Clinton	A	12	12	5	0	79	320	66	36	28	7	2	2	3	25	0	91	5	2	4	5	.444	0	0- -	—	3.19
Rancho Cuca	A+	6	6	0	0	38	168	42	23	23	6	2	1	2	16	0	39	2	0	3	2	.600	0	0- -	—	5.45
1998 Rancho Cuca	A+	4	4	0	0	21.2	91	22	11	9	1	0	1	1	6	0	16	3	0	1	1	.500	0	0- -	—	3.74
Mobile	AA	12	8	0	2	48	217	51	34	29	7	3	0	3	26	0	39	8	0	5	2	.714	0	1- -	—	4.50
1999 Mobile	AA	41	0	0	21	51	240	60	33	31	2	3	3	5	25	1	38	3	0	1	2	.333	0	6- -	—	5.47
1999 San Diego	NL	7	0	0	2	5	33	13	12	12	1	2	0	0	3	2	4	0	0	0	1	.000	0	0-0	0	21.60

Edwards Guzman

Bats: Left **Throws:** Right **Pos:** PH/PR-8; 3B-5; C-1
Ht: 5'10" **Wt:** 205 **Born:** 9/11/76 **Age:** 23

							BATTING											BASERUNNING				PERCENTAGES		
Year Team	Lg	G	AB	H	2B	3B	HR	(Hm	Rd)	TB	R	RBI	TBB	IBB	SO	HBP	SH	SF	SB	CS	SB%	GDP	Avg	OBP	SLG
1996 San Jose	A+	106	367	99	19	5	1	—	—	131	41	40	39	4	60	5	6	5	3	5	.38	6	.270	.344	.357
1997 Shreveport	AA	118	380	108	15	4	3	—	—	140	52	42	33	4	57	1	5	3	1	1	.75	6	.284	.341	.368
1998 Fresno	AAA	102	325	99	17	0	9	—	—	143	50	48	24	4	47	3	3	1	1	0	1.00	4	.305	.357	.440
1999 Fresno	AAA	90	358	98	13	0	7	—	—	132	48	48	17	0	50	3	4	1	6	5	.55	11	.274	.309	.369
1999 San Francisco	NL	14	15	0	0	0	0	(0	0)	0	0	0	0	0	4	0	1	0	0	0	.00	0	.000	.000	.000

Juan Guzman

Pitches: Right **Bats:** Right **Pos:** SP-33
Ht: 5'11" **Wt:** 195 **Born:** 10/28/66 **Age:** 33

			HOW MUCH HE PITCHED						WHAT HE GAVE UP									THE RESULTS					
Year Team	Lg	G	GS	CG	GF	IP	BFP	H	R	ER	HR	SH	SF	HB	TBB	IBB	SO	WP	Bk	W	L	Pct.	ShO	Sv-Op	Hld	ERA
1991 Toronto	AL	23	23	1	0	138.2	574	98	53	46	6	2	5	4	66	0	123	10	0	10	3	.769	0	0-0	0	2.99
1992 Toronto	AL	28	28	1	0	180.2	733	135	56	53	6	5	3	1	72	2	165	14	2	16	5	.762	0	0-0	0	2.64
1993 Toronto	AL	33	33	2	0	221	963	211	107	98	17	5	9	3	110	2	194	26	1	14	3	.824	1	0-0	0	3.99
1994 Toronto	AL	25	25	2	0	147.1	671	165	102	93	20	1	6	3	76	1	124	13	1	12	11	.522	0	0-0	0	5.68
1995 Toronto	AL	24	24	3	0	135.1	619	151	101	95	13	3	2	3	73	6	94	8	0	4	14	.222	0	0-0	0	6.32
1996 Toronto	AL	27	27	4	0	187.2	756	158	68	61	20	2	2	7	53	3	165	7	0	11	8	.579	1	0-0	0	2.93
1997 Toronto	AL	13	13	0	0	60	261	48	42	33	14	1	2	2	31	0	52	4	0	3	6	.333	0	0-0	0	4.95
1998 Tor-Bal	AL	33	33	2	0	211	918	193	117	102	22	5	5	8	98	2	168	11	0	10	16	.385	0	0-0	0	4.35
1999 Bal-Cin		33	33	2	0	200	864	194	96	83	28	7	4	4	86	6	155	12	2	11	12	.478	1	0-0	0	3.74
1998 Toronto	AL	22	22	2	0	145	632	133	83	71	19	2	3	6	65	1	113	6	0	6	12	.333	0	0-0	0	4.41
Baltimore	AL	11	11	0	0	66	286	60	34	31	4	0	2	2	33	1	55	5	0	4	4	.500	0	0-0	0	4.23
1999 Baltimore	AL	21	21	1	0	122.2	544	124	63	57	18	4	3	3	65	3	95	7	2	5	9	.357	1	0-0	0	4.18
Cincinnati	NL	12	12	1	0	77.1	320	70	33	26	10	3	1	1	21	3	60	5	0	6	3	.667	0	0-0	0	3.03
9 ML YEARS		239	239	17	0	1481.2	6359	1353	742	664	147	28	38	35	665	22	1240	105	6	91	78	.538	3	0-0	0	4.03

Tony Gwynn

Bats: Left **Throws:** Left **Pos:** RF-104; PH/PR-5; DH-2
Ht: 5'11" **Wt:** 220 **Born:** 5/9/60 **Age:** 40

							BATTING											BASERUNNING				PERCENTAGES		
Year Team	Lg	G	AB	H	2B	3B	HR	(Hm	Rd)	TB	R	RBI	TBB	IBB	SO	HBP	SH	SF	SB	CS	SB%	GDP	Avg	OBP	SLG
1982 San Diego	NL	54	190	55	12	2	1	(0	1)	74	33	17	14	0	16	0	4	1	8	3	.73	5	.289	.337	.389
1983 San Diego	NL	86	304	94	12	2	1	(0	1)	113	34	37	23	5	21	0	4	3	7	4	.64	9	.309	.355	.372
1984 San Diego	NL	158	606	213	21	10	5	(3	2)	269	88	71	59	13	23	2	6	2	33	18	.65	15	.351	.410	.444
1985 San Diego	NL	154	622	197	29	5	6	(3	3)	254	90	46	45	4	33	2	1	1	14	11	.56	17	.317	.364	.408
1986 San Diego	NL	160	642	211	33	7	14	(8	6)	300	107	59	52	11	35	3	2	2	37	9	.80	20	.329	.381	.467
1987 San Diego	NL	157	589	218	36	13	7	(5	2)	301	119	54	82	26	35	3	2	4	56	12	.82	13	.370	.447	.511
1988 San Diego	NL	133	521	163	22	5	7	(3	4)	216	64	70	51	13	40	0	4	2	26	11	.70	11	.313	.373	.415
1989 San Diego	NL	158	604	203	27	7	4	(2	2)	256	82	62	56	16	30	1	11	7	40	16	.71	12	.336	.389	.424
1990 San Diego	NL	141	573	177	29	10	4	(2	2)	238	79	72	44	20	23	1	7	4	17	8	.68	13	.309	.357	.415
1991 San Diego	NL	134	530	168	27	11	4	(1	3)	229	69	62	34	8	19	0	0	5	8	8	.50	11	.317	.355	.432
1992 San Diego	NL	128	520	165	27	3	6	(4	2)	216	77	41	46	12	16	0	0	3	3	6	.33	13	.317	.371	.415
1993 San Diego	NL	122	489	175	41	3	7	(4	3)	243	70	59	36	11	19	1	1	7	14	1	.93	18	.358	.398	.497
1994 San Diego	NL	110	419	165	35	1	12	(4	8)	238	79	64	48	16	19	2	1	5	5	0	1.00	20	.394	.454	.568
1995 San Diego	NL	135	535	197	33	1	9	(5	4)	259	82	90	35	10	15	1	0	6	17	5	.77	20	.368	.404	.484
1996 San Diego	NL	116	451	159	27	2	3	(2	1)	199	67	50	39	12	17	1	1	6	11	4	.73	17	.353	.400	.441
1997 San Diego	NL	149	592	220	49	2	17	(8	9)	324	97	119	43	12	28	3	1	12	12	5	.71	12	.372	.409	.547

94

Year Team	Lg	G	AB	H	2B	3B	HR	(Hm	Rd)	TB	R	RBI	TBB	IBB	SO	HBP	SH	SF	SB	CS	SB%	GDP	Avg	OBP	SLG
1998 San Diego	NL	127	461	148	35	0	16	(5	11)	231	65	69	35	6	18	1	0	8	3	1	.75	14	.321	.364	.501
1999 San Diego	NL	111	411	139	27	0	10	(5	5)	196	59	62	29	5	14	2	0	4	7	2	.78	15	.338	.381	.477
18 ML YEARS		2333	9059	3067	522	84	133	(65	68)	4156	1361	1104	771	200	421	23	45	82	318	124	.72	255	.339	.389	.459

Yamid Haad

Bats: Right **Throws:** Right **Pos:** PH/PR-1 Ht: 6'2" Wt: 204 Born: 9/2/77 Age: 22

Year Team	Lg	G	AB	H	2B	3B	HR	(Hm	Rd)	TB	R	RBI	TBB	IBB	SO	HBP	SH	SF	SB	CS	SB%	GDP	Avg	OBP	SLG
1997 Erie	A-	43	155	45	7	3	1	—	—	61	27	19	7	0	27	0	1	6	3	3	.50	5	.290	.310	.394
1998 Lynchburg	A+	88	299	76	8	2	5	—	—	103	32	34	13	0	54	3	4	4	1	7	.13	11	.254	.288	.344
1999 Lynchburg	A+	59	209	53	11	1	5	—	—	81	31	33	33	1	42	1	2	3	5	2	.71	8	.254	.354	.388
Altoona	AA	43	137	25	3	0	6	—	—	46	20	10	19	0	32	0	0	1	7	2	.78	4	.182	.280	.336
1999 Pittsburgh	NL	1	1	0	0	0	0	(0	0)	0	0	0	0	0	0	0	0	0	0	0	.00	0	.000	.000	.000

Luther Hackman

Pitches: Right **Bats:** Right **Pos:** SP-3; RP-2 Ht: 6'4" Wt: 195 Born: 10/10/74 Age: 25

Year Team	Lg	G	GS	CG	GF	IP	BFP	H	R	ER	HR	SH	SF	HB	TBB	IBB	SO	WP	Bk	W	L	Pct.	ShO	Sv-Op	Hld	ERA
1994 Rockies	R	12	12	0	0	55.2	234	50	21	13	1	0	0	1	16	0	63	5	1	1	3	.250	0	0- --	—	2.10
1995 Asheville	A	28	28	0	0	165	710	162	95	85	11	3	3	14	65	0	108	9	7	11	11	.500	0	0- --	—	4.64
1996 Salem	A+	21	21	1	0	110.1	484	93	60	52	2	4	7	5	69	1	83	6	2	5	7	.417	0	0- --	—	4.24
1997 New Haven	AA	10	10	0	0	50.2	241	58	49	44	11	5	2	5	34	1	34	4	3	0	6	.000	0	0- --	—	7.82
Salem	A+	15	15	2	0	80.2	384	99	60	52	14	4	5	9	37	0	59	8	0	1	4	.200	0	0- --	—	5.80
1998 New Haven	AA	28	23	1	2	139	640	169	102	84	18	7	7	10	54	1	90	10	2	3	12	.200	0	0- --	—	5.44
1999 Carolina	AA	11	10	0	0	62.1	271	53	33	28	4	2	1	4	28	0	50	4	0	4	3	.571	0	0- --	—	4.04
Colo Sprngs	AAA	15	15	1	0	101	445	106	49	42	7	4	3	6	44	2	88	2	2	7	6	.538	1	0- --	—	3.74
1999 Colorado	NL	5	3	0	0	16	84	26	19	19	5	2	0	0	12	0	10	0	0	1	2	.333	0	0-0	0	10.69

Jerry Hairston Jr.

Bats: Right **Throws:** Right **Pos:** 2B-50; PH/PR-1 Ht: 5'10" Wt: 175 Born: 5/29/76 Age: 24

Year Team	Lg	G	AB	H	2B	3B	HR	(Hm	Rd)	TB	R	RBI	TBB	IBB	SO	HBP	SH	SF	SB	CS	SB%	GDP	Avg	OBP	SLG
1997 Bluefield	R+	12	221	73	14	4	2	—	—	100	44	36	21	0	29	10	4	2	13	9	.59	4	.330	.409	.452
1998 Frederick	A+	80	293	83	22	3	5	—	—	126	56	33	28	3	32	12	1	3	13	7	.65	4	.283	.366	.430
Bowie	AA	55	221	72	12	3	5	—	—	105	42	37	20	0	25	5	2	1	6	4	.60	5	.326	.393	.475
1999 Rochester	AAA	107	413	120	24	5	7	—	—	175	65	48	30	0	50	19	4	3	19	10	.66	9	.291	.363	.424
1998 Baltimore	AL	6	7	0	0	0	0	(0	0)	0	2	0	0	0	1	0	0	0	0	0	.00	0	.000	.000	.000
1999 Baltimore	AL	50	175	47	12	1	4	(1	3)	73	26	17	11	0	24	3	4	0	9	4	.69	2	.269	.323	.417
2 ML YEARS		56	182	47	12	1	4	(1	3)	73	28	17	11	0	25	3	4	0	9	4	.69	2	.258	.311	.401

John Halama

Pitches: Left **Bats:** Left **Pos:** SP-24; RP-14 Ht: 6'5" Wt: 200 Born: 2/22/72 Age: 28

Year Team	Lg	G	GS	CG	GF	IP	BFP	H	R	ER	HR	SH	SF	HB	TBB	IBB	SO	WP	Bk	W	L	Pct.	ShO	Sv-Op	Hld	ERA
1994 Auburn	A-	6	3	0	3	28	107	18	5	4	1	2	0	0	5	0	27	1	1	4	1	.800	0	1- --	—	1.29
Quad City	A	9	9	1	0	51.1	222	63	31	26	2	3	0	2	18	1	37	3	0	3	4	.429	1	0- --	—	4.56
1995 Quad City	A	55	0	0	26	62.1	241	48	16	14	7	2	1	3	22	1	56	1	0	1	2	.333	0	2- --	—	2.02
1996 Jackson	AA	27	27	0	0	162.2	691	151	77	58	10	7	7	8	59	0	110	7	0	9	10	.474	0	0- --	—	3.21
1997 New Orleans	AAA	26	24	1	2	171	673	150	57	49	9	4	7	1	32	1	126	2	2	13	3	.813	0	0- --	—	2.58
1998 New Orleans	AAA	17	17	4	0	121	488	118	48	43	11	3	4	3	16	1	86	3	3	12	3	.800	1	0- --	—	3.20
1998 Houston	NL	6	6	0	0	32.1	147	37	21	21	0	3	4	2	13	0	21	2	1	1	1	.500	0	0-0	0	5.85
1999 Seattle	AL	38	24	1	7	179	763	193	88	84	20	5	9	7	56	3	105	4	0	11	10	.524	1	0-0	1	4.22
2 ML YEARS		44	30	1	7	211.1	910	230	109	105	20	8	13	9	69	3	126	6	1	12	11	.522	1	0-0	1	4.47

Darren Hall

Pitches: Right **Bats:** Right **Pos:** RP Ht: 6'3" Wt: 207 Born: 7/14/64 Age: 35

Year Team	Lg	G	GS	CG	GF	IP	BFP	H	R	ER	HR	SH	SF	HB	TBB	IBB	SO	WP	Bk	W	L	Pct.	ShO	Sv-Op	Hld	ERA
1994 Toronto	AL	30	0	0	28	31.2	131	26	12	12	3	1	0	1	14	1	28	1	0	2	3	.400	0	17-20	1	3.41
1995 Toronto	AL	17	0	0	11	16.1	77	21	9	8	2	0	0	0	9	0	11	0	0	0	2	.000	0	3-4	2	4.41
1996 Los Angeles	NL	9	0	0	3	12	53	13	9	8	2	0	0	0	5	0	12	0	0	0	1	.000	0	0-1	2	6.00
1997 Los Angeles	NL	63	0	0	20	54.2	233	58	15	14	3	1	1	0	26	7	39	0	0	3	2	.600	0	2-5	15	2.30
1998 Los Angeles	NL	11	0	0	2	11.1	56	17	14	13	2	0	1	0	5	0	8	0	0	0	3	.000	0	0-1	0	10.32
5 ML YEARS		130	0	0	64	126	550	135	59	55	12	2	2	1	59	8	98	1	0	5	12	.294	0	22-31	20	3.93

Roy Halladay

Pitches: Right **Bats:** Right **Pos:** SP-18; RP-18   **Ht:** 6'6" **Wt:** 205 **Born:** 5/14/77 **Age:** 23

		HOW MUCH HE PITCHED						WHAT HE GAVE UP											THE RESULTS						
Year Team	Lg	G	GS	CG	GF	IP	BFP	H	R	ER	HR	SH	SF	HB	TBB	IBB	SO	WP	Bk	W	L	Pct.	ShO	Sv-Op	Hld	ERA
1995 Blue Jays	R	10	8	0	1	50.1	203	35	25	19	4	2	0	1	16	0	48	9	2	3	5	.375	0	0--	—	3.40
1996 Dunedin	A+	27	27	2	0	164.2	688	158	75	50	7	5	1	6	46	0	109	1	2	15	7	.682	2	0--	—	2.73
1997 Knoxville	AA	7	7	0	0	36.2	165	46	26	22	4	1	0	0	11	0	30	4	0	2	3	.400	0	0--	—	5.40
Syracuse	AAA	22	22	2	0	125.2	537	132	74	64	13	4	1	1	53	1	64	8	3	7	10	.412	2	0--	—	4.58
1998 Syracuse	AAA	21	21	1	0	116.1	500	107	52	49	11	2	2	8	53	3	71	9	0	9	5	.643	1	0--	—	3.79
1998 Toronto	AL	2	2	1	0	14	53	9	4	3	2	0	0	0	2	0	13	0	0	1	0	1.000	0	0-0	0	1.93
1999 Toronto	AL	36	18	1	2	149.1	668	156	76	65	19	3	4	4	79	1	82	6	0	8	7	.533	1	1-1	2	3.92
2 ML YEARS		38	20	2	2	163.1	721	165	80	68	21	3	4	4	81	1	95	6	0	9	7	.563	1	1-1	2	3.75

Shane Halter

Bats: R **Throws:** R **Pos:** PH/PR-5; SS-1; CF-1; RF-1   **Ht:** 6'0" **Wt:** 180 **Born:** 11/8/69 **Age:** 30

		BATTING															BASERUNNING				PERCENTAGES		
Year Team	Lg	G	AB	H	2B	3B	HR	(Hm | Rd)	TB	R	RBI	TBB	IBB	SO	HBP	SH	SF	SB	CS	SB%	GDP	Avg	OBP	SLG
1999 Norfolk *	AAA	127	474	130	22	3	6	—	—	176	77	35	60	0	90	0	17	3	19	18	.51	10	.274	.354	.371
1997 Kansas City	AL	74	123	34	5	1	2	(1 | 1)	47	16	10	10	0	28	2	4	0	4	3	.57	1	.276	.341	.382
1998 Kansas City	AL	86	204	45	12	0	2	(0 | 2)	63	17	13	12	0	38	1	7	2	2	5	.29	3	.221	.265	.309
1999 New York	NL	7	0	0	0	0	0	(0 | 0)	0	0	0	0	0	0	0	0	0	0	0	.00	0	.000	.000	.000
3 ML YEARS		167	327	79	17	1	4	(1 | 3)	110	33	23	22	0	66	3	11	2	6	8	.43	4	.242	.294	.336

Darryl Hamilton

Bats: Left **Throws:** Right **Pos:** CF-134; PH/PR-16   **Ht:** 6'1" **Wt:** 192 **Born:** 12/3/64 **Age:** 35

		BATTING															BASERUNNING				PERCENTAGES		
Year Team	Lg	G	AB	H	2B	3B	HR	(Hm | Rd)	TB	R	RBI	TBB	IBB	SO	HBP	SH	SF	SB	CS	SB%	GDP	Avg	OBP	SLG
1988 Milwaukee	AL	44	103	19	4	0	1	(1 | 0)	26	14	11	12	0	9	1	0	1	7	3	.70	2	.184	.274	.252
1990 Milwaukee	AL	89	156	46	5	0	1	(1 | 0)	54	27	18	9	0	12	0	3	0	10	3	.77	2	.295	.333	.346
1991 Milwaukee	AL	122	405	126	15	6	1	(0 | 1)	156	64	57	33	2	38	0	7	3	16	6	.73	10	.311	.361	.385
1992 Milwaukee	AL	128	470	140	19	7	5	(1 | 4)	188	67	62	45	0	42	1	4	7	41	14	.75	10	.298	.356	.400
1993 Milwaukee	AL	135	520	161	21	1	9	(5 | 4)	211	74	48	45	5	62	3	4	1	21	13	.62	9	.310	.367	.406
1994 Milwaukee	AL	36	141	37	10	1	1	(0 | 1)	52	23	13	15	1	17	0	2	1	3	0	1.00	2	.262	.331	.369
1995 Milwaukee	AL	112	398	108	20	6	5	(3 | 2)	155	54	44	47	3	35	3	8	3	11	1	.92	9	.271	.350	.389
1996 Texas	AL	148	627	184	29	4	6	(2 | 4)	239	94	51	54	4	66	2	7	6	15	5	.75	15	.293	.348	.381
1997 San Francisco	NL	125	460	124	23	3	5	(1 | 4)	168	78	43	61	1	61	0	6	2	15	10	.60	6	.270	.354	.365
1998 SF-Col	NL	148	561	173	28	3	6	(3 | 3)	225	95	51	82	1	73	3	12	3	13	9	.59	6	.308	.398	.401
1999 Col-NYM	NL	146	505	159	19	4	5	(2 | 3)	201	82	45	57	0	39	2	3	1	6	3	.67	6	.315	.386	.422
1998 San Francisco	NL	97	367	108	19	2	1	(1 | 0)	134	65	26	59	0	53	2	6	2	9	8	.53	6	.294	.393	.365
Colorado	NL	51	194	65	9	1	5	(2 | 3)	91	30	25	23	1	20	1	6	1	4	1	.80	0	.335	.406	.469
1999 Colorado	NL	91	337	102	11	3	4	(2 | 2)	131	63	24	38	0	21	1	2	1	4	5	.44	7	.303	.374	.389
New York	NL	55	168	57	8	1	5	(3 | 2)	82	19	21	19	0	18	1	1	0	2	3	.40	2	.339	.410	.488
11 ML YEARS		1233	4346	1277	193	35	49	(22 | 27)	1687	672	443	460	17	454	15	56	28	158	72	.69	80	.294	.361	.388

Joey Hamilton

Pitches: Right **Bats:** Right **Pos:** SP-18; RP-4   **Ht:** 6'4" **Wt:** 230 **Born:** 9/9/70 **Age:** 29

		HOW MUCH HE PITCHED						WHAT HE GAVE UP											THE RESULTS						
Year Team	Lg	G	GS	CG	GF	IP	BFP	H	R	ER	HR	SH	SF	HB	TBB	IBB	SO	WP	Bk	W	L	Pct.	ShO	Sv-Op	Hld	ERA
1999 Syracuse *	AAA	3	3	0	0	12.1	57	15	8	7	2	0	2	2	5	0	9	0	0	1	0	.000	0	0--	—	5.11
1994 San Diego	NL	16	16	1	0	108.2	447	98	40	36	7	4	2	6	29	3	61	6	0	9	6	.600	1	0-0	0	2.98
1995 San Diego	NL	31	30	2	1	204.1	850	189	89	70	17	12	4	11	56	5	123	2	0	6	9	.400	2	0-0	0	3.08
1996 San Diego	NL	34	33	3	0	211.2	908	206	100	98	19	6	5	9	83	3	184	14	1	15	9	.625	1	0-0	1	4.17
1997 San Diego	NL	31	29	1	1	192.2	831	199	100	91	22	8	8	12	69	2	124	7	0	12	7	.632	0	0-0	0	4.25
1998 San Diego	NL	34	34	0	0	217.1	958	220	113	103	15	13	6	8	106	10	147	4	0	13	13	.500	0	0-0	0	4.27
1999 Toronto	AL	22	18	0	0	98	440	118	73	71	13	0	2	3	39	0	56	4	1	7	8	.467	0	0-0	1	6.52
6 ML YEARS		168	160	7	3	1032.2	4434	1030	515	469	93	43	27	49	382	23	695	37	2	62	52	.544	4	0-0	2	4.09

Jeffrey Hammonds

Bats: R **Throws:** R **Pos:** RF-53; LF-46; PH/PR-26; CF-21   **Ht:** 6'0" **Wt:** 195 **Born:** 3/5/71 **Age:** 29

		BATTING															BASERUNNING				PERCENTAGES		
Year Team	Lg	G	AB	H	2B	3B	HR	(Hm | Rd)	TB	R	RBI	TBB	IBB	SO	HBP	SH	SF	SB	CS	SB%	GDP	Avg	OBP	SLG
1993 Baltimore	AL	33	105	32	8	0	3	(2 | 1)	49	10	19	2	1	16	0	1	2	4	0	1.00	3	.305	.312	.467
1994 Baltimore	AL	68	250	74	18	2	8	(6 | 2)	120	45	31	17	1	39	2	0	5	5	0	1.00	3	.296	.339	.480
1995 Baltimore	AL	57	178	43	9	1	4	(2 | 2)	66	18	23	9	0	30	1	1	2	4	2	.67	3	.242	.279	.371
1996 Baltimore	AL	71	248	56	10	1	9	(3 | 6)	95	38	27	23	1	53	4	6	1	3	3	.50	7	.226	.301	.383
1997 Baltimore	AL	118	397	105	19	3	21	(9 | 12)	193	71	55	32	1	73	3	0	2	15	1	.94	6	.264	.323	.486
1998 Bal-Cin		89	257	72	16	2	6	(1 | 5)	110	50	39	39	1	56	3	3	4	8	3	.73	2	.280	.376	.428
1999 Cincinnati	NL	123	262	73	13	0	17	(5 | 12)	137	43	41	27	0	64	1	2	1	5	2	.33	4	.279	.347	.523
1998 Baltimore	AL	63	171	46	12	1	6	(1 | 5)	78	36	28	26	1	38	3	0	3	7	2	.78	2	.269	.369	.456
Cincinnati	NL	26	86	26	4	1	0	(0 | 0)	32	14	11	13	0	18	0	3	1	1	1	.50	0	.302	.390	.372
7 ML YEARS		559	1697	455	93	9	68	(28 | 40)	770	275	235	149	5	331	14	13	17	42	15	.74	28	.268	.329	.454

Mike Hampton

Pitches: Left **Bats:** Right **Pos:** SP-34   **Ht:** 5'10" **Wt:** 180 **Born:** 9/9/72 **Age:** 27

		HOW MUCH HE PITCHED						WHAT HE GAVE UP											THE RESULTS						
Year Team	Lg	G	GS	CG	GF	IP	BFP	H	R	ER	HR	SH	SF	HB	TBB	IBB	SO	WP	Bk	W	L	Pct.	ShO	Sv-Op	Hld	ERA
1993 Seattle	AL	13	3	0	2	17	95	28	20	18	3	1	1	0	17	3	8	1	1	1	3	.250	0	1-1	2	9.53
1994 Houston	NL	44	0	0	7	41.1	181	46	19	17	4	0	0	2	16	1	24	5	1	2	1	.667	0	0-1	10	3.70
1995 Houston	NL	24	24	0	0	150.2	641	141	73	56	13	11	5	4	49	3	115	3	1	9	8	.529	0	0-0	0	3.35
1996 Houston	NL	27	27	2	0	160.1	691	175	79	64	12	10	3	3	49	1	101	7	2	10	10	.500	1	0-0	0	3.59
1997 Houston	NL	34	34	7	0	223	941	217	105	95	16	11	7	2	77	2	139	6	1	15	10	.600	2	0-0	0	3.83
1998 Houston	NL	32	32	1	0	211.2	917	227	92	79	18	7	7	5	81	1	137	4	1	11	7	.611	1	0-0	0	3.36
1999 Houston	NL	34	34	3	0	239	979	206	86	77	12	10	9	5	101	2	177	9	0	22	4	.846	2	0-0	0	2.90
7 ML YEARS		208	154	13	9	1043	4445	1040	474	406	78	50	32	21	390	13	701	35	8	70	43	.619	6	1-2	12	3.50

Chris Haney

Pitches: Left **Bats:** Left **Pos:** RP-9; SP-4   **Ht:** 6'3" **Wt:** 210 **Born:** 11/16/68 **Age:** 31

		HOW MUCH HE PITCHED						WHAT HE GAVE UP											THE RESULTS						
Year Team	Lg	G	GS	CG	GF	IP	BFP	H	R	ER	HR	SH	SF	HB	TBB	IBB	SO	WP	Bk	W	L	Pct.	ShO	Sv-Op	Hld	ERA
1999 Buffalo *	AAA	13	10	0	0	58.2	247	50	25	21	4	6	3	1	22	1	37	4	1	2	5	.286	0	0 -	—	3.22
1991 Montreal	NL	16	16	0	0	84.2	387	94	49	38	6	6	1	1	43	1	51	9	0	3	7	.300	0	0-0	0	4.04
1992 Mon-KC		16	13	2	2	80	339	75	43	41	11	0	6	4	26	2	54	5	1	4	6	.400	2	0-0	0	4.61
1993 Kansas City	AL	23	23	1	0	124	556	141	87	83	13	4	3	3	53	2	65	6	1	9	9	.500	1	0-0	0	6.02
1994 Kansas City	AL	6	6	0	0	28.1	127	36	25	23	2	3	4	1	11	1	18	2	0	2	2	.500	0	0-0	0	7.31
1995 Kansas City	AL	16	13	1	0	81.1	338	78	35	33	7	1	4	2	33	0	31	2	0	3	4	.429	0	0-0	2	3.65
1996 Kansas City	AL	35	35	4	0	228	988	267	136	119	29	5	8	6	51	0	115	8	0	10	14	.417	1	0-0	0	4.70
1997 Kansas City	AL	8	3	0	1	24.2	110	29	16	12	1	2	1	2	5	2	16	1	0	1	2	.333	0	0-0	1	4.38
1998 KC-ChC		38	12	0	2	102.1	469	128	82	80	20	2	11	5	37	0	55	4	1	6	6	.500	0	0-1	0	7.04
1999 Cleveland	AL	13	4	0	1	40.1	178	43	22	21	3	0	0	3	16	0	22	0	0	0	0	.000	0	0-0	0	4.69
1992 Montreal	NL	9	6	1	2	38	165	40	25	23	6	0	3	4	10	0	27	5	1	2	3	.400	1	0-0	0	5.45
Kansas City	AL	7	7	1	0	42	174	35	18	18	5	0	3	0	16	2	27	0	0	2	3	.400	1	0-0	0	3.86
1998 Kansas City	AL	33	12	0	2	97.1	450	125	78	76	18	2	11	5	36	0	51	4	1	6	6	.500	0	0-1	0	7.03
Chicago	NL	5	0	0	0	5	19	3	4	4	2	0	0	0	1	0	4	0	0	0	0	.000	0	0-0	0	7.20
9 ML YEARS		171	125	8	6	793.2	3492	891	495	450	92	22	39	27	275	8	427	37	3	38	52	.422	4	0-1	3	5.10

Greg Hansell

Pitches: Right **Bats:** Right **Pos:** RP-33   **Ht:** 6'5" **Wt:** 215 **Born:** 3/12/71 **Age:** 29

		HOW MUCH HE PITCHED						WHAT HE GAVE UP											THE RESULTS						
Year Team	Lg	G	GS	CG	GF	IP	BFP	H	R	ER	HR	SH	SF	HB	TBB	IBB	SO	WP	Bk	W	L	Pct.	ShO	Sv-Op	Hld	ERA
1999 Nashville *	AAA	22	0	0	10	27	110	18	8	6	2	2	3	1	9	1	36	4	0	3	3	.500	0	2 -	—	2.00
1995 Los Angeles	NL	20	0	0	7	19.1	93	29	17	16	5	1	1	2	6	1	13	0	0	0	1	.000	0	0-1	1	7.45
1996 Minnesota	AL	50	0	0	23	74.1	329	83	48	47	14	3	2	2	31	1	46	9	1	3	0	1.000	0	3-4	3	5.69
1997 Milwaukee	AL	3	0	0	1	4.2	21	5	5	5	1	0	0	1	1	0	5	0	0	0	0	.000	0	0-0	0	9.64
1999 Pittsburgh	NL	33	0	0	9	39.1	168	42	20	17	5	3	1	3	11	3	34	2	0	1	3	.250	0	0-3	4	3.89
4 ML YEARS		106	0	0	40	137.2	611	159	90	85	25	7	4	8	49	5	98	11	1	4	4	.500	0	3-8	8	5.56

Dave Hansen

Bats: L **Throws:** R **Pos:** PH/PR-69; 1B-20; 3B-13; DH-2; RF-2   **Ht:** 6'0" **Wt:** 195 **Born:** 11/24/68 **Age:** 31

		BATTING																BASERUNNING				PERCENTAGES		
Year Team	Lg	G	AB	H	2B	3B	HR	(Hm	Rd)	TB	R	RBI	TBB	IBB	SO	HBP	SH	SF	SB	CS	SB%	GDP	Avg	OBP	SLG
1990 Los Angeles	NL	5	7	1	0	0	0	(0	0)	1	0	1	0	0	3	0	0	0	0	0	.00	0	.143	.143	.143
1991 Los Angeles	NL	53	56	15	4	0	1	(0	1)	22	3	5	2	0	12	0	0	0	1	0	1.00	2	.268	.293	.393
1992 Los Angeles	NL	132	341	73	11	0	6	(1	5)	102	30	22	34	3	49	1	0	2	0	2	.00	9	.214	.286	.299
1993 Los Angeles	NL	84	105	38	3	0	4	(2	2)	53	13	30	21	3	13	0	0	1	0	1	.00	0	.362	.465	.505
1994 Los Angeles	NL	40	44	15	3	0	0	(0	0)	18	3	5	5	0	5	0	0	0	0	0	.00	0	.341	.408	.409
1995 Los Angeles	NL	100	181	52	10	0	1	(0	1)	65	19	14	28	4	28	1	0	1	0	0	.00	4	.287	.384	.359
1996 Los Angeles	NL	80	104	23	1	0	0	(0	0)	24	7	6	11	1	22	0	0	1	0	0	.00	4	.221	.293	.231
1997 Chicago	NL	90	151	47	8	2	3	(1	2)	68	19	21	31	1	32	1	2	1	1	2	.33	0	.311	.429	.450
1999 Los Angeles	NL	100	107	27	8	1	2	(2	0)	43	14	17	26	0	20	2	0	1	0	0	.00	2	.252	.404	.402
9 ML YEARS		684	1096	291	48	3	17	(6	11)	396	108	121	158	12	184	5	2	7	2	5	.29	21	.266	.359	.361

Jed Hansen

Bats: R **Throws:** R **Pos:** 2B-21; PH/PR-13; SS-10; 3B-4; DH-3; CF-2; 1B-1   **Ht:** 6'1" **Wt:** 195 **Born:** 8/19/72 **Age:** 27

		BATTING																BASERUNNING				PERCENTAGES		
Year Team	Lg	G	AB	H	2B	3B	HR	(Hm	Rd)	TB	R	RBI	TBB	IBB	SO	HBP	SH	SF	SB	CS	SB%	GDP	Avg	OBP	SLG
1994 Eugene	A-	66	235	57	8	2	3	—	—	78	26	17	24	2	56	8	2	1	6	4	.60	1	.243	.332	.332
1995 Springfield	A	122	414	107	27	7	9	—	—	175	86	50	78	0	73	7	6	1	44	10	.81	8	.258	.384	.423
1996 Wichita	AA	99	405	116	27	4	12	—	—	187	60	50	29	0	72	4	4	2	14	8	.64	6	.286	.339	.462
Omaha	AAA	29	99	23	4	0	3	—	—	36	14	9	12	0	22	3	1	1	2	0	1.00	1	.232	.330	.364
1997 Omaha	AAA	114	380	102	20	2	11	—	—	159	43	44	32	0	78	2	5	2	8	1	.89	9	.268	.327	.418
1998 Omaha	AAA	127	417	116	19	7	16	—	—	197	63	56	44	0	125	4	4	7	17	9	.65	7	.278	.347	.472
1999 Omaha	AAA	54	175	48	8	5	7	—	—	87	35	22	32	2	72	3	3	0	8	3	.73	2	.274	.395	.497
1997 Kansas City	AL	34	94	29	6	1	1	(1	0)	40	11	14	13	0	29	1	2	1	3	2	.60	2	.309	.394	.426
1998 Kansas City	AL	4	3	0	0	0	0	(0	0)	0	0	0	0	0	3	0	0	0	0	0	.00	0	.000	.000	.000
1999 Kansas City	AL	49	79	16	1	0	3	(3	0)	26	16	5	10	0	32	0	4	1	0	1	.00	0	.203	.289	.329
3 ML YEARS		87	176	45	7	1	4	(4	0)	66	27	19	23	0	64	1	6	2	3	3	.50	2	.256	.342	.375

Tim Harikkala

Pitches: Right **Bats:** Right **Pos:** RP-7   **Ht:** 6'2" **Wt:** 185 **Born:** 7/15/71 **Age:** 28

			HOW MUCH HE PITCHED						WHAT HE GAVE UP										THE RESULTS					
Year Team	Lg	G	GS	CG	GF	IP	BFP	H	R	ER	HR	SH	SF	HB	TBB	IBB	SO	WP	Bk	W	L	Pct.	ShO	Sv-Op	Hld	ERA
1992 Bellingham	A-	15	2	0	2	33.1	145	37	15	10	2	3	2	0	16	0	18	1	2	2	0	1.000	0	1- -	—	2.70
1993 Bellingham	A-	4	0	0	0	8	30	3	1	1	0	0	0	1	2	0	12	0	0	1	0	1.000	0	0- -	—	1.13
Appleton	A	15	4	0	5	38.2	175	50	30	28	3	2	1	2	12	2	33	4	3	3	3	.500	0	0- -	—	6.52
1994 Appleton	A	13	13	3	0	93.2	373	69	31	20	6	2	3	5	24	0	63	5	0	8	3	.727	0	0- -	—	1.92
Riverside	A+	4	4	0	0	29	108	16	6	2	1	0	1	0	10	0	30	1	0	4	0	1.000	0	0- -	—	0.62
Jacksonville	AA	9	9	0	0	54.1	245	70	30	24	4	1	3	1	19	0	22	4	0	4	1	.800	0	0- -	—	3.98
1995 Tacoma	AAA	25	24	4	0	146.1	638	151	78	69	13	3	4	2	55	3	73	7	0	5	12	.294	1	0- -	—	4.24
1996 Tacoma	AAA	27	27	1	0	158.1	715	204	98	85	12	3	6	5	48	2	115	5	1	8	12	.400	1	0- -	—	4.83
1997 Tacoma	AAA	21	21	0	0	113.1	538	160	93	81	11	3	5	4	50	2	86	7	0	6	8	.429	0	0- -	—	6.43
Memphis	AA	5	5	1	0	33.2	146	39	18	14	3	0	1	3	4	0	26	1	0	3	1	.750	0	0- -	—	3.74
1998 Orlando	AA	15	15	3	0	103.1	429	112	56	52	9	5	2	7	14	0	55	0	0	5	7	.417	2	0- -	—	4.53
Tacoma	AAA	18	4	1	9	57	257	74	32	31	6	1	1	1	13	0	44	0	0	2	3	.400	1	1- -	—	4.89
1999 Pawtucket	AAA	14	1	0	4	30	141	44	19	18	2	0	1	2	7	1	19	0	0	1	2	.333	0	0- -	—	5.40
1995 Seattle	AL	1	0	0	1	3.1	18	7	6	6	1	0	0	0	1	0	1	0	0	0	0	.000	0	0-0	0	16.20
1996 Seattle	AL	1	1	0	0	4.1	20	4	6	6	1	1	0	1	2	0	1	0	0	0	1	.000	0	0-0	0	12.46
1999 Boston	AL	7	0	0	2	13	58	15	9	9	0	2	0	1	6	1	7	1	0	1	1	.500	0	0-0	0	6.23
3 ML YEARS		9	1	0	3	20.2	96	26	21	21	2	3	0	2	9	1	9	1	0	1	2	.333	0	0-0	0	9.15

Pete Harnisch

Pitches: Right **Bats:** Right **Pos:** SP-33   **Ht:** 6'0" **Wt:** 228 **Born:** 9/23/66 **Age:** 33

			HOW MUCH HE PITCHED						WHAT HE GAVE UP									THE RESULTS					
Year Team	Lg	G	GS	CG	GF	IP	BFP	H	R	ER	HR	SH	SF	HB	TBB	IBB	SO	WP	Bk	W	L	Pct.	ShO	Sv-Op	Hld	ERA
1988 Baltimore	AL	2	2	0	0	13	61	13	8	8	1	2	0	0	9	1	10	1	0	0	2	.000	0	0-0	0	5.54
1989 Baltimore	AL	18	17	2	1	103.1	468	97	55	53	10	4	5	5	64	3	70	5	1	5	9	.357	0	0-0	0	4.62
1990 Baltimore	AL	31	31	3	0	188.2	821	189	96	91	17	6	5	1	86	5	122	2	2	11	11	.500	0	0-0	0	4.34
1991 Houston	NL	33	33	4	0	216.2	900	169	71	65	14	9	7	5	83	3	172	5	2	12	9	.571	2	0-0	0	2.70
1992 Houston	NL	34	34	0	0	206.2	859	182	92	85	18	5	5	5	64	3	164	4	1	9	10	.474	0	0-0	0	3.70
1993 Houston	NL	33	33	5	0	217.2	896	171	84	72	20	9	4	6	79	5	185	3	1	16	9	.640	4	0-0	0	2.98
1994 Houston	NL	17	17	1	0	95	419	100	59	57	13	3	2	3	39	1	62	2	0	8	5	.615	0	0-0	0	5.40
1995 New York	NL	18	18	0	0	110	462	111	55	45	13	4	6	3	24	4	82	0	1	2	8	.200	0	0-0	0	3.68
1996 New York	NL	31	31	2	0	194.2	839	195	103	91	30	13	9	7	61	5	114	7	3	8	12	.400	1	0-0	0	4.21
1997 NYM-Mil		10	8	0	0	39.2	186	48	33	31	6	0	2	1	23	1	22	2	0	1	2	.333	0	0-0	0	7.03
1998 Cincinnati	NL	32	32	2	0	209	854	176	79	73	24	8	5	6	64	4	157	4	1	14	7	.667	1	0-0	0	3.14
1999 Cincinnati	NL	33	33	2	0	198.1	833	190	86	81	25	10	6	5	57	2	120	3	0	16	10	.615	2	0-0	0	3.68
1997 New York	NL	6	5	0	0	25.2	121	35	24	23	5	0	2	1	11	1	12	1	0	0	1	.000	0	0-0	0	8.06
Milwaukee	AL	4	3	0	0	14	65	13	9	8	1	0	0	0	12	0	10	1	0	1	1	.500	0	0-0	0	5.14
12 ML YEARS		292	289	21	1	1792.2	7598	1641	821	752	191	73	56	47	653	37	1280	38	12	102	94	.520	10	0-0	0	3.78

Lenny Harris

Bats: L **Throws:** R **Pos:** PH/PR-74; 2B-24; RF-13; 3B-7; LF-3; DH-2   **Ht:** 5'10" **Wt:** 225 **Born:** 10/28/64 **Age:** 35

			BATTING															BASERUNNING				PERCENTAGES		
Year Team	Lg	G	AB	H	2B	3B	HR	(Hm	Rd)	TB	R	RBI	TBB	IBB	SO	HBP	SH	SF	SB	CS	SB%	GDP	Avg	OBP	SLG
1988 Cincinnati	NL	16	43	16	1	0	0	(0	0)	17	7	8	5	0	4	0	1	2	4	1	.80	0	.372	.420	.395
1989 Cin-LA	NL	115	335	79	10	1	3	(1	2)	100	36	26	20	0	33	2	1	0	14	9	.61	14	.236	.283	.299
1990 Los Angeles	NL	137	431	131	16	4	2	(0	2)	161	61	29	29	2	31	1	3	1	15	10	.60	8	.304	.348	.374
1991 Los Angeles	NL	145	429	123	16	1	3	(1	2)	150	59	38	37	5	32	5	12	2	12	3	.80	16	.287	.349	.350
1992 Los Angeles	NL	135	347	94	11	0	0	(0	0)	105	28	30	24	3	24	1	6	2	19	7	.73	10	.271	.318	.303
1993 Los Angeles	NL	107	160	38	6	1	2	(0	2)	52	20	11	15	4	15	0	1	0	3	1	.75	4	.238	.303	.325
1994 Cincinnati	NL	66	100	31	3	1	0	(0	0)	36	13	14	5	0	13	0	0	1	7	2	.78	0	.310	.340	.360
1995 Cincinnati	NL	101	197	41	8	3	2	(0	2)	61	32	16	14	0	20	0	3	1	10	1	.91	6	.208	.259	.310
1996 Cincinnati	NL	125	302	86	17	2	5	(2	3)	122	33	32	21	1	31	1	6	3	14	6	.70	3	.285	.330	.404
1997 Cincinnati	NL	120	238	65	13	1	3	(2	1)	89	32	28	18	1	18	2	3	2	4	3	.57	10	.273	.327	.374
1998 Cin-NYM	NL	132	290	75	15	0	6	(2	4)	108	30	27	17	3	21	2	4	4	6	5	.55	13	.259	.300	.372
1999 Col-Ari	NL	110	187	58	13	0	1	(1	0)	74	17	20	6	0	7	0	0	1	2	1	.67	7	.310	.330	.396
1989 Los Angeles	NL	61	188	42	4	0	2	(0	2)	52	17	11	9	0	20	1	1	0	10	6	.63	5	.223	.263	.277
Los Angeles	NL	54	147	37	6	1	1	(1	0)	48	19	15	11	0	13	1	0	0	4	3	.57	9	.252	.308	.327
1998 Cincinnati	NL	57	122	36	8	0	0	(0	0)	44	12	10	8	2	9	1	0	2	1	3	.25	8	.295	.338	.361
New York	NL	75	168	39	7	0	6	(2	4)	64	18	17	9	1	12	1	4	2	5	2	.71	5	.232	.272	.381
1999 Colorado	NL	91	158	47	12	0	0	(0	0)	59	15	13	6	0	6	0	0	1	1	1	.50	7	.297	.323	.373
Arizona	NL	19	29	11	1	0	1	(1	0)	15	2	7	0	0	1	0	0	1	1	0	1.00	0	.379	.367	.517
12 ML YEARS		1309	3059	837	129	14	27	(9	18)	1075	368	279	211	19	249	14	40	19	110	49	.69	91	.274	.322	.351

Reggie Harris

Pitches: Right **Bats:** Right **Pos:** RP-8   **Ht:** 6'1" **Wt:** 217 **Born:** 8/12/68 **Age:** 31

			HOW MUCH HE PITCHED						WHAT HE GAVE UP										THE RESULTS					
Year Team	Lg	G	GS	CG	GF	IP	BFP	H	R	ER	HR	SH	SF	HB	TBB	IBB	SO	WP	Bk	W	L	Pct.	ShO	Sv-Op	Hld	ERA
1999 Louisville *	AAA	41	0	0	37	40	182	43	21	21	7	0	2	3	20	1	45	5	0	3	4	.429	0	16- -	—	4.73
1990 Oakland	AL	16	1	0	9	41.1	168	25	16	16	5	1	2	2	21	1	31	2	0	1	0	1.000	0	0-0	0	3.48
1991 Oakland	AL	2	0	0	1	3	15	5	4	4	0	0	1	0	3	1	2	2	0	0	0	.000	0	0-0	0	12.00
1996 Boston	AL	4	0	0	1	4.1	24	7	6	6	2	0	0	1	5	0	4	0	0	0	0	.000	0	0-1	0	12.46
1997 Philadelphia	NL	50	0	0	13	54.1	264	55	33	32	1	3	4	5	43	1	45	5	1	1	3	.250	0	0-0	1	5.30
1998 Houston	NL	6	0	0	2	6	26	6	4	4	1	0	1	0	2	0	2	0	0	0	0	.000	0	0-0	1	6.00

Year Team	Lg	G	GS	CG	GF	IP	BFP	H	R	ER	HR	SH	SF	HB	TBB	IBB	SO	WP	Bk	W	L	Pct.	ShO	Sv-Op	Hld	ERA
				HOW MUCH HE PITCHED						**WHAT HE GAVE UP**												**THE RESULTS**				
1999 Milwaukee	NL	8	0	0	2	12	53	8	4	4	1	0	1	2	7	0	11	2	0	0	0	.000	0	0-0		3.00
6 ML YEARS		86	1	0	28	121	550	106	67	66	10	4	9	10	81	3	95	11	1	2	3	.400	0	0-1	2	4.91

Chad Harville

Pitches: Right **Bats:** Right **Pos:** RP-15   **Ht:** 5'9" **Wt:** 180 **Born:** 9/16/76 **Age:** 23

Year Team	Lg	G	GS	CG	GF	IP	BFP	H	R	ER	HR	SH	SF	HB	TBB	IBB	SO	WP	Bk	W	L	Pct.	ShO	Sv-Op	Hld	ERA
				HOW MUCH HE PITCHED						**WHAT HE GAVE UP**												**THE RESULTS**				
1997 Sou Oregon	A-	3	0	0	1	5	23	3	0	0	0	1	0	2	3	0	6	0	0	1	0	1.000	0	0--	—	0.00
Visalia	A+	14	0	0	1	18.2	92	25	14	12	2	1	1	0	13	1	24	1	3	0	0	.000	0	0--	—	5.79
1998 Visalia	A+	24	7	0	12	69	294	59	25	23	0	0	2	5	31	0	76	6	2	4	3	.571	0	4--	—	3.00
Huntsville	AA	12	0	0	10	14.2	63	6	4	4	0	0	1	1	13	1	24	1	0	0	0	.000	0	8--	—	2.45
1999 Midland	AA	17	0	0	16	22.1	90	13	6	5	1	0	1	1	9	0	35	2	0	2	0	1.000	0	7--	—	2.01
Vancouver	AAA	22	0	0	19	25.2	114	24	5	5	0	0	0	3	11	1	36	4	0	1	0	1.000	0	11--	—	1.75
1999 Oakland	AL	15	0	0	8	14.1	69	18	11	11	2	0	1	0	10	1	15	3	1	0	2	.000	0	0-0	0	6.91

Shigetoshi Hasegawa

Pitches: Right **Bats:** Right **Pos:** RP-63; SP-1   **Ht:** 5'11" **Wt:** 171 **Born:** 8/1/68 **Age:** 31

Year Team	Lg	G	GS	CG	GF	IP	BFP	H	R	ER	HR	SH	SF	HB	TBB	IBB	SO	WP	Bk	W	L	Pct.	ShO	Sv-Op	Hld	ERA
				HOW MUCH HE PITCHED						**WHAT HE GAVE UP**												**THE RESULTS**				
1997 Anaheim	AL	50	7	0	17	116.2	497	118	60	51	14	5	5	3	46	6	83	2	1	3	7	.300	0	0-1	3	3.93
1998 Anaheim	AL	61	0	0	20	97.1	401	86	37	34	14	4	6	2	32	2	73	5	2	8	3	.727	0	5-7	10	3.14
1999 Anaheim	AL	64	1	0	26	77	333	80	45	42	14	3	4	2	34	2	44	4	0	4	6	.400	0	2-5	6	4.91
3 ML YEARS		175	8	0	63	291	1231	284	142	127	42	12	15	7	112	10	200	11	3	15	16	.484	0	7-13	19	3.93

Bill Haselman

Bats: Right **Throws:** Right **Pos:** C-39; DH-9; PH/PR-6   **Ht:** 6'3" **Wt:** 223 **Born:** 5/25/66 **Age:** 34

Year Team	Lg	G	AB	H	2B	3B	HR	(Hm	Rd)	TB	R	RBI	TBB	IBB	SO	HBP	SH	SF	SB	CS	SB%	GDP	Avg	OBP	SLG
							BATTING													**BASERUNNING**			**PERCENTAGES**		
1990 Texas	AL	7	13	2	0	0	0	(0	0)	2	0	3	1	0	5	0	0	0	0	0	.00	0	.154	.214	.154
1992 Seattle	AL	8	19	5	0	0	0	(0	0)	5	1	0	0	0	7	0	0	0	0	0	.00	1	.263	.263	.263
1993 Seattle	AL	58	137	35	8	0	5	(3	2)	58	21	16	12	0	19	1	2	2	2	1	.67	5	.255	.316	.423
1994 Seattle	AL	38	83	16	7	1	1	(1	0)	28	11	8	3	0	11	1	1	0	1	0	1.00	1	.193	.230	.337
1995 Boston	AL	64	152	37	6	1	5	(3	2)	60	22	23	17	0	30	2	0	3	0	2	.00	4	.243	.322	.395
1996 Boston	AL	77	237	65	13	1	8	(5	3)	104	33	34	19	3	52	1	0	0	4	2	.67	13	.274	.331	.439
1997 Boston	AL	67	212	50	15	0	6	(3	3)	83	22	26	15	2	44	2	1	2	0	2	.00	8	.236	.290	.392
1998 Texas	AL	40	105	33	6	0	6	(4	2)	57	11	17	3	0	17	0	0	2	0	0	.00	2	.314	.327	.543
1999 Detroit	AL	48	143	39	8	0	4	(2	2)	59	13	14	10	1	26	0	0	0	2	0	1.00	4	.273	.320	.413
9 ML YEARS		407	1101	282	63	3	35	(21	14)	456	134	141	80	6	211	7	4	9	9	7	.56	39	.256	.308	.414

Scott Hatteberg

Bats: Left **Throws:** Right **Pos:** C-23; DH-6; PH/PR-4   **Ht:** 6'1" **Wt:** 205 **Born:** 12/14/69 **Age:** 30

Year Team	Lg	G	AB	H	2B	3B	HR	(Hm	Rd)	TB	R	RBI	TBB	IBB	SO	HBP	SH	SF	SB	CS	SB%	GDP	Avg	OBP	SLG
							BATTING													**BASERUNNING**			**PERCENTAGES**		
1999 Red Sox *	R	6	15	6	2	0	1	—	—	11	4	6	7	0	1	0	0	0	0	0	.00	1	.400	.591	.733
Sarasota *	A+	1	1	1	0	0	0	—	—	1	0	1	0	0	0	1	0	0	0	0	.00	0	1.000	1.000	1.000
Pawtucket *	AAA	10	34	6	2	0	0	—	—	8	3	4	4	0	6	0	0	0	0	0	.00	2	.176	.263	.235
1995 Boston	AL	2	2	1	0	0	0	(0	0)	1	1	0	0	0	0	0	0	0	0	0	.00	1	.500	.500	.500
1996 Boston	AL	10	11	2	0	0	0	(0	0)	3	3	0	3	0	2	0	0	0	0	0	.00	0	.182	.357	.273
1997 Boston	AL	114	350	97	23	1	10	(5	5)	152	46	44	40	2	70	2	2	1	0	1	.00	11	.277	.354	.434
1998 Boston	AL	112	359	99	23	1	12	(4	8)	160	46	43	43	3	58	5	0	3	0	0	.00	11	.276	.359	.446
1999 Boston	AL	30	80	22	5	0	1	(1	0)	30	12	11	18	0	14	1	0	1	0	0	.00	2	.275	.410	.375
5 ML YEARS		268	802	221	52	2	23	(10	13)	346	108	98	104	5	144	8	2	5	0	1	.00	27	.276	.362	.431

LaTroy Hawkins

Pitches: Right **Bats:** Right **Pos:** SP-33   **Ht:** 6'5" **Wt:** 204 **Born:** 12/21/72 **Age:** 27

Year Team	Lg	G	GS	CG	GF	IP	BFP	H	R	ER	HR	SH	SF	HB	TBB	IBB	SO	WP	Bk	W	L	Pct.	ShO	Sv-Op	Hld	ERA
				HOW MUCH HE PITCHED						**WHAT HE GAVE UP**												**THE RESULTS**				
1995 Minnesota	AL	6	6	1	0	27	131	39	29	26	3	0	3	1	12	0	9	1	1	2	3	.400	0	0-0	0	8.67
1996 Minnesota	AL	7	6	0	1	26.1	124	42	24	24	8	1	1	0	9	0	24	1	1	1	1	.500	0	0-0	0	8.20
1997 Minnesota	AL	20	20	0	0	103.1	478	134	71	67	19	2	2	4	47	0	58	6	3	6	12	.333	0	0-0	0	5.84
1998 Minnesota	AL	33	33	0	0	190.1	840	227	114	111	27	4	10	5	61	1	105	10	2	7	14	.333	0	0-0	0	5.25
1999 Minnesota	AL	33	33	1	0	174.1	803	238	136	129	29	1	5	1	60	2	103	9	0	10	14	.417	0	0-0	0	6.66
5 ML YEARS		99	98	2	1	521.1	2376	680	386	357	86	8	21	11	189	3	299	27	7	26	44	.371	0	0-0	0	6.16

Charlie Hayes

Bats: R **Throws:** R **Pos:** 3B-55; PH/PR-24; 1B-20; DH-2; LF-1   **Ht:** 6'0" **Wt:** 215 **Born:** 5/29/65 **Age:** 35

Year Team	Lg	G	AB	H	2B	3B	HR	(Hm	Rd)	TB	R	RBI	TBB	IBB	SO	HBP	SH	SF	SB	CS	SB%	GDP	Avg	OBP	SLG
							BATTING													**BASERUNNING**			**PERCENTAGES**		
1988 San Francisco	NL	7	11	1	0	0	0	(0	0)	1	0	0	0	0	3	0	0	0	0	0	.00	0	.091	.091	.091

Year Team	Lg	G	AB	H	2B	3B	HR	(Hm	Rd)	TB	R	RBI	TBB	IBB	SO	HBP	SH	SF	SB	CS	SB%	GDP	Avg	OBP	SLG
1989 SF-Phi	NL	87	304	78	15	1	8	(3	5)	119	26	43	11	1	50	0	2	3	3	1	.75	6	.257	.280	.391
1990 Philadelphia	NL	152	561	145	20	0	10	(3	7)	195	56	57	28	3	91	2	0	6	4	4	.50	12	.258	.293	.348
1991 Philadelphia	NL	142	460	106	23	1	12	(6	6)	167	34	53	16	3	75	1	2	1	3	3	.50	13	.230	.257	.363
1992 New York	AL	142	509	131	19	2	18	(7	11)	208	52	66	28	0	100	3	3	6	3	5	.38	12	.257	.297	.409
1993 Colorado	NL	157	573	175	45	2	25	(17	8)	299	89	98	43	6	82	5	1	8	11	6	.65	25	.305	.355	.522
1994 Colorado	NL	113	423	122	23	4	10	(4	6)	183	46	50	36	4	71	3	0	1	3	6	.33	11	.288	.348	.433
1995 Philadelphia	NL	141	529	146	30	3	11	(6	5)	215	58	85	50	2	88	4	0	6	5	1	.83	22	.276	.340	.406
1996 Pit-NYY	NL	148	526	133	24	2	12	(5	7)	197	58	75	37	4	90	0	3	3	6	0	1.00	17	.253	.300	.375
1997 New York	AL	100	353	91	16	0	11	(5	6)	140	39	53	40	2	66	1	0	4	3	2	.60	13	.258	.332	.397
1998 San Francisco	NL	111	329	94	8	0	12	(7	5)	138	39	62	34	0	61	0	1	2	2	1	.67	4	.286	.351	.419
1999 San Francisco	NL	95	264	54	9	1	6	(2	4)	83	33	48	33	0	41	1	0	3	3	1	.75	8	.205	.292	.314
1989 San Francisco	NL	3	5	1	0	0	0	(0	0)	1	0	0	0	0	1	0	0	0	0	0	.00	0	.200	.200	.200
Philadelphia	NL	84	299	77	15	1	8	(3	5)	118	26	43	11	1	49	0	2	3	3	1	.75	6	.258	.281	.395
1996 Pittsburgh	NL	128	459	114	21	2	10	(5	5)	169	51	62	36	4	78	0	2	3	6	0	1.00	16	.248	.301	.368
New York	AL	20	67	19	3	0	2	(0	2)	28	7	13	1	0	12	0	1	0	0	0	.00	1	.284	.294	.418
12 ML YEARS		1395	4842	1276	232	16	135	(65	70)	1945	530	690	356	25	818	20	12	43	46	30	.61	143	.264	.314	.402

Jimmy Haynes

Pitches: Right Bats: Right Pos: SP-25; RP-5 Ht: 6'4" Wt: 203 Born: 9/5/72 Age: 27

Year Team	Lg	G	GS	CG	GF	IP	BFP	H	R	ER	HR	SH	SF	HB	TBB	IBB	SO	WP	Bk	W	L	Pct.	ShO	Sv-Op	Hld	ERA
1995 Baltimore	AL	4	3	0	0	24	94	11	6	6	2	1	0	0	12	1	22	0	0	2	1	.667	0	0-0	0	2.25
1996 Baltimore	AL	26	11	0	8	89	435	122	84	82	14	4	5	2	58	1	65	5	0	3	6	.333	0	1-1	0	8.29
1997 Oakland	AL	13	13	0	0	73.1	329	74	38	36	7	1	4	2	40	1	65	4	1	3	6	.333	0	0-0	0	4.42
1998 Oakland	AL	33	33	1	0	194.1	875	229	124	110	25	5	9	5	88	4	134	11	0	11	9	.550	1	0-0	0	5.09
1999 Oakland	AL	30	25	0	2	142	652	158	112	100	21	4	5	2	80	3	93	7	2	7	12	.368	0	0-0	0	6.34
5 ML YEARS		106	85	1	10	522.2	2385	594	364	334	69	15	23	11	278	10	379	27	3	26	34	.433	1	1-1	0	5.75

Rick Heiserman

Pitches: Right Bats: Right Pos: RP-3 Ht: 6'7" Wt: 225 Born: 2/22/73 Age: 27

Year Team	Lg	G	GS	CG	GF	IP	BFP	H	R	ER	HR	SH	SF	HB	TBB	IBB	SO	WP	Bk	W	L	Pct.	ShO	Sv-Op	Hld	ERA
1994 Watertown	A-	7	0	0	2	11.2	48	6	3	3	0	0	1	1	5	0	6	2	2	1	0	1.000	0	0--	—	2.31
1995 Kinston	A+	19	19	1	0	113	470	97	55	47	13	3	4	9	42	1	86	6	1	9	3	.750	0	0--	—	3.74
St. Pete	A+	6	5	0	1	28	118	28	18	17	2	0	2	1	11	0	18	4	0	2	3	.400	0	0--	—	5.46
1996 St. Pete	A+	26	26	1	0	155.1	663	168	68	56	8	6	3	9	41	0	104	4	0	10	8	.556	1	0--	—	3.24
1997 Arkansas	AA	34	20	1	9	131.2	569	151	73	61	19	6	2	8	36	2	90	8	0	5	8	.385	1	4--	—	4.17
Louisville	AAA	1	0	0	1	2	10	2	1	1	1	0	0	0	1	0	0	0	0	0	0	.000	0	0--	—	4.50
1998 Arkansas	AA	18	0	0	18	16.1	76	20	11	9	1	1	0	1	5	0	9	2	0	0	3	.000	0	9--	—	4.96
Memphis	AAA	40	0	0	16	40.1	185	54	21	18	2	2	1	2	14	1	28	1	0	3	4	.400	0	6--	—	4.02
1999 Memphis	AAA	52	0	0	38	61.2	266	67	37	35	7	1	1	4	21	1	57	6	0	2	3	.400	0	20--	—	5.11
1999 St. Louis	NL	3	0	0	0	4.1	24	8	4	4	2	0	0	0	4	0	4	2	0	0	0	.000	0	0-0	1	8.31

Rick Helling

Pitches: Right Bats: Right Pos: SP-35 Ht: 6'3" Wt: 220 Born: 12/15/70 Age: 29

Year Team	Lg	G	GS	CG	GF	IP	BFP	H	R	ER	HR	SH	SF	HB	TBB	IBB	SO	WP	Bk	W	L	Pct.	ShO	Sv-Op	Hld	ERA
1994 Texas	AL	9	9	1	0	52	228	62	34	34	14	0	0	0	18	0	25	4	1	3	2	.600	0	0-0	0	5.88
1995 Texas	AL	3	3	0	0	12.1	62	17	11	9	2	0	2	2	8	0	5	0	0	0	2	.000	0	0-0	0	6.57
1996 Tex-Fla		11	6	0	2	48	198	37	23	23	9	1	1	0	16	0	42	1	1	3	3	.500	0	0-0	0	4.31
1997 Fla-Tex		41	16	0	9	131	550	108	67	65	17	3	9	6	69	2	99	3	0	5	9	.357	0	0-1	6	4.47
1998 Texas	AL	33	33	4	0	216.1	922	209	109	106	27	6	10	1	78	6	164	10	0	20	7	.741	2	0-0	0	4.41
1999 Texas	AL	35	35	3	0	219.1	943	228	127	118	41	5	10	6	85	5	131	8	0	13	11	.542	0	0-0	0	4.84
1996 Texas	AL	6	2	0	2	20.1	92	23	17	17	7	0	1	0	9	0	16	1	0	1	2	.333	0	0-0	1	7.52
Florida	NL	5	4	0	0	27.2	106	14	6	6	2	1	0	0	7	0	26	0	1	2	1	.667	0	0-0	0	1.95
1997 Florida	NL	31	8	0	8	76	324	61	38	37	12	2	7	4	48	2	53	0	0	2	6	.250	0	0-1	6	4.38
Texas	AL	10	8	0	1	55	226	47	29	28	5	1	2	2	21	0	46	3	0	3	3	.500	0	0-0	0	4.58
6 ML YEARS		132	102	8	11	679	2903	661	371	355	110	15	32	15	274	13	466	26	2	44	34	.564	3	0-1	7	4.71

Todd Helton

Bats: Left Throws: Left Pos: 1B-156; PH/PR-7 Ht: 6'2" Wt: 206 Born: 8/20/73 Age: 26

Year Team	Lg	G	AB	H	2B	3B	HR	(Hm	Rd)	TB	R	RBI	TBB	IBB	SO	HBP	SH	SF	SB	CS	SB%	GDP	Avg	OBP	SLG
1997 Colorado	NL	35	93	26	2	1	5	(3	2)	45	13	11	8	0	11	0	0	0	0	1	.00	1	.280	.337	.484
1998 Colorado	NL	152	530	167	37	1	25	(13	12)	281	78	97	53	5	54	6	1	5	3	3	.50	15	.315	.380	.530
1999 Colorado	NL	159	578	185	39	5	35	(23	12)	339	114	113	68	6	77	6	0	4	7	6	.54	14	.320	.395	.587
3 ML YEARS		346	1201	378	78	7	65	(39	26)	665	205	221	129	11	142	12	1	9	10	10	.50	30	.315	.384	.554

Bret Hemphill

Bats: Both   **Throws:** Right   **Pos:** C-12   **Ht:** 6'3"   **Wt:** 210   **Born:** 12/17/71   **Age:** 28

Year Team	Lg	G	AB	H	2B	3B	HR	(Hm	Rd)	TB	R	RBI	TBB	IBB	SO	HBP	SH	SF	SB	CS	SB%	GDP	Avg	OBP	SLG
1994 Boise	A-	71	252	74	16	1	3	—	—	101	44	36	40	2	53	1	1	6	1	1	.50	6	.294	.385	.401
1995 Lk Elsinore	A+	45	146	29	7	0	1	—	—	39	12	17	18	0	36	3	0	3	2	1	.67	4	.199	.294	.267
Cedar Rapds	A	72	234	59	11	1	8	—	—	96	36	28	21	0	54	4	1	4	0	2	.00	5	.252	.319	.410
1996 Lk Elsinore	A+	108	399	105	21	3	17	—	—	183	64	64	52	1	93	4	6	1	4	3	.57	7	.263	.353	.459
1997 Midland	AA	78	266	82	15	2	10	—	—	131	46	63	47	2	56	1	1	5	0	2	.00	6	.308	.417	.492
1998 Vancouver	AAA	47	155	39	10	2	4	—	—	65	16	12	12	0	33	0	0	0	0	1	.00	4	.252	.305	.419
1999 Edmonton	AAA	74	246	77	16	1	7	—	—	116	29	31	31	0	58	4	7	2	1	0	1.00	8	.313	.396	.472
1999 Anaheim	AL	12	21	3	0	0	0	(0	0)	3	3	2	4	0	4	0	1	1	0	0	.00	1	.143	.269	.143

Rickey Henderson

Bats: Right   **Throws:** Left   **Pos:** LF-116; PH/PR-5; DH-1   **Ht:** 5'10"   **Wt:** 190   **Born:** 12/25/58   **Age:** 41

Year Team	Lg	G	AB	H	2B	3B	HR	(Hm	Rd)	TB	R	RBI	TBB	IBB	SO	HBP	SH	SF	SB	CS	SB%	GDP	Avg	OBP	SLG
1979 Oakland	AL	89	351	96	13	3	1	(1	0)	118	49	26	34	0	39	2	8	3	33	11	.75	4	.274	.338	.336
1980 Oakland	AL	158	591	179	22	4	9	(3	6)	236	111	53	117	7	54	5	6	3	100	26	.79	6	.303	.420	.399
1981 Oakland	AL	108	423	135	18	7	6	(5	1)	185	89	35	64	4	68	2	0	4	56	22	.72	7	.319	.408	.437
1982 Oakland	AL	149	536	143	24	4	10	(5	5)	205	119	51	116	1	94	2	0	2	130	42	.76	5	.267	.398	.382
1983 Oakland	AL	145	513	150	25	7	9	(5	4)	216	105	48	103	8	80	4	1	1	108	19	.85	11	.292	.414	.421
1984 Oakland	AL	142	502	147	27	4	16	(7	9)	230	113	58	86	1	81	5	1	3	66	18	.79	7	.293	.399	.458
1985 New York	AL	143	547	172	28	5	24	(8	16)	282	146	72	99	1	65	3	0	5	80	10	.89	8	.314	.419	.516
1986 New York	AL	153	608	160	31	5	28	(13	15)	285	130	74	89	2	81	2	0	2	87	18	.83	12	.263	.358	.469
1987 New York	AL	95	358	104	17	3	17	(10	7)	178	78	37	80	1	52	2	0	0	41	8	.84	10	.291	.423	.497
1988 New York	AL	140	554	169	30	2	6	(2	4)	221	118	50	82	1	54	3	2	6	93	13	.88	6	.305	.394	.399
1989 NYY-Oak	AL	150	541	148	26	3	12	(7	5)	216	113	57	126	5	68	3	0	4	77	14	.85	8	.274	.411	.399
1990 Oakland	AL	136	489	159	33	3	28	(8	20)	282	119	61	97	2	60	4	2	2	65	10	.87	13	.325	.439	.577
1991 Oakland	AL	134	470	126	17	1	18	(8	10)	199	105	57	98	7	73	7	0	3	58	18	.76	7	.268	.400	.423
1992 Oakland	AL	117	396	112	18	3	15	(10	5)	181	77	46	95	5	56	6	0	3	48	11	.81	5	.283	.426	.457
1993 Oak-Tor	AL	134	481	139	22	2	21	(10	11)	228	114	59	120	7	65	4	1	4	53	8	.87	9	.289	.432	.474
1994 Oakland	AL	87	296	77	13	0	6	(4	2)	108	66	20	72	1	45	5	1	2	22	7	.76	0	.260	.411	.365
1995 Oakland	AL	112	407	122	31	1	9	(3	6)	182	67	54	72	2	66	4	1	3	32	10	.76	8	.300	.407	.447
1996 San Diego	NL	148	465	112	17	2	9	(6	3)	160	110	29	125	2	90	10	0	2	37	15	.71	5	.241	.410	.344
1997 SD-Ana	AL	120	403	100	14	0	8	(6	2)	138	84	34	97	2	85	6	1	2	45	8	.85	10	.248	.400	.342
1998 Oakland	AL	152	542	128	16	1	14	(6	8)	188	101	57	118	0	114	5	2	3	66	13	.84	5	.236	.376	.347
1999 New York	NL	121	438	138	30	0	12	(1	11)	204	89	42	82	1	82	2	1	3	37	14	.73	4	.315	.423	.466
1989 New York	AL	65	235	58	13	1	3	(1	2)	82	41	22	56	0	29	1	0	1	25	8	.76	0	.247	.392	.349
Oakland	AL	85	306	90	13	2	9	(6	3)	134	72	35	70	5	39	2	0	3	52	6	.90	8	.294	.425	.438
1993 Oakland	AL	90	318	104	19	1	17	(8	9)	176	77	47	85	6	46	2	0	2	31	6	.84	8	.327	.469	.553
Toronto	AL	44	163	35	3	1	4	(2	2)	52	37	12	35	1	19	2	1	2	22	2	.92	1	.215	.356	.319
1997 San Diego	NL	88	288	79	11	0	6	(5	1)	108	63	27	71	2	62	4	0	2	29	4	.88	7	.274	.422	.375
Anaheim	AL	32	115	21	3	0	2	(1	1)	30	21	7	26	0	23	2	1	0	16	4	.80	3	.183	.343	.261
21 ML YEARS		2733	9911	2816	472	60	278	(128	150)	4242	2103	1020	1972	60	1472	86	27	60	1334	315	.81	150	.284	.405	.428

Butch Henry

Pitches: Left   **Bats:** Left   **Pos:** SP-4; RP-3   **Ht:** 6'1"   **Wt:** 205   **Born:** 10/7/68   **Age:** 31

Year Team	Lg	G	GS	CG	GF	IP	BFP	H	R	ER	HR	SH	SF	HB	TBB	IBB	SO	WP	Bk	W	L	Pct.	ShO	Sv-Op	Hld	ERA
1999 Tacoma *	AAA	3	3	0	0	5	18	4	0	0	0	0	0	0	1	0	3	0	0	2	0	1.000	0	0--	—	0.00
1992 Houston	NL	28	28	2	0	165.2	710	185	81	74	16	12	7	1	41	7	96	2	2	6	9	.400	1	0-0	0	4.02
1993 Col-Mon	NL	30	16	1	4	103	467	135	76	70	15	6	6	1	28	2	47	1	0	3	9	.250	0	0-0	0	6.12
1994 Montreal	NL	24	15	0	1	107.1	433	97	30	29	10	5	3	2	20	1	70	1	0	8	3	.727	0	1-1	2	2.43
1995 Montreal	NL	21	21	1	0	126.2	524	133	47	40	11	7	3	2	28	3	60	0	1	7	9	.438	1	0-0	0	2.84
1997 Boston	AL	36	5	0	13	84.1	345	89	36	33	6	2	3	0	19	2	51	0	0	7	3	.700	0	6-8	4	3.52
1998 Boston	AL	2	2	0	0	9	38	8	4	4	2	0	0	1	3	0	6	0	0	0	0	.000	0	0-0	0	4.00
1999 Seattle	AL	9	0	0	0	25	112	32	15	14	1	0	1	2	10	0	15	0	0	2	0	1.000	0	0-0	1	5.04
1993 Colorado	NL	20	15	1	1	84.2	390	117	66	62	14	6	5	1	24	2	39	1	0	8	2	.200	0	0-0	0	6.59
Montreal	NL	10	1	0	3	18.1	77	18	10	8	1	0	1	0	4	0	8	0	0	1	1	.500	0	0-0	0	3.93
7 ML YEARS		148	91	4	18	621	2629	677	289	264	61	32	23	9	149	15	345	4	3	33	33	.500	2	7-9	7	3.83

Doug Henry

Pitches: Right   **Bats:** Right   **Pos:** RP-35   **Ht:** 6'4"   **Wt:** 205   **Born:** 12/10/63   **Age:** 36

Year Team	Lg	G	GS	CG	GF	IP	BFP	H	R	ER	HR	SH	SF	HB	TBB	IBB	SO	WP	Bk	W	L	Pct.	ShO	Sv-Op	Hld	ERA
1999 New Orleans *	AAA	4	0	0	1	4	20	4	2	2	0	0	0	1	3	0	3	1	0	0	0	.000	0	0--	—	4.50
Jackson *	AA	2	1	0	1	2	10	2	1	1	0	0	0	0	1	0	3	0	0	0	1	.000	0	0--	—	4.50
1991 Milwaukee	AL	32	0	0	25	36	137	16	4	4	1	1	2	0	14	1	28	0	0	2	1	.667	0	15-16	3	1.00
1992 Milwaukee	AL	68	0	0	56	65	277	64	34	29	6	1	2	0	24	4	52	4	0	1	4	.200	0	29-33	1	4.02
1993 Milwaukee	AL	54	0	0	41	55	260	67	37	34	7	5	4	3	25	8	38	4	0	4	4	.500	0	17-24	0	5.56
1994 Milwaukee	AL	25	0	0	7	31.1	143	32	17	16	7	1	0	1	23	1	20	3	0	2	3	.400	0	0-0	4	4.60
1995 New York	NL	51	0	0	20	67	273	48	23	22	7	3	2	1	25	6	62	6	1	3	6	.333	0	4-7	6	2.96
1996 New York	NL	58	0	0	33	75	343	82	48	39	7	3	3	1	36	6	58	6	1	2	8	.200	0	9-14	8	4.68
1997 San Francisco	NL	75	0	0	25	70.2	317	70	45	37	5	4	3	1	41	6	69	3	0	4	5	.444	0	3-6	21	4.71
1998 Houston	NL	59	0	0	25	71	296	55	25	24	9	3	3	0	35	5	59	7	0	8	2	.800	0	2-5	11	3.04

			HOW MUCH HE PITCHED				WHAT HE GAVE UP										THE RESULTS						
Year Team	Lg	G	GS	CG	GF	IP	BFP	H	R	ER	HR	SH	SF	HB	TBB	IBB	SO	WP	Bk	W	L	Pct.	ShO	Sv-Op	Hld	ERA
1999 Houston	NL	35	0	0	17	40.2	188	45	24	21	8	1	0	3	24	0	36	0	0	2	3	.400	0	2-4	2	4.65
9 ML YEARS		457	0	0	249	511.2	2234	479	257	226	57	22	19	10	247	37	422	33	2	28	36	.438	0	81-109	56	3.98

Pat Hentgen

Pitches: Right **Bats:** Right **Pos:** SP-34   **Ht:** 6'2" **Wt:** 195 **Born:** 11/13/68 **Age:** 31

			HOW MUCH HE PITCHED				WHAT HE GAVE UP										THE RESULTS						
Year Team	Lg	G	GS	CG	GF	IP	BFP	H	R	ER	HR	SH	SF	HB	TBB	IBB	SO	WP	Bk	W	L	Pct.	ShO	Sv-Op	Hld	ERA
1991 Toronto	AL	3	1	0	1	7.1	30	5	2	2	1	1	0	2	3	0	3	1	0	0	0	.000	0	0-0	0	2.45
1992 Toronto	AL	28	2	0	10	50.1	229	49	30	30	7	2	2	0	32	5	39	2	1	5	2	.714	0	0-1	1	5.36
1993 Toronto	AL	34	32	3	0	216.1	926	215	103	93	27	6	5	7	74	0	122	11	1	19	9	.679	0	0-0	0	3.87
1994 Toronto	AL	24	24	6	0	174.2	728	158	74	66	21	6	3	3	59	1	147	5	1	13	8	.619	3	0-0	0	3.40
1995 Toronto	AL	30	30	2	0	200.2	913	236	129	114	24	2	1	5	90	6	135	7	2	10	14	.417	0	0-0	0	5.11
1996 Toronto	AL	35	35	10	0	265.2	1100	238	105	95	20	5	8	5	94	3	177	8	0	20	10	.667	3	0-0	0	3.22
1997 Toronto	AL	35	35	9	0	264	1085	253	116	108	31	9	3	7	71	2	160	6	2	15	10	.600	3	0-0	0	3.68
1998 Toronto	AL	29	29	0	0	177.2	795	208	109	102	28	5	7	5	69	1	94	7	1	12	11	.522	0	0-0	0	5.17
1999 Toronto	AL	34	34	1	0	199	869	225	115	106	32	3	11	3	65	1	118	8	1	11	12	.478	0	0-0	0	4.79
9 ML YEARS		252	222	31	11	1555.2	6675	1587	783	716	191	39	40	37	557	19	995	55	9	105	76	.580	9	0-1	1	4.14

Felix Heredia

Pitches: Left **Bats:** Left **Pos:** RP-69   **Ht:** 6'0" **Wt:** 180 **Born:** 6/18/76 **Age:** 24

			HOW MUCH HE PITCHED				WHAT HE GAVE UP										THE RESULTS						
Year Team	Lg	G	GS	CG	GF	IP	BFP	H	R	ER	HR	SH	SF	HB	TBB	IBB	SO	WP	Bk	W	L	Pct.	ShO	Sv-Op	Hld	ERA
1996 Florida	NL	21	0	0	5	16.2	78	21	8	8	1	0	1	0	10	1	10	2	0	1	1	.500	0	0-0	2	4.32
1997 Florida	NL	56	0	0	10	56.2	259	53	30	27	3	2	2	5	30	1	54	2	0	5	3	.625	0	0-1	7	4.29
1998 Fla-ChC	NL	71	2	0	18	58.2	268	57	39	33	2	1	2	1	38	3	54	6	1	3	3	.500	0	2-5	17	5.06
1999 Chicago	NL	69	0	0	15	52	237	56	35	28	7	1	4	1	25	2	50	2	0	1	1	.750	0	1-7	12	4.85
1998 Florida	NL	41	2	0	12	41	194	38	30	25	1	1	2	1	32	2	38	5	1	0	3	.000	0	2-3	9	5.49
Chicago	NL	30	0	0	6	17.2	74	19	9	8	1	0	0	0	6	1	16	1	0	3	0	1.000	0	0-2	8	4.08
4 ML YEARS		217	2	0	48	184	842	187	112	96	13	4	9	7	103	7	168	12	1	12	8	.600	0	3-13	38	4.70

Gil Heredia

Pitches: Right **Bats:** Right **Pos:** SP-33   **Ht:** 6'1" **Wt:** 221 **Born:** 10/26/65 **Age:** 34

			HOW MUCH HE PITCHED				WHAT HE GAVE UP										THE RESULTS						
Year Team	Lg	G	GS	CG	GF	IP	BFP	H	R	ER	HR	SH	SF	HB	TBB	IBB	SO	WP	Bk	W	L	Pct.	ShO	Sv-Op	Hld	ERA
1991 San Francisco	NL	7	4	0	1	33	126	27	14	14	4	2	1	0	7	2	13	1	0	2	0	.000	0	0-0	0	3.82
1992 SF-Mon	NL	20	5	0	4	44.2	187	44	23	21	4	2	1	1	20	1	22	1	0	2	3	.400	0	0-0	1	4.23
1993 Montreal	NL	20	9	1	2	57.1	246	66	28	25	4	4	1	2	14	2	40	0	0	4	2	.667	0	2-3	1	3.92
1994 Montreal	NL	39	3	0	8	75.1	325	85	34	29	7	3	4	2	13	3	62	4	1	6	3	.667	0	0-0	5	3.46
1995 Montreal	NL	40	18	0	5	119	509	137	60	57	7	9	4	5	21	1	74	1	0	5	6	.455	0	1-3	1	4.31
1996 Texas	AL	44	0	0	21	73.1	320	91	50	48	12	1	2	1	14	2	43	2	0	2	5	.286	0	1-4	7	5.89
1998 Oakland	AL	8	6	0	2	42.2	175	43	14	13	4	1	0	3	3	0	27	0	0	3	3	.500	0	0-0	0	2.74
1999 Oakland	AL	33	33	1	0	200.1	852	228	119	107	22	3	0	8	34	4	117	2	1	13	8	.619	0	0-0	0	4.81
1992 San Francisco	NL	13	4	0	3	30	132	32	20	18	3	0	0	1	16	1	15	1	0	2	3	.400	0	0-0	1	5.40
Montreal	NL	7	1	0	1	14.2	55	12	3	3	1	2	1	0	4	0	7	0	0	0	0	.000	0	0-0	0	1.84
8 ML YEARS		211	78	2	43	645.2	2740	721	342	314	64	25	13	22	126	15	398	11	2	35	32	.522	0	4-10	15	4.38

Matt Herges

Pitches: Right **Bats:** Left **Pos:** RP-17   **Ht:** 6'0" **Wt:** 200 **Born:** 4/1/70 **Age:** 30

			HOW MUCH HE PITCHED				WHAT HE GAVE UP										THE RESULTS						
Year Team	Lg	G	GS	CG	GF	IP	BFP	H	R	ER	HR	SH	SF	HB	TBB	IBB	SO	WP	Bk	W	L	Pct.	ShO	Sv-Op	Hld	ERA
1992 Yakima	A-	27	0	0	23	44.2	194	33	21	16	2	1	0	3	24	1	57	2	3	2	3	.400	0	9- -		3.22
1993 Bakersfield	A+	51	0	0	17	90.1	403	70	49	37	6	6	4	10	56	6	84	4	3	2	6	.250	0	2- -		3.69
1994 Vero Beach	A+	48	3	1	12	111	476	115	45	41	8	8	2	4	33	3	61	3	3	8	9	.471	0	3- -		3.32
1995 San Antonio	AA	19	0	0	13	27.2	130	34	16	15	2	3	0	0	16	1	18	3	0	0	3	.000	0	8- -		4.88
San Berndno	A+	22	2	0	4	51.2	231	58	29	21	3	2	1	2	15	0	35	0	0	5	2	.714	0	1- -		3.66
1996 San Antonio	AA	30	6	0	10	83	355	83	38	25	3	2	5	2	28	0	45	5	1	3	2	.600	0	3- -		2.71
Albuquerque	AAA	10	4	2	1	34.2	140	33	11	10	2	2	2	0	14	0	15	1	0	4	1	.800	1	0- -		2.60
1997 Albuquerque	AAA	31	12	0	5	85	417	120	92	84	13	5	4	9	46	1	61	5	0	0	8	.000	0	0- -		8.89
San Antonio	AA	4	3	0	0	15.1	74	22	15	15	2	0	0	2	10	0	12	3	0	0	1	.000	0	0- -		8.80
1998 San Antonio	AA	3	0	0	0	6	21	3	0	0	0	0	0	0	2	0	3	0	0	0	0	.000	0	0- -		0.00
Albuquerque	AAA	34	8	0	9	88.1	406	115	64	56	9	6	4	5	37	1	75	4	0	3	5	.375	0	0- -		5.71
1999 Albuquerque	AAA	21	21	2	0	131.1	563	135	82	69	17	7	5	7	47	0	88	4	0	8	3	.727	0	0- -		4.73
1999 Los Angeles	NL	17	0	0	9	24.1	104	24	13	11	5	1	0	1	8	0	18	0	0	0	2	.000	0	0-2	1	4.07

Chad Hermansen

Bats: R **Throws:** R **Pos:** CF-9; RF-6; LF-3; PH/PR-2   **Ht:** 6'2" **Wt:** 185 **Born:** 9/10/77 **Age:** 22

			BATTING																BASERUNNING				PERCENTAGES		
Year Team	Lg	G	AB	H	2B	3B	HR	(Hm	Rd)	TB	R	RBI	TBB	IBB	SO	HBP	SH	SF	SB	CS	SB%	GDP	Avg	OBP	SLG
1995 Pirates	R	24	92	28	10	1	3	—	—	49	14	17	9	1	19	0	0	1	0	0	.00	2	.304	.363	.533
Erie	A-	44	165	45	8	3	6	—	—	77	30	25	18	0	39	4	0	2	4	2	.67	6	.273	.354	.467
1996 Augusta	A	62	226	57	11	3	14	—	—	116	41	41	38	5	65	8	0	1	11	3	.79	1	.252	.377	.513

Year Team	Lg	G	AB	H	2B	3B	HR	(Hm	Rd)	TB	R	RBI	TBB	IBB	SO	HBP	SH	SF	SB	CS	SB%	GDP	Avg	OBP	SLG
Lynchburg	A+	66	251	69	11	3	10	—	—	116	40	46	29	1	56	3	0	4	5	1	.83	8	.275	.352	.462
1997 Carolina	AA	129	487	134	31	4	20	—	—	233	87	70	69	5	136	10	0	5	18	6	.75	3	.275	.373	.478
1998 Nashville	AAA	126	458	118	26	5	28	—	—	238	81	78	50	0	152	4	0	3	21	4	.84	3	.258	.334	.520
1999 Nashville	AAA	125	496	134	27	3	32	—	—	263	89	97	35	1	119	4	0	4	19	10	.66	9	.270	.321	.530
1999 Pittsburgh	NL	19	60	14	3	0	1	(0	1)	20	5	1	7	1	19	1	1	0	2	2	.50	0	.233	.324	.333

Dustin Hermanson

Pitches: Right **Bats:** Right **Pos:** SP-34   **Ht:** 6'3" **Wt:** 205 **Born:** 12/21/72 **Age:** 27

Year Team	Lg	G	GS	CG	GF	IP	BFP	H	R	ER	HR	SH	SF	HB	TBB	IBB	SO	WP	Bk	W	L	Pct.	ShO	Sv-Op	Hld	ERA
1995 San Diego	NL	26	0	0	6	31.2	151	35	26	24	8	3	0	1	22	1	19	3	0	3	1	.750	0	0-0	1	6.82
1996 San Diego	NL	8	0	0	4	13.2	62	18	15	13	3	2	3	0	4	0	11	0	1	1	0	1.000	0	0-0	0	8.56
1997 Montreal	NL	32	28	1	0	158.1	656	134	68	65	15	10	6	1	66	2	136	4	1	8	8	.500	1	0-0	0	3.69
1998 Montreal	NL	32	30	1	0	187	768	163	80	65	21	9	3	3	56	3	154	4	3	14	11	.560	1	0-0	1	3.13
1999 Montreal	NL	34	34	0	0	216.1	928	225	110	101	20	16	7	7	69	4	145	4	1	9	14	.391	0	0-0	0	4.20
5 ML YEARS		132	92	2	10	607	2565	575	299	268	67	40	19	12	217	10	465	15	6	35	34	.507	1	0-0	2	3.97

Carlos Hernandez

Bats: Right **Throws:** Right **Pos:** C   **Ht:** 5'10" **Wt:** 215 **Born:** 5/24/67 **Age:** 33

Year Team	Lg	G	AB	H	2B	3B	HR	(Hm	Rd)	TB	R	RBI	TBB	IBB	SO	HBP	SH	SF	SB	CS	SB%	GDP	Avg	OBP	SLG
1990 Los Angeles	NL	10	20	4	1	0	0	(0	0)	5	2	1	0	0	2	0	0	0	0	0	.00	0	.200	.200	.250
1991 Los Angeles	NL	15	14	3	1	0	0	(0	0)	4	1	1	0	0	5	1	0	1	1	0	1.00	2	.214	.250	.286
1992 Los Angeles	NL	69	173	45	4	0	3	(1	2)	58	11	17	11	1	21	4	0	2	0	1	.00	8	.260	.316	.335
1993 Los Angeles	NL	50	99	25	5	0	2	(1	1)	36	6	7	2	0	11	0	1	0	0	0	.00	0	.253	.267	.364
1994 Los Angeles	NL	32	64	14	2	0	2	(0	2)	22	6	6	1	0	14	0	0	0	0	0	.00	0	.219	.231	.344
1995 Los Angeles	NL	45	94	14	1	0	2	(1	1)	21	3	8	7	0	25	1	1	0	0	0	.00	5	.149	.216	.223
1996 Los Angeles	NL	13	14	4	0	0	0	(0	0)	4	1	0	2	0	2	0	0	0	0	0	.00	0	.286	.375	.286
1997 San Diego	NL	50	134	42	7	1	3	(2	1)	60	15	14	3	0	27	0	1	0	2	0	.00	5	.313	.328	.448
1998 San Diego	NL	129	390	102	15	0	9	(7	2)	144	34	52	16	2	54	9	0	2	2	2	.50	19	.262	.305	.369
9 ML YEARS		413	1002	253	36	1	21	(12	9)	354	79	106	42	3	161	15	3	5	3	5	.38	39	.252	.291	.353

Carlos Hernandez

Bats: Right **Throws:** Right **Pos:** PH/PR-10; 2B-7; SS-2   **Ht:** 5'9" **Wt:** 175 **Born:** 12/12/75 **Age:** 24

Year Team	Lg	G	AB	H	2B	3B	HR	(Hm	Rd)	TB	R	RBI	TBB	IBB	SO	HBP	SH	SF	SB	CS	SB%	GDP	Avg	OBP	SLG
1994 Astros	R	51	192	62	10	1	0	—	—	74	45	23	19	0	22	4	2	1	25	7	.78	1	.323	.394	.385
1995 Quad City	A	126	470	122	19	6	4	—	—	165	74	40	39	1	68	11	9	1	58	21	.73	4	.260	.330	.351
1996 Quad City	A	112	456	123	15	7	5	—	—	167	67	49	27	0	71	4	9	5	41	14	.75	6	.270	.313	.366
1997 Jackson	AA	92	363	106	12	1	4	—	—	132	62	33	33	2	59	4	6	3	17	8	.68	7	.292	.355	.364
1998 New Orleans	AAA	134	494	147	23	2	1	—	—	177	64	54	21	3	81	12	7	1	29	11	.73	10	.298	.341	.358
1999 New Orleans	AAA	94	355	104	14	0	0	—	—	118	56	43	27	1	65	10	3	3	22	13	.63	5	.293	.357	.332
1999 Houston	NL	16	14	2	0	0	0	(0	0)	2	1	0	1	0	6	0	0	1	3	1	.75	0	.143	.143	.143

Jose Hernandez

Bats: R **Throws:** R **Pos:** SS-137; CF-14; LF-7; PH/PR-5; 1B-2; RF-2   **Ht:** 6'1" **Wt:** 180 **Born:** 7/14/69 **Age:** 30

Year Team	Lg	G	AB	H	2B	3B	HR	(Hm	Rd)	TB	R	RBI	TBB	IBB	SO	HBP	SH	SF	SB	CS	SB%	GDP	Avg	OBP	SLG
1991 Texas	AL	45	98	18	2	1	0	(0	0)	22	8	4	3	0	31	0	6	0	1	0	.00	1	.184	.208	.224
1992 Cleveland	AL	3	4	0	0	0	0	(0	0)	0	0	0	0	0	2	0	0	0	0	0	.00	0	.000	.000	.000
1994 Chicago	NL	56	132	32	2	3	1	—	—	43	18	9	8	0	29	1	5	0	2	2	.50	4	.242	.291	.326
1995 Chicago	NL	93	245	60	11	4	13	(6	7)	118	37	40	13	3	69	0	8	2	1	0	1.00	8	.245	.281	.482
1996 Chicago	NL	131	331	80	14	1	10	(4	6)	126	52	41	24	4	97	1	5	2	4	0	1.00	10	.242	.293	.381
1997 Chicago	NL	121	183	50	8	5	7	(4	3)	89	33	26	14	2	42	0	1	1	2	5	.29	5	.273	.323	.486
1998 Chicago	NL	149	488	124	23	7	23	(11	12)	230	76	75	40	3	140	1	2	2	4	6	.40	12	.254	.311	.471
1999 ChC-Atl	NL	147	508	135	20	2	19	(6	13)	216	79	62	52	6	145	5	2	1	11	3	.79	10	.266	.339	.425
1999 Chicago	NL	99	342	93	12	2	15	(5	10)	154	57	43	40	3	101	5	1	0	7	2	.78	5	.272	.357	.450
Atlanta	NL	48	166	42	8	0	4	(1	3)	62	22	19	12	3	44	0	1	1	4	1	.80	5	.253	.302	.373
8 ML YEARS		745	1989	499	80	23	73	(31	42)	844	303	257	154	18	555	8	29	8	24	17	.59	51	.251	.306	.424

Livan Hernandez

Pitches: Right **Bats:** Right **Pos:** SP-30   **Ht:** 6'2" **Wt:** 225 **Born:** 2/20/75 **Age:** 25

Year Team	Lg	G	GS	CG	GF	IP	BFP	H	R	ER	HR	SH	SF	HB	TBB	IBB	SO	WP	Bk	W	L	Pct.	ShO	Sv-Op	Hld	ERA
1996 Florida	NL	1	0	0	0	3	13	3	0	0	0	0	0	0	2	0	2	0	0	0	0	.000	0	0-0	0	0.00
1997 Florida	NL	17	17	0	0	96.1	405	81	39	34	5	4	7	3	38	1	72	0	0	9	3	.750	0	0-0	0	3.18
1998 Florida	NL	33	33	9	0	234.1	1040	265	133	123	37	8	5	6	104	8	162	4	3	10	12	.455	0	0-0	0	4.72
1999 Fla-SF	NL	30	30	2	0	199.2	886	227	110	103	23	7	6	2	76	5	144	2	2	8	12	.400	0	0-0	0	4.64
1999 Florida	NL	20	20	2	0	136	612	161	78	72	17	3	4	2	55	3	97	2	1	5	9	.357	0	0-0	0	4.76
San Francisco	NL	10	10	0	0	63.2	274	66	32	31	6	4	2	0	21	2	47	0	1	3	3	.500	0	0-0	0	4.38
4 ML YEARS		81	80	11	0	533.1	2344	576	282	260	65	19	18	11	220	14	380	6	5	27	27	.500	0	0-0	0	4.39

Orlando Hernandez

Pitches: Right **Bats:** Right **Pos:** SP-33 **Ht:** 6'2" **Wt:** 210 **Born:** 10/11/65 **Age:** 34

			HOW MUCH HE PITCHED					WHAT HE GAVE UP										THE RESULTS					
Year Team	Lg	G	GS	CG	GF	IP	BFP	H	R	ER	HR	SH	SF	HB	TBB	IBB	SO	WP	Bk	W	L	Pct.	ShO	Sv-Op	Hld	ERA
1998 Tampa	A+	2	2	0	0	9	37	3	2	1	0	0	0	4	3	0	15	1	0	1	1	.500	0	0- -	—	1.00
Columbus	AAA	7	7	0	0	42.1	182	41	19	18	2	2	1	5	17	0	59	1	0	6	0	1.000	0	0- -	—	3.83
1998 New York	AL	21	21	3	0	141	574	113	53	49	11	3	5	6	52	1	131	5	2	12	4	.750	1	0-0	0	3.13
1999 New York	AL	33	33	2	0	214.1	910	187	108	98	24	3	11	8	87	2	157	4	0	17	9	.654	1	0-0	0	4.12
2 ML YEARS		54	54	5	0	355.1	1484	300	161	147	35	6	16	14	139	3	288	9	2	29	13	.690	2	0-0	0	3.72

Ramon Hernandez

Bats: Right **Throws:** Right **Pos:** C-40 **Ht:** 6'0" **Wt:** 227 **Born:** 5/20/76 **Age:** 24

					BATTING													BASERUNNING				PERCENTAGES		
Year Team	Lg	G	AB	H	2B	3B	HR	(Hm	Rd)	TB	R	RBI	TBB	IBB	SO	HBP	SH	SF	SB	CS	SB%	GDP	Avg	OBP	SLG
1995 Athletics	R	48	143	52	9	6	4	—	—	85	37	37	39	1	16	8	0	4	6	2	.75	3	.364	.510	.594
1996 W Michigan	A	123	447	114	26	2	12	—	—	180	62	68	69	1	62	4	1	7	2	3	.40	22	.255	.355	.403
1997 Visalia	A+	86	332	120	21	2	15	—	—	190	57	85	35	1	47	9	0	8	2	4	.33	5	.361	.427	.572
Huntsville	AA	44	161	31	3	0	4	—	—	46	27	24	18	0	23	3	0	3	0	0	.00	8	.193	.281	.286
1998 Huntsville	AA	127	479	142	24	1	15	—	—	213	83	98	57	2	61	19	2	6	4	5	.44	15	.296	.389	.445
1999 Vancouver	AAA	77	291	76	11	3	13	—	—	132	38	55	23	1	37	7	2	4	1	2	.33	13	.261	.326	.454
1999 Oakland	AL	40	136	38	7	0	3	(1	2)	54	13	21	18	0	11	1	1	2	1	0	1.00	5	.279	.363	.397

Roberto Hernandez

Pitches: Right **Bats:** Right **Pos:** RP-72 **Ht:** 6'4" **Wt:** 250 **Born:** 11/11/64 **Age:** 35

				HOW MUCH HE PITCHED				WHAT HE GAVE UP											THE RESULTS					
Year Team	Lg	G	GS	CG	GF	IP	BFP	H	R	ER	HR	SH	SF	HB	TBB	IBB	SO	WP	Bk	W	L	Pct.	ShO	Sv-Op	Hld	ERA
1991 Chicago	AL	9	3	0	1	15	69	18	15	13	1	0	0	0	7	0	6	1	0	1	0	1.000	0	0-0	0	7.80
1992 Chicago	AL	43	0	0	27	71	277	45	15	13	4	0	3	4	20	1	68	2	0	7	3	.700	0	12-16	6	1.65
1993 Chicago	AL	70	0	0	67	78.2	314	66	21	20	6	2	2	0	20	1	71	2	0	3	4	.429	0	38-44	5	2.29
1994 Chicago	AL	45	0	0	43	47.2	206	44	29	26	5	0	1	1	19	1	50	1	0	4	4	.500	0	14-20	4	4.91
1995 Chicago	AL	60	0	0	57	59.2	272	63	30	26	9	4	0	3	28	4	84	1	0	3	7	.300	0	32-42	0	3.92
1996 Chicago	AL	72	0	0	61	84.2	355	65	21	18	2	2	2	0	38	5	85	6	0	6	5	.545	0	38-46	0	1.91
1997 CWS-SF		74	0	0	50	80.2	340	67	24	22	7	2	1	1	38	5	82	3	0	10	3	.769	0	31-39	9	2.45
1998 Tampa Bay	AL	67	0	0	58	71.1	310	55	33	32	5	4	0	5	41	4	55	1	0	2	6	.250	0	26-35	0	4.04
1999 Tampa Bay	AL	72	0	0	66	73.1	321	68	27	25	1	2	3	4	33	1	69	3	0	2	3	.400	0	43-47	0	3.07
1997 Chicago	AL	46	0	0	43	48	203	38	15	13	5	1	1	1	24	4	47	2	0	5	1	.833	0	27-31	0	2.44
San Francisco	NL	28	0	0	7	32.2	137	29	9	9	2	1	0	0	14	1	35	1	0	5	2	.714	0	4-8	9	2.48
9 ML YEARS		512	3	0	430	582	2464	491	215	195	40	16	12	18	244	22	570	20	0	38	35	.521	0	234-289	15	3.02

Orel Hershiser

Pitches: Right **Bats:** Right **Pos:** SP-32 **Ht:** 6'3" **Wt:** 195 **Born:** 9/16/58 **Age:** 41

				HOW MUCH HE PITCHED				WHAT HE GAVE UP											THE RESULTS					
Year Team	Lg	G	GS	CG	GF	IP	BFP	H	R	ER	HR	SH	SF	HB	TBB	IBB	SO	WP	Bk	W	L	Pct.	ShO	Sv-Op	Hld	ERA
1983 Los Angeles	NL	8	0	0	4	8	37	7	6	3	1	1	0	0	6	0	5	1	0	0	0	.000	0	1-1	0	3.38
1984 Los Angeles	NL	45	20	8	10	189.2	771	160	65	56	9	2	3	4	50	8	150	8	1	11	8	.579	4	2-3	0	2.66
1985 Los Angeles	NL	36	34	9	1	239.2	953	179	72	54	8	5	4	6	68	5	157	5	0	19	3	.864	5	0-0	0	2.03
1986 Los Angeles	NL	35	35	8	0	231.1	988	213	112	99	13	14	6	3	86	11	153	12	3	14	14	.500	1	0-0	0	3.85
1987 Los Angeles	NL	37	35	10	2	264.2	1093	247	105	90	17	8	2	9	74	5	190	11	2	16	16	.500	1	1-1	0	3.06
1988 Los Angeles	NL	35	34	15	1	267	1068	208	73	67	18	9	6	4	73	10	178	6	5	23	8	.742	8	1-1	0	2.26
1989 Los Angeles	NL	35	33	8	0	256.2	1047	226	75	66	9	19	6	3	77	14	178	8	4	15	15	.500	4	0-0	0	2.31
1990 Los Angeles	NL	4	4	0	0	25.1	106	26	12	12	1	1	0	1	4	0	16	0	1	1	1	.500	0	0-0	0	4.26
1991 Los Angeles	NL	21	21	0	0	112	473	112	43	43	3	2	1	5	32	6	73	2	4	7	2	.778	0	0-0	0	3.46
1992 Los Angeles	NL	33	33	1	0	210.2	910	209	101	86	15	15	6	8	69	13	130	10	0	10	15	.400	0	0-0	0	3.67
1993 Los Angeles	NL	33	33	5	0	215.2	913	201	86	86	17	12	4	7	72	13	141	7	0	12	14	.462	1	0-0	0	3.59
1994 Los Angeles	NL	21	21	1	0	135.1	575	146	67	57	15	4	3	2	42	6	72	6	2	6	6	.500	0	0-0	0	3.79
1995 Cleveland	AL	26	26	1	0	167.1	683	151	76	72	21	3	4	5	51	1	111	3	0	16	6	.727	1	0-0	0	3.87
1996 Cleveland	AL	33	33	1	0	206	908	238	115	97	21	5	4	12	58	4	125	11	1	15	9	.625	0	0-0	0	4.24
1997 Cleveland	AL	32	32	1	0	195.1	826	199	105	97	26	6	8	11	69	2	107	11	0	14	6	.700	0	0-0	0	4.47
1998 San Francisco	NL	34	34	0	0	202	887	200	105	99	22	12	5	13	85	7	126	12	0	11	10	.524	0	0-0	0	4.41
1999 New York	NL	32	32	0	0	179	776	175	92	91	14	6	8	11	77	2	89	6	0	13	12	.520	0	0-0	0	4.58
17 ML YEARS		500	460	68	18	3105.2	13014	2897	1330	1175	230	124	70	106	993	107	2001	119	23	203	145	.583	25	5-6	0	3.41

Richard Hidalgo

Bats: R **Throws:** R **Pos:** LF-97; CF-30; RF-3; PH/PR-2 **Ht:** 6'3" **Wt:** 190 **Born:** 7/2/75 **Age:** 24

					BATTING													BASERUNNING				PERCENTAGES		
Year Team	Lg	G	AB	H	2B	3B	HR	(Hm	Rd)	TB	R	RBI	TBB	IBB	SO	HBP	SH	SF	SB	CS	SB%	GDP	Avg	OBP	SLG
1997 Houston	NL	19	62	19	5	0	2	(0	2)	30	8	6	4	0	18	1	0	0	1	0	1.00	0	.306	.358	.484
1998 Houston	NL	74	211	64	15	0	7	(3	4)	100	31	35	17	0	37	2	0	4	3	3	.50	5	.303	.355	.474
1999 Houston	NL	108	383	87	25	2	15	(5	10)	161	49	56	56	2	73	4	0	5	8	5	.62	5	.227	.328	.420
3 ML YEARS		201	656	170	45	2	24	(8	16)	291	88	97	77	2	128	7	0	9	12	8	.60	10	.259	.339	.444

Bob Higginson

Bats: Left **Throws:** Right **Pos:** RF-88; DH-17; PH/PR-3   **Ht:** 5'11" **Wt:** 195 **Born:** 8/18/70 **Age:** 29

Year Team	Lg	G	AB	H	2B	3B	HR	(Hm	Rd)	TB	R	RBI	TBB	IBB	SO	HBP	SH	SF	SB	CS	SB%	GDP	Avg	OBP	SLG
1995 Detroit	AL	131	410	92	17	5	14	(10	4)	161	61	43	62	3	107	5	2	7	6	4	.60	5	.224	.329	.393
1996 Detroit	AL	130	440	141	35	0	26	(15	11)	254	75	81	65	7	66	1	3	6	6	3	.67	7	.320	.404	.577
1997 Detroit	AL	146	546	163	30	5	27	(16	11)	284	94	101	70	2	85	3	0	4	12	7	.63	10	.299	.379	.520
1998 Detroit	AL	157	612	174	37	4	25	(10	15)	294	92	85	63	2	101	6	0	4	3	3	.50	16	.284	.355	.480
1999 Detroit	AL	107	377	90	18	0	12	(8	4)	144	51	46	64	2	66	2	0	2	4	6	.40	2	.239	.351	.382
5 ML YEARS		671	2385	660	137	14	104	(59	45)	1137	373	356	324	16	425	17	5	23	31	23	.57	40	.277	.364	.477

Erik Hiljus

Pitches: Right **Bats:** Right **Pos:** RP-6   **Ht:** 6'5" **Wt:** 230 **Born:** 12/25/72 **Age:** 27

Year Team	Lg	G	GS	CG	GF	IP	BFP	H	R	ER	HR	SH	SF	HB	TBB	IBB	SO	WP	Bk	W	L	Pct.	ShO	Sv-Op	Hld	ERA
1991 Mets	R	9	9	1	0	38	183	31	27	18	1	0	1	1	37	0	38	5	1	2	3	.400	1	0- -	—	4.26
1992 Kingsport	R+	12	11	0	1	70.2	317	66	49	40	5	2	2	2	40	0	63	7	2	3	6	.333	0	0- -	—	5.09
1993 Capital Cty	A	27	27	1	0	145.2	640	114	76	70	8	2	7	4	111	1	157	17	4	7	10	.412	0	0- -	—	4.32
1994 St. Lucie	A+	26	26	3	0	160.2	709	159	85	71	8	6	10	5	90	3	140	10	8	11	10	.524	1	0- -	—	3.98
1995 St. Lucie	A+	17	17	0	0	111.1	453	85	46	37	4	6	5	3	50	2	98	10	6	8	4	.667	0	0- -	—	2.99
Binghamton	AA	10	10	0	0	55.1	252	60	38	36	8	2	1	1	32	1	40	4	2	2	4	.333	0	0- -	—	5.86
1996 Arkansas	AA	10	10	0	0	45.2	221	62	37	31	6	3	2	0	30	1	21	4	0	3	5	.375	0	0- -	—	6.11
1998 Jacksnville	AA	42	0	0	17	65.2	280	49	31	27	7	2	3	0	35	0	85	4	0	2	3	.400	0	2- -	—	3.70
1999 Lakeland	A+	3	0	0	1	4	15	4	1	1	0	0	0	0	0	0	9	0	1	0	0	.000	0	0- -	—	2.25
Jacksnville	AA	10	0	0	3	17.1	65	5	4	2	1	3	1	1	5	0	28	1	1	1	0	1.000	0	0- -	—	1.04
Toledo	AAA	33	0	0	9	59.1	239	49	31	29	5	5	2	2	16	0	73	5	0	2	3	.400	0	5- -	—	4.40
1999 Detroit	AL	6	0	0	0	8.2	35	7	5	5	2	0	1	0	5	0	1	0	0	0	0	.000	0	0-0	1	5.19

Glenallen Hill

Bats: R **Throws:** R **Pos:** PH/PR-39; LF-37; RF-26; DH-4   **Ht:** 6'2" **Wt:** 230 **Born:** 3/22/65 **Age:** 35

Year Team	Lg	G	AB	H	2B	3B	HR	(Hm	Rd)	TB	R	RBI	TBB	IBB	SO	HBP	SH	SF	SB	CS	SB%	GDP	Avg	OBP	SLG
1989 Toronto	AL	19	52	15	0	0	1	(1	0)	18	4	7	3	0	12	0	0	0	2	1	.67	0	.288	.327	.346
1990 Toronto	AL	84	260	60	11	3	12	(7	5)	113	47	32	18	0	62	0	0	0	8	3	.73	5	.231	.281	.435
1991 Tor-Cle	AL	72	221	57	8	2	8	(3	5)	93	29	25	23	0	54	0	1	3	6	4	.60	7	.258	.324	.421
1992 Cleveland	AL	102	369	89	16	1	18	(7	11)	161	38	49	20	0	73	4	0	1	9	6	.60	11	.241	.287	.436
1993 Cle-ChC		97	261	69	14	2	15	(5	10)	132	33	47	17	1	71	1	1	4	8	3	.73	4	.264	.307	.506
1994 Chicago	NL	89	269	80	12	1	10	(7	3)	124	48	38	29	0	57	0	0	1	19	6	.76	5	.297	.365	.461
1995 San Francisco	NL	132	497	131	29	4	24	(13	11)	240	71	86	39	4	98	1	0	2	25	5	.83	11	.264	.317	.483
1996 San Francisco	NL	98	379	106	26	0	19	(9	10)	189	56	67	33	3	95	6	0	3	6	3	.67	6	.280	.344	.499
1997 San Francisco	NL	128	398	104	28	4	11	(3	8)	173	47	64	19	0	87	4	0	7	7	4	.64	8	.261	.297	.435
1998 Sea-ChC		122	390	121	25	2	20	(11	9)	210	63	56	28	2	79	3	0	1	1	1	.50	16	.310	.360	.538
1999 Chicago	NL	99	253	76	9	1	20	(11	9)	147	43	55	22	1	61	0	0	3	5	1	.83	7	.300	.353	.581
1991 Toronto	AL	35	99	25	5	2	3	(2	1)	43	14	11	7	0	24	0	0	2	2	2	.50	2	.253	.296	.434
Cleveland		37	122	32	3	0	5	(1	4)	50	15	14	16	0	30	0	1	1	4	2	.67	5	.262	.345	.410
1993 Cleveland	AL	66	174	39	7	2	5	(0	5)	65	19	25	11	1	50	1	1	4	7	3	.70	3	.224	.268	.374
Chicago	NL	31	87	30	7	0	10	(5	5)	67	14	22	6	0	21	0	0	0	1	0	1.00	1	.345	.387	.770
1998 Seattle	AL	74	259	75	20	2	12	(5	7)	135	37	33	14	1	45	3	0	1	1	1	.50	13	.290	.332	.521
Chicago	NL	48	131	46	5	0	8	(6	2)	75	26	23	14	1	34	0	0	0	0	0		3	.351	.414	.573
11 ML YEARS		1042	3349	908	178	20	158	(73	85)	1600	479	526	251	11	749	19	2	25	96	37	.72	80	.271	.323	.478

Ken Hill

Pitches: Right **Bats:** Right **Pos:** SP-22; RP-4   **Ht:** 6'2" **Wt:** 214 **Born:** 12/14/65 **Age:** 34

Year Team	Lg	G	GS	CG	GF	IP	BFP	H	R	ER	HR	SH	SF	HB	TBB	IBB	SO	WP	Bk	W	L	Pct.	ShO	Sv-Op	Hld	ERA
1988 St. Louis	NL	4	1	0	0	14	62	16	9	8	0	0	0	0	6	0	6	1	0	0	1	.000	0	0-0	0	5.14
1989 St. Louis	NL	33	33	2	0	196.2	862	186	92	83	9	14	5	5	99	6	112	11	2	7	15	.318	1	0-0	0	3.80
1990 St. Louis	NL	17	14	1	1	78.2	343	79	49	48	7	5	5	1	33	1	58	5	0	5	6	.455	0	0-0	1	5.49
1991 St. Louis	NL	30	30	0	0	181.1	743	147	76	72	15	7	7	6	67	4	121	7	1	11	10	.524	0	0-0	0	3.57
1992 Montreal	NL	33	33	3	0	218	908	187	76	65	13	15	3	3	75	4	150	11	4	16	9	.640	3	0-0	0	2.68
1993 Montreal	NL	28	28	2	0	183.2	780	163	84	66	7	9	7	6	74	7	90	6	2	9	7	.563	0	0-0	0	3.23
1994 Montreal	NL	23	23	2	0	154.2	647	145	61	57	12	6	6	6	44	7	85	3	0	16	5	.762	1	0-0	0	3.32
1995 StL-Cle		30	29	1	0	185	817	202	107	95	21	12	3	1	77	4	98	6	0	10	8	.556	0	0-0	0	4.62
1996 Texas	AL	35	35	7	0	250.2	1061	250	110	101	19	4	7	4	95	3	170	5	4	16	10	.615	3	0-0	0	3.63
1997 Tex-Ana	AL	31	31	1	0	190	833	194	103	96	19	3	7	3	95	3	106	7	0	9	12	.429	0	0-0	0	4.55
1998 Anaheim	AL	19	19	0	0	103	458	123	60	57	6	7	5	3	47	0	57	3	0	9	6	.600	0	0-0	0	4.98
1999 Anaheim	AL	26	22	0	0	128.1	569	129	72	68	14	3	8	4	76	1	76	5	0	4	11	.267	0	0-0	0	4.77
1995 St. Louis	NL	18	18	0	0	110.1	493	125	71	62	16	9	2	0	45	4	50	3	0	6	7	.462	0	0-0	0	5.06
Cleveland	AL	12	11	1	0	74.2	324	77	36	33	5	3	1	1	32	0	48	3	0	4	1	.800	0	0-0	0	3.98
1997 Texas	AL	19	19	0	0	111	499	129	69	64	11	2	6	2	56	3	68	5	0	5	8	.385	0	0-0	0	5.19
Anaheim	AL	12	12	1	0	79	334	65	34	32	8	1	1	1	39	0	38	2	0	4	4	.500	0	0-0	0	3.65
12 ML YEARS		309	298	19	3	1884	8083	1821	899	816	142	85	63	44	788	40	1129	70	13	112	100	.528	8	0-0	2	3.90

A.J. Hinch

Bats: Right **Throws:** Right **Pos:** C-73; PH/PR-4   **Ht:** 6'1" **Wt:** 207 **Born:** 5/15/74 **Age:** 26

Year Team	Lg	G	AB	H	2B	3B	HR	(Hm	Rd)	TB	R	RBI	TBB	IBB	SO	HBP	SH	SF	SB	CS	SB%	GDP	Avg	OBP	SLG
1997 Modesto	A+	95	333	103	25	3	20	—	—	194	70	73	42	3	68	11	4	4	8	3	.73	9	.309	.400	.583
Edmonton	AAA	39	125	47	7	0	4	—	—	66	23	24	20	1	13	3	0	0	2	0	1.00	7	.376	.473	.528
1999 Vancouver	AAA	15	61	23	3	0	2	—	—	32	9	7	3	1	12	1	0	0	1	1	.50	0	.377	.415	.525
1998 Oakland	AL	120	337	78	10	0	9	(4	5)	115	34	35	30	0	89	4	13	7	3	0	1.00	6	.231	.296	.341
1999 Oakland	AL	76	205	44	4	1	7	(3	4)	71	26	24	11	0	41	2	9	1	6	2	.75	4	.215	.260	.346
2 ML YEARS		196	542	122	14	1	16	(7	9)	186	60	59	41	0	130	6	22	8	9	2	.82	10	.225	.283	.343

Brett Hinchliffe

Pitches: Right **Bats:** Right **Pos:** RP-7; SP-4   **Ht:** 6'5" **Wt:** 190 **Born:** 7/21/74 **Age:** 25

Year Team	Lg	G	GS	CG	GF	IP	BFP	H	R	ER	HR	SH	SF	HB	TBB	IBB	SO	WP	Bk	W	L	Pct.	ShO	Sv-Op	Hld	ERA
1992 Mariners	R	24	0	0	20	35	161	42	17	9	0	3	0	3	9	0	26	1	1	5	4	.556	0	3- -	—	2.31
1993 Mariners	R	10	9	0	0	44.1	190	55	32	25	4	1	3	3	5	0	29	4	1	0	4	.000	0	0- -	—	5.08
1994 Appleton	A	27	27	3	0	173.2	721	140	79	62	16	7	4	10	50	4	160	5	2	11	7	.611	1	0- -	—	3.21
1995 Riverside	A+	15	15	0	0	77.2	373	110	69	57	10	5	3	8	35	3	68	4	0	3	8	.273	0	0- -	—	6.61
1996 Lancaster	A+	27	26	0	0	163.1	731	179	105	77	19	6	5	9	64	1	146	10	1	11	10	.524	0	0- -	—	4.24
1997 Memphis	AA	24	24	5	0	145.2	627	159	81	72	20	3	4	9	45	2	107	2	1	10	10	.500	1	0- -	—	4.45
1998 Lancaster	A+	3	3	0	0	17	62	8	5	3	2	0	0	0	5	0	26	1	0	1	1	.500	0	0- -	—	1.59
Tacoma	AAA	25	25	2	0	159.2	681	132	80	71	22	1	5	4	88	2	100	4	2	10	8	.556	1	0- -	—	4.00
1999 Tacoma	AAA	21	21	3	0	131	563	141	78	75	17	4	5	5	44	1	107	9	0	9	7	.563	0	0- -	—	5.15
1999 Seattle	AL	11	4	0	2	30.2	153	41	31	30	10	1	0	4	21	0	14	2	0	0	4	.000	0	0-0	0	8.80

Sterling Hitchcock

Pitches: Left **Bats:** Left **Pos:** SP-33   **Ht:** 6'0" **Wt:** 205 **Born:** 4/29/71 **Age:** 29

Year Team	Lg	G	GS	CG	GF	IP	BFP	H	R	ER	HR	SH	SF	HB	TBB	IBB	SO	WP	Bk	W	L	Pct.	ShO	Sv-Op	Hld	ERA
1992 New York	AL	3	3	0	0	13	68	23	12	12	2	0	0	1	6	0	6	0	0	0	2	.000	0	0-0	0	8.31
1993 New York	AL	6	6	0	0	31	135	32	18	16	4	0	2	1	14	1	26	3	2	1	2	.333	0	0-0	0	4.65
1994 New York	AL	23	5	1	4	49.1	218	48	24	23	3	1	7	0	29	1	37	5	0	4	1	.800	0	2-2	3	4.20
1995 New York	AL	27	27	4	0	168.1	719	155	91	88	22	5	9	5	68	1	121	5	2	11	10	.524	1	0-0	0	4.70
1996 Seattle	AL	35	35	0	0	196.2	885	245	131	117	27	3	8	7	73	4	132	4	1	13	9	.591	0	0-0	0	5.35
1997 San Diego	NL	32	28	1	1	161	693	172	102	93	24	7	4	4	55	2	106	6	2	10	11	.476	0	0-0	0	5.20
1998 San Diego	NL	39	27	2	3	176.1	743	169	83	77	29	9	3	9	48	2	158	11	1	9	7	.563	1	1-2	3	3.93
1999 San Diego	NL	33	33	1	0	205.2	892	202	99	94	29	9	6	5	76	6	194	15	2	12	14	.462	0	0-0	0	4.11
8 ML YEARS		198	164	9	8	1001.1	4353	1046	560	520	140	34	39	32	369	17	780	49	10	60	56	.517	2	3-4	6	4.67

Denny Hocking

Bats: B **Throws:** R **Pos:** SS-61; 2B-56; PH/PR-27; LF-17; RF-13; CF-11; 3B-6; 1B-2   **Ht:** 5'10" **Wt:** 183 **Born:** 4/2/70 **Age:** 30

Year Team	Lg	G	AB	H	2B	3B	HR	(Hm	Rd)	TB	R	RBI	TBB	IBB	SO	HBP	SH	SF	SB	CS	SB%	GDP	Avg	OBP	SLG
1993 Minnesota	AL	15	36	5	1	0	0	(0	0)	6	7	0	6	0	8	0	0	0	1	0	1.00	1	.139	.262	.167
1994 Minnesota	AL	11	31	10	3	0	0	(0	0)	13	3	2	0	0	4	0	0	0	2	0	1.00	1	.323	.323	.419
1995 Minnesota	AL	9	25	5	0	2	0	(0	0)	9	4	3	2	1	2	0	1	0	1	0	1.00	1	.200	.259	.360
1996 Minnesota	AL	49	127	25	6	0	1	(0	1)	34	16	10	8	0	24	0	1	1	3	3	.50	3	.197	.243	.268
1997 Minnesota	AL	115	253	65	12	4	2	(0	2)	91	28	25	18	0	51	1	5	1	3	5	.38	6	.257	.308	.360
1998 Minnesota	AL	110	198	40	6	1	3	(1	2)	57	32	15	16	1	44	0	3	2	2	1	.67	2	.202	.259	.288
1999 Minnesota	AL	136	386	103	18	2	7	(2	5)	146	47	41	22	1	54	3	4	6	11	7	.61	10	.267	.307	.378
7 ML YEARS		445	1056	253	46	9	13	(3	10)	356	137	96	72	3	187	4	14	10	23	16	.59	24	.240	.288	.337

Trevor Hoffman

Pitches: Right **Bats:** Right **Pos:** RP-64   **Ht:** 6'0" **Wt:** 215 **Born:** 10/13/67 **Age:** 32

Year Team	Lg	G	GS	CG	GF	IP	BFP	H	R	ER	HR	SH	SF	HB	TBB	IBB	SO	WP	Bk	W	L	Pct.	ShO	Sv-Op	Hld	ERA
1993 Fla-SD	NL	67	0	0	26	90	391	80	43	39	10	4	5	1	39	13	79	5	0	4	6	.400	0	5-8	15	3.90
1994 San Diego	NL	47	0	0	41	56	225	39	16	16	4	1	2	0	20	6	68	3	0	4	4	.500	0	20-23	1	2.57
1995 San Diego	NL	55	0	0	51	53.1	218	48	25	23	10	0	0	0	14	3	52	1	0	7	4	.636	0	31-38	0	3.88
1996 San Diego	NL	70	0	0	62	88	348	50	23	22	6	2	2	2	31	5	111	2	0	9	5	.643	0	42-49	0	2.25
1997 San Diego	NL	70	0	0	59	81.1	322	59	25	24	9	2	1	0	24	4	111	7	0	6	4	.600	0	37-44	0	2.66
1998 San Diego	NL	66	0	0	61	73	274	41	12	12	2	3	0	1	21	2	86	8	0	4	2	.667	0	53-54	0	1.48
1999 San Diego	NL	64	0	0	54	67.1	263	48	23	16	5	1	3	0	15	2	73	4	0	2	3	.400	0	40-43	0	2.14
1993 Florida	NL	28	0	0	13	35.2	152	24	13	13	5	2	1	0	19	7	26	3	0	2	2	.500	0	2-3	8	3.28
San Diego	NL	39	0	0	13	54.1	239	56	30	26	5	2	4	1	20	6	53	2	0	2	4	.333	0	3-5	7	4.31
7 ML YEARS		439	0	0	354	509	2041	365	167	152	46	13	13	4	164	35	580	30	0	36	28	.563	0	228-259	16	2.69

106

Ray Holbert

Bats: R **Throws:** R **Pos:** SS-22; 2B-11; PH/PR-4; 3B-1   **Ht:** 6'0" **Wt:** 185 **Born:** 9/25/70 **Age:** 29

Year Team	Lg	G	AB	H	2B	3B	HR	(Hm	Rd)	TB	R	RBI	TBB	IBB	SO	HBP	SH	SF	SB	CS	SB%	GDP	Avg	OBP	SLG
1988 Padres	R	49	170	44	1	0	3	—	—	54	38	19	37	0	32	2	1	0	20	7	.74	4	.259	.397	.318
1989 Waterloo	A	117	354	55	7	1	0	—	—	64	37	20	41	0	99	2	7	1	13	13	.50	9	.155	.246	.181
1990 Waterloo	A	133	411	84	10	1	3	—	—	105	51	37	51	0	117	4	9	1	16	16	.50	10	.204	.298	.255
1991 High Desert	A+	122	386	102	14	2	4	—	—	132	76	51	56	1	83	6	9	3	19	6	.76	10	.264	.364	.342
1992 Wichita	AA	95	304	86	7	3	2	—	—	105	46	23	42	2	68	1	3	1	26	8	.76	7	.283	.371	.345
1993 Wichita	AA	112	388	101	13	5	5	—	—	139	56	48	54	0	87	2	3	9	30	17	.64	6	.260	.347	.358
1994 Las Vegas	AAA	118	426	128	21	5	8	—	—	183	68	52	50	2	99	2	10	4	27	11	.71	8	.300	.373	.430
1995 Las Vegas	AAA	9	26	3	1	0	0	—	—	4	3	3	5	0	10	0	0	0	1	1	.50	1	.115	.258	.154
1996 Tucson	AAA	28	97	24	3	2	0	—	—	31	13	10	7	0	19	2	0	1	4	1	.80	3	.247	.308	.320
1997 Toledo	AAA	109	372	90	18	7	7	—	—	143	43	37	32	0	109	4	7	2	16	7	.70	7	.242	.307	.384
1998 Richmond	AAA	1	1	0	0	0	0	—	—	0	1	0	2	0	1	0	0	0	0	0	.00	0	.000	.667	.000
Ottawa	AAA	86	266	82	17	4	2	—	—	113	38	25	29	3	66	0	4	0	10	5	.67	2	.308	.376	.425
1999 Royals	R	5	16	3	2	0	0	—	—	5	5	1	1	0	4	0	1	0	1	0	1.00	1	.188	.235	.313
Omaha	AAA	33	128	38	14	0	4	—	—	54	26	12	12	0	35	0	0	1	13	4	.76	1	.297	.355	.422
1994 San Diego	NL	5	5	1	0	0	0	(0	0)	1	1	0	0	0	4	0	0	0	0	0	.00	0	.200	.200	.200
1995 San Diego	NL	63	73	13	2	1	2	(1	1)	23	11	5	8	1	20	2	3	0	4	0	1.00	3	.178	.277	.315
1998 Atl-Mon	NL	10	20	2	0	0	0	(0	0)	2	2	1	2	0	5	0	0	1	0	0	.00	0	.100	.174	.100
1999 Kansas City	AL	34	100	28	3	0	0	(0	0)	31	14	5	8	0	20	0	6	1	7	4	.64	4	.280	.330	.310
1998 Atlanta	NL	8	15	2	0	0	0	(0	0)	2	2	1	2	0	4	0	0	1	0	0	.00	0	.133	.222	.133
Montreal	NL	2	5	0	0	0	0	(0	0)	0	0	0	0	0	1	0	0	0	0	0	.00	0	.000	.000	.000
4 ML YEARS		112	198	44	5	1	2	(1	1)	57	28	11	18	1	49	2	9	2	11	4	.73	7	.222	.291	.288

Todd Hollandsworth

Bats: L **Throws:** L **Pos:** CF-34; PH/PR-28; LF-27; 1B-13; RF-9   **Ht:** 6'2" **Wt:** 215 **Born:** 4/20/73 **Age:** 27

Year Team	Lg	G	AB	H	2B	3B	HR	(Hm	Rd)	TB	R	RBI	TBB	IBB	SO	HBP	SH	SF	SB	CS	SB%	GDP	Avg	OBP	SLG
1999 San Berndno *	A+	4	13	5	2	0	0	—	—	7	3	3	2	0	4	1	0	0	0	1	.00	1	.385	.500	.538
1995 Los Angeles	NL	41	103	24	2	0	5	(2	3)	41	16	13	10	2	29	1	0	1	2	1	.67	1	.233	.304	.398
1996 Los Angeles	NL	149	478	139	26	4	12	(2	10)	209	64	59	41	1	93	2	3	2	21	6	.78	2	.291	.348	.437
1997 Los Angeles	NL	106	296	73	20	2	4	(1	3)	109	39	31	17	2	60	0	2	2	5	5	.50	8	.247	.286	.368
1998 Los Angeles	NL	55	175	47	6	4	3	(1	2)	70	23	20	9	0	42	1	2	0	4	3	.57	2	.269	.308	.400
1999 Los Angeles	NL	92	261	74	12	2	9	(5	4)	117	39	32	24	1	61	1	0	1	5	2	.71	2	.284	.345	.448
5 ML YEARS		443	1313	357	66	12	33	(12	21)	546	181	155	101	6	285	5	7	6	37	17	.69	15	.272	.325	.416

Dave Hollins

Bats: Both **Throws:** Right **Pos:** DH-23; PH/PR-4   **Ht:** 6'1" **Wt:** 232 **Born:** 5/25/66 **Age:** 34

Year Team	Lg	G	AB	H	2B	3B	HR	(Hm	Rd)	TB	R	RBI	TBB	IBB	SO	HBP	SH	SF	SB	CS	SB%	GDP	Avg	OBP	SLG
1999 Syracuse *	AAA	4	15	3	1	0	0	—	—	4	2	1	1	0	5	1	0	0	0	0	.00	0	.200	.294	.267
Charlotte *	AAA	63	199	63	18	0	8	—	—	105	49	33	33	2	37	13	0	4	5	1	.83	4	.317	.438	.528
1990 Philadelphia	NL	72	114	21	0	0	5	(2	3)	36	14	15	10	3	28	1	0	2	0	0	.00	1	.184	.252	.316
1991 Philadelphia	NL	56	151	45	10	2	6	(3	3)	77	18	21	17	1	26	3	0	1	1	1	.50	2	.298	.378	.510
1992 Philadelphia	NL	156	586	158	28	4	27	(14	13)	275	104	93	76	4	110	19	0	4	9	6	.60	8	.270	.369	.469
1993 Philadelphia	NL	143	543	148	30	4	18	(9	9)	240	104	93	85	5	109	5	0	7	2	3	.40	15	.273	.372	.442
1994 Philadelphia	NL	44	162	36	7	1	4	(1	3)	57	28	26	23	0	32	4	0	3	1	0	1.00	6	.222	.328	.352
1995 Phi-Bos		70	218	49	12	2	7	(5	2)	86	48	26	57	4	45	5	0	4	1	1	.50	4	.225	.391	.394
1996 Min-Sea	AL	149	516	135	29	0	16	(7	9)	212	88	78	84	7	117	13	1	2	6	6	.50	11	.262	.377	.411
1997 Anaheim	AL	149	572	165	29	2	16	(15	1)	246	101	85	62	2	124	8	1	5	16	6	.73	12	.288	.363	.430
1998 Anaheim	AL	101	363	88	16	2	11	(4	7)	141	60	39	44	2	69	7	2	2	11	3	.79	5	.242	.334	.388
1999 Toronto	AL	27	99	22	5	0	2	(1	1)	33	12	6	5	0	22	0	0	0	0	0	.00	2	.222	.260	.333
1995 Philadelphia	NL	65	205	47	12	2	7	(5	2)	84	46	25	53	4	38	5	0	4	1	1	.50	4	.229	.393	.410
Boston	AL	5	13	2	0	0	0	(0	0)	2	2	1	4	0	7	0	0	0	0	0	.00	0	.154	.353	.154
1996 Minnesota	AL	121	422	102	26	0	13	(6	7)	167	71	53	71	5	102	10	0	0	6	4	.60	9	.242	.364	.396
Seattle	AL	28	94	33	3	0	3	(1	2)	45	17	25	13	2	15	3	1	2	0	2	.00	2	.351	.438	.479
10 ML YEARS		967	3324	867	166	17	112	(61	51)	1403	577	482	463	28	682	65	4	30	47	26	.64	66	.261	.359	.422

Darren Holmes

Pitches: Right **Bats:** Right **Pos:** RP-44   **Ht:** 6'0" **Wt:** 202 **Born:** 4/25/66 **Age:** 34

		HOW MUCH HE PITCHED						WHAT HE GAVE UP											THE RESULTS						
Year Team	Lg	G	GS	CG	GF	IP	BFP	H	R	ER	HR	SH	SF	HB	TBB	IBB	SO	WP	Bk	W	L	Pct.	ShO	Sv-Op	Hld	ERA
1999 Diamondbcks *	R	2	2	0	0	2.2	9	1	0	0	0	0	0	0	0	0	4	0	0	0	0	.000	0	0- –	—	0.00
Tucson *	AAA	1	1	0	0	1	3	0	0	0	0	0	0	0	1	0	0	0	0	0	0	.000	0	0- –	—	0.00
1990 Los Angeles	NL	14	0	0	1	17.1	77	15	10	10	1	1	2	0	11	3	19	1	0	0	1	.000	0	0-0	—	5.19
1991 Milwaukee	AL	40	0	0	9	76.1	344	90	43	40	6	8	3	1	27	1	59	6	0	1	4	.200	0	3-6	3	4.72
1992 Milwaukee	AL	41	0	0	25	42.1	173	35	12	12	1	4	0	2	11	4	31	0	0	4	4	.500	0	6-8	2	2.55
1993 Colorado	NL	62	0	0	51	66.2	274	56	31	30	6	0	0	2	20	1	60	2	1	3	3	.500	0	25-29	2	4.05
1994 Colorado	NL	29	0	0	14	28.1	142	35	25	20	5	4	1	1	24	4	33	2	0	0	3	.000	0	3-8	3	6.35
1995 Colorado	NL	68	0	0	33	66.2	286	59	26	24	3	5	3	1	28	3	61	7	1	6	1	.857	0	14-18	13	3.24
1996 Colorado	NL	62	0	0	21	77.0	333	77	41	34	8	2	1	1	28	2	73	2	0	5	4	.556	0	1-8	7	3.97
1997 Colorado	NL	42	6	0	10	89.1	406	113	58	53	12	6	4	0	36	3	70	4	0	9	2	.818	0	3-4	5	5.34
1998 New York	AL	34	0	0	13	51.1	215	53	19	19	4	0	3	2	14	3	31	1	0	0	3	.000	0	2-3	2	3.33
1999 Arizona	NL	44	0	0	9	48.2	219	50	21	20	3	2	0	1	25	8	35	0	2	4	3	.571	0	0-2	4	3.70
10 ML YEARS		436	6	0	186	564	2469	584	286	262	49	32	17	11	224	32	472	25	4	32	28	.533	0	57-86	41	4.18

Chris Holt

Pitches: Right **Bats:** Right **Pos:** SP-26; RP-6   **Ht:** 6'4" **Wt:** 205 **Born:** 9/18/71 **Age:** 28

Year Team	Lg	G	GS	CG	GF	IP	BFP	H	R	ER	HR	SH	SF	HB	TBB	IBB	SO	WP	Bk	W	L	Pct.	ShO	Sv-Op	Hld	ERA
1996 Houston	NL	4	0	0	3	4.2	22	5	3	3	0	0	0	0	3	1	0	1	0	0	1	.000	0	0-0	0	5.79
1997 Houston	NL	33	32	0	0	209.2	883	211	98	82	17	7	5	8	61	4	95	1	0	8	12	.400	0	0-0	0	3.52
1999 Houston	NL	32	26	0	2	164	720	193	92	85	12	9	8	8	57	1	115	5	0	5	13	.278	0	1-2	0	4.66
3 ML YEARS		69	58	0	5	378.1	1625	409	193	170	29	16	13	16	121	6	210	7	0	13	26	.333	0	1-2	0	4.04

Mike Holtz

Pitches: Left **Bats:** Left **Pos:** RP-28   **Ht:** 5'9" **Wt:** 180 **Born:** 10/10/72 **Age:** 27

Year Team	Lg	G	GS	CG	GF	IP	BFP	H	R	ER	HR	SH	SF	HB	TBB	IBB	SO	WP	Bk	W	L	Pct.	ShO	Sv-Op	Hld	ERA
1999 Edmonton *	AAA	20	0	0	8	27.1	111	20	7	7	4	1	0	0	11	1	39	1	0	2	1	.667	0	1- -	—	2.30
1996 California	AL	30	0	0	8	29.1	127	21	11	8	1	1	1	3	19	2	31	1	0	3	3	.500	0	0-0	5	2.45
1997 Anaheim	AL	66	0	0	11	43.1	187	38	21	16	7	1	2	2	15	4	40	1	0	3	4	.429	0	2-8	14	3.32
1998 Anaheim	AL	53	0	0	9	30.1	137	38	16	16	0	1	2	1	15	1	29	4	0	2	2	.500	0	1-2	13	4.75
1999 Anaheim	AL	28	0	0	9	22.1	106	26	20	20	3	1	0	2	15	1	17	3	0	2	3	.400	0	0-0	1	8.06
4 ML YEARS		177	0	0	37	125.1	557	123	68	60	11	4	5	8	64	8	117	9	0	10	12	.455	0	3-10	33	4.31

Tyler Houston

Bats: L **Throws:** R **Pos:** 3B-73; PH/PR-31; C-19; 1B-2; RF-1   **Ht:** 6'1" **Wt:** 210 **Born:** 1/17/71 **Age:** 29

							BATTING												BASERUNNING				PERCENTAGES		
Year Team	Lg	G	AB	H	2B	3B	HR	(Hm	Rd)	TB	R	RBI	TBB	IBB	SO	HBP	SH	SF	SB	CS	SB%	GDP	Avg	OBP	SLG
1996 Atl-ChC	NL	79	142	45	9	1	3	(1	2)	65	21	27	9	1	27	0	0	0	3	2	.60	5	.317	.358	.458
1997 Chicago	NL	72	196	51	10	0	2	(0	2)	67	15	28	9	1	35	0	0	0	1	0	1.00	4	.260	.290	.342
1998 Chicago	NL	95	255	65	7	1	9	(4	5)	101	26	33	13	1	53	0	1	1	2	2	.50	6	.255	.290	.396
1999 ChC-Cle		113	276	62	10	1	10	(2	8)	104	28	30	31	4	78	0	1	1	1	1	.50	7	.225	.302	.377
1996 Atlanta	NL	33	27	6	2	1	1	(1	0)	13	3	8	1	0	9	0	0	0	0	0	.00	1	.222	.250	.481
Chicago	NL	46	115	39	7	0	2	(0	2)	52	18	19	8	1	18	0	0	0	3	2	.60	4	.339	.382	.452
1999 Chicago	NL	100	249	58	9	1	9	(2	7)	96	26	27	28	4	67	0	1	1	1	1	.50	7	.233	.309	.386
Cleveland	AL	13	27	4	1	0	1	(0	1)	8	2	3	3	0	11	0	0	0	0	0	.00	0	.148	.233	.296
4 ML YEARS		359	869	223	36	3	24	(7	17)	337	90	118	62	7	193	0	2	4	7	5	.58	22	.257	.305	.388

David Howard

Bats: B **Throws:** R **Pos:** PH/PR-18; SS-13; 1B-9; 2B-9; 3B-4; LF-3; CF-1; RF-1   **Ht:** 6'0" **Wt:** 175 **Born:** 2/26/67 **Age:** 33

							BATTING												BASERUNNING				PERCENTAGES		
Year Team	Lg	G	AB	H	2B	3B	HR	(Hm	Rd)	TB	R	RBI	TBB	IBB	SO	HBP	SH	SF	SB	CS	SB%	GDP	Avg	OBP	SLG
1999 Memphis *	AAA	8	19	5	0	0	0	—	—	5	3	2	1	0	6	1	0	0	2	0	1.00	0	.263	.318	.263
1991 Kansas City	AL	94	236	51	7	0	1	(0	1)	61	20	17	16	0	45	1	9	2	3	2	.60	1	.216	.267	.258
1992 Kansas City	AL	74	219	49	6	2	1	(1	0)	62	19	18	15	0	43	0	8	2	3	4	.43	3	.224	.271	.283
1993 Kansas City	AL	15	24	8	0	1	0	(0	0)	10	5	2	2	0	5	0	2	1	1	0	1.00	0	.333	.370	.417
1994 Kansas City	AL	46	83	19	4	0	1	(0	1)	26	9	13	11	0	23	0	3	3	3	2	.60	1	.229	.309	.313
1995 Kansas City	AL	95	255	62	13	4	0	(0	0)	83	23	19	24	1	41	1	6	1	6	1	.86	7	.243	.310	.325
1996 Kansas City	AL	143	420	92	14	5	4	(3	1)	128	51	48	40	0	74	4	17	4	5	6	.45	6	.219	.291	.305
1997 Kansas City	AL	80	162	39	8	1	1	(0	1)	52	24	13	10	1	31	1	3	1	2	2	.50	1	.241	.287	.321
1998 St. Louis	NL	46	102	25	1	1	2	(2	0)	34	15	12	12	2	22	0	2	1	0	0	.00	2	.245	.322	.333
1999 St. Louis	NL	52	82	17	4	0	1	(1	0)	24	3	6	7	3	27	2	1	0	0	2	.00	0	.207	.286	.293
9 ML YEARS		645	1583	362	57	14	11	(7	4)	480	169	148	137	7	311	9	51	15	23	19	.55	21	.229	.291	.303

Thomas Howard

Bats: B **Throws:** R **Pos:** PH/PR-52; RF-45; LF-3; DH-1   **Ht:** 6'2" **Wt:** 205 **Born:** 12/11/64 **Age:** 35

							BATTING												BASERUNNING				PERCENTAGES		
Year Team	Lg	G	AB	H	2B	3B	HR	(Hm	Rd)	TB	R	RBI	TBB	IBB	SO	HBP	SH	SF	SB	CS	SB%	GDP	Avg	OBP	SLG
1999 Memphis *	AAA	35	119	43	10	2	2	—	—	63	24	21	13	0	21	1	0	2	1	2	.33	2	.361	.425	.529
1990 San Diego	NL	20	44	12	2	0	0	(0	0)	14	4	0	0	0	11	0	1	0	0	1	.00	1	.273	.273	.318
1991 San Diego	NL	106	281	70	12	3	4	(4	0)	100	30	22	24	4	57	1	2	1	10	7	.59	4	.249	.309	.356
1992 SD-Cle		122	361	100	15	2	2	(1	1)	125	37	32	17	1	60	0	11	2	15	8	.65	4	.277	.308	.346
1993 Cle-Cin		112	319	81	15	3	7	(5	2)	123	48	36	24	0	63	0	0	5	10	7	.59	9	.254	.302	.386
1994 Cincinnati	NL	83	178	47	11	0	5	(4	1)	73	24	24	10	1	30	0	3	1	4	2	.67	2	.264	.302	.410
1995 Cincinnati	NL	113	281	85	15	2	3	(1	2)	113	42	26	20	0	37	1	1	1	17	8	.68	3	.302	.350	.402
1996 Cincinnati	NL	121	360	98	19	10	6	(1	5)	155	50	42	17	3	51	3	2	4	6	5	.55	5	.272	.307	.431
1997 Houston	NL	107	255	63	16	1	3	(0	3)	90	24	22	26	1	48	3	1	1	1	2	.33	5	.247	.323	.353
1998 Los Angeles	NL	47	76	14	4	0	2	(1	1)	24	9	4	3	0	15	0	0	0	1	0	1.00	2	.184	.215	.316
1999 St. Louis	NL	98	195	57	10	0	6	(3	3)	85	16	28	17	0	26	2	0	1	1	1	.50	3	.292	.353	.436
1992 San Diego	NL	5	3	1	0	0	0	(0	0)	1	1	0	0	0	0	0	1	0	0	0	.00	0	.333	.333	.333
Cleveland	AL	117	358	99	15	2	2	(1	1)	124	36	32	17	1	60	0	10	2	15	8	.65	4	.277	.308	.346
1993 Cleveland	AL	74	178	42	7	0	3	(3	0)	58	26	23	12	0	42	0	0	4	5	1	.83	5	.236	.278	.326
Cincinnati	NL	38	141	39	8	3	4	(2	2)	65	22	13	12	0	21	0	0	1	5	6	.45	4	.277	.331	.461
10 ML YEARS		929	2350	627	119	21	38	(20	18)	902	284	236	158	10	398	10	21	16	65	41	.61	36	.267	.314	.384

Jack Howell

Bats: L **Throws:** R **Pos:** PH/PR-30; 1B-5; 3B-3; DH-2   **Ht:** 6'0" **Wt:** 190 **Born:** 8/18/61 **Age:** 38

Year Team	Lg	G	AB	H	2B	3B	HR	(Hm	Rd)	TB	R	RBI	TBB	IBB	SO	HBP	SH	SF	SB	CS	SB%	GDP	Avg	OBP	SLG
1999 Jackson *	AA	3	8	3	1	0	2	—	—	10	2	3	0	0	2	0	0	0	0	0	.00	0	.375	.375	1.250
1985 California	AL	43	137	27	4	0	5	(2	3)	46	19	18	16	2	33	0	4	1	1	1	.50	1	.197	.279	.336
1986 California	AL	63	151	41	14	2	4	(1	3)	71	26	21	19	0	28	0	3	2	2	0	1.00	1	.272	.349	.470
1987 California	AL	138	449	110	18	5	23	(15	8)	207	64	64	57	4	118	2	1	2	4	3	.57	7	.245	.331	.461
1988 California	AL	154	500	127	32	2	16	(9	7)	211	59	63	46	8	130	6	4	2	2	6	.25	8	.254	.323	.422
1989 California	AL	144	474	108	19	4	20	(9	11)	195	56	52	52	9	125	3	3	1	0	3	.00	8	.228	.308	.411
1990 California	AL	105	316	72	19	1	8	(3	5)	117	35	33	46	5	61	1	1	2	3	0	1.00	3	.228	.326	.370
1991 Cal-SD		90	241	50	5	1	8	(3	5)	81	35	23	29	1	44	0	1	0	1	1	.50	2	.207	.293	.336
1996 Anaheim	AL	66	126	34	4	1	8	(4	4)	64	20	21	10	0	30	0	0	0	0	1	.00	3	.270	.324	.508
1997 Anaheim	AL	77	174	45	7	0	14	(5	9)	94	25	34	13	2	36	0	1	3	1	0	1.00	4	.259	.305	.540
1998 Houston	NL	24	38	11	5	0	1	(1	0)	19	4	7	4	0	12	0	0	0	0	0	.00	1	.289	.357	.500
1999 Houston	NL	37	33	7	2	0	1	(0	1)	12	2	1	8	0	9	0	0	0	0	0	.00	1	.212	.366	.364
1991 California	AL	32	81	17	2	0	2	(0	2)	25	11	7	11	0	11	0	0	0	1	1	.50	1	.210	.304	.309
San Diego	NL	58	160	33	3	1	6	(3	3)	56	24	16	18	1	33	0	1	0	0	0	.00	1	.206	.287	.350
11 ML YEARS		941	2639	632	129	16	108	(52	56)	1117	345	337	300	31	626	12	18	13	14	15	.48	39	.239	.318	.423

Bob Howry

Pitches: Right **Bats:** Left **Pos:** RP-69   **Ht:** 6'5" **Wt:** 220 **Born:** 8/4/73 **Age:** 26

Year Team	Lg	G	GS	CG	GF	IP	BFP	H	R	ER	HR	SH	SF	HB	TBB	IBB	SO	WP	Bk	W	L	Pct.	ShO	Sv-Op	Hld	ERA
1994 Everett	A-	5	5	0	0	19	97	29	19	15	3	0	1	1	10	2	16	5	0	0	4	.000	0	0- -	—	7.11
Clinton	A	9	8	0	0	49.1	219	61	29	23	1	3	4	3	16	0	22	4	2	1	3	.250	0	0- -	—	4.20
1995 San Jose	A+	27	25	1	1	165.1	695	171	79	65	6	12	4	8	54	0	107	7	3	12	10	.545	0	0- -	—	3.54
1996 Shreveport	AA	27	27	0	0	156.2	682	163	90	81	17	6	4	9	56	3	57	3	1	10	8	.556	0	0- -	—	4.65
1997 Shreveport	AA	48	0	0	39	55	240	58	35	30	6	1	3	0	21	0	43	3	1	6	3	.667	0	22- -	—	4.91
Birmingham	AA	12	0	0	6	12.2	54	16	4	4	1	0	0	0	3	0	3	0	0	0	0	.000	0	2- -	—	2.84
1998 Calgary	AAA	23	0	0	11	31.2	130	25	12	12	2	2	0	2	10	3	22	4	0	1	2	.333	0	5- -	—	3.41
1998 Chicago	AL	44	0	0	15	54.1	217	37	20	19	7	2	3	2	19	2	51	2	0	0	3	.000	0	9-11	19	3.15
1999 Chicago	AL	69	0	0	54	67.2	298	58	34	27	8	3	1	3	38	3	80	3	1	5	3	.625	0	28-34	1	3.59
2 ML YEARS		113	0	0	69	122	515	95	54	46	15	5	4	5	57	5	131	5	1	5	6	.455	0	37-45	20	3.39

Trenidad Hubbard

Bats: R **Throws:** R **Pos:** PH/PR-42; LF-29; CF-19; RF-3; C-1; 2B-1   **Ht:** 5'9" **Wt:** 185 **Born:** 5/11/66 **Age:** 34

Year Team	Lg	G	AB	H	2B	3B	HR	(Hm	Rd)	TB	R	RBI	TBB	IBB	SO	HBP	SH	SF	SB	CS	SB%	GDP	Avg	OBP	SLG
1999 Albuquerque *	AAA	32	123	41	8	2	5	—	—	68	24	24	16	1	27	0	0	3	16	4	.80	4	.333	.401	.553
1994 Colorado	NL	18	25	7	1	1	1	(1	0)	13	3	3	3	0	4	0	0	0	0	0	.00	1	.280	.357	.520
1995 Colorado	NL	24	58	18	4	0	3	(2	1)	31	13	9	8	0	6	0	1	0	2	1	.67	2	.310	.394	.534
1996 Col-SF	NL	55	89	19	5	2	2	(2	0)	34	15	14	11	0	27	1	0	0	2	0	1.00	3	.213	.307	.382
1997 Cleveland	AL	7	12	3	1	0	0	(0	0)	4	3	0	1	0	3	0	0	0	2	0	1.00	0	.250	.308	.333
1998 Los Angeles	NL	94	208	62	9	1	7	(2	5)	94	29	18	18	0	46	3	3	3	9	5	.64	5	.298	.358	.452
1999 Los Angeles	NL	82	105	33	5	0	1	(0	1)	41	23	13	13	1	24	0	1	1	4	3	.57	2	.314	.387	.390
1996 Colorado	NL	45	60	13	5	1	1	(1	0)	23	12	12	9	0	22	1	0	0	2	0	1.00	1	.217	.329	.383
San Francisco	NL	10	29	6	0	1	1	(1	0)	11	3	2	2	0	5	0	0	0	0	0	.00	2	.207	.258	.379
6 ML YEARS		280	497	142	25	4	14	(7	7)	217	86	57	54	1	110	4	5	4	19	9	.68	13	.286	.358	.437

John Hudek

Pitches: Right **Bats:** Both **Pos:** RP-20   **Ht:** 6'3" **Wt:** 205 **Born:** 8/8/66 **Age:** 33

Year Team	Lg	G	GS	CG	GF	IP	BFP	H	R	ER	HR	SH	SF	HB	TBB	IBB	SO	WP	Bk	W	L	Pct.	ShO	Sv-Op	Hld	ERA
1999 Richmond *	AAA	12	0	0	5	11.1	53	14	8	8	0	0	1	0	5	0	17	1	0	0	0	.000	0	0- -	—	6.35
Syracuse *	AAA	12	0	0	6	18	78	17	12	11	3	3	1	0	8	1	15	1	0	0	2	.000	0	1- -	—	5.50
1994 Houston	NL	42	0	0	33	39.1	159	24	14	13	5	0	2	1	18	2	39	0	0	2	2	.000	0	16-18	1	2.97
1995 Houston	NL	19	0	0	16	20	83	19	12	12	3	1	0	0	5	0	29	2	0	2	2	.500	0	7-9	0	5.40
1996 Houston	NL	15	0	0	6	16	65	12	5	5	2	2	0	0	5	2	14	1	1	0	1	.000	0	2-2	1	2.81
1997 Houston	NL	40	0	0	20	40.2	188	38	27	27	8	1	0	3	33	2	36	4	0	1	3	.250	0	4-8	2	5.98
1998 NYM-Cin	NL	58	0	0	23	64	289	50	27	22	8	5	5	4	47	4	68	1	0	5	6	.455	0	0-1	6	3.09
1999 Cin-Atl-Tor	NL	20	0	0	13	21.1	112	33	22	20	3	0	2	1	15	0	20	0	0	0	1	.000	0	0-1	0	8.44
1998 New York	NL	28	0	0	15	27	123	23	13	12	2	3	2	2	19	3	28	0	0	1	4	.200	0	0-0	1	4.00
Cincinnati	NL	30	0	0	8	37	166	27	14	10	6	2	3	2	28	1	40	1	0	4	2	.667	0	0-1	6	2.43
1999 Cincinnati	NL	2	0	0	0	1	9	4	3	3	1	0	0	0	3	0	0	0	0	0	0	.000	0	0-0	0	27.00
Atlanta	NL	15	0	0	12	16.2	84	21	14	12	1	0	1	1	11	0	18	0	0	0	0	.000	0	0-0	1	6.48
Toronto	AL	3	0	0	1	3.2	19	8	5	5	1	0	1	0	1	0	2	0	0	0	0	.000	0	0-0	0	12.27
6 ML YEARS		194	0	0	111	201.1	896	176	107	99	29	9	9	9	123	10	206	8	1	10	15	.400	0	29-39	10	4.43

Tim Hudson

Pitches: Right **Bats:** Right **Pos:** SP-21   **Ht:** 6'0" **Wt:** 160 **Born:** 7/14/75 **Age:** 24

Year Team	Lg	G	GS	CG	GF	IP	BFP	H	R	ER	HR	SH	SF	HB	TBB	IBB	SO	WP	Bk	W	L	Pct.	ShO	Sv-Op	Hld	ERA
1997 Sou Oregon	A-	8	4	0	1	28.2	111	12	8	8	0	0	1	1	15	2	37	3	2	3	1	.750	0	0- -	—	2.51

		HOW MUCH HE PITCHED				WHAT HE GAVE UP								THE RESULTS						
Year Team	Lg	G GS CG GF	IP	BFP	H	R	ER	HR SH SF HB	TBB IBB	SO WP Bk	W	L	Pct.	ShO	Sv-Op	Hld	ERA
1998 Modesto	A+	8 5 0 2	37.2	150	19	10	7	0 2 0 2	18 0	48 2 1	4	0	1.000	0	0--	—	1.67
Huntsville	AA	22 22 2 0	134.2	603	136	84	68	13 7 8 13	71 2	104 13 1	10	9	.526	0	0--	—	4.54
1999 Midland	AA	3 3 0 0	18	63	9	1	1	0 1 0 0	3 0	18 0 0	3	0	1.000	0	0--	—	0.50
Vancouver	AAA	8 8 0 0	49	202	38	16	12	2 0 1 1	21 0	61 2 0	4	0	1.000	0	0--	—	2.20
1999 Oakland	AL	21 21 1 0	136.1	580	121	56	49	8 1 2 4	62 2	132 6 0	11	2	.846	0	0-0	0	3.23

Bobby Hughes

Bats: Right **Throws:** Right **Pos:** C-44; PH/PR-8; DH-1   **Ht:** 6'4" **Wt:** 229 **Born:** 4/10/71 **Age:** 29

		BATTING														BASERUNNING				PERCENTAGES		
Year Team	Lg	G	AB	H	2B	3B	HR	(Hm	Rd)	TB	R	RBI	TBB	IBB	SO	HBP	SH	SF	SB	CS	SB%	GDP	Avg	OBP	SLG
1992 Helena	R+	11	40	7	1	1	0	—	—	10	5	6	4	0	14	2	0	0	0	0	.00	0	.175	.283	.250
1993 Beloit	A	98	321	89	11	3	17	—	—	157	42	56	23	0	77	6	5	0	1	3	.25	2	.277	.337	.489
1994 El Paso	AA	12	36	10	4	1	0	—	—	16	3	12	5	0	7	1	0	2	0	1	.00	1	.278	.364	.444
Stockton	A+	95	322	81	24	3	11	—	—	144	54	53	33	0	83	9	1	2	2	1	.67	8	.252	.336	.447
1995 Stockton	A+	52	179	42	9	2	8	—	—	79	22	31	17	1	41	1	0	3	2	2	.50	10	.235	.300	.441
El Paso	AA	51	173	46	12	0	7	—	—	79	11	27	12	1	30	2	0	2	0	2	.00	4	.266	.317	.457
1996 New Orleans	AAA	37	125	25	5	0	4	—	—	42	11	15	4	0	31	3	0	0	1	1	.50	2	.200	.242	.336
El Paso	AA	67	237	72	18	1	15	—	—	137	43	39	30	1	40	2	0	3	3	3	.50	5	.304	.382	.578
1997 El Paso	AA	89	290	90	29	2	7	—	—	144	43	51	24	1	46	9	0	4	0	0	.00	9	.310	.376	.497
1999 Louisville	AAA	10	32	6	2	0	1	—	—	11	5	2	2	0	7	1	0	0	0	0	.00	0	.188	.257	.344
1998 Milwaukee	NL	85	218	50	7	2	9	(4	5)	88	28	29	16	1	54	1	1	1	1	2	.33	3	.229	.284	.404
1999 Milwaukee	NL	48	101	26	2	0	3	—	—	37	10	8	5	0	28	0	0	0	0	0	.00	3	.257	.292	.366
2 ML YEARS		133	319	76	9	2	12	(4	8)	125	38	37	21	1	82	1	1	1	1	2	.33	6	.238	.287	.392

Todd Hundley

Bats: Left **Throws:** Right **Pos:** C-108; PH/PR-12   **Ht:** 5'11" **Wt:** 199 **Born:** 5/27/69 **Age:** 31

		BATTING														BASERUNNING				PERCENTAGES		
Year Team	Lg	G	AB	H	2B	3B	HR	(Hm | Rd)	TB	R	RBI	TBB	IBB	SO	HBP	SH	SF	SB	CS	SB%	GDP	Avg	OBP	SLG
1990 New York	NL	36	67	14	6	0	0	(0 | 0)	20	8	2	6	0	18	0	1	0	0	0	.00	1	.209	.274	.299
1991 New York	NL	21	60	8	0	1	1	(1 | 0)	13	5	7	6	0	14	1	1	1	0	0	.00	3	.133	.221	.217
1992 New York	NL	123	358	75	17	0	7	(2 | 5)	113	32	32	19	4	76	4	7	2	3	0	1.00	8	.209	.256	.316
1993 New York	NL	130	417	95	17	2	11	(5 | 6)	149	40	53	23	7	62	2	2	4	1	1	.50	10	.228	.269	.357
1994 New York	NL	91	291	69	10	1	16	(8 | 8)	129	45	42	25	4	73	3	3	1	2	1	.67	9	.237	.303	.443
1995 New York	NL	90	275	77	11	0	15	(6 | 9)	133	39	51	42	5	64	5	1	3	1	0	1.00	4	.280	.382	.484
1996 New York	NL	153	540	140	32	1	41	(20 | 21)	297	85	112	79	15	146	3	0	2	1	3	.25	9	.259	.356	.550
1997 New York	NL	132	417	114	21	2	30	(14 | 16)	229	78	86	83	16	116	3	0	5	2	3	.40	10	.273	.394	.549
1998 New York	NL	53	124	20	4	0	3	(1 | 2)	33	8	12	16	0	55	1	0	1	1	1	.50	0	.161	.261	.266
1999 Los Angeles	NL	114	376	78	14	0	24	(10 | 14)	164	49	55	44	3	113	4	1	3	3	0	1.00	5	.207	.295	.436
10 ML YEARS		943	2925	690	132	7	148	(67 | 81)	1280	389	452	343	54	737	26	16	22	14	9	.61	53	.236	.319	.438

Brian Hunter

Bats: Right **Throws:** Left **Pos:** 1B-101; PH/PR-36; LF-8   **Ht:** 6'0" **Wt:** 225 **Born:** 3/4/68 **Age:** 32

		BATTING														BASERUNNING				PERCENTAGES		
Year Team	Lg	G	AB	H	2B	3B	HR	(Hm | Rd)	TB	R	RBI	TBB	IBB	SO	HBP	SH	SF	SB	CS	SB%	GDP	Avg	OBP	SLG
1991 Atlanta	NL	97	271	68	16	1	12	(7 | 5)	122	32	50	17	0	48	1	0	2	0	2	.00	6	.251	.296	.450
1992 Atlanta	NL	102	238	57	13	2	14	(9 | 5)	116	34	41	21	3	50	0	1	8	1	2	.33	2	.239	.292	.487
1993 Atlanta	NL	37	80	11	3	1	0	(0 | 0)	16	4	8	2	1	15	0	0	3	0	0	.00	1	.138	.153	.200
1994 Pit-Cin	NL	85	256	60	16	1	15	(4 | 11)	123	34	57	17	2	56	0	0	5	0	0	.00	3	.234	.277	.480
1995 Cincinnati	NL	40	79	17	6	0	1	(0 | 1)	26	9	9	11	1	21	1	0	2	2	1	.67	2	.215	.312	.329
1996 Seattle	AL	75	198	53	10	0	7	(2 | 5)	84	21	28	15	2	43	4	1	3	0	1	.00	6	.268	.327	.424
1998 St. Louis	NL	62	112	23	9	1	4	(2 | 2)	46	11	13	7	0	23	1	3	0	1	1	.50	4	.205	.258	.411
1999 Atlanta	NL	114	181	45	12	1	6	(2 | 4)	77	28	30	31	1	40	4	5	2	0	1	.00	6	.249	.367	.425
1994 Pittsburgh	NL	76	233	53	15	1	11	(4 | 7)	103	28	47	15	2	55	0	0	4	0	0	.00	3	.227	.270	.442
Cincinnati	NL	9	23	7	1	0	4	(0 | 4)	20	6	10	2	0	1	0	0	1	0	0	.00	0	.304	.346	.870
8 ML YEARS		612	1415	334	85	7	59	(26 | 33)	610	173	236	121	10	296	11	10	25	4	8	.33	30	.236	.296	.431

Brian Hunter

Bats: Right **Throws:** Right **Pos:** LF-119; CF-37; PH/PR-4   **Ht:** 6'3" **Wt:** 180 **Born:** 3/5/71 **Age:** 29

		BATTING														BASERUNNING				PERCENTAGES		
Year Team	Lg	G	AB	H	2B	3B	HR	(Hm | Rd)	TB	R	RBI	TBB	IBB	SO	HBP	SH	SF	SB	CS	SB%	GDP	Avg	OBP	SLG
1994 Houston	NL	6	24	6	1	0	0	(0 | 0)	7	2	0	1	0	6	0	1	0	2	1	.67	0	.250	.280	.292
1995 Houston	NL	78	321	97	14	5	2	(0 | 2)	127	52	28	21	0	52	2	2	3	24	7	.77	2	.302	.346	.396
1996 Houston	NL	132	526	145	27	2	5	(1 | 4)	191	74	35	17	0	92	2	1	7	35	9	.80	6	.276	.297	.363
1997 Detroit	AL	162	658	177	29	7	4	(2 | 2)	232	112	45	66	1	121	1	8	5	74	18	.80	13	.269	.334	.353
1998 Detroit	AL	142	595	151	29	3	4	(1 | 3)	198	67	36	36	0	94	2	2	1	42	12	.78	8	.254	.298	.333
1999 Det-Sea	AL	139	539	125	13	6	4	(0 | 4)	162	79	34	37	0	91	2	4	7	44	8	.85	8	.232	.280	.301
1999 Detroit	AL	18	55	13	2	1	0	(0 | 0)	17	8	0	5	0	11	1	1	0	0	3	.00	0	.236	.311	.309
Seattle	AL	121	484	112	11	5	4	(0 | 4)	145	71	34	32	0	80	1	3	7	44	5	.90	8	.231	.277	.300
6 ML YEARS		659	2663	701	113	23	19	(4 | 15)	917	386	178	178	1	456	9	18	23	221	55	.80	37	.263	.309	.344

Torii Hunter

Bats: R **Throws:** R **Pos:** CF-107; LF-16; RF-14; PH/PR-11   **Ht:** 6'2" **Wt:** 205 **Born:** 7/18/75 **Age:** 24

								BATTING										BASERUNNING				PERCENTAGES		
Year Team	Lg	G	AB	H	2B	3B	HR	(Hm | Rd)	TB	R	RBI	TBB	IBB	SO	HBP	SH	SF	SB	CS	SB%	GDP	Avg	OBP	SLG
1993 Twins	R	28	100	19	3	0	0	—	—	22	6	8	4	0	23	9	1	0	4	2	.67	1	.190	.283	.220
1994 Fort Wayne	A	91	335	98	17	1	10	—	—	147	57	50	25	1	80	10	0	2	8	10	.44	5	.293	.358	.439
1995 Fort Myers	A+	113	391	96	15	2	7	—	—	136	64	36	38	1	77	12	5	1	7	4	.64	8	.246	.330	.348
1996 Fort Myers	A+	4	16	3	0	0	0	—	—	3	1	1	2	0	5	0	0	0	1	1	.50	0	.188	.278	.188
Hardware Cy	AA	99	342	90	20	3	7	—	—	137	49	33	28	1	60	7	9	1	7	7	.50	7	.263	.331	.401
1997 New Britain	AA	127	471	109	22	2	8	—	—	159	57	56	47	1	94	3	6	1	8	8	.50	6	.231	.305	.338
1998 New Britain	AA	82	308	87	24	3	6	—	—	135	42	32	19	1	64	4	4	3	11	9	.55	2	.282	.329	.438
Salt Lake	AAA	26	92	31	7	0	4	—	—	50	15	20	1	0	13	1	2	1	2	2	.50	3	.337	.347	.543
1997 Minnesota	AL	1	0	0	0	0	0	(0 | 0)	0	0	0	0	0	0	0	0	0	0	0	.00	0	.000	.000	.000
1998 Minnesota	AL	6	17	4	0	0	0	(0 | 0)	5	0	2	2	0	6	0	0	0	0	1	.00	1	.235	.316	.294
1999 Minnesota	AL	135	384	98	17	2	9	(2 | 7)	146	52	35	26	1	72	6	1	5	10	6	.63	9	.255	.309	.380
3 ML YEARS		142	401	102	18	2	9	(2 | 7)	151	52	37	28	1	78	6	1	5	10	7	.59	10	.254	.309	.377

Butch Huskey

Bats: R **Throws:** R **Pos:** DH-44; LF-32; RF-26; PH/PR-22; 1B-10; 3B-3   **Ht:** 6'3" **Wt:** 244 **Born:** 11/10/71 **Age:** 28

								BATTING										BASERUNNING				PERCENTAGES		
Year Team	Lg	G	AB	H	2B	3B	HR	(Hm	Rd)	TB	R	RBI	TBB	IBB	SO	HBP	SH	SF	SB	CS	SB%	GDP	Avg	OBP	SLG
1993 New York	NL	13	41	6	1	0	0	(0	0)	7	2	3	1	1	13	0	0	2	0	0	.00	0	.146	.159	.171
1995 New York	NL	28	90	17	1	0	3	(2	1)	27	8	11	10	0	16	0	1	1	1	0	1.00	3	.189	.267	.300
1996 New York	NL	118	414	115	16	2	15	(9	6)	180	43	60	27	3	77	0	0	4	1	2	.33	10	.278	.319	.435
1997 New York	NL	142	471	135	26	2	24	(7	17)	237	61	81	25	5	84	1	0	8	8	5	.62	21	.287	.319	.503
1998 New York	NL	113	369	93	18	0	13	(4	9)	150	43	59	26	3	66	1	2	4	7	6	.54	13	.252	.300	.407
1999 Sea-Bos	AL	119	386	109	15	0	22	(9	13)	190	62	77	34	1	65	0	0	3	3	1	.75	9	.282	.338	.492
1999 Seattle	AL	74	262	76	9	0	15	(7	8)	130	44	49	27	0	45	0	0	3	3	1	.75	3	.290	.353	.496
Boston	AL	45	124	33	6	0	7	(2	5)	60	18	28	7	1	20	0	0	0	0	0	.00	6	.266	.305	.484
6 ML YEARS		533	1771	475	77	4	77	(31	46)	791	219	291	123	13	321	2	3	22	20	14	.59	56	.268	.313	.447

Jeff Huson

Bats: L **Throws:** R **Pos:** 2B-41; PH/PR-35; SS-22; 3B-9; 1B-8; DH-7; LF-2   **Ht:** 6'3" **Wt:** 180 **Born:** 8/15/64 **Age:** 35

								BATTING										BASERUNNING				PERCENTAGES		
Year Team	Lg	G	AB	H	2B	3B	HR	(Hm	Rd)	TB	R	RBI	TBB	IBB	SO	HBP	SH	SF	SB	CS	SB%	GDP	Avg	OBP	SLG
1988 Montreal	NL	20	42	13	2	0	0	(0	0)	15	7	3	4	2	3	0	0	0	2	1	.67	2	.310	.370	.357
1989 Montreal	NL	32	74	12	5	0	0	(0	0)	17	1	2	6	3	6	0	3	0	3	0	1.00	6	.162	.225	.230
1990 Texas	AL	145	396	95	12	2	0	(0	0)	111	57	28	46	0	54	2	7	3	12	4	.75	8	.240	.320	.280
1991 Texas	AL	119	268	57	8	3	2	(1	1)	77	36	26	39	0	32	0	9	1	8	3	.73	6	.213	.312	.287
1992 Texas	AL	123	318	83	14	3	4	(0	4)	115	49	24	41	2	43	1	8	6	18	6	.75	7	.261	.342	.362
1993 Texas	AL	23	45	6	1	1	0	(0	0)	9	3	2	0	0	10	0	1	0	0	0	.00	0	.133	.133	.200
1995 Baltimore	AL	66	161	40	4	2	1	(0	1)	51	24	19	15	1	20	1	2	1	5	4	.56	4	.248	.315	.317
1996 Baltimore	AL	17	28	9	1	0	0	(0	0)	10	5	2	1	0	3	0	0	0	0	0	.00	0	.321	.333	.357
1997 Milwaukee	AL	84	143	29	3	0	0	(0	0)	32	12	11	5	0	15	2	2	1	3	0	1.00	7	.203	.238	.224
1998 Seattle	AL	31	49	8	1	0	1	(0	1)	12	8	4	5	0	6	0	0	0	1	1	.50	1	.163	.241	.245
1999 Anaheim	AL	97	225	59	7	1	0	(0	0)	68	21	18	16	0	27	0	1	3	10	1	.91	9	.262	.307	.302
11 ML YEARS		757	1749	411	58	12	8	(1	7)	517	223	139	178	8	219	6	33	16	62	20	.76	49	.235	.305	.296

Tim Hyers

Bats: L **Throws:** L **Pos:** PH/PR-35; 1B-14; LF-12; RF-4; DH-1   **Ht:** 6'1" **Wt:** 195 **Born:** 10/3/71 **Age:** 28

								BATTING										BASERUNNING				PERCENTAGES		
Year Team	Lg	G	AB	H	2B	3B	HR	(Hm	Rd)	TB	R	RBI	TBB	IBB	SO	HBP	SH	SF	SB	CS	SB%	GDP	Avg	OBP	SLG
1999 Calgary *	AAA	51	179	48	12	0	4	—	—	72	25	20	14	1	22	0	0	1	1	1	.50	6	.268	.320	.402
1994 San Diego	NL	52	118	30	3	0	0	(0	0)	33	13	7	9	0	15	0	2	0	3	0	1.00	1	.254	.307	.280
1995 San Diego	NL	6	5	0	0	0	0	(0	0)	0	0	0	0	0	1	0	0	0	0	0	.00	1	.000	.000	.000
1996 Detroit	AL	17	26	2	1	0	0	(0	0)	3	1	0	4	2	5	0	0	0	0	0	.00	1	.077	.200	.115
1999 Florida	NL	58	81	18	4	1	2	(0	2)	30	8	12	14	0	11	0	0	1	0	0	.00	1	.222	.333	.370
4 ML YEARS		133	230	50	8	1	2	(0	2)	66	22	19	27	2	32	0	2	1	3	0	1.00	4	.217	.298	.287

Raul Ibanez

Bats: L **Throws:** R **Pos:** RF-39; PH/PR-29; LF-22; 1B-21; DH-1; C-1   **Ht:** 6'2" **Wt:** 200 **Born:** 6/2/72 **Age:** 28

								BATTING										BASERUNNING				PERCENTAGES		
Year Team	Lg	G	AB	H	2B	3B	HR	(Hm	Rd)	TB	R	RBI	TBB	IBB	SO	HBP	SH	SF	SB	CS	SB%	GDP	Avg	OBP	SLG
1999 Tacoma *	AAA	8	31	11	1	0	3	—	—	21	6	5	1	0	7	0	0	0	1	1	.50	0	.355	.375	.677
1996 Seattle	AL	4	5	0	0	0	0	(0	0)	0	0	0	0	0	1	1	0	0	0	0	.00	0	.000	.167	.000
1997 Seattle	AL	11	26	4	0	1	1	(1	0)	9	3	4	0	0	6	0	0	0	0	0	.00	0	.154	.154	.346
1998 Seattle	AL	37	98	25	7	1	2	(1	1)	40	12	12	5	0	22	0	0	0	0	0	.00	4	.255	.291	.408
1999 Seattle	AL	87	209	54	7	0	9	(3	6)	88	23	27	17	1	32	0	0	1	5	1	.83	4	.258	.313	.421
4 ML YEARS		139	338	83	14	2	12	(5	7)	137	38	43	22	1	61	1	0	1	5	1	.83	8	.246	.293	.405

Hideki Irabu

Pitches: Right **Bats:** Right **Pos:** SP-27; RP-5 **Ht:** 6'4" **Wt:** 240 **Born:** 5/5/69 **Age:** 31

Year Team	Lg	G	GS	CG	GF	IP	BFP	H	R	ER	HR	SH	SF	HB	TBB	IBB	SO	WP	Bk	W	L	Pct.	ShO	Sv-Op	Hld	ERA
1997 New York	AL	13	9	0	0	53.1	246	69	47	42	15	1	2	1	20	0	56	4	3	5	4	.556	0	0-0	1	7.09
1998 New York	AL	29	28	2	0	173	732	148	79	78	27	6	6	9	76	1	126	6	1	13	9	.591	1	0-0	0	4.06
1999 New York	AL	32	27	2	2	169.1	733	180	98	91	26	2	4	6	46	0	133	7	0	11	7	.611	1	0-0	0	4.84
3 ML YEARS		74	64	4	2	395.2	1711	397	224	211	68	9	12	16	142	1	315	17	4	29	20	.592	2	0-0	1	4.80

Jason Isringhausen

Pitches: Right **Bats:** Right **Pos:** RP-28; SP-5 **Ht:** 6'3" **Wt:** 210 **Born:** 9/7/72 **Age:** 27

Year Team	Lg	G	GS	CG	GF	IP	BFP	H	R	ER	HR	SH	SF	HB	TBB	IBB	SO	WP	Bk	W	L	Pct.	ShO	Sv-Op	Hld	ERA
1999 Norfolk *	AAA	12	8	0	1	51	203	33	18	13	4	1	0	1	20	0	51	0	1	3	1	.750	0	0--	—	2.29
1995 New York	NL	14	14	1	0	93	385	88	29	29	6	3	3	2	31	2	55	4	1	9	2	.818	0	0-0	0	2.81
1996 New York	NL	27	27	0	0	171.2	766	190	103	91	13	7	9	8	73	5	114	14	0	6	14	.300	1	0-0	0	4.77
1997 New York	NL	6	6	0	0	29.2	145	40	27	25	3	1	2	1	22	0	25	3	0	2	2	.500	0	0-0	0	7.58
1999 NYM-Oak		33	5	0	20	64.2	286	64	35	34	9	0	1	3	34	4	51	4	0	1	4	.200	0	9-9	0	4.73
1999 New York	NL	13	5	0	2	39.1	179	43	29	28	7	0	1	2	22	2	31	2	0	1	3	.250	0	1-1	0	6.41
Oakland	AL	20	0	0	18	25.1	107	21	6	6	2	0	0	1	12	2	20	2	0	0	1	.000	0	8-8	0	2.13
4 ML YEARS		80	52	3	20	359	1582	382	194	179	31	11	15	14	160	11	245	25	1	18	22	.450	1	9-9	0	4.49

Damian Jackson

Bats: R **Throws:** R **Pos:** SS-100; 2B-21; PH/PR-18; LF-2; RF-1 **Ht:** 5'11" **Wt:** 185 **Born:** 8/16/73 **Age:** 26

Year Team	Lg	G	AB	H	2B	3B	HR	(Hm	Rd)	TB	R	RBI	TBB	IBB	SO	HBP	SH	SF	SB	CS	SB%	GDP	Avg	OBP	SLG
1996 Cleveland	AL	5	10	3	2	0	0	(0	0)	5	2	1	1	0	4	0	0	0	0	0	.00	0	.300	.364	.500
1997 Cle-Cin		20	36	7	2	1	1	(0	1)	14	8	2	4	1	8	1	1	0	2	1	.67	0	.194	.293	.389
1998 Cincinnati	NL	13	38	12	5	0	0	(0	0)	17	4	7	6	0	4	0	0	1	2	0	1.00	1	.316	.400	.447
1999 San Diego	NL	133	388	87	20	2	9	(6	3)	138	56	39	53	3	105	3	0	3	34	10	.77	2	.224	.320	.356
1997 Cleveland	AL	8	9	1	0	0	0	(0	0)	1	2	0	0	0	1	1	0	0	1	0	1.00	0	.111	.200	.111
Cincinnati	NL	12	27	6	2	1	1	(0	1)	13	6	2	4	1	7	0	1	0	1	1	.50	0	.222	.323	.481
4 ML YEARS		171	472	109	29	3	10	(6	4)	174	70	49	64	4	121	4	1	4	38	11	.78	3	.231	.325	.369

Darrin Jackson

Bats: R **Throws:** R **Pos:** LF-46; CF-25; PH/PR-24; DH-3; RF-3 **Ht:** 6'0" **Wt:** 198 **Born:** 8/22/63 **Age:** 36

Year Team	Lg	G	AB	H	2B	3B	HR	(Hm	Rd)	TB	R	RBI	TBB	IBB	SO	HBP	SH	SF	SB	CS	SB%	GDP	Avg	OBP	SLG
1985 Chicago	NL	5	11	1	0	0	0	(0	0)	1	0	0	0	0	3	0	0	0	0	0	.00	0	.091	.091	.091
1987 Chicago	NL	7	5	4	1	0	0	(0	0)	5	2	0	0	0	0	0	0	0	0	0	.00	0	.800	.800	1.000
1988 Chicago	NL	100	188	50	11	3	6	(3	3)	85	29	20	5	1	28	1	2	1	4	1	.80	3	.266	.287	.452
1989 ChC-SD	NL	70	170	37	7	0	4	(1	3)	56	17	20	13	5	34	0	0	2	1	4	.20	2	.218	.270	.329
1990 San Diego	NL	58	113	29	3	0	3	(1	2)	41	10	9	5	1	24	0	1	1	3	0	1.00	1	.257	.286	.363
1991 San Diego	NL	122	359	94	12	1	21	(12	9)	171	51	49	27	2	66	2	3	3	5	3	.63	5	.262	.315	.476
1992 San Diego	NL	155	587	146	23	5	17	(11	6)	230	72	70	26	4	106	4	6	5	14	3	.82	21	.249	.283	.392
1993 Tor-NYM		77	263	55	9	0	6	(4	2)	82	19	26	10	0	75	0	6	1	0	2	.00	9	.209	.237	.312
1994 Chicago	AL	104	369	115	17	3	10	(4	6)	168	43	51	27	3	56	3	2	2	7	1	.88	5	.312	.362	.455
1997 Min-Mil		75	211	55	9	1	4	(4	1)	81	26	36	6	0	31	0	5	2	4	1	.80	5	.261	.279	.384
1998 Milwaukee	NL	114	204	49	13	1	4	(2	2)	76	20	20	9	0	37	1	0	0	1	1	.50	5	.240	.276	.373
1999 Chicago	AL	73	149	41	9	1	4	(1	3)	64	22	16	3	0	20	0	2	1	4	1	.80	4	.275	.288	.430
1989 Chicago	NL	45	83	19	4	0	1	(0	1)	26	7	8	6	1	17	0	0	0	1	2	.33	1	.229	.281	.313
San Diego	NL	25	87	18	3	0	3	(1	2)	30	10	12	7	4	17	0	0	2	0	2	.00	1	.207	.260	.345
1993 Toronto	AL	46	176	38	8	0	5	(4	1)	61	15	19	8	0	53	0	5	0	0	2	.00	9	.216	.250	.347
New York	NL	31	87	17	1	0	1	(0	1)	21	4	7	2	0	22	0	1	1	0	0	.00	0	.195	.211	.241
1997 Minnesota	NL	49	130	33	2	1	3	(3	0)	46	19	21	4	0	21	0	3	2	2	1	1.00	2	.254	.272	.354
Milwaukee	AL	26	81	22	7	0	2	(1	1)	35	7	15	2	0	10	0	2	0	2	1	.67	3	.272	.289	.432
12 ML YEARS		960	2629	676	114	15	80	(43	37)	1060	311	317	131	16	480	11	27	18	43	17	.72	60	.257	.293	.403

Mike Jackson

Pitches: Right **Bats:** Right **Pos:** RP-72 **Ht:** 6'2" **Wt:** 225 **Born:** 12/22/64 **Age:** 35

Year Team	Lg	G	GS	CG	GF	IP	BFP	H	R	ER	HR	SH	SF	HB	TBB	IBB	SO	WP	Bk	W	L	Pct.	ShO	Sv-Op	Hld	ERA
1986 Philadelphia	NL	9	0	0	4	13.1	54	12	5	5	2	0	0	2	4	1	3	0	0	0	0	.000	0	0-1	0	3.38
1987 Philadelphia	NL	55	7	0	8	109.1	468	88	55	51	16	3	4	3	56	6	93	6	8	3	10	.231	0	1-2	6	4.20
1988 Seattle	AL	62	0	0	29	99.1	412	74	37	29	10	3	10	2	43	10	76	6	6	6	5	.545	0	4-11	10	2.63
1989 Seattle	AL	65	0	0	27	99.1	431	81	43	35	8	6	2	6	54	6	94	1	2	4	6	.400	0	7-10	9	3.17
1990 Seattle	AL	63	0	0	28	77.1	338	64	42	39	8	8	5	2	44	12	69	9	2	5	7	.417	0	3-12	13	4.54
1991 Seattle	AL	72	0	0	35	88.2	363	64	35	32	5	4	0	6	34	11	74	3	0	7	7	.500	0	14-22	9	3.25
1992 San Francisco	NL	67	0	0	24	82	346	76	35	34	7	5	2	4	33	10	80	1	0	6	6	.500	0	2-3	9	3.73
1993 San Francisco	NL	81	0	0	17	77.1	317	58	28	26	7	4	2	3	24	6	70	2	2	6	6	.500	0	1-6	34	3.03
1994 San Francisco	NL	36	0	0	12	42.1	158	23	8	7	4	4	1	2	11	0	51	0	0	3	2	.600	0	4-6	9	1.49
1995 Cincinnati	NL	40	0	0	10	49	200	38	13	13	5	1	1	1	19	1	41	1	1	6	1	.857	0	2-4	9	2.39
1996 Seattle	AL	73	0	0	23	72	302	61	32	29	11	0	1	6	24	3	70	2	0	1	1	.500	0	6-8	15	3.63
1997 Cleveland	AL	71	0	0	38	75	313	59	31	27	3	3	3	4	29	5	74	4	0	2	5	.286	0	15-17	14	3.24

Year Team	Lg	HOW MUCH HE PITCHED						WHAT HE GAVE UP										THE RESULTS						
		G	GS	CG	GF	IP	BFP	H	R	ER	HR	SH	SF	HB	TBB	IBB	SO	WP	Bk	W	L	Pct.	ShO	Sv-Op	Hld	ERA
1998 Cleveland	AL	69	0	0	57	64	239	43	11	11	4	1	0	4	13	0	55	1	3	1	1	.500	0	40-45	1	1.55
1999 Cleveland	AL	72	0	0	65	68.2	291	60	32	31	11	2	2	2	26	1	55	0	1	3	4	.429	0	39-43	0	4.06
14 ML YEARS		835	7	0	377	1017.2	4232	801	409	369	101	44	33	47	414	72	905	34	25	53	61	.465	0	138-190	138	3.26

Ryan Jackson

Bats: L Throws: L Pos: 1B-29; PH/PR-7; LF-1   **Ht:** 6'3"   **Wt:** 185   **Born:** 11/11/71   **Age:** 28

Year Team	Lg	BATTING																	BASERUNNING				PERCENTAGES		
		G	AB	H	2B	3B	HR	(Hm	Rd)	TB	R	RBI	TBB	IBB	SO	HBP	SH	SF	SB	CS	SB%	GDP	Avg	OBP	SLG
1994 Elmira	A-	72	276	80	18	1	6	—	—	118	46	41	22	1	40	1	0	6	4	3	.57	2	.290	.338	.428
1995 Kane County	A	132	471	138	39	6	10	—	—	219	78	82	67	7	74	4	0	5	13	8	.62	9	.293	.382	.465
1996 Marlins	R	7	25	9	0	0	0	—	—	9	5	5	1	0	3	1	0	0	2	0	1.00	6	.360	.407	.360
Brevard Cty	A+	6	26	8	2	0	1	—	—	13	4	4	1	0	7	0	0	0	1	0	1.00	1	.308	.333	.500
1997 Portland	AA	134	491	153	28	4	26	—	—	267	87	98	51	2	85	3	1	0	2	5	.29	6	.312	.380	.544
1998 Charlotte	AAA	13	50	19	4	0	2	—	—	29	5	11	4	0	14	0	0	0	2	0	1.00	1	.380	.426	.580
1999 Tacoma	AAA	105	409	126	25	2	8	—	—	179	57	62	36	5	64	1	1	7	12	3	.80	9	.308	.360	.438
1998 Florida	NL	111	260	65	15	1	5	(3	2)	97	26	31	20	0	73	1	2	1	1	1	.50	3	.250	.305	.373
1999 Seattle	AL	32	68	16	3	0	0	(0	0)	19	4	10	6	0	19	1	0	2	3	3	.50	3	.235	.299	.279
2 ML YEARS		143	328	81	18	1	5	(3	2)	116	30	41	26	0	92	2	2	3	4	4	.50	6	.247	.304	.354

John Jaha

Bats: Right Throws: Right Pos: DH-121; PH/PR-16; 1B-8   **Ht:** 6'1"   **Wt:** 224   **Born:** 5/27/66   **Age:** 34

Year Team	Lg	BATTING																	BASERUNNING				PERCENTAGES		
		G	AB	H	2B	3B	HR	(Hm	Rd)	TB	R	RBI	TBB	IBB	SO	HBP	SH	SF	SB	CS	SB%	GDP	Avg	OBP	SLG
1992 Milwaukee	AL	47	133	30	3	1	2	(1	1)	41	17	10	12	1	30	2	1	4	10	0	1.00	1	.226	.291	.308
1993 Milwaukee	AL	153	515	136	21	0	19	(5	14)	214	78	70	51	4	109	8	4	4	13	9	.59	6	.264	.337	.416
1994 Milwaukee	AL	84	291	70	14	0	12	(5	7)	120	45	39	32	3	75	10	1	4	3	3	.50	8	.241	.332	.412
1995 Milwaukee	AL	88	316	99	20	2	20	(8	12)	183	59	65	36	0	66	4	0	1	2	1	.67	8	.313	.389	.579
1996 Milwaukee	AL	148	543	163	28	1	34	(17	17)	295	108	118	85	1	118	5	0	3	3	1	.75	16	.300	.398	.543
1997 Milwaukee	AL	46	162	40	7	0	11	(1	10)	80	25	26	25	1	40	3	0	2	1	0	1.00	6	.247	.354	.494
1998 Milwaukee	NL	73	216	45	6	1	7	(2	5)	74	29	38	49	3	66	6	0	2	1	3	.25	5	.208	.366	.343
1999 Oakland	AL	142	457	126	23	0	35	(18	17)	254	93	111	101	2	129	9	0	3	2	0	1.00	14	.276	.414	.556
8 ML YEARS		781	2633	709	122	5	140	(57	83)	1261	454	477	391	15	633	47	6	23	35	17	.67	64	.269	.371	.479

Kevin Jarvis

Pitches: Right Bats: Left Pos: RP-3; SP-1   **Ht:** 6'2"   **Wt:** 200   **Born:** 8/1/69   **Age:** 30

Year Team	Lg	HOW MUCH HE PITCHED						WHAT HE GAVE UP										THE RESULTS						
		G	GS	CG	GF	IP	BFP	H	R	ER	HR	SH	SF	HB	TBB	IBB	SO	WP	Bk	W	L	Pct.	ShO	Sv-Op	Hld	ERA
1999 Modesto *	A+	2	2	0	0	7	26	4	1	1	0	1	0	0	1	0	10	0	0	0	0	.000	0	0- -	—	1.29
Vancouver *	AAA	17	16	2	0	103	439	110	47	41	14	3	1	2	26	0	64	4	0	10	2	.833	1	0- -	—	3.58
1994 Cincinnati	NL	6	3	0	0	17.2	79	22	14	14	4	1	0	0	5	0	10	1	0	1	1	.500	0	0-0	0	7.13
1995 Cincinnati	NL	19	11	1	2	79	354	91	56	50	13	2	5	3	32	2	33	2	0	3	4	.429	1	0-0	0	5.70
1996 Cincinnati	NL	24	20	2	2	120.1	552	152	93	80	17	6	2	2	43	5	63	3	0	8	9	.471	1	0-0	0	5.98
1997 Cin-Min-Det		32	5	0	13	68	329	99	62	58	17	2	1	1	29	0	48	4	0	0	4	.000	0	1-1	0	7.68
1999 Oakland	AL	4	1	0	0	14	75	28	19	18	6	0	1	1	6	0	11	0	0	0	0	.000	0	0-0	0	11.57
1997 Cincinnati	NL	9	0	0	3	13.1	70	21	16	15	4	1	0	1	7	0	12	2	0	0	1	.000	0	1-1	0	10.13
Minnesota	AL	6	2	0	1	13	70	23	18	18	4	0	0	0	8	0	9	2	0	0	0	.000	0	0-0	0	12.46
Detroit	AL	17	3	0	9	41.2	189	55	28	25	9	1	1	0	14	0	27	0	0	0	3	.000	0	0-0	0	5.40
5 ML YEARS		85	40	3	17	299	1389	392	244	220	57	11	9	7	115	7	165	10	0	12	19	.387	2	1-1	0	6.62

Stan Javier

Bats: B Throws: R Pos: LF-57; RF-52; PH/PR-24; CF-10; DH-1   **Ht:** 6'0"   **Wt:** 202   **Born:** 1/9/64   **Age:** 36

Year Team	Lg	BATTING																	BASERUNNING				PERCENTAGES		
		G	AB	H	2B	3B	HR	(Hm	Rd)	TB	R	RBI	TBB	IBB	SO	HBP	SH	SF	SB	CS	SB%	GDP	Avg	OBP	SLG
1984 New York	AL	7	7	1	0	0	0	(0	0)	1	1	0	0	0	1	0	0	0	0	0	.00	0	.143	.143	.143
1986 Oakland	AL	59	114	23	8	0	0	(0	0)	31	13	8	16	0	27	1	0	0	8	0	1.00	2	.202	.305	.272
1987 Oakland	AL	81	151	28	3	1	2	(1	1)	39	22	9	19	3	33	0	6	0	3	2	.60	2	.185	.276	.258
1988 Oakland	AL	125	397	102	13	3	2	(0	2)	127	49	35	32	1	63	2	6	3	20	1	.95	13	.257	.313	.320
1989 Oakland	AL	112	310	77	12	3	1	(1	0)	98	42	28	31	1	45	1	4	2	12	2	.86	6	.248	.317	.316
1990 Oak-LA		123	309	92	9	6	3	(1	2)	122	60	27	40	2	50	0	6	2	15	7	.68	6	.298	.376	.395
1991 Los Angeles	NL	121	176	36	5	3	1	(1	0)	50	21	11	16	0	36	0	3	2	7	1	.88	4	.205	.268	.284
1992 LA-Phi	NL	130	334	83	17	1	1	(1	0)	105	42	29	37	2	54	3	3	2	18	3	.86	4	.249	.327	.314
1993 California	AL	92	237	69	10	4	3	(0	3)	96	33	28	27	1	33	1	1	3	12	2	.86	7	.291	.362	.405
1994 Oakland	AL	109	419	114	23	0	10	(1	9)	167	75	44	49	1	76	2	7	3	24	7	.77	7	.272	.349	.399
1995 Oakland	AL	130	442	123	20	2	8	(3	5)	171	81	56	49	3	63	4	5	4	36	5	.88	8	.278	.353	.387
1996 San Francisco	NL	71	274	74	25	0	2	(1	1)	105	44	22	25	0	51	2	5	0	14	2	.88	4	.270	.336	.383
1997 San Francisco	NL	142	440	126	16	4	8	(6	2)	174	69	50	56	1	70	5	2	7	25	3	.89	5	.286	.368	.395
1998 San Francisco	NL	135	417	121	13	5	4	(1	3)	156	63	49	65	4	63	1	4	3	21	5	.81	13	.290	.385	.374
1999 SF-Hou	NL	132	397	113	19	2	3	(2	1)	145	61	34	38	4	63	1	8	2	16	7	.70	6	.285	.347	.365
1990 Oakland	AL	19	33	8	0	2	0	(0	0)	12	4	3	3	0	6	0	0	0	0	0	.00	0	.242	.306	.364
Los Angeles	NL	104	276	84	9	4	3	(1	2)	110	56	24	37	2	44	0	6	2	15	7	.68	6	.304	.384	.399
1992 Los Angeles	NL	56	58	11	3	0	1	(1	0)	17	6	5	6	2	11	1	1	0	1	2	.33	0	.190	.277	.293
Philadelphia	NL	74	276	72	14	1	0	(0	0)	88	36	24	31	0	43	2	2	2	17	1	.94	4	.261	.338	.319
1999 San Francisco	NL	112	333	92	15	1	3	(2	1)	118	49	30	29	4	55	1	7	1	13	6	.68	4	.276	.335	.354

Gregg Jefferies

Year Team	Lg	G	AB	H	2B	3B	HR	(Hm	Rd)	TB	R	RBI	TBB	IBB	SO	HBP	SH	SF	SB	CS	SB%	GDP	Avg	OBP	SLG
Houston	NL	20	64	21	4	1	0	(0	0)	27	12	4	9	0	8	0	1	1	3	1	.75	2	.328	.405	.422
15 ML YEARS		1569	4424	1182	193	34	48	(18	30)	1587	676	430	500	23	728	23	60	33	231	47	.83	87	.267	.342	.359

Bats: B **Throws:** R **Pos:** DH-45; PH/PR-22; 1B-3; 2B-2; LF-2   **Ht:** 5'10" **Wt:** 185 **Born:** 8/1/67 **Age:** 32

Year Team	Lg	G	AB	H	2B	3B	HR	(Hm	Rd)	TB	R	RBI	TBB	IBB	SO	HBP	SH	SF	SB	CS	SB%	GDP	Avg	OBP	SLG
1999 Toledo *	AAA	2	8	2	0	0	0	—	—	2	0	0	0	0	2	0	0	0	0	0	.00	0	.250	.250	.250
1987 New York	NL	6	6	3	1	0	0	(0	0)	4	0	2	0	0	0	0	0	0	0	0	.00	0	.500	.500	.667
1988 New York	NL	29	109	35	8	2	6	(3	3)	65	19	17	8	0	10	0	0	1	5	1	.83	1	.321	.364	.596
1989 New York	NL	141	508	131	28	2	12	(7	5)	199	72	56	39	8	46	5	2	5	21	6	.78	16	.258	.314	.392
1990 New York	NL	153	604	171	40	3	15	(9	6)	262	96	68	46	2	40	5	0	4	11	2	.85	12	.283	.337	.434
1991 New York	NL	136	486	132	19	2	9	(5	4)	182	59	62	47	2	38	2	1	3	26	5	.84	12	.272	.336	.374
1992 Kansas City	AL	152	604	172	36	3	10	(3	7)	244	66	75	43	4	29	1	0	9	19	9	.68	24	.285	.329	.404
1993 St. Louis	NL	142	544	186	24	3	16	(10	6)	264	89	83	62	7	32	2	0	4	46	9	.84	15	.342	.408	.485
1994 St. Louis	NL	103	397	129	27	1	12	(7	5)	194	52	55	45	12	26	1	0	4	12	5	.71	9	.325	.391	.489
1995 Philadelphia	NL	114	480	147	31	2	11	(4	7)	215	69	56	35	5	26	0	0	6	9	5	.64	15	.306	.349	.448
1996 Philadelphia	NL	104	404	118	17	3	7	(4	3)	162	59	51	36	6	21	1	0	5	20	6	.77	9	.292	.348	.401
1997 Philadelphia	NL	130	476	122	25	3	11	(2	9)	186	68	48	53	7	27	2	0	0	12	6	.67	8	.256	.333	.391
1998 Phi-Ana		144	555	167	28	3	9	(3	6)	228	72	58	29	4	32	1	1	6	12	3	.80	19	.301	.333	.411
1999 Detroit	AL	70	205	41	8	0	6	(5	1)	67	22	18	13	1	11	4	0	3	3	4	.43	9	.200	.258	.327
1998 Philadelphia	NL	125	483	142	22	3	8	(3	6)	194	65	48	29	4	27	1	1	6	11	3	.79	17	.294	.331	.402
Anaheim	AL	19	72	25	6	0	1	(0	1)	34	7	10	0	0	5	0	0	0	1	0	1.00	2	.347	.347	.472
13 ML YEARS		1424	5378	1554	292	27	124	(62	62)	2272	743	649	456	58	338	24	4	50	196	61	.76	149	.289	.344	.422

Reggie Jefferson

Bats: Left **Throws:** Left **Pos:** DH-58; PH/PR-30; 1B-2   **Ht:** 6'4" **Wt:** 215 **Born:** 9/25/68 **Age:** 31

Year Team	Lg	G	AB	H	2B	3B	HR	(Hm	Rd)	TB	R	RBI	TBB	IBB	SO	HBP	SH	SF	SB	CS	SB%	GDP	Avg	OBP	SLG
1999 Sarasota *	A+	3	14	6	2	0	1	—	—	11	4	2	1	0	2	0	0	0	0	0	.00	0	.429	.467	.786
Pawtucket *	AAA	3	10	0	0	0	0	—	—	0	1	0	2	0	3	1	0	0	0	0	.00	0	.000	.231	.000
1991 Cin-Cle		31	108	21	3	0	3	(2	1)	33	11	13	4	0	24	0	0	1	0	0	.00	1	.194	.221	.306
1992 Cleveland	AL	24	89	30	6	2	1	(1	0)	43	8	6	1	0	17	1	0	0	0	0	.00	2	.337	.352	.483
1993 Cleveland	AL	113	366	91	11	2	10	(4	6)	136	35	34	28	7	78	5	3	1	1	3	.25	7	.249	.310	.372
1994 Seattle	AL	63	162	53	11	0	8	(4	4)	88	24	32	17	5	32	1	0	0	0	0	.00	6	.327	.392	.543
1995 Boston	AL	46	121	35	8	0	5	(1	4)	58	21	26	9	1	24	0	0	2	0	0	.00	3	.289	.333	.479
1996 Boston	AL	122	386	134	30	4	19	(12	7)	229	67	74	25	5	89	3	0	4	0	0	.00	11	.347	.388	.593
1997 Boston	AL	136	489	156	33	1	13	(6	7)	230	74	67	24	5	93	7	1	3	1	2	.33	17	.319	.358	.470
1998 Boston	AL	62	196	60	16	1	8	(2	6)	102	24	31	21	2	40	1	0	1	0	0	.00	9	.306	.374	.520
1999 Boston	AL	83	206	57	13	1	5	(1	4)	87	21	17	17	0	54	2	0	0	0	0	.00	9	.277	.338	.422
1991 Cincinnati	NL	5	7	1	0	0	1	(1	0)	4	1	1	1	0	2	0	0	0	0	0	.00	0	.143	.250	.571
Cleveland	AL	26	101	20	3	0	2	(1	1)	29	10	12	3	0	22	0	0	1	0	0	.00	1	.198	.219	.287
9 ML YEARS		680	2123	637	131	11	72	(33	39)	1006	285	300	146	25	451	20	4	13	2	5	.29	63	.300	.349	.474

Geoff Jenkins

Bats: Left **Throws:** Right **Pos:** LF-128; PH/PR-13   **Ht:** 6'1" **Wt:** 204 **Born:** 7/21/74 **Age:** 25

Year Team	Lg	G	AB	H	2B	3B	HR	(Hm	Rd)	TB	R	RBI	TBB	IBB	SO	HBP	SH	SF	SB	CS	SB%	GDP	Avg	OBP	SLG
1995 Helena	R+	7	28	9	0	1	0	—	—	11	2	9	3	0	11	0	0	1	0	2	.00	0	.321	.375	.393
Stockton	A+	13	47	12	2	0	3	—	—	23	13	12	10	0	12	0	0	2	2	0	1.00	0	.255	.373	.489
El Paso	AA	22	79	22	4	2	1	—	—	33	12	13	8	0	23	0	0	1	3	1	.75	1	.278	.341	.418
1996 El Paso	AA	22	77	22	5	4	1	—	—	38	17	11	12	1	21	2	0	1	1	2	.33	2	.286	.391	.494
Stockton	A+	37	138	48	8	4	3	—	—	73	27	25	20	1	32	3	1	3	3	3	.50	3	.348	.433	.529
1997 Tucson	AAA	93	347	82	24	3	10	—	—	142	44	56	33	1	87	3	0	0	0	2	.00	7	.236	.308	.409
1998 Louisville	AAA	55	215	71	10	4	7	—	—	110	38	52	14	3	39	5	0	2	1	1	.50	6	.330	.381	.512
1998 Milwaukee	NL	84	262	60	12	1	9	(4	5)	101	33	28	20	4	61	2	0	1	1	3	.25	7	.229	.288	.385
1999 Milwaukee	NL	135	447	140	43	3	21	(10	11)	252	70	82	35	7	87	7	3	1	5	1	.83	10	.313	.371	.564
2 ML YEARS		219	709	200	55	4	30	(14	16)	353	103	110	55	11	148	9	3	2	6	4	.60	17	.282	.341	.498

Robin Jennings

Bats: Left **Throws:** Left **Pos:** PH/PR-5   **Ht:** 6'2" **Wt:** 210 **Born:** 4/11/72 **Age:** 28

Year Team	Lg	G	AB	H	2B	3B	HR	(Hm	Rd)	TB	R	RBI	TBB	IBB	SO	HBP	SH	SF	SB	CS	SB%	GDP	Avg	OBP	SLG
1992 Geneva	A-	72	275	82	12	2	7	—	—	119	39	47	20	5	43	2	0	0	10	3	.77	7	.298	.350	.433
1993 Peoria	A	132	474	146	29	5	3	—	—	194	65	65	46	2	73	4	5	3	11	11	.50	9	.308	.372	.409
1994 Daytona	A+	128	476	133	24	5	8	—	—	191	64	60	45	5	54	4	4	4	2	10	.17	13	.279	.344	.401
1995 Orlando	AA	132	490	145	27	7	17	—	—	237	71	79	44	5	61	4	0	5	7	14	.33	11	.296	.355	.484
1996 Iowa	AAA	86	331	94	15	6	18	—	—	175	53	56	32	1	53	1	0	3	2	0	1.00	6	.284	.346	.529
1997 Iowa	AAA	126	464	128	25	5	20	—	—	223	67	71	56	5	73	5	0	2	5	3	.63	7	.276	.359	.481
1998 West Tenn	AA	2	6	0	0	0	0	—	—	0	0	0	0	0	2	0	0	0	0	0	.00	0	.000	.000	.000
Iowa	AAA	81	298	74	23	2	16	—	—	149	57	42	33	1	49	6	1	0	4	4	.50	9	.248	.335	.500
1999 West Tenn	AA	13	53	17	3	0	5	—	—	35	11	17	5	0	7	1	0	2	1	0	1.00	2	.321	.377	.660
Iowa	AAA	67	259	80	20	5	9	—	—	137	47	43	25	0	34	1	0	0	6	4	.60	7	.309	.372	.529

Year Team	Lg	G	AB	H	2B	3B	HR	(Hm	Rd)	TB	R	RBI	TBB	IBB	SO	HBP	SH	SF	SB	CS	SB%	GDP	Avg	OBP	SLG
1996 Chicago	NL	31	58	13	5	0	0	(0	0)	18	7	4	3	0	9	1	0	0	1	0	1.00	1	.224	.274	.310
1997 Chicago	NL	9	18	3	1	0	0	(0	0)	4	1	2	0	0	2	0	0	1	0	0	.00	0	.167	.158	.222
1999 Chicago	NL	5	5	1	0	0	0	(0	0)	1	0	0	0	0	2	0	0	0	0	0	.00	0	.200	.200	.200
3 ML YEARS		45	81	17	6	0	0	(0	0)	23	8	6	3	0	13	1	0	1	1	0	1.00	1	.210	.244	.284

Marcus Jensen

Bats: Both **Throws:** Right **Pos:** C-14; PH/PR-4   **Ht:** 6'4" **Wt:** 204 **Born:** 12/14/72 **Age:** 27

Year Team	Lg	G	AB	H	2B	3B	HR	(Hm	Rd)	TB	R	RBI	TBB	IBB	SO	HBP	SH	SF	SB	CS	SB%	GDP	Avg	OBP	SLG
1990 Everett	A-	51	171	29	3	0	2	—	—	38	21	12	24	0	60	5	0	0	0	1	.00	3	.170	.290	.222
1991 Giants	R	48	155	44	8	3	2	—	—	64	28	30	34	3	22	5	0	4	4	2	.67	2	.284	.419	.413
1992 Clinton	A	86	264	62	14	0	4	—	—	88	35	33	54	3	87	4	1	2	4	2	.67	5	.235	.370	.333
1993 Clinton	A	104	324	85	24	2	11	—	—	146	53	56	66	5	98	4	0	4	1	2	.33	5	.262	.389	.451
1994 San Jose	A+	118	418	101	18	0	7	—	—	140	56	47	61	5	100	8	2	6	1	1	.50	9	.242	.345	.335
1995 Shreveport	AA	95	321	91	22	8	4	—	—	141	55	45	41	1	68	3	5	8	0	0	.00	4	.283	.362	.439
1996 Phoenix	AAA	120	405	107	22	4	5	—	—	152	41	53	44	4	95	3	2	4	1	1	.50	10	.264	.338	.375
1997 Toledo	AAA	24	80	14	5	0	0	—	—	19	5	9	9	0	25	0	2	0	0	0	.00	0	.175	.258	.238
1998 Louisville	AAA	74	230	52	13	0	10	—	—	95	29	33	33	1	64	1	0	0	0	3	.00	5	.226	.326	.413
1999 Memphis	AAA	72	237	69	19	4	8	—	—	120	38	44	30	0	59	4	0	1	0	0	.00	3	.291	.379	.506
1996 San Francisco	NL	9	19	4	1	0	0	(0	0)	5	4	4	8	0	7	0	0	0	0	0	.00	1	.211	.444	.263
1997 SF-Det		38	85	13	2	0	1	(1	0)	18	6	4	8	1	28	0	0	0	0	0	.00	2	.153	.226	.212
1998 Milwaukee	NL	2	2	0	0	0	0	(0	0)	0	0	0	0	0	2	0	0	0	0	0	.00	0	.000	.000	.000
1999 St. Louis	NL	16	34	8	5	0	1	(0	1)	16	5	1	6	1	12	0	2	0	0	0	.00	0	.235	.350	.471
1997 San Francisco	NL	30	74	11	2	0	1	(1	0)	16	5	3	7	1	23	0	0	0	0	0	.00	2	.149	.222	.216
Detroit	AL	8	11	2	0	0	0	(0	0)	2	1	1	1	0	5	0	0	0	0	0	.00	0	.182	.250	.182
4 ML YEARS		65	140	25	8	0	2	(1	1)	39	15	9	22	2	49	0	2	0	0	0	.00	4	.179	.290	.279

Derek Jeter

Bats: Right **Throws:** Right **Pos:** SS-158   **Ht:** 6'3" **Wt:** 195 **Born:** 6/26/74 **Age:** 26

Year Team	Lg	G	AB	H	2B	3B	HR	(Hm	Rd)	TB	R	RBI	TBB	IBB	SO	HBP	SH	SF	SB	CS	SB%	GDP	Avg	OBP	SLG
1995 New York	AL	15	48	12	4	1	0	(0	0)	18	5	7	3	0	11	0	0	0	0	0	.00	0	.250	.294	.375
1996 New York	AL	157	582	183	25	6	10	(3	7)	250	104	78	48	1	102	9	6	9	14	7	.67	13	.314	.370	.430
1997 New York	AL	159	654	190	31	7	10	(5	5)	265	116	70	74	0	125	10	8	2	23	12	.66	14	.291	.370	.405
1998 New York	AL	149	626	203	25	8	19	(9	10)	301	127	84	57	1	119	5	3	3	30	6	.83	13	.324	.384	.481
1999 New York	AL	158	627	**219**	37	9	24	(15	9)	346	134	102	91	5	116	12	3	4	19	8	.70	12	.349	.438	.552
5 ML YEARS		638	2537	807	122	31	63	(32	31)	1180	486	341	273	7	473	36	20	20	86	33	.72	52	.318	.389	.465

D'Angelo Jimenez

Bats: Both **Throws:** Right **Pos:** 3B-6; 2B-1; PH/PR-1   **Ht:** 6'0" **Wt:** 160 **Born:** 12/21/77 **Age:** 22

Year Team	Lg	G	AB	H	2B	3B	HR	(Hm	Rd)	TB	R	RBI	TBB	IBB	SO	HBP	SH	SF	SB	CS	SB%	GDP	Avg	OBP	SLG
1995 Yankees	R	57	214	60	14	8	2	—	—	96	41	28	23	1	31	1	3	4	6	3	.67	4	.280	.347	.449
1996 Greensboro	A	138	537	131	25	5	6	—	—	184	68	48	56	2	113	3	4	3	15	17	.47	7	.244	.317	.343
1997 Columbus	AAA	2	7	1	0	0	0	—	—	1	1	1	0	0	1	0	0	1	0	0	.00	1	.143	.125	.143
Tampa	A+	94	352	99	14	6	6	—	—	143	52	48	50	4	50	2	3	6	8	14	.36	3	.281	.368	.406
1998 Norwich	AA	40	152	41	6	2	2	—	—	57	21	21	25	1	26	2	2	1	5	5	.50	3	.270	.378	.375
Columbus	AAA	91	344	88	19	4	8	—	—	139	55	51	46	0	67	1	1	5	6	6	.50	7	.256	.341	.404
1999 Columbus	AAA	126	526	172	32	5	15	—	—	259	97	88	59	1	75	1	6	6	26	14	.65	8	.327	.392	.492
1999 New York	AL	7	20	8	2	0	0	(0	0)	10	3	4	3	0	4	0	0	0	0	0	.00	0	.400	.478	.500

Jose Jimenez

Pitches: Right **Bats:** Right **Pos:** SP-28; RP-1   **Ht:** 6'3" **Wt:** 190 **Born:** 7/7/73 **Age:** 26

Year Team	Lg	G	GS	CG	GF	IP	BFP	H	R	ER	HR	SH	SF	HB	TBB	IBB	SO	WP	Bk	W	L	Pct.	ShO	Sv-Op	Hld	ERA
1995 Johnson Cy	R+	14	14	1	0	90.1	380	81	48	35	3	3	1	5	25	0	85	7	1	5	7	.417	1	0- -	—	3.49
1996 Peoria	A	28	27	3	0	172.1	720	158	75	56	6	5	6	9	53	0	129	8	1	12	9	.571	1	0- -	—	2.92
1997 Pr William	A+	24	24	2	0	145.2	609	128	73	50	12	2	2	9	42	2	81	10	2	9	7	.563	0	0- -	—	3.09
1998 Arkansas	AA	26	26	1	0	179.2	743	156	71	62	9	6	4	12	68	1	88	13	0	15	6	.714	1	0- -	—	3.11
1999 Memphis	AAA	4	4	0	0	26.2	113	30	10	9	0	2	1	2	9	0	18	0	0	2	2	.500	0	0- -	—	3.04
1998 St. Louis	NL	4	3	0	0	21.1	94	22	8	7	0	1	1	0	8	0	12	0	0	3	0	1.000	0	0-0	0	2.95
1999 St. Louis	NL	29	28	2	0	163	727	173	114	106	16	10	6	11	71	2	113	10	1	5	14	.263	2	0-1	0	5.85
2 ML YEARS		33	31	2	0	184.1	821	195	122	113	16	11	7	11	79	2	125	10	1	8	14	.364	2	0-1	0	5.52

Doug Johns

Pitches: Left **Bats:** Right **Pos:** RP-27; SP-5   **Ht:** 6'2" **Wt:** 195 **Born:** 12/19/67 **Age:** 32

Year Team	Lg	G	GS	CG	GF	IP	BFP	H	R	ER	HR	SH	SF	HB	TBB	IBB	SO	WP	Bk	W	L	Pct.	ShO	Sv-Op	Hld	ERA
1999 Rochester *	AAA	6	6	1	0	29.2	130	34	20	16	3	0	1	6	8	0	18	0	1	1	1	.500	0	—	—	4.85
1995 Oakland	AL	11	9	1	1	54.2	229	44	32	28	5	2	1	5	26	1	25	5	1	5	3	.625	1	0-0	0	4.61
1996 Oakland	AL	40	23	1	4	158	710	187	112	105	21	2	3	6	69	5	71	9	0	6	12	.333	0	1-2	0	5.98

		HOW MUCH HE PITCHED						WHAT HE GAVE UP										THE RESULTS					
Year Team	Lg	G GS CG GF	IP	BFP	H R ER	HR SH SF HB	TBB IBB	SO	WP	Bk	W L	Pct.	ShO	Sv-Op	Hld	ERA
1998 Baltimore	AL	31 10 0 5	86.2	382	108 46 44	9 4 6 4	32 2	34	3	0	3 3	.500	0	1-1	2	4.57
1999 Baltimore	AL	32 5 0 2	86.2	368	81 45 43	9 1 7 8	25 2	50	1	0	6 4	.600	0	0-0	7	4.47
4 ML YEARS		114 47 2 12	386	1689	420 235 220	44 9 17 23	152 10	180	18	1	20 22	.476	1	2-3	9	5.13

Brian Johnson

Bats: Right Throws: Right Pos: C-39; PH/PR-14   Ht: 6'2" Wt: 210 Born: 1/8/68 Age: 32

		BATTING																	BASERUNNING				PERCENTAGES		
Year Team	Lg	G	AB	H	2B	3B	HR	(Hm	Rd)	TB	R	RBI	TBB	IBB	SO	HBP	SH	SF	SB	CS	SB%	GDP	Avg	OBP	SLG
1999 Indianapols *	AAA	6	19	4	3	0	0	(—	—)	7	2	4	1	0	3	0	0	0	0	0	.00	4	.211	.250	.368
1994 San Diego	NL	36	93	23	4	1	3	(3	0)	38	7	16	5	0	21	0	2	1	0	0	.00	4	.247	.283	.409
1995 San Diego	NL	68	207	52	9	0	3	(1	2)	70	20	29	11	2	39	1	1	4	0	0	.00	2	.251	.287	.338
1996 San Diego	NL	82	243	66	13	1	8	(3	5)	105	18	35	4	2	36	4	2	4	0	0	.00	8	.272	.290	.432
1997 Det-SF		101	318	83	13	3	13	(8	5)	141	32	45	19	8	45	2	5	4	1	1	.50	11	.261	.303	.443
1998 San Francisco	NL	99	308	73	8	1	13	(7	6)	122	34	34	28	4	67	5	4	1	0	2	.00	11	.237	.310	.396
1999 Cincinnati	NL	45	117	27	7	0	5	(3	2)	49	12	18	9	0	31	0	1	0	0	0	.00	2	.231	.286	.419
1997 Detroit	AL	45	139	33	6	1	2	(2	0)	47	13	18	5	1	19	0	2	1	1	0	1.00	3	.237	.262	.338
San Francisco	NL	56	179	50	7	2	11	(6	5)	94	19	27	14	7	26	2	3	3	0	1	.00	8	.279	.333	.525
6 ML YEARS		431	1286	324	54	6	45	(25	20)	525	123	177	76	16	239	12	15	14	1	3	.25	38	.252	.297	.408

Charles Johnson

Bats: Right Throws: Right Pos: C-135; PH/PR-4   Ht: 6'2" Wt: 220 Born: 7/20/71 Age: 28

		BATTING																	BASERUNNING				PERCENTAGES		
Year Team	Lg	G	AB	H	2B	3B	HR	(Hm	Rd)	TB	R	RBI	TBB	IBB	SO	HBP	SH	SF	SB	CS	SB%	GDP	Avg	OBP	SLG
1994 Florida	NL	4	11	5	1	0	1	(1	0)	9	5	4	1	0	4	0	0	1	0	0	.00	1	.455	.462	.818
1995 Florida	NL	97	315	79	15	1	11	(3	8)	129	40	39	46	2	71	4	4	2	0	2	.00	11	.251	.351	.410
1996 Florida	NL	120	386	84	13	1	13	(9	4)	138	34	37	40	6	91	2	2	4	1	0	1.00	20	.218	.292	.358
1997 Florida	NL	124	416	104	26	1	19	(7	12)	189	43	63	60	6	109	3	3	2	0	2	.00	13	.250	.347	.454
1998 Fla-LA	NL	133	459	100	18	0	19	(14	5)	175	44	58	45	1	129	1	0	1	0	2	.00	12	.218	.289	.381
1999 Baltimore	AL	135	426	107	19	1	16	(8	8)	176	58	54	55	2	107	4	4	3	0	0	.00	13	.251	.340	.413
1998 Florida	NL	31	113	25	5	0	7	(5	2)	51	13	23	16	0	30	0	0	1	0	1	.00	3	.221	.315	.451
Los Angeles	NL	102	346	75	13	0	12	(9	3)	124	31	35	29	1	99	1	0	0	0	0	.00	9	.217	.279	.358
6 ML YEARS		613	2013	479	92	4	79	(42	37)	816	224	255	247	17	511	14	13	13	1	6	.14	70	.238	.324	.405

Jason Johnson

Pitches: Right Bats: Right Pos: SP-21; RP-1   Ht: 6'6" Wt: 220 Born: 10/27/73 Age: 26

		HOW MUCH HE PITCHED						WHAT HE GAVE UP										THE RESULTS					
Year Team	Lg	G GS CG GF	IP	BFP	H R ER	HR SH SF HB	TBB IBB	SO	WP	Bk	W L	Pct.	ShO	Sv-Op	Hld	ERA
1999 Rochester *	AAA	8 8 0 0	44.1	194	35 19 18	6 0 1 1	27 0	47	2	1	4 2	.667	0	0--	—	3.65
1997 Pittsburgh	NL	3 0 0 0	6	27	10 4 4	2 1 0 0	1 0	3	0	0	0 0	.000	0	0-0	0	6.00
1998 Tampa Bay	AL	13 13 0 0	60	274	74 38 38	9 1 1 3	27 0	36	2	0	2 5	.286	0	0-0	0	5.70
1999 Baltimore	AL	22 21 0 0	115.1	515	120 74 70	16 2 4 3	55 0	71	5	1	8 7	.533	0	0-0	0	5.46
3 ML YEARS		38 34 0 0	181.1	816	204 116 112	27 3 6 6	83 0	110	7	1	10 12	.455	0	0-0	0	5.56

Jonathan Johnson

Pitches: Right Bats: Right Pos: RP-1   Ht: 6'0" Wt: 180 Born: 7/16/74 Age: 25

		HOW MUCH HE PITCHED						WHAT HE GAVE UP										THE RESULTS					
Year Team	Lg	G GS CG GF	IP	BFP	H R ER	HR SH SF HB	TBB IBB	SO	WP	Bk	W L	Pct.	ShO	Sv-Op	Hld	ERA
1995 Charlotte	A+	8 7 1 0	43.1	178	34 14 13	2 2 0 1	16 0	25	3	3	1 5	.167	0	0--	—	2.70
1996 Okla City	AAA	1 1 1 0	9	29	2 0 0	0 0 0 0	1 0	6	0	0	1 0	1.000	1	0--	—	0.00
Tulsa	AA	26 25 6 1	174.1	728	176 86 69	15 3 5 6	41 1	97	2	3	13 10	.565	0	0--	—	3.56
1997 Okla City	AAA	13 12 1 0	58	276	83 54 47	6 1 3 1	29 3	33	2	1	1 8	.111	0	1--	—	7.29
Tulsa	AA	10 10 4 0	71.2	297	70 35 28	3 1 3 2	15 0	47	4	0	5 4	.556	0	0--	—	3.52
1998 Charlotte	A+	3 3 0 0	11.2	51	10 6 6	2 0 1 2	4 0	11	0	0	0 2	.000	0	0--	—	4.63
Oklahoma	AAA	19 18 1 1	112	474	109 66 61	15 0 4 11	32 0	94	6	2	6 6	.500	1	0--	—	4.90
1999 Rangers	R	1 1 0 0	5	18	3 1 1	0 0 0 0	0 0	5	0	0	0 0	.000	0	0--	—	1.80
Tulsa	AA	1 1 0 0	5.2	28	12 6 6	3 1 1 0	4 0	8	0	0	0 0	.000	0	0--	—	9.53
Oklahoma	AAA	21 8 0 5	67.2	308	91 53 47	9 2 3 2	23 0	38	6	0	8 4	.667	0	2--	—	6.25
1998 Texas	AL	1 1 0 0	4.1	22	5 4 4	0 0 1 0	5 0	3	0	0	0 0	.000	0	0-0	0	8.31
1999 Texas	AL	1 0 0 0	3	21	9 5 5	0 0 1 1	2 0	3	0	0	0 0	.000	0	0-0	0	15.00
2 ML YEARS		2 1 0 0	7.1	43	14 9 9	0 0 2 1	7 0	6	0	0	0 0	.000	0	0-0	0	11.05

Lance Johnson

Bats: Left Throws: Left Pos: CF-91; PH/PR-10   Ht: 5'11" Wt: 165 Born: 7/6/63 Age: 36

		BATTING																	BASERUNNING				PERCENTAGES		
Year Team	Lg	G	AB	H	2B	3B	HR	(Hm	Rd)	TB	R	RBI	TBB	IBB	SO	HBP	SH	SF	SB	CS	SB%	GDP	Avg	OBP	SLG
1987 St. Louis	NL	33	59	13	2	1	0	(0	0)	17	4	7	4	1	6	0	0	0	6	1	.86	2	.220	.270	.288
1988 Chicago	AL	33	124	23	4	1	0	(0	0)	29	11	6	6	0	11	0	2	0	6	2	.75	1	.185	.223	.234
1989 Chicago	AL	50	180	54	8	2	0	(0	0)	66	28	16	17	0	24	0	2	0	16	3	.84	1	.300	.360	.367
1990 Chicago	AL	151	541	154	18	9	1	(0	1)	193	76	51	33	2	45	1	8	4	36	22	.62	12	.285	.325	.357
1991 Chicago	AL	160	588	161	14	13	0	(0	0)	201	72	49	26	2	58	1	6	3	26	11	.70	14	.274	.304	.342
1992 Chicago	AL	157	567	158	15	12	3	(2	1)	206	67	47	34	4	33	1	4	5	41	14	.75	20	.279	.318	.363

Year Team	Lg	G	AB	H	2B	3B	HR	(Hm	Rd)	TB	R	RBI	TBB	IBB	SO	HBP	SH	SF	SB	CS	SB%	GDP	Avg	OBP	SLG
1993 Chicago	AL	147	540	168	18	14	0	(0	0)	214	75	47	36	1	33	0	3	0	35	7	.83	10	.311	.354	.396
1994 Chicago	AL	106	412	114	11	14	3	(1	2)	162	56	54	26	5	23	2	0	3	26	6	.81	8	.277	.321	.393
1995 Chicago	AL	142	607	186	18	12	10	(2	8)	258	98	57	32	2	31	1	2	3	40	6	.87	7	.306	.341	.425
1996 New York	NL	160	682	227	31	21	9	(1	8)	327	117	69	33	8	40	1	3	5	50	12	.81	8	.333	.362	.479
1997 NYM-ChC	NL	111	410	126	16	8	5	(4	1)	173	60	39	42	3	31	0	0	2	20	12	.63	8	.307	.370	.422
1998 Chicago	NL	85	304	85	8	4	2	(1	1)	107	51	21	26	1	22	0	1	1	10	6	.63	8	.280	.335	.352
1999 Chicago	NL	95	335	87	11	6	1	(1	0)	113	46	21	37	0	20	0	4	1	13	3	.81	6	.260	.332	.337
1997 New York	NL	72	265	82	10	6	1	(1	0)	107	43	24	33	2	21	0	0	1	15	10	.60	6	.309	.385	.404
Chicago	NL	39	145	44	6	2	4	(3	1)	66	17	15	9	1	10	0	0	1	5	2	.71	2	.303	.342	.455
13 ML YEARS		1430	5349	1556	174	117	34	(12	22)	2066	761	484	352	29	377	7	35	27	325	105	.76	102	.291	.334	.386

Mark Johnson

Bats: Left **Throws:** Right **Pos:** C-72; DH-1; PH/PR-1   **Ht:** 6'0" **Wt:** 185 **Born:** 9/12/75 **Age:** 24

Year Team	Lg	G	AB	H	2B	3B	HR	(Hm	Rd)	TB	R	RBI	TBB	IBB	SO	HBP	SH	SF	SB	CS	SB%	GDP	Avg	OBP	SLG
1994 White Sox	R	32	87	21	5	0	0	—	—	26	10	14	14	0	15	3	0	0	1	1	.50	0	.241	.365	.299
1995 Hickory	A	107	319	58	9	0	2	—	—	73	31	17	59	1	52	3	2	2	3	5	.38	4	.182	.313	.229
1996 South Bend	A	67	214	55	14	3	2	—	—	81	29	27	39	2	25	1	4	4	3	3	.50	8	.257	.368	.379
Pr William	A+	18	58	14	3	0	0	—	—	17	9	3	13	0	6	1	0	0	0	0	.00	0	.241	.389	.293
1997 Winston-Sal	A+	120	375	95	27	4	4	—	—	142	59	46	106	2	85	5	0	5	4	2	.67	7	.253	.420	.379
1998 Birmingham	AA	117	382	108	17	3	9	—	—	158	68	59	105	2	72	6	0	1	0	1	.00	5	.283	.443	.414
1998 Chicago	AL	7	23	2	0	2	0	(0	0)	6	2	1	1	0	8	0	0	0	0	0	.00	0	.087	.125	.261
1999 Chicago	AL	73	207	47	11	0	4	(2	2)	70	27	16	36	0	58	2	1	2	3	1	.75	2	.227	.344	.338
2 ML YEARS		80	230	49	11	2	4	(2	2)	76	29	17	37	0	66	2	1	2	3	1	.75	2	.213	.325	.330

Mike Johnson

Pitches: Right **Bats:** Right **Pos:** RP-2; SP-1   **Ht:** 6'2" **Wt:** 170 **Born:** 10/3/75 **Age:** 24

Year Team	Lg	G	GS	CG	GF	IP	BFP	H	R	ER	HR	SH	SF	HB	TBB	IBB	SO	WP	Bk	W	L	Pct.	ShO	Sv-Op	Hld	ERA
1999 Ottawa *	AAA	28	27	0	1	147.1	673	174	105	88	24	5	4	7	63	0	120	7	0	6	12	.333	0	0- -		5.38
1997 Bal-Mon		25	16	0	5	89.2	403	106	70	68	20	2	4	1	37	4	57	5	0	2	6	.250	0	2-2		6.83
1998 Montreal	NL	2	2	0	0	7.1	40	16	12	12	4	0	0	1	2	0	4	0	0	0	2	.000	0	0-0		14.73
1999 Montreal	NL	3	1	0	0	8.1	44	12	8	8	2	0	0	0	7	1	6	2	0	0	0	.000	0	0-0		8.64
1997 Baltimore	AL	14	5	0	5	39.2	183	52	36	35	12	0	2	1	16	2	29	1	0	0	1	.000	0	2-2		7.94
Montreal	NL	11	11	0	0	50	220	54	34	33	8	2	2	0	21	2	28	4	0	2	5	.286	0	0-0		5.94
3 ML YEARS		30	19	0	5	105.1	487	134	90	88	26	4	4	2	46	5	67	7	0	2	8	.200	0	2-2		7.52

Randy Johnson

Pitches: Left **Bats:** Right **Pos:** SP-35   **Ht:** 6'10" **Wt:** 230 **Born:** 9/10/63 **Age:** 36

Year Team	Lg	G	GS	CG	GF	IP	BFP	H	R	ER	HR	SH	SF	HB	TBB	IBB	SO	WP	Bk	W	L	Pct.	ShO	Sv-Op	Hld	ERA
1988 Montreal	NL	4	4	1	0	26	109	23	8	7	3	0	0	0	7	0	25	3	0	3	0	1.000	0	0-0	0	2.42
1989 Mon-Sea		29	28	2	1	160.2	715	147	100	86	13	10	13	3	96	2	130	7	7	7	13	.350	0	0-0	0	4.82
1990 Seattle	AL	33	33	5	0	219.2	944	174	103	89	26	7	6	5	120	2	194	4	2	14	11	.560	2	0-0	0	3.65
1991 Seattle	AL	33	33	2	0	201.1	889	151	96	89	15	9	8	12	152	0	228	12	2	13	10	.565	1	0-0	0	3.98
1992 Seattle	AL	31	31	6	0	210.1	922	154	104	88	13	3	8	18	144	1	241	13	1	12	14	.462	2	0-0	0	3.77
1993 Seattle	AL	35	34	10	1	255.1	1043	185	97	92	22	8	7	16	99	1	308	8	2	19	8	.704	3	1-1	0	3.24
1994 Seattle	AL	23	23	9	0	172	694	132	65	61	14	3	1	6	72	2	204	5	0	13	6	.684	4	0-0	0	3.19
1995 Seattle	AL	30	30	6	0	214.1	866	159	65	59	12	2	1	6	65	1	294	5	2	18	2	.900	3	0-0	0	2.48
1996 Seattle	AL	14	8	0	2	61.1	256	48	27	25	8	1	0	2	25	0	85	3	1	5	0	1.000	0	1-2	0	3.67
1997 Seattle	AL	30	29	5	0	213	852	147	60	54	20	4	1	10	77	2	291	4	0	20	4	.833	2	0-0	0	2.28
1998 Sea-Hou		34	34	10	0	244.1	1014	203	102	89	23	5	2	14	86	1	329	7	2	19	11	.633	6	0-0	0	3.28
1999 Arizona	NL	35	35	12	0	271.2	1079	207	86	75	30	4	3	9	70	3	364	4	2	17	9	.654	2	0-0	0	2.48
1989 Montreal	NL	7	6	0	1	29.2	143	29	25	22	2	3	4	0	26	1	26	2	2	0	4	.000	0	0-0	0	6.67
Seattle	AL	22	22	2	0	131	572	118	75	64	11	7	9	3	70	1	104	5	5	7	9	.438	0	0-0	0	4.40
1998 Seattle	AL	23	23	6	0	160	685	146	90	77	19	5	1	11	60	0	213	7	2	9	10	.474	2	0-0	0	4.33
Houston	NL	11	11	4	0	84.1	329	57	12	12	4	0	1	3	26	1	116	0	0	10	1	.909	4	0-0	0	1.28
12 ML YEARS		331	322	68	4	2250	9381	1730	913	814	199	56	50	101	1013	15	2693	75	21	160	88	.645	25	2-3	0	3.26

Russ Johnson

Bats: R **Throws:** R **Pos:** PH/PR-42; 3B-36; 2B-15; SS-2   **Ht:** 5'10" **Wt:** 180 **Born:** 2/22/73 **Age:** 27

Year Team	Lg	G	AB	H	2B	3B	HR	(Hm	Rd)	TB	R	RBI	TBB	IBB	SO	HBP	SH	SF	SB	CS	SB%	GDP	Avg	OBP	SLG
1995 Jackson	AA	132	475	118	16	2	9	—	—	165	65	53	50	1	60	8	2	5	10	5	.67	11	.248	.327	.347
1996 Jackson	AA	132	496	154	24	5	15	—	—	233	86	74	56	1	50	3	5	3	9	4	.69	16	.310	.382	.470
1997 New Orleans	AAA	122	445	123	16	6	4	—	—	163	72	49	66	1	78	1	2	7	7	4	.64	10	.276	.370	.366
1998 New Orleans	AAA	122	443	140	28	2	7	—	—	193	95	52	90	2	64	5	4	6	11	11	.50	10	.309	.424	.426
1999 New Orleans	AAA	22	77	27	6	0	1	—	—	36	17	12	16	0	13	1	0	0	1	3	.25	2	.351	.468	.468
1997 Houston	NL	21	60	18	1	0	2	(2	0)	25	7	9	6	0	14	0	1	0	1	1	.50	2	.300	.364	.417
1998 Houston	NL	8	13	3	1	0	0	(0	0)	4	2	0	1	0	5	1	0	0	1	0	1.00	1	.231	.333	.308
1999 Houston	NL	83	156	44	10	0	5	(2	3)	69	24	23	20	0	31	0	4	3	2	3	.40	3	.282	.358	.442
3 ML YEARS		112	229	65	12	0	7	(4	3)	98	33	32	27	0	50	1	5	3	4	4	.50	6	.284	.358	.428

John Johnstone

Pitches: Right Bats: Right Pos: RP-62 Ht: 6'3" Wt: 210 Born: 11/25/68 Age: 31

Year Team	Lg	G	GS	CG	GF	IP	BFP	H	R	ER	HR	SH	SF	HB	TBB	IBB	SO	WP	Bk	W	L	Pct.	ShO	Sv-Op	Hld	ERA
1993 Florida	NL	7	0	0	3	10.2	54	16	8	7	1	0	0	0	7	0	5	1	0	0	2	.000	0	0-0	0	5.91
1994 Florida	NL	17	0	0	7	21.1	105	23	20	14	4	1	0	1	16	5	23	0	0	1	2	.333	0	0-0	3	5.91
1995 Florida	NL	4	0	0	0	4.2	23	7	2	2	1	0	0	0	2	1	3	0	0	0	0	.000	0	0-0	0	3.86
1996 Houston	NL	9	0	0	6	13	60	17	8	8	2	0	2	0	5	0	5	0	0	1	0	1.000	0	0-0	0	5.54
1997 SF-Oak		18	0	0	3	25	112	22	9	9	1	2	4	4	14	0	19	0	0	0	0	.000	0	0-0	1	3.24
1998 San Francisco	NL	70	0	0	13	88	370	72	32	30	10	4	5	1	38	8	86	4	0	6	5	.545	0	0-1	15	3.07
1999 San Francisco	NL	62	0	0	11	65.2	262	48	24	19	8	4	0	1	20	5	56	2	1	4	6	.400	0	3-7	28	2.60
1997 San Francisco	NL	13	0	0	2	18.2	80	15	7	7	1	2	3	4	7	0	15	0	0	0	0	.000	0	0-0	1	3.38
Oakland	AL	5	0	0	1	6.1	32	7	2	2	0	0	1	0	7	0	4	0	0	0	0	.000	0	0-0	0	2.84
7 ML YEARS		187	0	0	43	228.1	986	205	103	89	27	11	11	7	102	19	197	7	1	12	15	.444	0	3-8	47	3.51

Andruw Jones

Bats: Right Throws: Right Pos: CF-162 Ht: 6'1" Wt: 185 Born: 4/23/77 Age: 23

Year Team	Lg	G	AB	H	2B	3B	HR	(Hm	Rd)	TB	R	RBI	TBB	IBB	SO	HBP	SH	SF	SB	CS	SB%	GDP	Avg	OBP	SLG
1996 Atlanta	NL	31	106	23	7	1	5	(3	2)	47	11	13	7	0	29	0	0	0	3	0	1.00	1	.217	.265	.443
1997 Atlanta	NL	153	399	92	18	1	18	(5	13)	166	60	70	56	2	107	4	5	3	20	11	.65	11	.231	.329	.416
1998 Atlanta	NL	159	582	158	33	8	31	(16	15)	300	89	90	40	8	129	4	1	4	27	4	.87	10	.271	.321	.515
1999 Atlanta	NL	162	592	163	35	5	26	(10	16)	286	97	84	76	11	103	9	0	2	24	12	.67	12	.275	.365	.483
4 ML YEARS		505	1679	436	93	15	80	(34	46)	799	257	257	179	21	368	17	6	9	74	27	.73	34	.260	.335	.476

Bobby Jones

Pitches: Right Bats: Right Pos: SP-9; RP-3 Ht: 6'4" Wt: 225 Born: 2/10/70 Age: 30

Year Team	Lg	G	GS	CG	GF	IP	BFP	H	R	ER	HR	SH	SF	HB	TBB	IBB	SO	WP	Bk	W	L	Pct.	ShO	Sv-Op	Hld	ERA
1999 Norfolk *	AAA	2	2	0	0	11	47	11	3	3	2	0	0	1	3	0	8	0	0	2	0	1.000	0	0--	—	2.45
Binghamton *	AA	3	3	0	0	11.2	50	11	5	5	3	0	0	0	5	0	12	1	0	1	2	.333	0	0--	—	3.86
1993 New York	NL	9	9	0	0	61.2	265	61	35	25	6	5	3	2	22	3	35	1	0	2	4	.333	0	0-0	0	3.65
1994 New York	NL	24	24	1	0	160	685	157	75	56	10	11	4	4	56	9	80	1	3	12	7	.632	1	0-0	0	3.15
1995 New York	NL	30	30	3	0	195.2	839	209	107	91	20	11	6	7	53	6	127	2	1	10	10	.500	1	0-0	0	4.19
1996 New York	NL	31	31	3	0	195.2	826	219	102	96	26	12	5	3	46	6	116	2	0	12	8	.600	1	0-0	0	4.42
1997 New York	NL	30	30	2	0	193.1	806	177	88	78	24	6	4	2	63	3	125	3	1	15	9	.625	1	0-0	0	3.63
1998 New York	NL	30	30	0	0	195.1	804	192	94	88	23	4	7	8	53	2	115	2	2	9	9	.500	0	0-0	0	4.05
1999 New York	NL	12	9	0	0	59.1	253	69	37	37	3	3	3	2	11	0	31	0	0	3	3	.500	0	0-0	0	5.61
7 ML YEARS		166	163	9	0	1061	4478	1084	538	471	112	52	32	28	304	29	629	11	7	63	50	.558	4	0-0	0	4.00

Bobby Jones

Pitches: Left Bats: Right Pos: SP-20; RP-10 Ht: 6'0" Wt: 178 Born: 4/11/72 Age: 28

Year Team	Lg	G	GS	CG	GF	IP	BFP	H	R	ER	HR	SH	SF	HB	TBB	IBB	SO	WP	Bk	W	L	Pct.	ShO	Sv-Op	Hld	ERA
1999 Colo Sprngs *	AAA	3	3	0	0	16.2	82	17	13	10	1	0	0	3	15	0	14	1	0	2	1	.667	0	0--	—	5.40
1997 Colorado	NL	4	4	0	0	19.1	96	30	18	18	2	2	3	0	12	0	5	0	0	1	1	.500	0	0-0	0	8.38
1998 Colorado	NL	35	20	1	1	141.1	630	153	87	82	12	9	6	6	66	0	109	4	1	7	8	.467	0	0-0	1	5.22
1999 Colorado	NL	30	20	0	1	112.1	546	132	91	79	24	7	4	6	77	0	74	4	0	6	10	.375	0	0-0	1	6.33
3 ML YEARS		69	44	1	2	273	1272	315	196	179	38	18	13	12	155	0	188	8	1	14	19	.424	0	0-0	1	5.90

Chipper Jones

Bats: Both Throws: Right Pos: 3B-157; SS-1 Ht: 6'4" Wt: 210 Born: 4/24/72 Age: 28

Year Team	Lg	G	AB	H	2B	3B	HR	(Hm	Rd)	TB	R	RBI	TBB	IBB	SO	HBP	SH	SF	SB	CS	SB%	GDP	Avg	OBP	SLG
1993 Atlanta	NL	8	3	2	1	0	0	(0	0)	3	2	0	1	0	1	0	0	0	0	0	.00	0	.667	.750	1.000
1995 Atlanta	NL	140	524	139	22	3	23	(15	8)	236	87	86	73	1	99	0	1	4	8	4	.67	10	.265	.353	.450
1996 Atlanta	NL	157	598	185	32	5	30	(18	12)	317	114	110	87	0	88	0	1	7	14	1	.93	14	.309	.393	.530
1997 Atlanta	NL	157	597	176	41	3	21	(7	14)	286	100	111	76	8	88	0	0	6	20	5	.80	19	.295	.371	.479
1998 Atlanta	NL	160	601	188	29	5	34	(17	17)	329	123	107	96	1	93	1	1	8	16	6	.73	17	.313	.404	.547
1999 Atlanta	NL	157	567	181	41	1	45	(25	20)	359	116	110	126	18	94	2	0	6	25	3	.89	20	.319	.441	.633
6 ML YEARS		779	2890	871	166	17	153	(82	71)	1530	542	524	459	28	463	3	3	31	83	19	.81	80	.301	.394	.529

Doug Jones

Pitches: Right Bats: Right Pos: RP-70 Ht: 6'2" Wt: 224 Born: 6/24/57 Age: 43

Year Team	Lg	G	GS	CG	GF	IP	BFP	H	R	ER	HR	SH	SF	HB	TBB	IBB	SO	WP	Bk	W	L	Pct.	ShO	Sv-Op	Hld	ERA
1982 Milwaukee	AL	4	0	0	2	2.2	14	5	3	3	1	0	0	1	0	0	1	0	0	0	0	.000	0	0-0	0	10.13
1986 Cleveland	AL	11	0	0	5	18	79	18	5	5	0	1	1	1	6	1	12	0	0	1	0	1.000	0	1-3	0	2.50
1987 Cleveland	AL	49	0	0	29	91.1	400	101	45	32	4	5	5	6	24	5	87	0	0	6	5	.545	0	8-12	1	3.15
1988 Cleveland	AL	51	0	0	46	83.1	328	69	26	21	1	3	0	2	16	3	72	2	3	3	4	.429	0	37-43	0	2.27
1989 Cleveland	AL	59	0	0	53	80.2	331	76	25	21	4	8	6	1	13	4	65	1	1	7	10	.412	0	32-41	0	2.34
1990 Cleveland	AL	66	0	0	64	84.1	331	66	26	24	5	2	2	2	22	4	55	2	0	5	5	.500	0	43-51	0	2.56

Year Team	Lg	G	GS	CG	GF	IP	BFP	H	R	ER	HR	SH	SF	HB	TBB	IBB	SO	WP	Bk	W	L	Pct.	ShO	Sv-Op	Hld	ERA
1991 Cleveland	AL	36	4	0	29	63.1	293	87	42	39	7	2	0	5	17	5	48	1	0	4	8	.333	0	7-12	0	5.54
1992 Houston	NL	80	0	0	70	111.2	440	96	29	23	5	9	0	5	17	5	93	2	1	11	8	.579	0	36-42	0	1.85
1993 Houston	NL	71	0	0	60	85.1	381	102	46	43	7	9	4	5	21	6	66	3	0	4	10	.286	0	26-34	1	4.54
1994 Philadelphia	NL	47	0	0	42	54	226	55	14	13	2	4	0	0	6	0	38	1	0	2	4	.333	0	27-29	0	2.17
1995 Baltimore	AL	52	0	0	47	46.2	211	55	30	26	6	1	0	2	16	2	42	0	0	0	4	.000	0	22-25	0	5.01
1996 ChC-Mil		52	0	0	21	64	282	72	33	30	7	1	2	3	20	6	60	1	0	7	2	.778	0	3-11	2	4.22
1997 Milwaukee	AL	75	0	0	73	80.1	307	62	20	18	4	1	5	3	9	1	82	0	0	6	6	.500	0	36-38	0	2.02
1998 Mil-Cle		69	0	0	42	85.1	372	99	44	43	17	5	6	4	17	4	71	0	1	4	6	.400	0	13-22	5	4.54
1999 Oakland	AL	70	0	0	35	104	430	106	43	41	10	3	3	3	24	1	63	2	0	5	5	.500	0	10-16	11	3.55
1996 Chicago	NL	28	0	0	13	32.1	143	41	20	18	4	1	0	1	7	4	26	0	0	2	2	.500	0	2-7	0	5.01
Milwaukee	AL	24	0	0	8	31.2	139	31	13	12	3	0	2	2	13	2	34	1	0	5	0	1.000	0	1-4	2	3.41
1998 Milwaukee	NL	46	0	0	34	54	239	65	32	31	15	3	3	4	11	1	43	0	0	3	4	.429	0	12-20	1	5.17
Cleveland	AL	23	0	0	8	31.1	133	34	12	12	2	2	3	0	6	3	28	0	1	1	2	.333	0	1-2	4	3.45
15 ML YEARS		792	4	0	618	1055	4435	1069	431	382	80	54	36	37	229	49	855	17	6	65	77	.458	0	301-379	20	3.26

Jacque Jones

Bats: L **Throws:** L **Pos:** CF-82; RF-19; PH/PR-8; LF-1 **Ht:** 5'10" **Wt:** 175 **Born:** 4/25/75 **Age:** 25

Year Team	Lg	G	AB	H	2B	3B	HR	(Hm	Rd)	TB	R	RBI	TBB	IBB	SO	HBP	SH	SF	SB	CS	SB%	GDP	Avg	OBP	SLG
1996 Fort Myers	A+	1	3	2	1	0	0	—	—	3	0	1	0	0	0	0	0	0	0	1	.00	0	.667	.667	1.000
1997 Fort Myers	A+	131	539	160	33	6	15	—	—	250	84	82	33	3	110	3	0	2	24	12	.67	9	.297	.340	.464
1998 New Britain	AA	134	518	155	39	3	21	—	—	263	78	85	37	8	134	4	4	3	18	11	.62	4	.299	.349	.508
1999 Salt Lake	AAA	52	198	59	13	2	4	—	—	88	32	26	9	1	36	0	1	2	9	2	.82	5	.298	.325	.444
1999 Minnesota	AL	95	322	93	24	2	9	(5	4)	148	54	44	17	1	63	4	1	3	3	4	.43	7	.289	.329	.460

Terry Jones

Bats: Both **Throws:** Right **Pos:** CF-12; LF-5; PH/PR-1 **Ht:** 5'10" **Wt:** 165 **Born:** 2/15/71 **Age:** 29

Year Team	Lg	G	AB	H	2B	3B	HR	(Hm	Rd)	TB	R	RBI	TBB	IBB	SO	HBP	SH	SF	SB	CS	SB%	GDP	Avg	OBP	SLG
1999 Ottawa *	AAA	88	332	87	17	2	0	—	—	108	49	23	24	0	66	1	7	3	30	10	.75	6	.262	.311	.325
1996 Colorado	NL	12	10	3	0	0	0	(0	0)	3	6	1	0	0	3	0	0	0	0	0	.00	0	.300	.273	.300
1998 Montreal	NL	60	212	46	7	2	1	(1	0)	60	30	15	21	1	46	0	15	0	16	4	.80	2	.217	.288	.283
1999 Montreal	NL	17	63	17	1	1	0	(0	0)	20	4	3	3	0	14	0	0	1	1	2	.33	0	.270	.303	.317
3 ML YEARS		89	285	66	8	3	1	(1	0)	83	40	19	24	1	63	0	15	1	17	6	.74	2	.232	.290	.291

Todd Jones

Pitches: Right **Bats:** Left **Pos:** RP-65 **Ht:** 6'3" **Wt:** 230 **Born:** 4/24/68 **Age:** 32

Year Team	Lg	G	GS	CG	GF	IP	BFP	H	R	ER	HR	SH	SF	HB	TBB	IBB	SO	WP	Bk	W	L	Pct.	ShO	Sv-Op	Hld	ERA
1993 Houston	NL	27	0	0	8	37.1	150	28	14	13	4	2	1	1	15	2	25	1	1	1	2	.333	0	2-3	6	3.13
1994 Houston	NL	48	0	0	20	72.2	288	52	23	22	3	3	1	1	26	4	63	1	0	5	2	.714	0	5-9	8	2.72
1995 Houston	NL	68	0	0	40	99.2	442	89	38	34	8	5	4	6	52	17	96	5	0	6	5	.545	0	15-20	8	3.07
1996 Houston	NL	51	0	0	37	57.1	263	61	30	28	5	2	1	5	32	6	44	3	0	6	3	.667	0	17-23	1	4.40
1997 Detroit	AL	68	0	0	51	70	301	60	29	24	3	1	4	1	35	2	70	7	0	5	4	.556	0	31-36	5	3.09
1998 Detroit	AL	65	0	0	53	63.1	279	58	38	35	7	2	6	2	36	4	57	5	0	1	4	.200	0	28-32	0	4.97
1999 Detroit	AL	65	0	0	62	66.1	287	64	30	28	7	3	1	1	35	1	64	2	0	4	4	.500	0	30-35	0	3.80
7 ML YEARS		392	0	0	271	466.2	2010	412	202	184	37	18	18	17	231	36	419	24	1	28	24	.538	0	128-158	28	3.55

Brian Jordan

Bats: Right **Throws:** Right **Pos:** RF-150; PH/PR-4 **Ht:** 6'1" **Wt:** 205 **Born:** 3/29/67 **Age:** 33

Year Team	Lg	G	AB	H	2B	3B	HR	(Hm	Rd)	TB	R	RBI	TBB	IBB	SO	HBP	SH	SF	SB	CS	SB%	GDP	Avg	OBP	SLG
1992 St. Louis	NL	55	193	46	9	4	5	(3	2)	72	17	22	10	1	48	1	0	0	7	2	.78	6	.207	.250	.373
1993 St. Louis	NL	67	223	69	10	6	10	(4	6)	121	33	44	12	0	35	4	0	3	6	6	.50	6	.309	.351	.543
1994 St. Louis	NL	53	178	46	8	2	5	(4	1)	73	14	15	16	0	40	1	0	2	4	3	.57	6	.258	.320	.410
1995 St. Louis	NL	131	490	145	20	4	22	(14	8)	239	83	81	22	4	79	11	0	2	24	9	.73	5	.296	.339	.488
1996 St. Louis	NL	140	513	159	36	1	17	(3	14)	248	82	104	29	4	84	7	2	9	22	5	.81	6	.310	.349	.483
1997 St. Louis	NL	47	145	34	5	0	0	(0	0)	39	17	10	10	1	21	6	0	0	6	1	.86	4	.234	.311	.269
1998 St. Louis	NL	150	564	178	34	7	25	(9	16)	301	100	91	40	1	66	9	0	4	17	5	.77	18	.316	.368	.534
1999 Atlanta	NL	153	576	163	28	4	23	(11	12)	268	100	115	51	2	81	9	0	9	13	8	.62	9	.283	.346	.465
8 ML YEARS		796	2882	834	150	28	107	(48	59)	1361	446	482	190	13	454	48	2	29	99	39	.72	60	.289	.340	.472

Kevin Jordan

Bats: R **Throws:** R **Pos:** 3B-62; 2B-33; PH/PR-30; 1B-13 **Ht:** 6'1" **Wt:** 206 **Born:** 10/9/69 **Age:** 30

Year Team	Lg	G	AB	H	2B	3B	HR	(Hm	Rd)	TB	R	RBI	TBB	IBB	SO	HBP	SH	SF	SB	CS	SB%	GDP	Avg	OBP	SLG
1995 Philadelphia	NL	24	54	10	1	0	2	(1	1)	17	6	6	2	1	9	1	0	0	0	0	.00	3	.185	.228	.315
1996 Philadelphia	NL	43	131	37	10	0	3	(2	1)	56	15	12	5	0	20	1	3	2	2	1	.67	0	.282	.309	.427
1997 Philadelphia	NL	84	177	47	8	0	6	(4	2)	73	19	30	3	0	26	0	0	3	0	1	.00	5	.266	.273	.412
1998 Philadelphia	NL	112	250	69	13	0	2	(1	1)	88	23	27	8	1	30	2	0	1	0	0	.00	5	.276	.303	.352
1999 Philadelphia	NL	120	347	99	17	3	4	(2	2)	134	36	51	24	1	34	6	0	3	2	0	.00	12	.285	.339	.386
5 ML YEARS		383	959	262	49	3	17	(10	7)	368	99	126	42	3	119	10	3	9	2	2	.50	25	.273	.308	.384

Wally Joyner

Bats: Left **Throws:** Left **Pos:** 1B-105; PH/PR-8; DH-1 **Ht:** 6'2" **Wt:** 200 **Born:** 6/16/62 **Age:** 38

							BATTING												BASERUNNING				PERCENTAGES		
Year Team	Lg	G	AB	H	2B	3B	HR	(Hm	Rd)	TB	R	RBI	TBB	IBB	SO	HBP	SH	SF	SB	CS	SB%	GDP	Avg	OBP	SLG
1999 Las Vegas *	AAA	6	17	4	0	0	0	—	—	4	4	2	3	0	2	1	0	0	0	0	.00	2	.235	.381	.235
1986 California	AL	154	593	172	27	3	22	(11	11)	271	82	100	57	0	58	2	10	12	5	2	.71	11	.290	.348	.457
1987 California	AL	149	564	161	33	1	34	(19	15)	298	100	117	72	12	64	5	2	10	8	2	.80	14	.285	.366	.528
1988 California	AL	158	597	176	31	2	13	(6	7)	250	81	85	55	14	51	5	0	6	8	2	.80	16	.295	.356	.419
1989 California	AL	159	593	167	30	2	16	(8	8)	249	78	79	46	7	58	6	1	8	3	2	.60	15	.282	.335	.420
1990 California	AL	83	310	83	15	0	8	(5	3)	122	35	41	41	4	34	1	1	5	2	1	.67	10	.268	.350	.394
1991 California	AL	143	551	166	34	3	21	(10	11)	269	79	96	52	4	66	1	2	5	2	0	1.00	11	.301	.360	.488
1992 Kansas City	AL	149	572	154	36	2	9	(1	8)	221	66	66	55	4	50	4	0	2	11	5	.69	19	.269	.336	.386
1993 Kansas City	AL	141	497	145	36	3	15	(4	11)	232	83	65	66	13	67	3	2	5	5	9	.36	6	.292	.375	.467
1994 Kansas City	AL	97	363	113	20	3	8	(2	6)	163	52	57	47	3	43	0	2	5	3	2	.60	12	.311	.386	.449
1995 Kansas City	AL	131	465	144	28	0	12	(6	6)	208	69	83	69	10	65	2	5	9	3	2	.60	10	.310	.394	.447
1996 San Diego	NL	121	433	120	29	1	8	(5	3)	175	59	65	69	8	71	3	1	4	5	3	.63	6	.277	.377	.404
1997 San Diego	NL	135	455	149	29	2	13	(6	7)	221	59	83	51	5	51	2	0	10	3	5	.38	14	.327	.390	.486
1998 San Diego	NL	131	439	131	30	1	12	(4	8)	199	58	80	51	8	44	1	0	3	1	2	.33	11	.298	.370	.453
1999 San Diego	NL	110	323	80	14	2	5	(2	3)	113	34	43	58	6	54	2	0	3	0	1	.00	8	.248	.363	.350
14 ML YEARS		1861	6755	1961	392	25	196	(89	107)	2991	935	1060	789	106	776	37	26	87	59	38	.61	163	.290	.363	.443

Mike Judd

Pitches: Right **Bats:** Right **Pos:** SP-4; RP-3 **Ht:** 6'1" **Wt:** 217 **Born:** 6/30/75 **Age:** 25

		HOW MUCH HE PITCHED						WHAT HE GAVE UP											THE RESULTS					
Year Team	Lg	G	GS	CG	GF	IP	BFP	H	R	ER	HR	SH	SF	HB	TBB	IBB	SO	WP	Bk	W	L	Pct.	ShO	Sv-Op	Hld	ERA
1995 Yankees	R	21	0	0	18	32.1	123	18	5	4	0	0	0	4	6	0	30	4	0	1	1	.500	0	8-—	—	1.11
Greensboro	A	1	0	0	1	2.2	11	2	0	0	0	0	0	0	0	0	1	0	0	0	0	.000	0	0-—	—	0.00
1996 Greensboro	A	29	0	0	26	28.1	119	22	14	12	2	2	0	2	8	3	36	2	1	2	2	.500	0	10-—	—	3.81
Savannah	A	15	8	1	7	55.1	220	40	21	15	2	2	0	2	15	0	62	9	0	4	2	.667	0	3-—	—	2.44
1997 Vero Beach	A+	14	14	1	0	86.2	361	67	37	34	4	3	3	1	39	1	104	4	1	6	5	.545	0	0-—	—	3.53
San Antonio	AA	12	12	0	0	79	323	69	27	24	0	0	2	3	33	0	65	8	2	4	2	.667	0	0-—	—	2.73
1998 Albuquerque	AAA	17	17	3	0	94.2	424	98	62	48	17	4	2	6	44	0	77	6	3	5	7	.417	1	0-—	—	4.56
1999 Albuquerque	AAA	21	21	1	0	110.2	507	132	90	82	22	3	1	7	47	1	122	9	0	8	7	.533	0	0-—	—	6.67
1997 Los Angeles	NL	1	0	0	0	2.2	11	4	0	0	0	0	0	0	0	0	4	0	0	0	0	.000	0	0-0	—	0.00
1998 Los Angeles	NL	7	0	0	3	11.1	63	19	19	19	4	2	0	1	9	1	14	0	0	0	0	.000	0	0-0	0	15.09
1999 Los Angeles	NL	7	4	0	0	28	120	30	17	17	4	0	0	1	12	0	22	3	0	3	1	.750	0	0-0	0	5.46
3 ML YEARS		15	4	0	3	42	194	53	36	36	8	2	0	2	21	1	40	3	0	3	1	.750	0	0-0	0	7.71

Jeff Juden

Pitches: Right **Bats:** Both **Pos:** SP-1; RP-1 **Ht:** 6'8" **Wt:** 265 **Born:** 1/19/71 **Age:** 29

		HOW MUCH HE PITCHED						WHAT HE GAVE UP											THE RESULTS					
Year Team	Lg	G	GS	CG	GF	IP	BFP	H	R	ER	HR	SH	SF	HB	TBB	IBB	SO	WP	Bk	W	L	Pct.	ShO	Sv-Op	Hld	ERA
1999 Columbus *	AAA	27	26	4	0	176.1	768	164	124	109	24	6	7	17	76	2	151	14	4	11	12	.478	1	0-—	—	5.56
1991 Houston	NL	4	3	0	0	18	81	19	14	12	3	2	3	0	7	1	11	0	1	0	2	.000	0	0-0	0	6.00
1993 Houston	NL	2	0	0	1	5	23	4	3	3	1	0	1	0	4	1	7	0	0	0	0	.000	0	0-0	0	5.40
1994 Philadelphia	NL	6	5	0	0	27.2	121	29	25	19	4	1	2	1	12	0	22	0	2	1	4	.200	0	0-0	0	6.18
1995 Philadelphia	NL	13	10	1	0	62.2	271	53	31	28	6	5	4	5	31	0	47	4	1	2	4	.333	0	0-0	0	4.02
1996 SF-Mon	NL	58	0	0	16	74.1	318	61	35	27	8	3	3	5	34	2	61	5	0	5	0	1.000	0	0-0	0	3.27
1997 Mon-Cle		30	27	3	0	161.1	706	157	85	80	23	7	6	10	72	2	136	8	1	11	6	.647	0	0-0	0	4.46
1998 Mil-Ana		32	30	2	1	178.1	801	182	123	115	27	9	7	12	84	0	148	10	0	8	14	.364	0	0-0	0	5.80
1999 New York	AL	2	1	0	0	5.2	29	5	9	1	1	0	0	1	3	0	9	0	0	0	1	.000	0	0-0	0	1.59
1996 San Francisco	NL	36	0	0	9	41.2	180	39	23	19	7	1	2	1	20	2	35	3	0	4	0	1.000	0	0-0	3	4.10
Montreal	NL	22	0	0	7	32.2	138	22	12	8	1	2	1	4	14	0	26	2	0	1	0	1.000	0	0-0	0	2.20
1997 Montreal	NL	22	22	3	0	130	565	125	64	61	17	5	4	9	57	2	107	7	1	11	5	.688	0	0-0	0	4.22
Cleveland	AL	8	5	0	0	31.1	141	32	21	19	6	2	2	1	15	0	29	1	0	0	1	.000	0	0-0	0	5.46
1998 Milwaukee	NL	24	24	2	0	138.1	629	149	91	85	20	9	7	10	66	0	109	6	0	7	11	.389	0	0-0	0	5.53
Anaheim	AL	8	6	0	1	40	172	33	32	30	7	0	0	2	18	0	39	4	0	1	3	.250	0	0-0	0	6.75
8 ML YEARS		147	76	6	18	533	2350	510	325	285	73	27	26	34	247	6	441	27	5	27	32	.458	0	0-0	3	4.81

David Justice

Bats: L **Throws:** L **Pos:** LF-79; DH-34; RF-15; PH/PR-8 **Ht:** 6'3" **Wt:** 200 **Born:** 4/14/66 **Age:** 34

							BATTING												BASERUNNING				PERCENTAGES		
Year Team	Lg	G	AB	H	2B	3B	HR	(Hm	Rd)	TB	R	RBI	TBB	IBB	SO	HBP	SH	SF	SB	CS	SB%	GDP	Avg	OBP	SLG
1989 Atlanta	NL	16	51	12	3	0	1	(1	0)	18	7	3	3	1	9	1	1	0	2	1	.67	1	.235	.291	.353
1990 Atlanta	NL	127	439	124	23	2	28	(19	9)	235	76	78	64	4	92	0	0	1	11	6	.65	2	.282	.373	.535
1991 Atlanta	NL	109	396	109	25	1	21	(11	10)	199	67	87	65	9	81	3	0	5	8	8	.50	4	.275	.377	.503
1992 Atlanta	NL	144	484	124	19	5	21	(10	11)	216	78	72	79	8	85	2	0	6	2	4	.33	1	.256	.359	.446
1993 Atlanta	NL	157	585	158	15	4	40	(18	22)	301	90	120	78	12	90	3	0	4	3	5	.38	9	.270	.357	.515
1994 Atlanta	NL	104	352	110	16	2	19	(9	10)	187	61	59	69	5	45	2	0	1	2	4	.33	8	.313	.427	.531
1995 Atlanta	NL	120	411	104	17	2	24	(15	9)	197	73	78	73	5	68	2	0	5	4	2	.67	5	.253	.365	.479
1996 Atlanta	NL	40	140	45	9	0	6	(5	1)	72	23	25	21	1	22	1	0	2	1	1	.50	5	.321	.409	.514
1997 Cleveland	AL	139	495	163	31	1	33	(17	16)	295	84	101	80	11	79	0	0	7	3	5	.38	12	.329	.418	.596
1998 Cleveland	AL	146	540	151	39	2	21	(7	14)	257	94	88	76	7	98	0	0	9	9	3	.75	9	.280	.363	.476
1999 Cleveland	AL	133	429	123	18	0	21	(11	10)	204	75	88	94	11	90	2	0	5	1	3	.25	14	.287	.413	.476
11 ML YEARS		1235	4322	1223	215	19	235	(123	112)	2181	728	799	702	74	759	16	1	45	46	42	.52	70	.283	.382	.505

Scott Kamieniecki

Pitches: Right **Bats:** Right **Pos:** RP-40; SP-3   **Ht:** 6'0" **Wt:** 200 **Born:** 4/19/64 **Age:** 36

Year Team	Lg	HOW MUCH HE PITCHED						WHAT HE GAVE UP										THE RESULTS						
		G	GS	CG	GF	IP	BFP	H	R	ER	HR	SH	SF	HB	TBB	IBB	SO	WP	Bk	W	L	Pct.	ShO	Sv-Op	Hld	ERA
1999 Bowie *	AA	1	1	0	0	5	18	6	2	2	0	0	0	0	0	0	1	0	0	0	1	.000	0	0--	—	3.60
Frederick *	A+	1	1	0	0	4	14	0	0	0	0	0	0	0	1	0	3	0	0	0	0	.000	0	0--	—	0.00
Rochester *	AAA	4	4	0	0	23	95	23	13	13	5	0	1	1	6	0	14	0	0	1	2	.333	0	0--	—	5.09
1991 New York	AL	9	9	0	0	55.1	239	54	24	24	8	2	1	3	22	1	34	1	0	4	4	.500	0	0-0	0	3.90
1992 New York	AL	28	28	4	0	188	804	193	100	91	13	3	5	5	74	9	88	9	1	6	14	.300	0	0-0	0	4.36
1993 New York	AL	30	20	2	4	154.1	659	163	73	70	17	3	5	3	59	7	72	2	0	10	7	.588	0	1-1	0	4.08
1994 New York	AL	22	16	1	2	117.1	509	115	53	49	13	4	3	3	59	5	71	4	0	8	6	.571	0	0-0	1	3.76
1995 New York	AL	17	16	1	1	89.2	391	83	43	40	8	1	0	3	49	1	43	4	0	7	6	.538	0	0-0	0	4.01
1996 New York	AL	7	5	0	0	22.2	120	36	30	28	6	0	0	2	19	1	15	1	0	1	2	.333	0	0-1	0	11.12
1997 Baltimore	AL	30	30	0	0	179.1	764	179	83	80	20	1	6	4	67	2	109	5	0	10	6	.625	0	0-0	0	4.01
1998 Baltimore	AL	12	11	0	1	54.2	249	67	41	41	7	3	2	4	26	0	25	2	0	2	6	.250	0	0-0	0	6.75
1999 Baltimore	AL	43	3	0	18	56.1	248	52	32	31	4	4	3	4	29	2	39	4	0	2	4	.333	0	2-2	11	4.95
9 ML YEARS		198	138	8	26	917.2	3983	942	479	454	96	21	25	31	404	28	496	32	1	50	55	.476	0	3-4	12	4.45

Gabe Kapler

Bats: R **Throws:** R **Pos:** CF-114; RF-32; PH/PR-4; DH-2   **Ht:** 6'2" **Wt:** 208 **Born:** 8/31/75 **Age:** 24

Year Team	Lg	BATTING																	BASERUNNING				PERCENTAGES		
		G	AB	H	2B	3B	HR	(Hm	Rd)	TB	R	RBI	TBB	IBB	SO	HBP	SH	SF	SB	CS	SB%	GDP	Avg	OBP	SLG
1995 Jamestown	A-	63	236	68	19	4	4	—	—	107	38	34	23	0	37	2	0	4	1	2	.33	4	.288	.351	.453
1996 Fayetteville	A	138	524	157	45	0	26	—	—	280	81	99	62	6	73	7	3	5	14	4	.78	6	.300	.378	.534
1997 Lakeland	A+	137	519	153	40	6	19	—	—	262	87	87	54	4	68	5	0	10	8	6	.57	8	.295	.361	.505
1998 Jacksnville	AA	139	547	176	47	6	28	—	—	319	113	146	66	5	93	5	0	11	6	4	.60	6	.322	.393	.583
1999 Toledo	AAA	14	54	17	6	2	3	—	—	36	11	14	9	1	10	0	0	2	0	1	.00	0	.315	.400	.667
1998 Detroit	AL	7	25	5	0	1	0	(0	0)	7	3	0	1	0	4	0	0	0	2	0	1.00	0	.200	.231	.280
1999 Detroit	AL	130	416	102	22	4	18	(12	6)	186	60	49	42	0	74	2	4	4	11	5	.69	7	.245	.315	.447
2 ML YEARS		137	441	107	22	5	18	(12	6)	193	63	49	43	0	78	2	4	4	13	5	.72	7	.243	.310	.438

Matt Karchner

Pitches: Right **Bats:** Right **Pos:** RP-16   **Ht:** 6'4" **Wt:** 215 **Born:** 6/28/67 **Age:** 33

Year Team	Lg	HOW MUCH HE PITCHED						WHAT HE GAVE UP											THE RESULTS						
		G	GS	CG	GF	IP	BFP	H	R	ER	HR	SH	SF	HB	TBB	IBB	SO	WP	Bk	W	L	Pct.	ShO	Sv-Op	Hld	ERA
1999 Iowa *	AAA	5	1	0	0	5.2	24	6	4	4	1	0	1	1	1	0	6	0	0	0	0	.000	0	0--	—	6.35
1995 Chicago	AL	31	0	0	10	32	137	33	8	6	2	0	4	1	12	2	24	1	0	4	2	.667	0	0-0	13	1.69
1996 Chicago	AL	50	0	0	13	59.1	278	61	42	38	10	2	4	2	41	8	46	4	0	7	4	.636	0	1-9	13	5.76
1997 Chicago	AL	52	0	0	25	52.2	224	50	18	17	4	3	1	0	26	4	30	6	0	3	1	.750	0	15-16	12	2.91
1998 CWS-ChC	AL	61	0	0	26	64.2	299	63	39	37	8	5	4	7	33	8	52	1	0	5	5	.500	0	11-18	10	5.15
1999 Chicago	NL	16	0	0	2	18	80	16	5	5	3	1	0	2	9	0	9	1	0	1	0	1.000	0	0-1	2	2.50
1998 Chicago	AL	32	0	0	23	36.2	167	33	21	21	2	3	4	5	19	6	30	0	0	2	4	.333	0	11-15	1	5.15
Chicago	NL	29	0	0	3	28	132	30	18	16	6	2	0	2	14	2	22	1	0	3	1	.750	0	0-3	9	5.14
5 ML YEARS		210	0	0	76	226.2	1018	223	112	103	27	11	13	12	121	22	161	13	0	20	12	.625	0	27-44	50	4.09

Scott Karl

Pitches: Left **Bats:** Left **Pos:** SP-33   **Ht:** 6'2" **Wt:** 209 **Born:** 8/9/71 **Age:** 28

Year Team	Lg	HOW MUCH HE PITCHED						WHAT HE GAVE UP											THE RESULTS						
		G	GS	CG	GF	IP	BFP	H	R	ER	HR	SH	SF	HB	TBB	IBB	SO	WP	Bk	W	L	Pct.	ShO	Sv-Op	Hld	ERA
1995 Milwaukee	AL	25	18	1	3	124	548	141	65	57	10	3	3	3	50	6	59	0	0	6	7	.462	0	0-0	1	4.14
1996 Milwaukee	AL	32	32	3	0	207.1	905	220	124	112	29	2	7	11	72	0	121	5	1	13	9	.591	1	0-0	0	4.86
1997 Milwaukee	AL	32	32	1	0	193.1	839	212	103	96	23	5	2	4	67	1	119	6	0	10	13	.435	0	0-0	0	4.47
1998 Milwaukee	NL	32	32	1	0	192.1	843	219	104	94	21	14	3	4	66	4	102	6	0	11	11	.476	0	0-0	0	4.40
1999 Milwaukee	NL	33	33	0	0	197.2	885	246	121	105	21	12	7	8	69	4	74	4	2	11	11	.500	0	0-0	0	4.78
5 ML YEARS		155	148	5	3	914.2	4020	1038	517	464	104	36	22	30	324	15	475	21	3	50	51	.495	1	0-0	1	4.57

Eric Karros

Bats: Right **Throws:** Right **Pos:** 1B-151; PH/PR-2   **Ht:** 6'4" **Wt:** 226 **Born:** 11/4/67 **Age:** 32

Year Team	Lg	BATTING																	BASERUNNING				PERCENTAGES		
		G	AB	H	2B	3B	HR	(Hm	Rd)	TB	R	RBI	TBB	IBB	SO	HBP	SH	SF	SB	CS	SB%	GDP	Avg	OBP	SLG
1991 Los Angeles	NL	14	14	1	1	0	0	(0	0)	2	0	1	1	0	6	0	0	0	0	0	.00	0	.071	.133	.143
1992 Los Angeles	NL	149	545	140	30	1	20	(6	14)	232	63	88	37	3	103	2	0	5	2	4	.33	15	.257	.304	.426
1993 Los Angeles	NL	158	619	153	27	2	23	(13	10)	253	74	80	34	1	82	2	0	3	0	1	.00	17	.247	.287	.409
1994 Los Angeles	NL	111	406	108	21	1	14	(5	9)	173	51	46	29	1	53	2	0	11	2	0	1.00	13	.266	.310	.426
1995 Los Angeles	NL	143	551	164	29	3	32	(19	13)	295	83	105	61	4	115	4	0	4	4	4	.50	14	.298	.369	.535
1996 Los Angeles	NL	154	608	158	29	1	34	(16	18)	291	84	111	53	2	121	1	0	8	8	0	1.00	27	.260	.316	.479
1997 Los Angeles	NL	162	628	167	28	0	31	(13	18)	288	86	104	61	2	116	2	0	7	15	7	.68	10	.266	.329	.459
1998 Los Angeles	NL	139	507	150	20	1	23	(9	14)	241	59	87	47	1	93	3	0	7	7	2	.78	7	.296	.355	.475
1999 Los Angeles	NL	153	578	176	40	0	34	(17	17)	318	74	112	53	0	119	2	0	6	8	5	.62	18	.304	.362	.550
9 ML YEARS		1183	4456	1217	225	9	211	(98	113)	2093	574	734	376	14	808	18	0	53	46	23	.67	121	.273	.329	.470

121

Steve Karsay

Pitches: Right **Bats:** Right **Pos:** RP-47; SP-3 **Ht:** 6'3" **Wt:** 209 **Born:** 3/24/72 **Age:** 28

Year Team	Lg	G	GS	CG	GF	IP	BFP	H	R	ER	HR	SH	SF	HB	TBB	IBB	SO	WP	Bk	W	L	Pct.	ShO	Sv-Op	Hld	ERA
1993 Oakland	AL	8	8	0	0	49	210	49	23	22	4	0	2	2	16	1	33	1	0	3	3	.500	0	0-0	0	4.04
1994 Oakland	AL	4	4	1	0	28	115	26	8	8	1	2	1	1	8	0	15	0	0	1	1	.500	0	0-0	0	2.57
1997 Oakland	AL	24	24	0	0	132.2	609	166	92	85	20	2	5	9	47	3	92	7	0	3	12	.200	0	0-0	0	5.77
1998 Cleveland	AL	11	1	0	4	24.1	111	31	16	16	3	1	2	2	6	1	13	2	0	0	2	.000	0	0-0	2	5.92
1999 Cleveland	AL	50	3	0	13	78.2	324	71	29	26	6	2	3	2	30	3	68	5	0	10	2	.833	0	1-3	9	2.97
5 ML YEARS		97	40	1	17	312.2	1369	343	168	157	34	7	13	16	107	8	221	15	0	17	20	.459	0	1-3	11	4.52

Mike Kelly

Bats: Right **Throws:** Right **Pos:** RF-1; PH/PR-1 **Ht:** 6'4" **Wt:** 195 **Born:** 6/2/70 **Age:** 30

Year Team	Lg	G	AB	H	2B	3B	HR	(Hm	Rd)	TB	R	RBI	TBB	IBB	SO	HBP	SH	SF	SB	CS	SB%	GDP	Avg	OBP	SLG
1999 Colo Sprngs *	AAA	114	394	109	27	3	9	(—	—)	169	69	50	57	1	93	11	1	2	10	7	.59	4	.277	.381	.429
1994 Atlanta	NL	30	77	21	10	1	2	(0	2)	39	14	9	2	0	17	1	0	0	0	1	.00	1	.273	.300	.506
1995 Atlanta	NL	97	137	26	6	1	3	(0	3)	43	26	17	11	0	49	2	2	1	7	3	.70	2	.190	.258	.314
1996 Cincinnati	NL	19	49	9	4	0	1	(0	1)	16	5	7	9	0	11	2	0	0	4	0	1.00	2	.184	.333	.327
1997 Cincinnati	NL	73	140	41	13	2	6	(3	3)	76	27	19	10	0	30	0	0	1	6	1	.86	3	.293	.338	.543
1998 Tampa Bay	AL	106	279	67	11	2	10	(4	6)	112	39	33	22	1	80	0	1	1	13	6	.68	0	.240	.295	.421
1999 Colorado	NL	2	2	1	1	0	0	(0	0)	2	0	1	0	0	0	0	0	0	0	0	.00	0	.500	.500	1.000
6 ML YEARS		327	684	165	45	6	22	(7	15)	288	111	86	54	1	187	5	3	3	30	11	.73	16	.241	.300	.421

Pat Kelly

Bats: Right **Throws:** Right **Pos:** 2B-35; PH/PR-3; DH-2 **Ht:** 6'0" **Wt:** 182 **Born:** 10/14/67 **Age:** 32

Year Team	Lg	G	AB	H	2B	3B	HR	(Hm	Rd)	TB	R	RBI	TBB	IBB	SO	HBP	SH	SF	SB	CS	SB%	GDP	Avg	OBP	SLG
1991 New York	AL	96	298	72	12	4	3	(3	0)	101	35	23	15	0	52	5	2	2	12	1	.92	5	.242	.288	.339
1992 New York	AL	106	318	72	22	2	7	(3	4)	119	38	27	25	1	72	10	6	3	8	5	.62	6	.226	.301	.374
1993 New York	AL	127	406	111	24	1	7	(4	3)	158	49	51	24	0	68	5	10	6	14	11	.56	9	.273	.317	.389
1994 New York	AL	93	286	80	21	2	3	(1	2)	114	35	41	19	1	51	5	14	5	6	5	.55	10	.280	.330	.399
1995 New York	AL	89	270	64	12	1	4	(1	3)	90	32	29	23	0	65	5	10	2	8	3	.73	5	.237	.307	.333
1996 New York	AL	13	21	3	0	0	0	(0	0)	3	4	2	2	0	9	0	0	0	0	1	.00	1	.143	.217	.143
1997 New York	AL	67	120	29	6	1	2	(1	1)	43	25	10	14	1	37	1	2	1	8	1	.89	4	.242	.324	.358
1998 St. Louis	NL	53	153	33	5	0	4	(3	1)	50	18	14	13	0	48	2	1	1	5	1	.83	3	.216	.284	.327
1999 Toronto	AL	37	116	31	7	0	6	(5	1)	56	17	20	10	0	23	0	1	3	1	1	.00	1	.267	.318	.483
9 ML YEARS		681	1988	495	109	11	36	(21	15)	734	253	217	145	3	425	33	46	23	61	29	.68	44	.249	.307	.369

Roberto Kelly

Bats: R **Throws:** R **Pos:** CF-37; RF-37; LF-18; PH/PR-10 **Ht:** 6'2" **Wt:** 198 **Born:** 10/1/64 **Age:** 35

Year Team	Lg	G	AB	H	2B	3B	HR	(Hm	Rd)	TB	R	RBI	TBB	IBB	SO	HBP	SH	SF	SB	CS	SB%	GDP	Avg	OBP	SLG
1987 New York	AL	23	52	14	3	0	1	(0	1)	20	12	7	5	0	15	0	1	1	9	3	.75	0	.269	.328	.385
1988 New York	AL	38	77	19	4	1	1	(1	0)	28	9	7	3	0	15	0	3	1	5	2	.71	0	.247	.272	.364
1989 New York	AL	137	441	133	18	3	9	(2	7)	184	65	48	41	3	89	6	8	0	35	12	.74	9	.302	.369	.417
1990 New York	AL	162	641	183	32	4	15	(5	10)	268	85	61	33	0	148	4	4	4	42	17	.71	7	.285	.323	.418
1991 New York	AL	126	486	130	22	2	20	(11	9)	216	68	69	45	2	77	5	2	5	32	9	.78	14	.267	.333	.444
1992 New York	AL	152	580	158	31	2	10	(6	4)	223	81	66	41	4	96	4	1	6	28	5	.85	19	.272	.322	.384
1993 Cincinnati	NL	78	320	102	17	3	9	(4	5)	152	44	35	17	0	43	2	0	3	21	5	.81	10	.319	.354	.475
1994 Cin-Atl	NL	110	434	127	23	3	9	(4	5)	183	73	45	35	1	71	3	0	3	19	11	.63	8	.293	.347	.422
1995 Mon-LA	NL	136	504	140	23	2	7	(2	5)	188	58	57	22	6	79	6	0	7	19	10	.66	14	.278	.312	.373
1996 Minnesota	AL	98	322	104	17	4	6	(3	3)	147	41	47	23	0	53	7	0	5	10	2	.83	17	.323	.375	.457
1997 Min-Sea	AL	105	368	107	26	2	12	(8	4)	173	58	59	22	0	67	3	2	3	9	5	.64	6	.291	.333	.470
1998 Texas	AL	75	257	83	7	3	16	(6	10)	144	48	46	8	0	46	3	1	1	0	2	.00	4	.323	.349	.560
1999 Texas	AL	87	290	87	17	1	8	(4	4)	130	41	37	21	0	57	5	0	2	6	1	.86	5	.300	.355	.448
1994 Cincinnati	NL	47	179	54	8	0	3	(1	2)	71	29	21	11	1	35	3	0	1	9	8	.53	3	.302	.351	.397
Atlanta	NL	63	255	73	15	3	6	(3	3)	112	44	24	24	0	36	0	0	2	10	3	.77	5	.286	.345	.424
1995 Montreal	NL	24	95	26	4	0	1	(0	3)	33	11	9	7	1	14	2	0	0	4	3	.57	4	.274	.337	.347
Los Angeles	NL	112	409	114	19	2	6	(2	2)	155	47	48	15	5	65	4	0	7	15	7	.68	10	.279	.306	.379
1997 Minnesota	AL	75	247	71	19	2	5	(5	0)	109	39	37	17	0	50	2	1	2	7	4	.64	4	.287	.336	.441
Seattle	AL	30	121	36	7	0	7	(3	4)	64	19	22	5	0	17	1	1	1	2	1	.67	2	.298	.328	.529
13 ML YEARS		1327	4772	1387	240	30	123	(56	67)	2056	683	584	316	16	856	48	22	41	235	84	.74	113	.291	.338	.431

Jason Kendall

Bats: Right **Throws:** Right **Pos:** C-75; PH/PR-3 **Ht:** 6'0" **Wt:** 193 **Born:** 6/26/74 **Age:** 26

Year Team	Lg	G	AB	H	2B	3B	HR	(Hm	Rd)	TB	R	RBI	TBB	IBB	SO	HBP	SH	SF	SB	CS	SB%	GDP	Avg	OBP	SLG
1996 Pittsburgh	NL	130	414	124	23	5	3	(2	1)	166	54	42	35	11	30	15	3	4	5	2	.71	7	.300	.372	.401
1997 Pittsburgh	NL	144	486	143	36	4	8	(5	3)	211	71	49	49	2	53	31	1	5	18	6	.75	11	.294	.391	.434
1998 Pittsburgh	NL	149	535	175	36	3	12	(6	6)	253	95	75	51	3	51	31	2	8	26	5	.84	6	.327	.411	.473
1999 Pittsburgh	NL	78	280	93	20	3	8	(5	3)	143	61	41	38	3	32	12	0	4	22	3	.88	8	.332	.428	.511
4 ML YEARS		501	1715	535	115	15	31	(18	13)	773	281	207	173	19	166	89	6	21	71	16	.82	32	.312	.399	.451

Adam Kennedy

Bats: Left **Throws:** Right **Pos:** 2B-29; PH/PR-6   **Ht:** 6'1" **Wt:** 180 **Born:** 1/10/76 **Age:** 24

Year Team	Lg	G	AB	H	2B	3B	HR	(Hm	Rd)	TB	R	RBI	TBB	IBB	SO	HBP	SH	SF	SB	CS	SB%	GDP	Avg	OBP	SLG
1997 New Jersey	A-	29	114	39	6	3	0	—	—	51	20	19	13	0	10	2	1	2	9	1	.90	3	.342	.412	.447
Pr William	A+	35	154	48	9	3	1	—	—	66	24	27	6	1	17	2	1	0	4	3	.57	3	.312	.346	.429
1998 Pr William	A+	17	69	18	6	0	0	—	—	24	9	7	5	0	12	0	0	1	5	2	.71	1	.261	.307	.348
Arkansas	AA	52	205	57	11	4	6	—	—	90	35	24	8	0	21	2	3	3	6	2	.75	4	.278	.307	.439
Memphis	AAA	74	305	93	22	7	4	—	—	141	36	41	12	0	42	1	5	2	15	4	.79	3	.305	.331	.462
1999 Memphis	AAA	91	367	120	22	4	10	—	—	180	69	63	29	0	36	4	0	5	20	6	.77	7	.327	.378	.490
1999 St. Louis	NL	33	102	26	10	1	1	(1	0)	41	12	16	3	0	8	2	1	2	0	1	.00	1	.255	.284	.402

Jeff Kent

Bats: Right **Throws:** Right **Pos:** 2B-133; PH/PR-5; 1B-1   **Ht:** 6'1" **Wt:** 205 **Born:** 3/7/68 **Age:** 32

Year Team	Lg	G	AB	H	2B	3B	HR	(Hm	Rd)	TB	R	RBI	TBB	IBB	SO	HBP	SH	SF	SB	CS	SB%	GDP	Avg	OBP	SLG
1992 Tor-NYM		102	305	73	21	2	11	(4	7)	131	52	50	27	0	76	7	0	4	2	3	.40	5	.239	.312	.430
1993 New York	NL	140	496	134	24	0	21	(9	12)	221	65	80	30	2	88	8	6	4	4	4	.50	11	.270	.320	.446
1994 New York	NL	107	415	121	24	5	14	(10	4)	197	53	68	23	3	84	10	1	3	1	4	.20	7	.292	.341	.475
1995 New York	NL	125	472	131	22	3	20	(11	9)	219	65	65	29	3	89	8	1	4	3	3	.50	9	.278	.327	.464
1996 NYM-Cle		128	437	124	27	1	12	(4	8)	189	61	55	31	1	78	2	1	6	6	4	.60	8	.284	.330	.432
1997 San Francisco	NL	155	580	145	38	2	29	(13	16)	274	90	121	48	6	133	13	0	10	11	3	.79	14	.250	.316	.472
1998 San Francisco	NL	137	526	156	37	3	31	(17	14)	292	94	128	48	4	110	9	1	10	9	4	.69	16	.297	.359	.555
1999 San Francisco	NL	138	511	148	40	2	23	(11	12)	261	86	101	61	3	112	5	0	8	13	6	.68	12	.290	.366	.511
1992 Toronto	AL	65	192	46	13	1	8	(2	6)	85	36	35	20	0	47	6	0	4	2	1	.67	3	.240	.324	.443
New York	NL	37	113	27	8	1	3	(2	1)	46	16	15	7	0	29	1	0	0	0	2	.00	2	.239	.289	.407
1996 New York	NL	89	335	97	20	1	9	(2	7)	146	45	39	21	1	56	1	1	3	4	3	.57	7	.290	.331	.436
Cleveland	AL	39	102	27	7	0	3	(2	1)	43	16	16	10	0	22	1	0	3	2	1	.67	1	.265	.328	.422
8 ML YEARS		1032	3742	1032	233	18	161	(79	82)	1784	566	668	297	22	770	62	10	49	49	31	.61	82	.276	.335	.477

Masao Kida

Pitches: Right **Bats:** Right **Pos:** RP-49   **Ht:** 6'3" **Wt:** 210 **Born:** 9/12/68 **Age:** 31

Year Team	Lg	G	GS	CG	GF	IP	BFP	H	R	ER	HR	SH	SF	HB	TBB	IBB	SO	WP	Bk	W	L	Pct.	ShO	Sv-Op	Hld	ERA
1999 Toledo	AAA	3	0	0	1	5.2	23	6	2	2	2	0	0	0	1	0	4	0	0	0	0	.000	0	0- -	—	3.18
1999 Detroit	AL	49	0	0	21	64.2	292	73	48	45	6	1	4	4	30	3	50	7	0	1	0	1.000	0	1-1	4	6.26

Darryl Kile

Pitches: Right **Bats:** Right **Pos:** SP-32   **Ht:** 6'5" **Wt:** 212 **Born:** 12/2/68 **Age:** 31

Year Team	Lg	G	GS	CG	GF	IP	BFP	H	R	ER	HR	SH	SF	HB	TBB	IBB	SO	WP	Bk	W	L	Pct.	ShO	Sv-Op	Hld	ERA
1991 Houston	NL	37	22	0	5	153.2	689	144	81	63	16	9	5	6	84	4	100	5	4	7	11	.389	0	0-1	0	3.69
1992 Houston	NL	22	22	2	0	125.1	554	124	61	55	8	5	6	4	63	4	90	3	4	5	10	.333	0	0-0	0	3.95
1993 Houston	NL	32	26	4	0	171.2	733	152	73	67	12	5	7	15	69	1	141	9	3	15	8	.652	2	0-0	0	3.51
1994 Houston	NL	24	24	0	0	147.2	664	153	84	75	13	14	2	9	82	6	105	10	0	9	6	.600	0	0-0	0	4.57
1995 Houston	NL	25	21	0	1	127	570	114	81	70	5	7	3	12	73	2	113	11	1	4	12	.250	0	0-0	0	4.96
1996 Houston	NL	35	33	4	1	219	975	233	102	16	10	9	16	97	8	219	13	3	12	11	.522	0	0-0	0	4.19
1997 Houston	NL	34	34	6	0	255.2	1056	208	87	73	19	17	10	10	94	2	205	7	1	19	7	.731	4	0-0	0	2.57
1998 Colorado	NL	36	35	4	0	230.1	1020	257	141	133	28	15	8	7	96	4	158	12	0	13	17	.433	1	0-0	0	5.20
1999 Colorado	NL	32	32	1	0	190.2	888	225	150	140	33	9	9	6	109	5	116	13	1	8	13	.381	0	0-0	0	6.61
9 ML YEARS		277	249	21	8	1621	7149	1610	871	778	150	91	59	85	767	36	1247	83	17	92	95	.492	7	0-1	0	4.32

Byung-Hyun Kim

Pitches: Right **Bats:** Right **Pos:** RP-25   **Ht:** 5'11" **Wt:** 176 **Born:** 1/21/79 **Age:** 21

Year Team	Lg	G	GS	CG	GF	IP	BFP	H	R	ER	HR	SH	SF	HB	TBB	IBB	SO	WP	Bk	W	L	Pct.	ShO	Sv-Op	Hld	ERA
1999 El Paso	AA	10	0	0	3	21.1	81	6	5	5	0	3	1	3	9	0	32	0	2	2	0	1.000	0	0- -	—	2.11
Diamondbcks	R	1	1	0	0	2	7	0	0	0	0	0	0	0	1	0	2	0	0	0	0	.000	0	0- -	—	0.00
Tucson	AAA	11	3	0	3	30	123	21	9	8	2	0	0	1	15	1	40	1	3	4	0	1.000	0	1- -	—	2.40
1999 Arizona	NL	25	0	0	10	27.1	121	20	15	14	2	1	0	5	20	2	31	4	1	1	2	.333	0	1-4	3	4.61

Curtis King

Pitches: Right **Bats:** Right **Pos:** RP-2   **Ht:** 6'5" **Wt:** 205 **Born:** 10/25/70 **Age:** 29

Year Team	Lg	G	GS	CG	GF	IP	BFP	H	R	ER	HR	SH	SF	HB	TBB	IBB	SO	WP	Bk	W	L	Pct.	ShO	Sv-Op	Hld	ERA
1999 Memphis *	AAA	27	3	0	13	31	124	21	13	9	2	2	1	1	10	2	25	0	0	2	2	.500	0	7- -	—	2.61
1997 St. Louis	NL	30	0	0	13	29.1	136	38	14	9	0	4	3	1	11	0	13	2	0	4	2	.667	0	0-3	10	2.76
1998 St. Louis	NL	36	0	0	11	51	218	50	20	20	5	2	2	3	20	4	28	0	0	2	0	1.000	0	2-8	3	3.53
1999 St. Louis	NL	2	0	0	1	1	6	3	2	2	0	0	0	0	0	0	1	0	0	0	0	.000	0	0-0	0	18.00
3 ML YEARS		68	0	0	20	81.1	360	91	36	31	5	6	5	4	31	4	42	2	1	6	2	.750	0	2-11	13	3.43

Jeff King

Bats: Right **Throws:** Right **Pos:** 1B-20; DH-1   **Ht:** 6'1" **Wt:** 190 **Born:** 12/26/64 **Age:** 35

								BATTING											BASERUNNING				PERCENTAGES		
Year Team	Lg	G	AB	H	2B	3B	HR	(Hm	Rd)	TB	R	RBI	TBB	IBB	SO	HBP	SH	SF	SB	CS	SB%	GDP	Avg	OBP	SLG
1989 Pittsburgh	NL	75	215	42	13	3	5	(3	2)	76	31	19	20	1	34	2	2	4	4	2	.67	3	.195	.266	.353
1990 Pittsburgh	NL	127	371	91	17	1	14	(9	5)	152	46	53	21	1	50	1	2	7	3	3	.50	12	.245	.283	.410
1991 Pittsburgh	NL	33	109	26	1	1	4	(3	1)	41	16	18	14	3	15	1	0	1	3	1	.75	3	.239	.328	.376
1992 Pittsburgh	NL	130	480	111	21	2	14	(6	8)	178	56	65	27	3	56	2	8	5	4	6	.40	8	.231	.272	.371
1993 Pittsburgh	NL	158	611	180	35	3	9	(4	5)	248	82	98	59	4	54	4	1	8	8	6	.57	17	.295	.356	.406
1994 Pittsburgh	NL	94	339	89	23	0	5	(2	3)	127	36	42	30	1	38	0	2	7	3	2	.60	7	.263	.316	.375
1995 Pittsburgh	NL	122	445	118	27	2	18	(7	11)	203	61	87	55	5	63	1	0	8	7	4	.64	10	.265	.342	.456
1996 Pittsburgh	NL	155	591	160	36	4	30	(14	16)	294	91	111	70	3	95	2	1	8	15	1	.94	17	.271	.346	.497
1997 Kansas City	AL	155	543	129	30	1	28	(11	17)	245	84	112	89	4	96	2	1	12	16	5	.76	9	.238	.341	.451
1998 Kansas City	AL	131	486	128	17	1	24	(13	11)	219	83	93	42	1	73	2	0	10	10	2	.83	10	.263	.319	.451
1999 Kansas City	AL	21	72	17	2	0	3	(2	1)	28	14	11	15	1	10	3	0	1	2	0	1.00	1	.236	.385	.389
11 ML YEARS		1201	4262	1091	222	18	154	(74	80)	1811	600	709	442	27	584	20	17	71	75	32	.70	97	.256	.324	.425

Ray King

Pitches: Left **Bats:** Left **Pos:** RP-10   **Ht:** 6'1" **Wt:** 225 **Born:** 1/15/74 **Age:** 26

		HOW MUCH HE PITCHED						WHAT HE GAVE UP												THE RESULTS						
Year Team	Lg	G	GS	CG	GF	IP	BFP	H	R	ER	HR	SH	SF	HB	TBB	IBB	SO	WP	Bk	W	L	Pct.	ShO	Sv-Op	Hld	ERA
1995 Billings	R+	28	0	0	15	43	169	31	11	8	1	2	0	0	15	3	43	1	1	3	0	1.000	0	5--	—	1.67
1996 Macon	A	18	10	1	2	70.2	286	63	34	22	4	0	0	0	20	0	63	2	1	3	5	.375	0	0--	—	2.80
Durham	A+	14	14	2	0	82.2	364	104	54	41	3	4	4	3	15	2	52	2	1	3	6	.333	0	0--	—	4.46
1997 Greenville	AA	12	9	0	0	65.2	305	85	53	50	9	0	1	0	24	2	42	4	0	5	5	.500	0	0--	—	6.85
Durham	A+	24	6	0	6	71.2	335	89	54	43	6	7	1	4	26	4	60	4	0	6	9	.400	0	3--	—	5.40
1998 West Tenn	AA	25	0	0	8	29.2	121	23	9	8	1	1	1	1	10	0	26	2	0	1	2	.333	0	3--	—	2.43
Iowa	AAA	37	0	0	7	32.1	143	36	20	18	4	1	0	0	15	1	26	4	0	1	3	.250	0	2--	—	5.01
1999 Iowa	AAA	37	0	0	19	43	183	31	11	9	1	2	2	2	22	3	41	2	0	4	4	.500	0	2--	—	1.88
1999 Chicago	NL	10	0	0	0	10.2	50	11	8	7	2	1	0	1	10	0	5	1	0	0	0	.000	0	0-0	2	5.91

Gene Kingsale

Bats: Both **Throws:** Right **Pos:** CF-24; PH/PR-3; DH-2   **Ht:** 6'3" **Wt:** 194 **Born:** 8/20/76 **Age:** 23

								BATTING											BASERUNNING				PERCENTAGES		
Year Team	Lg	G	AB	H	2B	3B	HR	(Hm	Rd)	TB	R	RBI	TBB	IBB	SO	HBP	SH	SF	SB	CS	SB%	GDP	Avg	OBP	SLG
1994 Orioles	R	50	168	52	2	3	0	—	—	60	26	9	18	0	24	2	1	1	15	8	.65	1	.310	.381	.357
1995 Bluefield	R+	47	171	54	11	2	0	—	—	69	45	16	27	0	31	5	4	2	20	8	.71	0	.316	.420	.404
1996 Frederick	A+	49	166	45	6	4	0	—	—	59	26	9	19	1	32	6	3	2	23	4	.85	1	.271	.363	.355
1997 Orioles	R	6	17	5	0	0	0	—	—	5	2	0	2	0	2	1	0	0	1	0	1.00	0	.294	.400	.294
Bowie	AA	13	46	19	6	0	0	—	—	25	8	4	5	0	4	1	1	0	5	1	.83	2	.413	.481	.543
1998 Rochester	AAA	18	55	12	1	1	0	—	—	15	3	2	4	0	8	1	1	0	3	3	.50	3	.218	.283	.273
Bowie	AA	111	427	112	11	5	1	—	—	136	69	34	48	2	79	12	10	4	29	12	.71	6	.262	.350	.319
1999 Bowie	AA	67	268	63	11	4	3	—	—	91	43	23	33	0	46	1	6	2	13	10	.57	4	.235	.319	.340
Rochester	AAA	48	191	59	9	0	2	—	—	74	31	20	13	0	23	3	3	1	10	9	.53	2	.309	.361	.387
1996 Baltimore	AL	3	0	0	0	0	0	(0	0)	0	0	0	0	0	0	0	0	0	0	0	.00	0	.000	.000	.000
1998 Baltimore	AL	11	2	0	0	0	0	(0	0)	0	1	0	0	0	1	0	0	0	0	0	.00	0	.000	.000	.000
1999 Baltimore	AL	28	85	21	2	0	0	—	—	23	9	7	5	0	13	2	2	1	1	3	.25	3	.247	.301	.271
3 ML YEARS		42	87	21	2	0	0	(0	0)	23	10	7	5	0	14	2	2	1	1	3	.25	3	.241	.295	.264

Mike Kinkade

Bats: R **Throws:** R **Pos:** PH/PR-13; LF-12; RF-8; 3B-3; C-1; 1B-1   **Ht:** 6'1" **Wt:** 210 **Born:** 5/6/73 **Age:** 27

								BATTING											BASERUNNING				PERCENTAGES		
Year Team	Lg	G	AB	H	2B	3B	HR	(Hm	Rd)	TB	R	RBI	TBB	IBB	SO	HBP	SH	SF	SB	CS	SB%	GDP	Avg	OBP	SLG
1995 Helena	R+	69	266	94	19	1	4	—	—	127	76	39	43	2	38	10	0	6	26	9	.74	6	.353	.452	.477
1996 Beloit	A	135	499	151	33	4	15	—	—	237	105	100	47	7	69	32	3	6	23	12	.66	10	.303	.394	.475
1997 El Paso	AA	125	468	180	35	12	12	—	—	275	112	109	52	0	66	13	1	6	17	4	.81	13	.385	.455	.588
1998 Louisville	AAA	80	291	90	24	6	7	—	—	147	57	46	36	1	52	6	1	2	10	2	.83	7	.309	.394	.505
Norfolk	AAA	30	125	35	5	0	1	—	—	43	12	18	3	0	24	5	1	2	6	1	.86	5	.280	.319	.344
1999 Norfolk	AAA	84	312	96	20	2	7	—	—	141	53	49	21	2	31	5	0	2	7	1	.88	9	.308	.359	.452
1998 New York	NL	3	2	0	0	0	0	(0	0)	0	2	0	0	0	0	0	0	0	0	0	.00	0	.000	.000	.000
1999 New York	NL	28	46	9	2	1	2	(1	1)	19	3	6	3	0	9	2	0	0	1	0	1.00	1	.196	.275	.413
2 ML YEARS		31	48	9	2	1	2	(1	1)	19	5	6	3	0	9	2	0	0	1	0	1.00	1	.188	.264	.396

Danny Klassen

Bats: Right **Throws:** Right **Pos:** PH/PR-1   **Ht:** 6'0" **Wt:** 175 **Born:** 9/22/75 **Age:** 24

								BATTING											BASERUNNING				PERCENTAGES		
Year Team	Lg	G	AB	H	2B	3B	HR	(Hm	Rd)	TB	R	RBI	TBB	IBB	SO	HBP	SH	SF	SB	CS	SB%	GDP	Avg	OBP	SLG
1993 Brewers	R	38	117	26	5	0	2	—	—	37	26	20	24	3	28	8	1	4	14	3	.82	2	.222	.379	.316
Helena	R+	18	45	9	1	0	0	—	—	10	8	3	7	0	11	2	1	0	2	1	.67	2	.200	.333	.222
1994 Beloit	A	133	446	119	20	3	6	—	—	163	61	54	58	0	123	12	17	3	28	14	.67	3	.260	.356	.356
1995 Beloit	A	59	218	60	15	2	2	—	—	85	27	25	16	0	43	4	0	3	12	4	.75	4	.275	.332	.390
1996 Stockton	A+	118	432	116	22	4	2	—	—	152	58	46	34	0	77	10	5	2	14	8	.64	12	.269	.335	.352
1997 El Paso	AA	135	519	172	30	6	14	—	—	256	112	81	48	1	104	10	4	4	16	9	.64	13	.331	.396	.493
1998 Tucson	AAA	73	281	82	25	2	10	—	—	141	47	47	19	1	54	6	0	5	6	2	.75	11	.292	.344	.502

BATTING																			BASERUNNING				PERCENTAGES		
Year Team	Lg	G	AB	H	2B	3B	HR	(Hm	Rd)	TB	R	RBI	TBB	IBB	SO	HBP	SH	SF	SB	CS	SB%	GDP	Avg	OBP	SLG
1999 Diamondbcks	R	6	17	4	1	0	0	—	—	5	2	1	1	0	4	0	0	0	0	0	.00	1	.235	.278	.294
Tucson	AAA	64	245	66	16	3	6	—	—	106	38	33	20	1	51	1	0	2	5	3	.63	5	.269	.325	.433
1998 Arizona	NL	29	108	21	2	1	3	(3	0)	34	12	8	9	0	33	1	0	0	1	1	.50	5	.194	.263	.315
1999 Arizona	NL	1	1	1	0	0	0	(0	0)	1	0	0	0	0	0	0	0	0	0	0	.00	0	1.000	1.000	1.000
2 ML YEARS		30	109	22	2	1	3	(3	0)	35	12	8	9	0	33	1	0	0	1	1	.50	5	.202	.269	.321

Ryan Klesko

Bats: L **Throws:** L **Pos:** 1B-75; LF-53; PH/PR-15; DH-1   **Ht:** 6'3" **Wt:** 220 **Born:** 6/12/71 **Age:** 29

BATTING																			BASERUNNING				PERCENTAGES		
Year Team	Lg	G	AB	H	2B	3B	HR	(Hm	Rd)	TB	R	RBI	TBB	IBB	SO	HBP	SH	SF	SB	CS	SB%	GDP	Avg	OBP	SLG
1992 Atlanta	NL	13	14	0	0	0	0	(0	0)	0	0	1	0	0	5	1	0	0	0	0	.00	0	.000	.067	.000
1993 Atlanta	NL	22	17	6	1	0	2	(2	0)	13	3	5	3	1	4	0	0	0	0	0	.00	0	.353	.450	.765
1994 Atlanta	NL	92	245	68	13	3	17	(7	10)	138	42	47	26	3	48	1	0	4	1	0	1.00	8	.278	.344	.563
1995 Atlanta	NL	107	329	102	25	2	23	(15	8)	200	48	70	47	10	72	2	0	3	5	4	.56	8	.310	.396	.608
1996 Atlanta	NL	153	528	149	21	4	34	(20	14)	280	90	93	68	10	129	2	0	4	6	3	.67	10	.282	.364	.530
1997 Atlanta	NL	143	467	122	23	6	24	(10	14)	229	67	84	48	5	130	4	1	2	4	4	.50	12	.261	.334	.490
1998 Atlanta	NL	129	427	117	29	1	18	(8	10)	202	69	70	56	5	66	3	0	4	5	3	.63	9	.274	.359	.473
1999 Atlanta	NL	133	404	120	28	2	21	(12	9)	215	55	80	53	8	69	2	0	7	5	2	.71	6	.297	.376	.532
8 ML YEARS		792	2431	684	140	18	139	(74	65)	1277	374	450	301	42	523	15	1	24	26	16	.62	53	.281	.361	.525

Steve Kline

Pitches: Left **Bats:** Both **Pos:** RP-82   **Ht:** 6'0" **Wt:** 210 **Born:** 8/22/72 **Age:** 27

HOW MUCH HE PITCHED							WHAT HE GAVE UP											THE RESULTS						
Year Team	Lg	G	GS	CG	GF	IP	BFP	H	R	ER	HR	SH	SF	HB	TBB	IBB	SO	WP	Bk	W	L	Pct.	ShO	Sv-Op	Hld	ERA
1997 Cle-Mon		46	1	0	7	52.2	248	73	37	35	10	4	2	2	23	4	37	4	1	4	4	.500	0	0-3	5	5.98
1998 Montreal	NL	78	0	0	18	71.2	319	62	25	22	4	1	2	3	41	7	76	5	0	3	6	.333	0	1-2	18	2.76
1999 Montreal	NL	82	0	0	18	69.2	297	56	32	29	8	3	1	3	33	6	69	2	0	7	4	.636	0	0-2	16	3.75
1997 Cleveland	AL	20	1	0	0	26.1	130	42	19	17	6	1	0	1	13	1	17	3	1	3	1	.750	0	0-2	4	5.81
Montreal	NL	26	0	0	7	26.1	118	31	18	18	4	3	1	2	10	3	20	1	0	1	3	.250	0	0-1	1	6.15
3 ML YEARS		206	1	0	43	194	864	191	94	86	22	8	5	8	97	17	182	11	1	14	14	.500	0	1-7	39	3.99

Chuck Knoblauch

Bats: Right **Throws:** Right **Pos:** 2B-150   **Ht:** 5'9" **Wt:** 170 **Born:** 7/7/68 **Age:** 31

BATTING																			BASERUNNING				PERCENTAGES		
Year Team	Lg	G	AB	H	2B	3B	HR	(Hm	Rd)	TB	R	RBI	TBB	IBB	SO	HBP	SH	SF	SB	CS	SB%	GDP	Avg	OBP	SLG
1991 Minnesota	AL	151	565	159	24	6	1	(1	0)	198	78	50	59	0	40	4	1	5	25	5	.83	8	.281	.351	.350
1992 Minnesota	AL	155	600	178	19	6	2	(0	2)	215	104	56	88	1	60	5	2	12	34	13	.72	8	.297	.384	.358
1993 Minnesota	AL	153	602	167	27	4	2	(2	0)	208	82	41	65	1	44	9	4	5	29	11	.73	11	.277	.354	.346
1994 Minnesota	AL	109	445	139	45	3	5	(1	4)	205	85	51	41	2	56	10	0	3	35	6	.85	13	.312	.381	.461
1995 Minnesota	AL	136	538	179	34	8	11	(4	7)	262	107	63	78	3	95	10	0	3	46	18	.72	15	.333	.424	.487
1996 Minnesota	AL	153	578	197	35	14	13	(7	6)	299	140	72	98	6	74	19	0	6	45	14	.76	9	.341	.448	.517
1997 Minnesota	AL	156	611	178	26	10	9	(2	7)	251	117	58	84	6	84	17	4	6	62	10	.86	11	.291	.390	.411
1998 New York	AL	150	603	160	25	4	17	(5	12)	244	117	64	76	1	70	18	2	7	31	12	.72	13	.265	.361	.405
1999 New York	AL	150	603	176	36	4	18	(11	7)	274	120	68	83	0	57	21	3	5	28	9	.76	7	.292	.393	.454
9 ML YEARS		1313	5145	1533	271	59	78	(33	45)	2156	950	523	672	20	580	113	12	50	335	98	.77	95	.298	.388	.419

Randy Knorr

Bats: Right **Throws:** Right **Pos:** C-11; PH/PR-3   **Ht:** 6'2" **Wt:** 215 **Born:** 11/12/68 **Age:** 31

BATTING																			BASERUNNING				PERCENTAGES		
Year Team	Lg	G	AB	H	2B	3B	HR	(Hm	Rd)	TB	R	RBI	TBB	IBB	SO	HBP	SH	SF	SB	CS	SB%	GDP	Avg	OBP	SLG
1999 New Orleans *	AAA	77	270	95	22	1	11	—	—	152	33	41	20	1	41	1	0	3	0	1	.00	5	.352	.395	.563
1991 Toronto	AL	3	1	0	0	0	0	(0	0)	0	0	0	1	0	1	0	0	0	0	0	.00	0	.000	.500	.000
1992 Toronto	AL	8	19	5	0	0	1	(0	1)	8	1	2	1	1	5	0	0	0	0	0	.00	0	.263	.300	.421
1993 Toronto	AL	39	101	25	3	2	4	(2	2)	44	11	20	9	0	29	0	2	0	0	0	.00	2	.248	.309	.436
1994 Toronto	AL	40	124	30	2	0	7	(4	3)	53	20	19	10	0	35	1	0	1	0	0	.00	7	.242	.301	.427
1995 Toronto	AL	45	132	28	8	0	3	(2	1)	45	18	16	11	0	28	0	1	0	0	0	.00	5	.212	.273	.341
1996 Houston	NL	37	87	17	5	0	1	(1	0)	25	7	7	5	2	18	1	0	1	0	1	.00	5	.195	.245	.287
1997 Houston	NL	4	8	3	0	0	1	(1	0)	6	1	1	0	0	2	0	0	0	0	0	.00	0	.375	.375	.750
1998 Florida	NL	15	49	10	4	1	2	(0	2)	22	4	11	1	0	10	0	0	1	0	0	.00	0	.204	.216	.449
1999 Houston	NL	13	30	5	1	0	0	(0	0)	6	2	0	1	0	8	0	0	0	0	0	.00	1	.167	.194	.200
9 ML YEARS		204	551	123	23	3	19	(10	9)	209	64	76	39	3	136	2	3	3	0	1	.00	16	.223	.276	.379

Billy Koch

Pitches: Right **Bats:** Right **Pos:** RP-56   **Ht:** 6'3" **Wt:** 218 **Born:** 12/14/74 **Age:** 25

HOW MUCH HE PITCHED							WHAT HE GAVE UP											THE RESULTS						
Year Team	Lg	G	GS	CG	GF	IP	BFP	H	R	ER	HR	SH	SF	HB	TBB	IBB	SO	WP	Bk	W	L	Pct.	ShO	Sv-Op	Hld	ERA
1997 Dunedin	A+	3	3	0	0	21.2	88	27	10	5	1	1	1	0	3	0	20	1	1	0	1	.000	0	0--	—	2.08
1998 Dunedin	A+	25	25	0	0	124.2	528	120	65	52	8	2	2	7	41	0	108	4	3	14	7	.667	0	0--	—	3.75
Syracuse	AAA	2	2	0	0	5.2	31	9	9	9	1	0	1	0	5	0	9	0	1	0	0	.000	0	0--	—	14.29
1999 Syracuse	AAA	5	5	0	0	25.2	111	27	11	11	3	0	1	2	10	0	22	0	2	3	0	1.000	0	0--	—	3.86
1999 Toronto	AL	56	0	0	48	63.2	272	55	26	24	5	4	1	3	30	5	57	0	0	0	5	.000	0	31-35	0	3.39

Danny Kolb

Pitches: Right Bats: Right Pos: RP-16   Ht: 6'4" Wt: 185 Born: 3/29/75 Age: 25

		HOW MUCH HE PITCHED						WHAT HE GAVE UP												THE RESULTS						
Year Team	Lg	G	GS	CG	GF	IP	BFP	H	R	ER	HR	SH	SF	HB	TBB	IBB	SO	WP	Bk	W	L	Pct.	ShO	Sv-Op	Hld	ERA
1995 Rangers	R	12	11	0	0	53	219	38	22	13	0	0	2	3	28	0	46	8	2	1	7	.125	0	0--	—	2.21
1996 Chston-SC	A	20	20	4	0	126	514	80	50	36	5	6	0	6	60	2	127	22	4	8	6	.571	2	0--	—	2.57
Charlotte	A+	6	6	0	0	38	162	38	18	18	1	1	0	1	14	0	28	2	0	2	2	.500	0	0--	—	4.26
Tulsa	AA	2	2	0	0	11.2	45	5	1	1	0	0	0	1	8	0	7	0	0	1	0	1.000	0	0--	—	0.77
1997 Tulsa	AA	2	2	0	0	11.1	50	7	7	6	1	0	0	0	11	0	6	4	0	0	0	.000	0	0--	—	4.76
Charlotte	A+	24	23	3	0	133	600	146	91	72	10	8	5	8	62	1	83	12	0	4	10	.286	0	0--	—	4.87
1998 Tulsa	AA	28	28	2	0	162.1	730	187	104	87	11	3	5	8	76	1	83	8	1	12	11	.522	0	0--	—	4.82
Oklahoma	AAA	1	0	0	1	1	5	1	0	0	0	0	0	0	1	0	0	0	0	0	0	.000	0	0--	—	0.00
1999 Tulsa	AA	7	7	1	0	38.2	170	38	16	12	0	3	1	2	18	0	32	2	0	1	2	.333	1	0--	—	2.79
Oklahoma	AAA	11	8	0	2	60	261	74	35	34	4	2	0	1	27	0	21	2	0	5	3	.625	0	0--	—	5.10
1999 Texas	AL	16	0	0	6	31	139	33	18	16	2	0	1		15	0	15	2	0	2	1	.667	0	0-0	0	4.65

Paul Konerko

Bats: R Throws: R Pos: 1B-92; DH-46; PH/PR-9; 3B-1   Ht: 6'3" Wt: 211 Born: 3/5/76 Age: 24

		BATTING																	BASERUNNING				PERCENTAGES		
Year Team	Lg	G	AB	H	2B	3B	HR	(Hm	Rd)	TB	R	RBI	TBB	IBB	SO	HBP	SH	SF	SB	CS	SB%	GDP	Avg	OBP	SLG
1997 Los Angeles	NL	6	7	1	0	0	0	(0	0)	1	0	0	1	0	2	0	0	0	0	0	.00	1	.143	.250	.143
1998 LA-Cin	NL	75	217	47	4	0	7	(2	5)	72	21	29	16	0	40	3	0	3	0	1	.00	10	.217	.276	.332
1999 Chicago	AL	142	513	151	31	4	24	(16	8)	262	71	81	45	0	68	2	1	3	0	1	.00	19	.294	.352	.511
1998 Los Angeles	NL	49	144	31	1	0	4	(2	2)	44	14	16	10	0	30	2	0	2	0	1	.00	5	.215	.272	.306
Cincinnati	NL	26	73	16	3	0	3	(0	3)	28	7	13	6	0	10	1	0	1	0	0	.00	5	.219	.284	.384
3 ML YEARS		223	737	199	35	4	31	(18	13)	335	92	110	62	0	110	5	1	6	1	1	.50	30	.270	.328	.455

Corey Koskie

Bats: L Throws: R Pos: 3B-79; RF-25; PH/PR-15; DH-12   Ht: 6'3" Wt: 217 Born: 6/28/73 Age: 27

		BATTING																	BASERUNNING				PERCENTAGES		
Year Team	Lg	G	AB	H	2B	3B	HR	(Hm	Rd)	TB	R	RBI	TBB	IBB	SO	HBP	SH	SF	SB	CS	SB%	GDP	Avg	OBP	SLG
1994 Elizabethtn	R+	34	107	25	2	1	3	—	—	38	13	10	18	0	27	2	0	0	0	0	.00	3	.234	.354	.355
1995 Fort Wayne	A	123	462	143	37	5	16	—	—	238	64	78	38	3	79	9	1	5	2	4	.33	10	.310	.370	.515
1996 Fort Myers	A+	95	338	88	19	4	9	—	—	142	43	55	40	0	76	1	1	3	1	1	.50	4	.260	.338	.420
1997 New Britain	AA	131	437	125	26	6	23	—	—	232	88	79	90	10	106	7	0	2	9	5	.64	13	.286	.414	.531
1998 Salt Lake	AAA	135	505	152	32	5	26	—	—	272	91	105	51	4	104	8	0	10	15	7	.68	17	.301	.368	.539
1998 Minnesota	AL	11	29	4	0	0	1	(1	0)	7	2	2	2	0	10	0	0	0	0	0	.00	0	.138	.194	.241
1999 Minnesota	AL	117	342	106	21	0	11	(4	7)	160	42	58	40	4	72	5	2	3	4	4	.50	6	.310	.387	.468
2 ML YEARS		128	371	110	21	0	12	(5	7)	167	44	60	42	4	82	5	2	3	4	4	.50	6	.296	.373	.450

Mark Kotsay

Bats: L Throws: L Pos: RF-129; 1B-19; PH/PR-16   Ht: 6'0" Wt: 190 Born: 12/2/75 Age: 24

		BATTING																	BASERUNNING				PERCENTAGES		
Year Team	Lg	G	AB	H	2B	3B	HR	(Hm	Rd)	TB	R	RBI	TBB	IBB	SO	HBP	SH	SF	SB	CS	SB%	GDP	Avg	OBP	SLG
1997 Florida	NL	14	52	10	1	1	0	(0	0)	13	5	4	4	0	7	0	1	0	3	0	1.00	1	.192	.250	.250
1998 Florida	NL	154	578	161	25	7	11	(5	6)	233	72	68	34	2	68	1	7	3	10	5	.67	17	.279	.318	.403
1999 Florida	NL	148	495	134	23	9	8	(5	3)	199	57	50	29	5	50	0	2	9	7	6	.54	11	.271	.306	.402
3 ML YEARS		316	1125	305	49	17	19	(10	9)	445	134	122	67	7	118	1	10	12	20	11	.65	29	.271	.310	.396

Chad Kreuter

Bats: Both Throws: Right Pos: C-101; PH/PR-7; DH-1   Ht: 6'2" Wt: 200 Born: 8/26/64 Age: 35

		BATTING																	BASERUNNING				PERCENTAGES		
Year Team	Lg	G	AB	H	2B	3B	HR	(Hm	Rd)	TB	R	RBI	TBB	IBB	SO	HBP	SH	SF	SB	CS	SB%	GDP	Avg	OBP	SLG
1988 Texas	AL	16	51	14	2	1	1	(0	1)	21	3	5	7	0	13	0	0	0	0	0	.00	1	.275	.362	.412
1989 Texas	AL	87	158	24	3	0	5	(2	3)	42	16	9	27	0	40	0	6	1	0	1	.00	4	.152	.274	.266
1990 Texas	AL	22	22	1	1	0	0	(0	0)	2	2	2	8	0	9	0	1	1	0	0	.00	0	.045	.290	.091
1991 Texas	AL	3	4	0	0	0	0	(0	0)	0	0	0	0	0	1	0	0	0	0	0	.00	0	.000	.000	.000
1992 Detroit	AL	67	190	48	9	0	2	(2	0)	63	22	16	20	1	38	0	3	2	0	1	.00	8	.253	.321	.332
1993 Detroit	AL	119	374	107	23	3	15	(9	6)	181	59	51	49	4	92	3	2	3	2	1	.67	5	.286	.371	.484
1994 Detroit	AL	65	170	38	8	0	1	(1	0)	49	17	19	28	0	36	0	2	4	0	1	.00	3	.224	.327	.288
1995 Seattle	AL	26	75	17	5	0	1	(0	1)	25	12	8	5	0	22	2	1	0	0	0	.00	0	.227	.293	.333
1996 Chicago	AL	46	114	25	8	0	3	(2	1)	42	14	18	13	0	29	2	2	1	0	0	.00	3	.219	.308	.368
1997 CWS-Ana	AL	89	255	59	9	2	5	(3	2)	87	25	21	29	0	66	0	1	0	0	3	.00	7	.231	.310	.341
1998 CWS-Ana	AL	96	252	63	10	1	2	(2	0)	81	27	33	33	1	49	3	5	1	1	0	1.00	8	.250	.343	.321
1999 Kansas City	AL	107	324	73	15	0	5	(2	3)	103	31	35	34	1	65	6	2	2	0	0	.00	16	.225	.309	.318
1997 Chicago	AL	19	37	8	2	1	1	(1	0)	15	6	3	8	0	9	0	0	0	0	1	.00	0	.216	.356	.405
Anaheim	AL	70	218	51	7	1	4	(2	2)	72	19	18	21	0	57	0	1	0	0	2	.00	7	.234	.301	.330
1998 Chicago	AL	93	245	62	9	1	2	(2	0)	79	26	33	32	1	49	3	5	1	1	0	1.00	8	.253	.345	.321
Anaheim	AL	3	7	1	0	0	0	(0	0)	2	1	0	1	0	4	0	0	0	0	0	.00	0	.143	.250	.286
12 ML YEARS		743	1989	469	93	7	40	(23	17)	696	228	217	253	7	460	16	25	15	3	7	.30	54	.236	.325	.350

Jeff Kubenka

Pitches: Left **Bats:** Right **Pos:** RP-6 **Ht:** 6'1" **Wt:** 191 **Born:** 8/24/74 **Age:** 25

| | | HOW MUCH HE PITCHED | | | | | | WHAT HE GAVE UP | | | | | | | | | | | | THE RESULTS | | | | | | |
Year Team	Lg	G	GS	CG	GF	IP	BFP	H	R	ER	HR	SH	SF	HB	TBB	IBB	SO	WP	Bk	W	L	Pct.	ShO	Sv-Op	Hld	ERA
1996 Yakima	A-	28	0	0	24	32.1	127	20	11	9	2	0	0	0	10	1	61	4	1	5	1	.833	0	14--	—	2.51
1997 San Berndno	A+	34	0	0	32	39	152	24	4	4	1	4	2	1	11	1	62	3	0	5	1	.833	0	19--	—	0.92
Albuquerque	AAA	8	0	0	6	7.1	37	11	9	7	2	0	0	0	2	0	10	3	0	0	2	.000	0	2--	—	8.59
San Antonio	AA	19	0	0	17	25.2	93	10	2	2	1	0	1	0	6	0	38	1	0	3	0	1.000	0	4--	—	0.70
1998 San Antonio	AA	9	0	0	6	9	47	10	11	7	2	0	1	1	7	0	10	3	1	0	0	.000	0	0--	—	7.00
Albuquerque	AAA	28	0	0	22	40.1	163	32	11	11	1	1	3	0	12	2	40	1	0	2	5	.286	0	9--	—	2.45
1999 Albuquerque	AAA	51	0	0	27	67	283	60	30	22	6	3	2	4	22	3	63	4	0	4	4	.500	0	11--	—	2.96
1998 Los Angeles	NL	6	0	0	2	9.1	40	4	1	1	0	2	1	0	8	0	10	1	0	1	0	1.000	0	0-1	2	0.96
1999 Los Angeles	NL	6	0	0	2	7.2	42	13	12	10	1	2	1	0	4	0	2	0	0	0	1	.000	0	0-0	0	11.74
2 ML YEARS		12	0	0	4	17	82	17	13	11	1	4	2	0	12	0	12	1	0	1	1	.500	0	0-1	2	5.82

Tim Kubinski

Pitches: Left **Bats:** Left **Pos:** RP-14 **Ht:** 6'4" **Wt:** 205 **Born:** 1/20/72 **Age:** 28

| | | HOW MUCH HE PITCHED | | | | | | WHAT HE GAVE UP | | | | | | | | | | | | THE RESULTS | | | | | | |
Year Team	Lg	G	GS	CG	GF	IP	BFP	H	R	ER	HR	SH	SF	HB	TBB	IBB	SO	WP	Bk	W	L	Pct.	ShO	Sv-Op	Hld	ERA
1993 Athletics	R	1	1	0	0	3	13	5	2	2	1	0	0	0	0	0	3	0	0	0	1	.000	0	0--	—	6.00
Sou Oregon	A-	12	12	1	0	70	294	67	36	22	4	2	2	6	18	0	51	2	2	5	5	.500	0	0--	—	2.83
1994 W Michigan	A	30	23	1	4	158.2	677	168	82	64	8	13	4	7	36	0	126	8	10	14	6	.700	0	0--	—	3.63
1995 Edmonton	AAA	6	5	0	0	32	136	34	18	17	4	0	0	4	10	0	12	0	4	1	2	.333	0	0--	—	4.78
Modesto	A+	25	17	0	4	109	485	126	73	60	12	6	5	8	24	0	83	10	1	6	10	.375	0	2--	—	4.95
1996 Huntsville	AA	43	3	0	15	102	418	84	41	27	7	4	3	3	36	6	78	8	3	8	7	.533	0	3--	—	2.38
Edmonton	AAA	1	0	0	1	1	4	1	0	0	0	0	0	0	1	0	0	0	0	0	0	.000	0	0--	—	0.00
1997 Edmonton	AAA	47	0	0	17	76	315	64	39	38	8	6	1	1	34	4	53	7	2	4	4	.500	0	7--	—	4.50
1998 Edmonton	AAA	57	1	0	23	75.1	321	77	40	38	8	2	3	3	22	3	54	3	1	1	6	.545	0	2--	—	4.54
1999 Vancouver	AAA	46	1	0	17	73.1	314	70	30	28	2	6	2	2	27	3	56	5	2	5	3	.625	0	6--	—	3.44
1997 Oakland	AL	11	0	0	3	12.2	56	12	9	8	2	0	2	1	6	1	10	0	0	0	0	.000	0	0-0	1	5.68
1999 Oakland	AL	14	0	0	4	12.1	57	14	8	8	3	0	1	1	5	1	7	0	0	0	0	.000	0	0-1	1	5.84
2 ML YEARS		25	0	0	7	25	113	26	17	16	5	0	3	2	11	2	17	0	0	0	0	.000	0	0-1	2	5.76

Tim Laker

Bats: Right **Throws:** Right **Pos:** PH/PR-5; C-2 **Ht:** 6'3" **Wt:** 200 **Born:** 11/27/69 **Age:** 30

| | | BATTING | | | | | | | | | | | | | | | | | BASERUNNING | | | | PERCENTAGES | | |
Year Team	Lg	G	AB	H	2B	3B	HR	(Hm	Rd)	TB	R	RBI	TBB	IBB	SO	HBP	SH	SF	SB	CS	SB%	GDP	Avg	OBP	SLG
1999 Nashville *	AAA	112	405	109	29	3	12	--	--	180	48	65	29	2	68	4	0	3	3	0	1.00	10	.269	.322	.444
1992 Montreal	NL	28	46	10	3	0	0	(0	0)	13	8	4	2	0	14	0	0	1	1	1	.50	1	.217	.250	.283
1993 Montreal	NL	43	86	17	2	1	0	(0	0)	21	3	7	2	0	16	1	3	1	2	0	1.00	2	.198	.222	.244
1995 Montreal	NL	64	141	33	8	1	3	(1	2)	52	17	20	14	4	38	1	1	1	0	1	.00	5	.234	.306	.369
1997 Baltimore	AL	7	14	0	0	0	0	(0	0)	0	0	1	2	0	9	0	1	1	0	0	.00	1	.000	.118	.000
1998 TB-Pit		17	29	10	1	0	1	(0	1)	14	3	2	2	0	4	0	0	1	0	1	.00	1	.345	.375	.483
1999 Pittsburgh	NL	6	9	3	0	0	0			3	0	0	0	0	2	0	0	0	0	0	.00	1	.333	.333	.333
1998 Tampa Bay	AL	3	5	1	0	0	0	(0	0)	1	1	0	1	0	1	0	0	0	0	1	.00	0	.200	.333	.200
Pittsburgh	NL	14	24	9	1	0	1	(0	1)	13	2	2	1	0	3	0	0	1	0	0	.00	1	.375	.385	.542
6 ML YEARS		165	325	73	14	2	4	(1	3)	100	31	34	22	4	83	2	5	4	3	3	.50	9	.225	.275	.317

David Lamb

Bats: B **Throws:** R **Pos:** SS-35; 2B-15; PH/PR-13; DH-3 **Ht:** 6'2" **Wt:** 190 **Born:** 6/6/75 **Age:** 25

| | | BATTING | | | | | | | | | | | | | | | | | BASERUNNING | | | | PERCENTAGES | | |
Year Team	Lg	G	AB	H	2B	3B	HR	(Hm	Rd)	TB	R	RBI	TBB	IBB	SO	HBP	SH	SF	SB	CS	SB%	GDP	Avg	OBP	SLG
1993 Orioles	R	16	56	10	1	0	0	--	--	11	4	6	10	0	8	0	0	0	2	0	1.00	1	.179	.303	.196
1994 Albany	A	92	308	74	9	2	0	--	--	87	37	29	32	0	40	2	6	0	4	1	.80	4	.240	.316	.282
1995 Bowie	AA	1	4	1	0	0	0	--	--	1	0	1	0	0	1	0	0	0	0	0	.00	0	.250	.250	.250
Frederick	A+	124	436	97	14	2	2	--	--	121	39	34	38	5	81	10	8	5	6	7	.46	10	.222	.297	.278
1996 High Desert	A+	116	460	118	24	3	3	--	--	157	63	55	50	1	68	10	5	2	5	6	.45	19	.257	.341	.341
1997 Frederick	A+	70	249	65	21	1	2	--	--	94	30	39	25	2	32	6	3	3	3	1	.75	10	.261	.339	.378
Bowie	AA	73	269	89	20	2	4	--	--	125	46	38	34	0	35	4	4	4	0	0	.00	3	.331	.408	.465
1998 Bowie	AA	66	241	73	10	1	2	--	--	91	29	25	27	1	33	1	4	1	1	3	.25	4	.303	.374	.378
Rochester	AAA	48	178	53	7	1	1	--	--	65	24	16	17	1	25	3	1	2	1	5	.17	4	.298	.365	.365
1999 Durham	AAA	7	30	7	3	0	0	--	--	10	7	7	2	0	4	0	2	1	0	1	.00	0	.233	.273	.333
1999 Tampa Bay	AL	55	124	28	5	1	1	(0	1)	38	18	13	10	0	18	0	0	0	0	1	.00	4	.226	.284	.306

Tom Lampkin

Bats: L **Throws:** R **Pos:** C-56; PH/PR-24; DH-2; LF-2 **Ht:** 5'11" **Wt:** 195 **Born:** 3/4/64 **Age:** 36

| | | BATTING | | | | | | | | | | | | | | | | | BASERUNNING | | | | PERCENTAGES | | |
Year Team	Lg	G	AB	H	2B	3B	HR	(Hm	Rd)	TB	R	RBI	TBB	IBB	SO	HBP	SH	SF	SB	CS	SB%	GDP	Avg	OBP	SLG
1988 Cleveland	AL	4	4	0	0	0	0	(0	0)	0	0	0	1	0	0	0	0	0	0	0	.00	1	.000	.200	.000
1990 San Diego	NL	26	63	14	0	1	1	(1	0)	19	4	4	4	1	9	0	0	0	0	1	.00	2	.222	.269	.302
1991 San Diego	NL	38	58	11	3	1	0	(0	0)	16	4	3	3	0	9	0	0	0	0	0	.00	0	.190	.230	.276
1992 San Diego	NL	9	17	4	0	0	0	(0	0)	4	3	0	6	0	1	1	0	0	2	0	1.00	0	.235	.458	.235
1993 Milwaukee	AL	73	162	32	8	0	4	(1	3)	52	22	25	20	3	26	1	0	2	7	3	.70	2	.198	.280	.321
1995 San Francisco	NL	65	76	21	0	0	1	(1	0)	26	8	9	9	1	8	1	0	0	2	0	1.00	1	.276	.360	.342

Year Team	Lg	G	AB	H	2B	3B	HR	(Hm	Rd)	TB	R	RBI	TBB	IBB	SO	HBP	SH	SF	SB	CS	SB%	GDP	Avg	OBP	SLG
1996 San Francisco	NL	66	177	41	8	0	6	(5	1)	67	26	29	20	2	22	5	0	2	1	5	.17	2	.232	.324	.379
1997 St. Louis	NL	108	229	56	8	1	7	(2	5)	87	28	22	28	5	30	4	4	2	2	1	.67	8	.245	.335	.380
1998 St. Louis	NL	93	216	50	12	1	6	(4	2)	82	25	28	24	5	32	7	1	0	3	2	.60	5	.231	.328	.380
1999 Seattle	AL	76	206	60	11	2	9	(5	4)	102	29	34	13	1	32	5	1	2	1	3	.25	2	.291	.345	.495
10 ML YEARS		558	1208	289	52	6	34	(19	15)	455	149	154	128	18	169	23	8	10	18	15	.55	23	.239	.321	.377

Mark Langston

Pitches: Left Bats: Right Pos: RP-20; SP-5 Ht: 6'2" Wt: 185 Born: 8/20/60 Age: 39

Year Team	Lg	G	GS	CG	GF	IP	BFP	H	R	ER	HR	SH	SF	HB	TBB	IBB	SO	WP	Bk	W	L	Pct.	ShO	Sv-Op	Hld	ERA
1999 Buffalo *	AAA	4	4	0	0	18.2	77	16	9	8	4	0	0	0	8	0	11	0	0	0	1	.000	0	0--	—	3.86
1984 Seattle	AL	35	33	5	0	225	965	188	99	85	16	13	7	8	118	5	204	4	2	17	10	.630	2	0--	—	3.40
1985 Seattle	AL	24	24	2	0	126.2	577	122	85	77	22	3	2	2	91	2	72	3	3	7	14	.333	0	0-0	0	5.47
1986 Seattle	AL	37	36	9	1	239.1	1057	234	142	129	30	5	8	4	123	1	245	10	3	12	14	.462	0	0--	—	4.85
1987 Seattle	AL	35	35	14	0	272	1152	242	132	116	30	12	6	5	114	0	262	9	2	19	13	.594	3	0-0	0	3.84
1988 Seattle	AL	35	35	9	0	261.1	1078	222	100	97	32	6	5	3	110	2	235	7	4	15	11	.577	3	0-0	0	3.34
1989 Sea-Mon		34	34	8	0	250	1037	198	87	76	16	9	7	4	112	6	235	6	4	16	14	.533	5	0-0	0	2.74
1990 California	AL	33	33	5	0	223	950	215	120	109	13	6	6	5	104	1	195	8	0	10	17	.370	1	0-0	0	4.40
1991 California	AL	34	34	7	0	246.1	992	190	89	82	30	4	6	2	96	3	183	6	0	19	8	.704	2	0-0	0	3.00
1992 California	AL	32	32	9	0	229	941	206	103	93	14	4	5	6	74	2	174	5	0	13	14	.481	2	0-0	0	3.66
1993 California	AL	35	35	7	0	256.1	1039	220	100	91	22	3	8	1	85	2	196	10	2	16	11	.593	0	0-0	0	3.20
1994 California	AL	18	18	2	0	119.1	517	121	67	62	19	3	8	0	54	1	109	6	0	7	8	.467	1	0-0	0	4.68
1995 California	AL	31	31	2	0	200.1	859	212	109	103	21	11	3	3	64	1	142	5	1	15	7	.682	1	0-0	0	4.63
1996 California	AL	18	18	2	0	123.1	518	116	68	66	18	0	2	2	45	0	83	4	0	6	5	.545	0	0-0	0	4.82
1997 Anaheim	AL	9	9	0	0	47.2	226	61	34	31	8	2	2	0	29	1	30	1	0	2	4	.333	0	0-0	0	5.85
1998 San Diego	NL	22	16	0	0	81.1	380	107	55	53	11	5	4	1	41	1	56	3	1	4	6	.400	0	0-1	2	5.86
1999 Cleveland	AL	25	5	0	0	61.2	274	69	40	36	9	3	2	0	29	6	43	2	0	1	2	.333	0	0-1	0	5.25
1989 Seattle	AL	10	10	2	0	73.1	297	60	30	29	3	0	3	4	19	0	60	1	2	4	5	.444	1	0-0	0	3.56
Montreal	NL	24	24	6	0	176.2	740	138	57	47	13	9	4	0	93	6	175	5	2	12	9	.571	4	0-0	0	2.39
16 ML YEARS		457	428	81	3	2962.2	12562	2723	1438	1306	311	89	81	46	1289	34	2464	89	22	179	158	.531	18	0--	—	3.97

Ray Lankford

Bats: L Throws: L Pos: LF-105; PH/PR-15; CF-2; DH-1 Ht: 5'11" Wt: 200 Born: 6/5/67 Age: 33

Year Team	Lg	G	AB	H	2B	3B	HR	(Hm	Rd)	TB	R	RBI	TBB	IBB	SO	HBP	SH	SF	SB	CS	SB%	GDP	Avg	OBP	SLG
1990 St. Louis	NL	39	126	36	10	1	3	(2	1)	57	12	12	13	0	27	0	0	0	8	2	.80	1	.286	.353	.452
1991 St. Louis	NL	151	566	142	23	15	9	(4	5)	222	83	69	41	1	114	1	4	3	44	20	.69	4	.251	.301	.392
1992 St. Louis	NL	153	598	175	40	6	20	(13	7)	287	87	86	72	6	147	5	2	5	42	24	.64	5	.293	.371	.480
1993 St. Louis	NL	127	407	97	17	3	7	(6	1)	141	64	45	81	7	111	3	1	3	14	14	.50	5	.238	.366	.346
1994 St. Louis	NL	109	416	111	25	5	19	(8	11)	203	89	57	58	3	113	4	0	4	11	10	.52	0	.267	.359	.488
1995 St. Louis	NL	132	483	134	35	2	25	(16	9)	248	81	82	63	6	110	2	0	5	24	8	.75	10	.277	.360	.513
1996 St. Louis	NL	149	545	150	36	8	21	(8	13)	265	100	86	79	10	133	3	1	7	35	7	.83	12	.275	.366	.486
1997 St. Louis	NL	133	465	137	36	3	31	(10	21)	272	94	98	95	10	125	0	0	5	21	11	.66	9	.295	.411	.585
1998 St. Louis	NL	154	533	156	37	1	31	(20	11)	288	94	105	86	5	151	3	0	4	26	5	.84	4	.293	.391	.540
1999 St. Louis	NL	122	422	129	32	1	15	(8	7)	208	77	63	49	3	110	3	0	2	14	4	.78	6	.306	.380	.480
10 ML YEARS		1269	4561	1267	291	45	181	(95	86)	2191	781	703	637	51	1141	24	8	38	239	105	.69	56	.278	.367	.480

Mike Lansing

Bats: Right Throws: Right Pos: 2B-35 Ht: 6'0" Wt: 195 Born: 4/3/68 Age: 32

Year Team	Lg	G	AB	H	2B	3B	HR	(Hm	Rd)	TB	R	RBI	TBB	IBB	SO	HBP	SH	SF	SB	CS	SB%	GDP	Avg	OBP	SLG
1993 Montreal	NL	141	491	141	19	1	3	(1	2)	181	64	45	46	2	56	5	10	3	23	5	.82	16	.287	.352	.369
1994 Montreal	NL	106	394	105	21	2	5	(3	2)	145	44	35	30	3	37	7	2	2	12	8	.60	10	.266	.328	.368
1995 Montreal	NL	127	467	119	30	2	10	(4	6)	183	47	62	28	2	65	3	1	3	27	4	.87	14	.255	.299	.392
1996 Montreal	NL	159	641	183	40	2	11	(3	8)	260	99	53	44	1	85	10	9	1	23	8	.74	19	.285	.341	.406
1997 Montreal	NL	144	572	161	45	2	20	(11	9)	270	86	70	45	2	92	5	6	3	11	5	.69	9	.281	.338	.472
1998 Colorado	NL	153	584	161	39	2	12	(7	5)	240	73	66	39	4	88	5	7	3	10	3	.77	18	.276	.325	.411
1999 Colorado	NL	35	145	45	9	0	4	(2	2)	66	24	15	7	0	22	1	1	1	2	0	1.00	5	.310	.344	.455
7 ML YEARS		865	3294	915	213	11	65	(31	34)	1345	437	346	239	14	445	36	36	16	108	33	.77	89	.278	.332	.408

Barry Larkin

Bats: Right Throws: Right Pos: SS-161 Ht: 6'0" Wt: 185 Born: 4/28/64 Age: 36

Year Team	Lg	G	AB	H	2B	3B	HR	(Hm	Rd)	TB	R	RBI	TBB	IBB	SO	HBP	SH	SF	SB	CS	SB%	GDP	Avg	OBP	SLG
1986 Cincinnati	NL	41	159	45	4	3	3	(3	0)	64	27	19	9	1	21	0	0	1	8	0	1.00	2	.283	.320	.403
1987 Cincinnati	NL	125	439	107	16	2	12	(6	6)	163	64	43	36	3	52	5	5	3	21	6	.78	8	.244	.306	.371
1988 Cincinnati	NL	151	588	174	32	5	12	(9	3)	252	91	56	41	3	24	8	10	5	40	7	.85	7	.296	.347	.429
1989 Cincinnati	NL	97	325	111	14	4	4	(1	3)	145	47	36	20	5	23	2	2	8	10	5	.67	7	.342	.375	.446
1990 Cincinnati	NL	158	614	185	25	6	7	(4	3)	243	85	67	49	3	49	7	7	4	30	5	.86	14	.301	.358	.396
1991 Cincinnati	NL	123	464	140	27	4	20	(16	4)	235	88	69	55	1	64	3	3	2	24	6	.80	7	.302	.378	.506
1992 Cincinnati	NL	140	533	162	32	6	12	(8	4)	242	76	78	63	8	58	4	2	7	15	4	.79	13	.304	.377	.454
1993 Cincinnati	NL	100	384	121	20	3	8	(4	4)	171	57	51	51	6	33	1	1	3	14	1	.93	13	.315	.394	.445
1994 Cincinnati	NL	110	427	119	23	5	9	(3	6)	179	78	52	64	3	58	0	5	5	26	2	.93	6	.279	.369	.419

BATTING																	BASERUNNING				PERCENTAGES		
Year Team	Lg	G	AB	H	2B	3B	HR	(Hm | Rd)	TB	R	RBI	TBB	IBB	SO	HBP	SH	SF	SB	CS	SB%	GDP	Avg	OBP	SLG
1995 Cincinnati	NL	131	496	158	29	6	15	(8 | 7)	244	98	66	61	2	49	3	3	4	51	5	.91	6	.319	.394	.492
1996 Cincinnati	NL	152	517	154	32	4	33	(14 | 19)	293	117	89	96	3	52	7	0	7	36	10	.78	20	.298	.410	.567
1997 Cincinnati	NL	73	224	71	17	3	4	(0 | 4)	106	34	20	47	6	24	3	1	1	14	3	.82	3	.317	.440	.473
1998 Cincinnati	NL	145	538	166	34	10	17	(8 | 9)	271	93	72	79	5	69	2	4	3	26	3	.90	12	.309	.397	.504
1999 Cincinnati	NL	161	583	171	30	4	12	(7 | 5)	245	108	75	93	5	57	2	5	4	30	8	.79	12	.293	.390	.420
14 ML YEARS		1707	6291	1884	335	65	168	(91 | 77)	2853	1063	793	764	54	633	47	48	57	345	65	.84	130	.299	.376	.454

Jason LaRue

Bats: Right **Throws:** Right **Pos:** C-35; PH/PR-1   **Ht:** 5'11" **Wt:** 200 **Born:** 3/19/74 **Age:** 26

BATTING																	BASERUNNING				PERCENTAGES		
Year Team	Lg	G	AB	H	2B	3B	HR	(Hm | Rd)	TB	R	RBI	TBB	IBB	SO	HBP	SH	SF	SB	CS	SB%	GDP	Avg	OBP	SLG
1995 Billings	R+	58	183	50	8	1	5	—	—	75	35	31	16	2	28	12	2	2	3	5	.38	2	.273	.366	.410
1996 Chstn-WV	A	37	123	26	8	0	2	—	—	40	17	14	11	0	28	2	1	0	3	0	1.00	2	.211	.287	.325
1997 Chstn-WV	A	132	473	149	50	3	8	—	—	229	78	81	47	0	90	5	1	8	14	4	.78	8	.315	.377	.484
1998 Indianapls	AAA	15	51	12	4	0	0	—	—	16	5	5	4	1	8	0	0	1	0	1	.00	2	.235	.286	.314
Chattanooga	AA	105	386	141	39	8	14	—	—	238	71	82	40	0	60	10	1	9	4	3	.57	13	.365	.429	.617
1999 Indianapls	AAA	70	263	66	12	2	12	—	—	118	42	37	15	1	52	4	0	0	0	3	.00	13	.251	.299	.449
1999 Cincinnati	NL	36	90	19	7	0	3	(1 | 2)	35	12	10	11	1	32	2	0	0	4	1	.80	4	.211	.311	.389

Chris Latham

Bats: B **Throws:** R **Pos:** LF-6; CF-5; RF-4; PH/PR-4   **Ht:** 6'0" **Wt:** 198 **Born:** 5/26/73 **Age:** 27

BATTING																	BASERUNNING				PERCENTAGES		
Year Team	Lg	G	AB	H	2B	3B	HR	(Hm | Rd)	TB	R	RBI	TBB	IBB	SO	HBP	SH	SF	SB	CS	SB%	GDP	Avg	OBP	SLG
1991 Dodgers	R	43	109	26	2	1	0	—	—	30	17	11	16	0	45	0	0	1	14	4	.78	0	.239	.333	.275
1992 Great Falls	R+	17	37	12	2	0	0	—	—	14	8	3	8	0	8	0	0	0	1	1	.50	0	.324	.444	.378
Dodgers	R	14	48	11	2	0	0	—	—	13	4	2	5	1	17	0	1	1	2	3	.40	0	.229	.296	.271
1993 Yakima	A-	54	192	50	2	6	4	—	—	76	46	17	39	0	53	1	0	0	24	9	.73	2	.260	.388	.396
Bakersfield	A+	6	27	5	1	0	0	—	—	6	1	3	4	0	5	0	0	0	2	2	.50	0	.185	.290	.222
1994 Bakersfield	A+	52	191	41	5	2	2	—	—	56	29	15	28	1	49	2	4	0	28	7	.80	2	.215	.321	.293
Yakima	A-	71	288	98	19	8	5	—	—	148	69	32	55	7	66	2	3	0	33	20	.62	1	.340	.449	.514
1995 Vero Beach	A+	71	259	74	13	4	6	—	—	113	53	39	56	4	54	2	2	3	42	11	.79	2	.286	.413	.436
San Antonio	AA	58	214	64	14	5	9	—	—	115	38	37	33	0	59	2	1	1	11	11	.50	2	.299	.396	.537
Albuquerque	AAA	5	18	3	0	1	0	—	—	5	2	3	1	0	4	0	0	1	1	0	1.00	0	.167	.200	.278
1996 Salt Lake	AAA	115	376	103	16	6	9	—	—	158	59	50	36	1	91	2	4	3	26	9	.74	5	.274	.338	.420
1997 Salt Lake	AAA	118	492	152	22	5	8	—	—	208	78	58	58	0	110	4	4	1	21	19	.53	8	.309	.386	.423
1998 Salt Lake	AAA	97	377	122	21	4	11	—	—	184	81	51	56	0	99	1	4	0	29	5	.85	5	.324	.412	.488
1999 Salt Lake	AAA	94	382	123	24	8	15	—	—	208	93	51	54	2	95	1	4	2	18	13	.58	5	.322	.405	.545
1997 Minnesota	AL	15	22	4	1	0	0	(0 | 0)	5	4	1	0	0	8	0	0	0	0	0	.00	0	.182	.182	.227
1998 Minnesota	AL	34	94	15	1	0	1	(1 | 0)	19	14	5	13	0	36	0	1	0	4	2	.67	0	.160	.262	.202
1999 Minnesota	AL	14	22	2	0	0	0	(0 | 0)	2	1	3	0	0	13	0	0	2	0	0	.00	0	.091	.083	.091
3 ML YEARS		63	138	21	2	0	1	(1 | 0)	26	19	9	13	0	57	0	1	2	4	2	.67	0	.152	.222	.188

Matt Lawton

Bats: L **Throws:** R **Pos:** RF-103; LF-10; PH/PR-9; DH-6; CF-6   **Ht:** 5'10" **Wt:** 186 **Born:** 11/3/71 **Age:** 28

BATTING																	BASERUNNING				PERCENTAGES		
Year Team	Lg	G	AB	H	2B	3B	HR	(Hm | Rd)	TB	R	RBI	TBB	IBB	SO	HBP	SH	SF	SB	CS	SB%	GDP	Avg	OBP	SLG
1999 Fort Myers *	A+	4	14	8	1	0	0	—	—	9	3	2	3	0	1	0	0	0	1	0	1.00	0	.571	.647	.643
Twins *	R	1	4	1	0	0	0	—	—	1	0	1	0	0	2	0	0	0	0	0	.00	0	.250	.250	.250
1995 Minnesota	AL	21	60	19	4	1	1	(1 | 0)	28	11	12	7	0	11	3	0	0	1	1	.50	1	.317	.414	.467
1996 Minnesota	AL	79	252	65	7	1	6	(1 | 5)	92	34	42	28	1	28	4	0	2	4	4	.50	6	.258	.339	.365
1997 Minnesota	AL	142	460	114	29	3	14	(8 | 6)	191	74	60	76	3	81	10	1	1	7	4	.64	7	.248	.366	.415
1998 Minnesota	AL	152	557	155	36	6	21	(11 | 10)	266	91	77	86	6	64	15	0	4	16	8	.67	10	.278	.387	.478
1999 Minnesota	AL	118	406	105	18	0	7	(2 | 5)	144	58	54	57	7	42	6	0	7	26	4	.87	11	.259	.353	.355
5 ML YEARS		512	1735	458	94	11	49	(23 | 26)	721	268	245	254	17	226	38	1	14	54	21	.72	35	.264	.367	.416

Brett Laxton

Pitches: Right **Bats:** Left **Pos:** SP-2; RP-1   **Ht:** 6'2" **Wt:** 205 **Born:** 10/5/73 **Age:** 26

HOW MUCH HE PITCHED							WHAT HE GAVE UP											THE RESULTS					
Year Team	Lg	G	GS	CG	GF	IP	BFP	H	R	ER	HR	SH	SF	HB	TBB	IBB	SO	WP	Bk	W	L	Pct.	ShO	Sv-Op	Hld	ERA
1996 Sou Oregon	A-	13	8	0	1	32.2	162	39	34	28	4	1	1	3	26	1	38	5	3	0	5	.000	0	0- -	—	7.71
1997 Visalia	A+	29	22	0	2	138.2	606	141	62	46	7	4	0	11	50	0	121	14	0	11	5	.688	0	0- -	—	2.99
1998 Huntsville	AA	21	21	0	0	129.2	570	109	64	49	4	3	6	10	79	0	82	8	0	11	4	.733	0	0- -	—	3.40
Edmonton	AAA	8	8	0	0	46.1	204	45	35	34	6	1	3	5	24	2	21	7	0	2	4	.333	0	0- -	—	6.60
1999 Vancouver	AAA	25	25	3	0	161.1	662	158	68	62	8	5	4	6	49	0	112	10	0	13	8	.619	1	0- -	—	3.46
1999 Oakland	AL	3	2	0	0	9.2	50	12	12	8	1	0	3	2	7	1	9	3	0	0	1	.000	0	0-0	0	7.45

Ricky Ledee

Bats: L **Throws:** L **Pos:** LF-69; PH/PR-17; CF-6; DH-5; RF-3   **Ht:** 6'1" **Wt:** 160 **Born:** 11/22/73 **Age:** 26

BATTING																	BASERUNNING				PERCENTAGES		
Year Team	Lg	G	AB	H	2B	3B	HR	(Hm | Rd)	TB	R	RBI	TBB	IBB	SO	HBP	SH	SF	SB	CS	SB%	GDP	Avg	OBP	SLG
1990 Yankees	R	19	37	4	2	0	0	—	—	6	5	1	6	0	18	0	0	0	2	0	1.00	1	.108	.233	.162

Year Team	Lg	G	AB	H	2B	3B	HR	(Hm	Rd)	TB	R	RBI	TBB	IBB	SO	HBP	SH	SF	SB	CS	SB%	GDP	Avg	OBP	SLG
1991 Yankees	R	47	165	44	6	2	0	—	—	54	22	18	22	0	41	0	0	1	3	1	.75	3	.267	.351	.327
1992 Yankees	R	52	179	41	9	2	2	—	—	60	25	23	24	1	47	1	0	1	1	4	.20	2	.229	.322	.335
1993 Oneonta	A-	52	192	49	7	6	8	—	—	92	32	20	25	0	46	2	1	0	7	5	.58	2	.255	.347	.479
1994 Greensboro	A	134	484	121	23	9	22	—	—	228	87	71	91	4	126	4	3	6	10	11	.48	7	.250	.369	.471
1995 Greensboro	A	89	335	90	16	6	14	—	—	160	65	49	51	6	66	2	0	1	10	4	.71	3	.269	.368	.478
1996 Norwich	AA	39	137	50	11	1	8	—	—	87	27	37	16	0	25	1	1	5	2	2	.50	4	.365	.421	.635
Columbus	AAA	96	358	101	22	6	21	—	—	198	79	64	44	2	95	1	0	2	6	3	.67	4	.282	.360	.553
1997 Yankees	R	7	21	7	1	0	0	—	—	8	3	2	2	1	4	1	0	0	0	0	.00	1	.333	.417	.381
Columbus	AAA	43	170	52	12	1	10	—	—	96	38	39	21	0	49	1	0	0	4	0	1.00	5	.306	.385	.565
1998 Columbus	AAA	96	360	102	21	1	19	—	—	182	70	41	54	5	108	4	1	5	7	2	.78	7	.283	.378	.506
1999 Columbus	AAA	30	115	29	7	1	4	—	—	50	18	15	17	1	29	0	1	1	4	2	.67	1	.252	.346	.435
1998 New York	AL	42	79	19	5	2	1	(0	1)	31	13	12	7	0	29	0	0	1	3	1	.75	1	.241	.299	.392
1999 New York	AL	88	250	69	13	5	9	(4	5)	119	45	40	28	5	73	0	0	2	4	3	.57	2	.276	.346	.476
2 ML YEARS		130	329	88	18	7	10	(4	6)	150	58	52	35	5	102	0	0	3	7	4	.64	3	.267	.335	.456

Aaron Ledesma

Bats: R **Throws:** R **Pos:** SS-50; 3B-26; 2B-17; PH/PR-7; 1B-4; DH-1   **Ht:** 6'2" **Wt:** 210 **Born:** 6/3/71 **Age:** 29

Year Team	Lg	G	AB	H	2B	3B	HR	(Hm	Rd)	TB	R	RBI	TBB	IBB	SO	HBP	SH	SF	SB	CS	SB%	GDP	Avg	OBP	SLG
1999 St. Pete *	A+	2	7	1	1	0	0	—	—	2	0	0	1	0	1	0	0	0	0	0	.00	1	.143	.250	.286
Durham *	AAA	2	10	1	0	0	0	—	—	1	0	0	0	0	1	0	0	0	0	0	.00		.100	.100	.100
1995 New York	NL	21	33	8	0	0	0	(0	0)	8	4	3	6	1	7	0	0	0	0	0	.00	2	.242	.359	.242
1997 Baltimore	AL	43	88	31	5	1	2	(1	1)	44	24	11	13	0	9	1	1	1	1	0	1.00	1	.352	.437	.500
1998 Tampa Bay	AL	95	299	97	16	3	0	(0	0)	119	30	29	9	1	51	1	4	2	9	7	.56	8	.324	.344	.398
1999 Tampa Bay	AL	93	294	78	15	0	0	(0	0)	93	32	30	14	1	35	3	1	0	1	1	.50	14	.265	.305	.316
4 ML YEARS		252	714	214	36	4	2	(1	1)	264	90	73	42	3	102	5	6	3	11	8	.58	25	.300	.342	.370

Carlos Lee

Bats: R **Throws:** R **Pos:** LF-105; DH-16; 1B-5; PH/PR-2   **Ht:** 6'2" **Wt:** 220 **Born:** 6/20/76 **Age:** 24

Year Team	Lg	G	AB	H	2B	3B	HR	(Hm	Rd)	TB	R	RBI	TBB	IBB	SO	HBP	SH	SF	SB	CS	SB%	GDP	Avg	OBP	SLG
1994 White Sox	R	29	56	7	1	0	0	—	—	8	6	1	4	0	8	0	0	0	0	1	.00	1	.125	.183	.143
1995 Hickory	A	63	218	54	9	1	4	—	—	77	18	30	8	2	34	1	0	0	1	5	.17	7	.248	.278	.353
Bristol	R+	67	269	93	17	1	7	—	—	133	43	45	8	3	34	2	0	3	7	7	.71	6	.346	.365	.494
1996 Hickory	A	119	480	150	23	6	8	—	—	209	65	70	23	5	50	0	0	11	18	13	.58	15	.313	.337	.435
1997 Winston-Sal	A+	139	546	173	50	4	17	—	—	282	81	82	36	2	65	2	2	7	11	5	.69	12	.317	.357	.516
1998 Birmingham	AA	138	549	166	33	2	21	—	—	266	77	106	39	2	55	2	0	2	11	5	.69	32	.302	.350	.485
1999 Charlotte	AAA	25	94	33	5	0	4	—	—	50	16	20	8	1	14	1	0	3	2	1	.67	3	.351	.396	.532
1999 Chicago	AL	127	492	144	32	2	16	(10	6)	228	66	84	13	0	72	4	1	7	4	2	.67	11	.293	.312	.463

Corey Lee

Pitches: Left **Bats:** Left **Pos:** RP-1   **Ht:** 6'2" **Wt:** 180 **Born:** 12/26/74 **Age:** 25

Year Team	Lg	G	GS	CG	GF	IP	BFP	H	R	ER	HR	SH	SF	HB	TBB	IBB	SO	WP	Bk	W	L	Pct.	ShO	Sv-Op	Hld	ERA
1996 Hudson Val	A-	9	9	0	0	54.2	226	42	24	20	1	2	3	1	21	1	59	1	2	1	4	.200	0	0-—	—	3.29
1997 Charlotte	A+	23	23	6	0	160.2	654	132	66	62	9	5	3	7	60	1	147	7	0	15	5	.750	2	0-—	—	3.47
1998 Tulsa	AA	26	25	1	0	143.2	625	105	81	72	16	3	5	5	102	1	132	12	1	10	9	.526	0	0-—	—	4.51
1999 Tulsa	AA	22	22	0	0	127.2	549	132	76	63	11	1	1	4	44	0	121	3	1	8	5	.615	0	0-—	—	4.44
Oklahoma	AAA	4	4	0	0	26.2	105	21	6	6	2	0	0	4	8	0	25	2	0	3	0	1.000	0	0-—	—	2.03
1999 Texas	AL	1	0	0	1	1	6	2	3	3	1	0	0	0	1	0	0	0	0	0	1	.000	0	0-0	0	27.00

David Lee

Pitches: Right **Bats:** Right **Pos:** RP-36   **Ht:** 6'1" **Wt:** 202 **Born:** 3/12/73 **Age:** 27

Year Team	Lg	G	GS	CG	GF	IP	BFP	H	R	ER	HR	SH	SF	HB	TBB	IBB	SO	WP	Bk	W	L	Pct.	ShO	Sv-Op	Hld	ERA
1996 Portland	A-	17	0	0	16	23	99	13	3	2	1	0	3	16	3	24	1	0	5	1	.833	0	7-—	—	0.78
Salem	A+	8	0	0	5	12	56	14	6	3	1	0	0	2	6	0	10	2	0	0	2	.000	0	1-—	—	2.25
1997 Asheville	A	51	0	0	49	53	239	61	30	24	5	3	1	1	23	0	59	4	0	4	8	.333	0	22-—	—	4.08
1998 Salem	A+	54	0	0	52	57.1	244	57	26	24	2	4	4	3	15	1	54	3	1	3	5	.375	0	25-—	—	3.77
1999 Carolina	AA	16	0	0	15	17.1	63	8	3	2	1	0	0	1	3	0	16	0	0	0	0	.000	0	10-—	—	1.04
Colo Sprngs	AAA	6	0	0	0	5.2	20	0	0	0	0	0	0	0	1	0	7	2	0	0	0	.000	0	3-—	—	0.00
1999 Colorado	NL	36	0	0	11	49	212	43	21	20	4	3	2	4	29	1	38	3	1	3	2	.600	0	0-0	2	3.67

Derrek Lee

Bats: Right **Throws:** Right **Pos:** 1B-66; PH/PR-5   **Ht:** 6'5" **Wt:** 225 **Born:** 9/6/75 **Age:** 24

Year Team	Lg	G	AB	H	2B	3B	HR	(Hm	Rd)	TB	R	RBI	TBB	IBB	SO	HBP	SH	SF	SB	CS	SB%	GDP	Avg	OBP	SLG
1999 Calgary *	AAA	89	339	96	20	1	19	—	—	175	60	73	30	2	90	4	0	4	3	4	.43	7	.283	.345	.516
1997 San Diego	NL	22	54	14	3	0	1	(0	1)	20	9	4	9	0	24	0	0	0	0	0	.00	1	.259	.365	.370
1998 Florida	NL	141	454	106	29	4	17	(4	13)	188	62	74	47	1	120	10	0	2	5	2	.71	12	.233	.318	.414
1999 Florida	NL	70	218	45	9	1	5	(0	5)	71	21	20	17	1	70	0	0	1	2	1	.67	3	.206	.263	.326
3 ML YEARS		233	726	165	41	2	23	(4	19)	279	92	98	73	2	214	10	0	3	7	3	.70	16	.227	.305	.384

Travis Lee

Bats: Left **Throws:** Left **Pos:** 1B-114; PH/PR-14; RF-2 **Ht:** 6'3" **Wt:** 214 **Born:** 5/26/75 **Age:** 25

Year Team	Lg	G	AB	H	2B	3B	HR	(Hm	Rd)	TB	R	RBI	TBB	IBB	SO	HBP	SH	SF	SB	CS	SB%	GDP	Avg	OBP	SLG
1997 High Desert	A+	61	226	82	18	1	18	—	—	156	63	63	47	6	36	3	0	3	5	1	.83	8	.363	.473	.690
Tucson	AAA	59	227	68	16	2	14	—	—	130	42	46	31	2	46	2	0	1	2	0	1.00	10	.300	.387	.573
1998 Arizona	NL	146	562	151	20	2	22	(12	10)	241	71	72	67	5	123	0	0	1	8	1	.89	13	.269	.346	.429
1999 Arizona	NL	120	375	89	16	2	9	(7	2)	136	57	50	58	4	50	0	0	3	17	3	.85	10	.237	.337	.363
2 ML YEARS		266	937	240	36	4	31	(19	12)	377	128	122	125	9	173	0	0	4	25	4	.86	23	.256	.342	.402

Al Leiter

Pitches: Left **Bats:** Left **Pos:** SP-32 **Ht:** 6'3" **Wt:** 220 **Born:** 10/23/65 **Age:** 34

Year Team	Lg	G	GS	CG	GF	IP	BFP	H	R	ER	HR	SH	SF	HB	TBB	IBB	SO	WP	Bk	W	L	Pct.	ShO	Sv-Op	Hld	ERA
1987 New York	AL	4	4	0	0	22.2	104	24	16	16	2	1	0	0	15	0	28	4	0	2	2	.500	0	0-0	0	6.35
1988 New York	AL	14	14	0	0	57.1	251	49	27	25	7	1	0	5	33	0	60	1	4	4	4	.500	0	0-0	0	3.92
1989 NYY-Tor	AL	5	5	0	0	33.1	154	32	23	21	2	1	1	2	23	0	26	2	1	1	2	.333	0	0-0	0	5.67
1990 Toronto	AL	4	0	0	2	6.1	22	1	0	0	0	0	0	0	2	0	5	0	0	0	0	.000	0	0-0	0	0.00
1991 Toronto	AL	3	0	0	1	1.2	13	3	5	5	0	1	0	0	5	0	1	0	0	0	0	.000	0	0-0	0	27.00
1992 Toronto	AL	1	0	0	0	1	7	1	1	1	0	0	0	0	2	0	0	0	0	0	0	.000	0	0-0	0	9.00
1993 Toronto	AL	34	12	1	4	105	454	93	52	48	8	3	3	4	56	2	66	2	2	9	6	.600	1	2-3	3	4.11
1994 Toronto	AL	20	20	1	0	111.2	516	125	68	63	6	3	8	2	65	3	100	7	5	6	7	.462	0	0-0	0	5.08
1995 Toronto	AL	28	28	2	0	183	805	162	80	74	15	6	4	6	108	1	153	14	0	11	11	.500	1	0-0	0	3.64
1996 Florida	NL	33	33	2	0	215.1	896	153	74	70	14	7	3	11	119	3	200	5	0	16	12	.571	1	0-0	0	2.93
1997 Florida	NL	27	27	0	0	151.1	668	133	78	73	13	10	3	12	91	4	132	2	0	11	9	.550	0	0-0	0	4.34
1998 New York	NL	28	28	4	0	193	789	151	55	53	8	6	2	11	71	2	174	4	1	17	6	.739	2	0-0	0	2.47
1999 New York	NL	32	32	1	0	213	923	209	107	100	19	13	10	9	93	8	162	4	1	13	12	.520	1	0-0	0	4.23
1989 New York	AL	4	4	0	0	26.2	123	23	20	18	1	1	1	2	21	0	22	1	1	1	2	.333	0	0-0	0	6.08
Toronto	AL	1	1	0	0	6.2	31	9	3	3	1	0	0	0	2	0	4	1	0	0	0	.000	0	0-0	0	4.05
13 ML YEARS		233	203	11	7	1294.2	5602	1136	586	549	94	52	34	62	683	23	1107	45	14	90	71	.559	6	2-3	3	3.82

Mark Leiter

Pitches: Right **Bats:** Right **Pos:** RP-2 **Ht:** 6'3" **Wt:** 220 **Born:** 4/13/63 **Age:** 37

Year Team	Lg	G	GS	CG	GF	IP	BFP	H	R	ER	HR	SH	SF	HB	TBB	IBB	SO	WP	Bk	W	L	Pct.	ShO	Sv-Op	Hld	ERA
1999 Tacoma *	AAA	1	1	0	0	2	7	2	1	1	0	0	0	0	0	0	3	0	0	0	0	.000	0	0--	—	4.50
1990 New York	AL	8	3	0	2	26.1	119	33	20	20	5	2	1	2	9	0	21	0	0	1	1	.500	0	0-0	0	6.84
1991 Detroit	AL	38	15	1	7	134.2	578	125	66	63	16	5	6	6	50	4	103	2	0	9	7	.563	0	1-2	2	4.21
1992 Detroit	AL	35	14	1	7	112	475	116	57	52	9	2	8	3	43	5	75	3	0	8	5	.615	0	0-0	3	4.18
1993 Detroit	AL	27	13	1	4	106.2	471	111	61	56	17	3	5	3	44	5	70	5	0	6	6	.500	0	0-1	1	4.73
1994 California	AL	40	7	0	15	95.1	425	99	56	50	13	4	4	9	35	6	71	2	0	4	7	.364	0	2-3	3	4.72
1995 San Francisco	NL	30	29	7	0	195.2	817	185	91	83	19	10	6	17	55	4	129	9	3	10	12	.455	1	0-0	0	3.82
1996 SF-Mon	NL	35	34	2	0	205	904	219	128	112	37	12	6	16	69	8	164	6	4	8	12	.400	0	0-0	0	4.92
1997 Philadelphia	NL	31	31	3	0	182.2	832	216	132	115	25	11	8	9	64	4	148	11	2	10	17	.370	0	0-0	0	5.67
1998 Philadelphia	NL	69	0	0	50	88.2	378	67	36	35	8	9	4	8	47	5	84	5	0	7	5	.583	0	23-35	1	3.55
1999 Seattle	AL	2	0	0	0	1.1	6	2	1	1	0	0	0	0	0	0	1	0	0	0	0	.000	0	0-0	0	6.75
1996 San Francisco	NL	23	22	1	0	135.1	602	151	93	78	25	7	3	9	50	7	118	2	3	4	10	.286	0	0-0	0	5.19
Montreal	NL	12	12	1	0	69.2	302	68	35	34	12	5	3	7	19	1	46	4	1	4	2	.667	0	0-0	0	4.39
10 ML YEARS		315	146	15	85	1148.1	5005	1173	648	587	149	58	48	73	416	41	866	43	9	63	72	.467	1	26-41	10	4.60

Scott Leius

Bats: R **Throws:** R **Pos:** PH/PR-14; 1B-13; 3B-10; DH-6; SS-2; 2B-1 **Ht:** 6'3" **Wt:** 200 **Born:** 9/24/65 **Age:** 34

Year Team	Lg	G	AB	H	2B	3B	HR	(Hm	Rd)	TB	R	RBI	TBB	IBB	SO	HBP	SH	SF	SB	CS	SB%	GDP	Avg	OBP	SLG
1990 Minnesota	AL	14	25	6	1	0	1	(0	1)	10	4	4	2	0	2	0	1	0	0	0	.00	2	.240	.296	.400
1991 Minnesota	AL	109	199	57	7	2	5	(2	3)	83	35	20	30	1	35	0	5	1	5	5	.50	4	.286	.378	.417
1992 Minnesota	AL	129	409	102	18	2	2	(2	0)	130	50	35	34	0	61	1	5	0	6	5	.55	10	.249	.309	.318
1993 Minnesota	AL	10	18	3	0	0	0	(0	0)	3	4	2	2	0	4	0	0	0	0	0	.00	1	.167	.227	.167
1994 Minnesota	AL	97	350	86	16	1	14	(7	7)	146	57	49	37	0	58	1	1	2	2	4	.33	9	.246	.318	.417
1995 Minnesota	AL	117	372	92	16	5	4	(2	2)	130	51	45	49	3	54	2	0	4	2	1	.67	14	.247	.335	.349
1996 Cleveland	AL	27	43	6	4	0	1	(0	1)	13	3	3	2	0	8	0	1	0	0	0	.00	2	.140	.178	.302
1998 Kansas City	AL	17	46	8	0	0	0	(0	0)	8	2	4	1	0	6	0	0	0	0	0	.00	0	.174	.191	.174
1999 Kansas City	AL	37	74	15	1	0	1	(0	1)	19	8	10	4	0	8	1	0	3	1	0	1.00	2	.203	.244	.257
9 ML YEARS		557	1536	375	63	10	28	(13	15)	542	214	172	161	4	236	5	13	12	16	15	.52	44	.244	.316	.353

Patrick Lennon

Bats: Right **Throws:** Right **Pos:** LF-5; RF-4; PH/PR-1 **Ht:** 6'2" **Wt:** 200 **Born:** 4/27/68 **Age:** 32

Year Team	Lg	G	AB	H	2B	3B	HR	(Hm	Rd)	TB	R	RBI	TBB	IBB	SO	HBP	SH	SF	SB	CS	SB%	GDP	Avg	OBP	SLG
1999 Syracuse *	AAA	37	134	45	5	0	9	—	—	77	26	33	22	0	40	1	0	1	3	3	.50	2	.336	.430	.575
Toledo *	AAA	74	280	74	16	1	21	—	—	155	49	50	33	0	66	2	0	1	1	2	.33	10	.264	.345	.554
1991 Seattle	AL	9	8	1	1	0	0	(0	0)	2	2	1	3	0	1	0	0	0	0	0	.00	0	.125	.364	.250
1992 Seattle	AL	1	2	0	0	0	0	(0	0)	0	0	0	0	0	0	0	0	0	0	0	.00	0	.000	.000	.000
1996 Kansas City	AL	14	30	7	3	0	0	(0	0)	10	5	1	7	0	10	0	0	0	0	0	.00	0	.233	.378	.333

Year Team	Lg	G	AB	H	2B	3B	HR	(Hm	Rd)	TB	R	RBI	TBB	IBB	SO	HBP	SH	SF	SB	CS	SB%	GDP	Avg	OBP	SLG
1997 Oakland	AL	56	116	34	6	1	1	(1	0)	45	14	14	15	0	35	0	0	0	0	1	.00	3	.293	.374	.388
1998 Toronto	AL	2	4	2	2	0	0	(0	0)	4	1	0	0	0	1	0	0	0	0	0	.00	0	.500	.500	1.000
1999 Toronto	AL	9	29	6	2	0	1	(0	1)	11	3	6	2	0	12	1	0	0	0	0	.00	0	.207	.281	.379
6 ML YEARS		91	189	50	14	1	2	(1	1)	72	25	22	27	0	59	1	0	0	0	1	.00	3	.265	.359	.381

Curt Leskanic

Pitches: Right **Bats:** Right **Pos:** RP-63   **Ht:** 6'0" **Wt:** 186 **Born:** 4/2/68 **Age:** 32

Year Team	Lg	G	GS	CG	GF	IP	BFP	H	R	ER	HR	SH	SF	HB	TBB	IBB	SO	WP	Bk	W	L	Pct.	ShO	Sv-Op	Hld	ERA
1993 Colorado	NL	18	8	0	1	57	260	59	40	34	7	5	4	2	27	1	30	8	2	1	5	.167	0	0-0	0	5.37
1994 Colorado	NL	8	3	0	2	22.1	98	27	14	14	2	2	0	0	10	0	17	2	0	1	1	.500	0	0-0	0	5.64
1995 Colorado	NL	76	0	0	27	98	406	83	38	37	7	3	2	0	33	1	107	6	1	6	3	.667	0	10-16	19	3.40
1996 Colorado	NL	70	0	0	32	73.2	334	82	51	51	12	3	3	2	38	1	76	6	2	7	5	.583	0	6-10	9	6.23
1997 Colorado	NL	55	0	0	23	58.1	248	59	36	36	8	2	4	0	24	0	53	4	0	4	0	1.000	0	2-4	6	5.55
1998 Colorado	NL	66	0	0	20	75.2	332	75	37	37	9	0	0	1	40	2	55	3	1	6	4	.600	0	2-5	12	4.40
1999 Colorado	NL	63	0	0	5	85	382	87	54	48	7	5	3	5	49	4	77	5	0	6	2	.750	0	0-3	8	5.08
7 ML YEARS		356	11	0	110	470	2060	472	270	257	52	20	16	10	221	9	415	34	6	31	20	.608	0	20-38	54	4.92

Al Levine

Pitches: Right **Bats:** Left **Pos:** RP-49; SP-1   **Ht:** 6'3" **Wt:** 180 **Born:** 5/22/68 **Age:** 32

Year Team	Lg	G	GS	CG	GF	IP	BFP	H	R	ER	HR	SH	SF	HB	TBB	IBB	SO	WP	Bk	W	L	Pct.	ShO	Sv-Op	Hld	ERA
1996 Chicago	AL	16	0	0	5	18.1	85	22	14	11	1	0	1	1	7	1	12	0	0	0	1	.000	0	0-1	0	5.40
1997 Chicago	AL	25	0	0	6	27.1	133	35	22	21	4	1	2	2	16	1	22	2	0	2	2	.500	0	0-1	3	6.91
1998 Texas	AL	30	0	0	11	58	251	68	30	29	6	1	3	0	16	1	19	5	0	1	1	1.000	0	0-0	4	4.50
1999 Anaheim	AL	50	1	0	12	85	349	76	40	32	13	2	7	3	29	2	37	3	0	1	1	.500	0	0-1	3	3.39
4 ML YEARS		121	1	0	34	188.2	818	201	106	93	24	4	13	6	68	5	90	10	0	3	5	.375	0	0-3	6	4.44

Jesse Levis

Bats: Left **Throws:** Right **Pos:** C-9; PH/PR-1   **Ht:** 5'9" **Wt:** 200 **Born:** 4/14/68 **Age:** 32

Year Team	Lg	G	AB	H	2B	3B	HR	(Hm	Rd)	TB	R	RBI	TBB	IBB	SO	HBP	SH	SF	SB	CS	SB%	GDP	Avg	OBP	SLG
1999 Orlando *	AA	13	48	19	7	0	1	—	—	29	6	11	6	0	4	0	0	1	0	0	.00	0	.396	.455	.604
Durham *	AAA	27	94	31	5	0	1	—	—	39	20	8	15	1	9	2	0	1	0	0	.00	4	.330	.429	.415
1992 Cleveland	AL	28	43	12	4	0	1	(0	1)	19	2	3	0	0	5	0	0	0	0	0	.00	1	.279	.279	.442
1993 Cleveland	AL	31	63	11	2	0	0	(0	0)	13	7	4	2	0	10	0	1	1	0	0	.00	0	.175	.197	.206
1994 Cleveland	AL	1	1	0	0	0	0	(0	0)	1	0	0	0	0	0	0	0	0	0	0	.00	0	1.000	1.000	1.000
1995 Cleveland	AL	12	18	6	2	0	0	(0	0)	8	1	3	1	0	0	1	0	2	0	0	.00	0	.333	.333	.444
1996 Milwaukee	AL	104	233	55	6	1	1	(0	1)	66	27	21	38	0	15	2	1	0	0	0	.00	7	.236	.348	.283
1997 Milwaukee	AL	99	200	57	7	0	1	(1	0)	67	19	19	24	0	17	1	5	2	1	0	1.00	4	.285	.361	.335
1998 Milwaukee	NL	22	37	13	0	0	0	(0	0)	13	4	4	7	2	6	2	1	1	1	0	1.00	4	.351	.468	.351
1999 Cleveland	AL	10	26	4	0	0	0	(0	0)	4	0	3	1	0	6	0	0	0	0	0	.00	0	.154	.214	.308
8 ML YEARS		307	621	159	21	1	3	(1	2)	191	60	57	73	2	59	6	10	6	2	0	1.00	17	.256	.337	.308

Darren Lewis

Bats: R **Throws:** R **Pos:** CF-88; RF-51; PH/PR-6; DH-2   **Ht:** 6'0" **Wt:** 190 **Born:** 8/28/67 **Age:** 32

Year Team	Lg	G	AB	H	2B	3B	HR	(Hm	Rd)	TB	R	RBI	TBB	IBB	SO	HBP	SH	SF	SB	CS	SB%	GDP	Avg	OBP	SLG
1990 Oakland	AL	25	35	8	0	0	0	(0	0)	8	4	1	7	0	4	1	3	0	2	0	1.00	2	.229	.372	.229
1991 San Francisco	NL	72	222	55	5	3	1	(0	1)	69	41	15	36	0	30	2	7	0	13	7	.65	1	.248	.358	.311
1992 San Francisco	NL	100	320	74	8	1	1	(1	0)	87	38	18	29	0	46	1	10	2	28	8	.78	3	.231	.295	.272
1993 San Francisco	NL	136	522	132	17	7	2	(2	0)	169	84	48	30	0	40	7	12	1	46	15	.75	4	.253	.302	.324
1994 San Francisco	NL	114	451	116	15	9	4	(4	0)	161	70	29	53	0	50	4	4	1	30	13	.70	6	.257	.340	.357
1995 SF-Cin	NL	132	472	118	13	3	1	(1	0)	140	66	24	34	0	57	8	12	1	32	18	.64	9	.250	.311	.297
1996 Chicago	AL	141	337	77	12	2	4	(0	4)	105	55	53	45	1	40	3	15	5	21	5	.81	9	.228	.321	.312
1997 CWS-LA		107	154	41	4	1	1	(0	1)	50	22	15	17	0	31	0	7	0	14	6	.70	3	.266	.339	.325
1998 Boston	AL	155	585	157	25	3	8	(5	3)	212	95	63	70	0	94	8	2	5	29	12	.71	12	.268	.352	.362
1999 Boston	AL	135	470	113	14	6	2	(1	1)	145	63	40	45	0	52	5	14	4	16	10	.62	5	.240	.311	.309
1995 San Francisco	NL	74	309	78	10	3	1	(1	0)	97	47	16	17	0	37	6	7	1	21	7	.75	6	.252	.303	.314
Cincinnati	NL	58	163	40	3	0	0	(0	0)	43	19	8	17	0	20	2	5	0	11	11	.50	3	.245	.324	.264
1997 Chicago	NL	81	77	18	1	0	0	(0	0)	19	15	5	11	0	14	0	5	0	11	4	.73	2	.234	.330	.247
Los Angeles	NL	26	77	23	3	1	1	(0	1)	31	7	10	6	0	17	0	2	0	3	2	.60	1	.299	.349	.403
10 ML YEARS		1117	3568	891	113	35	24	(14	10)	1146	538	306	366	1	444	39	86	19	231	94	.71	54	.250	.325	.321

Mark Lewis

Bats: Right **Throws:** Right **Pos:** 3B-52; PH/PR-36; 2B-2   **Ht:** 6'1" **Wt:** 195 **Born:** 11/30/69 **Age:** 30

Year Team	Lg	G	AB	H	2B	3B	HR	(Hm	Rd)	TB	R	RBI	TBB	IBB	SO	HBP	SH	SF	SB	CS	SB%	GDP	Avg	OBP	SLG
1991 Cleveland	AL	84	314	83	15	1	0	(0	0)	100	29	30	15	0	45	0	2	5	2	2	.50	12	.264	.293	.318
1992 Cleveland	AL	122	413	109	21	0	5	(2	3)	145	44	30	25	1	69	3	1	4	4	5	.44	12	.264	.308	.351
1993 Cleveland	AL	14	52	13	2	0	1	(1	0)	18	6	5	0	0	7	0	1	0	3	0	1.00	1	.250	.250	.346

BATTING																		BASERUNNING				PERCENTAGES		
Year Team	Lg	G	AB	H	2B	3B	HR	(Hm Rd)	TB	R	RBI	TBB	IBB	SO	HBP	SH	SF	SB	CS	SB%	GDP	Avg	OBP	SLG
1994 Cleveland	AL	20	73	15	5	0	1	(1 0)	23	6	8	2	0	13	0	1	0	1	0	1.00	2	.205	.227	.315
1995 Cincinnati	NL	81	171	58	13	1	3	(1 2)	82	25	30	21	2	33	0	0	2	0	3	.00	1	.339	.407	.480
1996 Detroit	AL	145	545	147	30	3	11	(8 3)	216	69	55	42	0	109	4	3	4	6	1	.86	12	.270	.326	.396
1997 San Francisco	NL	118	341	91	14	6	10	(4 6)	147	50	42	23	2	62	4	1	3	3	2	.60	8	.267	.318	.431
1998 Philadelphia	NL	142	518	129	21	2	9	(4 5)	181	52	54	48	2	111	3	3	8	3	3	.50	17	.249	.312	.349
1999 Cincinnati	NL	88	173	44	16	0	6	(2 4)	78	18	28	7	1	24	0	2	2	0	0	.00	8	.254	.280	.451
9 ML YEARS		814	2600	689	137	13	46	(23 23)	990	299	282	183	8	473	15	15	27	22	16	.58	73	.265	.314	.381

Jim Leyritz

Bats: R **Throws:** R **Pos:** PH/PR-29; 1B-28; C-25; DH-14; 3B-2   Ht: 5'11" **Wt:** 220 **Born:** 12/27/63 **Age:** 36

BATTING																		BASERUNNING				PERCENTAGES		
Year Team	Lg	G	AB	H	2B	3B	HR	(Hm Rd)	TB	R	RBI	TBB	IBB	SO	HBP	SH	SF	SB	CS	SB%	GDP	Avg	OBP	SLG
1999 Rancho Cuca *	A+	1	4	0	0	0	0	(— —)	0	0	0	0	0	1	0	0	0	0	0	.00	0	.000	.000	.000
Las Vegas *	AAA	2	8	0	0	0	0	(— —)	0	0	0	0	0	5	0	0	0	0	0	.00	0	.000	.000	.000
1990 New York	AL	92	303	78	13	1	5	(1 4)	108	28	25	27	1	51	7	1	1	2	3	.40	11	.257	.331	.356
1991 New York	AL	32	77	14	3	0	0	(0 0)	17	8	4	13	0	15	0	1	0	0	1	.00	0	.182	.300	.221
1992 New York	AL	63	144	37	6	0	7	(3 4)	64	17	26	14	1	22	6	0	3	0	1	.00	2	.257	.341	.444
1993 New York	AL	95	259	80	14	0	14	(6 8)	136	43	53	37	3	59	8	0	1	0	0	.00	12	.309	.410	.525
1994 New York	AL	75	249	66	12	0	17	(4 13)	129	47	58	35	1	61	6	0	3	0	0	.00	9	.265	.365	.518
1995 New York	AL	77	264	71	12	0	7	(3 4)	104	37	37	37	2	73	8	0	1	1	1	.50	4	.269	.374	.394
1996 New York	AL	88	265	70	10	0	7	(3 4)	101	23	40	30	3	68	9	2	3	2	0	1.00	11	.264	.355	.381
1997 Ana-Tex	AL	121	379	105	11	0	11	(3 8)	149	58	64	60	2	78	6	4	6	2	1	.67	13	.277	.379	.393
1998 Bos-SD		114	272	75	16	0	12	(7 5)	127	34	42	42	1	74	9	0	5	0	0	.00	6	.276	.384	.467
1999 SD-NYY		81	200	47	9	1	8	(4 4)	82	25	26	28	2	54	4	0	1	0	0	.00	7	.235	.339	.410
1997 Anaheim	AL	84	294	81	7	0	11	(3 8)	121	47	50	37	2	56	3	3	5	1	1	.50	11	.276	.357	.412
Texas		37	85	24	4	0	0	(0 0)	28	11	14	23	0	22	3	1	1	1	0	1.00	2	.282	.446	.329
1998 Boston	AL	52	129	37	6	0	8	(6 2)	67	17	24	21	1	34	2	0	4	0	0	.00	4	.287	.385	.519
San Diego	NL	62	143	38	10	0	4	(1 3)	60	17	18	21	0	40	7	0	1	0	0	.00	2	.266	.384	.420
1999 San Diego	NL	50	134	32	5	0	8	(4 4)	61	17	21	15	1	37	4	0	1	0	0	.00	3	.239	.331	.455
New York		31	66	15	4	1	0	(0 0)	21	8	5	13	1	17	0	0	0	0	0	.00	4	.227	.354	.318
10 ML YEARS		838	2412	643	106	2	88	(34 54)	1017	320	375	323	16	555	63	8	24	7	7	.50	75	.267	.365	.422

Cory Lidle

Pitches: Right **Bats:** Right **Pos:** RP-4; SP-1   Ht: 5'11" **Wt:** 180 **Born:** 3/22/72 **Age:** 28

HOW MUCH HE PITCHED								WHAT HE GAVE UP												THE RESULTS						
Year Team	Lg	G	GS	CG	GF	IP	BFP	H	R	ER	HR	SH	SF	HB	TBB	IBB	SO	WP	Bk	W	L	Pct.	ShO	Sv-Op	Hld	ERA
1991 Twins	R	4	0	0	1	4.2	19	5	3	3	0	0	0	0	0	0	5	1	2	1	1	.500	0	0--	—	5.79
1992 Elizabethtn	R+	19	2	0	11	43.2	190	40	29	18	2	0	2	0	21	0	32	3	1	2	1	.667	0	6--	—	3.71
1993 Pocatello	R+	17	16	3	1	106.2	463	104	59	49	6	1	4	5	54	0	91	14	1	8	4	.667	0	1--	—	4.13
1994 Stockton	A+	25	1	0	12	42.2	200	60	32	21	2	0	0	1	13	1	38	1	0	1	2	.333	0	4--	—	4.43
Beloit	A	13	9	1	0	69	279	65	24	20	4	1	0	2	11	0	62	6	0	3	4	.429	1	0--	—	2.61
1995 El Paso	AA	45	9	0	12	109.2	480	126	52	41	6	6	1	6	36	3	78	6	0	5	4	.556	0	2--	—	3.36
1996 Binghamton	AA	27	27	6	0	190.1	779	186	78	70	13	6	2	3	49	4	141	14	3	14	10	.583	1	0--	—	3.31
1997 Norfolk	AAA	7	7	1	0	42	181	46	20	17	1	4	1	1	10	0	34	0	0	4	2	.667	0	0--	—	3.64
1998 High Desert	A+	1	1	0	0	2.2	13	2	1	0	0	0	0	0	2	0	6	0	0	0	0	.000	0	0--	—	0.00
Tucson	AAA	1	1	0	0	4.2	18	2	0	0	0	0	0	0	2	0	2	0	0	0	0	.000	0	0--	—	0.00
1999 St. Pete	A+	2	2	0	0	5	19	2	0	0	0	0	0	0	2	0	1	0	0	0	0	.000	0	0--	—	0.00
Durham	AAA	3	2	0	0	5.2	26	3	3	3	0	0	0	0	1	0	6	1	0	0	0	.000	0	0--	—	4.76
1997 New York	NL	54	2	0	20	81.2	345	86	38	32	7	4	4	3	20	4	54	2	0	7	2	.778	0	2-3	9	3.53
1999 Tampa Bay	AL	5	1	0	1	5	24	8	4	4	0	0	0	0	2	0	4	0	0	1	0	1.000	0	0-0	0	7.20
2 ML YEARS		59	3	0	21	86.2	369	94	42	36	7	4	4	3	22	4	58	2	0	8	2	.800	0	2-3	9	3.74

Jon Lieber

Pitches: Right **Bats:** Left **Pos:** SP-31   Ht: 6'3" **Wt:** 225 **Born:** 4/2/70 **Age:** 30

HOW MUCH HE PITCHED								WHAT HE GAVE UP												THE RESULTS						
Year Team	Lg	G	GS	CG	GF	IP	BFP	H	R	ER	HR	SH	SF	HB	TBB	IBB	SO	WP	Bk	W	L	Pct.	ShO	Sv-Op	Hld	ERA
1994 Pittsburgh	NL	17	17	1	0	108.2	460	116	62	45	12	3	3	1	25	3	71	2	3	6	7	.462	0	0-0	0	3.73
1995 Pittsburgh	NL	21	12	0	3	72.2	327	103	56	51	7	5	6	4	14	0	45	3	0	4	7	.364	0	0-1	3	6.32
1996 Pittsburgh	NL	51	15	0	6	142	600	156	70	63	19	7	2	3	28	2	94	0	0	9	5	.643	0	1-4	9	3.99
1997 Pittsburgh	NL	33	32	1	0	188.1	799	193	102	94	23	6	7	1	51	8	160	3	1	11	14	.440	0	0-0	0	4.49
1998 Pittsburgh	NL	29	28	2	1	171	731	182	93	78	23	7	4	3	40	4	138	0	3	8	14	.364	0	1-1	0	4.11
1999 Chicago	NL	31	31	3	0	203.1	875	226	107	92	28	7	11	1	46	6	186	2	2	10	11	.476	1	0-0	0	4.07
6 ML YEARS		182	135	7	10	886	3792	976	490	423	112	35	33	13	204	23	694	10	9	48	58	.453	1	2-6	12	4.30

Mike Lieberthal

Bats: Right **Throws:** Right **Pos:** C-143; PH/PR-4   Ht: 6'0" **Wt:** 185 **Born:** 1/18/72 **Age:** 28

BATTING																		BASERUNNING				PERCENTAGES		
Year Team	Lg	G	AB	H	2B	3B	HR	(Hm Rd)	TB	R	RBI	TBB	IBB	SO	HBP	SH	SF	SB	CS	SB%	GDP	Avg	OBP	SLG
1994 Philadelphia	NL	24	79	21	3	1	1	(1 0)	29	6	5	3	0	5	1	1	0	0	0	.00	4	.266	.301	.367
1995 Philadelphia	NL	16	47	12	2	0	0	(0 0)	14	1	4	5	0	5	0	2	0	0	0	.00	1	.255	.327	.298
1996 Philadelphia	NL	50	166	42	8	0	7	(4 3)	71	21	23	10	0	30	2	0	4	0	0	.00	4	.253	.297	.428
1997 Philadelphia	NL	134	455	112	27	1	20	(11 9)	201	59	77	44	1	76	4	0	7	3	4	.43	10	.246	.314	.442
1998 Philadelphia	NL	86	313	80	15	3	8	(5 3)	125	39	45	17	1	44	7	0	5	2	1	.67	4	.256	.304	.399

Year Team	Lg	G	AB	H	2B	3B	HR	(Hm	Rd)	TB	R	RBI	TBB	IBB	SO	HBP	SH	SF	SB	CS	SB%	GDP	Avg	OBP	SLG
1999 Philadelphia	NL	145	510	153	33	1	31	(10	21)	281	84	96	44	7	86	11	1	8	0	0	.00	15	.300	.363	.551
6 ML YEARS		455	1570	420	88	6	67	(31	36)	721	210	250	123	9	246	25	4	24	5	5	.50	38	.268	.326	.459

Jeff Liefer

Bats: L **Throws:** R **Pos:** 1B-15; LF-14; PH/PR-9; DH-7; RF-3   **Ht:** 6'3" **Wt:** 195 **Born:** 8/17/74 **Age:** 25

Year Team	Lg	G	AB	H	2B	3B	HR	(Hm	Rd)	TB	R	RBI	TBB	IBB	SO	HBP	SH	SF	SB	CS	SB%	GDP	Avg	OBP	SLG
1996 South Bend	A	74	277	90	14	0	15	—	—	149	60	58	30	3	62	5	0	4	6	5	.55	3	.325	.396	.538
Pr William	A+	37	147	33	6	0	1	—	—	42	17	13	11	2	27	0	0	1	0	0	.00	6	.224	.277	.286
1997 Birmingham	AA	119	474	113	24	9	15	—	—	200	67	71	38	3	115	7	1	4	2	0	1.00	10	.238	.302	.422
1998 Birmingham	AA	127	471	137	33	6	21	—	—	245	84	89	60	6	125	9	0	1	1	2	.33	9	.291	.381	.520
Calgary	AAA	8	31	8	3	0	1	—	—	14	3	10	2	0	12	0	0	0	0	0	.00	1	.258	.303	.452
1999 Charlotte	AAA	46	171	58	17	1	9	—	—	104	36	34	21	3	26	1	1	1	2	1	.67	3	.339	.412	.608
1999 Chicago	AL	45	113	28	7	1	0	(0	0)	37	8	14	8	0	28	0	0	1	2	0	1.00	3	.248	.295	.327

Kerry Ligtenberg

Pitches: Right **Bats:** Right **Pos:** RP   **Ht:** 6'2" **Wt:** 215 **Born:** 5/11/71 **Age:** 29

Year Team	Lg	G	GS	CG	GF	IP	BFP	H	R	ER	HR	SH	SF	HB	TBB	IBB	SO	WP	Bk	W	L	Pct.	ShO	Sv-Op	Hld	ERA
1997 Atlanta	NL	15	0	0	9	15	61	12	5	5	4	0	0	0	4	2	19	0	0	1	0	1.000	0	1-1	0	3.00
1998 Atlanta	NL	75	0	0	56	73	290	51	24	22	6	1	1	0	24	1	79	3	0	3	2	.600	0	30-34	11	2.71
2 ML YEARS		90	0	0	65	88	351	63	29	27	10	1	1	0	28	3	98	3	0	4	2	.667	0	31-35	11	2.76

Ted Lilly

Pitches: Left **Bats:** Left **Pos:** RP-6; SP-3   **Ht:** 6'1" **Wt:** 177 **Born:** 1/4/76 **Age:** 24

Year Team	Lg	G	GS	CG	GF	IP	BFP	H	R	ER	HR	SH	SF	HB	TBB	IBB	SO	WP	Bk	W	L	Pct.	ShO	Sv-Op	Hld	ERA
1996 Yakima	A-	13	8	0	1	53.2	200	25	9	5	0	0	0	1	14	1	75	0	2	4	0	1.000	0	0--	—	0.84
1997 San Berndno	A+	23	21	2	0	134.2	540	116	52	42	9	5	3	4	32	0	158	7	5	7	8	.467	1	0--	—	2.81
1998 San Antonio	AA	17	17	0	0	111.2	471	114	50	41	8	1	2	1	37	0	96	4	3	8	4	.667	0	0--	—	3.30
Albuquerque	AAA	5	5	0	0	31	135	39	20	17	3	0	0	0	9	0	25	1	2	1	3	.250	0	0--	—	4.94
Ottawa	AAA	7	7	0	0	39	182	45	28	21	8	1	1	0	19	0	49	0	0	2	2	.500	0	0--	—	4.85
1999 Ottawa	AAA	16	16	0	0	89	364	81	40	38	12	1	2	2	23	0	78	1	2	8	5	.615	0	0--	—	3.84
1999 Montreal	NL	9	3	0	1	23.2	110	30	20	20	7	0	1	3	9	0	28	1	0	0	1	.000	0	0-0	—	7.61

Jose Lima

Pitches: Right **Bats:** Right **Pos:** SP-35   **Ht:** 6'2" **Wt:** 205 **Born:** 9/30/72 **Age:** 27

Year Team	Lg	G	GS	CG	GF	IP	BFP	H	R	ER	HR	SH	SF	HB	TBB	IBB	SO	WP	Bk	W	L	Pct.	ShO	Sv-Op	Hld	ERA
1994 Detroit	AL	3	1	0	0	6.2	34	11	10	10	2	0	0	0	3	1	7	1	0	0	1	.000	0	0-0	0	13.50
1995 Detroit	AL	15	15	0	0	73.2	320	85	52	50	10	2	1	4	18	4	37	5	0	3	9	.250	0	0-0	0	6.11
1996 Detroit	AL	39	4	0	15	72.2	329	87	48	46	13	5	3	5	22	4	59	3	0	5	6	.455	0	3-7	6	5.70
1997 Houston	NL	52	1	0	15	75	321	79	45	44	9	6	3	5	16	2	63	2	0	1	6	.143	0	2-2	3	5.28
1998 Houston	NL	33	33	3	0	233.1	950	229	100	96	34	11	5	7	32	1	169	4	0	16	8	.667	1	0-0	0	3.70
1999 Houston	NL	35	35	3	0	246.1	1024	256	108	98	30	5	7	2	44	2	187	8	0	21	10	.677	0	0-0	0	3.58
6 ML YEARS		177	89	6	31	707.2	2978	747	363	344	98	29	19	23	135	14	522	23	0	46	40	.535	1	5-9	9	4.37

Mike Lincoln

Pitches: Right **Bats:** Right **Pos:** SP-15; RP-3   **Ht:** 6'2" **Wt:** 211 **Born:** 4/10/75 **Age:** 25

Year Team	Lg	G	GS	CG	GF	IP	BFP	H	R	ER	HR	SH	SF	HB	TBB	IBB	SO	WP	Bk	W	L	Pct.	ShO	Sv-Op	Hld	ERA
1996 Fort Myers	A+	12	11	0	0	59.2	263	64	31	27	5	2	4	3	25	0	24	4	1	5	2	.714	0	0--	—	4.07
1997 Fort Myers	A+	20	20	1	0	134	553	130	41	34	4	5	3	4	25	0	75	4	2	13	4	.765	1	0--	—	2.28
1998 New Britain	AA	26	26	1	0	173.1	720	180	80	62	13	8	5	5	35	0	109	5	1	15	7	.682	0	0--	—	3.22
1999 Salt Lake	AAA	9	9	0	0	59	274	82	52	51	12	1	5	2	21	0	39	2	0	5	2	.714	0	0--	—	7.78
1999 Minnesota	AL	18	15	0	0	76.1	353	102	59	58	11	2	6	1	26	0	27	4	0	3	10	.231	0	0-0	1	6.84

Cole Liniak

Bats: Right **Throws:** Right **Pos:** 3B-10; PH/PR-2   **Ht:** 6'1" **Wt:** 195 **Born:** 8/23/76 **Age:** 23

Year Team	Lg	G	AB	H	2B	3B	HR	(Hm	Rd)	TB	R	RBI	TBB	IBB	SO	HBP	SH	SF	SB	CS	SB%	GDP	Avg	OBP	SLG
1995 Red Sox	R	23	79	21	7	0	1	—	—	31	9	8	4	0	8	1	2	0	2	0	1.00	2	.266	.310	.392
1996 Michigan	A	121	437	115	26	2	3	—	—	154	65	46	59	1	59	10	3	8	7	6	.54	12	.263	.358	.352
1997 Sarasota	A+	64	217	73	16	0	6	—	—	107	32	42	22	1	31	3	3	2	1	2	.33	2	.336	.402	.493
Trenton	AA	53	200	56	11	0	2	—	—	73	20	18	17	0	29	1	3	1	0	1	.00	6	.280	.338	.365
1998 Red Sox	R	2	8	0	0	0	0	—	—	0	1	0	0	0	1	1	0	0	0	0	.00	0	.000	.111	.000
Pawtucket	AAA	112	429	112	31	1	17	—	—	196	65	59	39	1	71	5	4	3	4	4	.50	11	.261	.328	.440
1999 Pawtucket	AAA	95	348	92	25	0	12	—	—	153	55	42	40	1	57	1	3	1	0	5	.00	7	.264	.341	.440
1999 Chicago	NL	12	29	7	2	0	0	(0	0)	9	3	2	1	0	4	0	0	0	0	1	.00	2	.241	.267	.310

134

Doug Linton

Pitches: Right Bats: Right Pos: SP-8; RP-6   Ht: 6'1" Wt: 190 Born: 2/9/65 Age: 35

Year Team	Lg	G	GS	CG	GF	IP	BFP	H	R	ER	HR	SH	SF	HB	TBB	IBB	SO	WP	Bk	W	L	Pct.	ShO	Sv-Op	Hld	ERA
1999 Rochester *	AAA	18	18	1	0	118.1	510	120	58	48	13	3	4	10	27	1	97	3	0	7	5	.583	0	0--	—	3.65
1992 Toronto	AL	8	3	0	2	24	116	31	23	23	5	1	2	0	17	0	16	2	0	1	3	.250	0	0-0	0	8.63
1993 Tor-Cal	AL	23	1	0	6	36.2	178	46	30	30	8	0	3	1	23	1	23	2	0	2	1	.667	0	0-1	0	7.36
1994 New York	NL	32	3	0	8	50.1	241	74	27	25	4	3	1	0	20	3	29	2	0	6	2	.750	0	0-0	0	4.47
1995 Kansas City	AL	7	2	0	0	22.1	98	22	21	18	4	0	0	2	10	1	13	0	0	0	1	.000	0	0-0	0	7.25
1996 Kansas City	AL	21	18	0	0	104	452	111	65	58	18	6	2	8	26	1	87	3	1	7	9	.438	0	0-0	1	5.02
1999 Baltimore	AL	14	8	0	0	59	264	69	41	39	14	4	0	2	25	1	31	4	0	1	4	.200	0	0-0	0	5.95
1993 Toronto	AL	4	1	0	0	11	55	11	8	8	0	0	2	1	9	0	4	0	0	0	1	.000	0	0-0	0	6.55
California	AL	19	0	0	6	25.2	123	35	22	22	8	0	1	0	14	1	19	2	0	2	0	1.000	0	0-1	0	7.71
6 ML YEARS		105	35	0	16	296.1	1349	353	207	193	48	14	8	13	121	7	199	13	1	17	20	.459	0	0-1	1	5.86

Felipe Lira

Pitches: Right Bats: Right Pos: RP-2   Ht: 6'1" Wt: 205 Born: 4/26/72 Age: 28

Year Team	Lg	G	GS	CG	GF	IP	BFP	H	R	ER	HR	SH	SF	HB	TBB	IBB	SO	WP	Bk	W	L	Pct.	ShO	Sv-Op	Hld	ERA
1999 Toledo *	AAA	30	17	0	7	114	527	163	97	85	25	3	4	4	35	3	70	3	0	2	11	.154	0	1--	—	6.71
1995 Detroit	AL	37	22	0	7	146.1	635	151	74	70	17	4	9	8	56	7	89	5	1	9	13	.409	0	1-3	1	4.31
1996 Detroit	AL	32	32	3	0	194.2	850	204	123	113	30	5	11	10	66	2	113	7	0	6	14	.300	2	0-0	1	5.22
1997 Det-Sea	AL	28	18	1	3	110.2	516	132	82	78	18	2	4	6	55	2	73	7	0	5	11	.313	1	0-0	1	6.34
1998 Seattle	AL	7	0	0	3	15.2	75	22	10	8	5	0	1	0	5	0	16	1	0	1	0	1.000	0	0-0	0	4.60
1999 Detroit	AL	2	0	0	0	3.1	20	7	5	4	2	0	0	0	2	0	3	0	0	0	0	.000	0	0-0	0	10.80
1997 Detroit	AL	20	15	1	1	92	415	101	61	59	15	2	2	2	45	2	64	7	0	5	7	.417	1	0-0	1	5.77
Seattle	AL	8	3	0	2	18.2	101	31	21	19	3	0	2	4	10	0	9	0	0	0	4	.000	0	0-0	1	9.16
5 ML YEARS		106	72	4	13	470.2	2096	516	294	273	72	11	25	24	184	11	294	20	1	21	38	.356	3	1-3	2	5.22

Graeme Lloyd

Pitches: Left Bats: Left Pos: RP-74   Ht: 6'7" Wt: 234 Born: 4/9/67 Age: 33

Year Team	Lg	G	GS	CG	GF	IP	BFP	H	R	ER	HR	SH	SF	HB	TBB	IBB	SO	WP	Bk	W	L	Pct.	ShO	Sv-Op	Hld	ERA
1993 Milwaukee	AL	55	0	0	12	63.2	269	64	24	20	5	1	2	3	13	3	31	4	0	3	4	.429	0	0-4	6	2.83
1994 Milwaukee	AL	43	0	0	21	47	203	49	28	27	4	1	2	3	15	6	31	2	0	2	3	.400	0	3-6	3	5.17
1995 Milwaukee	AL	33	0	0	14	32	127	28	16	16	4	1	4	0	8	2	13	3	0	0	5	.000	0	4-6	9	4.50
1996 Mil-NYY	AL	65	0	0	15	56.2	252	61	30	27	4	5	3	1	22	4	30	4	0	2	6	.250	0	0-5	17	4.29
1997 New York	AL	46	0	0	17	49	217	55	24	18	6	3	5	1	20	7	26	3	0	1	1	.500	0	1-1	2	3.31
1998 New York	AL	50	0	0	8	37.2	145	26	10	7	3	0	1	2	6	2	20	2	0	3	0	1.000	0	0-2	9	1.67
1999 Toronto	AL	74	0	0	25	72	301	68	36	29	11	1	1	4	23	4	47	1	0	5	3	.625	0	3-9	22	3.63
1996 Milwaukee	AL	52	0	0	15	51	217	49	19	16	3	5	1	1	17	3	24	0	0	2	4	.333	0	0-3	15	2.82
New York	AL	13	0	0	0	5.2	35	12	11	11	1	0	2	0	5	1	6	4	0	0	2	.000	0	0-2	2	17.47
7 ML YEARS		366	0	0	112	358	1514	351	168	144	37	12	18	14	107	28	198	19	0	16	22	.421	0	11-33	68	3.62

Esteban Loaiza

Pitches: Right Bats: Right Pos: SP-15; RP-15   Ht: 6'3" Wt: 205 Born: 12/31/71 Age: 28

Year Team	Lg	G	GS	CG	GF	IP	BFP	H	R	ER	HR	SH	SF	HB	TBB	IBB	SO	WP	Bk	W	L	Pct.	ShO	Sv-Op	Hld	ERA
1999 Oklahoma *	AAA	2	2	0	0	4.1	19	3	0	0	0	0	0	0	3	0	6	0	0	0	0	.000	0	0--	—	0.00
1995 Pittsburgh	NL	32	31	1	0	172.2	762	205	115	99	21	10	9	5	55	3	85	6	1	8	9	.471	0	0-0	0	5.16
1996 Pittsburgh	NL	10	10	1	0	52.2	236	65	32	29	11	3	1	2	19	2	32	0	0	2	3	.400	1	0-0	0	4.96
1997 Pittsburgh	NL	33	32	1	0	196.1	851	214	99	90	17	10	7	12	56	9	122	2	3	11	11	.500	0	0-0	0	4.13
1998 Pit-Tex		35	28	1	3	171	751	199	107	98	28	7	12	5	52	4	108	4	2	9	11	.450	0	0-1	0	5.16
1999 Texas	AL	30	15	0	4	120.1	517	128	65	61	10	7	4	0	40	2	77	2	0	9	5	.643	0	0-0	0	4.56
1998 Pittsburgh	NL	21	14	0	3	91.2	394	96	50	46	13	5	7	3	30	1	53	1	2	6	5	.545	0	0-1	0	4.52
Texas	AL	14	14	1	0	79.1	357	103	57	52	15	2	5	2	22	3	55	3	0	3	6	.333	0	0-0	0	5.90
5 ML YEARS		140	116	4	7	713	3117	811	418	377	87	37	33	24	222	20	424	14	6	39	39	.500	1	0-1	0	4.76

Keith Lockhart

Bats: L Throws: R Pos: PH/PR-76; 2B-25; 3B-10; DH-4   Ht: 5'10" Wt: 170 Born: 11/10/64 Age: 35

Year Team	Lg	G	AB	H	2B	3B	HR	(Hm	Rd)	TB	R	RBI	TBB	IBB	SO	HBP	SH	SF	SB	CS	SB%	GDP	Avg	OBP	SLG
1994 San Diego	NL	27	43	9	0	0	2	(2	0)	15	4	6	4	0	10	1	1	1	1	0	1.00	1	.209	.286	.349
1995 Kansas City	AL	94	274	88	19	3	6	(3	3)	131	41	33	14	2	21	4	1	7	8	1	.89	2	.321	.355	.478
1996 Kansas City	AL	138	433	118	33	3	7	(4	3)	178	49	55	30	4	40	2	1	5	11	6	.65	7	.273	.319	.411
1997 Atlanta	NL	96	147	41	5	3	6	(3	3)	70	25	32	14	0	17	1	3	4	2	0	.00	4	.279	.337	.476
1998 Atlanta	NL	109	366	94	21	4	9	(4	5)	142	50	37	29	0	37	1	2	3	2	2	.50	2	.257	.311	.388
1999 Atlanta	NL	108	161	42	3	1	1	(0	1)	50	20	21	19	0	21	1	0	3	3	1	.75	2	.261	.337	.311
6 ML YEARS		572	1424	392	81	10	31	(16	15)	586	189	184	110	6	146	10	8	23	25	10	.71	19	.275	.327	.412

Paul LoDuca

Bats: Right **Throws:** Right **Pos:** C-34; PH/PR-4   **Ht:** 5'10" **Wt:** 185 **Born:** 4/12/72 **Age:** 28

Year Team	Lg	G	AB	H	2B	3B	HR	(Hm	Rd)	TB	R	RBI	TBB	IBB	SO	HBP	SH	SF	SB	CS	SB%	GDP	Avg	OBP	SLG
1993 Vero Beach	A+	39	134	42	6	0	0	—	—	48	17	13	13	0	22	2	0	1	0	0	.00	2	.313	.380	.358
1994 Bakersfield	A+	123	455	141	32	1	6	—	—	193	65	68	52	2	49	3	0	4	16	9	.64	5	.310	.381	.424
1995 San Antonio	AA	61	199	49	8	0	1	—	—	60	27	8	26	0	25	2	0	0	5	5	.50	12	.246	.339	.302
1996 Vero Beach	A+	124	439	134	22	0	3	—	—	165	54	66	70	2	38	2	0	4	8	2	.80	14	.305	.400	.376
1997 San Antonio	AA	105	385	126	28	2	7	—	—	179	63	69	46	3	27	3	4	5	16	8	.67	17	.327	.399	.465
1998 Albuquerque	AAA	126	451	144	30	3	8	—	—	204	69	58	59	2	40	5	7	6	19	7	.73	20	.319	.399	.452
1999 Albuquerque	AAA	26	76	28	9	0	1	—	—	40	17	8	10	0	1	0	6	0	1	1	.50	0	.368	.478	.526
1998 Los Angeles	NL	6	14	4	1	0	0	(0	0)	5	2	1	0	0	1	0	0	0	0	0	.00	0	.286	.286	.357
1999 Los Angeles	NL	36	95	22	1	0	3	(1	2)	32	11	11	10	4	9	2	1	2	1	2	.33	3	.232	.312	.337
2 ML YEARS		42	109	26	2	0	3	(1	2)	37	13	12	10	4	10	2	1	2	1	2	.33	3	.239	.309	.339

Carlton Loewer

Pitches: Right **Bats:** Right **Pos:** SP-13; RP-7   **Ht:** 6'6" **Wt:** 200 **Born:** 9/24/73 **Age:** 26

Year Team	Lg	G	GS	CG	GF	IP	BFP	H	R	ER	HR	SH	SF	HB	TBB	IBB	SO	WP	Bk	W	L	Pct.	ShO	Sv-Op	Hld	ERA
1995 Clearwater	A+	20	20	1	0	114.2	502	124	59	42	6	3	5	5	36	0	83	7	3	7	5	.583	0	0--	—	3.30
Reading	AA	8	8	0	0	50	212	42	17	12	3	1	0	1	31	0	35	4	0	4	1	.800	0	0--	—	2.16
1996 Reading	AA	27	27	3	0	171	753	191	115	100	24	7	3	8	57	3	119	9	1	7	10	.412	1	0--	—	5.26
1997 Scranton-WB	AAA	29	29	4	0	184	797	198	120	94	20	8	4	7	50	6	152	3	0	5	13	.278	0	0--	—	4.60
1998 Scranton-WB	AAA	12	12	5	0	94	385	89	34	30	5	5	2	5	22	0	69	3	0	7	3	.700	2	0--	—	2.87
1999 Phillies	R	1	1	0	0	2	8	2	0	0	0	0	0	0	0	0	2	1	0	0	0	.000	0	0--	—	0.00
Clearwater	A+	3	3	0	0	7	31	10	6	6	0	0	0	0	1	0	5	2	0	0	2	.000	0	0--	—	7.71
1998 Philadelphia	NL	21	21	1	0	122.2	549	154	86	83	18	5	8	3	39	1	58	4	0	7	8	.467	1	0-0	—	6.09
1999 Philadelphia	NL	20	13	2	2	89.2	385	100	54	51	9	5	6	0	26	0	48	3	0	2	6	.250	0	0-0	—	5.12
2 ML YEARS		41	34	3	2	212.1	934	254	140	134	27	10	14	3	65	1	106	7	0	9	14	.391	1	0-0	1	5.68

Kenny Lofton

Bats: Left **Throws:** Left **Pos:** CF-119; PH/PR-2; DH-1   **Ht:** 6'0" **Wt:** 190 **Born:** 5/31/67 **Age:** 33

Year Team	Lg	G	AB	H	2B	3B	HR	(Hm	Rd)	TB	R	RBI	TBB	IBB	SO	HBP	SH	SF	SB	CS	SB%	GDP	Avg	OBP	SLG
1991 Houston	NL	20	74	15	1	0	0	(0	0)	16	9	0	5	0	19	0	0	0	2	1	.67	0	.203	.253	.216
1992 Cleveland	AL	148	576	164	15	8	5	(3	2)	210	96	42	68	3	54	2	4	1	66	12	.85	7	.285	.362	.365
1993 Cleveland	AL	148	569	185	28	8	1	(1	0)	232	116	42	81	6	83	1	2	4	70	14	.83	8	.325	.408	.408
1994 Cleveland	AL	112	459	160	32	9	12	(10	2)	246	105	57	52	5	56	2	4	6	60	12	.83	5	.349	.412	.536
1995 Cleveland	AL	118	481	149	22	13	7	(5	2)	218	93	53	40	6	49	1	4	3	54	15	.78	6	.310	.362	.453
1996 Cleveland	AL	154	662	210	35	4	14	(7	7)	295	132	67	61	3	82	0	7	6	75	17	.82	7	.317	.372	.446
1997 Atlanta	NL	122	493	164	20	6	5	(3	2)	211	90	48	64	5	83	2	2	3	27	20	.57	10	.333	.409	.428
1998 Cleveland	AL	154	600	169	31	6	12	(6	6)	248	101	64	87	1	80	2	3	6	54	10	.84	7	.282	.371	.413
1999 Cleveland	AL	120	465	140	28	6	7	(1	6)	201	110	39	79	2	84	6	5	5	25	6	.81	6	.301	.405	.432
9 ML YEARS		1096	4379	1356	212	60	63	(36	27)	1877	852	412	537	31	590	16	31	34	433	107	.80	56	.310	.384	.429

Rich Loiselle

Pitches: Right **Bats:** Right **Pos:** RP-13   **Ht:** 6'5" **Wt:** 245 **Born:** 1/12/72 **Age:** 28

Year Team	Lg	G	GS	CG	GF	IP	BFP	H	R	ER	HR	SH	SF	HB	TBB	IBB	SO	WP	Bk	W	L	Pct.	ShO	Sv-Op	Hld	ERA
1996 Pittsburgh	NL	5	3	0	0	20.2	90	22	8	7	3	0	0	0	8	1	9	3	0	1	0	1.000	0	0-0	1	3.05
1997 Pittsburgh	NL	72	0	0	58	72.2	312	76	29	25	7	2	2	1	24	3	66	4	0	1	5	.167	0	29-34	5	3.10
1998 Pittsburgh	NL	54	0	0	43	55	258	56	26	21	2	5	1	2	36	9	48	0	0	2	7	.222	0	19-27	1	3.44
1999 Pittsburgh	NL	13	0	0	6	15.1	69	16	9	9	2	1	0	2	9	2	14	1	0	3	2	.600	0	0-1	3	5.28
4 ML YEARS		144	3	0	107	163.2	729	170	72	62	14	8	3	5	77	15	137	8	0	7	14	.333	0	48-62	10	3.41

Steve Lomasney

Bats: Right **Throws:** Right **Pos:** C-1   **Ht:** 6'0" **Wt:** 195 **Born:** 8/29/77 **Age:** 22

Year Team	Lg	G	AB	H	2B	3B	HR	(Hm	Rd)	TB	R	RBI	TBB	IBB	SO	HBP	SH	SF	SB	CS	SB%	GDP	Avg	OBP	SLG
1995 Red Sox	R	29	92	15	6	0	0	—	—	21	10	7	8	1	16	5	1	0	2	1	.67	0	.163	.267	.228
1996 Lowell	A-	59	173	24	10	0	4	—	—	46	26	21	42	0	63	2	0	0	2	0	1.00	2	.139	.313	.266
1997 Michigan	A	102	324	89	27	3	12	—	—	158	50	51	32	0	98	9	3	3	3	4	.43	8	.275	.353	.488
1998 Sarasota	A+	122	443	106	22	1	22	—	—	196	74	63	59	3	145	16	1	2	13	4	.76	7	.239	.348	.442
1999 Sarasota	A+	55	189	51	10	0	8	—	—	85	35	28	26	0	57	8	0	0	5	2	.71	2	.270	.381	.450
Trenton	AA	47	151	37	6	0	12	—	—	79	24	31	31	2	44	9	1	1	7	5	.58	5	.245	.401	.523
1999 Boston	AL	1	2	0	0	0	0	(0	0)	0	0	0	0	0	2	0	0	0	0	0	.00	0	.000	.000	.000

George Lombard

Bats: Left **Throws:** Right **Pos:** PH/PR-3; LF-2; RF-2   **Ht:** 6'0" **Wt:** 212 **Born:** 9/14/75 **Age:** 24

Year Team	Lg	G	AB	H	2B	3B	HR	(Hm	Rd)	TB	R	RBI	TBB	IBB	SO	HBP	SH	SF	SB	CS	SB%	GDP	Avg	OBP	SLG
1994 Braves	R	40	129	18	2	0	0	—	—	20	10	5	18	0	47	3	0	0	10	4	.71	1	.140	.260	.155

Year Team	Lg	G	AB	H	2B	3B	HR	(Hm	Rd)	TB	R	RBI	TBB	IBB	SO	HBP	SH	SF	SB	CS	SB%	GDP	Avg	OBP	SLG
1995 Macon	A	49	180	37	6	1	3	—	—	54	32	16	27	3	44	5	1	0	16	4	.80	4	.206	.325	.300
Eugene	A-	68	262	66	5	3	5	—	—	92	38	19	23	0	91	5	2	1	35	13	.73	0	.252	.323	.351
1996 Macon	A	116	444	109	16	8	15	—	—	186	76	51	36	0	122	7	8	2	24	17	.59	4	.245	.311	.419
1997 Durham	A+	131	462	122	25	7	14	—	—	203	65	72	66	9	145	9	2	2	35	7	.83	4	.264	.365	.439
1998 Greenville	AA	122	422	130	25	4	22	—	—	229	84	65	71	10	140	5	5	4	35	5	.88	2	.308	.410	.543
1999 Richmond	AAA	74	233	48	11	3	7	—	—	86	25	29	35	2	98	3	0	0	21	6	.78	2	.206	.317	.369
1998 Atlanta	NL	6	6	2	0	0	1	(0	1)	5	2	1	0	0	1	0	0	0	1	0	1.00	0	.333	.333	.833
1999 Atlanta	NL	6	6	2	0	0	0	(0	0)	2	1	0	1	0	2	0	0	0	2	0	1.00	0	.333	.429	.333
2 ML YEARS		12	12	4	0	0	1	(0	1)	7	3	1	1	0	3	0	0	0	3	0	1.00	0	.333	.385	.583

Terrence Long

Bats: Left **Throws:** Left **Pos:** PH/PR-3   **Ht:** 6'1" **Wt:** 190 **Born:** 2/29/76 **Age:** 24

Year Team	Lg	G	AB	H	2B	3B	HR	(Hm	Rd)	TB	R	RBI	TBB	IBB	SO	HBP	SH	SF	SB	CS	SB%	GDP	Avg	OBP	SLG
1994 Kingsport	R+	60	215	50	9	2	12	—	—	99	39	39	32	0	52	4	0	2	9	3	.75	2	.233	.340	.460
1995 Capital Cty	A	55	178	35	1	2	2	—	—	46	27	13	28	4	43	1	1	0	8	5	.62	3	.197	.309	.258
Pittsfield	A-	51	187	48	9	4	4	—	—	77	24	31	18	2	36	1	1	1	11	4	.73	2	.257	.324	.412
1996 Capital Cty	A	123	473	136	26	9	12	—	—	216	66	78	36	3	120	5	1	4	32	7	.82	9	.288	.342	.457
1997 St. Lucie	A+	126	470	118	29	7	8	—	—	185	52	61	40	4	102	2	0	4	24	8	.75	6	.251	.310	.394
1998 Binghamton	AA	130	455	135	20	10	16	—	—	223	69	58	62	6	105	2	4	2	23	11	.68	6	.297	.380	.490
1999 Norfolk	AAA	78	304	99	20	4	7	—	—	148	41	47	23	4	41	1	0	1	14	6	.70	6	.326	.374	.487
Vancouver	AAA	40	154	38	6	2	2	—	—	54	16	21	10	2	29	1	0	0	7	4	.64	4	.247	.297	.351
1999 New York	NL	3	3	0	0	0	0	(0	0)	0	0	0	0	0	2	0	0	0	0	0	.00	1	.000	.000	.000

Braden Looper

Pitches: Right **Bats:** Right **Pos:** RP-72   **Ht:** 6'5" **Wt:** 225 **Born:** 10/28/74 **Age:** 25

		HOW MUCH HE PITCHED					WHAT HE GAVE UP										THE RESULTS						
Year Team	Lg	G	GS	CG	GF	IP	BFP	H	R	ER	HR	SH	SF	HB	TBB	IBB	SO	WP	Bk	W	L	Pct.	ShO	Sv-Op	Hld	ERA
1997 Pr William	A+	12	12	0	0	64.1	287	71	38	32	6	1	1	3	25	0	58	1	2	3	6	.333	0	0--		4.48
Arkansas	AA	19	0	0	14	21.1	94	24	14	14	2	1	1	1	7	2	20	1	2	1	2	.200	0	5--		5.91
1998 Memphis	AAA	40	0	0	32	40.2	177	43	16	14	3	2	1	2	13	1	43	3	0	2	3	.400	0	20--		3.10
1998 St. Louis	NL	4	0	0	3	3.1	16	5	4	2	1	0	1	0	1	0	4	1	0	0	0	.000	0	0-2	0	5.40
1999 Florida	NL	72	0	0	22	83	370	96	43	35	7	5	5	1	31	6	50	2	2	3	3	.500	0	0-4	8	3.80
2 ML YEARS		76	0	0	25	86.1	386	101	47	37	8	5	6	1	32	6	54	3	2	3	4	.429	0	0-6	8	3.86

Albie Lopez

Pitches: Right **Bats:** Right **Pos:** RP-51   **Ht:** 6'2" **Wt:** 240 **Born:** 8/18/71 **Age:** 28

		HOW MUCH HE PITCHED					WHAT HE GAVE UP										THE RESULTS						
Year Team	Lg	G	GS	CG	GF	IP	BFP	H	R	ER	HR	SH	SF	HB	TBB	IBB	SO	WP	Bk	W	L	Pct.	ShO	Sv-Op	Hld	ERA
1999 St. Pete *	A+	2	1	0	0	3.1	17	7	5	2	0	0	0	0	0	0	3	0	0	0	0	.000	0	0--		5.40
1993 Cleveland	AL	9	9	0	0	49.2	222	49	34	33	7	1	1	1	32	1	25	0	0	3	1	.750	0	0-0	0	5.98
1994 Cleveland	AL	4	4	1	0	17	76	20	11	8	3	0	0	1	6	0	18	3	0	1	2	.333	1	0-0	0	4.24
1995 Cleveland	AL	6	2	0	0	23	92	17	8	8	4	0	1	1	7	1	22	2	0	0	0	.000	0	0-0	0	3.13
1996 Cleveland	AL	13	10	0	0	62	282	80	47	44	14	0	1	2	22	1	45	2	0	5	4	.556	0	0-0	0	6.39
1997 Cleveland	AL	37	6	0	10	76.2	364	101	61	59	11	3	2	4	40	9	63	5	0	3	7	.300	0	0-1	4	6.93
1998 Tampa Bay	AL	54	0	0	12	79.2	335	73	31	23	7	4	3	3	32	4	62	5	0	7	4	.636	0	1-5	4	2.60
1999 Tampa Bay	AL	51	0	0	14	64	281	66	40	33	8	1	4	1	24	2	37	3	0	3	2	.600	0	1-3	12	4.64
7 ML YEARS		174	31	1	36	372	1652	406	232	208	54	9	12	13	163	18	272	20	0	22	20	.524	1	2-9	20	5.03

Javy Lopez

Bats: Right **Throws:** Right **Pos:** C-60; PH/PR-5; DH-4   **Ht:** 6'3" **Wt:** 200 **Born:** 11/5/70 **Age:** 29

Year Team	Lg	G	AB	H	2B	3B	HR	(Hm	Rd)	TB	R	RBI	TBB	IBB	SO	HBP	SH	SF	SB	CS	SB%	GDP	Avg	OBP	SLG
1992 Atlanta	NL	9	16	6	2	0	0	(0	0)	8	3	2	0	0	1	0	0	0	0	0	.00	0	.375	.375	.500
1993 Atlanta	NL	8	16	6	1	1	1	(0	1)	12	1	2	0	0	2	1	0	0	0	0	.00	0	.375	.412	.750
1994 Atlanta	NL	80	277	68	9	0	13	(4	9)	116	27	35	17	0	61	5	2	2	0	2	.00	12	.245	.299	.419
1995 Atlanta	NL	100	333	105	11	4	14	(8	6)	166	37	51	14	0	57	2	0	3	0	1	.00	13	.315	.344	.498
1996 Atlanta	NL	138	489	138	19	1	23	(10	13)	228	56	69	28	5	84	3	1	5	1	6	.14	17	.282	.322	.466
1997 Atlanta	NL	123	414	122	28	1	23	(11	12)	221	52	68	40	10	82	5	1	4	1	1	.50	9	.295	.361	.534
1998 Atlanta	NL	133	489	139	21	1	34	(18	16)	264	73	106	30	1	85	6	1	8	5	3	.63	22	.284	.328	.540
1999 Atlanta	NL	65	246	78	18	1	11	(1	10)	131	34	45	20	2	41	3	0	0	0	3	.00	6	.317	.375	.533
8 ML YEARS		656	2280	662	109	9	119	(52	67)	1146	283	378	149	18	413	25	5	22	7	16	.30	79	.290	.338	.503

Luis Lopez

Bats: B **Throws:** R **Pos:** PH/PR-35; SS-33; 2B-16; 3B-9   **Ht:** 5'11" **Wt:** 166 **Born:** 9/4/70 **Age:** 29

Year Team	Lg	G	AB	H	2B	3B	HR	(Hm	Rd)	TB	R	RBI	TBB	IBB	SO	HBP	SH	SF	SB	CS	SB%	GDP	Avg	OBP	SLG
1993 San Diego	NL	17	43	5	1	0	0	(0	0)	6	1	1	0	0	8	0	0	1	0	0	.00	0	.116	.114	.140
1994 San Diego	NL	77	235	65	16	1	2	(2	0)	89	29	20	15	2	39	3	2	2	3	2	.60	7	.277	.325	.379
1996 San Diego	NL	63	139	25	3	0	2	(1	1)	34	10	11	9	1	35	1	1	1	0	0	.00	7	.180	.233	.245
1997 New York	NL	78	178	48	12	1	1	(1	0)	65	19	19	12	2	42	4	2	0	2	4	.33	2	.270	.330	.365

			BATTING													BASERUNNING				PERCENTAGES		
Year Team	Lg	G	AB	H	2B	3B	HR	(Hm | Rd)	TB	R	RBI	TBB	IBB	SO	HBP	SH	SF	SB	CS	SB%	GDP	Avg	OBP	SLG
1998 New York	NL	117	266	67	13	2	2	(1 | 1)	90	37	22	20	3	60	4	3	2	2	2	.50	10	.252	.312	.338
1999 New York	NL	68	104	22	4	0	2	(1 | 1)	32	11	13	12	0	33	3	1	1	1	1	.50	1	.212	.308	.308
6 ML YEARS		420	965	232	49	4	9	(6 | 3)	316	107	86	68	8	217	15	9	7	8	9	.47	27	.240	.299	.327

Mendy Lopez

Bats: Right **Throws:** Right **Pos:** 2B-6; SS-1; PH/PR-1   **Ht:** 6'2" **Wt:** 190 **Born:** 10/15/74 **Age:** 25

			BATTING													BASERUNNING				PERCENTAGES		
Year Team	Lg	G	AB	H	2B	3B	HR	(Hm	Rd)	TB	R	RBI	TBB	IBB	SO	HBP	SH	SF	SB	CS	SB%	GDP	Avg	OBP	SLG
1994 Royals	R	59	235	85	19	3	5	—	—	125	56	50	22	0	27	3	2	5	19	2	.90	5	.362	.415	.532
1995 Wilmington	A+	130	428	116	29	3	2	—	—	157	42	36	28	0	73	5	7	2	18	10	.64	12	.271	.322	.367
1996 Wichita	AA	93	327	92	20	5	6	—	—	140	47	32	26	1	67	4	2	1	14	4	.78	6	.281	.341	.428
1997 Omaha	AAA	17	52	12	2	0	1	—	—	17	6	6	8	0	21	0	1	0	0	0	.00	0	.231	.333	.327
Wichita	AA	101	357	83	16	3	5	—	—	120	56	42	36	0	70	3	5	5	7	5	.58	3	.232	.304	.336
1998 Omaha	AAA	60	195	35	6	1	3	—	—	52	18	14	18	0	44	1	3	0	2	3	.40	5	.179	.252	.267
1999 Royals	R	3	5	1	1	0	0	—	—	2	0	2	3	0	1	1	0	1	0	0	.00	0	.200	.500	.400
Omaha	AAA	61	222	69	8	0	12	—	—	113	41	40	18	1	41	0	2	1	2	2	.50	5	.311	.361	.509
1998 Kansas City	AL	74	206	50	10	2	1	(1	0)	67	18	15	12	0	40	1	5	1	5	2	.71	6	.243	.286	.325
1999 Kansas City	AL	7	20	8	0	1	0	(0	0)	10	2	3	0	0	5	1	0	0	0	0	.00	0	.400	.429	.500
2 ML YEARS		81	226	58	10	3	1	(1	0)	77	20	18	12	0	45	2	5	1	5	2	.71	6	.257	.299	.341

Mark Loretta

Bats: R **Throws:** R **Pos:** SS-74; 1B-66; 2B-17; 3B-14; PH/PR-8   **Ht:** 6'0" **Wt:** 180 **Born:** 8/14/71 **Age:** 28

			BATTING													BASERUNNING				PERCENTAGES		
Year Team	Lg	G	AB	H	2B	3B	HR	(Hm | Rd)	TB	R	RBI	TBB	IBB	SO	HBP	SH	SF	SB	CS	SB%	GDP	Avg	OBP	SLG
1995 Milwaukee	AL	19	50	13	3	0	1	(0 | 1)	19	13	3	4	0	7	1	1	0	1	1	.50	1	.260	.327	.380
1996 Milwaukee	AL	73	154	43	3	0	1	(0 | 1)	49	20	13	14	0	15	0	2	0	2	1	.67	7	.279	.339	.318
1997 Milwaukee	AL	132	418	120	17	5	5	(2 | 3)	162	56	47	47	2	60	2	5	10	5	5	.50	15	.287	.354	.388
1998 Milwaukee	NL	140	434	137	29	4	6	(3 | 3)	184	55	54	42	1	47	7	4	4	9	6	.60	14	.316	.382	.424
1999 Milwaukee	NL	153	587	170	34	5	5	(2 | 3)	229	93	67	52	1	59	10	9	6	4	1	.80	14	.290	.354	.390
5 ML YEARS		517	1643	483	86	10	18	(7 | 11)	643	237	184	159	4	188	20	21	20	21	14	.60	51	.294	.359	.391

Andrew Lorraine

Pitches: Left **Bats:** Left **Pos:** SP-11   **Ht:** 6'3" **Wt:** 205 **Born:** 8/11/72 **Age:** 27

		HOW MUCH HE PITCHED					WHAT HE GAVE UP											THE RESULTS					
Year Team	Lg	G	GS	CG	GF	IP	BFP	H	R	ER	HR	SH	SF	HB	TBB	IBB	SO	WP	Bk	W	L	Pct.	ShO	Sv-Op	Hld	ERA
1999 Iowa *	AAA	22	21	1	0	143	603	149	67	59	16	4	2	6	34	0	96	5	0	9	8	.529	0	0- -	—	3.71
1994 California	AL	4	3	0	0	18.2	96	30	23	22	7	2	1	0	11	0	10	0	0	0	2	.000	0	0-0	0	10.61
1995 Chicago	AL	5	0	0	2	8	30	3	3	3	0	0	0	1	2	0	5	0	0	0	0	.000	0	0-0	1	3.38
1997 Oakland	AL	12	6	0	1	29.2	146	45	22	21	2	0	3	1	15	0	18	0	0	3	1	.750	0	0-0	1	6.37
1998 Seattle	AL	4	0	0	1	3.2	16	3	1	1	0	0	0	0	4	0	0	1	0	0	0	.000	0	0-0	1	2.45
1999 Chicago	NL	11	11	2	0	61.2	272	71	42	38	9	6	2	0	22	3	40	3	0	2	5	.286	1	0-0	0	5.55
5 ML YEARS		36	20	2	4	121.2	560	152	91	85	18	8	6	2	54	3	73	4	0	5	8	.385	1	0-0	2	6.29

Torey Lovullo

Bats: Both **Throws:** Right **Pos:** 1B-6; 2B-6; PH/PR-6   **Ht:** 6'0" **Wt:** 185 **Born:** 7/25/65 **Age:** 34

			BATTING													BASERUNNING				PERCENTAGES		
Year Team	Lg	G	AB	H	2B	3B	HR	(Hm	Rd)	TB	R	RBI	TBB	IBB	SO	HBP	SH	SF	SB	CS	SB%	GDP	Avg	OBP	SLG
1999 Scranton-WB *	AAA	139	519	145	36	3	21	—	—	250	90	106	78	10	89	3	1	9	3	4	.43	12	.279	.371	.482
1988 Detroit	AL	12	21	8	1	1	1	(0	1)	14	2	2	1	0	2	0	1	0	0	0	.00	1	.381	.409	.667
1989 Detroit	AL	29	87	10	2	0	1	(0	1)	15	8	4	14	0	20	0	1	2	0	0	.00	3	.115	.233	.172
1991 New York	AL	22	51	9	2	0	0	(0	0)	11	0	2	5	1	7	0	3	0	0	0	.00	0	.176	.250	.216
1993 California	AL	116	367	92	20	0	6	(4	2)	130	42	30	36	1	49	1	3	2	7	6	.54	8	.251	.318	.354
1994 Seattle	AL	36	72	16	5	0	2	(2	0)	27	9	7	9	1	13	0	4	0	1	0	1.00	2	.222	.309	.375
1996 Oakland	AL	65	82	18	4	0	3	(0	3)	31	15	9	11	0	17	2	3	1	1	2	.33	0	.220	.323	.378
1998 Cleveland	AL	6	19	4	1	0	0	(0	0)	5	1	1	1	0	2	0	1	0	0	0	.00	1	.211	.250	.263
1999 Philadelphia	NL	17	38	8	0	0	2	(2	0)	14	3	5	3	0	11	0	0	0	0	0	.00	1	.211	.268	.368
8 ML YEARS		303	737	165	35	1	15	(8	7)	247	80	60	80	3	121	3	12	5	9	8	.53	16	.224	.301	.335

Derek Lowe

Pitches: Right **Bats:** Right **Pos:** RP-74   **Ht:** 6'6" **Wt:** 200 **Born:** 6/1/73 **Age:** 27

		HOW MUCH HE PITCHED					WHAT HE GAVE UP											THE RESULTS					
Year Team	Lg	G	GS	CG	GF	IP	BFP	H	R	ER	HR	SH	SF	HB	TBB	IBB	SO	WP	Bk	W	L	Pct.	ShO	Sv-Op	Hld	ERA
1997 Sea-Bos	AL	20	9	0	1	69	298	74	49	47	11	4	2	4	23	3	52	2	0	2	6	.250	0	0-2	1	6.13
1998 Boston	AL	63	10	0	8	123	527	126	65	55	5	4	5	4	42	5	77	8	0	3	9	.250	0	4-9	12	4.02
1999 Boston	AL	74	0	0	32	109.1	436	84	35	32	7	1	2	4	25	1	80	1	0	6	3	.667	0	15-20	22	2.63
1997 Seattle	AL	12	9	0	1	53	234	59	43	41	11	2	1	2	20	2	39	2	0	2	4	.333	0	0-0	0	6.96
Boston	AL	8	0	0	0	16	64	15	6	6	0	2	1	2	3	1	13	0	0	0	2	.000	0	0-2	1	3.38
3 ML YEARS		157	19	0	41	301.1	1261	284	149	134	23	9	9	12	90	9	209	11	0	11	18	.379	0	19-31	35	4.00

138

Sean Lowe

Pitches: Right **Bats:** Right **Pos:** RP-64 **Ht:** 6'2" **Wt:** 205 **Born:** 3/29/71 **Age:** 29

		HOW MUCH HE PITCHED						WHAT HE GAVE UP										THE RESULTS					
Year Team	Lg	G	GS	CG	GF	IP	BFP	H	R	ER	HR	SH	SF	HB	TBB	IBB	SO	WP	Bk	W	L	Pct.	ShO	Sv-Op	Hld	ERA
1992 Hamilton	A-	5	5	0	0	28	109	14	8	5	0	0	0	1	14	0	22	1	1	2	0	1.000	0	0--	—	1.61
1993 St. Pete	A+	25	25	0	0	132.2	594	152	80	63	6	2	5	6	62	1	87	4	5	6	11	.353	0	0--	—	4.27
1994 St. Pete	A+	21	21	0	0	114	488	119	51	44	6	3	2	5	37	0	92	3	0	5	6	.455	0	0--	—	3.47
Arkansas	AA	3	3	0	0	19.1	76	13	3	3	0	2	0	0	8	0	11	0	0	2	1	.667	0	0--	—	1.40
1995 Arkansas	AA	24	24	0	0	129	578	143	84	70	2	5	4	5	64	0	77	9	0	9	8	.529	0	0--	—	4.88
1996 Arkansas	AA	6	6	0	0	33	150	32	24	22	2	1	1	2	15	1	25	1	0	2	3	.400	0	0--	—	6.00
Louisville	AAA	25	18	0	1	115	515	127	72	60	7	4	6	7	51	7	76	6	0	8	9	.471	0	0--	—	4.70
1997 Louisville	AAA	26	23	1	2	131.2	581	142	74	64	13	3	3	10	53	4	117	5	2	6	10	.375	0	1--	—	4.37
1998 Memphis	AAA	25	21	0	0	153	637	147	57	54	17	6	1	4	61	1	114	2	0	12	8	.600	0	0--	—	3.18
1997 St. Louis	NL	6	4	0	1	17.1	89	27	21	18	2	1	2	1	10	0	8	0	0	0	2	.000	0	0-0	0	9.35
1998 St. Louis	NL	4	1	0	2	5.1	31	11	9	9	1	1	0	0	5	0	2	0	0	0	3	.000	0	0-0	0	15.19
1999 Chicago	AL	64	0	0	13	95.2	406	90	39	39	10	3	9	4	46	1	62	4	0	4	1	.800	0	0-3	6	3.67
3 ML YEARS		74	5	0	16	118.1	526	128	69	66	13	5	11	5	61	1	72	4	0	4	6	.400	0	0-3	6	5.02

Mike Lowell

Bats: Right **Throws:** Right **Pos:** 3B-83; PH/PR-15 **Ht:** 6'4" **Wt:** 205 **Born:** 2/24/74 **Age:** 26

		BATTING															BASERUNNING				PERCENTAGES		
Year Team	Lg	G	AB	H	2B	3B	HR	(Hm | Rd)	TB	R	RBI	TBB	IBB	SO	HBP	SH	SF	SB	CS	SB%	GDP	Avg	OBP	SLG
1995 Oneonta	A-	72	281	73	18	0	1	—	—	94	36	27	23	0	34	3	0	6	3	1	.75	5	.260	.316	.335
1996 Greensboro	A	113	433	122	33	0	8	—	—	179	58	64	46	0	43	4	2	2	10	3	.77	7	.282	.355	.413
Tampa	A+	24	78	22	5	0	0	—	—	27	8	11	3	0	13	0	1	3	1	1	.50	2	.282	.298	.346
1997 Norwich	AA	78	285	98	17	0	15	—	—	160	60	47	48	1	30	4	1	5	2	1	.67	11	.344	.439	.561
Columbus	AAA	57	210	58	13	1	15	—	—	118	36	45	23	0	34	3	1	6	2	4	.33	6	.276	.347	.562
1998 Columbus	AAA	126	510	155	34	3	26	—	—	273	79	99	37	2	85	6	0	5	4	0	1.00	10	.304	.355	.535
1999 Calgary	AAA	24	83	26	3	0	2	—	—	35	11	9	8	0	19	0	0	0	0	0	.00	0	.313	.374	.422
1998 New York	AL	8	15	4	0	0	0	(0 | 0)	4	1	0	0	0	1	0	0	0	0	0	.00	0	.267	.267	.267
1999 Florida	NL	97	308	78	15	0	12	(7 | 5)	129	32	47	26	1	69	5	0	5	0	0	.00	8	.253	.317	.419
2 ML YEARS		105	323	82	15	0	12	(7 | 5)	133	33	47	26	1	70	5	0	5	0	0	.00	8	.254	.315	.412

Terrell Lowery

Bats: R **Throws:** R **Pos:** CF-36; LF-29; PH/PR-7; DH-1; RF-1 **Ht:** 6'3" **Wt:** 195 **Born:** 10/25/70 **Age:** 29

		BATTING															BASERUNNING				PERCENTAGES		
Year Team	Lg	G	AB	H	2B	3B	HR	(Hm | Rd)	TB	R	RBI	TBB	IBB	SO	HBP	SH	SF	SB	CS	SB%	GDP	Avg	OBP	SLG
1991 Butte	R+	54	214	64	10	7	3	—	—	97	38	33	29	0	44	1	0	2	23	12	.66	2	.299	.382	.453
1993 Charlotte	A+	65	257	77	7	9	3	—	—	111	46	36	46	2	47	2	1	1	14	15	.48	2	.300	.408	.432
Tulsa	AA	66	258	62	5	1	3	—	—	78	29	14	28	1	50	1	1	1	10	12	.45	5	.240	.316	.302
1994 Tulsa	AA	129	496	142	34	8	8	—	—	216	89	54	59	0	113	5	5	5	33	15	.69	7	.286	.365	.435
1995 Rangers	R	10	34	9	3	1	3	—	—	23	10	7	6	0	7	0	0	1	1	0	1.00	1	.265	.375	.676
Charlotte	A+	11	35	9	2	2	0	—	—	15	4	4	6	0	6	1	0	0	1	0	1.00	2	.257	.381	.429
1996 Binghamton	AA	62	211	58	13	4	7	—	—	100	34	32	44	2	44	2	2	3	6	5	.45	4	.275	.400	.474
Norfolk	AAA	62	193	45	7	2	4	—	—	68	25	21	22	0	44	1	3	2	6	3	.67	1	.233	.312	.352
1997 Iowa	AAA	110	386	116	28	3	17	—	—	201	69	71	65	2	97	1	1	2	8	8	.53	8	.301	.401	.521
1998 Iowa	AAA	65	246	73	14	1	12	—	—	125	41	49	27	0	63	2	1	2	5	2	.71	10	.297	.368	.508
1999 Durham	AAA	71	275	92	20	5	15	—	—	167	69	57	43	1	62	1	8	2	10	5	.67	3	.335	.424	.607
1997 Chicago	NL	9	14	4	0	0	0	(0 | 0)	4	2	0	3	0	3	0	0	0	1	0	1.00	0	.286	.412	.286
1998 Chicago	NL	24	15	3	1	0	0	(0 | 0)	4	2	1	3	0	7	0	0	0	0	2	.00	0	.200	.333	.267
1999 Tampa Bay	AL	66	185	48	15	1	2	(0 | 2)	71	25	17	19	0	53	1	0	1	1	0	.00	1	.259	.330	.384
3 ML YEARS		99	214	55	16	1	2	(0 | 2)	79	29	18	25	0	63	1	0	1	1	2	.33	1	.257	.336	.369

Eric Ludwick

Pitches: Right **Bats:** Right **Pos:** RP-1 **Ht:** 6'5" **Wt:** 210 **Born:** 12/14/71 **Age:** 28

		HOW MUCH HE PITCHED						WHAT HE GAVE UP										THE RESULTS					
Year Team	Lg	G	GS	CG	GF	IP	BFP	H	R	ER	HR	SH	SF	HB	TBB	IBB	SO	WP	Bk	W	L	Pct.	ShO	Sv-Op	Hld	ERA
1999 Calgary *	AAA	48	0	0	44	58.1	270	65	33	25	5	3	1	2	36	4	61	1	0	11	6	.647	0	14--	—	3.86
1996 St. Louis	NL	6	1	0	2	10	45	11	11	10	4	0	1	1	3	0	12	0	0	0	1	.000	0	0-0	0	9.00
1997 StL-Oak		11	5	0	3	30.2	152	44	31	29	8	2	0	1	22	1	21	0	0	1	5	.167	0	0-0	0	8.51
1998 Florida	NL	13	6	0	0	32.2	159	46	31	27	7	2	2	0	17	1	27	2	0	1	4	.200	0	0-1	0	7.44
1999 Toronto	AL	1	0	0	0	1	8	3	3	3	0	0	0	0	2	0	0	0	0	0	0	.000	0	0-0	0	27.00
1997 St. Louis	NL	5	0	0	3	6.2	36	12	7	7	1	0	0	0	6	0	7	0	0	0	1	.000	0	0-0	0	9.45
Oakland	AL	6	5	0	0	24	116	32	24	22	7	2	0	1	16	1	14	0	0	1	4	.200	0	0-0	0	8.25
4 ML YEARS		31	12	0	5	74.1	364	104	76	69	19	4	3	2	44	2	60	2	0	2	10	.167	0	0-1	0	8.35

Larry Luebbers

Pitches: Right **Bats:** Right **Pos:** SP-8 **Ht:** 6'6" **Wt:** 205 **Born:** 10/11/69 **Age:** 30

		HOW MUCH HE PITCHED						WHAT HE GAVE UP										THE RESULTS					
Year Team	Lg	G	GS	CG	GF	IP	BFP	H	R	ER	HR	SH	SF	HB	TBB	IBB	SO	WP	Bk	W	L	Pct.	ShO	Sv-Op	Hld	ERA
1990 Billings	R+	13	13	1	0	72.1	319	74	46	36	3	2	3	6	31	0	48	7	1	5	4	.556	1	0--	—	4.48
1991 Cedar Rapids	A	28	28	3	0	184.2	781	177	85	64	8	12	6	10	64	5	98	11	4	8	10	.444	3	0--	—	3.12
1992 Cedar Rapids	A	14	14	1	0	82.1	355	71	33	24	2	4	3	8	33	0	56	1	1	7	0	1.000	0	0--	—	2.62
Chattanooga	AA	14	14	1	0	87.1	368	86	34	22	5	2	1	4	34	1	56	5	2	6	5	.545	1	0--	—	2.27

139

Year Team	Lg	G	GS	CG	GF	IP	BFP	H	R	ER	HR	SH	SF	HB	TBB	IBB	SO	WP	Bk	W	L	Pct.	ShO	Sv-Op	Hld	ERA
1993 Indianapols	AAA	15	15	0	0	84.1	380	81	45	39	7	6	2	6	47	5	51	1	0	4	7	.364	0	0--	—	4.16
1994 Iowa	AAA	27	26	0	0	138.2	630	149	100	93	22	4	7	5	87	3	90	7	4	10	12	.455	0	0--	—	6.04
1995 Chattanooga	AA	28	21	0	4	118	514	112	71	61	7	6	6	7	59	1	87	1	0	10	6	.625	0	0--	—	4.65
1996 Chattanooga	AA	11	11	0	0	69.1	292	64	32	28	6	3	1	3	26	0	38	5	0	3	5	.375	0	0--	—	3.63
Indianapols	AAA	14	11	0	0	71.1	301	76	44	31	8	1	2	1	23	2	35	1	0	5	4	.556	0	0--	—	3.91
1997 Richmond	AAA	27	26	2	1	144	634	180	101	86	20	2	6	3	44	2	91	6	0	3	14	.176	0	0--	—	5.38
1998 Memphis	AAA	29	29	2	0	173.1	732	183	90	79	23	5	2	7	47	1	110	2	0	11	11	.500	2	0--	—	4.10
1999 Memphis	AAA	21	19	1	0	129.2	547	134	61	58	15	7	3	5	33	1	84	3	0	13	4	.765	1	0--	—	4.03
1993 Cincinnati	NL	14	14	0	0	77.1	332	74	49	39	7	4	5	1	38	3	38	4	0	2	5	.286	0	0-0	0	4.54
1999 St. Louis	NL	8	8	1	0	45.2	199	46	27	26	8	4	0	3	16	0	16	1	1	3	3	.500	0	0-0	0	5.12
2 ML YEARS		22	22	1	0	123	531	120	76	65	15	8	5	4	54	3	54	5	1	5	8	.385	0	0-0	0	4.76

Matt Luke

Bats: L **Throws:** L **Pos:** PH/PR-10; 1B-4; RF-4; LF-2   **Ht:** 6'5" **Wt:** 220 **Born:** 2/26/71 **Age:** 29

Year Team	Lg	G	AB	H	2B	3B	HR	(Hm	Rd)	TB	R	RBI	TBB	IBB	SO	HBP	SH	SF	SB	CS	SB%	GDP	Avg	OBP	SLG
1999 Edmonton *	AAA	6	21	9	2	1	5	—	—	28	7	15	6	1	4	0	0	0	0	0	.00	1	.429	.556	1.333
Lk Elsinore *	A+	13	53	18	5	3	0	—	—	29	10	7	7	1	14	0	0	0	2	1	1.00	0	.340	.426	.547
1996 New York	AL	1	0	0	0	0	0	(0	0)	0	1	0	0	0	0	0	0	0	0	0	.00	0	.000	.000	.000
1998 LA-Cle	AL	104	239	56	12	1	12	(7	5)	106	34	34	17	2	60	1	1	1	2	1	.67	4	.234	.287	.444
1999 Anaheim	AL	18	30	9	0	0	3	(0	3)	18	4	6	2	0	10	0	0	0	0	0	.00	2	.300	.344	.600
1998 Los Angeles	NL	102	237	56	12	1	12	(7	5)	106	34	34	17	2	60	1	1	1	2	1	.67	4	.236	.289	.447
Cleveland	AL	2	2	0	0	0	0	(0	0)	0	0	0	0	0	0	0	0	0	0	0	.00	0	.000	.000	.000
3 ML YEARS		123	269	65	12	1	15	(7	8)	124	39	40	19	2	70	1	1	1	2	1	.67	6	.242	.293	.461

David Lundquist

Pitches: Right **Bats:** Right **Pos:** RP-17   **Ht:** 6'2" **Wt:** 200 **Born:** 6/4/73 **Age:** 27

Year Team	Lg	G	GS	CG	GF	IP	BFP	H	R	ER	HR	SH	SF	HB	TBB	IBB	SO	WP	Bk	W	L	Pct.	ShO	Sv-Op	Hld	ERA
1993 White Sox	R	11	10	0	0	63	267	70	26	22	0	1	1	4	15	0	40	2	2	5	3	.625	0	0--	—	3.14
1994 Hickory	A	27	27	3	0	178.2	759	170	88	69	15	4	3	12	43	0	133	8	2	13	10	.565	2	0--	—	3.48
1995 South Bend	A	18	18	5	0	118	492	107	54	47	4	7	3	5	38	0	60	3	0	8	4	.667	1	0--	—	3.58
1996 White Sox	R	3	3	0	0	13.2	49	8	4	4	1	0	0	0	2	0	16	0	0	1	1	.500	0	0--	—	2.63
Pr William	A+	5	5	0	0	27	125	31	17	17	2	1	0	1	14	1	23	2	1	0	2	.000	0	0--	—	5.67
1997 Winston-Sal	A+	20	6	0	6	48	228	65	41	36	7	1	2	3	23	3	39	2	2	3	1	.750	0	0--	—	6.75
Birmingham	AA	7	0	0	5	13.1	73	26	20	13	3	0	1	0	5	0	15	0	0	0	0	.000	0	0--	—	8.78
1998 Winston-Sal	A+	6	0	0	2	10.2	42	9	4	3	0	1	0	0	3	0	9	0	0	1	0	1.000	0	0--	—	2.53
Birmingham	AA	33	0	0	21	41	165	28	15	15	1	2	1	2	15	1	41	1	0	1	1	.500	0	10--	—	3.29
Calgary	AAA	12	0	0	8	15	64	12	6	6	0	0	2	1	7	0	12	1	0	3	0	1.000	0	2--	—	3.60
1999 Charlotte	AAA	3	0	0	1	3.2	14	3	0	0	0	0	0	0	1	0	4	1	0	0	0	.000	0	0--	—	0.00
1999 Chicago	AL	17	0	0	7	22	106	28	21	21	3	2	1		12	0	18	0	0	1	1	.500	0	0-0	0	8.59

John Mabry

Bats: L **Throws:** R **Pos:** RF-35; 3B-24; 1B-20; PH/PR-9; LF-7; CF-2; DH-1   **Ht:** 6'4" **Wt:** 210 **Born:** 10/17/70 **Age:** 29

Year Team	Lg	G	AB	H	2B	3B	HR	(Hm	Rd)	TB	R	RBI	TBB	IBB	SO	HBP	SH	SF	SB	CS	SB%	GDP	Avg	OBP	SLG
1994 St. Louis	NL	6	23	7	3	0	0	(0	0)	10	2	3	2	0	4	0	0	0	0	0	.00	0	.304	.360	.435
1995 St. Louis	NL	129	388	119	21	1	5	(2	3)	157	35	41	24	5	45	2	0	4	0	3	.00	6	.307	.347	.405
1996 St. Louis	NL	151	543	161	30	2	13	(3	10)	234	63	74	37	11	84	3	3	5	3	2	.60	21	.297	.342	.431
1997 St. Louis	NL	116	388	110	19	0	5	(5	0)	144	40	36	39	9	77	3	2	2	0	1	.00	11	.284	.352	.371
1998 St. Louis	NL	142	377	94	22	0	9	(5	4)	143	41	46	30	6	76	1	3	2	0	2	.00	6	.249	.305	.379
1999 Seattle	AL	87	262	64	14	0	9	(5	4)	105	34	33	20	1	60	0	2	1	2	1	.67	6	.244	.297	.401
6 ML YEARS		631	1981	555	109	3	41	(19	22)	793	215	233	152	32	346	9	10	14	5	9	.36	50	.280	.332	.400

Mike Macfarlane

Bats: Right **Throws:** Right **Pos:** C-79; PH/PR-6; DH-1   **Ht:** 6'1" **Wt:** 210 **Born:** 4/12/64 **Age:** 36

Year Team	Lg	G	AB	H	2B	3B	HR	(Hm	Rd)	TB	R	RBI	TBB	IBB	SO	HBP	SH	SF	SB	CS	SB%	GDP	Avg	OBP	SLG
1987 Kansas City	AL	8	19	4	1	0	0	(0	0)	5	0	3	2	0	2	0	0	0	0	0	.00	1	.211	.286	.263
1988 Kansas City	AL	70	211	56	15	0	4	(2	2)	83	25	26	21	2	37	1	1	2	0	0	.00	8	.265	.332	.393
1989 Kansas City	AL	69	157	35	6	0	2	(0	2)	47	13	19	7	0	27	2	0	1	0	0	.00	8	.223	.263	.299
1990 Kansas City	AL	124	400	102	24	4	6	(1	5)	152	37	58	25	2	69	7	1	6	1	0	1.00	9	.255	.306	.380
1991 Kansas City	AL	84	267	74	18	2	13	(6	7)	135	34	41	17	0	52	6	1	4	1	0	1.00	4	.277	.330	.506
1992 Kansas City	AL	129	402	94	28	3	17	(7	10)	179	51	48	30	2	89	15	1	2	1	5	.17	8	.234	.310	.445
1993 Kansas City	AL	117	388	106	27	0	20	(7	13)	193	55	67	40	2	83	16	1	6	2	5	.29	8	.273	.360	.497
1994 Kansas City	AL	92	314	80	17	3	14	(9	5)	145	53	47	35	1	71	18	0	3	1	0	1.00	9	.255	.359	.462
1995 Boston	AL	115	364	82	18	1	15	(7	8)	147	45	51	38	0	78	14	0	4	2	1	.67	9	.225	.319	.404
1996 Kansas City	AL	112	379	104	24	2	19	(9	10)	189	58	54	31	5	57	7	0	2	3	3	.50	4	.274	.339	.499
1997 Kansas City	AL	82	257	61	14	2	8	(5	3)	103	34	35	24	3	47	6	3	1	0	2	.00	4	.237	.316	.401
1998 KC-Oak	AL	81	218	53	12	0	7	(5	2)	86	29	34	12	0	36	4	1	3	1	0	1.00	3	.243	.291	.394
1999 Oakland	AL	81	226	55	17	0	4	(0	4)	84	24	31	13	0	52	1	1	5	0	0	.00	7	.243	.282	.372
1998 Kansas City	AL	3	11	1	0	0	0	(0	0)	1	1	0	0	0	2	0	0	0	0	0	.00	0	.091	.091	.091
Oakland	AL	78	207	52	12	0	7	(5	2)	85	28	34	12	0	34	4	1	3	1	0	1.00	3	.251	.301	.411
13 ML YEARS		1164	3602	906	221	17	129	(58	71)	1548	458	514	295	17	700	97	10	39	12	16	.43	79	.252	.322	.430

Robert Machado

Bats: Right **Throws:** Right **Pos:** C-17; PH/PR-2

Ht: 6'1" **Wt:** 205 **Born:** 6/3/73 **Age:** 27

Year Team	Lg	G	AB	H	2B	3B	HR	(Hm	Rd)	TB	R	RBI	TBB	IBB	SO	HBP	SH	SF	SB	CS	SB%	GDP	Avg	OBP	SLG
1999 Charlotte *	AAA	16	54	11	3	0	2	—	—	20	4	7	4	0	13	2	0	0	0	0	.00	3	.204	.283	.370
Ottawa *	AAA	21	75	17	5	0	0	—	—	22	6	3	0	0	13	2	1	0	0	1	.00	2	.227	.247	.293
1996 Chicago	AL	4	6	4	1	0	0	(0	0)	5	1	2	0	0	0	0	0	0	0	0	.00	1	.667	.667	.833
1997 Chicago	AL	10	15	3	0	1	0	(0	0)	5	1	2	1	0	6	0	1	0	0	0	.00	0	.200	.250	.333
1998 Chicago	AL	34	111	23	6	0	3	(2	1)	38	14	15	7	0	22	0	3	0	0	0	.00	3	.207	.254	.342
1999 Montreal	NL	17	22	4	1	0	0	(0	0)	5	3	0	2	0	6	0	0	0	0	0	.00	0	.182	.250	.227
4 ML YEARS		65	154	34	8	1	3	(2	1)	53	19	19	10	0	34	0	4	0	0	0	.00	4	.221	.268	.344

Jose Macias

Bats: Both **Throws:** Right **Pos:** PH/PR-4; 2B-1

Ht: 5'10" **Wt:** 173 **Born:** 1/25/74 **Age:** 26

Year Team	Lg	G	AB	H	2B	3B	HR	(Hm	Rd)	TB	R	RBI	TBB	IBB	SO	HBP	SH	SF	SB	CS	SB%	GDP	Avg	OBP	SLG
1994 Expos	R	31	104	28	8	2	1	—	—	43	23	6	14	0	15	0	0	0	4	1	.80	3	.269	.356	.413
1995 Vermont	A-	53	176	42	4	2	0	—	—	50	24	9	19	0	19	2	2	0	11	7	.61	3	.239	.320	.284
1996 Delmarva	A	116	369	91	13	4	1	—	—	115	64	33	56	1	48	6	7	2	38	15	.72	2	.247	.353	.312
1997 Lakeland	A+	122	424	113	18	2	2	—	—	141	54	21	52	1	33	2	8	2	10	14	.42	10	.267	.348	.333
1998 Jacksnville	AA	128	511	156	28	10	12	—	—	240	82	71	52	2	46	4	3	3	9	4	.69	8	.305	.372	.470
1999 Toledo	AAA	112	438	107	18	8	2	—	—	147	44	36	36	0	60	4	5	2	10	5	.67	8	.244	.306	.336
1999 Detroit	AL	5	4	1	0	0	1	(1	0)	4	2	2	0	0	1	0	0	0	0	0	.00	0	.250	.250	1.000

Greg Maddux

Pitches: Right **Bats:** Right **Pos:** SP-33

Ht: 6'0" **Wt:** 185 **Born:** 4/14/66 **Age:** 34

Year Team	Lg	G	GS	CG	GF	IP	BFP	H	R	ER	HR	SH	SF	HB	TBB	IBB	SO	WP	Bk	W	L	Pct.	ShO	Sv-Op	Hld	ERA
1986 Chicago	NL	6	5	1	1	31	144	44	20	19	3	1	0	1	11	2	20	2	0	2	4	.333	0	0-0	0	5.52
1987 Chicago	NL	30	27	1	2	155.2	701	181	111	97	17	7	1	4	74	13	101	4	7	6	14	.300	1	0-0	0	5.61
1988 Chicago	NL	34	34	9	0	249	1047	230	97	88	13	11	2	9	81	16	140	3	6	18	8	.692	3	0-0	0	3.18
1989 Chicago	NL	35	35	7	0	238.1	1002	222	90	78	13	18	6	6	82	13	135	5	3	19	12	.613	1	0-0	0	2.95
1990 Chicago	NL	35	35	8	0	237	1011	242	116	91	11	18	5	4	71	10	144	3	3	15	15	.500	2	0-0	0	3.46
1991 Chicago	NL	37	37	7	0	263	1070	232	113	98	18	16	3	6	66	9	198	6	3	15	11	.577	2	0-0	0	3.35
1992 Chicago	NL	35	35	9	0	268	1061	201	68	65	7	15	3	14	70	7	199	5	0	20	11	.645	4	0-0	0	2.18
1993 Atlanta	NL	36	36	8	0	267	1064	228	85	70	14	15	7	6	52	7	197	5	1	20	10	.667	1	0-0	0	2.36
1994 Atlanta	NL	25	25	10	0	202	774	150	44	35	4	6	5	6	31	3	156	3	1	16	6	.727	3	0-0	0	1.56
1995 Atlanta	NL	28	28	10	0	209.2	785	147	39	38	8	9	1	4	23	3	181	1	0	19	2	.905	3	0-0	0	1.63
1996 Atlanta	NL	35	35	5	0	245	978	225	85	74	11	8	5	3	28	11	172	4	0	15	11	.577	1	0-0	0	2.72
1997 Atlanta	NL	33	33	5	0	232.2	893	200	58	57	9	11	7	6	20	6	177	0	0	19	4	.826	2	0-0	0	2.20
1998 Atlanta	NL	34	34	9	0	251	987	201	75	62	13	15	5	7	45	10	204	4	0	18	9	.667	5	0-0	0	2.22
1999 Atlanta	NL	33	33	4	0	219.1	940	258	103	87	16	15	5	4	37	8	136	1	0	19	9	.679	0	0-0	0	3.57
14 ML YEARS		436	432	93	3	3068.2	12457	2761	1104	959	157	165	55	80	691	118	2160	46	24	221	126	.637	28	0-0	0	2.81

Mike Maddux

Pitches: Right **Bats:** Left **Pos:** RP-53

Ht: 6'2" **Wt:** 185 **Born:** 8/27/61 **Age:** 38

Year Team	Lg	G	GS	CG	GF	IP	BFP	H	R	ER	HR	SH	SF	HB	TBB	IBB	SO	WP	Bk	W	L	Pct.	ShO	Sv-Op	Hld	ERA
1999 San Berndno *	A+	5	0	0	2	9	35	8	4	3	0	1	1	0	2	0	10	2	1	0	0	.000	0	2- —	1	3.00
1986 Philadelphia	NL	16	16	0	0	78	351	88	56	47	6	3	3	3	34	4	44	4	2	3	7	.300	0	0-0	0	5.42
1987 Philadelphia	NL	7	2	0	0	17	72	17	5	5	0	0	0	0	5	0	15	1	0	2	0	1.000	0	0-0	0	2.65
1988 Philadelphia	NL	25	11	0	4	88.2	380	91	41	37	6	7	3	5	34	4	59	4	2	4	3	.571	0	0-0	0	3.76
1989 Philadelphia	NL	16	4	2	1	43.2	191	52	29	25	3	3	1	2	14	3	26	3	1	1	3	.250	1	1-1	2	5.15
1990 Los Angeles	NL	11	2	0	3	20.2	88	24	15	15	3	0	1	1	4	0	11	2	0	0	0	1.000	0	0-0	1	6.53
1991 San Diego	NL	64	1	0	27	98.2	388	78	30	27	4	5	2	1	27	3	57	5	0	7	2	.778	0	5-7	9	2.46
1992 San Diego	NL	50	1	0	14	79.2	330	71	25	21	2	2	3	0	24	4	60	4	1	2	2	.500	0	5-9	8	2.37
1993 New York	NL	58	0	0	31	75	320	67	34	30	3	7	6	4	27	7	57	4	1	3	8	.273	0	5-11	3	3.60
1994 New York	NL	27	0	0	12	44	186	45	25	25	7	0	2	0	13	4	32	2	0	2	1	.667	0	2-4	1	5.11
1995 Pit-Bos		44	4	0	7	98.2	409	100	49	45	5	1	4	2	18	4	69	6	0	5	1	.833	0	1-1	6	4.10
1996 Boston	AL	23	7	0	2	64.1	295	76	37	32	12	3	2	5	27	2	32	1	0	3	2	.600	0	0-0	2	4.48
1997 Seattle	AL	6	0	0	1	10.2	59	20	12	12	1	0	0	1	8	2	7	1	0	1	0	1.000	0	0-0	0	10.13
1998 Montreal	NL	51	0	0	20	55.2	228	50	24	23	3	3	3	1	15	1	33	3	1	3	4	.429	0	1-2	7	3.72
1999 Mon-LA	NL	53	0	0	21	59.2	260	63	26	25	6	2	2	5	22	2	45	1	0	1	1	.500	0	0-0	10	3.77
1995 Pittsburgh	NL	8	0	0	1	9	42	14	9	9	0	0	0	2	3	1	4	1	0	1	0	1.000	0	0-0	2	9.00
Boston	AL	36	4	0	6	89.2	367	86	40	36	5	1	1	2	15	3	65	5	0	4	1	.800	0	1-1	4	3.61
1999 Montreal	NL	4	0	0	2	5	26	9	5	5	1	0	0	1	3	0	4	0	0	0	0	.000	0	0-0	0	9.00
Los Angeles	NL	49	0	0	19	54.2	234	54	21	20	5	2	2	4	19	2	41	1	0	1	1	.500	0	0-0	10	3.29
14 ML YEARS		451	48	2	143	834.1	3557	842	408	369	61	36	29	30	272	40	547	41	8	37	35	.514	1	20-35	49	3.98

Dave Magadan

Bats: Left **Throws:** Right **Pos:** 3B-52; 1B-42; PH/PR-41

Ht: 6'4" **Wt:** 215 **Born:** 9/30/62 **Age:** 37

Year Team	Lg	G	AB	H	2B	3B	HR	(Hm	Rd)	TB	R	RBI	TBB	IBB	SO	HBP	SH	SF	SB	CS	SB%	GDP	Avg	OBP	SLG
1986 New York	NL	10	18	8	0	0	0	(0	0)	8	3	3	3	0	1	0	0	0	0	0	.00	1	.444	.524	.444
1987 New York	NL	85	192	61	13	1	3	(2	1)	85	21	24	22	2	22	0	1	1	0	0	.00	5	.318	.386	.443

Year Team	Lg	G	AB	H	2B	3B	HR	(Hm	Rd)	TB	R	RBI	TBB	IBB	SO	HBP	SH	SF	SB	CS	SB%	GDP	Avg	OBP	SLG
1988 New York	NL	112	314	87	15	0	1	(1	0)	105	39	35	60	4	39	2	1	3	0	1	.00	9	.277	.393	.334
1989 New York	NL	127	374	107	22	3	4	(3	1)	147	47	41	49	6	37	1	1	4	1	0	1.00	2	.286	.367	.393
1990 New York	NL	144	451	148	28	6	6	(2	4)	206	74	72	74	4	55	2	4	10	2	1	.67	11	.328	.417	.457
1991 New York	NL	124	418	108	23	0	4	(2	2)	143	58	51	83	3	50	2	7	7	1	1	.50	5	.258	.378	.342
1992 New York	NL	99	321	91	9	1	3	(2	1)	111	33	28	56	3	44	0	2	0	1	0	1.00	6	.283	.390	.346
1993 Fla-Sea		137	455	124	23	0	5	(3	2)	162	49	50	80	7	63	1	2	6	2	1	.67	12	.273	.378	.356
1994 Florida	NL	74	211	58	7	0	1	(1	0)	68	30	17	39	0	25	1	0	3	0	0	.00	8	.275	.386	.322
1995 Houston	NL	127	348	109	24	0	2	(0	2)	139	44	51	71	9	56	0	1	2	2	1	.67	9	.313	.428	.399
1996 Chicago	NL	78	169	43	10	0	3	(2	1)	62	23	17	29	3	23	0	1	2	0	2	.00	3	.254	.360	.367
1997 Oakland	AL	128	271	82	10	1	4	(2	2)	106	38	30	50	1	40	2	4	1	1	0	1.00	7	.303	.414	.391
1998 Oakland	AL	35	109	35	8	0	1	(0	1)	46	12	13	13	1	12	0	0	1	0	1	.00	5	.321	.390	.422
1999 San Diego	NL	116	248	68	12	1	2	(1	1)	88	20	30	45	2	36	0	0	7	1	3	.25	10	.274	.377	.355
1993 Florida	NL	66	227	65	12	0	4	(3	1)	89	22	29	44	4	30	1	0	3	0	1	.00	3	.286	.400	.392
Seattle	AL	71	228	59	11	0	1	(0	1)	73	27	21	36	3	33	0	2	3	2	0	1.00	9	.259	.356	.320
14 ML YEARS		1396	3899	1129	204	13	39	(21	18)	1476	491	462	674	45	503	11	24	47	11	11	.50	93	.290	.392	.379

Wendell Magee

Bats: R **Throws:** R **Pos:** PH/PR-10; CF-2; LF-1; RF-1   **Ht:** 6'0" **Wt:** 220 **Born:** 8/3/72 **Age:** 27

Year Team	Lg	G	AB	H	2B	3B	HR	(Hm	Rd)	TB	R	RBI	TBB	IBB	SO	HBP	SH	SF	SB	CS	SB%	GDP	Avg	OBP	SLG
1999 Scranton-WB *	AAA	142	566	160	34	2	20	—	—	258	95	79	55	0	124	2	1	5	10	8	.56	12	.283	.346	.456
1996 Philadelphia	NL	38	142	29	7	0	2	(2	0)	42	9	14	9	0	33	0	0	0	0	0	.00	2	.204	.252	.296
1997 Philadelphia	NL	38	115	23	4	0	1	(0	1)	30	7	9	9	1	20	0	0	2	1	4	.20	8	.200	.254	.261
1998 Philadelphia	NL	20	75	22	6	1	1	(0	1)	33	9	11	7	0	11	0	0	0	0	0	.00	4	.293	.354	.440
1999 Philadelphia	NL	12	14	5	1	0	2	(1	1)	12	4	5	1	0	4	0	0	0	0	0	.00	1	.357	.400	.857
4 ML YEARS		108	346	79	18	1	6	(3	3)	117	29	39	26	1	68	0	0	2	1	4	.20	15	.228	.281	.338

Mike Magnante

Pitches: Left **Bats:** Left **Pos:** RP-53   **Ht:** 6'1" **Wt:** 185 **Born:** 6/17/65 **Age:** 35

Year Team	Lg	G	GS	CG	GF	IP	BFP	H	R	ER	HR	SH	SF	HB	TBB	IBB	SO	WP	Bk	W	L	Pct.	ShO	Sv-Op	Hld	ERA
1991 Kansas City	AL	38	0	0	10	55	236	55	19	15	3	2	1	0	23	3	42	1	0	0	1	.000	0	0-0	2	2.45
1992 Kansas City	AL	44	12	0	11	89.1	403	115	53	49	5	5	7	2	35	5	31	2	0	4	9	.308	0	0-3	4	4.94
1993 Kansas City	AL	7	6	0	0	35.1	145	37	16	16	3	1	1	1	11	1	16	1	0	1	2	.333	0	0-0	0	4.08
1994 Kansas City	AL	36	1	0	10	47	211	55	27	24	5	2	3	0	16	1	21	3	0	2	3	.400	0	0-0	6	4.60
1995 Kansas City	AL	28	0	0	7	44.2	190	45	23	21	6	2	2	2	16	1	28	2	0	1	1	.500	0	0-1	5	4.23
1996 Kansas City	AL	38	0	0	9	54	238	58	38	34	5	0	4	4	24	1	32	3	0	2	2	.500	0	0-1	5	5.67
1997 Houston	NL	40	0	0	14	47.2	191	39	16	12	2	3	2	0	11	2	43	2	2	3	1	.750	0	1-5	3	2.27
1998 Houston	NL	48	0	0	20	51.2	237	56	28	28	2	3	1	4	26	4	39	3	0	4	7	.364	0	2-4	4	4.88
1999 Anaheim	AL	53	0	0	13	69.1	299	68	30	26	2	0	7	3	29	4	44	3	1	5	2	.714	0	0-3	4	3.38
9 ML YEARS		332	19	0	94	494	2150	528	250	225	33	18	28	16	191	22	296	20	3	22	28	.440	0	3-17	32	4.10

Ron Mahay

Pitches: Left **Bats:** Left **Pos:** RP-5; SP-1   **Ht:** 6'2" **Wt:** 189 **Born:** 6/28/71 **Age:** 29

Year Team	Lg	G	GS	CG	GF	IP	BFP	H	R	ER	HR	SH	SF	HB	TBB	IBB	SO	WP	Bk	W	L	Pct.	ShO	Sv-Op	Hld	ERA
1999 Vancouver *	AAA	32	15	0	4	107	466	116	57	51	12	1	5	0	45	0	73	5	0	7	2	.778	0	0- -	—	4.29
1997 Boston	AL	28	0	0	7	25	105	19	7	7	3	1	0	0	11	0	22	3	0	3	0	1.000	0	0-1	5	2.52
1998 Boston	AL	29	0	0	6	26	120	26	16	10	2	0	4	2	15	1	14	3	0	1	1	.500	0	1-2	7	3.46
1999 Oakland	AL	6	1	0	2	19.1	68	8	4	4	2	0	0	0	3	0	15	0	0	2	0	1.000	0	1-1	0	1.86
3 ML YEARS		63	1	0	15	70.1	293	53	27	21	7	1	4	2	29	1	51	6	0	6	1	.857	0	2-4	12	2.69

Pat Mahomes

Pitches: Right **Bats:** Right **Pos:** RP-39   **Ht:** 6'4" **Wt:** 212 **Born:** 8/9/70 **Age:** 29

Year Team	Lg	G	GS	CG	GF	IP	BFP	H	R	ER	HR	SH	SF	HB	TBB	IBB	SO	WP	Bk	W	L	Pct.	ShO	Sv-Op	Hld	ERA
1999 Norfolk *	AAA	6	6	0	0	38.2	164	38	17	15	6	0	1	0	12	1	24	1	0	4	1	.800	0	0- -	—	3.49
1992 Minnesota	AL	14	13	0	1	69.2	302	73	41	39	5	0	3	0	37	0	44	2	1	3	4	.429	0	0-0	0	5.04
1993 Minnesota	AL	12	5	0	4	37.1	173	47	34	32	8	1	3	1	16	0	23	3	0	1	5	.167	0	0-0	0	7.71
1994 Minnesota	AL	21	21	0	0	120	517	121	68	63	22	1	4	1	62	1	53	3	0	9	5	.643	0	0-0	0	4.73
1995 Minnesota	AL	47	7	0	16	94.2	423	100	74	67	22	3	2	2	47	1	67	6	0	4	10	.286	0	3-7	9	6.37
1996 Min-Bos	AL	31	5	0	10	57.1	271	72	46	44	13	2	2	0	33	0	36	2	0	3	4	.429	0	2-2	6	6.91
1997 Boston	AL	10	0	0	2	10	54	15	10	9	2	0	1	2	10	1	5	1	0	1	0	1.000	0	0-0	1	8.10
1999 New York	NL	39	0	0	12	63.2	265	44	26	26	1	1	2	2	37	5	51	2	0	8	0	1.000	0	0-1	1	3.68
1996 Minnesota	AL	20	5	0	5	45	220	63	38	36	10	0	2	0	27	0	30	2	0	1	4	.200	0	0-0	3	7.20
Boston	AL	11	0	0	5	12.1	51	9	8	8	3	2	0	0	6	0	6	0	0	2	0	1.000	0	2-2	3	5.84
7 ML YEARS		174	51	0	45	452.2	2005	472	299	280	79	8	17	8	242	8	279	19	1	29	28	.509	0	5-10	15	5.57

Matt Mantei

Pitches: Right **Bats:** Right **Pos:** RP-65   **Ht:** 6'1" **Wt:** 190 **Born:** 7/7/73 **Age:** 26

Year Team	Lg	HOW MUCH HE PITCHED						WHAT HE GAVE UP										THE RESULTS					
		G	GS	CG	GF	IP	BFP	H	R	ER	HR	SH	SF	HB	TBB	IBB	SO	WP	Bk	W	L	Pct.	ShO	Sv-Op	Hld	ERA
1995 Florida	NL	12	0	0	3	13.1	64	12	8	7	1	1	1	0	13	0	15	1	0	0	1	.000	0	0-0	0	4.73
1996 Florida	NL	14	0	0	1	18.1	89	13	13	13	2	1	0	1	21	1	25	2	0	1	0	1.000	0	0-1	0	6.38
1998 Florida	NL	42	0	0	23	54.2	224	38	19	18	1	3	4	7	23	3	63	0	0	3	4	.429	0	9-12	2	2.96
1999 Fla-Ari	NL	65	0	0	60	65.1	284	44	21	20	5	1	1	5	44	1	99	2	0	1	3	.250	0	32-37	0	2.76
1999 Florida	NL	35	0	0	32	36.1	157	24	11	11	4	0	1	2	25	1	50	0	0	1	2	.333	0	10-12	0	2.72
Arizona	NL	30	0	0	28	29	127	20	10	9	1	1	0	3	19	0	49	2	0	0	1	.000	0	22-25	0	2.79
4 ML YEARS		133	0	0	87	151.2	661	107	61	58	9	6	6	13	101	5	202	5	0	5	8	.385	0	41-50	2	3.44

Jeff Manto

Bats: Right **Throws:** Right **Pos:** 3B-11; PH/PR-6; 1B-4   **Ht:** 6'3" **Wt:** 210 **Born:** 8/23/64 **Age:** 35

Year Team	Lg	BATTING																	BASERUNNING				PERCENTAGES		
		G	AB	H	2B	3B	HR	(Hm	Rd)	TB	R	RBI	TBB	IBB	SO	HBP	SH	SF	SB	CS	SB%	GDP	Avg	OBP	SLG
1999 Buffalo *	AAA	66	203	60	9	0	23	—	—	138	47	44	66	1	47	3	0	1	3	1	.75	4	.296	.473	.680
1990 Cleveland	AL	30	76	17	5	1	2	(1	1)	30	12	14	21	1	18	0	0	0	0	1	.00	0	.224	.392	.395
1991 Cleveland	AL	47	128	27	7	0	2	(0	2)	40	15	13	14	0	22	4	1	1	2	0	1.00	3	.211	.306	.313
1993 Philadelphia	NL	8	18	1	0	0	0	(0	0)	1	0	0	0	0	3	1	0	0	0	0	.00	0	.056	.105	.056
1995 Baltimore	AL	89	254	65	9	0	17	(12	5)	125	31	38	24	0	69	2	0	0	0	3	.00	6	.256	.325	.492
1996 Bos-Sea	AL	43	102	20	6	1	3	(3	0)	37	15	10	17	0	24	1	0	0	0	1	.00	2	.196	.317	.363
1997 Cleveland	AL	16	30	8	3	0	2	(2	0)	17	3	7	1	0	10	0	0	0	0	0	.00	0	.267	.290	.567
1998 Cle-Det	AL	31	67	16	3	0	3	(1	2)	28	14	9	5	0	21	1	0	0	1	1	.50	5	.239	.301	.418
1999 Cle-NYY	AL	18	33	6	0	0	1	(1	0)	9	5	2	13	0	15	0	1	0	0	0	.00	0	.182	.413	.273
1996 Boston	AL	22	48	10	3	1	2	(2	0)	21	8	6	8	0	12	1	0	0	0	0	.00	0	.208	.333	.438
Seattle	AL	21	54	10	3	0	1	(1	0)	16	7	4	9	0	12	0	0	0	0	1	.00	2	.185	.302	.296
1998 Cleveland	AL	15	37	8	1	0	2	(1	1)	15	8	6	2	0	10	0	0	0	0	1	.00	1	.216	.256	.405
Detroit	AL	16	30	8	2	0	1	(0	1)	13	6	3	3	0	11	1	0	0	1	0	1.00	4	.267	.353	.433
1999 Cleveland	AL	12	25	5	0	0	1	(1	0)	8	5	2	11	0	11	0	1	0	0	0	.00	0	.200	.444	.320
New York	AL	6	8	1	0	0	0	(0	0)	1	0	0	2	0	4	0	0	0	0	0	.00	0	.125	.300	.125
8 ML YEARS		282	708	160	33	2	30	(20	10)	287	95	93	95	1	182	9	2	1	3	6	.33	18	.226	.325	.405

Kirt Manwaring

Bats: Right **Throws:** Right **Pos:** C-44; PH/PR-4; DH-1   **Ht:** 5'11" **Wt:** 198 **Born:** 7/15/65 **Age:** 34

Year Team	Lg	BATTING																	BASERUNNING				PERCENTAGES		
		G	AB	H	2B	3B	HR	(Hm	Rd)	TB	R	RBI	TBB	IBB	SO	HBP	SH	SF	SB	CS	SB%	GDP	Avg	OBP	SLG
1999 Colo Sprngs *	AAA	7	22	5	0	0	1	—	—	8	3	2	1	0	2	0	0	0	0	0	.00	1	.227	.261	.364
1987 San Francisco	NL	6	7	1	0	0	0	(0	0)	1	0	0	0	0	1	1	0	0	0	0	.00	1	.143	.250	.143
1988 San Francisco	NL	40	116	29	7	1	0	(0	1)	39	12	15	2	0	21	3	1	1	0	1	.00	1	.250	.279	.336
1989 San Francisco	NL	85	200	42	4	2	0	(0	0)	50	14	18	11	1	28	4	7	1	2	1	.67	5	.210	.264	.250
1990 San Francisco	NL	8	13	2	0	1	0	(0	0)	4	0	1	0	0	3	0	0	0	0	0	.00	0	.154	.154	.308
1991 San Francisco	NL	67	178	40	9	0	0	(0	0)	49	16	19	9	0	22	3	7	2	1	1	.50	2	.225	.271	.275
1992 San Francisco	NL	109	349	85	10	5	4	(1	3)	117	24	26	29	0	42	5	6	0	2	1	.67	12	.244	.311	.335
1993 San Francisco	NL	130	432	119	15	1	5	(3	2)	151	48	49	41	13	76	6	5	2	1	3	.25	14	.275	.345	.350
1994 San Francisco	NL	97	316	79	17	1	1	(0	1)	101	30	29	25	3	50	3	4	3	1	1	.50	10	.250	.308	.320
1995 San Francisco	NL	118	379	95	15	2	4	(4	0)	126	21	36	27	6	72	10	4	4	1	0	1.00	6	.251	.314	.332
1996 SF-Hou	NL	86	227	52	9	0	1	(1	0)	64	14	18	19	1	40	5	2	2	0	1	.00	4	.229	.300	.282
1997 Colorado	NL	104	337	76	6	4	1	(1	0)	93	22	27	30	0	78	2	4	2	1	5	.17	10	.226	.291	.276
1998 Colorado	NL	110	291	72	12	3	2	(1	1)	96	30	26	38	3	49	3	2	1	1	5	.17	11	.247	.339	.330
1999 Colorado	NL	48	137	41	7	1	2	(1	1)	56	17	14	12	1	23	5	0	1	0	0	.00	4	.299	.374	.409
1996 San Francisco	NL	49	145	34	6	0	1	(1	0)	43	9	14	16	1	24	3	1	0	0	1	.00	2	.234	.319	.297
Houston	NL	37	82	18	3	0	0	(0	0)	21	5	4	3	0	16	2	1	0	0	0	.00	2	.220	.264	.256
13 ML YEARS		1008	2982	733	111	20	21	(12	9)	947	248	278	243	28	505	50	42	19	10	19	.34	82	.246	.311	.318

Josias Manzanillo

Pitches: Right **Bats:** Right **Pos:** RP-12   **Ht:** 6'0" **Wt:** 190 **Born:** 10/16/67 **Age:** 32

Year Team	Lg	HOW MUCH HE PITCHED						WHAT HE GAVE UP											THE RESULTS					
		G	GS	CG	GF	IP	BFP	H	R	ER	HR	SH	SF	HB	TBB	IBB	SO	WP	Bk	W	L	Pct.	ShO	Sv-Op	Hld	ERA
1991 Boston	AL	1	0	0	1	1	8	2	2	2	0	0	0	0	3	0	1	0	0	0	0	.000	0	0-0	0	18.00
1993 Mil-NYM		16	1	0	6	29	140	30	27	22	2	3	3	2	19	3	21	1	0	1	1	.500	0	1-2	0	6.83
1994 New York	NL	37	0	0	14	47.1	186	34	15	14	4	0	0	3	13	2	48	2	0	3	2	.600	0	2-5	11	2.66
1995 NYM-NYY		23	0	0	8	33.1	154	37	19	18	4	2	1	2	15	4	25	6	0	1	2	.333	0	0-0	0	4.86
1997 Seattle	AL	16	0	0	4	18.1	88	19	13	11	3	0	2	0	17	1	18	2	0	0	1	.000	0	0-1	1	5.40
1999 New York	NL	12	0	0	1	18.2	80	19	12	12	5	1	1	2	4	1	25	0	0	0	0	.000	0	0-0	1	5.79
1993 Milwaukee	AL	10	1	0	4	17	86	22	20	18	1	2	2	2	10	3	10	1	0	1	1	.500	0	1-2	0	9.53
New York	NL	6	0	0	2	12	54	8	7	4	1	1	1	0	9	0	11	0	0	0	0	.000	0	0-0	0	3.00
1995 New York	NL	12	0	0	4	16	73	18	15	14	3	0	1	0	6	2	14	5	0	1	2	.333	0	0-0	0	7.88
New York	AL	11	0	0	4	17.1	81	19	4	4	1	2	0	2	9	2	11	1	0	0	0	.000	0	0-0	0	2.08
6 ML YEARS		105	1	0	34	147.2	656	141	88	79	18	6	7	9	71	11	138	11	0	5	6	.455	0	3-8	13	4.81

Eli Marrero

Bats: Right **Throws:** Right **Pos:** C-96; 1B-20; PH/PR-19 **Ht:** 6'1" **Wt:** 180 **Born:** 11/17/73 **Age:** 26

Year Team	Lg	G	AB	H	2B	3B	HR	(Hm	Rd)	TB	R	RBI	TBB	IBB	SO	HBP	SH	SF	SB	CS	SB%	GDP	Avg	OBP	SLG
1997 St. Louis	NL	17	45	11	2	0	2	(0	2)	19	4	7	2	1	13	0	0	1	4	0	1.00	1	.244	.271	.422
1998 St. Louis	NL	83	254	62	18	1	4	(2	2)	94	28	20	28	5	42	0	1	1	6	2	.75	5	.244	.318	.370
1999 St. Louis	NL	114	317	61	13	1	6	(3	3)	94	32	34	18	4	56	1	4	3	11	2	.85	14	.192	.236	.297
3 ML YEARS		214	616	134	33	2	12	(5	7)	207	64	61	48	10	111	1	5	5	21	4	.84	20	.218	.273	.336

Damaso Marte

Pitches: Left **Bats:** Left **Pos:** RP-5 **Ht:** 6'0" **Wt:** 170 **Born:** 2/14/75 **Age:** 25

		HOW MUCH HE PITCHED						WHAT HE GAVE UP											THE RESULTS						
Year Team	Lg	G	GS	CG	GF	IP	BFP	H	R	ER	HR	SH	SF	HB	TBB	IBB	SO	WP	Bk	W	L	Pct.	ShO	Sv-Op	Hld	ERA
1995 Everett	A-	11	5	0	1	36.2	141	25	11	9	2	1	1	1	10	0	39	3	0	2	2	.500	0	0- -	—	2.21
1996 Wisconsin	A	26	26	2	0	142.1	626	134	82	71	8	1	3	6	75	5	115	4	3	8	6	.571	1	0- -	—	4.49
1997 Lancaster	A+	25	25	2	0	139.1	609	144	75	64	15	4	4	8	62	1	127	8	4	8	8	.500	1	0- -	—	4.13
1998 Orlando	AA	22	20	0	0	121.1	541	136	82	71	14	2	6	2	47	0	99	6	2	7	6	.538	0	0- -	—	5.27
1999 Tacoma	AAA	31	11	0	4	73.2	335	79	43	42	13	1	1	2	40	1	59	1	2	3	3	.500	0	0- -	—	5.13
1999 Seattle	AL	5	0	0	2	8.2	47	16	9	9	3	0	0	0	6	0	3	0	0	0	1	.000	0	0-0	0	9.35

Al Martin

Bats: Left **Throws:** Left **Pos:** LF-134; PH/PR-13 **Ht:** 6'2" **Wt:** 214 **Born:** 11/24/67 **Age:** 32

Year Team	Lg	G	AB	H	2B	3B	HR	(Hm	Rd)	TB	R	RBI	TBB	IBB	SO	HBP	SH	SF	SB	CS	SB%	GDP	Avg	OBP	SLG
1992 Pittsburgh	NL	12	12	2	0	1	0	(0	0)	4	1	2	0	0	5	0	0	1	0	0	.00	0	.167	.154	.333
1993 Pittsburgh	NL	143	480	135	26	8	18	(15	3)	231	85	64	42	5	122	1	2	3	16	9	.64	5	.281	.338	.481
1994 Pittsburgh	NL	82	276	79	12	4	9	(6	3)	126	48	33	34	3	56	2	0	1	15	6	.71	3	.286	.367	.457
1995 Pittsburgh	NL	124	439	124	25	3	13	(8	5)	194	70	41	44	6	92	2	1	0	20	11	.65	5	.282	.351	.442
1996 Pittsburgh	NL	155	630	189	40	1	18	(8	10)	285	101	72	54	2	116	2	1	7	38	12	.76	9	.300	.354	.452
1997 Pittsburgh	NL	113	423	123	24	7	13	(8	5)	200	64	59	45	7	83	3	1	5	23	7	.77	7	.291	.359	.473
1998 Pittsburgh	NL	125	440	105	15	2	12	(5	7)	160	57	47	32	2	91	5	0	2	20	3	.87	13	.239	.296	.364
1999 Pittsburgh	NL	143	541	150	36	8	24	(12	12)	274	97	63	49	5	119	1	0	2	20	3	.87	8	.277	.337	.506
8 ML YEARS		897	3241	907	178	34	107	(62	45)	1474	523	381	300	30	684	16	5	21	152	51	.75	50	.280	.342	.455

Norberto Martin

Bats: Right **Throws:** Right **Pos:** 2B-8; SS-1 **Ht:** 5'10" **Wt:** 182 **Born:** 12/10/66 **Age:** 33

Year Team	Lg	G	AB	H	2B	3B	HR	(Hm	Rd)	TB	R	RBI	TBB	IBB	SO	HBP	SH	SF	SB	CS	SB%	GDP	Avg	OBP	SLG
1999 Syracuse *	AAA	81	319	94	11	2	5	—	—	124	45	34	12	0	33	2	3	2	14	1	.93	9	.295	.322	.389
1993 Chicago	AL	8	14	5	0	0	0	(0	0)	5	3	2	1	0	1	0	0	0	0	0	.00	0	.357	.400	.357
1994 Chicago	AL	45	131	36	7	1	1	(0	1)	48	19	16	9	0	16	0	3	2	4	2	.67	3	.275	.317	.366
1995 Chicago	AL	72	160	43	7	4	2	(1	1)	64	17	17	3	0	25	1	2	3	5	0	1.00	5	.269	.281	.400
1996 Chicago	AL	70	140	49	7	0	1	(0	1)	59	30	14	6	0	17	0	4	1	10	2	.83	4	.350	.374	.421
1997 Chicago	AL	71	213	64	7	1	2	(1	1)	79	24	27	6	0	31	0	0	0	1	4	.20	7	.300	.320	.371
1998 Anaheim	AL	79	195	42	2	0	1	(0	1)	47	20	13	6	0	29	0	3	2	3	1	.75	9	.215	.236	.241
1999 Toronto	AL	9	27	6	2	0	0	(0	0)	8	3	0	4	0	4	2	0	0	0	0	.00	0	.222	.364	.296
7 ML YEARS		354	880	245	32	6	7	(2	5)	310	116	89	35	0	123	3	12	8	23	9	.72	24	.278	.306	.352

Tom Martin

Pitches: Left **Bats:** Left **Pos:** RP-6 **Ht:** 6'1" **Wt:** 200 **Born:** 5/21/70 **Age:** 30

		HOW MUCH HE PITCHED						WHAT HE GAVE UP											THE RESULTS						
Year Team	Lg	G	GS	CG	GF	IP	BFP	H	R	ER	HR	SH	SF	HB	TBB	IBB	SO	WP	Bk	W	L	Pct.	ShO	Sv-Op	Hld	ERA
1999 Akron *	AA	3	3	0	0	9	34	4	1	1	0	1	0	1	3	0	9	0	0	0	0	.000	0	0- -	—	1.00
Buffalo *	AAA	5	0	0	1	6	25	5	2	2	1	0	0	0	1	0	6	0	0	1	0	1.000	0	0- -	—	3.00
1997 Houston	NL	55	0	0	18	56	236	52	13	13	2	6	1	1	23	2	36	3	0	5	3	.625	0	2-3	7	2.09
1998 Cleveland	AL	14	0	0	1	14.2	85	29	21	21	3	1	1	0	12	0	9	2	0	1	1	.500	0	0-0	3	12.89
1999 Cleveland	AL	6	0	0	0	9.1	44	13	9	9	2	0	1	0	3	1	8	0	0	0	1	.000	0	0-0	0	8.68
3 ML YEARS		75	0	0	19	80	365	94	43	43	7	7	3	1	38	3	53	5	0	6	5	.545	0	2-3	10	4.84

Dave Martinez

Bats: L **Throws:** L **Pos:** RF-93; CF-52; PH/PR-4; LF-2 **Ht:** 5'10" **Wt:** 190 **Born:** 9/26/64 **Age:** 35

Year Team	Lg	G	AB	H	2B	3B	HR	(Hm	Rd)	TB	R	RBI	TBB	IBB	SO	HBP	SH	SF	SB	CS	SB%	GDP	Avg	OBP	SLG
1986 Chicago	NL	53	108	15	1	1	1	(1	0)	21	13	7	6	0	22	1	0	1	4	2	.67	1	.139	.190	.194
1987 Chicago	NL	142	459	134	18	8	8	(5	3)	192	70	36	57	4	96	2	1	4	16	8	.67	4	.292	.372	.418
1988 ChC-Mon	NL	138	447	114	13	6	6	(2	4)	157	51	46	38	8	94	2	2	5	23	9	.72	3	.255	.313	.351
1989 Montreal	NL	126	361	99	16	7	3	(1	2)	138	41	27	27	2	57	0	7	1	23	4	.85	1	.274	.324	.382
1990 Montreal	NL	118	391	109	13	5	11	(5	6)	165	60	39	24	2	48	1	3	2	13	11	.54	3	.279	.321	.422
1991 Montreal	NL	124	396	117	18	5	7	(3	4)	166	47	42	20	3	54	3	5	3	16	7	.70	3	.295	.332	.419
1992 Cincinnati	NL	135	393	100	20	5	3	(3	0)	139	47	31	42	4	54	0	6	4	12	8	.60	6	.254	.323	.354
1993 San Francisco	NL	91	241	58	12	1	5	(1	4)	87	28	27	27	3	39	0	0	0	6	3	.67	5	.241	.317	.361
1994 San Francisco	NL	97	235	58	9	3	4	(1	3)	85	23	27	21	1	22	2	2	0	3	4	.43	6	.247	.314	.362

Year Team	Lg	G	AB	H	2B	3B	HR	(Hm	Rd)	TB	R	RBI	TBB	IBB	SO	HBP	SH	SF	SB	CS	SB%	GDP	Avg	OBP	SLG
								BATTING											**BASERUNNING**				**PERCENTAGES**		
1995 Chicago	AL	119	303	93	16	4	5	(2	3)	132	49	37	32	2	41	1	9	4	8	2	.80	6	.307	.371	.436
1996 Chicago	AL	146	440	140	20	8	10	(3	7)	206	85	53	52	1	52	3	2	1	15	7	.68	4	.318	.393	.468
1997 Chicago	AL	145	504	144	16	6	12	(5	7)	208	78	55	55	7	69	3	5	6	12	6	.67	4	.286	.356	.413
1998 Tampa Bay	AL	90	309	79	11	0	3	(2	1)	99	31	20	35	4	52	2	0	1	8	7	.53	5	.256	.334	.320
1999 Tampa Bay	AL	143	514	146	25	5	6	(2	4)	199	79	66	60	3	76	5	10	5	13	6	.68	6	.284	.361	.387
1988 Chicago	NL	75	256	65	10	1	4	(2	2)	89	27	34	21	5	46	2	0	4	7	3	.70	2	.254	.311	.348
Montreal		63	191	49	3	5	2	(0	2)	68	24	12	17	3	48	0	2	1	16	6	.73	1	.257	.316	.356
14 ML YEARS		1667	5101	1406	208	64	84	(36	48)	1994	702	513	496	44	776	25	52	34	172	84	.67	62	.276	.341	.391

Edgar Martinez

Bats: Right **Throws:** Right **Pos:** DH-134; 1B-5; PH/PR-3 **Ht:** 5'11" **Wt:** 200 **Born:** 1/2/63 **Age:** 37

Year Team	Lg	G	AB	H	2B	3B	HR	(Hm	Rd)	TB	R	RBI	TBB	IBB	SO	HBP	SH	SF	SB	CS	SB%	GDP	Avg	OBP	SLG
								BATTING											**BASERUNNING**				**PERCENTAGES**		
1987 Seattle	AL	13	43	16	5	2	0	(0	0)	25	6	5	2	0	5	1	0	0	0	0	.00	0	.372	.413	.581
1988 Seattle	AL	14	32	9	4	0	0	(0	0)	13	0	5	4	0	7	0	1	1	0	0	.00	0	.281	.351	.406
1989 Seattle	AL	65	171	41	5	0	2	(0	2)	52	20	20	17	1	26	3	2	3	2	1	.67	3	.240	.314	.304
1990 Seattle	AL	144	487	147	27	2	11	(8	3)	211	71	49	74	3	62	5	1	3	1	4	.20	13	.302	.397	.433
1991 Seattle	AL	150	544	167	35	1	14	(8	6)	246	98	52	84	9	72	8	2	4	0	3	.00	19	.307	.405	.452
1992 Seattle	AL	135	528	181	46	3	18	(11	7)	287	100	73	54	2	61	4	1	5	14	4	.78	15	.343	.404	.544
1993 Seattle	AL	42	135	32	7	0	4	(1	3)	51	20	13	28	1	19	0	1	1	0	0	.00	4	.237	.366	.378
1994 Seattle	AL	89	326	93	23	1	13	(4	9)	157	47	51	53	3	42	3	2	3	6	2	.75	2	.285	.387	.482
1995 Seattle	AL	145	511	182	52	0	29	(16	13)	321	121	113	116	19	87	8	0	4	4	3	.57	11	.356	.479	.628
1996 Seattle	AL	139	499	163	52	2	26	(14	12)	297	121	103	123	12	84	8	0	4	3	3	.50	15	.327	.464	.595
1997 Seattle	AL	155	542	179	35	1	28	(12	16)	300	104	108	119	11	86	11	0	6	2	4	.33	21	.330	.456	.554
1998 Seattle	AL	154	556	179	46	1	29	(17	12)	314	86	102	106	4	96	3	0	7	1	1	.50	13	.322	.429	.565
1999 Seattle	AL	142	502	169	35	1	24	(12	12)	278	86	86	97	6	99	6	0	3	7	2	.78	12	.337	.447	.554
13 ML YEARS		1387	4876	1558	372	14	198	(98	100)	2552	880	780	877	71	746	60	10	44	40	27	.60	128	.320	.426	.523

Felix Martinez

Bats: Both **Throws:** Right **Pos:** PH/PR-4; SS-2; 2B-1 **Ht:** 6'0" **Wt:** 180 **Born:** 5/18/74 **Age:** 26

Year Team	Lg	G	AB	H	2B	3B	HR	(Hm	Rd)	TB	R	RBI	TBB	IBB	SO	HBP	SH	SF	SB	CS	SB%	GDP	Avg	OBP	SLG
								BATTING											**BASERUNNING**				**PERCENTAGES**		
1993 Royals	R	57	165	42	5	1	0	—	—	49	23	12	17	0	26	3	1	0	22	5	.81	2	.255	.335	.297
1994 Wilmington	A+	117	400	107	16	4	2	—	—	137	65	43	30	0	91	3	12	2	19	8	.70	10	.268	.322	.343
1995 Wichita	AA	127	426	112	15	3	3	—	—	142	53	30	31	0	71	6	4	1	44	20	.69	5	.263	.321	.333
1996 Omaha	AAA	118	395	93	13	3	5	—	—	127	54	35	44	0	79	5	10	0	18	10	.64	11	.235	.320	.322
1997 Omaha	AAA	112	410	104	19	4	2	—	—	137	55	36	29	0	86	7	5	1	21	11	.66	11	.254	.313	.334
1998 Omaha	AAA	51	164	41	8	3	2	—	—	61	27	16	15	0	40	1	5	1	6	2	.75	1	.250	.315	.372
1999 Omaha	AAA	8	23	7	5	0	0	—	—	12	2	2	2	0	6	0	1	0	1	0	.00	0	.304	.360	.522
Wichita	AA	87	327	88	22	2	4	—	—	126	57	37	37	0	43	3	8	3	19	12	.61	8	.269	.346	.385
1997 Kansas City	AL	16	31	7	1	1	0	(0	0)	10	3	3	6	0	8	0	1	0	0	0	.00	1	.226	.351	.323
1998 Kansas City	AL	34	85	11	1	1	0	(0	0)	14	7	5	5	0	21	1	4	0	3	1	.75	1	.129	.187	.165
1999 Kansas City	AL	6	7	1	0	0	0	(0	0)	1	1	0	0	0	0	0	0	0	0	0	.00	1	.143	.143	.143
3 ML YEARS		56	123	19	2	2	0	(0	0)	25	11	8	11	0	29	1	5	0	3	1	.75	3	.154	.230	.203

Manny Martinez

Bats: Right **Throws:** Right **Pos:** CF-126; PH/PR-22; RF-1 **Ht:** 6'2" **Wt:** 185 **Born:** 10/3/70 **Age:** 29

Year Team	Lg	G	AB	H	2B	3B	HR	(Hm	Rd)	TB	R	RBI	TBB	IBB	SO	HBP	SH	SF	SB	CS	SB%	GDP	Avg	OBP	SLG
								BATTING											**BASERUNNING**				**PERCENTAGES**		
1996 Sea-Phi		22	53	12	2	3	0	(0	0)	20	5	3	4	0	16	1	1	0	4	1	.80	2	.226	.293	.377
1998 Pittsburgh	NL	73	180	45	11	2	6	(5	1)	78	21	24	9	0	44	2	3	2	0	3	.00	3	.250	.290	.433
1999 Montreal	NL	137	331	81	12	7	2	(1	1)	113	48	26	17	0	51	0	6	3	19	6	.76	5	.245	.279	.341
1996 Seattle	AL	9	17	4	2	1	0	(0	0)	8	3	3	3	0	5	0	0	0	2	0	1.00	1	.235	.350	.471
Philadelphia	NL	13	36	8	0	2	0	(0	0)	12	2	0	1	0	11	1	1	0	2	1	.67	1	.222	.263	.333
3 ML YEARS		232	564	138	25	12	8	(6	2)	211	74	53	30	0	111	3	10	5	23	10	.70	10	.245	.284	.374

Pedro Martinez

Pitches: Right **Bats:** Right **Pos:** SP-29; RP-2 **Ht:** 5'11" **Wt:** 170 **Born:** 10/25/71 **Age:** 28

Year Team	Lg	G	GS	CG	GF	IP	BFP	H	R	ER	HR	SH	SF	HB	TBB	IBB	SO	WP	Bk	W	L	Pct.	ShO	Sv-Op	Hld	ERA
				HOW MUCH HE PITCHED							**WHAT HE GAVE UP**											**THE RESULTS**				
1992 Los Angeles	NL	2	1	0	1	8	31	6	2	2	0	0	0	0	1	0	8	0	0	0	1	.000	0	0-0	0	2.25
1993 Los Angeles	NL	65	2	0	20	107	444	76	34	31	5	0	5	4	57	4	119	3	1	10	5	.667	0	2-3	14	2.61
1994 Montreal	NL	24	23	1	1	144.2	584	115	58	55	11	2	3	11	45	3	142	6	0	11	5	.688	1	1-1	0	3.42
1995 Montreal	NL	30	30	2	0	194.2	784	158	79	76	21	7	3	11	66	1	174	5	2	14	10	.583	2	0-0	0	3.51
1996 Montreal	NL	33	33	4	0	216.2	901	189	100	89	19	9	6	3	70	3	222	6	0	13	10	.565	1	0-0	0	3.70
1997 Montreal	NL	31	31	13	0	241.1	947	158	65	51	16	9	1	9	67	5	305	3	1	17	8	.680	4	0-0	0	1.90
1998 Boston	AL	33	33	3	0	233.2	951	188	82	75	26	4	7	8	67	3	251	9	0	19	7	.731	2	0-0	0	2.89
1999 Boston	AL	31	29	5	1	213.1	835	160	56	49	9	3	6	9	37	1	313	6	0	23	4	.852	1	0-0	0	2.07
8 ML YEARS		249	182	28	23	1359.1	5477	1050	476	428	107	34	31	55	410	20	1534	38	4	107	50	.682	11	3-4	14	2.83

Ramon Martinez

Pitches: Right **Bats:** Both **Pos:** SP-4   **Ht:** 6'4" **Wt:** 184 **Born:** 3/22/68 **Age:** 32

		HOW MUCH HE PITCHED						WHAT HE GAVE UP											THE RESULTS					
Year Team	Lg	G	GS	CG	GF	IP	BFP	H	R	ER	HR	SH	SF	HB	TBB	IBB	SO	WP	Bk	W	L	Pct.	ShO	Sv-Op	Hld	ERA
1999 Lowell *	A-	1	1	0	0	2	7	0	0	0	0	0	0	0	0	0	3	0	0	0	0	.000	0	0- -	—	0.00
Red Sox *	R	4	4	0	0	13	51	9	4	2	1	1	1	1	3	0	15	0	1	1	0	1.000	0	0- -	—	1.38
Sarasota *	A+	3	3	0	0	12	54	11	7	4	1	2	1	2	7	0	9	1	0	1	0	1.000	0	0- -	—	3.00
Pawtucket *	AAA	2	2	0	0	9	43	10	9	9	4	0	0	1	6	0	7	1	0	0	1	.000	0	0- -	—	9.00
1988 Los Angeles	NL	9	6	0	0	35.2	151	27	17	15	0	4	0	0	22	1	23	1	0	1	3	.250	0	0-0	1	3.79
1989 Los Angeles	NL	15	15	2	0	98.2	410	79	39	35	11	4	0	5	41	1	89	1	0	6	4	.600	2	0-0	0	3.19
1990 Los Angeles	NL	33	33	12	0	234.1	950	191	89	76	22	7	5	4	67	5	223	3	3	20	6	.769	3	0-0	0	2.92
1991 Los Angeles	NL	33	33	6	0	220.1	916	190	89	80	18	8	4	7	69	4	150	6	0	17	13	.567	4	0-0	0	3.27
1992 Los Angeles	NL	25	25	1	0	150.2	662	141	82	67	11	12	1	5	69	4	101	9	0	8	11	.421	1	0-0	0	4.00
1993 Los Angeles	NL	32	32	4	0	211.2	918	202	88	81	15	12	5	4	104	9	127	2	2	10	12	.455	3	0-0	0	3.44
1994 Los Angeles	NL	24	24	4	0	170	718	160	83	75	18	6	8	6	56	2	119	2	0	12	7	.632	3	0-0	0	3.97
1995 Los Angeles	NL	30	30	4	0	206.1	859	176	95	84	19	7	5	5	81	5	138	3	0	17	7	.708	2	0-0	0	3.66
1996 Los Angeles	NL	28	27	2	1	168.2	732	153	76	64	12	7	6	8	86	5	133	2	1	15	6	.714	2	0-0	0	3.42
1997 Los Angeles	NL	22	22	1	0	133.2	590	123	64	54	14	5	4	6	68	1	120	1	1	10	5	.667	0	0-0	0	3.64
1998 Los Angeles	NL	15	15	1	0	101.2	418	76	41	32	8	2	3	3	41	1	91	2	0	7	3	.700	1	0-0	0	2.83
1999 Boston	AL	4	4	0	0	20.2	84	14	8	7	2	0	1	2	8	0	15	0	0	2	1	.667	0	0-0	0	3.05
12 ML YEARS		270	266	37	1	1752.1	7408	1532	771	670	150	74	42	55	712	38	1329	32	7	125	78	.616	20	0-0	1	3.44

Ramon Martinez

Bats: R **Throws:** R **Pos:** 2B-27; PH/PR-18; SS-12; 3B-11; DH-1   **Ht:** 6'1" **Wt:** 187 **Born:** 10/10/72 **Age:** 27

		BATTING																	BASERUNNING				PERCENTAGES		
Year Team	Lg	G	AB	H	2B	3B	HR	(Hm	Rd)	TB	R	RBI	TBB	IBB	SO	HBP	SH	SF	SB	CS	SB%	GDP	Avg	OBP	SLG
1993 Royals	R	37	97	23	5	0	0	—	—	28	16	9	8	0	6	2	2	2	3	0	1.00	5	.237	.303	.289
Wilmington	A+	24	75	19	4	0	0	—	—	23	8	6	11	0	9	1	3	1	1	4	.20	2	.253	.352	.307
1994 Rockford	A	6	18	5	0	0	0	—	—	5	3	3	4	0	2	0	1	0	1	0	1.00	1	.278	.409	.278
Wilmington	A+	90	325	87	13	2	2	—	—	110	40	35	35	0	25	4	20	5	6	3	.67	14	.268	.341	.338
1995 Wichita	AA	103	393	108	20	2	3	—	—	141	58	51	42	1	50	4	18	9	11	8	.58	11	.275	.344	.359
1996 Omaha	AAA	85	320	81	12	3	6	—	—	117	35	41	21	1	34	3	13	0	3	2	.60	6	.253	.305	.366
Wichita	AA	26	93	32	4	1	1	—	—	41	16	8	7	0	8	0	7	0	4	1	.80	4	.344	.390	.441
1997 Phoenix	AAA	18	57	16	2	0	1	—	—	21	6	7	5	0	9	0	1	1	1	0	1.00	1	.281	.333	.368
Shreveport	AA	105	404	129	32	4	5	—	—	184	72	54	40	1	48	3	4	3	4	5	.44	6	.319	.382	.455
1998 Fresno	AAA	98	364	114	21	2	14	—	—	181	58	60	38	3	42	2	4	7	0	3	.00	11	.313	.375	.497
1999 Fresno	AAA	29	114	37	7	1	2	—	—	52	13	17	10	1	17	0	0	1	2	0	1.00	2	.325	.376	.456
1998 San Francisco	NL	19	19	6	1	0	0	(0	0)	7	4	0	4	0	2	0	1	0	0	0	.00	0	.316	.435	.368
1999 San Francisco	NL	61	144	38	6	0	5	(3	2)	59	21	19	14	0	17	0	6	1	1	2	.33	2	.264	.327	.410
2 ML YEARS		80	163	44	7	0	5	(3	2)	66	25	19	18	0	19	0	7	1	1	2	.33	2	.270	.341	.405

Sandy Martinez

Bats: Left **Throws:** Right **Pos:** C-12; PH/PR-6   **Ht:** 6'2" **Wt:** 215 **Born:** 10/3/72 **Age:** 27

		BATTING																	BASERUNNING				PERCENTAGES		
Year Team	Lg	G	AB	H	2B	3B	HR	(Hm	Rd)	TB	R	RBI	TBB	IBB	SO	HBP	SH	SF	SB	CS	SB%	GDP	Avg	OBP	SLG
1999 Iowa *	AAA	36	125	29	6	0	2	—	—	41	8	18	5	1	29	0	0	2	1	0	1.00	2	.232	.258	.328
1995 Toronto	AL	62	191	46	12	0	2	(1	1)	64	12	25	7	0	45	1	0	1	0	0	.00	1	.241	.270	.335
1996 Toronto	AL	76	229	52	9	3	3	(2	1)	76	17	18	16	0	58	4	1	1	0	0	.00	4	.227	.288	.332
1997 Toronto	AL	3	2	0	0	0	0	(0	0)	0	1	0	1	0	1	0	0	0	0	0	.00	0	.000	.333	.000
1998 Chicago	NL	45	87	23	9	1	0	(0	0)	34	7	7	13	0	21	1	0	1	1	0	1.00	3	.264	.363	.391
1999 Chicago	NL	17	30	5	0	0	1	(0	1)	8	1	1	0	0	11	0	0	0	0	0	.00	0	.167	.167	.267
5 ML YEARS		203	539	126	30	4	6	(3	3)	182	38	51	37	0	136	6	1	3	1	0	1.00	8	.234	.289	.338

Tino Martinez

Bats: Left **Throws:** Right **Pos:** 1B-158; PH/PR-4   **Ht:** 6'2" **Wt:** 210 **Born:** 12/7/67 **Age:** 32

		BATTING																	BASERUNNING				PERCENTAGES		
Year Team	Lg	G	AB	H	2B	3B	HR	(Hm	Rd)	TB	R	RBI	TBB	IBB	SO	HBP	SH	SF	SB	CS	SB%	GDP	Avg	OBP	SLG
1990 Seattle	AL	24	68	15	4	0	0	(0	0)	19	4	5	9	0	9	0	0	1	0	0	.00	0	.221	.308	.279
1991 Seattle	AL	36	112	23	2	0	4	(3	1)	37	11	9	11	0	24	0	0	2	0	0	.00	2	.205	.272	.330
1992 Seattle	AL	136	460	118	19	2	16	(10	6)	189	53	66	42	9	77	2	1	8	2	1	.67	24	.257	.316	.411
1993 Seattle	AL	109	408	108	25	1	17	(8	9)	186	48	60	45	9	56	5	3	3	0	3	.00	7	.265	.343	.456
1994 Seattle	AL	97	329	86	21	0	20	(8	12)	167	42	61	29	2	52	1	4	3	1	2	.33	9	.261	.320	.508
1995 Seattle	AL	141	519	152	35	3	31	(14	17)	286	92	111	62	15	91	4	2	6	0	0	.00	10	.293	.369	.551
1996 New York	AL	155	595	174	28	0	25	(9	16)	277	82	117	68	4	85	2	1	5	2	1	.67	18	.292	.364	.466
1997 New York	AL	158	594	176	31	2	44	(18	26)	343	96	141	75	14	75	3	0	13	3	1	.75	15	.296	.371	.577
1998 New York	AL	142	531	149	33	1	28	(12	16)	268	92	123	61	3	83	6	0	10	2	1	.67	18	.281	.355	.505
1999 New York	AL	159	589	155	27	2	28	(7	21)	270	95	105	69	7	86	3	0	4	3	4	.43	14	.263	.341	.458
10 ML YEARS		1157	4205	1156	225	11	213	(90	123)	2042	615	798	471	63	638	26	11	55	13	13	.50	117	.275	.347	.486

Onan Masaoka

Pitches: Left **Bats:** Right **Pos:** RP-54   **Ht:** 6'0" **Wt:** 188 **Born:** 10/27/77 **Age:** 22

		HOW MUCH HE PITCHED						WHAT HE GAVE UP											THE RESULTS					
Year Team	Lg	G	GS	CG	GF	IP	BFP	H	R	ER	HR	SH	SF	HB	TBB	IBB	SO	WP	Bk	W	L	Pct.	ShO	Sv-Op	Hld	ERA
1995 Yakima	A-	15	7	0	5	49.1	225	28	25	20	2	1	0	4	47	0	75	12	4	2	4	.333	0	3- -	—	3.65

Year Team	Lg	G	GS	CG	GF	IP	BFP	H	R	ER	HR	SH	SF	HB	TBB	IBB	SO	WP	Bk	W	L	Pct.	ShO	Sv-Op	Hld	ERA
		HOW MUCH HE PITCHED						WHAT HE GAVE UP												THE RESULTS						
1996 Savannah	A	13	13	0	0	65	283	55	35	31	7	1	0	6	35	0	80	3	2	2	5	.286	0	0--	—	4.29
1997 Vero Beach	A+	28	24	2	3	148.2	612	113	72	64	16	6	4	10	55	1	132	10	1	6	8	.429	1	1--	—	3.87
1998 San Antonio	AA	27	20	1	2	110	500	114	79	65	11	2	5	6	63	0	94	3	1	6	6	.500	1	1--	—	5.32
1999 Los Angeles	NL	54	0	0	12	66.2	300	55	33	32	8	1	2	2	47	3	61	3	0	2	4	.333	0	1-2	5	4.32

Ruben Mateo

Bats: Right **Throws:** Right **Pos:** CF-31; DH-1; PH/PR-1 **Ht:** 6'0" **Wt:** 170 **Born:** 2/10/78 **Age:** 22

Year Team	Lg	G	AB	H	2B	3B	HR	Hm	Rd	TB	R	RBI	TBB	IBB	SO	HBP	SH	SF	SB	CS	SB%	GDP	Avg	OBP	SLG
		BATTING																	BASERUNNING				PERCENTAGES		
1996 Chston-SC	A	134	496	129	30	8	8	—	—	199	65	58	26	1	78	12	2	7	30	9	.77	8	.260	.309	.401
1997 Charlotte	A+	99	385	121	23	8	12	—	—	196	63	67	22	0	55	6	1	2	20	5	.80	16	.314	.359	.509
1998 Charlotte	A+	1	4	0	0	0	0	—	—	0	0	1	0	0	1	0	0	0	0	0	.00	0	.000	.000	.000
Tulsa	AA	107	433	134	32	3	18	—	—	226	79	75	30	1	56	15	3	4	18	8	.69	7	.309	.371	.522
1999 Oklahoma	AAA	63	253	85	12	0	18	—	—	151	53	62	14	6	36	8	0	3	6	3	.67	5	.336	.385	.597
1999 Texas	AL	32	122	29	9	1	5	(2	3)	55	16	18	4	0	28	1	0	0	3	0	1.00	2	.238	.268	.451

Mike Matheny

Bats: Right **Throws:** Right **Pos:** C-57 **Ht:** 6'3" **Wt:** 205 **Born:** 9/22/70 **Age:** 29

Year Team	Lg	G	AB	H	2B	3B	HR	Hm	Rd	TB	R	RBI	TBB	IBB	SO	HBP	SH	SF	SB	CS	SB%	GDP	Avg	OBP	SLG
		BATTING																	BASERUNNING				PERCENTAGES		
1994 Milwaukee	AL	28	53	12	3	0	1	(1	0)	18	3	2	3	0	13	2	1	0	0	1	.00	1	.226	.293	.340
1995 Milwaukee	AL	80	166	41	9	1	0	(0	0)	52	13	21	12	0	28	2	1	0	2	1	.67	3	.247	.306	.313
1996 Milwaukee	AL	106	313	64	15	2	8	(5	3)	107	31	46	14	0	80	3	7	4	3	2	.60	9	.204	.243	.342
1997 Milwaukee	AL	123	320	78	16	1	4	(2	2)	108	29	32	17	0	68	7	9	3	0	1	.00	9	.244	.294	.338
1998 Milwaukee	NL	108	320	76	13	0	6	(4	2)	107	24	27	11	0	63	7	3	0	1	0	1.00	6	.238	.278	.334
1999 Toronto	AL	57	163	35	6	0	3	(1	2)	50	16	17	12	0	37	1	2	1	0	0	.00	3	.215	.271	.307
6 ML YEARS		502	1335	306	62	4	22	(13	9)	442	116	145	69	0	289	22	23	8	6	5	.55	31	.229	.277	.331

T.J. Mathews

Pitches: Right **Bats:** Right **Pos:** RP-50 **Ht:** 6'1" **Wt:** 214 **Born:** 1/19/70 **Age:** 30

Year Team	Lg	G	GS	CG	GF	IP	BFP	H	R	ER	HR	SH	SF	HB	TBB	IBB	SO	WP	Bk	W	L	Pct.	ShO	Sv-Op	Hld	ERA
		HOW MUCH HE PITCHED						WHAT HE GAVE UP												THE RESULTS						
1999 Vancouver *	AAA	1	1	0	0	1	4	1	1	1	0	0	1	0	0	0	1	0	0	0	0	.000	0	0--	—	9.00
1995 St. Louis	NL	23	0	0	12	29.2	120	21	7	5	1	4	0	0	11	1	28	2	0	1	1	.500	0	2-2	7	1.52
1996 St. Louis	NL	67	0	0	23	83.2	345	62	32	28	8	5	0	2	32	4	80	1	0	2	6	.250	0	6-11	9	3.01
1997 StL-Oak		64	0	0	26	74.2	329	75	32	25	9	8	1	2	30	4	70	1	0	10	6	.625	0	3-9	12	3.01
1998 Oakland	AL	66	0	0	15	72.2	319	71	44	37	6	2	9	4	29	3	53	1	0	7	4	.636	0	1-4	19	4.58
1999 Oakland	AL	50	0	0	15	59	242	46	28	25	9	5	1	2	20	4	42	2	0	4	5	.643	0	3-5	17	3.81
1997 St. Louis	NL	40	0	0	12	46	197	41	14	11	4	6	0	1	18	3	46	1	0	4	4	.500	0	0-3	8	2.15
Oakland	AL	24	0	0	14	28.2	132	34	18	14	5	2	1	1	12	1	24	0	0	6	2	.750	0	3-6	4	4.40
5 ML YEARS		270	0	0	91	319.2	1355	275	143	120	33	24	11	10	122	16	273	7	0	29	22	.569	0	15-31	64	3.38

Terry Mathews

Pitches: Right **Bats:** Left **Pos:** RP-23; SP-1 **Ht:** 6'2" **Wt:** 225 **Born:** 10/5/64 **Age:** 35

Year Team	Lg	G	GS	CG	GF	IP	BFP	H	R	ER	HR	SH	SF	HB	TBB	IBB	SO	WP	Bk	W	L	Pct.	ShO	Sv-Op	Hld	ERA
		HOW MUCH HE PITCHED						WHAT HE GAVE UP												THE RESULTS						
1999 Royals *	R	1	1	0	0	2	6	0	0	0	0	0	0	0	0	2	0	0	0	0	0	.000	0	0--	—	0.00
Wichita *	AA	1	0	0	0	2	8	2	1	1	0	0	0	0	0	2	0	0	0	0	0	.000	0	0--	—	4.50
Omaha *	AAA	7	0	0	0	16.1	60	11	4	3	1	0	0	0	5	0	11	2	0	0	1	0	1.000	0	0--	—	1.65
1991 Texas	AL	34	2	0	8	57.1	236	54	24	23	5	2	0	1	18	3	51	5	0	4	0	1.000	0	1-3	2	3.61
1992 Texas	AL	40	0	0	11	42.1	199	48	29	28	4	1	3	1	31	3	26	2	1	2	4	.333	0	0-4	6	5.95
1994 Florida	NL	24	2	0	5	43	179	45	16	16	4	1	0	1	9	1	21	1	0	2	1	.667	0	0-1	3	3.35
1995 Florida	NL	57	0	0	14	82.2	332	70	32	31	9	5	1	1	27	4	72	3	0	4	4	.500	0	3-7	11	3.38
1996 Fla-Bal		71	0	0	24	73.2	326	79	40	37	10	3	1	1	34	5	62	0	0	4	6	.400	0	4-6	15	4.52
1997 Baltimore	AL	57	0	0	19	63.1	285	63	35	31	8	9	4	0	36	2	39	3	0	4	4	.500	0	1-2	8	4.41
1998 Baltimore	AL	21	0	0	2	20.1	90	26	15	14	6	5	1	0	8	3	10	0	0	0	1	.000	0	0-1	1	6.20
1999 Kansas City	AL	24	1	0	7	39	175	44	21	19	4	0	4	2	17	1	19	0	0	2	1	.667	0	1-3	3	4.38
1996 Florida	NL	57	0	0	19	55	247	59	33	30	7	2	1	1	27	5	49	0	0	2	4	.333	0	4-5	11	4.91
Baltimore	AL	20	0	0	5	18.2	79	20	7	7	3	1	0	0	7	0	13	0	0	2	2	.500	0	0-1	4	3.38
8 ML YEARS		324	5	0	90	421.2	1822	429	212	199	50	26	14	7	180	22	300	14	1	22	21	.512	0	10-27	49	4.25

Pascual Matos

Bats: Right **Throws:** Right **Pos:** C-5; PH/PR-2 **Ht:** 6'2" **Wt:** 160 **Born:** 12/23/74 **Age:** 25

Year Team	Lg	G	AB	H	2B	3B	HR	Hm	Rd	TB	R	RBI	TBB	IBB	SO	HBP	SH	SF	SB	CS	SB%	GDP	Avg	OBP	SLG
		BATTING																	BASERUNNING				PERCENTAGES		
1992 Braves	R	13	33	5	1	0	0	—	—	6	3	0	10	1	12	0	0	0	0	1	.00	1	.152	.349	.182
1993 Braves	R	36	119	27	5	1	0	—	—	34	12	15	3	0	32	2	1	1	3	1	.75	1	.227	.256	.286
1994 Macon	A	11	29	5	2	0	0	—	—	7	1	2	0	0	10	1	0	0	1	0	1.00	0	.172	.200	.241
Idaho Falls	R+	43	157	40	7	1	7	—	—	70	22	29	2	0	39	0	1	2	7	2	.78	7	.255	.261	.446
1995 Macon	A	72	238	44	11	1	5	—	—	72	23	26	11	0	86	1	0	0	2	2	.50	4	.185	.224	.303
1996 Durham	A+	67	219	49	9	3	6	—	—	82	24	28	7	0	70	3	0	0	6	0	1.00	1	.224	.257	.374

Year Team	Lg	G	AB	H	2B	3B	HR	(Hm	Rd)	TB	R	RBI	TBB	IBB	SO	HBP	SH	SF	SB	CS	SB%	GDP	Avg	OBP	SLG
					BATTING														**BASERUNNING**				**PERCENTAGES**		
1997 Durham	A+	117	430	104	18	3	18	—	—	182	51	50	14	3	122	2	0	1	4	5	.44	12	.242	.268	.423
1998 Greenville	AA	98	338	84	16	1	12	—	—	138	40	58	14	2	102	4	3	2	4	1	.80	6	.249	.285	.408
1999 Richmond	AAA	66	224	47	7	0	3	—	—	63	17	21	6	0	47	1	3	2	3	1	.75	6	.210	.232	.281
1999 Atlanta	NL	6	8	1	0	0	0	(0	0)	1	0	2	0	0	1	0	0	0	0	0	.00	1	.125	.125	.125

Gary Matthews Jr.

Bats: B **Throws:** R **Pos:** RF-10; PH/PR-10; LF-6; CF-2   **Ht:** 6'3" **Wt:** 200 **Born:** 8/25/74 **Age:** 25

Year Team	Lg	G	AB	H	2B	3B	HR	(Hm	Rd)	TB	R	RBI	TBB	IBB	SO	HBP	SH	SF	SB	CS	SB%	GDP	Avg	OBP	SLG
1994 Spokane	A-	52	191	40	6	1	0	—	—	48	23	18	19	1	58	2	0	1	3	5	.38	4	.209	.286	.251
1995 Clinton	A	128	421	100	18	4	2	—	—	132	57	40	68	1	109	6	3	3	28	8	.78	8	.238	.349	.314
1996 Rancho Cuca	A+	123	435	118	21	11	7	—	—	182	65	54	60	1	102	6	4	2	7	8	.47	11	.271	.366	.418
1997 Rancho Cuca	A+	69	268	81	15	4	8	—	—	128	66	40	49	2	57	3	0	0	10	4	.71	4	.302	.416	.478
Mobile	AA	28	90	22	4	1	2	—	—	34	14	12	15	1	29	1	0	2	3	1	.75	1	.244	.352	.378
1998 Mobile	AA	72	254	78	15	4	7	—	—	122	62	51	55	2	50	1	0	3	11	1	.92	6	.307	.428	.480
1999 Las Vegas	AAA	121	422	108	22	3	9	—	—	163	57	52	58	0	104	7	0	4	17	6	.74	13	.256	.352	.386
1999 San Diego	NL	23	36	8	0	0	0	(0	0)	8	4	7	9	0	9	0	0	0	2	0	1.00	1	.222	.378	.222

Derrick May

Bats: L **Throws:** R **Pos:** PH/PR-16; DH-9; RF-3; LF-2   **Ht:** 6'4" **Wt:** 235 **Born:** 7/14/68 **Age:** 31

Year Team	Lg	G	AB	H	2B	3B	HR	(Hm	Rd)	TB	R	RBI	TBB	IBB	SO	HBP	SH	SF	SB	CS	SB%	GDP	Avg	OBP	SLG
1999 Rochester *	AAA	71	295	82	19	3	5	—	—	122	39	43	22	1	28	1	0	2	4	2	.67	10	.278	.328	.414
1990 Chicago	NL	17	61	15	3	0	1	(1	0)	21	8	11	2	0	7	0	0	0	1	0	1.00	1	.246	.270	.344
1991 Chicago	NL	15	22	5	2	0	1	(1	0)	10	4	3	2	0	1	0	0	0	0	0	.00	1	.227	.280	.455
1992 Chicago	NL	124	351	96	11	0	8	(3	5)	131	33	45	14	4	40	3	2	1	5	3	.63	10	.274	.306	.373
1993 Chicago	NL	128	465	137	25	2	10	(3	7)	196	62	77	31	6	41	1	0	6	10	3	.77	15	.295	.336	.422
1994 Chicago	NL	100	345	98	19	2	8	(5	3)	145	43	51	30	4	34	0	1	2	3	2	.60	11	.284	.340	.420
1995 Mil-Hou		110	319	90	18	2	9	(4	5)	139	44	50	24	0	42	2	0	3	5	1	.83	5	.282	.333	.436
1996 Houston	NL	109	259	65	12	3	5	(2	3)	98	24	33	30	8	33	2	0	3	2	2	.50	3	.251	.330	.378
1997 Philadelphia	NL	83	149	34	5	1	1	(0	1)	44	8	13	8	3	26	0	0	1	4	1	.80	4	.228	.266	.295
1998 Montreal	NL	85	180	43	8	0	5	(1	4)	66	13	15	11	1	24	0	0	1	0	0	.00	5	.239	.281	.367
1999 Baltimore	AL	26	49	13	0	0	4	(0	2)	25	5	12	4	0	6	0	0	1	0	0	.00	0	.265	.315	.510
1995 Milwaukee	AL	32	113	28	3	1	1	(1	0)	36	15	9	5	0	18	1	0	0	1	0	1.00	1	.248	.286	.319
Houston	NL	78	206	62	15	1	8	(3	5)	103	29	41	19	0	24	1	0	3	5	1	.83	4	.301	.358	.500
10 ML YEARS		797	2200	596	103	10	52	(22	30)	875	244	310	156	26	254	8	3	19	30	12	.71	57	.271	.319	.398

Brent Mayne

Bats: Left **Throws:** Right **Pos:** C-105; PH/PR-24   **Ht:** 6'1" **Wt:** 192 **Born:** 4/19/68 **Age:** 32

Year Team	Lg	G	AB	H	2B	3B	HR	(Hm	Rd)	TB	R	RBI	TBB	IBB	SO	HBP	SH	SF	SB	CS	SB%	GDP	Avg	OBP	SLG
1990 Kansas City	AL	5	13	3	0	0	0	(0	0)	3	2	1	3	0	3	0	0	0	0	1	.00	0	.231	.375	.231
1991 Kansas City	AL	85	231	58	8	0	3	(2	1)	75	22	31	23	4	42	0	2	3	2	4	.33	6	.251	.315	.325
1992 Kansas City	AL	82	213	48	10	0	0	(0	0)	58	16	18	11	0	26	0	2	3	0	4	.00	5	.225	.260	.272
1993 Kansas City	AL	71	205	52	9	1	2	(0	2)	69	22	22	18	7	31	1	3	0	3	2	.60	6	.254	.317	.337
1994 Kansas City	AL	46	144	37	5	1	2	(1	1)	50	19	20	14	1	27	0	0	0	1	0	1.00	3	.257	.323	.347
1995 Kansas City	AL	110	307	77	18	1	1	(1	0)	100	23	27	25	1	41	3	11	1	0	1	.00	16	.251	.313	.326
1996 New York	NL	70	99	26	6	0	1	(0	1)	35	9	6	12	1	22	0	2	0	0	1	.00	4	.263	.342	.354
1997 Oakland	AL	85	256	74	12	0	6	(4	2)	104	29	22	18	1	33	4	2	2	1	0	1.00	8	.289	.343	.406
1998 San Francisco	NL	94	275	75	15	0	3	(0	3)	99	26	32	37	3	47	1	2	2	2	1	.67	8	.273	.359	.360
1999 San Francisco	NL	117	322	97	32	0	2	(1	1)	135	39	39	43	5	65	5	1	3	2	2	.50	16	.301	.389	.419
10 ML YEARS		765	2065	547	115	3	20	(9	11)	728	207	218	204	23	337	14	25	14	11	16	.41	70	.265	.333	.353

Joe Mays

Pitches: Right **Bats:** Both **Pos:** RP-29; SP-20   **Ht:** 6'1" **Wt:** 185 **Born:** 12/10/75 **Age:** 24

Year Team	Lg	G	GS	CG	GF	IP	BFP	H	R	ER	HR	SH	SF	HB	TBB	IBB	SO	WP	Bk	W	L	Pct.	ShO	Sv-Op	Hld	ERA
1995 Mariners	R	10	10	0	0	44.1	189	41	24	16	0	2	2	1	18	0	44	7	1	2	3	.400	0	0--	—	3.25
1996 Everett	A-	13	10	0	0	64.1	271	55	33	22	3	3	2	2	22	0	56	9	1	4	4	.500	0	0--	—	3.08
1997 Wisconsin	A	13	13	1	0	81.2	322	62	20	19	3	1	2	6	23	1	79	1	0	7	3	.750	0	0--	—	2.09
Lancaster	A+	15	15	1	0	96.1	420	108	55	52	9	2	6	5	34	0	82	2	0	7	4	.636	0	0--	—	4.86
1998 Fort Myers	A+	16	15	0	0	94.2	409	101	45	32	7	5	2	5	23	0	83	4	0	7	2	.778	0	0--	—	3.04
New Britain	AA	11	10	0	0	57.2	258	63	40	32	4	2	3	1	21	0	45	2	1	5	3	.625	0	0--	—	4.99
1999 Minnesota	AL	49	20	2	8	171	746	179	92	83	24	7	6	2	67	2	115	6	0	6	11	.353	1	0-0	2	4.37

Quinton McCracken

Bats: Both **Throws:** Right **Pos:** LF-26; CF-20; PH/PR-2   **Ht:** 5'9" **Wt:** 173 **Born:** 8/16/70 **Age:** 29

Year Team	Lg	G	AB	H	2B	3B	HR	(Hm	Rd)	TB	R	RBI	TBB	IBB	SO	HBP	SH	SF	SB	CS	SB%	GDP	Avg	OBP	SLG
1995 Colorado	NL	3	1	0	0	0	0	(0	0)	0	0	0	0	0	1	0	0	0	0	0	.00	0	.000	.000	.000
1996 Colorado	NL	124	283	82	13	6	3	(2	1)	116	50	40	32	4	62	1	12	1	17	6	.74	5	.290	.363	.410

		BATTING																		BASERUNNING				PERCENTAGES		
Year Team	Lg	G	AB	H	2B	3B	HR	(Hm	Rd)	TB	R	RBI	TBB	IBB	SO	HBP	SH	SF	SB	CS	SB%	GDP	Avg	OBP	SLG
1997 Colorado	NL	147	325	95	11	1	3	(1	2)	117	69	36	42	0	62	1	6	1	28	11	.72	6	.292	.374	.360
1998 Tampa Bay	AL	155	614	179	38	7	7	(5	2)	252	77	59	41	1	107	3	9	8	19	10	.66	12	.292	.335	.410
1999 Tampa Bay	AL	40	148	37	6	1	1	(1	0)	48	20	18	14	0	23	1	1	1	6	5	.55	7	.250	.317	.324
5 ML YEARS		469	1371	393	68	15	14	(9	5)	533	216	153	129	5	255	6	28	11	70	32	.69	30	.287	.348	.389

Jeff McCurry

Pitches: Right **Bats:** Right **Pos:** RP-5   **Ht:** 6'6" **Wt:** 225 **Born:** 1/21/70 **Age:** 30

		HOW MUCH HE PITCHED						WHAT HE GAVE UP												THE RESULTS					
Year Team	Lg	G	GS	CG	GF	IP	BFP	H	R	ER	HR	SH	SF	HB	TBB	IBB	SO	WP	Bk	W	L	Pct.	ShO	Sv-Op	Hld	ERA
1999 New Orleans *	AAA	40	0	0	37	43.1	197	48	23	20	3	4	2	3	14	5	26	3	0	0	7	.000	0	14--	--	4.15
1995 Pittsburgh	NL	55	0	0	10	61	282	82	38	34	9	4	0	5	30	4	27	2	0	1	4	.200	0	1-2	5	5.02
1996 Detroit	AL	2	0	0	1	3.1	21	9	9	9	3	0	0	0	2	0	0	0	0	0	0	.000	0	0-0	0	24.30
1997 Colorado	NL	33	0	0	14	40.2	179	43	22	20	7	3	1	0	20	0	19	2	0	1	4	.200	0	0-2	4	4.43
1998 Pittsburgh	NL	16	0	0	8	19.1	87	24	14	14	4	2	1	1	9	0	11	0	0	1	3	.250	0	0-0	0	6.52
1999 Houston	NL	5	0	0	1	4	25	11	8	7	1	0	0	0	2	0	3	0	0	0	1	.000	0	0-0	0	15.75
5 ML YEARS		111	0	0	34	128.1	594	169	91	84	24	9	2	6	63	4	60	4	0	3	12	.200	0	1-4	9	5.89

Jason McDonald

Bats: B **Throws:** R **Pos:** CF-53; LF-31; PH/PR-26; RF-13; DH-5; 2B-1   **Ht:** 5'7" **Wt:** 190 **Born:** 3/20/72 **Age:** 28

		BATTING																		BASERUNNING				PERCENTAGES		
Year Team	Lg	G	AB	H	2B	3B	HR	(Hm	Rd)	TB	R	RBI	TBB	IBB	SO	HBP	SH	SF	SB	CS	SB%	GDP	Avg	OBP	SLG
1999 Vancouver *	AAA	32	129	42	9	1	4	(—	—)	65	27	18	19	1	33	2	2	0	8	5	.62	0	.326	.420	.504
1997 Oakland	AL	78	236	62	11	4	4	(1	3)	93	47	14	36	0	49	1	2	1	13	8	.62	0	.263	.361	.394
1998 Oakland	AL	70	175	44	9	0	1	(1	0)	56	25	16	27	0	33	3	6	1	10	4	.71	2	.251	.359	.320
1999 Oakland	AL	100	187	39	2	1	3	(0	3)	52	26	8	25	0	48	3	4	1	6	3	.67	2	.209	.310	.278
3 ML YEARS		248	598	145	22	5	8	(2	6)	201	98	38	88	0	130	7	12	3	29	15	.66	4	.242	.345	.336

John McDonald

Bats: Right **Throws:** Right **Pos:** 2B-7; PH/PR-7; SS-6   **Ht:** 5'11" **Wt:** 175 **Born:** 9/24/74 **Age:** 25

		BATTING																		BASERUNNING				PERCENTAGES		
Year Team	Lg	G	AB	H	2B	3B	HR	(Hm	Rd)	TB	R	RBI	TBB	IBB	SO	HBP	SH	SF	SB	CS	SB%	GDP	Avg	OBP	SLG
1996 Watertown	A-	75	278	75	11	0	2	—	—	92	48	26	32	0	49	5	11	1	11	1	.92	3	.270	.354	.331
1997 Kinston	A+	130	541	140	27	3	5	—	—	188	77	53	51	0	75	2	7	2	6	5	.55	12	.259	.324	.348
1998 Akron	AA	132	514	118	18	2	2	—	—	146	68	43	43	0	61	6	11	6	17	6	.74	7	.230	.293	.284
1999 Akron	AA	55	226	67	12	0	1	—	—	82	31	26	19	0	26	2	2	4	7	3	.70	5	.296	.351	.363
Buffalo	AAA	66	237	75	12	1	0	—	—	89	30	25	11	0	23	2	5	2	6	3	.67	5	.316	.349	.376
1999 Cleveland	AL	18	21	7	0	0	0	(0	0)	7	2	0	0	0	3	0	0	0	0	1	.00	2	.333	.333	.333

Jack McDowell

Pitches: Right **Bats:** Right **Pos:** SP-4   **Ht:** 6'5" **Wt:** 190 **Born:** 1/16/66 **Age:** 34

		HOW MUCH HE PITCHED						WHAT HE GAVE UP												THE RESULTS					
Year Team	Lg	G	GS	CG	GF	IP	BFP	H	R	ER	HR	SH	SF	HB	TBB	IBB	SO	WP	Bk	W	L	Pct.	ShO	Sv-Op	Hld	ERA
1999 Edmonton *	AAA	2	2	0	0	11	47	12	7	7	1	1	0	0	3	0	2	0	0	1	0	1.000	0	0--	--	5.73
Lk Elsinore *	A+	1	1	0	0	7.1	33	11	7	6	2	0	0	0	1	0	7	0	0	1	0	1.000	0	0--	--	7.36
1987 Chicago	AL	4	4	0	0	28	103	16	6	6	1	0	0	2	6	0	15	0	0	3	0	1.000	0	0-0	0	1.93
1988 Chicago	AL	26	26	1	0	158.2	687	147	85	70	12	6	7	7	68	5	84	11	1	5	10	.333	0	0-0	0	3.97
1990 Chicago	AL	33	33	4	0	205	866	189	93	87	20	1	5	7	77	0	165	7	1	14	9	.609	0	0-0	0	3.82
1991 Chicago	AL	35	35	15	0	253.2	1028	212	97	96	19	8	4	4	82	2	191	10	1	17	10	.630	3	0-0	0	3.41
1992 Chicago	AL	34	34	13	0	260.2	1079	247	95	92	21	8	6	7	75	9	178	6	0	20	10	.667	1	0-0	0	3.18
1993 Chicago	AL	34	34	10	0	256.2	1067	261	104	96	20	8	6	3	69	6	158	8	1	22	10	.688	4	0-0	0	3.37
1994 Chicago	AL	25	25	6	0	181	755	186	82	75	12	4	4	5	42	2	127	4	0	10	9	.526	2	0-0	0	3.73
1995 New York	AL	30	30	8	0	217.2	927	211	106	95	25	8	6	5	78	1	157	9	1	15	10	.600	2	0-0	0	3.93
1996 Cleveland	AL	30	30	5	0	192	846	214	119	109	22	10	5	4	67	2	141	5	0	13	9	.591	1	0-0	0	5.11
1997 Cleveland	AL	8	6	0	0	40.2	181	44	25	23	6	4	2	1	18	1	38	1	0	3	3	.500	0	0-0	0	5.09
1998 Anaheim	AL	14	14	0	0	76	334	96	45	43	11	3	2	1	19	1	45	2	0	5	3	.625	0	0-0	0	5.09
1999 Anaheim	AL	4	4	0	0	19	93	31	17	17	4	1	1	2	5	0	12	0	0	4	0	1.000	0	0-0	0	8.05
12 ML YEARS		277	275	62	0	1889	7966	1854	874	809	173	61	48	48	606	29	1311	63	5	127	87	.593	13	0-0		3.85

Chuck McElroy

Pitches: Left **Bats:** Left **Pos:** RP-56   **Ht:** 6'0" **Wt:** 205 **Born:** 10/1/67 **Age:** 32

		HOW MUCH HE PITCHED						WHAT HE GAVE UP												THE RESULTS					
Year Team	Lg	G	GS	CG	GF	IP	BFP	H	R	ER	HR	SH	SF	HB	TBB	IBB	SO	WP	Bk	W	L	Pct.	ShO	Sv-Op	Hld	ERA
1989 Philadelphia	NL	11	0	0	4	10.1	46	12	2	2	1	0	0	0	4	1	8	0	0	0	0	.000	0	0-0	0	1.74
1990 Philadelphia	NL	16	0	0	8	14	76	24	13	12	0	1	0	1	10	2	16	0	0	0	1	.000	0	0-0	0	7.71
1991 Chicago	NL	71	0	0	12	101.1	419	73	33	22	7	9	6	0	57	7	92	1	0	6	2	.750	0	3-6	10	1.95
1992 Chicago	NL	72	0	0	30	83.2	369	73	40	33	5	5	5	1	51	10	83	3	0	4	7	.364	0	6-11	3	3.55
1993 Chicago	NL	49	0	0	11	47.1	214	51	30	24	4	5	1	1	25	5	31	3	0	2	2	.500	0	0-0	0	4.56
1994 Cincinnati	NL	52	0	0	13	57.2	230	52	15	15	3	2	0	0	15	2	38	4	0	1	2	.333	0	5-11	10	2.34
1995 Cincinnati	NL	44	0	0	11	40.1	178	46	29	27	5	1	3	1	15	3	27	1	0	3	4	.429	0	0-3	3	6.02
1996 Cin-Cal		52	0	0	12	49	210	45	22	21	4	1	1	2	23	3	45	1	0	7	1	.875	0	0-2	7	3.86
1997 Ana-CWS	AL	61	0	0	16	75	320	73	36	32	5	3	3	2	22	1	62	1	0	1	3	.250	0	1-6	15	3.84

(Pitching)

		HOW MUCH HE PITCHED						WHAT HE GAVE UP												THE RESULTS						
Year Team	Lg	G	GS	CG	GF	IP	BFP	H	R	ER	HR	SH	SF	HB	TBB	IBB	SO	WP	Bk	W	L	Pct.	ShO	Sv-Op	Hld	ERA
1998 Colorado	NL	78	0	0	27	68.1	281	68	23	22	3	0	3	0	24	0	61	0	0	6	4	.600	0	2-6	19	2.90
1999 Col-NYM	NL	56	0	0	19	54	251	60	34	33	9	1	3	1	36	4	44	5	0	3	1	.750	0	0-3	5	5.50
1996 Cincinnati	NL	12	0	0	1	12.1	59	13	10	9	2	0	0	0	10	1	13	0	0	2	0	1.000	0	0-0	1	6.57
California	AL	40	0	0	11	36.2	151	32	12	12	2	1	1	2	13	2	32	1	0	5	1	.833	0	0-2	6	2.95
1997 Anaheim	AL	13	0	0	3	15.2	66	17	7	6	2	0	0	0	3	0	18	0	0	0	0	.000	0	0-2	4	3.45
Chicago	AL	48	0	0	13	59.1	254	56	29	26	3	3	3	2	19	1	44	1	0	1	3	.250	0	1-4	11	3.94
1999 Colorado	NL	41	0	0	12	40.2	192	48	29	28	9	0	2	0	28	3	37	4	0	3	1	.750	0	0-3	5	6.20
New York	NL	15	0	0	7	13.1	59	12	5	5	0	1	1	0	8	1	7	1	0	0	0	.000	0	0-0	1	3.38
11 ML YEARS		562	0	0	163	601	2594	577	277	243	46	27	26	7	282	38	507	19	0	33	27	.550	0	17-48	76	3.64

Joe McEwing

Bats: R **Throws:** R **Pos:** 2B-96; LF-32; CF-23; RF-19; PH/PR-13; 3B-6; 1B-2; SS-1 **Ht:** 5'11" **Wt:** 170 **Born:** 10/19/72 **Age:** 27

		BATTING																	BASERUNNING				PERCENTAGES		
Year Team	Lg	G	AB	H	2B	3B	HR	(Hm	Rd)	TB	R	RBI	TBB	IBB	SO	HBP	SH	SF	SB	CS	SB%	GDP	Avg	OBP	SLG
1992 Cardinals	R	55	211	71	4	2	0	—	—	79	55	13	24	0	18	5	1	1	23	7	.77	1	.336	.415	.374
1993 Savannah	A	138	511	127	35	1	0	—	—	164	94	43	89	0	73	4	15	4	22	9	.71	7	.249	.362	.321
1994 Madison	A	90	346	112	24	2	4	—	—	152	58	47	32	4	53	1	5	3	18	15	.55	5	.324	.380	.439
St. Pete	A+	50	197	49	7	0	1	—	—	59	22	20	19	0	32	1	4	3	8	4	.67	4	.249	.314	.299
1995 St. Pete	A+	75	281	64	13	0	1	—	—	80	33	23	25	3	49	1	6	4	2	3	.40	5	.228	.289	.285
Arkansas	AA	42	121	30	4	0	2	—	—	40	16	12	9	2	13	1	6	0	3	2	.60	4	.248	.305	.331
1996 Arkansas	AA	106	216	45	7	3	2	—	—	64	27	14	13	0	32	0	5	1	2	4	.33	8	.208	.252	.296
1997 Arkansas	AA	103	263	68	6	3	4	—	—	92	33	35	19	4	39	1	3	2	4	4	.33	6	.259	.309	.350
1998 Arkansas	AA	60	223	79	21	4	9	—	—	135	45	46	21	4	18	1	1	2	4	2	.67	2	.354	.409	.605
Memphis	AAA	78	329	110	30	7	6	—	—	172	52	46	21	0	39	3	1	1	11	10	.52	4	.334	.379	.523
1998 St. Louis	NL	10	20	4	1	0	0	(0	0)	5	5	1	1	0	3	1	1	0	0	1	.00	0	.200	.273	.250
1999 St. Louis	NL	152	513	141	28	4	9	(5	4)	204	65	44	41	8	87	6	9	5	7	4	.64	3	.275	.333	.398
2 ML YEARS		162	533	145	29	4	9	(5	4)	209	70	44	42	8	90	7	10	5	7	5	.58	3	.272	.330	.392

Willie McGee

Bats: B **Throws:** R **Pos:** PH/PR-57; RF-43; LF-30; CF-19; 1B-3 **Ht:** 6'1" **Wt:** 190 **Born:** 11/2/58 **Age:** 41

		BATTING																	BASERUNNING				PERCENTAGES		
Year Team	Lg	G	AB	H	2B	3B	HR	(Hm	Rd)	TB	R	RBI	TBB	IBB	SO	HBP	SH	SF	SB	CS	SB%	GDP	Avg	OBP	SLG
1982 St. Louis	NL	123	422	125	12	8	4	(2	2)	165	43	56	12	2	58	2	2	1	24	12	.67	9	.296	.318	.391
1983 St. Louis	NL	147	601	172	22	8	5	(4	1)	225	75	75	26	2	98	0	1	3	39	8	.83	8	.286	.314	.374
1984 St. Louis	NL	145	571	166	19	11	6	(2	4)	225	82	50	29	2	80	1	0	5	43	10	.81	12	.291	.325	.394
1985 St. Louis	NL	152	612	216	26	18	10	(3	7)	308	114	82	34	2	86	0	1	5	56	16	.78	3	.353	.384	.503
1986 St. Louis	NL	124	497	127	22	7	7	(7	0)	184	65	48	37	7	82	1	0	4	19	16	.54	8	.256	.306	.370
1987 St. Louis	NL	153	620	177	37	11	11	(6	5)	269	76	105	24	5	90	2	1	5	16	4	.80	24	.285	.312	.434
1988 St. Louis	NL	137	562	164	24	6	3	(1	2)	209	73	50	32	5	84	1	2	3	41	6	.87	10	.292	.329	.372
1989 St. Louis	NL	58	199	47	10	2	3	(1	2)	70	23	17	10	0	34	1	0	1	8	6	.57	2	.236	.275	.352
1990 StL-Oak		154	614	199	35	7	3	(1	2)	257	99	77	48	6	104	1	0	2	31	9	.78	13	.324	.373	.419
1991 San Francisco	NL	131	497	155	30	3	4	(2	2)	203	67	43	34	3	74	2	8	2	17	9	.65	11	.312	.357	.408
1992 San Francisco	NL	138	474	141	20	2	1	(0	1)	168	56	36	29	3	88	1	5	1	13	4	.76	7	.297	.339	.354
1993 San Francisco	NL	130	475	143	28	1	4	(0	4)	185	53	46	38	7	67	1	3	2	10	9	.53	12	.301	.353	.389
1994 San Francisco	NL	45	156	44	3	0	5	(2	3)	62	19	23	15	2	24	0	1	4	3	0	1.00	8	.282	.337	.397
1995 Boston	AL	67	200	57	11	3	2	(1	1)	80	32	15	9	0	41	0	5	3	5	2	.71	5	.285	.311	.400
1996 St. Louis	NL	123	309	95	15	2	5	(2	3)	129	52	41	18	2	60	2	1	1	5	2	.71	8	.307	.348	.417
1997 St. Louis	NL	122	300	90	19	4	3	(2	1)	126	29	38	22	2	59	0	0	1	8	2	.80	6	.300	.347	.420
1998 St. Louis	NL	120	269	68	10	1	3	(0	3)	89	27	34	14	5	49	0	0	3	7	2	.78	6	.253	.287	.331
1999 St. Louis	NL	132	271	68	7	0	0	(0	0)	75	25	20	17	3	60	0	0	2	4	4	.64	5	.251	.293	.277
1990 St. Louis	NL	125	501	168	32	5	3	(1	2)	219	76	62	38	6	86	1	0	2	28	9	.76	9	.335	.382	.437
Oakland	AL	29	113	31	3	2	0	(0	0)	38	23	15	10	0	18	0	0	0	3	0	1.00	4	.274	.333	.336
18 ML YEARS		2201	7649	2254	350	94	79	(36	43)	3029	1010	856	448	58	1238	15	30	46	352	121	.74	157	.295	.333	.396

Kevin McGlinchy

Pitches: Right **Bats:** Right **Pos:** RP-64 **Ht:** 6'5" **Wt:** 220 **Born:** 6/28/77 **Age:** 23

		HOW MUCH HE PITCHED						WHAT HE GAVE UP												THE RESULTS						
Year Team	Lg	G	GS	CG	GF	IP	BFP	H	R	ER	HR	SH	SF	HB	TBB	IBB	SO	WP	Bk	W	L	Pct.	ShO	Sv-Op	Hld	ERA
1996 Danville	R+	13	13	0	0	72	283	52	21	9	2	1	2	2	11	0	77	4	4	3	2	.600	0	0--	—	1.13
Eugene	A-	2	2	0	0	6.2	31	7	5	4	2	1	0	0	1	0	5	0	0	0	0	.000	0	0--	—	5.40
1997 Durham	A+	26	26	0	0	139.2	595	145	78	76	14	2	4	9	39	2	113	4	2	3	7	.300	0	0--	—	4.90
1998 Danville	A+	22	22	1	0	142.1	566	122	55	46	7	6	3	6	29	0	129	1	0	9	8	.529	0	0--	—	2.91
Greenville	AA	6	6	0	0	33	144	35	19	19	5	1	1	1	15	1	20	0	0	1	1	.500	0	0--	—	5.18
1999 Atlanta	NL	64	0	0	21	70.1	298	66	25	22	6	4	4	1	30	7	67	1	0	7	3	.700	0	0-2	7	2.82

Fred McGriff

Bats: Left **Throws:** Left **Pos:** 1B-125; DH-18; PH/PR-2 **Ht:** 6'3" **Wt:** 215 **Born:** 10/31/63 **Age:** 36

		BATTING																	BASERUNNING				PERCENTAGES		
Year Team	Lg	G	AB	H	2B	3B	HR	(Hm	Rd)	TB	R	RBI	TBB	IBB	SO	HBP	SH	SF	SB	CS	SB%	GDP	Avg	OBP	SLG
1986 Toronto	AL	3	5	1	0	0	0	(0	0)	1	1	0	0	0	2	0	0	0	0	0	.00	0	.200	.200	.200
1987 Toronto	AL	107	295	73	16	0	20	(7	13)	149	58	43	60	4	104	1	0	0	3	2	.60	3	.247	.376	.505
1988 Toronto	AL	154	536	151	35	4	34	(18	16)	296	100	82	79	3	149	4	0	4	6	1	.86	15	.282	.376	.552
1989 Toronto	AL	161	551	148	27	3	36	(18	18)	289	98	92	119	12	132	4	1	5	7	4	.64	14	.269	.399	.525

150

Year Team	Lg	G	AB	H	2B	3B	HR	(Hm	Rd)	TB	R	RBI	TBB	IBB	SO	HBP	SH	SF	SB	CS	SB%	GDP	Avg	OBP	SLG
1990 Toronto	AL	153	557	167	21	1	35	(14	21)	295	91	88	94	12	108	2	1	4	5	3	.63	7	.300	.400	.530
1991 San Diego	NL	153	528	147	19	1	31	(18	13)	261	84	106	105	26	135	2	0	7	4	1	.80	14	.278	.396	.494
1992 San Diego	NL	152	531	152	30	4	35	(21	14)	295	79	104	96	23	108	1	0	4	8	6	.57	14	.286	.394	.556
1993 SD-Atl	NL	151	557	162	29	2	37	(15	22)	306	111	101	76	6	106	2	0	5	3	3	.63	14	.291	.375	.549
1994 Atlanta	NL	113	424	135	25	1	34	(13	21)	264	81	94	50	8	76	1	0	3	7	3	.70	8	.318	.389	.623
1995 Atlanta	NL	144	528	148	27	1	27	(15	12)	258	85	93	65	6	99	5	0	6	3	6	.33	19	.280	.361	.489
1996 Atlanta	NL	159	617	182	37	1	28	(17	11)	305	81	107	68	12	116	2	0	4	7	3	.70	20	.295	.365	.494
1997 Atlanta	NL	152	564	156	25	1	22	(8	14)	249	77	97	68	4	112	4	0	5	5	0	1.00	22	.277	.356	.441
1998 Tampa Bay	AL	151	564	160	33	0	19	(14	5)	250	73	81	79	9	118	2	0	4	7	2	.78	14	.284	.371	.443
1999 Tampa Bay	AL	144	529	164	30	1	32	(18	14)	292	75	104	86	11	107	1	0	4	5	0	1.00	12	.310	.405	.552
1993 San Diego	NL	83	302	83	11	1	18	(7	11)	150	52	46	42	4	55	1	0	4	4	3	.57	9	.275	.361	.497
Atlanta	NL	68	255	79	18	1	19	(8	11)	156	59	55	34	2	51	1	0	1	—				.310	.392	.612
14 ML YEARS		1897	6786	1946	354	20	390	(196	194)	3510	1094	1192	1045	136	1472	31	2	55	68	34	.67	176	.287	.382	.517

Ryan McGuire

Bats: L **Throws:** L **Pos:** 1B-58; PH/PR-21; LF-16; RF-7; CF-1   **Ht:** 6'1" **Wt:** 215 **Born:** 11/23/71 **Age:** 28

Year Team	Lg	G	AB	H	2B	3B	HR	(Hm	Rd)	TB	R	RBI	TBB	IBB	SO	HBP	SH	SF	SB	CS	SB%	GDP	Avg	OBP	SLG
1999 Ottawa *	AAA	53	183	46	6	1	4	—	—	66	23	27	35	3	37	0	0	3	1	3	.25	5	.251	.367	.361
1997 Montreal	NL	84	199	51	15	2	3	(2	1)	79	22	17	19	1	34	0	3	1	1	4	.20	3	.256	.320	.397
1998 Montreal	NL	130	210	39	9	0	1	(1	0)	51	17	10	32	0	55	0	1	1	0	0	.00	9	.186	.292	.243
1999 Montreal	NL	88	140	31	7	2	2	(1	1)	48	17	18	27	0	33	0	3	0	1	1	.50	9	.221	.347	.343
3 ML YEARS		302	549	121	31	4	6	(4	2)	178	56	45	78	1	122	0	7	2	2	5	.29	21	.220	.316	.324

Mark McGwire

Bats: Right **Throws:** Right **Pos:** 1B-151; PH/PR-2   **Ht:** 6'5" **Wt:** 250 **Born:** 10/1/63 **Age:** 36

Year Team	Lg	G	AB	H	2B	3B	HR	(Hm	Rd)	TB	R	RBI	TBB	IBB	SO	HBP	SH	SF	SB	CS	SB%	GDP	Avg	OBP	SLG
1986 Oakland	AL	18	53	10	1	0	3	(1	2)	20	10	9	4	0	18	1	0	0	0	1	.00	0	.189	.259	.377
1987 Oakland	AL	151	557	161	28	4	49	(21	28)	344	97	118	71	8	131	5	0	8	1	1	.50	6	.289	.370	.618
1988 Oakland	AL	155	550	143	22	1	32	(12	20)	263	87	99	76	4	117	4	1	4	0	0	.00	15	.260	.352	.478
1989 Oakland	AL	143	490	113	17	0	33	(12	21)	229	74	95	83	5	94	3	0	11	1	1	.50	23	.231	.339	.467
1990 Oakland	AL	156	523	123	16	0	39	(14	25)	256	87	108	110	9	116	7	1	9	2	1	.67	13	.235	.370	.489
1991 Oakland	AL	154	483	97	22	0	22	(15	7)	185	62	75	93	3	116	3	1	5	2	1	.67	13	.201	.330	.383
1992 Oakland	AL	139	467	125	22	0	42	(24	18)	273	87	104	90	12	105	5	0	9	0	1	.00	10	.268	.385	.585
1993 Oakland	AL	27	84	28	6	0	9	(5	4)	61	16	24	21	5	19	1	0	1	0	1	.00	0	.333	.467	.726
1994 Oakland	AL	47	135	34	3	0	9	(6	3)	64	26	25	37	3	40	0	0	3	0	0	.00	3	.252	.413	.474
1995 Oakland	AL	104	317	87	13	0	39	(15	24)	217	75	90	88	5	77	11	0	6	1	1	.50	9	.274	.441	.685
1996 Oakland	AL	130	423	132	21	0	52	(24	28)	309	104	113	116	16	112	8	0	1	0	0	.00	14	.312	.467	.730
1997 Oak-StL		156	540	148	27	0	58	(30	28)	349	86	123	101	16	159	9	0	7	3	0	1.00	9	.274	.393	.646
1998 St. Louis	NL	155	509	152	21	0	70	(38	32)	383	130	147	162	28	155	6	0	4	1	0	1.00	8	.299	.470	.752
1999 St. Louis	NL	153	521	145	21	1	65	(37	28)	363	118	147	133	21	141	2	0	5	0	0	.00	12	.278	.424	.697
1997 Oakland	AL	105	366	104	24	0	34	(17	17)	230	48	81	58	8	98	4	0	5	1	0	1.00	9	.284	.383	.628
St. Louis	NL	51	174	44	3	0	24	(13	11)	119	38	42	43	8	61	5	0	2	2	0	1.00	0	.253	.411	.684
14 ML YEARS		1688	5652	1498	240	6	522	(254	268)	3316	1059	1277	1185	135	1400	65	3	70	11	8	.58	135	.265	.394	.587

Mark McLemore

Bats: B **Throws:** R **Pos:** 2B-135; RF-7; LF-4; PH/PR-4; DH-1   **Ht:** 5'11" **Wt:** 207 **Born:** 10/4/64 **Age:** 35

Year Team	Lg	G	AB	H	2B	3B	HR	(Hm	Rd)	TB	R	RBI	TBB	IBB	SO	HBP	SH	SF	SB	CS	SB%	GDP	Avg	OBP	SLG
1986 California	AL	5	4	0	0	0	0	(0	0)	0	0	0	1	0	2	0	1	0	0	1	.00	0	.000	.200	.000
1987 California	AL	138	433	102	13	3	3	(0	3)	130	61	41	48	0	72	0	15	3	25	8	.76	7	.236	.310	.300
1988 California	AL	77	233	56	11	2	2	(1	1)	77	38	16	25	0	28	0	5	2	13	7	.65	6	.240	.312	.330
1989 California	AL	32	103	25	3	1	0	(0	0)	30	12	14	7	0	19	1	3	1	6	1	.86	2	.243	.295	.291
1990 Cal-Cle	AL	28	60	9	2	0	0	(0	0)	11	6	2	4	0	15	0	1	0	1	0	1.00	1	.150	.203	.183
1991 Houston	NL	21	61	9	1	0	0	(0	0)	10	6	2	6	0	13	0	0	1	0	1	.00	1	.148	.221	.164
1992 Baltimore	AL	101	228	56	7	2	0	(0	0)	67	40	27	21	1	26	0	6	1	11	5	.69	6	.246	.308	.294
1993 Baltimore	AL	148	581	165	27	5	4	(2	2)	214	81	72	64	4	92	1	11	6	21	15	.58	21	.284	.353	.368
1994 Baltimore	AL	104	343	88	11	1	3	(2	1)	110	44	29	51	3	50	1	4	1	20	5	.80	7	.257	.354	.321
1995 Texas	AL	129	467	122	20	5	5	(3	2)	167	73	41	59	6	71	3	10	3	21	11	.66	10	.261	.346	.358
1996 Texas	AL	147	517	150	23	4	5	(3	2)	196	84	46	87	5	69	0	2	5	27	10	.73	16	.290	.389	.379
1997 Texas	AL	89	349	91	17	2	1	(0	1)	115	47	25	40	1	54	2	6	2	7	5	.58	5	.261	.338	.330
1998 Texas	AL	126	461	114	15	1	5	(4	1)	146	79	53	89	1	64	2	12	3	12	4	.75	15	.247	.369	.317
1999 Texas	AL	144	566	155	20	7	6	(2	4)	207	105	45	83	2	79	0	9	6	16	8	.67	8	.274	.363	.366
1990 California	AL	20	48	7	2	0	0	(0	0)	9	4	2	4	0	9	0	1	0	1	0	1.00	1	.146	.212	.188
Cleveland	AL	8	12	2	0	0	0	(0	0)	2	2	0	0	0	6	0	0	0	0	0	.00	0	.167	.167	.167
14 ML YEARS		1289	4406	1142	170	33	34	(20	14)	1480	676	413	585	23	654	10	85	34	180	81	.69	105	.259	.345	.336

Greg McMichael

Pitches: Right **Bats:** Right **Pos:** RP-36   **Ht:** 6'3" **Wt:** 222 **Born:** 12/1/66 **Age:** 33

	HOW MUCH HE PITCHED						WHAT HE GAVE UP									THE RESULTS						
Year Team	Lg	G	GS	CG	GF	IP	BFP	H	R	ER	HR	SH	SF	HB	TBB	IBB	SO	WP	Bk	W	L	Pct.	ShO	Sv-Op	Hld	ERA
1999 Binghamton *	AA	2	2	0	0	3	13	2	1	0	0	0	0	0	1	0	5	0	0	0	0	.000	0	0- -	—	0.00

151

Year Team	Lg	G	GS	CG	GF	IP	BFP	H	R	ER	HR	SH	SF	HB	TBB	IBB	SO	WP	Bk	W	L	Pct.	ShO	Sv-Op	Hld	ERA
Norfolk *	AAA	3	1	0	0	3.1	16	4	1	1	0	0	0	0	3	0	4	0	0	0	0	.000	0	0--	--	2.70
1993 Atlanta	NL	74	0	0	40	91.2	365	68	22	21	3	4	2	0	29	4	89	6	1	2	3	.400	0	19-21	12	2.06
1994 Atlanta	NL	51	0	0	41	58.2	259	66	29	25	1	3	1	0	19	6	47	3	1	4	6	.400	0	21-31	1	3.84
1995 Atlanta	NL	67	0	0	16	80.2	337	64	27	25	8	5	0	0	32	9	74	3	0	7	2	.778	0	2-4	20	2.79
1996 Atlanta	NL	73	0	0	14	86.2	366	84	37	31	4	3	3	1	27	7	78	4	1	5	3	.625	0	2-8	18	3.22
1997 New York	NL	73	0	0	23	87.2	355	73	34	29	8	9	4	2	27	6	81	5	0	7	10	.412	0	7-18	19	2.98
1998 NYM-LA	NL	64	0	0	19	68	317	81	39	31	9	6	3	4	35	10	55	6	1	5	4	.556	0	2-7	10	4.10
1999 NYM-Oak		36	0	0	8	33.2	153	35	19	19	6	2	2	2	20	5	21	4	0	1	1	.500	0	0-1	7	5.08
1998 New York	NL	52	0	0	18	53.2	251	64	31	24	8	3	2	3	29	7	44	5	1	5	3	.625	0	1-4	8	4.02
Los Angeles	NL	12	0	0	1	14.1	66	17	8	7	1	3	1	1	6	3	11	1	0	0	1	.000	0	1-3	2	4.40
1999 New York	NL	19	0	0	4	18.2	84	20	10	10	3	1	1	0	8	3	18	4	0	1	1	.500	0	0-1	4	4.82
Oakland	AL	17	0	0	4	15	69	15	9	9	3	1	1	2	12	2	3	0	0	0	0	.000	0	0-0	3	5.40
7 ML YEARS		438	0	0	161	507	2152	471	207	181	39	32	15	9	189	47	445	31	4	31	29	.517	0	53-90	87	3.21

Brian McNichol

Pitches: Left **Bats:** Left **Pos:** SP-2; RP-2 **Ht:** 6'6" **Wt:** 215 **Born:** 5/20/74 **Age:** 26

Year Team	Lg	G	GS	CG	GF	IP	BFP	H	R	ER	HR	SH	SF	HB	TBB	IBB	SO	WP	Bk	W	L	Pct.	ShO	Sv-Op	Hld	ERA
1995 Williamsprt	A-	9	9	0	0	49.2	215	57	28	17	1	1	1	2	8	0	35	1	1	3	1	.750	0	0--	—	3.08
1996 Daytona	A+	8	7	0	0	34.2	162	39	24	18	4	0	1	0	14	0	22	1	0	1	2	.333	0	0--	—	4.67
Cubs	R	1	1	0	0	3.1	16	4	2	0	0	0	0	0	0	0	2	0	0	0	0	.000	0	0--	—	0.00
1997 Daytona	A+	6	6	0	0	39	161	32	14	10	1	1	2	3	10	1	40	1	0	2	2	.500	0	0--	—	2.31
Orlando	AA	22	22	0	0	119.1	544	153	89	77	18	3	7	2	42	6	97	9	0	7	10	.412	0	0--	—	5.81
1998 West Tenn	AA	28	26	4	0	179	753	170	88	74	14	5	6	7	62	5	168	9	1	12	9	.571	1	0--	—	3.72
Iowa	AAA	1	1	0	0	7	31	12	6	6	2	0	0	0	1	0	5	0	0	0	0	.000	0	0--	—	7.71
1999 Iowa	AAA	28	28	2	0	161.1	720	194	108	100	21	7	2	7	55	0	120	6	0	10	11	.476	1	0--	—	5.58
1999 Chicago	NL	4	2	0	1	10.2	54	15	8	8	4	0	1	1	7	0	12	0	0	0	2	.000	0	0-0	0	6.75

Brian McRae

Bats: B **Throws:** R **Pos:** CF-107; PH/PR-26; DH-15 **Ht:** 6'0" **Wt:** 195 **Born:** 8/27/67 **Age:** 32

Year Team	Lg	G	AB	H	2B	3B	HR	(Hm	Rd)	TB	R	RBI	TBB	IBB	SO	HBP	SH	SF	SB	CS	SB%	GDP	Avg	OBP	SLG
1990 Kansas City	AL	46	168	48	8	3	2	(1	1)	68	21	23	9	0	29	0	3	2	4	3	.57	5	.286	.318	.405
1991 Kansas City	AL	152	629	164	28	9	8	(3	5)	234	86	64	24	1	99	2	3	5	20	11	.65	12	.261	.288	.372
1992 Kansas City	AL	149	533	119	23	5	4	(2	2)	164	63	52	42	1	88	6	7	4	18	5	.78	10	.223	.285	.308
1993 Kansas City	AL	153	627	177	28	9	12	(5	7)	259	78	69	37	1	105	4	14	3	23	14	.62	8	.282	.325	.413
1994 Kansas City	AL	114	436	119	22	6	4	(2	2)	165	71	40	54	3	67	6	6	3	28	8	.78	3	.273	.359	.378
1995 Chicago	NL	137	580	167	38	7	12	(6	6)	255	92	48	47	1	92	7	3	1	27	8	.77	12	.288	.348	.440
1996 Chicago	NL	157	624	172	32	5	17	(9	8)	265	111	66	73	6	84	12	2	5	37	9	.80	11	.276	.360	.425
1997 ChC-NYM	NL	153	562	136	32	7	11	(6	5)	215	86	43	65	2	84	6	4	2	17	10	.63	13	.242	.326	.383
1998 New York	NL	159	552	146	36	5	21	(12	9)	255	79	79	80	3	90	5	3	5	20	11	.65	5	.264	.360	.462
1999 NYM-Col-Tor		134	403	88	17	2	12	(6	6)	145	47	48	57	2	86	9	1	2	2	7	.22	8	.218	.327	.360
1997 New York	NL	108	417	100	27	5	6	(4	2)	155	63	28	52	2	62	4	3	1	14	6	.70	11	.240	.329	.372
New York	NL	45	145	36	5	2	5	(2	3)	60	23	15	13	0	22	2	1	1	3	4	.43	2	.248	.317	.414
1999 New York	NL	96	298	66	12	1	8	(5	3)	104	35	36	39	1	57	5	0	2	2	6	.25	6	.221	.320	.349
Colorado	NL	7	23	6	2	0	1	(0	1)	11	1	1	2	0	7	2	0	0	0	0	.00	0	.261	.370	.478
Toronto	AL	31	82	16	3	1	3	(1	2)	30	11	11	16	1	22	2	1	0	0	1	.00	2	.195	.340	.366
10 ML YEARS		1354	5114	1336	264	58	103	(52	51)	2025	734	532	488	20	824	57	46	32	196	86	.70	87	.261	.331	.396

Brian Meadows

Pitches: Right **Bats:** Right **Pos:** SP-31 **Ht:** 6'4" **Wt:** 200 **Born:** 11/21/75 **Age:** 24

Year Team	Lg	G	GS	CG	GF	IP	BFP	H	R	ER	HR	SH	SF	HB	TBB	IBB	SO	WP	Bk	W	L	Pct.	ShO	Sv-Op	Hld	ERA
1994 Marlins	R	8	7	0	0	37	151	34	9	8	1	0	0	1	6	0	33	0	0	3	0	1.000	0	0--	—	1.95
1995 Kane County	A	26	26	1	0	147	646	163	90	69	11	8	4	12	41	0	103	3	2	9	9	.500	1	0--	—	4.22
1996 Brevard Cty	A+	24	23	3	1	146	600	129	73	58	13	3	4	10	25	1	69	4	1	8	7	.533	1	0--	—	3.58
Portland	AA	4	4	1	0	27	108	26	15	13	1	3	1	1	4	0	13	0	0	0	1	.000	0	0--	—	4.33
1997 Portland	AA	29	29	4	0	175.2	763	204	99	90	23	9	2	4	48	4	115	7	1	9	7	.563	0	0--	—	4.61
1998 Florida	NL	31	31	1	0	174.1	772	222	106	101	20	14	4	3	46	3	88	5	1	11	13	.458	0	0-0	0	5.21
1999 Florida	NL	31	31	0	0	178.1	795	214	117	111	31	16	8	5	57	5	72	4	1	11	15	.423	0	0-0	0	5.60
2 ML YEARS		62	62	1	0	352.2	1567	436	223	212	51	30	12	8	103	8	160	9	2	22	28	.440	0	0-0	0	5.41

Pat Meares

Bats: Right **Throws:** Right **Pos:** SS-21 **Ht:** 6'0" **Wt:** 187 **Born:** 9/6/68 **Age:** 31

Year Team	Lg	G	AB	H	2B	3B	HR	(Hm	Rd)	TB	R	RBI	TBB	IBB	SO	HBP	SH	SF	SB	CS	SB%	GDP	Avg	OBP	SLG
1999 Nashville *	AAA	5	18	3	0	0	0	—	—	3	3	0	1	0	3	1	0	0	1	0	1.00	0	.167	.250	.167
1993 Minnesota	AL	111	346	87	14	3	0	(0	0)	107	33	33	7	0	52	1	4	3	4	5	.44	11	.251	.266	.309
1994 Minnesota	AL	80	229	61	12	1	2	(0	2)	81	29	24	14	0	50	2	6	3	5	1	.83	3	.266	.310	.354
1995 Minnesota	AL	116	390	105	19	4	12	(3	9)	168	57	49	15	0	68	11	4	5	10	4	.71	17	.269	.311	.431
1996 Minnesota	AL	152	517	138	26	7	8	(3	5)	202	66	67	17	1	90	9	4	7	9	4	.69	19	.267	.298	.391
1997 Minnesota	AL	134	439	121	23	3	10	(5	5)	180	63	60	18	0	86	16	3	7	7	7	.50	9	.276	.323	.410
1998 Minnesota	AL	149	543	141	26	3	9	(2	7)	200	56	70	24	1	86	6	3	5	7	4	.64	12	.260	.296	.368

	BATTING																		BASERUNNING				PERCENTAGES		
Year Team	Lg	G	AB	H	2B	3B	HR	(Hm Rd)	TB	R	RBI	TBB	IBB	SO	HBP	SH	SF	SB	CS	SB%	GDP	Avg	OBP	SLG
1999 Pittsburgh	NL	21	91	28	4	0	0	(0 0)	32	15	7	9	0	20	2	2	0	0	0	.00	1	.308	.382	.352
7 ML YEARS		763	2555	681	124	21	41	(13 28)	970	319	310	104	2	452	47	26	30	42	25	.63	72	.267	.304	.380

Gil Meche

Pitches: Right **Bats:** Right **Pos:** SP-15; RP-1   **Ht:** 6'3" **Wt:** 180 **Born:** 9/8/78 **Age:** 21

		HOW MUCH HE PITCHED						WHAT HE GAVE UP										THE RESULTS						
Year Team	Lg	G	GS	CG	GF	IP	BFP	H	R	ER	HR	SH	SF	HB	TBB	IBB	SO	WP	Bk	W	L	Pct.	ShO	Sv-Op	Hld	ERA
1996 Mariners	R	2	0	0	0	3	13	4	2	2	0	0	0	0	1	0	4	0	0	0	1	.000	0	0--	—	6.00
1997 Everett	A-	12	12	1	0	74.2	316	75	40	33	7	3	2	3	24	0	62	7	0	3	4	.429	0	0--	—	3.98
Wisconsin	A	2	2	0	0	12	51	12	5	4	1	0	0	1	4	0	14	2	1	0	2	.000	0	0--	—	3.00
1998 Wisconsin	A	26	26	0	0	149	643	136	77	57	9	2	2	5	63	0	168	12	2	8	7	.533	0	0--	—	3.44
1999 New Haven	AA	10	10	0	0	59	250	51	24	20	3	2	1	0	26	0	56	4	0	3	4	.429	0	0--	—	3.05
Tacoma	AAA	6	6	0	0	31	135	31	12	11	3	0	2	1	13	0	24	2	0	2	2	.500	0	0--	—	3.19
1999 Seattle	AL	16	15	0	0	85.2	375	73	48	45	9	5	3	2	57	1	47	1	0	8	4	.667	0	0-0	0	4.73

Jim Mecir

Pitches: Right **Bats:** Both **Pos:** RP-17   **Ht:** 6'1" **Wt:** 210 **Born:** 5/16/70 **Age:** 30

		HOW MUCH HE PITCHED						WHAT HE GAVE UP										THE RESULTS						
Year Team	Lg	G	GS	CG	GF	IP	BFP	H	R	ER	HR	SH	SF	HB	TBB	IBB	SO	WP	Bk	W	L	Pct.	ShO	Sv-Op	Hld	ERA
1995 Seattle	AL	2	0	0	1	4.2	21	5	1	0	0	0	0	0	2	0	3	0	0	0	0	.000	0	0-0	0	0.00
1996 New York	AL	26	0	0	10	40.1	185	42	24	23	6	5	4	0	23	4	38	6	0	1	1	.500	0	0-0	0	5.13
1997 New York	AL	25	0	0	11	33.2	142	36	23	22	5	0	1	2	10	1	25	1	0	0	4	.000	0	0-1	1	5.88
1998 Tampa Bay	AL	68	0	0	23	84	343	68	30	29	6	3	2	3	33	5	77	2	0	7	2	.778	0	0-3	14	3.11
1999 Tampa Bay	AL	17	0	0	3	20.2	91	15	7	6	0	0	2	1	14	0	15	0	0	0	1	.000	0	0-2	6	2.61
5 ML YEARS		138	0	0	48	183.1	782	166	85	80	17	8	9	6	82	10	158	9	0	8	8	.500	0	0-6	21	3.93

Rafael Medina

Pitches: Right **Bats:** Right **Pos:** RP-20   **Ht:** 6'3" **Wt:** 240 **Born:** 2/15/75 **Age:** 25

		HOW MUCH HE PITCHED						WHAT HE GAVE UP										THE RESULTS						
Year Team	Lg	G	GS	CG	GF	IP	BFP	H	R	ER	HR	SH	SF	HB	TBB	IBB	SO	WP	Bk	W	L	Pct.	ShO	Sv-Op	Hld	ERA
1993 Yankees	R	5	5	0	0	27.1	107	16	6	2	0	1	1	1	12	0	21	1	1	2	0	1.000	0	0--	—	0.66
1994 Oneonta	A-	14	14	1	0	73.1	319	67	54	38	7	2	5	1	35	0	59	7	3	3	7	.300	0	0--	—	4.66
1995 Greensboro	A	19	19	1	0	98.2	418	86	48	44	8	0	5	6	38	0	108	6	3	4	4	.500	0	0--	—	4.01
Tampa	A+	6	6	0	0	30.1	131	29	12	8	0	0	0	1	12	0	25	0	2	2	2	.500	0	0--	—	2.37
1996 Norwich	AA	19	19	1	0	103	446	78	48	35	7	5	1	6	55	2	112	11	4	5	8	.385	0	0--	—	3.06
1997 Rancho Cuca	A+	3	3	0	0	18	68	13	4	4	1	1	0	0	5	0	14	1	0	2	0	1.000	0	0--	—	2.00
Las Vegas	AAA	13	13	0	0	66.2	321	90	60	56	12	1	1	2	39	1	50	8	2	4	5	.444	0	0--	—	7.56
1998 Charlotte	AAA	11	9	3	1	57.2	245	53	27	25	8	0	2	2	26	1	41	4	1	4	2	.667	1	0--	—	3.90
1999 Calgary	AAA	25	0	0	9	35	153	29	15	13	1	0	0	2	21	0	34	3	0	1	2	.333	0	1--	—	3.34
1998 Florida	NL	12	12	0	0	67.1	327	76	50	45	8	5	4	3	52	3	49	5	0	2	6	.250	0	0-0	0	6.01
1999 Florida	NL	20	0	0	4	23.1	110	20	15	15	3	1	0	1	20	2	16	2	1	1	1	.500	0	0-0	0	5.79
2 ML YEARS		32	12	0	4	90.2	437	96	65	60	11	6	4	4	72	5	65	7	1	3	7	.300	0	0-0	0	5.96

Mitch Meluskey

Bats: Both **Throws:** Right **Pos:** C-10   **Ht:** 6'0" **Wt:** 185 **Born:** 9/18/73 **Age:** 26

		BATTING																	BASERUNNING				PERCENTAGES		
Year Team	Lg	G	AB	H	2B	3B	HR	(Hm Rd)	TB	R	RBI	TBB	IBB	SO	HBP	SH	SF	SB	CS	SB%	GDP	Avg	OBP	SLG
1992 Burlington	R+	43	126	29	7	0	3	— —	45	23	16	29	0	36	0	0	2	3	0	1.00	0	.230	.369	.357
1993 Columbus	A	101	342	84	18	3	3	— —	117	36	47	35	4	69	4	4	7	1	1	.50	5	.246	.317	.342
1994 Kinston	A+	100	319	77	16	1	3	— —	104	36	41	49	0	62	2	2	4	3	4	.43	4	.241	.342	.326
1995 Kinston	A+	8	29	7	5	0	0	— —	12	5	2	2	0	9	0	0	0	0	0	.00	1	.241	.290	.414
Kissimmee	A+	78	261	56	18	1	3	— —	85	23	31	27	2	33	1	2	4	3	0	1.00	12	.215	.287	.326
1996 Kissimmee	A+	74	231	77	19	0	1	— —	99	29	31	29	5	26	1	1	5	1	1	.50	9	.333	.402	.429
Jackson	AA	38	134	42	11	0	0	— —	53	18	21	18	0	24	1	1	1	0	0	.00	6	.313	.396	.396
1997 Jackson	AA	73	241	82	18	0	14	— —	142	49	46	31	4	39	3	0	3	1	3	.25	7	.340	.417	.589
New Orleans	AA	51	172	43	7	0	3	— —	59	22	21	25	1	38	1	0	1	0	0	.00	6	.250	.347	.343
1998 New Orleans	AAA	121	397	140	41	0	17	— —	232	76	71	85	10	59	3	0	5	2	0	1.00	15	.353	.465	.584
1998 Houston	NL	8	8	2	1	0	0	(0 0)	3	1	0	1	0	4	0	0	0	0	0	.00	1	.250	.333	.375
1999 Houston	NL	10	33	7	1	0	1	(0 1)	11	4	3	5	1	6	0	0	0	1	0	1.00	1	.212	.316	.333
2 ML YEARS		18	41	9	2	0	1	(0 1)	14	5	3	6	1	10	0	0	0	1	0	1.00	2	.220	.319	.341

Ramiro Mendoza

Pitches: Right **Bats:** Right **Pos:** RP-47; SP-6   **Ht:** 6'2" **Wt:** 170 **Born:** 6/15/72 **Age:** 28

		HOW MUCH HE PITCHED						WHAT HE GAVE UP										THE RESULTS						
Year Team	Lg	G	GS	CG	GF	IP	BFP	H	R	ER	HR	SH	SF	HB	TBB	IBB	SO	WP	Bk	W	L	Pct.	ShO	Sv-Op	Hld	ERA
1996 New York	AL	12	11	0	0	53	249	80	43	40	5	1	1	4	10	1	34	2	1	4	5	.444	0	0-0	0	6.79
1997 New York	AL	39	15	0	9	133.2	578	157	67	63	15	3	5	5	28	2	82	2	1	8	6	.571	0	2-4	4	4.24
1998 New York	AL	41	14	1	6	130.1	548	131	50	47	9	6	7	9	30	6	56	3	0	10	2	.833	1	1-4	5	3.25
1999 New York	AL	53	6	0	15	123.2	536	141	68	59	13	6	4	3	27	3	80	2	0	9	9	.500	0	3-6	4	4.29
4 ML YEARS		145	46	1	30	440.2	1911	509	228	209	42	16	17	21	95	12	252	9	2	31	22	.585	1	6-14	13	4.27

Frank Menechino

Bats: R **Throws:** R **Pos:** PH/PR-6; SS-5; DH-3; 3B-1 **Ht:** 5'9" **Wt:** 175 **Born:** 1/7/71 **Age:** 29

Year Team	Lg	G	AB	H	2B	3B	HR	(Hm	Rd)	TB	R	RBI	TBB	IBB	SO	HBP	SH	SF	SB	CS	SB%	GDP	Avg	OBP	SLG
1993 White Sox	R	17	45	11	4	1	1	—	—	20	10	9	12	0	4	4	0	0	3	1	.75	1	.244	.443	.444
Hickory	A	50	178	50	6	3	4	—	—	74	35	19	33	0	28	4	1	1	11	2	.85	4	.281	.403	.416
1994 South Bend	A	106	379	113	21	5	5	—	—	159	77	48	78	1	70	9	3	2	15	8	.65	8	.298	.427	.420
1995 Pr William	A+	137	476	124	31	3	6	—	—	179	65	58	96	2	75	11	3	8	6	2	.75	17	.261	.391	.376
1996 Birmingham	AA	125	415	121	25	3	12	—	—	188	77	62	64	0	84	8	3	6	7	9	.44	5	.292	.391	.453
1997 Nashville	AAA	37	113	26	4	0	4	—	—	42	20	11	26	1	31	6	0	1	3	2	.60	2	.230	.397	.372
Birmingham	AA	90	318	95	28	4	12	—	—	167	78	60	79	0	77	11	1	6	7	3	.70	7	.299	.447	.525
1998 Edmonton	AAA	106	378	105	11	7	10	—	—	160	72	40	70	1	75	10	2	1	9	10	.47	11	.278	.403	.423
1999 Vancouver	AAA	130	501	155	31	9	15	—	—	249	103	88	73	7	97	9	1	5	4	5	.44	12	.309	.403	.497
1999 Oakland	AL	9	9	2	0	0	0	(0	0)	2	0	0	0	0	4	0	0	0	0	0	.00	0	.222	.222	.222

Orlando Merced

Bats: L **Throws:** R **Pos:** LF-44; PH/PR-43; 1B-7; DH-2 **Ht:** 6'1" **Wt:** 195 **Born:** 11/2/66 **Age:** 33

Year Team	Lg	G	AB	H	2B	3B	HR	(Hm	Rd)	TB	R	RBI	TBB	IBB	SO	HBP	SH	SF	SB	CS	SB%	GDP	Avg	OBP	SLG
1990 Pittsburgh	NL	25	24	5	1	0	0	(0	0)	6	3	0	1	0	9	0	0	0	0	0	.00	1	.208	.240	.250
1991 Pittsburgh	NL	120	411	113	17	2	10	(5	5)	164	83	50	64	4	81	1	1	3	8	4	.67	6	.275	.373	.399
1992 Pittsburgh	NL	134	405	100	28	5	6	(4	2)	156	50	60	52	8	63	2	1	5	5	4	.56	6	.247	.332	.385
1993 Pittsburgh	NL	137	447	140	26	4	8	(3	5)	198	68	70	77	10	64	1	0	2	3	3	.50	9	.313	.414	.443
1994 Pittsburgh	NL	108	386	105	21	3	9	(4	5)	159	48	51	42	5	58	1	0	2	4	1	.80	17	.272	.343	.412
1995 Pittsburgh	NL	132	487	146	29	4	15	(8	7)	228	75	83	52	9	74	1	0	5	7	2	.78	9	.300	.365	.468
1996 Pittsburgh	NL	120	453	130	24	1	17	(9	8)	207	69	80	51	5	74	0	0	3	8	4	.67	9	.287	.357	.457
1997 Toronto	AL	98	368	98	23	2	9	(3	6)	152	45	40	47	1	62	3	0	2	7	3	.70	6	.266	.352	.413
1998 Min-Bos-ChC		84	223	62	12	0	6	(4	2)	92	24	40	20	3	34	1	0	3	1	4	.20	6	.278	.336	.413
1999 Montreal	NL	93	194	52	12	1	8	(3	5)	90	25	26	26	0	27	0	0	1	2	1	.67	5	.268	.353	.464
1998 Minnesota	AL	63	204	59	12	0	5	(3	2)	86	22	33	17	3	29	1	0	1	1	4	.20	4	.289	.345	.422
Boston	AL	9	9	0	0	0	0	(0	0)	0	0	2	2	0	3	0	0	1	0	0	.00	0	.000	.167	.000
Chicago	NL	12	10	3	0	0	1	(1	0)	6	2	5	1	0	2	0	0	2	0	0	.00	2	.300	.333	.600
10 ML YEARS		1051	3398	951	193	22	88	(43	45)	1452	490	500	432	45	546	10	2	24	45	26	.63	74	.280	.361	.427

Kent Mercker

Pitches: Left **Bats:** Left **Pos:** SP-23; RP-7 **Ht:** 6'2" **Wt:** 200 **Born:** 2/1/68 **Age:** 32

Year Team	Lg	G	GS	CG	GF	IP	BFP	H	R	ER	HR	SH	SF	HB	TBB	IBB	SO	WP	Bk	W	L	Pct.	ShO	Sv-Op	Hld	ERA
1989 Atlanta	NL	2	1	0	1	4.1	26	8	6	6	0	0	0	0	6	0	4	0	0	0	0	.000	0	0-0	0	12.46
1990 Atlanta	NL	36	0	0	28	48.1	211	43	22	17	6	1	2	2	24	3	39	2	0	4	7	.364	0	7-10	0	3.17
1991 Atlanta	NL	50	4	0	28	73.1	306	56	23	21	5	2	2	1	35	3	62	5	0	5	3	.625	0	6-8	3	2.58
1992 Atlanta	NL	53	0	0	18	68.1	289	51	27	26	4	4	1	3	35	1	49	6	0	3	2	.600	0	6-9	6	3.42
1993 Atlanta	NL	43	6	0	9	66	283	52	24	21	2	0	0	2	36	3	59	5	1	3	1	.750	0	0-3	4	2.86
1994 Atlanta	NL	20	17	2	0	112.1	461	90	46	43	16	4	3	0	45	3	111	4	1	9	4	.692	1	0-0	0	3.45
1995 Atlanta	NL	29	26	0	1	143	622	140	73	66	16	8	7	3	61	2	102	6	2	7	8	.467	0	0-0	0	4.15
1996 Bal-Cle	AL	24	12	0	2	69.2	329	83	60	54	13	3	6	3	38	2	29	3	1	4	6	.400	0	0-0	2	6.98
1997 Cincinnati	NL	28	25	0	0	144.2	616	135	65	63	16	8	4	2	62	6	75	2	1	8	11	.421	0	0-0	0	3.92
1998 St. Louis	NL	30	29	0	1	161.2	716	199	99	91	11	10	9	3	53	4	72	6	4	11	11	.500	0	0-0	0	5.07
1999 StL-Bos		30	23	0	2	129.1	589	148	85	69	16	8	4	3	64	3	81	3	1	8	5	.615	0	0-0	0	4.80
1996 Baltimore	AL	14	12	0	0	58	283	73	56	50	12	3	4	3	35	1	22	3	1	3	6	.333	0	0-0	0	7.76
Cleveland	AL	10	0	0	2	11.2	46	10	4	4	1	0	2	0	3	1	7	0	0	1	0	1.000	0	0-0	2	3.09
1999 St. Louis	NL	25	18	0	2	103.2	476	125	73	59	16	8	3	2	51	3	64	3	1	6	5	.545	0	0-0	0	5.12
Boston	AL	5	5	0	0	25.2	113	23	12	10	0	0	1	1	13	0	17	0	0	2	0	1.000	0	0-0	0	3.51
11 ML YEARS		345	143	2	90	1021	4448	1005	530	477	105	48	38	22	459	30	683	41	12	62	58	.517	1	19-30	15	4.20

Lou Merloni

Bats: R **Throws:** R **Pos:** SS-24; 3B-9; 2B-8; PH/PR-5; DH-3; 1B-1; LF-1 **Ht:** 5'10" **Wt:** 200 **Born:** 4/6/71 **Age:** 29

Year Team	Lg	G	AB	H	2B	3B	HR	(Hm	Rd)	TB	R	RBI	TBB	IBB	SO	HBP	SH	SF	SB	CS	SB%	GDP	Avg	OBP	SLG
1993 Red Sox	R	4	14	5	1	0	0	—	—	6	4	1	1	0	1	1	0	0	1	1	.50	0	.357	.438	.429
Ft. Laud	A+	44	156	38	1	1	2	—	—	47	14	21	13	1	26	1	0	4	1	1	.50	6	.244	.299	.301
1994 Sarasota	A+	113	419	120	16	2	1	—	—	143	59	63	36	4	57	7	7	10	5	2	.71	11	.286	.345	.341
1995 Trenton	AA	93	318	88	16	1	1	—	—	109	42	30	39	3	50	11	11	2	7	7	.50	1	.277	.373	.343
1996 Trenton	AA	28	95	22	6	1	3	—	—	39	11	16	9	1	18	5	1	0	0	2	.00	2	.232	.330	.411
Red Sox	R	1	4	1	0	0	0	—	—	1	1	1	0	0	0	0	0	1	0	0	.00	0	.250	.200	.250
Pawtucket	AAA	38	115	29	6	0	1	—	—	38	19	12	10	0	20	3	4	0	0	1	.00	1	.252	.328	.330
1997 Trenton	AA	69	255	79	17	4	5	—	—	119	49	37	30	1	43	12	1	4	3	2	.60	4	.310	.402	.467
Pawtucket	AAA	49	165	49	10	0	5	—	—	74	24	24	15	2	20	4	1	1	2	2	.50	2	.297	.368	.448
1998 Pawtucket	AAA	27	88	34	3	1	8	—	—	63	17	22	16	0	13	8	1	0	2	2	.50	4	.386	.518	.716
Red Sox	R	1	1	0	0	0	0	—	—	0	0	0	0	0	0	0	0	0	0	0	.00	0	.000	.000	.000
1999 Pawtucket	AAA	66	229	64	14	1	7	—	—	101	45	36	30	0	38	0	0	1	1	1	.50	4	.279	.383	.441
1998 Boston	AL	39	96	27	6	0	1	(1	0)	36	10	15	7	1	20	2	1	0	1	0	1.00	0	.281	.343	.375
1999 Boston	AL	43	126	32	7	0	1	(0	1)	42	18	13	8	0	16	2	3	1	0	0	.00	6	.254	.307	.333
2 ML YEARS		82	222	59	13	0	2	(1	1)	78	28	28	15	1	36	4	4	1	1	0	1.00	7	.266	.322	.351

154

Jose Mesa

Pitches: Right **Bats:** Right **Pos:** RP-68 **Ht:** 6'3" **Wt:** 225 **Born:** 5/22/66 **Age:** 34

Year Team	Lg	G	GS	CG	GF	IP	BFP	H	R	ER	HR	SH	SF	HB	TBB	IBB	SO	WP	Bk	W	L	Pct.	ShO	Sv-Op	Hld	ERA
1987 Baltimore	AL	6	5	0	0	31.1	143	38	23	21	7	0	0	0	15	0	17	4	0	1	3	.250	0	0-0	1	6.03
1990 Baltimore	AL	7	7	0	0	46.2	202	37	20	20	2	2	2	1	27	2	24	1	1	3	2	.600	0	0-0	0	3.86
1991 Baltimore	AL	23	23	2	0	123.2	566	151	86	82	11	5	4	3	62	2	64	3	0	6	11	.353	1	0-0	0	5.97
1992 Bal-Cle	AL	28	27	1	1	160.2	700	169	86	82	14	2	5	4	70	1	62	2	0	7	12	.368	1	0-0	0	4.59
1993 Cleveland	AL	34	33	3	0	208.2	897	232	122	114	21	9	9	7	62	2	118	8	2	10	12	.455	0	0-0	0	4.92
1994 Cleveland	AL	51	0	0	22	73	315	71	33	31	3	3	4	3	26	7	63	3	0	7	5	.583	0	2-6	8	3.82
1995 Cleveland	AL	62	0	0	57	64	250	49	9	8	3	4	2	0	17	2	58	5	0	3	0	1.000	0	46-48	0	1.13
1996 Cleveland	AL	69	0	0	60	72.1	304	69	32	30	6	2	3	3	28	4	64	4	0	2	7	.222	0	39-44	0	3.73
1997 Cleveland	AL	66	0	0	38	82.1	356	83	28	22	7	2	2	3	28	3	69	1	0	4	4	.500	0	16-21	9	2.40
1998 Cle-SF	AL	76	0	0	36	84.2	383	91	50	43	8	6	2	4	38	5	63	10	0	8	7	.533	0	1-4	13	4.57
1999 Seattle	AL	68	0	0	60	68.2	325	84	42	38	11	2	4	4	40	4	42	7	0	4	6	.333	0	33-38	1	4.98
1992 Baltimore	AL	13	12	0	1	67.2	300	77	41	39	9	0	3	2	27	1	22	2	0	3	8	.273	0	0-0	0	5.19
Cleveland	AL	15	15	1	0	93	400	92	45	43	5	2	2	2	43	0	40	0	0	4	4	.500	1	0-0	0	4.16
1998 Cleveland	AL	44	0	0	18	54	244	61	36	31	7	2	2	4	20	3	35	0	0	3	4	.429	0	1-3	7	5.17
San Francisco	NL	32	0	0	18	30.2	139	30	14	12	1	4	0	0	18	2	28	8	0	5	3	.625	0	0-1	6	3.52
11 ML YEARS		490	95	6	274	1016	4441	1074	531	491	93	37	36	32	413	32	644	48	3	54	69	.439	2	137-161	32	4.35

Chad Meyers

Bats: R **Throws:** R **Pos:** 2B-32; CF-10; LF-4; PH/PR-2 **Ht:** 6'0" **Wt:** 185 **Born:** 8/8/75 **Age:** 24

Year Team	Lg	G	AB	H	2B	3B	HR	(Hm	Rd)	TB	R	RBI	TBB	IBB	SO	HBP	SH	SF	SB	CS	SB%	GDP	Avg	OBP	SLG
1996 Williamsprt	A-	67	230	56	9	2	2	—	—	75	46	26	33	0	39	5	2	1	27	6	.82	2	.243	.349	.326
1997 Rockford	A	125	439	132	28	4	4	—	—	180	89	58	74	5	72	10	6	7	54	16	.77	4	.301	.408	.410
1998 Daytona	A+	48	186	60	8	3	3	—	—	83	39	25	33	1	29	1	5	1	23	7	.77	1	.323	.436	.446
West Tenn	AA	77	293	79	14	0	0	—	—	93	63	26	58	0	43	4	1	0	37	9	.80	5	.270	.397	.317
1999 West Tenn	AA	64	238	69	19	2	3	—	—	101	45	29	26	0	40	10	0	0	22	8	.73	6	.290	.383	.424
Iowa	AAA	44	175	62	13	2	0	—	—	79	39	16	29	0	20	3	3	0	17	7	.71	1	.354	.454	.451
1999 Chicago	NL	43	142	33	9	0	0	(0	0)	42	17	4	9	1	27	3	2	0	4	2	.67	5	.232	.292	.296

Dan Miceli

Pitches: Right **Bats:** Right **Pos:** RP-66 **Ht:** 6'0" **Wt:** 216 **Born:** 9/9/70 **Age:** 29

Year Team	Lg	G	GS	CG	GF	IP	BFP	H	R	ER	HR	SH	SF	HB	TBB	IBB	SO	WP	Bk	W	L	Pct.	ShO	Sv-Op	Hld	ERA
1993 Pittsburgh	NL	9	0	0	1	5.1	25	6	3	3	0	0	0	0	3	0	4	0	1	0	0	.000	0	0-0	0	5.06
1994 Pittsburgh	NL	28	0	0	9	27.1	121	28	19	18	5	1	2	2	11	2	27	2	0	2	1	.667	0	2-3	4	5.93
1995 Pittsburgh	NL	58	0	0	51	58	264	61	30	30	7	2	4	4	28	5	56	4	0	4	4	.500	0	21-27	2	4.66
1996 Pittsburgh	NL	44	9	0	17	85.2	398	99	65	55	15	3	7	3	45	5	66	9	0	2	10	.167	0	1-1	4	5.78
1997 Detroit	AL	71	0	0	24	82.2	357	77	49	46	13	5	3	1	38	4	79	3	0	3	2	.600	0	3-8	11	5.01
1998 San Diego	NL	67	0	0	18	72.2	302	64	28	26	6	3	2	1	27	4	70	5	1	10	5	.667	0	2-8	20	3.22
1999 San Diego	NL	66	0	0	28	68.2	296	67	39	34	7	4	2	2	36	5	59	2	0	4	5	.444	0	2-4	9	4.46
7 ML YEARS		343	9	0	148	400.1	1763	402	233	212	53	18	20	13	188	25	361	25	2	25	27	.481	0	31-51	50	4.77

Doug Mientkiewicz

Bats: Left **Throws:** Right **Pos:** 1B-110; PH/PR-14 **Ht:** 6'2" **Wt:** 193 **Born:** 6/19/74 **Age:** 26

Year Team	Lg	G	AB	H	2B	3B	HR	(Hm	Rd)	TB	R	RBI	TBB	IBB	SO	HBP	SH	SF	SB	CS	SB%	GDP	Avg	OBP	SLG
1995 Fort Myers	A+	38	110	27	6	1	1	—	—	38	9	15	18	1	19	1	2	0	2	2	.50	1	.245	.357	.345
1996 Fort Myers	A+	133	492	143	36	4	5	—	—	202	69	79	66	3	47	3	4	5	12	2	.86	10	.291	.374	.411
1997 New Britain	AA	132	467	119	28	2	15	—	—	196	87	61	98	2	67	7	5	2	21	8	.72	6	.255	.390	.420
1998 New Britain	AA	139	502	162	45	0	16	—	—	255	96	88	96	7	58	6	0	7	11	4	.73	6	.323	.432	.508
1998 Minnesota	AL	8	25	5	1	0	0	(0	0)	6	1	2	4	0	3	0	0	0	1	1	.50	0	.200	.310	.240
1999 Minnesota	AL	118	327	75	21	3	2	(0	2)	108	34	32	43	3	51	4	3	2	1	1	.50	13	.229	.324	.330
2 ML YEARS		126	352	80	22	3	2	(0	2)	114	35	34	47	3	54	4	3	2	2	2	.50	13	.227	.323	.324

Matt Mieske

Bats: R **Throws:** R **Pos:** LF-36; PH/PR-28; RF-20; CF-3; DH-1 **Ht:** 6'0" **Wt:** 194 **Born:** 2/13/68 **Age:** 32

Year Team	Lg	G	AB	H	2B	3B	HR	(Hm	Rd)	TB	R	RBI	TBB	IBB	SO	HBP	SH	SF	SB	CS	SB%	GDP	Avg	OBP	SLG
1993 Milwaukee	AL	23	58	14	0	0	3	(1	2)	23	9	7	4	0	14	0	1	0	0	2	.00	2	.241	.290	.397
1994 Milwaukee	AL	84	259	67	13	1	10	(7	3)	112	39	38	21	0	62	3	2	1	3	5	.38	6	.259	.320	.432
1995 Milwaukee	AL	117	267	67	13	1	12	(3	9)	118	42	48	27	0	45	4	0	5	2	4	.33	8	.251	.323	.442
1996 Milwaukee	AL	127	374	104	24	3	14	(9	5)	176	46	64	26	2	76	2	1	6	1	5	.17	5	.278	.324	.471
1997 Milwaukee	AL	84	253	63	15	3	5	(1	4)	99	39	21	19	2	50	0	0	1	1	0	1.00	12	.249	.300	.391
1998 Chicago	NL	77	97	29	7	0	1	(1	0)	39	16	12	11	1	17	1	1	1	0	0	.00	4	.299	.373	.402
1999 Sea-Hou		78	150	46	5	0	9	(4	5)	78	24	29	8	2	31	0	1	2	0	0	.00	0	.307	.338	.520
1999 Seattle	AL	24	41	15	0	0	4	(3	1)	27	11	7	2	1	9	0	0	0	0	0	.00	0	.366	.395	.659
Houston		54	109	31	5	0	5	(1	4)	51	13	22	6	1	22	0	1	2	0	0	.00	0	.284	.316	.468
7 ML YEARS		590	1458	390	77	8	54	(26	28)	645	215	219	116	7	295	10	6	16	7	16	.30	41	.267	.323	.442

Kevin Millar

Bats: R **Throws:** R **Pos:** 1B-94; PH/PR-9; 3B-1; LF-1 **Ht:** 6'0" **Wt:** 185 **Born:** 9/24/71 **Age:** 28

		BATTING																BASERUNNING			PERCENTAGES		
Year Team	Lg	G	AB	H	2B	3B	HR	(Hm	Rd)	TB	R	RBI	TBB	IBB	SO	HBP	SH	SF	SB	CS	SB%	GDP	Avg	OBP	SLG
1994 Kane County	A	135	477	144	35	2	19	—	—	240	75	93	74	2	88	13	0	6	3	3	.50	12	.302	.405	.503
1995 Brevard Cty	A+	129	459	132	32	2	13	—	—	207	53	68	70	2	66	12	0	10	4	4	.50	8	.288	.388	.451
1996 Portland	AA	130	472	150	32	0	18	—	—	236	69	86	37	4	53	9	0	5	6	5	.55	13	.318	.375	.500
1997 Portland	AA	135	511	175	34	2	32	—	—	309	94	131	66	9	53	10	0	7	2	3	.40	11	.342	.423	.605
1998 Charlotte	AAA	14	46	15	3	0	4	—	—	30	14	15	9	0	7	2	0	1	1	0	1.00	3	.326	.448	.652
1999 Calgary	AAA	36	143	43	11	1	7	—	—	77	24	26	11	2	19	0	0	1	2	0	1.00	5	.301	.348	.538
1998 Florida	NL	2	2	1	0	0	0	(0	0)	1	1	0	1	0	0	0	0	0	0	0	.00	0	.500	.667	.500
1999 Florida	NL	105	351	100	17	4	9	(3	6)	152	48	67	40	2	64	7	1	8	1	0	1.00	7	.285	.362	.433
2 ML YEARS		107	353	101	17	4	9	(3	6)	153	49	67	41	2	64	7	1	8	1	0	1.00	7	.286	.364	.433

Damian Miller

Bats: Right **Throws:** Right **Pos:** C-86; PH/PR-1 **Ht:** 6'2" **Wt:** 212 **Born:** 10/13/69 **Age:** 30

		BATTING																BASERUNNING			PERCENTAGES		
Year Team	Lg	G	AB	H	2B	3B	HR	(Hm | Rd)	TB	R	RBI	TBB	IBB	SO	HBP	SH	SF	SB	CS	SB%	GDP	Avg	OBP	SLG
1997 Minnesota	AL	25	66	18	1	0	2	(1 | 1)	25	5	13	2	0	12	0	0	3	0	0	.00	2	.273	.282	.379
1998 Arizona	NL	57	168	48	14	2	3	(2 | 1)	75	17	14	11	2	43	2	2	0	1	0	1.00	2	.286	.337	.446
1999 Arizona	NL	86	296	80	19	0	11	(3 | 8)	132	35	47	19	3	78	2	0	3	0	0	.00	6	.270	.316	.446
3 ML YEARS		168	530	146	34	2	16	(6 | 10)	232	57	74	32	5	133	4	2	6	1	0	1.00	10	.275	.318	.438

Kurt Miller

Pitches: Right **Bats:** Right **Pos:** RP-4 **Ht:** 6'5" **Wt:** 225 **Born:** 8/24/72 **Age:** 27

		HOW MUCH HE PITCHED						WHAT HE GAVE UP											THE RESULTS					
Year Team	Lg	G	GS	CG	GF	IP	BFP	H	R	ER	HR	SH	SF	HB	TBB	IBB	SO	WP	Bk	W	L	Pct.	ShO	Sv-Op	Hld	ERA
1999 Iowa *	AAA	8	2	0	2	17.2	77	17	10	10	3	0	1	0	8	0	23	2	0	1	3	.250	0	1--	—	5.09
1994 Florida	NL	4	4	0	0	20	92	26	18	18	3	0	1	2	7	0	11	0	0	1	3	.250	0	0-0	0	8.10
1996 Florida	NL	26	5	0	6	46.1	222	57	41	35	5	4	1	2	33	8	30	1	1	1	3	.250	0	0-2	0	6.80
1997 Florida	NL	7	0	0	1	7.1	41	12	8	8	2	0	1	0	7	0	7	0	0	0	0	.000	0	0-0	0	9.82
1998 Chicago	NL	3	0	0	1	4	15	3	0	0	0	0	0	0	0	0	6	0	0	0	0	.000	0	0-0	0	0.00
1999 Chicago	NL	4	0	0	1	3	17	6	6	6	1	1	0	0	3	0	1	0	0	0	0	.000	0	0-0	1	18.00
5 ML YEARS		44	9	0	9	80.2	387	104	73	67	11	5	2	5	50	8	55	1	1	2	7	.222	0	0-2	1	7.48

Travis Miller

Pitches: Left **Bats:** Right **Pos:** RP-52 **Ht:** 6'3" **Wt:** 209 **Born:** 11/2/72 **Age:** 27

		HOW MUCH HE PITCHED						WHAT HE GAVE UP											THE RESULTS					
Year Team	Lg	G	GS	CG	GF	IP	BFP	H	R	ER	HR	SH	SF	HB	TBB	IBB	SO	WP	Bk	W	L	Pct.	ShO	Sv-Op	Hld	ERA
1999 Salt Lake *	AAA	16	0	0	9	18	75	16	7	5	1	0	0	0	6	0	19	2	0	1	2	.333	0	1--	—	2.50
1996 Minnesota	AL	7	7	0	0	26.1	126	45	29	27	7	1	0	0	9	0	15	0	0	1	2	.333	0	0-0	0	9.23
1997 Minnesota	AL	13	7	0	1	48.1	227	64	49	41	8	1	2	1	23	2	26	5	0	1	5	.167	0	0-0	0	7.63
1998 Minnesota	AL	14	0	0	2	23.1	104	25	10	10	3	0	1	0	11	1	23	2	0	0	2	.000	0	0-0	0	3.86
1999 Minnesota	AL	52	0	0	12	49.2	214	55	19	15	3	2	2	0	16	3	40	6	0	2	2	.500	0	0-2	8	2.72
4 ML YEARS		86	14	0	15	147.2	671	189	107	93	18	4	5	1	59	6	104	13	0	4	11	.267	0	0-2	8	5.67

Trever Miller

Pitches: Left **Bats:** Right **Pos:** RP-47 **Ht:** 6'4" **Wt:** 195 **Born:** 5/29/73 **Age:** 27

		HOW MUCH HE PITCHED						WHAT HE GAVE UP											THE RESULTS					
Year Team	Lg	G	GS	CG	GF	IP	BFP	H	R	ER	HR	SH	SF	HB	TBB	IBB	SO	WP	Bk	W	L	Pct.	ShO	Sv-Op	Hld	ERA
1996 Detroit	AL	5	4	0	0	16.2	88	28	17	17	3	2	2	2	9	0	8	0	0	0	4	.000	0	0-0	0	9.18
1998 Houston	NL	37	1	0	15	53.1	235	57	21	18	4	0	0	1	20	1	30	1	0	2	0	1.000	0	1-2	4	3.04
1999 Houston	NL	47	0	0	11	49.2	232	58	29	28	6	2	2	5	29	1	37	4	0	3	2	.600	0	1-1	4	5.07
3 ML YEARS		89	5	0	26	119.2	555	143	67	63	13	4	4	8	58	2	75	5	0	5	6	.455	0	2-3	5	4.74

Wade Miller

Pitches: Right **Bats:** Right **Pos:** RP-4; SP-1 **Ht:** 6'2" **Wt:** 185 **Born:** 9/13/76 **Age:** 23

		HOW MUCH HE PITCHED						WHAT HE GAVE UP											THE RESULTS					
Year Team	Lg	G	GS	CG	GF	IP	BFP	H	R	ER	HR	SH	SF	HB	TBB	IBB	SO	WP	Bk	W	L	Pct.	ShO	Sv-Op	Hld	ERA
1996 Astros	R	11	10	0	0	57	233	49	26	24	1	2	5	4	12	0	53	5	0	3	4	.429	0	0--	—	3.79
Auburn	A-	2	2	0	0	9	41	8	9	5	0	0	0	0	4	0	11	0	1	1	1	.500	0	0--	—	5.00
1997 Quad City	A	10	8	2	1	59	235	45	27	22	7	0	1	0	10	0	50	4	0	5	3	.625	0	0--	—	3.36
Kissimmee	A+	14	14	4	0	100	395	79	28	20	3	3	5	4	14	1	76	4	1	10	2	.833	1	0--	—	1.80
1998 Jackson	AA	10	10	0	0	62	262	49	23	16	7	1	0	4	27	2	48	3	1	5	0	1.000	0	0--	—	2.32
1999 New Orleans	AAA	26	26	2	0	162.1	704	156	85	79	16	6	2	4	64	0	135	10	1	11	9	.550	0	0--	—	4.38
1999 Houston	NL	5	1	0	2	10.1	52	17	11	11	4	0	0	0	5	0	8	0	0	0	1	.000	0	0-0	0	9.58

Alan Mills

Pitches: Right Bats: Both Pos: RP-68 Ht: 6'1" Wt: 195 Born: 10/18/66 Age: 33

Year Team	Lg	G	GS	CG	GF	IP	BFP	H	R	ER	HR	SH	SF	HB	TBB	IBB	SO	WP	Bk	W	L	Pct.	ShO	Sv-Op	Hld	ERA
1990 New York	AL	36	0	0	18	41.2	200	48	21	19	4	4	1	1	33	6	24	3	0	1	5	.167	0	0-2	3	4.10
1991 New York	AL	6	2	0	3	16.1	72	16	9	8	1	0	1	0	8	0	11	2	0	1	1	.500	0	0-0	0	4.41
1992 Baltimore	AL	35	3	0	12	103.1	428	78	33	30	5	6	5	1	54	10	60	2	0	10	4	.714	0	2-3	2	2.61
1993 Baltimore	AL	45	0	0	18	100.1	421	80	39	36	14	4	6	4	51	5	68	3	0	5	4	.556	0	4-7	4	3.23
1994 Baltimore	AL	47	0	0	16	45.1	199	43	26	26	7	1	1	2	24	2	44	2	0	3	3	.500	0	2-4	14	5.16
1995 Baltimore	AL	21	0	0	1	23	118	30	20	19	4	0	1	2	18	4	16	1	0	3	0	1.000	0	0-1	1	7.43
1996 Baltimore	AL	49	0	0	23	54.2	233	40	26	26	10	3	2	1	35	2	50	6	0	3	2	.600	0	3-8	9	4.28
1997 Baltimore	AL	39	0	0	11	38.2	192	41	23	21	5	4	1	1	33	1	32	2	0	3	4	.400	0	0-0	7	4.89
1998 Baltimore	AL	72	0	0	13	77	327	55	32	32	8	2	3	1	50	8	57	4	0	3	4	.429	0	2-5	19	3.74
1999 Los Angeles	NL	68	0	0	18	72.1	322	70	33	30	10	3	4	4	43	4	49	3	0	3	4	.429	0	0-5	18	3.73
10 ML YEARS		418	5	0	133	572.2	2512	501	262	247	68	27	25	17	349	42	411	28	0	34	30	.531	0	13-35	77	3.88

Kevin Millwood

Pitches: Right Bats: Right Pos: SP-33 Ht: 6'4" Wt: 220 Born: 12/24/74 Age: 25

Year Team	Lg	G	GS	CG	GF	IP	BFP	H	R	ER	HR	SH	SF	HB	TBB	IBB	SO	WP	Bk	W	L	Pct.	ShO	Sv-Op	Hld	ERA
1997 Atlanta	NL	12	8	0	2	51.1	227	55	26	23	1	3	5	2	21	1	42	1	0	5	3	.625	0	0-0	0	4.03
1998 Atlanta	NL	31	29	3	1	174.1	748	175	86	79	18	8	3	3	56	3	163	6	1	17	8	.680	1	0-0	1	4.08
1999 Atlanta	NL	33	33	2	0	228	906	168	80	68	24	9	3	4	59	2	205	5	0	18	7	.720	0	0-0	0	2.68
3 ML YEARS		76	70	5	3	453.2	1881	398	192	170	43	20	11	9	136	6	410	12	1	40	18	.690	1	0-0	1	3.37

Eric Milton

Pitches: Left Bats: Left Pos: SP-34 Ht: 6'3" Wt: 220 Born: 8/4/75 Age: 24

Year Team	Lg	G	GS	CG	GF	IP	BFP	H	R	ER	HR	SH	SF	HB	TBB	IBB	SO	WP	Bk	W	L	Pct.	ShO	Sv-Op	Hld	ERA
1997 Tampa	A+	14	14	1	0	93.1	371	78	35	32	8	2	1	3	14	0	95	4	3	8	3	.727	0	0--	—	3.09
Norwich	AA	14	14	1	0	77.2	322	59	29	27	2	1	4	0	36	0	67	3	4	6	3	.667	0	0--	—	3.13
1998 Minnesota	AL	32	32	1	0	172.1	772	195	113	108	25	2	6	2	70	0	107	1	0	8	14	.364	0	0-0	0	5.64
1999 Minnesota	AL	34	34	5	0	206.1	858	190	111	103	28	3	6	3	63	2	163	2	0	7	11	.389	2	0-0	0	4.49
2 ML YEARS		66	66	6	0	378.2	1630	385	224	211	53	5	12	5	133	2	270	3	0	15	25	.375	2	0-0	0	5.01

Ryan Minor

Bats: Right Throws: Right Pos: 3B-45; 1B-1; PH/PR-1 Ht: 6'7" Wt: 245 Born: 1/5/74 Age: 26

Year Team	Lg	G	AB	H	2B	3B	HR	(Hm	Rd)	TB	R	RBI	TBB	IBB	SO	HBP	SH	SF	SB	CS	SB%	GDP	Avg	OBP	SLG
1996 Bluefield	R+	25	87	22	6	0	4	—	—	40	14	9	7	0	32	3	0	0	1	0	1.00	0	.253	.330	.460
1997 Delmarva	A	134	488	150	42	1	24	—	—	266	83	97	51	2	102	15	0	4	7	3	.70	8	.307	.387	.545
1998 Bowie	AA	138	521	130	20	3	17	—	—	207	73	71	34	2	152	13	0	1	2	3	.40	13	.250	.311	.397
1999 Rochester	AAA	101	383	98	24	1	21	—	—	187	56	67	37	1	119	5	1	6	3	1	.75	8	.256	.325	.488
1998 Baltimore	AL	9	14	6	1	0	0	(0	0)	7	1	3	1	0	0	3	0	0	0	0	.00	0	.429	.429	.500
1999 Baltimore	AL	46	124	24	7	0	3	(3	0)	40	13	10	8	0	43	0	0	1	1	0	1.00	1	.194	.241	.323
2 ML YEARS		55	138	30	8	0	3	(3	0)	47	16	11	8	0	46	0	0	1	1	0	1.00	1	.217	.259	.341

Steve Mintz

Pitches: Right Bats: Left Pos: RP-3 Ht: 5'10" Wt: 195 Born: 11/24/68 Age: 31

Year Team	Lg	G	GS	CG	GF	IP	BFP	H	R	ER	HR	SH	SF	HB	TBB	IBB	SO	WP	Bk	W	L	Pct.	ShO	Sv-Op	Hld	ERA
1990 Yakima	A-	20	0	0	12	26	113	21	9	7	1	3	1	1	16	1	38	2	1	2	3	.400	0	3--	—	2.42
1991 Bakersfield	A+	28	11	0	6	92	419	85	56	44	2	5	4	4	58	1	101	6	1	6	6	.500	0	4--	—	4.30
1992 Vero Beach	A+	43	2	0	21	77.2	323	66	29	27	7	5	3	3	30	2	66	7	3	3	6	.333	0	6--	—	3.13
1993 New Britain	AA	43	1	0	20	69.1	287	52	22	16	3	5	1	2	30	5	51	7	0	2	4	.333	0	7--	—	2.08
1994 Phoenix	AAA	24	0	0	13	36	161	40	24	22	8	1	3	1	13	3	27	3	0	0	1	.000	0	5--	—	5.50
Shreveport	AA	30	0	0	12	65.1	261	45	29	16	5	2	1	2	22	1	42	8	0	10	2	.833	0	0--	—	2.20
1995 Phoenix	AAA	31	0	0	19	49	205	42	16	13	4	3	0	2	21	4	36	4	0	5	2	.714	0	7--	—	2.39
1996 Phoenix	AAA	59	0	0	45	57	256	63	39	34	6	1	3	2	25	3	35	5	2	3	5	.375	0	27--	—	5.37
1997 Las Vegas	AAA	27	0	0	16	34.2	171	50	31	31	7	1	2	2	17	3	28	2	0	5	2	.714	0	5--	—	8.05
1998 Nashville	AAA	56	0	0	18	72.2	334	85	48	44	7	4	4	3	32	2	45	3	0	4	4	.500	0	1--	—	5.45
1999 Erie	AA	26	0	0	14	32.1	135	26	12	8	3	1	1	2	12	0	33	0	0	1	1	.500	0	9--	—	2.23
Edmonton	AAA	31	0	0	27	30.2	127	31	11	8	2	0	1	2	6	0	17	2	0	4	3	.571	0	9--	—	2.35
1995 San Francisco	NL	14	0	0	3	19.1	96	26	16	16	4	2	1	2	12	3	7	0	0	1	2	.333	0	0-1	0	7.45
1999 Anaheim	AL	3	0	0	2	5	23	8	2	2	1	0	0	0	2	0	2	0	0	0	0	.000	0	0-0	0	3.60
2 ML YEARS		17	0	0	5	24.1	119	34	18	18	5	2	1	2	14	3	9	0	0	1	2	.333	0	0-1	0	6.66

Doug Mirabelli

Bats: Right Throws: Right Pos: C-30; PH/PR-5 Ht: 6'1" Wt: 218 Born: 10/18/70 Age: 29

Year Team	Lg	G	AB	H	2B	3B	HR	(Hm	Rd)	TB	R	RBI	TBB	IBB	SO	HBP	SH	SF	SB	CS	SB%	GDP	Avg	OBP	SLG
1992 San Jose	A+	53	177	41	11	1	0	—	—	54	30	21	24	0	18	4	2	2	1	3	.25	7	.232	.333	.305

157

First player (batting, continued)

Year Team	Lg	G	AB	H	2B	3B	HR	(Hm	Rd)	TB	R	RBI	TBB	IBB	SO	HBP	SH	SF	SB	CS	SB%	GDP	Avg	OBP	SLG
1993 San Jose	A+	113	371	100	19	2	1	—	—	126	58	48	72	1	55	4	2	4	0	4	.00	7	.270	.390	.340
1994 Shreveport	AA	85	255	56	8	0	4	—	—	76	23	24	36	5	48	0	2	0	3	1	.75	6	.220	.316	.298
1995 Phoenix	AAA	23	66	11	0	1	0	—	—	13	3	7	12	1	10	1	0	2	1	0	1.00	5	.167	.296	.197
Shreveport	AA	40	126	38	13	0	0	—	—	51	14	16	20	1	14	0	2	0	1	0	1.00	3	.302	.397	.405
1996 Phoenix	AAA	14	47	14	7	0	0	—	—	21	10	7	4	0	7	1	0	0	0	0	.00	1	.298	.365	.447
Shreveport	AA	115	380	112	23	0	21	—	—	198	60	70	76	0	49	6	1	1	0	1	.00	9	.295	.419	.521
1997 Phoenix	AAA	100	332	88	23	2	8	—	—	139	49	48	58	2	69	7	3	1	1	2	.33	9	.265	.384	.419
1998 Fresno	AAA	85	265	69	12	2	13	—	—	124	45	53	52	6	55	3	3	1	2	0	1.00	9	.260	.386	.468
1999 Fresno	AAA	86	320	100	24	1	14	—	—	168	63	51	48	2	56	1	0	5	8	2	.80	6	.313	.398	.525
1996 San Francisco	NL	9	18	4	1	0	0	(0	0)	5	2	1	3	0	4	0	0	0	0	0	.00	0	.222	.333	.278
1997 San Francisco	NL	6	7	1	0	0	0	(0	0)	1	0	0	1	0	3	0	0	0	0	0	.00	0	.143	.250	.143
1998 San Francisco	NL	10	17	4	2	0	1	(1	0)	9	2	4	2	0	6	0	0	0	0	0	.00	0	.235	.316	.529
1999 San Francisco	NL	33	87	22	6	0	1	(1	0)	31	10	10	9	1	25	1	0	1	0	0	.00	1	.253	.327	.356
4 ML YEARS		58	129	31	9	0	2	(2	0)	46	14	15	15	1	38	1	0	1	0	0	.00	1	.240	.322	.357

Dave Mlicki

Pitches: Right **Bats:** Right **Pos:** SP-31; RP-2   **Ht:** 6'4" **Wt:** 205 **Born:** 6/8/68 **Age:** 32

Year Team	Lg	G	GS	CG	GF	IP	BFP	H	R	ER	HR	SH	SF	HB	TBB	IBB	SO	WP	Bk	W	L	Pct.	ShO	Sv-Op	Hld	ERA
1992 Cleveland	AL	4	4	0	0	21.2	101	23	14	12	3	2	0	1	16	0	16	1	0	0	2	.000	0	0-0	0	4.98
1993 Cleveland	AL	3	3	0	0	13.1	58	11	6	5	2	0	0	0	6	0	7	2	0	0	0	.000	0	0-0	0	3.38
1995 New York	NL	29	25	0	1	160.2	696	160	82	76	23	8	5	4	54	2	123	5	1	9	7	.563	0	0-0	0	4.26
1996 New York	NL	51	2	0	16	90	393	95	46	33	9	8	3	6	33	8	83	7	0	6	7	.462	0	1-3	8	3.30
1997 New York	NL	32	32	1	0	193.2	838	194	89	86	21	3	6	5	76	7	157	5	1	8	12	.400	1	0-0	0	4.00
1998 NYM-LA	NL	30	30	3	0	181.1	789	188	102	92	23	8	7	7	63	5	117	10	0	8	7	.533	1	0-0	0	4.57
1999 LA-Det		33	31	2	0	199	883	219	112	102	25	3	8	12	72	1	120	1	0	14	13	.519	0	0-0	1	4.61
1998 New York	NL	10	10	1	0	57	264	68	38	36	8	2	3	5	25	4	39	4	0	1	4	.200	0	0-0	0	5.68
Los Angeles	NL	20	20	2	0	124.1	525	120	64	56	15	6	4	2	38	1	78	6	0	7	3	.700	1	0-0	0	4.05
1999 Los Angeles	NL	2	0	0	0	7.1	33	10	4	4	1	0	0	0	2	0	1	1	0	0	1	.000	0	0-0	1	4.91
Detroit	AL	31	31	2	0	191.2	850	209	108	98	24	3	8	12	70	1	119	0	0	14	12	.538	0	0-0	0	4.60
7 ML YEARS		182	127	6	17	859.2	3758	890	451	406	106	32	29	37	320	23	623	31	2	45	48	.484	2	1-3	9	4.25

Brian Moehler

Pitches: Right **Bats:** Right **Pos:** SP-32   **Ht:** 6'3" **Wt:** 235 **Born:** 12/31/71 **Age:** 28

Year Team	Lg	G	GS	CG	GF	IP	BFP	H	R	ER	HR	SH	SF	HB	TBB	IBB	SO	WP	Bk	W	L	Pct.	ShO	Sv-Op	Hld	ERA
1996 Detroit	AL	2	2	0	0	10.1	51	11	10	5	1	1	0	0	8	1	2	1	0	0	1	.000	0	0-0	0	4.35
1997 Detroit	AL	31	31	2	0	175.1	770	198	97	91	22	1	8	5	61	1	97	3	0	11	12	.478	1	0-0	0	4.67
1998 Detroit	AL	33	33	4	0	221.1	912	220	103	96	30	3	3	2	56	1	123	4	0	14	13	.519	3	0-0	0	3.90
1999 Detroit	AL	32	32	2	0	196.1	859	229	116	110	22	8	5	7	59	5	106	4	0	10	16	.385	2	0-0	0	5.04
4 ML YEARS		98	98	8	0	603.1	2592	658	326	302	75	13	16	14	184	8	328	12	0	35	42	.455	6	0-0	0	4.50

Mike Mohler

Pitches: Left **Bats:** Right **Pos:** RP-48   **Ht:** 6'2" **Wt:** 208 **Born:** 7/26/68 **Age:** 31

Year Team	Lg	G	GS	CG	GF	IP	BFP	H	R	ER	HR	SH	SF	HB	TBB	IBB	SO	WP	Bk	W	L	Pct.	ShO	Sv-Op	Hld	ERA
1999 Memphis *	AAA	10	0	0	2	14.2	64	16	5	5	0	0	0	0	5	1	17	0	0	2	1	.667	0	1--	—	3.07
1993 Oakland	AL	42	9	0	4	64.1	290	57	45	40	10	5	2	2	44	4	42	0	1	1	6	.143	0	0-1	1	5.60
1994 Oakland	AL	1	1	0	0	2.1	14	3	3	2	1	0	0	0	2	0	4	0	0	0	1	.000	0	0-0	0	7.71
1995 Oakland	AL	28	0	0	6	23.2	100	16	8	8	0	1	0	0	18	1	15	1	0	1	1	.500	0	1-2	4	3.04
1996 Oakland	AL	72	0	0	30	81	352	79	36	33	9	6	4	1	41	6	64	9	0	6	3	.667	0	7-13	13	3.67
1997 Oakland	AL	62	10	0	16	101.2	462	116	65	58	11	9	7	7	54	8	66	4	0	1	10	.091	0	1-4	11	5.13
1998 Oakland	AL	57	0	0	16	61	277	70	38	35	6	3	2	4	26	3	42	3	1	3	3	.500	0	0-1	8	5.16
1999 St. Louis	NL	48	0	0	16	49.1	211	47	26	24	3	1	1	1	23	2	31	1	0	1	1	.500	0	1-2	6	4.38
7 ML YEARS		310	20	0	88	383.1	1706	387	221	200	40	25	16	15	208	24	264	18	2	13	25	.342	0	10-23	43	4.70

Ben Molina

Bats: Right **Throws:** Right **Pos:** C-30; PH/PR-1   **Ht:** 5'11" **Wt:** 200 **Born:** 7/20/74 **Age:** 25

Year Team	Lg	G	AB	H	2B	3B	HR	(Hm	Rd)	TB	R	RBI	TBB	IBB	SO	HBP	SH	SF	SB	CS	SB%	GDP	Avg	OBP	SLG
1993 Angels	R	27	80	21	6	2	0	—	—	31	9	10	10	0	4	1	0	1	0	2	.00	1	.263	.348	.388
1994 Cedar Rapds	A	48	171	48	8	0	3	—	—	65	14	16	8	0	12	3	1	0	1	2	.33	3	.281	.324	.380
1995 Vancouver	AAA	1	2	0	0	0	0	—	—	0	0	0	0	0	1	0	0	0	0	0	.00	0	.000	.000	.000
Cedar Rapds	A	39	133	39	9	0	4	—	—	60	15	17	15	0	11	1	1	1	1	1	.50	4	.293	.367	.451
Lk Elsinore	A+	27	96	37	7	2	2	—	—	54	21	12	8	1	7	4	3	1	0	0	.00	2	.385	.450	.563
1996 Midland	AA	108	365	100	21	2	8	—	—	149	45	54	25	1	25	6	4	5	0	1	.00	16	.274	.327	.408
1997 Lk Elsinore	A+	36	149	42	10	2	4	—	—	68	18	33	7	2	9	0	0	3	0	1	.00	7	.282	.308	.456
Midland	AA	29	106	35	8	0	6	—	—	61	18	30	10	0	7	0	0	2	0	0	.00	7	.330	.381	.575
1998 Midland	AA	41	154	55	8	0	9	—	—	90	28	39	14	2	7	3	0	1	0	1	.00	7	.357	.419	.584
Vancouver	AAA	49	184	54	9	1	1	—	—	68	13	22	5	0	14	0	1	1	1	1	.50	6	.293	.311	.370
1999 Edmonton	AAA	65	241	69	16	0	7	—	—	106	28	41	15	1	17	6	1	4	1	2	.33	7	.286	.338	.440
1998 Anaheim	AL	2	1	0	0	0	0	(0	0)	0	0	0	0	0	0	0	0	0	0	0	.00	0	.000	.000	.000
1999 Anaheim	AL	31	101	26	5	0	1	(0	1)	34	8	10	6	0	6	2	0	0	0	1	.00	5	.257	.312	.337
2 ML YEARS		33	102	26	5	0	1	(0	1)	34	8	10	6	0	6	2	0	0	0	1	.00	5	.255	.309	.333

Gabe Molina

Pitches: Right Bats: Right Pos: RP-20 Ht: 5'11" Wt: 202 Born: 5/3/75 Age: 25

Year Team	Lg	G	GS	CG	GF	IP	BFP	H	R	ER	HR	SH	SF	HB	TBB	IBB	SO	WP	Bk	W	L	Pct.	ShO	Sv-Op	Hld	ERA
1996 Bluefield	R+	23	0	0	19	30	131	29	12	12	1	1	0	2	13	1	33	5	3	4	0	1.000	0	7--	—	3.60
1997 Delmarva	A	46	0	0	31	91	364	59	24	22	3	6	1	3	32	5	119	7	2	8	6	.571	0	7--	—	2.18
1998 Bowie	AA	47	0	0	38	61.2	256	48	24	24	5	3	1	1	27	0	75	5	1	3	2	.600	0	24--	—	3.36
1999 Rochester	AAA	45	0	0	36	57.1	241	45	22	20	3	2	1	2	23	1	58	6	1	2	2	.500	0	18--	—	3.14
1999 Baltimore	AL	20	0	0	7	23	102	22	19	17	4	0	0	0	16	1	14	4	0	1	2	.333	0	0-1	2	6.65

Jose Molina

Bats: Right Throws: Right Pos: C-10 Ht: 6'1" Wt: 195 Born: 6/3/75 Age: 25

Year Team	Lg	G	AB	H	2B	3B	HR	(Hm	Rd)	TB	R	RBI	TBB	IBB	SO	HBP	SH	SF	SB	CS	SB%	GDP	Avg	OBP	SLG
1993 Cubs	R	33	78	17	2	0	0	—	—	19	5	4	12	0	12	0	4	0	3	2	.60	2	.218	.322	.244
Daytona	A+	3	7	1	0	0	0	—	—	1	0	1	2	0	0	0	0	0	0	1	.00	0	.143	.333	.143
1994 Peoria	A	78	253	58	13	1	1	—	—	76	31	33	24	1	61	4	5	4	4	3	.57	5	.229	.302	.300
1995 Daytona	A+	82	233	55	9	1	1	—	—	69	27	19	29	0	53	7	2	2	1	0	1.00	7	.236	.336	.296
1996 Rockford	A	96	305	69	10	1	2	—	—	87	35	27	36	0	71	3	7	4	2	4	.33	8	.226	.310	.285
1997 Iowa	AAA	1	3	1	0	0	0	—	—	1	0	0	1	0	1	0	0	0	0	0	.00	0	.333	.500	.333
Daytona	A+	55	179	45	9	1	0	—	—	56	17	23	14	0	25	1	5	2	4	0	1.00	5	.251	.306	.313
Orlando	AA	37	99	17	3	0	1	—	—	23	10	15	12	5	28	2	1	3	0	1	.00	4	.172	.267	.232
1998 West Tenn	AA	109	320	71	10	1	2	—	—	89	33	28	32	1	74	3	10	3	1	5	.17	10	.222	.296	.278
1999 West Tenn	AA	14	35	6	3	0	0	—	—	9	2	5	2	0	14	0	1	0	0	0	.00	1	.171	.211	.257
Iowa	AAA	74	240	63	11	1	4	—	—	88	24	26	20	5	54	4	2	2	0	1	.00	3	.263	.327	.367
1999 Chicago	NL	10	19	5	1	0	0	(0	0)	6	3	1	2	1	4	0	0	0	0	0	.00	0	.263	.333	.316

Shane Monahan

Bats: L Throws: R Pos: PH/PR-9; LF-7; DH-3; RF-3 Ht: 6'0" Wt: 195 Born: 8/12/74 Age: 25

Year Team	Lg	G	AB	H	2B	3B	HR	(Hm	Rd)	TB	R	RBI	TBB	IBB	SO	HBP	SH	SF	SB	CS	SB%	GDP	Avg	OBP	SLG
1995 Wisconsin	A	59	233	66	9	6	1	—	—	90	34	32	11	0	40	2	7	3	9	2	.82	4	.283	.317	.386
1996 Lancaster	A+	132	585	164	31	12	14	—	—	261	107	97	30	2	124	4	3	8	19	5	.79	8	.280	.316	.446
1997 Memphis	AA	107	401	121	24	6	12	—	—	193	52	76	30	2	100	2	1	2	14	7	.67	4	.302	.352	.481
Tacoma	AAA	21	85	25	4	0	2	—	—	35	15	12	5	0	21	1	2	0	5	1	.83	4	.294	.341	.412
1998 Tacoma	AAA	69	277	69	8	5	4	—	—	99	32	33	19	3	47	0	4	2	6	4	.60	3	.249	.295	.357
1999 Tacoma	AAA	108	399	102	21	5	2	—	—	148	51	31	19	2	81	3	1	2	9	3	.75	4	.256	.293	.371
1998 Seattle	AL	62	211	51	8	1	4	(2	2)	73	17	28	8	0	53	0	4	0	1	2	.33	0	.242	.269	.346
1999 Seattle	AL	16	15	2	0	0	0	(0	0)	2	3	0	0	0	6	0	0	0	0	0	.00	0	.133	.133	.133
2 ML YEARS		78	226	53	8	1	4	(2	2)	75	20	28	8	0	59	0	4	0	1	2	.33	0	.235	.261	.332

Raul Mondesi

Bats: Right Throws: Right Pos: RF-158; PH/PR-3; CF-1 Ht: 5'11" Wt: 215 Born: 3/12/71 Age: 29

Year Team	Lg	G	AB	H	2B	3B	HR	(Hm	Rd)	TB	R	RBI	TBB	IBB	SO	HBP	SH	SF	SB	CS	SB%	GDP	Avg	OBP	SLG
1993 Los Angeles	NL	42	86	25	3	1	4	(2	2)	42	13	10	4	0	16	0	1	0	4	1	.80	1	.291	.322	.488
1994 Los Angeles	NL	112	434	133	27	8	16	(10	6)	224	63	56	16	5	78	2	0	2	11	8	.58	9	.306	.333	.516
1995 Los Angeles	NL	139	536	153	23	6	26	(13	13)	266	91	88	33	4	96	4	0	7	27	4	.87	6	.285	.328	.496
1996 Los Angeles	NL	157	634	188	40	7	24	(11	13)	314	98	88	32	9	122	5	0	2	14	7	.67	6	.297	.334	.495
1997 Los Angeles	NL	159	616	191	42	5	30	(16	14)	333	95	87	44	7	105	6	1	3	32	15	.68	11	.310	.360	.541
1998 Los Angeles	NL	148	580	162	26	5	30	(13	17)	288	85	90	30	4	112	3	0	4	16	10	.62	8	.279	.316	.497
1999 Los Angeles	NL	159	601	152	29	5	33	(18	15)	290	98	99	71	6	134	3	0	5	36	9	.80	4	.253	.332	.483
7 ML YEARS		916	3487	1004	190	37	163	(83	80)	1757	543	518	230	35	663	23	2	23	140	54	.72	45	.288	.334	.504

Jeff Montgomery

Pitches: Right Bats: Right Pos: RP-49 Ht: 5'11" Wt: 175 Born: 1/7/62 Age: 38

Year Team	Lg	G	GS	CG	GF	IP	BFP	H	R	ER	HR	SH	SF	HB	TBB	IBB	SO	WP	Bk	W	L	Pct.	ShO	Sv-Op	Hld	ERA
1999 Wichita *	AA	1	0	0	0	1	5	2	1	1	0	0	0	0	1	0	1	0	0	0	0	.000	0	0--	—	9.00
Omaha *	AAA	4	0	0	4	5	17	1	0	0	0	0	0	0	1	0	3	0	0	0	0	.000	0	1--	—	0.00
1987 Cincinnati	NL	14	1	0	6	19.1	89	25	15	14	2	0	0	0	9	1	13	1	1	2	2	.500	0	0-0	1	6.52
1988 Kansas City	AL	45	0	0	13	62.2	271	54	25	24	6	3	2	2	30	1	47	3	6	7	2	.778	0	1-3	9	3.45
1989 Kansas City	AL	63	0	0	39	92	363	66	16	14	3	1	1	2	25	4	94	6	1	7	3	.700	0	18-24	11	1.37
1990 Kansas City	AL	73	0	0	59	94.1	400	81	36	25	6	2	2	5	34	8	94	3	0	6	5	.545	0	24-34	7	2.39
1991 Kansas City	AL	67	0	0	55	90	376	83	32	29	6	6	2	2	28	2	77	6	0	4	4	.500	0	33-39	3	2.90
1992 Kansas City	AL	65	0	0	62	82.2	333	61	23	20	5	4	2	3	27	2	69	2	0	1	6	.143	0	39-46	0	2.18
1993 Kansas City	AL	69	0	0	63	87.1	347	65	22	22	3	5	1	2	23	4	66	3	0	7	5	.583	0	**45-51**	0	2.27
1994 Kansas City	AL	42	0	0	38	44.2	193	48	21	20	5	2	1	1	15	1	50	2	0	2	3	.400	0	27-32	0	4.03
1995 Kansas City	AL	54	0	0	46	65.2	275	60	27	25	7	5	5	2	25	4	49	1	1	2	3	.400	0	31-38	0	3.43
1996 Kansas City	AL	48	0	0	41	63.1	261	59	31	30	14	3	1	3	19	3	45	0	0	4	6	.400	0	24-34	0	4.26
1997 Kansas City	AL	55	0	0	37	59.1	245	53	24	23	9	4	2	0	18	5	48	5	0	1	4	.200	0	14-17	3	3.49
1998 Kansas City	AL	56	0	0	54	56	247	58	35	31	8	2	1	2	22	2	54	0	1	2	5	.286	0	36-41	0	4.98
1999 Kansas City	AL	49	0	0	36	51.1	237	72	40	39	7	2	2	2	23	1	27	1	0	1	4	.200	0	12-19	1	6.84
13 ML YEARS		700	1	0	549	868.2	3637	785	347	316	81	39	22	26	296	40	733	33	10	46	52	.469	0	304-378	35	3.27

159

Steve Montgomery

Pitches: Right **Bats:** Right **Pos:** RP-53 **Ht:** 6'4" **Wt:** 200 **Born:** 12/25/70 **Age:** 29

Year Team	Lg	G	GS	CG	GF	IP	BFP	H	R	ER	HR	SH	SF	HB	TBB	IBB	SO	WP	Bk	W	L	Pct.	ShO	Sv-Op	Hld	ERA
1999 Scranton-WB *	AAA	14	0	0	11	13	65	17	9	9	0	1	1	0	11	0	13	1	1	0	0	.000	0	7--	-	6.23
1996 Oakland	AL	8	0	0	0	13.2	71	18	14	14	5	0	0	0	13	2	8	3	0	1	0	1.000	0	0-0	-	9.22
1997 Oakland	AL	4	0	0	0	6.1	35	10	7	7	2	0	1	0	8	2	1	0	0	1	0	1.000	0	0-0	1	9.95
1999 Philadelphia	NL	53	0	0	21	64.2	268	54	25	24	10	1	0	0	31	3	55	4	0	1	5	.167	0	3-3	11	3.34
3 ML YEARS		65	0	0	21	84.2	374	82	46	45	17	1	1	0	52	7	64	7	0	2	6	.250	0	3-3	12	4.78

Melvin Mora

Bats: R **Throws:** R **Pos:** LF-28; PH/PR-27; CF-11; RF-8; 2B-4; 3B-3; SS-1 **Ht:** 5'10" **Wt:** 160 **Born:** 2/2/72 **Age:** 28

Year Team	Lg	G	AB	H	2B	3B	HR	(Hm	Rd)	TB	R	RBI	TBB	IBB	SO	HBP	SH	SF	SB	CS	SB%	GDP	Avg	OBP	SLG
1992 Astros	R	49	144	32	3	0	0	—	—	35	28	8	18	0	16	5	0	1	16	3	.84	2	.222	.327	.243
1993 Asheville	A	108	365	104	22	2	2	—	—	136	66	31	36	0	46	9	5	8	20	13	.61	7	.285	.356	.373
1994 Osceola	A+	118	425	120	29	4	8	—	—	181	57	46	37	1	60	10	3	3	22	11	.67	11	.282	.352	.426
1995 Jackson	AA	123	467	139	32	0	3	—	—	180	63	45	32	1	57	9	7	7	22	11	.67	11	.298	.350	.385
Tucson	AAA	2	5	3	0	1	0	—	—	5	3	1	2	1	0	0	0	0	1	0	1.00	0	.600	.714	1.000
1996 Tucson	AAA	62	228	64	11	2	3	—	—	88	35	26	17	1	27	1	3	4	3	5	.38	7	.281	.328	.386
Jackson	AA	70	255	73	6	1	5	—	—	96	36	23	14	1	23	6	1	2	4	7	.36	4	.286	.336	.376
1997 New Orleans	AAA	119	370	95	15	3	2	—	—	122	55	38	47	0	52	11	9	2	7	7	.50	7	.257	.356	.330
1998 St. Lucie	A+	17	55	15	0	0	0	—	—	15	5	8	5	0	9	0	0	1	1	1	.50	0	.273	.328	.273
Norfolk	AAA	11	28	5	1	0	0	—	—	6	5	2	5	0	7	0	2	0	0	0	.00	0	.179	.303	.214
1999 Norfolk	AAA	82	304	92	17	2	8	—	—	137	55	36	41	0	54	7	4	4	18	8	.69	8	.303	.393	.451
1999 New York	NL	66	31	5	0	0	0	(0	0)	5	6	1	4	0	7	1	3	0	2	1	.67	0	.161	.278	.161

Mickey Morandini

Bats: Left **Throws:** Right **Pos:** 2B-132; PH/PR-25 **Ht:** 5'11" **Wt:** 180 **Born:** 4/22/66 **Age:** 34

Year Team	Lg	G	AB	H	2B	3B	HR	(Hm	Rd)	TB	R	RBI	TBB	IBB	SO	HBP	SH	SF	SB	CS	SB%	GDP	Avg	OBP	SLG
1990 Philadelphia	NL	25	79	19	4	0	1	(1	0)	26	9	3	6	0	19	0	2	0	3	0	1.00	1	.241	.294	.329
1991 Philadelphia	NL	98	325	81	11	4	1	(1	0)	103	38	20	29	0	45	2	6	2	13	2	.87	7	.249	.313	.317
1992 Philadelphia	NL	127	422	112	8	8	3	(2	1)	145	47	30	25	2	64	0	6	2	8	3	.73	4	.265	.305	.344
1993 Philadelphia	NL	120	425	105	19	9	3	(2	1)	151	57	33	34	2	73	5	4	2	13	2	.87	7	.247	.309	.355
1994 Philadelphia	NL	87	274	80	16	5	2	(1	1)	112	40	26	34	5	33	4	4	0	10	5	.67	4	.292	.378	.409
1995 Philadelphia	NL	127	494	140	34	7	6	(3	3)	206	65	49	42	3	80	9	4	1	9	6	.60	11	.283	.350	.417
1996 Philadelphia	NL	140	539	135	24	6	3	(2	1)	180	64	32	49	0	87	9	5	4	26	5	.84	15	.250	.321	.334
1997 Philadelphia	NL	150	553	163	40	2	1	(1	0)	210	83	39	62	0	91	8	12	5	16	13	.55	8	.295	.371	.380
1998 Chicago	NL	154	582	172	20	4	8	(4	4)	224	93	53	72	4	84	9	4	2	13	1	.93	14	.296	.380	.385
1999 Chicago	NL	144	456	110	18	5	4	(3	1)	150	60	37	48	2	61	6	7	4	6	6	.50	10	.241	.319	.329
10 ML YEARS		1172	4149	1117	194	50	32	(20	12)	1507	556	322	401	18	637	52	54	22	117	43	.73	81	.269	.340	.363

Mike Mordecai

Bats: R **Throws:** R **Pos:** 2B-38; SS-38; 3B-32; PH/PR-13; 1B-1 **Ht:** 5'11" **Wt:** 180 **Born:** 12/13/67 **Age:** 32

Year Team	Lg	G	AB	H	2B	3B	HR	(Hm	Rd)	TB	R	RBI	TBB	IBB	SO	HBP	SH	SF	SB	CS	SB%	GDP	Avg	OBP	SLG
1994 Atlanta	NL	4	4	1	0	0	1	(1	0)	4	1	3	1	0	0	0	0	0	0	0	.00	0	.250	.400	1.000
1995 Atlanta	NL	69	75	21	6	0	3	(1	2)	36	10	11	9	0	16	0	2	1	0	0	.00	0	.280	.353	.480
1996 Atlanta	NL	66	108	26	5	0	2	(0	2)	37	12	8	9	1	24	0	4	1	1	0	1.00	1	.241	.297	.343
1997 Atlanta	NL	61	81	14	2	1	0	(0	0)	18	8	3	6	0	16	0	1	1	0	1	.00	4	.173	.227	.222
1998 Montreal	NL	73	119	24	4	2	3	(1	2)	41	12	10	9	0	20	0	2	0	1	0	1.00	1	.202	.258	.345
1999 Montreal	NL	109	226	53	10	2	5	(4	1)	82	29	25	20	1	31	1	1	2	2	5	.29	1	.235	.297	.363
6 ML YEARS		382	613	139	27	5	14	(7	7)	218	72	60	54	1	107	1	10	5	4	6	.40	8	.227	.288	.356

Orber Moreno

Pitches: Right **Bats:** Right **Pos:** RP-7 **Ht:** 6'2" **Wt:** 190 **Born:** 4/27/77 **Age:** 23

Year Team	Lg	G	GS	CG	GF	IP	BFP	H	R	ER	HR	SH	SF	HB	TBB	IBB	SO	WP	Bk	W	L	Pct.	ShO	Sv-Op	Hld	ERA
1995 Royals	R	8	3	0	1	22	89	15	9	6	0	0	0	2	7	0	21	2	0	1	1	.500	0	0--	-	2.45
1996 Royals	R	12	7	0	5	46.1	187	37	15	7	2	2	0	1	10	0	50	1	2	5	1	.833	0	1--	-	1.36
1997 Lansing	A	27	25	0	0	138.1	603	150	83	74	15	6	4	8	45	0	128	9	4	4	8	.333	0	0--	-	4.81
1998 Wilmington	A+	23	0	0	17	33	115	8	3	3	1	1	0	0	10	1	50	1	0	3	2	.600	0	7--	-	0.82
Wichita	AA	24	0	0	19	34.1	144	28	13	11	1	2	0	0	12	3	40	3	0	0	0	.000	0	7--	-	2.88
1999 Omaha	AAA	16	0	0	15	25.2	97	17	6	6	2	0	0	0	4	0	30	0	0	3	1	.750	0	4--	-	2.10
Royals	R	1	1	0	0	1	3	0	0	0	0	0	0	0	0	0	1	0	0	0	0	.000	0	0--	-	0.00
1999 Kansas City	AL	7	0	0	3	8	34	4	5	5	1	0	0	0	6	0	7	0	0	0	0	.000	0	0-1	1	5.63

Mike Morgan

Pitches: Right **Bats:** Right **Pos:** SP-25; RP-9   **Ht:** 6'2" **Wt:** 220 **Born:** 10/8/59 **Age:** 40

Year Team	Lg	G	GS	CG	GF	IP	BFP	H	R	ER	HR	SH	SF	HB	TBB	IBB	SO	WP	Bk	W	L	Pct.	ShO	Sv-Op	Hld	ERA
1978 Oakland	AL	3	3	1	0	12.1	60	19	12	10	1	1	0	0	8	0	0	0	0	0	3	.000	0	0-0	0	7.30
1979 Oakland	AL	13	13	2	0	77.1	368	102	57	51	7	4	4	3	50	0	17	7	0	2	10	.167	0	0-0	0	5.94
1982 New York	AL	30	23	2	2	150.1	661	167	77	73	15	2	4	2	67	5	71	6	0	7	11	.389	0	0-0	0	4.37
1983 Toronto	AL	16	4	0	2	45.1	198	48	26	26	6	0	1	0	21	0	22	3	0	0	3	.000	0	0-0	0	5.16
1985 Seattle	AL	2	2	0	0	6	33	11	8	8	2	0	0	0	5	0	2	1	0	1	1	.500	0	0-0	0	12.00
1986 Seattle	AL	37	33	9	2	216.1	951	243	122	109	24	7	3	4	86	3	116	8	1	11	17	.393	1	1-1	0	4.53
1987 Seattle	AL	34	31	8	2	207	898	245	117	107	25	8	5	5	53	3	85	11	0	12	17	.414	2	0-0	0	4.65
1988 Baltimore	AL	22	10	2	6	71.1	299	70	45	43	6	1	0	1	23	1	29	5	0	1	6	.143	0	1-1	0	5.43
1989 Los Angeles	NL	40	19	0	7	152.2	604	130	51	43	6	8	6	2	33	8	72	6	0	8	11	.421	0	0-1	1	2.53
1990 Los Angeles	NL	33	33	6	0	211	891	216	100	88	19	11	4	5	60	5	106	4	1	11	15	.423	4	0-0	0	3.75
1991 Los Angeles	NL	34	33	5	1	236.1	949	197	85	73	12	10	4	3	61	10	140	6	0	14	10	.583	1	1-1	0	2.78
1992 Chicago	NL	34	34	6	0	240	966	203	80	68	14	10	5	3	79	10	123	11	0	16	8	.667	1	0-0	0	2.55
1993 Chicago	NL	32	32	1	0	207.2	883	206	100	93	15	11	5	7	74	8	111	8	2	10	15	.400	1	0-0	0	4.03
1994 Chicago	NL	15	15	1	0	80.2	380	111	65	60	12	7	6	4	35	2	57	5	0	2	10	.167	0	0-0	0	6.69
1995 ChC-StL	NL	21	21	1	0	131.1	548	133	56	52	12	12	5	6	34	2	61	6	0	7	7	.500	0	0-0	0	3.56
1996 StL-Cin	NL	23	23	0	0	130.1	567	146	72	67	16	6	7	1	47	0	74	2	0	6	11	.353	0	0-0	0	4.63
1997 Cincinnati	NL	31	30	1	0	162	688	165	91	86	13	9	2	8	49	6	103	7	0	9	12	.429	0	0-0	1	4.78
1998 Min-ChC		23	22	0	0	120.2	524	138	62	56	21	3	3	8	39	2	60	1	0	4	3	.571	0	0-0	0	4.18
1999 Texas		34	25	1	1	140	632	184	108	97	25	3	5	7	48	2	61	3	1	13	10	.565	0	0-1	0	6.24
1995 Chicago	NL	4	4	0	0	24.2	100	19	8	6	2	2	0	1	9	1	15	0	0	2	1	.667	0	0-0	0	2.19
St. Louis	NL	17	17	1	0	106.2	448	114	48	46	10	10	5	5	25	1	46	6	0	5	6	.455	0	0-0	0	3.88
1996 St. Louis	NL	18	18	0	0	103	452	118	63	60	14	5	6	0	40	0	55	2	0	4	8	.333	0	0-0	0	5.24
Cincinnati	NL	5	5	0	0	27.1	115	28	9	7	2	1	1	1	7	0	19	0	0	2	3	.400	0	0-0	0	2.30
1998 Minnesota	AL	18	17	0	0	98	412	108	41	38	13	0	3	7	24	1	50	1	0	4	2	.667	0	0-0	0	3.49
Chicago	NL	5	5	0	0	22.2	112	30	21	18	8	3	0	1	15	1	10	0	0	0	1	.000	0	0-0	0	7.15
19 ML YEARS		477	406	46	23	2598.2	11100	2734	1334	1210	251	113	69	69	872	67	1310	100	5	134	180	.427	10	3-5	2	4.19

Alvin Morman

Pitches: Left **Bats:** Right **Pos:** RP-49   **Ht:** 6'3" **Wt:** 210 **Born:** 1/6/69 **Age:** 31

Year Team	Lg	G	GS	CG	GF	IP	BFP	H	R	ER	HR	SH	SF	HB	TBB	IBB	SO	WP	Bk	W	L	Pct.	ShO	Sv-Op	Hld	ERA
1999 Omaha *	AAA	8	1	0	3	14.1	51	8	5	5	3	1	0	0	15	0	15	0	0	0	0	.000	0	1- -	-	3.14
1996 Houston	NL	53	0	0	9	42	192	43	24	23	8	2	1	0	24	6	31	3	1	4	1	.800	0	0-2	7	4.93
1997 Cleveland	AL	34	0	0	7	18.1	86	19	13	12	2	0	1	1	14	3	13	1	0	0	0	.000	0	2-2	5	5.89
1998 Cle-SF		40	0	0	8	29	128	33	17	17	5	0	1	0	14	1	23	2	0	0	2	.000	0	0-2	9	5.28
1999 Kansas City	AL	49	0	0	2	53.1	246	66	27	24	6	0	4	4	23	0	31	1	0	2	4	.333	0	1-3	3	4.05
1998 Cleveland	AL	31	0	0	5	22	96	25	13	13	1	0	1	0	11	1	16	2	0	0	1	.000	0	0-1	9	5.32
San Francisco	NL	9	0	0	3	7	32	8	4	4	4	0	0	0	3	0	7	0	0	0	1	.000	0	0-1	0	5.14
4 ML YEARS		176	0	0	26	142.2	652	161	81	76	21	2	6	5	75	10	98	7	1	6	7	.462	0	3-9	24	4.79

Hal Morris

Bats: L **Throws:** L **Pos:** PH/PR-53; 1B-25; LF-4; DH-1   **Ht:** 6'2" **Wt:** 195 **Born:** 4/9/65 **Age:** 35

Year Team	Lg	G	AB	H	2B	3B	HR	(Hm	Rd)	TB	R	RBI	TBB	IBB	SO	HBP	SH	SF	SB	CS	SB%	GDP	Avg	OBP	SLG
1988 New York	AL	15	20	2	0	0	0	(0	0)	2	1	0	0	0	9	0	0	0	0	0	.00	0	.100	.100	.100
1989 New York	AL	15	18	5	0	0	0	(0	0)	5	2	4	1	0	4	0	0	0	0	0	.00	2	.278	.316	.278
1990 Cincinnati	NL	107	309	105	22	3	7	(3	4)	154	50	36	21	4	32	1	3	2	9	3	.75	12	.340	.381	.498
1991 Cincinnati	NL	136	478	152	33	1	14	(5	9)	229	72	59	46	7	61	1	5	7	10	4	.71	4	.318	.374	.479
1992 Cincinnati	NL	115	395	107	21	3	6	(3	3)	152	41	53	45	8	53	2	2	2	6	6	.50	12	.271	.347	.385
1993 Cincinnati	NL	101	379	120	18	0	7	(2	5)	159	48	49	34	4	51	2	0	6	2	2	.50	5	.317	.371	.420
1994 Cincinnati	NL	112	436	146	30	4	10	(5	5)	214	60	78	34	8	62	2	2	6	6	2	.75	16	.335	.385	.491
1995 Cincinnati	NL	101	359	100	25	2	11	(6	5)	162	53	51	29	7	58	1	1	1	1	1	.50	10	.279	.333	.451
1996 Cincinnati	NL	142	528	165	32	4	16	(7	9)	253	82	80	50	5	76	5	5	6	7	5	.58	12	.313	.374	.479
1997 Cincinnati	NL	96	333	92	20	1	1	(1	0)	117	42	33	23	2	43	3	4	1	3	1	.75	10	.276	.328	.351
1998 Kansas City	AL	127	472	146	27	2	1	(0	1)	180	50	40	32	6	52	1	4	7	1	0	1.00	15	.309	.350	.381
1999 Cincinnati	NL	80	102	29	9	0	0	(0	0)	38	10	16	10	0	21	0	0	0	0	0	.00	1	.284	.348	.373
12 ML YEARS		1147	3829	1169	237	20	73	(36	37)	1665	511	499	325	51	522	21	26	38	45	24	.65	99	.305	.360	.435

Jim Morris

Pitches: Left **Bats:** Left **Pos:** RP-5   **Ht:** 6'3" **Wt:** 215 **Born:** 1/19/64 **Age:** 36

Year Team	Lg	G	GS	CG	GF	IP	BFP	H	R	ER	HR	SH	SF	HB	TBB	IBB	SO	WP	Bk	W	L	Pct.	ShO	Sv-Op	Hld	ERA
1983 Paintsville	R+	13	13	2	0	67	—	58	50	38	11	—	—	0	42	0	75	13	1	3	6	.333	0	0- -	—	5.10
1984 Beloit	A	24	22	1	0	112.1	510	107	80	63	8	7	3	1	79	1	109	13	1	8	9	.471	0	0- -	—	5.05
1985 Beloit	A	1	0	0	1	3	9	0	0	0	0	0	0	0	0	0	4	0	0	0	0	.000	0	0- -	—	0.00
Stockton	A+	19	13	0	2	73	—	85	63	49	3	—	—	2	57	2	43	7	0	5	6	.455	0	0- -	—	6.04
1987 Stockton	A+	4	0	0	0	12	60	6	5	1	1	0	0	0	12	0	9	0	0	1	0	1.000	0	0- -	—	0.75
1989 Sarasota	A+	2	0	0	1	2.2	14	3	3	3	0	0	1	0	2	0	4	1	0	0	1	.000	0	0- -	—	10.13
1999 Orlando	AA	3	0	0	2	5	22	6	1	1	0	0	0	0	1	0	6	1	0	0	0	.000	0	1- -	—	1.80
Durham	AAA	18	0	0	5	23	103	21	14	14	3	0	0	1	19	0	16	2	0	3	1	.750	0	0- -	—	5.48
1999 Tampa Bay	AL	5	0	0	3	4.2	21	3	3	3	1	0	0	1	2	0	3	0	0	0	0	.000	0	0-0	0	5.79

161

Matt Morris

Pitches: Right **Bats:** Right **Pos:** SP Ht: 6'5" Wt: 210 Born: 8/9/74 Age: 25

Year Team	Lg	G	GS	CG	GF	IP	BFP	H	R	ER	HR	SH	SF	HB	TBB	IBB	SO	WP	Bk	W	L	Pct.	ShO	Sv-Op	Hld	ERA
1997 St. Louis	NL	33	33	3	0	217	900	208	88	77	12	11	7	7	69	2	149	5	3	12	9	.571	0	0-0	0	3.19
1998 St. Louis	NL	17	17	2	0	113.2	468	101	37	32	8	6	1	3	42	6	79	3	0	7	5	.583	1	0-0	0	2.53
2 ML YEARS		50	50	5	0	330.2	1368	309	125	109	20	17	8	10	111	8	228	8	3	19	14	.576	1	0-0	0	2.97

Warren Morris

Bats: Left **Throws:** Right **Pos:** 2B-144; PH/PR-5 Ht: 5'11" Wt: 185 Born: 1/11/74 Age: 26

Year Team	Lg	G	AB	H	2B	3B	HR	(Hm	Rd)	TB	R	RBI	TBB	IBB	SO	HBP	SH	SF	SB	CS	SB%	GDP	Avg	OBP	SLG
1997 Charlotte	A+	128	494	151	27	9	12	—	—	232	78	75	62	3	100	7	3	1	16	5	.76	6	.306	.390	.470
Okla City	AAA	8	32	7	1	0	1	—	—	11	3	3	3	0	5	0	0	0	0	0	.00	0	.219	.286	.344
1998 Tulsa	AA	95	390	129	22	5	14	—	—	203	59	73	43	2	63	4	1	2	12	7	.63	11	.331	.401	.521
Carolina	AA	44	151	50	8	3	5	—	—	79	28	30	24	1	34	1	0	3	5	2	.71	2	.331	.419	.523
1999 Pittsburgh	NL	147	511	147	20	3	15	(9	6)	218	65	73	59	3	88	2	4	5	3	7	.30	12	.288	.360	.427

Guillermo Mota

Pitches: Right **Bats:** Right **Pos:** RP-51 Ht: 6'6" Wt: 200 Born: 7/25/73 Age: 26

Year Team	Lg	G	GS	CG	GF	IP	BFP	H	R	ER	HR	SH	SF	HB	TBB	IBB	SO	WP	Bk	W	L	Pct.	ShO	Sv-Op	Hld	ERA
1997 Cape Fear	A	25	23	0	0	126	528	135	65	61	8	2	3	4	33	0	112	1	2	5	10	.333	0	0--	—	4.36
1998 Jupiter	A+	20	0	0	13	41	149	18	6	3	0	2	1	2	6	0	27	0	0	3	2	.600	0	2--	—	0.66
Harrisburg	AA	12	0	0	9	17	60	10	2	2	0	0	0	0	2	0	19	2	0	2	0	1.000	0	4--	—	1.06
1999 Ottawa	AAA	14	0	0	10	19	76	16	6	4	0	2	0	1	5	0	17	0	0	2	0	1.000	0	5--	—	1.89
1999 Montreal	NL	51	0	0	18	55.1	243	54	24	18	5	3	3	2	25	3	27	1	1	2	4	.333	0	0-1	3	2.93

James Mouton

Bats: R **Throws:** R **Pos:** PH/PR-49; LF-32; CF-16; RF-11; DH-1 Ht: 5'9" Wt: 175 Born: 12/29/68 Age: 31

Year Team	Lg	G	AB	H	2B	3B	HR	(Hm	Rd)	TB	R	RBI	TBB	IBB	SO	HBP	SH	SF	SB	CS	SB%	GDP	Avg	OBP	SLG
1994 Houston	NL	99	310	76	11	0	2	(1	1)	93	43	16	27	0	69	5	2	1	24	5	.83	6	.245	.315	.300
1995 Houston	NL	104	298	78	18	2	4	(2	2)	112	42	27	25	1	59	4	3	1	25	8	.76	5	.262	.326	.376
1996 Houston	NL	122	300	79	15	1	3	(2	1)	105	40	34	38	2	55	0	2	3	21	9	.70	9	.263	.343	.350
1997 Houston	NL	86	180	38	9	1	3	(1	2)	58	24	23	18	0	30	2	2	2	9	7	.56	3	.211	.287	.322
1998 San Diego	NL	55	63	12	2	1	0	(0	0)	16	8	7	7	1	11	0	0	1	4	3	.57	3	.190	.268	.254
1999 Montreal	NL	95	122	32	5	1	2	(1	1)	45	18	13	18	1	31	2	3	1	6	2	.75	2	.262	.364	.369
6 ML YEARS		561	1273	315	60	6	14	(7	7)	429	175	120	133	5	255	13	12	9	89	34	.72	28	.247	.323	.337

Lyle Mouton

Bats: Right **Throws:** Right **Pos:** PH/PR-11; LF-2; RF-1 Ht: 6'4" Wt: 230 Born: 5/13/69 Age: 31

Year Team	Lg	G	AB	H	2B	3B	HR	(Hm	Rd)	TB	R	RBI	TBB	IBB	SO	HBP	SH	SF	SB	CS	SB%	GDP	Avg	OBP	SLG
1999 Rochester *	AAA	44	162	36	9	1	4	—	—	59	25	17	13	0	31	1	0	2	3	1	.75	6	.222	.281	.364
Louisville *	AAA	83	305	109	34	2	19	—	—	204	64	77	27	0	67	0	0	6	19	0	1.00	8	.357	.411	.669
1995 Chicago	AL	58	179	54	16	0	5	(4	1)	85	23	27	19	0	46	2	0	1	3	0	1.00	7	.302	.373	.475
1996 Chicago	AL	87	214	63	8	1	7	(4	3)	94	25	39	22	4	50	2	0	3	3	0	1.00	3	.294	.361	.439
1997 Chicago	AL	88	242	65	9	0	5	(4	1)	89	26	23	14	1	66	1	0	3	4	4	.50	8	.269	.308	.368
1998 Baltimore	AL	18	39	12	2	0	2	(0	2)	20	5	7	4	0	8	0	0	0	0	0	.00	0	.308	.372	.513
1999 Milwaukee	NL	14	17	3	1	0	1	(1	0)	7	2	3	2	0	3	0	0	0	0	0	.00	0	.176	.263	.412
5 ML YEARS		265	691	197	36	1	20	(13	7)	295	81	99	61	5	173	5	0	7	8	4	.67	18	.285	.344	.427

Jamie Moyer

Pitches: Left **Bats:** Left **Pos:** SP-32 Ht: 6'0" Wt: 170 Born: 11/18/62 Age: 37

Year Team	Lg	G	GS	CG	GF	IP	BFP	H	R	ER	HR	SH	SF	HB	TBB	IBB	SO	WP	Bk	W	L	Pct.	ShO	Sv-Op	Hld	ERA
1986 Chicago	NL	16	16	1	0	87.1	395	107	52	49	10	3	2	1	42	1	45	3	3	7	4	.636	0	0-0	0	5.05
1987 Chicago	NL	35	33	1	1	201	899	210	127	114	28	14	7	5	97	9	147	11	2	12	15	.444	0	0-0	0	5.10
1988 Chicago	NL	34	30	3	1	202	855	212	84	78	20	14	4	4	55	7	121	4	0	9	15	.375	1	0-2	0	3.48
1989 Texas	AL	15	15	1	0	76	337	84	51	41	10	1	4	2	33	0	44	1	0	4	9	.308	0	0-0	0	4.86
1990 Texas	AL	33	10	1	6	102.1	447	115	59	53	6	1	7	4	39	4	58	1	0	2	6	.250	0	0-0	1	4.66
1991 St. Louis	NL	8	7	0	1	31.1	142	38	21	20	5	4	2	1	16	0	20	2	1	0	5	.000	0	0-0	0	5.74
1993 Baltimore	AL	25	25	3	0	152	630	154	63	58	11	3	1	6	38	2	90	1	1	12	9	.571	1	0-0	0	3.43
1994 Baltimore	AL	23	23	0	0	149	631	158	81	79	23	5	2	2	38	3	87	1	0	5	7	.417	0	0-0	0	4.77
1995 Baltimore	AL	27	18	0	1	115.2	483	117	70	67	18	5	3	3	30	0	65	0	0	8	6	.571	0	0-0	0	5.21
1996 Bos-Sea	AL	34	21	0	1	160.2	703	177	86	71	23	7	6	2	46	5	79	3	1	13	3	.813	0	0-0	1	3.98
1997 Seattle	AL	30	30	2	0	188.2	787	187	82	81	21	6	1	7	43	2	113	3	0	17	5	.773	0	0-0	0	3.86
1998 Seattle	AL	34	34	4	0	234.1	974	234	99	92	23	4	3	10	42	2	158	0	1	15	9	.625	3	0-0	0	3.53
1999 Seattle	AL	32	32	4	0	228	945	235	108	98	23	6	2	9	48	1	137	3	0	14	8	.636	0	0-0	0	3.87
1996 Boston	AL	23	10	0	0	90	405	111	50	45	14	4	3	1	27	2	50	2	1	7	1	.875	0	0-0	0	4.50
Seattle	AL	11	11	0	0	70.2	298	66	36	26	9	3	3	1	19	3	29	1	0	6	2	.750	0	0-0	0	3.31
13 ML YEARS		346	294	20	13	1928.1	8228	2028	983	901	221	73	45	58	567	36	1164	36	9	118	101	.539	6	0-2	2	4.21

162

Bill Mueller

Bats: Both **Throws:** Right **Pos:** 3B-108; PH/PR-8; 2B-3   **Ht:** 5'10" **Wt:** 180 **Born:** 3/17/71 **Age:** 29

Year Team	Lg	G	AB	H	2B	3B	HR	(Hm	Rd)	TB	R	RBI	TBB	IBB	SO	HBP	SH	SF	SB	CS	SB%	GDP	Avg	OBP	SLG
1999 Fresno *	AAA	3	12	5	0	1	0	—	—	7	3	6	0	0	0	0	0	1	0	0	.00	0	.417	.385	.583
1996 San Francisco	NL	55	200	66	15	1	0	(0	0)	83	31	19	24	0	26	1	1	2	0	0	.00	1	.330	.401	.415
1997 San Francisco	NL	128	390	114	26	3	7	(5	2)	167	51	44	48	1	71	3	1	6	4	3	.57	10	.292	.369	.428
1998 San Francisco	NL	145	534	157	27	0	9	(1	8)	211	93	59	79	1	83	1	3	5	3	3	.50	12	.294	.383	.395
1999 San Francisco	NL	116	414	120	24	0	2	(1	1)	150	61	36	65	1	52	3	8	2	4	2	.67	11	.290	.388	.362
4 ML YEARS		444	1538	457	92	4	18	(7	11)	611	236	158	216	3	232	8	18	15	11	8	.58	34	.297	.383	.397

Terry Mulholland

Pitches: Left **Bats:** Right **Pos:** SP-24; RP-18   **Ht:** 6'3" **Wt:** 220 **Born:** 3/9/63 **Age:** 37

Year Team	Lg	G	GS	CG	GF	IP	BFP	H	R	ER	HR	SH	SF	HB	TBB	IBB	SO	WP	Bk	W	L	Pct.	ShO	Sv-Op	Hld	ERA
1986 San Francisco	NL	15	10	0	1	54.2	245	51	33	30	3	5	1	1	35	2	27	6	0	1	7	.125	0	0- -	—	4.94
1988 San Francisco	NL	9	6	2	1	46	191	50	20	19	3	5	0	1	7	0	18	1	0	2	1	.667	1	0-0	1	3.72
1989 SF-Phi	NL	25	18	2	4	115.1	513	137	66	63	8	7	1	4	36	3	66	3	0	4	7	.364	1	0-0	1	4.92
1990 Philadelphia	NL	33	26	6	2	180.2	746	172	78	67	15	7	12	2	42	7	75	7	2	9	10	.474	1	0-1	0	3.34
1991 Philadelphia	NL	34	34	8	0	232	956	231	100	93	15	11	6	3	49	2	142	3	0	16	13	.552	3	0-0	0	3.61
1992 Philadelphia	NL	32	32	12	0	229	937	227	101	97	14	10	7	3	46	3	125	3	0	13	11	.542	2	0-0	0	3.81
1993 Philadelphia	NL	29	28	7	0	191	786	177	80	69	20	5	4	3	40	2	116	5	0	12	9	.571	2	0-0	0	3.25
1994 New York	AL	24	19	2	4	120.2	542	150	94	87	24	3	4	3	37	1	72	5	0	6	7	.462	0	0-0	0	6.49
1995 San Francisco	NL	29	24	2	2	149	666	190	112	96	25	11	6	4	38	1	65	4	0	5	13	.278	0	0-0	0	5.80
1996 Phi-Sea	NL	33	33	3	0	202.2	871	232	112	105	22	11	8	5	49	4	86	6	0	13	11	.542	0	0-0	0	4.66
1997 ChC-SF	NL	40	27	1	5	186.2	794	190	100	88	24	17	4	11	51	3	99	3	0	6	13	.316	0	0-0	1	4.24
1998 Chicago	NL	70	6	0	14	112	476	100	49	36	7	5	3	4	39	7	72	4	0	6	5	.545	0	3-5	19	2.89
1999 ChC-Atl	NL	42	24	0	7	170.1	736	201	95	83	21	9	4	1	45	6	83	3	0	10	8	.556	0	1-1	4	4.39
1989 San Francisco	NL	5	1	0	2	11	51	15	5	5	0	0	0	0	4	0	6	0	0	0	0	.000	0	0-0	1	4.09
Philadelphia	NL	20	17	2	2	104.1	462	122	61	58	8	7	1	4	32	3	60	3	0	4	7	.364	1	0-0	0	5.00
1996 Philadelphia	NL	21	21	3	0	133.1	571	157	74	69	17	6	5	3	21	1	52	5	0	8	7	.533	0	0-0	0	4.66
Seattle	AL	12	12	0	0	69.1	300	75	38	36	5	5	3	2	28	3	34	1	0	5	4	.556	0	0-0	0	4.67
1997 Chicago	NL	25	25	1	0	157	668	162	79	71	20	13	3	9	45	2	74	2	0	6	12	.333	0	0-0	0	4.07
San Francisco	NL	15	2	0	5	29.2	126	28	21	17	4	4	1	2	6	1	25	1	0	0	1	.000	0	0-0	1	5.16
1999 Chicago	NL	26	16	0	4	110	485	137	71	63	16	6	3	1	32	4	44	2	0	6	6	.500	0	0-0	1	5.15
Atlanta	NL	16	8	0	3	60.1	251	64	24	20	5	3	1	0	13	2	39	1	0	4	2	.667	0	1-1	3	2.98
13 ML YEARS		415	287	45	40	1990	8459	2108	1040	933	201	106	60	45	514	41	1046	53	2	103	115	.472	10	4- -	—	4.22

Mike Munoz

Pitches: Left **Bats:** Left **Pos:** RP-56   **Ht:** 6'2" **Wt:** 198 **Born:** 7/12/65 **Age:** 34

Year Team	Lg	G	GS	CG	GF	IP	BFP	H	R	ER	HR	SH	SF	HB	TBB	IBB	SO	WP	Bk	W	L	Pct.	ShO	Sv-Op	Hld	ERA
1989 Los Angeles	NL	3	0	0	1	2.2	14	5	5	5	1	0	0	0	2	0	3	0	0	0	0	.000	0	0-0	0	16.88
1990 Los Angeles	NL	8	0	0	3	5.2	24	6	2	2	0	1	0	0	3	0	3	0	0	0	1	.000	0	0-1	2	3.18
1991 Detroit	AL	6	0	0	4	9.1	46	14	10	10	0	0	1	0	5	0	3	1	0	0	0	.000	0	0-0	0	9.64
1992 Detroit	AL	65	0	0	15	48	210	44	16	16	3	4	2	0	25	6	23	2	0	1	2	.333	0	2-3	15	3.00
1993 Det-Col		29	0	0	10	21	101	25	14	11	2	3	2	0	15	4	17	2	0	2	2	.500	0	0-2	4	4.71
1994 Colorado	NL	57	0	0	8	45.2	200	37	22	19	3	2	1	0	31	5	32	2	0	4	2	.667	0	1-2	12	3.74
1995 Colorado	NL	64	0	0	19	43.2	208	54	38	36	9	2	1	0	27	0	37	5	0	2	4	.333	0	2-4	12	7.42
1996 Colorado	NL	54	0	0	7	44.2	203	55	33	33	4	3	1	1	16	2	45	0	0	2	2	.500	0	0-3	6	6.65
1997 Colorado	NL	64	0	0	16	45.2	192	52	25	23	4	0	2	0	13	0	26	3	0	3	3	.500	0	2-2	19	4.53
1998 Colorado	NL	40	0	0	13	41.1	189	53	32	26	2	1	1	1	16	2	24	1	0	2	2	.500	0	3-4	1	5.66
1999 Texas	AL	56	0	0	11	52.2	221	52	24	23	5	1	3	1	18	2	27	2	0	2	1	.667	0	1-3	10	3.93
1993 Detroit	AL	8	0	0	3	3	19	4	2	2	1	0	0	0	6	1	1	0	0	0	1	.000	0	0-0	1	6.00
Colorado	NL	21	0	0	7	18	82	21	12	9	1	3	2	0	9	3	16	2	0	2	1	.667	0	0-2	3	4.50
11 ML YEARS		446	0	0	107	360.1	1608	397	221	204	33	17	15	4	171	21	239	18	0	18	19	.486	0	11-24	86	5.10

Peter Munro

Pitches: Right **Bats:** Right **Pos:** RP-29; SP-2   **Ht:** 6'2" **Wt:** 200 **Born:** 6/14/75 **Age:** 25

Year Team	Lg	G	GS	CG	GF	IP	BFP	H	R	ER	HR	SH	SF	HB	TBB	IBB	SO	WP	Bk	W	L	Pct.	ShO	Sv-Op	Hld	ERA
1995 Utica	A-	14	14	0	0	90	389	79	38	26	3	3	3	7	33	1	74	4	0	5	4	.556	0	0- -	—	2.60
1996 Sarasota	A+	27	25	2	1	155	667	153	76	62	4	3	2	7	62	1	115	7	1	11	6	.647	2	1- -	—	3.60
1997 Trenton	AA	22	22	1	0	116.1	506	113	76	64	12	10	6	8	47	0	109	6	3	7	10	.412	0	0- -	—	4.95
1998 Pawtucket	AAA	18	17	0	0	106.2	450	111	49	48	10	2	5	4	35	2	75	8	0	5	4	.556	0	0- -	—	4.05
Syracuse	AAA	8	8	0	0	44.2	213	58	42	37	7	2	0	2	23	2	42	4	0	2	5	.286	0	0- -	—	7.46
1999 Syracuse	AAA	18	11	0	3	69.2	312	70	29	24	6	0	3	4	33	1	68	3	0	6	1	.857	0	0- -	—	3.10
1999 Toronto	AL	31	2	0	9	55.1	250	70	38	37	6	1	4	2	23	0	38	3	0	0	2	.000	0	0-1	4	6.02

Calvin Murray

Bats: Right **Throws:** Right **Pos:** PH/PR-8; CF-6; LF-3   **Ht:** 5'11" **Wt:** 190 **Born:** 7/30/71 **Age:** 28

Year Team	Lg	G	AB	H	2B	3B	HR	(Hm	Rd)	TB	R	RBI	TBB	IBB	SO	HBP	SH	SF	SB	CS	SB%	GDP	Avg	OBP	SLG
1993 Shreveport	AA	37	138	26	6	0	0	—	—	32	15	6	14	0	29	2	3	1	12	6	.67	0	.188	.271	.232

Year Team	Lg	G	AB	H	2B	3B	HR	(Hm	Rd)	TB	R	RBI	TBB	IBB	SO	HBP	SH	SF	SB	CS	SB%	GDP	Avg	OBP	SLG
San Jose	A+	85	345	97	24	1	9	—	—	150	61	42	40	0	63	4	2	0	42	10	.81	4	.281	.362	.435
Phoenix	AAA	5	19	6	1	1	0	—	—	9	4	0	2	0	5	0	0	0	1	1	.50	0	.316	.381	.474
1994 Shreveport	AA	129	480	111	19	5	2	—	—	146	67	35	47	0	81	5	8	4	33	13	.72	4	.231	.304	.304
1995 Phoenix	AAA	13	50	9	1	0	4	—	—	22	8	10	4	0	6	0	1	1	2	2	.50	2	.180	.236	.440
Shreveport	AA	110	441	104	17	3	2	—	—	133	77	29	59	2	70	3	1	5	26	10	.72	5	.236	.329	.302
1996 Shreveport	AA	50	169	44	7	0	7	—	—	72	32	24	25	0	33	1	3	4	6	5	.55	5	.260	.352	.426
Phoenix	AAA	83	311	76	16	6	3	—	—	113	50	28	43	0	60	3	5	1	12	6	.67	1	.244	.341	.363
1997 Shreveport	AA	122	419	114	25	3	10	—	—	175	83	56	66	0	73	4	1	2	52	6	.90	7	.272	.375	.418
1998 Shreveport	AA	88	337	104	22	5	8	—	—	160	63	39	58	1	45	5	1	0	34	15	.69	8	.309	.418	.475
Fresno	AAA	33	90	21	3	1	3	—	—	35	16	5	12	0	18	0	1	0	3	1	.75	2	.233	.324	.389
1999 Fresno	AAA	130	548	183	31	7	23	—	—	297	122	73	49	3	88	3	4	4	42	14	.75	6	.334	.389	.542
1999 San Francisco	NL	15	19	5	2	0	0	(0	0)	7	1	5	2	0	4	0	0	0	1	0	1.00	0	.263	.333	.368

Dan Murray

Pitches: Right **Bats:** Right **Pos:** RP-5 — **Ht:** 6'1" **Wt:** 193 **Born:** 11/21/73 **Age:** 26

Year Team	Lg	G	GS	CG	GF	IP	BFP	H	R	ER	HR	SH	SF	HB	TBB	IBB	SO	WP	Bk	W	L	Pct.	ShO	Sv-Op	Hld	ERA
1995 Pittsfield	A-	22	0	0	19	32	145	24	17	7	1	2	0	1	16	3	34	3	0	0	6	.000	0	6--	—	1.97
1996 St. Lucie	A+	33	13	0	5	101.2	465	114	60	48	2	3	3	8	53	3	56	11	0	7	5	.583	0	0--	—	4.25
1997 St. Lucie	A+	30	24	4	3	156.1	682	150	75	60	4	5	3	10	55	3	91	13	0	12	10	.545	2	0--	—	3.45
1998 Binghamton	AA	27	27	1	0	164.1	681	153	64	58	13	3	2	8	54	2	159	5	0	11	6	.647	1	0--	—	3.18
1999 Norfolk	AAA	29	27	3	1	145	650	149	91	80	22	7	5	7	70	5	96	11	3	12	10	.545	1	0--	—	4.97
1999 NYM-KC		5	0	0	1	10.1	51	13	11	9	4	0	1	1	6	0	9	1	0	0	0	.000	0	0-0	0	7.84
1999 New York	NL	1	0	0	1	2	12	4	3	3	0	0	1	0	2	0	1	1	0	0	0	.000	0	0-0	0	13.50
Kansas City	AL	4	0	0	0	8.1	39	9	8	6	4	0	0	1	4	0	8	0	0	0	0	.000	0	0-0	0	6.48

Heath Murray

Pitches: Left **Bats:** Left **Pos:** RP-14; SP-8 — **Ht:** 6'4" **Wt:** 205 **Born:** 4/19/73 **Age:** 27

Year Team	Lg	G	GS	CG	GF	IP	BFP	H	R	ER	HR	SH	SF	HB	TBB	IBB	SO	WP	Bk	W	L	Pct.	ShO	Sv-Op	Hld	ERA
1994 Spokane	A-	15	15	2	0	99.1	408	101	46	32	6	6	2	5	18	0	78	4	3	5	6	.455	1	0--	—	2.90
1995 Rancho Cuca	A+	14	14	4	0	92.1	381	80	37	32	5	3	2	4	38	1	81	6	3	9	4	.692	2	0--	—	3.12
Memphis	AA	14	14	0	0	77.1	363	83	36	29	1	3	3	4	42	1	71	7	1	5	4	.556	0	0--	—	3.38
1996 Memphis	AA	27	27	1	0	174	728	154	83	62	13	4	3	6	60	2	156	7	3	13	9	.591	1	0--	—	3.21
1997 Las Vegas	AAA	19	19	2	0	109	493	142	72	66	10	1	2	5	41	1	99	8	1	6	8	.429	1	0--	—	5.45
1998 Las Vegas	AAA	27	27	3	0	162.1	726	191	103	90	13	9	5	8	62	3	121	6	3	9	11	.450	0	0--	—	4.99
1999 Las Vegas	AAA	15	15	0	0	82.1	366	99	45	39	5	1	3	2	32	0	65	4	0	5	4	.556	1	0--	—	4.26
1997 San Diego	NL	17	3	0	1	33.1	162	50	25	25	3	3	1	4	21	3	16	1	1	1	2	.333	0	0-0	1	6.75
1999 San Diego	NL	22	8	0	1	50	234	60	33	32	7	3	2	1	26	4	25	1	1	0	4	.000	0	0-0	0	5.76
2 ML YEARS		39	11	0	2	83.1	396	110	58	57	10	6	3	5	47	7	41	2	2	1	6	.143	0	0-0	1	6.16

Mike Mussina

Pitches: Right **Bats:** Both **Pos:** SP-31 — **Ht:** 6'2" **Wt:** 185 **Born:** 12/8/68 **Age:** 31

Year Team	Lg	G	GS	CG	GF	IP	BFP	H	R	ER	HR	SH	SF	HB	TBB	IBB	SO	WP	Bk	W	L	Pct.	ShO	Sv-Op	Hld	ERA
1991 Baltimore	AL	12	12	2	0	87.2	349	77	31	28	7	3	2	1	21	0	52	3	1	4	5	.444	0	0-0	0	2.87
1992 Baltimore	AL	32	32	8	0	241	957	212	70	68	16	13	6	2	48	2	130	6	0	18	5	.783	4	0-0	0	2.54
1993 Baltimore	AL	25	25	3	0	167.2	693	163	84	83	20	6	4	3	44	2	117	5	0	14	6	.700	2	0-0	0	4.46
1994 Baltimore	AL	24	24	3	0	176.1	712	163	63	60	19	3	9	1	42	1	99	0	0	16	5	.762	0	0-0	0	3.06
1995 Baltimore	AL	32	32	7	0	221.2	882	187	86	81	24	2	2	1	50	4	158	2	0	19	9	.679	4	0-0	0	3.29
1996 Baltimore	AL	36	36	4	0	243.1	1039	264	137	130	31	4	4	3	69	0	204	3	0	19	11	.633	1	0-0	0	4.81
1997 Baltimore	AL	33	33	4	0	224.2	905	197	87	80	27	3	2	3	54	3	218	5	0	15	8	.652	1	0-0	0	3.20
1998 Baltimore	AL	29	29	4	0	206.1	835	189	85	80	22	6	3	4	41	3	175	10	0	13	10	.565	2	0-0	0	3.49
1999 Baltimore	AL	31	31	4	0	203.1	842	207	88	79	16	9	7	1	52	0	172	2	0	18	7	.720	0	0-0	0	3.50
9 ML YEARS		254	254	39	0	1772	7214	1659	731	689	182	49	39	19	421	15	1325	36	1	136	66	.673	14	0-0	0	3.50

Greg Myers

Bats: Left **Throws:** Right **Pos:** C-72; PH/PR-16 — **Ht:** 6'2" **Wt:** 225 **Born:** 4/14/66 **Age:** 34

Year Team	Lg	G	AB	H	2B	3B	HR	(Hm	Rd)	TB	R	RBI	TBB	IBB	SO	HBP	SH	SF	SB	CS	SB%	GDP	Avg	OBP	SLG
1999 Rancho Cuca *	A+	3	3	0	0	0	0	—	—	0	0	0	1	0	1	0	0	0	0	0	.00	0	.000	.250	.000
1987 Toronto	AL	7	9	1	0	0	0	(0	0)	1	1	0	0	0	3	0	0	0	0	0	.00	2	.111	.111	.111
1989 Toronto	AL	17	44	5	2	0	0	(0	0)	7	0	1	2	0	9	0	0	0	0	1	.00	2	.114	.152	.159
1990 Toronto	AL	87	250	59	7	1	5	(3	2)	83	33	22	22	0	33	0	1	4	0	0	.00	12	.236	.293	.332
1991 Toronto	AL	107	309	81	22	0	8	(5	3)	127	25	36	21	4	45	0	0	3	0	0	.00	13	.262	.306	.411
1992 Tor-Cal	AL	30	78	18	7	0	1	(0	1)	28	4	13	5	0	11	0	1	2	0	0	.00	2	.231	.271	.359
1993 California	AL	108	290	74	10	0	7	(4	3)	105	27	40	17	2	47	2	3	3	3	3	.50	8	.255	.298	.362
1994 California	AL	45	126	31	6	0	2	(1	1)	43	10	8	10	3	27	0	5	1	0	2	.00	3	.246	.299	.341
1995 California	AL	85	273	71	12	2	9	(6	3)	114	35	38	17	3	49	1	1	2	1	1	.50	7	.260	.304	.418
1996 Minnesota	AL	97	329	94	22	3	6	(3	3)	140	37	47	19	3	52	0	0	5	0	0	.00	11	.286	.320	.426
1997 Min-Atl	AL	71	174	45	11	1	5	(3	2)	73	24	29	17	2	32	0	0	2	0	0	.00	4	.259	.321	.420
1998 San Diego	NL	69	171	42	10	0	4	(1	3)	64	19	20	17	1	36	0	0	1	0	1	.00	6	.246	.312	.374
1999 SD-Atl	NL	84	200	53	6	0	5	(3	2)	74	19	24	26	4	30	0	0	1	0	0	.00	6	.265	.348	.370

				BATTING																BASERUNNING				PERCENTAGES		
Year Team	Lg	G	AB	H	2B	3B	HR	(Hm Rd)	TB	R	RBI	TBB	IBB	SO	HBP	SH	SF	SB	CS	SB%	GDP	Avg	OBP	SLG
1992 Toronto	AL	22	61	14	6	0	1	(0 1)	23	4	13	5	0	5	0	0	2	0	0	.00	2	.230	.279	.377
California	AL	8	17	4	1	0	0	(0 0)	5	0	0	0	0	6	0	1	0	0	0	.00	0	.235	.235	.294
1997 Minnesota	AL	62	165	44	11	1	5	(3 2)	72	24	28	16	2	29	0	0	2	0	0	.00	4	.267	.328	.436
Atlanta	NL	9	9	1	0	0	0	(0 0)	1	0	1	1	0	3	0	0	0	0	0	.00	0	.111	.200	.111
1999 San Diego	NL	50	128	37	4	0	3	(2 1)	50	9	15	13	2	14	0	0	0	0	0	.00	5	.289	.355	.391
Atlanta	NL	34	72	16	2	0	2	(1 1)	24	10	9	13	2	16	0	0	1	0	0	.00	1	.222	.337	.333
12 ML YEARS		807	2253	574	115	7	52	(29 23)	859	234	278	173	22	374	3	11	24	3	9	.25	73	.255	.306	.381

Mike Myers

Pitches: Left Bats: Left Pos: RP-71 Ht: 6'4" Wt: 214 Born: 6/26/69 Age: 31

		HOW MUCH HE PITCHED						WHAT HE GAVE UP											THE RESULTS						
Year Team	Lg	G	GS	CG	GF	IP	BFP	H	R	ER	HR	SH	SF	HB	TBB	IBB	SO	WP	Bk	W	L	Pct.	ShO	Sv-Op	Hld	ERA
1995 Fla-Det		13	0	0	5	8.1	42	11	7	7	1	0	1	2	7	0	4	0	0	1	0	1.000	0	0-1	1	7.56
1996 Detroit	AL	83	0	0	25	64.2	298	70	41	36	6	2	1	4	34	8	69	2	0	1	5	.167	0	6-8	17	5.01
1997 Detroit	AL	88	0	0	23	53.2	246	58	36	34	12	4	3	2	25	2	50	0	0	0	4	.000	0	2-5	18	5.70
1998 Milwaukee	NL	70	0	0	14	50	211	44	19	15	5	4	2	6	22	1	40	2	1	2	2	.500	0	1-3	23	2.70
1999 Milwaukee	NL	71	0	0	14	41.1	179	46	24	24	7	5	0	3	13	1	35	1	0	2	1	.667	0	0-3	14	5.23
1995 Florida	NL	2	0	0	2	2	9	1	0	0	0	1	0	0	3	0	0	0	0	0	0	.000	0	0-0	0	0.00
Detroit	AL	11	0	0	3	6.1	33	10	7	7	1	0	1	2	4	0	4	0	0	1	0	1.000	0	0-1	1	9.95
5 ML YEARS		325	0	0	81	218	976	229	127	116	31	15	7	17	101	12	198	5	1	6	12	.333	0	9-20	73	4.79

Randy Myers

Pitches: Left Bats: Left Pos: RP Ht: 6'1" Wt: 210 Born: 9/19/62 Age: 37

		HOW MUCH HE PITCHED						WHAT HE GAVE UP											THE RESULTS						
Year Team	Lg	G	GS	CG	GF	IP	BFP	H	R	ER	HR	SH	SF	HB	TBB	IBB	SO	WP	Bk	W	L	Pct.	ShO	Sv-Op	Hld	ERA
1985 New York	NL	1	0	0	1	2	7	0	0	0	0	0	0	0	1	0	2	0	0	0	0	.000	0	0-0	0	0.00
1986 New York	NL	10	0	0	5	10.2	53	11	5	5	1	0	0	1	9	1	13	0	0	0	0	.000	0	0-0	4	4.22
1987 New York	NL	54	0	0	18	75	314	61	36	33	6	7	6	0	30	5	92	3	0	3	6	.333	0	6-9	7	3.96
1988 New York	NL	55	0	0	44	68	261	45	15	13	5	3	2	2	17	2	69	2	0	7	3	.700	0	26-29	3	1.72
1989 New York	NL	65	0	0	47	84.1	349	62	23	22	4	6	2	0	40	4	88	3	0	7	4	.636	0	24-29	2	2.35
1990 Cincinnati	NL	66	0	0	59	86.2	353	59	24	20	6	4	2	3	38	8	98	2	1	4	6	.400	0	31-37	0	2.08
1991 Cincinnati	NL	58	12	1	18	132	575	116	61	52	8	8	6	1	80	5	108	2	1	6	13	.316	0	6-10	8	3.55
1992 San Diego	NL	66	0	0	57	79.2	348	84	38	38	7	7	5	1	34	3	66	5	0	3	6	.333	0	38-46	0	4.29
1993 Chicago	NL	73	0	0	69	75.1	313	65	26	26	7	1	2	1	26	2	86	3	0	2	4	.333	0	53-59	0	3.11
1994 Chicago	NL	38	0	0	34	40.1	174	40	18	17	3	3	1	0	16	1	32	2	0	1	5	.167	0	21-26	0	3.79
1995 Chicago	NL	57	0	0	47	55.2	240	49	25	24	7	2	3	0	28	1	59	0	0	1	2	.333	0	38-44	0	3.88
1996 Baltimore	AL	62	0	0	50	58.2	262	60	24	23	7	3	3	1	29	4	74	3	0	4	4	.500	0	31-38	2	3.53
1997 Baltimore	AL	61	0	0	57	59.2	241	47	12	10	2	2	0	0	22	2	56	3	0	2	3	.400	0	45-46	2	1.51
1998 Tor-SD		62	0	0	42	56.2	254	59	31	31	6	4	1	2	26	5	41	4	0	4	7	.364	0	28-34	8	4.92
1998 Toronto	AL	41	0	0	37	42.1	190	44	21	21	4	2	1	2	19	4	32	2	0	3	4	.429	0	28-33	0	4.46
San Diego	NL	21	0	0	5	14.1	64	15	10	10	2	2	0	0	7	1	9	2	0	1	3	.250	0	0-1	8	6.28
14 ML YEARS		728	12	1	548	884.2	3744	758	338	314	69	50	33	12	396	43	884	32	2	44	63	.411	0	347-407	32	3.19

Rodney Myers

Pitches: Right Bats: Right Pos: RP-46 Ht: 6'1" Wt: 205 Born: 6/26/69 Age: 31

		HOW MUCH HE PITCHED						WHAT HE GAVE UP											THE RESULTS						
Year Team	Lg	G	GS	CG	GF	IP	BFP	H	R	ER	HR	SH	SF	HB	TBB	IBB	SO	WP	Bk	W	L	Pct.	ShO	Sv-Op	Hld	ERA
1999 Iowa *	AAA	20	1	0	14	31	131	29	16	14	3	2	1	0	11	3	24	0	0	2	4	.333	0	2--	1	4.06
1996 Chicago	NL	45	0	0	8	67.1	298	61	38	35	6	1	5	3	38	3	50	4	1	2	1	.667	0	0-0	1	4.68
1997 Chicago	NL	5	1	0	2	9	44	12	6	6	1	0	0	1	7	1	6	0	0	0	0	.000	0	0-0	0	6.00
1998 Chicago	NL	12	0	0	3	18	82	26	14	14	3	0	0	0	6	0	15	1	0	0	0	.000	0	0-1	0	7.00
1999 Chicago	NL	46	0	0	5	63.2	278	71	34	31	10	4	2	1	25	2	41	2	0	3	1	.750	0	0-1	8	4.38
4 ML YEARS		108	1	0	18	158	702	170	92	86	20	5	7	5	76	6	112	7	1	5	2	.714	0	0-2	9	4.90

Aaron Myette

Pitches: Right Bats: Right Pos: SP-3; RP-1 Ht: 6'4" Wt: 195 Born: 9/26/77 Age: 22

		HOW MUCH HE PITCHED						WHAT HE GAVE UP											THE RESULTS						
Year Team	Lg	G	GS	CG	GF	IP	BFP	H	R	ER	HR	SH	SF	HB	TBB	IBB	SO	WP	Bk	W	L	Pct.	ShO	Sv-Op	Hld	ERA
1997 Bristol	R+	9	8	1	0	47.1	215	39	28	19	9	0	0	7	20	0	50	2	1	4	3	.571	0	0--	--	3.61
Hickory	A	5	5	0	0	31.2	121	19	6	4	1	1	0	2	11	0	27	2	1	3	1	.750	0	0--	--	1.14
1998 Hickory	A	17	17	0	0	102	421	84	43	28	4	2	3	8	30	0	103	5	2	9	4	.692	0	0--	--	2.47
Winston-Sal	A+	6	6	1	0	44.2	178	32	14	10	4	1	0	1	14	0	54	0	0	4	2	.667	1	0--	--	2.01
1999 Birmingham	AA	28	28	0	0	164.2	711	138	76	67	19	2	3	15	77	0	135	6	1	12	7	.632	0	0--	--	3.66
1999 Chicago	AL	4	3	0	0	15.2	80	17	11	11	2	0	0	2	14	1	11	2	0	0	2	.000	0	0-0	0	6.32

Charles Nagy

Pitches: Right Bats: Left Pos: SP-32; RP-1 Ht: 6'3" Wt: 200 Born: 5/5/67 Age: 33

		HOW MUCH HE PITCHED						WHAT HE GAVE UP											THE RESULTS						
Year Team	Lg	G	GS	CG	GF	IP	BFP	H	R	ER	HR	SH	SF	HB	TBB	IBB	SO	WP	Bk	W	L	Pct.	ShO	Sv-Op	Hld	ERA
1990 Cleveland	AL	9	8	0	1	45.2	208	58	31	30	7	1	1	1	21	1	26	1	1	2	4	.333	0	0-0	0	5.91
1991 Cleveland	AL	33	33	6	0	211.1	914	228	103	97	15	5	9	6	66	7	109	6	2	10	15	.400	1	0-0	0	4.13

(Top player — continued)

Year Team	Lg	G	GS	CG	GF	IP	BFP	H	R	ER	HR	SH	SF	HB	TBB	IBB	SO	WP	Bk	W	L	Pct.	ShO	Sv-Op	Hld	ERA
1992 Cleveland	AL	33	33	10	0	252	1018	245	91	83	11	6	9	2	57	1	169	7	0	17	10	.630	3	0-0	0	2.96
1993 Cleveland	AL	9	9	1	0	48.2	223	66	38	34	6	2	1	2	13	1	30	2	0	2	6	.250	0	0-0	0	6.29
1994 Cleveland	AL	23	23	3	0	169.1	717	175	76	65	15	2	2	5	48	1	108	5	1	10	8	.556	0	0-0	0	3.45
1995 Cleveland	AL	29	29	2	0	178	771	194	95	90	20	2	5	6	61	0	139	2	0	16	6	.727	1	0-0	0	4.55
1996 Cleveland	AL	32	32	5	0	222	921	217	89	84	21	2	4	3	61	2	167	7	0	17	5	.773	0	0-0	0	3.41
1997 Cleveland	AL	34	34	1	0	227	991	253	115	108	27	5	6	7	77	4	149	5	0	15	11	.577	1	0-0	0	4.28
1998 Cleveland	AL	33	33	2	0	210.1	930	250	139	122	34	8	6	9	66	12	120	3	0	15	10	.600	0	0-0	0	5.22
1999 Cleveland	AL	33	32	1	0	202	887	238	120	111	26	5	4	6	59	4	126	3	0	17	11	.607	0	0-0	0	4.95
10 ML YEARS		268	266	31	1	1766.1	7580	1924	897	824	182	38	47	47	529	33	1143	41	4	121	86	.585	6	0-0	0	4.20

Joe Nathan

Pitches: Right **Bats:** Right **Pos:** SP-14; RP-5   **Ht:** 6'4" **Wt:** 195 **Born:** 11/22/74 **Age:** 25

Year Team	Lg	G	GS	CG	GF	IP	BFP	H	R	ER	HR	SH	SF	HB	TBB	IBB	SO	WP	Bk	W	L	Pct.	ShO	Sv-Op	Hld	ERA
1997 Salem-Keizr	A-	18	5	0	4	62	254	53	22	17	7	4	2	4	26	0	44	2	0	2	1	.667	0	2--	—	2.47
1998 Shreveport	AA	4	4	0	0	15.1	74	20	15	15	4	0	0	2	9	0	10	0	0	1	3	.250	0	0--	—	8.80
San Jose	A+	22	22	0	0	122	506	100	51	45	13	1	1	10	48	0	118	1	0	8	6	.571	0	0--	—	3.32
1999 Shreveport	AA	2	2	0	0	8.2	38	5	4	3	0	1	1	1	7	0	7	2	1	0	1	.000	0	0--	—	3.12
Fresno	AAA	13	13	1	0	74.2	324	68	44	37	11	3	1	5	36	0	82	6	1	6	4	.600	0	0--	—	4.46
1999 San Francisco	NL	19	14	0	2	90.1	395	84	45	42	17	2	0	1	46	0	54	2	0	7	4	.636	0	1-1	0	4.18

Dan Naulty

Pitches: Right **Bats:** Right **Pos:** RP-33   **Ht:** 6'6" **Wt:** 224 **Born:** 1/6/70 **Age:** 30

Year Team	Lg	G	GS	CG	GF	IP	BFP	H	R	ER	HR	SH	SF	HB	TBB	IBB	SO	WP	Bk	W	L	Pct.	ShO	Sv-Op	Hld	ERA
1999 Columbus *	AAA	7	0	0	2	10.1	48	14	6	5	1	0	2	0	4	0	5	1	0	2	1	.667	0	0--	—	4.35
1996 Minnesota	AL	49	0	0	15	57	245	43	26	24	5	2	0	0	35	3	56	2	0	3	2	.600	0	4-9	4	3.79
1997 Minnesota	AL	29	0	0	8	30.2	128	29	20	20	8	0	4	0	10	0	23	3	0	1	1	.500	0	1-3	8	5.87
1998 Minnesota	AL	19	0	0	9	23.2	104	25	16	13	3	0	1	0	10	1	15	0	0	0	2	.000	0	0-1	0	4.94
1999 New York	AL	33	0	0	20	49.1	206	40	24	24	8	1	1	4	22	0	25	2	0	1	0	1.000	0	0-0	1	4.38
4 ML YEARS		130	0	0	52	160.2	683	137	86	81	24	3	6	4	77	4	119	7	0	5	5	.500	0	5-13	13	4.54

Jaime Navarro

Pitches: Right **Bats:** Right **Pos:** SP-27; RP-5   **Ht:** 6'4" **Wt:** 250 **Born:** 3/27/68 **Age:** 32

Year Team	Lg	G	GS	CG	GF	IP	BFP	H	R	ER	HR	SH	SF	HB	TBB	IBB	SO	WP	Bk	W	L	Pct.	ShO	Sv-Op	Hld	ERA
1989 Milwaukee	AL	19	17	1	1	109.2	470	119	47	38	6	5	2	1	32	3	56	3	0	7	8	.467	0	0-0	0	3.12
1990 Milwaukee	AL	32	32	3	0	149.1	654	176	83	74	11	4	5	4	41	3	75	6	5	8	7	.533	0	1-2	3	4.46
1991 Milwaukee	AL	34	34	10	0	234	1002	237	117	102	18	7	8	6	73	3	114	10	0	15	12	.556	2	0-0	0	3.92
1992 Milwaukee	AL	34	34	5	0	246	1004	224	98	91	14	9	13	6	64	4	100	6	0	17	11	.607	3	0-0	0	3.33
1993 Milwaukee	AL	35	34	5	0	214.1	955	254	135	127	21	6	17	11	73	4	114	11	0	11	12	.478	1	0-0	0	5.33
1994 Milwaukee	AL	29	10	0	7	89.2	411	115	71	66	10	2	4	4	35	4	65	3	0	4	9	.308	0	0-0	0	6.62
1995 Chicago	NL	29	29	1	0	200.1	837	194	79	73	19	2	3	6	56	7	128	1	0	14	6	.700	1	0-0	0	3.28
1996 Chicago	NL	35	35	4	0	236.2	1007	244	116	103	25	10	7	10	72	5	158	10	0	15	12	.556	1	0-0	0	3.92
1997 Chicago	AL	33	33	2	0	209.2	957	267	155	135	22	2	14	3	73	6	142	14	1	9	14	.391	0	0-0	0	5.79
1998 Chicago	AL	37	27	1	4	172.2	802	223	135	122	30	3	7	7	77	1	71	18	0	8	16	.333	0	1-1	0	6.36
1999 Chicago	AL	32	27	0	1	159.2	748	206	126	108	29	3	4	11	71	1	74	9	0	8	13	.381	0	0-0	0	6.09
11 ML YEARS		349	302	32	15	2022	8847	2259	1162	1039	205	53	84	66	667	41	1097	91	6	116	120	.492	8	2-3	3	4.62

Denny Neagle

Pitches: Left **Bats:** Left **Pos:** SP-19; RP-1   **Ht:** 6'3" **Wt:** 225 **Born:** 9/13/68 **Age:** 31

Year Team	Lg	G	GS	CG	GF	IP	BFP	H	R	ER	HR	SH	SF	HB	TBB	IBB	SO	WP	Bk	W	L	Pct.	ShO	Sv-Op	Hld	ERA
1999 Indianapols *	AAA	3	3	0	0	17.1	66	11	9	9	2	0	1	1	2	0	9	0	0	2	0	1.000	0	0--	—	4.67
1991 Minnesota	AL	7	3	0	2	20	92	28	9	9	3	0	0	0	7	2	14	1	0	0	1	.000	0	0-0	0	4.05
1992 Pittsburgh	NL	55	6	0	8	86.1	380	81	46	43	9	4	3	2	43	8	77	3	2	4	6	.400	0	2-4	5	4.48
1993 Pittsburgh	NL	50	7	0	13	81.1	360	82	49	48	10	1	1	3	37	3	73	5	0	3	5	.375	0	1-1	6	5.31
1994 Pittsburgh	NL	24	24	2	0	137	587	135	80	78	18	7	6	3	49	3	122	2	0	9	10	.474	0	0-0	0	5.12
1995 Pittsburgh	NL	31	31	2	0	209.2	876	221	91	80	20	13	6	3	45	3	150	6	0	13	8	.619	1	0-0	0	3.43
1996 Pit-Atl	NL	33	33	2	0	221.1	910	226	93	86	26	10	4	3	48	2	149	3	1	16	9	.640	0	0-0	0	3.50
1997 Atlanta	NL	34	34	4	0	233.1	947	204	87	77	18	12	6	6	49	5	172	3	0	20	5	.800	4	0-0	0	2.97
1998 Atlanta	NL	32	31	5	0	210.1	861	196	91	83	25	7	3	6	60	3	165	6	1	16	11	.593	2	0-0	0	3.55
1999 Cincinnati	NL	20	19	0	0	111.2	467	95	54	53	23	3	5	4	40	3	76	4	0	9	5	.643	0	0-0	0	4.27
1996 Pittsburgh	NL	27	27	1	0	182.2	745	186	67	62	21	9	3	3	34	2	131	2	1	14	6	.700	0	0-0	0	3.05
Atlanta	NL	6	6	1	0	38.2	165	40	26	24	5	1	1	0	14	0	18	1	0	2	3	.400	0	0-0	0	5.59
9 ML YEARS		286	188	18	23	1311	5480	1268	600	557	152	57	34	30	378	32	998	33	4	90	60	.600	7	3-5	11	3.82

Jeff Nelson

Pitches: Right **Bats:** Right **Pos:** RP-39 **Ht:** 6'8" **Wt:** 235 **Born:** 11/17/66 **Age:** 33

		HOW MUCH HE PITCHED						WHAT HE GAVE UP											THE RESULTS					
Year Team	Lg	G	GS	CG	GF	IP	BFP	H	R	ER	HR	SH	SF	HB	TBB	IBB	SO	WP	Bk	W	L	Pct.	ShO	Sv-Op	Hld	ERA
1999 Tampa *	A+	3	3	0	0	3	12	1	0	0	0	0	0	0	2	0	5	0	0	0	0	.000	0	0- -	—	0.00
Yankees *	R	2	2	0	0	2	8	1	0	0	0	0	0	0	1	0	3	0	0	0	0	.000	0	0- -	—	0.00
1992 Seattle	AL	66	0	0	27	81	352	71	34	31	7	9	3	6	44	12	46	2	0	1	7	.125	0	6-14	6	3.44
1993 Seattle	AL	71	0	0	13	60	269	57	30	29	5	2	4	8	34	10	61	2	0	5	3	.625	0	1-11	17	4.35
1994 Seattle	AL	28	0	0	7	42.1	185	35	18	13	3	1	1	8	20	4	44	2	0	0	0	.000	0	0-0	2	2.76
1995 Seattle	AL	62	0	0	24	78.2	318	58	21	19	4	5	3	6	27	5	96	1	0	7	3	.700	0	2-4	14	2.17
1996 New York	AL	73	0	0	27	74.1	328	75	38	36	6	3	1	2	36	1	91	4	0	4	4	.500	0	2-4	10	4.36
1997 New York	AL	77	0	0	22	78.2	327	53	32	25	7	7	2	4	37	12	81	4	0	3	7	.300	0	2-8	22	2.86
1998 New York	AL	45	0	0	13	40.1	192	44	18	17	1	1	3	8	22	4	35	2	0	5	3	.625	0	3-6	10	3.79
1999 New York	AL	39	0	0	8	30.1	139	27	14	14	2	2	2	3	22	2	35	2	1	2	1	.667	0	1-2	10	4.15
8 ML YEARS		461	0	0	141	485.2	2110	420	205	184	35	30	19	45	242	50	489	19	1	27	28	.491	0	17-49	91	3.41

Robb Nen

Pitches: Right **Bats:** Right **Pos:** RP-72 **Ht:** 6'5" **Wt:** 215 **Born:** 11/28/69 **Age:** 30

		HOW MUCH HE PITCHED						WHAT HE GAVE UP											THE RESULTS					
Year Team	Lg	G	GS	CG	GF	IP	BFP	H	R	ER	HR	SH	SF	HB	TBB	IBB	SO	WP	Bk	W	L	Pct.	ShO	Sv-Op	Hld	ERA
1993 Tex-Fla		24	4	0	5	56	272	63	45	42	6	1	2	0	46	0	39	6	1	2	1	.667	0	0-0	0	6.75
1994 Florida	NL	44	0	0	28	58	228	46	20	19	6	3	1	0	17	2	60	3	2	5	5	.500	0	15-15	1	2.95
1995 Florida	NL	62	0	0	54	65.2	279	62	26	24	6	0	1	1	23	3	68	2	0	0	0	.000	0	23-29	0	3.29
1996 Florida	NL	75	0	0	66	83	326	67	21	18	2	5	1	1	21	6	92	4	0	5	1	.833	0	35-42	0	1.95
1997 Florida	NL	73	0	0	65	74	332	72	35	32	7	1	3	0	40	7	81	5	0	9	3	.750	0	35-42	0	3.89
1998 San Francisco	NL	78	0	0	67	88.2	357	59	21	15	4	2	2	1	25	5	110	3	0	7	7	.500	0	40-45	0	1.52
1999 San Francisco	NL	72	0	0	64	72.1	320	79	36	32	8	5	1	0	27	3	77	5	0	3	8	.273	0	37-46	0	3.98
1993 Texas	AL	9	3	0	3	22.2	113	28	17	16	1	0	1	0	26	0	12	2	1	1	1	.500	0	0-0	0	6.35
Florida	NL	15	1	0	2	33.1	159	35	28	26	5	1	1	0	20	0	27	4	0	1	0	1.000	0	0-0	0	7.02
7 ML YEARS		428	4	0	349	497.2	2114	448	204	182	39	17	11	3	199	26	527	28	3	31	32	.492	0	185-219	1	3.29

Phil Nevin

Bats: R **Throws:** R **Pos:** 3B-67; C-31; PH/PR-24; 1B-11; RF-9; LF-5; DH-1 **Ht:** 6'2" **Wt:** 231 **Born:** 1/19/71 **Age:** 29

		BATTING															BASERUNNING				PERCENTAGES		
Year Team	Lg	G	AB	H	2B	3B	HR	(Hm | Rd)	TB	R	RBI	TBB	IBB	SO	HBP	SH	SF	SB	CS	SB%	GDP	Avg	OBP	SLG
1999 Las Vegas *	AAA	3	10	2	0	0	2	—	—	8	2	2	0	0	2	0	0	0	0	0	.00	1	.200	.200	.800
1995 Hou-Det		47	156	28	4	1	2	(2 | 0)	40	13	13	18	1	40	4	1	0	1	0	1.00	5	.179	.281	.256
1996 Detroit	AL	38	120	35	5	0	8	(3 | 5)	64	15	19	8	0	39	1	0	1	1	0	1.00	4	.292	.338	.533
1997 Detroit	AL	93	251	59	16	1	9	(4 | 5)	104	32	35	25	1	68	1	0	1	0	1	.00	5	.235	.306	.414
1998 Anaheim	AL	75	237	54	8	1	8	(3 | 5)	88	27	27	17	0	67	5	0	2	0	0	.00	6	.228	.291	.371
1999 San Diego	NL	128	383	103	27	0	24	(12 | 12)	202	52	85	51	1	82	1	1	5	1	0	1.00	7	.269	.352	.527
1995 Houston	NL	18	60	7	1	0	0	(0 | 0)	8	4	1	7	1	13	1	1	0	1	0	1.00	1	.117	.221	.133
Detroit	AL	29	96	21	3	1	2	(2 | 0)	32	9	12	11	0	27	3	0	0	0	0	.00	3	.219	.318	.333
5 ML YEARS		381	1147	279	60	3	51	(24 | 27)	498	139	179	119	3	296	12	2	9	3	1	.75	24	.243	.319	.434

David Newhan

Bats: Left **Throws:** Right **Pos:** 2B-19; PH/PR-13; 3B-1; 1B-1 **Ht:** 5'10" **Wt:** 180 **Born:** 9/7/73 **Age:** 26

		BATTING															BASERUNNING				PERCENTAGES		
Year Team	Lg	G	AB	H	2B	3B	HR	(Hm | Rd)	TB	R	RBI	TBB	IBB	SO	HBP	SH	SF	SB	CS	SB%	GDP	Avg	OBP	SLG
1995 Sou Oregon	A-	42	145	39	8	1	6	—	—	67	25	21	29	1	30	1	1	3	10	5	.67	2	.269	.388	.462
W Michigan	A	25	96	21	5	0	3	—	—	35	9	8	13	1	26	1	1	1	3	2	.60	2	.219	.315	.365
1996 Modesto	A+	117	455	137	27	3	25	—	—	245	96	75	62	1	106	2	6	2	17	8	.68	8	.301	.386	.538
1997 Visalia	A+	67	241	67	15	2	7	—	—	107	52	48	44	2	58	3	2	5	9	3	.75	5	.278	.389	.444
Huntsville	AA	57	212	67	13	2	5	—	—	99	40	35	28	2	59	2	1	2	5	5	.50	4	.316	.398	.467
1998 Mobile	AA	121	491	128	26	3	12	—	—	196	89	45	68	1	110	2	2	1	27	8	.77	8	.261	.352	.399
1999 Las Vegas	AAA	98	374	107	25	1	14	—	—	176	49	49	30	0	84	2	4	1	22	4	.85	8	.286	.342	.471
1999 San Diego	NL	32	43	6	1	0	2	(1 | 1)	13	7	6	1	0	11	0	0	0	2	1	.67	0	.140	.159	.302

Alan Newman

Pitches: Left **Bats:** Left **Pos:** RP-18 **Ht:** 6'6" **Wt:** 240 **Born:** 10/2/69 **Age:** 30

		HOW MUCH HE PITCHED						WHAT HE GAVE UP											THE RESULTS					
Year Team	Lg	G	GS	CG	GF	IP	BFP	H	R	ER	HR	SH	SF	HB	TBB	IBB	SO	WP	Bk	W	L	Pct.	ShO	Sv-Op	Hld	ERA
1988 Elizabethtn	R+	13	12	2	0	55.1	279	57	62	50	3	2	2	2	56	0	51	17	3	2	8	.200	0	0- -	—	8.13
1989 Kenosha	A	18	18	1	0	88.2	398	65	41	28	2	5	0	4	74	0	82	3	9	3	9	.250	0	0- -	—	2.84
1990 Kenosha	A	22	22	5	0	154	614	94	41	28	2	4	0	6	78	2	158	10	2	10	4	.714	1	0- -	—	1.64
Visalia	A+	5	5	0	0	36.1	155	29	15	9	0	3	2	1	22	0	42	1	0	3	1	.750	0	0- -	—	2.23
1991 Visalia	A+	15	15	0	0	92.1	411	86	49	36	2	4	0	6	49	2	79	11	0	6	5	.545	0	0- -	—	3.51
Orlando	AA	11	11	2	0	67	275	53	28	20	0	2	1	1	30	1	53	8	0	5	4	.556	0	0- -	—	2.69
1992 Orlando	AA	18	18	2	0	102	454	94	54	47	3	4	3	4	67	0	86	9	3	4	8	.333	1	0- -	—	4.15
1993 Nashville	AA	14	11	1	1	65.2	304	75	52	44	4	4	2	1	40	0	35	5	0	1	6	.143	0	0- -	—	6.03
Indianapolis	AAA	8	3	0	3	20	111	24	23	19	3	0	2	1	27	0	15	5	1	1	3	.250	0	0- -	—	8.55
1995 Alexandria	IND	23	21	5	1	137	612	141	87	79	9	13	0	2	74	2	129	12	0	10	8	.556	2	0- -	—	5.19
1996 Alexandria	IND	35	11	0	10	118.1	522	136	70	60	8	7	4	4	43	1	82	6	0	6	6	.500	0	2- -	—	4.56
1997 Birmingham	AA	44	0	0	33	72.1	314	55	34	20	4	2	0	4	40	4	64	9	0	7	3	.700	0	10- -	—	2.49

Year Team	Lg	G	GS	CG	GF	IP	BFP	H	R	ER	HR	SH	SF	HB	TBB	IBB	SO	WP	Bk	W	L	Pct.	ShO	Sv-Op	Hld	ERA
		HOW MUCH HE PITCHED						WHAT HE GAVE UP												THE RESULTS						
1998 Las Vegas	AAA	63	0	0	23	76.1	332	58	29	28	2	5	3	3	50	3	76	6	0	3	3	.500	0	7--	—	3.30
1999 Durham	AAA	50	0	0	7	80.1	316	59	24	20	2	2	2	3	20	0	76	3	1	10	0	1.000	0	0--	—	2.24
1999 Tampa Bay	AL	18	0	0	5	15.2	76	22	12	12	2	0	0	1	9	0	20	2	1	2	2	.500	0	0-1	0	6.89

Jose Nieves

Bats: Right **Throws:** Right **Pos:** SS-52; PH/PR-2 **Ht:** 6'1" **Wt:** 185 **Born:** 6/16/75 **Age:** 25

Year Team	Lg	G	AB	H	2B	3B	HR	(Hm	Rd)	TB	R	RBI	TBB	IBB	SO	HBP	SH	SF	SB	CS	SB%	GDP	Avg	OBP	SLG
		BATTING																	BASERUNNING				PERCENTAGES		
1995 Williamsprt	A-	69	276	59	13	1	4	—	—	86	46	44	21	1	39	6	0	3	11	10	.52	4	.214	.281	.312
1996 Rockford	A	113	396	96	20	4	5	—	—	139	55	57	33	1	59	5	4	3	17	9	.65	8	.242	.307	.351
1997 Daytona	A+	85	331	91	20	1	4	—	—	125	51	42	17	0	55	4	4	6	16	6	.73	7	.275	.313	.378
1998 West Tenn	AA	82	314	91	27	5	8	—	—	152	42	39	18	0	55	1	2	3	17	10	.63	9	.290	.327	.484
Iowa	AAA	19	75	19	4	0	0	—	—	23	7	4	2	0	11	0	0	0	1	1	.50	2	.253	.273	.307
1999 Iowa	AAA	104	392	105	25	3	11	—	—	169	55	59	24	2	65	4	6	4	11	8	.58	9	.268	.314	.431
1998 Chicago	NL	2	1	0	0	0	0	(0	0)	0	0	0	0	0	0	0	1	0	0	0	.00	0	.000	.000	.000
1999 Chicago	NL	54	181	45	9	1	2	(2	0)	62	16	18	8	0	25	4	3	3	0	2	.00	5	.249	.291	.343
2 ML YEARS		56	182	45	9	1	2	(2	0)	62	16	18	8	0	25	4	4	3	0	2	.00	5	.247	.289	.341

Dave Nilsson

Bats: Left **Throws:** Right **Pos:** C-101; PH/PR-18; DH-1 **Ht:** 6'3" **Wt:** 229 **Born:** 12/14/69 **Age:** 30

Year Team	Lg	G	AB	H	2B	3B	HR	(Hm	Rd)	TB	R	RBI	TBB	IBB	SO	HBP	SH	SF	SB	CS	SB%	GDP	Avg	OBP	SLG
		BATTING																	BASERUNNING				PERCENTAGES		
1992 Milwaukee	AL	51	164	38	8	0	4	(1	3)	58	15	25	17	1	18	0	2	0	2	2	.50	1	.232	.304	.354
1993 Milwaukee	AL	100	296	76	10	2	7	(5	2)	111	35	40	37	5	36	0	4	3	3	6	.33	10	.257	.336	.375
1994 Milwaukee	AL	109	397	109	28	3	12	(4	8)	179	51	69	34	9	61	0	1	8	1	0	1.00	1	.275	.326	.451
1995 Milwaukee	AL	81	263	73	12	1	12	(7	5)	123	41	53	24	4	41	2	0	5	2	0	1.00	9	.278	.337	.468
1996 Milwaukee	AL	123	453	150	33	2	17	(13	4)	238	81	84	57	6	68	3	0	3	2	3	.40	4	.331	.407	.525
1997 Milwaukee	AL	156	554	154	33	0	20	(5	15)	247	71	81	65	8	88	2	1	7	2	3	.40	7	.278	.352	.446
1998 Milwaukee	NL	102	309	83	14	1	12	(6	6)	135	39	56	33	1	48	1	2	2	2	2	.50	12	.269	.339	.437
1999 Milwaukee	NL	115	343	106	19	1	21	(9	12)	190	56	62	53	6	64	2	2	4	1	2	.33	7	.309	.400	.554
8 ML YEARS		837	2779	789	157	10	105	(40	65)	1281	389	470	320	40	424	10	12	32	15	18	.45	57	.284	.356	.461

C.J. Nitkowski

Pitches: Left **Bats:** Left **Pos:** RP-61; SP-7 **Ht:** 6'3" **Wt:** 205 **Born:** 3/9/73 **Age:** 27

Year Team	Lg	G	GS	CG	GF	IP	BFP	H	R	ER	HR	SH	SF	HB	TBB	IBB	SO	WP	Bk	W	L	Pct.	ShO	Sv-Op	Hld	ERA
		HOW MUCH HE PITCHED						WHAT HE GAVE UP												THE RESULTS						
1995 Cin-Det		20	18	0	0	71.2	338	94	57	53	11	2	4	5	35	3	31	2	2	2	7	.222	0	0-1	0	6.66
1996 Detroit	AL	11	8	0	0	45.2	234	62	44	41	7	0	2	7	38	1	36	2	0	2	3	.400	0	0-0	0	8.08
1998 Houston	NL	43	0	0	11	59.2	250	49	27	25	4	4	2	6	23	2	44	3	1	3	3	.500	0	3-5	8	3.77
1999 Detroit	AL	68	7	0	7	81.2	349	63	44	39	11	1	4	3	45	3	66	4	3	4	5	.444	0	0-0	11	4.30
1995 Cincinnati	NL	9	7	0	0	32.1	154	41	25	22	4	2	1	2	15	1	18	1	2	1	3	.250	0	0-1	0	6.12
Detroit	AL	11	11	0	0	39.1	184	53	32	31	7	0	3	3	20	2	13	1	0	1	4	.200	0	0-0	0	7.09
4 ML YEARS		142	33	0	18	258.2	1171	268	172	158	33	7	12	21	141	9	177	11	6	11	18	.379	0	3-6	19	5.50

Otis Nixon

Bats: Both **Throws:** Right **Pos:** LF-50; PH/PR-36; CF-5 **Ht:** 6'2" **Wt:** 180 **Born:** 1/9/59 **Age:** 41

Year Team	Lg	G	AB	H	2B	3B	HR	(Hm	Rd)	TB	R	RBI	TBB	IBB	SO	HBP	SH	SF	SB	CS	SB%	GDP	Avg	OBP	SLG
		BATTING																	BASERUNNING				PERCENTAGES		
1983 New York	AL	13	14	2	0	0	0	(0	0)	2	2	0	1	0	5	0	0	0	2	0	1.00	0	.143	.200	.143
1984 Cleveland	AL	49	91	14	0	0	0	(0	0)	14	16	1	8	0	11	0	3	1	12	6	.67	2	.154	.220	.154
1985 Cleveland	AL	104	162	38	4	0	3	(1	2)	51	34	9	8	0	27	0	4	0	20	11	.65	2	.235	.271	.315
1986 Cleveland	AL	105	95	25	4	1	0	(0	0)	31	33	8	13	0	12	0	2	0	23	6	.79	1	.263	.352	.326
1987 Cleveland	AL	19	17	1	0	0	0	(0	0)	1	2	1	3	0	4	0	0	0	2	3	.40	0	.059	.200	.059
1988 Montreal	NL	90	271	66	8	2	0	(0	0)	78	47	15	28	0	42	0	4	2	46	13	.78	0	.244	.312	.288
1989 Montreal	NL	126	258	56	7	2	0	(0	0)	67	41	21	33	1	36	0	2	0	37	12	.76	4	.217	.306	.260
1990 Montreal	NL	119	231	58	6	2	1	(0	1)	71	46	20	28	0	33	0	3	1	50	13	.79	2	.251	.331	.307
1991 Atlanta	NL	124	401	119	10	1	0	(0	0)	131	81	26	47	3	40	2	7	3	72	21	.77	5	.297	.371	.327
1992 Atlanta	NL	120	456	134	14	2	2	(1	1)	158	79	22	39	0	54	0	5	2	41	18	.69	4	.294	.348	.346
1993 Atlanta	NL	134	461	124	12	3	1	(1	0)	145	77	24	61	2	63	0	5	5	47	13	.78	10	.269	.351	.315
1994 Boston	AL	103	398	109	15	1	0	(0	0)	126	60	25	55	1	65	0	6	2	42	10	.81	0	.274	.360	.317
1995 Texas	AL	139	589	174	21	2	0	(0	0)	199	87	45	58	1	85	0	6	3	50	21	.70	6	.295	.357	.338
1996 Toronto	AL	125	496	142	15	1	1	(1	0)	162	87	29	71	1	68	1	7	0	54	13	.81	9	.286	.377	.327
1997 Tor-LA		145	576	153	18	3	2	(0	2)	183	84	44	65	0	78	0	8	6	59	12	.83	12	.266	.337	.318
1998 Minnesota	AL	110	448	133	6	6	1	(0	0)	154	71	20	44	0	56	2	4	2	37	7	.84	14	.297	.360	.344
1999 Atlanta	NL	84	151	31	2	1	0	(0	0)	35	31	8	23	1	15	0	1	1	26	7	.79	1	.205	.309	.232
1997 Toronto	AL	103	401	105	12	1	1	(0	1)	122	54	26	52	0	54	0	6	5	47	10	.82	10	.262	.343	.318
Los Angeles	NL	42	175	48	6	2	1	(0	0)	61	30	18	13	0	24	0	2	1	12	2	.86	2	.274	.323	.349
17 ML YEARS		1709	5115	1379	142	27	11	(5	6)	1608	878	318	585	10	694	5	67	28	620	186	.77	72	.270	.343	.314

Trot Nixon

Bats: Left **Throws:** Left **Pos:** RF-121; PH/PR-6 **Ht:** 6'2" **Wt:** 200 **Born:** 4/11/74 **Age:** 26

Year Team	Lg	G	AB	H	2B	3B	HR	(Hm	Rd)	TB	R	RBI	TBB	IBB	SO	HBP	SH	SF	SB	CS	SB%	GDP	Avg	OBP	SLG
1994 Lynchburg	A+	71	264	65	12	0	12	—	—	113	33	43	44	1	53	3	1	3	10	3	.77	5	.246	.357	.428
1995 Sarasota	A+	73	264	80	11	4	5	—	—	114	43	39	45	3	46	1	0	2	7	5	.58	5	.303	.404	.432
Trenton	AA	25	94	15	3	1	2	—	—	26	9	8	7	0	20	0	2	2	2	1	.67	0	.160	.214	.277
1996 Trenton	AA	123	438	110	11	4	11	—	—	162	55	63	50	3	65	3	6	5	7	9	.44	6	.251	.329	.370
1997 Pawtucket	AAA	130	475	116	18	3	20	—	—	200	80	61	63	2	86	1	9	4	11	4	.73	11	.244	.331	.421
1998 Pawtucket	AAA	135	509	158	26	4	23	—	—	261	97	74	76	6	81	5	0	7	26	13	.67	10	.310	.400	.513
1996 Boston	AL	2	4	2	1	0	0	(0	0)	3	2	0	0	0	1	0	0	0	1	0	1.00	0	.500	.500	.750
1998 Boston	AL	3	27	7	1	0	0	(0	0)	8	3	0	1	0	3	0	0	0	0	0	.00	0	.259	.286	.296
1999 Boston	AL	124	381	103	22	5	15	(3	12)	180	67	52	53	1	75	3	2	8	3	1	.75	7	.270	.357	.472
3 ML YEARS		139	412	112	24	5	15	(3	12)	191	72	52	54	1	79	3	2	8	4	1	.80	7	.272	.354	.464

Hideo Nomo

Pitches: Right **Bats:** Right **Pos:** SP-28 **Ht:** 6'2" **Wt:** 220 **Born:** 8/31/68 **Age:** 31

Year Team	Lg	G	GS	CG	GF	IP	BFP	H	R	ER	HR	SH	SF	HB	TBB	IBB	SO	WP	Bk	W	L	Pct.	ShO	Sv-Op	Hld	ERA
1999 Iowa *	AAA	3	3	0	0	17	72	12	7	7	1	0	0	0	12	0	18	3	0	1	1	.500	0	0--	—	3.71
Huntsville *	AA	1	1	0	0	7	24	5	0	0	0	0	0	0	1	0	7	0	0	1	0	1.000	0	0--	—	0.00
1995 Los Angeles	NL	28	28	4	0	191.1	780	124	63	54	14	11	4	5	78	2	236	19	5	13	6	.684	3	0-0	0	2.54
1996 Los Angeles	NL	33	33	3	0	228.1	932	180	93	81	23	12	6	2	85	6	234	11	3	16	11	.593	2	0-0	0	3.19
1997 Los Angeles	NL	33	33	1	0	207.1	904	193	104	98	23	7	1	9	92	2	233	10	4	14	12	.538	0	0-0	0	4.25
1998 LA-NYM	NL	29	28	3	0	157.1	687	130	88	86	19	8	5	4	94	2	167	13	4	6	12	.333	0	0-0	0	4.92
1999 Milwaukee	NL	28	28	0	0	176.1	767	173	96	89	27	5	5	3	78	2	161	10	1	12	8	.600	0	0-0	0	4.54
1998 Los Angeles	NL	12	12	2	0	67.2	295	57	39	38	8	2	2	3	38	0	73	4	1	2	7	.222	0	0-0	0	5.05
New York	NL	17	16	1	0	89.2	392	73	49	48	11	6	3	1	56	2	94	9	3	4	5	.444	0	0-0	0	4.82
5 ML YEARS		151	150	11	0	960.2	4070	800	444	408	106	43	21	23	427	14	1031	63	17	61	49	.555	5	0-0	0	3.82

Greg Norton

Bats: B **Throws:** R **Pos:** 3B-120; 1B-26; PH/PR-7; DH-1 **Ht:** 6'1" **Wt:** 205 **Born:** 7/6/72 **Age:** 27

Year Team	Lg	G	AB	H	2B	3B	HR	(Hm	Rd)	TB	R	RBI	TBB	IBB	SO	HBP	SH	SF	SB	CS	SB%	GDP	Avg	OBP	SLG
1996 Chicago	AL	11	23	5	0	0	2	(0	2)	11	4	3	4	0	6	0	0	0	0	1	.00	0	.217	.333	.478
1997 Chicago	AL	18	34	9	2	2	0	(0	0)	15	5	1	2	0	8	0	1	0	0	0	.00	0	.265	.306	.441
1998 Chicago	AL	105	299	71	17	2	9	(6	3)	119	38	36	26	1	77	2	1	2	3	3	.50	11	.237	.301	.398
1999 Chicago	AL	132	436	111	26	0	16	(5	11)	185	62	50	69	3	93	2	1	2	4	4	.50	11	.255	.358	.424
4 ML YEARS		266	792	196	45	4	27	(11	16)	330	109	90	101	4	184	4	3	4	7	8	.47	22	.247	.334	.417

Abraham Nunez

Bats: Both **Throws:** Right **Pos:** SS-65; PH/PR-15; 2B-14 **Ht:** 5'11" **Wt:** 175 **Born:** 3/16/76 **Age:** 24

Year Team	Lg	G	AB	H	2B	3B	HR	(Hm	Rd)	TB	R	RBI	TBB	IBB	SO	HBP	SH	SF	SB	CS	SB%	GDP	Avg	OBP	SLG
1996 St.Cathrnes	A-	75	297	83	6	4	3	—	—	106	43	26	31	0	43	4	8	2	37	14	.73	2	.279	.353	.357
1997 Lynchburg	A+	78	304	79	9	4	3	—	—	105	45	32	23	0	47	1	9	1	29	14	.67	5	.260	.313	.345
Carolina	AA	47	198	65	6	1	1	—	—	76	31	14	20	1	28	0	2	3	10	5	.67	2	.328	.385	.384
1998 Lynchburg	A+	5	18	4	1	0	0	—	—	5	2	2	3	0	1	0	0	1	1	0	1.00	1	.222	.333	.278
Nashville	AAA	94	366	91	12	3	3	—	—	118	50	32	39	0	73	5	2	1	16	8	.67	9	.249	.328	.322
1999 Nashville	AAA	15	58	18	0	0	0	—	—	18	12	3	5	0	8	0	0	1	0	0	1.00	0	.310	.365	.310
1997 Pittsburgh	NL	19	40	9	2	2	0	(0	0)	15	3	6	3	0	10	1	0	1	1	0	1.00	1	.225	.289	.375
1998 Pittsburgh	NL	24	52	10	2	0	1	(0	1)	15	6	2	12	0	14	0	3	0	4	2	.67	1	.192	.344	.288
1999 Pittsburgh	NL	90	259	57	8	0	0	(0	0)	65	25	17	28	0	54	1	13	0	9	1	.90	2	.220	.299	.251
3 ML YEARS		133	351	76	12	2	1	(0	1)	95	34	25	43	0	78	2	16	1	14	3	.82	4	.217	.305	.271

Vladimir Nunez

Pitches: Right **Bats:** Right **Pos:** RP-32; SP-12 **Ht:** 6'4" **Wt:** 224 **Born:** 3/15/75 **Age:** 25

Year Team	Lg	G	GS	CG	GF	IP	BFP	H	R	ER	HR	SH	SF	HB	TBB	IBB	SO	WP	Bk	W	L	Pct.	ShO	Sv-Op	Hld	ERA
1996 Visalia	A+	12	10	0	0	53	233	64	45	32	10	1	3	3	17	0	37	3	2	1	6	.143	0	0--	—	5.43
Lethbridge	R+	14	13	0	0	85	342	78	25	21	4	1	1	9	10	0	93	6	0	10	0	1.000	0	0--	—	2.22
1997 High Desert	A+	28	28	1	0	158.1	682	169	102	91	36	1	3	14	40	1	142	10	2	8	5	.615	1	0--	—	5.17
1998 Tucson	AAA	31	13	1	8	95.1	422	103	58	52	12	2	4	7	37	0	78	5	0	4	4	.500	0	2--	—	4.91
1999 Tucson	AAA	3	0	0	1	2.2	11	5	2	2	0	0	0	0	0	0	3	0	0	1	0	1.000	0	0--	—	6.75
1998 Arizona	NL	4	0	0	2	5.1	29	7	6	6	1	0	0	1	2	0	2	0	1	0	0	.000	0	0-0	0	10.13
1999 Ari-Fla	NL	44	12	0	12	108.2	463	95	63	49	11	7	6	4	54	6	86	8	1	7	10	.412	0	1-3	4	4.06
1999 Arizona	NL	27	0	0	11	34	146	29	15	11	2	2	3	1	20	5	28	3	0	3	2	.600	0	1-2	3	2.91
Florida	NL	17	12	0	1	74.2	317	66	48	38	9	5	3	3	34	1	58	5	1	4	8	.333	0	0-1	1	4.58
2 ML YEARS		48	12	0	14	114	488	102	69	55	11	7	7	4	56	6	88	8	2	7	10	.412	0	1-3	4	4.34

169

Jon Nunnally

Bats: L **Throws:** R **Pos:** PH/PR-8; DH-3; LF-1; RF-1   **Ht:** 5'10" **Wt:** 190 **Born:** 11/9/71 **Age:** 28

Year Team	Lg	G	AB	H	2B	3B	HR	(Hm	Rd)	TB	R	RBI	TBB	IBB	SO	HBP	SH	SF	SB	CS	SB%	GDP	Avg	OBP	SLG
1999 Pawtucket *	AAA	133	494	132	24	3	23	—	—	231	90	76	85	5	103	3	1	7	26	4	.87	7	.267	.374	.468
1995 Kansas City	AL	119	303	74	15	6	14	(6	8)	143	51	42	51	5	86	2	4	0	6	4	.60	4	.244	.357	.472
1996 Kansas City	AL	35	90	19	5	1	5	(2	3)	41	16	17	13	2	25	0	0	1	0	0	.00	0	.211	.308	.456
1997 KC-Cin		78	230	71	12	4	14	(7	7)	133	46	39	31	0	58	2	1	1	7	3	.70	2	.309	.394	.578
1998 Cincinnati	NL	74	174	36	9	0	7	(2	5)	66	29	20	34	3	38	1	1	3	3	4	.43	4	.207	.335	.379
1999 Boston	AL	10	14	4	1	0	0	(0	0)	5	4	1	0	0	6	0	0	0	0	0	.00	0	.286	.286	.357
1997 Kansas City	AL	13	29	7	0	1	1	(1	0)	12	8	4	5	0	7	0	0	0	0	0	.00	0	.241	.353	.414
Cincinnati	NL	65	201	64	12	3	13	(6	7)	121	38	35	26	0	51	2	1	1	7	3	.70	2	.318	.400	.602
5 ML YEARS		316	811	204	42	11	40	(17	23)	388	146	119	129	10	213	5	6	5	16	11	.59	10	.252	.356	.478

Charlie O'Brien

Bats: Right **Throws:** Right **Pos:** C-27; PH/PR-1   **Ht:** 6'2" **Wt:** 205 **Born:** 5/1/61 **Age:** 39

Year Team	Lg	G	AB	H	2B	3B	HR	(Hm	Rd)	TB	R	RBI	TBB	IBB	SO	HBP	SH	SF	SB	CS	SB%	GDP	Avg	OBP	SLG
1985 Oakland	AL	16	11	3	1	0	0	(0	0)	4	3	1	3	0	3	0	0	0	0	0	.00	0	.273	.429	.364
1987 Milwaukee	AL	10	35	7	3	1	0	(0	0)	12	2	0	4	0	4	0	1	0	0	1	.00	0	.200	.282	.343
1988 Milwaukee	AL	40	118	26	6	0	2	(2	0)	38	12	9	5	0	16	0	4	0	0	1	.00	3	.220	.252	.322
1989 Milwaukee	AL	62	188	44	10	0	6	(4	2)	72	22	35	21	1	11	9	8	0	0	0	.00	11	.234	.339	.383
1990 Mil-NYM		74	213	38	10	2	0	(0	0)	52	17	20	21	3	34	3	10	2	0	0	.00	4	.178	.259	.244
1991 New York	NL	69	168	31	6	0	2	(1	1)	43	16	14	17	1	25	4	0	2	0	0	.00	4	.185	.272	.256
1992 New York	NL	68	156	33	12	0	2	(1	1)	51	15	13	16	1	18	1	4	0	0	1	.00	4	.212	.289	.327
1993 New York	NL	67	188	48	11	0	4	(1	3)	71	15	23	14	1	14	2	3	1	1	1	.50	3	.255	.312	.378
1994 Atlanta	NL	51	152	37	11	0	8	(6	2)	72	24	28	15	2	24	3	1	1	0	0	.00	5	.243	.322	.474
1995 Atlanta	NL	67	198	45	7	0	9	(4	5)	79	18	23	29	2	40	6	0	0	1	1	.00	8	.227	.343	.399
1996 Toronto	AL	109	324	77	17	0	13	(8	5)	133	33	44	29	1	68	17	3	2	0	1	.00	6	.238	.331	.410
1997 Toronto	AL	69	225	49	15	1	4	(2	2)	78	22	27	22	1	45	11	3	6	0	2	.00	6	.218	.311	.347
1998 CWS-Ana	AL	62	175	45	9	0	4	(0	4)	66	13	18	10	0	33	2	3	3	0	0	.00	4	.257	.300	.377
1999 Anaheim	AL	27	62	6	0	0	1	(0	1)	9	3	4	1	0	12	2	1	1	0	0	.00	1	.097	.136	.145
1990 Milwaukee	AL	46	145	27	7	2	0	(0	0)	38	11	11	11	1	26	2	8	0	0	0	.00	3	.186	.253	.262
New York	NL	28	68	11	3	0	0	(0	0)	14	6	9	10	2	8	1	2	2	0	0	.00	1	.162	.272	.206
1998 Chicago	AL	57	164	43	9	0	4	(0	4)	64	12	18	9	0	31	2	3	3	0	0	.00	3	.262	.303	.390
Anaheim	AL	5	11	2	0	0	0	(0	0)	2	1	0	1	0	2	0	0	0	0	0	.00	1	.182	.250	.182
14 ML YEARS		791	2213	489	118	4	55	(29	26)	780	215	259	207	13	347	60	41	18	1	10	.09	62	.221	.303	.352

Alex Ochoa

Bats: R **Throws:** R **Pos:** LF-50; PH/PR-42; RF-31; CF-9; DH-1   **Ht:** 6'0" **Wt:** 195 **Born:** 3/29/72 **Age:** 28

Year Team	Lg	G	AB	H	2B	3B	HR	(Hm	Rd)	TB	R	RBI	TBB	IBB	SO	HBP	SH	SF	SB	CS	SB%	GDP	Avg	OBP	SLG
1995 New York	NL	11	37	11	1	0	0	(0	0)	12	7	0	2	0	10	0	0	0	1	0	1.00	1	.297	.333	.324
1996 New York	NL	82	282	83	19	3	4	(1	3)	120	37	33	17	0	30	2	0	3	4	3	.57	2	.294	.336	.426
1997 New York	NL	113	238	58	14	4	1	(1	0)	83	31	22	18	0	32	2	2	2	3	4	.43	4	.244	.300	.349
1998 Minnesota	AL	94	249	64	14	2	2	(1	1)	88	35	25	10	0	35	1	0	0	6	3	.67	7	.257	.288	.353
1999 Milwaukee	NL	119	277	83	16	3	8	(8	0)	129	47	40	45	2	43	5	0	2	6	4	.60	6	.300	.404	.466
5 ML YEARS		419	1083	299	64	9	17	(11	6)	432	157	120	92	2	150	10	2	7	20	14	.59	21	.276	.336	.399

Jose Offerman

Bats: B **Throws:** R **Pos:** 2B-128; DH-17; 1B-8; PH/PR-1   **Ht:** 6'0" **Wt:** 190 **Born:** 11/8/68 **Age:** 31

Year Team	Lg	G	AB	H	2B	3B	HR	(Hm	Rd)	TB	R	RBI	TBB	IBB	SO	HBP	SH	SF	SB	CS	SB%	GDP	Avg	OBP	SLG
1990 Los Angeles	NL	29	58	9	0	0	1	(1	0)	12	7	7	4	1	14	0	1	0	1	0	1.00	0	.155	.210	.207
1991 Los Angeles	NL	52	113	22	2	0	0	(0	0)	24	10	3	25	2	32	1	1	0	3	2	.60	5	.195	.345	.212
1992 Los Angeles	NL	149	534	139	20	8	1	(1	0)	178	67	30	57	4	98	0	5	2	23	16	.59	5	.260	.331	.333
1993 Los Angeles	NL	158	590	159	21	6	1	(1	0)	195	77	62	71	7	75	2	25	8	30	13	.70	12	.269	.346	.331
1994 Los Angeles	NL	72	243	51	8	4	1	(0	1)	70	27	25	38	4	38	0	6	2	2	1	.67	6	.210	.314	.288
1995 Los Angeles	NL	119	429	123	14	6	4	(2	2)	161	69	33	69	0	67	3	10	0	2	7	.22	5	.287	.389	.375
1996 Kansas City	AL	151	561	170	33	8	5	(1	4)	234	85	47	74	3	98	1	7	2	24	10	.71	9	.303	.384	.417
1997 Kansas City	AL	106	424	126	23	6	2	(2	0)	167	59	39	41	3	64	0	6	0	9	10	.47	5	.297	.359	.394
1998 Kansas City	AL	158	607	191	28	13	7	(4	3)	266	102	66	89	1	96	5	2	6	45	12	.79	7	.315	.403	.438
1999 Boston	AL	149	586	172	37	11	8	(5	3)	255	107	69	96	5	79	2	2	7	18	12	.60	11	.294	.391	.435
10 ML YEARS		1143	4145	1162	186	62	30	(17	13)	1562	610	381	564	30	661	14	65	27	157	83	.65	65	.280	.366	.377

Chad Ogea

Pitches: Right **Bats:** Right **Pos:** SP-28; RP-8   **Ht:** 6'2" **Wt:** 220 **Born:** 11/9/70 **Age:** 29

		HOW MUCH HE PITCHED						WHAT HE GAVE UP												THE RESULTS						
Year Team	Lg	G	GS	CG	GF	IP	BFP	H	R	ER	HR	SH	SF	HB	TBB	IBB	SO	WP	Bk	W	L	Pct.	ShO	Sv-Op	Hld	ERA
1994 Cleveland	AL	4	1	0	0	16.1	80	21	11	11	2	0	0	1	10	2	11	0	0	0	1	.000	0	0-0	0	6.06
1995 Cleveland	AL	20	14	1	3	106.1	442	95	38	36	11	0	5	1	29	0	57	3	1	8	3	.727	0	0-0	0	3.05
1996 Cleveland	AL	29	21	1	2	146.2	620	151	82	78	22	3	3	5	42	3	101	2	0	10	6	.625	1	0-0	0	4.79
1997 Cleveland	AL	21	21	1	0	126.1	552	139	79	70	13	3	5	5	47	4	80	4	2	8	9	.471	0	0-0	0	4.99
1998 Cleveland	AL	19	9	0	1	69	307	74	44	43	9	1	3	7	25	1	43	0	0	5	4	.556	0	0-1	1	5.61

		HOW MUCH HE PITCHED					WHAT HE GAVE UP									THE RESULTS					
Year Team	Lg	G	GS	CG	GF	IP	BFP	H	R	ER	HR	SH	SF	HB	TBB	IBB	SO	WP	Bk	W	L	Pct.	ShO	Sv-Op	Hld	ERA
1999 Philadelphia	NL	36	28	0	3	168	746	192	110	105	36	10	4	4	61	1	77	5	2	6	12	.333	0	0-0	0	5.63
6 ML YEARS		129	94	3	9	632.2	2747	672	364	343	93	17	20	23	214	11	369	14	5	37	35	.514	1	0-1	1	4.88

Tomokazu Ohka

Pitches: Right **Bats:** Right **Pos:** RP-6; SP-2   **Ht:** 6'1" **Wt:** 179 **Born:** 3/18/76 **Age:** 24

		HOW MUCH HE PITCHED					WHAT HE GAVE UP									THE RESULTS					
Year Team	Lg	G	GS	CG	GF	IP	BFP	H	R	ER	HR	SH	SF	HB	TBB	IBB	SO	WP	Bk	W	L	Pct.	ShO	Sv-Op	Hld	ERA
1999 Trenton	AA	12	12	0	0	72	298	63	26	24	9	0	0	3	25	0	53	3	0	8	0	1.000	0	0--	—	3.00
Pawtucket	AAA	12	12	1	0	68.1	274	60	19	12	5	1	1	0	11	0	63	1	0	7	0	1.000	1	0--	—	1.58
1999 Boston	AL	8	2	0	3	13	65	21	12	9	2	0	1	0	6	0	8	0	0	1	2	.333	0	0-0	0	6.23

Kirt Ojala

Pitches: Left **Bats:** Left **Pos:** RP-7; SP-1   **Ht:** 6'2" **Wt:** 215 **Born:** 12/24/68 **Age:** 31

		HOW MUCH HE PITCHED					WHAT HE GAVE UP									THE RESULTS					
Year Team	Lg	G	GS	CG	GF	IP	BFP	H	R	ER	HR	SH	SF	HB	TBB	IBB	SO	WP	Bk	W	L	Pct.	ShO	Sv-Op	Hld	ERA
1999 Calgary *	AAA	16	14	1	0	78.2	381	110	70	63	12	4	5	2	44	0	54	6	0	3	8	.273	0	0--	—	7.21
1997 Florida	NL	7	5	0	1	28.2	130	28	10	10	4	0	1	0	18	0	19	0	0	1	2	.333	0	0-0	0	3.14
1998 Florida	NL	41	13	1	4	125	554	128	71	59	14	10	2	4	59	4	75	6	0	2	7	.222	0	0-0	1	4.25
1999 Florida	NL	8	1	0	2	10.2	56	21	17	17	1	0	2	0	6	0	5	0	0	0	1	.000	0	0-0	0	14.34
3 ML YEARS		56	19	1	7	164.1	740	177	98	86	19	10	5	4	83	4	99	6	0	3	10	.231	0	0-0	1	4.71

Troy O'Leary

Bats: Left **Throws:** Left **Pos:** LF-157; RF-2; PH/PR-1   **Ht:** 6'0" **Wt:** 200 **Born:** 8/4/69 **Age:** 30

		BATTING																BASERUNNING				PERCENTAGES		
Year Team	Lg	G	AB	H	2B	3B	HR	(Hm	Rd)	TB	R	RBI	TBB	IBB	SO	HBP	SH	SF	SB	CS	SB%	GDP	Avg	OBP	SLG
1993 Milwaukee	AL	19	41	12	3	0	0	(0	0)	15	3	3	5	0	9	0	3	0	0	0	.00	1	.293	.370	.366
1994 Milwaukee	AL	27	66	18	1	1	2	(0	2)	27	9	7	5	0	12	1	0	1	1	1	.50	0	.273	.329	.409
1995 Boston	AL	112	399	123	31	6	10	(5	5)	196	60	49	29	4	64	1	3	2	5	3	.63	8	.308	.355	.491
1996 Boston	AL	149	497	129	28	5	15	(10	5)	212	68	81	47	3	80	4	1	3	3	2	.60	13	.260	.327	.427
1997 Boston	AL	146	499	154	32	4	15	(5	10)	239	65	80	39	7	70	2	1	4	0	5	.00	13	.309	.358	.479
1998 Boston	AL	156	611	165	36	8	23	(12	11)	286	95	83	36	2	108	5	0	5	2	2	.50	17	.270	.314	.468
1999 Boston	AL	157	596	167	36	4	28	(13	15)	295	84	103	56	5	91	4	0	5	1	2	.33	21	.280	.343	.495
7 ML YEARS		766	2709	768	167	28	93	(45	48)	1270	384	406	217	21	434	17	8	20	12	15	.44	73	.283	.338	.469

John Olerud

Bats: Left **Throws:** Left **Pos:** 1B-160; PH/PR-2   **Ht:** 6'5" **Wt:** 220 **Born:** 8/5/68 **Age:** 31

		BATTING																BASERUNNING				PERCENTAGES		
Year Team	Lg	G	AB	H	2B	3B	HR	(Hm	Rd)	TB	R	RBI	TBB	IBB	SO	HBP	SH	SF	SB	CS	SB%	GDP	Avg	OBP	SLG
1989 Toronto	AL	6	8	3	0	0	0	(0	0)	3	2	0	0	0	1	0	0	0	0	0	.00	0	.375	.375	.375
1990 Toronto	AL	111	358	95	15	1	14	(11	3)	154	43	48	57	6	75	1	1	4	0	2	.00	5	.265	.364	.430
1991 Toronto	AL	139	454	116	30	1	17	(7	10)	199	64	68	68	9	84	6	3	10	0	2	.00	12	.256	.353	.438
1992 Toronto	AL	138	458	130	28	0	16	(4	12)	206	68	66	70	11	61	1	1	7	1	0	1.00	15	.284	.375	.450
1993 Toronto	AL	158	551	200	54	2	24	(9	15)	330	109	107	114	33	65	7	0	7	0	2	.00	12	.363	.473	.599
1994 Toronto	AL	108	384	114	29	2	12	(6	6)	183	47	67	61	12	53	3	0	5	1	2	.33	11	.297	.393	.477
1995 Toronto	AL	135	492	143	32	0	8	(1	7)	199	72	54	84	10	54	4	0	1	0	0	.00	17	.291	.398	.404
1996 Toronto	AL	125	398	109	25	0	18	(9	9)	188	59	61	60	6	37	10	0	1	1	0	1.00	10	.274	.382	.472
1997 New York	NL	154	524	154	34	1	22	(13	9)	256	90	102	85	5	67	13	0	8	0	0	.00	19	.294	.400	.489
1998 New York	NL	160	557	197	36	4	22	(13	9)	307	91	93	96	11	73	4	1	7	2	2	.50	15	.354	.447	.551
1999 New York	NL	162	581	173	39	0	19	(11	8)	269	107	96	125	5	66	11	0	6	3	0	1.00	22	.298	.427	.463
11 ML YEARS		1396	4765	1434	322	11	172	(84	88)	2294	752	762	820	108	636	60	6	56	8	10	.44	138	.301	.406	.481

Omar Olivares

Pitches: Right **Bats:** Right **Pos:** SP-32   **Ht:** 6'1" **Wt:** 205 **Born:** 7/6/67 **Age:** 32

		HOW MUCH HE PITCHED					WHAT HE GAVE UP									THE RESULTS					
Year Team	Lg	G	GS	CG	GF	IP	BFP	H	R	ER	HR	SH	SF	HB	TBB	IBB	SO	WP	Bk	W	L	Pct.	ShO	Sv-Op	Hld	ERA
1990 St. Louis	NL	9	6	0	0	49.1	201	45	17	16	2	1	0	2	17	0	20	1	1	1	1	.500	0	0-0	1	2.92
1991 St. Louis	NL	28	24	0	2	167.1	688	148	72	69	13	11	2	5	61	1	91	3	1	11	7	.611	0	1-1	0	3.71
1992 St. Louis	NL	32	30	1	1	197	818	189	84	84	20	8	7	4	63	5	124	2	0	9	9	.500	0	0-0	0	3.84
1993 St. Louis	NL	58	9	0	11	118.2	537	134	60	55	10	4	4	9	54	7	63	4	3	5	3	.625	0	1-5	2	4.17
1994 St. Louis	NL	14	12	1	2	73.2	333	84	53	47	10	3	3	4	37	0	26	5	0	3	4	.429	0	1-1	0	5.74
1995 Col-Phi	NL	16	6	0	4	41.2	195	55	34	32	5	2	2	3	23	0	22	4	0	1	4	.200	0	0-0	0	6.91
1996 Detroit	AL	25	25	4	0	160	708	169	90	87	16	3	6	9	75	4	81	4	1	7	11	.389	0	0-0	0	4.89
1997 Det-Sea	AL	32	31	3	0	177.1	794	191	109	98	18	2	7	13	81	4	103	5	0	6	10	.375	2	0-0	0	4.97
1998 Anaheim	AL	37	26	1	6	183	805	189	92	82	19	6	4	5	91	1	112	5	0	9	9	.500	0	0-0	0	4.03
1999 Ana-Oak	AL	32	32	4	0	205.2	885	217	105	95	19	3	7	9	81	0	85	6	0	15	11	.577	0	0-0	0	4.16
1995 Colorado	NL	11	6	0	1	31.2	155	44	28	26	4	1	1	2	21	0	15	4	0	1	3	.250	0	0-0	0	7.39
Philadelphia	NL	5	0	0	3	10	44	11	6	6	1	1	1	1	2	0	7	0	0	0	1	.000	0	0-0	0	5.40
1997 Detroit	AL	19	19	3	0	115	502	110	68	60	8	2	4	9	53	1	74	5	0	5	6	.455	2	0-0	0	4.70
Seattle	AL	13	12	0	0	62.1	292	81	41	38	10	0	3	4	28	3	29	0	0	1	4	.200	0	0-0	0	5.49
1999 Anaheim	AL	20	20	3	0	131	558	135	62	59	11	3	5	6	49	0	49	4	0	8	9	.471	0	0-0	0	4.05
Oakland	AL	12	12	1	0	74.2	327	82	43	36	8	0	2	3	32	0	36	2	0	7	2	.778	0	0-0	0	4.34
10 ML YEARS		283	201	14	26	1373.2	5964	1421	716	665	132	43	42	63	583	22	727	39	6	67	69	.493	2	3-7	3	4.36

171

Darren Oliver

Pitches: Left **Bats:** Right **Pos:** SP-30   Ht: 6'2" **Wt:** 210 **Born:** 10/6/70 **Age:** 29

		HOW MUCH HE PITCHED							WHAT HE GAVE UP											THE RESULTS					
Year Team	Lg	G	GS	CG	GF	IP	BFP	H	R	ER	HR	SH	SF	HB	TBB	IBB	SO	WP	Bk	W	L	Pct.	ShO	Sv-Op	Hld	ERA
1993 Texas	AL	2	0	0	0	3.1	14	2	1	1	1	0	0	0	1	1	4	0	0	0	0	.000	0	0-0	0	2.70
1994 Texas	AL	43	0	0	10	50	226	40	24	19	4	6	0	6	35	4	50	2	2	4	0	1.000	0	2-3	9	3.42
1995 Texas	AL	17	7	0	2	49	222	47	25	23	3	5	1	1	32	1	39	4	0	4	2	.667	0	0-0	0	4.22
1996 Texas	AL	30	30	1	0	173.2	777	190	97	90	20	2	7	10	76	3	112	5	1	14	6	.700	0	0-0	0	4.66
1997 Texas	AL	32	32	3	0	201.1	887	213	111	94	29	2	5	11	82	3	104	7	0	13	12	.520	1	0-0	0	4.20
1998 Tex-StL		29	29	2	0	160.1	749	204	115	102	18	8	8	10	66	2	87	7	4	10	11	.476	0	0-0	0	5.73
1999 St. Louis	NL	30	30	2	0	196.1	842	197	96	93	16	11	4	11	74	4	119	6	2	9	9	.500	1	0-0	0	4.26
1998 Detroit	AL	19	19	2	0	103.1	493	140	84	75	11	3	6	10	43	1	58	6	1	6	7	.462	0	0-0	0	6.53
St. Louis	NL	10	10	0	0	57	256	64	31	27	7	5	2	0	23	1	29	1	3	4	4	.500	0	0-0	0	4.26
7 ML YEARS		183	128	8	12	834	3717	893	469	422	91	34	25	49	366	18	515	31	9	54	40	.574	3	2-3	9	4.55

Joe Oliver

Bats: Right **Throws:** Right **Pos:** C-44; PH/PR-1   Ht: 6'3" **Wt:** 220 **Born:** 7/24/65 **Age:** 34

		BATTING																	BASERUNNING				PERCENTAGES		
Year Team	Lg	G	AB	H	2B	3B	HR	(Hm	Rd)	TB	R	RBI	TBB	IBB	SO	HBP	SH	SF	SB	CS	SB%	GDP	Avg	OBP	SLG
1999 Durham *	AAA	57	219	66	18	1	7	—	—	107	27	43	7	0	50	2	1	3	1	0	1.00	7	.301	.325	.489
1989 Cincinnati	NL	49	151	41	8	0	3	(1	2)	58	13	23	6	1	28	1	1	2	0	0	.00	3	.272	.300	.384
1990 Cincinnati	NL	121	364	84	23	0	8	(3	5)	131	34	52	37	15	75	2	5	1	1	1	.50	6	.231	.304	.360
1991 Cincinnati	NL	94	269	58	11	0	11	(7	4)	102	21	41	18	5	53	0	4	0	0	0	.00	14	.216	.265	.379
1992 Cincinnati	NL	143	485	131	25	1	10	(7	3)	188	42	57	35	19	75	1	6	7	2	3	.40	12	.270	.316	.388
1993 Cincinnati	NL	139	482	115	28	0	14	(7	7)	185	40	75	27	2	91	1	2	9	0	0	.00	13	.239	.276	.384
1994 Cincinnati	NL	6	19	4	0	0	1	(1	0)	7	1	5	2	1	3	0	0	0	0	0	.00	1	.211	.286	.368
1995 Milwaukee	AL	97	337	92	20	0	12	(4	8)	148	43	51	27	1	66	3	2	0	2	4	.33	11	.273	.332	.439
1996 Cincinnati	NL	106	289	70	12	1	11	(6	5)	117	31	46	28	6	54	2	3	3	2	0	1.00	8	.242	.311	.405
1997 Cincinnati	NL	111	349	90	13	0	14	(7	7)	145	28	43	25	1	58	5	2	5	1	3	.25	7	.258	.313	.415
1998 Det-Sea	AL	79	240	54	11	0	6	(3	3)	83	20	32	17	0	48	0	2	4	1	1	.50	8	.225	.272	.346
1999 Pittsburgh	NL	45	134	27	8	0	1	(1	0)	38	10	13	10	0	33	0	0	1	2	0	1.00	4	.201	.253	.284
1998 Detroit	AL	50	155	35	8	0	4	(2	2)	55	8	22	7	0	33	0	0	4	0	1	.00	5	.226	.253	.355
Seattle	AL	29	85	19	3	0	2	(1	1)	28	12	10	10	0	15	0	2	0	1	0	1.00	3	.224	.305	.329
11 ML YEARS		990	3119	766	159	2	91	(47	44)	1202	283	438	232	51	584	15	27	33	11	12	.48	87	.246	.298	.385

Gregg Olson

Pitches: Right **Bats:** Right **Pos:** RP-61   Ht: 6'4" **Wt:** 208 **Born:** 10/11/66 **Age:** 33

		HOW MUCH HE PITCHED							WHAT HE GAVE UP											THE RESULTS					
Year Team	Lg	G	GS	CG	GF	IP	BFP	H	R	ER	HR	SH	SF	HB	TBB	IBB	SO	WP	Bk	W	L	Pct.	ShO	Sv-Op	Hld	ERA
1988 Baltimore	AL	10	0	0	4	11	51	10	4	4	1	0	0	0	10	1	9	0	1	1	1	.500	0	0-1	1	3.27
1989 Baltimore	AL	64	0	0	52	85	356	57	17	16	1	4	1	1	46	10	90	9	3	5	2	.714	0	27-33	1	1.69
1990 Baltimore	AL	64	0	0	58	74.1	305	57	20	20	3	1	2	3	31	3	74	5	0	6	5	.545	0	37-42	0	2.42
1991 Baltimore	AL	72	0	0	62	73.2	319	74	28	26	1	5	1	1	29	5	72	8	1	4	6	.400	0	31-39	1	3.18
1992 Baltimore	AL	60	0	0	56	61.1	244	46	14	14	3	0	2	0	24	0	58	4	0	1	5	.167	0	36-44	0	2.05
1993 Baltimore	AL	50	0	0	45	45	188	37	9	8	1	2	2	0	18	3	44	5	0	0	2	.000	0	29-35	0	1.60
1994 Atlanta	NL	16	0	0	6	14.2	77	19	15	15	1	2	1	1	13	3	10	0	2	0	2	.000	0	1-1	1	9.20
1995 Cle-KC	AL	23	0	0	12	33	141	28	15	15	4	1	2	0	19	2	21	1	0	3	3	.500	0	3-5	2	4.09
1996 Det-Hou		52	0	0	30	52.1	243	55	30	29	7	1	1	1	35	6	37	6	0	4	0	1.000	0	8-10	1	4.99
1997 Min-KC	AL	45	0	0	18	50	226	58	35	31	3	2	1	1	28	4	34	1	0	4	3	.571	0	1-4	5	5.58
1998 Arizona	NL	64	0	0	49	68.2	281	56	25	23	4	3	1	1	25	1	55	2	0	3	4	.429	0	30-34	1	3.01
1999 Arizona	NL	61	0	0	36	60.2	257	54	28	25	9	1	2	2	25	2	45	1	0	9	4	.692	0	14-23	9	3.71
1995 Cleveland	AL	3	0	0	2	2.2	14	5	4	4	1	0	0	0	2	0	0	0	0	0	0	.000	0	0-0	0	13.50
Kansas City	AL	20	0	0	10	30.1	127	23	11	11	3	1	2	0	17	2	21	1	0	3	3	.500	0	3-5	2	3.26
1996 Detroit	AL	43	0	0	28	43	196	43	25	24	6	1	0	1	28	4	29	5	0	3	0	1.000	0	8-10	1	5.02
Houston	NL	9	0	0	2	9.1	47	12	5	5	1	0	1	0	7	2	8	1	0	1	0	1.000	0	0-0	0	4.82
1997 Minnesota	AL	11	0	0	5	8.1	55	19	17	17	0	0	0	1	11	1	6	0	0	0	0	.000	0	0-0	1	18.36
Kansas City	AL	34	0	0	13	41.2	171	39	18	14	3	2	1	0	17	3	28	1	0	4	3	.571	0	1-4	4	3.02
12 ML YEARS		581	0	0	428	629.2	2688	551	240	226	38	22	16	11	303	40	549	42	7	40	37	.519	0	217-271	21	3.23

Paul O'Neill

Bats: Left **Throws:** Left **Pos:** RF-151; PH/PR-3   Ht: 6'4" **Wt:** 215 **Born:** 2/25/63 **Age:** 37

		BATTING																	BASERUNNING				PERCENTAGES		
Year Team	Lg	G	AB	H	2B	3B	HR	(Hm	Rd)	TB	R	RBI	TBB	IBB	SO	HBP	SH	SF	SB	CS	SB%	GDP	Avg	OBP	SLG
1985 Cincinnati	NL	5	12	4	1	0	0	(0	0)	5	1	1	0	0	2	0	0	0	0	0	.00	0	.333	.333	.417
1986 Cincinnati	NL	3	2	0	0	0	0	(0	0)	0	0	1	0	0	1	0	0	0	0	0	.00	0	.000	.333	.000
1987 Cincinnati	NL	84	160	41	14	1	7	(4	3)	78	24	28	18	1	29	0	0	1	2	1	.67	5	.256	.331	.488
1988 Cincinnati	NL	145	485	122	25	3	16	(12	4)	201	58	73	38	5	65	2	3	5	8	6	.57	7	.252	.306	.414
1989 Cincinnati	NL	117	428	118	24	2	15	(11	4)	191	49	74	46	8	64	2	0	4	20	5	.80	7	.276	.346	.446
1990 Cincinnati	NL	145	503	136	28	0	16	(10	6)	212	59	78	53	13	103	2	1	5	13	11	.54	12	.270	.339	.421
1991 Cincinnati	NL	152	532	136	36	0	28	(20	8)	256	71	91	73	14	107	1	0	1	12	7	.63	8	.256	.346	.481
1992 Cincinnati	NL	148	496	122	19	1	14	(6	8)	185	59	66	77	15	85	2	3	6	6	3	.67	10	.246	.346	.373
1993 New York	AL	141	498	155	34	1	20	(8	12)	251	71	75	44	5	69	2	0	3	2	4	.33	13	.311	.367	.504
1994 New York	AL	103	368	132	25	1	21	(10	11)	222	68	83	72	13	56	0	0	3	5	4	.56	16	**.359**	.460	.603
1995 New York	AL	127	460	138	30	4	22	(12	10)	242	82	96	71	8	76	1	0	11	1	2	.33	**25**	.300	.387	.526
1996 New York	AL	150	546	165	35	1	19	(7	12)	259	89	91	102	8	76	4	0	8	0	1	.00	21	.302	.411	.474
1997 New York	AL	149	553	179	42	0	21	(10	11)	284	89	117	75	8	92	0	0	9	10	7	.59	16	.324	.399	.514

172

			BATTING																BASERUNNING				PERCENTAGES		
Year Team	Lg	G	AB	H	2B	3B	HR	(Hm	Rd)	TB	R	RBI	TBB	IBB	SO	HBP	SH	SF	SB	CS	SB%	GDP	Avg	OBP	SLG
1998 New York	AL	152	602	191	40	2	24	(10	14)	307	95	116	57	2	103	2	0	11	15	1	.94	**22**	.317	.372	.510
1999 New York	AL	153	597	170	39	4	19	(9	10)	274	70	110	66	1	89	2	0	10	11	9	.55	24	.285	.353	.459
15 ML YEARS		1774	6242	1809	392	20	242	(129	113)	2967	885	1099	793	101	1017	20	7	76	105	61	.63	184	.290	.368	.475

Mike Oquist

Pitches: Right **Bats:** Right **Pos:** SP-24; RP-4   **Ht:** 6'2" **Wt:** 190 **Born:** 5/30/68 **Age:** 32

		HOW MUCH HE PITCHED						WHAT HE GAVE UP										THE RESULTS					
Year Team	Lg	G	GS	CG	GF	IP	BFP	H	R	ER	HR	SH	SF	HB	TBB	IBB	SO	WP	Bk	W	L	Pct.	ShO	Sv-Op	Hld	ERA
1999 Vancouver *	AAA	1	1	0	0	6	22	2	0	0	0	0	0	0	1	0	2	1	0	0	1	1.000	0	0- -	0	0.00
1993 Baltimore	AL	5	0	0	2	11.2	50	12	5	5	0	0	0	0	4	1	8	0	0	0	0	.000	0	0-0	0	3.86
1994 Baltimore	AL	15	9	0	3	58.1	278	75	41	40	7	3	4	6	30	4	39	3	0	3	3	.500	0	0-0	0	6.17
1995 Baltimore	AL	27	0	0	8	54	255	51	27	25	6	1	4	2	41	3	27	2	0	2	1	.667	0	0-1	0	4.17
1996 San Diego	NL	8	0	0	3	7.2	30	6	2	2	0	0	0	0	4	2	4	1	0	0	0	.000	0	0-0	0	2.35
1997 Oakland	AL	19	17	1	0	107.2	473	111	62	60	15	3	3	6	43	3	72	2	0	4	6	.400	0	0-0	0	5.02
1998 Oakland	AL	31	29	0	2	175	777	210	125	121	27	5	6	5	57	1	112	4	0	7	11	.389	0	0-0	0	6.22
1999 Oakland	AL	28	24	0	1	140.2	629	158	86	84	18	3	1	2	64	5	89	2	0	9	10	.474	0	0-0	0	5.37
7 ML YEARS		133	79	1	13	555	2492	623	348	337	73	15	18	21	243	19	351	14	0	25	31	.446	0	0-1	0	5.46

Luis Ordaz

Bats: R **Throws:** R **Pos:** SS-8; PH/PR-3; 2B-1; 3B-1   **Ht:** 5'11" **Wt:** 170 **Born:** 8/12/75 **Age:** 24

					BATTING														BASERUNNING				PERCENTAGES		
Year Team	Lg	G	AB	H	2B	3B	HR	(Hm	Rd)	TB	R	RBI	TBB	IBB	SO	HBP	SH	SF	SB	CS	SB%	GDP	Avg	OBP	SLG
1999 Memphis *	AAA	107	362	103	25	4	1	—	—	139	31	45	24	2	40	4	3	9	4	3	.43	12	.285	.328	.384
1997 St. Louis	NL	12	22	6	1	0	0	(0	0)	7	3	1	1	0	2	0	0	0	3	0	1.00	0	.273	.304	.318
1998 St. Louis	NL	57	153	31	5	0	0	(0	0)	36	9	8	12	1	18	0	4	0	2	0	1.00	3	.203	.261	.235
1999 St. Louis	NL	10	9	1	0	0	0	(0	0)	1	3	2	1	0	2	0	1	0	1	0	1.00	0	.111	.200	.111
3 ML YEARS		79	184	38	6	0	0	(0	0)	44	15	11	14	1	22	0	5	0	6	0	1.00	3	.207	.263	.239

Magglio Ordonez

Bats: Right **Throws:** Right **Pos:** RF-153; DH-2; PH/PR-2   **Ht:** 6'0" **Wt:** 200 **Born:** 1/28/74 **Age:** 26

					BATTING														BASERUNNING				PERCENTAGES		
Year Team	Lg	G	AB	H	2B	3B	HR	(Hm	Rd)	TB	R	RBI	TBB	IBB	SO	HBP	SH	SF	SB	CS	SB%	GDP	Avg	OBP	SLG
1997 Chicago	AL	21	69	22	6	0	4	(2	2)	40	12	11	2	0	8	0	1	0	1	2	.33	1	.319	.338	.580
1998 Chicago	AL	145	535	151	25	2	14	(8	6)	222	70	65	28	1	53	9	2	4	9	7	.56	19	.282	.326	.415
1999 Chicago	AL	157	624	188	34	3	30	(16	14)	318	100	117	47	4	64	1	0	5	13	6	.68	24	.301	.349	.510
3 ML YEARS		323	1228	361	65	5	48	(26	22)	580	182	193	77	5	125	10	3	9	23	15	.61	44	.294	.338	.472

Rey Ordonez

Bats: Right **Throws:** Right **Pos:** SS-154; PH/PR-1   **Ht:** 5'9" **Wt:** 159 **Born:** 11/11/72 **Age:** 27

					BATTING														BASERUNNING				PERCENTAGES		
Year Team	Lg	G	AB	H	2B	3B	HR	(Hm	Rd)	TB	R	RBI	TBB	IBB	SO	HBP	SH	SF	SB	CS	SB%	GDP	Avg	OBP	SLG
1996 New York	NL	151	502	129	12	4	1	(0	1)	152	51	30	22	12	53	1	4	1	1	3	.25	12	.257	.289	.303
1997 New York	NL	120	356	77	5	3	1	(1	0)	91	35	33	18	3	36	1	14	2	11	5	.69	10	.216	.255	.256
1998 New York	NL	153	505	124	20	2	1	(0	1)	151	46	42	23	7	60	1	15	4	3	6	.33	11	.246	.278	.299
1999 New York	NL	154	520	134	24	2	1	(0	1)	165	49	60	49	12	59	1	11	7	8	4	.67	16	.258	.319	.317
4 ML YEARS		578	1883	464	61	11	4	(2	2)	559	181	165	112	34	208	4	44	14	23	18	.56	49	.246	.288	.297

Kevin Orie

Bats: Right **Throws:** Right **Pos:** 3B-64; PH/PR-12; 1B-1   **Ht:** 6'4" **Wt:** 215 **Born:** 9/1/72 **Age:** 27

					BATTING														BASERUNNING				PERCENTAGES		
Year Team	Lg	G	AB	H	2B	3B	HR	(Hm	Rd)	TB	R	RBI	TBB	IBB	SO	HBP	SH	SF	SB	CS	SB%	GDP	Avg	OBP	SLG
1999 Calgary *	AAA	23	72	23	9	0	3	—	—	41	10	8	13	0	7	1	0	0	0	0	.00	0	.319	.430	.569
1997 Chicago	NL	114	364	100	23	5	8	(6	2)	157	40	44	39	3	57	5	3	4	2	2	.50	13	.275	.350	.431
1998 ChC-Fla	NL	112	379	83	22	1	8	(2	6)	131	47	38	32	2	59	8	2	4	2	1	.67	8	.219	.291	.346
1999 Florida	NL	77	240	61	16	0	6	(1	5)	95	26	29	22	1	43	3	0	2	1	0	1.00	8	.254	.322	.396
1998 Chicago	NL	64	204	37	14	0	2	(1	1)	57	24	21	18	0	35	3	1	4	1	1	.50	4	.181	.253	.279
Florida	NL	48	175	46	8	1	6	(1	5)	74	23	17	14	2	24	5	1	0	1	0	1.00	4	.263	.335	.423
3 ML YEARS		303	983	244	61	6	22	(9	13)	383	113	111	93	6	159	16	5	10	5	3	.63	29	.248	.320	.390

Jesse Orosco

Pitches: Left **Bats:** Right **Pos:** RP-65   **Ht:** 6'2" **Wt:** 205 **Born:** 4/21/57 **Age:** 43

		HOW MUCH HE PITCHED						WHAT HE GAVE UP										THE RESULTS					
Year Team	Lg	G	GS	CG	GF	IP	BFP	H	R	ER	HR	SH	SF	HB	TBB	IBB	SO	WP	Bk	W	L	Pct.	ShO	Sv-Op	Hld	ERA
1979 New York	NL	18	2	0	6	35	154	33	20	19	4	3	0	2	22	0	22	0	0	1	2	.333	0	0-0	0	4.89
1981 New York	NL	8	0	0	4	17.1	69	13	4	3	2	2	0	0	6	2	18	0	1	0	1	.000	0	1-1	0	1.56
1982 New York	NL	54	2	0	22	109.1	432	92	37	33	7	5	4	2	40	2	89	3	2	4	10	.286	0	4-5	5	2.72
1983 New York	NL	62	0	0	42	110	432	76	27	18	3	4	3	1	38	7	84	1	2	13	7	.650	0	17-22	1	1.47
1984 New York	NL	60	0	0	52	87	355	58	29	25	7	3	3	2	34	6	85	1	1	10	6	.625	0	31-38	0	2.59
1985 New York	NL	54	0	0	39	79	331	66	26	24	6	1	1	0	34	7	68	4	0	8	6	.571	0	17-25	1	2.73

Year Team	Lg	G	GS	CG	GF	IP	BFP	H	R	ER	HR	SH	SF	HB	TBB	IBB	SO	WP	Bk	W	L	Pct.	ShO	Sv-Op	Hld	ERA
1986 New York	NL	58	0	0	40	81	338	64	23	21	6	2	3	3	35	3	62	2	0	8	6	.571	0	21-29	1	2.33
1987 New York	NL	58	0	0	41	77	335	78	41	38	5	5	4	2	31	9	78	2	0	3	9	.250	0	16-22	4	4.44
1988 Los Angeles	NL	55	0	0	21	53	229	41	18	16	4	3	3	2	30	3	43	1	0	3	2	.600	0	9-15	14	2.72
1989 Cleveland	AL	69	0	0	29	78	312	54	20	18	7	8	3	2	26	4	79	0	0	3	4	.429	0	3-7	12	2.08
1990 Cleveland	AL	55	0	0	28	64.2	289	58	35	28	9	5	3	0	38	7	55	1	0	5	4	.556	0	2-3	2	3.90
1991 Cleveland	AL	47	0	0	20	45.2	202	52	20	19	4	1	3	1	15	8	36	1	1	2	0	1.000	0	0-0	3	3.74
1992 Milwaukee	AL	59	0	0	14	39	158	33	15	14	5	0	2	1	13	1	40	2	0	3	1	.750	0	1-2	11	3.23
1993 Milwaukee	AL	57	0	0	27	56.2	233	47	25	20	2	1	2	3	17	3	67	3	1	3	5	.375	0	8-13	11	3.18
1994 Milwaukee	AL	40	0	0	5	39	174	32	26	22	4	0	2	2	26	2	36	0	0	3	1	.750	0	0-4	8	5.08
1995 Baltimore	AL	65	0	0	23	49.2	200	28	19	18	4	2	4	1	27	7	58	2	1	2	4	.333	0	3-6	15	3.26
1996 Baltimore	AL	66	0	0	10	55.2	236	42	22	21	5	2	1	2	28	4	52	2	0	3	1	.750	0	0-3	19	3.40
1997 Baltimore	AL	71	0	0	12	50.1	205	29	13	13	6	1	2	0	30	0	46	1	1	6	3	.667	0	0-4	21	2.32
1998 Baltimore	AL	69	0	0	26	56.2	243	46	20	20	6	4	2	1	28	1	50	3	1	4	1	.800	0	7-9	9	3.18
1999 Baltimore	AL	65	0	0	12	32	144	28	21	19	5	2	3	2	20	3	35	2	0	0	2	.000	0	1-4	12	5.34
20 ML YEARS		1090	4	0	473	1216	5090	970	461	409	101	54	48	29	538	79	1103	31	11	84	75	.528	0	141-212	149	3.03

David Ortiz

Bats: Left **Throws:** Left **Pos:** DH-5; PH/PR-5; 1B-1 | **Ht:** 6'4" **Wt:** 230 **Born:** 11/18/75 **Age:** 24

Year Team	Lg	G	AB	H	2B	3B	HR	(Hm	Rd)	TB	R	RBI	TBB	IBB	SO	HBP	SH	SF	SB	CS	SB%	GDP	Avg	OBP	SLG
1999 Salt Lake *	AAA	130	476	150	35	3	30	—	—	281	85	110	79	5	105	3	0	5	2	2	.50	8	.315	.412	.590
1997 Minnesota	AL	15	49	16	3	0	1	(0	1)	22	10	6	2	0	19	0	0	0	0	0	.00	1	.327	.353	.449
1998 Minnesota	AL	86	278	77	20	0	9	(2	7)	124	47	46	39	3	72	5	0	4	1	0	1.00	8	.277	.371	.446
1999 Minnesota	AL	10	20	0	0	0	0	(0	0)	0	1	0	5	0	12	0	0	0	0	0	.00	2	.000	.200	.000
3 ML YEARS		111	347	93	23	0	10	(2	8)	146	58	52	46	3	103	5	0	4	1	0	1.00	11	.268	.358	.421

Ramon Ortiz

Pitches: Right **Bats:** Right **Pos:** SP-9 | **Ht:** 6'0" **Wt:** 165 **Born:** 5/23/76 **Age:** 24

Year Team	Lg	G	GS	CG	GF	IP	BFP	H	R	ER	HR	SH	SF	HB	TBB	IBB	SO	WP	Bk	W	L	Pct.	ShO	Sv-Op	Hld	ERA
1996 Angels	R	16	8	2	5	68	285	55	28	16	5	0	1	2	27	0	78	5	2	5	4	.556	2	1--	—	2.12
Boise	A-	3	3	0	0	19.2	89	21	10	8	3	2	0	1	6	0	18	0	1	1	1	.500	0	0--	—	3.66
1997 Cedar Rapds	A	27	27	8	0	181	740	156	78	72	22	2	1	7	53	0	225	14	5	11	10	.524	4	0--	—	3.58
1998 Midland	AA	7	7	0	0	47	202	50	31	29	10	1	2	1	16	0	53	3	1	2	1	.667	0	0--	—	5.55
1999 Erie	AA	15	15	2	0	102	419	88	38	32	12	3	2	2	40	0	86	1	0	9	4	.692	2	0--	—	2.82
Edmonton	AAA	9	9	0	0	53.1	224	46	26	24	7	0	0	2	19	0	64	6	2	5	3	.625	0	0--	—	4.05
1999 Anaheim	AL	9	9	0	0	48.1	218	50	35	35	7	0	2	2	25	0	44	2	2	2	3	.400	0	0-0	0	6.52

Russ Ortiz

Pitches: Right **Bats:** Right **Pos:** SP-33 | **Ht:** 6'1" **Wt:** 210 **Born:** 6/5/74 **Age:** 26

Year Team	Lg	G	GS	CG	GF	IP	BFP	H	R	ER	HR	SH	SF	HB	TBB	IBB	SO	WP	Bk	W	L	Pct.	ShO	Sv-Op	Hld	ERA
1995 Bellingham	A-	25	0	0	20	34.1	131	19	4	2	1	0	1	0	13	0	55	2	1	2	0	1.000	0	11--	—	0.52
San Jose	A+	5	0	0	5	6	24	4	1	1	0	0	1	0	2	0	7	0	0	1	0	.000	0	0--	—	1.50
1996 San Jose	A+	34	0	0	31	36.2	145	16	2	1	0	0	0	2	20	0	63	0	0	0	0	.000	0	23--	—	0.25
Shreveport	AA	26	0	0	20	26.2	123	22	14	12	0	0	0	2	21	3	29	1	0	1	2	.333	0	13--	—	4.05
1997 Shreveport	AA	12	12	0	0	56.2	249	52	28	26	3	4	1	1	37	0	50	2	1	2	3	.400	0	0--	—	4.13
Phoenix	AAA	14	14	0	0	85	376	96	57	52	11	2	3	2	34	0	70	3	1	4	3	.571	0	0--	—	5.51
1998 Fresno	AAA	10	10	0	0	50.2	209	35	10	9	3	5	1	4	22	0	59	1	0	3	1	.750	0	0--	—	1.60
1998 San Francisco	NL	22	13	0	3	88.1	394	90	51	49	11	5	4	4	46	1	75	3	0	4	4	.500	0	0-0	1	4.99
1999 San Francisco	NL	33	33	3	0	207.2	922	189	109	88	24	11	6	6	125	5	164	13	0	18	9	.667	0	0-0	0	3.81
2 ML YEARS		55	46	3	3	296	1316	279	160	137	35	16	10	10	171	6	239	16	0	22	13	.629	0	0-0	1	4.17

Donovan Osborne

Pitches: Left **Bats:** Left **Pos:** SP-6 | **Ht:** 6'2" **Wt:** 210 **Born:** 6/21/69 **Age:** 31

Year Team	Lg	G	GS	CG	GF	IP	BFP	H	R	ER	HR	SH	SF	HB	TBB	IBB	SO	WP	Bk	W	L	Pct.	ShO	Sv-Op	Hld	ERA
1992 St. Louis	NL	34	29	0	2	179	754	193	91	75	14	7	4	2	38	2	104	6	0	11	9	.550	0	0-0	1	3.77
1993 St. Louis	NL	26	26	1	0	155.2	657	153	73	65	18	6	2	7	47	4	83	4	0	10	7	.588	0	0-0	0	3.76
1995 St. Louis	NL	19	19	0	0	113.1	477	112	58	48	17	8	3	2	34	2	82	0	0	4	6	.400	0	0-0	0	3.81
1996 St. Louis	NL	30	30	2	0	198.2	822	191	87	78	22	7	4	1	57	5	134	6	1	13	9	.591	1	0-0	0	3.53
1997 St. Louis	NL	14	14	0	0	80.1	337	84	46	44	10	3	3	1	23	2	51	1	0	3	7	.300	0	0-0	0	4.93
1998 St. Louis	NL	14	14	1	0	83.2	358	84	42	38	11	3	4	1	22	2	60	1	0	5	4	.556	1	0-0	0	4.09
1999 St. Louis	NL	6	6	0	0	29.1	130	34	18	18	4	3	1	2	10	0	21	1	0	1	3	.250	0	0-0	0	5.52
7 ML YEARS		143	138	4	2	840	3535	851	415	366	96	37	21	16	231	17	535	19	1	47	45	.511	2	0-0	1	3.92

Keith Osik

Bats: Right **Throws:** Right **Pos:** C-50; PH/PR-16; P-1 | **Ht:** 6'0" **Wt:** 198 **Born:** 10/22/68 **Age:** 31

Year Team	Lg	G	AB	H	2B	3B	HR	(Hm	Rd)	TB	R	RBI	TBB	IBB	SO	HBP	SH	SF	SB	CS	SB%	GDP	Avg	OBP	SLG
1999 Nashville *	AAA	4	11	1	0	0	0	—	—	1	0	0	1	0	1	0	0	0	0	0	.00	0	.091	.167	.091

Year Team	Lg	G	AB	H	2B	3B	HR	(Hm	Rd)	TB	R	RBI	TBB	IBB	SO	HBP	SH	SF	SB	CS	SB%	GDP	Avg	OBP	SLG
1996 Pittsburgh	NL	48	140	41	14	1	1	(0	1)	60	18	14	14	1	22	1	1	0	3	0	1.00	3	.293	.361	.429
1997 Pittsburgh	NL	49	105	27	9	1	0	(0	0)	38	10	7	9	1	21	1	2	0	0	1	.00	1	.257	.322	.362
1998 Pittsburgh	NL	39	98	21	4	0	0	(0	0)	25	8	7	13	2	16	2	2	1	1	2	.33	4	.214	.316	.255
1999 Pittsburgh	NL	66	167	31	3	1	2	(1	1)	42	12	13	11	0	30	1	1	1	0	0	.00	8	.186	.239	.251
4 ML YEARS		202	510	120	30	3	3	(1	2)	165	48	41	47	4	89	5	6	2	2	3	.40	16	.235	.305	.324

Antonio Osuna

Pitches: Right **Bats:** Right **Pos:** RP-5   **Ht:** 5'11" **Wt:** 206 **Born:** 4/12/73 **Age:** 27

Year Team	Lg	G	GS	CG	GF	IP	BFP	H	R	ER	HR	SH	SF	HB	TBB	IBB	SO	WP	Bk	W	L	Pct.	ShO	Sv-Op	Hld	ERA
1999 San Berndno *	A+	13	4	0	0	19.1	82	19	6	5	0	1	1	1	6	0	27	0	0	0	0	.000	0	0--	—	2.33
1995 Los Angeles	NL	39	0	0	8	44.2	186	39	22	22	5	2	1	1	20	2	46	1	0	2	4	.333	0	0-2	11	4.43
1996 Los Angeles	NL	73	0	0	21	84	342	65	33	28	6	7	5	2	32	12	85	3	0	9	6	.600	0	4-9	16	3.00
1997 Los Angeles	NL	48	0	0	18	61.2	245	46	15	15	6	4	1	1	19	2	68	2	0	3	4	.429	0	0-0	10	2.19
1998 Los Angeles	NL	54	0	0	25	64.2	272	50	26	22	8	2	2	2	32	0	72	1	0	7	1	.875	0	6-11	12	3.06
1999 Los Angeles	NL	5	0	0	1	4.2	22	4	5	4	0	0	0	1	3	0	5	1	0	0	0	.000	0	0-0	2	7.71
5 ML YEARS		219	0	0	73	259.2	1067	204	101	91	25	15	9	7	106	16	276	8	2	21	15	.583	0	10-22	51	3.15

Willis Otanez

Bats: R **Throws:** R **Pos:** 3B-46; 1B-18; PH/PR-14; DH-5   **Ht:** 6'1" **Wt:** 213 **Born:** 4/19/73 **Age:** 27

Year Team	Lg	G	AB	H	2B	3B	HR	(Hm	Rd)	TB	R	RBI	TBB	IBB	SO	HBP	SH	SF	SB	CS	SB%	GDP	Avg	OBP	SLG
1991 Great Falls	R+	58	222	64	9	2	6	—	—	95	38	39	19	0	34	2	1	4	3	3	.50	7	.288	.344	.428
1992 Vero Beach	A+	117	390	86	18	0	3	—	—	113	27	27	24	0	60	4	5	3	2	4	.33	10	.221	.271	.290
1993 Bakersfield	A+	95	325	85	11	2	10	—	—	130	34	39	29	1	63	2	4	2	1	4	.20	9	.262	.324	.400
1994 Vero Beach	A+	131	476	132	27	1	19	—	—	218	77	72	53	2	98	4	0	7	4	2	.67	10	.277	.350	.458
1995 Vero Beach	A+	92	354	92	24	0	10	—	—	146	39	53	28	3	59	2	0	5	1	1	.50	15	.260	.314	.412
San Antonio	AA	27	100	24	4	1	1	—	—	33	8	7	6	0	25	0	0	2	1	0	1.00	3	.240	.278	.330
1996 Bowie	AA	138	506	134	27	2	24	—	—	237	60	75	45	2	97	1	2	5	3	7	.30	17	.265	.323	.468
1997 Orioles	R	8	25	8	2	0	2	—	—	16	5	3	2	0	4	1	0	0	0	0	.00	1	.320	.393	.640
Bowie	AA	19	78	26	9	0	3	—	—	44	13	13	9	0	19	0	0	1	0	1	.00	3	.333	.398	.564
Rochester	AAA	49	168	35	9	0	5	—	—	59	20	25	15	0	35	0	0	3	0	0	.00	8	.208	.269	.351
1998 Rochester	AAA	124	481	137	24	2	27	—	—	246	87	100	41	6	104	6	1	8	1	0	1.00	8	.285	.343	.511
1998 Baltimore	AL	3	5	1	0	0	0	(0	0)	1	0	0	0	0	2	0	0	0	0	0	.00	0	.200	.200	.200
1999 Bal-Tor	AL	71	207	49	11	0	7	(2	5)	81	28	24	15	0	46	2	1	1	0	0	.00	6	.237	.293	.391
1999 Baltimore	AL	29	80	17	3	0	2	(1	1)	26	7	11	6	0	16	1	1	1	0	0	.00	3	.213	.273	.325
Toronto	AL	42	127	32	8	0	5	(1	4)	55	21	13	9	0	30	1	0	0	0	0	.00	3	.252	.307	.433
2 ML YEARS		74	212	50	11	0	7	(2	5)	82	28	24	15	0	48	2	1	1	0	0	.00	6	.236	.291	.387

Eric Owens

Bats: R **Throws:** R **Pos:** LF-69; CF-47; PH/PR-34; RF-27; 1B-12; 3B-4; 2B-1   **Ht:** 6'0" **Wt:** 198 **Born:** 2/3/71 **Age:** 29

Year Team	Lg	G	AB	H	2B	3B	HR	(Hm	Rd)	TB	R	RBI	TBB	IBB	SO	HBP	SH	SF	SB	CS	SB%	GDP	Avg	OBP	SLG
1995 Cincinnati	NL	2	2	2	0	0	0	(0	0)	2	0	1	0	0	0	0	1	0	0	0	.00	0	1.000	1.000	1.000
1996 Cincinnati	NL	88	205	41	6	0	0	(0	0)	47	26	9	23	1	38	1	1	2	16	2	.89	2	.200	.281	.229
1997 Cincinnati	NL	27	57	15	0	0	0	(0	0)	15	8	3	4	0	11	0	0	0	3	2	.60	2	.263	.311	.263
1998 Milwaukee	NL	34	40	5	2	0	1	(1	0)	10	5	4	2	0	6	0	1	0	0	0	.00	3	.125	.167	.250
1999 San Diego	NL	149	440	117	22	3	9	(2	7)	172	55	61	38	2	50	3	2	2	33	7	.83	12	.266	.327	.391
5 ML YEARS		300	744	180	30	3	10	(2	8)	246	94	78	67	3	105	4	5	4	52	11	.83	19	.242	.306	.331

Vicente Padilla

Pitches: Right **Bats:** Right **Pos:** RP-5   **Ht:** 6'2" **Wt:** 200 **Born:** 9/27/77 **Age:** 22

Year Team	Lg	G	GS	CG	GF	IP	BFP	H	R	ER	HR	SH	SF	HB	TBB	IBB	SO	WP	Bk	W	L	Pct.	ShO	Sv-Op	Hld	ERA
1999 High Desert	A+	9	9	0	0	50.2	220	50	27	21	3	1	2	1	17	0	55	2	2	4	1	.800	0	0--	—	3.73
Tucson	AAA	18	14	0	0	93.2	405	107	47	39	6	5	2	7	24	7	58	0	1	7	4	.636	0	0--	—	3.75
1999 Arizona	NL	5	0	0	2	2.2	19	7	5	5	1	1	0	0	3	0	0	0	0	0	1	.000	0	0-1	1	16.88

Lance Painter

Pitches: Left **Bats:** Left **Pos:** RP-52; SP-4   **Ht:** 6'1" **Wt:** 197 **Born:** 7/21/67 **Age:** 32

Year Team	Lg	G	GS	CG	GF	IP	BFP	H	R	ER	HR	SH	SF	HB	TBB	IBB	SO	WP	Bk	W	L	Pct.	ShO	Sv-Op	Hld	ERA
1999 Arkansas *	AA	1	1	0	0	2	7	1	0	0	0	0	0	0	0	0	4	0	0	0	0	.000	0	0--	—	0.00
1993 Colorado	NL	10	6	1	2	39	166	52	26	26	5	1	0	0	9	0	16	2	0	2	2	.500	0	0-0	0	6.00
1994 Colorado	NL	15	14	0	1	73.2	336	91	51	50	9	3	5	1	26	2	41	3	1	4	6	.400	0	0-0	0	6.11
1995 Colorado	NL	33	1	0	7	45.1	198	55	23	22	9	0	0	2	10	0	36	4	1	3	0	1.000	0	1-1	4	4.37
1996 Colorado	NL	34	1	0	4	50.2	234	56	37	33	12	3	3	3	25	3	48	1	0	4	2	.667	0	0-1	4	5.86
1997 St. Louis	NL	14	0	0	4	17	69	13	9	9	1	0	0	0	8	2	11	0	0	1	1	.500	0	0-0	3	4.76
1998 St. Louis	NL	65	0	0	9	47.1	207	42	24	21	5	4	2	4	28	3	39	2	0	4	0	1.000	0	1-2	21	3.99
1999 St. Louis	NL	56	4	0	10	63.1	272	63	37	34	6	4	3	2	25	1	56	4	0	5	4	.444	0	1-3	10	4.83
7 ML YEARS		227	26	1	37	336.1	1482	372	207	195	47	15	13	12	131	11	247	16	2	22	16	.579	0	3-7	42	5.22

Orlando Palmeiro

Bats: L **Throws:** L **Pos:** LF-60; RF-35; PH/PR-17; DH-10; CF-1 **Ht:** 5'11" **Wt:** 175 **Born:** 1/19/69 **Age:** 31

Year Team	Lg	G	AB	H	2B	3B	HR	(Hm	Rd)	TB	R	RBI	TBB	IBB	SO	HBP	SH	SF	SB	CS	SB%	GDP	Avg	OBP	SLG
1995 California	AL	15	20	7	0	0	0	(0	0)	7	3	1	1	0	1	0	0	0	0	0	.00	0	.350	.381	.350
1996 California	AL	50	87	25	6	1	0	(0	0)	33	6	6	8	1	13	2	1	0	0	1	.00	1	.287	.361	.379
1997 Anaheim	AL	74	134	29	2	2	0	(0	0)	35	19	8	17	1	11	1	3	1	2	2	.50	4	.216	.307	.261
1998 Anaheim	AL	75	165	53	7	2	0	(0	0)	64	28	21	20	1	11	0	7	0	5	4	.56	2	.321	.395	.388
1999 Anaheim	AL	109	317	88	12	1	1	(0	1)	105	46	23	39	1	30	6	6	3	5	5	.50	4	.278	.364	.331
5 ML YEARS		323	723	202	27	6	1	(0	1)	244	102	59	85	4	66	9	17	4	12	12	.50	11	.279	.361	.337

Rafael Palmeiro

Bats: Left **Throws:** Left **Pos:** DH-128; 1B-28; PH/PR-2 **Ht:** 6'0" **Wt:** 190 **Born:** 9/24/64 **Age:** 35

Year Team	Lg	G	AB	H	2B	3B	HR	(Hm	Rd)	TB	R	RBI	TBB	IBB	SO	HBP	SH	SF	SB	CS	SB%	GDP	Avg	OBP	SLG
1986 Chicago	NL	22	73	18	4	0	3	(1	2)	31	9	12	4	0	6	1	0	0	1	1	.50	4	.247	.295	.425
1987 Chicago	NL	84	221	61	15	1	14	(5	9)	120	32	30	20	1	26	1	0	2	2	2	.50	4	.276	.336	.543
1988 Chicago	NL	152	580	178	41	5	8	(8	0)	253	75	53	38	6	34	3	2	6	12	2	.86	11	.307	.349	.436
1989 Texas	AL	156	559	154	23	4	8	(4	4)	209	76	64	63	3	48	6	2	2	4	3	.57	18	.275	.354	.374
1990 Texas	AL	154	598	191	35	6	14	(9	5)	280	72	89	40	6	59	3	2	8	3	3	.50	24	.319	.361	.468
1991 Texas	AL	159	631	203	49	3	26	(12	14)	336	115	88	68	10	72	6	2	7	4	3	.57	17	.322	.389	.532
1992 Texas	AL	159	608	163	27	4	22	(8	14)	264	84	85	72	8	83	10	5	6	2	3	.40	10	.268	.352	.434
1993 Texas	AL	160	597	176	40	2	37	(22	15)	331	124	105	73	22	85	5	2	9	22	3	.88	8	.295	.371	.554
1994 Baltimore	AL	111	436	139	32	0	23	(11	12)	240	82	76	54	1	63	2	0	6	7	3	.70	11	.319	.392	.550
1995 Baltimore	AL	143	554	172	30	2	39	(21	18)	323	89	104	62	5	65	3	0	5	3	1	.75	12	.310	.380	.583
1996 Baltimore	AL	162	626	181	40	2	39	(21	18)	342	110	142	95	12	96	3	0	8	8	0	1.00	9	.289	.381	.546
1997 Baltimore	AL	158	614	156	24	2	38	(20	18)	298	95	110	67	7	109	5	0	6	5	2	.71	14	.254	.329	.485
1998 Baltimore	AL	162	619	183	36	1	43	(25	18)	350	98	121	79	8	91	7	0	4	11	7	.61	14	.296	.379	.565
1999 Texas	AL	158	565	183	30	1	47	(28	19)	356	96	148	97	14	69	3	0	9	2	4	.33	13	.324	.420	.630
14 ML YEARS		1940	7281	2158	426	33	361	(195	166)	3733	1157	1227	832	103	906	58	15	78	86	37	.70	169	.296	.369	.513

Dean Palmer

Bats: Right **Throws:** Right **Pos:** 3B-141; DH-9 **Ht:** 6'1" **Wt:** 210 **Born:** 12/27/68 **Age:** 31

Year Team	Lg	G	AB	H	2B	3B	HR	(Hm	Rd)	TB	R	RBI	TBB	IBB	SO	HBP	SH	SF	SB	CS	SB%	GDP	Avg	OBP	SLG
1989 Texas	AL	16	19	2	2	0	0	(0	0)	4	0	1	0	0	12	0	0	1	0	0	.00	0	.105	.100	.211
1991 Texas	AL	81	268	50	9	2	15	(6	9)	108	38	37	32	0	98	3	1	0	0	2	.00	4	.187	.281	.403
1992 Texas	AL	152	541	124	25	0	26	(11	15)	227	74	72	62	2	154	4	2	4	10	4	.71	9	.229	.311	.420
1993 Texas	AL	148	519	127	31	2	33	(12	21)	261	88	96	53	4	154	8	0	5	11	10	.52	5	.245	.321	.503
1994 Texas	AL	93	342	84	14	2	19	(11	8)	159	50	59	26	0	89	2	0	1	3	4	.43	7	.246	.302	.465
1995 Texas	AL	36	119	40	6	0	9	(5	4)	73	30	24	21	1	21	4	0	1	1	1	.50	2	.336	.448	.613
1996 Texas	AL	154	582	163	26	2	38	(19	19)	307	98	107	59	4	145	5	0	6	2	0	1.00	15	.280	.348	.527
1997 Tex-KC	AL	143	542	139	31	1	23	(10	13)	241	70	86	41	2	134	3	1	5	2	2	.50	7	.256	.310	.445
1998 Kansas City	AL	152	572	159	27	2	34	(21	13)	292	84	119	48	3	134	6	0	13	8	2	.80	18	.278	.333	.510
1999 Detroit	AL	150	560	147	25	2	38	(24	14)	290	92	100	57	3	153	10	0	4	3	3	.50	12	.263	.339	.518
1997 Texas	AL	94	355	87	21	0	14	(6	8)	150	47	55	26	2	84	1	1	3	1	0	1.00	4	.245	.296	.423
Kansas City	AL	49	187	52	10	1	9	(4	5)	91	23	31	15	0	50	2	0	2	1	2	.33	3	.278	.335	.487
10 ML YEARS		1125	4064	1035	196	13	235	(119	116)	1962	624	701	399	19	1094	45	4	40	40	28	.59	79	.255	.325	.483

Jose Paniagua

Pitches: Right **Bats:** Right **Pos:** RP-59 **Ht:** 6'2" **Wt:** 185 **Born:** 8/20/73 **Age:** 26

		HOW MUCH HE PITCHED						WHAT HE GAVE UP										THE RESULTS						
Year Team	Lg	G	GS	CG	GF	IP	BFP	H	R	ER	HR	SH	SF	HB	TBB	IBB	SO	WP	Bk	W	L	Pct.	ShO	Sv-Op	Hld	ERA
1996 Montreal	NL	13	11	0	0	51	223	55	24	20	7	1	1	3	23	0	27	2	2	2	4	.333	0	0-0	0	3.53
1997 Montreal	NL	9	3	0	0	18	100	29	24	24	2	1	1	4	16	1	8	1	0	1	2	.333	0	0-0	0	12.00
1998 Seattle	AL	18	0	0	2	22	83	15	5	5	3	0	0	3	5	0	16	2	0	2	0	1.000	0	1-2	6	2.05
1999 Seattle	AL	59	0	0	16	77.2	350	75	37	35	5	4	3	7	52	4	74	6	0	6	11	.353	0	3-12	16	4.06
4 ML YEARS		99	14	0	18	168.2	756	174	90	84	17	6	5	17	96	5	125	11	2	11	17	.393	0	4-14	22	4.48

Craig Paquette

Bats: R **Throws:** R **Pos:** RF-25; 3B-10; 2B-7; 1B-6; PH/PR-6; LF-3 **Ht:** 6'0" **Wt:** 190 **Born:** 3/28/69 **Age:** 31

Year Team	Lg	G	AB	H	2B	3B	HR	(Hm	Rd)	TB	R	RBI	TBB	IBB	SO	HBP	SH	SF	SB	CS	SB%	GDP	Avg	OBP	SLG
1999 Norfolk *	AAA	70	283	77	20	3	15	(—	—)	148	40	54	10	1	47	3	0	6	3	0	1.00	4	.272	.298	.523
1993 Oakland	AL	105	393	86	20	4	12	(8	4)	150	35	46	14	2	108	0	1	1	4	2	.67	7	.219	.245	.382
1994 Oakland	AL	14	49	7	2	0	0	(0	0)	9	0	0	0	0	14	0	1	0	1	0	1.00	0	.143	.143	.184
1995 Oakland	AL	105	283	64	13	1	13	(8	5)	118	42	49	12	0	88	1	3	5	5	2	.71	5	.226	.256	.417
1996 Kansas City	AL	118	429	111	15	1	22	(12	10)	194	61	67	23	2	101	2	3	5	5	3	.63	11	.259	.296	.452
1997 Kansas City	AL	77	252	56	11	1	8	(7	1)	99	26	33	10	0	57	2	1	2	2	2	.50	13	.230	.263	.393
1998 New York	NL	7	19	5	2	0	0	(0	0)	7	3	0	0	0	6	0	0	0	1	0	1.00	3	.263	.263	.368
1999 St. Louis	NL	48	157	45	6	0	10	(7	3)	81	21	37	6	0	38	0	1	2	1	0	1.00	6	.287	.309	.516
7 ML YEARS		474	1582	376	73	7	65	(42	23)	658	188	232	65	4	412	5	10	15	19	9	.68	45	.238	.268	.416

176

Chan Ho Park

Pitches: Right Bats: Right Pos: SP-33   Ht: 6'2" Wt: 204 Born: 6/30/73 Age: 27

Year Team	Lg	G	GS	CG	GF	IP	BFP	H	R	ER	HR	SH	SF	HB	TBB	IBB	SO	WP	Bk	W	L	Pct.	ShO	Sv-Op	Hld	ERA
1994 Los Angeles	NL	2	0	0	1	4	23	5	5	5	1	0	0	1	5	0	6	0	0	0	0	.000	0	0-0	0	11.25
1995 Los Angeles	NL	2	1	0	0	4	16	2	2	2	1	0	0	0	2	0	7	0	1	0	0	.000	0	0-0	0	4.50
1996 Los Angeles	NL	48	10	0	7	108.2	477	82	48	44	7	8	1	4	71	3	119	4	3	5	5	.500	0	0-0	4	3.64
1997 Los Angeles	NL	32	29	2	1	192	792	149	80	72	24	9	5	8	70	1	166	4	1	14	8	.636	0	0-0	0	3.38
1998 Los Angeles	NL	34	34	2	0	220.2	946	199	101	91	16	11	10	11	97	1	191	6	2	15	9	.625	0	0-0	0	3.71
1999 Los Angeles	NL	33	33	0	0	194.1	883	208	120	113	31	10	5	14	100	4	174	11	1	13	11	.542	0	0-0	0	5.23
6 ML YEARS		151	107	4	9	723.2	3137	645	356	327	80	38	21	38	345	9	663	25	8	47	33	.588	0	0-0	4	4.07

Jim Parque

Pitches: Left Bats: Left Pos: SP-30; RP-1   Ht: 5'11" Wt: 165 Born: 2/8/76 Age: 24

Year Team	Lg	G	GS	CG	GF	IP	BFP	H	R	ER	HR	SH	SF	HB	TBB	IBB	SO	WP	Bk	W	L	Pct.	ShO	Sv-Op	Hld	ERA
1997 Winston-Sal	A+	11	11	0	0	61.2	231	29	19	19	3	0	1	0	23	0	76	2	2	7	2	.778	0	0- -	—	2.77
Nashville	AAA	2	2	0	0	10.2	49	9	5	5	0	0	1	0	9	0	5	1	0	1	0	1.000	0	0- -	—	4.22
1998 Calgary	AAA	8	8	0	0	48	213	49	26	21	7	0	1	1	25	0	31	1	3	2	3	.400	0	0- -	—	3.94
1998 Chicago	AL	24	19	1	0	113	507	135	72	64	14	1	0	6	49	0	77	0	3	7	5	.583	0	0-0	0	5.10
1999 Chicago	AL	31	30	1	0	173.2	804	210	111	99	23	5	8	10	79	2	111	3	2	9	15	.375	0	0-0	0	5.13
2 ML YEARS		52	51	1	0	286.2	1311	345	183	163	37	6	8	16	128	2	188	3	5	16	20	.444	0	0-0	0	5.12

Steve Parris

Pitches: Right Bats: Right Pos: SP-21; RP-1   Ht: 6'0" Wt: 195 Born: 12/17/67 Age: 32

Year Team	Lg	G	GS	CG	GF	IP	BFP	H	R	ER	HR	SH	SF	HB	TBB	IBB	SO	WP	Bk	W	L	Pct.	ShO	Sv-Op	Hld	ERA
1999 Indianapols *	AAA	6	6	0	0	35.2	148	39	16	16	5	0	4	1	9	1	31	0	0	0	2	.000	0	0- -	—	4.04
1995 Pittsburgh	NL	15	15	1	0	82	360	89	49	49	12	3	2	7	33	1	61	4	0	6	6	.500	1	0-0	0	5.38
1996 Pittsburgh	NL	8	4	0	3	26.1	123	35	22	21	4	1	1	1	11	0	27	2	0	0	3	.000	0	0-0	0	7.18
1998 Cincinnati	NL	18	16	1	0	99	421	89	44	41	9	7	1	4	32	3	77	1	1	6	5	.545	1	0-0	0	3.73
1999 Cincinnati	NL	22	21	2	0	128.2	545	124	59	50	16	7	3	6	52	4	86	3	0	11	4	.733	1	0-0	0	3.50
4 ML YEARS		63	56	4	3	336	1449	337	174	161	41	18	7	18	128	8	251	10	1	23	18	.561	3	0-0	0	4.31

Bronswell Patrick

Pitches: Right Bats: Right Pos: RP-6   Ht: 6'1" Wt: 237 Born: 9/16/70 Age: 29

Year Team	Lg	G	GS	CG	GF	IP	BFP	H	R	ER	HR	SH	SF	HB	TBB	IBB	SO	WP	Bk	W	L	Pct.	ShO	Sv-Op	Hld	ERA
1988 Athletics	R	14	13	2	0	96.1	390	99	37	32	7	1	2	2	16	1	64	1	2	8	3	.727	0	0- -	—	2.99
1989 Madison	A	12	10	0	1	54.1	238	62	29	22	3	2	0	0	14	0	32	3	2	2	5	.286	0	0- -	—	3.64
1990 Modesto	A+	14	14	0	0	74.2	340	92	58	43	10	3	1	4	32	0	37	5	1	3	7	.300	0	0- -	—	5.18
Madison	A	13	12	3	0	80	337	88	44	32	6	5	4	1	19	0	40	3	0	3	7	.300	0	0- -	—	3.60
1991 Modesto	A+	28	26	3	1	169.2	716	158	77	61	9	4	4	1	60	4	95	7	0	12	12	.500	1	0- -	—	3.24
1992 Huntsville	AA	29	29	3	0	179.1	758	187	84	75	20	1	3	4	46	0	98	3	0	13	7	.650	0	0- -	—	3.76
1993 Tacoma	AAA	35	13	1	12	104.2	496	156	87	82	12	3	12	4	42	3	56	3	0	3	8	.273	0	1- -	—	7.05
1994 Huntsville	AA	7	3	0	1	27.2	120	31	11	9	2	1	0	2	10	0	16	1	1	2	0	1.000	0	1- -	—	2.93
Tacoma	AAA	30	0	9	0	47.1	208	50	31	25	5	3	1	0	20	2	38	2	0	1	1	.500	0	2- -	—	4.75
1995 Tucson	AAA	43	4	0	10	81.2	352	91	42	38	3	2	3	1	21	1	62	4	0	5	1	.833	0	1- -	—	4.19
1996 Tucson	AAA	33	15	0	2	118	521	137	59	46	7	1	14	0	33	4	82	1	0	7	3	.700	0	1- -	—	3.51
1997 New Orleans	AAA	30	12	1	10	100.2	426	108	45	36	10	6	2	0	30	4	88	5	0	6	5	.545	1	0- -	—	3.22
1998 Louisville	AAA	6	6	0	0	37.2	167	43	21	18	6	0	1	1	9	0	28	3	0	3	1	.750	0	0- -	—	4.30
1999 Fresno	AAA	28	28	1	0	164	719	194	116	89	33	5	5	3	42	0	142	2	1	14	11	.560	0	0- -	—	4.88
1998 Milwaukee	NL	32	3	0	8	78.2	334	83	43	41	9	4	3	0	29	1	49	2	0	4	1	.800	0	0-0	0	4.69
1999 San Francisco	NL	6	0	0	2	5.1	28	9	7	6	1	0	1	0	3	0	6	0	0	1	0	1.000	0	1-1	1	10.13
2 ML YEARS		38	3	0	10	84	362	92	50	47	10	4	4	0	32	1	55	2	0	5	1	.833	0	1-1	1	5.04

Danny Patterson

Pitches: Right Bats: Right Pos: RP-53   Ht: 6'0" Wt: 225 Born: 2/17/71 Age: 29

Year Team	Lg	G	GS	CG	GF	IP	BFP	H	R	ER	HR	SH	SF	HB	TBB	IBB	SO	WP	Bk	W	L	Pct.	ShO	Sv-Op	Hld	ERA
1999 Oklahoma *	AAA	2	0	0	1	3	11	0	0	0	0	0	0	0	1	0	4	0	0	1	0	1.000	0	0- -	—	0.00
1996 Texas	AL	7	0	0	5	8.2	38	10	4	0	0	0	0	0	3	1	5	0	0	0	0	.000	0	0-0	0	0.00
1997 Texas	AL	54	0	0	17	71	296	70	29	27	3	4	3	0	23	4	69	7	1	10	6	.625	0	1-8	9	3.42
1998 Texas	AL	56	0	0	21	60.2	257	64	31	30	11	1	1	2	19	2	33	3	0	2	5	.286	0	2-2	19	4.45
1999 Texas	AL	53	0	0	18	60.1	275	77	38	38	5	0	2	1	19	3	43	2	0	2	0	1.000	0	0-1	4	5.67
4 ML YEARS		170	0	0	61	200.2	866	221	102	95	19	5	6	3	64	10	150	12	1	14	11	.560	0	3-11	32	4.26

Josh Paul

Bats: Right Throws: Right Pos: C-6   Ht: 6'1" Wt: 185 Born: 5/19/75 Age: 25

Year Team	Lg	G	AB	H	2B	3B	HR	(Hm	Rd)	TB	R	RBI	TBB	IBB	SO	HBP	SH	SF	SB	CS	SB%	GDP	Avg	OBP	SLG
1996 White Sox	R	1	0	0	0	0	0	—	—	0	0	0	1	0	0	0	0	0	0	0	.00	0	.000	1.000	.000

177

Year Team	Lg	G	AB	H	2B	3B	HR	(Hm Rd)	TB	R	RBI	TBB	IBB	SO	HBP	SH	SF	SB	CS	SB%	GDP	Avg	OBP	SLG
Hickory	A	59	226	74	16	0	8	— —	114	41	37	21	3	53	1	3	1	13	4	.76	2	.327	.386	.504
1997 White Sox	R	5	14	6	0	1	0	— —	8	3	0	1	0	3	0	1	0	1	0	1.00	1	.429	.467	.571
Birmingham	AA	34	115	34	5	0	1	— —	42	18	16	12	0	25	1	3	0	6	2	.75	4	.296	.367	.365
1998 Winston-Sal	A+	123	444	113	20	7	11	— —	180	66	63	38	2	91	5	7	2	20	8	.71	11	.255	.319	.405
1999 Birmingham	AA	93	319	89	19	3	4	— —	126	47	42	29	1	68	5	3	4	6	6	.50	6	.279	.345	.395
1999 Chicago	AL	6	18	4	1	0	0	(0 0)	5	2	1	0	0	4	0	0	0	0	0	.00	0	.222	.222	.278

Carl Pavano

Pitches: Right **Bats:** Right **Pos:** SP-18; RP-1 — **Ht:** 6'5" **Wt:** 225 **Born:** 1/8/76 **Age:** 24

Year Team	Lg	G	GS	CG	GF	IP	BFP	H	R	ER	HR	SH	SF	HB	TBB	IBB	SO	WP	Bk	W	L	Pct.	ShO	Sv-Op	Hld	ERA
1994 Red Sox	R	9	7	0	0	44	176	31	14	9	1	0	1	1	7	0	47	4	1	4	3	.571	0	0--	—	1.84
1995 Michigan	A	22	22	1	0	141.1	591	118	63	54	7	6	7	6	52	0	138	9	0	6	6	.500	0	0--	—	3.44
1996 Trenton	AA	27	26	6	1	185	741	154	66	54	16	5	7	11	47	2	146	7	1	16	5	.762	2	0--	—	2.63
1997 Pawtucket	AAA	23	23	3	0	161.2	663	148	62	56	13	1	3	6	34	2	147	7	1	11	6	.647	0	0--	—	3.12
1998 Jupiter	A+	4	4	0	0	15	63	20	11	11	1	0	0	0	3	0	14	0	0	0	0	.000	0	0--	—	6.60
Ottawa	AAA	3	3	0	0	18.2	75	12	5	5	1	0	0	5	7	0	14	1	0	1	0	1.000	0	0--	—	2.41
1999 Ottawa	AAA	2	2	0	0	5	23	7	5	5	1	0	1	0	3	0	3	0	0	0	1	.000	0	0--	—	9.00
1998 Montreal	NL	24	23	0	0	134.2	580	130	63	63	18	5	6	8	43	1	83	1	0	6	9	.400	0	0-0	0	4.21
1999 Montreal	NL	19	18	1	0	104	457	117	66	65	8	5	2	4	35	1	70	1	3	6	8	.429	1	0-0	0	5.63
2 ML YEARS		43	41	1	0	238.2	1037	247	136	128	26	10	8	12	78	2	153	2	3	12	17	.414	1	0-0	0	4.83

Jay Payton

Bats: Right **Throws:** Right **Pos:** PH/PR-11; LF-5; CF-2 — **Ht:** 5'10" **Wt:** 185 **Born:** 11/22/72 **Age:** 27

Year Team	Lg	G	AB	H	2B	3B	HR	(Hm Rd)	TB	R	RBI	TBB	IBB	SO	HBP	SH	SF	SB	CS	SB%	GDP	Avg	OBP	SLG
1994 Pittsfield	A-	58	219	80	16	2	3	— —	109	47	37	23	2	18	9	0	4	10	2	.83	1	.365	.439	.498
Binghamton	AA	8	25	7	1	0	0	— —	8	3	1	2	0	3	1	0	0	1	1	.50	1	.280	.357	.320
1995 Binghamton	AA	85	357	123	20	3	14	— —	191	59	54	29	2	32	2	0	2	16	7	.70	11	.345	.395	.535
Norfolk	AAA	50	196	47	11	4	4	— —	78	33	30	11	0	22	2	4	2	11	3	.79	5	.240	.284	.398
1996 Mets	R	3	13	5	1	0	1	— —	9	3	2	0	0	1	0	0	0	1	0	1.00	0	.385	.385	.692
Binghamton	AA	4	10	2	0	0	0	— —	2	0	2	2	1	2	0	0	2	0	1	.00	0	.200	.286	.200
St. Lucie	A+	9	26	8	2	0	0	— —	10	4	1	4	1	5	0	0	0	2	1	.67	1	.308	.400	.385
Norfolk	AAA	55	153	47	6	3	6	— —	77	30	26	11	1	25	3	0	1	10	1	.91	3	.307	.363	.503
1998 St. Lucie	A+	3	7	1	0	0	0	— —	1	0	0	3	2	1	0	0	0	0	0	.00	0	.143	.400	.143
Norfolk	AAA	82	322	84	14	4	8	— —	130	45	30	26	0	50	1	1	0	12	7	.63	5	.261	.318	.404
1999 St. Lucie	A+	7	26	9	1	1	0	— —	12	3	3	4	0	5	0	0	0	1	0	1.00	1	.346	.433	.462
Norfolk	AAA	38	144	56	13	2	8	— —	97	27	35	12	1	13	1	0	1	2	2	.50	2	.389	.437	.674
1998 New York	NL	15	22	7	1	0	0	(0 0)	8	2	0	1	0	4	0	0	0	0	0	.00	0	.318	.348	.364
1999 New York	NL	13	8	2	1	0	0	(0 0)	3	1	1	0	0	2	1	0	0	1	2	.33	0	.250	.333	.375
2 ML YEARS		28	30	9	2	0	0	(0 0)	11	3	1	1	0	6	1	0	0	1	2	.33	0	.300	.344	.367

Angel Pena

Bats: Right **Throws:** Right **Pos:** C-43; PH/PR-1 — **Ht:** 5'10" **Wt:** 228 **Born:** 2/16/75 **Age:** 25

Year Team	Lg	G	AB	H	2B	3B	HR	(Hm Rd)	TB	R	RBI	TBB	IBB	SO	HBP	SH	SF	SB	CS	SB%	GDP	Avg	OBP	SLG
1995 Great Falls	R+	49	138	40	11	1	4	— —	65	24	15	21	2	32	3	0	3	2	1	.67	5	.290	.388	.471
1996 Savannah	A	36	127	26	4	0	6	— —	48	13	16	7	1	37	0	1	0	1	1	.50	1	.205	.246	.378
1997 San Berndno	A+	86	322	89	22	4	16	— —	167	53	64	32	4	84	2	0	2	3	5	.38	9	.276	.344	.519
1998 San Antonio	AA	126	483	162	32	2	22	— —	264	81	105	48	3	80	6	3	2	9	5	.64	7	.335	.401	.547
1999 Albuquerque	AAA	34	127	37	10	1	1	— —	52	15	24	10	0	24	0	0	0	3	2	.60	1	.291	.343	.409
1998 Los Angeles	NL	6	13	3	0	0	0	(0 0)	3	1	0	0	0	6	0	0	0	0	0	.00	0	.231	.231	.231
1999 Los Angeles	NL	43	120	25	6	0	4	(2 2)	43	14	21	12	0	24	0	1	2	0	1	.00	6	.208	.276	.358
2 ML YEARS		49	133	28	6	0	4	(2 2)	46	15	21	12	0	30	0	1	2	0	1	.00	6	.211	.272	.346

Jesus Pena

Pitches: Left **Bats:** Left **Pos:** RP-26 — **Ht:** 6'0" **Wt:** 170 **Born:** 3/8/75 **Age:** 25

Year Team	Lg	G	GS	CG	GF	IP	BFP	H	R	ER	HR	SH	SF	HB	TBB	IBB	SO	WP	Bk	W	L	Pct.	ShO	Sv-Op	Hld	ERA
1995 Erie	A-	3	3	0	0	10.2	56	18	16	15	1	1	0	2	7	0	5	0	1	0	3	.000	0	0--	—	12.66
Pirates	R	7	6	0	0	35	138	20	11	10	0	0	0	0	19	0	36	4	0	0	0	.000	0	0--	—	2.57
1996 Erie	A-	21	3	0	5	35.2	164	32	24	19	3	2	0	2	24	1	34	2	0	2	5	.286	0	0--	—	4.79
1997 Hickory	A	43	0	0	32	65	263	55	24	16	3	4	3	0	19	1	57	3	0	5	3	.625	0	8--	—	2.22
1998 Winston-Sal	A+	23	0	0	13	31.2	125	20	11	11	2	2	2	1	12	1	37	0	1	3	4	.429	0	7--	—	3.13
Birmingham	AA	22	0	0	12	23.1	100	20	12	10	3	2	1	0	10	0	28	2	2	0	2	.000	0	2--	—	3.86
1999 Birmingham	AA	40	0	0	18	45.2	183	31	12	12	2	1	1	0	18	1	49	2	1	3	2	.600	0	5--	—	2.36
1999 Chicago	AL	26	0	0	1	20.1	106	21	15	12	1	3	0	1	23	5	20	3	0	0	0	.000	0	0-1	2	5.31

Juan Pena

Pitches: Right **Bats:** Right **Pos:** SP-2   **Ht:** 6'5" **Wt:** 215 **Born:** 6/27/77 **Age:** 23

Year Team	Lg	G	GS	CG	GF	IP	BFP	H	R	ER	HR	SH	SF	HB	TBB	IBB	SO	WP	Bk	W	L	Pct.	ShO	Sv-Op	Hld	ERA
1995 Red Sox	R	13	4	2	6	55.1	217	41	17	12	2	1	2	1	6	0	47	2	1	3	2	.600	1	1--	—	1.95
Sarasota	A+	2	2	0	0	7.1	35	8	4	4	0	0	0	2	3	0	5	1	1	1	1	.500	0	0--	—	4.91
1996 Michigan	A	26	26	4	1	187.2	743	149	70	62	16	9	5	10	34	2	156	10	2	12	10	.545	0	0--	—	2.97
1997 Sarasota	A+	13	13	3	0	91.1	359	67	39	30	8	1	2	2	23	1	88	1	0	4	6	.400	0	0--	—	2.96
Trenton	AA	16	14	0	2	97	418	98	56	51	13	6	3	2	31	0	79	5	1	5	6	.455	1	0--	—	4.73
1998 Pawtucket	AAA	24	23	1	0	139.2	606	141	73	68	17	4	2	8	51	3	146	14	2	8	10	.444	1	0--	—	4.38
1999 Red Sox	R	1	1	0	0	2	7	0	0	0	0	0	0	0	0	0	4	0	0	0	0	.000	0	0--	—	0.00
Sarasota	A+	2	2	0	0	6.1	28	12	6	5	0	0	0	0	0	0	5	1	0	0	1	.000	0	0--	—	7.11
Pawtucket	AAA	10	10	0	0	48	206	44	28	22	8	0	0	4	13	0	61	1	3	4	2	.667	0	0--	—	4.13
1999 Boston	AL	2	2	0	0	13	49	9	1	1	0	0	0	0	3	0	15	0	0	2	0	1.000	0	0-0	0	0.69

Troy Percival

Pitches: Right **Bats:** Right **Pos:** RP-60   **Ht:** 6'3" **Wt:** 230 **Born:** 8/9/69 **Age:** 30

Year Team	Lg	G	GS	CG	GF	IP	BFP	H	R	ER	HR	SH	SF	HB	TBB	IBB	SO	WP	Bk	W	L	Pct.	ShO	Sv-Op	Hld	ERA
1995 California	AL	62	0	0	16	74	284	37	19	16	6	4	1	1	26	2	94	2	2	3	2	.600	0	3-6	29	1.95
1996 California	AL	62	0	0	52	74	291	38	20	19	8	2	1	2	31	4	100	2	0	0	2	.000	0	36-39	2	2.31
1997 Anaheim	AL	55	0	0	46	52	224	40	20	20	6	1	2	4	22	2	72	5	0	5	5	.500	0	27-31	0	3.46
1998 Anaheim	AL	67	0	0	60	66.2	287	45	31	27	5	3	2	3	37	4	87	3	0	2	7	.222	0	42-48	0	3.65
1999 Anaheim	AL	60	0	0	50	57	230	38	24	24	9	0	1	3	22	0	58	3	0	4	6	.400	0	31-39	0	3.79
5 ML YEARS		306	0	0	224	323.2	1316	198	114	106	34	10	7	13	138	12	411	15	2	14	22	.389	0	139-163	31	2.95

Carlos Perez

Pitches: Left **Bats:** Left **Pos:** SP-16; RP-1   **Ht:** 6'3" **Wt:** 210 **Born:** 1/14/71 **Age:** 29

Year Team	Lg	G	GS	CG	GF	IP	BFP	H	R	ER	HR	SH	SF	HB	TBB	IBB	SO	WP	Bk	W	L	Pct.	ShO	Sv-Op	Hld	ERA
1999 Albuquerque * AAA		6	6	0	0	38	168	46	28	25	6	2	1	3	10	0	14	0	1	3	3	.500	0	0--	—	5.92
1995 Montreal	NL	28	23	2	2	141.1	592	142	61	58	18	6	1	5	28	2	106	8	4	10	8	.556	1	0-0	1	3.69
1997 Montreal	NL	33	32	8	0	206.2	857	206	109	89	21	5	7	4	48	1	110	2	1	12	13	.480	5	0-0	0	3.88
1998 Mon-LA	NL	34	34	7	0	241	1009	244	109	96	21	14	3	3	63	4	128	7	1	11	14	.440	2	0-0	0	3.59
1999 Los Angeles	NL	17	16	0	0	89.2	420	116	77	74	23	6	3	6	39	1	40	2	3	2	10	.167	0	0-0	0	7.43
1998 Montreal	NL	23	23	3	0	163.1	690	177	79	68	12	11	3	3	33	3	82	5	1	7	10	.412	0	0-0	0	3.75
Los Angeles	NL	11	11	4	0	77.2	319	67	30	28	9	3	0	0	30	1	46	2	0	4	4	.500	2	0-0	0	3.24
4 ML YEARS		112	105	17	2	678.2	2878	708	356	317	83	31	14	18	178	8	384	19	9	35	45	.438	8	0-0	1	4.20

Eddie Perez

Bats: Right **Throws:** Right **Pos:** C-98; PH/PR-9; 1B-2   **Ht:** 6'1" **Wt:** 185 **Born:** 5/4/68 **Age:** 32

Year Team	Lg	G	AB	H	2B	3B	HR	(Hm	Rd)	TB	R	RBI	TBB	IBB	SO	HBP	SH	SF	SB	CS	SB%	GDP	Avg	OBP	SLG
1995 Atlanta	NL	7	13	4	1	0	1	(0	1)	8	1	4	0	0	2	0	0	0	0	0	.00	0	.308	.308	.615
1996 Atlanta	NL	68	156	40	9	1	4	(2	2)	63	19	17	8	0	19	1	0	2	0	0	.00	6	.256	.293	.404
1997 Atlanta	NL	73	191	41	5	0	6	(4	2)	64	20	18	10	0	35	2	1	2	0	1	.00	8	.215	.259	.335
1998 Atlanta	NL	61	149	50	12	0	6	(3	3)	80	18	32	15	0	28	2	1	0	1	1	.50	3	.336	.404	.537
1999 Atlanta	NL	104	309	77	17	0	7	(0	7)	115	30	30	17	4	40	6	4	3	0	1	.00	9	.249	.299	.372
5 ML YEARS		313	818	212	44	1	24	(9	15)	330	88	101	50	4	124	11	6	7	1	3	.25	26	.259	.308	.403

Eduardo Perez

Bats: Right **Throws:** Right **Pos:** PH/PR-11; LF-6; 1B-5   **Ht:** 6'4" **Wt:** 215 **Born:** 9/11/69 **Age:** 30

Year Team	Lg	G	AB	H	2B	3B	HR	(Hm	Rd)	TB	R	RBI	TBB	IBB	SO	HBP	SH	SF	SB	CS	SB%	GDP	Avg	OBP	SLG
1999 Memphis *	AAA	119	416	133	31	0	18	—	—	218	67	82	45	4	92	6	0	1	7	8	.47	11	.320	.393	.524
1993 California	AL	52	180	45	6	2	4	(2	2)	67	16	30	9	0	39	0	1	1	5	4	.56	4	.250	.292	.372
1994 California	AL	38	129	27	7	0	5	(3	2)	49	10	16	12	1	29	0	1	1	3	0	1.00	5	.209	.275	.380
1995 California	AL	29	71	12	4	1	1	(0	1)	21	9	7	12	0	9	2	0	1	0	2	.00	3	.169	.302	.296
1996 Cincinnati	NL	18	36	8	0	0	3	(3	0)	17	8	5	5	1	9	0	0	0	0	0	.00	2	.222	.317	.472
1997 Cincinnati	NL	106	297	75	18	0	16	(7	9)	141	44	52	29	1	76	2	0	2	5	1	.83	6	.253	.321	.475
1998 Cincinnati	NL	84	172	41	4	0	4	(1	3)	57	20	30	21	2	45	2	1	2	0	1	.00	2	.238	.325	.331
1999 St. Louis	NL	21	32	11	2	0	1	(0	1)	16	6	9	7	0	6	0	0	0	0	0	.00	0	.344	.462	.500
7 ML YEARS		348	917	219	41	3	34	(16	18)	368	113	149	95	5	213	8	2	7	13	8	.62	22	.239	.314	.401

Neifi Perez

Bats: Both **Throws:** Right **Pos:** SS-157   **Ht:** 6'0" **Wt:** 175 **Born:** 2/2/75 **Age:** 25

Year Team	Lg	G	AB	H	2B	3B	HR	(Hm	Rd)	TB	R	RBI	TBB	IBB	SO	HBP	SH	SF	SB	CS	SB%	GDP	Avg	OBP	SLG
1996 Colorado	NL	17	45	7	2	0	0	(0	0)	9	4	3	0	0	8	0	1	0	2	2	.50	2	.156	.156	.200
1997 Colorado	NL	83	313	91	13	10	5	(3	2)	139	46	31	21	4	43	1	5	4	4	3	.57	3	.291	.333	.444
1998 Colorado	NL	162	647	177	25	9	9	(6	3)	247	80	59	38	0	70	1	22	4	5	6	.45	8	.274	.315	.382
1999 Colorado	NL	157	690	193	27	11	12	(8	4)	278	108	70	28	0	54	1	9	4	13	5	.72	4	.280	.307	.403
4 ML YEARS		419	1695	468	67	30	26	(17	9)	673	238	163	87	4	175	3	37	12	24	16	.60	17	.276	.311	.397

Odalis Perez

Pitches: Left **Bats:** Left **Pos:** SP-17; RP-1   **Ht:** 6'0" **Wt:** 150 **Born:** 6/7/78 **Age:** 22

Year Team	Lg	G	GS	CG	GF	IP	BFP	H	R	ER	HR	SH	SF	HB	TBB	IBB	SO	WP	Bk	W	L	Pct.	ShO	Sv-Op	Hld	ERA
1995 Braves	R	12	12	1	0	65	264	48	22	16	0	3	0	3	18	0	62	7	3	3	5	.375	1	0--	—	2.22
1996 Eugene	A-	10	6	0	0	23.2	110	26	16	10	2	2	0	0	11	0	38	3	0	2	1	.667	0	0--	—	3.80
1997 Macon	A	36	0	0	12	87.1	358	67	31	16	4	4	1	5	27	1	100	3	0	4	5	.444	0	5--	—	1.65
1998 Greenville	AA	23	21	0	0	132	558	127	67	59	15	3	3	2	53	2	143	4	1	6	5	.545	0	0--	—	4.02
Richmond	AAA	13	0	0	10	24.1	100	26	10	8	4	1	0	0	7	1	22	2	0	1	2	.333	0	3--	—	2.96
1998 Atlanta	NL	10	0	0	0	10.2	45	10	5	5	1	0	0	0	4	0	5	0	0	0	1	.000	0	0-1	5	4.22
1999 Atlanta	NL	18	17	0	0	93	424	100	65	62	12	3	4	1	53	2	82	5	3	4	6	.400	0	0-0	0	6.00
2 ML YEARS		28	17	0	0	103.2	469	110	70	67	13	3	4	1	57	2	87	5	3	4	7	.364	0	0-1	5	5.82

Yorkis Perez

Pitches: Left **Bats:** Both **Pos:** RP-35   **Ht:** 6'0" **Wt:** 210 **Born:** 9/30/67 **Age:** 32

Year Team	Lg	G	GS	CG	GF	IP	BFP	H	R	ER	HR	SH	SF	HB	TBB	IBB	SO	WP	Bk	W	L	Pct.	ShO	Sv-Op	Hld	ERA
1991 Chicago	NL	3	0	0	0	3	16	2	1	1	0	0	2	0	2	0	3	2	0	1	0	1.000	0	0-1	0	2.08
1994 Florida	NL	44	0	0	11	40.2	167	33	18	16	4	2	0	1	14	3	41	4	1	3	0	1.000	0	0-2	15	3.54
1995 Florida	NL	69	0	0	11	46.2	205	35	29	27	6	2	1	2	28	4	47	2	0	2	6	.250	0	1-4	16	5.21
1996 Florida	NL	64	0	0	15	47.2	222	51	28	28	2	2	2	1	31	4	47	2	0	3	4	.429	0	0-2	10	5.29
1997 New York	NL	9	0	0	1	8.2	45	15	8	8	2	0	1	0	4	0	7	1	0	0	1	.000	0	0-1	1	8.31
1998 Philadelphia	NL	57	0	0	7	52	221	40	23	22	3	2	3	0	25	4	42	7	0	0	2	.000	0	0-0	13	3.81
1999 Philadelphia	NL	35	0	0	4	32	137	29	15	14	4	2	1	0	15	1	26	5	0	3	1	.750	0	0-1	5	3.94
7 ML YEARS		281	0	0	49	232	1013	205	122	116	21	10	10	4	119	12	213	23	1	12	14	.462	0	1-11	60	4.50

Matt Perisho

Pitches: Left **Bats:** Left **Pos:** RP-3; SP-1   **Ht:** 6'0" **Wt:** 205 **Born:** 6/8/75 **Age:** 25

Year Team	Lg	G	GS	CG	GF	IP	BFP	H	R	ER	HR	SH	SF	HB	TBB	IBB	SO	WP	Bk	W	L	Pct.	ShO	Sv-Op	Hld	ERA
1999 Oklahoma *	AAA	27	27	2	0	156.1	681	160	86	80	14	2	5	3	78	1	150	6	0	15	7	.682	0	0--	—	4.61
1997 Anaheim	AL	11	8	0	2	45	217	59	34	30	6	2	2	3	28	0	35	5	2	0	2	.000	0	0-0	0	6.00
1998 Texas	AL	2	2	0	0	5	40	15	17	15	2	0	0	2	8	0	2	0	0	0	2	.000	0	0-0	0	27.00
1999 Texas	AL	4	1	0	3	10.1	40	8	3	3	0	0	0	0	2	1	17	1	0	0	0	.000	0	0-0	0	2.61
3 ML YEARS		17	11	0	5	60.1	297	82	54	48	8	2	2	5	38	1	54	6	2	0	4	.000	0	0-0	0	7.16

Dan Perkins

Pitches: Right **Bats:** Right **Pos:** RP-17; SP-12   **Ht:** 6'2" **Wt:** 193 **Born:** 3/15/75 **Age:** 25

Year Team	Lg	G	GS	CG	GF	IP	BFP	H	R	ER	HR	SH	SF	HB	TBB	IBB	SO	WP	Bk	W	L	Pct.	ShO	Sv-Op	Hld	ERA
1993 Elizabethtn	R+	10	10	0	0	45	210	46	33	25	3	1	1	5	25	0	30	5	1	3	3	.500	0	0--	—	5.00
1994 Fort Wayne	A	12	12	0	0	50.2	229	61	38	35	3	3	1	4	22	1	34	4	1	1	8	.111	0	0--	—	6.22
Elizabethtn	R+	10	9	1	0	54		51	31	22	2	2	1	7	14	0	34	9	1	0	2	.000	0	0--	—	3.67
1995 Fort Wayne	A	29	22	0	2	121.1	562	133	86	74	3	3	4	13	69	1	89	22	2	7	12	.368	0	0--	—	5.49
1996 Fort Myers	A+	39	13	3	10	136.2	557	125	52	45	5	4	6	11	37	1	111	9	1	13	7	.650	1	2--	—	2.96
1997 New Britain	AA	24	24	2	0	144.2	644	158	94	79	17	8	2	11	53	1	114	10	0	7	10	.412	0	0--	—	4.91
1998 New Britain	AA	20	19	1	0	117.2	508	140	64	52	8	3	3	3	31	1	79	6	0	13	5	.722	0	0--	—	3.98
Salt Lake	AAA	7	7	1	0	46.2	205	48	30	25	8	0	2	2	20	1	33	2	0	5	0	1.000	0	0--	—	4.82
1999 Salt Lake	AAA	3	2	0	0	12.2	57	11	6	6	3	0	0	2	4	0	7	3	0	0	0	.000	0	0--	—	4.26
1999 Minnesota	AL	29	12	0	7	86.2	413	117	69	63	14	2	4	5	43	0	44	6	2	1	7	.125	0	0-0	0	6.54

Herbert Perry

Bats: R **Throws:** R **Pos:** 3B-42; 1B-14; PH/PR-7; LF-6; DH-5   **Ht:** 6'2" **Wt:** 220 **Born:** 9/15/69 **Age:** 30

Year Team	Lg	G	AB	H	2B	3B	HR	(Hm	Rd)	TB	R	RBI	TBB	IBB	SO	HBP	SH	SF	SB	CS	SB%	GDP	Avg	OBP	SLG
1999 Durham *	AAA	27	103	32	8	0	5	(—	—)	55	21	20	6	0	21	2	0	0	0	0	.00	3	.311	.360	.534
1994 Cleveland	AL	4	9	1	0	0	0	(0	0)	1	1	1	3	1	1	1	0	1	0	0	.00	0	.111	.357	.111
1995 Cleveland	AL	52	162	51	13	1	3	(3	0)	75	23	23	13	0	28	4	3	2	1	3	.25	5	.315	.376	.463
1996 Cleveland	AL	7	12	1	1	0	0	(0	0)	2	1	0	1	0	2	0	0	0	0	1	1.00	0	.083	.154	.167
1999 Tampa Bay	AL	66	209	53	10	1	6	(5	1)	83	29	32	16	1	42	10	0	4	0	0	.00	13	.254	.331	.397
4 ML YEARS		129	392	106	24	2	9	(8	1)	161	54	56	33	2	73	15	3	7	2	3	.40	18	.270	.345	.411

Robert Person

Pitches: Right **Bats:** Right **Pos:** SP-22; RP-20   **Ht:** 6'0" **Wt:** 190 **Born:** 10/6/69 **Age:** 30

Year Team	Lg	G	GS	CG	GF	IP	BFP	H	R	ER	HR	SH	SF	HB	TBB	IBB	SO	WP	Bk	W	L	Pct.	ShO	Sv-Op	Hld	ERA
1999 Dunedin *	A+	1	1	0	0	3	12	4	1	1	0	0	1	0	1	0	3	0	0	0	0	.000	0	0--	—	3.00
1995 New York	NL	3	1	0	0	12	44	5	1	1	1	0	0	0	2	0	10	0	0	1	0	1.000	0	0-0	0	0.75
1996 New York	NL	27	13	0	1	89.2	390	86	50	45	16	1	4	2	35	3	76	3	0	4	5	.444	0	0-0	1	4.52
1997 Toronto	AL	23	22	0	0	126	566	125	86	80	19	4	6	5	60	2	99	7	0	5	10	.333	0	0-0	0	5.61
1998 Toronto	AL	27	0	0	14	38.1	184	45	31	30	9	2	5	2	22	1	31	0	0	3	1	.750	0	6-8	0	7.04
1999 Tor-Phi		42	22	0	8	148	659	139	84	77	24	7	6	6	85	2	139	5	1	10	7	.588	0	2-2	0	4.68

Year Team	Lg	G	GS	CG	GF	IP	BFP	H	R	ER	HR	SH	SF	HB	TBB	IBB	SO	WP	Bk	W	L	Pct.	ShO	Sv-Op	Hld	ERA
1999 Toronto	AL	11	0	0	7	11	60	9	12	12	1	0	2	4	15	1	12	2	0	0	2	.000	0	2-2	1	9.82
Philadelphia	NL	31	22	0	1	137	599	130	72	65	23	7	4	2	70	1	127	3	1	10	5	.667	0	0-0	0	4.27
5 ML YEARS		122	58	0	23	416.1	1843	400	252	233	69	14	21	15	204	8	355	15	1	23	23	.500	0	8-10	2	5.04

Chris Peters

Pitches: Left **Bats:** Left **Pos:** SP-11; RP-8   **Ht:** 6'1" **Wt:** 165 **Born:** 1/28/72 **Age:** 28

Year Team	Lg	G	GS	CG	GF	IP	BFP	H	R	ER	HR	SH	SF	HB	TBB	IBB	SO	WP	Bk	W	L	Pct.	ShO	Sv-Op	Hld	ERA
1999 Nashville *	AAA	11	9	0	1	49.1	214	54	18	12	1	0	1	1	15	1	34	3	0	1	1	.750	0	1- -	—	2.19
1996 Pittsburgh	NL	16	10	0	0	64	283	72	43	40	9	3	3	1	25	0	28	4	0	2	4	.333	0	0-0	2	5.63
1997 Pittsburgh	NL	31	1	0	5	37.1	167	38	23	19	6	5	1	3	21	4	17	4	0	2	2	.500	0	0-1	2	4.58
1998 Pittsburgh	NL	39	21	1	7	148	630	142	63	57	13	4	5	3	55	4	103	4	1	8	10	.444	0	1-1	2	3.47
1999 Pittsburgh	NL	19	11	0	2	71	343	98	59	52	17	4	4	4	27	0	46	2	1	5	4	.556	0	0-0	1	6.59
4 ML YEARS		105	43	1	14	320.1	1423	350	188	168	45	16	13	11	128	8	194	14	2	17	20	.459	0	1-2	7	4.72

Chris Petersen

Bats: Right **Throws:** Right **Pos:** 2B-6; SS-1; PH/PR-1   **Ht:** 5'11" **Wt:** 180 **Born:** 11/6/70 **Age:** 29

Year Team	Lg	G	AB	H	2B	3B	HR	(Hm	Rd)	TB	R	RBI	TBB	IBB	SO	HBP	SH	SF	SB	CS	SB%	GDP	Avg	OBP	SLG
1992 Geneva	A-	71	244	55	8	0	1	—	—	66	36	23	32	0	69	4	9	2	11	7	.61	4	.225	.323	.270
1993 Daytona	A+	130	473	101	10	0	0	—	—	111	66	28	58	0	105	9	17	1	19	11	.63	10	.214	.311	.235
1994 Orlando	AA	117	376	85	12	3	1	—	—	106	34	26	37	0	89	2	16	1	8	11	.42	7	.226	.298	.282
1995 Orlando	AA	125	382	81	10	3	4	—	—	109	48	36	45	3	97	4	5	3	7	3	.70	14	.212	.300	.285
1996 Orlando	AA	47	152	45	3	4	2	—	—	62	21	12	18	0	31	5	0	1	3	5	.38	5	.296	.386	.408
Iowa	AAA	63	194	48	6	3	2	—	—	66	12	23	12	1	46	1	2	1	2	1	.33	4	.247	.293	.340
1997 Iowa	AAA	119	391	94	16	2	3	—	—	123	49	33	32	4	89	6	4	3	1	6	.14	15	.240	.306	.315
1998 Iowa	AAA	118	389	91	16	2	8	—	—	135	54	41	21	3	100	7	5	2	4	4	.33	12	.234	.284	.347
1999 Colo Sprngs	AAA	107	370	96	21	1	6	—	—	137	56	34	29	1	85	7	3	2	4	0	1.00	12	.259	.324	.370
1999 Colorado	NL	7	13	2	0	0	0	(0	0)	2	1	2	2	0	3	0	0	0	0	0	.00	0	.154	.267	.154

Kyle Peterson

Pitches: Right **Bats:** Left **Pos:** SP-12; RP-5   **Ht:** 6'3" **Wt:** 215 **Born:** 4/9/76 **Age:** 24

Year Team	Lg	G	GS	CG	GF	IP	BFP	H	R	ER	HR	SH	SF	HB	TBB	IBB	SO	WP	Bk	W	L	Pct.	ShO	Sv-Op	Hld	ERA
1997 Ogden	R+	3	3	0	0	10.1	40	5	2	1	1	0	0	1	4	0	11	0	0	0	0	.000	0	0- -	—	0.87
1998 Stockton	A+	17	17	0	0	96.1	430	99	54	38	4	6	1	8	33	0	109	5	5	4	7	.364	0	0- -	—	3.55
El Paso	AA	7	7	1	0	43	187	41	24	21	2	2	2	1	16	0	33	1	0	3	2	.600	0	0- -	—	4.40
Louisville	AAA	1	1	0	0	5.2	27	8	5	5	0	0	0	0	2	0	4	0	0	1	0	1.000	0	0- -	—	7.94
1999 Louisville	AAA	18	18	1	0	109	466	90	52	43	13	3	3	6	42	1	95	5	2	7	6	.538	1	0- -	—	3.55
1999 Milwaukee	NL	17	12	0	2	77	341	87	46	39	3	4	3	4	25	2	34	1	0	4	7	.364	0	0-1	0	4.56

Mark Petkovsek

Pitches: Right **Bats:** Right **Pos:** RP-64   **Ht:** 6'0" **Wt:** 195 **Born:** 11/18/65 **Age:** 34

Year Team	Lg	G	GS	CG	GF	IP	BFP	H	R	ER	HR	SH	SF	HB	TBB	IBB	SO	WP	Bk	W	L	Pct.	ShO	Sv-Op	Hld	ERA
1991 Texas	AL	4	1	0	1	9.1	53	21	16	15	4	0	1	0	4	0	6	2	0	0	1	.000	0	0-0	0	14.46
1993 Pittsburgh	NL	26	0	0	8	32.1	145	43	25	25	7	4	1	0	9	2	14	4	0	3	0	1.000	0	0-0	0	6.96
1995 St. Louis	NL	26	21	1	1	137.1	569	136	71	61	11	4	4	6	35	3	71	1	1	6	6	.500	1	0-0	0	4.00
1996 St. Louis	NL	48	6	0	7	88.2	377	83	37	35	9	5	1	5	35	2	45	2	1	11	2	.846	0	0-3	10	3.55
1997 St. Louis	NL	55	2	0	19	96	414	109	61	54	14	2	2	6	31	4	51	2	0	4	7	.364	0	2-2	5	5.06
1998 St. Louis	NL	48	10	0	7	105.2	476	131	63	56	9	9	3	8	36	3	55	1	1	7	4	.636	0	0-5	6	4.77
1999 Anaheim	AL	64	0	0	18	83	349	85	37	32	6	5	5	2	21	2	43	3	1	10	4	.714	0	1-4	12	3.47
7 ML YEARS		271	40	1	61	552.1	2383	608	310	278	60	29	17	27	171	16	285	15	4	41	24	.631	1	3-14	33	4.53

Ben Petrick

Bats: Right **Throws:** Right **Pos:** C-19   **Ht:** 6'0" **Wt:** 199 **Born:** 4/7/77 **Age:** 23

Year Team	Lg	G	AB	H	2B	3B	HR	(Hm	Rd)	TB	R	RBI	TBB	IBB	SO	HBP	SH	SF	SB	CS	SB%	GDP	Avg	OBP	SLG
1996 Asheville	A	122	446	105	24	2	14	—	—	175	74	52	75	1	98	5	2	3	19	9	.68	5	.235	.350	.392
1997 Salem	A+	121	412	102	23	3	15	—	—	176	68	56	62	2	100	2	4	2	30	11	.73	6	.248	.347	.427
1998 New Haven	AA	106	349	83	21	3	18	—	—	164	52	50	56	1	89	3	0	5	7	7	.50	5	.238	.345	.470
1999 Carolina	AA	20	68	21	5	1	4	—	—	40	18	22	9	0	15	1	0	2	3	1	.75	0	.309	.388	.588
Colo Sprngs	AAA	84	282	88	16	5	19	—	—	171	56	64	44	1	58	3	0	6	9	6	.60	4	.312	.403	.606
1999 Colorado	NL	19	62	20	3	0	4	(4	0)	35	13	12	10	0	13	0	0	0	1	0	1.00	1	.323	.417	.565

Andy Pettitte

Pitches: Left   Bats: Left   Pos: SP-31   Ht: 6'5"   Wt: 225   Born: 6/15/72   Age: 28

Year Team	Lg	G	GS	CG	GF	IP	BFP	H	R	ER	HR	SH	SF	HB	TBB	IBB	SO	WP	Bk	W	L	Pct.	ShO	Sv-Op	Hld	ERA
1999 Tampa *	A+	1	1	0	0	5	20	4	0	0	0	0	0	0	2	0	8	0	0	1	0	1.000	0	0- --	0	0.00
1995 New York	AL	31	26	3	1	175	745	183	86	81	15	4	5	1	63	3	114	8	1	12	9	.571	0	0-0	0	4.17
1996 New York	AL	35	34	2	1	221	929	229	105	95	23	7	3	3	72	2	162	6	1	21	8	.724	0	0-0	0	3.87
1997 New York	AL	35	35	4	0	240.1	986	233	86	77	7	6	2	3	65	0	166	7	0	18	7	.720	1	0-0	0	2.88
1998 New York	AL	33	32	5	0	216.1	932	226	110	102	20	6	7	6	87	1	146	5	0	16	11	.593	0	0-0	0	4.24
1999 New York	AL	31	31	0	0	191.2	851	216	105	100	20	6	6	3	89	3	121	3	1	14	11	.560	0	0-0	0	4.70
5 ML YEARS		165	158	14	2	1044.1	4443	1087	492	455	85	29	23	16	376	9	709	29	3	81	46	.638	1	0-0	0	3.92

J.R. Phillips

Bats: L Throws: L Pos: PH/PR-17; RF-6; 1B-4; LF-1   Ht: 6'1"   Wt: 205   Born: 4/29/70   Age: 30

Year Team	Lg	G	AB	H	2B	3B	HR	(Hm	Rd)	TB	R	RBI	TBB	IBB	SO	HBP	SH	SF	SB	CS	SB%	GDP	Avg	OBP	SLG
1999 Colo Sprngs *	AAA	124	479	149	22	0	41	—	—	294	87	100	54	6	143	1	0	3	4	3	.57	13	.311	.380	.614
1993 San Francisco	NL	11	16	5	1	1	1	(0	1)	11	1	4	0	0	5	0	0	0	0	0	.00	0	.313	.313	.688
1994 San Francisco	NL	15	38	5	0	0	1	(0	1)	8	1	3	1	0	13	0	0	1	1	0	1.00	1	.132	.150	.211
1995 San Francisco	NL	92	231	45	9	0	9	(5	4)	81	27	28	19	2	69	0	2	0	1	1	.50	3	.195	.256	.351
1996 SF-Phi	NL	50	104	17	5	0	7	(4	3)	43	12	15	11	1	51	1	0	0	0	0	.00	0	.163	.250	.413
1997 Houston	NL	13	15	2	0	0	1	(1	0)	5	2	4	0	0	7	0	0	1	0	0	.00	0	.133	.125	.333
1998 Houston	NL	36	58	11	0	0	2	(0	2)	17	4	9	7	1	22	0	0	0	0	0	.00	1	.190	.277	.293
1999 Colorado	NL	25	39	9	4	0	2	(1	1)	19	5	4	0	0	13	1	0	0	0	0	.00	0	.231	.250	.487
1996 San Francisco	NL	15	25	5	0	0	2	(0	2)	11	3	5	1	0	13	0	0	0	0	0	.00	0	.200	.231	.440
Philadelphia	NL	35	79	12	5	0	5	(4	1)	32	9	10	10	1	38	1	0	0	0	0	.00	0	.152	.256	.405
7 ML YEARS		242	501	94	19	1	23	(11	12)	184	52	67	38	4	180	2	2	2	2	1	.67	6	.188	.247	.367

Jason Phillips

Pitches: Right   Bats: Right   Pos: RP-6   Ht: 6'6"   Wt: 225   Born: 3/22/74   Age: 26

Year Team	Lg	G	GS	CG	GF	IP	BFP	H	R	ER	HR	SH	SF	HB	TBB	IBB	SO	WP	Bk	W	L	Pct.	ShO	Sv-Op	Hld	ERA
1992 Pirates	R	4	4	0	0	17	88	21	21	16	0	1	1	0	13	0	10	4	4	1	2	.333	0	0- --	—	8.47
1993 Welland	A-	14	14	0	0	71.1	323	60	44	28	2	1	2	9	36	0	66	15	4	6	4	.600	1	0- --	—	3.53
1994 Augusta	A	23	23	1	0	108.1	531	118	97	81	4	3	4	12	88	1	108	21	3	6	12	.333	1	0- --	—	6.73
1995 Augusta	A	30	6	0	3	80	354	76	46	32	2	2	2	0	53	1	65	10	0	4	3	.571	0	0- --	—	3.60
1996 Augusta	A	14	14	1	0	89.2	366	79	35	24	3	2	3	6	29	1	75	9	1	5	4	.556	0	0- --	—	2.41
Lynchburg	A+	13	13	1	0	73.2	343	82	47	37	3	2	2	5	35	0	63	6	1	5	6	.455	0	0- --	—	4.52
1997 Lynchburg	A+	23	23	2	0	138.2	577	129	66	58	10	4	2	6	35	0	140	9	1	11	6	.647	1	0- --	—	3.76
Carolina	AA	4	4	2	0	31	127	21	8	8	1	1	2	4	9	0	22	2	0	1	2	.333	1	0- --	—	2.32
1998 Carolina	AA	25	25	1	0	151	663	161	89	79	14	8	1	9	52	3	114	10	3	7	13	.350	1	0- --	—	4.71
Nashville	AAA	5	5	0	0	31.1	136	38	10	9	3	3	0	1	12	0	21	3	0	2	0	1.000	0	0- --	—	2.59
1999 Nashville	AAA	1	1	0	0	3	19	6	6	5	0	0	0	0	5	1	5	1	0	0	0	.000	0	0- --	—	15.00
1999 Pittsburgh	NL	6	0	0	0	7	37	11	9	9	2	2	1	0	6	1	7	2	0	0	0	.000	0	0-0	0	11.57

Tony Phillips

Bats: B Throws: R Pos: 2B-66; CF-32; LF-28; RF-15; PH/PR-4; 3B-2; DH-1; SS-1   Ht: 5'10"   Wt: 175   Born: 4/25/59   Age: 41

Year Team	Lg	G	AB	H	2B	3B	HR	(Hm	Rd)	TB	R	RBI	TBB	IBB	SO	HBP	SH	SF	SB	CS	SB%	GDP	Avg	OBP	SLG
1982 Oakland	AL	40	81	17	2	2	0	(0	0)	23	11	8	12	0	26	2	5	0	2	3	.40	0	.210	.326	.284
1983 Oakland	AL	148	412	102	12	3	4	(1	3)	132	54	35	48	1	70	2	11	3	16	5	.76	5	.248	.327	.320
1984 Oakland	AL	154	451	120	24	3	4	(2	2)	162	62	37	42	1	86	0	7	5	10	6	.63	5	.266	.325	.359
1985 Oakland	AL	42	161	45	12	2	4	(2	2)	73	23	17	13	0	34	0	1	1	3	2	.60	1	.280	.331	.453
1986 Oakland	AL	118	441	113	14	5	5	(3	2)	152	76	52	76	0	82	3	9	3	15	10	.60	2	.256	.367	.345
1987 Oakland	AL	111	379	91	20	0	10	(5	5)	141	48	46	57	1	76	0	2	3	7	6	.54	9	.240	.337	.372
1988 Oakland	AL	79	212	43	8	4	2	(2	0)	65	32	17	36	0	50	1	1	1	0	2	.00	6	.203	.320	.307
1989 Oakland	AL	143	451	118	15	6	4	(2	2)	157	48	47	58	2	66	3	5	7	3	8	.27	17	.262	.345	.348
1990 Detroit	AL	152	573	144	23	5	8	(4	4)	201	97	55	99	0	85	4	9	2	19	9	.68	10	.251	.364	.351
1991 Detroit	AL	146	564	160	28	4	17	(9	8)	247	87	72	79	5	95	3	3	6	10	5	.67	8	.284	.371	.438
1992 Detroit	AL	159	606	167	32	3	10	(3	7)	235	114	64	114	2	93	1	5	7	12	10	.55	13	.276	.387	.388
1993 Detroit	AL	151	566	177	27	0	7	(3	4)	225	113	57	132	5	102	4	1	4	16	11	.59	11	.313	.443	.398
1994 Detroit	AL	114	438	123	19	3	19	(12	7)	205	91	61	95	3	105	2	0	3	13	5	.72	8	.281	.409	.468
1995 California	AL	139	525	137	21	1	27	(13	14)	241	119	61	113	6	135	3	1	1	13	10	.57	5	.261	.394	.459
1996 Chicago	AL	153	581	161	29	3	12	(6	6)	232	119	63	125	9	132	4	1	8	13	8	.62	6	.277	.404	.399
1997 CWS-Ana	AL	141	534	147	34	2	8	(5	3)	209	96	57	102	5	118	3	5	4	13	10	.57	11	.275	.392	.391
1998 Tor-NYM	AL	65	236	59	16	0	4	(3	1)	87	34	21	47	1	50	2	1	3	1	1	.50	3	.250	.375	.369
1999 Oakland	AL	106	406	99	24	4	15	(5	10)	176	76	49	71	3	94	5	0	2	11	3	.79	7	.244	.362	.433
1997 Chicago	AL	36	129	40	6	0	2	(1	1)	52	23	9	29	0	29	1	2	0	4	1	.80	3	.310	.440	.403
Anaheim	AL	105	405	107	28	2	6	(4	2)	157	73	48	73	5	89	2	3	4	9	9	.50	8	.264	.376	.388
1998 Toronto	AL	13	48	17	5	0	1	(0	1)	25	9	7	9	1	6	2	0	1	0	0	.00	2	.354	.467	.521
New York	NL	52	188	42	11	0	3	(3	0)	62	25	14	38	0	44	0	1	2	1	1	.50	1	.223	.351	.330
18 ML YEARS		2161	7617	2023	360	50	160	(80	80)	2963	1300	819	1319	44	1499	42	69	63	177	114	.61	127	.266	.374	.389

Mike Piazza

Bats: Right Throws: Right Pos: C-137; PH/PR-4; DH-1　　　　Ht: 6'3" Wt: 215 Born: 9/4/68 Age: 31

Year Team	Lg	G	AB	H	2B	3B	HR	(Hm	Rd)	TB	R	RBI	TBB	IBB	SO	HBP	SH	SF	SB	CS	SB%	GDP	Avg	OBP	SLG
1992 Los Angeles	NL	21	69	16	3	0	1	(1	0)	22	5	7	4	0	12	1	0	0	0	0	.00	1	.232	.284	.319
1993 Los Angeles	NL	149	547	174	24	2	35	(21	14)	307	81	112	46	6	86	3	0	6	3	4	.43	10	.318	.370	.561
1994 Los Angeles	NL	107	405	129	18	0	24	(13	11)	219	64	92	33	10	65	1	0	2	1	3	.25	11	.319	.370	.541
1995 Los Angeles	NL	112	434	150	17	0	32	(9	23)	263	82	93	39	10	80	1	0	1	1	0	1.00	10	.346	.400	.606
1996 Los Angeles	NL	148	547	184	16	0	36	(14	22)	308	87	105	81	21	93	1	0	2	0	3	.00	21	.336	.422	.563
1997 Los Angeles	NL	152	556	201	32	1	40	(22	18)	355	104	124	69	11	77	3	0	5	5	1	.83	19	.362	.431	.638
1998 LA-Fla-NYM	NL	151	561	184	38	1	32	(15	17)	320	88	111	58	14	80	2	0	5	1	0	1.00	15	.328	.390	.570
1999 New York	NL	141	534	162	25	0	40	(18	22)	307	100	124	51	11	70	1	0	7	2	2	.50	27	.303	.361	.575
1998 Los Angeles	NL	37	149	42	5	0	9	(5	4)	74	20	30	11	4	27	0	0	1	0	0	.00	3	.282	.329	.497
Florida	NL	5	18	5	0	0	1	(0	0)	7	1	5	0	0	0	0	0	1	0	0	.00	0	.278	.263	.389
New York	NL	109	394	137	33	0	23	(10	13)	239	67	76	47	10	53	2	0	3	1	0	1.00	12	.348	.417	.607
8 ML YEARS		981	3653	1200	173	4	240	(113	127)	2101	611	768	381	83	563	13	0	28	13	13	.50	114	.328	.391	.575

Calvin Pickering

Bats: Left Throws: Left Pos: PH/PR-12; 1B-8; DH-7　　　　Ht: 6'5" Wt: 278 Born: 9/29/76 Age: 23

Year Team	Lg	G	AB	H	2B	3B	HR	(Hm	Rd)	TB	R	RBI	TBB	IBB	SO	HBP	SH	SF	SB	CS	SB%	GDP	Avg	OBP	SLG
1995 Orioles	R	15	60	30	10	0	1	—	—	43	8	22	2	0	6	0	0	1	0	0	.00	3	.500	.508	.717
1996 Bluefield	R+	60	200	65	14	1	18	—	—	135	45	66	28	4	64	2	0	1	8	2	.80	4	.325	.411	.675
1997 Delmarva	A	122	444	138	31	1	25	—	—	246	88	79	53	2	139	9	0	1	6	3	.67	14	.311	.394	.554
1998 Bowie	AA	139	448	151	28	2	31	—	—	276	93	114	98	16	119	11	0	2	4	6	.40	20	.309	.434	.566
1999 Rochester	AAA	103	372	106	20	0	16	—	—	174	63	63	60	6	99	11	0	4	1	3	.25	10	.285	.394	.468
1998 Baltimore	AL	9	21	5	0	0	2	(1	1)	11	4	3	3	0	4	0	0	0	1	0	1.00	2	.238	.333	.524
1999 Baltimore	AL	23	40	5	1	0	1	(1	0)	9	4	5	11	0	16	0	0	0	0	0	.00	1	.125	.314	.225
2 ML YEARS		32	61	10	1	0	3	(2	1)	20	8	8	14	0	20	0	0	0	1	0	1.00	3	.164	.320	.328

A.J. Pierzynski

Bats: Left Throws: Right Pos: C-9　　　　Ht: 6'3" Wt: 220 Born: 12/30/76 Age: 23

Year Team	Lg	G	AB	H	2B	3B	HR	(Hm	Rd)	TB	R	RBI	TBB	IBB	SO	HBP	SH	SF	SB	CS	SB%	GDP	Avg	OBP	SLG
1994 Twins	R	43	152	44	8	1	1	—	—	57	21	19	12	0	19	0	0	2	0	2	.00	3	.289	.337	.375
1995 Fort Wayne	A	22	84	26	5	1	2	—	—	39	10	14	2	0	10	0	0	1	0	0	.00	1	.310	.322	.464
Elizabethtn	R+	56	205	68	13	1	7	—	—	104	29	45	14	1	23	0	0	1	0	2	.00	6	.332	.373	.507
1996 Fort Wayne	A	114	431	118	30	3	7	—	—	175	48	70	22	1	53	2	0	6	0	4	.00	10	.274	.308	.406
1997 Fort Myers	A+	118	412	115	23	1	9	—	—	167	49	64	16	1	59	6	1	4	2	1	.67	9	.279	.313	.405
1998 New Britain	AA	59	212	63	11	0	3	—	—	83	30	17	10	4	25	2	0	2	0	2	.00	4	.297	.333	.392
Salt Lake	AAA	59	208	53	7	2	7	—	—	85	29	30	9	2	24	0	2	1	3	1	.75	4	.255	.284	.409
1999 Salt Lake	AAA	67	228	59	10	0	1	—	—	72	29	25	16	0	29	0	2	0	0	0	.00	11	.259	.307	.316
1998 Minnesota	AL	7	10	3	0	0	0	(0	0)	3	1	1	1	0	2	1	0	1	0	0	.00	0	.300	.385	.300
1999 Minnesota	AL	9	22	6	2	0	0	(0	0)	8	3	3	1	0	4	1	0	0	0	0	.00	0	.273	.333	.364
2 ML YEARS		16	32	9	2	0	0	(0	0)	11	4	4	2	0	6	2	0	1	0	0	.00	0	.281	.351	.344

Marc Pisciotta

Pitches: Right Bats: Right Pos: RP-8　　　　Ht: 6'5" Wt: 225 Born: 8/7/70 Age: 29

Year Team	Lg	G	GS	CG	GF	IP	BFP	H	R	ER	HR	SH	SF	HB	TBB	IBB	SO	WP	Bk	W	L	Pct.	ShO	Sv-Op	Hld	ERA
1999 Richmond *	AAA	23	0	0	3	35.2	153	34	25	24	3	2	3	0	17	3	27	3	0	3	2	.600	0	0--	—	6.06
Omaha *	AAA	10	0	0	5	13.2	67	18	18	17	3	0	2	1	11	1	8	2	0	0	1	.000	0	0--	—	11.20
1997 Chicago	NL	24	0	0	7	28.1	119	20	10	10	1	1	1	1	16	0	21	2	0	3	1	.750	0	0-1	10	3.18
1998 Chicago	NL	43	0	0	12	44	206	44	21	20	4	1	1	2	32	3	31	6	0	1	2	.333	0	0-0	7	4.09
1999 Kansas City	AL	8	0	0	3	8.1	42	9	8	8	1	0	2	0	10	0	3	1	1	0	2	.000	0	0-0	0	8.64
3 ML YEARS		75	0	0	22	80.2	367	73	39	38	6	2	2	3	58	3	55	9	1	4	5	.444	0	0-1	17	4.24

Jim Pittsley

Pitches: Right Bats: Right Pos: RP-15; SP-5　　　　Ht: 6'7" Wt: 230 Born: 4/3/74 Age: 26

Year Team	Lg	G	GS	CG	GF	IP	BFP	H	R	ER	HR	SH	SF	HB	TBB	IBB	SO	WP	Bk	W	L	Pct.	ShO	Sv-Op	Hld	ERA
1999 Louisville *	AAA	8	8	0	0	39	187	55	42	38	8	1	3	2	16	0	26	4	0	2	4	.333	0	0--	—	8.77
1995 Kansas City	AL	1	1	0	0	3.1	17	7	5	5	3	0	0	0	1	0	0	0	0	0	0	.000	0	0-0	0	13.50
1997 Kansas City	AL	21	21	0	0	112	501	120	72	68	15	2	6	6	54	1	52	3	0	5	8	.385	0	0-0	0	5.46
1998 KC-Mil	AL	39	2	0	11	68.1	320	88	56	50	13	3	5	2	37	1	44	6	0	1	1	.500	0	0-0	1	6.59
1999 Kansas City	AL	20	5	0	5	42	200	53	34	28	5	0	2	2	25	0	20	4	0	1	3	.250	0	0-1	3	6.00
1999 Kansas City	AL	5	5	0	0	23.1	115	33	22	18	2	0	1	1	15	0	7	2	0	1	2	.333	0	0-0	0	6.94
Milwaukee	NL	15	0	0	5	18.2	85	20	12	10	3	0	1	1	10	0	13	2	0	0	1	.000	0	0-1	3	4.82
4 ML YEARS		81	29	0	16	225.2	1038	268	167	151	36	5	13	10	117	2	116	13	0	7	12	.368	0	0-1	4	6.02

Dan Plesac

Pitches: Left **Bats:** Left **Pos:** RP-64 **Ht:** 6'5" **Wt:** 217 **Born:** 2/4/62 **Age:** 38

	HOW MUCH HE PITCHED						WHAT HE GAVE UP									THE RESULTS						
Year Team	Lg	G	GS	CG	GF	IP	BFP	H	R	ER	HR	SH	SF	HB	TBB	IBB	SO	WP	Bk	W	L	Pct.	ShO	Sv-Op	Hld	ERA
1986 Milwaukee	AL	51	0	0	33	91	377	81	34	30	5	6	5	0	29	1	75	4	0	10	7	.588	0	14-20	5	2.97
1987 Milwaukee	AL	57	0	0	47	79.1	325	63	30	23	8	1	2	3	23	1	89	6	0	5	6	.455	0	23-36	0	2.61
1988 Milwaukee	AL	50	0	0	48	52.1	211	46	14	14	2	2	2	0	12	2	52	4	6	1	2	.333	0	30-35	0	2.41
1989 Milwaukee	AL	52	0	0	51	61.1	242	47	16	16	6	0	4	0	17	1	52	0	0	3	4	.429	0	33-40	0	2.35
1990 Milwaukee	AL	66	0	0	52	69	299	67	36	34	5	2	2	3	31	6	65	2	0	3	7	.300	0	24-34	2	4.43
1991 Milwaukee	AL	45	10	0	25	92.1	402	92	49	44	12	3	7	3	39	1	61	2	1	2	7	.222	0	8-12	1	4.29
1992 Milwaukee	AL	44	4	0	13	79	330	64	28	26	5	8	4	3	35	5	54	3	1	5	4	.556	0	1-3	1	2.96
1993 Chicago	NL	57	0	0	12	62.2	276	74	37	33	10	4	3	0	21	6	47	5	2	2	1	.667	0	0-2	12	4.74
1994 Chicago	NL	54	0	0	14	54.2	235	61	30	28	9	1	1	1	13	0	53	0	0	2	3	.400	0	1-3	14	4.61
1995 Pittsburgh	NL	58	0	0	16	60.1	259	53	26	24	3	4	3	1	27	7	57	1	0	4	4	.500	0	3-5	11	3.58
1996 Pittsburgh	NL	73	0	0	30	70.1	300	67	35	32	4	2	3	0	24	6	76	4	0	6	5	.545	0	11-17	11	4.09
1997 Toronto	AL	73	0	0	18	50.1	215	47	22	20	8	2	1	0	19	4	61	2	0	2	4	.333	0	1-5	27	3.58
1998 Toronto	AL	78	0	0	16	50	203	41	23	21	4	0	3	1	16	1	55	0	0	4	3	.571	0	4-5	27	3.78
1999 Tor-Ari		64	0	0	11	44.1	198	50	30	29	7	4	1	0	17	2	53	3	0	4	4	.333	0	1-3	15	5.89
1999 Toronto	AL	30	0	0	5	22.2	104	28	21	21	4	3	1	0	9	1	26	2	0	0	3	.000	0	0-2	9	8.34
Arizona	NL	34	0	0	6	21.2	94	22	9	8	3	1	0	0	8	1	27	1	0	2	1	.667	0	1-1	6	3.32
14 ML YEARS		822	14	0	386	917	3872	853	410	374	88	39	39	15	323	43	850	36	10	51	61	.455	0	154-220	126	3.67

Eric Plunk

Pitches: Right **Bats:** Right **Pos:** RP-68 **Ht:** 6'6" **Wt:** 220 **Born:** 9/3/63 **Age:** 36

	HOW MUCH HE PITCHED						WHAT HE GAVE UP									THE RESULTS						
Year Team	Lg	G	GS	CG	GF	IP	BFP	H	R	ER	HR	SH	SF	HB	TBB	IBB	SO	WP	Bk	W	L	Pct.	ShO	Sv-Op	Hld	ERA
1986 Oakland	AL	26	15	0	2	120.1	537	91	75	71	14	2	3	5	102	2	98	9	6	4	7	.364	0	0- -	—	5.31
1987 Oakland	AL	32	11	0	11	95	432	91	53	50	8	3	5	2	62	3	90	5	2	4	6	.400	0	2-5	1	4.74
1988 Oakland	AL	49	0	0	22	78	331	62	27	26	6	3	2	1	39	4	79	4	7	7	2	.778	0	5-9	5	3.00
1989 Oak-NYY	AL	50	7	0	17	104.1	445	82	43	38	10	3	4	1	64	2	85	10	3	8	6	.571	0	1-3	7	3.28
1990 New York	AL	47	0	0	16	72.2	310	58	27	22	6	7	0	2	43	4	67	4	2	6	3	.667	0	0-1	3	2.72
1991 New York	AL	43	8	0	16	111.2	521	128	69	59	18	6	4	1	62	1	103	6	2	2	5	.286	0	0-0	2	4.76
1992 Cleveland	AL	58	0	0	20	71.2	309	61	31	29	5	3	2	0	38	2	50	5	0	9	6	.600	0	4-8	7	3.64
1993 Cleveland	AL	70	0	0	40	71	306	61	29	22	5	4	2	0	30	4	77	6	0	4	5	.444	0	15-18	16	2.79
1994 Cleveland	AL	41	0	0	18	71	306	61	25	20	3	2	1	2	37	5	73	7	0	7	2	.778	0	3-7	8	2.54
1995 Cleveland	AL	56	0	0	22	64	263	48	19	19	5	2	2	4	27	2	71	3	0	6	2	.750	0	2-5	10	2.67
1996 Cleveland	AL	56	0	0	12	77.2	318	56	21	21	6	1	4	3	34	2	85	4	1	3	2	.600	0	2-3	15	2.43
1997 Cleveland	AL	55	0	0	22	65.2	293	62	37	34	12	1	2	1	36	7	66	6	0	4	5	.444	0	0-2	10	4.66
1998 Cle-Mil		63	0	0	13	72.2	321	77	37	35	9	4	4	5	30	2	74	1	0	4	3	.571	0	1-6	14	4.33
1999 Milwaukee	NL	68	0	0	13	75.1	338	71	44	42	15	5	2	5	43	5	63	5	1	4	4	.500	0	0-3	17	5.02
1989 Oakland	AL	23	0	0	12	28.2	113	17	7	7	1	1	0	1	12	0	24	4	0	1	1	.500	0	1-3	5	2.20
New York	AL	27	7	0	5	75.2	332	65	36	31	9	2	4	0	52	2	61	6	3	7	5	.583	0	0-0	2	3.69
1998 Cleveland	AL	37	0	0	6	41	178	44	23	22	6	3	2	2	15	1	38	0	0	3	1	.750	0	0-3	7	4.83
Milwaukee	NL	26	0	0	7	31.2	143	33	14	13	3	1	2	3	15	1	36	1	0	1	2	.333	0	1-3	5	3.69
14 ML YEARS		714	41	0	234	1151	5030	1009	537	488	122	46	37	32	647	45	1081	75	24	72	58	.554	0	35- -	—	3.82

Placido Polanco

Bats: R **Throws:** R **Pos:** 2B-66; PH/PR-16; 3B-9; SS-9 **Ht:** 5'10" **Wt:** 168 **Born:** 10/10/75 **Age:** 24

	BATTING																	BASERUNNING				PERCENTAGES		
Year Team	Lg	G	AB	H	2B	3B	HR	(Hm	Rd)	TB	R	RBI	TBB	IBB	SO	HBP	SH	SF	SB	CS	SB%	GDP	Avg	OBP	SLG
1994 Cardinals	R	32	127	27	4	0	1	—	—	34	17	10	7	0	15	1	0	0	4	2	.67	2	.213	.259	.268
1995 Peoria	A	103	361	96	7	4	2	—	—	117	43	41	18	0	30	2	11	2	7	6	.54	8	.266	.303	.324
1996 St. Pete	A+	137	540	157	29	5	0	—	—	196	65	51	24	1	34	5	6	7	4	4	.50	31	.291	.323	.363
1997 Arkansas	AA	129	508	148	16	3	2	—	—	176	71	51	29	1	51	3	6	3	19	5	.79	11	.291	.331	.346
1998 Memphis	AAA	70	246	69	19	1	1	—	—	93	36	21	16	1	15	3	4	1	6	3	.67	8	.280	.331	.378
1999 Memphis	AAA	29	120	33	4	1	0	—	—	39	18	10	3	0	11	1	0	1	2	0	1.00	7	.275	.296	.325
1998 St. Louis	NL	45	114	29	3	2	1	(1	0)	39	10	11	5	0	9	1	2	0	2	0	1.00	1	.254	.292	.342
1999 St. Louis	NL	88	220	61	9	3	1	(0	1)	79	24	19	15	1	24	0	3	2	1	3	.25	7	.277	.321	.359
2 ML YEARS		133	334	90	12	5	2	(1	1)	118	34	30	20	1	33	1	5	2	3	3	.50	8	.269	.311	.353

Cliff Politte

Pitches: Right **Bats:** Right **Pos:** RP-13 **Ht:** 5'11" **Wt:** 185 **Born:** 2/27/74 **Age:** 26

	HOW MUCH HE PITCHED						WHAT HE GAVE UP									THE RESULTS						
Year Team	Lg	G	GS	CG	GF	IP	BFP	H	R	ER	HR	SH	SF	HB	TBB	IBB	SO	WP	Bk	W	L	Pct.	ShO	Sv-Op	Hld	ERA
1996 Peoria	A	25	25	0	0	149.2	603	108	50	43	8	3	2	7	47	0	151	5	1	14	6	.700	0	0- -	—	2.59
1997 Pr William	A+	19	19	0	0	120.1	475	89	37	30	11	0	3	2	31	0	118	2	2	11	1	.917	0	0- -	—	2.24
Arkansas	AA	6	6	0	0	37.2	152	35	15	9	3	6	1	0	9	1	26	0	0	4	1	.800	0	0- -	—	2.15
1998 Memphis	AAA	10	10	0	0	50.2	244	71	46	43	10	3	2	0	24	0	42	3	0	1	4	.200	0	0- -	—	7.64
Arkansas	AA	10	10	1	0	67	265	56	25	22	6	3	1	1	16	0	61	0	0	5	3	.625	1	0- -	—	2.96
1999 Reading	AA	37	13	1	16	109	460	112	45	44	12	6	1	5	33	3	97	4	0	9	8	.529	0	5- -	—	3.63
1998 St. Louis	NL	8	8	0	0	37	172	45	32	26	6	3	1	1	18	0	22	2	1	2	3	.400	0	0-0	0	6.32
1999 Philadelphia	NL	13	0	0	0	17.2	85	19	14	14	2	1	0	0	15	0	15	2	0	1	0	1.000	0	0-0	1	7.13
2 ML YEARS		21	8	0	0	54.2	257	64	46	40	8	4	1	1	33	0	37	4	1	3	3	.500	0	0-0	1	6.59

Luis Polonia

Bats: L **Throws:** L **Pos:** DH-43; LF-31; RF-10; PH/PR-6   **Ht:** 5'8" **Wt:** 160 **Born:** 12/10/64 **Age:** 35

Year Team	Lg	G	AB	H	2B	3B	HR	(Hm	Rd)	TB	R	RBI	TBB	IBB	SO	HBP	SH	SF	SB	CS	SB%	GDP	Avg	OBP	SLG
1999 Toledo *	AAA	42	161	52	7	1	3	—	—	70	20	22	10	1	28	0	0	0	13	3	.81	2	.323	.363	.435
1987 Oakland	AL	125	435	125	16	10	4	(1	3)	173	78	49	32	1	64	0	1	1	29	7	.81	4	.287	.335	.398
1988 Oakland	AL	84	288	84	11	4	2	(1	1)	109	51	27	21	0	40	0	2	2	24	9	.73	3	.292	.338	.378
1989 Oak-NYY	AL	125	433	130	17	6	3	(1	2)	168	70	46	25	1	44	2	2	4	22	8	.73	13	.300	.338	.388
1990 NYY-Cal	AL	120	403	135	7	9	2	(2	0)	166	52	35	25	1	43	1	3	4	21	14	.60	9	.335	.372	.412
1991 California	AL	150	604	179	28	8	2	(1	1)	229	92	50	52	4	74	1	2	3	48	23	.68	11	.296	.352	.379
1992 California	AL	149	577	165	17	4	0	(0	0)	190	83	35	45	6	64	1	8	4	51	21	.71	18	.286	.337	.329
1993 California	AL	152	576	156	17	6	1	(0	1)	188	75	32	48	7	53	2	8	3	55	24	.70	7	.271	.328	.326
1994 New York	AL	95	350	109	21	6	1	(0	1)	145	62	36	37	1	36	4	2	1	20	12	.63	7	.311	.383	.414
1995 NYY-Atl	AL	95	291	76	16	3	2	(2	0)	104	43	17	28	1	38	0	3	4	13	4	.76	3	.261	.322	.357
1996 Bal-Atl	AL	80	206	55	4	1	2	(2	0)	67	28	16	11	0	23	1	1	1	9	7	.56	10	.267	.306	.325
1999 Detroit	AL	87	333	108	21	8	10	(8	2)	175	46	32	16	0	32	2	2	2	17	9	.65	2	.324	.357	.526
1989 Oakland	AL	59	206	59	6	4	1	(0	1)	76	31	17	9	0	15	0	2	1	13	4	.76	5	.286	.315	.369
New York	AL	66	227	71	11	2	2	(1	1)	92	39	29	16	1	29	2	0	3	9	4	.69	8	.313	.359	.405
1990 New York	AL	11	22	7	0	0	0	(0	0)	7	2	3	0	0	1	0	0	1	1	0	1.00	1	.318	.304	.318
California	AL	109	381	128	7	9	2	(2	0)	159	50	32	25	1	42	1	3	3	20	14	.59	8	.336	.376	.417
1995 New York	AL	67	238	62	9	3	2	(2	0)	83	37	15	25	1	29	0	2	4	10	4	.71	3	.261	.326	.349
Atlanta	NL	28	53	14	7	0	0	(0	0)	21	6	2	3	0	9	0	1	0	3	0	1.00	0	.264	.304	.396
1996 Baltimore	AL	58	175	42	4	1	2	(2	0)	54	25	14	10	0	20	1	1	0	8	6	.57	10	.240	.285	.309
Atlanta	NL	22	31	13	0	0	0	(0	0)	13	3	2	1	0	3	0	0	1	1	1	.50	0	.419	.424	.419
11 ML YEARS		1262	4496	1322	175	65	29	(18	11)	1714	680	375	340	22	511	14	34	29	309	138	.69	87	.294	.344	.381

Sidney Ponson

Pitches: Right **Bats:** Right **Pos:** SP-32   **Ht:** 6'1" **Wt:** 225 **Born:** 11/2/76 **Age:** 23

Year Team	Lg	G	GS	CG	GF	IP	BFP	H	R	ER	HR	SH	SF	HB	TBB	IBB	SO	WP	Bk	W	L	Pct.	ShO	Sv-Op	Hld	ERA
1994 Orioles	R	12	10	1	0	73	300	68	30	24	5	1	3	2	17	0	53	2	4	4	3	.571	0	0--	—	2.96
1995 Bluefield	R+	13	13	0	0	77.2	324	79	44	36	7	1	2	1	16	0	56	4	3	6	3	.667	0	0--	—	4.17
1996 Frederick	A+	18	16	3	2	107	443	98	56	41	6	3	4	5	28	0	110	6	3	7	6	.538	0	0--	—	3.45
1997 Bowie	AA	13	13	1	0	74.2	328	77	51	45	11	4	3	3	32	2	56	1	1	2	7	.222	1	0--	—	5.42
Orioles	R	1	0	0	0	2	6	0	0	0	0	0	0	0	0	0	1	0	0	1	0	1.000	0	0--	—	0.00
1998 Rochester	AAA	1	1	0	0	5	20	4	0	0	0	0	0	0	0	0	3	0	0	1	0	1.000	0	0--	—	0.00
1998 Baltimore	AL	31	20	0	5	135	588	157	82	79	19	3	4	3	42	2	85	4	1	8	9	.471	0	1-2	0	5.27
1999 Baltimore	AL	32	32	6	0	210	897	227	118	110	35	4	7	1	80	2	112	4	0	12	12	.500	0	0-0	0	4.71
2 ML YEARS		63	52	6	5	345	1485	384	200	189	54	7	11	4	122	4	197	8	1	20	21	.488	0	1-2	0	4.93

Jim Poole

Pitches: Left **Bats:** Left **Pos:** RP-54   **Ht:** 6'2" **Wt:** 195 **Born:** 4/28/66 **Age:** 34

Year Team	Lg	G	GS	CG	GF	IP	BFP	H	R	ER	HR	SH	SF	HB	TBB	IBB	SO	WP	Bk	W	L	Pct.	ShO	Sv-Op	Hld	ERA
1999 Akron *	AA	2	0	0	0	2.2	7	0	0	0	0	0	0	0	0	0	4	1	0	0	0	.000	0	0--	—	0.00
1990 Los Angeles	NL	16	0	0	4	10.2	46	7	5	5	1	0	0	0	8	4	6	1	0	0	0	.000	0	0-0	2	4.22
1991 Tex-Bal	AL	29	0	0	5	42	166	29	14	11	3	3	3	0	12	2	38	2	0	3	2	.600	0	1-1	4	2.36
1992 Baltimore	AL	6	0	0	1	3.1	14	3	3	0	0	0	0	0	1	0	3	0	0	0	0	.000	0	0-1	0	0.00
1993 Baltimore	AL	55	0	0	11	50.1	197	30	18	12	2	3	2	0	21	5	29	0	0	2	1	.667	0	2-3	14	2.15
1994 Baltimore	AL	38	0	0	10	20.1	100	32	15	15	4	0	3	0	11	2	18	1	0	1	0	1.000	0	0-2	10	6.64
1995 Cleveland	AL	42	0	0	9	50.1	206	40	22	21	7	1	2	2	17	0	41	2	1	3	3	.500	0	0-0	6	3.75
1996 Cle-SF		67	0	0	13	50.1	218	44	22	16	5	3	1	1	27	7	38	3	0	6	1	.857	0	0-4	10	2.86
1997 San Francisco	NL	63	0	0	11	49.1	242	73	44	39	6	4	2	4	25	4	26	5	0	3	1	.750	0	0-0	9	7.11
1998 SF-Cle		38	0	0	9	39.1	174	47	24	23	5	4	1	1	12	6	27	2	0	1	3	.250	0	0-3	6	5.26
1999 Phi-Cle		54	0	0	12	36.1	173	50	22	19	3	1	1	3	18	2	22	4	1	2	1	.667	0	1-2	12	4.71
1991 Texas	AL	5	0	0	2	6	31	10	4	3	0	1	0	0	3	0	4	0	0	0	0	.000	0	1-1	0	4.50
Baltimore	AL	24	0	0	3	36	135	19	10	8	3	3	2	0	9	2	34	2	0	3	2	.600	0	0-0	4	2.00
1996 Cleveland	AL	32	0	0	8	26.2	121	29	15	9	3	0	1	0	14	4	19	2	0	4	0	1.000	0	0-1	5	3.04
San Francisco	NL	35	0	0	5	23.2	97	15	7	7	2	3	0	1	13	3	19	1	0	2	1	.667	0	0-3	5	2.66
1998 San Francisco	NL	26	0	0	8	32.1	140	38	20	19	5	4	1	0	9	5	16	2	0	1	3	.250	0	0-2	3	5.29
Cleveland	AL	12	0	0	1	7	34	9	4	4	0	0	0	1	3	1	11	0	0	0	0	.000	0	0-1	3	5.14
1999 Philadelphia	NL	51	0	0	12	35.1	166	48	20	17	3	1	0	3	15	1	22	4	1	1	1	.500	0	1-2	12	4.33
Cleveland	AL	3	0	0	0	1	7	2	2	2	0	0	0	0	3	1	0	0	0	1	0	1.000	0	0-0	0	18.00
10 ML YEARS		408	0	0	85	352.1	1536	355	189	161	36	19	15	11	152	32	248	20	2	21	12	.636	0	4-16	73	4.11

Bo Porter

Bats: R **Throws:** R **Pos:** LF-16; PH/PR-11; CF-5; RF-3   **Ht:** 6'2" **Wt:** 195 **Born:** 7/5/72 **Age:** 27

Year Team	Lg	G	AB	H	2B	3B	HR	(Hm	Rd)	TB	R	RBI	TBB	IBB	SO	HBP	SH	SF	SB	CS	SB%	GDP	Avg	OBP	SLG
1994 Peoria	A	66	221	60	11	2	6	—	—	93	40	29	24	0	59	2	6	4	6	5	.55	5	.271	.348	.421
1995 Daytona	A+	113	336	73	12	2	3	—	—	98	54	19	32	0	104	0	4	3	22	10	.69	5	.217	.287	.292
1996 Daytona	A+	20	63	11	4	1	0	—	—	17	9	6	6	0	24	0	0	2	5	1	.83	0	.175	.239	.270
Rockford	A	105	378	91	22	3	7	—	—	140	83	44	72	1	107	1	3	4	30	14	.68	5	.241	.360	.370
1997 Daytona	A+	122	440	135	20	6	17	—	—	218	87	65	61	1	115	3	1	3	23	13	.64	8	.307	.393	.495
Orlando	AA	8	31	8	1	0	1	—	—	12	4	3	0	0	11	1	0	0	1	1	.00	1	.258	.281	.387
1998 West Tenn	AA	125	464	134	26	11	10	—	—	212	91	68	82	4	117	6	3	5	50	17	.75	9	.289	.399	.457

Year Team	Lg	G	AB	H	2B	3B	HR	(Hm	Rd)	TB	R	RBI	TBB	IBB	SO	HBP	SH	SF	SB	CS	SB%	GDP	Avg	OBP	SLG
Iowa	AAA	4	11	4	1	0	0	—	—	5	2	3	4	0	4	0	0	0	1	2	.33	0	.364	.533	.455
1999 Iowa	AAA	111	414	121	24	2	27	—	—	230	86	64	65	0	121	8	1	3	15	17	.47	7	.292	.396	.556
1999 Chicago	NL	24	26	5	1	0	0	(0	0)	6	2	0	2	0	13	0	1	0	0	0	.00	1	.192	.250	.231

Mark Portugal

Pitches: Right **Bats:** Right **Pos:** SP-27; RP-4

Ht: 6'0" **Wt:** 215 **Born:** 10/30/62 **Age:** 37

Year Team	Lg	G	GS	CG	GF	IP	BFP	H	R	ER	HR	SH	SF	HB	TBB	IBB	SO	WP	Bk	W	L	Pct.	ShO	Sv-Op	Hld	ERA
1985 Minnesota	AL	6	4	0	0	24.1	105	24	16	15	3	0	2	0	14	0	12	1	1	1	3	.250	0	0-0	1	5.55
1986 Minnesota	AL	27	15	3	7	112.2	481	112	56	54	10	5	3	1	50	1	67	5	0	6	10	.375	0	1-2	2	4.31
1987 Minnesota	AL	13	7	0	3	44	204	58	40	38	13	0	1	1	24	1	28	2	0	1	3	.250	0	0-1	0	7.77
1988 Minnesota	AL	26	0	0	9	57.2	242	60	30	29	11	2	3	1	17	1	31	2	2	3	3	.500	0	3-4	0	4.53
1989 Houston	NL	20	15	2	1	108	440	91	34	33	7	8	1	2	37	0	86	3	0	7	1	.875	1	0-0	1	2.75
1990 Houston	NL	32	32	1	0	196.2	831	187	90	79	21	7	6	4	67	4	136	6	0	11	10	.524	0	0-0	0	3.62
1991 Houston	NL	32	27	1	3	168.1	710	163	91	84	19	6	6	2	59	5	120	4	1	10	12	.455	0	1-2	1	4.49
1992 Houston	NL	18	16	1	0	101.1	405	76	32	30	7	5	1	1	41	3	62	1	1	6	3	.667	0	0-0	0	2.66
1993 Houston	NL	33	33	1	0	208	876	194	75	64	10	11	3	4	77	3	131	9	2	18	4	**.818**	1	0-0	0	2.77
1994 San Francisco	NL	21	21	1	0	137.1	580	135	68	60	17	6	4	6	45	2	87	5	0	10	8	.556	0	0-0	0	3.93
1995 SF-Cin	NL	31	31	1	0	181.2	775	185	91	81	17	9	1	4	56	2	96	7	0	11	10	.524	0	0-0	0	4.01
1996 Cincinnati	NL	27	26	1	0	156	646	146	77	69	20	7	6	2	42	2	93	6	0	8	9	.471	0	0-0	0	3.98
1997 Philadelphia	NL	3	3	0	0	13.2	60	17	8	7	0	1	1	0	5	0	2	0	0	2	2	.000	0	0-0	0	4.61
1998 Philadelphia	NL	26	26	3	0	166.1	704	186	88	82	26	8	2	4	32	2	104	4	0	10	5	.667	0	0-0	0	4.44
1999 Boston	AL	31	27	1	1	150.1	667	179	100	92	28	3	6	4	41	1	79	2	0	7	12	.368	0	0-0	0	5.51
1995 San Francisco	NL	17	17	1	0	104	443	106	56	48	10	5	0	2	34	2	63	2	0	5	5	.500	0	0-0	0	4.15
Cincinnati	NL	14	14	0	0	77.2	330	79	35	33	7	4	1	2	22	0	33	5	0	6	5	.545	0	0-0	0	3.82
15 ML YEARS		346	283	16	24	1826.1	7726	1813	896	817	209	78	46	36	607	27	1134	57	7	109	95	.534	4	5-9	4	4.03

Mike Porzio

Pitches: Left **Bats:** Left **Pos:** RP-16

Ht: 6'3" **Wt:** 208 **Born:** 8/20/72 **Age:** 27

Year Team	Lg	G	GS	CG	GF	IP	BFP	H	R	ER	HR	SH	SF	HB	TBB	IBB	SO	WP	Bk	W	L	Pct.	ShO	Sv-Op	Hld	ERA
1993 Cubs	R	10	8	0	2	42.1	200	42	26	18	1	3	2	3	30	0	30	1	2	1	3	.250	0	0--	0	3.83
1994 Cubs	R	7	0	0	6	13.2	64	19	10	9	0	0	0	1	6	0	5	0	0	0	3	.000	0	1--	0	5.93
1995 Mobile	IND	16	2	0	4	28.1	131	32	19	17	2	4	1	3	13	2	15	2	0	0	3	.000	0	0--	0	5.40
Ogden	R+	8	8	2	0	48	220	66	39	34	4	0	3	2	15	0	26	6	0	4	3	.571	0	0--	0	6.38
1996 Tennessee	IND	15	15	3	0	98.2	428	94	55	40	9	2	4	9	30	1	54	4	0	7	4	.636	0	0--	0	3.65
1997 Sioux City	IND	27	5	1	6	61.1	284	75	32	29	6	0	3	5	27	1	63	2	0	2	2	.500	1	0--	0	4.26
1998 Danville	A+	26	11	1	8	97	384	74	34	27	7	5	3	1	30	5	95	1	0	3	2	.600	0	2--	0	2.51
Salem	A+	7	7	0	0	42.1	173	40	20	13	6	1	0	2	12	0	46	1	0	2	3	.400	0	0--	0	2.76
1999 Colo Sprngs	AAA	35	0	0	6	42.2	198	44	16	16	5	3	0	3	30	4	33	4	1	5	1	.833	0	0--	0	3.38
1999 Colorado	NL	16	0	0	3	14.2	75	21	14	14	1	0	0	0	10	0	10	0	0	0	0	.000	0	0-0	0	8.59

Jorge Posada

Bats: B **Throws:** R **Pos:** C-109; PH/PR-12; DH-1; 1B-1

Ht: 6'2" **Wt:** 205 **Born:** 8/17/71 **Age:** 28

Year Team	Lg	G	AB	H	2B	3B	HR	(Hm	Rd)	TB	R	RBI	TBB	IBB	SO	HBP	SH	SF	SB	CS	SB%	GDP	Avg	OBP	SLG
1995 New York	AL	1	0	0	0	0	0	(0	0)	0	0	0	0	0	0	0	0	0	0	0	.00	0	.000	.000	.000
1996 New York	AL	8	14	1	0	0	0	(0	0)	1	1	0	1	0	6	0	0	0	0	0	.00	1	.071	.133	.071
1997 New York	AL	60	188	47	12	0	6	(2	4)	77	29	25	30	2	33	3	1	2	1	2	.33	2	.250	.359	.410
1998 New York	AL	111	358	96	23	0	17	(6	11)	170	56	63	47	7	92	0	0	4	0	1	.00	14	.268	.350	.475
1999 New York	AL	112	379	93	19	2	12	(4	8)	152	50	57	53	2	91	3	0	2	1	0	1.00	9	.245	.341	.401
5 ML YEARS		292	939	237	54	2	35	(12	23)	400	136	145	131	11	222	6	1	8	2	3	.40	26	.252	.345	.426

Scott Pose

Bats: L **Throws:** R **Pos:** PH/PR-56; DH-18; LF-18; RF-6; CF-1

Ht: 5'11" **Wt:** 190 **Born:** 2/11/67 **Age:** 33

Year Team	Lg	G	AB	H	2B	3B	HR	(Hm	Rd)	TB	R	RBI	TBB	IBB	SO	HBP	SH	SF	SB	CS	SB%	GDP	Avg	OBP	SLG
1993 Florida	NL	15	41	8	2	0	0	(0	0)	10	0	3	2	0	4	0	0	0	0	2	.00	0	.195	.233	.244
1997 New York	AL	54	87	19	2	1	0	(0	0)	23	19	5	9	0	11	0	0	0	3	1	.75	1	.218	.292	.264
1999 Kansas City	AL	86	137	39	3	0	0	(0	0)	42	27	12	21	1	22	0	0	1	6	2	.75	3	.285	.377	.307
3 ML YEARS		155	265	66	7	1	0	(0	0)	75	46	20	32	1	37	0	0	1	9	5	.64	4	.249	.329	.283

Lou Pote

Pitches: Right **Bats:** Right **Pos:** RP-20

Ht: 6'3" **Wt:** 190 **Born:** 8/27/71 **Age:** 28

Year Team	Lg	G	GS	CG	GF	IP	BFP	H	R	ER	HR	SH	SF	HB	TBB	IBB	SO	WP	Bk	W	L	Pct.	ShO	Sv-Op	Hld	ERA
1991 Giants	R	8	8	0	0	42.1	184	38	23	12	0	1	0	1	18	0	41	5	0	2	3	.400	0	0--	—	2.55
Everett	A-	5	4	0	0	28.2	117	24	8	8	2	0	1	2	7	0	26	2	0	2	0	1.000	0	0--	—	2.51
1992 Shreveport	AA	20	3	0	9	37.2	146	20	7	4	1	3	1	1	15	2	26	3	0	4	2	.667	0	0--	—	0.96
San Jose	A+	4	3	0	1	9.2	46	11	5	5	0	1	1	0	7	0	8	3	0	1	1	.000	0	0--	—	4.66
1993 Shreveport	AA	19	19	0	0	108.1	458	111	53	49	10	1	3	1	45	1	81	3	1	8	7	.533	0	0--	—	4.07

Year Team	Lg	G	GS	CG	GF	IP	BFP	H	R	ER	HR	SH	SF	HB	TBB	IBB	SO	WP	Bk	W	L	Pct.	ShO	Sv-Op	Hld	ERA
1994 Giants	R	4	4	0	0	19.2	73	9	0	0	1	0	0	0	6	0	30	0	0	1	0	1.000	0	0--	—	0.00
Shreveport	AA	5	5	0	0	28.2	122	31	11	9	2	2	2	0	7	0	15	1	1	2	2	.500	0	0--	—	2.83
1995 San Jose	AA	28	0	0	11	50.2	226	53	41	30	8	4	1	0	26	1	30	4	0	2	2	.500	0	3--	—	5.33
Harrisburg	AA	9	4	0	2	28.1	123	32	17	17	.3	0	2	1	7	0	24	1	0	1	0	1.000	0	0--	—	5.40
1996 Harrisburg	AA	25	18	0	3	104.2	467	114	66	59	15	3	2	2	48	2	61	8	0	1	7	.125	0	1--	—	5.07
1997 Arkansas	AA	7	3	0	1	23.1	94	15	10	4	1	1	0	0	8	0	21	2	0	0	0	.000	0	0--	—	1.54
1998 Midland	AA	32	19	6	7	154.1	700	194	110	91	18	5	6	6	54	1	117	8	0	8	10	.444	1	0--	—	5.31
1999 Edmonton	AAA	24	23	3	1	150	637	171	80	75	19	2	2	2	41	0	118	6	0	7	9	.438	0	0--	—	4.50
1999 Anaheim	AL	20	0	0	10	29.1	118	23	9	7	1	1	0	0	12	1	20	1	0	1	1	.500	0	3-3	3	2.15

Dante Powell

Bats: Right **Throws:** Right **Pos:** PH/PR-12; CF-8; RF-7   **Ht:** 6'2" **Wt:** 185 **Born:** 8/25/73 **Age:** 26

Year Team	Lg	G	AB	H	2B	3B	HR	(Hm	Rd)	TB	R	RBI	TBB	IBB	SO	HBP	SH	SF	SB	CS	SB%	GDP	Avg	OBP	SLG
1994 Everett	A-	41	165	51	15	1	5	—	—	83	31	25	19	1	47	4	0	2	27	1	.96	1	.309	.389	.503
San Jose	A+	1	4	2	0	1	0	—	—	4	0	0	0	0	1	0	0	0	0	0	.00	0	.500	.500	1.000
1995 San Jose	A+	135	505	125	23	8	10	—	—	194	74	70	46	2	131	3	1	4	43	12	.78	8	.248	.312	.384
Phoenix	AAA	2	8	2	0	1	0	—	—	4	0	0	0	2	0	3	0	0	0	1	.00	0	.250	.400	.500
1996 Shreveport	AA	135	508	142	27	2	21	—	—	236	92	78	72	4	92	3	1	2	43	23	.65	6	.280	.371	.465
1997 Phoenix	AAA	108	452	109	24	4	11	—	—	174	91	42	52	1	105	3	3	0	34	10	.77	9	.241	.323	.385
1998 Fresno	AAA	134	448	103	17	3	14	—	—	168	83	52	71	1	138	14	3	4	41	9	.82	6	.230	.350	.375
1999 Tucson	AAA	51	187	62	14	2	7	—	—	101	29	30	14	0	38	1	3	0	22	6	.79	0	.332	.381	.540
1997 San Francisco	NL	27	39	12	1	0	1	(1	0)	16	8	3	4	0	11	0	1	0	1	1	.50	0	.308	.372	.410
1998 San Francisco	NL	8	4	2	0	0	1	(1	0)	5	2	1	3	0	0	0	0	0	0	0	.00	0	.500	.714	1.250
1999 Arizona	NL	22	25	4	3	0	0	(1	0)	7	4	1	2	0	6	0	1	0	2	1	.67	0	.160	.222	.280
3 ML YEARS		57	68	18	4	0	2	(2	0)	28	14	5	9	0	17	0	2	0	3	2	.60	0	.265	.351	.412

Jay Powell

Pitches: Right **Bats:** Right **Pos:** RP-67   **Ht:** 6'4" **Wt:** 225 **Born:** 1/9/72 **Age:** 28

Year Team	Lg	G	GS	CG	GF	IP	BFP	H	R	ER	HR	SH	SF	HB	TBB	IBB	SO	WP	Bk	W	L	Pct.	ShO	Sv-Op	Hld	ERA
1995 Florida	NL	9	0	0	1	8.1	38	7	2	1	0	1	0	2	6	1	4	0	0	0	0	.000	0	0-0	2	1.08
1996 Florida	NL	67	0	0	16	71.1	321	71	44	36	5	2	1	4	36	1	52	3	0	3	5	.571	0	2-5	10	4.54
1997 Florida	NL	74	0	0	23	79.2	337	71	35	29	3	6	4	4	30	3	65	3	0	7	2	.778	0	2-4	24	3.28
1998 Fla-Hou	NL	62	0	0	35	70.1	302	58	28	26	6	3	1	3	37	9	62	1	0	7	7	.500	0	7-11	3	3.33
1999 Houston	NL	67	0	0	26	75	341	82	38	36	3	5	2	3	40	4	77	5	0	4	5	.556	0	4-7	16	4.32
1998 Florida	NL	33	0	0	26	36.1	165	36	19	17	5	3	1	2	22	6	24	1	0	4	4	.500	0	3-6	0	4.21
Houston		29	0	0	9	34	137	22	9	9	1	0	0	1	15	3	38	0	0	3	3	.500	0	4-5	3	2.38
5 ML YEARS		279	0	0	101	304.2	1339	289	144	128	17	17	8	16	149	18	260	12	0	23	16	.590	0	15-27	55	3.78

Jeremy Powell

Pitches: Right **Bats:** Right **Pos:** SP-17   **Ht:** 6'6" **Wt:** 225 **Born:** 6/18/76 **Age:** 24

Year Team	Lg	G	GS	CG	GF	IP	BFP	H	R	ER	HR	SH	SF	HB	TBB	IBB	SO	WP	Bk	W	L	Pct.	ShO	Sv-Op	Hld	ERA
1994 Expos	R	9	9	1	0	43	171	37	16	14	1	0	1	2	14	0	36	2	2	2	2	.500	0	0--	—	2.93
1995 Albany	A	1	1	0	0	5.2	20	4	1	1	0	0	0	0	1	0	6	1	0	1	0	1.000	0	0--	—	1.59
Vermont	A-	15	15	0	0	87	373	88	48	42	5	2	2	6	34	1	47	6	2	5	5	.500	0	0--	—	4.34
1996 Delmarva	A	27	27	1	0	157.2	665	127	68	53	9	1	6	15	66	0	109	11	4	12	9	.571	0	0--	—	3.03
1997 Wst Plm Bch	A+	26	26	1	0	155	675	162	75	52	3	9	5	12	62	0	121	12	2	9	10	.474	0	0--	—	3.02
1998 Oklahoma	AAA	1	0	0	0	2	13	3	5	3	1	0	0	1	2	0	4	0	0	0	0	.000	0	0--	—	13.50
Harrisburg	AA	22	22	1	0	131.2	546	115	54	44	13	7	2	9	37	0	77	6	1	9	7	.563	0	0--	—	3.01
1999 Ottawa	AAA	16	16	0	0	91	382	85	37	30	5	3	3	4	37	0	72	6	0	3	5	.375	0	0--	—	2.97
1998 Montreal	NL	7	6	0	1	25	112	27	25	22	5	2	2	4	11	0	14	0	0	1	5	.167	0	0-0	0	7.92
1999 Montreal	NL	17	17	0	0	97	438	113	60	51	14	9	3	8	44	2	44	4	1	4	8	.333	0	0-0	0	4.73
2 ML YEARS		24	23	0	1	122	550	140	85	73	19	11	5	12	55	2	58	4	1	5	13	.278	0	0-0	0	5.39

Todd Pratt

Bats: R **Throws:** R **Pos:** C-52; PH/PR-28; 1B-1; LF-1   **Ht:** 6'3" **Wt:** 230 **Born:** 2/9/67 **Age:** 33

Year Team	Lg	G	AB	H	2B	3B	HR	(Hm	Rd)	TB	R	RBI	TBB	IBB	SO	HBP	SH	SF	SB	CS	SB%	GDP	Avg	OBP	SLG
1992 Philadelphia	NL	16	46	13	1	0	2	(2	0)	20	6	10	4	0	12	0	0	0	0	0	.00	2	.283	.340	.435
1993 Philadelphia	NL	33	87	25	6	0	5	(4	1)	46	8	13	5	0	19	1	1	1	0	0	.00	2	.287	.330	.529
1994 Philadelphia	NL	28	102	20	6	1	2	(1	1)	34	10	9	12	0	29	0	0	1	0	1	.00	0	.196	.281	.333
1995 Chicago	NL	25	60	8	2	0	0	(0	0)	10	3	4	6	1	21	0	0	1	0	0	.00	3	.133	.209	.167
1997 New York	NL	39	106	30	6	0	2	(1	1)	42	19	19	13	0	32	2	0	0	0	1	.00	1	.283	.372	.396
1998 New York	NL	41	69	19	9	1	2	(1	1)	36	9	18	2	0	20	0	0	0	0	0	.00	0	.275	.296	.522
1999 New York	NL	71	140	41	4	0	3	(1	2)	54	18	21	15	0	32	3	0	2	2	0	1.00	1	.293	.369	.386
7 ML YEARS		253	610	156	34	2	16	(10	6)	242	66	94	57	1	165	6	1	4	2	2	.50	10	.256	.323	.397

Tom Prince

Bats: Right **Throws:** Right **Pos:** C-4 **Ht:** 5'11" **Wt:** 206 **Born:** 8/13/64 **Age:** 35

Year Team	Lg	G	AB	H	2B	3B	HR	(Hm	Rd)	TB	R	RBI	TBB	IBB	SO	HBP	SH	SF	SB	CS	SB%	GDP	Avg	OBP	SLG
1999 Phillies *	R	7	21	5	3	0	0	—	—	8	3	3	4	1	0	1	0	0	0	0	.00	0	.238	.385	.381
Clearwater *	A+	9	33	12	0	0	2	—	—	18	5	9	3	0	3	1	1	0	1	0	1.00	1	.364	.432	.545
Scranton-WB *	AAA	7	22	2	0	0	1	—	—	5	2	1	3	0	5	1	1	0	1	0	1.00	0	.091	.231	.227
1987 Pittsburgh	NL	4	9	2	1	0	1	(0	1)	6	1	2	0	0	2	0	0	0	0	0	.00	0	.222	.222	.667
1988 Pittsburgh	NL	29	74	13	2	0	0	(0	0)	15	3	6	4	0	15	0	2	0	0	0	.00	5	.176	.218	.203
1989 Pittsburgh	NL	21	52	7	4	0	0	(0	0)	11	1	5	6	1	12	0	0	1	1	1	.50	1	.135	.220	.212
1990 Pittsburgh	NL	4	10	1	0	0	0	(0	0)	1	1	0	1	0	2	0	0	0	1	0	.00	0	.100	.182	.100
1991 Pittsburgh	NL	26	34	9	3	0	1	(0	1)	15	4	2	7	0	3	1	0	0	0	0	.00	3	.265	.405	.441
1992 Pittsburgh	NL	27	44	4	2	0	0	(0	0)	6	1	5	6	0	9	0	0	2	1	1	.50	0	.091	.192	.136
1993 Pittsburgh	NL	66	179	35	14	0	2	(2	0)	55	14	24	13	2	38	7	2	3	1	1	.50	5	.196	.272	.307
1994 Los Angeles	NL	3	6	2	0	0	0	(0	0)	2	2	1	1	0	3	0	0	0	0	0	.00	0	.333	.429	.333
1995 Los Angeles	NL	18	40	8	2	1	1	(0	1)	15	3	4	4	0	10	0	0	0	0	0	.00	0	.200	.273	.375
1996 Los Angeles	NL	40	64	19	6	0	1	(0	1)	28	6	11	6	2	15	2	3	2	0	0	.00	0	.297	.365	.438
1997 Los Angeles	NL	47	100	22	5	0	3	(2	1)	36	17	14	5	0	15	3	4	1	0	0	.00	2	.220	.275	.360
1998 Los Angeles	NL	37	81	15	5	1	0	(0	0)	22	7	5	7	1	24	2	2	0	0	0	.00	1	.185	.267	.272
1999 Philadelphia	NL	4	6	1	0	0	0	(0	0)	1	1	0	1	0	1	0	0	0	0	0	.00	1	.167	.286	.167
13 ML YEARS		326	699	138	44	2	9	(4	5)	213	61	79	61	6	149	15	13	9	3	4	.43	19	.197	.273	.305

Chris Pritchett

Bats: Left **Throws:** Right **Pos:** 1B-15; DH-5; PH/PR-5 **Ht:** 6'4" **Wt:** 212 **Born:** 1/31/70 **Age:** 30

Year Team	Lg	G	AB	H	2B	3B	HR	(Hm	Rd)	TB	R	RBI	TBB	IBB	SO	HBP	SH	SF	SB	CS	SB%	GDP	Avg	OBP	SLG
1991 Boise	A-	70	255	68	10	3	9	—	—	111	41	50	47	3	41	2	0	3	1	0	1.00	7	.267	.381	.435
1992 Quad City	A	128	448	130	19	1	13	—	—	190	79	72	71	6	88	5	2	5	9	4	.69	7	.290	.389	.424
1993 Midland	AA	127	464	143	30	6	2	—	—	191	61	66	61	2	72	2	6	7	5	7	.30	17	.308	.386	.412
1994 Midland	AA	127	460	142	25	4	6	—	—	193	86	91	92	9	87	2	3	7	5	3	.63	8	.309	.421	.420
1995 Vancouver	AAA	123	434	120	27	4	8	—	—	179	66	53	56	6	79	5	2	1	2	3	.40	7	.276	.365	.412
1996 Vancouver	AAA	130	485	143	39	1	16	—	—	232	78	73	71	11	96	6	0	6	5	4	.56	7	.295	.387	.478
1997 Vancouver	AAA	109	383	107	30	3	7	—	—	164	60	47	42	6	72	5	5	2	5	3	.63	9	.279	.356	.428
1998 Vancouver	AAA	104	374	97	21	1	7	—	—	141	42	41	37	3	72	0	3	5	2	2	.50	14	.259	.322	.377
1999 Edmonton	AAA	96	348	97	15	1	12	—	—	150	60	45	47	3	70	3	1	2	1	1	.50	7	.279	.368	.431
1996 California	AL	5	13	2	0	0	0	(0	0)	2	1	1	0	0	3	0	0	0	0	0	.00	0	.154	.154	.154
1998 Anaheim	AL	31	80	23	2	1	2	(0	2)	33	12	8	4	0	16	0	0	1	2	0	1.00	3	.288	.321	.412
1999 Anaheim	AL	20	45	7	1	0	1	(1	0)	11	3	2	2	0	9	0	1	1	1	1	.50	0	.156	.188	.244
3 ML YEARS		56	138	32	3	1	3	(1	2)	46	16	11	6	0	28	0	1	2	3	1	.75	3	.232	.262	.333

Bill Pulsipher

Pitches: Left **Bats:** Left **Pos:** SP-16; RP-3 **Ht:** 6'3" **Wt:** 200 **Born:** 10/9/73 **Age:** 26

Year Team	Lg	G	GS	CG	GF	IP	BFP	H	R	ER	HR	SH	SF	HB	TBB	IBB	SO	WP	Bk	W	L	Pct.	ShO	Sv-Op	Hld	ERA
1999 Louisville *	AAA	6	6	0	0	27.1	121	22	14	13	1	2	0	0	19	0	21	1	0	0	2	.000	0	0--	—	4.28
1995 New York	NL	17	17	2	0	126.2	530	122	58	56	11	2	1	4	45	0	81	2	1	5	7	.417	0	0-0	0	3.98
1998 NYM-Mil	NL	26	11	0	2	72.1	320	86	41	41	8	4	4	1	31	4	51	2	2	3	4	.429	0	0-1	2	5.10
1999 Milwaukee	NL	19	16	0	1	87.1	398	100	65	58	19	6	4	2	36	2	42	4	0	5	6	.455	0	0-0	0	5.98
1998 New York	NL	15	1	0	1	14.1	68	23	11	11	2	1	0	0	5	1	13	0	0	0	0	.000	0	0-1	2	6.91
Milwaukee	NL	11	10	0	1	58	252	63	30	30	6	3	4	1	26	3	38	2	2	3	4	.429	0	0-0	0	4.66
3 ML YEARS		62	44	2	3	286.1	1248	308	164	155	38	12	9	7	112	6	174	8	3	13	17	.433	0	0-1	2	4.87

Paul Quantrill

Pitches: Right **Bats:** Left **Pos:** RP-41 **Ht:** 6'1" **Wt:** 180 **Born:** 11/3/68 **Age:** 31

Year Team	Lg	G	GS	CG	GF	IP	BFP	H	R	ER	HR	SH	SF	HB	TBB	IBB	SO	WP	Bk	W	L	Pct.	ShO	Sv-Op	Hld	ERA
1999 Dunedin *	A+	5	4	0	0	6	22	5	3	3	1	0	0	0	1	0	2	0	0	0	1	.000	0	0--	—	4.50
Syracuse *	AAA	2	0	0	0	2	6	1	0	0	0	0	0	0	1	0	1	0	0	0	0	.000	0	0--	—	0.00
1992 Boston	AL	27	0	0	10	49.1	213	55	18	12	1	4	2	1	15	5	24	1	0	2	3	.400	0	1-5	3	2.19
1993 Boston	AL	49	14	1	8	138	594	151	73	60	13	4	2	2	44	14	66	0	1	6	12	.333	1	1-2	3	3.91
1994 Bos-Phi		35	1	0	9	53	236	64	31	29	7	5	3	5	15	4	28	0	2	3	3	.500	0	1-4	3	4.92
1995 Philadelphia	NL	33	29	0	1	179.1	784	212	102	93	20	9	6	6	44	3	103	0	3	11	12	.478	0	0-0	0	4.67
1996 Toronto	AL	38	20	0	7	134.1	609	172	90	81	27	5	7	2	51	3	86	1	1	5	14	.263	0	0-2	1	5.43
1997 Toronto	AL	77	0	0	29	88	373	103	25	19	5	5	3	1	17	3	56	1	0	6	7	.462	0	5-10	16	1.94
1998 Toronto	AL	82	0	0	32	80	345	88	26	23	5	7	4	3	22	6	59	1	0	3	4	.429	0	7-14	27	2.59
1999 Toronto	AL	41	0	0	13	48.2	212	53	19	18	5	1	2	4	17	1	28	0	0	3	2	.600	0	0-4	8	3.33
1994 Boston	AL	17	0	0	4	23	101	25	10	9	4	2	2	2	5	1	15	0	0	1	1	.500	0	0-2	2	3.52
Philadelphia	NL	18	1	0	5	30	135	39	21	20	3	3	1	3	10	3	13	0	2	2	2	.500	0	1-2	1	6.00
8 ML YEARS		382	64	1	109	770.2	3366	898	384	335	83	40	29	24	225	39	450	4	7	39	57	.406	1	15-41	61	3.91

Mark Quinn

Bats: R **Throws:** R **Pos:** LF-15; DH-1; RF-1; PH/PR-1   **Ht:** 6'1" **Wt:** 175 **Born:** 5/21/74 **Age:** 26

Year Team	Lg	G	AB	H	2B	3B	HR	(Hm	Rd)	TB	R	RBI	TBB	IBB	SO	HBP	SH	SF	SB	CS	SB%	GDP	Avg	OBP	SLG
1995 Spokane	A-	44	162	46	12	2	6	—	—	80	28	37	15	0	28	5	0	3	0	1	.00	5	.284	.357	.494
1996 Lansing	A	113	437	132	23	3	9	—	—	188	63	71	43	2	54	5	0	6	14	8	.64	12	.302	.367	.430
1997 Wilmington	A+	87	299	92	22	3	16	—	—	168	51	71	42	4	47	8	0	6	3	2	.60	10	.308	.400	.562
Wichita	AA	26	96	36	13	0	2	—	—	55	26	19	15	0	19	3	0	0	1	1	.50	2	.375	.474	.573
1998 Wichita	AA	100	372	130	26	6	16	—	—	216	82	84	43	1	54	10	0	7	4	1	.80	5	.349	.424	.581
1999 Omaha	AAA	107	428	154	27	0	25	—	—	256	67	84	28	3	69	10	0	1	7	9	.44	9	.360	.409	.598
1999 Kansas City	AL	17	60	20	4	1	6	(2	4)	44	11	18	4	0	11	1	0	0	1	0	1.00	1	.333	.385	.733

Scott Radinsky

Pitches: Left **Bats:** Left **Pos:** RP-43   **Ht:** 6'3" **Wt:** 215 **Born:** 3/3/68 **Age:** 32

Year Team	Lg	G	GS	CG	GF	IP	BFP	H	R	ER	HR	SH	SF	HB	TBB	IBB	SO	WP	Bk	W	L	Pct.	ShO	Sv-Op	Hld	ERA
1990 Chicago	AL	62	0	0	18	52.1	237	47	29	28	1	2	2	2	36	1	46	2	1	6	1	.857	0	4-5	10	4.82
1991 Chicago	AL	67	0	0	19	71.1	289	53	18	16	4	4	4	1	23	2	49	0	0	5	5	.500	0	8-15	15	2.02
1992 Chicago	AL	68	0	0	33	59.1	261	54	21	18	3	2	1	2	34	5	48	3	0	3	7	.300	0	15-23	16	2.73
1993 Chicago	AL	73	0	0	24	54.2	250	61	33	26	3	2	0	1	19	3	44	0	4	8	2	.800	0	4-5	12	4.28
1995 Chicago	AL	46	0	0	10	38	171	46	23	23	7	1	4	0	17	4	14	0	0	2	1	.667	0	1-3	8	5.45
1996 Los Angeles	NL	58	0	0	19	52.1	221	52	19	14	2	4	3	0	17	5	48	0	3	5	1	.833	0	1-4	7	2.41
1997 Los Angeles	NL	75	0	0	14	62.1	258	54	22	20	4	3	4	1	21	5	44	0	0	5	1	.833	0	3-5	26	2.89
1998 Los Angeles	NL	62	0	0	30	61.2	264	63	21	18	5	6	2	4	20	1	45	0	3	6	6	.500	0	13-24	8	2.63
1999 St. Louis	NL	43	0	0	13	27.2	126	27	16	15	2	2	5	1	18	3	17	3	1	2	1	.667	0	3-3	11	4.88
9 ML YEARS		554	0	0	180	479.2	2077	457	202	178	31	26	25	12	205	29	355	8	12	42	25	.627	0	52-87	113	3.34

Brad Radke

Pitches: Right **Bats:** Right **Pos:** SP-33   **Ht:** 6'2" **Wt:** 188 **Born:** 10/27/72 **Age:** 27

Year Team	Lg	G	GS	CG	GF	IP	BFP	H	R	ER	HR	SH	SF	HB	TBB	IBB	SO	WP	Bk	W	L	Pct.	ShO	Sv-Op	Hld	ERA
1995 Minnesota	AL	29	28	2	0	181	772	195	112	107	32	2	9	4	47	0	75	4	0	11	14	.440	0	0-0	0	5.32
1996 Minnesota	AL	35	35	3	0	232	973	231	125	115	40	5	4	6	57	2	148	1	0	11	16	.407	0	0-0	0	4.46
1997 Minnesota	AL	35	35	4	0	239.2	989	238	114	103	28	2	9	3	48	2	174	1	1	20	10	.667	0	0-0	0	3.87
1998 Minnesota	AL	32	32	5	0	213.2	904	238	109	102	23	9	3	9	43	1	146	3	1	12	14	.462	1	0-0	0	4.30
1999 Minnesota	AL	33	33	4	0	218.2	910	239	97	91	28	5	5	1	44	0	121	4	0	12	14	.462	0	0-0	0	3.75
5 ML YEARS		164	163	18	0	1085	4548	1141	557	518	151	23	32	21	239	4	664	13	2	66	68	.493	3	0-0	0	4.30

Rob Radlosky

Pitches: Right **Bats:** Right **Pos:** RP-7   **Ht:** 6'2" **Wt:** 192 **Born:** 1/7/74 **Age:** 26

Year Team	Lg	G	GS	CG	GF	IP	BFP	H	R	ER	HR	SH	SF	HB	TBB	IBB	SO	WP	Bk	W	L	Pct.	ShO	Sv-Op	Hld	ERA
1994 Twins	R	11	11	0	0	56.1	234	54	28	21	1	0	3	3	19	0	52	4	7	3	4	.429	0	0--	—	3.36
1995 Fort Wayne	A	30	18	1	5	120.2	522	111	64	54	11	7	5	11	55	2	102	5	2	11	8	.579	0	0--	—	4.03
1996 Fort Myers	A+	28	16	1	5	104	467	116	70	63	11	2	3	9	46	0	80	10	0	4	6	.400	1	1--	—	5.45
1997 Fort Myers	A+	23	22	3	1	128.1	510	87	42	37	10	5	4	5	37	0	109	2	0	9	5	.643	1	0--	—	2.59
1998 New Britain	AA	27	19	0	0	132	552	127	61	59	16	6	2	6	37	0	117	7	0	10	3	.769	0	0--	—	4.02
1999 Salt Lake	AAA	22	20	1	1	101.1	440	98	49	44	12	2	4	6	38	1	68	2	0	4	6	.667	0	0--	—	3.91
1999 Minnesota	AL	7	0	0	2	8.2	45	15	12	12	7	0	0	1	4	0	3	1	0	0	1	.000	0	0-1	0	12.46

Steve Rain

Pitches: Right **Bats:** Right **Pos:** RP-16   **Ht:** 6'6" **Wt:** 250 **Born:** 6/2/75 **Age:** 25

Year Team	Lg	G	GS	CG	GF	IP	BFP	H	R	ER	HR	SH	SF	HB	TBB	IBB	SO	WP	Bk	W	L	Pct.	ShO	Sv-Op	Hld	ERA
1993 Cubs	R	10	6	0	3	37	162	37	26	16	0	1	1	2	17	0	29	5	1	1	3	.250	0	0--	—	3.89
1994 Huntington	R+	14	10	1	1	68	272	55	26	20	2	2	2	2	19	0	55	4	4	3	3	.500	1	0--	—	2.65
1995 Rockford	A	53	0	0	51	59.1	234	38	12	8	0	3	2	2	23	3	66	8	0	5	2	.714	0	23--	—	1.21
1996 Orlando	AA	35	0	0	29	38.2	163	32	15	11	4	0	0	3	12	1	48	2	1	1	0	1.000	0	10--	—	2.56
Iowa	AAA	26	0	0	26	26	103	17	9	9	3	3	3	0	8	3	23	1	0	2	1	.667	0	10--	—	3.12
1997 Iowa	AAA	40	0	0	17	44.1	217	51	30	29	8	2	1	0	34	4	50	4	1	7	1	.875	0	1--	—	5.89
Orlando	AA	14	0	0	12	14.2	69	16	7	7	5	2	0	1	8	0	11	0	0	1	2	.333	0	4--	—	3.07
1998 Iowa	AAA	29	14	1	4	103.2	487	118	82	77	14	6	2	7	64	0	83	16	0	4	6	.400	0	0--	—	6.68
1999 West Tenn	AA	40	0	0	39	45.1	188	32	9	8	3	0	2	1	16	3	55	5	1	3	1	.750	0	24--	—	1.59
Iowa	AAA	8	0	0	7	9	38	7	2	2	1	0	0	0	4	0	9	0	0	1	0	1.000	0	2--	—	2.00
1999 Chicago	NL	16	0	0	5	14.2	79	28	17	15	1	3	1	1	7	0	12	1	0	0	1	.000	0	0-0	0	9.20

Tim Raines

Bats: B **Throws:** R **Pos:** LF-38; PH/PR-25; DH-3; CF-1   **Ht:** 5'8" **Wt:** 190 **Born:** 9/16/59 **Age:** 40

Year Team	Lg	G	AB	H	2B	3B	HR	(Hm	Rd)	TB	R	RBI	TBB	IBB	SO	HBP	SH	SF	SB	CS	SB%	GDP	Avg	OBP	SLG
1979 Montreal	NL	6	0	0	0	0	0	(0	0)	0	3	0	0	0	0	0	0	0	2	0	1.00	0	.000	.000	.000
1980 Montreal	NL	15	20	1	0	0	0	(0	0)	1	5	0	6	0	3	0	1	0	5	0	1.00	0	.050	.269	.050

Year Team	Lg	G	AB	H	2B	3B	HR	(Hm	Rd)	TB	R	RBI	TBB	IBB	SO	HBP	SH	SF	SB	CS	SB%	GDP	Avg	OBP	SLG
1981 Montreal	NL	88	313	95	13	7	5	(3	2)	137	61	37	45	5	31	2	0	3	71	11	.87	7	.304	.391	.438
1982 Montreal	NL	156	647	179	32	8	4	(1	3)	239	90	43	75	9	83	2	6	1	78	16	.83	6	.277	.353	.369
1983 Montreal	NL	156	615	183	32	8	11	(5	6)	264	133	71	97	9	70	2	2	4	90	14	.87	12	.298	.393	.429
1984 Montreal	NL	160	622	192	38	9	8	(2	6)	272	106	60	87	7	69	2	3	4	75	10	.88	7	.309	.393	.437
1985 Montreal	NL	150	575	184	30	13	11	(4	7)	273	115	41	81	13	60	3	3	3	70	9	.89	9	.320	.405	.475
1986 Montreal	NL	151	580	194	35	10	9	(4	5)	276	91	62	78	9	60	2	1	3	70	9	.89	6	.334	.413	.476
1987 Montreal	NL	139	530	175	34	8	18	(9	9)	279	123	68	90	26	52	4	0	3	50	5	.91	9	.330	.429	.526
1988 Montreal	NL	109	429	116	19	7	12	(5	7)	185	66	48	53	14	44	2	0	4	33	7	.83	8	.270	.350	.431
1989 Montreal	NL	145	517	148	29	6	9	(6	3)	216	76	60	93	18	48	3	0	5	41	9	.82	8	.286	.395	.418
1990 Montreal	NL	130	457	131	11	5	9	(6	3)	179	65	62	70	8	43	3	0	8	49	16	.75	9	.287	.379	.392
1991 Chicago	AL	155	609	163	20	6	5	(1	4)	210	102	50	83	9	68	5	9	3	45	6	.88	5	.268	.359	.345
1992 Chicago	AL	144	551	162	22	9	7	(4	3)	223	102	54	81	4	48	0	4	8	21	7	.75	7	.294	.380	.405
1993 Chicago	AL	115	415	127	16	4	16	(7	9)	199	75	54	64	4	35	3	2	2	21	7	.75	1	.306	.401	.480
1994 Chicago	AL	101	384	102	15	5	10	(5	5)	157	80	52	61	3	43	1	4	3	13	1	1.00	10	.266	.365	.409
1995 Chicago	AL	133	502	143	25	4	12	(6	6)	212	81	67	70	3	52	3	3	3	13	2	.87	8	.285	.374	.422
1996 New York	AL	59	201	57	10	0	9	(7	2)	94	45	33	34	1	29	1	0	1	10	1	.91	5	.284	.383	.468
1997 New York	AL	74	271	87	20	2	4	(3	1)	123	56	38	41	0	34	0	0	6	8	5	.62	4	.321	.403	.454
1998 New York	AL	109	321	93	13	1	5	(2	3)	123	53	47	55	1	49	3	0	3	8	3	.73	5	.290	.395	.383
1999 Oakland	AL	58	135	29	5	0	4	(2	2)	46	20	17	26	1	17	0	1	2	4	1	.80	5	.215	.337	.341
21 ML YEARS		2353	8694	2561	419	112	168	(82	86)	3708	1548	964	1290	144	938	41	39	72	807	146	.85	137	.295	.385	.427

Jason Rakers

Pitches: Right Bats: Right Pos: RP-1

Ht: 6'2" Wt: 200 Born: 6/29/73 Age: 27

Year Team	Lg	G	GS	CG	GF	IP	BFP	H	R	ER	HR	SH	SF	HB	TBB	IBB	SO	WP	Bk	W	L	Pct.	ShO	Sv-Op	Hld	ERA
1995 Watertown	A-	14	14	1	0	75	315	72	27	25	3	0	2	0	24	1	73	6	2	4	3	.571	1	0--	—	3.00
1996 Columbus	A	14	14	1	0	77.1	319	84	37	31	5	1	1	3	17	0	64	8	1	5	4	.556	1	0--	—	3.61
1997 Kinston	A+	17	17	2	0	102.2	405	93	41	35	10	1	0	1	18	0	105	2	1	8	5	.615	2	0--	—	3.07
Buffalo	AAA	1	1	0	0	7	26	5	0	0	0	0	0	0	1	0	3	0	1	1	0	1.000	1	0--	—	0.00
Akron	AA	7	7	1	0	41	168	36	21	20	3	1	2	4	11	0	31	1	0	1	4	.200	1	0--	—	4.39
1998 Akron	AA	5	5	0	0	31.1	130	35	10	9	2	2	1	0	7	0	27	2	0	3	1	.750	0	0--	—	2.59
Buffalo	AAA	21	21	1	0	126	542	134	70	64	13	2	6	8	38	0	89	7	1	8	6	.571	0	0--	—	4.57
1999 Buffalo	AAA	23	20	1	1	131.2	577	151	83	72	17	4	2	6	31	2	85	4	3	7	8	.467	0	0--	—	4.92
1998 Cleveland	AL	1	0	0	1	1	6	0	1	1	0	0	1	0	3	0	0	0	0	0	0	.000	0	0-0	0	9.00
1999 Cleveland	AL	1	0	0	0	2	9	2	1	1	1	0	0	0	1	0	0	0	0	0	0	.000	0	0-0	0	4.50
2 ML YEARS		2	0	0	1	3	15	2	2	2	1	0	1	0	4	0	0	0	0	0	0	.000	0	0-0	0	6.00

Alex Ramirez

Bats: R Throws: R Pos: RF-23; DH-14; PH/PR-9; LF-5; CF-1

Ht: 5'11" Wt: 190 Born: 10/3/74 Age: 25

Year Team	Lg	G	AB	H	2B	3B	HR	(Hm	Rd)	TB	R	RBI	TBB	IBB	SO	HBP	SH	SF	SB	CS	SB%	GDP	Avg	OBP	SLG
1993 Burlington	R+	64	252	68	14	4	13	—	—	129	44	54	13	1	52	4	0	3	12	8	.60	4	.270	.313	.512
Kinston	A+	3	12	2	0	0	0	—	—	2	0	1	0	0	5	0	0	0	0	1	.00	0	.167	.167	.167
1994 Columbus	A	125	458	115	23	3	18	—	—	198	64	57	26	0	100	4	0	4	7	5	.58	11	.251	.295	.432
1995 Bakersfield	A+	98	406	131	25	2	10	—	—	190	56	52	18	1	76	3	0	1	13	9	.59	9	.323	.355	.468
Canton-Akrn	AA	33	133	33	3	4	1	—	—	47	15	11	5	1	24	0	1	1	3	5	.38	5	.248	.273	.353
1996 Canton-Akrn	AA	131	513	169	28	12	14	—	—	263	79	85	16	1	74	3	1	1	18	10	.64	8	.329	.353	.513
1997 Buffalo	AAA	119	416	119	19	8	11	—	—	187	59	44	24	0	95	4	6	3	10	5	.67	9	.286	.329	.450
1998 Buffalo	AAA	121	521	156	21	8	34	—	—	295	94	103	16	4	101	5	0	4	6	4	.60	11	.299	.324	.566
1999 Buffalo	AAA	75	305	93	20	2	12	—	—	153	50	50	17	2	52	4	0	4	5	5	.50	0	.305	.345	.502
1998 Cleveland	AL	3	8	1	0	0	0	(0	0)	1	1	0	0	0	3	0	0	0	0	0	.00	0	.125	.125	.125
1999 Cleveland	AL	48	97	29	6	1	3	(2	1)	46	11	18	3	0	26	1	1	0	1	1	.50	1	.299	.327	.474
2 ML YEARS		51	105	30	6	1	3	(2	1)	47	12	18	3	0	29	1	1	0	1	1	.50	1	.286	.312	.448

Aramis Ramirez

Bats: Right Throws: Right Pos: 3B-17; PH/PR-1

Ht: 6'1" Wt: 215 Born: 6/25/78 Age: 22

Year Team	Lg	G	AB	H	2B	3B	HR	(Hm	Rd)	TB	R	RBI	TBB	IBB	SO	HBP	SH	SF	SB	CS	SB%	GDP	Avg	OBP	SLG
1996 Erie	A-	61	223	68	14	4	9	—	—	117	37	42	31	1	41	7	0	2	0	0	.00	7	.305	.403	.525
Augusta	A	6	20	4	1	0	1	—	—	8	3	2	1	0	7	2	0	0	2	0	.00	0	.200	.304	.400
1997 Lynchburg	A+	137	482	134	24	2	29	—	—	249	85	114	80	9	103	12	0	5	5	3	.63	12	.278	.390	.517
1998 Nashville	AAA	47	168	46	10	0	5	—	—	71	19	18	24	0	28	4	0	2	0	2	.00	3	.274	.374	.423
1999 Nashville	AAA	131	460	151	35	1	21	—	—	251	92	74	73	6	56	9	0	6	5	3	.63	11	.328	.425	.546
1998 Pittsburgh	NL	72	251	59	9	1	6	(3	3)	88	23	24	18	0	72	4	1	1	0	1	.00	0	.235	.296	.351
1999 Pittsburgh	NL	18	56	10	2	1	0	(0	0)	14	2	7	6	0	9	0	1	1	0	0	.00	3	.179	.254	.250
2 ML YEARS		90	307	69	11	2	6	(3	3)	102	25	31	24	0	81	4	2	2	0	1	.00	3	.225	.288	.332

Hector Ramirez

Pitches: Right Bats: Right Pos: RP-15

Ht: 6'3" Wt: 218 Born: 12/15/71 Age: 28

Year Team	Lg	G	GS	CG	GF	IP	BFP	H	R	ER	HR	SH	SF	HB	TBB	IBB	SO	WP	Bk	W	L	Pct.	ShO	Sv-Op	Hld	ERA
1989 Mets	R	15	5	0	8	42	189	35	29	21	0	0	3	3	24	1	14	8	2	0	5	.000	0	0--	—	4.50
1990 Mets	R	11	8	1	1	50.2	226	54	34	23	2	1	1	4	21	1	43	2	2	3	5	.375	0	0--	—	4.09

Year Team	Lg	G	GS	CG	GF	IP	BFP	H	R	ER	HR	SH	SF	HB	TBB	IBB	SO	WP	Bk	W	L	Pct.	ShO	Sv-Op	Hld	ERA
		HOW MUCH HE PITCHED						**WHAT HE GAVE UP**												**THE RESULTS**						
1991 Kingsport	R+	14	13	1	0	85	364	83	39	24	5	0	5	4	28	2	64	9	0	8	2	.800	0	0--	—	2.54
1992 Columbia	A	17	17	1	0	94.2	404	93	50	38	5	3	3	3	33	1	53	4	3	5	4	.556	0	0--	—	3.61
1993 Mets	R	1	1	0	0	7	26	5	1	0	0	0	0	0	1	0	6	0	0	1	0	1.000	0	0--	—	0.00
Capital Cty	A	14	14	0	0	64	294	86	51	38	2	3	4	2	23	0	42	7	0	4	6	.400	0	0--	—	5.34
1994 St. Lucie	A+	27	27	6	0	194	802	202	86	74	10	10	6	5	50	2	110	6	8	11	12	.478	1	0--	—	3.43
1995 Binghamton	AA	20	20	2	0	123.1	534	127	69	63	12	2	2	3	48	2	63	3	5	4	12	.250	0	0--	—	4.60
1996 Norfolk	AAA	3	1	0	1	10.2	49	13	7	4	1	1	1	0	3	0	8	1	0	1	0	1.000	0	0--	—	3.38
Binghamton	AA	38	0	0	17	56	245	51	34	32	3	5	3	6	23	5	49	4	2	1	5	.167	0	6--	—	5.14
1997 Rochester	AAA	39	9	0	15	102.2	456	114	65	56	11	1	8	7	38	2	50	11	3	8	7	.533	0	3--	—	4.91
1998 Charlotte	AAA	55	0	0	21	86.2	385	106	68	65	15	3	4	0	30	1	50	8	0	3	3	.500	0	3--	—	6.75
1999 Louisville	AAA	58	0	0	26	94.2	398	91	45	40	13	4	2	2	33	0	55	4	0	3	3	.500	0	9--	—	3.80
1999 Milwaukee	NL	15	0	0	5	21	88	19	8	8	1	0	0	0	11	2	9	0	1	1	2	.333	0	0-3	5	3.43

Julio Ramirez

Bats: Right Throws: Right Pos: CF-11; PH/PR-4   Ht: 5'11" Wt: 170 Born: 8/10/77 Age: 22

Year Team	Lg	G	AB	H	2B	3B	HR	(Hm	Rd)	TB	R	RBI	TBB	IBB	SO	HBP	SH	SF	SB	CS	SB%	GDP	Avg	OBP	SLG
		BATTING																	**BASERUNNING**				**PERCENTAGES**		
1995 Marlins	R	48	204	58	9	4	2	—	—	81	35	13	13	0	42	1	1	0	17	6	.74	2	.284	.330	.397
1996 Brevard Cty	A+	17	61	15	0	1	0	—	—	17	11	2	4	0	18	0	0	1	2	3	.40	1	.246	.288	.279
Marlins	R	42	171	49	5	3	0	—	—	60	33	15	14	0	34	3	1	0	25	8	.76	0	.287	.351	.351
1997 Kane County	A	99	376	96	18	7	14	—	—	170	70	53	37	1	122	5	14	2	41	6	.87	1	.255	.329	.452
1998 Brevard Cty	A+	135	559	156	20	12	13	—	—	239	90	58	45	2	147	4	3	2	71	27	.72	3	.279	.336	.428
1999 Portland	AA	138	568	148	30	10	13	—	—	237	87	64	39	1	150	2	5	5	64	14	.82	5	.261	.308	.417
1999 Florida	NL	15	21	3	1	0	0	(0	0)	4	3	2	1	0	6	0	0	0	0	1	.00	0	.143	.182	.190

Manny Ramirez

Bats: Right Throws: Right Pos: RF-146; DH-2; PH/PR-1   Ht: 6'0" Wt: 205 Born: 5/30/72 Age: 28

Year Team	Lg	G	AB	H	2B	3B	HR	(Hm	Rd)	TB	R	RBI	TBB	IBB	SO	HBP	SH	SF	SB	CS	SB%	GDP	Avg	OBP	SLG
		BATTING																	**BASERUNNING**				**PERCENTAGES**		
1993 Cleveland	AL	22	53	9	1	0	2	(1	1)	16	5	5	2	0	8	0	0	0	0	0	.00	3	.170	.200	.302
1994 Cleveland	AL	91	290	78	22	0	17	(9	8)	151	51	60	42	4	72	0	0	4	4	2	.67	6	.269	.357	.521
1995 Cleveland	AL	137	484	149	26	1	31	(12	19)	270	85	107	75	6	112	5	2	5	6	6	.50	13	.308	.402	.558
1996 Cleveland	AL	152	550	170	45	3	33	(19	14)	320	94	112	85	8	104	3	0	4	8	5	.62	18	.309	.399	.582
1997 Cleveland	AL	150	561	184	40	0	26	(14	12)	302	99	88	79	5	115	7	0	4	2	3	.40	19	.328	.415	.538
1998 Cleveland	AL	150	571	168	35	2	45	(22	23)	342	108	145	76	6	121	6	0	10	5	3	.63	18	.294	.377	.599
1999 Cleveland	AL	147	522	174	34	3	44	(21	23)	346	131	**165**	96	9	131	13	0	9	2	4	.33	12	.333	.442	**.663**
7 ML YEARS		849	3031	932	203	9	198	(100	98)	1747	573	682	455	38	663	34	2	41	27	23	.54	89	.307	.399	.576

Roberto Ramirez

Pitches: Left Bats: Left Pos: RP-28; SP-4   Ht: 5'11" Wt: 170 Born: 8/17/72 Age: 27

Year Team	Lg	G	GS	CG	GF	IP	BFP	H	R	ER	HR	SH	SF	HB	TBB	IBB	SO	WP	Bk	W	L	Pct.	ShO	Sv-Op	Hld	ERA
		HOW MUCH HE PITCHED						**WHAT HE GAVE UP**												**THE RESULTS**						
1990 Pirates	R	11	3	0	0	33.2	133	20	4	2	1	0	0	1	18	0	27	1	1	2	1	.667	0	0--	—	0.53
1991 Welland	A-	16	12	0	0	74.1	316	66	43	34	7	2	2	2	35	0	71	3	3	2	6	.250	0	1--	—	4.12
1994 Carolina	AA	6	6	0	0	27.1	129	38	19	16	2	3	0	1	8	0	21	1	0	0	1	.000	0	0--	—	5.27
1998 Las Vegas	AAA	26	1	0	7	29.2	120	23	14	8	2	2	1	0	10	2	33	2	0	1	1	.500	0	2--	—	2.43
1999 Colo Sprngs	AAA	10	10	0	0	61.2	258	64	26	24	6	1	1	2	17	1	55	0	1	3	2	.600	0	0--	—	3.50
1998 San Diego	NL	21	0	0	4	14.2	70	12	13	10	4	1	0	0	12	1	17	3	1	1	0	1.000	0	0-0	6	6.14
1999 Colorado	NL	32	4	0	6	40.1	209	68	42	37	8	2	0	0	22	2	32	4	0	1	5	.167	0	1-1	3	8.26
2 ML YEARS		53	4	0	10	55	279	80	55	47	12	3	0	0	34	3	49	7	1	2	5	.286	0	1-1	9	7.69

Rob Ramsay

Pitches: Left Bats: Left Pos: SP-3; RP-3   Ht: 6'5" Wt: 220 Born: 12/3/73 Age: 26

Year Team	Lg	G	GS	CG	GF	IP	BFP	H	R	ER	HR	SH	SF	HB	TBB	IBB	SO	WP	Bk	W	L	Pct.	ShO	Sv-Op	Hld	ERA
		HOW MUCH HE PITCHED						**WHAT HE GAVE UP**												**THE RESULTS**						
1996 Red Sox	R	2	0	0	1	3.2	19	5	2	2	0	0	0	1	3	0	5	0	0	0	1	.000	0	0--	—	4.91
Sarasota	A+	12	7	0	0	34	165	42	23	23	1	1	1	1	27	0	32	2	2	2	2	.500	0	0--	—	6.09
1997 Sarasota	A+	23	22	1	0	135.2	603	134	90	72	16	1	3	5	63	0	115	7	0	9	9	.500	0	0--	—	4.78
1998 Trenton	AA	27	27	1	0	162.2	659	137	67	63	10	5	5	3	50	1	166	8	3	12	6	.667	1	0--	—	3.49
1999 Pawtucket	AAA	20	20	0	0	114.1	498	114	81	68	21	9	4	4	36	1	79	5	0	6	6	.500	0	0--	—	5.35
Tacoma	AAA	5	5	0	0	33.1	130	20	6	4	2	0	1	0	14	1	37	1	0	4	1	.800	0	0--	—	1.08
1999 Seattle	AL	6	3	0	1	18.1	81	23	13	13	3	0	1	0	9	1	11	1	0	0	2	.000	0	0-0	0	6.38

Joe Randa

Bats: Right Throws: Right Pos: 3B-156   Ht: 5'11" Wt: 190 Born: 12/18/69 Age: 30

Year Team	Lg	G	AB	H	2B	3B	HR	(Hm	Rd)	TB	R	RBI	TBB	IBB	SO	HBP	SH	SF	SB	CS	SB%	GDP	Avg	OBP	SLG
		BATTING																	**BASERUNNING**				**PERCENTAGES**		
1995 Kansas City	AL	34	70	12	2	0	1	(1	0)	17	6	5	6	0	17	0	0	0	0	1	.00	2	.171	.237	.243
1996 Kansas City	AL	110	337	102	24	1	6	(2	4)	146	36	47	26	4	47	1	2	4	13	4	.76	10	.303	.351	.433
1997 Pittsburgh	NL	126	443	134	27	9	7	(5	2)	200	58	60	41	1	64	6	4	5	4	2	.67	10	.302	.366	.451
1998 Detroit	AL	138	460	117	21	2	9	(3	6)	169	56	50	41	0	70	7	3	3	8	7	.53	9	.254	.323	.367

		BATTING																			BASERUNNING				PERCENTAGES		
Year Team	Lg	G	AB	H	2B	3B	HR	(Hm	Rd)	TB	R	RBI	TBB	IBB	SO	HBP	SH	SF		SB	CS	SB%	GDP		Avg	OBP	SLG
1999 Kansas City	AL	156	628	197	36	8	16	(7	9)	297	92	84	50	4	80	3	1	7		5	4	.56	15		.314	.363	.473
5 ML YEARS		564	1938	562	110	20	39	(18	21)	829	248	246	164	10	278	17	10	19		30	18	.63	46		.290	.348	.428

Pat Rapp

Pitches: Right **Bats:** Right **Pos:** SP-26; RP-11 **Ht:** 6'3" **Wt:** 215 **Born:** 7/13/67 **Age:** 32

		HOW MUCH HE PITCHED						WHAT HE GAVE UP										THE RESULTS						
Year Team	Lg	G	GS	CG	GF	IP	BFP	H	R	ER	HR	SH	SF	HB	TBB	IBB	SO	WP	Bk	W	L	Pct.	ShO	Sv-Op	Hld	ERA
1992 San Francisco	NL	3	2	0	1	10	43	8	8	8	0	2	0	1	6	1	3	0	0	0	2	.000	0	0-0	0	7.20
1993 Florida	NL	16	16	1	0	94	412	101	49	42	7	8	4	2	39	1	57	6	0	4	6	.400	0	0-0	0	4.02
1994 Florida	NL	24	23	2	1	133.1	584	132	67	57	13	8	4	7	69	3	75	5	1	7	8	.467	1	0-0	0	3.85
1995 Florida	NL	28	28	3	0	167.1	716	158	72	64	10	8	0	7	76	2	102	7	0	14	7	.667	2	0-0	0	3.44
1996 Florida	NL	30	29	0	1	162.1	728	184	95	92	12	15	8	3	91	6	86	13	0	8	16	.333	0	0-0	0	5.10
1997 Fla-SF	NL	27	25	1	0	141.2	638	158	83	76	16	6	6	5	72	4	92	8	0	5	8	.385	1	0-0	0	4.83
1998 Kansas City	AL	32	32	1	0	188.1	855	208	117	111	24	3	6	10	107	7	132	14	0	12	13	.480	1	0-0	0	5.30
1999 Boston	AL	37	26	0	3	146.1	638	147	78	67	13	3	0	7	69	1	90	5	0	6	7	.462	0	0-0	1	4.12
1997 Minnesota	NL	19	19	1	0	108.2	484	121	59	54	11	4	3	3	51	3	64	5	0	4	6	.400	1	0-0	0	4.47
San Francisco	NL	8	6	0	0	33	154	37	24	22	5	2	3	2	21	1	28	3	0	1	2	.333	0	0-0	0	6.00
8 ML YEARS		197	181	8	6	1043.1	4614	1096	569	517	95	53	28	42	529	25	637	58	1	56	67	.455	5	0-0	1	4.46

Gary Rath

Pitches: Left **Bats:** Left **Pos:** RP-4; SP-1 **Ht:** 6'2" **Wt:** 186 **Born:** 1/10/73 **Age:** 27

		HOW MUCH HE PITCHED						WHAT HE GAVE UP										THE RESULTS						
Year Team	Lg	G	GS	CG	GF	IP	BFP	H	R	ER	HR	SH	SF	HB	TBB	IBB	SO	WP	Bk	W	L	Pct.	ShO	Sv-Op	Hld	ERA
1994 Vero Beach	A+	13	11	0	0	62.2	261	55	26	19	3	3	3	2	23	0	50	4	0	5	6	.455	0	0--	—	2.73
1995 San Antonio	AA	18	18	3	0	117	483	96	42	36	6	3	2	4	48	0	81	4	2	13	3	.813	1	0--	—	2.77
Albuquerque	AAA	8	8	0	0	39	178	46	31	22	4	1	1	2	20	0	23	2	0	3	5	.375	0	0--	—	5.08
1996 Albuquerque	AAA	30	30	1	0	180.1	784	177	97	84	13	9	4	3	89	8	125	8	0	10	11	.476	1	0--	—	4.19
1997 Albuquerque	AAA	24	24	0	0	132.1	615	177	107	89	17	7	4	4	49	1	100	7	0	7	11	.389	1	0--	—	6.05
1998 Albuquerque	AAA	28	24	1	3	157.1	687	184	91	79	17	5	1	4	52	1	119	2	0	9	7	.563	0	1--	—	4.52
1999 Salt Lake	AAA	20	18	1	1	99.1	454	129	76	62	12	7	7	1	27	1	67	7	0	3	8	.273	0	0--	—	5.62
1998 Los Angeles	NL	3	0	0	1	3.1	15	3	4	4	1	1	0	0	2	0	4	0	0	0	0	.000	0	0-0	0	10.80
1999 Minnesota	AL	5	1	0	1	4.2	25	6	6	6	1	0	0	0	5	0	1	2	1	0	1	.000	0	0-0	0	11.57
2 ML YEARS		8	1	0	2	8	40	9	10	10	2	1	0	0	7	0	5	2	1	0	1	.000	0	0-0	0	11.25

Ken Ray

Pitches: Right **Bats:** Right **Pos:** RP-13 **Ht:** 6'2" **Wt:** 200 **Born:** 11/27/74 **Age:** 25

		HOW MUCH HE PITCHED						WHAT HE GAVE UP										THE RESULTS						
Year Team	Lg	G	GS	CG	GF	IP	BFP	H	R	ER	HR	SH	SF	HB	TBB	IBB	SO	WP	Bk	W	L	Pct.	ShO	Sv-Op	Hld	ERA
1993 Royals	R	13	7	0	3	47.1	204	44	21	12	1	1	3	0	17	0	45	6	0	2	3	.400	0	0--	—	2.28
1994 Rockford	A	27	18	0	6	128.2	516	94	34	26	5	4	1	0	56	2	128	18	2	10	4	.714	0	3--	—	1.82
1995 Wilmington	A+	13	13	0	0	77	320	74	32	23	3	3	3	1	22	2	63	17	2	6	4	.600	0	0--	—	2.69
Wichita	AA	14	14	0	0	75.1	342	83	55	50	7	1	0	1	46	0	53	8	1	4	5	.444	0	0--	—	5.97
1996 Wichita	AA	22	22	1	0	120.2	553	151	94	82	17	5	6	1	57	1	79	15	1	4	12	.250	0	0--	—	6.12
1997 Omaha	AAA	25	21	2	1	113	516	131	86	80	21	2	5	4	63	2	96	8	1	5	12	.294	0	0--	—	6.37
1998 Wichita	AA	24	21	0	0	117.2	530	149	79	68	7	5	5	3	47	2	71	1	0	10	5	.667	0	0--	—	5.20
1999 Wichita	AA	14	0	0	13	21.1	90	23	12	12	2	1	0	1	10	0	18	1	1	0	0	.000	0	7--	—	5.06
Omaha	AAA	27	0	0	23	43.1	184	41	27	25	9	1	2	1	12	1	36	3	0	1	0	1.000	0	8--	—	5.19
1999 Kansas City	AL	13	0	0	4	11.1	57	23	12	11	2	0	0	1	6	0	0	0	0	1	0	1.000	0	0-0	1	8.74

Jeff Reboulet

Bats: R **Throws:** R **Pos:** 3B-56; 2B-36; PH/PR-21; SS-10 **Ht:** 6'0" **Wt:** 175 **Born:** 4/30/64 **Age:** 36

		BATTING																			BASERUNNING				PERCENTAGES		
Year Team	Lg	G	AB	H	2B	3B	HR	(Hm	Rd)	TB	R	RBI	TBB	IBB	SO	HBP	SH	SF		SB	CS	SB%	GDP		Avg	OBP	SLG
1992 Minnesota	AL	73	137	26	7	1	1	(1	0)	38	15	16	23	0	26	1	7	0		3	2	.60	6		.190	.311	.277
1993 Minnesota	AL	109	240	62	8	0	1	(0	1)	73	33	15	35	2	37	2	5	1		5	5	.50	6		.258	.356	.304
1994 Minnesota	AL	74	189	49	11	1	3	(2	1)	71	28	23	18	0	23	1	2	0		0	0	.00	6		.259	.327	.376
1995 Minnesota	AL	87	216	63	11	0	4	(1	3)	86	39	23	27	0	34	1	2	0		1	2	.33	3		.292	.373	.398
1996 Minnesota	AL	107	234	52	9	0	0	(0	0)	61	20	23	25	1	34	1	4	2		4	2	.67	10		.222	.298	.261
1997 Baltimore	AL	99	228	54	9	0	4	(2	2)	75	26	27	23	0	44	1	11	2		3	0	1.00	3		.237	.307	.329
1998 Baltimore	AL	79	126	31	6	0	1	(1	0)	40	20	8	19	0	34	2	7	1		0	1	.00	3		.246	.351	.317
1999 Baltimore	AL	99	154	25	4	0	0	(0	0)	29	25	4	33	0	29	2	3	0		1	0	1.00	1		.162	.317	.188
8 ML YEARS		727	1524	362	65	2	14	(7	7)	473	206	139	203	1	261	11	41	6		17	12	.59	32		.238	.330	.310

Mark Redman

Pitches: Left **Bats:** Left **Pos:** RP-4; SP-1 **Ht:** 6'5" **Wt:** 220 **Born:** 1/5/74 **Age:** 26

		HOW MUCH HE PITCHED						WHAT HE GAVE UP										THE RESULTS						
Year Team	Lg	G	GS	CG	GF	IP	BFP	H	R	ER	HR	SH	SF	HB	TBB	IBB	SO	WP	Bk	W	L	Pct.	ShO	Sv-Op	Hld	ERA
1995 Fort Myers	A+	8	5	0	0	32.2	134	28	13	10	4	1	2	1	13	0	26	2	0	2	1	.667	0	0--	—	2.76
1996 Fort Myers	A+	13	13	1	0	82.2	335	63	24	17	1	6	3	5	34	0	75	4	1	3	4	.429	0	0--	—	1.85
Hardware Cy	AA	16	16	3	0	106.1	467	101	51	45	5	1	6	8	50	1	96	4	0	7	7	.500	0	0--	—	3.81
Salt Lake	AAA	1	1	0	0	4	21	7	4	4	1	0	0	1	2	0	4	0	0	0	0	.000	0	0--	—	9.00

Year Team	Lg	G	GS	CG	GF	IP	BFP	H	R	ER	HR	SH	SF	HB	TBB	IBB	SO	WP	Bk	W	L	Pct.	ShO	Sv-Op	Hld	ERA
1997 Salt Lake	AAA	29	28	0	1	158.1	739	204	123	111	19	3	6	4	80	3	125	12	2	8	15	.348	0	1--	—	6.31
1998 New Britain	AA	8	8	0	0	47.1	190	40	11	8	3	1	0	3	17	0	51	1	1	4	2	.667	0	0--	—	1.52
Salt Lake	AAA	19	18	0	1	99.1	446	111	75	61	13	2	5	5	41	1	88	3	3	6	7	.462	0	0--	—	5.53
1999 Salt Lake	AAA	24	24	1	0	133.2	583	141	87	75	12	5	4	4	51	1	114	3	0	9	9	.500	0	0--	—	5.05
1999 Minnesota	AL	5	1	0	0	12.2	65	17	13	12	3	0	0	1	7	0	11	0	0	1	0	1.000	0	0-0	0	8.53

Mike Redmond

Bats: Right **Throws:** Right **Pos:** C-82; PH/PR-3   **Ht:** 6'1" **Wt:** 185 **Born:** 5/5/71 **Age:** 29

Year Team	Lg	G	AB	H	2B	3B	HR	(Hm	Rd)	TB	R	RBI	TBB	IBB	SO	HBP	SH	SF	SB	CS	SB%	GDP	Avg	OBP	SLG
1993 Kane County	A	43	100	20	2	0	0	—	—	22	10	10	6	0	17	4	2	0	2	0	1.00	1	.200	.273	.220
1994 Kane County	A	92	306	83	10	0	1	—	—	96	39	24	26	0	31	9	6	2	3	4	.43	10	.271	.344	.314
Brevard Cty	A+	12	42	11	4	0	0	—	—	15	4	2	3	0	4	1	0	0	0	0	.00	1	.262	.326	.357
1995 Portland	AA	105	333	85	11	1	3	—	—	107	37	39	22	2	27	3	4	3	2	2	.50	9	.255	.305	.321
1996 Portland	AA	120	394	113	22	0	4	—	—	147	43	44	26	2	45	5	5	5	3	4	.43	12	.287	.335	.373
1997 Charlotte	AAA	22	61	13	5	1	1	—	—	23	8	2	1	1	10	3	2	0	0	1	.00	1	.213	.262	.377
Marlins	R	16	55	19	3	0	0	—	—	22	7	5	9	0	5	3	0	0	2	0	1.00	1	.345	.463	.400
Brevard Cty	A+	5	17	0	0	0	0	—	—	0	2	0	2	0	2	0	0	0	0	0	.00	0	.000	.105	.000
1998 Portland	AA	8	28	9	4	0	1	—	—	16	7	7	2	0	2	2	1	0	0	0	.00	2	.321	.406	.571
Charlotte	AAA	18	58	14	2	0	2	—	—	22	4	7	0	0	3	1	0	2	0	0	.00	3	.241	.246	.379
1998 Florida	NL	37	118	39	9	0	2	(1	1)	54	10	12	5	2	16	2	4	0	0	0	.00	6	.331	.368	.458
1999 Florida	NL	84	242	73	9	0	1	(0	1)	85	22	27	26	2	34	5	5	0	0	0	.00	8	.302	.381	.351
2 ML YEARS		121	360	112	18	0	3	(1	2)	139	32	39	31	4	50	7	9	0	0	0	.00	14	.311	.377	.386

Jeff Reed

Bats: L **Throws:** R **Pos:** C-85; PH/PR-29; DH-1; 3B-1   **Ht:** 6'2" **Wt:** 202 **Born:** 11/12/62 **Age:** 37

Year Team	Lg	G	AB	H	2B	3B	HR	(Hm	Rd)	TB	R	RBI	TBB	IBB	SO	HBP	SH	SF	SB	CS	SB%	GDP	Avg	OBP	SLG
1984 Minnesota	AL	18	21	3	3	0	0	(0	0)	6	3	1	2	0	6	0	1	0	0	0	.00	0	.143	.217	.286
1985 Minnesota	AL	7	10	2	0	0	0	(0	0)	2	2	0	0	0	3	0	0	0	0	0	.00	0	.200	.200	.200
1986 Minnesota	AL	68	165	39	6	1	2	(1	1)	53	13	9	16	0	19	1	3	0	1	0	1.00	6	.236	.308	.321
1987 Montreal	NL	75	207	44	11	0	1	(1	0)	58	15	21	12	1	20	1	4	4	0	1	.00	8	.213	.254	.280
1988 Mon-Cin	NL	92	265	60	9	2	1	(1	0)	76	20	16	28	1	41	0	1	1	1	0	1.00	5	.226	.299	.287
1989 Cincinnati	NL	102	287	64	11	0	3	(1	2)	84	16	23	34	5	46	2	3	4	0	0	.00	6	.223	.306	.293
1990 Cincinnati	NL	72	175	44	8	1	3	(2	1)	63	12	16	24	5	26	0	5	1	0	0	.00	4	.251	.340	.360
1991 Cincinnati	NL	91	270	72	15	2	3	(1	2)	100	20	31	23	3	38	1	1	5	0	1	.00	6	.267	.321	.370
1992 Cincinnati	NL	15	25	4	0	0	0	(0	0)	4	2	2	1	1	4	0	0	0	0	0	.00	1	.160	.192	.160
1993 San Francisco	NL	66	119	31	3	0	6	(5	1)	52	10	12	16	4	22	0	0	1	0	1	.00	2	.261	.346	.437
1994 San Francisco	NL	50	103	18	3	0	1	(0	1)	24	11	7	11	4	21	0	0	0	0	0	.00	3	.175	.254	.233
1995 San Francisco	NL	66	113	30	2	0	0	(0	0)	32	12	9	20	3	17	0	1	0	0	0	.00	3	.265	.376	.283
1996 Colorado	NL	116	341	97	20	1	8	(7	1)	143	34	37	43	8	65	2	2	6	2	2	.50	8	.284	.365	.419
1997 Colorado	NL	90	256	76	10	0	17	(9	8)	137	43	47	35	1	55	2	5	0	2	1	.67	6	.297	.386	.535
1998 Colorado	NL	113	259	75	17	1	9	(6	3)	121	43	39	37	4	57	1	3	3	0	0	.00	6	.290	.377	.467
1999 Col-ChC	NL	103	256	66	16	2	3	(0	3)	95	29	28	45	1	58	3	0	2	1	2	.33	7	.258	.373	.371
1988 Montreal	NL	43	123	27	3	2	0	(0	0)	34	10	9	13	1	22	0	1	1	1	0	1.00	3	.220	.292	.276
Cincinnati	NL	49	142	33	6	0	1	(1	0)	42	10	7	15	0	19	0	0	0	0	0	.00	2	.232	.306	.296
1999 Colorado	NL	46	106	27	5	0	2	(0	2)	38	11	11	17	1	24	1	0	1	0	0	.00	3	.255	.360	.358
Chicago	NL	57	150	39	11	2	1	(0	1)	57	18	17	28	0	34	2	0	1	1	1	.50	4	.260	.381	.380
16 ML YEARS		1144	2872	725	134	10	57	(34	23)	1050	285	298	347	41	498	13	33	24	7	8	.47	69	.252	.333	.366

Rick Reed

Pitches: Right **Bats:** Right **Pos:** SP-26   **Ht:** 6'1" **Wt:** 195 **Born:** 8/16/65 **Age:** 34

Year Team	Lg	G	GS	CG	GF	IP	BFP	H	R	ER	HR	SH	SF	HB	TBB	IBB	SO	WP	Bk	W	L	Pct.	ShO	Sv-Op	Hld	ERA
1999 Norfolk *	AAA	1	1	0	0	3	21	10	9	9	1	0	1	0	2	0	2	0	0	0	1	.000	0	0--	—	27.00
Binghamton *	AA	1	1	0	0	5	17	1	1	1	1	0	0	0	1	0	5	0	0	0	0	.000	0	0--	—	1.80
1988 Pittsburgh	NL	2	2	0	0	12	47	10	4	4	1	2	0	0	2	0	6	0	0	1	0	1.000	0	0-0	0	3.00
1989 Pittsburgh	NL	15	7	0	2	54.2	232	62	35	34	5	2	3	2	11	3	34	0	3	1	4	.200	0	0-0	0	5.60
1990 Pittsburgh	NL	13	8	1	2	53.2	238	62	32	26	6	2	1	1	12	6	27	0	0	2	3	.400	1	1-1	1	4.36
1991 Pittsburgh	NL	1	1	0	0	4.1	21	8	6	5	1	0	0	0	1	0	2	0	0	0	0	.000	0	0-0	0	10.38
1992 Kansas City	AL	19	18	1	0	100.1	419	105	47	41	10	2	5	5	20	3	49	0	0	3	7	.300	0	0-0	0	3.68
1993 KC-Tex	AL	3	0	0	0	7.2	36	12	5	5	1	0	0	2	2	0	5	0	0	1	0	1.000	0	0-0	0	5.87
1994 Texas	AL	4	3	0	0	16.2	75	17	13	11	3	0	0	1	7	0	12	0	0	1	1	.500	0	0-0	0	5.94
1995 Cincinnati	NL	4	3	0	0	17	70	18	12	11	5	1	0	0	3	0	10	0	0	0	0	.000	0	0-0	0	5.82
1997 New York	NL	33	31	2	0	208.1	824	186	76	67	19	7	3	5	31	4	113	0	1	13	9	.591	2	0-0	0	2.89
1998 New York	NL	31	31	2	0	212.1	845	208	84	82	30	8	5	6	29	2	153	0	0	16	11	.593	1	0-0	0	3.48
1999 New York	NL	26	26	1	0	149.1	622	163	77	76	23	6	3	1	47	2	104	1	0	11	5	.688	1	0-0	0	4.58
1993 Kansas City	AL	1	0	0	0	3.2	18	6	4	4	0	0	0	1	1	0	3	0	0	0	0	.000	0	0-0	0	9.82
Texas	AL	2	0	0	0	4	18	6	1	1	1	0	0	1	1	0	2	0	0	1	0	1.000	0	0-0	0	2.25
11 ML YEARS		151	130	7	5	836.1	3444	851	391	362	104	30	20	23	165	20	515	2	3	49	40	.551	4	1-1	1	3.90

Steve Reed

Pitches: Right **Bats:** Right **Pos:** RP-63 **Ht:** 6'2" **Wt:** 212 **Born:** 3/11/66 **Age:** 34

Year Team	Lg	G	GS	CG	GF	IP	BFP	H	R	ER	HR	SH	SF	HB	TBB	IBB	SO	WP	Bk	W	L	Pct.	ShO	Sv-Op	Hld	ERA
1992 San Francisco	NL	18	0	0	2	15.2	63	13	5	4	2	0	0	1	3	0	11	0	0	1	0	1.000	0	0-0	1	2.30
1993 Colorado	NL	64	0	0	14	84.1	347	80	47	42	13	2	3	3	30	5	51	1	0	9	5	.643	0	3-6	9	4.48
1994 Colorado	NL	61	0	0	11	64	297	79	33	28	9	0	7	6	26	3	51	1	0	3	2	.600	0	3-10	14	3.94
1995 Colorado	NL	71	0	0	15	84	327	61	24	20	8	3	1	1	21	3	79	0	2	5	2	.714	0	3-6	11	2.14
1996 Colorado	NL	70	0	0	7	75	307	66	38	33	11	2	4	6	19	0	51	1	0	4	3	.571	0	0-6	22	3.96
1997 Colorado	NL	63	0	0	23	62.1	260	49	28	28	10	3	1	5	27	1	43	0	0	4	6	.400	0	6-13	10	4.04
1998 SF-Cle		70	0	0	19	80.1	322	56	29	28	8	2	0	5	27	5	73	0	0	4	3	.571	0	1-6	21	3.14
1999 Cleveland	AL	63	0	0	15	61.2	274	69	33	29	10	4	5	3	20	5	44	2	0	3	2	.600	0	0-3	8	4.23
1998 San Francisco	NL	50	0	0	14	54.2	213	30	10	9	4	2	0	4	19	5	50	0	0	2	1	.667	0	1-5	13	1.48
Cleveland	AL	20	0	0	5	25.2	109	26	19	19	4	0	0	1	8	0	23	0	0	2	2	.500	0	0-1	8	6.66
8 ML YEARS		480	0	0	106	527.1	2197	473	237	212	71	16	21	30	173	22	403	5	2	33	23	.589	0	16-50	96	3.62

Pokey Reese

Bats: Right **Throws:** Right **Pos:** 2B-146; SS-16; PH/PR-1 **Ht:** 5'11" **Wt:** 180 **Born:** 6/10/73 **Age:** 27

Year Team	Lg	G	AB	H	2B	3B	HR	(Hm	Rd)	TB	R	RBI	TBB	IBB	SO	HBP	SH	SF	SB	CS	SB%	GDP	Avg	OBP	SLG
1997 Cincinnati	NL	128	397	87	15	4	4	(3	1)	114	48	24	31	2	82	5	4	0	25	7	.78	1	.219	.284	.287
1998 Cincinnati	NL	59	133	34	2	2	1	(0	1)	43	20	16	14	1	28	0	2	2	3	2	.60	3	.256	.322	.323
1999 Cincinnati	NL	149	585	167	37	5	10	(5	5)	244	85	52	35	3	81	6	5	5	38	7	.84	9	.285	.330	.417
3 ML YEARS		336	1115	288	54	7	15	(8	7)	401	153	94	80	6	191	11	11	7	66	16	.80	13	.258	.312	.360

Dan Reichert

Pitches: Right **Bats:** Right **Pos:** SP-8 **Ht:** 6'3" **Wt:** 175 **Born:** 7/12/76 **Age:** 23

Year Team	Lg	G	GS	CG	GF	IP	BFP	H	R	ER	HR	SH	SF	HB	TBB	IBB	SO	WP	Bk	W	L	Pct.	ShO	Sv-Op	Hld	ERA
1997 Spokane	A-	9	9	0	0	38	178	40	25	12	2	0	2	3	16	0	39	2	2	3	4	.429	0	0--	—	2.84
1998 Wichita	AA	8	8	0	0	36	186	52	40	39	7	1	1	4	29	1	24	2	1	1	4	.200	0	0--	—	9.75
Lansing	A	13	6	0	1	35.2	152	25	16	13	0	1	2	3	20	0	35	4	1	1	1	.500	0	0--	—	3.28
Wilmington	A+	2	2	0	0	14	55	13	5	5	0	0	0	0	4	0	10	5	0	2	0	1.000	0	0--	—	3.21
Omaha	AAA	3	3	0	0	17.1	68	14	10	9	2	0	2	1	2	0	11	1	0	1	1	.500	0	0--	—	4.67
1999 Omaha	AAA	17	17	1	0	111.2	464	92	51	46	9	2	2	6	50	0	123	9	0	9	2	.818	0	0--	—	3.71
1999 Kansas City	AL	8	8	0	0	36.2	183	48	38	37	2	1	1	2	32	1	20	1	0	2	2	.500	0	0-0	0	9.08

Bryan Rekar

Pitches: Right **Bats:** Right **Pos:** RP-15; SP-12 **Ht:** 6'3" **Wt:** 220 **Born:** 6/3/72 **Age:** 28

Year Team	Lg	G	GS	CG	GF	IP	BFP	H	R	ER	HR	SH	SF	HB	TBB	IBB	SO	WP	Bk	W	L	Pct.	ShO	Sv-Op	Hld	ERA
1999 Durham *	AAA	6	5	0	1	35	142	29	15	15	3	1	0	1	8	0	26	3	0	4	1	.800	0	0--	—	3.86
1995 Colorado	NL	15	14	1	0	85	375	95	51	47	11	7	4	3	24	2	60	3	2	4	6	.400	0	0-0	1	4.98
1996 Colorado	NL	14	11	0	0	58.1	289	87	61	58	11	3	3	5	26	1	25	4	0	2	4	.333	0	0-1	0	8.95
1997 Colorado	NL	2	2	0	0	9.1	46	11	7	6	3	1	0	0	6	0	4	0	0	1	0	1.000	0	0-0	0	5.79
1998 Tampa Bay	AL	16	15	1	1	86.2	369	95	56	48	16	1	8	2	21	0	55	1	0	2	8	.200	0	0-0	0	4.98
1999 Tampa Bay	AL	27	12	0	2	94.2	437	121	68	61	14	3	2	5	41	2	55	4	0	6	6	.500	0	0-0	1	5.80
5 ML YEARS		74	54	2	3	334	1516	409	243	220	55	15	17	15	118	5	199	12	2	15	24	.385	0	0-1	2	5.93

Desi Relaford

Bats: Both **Throws:** Right **Pos:** SS-63; PH/PR-3 **Ht:** 5'9" **Wt:** 175 **Born:** 9/16/73 **Age:** 26

Year Team	Lg	G	AB	H	2B	3B	HR	(Hm	Rd)	TB	R	RBI	TBB	IBB	SO	HBP	SH	SF	SB	CS	SB%	GDP	Avg	OBP	SLG
1999 Clearwater *	A+	2	7	2	0	0	0	(0	0)	2	1	1	0	1	0	0	0	0	0	0	.00	1	.286	.375	.286
1996 Philadelphia	NL	15	40	7	2	0	0	(0	0)	9	2	1	3	0	9	0	1	0	1	0	1.00	1	.175	.233	.225
1997 Philadelphia	NL	15	38	7	1	2	0	(0	0)	12	3	6	5	0	6	0	1	0	1	0	1.00	0	.184	.279	.316
1998 Philadelphia	NL	142	494	121	25	3	5	(4	1)	167	45	41	33	4	87	3	10	6	9	5	.64	9	.245	.293	.338
1999 Philadelphia	NL	65	211	51	11	2	1	(0	1)	69	31	26	19	2	34	6	6	0	4	3	.57	5	.242	.322	.327
4 ML YEARS		237	783	186	39	7	6	(4	2)	257	81	74	60	6	136	9	18	6	17	8	.68	15	.238	.297	.328

Mike Remlinger

Pitches: Left **Bats:** Left **Pos:** RP-73 **Ht:** 6'1" **Wt:** 210 **Born:** 3/23/66 **Age:** 34

Year Team	Lg	G	GS	CG	GF	IP	BFP	H	R	ER	HR	SH	SF	HB	TBB	IBB	SO	WP	Bk	W	L	Pct.	ShO	Sv-Op	Hld	ERA
1991 San Francisco	NL	8	6	1	1	35	159	36	17	17	5	1	1	0	20	1	19	2	1	2	1	.667	1	0-0	0	4.37
1994 New York	NL	10	9	0	0	54.2	252	55	30	28	9	2	3	1	35	4	33	3	0	1	5	.167	0	0-0	0	4.61
1995 NYM-Cin	NL	7	0	0	4	6.2	34	9	6	5	1	1	0	0	5	0	7	0	0	0	1	.000	0	0-1	0	6.75
1996 Cincinnati	NL	19	4	0	2	27.1	125	24	17	17	4	3	1	3	19	2	19	2	2	0	1	.000	0	0-0	1	5.60
1997 Cincinnati	NL	69	12	2	10	124	525	100	61	57	11	6	4	7	60	6	145	12	2	8	8	.500	0	2-2	14	4.14
1998 Cincinnati	NL	35	28	1	0	164.1	727	164	96	88	23	12	7	5	87	1	144	11	1	8	15	.348	1	0-0	0	4.82
1999 Atlanta	NL	73	0	0	14	83.2	346	66	24	22	9	7	1	5	35	5	81	5	0	10	1	.909	0	1-3	21	2.37
1995 New York	NL	5	0	0	4	5.2	27	7	5	4	1	1	0	0	2	0	6	0	0	0	1	.000	0	0-1	0	6.35

Year Team	Lg	G	GS	CG	GF	IP	BFP	H	R	ER	HR	SH	SF	HB	TBB	IBB	SO	WP	Bk	W	L	Pct.	ShO	Sv-Op	Hld	ERA
Cincinnati	NL	2	0	0	0	1	7	2	1	1	0	0	0	0	3	0	1	0	0	0	0	.000	0	0-0	0	9.00
7 ML YEARS		221	59	4	31	495.2	2164	454	251	234	62	27	17	17	261	19	448	35	6	29	32	.475	2	3-6	37	4.25

Edgar Renteria

Bats: Right **Throws:** Right **Pos:** SS-151; PH/PR-8   **Ht:** 6'1" **Wt:** 180 **Born:** 8/7/75 **Age:** 24

Year Team	Lg	G	AB	H	2B	3B	HR	(Hm	Rd)	TB	R	RBI	TBB	IBB	SO	HBP	SH	SF	SB	CS	SB%	GDP	Avg	OBP	SLG
1996 Florida	NL	106	431	133	18	3	5	(2	3)	172	68	31	33	0	68	2	2	3	16	2	.89	12	.309	.358	.399
1997 Florida	NL	154	617	171	21	3	4	(3	1)	210	90	52	45	1	108	4	19	6	32	15	.68	17	.277	.327	.340
1998 Florida	NL	133	517	146	18	2	3	(2	1)	177	79	31	48	1	78	4	9	2	41	9	.65	13	.282	.347	.342
1999 St. Louis	NL	154	585	161	36	2	11	(6	5)	234	92	63	53	0	82	2	6	7	37	8	.82	16	.275	.334	.400
4 ML YEARS		547	2150	611	93	10	23	(13	10)	793	329	177	179	2	336	12	36	18	126	47	.73	58	.284	.340	.369

Al Reyes

Pitches: Right **Bats:** Right **Pos:** RP-53   **Ht:** 6'1" **Wt:** 206 **Born:** 4/10/71 **Age:** 29

Year Team	Lg	G	GS	CG	GF	IP	BFP	H	R	ER	HR	SH	SF	HB	TBB	IBB	SO	WP	Bk	W	L	Pct.	ShO	Sv-Op	Hld	ERA
1999 Louisville *	AAA	6	0	0	1	9.2	50	12	9	9	0	1	3	4	7	2	8	1	0	0	2	.000	0	0--	—	8.38
1995 Milwaukee	AL	27	0	0	13	33.1	138	19	9	9	3	1	2	3	18	2	29	0	0	1	1	.500	0	1-1	4	2.43
1996 Milwaukee	AL	5	0	0	2	5.2	27	8	5	5	1	0	0	0	2	0	2	2	0	1	0	1.000	0	0-0	0	7.94
1997 Milwaukee	AL	19	0	0	7	29.2	131	32	19	18	4	2	0	3	9	0	28	1	0	1	2	.333	0	1-1	1	5.46
1998 Milwaukee	NL	50	0	0	13	57	253	55	26	25	9	2	1	2	31	1	58	2	0	5	1	.833	0	0-1	10	3.95
1999 Mil-Bal		53	0	0	12	65.2	287	50	33	33	9	4	3	6	41	3	67	3	0	4	3	.571	0	0-4	6	4.52
1999 Milwaukee	NL	26	0	0	6	36	161	27	17	17	5	1	1	3	25	1	39	2	0	2	0	1.000	0	0-1	2	4.25
Baltimore	AL	27	0	0	6	29.2	126	23	16	16	4	3	2	3	16	2	28	1	0	2	3	.400	0	0-3	4	4.85
5 ML YEARS		154	0	0	47	191.1	836	164	92	90	26	9	6	14	101	6	184	8	0	12	7	.632	0	2-7	21	4.23

Carlos Reyes

Pitches: Right **Bats:** Both **Pos:** RP-65   **Ht:** 6'0" **Wt:** 190 **Born:** 4/4/69 **Age:** 31

Year Team	Lg	G	GS	CG	GF	IP	BFP	H	R	ER	HR	SH	SF	HB	TBB	IBB	SO	WP	Bk	W	L	Pct.	ShO	Sv-Op	Hld	ERA
1994 Oakland	AL	27	9	0	8	78	344	71	38	36	10	2	3	2	44	1	57	3	0	3	3	.000	0	1-1	0	4.15
1995 Oakland	AL	40	1	0	19	69	306	71	43	39	10	4	0	5	28	4	48	5	0	4	6	.400	0	0-1	4	5.09
1996 Oakland	AL	46	10	0	14	122.1	550	134	71	65	19	2	8	2	61	8	78	2	1	7	10	.412	0	0-0	1	4.78
1997 Oakland	AL	37	6	0	9	77.1	352	101	52	50	13	3	2	2	25	2	43	2	1	3	4	.429	0	0-1	1	5.82
1998 SD-Bos		46	0	0	18	66	267	58	26	26	6	2	2	3	20	2	47	3	1	3	3	.500	0	1-2	3	3.55
1999 San Diego	NL	65	0	0	23	77.1	331	76	38	32	11	5	3	0	24	4	57	7	1	2	4	.333	0	1-2	6	3.72
1998 San Diego	NL	22	0	0	8	27.2	109	23	11	11	4	2	1	2	6	0	24	0	1	2	2	.500	0	1-2	1	3.58
Boston	AL	24	0	0	10	38.1	158	35	15	15	2	0	1	1	14	2	23	3	0	1	1	.500	0	0-0	2	3.52
6 ML YEARS		261	26	0	91	490	2150	511	268	248	69	18	18	14	202	21	330	22	4	19	30	.388	0	3-7	15	4.56

Dennys Reyes

Pitches: Left **Bats:** Right **Pos:** RP-64; SP-1   **Ht:** 6'3" **Wt:** 246 **Born:** 4/19/77 **Age:** 23

Year Team	Lg	G	GS	CG	GF	IP	BFP	H	R	ER	HR	SH	SF	HB	TBB	IBB	SO	WP	Bk	W	L	Pct.	ShO	Sv-Op	Hld	ERA
1997 Los Angeles	NL	14	5	0	0	47	207	51	21	20	4	5	1	1	18	3	36	2	1	2	3	.400	0	0-0	0	3.83
1998 LA-Cin	NL	19	10	0	4	67.1	300	62	36	34	3	7	2	1	47	5	77	6	1	3	5	.375	0	0-0	0	4.54
1999 Cincinnati	NL	65	1	0	12	61.2	277	53	30	26	5	4	3	3	39	1	72	5	1	2	2	.500	0	2-3	14	3.79
1998 Los Angeles	NL	11	3	0	4	28.2	130	27	17	15	1	3	1	0	20	4	33	1	1	0	4	.000	0	0-0	0	4.71
Cincinnati	NL	8	7	0	0	38.2	170	35	19	19	2	4	1	1	27	1	44	5	0	3	1	.750	0	0-0	0	4.42
3 ML YEARS		98	16	0	16	176	784	166	87	80	12	16	6	5	104	9	185	13	3	7	10	.412	0	2-3	14	4.09

Shane Reynolds

Pitches: Right **Bats:** Right **Pos:** SP-35   **Ht:** 6'3" **Wt:** 210 **Born:** 3/26/68 **Age:** 32

Year Team	Lg	G	GS	CG	GF	IP	BFP	H	R	ER	HR	SH	SF	HB	TBB	IBB	SO	WP	Bk	W	L	Pct.	ShO	Sv-Op	Hld	ERA
1992 Houston	NL	8	5	0	0	25.1	122	42	22	20	2	6	1	0	6	1	10	1	1	1	3	.250	0	0-0	0	7.11
1993 Houston	NL	5	1	0	0	11	49	11	4	1	0	0	0	0	6	1	10	0	0	0	0	.000	0	0-0	0	0.82
1994 Houston	NL	33	14	1	5	124	517	128	46	42	10	4	0	6	21	3	110	3	2	8	5	.615	1	0-0	5	3.05
1995 Houston	NL	30	30	3	0	189.1	792	196	87	73	15	8	0	2	37	6	175	7	1	10	11	.476	2	0-0	0	3.47
1996 Houston	NL	35	35	4	0	239	981	227	103	97	20	11	7	8	44	3	204	5	1	16	10	.615	1	0-0	0	3.65
1997 Houston	NL	30	30	2	0	181	773	189	92	85	19	9	5	3	47	5	152	5	2	9	10	.474	0	0-0	0	4.23
1998 Houston	NL	35	35	3	0	233.1	986	257	99	91	25	5	7	2	53	2	209	5	0	19	8	.704	1	0-0	0	3.51
1999 Houston	NL	35	35	4	0	231.2	963	250	108	99	23	11	5	1	37	4	197	4	0	16	14	.533	2	0-0	0	3.85
8 ML YEARS		211	185	17	5	1234.2	5183	1300	561	508	114	54	25	22	251	21	1067	30	7	79	61	.564	7	0-0	5	3.70

Armando Reynoso

Pitches: Right **Bats:** Right **Pos:** SP-27; RP-4   **Ht:** 6'0" **Wt:** 204 **Born:** 5/1/66 **Age:** 34

Year Team	Lg	G	GS	CG	GF	IP	BFP	H	R	ER	HR	SH	SF	HB	TBB	IBB	SO	WP	Bk	W	L	Pct.	ShO	Sv-Op	Hld	ERA
1991 Atlanta	NL	6	5	0	1	23.1	103	26	18	16	4	3	0	3	10	1	10	2	0	2	1	.667	0	0-0	0	6.17
1992 Atlanta	NL	3	1	0	1	7.2	32	11	4	4	2	1	0	1	2	1	2	0	0	1	0	1.000	0	1-1	0	4.70
1993 Colorado	NL	30	30	4	0	189	830	206	101	84	22	5	8	9	63	7	117	7	6	12	11	.522	0	0-0	0	4.00
1994 Colorado	NL	9	9	1	0	52.1	226	54	30	28	5	2	2	6	22	1	25	2	2	3	4	.429	0	0-0	0	4.82
1995 Colorado	NL	20	18	0	0	93	418	116	61	55	12	8	2	5	36	3	40	2	0	7	7	.500	0	0-0	0	5.32
1996 Colorado	NL	30	30	0	0	168.2	733	195	97	93	27	3	3	9	49	0	88	4	3	8	9	.471	0	0-0	0	4.96
1997 New York	NL	16	16	1	0	91.1	388	95	47	46	7	3	5	6	29	4	47	4	1	6	3	.667	1	0-0	0	4.53
1998 New York	NL	11	11	0	0	68.1	292	64	31	29	4	4	1	5	32	3	40	2	2	7	3	.700	0	0-0	0	3.82
1999 Arizona	NL	31	27	0	1	167	730	178	90	81	20	6	6	6	67	7	79	7	1	10	6	.625	0	0-0	1	4.37
9 ML YEARS		156	147	6	3	860.2	3752	945	479	436	103	35	27	50	310	27	448	30	15	56	44	.560	1	1-1		4.56

Arthur Rhodes

Pitches: Left **Bats:** Left **Pos:** RP-43   **Ht:** 6'2" **Wt:** 205 **Born:** 10/24/69 **Age:** 30

Year Team	Lg	G	GS	CG	GF	IP	BFP	H	R	ER	HR	SH	SF	HB	TBB	IBB	SO	WP	Bk	W	L	Pct.	ShO	Sv-Op	Hld	ERA
1991 Baltimore	AL	8	8	0	0	36	174	47	35	32	4	1	3	0	23	0	23	2	0	0	3	.000	0	0-0	0	8.00
1992 Baltimore	AL	15	15	2	0	94.1	394	87	39	38	6	5	1	1	38	2	77	2	1	7	5	.583	1	0-0	0	3.63
1993 Baltimore	AL	17	17	0	0	85.2	387	91	62	62	16	2	3	1	49	1	49	2	0	5	6	.455	0	0-0	0	6.51
1994 Baltimore	AL	10	10	3	0	52.2	238	51	34	34	8	2	3	2	30	1	47	3	0	3	5	.375	2	0-0	0	5.81
1995 Baltimore	AL	19	9	0	3	75.1	336	68	53	52	13	4	0	0	48	1	77	3	1	2	5	.286	0	0-1	0	6.21
1996 Baltimore	AL	28	2	0	5	53	224	48	28	24	6	1	1	0	23	3	62	0	0	9	1	.900	0	1-1	2	4.08
1997 Baltimore	AL	53	0	0	6	95.1	378	75	32	32	9	0	4	4	26	5	102	2	0	10	3	.769	0	1-2	9	3.02
1998 Baltimore	AL	45	0	0	10	77	321	65	30	30	8	2	5	1	34	2	83	1	1	4	4	.500	0	4-8	10	3.51
1999 Baltimore	AL	43	0	0	11	53	244	43	37	32	9	2	2	0	45	6	59	4	0	3	4	.429	0	3-5	5	5.43
9 ML YEARS		238	61	5	35	622.1	2696	575	350	336	79	19	22	9	316	21	579	19	3	43	36	.544	3	9-17	26	4.86

Brad Rigby

Pitches: Right **Bats:** Right **Pos:** RP-49   **Ht:** 6'6" **Wt:** 214 **Born:** 5/14/73 **Age:** 27

Year Team	Lg	G	GS	CG	GF	IP	BFP	H	R	ER	HR	SH	SF	HB	TBB	IBB	SO	WP	Bk	W	L	Pct.	ShO	Sv-Op	Hld	ERA
1994 Modesto	A+	11	1	0	3	23.2	101	20	10	10	0	1	1	2	10	1	28	1	0	2	1	.667	0	2--		3.80
1995 Modesto	A+	31	23	0	4	154.2	653	135	79	66	5	2	7	12	48	0	145	8	2	11	4	.733	0	2--		3.84
1996 Huntsville	AA	26	26	3	0	159.1	682	161	89	70	13	3	3	7	59	8	127	13	2	9	12	.429	0	0--		3.95
1997 Edmonton	AAA	15	15	0	0	82.1	370	95	49	40	10	3	3	3	26	4	49	5	0	8	4	.667	0	0--		4.37
1998 Edmonton	AAA	13	13	0	0	69.2	310	86	52	46	5	2	6	3	17	0	34	3	1	5	6	.455	0	0--		5.94
1999 Vancouver	AAA	1	1	0	0	4.2	23	6	3	1	0	0	0	0	2	0	6	0	0	0	1	.000	0	0--		1.93
1997 Oakland	AL	14	14	0	0	77.2	339	92	44	42	14	2	8	2	22	2	34	3	0	1	7	.125	0	0-0	0	4.87
1999 Oak-KC	AL	49	0	0	11	83.2	382	102	51	47	11	2	5	7	31	7	36	6	0	4	6	.400	0	0-2	5	5.06
1999 Oakland	AL	29	0	0	5	62.1	278	69	31	30	5	1	3	5	26	7	26	3	0	3	4	.429	0	0-1	4	4.33
Kansas City	AL	20	0	0	6	21.1	104	33	20	17	6	1	2	2	5	0	10	3	0	1	2	.333	0	0-1	3	7.17
2 ML YEARS		63	14	0	11	161.1	721	194	95	89	25	4	13	9	53	9	70	9	0	5	13	.278	0	0-2	5	4.96

Matt Riley

Pitches: Left **Bats:** Left **Pos:** SP-3   **Ht:** 6'1" **Wt:** 201 **Born:** 8/2/79 **Age:** 20

Year Team	Lg	G	GS	CG	GF	IP	BFP	H	R	ER	HR	SH	SF	HB	TBB	IBB	SO	WP	Bk	W	L	Pct.	ShO	Sv-Op	Hld	ERA
1998 Delmarva	A	16	14	0	0	83	324	42	19	11	0	2	1	0	44	0	136	9	3	5	4	.556	0	0--	—	1.19
1999 Frederick	A+	8	8	0	0	51.2	200	34	19	15	5	3	0	1	14	0	58	1	1	3	2	.600	0	0--	—	2.61
Bowie	AA	20	20	3	0	125.2	520	113	53	45	13	2	3	5	42	0	131	10	4	10	6	.625	0	0--	—	3.22
1999 Baltimore	AL	3	3	0	0	11	59	17	9	9	4	0	1	0	13	0	6	0	2	0	0	.000	0	0-0	0	7.36

Ricky Rincon

Pitches: Left **Bats:** Left **Pos:** RP-59   **Ht:** 5'10" **Wt:** 188 **Born:** 4/13/70 **Age:** 30

Year Team	Lg	G	GS	CG	GF	IP	BFP	H	R	ER	HR	SH	SF	HB	TBB	IBB	SO	WP	Bk	W	L	Pct.	ShO	Sv-Op	Hld	ERA
1999 Akron *	AA	2	2	0	0	1.2	8	2	1	1	1	0	0	0	0	0	2	0	0	0	0	.000	0	0--	—	5.40
1997 Pittsburgh	NL	62	0	0	23	60	254	51	26	23	5	5	1	2	24	6	71	2	3	4	8	.333	0	4-6	18	3.45
1998 Pittsburgh	NL	60	0	0	27	65	272	50	31	21	6	1	2	0	29	2	64	2	0	0	2	.000	0	14-17	11	2.91
1999 Cleveland	AL	59	0	0	14	44.2	193	41	22	22	6	2	1	1	24	5	30	2	1	2	3	.400	0	0-2	11	4.43
3 ML YEARS		181	0	0	64	169.2	719	142	79	66	17	8	4	3	77	13	165	6	4	6	13	.316	0	18-25	40	3.50

Armando Rios

Bats: L **Throws:** L **Pos:** RF-39; PH/PR-22; LF-14; CF-2   **Ht:** 5'9" **Wt:** 185 **Born:** 9/13/71 **Age:** 28

Year Team	Lg	G	AB	H	2B	3B	HR	(Hm	Rd)	TB	R	RBI	TBB	IBB	SO	HBP	SH	SF	SB	CS	SB%	GDP	Avg	OBP	SLG
1994 Clinton	A	119	407	120	23	4	8	--	--	175	67	60	59	2	69	4	1	7	16	12	.57	7	.295	.384	.430
1995 San Jose	A+	128	488	143	34	3	8	--	--	207	76	75	74	3	75	1	4	7	51	10	.84	8	.293	.382	.424
1996 Shreveport	AA	92	329	93	22	2	12	--	--	155	62	49	44	3	42	1	3	4	9	9	.50	2	.283	.365	.471

Year Team	Lg	G	AB	H	2B	3B	HR	(Hm	Rd)	TB	R	RBI	TBB	IBB	SO	HBP	SH	SF	SB	CS	SB%	GDP	Avg	OBP	SLG
							BATTING													**BASERUNNING**				**PERCENTAGES**		
1997 Shreveport	AA	127	461	133	30	6	14	—	—	217	86	79	63	1	85	0	4	6	17	7	.71	11	.289	.370	.471
1998 Fresno	AAA	125	445	134	23	1	26	—	—	237	85	103	55	4	73	3	4	5	17	5	.77	9	.301	.378	.533
1999 Fresno	AAA	31	109	30	3	0	4	—	—	45	24	21	11	0	22	4	0	0	3	1	.75	2	.275	.363	.413
1998 San Francisco	NL	12	7	4	0	0	2	(0	2)	10	3	3	3	0	2	0	0	0	0	0	.00	0	.571	.700	1.429
1999 San Francisco	NL	72	150	49	9	0	7	(4	3)	79	32	29	24	1	35	1	1	1	7	4	.64	3	.327	.420	.527
2 ML YEARS		84	157	53	9	0	9	(4	5)	89	35	32	27	1	37	1	1	1	7	4	.64	3	.338	.435	.567

Cal Ripken Jr.

Bats: Right **Throws:** Right **Pos:** 3B-85; PH/PR-1   **Ht:** 6'4" **Wt:** 220 **Born:** 8/24/60 **Age:** 39

Year Team	Lg	G	AB	H	2B	3B	HR	(Hm	Rd)	TB	R	RBI	TBB	IBB	SO	HBP	SH	SF	SB	CS	SB%	GDP	Avg	OBP	SLG
							BATTING													**BASERUNNING**				**PERCENTAGES**		
1981 Baltimore	AL	23	39	5	0	0	0	(0	0)	5	1	0	1	0	8	0	0	0	0	0	.00	4	.128	.150	.128
1982 Baltimore	AL	160	598	158	32	5	28	(11	17)	284	90	93	46	3	95	3	2	6	3	3	.50	16	.264	.317	.475
1983 Baltimore	AL	162	663	211	47	2	27	(12	15)	343	121	102	58	0	97	0	0	5	0	4	.00	24	.318	.371	.517
1984 Baltimore	AL	162	641	195	37	7	27	(16	11)	327	103	86	71	1	89	2	0	2	2	1	.67	16	.304	.374	.510
1985 Baltimore	AL	161	642	181	32	5	26	(15	11)	301	116	110	67	1	68	1	0	8	2	3	.40	32	.282	.347	.469
1986 Baltimore	AL	162	627	177	35	1	25	(10	15)	289	98	81	70	5	60	4	0	6	4	2	.67	19	.282	.355	.461
1987 Baltimore	AL	162	624	157	28	3	27	(17	10)	272	97	98	81	0	77	1	0	11	3	5	.38	19	.252	.333	.436
1988 Baltimore	AL	161	575	152	25	1	23	(11	12)	248	87	81	102	7	69	2	0	10	2	2	.50	10	.264	.372	.431
1989 Baltimore	AL	162	646	166	30	0	21	(13	8)	259	80	93	57	5	72	3	0	6	3	2	.60	22	.257	.317	.401
1990 Baltimore	AL	161	600	150	28	4	21	(13	8)	249	78	84	82	18	66	5	1	7	3	1	.75	12	.250	.341	.415
1991 Baltimore	AL	162	650	210	46	5	34	(16	18)	368	99	114	53	15	46	5	0	9	6	1	.86	19	.323	.374	.566
1992 Baltimore	AL	162	637	160	29	1	14	(5	9)	233	73	72	64	14	50	7	0	7	4	3	.57	13	.251	.323	.366
1993 Baltimore	AL	162	641	165	26	3	24	(14	10)	269	87	90	65	19	58	6	0	6	1	4	.20	17	.257	.329	.420
1994 Baltimore	AL	112	444	140	19	3	13	(5	8)	204	71	75	32	3	41	4	0	4	1	0	1.00	17	.315	.364	.459
1995 Baltimore	AL	144	550	144	33	2	17	(10	7)	232	71	88	52	6	59	2	1	8	0	1	.00	15	.262	.324	.422
1996 Baltimore	AL	163	640	178	40	1	26	(10	16)	298	94	102	59	3	78	4	0	4	1	2	.33	28	.278	.341	.466
1997 Baltimore	AL	162	615	166	30	0	17	(10	7)	247	79	84	56	3	73	5	0	10	1	0	1.00	19	.270	.331	.402
1998 Baltimore	AL	161	601	163	27	1	14	(8	6)	234	65	61	51	0	68	4	1	2	0	2	.00	9	.271	.331	.389
1999 Baltimore	AL	86	332	113	27	0	18	(12	6)	194	51	57	13	3	31	3	3	3	0	1	.00	14	.340	.368	.584
19 ML YEARS		2790	10765	2991	571	44	402	(203	199)	4856	1561	1571	1080	106	1205	61	8	114	36	37	.49	325	.278	.344	.451

David Riske

Pitches: Right **Bats:** Right **Pos:** RP-12   **Ht:** 6'2" **Wt:** 175 **Born:** 10/23/76 **Age:** 23

Year Team	Lg	G	GS	CG	GF	IP	BFP	H	R	ER	HR	SH	SF	HB	TBB	IBB	SO	WP	Bk	W	L	Pct.	ShO	Sv-Op	Hld	ERA
			HOW MUCH HE PITCHED								**WHAT HE GAVE UP**											**THE RESULTS**				
1997 Kinston	A+	39	0	0	23	72	299	58	22	18	3	6	1	2	33	4	90	0	0	4	4	.500	0	4--	—	2.25
1998 Kinston	A+	53	0	0	50	54	218	48	15	14	4	2	1	1	15	0	67	1	0	1	1	.500	0	33--	—	2.33
Akron	AA	2	0	0	1	3	11	1	0	0	0	0	0	0	1	0	5	0	0	0	0	.000	0	1--	—	0.00
1999 Akron	AA	23	0	0	22	23.2	90	5	6	5	1	0	2	0	13	0	33	1	0	0	0	.000	0	12--	—	1.90
Buffalo	AAA	23	0	0	19	27.2	101	14	3	2	0	1	0	0	7	0	22	0	0	3	0	1.000	0	6--	—	0.65
1999 Cleveland	AL	12	0	0	3	14	68	20	15	13	2	1	1	0	6	0	16	0	0	1	1	.500	0	0-1	0	8.36

Todd Ritchie

Pitches: Right **Bats:** Right **Pos:** SP-26; RP-2   **Ht:** 6'3" **Wt:** 215 **Born:** 11/7/71 **Age:** 28

Year Team	Lg	G	GS	CG	GF	IP	BFP	H	R	ER	HR	SH	SF	HB	TBB	IBB	SO	WP	Bk	W	L	Pct.	ShO	Sv-Op	Hld	ERA
			HOW MUCH HE PITCHED								**WHAT HE GAVE UP**											**THE RESULTS**				
1999 Nashville *	AAA	1	1	0	0	5	22	6	1	1	0	1	0	0	1	0	2	0	0	0	0	.000	0	0--	—	1.80
1997 Minnesota	AL	42	0	0	19	74.2	331	87	41	38	11	0	1	2	28	0	44	11	0	2	3	.400	0	0-2	3	4.58
1998 Minnesota	AL	15	0	0	7	24	113	30	17	15	1	0	0	0	9	0	21	3	0	0	0	.000	0	0-0	0	5.63
1999 Pittsburgh	NL	28	26	2	0	172.1	715	169	79	67	17	3	2	4	54	3	107	7	0	15	9	.625	0	0-0	1	3.50
3 ML YEARS		85	26	2	26	271	1159	286	137	120	29	3	3	6	91	3	172	21	0	17	12	.586	0	0-2	4	3.99

Mariano Rivera

Pitches: Right **Bats:** Right **Pos:** RP-66   **Ht:** 6'2" **Wt:** 170 **Born:** 11/29/69 **Age:** 30

Year Team	Lg	G	GS	CG	GF	IP	BFP	H	R	ER	HR	SH	SF	HB	TBB	IBB	SO	WP	Bk	W	L	Pct.	ShO	Sv-Op	Hld	ERA
			HOW MUCH HE PITCHED								**WHAT HE GAVE UP**											**THE RESULTS**				
1995 New York	AL	19	10	0	2	67	301	71	43	41	11	0	2	2	30	0	51	0	1	5	3	.625	0	0-1	0	5.51
1996 New York	AL	61	0	0	14	107.2	425	73	25	25	1	2	1	2	34	3	130	1	0	8	3	.727	0	5-8	27	2.09
1997 New York	AL	66	0	0	56	71.2	301	65	17	15	5	3	4	0	20	6	68	2	0	6	4	.600	0	43-52	0	1.88
1998 New York	AL	54	0	0	49	61.1	246	48	13	13	3	2	3	1	17	1	36	0	0	3	0	1.000	0	36-41	0	1.91
1999 New York	AL	66	0	0	63	69	268	43	15	14	2	0	2	3	18	3	52	2	1	4	3	.571	0	45-49	0	1.83
5 ML YEARS		266	10	0	184	376.2	1541	300	113	108	22	7	12	8	119	13	337	5	2	26	13	.667	0	129-151	27	2.58

Roberto Rivera

Pitches: Left **Bats:** Left **Pos:** RP-12   **Ht:** 6'0" **Wt:** 200 **Born:** 1/1/69 **Age:** 31

Year Team	Lg	G	GS	CG	GF	IP	BFP	H	R	ER	HR	SH	SF	HB	TBB	IBB	SO	WP	Bk	W	L	Pct.	ShO	Sv-Op	Hld	ERA
			HOW MUCH HE PITCHED								**WHAT HE GAVE UP**											**THE RESULTS**				
1988 Indians	R	14	12	1	1	69.1	295	64	32	25	2	2	4	3	21	1	38	2	4	6	5	.545	1	0--	—	3.25
1989 Burlington	R+	18	2	1	8	51.1	214	44	24	20	4	4	2	1	16	3	42	0	2	3	4	.429	0	2--	—	3.51
1990 Watertown	A-	14	13	2	0	85	345	85	43	34	9	2	1	1	10	3	63	2	0	4	4	.500	1	0--	—	3.60

Year Team	Lg	G	GS	CG	GF	IP	BFP	H	R	ER	HR	SH	SF	HB	TBB	IBB	SO	WP	Bk	W	L	Pct.	ShO	Sv-Op	Hld	ERA
1991 Columbus	A	30	1	0	17	49	207	48	15	9	1	2	0	2	12	3	36	2	2	7	1	.875	0	3- -	—	1.65
Kinston	A+	10	0	0	5	10.1	46	10	6	5	1	1	1	0	2	0	9	0	0	1	0	1.000	0	0- -	—	4.35
1992 Kinston	A+	24	8	4	5	88.2	353	83	35	32	7	3	3	3	11	3	56	4	0	3	5	.375	0	1- -	—	3.25
1993 Canton-Akrn	AA	8	0	0	4	14.1	68	22	8	8	0	0	0	2	3	0	6	0	2	0	1	.000	0	0- -	—	5.02
Kinston	A+	19	1	0	9	35	150	44	26	24	4	1	2	1	4	0	32	0	0	2	3	.400	0	0- -	—	6.17
1994 Peoria	A	14	0	0	6	19.1	90	27	6	5	1	2	0	3	3	1	13	2	0	3	1	.750	0	0- -	—	2.33
Orlando	AA	34	0	0	19	45.2	192	45	14	14	1	2	0	2	11	0	31	2	0	3	2	.600	0	4- -	—	2.76
1995 Orlando	AA	49	0	0	14	68	257	50	18	18	4	0	4	0	11	3	34	3	1	6	2	.750	0	6- -	—	2.38
1996 Orlando	AA	9	0	0	4	17	81	20	13	12	2	2	0	2	8	5	14	1	0	1	2	.333	0	1- -	—	6.35
Iowa	AAA	35	0	0	13	33.1	130	26	10	10	3	3	0	0	8	1	18	0	0	1	0	1.000	0	2- -	—	2.70
1998 New Orleans	AAA	54	0	0	21	62.1	254	59	22	17	5	10	3	1	15	3	38	1	0	5	4	.556	0	5- -	—	2.45
1999 Las Vegas	AAA	20	3	0	7	33.2	175	61	39	38	6	2	3	3	14	0	25	2	0	1	2	.333	0	0- -	—	10.16
1995 Chicago	NL	7	0	0	2	5	23	8	3	3	1	0	0	0	2	0	2	0	0	0	0	.000	0	0-0	0	5.40
1999 San Diego	NL	12	0	0	3	7	30	6	4	3	1	1	1	0	3	0	3	1	0	1	2	.333	0	0-0	1	3.86
2 ML YEARS		19	0	0	5	12	53	14	7	6	2	1	1	0	5	0	5	1	0	1	2	.333	0	0-0	1	4.50

Ruben Rivera

Bats: Right Throws: Right Pos: CF-143; PH/PR-19   Ht: 6'3" Wt: 208 Born: 11/14/73 Age: 26

Year Team	Lg	G	AB	H	2B	3B	HR	(Hm	Rd)	TB	R	RBI	TBB	IBB	SO	HBP	SH	SF	SB	CS	SB%	GDP	Avg	OBP	SLG
1995 New York	AL	5	1	0	0	0	0	(0	0)	0	0	0	0	0	1	0	0	0	0	0	.00	0	.000	.000	.000
1996 New York	AL	46	88	25	6	1	2	(0	2)	39	17	16	13	0	26	2	1	2	6	2	.75	1	.284	.381	.443
1997 San Diego	NL	17	20	5	1	0	0	(0	0)	6	2	1	2	0	9	0	0	0	2	1	.67	0	.250	.318	.300
1998 San Diego	NL	95	172	36	7	2	6	(2	4)	65	31	29	28	0	52	2	1	1	5	1	.83	1	.209	.325	.378
1999 San Diego	NL	147	411	80	16	1	23	(10	13)	167	65	48	55	1	143	5	0	4	18	7	.72	9	.195	.295	.406
5 ML YEARS		310	692	146	30	4	31	(12	19)	277	115	94	98	1	231	9	2	7	31	11	.74	11	.211	.314	.400

Todd Rizzo

Pitches: Left Bats: Right Pos: RP-3   Ht: 6'2" Wt: 220 Born: 5/24/71 Age: 29

Year Team	Lg	G	GS	CG	GF	IP	BFP	H	R	ER	HR	SH	SF	HB	TBB	IBB	SO	WP	Bk	W	L	Pct.	ShO	Sv-Op	Hld	ERA
1992 Yakima	A-	15	0	0	8	26	121	21	13	13	3	0	1	2	24	0	26	6	0	2	0	1.000	0	0- -	—	4.50
Dodgers	R	3	1	0	1	7	31	4	4	3	0	0	0	1	8	0	7	0	0	0	1	.000	0	0- -	—	3.86
1995 Pr William	A+	36	0	0	10	68	307	68	30	21	2	2	1	3	39	8	59	13	0	3	5	.375	0	1- -	—	2.78
1996 Birmingham	AA	46	0	0	19	68.2	300	61	28	21	0	3	2	1	40	7	48	7	0	4	4	.500	0	10- -	—	2.75
1997 Nashville	AAA	54	0	0	23	70.2	318	63	39	28	6	3	1	3	33	3	60	9	0	4	5	.444	0	6- -	—	3.57
1998 Calgary	AAA	50	0	0	19	72	358	102	62	54	6	3	3	3	39	3	58	10	1	7	3	.700	0	4- -	—	6.75
1999 Charlotte	AAA	53	0	0	16	71	308	68	37	32	5	6	5	2	31	2	46	6	0	4	5	.444	0	8- -	—	4.06
1998 Chicago	AL	9	0	0	1	6.2	38	12	12	10	0	1	0	1	6	0	3	2	0	0	0	.000	0	0-0	0	13.50
1999 Chicago	AL	3	0	0	2	1.1	12	4	2	1	0	0	1	0	3	1	2	0	0	0	0	.000	0	0-0	0	6.75
2 ML YEARS		12	0	0	3	8	50	16	14	11	0	1	1	0	9	1	5	2	0	0	2	.000	0	0-0	0	12.38

David Roberts

Bats: Left Throws: Left Pos: CF-38; PH/PR-4; LF-1   Ht: 5'10" Wt: 172 Born: 5/31/72 Age: 28

Year Team	Lg	G	AB	H	2B	3B	HR	(Hm	Rd)	TB	R	RBI	TBB	IBB	SO	HBP	SH	SF	SB	CS	SB%	GDP	Avg	OBP	SLG
1994 Jamestown	A-	54	178	52	7	2	0	—	—	63	33	12	29	4	27	1	3	1	12	8	.60	0	.292	.392	.354
1995 Lakeland	A+	92	357	108	10	5	3	—	—	137	67	30	39	2	43	1	2	1	30	8	.79	7	.303	.371	.384
1996 Visalia	A+	126	482	131	24	7	5	—	—	184	112	37	98	0	105	1	3	7	65	21	.76	6	.272	.391	.382
Jacksnville	AA	3	9	2	0	0	0	—	—	2	0	0	1	0	0	0	0	0	1	1	.00	0	.222	.300	.222
1997 Jacksnville	AA	105	415	123	24	2	4	—	—	163	76	41	45	1	62	2	9	2	23	5	.82	5	.296	.366	.393
1998 Jacksnville	AA	69	279	91	14	5	5	—	—	130	71	42	53	1	59	3	3	4	21	9	.70	4	.326	.434	.466
Buffalo	AAA	5	15	2	0	0	0	—	—	2	2	2	0	0	3	0	0	1	2	0	1.00	0	.133	.125	.133
Akron	AA	56	227	82	10	5	7	—	—	123	49	33	35	5	30	1	5	1	28	6	.82	3	.361	.447	.542
1999 Buffalo	AAA	89	350	95	17	10	0	—	—	132	65	38	43	1	52	2	8	4	39	3	.93	1	.271	.351	.377
1999 Cleveland	AL	41	143	34	4	0	2	(1	1)	44	26	12	9	0	16	0	3	1	11	3	.79	4	.238	.281	.308

Willis Roberts

Pitches: Right Bats: Right Pos: RP-1   Ht: 6'3" Wt: 175 Born: 6/19/75 Age: 25

Year Team	Lg	G	GS	CG	GF	IP	BFP	H	R	ER	HR	SH	SF	HB	TBB	IBB	SO	WP	Bk	W	L	Pct.	ShO	Sv-Op	Hld	ERA
1993 Bristol	R+	10	2	0	2	26	116	24	16	4	0	2	0	1	11	0	23	2	0	2	3	.400	0	1- -	—	1.38
1994 Bristol	R+	4	4	0	0	20.2	81	9	9	9	1	0	1	2	8	0	17	2	0	1	2	.333	0	0- -	—	3.92
1995 Fayettevlle	A	17	15	0	0	80	339	72	33	24	2	1	2	6	40	0	52	15	3	6	3	.667	0	0- -	—	2.70
1996 Lakeland	A+	23	22	2	0	149.1	636	133	60	48	5	8	9	9	69	0	105	13	3	9	7	.563	0	0- -	—	2.89
1997 Jacksnville	AA	26	26	2	0	149	685	181	120	104	18	6	7	6	64	0	86	6	6	6	15	.286	0	0- -	—	6.28
1998 Jacksnville	AA	12	2	0	5	24.2	105	21	10	6	0	2	0	3	10	1	15	1	0	1	1	.750	0	0- -	—	2.19
Toledo	AAA	39	0	0	16	54.2	248	63	33	28	4	3	1	2	28	2	40	4	1	3	3	.500	0	2- -	—	4.61
1999 Toledo	AAA	31	12	2	9	92	433	112	68	64	10	3	3	3	59	3	52	5	4	5	8	.385	0	0- -	—	6.26
1999 Detroit	AL	1	0	0	0	1.1	8	3	4	2	0	0	1	1	0	0	0	0	0	0	0	.000	0	0-0	0	13.50

Kerry Robinson

Bats: Left **Throws:** Left **Pos:** PH/PR-7; LF-2   **Ht:** 6'0" **Wt:** 175 **Born:** 10/3/73 **Age:** 26

		BATTING																	BASERUNNING				PERCENTAGES		
Year Team	Lg	G	AB	H	2B	3B	HR	(Hm	Rd)	TB	R	RBI	TBB	IBB	SO	HBP	SH	SF	SB	CS	SB%	GDP	Avg	OBP	SLG
1995 Johnson Cy	R+	60	250	74	12	8	1	—	—	105	44	26	16	1	30	0	3	2	14	10	.58	3	.296	.336	.420
1996 Peoria	A	123	440	158	17	14	2	—	—	209	98	47	51	5	51	3	4	8	50	26	.66	2	.359	.422	.475
1997 Arkansas	AA	136	523	168	16	3	2	—	—	196	80	62	54	1	64	2	5	2	40	23	.63	7	.321	.386	.375
Louisville	AAA	2	9	1	0	0	0	—	—	1	0	0	0	0	1	0	0	0	0	0	.00	0	.111	.111	.111
1998 Orlando	AA	72	309	83	7	5	2	—	—	106	45	26	27	0	28	0	4	2	28	9	.76	6	.269	.325	.343
Durham	AAA	58	242	73	7	4	1	—	—	91	28	28	23	0	30	0	2	1	18	11	.62	1	.302	.361	.376
1999 Tacoma	AAA	79	335	108	16	9	0	—	—	142	53	34	14	0	44	0	3	2	30	7	.81	4	.322	.348	.424
Indianapolis	AAA	34	129	34	3	2	1	—	—	44	24	14	4	0	12	1	4	3	14	4	.78	2	.264	.285	.341
1998 Tampa Bay	AL	2	3	0	0	0	0	(0	0)	0	0	0	0	0	1	0	0	0	0	0	.00	0	.000	.000	.000
1999 Cincinnati	NL	9	1	0	0	0	0	(0	0)	0	4	0	0	0	1	0	0	0	0	1	.00	0	.000	.000	.000
2 ML YEARS		11	4	0	0	0	0	0	0	0	4	0	0	0	2	0	0	0	0	1	.00	0	.000	.000	.000

John Rocker

Pitches: Left **Bats:** Right **Pos:** RP-74   **Ht:** 6'4" **Wt:** 225 **Born:** 10/17/74 **Age:** 25

		HOW MUCH HE PITCHED						WHAT HE GAVE UP												THE RESULTS						
Year Team	Lg	G	GS	CG	GF	IP	BFP	H	R	ER	HR	SH	SF	HB	TBB	IBB	SO	WP	Bk	W	L	Pct.	ShO	Sv-Op	Hld	ERA
1994 Danville	R+	12	12	1	0	63.2	285	50	36	25	4	3	4	6	38	1	72	13	4	1	5	.167	0	0--	—	3.53
1995 Macon	A	16	16	0	0	86	375	86	50	43	5	1	1	4	52	0	61	5	1	4	4	.500	0	0--	—	4.50
Eugene	A-	12	12	0	0	59.1	260	45	40	34	4	1	1	2	36	0	74	7	2	1	5	.167	0	0--	—	5.16
1996 Macon	A	20	19	2	1	106.1	453	85	60	46	7	1	4	6	63	1	107	12	3	5	3	.625	2	0--	—	3.89
Durham	A+	9	9	0	0	58.1	245	63	24	22	4	0	1	0	25	0	43	4	0	4	3	.571	0	0--	—	3.39
1997 Durham	A+	11	1	0	3	35.1	157	33	21	17	3	2	1	2	22	0	39	5	1	1	1	.500	0	0--	—	4.33
Greenville	AA	22	18	0	1	113	507	119	69	61	12	3	1	0	61	0	96	17	2	5	6	.455	0	0--	—	4.86
1998 Richmond	AAA	9	0		4	19	81	13	4	3	1	1	0	0	10	0	22	1	1	1	1	.500	0	1--	—	1.42
1998 Atlanta	NL	47	0	0	16	38	156	22	10	9	4	3	0	3	22	4	42	6	0	1	3	.250	0	2-4	15	2.13
1999 Atlanta	NL	74	0	0	61	72.1	301	47	24	20	5	2	0	0	37	4	104	7	0	4	5	.444	0	38-45	0	2.49
2 ML YEARS		121	0	0	77	110.1	457	69	34	29	9	5	0	4	59	8	146	13	0	5	8	.385	0	40-49	15	2.37

Alex Rodriguez

Bats: Right **Throws:** Right **Pos:** SS-129   **Ht:** 6'3" **Wt:** 195 **Born:** 7/27/75 **Age:** 24

		BATTING																	BASERUNNING				PERCENTAGES		
Year Team	Lg	G	AB	H	2B	3B	HR	(Hm	Rd)	TB	R	RBI	TBB	IBB	SO	HBP	SH	SF	SB	CS	SB%	GDP	Avg	OBP	SLG
1994 Seattle	AL	17	54	11	0	0	0	(0	0)	11	4	2	3	0	20	0	1	1	3	0	1.00	0	.204	.241	.204
1995 Seattle	AL	48	142	33	6	2	5	(1	4)	58	15	19	6	0	42	0	1	0	4	2	.67	0	.232	.264	.408
1996 Seattle	AL	146	601	215	54	1	36	(18	18)	379	141	123	59	1	104	4	6	7	15	4	.79	15	.358	.414	.631
1997 Seattle	AL	141	587	176	40	3	23	(16	7)	291	100	84	41	1	99	5	4	1	29	6	.83	14	.300	.350	.496
1998 Seattle	AL	161	686	213	35	5	42	(16	24)	384	123	124	45	0	121	10	3	4	46	13	.78	12	.310	.360	.560
1999 Seattle	AL	129	502	143	25	0	42	(20	22)	294	110	111	56	2	109	5	1	8	21	7	.75	12	.285	.357	.586
6 ML YEARS		642	2572	791	160	11	148	(73	75)	1417	493	463	210	4	495	24	16	21	118	32	.79	53	.308	.363	.551

Felix Rodriguez

Pitches: Right **Bats:** Right **Pos:** RP-47   **Ht:** 6'1" **Wt:** 190 **Born:** 12/5/72 **Age:** 27

		HOW MUCH HE PITCHED						WHAT HE GAVE UP												THE RESULTS						
Year Team	Lg	G	GS	CG	GF	IP	BFP	H	R	ER	HR	SH	SF	HB	TBB	IBB	SO	WP	Bk	W	L	Pct.	ShO	Sv-Op	Hld	ERA
1995 Los Angeles	NL	11	0	0	5	10.2	45	11	3	3	2	0	0	0	5	0	5	0	0	1	1	.500	0	0-1	0	2.53
1997 Cincinnati	NL	26	1	0	13	46	212	48	23	22	2	0	1	6	28	2	34	4	1	0	0	.000	0	0-0	0	4.30
1998 Arizona	NL	43	0	0	23	44	207	44	31	30	5	4	3	1	29	1	36	5	2	0	2	.000	0	5-8	0	6.14
1999 San Francisco	NL	47	0	0	26	66.1	292	67	32	28	6	2	3	2	29	2	55	2	0	2	3	.400	0	0-1	3	3.80
4 ML YEARS		127	1	0	67	167	756	170	89	83	15	6	7	9	91	5	130	11	3	3	6	.333	0	5-10	3	4.47

Frank Rodriguez

Pitches: Right **Bats:** Right **Pos:** RP-23; SP-5   **Ht:** 6'0" **Wt:** 210 **Born:** 12/11/72 **Age:** 27

		HOW MUCH HE PITCHED						WHAT HE GAVE UP												THE RESULTS						
Year Team	Lg	G	GS	CG	GF	IP	BFP	H	R	ER	HR	SH	SF	HB	TBB	IBB	SO	WP	Bk	W	L	Pct.	ShO	Sv-Op	Hld	ERA
1999 Salt Lake *	AAA	9	9	1	0	43	191	40	34	32	8	1	2	6	14	0	33	2	0	3	4	.429	0	0--	—	6.70
1995 Bos-Min	AL	25	18	0	1	105.2	478	114	83	72	11	4	5		57	1	59	9	0	5	8	.385	0	0-0	1	6.13
1996 Minnesota	AL	38	33	3	4	206.2	899	218	129	116	27	6	8	5	78	1	110	2	0	13	14	.481	0	2-2	0	5.05
1997 Minnesota	AL	43	15	0	5	142.1	635	147	82	73	12	4	2	4	60	9	65	6	0	3	6	.333	0	0-2	4	4.62
1998 Minnesota	AL	20	11	0	4	70	329	88	58	51	6	1	5	3	30	0	62	6	1	4	6	.400	0	0-0	0	6.56
1999 Seattle	AL	28	5	0	10	73.1	334	94	47	46	11	0	1	4	30	2	47	1	0	2	4	.333	0	3-4	3	5.65
1995 Boston	AL	9	2	0	1	15.1	75	21	19	18	3	0	2	0	10	1	14	4	0	2	0	.000	0	0-0	1	10.57
Minnesota	AL	16	16	0	0	90.1	403	93	64	54	8	1	4	5	47	0	45	5	0	5	6	.455	0	0-0	0	5.38
5 ML YEARS		154	82	3	24	598	2653	661	399	358	67	12	20	21	255	13	343	24	1	27	38	.415	0	5-8	8	5.39

Henry Rodriguez

Bats: Left **Throws:** Left **Pos:** LF-122; PH/PR-7; DH-2　　　　　**Ht:** 6'2" **Wt:** 220 **Born:** 11/8/67 **Age:** 32

Year Team	Lg	G	AB	H	2B	3B	HR	(Hm	Rd)	TB	R	RBI	TBB	IBB	SO	HBP	SH	SF	SB	CS	SB%	GDP	Avg	OBP	SLG
1992 Los Angeles	NL	53	146	32	7	0	3	(2	1)	48	11	14	8	0	30	0	1	1	0	0	.00	2	.219	.258	.329
1993 Los Angeles	NL	76	176	39	10	0	8	(5	3)	73	20	23	11	2	39	0	0	1	1	0	1.00	1	.222	.266	.415
1994 Los Angeles	NL	104	306	82	14	2	8	(5	3)	124	33	49	17	2	58	2	1	4	0	1	.00	9	.268	.307	.405
1995 LA-Mon	NL	45	138	33	4	1	2	(1	1)	45	13	15	11	2	28	0	0	1	0	1	.00	5	.239	.293	.326
1996 Montreal	NL	145	532	147	42	1	36	(20	16)	299	81	103	37	7	160	3	0	4	2	0	1.00	10	.276	.325	.562
1997 Montreal	NL	132	476	116	28	3	26	(14	12)	228	55	83	42	5	149	2	0	3	3	3	.50	6	.244	.306	.479
1998 Chicago	NL	128	415	104	21	1	31	(16	15)	220	56	85	54	7	113	0	0	4	1	3	.25	6	.251	.334	.530
1999 Chicago	NL	130	447	136	29	0	26	(14	12)	243	72	87	56	6	113	0	0	1	2	4	.33	9	.304	.381	.544
1995 Los Angeles	NL	21	80	21	4	1	1	(0	1)	30	6	10	5	2	17	0	0	1	0	1	.00	3	.263	.306	.375
Montreal	NL	24	58	12	0	0	1	(1	0)	15	7	5	6	0	11	0	0	0	0	0	.00	2	.207	.277	.259
8 ML YEARS		813	2636	689	155	8	140	(77	63)	1280	341	459	236	31	690	7	2	19	9	12	.43	48	.261	.322	.486

Ivan Rodriguez

Bats: Right **Throws:** Right **Pos:** C-141; PH/PR-2; DH-1　　　　　**Ht:** 5'9" **Wt:** 205 **Born:** 11/30/71 **Age:** 28

Year Team	Lg	G	AB	H	2B	3B	HR	(Hm	Rd)	TB	R	RBI	TBB	IBB	SO	HBP	SH	SF	SB	CS	SB%	GDP	Avg	OBP	SLG
1991 Texas	AL	88	280	74	16	0	3	(3	0)	99	24	27	5	0	42	0	2	1	0	1	.00	10	.264	.276	.354
1992 Texas	AL	123	420	109	16	1	8	(4	4)	151	39	37	24	2	73	1	7	2	0	0	.00	15	.260	.300	.360
1993 Texas	AL	137	473	129	28	4	10	(7	3)	195	56	66	29	3	70	4	5	8	8	7	.53	16	.273	.315	.412
1994 Texas	AL	99	363	108	19	1	16	(7	9)	177	56	57	31	5	42	7	0	4	6	3	.67	10	.298	.360	.488
1995 Texas	AL	130	492	149	32	2	12	(5	7)	221	56	67	16	2	48	4	0	5	0	2	.00	11	.303	.327	.449
1996 Texas	AL	153	639	192	47	3	19	(10	9)	302	116	86	38	7	55	4	0	4	5	0	1.00	15	.300	.342	.473
1997 Texas	AL	150	597	187	34	4	20	(12	8)	289	98	77	38	7	89	8	1	4	7	3	.70	18	.313	.360	.484
1998 Texas	AL	145	579	186	40	4	21	(12	9)	297	88	91	32	4	88	3	0	3	9	0	1.00	18	.321	.358	.513
1999 Texas	AL	144	600	199	29	1	35	(12	23)	335	116	113	24	2	64	1	0	5	25	12	.68	31	.332	.356	.558
9 ML YEARS		1169	4443	1333	261	20	144	(72	72)	2066	649	621	237	32	571	32	15	36	60	28	.68	144	.300	.337	.465

Liu Rodriguez

Bats: B **Throws:** R **Pos:** 2B-22; SS-14; PH/PR-5; DH-2; 3B-1　　　　　**Ht:** 5'9" **Wt:** 170 **Born:** 11/5/76 **Age:** 23

Year Team	Lg	G	AB	H	2B	3B	HR	(Hm	Rd)	TB	R	RBI	TBB	IBB	SO	HBP	SH	SF	SB	CS	SB%	GDP	Avg	OBP	SLG
1995 White Sox	R	36	119	27	6	1	1	—	—	38	18	11	23	0	19	0	2	0	4	2	.67	2	.227	.352	.319
1996 Hickory	A	122	430	107	18	0	0	—	—	125	57	30	60	2	77	9	8	2	15	14	.52	3	.249	.351	.291
1997 Hickory	A	129	450	130	21	6	1	—	—	166	72	62	65	0	56	5	10	7	12	13	.48	13	.289	.380	.369
1998 Winston-Sal	A+	112	420	117	27	3	2	—	—	156	62	43	45	0	40	9	10	7	15	10	.60	13	.279	.356	.371
1999 Birmingham	AA	64	244	71	11	1	3	—	—	93	42	37	22	0	35	3	8	3	5	3	.63	2	.291	.353	.381
1999 Chicago	AL	39	93	22	2	2	1	(0	1)	31	8	12	12	0	11	3	3	0	0	0	.00	5	.237	.343	.333

Nerio Rodriguez

Pitches: Right **Bats:** Right **Pos:** RP-2　　　　　**Ht:** 6'1" **Wt:** 195 **Born:** 3/22/73 **Age:** 27

		HOW MUCH HE PITCHED						WHAT HE GAVE UP											THE RESULTS					
Year Team	Lg	G	GS	CG	GF	IP	BFP	H	R	ER	HR	SH	SF	HB	TBB	IBB	SO	WP	Bk	W	L	Pct.	ShO	Sv-Op	Hld	ERA
1999 Syracuse *	AAA	27	27	1	0	162.2	688	161	84	82	17	3	5	7	53	0	137	5	2	10	8	.556	1	0- -	—	4.54
1996 Baltimore	AL	8	1	0	2	16.2	77	18	11	8	2	0	1	1	7	0	12	0	0	0	1	.000	0	0-0	0	4.32
1997 Baltimore	AL	6	2	0	1	22	98	21	15	12	2	1	4	1	8	0	11	1	0	2	1	.667	0	0-1	0	4.91
1998 Bal-Tor	AL	13	4	0	3	27.1	133	35	26	26	1	0	2	1	17	0	11	1	0	2	3	.400	0	0-0	0	8.56
1999 Toronto	AL	2	0	0	1	2	10	2	3	3	2	0	0	0	2	0	2	0	0	0	1	.000	0	0-0	0	13.50
1998 Baltimore	AL	6	4	0	0	19	89	25	17	17	0	0	2	0	9	0	8	1	0	1	3	.250	0	0-0	0	8.05
Toronto	AL	7	0	0	3	8.1	44	10	9	9	1	0	0	1	8	0	3	0	0	1	0	1.000	0	0-0	0	9.72
4 ML YEARS		29	7	0	7	68	318	76	55	49	7	1	7	3	34	0	36	2	0	4	6	.400	0	0-1	0	6.49

Rich Rodriguez

Pitches: Left **Bats:** Left **Pos:** RP-62　　　　　**Ht:** 6'0" **Wt:** 205 **Born:** 3/1/63 **Age:** 37

		HOW MUCH HE PITCHED						WHAT HE GAVE UP											THE RESULTS					
Year Team	Lg	G	GS	CG	GF	IP	BFP	H	R	ER	HR	SH	SF	HB	TBB	IBB	SO	WP	Bk	W	L	Pct.	ShO	Sv-Op	Hld	ERA
1990 San Diego	NL	32	0	0	15	47.2	201	52	17	15	2	2	1	1	16	4	22	1	1	1	1	.500	0	1-1	3	2.83
1991 San Diego	NL	64	1	0	19	80	335	66	31	29	8	7	2	0	44	8	40	4	1	3	1	.750	0	0-2	8	3.26
1992 San Diego	NL	61	1	0	15	91	369	77	28	24	4	2	2	0	29	4	64	1	1	6	3	.667	0	0-1	5	2.37
1993 SD-Fla	NL	70	0	0	21	76	331	73	38	32	10	5	0	2	33	8	43	3	0	2	4	.333	0	3-7	10	3.79
1994 St. Louis	NL	56	0	0	15	60.1	260	62	30	27	6	2	1	1	26	4	43	4	0	3	5	.375	0	0-3	15	4.03
1995 St. Louis	NL	1	0	0	0	1.2	4	0	0	0	0	0	0	0	0	0	0	0	0	0	0	.000	0	0-0	0	0.00
1997 San Francisco	NL	71	0	0	15	65.1	271	65	24	23	7	3	0	1	21	4	32	0	0	4	3	.571	0	1-5	14	3.17
1998 San Francisco	NL	68	0	0	11	65.2	278	69	28	27	7	2	2	0	20	5	44	3	0	4	0	1.000	0	2-6	22	3.70
1999 San Francisco	NL	62	0	0	8	56.2	255	60	33	33	8	5	2	1	28	5	44	1	0	3	0	1.000	0	0-2	11	5.24
1993 San Diego	NL	34	0	0	10	30	133	34	15	11	2	2	0	1	9	3	22	1	0	2	3	.400	0	2-5	8	3.30
Florida	NL	36	0	0	11	46	198	39	23	21	8	3	0	1	24	5	21	2	0	0	1	.000	0	1-2	2	4.11
9 ML YEARS		485	2	0	119	544.1	2304	524	229	210	52	28	10	6	217	42	332	17	3	26	17	.605	0	7-27	88	3.47

Kenny Rogers

Pitches: Left **Bats:** Left **Pos:** SP-31   **Ht:** 6'1" **Wt:** 217 **Born:** 11/10/64 **Age:** 35

Year Team	Lg	G	GS	CG	GF	IP	BFP	H	R	ER	HR	SH	SF	HB	TBB	IBB	SO	WP	Bk	W	L	Pct.	ShO	Sv-Op	Hld	ERA
1989 Texas	AL	73	0	0	24	73.2	314	60	28	24	2	6	3	4	42	9	63	6	0	3	4	.429	0	2-5	16	2.93
1990 Texas	AL	69	3	0	46	97.2	428	93	40	34	6	7	4	1	42	5	74	5	0	10	6	.625	0	15-23	6	3.13
1991 Texas	AL	63	9	0	20	109.2	511	121	80	66	14	9	5	6	61	7	73	3	1	10	10	.500	0	5-6	11	5.42
1992 Texas	AL	81	0	0	38	78.2	337	80	32	27	7	4	1	0	26	8	70	4	1	3	6	.333	0	6-10	16	3.09
1993 Texas	AL	35	33	5	0	208.1	885	210	108	95	18	7	5	4	71	2	140	6	5	16	10	.615	0	0-0	1	4.10
1994 Texas	AL	24	24	6	0	167.1	714	169	93	83	24	3	6	3	52	1	120	3	1	11	8	.579	2	0-0	0	4.46
1995 Texas	AL	31	31	3	0	208	877	192	87	78	26	3	5	2	76	1	140	8	1	17	7	.708	1	0-0	0	3.38
1996 New York	AL	30	30	2	0	179	786	179	97	93	16	6	3	8	83	2	92	5	0	12	8	.600	1	0-0	0	4.68
1997 New York	AL	31	22	1	4	145	651	161	100	91	18	2	4	7	62	1	78	2	2	6	7	.462	0	0-0	1	5.65
1998 Oakland	AL	34	34	7	0	238.2	970	215	96	84	19	4	5	7	67	0	138	5	2	16	8	.667	1	0-0	0	3.17
1999 Oak-NYM		31	31	5	0	195.1	845	206	101	91	16	7	7	13	69	1	126	4	1	10	4	.714	1	0-0	0	4.19
1999 Oakland	AL	19	19	3	0	119.1	528	135	66	57	8	4	6	9	41	0	68	3	1	5	3	.625	0	0-0	0	4.30
New York	NL	12	12	2	0	76	317	71	35	34	8	3	1	4	28	1	58	1	0	5	1	.833	1	0-0	0	4.03
11 ML YEARS		502	217	29	132	1701.1	7318	1686	862	766	166	58	48	55	651	37	1114	51	14	114	78	.594	6	28-44	51	4.05

Mel Rojas

Pitches: Right **Bats:** Right **Pos:** RP-13   **Ht:** 5'11" **Wt:** 212 **Born:** 12/10/66 **Age:** 33

Year Team	Lg	G	GS	CG	GF	IP	BFP	H	R	ER	HR	SH	SF	HB	TBB	IBB	SO	WP	Bk	W	L	Pct.	ShO	Sv-Op	Hld	ERA
1999 Ottawa *	AAA	12	0	0	6	21	99	25	13	12	3	0	0	1	12	0	16	3	0	0	1	.000	0	2--	—	5.14
1990 Montreal	NL	23	0	0	5	40	173	34	17	16	5	2	0	2	24	4	26	2	0	3	1	.750	0	1-2	1	3.60
1991 Montreal	NL	37	0	0	13	48	200	42	21	20	4	0	2	1	13	1	37	3	0	3	3	.500	0	6-9	7	3.75
1992 Montreal	NL	68	0	0	26	100.2	399	71	17	16	2	4	2	2	34	8	70	2	0	7	1	.875	0	10-11	13	1.43
1993 Montreal	NL	66	0	0	25	88.1	378	80	39	29	6	8	6	4	30	3	48	5	0	5	8	.385	0	10-19	14	2.95
1994 Montreal	NL	58	0	0	27	84	341	71	35	31	11	2	1	4	21	0	84	3	0	3	2	.600	0	16-18	19	3.32
1995 Montreal	NL	59	0	0	48	67.2	302	69	32	31	2	2	1	7	29	4	61	6	0	1	4	.200	0	30-39	3	4.12
1996 Montreal	NL	74	0	0	64	81	326	56	30	29	5	2	4	2	28	3	92	3	0	7	4	.636	0	36-40	1	3.22
1997 ChC-NYM	NL	77	0	0	50	85.1	370	78	47	44	15	2	2	7	36	2	93	3	0	0	6	.000	0	15-22	7	4.64
1998 New York	NL	50	0	0	19	58	262	68	39	39	9	4	2	3	30	5	41	2	0	5	2	.714	0	2-6	7	6.05
1999 LA-Det-Mon		13	0	0	5	14	79	22	28	28	6	0	2	5	9	1	10	1	0	0	0	.000	0	0-0	1	18.00
1997 Chicago	NL	54	0	0	38	59	259	54	30	29	11	2	1	5	30	1	61	2	0	0	4	.000	0	13-19	2	4.42
New York	NL	23	0	0	12	26.1	111	24	17	15	4	0	1	2	6	1	32	1	0	0	2	.000	0	2-3	5	5.13
1999 Los Angeles	NL	5	0	0	2	5	23	5	7	7	3	0	0	0	3	1	3	0	0	0	0	.000	0	0-0	0	12.60
Detroit	AL	5	0	0	2	6.1	39	12	16	16	3	0	1	3	4	0	6	0	0	0	0	.000	0	0-0	1	22.74
Montreal	NL	3	0	0	1	2.2	17	5	5	5	0	0	1	2	2	0	1	1	0	0	0	.000	0	0-0	0	16.88
10 ML YEARS		525	0	0	282	667	2830	591	305	283	65	26	22	37	254	31	562	30	0	34	31	.523	0	126-166	73	3.82

Scott Rolen

Bats: Right **Throws:** Right **Pos:** 3B-112; PH/PR-1   **Ht:** 6'4" **Wt:** 225 **Born:** 4/4/75 **Age:** 25

Year Team	Lg	G	AB	H	2B	3B	HR	(Hm	Rd)	TB	R	RBI	TBB	IBB	SO	HBP	SH	SF	SB	CS	SB%	GDP	Avg	OBP	SLG
1996 Philadelphia	NL	37	130	33	7	0	4	(2	2)	52	10	18	13	0	27	1	0	2	0	2	.00	4	.254	.322	.400
1997 Philadelphia	NL	156	561	159	35	3	21	(10	10)	263	93	92	76	4	138	13	0	7	16	6	.73	6	.283	.377	.469
1998 Philadelphia	NL	160	601	174	45	4	31	(19	12)	320	120	110	93	6	141	11	0	6	14	7	.67	10	.290	.391	.532
1999 Philadelphia	NL	112	421	113	28	1	26	(9	17)	221	74	77	67	2	114	3	0	6	12	2	.86	8	.268	.368	.525
4 ML YEARS		465	1713	479	115	8	82	(41	41)	856	297	297	249	12	420	28	0	21	42	17	.71	28	.280	.376	.500

Mike Romano

Pitches: Right **Bats:** Right **Pos:** RP-3   **Ht:** 6'1" **Wt:** 190 **Born:** 3/3/72 **Age:** 28

Year Team	Lg	G	GS	CG	GF	IP	BFP	H	R	ER	HR	SH	SF	HB	TBB	IBB	SO	WP	Bk	W	L	Pct.	ShO	Sv-Op	Hld	ERA
1993 Medcine Hat	R+	9	8	0	0	41	175	34	20	12	1	0	0	7	11	0	28	3	0	4	1	.800	0	0--	—	2.63
1994 Hagerstown	A	18	18	2	0	108.1	453	91	47	37	10	2	3	9	40	0	90	5	2	10	2	.833	0	0--	—	3.07
1995 Dunedin	A+	28	26	1	1	150.1	654	141	79	69	15	4	3	11	75	0	102	5	3	11	7	.611	1	0--	—	4.13
1996 Knoxville	AA	34	21	0	5	130	600	148	98	72	17	5	8	5	72	1	92	5	2	9	9	.500	0	1--	—	4.98
1997 Syracuse	AAA	40	12	0	9	108	487	100	56	51	10	1	3	6	74	2	83	7	0	2	4	.333	0	0--	—	4.25
1998 Syracuse	AAA	27	13	1	7	117.1	516	131	66	54	13	0	2	3	53	3	69	6	0	8	6	.571	0	1--	—	4.14
1999 Syracuse	AAA	29	28	2	0	174.1	756	160	90	80	21	4	4	8	84	2	104	8	1	12	8	.600	0	0--	—	4.13
1999 Toronto	AL	3	0	0	1	5.1	28	8	8	7	1	0	1	0	5	0	3	1	0	0	0	.000	0	0-0	0	11.81

J.C. Romero

Pitches: Left **Bats:** Both **Pos:** RP-5   **Ht:** 5'11" **Wt:** 193 **Born:** 6/4/76 **Age:** 24

Year Team	Lg	G	GS	CG	GF	IP	BFP	H	R	ER	HR	SH	SF	HB	TBB	IBB	SO	WP	Bk	W	L	Pct.	ShO	Sv-Op	Hld	ERA
1997 Elizabethtn	R+	18	0	0	12	24	110	27	16	13	4	1	0	4	7	0	29	0	4	3	2	.800	0	3--	—	4.88
Fort Myers	A+	7	1	0	3	12.1	50	11	6	6	1	0	0	1	4	0	9	0	0	1	1	.500	0	0--	—	4.38
1998 New Britain	AA	51	1	0	14	78	324	48	28	19	3	6	2	4	43	3	79	13	0	6	3	.667	0	2--	—	2.19
1999 New Britain	AA	36	1	0	17	53	244	51	25	20	6	3	2	4	34	0	53	2	1	4	4	.500	0	7--	—	3.40
Salt Lake	AAA	15	0	0	7	19.2	89	18	11	7	1	1	1	1	14	0	20	3	0	4	1	.800	0	1--	—	3.20
1999 Minnesota	AL	5	0	0	3	9.2	39	13	4	4	0	0	0	0	0	0	4	0	0	0	0	.000	0	0-0	0	3.72

Rafael Roque

Pitches: Left **Bats:** Left **Pos:** RP-34; SP-9   **Ht:** 6'4" **Wt:** 189 **Born:** 10/27/73 **Age:** 26

Year Team	Lg	G	GS	CG	GF	IP	BFP	H	R	ER	HR	SH	SF	HB	TBB	IBB	SO	WP	Bk	W	L	Pct.	ShO	Sv-Op	Hld	ERA
1992 Mets	R	20	0	0	18	33.2	149	28	13	8	0	4	0	1	16	2	33	3	1	3	1	.750	0	8--	—	2.14
1993 Kingsport	R+	14	7	0	4	45.1	222	58	44	31	9	3	2	7	26	0	36	8	1	1	3	.250	0	0--	—	6.15
1994 St. Lucie	A+	2	0	0	2	3	15	2	1	0	0	1	1	1	3	1	2	0	0	0	0	.000	0	0--	—	0.00
Capital Cty	A	15	15	1	0	86.1	353	73	26	23	6	1	3	4	30	1	74	7	1	6	3	.667	0	0--	—	2.40
1995 St. Lucie	A+	24	24	2	0	136.2	582	114	65	54	7	2	4	4	72	1	81	11	4	6	9	.400	1	0--	—	3.56
1996 Binghamton	AA	13	13	0	0	60.2	291	71	57	49	8	2	1	2	39	0	46	4	0	0	4	.000	0	0--	—	7.27
St. Lucie	A+	14	12	1	1	76.1	311	57	22	18	2	5	0	3	39	0	59	8	0	6	4	.600	0	0--	—	2.12
1997 Binghamton	AA	16	0	0	5	26.1	126	35	26	20	7	2	0	1	17	1	23	1	0	1	1	.500	0	0--	—	6.84
St. Lucie	A+	17	13	1	1	77.2	325	81	42	37	8	3	4	1	25	0	54	2	1	2	10	.167	0	0--	—	4.29
1998 El Paso	AA	16	16	1	0	94	432	113	56	46	8	2	0	4	35	2	70	4	0	5	6	.455	0	0--	—	4.40
Louisville	AAA	9	8	0	0	49.2	207	42	21	20	2	2	2	4	19	1	43	1	0	5	2	.714	0	0--	—	3.62
1999 Louisville	AAA	2	2	0	0	10	35	4	0	0	0	1	0	1	3	0	3	0	0	1	0	1.000	0	0--	—	0.00
1998 Milwaukee	NL	9	9	0	0	48	206	42	28	26	9	4	0	1	24	0	34	3	1	4	2	.667	0	0-0	0	4.88
1999 Milwaukee	NL	43	9	0	7	84.1	386	96	52	50	16	1	3	4	42	1	66	4	1	1	6	.143	0	1-2	8	5.34
2 ML YEARS		52	18	0	7	132.1	592	138	80	76	25	5	3	5	66	1	100	7	2	5	8	.385	0	1-2	8	5.17

Jose Rosado

Pitches: Left **Bats:** Left **Pos:** SP-33   **Ht:** 6'0" **Wt:** 185 **Born:** 11/9/74 **Age:** 25

Year Team	Lg	G	GS	CG	GF	IP	BFP	H	R	ER	HR	SH	SF	HB	TBB	IBB	SO	WP	Bk	W	L	Pct.	ShO	Sv-Op	Hld	ERA
1996 Kansas City	AL	16	16	2	0	106.2	441	101	39	38	7	1	4	4	26	1	64	5	1	8	6	.571	0	0-0	0	3.21
1997 Kansas City	AL	33	33	2	0	203.1	881	208	117	106	26	6	11	4	73	3	129	4	2	9	12	.429	0	0-0	0	4.69
1998 Kansas City	AL	38	25	2	1	174.2	757	180	106	91	25	1	3	5	57	2	135	6	1	8	11	.421	1	1-1	2	4.69
1999 Kansas City	AL	33	33	5	0	208	882	197	103	89	24	8	4	5	72	1	141	9	0	10	14	.417	0	0-0	0	3.85
4 ML YEARS		120	107	11	1	692.2	2961	686	365	324	82	16	22	18	228	7	469	24	4	35	43	.449	2	1-1	2	4.21

Brian Rose

Pitches: Right **Bats:** Right **Pos:** SP-18; RP-4   **Ht:** 6'3" **Wt:** 215 **Born:** 2/13/76 **Age:** 24

Year Team	Lg	G	GS	CG	GF	IP	BFP	H	R	ER	HR	SH	SF	HB	TBB	IBB	SO	WP	Bk	W	L	Pct.	ShO	Sv-Op	Hld	ERA
1995 Michigan	A	21	20	2	0	136	561	127	63	52	5	3	1	9	31	0	105	4	0	8	5	.615	0	0--	—	3.44
1996 Trenton	AA	27	27	4	0	163.2	687	157	82	73	21	6	4	13	45	3	115	1	1	12	7	.632	2	0--	—	4.01
1997 Pawtucket	AAA	27	26	3	0	190.2	787	188	74	64	21	1	5	7	46	2	116	5	0	17	5	.773	0	0--	—	3.02
1998 Pawtucket	AAA	6	6	0	0	17.2	84	24	19	15	5	0	0	2	4	0	17	0	0	0	3	.000	0	0--	—	7.64
1999 Pawtucket	AAA	7	7	0	0	28	117	28	10	9	6	0	0	0	8	0	30	0	0	2	1	.667	0	0--	—	2.89
1997 Boston	AL	1	1	0	0	3	16	5	4	4	0	0	0	0	2	0	3	0	0	0	0	.000	0	0-0	0	12.00
1998 Boston	AL	8	8	0	0	37.2	168	43	32	29	9	0	1	2	14	0	18	0	0	1	4	.200	0	0-0	0	6.93
1999 Boston	AL	22	18	0	1	98	433	112	59	53	19	2	0	2	29	2	51	0	0	7	6	.538	0	0-0	0	4.87
3 ML YEARS		31	27	0	1	138.2	617	160	95	86	28	2	1	4	45	2	72	0	0	8	10	.444	0	0-0	0	5.58

John Roskos

Bats: Right **Throws:** Right **Pos:** PH/PR-12; C-1   **Ht:** 5'11" **Wt:** 195 **Born:** 11/19/74 **Age:** 25

Year Team	Lg	G	AB	H	2B	3B	HR	(Hm	Rd)	TB	R	RBI	TBB	IBB	SO	HBP	SH	SF	SB	CS	SB%	GDP	Avg	OBP	SLG
1993 Marlins	R	11	40	7	1	0	1	—	—	11	6	3	5	0	11	1	0	0	1	1	.50	0	.175	.283	.275
1994 Elmira	A-	39	136	38	7	1	4	—	—	57	11	23	27	0	37	0	0	2	0	1	.00	0	.279	.394	.419
1995 Kane County	A	114	418	124	36	3	12	—	—	202	74	88	42	1	86	6	0	6	2	0	1.00	6	.297	.364	.483
1996 Portland	AA	121	396	109	26	3	9	—	—	168	53	58	67	4	102	5	0	2	3	4	.43	5	.275	.385	.424
1997 Portland	AA	123	451	139	31	1	24	—	—	244	66	84	50	2	81	0	2	6	4	6	.40	17	.308	.373	.541
1998 Charlotte	AAA	115	416	118	23	1	10	—	—	173	54	62	43	0	84	3	0	1	0	0	.00	15	.284	.353	.416
1999 Calgary	AAA	134	506	162	44	0	24	—	—	278	85	90	52	2	112	3	0	9	2	1	.67	18	.320	.381	.549
1998 Florida	NL	10	10	1	0	0	0	(0	0)	1	1	0	0	0	5	0	0	0	0	0	.00	0	.100	.100	.100
1999 Florida	NL	13	12	2	2	0	0	(0	0)	4	0	1	1	0	7	0	0	0	0	0	.00	0	.167	.231	.333
2 ML YEARS		23	22	3	2	0	0	(0	0)	5	1	1	1	0	12	0	0	0	0	0	.00	0	.136	.174	.227

Kirk Rueter

Pitches: Left **Bats:** Left **Pos:** SP-33   **Ht:** 6'2" **Wt:** 205 **Born:** 12/1/70 **Age:** 29

Year Team	Lg	G	GS	CG	GF	IP	BFP	H	R	ER	HR	SH	SF	HB	TBB	IBB	SO	WP	Bk	W	L	Pct.	ShO	Sv-Op	Hld	ERA
1993 Montreal	NL	14	14	1	0	85.2	341	85	33	26	5	1	0	0	18	1	31	0	0	8	0	1.000	0	0-0	0	2.73
1994 Montreal	NL	20	20	0	0	92.1	397	106	60	53	11	6	6	2	23	1	50	2	0	7	3	.700	0	0-0	0	5.17
1995 Montreal	NL	9	9	1	0	47.1	184	38	17	17	3	4	0	1	9	0	28	0	0	5	3	.625	1	0-0	0	3.23
1996 Mon-SF	NL	20	19	0	0	102	430	109	50	45	12	4	1	2	27	0	46	2	0	6	8	.429	0	0-0	0	3.97
1997 San Francisco	NL	32	32	0	0	190.2	802	194	83	73	17	10	6	1	51	8	115	3	0	13	6	.684	0	0-0	0	3.45
1998 San Francisco	NL	33	33	1	0	187.2	806	193	100	91	27	5	8	7	57	3	102	6	0	16	9	.640	0	0-0	0	4.36
1999 San Francisco	NL	33	33	0	0	184.2	804	219	118	111	28	6	4	2	55	2	94	2	0	15	10	.600	0	0-0	0	5.41
1996 Montreal	NL	16	16	0	0	78.2	338	91	44	40	12	4	1	2	22	0	30	0	0	5	6	.455	0	0-0	0	4.58
San Francisco	NL	4	3	0	0	23.1	92	18	6	5	0	0	0	0	5	0	16	2	0	1	2	.333	0	0-0	0	1.93
7 ML YEARS		161	160	4	0	890.1	3764	944	461	416	103	36	25	15	240	15	466	15	0	70	39	.642	1	0-0	0	4.21

Sean Runyan

Pitches: Left **Bats:** Left **Pos:** RP-12   **Ht:** 6'3" **Wt:** 210 **Born:** 6/21/74 **Age:** 26

Year Team	Lg	G	GS	CG	GF	IP	BFP	H	R	ER	HR	SH	SF	HB	TBB	IBB	SO	WP	Bk	W	L	Pct.	ShO	Sv-Op	Hld	ERA
1992 Astros	R	10	10	0	0	45	203	54	19	16	0	1	0	5	16	0	30	8	1	3	3	.500	0	0--	—	3.20
1993 Astros	R	12	12	0	0	66.1	302	66	35	22	2	1	3	2	24	0	52	4	0	4	3	.571	0	0--	—	2.98
1994 Auburn	A-	14	14	2	0	95.1	396	90	49	37	5	1	1	2	19	0	66	12	1	7	5	.583	1	0--	—	3.49
1995 Quad City	A	22	11	0	2	76.1	327	67	37	31	10	1	2	3	29	0	65	4	0	4	6	.400	0	0--	—	3.66
1996 Quad City	A	29	17	0	3	132.1	551	128	61	57	10	1	5	14	30	0	104	4	1	9	4	.692	0	0--	—	3.88
1997 Mobile	AA	40	1	0	15	61.2	261	54	25	16	4	2	1	3	28	3	52	1	1	5	2	.714	0	1--	—	2.34
1999 Toledo	AAA	10	0	0	2	10.1	45	7	4	4	1	0	0	2	6	0	7	0	0	0	0	.000	0	0--	—	3.48
1998 Detroit	AL	**88**	0	0	11	50.1	223	47	23	20	7	2	7	2	28	3	39	5	0	1	4	.200	0	1-3	11	3.58
1999 Detroit	AL	12	0	0	2	10.2	45	9	4	4	2	1	2	1	3	1	6	2	0	0	1	.000	0	0-0	1	3.38
2 ML YEARS		100	0	0	13	61	268	56	27	24	9	3	9	3	31	4	45	7	0	1	5	.167	0	1-3	12	3.54

Ryan Rupe

Pitches: Right **Bats:** Right **Pos:** SP-24   **Ht:** 6'5" **Wt:** 230 **Born:** 3/31/75 **Age:** 25

Year Team	Lg	G	GS	CG	GF	IP	BFP	H	R	ER	HR	SH	SF	HB	TBB	IBB	SO	WP	Bk	W	L	Pct.	ShO	Sv-Op	Hld	ERA
1998 Hudson Val	A-	3	3	0	0	13.1	50	8	1	1	0	1	0	0	2	0	18	1	0	1	0	1.000	0	0--	—	0.68
Chston-SC	A	10	10	0	0	56.1	215	33	18	15	3	0	1	6	9	0	62	3	0	6	1	.857	0	0--	—	2.40
1999 Orlando	AA	5	5	0	0	26.1	109	18	13	8	1	0	0	2	6	0	22	1	1	2	2	.500	0	0--	—	2.73
1999 Tampa Bay	AL	24	24	0	0	142.1	614	136	81	72	17	1	7	12	57	2	97	4	1	8	9	.471	0	0-0	0	4.55

Glendon Rusch

Pitches: Left **Bats:** Left **Pos:** RP-4   **Ht:** 6'1" **Wt:** 200 **Born:** 11/7/74 **Age:** 25

Year Team	Lg	G	GS	CG	GF	IP	BFP	H	R	ER	HR	SH	SF	HB	TBB	IBB	SO	WP	Bk	W	L	Pct.	ShO	Sv-Op	Hld	ERA
1999 Royals *	R	2	2	0	0	6	25	3	1	1	0	0	0	0	3	0	9	1	0	0	0	.000	0	0--	—	1.50
Omaha *	AAA	20	20	1	0	114	511	143	68	56	10	3	4	5	33	0	102	3	0	4	7	.364	0	0--	—	4.42
1997 Kansas City	AL	30	27	1	0	170.1	758	206	111	104	28	8	7	7	52	0	116	0	1	6	9	.400	0	0-0	0	5.50
1998 Kansas City	AL	29	24	1	2	154.2	686	191	104	101	22	1	2	4	50	0	94	1	0	6	15	.286	1	1-1	0	5.88
1999 KC-NYM		4	0	0	2	5	26	8	7	7	1	0	0	1	3	0	4	0	0	0	1	.000	0	0-0	0	12.60
1999 Kansas City	AL	3	0	0	1	4	23	7	7	7	1	0	0	1	3	0	4	0	0	0	1	.000	0	0-0	0	15.75
New York	NL	1	0	0	1	1	3	1	0	0	0	0	0	0	0	0	0	0	0	0	0	.000	0	0-0	0	0.00
3 ML YEARS		63	51	2	4	330	1470	405	222	212	51	9	9	12	105	0	214	1	1	12	25	.324	1	1-1	0	5.78

B.J. Ryan

Pitches: Left **Bats:** Left **Pos:** RP-14   **Ht:** 6'6" **Wt:** 230 **Born:** 12/28/75 **Age:** 24

Year Team	Lg	G	GS	CG	GF	IP	BFP	H	R	ER	HR	SH	SF	HB	TBB	IBB	SO	WP	Bk	W	L	Pct.	ShO	Sv-Op	Hld	ERA
1998 Billings	R+	14	0	0	11	18.2	76	15	4	4	0	0	0	0	5	0	25	0	3	2	1	.667	0	4--	—	1.93
Chstn-WV	A	3	0	0	3	4.1	15	1	1	1	0	1	0	0	1	0	5	1	0	0	0	.000	0	2--	—	2.08
Chattanooga	AA	16	0	0	6	16.1	67	13	4	4	0	1	1	0	6	0	21	0	0	1	0	1.000	0	4--	—	2.20
1999 Chattanooga	AA	35	0	0	23	41.2	172	33	13	12	1	2	1	0	17	0	46	2	2	2	1	.667	0	6--	—	2.59
Indianapolis	AAA	11	0	0	4	9	37	9	4	4	0	0	0	0	3	1	12	1	0	1	0	1.000	0	0--	—	4.00
Rochester	AAA	11	0	0	3	14.1	55	8	4	4	2	1	0	0	4	1	20	1	0	0	0	.000	0	1--	—	2.51
1999 Cin-Bal		14	0	0	3	20.1	82	13	7	7	0	0	1	0	13	1	29	1	0	1	0	1.000	0	0-0	0	3.10
1999 Cincinnati	NL	1	0	0	0	2	9	4	1	1	0	0	0	0	1	0	1	0	0	0	0	.000	0	0-0	0	4.50
Baltimore	AL	13	0	0	3	18.1	73	9	6	6	0	0	1	0	12	1	28	1	0	1	0	1.000	0	0-0	0	2.95

Jason Ryan

Pitches: Right **Bats:** Both **Pos:** SP-8   **Ht:** 6'3" **Wt:** 185 **Born:** 1/23/76 **Age:** 24

Year Team	Lg	G	GS	CG	GF	IP	BFP	H	R	ER	HR	SH	SF	HB	TBB	IBB	SO	WP	Bk	W	L	Pct.	ShO	Sv-Op	Hld	ERA
1994 Cubs	R	7	7	0	0	33	143	32	19	15	2	1	1	2	4	0	30	5	0	1	2	.333	0	0--	—	4.09
Huntington	R+	4	4	1	0	26	93	7	1	1	0	1	0	1	8	0	32	0	0	2	0	1.000	1	0--	—	0.35
Orlando	AA	2	2	0	0	11	45	6	3	3	1	0	0	1	6	0	12	0	0	2	0	1.000	0	0--	—	2.45
1995 Daytona	A+	26	26	0	0	134.2	579	128	61	52	10	3	2	9	54	0	98	13	1	11	5	.688	0	0--	—	3.48
1996 Orlando	AA	7	7	0	0	34.2	169	39	30	22	6	1	0	4	24	0	25	2	0	2	5	.286	0	0--	—	5.71
Daytona	A+	17	10	0	3	67	298	72	42	39	8	5	2	4	33	0	49	1	0	1	8	.111	0	1--	—	5.24
1997 Daytona	A+	27	27	5	0	170.1	740	168	105	84	22	3	10	6	55	2	140	12	0	9	8	.529	0	0--	—	4.44
1998 West Tenn	AA	30	25	2	3	147.2	661	172	97	80	20	7	4	10	57	3	121	10	1	3	13	.188	0	0--	—	4.88
1999 West Tenn	AA	8	7	0	0	44.2	185	29	12	7	1	1	1	4	15	1	53	1	0	5	0	1.000	0	0--	—	1.41
New Britain	AA	8	8	0	0	50.2	217	48	29	27	6	1	0	1	24	0	42	3	0	2	4	.333	0	0--	—	4.80
Salt Lake	AAA	9	9	0	0	54.1	240	57	36	31	8	1	3	1	24	0	34	0	0	4	4	.500	0	0--	—	5.13
1999 Minnesota	AL	8	8	1	0	40.2	182	46	23	22	9	0	1	3	17	0	15	0	0	1	4	.200	0	0-0	0	4.87

Ken Ryan

Pitches: Right **Bats:** Right **Pos:** RP-15   **Ht:** 6'3" **Wt:** 225 **Born:** 10/24/68 **Age:** 31

Year Team	Lg	G	GS	CG	GF	IP	BFP	H	R	ER	HR	SH	SF	HB	TBB	IBB	SO	WP	Bk	W	L	Pct.	ShO	Sv-Op	Hld	ERA
1999 Scranton-WB *	AAA	31	0	0	18	41.1	197	54	30	26	2	3	3	0	19	2	33	1	0	2	2	.500	0	6--	—	5.66
Nashville *	AAA	6	0	0	2	7	35	7	3	3	1	1	0	1	8	1	9	1	0	1	1	.500	0	0--	—	3.86
1992 Boston	AL	7	0	0	6	7	30	4	5	5	2	1	1	0	5	0	5	0	0	0	0	.000	0	1-1	0	6.43
1993 Boston	AL	47	0	0	26	50	223	43	23	20	2	4	4	3	29	5	49	3	0	7	2	.778	0	1-4	3	3.60
1994 Boston	AL	42	0	0	26	48	202	46	14	13	1	4	0	1	17	3	32	2	0	2	3	.400	0	13-16	5	2.44
1995 Boston	AL	28	0	0	20	32.2	153	34	20	18	4	1	0	1	24	6	34	1	0	0	4	.000	0	7-10	0	4.96
1996 Philadelphia	NL	62	0	0	26	89	370	71	32	24	4	5	0	1	45	8	70	4	3	3	5	.375	0	8-13	15	2.43
1997 Philadelphia	NL	22	0	0	10	20.2	108	31	23	22	5	1	2	2	13	1	10	0	0	1	0	1.000	0	0-0	2	9.58
1998 Philadelphia	NL	17	1	0	6	12	108	21	12	11	1	2	2	1	20	1	16	4	0	0	0	.000	0	0-0	1	4.37
1999 Philadelphia	NL	15	0	0	5	15.2	71	16	11	11	2	0	0	0	11	2	9	1	0	1	2	.333	0	0-0	1	6.32
8 ML YEARS		240	1	0	125	285.2	1265	266	140	124	21	18	9	9	164	26	225	15	3	14	16	.467	0	30-44	26	3.91

Rob Ryan

Bats: Left **Throws:** Left **Pos:** PH/PR-16; RF-4; LF-1   **Ht:** 5'11" **Wt:** 190 **Born:** 6/24/73 **Age:** 27

Year Team	Lg	G	AB	H	2B	3B	HR	(Hm	Rd)	TB	R	RBI	TBB	IBB	SO	HBP	SH	SF	SB	CS	SB%	GDP	Avg	OBP	SLG
1996 Lethbridge	R+	59	211	64	8	1	4	—	—	86	55	37	43	1	33	2	5	3	23	6	.79	2	.303	.421	.408
1997 South Bend	A	121	421	132	35	5	8	—	—	201	71	73	89	5	58	2	0	5	12	1	.92	7	.314	.431	.477
1998 Tucson	AAA	116	394	125	18	2	17	—	—	198	71	66	63	3	61	10	0	5	9	3	.75	5	.317	.419	.503
1999 Tucson	AAA	117	414	120	30	5	19	—	—	217	72	88	56	2	70	12	0	5	4	3	.57	13	.290	.386	.524
1999 Arizona	NL	20	29	7	1	0	2	(1	1)	14	4	5	1	0	8	0	0	0	0	0	.00	0	.241	.267	.483

Erik Sabel

Pitches: Right **Bats:** Right **Pos:** RP-7   **Ht:** 6'2" **Wt:** 185 **Born:** 10/14/74 **Age:** 25

Year Team	Lg	G	GS	CG	GF	IP	BFP	H	R	ER	HR	SH	SF	HB	TBB	IBB	SO	WP	Bk	W	L	Pct.	ShO	Sv-Op	Hld	ERA
1996 Lethbridge	R+	20	3	0	5	42	184	43	23	13	3	1	1	3	7	0	41	4	0	1	4	.200	0	1--	—	2.79
1997 High Desert	A+	31	22	0	4	143.2	646	174	101	85	21	10	6	10	40	0	86	6	0	11	11	.500	0	1--	—	5.32
1998 High Desert	A+	14	0	0	9	22.2	100	25	8	8	2	1	0	0	4	3	18	0	0	1	0	1.000	0	4--	—	3.18
Tucson	AAA	7	0	0	1	10.1	53	17	10	10	0	2	1	1	5	1	7	1	0	1	0	1.000	0	0--	—	8.71
Tulsa	AA	24	2	0	7	56.1	226	46	24	20	6	0	0	2	13	1	33	6	0	7	0	1.000	0	2--	—	3.20
1999 El Paso	AA	8	1	0	4	10	49	16	9	7	1	0	0	0	4	0	7	0	0	1	0	1.000	0	1--	—	6.30
Tucson	AAA	22	9	0	8	72.2	306	79	36	27	4	5	1	1	24	4	38	3	0	5	2	.714	0	2--	—	3.34
1999 Arizona	NL	7	0	0	1	9.2	48	12	7	7	1	0	2	1	6	2	6	1	0	0	0	.000	0	0-0	0	6.52

Bret Saberhagen

Pitches: Right **Bats:** Right **Pos:** SP-22   **Ht:** 6'1" **Wt:** 200 **Born:** 4/11/64 **Age:** 36

Year Team	Lg	G	GS	CG	GF	IP	BFP	H	R	ER	HR	SH	SF	HB	TBB	IBB	SO	WP	Bk	W	L	Pct.	ShO	Sv-Op	Hld	ERA
1999 Trenton *	AA	1	1	0	0	6	19	2	0	0	0	0	0	0	0	0	5	0	0	1	0	1.000	0	0--	—	0.00
1984 Kansas City	AL	38	18	2	9	157.2	634	138	71	61	13	8	5	2	36	4	73	7	1	10	11	.476	1	1--	—	3.48
1985 Kansas City	AL	32	32	10	0	235.1	931	211	79	75	19	9	7	1	38	1	158	1	3	20	6	.769	1	0-0	0	2.87
1986 Kansas City	AL	30	25	4	4	156	652	165	77	72	15	3	3	2	29	1	112	1	1	7	12	.368	2	0--	—	4.15
1987 Kansas City	AL	33	33	15	0	257	1048	246	99	96	27	8	4	5	53	2	163	6	1	18	10	.643	4	0-0	0	3.36
1988 Kansas City	AL	35	35	9	0	260.2	1089	271	122	110	18	8	10	4	59	5	171	9	0	14	16	.467	0	0-0	0	3.80
1989 Kansas City	AL	36	35	12	0	262.1	1021	209	74	63	13	9	6	2	43	6	193	8	1	23	6	.793	4	0-0	0	2.16
1990 Kansas City	AL	20	20	5	0	135	552	146	52	49	9	4	4	1	28	1	87	1	0	5	9	.357	0	0-0	0	3.27
1991 Kansas City	AL	28	28	7	0	196.1	789	165	76	67	12	8	3	9	45	5	136	8	1	13	8	.619	2	0-0	0	3.07
1992 New York	NL	17	15	1	0	97.2	397	84	39	38	6	3	3	4	27	1	81	1	2	3	5	.375	1	0-1	0	3.50
1993 New York	NL	19	19	4	0	139.1	556	131	55	51	11	6	6	3	17	4	93	2	2	7	7	.500	1	0-0	0	3.29
1994 New York	NL	24	24	4	0	177.1	696	169	58	54	13	9	5	4	13	0	143	0	0	14	4	.778	1	0-0	0	2.74
1995 NYM-Col	NL	25	25	3	0	153	658	165	78	71	21	7	3	10	33	3	100	3	0	7	6	.538	0	0-0	0	4.18
1997 Boston	AL	6	6	0	0	26	120	30	20	19	5	1	3	2	10	0	14	1	0	0	1	.000	0	0-0	0	6.58
1998 Boston	AL	31	31	0	0	175	725	181	82	77	22	2	3	6	29	1	100	4	0	15	8	.652	0	0-0	0	3.96
1999 Boston	AL	22	22	0	0	119	480	122	43	39	11	4	2	2	11	0	81	0	0	10	6	.625	0	0-0	0	2.95
1995 New York	NL	16	16	3	0	110	452	105	45	41	13	5	3	5	20	2	71	2	0	5	5	.500	0	0-0	0	3.35
Colorado	NL	9	9	0	0	43	206	60	33	30	8	2	0	5	13	1	29	1	0	2	1	.667	0	0-0	0	6.28
15 ML YEARS		396	368	76	13	2547.2	10357	2433	1025	942	215	89	68	58	471	34	1705	53	12	166	115	.591	16	1--	—	3.33

Donnie Sadler

Bats: R **Throws:** R **Pos:** SS-14; PH/PR-12; 2B-10; 3B-9; CF-6; DH-4; LF-1; RF-1   **Ht:** 5'6" **Wt:** 175 **Born:** 6/17/75 **Age:** 25

Year Team	Lg	G	AB	H	2B	3B	HR	(Hm	Rd)	TB	R	RBI	TBB	IBB	SO	HBP	SH	SF	SB	CS	SB%	GDP	Avg	OBP	SLG
1994 Red Sox	R	53	206	56	8	6	1	—	—	79	52	16	23	0	27	3	1	3	32	8	.80	1	.272	.349	.383
1995 Michigan	A	118	438	124	25	8	9	—	—	192	103	55	79	0	85	6	3	4	41	13	.76	5	.283	.397	.438
1996 Trenton	AA	115	454	121	20	8	6	—	—	175	68	46	38	3	75	6	6	3	34	8	.81	6	.267	.329	.385
1997 Pawtucket	AAA	125	481	102	18	2	11	—	—	157	74	36	57	0	121	2	3	6	20	14	.59	11	.212	.295	.326
1998 Pawtucket	AAA	36	131	29	5	1	2	—	—	42	25	10	26	0	23	0	1	1	11	1	.92	1	.221	.348	.321
1999 Red Sox	R	4	13	5	2	0	0	—	—	7	2	1	2	0	1	0	0	0	0	0	.00	0	.385	.467	.538
Pawtucket	AAA	43	172	50	12	4	1	—	—	73	23	17	16	1	36	3	2	0	4	2	.67	3	.291	.361	.424

Year Team	Lg	G	AB	H	2B	3B	HR	(Hm	Rd)	TB	R	RBI	TBB	IBB	SO	HBP	SH	SF	SB	CS	SB%	GDP	Avg	OBP	SLG
1998 Boston	AL	58	124	28	4	4	3	(0	3)	49	21	15	6	0	28	3	5	1	4	0	1.00	1	.226	.276	.395
1999 Boston	AL	49	107	30	5	1	0	(0	0)	37	18	4	5	0	20	0	3	0	2	1	.67	1	.280	.313	.346
2 ML YEARS		107	231	58	9	5	3	(0	3)	86	39	19	11	0	48	3	8	1	6	1	.86	2	.251	.293	.372

Olmedo Saenz

Bats: R **Throws:** R **Pos:** 3B-56; 1B-28; PH/PR-25; DH-8 **Ht:** 6'0" **Wt:** 185 **Born:** 10/8/70 **Age:** 29

Year Team	Lg	G	AB	H	2B	3B	HR	(Hm	Rd)	TB	R	RBI	TBB	IBB	SO	HBP	SH	SF	SB	CS	SB%	GDP	Avg	OBP	SLG
1991 Sarasota	A+	5	19	2	0	1	0	—	—	4	1	2	2	0	0	0	0	0	0	1	.00	1	.105	.190	.211
South Bend	A	56	192	47	10	1	2	—	—	65	23	22	21	0	48	5	1	2	5	3	.63	3	.245	.332	.339
1992 South Bend	A	132	493	121	26	4	7	—	—	176	66	59	36	4	52	11	2	3	6	4	.60	15	.245	.309	.357
1993 South Bend	A	13	50	18	4	1	0	—	—	24	3	7	7	0	7	0	0	0	1	1	.50	1	.360	.439	.480
Sarasota	A+	33	121	31	9	4	0	—	—	48	13	27	9	0	18	2	1	1	3	1	.75	1	.256	.316	.397
Birmingham	AA	49	173	60	17	2	6	—	—	99	30	29	20	2	21	5	0	1	2	1	.67	7	.347	.427	.572
1994 Nashville	AAA	107	383	100	27	2	12	—	—	167	48	59	30	0	57	9	2	5	3	2	.60	5	.261	.326	.436
1995 Nashville	AAA	111	415	126	26	1	13	—	—	193	60	74	45	1	60	12	3	3	2	0	.00	11	.304	.385	.465
1996 Nashville	AAA	134	476	124	29	1	18	—	—	209	86	63	53	1	80	13	2	1	4	2	.67	5	.261	.350	.439
1997 White Sox	R	2	1	1	1	0	0	—	—	2	0	0	0	0	0	1	0	0	0	0	.00	0	1.000	1.000	2.000
1998 Calgary	AAA	124	466	146	29	0	29	—	—	262	89	102	45	3	49	22	0	7	3	3	.50	16	.313	.394	.562
1999 Vancouver	AAA	2	5	3	1	0	0	—	—	4	1	2	0	0	1	0	1	0	0	0	.00	0	.600	.571	.800
1994 Chicago	AL	5	14	2	0	1	0	(0	0)	4	2	0	0	0	5	0	1	0	0	0	.00	1	.143	.143	.286
1999 Oakland	AL	97	255	70	18	0	11	(8	3)	121	41	41	22	1	47	15	0	3	1	1	.50	6	.275	.363	.475
2 ML YEARS		102	269	72	18	1	11	(8	3)	125	43	41	22	1	52	15	1	3	1	1	.50	7	.268	.353	.465

Tim Salmon

Bats: Right **Throws:** Right **Pos:** RF-89; DH-7; PH/PR-2 **Ht:** 6'3" **Wt:** 241 **Born:** 8/24/68 **Age:** 31

Year Team	Lg	G	AB	H	2B	3B	HR	(Hm	Rd)	TB	R	RBI	TBB	IBB	SO	HBP	SH	SF	SB	CS	SB%	GDP	Avg	OBP	SLG
1999 Lk Elsinore *	A+	1	5	3	2	0	0	—	—	5	0	2	0	0	1	0	0	0	0	0	.00	0	.600	.600	1.000
1992 California	AL	23	79	14	1	0	2	(1	1)	21	8	6	11	1	23	1	0	1	1	1	.50	1	.177	.283	.266
1993 California	AL	142	515	146	35	1	31	(23	8)	276	93	95	82	5	135	5	0	8	5	6	.45	6	.283	.382	.536
1994 California	AL	100	373	107	18	2	23	(12	11)	198	67	70	54	2	102	5	0	3	1	3	.25	3	.287	.382	.531
1995 California	AL	143	537	177	34	3	34	(15	19)	319	111	105	91	2	111	6	0	4	5	5	.50	9	.330	.429	.594
1996 California	AL	156	581	166	27	4	30	(18	12)	291	90	98	93	7	125	4	0	3	4	2	.67	8	.286	.386	.501
1997 Anaheim	AL	157	582	172	28	1	33	(17	16)	301	95	129	95	5	142	7	0	11	9	12	.43	7	.296	.394	.517
1998 Anaheim	AL	136	463	139	24	1	26	(13	13)	247	84	88	90	5	100	3	0	10	0	1	.00	4	.300	.410	.533
1999 Anaheim	AL	98	353	94	24	2	17	(7	10)	173	60	69	63	2	82	0	0	6	4	1	.80	7	.266	.372	.490
8 ML YEARS		955	3483	1015	195	14	196	(106	90)	1826	608	660	579	29	820	31	0	46	29	31	.48	45	.291	.393	.524

Benj Sampson

Pitches: Left **Bats:** Right **Pos:** RP-26; SP-4 **Ht:** 6'2" **Wt:** 210 **Born:** 4/27/75 **Age:** 25

Year Team	Lg	G	GS	CG	GF	IP	BFP	H	R	ER	HR	SH	SF	HB	TBB	IBB	SO	WP	Bk	W	L	Pct.	ShO	Sv-Op	Hld	ERA
1993 Elizabethtn	R+	11	6	0	2	42.1	171	33	12	9	1	2	0	1	15	1	34	5	0	4	1	.800	0	1--	—	1.91
1994 Fort Wayne	A	25	25	0	0	139.2	617	149	72	59	10	7	5	5	60	0	111	5	4	6	9	.400	0	0--	—	3.80
1995 Fort Myers	A+	28	27	3	1	160	664	148	71	62	11	8	8	4	52	0	95	5	0	11	9	.550	2	0--	—	3.49
1996 Fort Myers	A+	11	11	2	0	70	282	55	28	27	5	1	2	1	26	0	65	1	0	7	1	.875	0	0--	—	3.47
Hardware Cy	AA	16	16	1	0	75.1	353	108	54	48	8	0	2	2	25	0	51	2	1	5	7	.417	0	0--	—	5.73
1997 New Britain	AA	25	20	0	1	118	498	112	56	55	12	2	5	1	49	1	92	4	2	10	6	.625	0	0--	—	4.19
1998 Salt Lake	AAA	28	28	0	0	161	726	198	99	92	24	4	6	2	52	0	132	8	4	10	7	.588	0	0--	—	5.14
1999 Salt Lake	AAA	3	3	0	0	15.2	72	25	16	14	3	0	2	1	1	0	7	1	0	1	1	.500	0	0--	—	8.04
1998 Minnesota	AL	5	2	0	1	17.1	67	10	3	3	0	0	2	1	6	0	16	2	0	1	0	1.000	0	0-0	—	1.56
1999 Minnesota	AL	30	4	0	2	71	345	107	65	64	17	1	5	0	34	3	56	2	2	3	2	.600	0	0-0	0	8.11
2 ML YEARS		35	6	0	3	88.1	412	117	68	67	17	1	7	1	40	3	72	4	2	4	2	.667	0	0-0	0	6.83

Jesus Sanchez

Pitches: Left **Bats:** Left **Pos:** RP-49; SP-10 **Ht:** 5'10" **Wt:** 155 **Born:** 10/11/74 **Age:** 25

Year Team	Lg	G	GS	CG	GF	IP	BFP	H	R	ER	HR	SH	SF	HB	TBB	IBB	SO	WP	Bk	W	L	Pct.	ShO	Sv-Op	Hld	ERA
1994 Kingsport	R+	13	12	3	0	87.1	346	61	27	19	2	1	1	4	24	0	71	7	1	7	4	.636	0	0--	—	1.96
1995 Capital Cty	A	27	27	4	0	169.2	705	154	76	59	9	2	5	7	58	0	177	10	4	9	7	.563	0	0--	—	3.13
1996 St. Lucie	A+	16	16	2	0	92	344	53	22	20	6	3	1	1	24	0	81	4	2	9	3	.750	1	0--	—	1.96
1997 Binghamton	AA	26	26	3	0	165.1	693	146	87	79	25	4	6	5	61	2	176	4	3	13	10	.565	0	0--	—	4.30
1999 Calgary	AAA	4	1	0	2	9.1	40	8	6	6	0	0	0	2	5	0	14	1	0	0	0	.000	0	1--	—	5.79
1998 Florida	NL	35	29	0	1	173	765	178	98	86	18	12	4	4	91	2	137	8	5	7	9	.438	0	0-1	0	4.47
1999 Florida	NL	59	10	0	8	76.1	362	84	53	51	16	2	7	4	60	11	62	5	2	5	7	.417	0	0-2	11	6.01
2 ML YEARS		94	39	0	9	249.1	1127	262	151	137	34	14	11	8	151	13	199	13	7	12	16	.429	0	0-3	11	4.95

Rey Sanchez

Bats: Right Throws: Right Pos: SS-134   Ht: 5'9" Wt: 170 Born: 10/5/67 Age: 32

							BATTING												BASERUNNING				PERCENTAGES		
Year Team	Lg	G	AB	H	2B	3B	HR	(Hm	Rd)	TB	R	RBI	TBB	IBB	SO	HBP	SH	SF	SB	CS	SB%	GDP	Avg	OBP	SLG
1991 Chicago	NL	13	23	6	0	0	0	(0	0)	6	1	2	4	0	3	0	0	0	0	0	.00	0	.261	.370	.261
1992 Chicago	NL	74	255	64	14	3	1	(1	0)	87	24	19	10	1	17	3	5	2	2	1	.67	7	.251	.285	.341
1993 Chicago	NL	105	344	97	11	2	0	(0	0)	112	35	28	15	7	22	3	9	2	1	1	.50	8	.282	.316	.326
1994 Chicago	NL	96	291	83	13	1	0	(0	0)	98	26	24	20	4	29	7	4	1	2	5	.29	9	.285	.345	.337
1995 Chicago	NL	114	428	119	22	2	3	(0	3)	154	57	27	14	2	48	1	8	2	6	4	.60	9	.278	.301	.360
1996 Chicago	NL	95	289	61	9	0	1	(1	0)	73	28	12	22	6	42	3	8	2	7	1	.88	6	.211	.272	.253
1997 ChC-NYY		135	343	94	21	0	2	(1	1)	121	35	27	16	2	47	1	9	1	4	6	.40	8	.274	.307	.353
1998 San Francisco	NL	109	316	90	14	2	2	(0	2)	114	44	30	16	0	47	4	1	2	0	0	.00	11	.285	.325	.361
1999 Kansas City	AL	134	479	141	18	6	2	(1	1)	177	66	56	22	2	48	4	10	3	11	5	.69	14	.294	.329	.370
1997 Chicago	NL	97	205	51	9	0	1	(1	0)	63	14	12	11	2	26	0	4	0	4	2	.67	7	.249	.287	.307
New York	AL	38	138	43	12	0	1	(0	1)	58	21	15	5	0	21	1	5	1	0	4	.00	4	.312	.338	.420
9 ML YEARS		875	2768	755	122	16	11	(4	7)	942	316	225	139	24	303	26	54	15	33	23	.59	72	.273	.312	.340

Anthony Sanders

Bats: Right Throws: Right Pos: DH-2; LF-1; PH/PR-1   Ht: 6'2" Wt: 200 Born: 3/2/74 Age: 26

							BATTING												BASERUNNING				PERCENTAGES		
Year Team	Lg	G	AB	H	2B	3B	HR	(Hm	Rd)	TB	R	RBI	TBB	IBB	SO	HBP	SH	SF	SB	CS	SB%	GDP	Avg	OBP	SLG
1993 Medcine Hat	R+	63	225	59	9	3	4	—	—	86	44	33	20	0	49	2	3	1	6	5	.55	2	.262	.327	.382
1994 St.Cathrnes	A-	74	258	66	17	3	6	—	—	107	36	45	27	0	53	1	4	2	8	7	.53	2	.256	.326	.415
1995 Hagerstown	A	133	512	119	28	1	8	—	—	173	72	48	52	0	103	5	9	5	26	14	.65	8	.232	.307	.338
1996 Dunedin	A+	102	417	108	25	0	17	—	—	184	75	50	34	0	93	6	0	0	16	12	.57	5	.259	.324	.441
Knoxville	AA	38	133	36	8	0	1	—	—	47	16	18	7	0	33	2	1	0	1	3	.25	0	.271	.317	.353
1997 Dunedin	A+	1	5	1	1	0	0	—	—	2	0	1	1	0	1	0	0	0	0	0	.00	0	.200	.333	.400
Knoxville	AA	111	429	114	20	4	26	—	—	220	68	69	44	3	121	3	4	4	20	12	.63	9	.266	.335	.513
1998 Syracuse	AAA	60	209	40	9	2	4	—	—	65	23	19	20	1	65	3	3	1	5	2	.71	3	.191	.270	.311
Knoxville	AA	6	25	10	2	0	4	—	—	24	9	9	2	0	6	0	0	0	1	0	.00	0	.400	.444	.960
1999 Syracuse	AAA	124	496	121	22	5	18	—	—	207	71	59	46	0	111	3	8	5	18	10	.64	6	.244	.309	.417
1999 Toronto	AL	3	7	2	1	0	0	(0	0)	3	1	2	0	0	2	0	0	0	0	0	.00	1	.286	.286	.429

Reggie Sanders

Bats: R Throws: R Pos: LF-97; RF-41; CF-15; PH/PR-4; DH-1   Ht: 6'1" Wt: 185 Born: 12/1/67 Age: 32

							BATTING												BASERUNNING				PERCENTAGES		
Year Team	Lg	G	AB	H	2B	3B	HR	(Hm	Rd)	TB	R	RBI	TBB	IBB	SO	HBP	SH	SF	SB	CS	SB%	GDP	Avg	OBP	SLG
1991 Cincinnati	NL	9	40	8	0	0	1	(0	1)	11	6	3	0	0	9	0	0	0	1	1	.50	1	.200	.200	.275
1992 Cincinnati	NL	116	385	104	26	6	12	(6	6)	178	62	36	48	2	98	4	0	1	16	7	.70	6	.270	.356	.462
1993 Cincinnati	NL	138	496	136	16	4	20	(8	12)	220	90	83	51	7	118	5	3	8	27	10	.73	10	.274	.343	.444
1994 Cincinnati	NL	107	400	105	20	8	17	(10	7)	192	66	62	41	1	114	8	1	3	21	9	.70	2	.263	.332	.480
1995 Cincinnati	NL	133	484	148	36	6	28	(9	19)	280	91	99	69	4	122	8	0	6	36	12	.75	9	.306	.397	.579
1996 Cincinnati	NL	81	287	72	17	1	14	(7	7)	133	49	33	44	4	86	2	0	1	24	8	.75	8	.251	.353	.463
1997 Cincinnati	NL	86	312	79	19	2	19	(11	8)	159	52	56	42	3	93	3	1	0	13	7	.65	9	.253	.347	.510
1998 Cincinnati	NL	135	481	129	18	6	14	(7	7)	201	83	59	51	2	137	7	4	2	20	9	.69	10	.268	.346	.418
1999 San Diego	NL	133	478	136	24	7	26	(11	15)	252	92	72	65	1	108	6	0	1	36	13	.73	10	.285	.376	.527
9 ML YEARS		938	3363	917	176	40	151	(69	82)	1626	591	503	411	24	885	37	9	22	194	76	.72	65	.273	.356	.483

Scott Sanders

Pitches: Right Bats: Right Pos: RP-61; SP-6   Ht: 6'4" Wt: 220 Born: 3/25/69 Age: 31

		HOW MUCH HE PITCHED						WHAT HE GAVE UP										THE RESULTS						
Year Team	Lg	G	GS	CG	GF	IP	BFP	H	R	ER	HR	SH	SF	HB	TBB	IBB	SO	WP	Bk	W	L	Pct.	ShO	Sv-Op	Hld	ERA
1993 San Diego	NL	9	9	0	0	52.1	231	54	32	24	4	1	2	1	23	1	37	0	1	3	3	.500	0	0-0	0	4.13
1994 San Diego	NL	23	20	0	2	111	485	103	63	59	10	6	5	5	48	4	109	10	1	4	8	.333	0	1-1	1	4.78
1995 San Diego	NL	17	15	1	0	90	383	79	46	43	14	2	2	2	31	4	88	6	1	5	5	.500	0	0-0	1	4.30
1996 San Diego	NL	46	16	0	6	144	594	117	58	54	10	7	7	2	48	5	157	7	0	9	5	.643	0	0-0	3	3.38
1997 Sea-Det	AL	47	20	1	15	139.2	626	152	92	91	30	3	10	4	62	6	120	8	0	6	14	.300	1	2-4	5	5.86
1998 Det-SD		26	2	0	8	40.1	188	57	39	33	6	4	0	0	11	3	32	2	0	3	3	.500	0	0-0	1	7.36
1999 Chicago	NL	67	6	0	16	104.1	469	112	69	64	19	8	3	0	53	8	89	5	1	4	7	.364	0	2-5	7	5.52
1997 Seattle	AL	33	6	0	15	65.1	309	73	48	47	16	2	5	3	38	5	62	4	0	3	6	.333	0	2-4	4	6.47
Detroit	AL	14	14	1	0	74.1	317	79	44	44	14	1	5	1	24	1	58	4	0	3	8	.273	1	0-0	1	5.33
1998 Detroit	AL	3	2	0	1	9.2	57	24	19	19	1	0	0	0	6	2	6	1	0	0	2	.000	0	0-0	0	17.69
San Diego	NL	23	0	0	7	30.2	131	33	20	14	5	4	0	0	5	1	26	1	0	3	1	.750	0	0-0	1	4.11
7 ML YEARS		235	88	2	47	681.2	2976	674	399	368	93	31	29	14	276	31	632	38	4	34	45	.430	1	5-10	17	4.86

Chance Sanford

Bats: Left Throws: Right Pos: PH/PR-4; 2B-2   Ht: 5'10" Wt: 175 Born: 6/2/72 Age: 28

							BATTING												BASERUNNING				PERCENTAGES		
Year Team	Lg	G	AB	H	2B	3B	HR	(Hm	Rd)	TB	R	RBI	TBB	IBB	SO	HBP	SH	SF	SB	CS	SB%	GDP	Avg	OBP	SLG
1992 Welland	A-	59	214	61	11	3	5	—	—	93	36	21	35	4	39	0	0	3	13	4	.76	2	.285	.381	.435
Augusta	A	14	46	5	1	0	0	—	—	6	3	2	3	0	10	1	0	0	0	2	.00	0	.109	.180	.130
1993 Salem	A+	115	428	109	21	5	10	—	—	170	54	37	33	0	80	1	3	2	11	10	.52	0	.255	.308	.397
1994 Salem	A+	127	474	130	32	6	19	—	—	231	81	78	56	0	95	2	1	4	12	6	.67	1	.274	.351	.487
1995 Carolina	AA	16	36	10	3	1	3	—	—	24	6	10	5	1	7	1	0	0	3	1	.75	0	.278	.381	.667

Year Team	Lg	G	AB	H	2B	3B	HR	(Hm	Rd)	TB	R	RBI	TBB	IBB	SO	HBP	SH	SF	SB	CS	SB%	GDP	Avg	OBP	SLG
Pirates	R	6	19	4	0	0	1	—	—	7	2	1	2	0	2	0	0	0	0	0	.00	0	.211	.286	.368
Lynchburg	A+	16	66	22	4	0	3	—	—	35	8	14	7	0	13	0	0	1	1	0	1.00	1	.333	.392	.530
1996 Carolina	AA	131	470	115	16	13	4	—	—	169	62	56	72	2	108	0	2	7	11	11	.50	9	.245	.341	.360
1997 Carolina	AA	44	149	39	10	2	9	—	—	80	30	36	20	1	39	2	2	4	3	1	.75	1	.262	.349	.537
Calgary	AAA	89	325	95	27	9	6	—	—	158	58	60	39	0	82	3	1	5	9	7	.56	5	.292	.368	.486
1998 Nashville	AAA	27	81	21	7	1	4	—	—	42	17	21	16	0	12	0	0	0	0	1	.00	1	.259	.381	.519
1999 Albuquerque	AAA	77	227	56	14	1	8	—	—	96	37	29	31	1	55	1	2	0	6	3	.67	5	.247	.340	.423
1998 Pittsburgh	NL	14	28	4	1	1	0	(0	0)	7	3	3	1	0	6	0	0	0	0	0	.00	1	.143	.172	.250
1999 Los Angeles	NL	5	8	2	0	0	0	(0	0)	2	1	2	0	0	1	0	0	0	0	0	.00	0	.250	.250	.250
2 ML YEARS		19	36	6	1	1	0	(0	0)	9	4	5	1	0	7	0	0	0	0	0	.00	1	.167	.189	.250

Julio Santana

Pitches: Right Bats: Right Pos: RP-17; SP-5   Ht: 6'0" Wt: 225 Born: 1/20/74 Age: 26

Year Team	Lg	G	GS	CG	GF	IP	BFP	H	R	ER	HR	SH	SF	HB	TBB	IBB	SO	WP	Bk	W	L	Pct.	ShO	Sv-Op	Hld	ERA
1997 Texas	AL	30	14	0	3	104	496	141	86	78	16	1	5	4	49	2	64	8	1	4	6	.400	0	0-1	1	6.75
1998 Tex-TB	AL	35	19	1	5	145.2	630	151	77	71	18	2	5	5	62	3	61	3	0	5	6	.455	0	0-0	0	4.39
1999 Tampa Bay	AL	22	5	0	7	55.1	261	66	49	45	10	1	1	7	32	0	34	0	0	1	4	.200	0	0-0	0	7.32
1998 Texas	AL	3	0	0	0	5.1	27	7	5	5	0	0	0	0	4	1	1	0	0	0	0	.000	0	0-0	0	8.44
Tampa Bay	AL	32	19	1	5	140.1	603	144	72	66	18	2	5	5	58	2	60	3	0	5	6	.455	0	0-0	0	4.23
3 ML YEARS		87	38	1	15	305	1387	358	212	194	44	4	11	16	143	5	159	11	1	10	16	.385	0	0-1	1	5.72

Marino Santana

Pitches: Right Bats: Right Pos: RP-3   Ht: 6'1" Wt: 175 Born: 5/10/72 Age: 28

Year Team	Lg	G	GS	CG	GF	IP	BFP	H	R	ER	HR	SH	SF	HB	TBB	IBB	SO	WP	Bk	W	L	Pct.	ShO	Sv-Op	Hld	ERA
1993 Bellingham	A-	15	0	0	8	21.2	117	27	19	14	3	0	1	0	22	1	24	4	2	0	1	.000	0	0- —		5.82
1994 Bellingham	A-	15	15	1	0	80	331	68	35	28	3	1	1	3	26	0	88	10	3	6	3	.667	0	0- —		3.15
1995 Wisconsin	A	15	15	2	0	96.2	368	57	26	19	5	2	1	2	25	0	110	6	0	8	3	.727	1	0- —		1.77
Riverside	A+	9	9	0	0	48	214	44	47	33	10	3	4	2	25	0	57	2	3	3	5	.375	0	0- —		6.19
1996 Lancaster	A+	28	28	1	0	157.1	688	164	105	88	26	5	8	8	57	0	167	18	6	8	15	.348	0	0- —		5.03
1997 Jacksnville	AA	39	0	0	10	74	317	55	28	27	8	1	1	4	43	0	98	13	1	4	1	.800	0	1- —		3.28
1998 Toledo	AAA	44	0	0	24	68.1	277	44	30	22	10	1	4	1	34	1	94	10	2	6	3	.667	0	7- —		2.90
1999 Pawtucket	AAA	25	0	0	10	39.2	171	28	15	13	5	0	3	2	17	3	45	7	3	2	3	.400	0	1- —		2.95
1998 Detroit	AL	7	0	0	2	7.1	39	9	3	3	1	1	0	1	8	2	10	3	0	0	0	.000	1	0-0	1	3.68
1999 Boston	AL	3	0	0	1	4	22	8	7	7	3	0	1	0	3	0	4	1	0	0	0	.000	0	0-0	0	15.75
2 ML YEARS		10	0	0	3	11.1	61	17	10	10	4	1	1	1	11	2	14	4	0	0	0	.000	0	0-0	1	7.94

F.P. Santangelo

Bats: B Throws: R Pos: CF-49; PH/PR-31; LF-26; 2B-11; RF-9; 3B-3; SS-1   Ht: 5'10" Wt: 180 Born: 10/24/67 Age: 32

Year Team	Lg	G	AB	H	2B	3B	HR	(Hm	Rd)	TB	R	RBI	TBB	IBB	SO	HBP	SH	SF	SB	CS	SB%	GDP	Avg	OBP	SLG
1995 Montreal	NL	35	98	29	5	1	1	(1	0)	39	11	9	12	0	9	2	1	0	1	1	.50	0	.296	.384	.398
1996 Montreal	NL	152	393	109	20	5	7	(5	2)	160	54	56	49	4	61	11	9	5	5	2	.71	6	.277	.369	.407
1997 Montreal	NL	130	350	87	19	5	5	(5	0)	131	56	31	50	1	73	25	12	3	8	5	.62	1	.249	.379	.374
1998 Montreal	NL	122	383	82	18	0	4	(2	2)	112	53	23	44	1	72	23	11	1	7	3	.70	5	.214	.330	.292
1999 San Francisco	NL	113	254	66	17	3	3	(2	1)	98	49	26	53	0	54	11	5	2	12	4	.75	1	.260	.406	.386
5 ML YEARS		552	1478	373	79	14	20	(15	5)	540	223	145	208	6	269	72	38	11	33	15	.69	13	.252	.369	.365

Benito Santiago

Bats: Right Throws: Right Pos: C-107; PH/PR-8; 1B-1   Ht: 6'1" Wt: 195 Born: 3/9/65 Age: 35

Year Team	Lg	G	AB	H	2B	3B	HR	(Hm	Rd)	TB	R	RBI	TBB	IBB	SO	HBP	SH	SF	SB	CS	SB%	GDP	Avg	OBP	SLG
1986 San Diego	NL	17	62	18	2	0	3	(2	1)	29	10	6	2	0	12	0	0	1	0	1	.00	0	.290	.308	.468
1987 San Diego	NL	146	546	164	33	2	18	(11	7)	255	64	79	16	2	112	5	1	4	21	12	.64	12	.300	.324	.467
1988 San Diego	NL	139	492	122	22	2	10	(3	7)	178	49	46	24	2	82	1	5	5	15	7	.68	18	.248	.282	.362
1989 San Diego	NL	129	462	109	16	3	16	(8	8)	179	50	62	26	6	89	1	3	2	11	6	.65	9	.236	.277	.387
1990 San Diego	NL	100	344	93	8	5	11	(5	6)	144	42	53	27	2	55	3	1	7	5	5	.50	4	.270	.323	.419
1991 San Diego	NL	152	580	155	22	3	17	(6	11)	234	60	87	23	5	114	4	0	7	8	10	.44	21	.267	.296	.403
1992 San Diego	NL	106	386	97	21	0	10	(8	2)	148	37	42	21	1	52	0	0	4	2	5	.29	14	.251	.287	.383
1993 Florida	NL	139	469	108	19	6	13	(6	7)	178	49	50	37	2	88	5	0	4	1	7	.59	9	.230	.291	.380
1994 Florida	NL	101	337	92	14	2	11	(4	7)	143	35	41	25	1	57	1	2	4	1	2	.33	11	.273	.322	.424
1995 Cincinnati	NL	81	266	76	20	0	11	(7	4)	129	40	44	24	1	48	4	0	2	2	2	.50	7	.286	.351	.485
1996 Philadelphia	NL	136	481	127	21	2	30	(8	22)	242	71	85	49	7	104	1	0	2	1	2	.33	10	.264	.332	.503
1997 Toronto	AL	97	341	83	10	0	13	(7	6)	132	31	42	17	1	80	2	1	5	1	0	1.00	10	.243	.279	.387
1998 Toronto	AL	15	29	9	5	0	0	(0	0)	14	3	4	1	0	6	0	0	0	0	0	.00	1	.310	.333	.483
1999 Chicago	NL	109	350	87	18	3	7	(2	5)	132	28	36	32	6	71	2	0	2	1	1	.50	12	.249	.313	.377
14 ML YEARS		1467	5145	1340	231	28	170	(77	93)	2137	569	677	324	36	970	29	13	49	79	58	.58	136	.260	.305	.415

Jose Santiago

Pitches: Right Bats: Right Pos: RP-34   Ht: 6'3" Wt: 215 Born: 11/5/74 Age: 25

Year Team	Lg	G	GS	CG	GF	IP	BFP	H	R	ER	HR	SH	SF	HB	TBB	IBB	SO	WP	Bk	W	L	Pct.	ShO	Sv-Op	Hld	ERA
1994 Royals	R	10	1	0	7	19	84	17	7	5	1	0	0	1	7	0	10	2	1	1	0	1.000	0	2--	—	2.37
1995 Spokane	A-	22	0	0	10	48.2	227	60	26	17	1	1	2	5	20	4	32	3	0	2	4	.333	0	1--	—	3.14
1996 Lansing	A	54	0	0	46	77	331	78	34	22	4	7	1	5	21	3	55	3	1	7	6	.538	0	19--	—	2.57
1997 Wilmington	A+	4	0	0	4	3.2	18	3	3	2	0	1	0	1	1	0	1	0	0	1	1	.500	0	2--	—	4.91
Lansing	A	9	0	0	6	13	57	10	6	3	0	0	1	0	1	0	8	0	0	1	0	1.000	0	1--	—	2.08
Wichita	AA	22	0	0	8	27	120	32	13	12	1	1	2	2	8	1	12	0	0	2	1	.667	0	3--	—	4.00
1998 Wichita	AA	52	0	0	41	72.1	316	79	36	29	9	6	1	1	27	7	31	1	0	3	4	.429	0	22--	—	3.61
Omaha	AAA	4	0	0	2	7.2	40	10	9	6	0	1	0	1	5	2	4	1	0	0	0	.000	0	1--	—	7.04
1999 Royals	R	3	3	0	0	5	16	1	1	1	0	0	0	0	0	0	4	0	0	0	0	.000	0	0--	—	1.80
Omaha	AAA	1	0	0	0	1.2	7	3	0	0	0	0	0	0	0	0	0	0	0	0	0	.000	0	0--	—	0.00
Wichita	AA	4	2	0	1	9	32	8	2	2	0	1	0	0	0	0	0	0	0	0	1	.000	0	0--	—	2.00
1997 Kansas City	AL	4	0	0	3	4.2	24	7	2	1	0	0	0	1	2	1	1	0	0	0	0	.000	0	0-0	0	1.93
1998 Kansas City	AL	2	0	0	2	2	9	4	2	2	0	0	0	0	0	0	2	0	0	0	0	.000	0	0-0	0	9.00
1999 Kansas City	AL	34	0	0	15	47.1	203	46	23	18	7	1	3	2	14	2	15	2	1	3	4	.429	0	2-3	4	3.42
3 ML YEARS		40	0	0	20	54	236	57	27	21	7	1	3	3	16	3	18	2	1	3	4	.429	0	2-3	4	3.50

Scott Sauerbeck

Pitches: Left Bats: Right Pos: RP-65   Ht: 6'3" Wt: 190 Born: 11/9/71 Age: 28

Year Team	Lg	G	GS	CG	GF	IP	BFP	H	R	ER	HR	SH	SF	HB	TBB	IBB	SO	WP	Bk	W	L	Pct.	ShO	Sv-Op	Hld	ERA
1994 Pittsfield	A-	21	0	0	9	48.1	200	39	16	11	0	3	1	1	19	2	39	4	0	3	1	.750	0	1--	—	2.05
1995 St. Lucie	A+	20	1	0	4	26.2	116	26	10	6	0	0	2	0	14	1	25	2	2	0	1	.000	0	0--	—	2.03
Capital Cty	A	19	0	0	13	33	139	28	14	12	2	2	0	1	14	1	33	3	1	5	4	.556	0	2--	—	3.27
1996 St. Lucie	A+	17	16	2	0	99.1	406	101	37	25	1	3	0	1	27	0	62	4	1	6	6	.500	2	0--	—	2.27
Binghamton	AA	8	8	2	0	46.2	191	48	24	18	4	1	2	1	12	0	30	0	0	3	3	.500	0	0--	—	3.47
1997 Norfolk	AAA	1	1	0	0	5	20	3	2	2	0	0	1	0	4	0	4	1	0	1	0	1.000	0	0--	—	3.60
Binghamton	AA	27	20	2	1	131.1	575	144	89	72	15	7	1	3	50	0	88	4	2	8	9	.471	0	0--	—	4.93
1998 Norfolk	AAA	27	27	2	0	160.1	701	178	82	70	8	7	2	3	68	1	119	8	2	7	13	.350	0	0--	—	3.93
1999 Pittsburgh	NL	65	0	0	16	67.2	287	53	19	15	6	4	0	4	38	5	55	3	0	4	1	.800	0	2-5	10	2.00

Tony Saunders

Pitches: Left Bats: Left Pos: SP-9   Ht: 6'2" Wt: 220 Born: 4/29/74 Age: 26

Year Team	Lg	G	GS	CG	GF	IP	BFP	H	R	ER	HR	SH	SF	HB	TBB	IBB	SO	WP	Bk	W	L	Pct.	ShO	Sv-Op	Hld	ERA
1999 Durham *	AAA	1	1	0	0	7	31	8	3	2	0	0	1	1	2	0	7	0	0	0	0	.000	0	0--	—	2.57
1997 Florida	NL	22	21	0	0	111.1	483	99	62	57	12	8	4	2	64	1	102	2	1	4	6	.400	0	0-0	0	4.61
1998 Tampa Bay	AL	31	31	2	0	192.1	855	191	95	88	15	6	10	7	111	1	172	2	1	6	15	.286	0	0-0	0	4.12
1999 Tampa Bay	AL	9	9	0	0	42	204	53	39	30	6	1	2	4	29	0	30	3	0	3	3	.500	0	0-0	0	6.43
3 ML YEARS		62	61	2	0	345.2	1542	343	196	175	33	15	16	13	204	2	304	7	2	13	24	.351	0	0-0	0	4.56

Steve Scarsone

Bats: R Throws: R Pos: SS-16; 1B-12; PH/PR-11; 2B-9; 3B-3; DH-2   Ht: 6'2" Wt: 195 Born: 4/11/66 Age: 34

Year Team	Lg	G	AB	H	2B	3B	HR	(Hm	Rd)	TB	R	RBI	TBB	IBB	SO	HBP	SH	SF	SB	CS	SB%	GDP	Avg	OBP	SLG
1999 Omaha *	AAA	18	58	10	1	0	5	—	—	26	9	7	7	0	21	0	0	1	1	0	1.00	2	.172	.258	.448
1992 Phi-Bal		18	30	5	0	0	0	(0	0)	5	3	0	2	0	12	0	1	0	0	0	.00	0	.167	.219	.167
1993 San Francisco	NL	44	103	26	9	0	2	(1	1)	41	16	15	4	0	32	0	4	1	0	1	.00	1	.252	.278	.398
1994 San Francisco	NL	52	103	28	8	0	2	(0	2)	42	21	13	10	1	20	0	3	2	0	2	.00	1	.272	.330	.408
1995 San Francisco	NL	80	233	62	10	3	11	(7	4)	111	33	29	18	0	82	6	3	1	3	2	.60	2	.266	.333	.476
1996 San Francisco	NL	105	283	62	12	1	5	(4	1)	91	28	23	25	0	91	2	8	1	2	3	.40	6	.219	.286	.322
1997 St. Louis	NL	5	10	1	0	0	0	(0	0)	1	0	0	2	0	5	0	0	0	1	0	1.00	0	.100	.250	.100
1999 Kansas City	AL	46	68	14	5	0	0	(0	0)	19	2	6	9	0	24	0	1	1	1	0	1.00	0	.206	.295	.279
1992 Philadelphia	NL	7	13	2	0	0	0	(0	0)	2	1	0	1	0	6	0	0	0	0	0	.00	0	.154	.214	.154
Baltimore	AL	11	17	3	0	0	0	(0	0)	3	2	0	1	0	6	0	1	0	0	0	.00	0	.176	.222	.176
7 ML YEARS		350	830	198	44	4	20	(12	8)	310	103	86	70	1	266	8	20	6	7	8	.47	9	.239	.302	.373

Aaron Scheffer

Pitches: Right Bats: Left Pos: RP-4   Ht: 6'2" Wt: 165 Born: 10/15/75 Age: 24

Year Team	Lg	G	GS	CG	GF	IP	BFP	H	R	ER	HR	SH	SF	HB	TBB	IBB	SO	WP	Bk	W	L	Pct.	ShO	Sv-Op	Hld	ERA
1994 Bellingham	A-	2	0	0	0	3	16	4	4	2	0	0	1	0	3	0	5	0	0	0	0	.000	0	0--	—	6.00
Mariners	R	24	0	0	20	32.1	127	18	11	7	1	1	1	2	10	0	26	4	1	2	2	.500	0	6--	—	1.95
1995 Wisconsin	A	9	0	0	6	13.2	65	17	14	10	2	1	0	0	5	1	8	2	0	1	0	1.000	0	0--	—	6.59
Everett	A-	24	0	0	9	43.1	185	44	23	18	4	1	0	2	16	1	38	2	1	2	5	.286	0	1--	—	3.74
1996 Wisconsin	A	45	1	0	28	67.2	292	55	35	28	5	2	2	3	34	4	89	16	5	8	1	.889	0	14--	—	3.72
1997 Lancaster	A+	37	3	0	9	92.2	410	93	58	56	17	4	3	7	42	1	103	10	0	11	3	.786	0	4--	—	5.44
1998 Lancaster	A+	25	0	0	19	43	189	46	19	15	0	2	1	1	12	3	65	5	0	2	2	.500	0	10--	—	3.14
Orlando	AA	19	0	0	11	32.2	132	23	8	8	3	0	0	1	13	0	33	1	1	1	0	1.000	0	5--	—	2.20
1999 New Haven	AA	10	0	0	4	17	79	19	9	7	3	1	0	1	8	0	24	1	0	2	0	1.000	0	0--	—	3.71
Tacoma	AAA	35	1	0	16	59.2	248	47	25	19	6	3	0	4	23	2	62	3	0	2	3	.400	0	9--	—	2.87
1999 Seattle	AL	4	0	0	3	4.2	24	6	5	1	0	0	1	0	3	0	4	0	0	0	0	.000	0	0-0	0	1.93

Curt Schilling

Pitches: Right Bats: Right Pos: SP-24   Ht: 6'4" Wt: 230 Born: 11/14/66 Age: 33

Year Team	Lg	G	GS	CG	GF	IP	BFP	H	R	ER	HR	SH	SF	HB	TBB	IBB	SO	WP	Bk	W	L	Pct.	ShO	Sv-Op	Hld	ERA
1988 Baltimore	AL	4	4	0	0	14.2	76	22	19	16	3	0	3	1	10	1	4	2	0	0	3	.000	0	0-0	0	9.82
1989 Baltimore	AL	5	1	0	0	8.2	38	10	6	6	2	0	0	0	3	0	6	1	0	0	1	.000	0	0-0	0	6.23
1990 Baltimore	AL	35	0	0	16	46	191	38	13	13	1	2	4	0	19	0	32	0	0	1	2	.333	0	3-9	5	2.54
1991 Houston	NL	56	0	0	34	75.2	336	79	35	32	2	5	1	0	39	7	71	4	1	3	5	.375	0	8-11	5	3.81
1992 Philadelphia	NL	42	26	10	10	226.1	895	165	67	59	11	7	8	1	59	4	147	4	0	14	11	.560	4	2-3	0	2.35
1993 Philadelphia	NL	34	34	7	0	235.1	982	234	114	105	23	9	7	4	57	6	186	9	3	16	7	.696	2	0-0	0	4.02
1994 Philadelphia	NL	13	13	1	0	82.1	360	87	42	41	10	6	1	3	28	3	58	3	1	2	8	.200	0	0-0	0	4.48
1995 Philadelphia	NL	17	17	1	0	116	473	96	52	46	12	5	2	3	26	2	114	0	1	7	5	.583	0	0-0	0	3.57
1996 Philadelphia	NL	26	26	8	0	183.1	732	149	69	65	16	6	4	3	50	5	182	5	0	9	10	.474	2	0-0	0	3.19
1997 Philadelphia	NL	35	35	7	0	254.1	1009	208	96	84	25	8	8	5	58	3	319	5	1	17	11	.607	2	0-0	0	2.97
1998 Philadelphia	NL	35	35	15	0	268.2	1089	236	101	97	23	14	7	6	61	3	300	12	0	15	14	.517	2	0-0	0	3.25
1999 Philadelphia	NL	24	24	8	0	180.1	735	159	74	71	25	11	3	5	44	0	152	4	0	15	6	.714	1	0-0	0	3.54
12 ML YEARS		326	215	57	60	1691.2	6916	1483	688	635	153	73	48	31	454	34	1571	49	7	99	83	.544	13	13-23	10	3.38

Jason Schmidt

Pitches: Right Bats: Right Pos: SP-33   Ht: 6'5" Wt: 211 Born: 1/29/73 Age: 27

Year Team	Lg	G	GS	CG	GF	IP	BFP	H	R	ER	HR	SH	SF	HB	TBB	IBB	SO	WP	Bk	W	L	Pct.	ShO	Sv-Op	Hld	ERA
1995 Atlanta	NL	9	2	0	1	25	119	27	17	16	2	2	4	1	18	3	19	1	0	2	2	.500	0	0-1	0	5.76
1996 Atl-Pit	NL	19	17	1	0	96.1	445	108	67	61	10	4	9	2	53	0	74	8	1	5	6	.455	0	0-0	0	5.70
1997 Pittsburgh	NL	32	32	2	0	187.2	825	193	106	96	16	10	3	9	76	2	136	8	0	10	9	.526	0	0-0	0	4.60
1998 Pittsburgh	NL	33	33	0	0	214.1	916	228	106	97	24	10	3	4	71	3	158	15	1	11	14	.440	0	0-0	0	4.07
1999 Pittsburgh	NL	33	33	2	0	212.2	937	219	110	99	24	7	7	3	85	4	148	6	4	13	11	.542	0	0-0	0	4.19
1996 Atlanta	NL	13	11	0	0	58.2	274	69	48	44	8	3	6	0	32	0	48	5	1	3	4	.429	0	0-0	0	6.75
Pittsburgh	NL	6	6	1	0	37.2	171	39	19	17	2	1	3	2	21	0	26	3	0	2	2	.500	0	0-0	0	4.06
5 ML YEARS		126	117	5	1	736	3242	775	406	369	76	33	26	19	303	12	535	38	6	41	42	.494	0	0-1	0	4.51

Scott Schoeneweis

Pitches: Left Bats: Left Pos: RP-31   Ht: 6'0" Wt: 186 Born: 10/2/73 Age: 26

Year Team	Lg	G	GS	CG	GF	IP	BFP	H	R	ER	HR	SH	SF	HB	TBB	IBB	SO	WP	Bk	W	L	Pct.	ShO	Sv-Op	Hld	ERA
1996 Lk Elsinore	A+	14	12	0	1	93.2	387	86	47	41	6	3	2	2	27	0	83	2	1	8	3	.727	0	0--	—	3.94
1997 Midland	AA	20	20	3	0	113.1	510	145	84	75	7	1	5	1	39	0	94	8	1	7	5	.583	0	0--	—	5.96
1998 Vancouver	AAA	27	27	2	0	180	787	188	102	90	18	6	5	9	59	0	133	9	1	11	8	.579	0	0--	—	4.50
1999 Edmonton	AAA	9	7	0	0	35.1	177	58	35	30	6	0	1	3	12	0	29	4	0	2	4	.333	0	0--	—	7.64
1999 Anaheim	AL	31	0	0	6	39.1	175	47	27	24	4	0	1	0	14	1	22	1	0	1	1	.500	0	0-0	3	5.49

Pete Schourek

Pitches: Left Bats: Left Pos: SP-17; RP-13   Ht: 6'5" Wt: 215 Born: 5/10/69 Age: 31

Year Team	Lg	G	GS	CG	GF	IP	BFP	H	R	ER	HR	SH	SF	HB	TBB	IBB	SO	WP	Bk	W	L	Pct.	ShO	Sv-Op	Hld	ERA
1991 New York	NL	35	8	1	7	86.1	385	82	46	41	7	5	4	2	43	4	67	1	0	5	4	.556	1	2-3	3	4.27
1992 New York	NL	22	21	0	0	136	578	137	60	55	9	4	4	2	44	6	60	4	2	6	8	.429	0	0-0	0	3.64
1993 New York	NL	41	18	0	6	128.1	586	168	90	85	13	3	8	3	45	7	72	1	2	5	12	.294	0	0-1	2	5.96
1994 Cincinnati	NL	22	10	0	3	81.1	354	90	39	37	11	6	2	3	29	4	69	0	0	7	2	.778	0	0-0	0	4.09
1995 Cincinnati	NL	29	29	2	0	190.1	754	158	72	68	17	4	4	8	45	3	160	1	1	18	7	.720	0	0-0	0	3.22
1996 Cincinnati	NL	12	12	0	0	67.1	300	79	48	45	7	3	4	3	24	1	54	3	0	4	5	.444	0	0-0	0	6.01
1997 Cincinnati	NL	18	17	0	0	84.2	371	78	59	51	18	4	1	4	38	0	59	2	0	5	8	.385	0	0-0	0	5.42
1998 Hou-Bos		25	23	0	0	124	537	127	64	61	17	5	7	5	50	1	95	7	0	8	9	.471	0	0-0	1	4.43
1999 Pittsburgh	NL	30	17	0	2	113	511	128	75	67	20	3	8	5	49	5	94	0	0	4	7	.364	0	0-0	0	5.34
1998 Houston	NL	15	15	0	0	80	354	82	43	40	10	5	4	4	36	0	59	5	0	7	6	.538	0	0-0	0	4.50
Boston	AL	10	8	0	0	44	183	45	21	21	7	0	3	1	14	1	36	2	0	1	3	.250	0	0-0	1	4.30
9 ML YEARS		234	155	3	18	1011.1	4380	1047	556	510	119	37	42	35	367	31	730	19	5	62	62	.500	1	2-4	6	4.54

Steve Schrenk

Pitches: Right Bats: Right Pos: RP-30; SP-2   Ht: 6'3" Wt: 185 Born: 11/20/68 Age: 31

Year Team	Lg	G	GS	CG	GF	IP	BFP	H	R	ER	HR	SH	SF	HB	TBB	IBB	SO	WP	Bk	W	L	Pct.	ShO	Sv-Op	Hld	ERA
1987 White Sox	R	8	6	1	0	28.1	115	23	10	3	0	3	0	2	12	0	19	2	1	1	2	.333	1	0--	—	0.95
1988 South Bend	A	21	18	1	1	90	417	95	63	50	4	0	3	13	37	0	58	7	2	3	7	.300	0	0--	—	5.00
1989 South Bend	A	16	16	1	0	79	353	71	44	38	6	2	0	8	44	1	49	9	0	5	2	.714	1	0--	—	4.33
1990 South Bend	A	20	14	2	2	103.2	419	79	44	34	7	3	3	11	25	0	92	7	1	7	6	.538	1	0--	—	2.95
1991 White Sox	R	11	7	0	2	37	144	30	20	12	0	1	0	5	6	0	39	1	0	1	3	.250	0	0--	—	2.92
1992 Sarasota	A+	25	22	4	2	154	621	130	48	35	1	4	6	7	40	2	113	7	6	15	2	.882	2	1--	—	2.05
Birmingham	AA	2	2	0	0	12.1	59	13	5	5	0	0	1	1	11	0	9	1	0	1	1	.500	0	0--	—	3.65
1993 Birmingham	AA	8	8	2	0	61.2	224	31	11	8	2	1	1	1	7	0	51	3	0	5	1	.833	1	0--	—	1.17
Nashville	AAA	21	20	0	0	122.1	526	117	61	53	11	5	2	3	47	3	78	6	3	6	8	.429	0	0--	—	3.90
1994 Nashville	AAA	29	28	2	0	178.2	769	175	82	69	15	10	4	6	69	3	134	14	1	14	6	.700	1	0--	—	3.48
1995 White Sox	R	2	2	0	0	7	27	5	2	0	0	0	0	0	0	0	6	0	0	1	0	1.000	0	0--	—	0.00
1996 Nashville	AAA	16	15	1	1	95.2	395	93	54	47	12	3	1	3	29	2	58	3	0	4	10	.286	0	0--	—	4.42

Year Team	Lg	G	GS	CG	GF	IP	BFP	H	R	ER	HR	SH	SF	HB	TBB	IBB	SO	WP	Bk	W	L	Pct.	ShO	Sv-Op	Hld	ERA
1997 Rochester	AAA	25	24	1	0	125.2	539	127	73	65	21	2	1	6	36	0	99	3	2	4	7	.364	0	0--	—	4.66
1998 Pawtucket	AAA	34	0	0	6	60.2	265	60	27	19	8	4	2	2	23	1	45	6	0	8	3	.727	0	1--	—	2.82
1999 Scranton-WB	AAA	32	0	0	13	43	185	38	17	14	2	3	2	0	21	6	34	2	0	3	1	.750	0	2--	—	2.93
1999 Philadelphia	NL	32	2	0	8	50.1	209	41	24	24	6	3	1	7	14	4	36	2	0	1	3	.250	0	1-1	1	4.29

Rudy Seanez

Pitches: Right **Bats:** Right **Pos:** RP-56 **Ht:** 5'11" **Wt:** 205 **Born:** 10/20/68 **Age:** 31

Year Team	Lg	G	GS	CG	GF	IP	BFP	H	R	ER	HR	SH	SF	HB	TBB	IBB	SO	WP	Bk	W	L	Pct.	ShO	Sv-Op	Hld	ERA
1989 Cleveland	AL	5	0	0	2	5	20	1	2	2	0	0	2	0	4	1	7	1	1	0	0	.000	0	0-0	0	3.60
1990 Cleveland	AL	24	0	0	12	27.1	127	22	17	17	2	0	1	1	25	1	24	5	0	2	1	.667	0	0-0	3	5.60
1991 Cleveland	AL	5	0	0	0	5	33	10	12	9	2	0	0	0	7	0	7	2	0	0	0	.000	0	0-1	0	16.20
1993 San Diego	NL	3	0	0	3	3.1	20	8	6	5	1	1	0	0	2	0	1	0	0	0	0	.000	0	0-0	0	13.50
1994 Los Angeles	NL	17	0	0	6	23.2	104	24	7	7	2	4	2	1	9	1	18	3	0	1	1	.500	0	0-1	1	2.66
1995 Los Angeles	NL	37	0	0	12	34.2	159	39	27	26	5	3	0	1	18	3	29	0	0	1	3	.250	0	3-4	6	6.75
1998 Atlanta	NL	34	0	0	8	36	148	25	13	11	2	1	2	1	16	0	50	2	0	4	1	.800	0	2-4	8	2.75
1999 Atlanta	NL	56	0	0	13	53.2	225	47	21	20	3	0	2	1	21	1	41	3	0	6	1	.857	0	3-8	18	3.35
8 ML YEARS		181	0	0	56	188.2	836	176	105	97	17	9	9	5	102	7	177	16	1	14	7	.667	0	8-18	36	4.63

Kevin Sefcik

Bats: R **Throws:** R **Pos:** PH/PR-57; LF-31; CF-19; RF-17; 2B-15 **Ht:** 5'10" **Wt:** 180 **Born:** 2/10/71 **Age:** 29

Year Team	Lg	G	AB	H	2B	3B	HR	(Hm	Rd)	TB	R	RBI	TBB	IBB	SO	HBP	SH	SF	SB	CS	SB%	GDP	Avg	OBP	SLG
1995 Philadelphia	NL	5	4	0	0	0	0	(0	0)	0	1	0	0	0	2	0	0	0	0	0	.00	0	.000	.000	.000
1996 Philadelphia	NL	44	116	33	5	3	0	(0	0)	44	10	9	9	3	16	2	1	2	3	0	1.00	4	.284	.341	.379
1997 Philadelphia	NL	61	119	32	3	0	2	(2	0)	41	11	6	4	0	9	1	7	0	1	2	.33	4	.269	.298	.345
1998 Philadelphia	NL	104	169	53	7	2	3	(2	1)	73	27	20	25	0	32	7	3	1	4	2	.67	3	.314	.421	.432
1999 Philadelphia	NL	111	209	58	15	3	1	(1	0)	82	28	11	29	0	24	1	3	0	9	4	.69	4	.278	.368	.392
5 ML YEARS		325	617	176	30	8	6	(5	1)	240	77	46	67	3	83	11	14	3	17	8	.68	15	.285	.364	.389

David Segui

Bats: Both **Throws:** Left **Pos:** 1B-94; DH-25; PH/PR-7 **Ht:** 6'1" **Wt:** 202 **Born:** 7/19/66 **Age:** 33

Year Team	Lg	G	AB	H	2B	3B	HR	(Hm	Rd)	TB	R	RBI	TBB	IBB	SO	HBP	SH	SF	SB	CS	SB%	GDP	Avg	OBP	SLG
1990 Baltimore	AL	40	123	30	7	0	2	(1	1)	43	14	15	11	2	15	1	1	0	0	0	.00	12	.244	.311	.350
1991 Baltimore	AL	86	212	59	7	0	2	(1	1)	72	15	22	12	2	19	0	3	1	1	1	.50	7	.278	.316	.340
1992 Baltimore	AL	115	189	44	9	0	1	(1	0)	56	21	17	20	3	23	0	2	0	1	0	1.00	4	.233	.306	.296
1993 Baltimore	AL	146	450	123	27	0	10	(6	4)	180	54	60	58	4	53	0	3	8	2	1	.67	18	.273	.351	.400
1994 New York	NL	92	336	81	17	1	10	(5	5)	130	46	43	33	6	43	1	1	3	0	0	.00	6	.241	.308	.387
1995 NYM-Mon	NL	130	456	141	25	4	12	(6	6)	210	68	68	40	5	47	3	8	3	2	7	.22	10	.309	.367	.461
1996 Montreal	NL	115	416	119	30	1	11	(6	5)	184	69	58	60	4	54	0	0	1	4	4	.50	8	.286	.375	.442
1997 Montreal	NL	125	459	141	22	3	21	(10	11)	232	75	68	57	12	66	1	0	6	1	0	1.00	9	.307	.380	.505
1998 Seattle	AL	143	522	159	36	1	19	(10	9)	254	79	84	49	4	80	0	0	3	1	.75	12	.305	.359	.487
1999 Sea-Tor	AL	121	440	131	27	3	14	(5	9)	206	57	52	40	4	60	1	1	4	2	2	.33	10	.298	.355	.468
1995 New York	NL	33	73	24	3	1	2	(2	0)	35	9	11	12	1	9	1	4	2	3	3	.25	2	.329	.420	.479
Montreal	NL	97	383	117	22	3	10	(4	6)	175	59	57	28	4	38	2	4	1	4	4	.20	8	.305	.355	.457
1999 Seattle	AL	90	345	101	22	3	9	(4	5)	156	43	39	32	4	43	1	1	3	1	2	.33	9	.293	.352	.452
Toronto	AL	31	95	30	5	0	5	(1	4)	50	14	13	8	0	17	0	0	1	0	0	.00	1	.316	.365	.526
10 ML YEARS		1113	3603	1028	207	13	102	(51	51)	1567	498	487	380	46	460	7	19	35	15	16	.48	96	.285	.352	.435

Fernando Seguignol

Bats: B **Throws:** R **Pos:** 1B-23; LF-6; PH/PR-6; RF-3 **Ht:** 6'5" **Wt:** 215 **Born:** 1/19/75 **Age:** 25

Year Team	Lg	G	AB	H	2B	3B	HR	(Hm	Rd)	TB	R	RBI	TBB	IBB	SO	HBP	SH	SF	SB	CS	SB%	GDP	Avg	OBP	SLG
1993 Yankees	R	45	161	35	3	3	2	—	—	50	16	20	9	0	37	5	0	0	2	0	1.00	6	.217	.280	.311
1994 Oneonta	A-	73	266	77	14	9	2	—	—	115	36	32	16	1	61	2	0	0	4	6	.40	6	.289	.335	.432
1995 Albany	A	121	457	95	22	2	12	—	—	157	59	66	28	3	141	6	1	6	12	8	.60	6	.208	.260	.344
1996 Delmarva	A	118	410	98	14	5	8	—	—	146	59	55	48	4	126	6	0	1	12	13	.48	5	.239	.327	.356
1997 Wst Plm Bch	A+	124	456	116	27	5	18	—	—	207	70	83	30	3	129	5	0	14	5	5	.50	1	.254	.299	.454
1998 Harrisburg	AA	80	281	81	13	0	25	—	—	169	54	69	29	4	77	6	0	1	6	1	.86	6	.288	.366	.601
Ottawa	AAA	16	45	16	8	0	6	—	—	54	16	16	12	0	43	1	1	1	0	0	.00	1	.257	.333	.495
1999 Ottawa	AAA	87	312	89	17	3	23	—	—	181	54	74	40	8	96	11	0	4	3	8	.27	9	.285	.381	.580
1998 Montreal	NL	16	42	11	4	0	2	(2	0)	21	6	3	3	0	15	0	0	1	0	0	.00	1	.262	.304	.500
1999 Montreal	NL	35	105	27	9	0	5	(3	2)	51	14	10	5	1	33	7	0	2	0	0	.00	1	.257	.328	.486
2 ML YEARS		51	147	38	13	0	7	(5	2)	72	20	13	8	1	48	7	0	3	0	0	.00	2	.259	.321	.490

Aaron Sele

Pitches: Right **Bats:** Right **Pos:** SP-33 **Ht:** 6'5" **Wt:** 220 **Born:** 6/25/70 **Age:** 30

Year Team	Lg	G	GS	CG	GF	IP	BFP	H	R	ER	HR	SH	SF	HB	TBB	IBB	SO	WP	Bk	W	L	Pct.	ShO	Sv-Op	Hld	ERA
1993 Boston	AL	18	18	0	0	111.2	484	100	42	34	5	2	5	7	48	2	93	5	0	7	2	.778	0	0-0	0	2.74

Year Team	Lg	G	GS	CG	GF	IP	BFP	H	R	ER	HR	SH	SF	HB	TBB	IBB	SO	WP	Bk	W	L	Pct.	ShO	Sv-Op	Hld	ERA
1994 Boston	AL	22	22	2	0	143.1	615	140	68	61	13	4	5	9	60	2	105	4	0	8	7	.533	0	0-0	0	3.83
1995 Boston	AL	6	6	0	0	32.1	146	32	14	11	3	1	1	3	14	0	21	3	0	3	1	.750	0	0-0	0	3.06
1996 Boston	AL	29	29	1	0	157.1	722	192	110	93	14	6	7	8	67	2	137	2	0	7	11	.389	0	0-0	0	5.32
1997 Boston	AL	33	33	1	0	177.1	810	196	115	106	25	5	7	15	80	4	122	7	0	13	12	.520	0	0-0	0	5.38
1998 Texas	AL	33	33	3	0	212.2	954	239	116	100	14	5	7	13	84	6	167	4	0	19	11	.633	2	0-0	0	4.23
1999 Texas	AL	33	33	2	0	205	920	244	115	109	21	1	3	12	70	3	186	4	0	18	9	.667	0	0-0	0	4.79
7 ML YEARS		174	174	9	0	1039.2	4651	1143	580	514	95	24	35	67	423	19	831	29	0	75	53	.586	4	0-0	0	4.45

Dan Serafini

Pitches: Left **Bats:** Both **Pos:** RP-38; SP-4 **Ht:** 6'1" **Wt:** 195 **Born:** 1/25/74 **Age:** 26

Year Team	Lg	G	GS	CG	GF	IP	BFP	H	R	ER	HR	SH	SF	HB	TBB	IBB	SO	WP	Bk	W	L	Pct.	ShO	Sv-Op	Hld	ERA
1999 Iowa *	AAA	2	2	0	0	13	56	12	6	4	1	1	0	0	5	0	11	0	0	0	0	.000	0	0- -	—	2.77
1996 Minnesota	AL	1	1	0	0	4.1	23	7	5	5	1	0	1	1	2	0	1	0	0	0	1	.000	0	0-0	0	10.38
1997 Minnesota	AL	6	4	1	1	26.1	111	27	11	10	1	1	0	0	11	0	15	1	0	2	1	.667	0	0-0	0	3.42
1998 Minnesota	AL	28	9	0	3	75	345	95	58	54	10	3	6	1	29	1	46	2	0	7	4	.636	0	0-0	2	6.48
1999 Chicago	NL	42	4	0	8	62.1	302	86	51	48	9	8	3	1	32	3	17	3	0	3	2	.600	0	1-1	5	6.93
4 ML YEARS		77	18	1	12	168	781	215	125	117	21	12	10	3	74	4	79	6	0	12	8	.600	0	1-1	7	6.27

Scott Servais

Bats: Right **Throws:** Right **Pos:** C-62; PH/PR-12; 1B-1 **Ht:** 6'2" **Wt:** 210 **Born:** 6/4/67 **Age:** 33

Year Team	Lg	G	AB	H	2B	3B	HR	(Hm	Rd)	TB	R	RBI	TBB	IBB	SO	HBP	SH	SF	SB	CS	SB%	GDP	Avg	OBP	SLG
1999 Fresno *	AAA	3	11	3	1	1	0	—	—	6	3	2	0	0	1	0	0	0	0	0	.00	0	.273	.273	.545
1991 Houston	NL	16	37	6	3	0	0	(0	0)	9	0	6	4	0	8	0	1	0	0	0	.00	0	.162	.244	.243
1992 Houston	NL	77	205	49	9	0	0	(0	0)	58	12	15	11	2	25	5	6	0	0	0	.00	7	.239	.294	.283
1993 Houston	NL	85	258	63	11	0	11	(5	6)	107	24	32	22	2	45	5	3	3	0	0	.00	6	.244	.313	.415
1994 Houston	NL	78	251	49	15	1	9	(3	6)	93	27	41	10	0	44	4	7	3	0	0	.00	6	.195	.235	.371
1995 Hou-ChC	NL	80	264	70	22	0	13	(8	5)	131	38	47	32	8	52	3	2	3	2	2	.50	9	.265	.348	.496
1996 Chicago	NL	129	445	118	20	0	11	(6	5)	171	42	63	30	1	75	14	3	7	0	2	.00	18	.265	.327	.384
1997 Chicago	NL	122	385	100	21	0	6	(4	2)	139	36	45	24	7	56	6	7	3	0	1	.00	7	.260	.311	.361
1998 Chicago	NL	113	325	72	15	1	7	(5	2)	110	35	36	26	6	51	5	3	1	1	0	1.00	12	.222	.289	.338
1999 San Francisco	NL	69	198	54	10	0	5	(0	5)	79	21	21	13	2	31	3	3	0	0	0	.00	7	.273	.327	.399
1995 Houston	NL	28	89	20	10	0	1	(1	0)	33	7	12	9	2	15	1	1	0	1	0	.00	4	.225	.300	.371
Chicago	NL	52	175	50	12	0	12	(7	5)	98	31	35	23	6	37	2	1	2	2	1	.67	5	.286	.371	.560
9 ML YEARS		769	2368	581	126	2	62	(31	31)	897	235	306	172	28	387	45	35	20	3	5	.38	72	.245	.306	.379

Scott Service

Pitches: Right **Bats:** Right **Pos:** RP-68 **Ht:** 6'6" **Wt:** 240 **Born:** 2/26/67 **Age:** 33

Year Team	Lg	G	GS	CG	GF	IP	BFP	H	R	ER	HR	SH	SF	HB	TBB	IBB	SO	WP	Bk	W	L	Pct.	ShO	Sv-Op	Hld	ERA
1988 Philadelphia	NL	5	0	0	1	5.1	23	7	1	1	0	0	0	1	1	0	6	0	0	0	0	.000	0	0-0	0	1.69
1992 Montreal	NL	5	0	0	0	7	41	15	11	11	1	0	0	1	5	0	11	0	0	0	0	.000	0	0-0	1	14.14
1993 Col-Cin	NL	29	0	0	7	46	197	44	24	22	6	2	4	2	16	4	43	0	0	2	2	.500	0	2-2	3	4.30
1994 Cincinnati	NL	6	0	0	2	7.1	35	8	9	6	2	2	0	0	3	0	5	0	0	1	2	.333	0	0-0	0	7.36
1995 San Francisco	NL	28	0	0	6	31	129	18	11	11	4	3	2	2	20	4	30	3	0	3	1	.750	0	0-0	7	3.19
1996 Cincinnati	NL	34	1	0	5	48	213	51	21	21	7	4	1	6	18	4	46	5	0	1	0	1.000	0	0-0	3	3.94
1997 Cin-KC	NL	16	0	0	3	22.1	95	28	16	16	2	2	1	6	6	0	22	2	0	3	0	.000	0	0-1	3	6.45
1998 Kansas City	AL	73	0	0	26	82.2	353	70	35	32	7	2	5	9	34	4	95	10	1	6	4	.600	0	4-8	18	3.48
1999 Kansas City	AL	68	0	0	29	75.1	352	87	51	51	13	4	7	3	42	8	68	3	0	5	5	.500	0	8-15	8	6.09
1993 Colorado	NL	3	0	0	0	4.2	24	8	5	5	1	0	2	1	1	0	3	0	0	0	0	.000	0	0-0	0	9.64
Cincinnati	NL	26	0	0	7	41.1	173	36	19	17	5	2	2	1	15	4	40	0	0	2	2	.500	0	2-2	3	3.70
1997 Cincinnati	NL	4	0	0	2	5.1	26	11	7	7	1	1	0	0	1	0	3	2	0	0	0	.000	0	0-0	1	11.81
Kansas City	AL	12	0	0	1	17	69	17	9	9	1	1	1	6	5	0	19	0	0	3	0	.000	0	0-1	2	4.76
9 ML YEARS		264	1	0	79	325	1438	328	179	171	42	19	20	23	145	24	326	23	1	18	17	.514	0	14-26	43	4.74

Richie Sexson

Bats: R **Throws:** R **Pos:** 1B-61; LF-48; DH-24; PH/PR-13; RF-3 **Ht:** 6'7" **Wt:** 210 **Born:** 12/29/74 **Age:** 25

Year Team	Lg	G	AB	H	2B	3B	HR	(Hm	Rd)	TB	R	RBI	TBB	IBB	SO	HBP	SH	SF	SB	CS	SB%	GDP	Avg	OBP	SLG
1997 Cleveland	AL	5	11	3	0	0	0	(0	0)	3	1	0	0	0	2	0	0	0	0	0	.00	2	.273	.273	.273
1998 Cleveland	AL	49	174	54	14	1	11	(9	2)	103	28	35	6	0	42	3	0	0	1	1	.50	3	.310	.344	.592
1999 Cleveland	AL	134	479	122	17	7	31	(18	13)	246	72	116	34	0	117	4	0	8	3	3	.50	19	.255	.305	.514
3 ML YEARS		188	664	179	31	8	42	(27	15)	352	101	151	40	0	161	7	0	8	4	4	.50	24	.270	.314	.530

Chris Sexton

Bats: R **Throws:** R **Pos:** 2B-10; PH/PR-10; CF-9; SS-6; LF-3; RF-1 **Ht:** 5'11" **Wt:** 178 **Born:** 8/3/71 **Age:** 28

Year Team	Lg	G	AB	H	2B	3B	HR	(Hm	Rd)	TB	R	RBI	TBB	IBB	SO	HBP	SH	SF	SB	CS	SB%	GDP	Avg	OBP	SLG
1993 Billings	R+	72	273	91	14	4	4	—	—	125	63	46	35	1	27	1	0	8	13	4	.76	6	.333	.401	.458
1994 Chstn-WV	A	133	467	140	21	4	5	—	—	184	82	59	91	3	67	2	6	6	18	11	.62	9	.300	.412	.394

Year Team	Lg	G	AB	H	2B	3B	HR	(Hm	Rd)	TB	R	RBI	TBB	IBB	SO	HBP	SH	SF	SB	CS	SB%	GDP	Avg	OBP	SLG
1995 Winston-Sal	A+	4	15	6	0	0	1	—	—	9	3	5	4	0	0	0	0	0	0	0	.00	0	.400	.526	.600
Salem	A+	123	461	123	16	6	4	—	—	163	81	32	93	2	55	1	12	1	14	11	.56	11	.267	.390	.354
New Haven	AA	1	3	0	0	0	0	—	—	0	0	0	0	0	0	0	0	0	0	0	.00	0	.000	.000	.000
1996 New Haven	AA	127	444	96	12	2	0	—	—	112	50	28	71	2	68	1	7	3	8	5	.62	10	.216	.324	.252
1997 New Haven	AA	98	360	107	22	4	1	—	—	140	65	38	62	0	37	2	11	4	8	16	.33	8	.297	.400	.389
Colo Sprngs	AAA	33	112	30	3	1	1	—	—	38	18	8	16	0	21	0	1	0	1	1	.50	4	.268	.359	.339
1998 Colo Sprngs	AAA	132	462	131	22	6	2	—	—	171	88	43	72	2	67	1	6	4	7	3	.70	17	.284	.378	.370
1999 Colo Sprngs	AAA	60	171	58	9	0	0	—	—	67	23	17	28	0	22	0	5	1	5	1	.83	7	.339	.430	.392
1999 Colorado	NL	35	59	14	0	1	1	(0	1)	19	9	7	11	1	10	0	0	0	4	2	.67	2	.237	.357	.322

Jon Shave

Bats: R Throws: R Pos: SS-24; 1B-9; 3B-6; PH/PR-4; DH-3; 2B-1   Ht: 6'0" Wt: 185 Born: 11/4/67 Age: 32

Year Team	Lg	G	AB	H	2B	3B	HR	(Hm	Rd)	TB	R	RBI	TBB	IBB	SO	HBP	SH	SF	SB	CS	SB%	GDP	Avg	OBP	SLG
1993 Texas	AL	17	47	15	2	0	0	(0	0)	17	3	7	0	0	8	0	3	2	1	3	.25	0	.319	.306	.362
1998 Minnesota	AL	19	40	10	3	0	1	(0	0)	16	7	5	3	0	10	0	0	0	1	2	.33	0	.250	.302	.400
1999 Texas	AL	43	73	21	4	0	0	(0	0)	25	10	9	5	0	17	2	3	0	1	0	1.00	0	.288	.350	.342
3 ML YEARS		79	160	46	9	0	1	(0	1)	58	20	21	8	0	35	2	6	2	3	5	.38	0	.288	.326	.363

Jeff Shaw

Pitches: Right Bats: Right Pos: RP-64   Ht: 6'2" Wt: 200 Born: 7/7/66 Age: 33

Year Team	Lg	G	GS	CG	GF	IP	BFP	H	R	ER	HR	SH	SF	HB	TBB	IBB	SO	WP	Bk	W	L	Pct.	ShO	Sv-Op	Hld	ERA
1990 Cleveland	AL	12	9	0	0	48.2	229	73	38	36	11	1	3	0	20	0	25	3	0	3	4	.429	0	0-0	0	6.66
1991 Cleveland	AL	29	1	0	9	72.1	311	72	34	27	6	1	4	4	27	5	31	6	0	0	5	.000	0	1-4	0	3.36
1992 Cleveland	AL	2	1	0	1	7.2	33	7	7	7	2	2	0	0	4	0	3	0	0	0	1	.000	0	0-0	0	8.22
1993 Montreal	NL	55	8	0	13	95.2	404	91	47	44	12	5	2	7	32	2	50	2	0	2	7	.222	0	0-1	4	4.14
1994 Montreal	NL	46	0	0	15	67.1	287	67	32	29	8	2	4	2	15	2	47	5	0	5	2	.714	0	1-2	10	3.88
1995 Mon-CWS		59	0	0	18	72	309	70	42	39	6	7	1	4	27	4	51	0	0	1	6	.143	0	3-5	6	4.88
1996 Cincinnati	NL	78	0	0	24	104.2	434	99	34	29	8	5	5	2	29	11	69	0	0	8	6	.571	0	4-11	22	2.49
1997 Cincinnati	NL	78	0	0	62	94.2	367	79	26	25	7	3	3	1	12	3	74	1	0	4	2	.667	0	42-49	5	2.38
1998 Cin-LA	NL	73	0	0	69	85	339	75	22	20	8	5	2	1	19	5	55	0	0	3	8	.273	0	48-57	0	2.12
1999 Los Angeles	NL	64	0	0	56	68	284	64	25	21	6	1	2	1	15	1	43	1	0	2	4	.333	0	34-39	0	2.78
1995 Montreal	NL	50	0	0	17	62.1	268	58	35	32	4	6	1	3	26	4	45	0	0	1	6	.143	0	3-5	4	4.62
Chicago	AL	9	0	0	1	9.2	41	12	7	7	2	1	0	1	1	0	6	0	0	0	0	.000	0	0-0	1	6.52
1998 Cincinnati	NL	39	0	0	35	49.2	192	40	11	10	2	4	2	1	12	4	29	0	0	2	4	.333	0	23-28	0	1.81
Los Angeles	NL	34	0	0	34	35.1	147	35	11	10	6	1	0	0	7	1	26	0	0	1	4	.200	0	25-29	0	2.55
10 ML YEARS		496	19	0	267	716	2997	697	307	277	74	32	26	22	200	33	448	18	0	28	45	.384	0	133-168	47	3.48

Andy Sheets

Bats: R Throws: R Pos: SS-76; PH/PR-9; 2B-7; 3B-1   Ht: 6'2" Wt: 180 Born: 11/19/71 Age: 28

Year Team	Lg	G	AB	H	2B	3B	HR	(Hm	Rd)	TB	R	RBI	TBB	IBB	SO	HBP	SH	SF	SB	CS	SB%	GDP	Avg	OBP	SLG
1999 Edmonton *	AAA	12	45	13	1	1	0	(1	3)	16	6	4	2	0	11	0	2	0	0	1	.00	0	.289	.319	.356
1996 Seattle	AL	47	110	21	8	0	0	(0	0)	29	18	9	10	0	41	1	2	1	2	0	1.00	2	.191	.262	.264
1997 Seattle	AL	32	89	22	3	0	4	(2	2)	37	18	9	7	0	34	0	5	1	2	0	1.00	0	.247	.299	.416
1998 San Diego	NL	88	194	47	5	3	7	(2	5)	79	31	29	21	3	62	1	2	1	7	2	.78	4	.242	.318	.407
1999 Anaheim	AL	87	244	48	10	0	3	(3	0)	67	22	29	14	0	59	0	6	5	1	2	.33	6	.197	.236	.275
4 ML YEARS		254	637	138	26	3	14	(7	7)	212	89	76	52	3	196	2	15	8	12	4	.75	13	.217	.275	.333

Gary Sheffield

Bats: Right Throws: Right Pos: LF-145; PH/PR-4; DH-3   Ht: 5'11" Wt: 205 Born: 11/18/68 Age: 31

Year Team	Lg	G	AB	H	2B	3B	HR	(Hm	Rd)	TB	R	RBI	TBB	IBB	SO	HBP	SH	SF	SB	CS	SB%	GDP	Avg	OBP	SLG
1988 Milwaukee	AL	24	80	19	1	0	4	(1	3)	32	12	12	7	0	7	0	1	1	3	1	.75	5	.238	.295	.400
1989 Milwaukee	AL	95	368	91	18	0	5	(2	3)	124	34	32	27	0	33	4	3	3	10	6	.63	4	.247	.303	.337
1990 Milwaukee	AL	125	487	143	30	1	10	(3	7)	205	67	67	44	1	41	3	4	9	25	10	.71	11	.294	.350	.421
1991 Milwaukee	AL	50	175	34	12	2	2	(0	2)	56	25	22	19	1	15	3	1	5	5	5	.50	3	.194	.277	.320
1992 San Diego	NL	146	557	184	34	3	33	(23	10)	323	87	100	48	5	40	6	0	7	5	6	.45	19	.330	.385	.580
1993 SD-Fla	NL	140	494	145	20	5	20	(10	10)	235	67	73	47	6	64	9	0	7	17	5	.77	11	.294	.361	.476
1994 Florida	NL	87	322	89	16	1	27	(15	12)	188	61	78	51	11	50	4	0	2	12	6	.67	10	.276	.380	.584
1995 Florida	NL	63	213	69	8	0	16	(4	12)	125	46	46	55	8	45	4	0	2	19	4	.83	3	.324	.467	.587
1996 Florida	NL	161	519	163	33	1	42	(19	23)	324	118	120	142	19	66	10	0	6	16	9	.64	16	.314	.465	.624
1997 Florida	NL	135	444	111	22	1	21	(13	8)	198	86	71	121	11	79	15	0	9	11	7	.61	7	.250	.424	.446
1998 Fla-LA	NL	130	437	132	27	2	22	(11	11)	229	73	85	95	12	46	8	0	9	22	7	.76	7	.302	.428	.524
1999 Los Angeles	NL	152	549	165	20	0	34	(15	19)	287	103	101	101	4	64	4	0	6	11	5	.69	10	.301	.407	.523
1993 San Diego	NL	68	258	76	12	2	10	(6	4)	122	34	36	18	0	30	3	0	3	5	1	.83	9	.295	.344	.473
Florida	NL	72	236	69	8	3	10	(4	6)	113	33	37	29	6	34	6	0	4	12	4	.75	2	.292	.378	.479
1998 Florida	NL	40	136	37	11	1	6	(6	0)	68	21	28	26	1	16	2	0	2	4	2	.67	3	.272	.392	.500
Los Angeles	NL	90	301	95	16	1	16	(5	11)	161	52	57	69	11	30	6	0	7	18	5	.78	4	.316	.444	.535
12 ML YEARS		1308	4645	1345	241	16	236	(118	118)	2326	779	807	757	78	550	72	9	65	156	71	.69	106	.290	.392	.501

Scott Sheldon

Bats: Right **Throws:** Right **Pos:** 3B-2 **Ht:** 6'3" **Wt:** 215 **Born:** 11/20/68 **Age:** 31

Year Team	Lg	G	AB	H	2B	3B	HR	(Hm	Rd)	TB	R	RBI	TBB	IBB	SO	HBP	SH	SF	SB	CS	SB%	GDP	Avg	OBP	SLG
1991 Sou Oregon	A-	65	229	58	10	3	0	—	—	74	34	24	23	0	44	2	3	1	9	5	.64	5	.253	.325	.323
1992 Madison	A	74	279	76	16	0	6	—	—	110	41	24	32	1	78	1	3	4	5	4	.56	2	.272	.345	.394
1993 Madison	A	131	428	91	22	1	8	—	—	139	67	67	49	3	121	8	3	8	8	7	.53	8	.213	.300	.325
1994 Huntsville	AA	91	268	62	10	1	0	—	—	74	31	28	28	1	69	7	7	3	7	1	.88	4	.231	.317	.276
1995 Edmonton	AAA	45	128	33	7	1	4	—	—	54	21	12	15	0	15	2	4	1	4	2	.67	0	.258	.342	.422
Huntsville	AA	66	235	51	10	2	4	—	—	77	25	15	23	0	60	1	3	1	5	0	1.00	7	.217	.288	.328
1996 Edmonton	AAA	98	350	105	27	3	10	—	—	168	61	60	43	3	83	4	3	4	5	3	.63	8	.300	.379	.480
1997 Edmonton	AAA	118	422	133	39	6	19	—	—	241	89	77	59	4	104	6	3	3	5	2	.71	11	.315	.404	.571
1998 Oklahoma	AAA	131	493	126	31	4	29	—	—	252	74	96	62	3	143	3	0	6	2	2	.50	7	.256	.339	.511
1999 Oklahoma	AAA	122	453	141	35	3	28	—	—	266	94	97	56	3	112	3	0	7	12	2	.86	11	.311	.385	.587
1997 Oakland	AL	13	24	6	0	0	1	(1	0)	9	2	1	1	0	6	1	1	0	0	0	.00	0	.250	.308	.375
1998 Texas	AL	7	16	2	0	0	0	(0	0)	2	0	1	1	0	6	0	0	0	0	0	.00	1	.125	.176	.125
1999 Texas	AL	2	1	0	0	0	0	(0	0)	0	0	0	0	0	0	0	0	0	0	0	.00	0	.000	.000	.000
3 ML YEARS		22	41	8	0	0	1	(1	0)	11	2	3	2	0	12	1	1	0	0	0	.00	1	.195	.250	.268

Paul Shuey

Pitches: Right **Bats:** Right **Pos:** RP-72 **Ht:** 6'3" **Wt:** 215 **Born:** 9/16/70 **Age:** 29

Year Team	Lg	G	GS	CG	GF	IP	BFP	H	R	ER	HR	SH	SF	HB	TBB	IBB	SO	WP	Bk	W	L	Pct.	ShO	Sv-Op	Hld	ERA
1999 Buffalo *	AAA	1	0	0	0	1	4	0	0	0	0	0	0	0	1	0	1	1	0	0	0	.000	0	0- -	—	0.00
1994 Cleveland	AL	14	0	0	11	11.2	62	14	11	11	1	0	0	0	12	1	16	4	0	0	1	.000	0	5-5	1	8.49
1995 Cleveland	AL	7	0	0	3	6.1	28	5	4	3	0	2	0	0	5	0	5	1	0	0	0	.000	0	0-0	0	4.26
1996 Cleveland	AL	42	0	0	18	53.2	225	45	19	17	6	1	3	0	26	3	44	3	1	5	2	.714	0	4-7	7	2.85
1997 Cleveland	AL	40	0	0	16	45	212	52	31	31	5	4	2	1	28	3	46	2	0	4	2	.667	0	2-3	4	6.20
1998 Cleveland	AL	43	0	0	16	51	222	44	19	17	6	2	0	3	25	5	58	3	0	5	4	.556	0	2-5	12	3.00
1999 Cleveland	AL	72	0	0	28	81.2	351	68	37	32	8	4	1	1	40	7	103	8	0	8	5	.615	0	6-12	19	3.53
6 ML YEARS		218	0	0	92	249.1	1100	228	121	111	26	13	6	5	136	19	272	21	1	22	16	.579	0	19-32	43	4.01

Anthony Shumaker

Pitches: Left **Bats:** Left **Pos:** SP-4; RP-4 **Ht:** 6'5" **Wt:** 223 **Born:** 5/14/73 **Age:** 27

Year Team	Lg	G	GS	CG	GF	IP	BFP	H	R	ER	HR	SH	SF	HB	TBB	IBB	SO	WP	Bk	W	L	Pct.	ShO	Sv-Op	Hld	ERA
1995 Martinsvlle	R+	6	4	0	0	28	120	31	16	14	1	2	0	1	8	0	26	3	0	1	3	.250	0	0- -	—	4.50
Batavia	A-	9	4	1	0	39	157	38	10	7	0	0	0	0	4	0	31	2	0	2	2	.500	1	0- -	—	1.62
1996 Piedmont	A	20	0	0	13	32.2	120	16	7	5	2	0	0	0	10	1	51	3	0	3	0	1.000	0	4- -	—	1.38
Clearwater	A+	31	0	0	13	29.1	137	42	18	18	1	3	0	0	12	5	25	1	0	5	3	.625	0	3- -	—	5.52
1997 Clearwater	A+	61	0	0	28	72	295	64	22	17	1	2	0	2	17	1	77	5	0	5	4	.556	0	9- -	—	2.13
1998 Reading	AA	38	21	0	9	166.2	689	152	75	62	20	9	7	4	44	2	129	3	0	7	10	.412	1	2- -	—	3.35
1999 Reading	AA	10	10	1	0	60.2	249	48	17	12	3	3	2	2	17	1	60	1	1	4	3	.571	0	0- -	—	1.78
Scranton-WB	AAA	14	14	0	0	89.2	403	119	60	57	15	3	6	2	32	2	49	2	0	3	5	.375	0	0- -	—	5.72
1999 Philadelphia	NL	8	4	0	2	22.2	105	23	17	15	3	2	0	1	14	0	17	1	1	0	3	.000	0	0-0	0	5.96

Terry Shumpert

Bats: R **Throws:** R **Pos:** 2B-54; PH/PR-22; 3B-14; CF-9; LF-6; RF-4; SS-2 **Ht:** 6'0" **Wt:** 195 **Born:** 8/16/66 **Age:** 33

Year Team	Lg	G	AB	H	2B	3B	HR	(Hm	Rd)	TB	R	RBI	TBB	IBB	SO	HBP	SH	SF	SB	CS	SB%	GDP	Avg	OBP	SLG
1999 Colo Spmgs *	AAA	29	79	30	8	1	6	—	—	58	15	17	4	0	9	0	1	0	3	1	.75	1	.380	.410	.734
1990 Kansas City	AL	32	91	25	6	1	0	(0	0)	33	7	8	2	0	17	1	0	2	3	3	.50	4	.275	.292	.363
1991 Kansas City	AL	144	369	80	16	4	5	(1	4)	119	45	34	30	0	75	5	10	3	17	11	.61	10	.217	.283	.322
1992 Kansas City	AL	36	94	14	5	1	1	(0	1)	24	6	11	3	0	17	0	2	0	2	2	.50	2	.149	.175	.255
1993 Kansas City	AL	8	10	1	0	0	0	(0	0)	1	0	0	2	0	2	0	0	0	1	0	1.00	0	.100	.250	.100
1994 Kansas City	AL	64	183	44	6	2	8	(2	6)	78	28	24	13	0	39	0	5	1	18	3	.86	0	.240	.289	.426
1995 Boston	AL	21	47	11	3	0	0	(0	0)	14	6	3	4	0	13	0	0	0	3	1	.75	0	.234	.294	.298
1996 Chicago	NL	27	31	7	1	0	2	(2	0)	14	5	6	2	0	11	1	0	1	0	0	.00	0	.226	.286	.452
1997 San Diego	NL	13	33	9	3	0	1	(0	1)	15	4	6	3	0	4	0	0	1	0	0	.00	1	.273	.324	.455
1998 Colorado	NL	23	26	6	1	0	1	(0	1)	10	3	2	2	0	8	0	0	0	0	0	.00	0	.231	.286	.385
1999 Colorado	NL	92	262	91	26	3	10	(8	2)	153	58	37	31	2	41	2	4	5	14	0	1.00	1	.347	.413	.584
10 ML YEARS		460	1146	288	67	11	28	(13	15)	461	162	131	92	2	227	9	21	13	58	21	.73	19	.251	.309	.402

Jose Silva

Pitches: Right **Bats:** Right **Pos:** RP-22; SP-12 **Ht:** 6'5" **Wt:** 227 **Born:** 12/19/73 **Age:** 26

Year Team	Lg	G	GS	CG	GF	IP	BFP	H	R	ER	HR	SH	SF	HB	TBB	IBB	SO	WP	Bk	W	L	Pct.	ShO	Sv-Op	Hld	ERA
1999 Nashville *	AAA	2	2	0	0	12	55	14	4	2	0	2	1	0	4	0	10	0	0	2	0	1.000	0	0- -	—	1.50
1996 Toronto	AL	2	0	0	0	2	11	5	3	3	1	0	0	0	0	0	0	0	0	0	0	.000	0	0-0	0	13.50
1997 Pittsburgh	NL	11	4	0	0	36.1	174	52	26	24	4	4	3	1	16	3	30	0	1	3	1	.667	0	0-0	0	5.94
1998 Pittsburgh	NL	18	18	1	0	100.1	425	104	55	49	7	5	5	1	30	2	64	2	2	6	7	.462	0	0-0	0	4.40
1999 Pittsburgh	NL	34	12	0	9	97.1	433	108	70	62	10	3	3	3	39	0	77	4	3	2	8	.200	0	4-5	2	5.73
4 ML YEARS		65	34	1	9	236	1043	269	154	138	22	12	11	5	85	5	171	6	6	10	16	.385	0	4-5	2	5.26

213

Dave Silvestri

Bats: Right **Throws:** Right **Pos:** 2B-1; SS-1; LF-1 **Ht:** 6'0" **Wt:** 196 **Born:** 9/29/67 **Age:** 32

Year Team	Lg	G	AB	H	2B	3B	HR	(Hm Rd)	TB	R	RBI	TBB	IBB	SO	HBP	SH	SF	SB	CS	SB%	GDP	Avg	OBP	SLG
1999 Durham *	AAA	1	3	0	0	0	0	— —	0	0	0	0	0	0	0	0	0	0	0	.00	0	.000	.000	.000
Edmonton *	AAA	79	318	101	18	0	6	— —	137	55	42	22	0	43	2	4	2	4	3	.57	12	.318	.363	.431
1992 New York	AL	7	13	4	0	2	0	(0 0)	8	3	1	0	0	3	0	0	0	0	0	.00	1	.308	.308	.615
1993 New York	AL	7	21	6	1	0	1	(0 1)	10	4	4	5	0	3	0	0	0	0	0	.00	1	.286	.423	.476
1994 New York	AL	12	18	2	0	1	1	(1 0)	7	3	2	4	0	9	0	0	1	0	0	.00	1	.111	.261	.389
1995 NYY-Mon		56	93	21	6	0	3	(0 3)	36	16	11	13	0	36	1	1	2	2	1	1.00	5	.226	.321	.387
1996 Montreal	NL	86	162	33	4	0	1	(0 1)	40	16	17	34	6	41	0	3	1	2	1	.67	5	.204	.340	.247
1997 Texas	AL	2	4	0	0	0	0	(0 0)	0	0	0	0	0	1	0	0	0	0	0	.00	0	.000	.000	.000
1998 Tampa Bay	AL	8	14	1	0	0	0	(0 0)	1	0	0	0	0	2	0	0	0	0	0	.00	1	.071	.071	.071
1999 Anaheim	AL	3	11	1	1	0	0	(0 0)	2	0	1	0	0	1	0	0	0	0	0	.00	1	.091	.091	.182
1995 New York	AL	17	21	2	0	0	1	(0 1)	5	4	4	4	0	9	1	0	1	0	0	.00	2	.095	.259	.238
Montreal	NL	39	72	19	6	0	2	(0 2)	31	12	7	9	0	27	0	1	1	2	0	1.00	2	.264	.341	.431
8 ML YEARS		181	336	68	12	3	5	(1 5)	104	42	36	56	6	96	1	4	4	4	2	.67	12	.202	.315	.310

Bill Simas

Pitches: Right **Bats:** Left **Pos:** RP-70 **Ht:** 6'3" **Wt:** 235 **Born:** 11/28/71 **Age:** 28

Year Team	Lg	G	GS	CG	GF	IP	BFP	H	R	ER	HR	SH	SF	HB	TBB	IBB	SO	WP	Bk	W	L	Pct.	ShO	Sv-Op	Hld	ERA
1995 Chicago	AL	14	0	0	4	14	66	15	5	4	1	0	0	1	10	2	16	1	0	1	1	.500	0	0-0	3	2.57
1996 Chicago	AL	64	0	0	16	72.2	328	75	39	37	5	1	2	3	39	6	65	0	0	2	8	.200	0	2-8	15	4.58
1997 Chicago	AL	40	0	0	11	41.1	193	46	23	19	6	1	1	2	24	3	38	2	0	3	1	.750	0	1-2	3	4.14
1998 Chicago	AL	60	0	0	41	70.2	287	54	29	28	12	2	0	1	22	4	56	1	0	4	3	.571	0	18-24	6	3.57
1999 Chicago	AL	70	0	0	21	72	324	73	36	30	6	4	4	6	32	6	41	4	1	6	3	.667	0	2-5	12	3.75
5 ML YEARS		248	0	0	93	270.2	1198	263	132	118	30	8	7	13	127	21	216	8	1	16	16	.500	0	23-39	39	3.92

Brian Simmons

Bats: B **Throws:** R **Pos:** LF-28; CF-11; PH/PR-11; RF-9; DH-3; C-1 **Ht:** 6'2" **Wt:** 190 **Born:** 9/4/73 **Age:** 26

Year Team	Lg	G	AB	H	2B	3B	HR	(Hm Rd)	TB	R	RBI	TBB	IBB	SO	HBP	SH	SF	SB	CS	SB%	GDP	Avg	OBP	SLG
1995 White Sox	R	5	17	3	1	0	1	— —	7	5	5	6	0	1	0	0	0	0	0	.00	1	.176	.391	.412
Hickory	A	41	163	31	6	1	2	— —	45	13	11	19	0	44	2	0	0	4	4	.50	2	.190	.283	.276
1996 South Bend	A	92	356	106	29	6	17	— —	198	73	58	48	2	69	2	1	4	14	9	.61	3	.298	.380	.556
Pr William	A+	33	131	26	4	3	4	— —	48	17	14	9	1	39	0	1	0	2	0	1.00	3	.198	.250	.366
1997 Birmingham	AA	138	546	143	28	12	15	— —	240	108	72	88	5	124	2	2	3	15	12	.56	10	.262	.365	.440
1998 White Sox	R	5	12	2	0	0	0	— —	2	1	0	1	0	1	0	0	0	0	0	.00	0	.167	.231	.167
Calgary	AAA	94	355	103	21	4	13	— —	171	72	51	41	1	82	1	3	3	10	6	.63	6	.290	.363	.482
1999 Charlotte	AAA	78	285	77	14	0	10	— —	121	53	44	37	1	60	5	1	1	8	2	.80	5	.270	.363	.425
1998 Chicago	AL	5	19	7	0	0	2	(0 2)	13	4	6	0	0	2	0	0	0	0	1	.00	0	.368	.368	.684
1999 Chicago	AL	54	126	29	3	3	4	(0 4)	50	14	17	9	0	30	0	0	0	4	0	1.00	3	.230	.281	.397
2 ML YEARS		59	145	36	3	3	6	(0 6)	63	18	23	9	0	32	0	0	0	4	1	.80	3	.248	.292	.434

Mike Simms

Bats: R **Throws:** R **Pos:** DH-2; PH/PR-2; 1B-1; RF-1 **Ht:** 6'4" **Wt:** 230 **Born:** 1/12/67 **Age:** 33

Year Team	Lg	G	AB	H	2B	3B	HR	(Hm Rd)	TB	R	RBI	TBB	IBB	SO	HBP	SH	SF	SB	CS	SB%	GDP	Avg	OBP	SLG
1999 Oklahoma *	AAA	22	73	20	1	0	2	— —	27	7	16	16	1	25	0	0	1	0	0	.00	3	.274	.400	.370
Charlotte *	A+	12	41	9	1	0	2	— —	16	7	9	8	0	3	1	0	1	0	0	.00	3	.220	.353	.390
1990 Houston	NL	12	13	4	1	0	1	(0 1)	8	3	2	0	0	4	0	0	0	0	0	.00	1	.308	.308	.615
1991 Houston	NL	49	123	25	5	0	3	(1 2)	39	18	16	18	0	38	0	0	2	1	0	1.00	4	.203	.301	.317
1992 Houston	NL	15	24	6	1	0	1	(0 1)	10	1	3	2	0	9	1	0	0	1	0	1.00	0	.250	.333	.417
1994 Houston	NL	6	12	1	1	0	0	(0 0)	2	1	0	0	0	5	0	0	0	1	0	1.00	0	.083	.083	.167
1995 Houston	NL	50	121	31	4	0	9	(5 4)	62	14	24	13	0	28	3	0	1	1	2	.33	3	.256	.341	.512
1996 Houston	NL	49	68	12	2	1	1	(1 0)	19	6	8	4	0	16	1	0	0	1	0	1.00	1	.176	.233	.279
1997 Texas	AL	59	111	28	8	0	5	(3 2)	51	13	22	8	1	27	0	0	2	0	1	.00	4	.252	.298	.459
1998 Texas	AL	86	186	55	11	0	16	(9 7)	114	36	46	24	0	47	3	0	2	0	0	.00	0	.296	.381	.613
1999 Texas	AL	4	2	1	0	0	0	(0 0)	1	0	0	0	0	0	0	0	0	0	0	.00	0	.500	.500	.500
9 ML YEARS		330	660	163	33	1	36	(19 17)	306	92	121	69	1	175	8	0	7	4	4	.50	15	.247	.323	.464

Randall Simon

Bats: Left **Throws:** Left **Pos:** 1B-70; PH/PR-23 **Ht:** 6'0" **Wt:** 180 **Born:** 5/26/75 **Age:** 25

Year Team	Lg	G	AB	H	2B	3B	HR	(Hm Rd)	TB	R	RBI	TBB	IBB	SO	HBP	SH	SF	SB	CS	SB%	GDP	Avg	OBP	SLG
1993 Danville	R+	61	232	59	17	1	3	— —	87	28	31	10	2	34	2	0	2	1	1	.50	4	.254	.289	.375
1994 Macon	A	106	358	105	23	1	10	— —	160	45	54	6	2	56	1	1	2	7	6	.54	7	.293	.305	.447
1995 Durham	A+	122	420	111	18	1	18	— —	185	56	79	36	14	63	5	0	5	6	5	.55	15	.264	.326	.440
1996 Greenville	AA	134	498	139	26	2	18	— —	223	74	77	37	7	61	4	0	4	1	9	.31	13	.279	.331	.480
1997 Richmond	AAA	133	519	160	45	1	14	— —	249	62	102	17	2	76	4	1	1	4	4	.50	22	.308	.335	.480
1998 Richmond	AAA	126	484	124	20	1	13	— —	185	52	70	24	3	62	2	0	6	4	4	.50	22	.256	.292	.382
1999 Richmond	AAA	15	59	16	4	0	1	— —	23	7	8	3	2	10	0	0	1	0	0	.00	1	.271	.302	.390
1997 Atlanta	NL	13	14	6	1	0	0	(0 0)	7	2	1	1	0	2	0	0	0	0	0	.00	1	.429	.467	.500

Year Team	Lg	BATTING G	AB	H	2B	3B	HR	(Hm	Rd)	TB	R	RBI	TBB	IBB	SO	HBP	SH	SF	BASERUNNING SB	CS	SB%	GDP	PERCENTAGES Avg	OBP	SLG
1998 Atlanta	NL	7	16	3	0	0	0	(0	0)	3	2	4	0	0	1	0	0	1	0	1	.00	0	.188	.176	.188
1999 Atlanta	NL	90	218	69	16	0	5	(2	3)	100	26	25	17	6	25	1	0	1	2	2	.50	10	.317	.367	.459
3 ML YEARS		110	248	78	17	0	5	(2	3)	110	30	30	18	6	28	1	0	2	2	2	.50	11	.315	.361	.444

Steve Sinclair

Pitches: Left Bats: Left Pos: RP-21 Ht: 6'2" Wt: 190 Born: 8/2/71 Age: 28

Year Team	Lg	HOW MUCH HE PITCHED G	GS	CG	GF	IP	BFP	WHAT HE GAVE UP H	R	ER	HR	SH	SF	HB	TBB	IBB	SO	WP	Bk	THE RESULTS W	L	Pct.	ShO	Sv-Op	Hld	ERA
1991 Medcine Hat	R+	12	0	0	8	14.2	76	17	15	11	1	1	0	3	11	0	14	0	0	0	1	.000	0	0--	—	6.75
1992 Blue Jays	R	5	4	0	0	23	92	23	10	7	2	0	0	0	5	0	18	1	0	1	2	.333	0	0--	—	2.74
Medcine Hat	R+	9	7	0	1	43	189	54	25	22	2	2	3	1	12	0	28	3	0	2	3	.400	0	0--	—	4.60
1993 Medcine Hat	R+	15	12	0	0	78.1	335	87	41	29	5	2	2	1	16	0	45	5	1	5	2	.714	0	0--	—	3.33
1994 Hagerstown	A	38	1	0	16	105	458	127	53	44	9	4	5	2	25	0	75	3	0	9	2	.818	0	3--	—	3.77
1995 Dunedin	A+	46	0	0	18	73	297	69	26	21	4	1	1	3	17	1	52	2	3	5	3	.625	0	2--	—	2.59
1996 Dunedin	A+	3	0	0	1	2.2	12	4	2	1	1	0	0	0	0	0	1	0	0	0	1	.000	0	0--	—	3.38
1997 Dunedin	A+	43	0	0	20	68.1	296	63	36	22	4	4	1	2	26	3	66	4	1	2	5	.286	0	3--	—	2.90
Syracuse	AAA	6	0	0	1	9	40	11	6	6	0	0	0	0	3	0	9	0	0	0	0	.000	0	0--	—	6.00
1998 Syracuse	AAA	43	1	0	16	49.2	204	37	15	12	2	1	2	1	23	2	45	0	0	3	1	.750	0	3--	—	2.17
1999 Syracuse	AAA	34	0	0	30	39.1	156	24	11	9	3	0	0	4	12	1	31	1	0	2	2	.500	0	18--	—	2.06
Tacoma	AAA	2	0	0	0	2	9	2	1	1	0	0	0	0	1	0	1	0	0	1	0	1.000	0	0--	—	4.50
1998 Toronto	AL	24	0	0	3	15	61	13	7	6	0	0	0	0	5	0	8	0	0	0	2	.000	0	0-2	3	3.60
1999 Tor-Sea	AL	21	0	0	6	19.1	95	22	16	14	5	0	0	2	14	2	18	0	0	0	1	.000	0	0-0	2	6.52
1999 Toronto	AL	3	0	0	1	5.2	28	7	8	8	4	0	0	1	4	0	3	0	0	0	0	.000	0	0-0	0	12.71
Seattle	AL	18	0	0	5	13.2	67	15	8	6	1	0	0	1	10	2	15	0	0	0	1	.000	0	0-0	2	3.95
2 ML YEARS		45	0	0	9	34.1	156	35	23	20	5	0	0	2	19	2	26	0	0	0	3	.000	0	0-2	5	5.24

Chris Singleton

Bats: L Throws: L Pos: CF-121; LF-11; PH/PR-7; DH-2; RF-1 Ht: 6'2" Wt: 195 Born: 8/15/72 Age: 27

Year Team	Lg	BATTING G	AB	H	2B	3B	HR	(Hm Rd)	TB	R	RBI	TBB	IBB	SO	HBP	SH	SF	BASERUNNING SB	CS	SB%	GDP	PERCENTAGES Avg	OBP	SLG
1993 Everett	A-	58	219	58	14	4	3	— —	89	39	18	18	0	46	1	5	1	14	3	.82	3	.265	.322	.406
1994 San Jose	A+	113	425	106	17	5	2	— —	139	51	49	27	0	62	3	5	3	19	6	.76	9	.249	.297	.327
1995 San Jose	A+	94	405	112	13	5	2	— —	141	55	31	17	1	49	5	5	1	33	13	.72	5	.277	.313	.348
1996 Shreveport	AA	129	500	149	31	9	5	— —	213	68	72	24	2	58	6	3	8	27	12	.69	12	.298	.333	.426
Phoenix	AAA	9	32	4	0	0	0	— —	4	3	0	1	0	2	0	1	0	0	0	.00	0	.125	.152	.125
1997 Shreveport	AA	126	464	147	26	10	9	— —	220	85	61	22	4	50	1	2	9	27	11	.71	7	.317	.343	.474
1998 Columbus	AAA	121	413	105	17	10	6	— —	160	55	45	27	0	78	4	7	4	9	3	.75	7	.254	.304	.387
1999 Chicago	AL	133	496	149	31	6	17	(5 12)	243	72	72	22	1	45	1	4	6	20	5	.80	10	.300	.328	.490

Mike Sirotka

Pitches: Left Bats: Left Pos: SP-32 Ht: 6'1" Wt: 200 Born: 5/13/71 Age: 29

Year Team	Lg	HOW MUCH HE PITCHED G	GS	CG	GF	IP	BFP	WHAT HE GAVE UP H	R	ER	HR	SH	SF	HB	TBB	IBB	SO	WP	Bk	THE RESULTS W	L	Pct.	ShO	Sv-Op	Hld	ERA
1995 Chicago	AL	6	6	0	0	34.1	152	39	16	16	2	1	3	0	17	0	19	2	0	1	2	.333	0	0-0	0	4.19
1996 Chicago	AL	15	4	0	2	26.1	122	34	27	21	3	0	2	0	12	0	11	1	0	1	2	.333	0	0-0	0	7.18
1997 Chicago	AL	7	4	0	1	32	130	36	9	8	4	0	0	1	5	1	24	0	0	3	0	1.000	0	0-0	1	2.25
1998 Chicago	AL	33	33	5	0	211.2	911	255	137	119	30	5	7	2	47	0	128	3	1	14	15	.483	0	0-0	0	5.06
1999 Chicago	AL	32	32	3	0	209	909	236	108	93	24	5	9	3	57	2	125	4	0	11	13	.458	1	0-0	0	4.00
5 ML YEARS		93	79	8	3	513.1	2224	600	297	257	63	11	21	6	138	3	307	10	1	30	32	.484	1	0-0	1	4.51

Heathcliff Slocumb

Pitches: Right Bats: Right Pos: RP-50 Ht: 6'3" Wt: 220 Born: 6/7/66 Age: 34

Year Team	Lg	HOW MUCH HE PITCHED G	GS	CG	GF	IP	BFP	WHAT HE GAVE UP H	R	ER	HR	SH	SF	HB	TBB	IBB	SO	WP	Bk	THE RESULTS W	L	Pct.	ShO	Sv-Op	Hld	ERA
1999 Memphis *	AAA	2	0	0	1	2	10	3	1	1	0	0	0	1	0	0	2	0	0	0	0	.000	0	0--	—	4.50
1991 Chicago	NL	52	0	0	21	62.2	274	53	29	24	3	6	6	3	30	6	34	9	0	2	1	.667	0	1-3	6	3.45
1992 Chicago	NL	30	0	0	11	36	174	52	27	26	3	2	2	1	21	3	27	1	0	0	3	.000	0	1-1	1	6.50
1993 ChC-Cle		30	0	0	9	38	164	35	19	17	3	1	3	0	20	2	22	0	0	4	1	.800	0	0-2	3	4.03
1994 Philadelphia	NL	52	0	0	16	72.1	322	75	32	23	0	2	4	2	28	4	58	9	0	5	1	.833	0	0-5	18	2.86
1995 Philadelphia	NL	61	0	0	54	65.1	289	64	26	21	2	4	0	1	35	3	63	3	0	5	6	.455	0	32-38	3	2.89
1996 Boston	AL	75	0	0	60	83.1	368	68	31	28	2	1	3	3	55	5	88	10	0	5	5	.500	0	31-39	2	3.02
1997 Bos-Sea	AL	76	0	0	61	75	353	84	45	43	6	4	2	4	49	5	64	10	0	0	9	.000	0	27-33	5	5.16
1998 Seattle	AL	57	0	0	29	67.2	313	72	40	40	5	4	2	1	44	1	51	10	0	2	5	.286	0	3-4	2	5.32
1999 Bal-StL	AL	50	0	0	19	62	287	64	28	26	5	4	1	3	39	7	60	4	0	3	2	.600	0	2-3	5	3.77
1993 Chicago	NL	10	0	0	4	10.2	42	7	5	4	0	0	1	0	4	0	4	0	0	1	0	1.000	0	0-0	2	3.38
Cleveland	AL	20	0	0	5	27.1	122	28	14	13	3	1	2	0	16	2	18	0	0	3	1	.750	0	0-2	1	4.28
1997 Boston	AL	49	0	0	37	46.2	227	58	32	30	4	2	2	3	34	4	36	6	0	0	5	.000	0	17-22	1	5.79
Seattle	AL	27	0	0	24	28.1	126	26	13	13	2	2	0	1	15	1	28	4	0	0	4	.000	0	10-11	2	4.13
1999 Baltimore	AL	10	0	0	7	8.2	49	15	12	12	2	0	0	2	9	2	12	1	0	0	0	.000	0	0-0	0	12.46
St. Louis	NL	40	0	0	12	53.1	238	49	16	14	3	4	1	1	30	5	48	3	0	3	2	.600	0	2-3	5	2.36
9 ML YEARS		483	0	0	280	562.1	2544	567	277	248	29	28	23	18	321	36	467	56	0	26	33	.441	0	97-128	43	3.97

Joe Slusarski

Pitches: Right **Bats:** Right **Pos:** RP-3 **Ht:** 6'4" **Wt:** 195 **Born:** 12/19/66 **Age:** 33

Year Team	Lg	G	GS	CG	GF	IP	BFP	H	R	ER	HR	SH	SF	HB	TBB	IBB	SO	WP	Bk	W	L	Pct.	ShO	Sv-Op	Hld	ERA
1999 New Orleans *	AAA	40	2	0	14	64.1	270	71	31	26	5	4	3	4	13	1	40	2	0	1	4	.200	0	1--	0	3.64
1991 Oakland	AL	20	19	1	0	109.1	486	121	69	64	14	0	3	4	52	1	60	4	0	5	7	.417	0	0-0	0	5.27
1992 Oakland	AL	15	14	0	1	76	338	85	52	46	15	1	5	6	27	0	38	0	1	5	5	.500	0	0-0	0	5.45
1993 Oakland	AL	2	1	0	0	8.2	43	9	5	5	1	2	0	0	11	3	1	0	0	0	0	.000	0	0-0	0	5.19
1995 Milwaukee	AL	12	0	0	6	15	73	21	11	9	3	1	1	2	6	1	6	0	0	1	1	.500	0	0-0	0	5.40
1999 Houston	NL	3	0	0	1	3.2	15	1	0	0	0	0	0	0	3	1	3	0	0	0	0	.000	0	0-0	0	0.00
5 ML YEARS		52	34	1	8	212.2	955	237	137	124	33	4	9	12	99	6	108	4	1	11	13	.458	0	0-0	0	5.25

J.D. Smart

Pitches: Right **Bats:** Right **Pos:** RP-29 **Ht:** 6'2" **Wt:** 185 **Born:** 11/12/73 **Age:** 26

Year Team	Lg	G	GS	CG	GF	IP	BFP	H	R	ER	HR	SH	SF	HB	TBB	IBB	SO	WP	Bk	W	L	Pct.	ShO	Sv-Op	Hld	ERA
1995 Expos	R	2	2	0	0	10.2	43	10	2	2	0	0	1	2	1	0	6	0	0	2	0	1.000	0	0--	—	1.69
Vermont	A-	5	5	0	0	27.2	118	29	9	7	1	1	3	3	7	0	21	0	0	1	1	.000	0	0--	—	2.28
1996 Delmarva	A	25	25	3	0	156.2	655	155	75	59	14	2	7	10	31	0	109	8	0	9	8	.529	2	0--	—	3.39
1997 Durham	A+	17	13	1	1	102	422	105	45	37	10	2	3	2	21	0	65	3	0	5	4	.556	0	1--	—	3.26
Harrisburg	AA	12	12	0	0	70.2	308	75	34	29	7	6	3	3	24	0	43	3	0	6	3	.667	0	0--	—	3.69
1998 Cape Fear	A	3	1	0	0	11	39	7	3	3	1	0	0	0	0	0	12	1	0	3	0	1.000	0	0--	—	2.45
Harrisburg	AA	14	11	2	2	77	311	67	23	21	2	3	1	3	18	0	47	3	1	3	5	.375	0	1--	—	2.45
Ottawa	AAA	6	6	0	0	35	149	34	22	19	3	2	2	2	11	0	16	0	0	2	3	.400	0	0--	—	4.89
1999 Ottawa	AAA	6	4	0	0	20.2	90	22	7	6	2	0	0	1	6	0	9	1	1	0	1	.000	0	0--	—	2.61
1999 Montreal	NL	29	0	0	6	52	223	56	30	29	4	2	1	0	17	0	21	0	0	0	0	.000	0	0-0	0	5.02

Bobby Smith

Bats: Right **Throws:** Right **Pos:** 3B-59; 2B-13; PH/PR-4 **Ht:** 6'3" **Wt:** 190 **Born:** 5/10/74 **Age:** 26

Year Team	Lg	G	AB	H	2B	3B	HR	(Hm	Rd)	TB	R	RBI	TBB	IBB	SO	HBP	SH	SF	SB	CS	SB%	GDP	Avg	OBP	SLG
1992 Braves	R	57	217	51	9	1	3	—	—	71	31	28	17	1	55	3	0	2	5	6	.45	5	.235	.297	.327
1993 Macon	A	108	384	94	16	7	4	—	—	136	53	38	23	1	81	5	0	1	12	8	.60	1	.245	.296	.354
1994 Durham	A+	127	478	127	27	2	12	—	—	194	49	71	41	1	112	4	1	0	18	7	.72	19	.266	.329	.406
1995 Greenville	AA	127	444	116	27	3	14	—	—	191	75	58	40	2	109	7	4	1	12	6	.67	12	.261	.331	.430
1996 Richmond	AAA	124	445	114	27	0	8	—	—	165	49	58	32	0	114	4	2	3	15	9	.63	12	.256	.310	.371
1997 Richmond	AAA	100	357	88	10	2	12	—	—	138	47	47	44	2	109	7	2	1	6	5	.55	4	.246	.340	.387
1999 Durham	AAA	57	225	75	15	3	14	—	—	138	52	47	27	0	61	4	0	3	13	4	.76	3	.333	.409	.613
1998 Tampa Bay	AL	117	370	102	15	3	11	(4	7)	156	44	55	34	0	110	6	2	4	5	3	.63	9	.276	.343	.422
1999 Tampa Bay	AL	68	199	36	4	1	3	(1	2)	51	18	19	16	0	64	1	2	1	4	4	.50	8	.181	.244	.256
2 ML YEARS		185	569	138	19	4	14	(5	9)	207	62	74	50	0	174	7	4	5	9	7	.56	17	.243	.309	.364

Dan Smith

Pitches: Right **Bats:** Right **Pos:** SP-17; RP-3 **Ht:** 6'3" **Wt:** 210 **Born:** 9/15/75 **Age:** 24

Year Team	Lg	G	GS	CG	GF	IP	BFP	H	R	ER	HR	SH	SF	HB	TBB	IBB	SO	WP	Bk	W	L	Pct.	ShO	Sv-Op	Hld	ERA
1993 Rangers	R	12	10	1	0	53.1	212	50	19	17	1	1	2	3	8	0	27	3	1	3	2	.600	0	0--	—	2.87
1994 Chston-SC	A	27	27	4	0	157.1	715	171	111	86	12	5	2	19	55	0	86	5	2	7	10	.412	0	0--	—	4.92
1995 Rangers	R	4	3	0	0	19	81	19	9	9	0	0	1	2	5	0	12	0	0	0	3	.000	0	0--	—	4.26
Charlotte	A+	9	9	1	0	58	242	53	23	19	4	1	2	3	16	0	34	1	0	5	1	.833	1	0--	—	2.95
1996 Charlotte	A+	18	18	1	0	87	403	100	61	49	6	5	4	3	38	0	55	3	0	3	7	.300	0	0--	—	5.07
1997 Charlotte	A+	26	25	2	0	160.2	705	169	93	79	17	6	4	11	66	1	113	9	0	8	10	.444	0	0--	—	4.43
1998 Tulsa	AA	26	25	1	0	153.1	675	162	101	99	27	1	7	11	58	1	105	9	1	13	9	.591	0	0--	—	5.81
Oklahoma	AAA	1	1	0	0	6	25	6	4	4	2	1	0	1	1	0	3	0	0	0	0	.000	0	0--	—	6.00
1999 Ottawa	AAA	11	11	0	0	71	298	61	31	29	7	3	0	7	27	0	59	3	0	5	4	.556	0	0--	—	3.68
1999 Montreal	NL	20	17	0	0	89.2	407	104	64	60	12	7	2	4	39	0	72	3	0	4	9	.308	0	0-1	0	6.02

John Smoltz

Pitches: Right **Bats:** Right **Pos:** SP-29 **Ht:** 6'3" **Wt:** 220 **Born:** 5/15/67 **Age:** 33

Year Team	Lg	G	GS	CG	GF	IP	BFP	H	R	ER	HR	SH	SF	HB	TBB	IBB	SO	WP	Bk	W	L	Pct.	ShO	Sv-Op	Hld	ERA
1999 Greenville *	AA	2	1	0	0	4	18	5	2	2	0	0	0	0	1	0	7	0	0	0	0	.000	0	0--	—	4.50
1988 Atlanta	NL	12	12	0	0	64	297	74	40	39	10	2	0	2	33	4	37	2	1	2	7	.222	0	0-0	0	5.48
1989 Atlanta	NL	29	29	5	0	208	847	160	79	68	15	10	7	2	72	2	168	8	3	12	11	.522	0	0-0	0	2.94
1990 Atlanta	NL	34	34	6	0	231.1	966	206	109	99	20	9	8	1	90	3	170	14	3	14	11	.560	2	0-0	0	3.85
1991 Atlanta	NL	36	36	5	0	229.2	947	206	101	97	16	9	9	3	77	1	148	20	2	14	13	.519	2	0-0	0	3.80
1992 Atlanta	NL	35	35	9	0	246.2	1021	206	90	78	17	7	8	5	80	5	215	17	1	15	12	.556	3	0-0	0	2.85
1993 Atlanta	NL	35	35	3	0	243.2	1028	208	104	98	23	13	4	6	100	12	208	13	1	15	11	.577	1	0-0	0	3.62
1994 Atlanta	NL	21	21	1	0	134.2	568	120	69	62	15	7	6	4	48	4	113	7	0	6	10	.375	0	0-0	0	4.14
1995 Atlanta	NL	29	29	2	0	192.2	808	166	76	68	15	13	5	4	72	6	193	13	0	12	7	.632	1	0-0	0	3.18
1996 Atlanta	NL	35	35	6	0	253.2	995	199	93	83	19	12	4	2	55	3	276	10	1	24	8	.750	2	0-0	0	2.94
1997 Atlanta	NL	35	35	7	0	256	1043	234	97	86	21	10	3	1	63	9	241	10	1	15	12	.556	2	0-0	0	3.02
1998 Atlanta	NL	26	26	2	0	167.2	681	145	58	54	10	4	2	4	44	2	173	3	1	17	3	.850	2	0-0	0	2.90
1999 Atlanta	NL	29	29	1	0	186.1	746	168	70	66	14	10	5	4	40	2	156	2	0	11	8	.579	1	0-0	0	3.19
12 ML YEARS		356	356	47	0	2414.1	9947	2092	986	898	195	106	61	38	774	55	2098	119	14	157	113	.581	14	0-0	0	3.35

J.T. Snow

Bats: Left **Throws:** Left **Pos:** 1B-160; PH/PR-5   **Ht:** 6'2" **Wt:** 202 **Born:** 2/26/68 **Age:** 32

Year Team	Lg	G	AB	H	2B	3B	HR	(Hm	Rd)	TB	R	RBI	TBB	IBB	SO	HBP	SH	SF	SB	CS	SB%	GDP	Avg	OBP	SLG
1992 New York	AL	7	14	2	1	0	0	(0	0)	3	1	2	5	1	5	0	0	0	0	0	.00	0	.143	.368	.214
1993 California	AL	129	419	101	18	2	16	(10	6)	171	60	57	55	4	88	2	7	6	3	0	1.00	10	.241	.328	.408
1994 California	AL	61	223	49	4	0	8	(7	1)	77	22	30	19	1	48	3	2	1	0	1	.00	2	.220	.289	.345
1995 California	AL	143	544	157	22	1	24	(14	10)	253	80	102	52	4	91	3	5	2	2	1	.67	16	.289	.353	.465
1996 California	AL	155	575	148	20	1	17	(8	9)	221	69	67	56	6	96	5	2	3	1	6	.14	19	.257	.327	.384
1997 San Francisco	NL	157	531	149	36	1	28	(14	14)	271	81	104	96	13	124	1	2	7	6	4	.60	8	.281	.387	.510
1998 San Francisco	NL	138	435	108	29	1	15	(9	6)	184	65	79	58	3	84	0	0	7	1	2	.33	12	.248	.332	.423
1999 San Francisco	NL	161	570	156	25	2	24	(7	17)	257	93	98	86	7	121	5	1	6	0	4	.00	16	.274	.370	.451
8 ML YEARS		951	3311	870	155	8	132	(69	63)	1437	471	539	427	39	657	19	19	32	13	18	.42	83	.263	.347	.434

John Snyder

Pitches: Right **Bats:** Right **Pos:** SP-25   **Ht:** 6'3" **Wt:** 200 **Born:** 8/16/74 **Age:** 25

Year Team	Lg	G	GS	CG	GF	IP	BFP	H	R	ER	HR	SH	SF	HB	TBB	IBB	SO	WP	Bk	W	L	Pct.	ShO	Sv-Op	Hld	ERA
1992 Angels	R	15	0	0	7	44	195	40	27	16	0	2	5	3	16	1	38	1	4	2	4	.333	0	3--	—	3.27
1993 Cedar Rapds	A	21	16	1	0	99	467	126	88	65	13	7	5	8	39	1	79	6	4	5	6	.455	1	0--	—	5.91
1994 Lk Elsinore	A+	26	26	2	0	159	698	181	101	79	16	5	5	6	56	0	108	11	2	10	11	.476	0	0--	—	4.47
1995 Midland	AA	21	21	4	0	133.1	591	158	93	85	12	3	6	10	48	1	81	7	3	8	9	.471	0	0--	—	5.74
Birmingham	AA	5	4	0	0	20.1	87	24	16	15	6	0	1	2	6	0	13	1	0	1	0	1.000	0	0--	—	6.64
1996 White Sox	R	4	4	0	0	16.1	58	5	3	3	1	1	0	0	4	0	23	0	0	1	0	1.000	0	0--	—	1.65
Birmingham	AA	9	9	0	0	54	236	59	35	29	10	2	2	1	16	1	58	4	3	3	5	.375	0	0--	—	4.83
1997 Birmingham	AA	20	20	2	0	114.1	510	130	76	59	9	1	3	6	43	0	90	6	2	7	8	.467	1	0--	—	4.64
1998 Calgary	AAA	15	15	1	0	97	429	112	49	47	11	5	2	5	34	1	63	2	2	7	3	.700	0	0--	—	4.36
1999 Charlotte	AAA	3	3	0	0	17	75	17	9	8	2	0	0	2	5	0	9	0	0	3	0	1.000	0	0--	—	4.24
1998 Chicago	AL	15	14	1	0	86.1	367	96	49	46	14	2	4	2	23	1	52	2	0	7	2	.778	0	0-0	0	4.80
1999 Chicago	AL	25	25	1	0	129.1	602	167	103	96	27	3	7	6	49	0	67	11	0	9	12	.429	0	0-0	0	6.68
2 ML YEARS		40	39	2	0	215.2	969	263	152	142	41	5	11	8	72	1	119	13	0	16	14	.533	0	0-0	0	5.93

Clint Sodowsky

Pitches: Right **Bats:** Left **Pos:** RP-2; SP-1   **Ht:** 6'4" **Wt:** 200 **Born:** 7/13/72 **Age:** 27

Year Team	Lg	G	GS	CG	GF	IP	BFP	H	R	ER	HR	SH	SF	HB	TBB	IBB	SO	WP	Bk	W	L	Pct.	ShO	Sv-Op	Hld	ERA
1999 Memphis *	AAA	19	13	2	3	80.1	350	85	55	43	14	4	1	4	32	0	52	6	2	4	5	.444	1	3--	—	4.82
1995 Detroit	AL	6	6	0	0	23.1	112	24	15	13	4	1	0	0	18	0	14	1	1	2	2	.500	0	0-0	0	5.01
1996 Detroit	AL	7	7	0	0	24.1	132	40	34	32	5	1	0	3	20	0	9	3	0	1	3	.250	0	0-0	0	11.84
1997 Pittsburgh	NL	45	0	0	8	52	236	49	22	21	6	1	2	2	34	7	51	6	0	2	2	.500	0	0-2	5	3.63
1998 Arizona	NL	45	6	0	10	77.2	357	86	56	49	5	5	2	7	39	5	42	4	2	3	6	.333	0	0-3	2	5.68
1999 St. Louis	NL	3	1	0	0	6.1	39	15	11	11	1	0	0	0	6	0	2	0	0	0	1	.000	0	0-0	0	15.63
5 ML YEARS		106	20	0	18	183.2	876	214	138	126	21	8	4	12	117	12	118	14	3	8	14	.364	0	0-5	7	6.17

Luis Sojo

Bats: R **Throws:** R **Pos:** 3B-20; 2B-16; PH/PR-9; SS-6; 1B-4; DH-2   **Ht:** 5'11" **Wt:** 175 **Born:** 1/3/66 **Age:** 34

Year Team	Lg	G	AB	H	2B	3B	HR	(Hm	Rd)	TB	R	RBI	TBB	IBB	SO	HBP	SH	SF	SB	CS	SB%	GDP	Avg	OBP	SLG
1990 Toronto	AL	33	80	18	3	0	1	(0	1)	24	14	9	5	0	5	0	0	0	1	1	.50	1	.225	.271	.300
1991 California	AL	113	364	94	14	1	3	(1	2)	119	38	20	14	0	26	5	19	0	4	2	.67	12	.258	.295	.327
1992 California	AL	106	368	100	12	3	7	(2	5)	139	37	43	14	0	24	1	7	1	7	11	.39	14	.272	.299	.378
1993 Toronto	AL	19	47	8	2	0	0	(0	0)	10	5	6	4	0	2	0	2	1	0	0	.00	3	.170	.231	.213
1994 Seattle	AL	63	213	59	9	2	6	(4	2)	90	32	22	8	0	25	2	3	1	2	1	.67	2	.277	.308	.423
1995 Seattle	AL	102	339	98	18	2	7	(4	3)	141	50	39	23	0	19	1	6	1	4	2	.67	6	.289	.335	.416
1996 Sea-NYY	AL	95	287	63	10	1	1	(1	0)	78	23	21	11	0	17	1	8	1	2	2	.50	10	.220	.250	.272
1997 New York	AL	77	215	66	6	1	2	(2	0)	80	27	25	16	0	14	1	5	2	3	1	.75	5	.307	.355	.372
1998 New York	AL	54	147	34	3	1	0	(0	0)	39	16	14	4	0	10	0	1	1	1	0	1.00	5	.231	.250	.265
1999 New York	AL	49	127	32	6	0	2	(1	1)	44	20	16	4	0	17	0	2	0	1	0	1.00	4	.252	.275	.346
1996 Seattle	AL	77	247	52	8	1	1	(1	0)	65	20	16	10	0	13	1	6	0	2	2	.50	8	.211	.244	.263
New York	AL	18	40	11	2	0	0	(0	0)	13	3	5	1	0	4	0	2	1	0	0	.00	2	.275	.286	.325
10 ML YEARS		711	2187	572	83	11	29	(15	14)	764	262	215	103	0	164	11	53	8	25	20	.56	65	.262	.297	.349

Alfonso Soriano

Bats: Right **Throws:** Right **Pos:** PH/PR-8; DH-6; SS-1   **Ht:** 6'1" **Wt:** 160 **Born:** 1/7/78 **Age:** 22

Year Team	Lg	G	AB	H	2B	3B	HR	(Hm	Rd)	TB	R	RBI	TBB	IBB	SO	HBP	SH	SF	SB	CS	SB%	GDP	Avg	OBP	SLG
1999 Norwich	AA	89	361	110	20	3	15	—	—	181	57	68	32	1	67	4	0	5	24	16	.60	9	.305	.363	.501
Yankees	R	5	19	5	2	0	1	—	—	10	7	5	1	0	3	1	0	1	0	0	.00	1	.263	.318	.526
Columbus	AAA	20	82	15	5	1	2	—	—	28	8	11	5	0	18	0	0	2	1	1	.50	1	.183	.225	.341
1999 New York	AL	9	8	1	0	0	1	(1	0)	4	2	1	0	0	3	0	0	0	0	1	.00	0	.125	.125	.500

Paul Sorrento

Bats: L Throws: R Pos: LF-57; 1B-27; PH/PR-14; DH-9   Ht: 6'2" Wt: 210 Born: 11/17/65 Age: 34

Year Team	Lg	G	AB	H	2B	3B	HR	(Hm	Rd)	TB	R	RBI	TBB	IBB	SO	HBP	SH	SF	SB	CS	SB%	GDP	Avg	OBP	SLG
1989 Minnesota	AL	14	21	5	0	0	0	(0	0)	5	2	1	5	1	4	0	0	1	0	0	.00	0	.238	.370	.238
1990 Minnesota	AL	41	121	25	4	1	5	(2	3)	46	11	13	12	0	31	1	0	1	1	1	.50	3	.207	.281	.380
1991 Minnesota	AL	26	47	12	2	0	4	(2	2)	26	6	13	4	2	11	0	0	0	0	0	.00	3	.255	.314	.553
1992 Cleveland	AL	140	458	123	24	1	18	(11	7)	203	52	60	51	7	89	1	1	3	0	3	.00	13	.269	.341	.443
1993 Cleveland	AL	148	463	119	26	1	18	(8	10)	201	75	65	58	11	121	2	0	4	3	1	.75	10	.257	.340	.434
1994 Cleveland	AL	95	322	90	14	0	14	(8	6)	146	43	62	34	6	68	0	1	3	0	1	.00	7	.280	.345	.453
1995 Cleveland	AL	104	323	76	14	0	25	(12	13)	165	50	79	51	6	71	0	0	4	1	1	.50	10	.235	.336	.511
1996 Seattle	AL	143	471	136	32	1	23	(13	10)	239	67	93	57	10	103	7	2	5	0	2	.00	10	.289	.370	.507
1997 Seattle	AL	146	457	121	19	0	31	(18	13)	235	68	80	51	9	112	3	0	2	0	2	.00	13	.269	.345	.514
1998 Tampa Bay	AL	137	435	98	27	0	17	(10	7)	176	40	57	54	1	133	3	0	3	2	3	.40	8	.225	.313	.405
1999 Tampa Bay	AL	99	294	69	14	1	11	(6	5)	118	40	42	49	1	101	4	0	1	1	1	.50	4	.235	.351	.401
11 ML YEARS		1093	3412	876	176	5	166	(90	76)	1560	454	565	426	54	844	21	4	27	8	15	.35	81	.257	.340	.457

Juan Sosa

Bats: R Throws: R Pos: PH/PR-6; CF-5; SS-2; LF-1   Ht: 6'1" Wt: 175 Born: 8/19/75 Age: 24

Year Team	Lg	G	AB	H	2B	3B	HR	(Hm	Rd)	TB	R	RBI	TBB	IBB	SO	HBP	SH	SF	SB	CS	SB%	GDP	Avg	OBP	SLG
1995 Vero Beach	A+	8	27	6	1	1	1	—	—	12	2	6	0	0	4	0	0	0	0	2	.00	0	.222	.222	.444
Yakima	A-	61	217	51	10	4	3	—	—	78	26	16	15	2	39	1	4	2	8	1	.89	4	.235	.285	.359
1996 Savannah	A	112	370	94	21	2	7	—	—	140	58	38	30	2	64	1	4	1	14	12	.54	9	.254	.311	.378
1997 Vero Beach	A+	92	250	55	5	2	5	—	—	79	32	29	14	0	39	2	3	3	20	8	.71	6	.220	.264	.316
1998 Salem	A+	133	529	147	20	12	8	—	—	215	88	47	43	1	83	4	7	4	64	16	.80	12	.278	.334	.406
1999 Carolina	AA	125	490	135	22	5	7	—	—	188	70	42	31	0	65	2	5	6	38	15	.72	12	.276	.318	.384
Colo Sprngs	AAA	6	28	11	1	1	1	—	—	17	3	5	0	0	1	0	0	0	1	0	1.00	2	.393	.393	.607
1999 Colorado	NL	11	9	2	0	0	0	(0	0)	2	3	0	2	0	2	0	0	0	0	0	.00	0	.222	.364	.222

Sammy Sosa

Bats: Right Throws: Right Pos: RF-146; CF-25   Ht: 6'0" Wt: 210 Born: 11/12/68 Age: 31

Year Team	Lg	G	AB	H	2B	3B	HR	(Hm	Rd)	TB	R	RBI	TBB	IBB	SO	HBP	SH	SF	SB	CS	SB%	GDP	Avg	OBP	SLG
1989 Tex-CWS	AL	58	183	47	8	0	4	(1	3)	67	27	13	11	2	47	2	5	2	7	5	.58	6	.257	.303	.366
1990 Chicago	AL	153	532	124	26	10	15	(10	5)	215	72	70	33	4	150	6	2	6	32	16	.67	10	.233	.282	.404
1991 Chicago	AL	116	316	64	10	1	10	(3	7)	106	39	33	14	2	98	2	5	1	13	6	.68	5	.203	.240	.335
1992 Chicago	NL	67	262	68	7	2	8	(4	4)	103	41	25	19	1	63	4	4	2	15	7	.68	4	.260	.317	.393
1993 Chicago	NL	159	598	156	25	5	33	(23	10)	290	92	93	38	6	135	4	0	1	36	11	.77	14	.261	.309	.485
1994 Chicago	NL	105	426	128	17	6	25	(11	14)	232	59	70	25	1	92	2	1	4	22	13	.63	7	.300	.339	.545
1995 Chicago	NL	144	564	151	17	3	36	(19	17)	282	89	119	58	11	134	5	0	2	34	7	.83	8	.268	.340	.500
1996 Chicago	NL	124	498	136	21	2	40	(26	14)	281	84	100	34	6	134	5	0	4	18	5	.78	14	.273	.323	.564
1997 Chicago	NL	162	642	161	31	4	36	(25	11)	308	90	119	45	9	174	2	0	5	22	12	.65	16	.251	.300	.480
1998 Chicago	NL	159	643	198	20	0	66	(35	31)	416	134	158	73	14	171	1	0	5	18	9	.67	20	.308	.377	.647
1999 Chicago	NL	162	625	180	24	2	63	(33	30)	397	114	141	78	8	171	3	0	6	7	8	.47	17	.288	.367	.635
1989 Texas	AL	25	84	20	3	0	1	(0	1)	26	8	3	0	0	20	0	4	0	0	2	.00	3	.238	.238	.310
Chicago	AL	33	99	27	5	0	3	(1	2)	41	19	10	11	2	27	2	1	2	7	3	.70	3	.273	.351	.414
11 ML YEARS		1409	5289	1413	206	35	336	(190	146)	2697	841	941	428	64	1369	36	17	38	224	99	.69	121	.267	.324	.510

Jeff Sparks

Pitches: Right Bats: Right Pos: RP-8   Ht: 6'3" Wt: 210 Born: 4/4/72 Age: 28

Year Team	Lg	G	GS	CG	GF	IP	BFP	H	R	ER	HR	SH	SF	HB	TBB	IBB	SO	WP	Bk	W	L	Pct.	ShO	Sv-Op	Hld	ERA
1995 Princeton	R+	16	6	0	7	39	172	32	19	14	2	0	1	0	27	2	49	2	1	2	0	1.000	0	2--	—	3.23
1996 Chattanooga	AA	3	0	0	0	2	10	5	1	1	0	0	0	1	1	0	2	0	0	0	0	.000	0	0--	—	4.50
Chstn-WV	A	46	3	0	14	89.1	394	79	51	47	4	4	4	9	46	6	94	10	1	2	7	.222	0	0--	—	4.74
1997 Burlington	A	22	9	0	5	61.1	281	61	49	39	7	2	3	0	39	1	72	6	1	2	5	.286	0	0--	—	5.72
1998 Winnipeg	IND	38	0	0	36	69	282	21	30	21	17	5	2	1	42	1	85	4	0	2	1	.667	0	17--	—	3.12
1999 Nashville	AAA	34	0	0	4	49.1	209	37	25	21	4	1	2	4	23	1	69	7	0	5	3	.625	0	0--	—	3.83
Durham	AAA	18	0	0	5	24	106	16	11	9	2	0	1	1	14	0	31	3	0	3	0	1.000	0	0--	—	3.38
1999 Tampa Bay	AL	8	0	0	2	10	49	6	6	6	1	1	0	1	12	1	17	1	0	0	0	.000	0	1-1	0	5.40

Steve Sparks

Pitches: Right Bats: Right Pos: SP-26; RP-2   Ht: 6'0" Wt: 180 Born: 7/2/65 Age: 34

Year Team	Lg	G	GS	CG	GF	IP	BFP	H	R	ER	HR	SH	SF	HB	TBB	IBB	SO	WP	Bk	W	L	Pct.	ShO	Sv-Op	Hld	ERA
1995 Milwaukee	AL	33	27	3	2	202	875	210	111	104	17	5	12	5	86	1	96	5	1	9	11	.450	0	0-0	0	4.63
1996 Milwaukee	AL	20	13	1	2	88.2	406	103	66	65	19	3	1	3	52	0	21	6	0	4	7	.364	0	0-0	0	6.60
1998 Anaheim	AL	22	20	0	1	128.2	562	130	66	62	14	2	3	6	58	0	90	6	0	9	4	.692	0	0-0	0	4.34
1999 Anaheim	AL	28	26	0	1	147.2	688	165	101	89	21	2	8	9	82	0	73	8	0	5	11	.313	0	0-0	0	5.42
4 ML YEARS		103	86	4	6	567	2531	608	344	320	71	12	24	22	278	1	280	25	1	27	33	.450	0	0-0	0	5.08

Tim Spehr

Bats: Right **Throws:** Right **Pos:** C-59; PH/PR-1   **Ht:** 6'2" **Wt:** 200 **Born:** 7/2/66 **Age:** 33

							BATTING												BASERUNNING				PERCENTAGES		
Year Team	Lg	G	AB	H	2B	3B	HR	(Hm	Rd)	TB	R	RBI	TBB	IBB	SO	HBP	SH	SF	SB	CS	SB%	GDP	Avg	OBP	SLG
1991 Kansas City	AL	37	74	14	5	0	3	(1	2)	28	7	14	9	0	18	1	3	1	1	0	1.00	2	.189	.282	.378
1993 Montreal	NL	53	87	20	6	0	2	(0	2)	32	14	10	6	1	20	1	3	2	2	0	1.00	0	.230	.281	.368
1994 Montreal	NL	52	36	9	3	1	0	(0	1)	14	8	5	4	0	11	0	1	0	2	0	1.00	0	.250	.325	.389
1995 Montreal	NL	41	35	9	5	0	1	(0	1)	17	4	3	6	0	7	0	3	0	0	0	.00	0	.257	.366	.486
1996 Montreal	NL	63	44	4	1	0	1	(0	1)	8	4	3	3	0	15	1	1	0	1	0	1.00	1	.091	.167	.182
1997 KC-Atl		25	49	9	1	0	2	(1	1)	16	5	6	2	0	16	1	0	0	1	0	1.00	1	.184	.231	.327
1998 NYM-KC		32	76	13	3	0	1	(1	0)	19	8	5	15	1	19	4	1	0	1	0	1.00	1	.171	.337	.250
1999 Kansas City	AL	60	155	32	7	0	9	(4	5)	66	26	26	22	0	47	6	2	2	1	0	1.00	2	.206	.324	.426
1997 Kansas City	AL	17	35	6	0	0	1	(0	1)	9	3	2	2	0	12	1	0	0	0	0	.00	0	.171	.237	.257
Atlanta	NL	8	14	3	1	0	1	(1	0)	7	2	4	0	0	4	0	0	0	1	0	1.00	1	.214	.214	.500
1998 New York	NL	21	51	7	1	0	0	(0	0)	8	3	3	7	1	16	2	0	0	1	0	1.00	0	.137	.267	.157
Kansas City		11	25	6	2	0	1	(1	0)	11	5	2	8	0	3	2	1	0	0	0	.00	1	.240	.457	.440
8 ML YEARS		363	556	110	31	1	19	(8	11)	200	76	72	67	2	153	14	14	5	9	0	1.00	6	.198	.298	.360

Justin Speier

Pitches: Right **Bats:** Right **Pos:** RP-19   **Ht:** 6'4" **Wt:** 205 **Born:** 11/6/73 **Age:** 26

		HOW MUCH HE PITCHED						WHAT HE GAVE UP										THE RESULTS						
Year Team	Lg	G	GS	CG	GF	IP	BFP	H	R	ER	HR	SH	SF	HB	TBB	IBB	SO	WP	Bk	W	L	Pct.	ShO	Sv-Op	Hld	ERA
1995 Williamsprt	A-	30	0	0	22	36.1	142	27	6	6	1	2	1	4	0	39	0	0		2	1	.667	0	12- -	—	1.49
1996 Daytona	A+	33	0	0	29	38.1	168	32	19	16	3	3	2	2	19	3	34	5	0	2	4	.333	0	13- -	—	3.76
Orlando	AA	24	0	0	19	26.1	110	23	7	6	2	1	1	2	5	1	14	0	0	4	1	.800	0	6- -	—	2.05
1997 Orlando	AA	50	0	0	20	78.1	328	77	46	39	8	4	2	3	23	0	63	2	2	6	5	.545	0	6- -	—	4.48
Iowa	AAA	8	0	0	4	12.1	41	5	0	0	1	0	0	1	0	9	0	0		2	0	1.000	0	1- -	—	0.00
1998 Iowa	AAA	45	0	0	33	51.2	226	52	31	29	10	3	0	5	19	1	49	6	0	3	3	.500	0	12- -	—	5.05
1999 Richmond	AAA	27	0	0	16	41.2	201	51	28	26	4	1	1	3	22	4	39	6	1	4	4	.333	0	3- -	—	5.62
1998 ChC-Fla	NL	19	0	0	10	20.2	99	27	20	20	7	2	1	0	13	1	17	3	0	0	3	.000	0	0-1	1	8.71
1999 Atlanta	NL	19	0	0	8	28.2	127	28	18	18	8	0	1	0	13	1	22	0	0	0	0	.000	0	0-0	0	5.65
1998 Chicago	NL	1	0	0	0	1.1	7	2	2	2	0	0	0	0	1	0	2	1	0	0	0	.000	0	0-0	0	13.50
Florida	NL	18	0	0	10	19.1	92	25	18	18	7	2	1	0	12	1	15	2	0	0	3	.000	0	0-1	1	8.38
2 ML YEARS		38	0	0	18	49.1	226	55	38	38	15	2	2	0	26	2	39	3	0	0	3	.000	0	0-1	1	6.93

Sean Spencer

Pitches: Left **Bats:** Left **Pos:** RP-2   **Ht:** 5'11" **Wt:** 185 **Born:** 5/29/75 **Age:** 25

		HOW MUCH HE PITCHED						WHAT HE GAVE UP										THE RESULTS						
Year Team	Lg	G	GS	CG	GF	IP	BFP	H	R	ER	HR	SH	SF	HB	TBB	IBB	SO	WP	Bk	W	L	Pct.	ShO	Sv-Op	Hld	ERA
1997 Lancaster	A+	39	0	0	32	60.1	227	41	12	11	4	4	1	2	15	0	72	2	0	2	3	.400	0	18- -	—	1.64
1998 Orlando	AA	37	0	0	32	42.2	178	33	18	14	3	3	1	1	18	1	43	5	1	2	1	.667	0	18- -	—	2.95
Tacoma	AAA	9	0	0	3	13	56	10	7	7	0	0	0	1	7	0	16	1	0	2	0	1.000	0	1- -	—	4.85
1999 Tacoma	AAA	44	0	0	28	49.1	205	41	21	19	6	1	0	1	23	2	53	4	0	2	1	.667	0	7- -	—	3.47
1999 Seattle	AL	2	0	0	0	1.2	12	5	4	4	0	0	0	0	3	0	2	0	0	0	0	.000	0	0-0	0	21.60

Shane Spencer

Bats: R **Throws:** R **Pos:** LF-46; RF-22; PH/PR-14; DH-3   **Ht:** 5'11" **Wt:** 210 **Born:** 2/20/72 **Age:** 28

							BATTING												BASERUNNING				PERCENTAGES		
Year Team	Lg	G	AB	H	2B	3B	HR	(Hm	Rd)	TB	R	RBI	TBB	IBB	SO	HBP	SH	SF	SB	CS	SB%	GDP	Avg	OBP	SLG
1990 Yankees	R	42	147	27	4	0	0	—	—	31	20	7	20	0	23	1	0	1	11	2	.85	3	.184	.284	.211
1991 Yankees	R	41	160	49	7	0	0	—	—	56	25	30	14	0	19	2	0	4	8	2	.80	6	.306	.361	.350
Oneonta	A-	18	53	13	2	1	0	—	—	17	10	3	10	0	9	1	3	0	2	2	.50	1	.245	.375	.321
1992 Greensboro	A	83	258	74	10	2	3	—	—	97	43	27	33	0	37	3	1	2	8	2	.80	12	.287	.372	.376
1993 Greensboro	A	122	431	116	35	2	12	—	—	191	89	80	52	0	62	3	0	8	14	2	.88	8	.269	.346	.443
1994 Tampa	A+	90	334	97	22	3	8	—	—	149	44	53	30	0	53	1	1	1	5	3	.63	8	.290	.350	.446
1995 Tampa	A+	134	500	150	31	3	16	—	—	235	87	88	61	2	60	7	2	3	14	8	.64	8	.300	.382	.470
1996 Norwich	AA	126	450	114	19	0	29	—	—	220	70	89	68	2	99	4	1	5	4	2	.67	6	.253	.353	.489
Columbus	AAA	9	31	11	4	0	3	—	—	24	7	6	5	0	5	1	0	0	0	1	.00	0	.355	.459	.774
1997 Columbus	AAA	125	452	109	34	4	30	—	—	241	78	86	71	1	105	4	1	5	0	2	.00	8	.241	.346	.533
1998 Columbus	AAA	87	342	110	29	1	18	—	—	195	66	67	41	0	59	3	0	2	1	3	.25	8	.322	.397	.570
1999 Columbus	AAA	14	50	18	2	0	2	—	—	26	17	10	9	0	8	0	0	0	1	3	.25	3	.360	.458	.520
1998 New York	AL	27	67	25	6	0	10	(8	2)	61	18	27	5	0	12	0	0	1	0	1	.00	0	.373	.411	.910
1999 New York	AL	71	205	48	8	0	8	(2	6)	80	25	20	18	0	51	2	0	1	0	4	.00	1	.234	.301	.390
2 ML YEARS		98	272	73	14	0	18	(10	8)	141	43	47	23	0	63	2	0	2	0	5	.00	1	.268	.328	.518

Stan Spencer

Pitches: Right **Bats:** Right **Pos:** SP-8; RP-1   **Ht:** 6'4" **Wt:** 223 **Born:** 8/7/69 **Age:** 30

		HOW MUCH HE PITCHED						WHAT HE GAVE UP										THE RESULTS						
Year Team	Lg	G	GS	CG	GF	IP	BFP	H	R	ER	HR	SH	SF	HB	TBB	IBB	SO	WP	Bk	W	L	Pct.	ShO	Sv-Op	Hld	ERA
1991 Harrisburg	AA	17	17	1	0	92	389	90	52	45	6	4	2	4	30	0	66	2	3	6	1	.857	0	0- -	—	4.40
1993 High Desert	A+	13	13	0	0	61.2	265	67	33	28	4	0	2	3	18	0	38	1	0	4	4	.500	0	0- -	—	4.09
1994 Brevard Cty	A+	6	5	0	1	20	84	20	9	7	0	0	1	1	6	0	22	1	0	1	0	1.000	0	0- -	—	3.15
Portland	AA	20	20	1	0	124	505	113	52	48	12	4	6	2	30	2	96	3	1	9	4	.692	0	0- -	—	3.48
1995 Charlotte	AAA	9	9	0	0	41.1	198	61	37	36	9	0	0	3	24	1	19	0	0	1	4	.200	0	0- -	—	7.84

Year Team	Lg	G	GS	CG	GF	IP	BFP	H	R	ER	HR	SH	SF	HB	TBB	IBB	SO	WP	Bk	W	L	Pct.	ShO	Sv-Op	Hld	ERA
	HOW MUCH HE PITCHED							WHAT HE GAVE UP												THE RESULTS						
Portland	AA	8	8	0	0	39	193	57	39	32	9	0	4	2	19	0	32	0	0	1	4	.200	0	0--	—	7.38
1997 Rancho Cuca	A+	7	7	0	0	40.1	164	37	18	15	6	0	1	2	5	0	46	1	0	3	1	.750	0	0--	—	3.35
Las Vegas	AAA	8	8	0	0	48	208	48	23	20	5	1	0	1	18	2	47	1	0	3	2	.600	0	0--	—	3.75
1998 Las Vegas	AAA	22	22	0	0	137.1	570	120	67	60	17	3	3	5	42	2	136	6	1	12	6	.667	0	0--	—	3.93
1999 Las Vegas	AAA	12	10	0	2	54.1	247	69	35	33	6	4	2	2	15	0	50	4	0	4	5	.556	0	0--	—	5.47
1998 San Diego	NL	6	5	0	0	30.2	124	29	16	16	5	0	0	1	4	0	31	0	0	1	0	1.000	0	0-0	0	4.70
1999 San Diego	NL	9	8	0	1	38.1	183	56	44	39	11	4	0	1	11	1	36	1	1	0	7	.000	0	0-0	0	9.16
2 ML YEARS		15	13	0	1	69	307	85	60	55	16	4	0	2	15	1	67	1	1	1	7	.125	0	0-0	0	7.17

Bill Spiers

Bats: L Throws: R Pos: 3B-71; LF-25; PH/PR-24; SS-13; RF-9; CF-7; 2B-4; 1B-1 Ht: 6'2" Wt: 190 Born: 6/5/66 Age: 34

Year Team	Lg	G	AB	H	2B	3B	HR	(Hm	Rd)	TB	R	RBI	TBB	IBB	SO	HBP	SH	SF	SB	CS	SB%	GDP	Avg	OBP	SLG
	BATTING																		BASERUNNING				PERCENTAGES		
1989 Milwaukee	AL	114	345	88	9	3	4	(1	3)	115	44	33	21	1	63	1	4	2	10	2	.83	2	.255	.298	.333
1990 Milwaukee	AL	112	363	88	15	3	2	(2	0)	115	44	36	16	0	45	1	6	3	11	6	.65	12	.242	.274	.317
1991 Milwaukee	AL	133	414	117	13	6	8	(1	7)	166	71	54	34	0	55	2	10	4	14	8	.64	9	.283	.337	.401
1992 Milwaukee	AL	12	16	5	2	0	0	(0	0)	7	2	2	1	0	4	0	1	0	1	1	.50	0	.313	.353	.438
1993 Milwaukee	AL	113	340	81	8	4	2	(2	0)	103	43	36	29	2	51	4	9	4	9	8	.53	11	.238	.302	.303
1994 Milwaukee	AL	73	214	54	10	1	0	(0	0)	66	27	17	19	1	42	1	3	0	7	1	.88	5	.252	.316	.308
1995 New York	NL	63	72	15	2	1	0	(0	0)	19	5	11	12	1	15	0	1	2	0	1	.00	1	.208	.314	.264
1996 Houston	NL	122	218	55	10	1	6	(3	3)	85	27	26	20	4	34	2	1	1	7	0	1.00	3	.252	.320	.390
1997 Houston	NL	132	291	93	27	4	4	(0	4)	140	51	48	61	6	42	1	1	1	10	5	.67	4	.320	.438	.481
1998 Houston	NL	123	384	105	27	4	4	(1	3)	152	66	43	45	0	62	5	1	2	11	2	.85	9	.273	.356	.396
1999 Houston	NL	127	393	113	18	5	4	(1	3)	153	56	39	47	2	45	0	3	1	10	5	.67	10	.288	.363	.389
11 ML YEARS		1124	3050	814	141	32	34	(11	23)	1121	436	345	305	17	458	17	40	20	90	39	.70	65	.267	.335	.368

Scott Spiezio

Bats: B Throws: R Pos: 2B-42; 3B-31; PH/PR-20; 1B-10; DH-6 Ht: 6'2" Wt: 225 Born: 9/21/72 Age: 27

Year Team	Lg	G	AB	H	2B	3B	HR	(Hm	Rd)	TB	R	RBI	TBB	IBB	SO	HBP	SH	SF	SB	CS	SB%	GDP	Avg	OBP	SLG
	BATTING																		BASERUNNING				PERCENTAGES		
1999 Vancouver *	AAA	28	105	41	7	1	6	—	—	68	27	27	15	2	16	2	0	0	0	0	.00	3	.390	.475	.648
1996 Oakland	AL	9	29	9	2	0	2	(1	1)	17	6	8	4	1	4	0	2	0	0	1	.00	1	.310	.394	.586
1997 Oakland	AL	147	538	131	28	4	14	(6	8)	209	58	65	44	2	75	1	3	4	9	3	.75	13	.243	.300	.388
1998 Oakland	AL	114	406	105	19	1	9	(6	3)	153	54	50	44	3	56	2	7	2	1	3	.25	10	.259	.333	.377
1999 Oakland	AL	89	247	60	24	0	8	(3	5)	108	31	33	29	3	36	2	1	3	0	0	.00	5	.243	.324	.437
4 ML YEARS		359	1220	305	73	5	33	(16	17)	487	149	156	121	9	171	5	13	9	10	7	.59	28	.250	.318	.399

Paul Spoljaric

Pitches: Left Bats: Right Pos: RP-37; SP-5 Ht: 6'3" Wt: 210 Born: 9/24/70 Age: 29

Year Team	Lg	G	GS	CG	GF	IP	BFP	H	R	ER	HR	SH	SF	HB	TBB	IBB	SO	WP	Bk	W	L	Pct.	ShO	Sv-Op	Hld	ERA
	HOW MUCH HE PITCHED							WHAT HE GAVE UP												THE RESULTS						
1994 Toronto	AL	2	1	0	0	2.1	21	5	10	10	3	0	0	0	9	1	2	0	0	0	1	.000	0	0-0	0	38.57
1996 Toronto	AL	28	0	0	12	38	163	30	17	13	6	1	1	2	19	1	38	0	0	2	2	.500	0	1-1	5	3.08
1997 Tor-Sea	AL	57	0	0	10	70.2	302	61	30	29	4	2	2	3	36	6	70	6	3	0	3	.000	0	3-5	10	3.69
1998 Seattle	AL	53	6	0	10	83.1	387	85	67	60	14	5	3	1	55	3	89	10	0	4	6	.400	0	0-2	9	6.48
1999 Phi-Tor	AL	42	5	0	8	73.1	346	85	65	51	10	6	4	3	39	2	73	1	0	2	5	.286	0	0-1	2	6.26
1997 Toronto	AL	37	0	0	10	48	198	37	17	17	3	1	2	2	21	4	43	5	1	0	3	.000	0	3-3	8	3.19
Seattle	AL	20	0	0	0	22.2	104	24	13	12	1	1	0	1	15	2	27	1	2	0	0	.000	0	0-2	2	4.76
1999 Philadelphia	NL	5	3	0	1	11.1	64	23	24	19	1	1	1	1	7	0	10	0	0	0	3	.000	0	0-0	0	15.09
Toronto	AL	37	2	0	7	62	282	62	41	32	9	5	3	2	32	2	63	1	0	2	2	.500	0	0-1	2	4.65
5 ML YEARS		182	12	0	40	267.2	1219	266	189	163	37	14	10	9	158	13	272	17	3	8	17	.320	0	4-9	26	5.48

Jerry Spradlin

Pitches: Right Bats: Both Pos: RP-63 Ht: 6'7" Wt: 246 Born: 6/14/67 Age: 33

Year Team	Lg	G	GS	CG	GF	IP	BFP	H	R	ER	HR	SH	SF	HB	TBB	IBB	SO	WP	Bk	W	L	Pct.	ShO	Sv-Op	Hld	ERA
	HOW MUCH HE PITCHED							WHAT HE GAVE UP												THE RESULTS						
1993 Cincinnati	NL	37	0	0	16	49	193	44	20	19	4	3	4	0	9	0	24	3	1	2	1	.667	0	2-3	0	3.49
1994 Cincinnati	NL	6	0	0	2	8	38	12	11	9	2	0	2	0	2	0	4	0	0	0	0	.000	0	0-0	0	10.13
1996 Cincinnati	NL	1	0	0	1	0.1	1	0	0	0	0	0	0	0	0	0	0	1	0	0	0	.000	0	0-0	0	0.00
1997 Philadelphia	NL	76	0	0	23	81.2	345	86	45	43	9	1	2	1	27	3	67	5	2	4	8	.333	0	1-5	18	4.74
1998 Philadelphia	NL	69	0	0	20	81.2	319	83	34	32	9	4	2	2	20	1	76	6	1	4	4	.500	0	1-4	5	3.53
1999 Cle-SF		63	0	0	15	61	286	65	37	33	5	1	0	10	32	6	54	2	0	3	1	.750	0	0-1	11	4.87
1999 Cleveland	AL	4	0	0	1	3	18	6	6	6	1	0	0	0	3	0	2	0	0	0	0	.000	0	0-0	0	18.00
San Francisco	NL	59	0	0	14	58	268	59	31	27	4	1	0	10	29	6	52	2	0	3	1	.750	0	0-1	11	4.19
6 ML YEARS		252	0	0	77	281.2	1182	270	147	136	29	9	10	13	90	10	225	17	4	13	14	.481	0	4-13	34	4.35

Ed Sprague

Bats: Right Throws: Right Pos: 3B-134; PH/PR-5 Ht: 6'2" Wt: 205 Born: 7/25/67 Age: 32

Year Team	Lg	G	AB	H	2B	3B	HR	(Hm	Rd)	TB	R	RBI	TBB	IBB	SO	HBP	SH	SF	SB	CS	SB%	GDP	Avg	OBP	SLG
	BATTING																		BASERUNNING				PERCENTAGES		
1991 Toronto	AL	61	160	44	7	0	4	(3	1)	63	17	20	19	2	43	3	0	1	0	3	.00	2	.275	.361	.394

		BATTING																BASERUNNING				PERCENTAGES		
Year Team	Lg	G	AB	H	2B	3B	HR	(Hm	Rd)	TB	R	RBI	TBB	IBB	SO	HBP	SH	SF	SB	CS	SB%	GDP	Avg	OBP	SLG
1992 Toronto	AL	22	47	11	2	0	1	(1	0)	16	6	7	3	0	7	0	0	0	0	0	.00	0	.234	.280	.340
1993 Toronto	AL	150	546	142	31	1	12	(8	4)	211	50	73	32	1	85	10	2	6	1	0	1.00	23	.260	.310	.386
1994 Toronto	AL	109	405	97	19	1	11	(6	5)	151	38	44	23	1	95	11	2	4	1	0	1.00	11	.240	.296	.373
1995 Toronto	AL	144	521	127	27	2	18	(12	6)	212	77	74	58	3	96	15	1	7	0	0	.00	19	.244	.333	.407
1996 Toronto	AL	159	591	146	35	2	36	(17	19)	293	88	101	60	3	146	12	0	7	0	0	.00	7	.247	.325	.496
1997 Toronto	AL	138	504	115	29	4	14	(5	9)	194	63	48	51	0	102	6	0	1	0	0	.00	10	.228	.306	.385
1998 Tor-Oak	AL	132	469	104	25	0	20	(9	11)	189	57	58	26	2	90	13	0	2	1	2	.33	16	.222	.280	.403
1999 Pittsburgh	NL	137	490	131	27	2	22	(10	12)	228	71	81	50	6	93	17	1	6	3	6	.33	12	.267	.352	.465
1998 Toronto	AL	105	382	91	20	0	17	(6	11)	162	49	51	24	1	73	11	0	2	0	2	.00	15	.238	.301	.424
Oakland	AL	27	87	13	5	0	3	(3	0)	27	8	7	2	1	17	2	0	0	1	0	1.00	1	.149	.187	.310
9 ML YEARS		1052	3733	917	202	12	138	(71	67)	1557	467	506	322	18	757	87	6	34	6	12	.33	100	.246	.318	.417

Dennis Springer

Pitches: Right **Bats:** Right **Pos:** SP-29; RP-9 **Ht:** 5'10" **Wt:** 185 **Born:** 2/12/65 **Age:** 35

		HOW MUCH HE PITCHED						WHAT HE GAVE UP												THE RESULTS				
Year Team	Lg	G	GS	CG	GF	IP	BFP	H	R	ER	HR	SH	SF	HB	TBB	IBB	SO	WP	Bk	W	L	Pct.	ShO	Sv-Op	Hld	ERA
1995 Philadelphia	NL	4	4	0	0	22.1	94	21	15	12	3	2	0	1	9	1	15	1	0	0	3	.000	0	0-0	0	4.84
1996 California	AL	20	15	2	3	94.2	413	91	65	58	24	0	1	6	43	0	64	1	0	5	6	.455	1	0-0	1	5.51
1997 Anaheim	AL	32	28	3	0	194.2	846	199	118	112	32	4	13	10	73	0	75	7	0	9	9	.500	1	0-0	1	5.18
1998 Tampa Bay	AL	29	17	1	8	115.2	517	120	77	70	21	1	2	12	60	1	46	6	0	3	11	.214	0	0-0	0	5.45
1999 Florida	NL	38	29	3	3	196.1	855	231	121	106	23	12	10	7	64	3	83	2	0	6	16	.273	2	1-1	1	4.86
5 ML YEARS		123	93	9	14	623.2	2725	662	396	358	103	19	26	36	249	5	283	17	0	23	45	.338	4	1-1	2	5.17

Russ Springer

Pitches: Right **Bats:** Right **Pos:** RP-49 **Ht:** 6'4" **Wt:** 205 **Born:** 11/7/68 **Age:** 31

		HOW MUCH HE PITCHED						WHAT HE GAVE UP												THE RESULTS				
Year Team	Lg	G	GS	CG	GF	IP	BFP	H	R	ER	HR	SH	SF	HB	TBB	IBB	SO	WP	Bk	W	L	Pct.	ShO	Sv-Op	Hld	ERA
1999 Richmond *	AAA	11	0	0	6	15.1	56	9	2	2	0	1	1	0	1	0	13	0	0	1	0	1.000	0	2- --		1.17
1992 New York	AL	14	0	0	5	16	75	18	11	11	0	0	1	0	10	0	12	0	0	0	0	.000	0	0-0	2	6.19
1993 California	AL	14	9	1	3	60	278	73	48	48	11	1	1	3	32	1	31	6	0	1	6	.143	0	0-0	1	7.20
1994 California	AL	18	5	0	6	45.2	198	53	28	28	9	1	1	0	14	0	28	2	0	2	2	.500	0	2-3	1	5.52
1995 Cal-Phi		33	6	0	6	78.1	350	82	48	46	16	2	2	7	35	4	70	2	0	1	2	.333	0	1-2	1	5.29
1996 Philadelphia	NL	51	7	0	12	96.2	437	106	60	50	12	5	3	1	38	6	94	5	0	3	10	.231	0	0-3	6	4.66
1997 Houston	NL	54	0	0	13	55.1	241	48	28	26	4	1	2	4	27	2	74	4	0	3	3	.500	0	3-7	9	4.23
1998 Ari-Atl	NL	48	0	0	14	52.2	232	51	26	24	4	2	1	1	30	4	56	5	0	5	4	.556	0	0-4	7	4.10
1999 Atlanta	NL	49	0	0	8	47.1	194	31	20	18	5	0	2	2	22	2	49	0	0	2	1	.667	0	1-1	8	3.42
1995 California	AL	19	6	0	3	51.2	238	60	37	35	11	1	0	5	25	1	38	1	0	1	2	.333	0	1-2	0	6.10
Philadelphia	NL	14	0	0	3	26.2	112	22	11	11	5	1	2	2	10	3	32	1	0	0	0	.000	0	0-0	1	3.71
1998 Arizona	NL	26	0	0	13	32.2	140	29	16	15	4	0	0	1	14	1	37	3	0	4	3	.571	0	0-3	1	4.13
Atlanta	NL	22	0	0	1	20	92	22	10	9	0	2	1	0	16	3	19	2	0	1	1	.500	0	0-1	6	4.05
8 ML YEARS		281	27	1	67	452	2005	462	269	251	61	12	12	19	208	19	414	24	0	17	28	.378	0	7-20	33	5.00

Matt Stairs

Bats: L **Throws:** R **Pos:** RF-139; DH-5; PH/PR-3; 1B-1; CF-1 **Ht:** 5'9" **Wt:** 217 **Born:** 2/27/68 **Age:** 32

		BATTING																	BASERUNNING				PERCENTAGES		
Year Team	Lg	G	AB	H	2B	3B	HR	(Hm	Rd)	TB	R	RBI	TBB	IBB	SO	HBP	SH	SF	SB	CS	SB%	GDP	Avg	OBP	SLG
1992 Montreal	NL	13	30	5	2	0	0	(0	0)	7	2	5	7	0	7	0	0	1	0	0	.00	0	.167	.316	.233
1993 Montreal	NL	6	8	3	1	0	0	(0	0)	4	1	2	0	0	1	0	0	0	0	0	.00	1	.375	.375	.500
1995 Boston	AL	39	88	23	7	1	1	(0	1)	35	8	17	4	0	14	1	1	1	0	1	.00	4	.261	.298	.398
1996 Oakland	AL	61	137	38	5	1	10	(5	5)	75	21	23	19	2	23	1	0	1	1	1	.50	2	.277	.367	.547
1997 Oakland	AL	133	352	105	19	4	27	(20	7)	205	62	73	50	1	60	3	1	4	3	2	.60	6	.298	.386	.582
1998 Oakland	AL	149	523	154	33	1	26	(16	10)	267	88	106	59	4	93	6	1	4	8	3	.73	13	.294	.370	.511
1999 Oakland	AL	146	531	137	26	3	38	(15	23)	283	94	102	89	6	124	1	0	1	2	7	.22	8	.258	.366	.533
7 ML YEARS		547	1669	465	93	6	102	(56	46)	876	276	328	228	13	322	13	3	12	14	14	.50	34	.279	.367	.525

Mike Stanley

Bats: R **Throws:** R **Pos:** 1B-111; PH/PR-23; DH-20 **Ht:** 6'0" **Wt:** 205 **Born:** 6/25/63 **Age:** 37

		BATTING																	BASERUNNING				PERCENTAGES		
Year Team	Lg	G	AB	H	2B	3B	HR	(Hm	Rd)	TB	R	RBI	TBB	IBB	SO	HBP	SH	SF	SB	CS	SB%	GDP	Avg	OBP	SLG
1986 Texas	AL	15	30	10	3	0	1	(0	1)	16	4	1	3	0	7	0	0	0	1	0	1.00	0	.333	.394	.533
1987 Texas	AL	78	216	59	8	1	6	(3	3)	87	34	37	31	0	48	1	1	4	3	0	1.00	6	.273	.361	.403
1988 Texas	AL	94	249	57	8	0	3	(1	2)	74	21	27	37	0	62	0	1	5	0	0	.00	6	.229	.323	.297
1989 Texas	AL	67	122	30	3	1	1	(1	0)	38	9	11	12	1	29	2	1	0	1	0	1.00	5	.246	.324	.311
1990 Texas	AL	103	189	47	8	1	2	(1	1)	63	21	19	30	2	25	0	6	1	1	0	1.00	4	.249	.350	.333
1991 Texas	AL	95	181	45	13	1	3	(1	2)	69	25	25	34	0	44	2	5	1	0	0	.00	4	.249	.372	.381
1992 New York	AL	68	173	43	7	0	8	(5	3)	74	24	27	33	0	45	1	0	0	0	0	.00	4	.249	.372	.428
1993 New York	AL	130	423	129	17	1	26	(17	9)	226	70	84	57	4	85	5	0	6	1	1	.50	10	.305	.389	.534
1994 New York	AL	82	290	87	20	0	17	(9	8)	158	54	57	39	2	56	2	0	2	0	0	.00	10	.300	.384	.545
1995 New York	AL	118	399	107	29	1	18	(13	5)	192	63	83	57	1	106	5	0	9	1	5	.14	14	.268	.360	.481
1996 Boston	AL	121	397	107	20	1	24	(10	14)	201	73	69	69	3	62	5	0	2	2	0	1.00	9	.270	.383	.506
1997 Bos-NYY	AL	125	347	103	25	0	16	(6	10)	176	61	65	54	4	72	6	0	8	0	1	.00	13	.297	.393	.507
1998 Tor-Bos	AL	145	497	127	25	0	29	(12	17)	239	74	79	82	5	129	7	0	7	3	1	.75	12	.256	.364	.481
1999 Boston	AL	136	427	120	22	0	19	(8	11)	199	59	72	70	3	94	11	0	4	0	0	.00	8	.281	.393	.466

221

		BATTING																	BASERUNNING				PERCENTAGES		
Year Team	Lg	G	AB	H	2B	3B	HR	(Hm	Rd)	TB	R	RBI	TBB	IBB	SO	HBP	SH	SF	SB	CS	SB%	GDP	Avg	OBP	SLG
1997 Boston	AL	97	260	78	17	0	13	(5	8)	134	45	53	39	0	50	6	0	7	0	1	.00	9	.300	.394	.515
New York	AL	28	87	25	8	0	3	(1	2)	42	16	12	15	4	22	0	0	1	0	0	.00	4	.287	.388	.483
1998 Toronto	AL	98	341	82	13	0	22	(11	11)	161	49	47	56	3	86	5	0	3	2	1	.67	6	.240	.353	.472
Boston	AL	47	156	45	12	0	7	(1	6)	78	25	32	26	2	43	2	0	4	1	0	1.00	6	.288	.388	.500
14 ML YEARS		1377	3940	1071	208	7	173	(86	87)	1812	592	656	608	25	864	47	14	49	13	4	.76	104	.272	.372	.460

Mike Stanton

Pitches: Left Bats: Left Pos: RP-72; SP-1   Ht: 6'1" Wt: 215 Born: 6/2/67 Age: 33

		HOW MUCH HE PITCHED						WHAT HE GAVE UP												THE RESULTS					
Year Team	Lg	G	GS	CG	GF	IP	BFP	H	R	ER	HR	SH	SF	HB	TBB	IBB	SO	WP	Bk	W	L	Pct.	ShO	Sv-Op	Hld	ERA
1989 Atlanta	NL	20	0	0	10	24	94	17	4	4	0	4	0	0	8	1	27	1	0	0	1	.000	0	7-8	2	1.50
1990 Atlanta	NL	7	0	0	4	7	42	16	16	14	1	1	0	1	4	2	7	1	0	0	3	.000	0	2-3	0	18.00
1991 Atlanta	NL	74	0	0	20	78	314	62	27	25	6	6	0	1	21	6	54	0	0	5	5	.500	0	7-10	15	2.88
1992 Atlanta	NL	65	0	0	23	63.2	264	59	32	29	6	1	2	2	20	2	44	3	0	5	4	.556	0	8-11	15	4.10
1993 Atlanta	NL	63	0	0	41	52	236	51	35	27	4	5	2	0	29	7	43	1	0	4	6	.400	0	27-33	5	4.67
1994 Atlanta	NL	49	0	0	15	45.2	197	41	18	18	2	2	1	3	26	3	35	1	0	3	1	.750	0	3-4	10	3.55
1995 Atl-Bos		48	0	0	22	40.1	178	48	23	19	6	2	1	1	14	2	23	2	1	2	1	.667	0	1-3	8	4.24
1996 Bos-Tex	AL	81	0	0	28	78.2	327	78	32	32	11	4	2	0	27	5	60	3	2	4	4	.500	0	1-6	22	3.66
1997 New York	AL	64	0	0	15	66.2	283	50	19	19	3	2	0	3	34	2	70	0	3	6	1	.857	0	3-5	26	2.57
1998 New York	AL	67	0	0	26	79	330	71	51	48	13	1	2	4	26	1	69	0	0	4	1	.800	0	6-10	18	5.47
1999 New York	AL	73	1	0	10	62.1	271	71	30	30	5	4	2	1	18	4	59	3	0	2	2	.500	0	0-5	21	4.33
1995 Atlanta	NL	26	0	0	10	19.1	94	31	14	12	3	2	1	1	6	2	13	1	1	1	1	.500	0	1-2	4	5.59
Boston	AL	22	0	0	12	21	84	17	9	7	3	0	0	0	8	0	10	1	0	1	0	1.000	0	0-1	4	3.00
1996 Boston	AL	59	0	0	19	56.1	239	58	24	24	9	3	2	0	23	4	46	3	2	4	3	.571	0	1-5	15	3.83
Texas	AL	22	0	0	9	22.1	88	20	8	8	2	1	0	0	4	1	14	0	0	0	1	.000	0	0-1	7	3.22
11 ML YEARS		611	1	0	214	597.1	2536	564	287	265	57	32	12	16	227	35	491	18	5	35	29	.547	0	65-98	142	3.99

Dennis Stark

Pitches: Right Bats: Right Pos: RP-5   Ht: 6'2" Wt: 210 Born: 10/27/74 Age: 25

		HOW MUCH HE PITCHED						WHAT HE GAVE UP												THE RESULTS					
Year Team	Lg	G	GS	CG	GF	IP	BFP	H	R	ER	HR	SH	SF	HB	TBB	IBB	SO	WP	Bk	W	L	Pct.	ShO	Sv-Op	Hld	ERA
1996 Everett	A-	12	4	0	4	30.1	133	25	19	15	2	3	1	1	17	0	49	5	1	1	3	.250	0	0- -	—	4.45
1997 Wisconsin	A	16	15	1	0	91.1	361	52	27	20	3	4	1	2	33	0	105	5	1	6	3	.667	0	0- -	—	1.97
Lancaster	A+	3	3	0	0	16.2	71	13	7	6	1	1	0	2	10	0	17	0	0	1	1	.500	0	0- -	—	3.24
1998 Lancaster	A+	5	5	0	0	21	100	18	12	10	1	1	0	1	17	0	21	0	0	1	2	.333	0	0- -	—	4.29
Mariners	R	3	1	0	0	8.1	36	9	2	2	0	0	0	0	2	0	13	0	0	0	0	.000	0	0- -	—	2.16
1999 New Haven	AA	26	26	2	0	147.1	646	151	82	72	14	6	2	13	62	0	103	7	1	9	11	.450	1	0- -	—	4.40
1999 Seattle	AL	5	0	0	2	6.1	31	10	8	7	0	0	0	0	4	0	4	0	0	0	0	.000	0	0-0	—	9.95

Blake Stein

Pitches: Right Bats: Right Pos: SP-12; RP-1   Ht: 6'7" Wt: 228 Born: 8/3/73 Age: 26

		HOW MUCH HE PITCHED						WHAT HE GAVE UP												THE RESULTS					
Year Team	Lg	G	GS	CG	GF	IP	BFP	H	R	ER	HR	SH	SF	HB	TBB	IBB	SO	WP	Bk	W	L	Pct.	ShO	Sv-Op	Hld	ERA
1994 Johnson Cy	R+	13	13	1	0	59.2	242	44	21	19	4	4	2	1	24	0	69	3	0	4	1	.800	0	0- -	—	2.87
1995 Peoria	A	27	27	1	0	139.2	596	122	69	59	12	1	4	5	61	0	133	2	1	10	6	.625	0	0- -	—	3.80
1996 St. Pete	A+	28	27	2	1	172	667	122	48	41	4	3	4	5	54	0	159	4	0	16	5	.762	1	1- -	—	2.15
1997 Arkansas	AA	22	22	1	0	133.2	557	128	67	63	17	5	1	1	49	2	114	5	0	8	7	.533	0	0- -	—	4.24
Huntsville	AA	7	7	0	0	34.2	157	36	24	22	3	0	1	0	20	1	25	6	0	3	2	.600	0	0- -	—	5.71
1998 Edmonton	AAA	5	4	0	0	23.1	104	22	13	9	1	1	0	0	11	0	31	1	0	3	1	.750	0	0- -	—	3.47
1999 Vancouver	AAA	19	19	0	0	109.2	451	94	54	50	9	1	4	0	43	0	111	7	1	4	2	.667	0	0- -	—	4.10
1998 Oakland	AL	24	20	1	0	117.1	538	117	92	83	22	1	2	5	71	3	89	15	0	5	9	.357	1	0-0	0	6.37
1999 Oak-KC	AL	13	12	0	0	73	327	65	38	37	11	2	1	7	47	1	47	3	0	1	2	.333	0	0-0	0	4.56
1999 Oakland	AL	1	1	0	0	2.2	19	6	5	5	1	0	0	0	6	0	4	1	0	0	0	.000	0	0-0	0	16.88
Kansas City	AL	12	11	0	0	70.1	308	59	33	32	10	2	1	7	41	1	43	2	0	1	2	.333	0	0-0	0	4.09
2 ML YEARS		37	32	1	0	190.1	865	182	130	120	33	3	3	12	118	4	136	18	0	6	11	.353	1	0-0	0	5.67

Terry Steinbach

Bats: Right Throws: Right Pos: C-96; PH/PR-5; DH-1   Ht: 6'1" Wt: 211 Born: 3/2/62 Age: 38

		BATTING																	BASERUNNING				PERCENTAGES		
Year Team	Lg	G	AB	H	2B	3B	HR	(Hm	Rd)	TB	R	RBI	TBB	IBB	SO	HBP	SH	SF	SB	CS	SB%	GDP	Avg	OBP	SLG
1986 Oakland	AL	6	15	5	0	0	2	(0	2)	11	3	4	1	0	0	0	0	0	0	0	.00	0	.333	.375	.733
1987 Oakland	AL	122	391	111	16	3	16	(6	10)	181	66	56	32	2	66	9	3	3	1	2	.33	10	.284	.349	.463
1988 Oakland	AL	104	351	93	19	1	9	(6	3)	141	42	51	33	2	47	6	3	5	3	0	1.00	13	.265	.334	.402
1989 Oakland	AL	130	454	124	13	1	7	(5	2)	160	37	42	30	2	66	2	2	3	1	2	.33	14	.273	.319	.352
1990 Oakland	AL	114	379	95	15	2	9	(3	6)	141	32	57	19	1	66	4	5	3	0	1	.00	11	.251	.291	.372
1991 Oakland	AL	129	456	125	31	1	6	(1	5)	176	50	67	22	4	70	7	0	9	2	2	.50	15	.274	.312	.386
1992 Oakland	AL	128	438	122	20	1	12	(3	9)	180	48	53	45	3	58	1	0	3	3	3	.50	20	.279	.345	.411
1993 Oakland	AL	104	389	111	19	1	10	(5	5)	162	47	43	25	1	65	3	0	1	3	3	.50	13	.285	.333	.416
1994 Oakland	AL	103	369	105	21	2	11	(5	6)	163	51	57	26	4	62	0	1	6	1	3	.25	15	.285	.327	.442
1995 Oakland	AL	114	406	113	26	1	15	(9	6)	186	43	65	25	4	74	3	1	4	1	3	.25	15	.278	.322	.458
1996 Oakland	AL	145	514	140	25	1	35	(16	19)	272	79	100	49	5	115	6	0	2	0	1	.00	16	.272	.342	.529
1997 Minnesota	AL	122	447	111	27	1	12	(6	6)	176	60	54	35	2	106	1	0	4	6	1	.86	14	.248	.302	.394
1998 Minnesota	AL	124	422	102	25	2	14	(6	8)	173	45	54	38	0	89	4	0	1	0	1	.00	16	.242	.310	.410

222

								BATTING												BASERUNNING				PERCENTAGES		
Year Team	Lg	G	AB	H	2B	3B	HR	(Hm	Rd)	TB	R	RBI	TBB	IBB	SO	HBP	SH	SF	SB	CS	SB%	GDP	Avg	OBP	SLG
1999 Minnesota	AL	101	338	96	16	4	4	(3	1)	132	35	42	38	1	54	2	0	2	2	2	.50	10	.284	.358	.391
14 ML YEARS		1546	5369	1453	273	21	162	(74	88)	2254	638	745	418	31	938	48	15	46	23	22	.51	177	.271	.326	.420

Garrett Stephenson

Pitches: Right **Bats:** Right **Pos:** SP-12; RP-6 **Ht:** 6'5" **Wt:** 208 **Born:** 1/2/72 **Age:** 28

		HOW MUCH HE PITCHED						WHAT HE GAVE UP											THE RESULTS					
Year Team	Lg	G	GS	CG	GF	IP	BFP	H	R	ER	HR	SH	SF	HB	TBB	IBB	SO	WP	Bk	W	L	Pct.	ShO	Sv-Op	Hld	ERA
1999 Arkansas *	AA	1	1	0	0	5.1	23	8	3	2	1	1	0	0	1	0	2	0	0	0	0	.000	0	0--	—	3.38
Memphis *	AAA	4	4	0	0	25.2	102	22	9	9	2	0	0	1	7	0	19	0	0	1	1	.500	0	0--	—	3.16
1996 Baltimore	AL	3	0	0	2	6.1	35	13	9	9	1	1	0	1	3	1	3	0	0	0	1	.000	0	0-0	0	12.79
1997 Philadelphia	NL	20	18	2	0	117	474	104	45	41	11	5	3	38	0	81	1	0	8	6	.571	0	0-0	0	3.15
1998 Philadelphia	NL	6	6	0	0	23	118	31	24	23	3	1	0	0	19	0	17	0	1	0	2	.000	0	0-0	0	9.00
1999 St. Louis	NL	18	12	0	1	85.1	371	90	43	40	11	5	5	5	29	1	59	0	0	6	3	.667	0	0-0	0	4.22
4 ML YEARS		47	36	2	3	231.2	998	238	121	113	26	9	10	9	89	2	160	1	1	14	12	.538	0	0-0	0	4.39

Dave Stevens

Pitches: Right **Bats:** Right **Pos:** RP-5 **Ht:** 6'3" **Wt:** 215 **Born:** 3/4/70 **Age:** 30

		HOW MUCH HE PITCHED						WHAT HE GAVE UP											THE RESULTS					
Year Team	Lg	G	GS	CG	GF	IP	BFP	H	R	ER	HR	SH	SF	HB	TBB	IBB	SO	WP	Bk	W	L	Pct.	ShO	Sv-Op	Hld	ERA
1999 Buffalo *	AAA	20	0	0	18	23.2	97	12	4	4	1	1	1	2	14	1	28	0	0	1	0	1.000	0	12--	—	1.52
Tacoma *	AAA	7	0	0	1	10	54	14	14	14	2	0	0	2	6	1	8	1	0	1	1	.500	0	0--	—	12.60
1994 Minnesota	AL	24	0	0	6	45	208	55	35	34	6	2	0	1	23	2	24	3	0	5	2	.714	0	0-0	1	6.80
1995 Minnesota	AL	56	0	0	34	65.2	302	74	40	37	14	4	5	1	32	1	47	2	0	5	4	.556	0	10-12	5	5.07
1996 Minnesota	AL	49	0	0	38	58	251	58	31	30	12	3	3	0	25	2	29	1	0	3	3	.500	0	11-16	0	4.66
1997 Min-ChC		16	6	0	0	32.1	174	54	34	33	8	0	1	1	26	0	29	1	3	1	5	.167	0	0-0	0	9.19
1998 Chicago	NL	31	0	0	13	38	169	42	20	20	6	4	1	1	17	5	31	1	1	1	2	.333	0	0-0	0	4.74
1999 Cleveland	AL	5	0	0	0	9	44	10	10	10	1	0	1	0	8	1	6	1	0	0	0	.000	0	0-0	0	10.00
1997 Minnesota	AL	6	6	0	0	23	124	41	23	23	8	0	0	0	17	0	16	1	2	1	3	.250	0	0-0	0	9.00
Chicago	NL	10	0	0	0	9.1	50	13	11	10	0	0	1	1	9	0	13	0	1	0	2	.000	0	0-0	0	9.64
6 ML YEARS		181	6	0	91	248	1148	293	170	164	47	13	11	4	131	11	166	9	4	15	16	.484	0	21-28	6	5.95

Lee Stevens

Bats: Left **Throws:** Left **Pos:** 1B-133; DH-8; PH/PR-6 **Ht:** 6'4" **Wt:** 235 **Born:** 7/10/67 **Age:** 32

								BATTING												BASERUNNING				PERCENTAGES		
Year Team	Lg	G	AB	H	2B	3B	HR	(Hm	Rd)	TB	R	RBI	TBB	IBB	SO	HBP	SH	SF	SB	CS	SB%	GDP	Avg	OBP	SLG
1990 California	AL	67	248	53	10	0	7	(4	3)	84	28	32	22	3	75	0	2	3	1	1	.50	8	.214	.275	.339
1991 California	AL	18	58	17	7	0	0	(0	0)	24	8	9	6	2	12	0	1	1	1	2	.33	0	.293	.354	.414
1992 California	AL	106	312	69	19	0	7	(2	5)	109	25	37	29	6	64	1	1	2	1	4	.20	4	.221	.288	.349
1996 Texas	AL	27	78	18	2	3	3	(2	1)	35	6	12	6	0	22	1	0	1	0	0	.00	2	.231	.291	.449
1997 Texas	AL	137	426	128	24	2	21	(12	9)	219	58	74	23	2	83	1	1	3	1	3	.25	18	.300	.336	.514
1998 Texas	AL	120	344	91	17	4	20	(13	7)	176	52	59	31	4	93	0	1	6	0	2	.00	6	.265	.324	.512
1999 Texas	AL	146	517	146	31	1	24	(10	14)	251	76	81	52	10	132	0	0	7	2	3	.40	19	.282	.344	.485
7 ML YEARS		621	1983	522	110	10	82	(43	39)	898	253	304	169	27	481	3	5	18	6	15	.29	57	.263	.319	.453

Shannon Stewart

Bats: R **Throws:** R **Pos:** LF-141; CF-7; DH-2; PH/PR-1 **Ht:** 6'1" **Wt:** 205 **Born:** 2/25/74 **Age:** 26

								BATTING												BASERUNNING				PERCENTAGES		
Year Team	Lg	G	AB	H	2B	3B	HR	(Hm	Rd)	TB	R	RBI	TBB	IBB	SO	HBP	SH	SF	SB	CS	SB%	GDP	Avg	OBP	SLG
1995 Toronto	AL	12	38	8	0	0	0	(0	0)	8	2	1	5	0	5	1	0	0	2	0	1.00	0	.211	.318	.211
1996 Toronto	AL	7	17	3	1	0	0	(0	0)	4	2	2	1	0	4	0	0	0	1	0	1.00	1	.176	.222	.235
1997 Toronto	AL	44	168	48	13	0	0	(0	0)	75	25	22	19	1	24	4	0	2	10	3	.77	3	.286	.368	.446
1998 Toronto	AL	144	516	144	29	3	12	(6	6)	215	90	55	67	1	77	15	6	1	51	18	.74	5	.279	.377	.417
1999 Toronto	AL	145	608	185	28	2	11	(4	7)	250	102	67	59	0	83	8	3	4	37	14	.73	12	.304	.371	.411
5 ML YEARS		352	1347	388	71	12	23	(10	13)	552	221	147	151	2	193	28	9	7	101	35	.74	21	.288	.370	.410

Kelly Stinnett

Bats: Right **Throws:** Right **Pos:** C-86; PH/PR-4 **Ht:** 5'11" **Wt:** 225 **Born:** 2/4/70 **Age:** 30

								BATTING												BASERUNNING				PERCENTAGES		
Year Team	Lg	G	AB	H	2B	3B	HR	(Hm	Rd)	TB	R	RBI	TBB	IBB	SO	HBP	SH	SF	SB	CS	SB%	GDP	Avg	OBP	SLG
1994 New York	NL	47	150	38	6	2	2	(0	2)	54	20	14	11	1	28	5	0	1	2	0	1.00	3	.253	.323	.360
1995 New York	NL	77	196	43	8	1	4	(1	3)	65	23	18	29	3	65	6	0	0	2	0	1.00	3	.219	.338	.332
1996 Milwaukee	AL	14	26	2	0	0	0	(0	0)	2	1	0	2	0	11	1	0	0	0	0	.00	0	.077	.172	.077
1997 Milwaukee	AL	30	36	9	4	0	0	(0	0)	13	2	3	3	0	9	0	0	0	0	0	.00	0	.250	.308	.361
1998 Arizona	NL	92	274	71	14	1	11	(5	6)	120	35	34	35	3	74	6	1	2	0	1	.00	9	.259	.353	.438
1999 Arizona	NL	88	284	66	13	0	14	(3	11)	121	36	38	24	2	83	5	2	2	2	1	.67	4	.232	.302	.426
6 ML YEARS		348	966	229	45	4	31	(9	22)	375	117	107	104	9	270	23	3	5	6	2	.75	19	.237	.324	.388

Kevin Stocker

Bats: Both **Throws:** Right **Pos:** SS-76; PH/PR-4 **Ht:** 6'1" **Wt:** 180 **Born:** 2/13/70 **Age:** 30

			BATTING															BASERUNNING			PERCENTAGES		
Year Team	Lg	G	AB	H	2B	3B	HR	(Hm	Rd)	TB	R	RBI	TBB	IBB	SO	HBP	SH	SF	SB	CS	SB%	GDP	Avg	OBP	SLG
1999 St. Pete *	A+	3	11	1	0	0	0	—	—	1	2	0	1	0	2	0	0	0	0	0	.00	0	.091	.167	.091
1993 Philadelphia	NL	70	259	84	12	3	2	(1	1)	108	46	31	30	11	43	8	4	1	5	0	1.00	8	.324	.409	.417
1994 Philadelphia	NL	82	271	74	11	2	2	(2	0)	95	38	28	44	8	41	7	4	4	2	2	.50	3	.273	.383	.351
1995 Philadelphia	NL	125	412	90	14	3	1	(1	0)	113	42	32	43	9	75	9	10	3	6	1	.86	7	.218	.304	.274
1996 Philadelphia	NL	119	394	100	22	6	5	(0	5)	149	46	41	43	9	89	8	3	4	6	4	.60	6	.254	.336	.378
1997 Philadelphia	NL	149	504	134	23	5	4	(2	2)	179	51	40	51	7	91	2	2	1	11	6	.65	14	.266	.335	.355
1998 Tampa Bay	AL	112	336	70	11	3	6	(4	2)	105	37	25	27	1	80	8	8	2	5	3	.63	7	.208	.282	.313
1999 Tampa Bay	AL	79	254	76	11	2	1	(1	0)	94	39	27	24	0	41	4	4	0	9	7	.56	4	.299	.369	.370
7 ML YEARS		736	2430	628	104	24	21	(11	10)	843	299	224	262	45	460	46	35	15	44	23	.66	49	.258	.340	.347

Todd Stottlemyre

Pitches: Right **Bats:** Left **Pos:** SP-17 **Ht:** 6'3" **Wt:** 200 **Born:** 5/20/65 **Age:** 35

		HOW MUCH HE PITCHED						WHAT HE GAVE UP										THE RESULTS						
Year Team	Lg	G	GS	CG	GF	IP	BFP	H	R	ER	HR	SH	SF	HB	TBB	IBB	SO	WP	Bk	W	L	Pct.	ShO	Sv-Op	Hld	ERA
1999 Diamondbcks *	R	3	3	1	0	17	64	11	1	1	0	0	0	0	1	0	25	0	0	2	0	1.000	0	0--	—	0.53
1988 Toronto	AL	28	16	0	2	98	443	109	70	62	15	5	3	4	46	5	67	2	3	4	8	.333	0	0-1	0	5.69
1989 Toronto	AL	27	18	0	4	127.2	545	137	56	55	11	3	7	5	44	4	63	4	1	7	7	.500	0	0-0	0	3.88
1990 Toronto	AL	33	33	4	0	203	866	214	101	98	18	3	5	8	69	4	115	6	1	13	17	.433	0	0-0	0	4.34
1991 Toronto	AL	34	34	1	0	219	921	194	97	92	21	0	8	12	75	3	116	4	0	15	8	.652	0	0-0	0	3.78
1992 Toronto	AL	28	27	6	0	174	755	175	99	87	20	2	11	10	63	4	98	7	0	12	11	.522	2	0-0	0	4.50
1993 Toronto	AL	30	28	1	0	176.2	786	204	107	95	11	5	11	3	69	5	98	7	1	11	12	.478	1	0-0	0	4.84
1994 Toronto	AL	26	19	3	5	140.2	605	149	67	66	19	4	5	7	48	2	105	0	0	7	7	.500	1	1-3	0	4.22
1995 Oakland	AL	31	31	2	0	209.2	920	228	117	106	26	4	4	6	80	7	205	11	0	14	7	.667	0	0-0	0	4.55
1996 St. Louis	NL	34	33	5	0	223.1	944	191	100	96	30	12	9	4	93	8	194	8	1	14	11	.560	2	0-0	0	3.87
1997 St. Louis	NL	28	28	0	0	181	761	155	86	78	16	8	5	12	65	3	160	6	0	12	9	.571	0	0-0	0	3.88
1998 StL-Tex		33	33	3	0	221.2	949	214	107	92	25	8	6	4	81	1	204	5	2	14	13	.519	0	0-0	0	3.74
1999 Arizona	NL	17	17	0	0	101.1	446	106	51	46	12	3	1	6	40	1	74	2	0	6	3	.667	0	0-0	0	4.09
1998 St. Louis	NL	23	23	3	0	161.1	674	146	74	63	20	7	3	4	51	0	147	4	2	9	9	.500	0	0-0	0	3.51
Texas	AL	10	10	0	0	60.1	275	68	33	29	5	1	3	0	30	1	57	1	0	5	4	.556	0	0-0	0	4.33
12 ML YEARS		349	317	25	11	2076	8941	2076	1058	973	224	57	75	81	773	47	1499	62	9	129	113	.533	6	1-4	0	4.22

Chris Stowers

Bats: Left **Throws:** Left **Pos:** PH/PR-3; CF-1; RF-1 **Ht:** 6'3" **Wt:** 195 **Born:** 8/18/74 **Age:** 25

			BATTING															BASERUNNING			PERCENTAGES		
Year Team	Lg	G	AB	H	2B	3B	HR	(Hm	Rd)	TB	R	RBI	TBB	IBB	SO	HBP	SH	SF	SB	CS	SB%	GDP	Avg	OBP	SLG
1996 Vermont	A-	72	282	90	21	9	7	—	—	150	58	44	21	6	37	2	0	0	16	5	.76	4	.319	.370	.532
1997 Wst Plm Bch	A+	111	414	113	15	5	4	—	—	150	56	30	30	5	77	7	2	2	19	14	.58	6	.273	.331	.362
Harrisburg	AA	19	59	17	4	2	0	—	—	25	9	5	2	1	11	0	1	0	3	1	.75	1	.288	.344	.424
1998 Harrisburg	AA	134	510	137	31	5	17	—	—	229	86	66	42	2	109	8	3	3	24	7	.77	7	.269	.332	.449
1999 Ottawa	AAA	118	431	102	17	4	5	—	—	142	60	37	39	2	92	4	3	2	28	9	.76	10	.237	.305	.329
1999 Montreal	NL	4	2	0	0	0	0	(0	0)	0	0	0	0	0	0	0	0	0	0	0	.00	0	.000	.000	.000

Darryl Strawberry

Bats: Left **Throws:** Left **Pos:** DH-17; PH/PR-9 **Ht:** 6'6" **Wt:** 215 **Born:** 3/12/62 **Age:** 38

			BATTING															BASERUNNING			PERCENTAGES		
Year Team	Lg	G	AB	H	2B	3B	HR	(Hm	Rd)	TB	R	RBI	TBB	IBB	SO	HBP	SH	SF	SB	CS	SB%	GDP	Avg	OBP	SLG
1999 Columbus *	AAA	21	73	21	5	1	4	—	—	40	12	15	11	1	13	0	0	2	1	2	.33	1	.288	.372	.548
1983 New York	NL	122	420	108	15	7	26	(10	16)	215	63	74	47	9	128	4	0	2	19	6	.76	5	.257	.336	.512
1984 New York	NL	147	522	131	27	4	26	(8	18)	244	75	97	75	15	131	0	1	4	27	8	.77	8	.251	.343	.467
1985 New York	NL	111	393	109	15	4	29	(14	15)	219	78	79	73	13	96	1	0	3	26	11	.70	9	.277	.389	.557
1986 New York	NL	136	475	123	27	5	27	(11	16)	241	76	93	72	9	141	6	0	0	28	12	.70	4	.259	.358	.507
1987 New York	NL	154	532	151	32	5	39	(20	19)	310	108	104	97	13	122	7	0	4	36	12	.75	4	.284	.398	.583
1988 New York	NL	153	543	146	27	3	39	(21	18)	296	101	101	85	21	127	3	0	9	29	14	.67	6	.269	.366	.545
1989 New York	NL	134	476	107	26	1	29	(15	14)	222	69	77	61	13	105	1	0	3	11	4	.73	6	.225	.312	.466
1990 New York	NL	152	542	150	18	1	37	(24	13)	281	92	108	70	15	110	4	0	5	15	8	.65	5	.277	.361	.518
1991 Los Angeles	NL	139	505	134	22	4	28	(14	14)	248	86	99	75	4	125	3	0	5	10	8	.56	8	.265	.361	.491
1992 Los Angeles	NL	43	156	37	8	0	5	(3	2)	60	20	25	19	4	34	1	0	1	3	1	.75	2	.237	.322	.385
1993 Los Angeles	NL	32	100	14	2	0	5	(3	2)	31	12	12	16	1	19	2	0	2	1	0	1.00	1	.140	.267	.310
1994 San Francisco	NL	29	92	22	3	1	4	(2	2)	39	13	17	19	4	22	0	0	2	0	3	.00	2	.239	.363	.424
1995 New York	AL	32	87	24	4	1	3	(3	0)	39	15	13	10	1	22	2	0	0	0	0	.00	0	.276	.364	.448
1996 New York	AL	63	202	53	13	0	11	(8	3)	99	35	36	31	5	55	1	0	3	6	5	.55	3	.262	.359	.490
1997 New York	AL	11	29	3	1	0	0	(0	0)	4	1	2	3	0	9	0	0	0	0	0	.00	2	.103	.188	.138
1998 New York	AL	101	295	73	11	2	24	(14	10)	160	44	57	46	4	90	3	0	1	8	7	.53	1	.247	.354	.542
1999 New York	AL	24	49	16	5	0	3	(1	2)	30	10	6	17	0	16	0	0	0	2	0	1.00	0	.327	.500	.612
17 ML YEARS		1583	5418	1401	256	38	335	(171	164)	2738	898	1000	816	131	1352	38	1	53	221	99	.69	64	.259	.357	.505

Scott Strickland

Pitches: Right **Bats:** Right **Pos:** RP-17 **Ht:** 5'11" **Wt:** 180 **Born:** 4/26/76 **Age:** 24

		HOW MUCH HE PITCHED					WHAT HE GAVE UP											THE RESULTS						
Year Team	Lg	G	GS	CG	GF	IP	BFP	H	R	ER	HR	SH	SF	HB	TBB	IBB	SO	WP	Bk	W	L	Pct.	ShO	Sv-Op	Hld	ERA
1997 Vermont	A-	15	9	1	5	61.1	255	56	27	26	5	3	2	6	20	0	69	3	1	5	2	.714	0	5--	—	3.82
Cape Fear	A	3	1	0	2	5.2	26	8	7	4	0	0	0	0	1	0	8	1	0	0	1	.000	0	1--	—	6.35
1998 Cape Fear	A	15	2	0	11	36.1	161	36	19	18	3	3	1	3	12	0	53	1	0	0	3	.000	0	4--	—	4.46
Jupiter	A+	22	11	0	7	69	282	64	28	26	5	4	2	1	20	0	51	0	1	4	3	.571	0	2--	—	3.39
1999 Jupiter	A+	12	1	0	7	25.2	103	21	11	10	1	1	1	2	4	1	33	1	0	1	1	.500	0	2--	—	3.51
Harrisburg	AA	14	1	0	6	29	117	25	8	8	1	1	0	1	10	0	36	0	0	1	1	.500	0	3--	—	2.48
Ottawa	AAA	19	0	0	12	27.2	116	23	5	5	0	0	1	1	11	2	34	1	0	3	0	1.000	0	5--	—	1.63
1999 Montreal	NL	17	0	0	5	18	78	15	10	9	3	2	0	0	11	0	23	0	0	0	1	.000	0	0-0	2	4.50

Everett Stull

Pitches: Right **Bats:** Right **Pos:** RP-1 **Ht:** 6'3" **Wt:** 200 **Born:** 8/24/71 **Age:** 28

		HOW MUCH HE PITCHED					WHAT HE GAVE UP											THE RESULTS						
Year Team	Lg	G	GS	CG	GF	IP	BFP	H	R	ER	HR	SH	SF	HB	TBB	IBB	SO	WP	Bk	W	L	Pct.	ShO	Sv-Op	Hld	ERA
1992 Jamestown	A-	14	14	0	0	63.1	303	52	49	38	2	2	3	3	61	0	64	18	4	3	5	.375	0	0--	—	5.40
1993 Burlington	A	15	15	1	0	82.1	366	68	44	35	8	2	1	3	59	0	85	11	4	4	9	.308	0	0--	—	3.83
1994 Wst Plm Bch	A+	27	26	3	0	147	627	116	60	54	3	7	3	12	78	0	165	15	6	10	10	.500	1	0--	—	3.31
1995 Harrisburg	AA	24	24	0	0	126.2	569	114	88	78	12	5	5	9	79	2	132	7	1	3	12	.200	0	0--	—	5.54
1996 Harrisburg	AA	14	14	0	0	80	345	64	31	28	8	3	2	2	52	1	81	6	0	6	3	.667	0	0--	—	3.15
Ottawa	AAA	13	13	1	0	69.2	331	87	57	49	7	3	3	3	39	1	69	5	0	2	6	.250	0	0--	—	6.33
1997 Ottawa	AAA	27	27	1	0	159.1	710	166	110	103	25	4	4	13	86	0	130	9	0	8	10	.444	0	0--	—	5.82
1998 Rochester	AAA	21	7	0	6	42.2	222	49	44	42	9	0	3	5	45	0	39	6	0	1	4	.200	0	0--	—	8.86
1999 Richmond	AAA	30	22	0	5	139	603	124	75	69	17	4	7	8	73	0	126	12	2	8	8	.500	0	0--	—	4.47
1997 Montreal	NL	3	0	0	1	3.1	21	7	7	6	1	1	0	0	4	0	2	0	0	0	1	.000	0	0-0	0	16.20
1999 Atlanta	NL	1	0	0	0	0.2	7	2	3	1	0	0	1	0	2	0	0	0	0	0	0	.000	0	0-0	0	13.50
2 ML YEARS		4	0	0	1	4	28	9	10	7	1	1	1	0	6	0	2	0	0	0	1	.000	0	0-0	0	15.75

Tanyon Sturtze

Pitches: Right **Bats:** Right **Pos:** SP-1 **Ht:** 6'5" **Wt:** 205 **Born:** 10/12/70 **Age:** 29

		HOW MUCH HE PITCHED					WHAT HE GAVE UP											THE RESULTS						
Year Team	Lg	G	GS	CG	GF	IP	BFP	H	R	ER	HR	SH	SF	HB	TBB	IBB	SO	WP	Bk	W	L	Pct.	ShO	Sv-Op	Hld	ERA
1999 Charlotte *	AAA	33	14	2	11	104.1	433	83	53	47	7	1	2	1	41	1	107	2	0	9	4	.692	1	3--	—	4.05
1995 Chicago	NL	2	0	0	0	2	9	2	2	2	1	0	0	0	1	0	0	0	0	0	0	.000	0	0-0	0	9.00
1996 Chicago	NL	6	0	0	3	11	51	16	11	11	3	0	0	0	5	0	7	0	0	1	0	1.000	0	0-0	0	9.00
1997 Texas	AL	9	5	0	1	32.2	155	45	30	30	6	0	4	0	18	0	18	1	1	1	1	.500	0	0-0	0	8.27
1999 Chicago	AL	1	1	0	0	6	22	4	0	0	0	0	0	0	2	0	2	0	0	0	0	.000	0	0-0	0	0.00
4 ML YEARS		18	6	0	4	51.2	237	67	43	43	10	0	4	0	26	0	27	1	1	2	1	.667	0	0-0	0	7.49

Chris Stynes

Bats: R **Throws:** R **Pos:** 2B-43; PH/PR-23; 3B-8; LF-4 **Ht:** 5'10" **Wt:** 185 **Born:** 1/19/73 **Age:** 27

		BATTING																		BASERUNNING			PERCENTAGES		
Year Team	Lg	G	AB	H	2B	3B	HR	(Hm	Rd)	TB	R	RBI	TBB	IBB	SO	HBP	SH	SF	SB	CS	SB%	GDP	Avg	OBP	SLG
1995 Kansas City	AL	22	35	6	1	0	0	(0	0)	7	7	2	4	0	3	0	0	0	0	0	.00	3	.171	.256	.200
1996 Kansas City	AL	36	92	27	6	0	0	(0	0)	33	8	6	2	0	5	0	1	0	5	2	.71	1	.293	.309	.359
1997 Cincinnati	NL	49	198	69	7	1	6	(2	4)	96	31	28	11	1	13	4	2	0	11	2	.85	1	.348	.394	.485
1998 Cincinnati	NL	123	347	88	10	1	6	(3	3)	118	52	27	32	1	36	4	4	1	15	1	.94	5	.254	.323	.340
1999 Cincinnati	NL	73	113	27	1	0	2	(1	1)	34	18	14	12	1	13	0	3	1	5	2	.71	2	.239	.310	.301
5 ML YEARS		303	785	217	25	2	14	(6	8)	288	116	77	61	3	70	8	10	2	36	7	.84	16	.276	.334	.367

Scott Sullivan

Pitches: Right **Bats:** Right **Pos:** RP-79 **Ht:** 6'3" **Wt:** 210 **Born:** 3/13/71 **Age:** 29

		HOW MUCH HE PITCHED					WHAT HE GAVE UP											THE RESULTS						
Year Team	Lg	G	GS	CG	GF	IP	BFP	H	R	ER	HR	SH	SF	HB	TBB	IBB	SO	WP	Bk	W	L	Pct.	ShO	Sv-Op	Hld	ERA
1995 Cincinnati	NL	3	0	0	1	3.2	17	4	2	2	0	1	0	0	2	0	2	0	0	0	0	.000	0	0-0	0	4.91
1996 Cincinnati	NL	7	0	0	4	8	35	7	2	2	0	1	0	1	5	0	3	1	0	0	0	.000	0	0-0	0	2.25
1997 Cincinnati	NL	59	0	0	15	97.1	402	79	36	35	12	3	3	7	30	8	96	7	1	5	3	.625	0	1-2	13	3.24
1998 Cincinnati	NL	67	0	0	13	102	440	98	62	59	14	3	4	9	36	4	86	4	0	5	5	.500	0	1-4	5	5.21
1999 Cincinnati	NL	79	0	0	16	113.2	470	88	41	38	10	4	4	8	47	4	78	6	1	5	4	.556	0	3-5	13	3.01
5 ML YEARS		215	0	0	49	324.2	1364	276	143	136	36	12	11	25	120	16	265	18	2	15	12	.556	0	5-11	31	3.77

Jeff Suppan

Pitches: Right **Bats:** Right **Pos:** SP-32 **Ht:** 6'2" **Wt:** 210 **Born:** 1/2/75 **Age:** 25

		HOW MUCH HE PITCHED					WHAT HE GAVE UP											THE RESULTS						
Year Team	Lg	G	GS	CG	GF	IP	BFP	H	R	ER	HR	SH	SF	HB	TBB	IBB	SO	WP	Bk	W	L	Pct.	ShO	Sv-Op	Hld	ERA
1995 Boston	AL	8	3	0	1	22.2	100	29	15	15	4	1	1	0	5	1	19	0	0	1	2	.333	0	0-0	1	5.96
1996 Boston	AL	8	4	0	2	22.2	107	29	19	19	3	1	4	1	13	0	13	3	0	1	1	.500	0	0-0	0	7.54
1997 Boston	AL	23	22	0	1	112.1	503	140	75	71	12	0	4	4	36	1	67	5	0	7	3	.700	0	0-0	0	5.69
1998 Ari-KC		17	14	1	2	78.2	345	91	56	50	13	3	2	1	22	1	51	2	0	1	7	.125	0	0-0	0	5.72
1999 Kansas City	AL	32	32	4	0	208.2	887	222	113	105	28	7	5	3	62	4	103	5	1	10	12	.455	1	0-0	0	4.53

			HOW MUCH HE PITCHED						WHAT HE GAVE UP										THE RESULTS						
Year Team	Lg	G	GS	CG	GF	IP	BFP	H	R	ER	HR	SH	SF	HB	TBB	IBB	SO	WP	Bk	W	L	Pct.	ShO	Sv-Op	Hld	ERA
1998 Arizona	NL	13	13	1	0	66	299	82	55	49	12	3	2	1	21	1	39	2	0	1	7	.125	0	0-0	0	6.68
Kansas City	AL	4	1	0	2	12.2	46	9	1	1	1	0	0	0	1	0	12	0	0	0	0	.000	0	0-0	0	0.71
5 ML YEARS		88	75	5	6	445	1942	511	278	260	60	12	16	9	138	7	253	15	1	20	25	.444	1	0-0	1	5.26

B.J. Surhoff

Bats: L **Throws:** R **Pos:** LF-148; DH-13; 3B-2; PH/PR-1   **Ht:** 6'1" **Wt:** 200 **Born:** 8/4/64 **Age:** 35

								BATTING												BASERUNNING				PERCENTAGES		
Year Team	Lg	G	AB	H	2B	3B	HR	(Hm	Rd)	TB	R	RBI	TBB	IBB	SO	HBP	SH	SF	SB	CS	SB%	GDP	Avg	OBP	SLG
1987 Milwaukee	AL	115	395	118	22	3	7	(5	2)	167	50	68	36	1	30	0	5	9	11	10	.52	13	.299	.350	.423
1988 Milwaukee	AL	139	493	121	21	0	5	(2	3)	157	47	38	31	9	49	3	11	3	21	6	.78	12	.245	.292	.318
1989 Milwaukee	AL	126	436	108	17	4	5	(3	2)	148	42	55	21	5	29	3	3	10	14	12	.54	8	.248	.287	.339
1990 Milwaukee	AL	135	474	131	21	4	6	(4	2)	178	55	59	41	5	37	1	7	7	18	7	.72	8	.276	.331	.376
1991 Milwaukee	AL	143	505	146	19	4	5	(3	2)	188	57	68	26	2	33	0	13	9	5	8	.38	21	.289	.319	.372
1992 Milwaukee	AL	139	480	121	19	1	4	(3	1)	154	63	62	46	8	41	2	5	10	14	8	.64	9	.252	.314	.321
1993 Milwaukee	AL	148	552	151	38	3	7	(4	3)	216	66	79	36	5	47	2	4	5	12	9	.57	9	.274	.318	.391
1994 Milwaukee	AL	40	134	35	11	2	5	(2	3)	65	20	22	16	0	14	0	2	2	1	0	1.00	5	.261	.336	.485
1995 Milwaukee	AL	117	415	133	26	3	13	(7	6)	204	72	73	37	4	43	4	2	4	7	3	.70	7	.320	.378	.492
1996 Baltimore	AL	143	537	157	27	6	21	(12	9)	259	74	82	47	8	79	3	2	1	0	1	.00	7	.292	.352	.482
1997 Baltimore	AL	147	528	150	30	4	18	(10	8)	242	80	88	49	14	60	5	3	10	1	1	.50	7	.284	.345	.458
1998 Baltimore	AL	162	573	160	34	1	22	(9	13)	262	79	92	49	9	81	1	1	10	9	7	.56	13	.279	.332	.457
1999 Baltimore	AL	162	673	207	38	1	28	(9	19)	331	104	107	43	1	78	2	1	8	5	1	.83	15	.308	.347	.492
13 ML YEARS		1716	6195	1738	323	36	146	(73	73)	2571	809	893	482	67	621	26	59	88	117	74	.61	134	.281	.331	.415

Larry Sutton

Bats: L **Throws:** L **Pos:** 1B-30; PH/PR-11; DH-5; RF-1   **Ht:** 6'0" **Wt:** 185 **Born:** 5/14/70 **Age:** 30

								BATTING												BASERUNNING				PERCENTAGES		
Year Team	Lg	G	AB	H	2B	3B	HR	(Hm	Rd)	TB	R	RBI	TBB	IBB	SO	HBP	SH	SF	SB	CS	SB%	GDP	Avg	OBP	SLG
1999 Royals *	R	9	31	8	2	0	1	—	—	13	7	6	7	0	6	1	0	0	0	0	.00	1	.258	.410	.419
Omaha *	AAA	39	148	41	8	1	3	—	—	60	28	12	27	2	24	1	1	1	4	1	.80	4	.277	.390	.405
1997 Kansas City	AL	27	69	20	2	0	2	(1	1)	28	9	8	5	0	12	0	1	0	0	0	.00	0	.290	.338	.406
1998 Kansas City	AL	111	310	76	14	2	5	(3	2)	109	29	42	29	3	46	3	4	5	3	3	.50	5	.245	.311	.352
1999 Kansas City	AL	43	102	23	6	0	2	(2	0)	35	14	15	13	0	17	0	1	2	1	0	1.00	4	.225	.308	.343
3 ML YEARS		181	481	119	22	2	9	(6	3)	172	52	65	47	3	75	3	6	7	4	3	.57	9	.247	.314	.358

Makoto Suzuki

Pitches: Right **Bats:** Right **Pos:** RP-25; SP-13   **Ht:** 6'3" **Wt:** 195 **Born:** 5/31/75 **Age:** 25

									WHAT HE GAVE UP											THE RESULTS						
Year Team	Lg	G	GS	CG	GF	IP	BFP	H	R	ER	HR	SH	SF	HB	TBB	IBB	SO	WP	Bk	W	L	Pct.	ShO	Sv-Op	Hld	ERA
1992 Salinas	A+	1	0	0	0	1	3	0	0	0	0	0	0	0	0	0	1	0	0	0	0	.000	0	0- -	—	0.00
1993 San Berndno	A+	48	1	0	35	80.2	351	59	37	33	5	3	2	2	56	4	87	12	2	4	4	.500	0	12- -	—	3.68
1994 Jacksnville	AA	8	0	0	1	12.2	58	15	4	4	1	0	1	0	6	0	10	0	0	1	0	1.000	0	1- -	—	2.84
1995 Mariners	R	4	3	0	0	4	19	5	4	3	1	0	0	1	0	0	3	0	0	1	0	1.000	0	0- -	—	6.75
Riverside	A+	6	0	0	1	7.2	39	10	4	4	0	0	1	0	6	0	6	2	0	1	1	.000	0	0- -	—	4.70
1996 Port City	AA	16	16	0	0	74.1	320	69	41	39	10	2	1	2	32	0	66	0	0	3	6	.333	0	0- -	—	4.72
Tacoma	AAA	13	2	0	6	22.1	110	31	19	18	3	2	0	0	12	2	14	3	0	0	3	.000	0	0- -	—	7.25
1997 Tacoma	AAA	32	10	0	7	83.1	384	79	60	55	13	2	1	0	64	1	63	6	1	4	9	.308	0	0- -	—	5.94
1998 Tacoma	AAA	28	21	2	1	131.2	578	130	70	64	19	2	3	5	70	0	117	8	0	9	10	.474	1	0- -	—	4.37
1996 Seattle	AL	1	0	0	0	1.1	8	2	3	3	0	0	0	0	2	1	1	0	0	0	0	.000	0	0-0	0	20.25
1998 Seattle	AL	6	5	0	0	26.1	127	34	23	21	3	0	0	0	15	0	19	0	0	1	2	.333	0	0-0	0	7.18
1999 Sea-KC	AL	38	13	0	6	110	510	124	92	83	16	2	3	7	64	3	68	11	0	2	5	.286	0	0-0	0	6.79
1999 Seattle	AL	16	4	0	3	42	207	47	47	44	7	0	3	4	34	2	32	2	0	0	2	.000	0	0-0	0	9.43
Kansas City	AL	22	9	0	3	68	303	77	45	39	9	2	0	3	30	1	36	9	0	2	3	.400	0	0-0	0	5.16
3 ML YEARS		45	18	0	6	137.2	645	160	118	107	19	2	3	7	81	4	88	11	0	3	7	.300	0	0-0	0	7.00

Dale Sveum

Bats: B **Throws:** R **Pos:** PH/PR-32; 3B-12; 1B-4; SS-4; 2B-2; LF-1   **Ht:** 6'3" **Wt:** 185 **Born:** 11/23/63 **Age:** 36

								BATTING												BASERUNNING				PERCENTAGES		
Year Team	Lg	G	AB	H	2B	3B	HR	(Hm	Rd)	TB	R	RBI	TBB	IBB	SO	HBP	SH	SF	SB	CS	SB%	GDP	Avg	OBP	SLG
1999 Tucson *	AAA	20	67	14	1	0	1	—	—	18	3	4	3	0	23	0	0	1	0	1	.00	3	.209	.239	.269
Nashville *	AAA	42	125	43	14	1	3	—	—	68	25	25	18	0	30	2	0	0	1	0	1.00	5	.344	.434	.544
1986 Milwaukee	AL	91	317	78	13	2	7	(4	3)	116	35	35	32	0	63	1	5	1	4	3	.57	7	.246	.316	.366
1987 Milwaukee	AL	153	535	135	27	3	25	(9	16)	243	86	95	40	4	133	1	5	5	2	6	.25	11	.252	.303	.454
1988 Milwaukee	AL	129	467	113	14	4	9	(2	7)	162	41	51	21	0	122	1	3	3	1	0	1.00	6	.242	.274	.347
1990 Milwaukee	AL	48	117	23	7	0	1	(1	0)	33	15	12	12	0	30	2	0	2	0	1	.00	2	.197	.278	.282
1991 Milwaukee	AL	90	266	64	19	1	4	(3	1)	97	33	43	32	0	78	1	5	4	2	4	.33	8	.241	.320	.365
1992 Phi-CWS		94	249	49	13	0	4	(1	3)	74	28	28	28	4	68	0	2	5	1	1	.50	6	.197	.273	.297
1993 Oakland	AL	30	79	14	2	1	2	(0	2)	24	12	6	16	1	21	0	1	0	0	0	.00	2	.177	.316	.304
1994 Seattle	AL	10	27	5	0	0	1	(0	1)	8	3	2	2	0	10	0	0	0	0	0	.00	1	.185	.241	.296
1996 Pittsburgh	NL	12	34	12	5	0	1	(0	1)	20	9	5	6	0	6	0	0	0	0	0	.00	0	.353	.450	.588
1997 Pittsburgh	NL	126	306	80	20	1	12	(5	7)	138	30	47	27	2	81	0	4	2	0	3	.00	8	.261	.319	.451
1998 New York	AL	30	58	9	0	0	0	(0	0)	9	6	3	4	0	16	0	0	2	0	0	.00	2	.155	.203	.155
1999 Pittsburgh	NL	49	71	15	5	1	3	(0	3)	31	7	13	7	1	28	0	1	1	0	0	.00	5	.211	.278	.437
1992 Philadelphia	NL	54	135	24	4	0	2	(0	2)	34	13	16	16	4	39	0	2	0	0	0	.00	5	.178	.261	.252

Year Team	Lg	G	AB	H	2B	3B	HR	(Hm	Rd)	TB	R	RBI	TBB	IBB	SO	HBP	SH	SF	SB	CS	SB%	GDP	Avg	OBP	SLG
						BATTING													BASERUNNING				PERCENTAGES		
Chicago	AL	40	114	25	9	0	2	(1	1)	40	15	12	12	0	29	0	2	3	1	1	.50	1	.219	.287	.351
12 ML YEARS		862	2526	597	125	13	69	(25	44)	955	305	340	227	12	656	6	26	25	10	18	.36	53	.236	.298	.378

Mark Sweeney

Bats: Left **Throws:** Left **Pos:** PH/PR-36; 1B-1; LF-1 **Ht:** 6'1" **Wt:** 215 **Born:** 10/26/69 **Age:** 30

Year Team	Lg	G	AB	H	2B	3B	HR	(Hm	Rd)	TB	R	RBI	TBB	IBB	SO	HBP	SH	SF	SB	CS	SB%	GDP	Avg	OBP	SLG
						BATTING													BASERUNNING				PERCENTAGES		
1999 Indianapolis *	AAA	86	311	100	17	1	12	—	—	155	66	51	59	4	40	4	0	3	3	2	.60	7	.322	.432	.498
1995 St. Louis	NL	37	77	21	2	0	2	(0	2)	29	5	13	10	0	15	0	1	2	1	1	.50	3	.273	.348	.377
1996 St. Louis	NL	98	170	45	9	0	3	(0	3)	63	32	22	33	2	29	1	5	0	3	0	1.00	4	.265	.387	.371
1997 StL-SD	NL	115	164	46	7	0	2	(2	0)	59	16	23	20	1	32	1	1	2	2	3	.40	3	.280	.358	.360
1998 San Diego	NL	122	192	45	8	3	2	(1	1)	65	17	15	26	0	37	1	0	3	1	2	.33	5	.234	.324	.339
1999 Cincinnati	NL	37	31	11	3	0	2	(1	1)	20	6	7	4	1	9	0	0	0	0	0	.00	2	.355	.429	.645
1997 St. Louis	NL	44	61	13	3	0	0	(0	0)	16	5	4	9	1	14	1	1	1	0	1	.00	2	.213	.319	.262
San Diego	NL	71	103	33	4	0	2	(2	0)	43	11	19	11	0	18	0	0	1	2	2	.50	1	.320	.383	.417
5 ML YEARS		409	634	168	29	3	11	(4	7)	236	76	80	93	4	122	3	7	7	7	6	.54	17	.265	.358	.372

Mike Sweeney

Bats: R **Throws:** R **Pos:** 1B-74; DH-71; C-4; PH/PR-4 **Ht:** 6'2" **Wt:** 215 **Born:** 7/22/73 **Age:** 26

Year Team	Lg	G	AB	H	2B	3B	HR	(Hm	Rd)	TB	R	RBI	TBB	IBB	SO	HBP	SH	SF	SB	CS	SB%	GDP	Avg	OBP	SLG
						BATTING													BASERUNNING				PERCENTAGES		
1995 Kansas City	AL	4	4	1	0	0	0	(0	0)	1	1	0	0	0	0	0	0	0	0	0	.00	0	.250	.250	.250
1996 Kansas City	AL	50	165	46	10	0	4	(1	3)	68	23	24	18	0	21	4	0	3	1	2	.33	7	.279	.358	.412
1997 Kansas City	AL	84	240	58	8	0	7	(5	2)	87	30	31	17	0	33	6	1	2	3	2	.60	8	.242	.306	.363
1998 Kansas City	AL	92	282	73	18	0	8	(6	2)	115	32	35	24	1	38	2	2	1	2	3	.40	7	.259	.320	.408
1999 Kansas City	AL	150	575	185	44	2	22	(10	12)	299	101	102	54	0	48	10	0	4	6	1	.86	21	.322	.387	.520
5 ML YEARS		380	1266	363	80	2	41	(22	19)	570	187	192	113	1	140	22	3	10	12	8	.60	43	.287	.353	.450

Greg Swindell

Pitches: Left **Bats:** Right **Pos:** RP-63 **Ht:** 6'3" **Wt:** 230 **Born:** 1/2/65 **Age:** 35

Year Team	Lg	G	GS	CG	GF	IP	BFP	H	R	ER	HR	SH	SF	HB	TBB	IBB	SO	WP	Bk	W	L	Pct.	ShO	Sv-Op	Hld	ERA
				HOW MUCH HE PITCHED							WHAT HE GAVE UP											THE RESULTS				
1986 Cleveland	AL	9	9	1	0	61.2	255	57	35	29	9	3	1	1	15	0	46	3	2	5	2	.714	0	0-0	0	4.23
1987 Cleveland	AL	16	15	4	0	102.1	441	112	62	58	18	4	3	1	37	1	97	0	1	3	8	.273	1	0-0	0	5.10
1988 Cleveland	AL	33	33	12	0	242	988	234	97	86	18	9	5	1	45	3	180	5	0	18	14	.563	4	0-0	0	3.20
1989 Cleveland	AL	28	28	5	0	184.1	749	170	71	69	16	4	4	0	51	1	129	3	1	13	6	.684	2	0-0	0	3.37
1990 Cleveland	AL	34	34	3	0	214.2	912	245	110	105	27	8	6	1	47	2	135	3	2	12	9	.571	0	0-0	0	4.40
1991 Cleveland	AL	33	33	7	0	238	971	241	112	92	21	13	8	3	31	1	169	3	1	9	16	.360	0	0-0	0	3.48
1992 Cincinnati	NL	31	30	5	0	213.2	867	210	72	64	14	9	7	2	41	4	138	3	2	12	8	.600	3	0-0	0	2.70
1993 Houston	NL	31	30	1	0	190.1	818	215	98	88	24	13	3	1	40	3	124	2	2	12	13	.480	1	0-0	0	4.16
1994 Houston	NL	24	24	1	0	148.1	623	175	80	72	20	9	7	1	26	2	74	1	1	8	9	.471	0	0-0	0	4.37
1995 Houston	NL	33	26	1	3	153	659	180	86	76	21	4	8	2	39	2	96	3	0	10	9	.526	1	0-2	0	4.47
1996 Hou-Cle		21	6	0	4	51.2	237	66	46	41	13	1	2	1	19	0	36	0	0	1	4	.200	0	0-2	1	7.14
1997 Minnesota	AL	65	1	0	12	115.2	460	102	46	46	12	2	3	2	25	3	75	0	0	7	4	.636	0	1-7	12	3.58
1998 Min-Bos	AL	81	0	0	15	90.1	385	92	40	36	13	4	2	3	31	3	63	3	0	5	6	.455	0	2-5	24	3.59
1999 Arizona	NL	63	0	0	15	64.2	261	54	19	18	8	4	0	1	21	1	51	0	0	4	0	1.000	0	1-2	19	2.51
1996 Houston	NL	8	4	0	3	23	116	35	25	20	5	0	1	1	11	0	15	0	0	0	3	.000	0	0-2	0	7.83
Cleveland	AL	13	2	0	1	28.2	121	31	21	21	8	1	1	0	8	0	21	0	0	1	1	.500	0	0-0	1	6.59
1998 Minnesota	AL	52	0	0	12	66.1	281	67	27	27	10	3	2	3	18	2	45	0	0	3	3	.500	0	2-4	18	3.66
Boston	AL	29	0	0	3	24	104	25	13	9	3	1	0	0	13	1	18	0	0	2	3	.400	0	0-1	6	3.38
14 ML YEARS		502	269	40	49	2070.2	8626	2153	974	880	234	87	59	20	468	26	1413	29	12	119	108	.524	12	4-18	57	3.82

Jeff Tam

Pitches: Right **Bats:** Right **Pos:** RP-10 **Ht:** 6'1" **Wt:** 202 **Born:** 8/19/70 **Age:** 29

Year Team	Lg	G	GS	CG	GF	IP	BFP	H	R	ER	HR	SH	SF	HB	TBB	IBB	SO	WP	Bk	W	L	Pct.	ShO	Sv-Op	Hld	ERA
				HOW MUCH HE PITCHED							WHAT HE GAVE UP											THE RESULTS				
1993 Pittsfield	A-	21	1	0	13	40.1	180	50	21	15	0	1	1	1	7	0	31	1	3	3	3	.500	0	0--	—	3.35
1994 Capital Cty	A	26	0	0	26	28	115	23	14	4	0	1	0	2	6	0	22	0	2	1	1	.500	0	18--	—	1.29
St. Lucie	A+	24	0	0	22	26.2	99	13	0	0	0	0	0	3	6	1	15	1	2	0	0	.000	0	16--	—	0.00
Binghamton	AA	4	0	0	1	6.2	35	9	6	6	0	1	0	1	5	0	7	0	0	0	0	.000	0	0--	—	8.10
1995 Mets	R	2	1	0	0	3	13	2	1	1	0	1	0	1	1	0	2	1	0	0	0	.000	0	0--	—	3.00
Binghamton	AA	14	0	0	7	18	83	20	11	9	1	2	1	4	4	2	9	3	0	0	2	.000	0	3--	—	4.50
1996 Binghamton	AA	49	0	0	18	62.2	241	51	19	17	6	2	1	2	16	3	48	2	4	6	2	.750	0	2--	—	2.44
1997 Norfolk	AAA	40	11	0	15	111.2	480	137	72	58	9	6	4	7	14	4	67	5	0	7	5	.583	0	6--	—	4.67
1998 Norfolk	AAA	45	0	0	24	64	239	42	14	13	3	3	2	3	6	0	54	0	0	3	3	.500	0	11--	—	1.83
1999 St. Lucie	A+	2	0	0	0	2.2	13	4	1	1	0	0	0	0	0	0	3	0	0	0	0	.000	0	0--	—	3.38
Norfolk	AAA	16	0	0	9	20.1	87	24	7	7	1	0	0	1	3	1	10	0	1	0	0	.000	0	3--	—	3.10
Buffalo	AAA	16	0	0	3	26	106	23	9	6	2	1	0	0	8	1	13	0	0	2	2	.500	0	2--	—	2.08
1998 New York	NL	15	0	0	5	14.1	60	13	10	10	2	0	0	2	4	1	6	0	0	1	1	.500	0	0-1	1	6.28
1999 Cle-NYM		10	0	0	3	11.2	47	8	7	7	3	1	0	0	4	1	8	0	0	0	0	.000	0	0-0	0	5.40
1999 Cleveland	AL	1	0	0	0	0.1	4	2	3	3	0	0	0	0	1	1	0	0	0	0	0	.000	0	0-0	0	81.00
New York	NL	9	0	0	3	11.1	43	6	4	4	3	1	0	0	3	0	8	0	0	0	0	.000	0	0-0	0	3.18
2 ML YEARS		25	0	0	8	26	107	21	17	17	5	1	0	2	8	2	16	0	0	1	1	.500	0	0-1	1	5.88

227

Kevin Tapani

Pitches: Right Bats: Right Pos: SP-23   Ht: 6'1" Wt: 195 Born: 2/18/64 Age: 36

		HOW MUCH HE PITCHED						WHAT HE GAVE UP										THE RESULTS					
Year Team	Lg	G	GS	CG	GF	IP	BFP	H	R	ER	HR	SH	SF	HB	TBB	IBB	SO	WP	Bk	W	L	Pct.	ShO	Sv-Op	Hld	ERA
1989 NYM-Min		8	5	0	1	40	169	39	18	17	3	1	2	0	12	1	23	0	1	2	2	.500	0	0-0	0	3.83
1990 Minnesota	AL	28	28	1	0	159.1	659	164	75	72	12	3	4	2	29	2	101	1	0	12	8	.600	1	0-0	0	4.07
1991 Minnesota	AL	34	34	4	0	244	974	225	84	81	23	9	6	2	40	0	135	3	3	16	9	.640	1	0-0	0	2.99
1992 Minnesota	AL	34	34	4	0	220	911	226	103	97	17	8	11	5	48	2	138	4	0	16	11	.593	1	0-0	0	3.97
1993 Minnesota	AL	36	35	3	0	225.2	964	243	123	111	21	3	5	6	57	1	150	4	0	12	15	.444	1	0-0	0	4.43
1994 Minnesota	AL	24	24	4	0	156	672	181	86	80	13	2	5	4	39	0	91	1	0	11	7	.611	1	0-0	0	4.62
1995 Min-LA		33	31	3	0	190.2	834	227	116	105	29	6	5	5	48	4	131	4	0	10	13	.435	0	0-0	0	4.96
1996 Chicago	AL	34	34	1	0	225.1	971	236	123	115	34	6	6	3	76	5	150	13	0	13	10	.565	0	0-0	0	4.59
1997 Chicago	NL	13	13	1	0	85	352	77	33	32	7	7	2	2	23	2	55	0	2	9	3	.750	1	0-0	0	3.39
1998 Chicago	NL	35	34	2	0	219	945	244	120	118	30	11	9	5	62	4	136	7	0	19	9	.679	2	0-0	0	4.85
1999 Chicago	NL	23	23	1	0	136	591	151	81	73	12	8	7	4	33	2	73	3	0	6	12	.333	0	0-0	0	4.83
1989 New York	NL	3	0	0	1	7.1	31	5	3	3	1	0	1	0	4	0	2	0	1	0	0	.000	0	0-0	0	3.68
Minnesota	AL	5	5	0	0	32.2	138	34	15	14	2	1	1	0	8	1	21	0	0	2	2	.500	0	0-0	0	3.86
1995 Minnesota	AL	20	20	3	0	133.2	579	155	79	73	21	3	3	4	34	2	88	3	0	6	11	.353	1	0-0	0	4.92
Los Angeles	NL	13	11	0	0	57	255	72	37	32	8	3	2	1	14	2	43	1	0	4	2	.667	0	0-0	0	5.05
11 ML YEARS		302	295	24	1	1901	8042	2013	962	901	201	64	62	38	467	23	1183	40	6	126	99	.560	9	0-0	0	4.27

Tony Tarasco

Bats: L Throws: R Pos: LF-9; RF-5; PH/PR-3; DH-1   Ht: 6'0" Wt: 205 Born: 12/9/70 Age: 29

		BATTING																BASERUNNING				PERCENTAGES		
Year Team	Lg	G	AB	H	2B	3B	HR	(Hm	Rd)	TB	R	RBI	TBB	IBB	SO	HBP	SH	SF	SB	CS	SB%	GDP	Avg	OBP	SLG
1999 Columbus *	AAA	95	346	102	23	0	19	—	—	182	72	61	49	6	39	2	0	3	9	5	.64	10	.295	.383	.526
1993 Atlanta	NL	24	35	8	2	0	0	(0	0)	10	6	2	0	0	5	1	0	1	0	1	.00	1	.229	.243	.286
1994 Atlanta	NL	87	132	36	6	0	5	(2	3)	57	16	19	9	1	17	0	0	3	5	0	1.00	5	.273	.313	.432
1995 Montreal	NL	126	438	109	18	4	14	(7	7)	177	64	40	51	12	78	2	3	1	24	3	.89	2	.249	.329	.404
1996 Baltimore	AL	31	84	20	3	0	1	(1	0)	26	14	9	7	0	15	0	1	0	5	3	.63	1	.238	.297	.310
1997 Baltimore	AL	100	166	34	8	1	7	(4	3)	65	26	26	25	1	33	1	1	0	2	2	.50	3	.205	.313	.392
1998 Cincinnati	NL	15	24	5	2	0	1	(1	0)	10	5	4	3	0	5	0	1	0	0	0	.00	1	.208	.296	.417
1999 New York	AL	14	31	5	2	0	0	(0	0)	7	5	3	3	0	5	0	0	1	1	0	1.00	1	.161	.229	.226
7 ML YEARS		397	910	217	41	5	28	(15	13)	352	136	103	98	14	158	4	6	6	37	9	.80	13	.238	.313	.387

Fernando Tatis

Bats: Right Throws: Right Pos: 3B-147; PH/PR-2   Ht: 5'10" Wt: 170 Born: 1/1/75 Age: 25

		BATTING																BASERUNNING				PERCENTAGES		
Year Team	Lg	G	AB	H	2B	3B	HR	(Hm	Rd)	TB	R	RBI	TBB	IBB	SO	HBP	SH	SF	SB	CS	SB%	GDP	Avg	OBP	SLG
1997 Texas	AL	60	223	57	9	0	8	(6	2)	90	29	29	14	0	42	0	2	2	3	0	1.00	6	.256	.297	.404
1998 Tex-StL		150	532	147	33	4	11	(6	5)	221	69	58	36	3	123	6	4	1	13	5	.72	16	.276	.329	.415
1999 St. Louis	NL	149	537	160	31	2	34	(16	18)	297	104	107	82	4	128	16	0	4	21	9	.70	11	.298	.404	.553
1998 St. Louis	AL	95	330	89	17	2	3	(1	2)	119	41	32	12	2	66	4	4	0	6	2	.75	10	.270	.303	.361
St. Louis	NL	55	202	58	16	2	8	(5	3)	102	28	26	24	1	57	2	0	1	7	3	.70	6	.287	.367	.505
3 ML YEARS		359	1292	364	73	6	53	(28	25)	608	202	194	132	7	293	22	6	7	37	14	.73	33	.282	.357	.471

Eddie Taubensee

Bats: Left Throws: Right Pos: C-124; PH/PR-7   Ht: 6'3" Wt: 230 Born: 10/31/68 Age: 31

		BATTING																BASERUNNING				PERCENTAGES		
Year Team	Lg	G	AB	H	2B	3B	HR	(Hm	Rd)	TB	R	RBI	TBB	IBB	SO	HBP	SH	SF	SB	CS	SB%	GDP	Avg	OBP	SLG
1991 Cleveland	AL	26	66	16	2	1	0	(0	0)	20	5	8	5	1	16	0	0	2	0	0	.00	1	.242	.288	.303
1992 Houston	NL	104	297	66	15	0	5	(2	3)	96	23	28	31	3	78	2	0	1	2	1	.67	4	.222	.299	.323
1993 Houston	NL	94	288	72	11	1	9	(4	5)	112	26	42	21	5	44	0	1	2	1	0	1.00	8	.250	.299	.389
1994 Hou-Cin	NL	66	187	53	8	2	8	(2	6)	89	29	21	15	2	31	0	1	2	2	0	1.00	3	.283	.333	.476
1995 Cincinnati	NL	80	218	62	14	2	9	(4	5)	107	32	44	22	2	52	2	1	1	2	2	.50	2	.284	.354	.491
1996 Cincinnati	NL	108	327	95	20	0	12	(6	6)	151	46	48	26	5	64	0	1	5	3	4	.43	4	.291	.338	.462
1997 Cincinnati	NL	108	254	68	18	0	10	(7	3)	116	26	34	22	2	66	1	1	5	0	1	.00	2	.268	.323	.457
1998 Cincinnati	NL	130	431	120	27	0	11	(8	3)	180	61	72	52	6	93	0	2	6	1	0	1.00	4	.278	.352	.418
1999 Cincinnati	NL	126	424	132	22	2	21	(8	13)	221	58	87	30	1	67	1	1	5	0	2	.00	12	.311	.354	.521
1994 Houston	NL	5	10	1	0	0	0	(0	0)	1	0	0	0	0	3	0	0	0	0	0	.00	1	.100	.100	.100
Cincinnati	NL	61	177	52	8	2	8	(2	6)	88	29	21	15	2	28	0	1	2	2	0	1.00	2	.294	.345	.497
9 ML YEARS		842	2492	684	137	8	85	(41	44)	1092	306	384	224	27	511	6	8	29	11	10	.52	40	.274	.332	.438

Julian Tavarez

Pitches: Right Bats: Left Pos: RP-47   Ht: 6'2" Wt: 190 Born: 5/22/73 Age: 27

		HOW MUCH HE PITCHED						WHAT HE GAVE UP										THE RESULTS					
Year Team	Lg	G	GS	CG	GF	IP	BFP	H	R	ER	HR	SH	SF	HB	TBB	IBB	SO	WP	Bk	W	L	Pct.	ShO	Sv-Op	Hld	ERA
1999 San Jose *	A+	1	1	0	0	4	12	1	0	0	0	0	0	0	1	0	3	0	0	0	0	.000	0	0- --	—	0.00
Fresno *	AAA	4	1	0	1	8	30	3	2	2	1	0	0	1	3	0	9	0	0	0	0	.000	0	0- --	—	2.25
1993 Cleveland	AL	8	7	0	0	37	172	53	29	27	7	0	1	2	13	2	19	3	1	2	2	.500	0	0-0	0	6.57
1994 Cleveland	AL	1	1	0	0	1.2	14	6	8	4	1	0	1	0	1	0	0	0	0	0	0	1.000	0	0-0	0	21.60
1995 Cleveland	AL	57	0	0	15	85	350	76	36	23	7	0	2	3	21	0	68	3	2	10	2	.833	0	0-4	19	2.44
1996 Cleveland	AL	51	4	0	13	80.2	353	101	49	48	9	5	4	1	22	5	46	1	0	4	7	.364	0	0-0	13	5.36
1997 San Francisco	NL	89	0	0	13	88.1	378	91	43	38	6	3	8	1	34	5	38	4	0	6	4	.600	0	0-3	26	3.87

228

Year Team	Lg	G	GS	CG	GF	IP	BFP	H	R	ER	HR	SH	SF	HB	TBB	IBB	SO	WP	Bk	W	L	Pct.	ShO	Sv-Op	Hld	ERA
1998 San Francisco	NL	60	0	0	12	85.1	374	96	41	36	5	5	3	8	36	11	52	1	1	5	3	.625	0	1-6	10	3.80
1999 San Francisco	NL	47	0	0	12	54.2	258	65	38	36	7	3	2	8	25	3	33	4	1	2	0	1.000	0	0-2	5	5.93
7 ML YEARS		313	12	0	65	432.2	1899	488	244	212	42	16	21	26	152	27	256	16	5	29	19	.604	0	1-15	73	4.41

Billy Taylor

Pitches: Right **Bats:** Right **Pos:** RP-61 **Ht:** 6'8" **Wt:** 235 **Born:** 10/16/61 **Age:** 38

Year Team	Lg	G	GS	CG	GF	IP	BFP	H	R	ER	HR	SH	SF	HB	TBB	IBB	SO	WP	Bk	W	L	Pct.	ShO	Sv-Op	Hld	ERA
1994 Oakland	AL	41	0	0	11	46.1	195	38	24	18	4	1	1	2	18	5	48	0	0	1	3	.250	0	1-3	2	3.50
1996 Oakland	AL	55	0	0	30	60.1	261	52	30	29	5	4	3	4	25	4	67	1	0	6	3	.667	0	17-19	4	4.33
1997 Oakland	AL	72	0	0	45	73	320	70	32	31	3	1	2	5	36	9	66	0	0	3	4	.429	0	23-30	7	3.82
1998 Oakland	AL	70	0	0	58	73	311	71	37	29	7	3	5	3	22	4	58	0	1	4	9	.308	0	33-37	0	3.58
1999 Oak-NYM		61	0	0	43	56.1	257	68	35	31	5	5	2	2	23	8	52	1	1	1	6	.143	0	26-34	1	4.95
1999 Oakland	AL	43	0	0	38	43	189	48	23	19	3	4	2	2	14	3	38	1	1	1	5	.167	0	26-33	0	3.98
New York	NL	18	0	0	5	13.1	68	20	12	12	2	1	0	0	9	5	14	0	0	0	1	.000	0	0-1	1	8.10
5 ML YEARS		299	0	0	187	309	1344	299	158	138	24	14	13	16	124	30	291	2	2	15	25	.375	0	100-123	14	4.02

Miguel Tejada

Bats: Right **Throws:** Right **Pos:** SS-159; PH/PR-2 **Ht:** 5'9" **Wt:** 188 **Born:** 5/25/76 **Age:** 24

Year Team	Lg	G	AB	H	2B	3B	HR	(Hm	Rd)	TB	R	RBI	TBB	IBB	SO	HBP	SH	SF	SB	CS	SB%	GDP	Avg	OBP	SLG
1997 Oakland	AL	26	99	20	3	2	2	(1	1)	33	10	10	2	0	22	3	0	0	2	0	1.00	1	.202	.240	.333
1998 Oakland	AL	105	365	85	20	1	11	(5	6)	140	53	45	28	0	86	7	4	3	5	6	.45	8	.233	.298	.384
1999 Oakland	AL	159	593	149	33	4	21	(12	9)	253	93	84	57	3	94	10	9	5	8	7	.53	11	.251	.325	.427
3 ML YEARS		290	1057	254	56	7	34	(18	16)	426	156	139	87	3	202	20	13	8	15	13	.54	22	.240	.308	.403

Michael Tejera

Pitches: Left **Bats:** Left **Pos:** RP-2; SP-1 **Ht:** 5'9" **Wt:** 175 **Born:** 10/18/76 **Age:** 23

Year Team	Lg	G	GS	CG	GF	IP	BFP	H	R	ER	HR	SH	SF	HB	TBB	IBB	SO	WP	Bk	W	L	Pct.	ShO	Sv-Op	Hld	ERA
1995 Marlins	R	11	3	0	4	34	142	28	13	10	2	4	1	2	16	1	28	3	0	3	1	.750	0	2--	—	2.65
1996 Marlins	R	2	0	0	0	5	21	6	2	2	0	0	0	0	0	0	2	0	0	1	0	1.000	0	0--	—	3.60
1997 Utica	A-	12	12	0	0	69.1	279	65	36	29	8	3	1	2	11	0	67	6	0	3	3	.500	0	0--	—	3.76
1998 Kane County	A	10	10	0	0	55.1	218	44	20	17	3	3	1	2	13	0	47	2	0	6	1	.857	0	0--	—	2.77
Portland	AA	18	18	2	0	107.1	466	113	55	49	15	3	1	4	36	2	97	4	0	9	5	.643	2	0--	—	4.11
1999 Calgary	AAA	2	2	0	0	9	49	19	14	12	2	1	1	1	4	0	5	1	0	0	2	.000	0	0--	—	12.00
Portland	AA	25	25	0	0	154.2	640	137	55	45	13	9	3	7	45	1	152	6	1	13	4	.765	1	0--	—	2.62
1999 Florida	NL	3	1	0	1	6.1	31	10	8	8	1	0	0	0	5	0	7	0	0	0	0	.000	0	0-0	0	11.37

Amaury Telemaco

Pitches: Right **Bats:** Right **Pos:** RP-49 **Ht:** 6'3" **Wt:** 225 **Born:** 1/19/74 **Age:** 26

Year Team	Lg	G	GS	CG	GF	IP	BFP	H	R	ER	HR	SH	SF	HB	TBB	IBB	SO	WP	Bk	W	L	Pct.	ShO	Sv-Op	Hld	ERA
1999 Tucson *	AAA	13	12	0	0	17.2	79	21	11	10	1	0	2	1	6	0	17	0	0	0	3	.000	0	0--	—	5.09
1996 Chicago	NL	25	17	0	2	97.1	427	108	67	59	20	5	3	3	31	2	64	3	0	5	7	.417	0	0-0	0	5.46
1997 Chicago	NL	10	5	0	2	38	169	47	26	26	4	2	1	0	11	0	29	1	0	0	3	.000	0	0-0	0	6.16
1998 ChC-Ari	NL	41	18	0	5	148.2	637	150	75	65	18	8	6	4	46	2	78	7	0	7	10	.412	0	0-0	1	3.93
1999 Ari-Phi	NL	49	0	0	10	53	234	52	34	34	10	4	1	2	26	4	43	5	0	4	0	1.000	0	0-1	3	5.77
1998 Chicago	NL	14	0	0	4	27.2	118	23	12	12	5	0	0	0	13	0	18	3	0	1	1	.500	0	0-0	1	3.90
1999 Arizona	NL	27	18	0	1	121	519	127	63	53	13	8	6	4	33	2	60	4	0	6	9	.400	0	0-0	0	3.94
Arizona	NL	5	0	0	3	6	28	7	5	5	2	1	0	0	6	1	2	0	0	1	0	1.000	0	0-0	0	7.50
Philadelphia	NL	44	0	0	7	47	206	45	29	29	8	3	1	2	20	3	41	5	0	3	0	1.000	0	0-1	3	5.55
4 ML YEARS		125	40	0	19	337	1467	357	202	184	52	19	11	9	114	8	214	16	0	16	20	.444	0	0-1	4	4.91

Anthony Telford

Pitches: Right **Bats:** Right **Pos:** RP-79 **Ht:** 6'0" **Wt:** 195 **Born:** 3/6/66 **Age:** 34

Year Team	Lg	G	GS	CG	GF	IP	BFP	H	R	ER	HR	SH	SF	HB	TBB	IBB	SO	WP	Bk	W	L	Pct.	ShO	Sv-Op	Hld	ERA
1990 Baltimore	AL	8	8	0	0	36.1	168	43	22	20	4	0	2	1	19	0	20	1	0	3	3	.500	0	0-0	0	4.95
1991 Baltimore	AL	9	1	0	4	26.2	109	27	12	12	3	0	1	0	6	1	24	1	0	0	0	.000	0	0-0	0	4.05
1993 Baltimore	AL	3	0	0	2	7.1	34	11	8	8	3	0	0	1	1	0	6	1	0	0	0	.000	0	0-0	0	9.82
1997 Montreal	NL	65	0	0	17	89	369	77	34	32	11	4	1	5	33	4	61	6	0	4	6	.400	0	1-5	11	3.24
1998 Montreal	NL	77	0	0	24	91	398	85	45	39	9	10	4	4	36	1	59	8	1	3	6	.333	0	1-5	8	3.86
1999 Montreal	NL	79	0	0	21	96	429	112	52	42	3	3	5	3	38	3	69	3	1	5	4	.556	0	2-9	18	3.94
6 ML YEARS		241	9	0	68	346.1	1507	355	173	153	33	17	13	14	133	9	239	20	2	15	19	.441	0	4-19	37	3.98

Jay Tessmer

Pitches: Right **Bats:** Right **Pos:** RP-6   **Ht:** 6'3" **Wt:** 190 **Born:** 12/26/71 **Age:** 28

Year Team	Lg	G	GS	CG	GF	IP	BFP	H	R	ER	HR	SH	SF	HB	TBB	IBB	SO	WP	Bk	W	L	Pct.	ShO	Sv-Op	Hld	ERA
1995 Oneonta	A-	34	0	0	33	38	156	27	8	4	0	0	0	3	12	2	52	3	2	2	0	1.000	0	20--	—	0.95
1996 Tampa	A+	68	0	0	63	97.1	381	68	18	16	2	6	0	6	19	3	104	1	0	12	4	.750	0	35--	—	1.48
1997 Norwich	AA	55	0	0	49	62.2	289	78	41	37	7	3	2	2	24	2	51	4	0	3	6	.333	0	17--	—	5.31
1998 Norwich	AA	45	0	0	44	49.2	208	50	8	6	0	3	0	0	13	5	57	0	1	3	4	.429	0	29--	—	1.09
Columbus	AAA	12	0	0	11	18.1	64	8	2	1	1	0	1	1	1	0	14	0	0	1	1	.500	0	5--	—	0.49
1999 Columbus	AAA	51	0	0	48	56.2	232	52	22	21	4	5	0	1	12	1	42	3	0	3	3	.500	0	28--	—	3.34
1998 New York	AL	7	0	0	3	8.2	33	4	3	3	1	0	1	0	4	0	6	1	0	1	0	1.000	0	0-0	1	3.12
1999 New York	AL	6	0	0	4	6.2	41	16	11	11	1	0	0	1	4	2	3	0	0	0	0	.000	0	0-0	0	14.85
2 ML YEARS		13	0	0	7	15.1	74	20	14	14	2	0	1	1	8	2	9	1	0	1	0	1.000	0	0-0	1	8.22

Frank Thomas

Bats: Right **Throws:** Right **Pos:** DH-83; 1B-49; PH/PR-3   **Ht:** 6'5" **Wt:** 270 **Born:** 5/27/68 **Age:** 32

Year Team	Lg	G	AB	H	2B	3B	HR	(Hm	Rd)	TB	R	RBI	TBB	IBB	SO	HBP	SH	SF	SB	CS	SB%	GDP	Avg	OBP	SLG
1990 Chicago	AL	60	191	63	11	3	7	(2	5)	101	39	31	44	0	54	2	0	3	0	1	.00	5	.330	.454	.529
1991 Chicago	AL	158	559	178	31	2	32	(24	8)	309	104	109	138	13	112	1	0	2	1	2	.33	20	.318	.453	.553
1992 Chicago	AL	160	573	185	46	2	24	(10	14)	307	108	115	122	6	88	5	0	11	6	3	.67	19	.323	.439	.536
1993 Chicago	AL	153	549	174	36	0	41	(26	15)	333	106	128	112	23	54	2	0	13	4	2	.67	10	.317	.426	.607
1994 Chicago	AL	113	399	141	34	1	38	(22	16)	291	106	101	109	12	61	2	0	7	2	3	.40	15	.353	.487	.729
1995 Chicago	AL	145	493	152	27	0	40	(15	25)	299	102	111	136	29	74	6	0	12	3	2	.60	14	.308	.454	.606
1996 Chicago	AL	141	527	184	26	0	40	(16	24)	330	110	134	109	26	70	5	0	8	1	1	.50	25	.349	.459	.626
1997 Chicago	AL	146	530	184	35	0	35	(16	19)	324	110	125	109	9	69	3	0	7	1	1	.50	15	.347	.456	.611
1998 Chicago	AL	160	585	155	35	2	29	(15	14)	281	109	109	110	2	93	6	0	11	7	0	1.00	14	.265	.381	.480
1999 Chicago	AL	135	486	148	36	0	15	(9	6)	229	74	77	87	13	66	9	0	8	3	3	.50	15	.305	.414	.471
10 ML YEARS		1371	4892	1564	317	10	301	(155	146)	2804	968	1040	1076	133	741	41	0	82	28	18	.61	152	.320	.440	.573

Jim Thome

Bats: Left **Throws:** Right **Pos:** 1B-111; DH-34; PH/PR-3   **Ht:** 6'4" **Wt:** 225 **Born:** 8/27/70 **Age:** 29

Year Team	Lg	G	AB	H	2B	3B	HR	(Hm	Rd)	TB	R	RBI	TBB	IBB	SO	HBP	SH	SF	SB	CS	SB%	GDP	Avg	OBP	SLG
1991 Cleveland	AL	27	98	25	4	2	1	(0	1)	36	7	9	5	1	16	1	0	0	1	1	.50	4	.255	.298	.367
1992 Cleveland	AL	40	117	24	3	1	2	(1	1)	35	8	12	10	2	34	2	0	2	2	0	1.00	3	.205	.275	.299
1993 Cleveland	AL	47	154	41	11	0	7	(5	2)	73	28	22	29	1	36	4	0	5	2	1	.67	3	.266	.385	.474
1994 Cleveland	AL	98	321	86	20	1	20	(10	10)	168	58	52	46	5	84	0	1	1	3	3	.50	11	.268	.359	.523
1995 Cleveland	AL	137	452	142	29	3	25	(13	12)	252	92	73	97	3	113	5	0	3	4	3	.57	8	.314	.438	.558
1996 Cleveland	AL	151	505	157	28	5	38	(18	20)	309	122	116	123	8	141	6	0	2	2	2	.50	13	.311	.450	.612
1997 Cleveland	AL	147	496	142	25	0	40	(17	23)	287	104	102	120	9	146	3	0	8	1	1	.50	9	.286	.423	.579
1998 Cleveland	AL	123	440	129	34	2	30	(18	12)	257	89	85	89	8	141	4	0	4	1	0	1.00	7	.293	.413	.584
1999 Cleveland	AL	146	494	137	27	2	33	(19	14)	267	101	108	127	13	171	4	0	4	0	0	.00	6	.277	.426	.540
9 ML YEARS		916	3077	883	181	16	196	(101	95)	1684	609	579	646	50	882	29	1	29	16	11	.59	64	.287	.412	.547

Justin Thompson

Pitches: Left **Bats:** Left **Pos:** SP-24   **Ht:** 6'4" **Wt:** 215 **Born:** 3/8/73 **Age:** 27

Year Team	Lg	G	GS	CG	GF	IP	BFP	H	R	ER	HR	SH	SF	HB	TBB	IBB	SO	WP	Bk	W	L	Pct.	ShO	Sv-Op	Hld	ERA
1996 Detroit	AL	11	11	0	0	59	267	62	35	30	7	0	2	2	31	2	44	1	0	1	6	.143	0	0-0	0	4.58
1997 Detroit	AL	32	32	4	0	223.1	891	188	82	75	20	5	10	2	66	1	151	4	0	15	11	.577	0	0-0	0	3.02
1998 Detroit	AL	34	34	5	0	222	946	227	114	100	20	10	6	2	79	4	149	4	0	11	15	.423	0	0-0	0	4.05
1999 Detroit	AL	24	24	0	0	142.2	626	152	85	81	24	1	7	4	59	1	83	2	0	9	11	.450	0	0-0	0	5.11
4 ML YEARS		101	101	9	0	647	2730	629	316	286	71	16	25	10	235	8	427	11	0	36	43	.456	0	0-0	0	3.98

Mark Thompson

Pitches: Right **Bats:** Right **Pos:** SP-5   **Ht:** 6'2" **Wt:** 213 **Born:** 4/7/71 **Age:** 29

Year Team	Lg	G	GS	CG	GF	IP	BFP	H	R	ER	HR	SH	SF	HB	TBB	IBB	SO	WP	Bk	W	L	Pct.	ShO	Sv-Op	Hld	ERA
1999 Indianapolis *	AAA	11	10	0	0	54.1	237	50	31	31	5	1	4	6	29	1	28	0	0	2	6	.250	0	0--	—	5.13
Memphis *	AAA	9	8	0	0	52	225	50	22	17	3	4	3	0	20	0	27	1	0	4	2	.667	0	0--	—	2.94
1994 Colorado	NL	2	2	0	0	9	49	16	9	9	2	0	0	1	8	0	5	0	0	1	1	.500	0	0-0	0	9.00
1995 Colorado	NL	21	5	0	0	51	240	73	42	37	7	4	4	1	22	2	30	2	0	2	3	.400	0	0-0	2	6.53
1996 Colorado	NL	34	28	3	2	169.2	763	189	109	100	25	10	3	13	74	1	99	1	1	9	11	.450	1	0-1	0	5.30
1997 Colorado	NL	6	6	0	0	29.2	146	40	27	26	8	3	2	4	13	0	9	1	0	3	3	.500	0	0-0	0	7.89
1998 Colorado	NL	6	6	0	0	23.1	116	36	22	20	8	2	2	5	12	0	14	1	0	1	2	.333	0	0-0	0	7.71
1999 St. Louis	NL	5	5	0	0	29.1	130	26	12	12	1	3	0	2	17	1	22	1	0	1	3	.250	0	0-0	0	2.76
6 ML YEARS		74	52	3	5	312	1444	380	221	201	51	22	11	26	146	4	179	5	2	17	23	.425	1	0-1	2	5.80

Ryan Thompson

Bats: R **Throws:** R **Pos:** PH/PR-6; CF-5; RF-3; LF-2   **Ht:** 6'3" **Wt:** 215 **Born:** 11/4/67 **Age:** 32

Year Team	Lg	G	AB	H	2B	3B	HR	(Hm	Rd)	TB	R	RBI	TBB	IBB	SO	HBP	SH	SF	SB	CS	SB%	GDP	Avg	OBP	SLG
1999 New Orleans *	AAA	112	404	125	23	2	16	—	—	200	60	58	37	0	78	2	0	2	4	9	.31	17	.309	.369	.495
1992 New York	NL	30	108	24	7	1	3	(3	0)	42	15	10	8	0	24	0	0	1	2	2	.50	2	.222	.274	.389
1993 New York	NL	80	288	72	19	2	11	(5	6)	128	34	26	19	4	81	3	5	1	2	7	.22	5	.250	.302	.444
1994 New York	NL	98	334	75	14	1	18	(5	13)	145	39	59	28	7	94	10	3	4	1	1	.50	8	.225	.301	.434
1995 New York	NL	75	267	67	13	0	7	(3	4)	101	39	31	19	1	77	4	0	4	3	1	.75	12	.251	.306	.378
1996 Cleveland	AL	8	22	7	0	0	1	(1	0)	10	2	5	1	0	6	0	0	0	0	0	.00	0	.318	.348	.455
1999 Houston	NL	12	20	4	1	0	1	(0	1)	8	2	5	2	0	7	0	0	0	0	0	.00	1	.200	.273	.400
6 ML YEARS		303	1039	249	54	4	41	(17	24)	434	131	136	77	12	289	17	8	10	8	11	.42	28	.240	.300	.418

John Thomson

Pitches: Right **Bats:** Right **Pos:** SP-13; RP-1   **Ht:** 6'3" **Wt:** 187 **Born:** 10/1/73 **Age:** 26

Year Team	Lg	G	GS	CG	GF	IP	BFP	H	R	ER	HR	SH	SF	HB	TBB	IBB	SO	WP	Bk	W	L	Pct.	ShO	Sv-Op	Hld	ERA
1999 Salem *	A+	1	1	0	0	2	10	4	2	2	0	0	0	0	0	0	2	0	0	0	1	.000	0	0--	—	9.00
Colo Sprngs *	AAA	5	5	1	0	20	98	36	25	21	3	2	1	0	8	0	19	1	1	0	2	.000	0	0--	—	9.45
1997 Colorado	NL	27	27	2	0	166.1	721	193	94	87	15	10	3	5	51	0	106	2	0	7	9	.438	1	0-0	0	4.71
1998 Colorado	NL	26	26	2	0	161	680	174	86	86	21	8	5	2	49	0	106	4	2	8	11	.421	0	0-0	0	4.81
1999 Colorado	NL	14	13	1	1	62.2	305	85	62	56	11	4	2	1	36	1	34	2	0	1	10	.091	0	0-0	0	8.04
3 ML YEARS		67	66	5	1	390	1706	452	242	229	47	22	10	8	136	1	246	8	2	16	30	.348	1	0-0	0	5.28

Mike Thurman

Pitches: Right **Bats:** Right **Pos:** SP-27; RP-2   **Ht:** 6'5" **Wt:** 210 **Born:** 7/22/73 **Age:** 26

Year Team	Lg	G	GS	CG	GF	IP	BFP	H	R	ER	HR	SH	SF	HB	TBB	IBB	SO	WP	Bk	W	L	Pct.	ShO	Sv-Op	Hld	ERA
1997 Montreal	NL	5	2	0	1	11.2	48	8	9	7	3	0	0	1	4	0	8	0	0	1	0	1.000	0	0-0	0	5.40
1998 Montreal	NL	14	13	0	1	67	287	60	38	35	7	2	4	3	26	2	32	3	0	4	5	.444	0	0-0	0	4.70
1999 Montreal	NL	29	27	0	1	146.2	627	140	84	66	17	8	3	7	52	4	85	4	1	7	11	.389	0	0-0	0	4.05
3 ML YEARS		48	42	0	3	225.1	962	208	131	108	27	10	7	11	82	6	125	7	1	12	16	.429	0	0-0	0	4.31

Mike Timlin

Pitches: Right **Bats:** Right **Pos:** RP-62   **Ht:** 6'4" **Wt:** 210 **Born:** 3/10/66 **Age:** 34

Year Team	Lg	G	GS	CG	GF	IP	BFP	H	R	ER	HR	SH	SF	HB	TBB	IBB	SO	WP	Bk	W	L	Pct.	ShO	Sv-Op	Hld	ERA
1991 Toronto	AL	63	3	0	17	108.1	463	94	43	38	6	6	2	1	50	11	85	5	0	11	6	.647	0	3-8	9	3.16
1992 Toronto	AL	26	0	0	14	43.2	190	45	23	20	0	2	1	1	20	5	35	0	0	0	2	.000	0	1-1	1	4.12
1993 Toronto	AL	54	0	0	27	55.2	254	63	32	29	7	1	3	1	27	3	49	1	0	4	2	.667	0	1-4	9	4.69
1994 Toronto	AL	34	0	0	16	40	179	41	25	23	5	0	0	2	20	0	38	3	0	0	1	.000	0	2-4	5	5.18
1995 Toronto	AL	31	0	0	19	42	179	38	13	10	1	3	0	2	17	5	36	3	1	4	3	.571	0	5-9	4	2.14
1996 Toronto	AL	59	0	0	56	56.2	230	47	25	23	4	2	3	2	18	4	52	3	1	1	6	.143	0	31-38	2	3.65
1997 Tor-Sea	AL	64	0	0	31	72.2	297	69	30	26	8	6	1	1	20	5	45	1	1	6	4	.600	0	10-18	9	3.22
1998 Seattle	AL	70	0	0	40	79.1	321	78	26	26	5	4	2	3	16	2	60	0	0	3	3	.500	0	19-24	6	2.95
1999 Baltimore	AL	62	0	0	52	63	261	51	30	25	9	1	1	5	23	3	50	1	0	3	9	.250	0	27-36	0	3.57
1997 Toronto	AL	38	0	0	26	47	190	41	17	15	6	4	1	1	15	4	36	1	1	3	2	.600	0	9-13	2	2.87
Seattle	AL	26	0	0	5	25.2	107	28	13	11	2	2	0	0	5	1	9	0	0	3	2	.600	0	1-5	7	3.86
9 ML YEARS		463	3	0	272	561.1	2374	526	247	220	45	25	13	18	211	38	450	17	2	32	36	.471	0	99-142	45	3.53

Ozzie Timmons

Bats: R **Throws:** R **Pos:** LF-12; PH/PR-12; DH-5; RF-5; 1B-1   **Ht:** 6'2" **Wt:** 225 **Born:** 9/18/70 **Age:** 29

Year Team	Lg	G	AB	H	2B	3B	HR	(Hm	Rd)	TB	R	RBI	TBB	IBB	SO	HBP	SH	SF	SB	CS	SB%	GDP	Avg	OBP	SLG
1999 Tacoma *	AAA	82	297	81	22	0	21	—	—	166	56	66	53	1	81	2	0	3	0	2	.00	9	.273	.383	.559
1995 Chicago	NL	77	171	45	10	1	8	(5	3)	81	30	28	13	2	32	0	0	1	3	0	1.00	8	.263	.314	.474
1996 Chicago	NL	65	140	28	4	0	7	(6	1)	53	18	16	15	0	30	1	1	0	1	0	1.00	1	.200	.282	.379
1997 Cincinnati	NL	6	9	3	1	0	0	(0	0)	4	1	0	0	0	1	0	0	0	0	0	.00	0	.333	.333	.444
1999 Seattle	AL	26	44	5	2	0	1	(0	1)	10	4	3	4	0	12	0	0	0	0	1	.00	0	.114	.188	.227
4 ML YEARS		174	364	81	17	1	16	(11	5)	148	53	47	32	2	75	1	1	1	4	1	.80	9	.223	.286	.407

Jorge Toca

Bats: Right **Throws:** Right **Pos:** PH/PR-3; 1B-1   **Ht:** 6'3" **Wt:** 202 **Born:** 1/7/75 **Age:** 25

Year Team	Lg	G	AB	H	2B	3B	HR	(Hm	Rd)	TB	R	RBI	TBB	IBB	SO	HBP	SH	SF	SB	CS	SB%	GDP	Avg	OBP	SLG
1999 Binghamton	AA	75	279	86	15	1	20	—	—	163	60	67	32	3	43	5	0	4	5	5	.50	9	.308	.384	.584
Norfolk	AAA	49	176	59	12	1	5	—	—	88	25	29	6	0	23	1	0	2	0	3	.00	9	.335	.357	.500
1999 New York	NL	4	3	1	0	0	0	(0	0)	1	0	0	0	0	2	0	0	0	0	0	.00	0	.333	.333	.333

Brett Tomko

Pitches: Right Bats: Right Pos: SP-26; RP-7   Ht: 6'4" Wt: 215 Born: 4/7/73 Age: 27

		HOW MUCH HE PITCHED						WHAT HE GAVE UP												THE RESULTS						
Year Team	Lg	G	GS	CG	GF	IP	BFP	H	R	ER	HR	SH	SF	HB	TBB	IBB	SO	WP	Bk	W	L	Pct.	ShO	Sv-Op	Hld	ERA
1999 Indianapols *	AAA	2	2	0	0	12.2	54	15	7	7	1	0	0	1	1	0	9	0	0	2	0	1.000	0	0--	—	4.97
1997 Cincinnati	NL	22	19	0	1	126	519	106	50	48	14	5	9	4	47	4	95	5	0	11	7	.611	0	0-0	0	3.43
1998 Cincinnati	NL	34	34	1	0	210.2	887	198	111	104	22	12	2	7	64	3	162	9	1	13	12	.520	0	0-0	0	4.44
1999 Cincinnati	NL	33	26	1	1	172	744	175	103	94	31	9	5	4	60	10	132	8	0	5	7	.417	0	0-0	1	4.92
3 ML YEARS		89	79	2	2	508.2	2150	479	264	246	67	26	16	15	171	17	389	22	1	29	26	.527	0	0-0	1	4.35

Steve Trachsel

Pitches: Right Bats: Right Pos: SP-34   Ht: 6'4" Wt: 205 Born: 10/31/70 Age: 29

		HOW MUCH HE PITCHED						WHAT HE GAVE UP												THE RESULTS						
Year Team	Lg	G	GS	CG	GF	IP	BFP	H	R	ER	HR	SH	SF	HB	TBB	IBB	SO	WP	Bk	W	L	Pct.	ShO	Sv-Op	Hld	ERA
1993 Chicago	NL	3	3	0	0	19.2	78	16	10	10	4	1	1	0	3	0	14	1	0	0	2	.000	0	0-0	0	4.58
1994 Chicago	NL	22	22	1	0	146	612	133	57	52	19	3	3	3	54	4	108	6	0	9	7	.563	0	0-0	0	3.21
1995 Chicago	NL	30	29	2	0	160.2	722	174	104	92	25	12	5	0	76	8	117	2	1	7	13	.350	0	0-0	0	5.15
1996 Chicago	NL	31	31	3	0	205	845	181	82	69	30	3	3	8	62	3	132	5	2	13	9	.591	2	0-0	0	3.03
1997 Chicago	NL	34	34	0	0	201.1	878	225	110	101	32	8	11	5	69	6	160	4	1	8	12	.400	0	0-0	0	4.51
1998 Chicago	NL	33	33	1	0	208	894	204	107	103	27	9	7	8	84	5	149	3	2	15	8	.652	0	0-0	0	4.46
1999 Chicago	NL	34	34	4	0	205.2	894	226	133	127	32	6	14	3	64	4	149	8	3	8	18	.308	0	0-0	0	5.56
7 ML YEARS		187	186	11	0	1146.1	4923	1159	603	554	169	42	44	27	412	30	829	29	9	60	69	.465	2	0-0	0	4.35

Bubba Trammell

Bats: R Throws: R Pos: LF-61; RF-20; DH-6; PH/PR-5   Ht: 6'2" Wt: 220 Born: 11/6/71 Age: 28

		BATTING																	BASERUNNING				PERCENTAGES		
Year Team	Lg	G	AB	H	2B	3B	HR	(Hm	Rd)	TB	R	RBI	TBB	IBB	SO	HBP	SH	SF	SB	CS	SB%	GDP	Avg	OBP	SLG
1999 Durham *	AAA	47	186	50	12	0	7	—	—	83	25	31	15	1	36	0	0	4	0	0	.00	1	.269	.317	.446
1997 Detroit	AL	44	123	28	5	0	4	(2	2)	45	14	13	15	0	35	0	0	2	3	1	.75	2	.228	.307	.366
1998 Tampa Bay	AL	59	199	57	18	1	12	(6	6)	113	28	35	16	0	45	0	0	1	0	2	.00	4	.286	.338	.568
1999 Tampa Bay	AL	82	283	82	19	0	14	(6	8)	143	49	39	43	1	37	1	0	1	0	2	.00	7	.290	.384	.505
3 ML YEARS		185	605	167	42	1	30	(14	16)	301	91	87	74	1	117	1	0	4	3	5	.38	13	.276	.354	.498

Chris Tremie

Bats: Right Throws: Right Pos: C-8; PH/PR-2   Ht: 6'0" Wt: 215 Born: 10/17/69 Age: 30

		BATTING																	BASERUNNING				PERCENTAGES		
Year Team	Lg	G	AB	H	2B	3B	HR	(Hm	Rd)	TB	R	RBI	TBB	IBB	SO	HBP	SH	SF	SB	CS	SB%	GDP	Avg	OBP	SLG
1992 Utica	A-	6	16	1	0	0	0	—	—	1	1	0	0	0	5	0	0	0	0	0	.00	0	.063	.063	.063
1993 White Sox	R	2	4	0	0	0	0	—	—	0	0	0	0	0	0	0	0	0	0	0	.00	0	.000	.000	.000
Sarasota	A+	14	37	6	1	0	0	—	—	7	2	5	2	0	4	3	0	0	0	0	.00	1	.162	.262	.189
Hickory	A	49	155	29	6	1	1	—	—	40	7	17	9	0	26	4	1	0	0	0	.00	5	.187	.250	.258
1994 Birmingham	AA	92	302	68	13	0	2	—	—	87	32	29	17	0	44	6	3	2	4	1	.80	3	.225	.278	.288
1995 Nashville	AAA	67	190	38	4	0	2	—	—	48	13	16	13	0	37	2	4	0	0	0	.00	6	.200	.259	.253
1996 Nashville	AAA	70	215	47	10	1	0	—	—	59	17	26	18	0	48	2	6	3	2	0	1.00	4	.219	.282	.274
1997 Reading	AA	97	295	60	11	1	2	—	—	79	20	31	36	0	61	5	5	5	0	5	.00	7	.203	.296	.268
1998 Oklahoma	AAA	78	247	55	10	0	0	—	—	65	35	12	24	0	47	5	4	1	1	1	.50	12	.223	.303	.263
1999 Nashville	AAA	47	121	30	7	0	3	—	—	46	20	16	14	0	29	2	3	2	4	0	1.00	4	.248	.331	.380
1995 Chicago	AL	10	24	4	0	0	0	(0	0)	4	0	1	0	2	0	1	0	0	0	0	.00	0	.167	.200	.167
1998 Texas	AL	2	3	1	1	0	0	(0	0)	2	2	0	1	0	1	0	0	0	0	0	.00	0	.333	.500	.667
1999 Pittsburgh	NL	9	14	1	0	0	0	(0	0)	1	1	1	2	0	4	0	0	0	0	0	.00	0	.071	.188	.071
3 ML YEARS		21	41	6	1	0	0	(0	0)	7	3	1	4	0	7	0	1	0	0	0	.00	0	.146	.222	.171

Mike Trombley

Pitches: Right Bats: Right Pos: RP-75   Ht: 6'2" Wt: 204 Born: 4/14/67 Age: 33

		HOW MUCH HE PITCHED						WHAT HE GAVE UP												THE RESULTS						
Year Team	Lg	G	GS	CG	GF	IP	BFP	H	R	ER	HR	SH	SF	HB	TBB	IBB	SO	WP	Bk	W	L	Pct.	ShO	Sv-Op	Hld	ERA
1992 Minnesota	AL	10	7	0	0	46.1	194	43	20	17	5	2	0	1	17	0	38	0	0	3	2	.600	0	0-0	0	3.30
1993 Minnesota	AL	44	10	0	8	114.1	506	131	72	62	15	3	7	3	41	4	85	5	0	6	6	.500	0	2-5	8	4.88
1994 Minnesota	AL	24	0	0	8	48.1	219	56	36	34	10	1	2	3	18	2	32	3	0	2	0	1.000	0	0-1	1	6.33
1995 Minnesota	AL	20	18	0	0	97.2	442	107	68	61	18	3	2	3	42	1	68	4	0	4	8	.333	0	0-0	0	5.62
1996 Minnesota	AL	43	0	0	19	68.2	292	61	24	23	2	0	3	5	25	8	57	4	0	5	1	.833	0	6-9	4	3.01
1997 Minnesota	AL	67	0	0	21	82.1	349	77	43	40	7	2	3	2	31	4	74	5	0	2	3	.400	0	1-1	11	4.37
1998 Minnesota	AL	77	1	0	17	96.2	413	90	41	39	16	2	1	5	41	3	89	6	1	6	5	.545	0	1-4	23	3.63
1999 Minnesota	AL	75	0	0	56	87.1	377	93	42	42	15	2	3	2	28	2	82	6	0	2	8	.200	0	24-30	50	4.33
8 ML YEARS		360	36	0	129	641.2	2792	658	346	318	88	15	21	24	243	24	525	33	1	30	33	.476	0	34-50	50	4.46

Michael Tucker

Bats: L Throws: R Pos: RF-107; PH/PR-29; CF-13   Ht: 6'2" Wt: 185 Born: 6/25/71 Age: 29

		BATTING																	BASERUNNING				PERCENTAGES		
Year Team	Lg	G	AB	H	2B	3B	HR	(Hm	Rd)	TB	R	RBI	TBB	IBB	SO	HBP	SH	SF	SB	CS	SB%	GDP	Avg	OBP	SLG
1995 Kansas City	AL	62	177	46	10	0	4	(1	3)	68	23	17	18	2	51	1	2	0	2	3	.40	3	.260	.332	.384
1996 Kansas City	AL	108	339	88	18	4	12	(2	10)	150	55	53	40	1	69	7	3	4	10	4	.71	7	.260	.346	.442

Year Team	Lg	G	AB	H	2B	3B	HR	(Hm	Rd)	TB	R	RBI	TBB	IBB	SO	HBP	SH	SF	SB	CS	SB%	GDP	Avg	OBP	SLG
1997 Atlanta	NL	138	499	141	25	7	14	(5	9)	222	80	56	44	0	116	6	4	1	12	7	.63	7	.283	.347	.445
1998 Atlanta	NL	130	414	101	27	3	13	(10	3)	173	54	46	49	10	112	3	1	2	8	3	.73	4	.244	.327	.418
1999 Cincinnati	NL	133	296	75	8	5	11	(5	6)	126	55	44	37	3	81	3	0	4	11	4	.73	5	.253	.338	.426
5 ML YEARS		571	1725	451	88	19	54	(23	31)	739	267	216	188	16	429	20	10	11	43	21	.67	26	.261	.339	.428

Chris Turner

Bats: Right **Throws:** Right **Pos:** C-12   **Ht:** 6'1" **Wt:** 190 **Born:** 3/23/69 **Age:** 31

							BATTING												BASERUNNING				PERCENTAGES		
Year Team	Lg	G	AB	H	2B	3B	HR	(Hm	Rd)	TB	R	RBI	TBB	IBB	SO	HBP	SH	SF	SB	CS	SB%	GDP	Avg	OBP	SLG
1999 Buffalo *	AAA	69	231	63	9	0	9	—	—	99	36	33	34	0	45	1	3	2	2	2	.50	10	.273	.366	.429
1993 California	AL	25	75	21	5	0	1	(0	1)	29	9	13	9	0	16	1	0	1	1	1	.50	1	.280	.360	.387
1994 California	AL	58	149	36	7	1	1	(1	0)	48	23	12	10	0	29	1	1	2	3	0	1.00	0	.242	.290	.322
1995 California	AL	5	10	1	0	0	0	(0	0)	1	0	1	0	0	3	0	0	0	0	0	.00	0	.100	.100	.100
1996 California	AL	4	3	1	0	0	0	(0	0)	1	1	1	1	0	0	0	0	0	0	0	.00	0	.333	.400	.333
1997 Anaheim	AL	13	23	6	1	1	1	(0	1)	12	4	2	5	0	8	0	1	0	0	0	.00	0	.261	.393	.522
1998 Kansas City	AL	4	9	0	0	0	0	(0	0)	0	0	0	0	0	4	1	0	0	0	0	.00	1	.000	.100	.000
1999 Cleveland	AL	12	21	4	0	0	0	(0	0)	4	3	0	1	0	8	0	0	0	1	0	1.00	0	.190	.227	.190
7 ML YEARS		121	290	69	13	2	3	(1	2)	95	40	29	26	0	68	3	2	4	5	1	.83	4	.238	.303	.328

Tim Unroe

Bats: R **Throws:** R **Pos:** PH/PR-12; DH-8; RF-8; LF-4; 3B-3; 2B-1   **Ht:** 6'3" **Wt:** 200 **Born:** 10/7/70 **Age:** 29

							BATTING												BASERUNNING				PERCENTAGES		
Year Team	Lg	G	AB	H	2B	3B	HR	(Hm	Rd)	TB	R	RBI	TBB	IBB	SO	HBP	SH	SF	SB	CS	SB%	GDP	Avg	OBP	SLG
1999 Edmonton *	AAA	10	44	17	5	1	5	—	—	39	10	18	5	0	9	0	0	0	0	0	.00	0	.386	.449	.886
Omaha *	AAA	5	22	5	0	0	1	—	—	8	4	2	0	0	5	0	0	0	0	0	.00	0	.227	.227	.364
1995 Milwaukee	AL	2	4	1	0	0	0	(0	0)	1	0	0	0	0	0	0	0	0	0	0	.00	0	.250	.250	.250
1996 Milwaukee	AL	14	16	3	0	0	0	(0	0)	3	5	0	4	0	5	0	0	0	0	1	.00	0	.188	.350	.188
1997 Milwaukee	AL	32	16	4	1	0	2	(1	1)	11	3	5	2	0	9	0	0	0	2	0	1.00	0	.250	.333	.688
1999 Anaheim	AL	27	54	13	2	0	1	(1	0)	18	5	6	4	0	16	1	0	0	0	0	.00	0	.241	.305	.333
4 ML YEARS		75	90	21	3	0	3	(2	1)	33	13	11	10	0	30	1	0	0	2	1	.67	0	.233	.317	.367

Ugueth Urbina

Pitches: Right **Bats:** Right **Pos:** RP-71   **Ht:** 6'2" **Wt:** 205 **Born:** 2/15/74 **Age:** 26

		HOW MUCH HE PITCHED					WHAT HE GAVE UP										THE RESULTS						
Year Team	Lg	G	GS	CG	GF	IP	BFP	H	R	ER	HR	SH	SF	HB	TBB	IBB	SO	WP	Bk	W	L	Pct.	ShO	Sv-Op	Hld	ERA
1995 Montreal	NL	7	4	0	0	23.1	109	26	17	16	6	2	0	0	14	1	15	2	0	2	2	.500	0	0-0	4	6.17
1996 Montreal	NL	33	17	0	2	114	484	102	54	47	18	1	3	1	44	4	108	3	1	10	5	.667	0	0-1	6	3.71
1997 Montreal	NL	63	0	0	50	64.1	276	52	29	27	9	3	0	1	29	2	84	2	0	5	8	.385	0	27-32	1	3.78
1998 Montreal	NL	64	0	0	59	69.1	272	37	11	10	2	2	1	0	33	2	94	3	2	6	3	.667	0	34-38	0	1.30
1999 Montreal	NL	71	0	0	62	75.2	323	59	35	31	6	1	2	0	36	6	100	6	0	6	6	.500	0	**41-50**	0	3.69
5 ML YEARS		238	21	0	173	346.2	1464	276	146	131	41	9	6	2	156	15	401	16	3	29	24	.547	0	102-121	7	3.40

Ismael Valdes

Pitches: Right **Bats:** Right **Pos:** SP-32   **Ht:** 6'3" **Wt:** 215 **Born:** 8/21/73 **Age:** 26

		HOW MUCH HE PITCHED					WHAT HE GAVE UP										THE RESULTS						
Year Team	Lg	G	GS	CG	GF	IP	BFP	H	R	ER	HR	SH	SF	HB	TBB	IBB	SO	WP	Bk	W	L	Pct.	ShO	Sv-Op	Hld	ERA
1994 Los Angeles	NL	21	1	0	7	28.1	115	21	10	10	2	3	0	0	10	2	28	1	2	3	1	.750	0	0-0	4	3.18
1995 Los Angeles	NL	33	27	6	1	197.2	804	168	76	67	17	10	5	1	51	5	150	1	3	13	11	.542	2	1-1	2	3.05
1996 Los Angeles	NL	33	33	0	0	225	945	219	94	83	20	7	7	3	54	10	173	1	5	15	7	.682	0	0-0	0	3.32
1997 Los Angeles	NL	30	30	0	0	196.2	795	171	68	58	16	11	3	3	47	1	140	2	2	10	11	.476	0	0-0	0	2.65
1998 Los Angeles	NL	27	27	2	0	174	745	171	82	77	17	5	3	2	66	4	122	4	2	11	10	.524	2	0-0	0	3.98
1999 Los Angeles	NL	32	32	2	0	203.1	871	213	97	90	32	9	8	6	58	2	143	6	0	9	14	.391	1	0-0	0	3.98
6 ML YEARS		176	150	10	8	1025	4275	963	427	385	104	45	26	15	286	24	756	16	14	61	54	.530	5	1-1	6	3.38

Javier Valentin

Bats: Both **Throws:** Right **Pos:** C-76; PH/PR-3   **Ht:** 5'10" **Wt:** 192 **Born:** 9/19/75 **Age:** 24

							BATTING												BASERUNNING				PERCENTAGES		
Year Team	Lg	G	AB	H	2B	3B	HR	(Hm	Rd)	TB	R	RBI	TBB	IBB	SO	HBP	SH	SF	SB	CS	SB%	GDP	Avg	OBP	SLG
1997 Minnesota	AL	4	7	2	0	0	0	(0	0)	2	1	0	0	0	3	0	0	0	0	0	.00	0	.286	.286	.286
1998 Minnesota	AL	55	162	32	7	1	3	(1	2)	50	11	18	11	1	30	0	3	1	0	0	.00	7	.198	.247	.309
1999 Minnesota	AL	78	218	54	12	1	5	(2	3)	83	22	28	22	0	39	1	1	5	0	0	.00	2	.248	.313	.381
3 ML YEARS		137	387	88	19	2	8	(3	5)	135	34	46	33	1	72	1	4	6	0	0	.00	9	.227	.286	.349

John Valentin

Bats: Right **Throws:** Right **Pos:** 3B-111; DH-1; PH/PR-1   **Ht:** 6'0" **Wt:** 185 **Born:** 2/18/67 **Age:** 33

							BATTING												BASERUNNING				PERCENTAGES		
Year Team	Lg	G	AB	H	2B	3B	HR	(Hm	Rd)	TB	R	RBI	TBB	IBB	SO	HBP	SH	SF	SB	CS	SB%	GDP	Avg	OBP	SLG
1992 Boston	AL	58	185	51	13	0	5	(1	4)	79	21	25	20	0	17	2	4	1	1	0	1.00	5	.276	.351	.427
1993 Boston	AL	144	468	130	40	3	11	(7	4)	209	50	66	49	2	77	2	16	4	3	4	.43	9	.278	.346	.447

233

Year Team	Lg	G	AB	H	2B	3B	HR	(Hm	Rd)	TB	R	RBI	TBB	IBB	SO	HBP	SH	SF	SB	CS	SB%	GDP	Avg	OBP	SLG
1994 Boston	AL	84	301	95	26	2	9	(6	3)	152	53	49	42	1	38	3	5	4	3	1	.75	3	.316	.400	.505
1995 Boston	AL	135	520	155	37	2	27	(11	16)	277	108	102	81	2	67	10	4	6	20	5	.80	7	.298	.399	.533
1996 Boston	AL	131	527	156	29	3	13	(9	4)	230	84	59	63	0	59	7	2	7	9	10	.47	15	.296	.374	.436
1997 Boston	AL	143	575	176	47	5	18	(11	7)	287	95	77	58	5	66	5	1	5	7	4	.64	21	.306	.372	.499
1998 Boston	AL	153	588	145	44	1	23	(11	12)	260	113	73	77	3	82	9	2	5	4	5	.44	9	.247	.340	.442
1999 Boston	AL	113	450	114	27	1	12	(5	7)	179	58	70	40	2	68	4	1	8	0	1	.00	11	.253	.315	.398
8 ML YEARS		961	3614	1022	263	17	118	(61	57)	1673	582	521	430	15	474	42	35	40	47	30	.61	80	.283	.362	.463

Jose Valentin

Bats: Both   Throws: Right   Pos: SS-85; PH/PR-6   Ht: 5'10" Wt: 173 Born: 10/12/69 Age: 30

Year Team	Lg	G	AB	H	2B	3B	HR	(Hm	Rd)	TB	R	RBI	TBB	IBB	SO	HBP	SH	SF	SB	CS	SB%	GDP	Avg	OBP	SLG
1999 Louisville *	AAA	6	20	5	0	0	3	—	—	14	6	3	4	0	3	0	0	0	0	1	.00	0	.250	.375	.700
1992 Milwaukee	AL	4	3	0	0	0	0	(0	0)	0	1	1	0	0	0	0	0	1	0	0	.00	0	.000	.000	.000
1993 Milwaukee	AL	19	53	13	1	2	1	(1	0)	21	10	7	7	1	16	1	2	0	1	0	1.00	1	.245	.344	.396
1994 Milwaukee	AL	97	285	68	19	0	11	(8	3)	120	47	46	38	1	75	2	4	2	12	3	.80	1	.239	.330	.421
1995 Milwaukee	AL	112	338	74	23	3	11	(3	8)	136	62	49	37	0	83	0	7	4	16	8	.67	0	.219	.293	.402
1996 Milwaukee	AL	154	552	143	33	7	24	(10	14)	262	90	95	66	9	145	0	6	4	17	4	.81	4	.259	.336	.475
1997 Milwaukee	AL	136	494	125	23	1	17	(3	14)	201	58	58	39	4	109	4	4	5	19	8	.70	5	.253	.310	.407
1998 Milwaukee	NL	151	428	96	24	0	16	(7	9)	168	65	49	63	8	105	1	2	3	10	7	.59	2	.224	.323	.393
1999 Milwaukee	NL	89	256	58	9	5	10	(3	7)	107	45	38	48	7	52	2	2	5	3	2	.60	3	.227	.347	.418
8 ML YEARS		762	2409	577	132	18	90	(36	54)	1015	378	343	298	30	585	10	27	24	78	32	.71	16	.240	.323	.421

John Vander Wal

Bats: L Throws: L Pos: PH/PR-66; LF-45; 1B-28; RF-3; DH-1   Ht: 6'2" Wt: 197 Born: 4/29/66 Age: 34

Year Team	Lg	G	AB	H	2B	3B	HR	(Hm	Rd)	TB	R	RBI	TBB	IBB	SO	HBP	SH	SF	SB	CS	SB%	GDP	Avg	OBP	SLG
1991 Montreal	NL	21	61	13	4	1	1	(0	1)	22	4	8	1	0	18	0	0	1	0	0	.00	2	.213	.222	.361
1992 Montreal	NL	105	213	51	8	2	4	(2	2)	75	21	20	24	2	36	0	0	0	3	0	1.00	1	.239	.316	.352
1993 Montreal	NL	106	215	50	7	4	5	(1	4)	80	34	30	27	2	30	1	0	1	6	3	.67	4	.233	.320	.372
1994 Colorado	NL	91	110	27	3	1	5	(1	4)	47	12	15	16	0	31	0	0	1	2	1	.67	4	.245	.339	.427
1995 Colorado	NL	105	101	35	8	1	5	(2	3)	60	15	21	16	5	23	0	0	1	1	1	.50	2	.347	.432	.594
1996 Colorado	NL	104	151	38	6	2	5	(5	0)	63	20	31	19	2	38	1	0	2	2	2	.50	1	.252	.335	.417
1997 Colorado	NL	76	92	16	2	0	1	(0	1)	21	7	11	10	0	33	0	0	0	1	1	.50	2	.174	.255	.228
1998 Col-SD	NL	109	129	36	13	1	5	(3	2)	66	21	20	22	0	34	0	0	1	0	0	.00	2	.279	.382	.512
1999 San Diego	NL	132	246	67	18	0	6	(2	4)	103	26	41	37	1	59	2	0	3	2	1	.67	5	.272	.368	.419
1998 Col	NL	89	104	30	10	1	5	(3	2)	57	18	20	16	0	29	0	0	1	0	0	.00	1	.288	.380	.548
San Diego	NL	20	25	6	3	0	0	(0	0)	9	3	0	6	0	5	0	0	0	0	0	.00	1	.240	.387	.360
9 ML YEARS		849	1318	333	69	12	37	(16	21)	537	160	197	172	12	302	4	0	10	17	9	.65	24	.253	.338	.407

Jason Varitek

Bats: Both   Throws: Right   Pos: C-140; PH/PR-8; DH-2   Ht: 6'2" Wt: 220 Born: 4/11/72 Age: 28

Year Team	Lg	G	AB	H	2B	3B	HR	(Hm	Rd)	TB	R	RBI	TBB	IBB	SO	HBP	SH	SF	SB	CS	SB%	GDP	Avg	OBP	SLG
1997 Boston	AL	1	1	0	0	0	0	(0	0)	0	0	0	0	0	0	0	0	0	0	0	.00	0	1.000	1.000	1.000
1998 Boston	AL	86	221	56	13	0	7	(1	6)	90	31	33	17	1	45	2	4	3	2	2	.50	8	.253	.309	.407
1999 Boston	AL	144	483	130	39	2	20	(12	8)	233	70	76	46	2	85	2	5	8	1	2	.33	13	.269	.330	.482
3 ML YEARS		231	705	187	52	2	27	(13	14)	324	101	109	63	3	130	4	9	11	3	4	.43	21	.265	.324	.460

Greg Vaughn

Bats: Right   Throws: Right   Pos: LF-144; DH-6; PH/PR-4   Ht: 6'0" Wt: 202 Born: 7/3/65 Age: 34

Year Team	Lg	G	AB	H	2B	3B	HR	(Hm	Rd)	TB	R	RBI	TBB	IBB	SO	HBP	SH	SF	SB	CS	SB%	GDP	Avg	OBP	SLG
1989 Milwaukee	AL	38	113	30	3	0	5	(1	4)	48	18	23	13	0	23	0	0	0	4	1	.80	0	.265	.336	.425
1990 Milwaukee	AL	120	382	84	26	2	17	(9	8)	165	51	61	33	1	91	1	7	6	7	4	.64	11	.220	.280	.432
1991 Milwaukee	AL	145	542	132	24	5	27	(16	11)	247	81	98	62	2	125	1	2	7	2	2	.50	5	.244	.319	.456
1992 Milwaukee	AL	141	501	114	18	2	23	(11	12)	205	77	78	60	1	123	5	2	5	15	15	.50	8	.228	.313	.409
1993 Milwaukee	AL	154	569	152	28	2	30	(12	18)	274	97	97	89	14	118	5	0	4	10	7	.59	6	.267	.369	.482
1994 Milwaukee	AL	95	370	94	24	1	19	(9	10)	177	59	55	51	6	93	1	0	1	9	5	.64	4	.254	.345	.478
1995 Milwaukee	AL	108	392	88	19	1	17	(8	9)	160	67	59	55	3	89	0	0	4	10	4	.71	10	.224	.317	.408
1996 Mil-SD		145	516	134	19	1	41	(22	19)	278	98	117	82	6	130	6	0	5	9	3	.75	7	.260	.365	.539
1997 San Diego	NL	120	361	78	10	0	18	(11	7)	142	60	57	56	1	110	2	0	3	7	4	.64	7	.216	.322	.393
1998 San Diego	NL	158	573	156	28	4	50	(23	27)	342	112	119	79	6	121	5	0	4	11	4	.73	7	.272	.363	.597
1999 Cincinnati	NL	153	550	135	20	2	45	(20	25)	294	104	118	85	3	137	3	0	5	15	2	.88	9	.245	.347	.535
1996 Milwaukee	AL	102	375	105	16	0	31	(16	15)	214	78	95	58	4	99	4	0	5	5	2	.71	6	.280	.378	.571
San Diego	NL	43	141	29	3	1	10	(6	4)	64	20	22	24	2	31	2	0	0	4	1	.80	1	.206	.329	.454
11 ML YEARS		1377	4869	1197	219	20	292	(142	150)	2332	824	882	665	43	1160	29	11	46	99	51	.66	76	.246	.337	.479

Mo Vaughn

Bats: Left **Throws:** Right **Pos:** 1B-72; DH-67 **Ht:** 6'1" **Wt:** 245 **Born:** 12/15/67 **Age:** 32

Year Team	Lg	G	AB	H	2B	3B	HR	(Hm	Rd)	TB	R	RBI	TBB	IBB	SO	HBP	SH	SF	SB	CS	SB%	GDP	Avg	OBP	SLG
1991 Boston	AL	74	219	57	12	0	4	(1	3)	81	21	32	26	2	43	2	0	4	2	1	.67	7	.260	.339	.370
1992 Boston	AL	113	355	83	16	2	13	(8	5)	142	42	57	47	7	67	3	0	3	3	3	.50	8	.234	.326	.400
1993 Boston	AL	152	539	160	34	1	29	(13	16)	283	86	101	79	23	130	8	0	7	4	3	.57	14	.297	.390	.525
1994 Boston	AL	111	394	122	25	1	26	(15	11)	227	65	82	57	20	112	10	0	2	4	4	.50	7	.310	.408	.576
1995 Boston	AL	140	550	165	28	3	39	(15	24)	316	98	126	68	17	150	14	0	4	11	4	.73	17	.300	.388	.575
1996 Boston	AL	161	635	207	29	1	44	(27	17)	370	118	143	95	19	154	14	0	8	2	0	1.00	17	.326	.420	.583
1997 Boston	AL	141	527	166	24	0	35	(20	15)	295	91	96	86	17	154	12	0	3	2	2	.50	10	.315	.420	.560
1998 Boston	AL	154	609	205	31	2	40	(19	21)	360	107	115	61	13	144	8	0	3	0	0	.00	13	.337	.402	.591
1999 Anaheim	AL	139	524	147	20	0	33	(16	17)	266	63	108	54	7	127	11	0	3	0	0	.00	11	.281	.358	.508
9 ML YEARS		1185	4352	1312	219	10	263	(134	129)	2340	691	860	573	125	1081	82	0	37	28	17	.62	104	.301	.390	.538

Javier Vazquez

Pitches: Right **Bats:** Right **Pos:** SP-26 **Ht:** 6'2" **Wt:** 190 **Born:** 7/25/76 **Age:** 23

| | | HOW MUCH HE PITCHED | | | | | | WHAT HE GAVE UP | | | | | | | | | | THE RESULTS | | | | | |
Year Team	Lg	G	GS	CG	GF	IP	BFP	H	R	ER	HR	SH	SF	HB	TBB	IBB	SO	WP	Bk	W	L	Pct.	ShO	Sv-Op	Hld	ERA
1994 Expos	R	15	11	1	0	67.2	260	37	25	19	0	1	2	3	15	0	56	9	2	5	2	.714	1	0--	—	2.53
1995 Albany	A	21	21	1	0	102.2	459	109	67	58	8	1	2	9	47	0	87	2	2	6	6	.500	0	0--	—	5.08
1996 Delmarva	A	27	27	1	0	164.1	668	138	64	49	12	1	1	7	57	0	173	12	2	14	3	.824	0	0--	—	2.68
1997 Wst Plm Bch	A+	19	19	1	0	112.2	461	98	40	27	8	1	2	6	28	0	100	2	2	6	3	.667	0	0--	—	2.16
Harrisburg	AA	6	6	1	0	42	155	15	5	5	2	0	1	2	12	0	47	2	0	4	0	1.000	0	0--	—	1.07
1999 Ottawa	AAA	7	7	0	0	42.2	183	45	24	23	7	2	2	2	16	0	46	0	0	4	2	.667	0	0--	—	4.85
1998 Montreal	NL	33	32	0	1	172.1	764	196	121	116	31	9	4	11	68	2	139	2	0	5	15	.250	0	0-0	0	6.06
1999 Montreal	NL	26	26	3	0	154.2	667	154	98	86	20	3	3	4	52	4	113	2	0	9	8	.529	1	0-0	0	5.00
2 ML YEARS		59	58	3	1	327	1431	350	219	202	51	12	7	15	120	6	252	4	0	14	23	.378	1	0-0	0	5.56

Jorge Velandia

Bats: R **Throws:** R **Pos:** 2B-52; PH/PR-15; SS-8; 3B-2; DH-1 **Ht:** 5'9" **Wt:** 185 **Born:** 1/12/75 **Age:** 25

Year Team	Lg	G	AB	H	2B	3B	HR	(Hm	Rd)	TB	R	RBI	TBB	IBB	SO	HBP	SH	SF	SB	CS	SB%	GDP	Avg	OBP	SLG
1992 Bristol	R+	45	119	24	6	1	0	—	—	32	20	9	15	0	16	0	3	0	3	2	.60	1	.202	.291	.269
1993 Fayetteville	A	37	106	17	4	0	0	—	—	21	15	11	13	0	21	3	0	2	5	0	1.00	3	.160	.266	.198
Niagara Fal	A-	72	212	41	11	0	1	—	—	55	30	22	19	0	48	0	3	2	22	4	.85	2	.193	.258	.259
1994 Lakeland	A+	22	60	14	4	0	0	—	—	18	8	3	6	0	14	0	3	1	0	2	.00	0	.233	.299	.300
Springfield	A	98	290	71	14	0	4	—	—	97	42	36	21	0	46	4	6	3	5	6	.45	8	.245	.302	.334
1995 Memphis	AA	63	186	38	10	2	4	—	—	64	23	17	14	2	37	1	1	1	0	2	.00	4	.204	.262	.344
Las Vegas	AAA	66	206	54	12	3	0	—	—	72	25	25	13	1	37	2	7	2	0	0	.00	5	.262	.309	.350
1996 Memphis	AA	122	392	94	19	0	9	—	—	140	42	48	31	3	65	3	5	8	3	7	.30	10	.240	.295	.357
1997 Las Vegas	AAA	114	405	110	15	2	3	—	—	138	46	35	29	3	62	4	8	1	13	3	.81	5	.272	.326	.341
1998 Edmonton	AAA	128	488	140	35	1	6	—	—	195	64	57	37	0	52	6	5	5	8	6	.57	19	.287	.341	.400
1997 San Diego	NL	14	29	3	2	0	0	(0	0)	5	0	0	1	0	7	0	0	0	0	0	.00	0	.103	.133	.172
1998 Oakland	AL	8	4	1	0	0	0	(0	0)	1	0	0	0	0	1	0	0	0	0	0	.00	0	.250	.250	.250
1999 Oakland	AL	63	48	9	1	0	0	(0	0)	10	4	2	2	0	13	1	0	0	2	0	1.00	0	.188	.235	.208
3 ML YEARS		85	81	13	3	0	0	(0	0)	16	4	2	3	0	21	1	0	0	2	0	1.00	0	.160	.200	.198

Randy Velarde

Bats: Right **Throws:** Right **Pos:** 2B-156 **Ht:** 6'0" **Wt:** 200 **Born:** 11/24/62 **Age:** 37

Year Team	Lg	G	AB	H	2B	3B	HR	(Hm	Rd)	TB	R	RBI	TBB	IBB	SO	HBP	SH	SF	SB	CS	SB%	GDP	Avg	OBP	SLG
1987 New York	AL	8	22	4	0	0	0	(0	0)	4	1	1	0	0	6	0	0	0	0	0	.00	1	.182	.182	.182
1988 New York	AL	48	115	20	6	0	5	(2	3)	41	18	12	8	0	24	2	0	0	1	1	.50	3	.174	.240	.357
1989 New York	AL	33	100	34	4	2	2	(1	1)	48	12	11	7	0	14	1	3	0	0	3	.00	0	.340	.389	.480
1990 New York	AL	95	229	48	6	2	5	(1	4)	73	21	19	20	0	53	1	2	1	0	3	.00	6	.210	.275	.319
1991 New York	AL	80	184	45	11	1	1	(0	1)	61	19	15	18	0	43	3	5	0	3	1	.75	6	.245	.322	.332
1992 New York	AL	121	412	112	24	1	7	(2	5)	159	57	46	38	1	78	2	4	5	7	2	.78	13	.272	.333	.386
1993 New York	AL	85	226	68	13	2	7	(4	3)	106	28	24	18	2	39	4	3	2	2	2	.50	12	.301	.360	.469
1994 New York	AL	77	280	78	16	1	9	(3	6)	123	47	34	22	0	61	4	2	2	4	2	.67	7	.279	.338	.439
1995 New York	AL	111	367	102	19	1	7	(2	5)	144	60	46	55	0	64	4	3	3	5	1	.83	9	.278	.375	.392
1996 California	AL	136	530	151	27	3	14	(8	6)	226	82	54	70	0	118	5	4	2	7	7	.50	7	.285	.372	.426
1997 Anaheim	AL	1	0	0	0	0	0	(0	0)	0	0	0	0	0	0	0	0	0	0	0	.00	0	.000	.000	.000
1998 Anaheim	AL	51	188	49	13	1	4	(1	3)	76	29	24	34	0	42	1	0	1	7	2	.78	8	.261	.375	.404
1999 Ana-Oak	AL	156	631	200	25	7	16	(8	8)	287	105	76	70	2	98	6	4	0	24	8	.75	19	.317	.390	.455
1999 Anaheim	AL	95	376	115	15	4	9	(4	5)	165	57	48	43	1	56	4	2	0	13	4	.76	8	.306	.383	.439
Oakland	AL	61	255	85	10	3	7	(4	3)	122	48	28	27	1	42	2	2	0	11	4	.73	11	.333	.401	.478
13 ML YEARS		1002	3284	911	164	21	77	(32	45)	1348	479	364	360	5	640	33	30	16	60	32	.65	91	.277	.353	.410

Mike Venafro

Pitches: Left **Bats:** Left **Pos:** RP-65 **Ht:** 5'10" **Wt:** 180 **Born:** 8/2/73 **Age:** 26

| | | HOW MUCH HE PITCHED | | | | | | WHAT HE GAVE UP | | | | | | | | | | THE RESULTS | | | | | |
Year Team	Lg	G	GS	CG	GF	IP	BFP	H	R	ER	HR	SH	SF	HB	TBB	IBB	SO	WP	Bk	W	L	Pct.	ShO	Sv-Op	Hld	ERA
1995 Hudson Val	A-	32	0	0	12	50.2	200	37	13	12	0	2	1	5	21	2	32	1	3	9	1	.900	0	2--	—	2.13

235

		HOW MUCH HE PITCHED						WHAT HE GAVE UP												THE RESULTS						
Year Team	Lg	G	GS	CG	GF	IP	BFP	H	R	ER	HR	SH	SF	HB	TBB	IBB	SO	WP	Bk	W	L	Pct.	ShO	Sv-Op	Hld	ERA
1996 Chston-SC	A	50	0	0	42	59	258	57	27	23	0	4	2	3	21	3	62	13	0	1	3	.250	0	19--	—	3.51
1997 Charlotte	A+	35	0	0	27	44.2	196	51	17	17	2	4	3	1	21	1	35	1	0	4	2	.667	0	10--	—	3.43
Tulsa	AA	11	0	0	9	15.2	75	13	12	6	1	0	2	2	12	0	13	1	0	0	1	.000	0	1--	—	3.45
1998 Tulsa	AA	46	0	0	39	52.1	223	42	21	18	5	3	1	1	26	0	45	3	0	3	4	.429	0	14--	—	3.10
Oklahoma	AAA	13	0	0	4	17	82	19	12	12	3	0	0	2	10	0	15	1	0	0	0	.000	0	0--	—	6.35
1999 Oklahoma	AAA	6	0	0	3	11.2	*46	16	7	7	2	0	0	0	0	0	7	0	0	0	0	.000	0	1--	—	5.40
1999 Texas	AL	65	0	0	11	68.1	283	63	29	25	4	5	2	3	22	0	37	0	0	3	2	.600	0	0-1	19	3.29

Robin Ventura

Bats: Left **Throws:** Right **Pos:** 3B-160; PH/PR-2; 1B-1 **Ht:** 6'1" **Wt:** 198 **Born:** 7/14/67 **Age:** 32

		BATTING																BASERUNNING				PERCENTAGES		
Year Team	Lg	G	AB	H	2B	3B	HR	(Hm	Rd)	TB	R	RBI	TBB	IBB	SO	HBP	SH	SF	SB	CS	SB%	GDP	Avg	OBP	SLG
1989 Chicago	AL	16	45	8	3	0	0	(0	0)	11	5	7	8	0	6	1	1	3	0	0	.00	1	.178	.298	.244
1990 Chicago	AL	150	493	123	17	1	5	(2	3)	157	48	54	55	2	53	1	13	3	1	4	.20	5	.249	.324	.318
1991 Chicago	AL	157	606	172	25	1	23	(16	7)	268	92	100	80	3	67	4	8	7	2	4	.33	22	.284	.367	.442
1992 Chicago	AL	157	592	167	*38	1	16	(7	9)	255	85	93	93	9	71	0	1	8	2	4	.33	14	.282	.375	.431
1993 Chicago	AL	157	554	145	27	1	22	(12	10)	240	85	94	105	16	82	3	1	6	1	6	.14	18	.262	.379	.433
1994 Chicago	AL	109	401	113	15	1	18	(8	10)	184	57	78	61	15	69	2	2	8	3	1	.75	8	.282	.373	.459
1995 Chicago	AL	135	492	145	22	0	26	(8	18)	245	79	93	75	11	98	1	1	8	4	3	.57	8	.295	.384	.498
1996 Chicago	AL	158	586	168	31	2	34	(13	21)	305	96	105	78	10	81	2	0	8	1	3	.25	15	.287	.368	.520
1997 Chicago	AL	54	183	48	10	1	6	(2	4)	78	27	26	34	5	21	0	0	3	0	0	.00	3	.262	.373	.426
1998 Chicago	AL	161	590	155	31	4	21	(15	6)	257	84	91	79	15	111	1	1	3	1	1	.50	10	.263	.349	.436
1999 New York	NL	161	588	177	38	0	32	(13	19)	311	88	120	74	10	109	3	1	5	1	1	.50	14	.301	.379	.529
11 ML YEARS		1415	5130	1421	257	12	203	(96	107)	2311	746	861	742	96	768	18	29	62	16	27	.37	121	.277	.366	.450

Quilvio Veras

Bats: Both **Throws:** Right **Pos:** 2B-119; PH/PR-14 **Ht:** 5'10" **Wt:** 183 **Born:** 4/3/71 **Age:** 29

		BATTING																BASERUNNING				PERCENTAGES		
Year Team	Lg	G	AB	H	2B	3B	HR	(Hm	Rd)	TB	R	RBI	TBB	IBB	SO	HBP	SH	SF	SB	CS	SB%	GDP	Avg	OBP	SLG
1995 Florida	NL	124	440	115	20	7	5	(2	3)	164	86	32	80	0	68	9	7	2	56	21	.73	7	.261	.384	.373
1996 Florida	NL	73	253	64	8	1	4	(1	3)	86	40	14	51	1	42	2	1	1	8	8	.50	3	.253	.381	.340
1997 San Diego	NL	145	539	143	23	1	3	(3	0)	177	74	45	72	0	84	7	9	4	33	12	.73	9	.265	.357	.328
1998 San Diego	NL	138	517	138	24	2	6	(5	1)	184	79	45	84	2	78	6	1	4	24	9	.73	6	.267	.373	.356
1999 San Diego	NL	132	475	133	25	2	6	(4	2)	180	95	41	65	0	88	2	1	2	30	17	.64	7	.280	.368	.379
5 ML YEARS		612	2224	593	100	13	24	(15	9)	791	374	177	352	3	360	26	19	13	151	67	.69	32	.267	.371	.356

Wilton Veras

Bats: Right **Throws:** Right **Pos:** 3B-35; PH/PR-1 **Ht:** 6'2" **Wt:** 186 **Born:** 1/19/78 **Age:** 22

		BATTING																BASERUNNING				PERCENTAGES		
Year Team	Lg	G	AB	H	2B	3B	HR	(Hm	Rd)	TB	R	RBI	TBB	IBB	SO	HBP	SH	SF	SB	CS	SB%	GDP	Avg	OBP	SLG
1995 Red Sox	R	31	91	24	1	0	0	—	—	25	7	5	7	0	9	3	0	0	1	2	.33	2	.264	.337	.275
1996 Lowell	A-	67	250	60	15	0	0	—	—	75	22	19	13	0	29	0	1	2	2	1	.67	9	.240	.275	.300
1997 Michigan	A	131	489	141	21	3	8	—	—	192	51	68	31	0	51	6	1	3	3	2	.60	19	.288	.336	.393
1998 Trenton	AA	126	470	137	27	4	16	—	—	220	70	67	15	1	66	6	6	5	5	4	.56	14	.291	.319	.468
1999 Trenton	AA	116	474	133	23	2	11	—	—	193	65	75	23	1	55	5	1	5	7	6	.54	23	.281	.318	.407
1999 Boston	AL	36	118	34	5	1	2	(0	2)	47	14	13	5	0	14	2	0	2	0	2	.00	5	.288	.323	.398

Dave Veres

Pitches: Right **Bats:** Right **Pos:** RP-73 **Ht:** 6'2" **Wt:** 220 **Born:** 10/19/66 **Age:** 33

		HOW MUCH HE PITCHED						WHAT HE GAVE UP												THE RESULTS						
Year Team	Lg	G	GS	CG	GF	IP	BFP	H	R	ER	HR	SH	SF	HB	TBB	IBB	SO	WP	Bk	W	L	Pct.	ShO	Sv-Op	Hld	ERA
1994 Houston	NL	32	0	0	7	41	168	39	13	11	4	0	2	1	7	3	28	2	0	3	3	.500	0	1-1	3	2.41
1995 Houston	NL	72	0	0	15	103.1	418	89	29	26	5	6	8	4	30	6	94	4	0	5	1	.833	0	1-3	19	2.26
1996 Montreal	NL	68	0	0	22	77.2	351	85	39	36	10	3	3	6	32	2	81	3	2	6	3	.667	0	4-6	15	4.17
1997 Montreal	NL	53	0	0	11	62	281	68	28	24	5	6	1	2	27	3	47	7	0	2	3	.400	0	1-4	10	3.48
1998 Colorado	NL	63	0	0	26	76.1	319	67	26	24	6	0	2	2	27	2	74	2	2	3	1	.750	0	8-13	8	2.83
1999 Colorado	NL	73	0	0	63	77	349	88	46	44	14	5	2	2	37	7	71	8	1	4	8	.333	0	31-39	0	5.14
6 ML YEARS		361	0	0	144	437.1	1886	436	181	165	44	20	18	17	160	23	395	26	5	23	19	.548	0	46-66	55	3.40

Jose Vidro

Bats: B **Throws:** R **Pos:** 2B-121; PH/PR-16; 1B-14; LF-3; 3B-2 **Ht:** 5'11" **Wt:** 190 **Born:** 8/27/74 **Age:** 25

		BATTING																BASERUNNING				PERCENTAGES		
Year Team	Lg	G	AB	H	2B	3B	HR	(Hm	Rd)	TB	R	RBI	TBB	IBB	SO	HBP	SH	SF	SB	CS	SB%	GDP	Avg	OBP	SLG
1997 Montreal	NL	67	169	42	12	1	2	(0	2)	62	19	17	11	0	20	2	0	3	1	0	1.00	1	.249	.297	.367
1998 Montreal	NL	83	205	45	12	0	0	(0	0)	57	24	18	27	0	33	4	6	3	2	2	.50	5	.220	.318	.278
1999 Montreal	NL	140	494	150	45	2	12	(5	7)	235	67	59	29	2	51	4	2	2	0	4	.00	12	.304	.346	.476
3 ML YEARS		290	868	237	69	3	14	(5	9)	354	110	94	67	2	104	10	8	8	3	6	.33	18	.273	.329	.408

236

Ron Villone

Pitches: Left **Bats:** Left **Pos:** SP-22; RP-7   **Ht:** 6'3" **Wt:** 237 **Born:** 1/16/70 **Age:** 30

Year Team	Lg	G	GS	CG	GF	IP	BFP	H	R	ER	HR	SH	SF	HB	TBB	IBB	SO	WP	Bk	W	L	Pct.	ShO	Sv-Op	Hld	ERA
1999 Indianapolis *	AAA	18	0	0	6	19	75	9	3	3	1	1	1	2	13	1	23	0	0	2	0	1.000	0	1- —	—	1.42
1995 Sea-SD		38	0	0	15	45	212	44	31	29	11	3	1	1	34	0	63	3	0	2	3	.400	0	1-5	6	5.80
1996 SD-Mil		44	0	0	19	43	182	31	15	15	6	0	2	5	25	0	38	2	0	1	1	.500	0	2-3	9	3.14
1997 Milwaukee	AL	50	0	0	15	52.2	238	54	23	20	4	2	0	1	36	2	40	3	0	1	0	1.000	0	0-2	8	3.42
1998 Cleveland	AL	25	0	0	6	27	129	30	18	18	3	2	2	2	22	0	15	0	0	0	0	.000	0	0-0	1	6.00
1999 Cincinnati	NL	29	22	0	2	142.2	610	114	70	67	8	9	3	5	73	2	97	6	0	9	7	.563	0	2-2	0	4.23
1995 Seattle	AL	19	0	0	7	19.1	101	20	19	17	6	3	0	1	23	0	26	1	0	0	2	.000	0	0-3	3	7.91
San Diego	NL	19	0	0	8	25.2	111	24	12	12	5	0	1	0	11	0	37	2	0	2	1	.667	0	1-2	3	4.21
1996 San Diego	NL	21	0	0	9	18.1	78	17	6	6	2	0	0	1	7	0	19	0	0	1	1	.500	0	0-1	4	2.95
Milwaukee	AL	23	0	0	10	24.2	104	14	9	9	4	0	2	4	18	0	19	2	0	0	0	.000	0	2-2	5	3.28
5 ML YEARS		186	22	0	57	310.1	1371	273	157	149	32	16	8	14	190	4	253	14	0	13	11	.542	0	5-12	24	4.32

Fernando Vina

Bats: Left **Throws:** Right **Pos:** 2B-37   **Ht:** 5'9" **Wt:** 170 **Born:** 4/16/69 **Age:** 31

Year Team	Lg	G	AB	H	2B	3B	HR	(Hm	Rd)	TB	R	RBI	TBB	IBB	SO	HBP	SH	SF	SB	CS	SB%	GDP	Avg	OBP	SLG
1999 Beloit *	A	2	10	2	1	0	0	—	—	3	1	0	0	0	2	0	0	0	0	1	.200	0	.200	.200	.300
1993 Seattle	AL	24	45	10	2	0	0	(0	0)	12	5	2	4	0	3	3	1	0	6	0	1.00	0	.222	.327	.267
1994 New York	NL	79	124	31	6	0	0	(0	0)	37	20	6	12	0	11	12	2	0	3	1	.75	4	.250	.372	.298
1995 Milwaukee	AL	113	288	74	7	7	3	(1	2)	104	46	29	22	0	28	9	4	2	6	3	.67	6	.257	.327	.361
1996 Milwaukee	AL	140	554	157	19	10	7	(3	4)	217	94	46	38	3	35	13	6	4	16	7	.70	15	.283	.342	.392
1997 Milwaukee	AL	79	324	89	12	2	4	(1	3)	117	37	28	12	1	23	7	2	3	8	7	.53	4	.275	.312	.361
1998 Milwaukee	NL	159	637	198	39	7	7	(2	5)	272	101	45	54	2	46	25	5	1	22	16	.58	7	.311	.386	.427
1999 Cincinnati	NL	37	154	41	7	0	1	(0	1)	51	17	16	14	0	6	4	3	2	5	2	.71	1	.266	.339	.331
7 ML YEARS		631	2126	600	92	26	22	(7	15)	810	320	172	156	6	152	73	23	12	66	36	.65	37	.282	.350	.381

Joe Vitiello

Bats: Right **Throws:** Right **Pos:** 1B-10; DH-2; PH/PR-1   **Ht:** 6'3" **Wt:** 230 **Born:** 4/11/70 **Age:** 30

Year Team	Lg	G	AB	H	2B	3B	HR	(Hm	Rd)	TB	R	RBI	TBB	IBB	SO	HBP	SH	SF	SB	CS	SB%	GDP	Avg	OBP	SLG
1999 Omaha *	AAA	122	447	142	33	0	28	—	—	259	70	98	66	2	84	4	0	4	3	4	.43	16	.318	.407	.579
1995 Kansas City	AL	53	130	33	4	0	7	(3	4)	58	13	21	8	0	25	4	0	0	0	0	.00	4	.254	.317	.446
1996 Kansas City	AL	85	257	62	15	1	8	(3	5)	103	29	40	38	2	69	3	0	3	2	0	1.00	12	.241	.342	.401
1997 Kansas City	AL	51	130	31	6	0	5	(4	1)	52	11	18	14	1	37	2	0	0	0	0	.00	2	.238	.322	.400
1998 Kansas City	AL	3	7	1	0	0	0	(0	0)	1	0	0	1	0	2	0	0	0	0	0	.00	0	.143	.250	.143
1999 Kansas City	AL	13	41	6	1	0	1	(0	1)	10	4	4	2	0	9	2	0	0	0	0	.00	2	.146	.222	.244
5 ML YEARS		205	565	133	26	1	21	(10	11)	224	57	83	63	3	142	11	0	3	2	0	1.00	20	.235	.322	.396

Jose Vizcaino

Bats: B **Throws:** R **Pos:** SS-44; 2B-30; PH/PR-24; 3B-9; LF-1   **Ht:** 6'1" **Wt:** 180 **Born:** 3/26/68 **Age:** 32

Year Team	Lg	G	AB	H	2B	3B	HR	(Hm	Rd)	TB	R	RBI	TBB	IBB	SO	HBP	SH	SF	SB	CS	SB%	GDP	Avg	OBP	SLG
1989 Los Angeles	NL	7	10	2	0	0	0	(0	0)	2	2	0	0	0	1	0	1	0	0	0	.00	0	.200	.200	.200
1990 Los Angeles	NL	37	51	14	1	1	0	(0	0)	17	3	2	4	1	8	0	0	0	1	1	.50	1	.275	.327	.333
1991 Chicago	NL	93	145	38	5	0	0	(0	0)	43	7	10	5	0	18	0	2	2	2	1	.67	1	.262	.283	.297
1992 Chicago	NL	86	285	64	10	4	1	(0	1)	85	25	17	14	2	35	0	5	1	3	0	1.00	4	.225	.260	.298
1993 Chicago	NL	151	551	158	19	4	4	(1	3)	197	74	54	46	2	71	3	8	9	12	9	.57	9	.287	.340	.358
1994 New York	NL	103	410	105	13	3	3	(1	2)	133	47	33	33	3	62	2	5	6	1	11	.08	5	.256	.310	.324
1995 New York	NL	135	509	146	21	5	3	(2	1)	186	66	56	35	4	76	1	13	3	8	3	.73	14	.287	.332	.365
1996 NYM-Cle		144	542	161	17	8	1	(0	1)	197	70	45	35	0	82	3	10	3	15	7	.68	8	.297	.341	.363
1997 San Francisco	NL	151	548	151	19	7	5	(1	4)	199	77	50	48	1	87	0	13	1	8	8	.50	13	.266	.323	.350
1998 Los Angeles	NL	67	237	62	9	0	3	(0	3)	80	30	29	17	0	35	1	10	2	7	3	.70	4	.262	.311	.338
1999 Los Angeles	NL	94	266	67	9	0	1	(1	0)	79	27	29	20	0	23	1	9	2	2	1	.67	9	.252	.304	.297
1996 New York	NL	96	363	110	12	6	1	(1	0)	137	47	32	28	0	58	3	6	2	9	5	.64	6	.303	.356	.377
Cleveland	AL	48	179	51	5	2	0	(0	0)	60	23	13	7	0	24	0	4	1	6	2	.75	2	.285	.310	.335
11 ML YEARS		1068	3574	968	123	32	21	(7	14)	1218	428	325	257	13	498	11	76	29	59	44	.57	68	.271	.319	.341

Luis Vizcaino

Pitches: Right **Bats:** Right **Pos:** RP-1   **Ht:** 6'1" **Wt:** 170 **Born:** 6/1/77 **Age:** 23

Year Team	Lg	G	GS	CG	GF	IP	BFP	H	R	ER	HR	SH	SF	HB	TBB	IBB	SO	WP	Bk	W	L	Pct.	ShO	Sv-Op	Hld	ERA
1996 Athletics	R	15	10	0	4	59.2	264	58	36	27	1	1	1	2	24	1	52	6	3	6	3	.667	0	1- —	—	4.07
1997 Modesto	A+	7	0	0	3	14.1	76	24	24	21	4	1	0	0	13	4	15	0	2	0	3	.000	0	0- —	—	13.19
Sou Oregon	A-	22	5	0	7	47.2	237	62	51	42	5	1	5	3	27	0	42	14	0	1	6	.143	0	0- —	—	7.93
1998 Modesto	A+	23	16	0	2	102	421	72	39	31	5	1	4	5	43	1	108	6	4	6	3	.667	0	0- —	—	2.74
Huntsville	AA	7	7	0	0	38.2	182	43	27	20	8	0	3	3	22	0	26	2	0	3	2	.600	0	0- —	—	4.66
1999 Midland	AA	25	19	0	1	104.2	473	120	74	68	18	1	3	3	48	2	88	6	0	8	7	.533	0	0- —	—	5.85
Vancouver	AAA	7	0	0	3	13	56	13	4	2	0	0	0	0	6	0	7	1	0	1	0	1.000	0	0- —	—	1.38
1999 Oakland	AL	1	0	0	1	3.1	16	3	2	2	1	0	0	0	3	0	2	1	0	0	0	.000	0	0-0	0	5.40

Omar Vizquel

Bats: Both   Throws: Right   Pos: SS-143; PH/PR-2; RF-1   Ht: 5'9"   Wt: 170   Born: 4/24/67   Age: 33

Year Team	Lg	G	AB	H	2B	3B	HR	(Hm	Rd)	TB	R	RBI	TBB	IBB	SO	HBP	SH	SF	SB	CS	SB%	GDP	Avg	OBP	SLG
1989 Seattle	AL	143	387	85	7	3	1	(1	0)	101	45	20	28	0	40	1	13	2	1	4	.20	6	.220	.273	.261
1990 Seattle	AL	81	255	63	3	2	2	(0	2)	76	19	18	18	0	22	0	10	2	4	1	.80	7	.247	.295	.298
1991 Seattle	AL	142	426	98	16	4	1	(1	0)	125	42	41	45	0	37	0	8	3	7	2	.78	8	.230	.302	.293
1992 Seattle	AL	136	483	142	20	4	0	(0	0)	170	49	21	32	0	38	2	9	1	15	13	.54	14	.294	.340	.352
1993 Seattle	AL	158	560	143	14	2	2	(1	1)	167	68	31	50	2	71	4	13	3	12	14	.46	7	.255	.319	.298
1994 Cleveland	AL	69	286	78	10	1	1	(0	1)	93	39	33	23	0	23	0	11	2	13	4	.76	4	.273	.325	.325
1995 Cleveland	AL	136	542	144	28	0	6	(3	3)	190	87	56	59	0	59	1	10	10	29	11	.73	6	.266	.333	.351
1996 Cleveland	AL	151	542	161	36	1	9	(2	7)	226	98	64	56	0	42	4	12	9	35	9	.80	10	.297	.362	.417
1997 Cleveland	AL	153	565	158	23	6	5	(3	2)	208	89	49	57	1	58	2	16	7	43	12	.78	16	.280	.347	.368
1998 Cleveland	AL	151	576	166	30	6	2	(0	2)	214	86	50	62	1	64	4	12	6	37	12	.76	10	.288	.358	.372
1999 Cleveland	AL	144	574	191	36	4	5	(3	2)	250	112	66	65	0	50	1	17	7	42	9	.82	8	.333	.397	.436
11 ML YEARS		1464	5196	1429	223	33	34	(14	20)	1820	734	449	495	4	504	19	131	47	238	91	.72	94	.275	.338	.350

Ed Vosberg

Pitches: Left   Bats: Left   Pos: RP-19   Ht: 6'1"   Wt: 210   Born: 9/28/61   Age: 38

Year Team	Lg	G	GS	CG	GF	IP	BFP	H	R	ER	HR	SH	SF	HB	TBB	IBB	SO	WP	Bk	W	L	Pct.	ShO	Sv-Op	Hld	ERA
1999 Las Vegas *	AAA	8	0	0	1	8.1	31	3	1	1	1	0	0	0	4	0	12	0	0	0	0	.000	0	1- -	—	1.08
Tucson *	AAA	26	0	0	16	34.2	127	26	5	3	0	1	0	0	8	1	30	2	0	1	0	1.000	0	7- -	—	0.78
1986 San Diego	NL	5	3	0	0	13.2	65	17	11	10	1	0	0	0	9	1	8	0	1	0	0	.000	0	0- -	—	6.59
1990 San Francisco	NL	18	0	0	5	24.1	104	21	16	15	3	2	0	0	12	2	12	0	0	1	1	.500	0	0-0	0	5.55
1994 Oakland	AL	16	0	0	2	13.2	56	16	7	6	2	1	0	0	5	0	12	1	1	0	2	.000	0	0-1	2	3.95
1995 Texas	AL	44	0	0	20	36	154	32	15	12	3	2	3	0	16	1	36	3	2	5	5	.500	0	4-8	5	3.00
1996 Texas	AL	52	0	0	21	44	195	51	17	16	4	2	1	0	21	4	32	1	2	1	1	.500	0	8-9	11	3.27
1997 Tex-Fla		59	0	0	22	53	239	59	30	26	3	2	4	5	21	6	37	2	1	2	3	.400	0	1-3	8	4.42
1999 SD-Ari	NL	19	0	0	3	11	60	22	12	10	1	2	2	2	3	0	8	1	0	0	1	.000	0	0-2	4	8.18
1997 Texas	AL	42	0	0	16	41	180	44	23	21	3	1	3	2	15	6	29	1	1	1	2	.333	0	0-1	5	4.61
Florida	NL	17	0	0	6	12	59	15	7	5	0	1	1	3	6	0	8	1	1	1	1	.500	0	1-2	3	3.75
1999 San Diego	NL	15	0	0	3	8.1	47	16	11	9	1	2	2	2	3	0	6	1	0	0	0	.000	0	0-2	4	9.72
Arizona	NL	4	0	0	0	2.2	13	6	1	1	0	0	0	0	0	0	2	0	0	0	1	.000	0	0-0	0	3.38
7 ML YEARS		213	3	0	73	195.2	873	218	108	95	17	11	10	7	87	14	145	8	7	9	14	.391	0	13- -	—	4.37

Billy Wagner

Pitches: Left   Bats: Left   Pos: RP-66   Ht: 5'11"   Wt: 180   Born: 7/25/71   Age: 28

Year Team	Lg	G	GS	CG	GF	IP	BFP	H	R	ER	HR	SH	SF	HB	TBB	IBB	SO	WP	Bk	W	L	Pct.	ShO	Sv-Op	Hld	ERA
1995 Houston	NL	1	0	0	0	0.1	1	0	0	0	0	0	0	0	0	0	0	0	0	0	0	.000	0	0-0	0	0.00
1996 Houston	NL	37	0	0	20	51.2	212	28	16	14	6	7	3	2	30	2	67	1	0	2	2	.500	0	9-13	3	2.44
1997 Houston	NL	62	0	0	49	66.1	277	49	23	21	5	3	1	3	30	1	106	3	0	7	8	.467	0	23-29	1	2.85
1998 Houston	NL	58	0	0	50	60	247	46	19	18	6	4	0	0	25	1	97	2	0	4	3	.571	0	30-35	1	2.70
1999 Houston	NL	66	0	0	55	74.2	286	35	14	13	5	2	1	1	23	1	124	2	0	4	1	.800	0	39-42	1	1.57
5 ML YEARS		224	0	0	174	253	1023	158	72	66	22	16	4	7	108	5	394	8	0	17	14	.548	0	101-119	6	2.35

Paul Wagner

Pitches: Right   Bats: Right   Pos: RP-3   Ht: 6'1"   Wt: 210   Born: 11/14/67   Age: 32

Year Team	Lg	G	GS	CG	GF	IP	BFP	H	R	ER	HR	SH	SF	HB	TBB	IBB	SO	WP	Bk	W	L	Pct.	ShO	Sv-Op	Hld	ERA
1999 Buffalo *	AAA	23	23	0	0	129.2	559	123	67	55	11	1	4	4	55	2	95	11	0	8	4	.667	0	0- -	—	3.82
1992 Pittsburgh	NL	6	1	0	1	13	52	9	1	1	0	0	0	0	5	0	5	1	0	2	0	1.000	0	0-0	0	0.69
1993 Pittsburgh	NL	44	17	1	9	141.1	599	143	72	67	15	6	7	1	42	2	114	12	0	8	8	.500	1	2-5	4	4.27
1994 Pittsburgh	NL	29	17	1	4	119.2	534	136	69	61	7	8	4	8	50	4	86	4	0	7	8	.467	0	0-0	2	4.59
1995 Pittsburgh	NL	33	25	3	1	165	725	174	96	88	18	7	2	7	72	7	120	8	0	5	16	.238	1	1-1	0	4.80
1996 Pittsburgh	NL	16	15	1	0	81.2	361	86	49	49	10	5	1	3	39	2	81	7	0	4	8	.333	0	0-0	0	5.40
1997 Pit-Mil		16	0	0	3	18	87	20	9	9	4	3	1	0	13	3	9	3	2	1	0	1.000	0	0-1	0	4.50
1998 Milwaukee	NL	13	9	0	1	55.2	261	67	49	44	10	5	2	1	31	1	37	3	0	1	5	.167	0	0-0	0	7.11
1999 Cleveland	AL	3	0	0	1	4.1	24	5	4	2	0	0	0	2	3	0	0	1	0	1	0	1.000	0	0-0	0	4.15
1997 Pittsburgh	NL	14	0	0	2	16	79	17	7	7	3	3	1	0	13	3	9	3	2	0	0	.000	0	0-1	0	3.94
Milwaukee	AL	2	0	0	1	2	8	3	2	2	1	0	0	0	0	0	0	0	0	1	0	1.000	0	0-0	0	9.00
8 ML YEARS		160	84	6	20	598.2	2643	640	349	321	64	34	17	22	255	19	452	38	2	29	45	.392	2	3-7	7	4.83

Dave Wainhouse

Pitches: Right   Bats: Left   Pos: RP-19   Ht: 6'2"   Wt: 196   Born: 11/7/67   Age: 32

Year Team	Lg	G	GS	CG	GF	IP	BFP	H	R	ER	HR	SH	SF	HB	TBB	IBB	SO	WP	Bk	W	L	Pct.	ShO	Sv-Op	Hld	ERA
1999 Colo Sprngs *	AAA	38	0	0	35	42.1	175	42	19	15	6	1	0	2	7	1	42	0	0	1	3	.250	0	22- -	—	3.19
1991 Montreal	NL	2	0	0	1	2.2	14	2	2	2	0	0	1	0	4	0	1	2	0	0	0	.000	0	0-0	0	6.75
1993 Seattle	AL	3	0	0	0	2.1	20	7	7	7	1	0	0	1	5	0	2	0	0	0	0	.000	0	0-0	0	27.00
1996 Pittsburgh	NL	17	0	0	6	23.2	101	22	16	15	3	1	2	0	10	1	16	2	0	1	0	1.000	0	0-0	0	5.70
1997 Pittsburgh	NL	25	0	0	6	28	137	34	28	25	2	3	1	3	17	0	21	1	1	0	1	.000	0	0-0	1	8.04
1998 Colorado	NL	10	0	0	3	11	51	15	6	6	1	0	0	2	5	0	3	0	0	1	0	1.000	0	0-1	0	4.91

Year Team	Lg	G	GS	CG	GF	IP	BFP	H	R	ER	HR	SH	SF	HB	TBB	IBB	SO	WP	Bk	W	L	Pct.	ShO	Sv-Op	Hld	ERA
1999 Colorado	NL	19	0	0	11	28.2	131	37	22	22	6	0	3	0	16	0	18	1	0	0	0	.000	0	0-0	0	6.91
6 ML YEARS		76	0	0	27	96.1	454	117	81	77	13	4	7	6	57	1	61	6	1	2	2	.500	0	0-1	2	7.19

Tim Wakefield

Pitches: Right **Bats:** Right **Pos:** RP-32; SP-17 **Ht:** 6'2" **Wt:** 210 **Born:** 8/2/66 **Age:** 33

Year Team	Lg	G	GS	CG	GF	IP	BFP	H	R	ER	HR	SH	SF	HB	TBB	IBB	SO	WP	Bk	W	L	Pct.	ShO	Sv-Op	Hld	ERA
1992 Pittsburgh	NL	13	13	4	0	92	373	76	26	22	3	6	4	1	35	1	51	3	1	8	1	.889	1	0-0	0	2.15
1993 Pittsburgh	NL	24	20	3	1	128.1	595	145	83	80	14	7	5	9	75	2	59	6	0	6	11	.353	2	0-0	0	5.61
1995 Boston	AL	27	27	6	0	195.1	804	163	76	64	22	3	7	9	68	0	119	11	0	16	8	.667	1	0-0	0	2.95
1996 Boston	AL	32	32	6	0	211.2	963	238	151	121	38	1	9	12	90	0	140	4	1	14	13	.519	0	0-0	0	5.14
1997 Boston	AL	35	29	4	2	201.1	866	193	109	95	24	3	7	16	87	5	151	6	0	12	15	.444	2	0-0	1	4.25
1998 Boston	AL	36	33	2	1	216	939	211	123	110	30	1	8	14	79	1	146	6	1	17	8	.680	0	0-0	0	4.58
1999 Boston	AL	49	17	0	28	140	635	146	93	79	19	1	8	5	72	2	104	1	0	6	11	.353	0	15-18	0	5.08
7 ML YEARS		216	171	25	32	1184.2	5175	1172	661	571	150	22	48	66	506	11	770	37	3	79	67	.541	6	15-18	1	4.34

Matt Walbeck

Bats: Both **Throws:** Right **Pos:** C-97; PH/PR-21; DH-1 **Ht:** 5'11" **Wt:** 206 **Born:** 10/2/69 **Age:** 30

Year Team	Lg	G	AB	H	2B	3B	HR	(Hm	Rd)	TB	R	RBI	TBB	IBB	SO	HBP	SH	SF	SB	CS	SB%	GDP	Avg	OBP	SLG
1993 Chicago	NL	11	30	6	2	0	1	(1	0)	11	2	6	1	0	6	0	0	0	0	0	.00	0	.200	.226	.367
1994 Minnesota	AL	97	338	69	12	0	5	(0	5)	96	31	35	17	1	37	2	1	1	1	1	.50	7	.204	.246	.284
1995 Minnesota	AL	115	393	101	18	1	1	(1	0)	124	40	44	25	2	71	1	1	2	3	1	.75	11	.257	.302	.316
1996 Minnesota	AL	63	215	48	10	0	2	(1	1)	64	25	24	9	0	34	0	1	2	3	1	.75	6	.223	.252	.298
1997 Detroit	AL	47	137	38	3	0	3	(1	2)	50	18	10	12	0	19	0	0	2	3	3	.50	4	.277	.331	.365
1998 Anaheim	AL	108	338	87	15	2	6	(3	3)	124	41	46	30	0	68	2	5	5	1	1	.50	9	.257	.317	.367
1999 Anaheim	AL	107	288	69	8	1	3	(1	2)	88	26	22	26	1	46	3	3	1	2	3	.40	12	.240	.308	.306
7 ML YEARS		548	1739	418	68	4	21	(8	13)	557	183	187	120	4	281	8	11	13	13	10	.57	49	.240	.290	.320

Larry Walker

Bats: Left **Throws:** Right **Pos:** RF-114; PH/PR-15; DH-1 **Ht:** 6'3" **Wt:** 237 **Born:** 12/1/66 **Age:** 33

Year Team	Lg	G	AB	H	2B	3B	HR	(Hm	Rd)	TB	R	RBI	TBB	IBB	SO	HBP	SH	SF	SB	CS	SB%	GDP	Avg	OBP	SLG
1989 Montreal	NL	20	47	8	0	0	0	(0	0)	8	4	4	5	0	13	1	3	0	1	1	.50	1	.170	.264	.170
1990 Montreal	NL	133	419	101	18	3	19	(9	10)	182	59	51	49	5	112	5	3	2	21	7	.75	8	.241	.326	.434
1991 Montreal	NL	137	487	141	30	2	16	(5	11)	223	59	64	42	2	102	5	1	4	14	9	.61	7	.290	.349	.458
1992 Montreal	NL	143	528	159	31	4	23	(13	10)	267	85	93	41	10	97	6	0	6	18	6	.75	9	.301	.353	.506
1993 Montreal	NL	138	490	130	24	5	22	(13	9)	230	85	86	80	20	76	6	0	6	29	7	.81	8	.265	.371	.469
1994 Montreal	NL	103	395	127	44	2	19	(7	12)	232	76	86	47	5	74	4	0	6	15	5	.75	8	.322	.394	.587
1995 Colorado	NL	131	494	151	31	5	36	(24	12)	300	96	101	49	13	72	14	0	5	16	3	.84	13	.306	.381	.607
1996 Colorado	NL	83	272	75	18	4	18	(12	6)	155	58	58	20	2	58	9	0	3	18	2	.90	7	.276	.342	.570
1997 Colorado	NL	153	568	208	46	4	49	(20	29)	409	143	130	78	14	90	14	0	4	33	8	.80	15	.366	.452	.720
1998 Colorado	NL	130	454	165	46	3	23	(17	6)	286	113	67	64	2	61	4	0	2	14	4	.78	11	.363	.445	.630
1999 Colorado	NL	127	438	166	26	4	37	(26	11)	311	108	115	57	8	52	12	0	6	11	4	.73	12	.379	.458	.710
11 ML YEARS		1298	4592	1431	314	36	262	(146	116)	2603	886	855	532	81	807	80	7	46	190	56	.77	98	.312	.389	.567

Todd Walker

Bats: Left **Throws:** Right **Pos:** 2B-103; DH-34; PH/PR-9 **Ht:** 6'0" **Wt:** 181 **Born:** 5/25/73 **Age:** 27

Year Team	Lg	G	AB	H	2B	3B	HR	(Hm	Rd)	TB	R	RBI	TBB	IBB	SO	HBP	SH	SF	SB	CS	SB%	GDP	Avg	OBP	SLG
1996 Minnesota	AL	25	82	21	6	0	0	(0	0)	27	8	6	4	0	13	0	0	3	2	0	1.00	4	.256	.281	.329
1997 Minnesota	AL	52	156	37	7	1	3	(1	2)	55	15	16	11	1	30	1	1	2	7	0	1.00	5	.237	.288	.353
1998 Minnesota	AL	143	528	167	41	3	12	(7	5)	250	85	62	47	9	65	2	0	4	19	7	.73	13	.316	.372	.473
1999 Minnesota	AL	143	531	148	37	4	6	(4	2)	211	62	46	52	5	83	1	0	2	18	10	.64	15	.279	.343	.397
4 ML YEARS		363	1297	373	91	8	21	(12	9)	543	170	130	114	15	191	4	1	11	46	17	.73	37	.288	.344	.419

Donne Wall

Pitches: Right **Bats:** Right **Pos:** RP-55 **Ht:** 6'1" **Wt:** 205 **Born:** 7/11/67 **Age:** 32

Year Team	Lg	G	GS	CG	GF	IP	BFP	H	R	ER	HR	SH	SF	HB	TBB	IBB	SO	WP	Bk	W	L	Pct.	ShO	Sv-Op	Hld	ERA
1995 Houston	NL	6	5	0	0	24.1	110	33	19	15	5	0	4	0	5	0	16	1	0	3	1	.750	0	0-0	1	5.55
1996 Houston	NL	26	23	2	1	150	643	170	84	76	17	4	5	6	34	3	99	3	2	9	8	.529	1	0-0	0	4.56
1997 Houston	NL	8	8	0	0	41.2	186	53	31	29	8	0	0	2	16	0	25	2	1	5	5	.286	0	0-0	0	6.26
1998 San Diego	NL	46	1	0	14	70.1	287	50	20	19	6	4	2	1	32	2	56	3	1	5	4	.556	0	1-4	16	2.43
1999 San Diego	NL	55	0	0	12	70.1	290	58	31	24	11	1	1	0	23	3	53	6	0	7	4	.636	0	0-6	18	3.07
5 ML YEARS		141	37	2	27	356.2	1516	364	185	163	47	9	10	9	110	8	249	15	4	26	22	.542	1	1-10	35	4.11

Derek Wallace

Pitches: Right **Bats:** Right **Pos:** RP-8 Ht: 6'3" Wt: 215 Born: 9/1/71 Age: 28

Year Team	Lg	G	GS	CG	GF	IP	BFP	H	R	ER	HR	SH	SF	HB	TBB	IBB	SO	WP	Bk	W	L	Pct.	ShO	Sv-Op	Hld	ERA
1992 Peoria	A	2	0	0	1	3.2	13	3	2	2	0	1	0	0	1	0	2	0	2	0	1	.000	0	0--	—	4.91
1993 Daytona	A+	14	12	0	1	79.1	342	85	50	37	6	6	2	2	23	2	34	5	11	5	6	.455	0	1--	—	4.20
Iowa	AAA	1	1	0	0	4	20	8	5	5	0	0	1	0	1	0	2	0	0	0	0	.000	0	0--	—	11.25
Orlando	AA	15	15	2	0	96.2	418	105	59	54	12	5	0	10	28	3	69	9	4	5	7	.417	0	0--	—	5.03
1994 Orlando	AA	33	12	1	19	89.1	391	95	61	57	11	3	4	10	31	3	49	6	4	2	9	.182	0	8--	—	5.74
Iowa	AAA	5	0	0	2	4.1	21	4	4	2	0	0	0	0	4	0	3	1	0	1	0	.000	0	1--	—	4.15
1995 Wichita	AA	26	0	0	18	43	188	51	23	21	5	1	1	2	13	4	24	3	0	4	3	.571	0	6--	—	4.40
Binghamton	AA	15	0	0	11	15.1	62	11	9	9	1	0	3	1	9	1	8	1	2	0	1	.000	0	2--	—	5.28
1996 Norfolk	AAA	49	0	0	39	57.2	227	37	20	11	4	2	2	1	17	1	52	0	1	5	2	.714	0	26--	—	1.72
1997 Norfolk	AAA	1	0	0	1	1	6	2	2	1	0	0	0	0	1	1	0	0	0	0	0	.000	0	0--	—	9.00
Mets	R	8	5	0	0	8	31	6	3	3	2	0	0	0	1	0	9	0	0	0	1	.000	0	0--	—	3.38
St. Lucie	A+	5	0	0	3	7	30	7	6	5	0	0	0	0	2	0	8	1	1	0	0	.000	0	0--	—	6.43
1998 Norfolk	AAA	54	0	0	44	60.1	265	58	31	26	3	3	3	1	27	3	50	4	0	5	2	.714	0	16--	—	3.88
1999 Norfolk	AAA	36	0	0	19	55	233	53	24	22	6	1	0	2	25	7	38	2	0	2	5	.286	0	7--	—	3.60
1996 New York	NL	19	0	0	11	24.2	115	29	12	11	2	1	0	0	14	2	15	2	0	2	3	.400	0	3-3	0	4.01
1999 Kansas City	AL	8	0	0	4	8.1	34	7	4	3	2	1	1	0	5	0	5	0	0	0	1	.000	0	0-0	1	3.24
2 ML YEARS		27	0	0	15	33	149	36	16	14	4	2	1	0	19	2	20	2	0	2	4	.333	0	3-3	1	3.82

Jeff Wallace

Pitches: Left **Bats:** Left **Pos:** RP-41 Ht: 6'2" Wt: 228 Born: 4/12/76 Age: 24

Year Team	Lg	G	GS	CG	GF	IP	BFP	H	R	ER	HR	SH	SF	HB	TBB	IBB	SO	WP	Bk	W	L	Pct.	ShO	Sv-Op	Hld	ERA
1995 Royals	R	12	7	0	3	44	177	28	20	6	0	1	1	1	15	0	51	3	2	5	3	.625	0	1--	—	1.23
1996 Lansing	A	30	21	0	2	122.1	560	140	79	72	10	8	3	7	66	0	84	12	7	4	9	.308	0	0--	—	5.30
1997 Lynchburg	A+	9	0	0	6	16.1	65	9	3	3	0	1	0	0	10	1	13	1	0	5	0	1.000	0	1--	—	1.65
Carolina	AA	38	0	0	15	43.1	207	43	37	26	3	5	0	1	36	3	39	9	1	4	8	.333	0	3--	—	5.40
1999 Nashville	AAA	15	0	0	7	14.1	68	18	15	14	3	1	0	2	8	1	14	1	0	2	2	.500	0	3--	—	8.79
1997 Pittsburgh	NL	11	0	0	1	12	50	8	2	1	0	1	1	0	8	1	14	1	0	0	0	.000	0	0-1	3	0.75
1999 Pittsburgh	NL	41	0	0	7	39	176	26	17	16	2	4	1	0	38	1	41	5	0	1	0	1.000	0	0-1	7	3.69
2 ML YEARS		52	0	0	8	51	226	34	19	17	2	5	2	0	46	2	55	6	0	1	0	1.000	0	0-2	10	3.00

Bryan Ward

Pitches: Left **Bats:** Left **Pos:** RP-40 Ht: 6'2" Wt: 205 Born: 1/25/72 Age: 28

Year Team	Lg	G	GS	CG	GF	IP	BFP	H	R	ER	HR	SH	SF	HB	TBB	IBB	SO	WP	Bk	W	L	Pct.	ShO	Sv-Op	Hld	ERA
1993 Elmira	A-	14	11	0	2	61.1	291	82	41	34	6	2	4	4	26	2	63	5	5	2	5	.286	0	0--	—	4.99
1994 Kane County	A	47	0	0	40	55.2	235	46	27	21	4	3	4	2	21	2	62	2	0	3	4	.429	0	11--	—	3.40
1995 Portland	AA	20	11	1	5	72	321	70	42	36	9	1	1	2	31	3	71	7	3	7	3	.700	1	2--	—	4.50
Brevard Cty	A+	11	11	0	0	72	296	68	27	23	5	4	0	2	17	0	65	1	1	5	1	.833	0	0--	—	2.88
1996 Portland	AA	28	25	2	0	146.2	633	170	97	80	23	9	6	7	32	3	124	0	2	9	9	.500	0	0--	—	4.91
1997 Portland	AA	12	12	0	0	76	316	71	39	33	17	2	2	2	19	1	69	6	0	6	3	.667	0	0--	—	3.91
Charlotte	AAA	15	14	2	0	75.1	349	102	62	58	17	5	4	4	30	4	48	5	1	2	9	.182	0	0--	—	6.93
1998 Birmingham	AA	29	0	0	24	42	187	33	19	11	0	2	3	1	25	3	40	5	0	2	3	.400	0	12--	—	2.36
1999 Charlotte	AAA	14	0	0	6	15.1	64	15	7	6	2	1	1	0	3	1	15	1	0	2	0	1.000	0	1--	—	3.52
1998 Chicago	AL	28	0	0	9	27	116	30	13	10	4	0	1	0	7	0	17	0	0	1	2	.333	0	1-4	3	3.33
1999 Chicago	AL	40	0	0	8	39.1	183	63	36	33	10	0	1	0	11	1	35	2	0	0	1	.000	0	0-0	3	7.55
2 ML YEARS		68	0	0	17	66.1	299	93	49	43	14	0	2	0	18	1	52	2	0	1	3	.250	0	1-4	6	5.83

Daryle Ward

Bats: L **Throws:** L **Pos:** LF-31; PH/PR-26; 1B-10; DH-3 Ht: 6'2" Wt: 230 Born: 6/27/75 Age: 25

Year Team	Lg	G	AB	H	2B	3B	HR	(Hm	Rd)	TB	R	RBI	TBB	IBB	SO	HBP	SH	SF	SB	CS	SB%	GDP	Avg	OBP	SLG
1994 Bristol	R+	48	161	43	6	0	5	—	—	64	17	30	19	4	33	0	1	1	5	1	.83	3	.267	.343	.398
1995 Fayetteville	A	137	524	149	32	0	14	—	—	223	75	106	46	11	111	5	0	7	1	2	.33	13	.284	.344	.426
1996 Toledo	AAA	6	23	4	0	0	0	—	—	4	1	1	0	0	3	0	0	0	0	0	.00	2	.174	.174	.174
Lakeland	A+	128	464	135	29	4	10	—	—	202	65	68	57	6	77	6	0	4	1	1	.50	9	.291	.373	.435
1997 Jackson	AA	114	422	139	25	0	19	—	—	221	72	90	46	4	68	3	0	1	4	2	.67	11	.329	.398	.524
New Orleans	AAA	14	48	18	1	0	2	—	—	25	4	8	7	1	7	0	0	0	0	0	.00	0	.375	.455	.521
1998 New Orleans	AAA	116	463	141	31	1	23	—	—	243	78	96	41	7	78	2	0	4	2	0	1.00	17	.305	.361	.525
1999 New Orleans	AAA	61	241	85	15	1	28	—	—	186	56	65	23	5	43	3	0	0	1	1	.50	3	.353	.416	.772
1998 Houston	NL	4	3	1	0	0	0	(0	0)	1	1	0	1	0	2	0	0	0	0	0	.00	0	.333	.500	.333
1999 Houston	NL	64	150	41	6	0	8	(2	6)	71	11	30	9	0	31	0	0	2	0	0	.00	3	.273	.311	.473
2 ML YEARS		68	153	42	6	0	8	(2	6)	72	12	30	10	0	33	0	0	2	0	0	.00	3	.275	.315	.471

Turner Ward

Bats: B **Throws:** R **Pos:** CF-24; PH/PR-23; RF-17; LF-5 Ht: 6'2" Wt: 204 Born: 4/11/65 Age: 35

Year Team	Lg	G	AB	H	2B	3B	HR	(Hm	Rd)	TB	R	RBI	TBB	IBB	SO	HBP	SH	SF	SB	CS	SB%	GDP	Avg	OBP	SLG
1999 Altoona *	AA	1	3	0	0	0	0	—	—	0	1	0	2	0	2	0	0	0	0	0	.00	0	.000	.400	.000
Nashville *	AAA	35	89	26	3	1	2	—	—	37	15	17	16	0	14	1	0	0	3	1	.75	1	.292	.406	.416

Year Team	Lg	G	AB	H	2B	3B	HR	(Hm	Rd)	TB	R	RBI	TBB	IBB	SO	HBP	SH	SF	SB	CS	SB%	GDP	Avg	OBP	SLG
Tucson *	AAA	12	40	15	2	0	2	—	—	23	9	8	7	0	4	1	0	0	4	1	.80	1	.375	.479	.575
1990 Cleveland	AL	14	46	16	2	1	1	(0	1)	23	10	10	3	0	8	0	0	0	3	0	1.00	1	.348	.388	.500
1991 Cle-Tor	AL	48	113	27	7	0	0	(0	0)	34	12	7	11	0	18	0	4	0	0	0	.00	2	.239	.306	.301
1992 Toronto	AL	18	29	10	3	0	1	(0	1)	16	7	3	4	0	4	0	0	0	1	0	.00	1	.345	.424	.552
1993 Toronto	AL	72	167	32	4	2	4	(2	2)	52	20	28	23	2	26	1	3	4	3	3	.50	7	.192	.287	.311
1994 Milwaukee	AL	102	367	85	15	2	9	(3	6)	131	55	45	52	4	68	3	0	5	6	2	.75	9	.232	.328	.357
1995 Milwaukee	AL	44	129	34	3	1	4	(3	1)	51	19	16	14	1	21	1	1	1	6	1	.86	2	.264	.338	.395
1996 Milwaukee	AL	43	67	12	2	1	2	(2	0)	22	7	10	13	0	17	0	1	1	3	0	1.00	3	.179	.309	.328
1997 Pittsburgh	NL	71	167	59	16	1	7	(5	2)	98	33	33	18	2	17	2	3	1	4	1	.80	1	.353	.420	.587
1998 Pittsburgh	NL	123	282	74	13	3	9	(6	3)	120	33	46	27	1	40	4	4	7	5	4	.56	4	.262	.328	.426
1999 Pit-Ari	NL	59	114	27	3	0	2	(2	0)	36	8	15	15	0	15	1	3	2	2	2	.50	2	.237	.326	.316
1991 Cleveland	AL	40	100	23	7	0	0	(0	0)	30	11	5	10	0	16	0	4	0	0	0	.00	1	.230	.300	.300
Toronto	AL	8	13	4	0	0	0	(0	0)	4	1	2	1	0	2	0	0	0	0	0	.00	1	.308	.357	.308
1999 Pittsburgh	NL	49	91	19	2	0	0	(0	0)	21	2	8	13	0	9	1	3	1	2	2	.50	2	.209	.311	.231
Arizona	NL	10	23	8	1	0	2	(2	0)	15	6	7	2	0	6	0	0	1	0	0	.00	0	.348	.385	.652
10 ML YEARS		594	1481	376	68	11	39	(23	16)	583	204	213	180	10	234	12	19	21	32	14	.70	32	.254	.335	.394

John Wasdin

Pitches: Right **Bats:** Right **Pos:** RP-45 **Ht:** 6'2" **Wt:** 195 **Born:** 8/5/72 **Age:** 27

Year Team	Lg	G	GS	CG	GF	IP	BFP	H	R	ER	HR	SH	SF	HB	TBB	IBB	SO	WP	Bk	W	L	Pct.	ShO	Sv-Op	Hld	ERA
1999 Pawtucket *	AAA	5	5	0	0	29.2	113	19	9	7	1	1	1	1	7	0	28	0	0	1	1	.500	0	0--	—	2.12
Red Sox *	R	1	1	0	0	2	7	1	0	0	0	0	0	0	0	0	4	0	0	0	0	.000	0	0--	—	0.00
1995 Oakland	AL	5	2	0	3	17.1	69	14	9	9	4	0	0	1	3	0	6	0	0	1	1	.500	0	0-0	0	4.67
1996 Oakland	AL	25	21	1	2	131.1	575	145	96	87	24	3	6	4	50	5	75	2	2	8	7	.533	0	0-1	0	5.96
1997 Boston	AL	53	7	0	10	124.2	534	121	68	61	18	4	7	3	38	4	84	4	0	4	6	.400	0	0-2	11	4.40
1998 Boston	AL	47	8	0	13	96	424	111	57	56	14	3	6	2	27	8	59	1	0	6	4	.600	0	0-1	4	5.25
1999 Boston	AL	45	0	0	17	74.1	302	66	38	34	14	2	2	0	18	0	57	2	0	8	3	.727	0	2-5	2	4.12
5 ML YEARS		175	38	1	45	443.2	1904	457	268	247	74	12	21	10	136	17	281	9	2	27	21	.563	0	2-9	17	5.01

Jarrod Washburn

Pitches: Left **Bats:** Left **Pos:** SP-10; RP-6 **Ht:** 6'1" **Wt:** 200 **Born:** 8/13/74 **Age:** 25

Year Team	Lg	G	GS	CG	GF	IP	BFP	H	R	ER	HR	SH	SF	HB	TBB	IBB	SO	WP	Bk	W	L	Pct.	ShO	Sv-Op	Hld	ERA
1995 Boise	A-	8	8	0	0	46	185	35	17	17	1	0	1	2	14	0	54	1	0	3	2	.600	0	0--	—	3.33
Cedar Rapds	A	3	3	0	0	18.1	79	17	7	7	1	2	1	3	7	0	20	1	0	0	1	.000	0	0--	—	3.44
1996 Lk Elsinore	A+	14	14	3	0	92.2	384	79	38	34	5	2	2	2	33	0	93	8	0	6	3	.667	0	0--	—	3.30
Vancouver	AAA	2	2	0	0	8.1	48	12	16	10	1	0	0	0	12	0	5	1	0	0	2	.000	0	0--	—	10.80
Midland	AA	13	13	1	0	88	361	77	44	43	11	1	2	5	25	0	58	1	1	5	6	.455	0	0--	—	4.40
1997 Midland	AA	29	29	5	0	189.1	818	211	115	101	23	7	4	9	65	0	146	9	1	15	12	.556	1	0--	—	4.80
Vancouver	AAA	1	1	0	0	5	21	4	2	2	0	0	0	0	2	0	6	2	0	0	0	.000	0	0--	—	3.60
1998 Midland	AA	1	1	0	0	8.2	40	13	8	6	2	1	0	0	2	0	8	0	0	0	1	.000	0	0--	—	6.23
Vancouver	AAA	14	14	2	0	91.2	402	91	44	44	7	5	1	5	43	0	66	5	0	4	5	.444	0	0--	—	4.32
1999 Edmonton	AAA	11	11	0	0	59	243	50	31	31	6	2	2	1	17	0	55	1	0	1	5	.167	0	0--	—	4.73
1998 Anaheim	AL	15	11	0	0	74	317	70	40	38	11	2	3	3	27	1	48	0	0	6	3	.667	0	0-0	1	4.62
1999 Anaheim	AL	16	10	0	0	61.2	264	61	36	36	6	1	2	1	26	0	39	2	0	4	5	.444	0	0-0	1	5.25
2 ML YEARS		31	21	0	3	135.2	581	131	76	74	17	3	5	4	53	1	87	2	0	10	8	.556	0	0-0	2	4.91

Pat Watkins

Bats: R **Throws:** R **Pos:** PH/PR-7; RF-5; LF-4; CF-1 **Ht:** 6'2" **Wt:** 195 **Born:** 9/2/72 **Age:** 27

Year Team	Lg	G	AB	H	2B	3B	HR	(Hm	Rd)	TB	R	RBI	TBB	IBB	SO	HBP	SH	SF	SB	CS	SB%	GDP	Avg	OBP	SLG
1999 Colo Sprngs *	AAA	12	30	10	1	0	0	—	—	11	4	2	2	0	6	0	0	1	0	0	.00	0	.333	.364	.367
Carolina *	AA	88	312	93	27	1	3	—	—	131	38	40	24	0	49	6	1	3	6	5	.55	3	.298	.357	.420
1997 Cincinnati	NL	17	29	6	2	0	0	(0	0)	8	2	0	0	0	5	0	1	0	1	0	1.00	1	.207	.207	.276
1998 Cincinnati	NL	83	147	39	8	1	2	(1	1)	55	11	15	8	0	26	1	2	4	1	3	.25	3	.265	.300	.374
1999 Colorado	NL	16	19	1	0	0	0	—	—	1	2	0	2	0	5	0	1	0	0	0	.00	1	.053	.143	.053
3 ML YEARS		116	195	46	10	1	2	(1	1)	64	15	15	10	0	36	1	4	4	2	3	.40	5	.236	.271	.328

Allen Watson

Pitches: Left **Bats:** Left **Pos:** RP-34; SP-4 **Ht:** 6'1" **Wt:** 212 **Born:** 11/18/70 **Age:** 29

Year Team	Lg	G	GS	CG	GF	IP	BFP	H	R	ER	HR	SH	SF	HB	TBB	IBB	SO	WP	Bk	W	L	Pct.	ShO	Sv-Op	Hld	ERA
1999 Columbus *	AAA	2	2	0	0	7.1	31	7	5	5	2	0	0	0	2	0	5	0	0	0	0	.000	0	0--	—	6.14
1993 St. Louis	NL	16	15	0	1	86	373	90	53	44	11	6	4	3	28	2	49	2	1	6	7	.462	0	0-1	0	4.60
1994 St. Louis	NL	22	22	0	0	115.2	523	130	73	71	15	7	0	8	53	0	74	2	2	6	5	.545	0	0-0	0	5.52
1995 St. Louis	NL	21	19	0	1	114.1	491	126	68	63	17	2	1	5	41	0	49	2	2	7	9	.438	0	0-0	0	4.96
1996 San Francisco	NL	29	29	2	0	185.2	793	189	105	95	28	**18**	9	5	69	2	128	9	2	8	12	.400	0	0-0	0	4.61
1997 Anaheim	AL	35	34	0	0	199	880	220	121	109	**37**	5	6	8	73	0	141	8	2	12	12	.500	0	0-0	0	4.93
1998 Anaheim	AL	28	14	1	4	92.1	421	122	67	62	12	0	6	3	34	0	64	6	1	6	7	.462	0	0-0	0	6.04
1999 NYM-Sea-NYY		38	4	0	14	77	329	72	35	30	13	3	5	1	35	3	64	4	0	6	3	.667	0	1-2	2	3.51
1999 New York	NL	14	4	0	6	39.2	173	36	18	18	5	3	4	1	22	3	32	2	0	2	2	.500	0	1-1	1	4.08
Seattle	AL	3	0	0	2	3	19	6	9	4	5	0	1	0	3	0	2	1	0	0	1	.000	0	0-0	0	12.00

Year Team	Lg	HOW MUCH HE PITCHED						WHAT HE GAVE UP												THE RESULTS						
		G	GS	CG	GF	IP	BFP	H	R	ER	HR	SH	SF	HB	TBB	IBB	SO	WP	Bk	W	L	Pct.	ShO	Sv-Op	Hld	ERA
New York	AL	21	0	0	6	34.1	137	30	8	8	3	0	0	0	10	0	30	1	0	4	0	1.000	0	0-1	1	2.10
7 ML YEARS		189	137	3	20	870	3810	949	522	474	133	41	31	33	333	7	569	33	10	51	55	.481	0	1-3	2	4.90

Dave Weathers

Pitches: Right **Bats:** Right **Pos:** RP-63   **Ht:** 6'3" **Wt:** 231 **Born:** 9/25/69 **Age:** 30

Year Team	Lg	HOW MUCH HE PITCHED						WHAT HE GAVE UP												THE RESULTS						
		G	GS	CG	GF	IP	BFP	H	R	ER	HR	SH	SF	HB	TBB	IBB	SO	WP	Bk	W	L	Pct.	ShO	Sv-Op	Hld	ERA
1991 Toronto	AL	15	0	0	4	14.2	79	15	9	8	1	2	1	2	17	3	13	0	0	1	0	1.000	0	0-0	1	4.91
1992 Toronto	AL	2	0	0	0	3.1	15	5	3	3	1	0	0	0	2	0	3	0	0	0	0	.000	0	0-0	0	8.10
1993 Florida	NL	14	6	0	2	45.2	202	57	26	26	3	2	0	1	13	1	34	6	0	2	3	.400	0	0-0	0	5.12
1994 Florida	NL	24	24	0	0	135	621	166	87	79	13	12	4	4	59	9	72	7	1	8	12	.400	0	0-0	0	5.27
1995 Florida	NL	28	15	0	0	90.1	419	104	68	60	8	7	3	5	52	3	60	3	0	4	5	.444	0	0-0	0	5.98
1996 Fla-NYY		42	12	0	9	88.2	409	108	60	54	8	5	2	6	42	5	53	3	0	2	4	.333	0	0-0	3	5.48
1997 NYY-Cle	AL	19	1	0	5	25.2	126	38	24	24	3	2	1	1	15	0	18	3	0	1	3	.250	0	0-1	0	8.42
1998 Cin-Mil	NL	44	9	0	9	110	492	130	69	60	6	6	2	3	41	3	94	7	2	6	5	.545	0	0-1	3	4.91
1999 Milwaukee	NL	63	0	0	14	93	414	102	49	48	14	4	4	2	38	3	74	1	1	7	4	.636	0	2-6	9	4.65
1996 Florida	NL	31	8	0	8	71.1	319	85	41	36	7	5	1	4	28	4	40	2	0	2	2	.500	0	0-0	3	4.54
New York	AL	11	4	0	1	17.1	90	23	19	18	1	0	1	2	14	1	13	1	0	0	2	.000	0	0-0	0	9.35
1997 New York	AL	10	0	0	3	9	47	15	10	10	1	0	0	0	7	0	4	2	0	0	1	.000	0	0-1	0	10.00
Cleveland	AL	9	1	0	2	16.2	79	23	14	14	2	2	1	1	8	0	14	1	0	1	2	.333	0	0-0	0	7.56
1998 Cincinnati	NL	16	9	0	0	62.1	294	86	47	43	3	4	1	1	27	2	51	5	1	2	4	.333	0	0-0	0	6.21
Milwaukee	NL	28	0	0	9	47.2	198	44	22	17	3	2	1	2	14	1	43	2	1	4	1	.800	0	0-1	3	3.21
9 ML YEARS		251	67	0	43	606.1	2777	725	395	362	57	40	17	24	279	27	421	30	4	31	36	.463	0	2-8	17	5.37

Eric Weaver

Pitches: Right **Bats:** Right **Pos:** RP-8   **Ht:** 6'5" **Wt:** 230 **Born:** 8/4/73 **Age:** 26

Year Team	Lg	HOW MUCH HE PITCHED						WHAT HE GAVE UP												THE RESULTS						
		G	GS	CG	GF	IP	BFP	H	R	ER	HR	SH	SF	HB	TBB	IBB	SO	WP	Bk	W	L	Pct.	ShO	Sv-Op	Hld	ERA
1992 Vero Beach	A+	19	18	1	0	89.2	394	73	52	41	7	5	6	1	57	0	73	17	2	4	11	.267	0	0--	—	4.12
1993 Bakersfield	A+	28	27	0	0	157.2	703	135	89	75	10	2	9	2	118	2	110	16	0	6	11	.353	0	0--	—	4.28
1994 Vero Beach	A+	7	7	0	0	24	109	28	20	18	3	0	0	1	9	1	22	1	0	1	3	.250	0	0--	—	6.75
1995 San Antonio	AA	27	26	1	1	141.2	635	147	83	64	10	9	7	7	72	1	105	8	2	8	11	.421	0	0--	—	4.07
1996 San Antonio	AA	18	18	1	0	122.2	509	106	51	45	6	7	2	3	44	0	69	2	1	10	5	.667	1	0--	—	3.30
Albuquerque	AAA	13	8	0	0	46.2	225	63	39	28	5	2	1	3	22	0	38	3	0	1	4	.200	0	0--	—	5.40
1997 San Antonio	AA	13	13	2	0	84.2	363	80	43	34	4	1	4	5	38	0	60	2	0	7	2	.778	1	0--	—	3.61
Albuquerque	AAA	21	8	0	5	68.2	335	101	53	49	6	3	4	2	38	1	54	4	0	0	3	.000	0	0--	—	6.42
1998 Albuquerque	AAA	46	0	0	26	61.2	277	65	41	38	7	2	2	3	32	2	63	2	0	2	5	.286	0	3--	—	5.55
1999 Tacoma	AAA	16	3	0	5	25.2	105	22	11	11	4	0	1	1	7	0	22	1	0	1	2	.333	0	1--	—	3.86
1998 Los Angeles	NL	7	0	0	4	9.2	35	5	1	1	1	1	0	0	6	0	5	0	0	2	0	1.000	0	0-0	0	0.93
1999 Seattle	AL	8	0	0	2	9.1	52	14	12	11	2	0	0	0	8	1	14	5	0	0	1	.000	0	0-1	0	10.61
2 ML YEARS		15	0	0	6	19	87	19	13	12	3	1	0	0	14	1	19	5	0	2	1	.667	0	0-1	0	5.68

Jeff Weaver

Pitches: Right **Bats:** Right **Pos:** SP-29; RP-1   **Ht:** 6'5" **Wt:** 200 **Born:** 8/22/76 **Age:** 23

Year Team	Lg	HOW MUCH HE PITCHED						WHAT HE GAVE UP												THE RESULTS						
		G	GS	CG	GF	IP	BFP	H	R	ER	HR	SH	SF	HB	TBB	IBB	SO	WP	Bk	W	L	Pct.	ShO	Sv-Op	Hld	ERA
1998 Jamestown	A-	3	3	0	0	12	44	6	4	2	0	0	0	1	1	0	12	0	1	1	0	1.000	0	0--	—	1.50
W Michigan	A	2	2	0	0	13	46	8	3	2	1	1	1	0	0	0	21	1	0	1	0	1.000	0	0--	—	1.38
1999 Jacksonville	AA	1	1	0	0	6	22	5	2	2	0	0	0	0	0	0	6	0	0	0	0	.000	0	0--	—	3.00
1999 Detroit	AL	30	29	0	1	163.2	717	176	104	101	27	5	5	17	56	2	114	0	0	9	12	.429	0	0-0	0	5.55

Lenny Webster

Bats: Right **Throws:** Right **Pos:** C-18; PH/PR-4; DH-2   **Ht:** 5'9" **Wt:** 200 **Born:** 2/10/65 **Age:** 35

Year Team	Lg	BATTING																			BASERUNNING				PERCENTAGES		
		G	AB	H	2B	3B	HR	(Hm	Rd)	TB	R	RBI	TBB	IBB	SO	HBP	SH	SF	SB	CS	SB%	GDP	Avg	OBP	SLG		
1999 Rochester *	AAA	13	43	13	5	0	3	—	—	27	8	9	4	0	8	0	0	1	0	0	.00	1	.302	.354	.628		
1989 Minnesota	AL	14	20	6	2	0	0	(0	0)	8	3	1	3	0	2	0	0	0	0	0	.00	0	.300	.391	.400		
1990 Minnesota	AL	2	6	2	1	0	0	(0	0)	3	1	0	1	0	1	0	0	0	0	0	.00	0	.333	.429	.500		
1991 Minnesota	AL	18	34	10	1	0	3	(1	2)	20	7	8	6	0	10	0	0	1	0	0	.00	2	.294	.390	.588		
1992 Minnesota	AL	53	118	33	10	1	1	(1	0)	48	10	13	9	0	11	0	2	0	0	0	.00	3	.280	.331	.407		
1993 Minnesota	AL	49	106	21	2	0	1	(1	0)	26	14	8	11	1	8	0	0	0	1	0	1.00	1	.198	.274	.245		
1994 Montreal	NL	57	143	39	10	0	5	(2	3)	64	13	23	16	1	24	6	1	0	0	0	.00	7	.273	.370	.448		
1995 Philadelphia	NL	49	150	40	9	0	4	(1	3)	61	18	14	16	0	27	0	1	0	0	0	.00	4	.267	.337	.407		
1996 Montreal	NL	78	174	40	10	0	2	(1	1)	56	18	17	25	2	21	2	1	1	0	0	.00	10	.230	.332	.322		
1997 Baltimore	AL	98	259	66	8	1	7	(3	4)	97	29	37	22	0	46	2	3	1	0	1	.00	10	.255	.317	.375		
1998 Baltimore	AL	108	309	88	16	0	10	(6	4)	134	37	46	15	0	38	0	3	1	0	0	.00	10	.285	.317	.434		
1999 Bal-Bos	AL	22	50	6	1	0	0	(0	0)	7	1	4	10	0	7	2	0	0	0	0	.00	1	.120	.290	.140		
1999 Baltimore	AL	16	36	6	1	0	0	(0	0)	7	1	3	8	0	5	1	0	0	0	0	.00	0	.167	.333	.194		
Boston	AL	6	14	0	0	0	0	(0	0)	0	0	1	2	0	2	1	0	0	0	0	.00	0	.000	.176	.000		
11 ML YEARS		548	1369	351	70	2	33	(16	17)	524	151	171	134	4	195	12	11	4	1	3	.25	48	.256	.327	.383		

John Wehner

Bats: R **Throws:** R **Pos:** PH/PR-20; LF-12; RF-6; 3B-2; SS-2; CF-2; 2B-1 **Ht:** 6'3" **Wt:** 206 **Born:** 6/29/67 **Age:** 33

Year Team	Lg	G	AB	H	2B	3B	HR	(Hm	Rd)	TB	R	RBI	TBB	IBB	SO	HBP	SH	SF	SB	CS	SB%	GDP	Avg	OBP	SLG
1999 Altoona *	AA	4	12	2	0	0	0	—	—	2	2	2	0	0	0	1	0	0	1	1	.50	0	.167	.231	.167
Nashville *	AAA	17	58	25	3	0	8	—	—	52	14	15	3	0	6	0	0	1	0	0	.00	1	.431	.452	.897
1991 Pittsburgh	NL	37	106	36	7	0	0	(0	0)	43	15	7	7	0	17	0	0	0	3	0	1.00	0	.340	.381	.406
1992 Pittsburgh	NL	55	123	22	6	0	0	(0	0)	28	11	4	12	2	22	0	2	0	3	0	1.00	4	.179	.252	.228
1993 Pittsburgh	NL	29	35	5	0	0	0	(0	0)	5	3	0	6	1	10	0	2	0	0	0	.00	0	.143	.268	.143
1994 Pittsburgh	NL	2	4	1	1	0	0	(0	0)	2	1	3	0	0	1	0	0	0	0	0	.00	0	.250	.250	.500
1995 Pittsburgh	NL	52	107	33	0	3	0	(0	0)	39	13	5	10	1	17	0	4	2	3	1	.75	2	.308	.361	.364
1996 Pittsburgh	NL	86	139	36	9	1	2	(1	1)	53	19	13	8	1	22	0	2	0	1	5	.17	3	.259	.299	.381
1997 Florida	NL	44	36	10	2	0	0	(0	0)	12	8	2	2	0	5	1	1	0	1	0	1.00	2	.278	.333	.333
1998 Florida	NL	53	88	20	2	0	0	(0	0)	22	10	5	7	0	12	0	0	1	1	0	1.00	3	.227	.281	.250
1999 Pittsburgh	NL	39	65	12	2	0	1	(0	0)	17	6	4	7	0	12	0	3	0	1	0	1.00	1	.185	.264	.262
9 ML YEARS		397	703	175	29	4	3	(1	2)	221	86	43	59	5	118	1	14	3	13	6	.68	15	.249	.307	.314

Walt Weiss

Bats: Both **Throws:** Right **Pos:** SS-102; PH/PR-13 **Ht:** 6'0" **Wt:** 188 **Born:** 11/28/63 **Age:** 36

Year Team	Lg	G	AB	H	2B	3B	HR	(Hm	Rd)	TB	R	RBI	TBB	IBB	SO	HBP	SH	SF	SB	CS	SB%	GDP	Avg	OBP	SLG
1987 Oakland	AL	16	26	12	4	0	0	(0	0)	16	3	1	2	0	2	0	1	0	1	2	.33	0	.462	.500	.615
1988 Oakland	AL	147	452	113	17	3	3	(0	3)	145	44	39	35	1	56	9	8	7	4	4	.50	9	.250	.312	.321
1989 Oakland	AL	84	236	55	11	0	3	(2	1)	75	30	21	21	0	39	1	5	0	6	1	.86	5	.233	.298	.318
1990 Oakland	AL	138	445	118	17	1	2	(1	1)	143	50	35	46	5	53	4	6	4	9	3	.75	7	.265	.337	.321
1991 Oakland	AL	40	133	30	6	1	0	(0	0)	38	15	13	12	0	14	0	1	2	6	0	1.00	3	.226	.286	.286
1992 Oakland	AL	103	316	67	5	2	0	(0	0)	76	36	21	43	1	39	1	11	4	6	3	.67	10	.212	.305	.241
1993 Florida	NL	158	500	133	14	2	1	(0	1)	154	50	39	79	13	73	3	5	4	7	3	.70	5	.266	.367	.308
1994 Colorado	NL	110	423	106	11	4	1	(1	0)	128	58	32	56	0	58	0	4	3	12	7	.63	6	.251	.336	.303
1995 Colorado	NL	137	427	111	17	3	1	(0	1)	137	65	25	98	8	57	5	6	1	15	3	.83	7	.260	.403	.321
1996 Colorado	NL	155	517	146	20	2	8	(5	3)	194	89	48	80	5	78	6	14	6	10	2	.83	9	.282	.381	.375
1997 Colorado	NL	121	393	106	23	5	4	(2	2)	151	52	38	66	3	56	2	7	1	5	2	.71	7	.270	.377	.384
1998 Atlanta	NL	96	347	97	18	2	0	(0	0)	119	64	27	59	0	53	3	12	3	7	1	.88	4	.280	.386	.343
1999 Atlanta	NL	110	279	63	13	4	2	(0	2)	90	38	29	35	1	48	3	6	4	7	3	.70	1	.226	.315	.323
13 ML YEARS		1415	4494	1157	176	29	25	(11	14)	1466	594	368	632	37	626	37	86	39	95	34	.74	73	.257	.351	.326

Bob Wells

Pitches: Right **Bats:** Right **Pos:** RP-76 **Ht:** 6'0" **Wt:** 200 **Born:** 11/1/66 **Age:** 33

Year Team	Lg	G	GS	CG	GF	IP	BFP	H	R	ER	HR	SH	SF	HB	TBB	IBB	SO	WP	Bk	W	L	Pct.	ShO	Sv-Op	Hld	ERA
1994 Phi-Sea		7	0	0	2	9	38	8	2	2	0	0	0	1	4	0	6	0	0	2	0	1.000	0	0-0	0	2.00
1995 Seattle	AL	30	4	0	3	76.2	358	88	51	49	11	1	5	3	39	3	38	1	0	4	3	.571	0	0-1	0	5.75
1996 Seattle	AL	36	16	1	6	130.2	574	141	78	77	25	3	4	6	46	5	94	0	0	12	7	.632	1	0-0	1	5.30
1997 Seattle	AL	46	1	0	19	67.1	304	88	49	43	11	1	2	3	18	1	51	1	0	2	0	1.000	0	2-4	5	5.75
1998 Seattle	AL	30	0	0	4	51.2	228	54	38	35	12	2	1	2	16	1	29	1	0	2	2	.500	0	0-1	1	6.10
1999 Minnesota	AL	76	0	0	18	87.1	364	79	41	37	8	5	3	5	28	4	44	4	0	8	3	.727	0	1-5	17	3.81
1994 Philadelphia	NL	6	0	0	2	5	21	4	1	1	0	0	0	1	3	0	3	0	0	1	0	1.000	0	0-0	0	1.80
Seattle	AL	1	0	0	0	4	17	4	1	1	0	0	0	0	1	0	3	0	0	1	0	1.000	0	0-0	0	2.25
6 ML YEARS		225	21	1	52	422.2	1866	458	259	243	67	12	15	20	151	14	262	7	0	30	15	.667	1	3-11	24	5.17

David Wells

Pitches: Left **Bats:** Left **Pos:** SP-34 **Ht:** 6'4" **Wt:** 225 **Born:** 5/20/63 **Age:** 37

Year Team	Lg	G	GS	CG	GF	IP	BFP	H	R	ER	HR	SH	SF	HB	TBB	IBB	SO	WP	Bk	W	L	Pct.	ShO	Sv-Op	Hld	ERA
1987 Toronto	AL	18	2	0	6	29.1	132	37	14	13	0	1	0	0	12	0	32	4	0	4	3	.571	0	1-2	3	3.99
1988 Toronto	AL	41	0	0	15	64.1	279	65	36	33	12	2	2	2	31	4	56	6	2	3	5	.375	0	4-6	4	4.62
1989 Toronto	AL	54	0	0	19	86.1	352	66	25	23	5	3	2	0	28	7	78	6	3	7	4	.636	0	2-9	8	2.40
1990 Toronto	AL	43	25	0	8	189	759	165	72	66	14	9	2	2	45	3	115	7	1	11	6	.647	0	3-3	3	3.14
1991 Toronto	AL	40	28	2	3	198.1	811	188	88	82	24	6	6	2	49	1	106	10	3	15	10	.600	0	1-2	3	3.72
1992 Toronto	AL	41	14	0	14	120	529	138	84	72	16	3	4	8	36	6	62	3	1	7	9	.438	0	2-4	3	5.40
1993 Detroit	AL	32	30	0	0	187	776	183	93	87	26	3	3	7	42	6	139	13	0	11	9	.550	0	0-0	1	4.19
1994 Detroit	AL	16	16	5	0	111.1	464	113	54	49	13	3	1	2	24	6	71	5	0	5	7	.417	1	0-0	0	3.96
1995 Det-Cin		29	29	6	0	203	839	194	88	73	23	7	3	2	53	9	133	7	2	16	8	.667	0	0-0	0	3.24
1996 Baltimore	AL	34	34	3	0	224.1	946	247	132	128	32	8	14	7	51	7	130	4	2	11	14	.440	0	0-0	0	5.14
1997 New York	AL	32	32	5	0	218	922	239	109	102	24	7	3	6	45	0	156	8	0	16	10	.615	2	0-0	0	4.21
1998 New York	AL	30	30	8	0	214.1	851	195	86	83	29	2	2	1	29	0	163	2	0	18	4	.818	5	0-0	0	3.49
1999 Toronto	AL	34	34	7	0	231.2	987	246	132	124	32	6	6	6	62	2	169	1	0	17	10	.630	1	0-0	0	4.82
1995 Detroit	AL	18	18	3	0	130.1	539	120	54	44	17	3	2	2	37	5	83	6	1	10	3	.769	0	0-0	0	3.04
Cincinnati	NL	11	11	3	0	72.2	300	74	34	29	6	4	1	0	16	4	50	1	1	6	5	.545	0	0-0	0	3.59
13 ML YEARS		444	274	36	65	2077	8647	2076	1013	935	250	60	48	45	507	56	1410	76	14	141	99	.588	9	13-26	30	4.05

Kip Wells

Pitches: Right **Bats:** Right **Pos:** SP-7   **Ht:** 6'3" **Wt:** 196 **Born:** 4/21/77 **Age:** 23

Year Team	Lg	G	GS	CG	GF	IP	BFP	H	R	ER	HR	SH	SF	HB	TBB	IBB	SO	WP	Bk	W	L	Pct.	ShO	Sv-Op	Hld	ERA
1999 Winston-Sal	A+	14	14	0	0	85.2	353	78	39	34	4	2	2	6	34	1	95	7	0	5	6	.455	0	0--	—	3.57
Birmingham	AA	11	11	0	0	70.1	283	49	24	23	5	0	0	4	31	0	44	1	1	8	2	.800	0	0--	—	2.94
1999 Chicago	AL	7	7	0	0	35.2	153	33	17	16	2	0	2	3	15	0	29	1	2	4	1	.800	0	0-0	0	4.04

Vernon Wells

Bats: Right **Throws:** Right **Pos:** CF-24   **Ht:** 6'1" **Wt:** 210 **Born:** 12/8/78 **Age:** 21

Year Team	Lg	G	AB	H	2B	3B	HR	(Hm	Rd)	TB	R	RBI	TBB	IBB	SO	HBP	SH	SF	SB	CS	SB%	GDP	Avg	OBP	SLG
1997 St.Cathrnes	A-	66	264	81	12	1	10	—	—	133	52	31	30	1	44	1	0	2	8	6	.57	2	.307	.377	.504
1998 Hagerstown	A	134	509	145	35	2	11	—	—	217	86	65	49	1	84	1	1	2	13	8	.62	8	.285	.348	.426
1999 Dunedin	A+	70	265	91	16	2	11	—	—	144	43	43	26	0	34	1	0	1	13	2	.87	6	.343	.403	.543
Knoxville	AA	26	106	36	6	2	3	—	—	55	18	17	12	1	15	0	0	2	6	2	.75	0	.340	.400	.519
Syracuse	AAA	33	129	40	8	1	4	—	—	62	20	21	10	0	22	1	0	3	5	1	.83	3	.310	.357	.481
1999 Toronto	AL	24	88	23	5	0	1	(1	0)	31	8	8	4	0	18	0	0	0	1	1	.50	6	.261	.293	.352

Turk Wendell

Pitches: Right **Bats:** Left **Pos:** RP-80   **Ht:** 6'2" **Wt:** 205 **Born:** 5/19/67 **Age:** 33

Year Team	Lg	G	GS	CG	GF	IP	BFP	H	R	ER	HR	SH	SF	HB	TBB	IBB	SO	WP	Bk	W	L	Pct.	ShO	Sv-Op	Hld	ERA
1993 Chicago	NL	7	4	0	1	22.2	98	24	13	11	0	2	0	0	8	1	15	1	1	1	2	.333	0	0-0	0	4.37
1994 Chicago	NL	6	2	0	1	14.1	76	22	20	19	3	2	1	0	10	1	9	1	0	0	1	.000	0	0-0	0	11.93
1995 Chicago	NL	43	0	0	17	60.1	270	71	35	33	11	3	3	2	24	4	50	1	0	3	1	.750	0	0-0	3	4.92
1996 Chicago	NL	70	0	0	49	79.1	339	58	26	25	8	3	1	3	44	4	75	3	2	4	5	.444	0	18-21	6	2.84
1997 ChC-NYM	NL	65	0	0	21	76.1	345	68	42	37	7	4	3	2	53	6	64	4	0	3	5	.375	0	5-7	2	4.36
1998 New York	NL	66	0	0	17	76.2	319	62	25	25	4	2	1	2	33	9	58	1	0	5	1	.833	0	4-8	11	2.93
1999 New York	NL	80	0	0	14	85.2	369	80	31	29	9	2	1	2	37	8	77	2	1	5	4	.556	0	3-6	21	3.05
1997 Chicago	NL	52	0	0	18	60	269	53	32	28	4	3	3	1	39	5	54	4	0	3	5	.375	0	4-5	2	4.20
New York	NL	13	0	0	3	16.1	76	15	10	9	3	1	0	1	14	1	10	0	0	0	0	.000	0	1-2	0	4.96
7 ML YEARS		337	6	0	120	415.1	1816	385	192	179	42	18	10	11	209	33	348	13	4	21	19	.525	0	30-42	43	3.88

Don Wengert

Pitches: Right **Bats:** Right **Pos:** RP-10; SP-1   **Ht:** 6'3" **Wt:** 205 **Born:** 11/6/69 **Age:** 30

Year Team	Lg	G	GS	CG	GF	IP	BFP	H	R	ER	HR	SH	SF	HB	TBB	IBB	SO	WP	Bk	W	L	Pct.	ShO	Sv-Op	Hld	ERA
1999 Omaha *	AAA	16	2	0	7	41	167	41	20	19	5	2	1	4	9	1	24	1	1	4	0	1.000	0	1--	—	4.17
Columbus *	AAA	6	2	0	0	15.1	73	25	13	13	4	0	0	1	3	1	5	1	0	0	1	.000	0	0--	—	7.63
Richmond *	AAA	1	1	0	0	6	25	7	3	3	1	1	0	1	0	0	3	1	0	0	0	.000	0	0--	—	4.50
1995 Oakland	AL	19	0	0	10	29.2	129	30	14	11	3	1	1	1	12	2	16	1	0	1	1	.500	0	0-0	1	3.34
1996 Oakland	AL	36	25	1	2	161.1	725	200	102	100	29	3	5	6	60	5	75	4	0	7	11	.389	1	0-0	3	5.58
1997 Oakland	AL	49	12	1	16	134	612	177	96	90	21	5	7	8	41	4	68	2	0	5	11	.313	0	2-3	0	6.04
1998 SD-ChC	NL	31	6	0	9	63.1	288	76	38	37	10	1	0	3	28	0	46	1	0	1	5	.167	0	1-1	0	5.26
1999 Kansas City	AL	11	1	0	2	24.1	116	41	26	25	6	0	2	0	5	0	10	0	0	0	1	.000	0	0-3	0	9.25
1998 San Diego	NL	10	0	0	3	13.2	64	21	9	9	2	0	0	0	5	0	5	0	0	0	0	.000	0	1-1	0	5.93
Chicago	NL	21	6	0	6	49.2	224	55	29	28	8	1	0	3	23	0	41	1	0	1	5	.167	0	0-0	0	5.07
5 ML YEARS		146	44	2	39	412.2	1870	524	276	263	69	10	15	18	146	11	215	8	0	14	29	.326	1	3-7	4	5.74

John Wetteland

Pitches: Right **Bats:** Right **Pos:** RP-62   **Ht:** 6'2" **Wt:** 215 **Born:** 8/21/66 **Age:** 33

Year Team	Lg	G	GS	CG	GF	IP	BFP	H	R	ER	HR	SH	SF	HB	TBB	IBB	SO	WP	Bk	W	L	Pct.	ShO	Sv-Op	Hld	ERA
1989 Los Angeles	NL	31	12	0	7	102.2	411	81	46	43	8	4	2	0	34	4	96	16	1	5	8	.385	0	1-1	1	3.77
1990 Los Angeles	NL	22	5	0	7	43	190	44	28	23	6	1	1	4	17	3	36	8	0	2	4	.333	0	0-1	0	4.81
1991 Los Angeles	NL	6	0	0	3	9	36	5	2	0	0	0	1	1	3	0	9	1	0	1	0	1.000	0	0-0	0	0.00
1992 Montreal	NL	67	0	0	58	83.1	347	64	27	27	6	5	1	4	36	3	99	4	0	4	4	.500	0	37-46	0	2.92
1993 Montreal	NL	70	0	0	58	85.1	344	58	17	13	3	5	1	2	28	3	113	7	0	9	3	.750	0	43-49	0	1.37
1994 Montreal	NL	52	0	0	43	63.2	261	46	22	20	5	5	4	3	21	4	68	0	0	4	6	.400	0	25-35	0	2.83
1995 New York	AL	60	0	0	56	61.1	233	40	22	20	6	1	2	0	14	2	66	1	0	1	5	.167	0	31-37	0	2.93
1996 New York	AL	62	0	0	58	63.2	265	54	23	20	9	1	2	0	21	4	69	1	0	2	3	.400	0	43-47	0	2.83
1997 Texas	AL	61	0	0	58	65	259	43	18	14	5	1	1	0	21	3	63	1	0	7	2	.778	0	31-37	0	1.94
1998 Texas	AL	63	0	0	59	62	249	47	17	14	6	2	2	0	14	1	72	1	0	3	1	.750	0	42-47	0	2.03
1999 Texas	AL	62	0	0	59	66	281	67	30	27	9	1	5	0	19	1	60	0	0	4	4	.500	0	43-50	0	3.68
11 ML YEARS		556	17	0	466	705	2876	549	252	221	63	26	22	14	228	28	751	40	1	42	40	.512	0	296-350	1	2.82

Dan Wheeler

Pitches: Right **Bats:** Right **Pos:** SP-6   **Ht:** 6'3" **Wt:** 222 **Born:** 12/10/77 **Age:** 22

Year Team	Lg	G	GS	CG	GF	IP	BFP	H	R	ER	HR	SH	SF	HB	TBB	IBB	SO	WP	Bk	W	L	Pct.	ShO	Sv-Op	Hld	ERA
1997 Hudson Val	A-	15	15	0	0	84	351	75	38	28	2	1	1	3	17	0	81	4	2	6	7	.462	0	0--	—	3.00

		HOW MUCH HE PITCHED						WHAT HE GAVE UP												THE RESULTS						
Year Team	Lg	G	GS	CG	GF	IP	BFP	H	R	ER	HR	SH	SF	HB	TBB	IBB	SO	WP	Bk	W	L	Pct.	ShO	Sv-Op	Hld	ERA
1998 Chston-SC	A	29	29	3	0	181	763	206	96	89	16	7	6	11	29	0	136	4	0	12	14	.462	1	0--	—	4.43
1999 Orlando	AA	9	9	0	0	58	236	56	27	21	7	0	2	4	8	0	53	1	1	3	0	1.000	0	0--	—	3.26
Durham	AAA	14	14	2	0	82.1	369	103	59	45	16	1	3	4	25	0	58	1	0	7	5	.583	1	0--	—	4.92
1999 Tampa Bay	AL	6	6	0	0	30.2	136	35	20	20	7	1	0	0	13	1	32	1	0	0	4	.000	0	0-0	0	5.87

Matt Whisenant

Pitches: Left **Bats:** Right **Pos:** RP-67 **Ht:** 6'3" **Wt:** 215 **Born:** 6/8/71 **Age:** 29

		HOW MUCH HE PITCHED						WHAT HE GAVE UP												THE RESULTS						
Year Team	Lg	G	GS	CG	GF	IP	BFP	H	R	ER	HR	SH	SF	HB	TBB	IBB	SO	WP	Bk	W	L	Pct.	ShO	Sv-Op	Hld	ERA
1997 Fla-KC		28	0	0	5	21.2	105	19	13	11	0	1	0	3	18	0	20	3	0	1	0	1.000	0	0-0	5	4.57
1998 Kansas City	AL	70	0	0	23	60.2	267	61	37	33	3	1	5	3	33	2	45	9	0	2	1	.667	0	2-5	16	4.90
1999 KC-SD		67	0	0	25	54.1	244	50	34	34	4	1	0	7	36	2	37	1	0	4	5	.444	0	1-5	11	5.63
1997 Florida	NL	4	0	0	2	2.2	19	4	6	5	0	1	0	0	6	0	4	0	0	0	0	.000	0	0-0	0	16.88
Kansas City		24	0	0	3	19	86	15	7	6	0	0	0	3	12	0	16	3	0	1	0	1.000	0	0-0	5	2.84
1999 Kansas City	AL	48	0	0	21	39.2	184	40	28	28	4	1	0	7	26	1	27	1	0	4	4	.500	0	1-4	6	6.35
San Diego	NL	19	0	0	4	14.2	60	10	6	6	0	0	0	0	10	1	10	0	0	0	1	.000	0	0-1	5	3.68
3 ML YEARS		165	0	0	53	136.2	616	130	84	78	7	3	5	13	87	4	102	13	0	7	6	.538	0	3-10	32	5.14

Devon White

Bats: Both **Throws:** Right **Pos:** CF-128; PH/PR-9; DH-1 **Ht:** 6'2" **Wt:** 190 **Born:** 12/29/62 **Age:** 37

		BATTING																	BASERUNNING				PERCENTAGES		
Year Team	Lg	G	AB	H	2B	3B	HR	(Hm	Rd)	TB	R	RBI	TBB	IBB	SO	HBP	SH	SF	SB	CS	SB%	GDP	Avg	OBP	SLG
1985 California	AL	21	7	1	0	0	0	(0	0)	1	7	0	1	0	3	1	0	0	3	1	.75	0	.143	.333	.143
1986 California	AL	29	51	12	1	1	1	(0	1)	18	8	3	6	0	8	0	0	0	6	0	1.00	0	.235	.316	.353
1987 California	AL	159	639	168	33	5	24	(11	13)	283	103	87	39	2	135	2	14	2	32	11	.74	8	.263	.306	.443
1988 California	AL	122	455	118	22	2	11	(3	8)	177	76	51	23	1	84	2	5	1	17	8	.68	5	.259	.297	.389
1989 California	AL	156	642	156	18	13	12	(9	3)	236	86	56	31	3	129	2	7	2	44	16	.73	12	.245	.282	.371
1990 California	AL	125	443	96	17	3	11	(6	5)	152	57	44	44	5	116	3	10	3	21	6	.78	6	.217	.290	.343
1991 Toronto	AL	156	642	181	40	10	17	(9	8)	292	110	60	55	1	135	7	5	6	33	10	.77	7	.282	.342	.455
1992 Toronto	AL	153	641	159	26	7	17	(7	10)	250	98	60	47	0	133	5	0	3	37	4	.90	9	.248	.303	.390
1993 Toronto	AL	146	598	163	42	6	15	(10	5)	262	116	52	57	1	127	7	3	3	34	4	**.89**	3	.273	.341	.438
1994 Toronto	AL	100	403	109	24	6	13	(5	8)	184	67	49	21	3	80	5	4	2	11	3	.79	4	.270	.313	.457
1995 Toronto	AL	101	427	121	23	5	10	(4	6)	184	61	53	29	1	97	5	1	3	11	2	.85	5	.283	.334	.431
1996 Florida	NL	146	552	151	37	6	17	(5	12)	251	77	84	38	6	99	8	4	9	22	6	.79	8	.274	.325	.455
1997 Florida	NL	74	265	65	13	1	6	(2	4)	98	37	34	32	2	65	7	0	4	13	5	.72	3	.245	.338	.370
1998 Arizona	NL	146	563	157	32	1	22	(11	11)	257	84	85	42	4	102	9	7	6	22	8	.73	9	.279	.335	.456
1999 Los Angeles	NL	134	474	127	20	2	14	(8	6)	193	60	68	39	2	88	11	0	2	19	5	.79	10	.268	.337	.407
15 ML YEARS		1768	6796	1784	348	68	190	(91	99)	2838	1047	786	504	31	1401	74	60	46	325	89	.79	89	.263	.318	.418

Gabe White

Pitches: Left **Bats:** Left **Pos:** RP-50 **Ht:** 6'2" **Wt:** 200 **Born:** 11/20/71 **Age:** 28

		HOW MUCH HE PITCHED						WHAT HE GAVE UP												THE RESULTS						
Year Team	Lg	G	GS	CG	GF	IP	BFP	H	R	ER	HR	SH	SF	HB	TBB	IBB	SO	WP	Bk	W	L	Pct.	ShO	Sv-Op	Hld	ERA
1994 Montreal	NL	7	5	0	2	23.2	106	24	16	16	4	1	1	1	11	0	17	0	0	1	1	.500	0	1-1	0	6.08
1995 Montreal	NL	19	1	0	8	25.2	115	26	21	20	7	2	3	1	9	0	25	0	0	1	2	.333	0	0-0	0	7.01
1997 Cincinnati	NL	12	6	0	2	41	168	39	20	20	6	3	2	1	8	1	25	0	0	2	2	.500	0	1-1	3	4.39
1998 Cincinnati	NL	69	3	0	29	98.2	404	86	46	44	17	2	2	1	27	6	83	3	0	5	5	.500	0	9-13	6	4.01
1999 Cincinnati	NL	50	0	0	18	61	261	68	31	30	13	2	1	2	14	1	61	0	0	1	2	.333	0	0-1	3	4.43
5 ML YEARS		157	15	0	59	250	1054	243	134	130	47	10	9	6	69	8	211	3	0	10	12	.455	0	11-16	12	4.68

Rick White

Pitches: Right **Bats:** Right **Pos:** RP-62; SP-1 **Ht:** 6'4" **Wt:** 230 **Born:** 12/23/68 **Age:** 31

		HOW MUCH HE PITCHED						WHAT HE GAVE UP												THE RESULTS						
Year Team	Lg	G	GS	CG	GF	IP	BFP	H	R	ER	HR	SH	SF	HB	TBB	IBB	SO	WP	Bk	W	L	Pct.	ShO	Sv-Op	Hld	ERA
1994 Pittsburgh	NL	43	5	0	23	75.1	317	79	35	32	9	7	5	6	17	3	38	2	2	4	5	.444	0	6-9	3	3.82
1995 Pittsburgh	NL	15	9	0	2	55	247	66	33	29	3	3	3	2	18	0	29	2	0	2	3	.400	0	0-0	0	4.75
1998 Tampa Bay	AL	38	3	0	12	68.2	289	66	32	29	8	0	3	2	23	2	39	3	0	2	6	.250	0	0-0	2	3.80
1999 Tampa Bay	AL	63	1	0	11	108	480	132	56	49	8	2	5	1	38	5	81	3	0	5	3	.625	0	0-2	4	4.08
4 ML YEARS		159	18	0	48	307	1333	343	156	139	28	12	16	11	96	10	187	10	2	13	17	.433	0	6-11	9	4.07

Rondell White

Bats: Right **Throws:** Right **Pos:** LF-102; CF-73; PH/PR-3 **Ht:** 6'0" **Wt:** 210 **Born:** 2/23/72 **Age:** 28

		BATTING																	BASERUNNING				PERCENTAGES		
Year Team	Lg	G	AB	H	2B	3B	HR	(Hm	Rd)	TB	R	RBI	TBB	IBB	SO	HBP	SH	SF	SB	CS	SB%	GDP	Avg	OBP	SLG
1993 Montreal	NL	23	73	19	3	1	2	(1	1)	30	9	15	7	0	16	0	2	1	1	2	.33	2	.260	.321	.411
1994 Montreal	NL	40	97	27	10	1	2	(1	1)	45	16	13	9	0	18	3	0	0	1	1	.50	1	.278	.358	.464
1995 Montreal	NL	130	474	140	33	4	13	(6	7)	220	87	57	41	1	87	6	0	4	25	5	.83	11	.295	.356	.464
1996 Montreal	NL	88	334	98	19	4	6	(2	4)	143	35	41	22	0	53	2	0	1	14	6	.70	11	.293	.340	.428
1997 Montreal	NL	151	592	160	29	5	28	(9	19)	283	84	82	31	3	111	10	1	4	16	8	.67	18	.270	.316	.478
1998 Montreal	NL	97	357	107	21	2	17	(9	8)	183	54	58	30	2	57	7	0	3	16	7	.70	7	.300	.363	.513
1999 Montreal	NL	138	539	168	26	6	22	(10	12)	272	83	64	32	2	85	11	0	6	10	6	.63	17	.312	.359	.505
7 ML YEARS		667	2466	719	141	23	90	(38	52)	1176	368	330	172	8	427	39	3	19	83	35	.70	67	.292	.345	.477

Mark Whiten

Bats: Both   **Throws:** Right   **Pos:** LF-5; CF-2; PH/PR-1   **Ht:** 6'3"   **Wt:** 235   **Born:** 11/25/66   **Age:** 33

								BATTING										BASERUNNING				PERCENTAGES		
Year Team	Lg	G	AB	H	2B	3B	HR	(Hm | Rd)	TB	R	RBI	TBB	IBB	SO	HBP	SH	SF	SB	CS	SB%	GDP	Avg	OBP	SLG
1999 Buffalo *	AAA	48	175	49	10	0	6	—	—	77	32	19	22	1	38	0	0	6	3	1	.75	6	.280	.360	.440
1990 Toronto	AL	33	88	24	1	1	2	(1 | 1)	33	12	7	7	0	14	0	0	1	2	0	1.00	2	.273	.323	.375
1991 Tor-Cle	AL	116	407	99	18	7	9	(4 | 5)	158	46	45	30	2	85	3	0	5	4	3	.57	13	.243	.297	.388
1992 Cleveland	AL	148	508	129	19	4	9	(6 | 3)	183	73	43	72	10	102	2	3	3	16	12	.57	12	.254	.347	.360
1993 St. Louis	NL	152	562	142	13	4	25	(12 | 13)	238	81	99	58	9	110	2	0	4	15	8	.65	11	.253	.323	.423
1994 St. Louis	NL	92	334	98	18	2	14	(6 | 8)	162	57	53	37	9	75	1	0	2	10	5	.67	8	.293	.364	.485
1995 Bos-Phi		92	320	77	13	1	12	(5 | 7)	128	51	47	39	1	86	1	0	1	8	0	1.00	9	.241	.324	.400
1996 Phi-Atl-Sea		136	412	108	20	1	22	(9 | 13)	196	76	71	70	6	127	3	0	1	17	9	.65	12	.262	.372	.476
1997 New York	AL	69	215	57	11	0	5	(4 | 1)	83	34	24	30	5	47	2	1	0	4	2	.67	5	.265	.360	.386
1998 Cleveland	AL	88	226	64	14	0	6	(3 | 3)	96	31	29	29	0	60	3	1	0	2	1	.67	7	.283	.372	.425
1999 Cleveland	AL	8	25	4	1	0	1	(0 | 1)	8	2	4	3	0	4	0	0	0	0	0	.00	1	.160	.250	.320
1991 Toronto	AL	46	149	33	4	3	2	(2 | 0)	49	12	19	11	1	35	1	0	3	0	1	.00	5	.221	.274	.329
Cleveland		70	258	66	14	4	7	(2 | 5)	109	34	26	19	1	50	2	0	2	4	2	.67	8	.256	.310	.422
1995 Boston		32	108	20	3	0	1	(0 | 1)	26	13	10	8	0	23	0	0	1	1	0	1.00	4	.185	.239	.241
Philadelphia	NL	60	212	57	10	1	11	(5 | 6)	102	38	37	31	1	63	1	0	0	7	0	1.00	4	.269	.365	.481
1996 Philadelphia	NL	60	182	43	8	0	7	(4 | 3)	72	33	21	33	2	62	1	0	0	13	3	.81	9	.236	.356	.396
Atlanta		36	90	23	5	1	3	(1 | 2)	39	12	17	16	0	25	0	0	1	2	5	.29	2	.256	.364	.433
Seattle	AL	40	140	42	7	0	12	(4 | 8)	85	31	33	21	4	40	2	0	0	2	1	.67	1	.300	.399	.607
10 ML YEARS		934	3097	802	128	20	105	(50 | 55)	1285	463	422	375	42	710	17	5	17	78	40	.66	81	.259	.341	.415

Matt Whiteside

Pitches: Right   **Bats:** Right   **Pos:** RP-10   **Ht:** 6'0"   **Wt:** 205   **Born:** 8/8/67   **Age:** 32

		HOW MUCH HE PITCHED						WHAT HE GAVE UP										THE RESULTS					
Year Team	Lg	G	GS	CG	GF	IP	BFP	H	R	ER	HR	SH	SF	HB	TBB	IBB	SO	WP	Bk	W	L	Pct.	ShO	Sv-Op	Hld	ERA
1999 Las Vegas *	AAA	47	3	1	23	89.2	398	99	59	51	13	1	4	3	29	3	88	2	0	9	5	.643	1	7--	—	5.12
1992 Texas	AL	20	0	0	8	28	118	26	8	6	1	0	1	0	11	2	13	2	0	1	1	.500	0	4-4	0	1.93
1993 Texas	AL	60	0	0	10	73	305	78	37	35	7	2	1	1	23	6	39	0	2	2	1	.667	0	1-5	14	4.32
1994 Texas	AL	47	0	0	16	61	272	68	40	34	6	3	2	1	28	3	37	1	0	2	2	.500	0	1-3	7	5.02
1995 Texas	AL	40	0	0	18	53	223	48	24	24	5	2	3	1	19	2	46	4	0	5	4	.556	0	3-4	7	4.08
1996 Texas	AL	14	0	0	7	32.1	148	43	24	24	8	1	2	0	11	1	15	1	0	0	0	.000	0	0-0	1	6.68
1997 Texas	AL	42	1	0	8	72.2	323	85	45	41	4	2	5	3	26	3	44	3	2	4	1	.800	0	0-4	2	5.08
1998 Philadelphia	NL	10	0	0	1	18	85	27	18	17	6	0	0	0	5	0	14	0	1	1	1	.500	0	0-0	0	8.50
1999 San Diego	NL	10	0	0	4	11	55	19	17	17	1	1	1	0	5	0	9	1	0	1	0	1.000	0	0-0	0	13.91
8 ML YEARS		243	1	0	72	349	1529	394	213	198	38	11	15	6	128	17	217	12	5	16	11	.593	0	9-20	31	5.11

Bob Wickman

Pitches: Right   **Bats:** Right   **Pos:** RP-71   **Ht:** 6'1"   **Wt:** 227   **Born:** 2/6/69   **Age:** 31

		HOW MUCH HE PITCHED						WHAT HE GAVE UP										THE RESULTS					
Year Team	Lg	G	GS	CG	GF	IP	BFP	H	R	ER	HR	SH	SF	HB	TBB	IBB	SO	WP	Bk	W	L	Pct.	ShO	Sv-Op	Hld	ERA
1992 New York	AL	8	8	0	0	50.1	213	51	25	23	2	1	3	0	20	0	21	3	0	6	1	.857	0	0-0	0	4.11
1993 New York	AL	41	19	1	9	140	629	156	82	72	13	4	1	5	69	7	70	2	0	14	4	.778	1	4-8	2	4.63
1994 New York	AL	53	0	0	19	70	286	54	26	24	3	0	5	1	27	3	56	2	0	5	4	.556	0	6-10	11	3.09
1995 New York	AL	63	1	0	14	80	347	77	38	36	6	4	1	5	33	3	51	2	0	2	4	.333	0	1-10	21	4.05
1996 NYY-Mil	AL	70	0	0	18	95.2	429	106	50	47	10	2	4	5	44	3	75	4	0	7	1	.875	0	0-4	10	4.42
1997 Milwaukee	AL	74	0	0	20	95.2	405	89	32	29	8	6	2	3	41	7	78	8	0	7	6	.538	0	1-5	28	2.73
1998 Milwaukee	NL	72	0	0	51	82.1	357	79	38	34	5	10	3	4	39	2	71	1	0	6	9	.400	0	25-32	9	3.72
1999 Milwaukee	NL	71	0	0	63	74.1	331	75	31	28	6	3	2	2	38	6	60	2	0	3	8	.273	0	37-45	0	3.39
1996 New York	AL	58	0	0	14	79	358	94	41	41	7	1	4	5	34	1	61	3	0	4	1	.800	0	0-3	6	4.67
Milwaukee		12	0	0	4	16.2	71	12	9	6	3	1	0	0	10	2	14	1	0	3	0	1.000	0	0-1	4	3.24
8 ML YEARS		452	28	1	194	688.1	2997	687	322	293	53	30	21	27	311	31	482	24	0	50	37	.575	1	74-114	81	3.83

Chris Widger

Bats: Right   **Throws:** Right   **Pos:** C-118; PH/PR-6   **Ht:** 6'3"   **Wt:** 215   **Born:** 5/21/71   **Age:** 29

								BATTING										BASERUNNING				PERCENTAGES		
Year Team	Lg	G	AB	H	2B	3B	HR	(Hm	Rd)	TB	R	RBI	TBB	IBB	SO	HBP	SH	SF	SB	CS	SB%	GDP	Avg	OBP	SLG
1995 Seattle	AL	23	45	9	0	0	1	(1	0)	12	2	2	3	0	11	0	0	1	0	0	.00	0	.200	.245	.267
1996 Seattle	AL	8	11	2	0	0	0	(0	0)	2	1	0	0	0	5	1	0	0	0	0	.00	0	.182	.250	.182
1997 Montreal	NL	91	278	65	20	3	7	(4	3)	112	30	37	22	1	59	1	2	2	2	0	1.00	7	.234	.290	.403
1998 Montreal	NL	125	417	97	18	1	15	(6	9)	162	36	53	29	2	85	0	0	4	6	1	.86	5	.233	.281	.388
1999 Montreal	NL	124	383	101	24	1	14	(11	3)	169	42	56	28	0	86	7	0	1	1	4	.20	5	.264	.325	.441
5 ML YEARS		371	1134	274	62	5	37	(22	15)	457	111	148	82	3	246	9	2	6	9	5	.64	17	.242	.297	.403

Marc Wilkins

Pitches: Right   **Bats:** Right   **Pos:** RP-46   **Ht:** 5'11"   **Wt:** 221   **Born:** 10/21/70   **Age:** 29

		HOW MUCH HE PITCHED						WHAT HE GAVE UP										THE RESULTS					
Year Team	Lg	G	GS	CG	GF	IP	BFP	H	R	ER	HR	SH	SF	HB	TBB	IBB	SO	WP	Bk	W	L	Pct.	ShO	Sv-Op	Hld	ERA
1999 Altoona *	AA	4	0	0	2	6	26	4	2	1	0	0	0	0	4	1	5	0	0	0	1	.000	0	0--	—	1.50
Nashville *	AAA	8	0	0	6	11.1	45	9	3	1	0	0	2	0	3	1	8	0	0	1	1	.500	0	3--	—	0.79
1996 Pittsburgh	NL	47	2	0	11	75	331	75	36	32	6	3	4	6	36	6	62	5	0	4	3	.571	0	1-5	4	3.84
1997 Pittsburgh	NL	70	0	0	21	75.2	310	65	33	31	7	4	0	4	33	2	47	5	0	9	5	.643	0	2-4	15	3.69

246

Year Team	Lg	G	GS	CG	GF	IP	BFP	H	R	ER	HR	SH	SF	HB	TBB	IBB	SO	WP	Bk	W	L	Pct.	ShO	Sv-Op	Hld	ERA
1998 Pittsburgh	NL	16	0	0	6	15.1	67	13	6	6	1	0	1	2	9	2	17	1	1	0	0	.000	0	0-1	4	3.52
1999 Pittsburgh	NL	46	0	0	14	51	227	49	28	24	3	4	2	4	26	1	44	4	1	2	3	.400	0	0-0	8	4.24
4 ML YEARS		179	2	0	52	217	935	202	103	93	17	11	7	16	104	11	170	15	2	15	11	.577	0	3-10	31	3.86

Rick Wilkins

Bats: Left **Throws:** Right **Pos:** PH/PR-3; C-1   **Ht:** 6'2" **Wt:** 215 **Born:** 6/4/67 **Age:** 33

								BATTING											BASERUNNING				PERCENTAGES		
Year Team	Lg	G	AB	H	2B	3B	HR	(Hm	Rd)	TB	R	RBI	TBB	IBB	SO	HBP	SH	SF	SB	CS	SB%	GDP	Avg	OBP	SLG
1999 Albuquerque *	AAA	92	300	76	8	1	8	—	—	110	39	33	29	2	87	1	2	2	1	8	.11	7	.253	.319	.367
1991 Chicago	NL	86	203	45	9	0	6	(2	4)	72	21	22	19	2	56	6	7	0	3	3	.50	3	.222	.307	.355
1992 Chicago	NL	83	244	66	9	1	8	(3	5)	101	20	22	28	7	53	0	1	1	0	2	.00	6	.270	.344	.414
1993 Chicago	NL	136	446	135	23	1	30	(10	20)	250	78	73	50	13	99	3	0	1	2	1	.67	6	.303	.376	.561
1994 Chicago	NL	100	313	71	25	2	7	(4	3)	121	44	39	40	5	86	2	1	2	4	3	.57	3	.227	.317	.387
1995 ChC-Hou	NL	65	202	41	3	0	7	(3	4)	65	30	19	46	2	61	1	0	2	0	0	.00	9	.203	.351	.322
1996 Hou-SF	NL	136	411	100	18	2	14	(6	8)	164	53	59	67	13	121	1	0	10	0	3	.00	5	.243	.344	.399
1997 SF-Sea		71	202	40	6	0	7	(2	5)	67	20	27	18	0	67	0	0	4	0	0	.00	0	.198	.259	.332
1998 Sea-NYM		24	56	10	1	1	1	(1	0)	16	8	5	6	0	16	0	0	1	0	0	.00	1	.179	.254	.286
1999 Los Angeles	NL	3	4	0	0	0	0	(0	0)	0	0	0	0	0	2	0	0	0	0	0	.00	0	.000	.000	.000
1995 Chicago	NL	50	162	31	2	0	6	(3	3)	51	24	14	36	1	51	1	0	1	0	0	.00	8	.191	.340	.315
Houston	NL	15	40	10	1	0	1	(0	1)	14	6	5	10	1	10	0	0	1	0	0	.00	1	.250	.392	.350
1996 Houston	NL	84	254	54	8	2	6	(3	3)	84	34	23	46	10	81	1	0	5	0	1	.00	1	.213	.330	.331
San Francisco	NL	52	157	46	10	0	8	(3	5)	80	19	36	21	3	40	0	0	5	0	2	.00	4	.293	.366	.510
1997 San Francisco	NL	66	190	37	5	0	6	(1	5)	60	18	23	17	0	65	0	0	3	0	0	.00	0	.195	.257	.316
Seattle	AL	5	12	3	1	0	1	(1	0)	7	2	4	1	0	2	0	0	1	0	0	.00	0	.250	.286	.583
1998 Seattle	AL	19	41	8	1	1	1	(1	0)	14	5	4	4	0	14	0	0	1	0	0	.00	1	.195	.261	.341
New York	NL	5	15	2	0	0	0	(0	0)	2	3	1	2	0	2	0	0	0	0	0	.00	0	.133	.235	.133
9 ML YEARS		704	2081	508	94	7	80	(31	49)	856	274	266	274	42	561	13	9	21	9	12	.43	33	.244	.333	.411

Bernie Williams

Bats: Both **Throws:** Right **Pos:** CF-155; PH/PR-4; DH-2   **Ht:** 6'2" **Wt:** 205 **Born:** 9/13/68 **Age:** 31

								BATTING											BASERUNNING				PERCENTAGES		
Year Team	Lg	G	AB	H	2B	3B	HR	(Hm	Rd)	TB	R	RBI	TBB	IBB	SO	HBP	SH	SF	SB	CS	SB%	GDP	Avg	OBP	SLG
1991 New York	AL	85	320	76	19	4	3	(1	2)	112	43	34	48	0	57	1	2	3	10	5	.64	4	.238	.336	.350
1992 New York	AL	62	261	73	14	2	5	(3	2)	106	39	26	29	1	36	1	2	0	7	6	.54	5	.280	.354	.406
1993 New York	AL	139	567	152	31	4	12	(5	7)	227	67	68	53	4	106	4	1	3	9	9	.50	17	.268	.333	.400
1994 New York	AL	108	408	118	29	1	12	(4	8)	185	80	57	61	2	54	3	1	2	16	9	.64	11	.289	.384	.453
1995 New York	AL	144	563	173	29	9	18	(7	11)	274	93	82	75	1	98	5	2	3	8	6	.57	12	.307	.392	.487
1996 New York	AL	143	551	168	26	7	29	(12	17)	295	108	102	82	8	72	0	1	7	17	4	.81	15	.305	.391	.535
1997 New York	AL	129	509	167	35	6	21	(13	8)	277	107	100	73	7	80	1	0	8	15	8	.65	10	.328	.408	.544
1998 New York	AL	128	499	169	30	5	26	(14	12)	287	101	97	74	9	81	1	0	4	15	9	.63	19	.339	.422	.575
1999 New York	AL	158	591	202	28	6	25	(11	14)	317	116	115	100	17	95	1	0	5	9	10	.47	11	.342	.435	.536
9 ML YEARS		1096	4269	1298	241	44	151	(70	81)	2080	754	681	595	49	679	17	9	35	106	66	.62	104	.304	.389	.487

Brian Williams

Pitches: Right **Bats:** Right **Pos:** RP-50   **Ht:** 6'2" **Wt:** 225 **Born:** 2/15/69 **Age:** 31

Year Team	Lg	G	GS	CG	GF	IP	BFP	H	R	ER	HR	SH	SF	HB	TBB	IBB	SO	WP	Bk	W	L	Pct.	ShO	Sv-Op	Hld	ERA
1991 Houston	NL	2	2	0	0	12	49	11	5	5	2	0	0	1	4	0	4	0	0	0	1	.000	0	0-0	0	3.75
1992 Houston	NL	16	16	0	0	96.1	413	92	44	42	10	7	3	0	42	1	54	2	1	7	6	.538	0	0-0	0	3.92
1993 Houston	NL	42	5	0	12	82	357	76	48	44	7	5	3	4	38	4	56	9	2	4	4	.500	0	3-6	2	4.83
1994 Houston	NL	20	13	0	2	78.1	384	112	64	50	9	7	5	4	41	4	49	3	1	6	5	.545	0	0-0	0	5.74
1995 San Diego	NL	44	6	0	7	72	337	79	54	48	3	7	1	8	38	4	75	7	1	3	10	.231	0	0-2	7	6.00
1996 Detroit	AL	40	17	2	17	121	579	145	107	91	21	5	6	6	85	2	72	8	0	3	10	.231	1	2-4	0	6.77
1997 Baltimore	AL	13	0	0	8	24	110	20	8	8	0	0	1	0	18	0	14	1	0	0	0	.000	0	0-1	0	3.00
1999 Houston	NL	50	0	0	15	67.1	303	69	35	33	4	5	4	5	35	2	53	7	0	2	1	.667	0	0-2	2	4.41
8 ML YEARS		227	59	2	61	553	2532	604	365	321	56	36	23	28	301	17	377	37	5	25	37	.403	1	5-15	12	5.22

Gerald Williams

Bats: R **Throws:** R **Pos:** LF-120; RF-32; PH/PR-29; CF-1   **Ht:** 6'2" **Wt:** 187 **Born:** 8/10/66 **Age:** 33

								BATTING											BASERUNNING				PERCENTAGES		
Year Team	Lg	G	AB	H	2B	3B	HR	(Hm	Rd)	TB	R	RBI	TBB	IBB	SO	HBP	SH	SF	SB	CS	SB%	GDP	Avg	OBP	SLG
1992 New York	AL	15	27	8	2	0	3	(2	1)	19	7	6	0	0	3	0	0	0	2	0	1.00	0	.296	.296	.704
1993 New York	AL	42	67	10	2	3	0	(0	0)	18	11	6	1	0	14	2	0	1	2	0	1.00	2	.149	.183	.269
1994 New York	AL	57	86	25	8	0	4	(2	2)	45	19	13	4	0	17	0	0	1	1	3	.25	6	.291	.319	.523
1995 New York	AL	100	182	45	18	2	6	(4	2)	85	33	28	22	1	34	1	0	3	4	2	.67	4	.247	.327	.467
1996 NYY-Mil	AL	125	325	82	19	4	5	(3	2)	124	43	34	19	3	57	5	3	5	10	9	.53	8	.252	.299	.382
1997 Milwaukee	AL	155	566	143	32	2	10	(3	7)	209	73	41	19	1	90	6	5	5	23	9	.72	9	.253	.282	.369
1998 Atlanta	NL	129	266	81	19	2	10	(5	5)	134	46	44	17	1	48	3	2	1	11	5	.69	5	.305	.352	.504
1999 Atlanta	NL	143	422	116	24	1	17	(10	7)	193	76	58	31	1	67	6	4	3	19	11	.63	8	.275	.335	.457
1996 New York	AL	99	233	63	15	4	5	(3	2)	101	37	30	15	2	39	4	1	5	7	8	.47	7	.270	.319	.433
Milwaukee	AL	26	92	19	4	0	0	(0	0)	23	6	4	4	1	18	1	2	0	3	1	.75	1	.207	.247	.250
8 ML YEARS		766	1941	510	124	14	55	(26	29)	827	308	240	115	2	330	23	14	18	72	39	.65	42	.263	.309	.426

Jeff Williams

Pitches: Left **Bats:** Right **Pos:** SP-3; RP-2 | **Ht:** 6'0" **Wt:** 185 **Born:** 6/6/72 **Age:** 28

Year Team	Lg	G	GS	CG	GF	IP	BFP	H	R	ER	HR	SH	SF	HB	TBB	IBB	SO	WP	Bk	W	L	Pct.	ShO	Sv-Op	Hld	ERA
1997 San Antonio	AA	5	5	0	0	28.1	119	30	17	17	2	2	2	0	7	0	14	3	1	2	1	.667	0	0--	—	5.40
San Berndno	A+	18	18	0	0	116	472	101	52	40	8	4	2	2	34	0	72	7	3	10	4	.714	0	0--	—	3.10
1998 San Antonio	AA	7	7	0	0	41.2	182	43	19	12	3	1	3	0	13	1	35	1	1	3	0	1.000	0	0--	—	2.59
Albuquerque	AAA	21	21	0	0	121	556	160	87	67	14	3	3	6	49	0	93	6	4	8	8	.500	0	0--	—	4.98
1999 Albuquerque	AAA	42	14	1	10	125.2	558	151	77	70	14	4	8	9	47	2	86	3	0	9	7	.563	1	4--	—	5.01
1999 Los Angeles	NL	5	3	0	1	17.2	73	12	10	8	2	1	0	0	9	0	7	0	0	2	0	1.000	0	0-0	0	4.08

Matt Williams

Bats: Right **Throws:** Right **Pos:** 3B-153; PH/PR-1 | **Ht:** 6'2" **Wt:** 214 **Born:** 11/28/65 **Age:** 34

Year Team	Lg	G	AB	H	2B	3B	HR	(Hm	Rd)	TB	R	RBI	TBB	IBB	SO	HBP	SH	SF	SB	CS	SB%	GDP	Avg	OBP	SLG
1987 San Francisco	NL	84	245	46	9	2	8	(5	3)	83	28	21	16	4	68	1	3	1	4	3	.57	5	.188	.240	.339
1988 San Francisco	NL	52	156	32	6	1	8	(7	1)	64	17	19	8	0	41	2	3	1	0	1	.00	7	.205	.251	.410
1989 San Francisco	NL	84	292	59	18	1	18	(10	8)	133	31	50	14	1	72	2	1	2	1	2	.33	5	.202	.242	.455
1990 San Francisco	NL	159	617	171	27	2	33	(20	13)	301	87	122	33	9	138	7	2	5	7	4	.64	13	.277	.319	.488
1991 San Francisco	NL	157	589	158	24	5	34	(17	17)	294	72	98	33	6	128	6	0	7	5	5	.50	11	.268	.310	.499
1992 San Francisco	NL	146	529	120	13	5	20	(9	11)	203	58	66	39	11	109	6	1	4	7	7	.50	15	.227	.286	.384
1993 San Francisco	NL	145	579	170	33	4	38	(19	19)	325	105	110	27	4	80	4	0	9	1	3	.25	12	.294	.325	.561
1994 San Francisco	NL	112	445	119	16	3	43	(20	23)	270	74	96	33	7	87	2	0	3	1	0	1.00	11	.267	.319	.607
1995 San Francisco	NL	76	283	95	17	1	23	(9	14)	183	53	65	30	8	58	2	0	3	2	0	1.00	8	.336	.399	.647
1996 San Francisco	NL	105	404	122	16	1	22	(13	9)	206	69	85	39	9	91	6	0	6	1	2	.33	10	.302	.367	.510
1997 Cleveland	AL	151	596	157	32	3	32	(7	25)	291	86	105	34	4	108	4	0	2	12	4	.75	14	.263	.307	.488
1998 Arizona	NL	135	510	136	26	1	20	(11	9)	224	72	71	43	8	102	3	0	1	5	1	.83	19	.267	.327	.439
1999 Arizona	NL	154	627	190	37	2	35	(17	18)	336	98	142	41	9	93	2	0	8	2	0	1.00	17	.303	.344	.536
13 ML YEARS		1560	5872	1575	274	31	334	(164	170)	2913	850	1050	390	80	1175	47	9	50	48	32	.60	147	.268	.316	.496

Mike Williams

Pitches: Right **Bats:** Right **Pos:** RP-58 | **Ht:** 6'2" **Wt:** 209 **Born:** 7/29/68 **Age:** 31

Year Team	Lg	G	GS	CG	GF	IP	BFP	H	R	ER	HR	SH	SF	HB	TBB	IBB	SO	WP	Bk	W	L	Pct.	ShO	Sv-Op	Hld	ERA
1992 Philadelphia	NL	5	5	1	0	28.2	121	29	20	17	3	1	1	0	7	0	.5	0	0	1	1	.500	0	0-0	0	5.34
1993 Philadelphia	NL	17	4	0	2	51	221	50	32	30	5	1	0	0	22	2	33	2	0	1	3	.250	0	0-0	0	5.29
1994 Philadelphia	NL	12	8	0	0	50.1	222	61	31	28	7	2	3	0	20	3	29	0	0	2	4	.333	0	0-0	0	5.01
1995 Philadelphia	NL	33	8	0	7	87.2	367	78	37	32	10	5	3	3	29	2	57	7	0	3	3	.500	0	0-0	1	3.29
1996 Philadelphia	NL	32	29	0	1	167	732	188	107	101	25	6	5	6	67	6	103	16	1	6	14	.300	0	0-0	0	5.44
1997 Kansas City	AL	10	0	0	4	14	70	20	11	10	1	0	1	1	8	1	10	0	0	0	2	.000	0	1-1	0	6.43
1998 Pittsburgh	NL	37	1	0	9	51	204	39	12	11	1	1	2	0	16	4	59	3	0	4	2	.667	0	0-1	1	1.94
1999 Pittsburgh	NL	58	0	0	50	58.1	269	63	36	33	9	2	1	1	37	7	76	4	0	3	4	.429	0	23-28	1	5.09
8 ML YEARS		204	55	1	75	508	2206	528	286	262	61	18	16	11	206	25	372	32	1	20	33	.377	0	24-30	10	4.64

Reggie Williams

Bats: B **Throws:** R **Pos:** RF-18; PH/PR-11; LF-4; DH-3; CF-3 | **Ht:** 6'1" **Wt:** 180 **Born:** 5/5/66 **Age:** 34

Year Team	Lg	G	AB	H	2B	3B	HR	(Hm	Rd)	TB	R	RBI	TBB	IBB	SO	HBP	SH	SF	SB	CS	SB%	GDP	Avg	OBP	SLG
1988 Everett	A-	60	223	56	8	1	3	—	—	75	52	29	47	0	43	3	0	2	36	10	.78	5	.251	.385	.336
1989 Clinton	A	68	236	46	9	2	3	—	—	68	38	18	29	0	66	3	5	1	14	9	.61	1	.195	.290	.288
Boise	A-	42	153	41	5	1	3	—	—	57	33	14	24	0	29	2	0	1	18	5	.78	2	.268	.372	.373
1990 Quad City	A	58	189	46	11	2	3	—	—	70	50	12	39	0	60	4	2	1	24	6	.80	2	.243	.382	.370
1991 Palm Spring	A+	14	44	13	1	0	1	—	—	17	10	2	21	0	15	1	1	0	6	5	.55	0	.295	.530	.386
Midland	AA	83	319	99	12	3	1	—	—	120	77	30	62	2	67	0	5	3	21	9	.70	3	.310	.419	.376
1992 Edmonton	AAA	139	519	141	26	9	3	—	—	194	96	64	88	2	110	3	7	8	44	14	.76	9	.272	.375	.374
1993 Vancouver	AAA	130	481	132	17	6	2	—	—	167	92	53	88	2	99	5	9	6	50	17	.75	7	.274	.388	.347
1994 Albuquerque	AAA	104	288	90	15	8	4	—	—	133	55	42	33	1	62	0	1	2	21	10	.68	6	.313	.381	.462
1995 Albuquerque	AAA	66	234	73	15	5	6	—	—	116	44	29	30	0	46	1	1	3	6	4	.60	3	.312	.388	.496
1996 Albuquerque	AAA	92	352	101	25	2	6	—	—	148	60	42	37	5	72	1	5	1	17	7	.71	6	.287	.355	.420
1997 Vancouver	AAA	12	40	10	3	0	2	—	—	19	10	5	6	0	13	0	0	0	3	2	.60	0	.250	.348	.475
1998 Vancouver	AAA	100	373	105	25	5	5	—	—	155	58	39	53	2	98	6	1	2	13	12	.52	2	.282	.378	.416
1999 Edmonton	AAA	35	137	43	9	1	6	—	—	72	25	31	16	1	29	0	0	2	3	2	.60	4	.314	.381	.526
1992 California	AL	14	26	6	1	1	0	(0	0)	9	5	2	1	0	10	0	0	2	0	2	.00	0	.231	.259	.346
1995 Los Angeles	NL	15	11	1	0	0	0	(0	0)	1	2	1	2	0	3	0	0	0	0	0	.00	0	.091	.231	.091
1998 Anaheim	AL	29	36	13	1	0	1	(0	1)	17	7	5	7	0	11	1	1	0	3	3	.50	0	.361	.477	.472
1999 Anaheim	AL	30	63	14	1	2	1	(0	1)	22	8	6	5	0	21	1	1	1	2	1	.67	3	.222	.286	.349
4 ML YEARS		88	136	34	3	3	2	(0	2)	49	22	14	15	0	45	2	2	1	5	6	.45	3	.250	.331	.360

Todd Williams

Pitches: Right **Bats:** Right **Pos:** RP-13 | **Ht:** 6'3" **Wt:** 210 **Born:** 2/13/71 **Age:** 29

Year Team	Lg	G	GS	CG	GF	IP	BFP	H	R	ER	HR	SH	SF	HB	TBB	IBB	SO	WP	Bk	W	L	Pct.	ShO	Sv-Op	Hld	ERA
1999 Indianapols *	AAA	38	0	0	33	42.1	174	38	24	24	3	2	2	5	13	0	35	7	0	1	3	.250	0	24--	—	5.10
Tacoma *	AAA	1	0	0	1	1.2	5	1	0	0	0	0	0	0	0	0	0	0	0	0	0	.000	0	1--	—	0.00

Year Team	Lg	G	GS	CG	GF	IP	BFP	H	R	ER	HR	SH	SF	HB	TBB	IBB	SO	WP	Bk	W	L	Pct.	ShO	Sv-Op	Hld	ERA
1995 Los Angeles	NL	16	0	0	5	19.1	83	19	11	11	3	3	1	0	7	2	8	0	0	2	2	.500	0	0-1	0	5.12
1998 Cincinnati	NL	6	0	0	2	9.1	50	15	8	8	1	0	0	0	6	0	4	0	0	0	1	.000	0	0-0	0	7.71
1999 Seattle	AL	13	0	0	7	9.2	47	11	5	5	1	1	0	1	7	0	7	0	0	0	0	.000	0	0-0	0	4.66
3 ML YEARS		35	0	0	14	38.1	180	45	24	24	5	4	1	1	20	2	19	0	0	2	3	.400	0	0-1	0	5.63

Woody Williams

Pitches: Right **Bats:** Right **Pos:** SP-33   **Ht:** 6'0" **Wt:** 195 **Born:** 8/19/66 **Age:** 33

		HOW MUCH HE PITCHED						WHAT HE GAVE UP												THE RESULTS						
Year Team	Lg	G	GS	CG	GF	IP	BFP	H	R	ER	HR	SH	SF	HB	TBB	IBB	SO	WP	Bk	W	L	Pct.	ShO	Sv-Op	Hld	ERA
1993 Toronto	AL	30	0	0	9	37	172	40	18	18	2	2	1	1	22	3	24	2	1	3	1	.750	0	0-2	4	4.38
1994 Toronto	AL	38	0	0	14	59.1	253	44	24	24	5	1	2	2	33	1	56	4	0	1	3	.250	0	0-0	5	3.64
1995 Toronto	AL	23	3	0	10	53.2	232	44	23	22	6	2	0	2	28	1	41	0	0	1	2	.333	0	0-1	1	3.69
1996 Toronto	AL	12	10	1	0	59	255	64	33	31	8	2	1	1	21	1	43	2	0	4	5	.444	0	0-0	0	4.73
1997 Toronto	AL	31	31	0	0	194.2	833	201	98	94	31	6	8	5	66	3	124	7	0	9	14	.391	0	0-0	0	4.35
1998 Toronto	AL	32	32	1	0	209.2	894	196	112	104	36	5	6	2	81	3	151	2	1	10	9	.526	1	0-0	0	4.46
1999 San Diego	NL	33	33	0	0	208.1	887	213	106	102	33	9	9	2	73	5	137	9	0	12	12	.500	0	0-0	0	4.41
7 ML YEARS		199	109	2	33	821.2	3526	802	414	395	121	27	27	15	324	17	576	26	2	40	46	.465	1	0-3	10	4.33

Scott Williamson

Pitches: Right **Bats:** Right **Pos:** RP-62   **Ht:** 6'0" **Wt:** 185 **Born:** 2/17/76 **Age:** 24

		HOW MUCH HE PITCHED						WHAT HE GAVE UP												THE RESULTS						
Year Team	Lg	G	GS	CG	GF	IP	BFP	H	R	ER	HR	SH	SF	HB	TBB	IBB	SO	WP	Bk	W	L	Pct.	ShO	Sv-Op	Hld	ERA
1997 Billings	R+	13	13	2	0	86	346	66	25	17	5	1	2	4	23	0	101	12	2	8	2	.800	1	0- -	—	1.78
1998 Chattanooga	AA	18	18	0	0	100	420	85	49	42	4	2	6	3	46	4	105	13	2	4	5	.444	0	0- -	—	3.78
Indianapolis	AAA	5	5	0	0	20.2	87	20	9	8	2	0	0	1	9	0	17	0	0	0	0	.000	0	0- -	—	3.48
1999 Cincinnati	NL	62	0	0	40	93.1	366	54	29	25	8	5	2	1	43	6	107	13	0	12	7	.632	0	19-26	5	2.41

Craig Wilson

Bats: R **Throws:** R **Pos:** 3B-72; SS-22; PH/PR-10; 2B-7; DH-1; 1B-1   **Ht:** 6'0" **Wt:** 185 **Born:** 9/3/70 **Age:** 29

		BATTING									BASERUNNING				PERCENTAGES		
Year Team	Lg	G	AB	H	2B	3B	HR	(Hm | Rd)	TB	R	RBI	TBB	IBB	SO	HBP	SH	SF	SB	CS	SB%	GDP	Avg	OBP	SLG

Year Team	Lg	G	AB	H	2B	3B	HR	(Hm	Rd)	TB	R	RBI	TBB	IBB	SO	HBP	SH	SF	SB	CS	SB%	GDP	Avg	OBP	SLG
1993 South Bend	A	132	455	118	27	2	5	—	—	164	56	59	49	2	50	8	7	6	4	4	.50	16	.259	.338	.360
1994 Pr William	A+	131	496	131	36	4	4	—	—	187	70	66	58	2	44	6	5	6	1	2	.33	16	.264	.345	.377
1995 Birmingham	AA	132	471	136	19	1	4	—	—	169	56	46	43	0	44	5	10	2	2	2	.50	21	.289	.353	.359
1996 Nashville	AAA	44	123	22	4	1	1	—	—	31	13	6	10	0	15	0	5	1	0	0	.00	6	.179	.239	.252
Birmingham	AA	58	202	57	9	0	3	—	—	75	36	26	40	1	28	1	6	4	1	1	.50	7	.282	.397	.371
1997 Nashville	AAA	137	453	123	20	2	6	—	—	165	71	42	48	1	31	1	12	0	4	4	.50	19	.272	.343	.364
1998 Calgary	AAA	120	432	132	21	1	14	—	—	197	67	69	37	1	41	3	9	5	4	2	.67	13	.306	.361	.456
1998 Chicago	AL	13	47	22	5	0	3	(1	2)	36	14	10	3	0	6	0	2	1	1	0	1.00	0	.468	.490	.766
1999 Chicago	AL	98	252	60	8	1	4	(0	4)	82	28	26	23	0	22	0	6	1	1	1	.50	5	.238	.301	.325
2 ML YEARS		111	299	82	13	1	7	(1	6)	118	42	36	26	0	28	0	8	2	2	1	.67	5	.274	.330	.395

Dan Wilson

Bats: Right **Throws:** Right **Pos:** C-121; PH/PR-8; 1B-5   **Ht:** 6'3" **Wt:** 190 **Born:** 3/25/69 **Age:** 31

Year Team	Lg	G	AB	H	2B	3B	HR	(Hm	Rd)	TB	R	RBI	TBB	IBB	SO	HBP	SH	SF	SB	CS	SB%	GDP	Avg	OBP	SLG
1992 Cincinnati	NL	12	25	9	1	0	0	(0	0)	10	2	3	3	0	8	0	0	0	0	0	.00	2	.360	.429	.400
1993 Cincinnati	NL	36	76	17	3	0	0	(0	0)	20	6	8	9	4	16	0	2	1	0	0	.00	3	.224	.302	.263
1994 Seattle	AL	91	282	61	14	2	3	(1	2)	88	24	27	10	0	57	1	8	2	1	2	.33	11	.216	.244	.312
1995 Seattle	AL	119	399	111	22	3	9	(5	4)	166	40	51	33	1	63	2	5	1	2	1	.67	12	.278	.336	.416
1996 Seattle	AL	138	491	140	24	0	18	(7	11)	218	51	83	32	2	88	3	9	5	1	2	.33	15	.285	.330	.444
1997 Seattle	AL	146	508	137	31	1	15	(9	6)	215	66	74	39	1	72	5	8	3	7	2	.78	12	.270	.326	.423
1998 Seattle	AL	96	325	82	17	1	9	(6	3)	128	39	44	24	0	56	5	8	6	2	1	.67	6	.252	.308	.394
1999 Seattle	AL	123	414	110	23	2	7	(3	4)	158	46	38	29	4	83	2	10	2	5	0	1.00	10	.266	.315	.382
8 ML YEARS		761	2520	667	135	9	61	(31	30)	1003	274	328	179	12	443	18	50	20	18	8	.69	70	.265	.316	.398

Enrique Wilson

Bats: B **Throws:** R **Pos:** 3B-61; SS-35; 2B-21; PH/PR-21; DH-1   **Ht:** 5'11" **Wt:** 170 **Born:** 7/27/75 **Age:** 24

Year Team	Lg	G	AB	H	2B	3B	HR	(Hm	Rd)	TB	R	RBI	TBB	IBB	SO	HBP	SH	SF	SB	CS	SB%	GDP	Avg	OBP	SLG
1992 Twins	R	13	44	15	1	0	0	—	—	16	12	8	4	0	4	4	0	1	3	0	1.00	0	.341	.384	.364
1993 Elizabethtn	R+	58	197	57	8	4	13	—	—	112	42	50	14	1	18	6	0	2	5	4	.56	1	.289	.352	.569
1994 Columbus	A	133	512	143	28	12	10	—	—	225	82	72	44	5	34	6	0	4	21	13	.62	7	.279	.341	.439
1995 Kinston	A+	117	464	124	24	7	6	—	—	180	55	52	25	2	38	2	4	10	18	19	.49	10	.267	.301	.388
1996 Canton-Akrn	AA	117	484	147	17	5	5	—	—	189	70	50	31	2	46	4	0	7	23	16	.59	9	.304	.346	.390
Buffalo	AAA	3	8	4	1	0	0	—	—	5	1	0	1	0	1	0	0	0	2	2	.50	1	.500	.556	.625
1997 Buffalo	AAA	118	451	138	20	3	11	—	—	197	78	39	42	2	41	5	4	4	9	8	.53	9	.306	.369	.437
1998 Buffalo	AAA	56	221	62	13	0	4	—	—	87	40	23	19	0	21	0	3	2	8	3	.73	6	.281	.335	.394
1997 Cleveland	AL	5	15	5	0	0	0	(0	0)	5	2	1	0	0	2	0	0	0	0	0	.00	0	.333	.333	.333
1998 Cleveland	AL	32	90	29	6	0	2	(1	1)	41	13	12	4	0	8	1	1	1	2	4	.33	1	.322	.354	.456
1999 Cleveland	AL	113	332	87	22	1	2	(1	1)	117	41	24	25	1	41	1	4	6	5	4	.56	12	.262	.310	.352
3 ML YEARS		150	437	121	28	1	4	(2	2)	163	56	37	29	1	51	2	5	7	7	8	.47	13	.277	.320	.373

Preston Wilson

Bats: R **Throws:** R **Pos:** CF-111; LF-23; RF-15; PH/PR-14   **Ht:** 6'2" **Wt:** 193 **Born:** 7/19/74 **Age:** 25

								BATTING												BASERUNNING				PERCENTAGES		
Year Team	Lg	G	AB	H	2B	3B	HR	(Hm	Rd)	TB	R	RBI	TBB	IBB	SO	HBP	SH	SF	SB	CS	SB%	GDP	Avg	OBP	SLG
1993 Kingsport	R+	66	259	60	9	0	16	—	—	117	44	48	24	0	75	3	1	1	6	2	.75	6	.232	.303	.452
Pittsfield	A-	8	29	16	5	1	1	—	—	26	6	12	2	0	7	1	0	1	1	0	1.00	0	.552	.576	.897
1994 Capital Cty	A	131	474	108	17	4	14	—	—	175	55	58	20	0	135	3	0	3	13	10	.57	4	.228	.262	.369
1995 Capital Cty	A	111	442	119	26	5	20	—	—	215	70	61	19	2	114	9	1	3	20	6	.77	4	.269	.311	.486
1996 St. Lucie	A+	23	85	15	3	0	1	—	—	21	6	7	8	0	21	2	0	0	1	1	.50	3	.176	.263	.247
1997 St. Lucie	A+	63	245	60	12	1	11	—	—	107	32	48	8	0	66	1	0	4	3	4	.43	4	.245	.267	.437
Binghamton	AA	70	259	74	12	1	19	—	—	145	37	47	21	0	71	2	0	3	7	1	.88	5	.286	.340	.560
1998 Norfolk	AAA	18	73	18	5	1	1	—	—	28	9	9	2	0	22	1	0	1	1	1	.50	2	.247	.273	.384
Charlotte	AAA	94	356	99	25	3	25	—	—	205	71	77	34	0	121	2	0	4	14	6	.70	6	.278	.341	.576
1998 NYM-Fla	NL	22	51	8	2	0	1	(1	0)	13	7	3	6	0	21	1	2	0	1	1	.50	0	.157	.259	.255
1999 Florida	NL	149	482	135	21	4	26	(8	18)	242	67	71	46	3	156	9	0	6	11	4	.73	15	.280	.350	.502
1998 New York	NL	8	20	6	2	0	0	(0	0)	8	3	2	2	0	8	0	0	0	1	1	.50	0	.300	.364	.400
Florida	NL	14	31	2	0	0	1	(1	0)	5	4	1	4	0	13	1	2	0	0	0	.00	0	.065	.194	.161
2 ML YEARS		171	533	143	23	4	27	(9	18)	255	74	74	52	3	177	10	2	6	12	5	.71	15	.268	.341	.478

Vance Wilson

Bats: Right **Throws:** Right **Pos:** C-1   **Ht:** 5'11" **Wt:** 190 **Born:** 3/17/73 **Age:** 27

								BATTING												BASERUNNING				PERCENTAGES		
Year Team	Lg	G	AB	H	2B	3B	HR	(Hm	Rd)	TB	R	RBI	TBB	IBB	SO	HBP	SH	SF	SB	CS	SB%	GDP	Avg	OBP	SLG
1994 Pittsfield	A-	44	166	51	12	0	2	—	—	69	22	20	5	2	27	5	0	2	4	1	.80	1	.307	.343	.416
1995 Capital Cty	A	91	324	81	11	0	6	—	—	110	34	32	19	1	45	8	1	2	4	3	.57	6	.250	.306	.340
1996 St. Lucie	A+	93	311	76	14	2	6	—	—	112	29	44	31	2	41	6	0	4	2	4	.33	7	.244	.321	.360
1997 Binghamton	AA	92	322	89	17	0	15	—	—	151	46	40	20	0	46	5	3	1	2	5	.29	6	.276	.328	.469
1998 Mets	R	10	28	10	5	0	2	—	—	21	5	9	0	0	0	1	0	1	0	1	.00	2	.357	.367	.750
St. Lucie	A+	4	16	1	0	0	0	—	—	1	0	0	0	0	5	0	0	0	0	0	.00	0	.063	.063	.063
Norfolk	AAA	46	154	40	3	0	4	—	—	55	18	16	9	0	29	1	3	0	0	3	.00	5	.260	.305	.357
1999 Norfolk	AAA	15	53	14	3	0	3	—	—	26	10	5	4	2	8	1	0	0	1	0	1.00	4	.264	.328	.491
1999 New York	NL	1	0	0	0	0	0	(0	0)	0	0	0	0	0	0	0	0	0	0	0	.00	0	.000	.000	.000

Joe Winkelsas

Pitches: Right **Bats:** Right **Pos:** RP-1   **Ht:** 6'3" **Wt:** 188 **Born:** 9/14/73 **Age:** 26

		HOW MUCH HE PITCHED						WHAT HE GAVE UP												THE RESULTS						
Year Team	Lg	G	GS	CG	GF	IP	BFP	H	R	ER	HR	SH	SF	HB	TBB	IBB	SO	WP	Bk	W	L	Pct.	ShO	Sv-Op	Hld	ERA
1996 Danville	R+	8	0	0	6	11.1	54	11	10	9	0	0	0	4	4	0	9	2	1	1	1	.500	0	2--		7.15
1997 Macon	A	38	0	0	15	62.2	242	44	17	14	1	3	0	4	13	0	45	4	2	3	2	.600	0	5--		2.01
Durham	A+	13	0	0	8	19	93	24	18	15	0	5	2	4	11	1	17	1	0	1	4	.200	0	1--		7.11
1998 Danville	A+	50	0	0	36	69	298	66	26	17	3	7	0	3	24	8	53	0	0	6	9	.400	0	22--		2.22
Greenville	AA	4	0	0	4	4.1	20	3	2	2	0	0	0	4	0	3	0	0	0	0	.000	0	0--		4.15
1999 Greenville	AA	55	0	0	40	62.1	280	71	32	26	5	2	0	2	30	6	38	3	1	4	4	.500	0	12--	—	3.75
1999 Atlanta	NL	1	0	0	0	0.1	6	4	2	2	0	1	0	0	1	1	0	0	0	0	0	.000	0	0-0	0	54.00

Randy Winn

Bats: Both **Throws:** Right **Pos:** CF-77; PH/PR-5   **Ht:** 6'2" **Wt:** 193 **Born:** 6/9/74 **Age:** 26

								BATTING												BASERUNNING				PERCENTAGES		
Year Team	Lg	G	AB	H	2B	3B	HR	(Hm	Rd)	TB	R	RBI	TBB	IBB	SO	HBP	SH	SF	SB	CS	SB%	GDP	Avg	OBP	SLG
1995 Elmira	A-	51	213	67	7	4	0	—	—	82	38	22	15	0	31	3	0	2	19	7	.73	1	.315	.365	.385
1996 Kane County	A	130	514	139	16	3	0	—	—	161	90	35	47	0	115	8	11	1	30	18	.63	3	.270	.340	.313
1997 Brevard Cty	A	36	143	45	8	2	0	—	—	57	26	15	16	1	28	5	2	1	16	8	.67	3	.315	.400	.399
Portland	AA	96	384	112	15	6	8	—	—	163	66	36	42	2	92	7	6	1	35	20	.64	4	.292	.371	.424
1998 Durham	AAA	29	123	35	5	2	1	—	—	47	25	16	15	0	24	0	4	0	10	4	.71	1	.285	.362	.382
1999 Durham	AAA	46	207	73	20	3	3	—	—	108	38	30	16	1	27	1	2	0	9	6	.60	2	.353	.402	.522
1998 Tampa Bay	AL	109	338	94	9	9	1	(0	1)	124	51	17	29	0	69	1	11	0	26	12	.68	2	.278	.337	.367
1999 Tampa Bay	AL	79	303	81	16	4	2	(2	0)	111	44	24	17	0	63	1	1	2	9	9	.50	3	.267	.307	.366
2 ML YEARS		188	641	175	25	13	3	(2	1)	235	95	41	46	0	132	2	12	2	35	21	.63	5	.273	.323	.367

Jay Witasick

Pitches: Right **Bats:** Right **Pos:** SP-28; RP-4   **Ht:** 6'4" **Wt:** 210 **Born:** 8/28/72 **Age:** 27

		HOW MUCH HE PITCHED						WHAT HE GAVE UP												THE RESULTS						
Year Team	Lg	G	GS	CG	GF	IP	BFP	H	R	ER	HR	SH	SF	HB	TBB	IBB	SO	WP	Bk	W	L	Pct.	ShO	Sv-Op	Hld	ERA
1996 Oakland	AL	12	0	0	6	13	55	12	9	9	5	0	1	0	5	0	12	2	0	1	1	.500	0	0-1	0	6.23
1997 Oakland	AL	8	0	0	1	11	53	14	7	7	2	1	0	0	6	0	8	0	0	0	0	.000	0	0-0	1	5.73
1998 Oakland	AL	7	3	0	1	27	131	36	24	19	9	0	0	0	15	1	29	2	0	1	3	.250	0	0-0	0	6.33
1999 Kansas City	AL	32	28	1	2	158.1	732	191	108	98	23	4	8	8	83	1	102	5	2	9	12	.429	1	0-0	0	5.57
4 ML YEARS		59	31	1	10	209.1	971	253	148	133	39	5	9	8	109	2	151	9	2	11	16	.407	1	0-1	0	5.72

Bobby Witt

Pitches: Right **Bats:** Right **Pos:** SP-32

Ht: 6'2" **Wt:** 215 **Born:** 5/11/64 **Age:** 36

Year Team	Lg	G	GS	CG	GF	IP	BFP	H	R	ER	HR	SH	SF	HB	TBB	IBB	SO	WP	Bk	W	L	Pct.	ShO	Sv-Op	Hld	ERA
1986 Texas	AL	31	31	0	0	157.2	741	130	104	96	18	3	9	3	143	2	174	22	3	11	9	.550	0	0-0	0	5.48
1987 Texas	AL	26	25	1	0	143	673	114	82	78	10	5	5	3	140	1	160	7	2	8	10	.444	0	0-0	0	4.91
1988 Texas	AL	22	22	13	0	174.1	736	134	83	76	13	7	6	1	101	2	148	16	8	8	10	.444	2	0-0	0	3.92
1989 Texas	AL	31	31	5	0	194.1	869	182	123	111	14	11	8	2	114	3	166	7	4	12	13	.480	1	0-0	0	5.14
1990 Texas	AL	33	32	7	1	222	954	197	98	83	12	5	6	4	110	3	221	11	2	17	10	.630	1	0-0	0	3.36
1991 Texas	AL	17	16	1	0	88.2	413	84	66	60	4	3	4	1	74	1	82	8	0	3	7	.300	1	0-0	0	6.09
1992 Tex-Oak	AL	31	31	0	0	193	848	183	99	92	16	7	10	2	114	2	125	9	1	10	14	.417	0	0-0	0	4.29
1993 Oakland	AL	35	33	5	0	220	950	226	112	103	16	9	8	3	91	5	131	8	1	14	13	.519	0	0-0	0	4.21
1994 Oakland	AL	24	24	5	0	135.2	618	151	88	76	22	2	7	5	70	4	111	6	1	8	10	.444	3	0-0	0	5.04
1995 Fla-Tex	AL	29	29	2	0	172	748	185	87	79	12	7	5	3	68	2	141	7	0	5	11	.313	0	0-0	0	4.13
1996 Texas	AL	33	32	2	1	199.2	903	235	129	120	28	2	7	2	96	3	157	4	1	16	12	.571	0	0-0	0	5.41
1997 Texas	AL	34	32	3	1	209	919	245	118	112	33	3	7	2	74	4	121	7	0	12	12	.500	0	0-0	0	4.82
1998 Tex-StL	AL	31	18	0	8	116.2	546	150	94	85	21	6	5	2	53	2	58	3	2	7	9	.438	0	0-0	0	6.56
1999 Tampa Bay	AL	32	32	3	0	180.1	815	213	130	117	23	7	8	3	96	1	123	9	1	7	15	.318	2	0-0	0	5.84
1992 Texas	AL	25	25	0	0	161.1	708	152	87	80	14	5	8	2	95	1	100	6	1	9	13	.409	0	0-0	0	4.46
Oakland	AL	6	6	0	0	31.2	140	31	12	12	2	2	2	0	19	1	25	3	0	1	1	.500	0	0-0	0	3.41
1995 Florida	NL	19	19	1	0	110.2	472	104	52	48	8	5	3	2	47	1	95	2	0	2	7	.222	0	0-0	0	3.90
Texas	AL	10	10	1	0	61.1	276	81	35	31	4	2	2	1	21	1	46	5	0	3	4	.429	0	0-0	0	4.55
1998 Texas	AL	14	13	0	0	69.1	329	95	62	59	14	2	4	0	33	1	30	2	1	5	4	.556	0	0-0	0	7.66
St. Louis	NL	17	5	0	8	47.1	217	55	32	26	7	4	1	2	20	1	28	1	1	2	5	.286	0	0-0	0	4.94
14 ML YEARS		409	388	47	11	2406.1	10733	2429	1413	1288	242	77	95	36	1344	35	1918	124	26	138	155	.471	11	0-0	0	4.82

Kevin Witt

Bats: Left **Throws:** Right **Pos:** DH-11; PH/PR-8

Ht: 6'4" **Wt:** 200 **Born:** 1/5/76 **Age:** 24

		BATTING																	BASERUNNING				PERCENTAGES		
Year Team	Lg	G	AB	H	2B	3B	HR	(Hm	Rd)	TB	R	RBI	TBB	IBB	SO	HBP	SH	SF	SB	CS	SB%	GDP	Avg	OBP	SLG
1994 Medcine Hat	R+	60	243	62	10	4	7	—	—	101	37	36	15	0	52	1	1	1	4	1	.80	3	.255	.300	.416
1995 Hagerstown	A	119	479	111	35	1	14	—	—	190	58	50	28	2	148	4	3	0	1	5	.17	5	.232	.280	.397
1996 Dunedin	A+	124	446	121	18	6	13	—	—	190	63	70	39	3	96	6	2	5	9	4	.69	9	.271	.335	.426
1997 Knoxville	AA	127	501	145	27	4	30	—	—	270	76	91	44	7	109	3	1	2	1	0	1.00	13	.289	.349	.539
1998 Syracuse	AAA	126	455	124	20	3	23	—	—	219	71	67	53	6	124	7	1	5	3	3	.50	5	.273	.354	.481
1999 Syracuse	AAA	114	421	117	24	3	24	—	—	219	72	71	64	10	109	3	2	2	0	0	.00	11	.278	.376	.520
1998 Toronto	AL	5	7	1	0	0	0	(0	0)	1	0	0	0	0	3	0	0	0	0	0	.00	0	.143	.143	.143
1999 Toronto	AL	15	34	7	1	0	1	(0	1)	11	3	5	2	0	9	0	1	0	0	0	.00	1	.206	.250	.324
2 ML YEARS		20	41	8	1	0	1	(0	1)	12	3	5	2	0	12	0	1	0	0	0	.00	1	.195	.233	.293

Mark Wohlers

Pitches: Right **Bats:** Right **Pos:** RP-2

Ht: 6'4" **Wt:** 207 **Born:** 1/23/70 **Age:** 30

Year Team	Lg	G	GS	CG	GF	IP	BFP	H	R	ER	HR	SH	SF	HB	TBB	IBB	SO	WP	Bk	W	L	Pct.	ShO	Sv-Op	Hld	ERA
1999 Indianapolis *	AAA	1	0	0	0	0.1	7	1	4	4	0	0	0	0	5	0	1	4	0	0	0	.000	0	0- -	—	108.00
Rockford *	A	2	0	0	0	2	9	1	1	1	0	0	0	0	2	0	4	0	0	0	0	.000	0	0- -	—	4.50
Chattanooga *	AA	2	0	0	0	1.2	9	1	3	3	1	0	0	0	3	0	3	3	0	0	0	.000	0	0- -	—	16.20
1991 Atlanta	NL	17	0	0	4	19.2	89	17	7	7	1	2	1	2	13	3	13	0	0	3	1	.750	0	2-4	2	3.20
1992 Atlanta	NL	32	0	0	16	35.1	140	28	11	10	0	5	1	1	14	4	17	1	0	1	2	.333	0	4-6	2	2.55
1993 Atlanta	NL	46	0	0	13	48	199	37	25	24	2	5	1	1	22	3	45	0	0	6	2	.750	0	0-0	12	4.50
1994 Atlanta	NL	51	0	0	15	51	236	51	35	26	1	4	6	0	33	9	58	2	0	7	2	.778	0	1-2	7	4.59
1995 Atlanta	NL	65	0	0	49	64.2	269	51	16	15	2	2	0	1	24	3	90	4	0	7	3	.700	0	25-29	2	2.09
1996 Atlanta	NL	77	0	0	64	77.1	323	71	30	26	8	2	2	2	21	3	100	10	0	2	4	.333	0	39-44	0	3.03
1997 Atlanta	NL	71	0	0	55	69.1	300	57	29	27	4	4	4	0	38	0	92	6	0	5	7	.417	0	33-40	1	3.50
1998 Atlanta	NL	27	0	0	17	20.1	113	18	23	23	2	1	0	1	33	0	22	7	0	0	1	.000	0	8-8	0	10.18
1999 Atlanta	NL	2	0	0	0	0.2	10	1	2	2	0	0	0	0	6	0	0	0	0	0	1	.000	0	0-0	0	27.00
9 ML YEARS		388	0	0	233	386.1	1679	331	178	160	20	26	15	8	204	25	437	30	0	31	22	.585	0	112-133	26	3.73

Bob Wolcott

Pitches: Right **Bats:** Right **Pos:** RP-4

Ht: 6'0" **Wt:** 190 **Born:** 9/8/73 **Age:** 26

Year Team	Lg	G	GS	CG	GF	IP	BFP	H	R	ER	HR	SH	SF	HB	TBB	IBB	SO	WP	Bk	W	L	Pct.	ShO	Sv-Op	Hld	ERA
1999 Pawtucket *	AAA	26	16	2	5	125.1	538	131	67	50	17	7	4	8	28	3	69	3	0	6	13	.316	0	2- -	—	3.59
1995 Seattle	AL	7	6	0	0	36.2	164	43	18	18	6	0	3	2	14	0	19	0	0	3	2	.600	0	0-0	0	4.42
1996 Seattle	AL	30	28	1	0	149.1	672	179	101	95	26	5	3	7	54	5	78	3	1	7	10	.412	0	0-0	0	5.73
1997 Seattle	AL	19	18	0	0	100	451	129	71	67	22	4	2	5	29	2	58	0	0	6	6	.455	0	0-0	0	6.03
1998 Arizona	NL	6	6	0	0	33	141	32	27	26	7	1	0	1	13	1	21	1	0	1	3	.250	0	0-0	0	7.09
1999 Boston	AL	4	0	0	1	6.2	29	8	6	6	1	0	1	1	3	0	2	0	0	0	0	.000	0	0-0	0	8.10
5 ML YEARS		66	58	1	1	325.2	1457	391	223	212	62	10	9	15	113	8	178	4	1	16	21	.432	0	0-0	0	5.86

Randy Wolf

Pitches: Left **Bats:** Left **Pos:** SP-21; RP-1 **Ht:** 6'0" **Wt:** 198 **Born:** 8/22/76 **Age:** 23

Year Team	Lg	G	GS	CG	GF	IP	BFP	H	R	ER	HR	SH	SF	HB	TBB	IBB	SO	WP	Bk	W	L	Pct.	ShO	Sv-Op	Hld	ERA
1997 Batavia	A-	7	7	0	0	40	153	29	8	7	1	0	1	2	8	0	53	0	0	4	0	1.000	0	0--	—	1.58
1998 Reading	AA	4	4	0	0	25	92	15	4	4	0	0	0	1	4	0	33	0	0	2	0	1.000	0	0--	—	1.44
Scranton-WB	AAA	24	23	1	0	148	650	167	88	76	16	2	10	4	48	4	118	6	1	9	7	.563	0	0--	—	4.62
1999 Scranton-WB	AAA	12	12	0	0	77.1	329	73	36	31	8	1	2	1	29	1	72	4	0	4	5	.444	0	0--	—	3.61
1999 Philadelphia	NL	22	21	0	0	121.2	552	126	78	75	20	5	1	5	67	0	116	4	0	6	9	.400	0	0-0	0	5.55

Tony Womack

Bats: L **Throws:** R **Pos:** RF-122; 2B-19; SS-19; CF-6; PH/PR-2 **Ht:** 5'9" **Wt:** 159 **Born:** 9/25/69 **Age:** 30

Year Team	Lg	G	AB	H	2B	3B	HR	(Hm	Rd)	TB	R	RBI	TBB	IBB	SO	HBP	SH	SF	SB	CS	SB%	GDP	Avg	OBP	SLG
1999 Tucson *	AAA	4	16	4	1	0	1			8	1	3	2	0	3	0	1	0	0	1	.00	2	.250	.333	.500
1993 Pittsburgh	NL	15	24	2	0	0	0	(0	0)	2	5	0	3	0	3	0	1	0	2	0	1.00	0	.083	.185	.083
1994 Pittsburgh	NL	5	12	4	0	0	0	(0	0)	4	4	1	2	0	3	0	0	0	0	0	.00	0	.333	.429	.333
1996 Pittsburgh	NL	17	30	10	3	1	0	(0	0)	15	11	7	6	0	1	1	3	0	2	0	1.00	0	.333	.459	.500
1997 Pittsburgh	NL	155	641	178	26	9	6	(5	1)	240	85	50	43	2	109	3	2	6	60	7	.90	6	.278	.326	.374
1998 Pittsburgh	NL	159	655	185	26	7	3	(2	1)	234	85	45	38	1	94	0	6	5	58	8	.88	4	.282	.319	.357
1999 Arizona	NL	144	614	170	25	10	4	(1	3)	227	111	41	52	0	68	2	9	7	72	13	.85	4	.277	.332	.370
6 ML YEARS		495	1976	549	80	27	13	(8	5)	722	301	144	144	3	278	6	21	12	194	28	.87	14	.278	.327	.365

Jason Wood

Bats: R **Throws:** R **Pos:** 3B-9; SS-9; 1B-5; PH/PR-3; DH-1; 2B-1 **Ht:** 6'1" **Wt:** 190 **Born:** 12/16/69 **Age:** 30

Year Team	Lg	G	AB	H	2B	3B	HR	(Hm	Rd)	TB	R	RBI	TBB	IBB	SO	HBP	SH	SF	SB	CS	SB%	GDP	Avg	OBP	SLG
1991 Sou Oregon	A-	44	142	44	3	4	1	—	—	64	30	23	28	0	30	2	2	3	5	2	.71	0	.310	.423	.451
1992 Modesto	A+	128	454	105	28	3	6	—	—	157	66	49	40	1	106	4	3	5	5	4	.56	15	.231	.296	.346
1993 Huntsville	AA	103	370	85	21	2	3	—	—	119	44	36	33	0	97	2	9	3	2	4	.33	7	.230	.294	.322
1994 Huntsville	AA	134	468	128	29	2	6	—	—	179	54	84	46	1	83	6	5	15	3	6	.33	9	.274	.336	.382
1995 Edmonton	AAA	127	421	99	20	5	2	—	—	135	49	50	29	3	72	3	6	12	1	4	.20	13	.235	.282	.321
1996 Huntsville	AA	133	491	128	21	1	20	—	—	211	77	84	72	2	87	5	2	11	2	5	.29	14	.261	.354	.430
Edmonton	AAA	3	12	0	0	0	0	—	—	0	0	0	5	0	6	0	0	0	0	1	.00	0	.000	.294	.000
1997 Edmonton	AAA	130	505	162	35	7	19	—	—	268	83	87	45	0	74	8	2	4	2	4	.33	11	.321	.383	.531
1998 Edmonton	AAA	80	307	86	20	0	18	—	—	160	52	73	37	1	71	2	0	6	1	1	.50	5	.280	.355	.521
Toledo	AAA	46	169	47	9	0	7	—	—	77	24	29	16	1	30	1	0	1	0	0	.00	5	.278	.342	.456
1999 Lakeland	A+	5	17	4	0	0	0	—	—	4	0	1	4	1	2	1	0	0	0	1	.00	0	.235	.409	.235
Toledo	AAA	48	185	53	11	0	6	—	—	82	34	24	22	0	43	1	0	2	0	2	.00	6	.286	.362	.443
1998 Oak-Det	AL	13	24	8	2	0	1	(0	1)	13	6	1	3	0	5	0	0	0	0	1	.00	0	.333	.407	.542
1999 Detroit	AL	27	44	7	1	0	1	(1	0)	11	5	8	2	0	13	0	1	0	0	0	.00	0	.159	.196	.250
1998 Oakland	AL	3	1	0	0	0	0	(0	0)	0	1	0	0	0	1	0	0	0	0	0	.00	0	.000	.000	.000
Detroit	AL	10	23	8	2	0	1	(0	1)	13	5	1	3	0	13	0	1	0	0	1	.00	0	.348	.423	.565
2 ML YEARS		40	68	15	3	0	2	(1	1)	24	11	9	5	0	18	0	1	0	0	1	.00	0	.221	.274	.353

Kerry Wood

Pitches: Right **Bats:** Right **Pos:** SP **Ht:** 6'5" **Wt:** 225 **Born:** 6/16/77 **Age:** 23

Year Team	Lg	G	GS	CG	GF	IP	BFP	H	R	ER	HR	SH	SF	HB	TBB	IBB	SO	WP	Bk	W	L	Pct.	ShO	Sv-Op	Hld	ERA
1995 Cubs	R	1	1	0	0	3	9	0	0	0	0	0	0	0	1	0	2	0	0	0	0	.000	0	0--	—	0.00
Williamsprt	A-	2	2	0	0	4.1	23	5	8	5	0	0	0	0	5	0	5	1	0	0	0	.000	0	0--	—	10.38
1996 Daytona	A+	22	22	0	0	114.1	495	72	51	37	6	5	4	14	70	0	136	10	7	10	2	.833	0	0--	—	2.91
1997 Orlando	AA	19	19	0	0	94	416	58	49	47	2	0	6	10	79	2	106	10	4	6	7	.462	0	0--	—	4.50
Iowa	AAA	10	10	0	0	57.2	254	35	35	30	2	3	0	6	52	0	80	8	2	4	2	.667	0	0--	—	4.68
1998 Iowa	AAA	1	1	0	0	5	17	1	0	0	0	0	0	0	2	0	11	0	0	1	0	1.000	0	0--	—	0.00
1998 Chicago	NL	26	26	1	0	166.2	699	117	69	63	14	2	4	11	85	1	233	6	3	13	6	.684	1	0-0	0	3.40

Brad Woodall

Pitches: Left **Bats:** Both **Pos:** SP-3; RP-3 **Ht:** 6'0" **Wt:** 175 **Born:** 6/25/69 **Age:** 31

Year Team	Lg	G	GS	CG	GF	IP	BFP	H	R	ER	HR	SH	SF	HB	TBB	IBB	SO	WP	Bk	W	L	Pct.	ShO	Sv-Op	Hld	ERA
1999 Iowa *	AAA	15	9	0	2	52.2	245	67	40	40	9	4	2	0	23	1	41	4	0	2	2	.500	0	1--	—	6.84
1994 Atlanta	NL	1	1	0	0	6	24	5	3	3	2	0	0	0	2	0	2	0	0	0	1	.000	0	0-0	0	4.50
1995 Atlanta	NL	9	0	0	3	10.1	52	13	10	7	1	1	1	0	8	1	5	1	0	1	1	.500	0	0-0	0	6.10
1996 Atlanta	NL	8	3	0	2	19.2	91	28	19	16	4	1	2	0	4	0	20	1	0	2	2	.500	0	0-0	0	7.32
1998 Milwaukee	NL	31	20	0	4	138	594	145	81	76	25	7	2	6	47	4	85	3	0	7	9	.438	0	0-0	1	4.96
1999 Chicago	NL	6	3	0	3	16	71	17	12	10	5	0	1	1	6	0	7	1	0	0	1	.000	0	0-0	1	5.63
5 ML YEARS		55	27	0	12	190	832	208	125	112	37	9	6	7	67	5	119	6	0	10	14	.417	0	0-0	1	5.31

Steve Woodard

Pitches: Right Bats: Left Pos: SP-29; RP-2 Ht: 6'4" Wt: 217 Born: 5/15/75 Age: 25

Year Team	Lg	HOW MUCH HE PITCHED						WHAT HE GAVE UP											THE RESULTS						
		G	GS	CG	GF	IP	BFP	H	R	ER	HR	SH	SF	HB	TBB	IBB	SO	WP	Bk	W	L	Pct.	ShO	Sv-Op	Hld	ERA
1997 Milwaukee	AL	7	7	0	0	36.2	153	39	25	21	5	0	0	2	6	0	32	0	0	3	3	.500	0	0-0	0	5.15
1998 Milwaukee	NL	34	26	0	2	165.2	692	170	83	77	19	2	4	9	33	4	135	3	2	10	12	.455	0	0-0	0	4.18
1999 Milwaukee	NL	31	29	2	0	185	801	219	101	93	23	9	4	6	36	7	119	4	1	11	8	.579	0	0-0	0	4.52
3 ML YEARS		72	62	2	2	387.1	1646	428	209	191	47	11	8	17	75	11	286	7	3	24	23	.511	0	0-0	0	4.44

Chris Woodward

Bats: Right Throws: Right Pos: SS-10; PH/PR-4; 3B-2 Ht: 6'0" Wt: 170 Born: 6/27/76 Age: 24

Year Team	Lg	BATTING																	BASERUNNING				PERCENTAGES		
		G	AB	H	2B	3B	HR	(Hm	Rd)	TB	R	RBI	TBB	IBB	SO	HBP	SH	SF	SB	CS	SB%	GDP	Avg	OBP	SLG
1995 Medcine Hat	R+	72	241	56	8	0	3	—	—	73	44	21	33	1	41	6	5	3	9	4	.69	1	.232	.336	.303
1996 Hagerstown	A	123	424	95	24	2	1	—	—	126	41	48	43	1	70	5	7	5	11	3	.79	1	.224	.300	.297
1997 Dunedin	A+	91	314	92	13	4	1	—	—	116	38	38	52	0	52	5	3	4	4	8	.33	3	.293	.397	.369
1998 Knoxville	AA	73	253	62	12	0	3	—	—	83	36	27	26	1	47	3	3	3	3	5	.38	4	.245	.319	.328
Syracuse	AAA	25	85	17	6	0	2	—	—	29	9	6	7	0	20	0	2	0	1	1	.50	4	.200	.261	.341
1999 Syracuse	AAA	75	281	82	20	3	1	—	—	111	46	20	38	1	49	1	1	0	4	1	.80	5	.292	.378	.395
1999 Toronto	AL	14	26	6	1	0	0	(0	0)	7	1	2	2	0	6	0	0	1	0	0	.00	1	.231	.276	.269

Tim Worrell

Pitches: Right Bats: Right Pos: RP-53 Ht: 6'4" Wt: 231 Born: 7/5/67 Age: 32

Year Team	Lg	HOW MUCH HE PITCHED						WHAT HE GAVE UP											THE RESULTS						
		G	GS	CG	GF	IP	BFP	H	R	ER	HR	SH	SF	HB	TBB	IBB	SO	WP	Bk	W	L	Pct.	ShO	Sv-Op	Hld	ERA
1999 Modesto *	A+	1	1	0	0	2	6	0	0	0	0	0	0	0	0	0	5	0	0	0	0	.000	0	0- —		0.00
1993 San Diego	NL	21	16	0	1	100.2	443	104	63	55	11	8	5	0	43	5	52	3	0	2	7	.222	0	0-0	1	4.92
1994 San Diego	NL	3	3	0	0	14.2	59	9	7	6	0	1	0	0	5	0	14	0	0	1	0	1.000	0	0-0	0	3.68
1995 San Diego	NL	9	0	0	4	13.1	63	16	7	7	2	1	0	1	6	0	13	1	0	1	0	1.000	0	0-0	0	4.73
1996 San Diego	NL	50	11	0	8	121	510	109	45	41	9	3	1	6	39	1	99	0	0	9	7	.563	0	1-2	10	3.05
1997 San Diego	NL	60	10	0	14	106.1	483	116	67	61	14	6	6	7	50	2	81	2	1	4	8	.333	0	3-7	16	5.16
1998 Det-Cle-Oak	AL	43	9	0	5	103	440	106	62	60	16	2	3	1	29	3	82	2	0	2	7	.222	0	0-3	6	5.24
1999 Oakland	AL	53	0	0	17	69.1	309	69	38	32	6	1	1	3	34	1	62	1	0	2	2	.500	0	0-5	5	4.15
1998 Detroit	AL	15	9	0	0	61.2	265	66	42	41	11	0	1	1	19	2	47	0	0	2	6	.250	0	0-1	0	5.98
Cleveland	AL	3	0	0	1	5.1	24	6	3	3	0	0	2	0	2	0	2	0	0	0	0	.000	0	0-0	0	5.06
Oakland	AL	25	0	0	4	36	151	34	17	16	5	2	0	0	8	1	33	2	0	0	1	.000	0	0-2	6	4.00
7 ML YEARS		239	49	0	49	528.1	2307	529	289	262	58	21	17	18	206	12	403	9	1	20	32	.385	0	4-17	38	4.46

Jamey Wright

Pitches: Right Bats: Right Pos: SP-16 Ht: 6'5" Wt: 221 Born: 12/24/74 Age: 25

Year Team	Lg	HOW MUCH HE PITCHED						WHAT HE GAVE UP											THE RESULTS						
		G	GS	CG	GF	IP	BFP	H	R	ER	HR	SH	SF	HB	TBB	IBB	SO	WP	Bk	W	L	Pct.	ShO	Sv-Op	Hld	ERA
1999 Colo Sprngs *	AAA	17	16	2	0	100.1	463	133	87	72	13	1	4	10	38	2	75	9	0	5	7	.417	0	0- —	—	6.46
1996 Colorado	NL	16	15	0	0	91.1	406	105	60	50	8	4	2	7	41	1	45	1	2	4	4	.500	0	0-0	1	4.93
1997 Colorado	NL	26	26	1	0	149.2	698	198	113	104	19	8	3	11	71	3	59	6	2	8	12	.400	0	0-0	0	6.25
1998 Colorado	NL	34	34	1	0	206.1	919	235	143	130	24	8	6	11	95	3	86	6	3	9	14	.391	0	0-0	0	5.67
1999 Colorado	NL	16	16	0	0	94.1	423	110	52	51	10	3	4	4	54	3	49	3	0	4	3	.571	0	0-0	0	4.87
4 ML YEARS		92	91	2	0	541.2	2446	648	368	335	61	23	15	33	261	10	239	16	7	25	33	.431	0	0-0	1	5.57

Jaret Wright

Pitches: Right Bats: Right Pos: SP-26 Ht: 6'2" Wt: 230 Born: 12/29/75 Age: 24

Year Team	Lg	HOW MUCH HE PITCHED						WHAT HE GAVE UP											THE RESULTS						
		G	GS	CG	GF	IP	BFP	H	R	ER	HR	SH	SF	HB	TBB	IBB	SO	WP	Bk	W	L	Pct.	ShO	Sv-Op	Hld	ERA
1999 Buffalo *	AAA	1	1	0	0	3	10	0	0	0	0	0	0	0	0	0	4	0	0	0	0	.000	0	0- —	—	0.00
Akron *	AA	1	1	0	0	5	19	3	0	0	0	0	0	0	1	0	6	0	0	1	0	1.000	0	0- —	—	0.00
1997 Cleveland	AL	16	16	0	0	90.1	388	81	45	44	9	3	4	5	35	0	63	1	0	8	3	.727	0	0-0	0	4.38
1998 Cleveland	AL	32	32	1	0	192.2	855	207	109	101	22	4	6	11	87	4	140	6	0	12	10	.545	0	0-0	0	4.72
1999 Cleveland	AL	26	26	0	0	133.2	609	144	99	90	18	3	3	7	77	1	91	4	0	8	10	.444	0	0-0	0	6.06
3 ML YEARS		74	74	1	0	416.2	1852	432	253	235	49	10	13	23	199	5	294	11	0	28	23	.549	1	0-0	0	5.08

Esteban Yan

Pitches: Right Bats: Right Pos: RP-49; SP-1 Ht: 6'4" Wt: 230 Born: 6/22/74 Age: 26

Year Team	Lg	HOW MUCH HE PITCHED						WHAT HE GAVE UP											THE RESULTS						
		G	GS	CG	GF	IP	BFP	H	R	ER	HR	SH	SF	HB	TBB	IBB	SO	WP	Bk	W	L	Pct.	ShO	Sv-Op	Hld	ERA
1999 St. Pete *	A+	2	2	0	0	4	15	1	0	0	0	0	0	0	0	0	0	0	0	0	0	.000	0	0- —	—	0.00
1996 Baltimore	AL	4	0	0	0	9.1	42	13	7	6	3	0	0	0	3	1	7	0	0	0	0	.000	0	0-0	0	5.79
1997 Baltimore	AL	3	2	0	0	9.2	58	20	18	17	3	0	1	2	7	0	4	1	0	0	1	.000	0	0-0	0	15.83
1998 Tampa Bay	AL	64	0	0	18	88.2	381	78	41	38	11	1	3	5	41	2	77	6	0	5	4	.556	0	1-5	8	3.86
1999 Tampa Bay	AL	50	1	0	15	61	286	77	41	40	8	6	3	9	32	4	46	2	0	3	4	.429	0	0-3	7	5.90
4 ML YEARS		121	3	0	35	168.2	767	188	107	101	25	7	7	16	83	7	134	9	0	8	9	.471	0	1-8	15	5.39

Ed Yarnall

Pitches: Left Bats: Left Pos: RP-3; SP-2 Ht: 6'3" Wt: 234 Born: 12/4/75 Age: 24

		HOW MUCH HE PITCHED						WHAT HE GAVE UP												THE RESULTS						
Year Team	Lg	G	GS	CG	GF	IP	BFP	H	R	ER	HR	SH	SF	HB	TBB	IBB	SO	WP	Bk	W	L	Pct.	ShO	Sv-Op	Hld	ERA
1997 St. Lucie	A+	18	18	2	0	105.1	435	93	33	29	5	2	1	2	30	0	114	2	4	5	8	.385	0	0--	—	2.48
Norfolk	AAA	1	1	0	0	5	29	11	8	8	1	0	0	0	7	2	2	0	0	0	1	.000	0	0--	—	14.40
Binghamton	AA	5	5	0	0	32.1	127	20	11	11	2	2	1	0	11	0	32	0	0	3	2	.600	0	0--	—	3.06
1998 Binghamton	AA	7	7	0	0	46.2	177	20	5	2	0	0	1	1	17	0	52	1	1	7	0	1.000	0	0--	—	0.39
Portland	AA	2	2	0	0	15.1	59	9	5	5	2	1	0	1	4	0	15	1	0	2	0	1.000	0	0--	—	2.93
Charlotte	AAA	15	13	2	0	69.2	331	79	60	48	11	5	3	3	39	4	47	2	1	4	5	.444	0	0--	—	6.20
1999 Columbus	AAA	23	23	1	0	145.1	611	136	61	56	5	3	8	3	57	0	146	2	1	13	4	.765	1	0--	—	3.47
1999 New York	AL	5	2	0	2	17	77	17	8	7	1	0	0	0	10	0	13	0	0	1	0	1.000	0	0-0	0	3.71

Masato Yoshii

Pitches: Right Bats: Right Pos: SP-29; RP-2 Ht: 6'2" Wt: 210 Born: 4/20/65 Age: 35

		HOW MUCH HE PITCHED						WHAT HE GAVE UP												THE RESULTS						
Year Team	Lg	G	GS	CG	GF	IP	BFP	H	R	ER	HR	SH	SF	HB	TBB	IBB	SO	WP	Bk	W	L	Pct.	ShO	Sv-Op	Hld	ERA
1998 New York	NL	29	29	1	0	171.2	724	166	79	75	22	9	4	6	53	5	117	5	1	6	8	.429	0	0-0	0	3.93
1999 New York	NL	31	29	1	1	174	723	168	86	85	25	7	6	6	58	3	105	1	0	12	8	.600	0	0-0	0	4.40
2 ML YEARS		60	58	2	1	345.2	1447	334	165	160	47	16	10	12	111	8	222	6	1	18	16	.529	0	0-0	0	4.17

Dmitri Young

Bats: B Throws: R Pos: RF-75; PH/PR-33; LF-23; 1B-9; DH-1 Ht: 6'2" Wt: 235 Born: 10/11/73 Age: 26

		BATTING																	BASERUNNING				PERCENTAGES		
Year Team	Lg	G	AB	H	2B	3B	HR	(Hm	Rd)	TB	R	RBI	TBB	IBB	SO	HBP	SH	SF	SB	CS	SB%	GDP	Avg	OBP	SLG
1996 St. Louis	NL	16	29	7	0	0	0	(0	0)	7	3	2	4	0	5	1	0	0	0	1	.00	1	.241	.353	.241
1997 St. Louis	NL	110	333	86	14	3	5	(2	3)	121	38	34	38	3	63	2	1	3	6	5	.55	8	.258	.335	.363
1998 Cincinnati	NL	144	536	166	48	1	14	(3	11)	258	81	83	47	4	94	2	0	5	2	4	.33	16	.310	.364	.481
1999 Cincinnati	NL	127	373	112	30	2	14	(9	5)	188	63	56	30	2	71	2	0	4	3	1	.75	11	.300	.352	.504
4 ML YEARS		397	1271	371	92	6	33	(14	19)	574	185	175	119	8	233	7	1	12	11	11	.50	36	.292	.353	.452

Eric Young

Bats: Right Throws: Right Pos: 2B-117; PH/PR-2 Ht: 5'9" Wt: 170 Born: 5/18/67 Age: 33

		BATTING																	BASERUNNING				PERCENTAGES		
Year Team	Lg	G	AB	H	2B	3B	HR	(Hm	Rd)	TB	R	RBI	TBB	IBB	SO	HBP	SH	SF	SB	CS	SB%	GDP	Avg	OBP	SLG
1999 San Berndno *	A+	3	12	3	0	0	0	—	—	3	0	0	0	0	0	2	0	0	0	0	.00	0	.250	.250	.250
1992 Los Angeles	NL	49	132	34	1	0	1	(0	1)	38	9	11	8	0	9	0	4	0	6	1	.86	3	.258	.300	.288
1993 Colorado	NL	144	490	132	16	8	3	(3	0)	173	82	42	63	3	41	4	4	4	42	19	.69	9	.269	.355	.353
1994 Colorado	NL	90	228	62	13	1	7	(6	1)	98	37	30	38	1	17	2	5	2	18	7	.72	3	.272	.378	.430
1995 Colorado	NL	120	366	116	21	9	6	(5	1)	173	68	36	49	3	29	5	3	1	35	12	.74	4	.317	.404	.473
1996 Colorado	NL	141	568	184	28	4	8	(7	1)	239	113	74	47	1	31	21	2	5	53	19	.74	9	.324	.393	.421
1997 Col-LA	NL	155	622	174	33	8	8	(2	6)	247	106	61	71	1	54	9	10	6	45	14	.76	18	.280	.359	.397
1998 Los Angeles	NL	117	452	129	24	1	8	(7	1)	179	78	43	45	0	32	5	9	2	42	13	.76	4	.285	.355	.396
1999 Los Angeles	NL	119	456	128	24	2	2	(2	0)	162	73	41	63	0	26	5	6	4	51	22	.70	12	.281	.371	.355
1997 Colorado	NL	118	468	132	29	6	6	(2	4)	191	78	45	57	0	37	5	8	5	32	12	.73	16	.282	.363	.408
Los Angeles	NL	37	154	42	4	2	2	(0	2)	56	28	16	14	1	17	4	2	1	13	2	.87	2	.273	.347	.364
8 ML YEARS		935	3314	959	155	33	43	(32	11)	1309	566	338	384	9	239	51	43	24	292	107	.73	62	.289	.369	.395

Ernie Young

Bats: Right Throws: Right Pos: RF-3; PH/PR-2; LF-1 Ht: 6'1" Wt: 234 Born: 7/8/69 Age: 30

		BATTING																	BASERUNNING				PERCENTAGES		
Year Team	Lg	G	AB	H	2B	3B	HR	(Hm	Rd)	TB	R	RBI	TBB	IBB	SO	HBP	SH	SF	SB	CS	SB%	GDP	Avg	OBP	SLG
1999 Tucson *	AAA	126	453	133	25	1	30	—	—	250	78	95	57	1	129	5	0	6	4	1	.80	9	.294	.374	.552
1994 Oakland	AL	11	30	2	1	0	0	(0	0)	3	2	3	1	0	8	0	0	0	0	0	.00	1	.067	.097	.100
1995 Oakland	AL	26	50	10	3	0	2	(2	0)	19	9	5	8	0	12	0	0	0	0	0	.00	1	.200	.310	.380
1996 Oakland	AL	141	462	112	19	4	19	(10	9)	196	72	64	52	1	118	7	3	4	7	5	.58	13	.242	.326	.424
1997 Oakland	AL	71	175	39	7	0	5	(3	2)	61	22	15	19	0	57	2	2	2	1	3	.25	6	.223	.303	.349
1998 Kansas City	AL	25	53	10	3	0	1	(0	1)	16	2	3	2	0	9	1	0	0	2	1	.67	3	.189	.232	.302
1999 Arizona	NL	6	11	2	0	0	0	(0	0)	2	1	0	3	0	2	1	0	0	0	0	.00	0	.182	.400	.182
6 ML YEARS		280	781	175	33	4	27	(15	12)	297	108	90	85	1	206	11	5	6	10	9	.53	24	.224	.307	.380

Kevin Young

Bats: Right Throws: Right Pos: 1B-155; PH/PR-2 Ht: 6'3" Wt: 224 Born: 6/16/69 Age: 31

		BATTING																	BASERUNNING				PERCENTAGES		
Year Team	Lg	G	AB	H	2B	3B	HR	(Hm	Rd)	TB	R	RBI	TBB	IBB	SO	HBP	SH	SF	SB	CS	SB%	GDP	Avg	OBP	SLG
1992 Pittsburgh	NL	10	7	4	0	0	0	(0	0)	4	2	4	2	0	0	0	0	0	0	1	1.00	0	.571	.667	.571
1993 Pittsburgh	NL	141	449	106	24	3	6	(6	0)	154	38	47	36	3	82	9	5	9	2	2	.50	10	.236	.300	.343
1994 Pittsburgh	NL	59	122	25	7	2	1	(1	0)	39	15	11	8	2	34	1	2	1	2	0	.00	3	.205	.258	.320
1995 Pittsburgh	NL	56	181	42	9	0	6	(5	1)	69	13	22	8	0	53	2	1	3	1	3	.25	5	.232	.268	.381
1996 Kansas City	AL	55	132	32	6	0	8	(4	4)	62	20	23	11	0	32	0	0	0	3	3	.50	2	.242	.301	.470
1997 Pittsburgh	NL	97	333	100	18	3	18	(11	7)	178	59	74	16	1	89	4	1	8	15	2	.85	6	.300	.332	.535
1998 Pittsburgh	NL	159	592	160	40	2	27	(15	12)	285	88	108	44	1	127	11	0	9	15	7	.68	20	.270	.328	.481

		BATTING																BASERUNNING				PERCENTAGES		
Year Team	Lg	G	AB	H	2B	3B	HR	(Hm | Rd)	TB	R	RBI	TBB	IBB	SO	HBP	SH	SF	SB	CS	SB%	GDP	Avg	OBP	SLG
1999 Pittsburgh	NL	156	584	174	41	6	26	(16 | 10)	305	103	106	75	5	124	12	0	4	22	10	.69	13	.298	.387	.522
8 ML YEARS		733	2400	643	145	16	92	(58 | 34)	1096	338	395	200	12	541	39	9	34	55	29	.65	59	.268	.330	.457

Gregg Zaun

Bats: Both **Throws:** Right **Pos:** C-37; PH/PR-11; DH-2 **Ht:** 5'10" **Wt:** 190 **Born:** 4/14/71 **Age:** 29

		BATTING																BASERUNNING				PERCENTAGES		
Year Team	Lg	G	AB	H	2B	3B	HR	(Hm | Rd)	TB	R	RBI	TBB	IBB	SO	HBP	SH	SF	SB	CS	SB%	GDP	Avg	OBP	SLG
1995 Baltimore	AL	40	104	27	5	0	3	(1 | 2)	41	18	14	16	0	14	0	2	0	1	1	.50	2	.260	.358	.394
1996 Bal-Fla		60	139	34	9	1	2	(1 | 1)	51	20	15	14	3	20	2	1	2	1	0	1.00	5	.245	.318	.367
1997 Florida	NL	58	143	43	10	2	2	(0 | 2)	63	21	20	26	4	18	2	1	0	1	0	1.00	3	.301	.415	.441
1998 Florida	NL	106	298	56	12	2	5	(2 | 3)	87	19	29	35	2	52	1	2	2	5	2	.71	7	.188	.274	.292
1999 Texas	AL	43	93	23	2	1	1	(0 | 1)	30	12	12	10	0	7	0	1	2	1	0	1.00	1	.247	.314	.323
1996 Baltimore	AL	50	108	25	8	1	1	(1 | 0)	38	16	13	11	2	15	2	0	2	0	0	.00	3	.231	.309	.352
Florida	NL	10	31	9	1	0	1	(0 | 1)	13	4	2	3	1	5	0	1	0	1	0	1.00	1	.290	.353	.419
5 ML YEARS		307	777	183	38	6	13	(4 | 9)	272	90	90	101	9	111	5	7	6	9	3	.75	19	.236	.325	.350

Todd Zeile

Bats: Right **Throws:** Right **Pos:** 3B-155; DH-1; 1B-1 **Ht:** 6'1" **Wt:** 200 **Born:** 9/9/65 **Age:** 34

		BATTING																BASERUNNING				PERCENTAGES		
Year Team	Lg	G	AB	H	2B	3B	HR	(Hm | Rd)	TB	R	RBI	TBB	IBB	SO	HBP	SH	SF	SB	CS	SB%	GDP	Avg	OBP	SLG
1989 St. Louis	NL	28	82	21	3	1	1	(0 | 1)	29	7	8	9	1	14	0	1	1	0	0	.00	1	.256	.326	.354
1990 St. Louis	NL	144	495	121	25	3	15	(8 | 7)	197	62	57	67	3	77	2	0	6	2	4	.33	11	.244	.333	.398
1991 St. Louis	NL	155	565	158	36	3	11	(7 | 4)	233	76	81	62	3	94	5	0	6	17	11	.61	15	.280	.353	.412
1992 St. Louis	NL	126	439	113	18	4	7	(4 | 3)	160	51	48	68	4	70	0	0	7	7	10	.41	11	.257	.352	.364
1993 St. Louis	NL	157	571	158	36	1	17	(8 | 9)	247	82	103	70	5	76	0	0	6	5	4	.56	15	.277	.352	.433
1994 St. Louis	NL	113	415	111	25	1	19	(9 | 10)	195	62	75	52	3	56	3	0	7	1	3	.25	13	.267	.348	.470
1995 StL-ChC	NL	113	426	105	22	0	14	(8 | 6)	169	50	52	34	1	76	4	4	5	1	0	1.00	13	.246	.305	.397
1996 Phi-Bal		163	617	162	32	0	25	(10 | 15)	269	78	99	82	4	104	1	0	4	1	1	.50	18	.263	.348	.436
1997 Los Angeles	NL	160	575	154	17	0	31	(17 | 14)	264	89	90	85	7	112	6	0	6	8	7	.53	18	.268	.365	.459
1998 LA-Fla-Tex		158	572	155	32	3	19	(7 | 12)	250	85	94	69	2	90	4	1	7	4	4	.50	12	.271	.350	.437
1999 Texas	AL	156	588	172	41	1	24	(13 | 11)	287	80	98	56	3	94	4	1	7	1	2	.33	20	.293	.354	.488
1995 St. Louis	NL	34	127	37	6	0	5	(2 | 3)	58	16	22	18	1	23	1	0	2	1	0	1.00	2	.291	.378	.457
Chicago	NL	79	299	68	16	0	9	(6 | 3)	111	34	30	16	0	53	3	4	3	0	0	.00	11	.227	.271	.371
1996 Philadelphia	NL	134	500	134	24	0	20	(9 | 11)	218	61	80	67	4	88	1	0	4	1	1	.50	16	.268	.353	.436
Baltimore	AL	29	117	28	8	0	5	(1 | 4)	51	17	19	15	0	16	0	0	0	0	0	.00	2	.239	.326	.436
1998 Los Angeles	NL	40	158	40	6	1	7	(1 | 6)	69	22	27	10	0	24	1	0	1	1	1	.50	5	.253	.300	.437
Florida	NL	66	234	68	12	1	6	(2 | 4)	100	37	39	31	2	34	2	0	3	2	3	.40	4	.291	.374	.427
Texas	AL	52	180	47	14	1	6	(4 | 2)	81	26	28	28	0	32	1	1	3	1	0	1.00	3	.261	.358	.450
11 ML YEARS		1473	5345	1430	287	17	183	(91 | 92)	2300	722	805	654	36	863	29	7	62	47	46	.51	147	.268	.347	.430

Jeff Zimmerman

Pitches: Right **Bats:** Right **Pos:** RP-65 **Ht:** 6'1" **Wt:** 200 **Born:** 8/9/72 **Age:** 27

		HOW MUCH HE PITCHED						WHAT HE GAVE UP											THE RESULTS					
Year Team	Lg	G	GS	CG	GF	IP	BFP	H	R	ER	HR	SH	SF	HB	TBB	IBB	SO	WP	Bk	W	L	Pct.	ShO	Sv-Op	Hld	ERA
1997 Winnipeg	IND	18	16	3	0	118	479	94	49	37	7	2	2	7	35	0	140	6	1	9	2	.818	0	0--	—	2.82
1998 Charlotte	A+	10	0	0	3	14.1	52	10	2	2	1	1	0	0	1	0	14	0	0	2	1	.667	0	0--	—	1.26
Tulsa	AA	41	0	0	28	63	249	38	16	9	5	2	3	0	20	3	67	3	2	3	1	.750	0	9--	—	1.29
1999 Oklahoma	AAA	2	0	0	2	3.2	10	0	0	0	0	0	0	0	0	0	2	0	0	1	0	1.000	0	1--	—	0.00
1999 Texas	AL	65	0	0	14	87.2	336	50	24	23	9	3	6	2	23	1	67	2	0	9	3	.750	0	3-7	24	2.36

Jordan Zimmerman

Pitches: Left **Bats:** Right **Pos:** RP-12 **Ht:** 6'0" **Wt:** 200 **Born:** 4/28/75 **Age:** 25

		HOW MUCH HE PITCHED						WHAT HE GAVE UP											THE RESULTS					
Year Team	Lg	G	GS	CG	GF	IP	BFP	H	R	ER	HR	SH	SF	HB	TBB	IBB	SO	WP	Bk	W	L	Pct.	ShO	Sv-Op	Hld	ERA
1997 Everett	A-	11	9	0	1	39	177	37	27	18	2	0	3	3	23	0	54	1	2	2	3	.400	0	0--	—	4.15
Wisconsin	A	3	3	0	0	17	75	18	11	11	0	0	1	0	10	0	18	2	0	0	1	.000	0	0--	—	5.82
1998 Mariners	R	5	3	0	1	12	55	14	6	4	1	0	0	2	7	0	11	0	0	1	0	1.000	0	0--	—	3.00
Lancaster	A+	3	3	0	0	16.2	74	21	9	9	2	0	0	0	8	0	8	1	0	1	0	1.000	0	0--	—	4.86
1999 Everett	A-	1	0	0	0	0.2	5	3	2	2	0	0	0	0	0	0	1	0	0	0	0	.000	0	0--	—	27.00
Tacoma	AAA	9	0	0	2	7	35	13	4	4	1	0	0	0	4	1	4	1	0	0	0	.000	0	0--	—	5.14
New Haven	AA	22	0	0	8	33.1	149	26	8	4	0	0	1	2	19	0	33	1	1	1	4	.200	0	2--	—	1.08
1999 Seattle	AL	12	0	0	2	8	41	14	8	7	0	0	0	1	4	0	3	1	0	0	0	.000	0	0-0	2	7.88

Eddie Zosky

Bats: Right **Throws:** Right **Pos:** 3B-4; PH/PR-4; 2B-2 **Ht:** 6'0" **Wt:** 175 **Born:** 2/10/68 **Age:** 32

		BATTING																BASERUNNING				PERCENTAGES		
Year Team	Lg	G	AB	H	2B	3B	HR	(Hm | Rd)	TB	R	RBI	TBB	IBB	SO	HBP	SH	SF	SB	CS	SB%	GDP	Avg	OBP	SLG
1989 Knoxville	AA	56	208	46	5	3	2	—	—	63	21	14	10	0	32	0	2	1	1	1	.50	4	.221	.256	.303
1990 Knoxville	AA	115	450	122	20	7	3	—	—	165	53	45	26	1	73	5	6	3	13	13	.19	7	.271	.316	.367
1991 Syracuse	AAA	119	511	135	18	4	6	—	—	179	69	39	35	1	82	5	7	5	9	4	.69	11	.264	.315	.350
1992 Syracuse	AAA	96	342	79	11	6	4	—	—	114	31	38	19	0	53	1	7	4	3	4	.43	10	.231	.270	.333

			BATTING																BASERUNNING				PERCENTAGES		
Year Team	Lg	G	AB	H	2B	3B	HR	(Hm	Rd)	TB	R	RBI	TBB	IBB	SO	HBP	SH	SF	SB	CS	SB%	GDP	Avg	OBP	SLG
1993 Hagerstown	A	5	20	2	0	0	0	—	—	2	2	1	2	0	1	0	0	1	0	0	.00	1	.100	.174	.100
Syracuse	AAA	28	93	20	5	0	0	—	—	25	9	8	1	0	20	4	2	3	0	1	.00	1	.215	.248	.269
1994 Syracuse	AAA	85	284	75	15	3	7	—	—	117	41	37	9	0	46	2	6	5	3	1	.75	8	.264	.287	.412
1995 Charlotte	AAA	92	312	77	15	2	3	—	—	105	27	42	7	0	48	1	5	1	2	3	.40	8	.247	.265	.337
1996 Orioles	R	1	3	1	1	0	0	—	—	2	1	0	1	0	0	0	0	0	0	0	.00	0	.333	.500	.667
Rochester	AAA	95	340	87	22	4	3	—	—	126	42	34	21	1	40	2	3	6	5	2	.71	8	.256	.298	.371
1997 Phoenix	AAA	86	241	67	10	4	9	—	—	112	38	45	16	2	38	1	1	2	3	3	.50	5	.278	.323	.465
1998 Louisville	AAA	90	257	63	12	1	8	—	—	101	36	35	15	2	47	1	4	1	1	3	.25	3	.245	.288	.393
1999 Louisville	AAA	116	415	122	22	3	12	—	—	186	60	47	23	0	68	3	4	3	5	1	.83	6	.294	.333	.448
1991 Toronto	AL	18	27	4	1	1	0	(0	0)	7	2	2	0	0	8	0	1	0	0	0	.00	1	.148	.148	.259
1992 Toronto	AL	8	7	2	0	1	0	(0	0)	4	1	1	0	0	2	0	0	1	0	0	.00	0	.286	.250	.571
1995 Florida	NL	6	5	1	0	0	0	(0	0)	1	0	0	0	0	0	0	0	0	0	0	.00	0	.200	.200	.200
1999 Milwaukee	NL	8	7	1	0	0	0	(0	0)	1	1	0	1	0	2	0	0	0	0	0	.00	0	.143	.250	.143
4 ML YEARS		40	46	8	1	2	0	(0	0)	13	4	3	1	0	12	0	1	1	0	0	.00	1	.174	.188	.283

1999 Team Statistics

All the statistics you need to know about your favorite team are here. Final standings, record breakdowns, team batting, pitching and fielding can be found in this section. Also included here are teams' records against the other league. American League teams have a split vs. NL teams and National League teams have a split vs. AL teams.

Keep in mind that hitting totals in each league will not necessarily mirror hitting totals allowed by that league's pitchers. For example, home runs hit in the American League may not equal the home runs allowed by American League pitchers. The reason is interleague play.

Some of the abbreviations need an explanation. They are:

LD1st = Last date team was in first place; **1st** = number of days team spent in first place (including days tied for the lead); **Lead** = largest first-place lead, if any, during the season; **LHS** = record in games started by opposing lefthanded pitchers; **RHS** = record in games started by opposing righthanded pitchers; **1-R** = record in games decided by one run; **5+R** = record in games decided by five or more runs.

1999 American League Final Standings

Overall

EAST Team	W-L	Pct	GB	LD1st	1st	Lead
New York Yankees	98-64	.605	—	10/3	146	8.5
Boston Red Sox*	94-68	.580	4	6/8	34	2.5
Toronto Blue Jays	84-78	.519	14	4/23	7	2
Baltimore Orioles	78-84	.481	20	4/6	3	0
Tampa Bay Devil Rays	69-93	.426	29	4/4	1	0

CENTRAL Team	W-L	Pct	GB	LD1st	1st	Lead
Cleveland Indians	97-65	.599	—	10/3	178	25.5
Chicago White Sox	75-86	.466	21.5	4/8	5	0.5
Detroit Tigers	69-92	.429	27.5	4/5	2	0
Kansas City Royals	64-97	.398	32.5	4/4	1	0
Minnesota Twins	63-97	.394	33	4/8	2	0

WEST Team	W-L	Pct	GB	LD1st	1st	Lead
Texas Rangers	95-67	.586	—	10/3	177	10
Oakland Athletics	87-75	.537	8	5/18	5	0.5
Seattle Mariners	79-83	.488	16	4/13	5	0
Anaheim Angels	70-92	.432	25	4/17	9	1

* represents playoff wild-card berth. Clinch Dates: Cleveland 9/8, Texas 9/26, Boston 9/29, New York 9/30.

East Division

Team	AT Home	Road	VERSUS East	Cent	West	NL	LHS	RHS	CONDITIONS Grass	Turf	Day	Night	XInn	RUNS 1-R	5+R	MONTHLY Apr	May	June	July	Aug	Sep	ALL-STAR Pre	Post
New York	48-33	50-31	31-18	31-22	27-15	9-9	19-14	79-50	83-58	15-6	34-24	64-40	7-2	22-12	31-19	14-7	15-13	17-9	16-11	19-10	17-14	52-34	46-30
Boston	49-32	45-36	28-21	36-20	24-15	6-12	18-17	76-51	83-57	11-11	38-22	56-46	4-4	21-20	32-18	11-11	20-8	14-13	11-15	18-11	20-10	49-39	45-29
Toronto	40-41	44-37	24-25	34-20	17-24	9-9	13-15	71-63	33-26	51-52	27-26	57-52	6-3	26-18	30-24	13-11	11-17	15-13	19-7	12-16	14-14	47-43	37-35
Baltimore	41-40	37-44	15-34	27-22	25-21	11-7	12-15	66-69	70-71	8-13	24-28	54-56	8-6	16-26	25-20	6-16	13-15	13-13	14-13	12-16	20-11	36-51	42-33
Tampa Bay	33-48	36-45	25-25	26-22	14-32	4-14	8-23	61-70	29-35	40-58	23-22	46-71	3-6	27-20	14-32	12-12	11-16	10-16	10-17	16-12	10-20	39-49	30-44

Central Division

Team	AT Home	Road	VERSUS East	Cent	West	NL	LHS	RHS	CONDITIONS Grass	Turf	Day	Night	XInn	RUNS 1-R	5+R	MONTHLY Apr	May	June	July	Aug	Sep	ALL-STAR Pre	Post
Cleveland	47-34	50-31	26-27	33-16	29-13	9-9	28-15	69-50	82-56	15-9	28-22	69-43	7-7	26-19	33-19	16-6	17-10	17-10	13-14	18-10	16-15	56-31	41-34
Chicago	38-42	37-44	25-29	24-23	17-25	9-9	16-11	59-75	62-80	13-6	24-29	51-57	6-9	20-19	25-32	11-9	11-16	15-13	11-16	14-17	13-15	42-43	33-43
Detroit	38-43	31-49	21-34	23-25	17-23	8-10	15-14	54-78	57-76	12-16	26-30	43-62	5-5	19-22	26-37	11-12	10-18	12-15	9-17	11-16	16-14	36-52	33-40
Kansas City	33-47	31-50	16-33	20-28	22-24	6-12	15-17	49-80	55-83	9-14	14-35	50-62	5-10	11-32	25-26	9-11	14-15	9-18	11-16	8-21	13-16	35-52	29-45
Minnesota	31-50	32-47	18-31	20-28	15-31	10-7	13-24	50-73	27-39	36-58	21-25	42-72	6-5	19-26	17-33	9-14	9-18	11-15	15-11	12-16	7-23	34-52	29-45

West Division

Team	AT Home	Road	VERSUS East	Cent	West	NL	LHS	RHS	CONDITIONS Grass	Turf	Day	Night	XInn	RUNS 1-R	5+R	MONTHLY Apr	May	June	July	Aug	Sep	ALL-STAR Pre	Post
Texas	51-30	44-37	29-26	35-17	21-16	10-8	20-10	75-57	74-64	21-3	17-18	78-49	6-2	24-16	36-20	13-10	17-10	15-13	16-9	18-12	16-13	48-39	47-28
Oakland	52-29	35-46	34-18	26-30	15-21	12-6	23-17	64-58	75-67	12-8	33-27	54-48	3-7	22-19	27-26	10-14	17-10	10-16	16-10	19-10	15-15	43-44	44-31
Seattle	43-38	36-45	24-27	31-25	17-20	7-11	13-22	66-61	49-59	30-24	24-23	55-60	5-6	20-23	25-36	11-12	15-12	13-14	11-15	16-13	13-17	42-45	37-38
Anaheim	37-44	33-48	20-36	24-28	20-16	6-12	19-19	51-73	62-81	8-11	17-28	53-64	4-8	23-25	17-31	11-12	13-15	11-15	8-17	8-21	19-12	41-45	29-47

Team vs. Team Breakdown

	NYY	Bos	Tor	Bal	TB	Cle	CWS	Det	KC	Min	Tex	Oak	Sea	Ana
New York Yankees	—	4	10	9	8	7	7	7	4	6	8	6	9	4
Boston Red Sox	8	—	9	7	4	8	7	7	8	6	4	4	7	9
Toronto Blue Jays	2	3	—	11	8	7	4	10	7	6	4	2	2	9
Baltimore Orioles	4	5	1	—	5	1	7	5	6	8	6	5	5	9
Tampa Bay Devil Rays	4	9	5	7	—	4	4	5	8	5	4	1	4	5
Cleveland Indians	3	4	5	9	5	—	9	8	7	9	3	10	7	9
Chicago White Sox	5	5	6	3	6	3	—	7	6	8	5	3	4	5
Detroit Tigers	5	5	2	5	4	5	5	—	7	6	5	4	3	5
Kansas City Royals	5	2	3	4	2	5	6	4	—	5	4	6	7	5
Minnesota Twins	4	4	4	1	5	3	3	6	8	—	0	7	4	4
Texas Rangers	4	5	6	6	8	7	5	5	6	12	—	7	8	6
Oakland Athletics	4	6	8	7	9	2	7	6	6	5	5	—	6	4
Seattle Mariners	1	3	7	5	8	3	8	7	5	8	5	6	—	6
Anaheim Angels	6	5	3	3	7	1	5	5	7	6	6	8	6	—

(read wins across and losses down)

1999 National League Final Standings

Overall

EAST						
Team	W-L	Pct	GB	LD1st	1st	Lead
Atlanta Braves	103-59	.636	—	10/4	159	8
New York Mets*	97-66	.595	6.5	8/21	30	2
Philadelphia Phillies	77-85	.475	26	4/6	3	0
Montreal Expos	68-94	.420	35	4/9	6	1
Florida Marlins	64-98	.395	39	4/6	3	0

CENTRAL						
Team	W-L	Pct	GB	LD1st	1st	Lead
Houston Astros	97-65	.599	—	10/4	135	6
Cincinnati Reds	96-67	.589	1.5	10/1	31	1
Pittsburgh Pirates	78-83	.484	18.5	4/13	6	1
St. Louis Cardinals	75-86	.466	21.5	4/29	22	2
Milwaukee Brewers	74-87	.460	22.5	4/7	4	0.5
Chicago Cubs	67-95	.414	30	4/9	4	0

WEST						
Team	W-L	Pct	GB	LD1st	1st	Lead
Arizona D'backs	100-62	.617	—	10/4	108	14
San Francisco Giants	86-76	.531	14	7/23	76	3.5
Los Angeles Dodgers	77-85	.475	23	4/10	4	0
San Diego Padres	74-88	.457	26	—	—	—
Colorado Rockies	72-90	.444	28	4/5	2	0.5

* represents playoff wild-card berth. Clinch Dates: Arizona 9/24, Atlanta 9/26, Houston 10/3, New York 10/4.

East Division

Team	AT Home	Road	VERSUS East	Cent	West	AL	LHS	RHS	CONDITIONS Grass	Turf	Day	Night	XInn	RUNS 1-R	5+R	MONTHLY Apr	May	June	July	Aug	Sep	ALL-STAR Pre	Post
Atlanta	56-25	47-34	35-16	35-13	24-21	9-9	29-15	74-44	88-48	15-11	29-17	74-42	17-5	29-21	27-17	15-7	16-13	16-11	16-12	21-7	19-9	55-34	48-25
New York	49-32	48-34	27-23	33-18	25-19	12-6	22-18	75-48	79-56	18-10	33-23	64-43	6-5	27-19	32-14	14-9	13-15	17-10	18-9	18-10	17-13	50-39	47-27
Philadelphia	41-40	36-45	28-22	22-28	16-28	11-7	19-22	58-63	27-35	50-50	25-25	52-60	4-9	25-19	26-28	11-11	14-13	15-12	17-11	10-17	10-21	46-40	31-45
Montreal	35-46	33-48	19-31	22-28	19-25	8-10	18-21	50-73	23-34	45-60	14-32	54-62	3-11	16-28	13-32	7-14	11-16	12-14	8-18	18-14	12-18	33-51	35-43
Florida	35-45	29-53	17-34	17-31	19-26	11-7	18-21	46-77	52-80	12-18	17-30	47-68	6-4	19-25	17-32	6-17	10-18	11-16	14-13	12-15	11-19	32-56	32-42

Central Division

Team	AT Home	Road	VERSUS East	Cent	West	AL	LHS	RHS	CONDITIONS Grass	Turf	Day	Night	XInn	RUNS 1-R	5+R	MONTHLY Apr	May	June	July	Aug	Sep	ALL-STAR Pre	Post
Houston	50-32	47-33	25-16	31-31	29-15	12-3	27-16	70-49	34-23	63-42	27-19	70-46	8-5	22-18	30-14	13-9	16-11	16-12	19-9	15-14	18-10	51-37	46-28
Cincinnati	45-37	51-30	22-20	38-25	29-14	7-8	27-17	69-50	36-20	60-47	33-24	63-43	9-4	21-24	26-12	9-12	16-10	18-9	16-12	17-12	20-12	49-36	47-31
Pittsburgh	45-36	33-47	19-22	30-32	22-21	7-8	17-30	61-53	24-34	54-49	25-22	53-61	9-4	20-22	22-24	9-12	17-12	13-13	11-16	16-14	12-16	43-44	35-39
St. Louis	38-42	37-44	16-25	27-34	25-19	7-8	17-29	58-57	64-70	11-16	25-28	50-58	9-8	26-27	18-12	12-9	13-15	12-16	15-12	12-17	11-17	43-45	32-41
Milwaukee	32-48	42-39	18-23	32-30	16-28	8-6	21-27	53-60	58-75	16-12	31-28	43-59	8-9	22-27	21-29	9-13	14-14	12-14	14-12	8-21	17-13	42-44	32-43
Chicago	34-47	33-48	18-23	28-34	15-29	6-9	25-22	42-73	58-76	9-19	41-49	26-46	5-6	26-24	16-35	10-10	17-10	10-17	11-16	6-24	13-18	41-44	26-51

West Division

Team	AT Home	Road	VERSUS East	Cent	West	AL	LHS	RHS	CONDITIONS Grass	Turf	Day	Night	XInn	RUNS 1-R	5+R	MONTHLY Apr	May	June	July	Aug	Sep	ALL-STAR Pre	Post
Arizona	52-29	48-33	33-12	27-24	33-18	7-8	32-16	68-46	89-51	11-11	26-14	74-48	11-10	24-24	32-9	13-11	18-10	12-14	16-11	20-8	21-8	48-41	52-21
San Francisco	49-32	37-44	23-21	32-21	24-26	7-8	18-28	68-48	71-63	15-13	40-34	46-42	7-7	29-19	23-22	16-8	11-16	16-11	13-13	15-13	15-15	50-38	36-38
Los Angeles	37-44	40-41	21-23	26-26	22-29	8-7	24-25	53-60	63-72	14-13	25-21	52-64	4-12	21-27	27-22	13-10	13-14	8-17	11-18	17-11	15-15	39-47	38-38
San Diego	46-35	28-53	18-26	20-33	25-25	11-4	15-32	59-56	68-72	6-16	24-32	50-56	6-6	28-25	17-21	9-13	10-17	18-9	12-15	12-18	13-16	43-44	31-44
Colorado	39-42	33-48	24-21	21-32	23-29	4-8	23-28	49-62	63-77	9-13	30-38	42-52	4-6	24-23	19-33	9-10	12-17	13-13	12-18	14-16	12-16	40-46	32-44

Team vs. Team Breakdown

	Atl	NYM	Phi	Mon	Fla	Hou	Cin	Pit	StL	Mil	ChC	Ari	SF	LA	SD	Col
Atlanta Braves	—	9	8	9	9	6	8	6	8	5	2	5	4	5	5	5
New York Mets	3	—	6	8	10	5	5	7	5	5	6	2	7	4	7	5
Philadelphia Phillies	5	6	—	6	11	1	3	3	4	4	7	1	2	3	6	4
Montreal Expos	4	5	6	—	4	2	3	3	5	4	5	3	4	4	5	3
Florida Marlins	4	3	2	8	—	2	1	3	3	5	3	1	4	7	3	4
Houston Astros	1	4	6	7	7	—	4	5	5	8	9	4	5	6	8	6
Cincinnati Reds	1	5	6	4	6	9	—	7	8	6	8	8	4	4	6	7
Pittsburgh Pirates	3	2	4	6	4	7	6	—	7	4	6	2	4	6	3	7
St. Louis Cardinals	1	5	5	4	7	4	5	5	—	6	5	4	3	6	7	5
Milwaukee Brewers	2	2	5	5	4	5	6	8	7	—	6	4	4	2	3	3
Chicago Cubs	5	3	2	2	6	3	5	7	7	6	—	2	1	2	6	4
Arizona Diamondbacks	4	7	8	6	8	5	1	5	4	5	7	—	9	7	11	6
San Francisco Giants	5	2	6	5	5	4	5	5	6	5	7	3	—	5	7	9
Los Angeles Dodgers	4	4	6	5	2	3	3	3	3	7	7	6	8	—	3	5
San Diego Padres	4	2	3	3	6	1	3	6	2	5	5	3	2	5	—	9
Colorado Rockies	4	4	5	6	5	2	2	2	4	5	6	5	7	4	8	—

(read wins across and losses down)

American League Batting

Tm	G	AB	H	2B	3B	HR	(Hm	Rd)	TB	R	RBI	TBB	IBB	SO	HBP	SH	SF	ShO	SB	CS	SB%	GDP	LOB	Avg	OBP	SLG
Cle	162	5634	1629	309	32	209	(110	99)	2629	1009	960	743	41	1099	55	54	67	3	147	50	.75	136	1234	.289	.373	.467
Tex	162	5651	1653	304	29	230	(103	127)	2705	945	897	611	41	937	29	35	62	7	111	54	.67	147	1176	.293	.361	.479
NYY	162	5568	1568	302	36	193	(84	109)	2521	900	855	718	47	978	55	22	53	6	104	57	.65	137	1244	.282	.366	.453
Oak	162	5519	1430	287	20	235	(112	123)	2462	893	845	770	32	1129	71	39	41	4	70	37	.65	129	1246	.259	.355	.446
Tor	162	5642	1580	337	14	212	(96	116)	2581	883	856	578	29	1077	76	28	45	8	119	48	.71	129	1177	.280	.352	.457
Sea	162	5572	1499	263	21	244	(122	122)	2536	859	825	610	38	1095	42	38	48	9	130	45	.74	114	1147	.269	.343	.455
KC	161	5624	1584	294	52	151	(74	77)	2435	856	800	535	25	932	64	46	56	4	127	39	.77	156	1165	.282	.348	.433
Bal	162	5637	1572	299	21	203	(98	105)	2522	851	804	615	34	890	61	41	55	8	107	46	.70	146	1241	.279	.353	.447
Bos	162	5579	1551	334	42	176	(80	96)	2497	836	808	597	27	928	55	34	56	5	67	39	.63	131	1213	.278	.350	.448
CWS	162	5644	1563	298	37	162	(77	85)	2421	777	742	499	22	810	34	40	45	7	110	50	.69	138	1157	.277	.337	.429
TB	162	5586	1531	272	29	145	(66	79)	2296	772	728	544	24	1042	64	30	48	7	73	49	.60	157	1169	.274	.343	.411
Det	161	5481	1433	289	34	212	(118	94)	2426	747	704	458	19	1049	82	35	39	12	108	70	.61	108	1061	.261	.326	.443
Ana	162	5494	1404	248	22	170	(74	84)	2170	711	673	511	24	1022	43	41	42	11	71	45	.61	135	1097	.256	.322	.395
Min	161	5495	1450	285	30	105	(47	58)	2110	686	643	500	28	978	49	24	56	10	118	60	.66	151	1118	.264	.328	.384
AL	1133	78126	21447	4121	419	2635	(1261	1374)	34311	11725	11140	8289	431	13966	780	507	713	101	1462	689	.68	1914	16445	.275	.347	.439

American League Pitching

Tm	G	CG	Rel	IP	BFP	H	R	ER	HR	SH	SF	HB	TBB	IBB	SO	WP	Bk	W	L	Pct.	ShO	Sv-Op	Hld	OAvg	OOBP	OSLG	ERA
Bos	162	6	412	1436.2	6120	1396	718	638	160	27	43	55	469	25	1131	28	0	94	68	.580	12	50-72	66	.253	.315	.398	4.00
NYY	162	6	359	1439.2	6233	1402	731	661	158	42	47	57	581	27	1111	49	4	98	64	.605	10	50-67	45	.255	.330	.400	4.13
Bal	162	17	393	1435.0	6259	1468	815	760	198	47	49	49	647	34	982	55	6	78	84	.481	11	33-58	47	.269	.348	.439	4.77
Ana	162	4	400	1431.1	6258	1472	826	762	177	36	65	56	624	17	877	65	5	70	92	.432	7	37-55	36	.269	.346	.427	4.79
Min	161	13	417	1423.1	6216	1591	845	791	208	32	48	28	487	22	927	57	6	63	97	.394	8	34-52	53	.283	.341	.464	5.00
Oak	162	6	406	1438.1	6309	1537	846	750	160	34	39	54	569	45	967	57	8	87	75	.537	5	48-73	66	.274	.344	.429	4.69
Tex	162	6	439	1436.1	6313	1626	859	809	186	34	52	40	509	23	979	50	2	95	67	.586	9	47-66	72	.286	.346	.459	5.07
Cle	162	3	466	1450.1	6374	1503	860	788	197	41	39	54	634	55	1120	54	3	97	65	.599	6	46-67	57	.268	.346	.438	4.89
Tor	162	14	377	1439.2	6368	1582	862	787	191	39	57	53	575	25	1009	55	4	84	78	.519	9	39-58	58	.280	.349	.451	4.92
CWS	162	6	409	1438.1	6452	1608	870	786	210	39	56	61	596	31	968	60	9	75	86	.466	6	39-56	48	.282	.353	.447	4.92
Det	161	4	421	1421.0	6286	1528	882	817	209	39	60	70	583	26	976	43	4	69	92	.429	6	33-42	57	.276	.349	.451	5.17
Sea	162	7	346	1433.2	6471	1613	905	834	191	34	54	71	684	39	980	63	3	79	83	.488	6	40-60	33	.287	.368	.454	5.24
TB	162	6	453	1433.0	6482	1606	913	805	172	42	53	79	695	25	1055	52	5	69	93	.426	5	45-62	48	.286	.370	.447	5.06
KC	161	11	416	1420.2	6387	1607	921	844	202	44	53	68	643	34	831	60	6	64	97	.398	3	29-59	44	.288	.365	.454	5.35
AL	1133	109	5714	20076.2	88528	21539	11853	10832	2619	530	715	795	8296	428	13913	748	65	1122	1141	.496	100	570-847	730	.275	.348	.440	4.86

American League Fielding

Team	G	PO	Ast	OFAst	E	(Throw	Field)	TC	DP	GDP Opp	GDP	GDP%	PB	OSB	OCS	OSB%	CPkof	PPkof	AVG
Baltimore	162	4305	1781	39	89	(35	54)	6175	191	243	158	.650	5	93	50	.65	3	2	.986
Minnesota	161	4270	1613	39	92	(43	49)	5975	150	221	121	.548	12	73	37	.66	1	5	.985
Cleveland	162	4351	1739	30	106	(47	59)	6196	154	212	127	.599	8	118	46	.72	4	0	.983
Anaheim	162	4294	1723	37	106	(58	48)	6123	156	216	132	.611	20	103	62	.62	0	10	.983
Toronto	162	4317	1664	29	106	(39	67)	6087	165	227	134	.590	13	124	53	.70	1	4	.983
Detroit	161	4263	1623	28	106	(39	67)	5992	156	233	135	.579	12	81	44	.65	0	5	.982
New York	162	4319	1577	29	111	(57	54)	6007	132	198	105	.530	18	131	48	.73	1	3	.982
Seattle	162	4301	1689	45	113	(56	57)	6103	182	252	152	.603	8	107	50	.68	2	5	.981
Texas	162	4309	1729	21	119	(43	76)	6157	169	239	147	.615	2	47	52	.47	10	3	.981
Oakland	162	4315	1700	33	122	(62	60)	6137	166	221	137	.620	18	110	51	.68	0	4	.980
Kansas City	161	4262	1727	47	125	(59	66)	6114	188	266	155	.583	10	111	49	.69	0	2	.980
Boston	162	4310	1548	25	127	(56	71)	5985	132	211	105	.498	31	159	58	.73	0	4	.979
Tampa Bay	162	4299	1776	31	135	(58	77)	6210	198	281	166	.591	12	101	69	.59	4	3	.978
Chicago	162	4315	1563	29	136	(68	68)	6014	149	223	122	.547	14	102	46	.69	0	6	.977
American League	1133	60230	23452	456	1593	(720	873)	85275	2288	3243	1896	.585	183	1460	715	.67	26	56	.981

National League Batting

	BATTING																			BASERUNNING					PERCENTAGES		
Tm	G	AB	H	2B	3B	HR	(Hm	Rd)	TB	R	RBI	TBB	IBB	SO	HBP	SH	SF	ShO	SB	CS	SB%	GDP	LOB	Avg	OBP	SLG
Ari	162	5658	1566	289	46	216	(101	115)	2595	908	865	588	52	1045	48	61	60	6	137	39	.78	94	1169	.277	.347	.459
Col	162	5717	1644	305	39	223	(144	79)	2696	906	863	508	31	863	43	54	46	3	70	43	.62	125	1144	.288	.348	.472
SF	162	5563	1507	307	18	188	(87	101)	2414	872	828	696	40	1028	60	87	42	2	109	56	.66	129	1230	.271	.356	.434
Cin	163	5649	1536	312	37	209	(97	112)	2549	865	820	569	37	1125	45	70	44	3	164	54	.75	107	1168	.272	.341	.451
NYM	163	5572	1553	297	14	181	(84	97)	2421	853	814	717	53	994	48	63	54	5	150	61	.71	149	1267	.279	.363	.434
Phi	162	5598	1539	302	44	161	(77	84)	2412	841	797	631	37	1081	46	70	41	7	125	35	.78	127	1221	.275	.351	.431
Atl	162	5569	1481	309	23	197	(86	111)	2427	840	791	608	62	962	53	74	47	6	148	66	.69	120	1155	.266	.341	.436
Hou	162	5485	1463	293	23	168	(65	103)	2306	823	784	728	56	1138	52	79	58	5	166	75	.69	127	1252	.267	.355	.420
Mil	161	5582	1524	299	30	165	(77	88)	2378	815	777	658	44	1065	55	87	51	6	81	33	.71	110	1276	.273	.353	.426
StL	161	5570	1461	274	27	194	(104	90)	2371	809	763	613	51	1202	51	75	44	4	134	48	.74	110	1188	.262	.338	.426
LA	162	5567	1480	253	23	187	(92	95)	2340	793	761	594	34	1030	52	74	51	6	167	68	.71	109	1173	.266	.339	.420
Pit	161	5468	1417	282	40	171	(91	80)	2292	775	735	573	40	1197	60	87	45	7	112	44	.72	111	1157	.259	.334	.419
ChC	162	5482	1411	255	35	189	(98	91)	2303	747	717	571	38	1170	39	65	44	7	60	44	.58	120	1130	.257	.329	.420
Mon	162	5559	1473	320	47	163	(84	79)	2376	718	680	438	39	939	53	71	28	8	70	51	.58	138	1094	.265	.323	.427
SD	162	5394	1360	256	22	153	(69	84)	2119	710	671	631	51	1169	35	36	40	10	174	67	.72	132	1139	.252	.332	.393
Fla	162	5578	1465	266	44	128	(48	80)	2203	691	655	479	30	1145	59	44	56	7	92	46	.67	119	1159	.263	.325	.395
NL	1296	89011	23880	4619	512	2893	(1404	1489)	38202	12966	12321	9602	675	17153	799	1097	751	92	1959	830	.70	1927	18922	.268	.342	.429

National League Pitching

HOW MUCH THEY PITCHED					WHAT THEY GAVE UP												THE RESULTS									
Tm	G	CG	Rel	IP	BFP	H	R	ER	HR	SH	SF	HB	TBB	IBB	SO	WP	Bk	W	L	Pct.	ShO	Sv-Op	Hld	OAvg	OOBP	OSLG	ERA
Atl	162	9	394	1471.0	6218	1398	661	593	142	74	41	26	507	55	1197	34	3	103	59	.636	9	45-63	58	.251	.314	.377	3.63
Hou	162	12	339	1458.2	6199	1485	675	620	128	60	49	40	478	17	1204	54	0	97	65	.599	8	48-63	36	.267	.326	.397	3.83
Ari	162	16	382	1467.1	6233	1387	676	615	176	46	30	49	543	48	1198	39	10	100	62	.617	9	42-65	58	.249	.320	.402	3.77
Cin	163	6	381	1462.0	6221	1309	711	647	190	71	43	45	636	46	1081	65	3	96	67	.589	11	55-76	38	.241	.324	.411	3.98
NYM	162	5	439	1456.2	6232	1372	711	691	167	57	51	52	617	53	1172	38	4	97	66	.595	7	49-66	66	.252	.331	.418	4.27
SD	162	5	403	1420.1	6147	1454	781	705	193	70	44	35	529	48	1078	73	5	74	88	.457	6	43-60	51	.266	.332	.429	4.47
Pit	161	8	425	1433.1	6272	1444	782	689	160	59	45	51	633	54	1083	54	10	78	83	.484	3	34-51	54	.263	.343	.420	4.33
LA	162	8	399	1453.0	6317	1438	787	718	192	56	34	62	594	26	1077	53	9	77	85	.475	6	37-53	54	.258	.334	.420	4.45
SF	162	6	450	1456.1	6430	1486	831	762	194	71	39	51	655	41	1076	62	7	86	76	.531	3	42-65	82	.265	.345	.423	4.71
StL	161	5	454	1445.1	6427	1519	838	761	161	85	48	63	667	38	1025	60	9	75	86	.466	3	38-62	75	.273	.355	.427	4.74
Phi	162	11	441	1438.1	6348	1494	846	787	212	69	44	58	627	24	1030	67	10	77	85	.475	6	32-45	49	.269	.347	.447	4.92
Fla	162	6	453	1435.2	6389	1560	852	781	171	69	69	54	655	53	943	46	12	64	98	.395	5	33-52	50	.281	.359	.441	4.90
Mon	162	8	442	1434.1	6321	1505	853	748	192	74	50	60	572	39	1043	46	8	68	94	.420	4	44-65	47	.270	.342	.418	4.69
Mil	161	2	453	1442.2	6477	1618	886	813	213	60	44	51	616	42	987	64	10	74	87	.460	5	40-67	68	.284	.356	.456	5.07
ChC	162	11	441	1430.2	6359	1619	920	837	221	79	66	27	529	48	980	59	9	67	95	.414	6	32-57	52	.286	.346	.467	5.27
Col	162	12	420	1429.0	6574	1700	1028	955	237	74	52	60	737	46	1032	70	3	72	90	.444	2	33-51	43	.301	.384	.499	6.01
NL	1296	128	6706	23134.2	101164	23788	12838	11722	2909	1074	749	784	9595	678	17206	884	112	1305	1286	.504	93	647-961	881	.267	.341	.428	4.56

National League Fielding

	FIELDING																	
Team	G	PO	Ast	OFAst	E	(Throw | Field)	TC	DP	GDP Opp	GDP	GDP%	PB	OSB	OCS	OSB%	CPkof	PPkof	AVG
New York	163	4370	1607	19	68	(39 | 29)	6045	147	196	125	.638	10	134	44	.75	0	8	.989
Philadelphia	162	4315	1598	30	100	(43 | 57)	6013	144	227	117	.515	13	94	35	.73	2	4	.983
Houston	162	4376	1730	38	106	(49 | 57)	6212	175	245	136	.555	9	94	43	.69	2	4	.983
Arizona	162	4402	1589	28	104	(49 | 55)	6095	132	193	102	.528	17	138	66	.68	0	13	.983
San Francisco	162	4369	1629	25	105	(42 | 63)	6103	155	212	116	.547	8	129	53	.71	0	1	.983
Cincinnati	163	4386	1552	32	105	(60 | 45)	6043	139	203	116	.571	11	124	34	.78	0	12	.983
Atlanta	162	4413	1657	33	111	(49 | 62)	6181	127	200	98	.490	10	108	45	.71	1	4	.982
Colorado	162	4287	1737	48	118	(46 | 72)	6142	189	270	157	.581	9	163	63	.72	0	6	.981
Florida	162	4307	1686	44	127	(47 | 80)	6120	150	226	124	.549	10	94	67	.58	5	7	.979
Milwaukee	161	4328	1669	31	127	(61 | 66)	6124	146	221	120	.543	13	177	44	.80	3	4	.979
San Diego	162	4261	1633	23	129	(64 | 65)	6023	151	228	131	.575	15	114	45	.72	1	3	.979
St. Louis	161	4336	1635	33	132	(55 | 77)	6103	163	200	119	.575	8	80	69	.54	1	6	.978
Los Angeles	162	4359	1725	20	137	(64 | 73)	6221	137	202	115	.569	13	156	56	.74	2	9	.978
Chicago	162	4292	1597	28	139	(61 | 78)	6028	135	200	113	.565	14	100	43	.70	2	3	.977
Pittsburgh	161	4300	1745	20	147	(58 | 89)	6192	179	243	149	.613	9	99	50	.66	0	13	.976
Montreal	162	4303	1618	42	160	(61 | 99)	6081	125	189	102	.540	16	157	47	.77	3	8	.974
National League	1296	69404	26407	494	1915	(848 | 1067)	97726	2394	3455	1940	.562	185	1961	804	.71	22	105	.980

1999 Fielding Statistics

Thanks to STATS, Inc., fielding statistics have come a long way since the days when all we had were games, putouts, assists, errors, fielding percentage and double plays. On the following pages, you'll see that we've added games started and defensive innings, as well as range factor. In the STATS *All-Time Major League Handbook*, range factor is calculated as (putouts plus assists) per game. On the following pages, we've used the formula (putouts plus assists) *per nine innings*, which is a bit more precise. The catchers have an additional section of special stats, where you'll find opponents' stolen base/caught stealing data and team ERA with a particular catcher behind the plate. Although these stats are unofficial, we don't expect that the official ones will be substantially different when they arrive in a few months.

First Basemen - Regulars

Player	Tm	G	GS	Inn	PO	A	E	DP	Pct.	Rng
Erstad, Darin	Ana	78	72	640.1	669	41	1	59	.999	—
Mientkiewicz, Doug	Min	110	95	845.0	882	50	3	75	.997	—
Lee, Travis	Ari	114	90	869.0	802	62	3	65	.997	—
Snow, J.T.	SF	160	150	1344.1	1221	122	6	123	.996	—
Casey, Sean	Cin	148	147	1297.0	1190	55	6	109	.995	—
Martinez, Tino	NYY	158	151	1342.0	1300	106	7	110	.995	—
Konerko, Paul	CWS	92	89	786.1	740	58	4	72	.995	—
Joyner, Wally	SD	105	88	779.1	731	66	4	83	.995	—
Segui, David	TOT	94	90	780.0	719	63	4	89	.995	—
Brogna, Rico	Phi	157	155	1352.1	1240	123	7	119	.995	—
Millar, Kevin	Fla	94	89	770.0	720	52	4	80	.995	—
Giambi, Jason	Oak	142	140	1208.2	1251	45	7	128	.995	—
Bagwell, Jeff	Hou	161	158	1401.2	1337	106	8	141	.994	—
Grace, Mark	ChC	160	157	1379.2	1335	93	8	115	.994	—
Thome, Jim	Cle	111	109	953.2	930	83	6	93	.994	—
Olerud, John	NYM	160	159	1384.2	1344	105	9	127	.994	—
Stevens, Lee	Tex	133	130	1151.0	1228	60	8	128	.994	—
Helton, Todd	Col	156	148	1310.0	1243	103	9	152	.993	—
Conine, Jeff	Bal	99	93	827.2	831	52	6	108	.993	—
Clark, Tony	Det	132	130	1147.2	1126	86	10	111	.992	—
Karros, Eric	LA	151	147	1302.1	1291	126	13	108	.991	—
Fullmer, Brad	Mon	94	92	767.1	700	41	7	48	.991	—
Delgado, Carlos	Tor	147	147	1305.0	1306	84	14	134	.990	—
McGwire, Mark	StL	151	150	1257.2	1181	80	13	119	.990	—
McGriff, Fred	TB	125	124	1065.2	1038	87	13	132	.989	—
Stanley, Mike	Bos	111	100	892.1	830	60	11	71	.988	—
Young, Kevin	Pit	155	153	1358.2	1413	97	23	148	.985	—
Sweeney, Mike	KC	74	73	630.2	584	41	12	76	.981	—
Average	—	127	122	1076.2	1042	76	8	104	.993	—

First Basemen - The Rest

Player	Tm	G	GS	Inn	PO	A	E	DP	Pct.	Rng
Abbott, Kurt	Col	8	7	48.2	57	3	0	6	1.000	—
Amaral, Rich	Bal	2	1	10.0	4	2	0	1	1.000	—
Andrews, Shane	Mon	18	14	118.0	122	7	2	12	.985	—
Andrews, Shane	ChC	1	0	0.0	0	0	0	0	.000	—
Baerga, Carlos	SD	2	0	2.1	0	0	0	0	.000	—
Banks, Brian	Mil	44	21	232.2	221	20	2	18	.992	—
Barker, Kevin	Mil	31	29	245.1	254	17	1	19	.996	—
Bell, David	Sea	4	2	18.1	15	1	0	2	1.000	—
Bellinger, Clay	NYY	8	0	10.0	7	1	0	1	1.000	—
Berkman, Lance	Hou	1	0	1.0	1	0	0	1	1.000	—
Berry, Sean	Mil	64	57	472.0	438	27	5	50	.989	—
Blowers, Mike	Sea	14	9	77.1	72	6	0	14	1.000	—
Boggs, Wade	TB	4	3	28.0	32	0	0	3	1.000	—
Bonilla, Bobby	NYM	4	2	23.0	23	2	1	2	.962	—
Brown, Brant	Pit	7	5	45.0	37	3	0	2	1.000	—
Buhner, Jay	Sea	1	1	9.0	9	0	0	1	1.000	—
Catalanotto, Frank	Det	32	24	219.1	219	11	0	29	1.000	—
Clark, Will	Bal	63	62	532.1	575	42	3	54	.995	—
Colbrunn, Greg	Ari	39	31	241.2	203	19	1	21	.996	—
Coomer, Ron	Min	71	63	541.1	518	47	2	57	.996	—
Cox, Steve	TB	4	3	28.0	19	1	0	5	1.000	—
Cromer, Tripp	LA	1	0	1.0	1	0	0	0	1.000	—
Cruz, Ivan	Pit	1	1	9.0	13	1	0	3	1.000	—
Daubach, Brian	Bos	61	56	482.1	418	35	8	35	.983	—

First Basemen - The Rest

Player	Tm	G	GS	Inn	PO	A	E	DP	Pct.	Rng
Davis, Tommy	Bal	1	0	2.0	2	0	0	0	1.000	—
Decker, Steve	Ana	6	4	31.0	30	4	0	2	1.000	—
Dunston, Shawon	StL	8	1	30.1	37	2	0	3	1.000	—
Durazo, Erubiel	Ari	44	41	356.2	324	20	0	25	1.000	—
Echevarria, Angel	Col	10	7	64.1	58	4	0	6	1.000	—
Edmonds, Jim	Ana	2	2	18.0	19	1	0	2	1.000	—
Fabregas, Jorge	Atl	1	0	1.0	0	1	0	0	1.000	—
Franco, Julio	TB	1	0	1.0	2	0	0	0	1.000	—
Franco, Matt	NYM	19	2	44.0	41	5	0	8	1.000	—
Gaetti, Gary	ChC	8	5	43.0	39	6	2	6	.957	—
Garcia, Carlos	SD	1	0	2.0	2	0	0	0	1.000	—
Garcia, Freddy	Pit	1	0	1.0	0	0	0	0	.000	—
Gates, Brent	Min	5	3	27.0	27	0	0	2	1.000	—
Giambi, Jeremy	KC	26	25	218.0	208	8	2	22	.991	—
Hansen, Dave	LA	20	3	51.2	52	4	1	6	.982	—
Hansen, Jed	KC	1	0	1.0	0	0	0	0	.000	—
Hayes, Charlie	SF	20	11	103.0	103	8	0	9	1.000	—
Hernandez, Jose	ChC	1	0	1.0	2	0	0	0	1.000	—
Hernandez, Jose	Atl	1	0	3.0	1	0	0	0	1.000	—
Hocking, Denny	Min	2	0	5.0	7	0	0	0	1.000	—
Hollandsworth, T.	LA	13	12	98.0	91	9	1	12	.990	—
Houston, Tyler	ChC	2	0	6.0	1	0	0	0	1.000	—
Howard, David	StL	9	2	30.1	33	1	0	4	1.000	—
Howell, Jack	Hou	5	1	15.0	9	2	0	4	1.000	—
Hunter, Brian	Atl	101	40	449.0	425	36	4	37	.991	—
Huskey, Butch	Sea	10	10	81.0	76	3	1	10	.988	—
Huson, Jeff	Ana	8	2	28.0	25	1	0	3	1.000	—
Hyers, Tim	Fla	14	7	64.2	71	3	0	6	1.000	—
Ibanez, Raul	Sea	21	18	140.0	147	7	2	18	.987	—
Jackson, Ryan	Sea	29	19	183.0	167	11	2	19	.989	—
Jaha, John	Oak	8	5	37.0	42	4	0	3	1.000	—
Jefferies, Gregg	Det	3	3	24.0	19	4	0	1	1.000	—
Jefferson, Reggie	Bos	2	0	5.0	8	1	0	0	1.000	—
Jordan, Kevin	Phi	13	5	56.1	55	4	0	6	1.000	—
Kent, Jeff	SF	1	1	7.0	7	2	0	2	1.000	—
King, Jeff	KC	20	20	173.1	188	15	2	21	.990	—
Kinkade, Mike	NYM	1	0	1.0	0	0	0	0	.000	—
Klesko, Ryan	Atl	75	66	529.2	493	30	6	37	.989	—
Kotsay, Mark	Fla	19	12	99.1	104	8	0	9	1.000	—
Ledesma, Aaron	TB	4	3	26.0	27	6	0	4	1.000	—
Lee, Carlos	CWS	5	4	29.0	24	4	1	3	.966	—
Lee, Derrek	Fla	66	54	499.2	463	47	3	44	.994	—
Leius, Scott	KC	13	7	63.1	61	6	2	13	.971	—
Leyritz, Jim	SD	19	14	129.1	116	7	2	10	.984	—
Leyritz, Jim	NYY	9	9	60.2	59	8	1	5	.985	—
Liefer, Jeff	CWS	15	12	107.0	96	11	0	11	1.000	—
Loretta, Mark	Mil	66	54	492.2	472	31	3	44	.994	—
Lovullo, Torey	Phi	6	2	29.2	22	5	0	3	1.000	—
Luke, Matt	Ana	4	2	23.0	20	4	0	5	1.000	—
Mabry, John	Sea	20	12	121.1	120	10	1	11	.992	—
Magadan, Dave	SD	42	19	183.1	186	15	3	19	.985	—
Manto, Jeff	Cle	1	0	4.0	5	0	0	0	1.000	—
Manto, Jeff	NYY	3	1	13.0	14	1	0	1	1.000	—
Marrero, Eli	StL	20	3	58.2	47	5	0	2	1.000	—
Martinez, Edgar	Sea	5	5	38.0	29	2	0	2	1.000	—
McEwing, Joe	StL	2	1	9.0	5	0	0	0	1.000	—
McGee, Willie	StL	3	1	11.0	9	0	0	0	1.000	—
McGuire, Ryan	Mon	58	26	281.1	267	37	1	19	.997	—

First Basemen - The Rest

Player	Tm	G	GS	Inn	PO	A	E	DP	Pct.	Rng
Merced, Orlando	Mon	7	2	23.2	21	1	2	2	.917	—
Merloni, Lou	Bos	1	1	8.0	9	1	1	0	.909	—
Minor, Ryan	Bal	1	1	8.0	10	1	1	1	.917	—
Mordecai, Mike	Mon	1	0	2.0	2	0	0	0	1.000	—
Morris, Hal	Cin	25	10	108.0	107	6	1	10	.991	—
Nevin, Phil	SD	11	10	78.1	74	9	1	5	.988	—
Newhan, David	SD	1	0	0.0	0	0	0	0	.000	—
Norton, Greg	CWS	26	7	90.2	67	3	2	9	.972	—
Offerman, Jose	Bos	8	5	49.0	48	3	0	7	1.000	—
Orie, Kevin	Fla	1	0	2.0	1	0	0	1	1.000	—
Ortiz, David	Min	1	0	5.0	7	0	0	1	1.000	—
Otanez, Willis	Bal	5	0	7.0	6	0	0	0	1.000	—
Otanez, Willis	Tor	13	11	107.0	89	7	0	11	1.000	—
Owens, Eric	SD	12	12	81.0	77	4	0	7	1.000	—
Palmeiro, Rafael	Tex	28	28	246.1	261	13	1	23	.996	—
Paquette, Craig	StL	6	1	27.1	19	3	0	1	1.000	—
Perez, Eddie	Atl	2	1	5.0	4	0	0	0	1.000	—
Perez, Eduardo	StL	5	2	21.0	18	2	1	2	.952	—
Perry, Herbert	TB	14	8	87.0	77	4	0	13	1.000	—
Phillips, J.R.	Col	4	0	6.0	3	0	0	1	1.000	—
Pickering, Calvin	Bal	8	5	48.0	48	2	2	8	.962	—
Posada, Jorge	NYY	1	1	8.0	4	1	0	1	1.000	—
Pratt, Todd	NYM	1	0	1.0	0	0	0	0	.000	—
Pritchett, Chris	Ana	15	8	93.0	96	8	1	8	.990	—
Saenz, Olmedo	Oak	28	12	134.2	153	12	1	11	.994	—
Santiago, Benito	ChC	1	0	1.0	2	0	0	0	1.000	—
Scarsone, Steve	KC	12	5	60.0	69	9	0	8	1.000	—
Segui, David	Sea	90	86	753.0	700	61	3	86	.996	—
Segui, David	Tor	4	4	27.0	19	2	1	3	.955	—
Seguignol, Fern.	Mon	23	21	174.2	172	11	2	20	.989	—
Servais, Scott	SF	1	0	2.0	1	0	0	0	1.000	—
Sexson, Richie	Cle	61	53	492.2	517	51	7	48	.988	—
Shave, Jon	Tex	9	4	37.0	43	1	0	7	1.000	—
Simms, Mike	Tex	1	0	1.0	1	0	0	0	1.000	—
Simon, Randall	Atl	70	55	483.1	462	27	3	38	.994	—
Sojo, Luis	NYY	4	0	6.0	8	0	0	0	1.000	—
Sorrento, Paul	TB	27	21	197.1	203	9	1	19	.995	—
Spiers, Bill	Hou	1	0	2.0	3	0	0	1	1.000	—
Spiezio, Scott	Oak	10	5	56.0	51	1	0	6	1.000	—
Stairs, Matt	Oak	1	0	2.0	2	0	0	0	1.000	—
Sutton, Larry	KC	30	22	196.1	215	14	3	19	.987	—
Sveum, Dale	Pit	4	2	19.2	23	2	0	5	1.000	—
Sweeney, Mark	Cin	1	0	2.0	2	0	0	1	1.000	—
Thomas, Frank	CWS	49	49	421.1	385	18	4	40	.990	—
Timmons, Ozzie	Sea	1	0	1.0	1	0	0	0	1.000	—
Toca, Jorge	NYM	1	0	1.0	2	0	0	0	1.000	—
Vander Wal, John	SD	28	19	164.2	156	8	1	14	.994	—
Vaughn, Mo	Ana	72	72	598.0	584	35	3	62	.995	—
Ventura, Robin	NYM	1	0	1.0	0	0	0	0	1.000	—
Vidro, Jose	Mon	14	7	67.1	59	5	2	7	.970	—
Vitiello, Joe	KC	10	9	78.0	65	7	0	11	1.000	—
Ward, Daryle	Hou	10	3	39.0	36	2	0	6	1.000	—
Wilson, Craig	CWS	1	0	4.0	4	0	0	0	1.000	—
Wilson, Dan	Sea	5	0	11.2	10	2	0	1	1.000	—
Wood, Jason	Det	5	4	30.0	35	0	1	3	.972	—
Young, Dmitri	Cin	9	6	55.0	56	1	0	5	1.000	—
Zeile, Todd	Tex	1	0	1.0	1	0	0	0	1.000	—

Second Basemen - Regulars

Player	Tm	G	GS	Inn	PO	A	E	DP	Pct.	Rng
Cairo, Miguel	TB	117	114	994.0	250	379	9	102	.986	5.70
Febles, Carlos	KC	122	122	1066.0	272	375	14	101	.979	5.46
Veras, Quilvio	SD	119	118	1003.0	273	334	12	79	.981	5.45
Reese, Pokey	Cin	146	144	1222.2	325	409	7	91	.991	5.40
McEwing, Joe	StL	96	85	733.2	202	238	9	51	.980	5.40
McLemore, Mark	Tex	135	132	1158.2	261	433	12	93	.983	5.39
Bush, Homer	Tor	109	107	951.2	220	350	9	81	.984	5.39
Easley, Damion	Det	147	141	1229.0	302	421	8	111	.989	5.29
Biggio, Craig	Hou	155	153	1351.1	359	430	12	117	.985	5.25
Velarde, Randy	TOT	156	156	1358.1	298	493	14	104	.983	5.24
Belliard, Ron	Mil	119	113	1007.2	247	331	13	75	.978	5.16
DeShields, Delino	Bal	93	87	750.2	178	249	10	54	.977	5.12
Durham, Ray	CWS	148	147	1263.2	305	412	19	100	.974	5.11
Bell, David	Sea	154	150	1307.2	313	426	17	118	.978	5.09
Alomar, Roberto	Cle	156	154	1306.1	270	466	6	102	.992	5.07
Morandini, Mickey	ChC	132	110	992.1	239	319	5	72	.991	5.06
Castillo, Luis	Fla	126	122	1068.1	257	343	15	75	.976	5.05
Anderson, Marlon	Phi	121	121	925.2	234	284	11	59	.979	5.04
Young, Eric	LA	117	116	974.1	217	320	9	62	.984	4.96
Morris, Warren	Pit	144	134	1215.2	263	403	14	102	.979	4.93
Kent, Jeff	SF	133	132	1125.0	279	325	10	90	.984	4.83
Boone, Bret	Atl	151	145	1296.2	270	424	13	78	.982	4.82
Walker, Todd	Min	103	99	829.1	168	270	7	54	.984	4.75
Vidro, Jose	Mon	121	115	951.2	208	293	9	62	.982	4.74
Knoblauch, Chuck	NYY	150	150	1316.2	254	425	26	67	.963	4.64
Alfonzo, Edgardo	NYM	158	158	1380.2	298	409	5	98	.993	4.61
Bell, Jay	Ari	148	145	1297.0	320	339	22	86	.968	4.57
Offerman, Jose	Bos	128	126	1096.2	237	318	14	70	.975	4.55
Average	—	132	128	1113.1	261	364	11	84	.981	5.06

Second Basemen - The Rest

Player	Tm	G	GS	Inn	PO	A	E	DP	Pct.	Rng
Abbott, Kurt	Col	66	58	489.2	124	145	3	34	.989	4.94
Alexander, Manny	ChC	17	7	63.2	21	17	3	4	.927	5.37
Alicea, Luis	Tex	37	30	276.2	60	87	3	19	.980	4.78
Amaral, Rich	Bal	2	0	2.0	0	0	0	0	.000	.00
Arias, Alex	Phi	1	1	5.0	0	0	0	0	.000	.00
Baerga, Carlos	SD	13	9	72.2	16	20	0	7	1.000	4.46
Baerga, Carlos	Cle	6	2	29.0	5	9	0	3	1.000	4.34
Bellinger, Clay	NYY	1	0	3.0	0	0	0	0	.000	.00
Benjamin, Mike	Pit	12	11	100.1	21	31	0	5	1.000	4.66
Berg, Dave	Fla	29	24	221.1	51	80	0	16	1.000	5.33
Blauser, Jeff	ChC	25	14	129.2	41	32	3	9	.961	5.07
Blum, Geoff	Mon	2	0	5.1	2	0	0	0	1.000	3.38
Bogar, Tim	Hou	1	0	3.0	1	2	0	1	1.000	9.00
Bournigal, Rafael	Sea	17	10	95.0	26	33	1	10	.983	5.59
Cabrera, Jolbert	Cle	6	0	10.0	4	4	0	1	1.000	7.20
Canizaro, Jay	SF	4	2	18.0	2	5	0	1	1.000	3.50
Castro, Juan	LA	1	0	3.0	1	4	0	1	1.000	15.00
Catalanotto, Frank	Det	32	19	179.0	24	61	3	7	.966	4.27
Cedeno, Domingo	Sea	1	0	7.0	1	2	0	0	1.000	3.86
Cedeno, Domingo	Phi	1	0	1.1	1	2	0	0	1.000	20.25
Cedeno, Roger	NYM	1	0	0.1	0	0	0	0	.000	.00
Clapinski, Chris	Fla	2	0	2.0	0	2	0	0	1.000	9.00
Collier, Lou	Mil	4	2	16.1	7	0	0	0	1.000	3.86
Coquillette, Trace	Mon	6	4	36.0	10	14	0	4	1.000	6.00

265

Second Basemen - The Rest

Player	Tm	G	GS	Inn	PO	A	E	DP	Pct.	Rng
Cora, Alex	LA	3	3	23.0	3	9	2	2	.857	4.70
Counsell, Craig	Fla	12	10	89.0	20	29	1	4	.980	4.96
Counsell, Craig	LA	38	23	228.1	54	85	1	13	.993	5.48
Cromer, Tripp	LA	9	4	41.0	7	18	0	5	1.000	5.49
Davidson, Cleatus	Min	6	5	42.0	13	23	1	7	.973	7.71
Delgado, Wilson	SF	15	4	68.0	17	9	1	2	.963	3.44
Diaz, Edwin	Ari	2	0	4.0	0	3	0	0	1.000	6.75
Doster, David	Phi	77	7	214.0	69	72	1	21	.993	5.93
Durrington, Trent	Ana	41	36	303.1	73	98	6	19	.966	5.07
Fernandez, Tony	Tor	1	0	3.0	0	2	0	0	1.000	6.00
Fonville, Chad	Bos	2	1	10.0	6	3	1	1	.900	8.10
Frias, Hanley	Ari	8	0	10.1	4	6	0	2	1.000	8.71
Frye, Jeff	Bos	26	21	205.0	41	56	2	9	.980	4.26
Garcia, Amaury	Fla	8	6	55.0	15	26	3	5	.932	6.71
Garcia, Jesse	Bal	6	3	32.0	7	8	0	3	1.000	4.22
Garcia, Luis	Det	1	0	1.0	0	0	0	0	.000	.00
Gates, Brent	Min	47	26	262.0	44	95	0	19	1.000	4.77
Giovanola, Ed	SD	19	8	95.0	26	28	1	9	.982	5.12
Gipson, Charles	Sea	3	0	6.0	1	1	0	1	1.000	3.00
Graffanino, Tony	TB	17	17	148.0	38	65	1	14	.990	6.26
Grebeck, Craig	Tor	17	16	136.1	32	39	3	7	.959	4.69
Guerrero, Wilton	Mon	54	36	334.1	65	98	12	17	.931	4.39
Guillen, Carlos	Sea	2	2	18.0	6	6	0	5	1.000	6.00
Guillen, Ozzie	Atl	1	0	3.0	1	0	0	0	1.000	3.00
Hairston Jr., Jerry	Bal	50	49	434.0	115	154	0	47	1.000	5.58
Hansen, Jed	KC	21	18	163.1	44	44	1	18	.989	4.85
Harris, Lenny	Col	24	16	141.1	46	51	8	19	.924	6.18
Hernandez, Carlos	Hou	7	0	18.0	5	11	0	3	1.000	8.00
Hocking, Denny	Min	56	31	290.0	77	85	1	22	.994	5.03
Holbert, Ray	KC	11	9	85.0	14	30	1	4	.978	4.66
Howard, David	StL	9	7	48.2	10	16	0	4	1.000	4.81
Hubbard, Trenidad	LA	1	0	1.0	0	0	0	0	.000	.00
Huson, Jeff	Ana	41	27	260.1	53	92	1	20	.993	5.01
Jackson, Damian	SD	21	18	152.0	37	44	1	13	.988	4.80
Jefferies, Gregg	Det	2	0	3.0	0	1	0	0	1.000	3.00
Jimenez, D'Angelo	NYY	1	0	7.0	1	1	0	0	1.000	2.57
Johnson, Russ	Hou	15	7	67.1	16	32	2	6	.960	6.42
Jordan, Kevin	Phi	33	20	179.0	56	67	2	22	.984	6.18
Kelly, Pat	Tor	35	32	280.1	60	92	6	17	.962	4.88
Kennedy, Adam	StL	29	26	226.2	68	64	4	14	.971	5.24
Lamb, David	TB	15	6	66.0	12	25	2	6	.949	5.05
Lansing, Mike	Col	35	35	302.1	91	98	2	40	.990	5.63
Ledesma, Aaron	TB	17	13	129.0	43	56	1	18	.990	6.91
Leius, Scott	KC	1	0	1.0	0	0	0	0	.000	.00
Lewis, Mark	Cin	2	0	4.1	0	1	1	0	.500	2.08
Lockhart, Keith	Atl	25	18	171.1	26	58	0	11	1.000	4.41
Lopez, Luis	NYM	16	5	66.2	8	20	1	5	.966	3.78
Lopez, Mendy	KC	6	6	49.0	11	16	0	5	1.000	4.96
Loretta, Mark	Mil	17	9	88.2	28	37	3	8	.956	6.60
Lovullo, Torey	Phi	6	5	39.0	14	8	0	1	1.000	5.08
Macias, Jose	Det	1	1	8.0	1	6	0	0	1.000	7.88
Martin, Norberto	Tor	8	7	67.2	9	29	1	8	.974	5.05
Martinez, Felix	KC	1	0	4.0	1	2	0	1	1.000	6.75
Martinez, Ramon	SF	27	18	176.0	50	68	1	15	.992	6.03
McDonald, Jason	Oak	1	0	1.0	0	0	0	0	1.000	9.00
McDonald, John	Cle	7	1	21.0	7	11	0	4	1.000	7.71
Merloni, Lou	Bos	8	7	62.0	17	20	2	4	.949	5.37
Meyers, Chad	ChC	32	31	245.0	49	68	2	13	.983	4.30

Second Basemen - The Rest

Player	Tm	G	GS	Inn	PO	A	E	DP	Pct.	Rng
Mora, Melvin	NYM	4	0	9.0	1	1	0	1	1.000	2.00
Mordecai, Mike	Mon	38	7	107.0	17	33	2	11	.962	4.21
Mueller, Bill	SF	3	0	6.0	2	0	0	0	1.000	3.00
Newhan, David	SD	19	9	94.2	28	36	2	10	.970	6.08
Nunez, Abraham	Pit	14	14	104.1	24	42	1	13	.985	5.69
Ordaz, Luis	StL	1	0	2.0	0	1	0	0	1.000	4.50
Owens, Eric	SD	1	0	3.0	1	0	0	0	1.000	3.00
Paquette, Craig	StL	7	4	37.2	10	15	1	4	.962	5.97
Petersen, Chris	Col	6	3	28.0	9	12	1	5	.955	6.75
Phillips, Tony	Oak	66	64	484.1	96	164	7	41	.974	4.83
Polanco, Placido	StL	66	39	396.2	116	123	5	32	.980	5.42
Reboulet, Jeff	Bal	36	23	216.1	54	83	1	21	.993	5.70
Rodriguez, Liu	CWS	22	14	145.2	25	41	1	6	.985	4.08
Sadler, Donnie	Bos	10	7	63.0	7	22	2	4	.935	4.14
Sanford, Chance	LA	2	1	9.0	1	1	0	0	1.000	2.00
Santangelo, F.P.	SF	11	6	63.1	13	21	0	1	1.000	4.83
Scarsone, Steve	KC	9	6	52.1	17	13	2	3	.938	5.16
Sefcik, Kevin	Phi	15	8	74.1	24	17	1	3	.976	4.96
Sexton, Chris	Col	10	4	55.0	19	18	2	3	.949	6.05
Shave, Jon	Tex	1	0	1.0	1	1	0	1	1.000	18.00
Sheets, Andy	Ana	7	3	31.0	6	7	1	0	.929	3.77
Shumpert, Terry	Col	54	46	412.2	102	151	3	35	.988	5.52
Silvestri, Dave	Ana	1	1	7.0	0	3	0	0	1.000	3.86
Smith, Bobby	TB	13	12	96.0	22	32	2	7	.964	5.06
Sojo, Luis	NYY	16	12	113.0	30	40	1	12	.986	5.58
Spiers, Bill	Hou	4	2	19.0	5	10	0	0	1.000	7.11
Spiezio, Scott	Oak	42	32	285.1	57	127	3	25	.984	5.80
Stynes, Chris	Cin	43	19	235.0	48	60	5	11	.956	4.14
Sveum, Dale	Pit	2	1	7.0	1	2	0	1	1.000	3.86
Unroe, Tim	Ana	1	0	1.0	0	0	0	0	.000	.00
Velandia, Jorge	Oak	52	5	138.0	36	57	1	13	.989	6.07
Velarde, Randy	Ana	95	95	828.2	191	307	7	61	.986	5.41
Velarde, Randy	Oak	61	61	529.2	107	186	7	43	.977	4.98
Vina, Fernando	Mil	37	37	324.0	84	104	1	31	.995	5.22
Vizcaino, Jose	LA	30	15	173.1	36	69	1	9	.991	5.45
Wehner, John	Pit	1	1	6.0	4	2	0	2	1.000	9.00
Wilson, Craig	CWS	7	1	29.0	6	9	1	1	.938	4.66
Wilson, Enrique	Cle	21	5	84.0	16	19	0	2	1.000	3.75
Womack, Tony	Ari	19	17	156.0	30	36	2	6	.971	3.81
Wood, Jason	Det	1	0	1.0	0	1	0	0	1.000	9.00
Zosky, Eddie	Mil	2	0	6.0	1	3	0	0	1.000	6.00

Third Basemen - Regulars

Player	Tm	G	GS	Inn	PO	A	E	DP	Pct.	Rng
Rolen, Scott	Phi	112	111	962.1	111	227	14	21	.960	3.16
Ventura, Robin	NYM	160	157	1356.0	123	320	9	33	.980	2.94
Cirillo, Jeff	Mil	155	154	1338.1	125	307	15	34	.966	2.91
Randa, Joe	KC	156	156	1355.1	119	314	22	28	.952	2.88
Williams, Matt	Ari	153	151	1358.0	123	299	10	30	.977	2.80
Valentin, John	Bos	111	110	952.1	84	208	14	16	.954	2.76
Boone, Aaron	Cin	136	129	1110.0	86	253	15	17	.958	2.75
Caminiti, Ken	Hou	75	73	629.0	52	138	14	17	.931	2.72
Norton, Greg	CWS	120	113	982.2	93	201	25	17	.922	2.69
Beltre, Adrian	LA	152	149	1320.2	121	274	29	24	.932	2.69
Mueller, Bill	SF	108	102	924.0	81	195	12	17	.958	2.69
Zeile, Todd	Tex	155	155	1354.1	104	294	25	23	.941	2.64

Third Basemen - Regulars

Player	Tm	G	GS	Inn	PO	A	E	DP	Pct.	Rng
Castilla, Vinny	Col	157	155	1351.1	96	299	19	32	.954	2.63
Sprague, Ed	Pit	134	132	1144.1	79	254	29	22	.920	2.62
Glaus, Troy	Ana	153	153	1344.0	114	277	19	25	.954	2.62
Koskie, Corey	Min	79	72	612.2	33	143	7	7	.962	2.59
Tatis, Fernando	StL	147	147	1278.2	100	267	16	30	.958	2.58
Brosius, Scott	NYY	132	130	1150.2	87	239	13	20	.962	2.55
Lowell, Mike	Fla	83	81	716.1	59	143	4	12	.981	2.54
Andrews, Shane	TOT	101	78	736.2	45	162	14	15	.937	2.53
Palmer, Dean	Det	141	140	1212.0	89	240	19	24	.945	2.44
Chavez, Eric	Oak	105	98	847.1	69	155	9	13	.961	2.38
Davis, Russ	Sea	124	120	1058.2	71	206	12	17	.958	2.35
Fryman, Travis	Cle	85	84	726.1	41	146	6	12	.969	2.32
Ripken Jr., Cal	Bal	85	85	700.0	36	142	13	11	.932	2.29
Fernandez, Tony	Tor	132	130	1108.2	65	211	18	21	.939	2.24
Jones, Chipper	Atl	157	157	1381.0	88	237	17	10	.950	2.12
Average	—	126	123	1074.1	84	227	15	20	.953	2.62

Third Basemen - The Rest

Player	Tm	G	GS	Inn	PO	A	E	DP	Pct.	Rng
Alexander, Manny	ChC	22	7	75.0	8	17	3	0	.893	3.00
Alicea, Luis	Tex	10	6	57.0	6	13	2	3	.905	3.00
Alvarez, Gabe	Det	2	0	6.0	0	1	0	0	1.000	1.50
Amaral, Rich	Bal	1	0	2.0	0	0	0	0	.000	.00
Andrews, Shane	Mon	82	60	576.2	37	127	12	9	.932	2.56
Andrews, Shane	ChC	19	18	160.0	8	35	2	6	.956	2.42
Arias, Alex	Phi	2	0	4.0	1	1	0	0	1.000	4.50
Arias, George	SD	50	45	379.1	35	93	8	4	.941	3.04
Baerga, Carlos	SD	13	7	71.1	5	10	2	2	.882	1.89
Baerga, Carlos	Cle	15	11	107.0	8	19	1	1	.964	2.27
Barrett, Michael	Mon	66	62	505.0	45	104	9	4	.943	2.66
Battle, Howard	Atl	6	0	23.0	2	4	0	1	1.000	2.35
Belliard, Ron	Mil	1	0	4.0	1	0	0	0	1.000	2.25
Bellinger, Clay	NYY	16	8	86.0	12	16	0	1	1.000	2.93
Benjamin, Mike	Pit	6	1	18.0	1	5	0	0	1.000	3.00
Berg, Dave	Fla	19	11	114.0	13	28	4	3	.911	3.24
Blake, Casey	Tor	14	8	90.2	12	23	0	4	1.000	3.47
Blauser, Jeff	ChC	18	12	113.1	7	19	3	0	.897	2.06
Blowers, Mike	Sea	4	2	23.1	2	5	1	1	.875	2.70
Bogar, Tim	Hou	12	9	74.2	6	20	0	1	1.000	3.13
Boggs, Wade	TB	74	72	573.2	45	100	9	14	.942	2.27
Borders, Pat	Cle	1	0	2.0	0	0	0	0	.000	.00
Bournigal, Rafael	Sea	8	4	42.0	5	4	1	0	.900	1.93
Branyan, Russ	Cle	8	7	56.0	6	18	1	0	.960	3.86
Catalanotto, Frank	Det	21	18	162.0	9	26	2	4	.946	1.94
Cedeno, Domingo	Sea	1	0	2.0	0	0	0	0	.000	.00
Clapinski, Chris	Fla	9	8	67.2	6	9	2	1	.882	2.00
Colbrunn, Greg	Ari	2	0	3.0	0	0	0	0	.000	.00
Collier, Lou	Mil	7	0	22.1	0	4	1	0	.800	1.61
Conine, Jeff	Bal	4	0	6.0	0	0	0	0	.000	.00
Coomer, Ron	Min	57	46	407.2	24	101	4	9	.969	2.76
Coquillette, Trace	Mon	11	10	86.1	3	14	1	1	.944	1.77
Cromer, Tripp	LA	2	1	13.0	2	1	0	0	1.000	2.08
Dalesandro, Mark	Tor	2	0	8.0	0	1	0	0	1.000	1.13
Daubach, Brian	Bos	4	0	2.0	0	0	0	0	.000	.00
Doster, David	Phi	6	0	15.2	3	7	0	1	1.000	5.74
Dunston, Shawon	StL	5	2	26.2	2	8	1	2	.909	3.38

Third Basemen - The Rest

Player	Tm	G	GS	Inn	PO	A	E	DP	Pct.	Rng
Dunston, Shawon	NYM	1	0	3.0	1	1	0	0	1.000	6.00
Fernandez, Jose	Mon	6	6	44.0	7	9	2	0	.889	3.27
Fox, Andy	Ari	12	8	73.1	5	15	2	2	.909	2.45
Franco, Matt	NYM	12	5	55.1	1	18	1	1	.950	3.09
Frye, Jeff	Bos	7	5	51.0	5	10	2	0	.882	2.65
Gaetti, Gary	ChC	81	65	574.2	35	140	7	8	.962	2.74
Garcia, Carlos	SD	4	3	21.1	4	3	2	0	.778	2.95
Garcia, Freddy	Pit	9	6	61.0	1	14	1	1	.938	2.21
Garcia, Jesse	Bal	2	1	11.0	0	1	0	0	1.000	0.82
Gates, Brent	Min	61	41	379.0	27	79	3	10	.972	2.52
Giambi, Jason	Oak	1	0	0.0	0	0	0	0	.000	.00
Giovanola, Ed	SD	25	3	42.1	4	11	1	0	.938	3.19
Gipson, Charles	Sea	17	17	136.1	13	45	1	4	.983	3.83
Graffanino, Tony	TB	1	0	1.0	0	0	0	0	.000	.00
Grebeck, Craig	Tor	2	1	9.0	1	0	0	0	1.000	1.00
Greene, Willie	Tor	7	5	52.2	4	7	1	0	.917	1.88
Gubanich, Creight.	Bos	1	0	7.0	1	3	0	0	1.000	5.14
Guillen, Ozzie	Atl	6	3	33.0	3	9	0	1	1.000	3.27
Gutierrez, Ricky	Hou	1	1	8.0	0	1	0	0	1.000	1.13
Guzman, Edwards	SF	5	2	20.2	2	7	0	0	1.000	3.92
Hansen, Dave	LA	13	7	72.0	5	13	2	0	.900	2.25
Hansen, Jed	KC	4	0	6.1	2	1	0	0	1.000	4.26
Harris, Lenny	Col	2	0	4.1	2	0	0	0	1.000	4.15
Harris, Lenny	Ari	5	3	33.0	3	5	0	2	1.000	2.18
Hayes, Charlie	SF	55	50	439.2	27	83	7	3	.940	2.25
Hocking, Denny	Min	6	2	24.0	1	5	0	1	1.000	2.25
Holbert, Ray	KC	1	0	1.0	0	0	0	0	.000	.00
Houston, Tyler	ChC	63	51	435.1	35	83	13	7	.901	2.44
Houston, Tyler	Cle	10	5	53.0	3	11	0	1	1.000	2.38
Howard, David	StL	4	3	28.1	3	6	0	1	1.000	2.86
Howell, Jack	Hou	3	1	9.1	1	3	0	0	1.000	3.86
Huskey, Butch	Sea	1	0	1.0	0	0	0	0	.000	.00
Huskey, Butch	Bos	2	1	10.0	1	1	0	0	1.000	1.80
Huson, Jeff	Ana	9	8	71.1	11	22	1	4	.971	4.16
Jimenez, D'Angelo	NYY	6	5	38.0	2	8	0	2	1.000	2.37
Johnson, Russ	Hou	36	23	220.2	16	52	4	8	.944	2.77
Jordan, Kevin	Phi	62	51	456.1	40	93	8	10	.943	2.62
Kinkade, Mike	NYM	3	0	8.0	1	1	0	0	1.000	2.25
Konerko, Paul	CWS	1	0	1.0	0	0	0	0	.000	.00
Ledesma, Aaron	TB	26	10	121.2	11	28	4	1	.907	2.88
Leius, Scott	KC	10	5	55.0	7	14	0	3	1.000	3.44
Lewis, Mark	Cin	52	30	314.0	21	54	5	7	.938	2.15
Leyritz, Jim	SD	1	0	1.0	0	0	0	0	.000	.00
Leyritz, Jim	NYY	1	1	9.0	2	2	1	0	.800	4.00
Liniak, Cole	ChC	10	9	71.1	8	8	0	1	1.000	2.02
Lockhart, Keith	Atl	10	2	34.0	1	6	1	1	.875	1.85
Lopez, Luis	NYM	9	0	22.1	3	3	1	1	.857	2.42
Loretta, Mark	Mil	14	7	73.0	11	16	3	2	.900	3.33
Mabry, John	Sea	24	19	170.1	21	34	8	0	.873	2.91
Magadan, Dave	SD	52	40	350.1	23	70	3	5	.969	2.39
Manto, Jeff	Cle	10	8	72.0	7	16	0	2	1.000	2.88
Manto, Jeff	NYY	1	0	1.0	0	0	0	0	.000	.00
Martinez, Ramon	SF	11	5	53.0	5	9	0	1	1.000	2.38
McEwing, Joe	StL	6	0	15.0	2	5	1	2	.875	4.20
Menechino, Frank	Oak	1	0	3.0	1	1	0	0	1.000	6.00
Merloni, Lou	Bos	9	6	62.0	6	17	3	1	.885	3.34
Millar, Kevin	Fla	1	1	9.0	0	2	0	0	1.000	2.00

Third Basemen - The Rest

Player	Tm	G	GS	Inn	PO	A	E	DP	Pct.	Rng
Minor, Ryan	Bal	45	38	326.0	25	79	4	8	.963	2.87
Mora, Melvin	NYM	3	1	12.0	2	5	0	1	1.000	5.25
Mordecai, Mike	Mon	32	24	219.1	15	47	1	4	.984	2.54
Nevin, Phil	SD	67	61	532.2	36	131	3	12	.982	2.82
Newhan, David	SD	1	0	1.0	0	0	0	0	.000	.00
Ordaz, Luis	StL	1	0	1.0	0	0	0	0	.000	.00
Orie, Kevin	Fla	64	61	528.2	51	120	7	8	.961	2.91
Otanez, Willis	Bal	22	20	173.0	16	28	4	2	.917	2.29
Otanez, Willis	Tor	24	18	166.0	16	25	2	6	.953	2.22
Owens, Eric	SD	4	3	21.0	1	4	2	0	.714	2.14
Paquette, Craig	StL	10	7	65.0	4	24	0	0	1.000	3.88
Perry, Herbert	TB	42	37	322.2	32	75	5	11	.955	2.98
Phillips, Tony	Oak	2	0	1.1	0	0	0	0	.000	.00
Polanco, Placido	StL	9	2	30.2	0	8	1	0	.889	2.35
Ramirez, Aramis	Pit	17	14	129.2	11	29	3	2	.930	2.78
Reboulet, Jeff	Bal	56	16	204.0	19	56	1	4	.987	3.31
Reed, Jeff	ChC	1	0	1.0	0	0	0	0	.000	.00
Rodriguez, Liu	CWS	1	0	1.0	0	0	0	0	.000	.00
Sadler, Donnie	Bos	9	6	58.0	7	6	3	0	.813	2.02
Saenz, Olmedo	Oak	56	43	382.0	27	79	7	12	.938	2.50
Santangelo, F.P.	SF	3	2	19.0	1	0	0	0	1.000	0.47
Scarsone, Steve	KC	3	0	3.0	0	0	0	0	.000	.00
Shave, Jon	Tex	6	1	22.0	2	6	1	1	.889	3.27
Sheets, Andy	Ana	1	0	2.0	0	1	1	0	.500	4.50
Sheldon, Scott	Tex	2	0	3.0	2	3	0	0	1.000	15.00
Shumpert, Terry	Col	14	7	73.1	6	12	1	3	.947	2.21
Smith, Bobby	TB	59	43	414.0	26	100	9	13	.933	2.74
Sojo, Luis	NYY	20	18	155.0	15	23	1	3	.974	2.21
Spiers, Bill	Hou	71	55	517.0	40	143	8	11	.958	3.19
Spiezio, Scott	Oak	31	21	202.0	16	35	4	1	.927	2.27
Stynes, Chris	Cin	8	4	38.0	2	11	1	0	.929	3.08
Surhoff, B.J.	Bal	2	2	13.0	1	5	0	0	1.000	4.15
Sveum, Dale	Pit	12	7	64.1	2	14	1	0	.941	2.24
Unroe, Tim	Ana	3	1	14.0	1	2	0	0	1.000	1.93
Velandia, Jorge	Oak	2	0	2.2	1	1	0	0	1.000	6.75
Veras, Wilton	Bos	35	34	294.1	23	56	6	7	.929	2.42
Vidro, Jose	Mon	2	0	3.0	1	0	0	0	1.000	3.00
Vizcaino, Jose	LA	9	5	47.1	2	13	0	2	1.000	2.85
Wehner, John	Pit	2	1	16.0	1	1	0	0	1.000	1.13
Wilson, Craig	CWS	72	49	453.2	47	108	5	10	.969	3.07
Wilson, Enrique	Cle	61	47	434.0	24	86	4	2	.965	2.28
Wood, Jason	Det	9	3	41.0	5	5	1	0	.909	2.20
Woodward, Chris	Tor	2	0	4.0	0	3	0	0	1.000	6.75
Zosky, Eddie	Mil	4	0	5.0	0	1	0	0	1.000	1.80

Shortstops - Regulars

Player	Tm	G	GS	Inn	PO	A	E	DP	Pct.	Rng
Sanchez, Rey	KC	134	131	1128.2	242	452	13	111	.982	5.53
Benjamin, Mike	Pit	93	81	730.2	140	298	8	77	.982	5.40
Bordick, Mike	Bal	159	155	1355.0	277	511	9	132	.989	5.23
Tejada, Miguel	Oak	159	156	1377.1	291	471	21	110	.973	4.98
Bogar, Tim	Hou	90	74	683.1	123	255	9	65	.977	4.98
Stocker, Kevin	TB	76	73	640.1	137	216	16	55	.957	4.96
Batista, Tony	TOT	141	136	1207.2	225	439	16	99	.976	4.95
DiSarcina, Gary	Ana	81	81	704.1	138	249	15	62	.963	4.95
Cabrera, Orlando	Mon	102	100	870.0	186	289	10	61	.979	4.91

Shortstops - Regulars

Player	Tm	G	GS	Inn	PO	A	E	DP	Pct.	Rng
Perez, Neifi	Col	157	156	1369.2	260	480	14	124	.981	4.86
Rodriguez, Alex	Sea	129	129	1114.2	213	382	14	103	.977	4.80
Clayton, Royce	Tex	133	133	1149.1	204	406	25	91	.961	4.78
Cruz, Deivi	Det	155	151	1300.1	230	453	12	106	.983	4.73
Guzman, Cristian	Min	131	126	1069.0	196	363	24	82	.959	4.71
Vizquel, Omar	Cle	143	140	1214.1	221	396	15	88	.976	4.57
Jackson, Damian	SD	100	86	777.1	136	258	25	57	.940	4.56
Gonzalez, Alex	Fla	135	130	1144.1	237	339	27	85	.955	4.53
Garciaparra, No.	Bos	134	133	1171.2	232	357	17	72	.972	4.52
Hernandez, Jose	TOT	137	123	1054.0	162	363	17	75	.969	4.48
Valentin, Jose	Mil	85	70	660.0	113	214	22	38	.937	4.46
Aurilia, Rich	SF	150	146	1281.0	218	411	28	97	.957	4.42
Renteria, Edgar	StL	151	140	1258.0	219	393	26	88	.959	4.38
Ordonez, Rey	NYM	154	151	1316.2	220	416	4	91	.994	4.35
Caruso, Mike	CWS	132	125	1114.2	183	348	24	86	.957	4.29
Gomez, Chris	SD	75	75	627.2	101	195	12	48	.961	4.24
Sheets, Andy	Ana	76	68	604.2	107	174	10	37	.966	4.18
Grudzielanek, Mark	LA	119	117	1028.0	171	306	13	66	.973	4.18
Larkin, Barry	Cin	161	160	1372.2	220	401	14	77	.978	4.07
Gutierrez, Ricky	Hou	80	78	674.2	102	203	9	37	.971	4.07
Weiss, Walt	Atl	102	74	692.0	108	203	12	41	.963	4.04
Jeter, Derek	NYY	158	158	1395.2	230	391	14	88	.978	4.00
Fox, Andy	Ari	82	68	622.1	95	181	12	33	.958	3.99
Arias, Alex	Phi	95	87	762.0	119	207	4	43	.988	3.85
Average	—	121	115	1014.0	183	333	15	76	.971	4.59

Shortstops - The Rest

Player	Tm	G	GS	Inn	PO	A	E	DP	Pct.	Rng
Abbott, Kurt	Col	3	1	14.0	3	3	1	2	.857	3.86
Alexander, Manny	ChC	30	16	148.1	27	54	1	9	.988	4.91
Barrett, Michael	Mon	2	0	3.0	0	1	0	0	1.000	3.00
Batista, Tony	Ari	43	38	347.0	60	130	4	27	.979	4.93
Batista, Tony	Tor	98	98	860.2	165	309	12	72	.975	4.96
Bell, David	Sea	1	0	2.0	1	0	0	0	1.000	4.50
Bell, Jay	Ari	1	0	0.1	0	0	0	0	.000	.00
Belliard, Ron	Mil	1	1	9.0	2	3	0	0	1.000	5.00
Bellinger, Clay	NYY	1	0	1.0	2	1	0	0	1.000	27.00
Berg, Dave	Fla	37	29	258.1	39	87	4	12	.969	4.39
Blauser, Jeff	ChC	22	14	123.2	21	43	1	7	.985	4.66
Blum, Geoff	Mon	42	40	321.2	47	83	10	11	.929	3.64
Boone, Aaron	Cin	6	0	14.0	1	5	0	2	1.000	3.86
Bournigal, Rafael	Sea	28	13	128.2	28	47	1	13	.987	5.25
Bush, Homer	Tor	18	18	159.0	26	54	7	5	.920	4.53
Castro, Juan	LA	1	0	1.1	0	0	0	0	.000	.00
Cedeno, Domingo	Sea	20	13	113.0	17	47	4	11	.941	5.10
Cedeno, Domingo	Phi	19	12	126.1	19	35	1	6	.982	3.85
Chavez, Eric	Oak	2	0	2.0	0	0	0	0	.000	.00
Clapinski, Chris	Fla	6	3	33.0	9	12	1	4	.955	5.73
Collier, Lou	Mil	31	20	182.0	21	52	4	7	.948	3.61
Cora, Alex	LA	8	3	37.1	10	11	0	2	1.000	5.06
Counsell, Craig	LA	2	0	3.0	0	1	0	0	1.000	3.00
Cromer, Tripp	LA	9	3	37.2	10	17	0	4	1.000	6.45
Davidson, Cleatus	Min	4	2	20.0	5	5	0	1	1.000	4.50
Davis, Russ	Sea	2	0	3.0	0	0	0	0	.000	.00
Dawkins, Travis	Cin	7	0	18.0	2	4	0	1	1.000	3.00
Delgado, Wilson	SF	20	9	99.2	22	33	4	10	.932	4.97

268

Shortstops - The Rest

Player	Tm	G	GS	Inn	PO	A	E	DP	Pct.	Rng
Dellaero, Jason	CWS	11	10	86.0	16	28	4	5	.917	4.60
DeRosa, Mark	Atl	2	0	7.0	2	2	0	0	1.000	5.14
Diaz, Edwin	Ari	2	2	14.0	4	2	0	0	1.000	3.86
Doster, David	Phi	5	3	32.0	6	9	0	3	1.000	4.22
Dransfeldt, Kelly	Tex	16	16	138.0	31	54	3	13	.966	5.54
Dunston, Shawon	StL	7	5	39.0	1	12	1	3	.929	3.00
Easley, Damion	Det	19	7	76.0	16	24	0	5	1.000	4.74
Frias, Hanley	Ari	53	36	348.0	42	95	5	16	.965	3.54
Frye, Jeff	Bos	2	2	15.0	6	5	0	1	1.000	6.60
Gaetti, Gary	ChC	1	0	2.0	0	1	0	0	1.000	4.50
Garcia, Jesse	Bal	7	4	41.0	9	13	0	5	1.000	4.83
Garcia, Luis	Det	7	1	15.2	3	2	0	0	1.000	2.87
Gates, Brent	Min	1	0	2.0	0	0	0	0	.000	.00
Giovanola, Ed	SD	7	1	15.1	6	8	0	2	1.000	8.22
Gipson, Charles	Sea	3	0	10.0	2	1	1	0	.750	2.70
Gonzalez, Alex	Tor	37	37	326.0	69	132	4	34	.980	5.55
Graffanino, Tony	TB	17	17	147.1	28	49	4	14	.951	4.70
Grebeck, Craig	Tor	4	3	30.0	9	6	2	3	.882	4.50
Guevara, Giomar	Sea	9	4	42.0	6	14	3	2	.870	4.29
Guillen, Carlos	Sea	3	3	20.1	6	9	1	1	.938	6.64
Guillen, Ozzie	Atl	53	45	421.0	54	137	7	29	.965	4.08
Halter, Shane	NYM	1	0	1.0	0	0	0	0	.000	.00
Hansen, Jed	KC	10	4	45.0	11	22	0	3	1.000	6.60
Hernandez, Carlos	Hou	2	0	3.1	2	0	1	0	.667	5.40
Hernandez, Jose	ChC	92	80	704.0	114	249	11	51	.971	4.64
Hernandez, Jose	Atl	45	43	350.0	48	114	6	24	.964	4.17
Hocking, Denny	Min	61	33	332.1	62	95	2	22	.987	4.25
Holbert, Ray	KC	22	19	167.2	31	46	1	16	.987	4.13
Howard, David	StL	13	7	60.2	10	18	1	2	.966	4.15
Huson, Jeff	Ana	22	12	114.1	14	32	3	7	.939	3.62
Johnson, Russ	Hou	2	1	10.0	1	4	1	1	.833	4.50
Jones, Chipper	Atl	1	0	1.0	0	1	0	0	1.000	9.00
Lamb, David	TB	35	22	223.1	46	75	7	28	.945	4.88
Ledesma, Aaron	TB	50	50	422.0	83	134	5	37	.977	4.63
Leius, Scott	KC	2	0	3.0	0	0	0	0	.000	.00
Lopez, Luis	NYM	33	11	132.0	23	45	2	8	.971	4.64
Lopez, Mendy	KC	1	0	1.0	0	0	0	0	.000	.00
Loretta, Mark	Mil	74	70	591.2	112	176	4	40	.986	4.38
Martin, Norberto	Tor	1	0	2.0	0	0	0	0	.000	.00
Martinez, Felix	KC	2	1	10.0	0	0	0	0	.000	.00
Martinez, Ramon	SF	12	7	74.2	11	25	5	4	.878	4.34
McDonald, John	Cle	6	1	21.0	1	10	1	1	.917	4.71
McEwing, Joe	StL	1	0	1.0	0	0	0	0	.000	.00
Meares, Pat	Pit	21	21	189.2	26	67	6	13	.939	4.41
Menechino, Frank	Oak	5	2	18.0	3	6	0	2	1.000	4.50
Merloni, Lou	Bos	24	17	162.0	36	50	4	12	.956	4.78
Mora, Melvin	NYM	1	1	7.0	0	1	0	0	1.000	1.29
Mordecai, Mike	Mon	38	22	239.2	38	75	4	20	.966	4.24
Nieves, Jose	ChC	52	52	452.2	67	162	16	29	.935	4.55
Nunez, Abraham	Pit	65	58	498.0	89	172	13	37	.953	4.72
Ordaz, Luis	StL	8	2	28.0	4	7	3	4	.786	3.54
Petersen, Chris	Col	1	1	11.1	3	4	0	1	1.000	5.56
Phillips, Tony	Oak	1	0	1.0	0	0	0	0	.000	.00
Polanco, Placido	StL	9	7	58.2	7	20	2	5	.931	4.14
Reboulet, Jeff	Bal	10	3	39.0	6	13	0	0	1.000	4.38
Reese, Pokey	Cin	16	3	57.1	15	16	0	4	1.000	4.87
Relaford, Desi	Phi	63	60	518.0	97	182	14	43	.952	4.85
Rodriguez, Liu	CWS	14	11	87.2	20	26	2	6	.958	4.72

Shortstops - The Rest

Player	Tm	G	GS	Inn	PO	A	E	DP	Pct.	Rng
Sadler, Donnie	Bos	14	10	88.0	18	22	3	5	.930	4.09
Santangelo, F.P.	SF	1	0	1.0	0	0	0	0	.000	.00
Scarsone, Steve	KC	16	6	65.1	15	27	1	7	.977	5.79
Sexton, Chris	Col	6	3	22.0	3	7	0	1	1.000	4.09
Shave, Jon	Tex	24	13	149.0	26	55	4	14	.953	4.89
Shumpert, Terry	Col	2	0	3.0	1	2	0	1	1.000	9.00
Silvestri, Dave	Ana	1	1	8.0	2	3	1	0	.833	5.63
Sojo, Luis	NYY	6	3	35.0	12	9	0	2	1.000	5.40
Soriano, Alfonso	NYY	1	1	8.0	0	1	1	1	.500	1.13
Sosa, Juan	Col	2	1	9.0	4	3	1	1	.875	7.00
Spiers, Bill	Hou	13	9	87.1	22	23	0	7	1.000	4.64
Sveum, Dale	Pit	4	1	13.0	1	5	0	1	1.000	4.15
Velandia, Jorge	Oak	8	4	40.0	9	21	2	4	.938	6.75
Vizcaino, Jose	LA	44	39	345.2	60	109	6	20	.966	4.40
Wehner, John	Pit	2	0	2.0	0	1	0	0	1.000	4.50
Wilson, Craig	CWS	22	16	150.0	29	38	1	8	.985	4.02
Wilson, Enrique	Cle	35	21	215.0	37	58	4	21	.960	3.98
Womack, Tony	Ari	19	18	135.2	16	40	1	5	.982	3.71
Wood, Jason	Det	9	2	29.0	2	7	2	1	.818	2.79
Woodward, Chris	Tor	10	6	61.1	8	23	2	2	.939	4.55

Left Fielders - Regulars

Player	Tm	G	GS	Inn	PO	A	E	DP	Pct.	Rng
Hunter, Brian L.	Sea	119	108	929.2	235	14	4	3	.984	2.41
Jenkins, Geoff	Mil	128	118	1012.1	250	14	7	4	.974	2.35
Damon, Johnny	KC	132	131	1148.2	288	7	4	0	.987	2.31
Allen, Chad	Min	133	129	1114.0	267	9	7	2	.975	2.23
Lankford, Ray	StL	105	103	883.2	210	6	3	0	.986	2.20
White, Rondell	Mon	102	66	624.2	148	3	7	1	.956	2.18
Hidalgo, Richard	Hou	97	73	704.0	155	13	0	2	1.000	2.15
Encarnacion, Juan	Det	118	107	949.0	216	10	7	2	.970	2.14
Gant, Ron	Phi	133	131	1118.2	260	7	2	2	.993	2.14
Lee, Carlos	CWS	105	105	859.1	201	3	4	0	.981	2.14
Surhoff, B.J.	Bal	148	145	1269.0	282	16	0	5	1.000	2.11
Rodriguez, Henry	ChC	122	120	981.1	222	7	6	1	.974	2.10
Vaughn, Greg	Cin	144	144	1191.1	264	8	4	2	.986	2.05
Greer, Rusty	Tex	145	145	1267.1	286	3	5	1	.983	2.05
Bonds, Barry	SF	96	95	794.1	177	4	3	2	.984	2.05
Grieve, Ben	Oak	131	127	989.2	220	5	3	1	.987	2.05
O'Leary, Troy	Bos	157	154	1357.2	296	9	2	3	.993	2.02
Sanders, Reggie	SD	97	88	706.0	150	4	5	0	.969	1.96
Gonzalez, Luis	Ari	148	146	1321.0	271	10	5	1	.983	1.91
Bichette, Dante	Col	144	144	1233.0	238	17	13	3	.951	1.87
Williams, Gerald	Atl	120	78	738.0	145	7	3	2	.981	1.85
Stewart, Shannon	Tor	141	136	1207.0	244	3	5	1	.980	1.84
Sheffield, Gary	LA	145	145	1222.1	235	7	7	1	.972	1.78
Justice, David	Cle	79	76	673.2	126	7	3	3	.978	1.78
Henderson, Rickey	NYM	116	113	889.0	168	0	2	0	.988	1.69
Martin, Al	Pit	134	125	1104.2	196	3	10	0	.952	1.62
Average	—	124	117	1011.0	221	7	4	1	.980	2.04

Left Fielders - The Rest

Player	Tm	G	GS	Inn	PO	A	E	DP	Pct.	Rng
Abbott, Jeff	CWS	17	17	136.0	25	0	1	0	.962	1.65
Agbayani, Benny	NYM	47	28	263.1	49	1	1	0	.980	1.71
Alicea, Luis	Tex	1	0	1.0	0	0	0	0	.000	.00
Allensworth, Jer.	NYM	10	2	32.2	10	0	0	0	1.000	2.76
Amaral, Rich	Bal	14	2	40.0	9	0	0	0	1.000	2.03
Anderson, Brady	Bal	9	9	76.0	17	0	0	0	1.000	2.01
Anderson, Garret	Ana	32	31	278.2	54	1	0	0	1.000	1.78
Aven, Bruce	Fla	78	62	546.0	137	2	2	0	.986	2.29
Banks, Brian	Mil	4	0	6.0	1	0	0	0	1.000	1.50
Barker, Glen	Hou	4	0	9.0	0	0	0	0	.000	.00
Barry, Jeff	Col	14	5	58.2	14	1	0	0	1.000	2.30
Bautista, Danny	Fla	22	11	104.0	44	0	3	0	.936	3.81
Becker, Rich	Mil	16	1	39.2	3	0	0	0	1.000	0.68
Becker, Rich	Oak	17	1	36.0	8	0	0	0	1.000	2.00
Bellinger, Clay	NYY	2	2	11.0	2	0	0	0	1.000	1.64
Benard, Marvin	SF	4	1	14.0	8	0	0	0	1.000	5.14
Berg, Dave	Fla	3	1	9.2	0	0	0	0	.000	.00
Bergeron, Peter	Mon	13	12	91.1	22	2	1	1	.960	2.36
Berkman, Lance	Hou	22	16	156.2	34	0	1	0	.971	1.95
Berroa, Geronimo	Tor	2	2	16.0	4	0	0	0	1.000	2.25
Biggio, Craig	Hou	6	3	25.1	6	1	0	0	1.000	2.49
Blanco, Henry	Col	1	0	1.0	0	0	0	0	.000	.00
Blauser, Jeff	ChC	1	0	1.0	1	0	0	0	1.000	9.00
Bonilla, Bobby	NYM	2	1	4.0	0	0	0	0	.000	.00
Bournigal, Rafael	Sea	1	0	0.0	0	0	0	0	.000	.00
Bragg, Darren	StL	22	14	125.2	20	3	0	1	1.000	1.65
Brown, Adrian	Pit	4	1	10.0	5	0	0	0	1.000	4.50
Brown, Dee	KC	3	3	26.0	12	1	1	0	.929	4.50
Brown, Emil	Pit	6	3	32.0	8	0	0	0	1.000	2.25
Brown, Roosevelt	ChC	13	10	81.0	12	0	1	0	.923	1.33
Brumfield, Jacob	LA	7	1	21.0	4	0	0	0	1.000	1.71
Brumfield, Jacob	Tor	10	8	85.0	15	3	0	0	1.000	1.91
Buford, Damon	Bos	5	5	39.0	8	2	0	0	1.000	2.31
Butler, Rich	TB	2	2	16.0	2	0	0	0	1.000	1.13
Butler, Rob	Tor	2	1	9.0	1	0	0	0	1.000	1.00
Cabrera, Jolbert	Cle	4	0	10.1	2	0	0	0	1.000	1.74
Cangelosi, John	Col	1	0	2.0	1	0	0	0	1.000	4.50
Canseco, Jose	TB	6	6	41.1	7	1	0	0	1.000	1.74
Cedeno, Roger	NYM	13	8	68.0	8	0	0	0	1.000	1.06
Clapinski, Chris	Fla	3	0	9.0	2	0	0	0	1.000	2.00
Clemente, Edgard	Col	2	0	2.2	0	0	0	0	.000	.00
Clyburn, Danny	TB	14	11	100.0	23	1	0	0	1.000	2.16
Colangelo, Mike	Ana	1	1	6.1	1	1	0	1	1.000	2.84
Coleman, Michael	Bos	1	0	7.0	0	0	0	0	.000	.00
Collier, Lou	Mil	9	3	26.1	14	0	0	0	1.000	4.78
Conine, Jeff	Bal	7	5	43.0	14	0	0	0	1.000	2.93
Cookson, Brent	LA	2	1	11.0	3	0	0	0	1.000	2.45
Cordero, Wil	Cle	29	29	251.0	51	0	1	0	.981	1.83
Cordova, Marty	Min	6	3	27.0	4	0	1	0	.800	1.33
Cox, Steve	TB	2	2	11.0	1	0	0	0	1.000	0.82
Cromer, Tripp	LA	1	0	2.0	0	0	0	0	.000	.00
Cruz, Jacob	Cle	11	9	76.0	14	0	0	0	1.000	1.66
Cruz, Jose	Tor	9	9	80.0	28	2	0	1	1.000	3.38
Cummings, Midre	Min	1	0	2.0	1	0	0	0	1.000	4.50
Curtis, Chad	NYY	72	47	459.0	83	2	1	0	.988	1.67
Daubach, Brian	Bos	2	0	4.0	2	0	0	0	1.000	4.50
DaVanon, Jeff	Ana	3	3	26.0	4	0	0	0	1.000	1.38
Dellucci, David	Ari	13	4	39.2	3	0	0	0	1.000	0.68

Left Fielders - The Rest

Player	Tm	G	GS	Inn	PO	A	E	DP	Pct.	Rng
Diaz, Alex	Hou	7	6	49.0	7	1	1	0	.889	1.47
Drew, J.D.	StL	1	1	4.0	2	0	0	0	1.000	4.50
Ducey, Rob	Phi	39	24	211.0	53	0	0	0	1.000	2.26
Dunston, Shawon	StL	9	7	51.0	10	0	0	0	1.000	1.76
Dunston, Shawon	NYM	9	2	34.0	9	0	1	0	.900	2.38
Dunwoody, Todd	Fla	8	5	50.0	11	0	1	0	.917	1.98
Echevarria, Angel	Col	20	8	75.2	16	0	0	0	1.000	1.90
Erstad, Darin	Ana	67	66	569.0	177	7	0	1	1.000	2.91
Everett, Carl	Hou	2	0	2.1	0	0	0	0	.000	.00
Floyd, Cliff	Fla	62	61	510.2	115	4	6	0	.952	2.10
Franco, Matt	NYM	15	5	56.0	11	0	0	0	1.000	1.77
Garcia, Freddy	Pit	17	17	128.0	35	0	0	0	1.000	2.46
Garcia, Freddy	Atl	1	1	5.0	0	0	0	0	.000	.00
Garcia, Karim	Det	35	25	225.0	54	3	0	0	1.000	2.28
Giambi, Jeremy	KC	5	4	31.0	5	0	0	0	1.000	1.45
Giles, Brian S.	Pit	8	6	58.0	10	1	0	0	1.000	1.71
Gilkey, Bernard	Ari	15	12	103.0	19	2	1	0	.955	1.83
Gipson, Charles	Sea	8	2	25.0	2	1	0	0	1.000	1.08
Goodwin, Curtis	ChC	36	0	69.1	25	0	0	0	1.000	3.25
Green, Scar.	Tex	3	1	11.0	2	0	0	0	1.000	1.64
Greene, Todd	Ana	5	5	39.0	3	0	0	0	1.000	0.69
Guerrero, Wilton	Mon	22	19	146.0	21	0	0	0	1.000	1.29
Hammonds, Jeffrey	Cin	46	3	115.2	34	1	0	0	1.000	2.72
Harris, Lenny	Col	3	2	18.0	2	0	0	0	1.000	1.00
Hayes, Charlie	SF	1	0	2.0	0	0	0	0	.000	.00
Hermansen, Chad	Pit	3	3	25.0	5	0	0	0	1.000	1.80
Hernandez, Jose	ChC	6	1	22.0	5	0	0	0	1.000	2.05
Hernandez, Jose	Atl	1	1	12.0	5	0	0	0	1.000	3.75
Hill, Glenallen	ChC	37	30	238.1	49	2	3	0	.944	1.93
Hocking, Denny	Min	17	8	78.0	15	2	0	0	1.000	1.96
Hollandsworth, T.	LA	27	11	126.2	33	0	2	0	.943	2.34
Howard, David	StL	3	1	13.0	1	0	0	0	1.000	0.69
Howard, Thomas	StL	3	1	17.0	3	0	0	0	1.000	1.59
Hubbard, Trenidad	LA	29	4	67.0	11	0	0	0	1.000	1.48
Hunter, Brian	Atl	8	0	32.2	10	0	0	0	1.000	2.76
Hunter, Torii	Min	16	13	117.1	19	1	0	0	1.000	1.53
Huskey, Butch	Sea	30	29	233.0	56	1	0	0	1.000	2.20
Huskey, Butch	Bos	2	1	12.0	1	0	0	0	1.000	0.75
Huson, Jeff	Ana	2	1	9.0	1	0	0	0	1.000	1.00
Hyers, Tim	Fla	12	5	57.2	13	0	0	0	1.000	2.03
Ibanez, Raul	Sea	22	7	87.0	24	1	0	0	1.000	2.59
Jackson, Damian	SD	2	0	5.2	0	1	0	0	1.000	1.59
Jackson, Darrin	CWS	46	10	145.0	38	1	1	0	.975	2.42
Jackson, Ryan	Sea	1	0	1.0	0	0	0	0	.000	.00
Javier, Stan	SF	51	45	424.2	89	2	2	1	.978	1.93
Javier, Stan	Hou	6	0	16.2	5	0	0	0	1.000	2.70
Jefferies, Gregg	Det	2	1	16.0	2	0	0	0	1.000	1.13
Jones, Jacque	Min	1	1	9.0	1	0	0	0	1.000	1.00
Jones, Terry	Mon	5	4	34.0	13	0	0	0	1.000	3.44
Kelly, Roberto	Tex	18	14	136.0	29	0	0	0	1.000	1.92
Kinkade, Mike	NYM	12	3	48.0	9	1	0	0	1.000	1.88
Klesko, Ryan	Atl	53	50	387.0	61	2	0	0	1.000	1.44
Lampkin, Tom	Sea	2	0	3.0	0	0	0	0	.000	.00
Latham, Chris	Min	6	2	25.0	3	0	0	0	1.000	1.08
Lawton, Matt	Min	10	5	51.0	14	0	0	0	1.000	2.47
Ledee, Ricky	NYY	69	63	541.0	130	2	8	0	.943	2.20
Lennon, Patrick	Tor	5	5	33.0	8	1	0	1	1.000	2.45
Liefer, Jeff	CWS	14	10	99.0	24	1	0	1	1.000	2.27

Left Fielders - The Rest

Player	Tm	G	GS	Inn	PO	A	E	DP	Pct.	Rng
Lombard, George	Atl	2	0	7.0	2	0	0	0	1.000	2.57
Lowery, Terrell	TB	29	12	152.1	38	0	1	0	.974	2.25
Luke, Matt	Ana	2	2	16.0	2	0	0	0	1.000	1.13
Mabry, John	Sea	7	6	48.0	17	2	0	0	1.000	3.56
Magee, Wendell	Phi	1	0	1.0	0	0	0	0	.000	.00
Martinez, Dave	TB	2	2	13.0	4	0	0	0	1.000	2.77
Matthews Jr., Gary	SD	6	2	25.1	4	0	0	0	1.000	1.42
May, Derrick	Bal	2	1	7.0	1	0	0	0	1.000	1.29
McCracken, Quin.	TB	26	16	166.1	34	1	0	0	1.000	1.89
McDonald, Jason	Oak	31	1	69.2	17	0	1	0	.944	2.20
McElroy, Chuck	NYM	1	0	1.0	1	0	0	0	1.000	9.00
McEwing, Joe	StL	32	16	157.2	37	1	1	0	.974	2.17
McGee, Willie	StL	30	9	135.0	31	0	2	0	.939	2.07
McGuire, Ryan	Mon	16	3	48.2	18	1	1	0	.950	3.51
McLemore, Mark	Tex	4	2	21.0	5	0	0	0	1.000	2.14
Merced, Orlando	Mon	44	41	297.0	74	3	3	0	.963	2.33
Merloni, Lou	Bos	1	0	1.0	0	0	0	0	.000	.00
Meyers, Chad	ChC	4	0	11.0	1	0	0	0	1.000	0.82
Mieske, Matt	Sea	6	2	23.0	6	0	0	0	1.000	2.35
Mieske, Matt	Hou	30	20	164.2	43	1	0	0	1.000	2.40
Millar, Kevin	Fla	1	1	7.0	1	0	0	0	1.000	1.29
Monahan, Shane	Sea	7	2	27.0	5	0	0	0	1.000	1.67
Mora, Melvin	NYM	28	0	45.0	10	0	0	0	1.000	2.00
Morris, Hal	Cin	4	2	18.0	3	0	0	0	1.000	1.50
Mouton, James	Mon	32	11	140.2	30	1	1	1	.969	1.98
Mouton, Lyle	Mil	2	2	16.0	1	0	0	0	1.000	0.56
Murray, Calvin	SF	3	0	5.0	0	0	0	0	.000	.00
Nevin, Phil	SD	5	0	14.0	3	0	0	0	1.000	1.93
Nixon, Otis	Atl	50	32	289.1	49	0	1	0	.980	1.52
Nunnally, Jon	Bos	1	1	8.0	0	0	0	0	.000	.00
Ochoa, Alex	Mil	50	37	342.1	74	1	0	0	1.000	1.97
Owens, Eric	SD	69	34	386.2	82	2	0	0	1.000	1.96
Palmeiro, Orlando	Ana	60	45	430.2	100	4	1	0	.990	2.17
Paquette, Craig	StL	3	3	19.2	2	0	0	0	1.000	0.92
Payton, Jay	NYM	5	0	7.2	2	0	0	0	1.000	2.35
Perez, Eduardo	StL	6	6	38.2	10	1	0	1	1.000	2.79
Perry, Herbert	TB	6	2	23.0	4	0	0	0	1.000	1.57
Phillips, J.R.	Col	1	1	7.0	1	0	0	0	1.000	1.29
Phillips, Tony	Oak	28	3	85.2	13	0	1	0	.929	1.37
Polonia, Luis	Det	31	29	231.0	52	3	1	0	.982	2.14
Porter, Bo	ChC	16	0	26.2	5	0	1	0	.833	1.69
Pose, Scott	KC	18	8	88.0	20	2	1	0	.957	2.25
Pratt, Todd	NYM	1	1	8.0	1	0	0	0	1.000	1.13
Quinn, Mark	KC	15	15	127.0	24	2	1	0	.963	1.84
Raines, Tim	Oak	38	30	257.1	60	0	0	0	1.000	2.10
Ramirez, Alex	Cle	5	3	26.0	6	0	0	0	1.000	2.08
Rios, Armando	SF	14	10	92.2	23	3	0	0	1.000	2.53
Roberts, David	Cle	1	0	5.0	2	0	0	0	1.000	3.60
Robinson, Kerry	Cin	2	0	5.0	0	0	0	0	.000	.00
Ryan, Rob	Ari	1	0	1.0	0	0	0	0	.000	.00
Sadler, Donnie	Bos	1	1	8.0	1	0	0	0	1.000	1.13
Sanders, Anthony	Tor	1	1	9.0	1	0	0	0	1.000	1.00
Santangelo, F.P.	SF	26	11	123.2	29	1	0	0	1.000	2.18
Sefcik, Kevin	Phi	31	7	107.2	24	1	0	0	1.000	2.09
Seguignol, Fern.	Mon	6	6	46.0	10	0	0	0	1.000	1.96
Sexson, Richie	Cle	48	40	366.1	60	3	0	0	1.000	1.55
Sexton, Chris	Col	3	0	3.0	1	0	0	0	1.000	3.00
Shumpert, Terry	Col	6	2	22.0	4	0	0	0	1.000	1.64

Left Fielders - The Rest

Player	Tm	G	GS	Inn	PO	A	E	DP	Pct.	Rng
Silvestri, Dave	Ana	1	1	8.0	1	0	0	0	1.000	1.13
Simmons, Brian	CWS	28	14	139.2	32	0	1	0	.970	2.06
Singleton, Chris	CWS	11	6	59.1	18	0	0	0	1.000	2.73
Sorrento, Paul	TB	57	55	441.1	87	2	4	1	.957	1.81
Sosa, Juan	Col	1	0	1.0	0	0	0	0	.000	.00
Spencer, Shane	NYY	46	41	359.2	81	4	0	2	1.000	2.13
Spiers, Bill	Hou	25	14	124.1	21	0	1	0	.955	1.52
Stynes, Chris	Cin	4	0	3.0	0	0	0	0	.000	.00
Sveum, Dale	Pit	1	0	3.0	2	0	0	0	1.000	6.00
Sweeney, Mark	Cin	1	0	1.0	1	0	0	0	1.000	9.00
Tarasco, Tony	NYY	9	9	69.0	11	0	0	0	1.000	1.43
Thompson, Ryan	Hou	2	0	3.0	0	0	0	0	.000	.00
Timmons, Ozzie	Sea	12	6	57.0	11	0	0	0	1.000	1.74
Trammell, Bubba	TB	61	54	468.2	105	2	1	1	.991	2.05
Unroe, Tim	Ana	4	4	24.0	6	0	0	0	1.000	2.25
Vander Wal, John	SD	45	38	282.2	69	2	0	1	1.000	2.26
Vidro, Jose	Mon	3	0	6.0	2	0	0	0	1.000	3.00
Vizcaino, Jose	LA	1	0	3.0	0	0	0	0	.000	.00
Ward, Daryle	Hou	31	30	203.2	33	1	2	0	.944	1.50
Ward, Turner	Pit	5	0	10.2	1	0	0	0	1.000	0.84
Watkins, Pat	Col	4	0	5.0	0	0	0	0	.000	.00
Wehner, John	Pit	12	6	62.0	10	0	1	0	.909	1.45
Whiten, Mark	Cle	5	5	42.0	10	1	0	0	1.000	2.36
Williams, Reggie	Ana	4	3	24.2	2	0	0	0	1.000	0.73
Wilson, Preston	Fla	23	16	141.2	39	2	1	0	.976	2.60
Young, Dmitri	Cin	23	14	128.0	28	1	1	0	.967	2.04
Young, Ernie	Ari	1	0	2.0	1	0	0	0	1.000	4.50

Center Fielders - Regulars

Player	Tm	G	GS	Inn	PO	A	E	DP	Pct.	Rng
Singleton, Chris	CWS	121	119	1036.1	355	9	4	3	.989	3.16
Jones, Andruw	Atl	162	162	1447.1	492	13	10	1	.981	3.15
Anderson, Garret	Ana	116	115	1011.2	340	5	3	1	.991	3.07
Johnson, Lance	ChC	91	77	716.2	235	6	3	1	.988	3.03
Hunter, Torii	Min	107	90	770.1	250	6	1	3	.996	2.99
Cruz, Jose	Tor	97	87	787.1	248	6	3	1	.988	2.90
Glanville, Doug	Phi	148	146	1267.2	385	13	8	3	.980	2.84
Martinez, Manny	Mon	126	77	761.0	231	9	8	0	.968	2.84
Rivera, Ruben	SD	143	110	1023.0	312	8	8	2	.976	2.82
Christenson, Ryan	Oak	104	73	692.0	213	3	7	1	.969	2.81
Wilson, Preston	Fla	111	105	896.1	269	8	7	1	.975	2.78
Drew, J.D.	StL	97	92	803.1	234	9	7	6	.972	2.72
Beltran, Carlos	KC	154	154	1352.2	395	16	12	2	.972	2.72
Lewis, Darren	Bos	88	85	739.2	222	1	2	1	.991	2.71
Griffey Jr., Ken	Sea	158	154	1315.0	385	10	9	5	.978	2.71
Cameron, Mike	Cin	146	142	1260.2	371	7	8	3	.979	2.71
Finley, Steve	Ari	155	144	1347.2	397	5	2	0	.995	2.68
Winn, Randy	TB	77	69	621.2	180	4	1	0	.995	2.66
Kapler, Gabe	Det	114	106	916.0	266	3	4	1	.985	2.64
Grissom, Marquis	Mil	149	145	1285.0	374	1	5	2	.987	2.63
Williams, Bernie	NYY	155	153	1354.2	381	9	5	3	.987	2.59
Buford, Damon	Bos	82	71	644.0	181	4	3	2	.984	2.59
Goodwin, Tom	Tex	107	104	916.0	258	4	0	0	.989	2.57
Hamilton, Darryl	TOT	134	124	1085.1	305	3	0	0	1.000	2.55
Benard, Marvin	SF	123	120	1056.0	291	5	4	1	.987	2.52
Lofton, Kenny	Cle	119	115	991.1	255	11	3	3	.989	2.41

Center Fielders - Regulars

Player	Tm	G	GS	Inn	PO	A	E	DP	Pct.	Rng
Anderson, Brady	Bal	129	125	1102.0	291	3	1	1	.997	2.40
Giles, Brian S.	Pit	108	107	924.1	238	6	2	2	.992	2.38
White, Devon	LA	128	121	1065.0	273	3	4	1	.986	2.33
Everett, Carl	Hou	118	116	986.0	237	10	5	3	.980	2.25
McRae, Brian	TOT	107	98	850.2	194	2	1	1	.995	2.07
Average	—	121	113	1000.2	292	6	4	1	.985	2.69

Center Fielders - The Rest

Player	Tm	G	GS	Inn	PO	A	E	DP	Pct.	Rng
Abbott, Kurt	Col	2	2	15.0	3	0	0	0	1.000	1.80
Agbayani, Benny	NYM	4	3	27.0	6	0	0	0	1.000	2.00
Allensworth, Jer.	NYM	14	5	59.0	14	0	0	0	1.000	2.14
Amaral, Rich	Bal	18	14	128.0	40	0	0	0	1.000	2.81
Aven, Bruce	Fla	9	5	54.0	15	0	0	0	1.000	2.50
Barker, Glen	Hou	46	8	166.2	47	1	1	1	.980	2.59
Barry, Jeff	Col	32	26	235.2	62	3	0	0	1.000	2.48
Bartee, Kimera	Det	38	20	204.0	66	0	1	0	.985	2.96
Bautista, Danny	Fla	18	10	101.1	45	0	0	0	1.000	4.00
Becker, Rich	Mil	19	12	108.1	36	1	1	0	.974	3.07
Becker, Rich	Oak	32	29	216.0	49	3	1	1	.981	2.17
Bergeron, Peter	Mon	3	0	7.0	5	0	0	0	1.000	6.43
Bragg, Darren	StL	43	31	295.1	79	2	0	0	1.000	2.47
Brown, Adrian	Pit	29	13	142.0	33	2	0	2	1.000	2.22
Brown, Brant	Pit	23	21	158.1	35	0	3	0	.921	1.99
Brown, Roosevelt	ChC	5	4	35.0	8	1	0	0	1.000	2.31
Brumfield, Jacob	LA	4	1	15.0	7	0	0	0	1.000	4.20
Brumfield, Jacob	Tor	36	31	281.2	90	2	2	0	.979	2.94
Cabrera, Jolbert	Cle	12	6	63.0	20	0	1	0	.952	2.86
Cedeno, Roger	NYM	21	18	142.1	36	1	0	1	1.000	2.34
Christensen, McK.	CWS	27	15	146.1	50	0	3	0	.943	3.08
Clemente, Edgard	Col	45	38	335.0	96	2	3	1	.970	2.63
Coleman, Michael	Bos	1	1	7.0	0	0	0	0	.000	.00
Cruz, Jacob	Cle	15	9	89.0	33	0	0	0	1.000	3.34
Curtis, Chad	NYY	6	4	39.0	11	0	0	0	1.000	2.54
Damon, Johnny	KC	8	6	55.0	10	0	0	0	1.000	1.64
Darr, Mike	SD	3	2	14.0	6	0	0	0	1.000	3.86
Davis, Eric	StL	3	0	8.1	5	0	0	0	1.000	5.40
Dellucci, David	Ari	4	2	24.2	6	0	0	0	1.000	2.19
Ducey, Rob	Phi	9	6	62.0	22	1	0	0	1.000	3.34
Dunston, Shawon	StL	11	9	69.1	22	1	0	0	1.000	2.99
Dunston, Shawon	NYM	16	13	117.2	32	1	0	0	1.000	2.52
Dunwoody, Todd	Fla	44	38	334.0	87	3	1	0	.989	2.43
Edmonds, Jim	Ana	42	42	375.2	119	4	1	1	.992	2.95
Encarnacion, Juan	Det	22	20	161.0	47	0	2	0	.959	2.63
Erstad, Darin	Ana	2	1	18.0	8	0	0	0	1.000	4.00
Gipson, Charles	Sea	9	1	22.0	14	2	0	0	1.000	6.55
Goodwin, Curtis	ChC	42	34	305.1	90	3	2	2	.979	2.74
Goodwin, Curtis	Tor	2	2	17.0	7	1	0	0	1.000	4.24
Green, Scar.	Tex	4	0	8.0	3	0	0	0	1.000	3.38
Halter, Shane	NYM	1	0	1.0	0	0	0	0	.000	.00
Hamilton, Darryl	Col	82	79	691.0	204	1	0	0	1.000	2.67
Hamilton, Darryl	NYM	52	45	394.1	100	2	0	0	1.000	2.33
Hammonds, Jeffrey	Cin	21	14	134.2	41	1	0	1	1.000	2.81
Hansen, Jed	KC	2	0	4.0	0	0	0	0	.000	.00
Hermansen, Chad	Pit	9	9	79.0	13	0	0	0	1.000	1.48

Center Fielders - The Rest

Player	Tm	G	GS	Inn	PO	A	E	DP	Pct.	Rng
Hernandez, Jose	ChC	14	10	77.0	16	0	0	0	1.000	1.87
Hidalgo, Richard	Hou	30	27	202.1	53	2	2	0	.965	2.45
Hocking, Denny	Min	11	4	42.0	12	1	0	0	1.000	2.79
Hollandsworth, T.	LA	34	30	262.0	76	1	0	0	1.000	2.65
Howard, David	StL	1	0	0.2	0	0	0	0	.000	.00
Hubbard, Trenidad	LA	19	10	110.0	31	0	0	0	1.000	2.54
Hunter, Brian L.	Det	18	15	140.0	49	1	0	0	1.000	3.21
Hunter, Brian L.	Sea	19	6	76.2	17	0	0	0	1.000	2.00
Jackson, Darrin	CWS	25	20	176.0	61	1	2	0	.969	3.17
Javier, Stan	SF	3	2	19.0	5	0	0	0	1.000	2.37
Javier, Stan	Hou	7	6	50.0	12	0	0	0	1.000	2.16
Jones, Jacque	Min	82	64	569.0	195	8	5	2	.976	3.21
Jones, Terry	Mon	12	12	97.0	34	2	0	0	1.000	3.34
Kelly, Roberto	Tex	37	27	246.2	61	3	1	1	.985	2.34
Kingsale, Gene	Bal	24	23	205.0	48	1	1	0	.980	2.15
Lankford, Ray	StL	2	0	9.0	4	0	0	0	1.000	4.00
Latham, Chris	Min	5	1	22.0	5	0	0	0	1.000	2.05
Lawton, Matt	Min	6	2	20.0	7	0	0	0	1.000	3.15
Ledee, Ricky	NYY	6	5	46.0	13	1	1	0	.933	2.74
Lowery, Terrell	TB	36	31	271.0	59	4	2	1	.969	2.09
Mabry, John	Sea	2	1	11.0	5	0	0	0	1.000	4.09
Magee, Wendell	Phi	1	0	10.0	5	0	0	0	1.000	4.50
Martinez, Dave	TB	52	42	378.0	91	2	1	0	.989	2.21
Mateo, Ruben	Tex	31	31	265.2	62	3	0	0	1.000	2.20
Matthews Jr., Gary	SD	2	1	10.2	4	0	0	0	1.000	3.38
McCracken, Quin.	TB	20	20	162.1	46	0	1	0	.979	2.55
McDonald, Jason	Oak	53	36	345.1	115	2	0	1	1.000	3.05
McEwing, Joe	StL	23	18	147.0	36	1	0	0	1.000	2.27
McGee, Willie	StL	19	11	112.1	29	1	0	1	1.000	2.40
McGuire, Ryan	Mon	1	0	1.0	0	0	0	0	.000	.00
McRae, Brian	NYM	87	78	688.1	152	1	1	0	.994	2.00
McRae, Brian	Col	7	7	55.1	14	0	0	0	1.000	2.28
McRae, Brian	Tor	13	13	107.0	28	1	0	1	1.000	2.44
Meyers, Chad	ChC	10	9	70.0	26	0	0	0	1.000	3.34
Mieske, Matt	Sea	3	0	9.0	4	0	0	0	1.000	4.00
Mondesi, Raul	LA	1	0	1.0	0	0	0	0	.000	.00
Mora, Melvin	NYM	11	1	23.0	7	0	0	0	1.000	2.74
Mouton, James	Mon	16	5	59.0	15	1	0	0	1.000	2.44
Murray, Calvin	SF	6	2	27.2	6	0	0	0	1.000	1.95
Nixon, Otis	Atl	5	0	19.0	3	0	0	0	1.000	1.42
Ochoa, Alex	Mil	9	4	49.1	12	1	1	0	.929	2.37
Owens, Eric	SD	47	36	275.1	83	2	2	1	.977	2.78
Palmeiro, Orlando	Ana	1	1	8.0	2	0	0	0	1.000	2.25
Payton, Jay	NYM	2	0	4.0	1	0	0	0	1.000	2.25
Phillips, Tony	Oak	32	24	182.0	54	4	3	1	.951	2.87
Porter, Bo	ChC	5	5	32.0	10	0	0	0	1.000	2.81
Pose, Scott	KC	1	1	9.0	1	0	0	0	1.000	1.00
Powell, Dante	Ari	8	4	44.0	9	0	0	0	1.000	1.84
Raines, Tim	Oak	1	0	1.0	1	0	0	0	1.000	9.00
Ramirez, Alex	Cle	1	0	2.0	1	0	0	0	1.000	4.50
Ramirez, Julio	Fla	11	4	50.0	19	0	1	0	.950	3.42
Rios, Armando	SF	2	1	12.0	4	0	0	0	1.000	3.00
Roberts, David	Cle	38	30	288.0	85	0	0	0	1.000	2.66
Sadler, Donnie	Bos	6	5	46.0	12	2	1	0	.933	2.74
Sanders, Reggie	SD	15	13	97.1	18	0	1	0	.947	1.66
Santangelo, F.P.	SF	49	37	341.2	93	3	1	1	.990	2.53
Sefcik, Kevin	Phi	19	9	98.2	21	0	1	0	.955	1.92
Sexton, Chris	Col	9	6	56.0	11	1	0	0	1.000	1.93

Center Fielders - The Rest

Player	Tm	G	GS	Inn	PO	A	E	DP	Pct.	Rng
Shumpert, Terry	Col	9	3	25.0	10	0	1	0	.909	3.60
Simmons, Brian	CWS	11	8	79.2	32	2	1	1	.971	3.84
Sosa, Juan	Col	5	0	8.0	2	0	0	0	1.000	2.25
Sosa, Sammy	ChC	25	23	194.2	77	3	1	0	.988	3.70
Spiers, Bill	Hou	7	5	33.2	8	0	0	0	1.000	2.14
Stairs, Matt	Oak	1	0	2.0	0	0	0	0	.000	.00
Stewart, Shannon	Tor	7	6	41.0	13	1	0	0	1.000	3.07
Stowers, Chris	Mon	1	0	2.0	1	0	0	0	1.000	4.50
Thompson, Ryan	Hou	5	1	20.0	3	1	0	1	1.000	1.80
Tucker, Michael	Cin	13	7	66.2	15	0	0	0	1.000	2.03
Ward, Turner	Pit	22	11	122.1	26	1	2	0	.931	1.99
Ward, Turner	Ari	2	2	17.0	7	0	0	0	1.000	3.71
Watkins, Pat	Col	1	1	8.0	8	0	0	0	1.000	9.00
Wehner, John	Pit	2	0	7.1	2	0	0	0	1.000	2.45
Wells, Vernon	Tor	24	23	205.0	51	4	0	1	1.000	2.37
White, Rondell	Mon	73	68	507.1	138	4	4	1	.973	2.52
Whiten, Mark	Cle	2	2	17.0	1	0	0	0	1.000	0.53
Williams, Gerald	Atl	1	0	4.2	0	0	0	0	.000	.00
Williams, Reggie	Ana	3	2	18.0	5	0	0	0	1.000	2.50
Womack, Tony	Ari	6	5	34.0	4	0	0	0	1.000	1.06

Right Fielders - Regulars

Player	Tm	G	GS	Inn	PO	A	E	DP	Pct.	Rng
Tucker, Michael	Cin	107	59	604.0	167	8	2	0	.989	2.61
Dye, Jermaine	KC	157	155	1358.2	362	17	6	6	.984	2.52
Kotsay, Mark	Fla	129	108	986.0	245	19	5	5	.981	2.44
Salmon, Tim	Ana	89	89	786.1	204	7	4	1	.981	2.42
Sosa, Sammy	ChC	146	139	1220.0	322	5	8	3	.976	2.41
Womack, Tony	Ari	122	102	954.0	243	8	2	2	.992	2.37
Cedeno, Roger	NYM	127	89	849.0	213	8	3	1	.987	2.34
Green, Shawn	Tor	152	152	1333.2	341	5	1	1	.997	2.33
Ordonez, Magglio	CWS	153	153	1341.1	332	12	3	4	.991	2.30
Guerrero, Vladimir	Mon	160	159	1378.1	332	15	19	3	.948	2.27
Burks, Ellis	SF	107	106	864.2	210	3	2	2	.991	2.22
Burnitz, Jeromy	Mil	127	127	1109.1	262	8	5	2	.982	2.19
Jordan, Brian	Atl	150	148	1281.0	295	9	3	3	.990	2.14
Lawton, Matt	Min	103	96	830.1	192	3	4	0	.980	2.11
Higginson, Bob	Det	88	87	759.0	175	2	3	0	.983	2.11
Mondesi, Raul	LA	158	155	1378.2	315	7	6	5	.982	2.10
O'Neill, Paul	NYY	151	150	1303.1	291	10	8	3	.974	2.08
Walker, Larry	Col	114	110	942.2	204	13	4	3	.982	2.07
Ramirez, Manny	Cle	146	145	1225.1	267	7	7	2	.975	2.01
Guillen, Jose	TOT	84	76	672.0	138	7	6	1	.960	1.94
Stairs, Matt	Oak	139	139	1209.2	245	13	5	1	.981	1.92
Martinez, Dave	TB	93	87	773.0	158	6	3	0	.982	1.91
Abreu, Bobby	Phi	146	145	1267.2	260	8	3	0	.989	1.90
Nixon, Trot	Bos	121	116	1025.2	210	3	7	1	.968	1.86
Gonzalez, Juan	Tex	131	130	1113.2	223	7	4	3	.983	1.86
Belle, Albert	Bal	154	154	1340.0	252	17	4	2	.985	1.81
Buhner, Jay	Sea	85	83	694.0	127	7	1	2	.993	1.74
Gwynn, Tony	SD	104	104	806.1	147	4	1	0	.993	1.67
Bell, Derek	Hou	126	123	1105.0	192	4	3	1	.985	1.60
Average	—	126	120	1052.0	238	8	4	1	.982	2.11

Right Fielders - The Rest

Player	Tm	G	GS	Inn	PO	A	E	DP	Pct.	Rng
Abbott, Kurt	Col	2	1	10.0	1	0	0	0	1.000	0.90
Agbayani, Benny	NYM	45	39	306.2	66	1	1	0	.985	1.97
Alexander, Manny	ChC	2	0	3.0	0	0	0	0	.000	.00
Allen, Chad	Min	1	0	1.0	0	0	0	0	.000	.00
Allensworth, Jer.	NYM	15	6	75.0	23	1	0	0	1.000	2.88
Alvarez, Gabe	Det	5	3	25.0	3	0	0	0	1.000	1.08
Amaral, Rich	Bal	19	4	55.0	17	0	0	0	1.000	2.78
Anderson, Garret	Ana	6	6	52.0	12	1	0	0	1.000	2.25
Aven, Bruce	Fla	24	17	135.0	29	2	1	1	.969	2.07
Banks, Brian	Mil	1	0	0.2	0	0	0	0	.000	.00
Barker, Glen	Hou	8	2	25.0	3	1	0	0	1.000	1.44
Barry, Jeff	Col	15	6	65.1	15	0	0	0	1.000	2.07
Bautista, Danny	Fla	31	26	208.2	51	3	0	0	1.000	2.33
Becker, Rich	Mil	17	11	112.0	23	2	1	1	.962	2.01
Becker, Rich	Oak	8	2	25.0	9	1	0	0	1.000	3.60
Benard, Marvin	SF	20	6	85.0	24	0	0	0	1.000	2.54
Berkman, Lance	Hou	8	5	47.0	8	0	1	0	.889	1.53
Bonilla, Bobby	NYM	23	22	157.0	36	2	1	0	.974	2.18
Bragg, Darren	StL	33	24	212.1	56	2	3	0	.951	2.46
Brown, Adrian	Pit	66	33	363.1	73	1	4	0	.949	1.83
Brown, Brant	Pit	59	55	419.1	115	4	0	0	1.000	2.55
Brown, Roosevelt	ChC	1	0	1.0	0	0	0	0	.000	.00
Brumfield, Jacob	Tor	8	5	59.1	20	0	1	0	.952	3.03
Butler, Rich	TB	4	3	29.0	6	0	0	0	1.000	1.86
Clemente, Edgard	Col	4	1	11.0	5	0	0	0	1.000	4.09
Clyburn, Danny	TB	10	7	64.2	16	2	0	1	1.000	2.51
Collier, Lou	Mil	1	0	1.0	0	0	0	0	.000	.00
Conine, Jeff	Bal	6	2	21.0	3	1	0	0	1.000	1.71
Cookson, Brent	LA	1	0	1.0	1	0	0	0	1.000	9.00
Coomer, Ron	Min	1	0	2.0	0	0	0	0	.000	.00
Cordova, Marty	Min	25	21	180.0	34	0	2	0	.944	1.70
Cromer, Tripp	LA	1	0	2.0	1	0	0	0	1.000	4.50
Cruz, Ivan	Pit	1	0	2.0	0	0	0	0	.000	.00
Cruz, Jacob	Cle	2	0	7.0	1	0	0	0	1.000	1.29
Cummings, Midre	Min	5	3	27.0	4	0	0	0	1.000	1.33
Curtis, Chad	NYY	3	1	10.0	4	0	0	0	1.000	3.60
Damon, Johnny	KC	3	3	24.0	4	1	0	0	1.000	1.88
Darr, Mike	SD	21	7	97.2	22	0	0	0	1.000	2.03
DaVanon, Jeff	Ana	2	1	10.0	1	0	0	0	1.000	0.90
Davis, Eric	StL	50	48	402.1	88	4	0	0	1.000	2.06
Dellucci, David	Ari	19	11	108.1	28	1	0	0	1.000	2.41
Diaz, Alex	Hou	1	1	7.0	1	0	0	0	1.000	1.29
Ducey, Rob	Phi	11	7	68.1	14	0	0	0	1.000	1.84
Dunston, Shawon	SD	4	3	24.0	6	0	0	0	1.000	2.25
Dunston, Shawon	NYM	5	0	10.1	2	0	0	0	1.000	1.74
Dunwoody, Todd	Fla	5	3	26.0	4	0	0	0	1.000	1.38
Echevarria, Angel	Col	31	22	190.0	47	3	1	1	.980	2.37
Encarnacion, Juan	Det	1	0	1.0	1	0	0	0	1.000	9.00
Everett, Carl	Hou	16	5	75.1	19	1	1	1	.952	2.39
Franco, Matt	NYM	3	1	12.0	2	0	0	0	1.000	1.50
Garcia, Freddy	Pit	7	6	43.0	8	0	1	0	.889	1.67
Garcia, Karim	Det	55	51	432.0	99	4	7	1	.936	2.15
Gibson, Derrick	Col	10	7	59.1	15	2	1	0	.941	2.43
Giles, Brian S.	Pit	25	23	206.0	46	1	1	0	.979	2.05
Gilkey, Bernard	Ari	40	37	284.2	71	1	2	0	.973	2.28
Gipson, Charles	Sea	15	1	27.0	3	2	1	0	.833	1.67
Green, Scar.	Tex	3	1	10.0	1	0	0	0	1.000	0.90
Greene, Todd	Ana	25	25	189.0	33	1	1	0	.971	1.62

Right Fielders - The Rest

Player	Tm	G	GS	Inn	PO	A	E	DP	Pct.	Rng
Greene, Willie	Tor	3	2	15.0	3	0	0	0	1.000	1.80
Grieve, Ben	Oak	8	5	49.0	12	1	0	0	1.000	2.39
Guillen, Jose	Pit	37	29	261.2	58	1	3	1	.952	2.03
Guillen, Jose	TB	47	47	410.1	80	6	3	0	.966	1.89
Halter, Shane	NYM	1	0	0.1	0	0	0	0	.000	.00
Hammonds, Jeffrey	Cin	53	37	332.2	82	3	0	1	1.000	2.30
Hansen, Dave	LA	2	0	2.0	1	0	0	0	1.000	4.50
Harris, Lenny	Col	11	5	54.1	10	2	1	1	.923	1.99
Harris, Lenny	Ari	2	1	8.2	3	0	0	0	1.000	3.12
Hermansen, Chad	Pit	6	5	47.0	11	0	0	0	1.000	2.11
Hernandez, Jose	ChC	2	0	2.0	3	0	0	0	1.000	13.50
Hidalgo, Richard	Hou	3	3	22.0	5	0	0	0	1.000	2.05
Hill, Glenallen	ChC	26	23	197.2	32	1	1	0	.971	1.50
Hocking, Denny	Min	13	7	66.1	19	2	0	0	1.000	2.85
Hollandsworth, T.	LA	9	5	51.0	11	1	0	0	1.000	2.12
Houston, Tyler	ChC	1	0	1.0	0	0	0	0	.000	.00
Howard, David	StL	1	1	5.2	2	0	0	0	1.000	3.18
Howard, Thomas	StL	45	37	312.0	73	0	1	0	.986	2.11
Hubbard, Trenidad	LA	3	2	18.1	7	1	1	0	.889	3.93
Hunter, Torii	Min	14	10	79.2	15	0	0	0	1.000	1.69
Huskey, Butch	Sea	24	22	179.0	46	0	0	0	1.000	2.31
Huskey, Butch	Bos	2	2	18.0	3	1	0	0	1.000	2.00
Hyers, Tim	Fla	4	1	11.0	2	0	0	0	1.000	1.64
Ibanez, Raul	Sea	39	22	217.0	59	0	1	0	.983	2.45
Jackson, Damian	SD	1	1	8.0	1	0	0	0	1.000	1.13
Jackson, Darrin	CWS	3	1	13.0	4	0	0	0	1.000	2.77
Javier, Stan	SF	42	29	267.0	63	2	2	1	.970	2.19
Javier, Stan	Hou	10	10	70.0	14	1	0	0	1.000	1.93
Jones, Jacque	Min	19	13	116.0	35	1	0	0	1.000	2.79
Justice, David	Cle	15	12	124.0	35	0	1	0	.972	2.54
Kapler, Gabe	Det	32	12	140.0	35	1	2	1	.947	2.31
Kelly, Mike	Col	1	0	4.0	0	0	0	0	.000	.00
Kelly, Roberto	Tex	37	27	273.0	66	1	2	1	.971	2.21
Kinkade, Mike	NYM	8	6	35.1	5	0	0	0	1.000	1.27
Koskie, Corey	Min	25	10	104.0	25	0	1	0	.962	2.16
Latham, Chris	Min	4	1	17.0	5	0	0	0	1.000	2.65
Ledee, Ricky	NYY	3	0	7.0	0	0	0	0	.000	.00
Lee, Travis	Ari	2	2	16.0	3	0	0	0	1.000	1.69
Lennon, Patrick	Tor	4	3	31.0	15	0	0	0	1.000	4.35
Lewis, Darren	Bos	51	44	385.0	87	3	0	1	1.000	2.10
Liefer, Jeff	CWS	3	1	17.0	4	0	0	0	1.000	2.12
Lombard, George	Atl	2	0	7.0	2	0	0	0	1.000	2.57
Lowery, Terrell	TB	1	0	2.0	0	0	0	0	.000	.00
Luke, Matt	Ana	4	3	18.0	6	0	0	0	1.000	3.00
Mabry, John	Sea	35	28	244.2	57	4	1	1	.984	2.24
Magee, Wendell	Phi	1	0	3.0	0	0	0	0	.000	.00
Martinez, Manny	Mon	1	1	7.0	3	1	0	1	1.000	5.14
Matthews Jr., Gary	SD	10	5	53.0	14	0	0	0	1.000	2.38
May, Derrick	Bal	3	2	19.0	6	1	0	0	1.000	3.32
McDonald, Jason	Oak	13	6	61.0	17	1	0	0	1.000	2.66
McEwing, Joe	StL	19	8	81.1	38	1	0	1	1.000	4.32
McGee, Willie	StL	43	18	226.2	43	1	1	0	.978	1.75
McGuire, Ryan	Mon	7	0	11.0	5	0	0	0	1.000	4.09
McLemore, Mark	Tex	7	4	38.2	9	0	0	0	1.000	2.09
Mieske, Matt	Sea	13	4	48.0	15	1	0	0	1.000	3.00
Mieske, Matt	Hou	7	4	41.1	11	0	0	0	1.000	2.40
Monahan, Shane	Sea	3	0	3.0	2	0	0	0	1.000	6.00
Mora, Melvin	NYM	8	0	10.2	1	0	0	0	1.000	0.84

Right Fielders - The Rest

Player	Tm	G	GS	Inn	PO	A	E	DP	Pct.	Rng
Mouton, James	Mon	11	1	25.0	5	0	0	0	1.000	1.80
Mouton, Lyle	Mil	1	0	1.0	0	0	0	0	.000	.00
Nevin, Phil	SD	9	5	50.0	8	0	0	0	1.000	1.44
Nunnally, Jon	Bos	1	0	1.0	0	0	0	0	.000	.00
O'Leary, Troy	Bos	2	0	2.0	0	0	0	0	.000	.00
Ochoa, Alex	Mil	31	23	218.2	47	3	2	0	.962	2.06
Owens, Eric	SD	27	13	138.0	34	0	0	0	1.000	2.22
Palmeiro, Orlando	Ana	35	21	211.0	52	2	0	0	1.000	2.30
Paquette, Craig	StL	25	22	181.0	40	0	2	0	.952	1.99
Phillips, J.R.	Col	6	5	40.0	10	3	1	2	.929	2.93
Phillips, Tony	Oak	15	10	93.2	18	0	2	0	.900	1.73
Polonia, Luis	Det	10	8	64.0	15	1	0	0	1.000	2.25
Porter, Bo	ChC	3	0	6.0	1	0	0	0	1.000	1.50
Pose, Scott	KC	6	2	28.0	8	1	0	0	1.000	2.89
Powell, Dante	Ari	7	1	18.1	4	0	1	0	.800	1.96
Quinn, Mark	KC	1	0	3.0	1	0	0	0	1.000	3.00
Ramirez, Alex	Cle	23	4	79.0	15	1	2	0	.889	1.82
Reed, Rick	NYM	1	0	0.1	0	0	0	0	.000	.00
Rios, Armando	SF	39	19	212.2	57	2	2	1	.967	2.50
Ryan, Rob	Ari	4	3	29.1	7	0	0	0	1.000	2.15
Sadler, Donnie	Bos	1	0	5.0	1	0	0	0	1.000	1.80
Sanders, Reggie	SD	41	26	254.1	66	0	0	0	1.000	2.34
Santangelo, F.P.	SF	9	2	27.0	8	0	0	0	1.000	2.67
Sefcik, Kevin	Phi	17	10	99.1	22	0	0	0	1.000	1.99
Seguignol, Fern.	Mon	3	1	12.0	1	0	0	0	1.000	0.75
Sexson, Richie	Cle	3	1	14.0	6	0	0	0	1.000	3.86
Sexton, Chris	Col	1	0	1.0	0	0	0	0	.000	.00
Shumpert, Terry	Col	4	3	27.1	6	0	0	0	1.000	1.98
Simmons, Brian	CWS	9	7	65.0	15	0	0	0	1.000	2.08
Simms, Mike	Tex	1	0	1.0	0	0	0	0	.000	.00
Singleton, Chris	CWS	1	0	2.0	3	0	0	0	1.000	13.50
Spencer, Shane	NYY	22	11	112.1	27	1	0	1	1.000	2.24
Spiers, Bill	Hou	9	7	51.0	11	0	0	0	1.000	1.94
Stowers, Chris	Mon	1	0	1.0	0	0	0	0	.000	.00
Sutton, Larry	KC	1	1	7.0	0	0	0	0	.000	.00
Tarasco, Tony	NYY	5	0	7.0	0	0	0	0	.000	.00
Thompson, Ryan	Hou	3	2	15.0	0	0	1	0	.000	.00
Timmons, Ozzie	Sea	5	2	21.0	1	0	0	0	1.000	0.43
Trammell, Bubba	TB	20	18	154.0	37	0	0	0	1.000	2.16
Unroe, Tim	Ana	8	7	59.0	7	1	0	0	1.000	1.22
Vander Wal, John	SD	3	1	13.0	2	0	0	0	1.000	1.38
Vizquel, Omar	Cle	1	0	1.0	0	0	0	0	.000	.00
Ward, Turner	Pit	13	6	58.2	14	0	0	0	1.000	2.15
Ward, Turner	Ari	4	2	22.0	4	0	0	0	1.000	1.64
Watkins, Pat	Col	5	2	24.0	2	0	0	0	1.000	0.75
Wehner, John	Pit	6	4	32.1	11	0	0	0	1.000	3.06
Williams, Gerald	Atl	32	14	183.0	43	2	0	0	1.000	2.21
Williams, Reggie	Ana	18	10	106.0	27	3	1	2	.968	2.55
Wilson, Preston	Fla	15	7	69.0	10	0	1	0	.909	1.30
Young, Dmitri	Cin	75	67	525.1	132	3	3	0	.978	2.31
Young, Ernie	Ari	3	3	26.0	9	1	0	1	1.000	3.46

Catchers - Regulars

Player	Tm	G	GS	Inn	PO	A	E	DP	PB	Pct.
Ausmus, Brad	Det	127	121	1080.2	754	56	2	5	7	.998
Fletcher, Darrin	Tor	113	106	935.0	638	42	2	4	10	.997
Lieberthal, Mike	Phi	143	138	1191.1	881	62	3	12	11	.997
Mayne, Brent	SF	105	85	774.0	597	47	3	9	2	.995
Wilson, Dan	Sea	121	113	995.0	743	46	4	7	3	.995
Eusebio, Tony	Hou	98	83	764.2	652	37	4	3	4	.994
Kreuter, Chad	KC	101	85	767.1	460	44	3	8	6	.994
Johnson, Charles	Bal	135	124	1093.0	770	66	5	14	3	.994
Posada, Jorge	NYY	109	98	885.2	705	46	5	7	17	.993
Flaherty, John	TB	115	112	990.2	726	87	6	12	4	.993
Rodriguez, Ivan	Tex	141	141	1208.1	850	83	7	13	1	.993
Perez, Eddie	Atl	98	85	758.0	616	48	5	7	4	.993
Blanco, Henry	Col	86	78	693.1	562	58	5	12	5	.992
Redmond, Mike	Fla	82	74	652.2	444	45	4	5	3	.992
Widger, Chris	Mon	118	105	887.2	662	54	6	6	8	.992
Nilsson, Dave	Mil	101	94	762.0	531	44	5	3	2	.991
Miller, Damian	Ari	86	78	715.1	622	61	6	9	11	.991
Steinbach, Terry	Min	96	96	811.2	539	30	5	5	5	.991
Castillo, Alberto	StL	91	74	660.1	514	38	5	10	5	.991
Santiago, Benito	ChC	107	95	841.1	560	43	6	8	10	.990
Stinnett, Kelly	Ari	86	79	707.0	549	37	6	7	5	.990
Fabregas, Jorge	TOT	82	67	612.0	425	52	5	2	4	.990
Varitek, Jason	Bos	140	130	1153.0	972	66	11	8	25	.990
Piazza, Mike	NYM	137	135	1156.2	953	47	11	5	7	.989
Walbeck, Matt	Ana	97	79	721.1	407	46	5	9	6	.989
Taubensee, Eddie	Cin	124	110	973.0	733	48	9	8	5	.989
Diaz, Einar	Cle	119	108	978.1	751	81	10	8	5	.988
Kendall, Jason	Pit	75	74	649.0	505	48	7	13	6	.988
Marrero, Eli	StL	96	77	696.2	490	42	7	12	2	.987
Fordyce, Brook	CWS	90	90	811.0	561	30	8	5	4	.987
Davis, Ben	SD	74	71	628.1	471	29	7	7	5	.986
Reed, Jeff	TOT	85	69	604.2	442	32	7	4	2	.985
Hundley, Todd	LA	108	99	878.2	681	51	16	5	7	.979
Average	—	106	96	849.1	629	49	6	7	6	.991

Catchers - The Rest

Player	Tm	G	GS	Inn	PO	A	E	DP	PB	Pct.
Alomar Jr., Sandy	Cle	35	35	296.0	257	10	7	2	1	.974
Bako, Paul	Hou	71	63	551.0	461	35	6	10	4	.988
Banks, Brian	Mil	40	22	219.1	148	14	3	3	5	.982
Barajas, Rod	Ari	5	5	45.0	30	1	0	0	1	1.000
Barrett, Michael	Mon	59	51	443.1	329	25	5	2	7	.986
Bennett, Gary	Phi	32	19	184.2	129	6	4	0	2	.971
Borders, Pat	Cle	5	5	41.0	32	1	2	0	2	.943
Borders, Pat	Tor	3	1	14.0	7	2	0	0	0	1.000
Brown, Kevin L.	Tor	2	2	18.0	10	1	0	0	0	1.000
Cancel, Robinson	Mil	15	12	105.1	84	12	2	2	0	.980
Castro, Ramon	Fla	24	22	179.2	105	17	1	1	3	.992
Cox, Darron	Mon	14	3	51.2	48	4	2	1	0	.963
Dalesandro, Mark	Tor	8	3	27.0	22	2	0	2	1	1.000
Davis, Tommy	Bal	4	1	11.0	9	1	1	0	0	.909
Decker, Steve	Ana	17	15	122.0	73	4	1	0	5	.987
DiFelice, Mike	TB	51	50	442.1	344	28	5	8	8	.987
Estalella, Bobby	Phi	7	4	46.1	38	2	1	0	0	.976
Fabregas, Jorge	Fla	78	66	595.0	404	52	5	2	4	.989

Catchers - The Rest

Player	Tm	G	GS	Inn	PO	A	E	DP	PB	Pct.
Fabregas, Jorge	Atl	4	1	17.0	21	0	0	0	0	1.000
Fasano, Sal	KC	23	20	176.2	143	8	0	0	1	1.000
Fick, Robert	Det	4	3	27.0	24	1	0	0	1	1.000
Figga, Mike	NYY	2	0	2.0	3	0	0	0	0	1.000
Figga, Mike	Bal	41	26	246.0	169	12	5	1	2	.973
Garcia, Guillermo	Fla	3	0	4.1	5	0	0	0	0	1.000
Girardi, Joe	NYY	65	64	551.0	452	34	8	5	1	.984
Gonzalez, Wiki	SD	17	17	151.2	109	15	1	2	1	.992
Greene, Charlie	Mil	31	13	136.2	104	8	1	0	1	.991
Greene, Todd	Ana	12	11	92.0	55	7	1	0	5	.984
Gubanich, Creight.	Bos	14	10	82.2	39	8	1	1	3	.979
Guzman, Edwards	SF	1	0	1.0	1	0	0	0	0	1.000
Haselman, Bill	Det	39	37	313.1	231	13	1	0	4	.996
Hatteberg, Scott	Bos	23	18	158.0	128	14	1	1	2	.993
Hemphill, Bret	Ana	12	7	69.0	36	6	2	1	1	.955
Hernandez, Ramon	Oak	40	39	341.0	274	19	6	5	2	.980
Hinch, A.J.	Oak	73	67	566.2	368	26	5	4	10	.987
Houston, Tyler	ChC	18	13	105.2	73	6	4	1	1	.952
Houston, Tyler	Cle	1	1	7.0	4	0	0	0	0	1.000
Hubbard, Trenidad	LA	1	0	3.0	1	0	0	0	0	1.000
Hughes, Bobby	Mil	44	20	219.1	149	15	2	2	5	.988
Ibanez, Raul	Sea	1	0	4.0	4	0	0	0	0	1.000
Jensen, Marcus	StL	14	10	88.1	72	9	1	1	1	.988
Johnson, Brian	Cin	39	26	248.1	201	11	1	2	4	.995
Johnson, Mark L.	CWS	72	67	581.1	413	33	3	6	10	.993
Kinkade, Mike	NYM	1	0	1.0	3	0	0	0	0	1.000
Knorr, Randy	Hou	11	7	64.0	54	3	0	0	1	1.000
Laker, Tim	Pit	2	1	9.0	9	0	0	0	0	1.000
Lampkin, Tom	Sea	56	49	434.2	292	27	5	5	5	.985
LaRue, Jason	Cin	35	27	240.2	179	15	2	0	2	.990
Levis, Jesse	Cle	9	7	66.1	53	3	0	0	0	1.000
Leyritz, Jim	SD	24	21	171.2	150	16	1	0	6	.994
Leyritz, Jim	NYY	1	0	1.0	0	0	0	0	0	.000
LoDuca, Paul	LA	34	27	248.0	178	21	2	3	0	.990
Lomasney, Steve	Bos	1	0	5.0	7	2	0	0	0	1.000
Lopez, Javy	Atl	60	56	494.2	413	29	4	3	6	.991
Macfarlane, Mike	Oak	79	56	530.2	351	43	1	8	6	.997
Machado, Robert	Mon	17	3	51.2	33	3	0	0	1	1.000
Manwaring, Kirt	Col	44	39	345.0	243	21	5	4	1	.981
Martinez, Sandy	ChC	12	5	55.2	45	2	2	0	0	.959
Matheny, Mike	Tor	57	50	445.0	346	33	2	8	2	.995
Matos, Pascual	Atl	5	1	14.0	13	1	0	0	0	1.000
Meluskey, Mitch	Hou	10	9	79.0	62	6	0	1	0	1.000
Mirabelli, Doug	SF	30	24	219.0	156	11	0	2	0	1.000
Molina, Ben	Ana	30	30	256.0	192	19	2	2	3	.991
Molina, Jose	ChC	10	7	57.0	44	5	0	1	1	1.000
Myers, Greg	SD	41	33	281.0	199	14	3	0	0	.986
Myers, Greg	Atl	31	19	187.1	166	12	1	2	0	.994
Nevin, Phil	SD	31	20	187.2	155	14	1	0	4	.994
O'Brien, Charlie	Ana	27	20	171.0	140	11	1	2	0	.993
Oliver, Joe	Pit	44	40	356.2	285	12	2	4	1	.993
Osik, Keith	Pit	50	43	382.2	289	22	1	4	1	.997
Paul, Josh	CWS	5	5	46.0	40	2	0	0	0	1.000
Pena, Angel	LA	43	36	321.1	233	26	3	5	6	.989
Petrick, Ben	Col	19	18	157.0	100	7	2	1	3	.982
Pierzynski, A.J.	Min	9	6	58.0	35	2	0	1	1	1.000
Pratt, Todd	NYM	52	28	298.0	262	13	1	1	3	.996
Prince, Tom	Phi	4	1	16.0	13	1	0	0	0	1.000

Catchers - The Rest

Player	Tm	G	GS	Inn	PO	A	E	DP	PB	Pct.
Reed, Jeff	Col	36	27	233.2	160	15	3	1	0	.983
Reed, Jeff	ChC	49	42	371.0	282	16	4	3	2	.987
Roskos, John	Fla	1	0	4.0	5	0	0	0	0	1.000
Servais, Scott	SF	62	53	462.1	362	23	3	5	6	.992
Spehr, Tim	KC	59	53	454.2	274	11	3	4	3	.990
Sweeney, Mike	KC	4	3	22.0	4	2	0	0	0	1.000
Tremie, Chris	Pit	8	3	36.0	29	2	0	0	1	1.000
Turner, Chris	Cle	12	6	61.2	50	3	2	0	0	.964
Valentin, Javier	Min	76	59	553.2	387	27	1	4	6	.998
Webster, Lenny	Bal	12	11	85.0	67	6	1	2	0	.986
Webster, Lenny	Bos	6	4	38.0	25	3	0	1	1	1.000
Wilkins, Rick	LA	1	0	2.0	1	0	0	0	0	1.000
Wilson, Vance	NYM	1	0	1.0	0	0	0	0	0	.000
Zaun, Gregg	Tex	37	21	228.0	165	15	3	0	1	.984

Catchers - Regulars - Special

Player	Tm	G	GS	Inn	SBA	CS	PCS	CS%	ER	CERA
Eusebio, Tony	Hou	98	83	764.2	59	20	2	.32	293	3.45
Perez, Eddie	Atl	98	85	758.0	75	23	2	.29	301	3.57
Miller, Damian	Ari	86	78	715.1	103	36	7	.30	292	3.67
Taubensee, Eddie	Cin	124	110	973.0	114	17	2	.13	410	3.79
Stinnett, Kelly	Ari	86	79	707.0	99	30	8	.24	304	3.87
Varitek, Jason	Bos	140	130	1153.0	170	46	4	.25	510	3.98
Posada, Jorge	NYY	109	98	885.2	104	29	8	.22	409	4.16
Piazza, Mike	NYM	137	135	1156.2	152	37	7	.21	565	4.40
Hundley, Todd	LA	99	89	878.2	139	32	9	.18	431	4.41
Redmond, Mike	Fla	82	74	652.2	74	28	3	.35	321	4.43
Marrero, Eli	StL	96	77	696.2	70	29	5	.37	353	4.56
Nilsson, Dave	Mil	101	94	762.0	131	27	8	.15	387	4.57
Mayne, Brent	SF	105	85	774.0	100	31	8	.25	395	4.59
Walbeck, Matt	Ana	97	79	721.1	89	30	3	.31	353	4.65
Kendall, Jason	Pit	75	74	649.0	69	30	5	.39	336	4.66
Steinbach, Terry	Min	96	96	811.2	62	15	0	.24	421	4.67
Johnson, Charles	Bal	135	124	1093.0	100	38	2	.37	572	4.71
Widger, Chris	Mon	118	105	887.2	130	29	3	.20	467	4.73
Davis, Ben	SD	74	71	628.1	65	20	3	.27	335	4.80
Diaz, Einar	Cle	119	108	978.1	111	39	1	.35	532	4.89
Santiago, Benito	ChC	107	95	841.1	67	25	2	.35	458	4.90
Lieberthal, Mike	Phi	143	138	1191.1	97	31	4	.29	649	4.90
Rodriguez, Ivan	Tex	141	141	1208.1	75	41	3	.53	663	4.94
Castillo, Alberto	StL	91	74	660.1	71	36	9	.44	368	5.02
Fletcher, Darrin	Tor	113	106	935.0	108	29	7	.22	523	5.03
Fordyce, Brook	CWS	103	90	811.0	88	27	10	.22	457	5.07
Ausmus, Brad	Det	127	121	1080.2	94	35	3	.35	617	5.14
Fabregas, Jorge	TOT	82	67	612.0	67	30	4	.41	357	5.25
Flaherty, John	TB	115	112	990.2	130	52	3	.39	581	5.28
Wilson, Dan	Sea	121	113	995.0	103	25	6	.20	605	5.47
Blanco, Henry	Col	86	78	693.1	98	39	2	.39	424	5.50
Kreuter, Chad	KC	101	85	767.1	104	36	6	.31	473	5.55
Reed, Jeff	TOT	85	69	604.2	103	24	2	.22	389	5.79
Average	**—**	106	96	849.1	97	30	4	.31	441	4.67

Catchers - The Rest - Special

Player	Tm	G	GS	Inn	SBA	CS	PCS	CS%	ER	CERA
Alomar Jr., Sandy	Cle	35	35	296.0	31	4	0	.13	154	4.68
Bako, Paul	Hou	71	63	551.0	54	19	1	.34	242	3.95
Banks, Brian	Mil	40	22	219.1	28	1	0	.04	122	5.01
Barajas, Rod	Ari	5	5	45.0	2	0	0	0	19	3.80
Barrett, Michael	Mon	59	51	443.1	70	16	2	.21	212	4.30
Bennett, Gary	Phi	32	19	184.2	23	3	1	.09	82	4.00
Borders, Pat	Cle	5	5	41.0	8	0	0	0	42	9.22
Borders, Pat	Tor	3	1	14.0	1	1	0	1.00	9	5.79
Brown, Kevin L.	Tor	2	2	18.0	2	1	0	.50	23	11.50
Cancel, Robinson	Mil	15	12	105.1	15	4	1	.21	86	7.35
Castro, Ramon	Fla	24	22	179.2	20	9	1	.42	95	4.76
Cox, Darron	Mon	14	3	51.2	3	1	0	.33	43	7.49
Dalesandro, Mark	Tor	8	3	27.0	6	2	0	.33	18	6.00
Davis, Tommy	Bal	4	1	11.0	3	1	0	.33	8	6.55
Decker, Steve	Ana	17	15	122.0	13	4	3	.10	61	4.50
DiFelice, Mike	TB	51	50	442.1	40	17	1	.41	224	4.56
Estalella, Bobby	Phi	7	4	46.1	8	1	0	.13	36	6.99
Fabregas, Jorge	Fla	78	66	595.0	67	30	4	.41	354	5.35

276

Catchers - The Rest - Special

Player	Tm	G	GS	Inn	SBA	CS	PCS	CS%	ER	CERA
Fabregas, Jorge	Atl	4	1	17.0	0	0	0	0	3	1.59
Fasano, Sal	KC	23	20	176.2	10	3	0	.30	86	4.38
Fick, Robert	Det	4	3	27.0	2	0	0	0	14	4.67
Figga, Mike	NYY	2	0	2.0	0	0	0	0	0	0.00
Figga, Mike	Bal	41	26	246.0	29	7	1	.21	121	4.43
Garcia, Guillermo	Fla	3	0	4.1	0	0	0	0	2	4.15
Girardi, Joe	NYY	65	64	551.0	75	19	4	.21	252	4.12
Gonzalez, Wiki	SD	17	17	151.2	11	8	1	.70	68	4.04
Greene, Charlie	Mil	31	13	136.2	21	4	0	.19	63	4.15
Greene, Todd	Ana	12	11	92.0	13	6	1	.42	54	5.28
Gubanich, Creigh.	Bos	14	10	82.2	11	3	0	.27	58	6.31
Guzman, Ed.	SF	1	0	1.0	0	0	0	0	0	0.00
Haselman, Bill	Det	39	37	313.1	29	9	3	.23	187	5.37
Hatteberg, Scott	Bos	23	18	158.0	29	6	2	.15	55	3.13
Hemphill, Bret	Ana	12	7	69.0	10	5	1	.44	38	4.96
Hernandez, Ra.	Oak	40	39	341.0	43	11	1	.24	184	4.86
Hinch, A.J.	Oak	73	67	566.2	57	15	5	.19	277	4.40
Houston, Tyler	ChC	18	13	105.2	17	3	0	.18	91	7.75
Houston, Tyler	Cle	1	1	7.0	1	0	0	0	6	7.71
Hubbard, Tren.	LA	1	0	3.0	0	0	0	0	0	0.00
Hughes, Bobby	Mil	44	20	219.1	26	8	4	.18	155	6.36
Ibanez, Raul	Sea	1	0	4.0	0	0	0	0	2	4.50
Jensen, Marcus	StL	14	10	88.1	8	4	0	.50	40	4.08
Johnson, Brian	Cin	39	26	248.1	21	7	1	.30	136	4.93
Johnson, Mark L.	CWS	72	67	581.1	55	19	5	.28	297	4.60
Kinkade, Mike	NYM	1	0	1.0	0	0	0	0	0	0.00
Knorr, Randy	Hou	11	7	64.0	8	0	0	0	39	5.48
Laker, Tim	Pit	2	1	9.0	1	0	0	0	5	5.00
Lampkin, Tom	Sea	56	49	434.2	54	25	6	.40	227	4.70
LaRue, Jason	Cin	35	27	240.2	23	10	2	.38	102	3.81
Levis, Jesse	Cle	9	7	66.1	6	1	0	.17	21	2.85
Leyritz, Jim	SD	24	21	171.2	31	5	2	.10	84	4.40
Leyritz, Jim	NYY	1	0	1.0	0	0	0	0	0	0.00
LoDuca, Paul	LA	34	27	248.0	30	10	2	.29	134	4.86
Lomasney, Steve	Bos	1	0	5.0	2	2	0	1.00	0	0.00
Lopez, Javy	Atl	60	56	494.2	61	15	5	.18	214	4.00
Macfarlane, Mike	Oak	79	56	530.2	61	25	1	.40	289	4.90
Machado, Robert	Mon	17	3	51.2	1	1	1	0	26	4.53
Manwaring, Kirt	Col	44	39	345.0	52	10	2	.16	255	6.65
Martinez, Sandy	ChC	12	5	55.2	1	0	0	0	39	6.31
Matheny, Mike	Tor	57	50	445.0	60	20	4	.29	214	4.33
Matos, Pascual	Atl	5	1	14.0	2	0	0	0	9	5.79
Meluskey, Mitch	Hou	10	9	79.0	16	4	0	.25	48	5.47
Mirabelli, Doug	SF	30	24	219.0	25	10	3	.32	105	4.32
Molina, Ben	Ana	30	30	256.0	25	10	2	.35	129	4.54
Molina, Jose	ChC	10	7	57.0	8	3	0	.38	31	4.89
Myers, Greg	SD	41	33	281.0	33	7	1	.19	116	3.72
Myers, Greg	Atl	31	19	187.1	15	7	0	.47	60	2.88
Nevin, Phil	SD	31	20	187.2	19	5	0	.26	102	4.89
O'Brien, Charlie	Ana	27	20	171.0	15	7	2	.38	107	5.63
Oliver, Joe	Pit	44	40	356.2	33	6	1	.16	155	3.91
Osik, Keith	Pit	50	43	382.2	39	12	1	.29	172	4.05
Paul, Josh	CWS	6	5	46.0	5	0	0	0	32	6.26
Pena, Angel	LA	43	36	321.1	43	14	4	.26	153	4.29
Petrick, Ben	Col	19	18	157.0	23	2	0	.09	105	6.02
Pierzynski, A.J.	Min	9	6	58.0	2	1	0	.50	48	7.45
Pratt, Todd	NYM	52	28	298.0	26	7	1	.24	126	3.81
Prince, Tom	Phi	4	1	16.0	1	0	0	0	20	11.25

Catchers - The Rest - Special

Player	Tm	G	GS	Inn	SBA	CS	PCS	CS%	ER	CERA
Reed, Jeff	Col	36	27	233.2	53	12	2	.20	171	6.59
Reed, Jeff	ChC	49	42	371.0	50	12	0	.24	218	5.29
Roskos, John	Fla	1	0	4.0	0	0	0	0	9	20.25
Servais, Scott	SF	62	53	462.1	57	12	3	.17	262	5.10
Spehr, Tim	KC	59	53	454.2	43	8	3	.13	271	5.36
Sweeney, Mike	KC	4	3	22.0	3	2	0	.67	14	5.73
Tremie, Chris	Pit	8	3	36.0	7	2	0	.29	21	5.25
Turner, Chris	Cle	12	6	61.2	7	2	1	.17	34	4.96
Valentin, Javier	Min	76	59	553.2	46	21	2	.43	323	5.25
Webster, Lenny	Bal	12	11	85.0	11	4	1	.30	59	6.25
Webster, Lenny	Bos	6	4	38.0	5	1	0	.20	15	3.55
Wilkins, Rick	LA	1	0	2.0	0	0	0	0	0	0.00
Wilson, Vance	NYM	1	0	1.0	0	0	0	0	0	0.00
Zaun, Gregg	Tex	37	21	228.0	24	11	1	.43	146	5.76

Pitchers Hitting & Fielding
and Hitters Pitching

If chicks really do dig guys who hit the longball, Greg Maddux is The Man on the Atlanta pitching staff with two homers in 1999. But Maddux and Tom Glavine might have to step aside. It's John Smoltz who may have the better chance at Heather Locklear's heart by virtue of his .274 average and .387 slugging percentage. Smoltz delivered four doubles and a homer, scored 11 runs and drove in seven.

The truth is, Alex Fernandez is the home-run king among pitchers, stroking three longballs in '99. The batting champ, however, is Cy Young Award candidate Mike Hampton, who batted .311 in 74 at-bats and contributed three doubles and three triples. He reached base at a .373 clip and slugged a whopping .432. Manager Larry Dierker had to be thinking about moving his stud hitter further up in the Houston lineup.

Hampton's teammate Shane Reynolds handled more chances in the field without committing an error than any other pitcher in baseball last season. He recorded 18 putouts and 41 assists en route to a 1.000 fielding percentage. In the American League, the leader in errorless chances was Brad Radke, who handled 57 opportunities without being tagged with a miscue.

Two hurlers demonstrated the advantage they have as lefthanders, as Wilson Alvarez and Kent Mercker were especially tough on potential basestealers. Alvarez thwarted 10 of 12 steal attempts, seven with help from his catcher and three others by his own throw to the bag on a stolen-base attempt. Mercker enjoyed similar success on 12 tries, retiring nine batters and picking off a 13th runner. A third lefty, Kenny Rogers, was successful stopping eight of 14 runners from stealing, five of them with his own toss to the bag on an attempted steal. He also picked off another four baserunners.

Among non-pitchers who took the mound in 1999, the Mets' Matt Franco led in appearances (two) and strikeouts (two).

Pitchers Hitting

	1999 Hitting														Career Hitting													
Pitcher, Team	Avg	OBP	SLG	AB	H	2B	3B	HR	R	RBI	BB	SO	SH	SB-CS	Avg	OBP	SLG	AB	H	2B	3B	HR	R	RBI	BB	SO	SH	SB-CS
Abbott, Jim, Mil	.095	.095	.095	21	2	0	0	0	0	3	0	10	3	0-0	.095	.095	.095	21	2	0	0	0	0	3	0	10	3	0-0
Abbott, Paul, Sea	.000	.000	.000	0	0	0	0	0	0	0	0	0	0	0-0	.000	.000	.000	0	0	0	0	0	0	0	0	0	0	0-0
Acevedo, Juan, StL	.050	.050	.050	20	1	0	0	0	0	0	0	16	2	0-0	.082	.111	.098	61	5	1	0	0	2	0	2	32	5	0-0
Adams, Terry, ChC	.000	.000	.000	2	0	0	0	0	0	0	0	2	0	0-0	.000	.083	.000	11	0	0	0	0	0	0	1	7	0	0-0
Aguilera, R., Min-ChC	.000	.000	.000	1	0	0	0	0	0	0	0	0	0	0-0	.201	.234	.288	139	28	3	0	3	12	11	6	37	16	0-0
Aldred, Scott, TB-Phi	.000	.000	.000	1	0	0	0	0	0	0	0	1	0	0-0	.000	.000	.000	1	0	0	0	0	0	0	0	1	0	0-0
Alfonseca, Antonio, Fla	.000	.000	.000	2	0	0	0	0	0	0	0	2	0	0-0	.000	.000	.000	9	0	0	0	0	0	0	0	7	0	0-0
Almanza, Armando, Fla	.000	.000	.000	3	0	0	0	0	0	0	0	2	0	0-0	.000	.000	.000	3	0	0	0	0	0	0	0	2	0	0-0
Almanzar, Carlos, SD	.000	.000	.000	1	0	0	0	0	0	0	0	1	0	0-0	.000	.000	.000	1	0	0	0	0	0	0	0	1	0	0-0
Almonte, Hector, Fla	.000	.000	.000	0	0	0	0	0	0	0	0	0	0	0-0	.000	.000	.000	0	0	0	0	0	0	0	0	0	0	0-0
Alvarez, Juan, Ana	.000	.000	.000	0	0	0	0	0	0	0	0	0	0	0-0	.000	.000	.000	0	0	0	0	0	0	0	0	0	0	0-0
Alvarez, Wilson, TB	.000	.000	.000	3	0	0	0	0	0	0	0	1	0	0-0	.103	.161	.103	29	3	0	0	0	1	1	2	8	1	0-0
Anderson, Brian, Ari	.132	.171	.263	38	5	0	1	1	4	2	2	10	1	1-0	.115	.155	.163	104	12	0	1	1	10	2	5	29	7	2-0
Anderson, Jimmy, Pit	.333	.333	.444	9	3	1	0	0	2	1	0	2	0	0-0	.333	.333	.444	9	3	1	0	0	2	1	0	2	0	0-0
Anderson, Matt, Det	.000	.000	.000	0	0	0	0	0	0	0	0	0	0	0-0	.000	.000	.000	0	0	0	0	0	0	0	0	0	0	0-0
Ankiel, Rick, StL	.100	.100	.100	10	1	0	0	0	0	0	0	3	1	0-0	.100	.100	.100	10	1	0	0	0	0	0	0	3	1	0-0
Appier, Kevin, KC-Oak	.000	.000	.000	2	0	0	0	0	0	0	0	1	0	0-0	.000	.000	.000	8	0	0	0	0	0	0	0	6	0	0-0
Armas Jr., Tony, Mon	.000	.000	.000	2	0	0	0	0	0	0	0	1	0	0-0	.000	.000	.000	2	0	0	0	0	0	0	0	1	0	0-0
Arnold, Jamie, LA	.200	.200	.200	10	2	0	0	0	1	1	0	3	1	0-0	.200	.200	.200	10	2	0	0	0	1	1	0	3	1	0-0
Arrojo, Rolando, TB	.000	.000	.000	0	0	0	0	0	0	0	0	0	0	0-0	.000	.000	.000	3	0	0	0	0	0	0	0	2	0	0-0
Ashby, Andy, SD	.129	.169	.161	62	8	2	0	0	3	2	3	25	7	0-0	.136	.159	.169	396	54	13	0	0	18	15	11	165	63	1-0
Assenmacher, P., Cle	.000	.000	.000	0	0	0	0	0	0	0	0	0	0	0-0	.083	.195	.111	36	3	1	0	0	3	0	5	12	7	0-0
Astacio, Pedro, Col	.233	.241	.279	86	20	2	1	0	5	7	1	24	7	0-0	.141	.150	.159	427	60	6	1	0	20	17	3	168	55	0-1
Avery, Steve, Cin	.077	.077	.077	26	2	0	0	0	1	1	0	11	2	0-0	.172	.192	.250	436	75	14	4	4	34	32	12	135	41	1-1
Ayala, B., Mon-ChC	.000	.000	.000	1	0	0	0	0	0	0	0	0	0	0-0	.065	.065	.097	31	2	1	0	0	2	1	0	13	3	0-1
Aybar, Manny, StL	.083	.083	.083	12	1	0	0	0	0	1	0	7	1	0-0	.167	.167	.217	60	10	0	0	1	4	5	0	25	2	0-0
Baldwin, James, CWS	.500	.500	1.500	2	1	0	1	0	1	1	0	1	0	0-0	.143	.143	.429	7	1	0	1	0	1	1	0	4	1	0-0
Bale, John, Tor	.000	.000	.000	0	0	0	0	0	0	0	0	0	0	0-0	.000	.000	.000	0	0	0	0	0	0	0	0	0	0	0-0
Barber, Brian, KC	.000	.000	.000	0	0	0	0	0	0	0	0	0	1	0-0	.125	.222	.125	8	1	0	0	0	0	0	1	2	1	0-0
Barker, Richie, ChC	.000	.000	.000	0	0	0	0	0	0	0	0	0	0	0-0	.000	.000	.000	0	0	0	0	0	0	0	0	0	0	0-0
Batista, Miguel, Mon	.200	.243	.314	35	7	1	0	1	6	3	2	19	4	0-0	.093	.117	.147	75	7	1	0	1	6	3	2	45	6	0-0
Beck, Rod, ChC-Bos	.000	.000	.000	0	0	0	0	0	0	0	0	0	0	0-0	.222	.222	.222	18	4	0	0	0	0	1	0	9	1	0-0
Belcher, Tim, Ana	.200	.200	.400	5	1	1	0	0	0	0	0	2	0	0-0	.124	.137	.162	388	48	9	0	2	19	25	2	147	42	0-1
Belinda, Stan, Cin	.250	.250	.250	4	1	0	0	0	0	0	0	1	0	0-0	.167	.231	.208	24	4	1	0	0	1	3	2	12	3	0-0
Beltran, Rigo, NYM-Col	.333	.333	.333	3	1	0	0	0	0	0	0	0	0	0-0	.182	.182	.273	11	2	1	0	0	1	0	0	1	0	0-0
Benes, Alan, StL	.000	.000	.000	0	0	0	0	0	0	0	0	0	0	0-0	.151	.165	.193	119	18	5	0	0	5	8	2	44	9	0-0
Benes, Andy, Ari	.155	.222	.207	58	9	0	0	1	6	5	4	17	10	0-0	.144	.187	.200	625	90	17	0	6	43	43	28	264	85	0-0
Benitez, Ar., NYM	.000	.000	.000	5	0	0	0	0	0	1	0	2	0	0-0	.000	.000	.000	5	0	0	0	0	0	1	0	2	0	0-0
Bennett, Joel, Phi	.000	.200	.000	4	0	0	0	0	1	0	1	1	1	0-0	.000	.200	.000	4	0	0	0	0	1	0	1	1	1	0-0
Bennett, Shayne, Mon	.000	.000	.000	2	0	0	0	0	0	0	0	1	0	0-0	.000	.182	.000	9	0	0	0	0	0	0	2	2	1	0-0
Benson, Kris, Pit	.154	.191	.200	65	10	3	0	0	7	7	3	24	6	0-0	.154	.191	.200	65	10	3	0	0	7	7	3	24	6	0-0
Bere, Jason, Cin-Mil	.318	.400	.318	22	7	0	0	0	3	1	2	9	2	0-0	.194	.275	.194	36	7	0	0	0	3	1	3	14	2	0-0
Bergman, S., Hou-Atl	.107	.107	.321	28	3	0	0	2	4	2	0	12	1	0-0	.107	.107	.198	131	14	3	0	3	10	11	0	58	12	0-0
Billingsley, Brent, Fla	.000	.000	.000	0	0	0	0	0	0	0	0	0	0	0-0	.000	.000	.000	0	0	0	0	0	0	0	0	0	0	0-0
Blair, Willie, Det	.000	.000	.000	1	0	0	0	0	0	0	0	0	0	0-0	.070	.107	.077	143	10	1	0	0	6	5	6	86	12	0-0
Bochtler, Doug, LA	.000	.000	.000	0	0	0	0	0	0	0	0	0	0	0-0	.000	.000	.000	2	0	0	0	0	0	0	0	0	0	0-0
Boehringer, Brian, SD	.063	.167	.063	16	1	0	0	0	0	0	2	9	2	0-0	.043	.154	.043	23	1	0	0	0	0	0	3	13	2	0-0
Bohanon, Brian, Col	.197	.250	.268	71	14	2	0	1	6	7	5	20	5	0-0	.218	.252	.279	147	32	4	1	1	7	16	7	48	10	0-0
Bones, Ricky, Bal	.000	.000	.000	0	0	0	0	0	1	0	0	0	0	0-0	.063	.167	.063	16	1	0	0	0	2	1	2	5	4	0-0
Borbon, Pedro, LA	.000	.000	.000	2	0	0	0	0	0	0	0	1	1	0-0	.250	.250	.250	4	1	0	0	0	0	0	0	1	1	0-0
Borkowski, Dave, Det	.000	.000	.000	3	0	0	0	0	0	1	0	2	0	0-0	.000	.000	.000	3	0	0	0	0	0	1	0	2	0	0-0
Bottalico, Ricky, StL	.000	.000	.000	3	0	0	0	0	0	0	0	1	0	0-0	.083	.083	.167	12	1	1	0	0	0	0	0	8	1	0-0
Bottenfield, Kent, StL	.148	.161	.197	61	9	3	0	0	4	5	1	26	8	0-0	.169	.184	.188	160	27	3	0	0	10	10	2	57	22	1-0
Bowie, Micah, Atl-ChC	.214	.267	.214	14	3	0	0	0	0	3	1	3	0	0-0	.214	.267	.214	14	3	0	0	0	0	3	1	3	0	0-0
Boyd, Jason, Pit	.000	.000	.000	1	0	0	0	0	0	0	0	1	0	0-0	.000	.000	.000	1	0	0	0	0	0	0	0	1	0	0-0
Bradford, Chad, CWS	.000	.000	.000	0	0	0	0	0	0	0	0	0	0	0-0	.000	.000	.000	0	0	0	0	0	0	0	0	0	0	0-0
Brantley, Jeff, Phi	.000	.000	.000	0	0	0	0	0	0	0	0	0	0	0-0	.118	.143	.132	68	8	1	0	0	5	5	2	23	11	0-0
Brewer, Billy, Phi	.000	.000	.000	0	0	0	0	0	0	0	0	0	0	0-0	.000	.000	.000	1	0	0	0	0	0	0	0	1	0	0-0
Brocail, Doug, Det	.000	.000	.000	0	0	0	0	0	0	0	0	0	0	0-0	.164	.164	.194	67	11	0	1	0	9	1	0	18	15	2-0
Brock, Chris, SF	.200	.263	.200	35	7	0	0	0	4	4	3	8	4	0-0	.184	.231	.184	49	9	0	0	0	4	5	3	10	4	0-0
Brower, Jim, Cle	.000	.000	.000	0	0	0	0	0	0	0	0	0	0	0-0	.000	.000	.000	0	0	0	0	0	0	0	0	0	0	0-0
Brown, Kevin, LA	.064	.086	.064	78	5	0	0	0	1	3	2	24	13	0-0	.130	.175	.146	308	40	5	0	0	10	20	17	106	30	0-0
Brownson, Mark, Col	.111	.111	.111	9	1	0	0	0	1	0	0	2	2	0-0	.071	.071	.071	14	1	0	0	0	1	0	0	2	2	0-0
Brunson, Will, Det	.000	.000	.000	0	0	0	0	0	0	0	0	0	0	0-0	.000	.000	.000	0	0	0	0	0	0	0	0	0	0	0-0
Buddie, Mike, NYY	.000	.000	.000	0	0	0	0	0	0	0	0	0	0	0-0	.000	.000	.000	0	0	0	0	0	0	0	0	0	0	0-0
Bullinger, Kirk, Bos	.000	.000	.000	0	0	0	0	0	0	0	0	0	0	0-0	.000	.000	.000	1	0	0	0	0	0	0	0	0	0	0-0
Bunch, Mel, Sea	.000	.000	.000	0	0	0	0	0	0	0	0	0	0	0-0	.000	.000	.000	0	0	0	0	0	0	0	0	0	0	0-0
Burba, Dave, Cle	.333	.500	.333	3	1	0	0	0	0	0	1	0	0	0-0	.145	.201	.203	172	25	1	0	3	9	12	10	71	17	0-0
Burkett, John, Tex	.000	.000	.000	2	0	0	0	0	0	0	0	2	0	0-0	.089	.131	.100	429	38	5	0	0	18	14	20	181	47	0-0
Burnett, A.J., Fla	.118	.118	.118	17	2	0	0	0	1	0	0	10	0	0-0	.118	.118	.118	17	2	0	0	0	1	0	0	10	0	0-0
Busby, Mike, StL	.000	.000	.000	0	0	0	0	0	0	0	0	0	0	0-0	.333	.400	.333	9	3	0	0	0	0	1	1	4	0	0-0
Byrd, Paul, Phi	.127	.200	.127	55	7	0	0	0	6	4	5	11	11	0-0	.145	.211	.145	83	12	0	0	0	7	6	6	20	13	0-0
Byrdak, Tim, KC	.500	.500	1.000	2	1	1	0	0	1	0	0	0	0	0-0	.500	.500	1.000	2	1	1	0	0	1	0	0	0	0	0-0
Cabrera, Jose, Hou	.000	.000	.000	0	0	0	0	0	0	0	0	0	0	0-0	.000	.000	.000	2	0	0	0	0	0	0	0	0	0	0-0
Callaway, Mickey, TB	.667	.667	.667	3	2	0	0	0	0	1	0	0	0	0-0	.667	.667	.667	3	2	0	0	0	0	1	0	0	0	0-0
Candiotti, T., Oak-Cle	.000	.000	.000	0	0	0	0	0	0	0	0	0	0	0-0	.117	.140	.134	299	35	5	0	0	11	12	7	71	52	0-0
Carlson, Dan, Ari	.000	.000	.000	0	0	0	0	0	0	0	0	0	0	0-0	.000	.000	.000	4	0	0	0	0	0	0	0	0	0	0-0
Carlyle, Buddy, SD	.222	.364	.222	9	2	0	0	0	1	1	2	3	0	0-0	.222	.364	.222	9	2	0	0	0	1	1	2	3	0	0-0
Carmona, Rafael, Sea	.000	.000	.000	0	0	0	0	0	0	0	0	0	0	0-0	.000	.000	.000	0	0	0	0	0	0	0	0	0	0	0-0
Carpenter, Chris, Tor	.000	.500	.000	1	0	0	0	0	0	0	1	1	0	0-0	.000	.333	.000	2	0	0	0	0	0	0	1	1	0	0-0
Carrasco, Hector, Min	.000	.000	.000	0	0	0	0	0	0	0	0	0	0	0-0	.056	.056	.056	18	1	0	0	0	0	0	0	12	0	0-0
Carter, Lance, KC	.000	.000	.000	0	0	0	0	0	0	0	0	0	0	0-0	.000	.000	.000	0	0	0	0	0	0	0	0	0	0	0-0
Castillo, Carlos, CWS	.000	.000	.000	0	0	0	0	0	0	0	0	0	0	0-0	.500	.500	.500	2	1	0	0	0	0	0	0	0	0	0-0

	1999 Hitting														Career Hitting													
Pitcher, Team	Avg	OBP	SLG	AB	H	2B	3B	HR	R	RBI	BB	SO	SH	SB-CS	Avg	OBP	SLG	AB	H	2B	3B	HR	R	RBI	BB	SO	SH	SB-CS
Cather, Mike, Atl	.000	.000	.000	0	0	0	0	0	0	0	0	0	0	0-0	.000	.000	.000	1	0	0	0	0	0	0	0	0	0	0-0
Charlton, Norm, TB	.000	.000	.000	0	0	0	0	0	0	0	0	0	0	0-0	.092	.151	.115	87	8	2	0	0	6	1	3	50	10	0-0
Checo, Robinson, LA	.333	.333	.333	3	1	0	0	0	0	2	0	2	1	0-0	.333	.333	.333	3	1	0	0	0	0	2	0	2	1	0-0
Chen, Bruce, Atl	.000	.000	.000	11	0	0	0	0	0	0	0	6	1	0-0	.056	.056	.056	18	1	0	0	0	0	1	0	10	3	0-0
Cho, Jin Ho, Bos	.000	.000	.000	1	0	0	0	0	0	0	0	0	0	0-0	.000	.000	.000	1	0	0	0	0	0	0	0	0	0	0-0
Chouinard, Bobby, Ari	.000	.000	.000	3	0	0	0	0	0	0	0	3	1	0-0	.000	.000	.000	5	0	0	0	0	0	0	0	4	1	0-0
Christiansen, Jason, Pit	.000	.000	.000	1	0	0	0	0	0	0	0	1	0	0-0	.100	.100	.100	10	1	0	0	0	0	1	0	7	1	0-0
Clark, Mark, Tex	.000	.000	.000	2	0	0	0	0	0	0	0	2	0	0-0	.058	.088	.083	242	14	3	0	1	7	9	8	106	29	0-0
Clemens, Roger, NYY	.000	.000	.000	4	0	0	0	0	0	0	0	3	1	0-0	.182	.308	.273	11	2	1	0	0	1	0	2	3	2	0-0
Clement, Matt, SD	.077	.143	.077	52	4	0	0	0	7	1	4	28	6	0-0	.074	.138	.074	54	4	0	0	0	7	1	4	30	8	0-0
Clontz, Brad, Pit	.000	.000	.000	3	0	0	0	0	0	0	0	2	0	0-0	.000	.167	.000	10	0	0	0	0	1	0	2	6	1	0-0
Cloude, Ken, Sea	.000	.000	.000	2	0	0	0	0	0	0	0	0	0	0-0	.000	.000	.000	7	0	0	0	0	0	0	0	0	0	0-0
Colon, Bartolo, Cle	.143	.143	.143	7	1	0	0	0	0	0	0	5	1	0-0	.200	.200	.200	10	2	0	0	0	0	1	0	7	1	0-0
Cone, David, NYY	.333	.333	.667	3	1	1	0	0	1	1	0	0	0	0-0	.153	.191	.176	404	62	9	0	0	28	22	16	88	37	0-1
Cook, Dennis, NYM	.000	.000	.000	1	0	0	0	0	0	0	0	1	0	0-0	.266	.286	.358	109	29	2	1	2	15	9	3	13	8	0-0
Cooper, Brian, Ana	.000	.000	.000	0	0	0	0	0	0	0	0	0	0	0-0	.000	.000	.000	0	0	0	0	0	0	0	0	0	0	0-0
Coppinger, R., Bal-Mil	.333	.333	.333	3	1	0	0	0	0	0	0	2	0	0-0	.333	.333	.333	3	1	0	0	0	0	0	0	2	0	0-0
Corbin, Archie, Fla	.000	.000	.000	1	0	0	0	0	0	0	0	1	0	0-0	.000	.000	.000	1	0	0	0	0	0	0	0	1	0	0-0
Cordero, Francisco, Det	.000	.000	.000	0	0	0	0	0	0	0	0	0	0	0-0	.000	.000	.000	0	0	0	0	0	0	0	0	0	0	0-0
Cordova, Francisco, Pit	.163	.196	.163	49	8	0	0	0	2	2	2	15	5	0-0	.122	.157	.138	196	24	1	1	0	8	5	8	77	17	0-0
Cormier, Rheal, Bos	.000	.000	.000	0	0	0	0	0	0	0	0	0	0	0-0	.185	.202	.217	184	34	4	1	0	14	12	3	43	28	0-0
Cornelius, Reid, Fla	.200	.200	.200	5	1	0	0	0	0	0	0	2	1	0-0	.120	.120	.120	25	3	0	0	0	0	0	0	9	1	0-0
Corsi, Jim, Bos-Bal	.000	.000	.000	0	0	0	0	0	0	0	0	0	0	0-0	.000	.000	.000	2	0	0	0	0	0	0	0	1	0	0-0
Cortes, David, Atl	.000	.000	.000	0	0	0	0	0	0	0	0	0	0	0-0	.000	.000	.000	0	0	0	0	0	0	0	0	0	0	0-0
Crabtree, Tim, Tex	.000	.000	.000	0	0	0	0	0	0	0	0	0	0	0-0	.000	.000	.000	1	0	0	0	0	0	0	0	0	0	0-0
Creek, Doug, ChC	.000	.000	.000	0	0	0	0	0	0	0	0	0	0	0-0	.250	.250	.250	4	1	0	0	0	1	0	0	2	3	0-0
Croushore, Rich, StL	.333	.500	.333	3	1	0	0	0	1	0	1	1	0	0-0	.333	.500	.333	3	1	0	0	0	1	0	1	1	2	0-0
Cruz, Nelson, Det	.000	.000	.000	0	0	0	0	0	0	0	0	0	0	0-0	.000	.000	.000	0	0	0	0	0	0	0	0	0	0	0-0
Cunnane, Will, SD	.000	.000	.000	3	0	0	0	0	0	0	0	1	0	0-0	.294	.368	.412	17	5	0	1	0	4	4	2	5	1	0-0
D'Amico, Jeff, Mil	.000	.000	.000	0	0	0	0	0	0	0	0	0	0	0-0	.000	.000	.000	4	0	0	0	0	0	0	0	3	1	0-0
Daal, Omar, Ari	.232	.254	.261	69	16	2	0	0	8	4	2	10	6	0-0	.168	.216	.183	131	22	2	0	0	11	6	8	32	11	0-0
Dale, Carl, Mil	.000	.000	.000	0	0	0	0	0	0	0	0	0	0	0-0	.000	.000	.000	0	0	0	0	0	0	0	0	0	0	0-0
Daneker, Pat, CWS	.000	.000	.000	2	0	0	0	0	0	0	0	1	0	0-0	.000	.000	.000	2	0	0	0	0	0	0	0	1	0	0-0
Darensbourg, Vic, Fla	.000	1.000	.000	0	0	0	0	0	0	0	1	0	0	0-0	.000	.200	.000	8	0	0	0	0	0	0	2	3	0	0-0
Davenport, Joe, CWS	.000	.000	.000	0	0	0	0	0	0	0	0	0	0	0-0	.000	.000	.000	0	0	0	0	0	0	0	0	0	0	0-0
Davey, Tom, Tor-Sea	.000	.000	.000	0	0	0	0	0	0	0	0	0	0	0-0	.000	.000	.000	0	0	0	0	0	0	0	0	0	0	0-0
Davis, Doug, Tex	.000	.000	.000	0	0	0	0	0	0	0	0	0	0	0-0	.000	.000	.000	0	0	0	0	0	0	0	0	0	0	0-0
DeHart, Rick, Mon	.000	.000	.000	0	0	0	0	0	0	0	0	0	0	0-0	.000	.000	.000	2	0	0	0	0	0	0	0	2	0	0-0
DeJean, Mike, Col	.000	.000	.000	2	0	0	0	0	0	0	0	1	0	0-0	.100	.100	.200	10	1	1	0	0	0	0	0	6	1	0-0
de los Santos, Val., Mil	.000	.000	.000	0	0	0	0	0	0	0	0	0	0	0-0	.000	.000	.000	0	0	0	0	0	0	0	0	0	0	0-0
del Toro, Miguel, SF	.000	.000	.000	4	0	0	0	0	0	0	0	3	1	0-0	.000	.000	.000	4	0	0	0	0	0	0	0	3	1	0-0
DeLucia, Rich, Cle	.000	.000	.000	0	0	0	0	0	0	0	0	0	0	0-0	.214	.313	.214	14	3	0	0	0	2	0	2	3	1	0-0
Dempster, Ryan, Fla	.102	.120	.122	49	5	1	0	0	5	2	1	22	1	0-0	.081	.095	.097	62	5	1	0	0	5	2	1	30	2	0-0
DePaula, Sean, Cle	.000	.000	.000	0	0	0	0	0	0	0	0	0	0	0-0	.000	.000	.000	0	0	0	0	0	0	0	0	0	0	0-0
Dipoto, Jerry, Col	.000	.167	.000	5	0	0	0	0	0	0	1	2	0	0-0	.048	.130	.048	21	1	0	0	0	0	0	2	11	1	0-0
Dotel, Octavio, NYM	.125	.276	.125	24	3	0	0	0	2	1	4	17	1	0-0	.125	.276	.125	24	3	0	0	0	2	1	4	17	1	0-0
Dougherty, Jim, Pit	.000	1.000	.000	0	0	0	0	0	0	0	1	0	0	0-0	.125	.222	.125	8	1	0	0	0	1	0	1	2	1	0-0
Dreifort, Darren, LA	.210	.246	.323	62	13	4	0	1	7	9	3	23	4	1-0	.213	.244	.295	122	26	4	0	2	17	12	5	52	10	1-0
Durbin, Chad, KC	.000	.000	.000	0	0	0	0	0	0	0	0	0	0	0-0	.000	.000	.000	0	0	0	0	0	0	0	0	0	0	0-0
Duvall, Mike, TB	.000	1.000	.000	0	0	0	0	0	0	0	1	0	0	0-0	.000	1.000	.000	0	0	0	0	0	0	0	1	0	0	0-0
Ebert, Derrin, Atl	.000	.000	.000	1	0	0	0	0	0	0	0	1	0	0-0	.000	.000	.000	1	0	0	0	0	0	0	0	1	0	0-0
Edmondson, Brian, Fla	.364	.364	.545	11	4	2	0	0	0	2	0	4	0	0-0	.174	.174	.261	23	4	2	0	0	0	2	0	9	1	0-0
Eiland, Dave, TB	.000	.000	.000	1	0	0	0	0	0	0	0	0	1	0-0	.091	.091	.227	22	2	0	0	1	2	2	0	8	5	0-0
Elarton, Scott, Hou	.192	.192	.192	26	5	0	0	0	1	1	0	10	7	0-0	.152	.152	.152	33	5	0	0	0	1	1	0	14	10	0-0
Eldred, Cal, Mil	.083	.154	.125	24	2	1	0	0	3	2	2	13	4	0-0	.102	.159	.136	59	6	2	0	0	4	4	4	32	10	0-1
Embree, Alan, SF	.000	.000	.000	0	0	0	0	0	0	0	0	0	0	0-0	.000	.500	.000	1	0	0	0	0	0	0	1	1	0	0-0
Erdos, Todd, NYY	.000	.000	.000	0	0	0	0	0	0	0	0	0	0	0-0	.000	.000	.000	1	0	0	0	0	0	0	0	1	0	0-0
Erickson, Scott, Bal	.000	.000	.000	6	0	0	0	0	0	0	0	2	1	0-0	.000	.286	.000	10	0	0	0	0	2	0	4	6	4	0-0
Escobar, Kelvim, Tor	.000	.000	.000	1	0	0	0	0	0	0	0	1	0	0-0	.000	.000	.000	1	0	0	0	0	0	0	0	1	0	0-0
Estes, Shawn, SF	.164	.215	.230	61	10	4	0	0	8	5	3	21	10	0-1	.159	.196	.200	195	31	5	0	1	23	9	6	72	31	0-1
Estrada, Horacio, Mil	.000	.000	.000	2	0	0	0	0	0	0	0	0	0	0-0	.000	.000	.000	2	0	0	0	0	0	0	0	0	0	0-0
Eyre, Scott, CWS	.000	.000	.000	0	0	0	0	0	0	0	0	0	0	0-0	.200	.200	.200	5	1	0	0	0	0	0	0	3	0	0-0
Falkenborg, Brian, Bal	.000	.000	.000	0	0	0	0	0	0	0	0	0	0	0-0	.000	.000	.000	0	0	0	0	0	0	0	0	0	0	0-0
Falteisek, Steve, Mil	.000	.000	.000	1	0	0	0	0	1	0	0	1	0	0-0	.000	.000	.000	3	0	0	0	0	1	0	0	3	1	0-0
Farnsworth, Kyle, ChC	.086	.158	.086	35	3	0	0	0	3	2	2	10	6	0-0	.086	.158	.086	35	3	0	0	0	3	2	2	10	6	0-0
Fassero, Jeff, Sea-Tex	.000	.000	.000	7	0	0	0	0	0	0	0	5	0	0-0	.077	.142	.095	222	17	2	1	0	15	5	17	125	39	1-0
Fernandez, Alex, Fla	.233	.233	.465	43	10	1	0	3	3	7	0	5	3	0-0	.183	.224	.330	109	20	7	0	3	6	11	6	25	10	0-0
Fetters, Mike, Bal	.000	.000	.000	0	0	0	0	0	0	0	0	0	0	0-0	.000	.000	.000	0	0	0	0	0	0	0	0	0	0	0-0
Finley, Chuck, Ana	.000	.000	.000	4	0	0	0	0	0	0	0	3	1	0-0	.000	.000	.000	14	0	0	0	0	1	0	0	8	1	0-0
Florie, Bryce, Det-Bos	.000	.000	.000	1	0	0	0	0	0	0	0	1	0	0-0	.111	.273	.111	9	1	0	0	0	0	0	2	5	1	0-0
Fossas, Tony, NYY	.000	.000	.000	0	0	0	0	0	0	0	0	0	0	0-0	.000	.000	.000	1	0	0	0	0	0	0	0	0	0	0-0
Foulke, Keith, CWS	.000	.000	.000	2	0	0	0	0	0	0	0	1	0	0-0	.133	.133	.133	15	2	0	0	0	0	0	0	5	2	0-0
Fox, Chad, Mil	.000	.000	.000	1	0	0	0	0	0	0	0	0	0	0-0	.000	.000	.000	4	0	0	0	0	0	0	0	2	1	0-0
Franco, John, NYM	.000	.000	.000	0	0	0	0	0	0	0	0	0	0	0-0	.091	.091	.091	33	3	0	0	0	2	1	0	13	3	0-0
Franklin, Ryan, Sea	.000	.000	.000	0	0	0	0	0	0	0	0	0	0	0-0	.000	.000	.000	0	0	0	0	0	0	0	0	0	0	0-0
Frascatore, J., Ari-Tor	.000	.000	.000	0	0	0	0	0	0	0	0	0	0	0-0	.059	.111	.059	17	1	0	0	0	0	0	1	12	1	0-0
Fussell, Chris, KC	.000	.000	.000	0	0	0	0	0	0	0	0	0	0	0-0	.000	.000	.000	0	0	0	0	0	0	0	0	0	0	0-0
Fyhrie, Mike, Ana	.000	.000	.000	0	0	0	0	0	0	0	0	0	0	0-0	.000	.000	.000	0	0	0	0	0	0	0	0	0	0	0-0
Gagne, Eric, LA	.200	.200	.200	10	2	0	0	0	1	1	0	3	0	0-0	.200	.200	.200	10	2	0	0	0	1	1	0	3	0	0-0
Gaillard, Eddie, TB	.000	.000	.000	0	0	0	0	0	0	0	0	0	0	0-0	.000	.000	.000	0	0	0	0	0	0	0	0	0	0	0-0
Garces, Rich, Bos	.000	.000	.000	0	0	0	0	0	0	0	0	0	0	0-0	.000	.000	.000	1	0	0	0	0	0	0	0	0	0	0-0
Garcia, Freddy, Sea	.250	.250	.250	4	1	0	0	0	0	1	0	1	2	0-0	.250	.250	.250	4	1	0	0	0	0	1	0	1	2	0-0
Garcia, Mike, Pit	.000	.000	.000	0	0	0	0	0	0	0	0	0	0	0-0	.000	.000	.000	0	0	0	0	0	0	0	0	0	0	0-0
Gardner, Mark, SF	.103	.167	.179	39	4	0	0	1	2	3	3	15	6	0-0	.129	.164	.152	442	57	3	2	1	20	21	15	176	50	0-0
Glavine, Tom, Atl	.138	.200	.154	65	9	1	0	0	3	4	5	17	7	0-0	.200	.251	.227	831	166	16	2	1	62	62	55	211	124	1-0
Glover, Gary, Tor	.000	.000	.000	0	0	0	0	0	0	0	0	0	0	0-0	.000	.000	.000	0	0	0	0	0	0	0	0	0	0	0-0

Pitcher, Team	1999 Hitting														Career Hitting													
	Avg	OBP	SLG	AB	H	2B	3B	HR	R	RBI	BB	SO	SH	SB-CS	Avg	OBP	SLG	AB	H	2B	3B	HR	R	RBI	BB	SO	SH	SB-CS
Glynn, Ryan, Tex	.000	.000	.000	1	0	0	0	0	0	0	0	0	0	0-0	.000	.000	.000	1	0	0	0	0	0	0	0	0	0	0-0
Gomes, Wayne, Phi	.000	.000	.000	1	0	0	0	0	0	0	0	1	0	0-0	.000	.167	.000	5	0	0	0	0	0	0	1	4	0	0-0
Gooden, Dwight, Cle	.500	.667	2.000	2	1	0	0	1	1	2	1	1	0	0-0	.196	.213	.263	738	145	15	5	8	60	67	14	134	85	1-1
Gordon, Tom, Bos	.000	.000	.000	0	0	0	0	0	0	0	0	0	0	0-0	.000	.000	.000	0	0	0	0	0	0	0	0	0	0	0-0
Grace, Mike, Phi	.000	.125	.000	7	0	0	0	0	1	0	1	4	3	0-0	.096	.165	.096	73	7	0	0	0	3	1	5	37	9	0-0
Grahe, Joe, Phi	.143	.250	.143	7	1	0	0	0	1	0	1	3	0	0-0	.316	.350	.368	19	6	1	0	0	2	2	1	6	6	0-0
Graterol, Beiker, Det	.000	.000	.000	0	0	0	0	0	0	0	0	0	0	0-0	.000	.000	.000	0	0	0	0	0	0	0	0	0	0	0-0
Graves, Danny, Cin	.000	.000	.000	5	0	0	0	0	0	0	0	2	0	0-0	.000	.000	.000	10	0	0	0	0	0	0	0	6	0	0-0
Greene, Rick, Cin	.000	.000	.000	2	0	0	0	0	0	0	0	2	0	0-0	.000	.000	.000	2	0	0	0	0	0	0	0	2	0	0-0
Grimsley, Jason, NYY	.000	.000	.000	0	0	0	0	0	0	0	0	0	0	0-0	.105	.171	.105	38	4	0	0	0	3	2	3	10	5	0-0
Groom, Buddy, Oak	.000	.000	.000	0	0	0	0	0	0	0	0	0	0	0-0	.000	.000	.000	0	0	0	0	0	0	0	0	0	0	0-0
Gross, Kip, Bos	.000	.000	.000	0	0	0	0	0	0	0	0	0	0	0-0	.167	.167	.167	24	4	0	0	0	2	2	0	6	4	0-0
Guardado, Eddie, Min	.000	.000	.000	0	0	0	0	0	0	0	0	0	0	0-0	.000	.000	.000	0	0	0	0	0	0	0	0	0	0	0-0
Gunderson, Eric, Tex	.000	.000	.000	0	0	0	0	0	0	0	0	0	0	0-0	.000	.143	.000	6	0	0	0	0	1	0	0	4	0	0-0
Guthrie, M., Bos-ChC	.000	.000	.000	0	0	0	0	0	0	0	0	0	0	0-0	.111	.111	.111	9	1	0	0	0	0	0	0	0	1	0-0
Guzman, Domingo, SD	.000	.000	.000	0	0	0	0	0	0	0	0	0	0	0-0	.000	.000	.000	0	0	0	0	0	0	0	0	0	0	0-0
Guzman, Juan, Bal-Cin	.125	.152	.125	32	4	0	0	0	1	3	1	14	3	0-0	.118	.143	.118	34	4	0	0	0	1	3	1	14	3	0-0
Hackman, Luther, Col	.200	.200	.200	5	1	0	0	0	1	0	0	3	0	0-0	.200	.200	.200	5	1	0	0	0	1	0	0	3	0	0-0
Halama, John, Sea	.200	.333	.400	5	1	1	0	0	1	0	1	2	0	0-0	.067	.222	.133	15	1	1	0	0	2	0	3	9	1	0-0
Halladay, Roy, Tor	.000	.000	.000	2	0	0	0	0	0	0	0	2	1	0-0	.000	.000	.000	2	0	0	0	0	0	0	0	2	1	0-0
Hamilton, Joey, Tor	.000	.000	.000	2	0	0	0	0	0	0	0	1	0	0-0	.117	.138	.177	300	35	4	1	4	16	20	8	152	32	0-0
Hampton, Mike, Hou	.311	.373	.432	74	23	3	3	0	10	10	7	18	5	0-0	.221	.292	.278	299	66	9	4	0	35	23	27	77	33	2-1
Haney, Chris, Cle	.000	.000	.000	0	0	0	0	0	0	0	0	0	0	0-0	.111	.111	.111	36	4	0	0	0	2	4	0	4	4	0-0
Hansell, Greg, Pit	.000	.000	.000	2	0	0	0	0	0	0	0	2	0	0-0	.000	.000	.000	2	0	0	0	0	0	0	0	2	0	0-0
Harikkala, Tim, Bos	.000	.000	.000	0	0	0	0	0	0	0	0	0	0	0-0	.000	.000	.000	0	0	0	0	0	0	0	0	0	0	0-0
Harnisch, Pete, Cin	.152	.164	.258	66	10	4	0	1	6	5	1	20	8	0-0	.120	.143	.161	459	55	16	0	1	34	21	12	131	55	0-2
Harris, Reggie, Mil	.000	.000	.000	1	0	0	0	0	0	0	0	1	0	0-0	.000	.000	.000	1	0	0	0	0	0	0	0	1	0	0-0
Harville, Chad, Oak	.000	.000	.000	0	0	0	0	0	0	0	0	0	0	0-0	.000	.000	.000	0	0	0	0	0	0	0	0	0	0	0-0
Hasegawa, Shig., Ana	.000	.000	.000	0	0	0	0	0	0	0	0	0	0	0-0	.000	.000	.000	0	0	0	0	0	0	0	0	0	0	0-0
Hawkins, LaTroy, Min	.000	.000	.000	2	0	0	0	0	0	0	0	1	0	0-0	.000	.000	.000	4	0	0	0	0	0	0	0	3	0	0-0
Haynes, Jimmy, Oak	.000	.000	.000	4	0	0	0	0	0	0	0	1	1	0-0	.000	.100	.000	9	0	0	0	0	1	0	1	5	1	0-0
Heiserman, Rick, StL	.000	.000	.000	1	0	0	0	0	0	0	0	0	0	0-0	.000	.000	.000	1	0	0	0	0	0	0	0	0	0	0-0
Helling, Rick, Tex	.000	.000	.000	2	0	0	0	0	0	0	0	2	0	0-0	.100	.100	.100	30	3	0	0	0	1	0	0	12	2	0-0
Henry, Butch, Sea	.000	.000	.000	0	0	0	0	0	0	0	0	0	0	0-0	.139	.166	.166	151	21	1	0	1	10	12	5	30	19	0-0
Henry, Doug, Hou	.000	.000	.000	1	0	0	0	0	0	0	0	1	0	0-0	.063	.063	.063	16	1	0	0	0	1	0	0	6	2	0-0
Hentgen, Pat, Tor	.167	.167	.167	6	1	0	0	0	0	0	0	4	0	0-0	.056	.056	.056	18	1	0	0	0	0	0	0	8	1	0-0
Heredia, Felix, ChC	.500	.500	.500	4	2	0	0	0	0	1	0	0	0	0-0	.333	.333	.333	9	3	0	0	0	0	1	0	2	1	0-0
Heredia, Gil, Oak	.000	.143	.000	6	0	0	0	0	0	0	1	1	1	0-0	.202	.230	.214	84	17	1	0	0	3	3	3	11	11	0-0
Herges, Matt, LA	.000	.000	.000	1	0	0	0	0	0	0	0	1	0	0-0	.000	.000	.000	1	0	0	0	0	0	0	0	1	0	0-0
Hermanson, Dus., Mon	.047	.090	.047	64	3	0	0	0	1	2	3	39	8	0-0	.085	.167	.134	164	14	2	0	2	9	5	15	92	18	0-0
Hernandez, Li., Fla-SF	.270	.288	.397	63	17	2	0	2	6	8	1	10	7	0-0	.223	.239	.297	175	39	7	0	2	12	16	2	36	11	0-0
Hernandez, Or., NYY	.333	.333	.333	3	1	0	0	0	1	0	0	0	0	0-0	.100	.100	.100	10	1	0	0	0	1	0	0	5	1	0-0
Hernandez, Ro., TB	.000	.000	.000	0	0	0	0	0	0	0	0	0	0	0-0	.500	.500	.500	2	1	0	0	0	0	0	0	1	0	0-0
Hershiser, Orel, NYM	.145	.154	.161	62	9	1	0	0	3	3	1	18	3	1-0	.203	.232	.244	803	163	29	2	0	65	50	27	180	101	8-3
Hiljus, Erik, Det	.000	.000	.000	0	0	0	0	0	0	0	0	0	0	0-0	.000	.000	.000	0	0	0	0	0	0	0	0	0	0	0-0
Hill, Ken, Ana	.000	.000	.000	3	0	0	0	0	0	0	0	0	0	0-0	.148	.208	.185	330	49	7	1	1	22	21	24	94	66	0-0
Hinchliffe, Brett, Sea	.000	.000	.000	0	0	0	0	0	0	0	0	0	0	0-0	.000	.000	.000	0	0	0	0	0	0	0	0	0	0	0-0
Hitchcock, Sterling, SD	.082	.125	.082	61	5	0	0	0	4	0	3	34	7	0-0	.106	.143	.106	161	17	0	0	0	13	3	7	85	20	0-1
Hoffman, Trevor, SD	.333	.333	.667	3	1	1	0	0	0	2	0	0	0	0-0	.138	.138	.207	29	4	2	0	0	1	5	0	9	2	0-0
Holmes, Darren, Ari	.000	.000	.000	2	0	0	0	0	0	0	0	2	0	0-0	.120	.148	.240	25	3	0	0	1	2	2	1	13	6	0-0
Holt, Chris, Hou	.067	.125	.067	45	3	0	0	0	3	2	3	14	7	0-0	.080	.111	.080	113	9	0	0	0	9	3	4	47	16	0-0
Holtz, Mike, Ana	.000	.000	.000	0	0	0	0	0	0	0	0	0	0	0-0	.000	.000	.000	1	0	0	0	0	0	0	0	1	0	0-0
Howry, Bob, CWS	.000	.000	.000	0	0	0	0	0	0	0	0	0	0	0-0	.000	.000	.000	0	0	0	0	0	0	0	0	0	0	0-0
Hudek, J., Cin-Atl-Tor	.000	.000	.000	1	0	0	0	0	0	0	0	1	0	0-0	.200	.200	.200	5	1	0	0	0	0	2	0	4	1	0-0
Hudson, Tim, Oak	.250	.400	.250	4	1	0	0	0	0	0	1	2	0	0-0	.250	.400	.250	4	1	0	0	0	0	0	1	2	0	0-0
Irabu, Hideki, NYY	.000	.200	.000	4	0	0	0	0	0	0	1	3	2	0-0	.111	.200	.111	9	1	0	0	0	0	0	1	6	3	0-0
Isringhaus'n, NYM-Oak	.083	.083	.167	12	1	1	0	0	2	1	0	4	1	0-0	.196	.238	.299	97	19	4	0	2	10	11	5	33	8	0-0
Jackson, Mike, Cle	.000	.000	.000	0	0	0	0	0	0	0	0	0	0	0-0	.185	.214	.259	27	5	2	0	0	3	1	1	4	4	0-0
Jarvis, Kevin, Oak	.000	.000	.000	0	0	0	0	0	0	0	0	0	0	0-0	.161	.175	.194	62	10	2	0	0	4	2	0	21	11	0-0
Jimenez, Jose, StL	.094	.094	.132	53	5	0	1	0	5	2	0	22	2	0-0	.085	.085	.119	59	5	0	1	0	5	3	0	26	4	0-0
Johns, Doug, Bal	.000	.000	.000	1	0	0	0	0	0	0	0	1	0	0-0	.667	.667	.667	3	2	0	0	0	2	0	0	1	0	0-0
Johnson, Jason, Bal	.000	.000	.000	2	0	0	0	0	0	0	0	1	0	0-0	.000	.000	.000	5	0	0	0	0	0	0	0	4	0	0-0
Johnson, Jon., Tex	.000	.000	.000	0	0	0	0	0	0	0	0	0	0	0-0	.000	.000	.000	0	0	0	0	0	0	0	0	0	0	0-0
Johnson, Mike, Mon	.250	.250	.250	4	1	0	0	0	1	0	0	1	0	0-0	.150	.150	.150	20	3	0	0	0	2	2	0	7	2	0-0
Johnson, Randy, Ari	.124	.124	.165	97	12	4	0	0	1	6	0	46	7	0-0	.112	.112	.145	152	17	5	0	0	4	8	0	74	12	0-0
Johnstone, John, SF	.000	.000	.000	0	0	0	0	0	0	0	0	0	0	0-0	.000	.000	.000	4	0	0	0	0	0	0	0	1	2	0-0
Jones, Bobby, NYM	.313	.313	.500	16	5	0	0	1	1	1	0	4	1	0-0	.143	.167	.172	308	44	6	0	1	18	14	9	114	54	0-0
Jones, Bobby M., Col	.148	.200	.185	27	4	1	0	0	3	4	2	7	4	0-0	.169	.198	.195	77	13	2	0	0	7	8	3	21	10	0-0
Jones, Doug, Oak	.000	.000	.000	0	0	0	0	0	0	0	0	0	0	0-0	.143	.250	.143	7	1	0	0	0	0	0	1	4	0	0-0
Jones, Todd, Det	.000	.000	.000	0	0	0	0	0	0	0	0	0	0	0-0	.273	.273	.364	11	3	1	0	0	1	0	0	1	0	0-0
Judd, Mike, LA	.000	.167	.000	5	0	0	0	0	0	0	1	1	3	0-0	.000	.125	.000	7	0	0	0	0	0	0	1	2	3	0-0
Juden, Jeff, NYY	.000	.000	.000	0	0	0	0	0	0	0	0	0	0	0-0	.109	.124	.160	119	13	3	0	1	5	13	1	60	11	0-0
Kamieniecki, Scott, Bal	.000	.000	.000	0	0	0	0	0	0	0	0	0	0	0-0	.000	.000	.000	2	0	0	0	0	0	0	0	2	0	0-0
Karchner, Matt, ChC	.000	.000	.000	0	0	0	0	0	0	0	0	0	0	0-0	.000	.000	.000	0	0	0	0	0	0	0	0	0	0	0-0
Karl, Scott, Mil	.183	.219	.317	60	11	2	0	2	5	7	3	17	12	0-0	.125	.172	.208	120	15	2	1	2	8	7	7	37	21	0-0
Karsay, Steve, Cle	.000	.000	.000	0	0	0	0	0	0	0	0	0	0	0-0	.000	.000	.000	0	0	0	0	0	1	0	0	0	0	0-0
Kida, Masao, Det	.000	.000	.000	0	0	0	0	0	0	0	0	0	0	0-0	.000	.000	.000	0	0	0	0	0	0	0	0	0	0	0-0
Kile, Darryl, Col	.135	.196	.135	52	7	0	0	0	3	4	4	20	8	0-0	.136	.187	.179	491	67	18	0	1	28	33	27	220	65	0-0
Kim, Byung-Hyun, Ari	.000	.000	.000	1	0	0	0	0	0	0	0	0	0	0-0	.000	.000	.000	1	0	0	0	0	0	0	0	0	0	0-0
King, Curtis, StL	.000	.000	.000	0	0	0	0	0	0	0	0	0	0	0-0	.000	.000	.000	6	0	0	0	0	0	0	0	2	0	0-0
King, Ray, ChC	.000	.000	.000	1	0	0	0	0	0	0	0	1	0	0-0	.000	.000	.000	1	0	0	0	0	0	0	0	1	0	0-0
Kline, Steve, Mon	.000	.000	.000	1	0	0	0	0	0	0	0	1	1	0-0	.000	.000	.000	6	0	0	0	0	0	0	0	3	2	0-0
Koch, Billy, Tor	.000	.000	.000	1	0	0	0	0	0	0	0	1	0	0-0	.000	.000	.000	1	0	0	0	0	0	0	0	1	0	0-0
Kolb, Danny, Tex	.000	.000	.000	0	0	0	0	0	0	0	0	0	0	0-0	.000	.000	.000	0	0	0	0	0	0	0	0	0	0	0-0
Kubenka, Jeff, LA	1.000	1.000	1.000	1	1	0	0	0	1	0	0	0	0	0-0	1.000	1.000	1.000	1	1	0	0	0	1	0	0	0	0	0-0
Kubinski, Tim, Oak	.000	.000	.000	0	0	0	0	0	0	0	0	0	0	0-0	.000	.000	.000	0	0	0	0	0	0	0	0	0	0	0-0

	1999 Hitting														Career Hitting													
Pitcher, Team	Avg	OBP	SLG	AB	H	2B	3B	HR	R	RBI	BB	SO	SH	SB-CS	Avg	OBP	SLG	AB	H	2B	3B	HR	R	RBI	BB	SO	SH	SB-CS
Langston, Mark, Cle	.500	.500	.500	2	1	0	0	0	0	0	0	1	0	0-0	.152	.168	.185	92	14	3	0	0	5	5	2	38	5	0-0
Laxton, Brett, Oak	.000	.000	.000	0	0	0	0	0	0	0	0	0	0	0-0	.000	.000	.000	0	0	0	0	0	0	0	0	0	0	0-0
Lee, Corey, Tex	.000	.000	.000	0	0	0	0	0	0	0	0	0	0	0-0	.000	.000	.000	0	0	0	0	0	0	0	0	0	0	0-0
Lee, David, Col	.200	.200	.200	5	1	0	0	0	1	0	0	2	0	0-0	.200	.200	.200	5	1	0	0	0	1	0	0	2	0	0-0
Leiter, Al, NYM	.105	.136	.140	57	6	2	0	0	1	5	2	29	11	0-0	.103	.161	.125	232	24	5	0	0	7	11	16	131	25	0-0
Leiter, Mark, Sea	.000	.000	.000	0	0	0	0	0	0	0	0	0	0	0-0	.110	.153	.116	181	20	1	0	0	8	14	9	98	28	0-0
Leskanic, Curt, Col	.500	.500	1.250	4	2	0	0	1	1	3	0	2	0	0-0	.194	.216	.361	36	7	3	0	1	4	7	1	15	5	0-0
Levine, Al, Ana	.000	.000	.000	0	0	0	0	0	0	0	0	0	0	0-0	.000	.000	.000	0	0	0	0	0	0	0	0	0	0	0-0
Lidle, Cory, TB	.000	.000	.000	0	0	0	0	0	0	0	0	0	0	0-0	.000	.167	.000	5	0	0	0	0	1	0	1	4	0	0-0
Lieber, Jon, ChC	.121	.188	.138	58	7	1	0	0	8	2	5	23	7	0-0	.131	.181	.162	260	34	8	0	0	19	14	16	105	21	0-0
Lilly, Ted, Mon	.200	.200	.200	5	1	0	0	0	0	0	0	1	1	0-0	.200	.200	.200	5	1	0	0	0	0	0	0	1	1	0-0
Lima, Jose, Hou	.080	.115	.080	75	6	0	0	0	4	2	3	24	13	0-0	.108	.135	.121	157	17	2	0	0	10	6	5	54	24	0-0
Lincoln, Mike, Min	.000	.000	.000	1	0	0	0	0	0	0	0	0	0	0-0	.000	.000	.000	1	0	0	0	0	0	0	0	0	0	0-0
Linton, Doug, Bal	.000	.000	.000	0	0	0	0	0	0	0	0	0	0	0-0	.000	.000	.000	7	0	0	0	0	0	0	0	3	2	0-0
Lira, Felipe, Det	.000	.000	.000	0	0	0	0	0	0	0	0	0	0	0-0	.000	.000	.000	0	0	0	0	0	0	0	0	0	0	0-0
Lloyd, Graeme, Tor	.000	.000	.000	0	0	0	0	0	0	0	0	0	0	0-0	.000	.000	.000	0	0	0	0	0	0	0	0	0	0	0-0
Loaiza, Esteban, Tex	.000	.000	.000	0	0	0	0	0	0	0	0	0	0	0-0	.184	.198	.209	158	29	2	1	0	11	11	3	35	23	0-0
Loewer, Carlton, Phi	.227	.261	.227	22	5	0	0	0	0	1	1	9	2	0-0	.140	.197	.140	57	8	0	0	0	4	2	4	19	7	0-0
Loiselle, Rich, Pit	.000	.000	.000	0	0	0	0	0	0	0	0	0	1	0-0	.222	.222	.333	9	2	1	0	0	0	2	0	4	2	0-0
Looper, Braden, Fla	.000	.000	.000	0	0	0	0	0	0	0	0	0	0	0-0	.000	.000	.000	0	0	0	0	0	0	0	0	0	0	0-0
Lopez, Albie, TB	.000	.000	.000	0	0	0	0	0	0	0	0	0	0	0-0	.000	.000	.000	2	0	0	0	0	0	0	0	1	0	0-0
Lorraine, Andrew, ChC	.133	.188	.200	15	2	1	0	0	1	0	1	9	4	0-0	.133	.188	.200	15	2	1	0	0	1	0	1	9	4	0-0
Lowe, Derek, Bos	.000	.000	.000	0	0	0	0	0	0	0	0	0	0	0-0	.000	.125	.000	7	0	0	0	0	0	0	1	5	0	0-0
Lowe, Sean, CWS	.000	.000	.000	0	0	0	0	0	0	0	0	0	0	0-0	.200	.200	.200	5	1	0	0	0	0	0	0	1	0	0-0
Ludwick, Eric, Tor	.000	.000	.000	0	0	0	0	0	0	0	0	0	0	0-0	.000	.000	.000	11	0	0	0	0	0	0	0	5	0	0-0
Luebbers, Larry, StL	.125	.176	.125	16	2	0	0	0	1	0	1	2	1	0-0	.200	.238	.225	40	8	1	0	0	2	0	1	10	2	0-0
Lundquist, David, CWS	.000	.000	.000	0	0	0	0	0	0	0	0	0	0	0-0	.000	.000	.000	0	0	0	0	0	0	0	0	0	0	0-0
Maddux, Greg, Atl	.172	.197	.313	64	11	1	1	2	7	7	1	18	13	0-0	.178	.199	.215	990	176	23	1	4	75	52	24	269	106	4-2
Maddux, Mike, Mon-LA	.000	.000	.000	0	0	0	0	0	0	0	0	0	0	0-0	.067	.125	.078	90	6	1	0	0	4	4	6	32	14	0-0
Magnante, Mike, Ana	.000	.000	.000	0	0	0	0	0	0	0	0	0	0	0-0	.400	.400	.400	5	2	0	0	0	0	1	0	2	0	0-0
Mahay, Ron, Oak	.000	.000	.000	0	0	0	0	0	0	0	0	0	0	0-0	.200	.273	.450	20	4	2	0	1	3	3	1	6	0	0-0
Mahomes, Pat, NYM	.313	.313	.500	16	5	3	0	0	2	3	0	6	0	0-0	.313	.313	.500	16	5	3	0	0	3	3	0	6	0	0-0
Mantei, Matt, Fla-Ari	.000	.000	.000	1	0	0	0	0	0	0	0	1	0	0-0	.200	.200	.200	5	1	0	0	0	0	0	0	2	0	0-0
Manzanillo, Jo., NYM	1.000	1.000	1.000	1	1	0	0	0	0	0	0	0	0	0-0	.143	.143	.143	7	1	0	0	0	0	0	0	3	1	0-0
Marte, Damaso, Sea	.000	.000	.000	0	0	0	0	0	0	0	0	0	0	0-0	.000	.000	.000	0	0	0	0	0	0	0	0	0	0	0-0
Martin, Tom, Cle	.000	.000	.000	0	0	0	0	0	0	0	0	0	0	0-0	.000	.000	.000	3	0	0	0	0	0	0	0	1	0	0-0
Martinez, Pedro, Bos	.000	.000	.000	2	0	0	0	0	0	0	0	1	0	0-0	.098	.140	.125	255	25	3	2	0	13	11	10	117	37	0-0
Martinez, Ramon, Bos	.000	.000	.000	0	0	0	0	0	0	0	0	0	0	0-0	.154	.164	.183	586	90	12	1	1	32	33	7	197	68	0-2
Masaoka, Onan, LA	.000	.000	.000	4	0	0	0	0	0	0	0	2	1	0-0	.000	.000	.000	4	0	0	0	0	0	0	0	2	1	0-0
Mathews, T.J., Oak	.000	.000	.000	0	0	0	0	0	0	0	0	0	0	0-0	.000	.000	.000	7	0	0	0	0	0	0	0	4	0	0-0
Mathews, Terry, KC	.000	.000	.000	1	0	0	0	0	0	0	0	1	0	0-0	.375	.375	.500	24	9	3	0	0	3	3	0	9	0	0-0
Mays, Joe, Min	.000	.400	.000	3	0	0	0	0	0	0	2	1	0	0-0	.000	.400	.000	3	0	0	0	0	0	0	2	1	0	0-0
McCurry, Jeff, Hou	.000	.000	.000	0	0	0	0	0	0	0	0	0	0	0-0	.000	.000	.000	4	0	0	0	0	0	0	0	2	0	0-0
McDowell, Jack, Ana	.000	.000	.000	0	0	0	0	0	0	0	0	0	0	0-0	.000	.000	.000	0	0	0	0	0	0	0	0	0	0	0-0
McElroy, C., Col-NYM	.000	.000	.000	1	0	0	0	0	0	0	0	0	1	0-0	.231	.231	.359	39	9	3	1	0	4	4	0	12	2	0-1
McGlinchy, Kevin, Atl	.000	.000	.000	2	0	0	0	0	0	0	0	1	0	0-0	.000	.000	.000	2	0	0	0	0	0	0	0	1	0	0-0
McMichael, NYM-Oak	.000	.000	.000	0	0	0	0	0	0	0	0	0	0	0-0	.133	.188	.133	15	2	0	0	0	0	0	1	7	0	0-0
McNichol, Brian, ChC	.000	.000	.000	2	0	0	0	0	0	0	0	1	1	0-0	.000	.000	.000	2	0	0	0	0	0	0	0	1	1	0-0
Meadows, Brian, Fla	.140	.173	.200	50	7	3	0	0	6	1	2	21	7	0-0	.135	.180	.163	104	14	3	0	0	10	4	6	40	9	0-0
Meche, Gil, Sea	.000	.000	.000	0	0	0	0	0	0	0	0	0	0	0-0	.000	.000	.000	0	0	0	0	0	0	0	0	0	0	0-0
Mecir, Jim, TB	.000	.000	.000	0	0	0	0	0	0	0	0	0	0	0-0	.000	.000	.000	1	0	0	0	0	0	0	0	0	0	0-0
Medina, Rafael, Fla	.000	.000	.000	0	0	0	0	0	0	0	0	0	0	0-0	.053	.053	.053	19	1	0	0	0	1	0	0	6	6	0-0
Mendoza, Ramiro, NYY	.000	.000	.000	0	0	0	0	0	0	0	0	0	0	0-0	.000	.000	.000	0	0	0	0	0	0	0	0	0	1	0-0
Mercker, Kent, StL-Bos	.179	.233	.214	28	5	1	0	0	5	2	2	10	4	0-0	.115	.152	.164	244	28	5	2	1	12	18	11	114	22	0-0
Mesa, Jose, Sea	.000	.000	.000	0	0	0	0	0	0	0	0	0	0	0-0	.000	1.000	.000	0	0	0	0	0	1	0	1	0	0	0-0
Miceli, Dan, SD	.000	.000	.000	1	0	0	0	0	0	0	0	1	0	0-0	.053	.053	.053	19	1	0	0	0	0	0	0	8	0	0-0
Miller, Kurt, ChC	.000	.000	.000	0	0	0	0	0	0	0	0	0	0	0-0	.286	.286	.286	14	4	0	0	0	1	2	0	2	2	0-0
Miller, Travis, Min	.000	.000	.000	0	0	0	0	0	0	0	0	0	0	0-0	.000	.000	.000	0	0	0	0	0	0	0	0	0	0	0-0
Miller, Trever, Hou	.000	.000	.000	3	0	0	0	0	0	0	0	1	2	0-0	.167	.167	.333	6	1	1	0	0	1	0	0	1	2	0-0
Miller, Wade, Hou	.000	.000	.000	1	0	0	0	0	0	0	0	1	0	0-0	.000	.000	.000	1	0	0	0	0	0	0	0	1	0	0-0
Mills, Alan, LA	.000	.000	.000	2	0	0	0	0	0	0	0	1	0	0-0	.000	.000	.000	2	0	0	0	0	0	0	0	1	0	0-0
Millwood, Kevin, Atl	.154	.175	.218	78	12	2	0	1	4	6	2	29	6	0-0	.114	.168	.157	140	16	3	0	1	5	7	9	59	13	0-0
Milton, Eric, Min	.000	.333	.000	2	0	0	0	0	0	0	1	1	0	0-0	.364	.417	.364	11	4	0	0	0	0	1	1	5	0	0-0
Mintz, Steve, Ana	.000	.000	.000	0	0	0	0	0	0	0	0	0	0	0-0	.000	.000	.000	3	0	0	0	0	0	0	0	3	0	0-0
Mlicki, Dave, LA-Det	.200	.429	.200	5	1	0	0	0	0	0	2	3	2	0-0	.118	.211	.145	152	18	4	0	0	9	5	18	55	27	0-0
Moehler, Brian, Det	.000	.500	.000	1	0	0	0	0	0	0	1	1	0	0-0	.000	.111	.000	8	0	0	0	0	1	0	1	5	0	0-0
Mohler, Mike, StL	.000	.000	.000	3	0	0	0	0	0	0	0	1	0	0-0	.000	.000	.000	3	0	0	0	0	0	0	0	1	0	0-0
Molina, Gabe, Bal	.000	.000	.000	0	0	0	0	0	0	0	0	0	0	0-0	.000	.000	.000	0	0	0	0	0	0	0	0	0	0	0-0
Montgomery, Jeff, KC	.000	.000	.000	0	0	0	0	0	0	0	0	0	0	0-0	.000	.000	.000	2	0	0	0	0	0	0	0	1	0	0-0
Montgomery, S., Phi	1.000	1.000	1.000	1	1	0	0	0	1	0	0	0	0	0-0	1.000	1.000	1.000	1	1	0	0	0	1	0	0	0	0	0-0
Moreno, Orber, KC	.000	.000	.000	0	0	0	0	0	0	0	0	0	0	0-0	.000	.000	.000	0	0	0	0	0	0	0	0	0	0	0-0
Morgan, Mike, Tex	.250	.250	.250	4	1	0	0	0	0	0	0	2	0	0-0	.098	.121	.108	481	47	3	1	0	13	14	12	146	58	0-0
Morman, Alvin, KC	.000	.000	.000	0	0	0	0	0	0	0	0	0	0	0-0	.000	.000	.000	1	0	0	0	0	0	0	0	0	0	0-0
Morris, Jim, TB	.000	.000	.000	0	0	0	0	0	0	0	0	0	0	0-0	.000	.000	.000	0	0	0	0	0	0	0	0	0	0	0-0
Mota, Guillermo, Mon	1.000	1.000	4.000	1	1	0	0	1	1	3	0	0	0	0-0	1.000	1.000	4.000	1	1	0	0	1	1	3	0	0	0	0-0
Moyer, Jamie, Sea	.500	.667	.500	2	1	0	0	0	0	0	1	1	1	0-0	.146	.218	.158	158	23	2	0	0	10	4	15	52	20	0-0
Mulholland, T., ChC-Atl	.104	.140	.104	48	5	0	0	0	2	3	2	21	5	0-0	.105	.126	.137	570	60	10	1	2	23	19	13	258	44	1-1
Munoz, Mike, Tex	.000	.000	.000	0	0	0	0	0	0	0	0	0	0	0-0	.143	.400	.286	7	1	1	0	0	2	1	3	6	1	0-0
Munro, Peter, Tor	.000	.000	.000	0	0	0	0	0	0	0	0	0	0	0-0	.000	.000	.000	0	0	0	0	0	0	0	0	0	0	0-0
Murray, Dan, NYM-KC	.000	.000	.000	0	0	0	0	0	0	0	0	0	0	0-0	.000	.000	.000	0	0	0	0	0	0	0	0	0	0	0-0
Murray, Heath, SD	.154	.214	.154	13	2	0	0	0	1	0	1	9	1	0-0	.105	.150	.105	19	2	0	0	0	1	0	1	10	1	0-0
Mussina, Mike, Bal	.273	.273	.364	11	3	1	0	0	1	4	0	1	0	0-0	.235	.235	.294	17	4	1	0	0	1	4	0	3	0	0-0
Myers, Mike, Mil	.000	.000	.000	1	0	0	0	0	0	0	0	1	0	0-0	.000	.000	.000	1	0	0	0	0	0	0	0	1	0	0-0
Myers, Rodney, ChC	.429	.429	.571	7	3	1	0	0	2	1	0	2	0	0-0	.231	.231	.308	13	3	1	0	0	2	1	0	7	0	0-0
Myette, Aaron, CWS	.000	.000	.000	0	0	0	0	0	0	0	0	0	0	0-0	.000	.000	.000	0	0	0	0	0	0	0	0	0	0	0-0
Nagy, Charles, Cle	.000	.000	.000	6	0	0	0	0	0	0	0	5	0	0-0	.063	.063	.063	16	1	0	0	0	1	0	0	10	0	0-0

	1999 Hitting														Career Hitting													
Pitcher, Team	Avg	OBP	SLG	AB	H	2B	3B	HR	R	RBI	BB	SO	SH	SB-CS	Avg	OBP	SLG	AB	H	2B	3B	HR	R	RBI	BB	SO	SH	SB-CS
Nathan, Joe, SF	.179	.233	.214	28	5	1	0	0	1	1	2	6	5	0-0	.179	.233	.214	28	5	1	0	0	1	1	2	6	5	0-0
Naulty, Dan, NYY	.000	.000	.000	0	0	0	0	0	0	0	0	0	0	0-0	.000	.000	.000	0	0	0	0	0	0	0	0	0	0	0-0
Navarro, Jaime, CWS	.000	.000	.000	3	0	0	0	0	0	0	0	1	1	0-0	.150	.161	.190	147	22	6	0	0	1	10	1	52	18	0-0
Neagle, Denny, Cin	.162	.184	.189	37	6	1	0	0	1	2	1	9	5	0-0	.149	.181	.191	382	57	7	0	3	19	31	15	119	53	0-1
Nelson, Jeff, NYY	.000	.000	.000	0	0	0	0	0	0	0	0	0	0	0-0	.000	.000	.000	1	0	0	0	0	0	0	0	0	1	0-0
Nen, Robb, SF	.000	.000	.000	0	0	0	0	0	0	0	0	0	0	0-0	.000	.000	.000	12	0	0	0	0	0	0	0	3	0	0-0
Newman, Alan, TB	.000	.000	.000	0	0	0	0	0	0	0	0	0	0	0-0	.000	.000	.000	0	0	0	0	0	0	0	0	0	0	0-0
Nitkowski, C.J., Det	.000	.000	.000	1	0	0	0	0	0	0	0	1	0	0-0	.133	.133	.133	15	2	0	0	0	1	1	0	10	1	0-0
Nomo, Hideo, Mil	.214	.228	.286	56	12	2	1	0	3	5	1	22	7	0-0	.152	.165	.203	316	48	11	1	1	13	19	5	142	31	0-0
Nunez, Vladimir, Ari-Fla	.143	.143	.143	28	4	0	0	0	0	2	0	6	2	0-0	.143	.143	.143	28	4	0	0	0	0	2	0	6	2	0-0
Ogea, Chad, Phi	.091	.167	.091	44	4	0	0	0	1	0	4	25	7	0-0	.087	.160	.087	46	4	0	0	0	1	0	4	26	9	0-0
Ohka, Tomokazu, Bos	.000	.000	.000	0	0	0	0	0	0	0	0	0	0	0-0	.000	.000	.000	0	0	0	0	0	0	0	0	0	0	0-0
Ojala, Kirt, Fla	.000	.000	.000	0	0	0	0	0	0	0	0	0	0	0-0	.121	.194	.152	33	4	1	0	0	2	3	3	12	3	0-0
Olivares, O., Ana-Oak	.333	.333	.500	6	2	1	0	0	0	0	0	1	1	0-0	.238	.258	.341	214	51	8	1	4	22	23	6	61	14	0-0
Oliver, Darren, StL	.274	.303	.329	73	20	4	0	0	7	6	3	23	8	0-0	.231	.266	.288	104	24	6	0	0	9	9	4	38	8	0-0
Olson, Gregg, Ari	.000	1.000	.000	0	0	0	0	0	0	0	1	0	0	0-0	.250	.400	1.000	4	1	0	0	1	1	2	1	3	0	0-0
Oquist, Mike, Oak	.000	.000	.000	2	0	0	0	0	0	0	0	1	0	0-0	.143	.143	.143	7	1	0	0	0	0	0	0	1	2	0-0
Orosco, Jesse, Bal	.000	.000	.000	0	0	0	0	0	0	0	0	0	0	0-0	.169	.250	.169	59	10	0	0	0	2	4	7	25	7	0-0
Ortiz, Ramon, Ana	.000	.000	.000	0	0	0	0	0	0	0	0	0	0	0-0	.000	.000	.000	0	0	0	0	0	0	0	0	0	0	0-0
Ortiz, Russ, SF	.197	.230	.268	71	14	2	0	1	7	8	3	17	7	0-0	.219	.257	.302	96	21	2	0	2	10	10	5	26	12	0-0
Osborne, Donovan, StL	.100	.100	.200	10	1	1	0	0	1	0	0	2	1	0-0	.164	.204	.223	256	42	10	1	1	18	19	12	86	28	1-1
Osuna, Antonio, LA	.000	.000	.000	0	0	0	0	0	0	0	0	0	0	0-0	.143	.222	.143	7	1	0	0	0	0	1	1	0	0	0-0
Padilla, Vicente, Ari	.000	.000	.000	0	0	0	0	0	0	0	0	0	0	0-0	.000	.000	.000	0	0	0	0	0	0	0	0	0	0	0-0
Painter, Lance, StL	.000	.000	.000	7	0	0	0	0	0	0	0	5	0	0-0	.156	.176	.219	64	10	2	1	0	6	5	2	33	8	0-0
Paniagua, Jose, Sea	.000	.000	.000	0	0	0	0	0	0	0	0	0	0	0-0	.000	.111	.000	16	0	0	0	0	1	0	2	10	1	0-0
Park, Chan Ho, LA	.153	.175	.186	59	9	2	0	0	4	6	2	26	6	0-0	.163	.197	.213	202	33	8	1	0	11	13	9	87	26	0-0
Parque, Jim, CWS	.400	.400	.400	5	2	0	0	0	0	0	0	1	1	0-0	.333	.333	.333	6	2	0	0	0	0	0	0	1	3	0-0
Parris, Steve, Cin	.158	.158	.158	38	6	0	0	0	1	4	0	11	5	0-0	.178	.186	.198	101	18	2	0	0	4	11	1	31	11	0-0
Patrick, Bronswell, SF	.000	.000	.000	1	0	0	0	0	0	0	0	1	0	0-0	.188	.278	.375	16	3	0	0	1	1	1	2	4	1	0-0
Patterson, Danny, Tex	.000	.000	.000	1	0	0	0	0	0	0	0	0	0	0-0	.000	.000	.000	1	0	0	0	0	0	0	0	0	0	0-0
Pavano, Carl, Mon	.061	.088	.061	33	2	0	0	0	1	2	1	14	5	0-0	.113	.125	.127	71	8	1	0	0	2	5	1	28	11	0-0
Pena, Jesus, CWS	.000	.000	.000	0	0	0	0	0	0	0	0	0	0	0-0	.000	.000	.000	0	0	0	0	0	0	0	0	0	0	0-0
Pena, Juan, Bos	.000	.000	.000	0	0	0	0	0	0	0	0	0	0	0-0	.000	.000	.000	0	0	0	0	0	0	0	0	0	0	0-0
Percival, Troy, Ana	.000	.000	.000	0	0	0	0	0	0	0	0	0	0	0-0	.000	.000	.000	1	0	0	0	0	0	0	0	1	0	0-0
Perez, Carlos, LA	.296	.345	.481	27	8	2	0	1	2	2	2	8	3	0-0	.174	.219	.275	207	36	7	1	4	11	12	12	92	26	0-0
Perez, Odalis, Atl	.133	.133	.133	30	4	0	0	0	1	3	0	10	4	0-0	.133	.133	.133	30	4	0	0	0	1	3	0	10	4	0-0
Perez, Yorkis, Phi	.000	.000	.000	2	0	0	0	0	0	0	0	2	0	0-0	.000	.000	.000	10	0	0	0	0	0	0	0	7	0	0-0
Perisho, Matt, Tex	.000	.000	.000	0	0	0	0	0	0	0	0	0	0	0-0	.000	.000	.000	1	0	0	0	0	0	0	0	1	0	0-0
Perkins, Dan, Min	.500	.500	.500	2	1	0	0	0	0	0	0	1	0	0-0	.500	.500	.500	2	1	0	0	0	0	0	0	1	0	0-0
Person, Robert, Tor-Phi	.073	.116	.073	41	3	0	0	0	3	1	1	23	4	0-0	.116	.153	.130	69	8	1	0	0	5	1	2	36	9	0-0
Peters, Chris, Pit	.273	.333	.273	22	6	0	0	0	5	1	2	10	1	1-0	.238	.264	.250	84	20	1	0	0	9	6	3	29	6	2-0
Peterson, Kyle, Mil	.136	.174	.136	22	3	0	0	0	2	1	1	9	2	0-0	.136	.174	.136	22	3	0	0	0	2	1	1	9	2	0-0
Petkovsek, Mark, Ana	.000	.000	.000	0	0	0	0	0	0	0	0	0	0	0-0	.163	.232	.174	86	14	1	0	0	10	3	7	18	6	0-0
Pettitte, Andy, NYY	.200	.333	.200	5	1	0	0	0	0	0	1	2	0	0-0	.111	.200	.111	9	1	0	0	0	0	0	1	5	2	0-0
Phillips, Jason, Pit	.000	.000	.000	0	0	0	0	0	0	0	0	0	0	0-0	.000	.000	.000	0	0	0	0	0	0	0	0	0	0	0-0
Pisciotta, Marc, KC	.000	.000	.000	0	0	0	0	0	0	0	0	0	0	0-0	.250	.250	.250	4	1	0	0	0	0	0	0	2	0	0-0
Pittsley, Jim, KC-Mil	.000	.500	.000	1	0	0	0	0	0	0	1	1	0	0-0	.200	.333	.400	5	1	1	0	0	0	0	1	4	1	0-0
Plesac, Dan, Tor-Ari	.000	.000	.000	1	0	0	0	0	0	0	0	1	0	0-0	.067	.067	.067	15	1	0	0	0	0	0	0	10	0	0-0
Plunk, Eric, Mil	.000	.000	.000	0	0	0	0	0	0	0	0	0	0	0-0	.000	.333	.000	2	0	0	0	0	1	0	1	2	0	0-0
Politte, Cliff, Phi	.000	.000	.000	0	0	0	0	0	0	0	0	0	0	0-0	.071	.133	.071	14	1	0	0	0	0	0	1	8	1	0-0
Ponson, Sidney, Bal	.000	.000	.000	3	0	0	0	0	0	0	0	0	1	0-0	.286	.286	.286	7	2	0	0	0	1	0	0	2	1	0-0
Poole, Jim, Phi-Cle	.000	.000	.000	2	0	0	0	0	0	0	0	1	0	0-0	.125	.125	.250	8	1	1	0	0	1	0	0	2	3	0-0
Portugal, Mark, Bos	.000	.000	.000	3	0	0	0	0	0	0	0	0	1	0-0	.198	.232	.260	450	89	20	1	2	33	36	20	87	54	0-0
Porzio, Mike, Col	.000	.000	.000	0	0	0	0	0	0	0	0	0	0	0-0	.000	.000	.000	0	0	0	0	0	0	0	0	0	0	0-0
Pote, Lou, Ana	.000	.000	.000	0	0	0	0	0	0	0	0	0	0	0-0	.000	.000	.000	0	0	0	0	0	0	0	0	0	0	0-0
Powell, Jay, Hou	.000	.000	.000	0	0	0	0	0	0	0	0	0	0	0-0	.200	.200	.200	10	2	0	0	0	0	1	0	6	1	0-0
Powell, Jeremy, Mon	.133	.212	.167	30	4	1	0	0	2	0	3	8	1	0-0	.111	.179	.139	36	4	1	0	0	2	0	3	11	1	0-0
Pulsipher, Bill, Mil	.143	.143	.143	21	3	0	0	0	1	0	0	14	8	0-0	.127	.174	.152	79	10	2	0	0	7	4	5	39	13	0-0
Quantrill, Paul, Tor	.000	.000	.000	0	0	0	0	0	0	0	0	0	0	0-0	.098	.141	.098	61	6	0	0	0	5	0	3	26	7	0-0
Radinsky, Scott, StL	.000	.000	.000	0	0	0	0	0	0	0	0	0	0	0-0	.000	.000	.000	5	0	0	0	0	0	0	0	4	0	0-0
Radke, Brad, Min	.000	.000	.000	5	0	0	0	0	0	0	0	2	0	0-0	.000	.000	.000	10	0	0	0	0	0	0	0	3	1	0-0
Radlosky, Rob, Min	.000	.000	.000	0	0	0	0	0	0	0	0	0	0	0-0	.000	.000	.000	0	0	0	0	0	0	0	0	0	0	0-0
Rain, Steve, ChC	.000	.000	.000	0	0	0	0	0	0	0	0	0	0	0-0	.000	.000	.000	0	0	0	0	0	0	0	0	0	0	0-0
Rakers, Jason, Cle	.000	.000	.000	0	0	0	0	0	0	0	0	0	0	0-0	.000	.000	.000	0	0	0	0	0	0	0	0	0	0	0-0
Ramirez, Hector, Mil	.000	.000	.000	3	0	0	0	0	0	0	0	2	0	0-0	.000	.000	.000	3	0	0	0	0	0	0	0	2	0	0-0
Ramirez, Roberto, Col	.143	.250	.143	7	1	0	0	0	1	0	0	0	1	0-0	.143	.250	.143	7	1	0	0	0	1	0	0	0	1	0-0
Ramsay, Rob, Sea	.000	.000	.000	0	0	0	0	0	0	0	0	0	0	0-0	.000	.000	.000	0	0	0	0	0	0	0	0	0	0	0-0
Rapp, Pat, Bos	.000	.000	.000	2	0	0	0	0	0	0	0	1	0	0-0	.121	.125	.151	239	29	4	0	1	10	13	1	90	21	0-0
Rath, Gary, Min	.000	.000	.000	0	0	0	0	0	0	0	0	0	0	0-0	.000	.000	.000	0	0	0	0	0	0	0	0	0	0	0-0
Ray, Ken, KC	.000	.000	.000	0	0	0	0	0	0	0	0	0	0	0-0	.000	.000	.000	0	0	0	0	0	0	0	0	0	0	0-0
Redman, Mark, Min	.000	.000	.000	0	0	0	0	0	0	0	0	0	0	0-0	.000	.000	.000	0	0	0	0	0	0	0	0	0	0	0-0
Reed, Rick, NYM	.244	.261	.289	45	11	2	0	0	2	5	1	14	8	0-0	.172	.209	.240	204	35	8	0	2	15	18	10	65	28	0-0
Reed, Steve, Cle	.000	.000	.000	0	0	0	0	0	0	0	0	0	0	0-0	.143	.143	.143	21	3	0	0	0	0	0	0	6	2	0-0
Reichert, Dan, KC	.333	.333	.333	3	1	0	0	0	0	0	0	2	1	0-0	.333	.333	.333	3	1	0	0	0	0	0	0	2	1	0-0
Rekar, Bryan, TB	.200	.200	.200	5	1	0	0	0	0	0	0	2	0	0-0	.140	.204	.160	50	7	1	0	0	4	0	4	23	5	0-1
Remlinger, Mike, Atl	.000	.000	.000	2	0	0	0	0	1	0	0	2	2	0-0	.079	.139	.109	101	8	3	0	0	5	8	7	31	19	0-1
Reyes, Al, Mil-Bal	.000	.000	.000	2	0	0	0	0	0	0	0	0	0	0-0	.143	.143	.143	7	1	0	0	0	1	0	0	4	0	0-0
Reyes, Carlos, SD	.000	.000	.000	1	0	0	0	0	0	0	0	1	0	0-0	.000	.000	.000	1	0	0	0	0	0	0	0	1	1	0-0
Reyes, Dennys, Cin	.000	.000	.000	4	0	0	0	0	0	0	0	3	0	0-0	.033	.065	.067	30	1	1	0	0	2	0	1	13	2	1-0
Reynolds, Shane, Hou	.167	.188	.242	66	11	2	0	1	4	14	2	27	17	0-0	.153	.179	.211	379	58	13	0	3	28	31	11	170	64	0-0
Reynoso, Armando, Ari	.163	.180	.204	49	8	2	0	0	3	2	1	26	8	0-0	.158	.197	.208	279	44	5	0	3	17	11	14	122	28	0-0
Rhodes, Arthur, Bal	.000	.000	.000	0	0	0	0	0	0	0	0	0	0	0-0	.333	.333	.333	3	1	0	0	0	0	0	0	2	0	0-0
Rigby, Brad, Oak-KC	.000	.000	.000	0	0	0	0	0	0	0	0	0	0	0-0	.000	.000	.000	3	0	0	0	0	0	0	0	2	0	0-0
Riley, Matt, Bal	.000	.000	.000	0	0	0	0	0	0	0	0	0	0	0-0	.000	.000	.000	0	0	0	0	0	0	0	0	0	0	0-0
Rincon, Ricky, Cle	.000	.000	.000	0	0	0	0	0	0	0	0	0	0	0-0	.000	.000	.000	3	0	0	0	0	0	0	0	1	1	0-0
Riske, David, Cle	.000	.000	.000	0	0	0	0	0	0	0	0	0	0	0-0	.000	.000	.000	0	0	0	0	0	0	0	0	0	0	0-0

	1999 Hitting														Career Hitting													
Pitcher, Team	Avg	OBP	SLG	AB	H	2B	3B	HR	R	RBI	BB	SO	SH	SB-CS	Avg	OBP	SLG	AB	H	2B	3B	HR	R	RBI	BB	SO	SH	SB-CS
Ritchie, Todd, Pit	.151	.167	.170	53	8	1	0	0	3	1	1	16	8	0-0	.145	.161	.164	55	8	1	0	0	3	1	1	17	8	0-0
Rivera, Mariano, NYY	.000	.000	.000	0	0	0	0	0	0	0	0	0	0	0-0	.000	.000	.000	0	0	0	0	0	0	0	0	0	0	0-0
Rivera, Roberto, SD	.000	.000	.000	0	0	0	0	0	0	0	0	0	0	0-0	.000	.000	.000	0	0	0	0	0	0	0	0	0	0	0-0
Rizzo, Todd, CWS	.000	.000	.000	0	0	0	0	0	0	0	0	0	0	0-0	.000	.000	.000	0	0	0	0	0	0	0	0	0	0	0-0
Roberts, Willis, Det	.000	.000	.000	0	0	0	0	0	0	0	0	0	0	0-0	.000	.000	.000	0	0	0	0	0	0	0	0	0	0	0-0
Rocker, John, Atl	.000	.000	.000	0	0	0	0	0	0	0	0	0	0	0-0	.000	.000	.000	0	0	0	0	0	0	0	0	0	0	0-0
Rodriguez, Felix, SF	.333	.429	1.000	6	2	1	0	1	3	3	0	1	1	0-0	.222	.300	.667	9	2	1	0	1	3	3	0	1	2	0-0
Rodriguez, Frank, Sea	.333	.333	.333	3	1	0	0	0	1	1	0	0	0	0-0	.250	.250	.250	4	1	0	0	0	1	1	0	0	0	0-0
Rodriguez, Nerio, Tor	.000	.000	.000	0	0	0	0	0	0	0	0	0	0	0-0	.000	.000	.000	0	0	0	0	0	0	0	0	0	0	0-0
Rodriguez, Rich, SF	1.000	1.000	1.000	1	1	0	0	0	1	1	0	0	1	0-0	.111	.200	.111	27	3	0	0	0	3	1	3	8	4	0-0
Rogers, K., Oak-NYM	.107	.167	.107	28	3	0	0	0	2	2	2	11	3	0-0	.086	.135	.086	35	3	0	0	0	3	2	2	13	3	0-0
Rojas, M., LA-Det-Mon	.000	.000	.000	0	0	0	0	0	0	0	0	0	0	0-0	.119	.119	.136	59	7	1	0	0	1	3	0	32	6	0-0
Romano, Mike, Tor	.000	.000	.000	0	0	0	0	0	0	0	0	0	0	0-0	.000	.000	.000	0	0	0	0	0	0	0	0	0	0	0-0
Romero, J.C., Min	.000	.000	.000	0	0	0	0	0	0	0	0	0	0	0-0	.000	.000	.000	0	0	0	0	0	0	0	0	0	0	0-0
Roque, Rafael, Mil	.059	.158	.059	17	1	0	0	0	0	0	2	10	1	0-0	.067	.125	.067	30	2	0	0	0	0	1	2	16	5	0-0
Rosado, Jose, KC	.000	.000	.000	5	0	0	0	0	0	0	0	4	0	0-0	.111	.111	.111	9	1	0	0	0	0	0	0	5	0	0-0
Rose, Brian, Bos	.000	.000	.000	2	0	0	0	0	0	0	0	0	1	0-0	.000	.000	.000	2	0	0	0	0	0	0	0	0	1	0-0
Rueter, Kirk, SF	.155	.194	.190	58	9	2	0	0	6	5	3	6	8	0-0	.141	.176	.151	298	42	3	0	0	21	21	13	61	38	0-1
Runyan, Sean, Det	.000	.000	.000	0	0	0	0	0	0	0	0	0	0	0-0	.000	.000	.000	0	0	0	0	0	0	0	0	0	0	0-0
Rupe, Ryan, TB	.000	.000	.000	4	0	0	0	0	0	0	0	1	0	0-0	.000	.000	.000	4	0	0	0	0	0	0	0	1	0	0-0
Rusch, Glen., KC-NYM	.000	.000	.000	0	0	0	0	0	0	0	0	0	0	0-0	.000	.000	.000	6	0	0	0	0	0	0	0	2	0	0-0
Ryan, B.J., Cin-Bal	.000	.000	.000	0	0	0	0	0	0	0	0	0	0	0-0	.000	.000	.000	0	0	0	0	0	0	0	0	0	0	0-0
Ryan, Jason, Min	.000	.000	.000	0	0	0	0	0	0	0	0	0	0	0-0	.000	.000	.000	0	0	0	0	0	0	0	0	0	0	0-0
Ryan, Ken, Phi	.000	.000	.000	0	0	0	0	0	0	0	0	0	0	0-0	.125	.125	.125	8	1	0	0	0	0	0	0	4	1	0-0
Sabel, Erik, Ari	.000	.000	.000	2	0	0	0	0	0	0	0	2	0	0-0	.000	.000	.000	2	0	0	0	0	0	0	0	2	0	0-0
Saberhagen, Bret, Bos	.000	.200	.000	4	0	0	0	0	0	0	1	2	0	0-0	.121	.177	.142	190	23	4	0	0	13	1	13	49	24	0-0
Sampson, Benj, Min	.000	.000	.000	3	0	0	0	0	0	0	0	2	0	0-0	.000	.000	.000	3	0	0	0	0	0	0	0	2	0	0-0
Sanchez, Jesus, Fla	.083	.154	.083	12	1	0	0	0	0	0	1	5	2	0-0	.125	.152	.156	64	8	0	1	0	2	1	2	20	6	0-0
Sanders, Scott, ChC	.278	.278	.389	18	5	2	0	0	0	1	0	6	2	0-0	.194	.224	.240	129	25	6	0	0	4	8	5	42	20	1-0
Santana, Julio, TB	1.000	1.000	1.000	1	1	0	0	0	0	1	0	0	0	0-0	.286	.286	.286	7	2	0	0	0	0	1	0	3	0	0-0
Santana, Marino, Bos	.000	.000	.000	0	0	0	0	0	0	0	0	0	0	0-0	.000	.000	.000	0	0	0	0	0	0	0	0	0	0	0-0
Santiago, Jose, KC	.000	.000	.000	0	0	0	0	0	0	0	0	0	0	0-0	.000	.000	.000	0	0	0	0	0	0	0	0	0	0	0-0
Sauerbeck, Scott, Pit	.000	.000	.000	1	0	0	0	0	0	0	0	1	1	0-0	.000	.000	.000	1	0	0	0	0	0	0	0	1	1	0-0
Saunders, Tony, TB	.000	.000	.000	0	0	0	0	0	0	0	0	0	0	0-0	.128	.171	.205	39	5	0	0	1	2	1	2	19	1	0-0
Scheffer, Aaron, Sea	.000	.000	.000	0	0	0	0	0	0	0	0	0	0	0-0	.000	.000	.000	0	0	0	0	0	0	0	0	0	0	0-0
Schilling, Curt, Phi	.100	.211	.160	50	5	1	1	0	5	3	7	28	9	0-0	.150	.177	.173	480	72	9	1	0	22	21	16	176	67	1-0
Schmidt, Jason, Pit	.083	.154	.083	60	5	0	0	0	2	1	5	33	12	0-0	.089	.137	.107	214	19	4	0	0	6	8	12	101	36	0-0
Schoeneweis, S., Ana	.000	.000	.000	0	0	0	0	0	0	0	0	0	0	0-0	.000	.000	.000	0	0	0	0	0	0	0	0	0	0	0-0
Schourek, Pete, Pit	.000	.107	.000	25	0	0	0	0	1	1	3	13	3	0-0	.158	.188	.196	265	42	4	0	2	15	20	10	80	37	2-0
Schrenk, Steve, Phi	.000	.000	.000	3	0	0	0	0	0	0	0	2	1	0-0	.000	.000	.000	3	0	0	0	0	0	0	0	2	1	0-0
Seanez, Rudy, Atl	.000	.500	.000	1	0	0	0	0	1	0	1	1	0	0-0	.000	.200	.000	4	0	0	0	0	1	0	1	4	0	0-0
Sele, Aaron, Tex	.000	.200	.000	4	0	0	0	0	0	0	1	2	1	0-0	.100	.182	.200	10	1	1	0	0	0	0	1	3	1	0-0
Serafini, Dan, ChC	.083	.267	.083	12	1	0	0	0	1	0	3	7	1	0-0	.077	.250	.077	13	1	0	0	0	1	0	3	8	1	0-0
Service, Scott, KC	.000	.000	.000	0	0	0	0	0	0	0	0	0	0	0-0	.063	.063	.063	16	1	0	0	0	0	1	0	9	0	0-0
Shaw, Jeff, LA	.000	.000	.000	0	0	0	0	0	0	0	0	0	0	0-0	.079	.167	.079	38	3	0	0	0	4	0	4	20	3	0-0
Shuey, Paul, Cle	.000	.000	.000	0	0	0	0	0	0	0	0	0	0	0-0	.000	.000	.000	2	0	0	0	0	0	0	0	1	0	0-0
Shumaker, An., Phi	.200	.333	.200	5	1	0	0	0	0	0	1	3	0	0-0	.200	.333	.200	5	1	0	0	0	0	0	1	3	0	0-0
Silva, Jose, Pit	.100	.100	.100	20	2	0	0	0	0	3	0	10	2	0-0	.074	.123	.093	54	4	1	0	0	1	3	2	24	10	0-0
Simas, Bill, CWS	.000	.000	.000	0	0	0	0	0	0	0	0	0	0	0-0	.000	.000	.000	0	0	0	0	0	0	0	0	0	0	0-0
Sinclair, Steve, Tor-Sea	.000	.000	.000	0	0	0	0	0	0	0	0	0	0	0-0	.000	.000	.000	0	0	0	0	0	0	0	0	0	0	0-0
Sirotka, Mike, CWS	.250	.250	.250	8	2	0	0	0	1	0	0	3	0	0-0	.154	.214	.154	13	2	0	0	0	1	0	1	4	0	0-0
Slocumb, H., Bal-StL	.000	.000	.000	0	0	0	0	0	0	0	0	0	0	0-0	.091	.091	.091	11	1	0	0	0	0	2	0	6	1	0-0
Slusarski, Joe, Hou	.000	.000	.000	0	0	0	0	0	0	0	0	0	0	0-0	.000	.000	.000	0	0	0	0	0	0	0	0	0	0	0-0
Smart, J.D., Mon	.000	.000	.000	3	0	0	0	0	0	0	0	0	0	0-0	.000	.000	.000	3	0	0	0	0	0	0	0	0	0	0-0
Smith, Dan, Mon	.083	.185	.083	24	2	0	0	0	3	1	3	15	3	0-0	.083	.185	.083	24	2	0	0	0	3	1	3	15	3	0-0
Smoltz, John, Atl	.274	.338	.387	62	17	4	0	1	11	7	5	28	4	0-0	.175	.249	.226	727	127	20	1	5	69	51	69	278	90	3-2
Snyder, John, CWS	.000	.000	.000	0	0	0	0	0	0	0	0	0	0	0-0	.000	.000	.000	0	0	0	0	0	0	0	0	0	0	0-0
Sodowsky, Clint, StL	.000	.000	.000	1	0	0	0	0	0	0	0	1	0	0-0	.308	.308	.385	13	4	1	0	0	2	0	0	3	1	0-0
Sparks, Jeff, TB	.000	.000	.000	0	0	0	0	0	0	0	0	0	0	0-0	.000	.000	.000	0	0	0	0	0	0	0	0	0	0	0-0
Sparks, Steve, Ana	.333	.333	.667	3	1	1	0	0	0	2	0	1	0	0-0	.250	.400	.500	4	1	1	0	0	1	2	1	1	1	0-0
Speier, Justin, Atl	.333	.333	.333	3	1	0	0	0	0	0	0	2	0	0-0	.333	.333	.333	3	1	0	0	0	0	0	0	2	0	0-0
Spencer, Sean, Sea	.000	.000	.000	0	0	0	0	0	0	0	0	0	0	0-0	.000	.000	.000	0	0	0	0	0	0	0	0	0	0	0-0
Spencer, Stan, SD	.000	.091	.000	10	0	0	0	0	0	0	0	3	1	0-0	.053	.100	.105	19	1	1	0	0	0	0	0	7	4	0-0
Spoljaric, Paul, Phi-Tor	.000	.000	.000	2	0	0	0	0	0	0	0	0	2	0-0	.000	.000	.000	3	0	0	0	0	0	0	0	0	2	0-0
Spradlin, Jerry, Cle-SF	.000	.000	.000	1	0	0	0	0	0	0	0	0	0	0-0	.200	.200	.400	5	1	1	0	0	0	0	0	2	0	0-0
Springer, Dennis, Fla	.120	.118	.140	50	6	1	0	0	2	2	0	17	3	0-0	.113	.111	.129	62	7	1	0	0	2	2	0	24	3	0-0
Springer, Russ, Atl	.000	.000	.000	0	0	0	0	0	0	0	0	0	0	0-0	.050	.050	.050	20	1	0	0	0	1	0	0	14	3	0-0
Stanton, Mike, NYY	.000	.000	.000	1	0	0	0	0	0	0	0	1	0	0-0	.462	.500	.538	13	6	1	0	0	1	2	1	2	1	0-0
Stark, Dennis, Sea	.000	.000	.000	0	0	0	0	0	0	0	0	0	0	0-0	.000	.000	.000	0	0	0	0	0	0	0	0	0	0	0-0
Stein, Blake, Oak-KC	.000	.000	.000	0	0	0	0	0	0	0	0	0	0	0-0	.000	.000	.000	5	0	0	0	0	0	0	0	4	1	0-0
Stephenson, Garr., StL	.074	.074	.111	27	2	1	0	0	1	0	0	5	3	0-0	.092	.119	.123	65	6	2	0	0	1	1	1	22	9	0-0
Stevens, Dave, Cle	.000	.000	.000	0	0	0	0	0	0	0	0	0	0	0-0	.200	.200	.200	5	1	0	0	0	0	0	0	2	0	0-0
Stottlemyre, Todd, Ari	.125	.243	.156	32	4	1	0	0	0	0	5	12	3	0-0	.213	.294	.246	207	44	5	1	0	17	7	24	77	22	1-1
Strickland, Scott, Mon	.000	.000	.000	0	0	0	0	0	0	0	0	0	0	0-0	.000	.000	.000	0	0	0	0	0	0	0	0	0	0	0-0
Stull, Everett, Atl	.000	.000	.000	0	0	0	0	0	0	0	0	0	0	0-0	.000	.000	.000	0	0	0	0	0	0	0	0	0	1	0-0
Sturtze, Tanyon, CWS	.000	.000	.000	0	0	0	0	0	0	0	0	0	0	0-0	.000	.000	.000	1	0	0	0	0	0	0	0	0	1	0-0
Sullivan, Scott, Cin	.000	.000	.000	15	0	0	0	0	1	0	0	11	0	0-0	.029	.029	.029	35	1	0	0	0	1	1	0	22	3	0-0
Suppan, Jeff, KC	.200	.200	.200	5	1	0	0	0	0	1	0	0	0	0-0	.241	.267	.241	29	7	0	0	0	1	2	0	7	1	1-0
Suzuki, Mak., Sea-KC	.000	.000	.000	0	0	0	0	0	0	0	0	0	0	0-0	.000	.000	.000	0	0	0	0	0	0	0	0	0	0	0-0
Swindell, Greg, Ari	.000	.000	.000	4	0	0	0	0	0	0	0	1	2	0-0	.189	.201	.230	244	46	10	0	0	10	13	4	56	35	0-0
Tam, Jeff, Cle-NYM	.000	.000	.000	0	0	0	0	0	0	0	0	0	0	0-0	.000	.000	.000	1	0	0	0	0	0	0	0	0	0	0-0
Tapani, Kevin, ChC	.051	.119	.077	39	2	1	0	0	1	3	3	21	5	0-0	.116	.179	.161	155	18	4	0	1	10	16	12	71	17	1-0
Tavarez, Julian, SF	.200	.200	.200	5	1	0	0	0	0	0	0	2	0	0-0	.133	.133	.133	15	2	0	0	0	0	0	0	7	1	0-0
Taylor, Billy, Oak-NYM	.000	.000	.000	0	0	0	0	0	0	0	0	0	0	0-0	.000	.000	.000	0	0	0	0	0	0	0	0	0	0	0-0
Tejera, Michael, Fla	.000	.000	.000	0	0	0	0	0	0	0	0	0	0	0-0	.000	.000	.000	0	0	0	0	0	0	0	0	0	0	0-0
Telemaco, A., Ari-Phi	.000	.000	.000	0	0	0	0	0	0	0	0	0	0	0-0	.110	.143	.151	73	8	1	1	0	3	3	3	37	5	0-0

1999 Hitting / Career Hitting

Pitcher, Team	1999 Hitting														Career Hitting													
	Avg	OBP	SLG	AB	H	2B	3B	HR	R	RBI	BB	SO	SH	SB-CS	Avg	OBP	SLG	AB	H	2B	3B	HR	R	RBI	BB	SO	SH	SB-CS
Telford, Anthony, Mon	.000	.333	.000	2	0	0	0	0	0	0	1	1	1	2	0-0	.190	.227	.238	21	4	1	0	0	0	3	1	4	3	0-0
Tessmer, Jay, NYY	.000	.000	.000	0	0	0	0	0	0	0	0	0	0	0-0	.000	.000	.000	0	0	0	0	0	0	0	0	0	0	0-0
Thompson, Justin, Det	.000	.000	.000	5	0	0	0	0	0	0	0	2	0	0-0	.071	.071	.071	14	1	0	0	0	1	0	0	6	0	0-0
Thompson, Mark, StL	.000	.000	.000	8	0	0	0	0	0	0	0	6	1	0-0	.158	.167	.228	101	16	4	0	1	7	3	1	46	10	0-0
Thomson, John, Col	.167	.250	.222	18	3	1	0	0	1	1	2	7	0	0-1	.165	.203	.174	115	19	1	0	0	7	8	6	53	15	0-1
Thurman, Mike, Mon	.025	.071	.025	40	1	0	0	0	1	0	1	31	4	0-0	.031	.087	.031	65	2	0	0	0	3	0	3	49	7	0-0
Timlin, Mike, Bal	.000	.000	.000	0	0	0	0	0	0	0	0	0	0	0-0	.000	.000	.000	0	0	0	0	0	0	0	0	0	0	0-0
Tomko, Brett, Cin	.213	.260	.255	47	10	2	0	0	3	2	3	17	8	0-0	.149	.191	.176	148	22	4	0	0	9	8	8	60	20	0-0
Trachsel, Steve, ChC	.111	.125	.127	63	7	1	0	0	4	0	1	25	7	1-0	.171	.211	.222	351	60	12	0	2	30	23	17	110	47	1-1
Trombley, Mike, Min	.000	.000	.000	0	0	0	0	0	0	0	0	0	0	0-0	.000	.000	.000	1	0	0	0	0	0	0	0	0	0	0-0
Urbina, Ugueth, Mon	.000	.000	.000	5	0	0	0	0	0	0	0	2	0	0-0	.098	.132	.098	51	5	0	0	0	3	1	2	30	3	0-0
Valdes, Ismael, LA	.086	.102	.086	58	5	0	0	0	1	2	1	18	10	1-0	.114	.141	.125	297	34	3	0	0	12	8	9	93	45	3-0
Vazquez, Javier, Mon	.286	.333	.333	42	12	2	0	0	4	5	3	8	8	0-0	.223	.260	.287	94	21	4	1	0	7	10	5	15	14	0-0
Venafro, Mike, Tex	.000	.000	.000	0	0	0	0	0	0	0	0	0	0	0-0	.000	.000	.000	0	0	0	0	0	0	0	0	0	0	0-0
Veres, Dave, Col	.000	.000	.000	1	0	0	0	0	0	0	0	0	0	0-0	.300	.333	.350	20	6	1	0	0	1	1	1	10	2	0-0
Villone, Ron, Cin	.070	.091	.070	43	3	0	0	0	0	0	1	10	5	0-0	.067	.087	.067	45	3	0	0	0	0	0	1	11	5	0-0
Vizcaino, Luis, Oak	.000	.000	.000	0	0	0	0	0	0	0	0	0	0	0-0	.000	.000	.000	0	0	0	0	0	0	0	0	0	0	0-0
Vosberg, Ed, SD-Ari	.000	.000	.000	0	0	0	0	0	0	0	0	0	0	0-0	.000	.000	.000	2	0	0	0	0	0	0	0	1	0	0-0
Wagner, Billy, Hou	.000	.000	.000	0	0	0	0	0	0	0	0	0	0	0-0	.111	.111	.111	9	1	0	0	0	0	0	0	4	0	0-0
Wagner, Paul, Cle	.000	.000	.000	0	0	0	0	0	0	0	0	0	0	0-0	.166	.199	.178	169	28	2	0	0	10	9	7	47	16	0-1
Wainhouse, Dave, Col	.000	.000	.000	1	0	0	0	0	0	0	0	0	0	0-0	.000	.000	.000	5	0	0	0	0	0	0	0	1	0	0-0
Wakefield, Tim, Bos	.000	.000	.000	3	0	0	0	0	0	0	0	3	0	0-0	.117	.139	.182	77	9	2	0	1	3	3	2	25	10	0-0
Wall, Donne, SD	.000	.000	.000	1	0	0	0	0	0	0	0	1	0	0-0	.179	.214	.194	67	12	1	0	0	5	1	3	21	12	0-0
Wallace, Derek, KC	.000	.000	.000	0	0	0	0	0	0	0	0	0	0	0-0	.000	.000	.000	0	0	0	0	0	0	0	0	0	0	0-0
Wallace, Jeff, Pit	.000	1.000	.000	0	0	0	0	0	0	0	1	0	0	0-0	.000	1.000	.000	0	0	0	0	0	0	0	1	0	0	0-0
Ward, Bryan, CWS	.000	1.000	.000	0	0	0	0	0	0	0	1	0	0	0-0	.000	1.000	.000	0	0	0	0	0	0	0	1	0	0	0-0
Wasdin, John, Bos	.000	.000	.000	0	0	0	0	0	0	0	0	0	0	0-0	.000	.000	.000	1	0	0	0	0	0	0	0	2	0	0-0
Washburn, Jarrod, Ana	.000	.000	.000	0	0	0	0	0	0	0	0	0	0	0-0	.000	.000	.000	0	0	0	0	0	0	0	0	0	0	0-0
Wats'n, NYM-Sea-NYY	.300	.300	.400	10	3	1	0	0	0	0	0	1	0	0-0	.257	.293	.343	175	45	13	1	0	13	19	9	22	13	0-0
Weathers, Dave, Mil	.143	.250	.143	7	1	0	0	0	1	0	1	4	0	0-0	.109	.154	.155	129	14	0	0	2	7	4	6	80	16	0-0
Weaver, Eric, Sea	.000	.000	.000	0	0	0	0	0	0	0	0	0	0	0-0	.000	.000	.000	1	0	0	0	0	0	0	0	0	0	0-0
Weaver, Jeff, Det	.500	.500	.750	4	2	1	0	0	2	0	0	1	1	0-0	.500	.500	.750	4	2	1	0	0	2	0	0	1	1	0-0
Wells, Bob, Min	.000	.000	.000	0	0	0	0	0	0	0	0	0	0	0-0	.000	1.000	.000	0	0	0	0	0	0	0	1	0	0	0-0
Wells, David, Tor	.000	.000	.000	6	0	0	0	0	0	0	0	0	1	0-0	.132	.132	.132	38	5	0	0	0	2	0	0	6	2	0-0
Wells, Kip, CWS	.000	.000	.000	0	0	0	0	0	0	0	0	0	0	0-0	.000	.000	.000	0	0	0	0	0	0	0	0	0	0	0-0
Wendell, Turk, NYM	.000	.143	.000	6	0	0	0	0	0	0	1	3	0	0-0	.061	.184	.061	33	2	0	0	0	1	0	5	16	1	0-0
Wengert, Don, KC	.000	.000	.000	0	0	0	0	0	0	0	0	0	0	0-0	.000	.059	.000	16	0	0	0	0	0	0	1	3	1	0-0
Wetteland, John, Tex	.000	.000	.000	0	0	0	0	0	0	0	0	0	0	0-0	.167	.167	.286	42	7	2	0	1	4	8	0	19	9	0-0
Wheeler, Dan, TB	.000	.000	.000	0	0	0	0	0	0	0	0	0	0	0-0	.000	.000	.000	0	0	0	0	0	0	0	0	0	0	0-0
Whisenant, M., KC-SD	.000	.000	.000	0	0	0	0	0	0	0	0	0	0	0-0	.091	.130	.091	22	2	0	0	0	0	1	1	14	8	0-0
White, Gabe, Cin	.000	.000	.000	0	0	0	0	0	0	0	0	0	0	0-0	.097	.125	.129	31	3	1	0	0	1	1	0	8	2	0-0
White, Rick, TB	.000	.000	.000	0	0	0	0	0	0	0	0	0	0	0-0	.000	.000	.000	2	0	0	0	0	0	0	0	2	0	0-0
Whiteside, Matt, SD	.000	.000	.000	0	0	0	0	0	0	0	0	0	0	0-0	.000	.000	.000	2	0	0	0	0	0	0	0	0	0	0-0
Wickman, Bob, Mil	.000	.000	.000	1	0	0	0	0	0	0	0	0	0	0-0	.143	.250	.143	14	2	0	0	0	1	2	2	10	1	0-0
Wilkins, Marc, Pit	.000	.000	.000	1	0	0	0	0	0	0	0	1	0	0-0	.169	.167	.205	83	14	3	0	0	5	8	0	26	15	0-0
Williams, Brian, Hou	.333	.333	.333	3	1	0	0	0	0	1	0	1	0	0-0	.200	.200	.200	5	1	0	0	0	2	0	1	4	1	0-0
Williams, Jeff, LA	.200	.333	.200	5	1	0	0	0	2	0	1	4	1	0-0	.200	.333	.200	5	1	0	0	0	2	0	1	4	1	0-0
Williams, Mike, Pit	.000	.000	.000	2	0	0	0	0	0	0	0	0	0	0-0	.160	.183	.179	106	17	2	0	0	7	7	3	32	24	1-0
Williams, Todd, Sea	.000	.000	.000	0	0	0	0	0	0	0	0	0	0	0-0	.250	.250	.250	4	1	0	0	0	0	0	0	2	0	0-0
Williams, Woody, SD	.178	.197	.233	73	13	4	0	0	4	6	2	19	4	0-1	.198	.214	.247	81	16	4	0	0	4	6	2	21	4	0-1
Williamson, Scott, Cin	.000	.125	.000	7	0	0	0	0	0	0	1	6	3	0-0	.000	.125	.000	7	0	0	0	0	0	0	1	6	3	0-0
Winkelsas, Joe, Atl	.000	.000	.000	0	0	0	0	0	0	0	0	0	0	0-0	.000	.000	.000	0	0	0	0	0	0	0	0	0	0	0-0
Witasick, Jay, KC	.000	.000	.000	5	0	0	0	0	0	0	0	4	0	0-0	.115	.145	.231	52	6	3	0	1	2	5	2	18	5	0-0
Witt, Bobby, TB	.000	.000	.000	2	0	0	0	0	0	0	0	1	0	0-0	.083	.083	.083	12	1	0	0	0	1	0	0	11	1	0-0
Wohlers, Mark, Atl	.000	.000	.000	0	0	0	0	0	0	0	0	0	0	0-0	.200	.200	.200	10	2	0	0	0	1	0	0	1	0	0-0
Wolcott, Bob, Bos	.000	.000	.000	0	0	0	0	0	0	0	0	0	0	0-0	.233	.281	.267	30	7	1	0	0	2	0	2	8	7	0-0
Wolf, Randy, Phi	.233	.281	.267	30	7	1	0	0	2	0	2	8	7	0-0	.233	.281	.267	30	7	1	0	0	2	0	2	8	7	0-0
Woodall, Brad, ChC	.500	.750	.500	2	1	0	0	0	2	0	0	0	0	0-0	.271	.364	.354	48	13	1	0	1	7	3	7	12	5	0-0
Woodard, Steve, Mil	.132	.220	.151	53	7	1	0	0	5	0	6	16	10	0-0	.136	.183	.165	103	14	3	0	0	6	4	6	28	12	0-0
Worrell, Tim, Oak	.000	.000	.000	0	0	0	0	0	0	0	0	0	0	0-0	.116	.164	.130	69	8	1	0	0	6	4	4	34	9	0-0
Wright, Jamey, Col	.125	.125	.156	32	4	1	0	0	0	2	0	13	3	0-0	.135	.175	.202	163	22	6	1	1	12	9	8	77	19	0-0
Wright, Jaret, Cle	.000	.000	.000	1	0	0	0	0	0	0	0	1	0	0-0	.273	.273	.273	11	3	0	0	0	2	1	0	4	2	0-0
Yan, Esteban, TB	.000	.000	.000	0	0	0	0	0	0	0	0	0	0	0-0	.000	.000	.000	0	0	0	0	0	0	0	0	0	0	0-0
Yarnall, Ed, NYY	.000	.000	.000	0	0	0	0	0	0	0	0	0	0	0-0	.000	.000	.000	0	0	0	0	0	0	0	0	0	0	0-0
Yoshii, Masato, NYM	.164	.164	.164	55	9	0	0	0	1	2	0	16	6	0-1	.117	.142	.126	103	12	1	0	0	4	5	3	43	14	0-1
Zimmerman, Jeff, Tex	.000	.000	.000	0	0	0	0	0	0	0	0	0	0	0-0	.000	.000	.000	0	0	0	0	0	0	0	0	0	0	0-0
Zimmerman, Jor., Sea	.000	.000	.000	0	0	0	0	0	0	0	0	0	0	0-0	.000	.000	.000	0	0	0	0	0	0	0	0	0	0	0-0

Pitchers Fielding and Holding Runners

1999 Fielding and Holding Runners

Pitcher, Team	G	Inn	PO	A	E	DP	Pct.	SBA	CS	PCS	PPO	CS%
Abbott, Jim, Mil	20	82.0	3	23	1	1	.963	22	1	6	0	.32
Abbott, Paul, Sea	25	72.2	7	8	0	1	1.000	3	1	0	0	.33
Acevedo, Juan, StL	50	102.1	5	7	2	0	.857	14	5	1	0	.43
Adams, Terry, ChC	52	65.0	8	6	1	0	.933	6	1	0	0	.17
Aguilera, Rick, Min-ChC	61	67.2	6	7	0	1	1.000	5	2	0	0	.40
Aldred, Scott, TB-Phi	66	56.2	2	8	0	0	1.000	8	2	1	0	.38
Alfonseca, Antonio, Fla	73	77.2	5	14	0	2	1.000	13	4	2	0	.46
Almanza, Armando, Fla	14	15.2	0	2	0	1	1.000	2	1	0	0	.50
Almanzar, Carlos, SD	28	37.1	2	3	2	1	.714	2	0	0	0	.00
Almonte, Hector, Fla	15	15.0	1	3	0	1	1.000	1	0	1	0	1.00
Alvarez, Juan, Ana	8	3.0	0	2	0	0	1.000	0	0	0	0	.00
Alvarez, Wilson, TB	28	160.0	2	24	3	1	.897	12	7	3	0	.83
Anderson, Brian, Ari	31	130.0	10	36	2	1	.958	6	0	0	4	.00
Anderson, Jimmy, Pit	13	29.1	1	5	0	2	1.000	3	0	0	0	.00
Anderson, Matt, Det	37	38.0	0	1	0	0	1.000	4	1	0	0	.25
Ankiel, Rick, StL	9	33.0	2	0	0	0	1.000	0	0	0	0	.00
Appier, Kevin, KC-Oak	34	209.0	13	21	1	2	.971	33	9	0	0	.27
Armas Jr., Tony, Mon	1	6.0	1	0	0	0	1.000	0	0	0	0	.00
Arnold, Jamie, LA	36	69.0	4	18	2	5	.917	10	3	0	0	.30
Arrojo, Rolando, TB	24	140.2	13	19	0	3	1.000	18	6	0	1	.33
Ashby, Andy, SD	31	206.0	14	35	2	4	.961	29	5	1	0	.21
Assenmacher, Paul, Cle	55	33.0	1	4	0	1	1.000	5	1	0	0	.20
Astacio, Pedro, Col	34	232.0	16	25	4	3	.911	38	14	0	0	.37
Avery, Steve, Cin	19	96.0	4	16	1	0	.952	20	2	1	3	.15
Ayala, Bobby, Mon-ChC	66	82.0	8	12	4	1	.833	15	2	1	0	.20
Aybar, Manny, StL	65	97.0	5	11	0	0	1.000	11	4	1	0	.45
Baldwin, James, CWS	35	199.1	12	21	2	0	.943	21	4	1	0	.24
Bale, John, Tor	1	2.0	0	0	0	0	.000	0	0	0	0	.00
Barber, Brian, KC	8	18.2	1	3	0	0	1.000	1	0	0	0	.00
Barker, Richie, ChC	5	5.0	1	0	0	0	1.000	2	0	0	0	.00
Batista, Miguel, Mon	39	134.2	5	20	2	1	.926	24	3	1	0	.17
Beck, Rod, ChC-Bos	43	44.0	5	6	0	0	1.000	6	1	0	0	.17
Belcher, Tim, Ana	24	132.1	11	15	2	1	.929	7	4	1	0	.71
Belinda, Stan, Cin	29	42.2	0	5	0	0	1.000	5	1	1	0	.40
Beltran, Rigo, NYM-Col	33	42.0	3	7	0	1	1.000	3	0	0	0	.00
Benes, Alan, StL	2	2.0	1	0	0	0	1.000	0	0	0	0	.00
Benes, Andy, Ari	33	198.1	13	15	2	1	.933	28	7	0	1	.25
Benitez, Armando, NYM	77	78.0	2	6	0	0	1.000	12	0	0	0	.00
Bennett, Joel, Phi	5	17.0	2	3	0	0	1.000	1	1	0	0	1.00
Bennett, Shayne, Mon	5	11.1	0	0	0	0	.000	2	1	0	0	.50
Benson, Kris, Pit	31	196.2	15	27	2	6	.955	24	7	0	0	.29
Bere, Jason, Cin-Mil	17	66.2	1	8	1	1	.900	12	3	0	1	.25
Bergman, S., Hou-Atl	25	105.1	4	10	0	1	1.000	10	1	0	0	.10
Billingsley, Brent, Fla	8	7.2	1	0	0	1	1.000	3	2	0	0	.67
Blair, Willie, Det	39	134.0	6	15	0	0	1.000	13	6	0	0	.46
Bochtler, Doug, LA	12	13.0	1	3	0	0	1.000	3	0	0	0	.00
Boehringer, Brian, SD	33	94.1	8	9	1	0	.944	12	4	0	1	.33
Bohanon, Brian, Col	33	197.1	7	29	1	2	.973	35	8	2	0	.29
Bones, Ricky, Bal	30	43.2	2	2	0	0	1.000	7	1	0	0	.14
Borbon, Pedro, LA	70	50.2	2	6	0	0	1.000	6	1	0	0	.17
Borkowski, Dave, Det	17	76.2	7	10	4	1	.810	8	2	0	3	.25
Bottalico, Ricky, StL	68	73.1	4	9	0	2	1.000	6	5	0	0	.83
Bottenfield, Kent, StL	31	190.1	10	30	0	3	1.000	8	3	0	4	.38
Bowie, Micah, Atl-ChC	14	51.0	0	6	1	0	.857	13	2	1	0	.23
Boyd, Jason, Pit	4	5.1	1	0	0	0	1.000	0	0	0	0	.00
Bradford, Chad, CWS	3	3.2	1	3	0	0	1.000	0	0	0	0	.00
Brantley, Jeff, Phi	10	8.2	0	1	0	0	1.000	0	0	0	0	.00
Brewer, Billy, Phi	25	25.2	0	1	0	0	1.000	1	0	1	0	1.00
Brocail, Doug, Det	70	82.0	11	6	0	1	1.000	5	3	0	0	.60
Brock, Chris, SF	19	106.2	11	9	1	2	.952	12	4	1	0	.42
Brower, Jim, Cle	9	25.2	1	2	0	0	1.000	5	0	0	0	.00
Brown, Kevin, LA	35	252.1	41	46	6	2	.935	26	5	2	1	.27
Brownson, Mark, Col	7	29.2	1	5	1	0	.857	6	0	1	0	.17
Brunson, Will, Det	17	12.0	0	3	0	1	1.000	1	0	0	0	.00
Buddie, Mike, NYY	2	2.0	0	0	0	0	.000	0	0	0	0	.00
Bullinger, Kirk, Bos	4	2.0	1	2	0	1	1.000	0	0	0	0	.00
Bunch, Mel, Sea	5	10.0	0	2	0	0	1.000	1	0	0	0	.00
Burba, Dave, Cle	34	220.0	20	29	1	4	.980	27	12	0	0	.44
Burkett, John, Tex	30	147.1	7	18	0	2	1.000	10	5	0	0	.50
Burnett, A.J., Fla	7	41.1	2	5	1	0	.875	9	3	1	0	.44
Busby, Mike, StL	15	17.2	1	2	0	1	1.000	2	0	0	1	.00
Byrd, Paul, Phi	32	199.2	10	25	6	3	.854	20	6	1	1	.35
Byrdak, Tim, KC	33	24.2	2	6	0	1	1.000	1	1	0	0	1.00
Cabrera, Jose, Hou	26	29.1	0	2	0	0	1.000	2	0	0	1	.00
Callaway, Mickey, TB	6	19.1	0	4	0	0	1.000	1	1	0	0	1.00
Candiotti, Tom, Oak-Cle	18	71.1	1	12	1	1	.929	13	2	0	0	.15
Carlson, Dan, Ari	2	4.0	0	0	0	0	.000	1	0	0	0	.00
Carlyle, Buddy, SD	7	37.2	0	3	0	1	1.000	6	1	0	0	.17
Carmona, Rafael, Sea	9	11.1	1	0	1	0	.500	0	0	0	0	.00
Carpenter, Chris, Tor	24	150.0	10	15	1	3	.962	9	6	0	0	.67
Carrasco, Hector, Min	39	49.0	5	0	1	0	.833	0	0	0	0	.00
Carter, Lance, KC	6	5.1	0	1	0	0	1.000	0	0	0	0	.00
Castillo, Carlos, CWS	18	41.0	1	5	0	0	1.000	7	1	1	1	.29

1999 Fielding and Holding Runners

Pitcher, Team	G	Inn	PO	A	E	DP	Pct.	SBA	CS	PCS	PPO	CS%
Cather, Mike, Atl	4	2.2	0	1	0	0	1.000	1	0	1	0	1.00
Charlton, Norm, TB	42	50.2	2	6	1	0	.889	7	3	0	0	.43
Checo, Robinson, LA	9	15.2	0	0	0	0	.000	0	0	0	0	.00
Chen, Bruce, Atl	16	51.0	0	3	1	0	.750	9	3	0	0	.33
Cho, Jin Ho, Bos	9	39.1	1	5	0	1	1.000	5	1	0	0	.20
Chouinard, Bobby, Ari	32	40.1	2	6	1	1	.889	6	1	0	0	.17
Christiansen, Jason, Pit	39	38.0	0	7	0	1	1.000	4	2	0	0	.50
Clark, Mark, Tex	15	74.1	3	4	1	1	.875	5	4	0	0	.80
Clemens, Roger, NYY	30	187.2	16	30	1	2	.979	28	9	2	1	.39
Clement, Matt, SD	31	180.2	12	12	2	0	.923	11	5	0	0	.45
Clontz, Brad, Pit	56	49.1	1	7	0	0	1.000	7	1	0	0	.14
Cloude, Ken, Sea	31	72.1	3	9	0	0	1.000	10	3	1	0	.40
Colon, Bartolo, Cle	32	205.0	20	31	2	4	.962	16	7	0	0	.44
Cone, David, NYY	31	193.1	7	12	1	1	.950	32	10	0	0	.31
Cook, Dennis, NYM	71	63.0	2	8	0	0	1.000	5	0	1	0	.20
Cooper, Brian, Ana	5	27.2	2	5	0	2	1.000	1	0	0	1	.00
Coppinger, R., Bal-Mil	40	58.1	5	1	1	0	.857	12	2	0	0	.17
Corbin, Archie, Fla	17	21.0	0	1	0	0	1.000	1	0	0	0	.00
Cordero, Francisco, Det	20	19.0	2	5	0	1	1.000	3	0	0	0	.00
Cordova, Francisco, Pit	27	160.2	14	25	1	2	.975	19	6	0	3	.32
Cormier, Rheal, Bos	60	63.1	1	7	1	1	.889	4	0	0	0	.00
Cornelius, Reid, Fla	5	19.1	0	5	0	0	1.000	3	1	0	0	.33
Corsi, Jim, Bos-Bal	36	37.1	3	8	0	0	1.000	5	2	0	0	.40
Cortes, David, Atl	4	3.2	0	1	1	0	.500	0	0	0	0	.00
Crabtree, Tim, Tex	68	65.0	6	4	0	0	1.000	6	4	0	0	.67
Creek, Doug, ChC	3	6.0	0	0	0	0	.000	1	0	0	0	.00
Croushore, Rich, StL	59	71.2	2	4	2	0	.750	12	4	0	0	.33
Cruz, Nelson, Det	29	66.2	8	17	2	0	.926	7	2	0	0	.29
Cunnane, Will, SD	24	31.0	1	4	0	0	1.000	7	2	0	0	.29
D'Amico, Jeff, Mil	1	1.0	0	0	0	0	.000	0	0	0	0	.00
Daal, Omar, Ari	32	214.2	13	34	2	2	.959	17	6	4	0	.59
Dale, Carl, Mil	4	4.0	0	0	0	0	.000	0	0	0	0	.00
Daneker, Pat, CWS	3	15.0	0	3	0	0	1.000	1	0	0	0	.00
Darensbourg, Vic, Fla	56	34.2	1	4	0	0	1.000	0	0	0	0	.00
Davenport, Joe, CWS	3	1.2	0	1	0	0	1.000	1	0	0	0	.00
Davey, Tom, Tor-Sea	45	65.0	4	6	2	1	.833	9	3	1	0	.44
Davis, Doug, Tex	2	2.2	0	1	0	0	1.000	0	0	0	0	.00
DeHart, Rick, Mon	3	1.2	0	0	0	0	.000	0	0	0	0	.00
DeJean, Mike, Col	56	61.0	4	11	0	2	1.000	17	2	0	0	.12
de los Santos, Val., Mil	7	8.1	0	2	0	0	1.000	1	0	1	0	1.00
del Toro, Miguel, SF	14	23.2	1	3	0	2	1.000	5	0	0	0	.00
DeLucia, Rich, Cle	6	9.1	0	0	0	0	.000	2	0	0	0	.00
Dempster, Ryan, Fla	25	147.0	10	15	1	4	.962	9	5	0	0	.56
DePaula, Sean, Cle	11	11.2	0	2	0	0	1.000	2	0	0	0	.00
Dipoto, Jerry, Col	63	86.2	4	11	1	0	.938	21	7	0	1	.33
Dotel, Octavio, NYM	19	85.1	8	9	1	0	.944	16	6	0	1	.38
Dougherty, Jim, Pit	2	2.0	0	0	0	0	.000	1	1	0	0	1.00
Dreifort, Darren, LA	30	178.2	18	26	3	2	.936	27	6	1	3	.26
Durbin, Chad, KC	1	2.1	0	0	0	0	.000	0	0	0	0	.00
Duvall, Mike, TB	40	40.0	5	4	1	2	.900	1	0	0	0	.00
Ebert, Derrin, Atl	5	8.0	0	2	0	0	1.000	0	0	0	0	.00
Edmondson, Brian, Fla	68	94.0	6	15	0	1	1.000	5	2	0	1	.40
Eiland, Dave, TB	21	80.1	5	15	0	1	1.000	10	3	0	0	.30
Elarton, Scott, Hou	42	124.0	4	8	0	0	1.000	6	2	0	0	.33
Eldred, Cal, Mil	20	82.0	5	3	0	0	1.000	13	3	0	0	.23
Embree, Alan, SF	68	58.2	2	3	0	0	1.000	13	1	1	0	.15
Erdos, Todd, NYY	4	7.0	0	1	0	0	1.000	0	0	0	0	.00
Erickson, Scott, Bal	34	230.1	24	42	2	5	.971	22	10	0	0	.45
Escobar, Kelvim, Tor	33	174.0	6	11	1	1	.944	32	11	0	2	.34
Estes, Shawn, SF	32	203.0	18	31	1	1	.980	26	4	6	0	.38
Estrada, Horacio, Mil	4	7.1	0	1	0	0	1.000	0	0	0	0	.00
Eyre, Scott, CWS	21	25.0	0	1	0	0	1.000	4	1	1	0	.50
Falkenborg, Brian, Bal	2	3.0	1	0	0	0	1.000	1	0	0	0	.00
Falteisek, Steve, Mil	10	12.0	0	0	0	0	.000	3	0	0	0	.00
Farnsworth, Kyle, ChC	27	130.0	9	13	4	1	.846	19	4	0	1	.21
Fassero, Jeff, Sea-Tex	37	156.1	4	29	0	2	1.000	29	3	3	0	.21
Fernandez, Alex, Fla	24	141.0	7	27	1	3	.971	9	3	0	0	.33
Fetters, Mike, Bal	27	31.0	2	4	3	0	.667	1	0	1	1	1.00
Finley, Chuck, Ana	33	213.1	7	28	3	1	.921	30	12	1	2	.43
Florie, Bryce, Det-Bos	41	81.1	2	12	3	1	.824	6	2	0	0	.33
Fossas, Tony, NYY	5	1.0	0	0	0	0	.000	0	0	0	0	.00
Foulke, Keith, CWS	67	105.1	5	13	1	0	.947	3	2	0	0	.67
Fox, Chad, Mil	6	6.2	2	0	0	0	1.000	3	0	0	0	.00
Franco, John, NYM	46	40.2	4	4	0	0	1.000	10	0	0	0	.00
Franklin, Ryan, Sea	6	11.1	1	1	0	1	1.000	0	0	0	0	.00
Frascatore, J., Ari-Tor	59	70.0	3	8	0	0	1.000	6	1	1	0	.33
Fussell, Chris, KC	17	56.0	2	6	3	3	.727	11	2	0	0	.18
Fyhrie, Mike, Ana	16	51.2	2	3	0	0	1.000	3	1	0	0	.33
Gagne, Eric, LA	5	30.0	2	0	0	0	1.000	3	1	0	0	.33
Gaillard, Eddie, TB	8	8.2	0	3	0	0	1.000	0	0	0	0	.00
Garces, Rich, Bos	30	40.2	5	6	0	0	1.000	8	1	0	0	.13
Garcia, Freddy, Sea	33	201.1	13	28	2	1	.953	33	7	0	2	.21
Garcia, Mike, Pit	7	7.0	0	0	0	0	.000	1	1	0	0	1.00

1999 Fielding and Holding Runners

Pitcher, Team	G	Inn	PO	A	E	DP	Pct.	SBA	CS	PCS	PPO	CS%
Gardner, Mark, SF	29	139.0	7	18	0	1	1.000	17	5	1	0	.35
Glavine, Tom, Atl	35	234.0	12	59	1	6	.986	17	3	1	0	.24
Glover, Gary, Tor	1	1.0	0	0	0	0	.000	0	0	0	0	.00
Glynn, Ryan, Tex	13	54.2	2	3	0	0	1.000	2	1	0	0	.50
Gomes, Wayne, Phi	73	74.0	4	5	0	0	1.000	14	1	0	0	.07
Gooden, Dwight, Cle	26	115.0	5	16	0	1	1.000	32	4	1	0	.16
Gordon, Tom, Bos	21	17.2	0	1	0	0	1.000	7	0	0	0	.00
Grace, Mike, Phi	27	55.0	5	5	0	0	1.000	11	3	0	0	.27
Grahe, Joe, Phi	13	32.2	3	5	0	1	1.000	2	2	0	0	1.00
Graterol, Beiker, Det	1	4.0	0	1	0	0	1.000	0	0	0	0	.00
Graves, Danny, Cin	75	111.0	7	21	0	3	1.000	6	1	0	0	.17
Greene, Rick, Cin	1	5.2	0	0	0	0	.000	0	0	0	0	.00
Grimsley, Jason, NYY	55	75.0	9	13	0	0	1.000	5	0	0	0	.00
Groom, Buddy, Oak	76	46.0	1	13	0	1	1.000	6	1	2	0	.50
Gross, Kip, Bos	11	12.2	0	1	0	0	1.000	0	0	0	0	.00
Guardado, Eddie, Min	63	48.0	0	9	1	1	.900	1	1	0	2	1.00
Gunderson, Eric, Tex	11	10.0	0	1	0	0	1.000	0	0	0	0	.00
Guthrie, Mark, Bos-ChC	57	58.2	1	7	0	0	1.000	10	2	2	0	.40
Guzman, Domingo, SD	7	5.0	1	3	1	0	.800	0	0	0	0	.00
Guzman, Juan, Bal-Cin	33	200.0	7	23	3	6	.909	38	10	0	0	.26
Hackman, Luther, Col	5	16.0	2	4	0	0	1.000	3	1	0	0	.33
Halama, John, Sea	38	179.0	7	32	2	4	.951	12	1	4	1	.42
Halladay, Roy, Tor	36	149.1	8	16	0	3	1.000	12	3	0	0	.25
Hamilton, Joey, Tor	22	98.0	4	10	0	0	1.000	7	4	0	0	.57
Hampton, Mike, Hou	34	239.0	12	41	3	4	.946	14	4	2	0	.43
Haney, Chris, Cle	13	40.1	4	3	1	1	.875	4	0	0	0	.00
Hansell, Greg, Pit	33	39.1	1	5	0	1	1.000	5	2	0	0	.40
Harikkala, Tim, Bos	7	13.0	0	2	0	0	1.000	3	2	0	0	.67
Harnisch, Pete, Cin	33	198.1	7	18	3	1	.893	16	3	0	1	.19
Harris, Reggie, Mil	8	12.0	1	0	0	1	1.000	1	0	0	0	.00
Harville, Chad, Oak	15	14.1	0	0	0	0	.000	3	1	0	0	.33
Hasegawa, Shig., Ana	64	77.0	5	14	0	1	1.000	6	2	1	0	.50
Hawkins, LaTroy, Min	33	174.1	7	18	1	3	.962	15	5	0	0	.33
Haynes, Jimmy, Oak	30	142.0	1	19	5	1	.800	12	4	0	0	.33
Heiserman, Rick, StL	3	4.1	1	0	0	1	1.000	0	0	0	0	.00
Helling, Rick, Tex	35	219.1	4	24	3	2	.903	27	11	3	1	.52
Henry, Butch, Sea	7	25.0	0	2	0	0	1.000	7	2	0	1	.29
Henry, Doug, Hou	35	40.2	2	5	1	0	.875	7	3	1	0	.57
Hentgen, Pat, Tor	34	199.0	15	22	3	4	.925	24	3	4	1	.29
Heredia, Felix, ChC	69	52.0	1	4	0	0	1.000	5	2	0	0	.40
Heredia, Gil, Oak	33	200.1	10	29	1	2	.975	21	9	1	2	.48
Herges, Matt, LA	17	24.1	2	2	0	0	1.000	1	1	0	0	1.00
Hermanson, Dus., Mon	34	216.1	20	21	0	1	1.000	24	4	0	3	.17
Hernandez, Liv., Fla-SF	30	199.2	18	34	1	2	.981	22	5	1	1	.27
Hernandez, Or., NYY	33	214.1	16	25	2	3	.953	27	7	1	0	.30
Hernandez, Rob., TB	72	73.1	4	10	1	1	.933	9	3	0	0	.33
Hershiser, Orel, NYM	32	179.0	19	35	3	1	.947	13	4	0	1	.31
Hiljus, Erik, Det	6	8.2	0	1	0	0	1.000	0	0	0	0	.00
Hill, Ken, Ana	26	128.1	6	25	0	3	1.000	26	4	1	1	.19
Hinchliffe, Brett, Sea	11	30.2	5	2	1	0	.875	2	1	0	0	.50
Hitchcock, Sterling, SD	33	205.2	7	24	1	0	.969	28	3	4	0	.25
Hoffman, Trevor, SD	64	67.1	3	5	0	0	1.000	2	0	0	0	.00
Holmes, Darren, Ari	44	48.2	6	5	1	1	.917	11	3	0	0	.27
Holt, Chris, Hou	32	164.0	14	16	1	2	.968	23	9	0	0	.39
Holtz, Mike, Ana	28	22.1	2	5	0	0	1.000	3	2	1	0	1.00
Howry, Bob, CWS	69	67.2	2	3	0	0	1.000	4	2	0	0	.50
Hudek, J., Cin-Atl-Tor	20	21.1	1	2	0	0	1.000	1	1	0	0	1.00
Hudson, Tim, Oak	23	136.1	10	22	1	3	.970	19	5	0	0	.26
Irabu, Hideki, NYY	32	169.1	2	13	0	0	1.000	23	3	1	0	.17
Isringhausen, NYM-Oak	33	64.2	4	9	1	1	.929	11	1	0	0	.09
Jackson, Mike, Cle	72	68.2	2	16	1	1	.947	3	0	0	0	.00
Jarvis, Kevin, Oak	4	14.0	2	1	0	0	1.000	2	1	0	0	.50
Jimenez, Jose, StL	29	163.0	10	29	1	2	.975	17	9	1	0	.59
Johns, Doug, Bal	32	86.2	10	11	0	0	1.000	3	0	0	0	.00
Johnson, Jason, Bal	22	115.1	4	11	2	1	.882	18	1	0	0	.06
Johnson, Jonathan, Tex	1	3.0	0	0	0	0	.000	2	0	0	0	.00
Johnson, Mike, Mon	3	8.1	1	1	0	0	1.000	0	0	0	0	.00
Johnson, Randy, Ari	35	271.2	4	28	5	2	.865	59	13	4	1	.29
Johnstone, John, SF	62	65.2	5	8	0	0	1.000	12	1	0	0	.08
Jones, Bobby, NYM	12	59.1	4	7	0	0	1.000	5	1	0	0	.20
Jones, Bobby M., Col	30	112.1	4	10	2	0	.875	20	4	0	0	.20
Jones, Doug, Oak	70	104.0	5	12	2	2	.895	6	1	0	0	.17
Jones, Todd, Det	65	66.1	2	5	1	0	.875	5	2	0	0	.40
Judd, Mike, LA	7	28.0	0	4	0	1	1.000	10	0	0	0	.00
Juden, Jeff, NYY	2	5.2	0	1	0	0	1.000	1	0	0	0	.00
Kamieniecki, Scott, Bal	43	56.1	5	16	0	1	1.000	5	1	1	1	.40
Karchner, Matt, ChC	16	18.0	1	1	0	0	1.000	1	0	0	0	.00
Karl, Scott, Mil	33	197.2	10	44	4	4	.931	14	4	1	1	.36
Karsay, Steve, Cle	50	78.2	8	10	3	1	.857	6	3	0	0	.50
Kida, Masao, Det	49	64.2	2	7	0	0	1.000	4	1	0	0	.25
Kile, Darryl, Col	32	190.2	10	24	1	2	.971	21	4	0	0	.19
Kim, Byung-Hyun, Ari	25	27.1	2	7	0	0	1.000	12	2	1	1	.25
King, Curtis, StL	2	1.0	0	0	0	0	.000	0	0	0	0	.00
King, Ray, ChC	10	10.2	0	1	0	0	1.000	0	0	0	0	.00
Kline, Steve, Mon	82	69.2	5	17	1	2	.957	8	0	1	0	.13
Koch, Billy, Tor	56	63.2	3	12	0	0	1.000	9	2	0	0	.22

1999 Fielding and Holding Runners

Pitcher, Team	G	Inn	PO	A	E	DP	Pct.	SBA	CS	PCS	PPO	CS%
Kolb, Danny, Tex	16	31.0	1	7	0	0	1.000	0	0	0	0	.00
Kubenka, Jeff, LA	6	7.2	0	3	0	0	1.000	2	0	0	0	.00
Kubinski, Tim, Oak	14	12.1	0	4	0	0	1.000	0	0	0	0	.00
Langston, Mark, Cle	25	61.2	7	8	2	1	.882	3	2	1	0	1.00
Laxton, Brett, Oak	3	9.2	0	1	1	0	.500	5	0	0	0	.00
Lee, Corey, Tex	1	1.0	0	0	0	0	.000	0	0	0	0	.00
Lee, David, Col	36	49.0	3	7	0	0	1.000	15	4	0	0	.27
Leiter, Al, NYM	32	213.0	3	18	4	1	.840	34	6	2	0	.24
Leiter, Mark, Sea	2	1.1	0	0	0	0	.000	0	0	0	0	.00
Leskanic, Curt, Col	63	85.0	6	13	3	1	.864	6	2	0	1	.33
Levine, Al, Ana	50	85.0	5	12	2	3	.895	8	4	0	0	.50
Lidle, Cory, TB	5	5.0	0	2	0	0	1.000	2	1	0	0	.50
Lieber, Jon, ChC	31	203.1	18	17	2	1	.946	9	4	0	0	.44
Lilly, Ted, Mon	9	23.2	0	3	0	0	1.000	3	1	0	0	.33
Lima, Jose, Hou	36	246.1	17	21	2	1	.950	19	7	0	1	.37
Lincoln, Mike, Min	18	76.1	5	12	0	0	1.000	3	2	0	0	.67
Linton, Doug, Bal	14	59.0	5	8	0	0	1.000	5	3	0	0	.60
Lira, Felipe, Det	2	3.1	1	0	0	0	1.000	0	0	0	0	.00
Lloyd, Graeme, Tor	74	72.0	1	4	0	0	1.000	5	0	2	0	.40
Loaiza, Esteban, Tex	30	120.1	8	17	0	0	1.000	5	4	0	0	.80
Loewer, Carlton, Phi	20	89.2	3	10	1	0	.929	7	3	0	1	.43
Loiselle, Rich, Pit	13	15.1	2	3	0	1	1.000	2	2	0	0	1.00
Looper, Braden, Fla	72	83.0	3	8	0	0	1.000	5	1	0	0	.20
Lopez, Albie, TB	51	64.0	3	7	1	1	.909	4	0	0	0	.00
Lorraine, Andrew, ChC	11	61.2	2	8	1	0	.909	8	4	0	0	.50
Lowe, Derek, Bos	74	109.1	8	14	0	1	1.000	7	1	0	0	.14
Lowe, Sean, CWS	64	95.2	5	14	0	1	1.000	9	1	3	3	.44
Ludwick, Eric, Tor	1	1.0	1	0	0	0	1.000	0	0	0	0	.00
Luebbers, Larry, StL	8	45.2	4	7	0	0	1.000	8	2	0	0	.25
Lundquist, David, CWS	17	22.0	1	2	0	0	1.000	3	1	0	0	.33
Maddux, Greg, Atl	33	219.1	29	58	4	3	.956	31	9	1	0	.32
Maddux, Mike, Mon-LA	53	59.2	5	6	1	1	.917	6	1	1	0	.33
Magnante, Mike, Ana	53	69.1	3	13	0	3	1.000	11	1	3	0	.36
Mahay, Ron, Oak	6	19.1	0	2	0	0	1.000	1	0	1	0	1.00
Mahomes, Pat, NYM	39	63.2	2	6	0	0	1.000	7	1	0	1	.14
Mantei, Matt, Fla-Ari	65	65.1	3	7	1	0	.909	8	2	0	0	.25
Manzanillo, Jo., NYM	12	18.2	1	2	0	0	1.000	1	1	0	0	1.00
Marte, Damaso, Sea	5	8.2	0	1	0	0	1.000	0	0	0	0	.00
Martin, Tom, Cle	6	9.1	0	0	0	0	.000	0	0	0	0	.00
Martinez, Pedro, Bos	31	213.1	13	15	1	0	.966	31	10	0	0	.32
Martinez, Ramon, Bos	4	20.2	1	2	0	1	1.000	3	1	0	0	.33
Masaoka, Onan, LA	54	66.2	1	4	1	0	.833	14	2	0	0	.14
Mathews, T.J., Oak	50	59.0	6	7	0	0	1.000	3	0	0	0	.00
Mathews, Terry, KC	24	39.0	4	4	0	0	1.000	3	1	0	1	.33
Mays, Joe, Min	49	171.0	17	23	1	2	.976	17	5	0	0	.29
McCurry, Jeff, Hou	5	4.0	0	0	0	0	.000	1	0	0	0	.00
McDowell, Jack, Ana	4	19.0	0	6	0	0	1.000	0	0	0	0	.00
McElroy, C., Col-NYM	57	54.0	3	8	0	1	1.000	10	1	2	0	.30
McGlinchy, Kevin, Atl	64	70.1	4	6	2	0	.833	15	7	0	0	.47
McMichael, NYM-Oak	36	33.2	2	2	0	0	1.000	10	1	0	0	.10
McNichol, Brian, ChC	4	10.2	0	0	0	0	.000	3	0	0	0	.00
Meadows, Brian, Fla	31	178.1	12	21	2	1	.943	17	6	0	0	.35
Meche, Gil, Sea	16	85.2	10	8	0	0	1.000	7	3	1	0	.57
Mecir, Jim, TB	17	20.2	1	4	0	0	1.000	1	0	0	0	.00
Medina, Rafael, Fla	20	23.1	1	1	0	0	1.000	2	0	0	0	.00
Mendoza, Ramiro, NYY	53	123.2	11	23	1	1	.971	6	1	0	0	.17
Mercker, Kent, StL-Bos	30	129.1	2	24	5	1	.839	12	5	4	1	.75
Mesa, Jose, Sea	68	68.2	11	7	1	2	.947	6	2	0	0	.33
Miceli, Dan, SD	66	68.2	4	6	1	0	.909	9	2	0	0	.22
Miller, Kurt, ChC	4	3.0	0	0	0	0	.000	0	0	0	0	.00
Miller, Travis, Min	52	49.2	3	8	0	0	1.000	3	0	1	0	.33
Miller, Trever, Hou	47	49.2	3	7	0	0	1.000	7	3	0	0	.43
Miller, Wade, Hou	5	10.1	0	2	0	0	1.000	1	0	0	0	.00
Mills, Alan, LA	68	72.1	3	7	2	2	.833	12	2	0	0	.17
Millwood, Kevin, Atl	33	228.0	13	20	2	0	.943	16	4	0	2	.25
Milton, Eric, Min	34	206.1	8	16	3	1	.889	12	5	1	0	.50
Mintz, Steve, Ana	3	5.0	0	0	0	0	.000	0	0	0	0	.00
Mlicki, Dave, LA-Det	33	199.0	15	18	3	2	.917	20	7	0	0	.35
Moehler, Brian, Det	32	196.1	18	31	0	2	1.000	22	3	1	1	.18
Mohler, Mike, StL	48	49.1	0	4	0	0	1.000	4	1	1	0	.50
Molina, Gabe, Bal	20	23.0	1	2	0	0	1.000	0	0	0	0	.00
Montgomery, Jeff, KC	49	51.1	3	9	0	2	1.000	13	5	0	0	.38
Montgomery, Steve, Phi	53	64.2	1	6	0	0	1.000	8	2	1	0	.38
Moreno, Orber, KC	7	8.0	1	1	0	0	1.000	1	0	0	0	.00
Morgan, Mike, Tex	34	140.0	7	26	2	3	.943	13	8	0	1	.62
Morman, Alvin, KC	49	53.1	4	10	1	1	.933	10	1	3	0	.40
Morris, Jim, TB	5	4.2	0	0	0	0	.000	0	0	0	0	.00
Mota, Guillermo, Mon	51	55.1	4	10	0	1	1.000	8	1	1	1	.25
Moyer, Jamie, Sea	32	228.0	15	47	2	9	.969	17	5	3	1	.47
Mulholland, T., ChC-Atl	42	170.1	8	30	5	1	.884	5	4	0	2	.80
Munoz, Mike, Tex	56	52.2	3	9	1	2	.923	0	0	0	0	.00
Munro, Peter, Tor	31	55.1	3	8	0	0	1.000	2	0	0	0	.00
Murray, Dan, NYM-KC	5	10.1	3	0	0	0	1.000	1	0	0	0	.00
Murray, Heath, SD	22	50.0	0	8	0	0	1.000	9	2	1	0	.33
Mussina, Mike, Bal	31	203.1	14	46	1	3	.984	9	5	0	0	.56
Myers, Mike, Mil	71	41.1	5	7	0	0	1.000	4	2	1	0	.75

1999 Fielding and Holding Runners

Pitcher, Team	G	Inn	PO	A	E	DP	Pct.	SBA	CS	PCS	PPO	CS%
Myers, Rodney, ChC	46	63.2	2	4	1	0	.857	3	2	0	0	.67
Myette, Aaron, CWS	4	15.2	0	1	0	0	1.000	2	0	0	0	.00
Nagy, Charles, Cle	33	202.0	21	33	1	3	.982	18	5	0	0	.28
Nathan, Joe, SF	19	90.1	3	11	0	0	1.000	8	2	0	0	.25
Naulty, Dan, NYY	33	49.1	2	9	0	0	1.000	6	1	0	0	.17
Navarro, Jaime, CWS	32	159.2	9	15	2	2	.923	28	4	2	0	.21
Neagle, Denny, Cin	20	111.2	2	5	0	1	1.000	7	2	0	0	.29
Nelson, Jeff, NYY	39	30.1	3	5	1	2	.889	9	0	0	0	.00
Nen, Robb, SF	72	72.1	2	10	2	1	.857	10	1	0	0	.10
Newman, Alan, TB	18	15.2	0	1	1	0	.500	3	1	0	0	.33
Nitkowski, C.J., Det	69	81.2	5	17	3	0	.880	8	3	1	0	.50
Nomo, Hideo, Mil	28	176.1	11	11	0	3	1.000	50	9	0	0	.18
Nunez, Vladimir, Ari-Fla	44	108.2	7	19	2	1	.929	22	7	1	2	.36
Ogea, Chad, Phi	36	168.0	8	16	1	1	.960	20	4	0	0	.20
Ohka, Tomokazu, Bos	8	13.0	0	3	0	0	1.000	1	0	0	0	.00
Ojala, Kirt, Fla	8	10.2	0	0	0	0	.000	1	1	0	0	1.00
Olivares, O., Ana-Oak	32	205.2	13	38	3	4	.944	19	7	1	4	.42
Oliver, Darren, StL	30	196.1	7	33	2	1	.952	24	5	6	0	.46
Olson, Gregg, Ari	61	60.2	4	9	0	0	1.000	8	3	0	0	.38
Oquist, Mike, Oak	28	140.2	1	17	1	3	.947	11	6	0	0	.55
Orosco, Jesse, Bal	65	32.0	2	5	1	0	.875	4	0	0	0	.00
Ortiz, Ramon, Ana	9	48.1	4	6	0	0	1.000	9	2	1	0	.33
Ortiz, Russ, SF	33	207.2	14	31	0	2	1.000	32	7	0	1	.22
Osborne, Donovan, StL	6	29.1	1	7	1	0	.889	4	3	0	0	.75
Osuna, Antonio, LA	5	4.2	0	1	0	0	1.000	2	0	0	0	.00
Padilla, Vicente, Ari	5	2.2	0	0	0	0	.000	0	0	0	0	.00
Painter, Lance, StL	56	63.1	3	12	1	1	.938	9	2	2	0	.44
Paniagua, Jose, Sea	59	77.2	7	5	1	0	.923	11	3	0	0	.27
Park, Chan Ho, LA	33	194.1	15	33	0	4	1.000	30	10	4	3	.47
Parque, Jim, CWS	31	173.2	6	21	1	1	.964	22	4	3	0	.32
Parris, Steve, Cin	22	128.2	8	17	1	6	.962	11	3	0	0	.27
Patrick, Bronswell, SF	6	5.1	0	1	1	0	.500	3	0	0	0	.00
Patterson, Danny, Tex	53	60.1	3	6	0	1	1.000	1	0	0	0	.00
Pavano, Carl, Mon	19	104.0	10	24	0	0	1.000	15	5	0	0	.33
Pena, Jesus, CWS	26	20.1	0	5	0	0	1.000	0	0	0	1	.00
Pena, Juan, Bos	2	13.0	3	1	0	0	1.000	2	1	0	0	.50
Percival, Troy, Ana	60	57.0	3	1	0	0	1.000	10	2	0	0	.20
Perez, Carlos, LA	17	89.2	4	15	2	0	.905	11	0	3	1	.27
Perez, Odalis, Atl	18	93.0	4	17	0	1	1.000	20	0	4	0	.20
Perez, Yorkis, Phi	35	32.0	1	0	0	0	1.000	2	0	0	0	.00
Perisho, Matt, Tex	4	10.1	0	2	0	0	1.000	0	0	0	0	.00
Perkins, Dan, Min	29	86.2	7	8	1	0	.938	10	3	0	1	.30
Person, Robert, Tor-Phi	42	148.0	8	13	1	0	.955	10	1	0	1	.10
Peters, Chris, Pit	19	71.0	5	14	0	0	1.000	6	2	0	0	.33
Peterson, Kyle, Mil	17	77.0	3	7	2	0	.833	13	2	0	0	.15
Petkovsek, Mark, Ana	64	83.0	5	16	1	1	.955	7	4	0	0	.57
Pettitte, Andy, NYY	31	191.2	5	38	2	3	.956	23	3	4	1	.30
Phillips, Jason, Pit	6	7.0	0	2	0	0	1.000	1	0	0	0	.00
Pisciotta, Marc, KC	8	8.1	0	2	1	0	.667	3	0	0	0	.00
Pittsley, Jim, KC-Mil	20	42.0	3	9	1	0	.923	5	2	0	0	.40
Plesac, Dan, Tor-Ari	64	44.1	1	6	0	0	1.000	2	0	0	0	.00
Plunk, Eric, Mil	68	75.1	0	6	1	0	.857	20	0	2	1	.10
Politte, Cliff, Phi	13	17.2	1	1	0	0	1.000	1	0	0	0	.00
Ponson, Sidney, Bal	32	210.0	12	26	2	6	.950	26	14	0	0	.54
Poole, Jim, Phi-Cle	54	36.1	1	3	1	0	.800	5	1	0	0	.20
Portugal, Mark, Bos	31	150.1	9	22	0	1	1.000	17	5	1	0	.35
Porzio, Mike, Col	16	14.2	0	3	0	0	1.000	0	0	0	0	.00
Pote, Lou, Ana	20	29.1	0	5	0	1	1.000	6	2	0	0	.33
Powell, Jay, Hou	67	75.0	1	7	2	0	.800	15	2	0	0	.13
Powell, Jeremy, Mon	17	97.0	9	13	1	0	.957	11	7	1	1	.73
Pulsipher, Bill, Mil	19	87.1	2	19	0	1	1.000	8	1	0	0	.13
Quantrill, Paul, Tor	41	48.2	2	9	0	1	1.000	5	2	0	0	.40
Radinsky, Scott, StL	43	27.2	1	4	1	1	.833	1	0	0	0	.00
Radke, Brad, Min	33	218.2	21	36	0	5	1.000	19	6	0	2	.32
Radlosky, Rob, Min	7	8.2	1	1	1	0	.667	1	0	0	0	.00
Rain, Steve, ChC	16	14.2	3	3	0	0	1.000	0	0	0	0	.00
Rakers, Jason, Cle	1	2.0	0	0	0	0	.000	0	0	0	0	.00
Ramirez, Hector, Mil	15	21.0	2	1	0	0	1.000	3	1	0	0	.33
Ramirez, Roberto, Col	32	40.1	2	5	0	1	1.000	6	0	0	0	.00
Ramsay, Rob, Sea	6	18.1	0	1	0	0	1.000	1	1	0	0	1.00
Rapp, Pat, Bos	37	146.1	7	15	0	2	1.000	34	7	0	0	.21
Rath, Gary, Min	5	4.2	0	1	0	0	1.000	0	0	0	0	.00
Ray, Ken, KC	13	11.1	1	3	0	2	1.000	1	0	0	0	.00
Redman, Mark, Min	5	12.2	2	0	0	0	1.000	1	0	0	0	.00
Reed, Rick, NYM	26	149.1	11	29	1	4	.976	13	5	0	1	.38
Reed, Steve, Cle	63	61.2	4	10	1	0	.933	1	0	0	0	.00
Reichert, Dan, KC	8	36.2	3	3	0	1	1.000	4	0	1	0	.25
Rekar, Bryan, TB	27	94.2	6	13	1	2	.950	9	4	0	0	.44
Remlinger, Mike, Atl	73	83.2	4	10	1	1	.933	5	1	0	0	.20
Reyes, Al, Mil-Bal	53	65.2	1	8	0	1	1.000	5	1	1	0	.40
Reyes, Carlos, SD	65	77.1	3	15	0	2	1.000	7	1	0	0	.14
Reyes, Dennys, Cin	65	61.2	0	5	1	0	.833	10	0	1	0	.10
Reynolds, Shane, Hou	35	231.2	18	41	0	3	1.000	17	4	0	1	.24
Reynoso, Armando, Ari	31	167.0	12	28	3	4	.930	14	6	0	4	.43
Rhodes, Arthur, Bal	43	53.0	0	6	0	0	1.000	4	0	0	0	.00
Rigby, Brad, Oak-KC	49	83.2	2	4	4	1	.600	10	2	0	0	.20
Riley, Matt, Bal	3	11.0	0	2	0	0	1.000	4	1	1	0	.50
Rincon, Ricky, Cle	59	44.2	1	10	0	1	1.000	2	0	0	0	.00
Riske, David, Cle	12	14.0	1	2	1	0	.750	0	0	0	0	.00
Ritchie, Todd, Pit	28	172.1	9	25	0	0	1.000	9	2	1	6	.33
Rivera, Mariano, NYY	66	69.0	12	10	0	2	1.000	4	0	0	0	.00
Rivera, Roberto, SD	12	7.0	0	3	0	0	1.000	4	0	0	0	.00
Rizzo, Todd, CWS	3	1.1	0	0	0	0	.000	0	0	0	0	.00
Roberts, Willis, Det	1	1.1	0	1	1	0	.500	0	0	0	1	.00
Rocker, John, Atl	74	72.1	1	10	0	0	1.000	4	1	0	0	.25
Rodriguez, Felix, SF	47	66.1	5	11	0	1	1.000	4	2	0	0	.50
Rodriguez, Frank, Sea	28	73.1	6	13	1	2	.950	6	2	0	0	.33
Rodriguez, Nerio, Tor	2	2.0	0	0	0	0	.000	0	0	0	0	.00
Rodriguez, Rich, SF	62	56.2	6	11	0	1	1.000	3	0	1	0	.33
Rogers, K., Oak-NYM	31	195.1	10	62	4	4	.947	14	3	5	4	.57
Rojas, Mel, LA-Det-Mon	13	14.0	0	3	0	0	1.000	3	0	0	0	.00
Romano, Mike, Tor	3	5.1	1	0	0	0	1.000	0	0	0	0	.00
Romero, J.C., Min	5	9.2	1	1	1	1	.667	0	0	0	0	.00
Roque, Rafael, Mil	43	84.1	3	14	2	0	.895	7	1	2	1	.43
Rosado, Jose, KC	33	208.0	7	27	2	1	.944	9	2	3	0	.56
Rose, Brian, Bos	22	98.0	6	18	1	2	.960	14	3	1	1	.29
Rueter, Kirk, SF	33	184.2	15	30	1	5	.978	12	6	2	0	.67
Runyan, Sean, Det	12	10.2	1	3	0	0	1.000	0	0	0	0	.00
Rupe, Ryan, TB	24	142.1	5	12	3	5	.850	26	6	0	1	.23
Rusch, Glen., KC-NYM	4	5.0	0	0	0	0	.000	0	0	0	0	.00
Ryan, B.J., Cin-Bal	14	20.1	0	1	0	0	1.000	0	0	0	0	.00
Ryan, Jason, Min	8	40.2	3	4	0	1	1.000	1	0	0	0	.00
Ryan, Ken, Phi	15	15.2	2	2	0	0	1.000	7	1	0	0	.14
Sabel, Erik, Ari	7	9.2	0	2	0	1	1.000	0	0	0	0	.00
Saberhagen, Bret, Bos	22	119.0	5	18	0	0	1.000	10	5	0	3	.50
Sampson, Benj, Min	30	71.0	3	4	0	0	1.000	14	3	0	0	.21
Sanchez, Jesus, Fla	59	76.1	7	8	0	1	1.000	7	2	2	3	.57
Sanders, Scott, ChC	67	104.1	5	12	3	2	.850	16	5	0	0	.31
Santana, Julio, TB	22	55.1	3	5	1	1	.889	11	5	0	0	.45
Santana, Marino, Bos	3	4.0	0	1	0	0	1.000	0	0	0	0	.00
Santiago, Jose, KC	34	47.1	4	4	0	0	1.000	2	2	0	0	1.00
Sauerbeck, Scott, Pit	65	67.2	4	8	0	1	1.000	5	3	0	0	.60
Saunders, Tony, TB	9	42.0	4	5	1	0	.900	2	1	0	0	.50
Scheffer, Aaron, Sea	4	4.2	0	0	1	0	.000	0	0	0	0	.00
Schilling, Curt, Phi	24	180.1	11	19	0	1	1.000	4	2	0	1	.50
Schmidt, Jason, Pit	33	212.2	10	16	2	0	.929	19	7	0	0	.37
Schoeneweis, S., Ana	31	39.1	1	10	0	1	1.000	1	1	0	0	1.00
Schourek, Pete, Pit	30	113.0	3	15	2	0	.900	15	1	3	1	.27
Schrenk, Steve, Phi	32	50.1	4	7	0	1	1.000	1	0	0	0	.00
Seanez, Rudy, Atl	56	53.2	4	5	0	0	1.000	2	1	0	0	.50
Sele, Aaron, Tex	33	205.0	8	30	2	2	.950	17	8	0	1	.47
Serafini, Dan, ChC	42	62.1	3	5	0	0	1.000	4	1	0	0	.25
Service, Scott, KC	68	75.1	2	3	1	0	.833	11	1	0	0	.09
Shaw, Jeff, LA	64	68.0	10	4	0	1	1.000	7	1	0	0	.14
Shuey, Paul, Cle	72	81.2	3	10	0	1	1.000	10	2	0	0	.20
Shumaker, An., Phi	8	22.2	0	5	1	0	.833	1	1	0	0	1.00
Silva, Jose, Pit	34	97.1	6	16	0	2	1.000	7	3	0	1	.43
Simas, Bill, CWS	70	72.0	7	6	0	1	1.000	5	1	0	1	.20
Sinclair, Steve, Tor-Sea	21	19.1	0	1	0	0	1.000	0	0	0	0	.00
Sirotka, Mike, CWS	32	209.0	5	24	4	0	.879	20	5	2	0	.35
Slocumb, H., Bal-StL	50	62.0	4	7	0	0	1.000	12	2	0	0	.17
Slusarski, Joe, Hou	3	3.2	0	0	0	0	.000	2	0	0	0	.00
Smart, J.D., Mon	29	52.0	2	8	0	1	1.000	3	0	0	1	.00
Smith, Dan, Mon	20	89.2	4	7	2	0	.846	11	4	1	0	.45
Smoltz, John, Atl	29	186.1	9	30	1	3	.975	16	7	0	1	.44
Snyder, John, CWS	25	129.1	10	16	0	1	1.000	9	3	0	0	.33
Sodowsky, Clint, StL	3	6.1	1	0	0	0	1.000	1	0	0	0	.00
Sparks, Jeff, TB	8	10.0	0	0	0	0	.000	1	0	0	0	.00
Sparks, Steve, Ana	29	147.2	7	35	3	4	.933	17	4	1	2	.29
Speier, Justin, Atl	19	28.2	5	2	0	0	1.000	4	0	0	0	.00
Spencer, Sean, Sea	2	1.2	0	0	0	0	.000	0	0	0	0	.00
Spencer, Stan, SD	9	38.1	3	2	0	0	1.000	12	1	0	0	.08
Spoljaric, Paul, Phi-Tor	42	73.1	1	9	2	0	.833	19	1	2	1	.16
Spradlin, Jerry, Cle-SF	63	61.0	2	4	2	1	.750	11	1	2	0	.27
Springer, Dennis, Fla	38	196.1	12	30	4	5	.913	34	17	0	2	.50
Springer, Russ, Atl	49	47.1	1	4	0	0	1.000	10	1	0	0	.10
Stanton, Mike, NYY	73	62.1	2	6	1	0	.889	4	0	1	1	.25
Stark, Dennis, Sea	5	6.1	0	0	0	0	.000	0	0	0	0	.00
Stein, Blake, Oak-KC	13	73.0	2	4	0	0	1.000	6	1	0	0	.17
Stephenson, Garr., StL	18	85.1	6	9	0	1	1.000	9	3	0	0	.33
Stevens, Dave, Cle	5	9.0	0	1	0	0	1.000	3	1	0	0	.33
Stottlemyre, Todd, Ari	17	101.1	8	12	1	1	.952	23	6	0	0	.26
Strickland, Scott, Mon	17	18.0	0	4	0	0	1.000	5	0	0	0	.00
Stull, Everett, Atl	1	0.2	0	0	0	0	.000	0	0	0	0	.00
Sturtze, Tanyon, CWS	1	6.0	0	1	0	1	1.000	0	0	0	0	.00
Sullivan, Scott, Cin	79	113.2	6	10	3	0	.842	13	8	1	0	.69
Suppan, Jeff, KC	32	208.2	16	27	1	0	.977	25	4	2	0	.24
Suzuki, Ma., Sea-KC	38	110.0	6	10	1	0	.941	21	6	1	1	.33
Swindell, Greg, Ari	63	64.2	3	10	0	1	1.000	7	2	4	0	.86
Tam, Jeff, Cle-NYM	10	11.2	3	2	0	0	1.000	0	0	0	0	.00
Tapani, Kevin, ChC	23	136.0	2	18	0	0	1.000	12	5	0	0	.42
Tavarez, Julian, SF	47	54.2	7	6	1	1	.929	8	3	0	0	.38

1999 Fielding and Holding Runners

Pitcher, Team	G	Inn	PO	A	E	DP	Pct.	SBA	CS	PCS	PPO	CS%
Taylor, Billy, Oak-NYM	61	56.1	1	7	0	0	1.000	14	3	0	0	.21
Tejera, Michael, Fla	3	6.1	1	3	0	2	1.000	1	0	1	0	1.00
Telemaco, A., Ari-Phi	49	53.0	5	8	1	0	.929	2	1	0	0	.50
Telford, Anthony, Mon	79	96.0	10	15	4	0	.862	7	1	0	0	.14
Tessmer, Jay, NYY	6	6.2	0	1	0	0	1.000	0	0	0	0	.00
Thompson, Justin, Det	24	142.2	5	11	1	1	.941	12	3	3	0	.50
Thompson, Mark, StL	5	29.1	3	4	0	0	1.000	3	2	0	0	.67
Thomson, John, Col	14	62.2	9	10	0	1	1.000	9	2	0	0	.22
Thurman, Mike, Mon	29	146.2	9	12	1	0	.955	32	7	0	0	.22
Timlin, Mike, Bal	62	63.0	5	8	3	1	.813	4	1	0	0	.25
Tomko, Brett, Cin	33	172.0	10	20	2	2	.938	21	3	0	0	.14
Trachsel, Steve, ChC	34	205.2	18	20	0	3	1.000	25	6	0	1	.24
Trombley, Mike, Min	75	87.1	8	9	0	0	1.000	3	0	0	0	.00
Urbina, Ugueth, Mon	71	75.2	5	2	0	0	1.000	21	1	0	0	.05
Valdes, Ismael, LA	32	203.1	12	33	1	1	.978	35	6	3	1	.26
Vazquez, Javier, Mon	26	154.2	9	33	0	1	1.000	16	4	1	2	.31
Venafro, Mike, Tex	65	68.1	2	18	0	0	1.000	2	0	0	0	.00
Veres, Dave, Col	73	77.0	7	5	0	0	1.000	9	2	1	0	.33
Villone, Ron, Cin	29	142.2	7	28	6	1	.854	9	1	1	5	.22
Vizcaino, Luis, Oak	1	3.1	0	0	0	0	.000	0	0	0	0	.00
Vosberg, Ed, SD-Ari	19	11.0	1	3	1	0	.800	0	0	0	0	.00
Wagner, Billy, Hou	66	74.2	2	5	0	1	1.000	6	0	0	0	.00
Wagner, Paul, Cle	3	4.1	1	0	0	0	1.000	0	0	0	0	.00
Wainhouse, Dave, Col	19	28.2	3	4	0	1	1.000	1	0	0	0	.00
Wakefield, Tim, Bos	49	140.0	7	12	1	1	.950	41	6	0	0	.15
Wall, Donne, SD	55	70.1	9	11	2	1	.909	3	1	0	2	.33
Wallace, Derek, KC	8	8.1	0	1	1	0	.500	1	1	0	0	1.00
Wallace, Jeff, Pit	41	39.0	0	3	0	0	1.000	5	1	1	0	.40
Ward, Bryan, CWS	40	39.1	0	6	0	0	1.000	4	0	1	0	.25
Wasdin, John, Bos	45	74.1	3	5	1	0	.889	7	2	0	0	.29
Washburn, Jarrod, Ana	16	61.2	2	5	0	3	1.000	6	1	1	0	.33
Watson, NYM-Sea-NYY	38	77.0	4	7	1	0	.917	14	1	3	1	.29
Weathers, Dave, Mil	63	93.0	6	13	0	0	1.000	17	2	0	1	.12
Weaver, Eric, Sea	8	9.1	0	1	1	0	.500	0	0	0	0	.00
Weaver, Jeff, Det	30	163.2	9	18	0	3	1.000	10	4	1	0	.50
Wells, Bob, Min	76	87.1	3	9	1	0	.923	9	5	0	2	.56
Wells, David, Tor	34	231.2	7	30	0	2	1.000	46	6	3	0	.20
Wells, Kip, CWS	7	35.2	4	3	2	0	.778	5	2	1	0	.60
Wendell, Turk, NYM	80	85.2	4	6	2	0	.833	10	3	2	0	.50
Wengert, Don, KC	11	24.1	0	3	0	0	1.000	2	2	0	0	1.00
Wetteland, John, Tex	62	66.0	1	5	1	0	.857	3	1	0	0	.33
Wheeler, Dan, TB	6	30.2	1	2	0	0	1.000	2	2	0	0	1.00
Whisenant, M., KC-SD	67	54.1	4	7	1	0	.917	4	1	0	0	.25
White, Gabe, Cin	50	61.0	1	2	0	0	1.000	3	1	0	0	.33
White, Rick, TB	63	108.0	6	16	2	1	.917	8	6	0	1	.75
Whiteside, Matt, SD	10	11.0	0	3	0	0	1.000	1	1	0	0	1.00
Wickman, Bob, Mil	71	74.1	6	15	4	2	.840	6	0	0	0	.00
Wilkins, Marc, Pit	46	51.0	2	11	0	0	1.000	8	2	1	0	.38
Williams, Brian, Hou	50	67.1	4	11	0	1	1.000	7	5	0	1	.71
Williams, Jeff, LA	5	17.2	1	3	0	1	1.000	5	2	1	0	.60
Williams, Mike, Pit	58	58.1	4	9	4	1	.765	8	0	1	2	.13
Williams, Todd, Sea	13	9.2	0	1	0	0	1.000	2	1	0	0	.50
Williams, Woody, SD	33	208.1	11	17	1	0	.966	16	9	1	0	.63
Williamson, Scott, Cin	62	93.1	2	7	1	1	.900	13	0	0	2	.00
Winkelsas, Joe, Atl	1	0.1	0	0	0	0	.000	0	0	0	0	.00
Witasick, Jay, KC	32	158.1	4	12	2	0	.889	14	3	0	0	.21
Witt, Bobby, TB	32	180.1	12	27	3	4	.929	32	10	1	0	.34
Wohlers, Mark, Atl	2	0.2	0	0	1	0	.000	2	0	0	0	.00
Wolcott, Bob, Bos	4	6.2	0	0	0	0	.000	1	1	0	0	1.00
Wolf, Randy, Phi	22	121.2	3	13	2	2	.889	1	1	0	0	1.00
Woodall, Brad, ChC	6	16.0	1	2	0	1	1.000	0	0	0	0	.00
Woodard, Steve, Mil	31	185.0	12	24	0	0	1.000	17	2	0	0	.12
Worrell, Tim, Oak	53	69.1	1	3	0	0	1.000	12	4	0	0	.33
Wright, Jamey, Col	16	94.1	9	18	1	2	.964	10	6	0	4	.60
Wright, Jaret, Cle	26	133.2	13	15	3	0	.903	23	7	0	0	.30
Yan, Esteban, TB	50	61.0	8	9	0	2	1.000	9	4	0	0	.44
Yarnall, Ed, NYY	5	17.0	0	4	0	0	1.000	5	2	1	0	.60
Yoshii, Masato, NYM	31	174.0	7	10	0	1	1.000	16	5	0	1	.31
Zimmerman, Jeff, Tex	65	87.2	3	7	0	0	1.000	5	2	0	0	.40
Zimmerman, Jor., Sea	12	8.0	0	1	0	0	1.000	0	0	0	0	.00

Hitters Pitching

Player	|	1999 Pitching											Career Pitching											
		G	W	L	Sv	IP	H	R	ER	BB	SO	ERA		G	W	L	Sv	IP	H	R	ER	BB	SO	ERA
Alexander, Manny		0	0	0	0	0.0	0	0	0	0	0	0.00		1	0	0	0	0.2	1	5	5	4	0	67.50
Benjamin, Mike		0	0	0	0	0.0	0	0	0	0	0	0.00		1	0	0	0	1.0	0	0	0	0	0	0.00
Boggs, Wade		1	0	0	0	1.1	3	1	1	0	1	6.75		2	0	0	0	2.1	3	1	1	1	2	3.86
Cangelosi, John		0	0	0	0	0.0	0	0	0	0	0	0.00		3	0	0	0	4.0	1	0	0	2	0	0.00
Canseco, Jose		0	0	0	0	0.0	0	0	0	0	0	0.00		1	0	0	0	1.0	2	3	3	3	0	27.00
Davis, Chili		0	0	0	0	0.0	0	0	0	0	0	0.00		1	0	0	0	2.0	0	0	0	0	0	0.00
Franco, Matt		2	0	0	0	1.1	3	2	2	3	2	13.50		2	0	0	0	1.1	3	2	2	3	2	13.50
Gaetti, Gary		1	0	0	0	1.0	2	2	2	1	1	18.00		3	0	0	0	2.1	5	2	2	1	1	7.71
Giovanola, Ed		1	0	0	0	1.1	1	0	0	2	0	0.00		1	0	0	0	1.1	1	0	0	2	0	0.00
Halter, Shane		0	0	0	0	0.0	0	0	0	0	0	0.00		1	0	0	0	1.0	1	0	0	0	0	0.00
Harris, Lenny		0	0	0	0	0.0	0	0	0	0	0	0.00		1	0	0	0	1.0	0	0	0	0	1	0.00
Howard, David		0	0	0	0	0.0	0	0	0	0	0	0.00		1	0	0	0	2.0	2	1	1	5	0	4.50
Jackson, Darrin		0	0	0	0	0.0	0	0	0	0	0	0.00		1	0	0	0	2.0	3	2	2	2	0	9.00
Martinez, Dave		0	0	0	0	0.0	0	0	0	0	0	0.00		2	0	0	0	1.1	2	2	2	4	0	13.50
O'Neill, Paul		0	0	0	0	0.0	0	0	0	0	0	0.00		1	0	0	0	2.0	2	3	3	4	2	13.50
Osik, Keith		1	0	0	0	1.0	2	4	4	2	1	36.00		1	0	0	0	1.0	2	4	4	2	1	36.00
Whiten, Mark		0	0	0	0	0.0	0	0	0	0	0	0.00		1	0	0	0	1.0	1	1	1	2	3	9.00

Park Data

Is Safeco Field less hitter-friendly than the Kingdome? How much did Wrigley Field and Tiger Stadium contribute to their respective teams' pitching woes? You'll find the answers on the following pages.

For each park, we show how the home team and its opponents performed, both at home and on the road with the exception being that we do not include data from interleague games. The differences in interleague opponents and ballparks would skew the data.

By comparing the per-game averages at the home park and on the road, we can evaluate the park's impact. We simply divide the home average by the road average and multiply the result by 100, generating a park index. If the home and road per-game averages are equal, the index equals 100, and we can conclude that the park had no impact. An index above 100 means that the park favors that particular statistic.

The indexes for at-bats, runs, hits, errors, and infield errors are determined on a per-game basis; all other stats are calculated on a per-at-bat basis. "E-infield" denotes infield *fielding* errors. "Alt" is the approximate elevation of the ballpark.

For most parks, data is presented both for 1999 and for the last three years overall. If the park's dimensions have changed over that time, however, we do not combine the data from its old and new configurations. At the end, you'll find a rankings section that shows which parks inflate runs, homers and batting average the most.

Anaheim Angels—Edison Int'l Field of Anaheim   Alt: 160 feet   Surface: Grass

	1999 Season							1998-1999						
	Home Games			Away Games			Index	Home Games			Away Games			Index
	Angels	Opp	Total	Angels	Opp	Total		Angels	Opp	Total	Angels	Opp	Total	
G	72	72	144	72	72	144	—	145	145	290	145	145	290	—
Avg	.252	.269	.261	.260	.267	.263	99	.258	.263	.261	.270	.270	.270	97
AB	2357	2499	4856	2521	2349	4870	100	4802	5021	9823	5152	4798	9950	99
R	314	377	691	333	351	684	101	641	739	1380	712	696	1408	98
H	595	671	1266	655	628	1283	99	1240	1321	2561	1391	1296	2687	95
2B	104	131	235	118	118	236	100	229	277	506	282	273	555	92
3B	13	10	23	7	15	22	105	30	20	50	15	26	41	124
HR	70	90	160	74	65	139	115	118	172	290	155	129	284	103
BB	235	288	523	217	277	494	106	458	580	1038	452	563	1015	104
SO	440	394	834	473	394	867	96	887	921	1808	947	850	1797	102
E	50	41	91	41	52	93	98	98	98	196	88	106	194	101
E-Infield	43	33	76	37	43	80	95	83	83	166	81	87	168	99
LHB-Avg	.270	.265	.267	.267	.257	.263	102	.276	.262	.269	.277	.268	.273	99
LHB-HR	37	45	82	38	21	59	141	62	76	138	82	49	131	105
RHB-Avg	.234	.271	.255	.252	.274	.264	97	.240	.264	.253	.264	.271	.268	95
RHB-HR	33	45	78	36	44	80	97	56	96	152	73	80	153	102

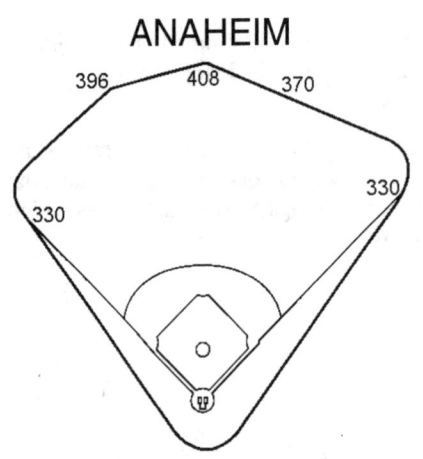

ANAHEIM

396   408   370

330

330

330

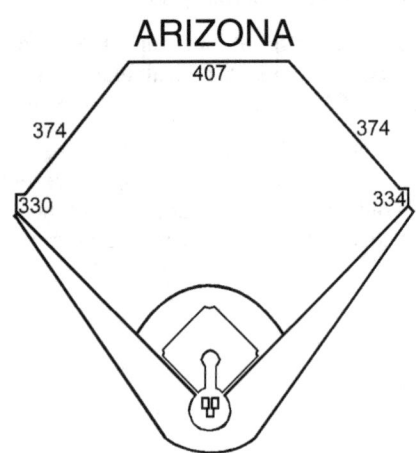

ARIZONA

407

374   374

330   334

Arizona Diamondbacks—BankOne Ballpark   Alt: 1090 feet   Surface: Grass

	1999 Season							1998-1999						
	Home Games			Away Games			Index	Home Games			Away Games			Index
	D'backs	Opp	Total	D'backs	Opp	Total		D'backs	Opp	Total	D'backs	Opp	Total	
G	75	75	150	72	72	144	—	148	148	296	148	148	296	—
Avg	.279	.250	.264	.277	.249	.263	100	.268	.257	.262	.254	.257	.255	103
AB	2534	2620	5154	2591	2432	5023	99	4977	5185	10162	5167	4905	10072	101
R	407	304	711	415	307	722	95	708	655	1363	701	686	1387	98
H	707	656	1363	717	606	1323	99	1333	1331	2664	1312	1260	2572	104
2B	129	126	255	131	109	240	104	228	249	477	247	227	474	100
3B	31	22	53	14	11	25	207	54	41	95	33	21	54	174
HR	93	74	167	100	85	185	88	159	155	314	173	174	347	90
BB	266	229	495	268	253	521	93	484	417	901	504	520	1024	87
SO	447	534	981	511	546	1057	90	958	926	1884	1145	986	2131	88
E	39	60	99	57	45	102	93	81	107	188	100	103	203	93
E-Infield	33	49	82	50	36	86	92	67	88	155	81	79	160	97
LHB-Avg	.282	.250	.271	.288	.257	.276	98	.269	.258	.264	.263	.264	.264	100
LHB-HR	45	18	63	45	23	68	92	70	45	115	75	50	125	92
RHB-Avg	.275	.250	.260	.265	.246	.254	102	.267	.256	.261	.244	.253	.249	105
RHB-HR	48	56	104	55	62	117	86	89	110	199	98	124	222	88

Atlanta Braves—Turner Field

Alt: 1050 feet **Surface:** Grass

| | 1999 Season | | | | | | | 1997-1999 | | | | | | |
| | Home Games | | | Away Games | | | | Home Games | | | Away Games | | | |
	Braves	Opp	Total	Braves	Opp	Total	Index	Braves	Opp	Total	Braves	Opp	Total	Index
G	72	72	144	72	72	144	—	220	220	440	217	217	434	—
Avg	.264	.234	.249	.270	.258	.264	94	.273	.238	.255	.265	.247	.256	100
AB	2358	2461	4819	2581	2457	5038	96	7234	7514	14748	7624	7197	14821	98
R	366	245	611	388	312	700	87	1088	768	1856	1123	827	1950	94
H	622	576	1198	696	633	1329	90	1976	1788	3764	2024	1775	3799	98
2B	139	92	231	135	112	247	98	381	306	687	403	305	708	98
3B	9	8	17	14	6	20	89	42	32	74	38	25	63	118
HR	78	61	139	101	56	157	93	239	158	397	286	157	443	90
BB	258	191	449	283	252	535	88	798	631	1429	796	653	1449	99
SO	390	555	945	461	518	979	101	1383	1672	3055	1469	1601	3070	100
E	52	62	114	48	55	103	111	157	181	338	128	174	302	110
E-Infield	44	50	94	42	45	87	108	132	145	277	108	145	253	108
LHB-Avg	.252	.226	.238	.281	.265	.273	87	.276	.233	.256	.268	.257	.263	97
LHB-HR	26	24	50	26	24	50	105	96	54	150	104	59	163	90
RHB-Avg	.270	.239	.254	.264	.253	.259	98	.271	.241	.255	.264	.241	.252	101
RHB-HR	52	37	89	75	32	107	87	143	104	247	182	98	280	90

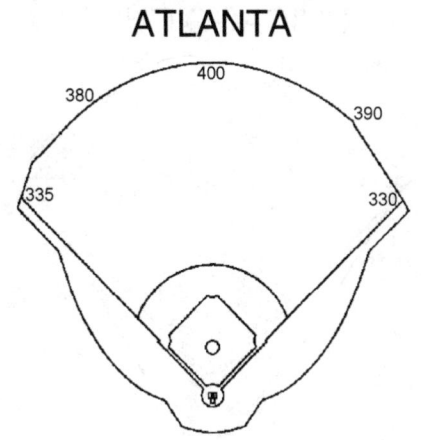

ATLANTA

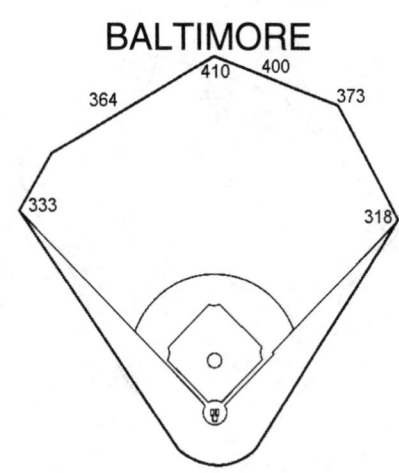

BALTIMORE

Baltimore Orioles—Oriole Park at Camden Yards

Alt: 20 feet **Surface:** Grass

| | 1999 Season | | | | | | | 1997-1999 | | | | | | |
| | Home Games | | | Away Games | | | | Home Games | | | Away Games | | | |
	Orioles	Opp	Total	Orioles	Opp	Total	Index	Orioles	Opp	Total	Orioles	Opp	Total	Index
G	72	72	144	72	72	144	—	217	217	434	220	220	440	—
Avg	.277	.264	.270	.272	.276	.274	99	.272	.258	.265	.274	.270	.272	97
AB	2429	2511	4940	2562	2362	4924	100	7268	7525	14793	7807	7335	15142	99
R	370	360	730	375	387	762	96	1070	1000	2070	1171	1059	2230	94
H	672	663	1335	698	652	1350	99	1975	1939	3914	2136	1981	4117	96
2B	126	97	223	139	142	281	79	341	323	664	446	399	845	80
3B	8	14	22	11	16	27	81	19	30	49	30	49	79	63
HR	85	92	177	92	96	188	94	277	242	519	272	244	516	103
BB	270	292	562	273	287	560	100	762	757	1519	855	808	1663	93
SO	394	459	853	408	420	828	103	1194	1479	2673	1263	1392	2655	103
E	43	45	88	41	46	87	101	120	120	240	130	144	274	89
E-Infield	39	39	78	40	39	79	99	102	107	209	111	115	226	94
LHB-Avg	.282	.248	.264	.283	.285	.284	93	.276	.249	.262	.282	.276	.279	94
LHB-HR	36	36	72	47	48	95	78	128	96	224	139	112	251	92
RHB-Avg	.273	.277	.275	.265	.268	.266	103	.268	.264	.266	.267	.265	.266	100
RHB-HR	49	56	105	45	48	93	110	149	146	295	133	132	265	113

Boston Red Sox—Fenway Park

Alt: 21 feet **Surface:** Grass

	1999 Season							1997-1999						
	Home Games			Away Games				Home Games			Away Games			
	Red Sox	Opp	Total	Red Sox	Opp	Total	Index	Red Sox	Opp	Total	Red Sox	Opp	Total	Index
G	72	72	144	72	72	144	—	217	217	434	220	220	440	—
Avg	.292	.253	.272	.274	.245	.260	105	.295	.263	.279	.276	.260	.268	104
AB	2413	2497	4910	2553	2389	4942	99	7409	7663	15072	7879	7347	15226	100
R	403	311	714	363	306	669	107	1182	1013	2195	1140	1044	2184	102
H	704	632	1336	700	585	1285	104	2186	2016	4202	2172	1907	4079	104
2B	159	128	287	145	120	265	109	500	426	926	439	362	801	117
3B	18	9	27	19	8	27	101	50	31	81	51	28	79	104
HR	68	64	132	89	73	162	82	236	192	428	281	227	508	85
BB	275	199	474	272	215	487	98	760	685	1445	732	751	1483	98
SO	389	531	920	428	481	909	102	1316	1500	2816	1386	1354	2740	104
E	68	48	116	40	45	85	136	180	136	316	143	141	284	113
E-Infield	56	42	98	39	31	70	140	159	116	275	131	109	240	116
LHB-Avg	.294	.262	.278	.265	.251	.258	108	.304	.274	.288	.272	.268	.270	107
LHB-HR	34	18	52	47	33	80	66	110	72	182	140	97	237	78
RHB-Avg	.289	.246	.267	.281	.239	.262	102	.288	.254	.271	.279	.253	.266	102
RHB-HR	34	46	80	42	40	82	98	126	120	246	141	130	271	92

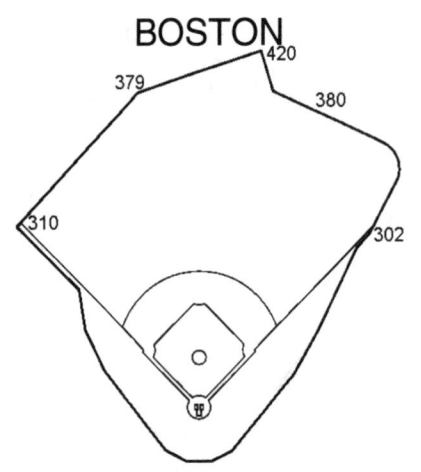

BOSTON
420
379
380
310
302

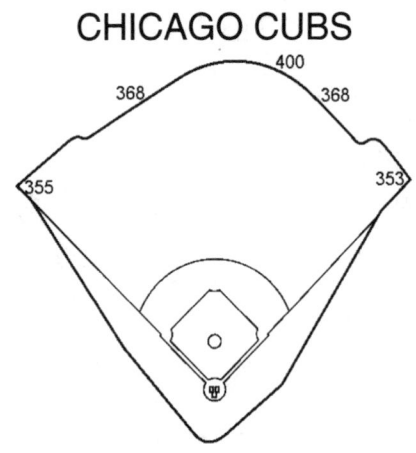

CHICAGO CUBS
400
368
368
355
353

Chicago Cubs—Wrigley Field

Alt: 595 feet **Surface:** Grass

	1999 Season							1997-1999						
	Home Games			Away Games				Home Games			Away Games			
	Cubs	Opp	Total	Cubs	Opp	Total	Index	Cubs	Opp	Total	Cubs	Opp	Total	Index
G	72	72	144	75	75	150	—	220	220	440	224	224	448	—
Avg	.266	.285	.276	.244	.281	.263	105	.272	.267	.270	.247	.274	.260	104
AB	2410	2604	5014	2561	2523	5084	103	7387	7805	15192	7763	7539	15302	101
R	352	429	781	320	405	725	112	1087	1122	2209	953	1128	2081	108
H	642	741	1383	626	709	1335	108	2011	2087	4098	1916	2068	3984	105
2B	125	132	257	108	124	232	112	349	388	737	352	416	768	97
3B	20	12	32	12	25	37	88	54	38	92	44	61	105	88
HR	88	111	199	85	91	176	115	260	293	553	221	247	468	119
BB	270	239	509	252	238	490	105	768	775	1543	709	766	1475	105
SO	504	471	975	561	426	987	100	1477	1592	3069	1637	1400	3037	102
E	66	45	111	56	45	101	114	158	160	318	161	152	313	103
E-Infield	51	38	89	48	37	85	109	126	135	261	130	134	264	101
LHB-Avg	.273	.304	.287	.252	.277	.263	109	.288	.277	.282	.258	.275	.266	106
LHB-HR	24	36	60	30	34	64	101	79	98	177	82	93	175	105
RHB-Avg	.261	.274	.268	.238	.283	.262	102	.261	.261	.261	.239	.274	.256	102
RHB-HR	64	75	139	55	57	112	121	181	195	376	139	154	293	126

Chicago White Sox—Comiskey Park

Alt: 595 feet **Surface:** Grass

| | 1999 Season | | | | | | | 1997-1999 | | | | | | |
| | Home Games | | | Away Games | | | | Home Games | | | Away Games | | | |
	White Sox	Opp	Total	White Sox	Opp	Total	Index	White Sox	Opp	Total	White Sox	Opp	Total	Index
G	72	72	144	72	72	144	—	221	221	442	216	216	432	—
Avg	.272	.281	.277	.278	.285	.282	98	.275	.273	.274	.273	.282	.277	99
AB	2423	2597	5020	2569	2447	5016	100	7304	7827	15131	7700	7368	15068	98
R	333	377	710	359	391	750	95	1089	1161	2250	1102	1206	2308	95
H	660	730	1390	715	698	1413	98	2012	2133	4145	2099	2075	4174	97
2B	119	125	244	149	125	274	89	382	408	790	388	392	780	101
3B	18	3	21	14	13	27	78	50	33	83	43	32	75	110
HR	71	93	164	72	92	164	100	231	253	484	237	282	519	93
BB	217	254	471	222	283	505	93	753	764	1517	724	819	1543	98
SO	337	421	758	383	416	799	95	1083	1315	2398	1250	1225	2475	96
E	56	52	108	54	61	115	94	173	148	321	186	173	359	87
E-Infield	49	41	90	46	51	97	93	145	119	264	159	141	300	86
LHB-Avg	.254	.272	.263	.276	.303	.289	91	.269	.279	.274	.274	.294	.284	96
LHB-HR	17	44	61	29	41	70	89	58	117	175	82	128	210	85
RHB-Avg	.286	.288	.287	.280	.272	.276	104	.281	.268	.274	.271	.272	.272	101
RHB-HR	54	49	103	43	51	94	108	173	136	309	155	154	309	98

CHICAGO WHITE SOX

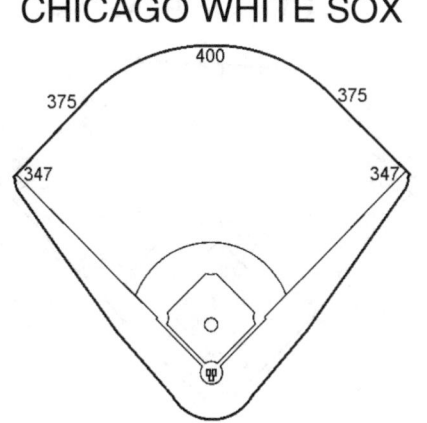

CINCINNATI

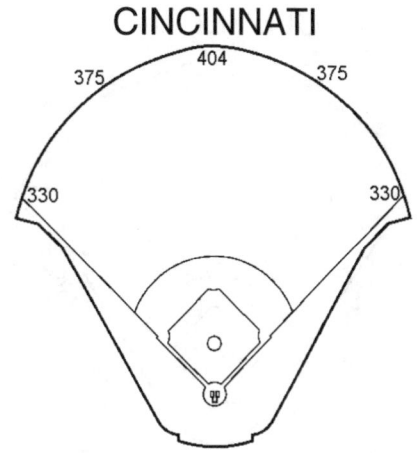

Cincinnati Reds—Cinergy Field

Alt: 550 feet **Surface:** Turf

| | 1999 Season | | | | | | | 1997-1999 | | | | | | |
| | Home Games | | | Away Games | | | | Home Games | | | Away Games | | | |
	Reds	Opp	Total	Reds	Opp	Total	Index	Reds	Opp	Total	Reds	Opp	Total	Index
G	76	76	152	72	72	144	—	221	221	442	223	223	446	—
Avg	.264	.239	.252	.276	.238	.258	98	.261	.244	.252	.261	.257	.259	97
AB	2531	2588	5119	2586	2315	4901	99	7300	7563	14863	7845	7344	15189	99
R	373	341	714	398	291	689	98	1026	1037	2063	1031	1003	2034	102
H	669	619	1288	713	551	1264	97	1905	1844	3749	2047	1884	3931	96
2B	132	149	281	148	121	269	100	395	440	835	402	386	788	108
3B	15	9	24	21	12	33	70	37	41	78	49	41	90	89
HR	92	103	195	99	67	166	112	220	256	476	230	225	455	107
BB	274	297	571	235	271	506	108	819	837	1656	731	779	1510	112
SO	493	519	1012	528	460	988	98	1443	1578	3021	1644	1451	3095	100
E	51	44	95	42	71	113	80	151	138	289	159	185	344	85
E-Infield	40	39	79	36	57	93	80	122	112	234	125	149	274	86
LHB-Avg	.276	.246	.259	.314	.252	.282	92	.263	.261	.262	.279	.260	.270	97
LHB-HR	31	31	62	34	26	60	101	85	86	171	88	70	158	113
RHB-Avg	.259	.235	.248	.257	.230	.245	101	.260	.233	.246	.249	.254	.252	98
RHB-HR	61	72	133	65	41	106	119	135	170	305	142	155	297	103

Cleveland Indians—Jacobs Field

Alt: 660 feet   Surface: Grass

| | 1999 Season | | | | | | | 1997-1999 | | | | | | |
| | Home Games | | | Away Games | | | | Home Games | | | Away Games | | | |
	Indians	Opp	Total	Indians	Opp	Total	Index	Indians	Opp	Total	Indians	Opp	Total	Index
G	72	72	144	72	72	144	—	220	220	440	216	216	432	—
Avg	.297	.278	.287	.283	.260	.272	106	.290	.279	.284	.274	.267	.270	105
AB	2433	2581	5014	2568	2399	4967	101	7413	7846	15259	7663	7285	14948	100
R	451	405	856	466	355	821	104	1258	1162	2420	1206	1065	2271	105
H	723	717	1440	728	623	1351	107	2153	2188	4341	2097	1945	4042	105
2B	127	153	280	158	122	280	99	407	441	848	445	372	817	102
3B	15	11	26	14	16	30	86	41	31	72	36	47	83	85
HR	96	98	194	89	77	166	116	280	256	536	286	247	533	99
BB	326	282	608	333	271	604	100	909	815	1724	880	783	1663	102
SO	473	527	1000	488	458	946	105	1337	1527	2864	1439	1358	2797	100
E	55	57	112	36	58	94	119	163	166	329	125	154	279	116
E-Infield	43	43	86	30	47	77	112	126	130	256	104	129	233	108
LHB-Avg	.293	.273	.283	.285	.258	.273	104	.296	.286	.291	.273	.271	.272	107
LHB-HR	40	50	90	41	35	76	115	127	132	259	130	112	242	104
RHB-Avg	.301	.282	.291	.282	.261	.271	107	.286	.272	.279	.275	.263	.269	104
RHB-HR	56	48	104	48	42	90	117	153	124	277	156	135	291	94

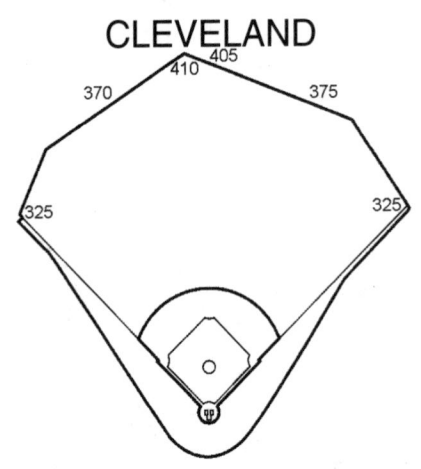

CLEVELAND
405
410
370   375
325   325

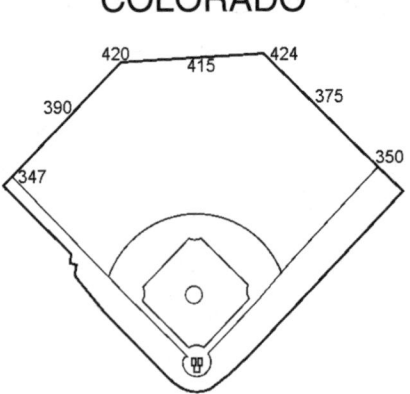

COLORADO
420   424
415
390   375
347   350

Colorado Rockies—Coors Field

Alt: 5280 feet   Surface: Grass

| | 1999 Season | | | | | | | 1997-1999 | | | | | | |
| | Home Games | | | Away Games | | | | Home Games | | | Away Games | | | |
	Rockies	Opp	Total	Rockies	Opp	Total	Index	Rockies	Opp	Total	Rockies	Opp	Total	Index
G	75	75	150	75	75	150	—	223	223	446	223	223	446	—
Avg	.328	.329	.329	.249	.271	.259	127	.325	.316	.320	.253	.273	.262	122
AB	2731	2790	5521	2575	2451	5026	110	7926	8180	16106	7625	7273	14898	108
R	532	581	1113	310	373	683	163	1503	1500	3003	932	1050	1982	152
H	895	919	1814	641	663	1304	139	2572	2581	5153	1926	1982	3908	132
2B	163	170	333	122	135	257	118	466	475	941	362	403	765	114
3B	26	22	48	11	15	26	168	66	66	132	40	49	89	137
HR	135	145	280	74	66	140	182	347	351	698	247	199	446	145
BB	247	356	603	221	324	545	101	756	842	1598	665	865	1530	97
SO	360	484	844	448	467	915	84	1148	1302	2450	1479	1298	2777	82
E	56	59	115	58	55	113	102	152	190	342	157	155	312	110
E-Infield	42	50	92	48	51	99	93	111	156	267	134	131	265	101
LHB-Avg	.356	.329	.343	.268	.296	.281	122	.344	.323	.333	.271	.289	.280	119
LHB-HR	58	50	108	31	23	54	187	126	139	265	100	86	186	130
RHB-Avg	.308	.330	.319	.235	.255	.245	130	.312	.310	.311	.241	.260	.250	124
RHB-HR	77	95	172	43	43	86	179	221	212	433	147	113	260	156

Detroit Tigers—Tiger Stadium

Alt: 585 feet **Surface:** Grass

| | 1999 Season | | | | | | | 1997-1999 | | | | | | |
| | Home Games | | | Away Games | | | | Home Games | | | Away Games | | | |
	Tigers	Opp	Total	Tigers	Opp	Total	Index	Tigers	Opp	Total	Tigers	Opp	Total	Index
G	72	72	144	71	71	142	—	217	217	434	219	219	438	—
Avg	.262	.268	.265	.262	.285	.273	97	.258	.265	.262	.265	.284	.274	96
AB	2391	2505	4896	2458	2381	4839	100	7210	7612	14822	7721	7380	15101	99
R	347	388	735	310	402	712	102	1035	1134	2169	983	1182	2165	101
H	627	672	1299	643	678	1321	97	1863	2014	3877	2043	2093	4136	95
2B	121	121	242	140	127	267	90	337	362	699	446	385	831	86
3B	19	14	33	11	10	21	155	46	42	88	37	49	86	104
HR	102	108	210	78	85	163	127	268	297	565	217	235	452	127
BB	213	259	472	189	252	441	106	718	783	1501	618	785	1403	109
SO	457	435	892	452	402	854	103	1444	1326	2770	1463	1255	2718	104
E	33	59	92	59	40	99	92	136	182	318	149	125	274	117
E-Infield	23	52	75	43	31	74	100	109	154	263	116	105	221	120
LHB-Avg	.265	.277	.272	.272	.299	.287	95	.266	.268	.267	.272	.293	.283	94
LHB-HR	38	58	96	32	51	83	116	126	135	261	105	123	228	120
RHB-Avg	.261	.261	.261	.256	.272	.263	99	.253	.262	.258	.260	.276	.267	96
RHB-HR	64	50	114	46	34	80	140	142	162	304	112	112	224	135

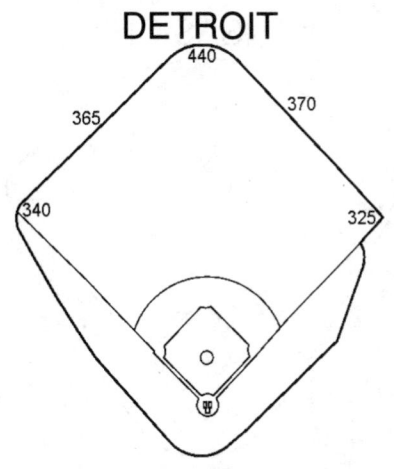

DETROIT
440
365
370
340
325

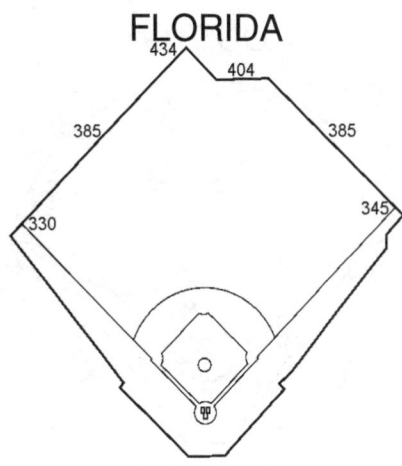

FLORIDA
434
404
385
385
330
345

Florida Marlins—Pro Player Stadium

Alt: 10 feet **Surface:** Grass

| | 1999 Season | | | | | | | 1997-1999 | | | | | | |
| | Home Games | | | Away Games | | | | Home Games | | | Away Games | | | |
	Marlins	Opp	Total	Marlins	Opp	Total	Index	Marlins	Opp	Total	Marlins	Opp	Total	Index
G	71	71	142	73	73	146	—	219	219	438	218	218	436	—
Avg	.260	.266	.263	.258	.297	.277	95	.256	.258	.257	.256	.290	.273	94
AB	2443	2501	4944	2496	2417	4913	103	7316	7600	14916	7562	7285	14847	100
R	287	336	623	294	426	720	89	909	1029	1938	940	1202	2142	90
H	634	665	1299	645	717	1362	98	1875	1962	3837	1933	2116	4049	94
2B	117	128	245	114	133	247	99	349	365	714	376	389	765	93
3B	24	22	46	15	14	29	158	57	62	119	42	57	99	120
HR	43	66	109	72	86	158	69	146	212	358	199	229	428	83
BB	235	288	523	189	309	498	104	829	902	1731	687	908	1595	108
SO	465	473	938	567	358	925	101	1432	1513	2945	1602	1289	2891	101
E	59	54	113	54	36	90	129	170	163	333	177	139	316	105
E-Infield	49	45	94	40	27	67	144	145	138	283	144	111	255	110
LHB-Avg	.248	.272	.262	.259	.305	.286	91	.256	.267	.261	.258	.303	.280	93
LHB-HR	10	30	40	13	47	60	63	44	80	124	58	91	149	80
RHB-Avg	.265	.261	.263	.258	.290	.272	97	.257	.253	.255	.254	.282	.268	95
RHB-HR	33	36	69	59	39	98	72	102	132	234	141	138	279	85

Houston Astros—The Astrodome

Alt: 40 feet   **Surface:** Turf

	1999 Season							1997-1999						
	Home Games			Away Games				Home Games			Away Games			
	Astros	Opp	Total	Astros	Opp	Total	Index	Astros	Opp	Total	Astros	Opp	Total	Index
G	76	76	152	71	71	142	—	221	221	442	221	221	442	—
Avg	.265	.256	.260	.266	.277	.271	96	.270	.248	.259	.266	.267	.267	97
AB	2493	2623	5116	2468	2431	4899	98	7353	7680	15033	7785	7490	15275	98
R	381	296	677	364	317	681	93	1112	829	1941	1132	953	2085	93
H	661	671	1332	656	674	1330	94	1982	1905	3887	2074	2003	4077	95
2B	150	126	276	119	122	241	110	448	383	831	413	347	760	111
3B	12	20	32	8	11	19	161	46	43	89	36	33	69	131
HR	61	49	110	90	67	157	67	187	165	352	234	210	444	81
BB	338	220	558	325	221	546	98	908	612	1520	910	723	1633	95
SO	534	627	1161	508	462	970	115	1504	1827	3331	1575	1415	2990	113
E	51	71	122	45	55	100	114	146	181	327	175	180	355	92
E-Infield	39	65	104	40	47	87	112	116	158	274	150	150	300	91
LHB-Avg	.281	.273	.276	.285	.276	.280	99	.271	.255	.261	.276	.269	.272	96
LHB-HR	22	22	44	31	28	59	71	40	65	105	54	79	133	78
RHB-Avg	.258	.245	.252	.258	.278	.267	94	.269	.244	.257	.263	.266	.265	97
RHB-HR	39	27	66	59	39	98	65	147	100	247	180	131	311	82

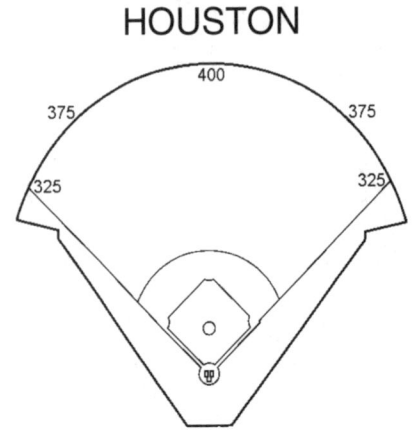

HOUSTON

400
375   375
325   325

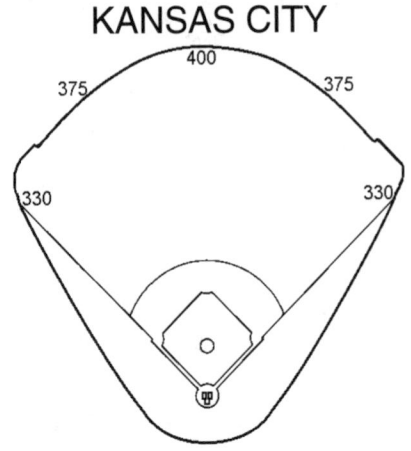

KANSAS CITY

400
375   375
330   330

Kansas City Royals—Ewing M. Kauffman Stadium

Alt: 750 feet   **Surface:** Grass

	1999 Season							1997-1999						
	Home Games			Away Games				Home Games			Away Games			
	Royals	Opp	Total	Royals	Opp	Total	Index	Royals	Opp	Total	Royals	Opp	Total	Index
G	71	71	142	72	72	144	—	217	217	434	217	217	434	—
Avg	.288	.284	.286	.273	.279	.276	104	.272	.283	.278	.265	.275	.270	103
AB	2451	2511	4962	2524	2412	4936	102	7419	7796	15215	7628	7296	14924	102
R	387	373	760	356	415	771	100	1048	1221	2269	1013	1143	2156	105
H	707	712	1419	688	672	1360	106	2015	2208	4223	2021	2008	4029	105
2B	119	104	223	134	112	246	90	332	349	681	393	362	755	88
3B	28	17	45	16	12	28	160	71	45	116	41	26	67	170
HR	71	81	152	65	95	160	95	212	273	485	181	257	438	109
BB	231	273	504	240	292	532	94	733	746	1479	668	829	1497	97
SO	387	344	731	428	389	817	89	1241	1216	2457	1406	1284	2690	90
E	49	62	111	61	59	120	94	146	154	300	152	162	314	96
E-Infield	38	51	89	51	49	100	90	120	129	249	129	139	268	93
LHB-Avg	.287	.305	.297	.272	.276	.274	108	.276	.289	.283	.270	.273	.272	104
LHB-HR	16	37	53	15	45	60	83	57	113	170	42	108	150	109
RHB-Avg	.289	.266	.278	.273	.280	.276	101	.269	.279	.274	.262	.276	.269	102
RHB-HR	55	44	99	50	50	100	102	155	160	315	139	149	288	109

Los Angeles Dodgers—Dodger Stadium

Alt: 340 feet **Surface:** Grass

	1999 Season							1997-1999						
	Home Games			Away Games				Home Games			Away Games			
	Dodgers	Opp	Total	Dodgers	Opp	Total	Index	Dodgers	Opp	Total	Dodgers	Opp	Total	Index
G	72	72	144	75	75	150	—	221	221	442	221	221	442	—
Avg	.266	.252	.259	.260	.266	.263	98	.262	.237	.249	.259	.261	.260	96
AB	2389	2502	4891	2650	2548	5198	98	7259	7555	14814	7766	7428	15194	97
R	323	354	677	383	366	749	94	936	875	1811	1033	1045	2078	87
H	636	631	1267	690	678	1368	96	1904	1788	3692	2008	1939	3947	94
2B	99	114	213	129	139	268	84	289	319	608	342	391	733	85
3B	8	7	15	13	19	32	50	32	17	49	44	60	104	48
HR	82	95	177	87	82	169	111	226	222	448	242	223	465	99
BB	252	254	506	289	290	579	93	679	741	1420	729	831	1560	93
SO	413	470	883	526	499	1025	92	1330	1579	2909	1555	1590	3145	95
E	68	53	121	58	66	124	102	176	164	340	176	191	367	93
E-Infield	58	41	99	49	56	105	98	155	133	288	147	148	295	98
LHB-Avg	.263	.256	.259	.227	.296	.270	96	.249	.249	.249	.242	.278	.264	94
LHB-HR	21	38	59	22	37	59	107	37	96	133	40	97	137	99
RHB-Avg	.267	.250	.259	.271	.243	.259	100	.267	.227	.249	.264	.248	.258	97
RHB-HR	61	57	118	65	45	110	114	189	126	315	202	126	328	99

LOS ANGELES

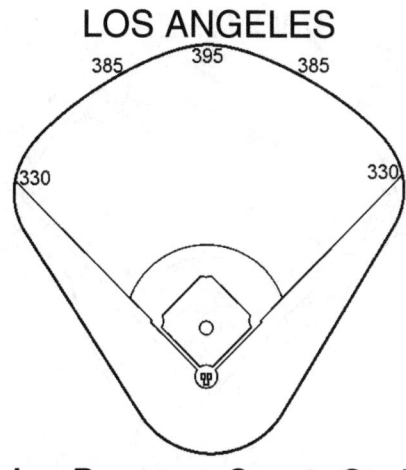

385 395 385
330 330

MILWAUKEE

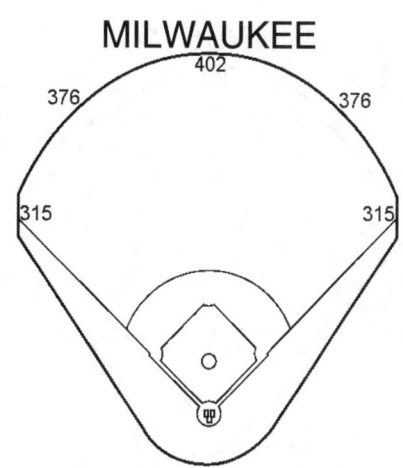

402
376 376
315 315

Milwaukee Brewers—County Stadium

Alt: 635 feet **Surface:** Grass

	1999 Season							1997-1999						
	Home Games			Away Games				Home Games			Away Games			
	Brewers	Opp	Total	Brewers	Opp	Total	Index	Brewers	Opp	Total	Brewers	Opp	Total	Index
G	72	72	144	75	75	150	—	221	221	442	220	220	440	—
Avg	.266	.286	.276	.274	.279	.277	100	.266	.276	.271	.261	.270	.266	102
AB	2405	2578	4983	2659	2592	5251	99	7374	7848	15222	7700	7357	15057	101
R	325	418	743	404	390	794	97	983	1151	2134	1012	1087	2099	101
H	640	737	1377	729	723	1452	99	1959	2164	4123	2012	1990	4002	103
2B	124	118	242	154	142	296	86	391	397	788	393	392	785	99
3B	9	13	22	16	19	35	66	33	35	68	34	49	83	81
HR	64	99	163	79	96	175	98	182	273	455	228	264	492	91
BB	287	272	559	308	300	608	97	799	767	1566	732	797	1529	101
SO	408	445	853	558	453	1011	89	1254	1412	2666	1541	1378	2919	90
E	46	43	89	64	52	116	80	157	146	303	159	145	304	99
E-Infield	37	32	69	51	41	92	78	123	116	239	129	118	247	96
LHB-Avg	.256	.281	.268	.277	.280	.278	96	.262	.270	.266	.263	.274	.268	99
LHB-HR	37	34	71	48	26	74	103	104	90	194	127	91	218	89
RHB-Avg	.273	.289	.281	.272	.278	.275	102	.268	.280	.274	.260	.268	.264	104
RHB-HR	27	65	92	31	70	101	95	78	183	261	101	173	274	93

Minnesota Twins—Hubert H. Humphrey Metrodome

Alt: 815 feet **Surface:** Turf

| | 1999 Season | | | | | | | 1997-1999 | | | | | | |
| | Home Games | | | Away Games | | | | Home Games | | | Away Games | | | |
	Twins	Opp	Total	Twins	Opp	Total	Index	Twins	Opp	Total	Twins	Opp	Total	Index
G	72	72	144	72	72	144	—	220	220	440	217	217	434	—
Avg	.264	.281	.273	.252	.279	.266	103	.271	.282	.277	.259	.284	.271	102
AB	2422	2618	5040	2468	2396	4864	104	7512	7992	15504	7580	7328	14908	103
R	307	403	710	278	349	627	113	1004	1190	2194	960	1112	2072	104
H	639	736	1375	623	669	1292	106	2037	2257	4294	1961	2080	4041	105
2B	144	171	315	114	115	229	133	424	481	905	368	405	773	113
3B	18	16	34	8	18	26	126	52	54	106	41	47	88	116
HR	39	97	136	50	82	132	99	138	270	408	175	253	428	92
BB	232	242	474	215	205	420	109	715	681	1396	659	625	1284	105
SO	440	439	879	437	389	826	103	1370	1337	2707	1320	1185	2505	104
E	53	48	101	34	53	87	116	142	155	297	133	161	294	100
E-Infield	40	42	82	27	50	77	106	115	129	244	104	146	250	96
LHB-Avg	.256	.281	.267	.248	.270	.257	104	.272	.284	.278	.250	.290	.269	103
LHB-HR	15	51	66	25	25	50	124	60	138	198	72	95	167	114
RHB-Avg	.273	.281	.278	.258	.285	.273	102	.270	.281	.276	.266	.280	.273	101
RHB-HR	24	46	70	25	57	82	84	78	132	210	103	158	261	77

MINNESOTA

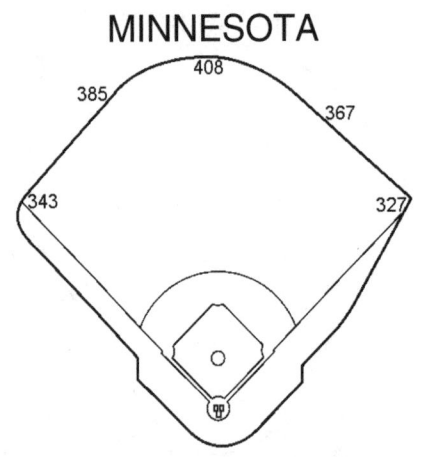

408
385
367
343
327

MONTREAL

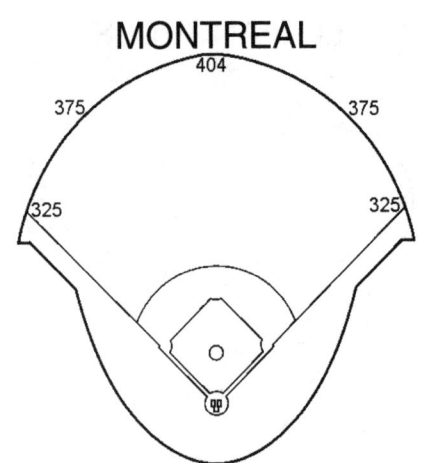

404
375
375
325
325

Montreal Expos—Olympic Stadium

Alt: 90 feet **Surface:** Turf

| | 1999 Season | | | | | | | 1997-1999 | | | | | | |
| | Home Games | | | Away Games | | | | Home Games | | | Away Games | | | |
	Expos	Opp	Total	Expos	Opp	Total	Index	Expos	Opp	Total	Expos	Opp	Total	Index
G	72	72	144	72	72	144	—	220	220	440	217	217	434	—
Avg	.269	.275	.272	.262	.270	.266	102	.259	.260	.260	.257	.265	.261	100
AB	2424	2551	4975	2536	2435	4971	100	7328	7703	15031	7542	7159	14701	101
R	334	409	743	310	369	679	109	935	1065	2000	924	1103	2027	97
H	651	702	1353	664	658	1322	102	1898	2006	3904	1935	1899	3834	100
2B	161	154	315	125	133	258	122	443	396	839	400	359	759	108
3B	20	15	35	23	11	34	103	53	47	100	51	40	91	107
HR	74	62	136	74	75	149	91	207	183	390	229	229	458	83
BB	203	256	459	186	257	443	104	616	742	1358	555	783	1338	99
SO	374	477	851	452	462	914	93	1353	1477	2830	1422	1398	2820	98
E	79	59	138	69	58	127	109	213	163	376	188	150	338	110
E-Infield	54	50	104	55	48	103	101	161	133	294	150	127	277	105
LHB-Avg	.293	.293	.293	.251	.271	.263	111	.263	.266	.265	.247	.265	.257	103
LHB-HR	13	21	34	23	31	54	63	58	67	125	77	90	167	72
RHB-Avg	.259	.262	.260	.266	.269	.268	97	.257	.256	.256	.262	.265	.263	97
RHB-HR	61	41	102	51	44	95	108	149	116	265	152	139	291	90

New York Mets—Shea Stadium

Alt: 20 feet **Surface:** Grass

| | 1999 Season | | | | | | | 1997-1999 | | | | | | |
| | Home Games | | | Away Games | | | | Home Games | | | Away Games | | | |
	Mets	Opp	Total	Mets	Opp	Total	Index	Mets	Opp	Total	Mets	Opp	Total	Index
G	72	72	144	73	73	146	—	220	220	440	218	218	436	—
Avg	.262	.253	.257	.293	.249	.272	95	.265	.251	.258	.269	.260	.265	97
AB	2363	2441	4804	2580	2384	4964	98	7276	7568	14844	7653	7230	14883	99
R	342	315	657	415	323	738	90	1038	904	1942	1066	943	2009	96
H	619	617	1236	757	594	1351	93	1927	1899	3826	2059	1883	3942	96
2B	104	136	240	163	132	295	84	369	396	765	409	399	808	95
3B	3	24	27	9	28	37	75	27	55	82	31	53	84	98
HR	70	64	134	91	80	171	81	196	190	386	223	219	442	88
BB	289	289	578	347	251	598	100	823	739	1562	838	728	1566	100
SO	419	567	986	466	495	961	106	1300	1582	2882	1462	1379	2841	102
E	30	52	82	28	46	74	112	134	151	285	126	138	264	107
E-Infield	24	43	67	25	38	63	108	107	123	230	100	112	212	108
LHB-Avg	.286	.256	.272	.291	.268	.281	97	.289	.259	.275	.270	.272	.271	101
LHB-HR	30	15	45	35	30	65	72	101	65	166	94	82	176	95
RHB-Avg	.244	.251	.248	.295	.239	.267	93	.246	.246	.246	.268	.253	.260	94
RHB-HR	40	49	89	56	50	106	86	95	125	220	129	137	266	83

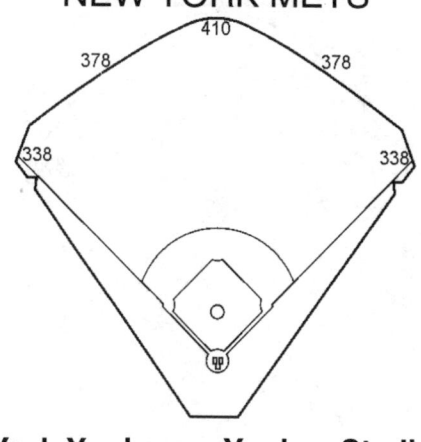

NEW YORK METS

410
378 378
338 338

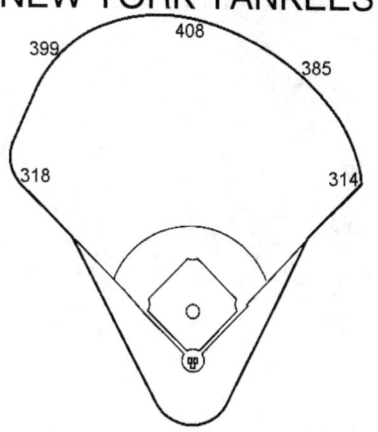

NEW YORK YANKEES

408
399 385
318 314

New York Yankees—Yankee Stadium

Alt: 55 feet **Surface:** Grass

| | 1999 Season | | | | | | | 1997-1999 | | | | | | |
| | Home Games | | | Away Games | | | | Home Games | | | Away Games | | | |
	Yankees	Opp	Total	Yankees	Opp	Total	Index	Yankees	Opp	Total	Yankees	Opp	Total	Index
G	72	72	144	72	72	144	—	215	215	430	222	222	444	—
Avg	.271	.239	.255	.294	.267	.281	91	.287	.247	.266	.290	.265	.278	96
AB	2388	2473	4861	2578	2420	4998	97	7240	7463	14703	8049	7511	15560	98
R	362	280	642	437	353	790	81	1164	868	2032	1355	1001	2356	89
H	647	592	1239	759	645	1404	88	2075	1841	3916	2335	1987	4322	94
2B	118	114	232	151	117	268	89	390	350	740	450	363	813	96
3B	12	10	22	20	16	36	63	36	30	66	46	39	85	82
HR	76	63	139	95	75	170	84	231	192	423	281	224	505	89
BB	325	259	584	309	249	558	108	895	671	1566	944	746	1690	98
SO	451	509	960	431	492	923	107	1253	1551	2804	1397	1460	2857	104
E	56	40	96	45	42	87	110	143	131	274	137	176	313	90
E-Infield	44	35	79	36	33	69	114	119	116	235	109	145	254	96
LHB-Avg	.259	.242	.250	.309	.268	.289	87	.283	.250	.267	.296	.275	.287	93
LHB-HR	37	33	70	50	41	91	79	119	90	209	154	107	261	86
RHB-Avg	.282	.237	.259	.282	.265	.274	94	.290	.245	.266	.285	.257	.271	98
RHB-HR	39	30	69	45	34	79	89	112	102	214	127	117	244	92

Oakland Athletics—Oakland-Alameda County Coliseum **Alt:** 25 feet **Surface:** Grass

	1999 Season							1997-1999						
	Home Games			Away Games			Index	Home Games			Away Games			Index
	Athletics	Opp	Total	Athletics	Opp	Total		Athletics	Opp	Total	Athletics	Opp	Total	
G	72	72	144	72	72	144	—	218	218	436	218	218	436	—
Avg	.267	.263	.265	.258	.292	.275	96	.261	.277	.270	.257	.292	.275	98
AB	2377	2529	4906	2542	2473	5015	98	7263	7789	15052	7645	7485	15130	99
R	402	355	757	404	417	821	92	1073	1143	2216	1120	1245	2365	94
H	634	664	1298	657	721	1378	94	1899	2160	4059	1968	2189	4157	98
2B	127	140	267	128	151	279	98	367	442	809	406	448	854	95
3B	12	11	23	7	18	25	94	29	34	63	20	64	84	75
HR	93	67	160	113	80	193	85	256	226	482	262	258	520	93
BB	320	251	571	355	246	601	97	884	757	1641	935	809	1744	95
SO	447	421	868	542	422	964	92	1400	1266	2666	1664	1244	2908	92
E	58	59	117	50	54	104	113	167	158	325	172	154	326	100
E-Infield	47	50	97	42	45	87	111	136	135	271	141	125	266	102
LHB-Avg	.269	.272	.271	.267	.274	.270	100	.277	.283	.280	.275	.290	.282	99
LHB-HR	53	28	81	69	29	98	82	133	108	241	128	107	235	99
RHB-Avg	.265	.253	.259	.250	.307	.279	93	.248	.273	.261	.243	.295	.268	97
RHB-HR	40	39	79	44	51	95	88	123	118	241	134	151	285	88

OAKLAND

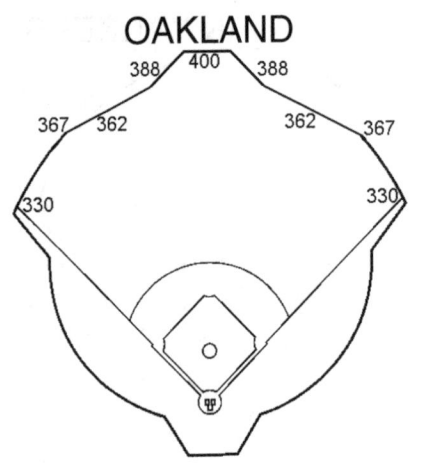

388 / 400 \ 388
367 / 362 | 362 \ 367
330 | | 330

PHILADELPHIA

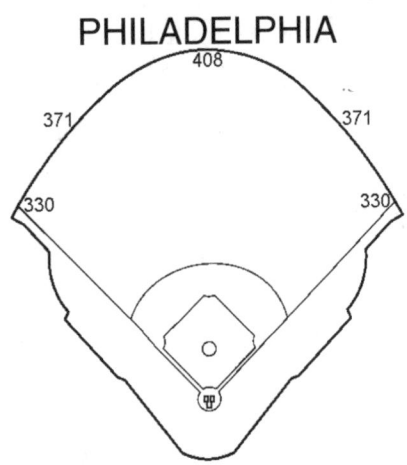

408
371 / | \ 371
330 | | 330

Philadelphia Phillies—Veterans Stadium **Alt:** 20 feet **Surface:** Turf

	1999 Season							1997-1999						
	Home Games			Away Games			Index	Home Games			Away Games			Index
	Phillies	Opp	Total	Phillies	Opp	Total		Phillies	Opp	Total	Phillies	Opp	Total	
G	72	72	144	72	72	144	—	220	220	440	217	217	434	—
Avg	.280	.256	.268	.264	.282	.273	98	.273	.260	.266	.253	.269	.261	102
AB	2471	2508	4979	2488	2404	4892	102	7402	7706	15108	7528	7210	14738	101
R	392	365	757	331	389	720	105	1072	1113	2185	902	1122	2024	106
H	693	641	1334	658	679	1337	100	2018	2002	4020	1908	1941	3849	103
2B	140	129	269	114	135	249	106	415	463	878	354	400	754	114
3B	21	9	30	17	15	32	92	57	46	103	43	48	91	110
HR	70	100	170	70	90	160	104	194	261	455	165	256	421	105
BB	300	304	604	254	251	505	118	809	801	1610	687	793	1480	106
SO	495	533	1028	467	399	866	117	1432	1694	3126	1450	1393	2843	107
E	33	46	79	57	47	104	76	125	160	285	166	155	321	88
E-Infield	31	36	67	48	36	84	80	107	119	226	140	124	264	84
LHB-Avg	.309	.267	.287	.250	.295	.273	105	.288	.267	.277	.255	.284	.269	103
LHB-HR	31	43	74	22	28	50	143	80	99	179	60	98	158	112
RHB-Avg	.263	.248	.256	.273	.274	.273	94	.262	.255	.258	.252	.258	.255	101
RHB-HR	39	57	96	48	62	110	87	114	162	276	105	158	263	101

Pittsburgh Pirates—Three Rivers Stadium

Alt: 730 feet   **Surface:** Turf

	1999 Season							1997-1999						
	Home Games			Away Games			Index	Home Games			Away Games			Index
	Pirates	Opp	Total	Pirates	Opp	Total		Pirates	Opp	Total	Pirates	Opp	Total	
G	75	75	150	71	71	142	—	220	220	440	223	223	446	—
Avg	.261	.250	.256	.249	.269	.259	99	.263	.257	.260	.251	.269	.260	100
AB	2456	2559	5015	2469	2401	4870	97	7242	7587	14829	7731	7479	15210	99
R	360	342	702	316	355	671	99	1021	1003	2024	933	1043	1976	104
H	642	640	1282	616	646	1262	96	1908	1953	3861	1939	2009	3948	99
2B	142	138	280	109	140	249	109	409	416	825	357	395	752	113
3B	21	11	32	17	18	35	89	70	37	107	48	46	94	117
HR	78	75	153	68	66	134	111	194	206	400	171	202	373	110
BB	270	276	546	255	302	557	95	684	753	1437	658	842	1500	98
SO	547	535	1082	555	448	1003	105	1545	1559	3104	1641	1413	3054	104
E	62	56	118	68	51	119	94	183	185	368	197	163	360	104
E-Infield	52	49	101	56	40	96	100	156	164	320	164	136	300	108
LHB-Avg	.276	.256	.267	.256	.282	.268	99	.268	.262	.265	.252	.294	.274	97
LHB-HR	48	33	81	41	27	68	115	83	91	174	69	87	156	116
RHB-Avg	.250	.247	.248	.244	.262	.253	98	.260	.254	.257	.250	.251	.251	103
RHB-HR	30	42	72	27	39	66	107	111	115	226	102	115	217	106

PITTSBURGH

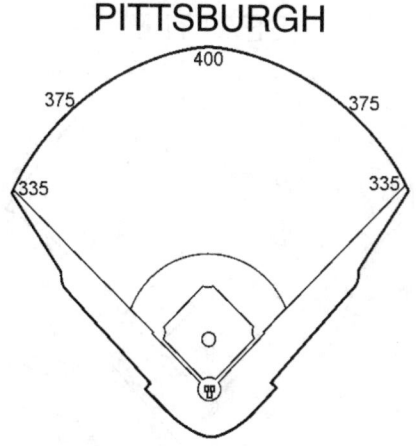

400
375   375
335   335

SAN DIEGO

405
370   370
327   330

San Diego Padres—Qualcomm Stadium

Alt: 20 feet   **Surface:** Grass

	1999 Season							1997-1999						
	Home Games			Away Games			Index	Home Games			Away Games			Index
	Padres	Opp	Total	Padres	Opp	Total		Padres	Opp	Total	Padres	Opp	Total	
G	71	71	142	76	76	152	—	217	217	434	225	225	450	—
Avg	.270	.252	.261	.239	.286	.262	99	.256	.249	.252	.258	.284	.271	93
AB	2344	2431	4775	2566	2535	5101	100	7185	7514	14699	7783	7609	15392	99
R	336	311	647	329	425	754	92	956	917	1873	1076	1177	2253	86
H	632	612	1244	614	725	1339	99	1839	1871	3710	2010	2160	4170	92
2B	106	114	220	127	120	247	95	326	315	641	404	403	807	83
3B	16	10	26	5	18	23	121	29	31	60	35	54	89	71
HR	65	78	143	81	100	181	84	207	218	425	228	233	461	97
BB	288	212	500	271	264	535	100	824	634	1458	841	799	1640	93
SO	503	500	1003	550	469	1019	105	1520	1621	3141	1555	1430	2985	110
E	54	56	110	65	52	117	101	151	160	311	179	153	332	97
E-Infield	48	46	94	54	43	97	104	130	134	264	149	126	275	100
LHB-Avg	.293	.256	.275	.255	.309	.282	97	.274	.254	.264	.280	.293	.286	92
LHB-HR	18	22	40	19	38	57	72	82	77	159	101	84	185	91
RHB-Avg	.252	.249	.251	.229	.271	.250	100	.241	.246	.243	.239	.277	.259	94
RHB-HR	47	56	103	62	62	124	92	125	141	266	127	149	276	100

San Francisco Giants—3Com Park

Alt: 65 feet **Surface:** Grass

	1999 Season							1997-1999						
	Home Games			Away Games			Index	Home Games			Away Games			Index
	Giants	Opp	Total	Giants	Opp	Total		Giants	Opp	Total	Giants	Opp	Total	
G	75	75	150	72	72	144	—	221	221	442	222	222	444	—
Avg	.263	.252	.257	.277	.280	.279	92	.265	.254	.259	.269	.274	.271	96
AB	2473	2626	5099	2560	2468	5028	97	7255	7679	14934	7883	7546	15429	97
R	360	340	700	424	411	835	80	1088	975	2063	1175	1160	2335	89
H	651	661	1312	709	692	1401	90	1923	1950	3873	2119	2068	4187	93
2B	126	113	239	142	128	270	87	362	334	696	411	386	797	90
3B	8	7	15	9	11	20	74	36	34	70	41	43	84	86
HR	82	94	176	93	87	180	96	230	238	468	238	236	474	102
BB	313	288	601	319	300	619	96	937	781	1718	909	834	1743	102
SO	498	561	1059	456	422	878	119	1460	1590	3050	1458	1341	2799	113
E	46	61	107	51	60	111	93	157	172	329	147	161	308	107
E-Infield	39	55	94	45	48	93	97	126	151	277	129	128	257	108
LHB-Avg	.274	.257	.266	.283	.287	.285	94	.279	.263	.272	.276	.274	.275	99
LHB-HR	37	37	74	41	25	66	105	111	87	198	112	70	182	112
RHB-Avg	.253	.249	.251	.272	.277	.274	91	.250	.249	.249	.261	.274	.268	93
RHB-HR	45	57	102	52	62	114	91	119	151	270	126	166	292	96

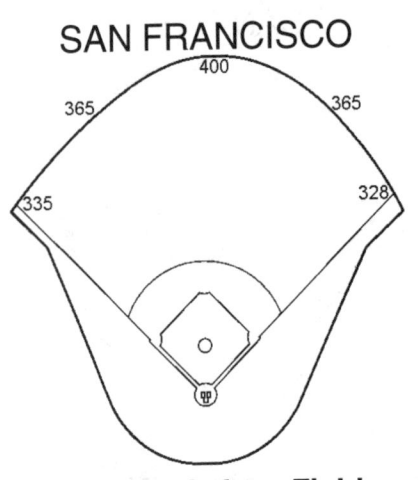

SAN FRANCISCO

400
365 / 365
335 / 328

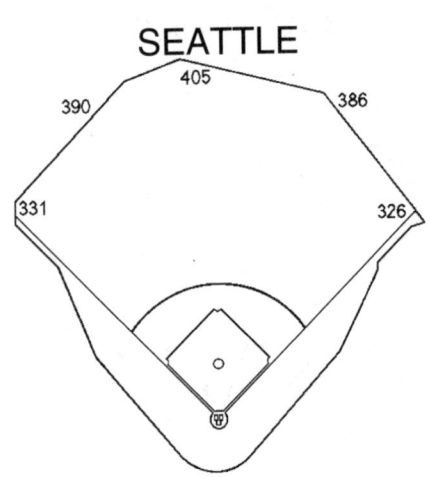

SEATTLE

405
390 / 386
331 / 326

Seattle Mariners—Safeco Field

Alt: -2 feet **Surface:** Grass

	1999 Season							1997-1999 (Kingdome)						
	Home Games			Away Games			Index	Home Games			Away Games			Index
	Mariners	Opp	Total	Mariners	Opp	Total		Mariners	Opp	Total	Mariners	Opp	Total	
G	36	36	72	33	33	66	—	182	182	364	184	184	368	—
Avg	.243	.247	.245	.253	.289	.270	91	.283	.275	.279	.278	.278	.278	100
AB	1155	1224	2379	1144	1119	2263	96	6212	6505	12717	6573	6265	12838	100
R	159	159	318	146	172	318	92	1030	1009	2039	1043	975	2018	102
H	281	302	583	289	323	612	87	1761	1786	3547	1826	1743	3569	100
2B	45	57	102	56	67	123	79	372	410	782	334	364	698	113
3B	3	5	8	4	10	14	54	23	20	43	31	29	60	72
HR	41	42	83	46	28	74	107	290	237	527	288	203	491	108
BB	142	131	273	119	139	258	101	714	699	1413	625	659	1284	111
SO	255	242	497	263	178	441	107	1215	1392	2607	1216	1183	2399	110
E	21	20	41	27	23	50	75	117	105	222	157	125	282	80
E-Infield	17	17	34	22	21	43	72	102	94	196	136	104	240	83
LHB-Avg	.254	.211	.229	.240	.296	.272	84	.282	.287	.285	.275	.304	.289	99
LHB-HR	20	13	33	12	15	27	118	110	105	215	116	90	206	104
RHB-Avg	.239	.269	.253	.258	.284	.269	94	.284	.267	.276	.280	.264	.272	101
RHB-HR	21	29	50	34	13	47	100	180	132	312	172	113	285	111

St. Louis Cardinals—Busch Stadium

Alt: 455 feet   **Surface:** Grass

	1999 Season							1997-1999						
	Home Games			Away Games				Home Games			Away Games			
	Cardinals	Opp	Total	Cardinals	Opp	Total	Index	Cardinals	Opp	Total	Cardinals	Opp	Total	Index
G	71	71	142	75	75	150	—	220	220	440	223	223	446	—
Avg	.258	.274	.266	.257	.275	.266	100	.262	.258	.260	.253	.275	.264	99
AB	2385	2529	4914	2620	2491	5111	102	7434	7791	15225	7759	7421	15180	102
R	341	385	726	380	362	742	103	1075	1041	2116	1042	1052	2094	102
H	615	692	1307	673	685	1358	102	1949	2011	3960	1962	2039	4001	100
2B	101	143	244	144	135	279	91	378	373	751	388	385	773	97
3B	11	9	20	16	21	37	56	42	29	71	48	53	101	70
HR	91	70	161	83	73	156	107	261	203	464	256	182	438	106
BB	284	307	591	284	299	583	105	890	813	1703	802	813	1615	105
SO	489	459	948	610	469	1079	91	1531	1461	2992	1774	1384	3158	94
E	71	50	121	51	69	120	107	201	136	337	163	158	321	106
E-Infield	60	42	102	43	51	94	115	165	109	274	132	123	255	109
LHB-Avg	.265	.269	.267	.246	.276	.262	102	.274	.255	.264	.263	.275	.270	98
LHB-HR	18	27	45	20	22	42	116	77	80	157	81	58	139	114
RHB-Avg	.255	.276	.265	.262	.274	.267	99	.255	.260	.258	.247	.274	.260	99
RHB-HR	73	43	116	63	51	114	104	184	123	307	175	124	299	102

ST. LOUIS

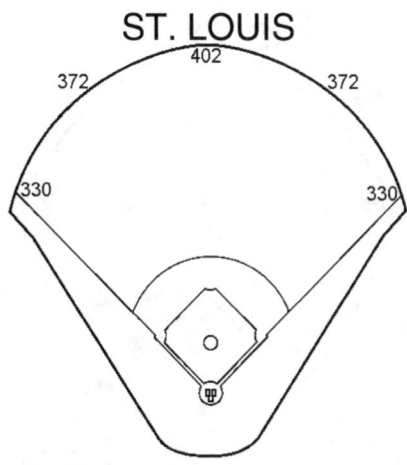

TAMPA BAY

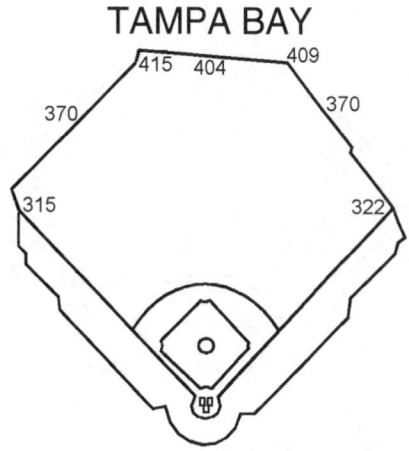

Tampa Bay Devil Rays—Tropicana Field

Alt: 15 feet   **Surface:** grass

	1999 Season							1998-1999						
	Home Games			Away Games				Home Games			Away Games			
	Devil Rays	Opp	Total	Devil Rays	Opp	Total	Index	Devil Rays	Opp	Total	Devil Rays	Opp	Total	Index
G	72	72	144	72	72	144	—	145	145	290	145	145	290	—
Avg	.270	.286	.278	.281	.279	.280	99	.263	.276	.270	.274	.268	.271	99
AB	2381	2543	4924	2567	2400	4967	99	4842	5117	9959	5100	4738	9838	101
R	331	403	734	367	380	747	98	623	759	1382	647	699	1346	103
H	642	727	1369	721	670	1391	98	1272	1412	2684	1399	1269	2668	101
2B	110	160	270	137	122	259	105	230	291	521	262	226	488	105
3B	10	17	27	14	11	25	109	26	27	53	37	25	62	84
HR	55	81	136	74	73	147	93	118	164	282	115	143	258	108
BB	244	290	534	239	320	559	96	455	570	1025	455	624	1079	94
SO	456	494	950	463	438	901	106	925	948	1873	967	893	1860	99
E	55	43	98	60	50	110	89	100	98	198	99	95	194	102
E-Infield	48	38	86	50	40	90	96	88	87	175	88	80	168	104
LHB-Avg	.290	.296	.293	.276	.276	.276	106	.271	.284	.277	.271	.271	.271	102
LHB-HR	25	38	63	24	37	61	109	68	69	137	39	67	106	127
RHB-Avg	.257	.278	.267	.284	.282	.283	94	.255	.270	.263	.277	.265	.271	97
RHB-HR	30	43	73	50	36	86	83	50	95	145	76	76	152	95

Texas Rangers—The Ballpark in Arlington

Alt: 551 feet **Surface:** Grass

| | 1999 Season | | | | | | | 1997-1999 | | | | | | |
| | Home Games | | | Away Games | | | Index | Home Games | | | Away Games | | | Index |
	Rangers	Opp	Total	Rangers	Opp	Total		Rangers	Opp	Total	Rangers	Opp	Total	
G	72	72	144	72	72	144	—	218	218	436	218	218	436	—
Avg	.304	.293	.298	.289	.287	.288	104	.297	.290	.294	.273	.283	.278	106
AB	2447	2615	5062	2576	2438	5014	101	7480	7893	15373	7733	7359	15092	102
R	427	407	834	424	355	779	107	1238	1212	2450	1175	1078	2253	109
H	743	765	1508	744	699	1443	105	2225	2289	4514	2108	2086	4194	108
2B	132	151	283	145	161	306	92	418	448	866	421	436	857	99
3B	19	18	37	9	18	27	136	54	59	113	25	49	74	150
HR	95	99	194	114	68	182	106	274	263	537	289	208	497	106
BB	278	211	489	259	237	496	98	769	696	1465	754	713	1467	98
SO	378	449	827	427	432	859	95	1317	1305	2622	1459	1300	2759	93
E	52	42	94	49	50	99	95	172	147	319	134	155	289	110
E-Infield	43	39	82	44	41	85	96	145	117	262	115	130	245	107
LHB-Avg	.293	.282	.287	.284	.287	.285	101	.297	.289	.293	.272	.280	.276	106
LHB-HR	48	45	93	47	37	84	119	121	127	248	114	103	217	116
RHB-Avg	.314	.301	.307	.293	.287	.290	106	.298	.291	.294	.273	.287	.280	105
RHB-HR	47	54	101	67	31	98	95	153	136	289	175	105	280	98

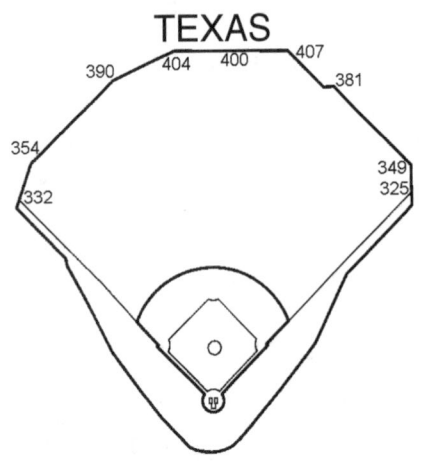

TEXAS

390 404 400 407 381 354 349 325 332

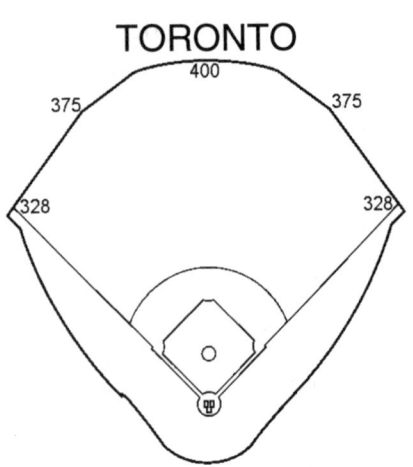

TORONTO

400 375 375 328 328

Toronto Blue Jays—SkyDome

Alt: 300 feet **Surface:** Turf

| | 1999 Season | | | | | | | 1997-1999 | | | | | | |
| | Home Games | | | Away Games | | | Index | Home Games | | | Away Games | | | Index |
	Blue Jays	Opp	Total	Blue Jays	Opp	Total		Blue Jays	Opp	Total	Blue Jays	Opp	Total	
G	72	72	144	72	72	144	—	217	217	434	221	221	442	—
Avg	.278	.287	.283	.285	.277	.281	101	.265	.259	.262	.264	.274	.269	97
AB	2426	2582	5008	2593	2436	5029	100	7222	7643	14865	7791	7436	15227	99
R	380	417	797	420	358	778	102	1062	1014	2076	1076	1078	2154	98
H	674	741	1415	738	675	1413	100	1912	1977	3889	2060	2034	4094	97
2B	156	172	328	151	119	270	122	434	446	880	410	397	807	112
3B	6	10	16	7	18	25	64	39	30	69	31	50	81	87
HR	86	88	174	105	87	192	91	241	218	459	275	264	539	87
BB	248	268	516	267	259	526	99	770	730	1500	705	799	1504	102
SO	470	450	920	477	449	926	100	1442	1506	2948	1526	1502	3028	100
E	46	30	76	42	52	94	81	158	118	276	127	171	298	94
E-Infield	41	26	67	38	44	82	82	132	97	229	108	145	253	92
LHB-Avg	.271	.304	.288	.274	.262	.269	107	.275	.258	.266	.271	.273	.272	98
LHB-HR	60	43	103	66	31	97	100	127	99	226	139	124	263	85
RHB-Avg	.284	.272	.278	.294	.287	.291	96	.257	.259	.258	.260	.274	.266	97
RHB-HR	26	45	71	39	56	95	79	114	119	233	136	140	276	89

1997-99 Ballpark Index Rankings—Runs per Game

	AMERICAN LEAGUE									NATIONAL LEAGUE								
	Home Games			Away Games						Home Games			Away Games				
	Gm	Team	Opp	Total	Gm	Team	Opp	Total	Index		Gm	Team	Opp	Total	Gm	Team	Opp	Total	Index
Tex	218	1238	1212	2450	218	1175	1078	2253	109	Col	223	1503	1500	3003	223	932	1050	1982	152
Cle	220	1258	1162	2420	216	1206	1065	2271	105	ChC	220	1087	1122	2209	224	953	1128	2081	108
KC	217	1048	1221	2269	217	1013	1143	2156	105	Phi	220	1072	1113	2185	217	902	1122	2024	106
Min	220	1004	1190	2194	217	960	1112	2072	104	Pit	220	1021	1003	2024	223	933	1043	1976	104
TB*	145	623	759	1382	145	647	699	1346	103	Cin	221	1026	1037	2063	223	1031	1003	2034	102
Bos	217	1182	1013	2195	220	1140	1044	2184	102	StL	220	1075	1041	2116	223	1042	1052	2094	102
Det	217	1035	1134	2169	219	983	1182	2165	101	Mil	221	983	1151	2134	220	1012	1087	2099	101
Ana*	145	641	739	1380	145	712	696	1408	98	Ari*	148	708	655	1363	148	701	686	1387	98
Tor	217	1062	1014	2076	221	1076	1078	2154	98	Mon	220	935	1065	2000	217	924	1103	2027	97
CWS	221	1089	1161	2250	216	1102	1206	2308	95	NYM	220	1038	904	1942	218	1066	943	2009	96
Bal	217	1070	1000	2070	220	1171	1059	2230	94	Atl	220	1088	768	1856	217	1123	827	1950	94
Oak	218	1073	1143	2216	218	1120	1245	2365	94	Hou	221	1112	829	1941	221	1132	953	2085	93
Sea**	36	159	159	318	33	146	172	318	92	Fla	219	909	1029	1938	218	940	1202	2142	90
NYY	215	1164	868	2032	222	1355	1001	2356	89	SF	221	1088	975	2063	222	1175	1160	2335	89
										LA	221	936	875	1811	221	1033	1045	2078	87
										SD	217	956	917	1873	225	1076	1177	2253	86

*—Current dimensions began 1998; **—Current dimensions began 1999

1997-99 Ballpark Index Rankings—Home Runs per At Bat

	AMERICAN LEAGUE									NATIONAL LEAGUE								
	Home Games			Away Games						Home Games			Away Games				
	Gm	Team	Opp	Total	Gm	Team	Opp	Total	Index		Gm	Team	Opp	Total	Gm	Team	Opp	Total	Index
Det	217	268	297	565	219	217	235	452	127	Col	223	347	351	698	223	247	199	446	145
KC	217	212	273	485	217	181	257	438	109	ChC	220	260	293	553	224	221	247	468	119
TB*	145	118	164	282	145	115	143	258	108	Pit	220	194	206	400	223	171	202	373	110
Sea**	36	41	42	83	33	46	28	74	107	Cin	221	220	256	476	223	230	225	455	107
Tex	218	274	263	537	218	289	208	497	106	StL	220	261	203	464	223	256	182	438	106
Ana*	145	118	172	290	145	155	129	284	103	Phi	220	194	261	455	217	165	256	421	105
Bal	217	277	242	519	220	272	244	516	103	SF	221	230	238	468	222	238	236	474	102
Cle	220	280	256	536	216	286	247	533	99	LA	221	226	222	448	221	242	223	465	99
Oak	218	256	226	482	218	262	258	520	93	SD	217	207	218	425	225	228	233	461	97
CWS	221	231	253	484	216	237	282	519	93	Mil	221	182	273	455	220	228	264	492	91
Min	220	138	270	408	217	175	253	428	92	Atl	220	239	158	397	217	286	157	443	90
NYY	215	231	192	423	222	281	224	505	89	Ari*	148	159	155	314	148	173	174	347	90
Tor	217	241	218	459	221	275	264	539	87	NYM	220	196	190	386	218	223	219	442	88
Bos	217	236	192	428	220	281	227	508	85	Mon	220	207	183	390	217	229	229	458	83
										Fla	219	146	212	358	218	199	229	428	83
										Hou	221	187	165	352	221	234	210	444	81

*—Current dimensions began 1998; **—Current dimensions began 1999

1997-99 Ballpark Index Rankings—Batting Average

	AMERICAN LEAGUE									NATIONAL LEAGUE								
	Home Games			Away Games						Home Games			Away Games				
	Gm	Team	Opp	Avg	Gm	Team	Opp	Avg	Index		Gm	Team	Opp	Avg	Gm	Team	Opp	Avg	Index
Tex	218	.297	.290	.294	218	.273	.283	.278	106	Col	223	.325	.316	.320	223	.253	.273	.262	122
Cle	220	.290	.279	.284	216	.274	.267	.270	105	ChC	220	.272	.267	.270	224	.247	.274	.260	104
Bos	217	.295	.263	.279	220	.276	.260	.268	104	Ari*	148	.268	.257	.262	148	.254	.257	.255	103
KC	217	.272	.283	.278	217	.265	.275	.270	103	Mil	221	.266	.276	.271	220	.261	.270	.266	102
Min	220	.271	.282	.277	217	.259	.284	.271	102	Phi	220	.273	.260	.266	217	.253	.269	.261	102
TB*	145	.263	.276	.270	145	.274	.268	.271	99	Pit	220	.263	.257	.260	223	.251	.269	.260	100
CWS	221	.275	.273	.274	216	.273	.282	.277	99	Mon	220	.259	.260	.260	217	.257	.265	.261	100
Oak	218	.261	.277	.270	218	.257	.292	.275	98	Atl	220	.273	.238	.255	217	.265	.247	.256	100
Bal	217	.272	.258	.265	220	.274	.270	.272	97	StL	220	.262	.258	.260	223	.253	.275	.264	99
Tor	217	.265	.259	.262	221	.264	.274	.269	97	Cin	221	.261	.244	.252	223	.261	.257	.259	97
Ana*	145	.258	.263	.261	145	.270	.270	.270	97	NYM	220	.265	.251	.258	218	.269	.260	.265	97
NYY	215	.287	.247	.266	222	.290	.265	.278	96	Hou	221	.270	.248	.259	221	.266	.267	.267	97
Det	217	.258	.265	.262	219	.265	.284	.274	96	LA	221	.262	.237	.249	221	.259	.261	.260	96
Sea**	36	.243	.247	.245	33	.253	.289	.270	91	SF	221	.265	.254	.259	222	.269	.274	.271	96
										Fla	219	.256	.258	.257	218	.256	.290	.273	94
										SD	217	.256	.249	.252	225	.258	.284	.271	93

*—Current dimensions began 1998; **—Current dimensions began 1999

1999 Lefty/Righty Statistics

These are the numbers that consume managers when they make out lineup cards and when the game is on the line. Late in close contests, managers constantly are making critical platoon decisions regarding pinch-hitters and relief pitchers.

In 1999, it seems lefthanded hurlers were better off not pitching to shortstops. The top two batting averages against lefties in the majors came courtesy of Mike Bordick (.402) and Nomar Garciaparra (.400). They were the only two regulars to break the .400 plateau while the National League leader versus southpaws was another shortstop, Mark Grudzielanek (.389).

Righthanded pitchers were best to avoid the New York Yankees, as Derek Jeter (.366) and Bernie Williams (.359) posted the two best batting averages against righties in the big leagues. In the National League, leading the way were a pair of first basemen, Sean Casey (.356) and Todd Helton (.349). We should also mention NL batting champion Larry Walker who batted .395 vs. righties but fell short of the 377-AB minimum. Had we used the "hypothetical at-bat" rule which gave Tony Gwynn the 1996 NL batting title, Walker would have come out on top.

Gaining the advantage in a lefty-righty situation obviously is more complicated than not pitching to a certain position or team. So check out the 1999 numbers that assisted big league managers every step of the way last season.

Batters vs. Lefthanded and Righthanded Pitchers

Batter	vs	Avg	AB	H	2B	3B	HR	BI	BB	SO	OBP	SLG
Abbott,Jeff	L	.300	20	6	0	0	1	4	4	3	.400	.450
Bats Right	R	.081	37	3	0	0	1	2	1	9	.105	.162
Abbott,Kurt	L	.272	92	25	8	0	2	12	6	23	.316	.424
Bats Right	R	.273	194	53	9	2	6	29	10	46	.307	.433
Abreu,Bobby	L	.298	141	42	10	0	0	20	29	40	.425	.369
Bats Left	R	.348	405	141	25	11	20	73	80	73	.453	.612
Agbayani,B	L	.298	104	31	11	0	5	11	13	30	.388	.548
Bats Right	R	.279	172	48	7	3	9	31	19	30	.347	.512
Alexander,M	L	.290	93	27	4	2	0	10	6	20	.330	.376
Bats Right	R	.250	84	21	7	0	0	5	4	18	.284	.333
Alfonzo,E	L	.268	138	37	9	0	6	20	23	22	.367	.464
Bats Right	R	.314	490	154	32	1	21	88	62	63	.390	.512
Alicea,Luis	L	.290	62	18	7	0	1	5	8	6	.371	.452
Bats Both	R	.147	102	15	3	0	2	12	20	26	.285	.235
Allen,Chad	L	.302	116	35	5	0	3	9	9	21	.349	.422
Bats Right	R	.268	365	98	16	3	7	37	28	68	.323	.386
Allensworth,J	L	.226	31	7	1	0	2	4	4	11	.306	.452
Bats Right	R	.214	42	9	1	0	1	5	5	12	.313	.310
Alomar,R	L	.338	145	49	10	1	6	21	19	31	.422	.545
Bats Both	R	.318	418	133	30	2	18	99	80	65	.422	.529
Alomar Jr.,S	L	.353	34	12	3	0	2	7	1	5	.371	.618
Bats Right	R	.291	103	30	10	0	4	18	3	18	.306	.505
Alvarez,Gabe	L	.200	15	3	1	0	0	0	3	2	.333	.267
Bats Right	R	.211	38	8	2	0	2	4	0	7	.211	.421
Amaral,Rich	L	.342	73	25	6	1	0	4	7	9	.407	.452
Bats Right	R	.203	64	13	2	0	0	7	8	11	.284	.234
Anderson,B	L	.237	93	22	2	0	4	20	12	25	.339	.387
Bats Left	R	.291	471	137	26	5	20	61	84	80	.416	.495
Anderson,G	L	.280	161	45	3	1	3	23	6	24	.302	.366
Bats Left	R	.312	459	143	33	1	18	57	28	57	.348	.505
Anderson,M	L	.297	64	19	5	1	0	10	3	11	.328	.406
Bats Left	R	.245	388	95	21	3	5	44	21	50	.286	.353
Andrews,Sh.	L	.231	91	21	2	0	4	9	17	29	.345	.385
Bats Right	R	.183	257	47	10	0	12	42	33	80	.276	.362
Arias,Alex	L	.253	95	24	7	0	0	9	13	4	.339	.326
Bats Right	R	.321	252	81	13	1	4	39	23	27	.386	.429
Arias,George	L	.239	67	16	3	0	3	7	2	22	.261	.418
Bats Right	R	.247	97	24	5	0	4	13	4	32	.277	.423
Aurilia,Rich	L	.296	142	42	5	0	5	22	14	12	.357	.437
Bats Right	R	.276	416	115	18	1	17	58	29	59	.328	.447
Ausmus,Brad	L	.264	72	19	5	0	0	8	9	12	.354	.333
Bats Right	R	.277	386	107	20	6	9	46	42	59	.367	.430
Aven,Bruce	L	.276	105	29	4	0	4	19	16	23	.382	.429
Bats Right	R	.293	276	81	15	2	8	51	28	59	.366	.449
Baerga,Carlos	L	.222	27	6	0	0	0	2	2	7	.276	.222
Bats Both	R	.245	110	27	1	0	3	8	8	17	.306	.336
Bagwell,Jeff	L	.354	130	46	8	0	9	26	33	30	.476	.623
Bats Right	R	.289	432	125	27	0	33	100	116	97	.448	.581
Baines,Harold	L	.302	53	16	3	0	3	17	3	10	.328	.528
Bats Left	R	.313	377	118	15	1	22	86	51	38	.395	.533
Bako,Paul	L	.167	18	3	2	0	0	1	2	7	.250	.278
Bats Left	R	.264	197	52	12	1	2	16	24	50	.339	.365
Banks,Brian	L	.222	54	12	2	0	1	5	7	18	.302	.315
Bats Both	R	.248	165	41	5	1	4	17	18	41	.322	.364
Barajas,Rod	L	.667	3	2	0	0	1	2	1	0	.750	1.667
Bats Right	R	.154	13	2	1	0	0	1	0	1	.154	.231
Barker,Glen	L	.304	23	7	0	0	0	2	2	8	.360	.304
Bats Both	R	.280	50	14	2	0	1	9	9	11	.393	.380
Barker,Kevin	L	.118	17	2	0	0	0	0	2	4	.211	.118
Bats Left	R	.310	100	31	3	0	3	23	7	15	.352	.430
Barrett,M	L	.267	116	31	10	1	2	14	6	10	.309	.422
Bats Right	R	.303	317	96	22	2	6	38	26	29	.358	.442
Barry,Jeff	L	.325	40	13	6	0	2	12	2	1	.349	.625
Bats Both	R	.250	128	32	10	0	3	14	17	28	.342	.398
Bartee,Kimera	L	.219	32	7	0	3	0	1	3	6	.286	.406
Bats Right	R	.178	45	8	1	0	0	2	6	14	.275	.200
Batista,Tony	L	.282	110	31	6	0	6	20	16	18	.371	.500
Bats Right	R	.276	409	113	24	1	25	80	22	78	.317	.523
Battle,Howard	L	.455	11	5	0	0	1	5	1	3	.500	.727
Bats Right	R	.167	6	1	0	0	0	0	1	0	.286	.167
Bautista,D	L	.277	65	18	1	1	1	6	2	11	.294	.369
Bats Right	R	.293	140	41	9	0	4	18	2	19	.308	.443
Becker,Rich	L	.158	19	3	0	0	0	2	2	8	.238	.158
Bats Left	R	.265	245	65	8	2	6	24	56	73	.406	.388
Bell,David	L	.220	118	26	6	0	3	15	16	21	.311	.347
Bats Right	R	.280	479	134	25	2	18	63	42	69	.336	.453
Bell,Derek	L	.303	122	37	6	0	5	23	12	18	.365	.475
Bats Right	R	.214	387	83	16	0	7	43	38	111	.288	.310
Bell,Jay	L	.339	168	57	12	3	12	38	43	30	.479	.661
Bats Right	R	.268	421	113	20	3	26	74	39	102	.327	.515
Belle,Albert	L	.367	98	36	7	0	11	27	27	15	.508	.776
Bats Right	R	.283	512	145	29	1	26	90	74	67	.377	.496
Belliard,Ron	L	.273	121	33	7	1	4	17	25	23	.397	.446
Bats Right	R	.304	336	102	22	3	4	41	39	36	.372	.423
Bellinger,C	L	.364	11	4	0	0	1	1	0	2	.364	.636
Bats Right	R	.147	34	5	2	0	0	1	1	8	.171	.206
Beltran,C	L	.273	132	36	5	2	7	19	9	39	.324	.500
Bats Both	R	.298	531	158	22	5	15	89	37	84	.341	.443
Beltre,Adrian	L	.230	135	31	7	1	1	15	22	38	.329	.319
Bats Right	R	.290	403	117	20	4	14	52	39	67	.361	.464
Benard,Marvin	L	.263	114	30	5	0	3	11	7	26	.320	.386
Bats Left	R	.297	448	133	31	5	13	53	48	71	.369	.475
Benjamin,Mike	L	.261	142	37	14	2	0	16	10	32	.312	.387
Bats Right	R	.239	226	54	12	5	1	21	10	58	.272	.350
Bennett,Gary	L	.273	22	6	0	0	0	4	1	3	.304	.273
Bats Right	R	.273	66	18	4	0	1	17	3	8	.296	.379
Berg,Dave	L	.241	83	20	6	0	0	3	6	15	.300	.313
Bats Right	R	.303	221	67	12	1	3	22	21	44	.366	.407
Bergeron,P	L	.000	1	0	0	0	0	0	1	1	.500	.000
Bats Left	R	.250	44	11	2	0	0	1	8	4	.365	.295

Batters vs. Lefthanded and Righthanded Pitchers

Batter	vs	Avg	AB	H	2B	3B	HR	BI	BB	SO	OBP	SLG	Batter	vs	Avg	AB	H	2B	3B	HR	BI	BB	SO	OBP	SLG
Berkman,Lan.	L	.154	13	2	0	0	0	0	2	5	.267	.154	Brown,Dee	L	.000	0	0	0	0	0	0	0	0	.000	.000
Bats Both	R	.250	80	20	2	0	4	15	10	16	.330	.425	Bats Left	R	.080	25	2	0	0	0	0	2	7	.148	.080
Berroa,G	L	.263	19	5	2	0	1	4	4	5	.391	.526	Brown,Emil	L	.250	4	1	1	0	0	0	0	2	.250	.500
Bats Right	R	.163	43	7	1	0	0	2	5	10	.280	.186	Bats Right	R	.100	10	1	0	0	0	0	0	1	.100	.100
Berry,Sean	L	.175	80	14	4	1	0	7	4	15	.212	.250	Brown,K	L	.000	2	0	0	0	0	1	0	0	.000	.000
Bats Right	R	.251	179	45	7	0	2	16	13	35	.311	.324	Bats Right	R	.571	7	4	2	0	0	0	0	3	.571	.857
Bichette,D	L	.313	166	52	10	1	8	33	19	18	.380	.530	Brown,R	L	.000	2	0	0	0	0	0	0	2	.000	.000
Bats Right	R	.293	427	125	28	1	26	100	35	66	.343	.546	Bats Left	R	.226	62	14	6	1	1	10	2	12	.246	.403
Biggio,Craig	L	.307	150	46	19	0	4	18	28	19	.410	.513	Brumfield,J	L	.306	49	15	2	2	1	7	3	7	.346	.490
Bats Right	R	.290	489	142	37	0	12	55	60	88	.378	.440	Bats Right	R	.217	138	30	6	2	1	13	16	37	.293	.312
Blake,Casey	L	.000	4	0	0	0	0	0	0	0	.000	.000	Buford,Damon	L	.245	110	27	4	1	1	15	11	23	.325	.327
Bats Right	R	.286	35	10	2	0	1	1	2	7	.324	.429	Bats Right	R	.241	187	45	11	1	5	23	10	51	.275	.390
Blanco,Henry	L	.222	99	22	6	1	3	13	13	9	.310	.394	Buhner,Jay	L	.266	64	17	1	0	8	16	22	17	.453	.656
Bats Right	R	.238	164	39	6	2	3	15	21	29	.326	.354	Bats Right	R	.208	202	42	10	0	6	22	47	83	.366	.347
Blauser,Jeff	L	.266	94	25	2	1	4	9	15	25	.384	.436	Burks,Ellis	L	.345	116	40	4	0	9	30	26	21	.465	.612
Bats Right	R	.217	106	23	3	1	5	17	11	27	.315	.406	Bats Right	R	.255	274	70	15	0	22	66	43	65	.363	.551
Blowers,Mike	L	.231	26	6	1	0	1	3	3	5	.310	.385	Burnitz,J	L	.247	162	40	12	1	11	41	35	46	.399	.537
Bats Right	R	.250	20	5	0	0	1	4	1	7	.286	.400	Bats Left	R	.282	305	86	21	1	22	62	56	78	.403	.574
Blum,Geoff	L	.190	21	4	2	0	2	2	4	3	.320	.571	Bush,Homer	L	.368	76	28	7	0	1	12	3	11	.400	.500
Bats Both	R	.250	112	28	5	2	6	16	13	22	.328	.491	Bats Right	R	.311	409	127	19	4	4	43	18	71	.345	.406
Bogar,Tim	L	.218	101	22	4	0	2	12	17	17	.331	.317	Butler,Rich	L	.000	4	0	0	0	0	0	1	1	.200	.000
Bats Right	R	.250	208	52	12	2	2	19	21	35	.326	.356	Bats Left	R	.188	16	3	1	0	0	0	1	3	.235	.250
Boggs,Wade	L	.277	47	13	2	0	1	5	3	4	.320	.383	Butler,Rob	L	.000	0	0	0	0	0	0	0	0	.000	.000
Bats Left	R	.306	245	75	12	1	1	24	35	19	.387	.376	Bats Left	R	.143	7	1	0	0	0	1	0	0	.250	.143
Bonds,Barry	L	.266	128	34	6	0	12	25	24	26	.394	.594	Cabrera,J	L	.208	24	5	1	0	0	0	1	5	.240	.250
Bats Left	R	.260	227	59	14	2	22	58	49	36	.387	.630	Bats Right	R	.154	13	2	0	0	0	0	0	3	.214	.154
Bonilla,Bobby	L	.129	31	4	0	0	2	7	6	5	.270	.323	Cabrera,O	L	.333	93	31	8	1	1	8	5	9	.367	.473
Bats Both	R	.170	88	15	5	0	2	11	13	11	.279	.295	Bats Right	R	.228	289	66	15	4	7	31	13	29	.269	.381
Boone,Aaron	L	.219	105	23	7	0	2	8	7	22	.281	.343	Cairo,Miguel	L	.384	86	33	4	0	0	5	5	2	.424	.430
Bats Right	R	.297	367	109	19	5	12	64	23	57	.344	.474	Bats Right	R	.274	379	104	11	5	3	31	19	44	.315	.354
Boone,Bret	L	.280	164	46	12	0	5	15	12	30	.339	.445	Cameron,Mike	L	.292	120	35	7	3	7	15	25	27	.418	.575
Bats Right	R	.241	444	107	26	1	15	48	35	82	.299	.405	Bats Right	R	.246	422	104	27	6	14	51	55	118	.338	.438
Borders,Pat	L	.316	19	6	0	1	1	6	1	2	.350	.579	Caminiti,Ken	L	.338	68	23	5	1	1	7	10	5	.420	.485
Bats Right	R	.200	15	3	0	0	0	0	0	3	.200	.200	Bats Both	R	.268	205	55	6	0	12	49	36	53	.375	.473
Bordick,Mike	L	.402	107	43	9	0	3	23	16	13	.472	.570	Cancel,R	L	.154	13	2	1	0	0	2	1	3	.214	.231
Bats Right	R	.252	524	132	26	7	7	54	38	89	.304	.368	Bats Right	R	.194	31	6	1	0	0	3	1	9	.242	.226
Bournigal,R	L	.353	17	6	2	0	1	5	1	1	.389	.647	Cangelosi,J	L	.000	1	0	0	0	0	0	0	1	.000	.000
Bats Right	R	.256	78	20	3	0	1	9	6	5	.302	.333	Bats Both	R	.200	5	1	1	0	0	0	0	3	.200	.400
Bragg,Darren	L	.230	61	14	1	0	1	4	9	14	.329	.295	Canizaro,Jay	L	.200	10	2	0	0	0	3	0	2	.200	.200
Bats Left	R	.269	212	57	11	1	5	22	35	53	.380	.401	Bats Right	R	.750	8	6	2	0	1	6	1	0	.778	1.375
Branyan,Russ	L	.000	5	0	0	0	0	0	0	4	.167	.000	Canseco,Jose	L	.292	89	26	7	0	8	26	12	30	.369	.640
Bats Left	R	.242	33	8	2	0	1	6	3	15	.306	.394	Bats Right	R	.276	341	94	11	1	26	69	46	105	.368	.543
Brogna,Rico	L	.263	186	49	8	3	9	33	13	47	.318	.484	Caruso,Mike	L	.266	109	29	4	0	0	6	6	10	.310	.303
Bats Left	R	.284	433	123	21	1	15	69	41	85	.343	.441	Bats Left	R	.245	420	103	7	4	2	29	14	26	.272	.295
Brosius,Scott	L	.194	108	21	3	0	10	23	12	16	.270	.500	Casey,Sean	L	.271	170	46	7	1	8	29	18	40	.361	.465
Bats Right	R	.263	365	96	23	1	7	48	27	58	.319	.389	Bats Left	R	.356	424	151	35	2	17	70	43	48	.415	.568
Brown,Adrian	L	.250	112	28	2	0	2	8	22	17	.373	.321	Castilla,V	L	.225	169	38	3	0	8	19	20	15	.307	.385
Bats Both	R	.289	114	33	3	2	2	9	11	22	.354	.404	Bats Right	R	.294	446	131	21	1	25	83	33	60	.340	.513
Brown,Brant	L	.213	47	10	1	1	0	1	0	16	.213	.277	Castillo,A	L	.174	86	15	2	0	0	1	11	21	.265	.198
Bats Left	R	.235	294	69	19	2	16	57	22	98	.293	.476	Bats Right	R	.308	169	52	6	0	4	30	13	27	.358	.414

Batters vs. Lefthanded and Righthanded Pitchers

Batter	vs	Avg	AB	H	2B	3B	HR	BI	BB	SO	OBP	SLG	Batter	vs	Avg	AB	H	2B	3B	HR	BI	BB	SO	OBP	SLG
Castillo,Luis	L	.310	100	31	8	1	0	8	15	15	.397	.410	Cordero,Wil	L	.255	55	14	5	0	2	6	7	7	.344	.455
Bats Both	R	.300	387	116	15	3	0	20	52	70	.381	.354	Bats Right	R	.317	139	44	10	0	6	26	8	30	.373	.518
Castro,Juan	L	.000	0	0	0	0	0	0	0	0	.000	.000	Cordova,Marty	L	.206	102	21	6	0	2	11	18	28	.333	.324
Bats Right	R	.000	1	0	0	0	0	0	0	1	.000	.000	Bats Right	R	.310	323	100	22	3	12	59	30	68	.375	.508
Castro,Ramon	L	.167	12	2	0	0	0	0	1	4	.231	.167	Counsell,C	L	.250	24	6	1	0	0	4	1	3	.259	.292
Bats Right	R	.182	55	10	4	0	2	4	9	10	.292	.364	Bats Left	R	.213	150	32	6	0	0	7	13	21	.276	.253
Catalanotto,F	L	.269	26	7	2	0	0	1	0	5	.286	.346	Cox,Darron	L	.273	11	3	0	0	1	1	0	2	.333	.545
Bats Left	R	.277	260	72	17	0	11	34	15	44	.331	.469	Bats Right	R	.214	14	3	1	0	0	1	0	3	.267	.286
Cedeno,D	L	.143	28	4	2	0	0	2	1	7	.172	.214	Cox,Steve	L	.250	4	1	1	0	0	0	0	1	.250	.500
Bats Both	R	.188	80	15	4	0	3	11	9	24	.278	.350	Bats Left	R	.200	15	3	0	0	0	0	0	1	.200	.200
Cedeno,Roger	L	.194	67	13	3	0	3	8	13	31	.325	.373	Cromer,Tripp	L	.286	14	4	0	0	1	3	3	4	.412	.500
Bats Both	R	.334	386	129	20	4	1	28	47	69	.409	.415	Bats Right	R	.158	38	6	0	0	1	5	2	6	.200	.237
Chavez,Eric	L	.184	49	9	3	0	0	3	8	7	.298	.245	Cruz,Deivi	L	.290	93	27	5	0	1	10	4	8	.320	.376
Bats Left	R	.257	307	79	18	2	13	47	38	49	.339	.456	Bats Right	R	.282	425	120	30	0	12	48	8	49	.298	.438
Christensen,M	L	.000	5	0	0	0	0	1	0	0	.000	.000	Cruz,Ivan	L	1.000	1	1	0	0	0	0	0	0	1.000	1.000
Bats Left	R	.250	48	12	1	0	1	5	4	7	.302	.333	Bats Left	R	.333	9	3	0	0	1	2	0	2	.333	.667
Christenson,R	L	.301	93	28	7	1	3	16	17	15	.405	.495	Cruz,Jacob	L	.615	13	8	0	0	1	5	2	1	.688	.846
Bats Right	R	.160	175	28	5	0	1	8	21	43	.250	.206	Bats Left	R	.280	75	21	5	1	2	12	3	12	.304	.453
Cirillo,Jeff	L	.323	158	51	10	0	9	33	26	17	.422	.557	Cruz,Jose	L	.275	80	22	7	0	2	10	9	11	.348	.438
Bats Right	R	.327	449	147	25	1	6	55	49	66	.393	.428	Bats Both	R	.230	269	62	12	3	12	35	55	80	.361	.431
Clapinski,C	L	.278	18	5	0	0	0	1	1	4	.350	.278	Cummings,M	L	.300	10	3	0	0	0	2	0	1	.273	.300
Bats Both	R	.211	38	8	1	2	0	1	8	8	.348	.342	Bats Left	R	.250	28	7	0	0	1	7	3	6	.323	.357
Clark,Tony	L	.262	107	28	4	0	7	19	6	27	.301	.495	Curtis,Chad	L	.297	74	22	3	0	1	6	20	15	.447	.378
Bats Both	R	.284	429	122	25	0	24	80	58	106	.375	.510	Bats Right	R	.240	121	29	3	0	4	18	23	20	.367	.364
Clark,Will	L	.192	52	10	1	0	0	3	2	9	.250	.212	Dalesandro,M	L	.000	5	0	0	0	0	1	0	0	.143	.000
Bats Left	R	.332	199	66	14	0	10	26	36	33	.429	.553	Bats Right	R	.227	22	5	0	0	0	0	0	2	.227	.227
Clayton,Royce	L	.306	98	30	5	1	5	23	9	20	.370	.531	Damon,Johnny	L	.329	140	46	8	0	1	20	10	17	.370	.407
Bats Right	R	.283	367	104	16	4	9	29	30	80	.340	.422	Bats Left	R	.300	443	133	31	9	13	57	57	33	.382	.499
Clemente,E	L	.327	52	17	5	1	3	7	4	13	.375	.635	Darr,Mike	L	.200	5	1	0	0	0	0	0	3	.200	.200
Bats Right	R	.218	110	24	5	1	5	18	3	33	.237	.418	Bats Left	R	.279	43	12	1	0	2	3	5	15	.354	.442
Clyburn,Danny	L	.235	34	8	1	0	1	1	1	10	.257	.353	Daubach,Brian	L	.273	44	12	2	0	1	9	6	6	.373	.386
Bats Right	R	.170	47	8	3	0	2	4	6	11	.278	.362	Bats Left	R	.297	337	100	31	3	20	64	30	86	.358	.585
Colangelo,M	L	.500	2	1	0	0	0	0	1	0	.667	.500	DaVanon,Jeff	L	.000	6	0	0	0	0	0	1	6	.143	.000
Bats Right	R	.000	0	0	0	0	0	0	0	0	.000	.000	Bats Both	R	.286	14	4	0	1	1	4	1	1	.333	.643
Colbrunn,Greg	L	.361	97	35	2	3	5	19	9	15	.417	.598	Davidson,C	L	.200	5	1	0	0	0	0	0	2	.200	.200
Bats Right	R	.237	38	9	3	0	0	5	3	8	.333	.316	Bats Both	R	.118	17	2	0	0	0	3	0	2	.118	.118
Coleman,M	L	.250	4	1	0	0	0	0	1	0	.400	.250	Davis,Ben	L	.239	67	16	4	0	1	11	8	16	.320	.343
Bats Right	R	.000	1	0	0	0	0	0	0	0	.000	.000	Bats Both	R	.246	199	49	10	1	4	19	17	54	.303	.367
Collier,Lou	L	.308	65	20	5	0	1	9	5	18	.347	.431	Davis,Chili	L	.267	146	39	5	0	6	24	20	23	.353	.425
Bats Right	R	.214	70	15	4	0	1	12	9	14	.304	.314	Bats Both	R	.270	330	89	20	1	13	54	53	77	.372	.455
Conine,Jeff	L	.280	93	26	5	1	5	15	8	11	.333	.516	Davis,Eric	L	.286	49	14	3	0	2	8	7	13	.375	.469
Bats Right	R	.293	351	103	26	0	8	60	22	29	.335	.436	Bats Right	R	.246	142	35	6	2	3	22	23	36	.353	.380
Cookson,Brent	L	.000	3	0	0	0	0	0	0	1	.000	.000	Davis,Russ	L	.298	104	31	6	0	8	18	4	23	.330	.587
Bats Right	R	.500	2	1	0	0	0	0	0	0	.500	.500	Bats Right	R	.229	328	75	11	1	13	41	28	88	.296	.387
Coomer,Ron	L	.278	115	32	7	0	5	15	10	20	.336	.470	Davis,Tommy	L	.000	0	0	0	0	0	0	0	0	.000	.000
Bats Right	R	.259	352	91	18	1	11	50	20	49	.298	.409	Bats Right	R	.167	6	1	0	0	0	2	0	2	.167	.167
Coquillette,T	L	.417	12	5	1	0	0	3	0	0	.462	.500	Dawkins,T	L	.000	0	0	0	0	0	0	0	0	.000	.000
Bats Right	R	.216	37	8	2	0	0	1	4	7	.293	.270	Bats Right	R	.250	4	1	0	0	0	0	0	3	.400	.250
Cora,Alex	L	.333	3	1	0	0	0	0	0	1	.333	.333	Decker,Steve	L	.143	28	4	1	0	0	2	5	2	.265	.179
Bats Left	R	.148	27	4	1	0	0	3	0	3	.179	.185	Bats Right	R	.314	35	11	5	0	0	3	8	7	.455	.457

Batters vs. Lefthanded and Righthanded Pitchers

Batter	vs	Avg	AB	H	2B	3B	HR	BI	BB	SO	OBP	SLG	Batter	vs	Avg	AB	H	2B	3B	HR	BI	BB	SO	OBP	SLG
Delgado,C	L	.309	152	47	9	0	12	33	23	42	.416	.605	Erstad,Darin	L	.274	157	43	6	1	5	19	8	30	.310	.420
Bats Left	R	.259	421	109	30	0	32	101	63	99	.363	.558	Bats Left	R	.245	428	105	16	4	8	34	39	71	.308	.357
Delgado,W	L	.333	24	8	1	1	0	1	1	2	.360	.458	Estalella,B	L	.333	3	1	0	0	0	0	0	1	.333	.333
Bats Both	R	.213	47	10	1	0	0	2	4	7	.288	.234	Bats Right	R	.133	15	2	0	0	0	1	4	6	.316	.133
Dellaero,J	L	.167	6	1	0	0	0	1	0	3	.143	.167	Eusebio,Tony	L	.333	117	39	6	0	4	16	17	26	.418	.487
Bats Both	R	.074	27	2	0	0	0	1	1	10	.107	.074	Bats Right	R	.238	206	49	9	0	0	17	23	41	.314	.282
Dellucci,D	L	.250	16	4	0	0	0	2	0	4	.250	.250	Everett,Carl	L	.325	117	38	4	0	4	20	7	21	.394	.462
Bats Left	R	.419	93	39	7	1	1	13	11	20	.495	.548	Bats Both	R	.326	347	113	29	3	21	88	43	73	.399	.608
DeRosa,Mark	L	.000	2	0	0	0	0	0	0	1	.000	.000	Fabregas,J	L	.300	20	6	0	1	0	4	3	3	.375	.400
Bats Right	R	.000	6	0	0	0	0	0	0	1	.000	.000	Bats Left	R	.190	211	40	10	1	3	17	23	24	.271	.289
DeShields,D	L	.171	41	7	0	0	1	3	2	11	.227	.244	Fasano,Sal	L	.375	8	3	0	0	1	2	1	2	.583	.750
Bats Left	R	.277	289	80	11	2	5	31	35	41	.354	.381	Bats Right	R	.212	52	11	2	0	4	14	6	15	.333	.481
Diaz,Alex	L	.222	18	4	1	0	0	1	2	6	.300	.278	Febles,Carlos	L	.278	97	27	6	1	2	12	7	21	.327	.423
Bats Both	R	.219	32	7	1	0	1	6	1	7	.242	.344	Bats Right	R	.250	356	89	16	8	8	41	40	70	.338	.407
Diaz,Edwin	L	.400	5	2	2	0	0	1	3	1	.625	.800	Fernandez,J	L	.000	1	0	0	0	0	0	0	0	.000	.000
Bats Right	R	.000	0	0	0	0	0	0	0	0	.000	.000	Bats Right	R	.217	23	5	2	0	0	1	1	7	.250	.304
Diaz,Einar	L	.213	94	20	4	0	2	7	6	14	.267	.319	Fernandez,T	L	.322	143	46	13	0	1	22	12	13	.374	.434
Bats Right	R	.302	298	90	17	1	1	25	17	27	.347	.376	Bats Both	R	.330	342	113	28	0	5	53	65	49	.447	.456
DiFelice,Mike	L	.286	49	14	1	0	2	9	3	6	.327	.429	Fick,Robert	L	.500	4	2	0	0	0	0	1	0	.600	.500
Bats Right	R	.315	130	41	10	0	4	18	5	17	.353	.485	Bats Left	R	.189	37	7	0	0	3	10	6	6	.295	.432
DiSarcina,G	L	.200	60	12	2	1	0	5	2	8	.226	.267	Figga,Mike	L	.182	11	2	1	0	0	0	0	3	.182	.273
Bats Right	R	.237	211	50	5	0	1	24	13	24	.286	.275	Bats Right	R	.227	75	17	3	0	1	5	2	24	.244	.307
Doster,David	L	.234	47	11	2	0	2	5	4	9	.294	.404	Finley,Steve	L	.259	189	49	10	1	10	38	16	28	.322	.481
Bats Right	R	.160	50	8	0	0	1	5	8	14	.271	.220	Bats Left	R	.267	401	107	22	9	24	65	47	66	.342	.546
Dransfeldt,K	L	.286	7	2	0	0	0	0	0	0	.286	.286	Flaherty,John	L	.175	80	14	2	0	1	4	3	11	.212	.238
Bats Right	R	.174	46	8	1	0	1	5	3	12	.224	.261	Bats Right	R	.301	366	110	17	0	13	67	16	53	.331	.454
Drew,J.D.	L	.264	106	28	4	2	5	12	10	24	.361	.481	Fletcher,D	L	.228	79	18	5	0	7	26	11	13	.344	.557
Bats Left	R	.233	262	61	12	4	8	27	40	53	.331	.401	Bats Right	R	.306	333	102	21	0	11	54	15	34	.338	.468
Ducey,Rob	L	.143	7	1	0	0	0	2	1	5	.250	.143	Floyd,Cliff	L	.305	59	18	4	0	4	9	5	13	.359	.576
Bats Left	R	.265	181	48	10	2	8	31	37	52	.388	.475	Bats Left	R	.302	192	58	15	1	7	40	25	34	.385	.500
Dunston,S	L	.340	94	32	7	0	1	14	2	12	.354	.447	Fonville,Chad	L	.000	2	0	0	0	0	0	2	0	.500	.000
Bats Right	R	.309	149	46	4	3	4	27	0	27	.327	.456	Bats Both	R	.000	0	0	0	0	0	0	0	0	.000	.000
Dunwoody,To.	L	.222	27	6	0	0	0	4	1	13	.250	.222	Fordyce,Brook	L	.333	93	31	5	0	4	18	5	9	.367	.516
Bats Left	R	.220	159	35	6	3	2	16	11	28	.273	.333	Bats Right	R	.283	240	68	20	1	5	31	16	39	.333	.438
Durazo,E	L	.222	18	4	0	0	3	7	7	5	.423	.722	Fox,Andy	L	.152	46	7	0	0	0	5	6	11	.273	.152
Bats Left	R	.343	137	47	4	2	8	23	19	38	.421	.577	Bats Left	R	.276	228	63	12	2	6	28	27	50	.367	.425
Durham,Ray	L	.301	136	41	3	4	3	13	22	22	.396	.449	Franco,Julio	L	.000	1	0	0	0	0	0	0	1	.000	.000
Bats Both	R	.294	476	140	27	4	10	47	51	83	.367	.431	Bats Right	R	.000	0	0	0	0	0	0	0	0	.000	.000
Durrington,T	L	.231	39	9	1	0	0	2	1	9	.250	.256	Franco,Matt	L	.000	7	0	0	0	0	0	0	2	.000	.000
Bats Right	R	.157	83	13	1	0	0	0	8	19	.231	.169	Bats Left	R	.248	125	31	5	0	4	21	28	19	.383	.384
Dye,Jermaine	L	.267	101	27	3	3	5	18	10	19	.333	.505	Frias,Hanley	L	.229	48	11	0	0	0	1	8	5	.339	.229
Bats Right	R	.300	507	152	41	5	22	101	48	100	.358	.531	Bats Both	R	.294	102	30	3	2	1	15	21	13	.415	.392
Easley,Damion	L	.291	86	25	6	0	4	9	14	13	.394	.500	Frye,Jeff	L	.273	33	9	1	0	0	2	5	4	.368	.303
Bats Right	R	.261	463	121	24	1	16	56	37	111	.336	.421	Bats Right	R	.284	81	23	2	0	1	10	9	7	.359	.346
Echevarria,A	L	.286	98	28	1	0	7	19	12	15	.369	.510	Fryman,Travis	L	.273	66	18	2	2	2	13	11	12	.367	.455
Bats Right	R	.301	93	28	6	0	4	16	5	19	.350	.495	Bats Right	R	.250	256	64	14	0	8	35	14	45	.292	.398
Edmonds,Jim	L	.190	63	12	4	0	0	5	11	17	.311	.317	Fullmer,Brad	L	.240	50	12	4	1	2	13	2	7	.264	.480
Bats Left	R	.277	141	39	13	2	5	18	17	28	.352	.504	Bats Left	R	.283	297	84	30	1	7	34	20	28	.330	.461
Encarnacion,J	L	.263	95	25	4	2	5	18	5	20	.314	.505	Gaetti,Gary	L	.220	118	26	4	1	3	14	12	16	.298	.347
Bats Right	R	.254	414	105	26	4	14	56	9	93	.280	.437	Bats Right	R	.191	162	31	5	0	6	32	9	35	.232	.333

Batters vs. Lefthanded and Righthanded Pitchers

Batter	vs	Avg	AB	H	2B	3B	HR	BI	BB	SO	OBP	SLG	Batter	vs	Avg	AB	H	2B	3B	HR	BI	BB	SO	OBP	SLG
Gant,Ron	L	.300	130	39	5	1	5	22	27	24	.421	.469	Gonzalez,W	L	.150	40	6	0	0	1	4	0	6	.150	.225
Bats Right	R	.246	386	95	22	4	12	55	58	88	.343	.417	Bats Right	R	.349	43	15	2	1	2	8	1	2	.378	.581
Garcia,Amaury	L	.286	14	4	0	0	2	2	1	6	.333	.714	Goodwin,C	L	.185	27	5	0	0	0	2	1	12	.214	.185
Bats Right	R	.200	10	2	0	1	0	0	2	5	.333	.400	Bats Left	R	.239	138	33	6	1	0	7	12	29	.298	.297
Garcia,Carlos	L	.111	9	1	0	0	0	0	1	3	.200	.111	Goodwin,Tom	L	.262	61	16	0	1	0	4	5	12	.313	.295
Bats Right	R	.500	2	1	0	0	0	0	0	0	.500	.500	Bats Left	R	.259	344	89	12	5	3	29	35	49	.325	.349
Garcia,Freddy	L	.267	86	23	3	0	6	16	4	26	.300	.512	Grace,Mark	L	.307	199	61	18	0	4	34	20	18	.364	.457
Bats Right	R	.174	46	8	2	0	1	8	1	16	.188	.283	Bats Left	R	.310	394	122	26	5	12	57	63	26	.402	.492
Garcia,G	L	.500	2	1	0	0	0	0	0	0	.500	.500	Graffanino,T	L	.367	30	11	3	1	0	5	4	2	.441	.533
Bats Right	R	.000	2	0	0	0	0	0	0	2	.000	.000	Bats Right	R	.300	100	30	6	3	2	14	5	20	.340	.480
Garcia,Jesse	L	.000	3	0	0	0	0	0	1	0	.250	.000	Grebeck,Craig	L	.310	29	9	3	0	0	4	1	3	.333	.414
Bats Right	R	.231	26	6	0	0	2	2	1	3	.259	.462	Bats Right	R	.381	84	32	4	0	0	6	14	10	.475	.429
Garcia,Karim	L	.289	38	11	0	1	1	5	3	11	.341	.421	Green,S	L	.286	7	2	0	0	0	0	0	2	.286	.286
Bats Left	R	.232	250	58	10	2	13	27	17	56	.280	.444	Bats Right	R	.333	6	2	0	0	0	0	1	0	.429	.333
Garcia,Luis	L	.000	2	0	0	0	0	0	0	0	.000	.000	Green,Shawn	L	.280	164	46	13	0	8	39	19	39	.376	.506
Bats Right	R	.143	7	1	1	0	0	0	0	2	.143	.286	Bats Left	R	.320	450	144	32	0	34	84	47	78	.386	.618
Garciaparra,N	L	.400	110	44	13	0	9	32	15	6	.476	.764	Greene,C	L	.188	16	3	0	0	0	0	3	5	.316	.188
Bats Right	R	.346	422	146	29	4	18	72	36	33	.403	.562	Bats Right	R	.192	26	5	1	0	0	1	2	6	.241	.231
Gates,Brent	L	.278	115	32	7	1	2	23	18	17	.370	.409	Greene,Todd	L	.253	95	24	8	0	2	16	2	17	.268	.400
Bats Both	R	.241	191	46	6	1	1	15	16	39	.301	.298	Bats Right	R	.239	226	54	12	0	12	26	10	46	.278	.451
Giambi,Jason	L	.282	181	51	12	0	8	37	26	32	.381	.481	Greene,Willie	L	.150	20	3	1	0	0	1	3	7	.261	.200
Bats Left	R	.330	394	130	24	1	25	86	79	74	.440	.586	Bats Left	R	.209	206	43	6	0	12	40	17	49	.267	.413
Giambi,Jeremy	L	.292	48	14	2	0	0	6	7	13	.382	.333	Greer,Rusty	L	.282	124	35	10	0	3	24	24	16	.411	.435
Bats Left	R	.283	240	68	11	1	3	28	33	54	.371	.375	Bats Left	R	.306	432	132	31	3	17	77	72	51	.403	.509
Gibson,D	L	.375	8	3	1	0	1	3	0	0	.444	.875	Grieve,Ben	L	.156	109	17	3	0	3	13	9	31	.240	.266
Bats Right	R	.100	20	2	0	0	1	3	0	7	.100	.250	Bats Left	R	.297	377	112	18	0	25	73	54	77	.391	.544
Giles,B	L	.299	177	53	10	1	9	28	27	30	.393	.520	Griffey Jr.,K	L	.229	170	39	5	1	8	27	20	36	.318	.412
Bats Left	R	.323	344	111	23	2	30	87	68	50	.430	.663	Bats Left	R	.307	436	134	21	2	40	107	71	72	.409	.640
Gilkey,B	L	.337	104	35	12	1	4	26	21	12	.438	.587	Grissom,M	L	.322	171	55	11	1	4	20	18	33	.384	.468
Bats Right	R	.250	100	25	4	0	4	13	8	30	.313	.410	Bats Right	R	.245	432	106	16	0	16	63	31	76	.293	.394
Giovanola,Ed	L	.167	12	2	0	0	0	0	2	3	.286	.167	Grudzielanek	L	.389	144	56	11	1	2	14	16	20	.451	.521
Bats Left	R	.196	46	9	0	1	0	3	7	5	.296	.239	Bats Right	R	.299	344	103	12	4	5	32	15	45	.343	.401
Gipson,C	L	.280	25	7	1	0	0	1	2	2	.333	.320	Gubanich,C	L	.292	24	7	2	0	0	5	2	8	.370	.375
Bats Right	R	.200	55	11	4	2	0	8	4	11	.267	.345	Bats Right	R	.261	23	6	0	1	1	6	1	5	.320	.478
Girardi,Joe	L	.184	49	9	3	0	0	4	2	5	.212	.245	Guerrero,V	L	.287	129	37	4	1	12	27	16	20	.363	.612
Bats Right	R	.256	160	41	13	1	2	23	8	21	.290	.388	Bats Right	R	.324	481	156	33	4	30	104	39	42	.383	.597
Glanville,D	L	.250	140	35	6	0	2	11	17	17	.340	.336	Guerrero,W	L	.330	97	32	7	3	1	11	3	17	.356	.495
Bats Right	R	.346	488	169	32	6	9	62	31	65	.386	.492	Bats Both	R	.275	218	60	8	4	1	20	10	21	.310	.362
Glaus,Troy	L	.216	116	25	10	0	5	17	17	28	.321	.431	Guevara,G	L	.000	0	0	0	0	0	0	0	0	.000	.000
Bats Right	R	.246	435	107	19	0	24	62	54	115	.334	.455	Bats Both	R	.250	12	3	2	0	0	2	0	2	.250	.417
Gomez,Chris	L	.294	68	20	5	0	0	7	9	11	.377	.368	Guillen,C	L	.143	7	1	0	0	0	1	1	3	.250	.143
Bats Right	R	.235	166	39	3	1	1	8	18	38	.312	.283	Bats Both	R	.167	12	2	0	0	1	2	0	3	.167	.417
Gonzalez,Alex	L	.268	41	11	3	0	1	3	1	7	.286	.415	Guillen,Jose	L	.304	79	24	10	0	0	8	5	19	.341	.430
Bats Right	R	.301	113	34	10	0	1	9	15	16	.397	.416	Bats Right	R	.234	209	49	6	0	3	23	15	38	.306	.306
Gonzalez,Alex	L	.254	114	29	7	1	3	13	2	32	.271	.412	Guillen,Ozzie	L	.280	50	14	3	0	0	4	4	5	.327	.340
Bats Right	R	.283	446	126	21	7	11	46	13	81	.318	.435	Bats Left	R	.231	182	42	13	0	1	16	11	12	.272	.319
Gonzalez,Juan	L	.342	114	39	6	0	9	23	13	21	.409	.632	Gutierrez,R	L	.379	66	25	2	3	0	8	11	12	.468	.500
Bats Right	R	.321	448	144	30	1	30	105	38	84	.371	.594	Bats Right	R	.223	202	45	5	2	1	17	26	33	.316	.282
Gonzalez,Luis	L	.327	165	54	14	1	3	32	23	24	.421	.479	Guzman,C	L	.296	115	34	7	1	1	8	7	24	.336	.400
Bats Left	R	.339	449	152	31	3	23	79	43	39	.396	.575	Bats Both	R	.200	305	61	5	2	0	18	15	66	.241	.230

Batters vs. Lefthanded and Righthanded Pitchers

Batter	vs	Avg	AB	H	2B	3B	HR	BI	BB	SO	OBP	SLG
Guzman,E	L	.000	1	0	0	0	0	0	0	0	.000	.000
Bats Left	R	.000	14	0	0	0	0	0	0	4	.000	.000
Gwynn,Tony	L	.324	139	45	5	0	6	26	8	8	.360	.489
Bats Left	R	.346	272	94	22	0	4	36	21	6	.392	.471
Haad,Yamid	L	.000	0	0	0	0	0	0	0	0	.000	.000
Bats Right	R	.000	1	0	0	0	0	0	0	0	.000	.000
Hairston Jr.,J	L	.333	27	9	3	1	1	3	1	6	.357	.630
Bats Right	R	.257	148	38	9	0	3	14	10	18	.317	.378
Halter,Shane	L	.000	0	0	0	0	0	0	0	0	.000	.000
Bats Right	R	.000	0	0	0	0	0	0	0	0	.000	.000
Hamilton,D	L	.286	147	42	3	0	2	9	12	15	.348	.347
Bats Left	R	.327	358	117	16	4	7	36	45	24	.401	.453
Hammonds,J	L	.300	140	42	8	0	8	17	12	30	.359	.529
Bats Right	R	.254	122	31	5	0	9	24	15	34	.333	.516
Hansen,Dave	L	.267	15	4	3	0	0	5	4	2	.450	.467
Bats Left	R	.250	92	23	5	1	2	12	22	18	.397	.391
Hansen,Jed	L	.222	18	4	0	0	0	1	2	9	.300	.222
Bats Right	R	.197	61	12	1	0	3	4	8	23	.286	.361
Harris,Lenny	L	.412	17	7	0	0	1	2	1	0	.444	.588
Bats Left	R	.300	170	51	13	0	0	18	5	7	.318	.376
Haselman,Bill	L	.308	39	12	1	0	1	4	4	7	.372	.410
Bats Right	R	.260	104	27	7	0	3	10	6	19	.300	.413
Hatteberg,S	L	.267	15	4	1	0	0	2	3	1	.389	.333
Bats Left	R	.277	65	18	4	0	1	9	15	13	.415	.385
Hayes,Charlie	L	.197	117	23	4	0	4	23	11	15	.264	.333
Bats Right	R	.211	147	31	5	1	2	25	22	26	.314	.299
Helton,Todd	L	.245	163	40	7	1	4	28	15	25	.319	.374
Bats Left	R	.349	415	145	32	4	31	85	53	52	.424	.670
Hemphill,Bret	L	.125	8	1	0	0	0	2	0	3	.111	.125
Bats Both	R	.154	13	2	0	0	0	0	4	1	.353	.154
Henderson,R	L	.343	105	36	7	0	6	9	28	17	.481	.581
Bats Right	R	.306	333	102	23	0	6	33	54	65	.403	.429
Hermansen,C	L	.278	18	5	1	0	1	1	3	2	.381	.500
Bats Right	R	.214	42	9	2	0	0	0	4	17	.298	.262
Hernandez,C	L	.000	2	0	0	0	0	0	0	0	.000	.000
Bats Right	R	.167	12	2	0	0	0	1	0	0	.167	.167
Hernandez,J	L	.292	168	49	9	1	8	24	18	45	.364	.500
Bats Right	R	.253	340	86	11	1	11	38	34	100	.327	.388
Hernandez,R	L	.357	42	15	3	0	3	12	8	1	.451	.643
Bats Right	R	.245	94	23	4	0	0	9	10	10	.321	.287
Hidalgo,R	L	.224	98	22	6	0	3	17	13	15	.313	.378
Bats Right	R	.228	285	65	19	2	12	39	43	58	.333	.435
Higginson,Bob	L	.265	83	22	1	0	2	10	18	19	.396	.349
Bats Left	R	.231	294	68	17	0	10	36	46	47	.337	.391
Hill,G	L	.358	106	38	5	1	4	16	9	26	.409	.538
Bats Right	R	.259	147	38	4	0	16	39	13	35	.313	.612
Hinch,A.J.	L	.224	49	11	0	0	1	3	1	7	.240	.286
Bats Right	R	.212	156	33	4	1	6	21	10	34	.266	.365
Hocking,Den.	L	.242	128	31	6	1	3	14	7	20	.285	.375
Bats Both	R	.279	258	72	12	1	4	27	15	34	.318	.380

Batter	vs	Avg	AB	H	2B	3B	HR	BI	BB	SO	OBP	SLG
Holbert,Ray	L	.235	17	4	0	0	0	0	0	2	.235	.235
Bats Right	R	.289	83	24	3	0	0	5	8	18	.348	.325
Hollandsworth	L	.310	29	9	0	0	2	6	2	9	.355	.517
Bats Left	R	.280	232	65	12	2	7	26	22	52	.344	.440
Hollins,Dave	L	.250	20	5	1	0	0	0	6	6	.250	.300
Bats Both	R	.215	79	17	4	0	2	6	5	16	.262	.342
Houston,Tyler	L	.207	29	6	2	0	1	2	2	11	.258	.379
Bats Left	R	.227	247	56	8	1	9	28	29	67	.307	.377
Howard,David	L	.226	31	7	2	0	0	1	1	8	.273	.290
Bats Both	R	.196	51	10	2	0	1	5	6	19	.293	.294
Howard,Thom.	L	.351	37	13	2	0	1	7	7	9	.444	.486
Bats Both	R	.278	158	44	8	0	5	21	10	17	.329	.424
Howell,Jack	L	.000	1	0	0	0	0	0	0	1	.000	.000
Bats Left	R	.219	32	7	2	0	1	1	8	8	.375	.375
Hubbard,T	L	.278	54	15	2	0	1	6	7	12	.361	.370
Bats Right	R	.353	51	18	3	0	0	7	6	12	.414	.412
Hughes,Bobby	L	.224	49	11	1	0	2	6	3	15	.269	.367
Bats Right	R	.288	52	15	1	0	1	2	2	13	.315	.365
Hundley,Todd	L	.105	57	6	1	0	0	5	8	25	.227	.123
Bats Left	R	.226	319	72	13	0	24	50	36	88	.307	.492
Hunter,Brian	L	.290	124	36	11	1	4	22	16	30	.379	.492
Bats Right	R	.158	57	9	1	0	2	8	15	10	.342	.281
Hunter,B	L	.186	102	19	2	0	0	1	6	13	.229	.206
Bats Right	R	.243	437	106	11	4	33	78	31	78	.292	.323
Hunter,Torii	L	.295	112	33	4	1	2	12	8	18	.344	.402
Bats Right	R	.239	272	65	13	1	7	23	18	54	.294	.371
Huskey,Butch	L	.327	110	36	3	0	9	29	14	13	.400	.600
Bats Right	R	.264	276	73	12	0	13	48	20	52	.312	.449
Huson,Jeff	L	.182	11	2	0	0	0	0	1	1	.250	.182
Bats Left	R	.266	214	57	7	1	0	18	15	26	.310	.308
Hyers,Tim	L	.375	16	6	2	0	0	1	1	4	.412	.500
Bats Left	R	.185	65	12	2	1	2	11	13	7	.316	.338
Ibanez,Raul	L	.238	21	5	1	0	1	2	4	3	.360	.429
Bats Left	R	.261	188	49	6	0	8	25	13	29	.307	.420
Jackson,D	L	.188	117	22	5	0	2	6	14	34	.275	.282
Bats Right	R	.240	271	65	15	2	7	33	39	71	.339	.387
Jackson,D	L	.351	77	27	6	1	4	15	2	4	.363	.610
Bats Right	R	.194	72	14	3	0	0	1	1	16	.205	.236
Jackson,Ryan	L	.333	9	3	0	0	0	2	0	5	.333	.333
Bats Right	R	.220	59	13	3	0	0	8	6	14	.294	.271
Jaha,John	L	.318	129	41	9	0	11	29	31	34	.451	.643
Bats Right	R	.259	328	85	14	0	24	82	70	95	.400	.521
Javier,Stan	L	.321	109	35	6	0	3	11	6	17	.362	.459
Bats Both	R	.271	288	78	13	2	0	23	32	46	.342	.330
Jefferies,G	L	.149	47	7	2	0	1	3	1	2	.160	.213
Bats Both	R	.215	158	34	6	0	5	15	12	9	.286	.348
Jefferson,R	L	.182	11	2	0	0	1	1	2	3	.308	.455
Bats Left	R	.282	195	55	13	1	4	16	15	51	.340	.421
Jenkins,Geoff	L	.259	85	22	6	0	2	15	6	19	.330	.400
Bats Left	R	.326	362	118	37	3	19	67	29	68	.381	.602

Batters vs. Lefthanded and Righthanded Pitchers

Batter	vs	Avg	AB	H	2B	3B	HR	BI	BB	SO	OBP	SLG
Jennings,R	L	.000	1	0	0	0	0	0	0	1	.000	.000
Bats Left	R	.250	4	1	0	0	0	0	0	1	.250	.250
Jensen,Mar.	L	.286	7	2	2	0	0	0	0	3	.286	.571
Bats Both	R	.222	27	6	3	0	1	1	6	9	.364	.444
Jeter,Derek	L	.282	124	35	6	0	5	18	16	26	.366	.452
Bats Right	R	.366	503	184	31	9	19	84	75	90	.455	.577
Jimenez,D	L	.750	4	3	0	0	0	1	0	1	.750	.750
Bats Both	R	.313	16	5	2	0	0	3	3	3	.421	.438
Johnson,Brian	L	.267	60	16	5	0	3	10	4	13	.313	.500
Bats Right	R	.193	57	11	2	0	2	8	5	18	.258	.333
Johnson,C	L	.355	62	22	1	1	3	9	8	15	.423	.548
Bats Right	R	.234	364	85	18	0	13	45	47	92	.326	.390
Johnson,Lance	L	.188	69	13	0	2	0	2	11	6	.300	.246
Bats Left	R	.278	266	74	11	4	1	19	26	14	.341	.361
Johnson,M	L	.250	36	9	3	0	1	2	4	15	.325	.417
Bats Left	R	.222	171	38	8	0	3	14	32	43	.348	.322
Johnson,Russ	L	.283	60	17	2	0	2	11	12	9	.392	.417
Bats Right	R	.281	96	27	8	0	3	12	8	22	.333	.458
Jones,Andruw	L	.270	141	38	8	2	6	20	21	28	.373	.482
Bats Right	R	.277	451	125	27	3	20	64	55	75	.363	.483
Jones,Chipper	L	.352	142	50	10	0	15	35	27	25	.450	.739
Bats Both	R	.308	425	131	31	1	30	75	99	69	.438	.598
Jones,Jacque	L	.222	36	8	2	0	1	8	0	7	.231	.361
Bats Left	R	.297	286	85	22	2	8	36	17	56	.342	.472
Jones,Terry	L	.167	6	1	1	0	0	1	0	0	.167	.333
Bats Both	R	.281	57	16	0	1	0	2	3	14	.317	.316
Jordan,Brian	L	.331	124	41	11	0	6	32	10	23	.380	.565
Bats Right	R	.270	452	122	17	4	17	83	41	58	.337	.438
Jordan,Kevin	L	.301	123	37	8	0	2	19	7	10	.341	.415
Bats Right	R	.277	224	62	9	3	2	32	17	24	.339	.371
Joyner,Wally	L	.247	81	20	2	2	3	16	10	11	.340	.432
Bats Left	R	.248	242	60	12	0	2	27	48	43	.370	.322
Justice,David	L	.248	101	25	1	0	5	19	16	30	.353	.406
Bats Left	R	.299	328	98	17	0	16	69	78	60	.431	.497
Kapler,Gabe	L	.280	75	21	5	2	4	11	8	11	.349	.560
Bats Right	R	.238	341	81	17	2	14	38	34	63	.307	.422
Karros,Eric	L	.308	146	45	7	0	11	34	21	27	.391	.582
Bats Right	R	.303	432	131	33	0	23	78	32	92	.351	.539
Kelly,Mike	L	.000	0	0	0	0	0	0	0	0	.000	.000
Bats Right	R	.500	2	1	1	0	0	1	0	0	.500	1.000
Kelly,Pat	L	.333	24	8	3	0	0	6	1	5	.321	.458
Bats Right	R	.250	92	23	4	0	6	14	9	18	.317	.489
Kelly,Roberto	L	.358	95	34	8	0	2	14	9	16	.421	.505
Bats Right	R	.272	195	53	9	1	6	23	12	41	.322	.421
Kendall,Jason	L	.271	59	16	2	0	4	9	12	6	.392	.508
Bats Right	R	.348	221	77	18	3	4	32	26	26	.438	.511
Kennedy,Ad.	L	.250	12	3	3	0	0	4	0	2	.308	.500
Bats Left	R	.256	90	23	7	1	1	12	3	6	.281	.389
Kent,Jeff	L	.273	132	36	12	1	7	30	15	30	.344	.538
Bats Right	R	.296	379	112	28	1	16	71	46	82	.373	.501
King,Jeff	L	.231	13	3	0	0	1	3	3	2	.353	.462
Bats Right	R	.237	59	14	2	0	2	8	12	8	.392	.373
Kingsale,Gene	L	.250	12	3	1	0	0	0	2	1	.357	.333
Bats Both	R	.247	73	18	1	0	0	7	3	12	.291	.260
Kinkade,Mike	L	.211	19	4	1	0	1	4	3	3	.318	.421
Bats Right	R	.185	27	5	1	1	1	2	0	6	.241	.407
Klassen,Danny	L	1.000	1	1	0	0	0	0	0	0	1.000	1.000
Bats Right	R	.000	0	0	0	0	0	0	0	0	.000	.000
Klesko,Ryan	L	.102	49	5	0	0	1	7	3	16	.179	.163
Bats Left	R	.324	355	115	28	2	20	73	50	53	.402	.583
Knoblauch,C	L	.272	114	31	11	1	4	17	20	12	.375	.491
Bats Right	R	.297	489	145	25	3	14	51	63	45	.398	.446
Knorr,Randy	L	.278	18	5	1	0	0	0	0	3	.278	.333
Bats Right	R	.000	12	0	0	0	0	0	1	5	.077	.000
Konerko,Paul	L	.319	116	37	3	2	5	23	8	16	.363	.509
Bats Right	R	.287	397	114	28	2	19	58	37	52	.349	.511
Koskie,Corey	L	.267	45	12	1	0	0	5	6	11	.358	.289
Bats Left	R	.316	297	94	20	0	11	53	34	61	.392	.495
Kotsay,Mark	L	.272	81	22	3	3	1	11	5	10	.314	.420
Bats Left	R	.271	414	112	20	6	7	39	24	40	.304	.399
Kreuter,Chad	L	.279	43	12	1	0	2	5	4	5	.340	.442
Bats Both	R	.217	281	61	14	0	3	30	30	60	.304	.299
Laker,Tim	L	.500	4	2	0	0	0	0	0	1	.500	.500
Bats Right	R	.200	5	1	0	0	0	0	0	1	.200	.200
Lamb,David	L	.167	24	4	1	0	0	5	3	3	.259	.208
Bats Both	R	.240	100	24	4	1	1	8	7	15	.290	.330
Lampkin,Tom	L	.296	27	8	0	0	0	4	0	6	.296	.296
Bats Left	R	.291	179	52	11	2	9	30	13	26	.352	.525
Lankford,Ray	L	.237	114	27	3	0	2	16	9	33	.298	.316
Bats Left	R	.331	308	102	29	1	13	47	40	77	.409	.558
Lansing,Mike	L	.340	53	18	5	0	1	5	4	9	.386	.491
Bats Right	R	.293	92	27	4	0	3	10	3	13	.320	.435
Larkin,Barry	L	.259	147	38	7	0	5	19	21	11	.349	.408
Bats Right	R	.305	436	133	23	4	7	56	72	46	.404	.424
LaRue,Jason	L	.162	37	6	2	0	2	5	4	18	.262	.378
Bats Right	R	.245	53	13	5	0	1	5	7	14	.344	.396
Latham,Chris	L	.000	3	0	0	0	0	0	0	3	.000	.000
Bats Both	R	.105	19	2	0	0	0	3	0	9	.095	.105
Lawton,Matt	L	.290	100	29	4	0	2	15	9	15	.357	.390
Bats Left	R	.248	306	76	14	0	5	39	48	27	.352	.343
Ledee,Ricky	L	.282	39	11	0	0	2	4	3	14	.333	.462
Bats Left	R	.275	211	58	12	5	7	36	25	59	.349	.479
Ledesma,Aa.	L	.262	65	17	4	0	0	7	7	7	.342	.323
Bats Right	R	.266	229	61	11	0	0	23	7	28	.294	.314
Lee,Carlos	L	.301	93	28	5	0	3	9	1	17	.302	.452
Bats Right	R	.291	399	116	27	2	13	75	12	55	.314	.466
Lee,Derek	L	.234	47	11	4	0	1	5	4	18	.294	.383
Bats Right	R	.199	171	34	5	1	4	15	13	52	.254	.310
Lee,Travis	L	.216	102	22	4	0	3	18	12	21	.293	.343
Bats Left	R	.245	273	67	12	2	6	32	46	29	.353	.370

Batters vs. Lefthanded and Righthanded Pitchers

Batter	vs	Avg	AB	H	2B	3B	HR	BI	BB	SO	OBP	SLG
Leius,Scott	L	.212	33	7	0	0	1	5	1	5	.235	.303
Bats Right	R	.195	41	8	1	0	0	5	3	3	.250	.220
Lennon,P	L	.200	5	1	0	0	0	1	0	2	.200	.200
Bats Right	R	.208	24	5	2	0	1	5	2	10	.296	.417
Levis,Jesse	L	.333	3	1	0	0	0	1	1	0	.600	.333
Bats Left	R	.130	23	3	0	0	0	2	0	6	.130	.130
Lewis,Darren	L	.229	140	32	2	1	1	14	8	11	.270	.279
Bats Right	R	.245	330	81	12	5	1	26	37	41	.327	.321
Lewis,Mark	L	.273	55	15	4	0	1	6	3	7	.310	.400
Bats Right	R	.246	118	29	12	0	5	22	4	17	.266	.475
Leyritz,Jim	L	.239	88	21	2	1	5	15	17	19	.364	.455
Bats Right	R	.232	112	26	7	0	3	11	11	35	.317	.375
Lieberthal,M	L	.377	122	46	9	0	10	29	16	15	.443	.697
Bats Right	R	.276	388	107	24	1	21	67	28	71	.337	.505
Liefer,Jeff	L	.125	8	1	1	0	0	2	1	3	.222	.250
Bats Left	R	.257	105	27	6	1	0	12	7	25	.301	.333
Liniak,Cole	L	.500	2	1	0	0	0	0	0	1	.500	.500
Bats Right	R	.222	27	6	2	0	0	2	1	3	.250	.296
Lockhart,K	L	.083	12	1	0	0	0	2	4	5	.313	.083
Bats Left	R	.275	149	41	3	1	1	19	15	16	.339	.329
LoDuca,Paul	L	.278	54	15	0	0	2	6	8	5	.375	.389
Bats Right	R	.171	41	7	1	0	1	5	2	4	.222	.268
Lofton,Kenny	L	.224	116	26	4	0	0	5	25	31	.364	.259
Bats Left	R	.327	349	114	24	6	7	34	54	53	.420	.490
Lomasney,S	L	.000	1	0	0	0	0	0	0	1	.000	.000
Bats Right	R	.000	1	0	0	0	0	0	0	1	.000	.000
Lombard,G	L	.333	3	1	0	0	0	0	0	0	.333	.333
Bats Left	R	.333	3	1	0	0	0	0	1	2	.500	.333
Long,Terrence	L	.000	0	0	0	0	0	0	0	0	.000	.000
Bats Left	R	.000	3	0	0	0	0	0	0	2	.000	.000
Lopez,Javy	L	.340	53	18	3	0	5	13	5	9	.397	.679
Bats Right	R	.311	193	60	15	1	6	32	15	32	.370	.492
Lopez,Luis	L	.174	23	4	0	0	1	4	2	2	.231	.304
Bats Both	R	.222	81	18	4	0	1	9	10	31	.330	.309
Lopez,Mendy	L	1.000	2	2	0	0	0	2	0	0	1.000	1.000
Bats Right	R	.333	18	6	0	1	0	1	0	5	.368	.444
Loretta,Mark	L	.300	160	48	11	1	0	17	21	15	.383	.381
Bats Right	R	.286	427	122	23	4	5	50	31	44	.343	.393
Lovullo,Torey	L	.263	19	5	0	0	1	3	0	4	.263	.421
Bats Right	R	.158	19	3	0	0	1	2	3	7	.273	.316
Lowell,Mike	L	.250	72	18	2	0	6	14	13	13	.356	.528
Bats Right	R	.254	236	60	13	0	6	33	13	56	.304	.386
Lowery,T	L	.231	52	12	4	0	1	3	6	13	.310	.365
Bats Right	R	.271	133	36	11	1	1	14	13	40	.338	.391
Luke,Matt	L	.111	9	1	0	0	1	1	0	5	.111	.444
Bats Left	R	.381	21	8	0	0	2	5	2	5	.435	.667
Mabry,John	L	.250	28	7	1	0	0	2	1	11	.276	.286
Bats Left	R	.244	234	57	13	0	9	31	19	49	.299	.415
Macfarlane,M	L	.319	47	15	7	0	1	7	1	7	.340	.532
Bats Right	R	.223	179	40	10	0	3	24	12	45	.267	.330

Batter	vs	Avg	AB	H	2B	3B	HR	BI	BB	SO	OBP	SLG
Machado,R	L	.000	6	0	0	0	0	0	0	3	.000	.000
Bats Right	R	.250	16	4	1	0	0	0	2	3	.333	.313
Macias,Jose	L	.000	0	0	0	0	0	0	0	0	.000	.000
Bats Both	R	.250	4	1	0	0	1	2	0	1	.250	1.000
Magadan,Dave	L	.211	38	8	1	0	0	3	11	5	.388	.237
Bats Left	R	.286	210	60	11	1	2	27	34	31	.375	.376
Magee,Wen.	L	.500	6	3	1	0	2	4	1	2	.571	1.667
Bats Right	R	.250	8	2	0	0	0	1	0	2	.250	.250
Manto,Jeff	L	.100	10	1	0	0	0	0	7	6	.471	.100
Bats Right	R	.217	23	5	0	0	1	2	6	9	.379	.348
Manwaring,K	L	.316	38	12	2	0	1	7	10	11	.460	.447
Bats Right	R	.293	99	29	5	1	1	7	2	12	.333	.394
Marrero,Eli	L	.203	74	15	3	0	1	7	6	16	.263	.284
Bats Right	R	.189	243	46	10	1	5	27	12	40	.228	.300
Martin,Al	L	.242	120	29	6	1	2	9	10	35	.305	.358
Bats Left	R	.287	421	121	30	7	22	54	39	84	.346	.549
Martin,N	L	.000	3	0	0	0	0	0	2	1	.400	.000
Bats Right	R	.250	24	6	2	0	0	0	2	3	.357	.333
Martinez,Dave	L	.239	88	21	2	0	1	14	9	22	.310	.295
Bats Left	R	.293	426	125	23	5	5	52	51	54	.372	.406
Martinez,E	L	.358	109	39	10	0	10	24	27	20	.478	.725
Bats Right	R	.331	393	130	25	1	14	62	70	79	.438	.506
Martinez,F	L	.000	1	0	0	0	0	0	0	0	.000	.000
Bats Both	R	.167	6	1	0	0	0	0	0	0	.167	.167
Martinez,M	L	.274	106	29	6	1	0	8	8	13	.322	.349
Bats Right	R	.231	225	52	6	6	2	18	9	38	.258	.338
Martinez,R	L	.259	54	14	3	0	2	7	3	9	.298	.426
Bats Right	R	.267	90	24	3	0	3	12	11	8	.343	.400
Martinez,S	L	.200	5	1	0	0	0	0	0	1	.200	.200
Bats Left	R	.160	25	4	0	0	1	1	0	10	.160	.280
Martinez,Tino	L	.261	180	47	7	1	7	31	14	33	.315	.428
Bats Left	R	.264	409	108	20	1	21	74	55	53	.353	.472
Mateo,Ruben	L	.350	20	7	2	1	1	4	2	4	.409	.700
Bats Right	R	.216	102	22	7	0	4	14	2	24	.238	.402
Matheny,Mike	L	.164	55	9	1	0	2	8	5	7	.246	.291
Bats Right	R	.241	108	26	5	0	1	9	7	30	.284	.315
Matos,Pascual	L	.000	3	0	0	0	0	0	0	0	.000	.000
Bats Right	R	.200	5	1	0	0	0	2	0	1	.200	.200
Matthews Jr.,G	L	.050	20	1	0	0	0	2	3	6	.174	.050
Bats Both	R	.438	16	7	0	0	0	5	6	3	.591	.438
May,Derrick	L	.000	0	0	0	0	0	0	0	0	.000	.000
Bats Left	R	.265	49	13	0	0	4	12	4	6	.315	.510
Mayne,Brent	L	.286	56	16	6	0	0	8	8	14	.388	.393
Bats Left	R	.305	266	81	26	0	2	31	35	51	.389	.425
McCracken,Q	L	.257	35	9	0	0	0	2	6	5	.366	.257
Bats Both	R	.248	113	28	6	1	1	16	8	18	.301	.345
McDonald,J	L	.222	54	12	0	0	1	4	5	12	.288	.278
Bats Both	R	.203	133	27	2	1	2	4	20	36	.318	.278
McDonald,Jo.	L	.286	7	2	0	0	0	0	0	2	.286	.286
Bats Right	R	.357	14	5	0	0	0	0	0	1	.357	.357

Batters vs. Lefthanded and Righthanded Pitchers

Batter	vs	Avg	AB	H	2B	3B	HR	BI	BB	SO	OBP	SLG	Batter	vs	Avg	AB	H	2B	3B	HR	BI	BB	SO	OBP	SLG
McEwing,Joe	L	.292	154	45	12	0	2	11	14	28	.353	.409	Mordecai,Mike	L	.254	67	17	3	0	2	7	6	6	.311	.388
Bats Right	R	.267	359	96	16	4	7	33	27	59	.324	.393	Bats Right	R	.226	159	36	7	2	3	18	14	25	.291	.352
McGee,Willie	L	.174	46	8	1	0	0	5	4	13	.235	.196	Morris,Hal	L	.286	21	6	3	0	0	3	1	4	.318	.429
Bats Both	R	.267	225	60	6	0	0	15	13	47	.305	.293	Bats Left	R	.284	81	23	6	0	0	13	9	17	.356	.358
McGriff,Fred	L	.236	148	35	5	1	8	25	18	42	.319	.446	Morris,Warren	L	.336	110	37	4	2	2	17	10	15	.393	.464
Bats Left	R	.339	381	129	25	0	24	79	68	65	.436	.593	Bats Left	R	.274	401	110	16	1	13	56	49	73	.352	.416
McGuire,Ryan	L	.278	18	5	3	0	0	2	2	4	.350	.444	Mouton,James	L	.281	57	16	5	1	0	7	8	13	.373	.404
Bats Left	R	.213	122	26	4	2	2	16	25	29	.347	.328	Bats Right	R	.246	65	16	0	0	2	6	10	18	.355	.338
McGwire,Mark	L	.254	122	31	7	0	16	30	36	32	.425	.705	Mouton,Lyle	L	.250	8	2	0	0	1	2	2	1	.400	.625
Bats Right	R	.286	399	114	14	1	49	117	97	109	.423	.694	Bats Right	R	.111	9	1	1	0	0	1	0	2	.111	.222
McLemore,Ma.	L	.163	104	17	3	0	1	4	13	22	.252	.221	Mueller,Bill	L	.248	113	28	4	0	2	14	15	13	.338	.336
Bats Both	R	.299	462	138	17	7	5	41	70	57	.388	.398	Bats Both	R	.306	301	92	20	0	0	22	50	39	.407	.372
McRae,Brian	L	.253	91	23	4	2	1	9	11	16	.340	.374	Murray,Calvin	L	.167	12	2	1	0	0	2	0	2	.167	.250
Bats Both	R	.208	312	65	13	0	11	39	46	70	.323	.356	Bats Right	R	.429	7	3	1	0	0	3	2	2	.556	.571
Meares,Pat	L	.341	44	15	1	0	0	3	3	6	.396	.364	Myers,Greg	L	.241	29	7	1	0	0	3	1	4	.267	.276
Bats Right	R	.277	47	13	3	0	0	4	6	14	.370	.340	Bats Left	R	.269	171	46	5	0	5	21	25	26	.360	.386
Meluskey,M	L	.333	6	2	1	0	0	1	0	2	.333	.500	Nevin,Phil	L	.270	137	37	8	0	11	38	27	34	.383	.569
Bats Both	R	.185	27	5	0	0	1	2	5	4	.313	.296	Bats Right	R	.268	246	66	19	0	13	47	24	48	.333	.504
Menechino,F	L	1.000	1	1	0	0	0	0	0	0	1.000	1.000	Newhan,David	L	.167	6	1	0	0	0	0	0	1	.167	.167
Bats Right	R	.125	8	1	0	0	0	0	0	4	.125	.125	Bats Left	R	.135	37	5	1	0	2	6	1	10	.158	.324
Merced,O	L	.300	10	3	1	0	0	1	2	2	.417	.400	Nieves,Jose	L	.311	45	14	4	0	1	4	4	7	.367	.467
Bats Left	R	.266	184	49	11	1	8	25	24	25	.349	.467	Bats Right	R	.228	136	31	5	1	1	14	4	18	.265	.301
Merloni,Lou	L	.184	49	9	3	0	1	7	2	7	.241	.306	Nilsson,Dave	L	.253	91	23	2	0	5	15	14	26	.352	.440
Bats Right	R	.299	77	23	4	0	0	6	6	9	.349	.351	Bats Left	R	.329	252	83	17	1	16	47	39	38	.418	.595
Meyers,Chad	L	.143	42	6	3	0	0	0	2	9	.200	.214	Nixon,Otis	L	.259	27	7	0	0	0	2	3	2	.333	.259
Bats Right	R	.270	100	27	6	0	0	4	7	18	.330	.330	Bats Both	R	.194	124	24	2	1	0	6	20	13	.303	.226
Mientkiewicz,D	L	.256	39	10	3	0	0	8	4	10	.341	.333	Nixon,Trot	L	.116	43	5	2	0	1	2	3	12	.204	.233
Bats Left	R	.226	288	65	18	3	2	24	39	41	.322	.330	Bats Left	R	.290	338	98	20	5	14	50	50	63	.376	.503
Mieske,Matt	L	.354	82	29	4	0	6	17	5	8	.391	.622	Norton,Greg	L	.203	74	15	3	0	0	3	11	20	.314	.243
Bats Right	R	.250	68	17	1	0	3	12	3	23	.274	.397	Bats Both	R	.265	362	96	23	0	16	47	58	73	.366	.461
Millar,Kevin	L	.290	93	27	5	1	3	19	14	20	.373	.462	Nunez,Ab.	L	.235	81	19	2	0	0	4	4	21	.271	.259
Bats Right	R	.283	258	73	12	3	6	48	26	44	.358	.422	Bats Both	R	.213	178	38	6	0	0	13	24	33	.310	.247
Miller,Damian	L	.320	103	33	12	0	5	17	8	22	.363	.583	Nunnally,Jon	L	.000	0	0	0	0	0	0	0	0	.000	.000
Bats Right	R	.244	193	47	7	0	6	30	11	56	.290	.373	Bats Left	R	.286	14	4	1	0	0	1	0	6	.286	.357
Minor,Ryan	L	.200	15	3	0	0	1	1	1	2	.250	.400	O'Brien,C	L	.267	15	4	0	0	1	4	0	2	.250	.467
Bats Right	R	.193	109	21	7	0	2	9	7	41	.239	.312	Bats Right	R	.043	47	2	0	0	0	0	1	10	.100	.043
Mirabelli,D	L	.240	25	6	3	0	1	1	4	6	.345	.480	O'Leary,Troy	L	.346	156	54	9	2	4	31	18	20	.415	.506
Bats Right	R	.258	62	16	3	0	0	9	5	19	.319	.306	Bats Left	R	.257	440	113	27	2	24	72	38	71	.318	.491
Molina,Ben	L	.263	19	5	1	0	1	5	2	1	.333	.474	O'Neill,Paul	L	.190	158	30	6	1	3	26	12	34	.246	.297
Bats Right	R	.256	82	21	4	0	0	5	4	5	.307	.305	Bats Left	R	.319	439	140	33	3	16	84	54	55	.390	.517
Molina,Jose	L	.200	5	1	0	0	0	1	0	2	.200	.200	Ochoa,Alex	L	.319	138	44	9	2	5	25	24	22	.418	.522
Bats Right	R	.286	14	4	1	0	0	0	2	2	.375	.357	Bats Right	R	.281	139	39	7	1	3	15	21	21	.390	.410
Monahan,Sh.	L	1.000	1	1	0	0	0	0	0	0	1.000	1.000	Offerman,Jose	L	.268	138	37	7	1	3	18	23	23	.377	.399
Bats Left	R	.071	14	1	0	0	0	0	0	6	.071	.071	Bats Both	R	.301	448	135	30	10	5	51	73	56	.395	.446
Mondesi,Raul	L	.273	139	38	7	1	6	20	27	23	.389	.468	Olerud,John	L	.247	166	41	7	0	2	20	31	24	.380	.325
Bats Right	R	.247	462	114	22	4	27	79	44	111	.314	.487	Bats Left	R	.318	415	132	32	0	17	76	94	42	.447	.518
Mora,Melvin	L	.118	17	2	0	0	0	1	2	2	.211	.118	Oliver,Joe	L	.214	42	9	3	0	1	6	4	12	.277	.357
Bats Right	R	.214	14	3	0	0	0	0	2	5	.353	.214	Bats Right	R	.196	92	18	5	0	0	7	6	21	.242	.250
Morandini,M	L	.155	97	15	4	2	0	2	11	16	.255	.237	Ordaz,Luis	L	.000	5	0	0	0	0	0	0	1	.000	.000
Bats Left	R	.265	359	95	14	3	4	35	37	45	.337	.354	Bats Right	R	.250	4	1	0	0	0	2	1	1	.400	.250

Batters vs. Lefthanded and Righthanded Pitchers

Batter	vs	Avg	AB	H	2B	3B	HR	BI	BB	SO	OBP	SLG	Batter	vs	Avg	AB	H	2B	3B	HR	BI	BB	SO	OBP	SLG
Ordonez,M	L	.320	103	33	7	0	3	15	11	14	.388	.476	Polanco,P	L	.346	81	28	6	1	1	7	7	7	.393	.481
Bats Right	R	.298	521	155	27	3	27	102	36	50	.340	.516	Bats Right	R	.237	139	33	3	2	0	12	8	17	.277	.288
Ordonez,Rey	L	.231	130	30	5	0	0	14	12	15	.295	.269	Polonia,Luis	L	.217	23	5	0	0	1	3	2	3	.280	.348
Bats Right	R	.267	390	104	19	2	1	46	37	44	.327	.333	Bats Left	R	.332	310	103	21	8	9	29	14	29	.363	.539
Orie,Kevin	L	.263	57	15	4	0	1	3	5	11	.323	.386	Porter,Bo	L	.133	15	2	1	0	0	0	1	7	.188	.200
Bats Right	R	.251	183	46	12	0	5	26	17	32	.322	.399	Bats Right	R	.273	11	3	0	0	0	0	1	6	.333	.273
Ortiz,David	L	.000	2	0	0	0	0	0	0	1	.000	.000	Posada,Jorge	L	.303	99	30	6	1	4	18	7	19	.349	.505
Bats Left	R	.000	18	0	0	0	0	0	5	11	.217	.000	Bats Both	R	.225	280	63	13	1	8	39	46	72	.338	.364
Osik,Keith	L	.213	61	13	2	0	0	6	1	10	.234	.246	Pose,Scott	L	.462	13	6	1	0	0	1	2	2	.533	.538
Bats Right	R	.170	106	18	1	1	2	7	10	20	.241	.255	Bats Left	R	.266	124	33	2	0	0	11	19	20	.361	.282
Otanez,Willis	L	.327	52	17	6	0	0	6	3	11	.364	.442	Powell,Dante	L	.111	18	2	2	0	0	1	2	4	.200	.222
Bats Right	R	.206	155	32	5	0	7	18	12	35	.271	.374	Bats Right	R	.286	7	2	1	0	0	0	0	2	.286	.429
Owens,Eric	L	.231	130	30	7	1	4	21	16	15	.318	.392	Pratt,Todd	L	.279	43	12	1	0	2	8	4	12	.347	.442
Bats Right	R	.281	310	87	15	2	5	40	22	35	.331	.390	Bats Right	R	.299	97	29	3	0	1	13	11	20	.378	.361
Palmeiro,O	L	.200	35	7	0	0	0	2	5	8	.341	.200	Prince,Tom	L	.000	3	0	0	0	0	0	1	1	.250	.000
Bats Left	R	.287	282	81	12	1	1	21	34	22	.368	.348	Bats Right	R	.333	3	1	0	0	0	0	0	0	.333	.333
Palmeiro,R	L	.274	146	40	8	0	11	40	16	23	.345	.555	Pritchett,C	L	.000	4	0	0	0	0	0	0	1	.000	.000
Bats Left	R	.341	419	143	22	1	36	108	81	46	.444	.656	Bats Left	R	.171	41	7	1	0	1	2	2	8	.205	.268
Palmer,Dean	L	.390	100	39	6	0	10	24	7	20	.432	.750	Quinn,Mark	L	.333	9	3	0	0	1	1	1	4	.400	.667
Bats Right	R	.235	460	108	19	2	28	76	50	133	.319	.467	Bats Right	R	.333	51	17	4	1	5	17	3	7	.382	.745
Paquette,C	L	.204	54	11	1	0	3	10	3	14	.241	.389	Raines,Tim	L	.234	64	15	3	0	3	11	12	10	.351	.422
Bats Right	R	.330	103	34	5	0	7	27	3	24	.346	.583	Bats Both	R	.197	71	14	2	0	1	6	14	7	.326	.268
Paul,Josh	L	.000	2	0	0	0	0	0	0	0	.000	.000	Ramirez,Alex	L	.286	49	14	3	0	2	10	2	12	.314	.469
Bats Right	R	.250	16	4	1	0	0	1	0	4	.250	.313	Bats Right	R	.313	48	15	3	1	1	8	1	14	.340	.479
Payton,Jay	L	.167	6	1	1	0	0	1	0	2	.167	.333	Ramirez,A	L	.200	10	2	0	0	0	2	0	1	.182	.200
Bats Right	R	.500	2	1	0	0	0	0	0	0	.667	.500	Bats Right	R	.174	46	8	2	1	0	5	6	8	.269	.261
Pena,Angel	L	.231	52	12	0	0	4	15	6	12	.300	.462	Ramirez,Julio	L	.083	12	1	0	0	0	0	1	4	.154	.083
Bats Right	R	.191	68	13	6	0	0	6	6	12	.257	.279	Bats Right	R	.222	9	2	1	0	0	2	0	2	.222	.333
Perez,Eddie	L	.267	101	27	7	0	1	6	8	15	.318	.366	Ramirez,Man.	L	.383	115	44	9	1	8	38	24	25	.493	.687
Bats Right	R	.240	208	50	10	0	6	24	9	25	.289	.375	Bats Right	R	.319	407	130	25	2	36	127	72	106	.427	.656
Perez,Eduardo	L	.375	16	6	2	0	0	4	5	1	.524	.500	Randa,Joe	L	.356	101	36	9	4	1	10	8	11	.393	.554
Bats Right	R	.313	16	5	0	0	1	5	2	5	.389	.500	Bats Right	R	.306	527	161	27	4	15	74	42	69	.358	.457
Perez,Neifi	L	.230	209	48	7	2	6	22	7	23	.257	.368	Reboulet,Jeff	L	.235	51	12	2	0	0	2	10	5	.361	.275
Bats Both	R	.301	481	145	20	9	6	48	21	31	.329	.418	Bats Right	R	.126	103	13	2	0	0	2	23	24	.297	.146
Perry,Herbert	L	.242	62	15	2	0	1	3	5	20	.309	.323	Redmond,Mike	L	.304	92	28	3	0	1	11	15	14	.407	.370
Bats Right	R	.259	147	38	8	1	5	29	11	22	.339	.429	Bats Right	R	.300	150	45	6	0	0	16	11	20	.364	.340
Petersen,C	L	.200	10	2	0	0	0	2	0	2	.200	.200	Reed,Jeff	L	.162	37	6	1	0	1	7	3	16	.225	.270
Bats Right	R	.000	3	0	0	0	0	0	2	1	.400	.000	Bats Left	R	.274	219	60	15	2	2	21	42	42	.395	.388
Petrick,Ben	L	.333	12	4	0	0	0	0	2	1	.429	.333	Reese,Pokey	L	.295	146	43	11	1	3	13	13	24	.350	.445
Bats Right	R	.320	50	16	3	0	4	12	8	12	.414	.620	Bats Right	R	.282	439	124	26	4	7	39	22	57	.323	.408
Phillips,J.R.	L	.000	1	0	0	0	0	0	0	0	.000	.000	Relaford,Desi	L	.250	44	11	3	0	0	7	5	5	.340	.318
Bats Left	R	.237	38	9	4	0	2	4	0	13	.256	.500	Bats Both	R	.240	167	40	8	2	1	19	14	29	.317	.329
Phillips,Tony	L	.196	92	18	7	1	0	3	16	15	.333	.293	Renteria,E	L	.250	140	35	11	1	2	16	22	19	.354	.386
Bats Both	R	.258	314	81	17	3	15	46	55	79	.370	.475	Bats Right	R	.283	445	126	25	1	9	47	31	63	.327	.404
Piazza,Mike	L	.298	131	39	4	0	11	27	21	12	.392	.580	Rios,Armando	L	.269	26	7	2	0	2	8	5	5	.406	.577
Bats Right	R	.305	403	123	21	0	29	97	30	58	.350	.573	Bats Left	R	.339	124	42	7	0	5	21	19	30	.424	.516
Pickering,C	L	.000	0	0	0	0	0	0	0	0	.000	.000	Ripken Jr.,C	L	.327	49	16	5	0	2	5	3	5	.365	.551
Bats Left	R	.125	40	5	1	0	1	5	11	16	.314	.225	Bats Right	R	.343	283	97	22	0	16	52	10	26	.368	.590
Pierzynski,A	L	.000	4	0	0	0	0	0	0	2	.000	.000	Rivera,Ruben	L	.200	140	28	9	0	8	18	16	48	.280	.436
Bats Left	R	.333	18	6	2	0	0	3	1	2	.400	.444	Bats Right	R	.192	271	52	7	1	15	30	39	95	.302	.391

Batters vs. Lefthanded and Righthanded Pitchers

Batter	vs	Avg	AB	H	2B	3B	HR	BI	BB	SO	OBP	SLG	Batter	vs	Avg	AB	H	2B	3B	HR	BI	BB	SO	OBP	SLG
Roberts,David	L	.222	36	8	2	0	0	1	2	6	.256	.278	Shave,Jon	L	.346	26	9	3	0	0	6	2	6	.433	.462
Bats Left	R	.243	107	26	2	0	2	11	7	10	.289	.318	Bats Right	R	.255	47	12	1	0	0	3	3	11	.300	.277
Robinson,K	L	.000	0	0	0	0	0	0	0	0	.000	.000	Sheets,Andy	L	.214	70	15	3	0	2	7	6	14	.273	.343
Bats Left	R	.000	1	0	0	0	0	0	0	1	.000	.000	Bats Right	R	.190	174	33	7	0	1	22	8	45	.220	.247
Rodriguez,A	L	.277	112	31	4	0	7	17	13	19	.352	.500	Sheffield,G	L	.336	146	49	7	0	8	33	26	9	.434	.548
Bats Right	R	.287	390	112	21	0	35	94	43	90	.359	.610	Bats Right	R	.288	403	116	13	0	26	68	75	55	.398	.514
Rodriguez,H	L	.237	139	33	5	0	8	18	16	42	.316	.446	Sheldon,Scott	L	.000	0	0	0	0	0	0	0	0	.000	.000
Bats Left	R	.334	308	103	24	0	18	69	40	71	.410	.588	Bats Right	R	.000	1	0	0	0	0	0	0	0	.000	.000
Rodriguez,I	L	.325	114	37	3	0	6	20	8	12	.366	.509	Shumpert,T	L	.395	86	34	8	1	3	8	12	15	.475	.616
Bats Right	R	.333	486	162	26	1	29	93	16	52	.353	.570	Bats Right	R	.324	176	57	18	2	7	29	19	26	.383	.568
Rodriguez,Liu	L	.273	22	6	1	1	0	1	6	4	.484	.409	Silvestri,D	L	.000	6	0	0	0	0	0	0	1	.000	.000
Bats Both	R	.225	71	16	1	1	1	11	6	7	.286	.310	Bats Both	R	.200	5	1	1	0	0	1	0	0	.200	.400
Rolen,Scott	L	.330	91	30	8	0	9	22	21	26	.452	.714	Simmons,Brian	L	.160	25	4	1	0	0	2	1	5	.192	.200
Bats Right	R	.252	330	83	20	1	17	55	46	88	.343	.473	Bats Both	R	.248	101	25	2	3	4	15	8	25	.303	.446
Roskos,John	L	.500	4	2	2	0	0	1	0	1	.500	1.000	Simms,Mike	L	.000	0	0	0	0	0	0	0	0	.000	.000
Bats Right	R	.000	8	0	0	0	0	0	1	6	.111	.000	Bats Right	R	.500	2	1	0	0	0	0	0	1	.500	.500
Ryan,Rob	L	.500	2	1	0	0	0	0	0	1	.500	.500	Simon,Randall	L	.222	18	4	1	0	1	4	0	2	.222	.444
Bats Left	R	.222	27	6	1	0	2	5	1	7	.250	.481	Bats Left	R	.325	200	65	15	0	4	21	17	23	.379	.460
Sadler,Donnie	L	.172	29	5	2	0	0	0	3	10	.250	.241	Singleton,C	L	.408	76	31	5	1	3	15	4	9	.432	.618
Bats Right	R	.321	78	25	3	1	0	4	2	10	.338	.385	Bats Left	R	.281	420	118	26	5	14	57	18	36	.309	.467
Saenz,Olmedo	L	.297	111	33	9	0	3	16	9	22	.375	.459	Smith,Bobby	L	.167	42	7	0	0	0	2	7	18	.286	.167
Bats Right	R	.257	144	37	9	0	8	25	13	25	.353	.486	Bats Right	R	.185	157	29	4	1	3	17	9	46	.232	.280
Salmon,Tim	L	.301	73	22	4	0	2	15	18	18	.430	.438	Snow,J.T.	L	.231	169	39	6	1	3	23	18	46	.313	.331
Bats Right	R	.257	280	72	20	2	15	54	45	64	.356	.504	Bats Left	R	.292	401	117	19	1	21	75	68	75	.394	.501
Sanchez,Rey	L	.326	95	31	3	2	0	8	4	7	.354	.400	Sojo,Luis	L	.348	23	8	2	0	1	4	0	2	.348	.565
Bats Right	R	.286	384	110	15	4	2	48	18	41	.323	.362	Bats Right	R	.231	104	24	4	0	1	12	4	15	.259	.298
Sanders,A	L	.286	7	2	1	0	0	2	0	2	.286	.429	Soriano,A	L	.250	4	1	0	0	1	1	0	1	.250	1.000
Bats Right	R	.000	0	0	0	0	0	0	0	0	.000	.000	Bats Right	R	.000	4	0	0	0	0	0	0	2	.000	.000
Sanders,R	L	.303	142	43	9	1	8	16	22	31	.396	.549	Sorrento,Paul	L	.289	38	11	2	0	2	5	6	11	.400	.500
Bats Right	R	.277	336	93	15	6	18	56	43	77	.368	.518	Bats Left	R	.227	256	58	12	1	9	37	43	90	.343	.387
Sanford,C	L	.000	0	0	0	0	0	0	0	0	.000	.000	Sosa,Juan	L	.000	3	0	0	0	0	0	1	2	.250	.000
Bats Left	R	.250	8	2	0	0	0	2	0	1	.250	.250	Bats Right	R	.333	6	2	0	0	0	0	1	0	.429	.333
Santangelo,F	L	.280	132	37	8	1	2	12	29	30	.438	.402	Sosa,Sammy	L	.313	163	51	9	1	18	37	23	46	.396	.712
Bats Right	R	.238	122	29	9	2	1	14	24	24	.371	.369	Bats Right	R	.279	462	129	15	1	45	104	55	125	.356	.608
Santiago,B	L	.250	132	33	6	0	5	21	12	26	.313	.409	Spehr,Tim	L	.146	48	7	0	0	2	5	6	12	.255	.271
Bats Right	R	.248	218	54	12	3	2	15	20	45	.314	.358	Bats Right	R	.234	107	25	7	0	7	21	16	35	.354	.495
Scarsone,S	L	.059	17	1	0	0	0	0	2	7	.158	.059	Spencer,Sh.	L	.289	83	24	4	0	5	8	5	24	.330	.518
Bats Right	R	.255	51	13	5	0	0	6	7	17	.339	.353	Bats Right	R	.197	122	24	4	0	3	12	13	27	.283	.303
Sefcik,Kevin	L	.341	91	31	8	1	1	6	13	7	.429	.484	Spiers,Bill	L	.375	40	15	3	0	0	10	4	6	.432	.450
Bats Right	R	.229	118	27	7	2	0	5	16	17	.321	.322	Bats Left	R	.278	353	98	15	5	4	29	43	39	.355	.382
Segui,David	L	.271	70	19	1	0	1	4	6	6	.333	.329	Spiezio,Scott	L	.229	70	16	6	0	1	7	8	17	.316	.357
Bats Both	R	.303	370	112	26	3	13	48	34	54	.359	.495	Bats Both	R	.249	177	44	18	0	7	26	21	19	.327	.469
Seguignol,F	L	.227	22	5	2	0	1	3	1	8	.292	.455	Sprague,Ed	L	.212	137	29	4	0	6	23	18	22	.311	.372
Bats Both	R	.265	83	22	7	0	4	7	4	25	.337	.494	Bats Right	R	.289	353	102	23	2	16	58	32	71	.368	.501
Servais,Scott	L	.303	89	27	3	0	3	9	6	14	.347	.438	Stairs,Matt	L	.236	165	39	9	0	8	26	27	46	.342	.436
Bats Right	R	.248	109	27	7	0	2	12	7	17	.311	.367	Bats Left	R	.268	366	98	17	3	30	76	62	78	.377	.577
Sexson,Richie	L	.277	137	38	3	3	11	35	13	33	.336	.584	Stanley,Mike	L	.302	126	38	7	0	8	22	23	24	.413	.548
Bats Right	R	.246	342	84	14	4	20	81	21	84	.292	.485	Bats Right	R	.272	301	82	15	0	11	50	47	70	.384	.432
Sexton,Chris	L	.324	34	11	0	1	1	6	8	5	.452	.471	Steinbach,T	L	.255	55	14	3	1	0	7	11	7	.379	.345
Bats Right	R	.120	25	3	0	0	0	1	3	5	.214	.120	Bats Right	R	.290	283	82	13	3	4	35	27	47	.354	.399

Batters vs. Lefthanded and Righthanded Pitchers

Batter	vs	Avg	AB	H	2B	3B	HR	BI	BB	SO	OBP	SLG
Stevens,Lee	L	.304	102	31	2	1	4	23	16	28	.398	.461
Bats Left	R	.277	415	115	29	0	20	58	36	104	.330	.492
Stewart,S	L	.369	103	38	6	0	1	12	14	18	.445	.456
Bats Right	R	.291	505	147	22	2	10	55	45	65	.355	.402
Stinnett,K	L	.303	66	20	4	0	3	10	5	21	.356	.500
Bats Right	R	.211	218	46	9	0	11	28	19	62	.285	.404
Stocker,Kevin	L	.246	61	15	3	0	0	5	6	6	.313	.295
Bats Both	R	.316	193	61	8	2	1	22	18	35	.386	.394
Stowers,Chris	L	.000	0	0	0	0	0	0	0	0	.000	.000
Bats Left	R	.000	2	0	0	0	0	0	0	0	.000	.000
Strawberry,D	L	.500	6	3	1	0	1	1	6	2	.750	1.167
Bats Left	R	.302	43	13	4	0	2	5	11	14	.444	.535
Stynes,Chris	L	.292	24	7	0	0	0	2	2	4	.346	.292
Bats Right	R	.225	89	20	1	0	2	12	10	9	.300	.303
Surhoff,B.J.	L	.327	159	52	7	1	7	36	5	27	.341	.516
Bats Left	R	.302	514	155	31	0	21	71	38	51	.349	.484
Sutton,Larry	L	.143	7	1	0	0	1	4	0	1	.143	.571
Bats Left	R	.232	95	22	6	0	1	11	13	16	.318	.326
Sveum,Dale	L	.333	15	5	2	0	2	7	0	5	.333	.867
Bats Both	R	.179	56	10	3	1	1	6	7	23	.266	.321
Sweeney,Mark	L	.000	0	0	0	0	0	0	1	0	1.000	.000
Bats Left	R	.355	31	11	3	0	2	7	3	9	.412	.645
Sweeney,Mike	L	.350	100	35	7	1	4	18	16	6	.440	.560
Bats Right	R	.316	475	150	37	1	18	84	38	42	.376	.512
Tarasco,Tony	L	.000	2	0	0	0	0	0	0	1	.000	.000
Bats Left	R	.172	29	5	2	0	0	3	3	4	.242	.241
Tatis,F	L	.290	138	40	9	1	10	29	18	36	.388	.587
Bats Right	R	.301	399	120	22	1	24	78	64	92	.409	.541
Taubensee,E	L	.333	60	20	3	0	2	11	3	7	.354	.483
Bats Left	R	.308	364	112	19	2	19	76	27	60	.354	.527
Tejada,Miguel	L	.271	140	38	12	0	4	20	20	21	.364	.443
Bats Right	R	.245	453	111	21	4	17	64	37	73	.312	.422
Thomas,Frank	L	.253	75	19	6	0	3	7	15	13	.387	.453
Bats Right	R	.314	411	129	30	0	12	70	72	53	.419	.474
Thome,Jim	L	.239	134	32	7	0	6	29	24	50	.363	.425
Bats Left	R	.292	360	105	20	2	27	79	103	121	.448	.583
Thompson,Ry.	L	.222	9	2	1	0	0	2	1	4	.300	.333
Bats Right	R	.182	11	2	0	0	1	3	1	3	.250	.455
Timmons,Ozz.	L	.103	29	3	2	0	0	1	2	6	.161	.172
Bats Right	R	.133	15	2	0	0	1	2	2	6	.235	.333
Toca,Jorge	L	.333	3	1	0	0	0	0	0	2	.333	.333
Bats Right	R	.000	0	0	0	0	0	0	0	0	.000	.000
Trammell,B	L	.227	66	15	8	0	4	9	14	7	.363	.530
Bats Right	R	.309	217	67	11	0	10	30	29	30	.391	.498
Tremie,Chris	L	.000	3	0	0	0	0	0	0	1	.000	.000
Bats Right	R	.091	11	1	0	0	0	1	2	3	.231	.091
Tucker,M	L	.154	39	6	1	1	2	7	3	18	.244	.385
Bats Left	R	.268	257	69	7	4	9	37	34	63	.353	.432
Turner,Chris	L	.100	10	1	0	0	0	0	0	6	.100	.100
Bats Right	R	.273	11	3	0	0	0	0	1	2	.333	.273

Batter	vs	Avg	AB	H	2B	3B	HR	BI	BB	SO	OBP	SLG
Unroe,Tim	L	.313	32	10	2	0	1	6	2	10	.371	.469
Bats Right	R	.136	22	3	0	0	0	0	2	6	.208	.136
Valentin,J	L	.317	63	20	1	0	1	8	5	5	.362	.381
Bats Both	R	.219	155	34	11	1	4	20	17	34	.294	.381
Valentin,John	L	.277	94	26	2	0	0	4	10	12	.346	.298
Bats Right	R	.247	356	88	25	1	12	66	30	56	.307	.424
Valentin,Jose	L	.253	75	19	3	0	1	11	10	17	.341	.333
Bats Both	R	.215	181	39	6	5	9	27	38	35	.350	.453
Vander Wal,J	L	.111	18	2	1	0	0	2	2	6	.200	.167
Bats Left	R	.285	228	65	17	0	6	39	35	53	.381	.439
Varitek,Jason	L	.282	103	29	8	0	3	19	9	15	.325	.447
Bats Both	R	.266	380	101	31	2	17	57	37	70	.332	.492
Vaughn,Greg	L	.262	141	37	3	1	11	32	36	34	.410	.532
Bats Right	R	.240	409	98	17	1	34	86	49	103	.323	.535
Vaughn,Mo	L	.336	152	51	7	0	11	48	23	36	.433	.599
Bats Left	R	.258	372	96	13	0	22	60	31	91	.325	.470
Velandia,J	L	.071	14	1	0	0	0	0	0	5	.133	.071
Bats Right	R	.235	34	8	1	0	0	2	2	8	.278	.265
Velarde,Randy	L	.348	141	49	6	1	4	20	24	17	.446	.489
Bats Right	R	.308	490	151	19	6	12	56	46	81	.373	.445
Ventura,Robin	L	.271	181	49	12	0	9	39	23	45	.351	.486
Bats Left	R	.314	407	128	26	0	23	81	51	64	.391	.548
Veras,Quilvio	L	.288	132	38	11	0	2	12	17	14	.373	.417
Bats Both	R	.277	343	95	14	2	4	29	48	74	.365	.364
Veras,Wilton	L	.262	42	11	1	1	1	3	1	5	.273	.405
Bats Right	R	.303	76	23	4	0	1	10	4	9	.349	.395
Vidro,Jose	L	.260	100	26	9	1	1	10	5	16	.292	.400
Bats Both	R	.315	394	124	36	1	11	49	24	35	.359	.495
Vina,Fernando	L	.341	44	15	3	0	0	6	5	3	.431	.409
Bats Left	R	.236	110	26	4	0	1	10	9	3	.301	.300
Vitiello,Joe	L	.071	14	1	0	0	0	0	0	6	.071	.071
Bats Right	R	.185	27	5	1	0	1	4	2	3	.290	.333
Vizcaino,Jose	L	.329	70	23	5	0	0	9	9	4	.413	.400
Bats Both	R	.224	196	44	4	0	1	20	11	19	.263	.260
Vizquel,Omar	L	.333	147	49	14	0	1	15	15	8	.390	.449
Bats Both	R	.333	427	142	22	4	4	51	50	42	.400	.431
Walbeck,Matt	L	.266	64	17	3	0	0	5	2	10	.288	.313
Bats Both	R	.232	224	52	5	1	3	17	24	36	.313	.304
Walker,Larry	L	.345	142	49	6	3	9	37	17	14	.424	.620
Bats Left	R	.395	296	117	20	1	28	78	40	38	.474	.753
Walker,Todd	L	.178	101	18	5	0	1	10	6	19	.231	.257
Bats Left	R	.302	430	130	32	4	5	36	46	64	.368	.430
Ward,Daryle	L	.250	12	3	1	0	1	3	1	7	.308	.583
Bats Left	R	.275	138	38	5	0	7	27	8	24	.311	.464
Ward,Turner	L	.209	43	9	1	0	0	9	5	5	.300	.233
Bats Both	R	.254	71	18	2	0	2	6	10	10	.341	.366
Watkins,Pat	L	.000	7	0	0	0	0	0	2	1	.222	.000
Bats Right	R	.083	12	1	0	0	0	0	0	4	.083	.083
Webster,Lenny	L	.143	21	3	0	0	0	3	5	3	.333	.143
Bats Right	R	.103	29	3	1	0	0	1	5	4	.257	.138

Batters vs. Lefthanded and Righthanded Pitchers

Batter	vs	Avg	AB	H	2B	3B	HR	BI	BB	SO	OBP	SLG
Wehner,John	L	.179	39	7	2	0	1	3	3	7	.238	.308
Bats Right	R	.192	26	5	0	0	0	1	4	5	.300	.192
Weiss,Walt	L	.200	75	15	3	0	2	7	10	15	.295	.320
Bats Both	R	.235	204	48	10	4	0	22	25	33	.322	.324
Wells,Vernon	L	.412	17	7	2	0	0	1	0	1	.412	.529
Bats Right	R	.225	71	16	3	0	1	7	4	17	.267	.310
White,Devon	L	.288	139	40	8	1	5	22	17	27	.367	.468
Bats Both	R	.260	335	87	12	1	9	46	22	61	.323	.382
White,Rondell	L	.374	123	46	7	2	8	22	9	17	.415	.659
Bats Right	R	.293	416	122	19	4	14	42	23	68	.342	.459
Whiten,Mark	L	.125	8	1	0	0	0	0	0	1	.125	.125
Bats Both	R	.176	17	3	1	0	1	4	3	3	.300	.412
Widger,Chris	L	.350	100	35	8	0	5	19	7	17	.393	.580
Bats Right	R	.233	283	66	16	1	9	37	21	69	.301	.392
Wilkins,Rick	L	.000	1	0	0	0	0	0	0	1	.000	.000
Bats Left	R	.000	3	0	0	0	0	0	0	1	.000	.000
Williams,B	L	.297	165	49	7	3	5	22	26	25	.393	.467
Bats Both	R	.359	426	153	21	3	20	93	74	70	.451	.563
Williams,G	L	.286	182	52	12	1	9	32	13	28	.333	.511
Bats Right	R	.267	240	64	12	0	8	36	20	39	.336	.417
Williams,Matt	L	.333	177	59	11	1	12	45	19	23	.396	.610
Bats Right	R	.291	450	131	26	1	23	97	22	70	.322	.507
Williams,R	L	.250	32	8	1	1	0	4	3	9	.324	.344
Bats Both	R	.194	31	6	0	1	1	2	2	12	.242	.355
Wilson,Craig	L	.286	70	20	1	1	1	5	7	5	.346	.371
Bats Right	R	.220	182	40	7	0	3	21	16	17	.283	.308
Wilson,Dan	L	.255	102	26	5	0	1	7	6	16	.296	.333
Bats Right	R	.269	312	84	18	2	6	31	23	67	.322	.397
Wilson,E	L	.255	110	28	7	0	1	5	5	14	.287	.345
Bats Both	R	.266	222	59	15	1	1	19	20	27	.321	.356
Wilson,P	L	.285	123	35	6	2	9	23	16	45	.366	.585
Bats Right	R	.279	359	100	15	2	17	48	30	111	.344	.474
Wilson,Vance	L	.000	0	0	0	0	0	0	0	0	.000	.000
Bats Right	R	.000	0	0	0	0	0	0	0	0	.000	.000
Winn,Randy	L	.238	80	19	1	1	1	2	2	13	.253	.313
Bats Both	R	.278	223	62	15	3	1	22	15	50	.325	.386
Witt,Kevin	L	.333	6	2	1	0	0	2	0	1	.333	.500
Bats Left	R	.179	28	5	0	0	1	3	2	8	.233	.286
Womack,Tony	L	.290	169	49	6	1	2	18	15	24	.348	.373
Bats Left	R	.272	445	121	19	9	2	23	37	44	.326	.369
Wood,Jason	L	.167	24	4	0	0	0	2	1	6	.200	.167
Bats Right	R	.150	20	3	1	0	1	6	1	7	.190	.350
Woodward,C	L	.111	9	1	0	0	0	0	1	2	.200	.111
Bats Right	R	.294	17	5	1	0	0	2	1	4	.316	.353
Young,Dmitri	L	.266	109	29	9	0	3	13	7	18	.308	.431
Bats Both	R	.314	264	83	21	2	11	43	23	53	.370	.534
Young,Eric	L	.295	132	39	7	1	1	11	26	11	.419	.386
Bats Right	R	.275	324	89	17	1	1	30	37	15	.351	.343
Young,Ernie	L	.200	10	2	0	0	0	0	2	2	.333	.200
Bats Right	R	.000	1	0	0	0	0	0	1	0	.667	.000

Batter	vs	Avg	AB	H	2B	3B	HR	BI	BB	SO	OBP	SLG
Young,Kevin	L	.308	159	49	13	4	5	25	17	25	.378	.535
Bats Right	R	.294	425	125	28	2	21	81	58	99	.390	.518
Zaun,Gregg	L	.211	19	4	0	0	0	0	4	1	.348	.211
Bats Both	R	.257	74	19	2	1	1	12	6	6	.305	.351
Zeile,Todd	L	.291	117	34	7	0	3	22	15	15	.378	.427
Bats Right	R	.293	471	138	34	1	21	76	41	79	.348	.503
Zosky,Eddie	L	.000	2	0	0	0	0	0	0	1	.000	.000
Bats Right	R	.200	5	1	0	0	0	0	1	1	.333	.200
AL	L	.274	—	—	—	—	—	—	—	—	.349	.432
	R	.275	—	—	—	—	—	—	—	—	.347	.441
NL	L	.268	—	—	—	—	—	—	—	—	.346	.431
	R	.268	—	—	—	—	—	—	—	—	.341	.429
MLB	L	.271	—	—	—	—	—	—	—	—	.347	.431
	R	.271	—	—	—	—	—	—	—	—	.344	.435

Pitchers vs. Lefthanded and Righthanded Batters

Pitcher	vs	Avg	AB	H	2B	3B	HR	BI	BB	SO	OBP	SLG
Abbott,Jim	L	.300	90	27	6	1	3	22	12	9	.379	.489
Throws Left	R	.323	257	83	12	0	11	41	30	28	.398	.498
Abbott,Paul	L	.159	138	22	3	1	3	18	24	46	.280	.261
Throws Right	R	.231	121	28	4	1	6	18	8	22	.275	.430
Acevedo,Juan	L	.275	149	41	8	2	6	19	23	18	.370	.477
Throws Right	R	.301	246	74	14	1	11	50	25	34	.368	.500
Adams,Terry	L	.186	102	19	5	0	3	10	12	36	.272	.324
Throws Right	R	.287	143	41	8	0	6	26	16	21	.352	.469
Aguilera,Rick	L	.292	96	28	3	1	4	13	7	13	.343	.469
Throws Right	R	.172	151	26	6	1	4	17	5	32	.203	.305
Aldred,Scott	L	.310	84	26	5	1	1	20	13	15	.400	.429
Throws Left	R	.254	130	33	7	1	1	20	16	26	.331	.346
Alfonseca,A	L	.270	126	34	5	1	1	11	12	17	.333	.349
Throws Right	R	.278	162	45	8	0	3	18	17	29	.359	.383
Almanza,A	L	.063	16	1	0	0	0	1	6	8	.348	.063
Throws Left	R	.194	36	7	1	0	1	3	3	12	.250	.306
Almanzar,C	L	.377	61	23	3	1	2	12	9	6	.465	.557
Throws Right	R	.275	91	25	4	0	4	19	6	24	.330	.451
Almonte,H	L	.455	22	10	0	0	1	5	2	2	.480	.591
Throws Right	R	.270	37	10	1	0	0	3	4	6	.341	.297
Alvarez,Juan	L	.167	6	1	0	0	0	1	3	2	.444	.167
Throws Left	R	.000	3	0	0	0	0	0	1	2	.250	.000
Alvarez,W	L	.276	116	32	5	0	7	21	11	18	.341	.500
Throws Left	R	.257	495	127	26	3	15	57	68	110	.351	.412
Anderson,B	L	.296	108	32	4	0	1	4	6	14	.333	.361
Throws Left	R	.275	408	112	18	3	17	51	22	61	.313	.458
Anderson,J	L	.231	26	6	1	0	1	5	3	1	.323	.385
Throws Left	R	.235	81	19	1	1	1	5	13	12	.340	.309
Anderson,Matt	L	.232	56	13	0	0	7	19	18	11	.413	.607
Throws Right	R	.233	86	20	6	0	1	14	17	21	.362	.337
Ankiel,Rick	L	.235	17	4	0	0	0	0	1	10	.316	.235
Throws Left	R	.212	104	22	3	1	2	11	13	29	.299	.317
Appier,Kevin	L	.297	411	122	26	4	11	48	57	69	.385	.460
Throws Right	R	.262	412	108	24	0	16	65	27	62	.312	.437
Armas Jr.,T	L	.250	8	2	2	0	0	1	2	0	.400	.500
Throws Right	R	.353	17	6	2	0	0	3	0	2	.333	.471
Arnold,Jamie	L	.345	113	39	11	0	2	21	16	13	.426	.496
Throws Right	R	.268	157	42	4	0	4	29	18	13	.365	.369
Arrojo,R	L	.315	302	95	19	5	16	50	39	51	.399	.570
Throws Right	R	.272	246	67	16	0	7	27	21	56	.350	.423
Ashby,Andy	L	.281	356	100	20	1	9	35	23	41	.327	.419
Throws Right	R	.240	434	104	17	0	17	50	31	91	.298	.396
Assenmacher	L	.227	66	15	1	0	3	11	6	18	.297	.379
Throws Left	R	.449	78	35	7	1	3	21	11	11	.511	.679
Astacio,Pedro	L	.306	409	125	33	5	13	54	48	92	.379	.506
Throws Right	R	.268	497	133	17	1	25	74	27	118	.312	.457
Avery,Steve	L	.211	76	16	6	0	2	17	23	8	.382	.368
Throws Left	R	.225	262	59	11	1	9	32	55	43	.358	.378
Ayala,Bobby	L	.244	131	32	12	0	3	24	20	37	.346	.405
Throws Right	R	.215	181	39	7	2	7	31	19	42	.304	.392

Pitcher	vs	Avg	AB	H	2B	3B	HR	BI	BB	SO	OBP	SLG
Aybar,Manny	L	.305	141	43	10	2	4	23	20	27	.393	.489
Throws Right	R	.252	242	61	11	0	9	43	16	47	.304	.409
Baldwin,James	L	.272	419	114	24	0	16	55	51	72	.353	.444
Throws Right	R	.285	368	105	19	2	18	50	30	51	.342	.495
Bale,John	L	.000	2	0	0	0	0	0	1	2	.333	.000
Throws Left	R	.333	6	2	1	0	1	3	1	2	.429	1.000
Barber,Brian	L	.350	40	14	5	0	1	4	4	6	.409	.550
Throws Right	R	.415	41	17	4	0	5	18	6	1	.500	.878
Barker,Richie	L	.375	8	3	2	0	0	2	3	0	.545	.625
Throws Right	R	.250	12	3	0	0	0	2	1	3	.286	.250
Batista,M	L	.339	239	81	18	1	2	27	32	30	.417	.448
Throws Right	R	.230	283	65	18	1	8	50	26	65	.298	.385
Beck,Rod	L	.286	77	22	4	1	1	9	9	9	.356	.403
Throws Right	R	.292	96	28	10	1	4	19	9	16	.355	.542
Belcher,Tim	L	.312	276	86	13	3	13	49	32	29	.383	.522
Throws Right	R	.318	258	82	19	2	14	44	14	23	.353	.570
Belinda,Stan	L	.258	66	17	5	0	5	17	8	15	.333	.561
Throws Right	R	.258	97	25	3	0	6	10	10	25	.333	.474
Beltran,Rigo	L	.342	73	25	8	0	2	10	8	19	.407	.534
Throws Left	R	.253	99	25	6	0	5	18	11	31	.333	.465
Benes,Alan	L	.000	2	0	0	0	0	0	0	0	.000	.000
Throws Right	R	.400	5	2	0	0	0	0	0	2	.400	.400
Benes,Andy	L	.273	366	100	13	2	14	52	35	57	.338	.434
Throws Right	R	.273	425	116	25	2	20	56	47	84	.347	.482
Benitez,A	L	.177	113	20	5	1	2	10	26	48	.331	.292
Throws Right	R	.127	158	20	3	1	2	11	15	80	.202	.196
Bennett,Joel	L	.286	28	8	1	0	2	3	3	5	.355	.536
Throws Right	R	.391	46	18	2	1	8	14	4	8	.440	1.000
Bennett,S	L	.500	22	11	3	1	1	8	1	3	.500	.864
Throws Right	R	.406	32	13	4	0	3	9	2	1	.457	.813
Benson,Kris	L	.277	339	94	16	2	7	40	53	54	.374	.398
Throws Right	R	.226	399	90	19	0	9	50	30	85	.285	.341
Bere,Jason	L	.267	131	35	7	0	1	17	17	27	.349	.344
Throws Right	R	.336	131	44	11	1	8	24	33	20	.473	.618
Bergman,Sean	L	.307	199	61	7	2	5	27	19	17	.367	.437
Throws Right	R	.343	216	74	12	2	4	31	10	27	.374	.472
Billingsley,B	L	.333	12	4	1	0	1	4	4	1	.500	.667
Throws Left	R	.412	17	7	1	0	2	9	6	2	.583	.824
Blair,Willie	L	.324	275	89	21	2	13	44	28	47	.391	.556
Throws Right	R	.292	274	80	20	0	16	47	16	35	.330	.540
Bochtler,Doug	L	.471	17	8	3	0	1	5	1	1	.526	.824
Throws Right	R	.094	32	3	1	0	2	3	5	6	.211	.313
Boehringer,B	L	.223	148	33	3	1	3	12	20	27	.310	.318
Throws Right	R	.298	215	64	5	0	7	26	15	37	.345	.419
Bohanon,Brian	L	.320	147	47	9	1	7	23	19	26	.422	.537
Throws Left	R	.301	628	189	43	3	23	112	73	94	.378	.489
Bones,Ricky	L	.349	86	30	7	2	3	16	9	9	.417	.581
Throws Right	R	.299	97	29	0	1	4	15	10	17	.367	.443
Borbon,Pedro	L	.156	90	14	2	0	2	8	20	22	.313	.244
Throws Left	R	.258	97	25	9	0	3	16	9	11	.315	.443

Pitchers vs. Lefthanded and Righthanded Batters

Pitcher	vs	Avg	AB	H	2B	3B	HR	BI	BB	SO	OBP	SLG
Borkowski,D	L	.303	142	43	7	1	3	26	23	20	.398	.430
Throws Right	R	.265	162	43	8	1	7	26	17	30	.348	.457
Bottalico,R	L	.310	113	35	10	2	3	18	21	26	.422	.513
Throws Right	R	.268	179	48	10	0	5	28	28	40	.373	.408
Bottenfield,K	L	.245	322	79	16	1	7	34	33	54	.319	.366
Throws Right	R	.290	407	118	27	5	14	51	56	70	.374	.484
Bowie,Micah	L	.455	33	15	5	0	1	13	3	3	.500	.697
Throws Left	R	.347	190	66	7	2	8	44	31	38	.438	.532
Boyd,Jason	L	.500	2	1	1	0	0	1	0	0	.333	1.000
Throws Right	R	.222	18	4	2	0	0	2	2	4	.333	.333
Bradford,Chad	L	.625	8	5	2	0	1	5	2	0	.700	1.250
Throws Right	R	.364	11	4	0	0	0	2	3	0	.500	.364
Brantley,Jeff	L	.083	12	1	0	0	0	2	3	5	.267	.083
Throws Right	R	.211	19	4	1	0	0	3	5	6	.360	.263
Brewer,Billy	L	.325	40	13	2	1	2	10	2	11	.357	.575
Throws Left	R	.274	62	17	4	0	2	11	12	17	.387	.435
Brocail,Doug	L	.213	141	30	5	0	5	14	15	36	.287	.355
Throws Right	R	.200	150	30	4	0	2	16	10	42	.267	.267
Brock,Chris	L	.318	223	71	12	0	7	32	28	31	.398	.466
Throws Right	R	.261	203	53	11	0	11	28	13	45	.309	.478
Brower,Jim	L	.286	42	12	1	0	4	7	7	7	.400	.595
Throws Right	R	.259	58	15	4	0	4	7	3	11	.290	.534
Brown,Kevin	L	.255	478	122	27	3	7	51	32	89	.305	.368
Throws Right	R	.189	466	88	11	3	12	40	27	132	.239	.303
Brownson,Ma.	L	.403	72	29	4	0	4	14	1	13	.419	.625
Throws Right	R	.241	54	13	0	0	4	7	7	8	.328	.463
Brunson,Will	L	.333	24	8	1	0	0	7	4	8	.400	.375
Throws Left	R	.400	25	10	3	0	3	8	2	1	.444	.880
Buddie,Mike	L	.000	2	0	0	0	0	0	0	0	.000	.000
Throws Right	R	.429	7	3	0	0	1	1	0	1	.429	.857
Bullinger,K	L	.000	1	0	0	0	0	0	1	0	.500	.000
Throws Right	R	.333	6	2	0	0	0	0	1	0	.429	.333
Bunch,Mel	L	.400	20	8	1	0	1	5	7	2	.556	.600
Throws Right	R	.444	27	12	2	0	2	10	0	2	.429	.741
Burba,Dave	L	.224	379	85	12	2	13	36	46	82	.316	.369
Throws Right	R	.279	452	126	29	2	17	67	50	92	.353	.465
Burkett,John	L	.280	307	86	14	1	7	31	23	53	.331	.401
Throws Right	R	.336	292	98	30	0	11	55	23	43	.386	.551
Burnett,A.J.	L	.269	67	18	6	0	2	6	8	12	.342	.448
Throws Right	R	.221	86	19	3	1	1	13	17	21	.343	.314
Busby,Mike	L	.240	25	6	1	0	2	8	9	2	.457	.520
Throws Right	R	.341	44	15	4	1	0	7	5	5	.420	.477
Byrd,Paul	L	.304	365	111	23	1	17	57	38	33	.373	.512
Throws Right	R	.230	409	94	20	1	17	48	32	73	.305	.408
Byrdak,Tim	L	.212	52	11	1	0	3	13	6	11	.293	.404
Throws Left	R	.404	52	21	1	0	2	13	14	6	.537	.538
Cabrera,Jose	L	.143	49	7	2	0	2	6	3	18	.189	.306
Throws Right	R	.241	58	14	3	0	1	10	6	10	.303	.345
Callaway,M	L	.455	33	15	3	1	1	3	10	4	.581	.697
Throws Right	R	.294	51	15	2	0	1	10	4	7	.339	.392

Pitcher	vs	Avg	AB	H	2B	3B	HR	BI	BB	SO	OBP	SLG
Candiotti,Tom	L	.244	123	30	7	2	4	17	16	16	.329	.431
Throws Right	R	.341	164	56	8	1	10	38	14	25	.397	.585
Carlson,Dan	L	.600	5	3	0	0	0	1	0	0	.600	.600
Throws Right	R	.154	13	2	0	0	0	1	0	3	.154	.154
Carlyle,Buddy	L	.323	62	20	8	1	3	13	10	13	.411	.629
Throws Right	R	.205	78	16	4	0	4	14	7	16	.284	.410
Carmona,R	L	.348	23	8	3	0	0	2	3	0	.407	.478
Throws Right	R	.476	21	10	2	0	3	8	6	0	.571	1.000
Carpenter,C	L	.299	278	83	19	2	11	33	21	45	.349	.500
Throws Right	R	.290	324	94	19	2	5	36	27	61	.344	.407
Carrasco,H	L	.297	64	19	5	0	2	10	6	15	.352	.469
Throws Right	R	.242	120	29	4	1	1	18	12	20	.316	.317
Carter,Lance	L	.200	5	1	0	0	1	1	1	0	.333	.800
Throws Right	R	.154	13	2	0	0	1	2	2	3	.267	.385
Castillo,C	L	.325	77	25	3	0	6	16	9	8	.395	.597
Throws Right	R	.230	87	20	2	0	4	8	5	15	.272	.391
Cather,Mike	L	.333	6	2	0	0	0	1	0	0	.333	.333
Throws Right	R	.500	6	3	0	0	2	3	1	0	.571	1.500
Charlton,Norm	L	.295	61	18	3	1	1	18	13	13	.421	.426
Throws Left	R	.238	130	31	9	1	3	20	23	32	.348	.392
Checo,R	L	.364	22	8	3	1	2	9	9	4	.548	.864
Throws Right	R	.320	50	16	3	0	3	14	4	7	.370	.560
Chen,Bruce	L	.222	45	10	1	0	3	9	7	8	.340	.444
Throws Left	R	.203	138	28	3		8	19	20	37	.306	.399
Cho,Jin Ho	L	.247	77	19	6	1	1	6	4	6	.282	.390
Throws Right	R	.325	80	26	4	0	6	20	4	10	.365	.600
Chouinard,B	L	.190	42	8	1	0	1	5	3	7	.244	.286
Throws Right	R	.232	99	23	5	0	2	13	9	16	.286	.343
Christiansen,J	L	.205	44	9	2	1	0	3	6	16	.314	.295
Throws Left	R	.193	88	17	4	0	2	10	16	19	.321	.307
Clark,Mark	L	.327	159	52	9	1	13	37	24	17	.409	.642
Throws Right	R	.331	154	51	19	0	4	26	10	27	.373	.532
Clemens,Rog.	L	.263	365	96	14	0	6	38	63	92	.377	.351
Throws Right	R	.259	343	89	18	1	14	52	27	71	.318	.440
Clement,Matt	L	.319	320	102	23	1	11	57	36	37	.386	.500
Throws Right	R	.235	375	88	14	0	7	31	50	98	.335	.328
Clontz,Brad	L	.435	46	20	4	0	3	7	9	6	.527	.717
Throws Right	R	.197	147	29	3	0	3	15	15	34	.283	.279
Cloude,Ken	L	.363	135	49	10	1	4	36	28	16	.479	.541
Throws Right	R	.333	171	57	14	2	6	32	18	19	.397	.424
Colon,Bartolo	L	.255	368	94	25	3	14	46	37	82	.324	.454
Throws Right	R	.229	398	91	15	1	10	39	39	79	.305	.347
Cone,David	L	.244	360	88	13	2	15	46	56	75	.353	.417
Throws Right	R	.214	355	76	24	0	6	34	34	102	.290	.332
Cook,Dennis	L	.211	71	15	2	1	0	6	7	12	.282	.268
Throws Left	R	.219	160	35	7	2	11	28	20	56	.306	.494
Cooper,Brian	L	.260	50	13	6	0	3	10	11	6	.403	.560
Throws Right	R	.196	51	10	3	2	0	4	7	9	.323	.333
Coppinger,R	L	.214	98	21	1	0	5	10	27	31	.384	.378
Throws Right	R	.307	127	39	4	1	8	30	15	25	.375	.543

Pitchers vs. Lefthanded and Righthanded Batters

Pitcher	vs	Avg	AB	H	2B	3B	HR	BI	BB	SO	OBP	SLG
Corbin,Archie	L	.316	38	12	1	0	1	6	3	12	.357	.421
Throws Right	R	.271	48	13	3	2	1	8	12	18	.426	.479
Cordero,F	L	.133	30	4	1	0	1	4	16	10	.426	.267
Throws Right	R	.405	37	15	3	1	1	8	2	9	.405	.622
Cordova,F	L	.281	285	80	18	3	7	29	34	27	.361	.439
Throws Right	R	.266	323	86	18	1	9	43	25	71	.319	.412
Cormier,Rheal	L	.198	96	19	6	0	1	18	6	14	.255	.292
Throws Left	R	.276	152	42	9	0	3	13	12	25	.339	.395
Cornelius,R	L	.161	31	5	0	0	0	3	3	6	.235	.161
Throws Right	R	.282	39	11	3	0	0	5	2	6	.317	.359
Corsi,Jim	L	.356	59	21	1	0	3	11	10	6	.457	.525
Throws Right	R	.238	80	19	3	0	3	10	10	16	.326	.388
Cortes,David	L	.333	3	1	0	0	0	0	3	0	.667	.333
Throws Right	R	.182	11	2	1	0	0	3	1	2	.250	.273
Crabtree,Tim	L	.224	98	22	2	0	1	10	9	21	.290	.276
Throws Right	R	.314	156	49	5	4	3	27	9	33	.353	.455
Creek,Doug	L	.143	7	1	0	0	1	4	3	2	.400	.571
Throws Left	R	.313	16	5	1	0	0	2	5	4	.455	.375
Croushore,R	L	.207	121	25	7	0	2	20	22	42	.326	.314
Throws Right	R	.279	154	43	10	0	7	31	21	46	.376	.481
Cruz,Nelson	L	.299	127	38	8	0	9	20	7	17	.336	.575
Throws Right	R	.265	136	36	4	1	2	25	16	29	.346	.353
Cunnane,Will	L	.421	38	16	1	1	2	6	6	5	.500	.658
Throws Right	R	.231	78	18	3	0	6	14	6	17	.286	.500
D'Amico,Jeff	L	.500	2	1	0	0	0	0	0	0	.500	.500
Throws Right	R	.000	2	0	0	0	0	0	0	1	.000	.000
Daal,Omar	L	.204	142	29	8	0	2	10	9	26	.266	.303
Throws Left	R	.242	656	159	33	5	19	74	70	122	.316	.395
Dale,Carl	L	.455	11	5	0	0	2	4	1	2	.500	1.000
Throws Right	R	.333	9	3	0	0	0	2	5	2	.600	.333
Daneker,Pat	L	.250	24	6	0	0	1	3	1	3	.280	.375
Throws Right	R	.258	31	8	1	1	0	5	5	2	.351	.355
Darensbourg,V	L	.264	72	19	5	1	2	20	8	11	.341	.444
Throws Left	R	.413	75	31	7	0	1	24	13	5	.516	.547
Davenport,Joe	L	.500	2	1	0	0	0	0	0	0	.500	.500
Throws Right	R	.000	3	0	0	0	0	0	2	0	.400	.000
Davey,Tom	L	.267	101	27	3	1	1	13	20	26	.395	.347
Throws Right	R	.238	147	35	12	1	4	24	20	33	.347	.415
Davis,Doug	L	.400	10	4	3	0	1	5	0	2	.400	1.000
Throws Left	R	.800	10	8	2	0	2	7	0	1	.800	1.600
DeHart,Rick	L	.333	6	2	1	0	1	1	1	0	.429	1.000
Throws Left	R	.800	5	4	1	0	1	3	2	1	.857	1.600
DeJean,Mike	L	.376	93	35	5	2	4	25	18	13	.477	.602
Throws Right	R	.310	155	48	6	1	9	29	14	18	.368	.535
de los Santos	L	.286	7	2	1	0	0	1	2	3	.444	.429
Throws Left	R	.357	28	10	2	0	1	6	5	2	.471	.536
del Toro,M	L	.300	30	9	3	0	2	6	3	6	.364	.600
Throws Right	R	.246	61	15	3	0	3	7	8	14	.333	.443
DeLucia,Rich	L	.400	20	8	3	0	2	5	4	3	.500	.850
Throws Right	R	.238	21	5	1	0	2	4	5	4	.385	.571
Dempster,Ry.	L	.282	262	74	12	0	12	33	45	53	.389	.466
Throws Right	R	.243	296	72	11	4	9	31	48	73	.352	.399
DePaula,Sean	L	.158	19	3	1	0	0	4	0	10	.158	.211
Throws Right	R	.238	21	5	2	0	0	0	3	8	.333	.333
Dipoto,Jerry	L	.284	148	42	9	1	2	18	13	36	.349	.399
Throws Right	R	.275	178	49	9	0	8	23	31	33	.377	.461
Dotel,Octavio	L	.210	138	29	7	2	2	15	28	38	.341	.333
Throws Right	R	.240	167	40	10	2	10	31	21	47	.338	.503
Dougherty,Jim	L	1.000	2	2	0	0	0	2	0	0	1.000	1.000
Throws Right	R	.143	7	1	1	0	0	0	3	1	.400	.286
Dreifort,D	L	.273	308	84	18	2	11	48	35	56	.351	.451
Throws Right	R	.250	372	93	13	1	9	42	41	84	.331	.363
Durbin,Chad	L	.250	4	1	0	0	0	0	0	2	.250	.250
Throws Right	R	.000	4	0	0	0	0	0	1	1	.200	.000
Duvall,Mike	L	.324	71	23	5	1	4	25	9	8	.410	.592
Throws Left	R	.267	86	23	7	0	1	12	18	10	.394	.384
Ebert,Derrin	L	.250	12	3	1	0	2	3	1	0	.308	.833
Throws Left	R	.333	18	6	2	0	0	2	4	4	.455	.444
Edmondson,B	L	.331	154	51	13	2	3	26	17	24	.399	.500
Throws Right	R	.261	211	55	13	1	8	31	27	34	.348	.445
Eiland,Dave	L	.279	154	43	11	0	3	17	19	29	.360	.409
Throws Right	R	.307	179	55	12	0	5	33	8	24	.339	.458
Elarton,Scott	L	.251	215	54	10	0	4	22	30	55	.341	.353
Throws Right	R	.227	251	57	12	1	4	33	13	66	.272	.331
Eldred,Cal	L	.357	157	56	8	4	5	31	18	28	.424	.554
Throws Right	R	.246	183	45	5	2	14	35	28	32	.343	.525
Embree,Alan	L	.200	90	18	2	0	4	17	13	23	.318	.356
Throws Left	R	.200	120	24	4	0	2	9	13	30	.276	.283
Erdos,Todd	L	.000	9	0	0	0	0	0	3	3	.250	.000
Throws Right	R	.294	17	5	0	0	2	5	1	1	.316	.647
Erickson,S	L	.270	440	119	20	2	14	62	66	44	.370	.420
Throws Right	R	.289	432	125	16	6	13	57	33	62	.345	.444
Escobar,K	L	.279	348	97	25	0	10	54	53	68	.373	.437
Throws Right	R	.306	346	106	27	0	9	44	28	61	.368	.462
Estes,Shawn	L	.270	122	33	4	1	4	12	14	24	.359	.418
Throws Left	R	.267	658	176	32	2	17	90	98	135	.363	.400
Estrada,H	L	.400	5	2	0	0	2	6	1	2	.500	1.600
Throws Left	R	.296	27	8	1	0	2	3	3	3	.367	.556
Eyre,Scott	L	.279	43	12	2	0	0	6	9	6	.396	.326
Throws Left	R	.377	69	26	4	1	6	18	6	11	.434	.725
Falkenborg,B	L	.200	5	1	0	0	0	0	2	0	.429	.200
Throws Right	R	.200	5	1	0	0	0	0	0	1	.200	.200
Falteisek,S	L	.353	17	6	0	0	0	2	0	1	.353	.353
Throws Right	R	.387	31	12	1	0	3	9	3	4	.429	.710
Farnsworth,K	L	.276	214	59	11	1	10	33	20	27	.338	.477
Throws Right	R	.268	302	81	11	1	18	44	32	43	.342	.490
Fassero,Jeff	L	.271	140	38	4	1	3	26	16	33	.348	.379
Throws Left	R	.330	515	170	40	2	32	102	67	81	.406	.602
Fernandez,A	L	.276	283	78	15	4	7	35	24	45	.331	.431
Throws Right	R	.225	253	57	11	3	3	23	17	46	.279	.328

Pitchers vs. Lefthanded and Righthanded Batters

Pitcher	vs	Avg	AB	H	2B	3B	HR	BI	BB	SO	OBP	SLG
Fetters,Mike	L	.296	54	16	2	2	3	10	8	9	.397	.574
Throws Right	R	.264	72	19	5	0	2	16	14	13	.391	.417
Finley,Chuck	L	.234	158	37	7	0	3	16	18	42	.324	.335
Throws Left	R	.249	643	160	32	2	20	83	76	158	.331	.398
Florie,Bryce	L	.364	151	55	7	2	7	32	16	24	.424	.576
Throws Right	R	.223	175	39	2	0	1	16	19	41	.303	.251
Fossas,Tony	L	.600	5	3	0	0	1	6	0	0	.600	1.200
Throws Left	R	.750	4	3	0	0	0	1	1	0	.800	.750
Foulke,Keith	L	.183	186	34	6	0	6	15	11	67	.232	.312
Throws Right	R	.192	198	38	12	0	5	14	10	56	.238	.328
Fox,Chad	L	.222	9	2	1	0	0	3	3	5	.417	.333
Throws Right	R	.409	22	9	1	1	1	5	1	7	.458	.682
Franco,John	L	.300	30	9	1	0	0	3	4	11	.405	.333
Throws Left	R	.244	127	31	8	1	1	12	15	30	.324	.346
Franklin,Ryan	L	.174	23	4	2	0	0	1	7	3	.367	.261
Throws Right	R	.316	19	6	2	0	2	5	1	3	.381	.737
Frascatore,J	L	.245	102	25	7	0	3	13	9	16	.310	.402
Throws Right	R	.294	163	48	11	1	8	33	12	21	.343	.521
Fussell,Chris	L	.316	95	30	5	0	4	21	28	18	.472	.495
Throws Right	R	.339	124	42	5	1	5	21	8	19	.390	.516
Fyhrie,Mike	L	.256	86	22	5	0	4	15	11	16	.340	.453
Throws Right	R	.307	127	39	8	0	4	19	10	10	.355	.465
Gagne,Eric	L	.196	51	10	2	0	1	1	3	12	.241	.294
Throws Right	R	.154	52	8	2	0	2	6	12	18	.313	.308
Gaillard,E	L	.385	13	5	1	0	1	4	3	4	.529	.692
Throws Right	R	.292	24	7	1	1	0	4	1	3	.320	.417
Garces,Rich	L	.197	66	13	5	0	0	2	10	6	.303	.273
Throws Right	R	.150	80	12	1	0	1	5	8	27	.227	.200
Garcia,Freddy	L	.255	424	108	19	2	12	42	54	91	.342	.394
Throws Right	R	.273	355	97	24	2	6	40	36	79	.347	.403
Garcia,Mike	L	.000	4	0	0	0	0	0	2	0	.333	.000
Throws Right	R	.111	18	2	0	0	1	1	1	9	.158	.278
Gardner,Mark	L	.279	226	63	7	0	11	31	27	31	.358	.456
Throws Right	R	.258	306	79	19	1	16	63	30	55	.329	.484
Glavine,Tom	L	.267	202	54	5	1	2	21	8	25	.306	.332
Throws Left	R	.292	702	205	31	1	16	87	75	113	.357	.407
Glover,Gary	L	.000	1	0	0	0	0	0	1	0	.500	.000
Throws Right	R	.000	1	0	0	0	0	0	0	0	.000	.000
Glynn,Ryan	L	.339	115	39	4	2	6	20	19	17	.433	.565
Throws Right	R	.291	110	32	7	1	4	21	16	22	.383	.482
Gomes,Wayne	L	.254	114	29	2	0	0	11	26	18	.397	.272
Throws Right	R	.255	161	41	7	1	5	22	30	40	.369	.404
Gooden,Dw.	L	.286	213	61	10	2	10	32	43	45	.413	.493
Throws Right	R	.277	238	66	14	0	8	42	24	43	.353	.437
Gordon,Tom	L	.300	30	9	2	0	0	6	8	9	.447	.367
Throws Right	R	.205	39	8	2	0	2	6	4	15	.295	.410
Grace,Mike	L	.368	95	35	5	1	1	16	15	8	.460	.474
Throws Right	R	.331	136	45	9	3	4	31	15	20	.408	.529
Grahe,Joe	L	.379	66	25	7	0	1	9	11	6	.457	.530
Throws Right	R	.234	64	15	4	0	0	7	6	10	.319	.297

Pitcher	vs	Avg	AB	H	2B	3B	HR	BI	BB	SO	OBP	SLG
Graterol,B	L	.600	5	3	0	0	2	5	3	1	.750	1.800
Throws Right	R	.091	11	1	0	0	1	2	1	1	.167	.364
Graves,Danny	L	.220	173	38	8	1	4	16	19	25	.294	.347
Throws Right	R	.233	223	52	8	2	6	28	30	44	.329	.368
Greene,Rick	L	.455	11	5	1	0	2	5	1	1	.500	1.091
Throws Right	R	.154	13	2	1	0	0	0	0	2	.154	.231
Grimsley,J	L	.167	114	19	3	1	2	11	16	19	.269	.263
Throws Right	R	.273	172	47	9	0	5	30	24	30	.369	.413
Groom,Buddy	L	.245	102	25	3	0	0	17	6	22	.294	.275
Throws Left	R	.315	73	23	4	0	1	10	12	10	.412	.411
Gross,Kip	L	.241	29	7	1	0	3	10	3	6	.343	.586
Throws Right	R	.381	21	8	2	0	0	1	5	3	.519	.476
Guardado,E	L	.176	74	13	8	0	2	9	8	30	.265	.365
Throws Left	R	.258	93	24	5	3	4	19	17	20	.375	.505
Gunderson,E	L	.391	23	9	3	0	1	6	1	2	.400	.652
Throws Left	R	.440	25	11	3	0	0	5	1	4	.462	.560
Guthrie,Mark	L	.313	80	25	8	0	2	13	6	17	.367	.488
Throws Left	R	.224	143	32	10	0	8	29	18	28	.309	.462
Guzman,D	L	.429	14	6	0	2	0	2	1	1	.467	.714
Throws Right	R	.500	14	7	2	1	1	6	2	3	.563	1.000
Guzman,Juan	L	.259	371	96	16	0	8	46	51	67	.346	.367
Throws Right	R	.251	391	98	19	3	20	42	35	88	.318	.466
Hackman,L	L	.357	42	15	1	2	4	11	8	4	.460	.762
Throws Right	R	.393	28	11	1	0	1	7	4	6	.469	.536
Halama,John	L	.286	175	50	11	0	5	23	20	32	.365	.434
Throws Left	R	.280	510	143	31	3	15	57	36	73	.329	.441
Halladay,Roy	L	.274	296	81	14	1	7	33	44	40	.370	.399
Throws Right	R	.266	282	75	15	2	12	44	35	42	.348	.461
Hamilton,Joey	L	.348	207	72	17	4	5	32	18	30	.400	.541
Throws Right	R	.243	189	46	8	0	8	33	21	26	.326	.413
Hampton,Mike	L	.149	141	21	1	0	2	9	12	28	.218	.199
Throws Left	R	.259	713	185	30	2	10	66	89	149	.342	.349
Haney,Chris	L	.289	38	11	0	2	2	10	3	7	.386	.553
Throws Left	R	.264	121	32	7	1	1	13	13	15	.336	.364
Hansell,Greg	L	.321	56	18	2	1	4	14	6	15	.391	.607
Throws Right	R	.255	94	24	5	0	1	15	5	19	.307	.340
Harikkala,Tim	L	.385	26	10	2	0	0	4	4	5	.467	.462
Throws Right	R	.217	23	5	2	0	0	6	2	2	.308	.304
Harnisch,Pete	L	.256	336	86	19	3	14	39	30	44	.315	.455
Throws Right	R	.249	418	104	21	3	11	42	27	76	.300	.392
Harris,Reggie	L	.300	10	3	0	0	0	1	2	2	.429	.300
Throws Right	R	.152	33	5	0	1	1	5	5	9	.282	.303
Harville,Chad	L	.280	25	7	3	0	1	3	4	1	.367	.520
Throws Right	R	.333	33	11	3	0	1	4	6	14	.436	.515
Hasegawa,S	L	.274	113	31	5	0	3	13	18	19	.368	.398
Throws Right	R	.277	177	49	7	0	11	33	16	25	.340	.503
Hawkins,L	L	.310	342	106	20	2	18	63	37	48	.374	.538
Throws Right	R	.335	394	132	20	2	11	52	23	55	.371	.480
Haynes,Jimmy	L	.283	307	87	22	1	6	44	45	49	.373	.420
Throws Right	R	.280	254	71	15	1	15	52	35	44	.367	.524

Pitchers vs. Lefthanded and Righthanded Batters

Pitcher	vs	Avg	AB	H	2B	3B	HR	BI	BB	SO	OBP	SLG	Pitcher	vs	Avg	AB	H	2B	3B	HR	BI	BB	SO	OBP	SLG
Heiserman,R	L	.167	6	1	0	0	0	0	4	0	.500	.167	Isringhausen,J	L	.221	113	25	5	1	4	10	17	22	.331	.389
Throws Right	R	.500	14	7	0	0	2	5	0	4	.500	.929	Throws Right	R	.289	135	39	9	2	5	23	17	29	.373	.496
Helling,Rick	L	.262	401	105	19	4	20	50	50	66	.343	.479	Jackson,Mike	L	.238	130	31	2	1	2	6	15	26	.320	.315
Throws Right	R	.282	436	123	30	4	21	62	35	65	.338	.514	Throws Right	R	.225	129	29	3	0	9	27	11	29	.289	.457
Henry,Butch	L	.233	30	7	1	0	0	1	7	5	.378	.267	Jarvis,Kevin	L	.355	31	11	1	0	2	6	4	7	.417	.581
Throws Left	R	.333	69	23	6	0	1	8	3	10	.373	.464	Throws Right	R	.472	36	17	6	1	4	15	2	4	.513	1.028
Henry,Doug	L	.315	73	23	4	2	3	11	14	19	.432	.548	Jimenez,Jose	L	.304	296	90	18	1	11	57	44	49	.397	.483
Throws Right	R	.253	87	22	3	2	5	14	10	17	.343	.506	Throws Right	R	.249	333	83	13	1	5	35	27	64	.317	.339
Hentgen,Pat	L	.306	395	121	24	4	18	60	35	56	.362	.524	Johns,Doug	L	.138	87	12	1	0	2	14	8	18	.245	.218
Throws Right	R	.265	392	104	18	1	14	46	30	62	.315	.423	Throws Left	R	.288	240	69	17	1	7	32	17	32	.336	.454
Heredia,Felix	L	.247	93	23	4	1	3	19	10	26	.324	.409	Johnson,Jason	L	.242	215	52	11	0	8	33	31	38	.333	.405
Throws Left	R	.292	113	33	8	0	4	22	15	24	.366	.469	Throws Right	R	.289	235	68	15	1	8	30	24	33	.361	.464
Heredia,Gil	L	.286	409	117	29	2	7	43	19	65	.319	.418	Johnson,J	L	.714	7	5	0	0	0	2	1	0	.667	.714
Throws Right	R	.279	398	111	23	3	15	57	15	52	.317	.465	Throws Right	R	.400	10	4	1	0	0	5	1	3	.500	.500
Herges,Matt	L	.250	36	9	2	0	3	6	2	8	.308	.556	Johnson,Mike	L	.429	14	6	2	0	1	4	2	0	.500	.786
Throws Right	R	.259	58	15	4	1	2	5	6	10	.328	.466	Throws Right	R	.261	23	6	1	0	1	4	5	6	.393	.435
Hermanson,D	L	.272	378	103	23	1	10	45	37	55	.339	.418	Johnson,Ra.	L	.103	87	9	0	1	0	3	8	35	.204	.126
Throws Right	R	.271	451	122	31	3	10	55	32	90	.323	.419	Throws Left	R	.219	906	198	28	3	30	74	62	329	.272	.355
Hernandez,L	L	.292	384	112	18	2	12	44	47	58	.368	.443	Johnstone,J	L	.193	88	17	1	1	4	8	8	20	.260	.364
Throws Right	R	.280	411	115	20	3	11	52	29	86	.327	.423	Throws Right	R	.208	149	31	10	0	4	12	12	36	.272	.356
Hernandez,O	L	.273	432	118	26	1	15	63	52	52	.352	.442	Jones,Bobby	L	.330	91	30	6	2	3	17	5	10	.367	.538
Throws Right	R	.187	369	69	19	4	9	29	35	105	.261	.333	Throws Right	R	.273	143	39	9	4	0	18	6	21	.303	.392
Hernandez,R	L	.241	141	34	6	1	0	16	17	40	.319	.298	Jones,B	L	.244	90	22	5	0	6	14	13	12	.333	.500
Throws Right	R	.248	137	34	3	0	1	13	16	29	.342	.292	Throws Left	R	.304	362	110	21	1	18	70	64	62	.415	.517
Hershiser,O	L	.282	291	82	20	7	9	39	51	27	.393	.491	Jones,Doug	L	.255	204	52	11	1	5	28	8	32	.284	.392
Throws Right	R	.243	383	93	15	2	5	37	26	62	.299	.332	Throws Right	R	.280	193	54	8	2	5	25	16	31	.340	.420
Hiljus,Erik	L	.273	11	3	0	0	2	4	2	0	.357	.818	Jones,Todd	L	.292	130	38	7	1	4	17	18	31	.378	.454
Throws Right	R	.222	18	4	1	1	0	4	3	1	.333	.389	Throws Right	R	.222	117	26	5	0	3	14	17	33	.324	.342
Hill,Ken	L	.240	246	59	13	0	7	32	48	33	.359	.378	Judd,Mike	L	.262	42	11	1	0	1	4	7	12	.367	.357
Throws Right	R	.302	232	70	10	3	7	29	28	43	.381	.461	Throws Right	R	.292	65	19	0	0	3	12	5	10	.352	.431
Hinchliffe,B	L	.316	57	18	4	0	4	11	9	8	.418	.596	Juden,Jeff	L	.300	10	3	1	0	1	5	1	3	.364	.700
Throws Right	R	.329	70	23	6	0	6	16	12	6	.447	.671	Throws Right	R	.133	15	2	1	0	0	3	2	6	.278	.200
Hitchcock,S	L	.253	158	40	7	3	7	18	11	39	.302	.468	Kamieniecki,S	L	.265	98	26	4	1	3	15	17	23	.379	.418
Throws Left	R	.254	638	162	28	4	22	72	65	155	.325	.414	Throws Right	R	.236	110	26	4	0	1	14	12	16	.320	.300
Hoffman,T	L	.215	107	23	1	1	1	12	12	36	.289	.271	Karchner,Matt	L	.200	25	5	2	0	1	2	4	3	.310	.400
Throws Right	R	.182	137	25	7	1	4	11	3	37	.199	.336	Throws Right	R	.256	43	11	0	0	2	5	5	6	.360	.395
Holmes,Darren	L	.258	66	17	2	1	2	11	14	15	.395	.409	Karl,Scott	L	.285	130	37	6	0	2	11	9	11	.359	.377
Throws Right	R	.264	125	33	11	4	1	14	11	20	.324	.440	Throws Left	R	.317	659	209	39	2	19	94	60	63	.372	.469
Holt,Chris	L	.307	309	95	20	1	4	31	34	50	.375	.417	Karsay,Steve	L	.209	134	28	8	2	2	11	17	37	.305	.343
Throws Right	R	.298	329	98	15	0	8	44	23	65	.352	.416	Throws Right	R	.281	153	43	7	0	4	23	13	31	.333	.405
Holtz,Mike	L	.237	38	9	3	0	1	4	9	10	.408	.395	Kida,Masao	L	.279	111	31	7	1	3	21	14	20	.362	.441
Throws Left	R	.340	50	17	3	0	2	12	6	7	.411	.520	Throws Right	R	.296	142	42	12	0	3	24	16	30	.373	.444
Howry,Bob	L	.226	133	30	5	1	3	19	24	45	.342	.346	Kile,Darryl	L	.318	359	114	20	6	16	79	53	53	.400	.540
Throws Right	R	.233	120	28	3	0	5	10	14	35	.328	.383	Throws Right	R	.281	395	111	14	5	17	55	56	63	.376	.471
Hudek,John	L	.250	40	10	2	0	1	9	6	4	.340	.375	Kim,B	L	.265	34	9	2	0	1	6	8	6	.444	.412
Throws Right	R	.426	54	23	4	0	2	16	9	16	.508	.611	Throws Right	R	.180	61	11	2	1	1	9	12	25	.333	.295
Hudson,Tim	L	.234	265	62	12	2	4	22	32	57	.318	.340	King,Curtis	L	.000	3	0	0	0	0	0	0	1	.000	.000
Throws Right	R	.240	246	59	12	0	4	24	30	75	.329	.337	Throws Right	R	1.000	3	3	0	0	0	0	0	0	1.000	1.000
Irabu,Hideki	L	.287	363	104	15	0	16	49	28	72	.339	.460	King,Ray	L	.308	13	4	2	0	0	2	5	2	.500	.462
Throws Right	R	.244	312	76	11	4	10	41	18	61	.292	.401	Throws Left	R	.280	25	7	1	0	2	7	5	3	.419	.560

Pitchers vs. Lefthanded and Righthanded Batters

Pitcher	vs	Avg	AB	H	2B	3B	HR	BI	BB	SO	OBP	SLG	Pitcher	vs	Avg	AB	H	2B	3B	HR	BI	BB	SO	OBP	SLG
Kline,Steve	L	.194	93	18	3	0	1	9	12	41	.306	.258	Lopez,Albie	L	.257	101	26	4	0	2	14	11	15	.330	.356
Throws Left	R	.232	164	38	9	0	7	17	21	28	.317	.415	Throws Right	R	.267	150	40	3	0	6	24	13	22	.321	.407
Koch,Billy	L	.209	115	24	5	0	3	12	14	27	.303	.330	Lorraine,A	L	.278	36	10	2	0	0	3	0	8	.270	.333
Throws Right	R	.261	119	31	7	0	2	13	16	30	.353	.370	Throws Left	R	.296	206	61	10	3	9	33	22	32	.362	.505
Kolb,Danny	L	.280	50	14	2	0	0	4	7	8	.379	.320	Lowe,Derek	L	.232	181	42	13	1	4	22	12	29	.282	.381
Throws Right	R	.260	73	19	1	0	2	7	8	7	.333	.356	Throws Right	R	.188	223	42	6	0	3	21	13	51	.242	.256
Kubenka,Jeff	L	.286	7	2	0	0	0	2	3	0	.500	.286	Lowe,Sean	L	.261	134	35	8	1	5	19	31	26	.386	.448
Throws Left	R	.393	28	11	1	0	1	7	1	2	.400	.536	Throws Right	R	.262	210	55	11	0	5	32	15	36	.319	.386
Kubinski,Tim	L	.250	20	5	1	0	1	4	3	5	.375	.450	Ludwick,Eric	L	.333	3	1	1	0	0	0	1	0	.500	.667
Throws Left	R	.300	30	9	1	1	2	7	2	2	.333	.600	Throws Right	R	.667	3	2	0	0	0	1	1	0	.750	.667
Langston,Mark	L	.254	71	18	2	0	4	16	4	15	.289	.451	Luebbers,L	L	.286	77	22	4	1	4	10	8	3	.360	.519
Throws Left	R	.302	169	51	13	2	5	26	25	28	.390	.491	Throws Right	R	.242	99	24	5	0	4	14	8	13	.312	.414
Laxton,Brett	L	.286	14	4	0	0	0	1	2	2	.353	.286	Lundquist,D	L	.308	39	12	5	0	2	10	5	9	.400	.590
Throws Right	R	.333	24	8	2	0	1	6	5	7	.455	.542	Throws Right	R	.320	50	16	1	0	1	8	7	9	.390	.400
Lee,Corey	L	.667	3	2	0	0	1	3	0	0	.667	1.667	Maddux,Greg	L	.300	410	123	17	3	8	51	20	69	.332	.415
Throws Left	R	.000	2	0	0	0	0	0	1	0	.333	.000	Throws Right	R	.288	469	135	21	2	8	46	17	67	.316	.392
Lee,David	L	.261	46	12	2	1	0	4	15	12	.438	.348	Maddux,Mike	L	.270	100	27	5	0	2	9	7	21	.315	.380
Throws Right	R	.242	128	31	5	0	4	16	14	26	.331	.375	Throws Right	R	.279	129	36	6	0	4	22	15	24	.373	.419
Leiter,Al	L	.260	123	32	6	1	2	17	18	31	.370	.374	Magnante,Mi.	L	.217	106	23	5	0	1	14	13	13	.306	.292
Throws Left	R	.262	675	177	40	3	17	83	75	131	.336	.406	Throws Left	R	.292	154	45	13	0	1	23	16	31	.354	.396
Leiter,Mark	L	.000	1	0	0	0	0	0	0	0	.000	.000	Mahay,Ron	L	.143	21	3	0	0	1	2	1	8	.182	.286
Throws Right	R	.400	5	2	2	0	0	2	0	1	.400	.800	Throws Left	R	.114	44	5	0	0	1	1	2	7	.152	.182
Leskanic,Curt	L	.300	110	33	9	1	3	25	17	27	.392	.482	Mahomes,Pat	L	.211	90	19	8	2	1	13	17	15	.339	.378
Throws Right	R	.257	210	54	12	2	4	32	32	50	.364	.390	Throws Right	R	.189	132	25	4	1	6	14	20	36	.299	.371
Levine,Al	L	.233	120	28	6	1	5	14	12	14	.301	.425	Mantei,Matt	L	.159	113	18	3	1	4	13	31	51	.345	.310
Throws Right	R	.255	188	48	10	1	8	30	17	23	.318	.447	Throws Right	R	.217	120	26	5	1	1	8	13	48	.312	.300
Lidle,Cory	L	.750	4	3	0	0	0	0	1	0	.800	.750	Manzanillo,J	L	.258	31	8	0	1	2	6	0	8	.258	.516
Throws Right	R	.278	18	5	2	0	0	1	1	4	.316	.389	Throws Right	R	.268	41	11	1	0	3	7	4	17	.354	.512
Lieber,Jon	L	.333	360	120	10	6	18	55	35	71	.388	.544	Marte,Damaso	L	.444	18	8	1	1	0	3	5	2	.565	.611
Throws Right	R	.236	450	106	14	2	10	40	11	115	.252	.342	Throws Left	R	.348	23	8	0	0	3	7	1	1	.375	.739
Lilly,Ted	L	.417	12	5	1	0	0	4	2	3	.500	.500	Martin,Tom	L	.286	14	4	1	1	0	2	1	3	.333	.500
Throws Left	R	.294	85	25	8	0	7	19	7	25	.362	.635	Throws Left	R	.346	26	9	2	0	2	7	2	5	.379	.654
Lima,Jose	L	.287	421	121	19	6	14	48	21	63	.319	.461	Martinez,P	L	.222	414	92	24	0	4	27	21	146	.266	.309
Throws Right	R	.248	545	135	31	2	16	54	23	124	.279	.400	Throws Right	R	.186	366	68	14	0	5	24	16	167	.227	.265
Lincoln,Mike	L	.358	162	58	16	3	6	26	16	14	.409	.605	Martinez,R	L	.182	33	6	2	0	1	3	6	9	.300	.333
Throws Right	R	.282	156	44	8	1	5	25	10	13	.324	.442	Throws Right	R	.200	40	8	2	0	1	4	2	6	.273	.325
Linton,Doug	L	.269	119	32	9	1	8	20	14	18	.356	.563	Masaoka,Onan	L	.217	92	20	2	1	2	11	18	20	.354	.326
Throws Right	R	.325	114	37	5	0	6	20	11	13	.384	.526	Throws Left	R	.224	156	35	9	1	6	22	29	41	.344	.410
Lira,Felipe	L	.364	11	4	0	0	1	3	0	2	.364	.636	Mathews,T.J.	L	.232	95	22	1	0	5	18	12	16	.315	.400
Throws Right	R	.429	7	3	1	0	1	3	2	1	.556	1.000	Throws Right	R	.202	119	24	7	0	4	17	8	26	.264	.361
Lloyd,Graeme	L	.269	108	29	3	1	6	17	7	24	.313	.481	Mathews,Terry	L	.274	62	17	3	0	1	10	7	6	.338	.371
Throws Left	R	.238	164	39	7	1	5	19	16	23	.319	.384	Throws Right	R	.300	90	27	5	2	3	16	10	13	.375	.500
Loaiza,E	L	.257	214	55	11	0	1	25	27	33	.335	.322	Mays,Joe	L	.255	322	82	16	2	15	43	33	60	.321	.457
Throws Right	R	.290	252	73	18	1	9	32	13	44	.325	.476	Throws Right	R	.284	342	97	19	2	9	46	34	55	.349	.430
Loewer,C	L	.301	156	47	8	2	4	22	12	20	.343	.455	McCurry,Jeff	L	.400	10	4	1	0	0	1	2	1	.500	.500
Throws Right	R	.276	192	53	7	0	5	28	14	28	.322	.391	Throws Right	R	.538	13	7	2	0	1	4	0	2	.538	.923
Loiselle,Rich	L	.150	20	3	0	1	0	3	6	5	.370	.250	McDowell,Jack	L	.378	45	17	1	0	2	7	5	9	.451	.533
Throws Right	R	.351	37	13	2	0	2	7	3	9	.415	.568	Throws Right	R	.359	39	14	3	0	2	7	0	3	.366	.590
Looper,Braden	L	.343	137	47	6	0	4	25	14	24	.401	.474	McElroy,Chuck	L	.266	79	21	6	0	4	20	12	18	.359	.494
Throws Right	R	.257	191	49	6	0	3	33	17	26	.315	.335	Throws Left	R	.298	131	39	7	2	5	30	24	26	.405	.496

Pitchers vs. Lefthanded and Righthanded Batters

Pitcher	vs	Avg	AB	H	2B	3B	HR	BI	BB	SO	OBP	SLG	Pitcher	vs	Avg	AB	H	2B	3B	HR	BI	BB	SO	OBP	SLG
McGlinchy,K	L	.229	96	22	3	2	3	9	9	26	.294	.396	Moreno,Orber	L	.111	9	1	0	1	0	0	4	2	.385	.333
Throws Right	R	.270	163	44	7	0	3	21	21	41	.351	.368	Throws Right	R	.158	19	3	1	0	1	3	2	5	.238	.368
McMichael,G	L	.245	49	12	3	0	2	3	10	12	.387	.429	Morgan,Mike	L	.318	274	87	13	4	14	47	31	32	.395	.547
Throws Right	R	.295	78	23	4	1	4	16	10	9	.371	.526	Throws Right	R	.329	295	97	22	3	11	49	17	29	.365	.536
McNichol,B	L	.143	7	1	0	0	0	1	1	3	.222	.143	Morman,Alvin	L	.293	92	27	5	0	2	10	11	16	.377	.413
Throws Left	R	.368	38	14	2	0	4	7	6	9	.467	.737	Throws Left	R	.317	123	39	6	2	4	19	12	15	.379	.496
Meadows,Bri.	L	.313	351	110	20	3	18	57	23	33	.356	.541	Morris,Jim	L	.000	4	0	0	0	0	0	2	0	.333	.000
Throws Right	R	.291	358	104	23	1	13	43	34	39	.353	.469	Throws Left	R	.214	14	3	0	1	1	3	0	3	.267	.571
Meche,Gil	L	.240	179	43	8	1	5	15	27	27	.341	.380	Mota,G	L	.250	88	22	6	0	3	9	12	14	.333	.420
Throws Right	R	.233	129	30	8	2	4	22	30	20	.377	.419	Throws Right	R	.262	122	32	8	0	2	15	13	13	.341	.377
Mecir,Jim	L	.214	28	6	1	0	0	5	5	7	.343	.250	Moyer,Jamie	L	.234	214	50	5	1	7	25	14	43	.287	.364
Throws Right	R	.200	45	9	2	1	0	3	9	8	.327	.289	Throws Left	R	.278	666	185	34	1	16	68	34	94	.319	.404
Medina,Rafael	L	.184	38	7	1	0	2	8	6	6	.311	.368	Mulholland,T	L	.290	145	42	6	2	4	21	13	22	.348	.441
Throws Right	R	.260	50	13	4	0	1	7	14	10	.422	.400	Throws Left	R	.299	532	159	29	1	17	58	32	61	.337	.453
Mendoza,R	L	.286	231	66	8	1	10	37	20	32	.340	.459	Munoz,Mike	L	.290	100	29	3	1	3	17	6	15	.330	.430
Throws Right	R	.283	265	75	14	4	3	26	7	48	.307	.400	Throws Left	R	.235	98	23	5	0	2	8	12	12	.315	.347
Mercker,Kent	L	.296	135	40	9	0	2	15	14	23	.364	.407	Munro,Peter	L	.269	108	29	7	1	0	16	12	23	.331	.352
Throws Left	R	.288	375	108	32	1	14	60	50	58	.372	.491	Throws Right	R	.366	112	41	6	1	6	23	11	15	.432	.598
Mesa,Jose	L	.331	157	52	3	0	8	31	26	20	.419	.503	Murray,Dan	L	.313	16	5	0	0	0	1	3	1	.450	.313
Throws Right	R	.271	118	32	1	0	3	14	14	22	.365	.356	Throws Right	R	.296	27	8	1	0	4	10	3	8	.355	.778
Miceli,Dan	L	.269	93	25	3	0	2	13	17	18	.378	.366	Murray,Heath	L	.320	50	16	3	0	1	7	4	7	.370	.440
Throws Right	R	.264	159	42	7	2	5	21	19	41	.348	.428	Throws Left	R	.289	152	44	7	1	6	24	22	18	.379	.467
Miller,Kurt	L	.750	4	3	1	0	0	1	0	0	.750	1.000	Mussina,Mike	L	.268	365	98	28	1	7	36	31	90	.324	.408
Throws Right	R	.333	9	3	1	1	1	5	3	1	.500	1.000	Throws Right	R	.267	408	109	21	6	9	39	21	82	.301	.414
Miller,Travis	L	.277	83	23	2	0	1	7	4	21	.307	.337	Myers,Mike	L	.188	80	15	2	1	2	10	11	26	.293	.313
Throws Left	R	.288	111	32	7	0	2	9	12	19	.355	.405	Throws Left	R	.397	78	31	4	0	5	15	2	9	.427	.641
Miller,Trever	L	.237	76	18	2	1	3	14	11	20	.363	.408	Myers,Rodney	L	.326	86	28	5	2	0	9	11	14	.402	.430
Throws Left	R	.339	118	40	8	1	3	19	18	17	.424	.500	Throws Right	R	.269	160	43	8	0	10	31	14	27	.328	.506
Miller,Wade	L	.273	22	6	0	0	2	4	3	5	.360	.545	Myette,Aaron	L	.364	33	12	3	0	2	7	10	9	.523	.636
Throws Right	R	.440	25	11	5	0	2	7	2	3	.481	.880	Throws Right	R	.161	31	5	3	0	0	3	4	2	.278	.258
Mills,Alan	L	.311	103	32	11	1	3	12	16	16	.416	.524	Nagy,Charles	L	.323	402	130	25	2	11	61	34	56	.378	.478
Throws Right	R	.230	165	38	9	0	7	29	27	33	.335	.412	Throws Right	R	.263	411	108	21	3	15	50	25	70	.309	.438
Millwood,K	L	.230	413	95	20	2	15	41	32	98	.292	.397	Nathan,Joe	L	.231	130	30	3	0	8	19	27	18	.363	.438
Throws Right	R	.175	418	73	16	0	9	33	27	107	.223	.278	Throws Right	R	.250	216	54	13	2	9	23	19	36	.314	.454
Milton,Eric	L	.253	154	39	7	0	7	19	12	43	.305	.435	Naulty,Dan	L	.208	77	16	3	1	2	11	5	10	.274	.351
Throws Left	R	.240	629	151	31	3	21	78	51	120	.298	.399	Throws Right	R	.238	101	24	8	0	6	18	17	15	.355	.495
Mintz,Steve	L	.222	9	2	1	0	0	1	1	1	.300	.333	Navarro,Jaime	L	.361	327	118	13	3	17	58	40	29	.431	.575
Throws Right	R	.500	12	6	2	0	1	1	1	1	.538	.917	Throws Right	R	.265	332	88	10	1	12	50	31	45	.342	.410
Mlicki,Dave	L	.276	355	98	15	3	13	51	46	52	.364	.445	Neagle,Denny	L	.198	81	16	4	0	4	10	10	10	.287	.395
Throws Right	R	.279	433	121	25	3	12	49	26	68	.327	.434	Throws Left	R	.237	334	79	27	0	19	40	30	66	.303	.488
Moehler,Brian	L	.296	392	116	23	3	15	58	38	64	.364	.485	Nelson,Jeff	L	.235	34	8	1	1	1	5	10	8	.435	.412
Throws Right	R	.291	388	113	14	3	7	41	21	42	.329	.397	Throws Right	R	.250	76	19	4	0	1	14	12	27	.352	.342
Mohler,Mike	L	.224	58	13	3	0	0	6	4	12	.286	.276	Nen,Robb	L	.354	130	46	7	1	5	23	15	27	.421	.538
Throws Left	R	.270	126	34	10	0	3	20	19	19	.363	.421	Throws Right	R	.210	157	33	6	0	3	17	12	50	.265	.306
Molina,Gabe	L	.303	33	10	1	0	1	3	5	3	.395	.424	Newman,Alan	L	.342	38	13	1	0	1	12	2	11	.375	.447
Throws Right	R	.226	53	12	3	0	3	14	11	11	.359	.453	Throws Left	R	.321	28	9	2	0	1	3	7	9	.472	.500
Montgomery,J	L	.379	95	36	8	0	2	20	11	7	.439	.526	Nitkowski,C	L	.210	105	22	2	0	5	19	14	31	.303	.371
Throws Right	R	.313	115	36	5	1	5	26	10	20	.375	.504	Throws Left	R	.215	191	41	8	0	6	20	31	35	.327	.351
Montgomery,S	L	.200	90	18	1	0	4	7	11	23	.287	.344	Nomo,Hideo	L	.279	319	89	20	3	11	40	36	83	.354	.464
Throws Right	R	.247	146	36	7	0	6	16	20	32	.337	.418	Throws Right	R	.235	357	84	16	1	16	49	42	78	.315	.420

Pitchers vs. Lefthanded and Righthanded Batters

Pitcher	vs	Avg	AB	H	2B	3B	HR	BI	BB	SO	OBP	SLG	Pitcher	vs	Avg	AB	H	2B	3B	HR	BI	BB	SO	OBP	SLG
Nunez,V	L	.268	153	41	11	1	6	21	34	31	.400	.471	Perez,Carlos	L	.333	96	32	4	0	8	18	6	11	.375	.625
Throws Right	R	.226	239	54	9	2	5	26	20	55	.289	.343	Throws Left	R	.311	270	84	18	2	15	52	33	29	.394	.559
Ogea,Chad	L	.320	281	90	25	1	16	54	28	19	.383	.587	Perez,Odalis	L	.333	51	17	4	0	3	11	6	11	.414	.588
Throws Right	R	.264	386	102	27	0	20	49	33	58	.324	.490	Throws Left	R	.266	312	83	17	1	9	40	47	71	.358	.413
Ohka,Tom.	L	.321	28	9	2	0	1	5	5	4	.424	.500	Perez,Yorkis	L	.250	48	12	4	0	1	8	5	11	.315	.396
Throws Right	R	.400	30	12	1	0	1	8	1	4	.406	.533	Throws Left	R	.239	71	17	4	0	3	10	10	15	.333	.423
Ojala,Kirt	L	.500	12	6	1	1	1	7	2	0	.571	1.000	Perisho,Matt	L	.364	11	4	2	0	0	0	0	2	.364	.545
Throws Left	R	.417	36	15	3	1	0	11	4	5	.452	.556	Throws Left	R	.148	27	4	3	0	0	3	2	15	.207	.259
Olivares,Omar	L	.263	392	103	25	3	12	53	49	34	.348	.434	Perkins,Dan	L	.283	166	47	11	0	7	29	26	22	.383	.476
Throws Right	R	.290	393	114	24	0	7	45	32	51	.348	.405	Throws Right	R	.363	193	70	20	3	7	37	17	22	.419	.606
Oliver,Darren	L	.325	126	41	7	0	2	15	13	18	.400	.429	Person,Robert	L	.273	249	68	14	3	12	42	44	60	.385	.498
Throws Left	R	.253	616	156	32	5	14	68	61	101	.327	.390	Throws Right	R	.232	306	71	14	4	12	38	41	79	.326	.422
Olson,Gregg	L	.300	90	27	5	0	3	13	9	18	.360	.456	Peters,Chris	L	.160	50	8	2	0	2	10	3	12	.214	.320
Throws Right	R	.197	137	27	3	0	6	23	16	27	.288	.350	Throws Left	R	.354	254	90	15	2	15	48	24	34	.413	.606
Oquist,Mike	L	.274	285	78	12	3	8	43	43	50	.369	.421	Peterson,Kyle	L	.301	136	41	6	2	2	16	11	13	.354	.419
Throws Right	R	.292	274	80	28	3	10	30	21	39	.346	.526	Throws Right	R	.272	169	46	7	1	1	22	14	21	.337	.343
Orosco,Jesse	L	.270	63	17	4	0	3	15	9	20	.355	.476	Petkovsek,M	L	.242	124	30	5	0	1	12	6	16	.288	.306
Throws Left	R	.204	54	11	2	1	2	11	11	15	.348	.389	Throws Right	R	.286	192	55	11	0	5	39	15	27	.330	.422
Ortiz,Ramon	L	.293	99	29	2	1	6	27	13	20	.374	.515	Pettitte,Andy	L	.275	149	41	7	0	8	29	19	27	.365	.483
Throws Right	R	.233	90	21	3	1	1	5	12	24	.330	.322	Throws Left	R	.293	598	175	42	4	12	62	70	94	.364	.436
Ortiz,Russ	L	.252	361	91	15	0	10	35	59	65	.357	.377	Phillips,J	L	.500	6	3	0	1	0	3	3	1	.667	.833
Throws Right	R	.237	413	98	18	3	14	61	66	99	.346	.397	Throws Right	R	.364	22	8	1	0	2	6	3	6	.423	.682
Osborne,D	L	.222	9	2	1	0	0	2	1	5	.273	.333	Pisciotta,M	L	.333	12	4	2	0	1	1	6	0	.556	.750
Throws Left	R	.305	105	32	6	1	4	14	9	16	.371	.495	Throws Right	R	.250	20	5	0	0	0	3	4	3	.375	.250
Osuna,Antonio	L	.000	6	0	0	0	0	0	2	3	.250	.000	Pittsley,Jim	L	.341	82	28	5	0	3	17	14	9	.434	.512
Throws Right	R	.333	12	4	2	0	0	3	1	2	.429	.500	Throws Right	R	.281	89	25	4	0	2	9	11	11	.366	.393
Padilla,V	L	.500	4	2	1	0	0	2	0	0	.500	.750	Plesac,Dan	L	.204	98	20	2	0	1	9	6	31	.250	.255
Throws Right	R	.455	11	5	1	0	1	6	3	0	.571	.818	Throws Left	R	.385	78	30	7	1	6	25	11	22	.456	.731
Painter,Lance	L	.222	90	20	4	0	3	11	11	20	.314	.367	Plunk,Eric	L	.264	91	24	9	1	4	15	19	15	.402	.516
Throws Left	R	.291	148	43	4	3	3	23	14	36	.349	.419	Throws Right	R	.245	192	47	8	2	11	32	24	48	.335	.479
Paniagua,Jose	L	.276	127	35	6	0	3	25	34	34	.429	.394	Politte,Cliff	L	.269	26	7	4	0	0	3	6	8	.406	.423
Throws Right	R	.255	157	40	7	1	2	21	18	40	.351	.350	Throws Right	R	.279	43	12	2	0	2	8	9	7	.404	.465
Park,Chan Ho	L	.358	344	123	26	2	18	58	58	47	.454	.602	Ponson,Sidney	L	.290	393	114	15	3	18	42	50	48	.366	.481
Throws Right	R	.207	410	85	19	3	13	50	42	127	.295	.363	Throws Right	R	.274	412	113	22	1	17	67	30	64	.324	.456
Parque,Jim	L	.325	157	51	6	0	5	24	19	32	.406	.459	Poole,Jim	L	.273	77	21	4	2	2	17	5	10	.337	.455
Throws Left	R	.292	545	159	21	2	18	75	60	79	.365	.437	Throws Left	R	.397	73	29	4	0	1	14	13	12	.488	.493
Parris,Steve	L	.301	209	63	14	2	6	23	23	24	.369	.474	Portugal,Mark	L	.280	293	82	14	4	11	41	27	38	.343	.468
Throws Right	R	.228	268	61	13	0	10	29	29	62	.315	.388	Throws Right	R	.303	320	97	14	1	17	49	14	41	.332	.513
Patrick,B	L	.200	5	1	0	0	0	2	2	0	.429	.200	Porzio,Mike	L	.318	22	7	3	0	1	2	5	4	.444	.591
Throws Right	R	.421	19	8	0	0	1	4	1	6	.429	.579	Throws Right	R	.333	42	14	2	1	4	11	5	6	.404	.714
Patterson,D	L	.349	86	30	10	1	0	18	12	10	.420	.488	Pote,Lou	L	.184	38	7	1	0	0	4	3	6	.244	.211
Throws Right	R	.281	167	47	11	3	5	26	7	33	.314	.473	Throws Right	R	.239	67	16	4	0	1	5	9	14	.329	.343
Pavano,Carl	L	.290	207	60	8	1	5	24	15	32	.344	.411	Powell,Jay	L	.304	125	38	9	2	3	20	21	28	.411	.480
Throws Right	R	.279	204	57	6	4	3	29	20	38	.347	.392	Throws Right	R	.265	166	44	4	1	0	20	19	49	.341	.301
Pena,Jesus	L	.233	43	10	1	0	1	6	9	12	.377	.326	Powell,Jeremy	L	.250	164	41	3	1	4	14	18	23	.321	.354
Throws Left	R	.289	38	11	1	0	2	11	14	8	.481	.474	Throws Right	R	.343	210	72	11	1	10	38	26	21	.433	.548
Pena,Juan	L	.192	26	5	1	0	0	1	2	8	.250	.231	Pulsipher,B	L	.329	76	25	4	1	5	15	6	10	.376	.605
Throws Right	R	.200	20	4	0	0	0	0	1	7	.238	.200	Throws Left	R	.275	273	75	8	1	14	40	30	32	.346	.465
Percival,Troy	L	.214	112	24	7	1	5	25	15	33	.310	.429	Quantrill,P	L	.261	69	18	2	1	3	9	6	15	.350	.449
Throws Right	R	.152	92	14	1	0	4	9	7	25	.228	.293	Throws Right	R	.294	119	35	7	0	2	19	11	13	.351	.403

Pitchers vs. Lefthanded and Righthanded Batters

Pitcher	vs	Avg	AB	H	2B	3B	HR	BI	BB	SO	OBP	SLG
Radinsky,S	L	.273	44	12	1	0	2	9	9	10	.400	.432
Throws Left	R	.268	56	15	4	1	0	13	9	7	.348	.375
Radke,Brad	L	.281	456	128	25	1	14	53	33	56	.329	.432
Throws Right	R	.278	399	111	23	3	14	41	11	65	.296	.456
Radlosky,Rob	L	.250	12	3	1	0	1	4	1	1	.308	.583
Throws Right	R	.429	28	12	2	0	6	11	3	2	.500	1.143
Rain,Steve	L	.423	26	11	1	0	1	7	3	5	.500	.577
Throws Right	R	.415	41	17	3	0	0	13	4	7	.457	.488
Rakers,Jason	L	.200	5	1	0	0	1	1	0	0	.200	.800
Throws Right	R	.333	3	1	0	0	0	0	1	0	.500	.333
Ramirez,H	L	.257	35	9	2	0	0	4	3	2	.316	.314
Throws Right	R	.238	42	10	2	0	1	9	8	7	.360	.357
Ramirez,R	L	.403	62	25	4	0	3	12	5	14	.448	.613
Throws Left	R	.350	123	43	11	2	5	28	17	18	.429	.593
Ramsay,Rob	L	.227	22	5	2	0	0	2	1	3	.261	.318
Throws Left	R	.367	49	18	5	0	3	12	8	8	.448	.653
Rapp,Pat	L	.263	289	76	13	3	6	33	29	44	.332	.391
Throws Right	R	.263	270	71	9	0	7	29	40	46	.370	.374
Rath,Gary	L	.200	5	1	1	0	0	0	2	1	.429	.400
Throws Left	R	.333	15	5	0	0	1	3	3	0	.444	.533
Ray,Ken	L	.385	13	5	2	0	1	3	2	0	.467	.769
Throws Right	R	.486	37	18	4	2	1	9	4	0	.548	.784
Redman,Mark	L	.385	13	5	2	0	0	2	2	4	.467	.538
Throws Left	R	.273	44	12	3	1	3	11	5	7	.360	.591
Reed,Rick	L	.296	250	74	17	2	13	34	30	49	.369	.536
Throws Right	R	.270	330	89	16	3	10	39	17	55	.307	.427
Reed,Steve	L	.264	87	23	5	0	7	19	11	12	.350	.563
Throws Right	R	.297	155	46	8	0	3	29	9	32	.335	.406
Reichert,Dan	L	.342	73	25	4	1	2	19	17	10	.462	.507
Throws Right	R	.311	74	23	2	0	0	9	15	10	.440	.338
Rekar,Bryan	L	.323	186	60	13	1	4	24	23	22	.398	.468
Throws Right	R	.305	200	61	9	1	10	34	18	33	.372	.510
Remlinger,M	L	.205	83	17	1	0	3	10	5	22	.256	.325
Throws Left	R	.219	224	49	7	2	6	11	30	59	.311	.348
Reyes,Al	L	.174	86	15	7	0	3	19	18	25	.339	.360
Throws Right	R	.238	147	35	6	1	6	29	23	42	.345	.415
Reyes,Carlos	L	.289	128	37	6	1	4	24	10	21	.338	.445
Throws Right	R	.228	171	39	4	0	7	26	14	36	.283	.374
Reyes,Dennys	L	.242	95	23	2	0	2	14	17	45	.368	.326
Throws Left	R	.226	133	30	8	0	3	19	22	27	.333	.353
Reynolds,S	L	.282	418	118	22	3	10	39	22	95	.316	.421
Throws Right	R	.269	491	132	23	5	13	57	15	102	.291	.415
Reynoso,A	L	.263	323	85	18	0	11	37	28	37	.323	.421
Throws Right	R	.289	322	93	18	0	9	44	39	42	.369	.429
Rhodes,Arthur	L	.206	68	14	4	0	1	9	13	16	.333	.309
Throws Left	R	.228	127	29	2	0	8	23	32	43	.379	.433
Rigby,Brad	L	.350	163	57	9	1	5	32	17	16	.412	.509
Throws Right	R	.259	174	45	9	0	6	30	14	20	.326	.414
Riley,Matt	L	.333	6	2	0	0	1	2	3	1	.556	.833
Throws Left	R	.385	39	15	3	1	3	7	10	5	.500	.744

Pitcher	vs	Avg	AB	H	2B	3B	HR	BI	BB	SO	OBP	SLG
Rincon,Ricky	L	.233	73	17	4	0	3	11	6	11	.288	.411
Throws Left	R	.261	92	24	3	1	3	9	18	19	.387	.413
Riske,David	L	.316	19	6	0	0	0	5	3	3	.391	.316
Throws Right	R	.341	41	14	5	0	2	10	3	13	.386	.610
Ritchie,Todd	L	.280	275	77	15	3	8	34	31	41	.352	.444
Throws Right	R	.244	377	92	23	0	9	35	23	66	.294	.377
Rivera,M	L	.143	140	20	1	0	1	8	9	24	.193	.171
Throws Right	R	.219	105	23	6	1	1	9	9	28	.297	.324
Rivera,R	L	.111	18	2	1	0	0	3	2	3	.190	.167
Throws Left	R	.571	7	4	1	0	1	1	1	0	.625	1.143
Rizzo,Todd	L	.750	4	3	2	0	0	0	1	1	.800	1.250
Throws Left	R	.250	4	1	0	0	0	1	2	1	.500	.250
Roberts,W	L	.400	5	2	0	0	0	4	0	0	.333	.400
Throws Right	R	1.000	1	1	0	0	0	0	0	0	1.000	1.000
Rocker,John	L	.140	57	8	0	0	2	11	3	27	.183	.246
Throws Left	R	.191	204	39	8	0	3	21	34	77	.310	.275
Rodriguez,F	L	.223	103	23	6	0	1	14	15	31	.319	.311
Throws Right	R	.288	153	44	8	0	5	30	14	24	.351	.438
Rodriguez,F	L	.322	146	47	5	1	7	28	23	20	.412	.514
Throws Right	R	.307	153	47	11	1	4	24	7	27	.354	.471
Rodriguez,N	L	.400	5	2	0	0	2	3	1	0	.500	1.600
Throws Right	R	.000	3	0	0	0	0	0	1	2	.250	.000
Rodriguez,R	L	.271	96	26	4	1	5	20	13	22	.355	.490
Throws Left	R	.276	123	34	8	0	3	19	15	22	.357	.415
Rogers,Kenny	L	.274	157	43	8	1	6	23	14	42	.343	.452
Throws Left	R	.275	592	163	28	0	10	64	55	84	.344	.373
Rojas,Mel	L	.320	25	8	2	0	3	12	6	3	.455	.760
Throws Right	R	.368	38	14	5	0	3	17	3	7	.457	.737
Romano,Mike	L	.364	11	4	0	0	0	4	4	2	.500	.364
Throws Right	R	.364	11	4	0	0	1	5	1	1	.417	.636
Romero,J.C.	L	.231	13	3	0	0	0	1	0	2	.231	.231
Throws Left	R	.385	26	10	4	0	0	3	0	2	.385	.538
Roque,Rafael	L	.308	91	28	3	0	2	13	10	16	.388	.407
Throws Left	R	.278	245	68	10	1	14	39	32	50	.362	.498
Rosado,Jose	L	.242	149	36	4	0	6	21	15	29	.319	.389
Throws Left	R	.250	644	161	30	3	18	68	57	112	.312	.390
Rose,Brian	L	.220	191	42	7	1	6	13	13	26	.270	.361
Throws Right	R	.335	209	70	13	2	13	44	16	25	.388	.603
Rueter,Kirk	L	.236	148	35	8	1	1	10	6	25	.265	.324
Throws Left	R	.312	589	184	35	3	27	99	49	69	.365	.520
Runyan,Sean	L	.235	17	4	0	0	1	3	1	3	.300	.412
Throws Left	R	.238	21	5	1	0	1	8	2	3	.292	.429
Rupe,Ryan	L	.261	245	64	23	3	8	38	36	47	.357	.478
Throws Right	R	.247	292	72	7	4	9	34	21	50	.315	.390
Rusch,Glen.	L	.375	8	3	0	0	0	1	3	2	.583	.375
Throws Left	R	.357	14	5	0	0	1	5	1	1	.357	.571
Ryan,B.J.	L	.192	26	5	0	0	0	6	2	16	.241	.192
Throws Left	R	.190	42	8	2	0	0	3	11	13	.358	.238
Ryan,Jason	L	.320	75	24	3	2	2	7	13	8	.422	.493
Throws Right	R	.256	86	22	5	0	7	13	4	7	.304	.558

Pitchers vs. Lefthanded and Righthanded Batters

Pitcher	vs	Avg	AB	H	2B	3B	HR	BI	BB	SO	OBP	SLG	Pitcher	vs	Avg	AB	H	2B	3B	HR	BI	BB	SO	OBP	SLG
Ryan,Ken	L	.125	16	2	0	0	0	0	5	6	.333	.125	Simas,Bill	L	.258	124	32	8	0	1	18	18	16	.359	.347
Throws Right	R	.318	44	14	1	0	2	11	6	3	.400	.477	Throws Right	R	.266	154	41	9	3	5	35	14	25	.337	.461
Sabel,Erik	L	.357	14	5	2	0	1	1	1	2	.400	.714	Sinclair,S	L	.226	31	7	2	0	1	4	8	7	.415	.387
Throws Right	R	.269	26	7	1	0	0	3	5	4	.424	.308	Throws Left	R	.313	48	15	6	0	4	10	6	11	.389	.688
Saberhagen,B	L	.276	210	58	14	2	3	15	2	34	.285	.405	Sirotka,Mike	L	.266	188	50	9	0	7	27	8	40	.298	.426
Throws Right	R	.255	251	64	14	2	8	25	9	47	.282	.422	Throws Left	R	.287	647	186	30	1	17	76	49	85	.336	.416
Sampson,Benj	L	.330	97	32	5	0	4	17	5	22	.356	.505	Slocumb,H	L	.297	101	30	6	1	0	9	21	24	.423	.376
Throws Right	R	.361	208	75	10	1	13	44	29	34	.433	.606	Throws Left	R	.245	139	34	5	1	5	24	18	36	.338	.403
Sanchez,Je.	L	.256	90	23	4	1	3	17	15	19	.367	.422	Slusarski,Joe	L	.000	4	0	0	0	0	0	2	0	.333	.000
Throws Left	R	.307	199	61	16	4	13	48	45	43	.430	.623	Throws Right	R	.125	8	1	1	0	0	0	1	3	.222	.250
Sanders,Scott	L	.299	137	41	6	1	7	19	31	22	.424	.511	Smart,J.D.	L	.295	88	26	7	1	2	18	11	7	.370	.466
Throws Right	R	.265	268	71	12	1	12	47	22	67	.320	.451	Throws Right	R	.261	115	30	7	0	2	21	6	14	.298	.374
Santana,Julio	L	.265	102	27	10	1	4	17	8	13	.339	.500	Smith,Dan	L	.322	146	47	6	1	8	26	22	30	.416	.541
Throws Right	R	.331	118	39	8	0	6	26	24	21	.455	.551	Throws Right	R	.273	209	57	11	2	4	32	17	42	.330	.402
Santana,M	L	.500	8	4	1	0	2	3	1	3	.556	1.375	Smoltz,John	L	.264	311	82	18	2	7	32	22	47	.315	.402
Throws Right	R	.400	10	4	0	0	1	5	2	1	.462	.700	Throws Right	R	.229	376	86	21	2	7	34	18	109	.266	.351
Santiago,Jose	L	.210	81	17	1	0	2	8	5	8	.250	.296	Snyder,John	L	.297	266	79	19	1	13	46	21	32	.349	.523
Throws Right	R	.284	102	29	4	0	5	24	9	7	.351	.471	Throws Right	R	.325	271	88	14	1	14	49	28	35	.391	.539
Sauerbeck,S	L	.167	90	15	1	0	5	20	10	27	.272	.344	Sodowsky,C	L	.429	14	6	0	0	1	4	1	1	.467	.643
Throws Left	R	.252	151	38	10	0	1	8	28	28	.372	.338	Throws Right	R	.474	19	9	1	1	0	8	5	1	.583	.632
Saunders,Tony	L	.279	43	12	1	0	1	8	7	9	.380	.372	Sparks,Jeff	L	.071	14	1	0	0	0	2	5	11	.316	.071
Throws Left	R	.328	125	41	12	0	5	22	22	21	.438	.544	Throws Right	R	.238	21	5	2	0	1	4	7	6	.448	.476
Scheffer,A	L	.333	9	3	0	0	0	4	3	1	.400	.333	Sparks,Steve	L	.293	280	82	18	3	9	38	46	35	.396	.475
Throws Right	R	.375	8	3	0	0	0	1	0	3	.444	.375	Throws Right	R	.270	307	83	13	0	12	51	36	38	.351	.430
Schilling,C	L	.249	334	83	13	2	12	37	20	83	.291	.407	Speier,Justin	L	.275	51	14	3	0	3	11	2	8	.302	.510
Throws Right	R	.225	338	76	15	0	13	34	24	69	.283	.385	Throws Right	R	.226	62	14	2	0	5	11	11	14	.338	.500
Schmidt,Jason	L	.288	379	109	20	7	17	58	47	74	.361	.512	Spencer,Sean	L	.333	3	1	0	0	0	0	0	1	.333	.333
Throws Right	R	.241	456	110	27	8	7	37	38	74	.303	.382	Throws Left	R	.667	6	4	1	0	0	2	3	1	.778	.833
Schoeneweis	L	.266	64	17	3	0	1	11	6	13	.329	.359	Spencer,Stan	L	.317	82	26	2	0	6	20	4	11	.349	.561
Throws Left	R	.313	96	30	5	1	3	16	8	9	.362	.479	Throws Right	R	.353	85	30	7	1	5	17	7	25	.409	.635
Schourek,Pete	L	.275	80	22	7	1	4	15	7	20	.351	.538	Spoljaric,P	L	.363	91	33	7	2	5	27	15	32	.453	.648
Throws Left	R	.290	366	106	31	1	16	53	42	74	.360	.511	Throws Left	R	.256	203	52	17	2	5	36	24	41	.338	.433
Schrenk,Steve	L	.283	60	17	4	1	4	11	7	8	.371	.583	Spradlin,J	L	.288	73	21	4	0	2	16	19	21	.447	.425
Throws Right	R	.194	124	24	1	0	2	11	7	28	.265	.250	Throws Right	R	.259	170	44	7	1	3	24	13	33	.340	.365
Seanez,Rudy	L	.239	88	21	1	0	3	9	5	12	.277	.352	Springer,D	L	.328	317	104	19	3	12	55	38	32	.401	.521
Throws Right	R	.230	113	26	5	0	0	11	16	29	.328	.274	Throws Right	R	.285	445	127	22	3	11	63	26	51	.326	.422
Sele,Aaron	L	.286	399	114	24	3	11	56	32	89	.343	.444	Springer,Russ	L	.154	65	10	2	0	3	10	9	21	.276	.323
Throws Right	R	.299	435	130	32	2	10	48	38	97	.365	.451	Throws Right	R	.204	103	21	6	1	2	13	13	28	.288	.340
Serafini,Dan	L	.282	85	24	3	0	4	16	11	9	.361	.459	Stanton,Mike	L	.256	90	23	7	0	2	15	9	28	.317	.400
Throws Left	R	.358	173	62	12	2	5	33	21	8	.426	.538	Throws Left	R	.308	156	48	7	2	3	18	9	31	.349	.436
Service,Scott	L	.339	118	40	7	3	7	25	24	20	.448	.627	Stark,Dennis	L	.462	13	6	1	0	0	3	1	1	.500	.538
Throws Right	R	.264	178	47	7	2	6	37	18	48	.330	.427	Throws Right	R	.286	14	4	1	0	0	0	3	3	.412	.357
Shaw,Jeff	L	.201	134	27	3	0	3	12	8	26	.245	.291	Stein,Blake	L	.256	133	34	6	1	6	18	29	22	.390	.451
Throws Right	R	.282	131	37	6	0	3	16	7	17	.321	.397	Throws Right	R	.226	137	31	6	0	5	18	18	25	.342	.380
Shuey,Paul	L	.223	139	31	9	0	3	20	20	41	.321	.353	Stephenson,G	L	.320	153	49	3	3	6	24	13	21	.375	.497
Throws Right	R	.223	166	37	8	1	5	22	20	62	.309	.373	Throws Right	R	.236	174	41	9	0	5	17	16	38	.308	.374
Shumaker,A	L	.250	20	5	0	0	0	1	3	5	.348	.250	Stevens,Dave	L	.294	17	5	2	0	1	4	3	3	.400	.588
Throws Right	R	.265	68	18	5	0	3	13	11	12	.375	.471	Throws Right	R	.278	18	5	2	0	0	4	5	3	.417	.389
Silva,Jose	L	.230	161	37	8	1	5	22	18	38	.309	.385	Stottlemyre,T	L	.312	170	53	11	1	6	22	18	26	.394	.494
Throws Right	R	.317	224	71	18	1	5	42	21	39	.378	.473	Throws Right	R	.235	226	53	11	1	6	26	22	48	.304	.372

Pitchers vs. Lefthanded and Righthanded Batters

Pitcher	vs	Avg	AB	H	2B	3B	HR	BI	BB	SO	OBP	SLG
Strickland,S	L	.400	20	8	0	0	3	6	7	2	.556	.850
Throws Right	R	.156	45	7	0	0	0	0	4	21	.224	.156
Stull,Everett	L	.500	4	2	0	0	0	3	1	0	.500	.500
Throws Right	R	.000	0	0	0	0	0	0	1	0	1.000	.000
Sturtze,T	L	.167	18	3	0	0	0	0	2	2	.250	.167
Throws Right	R	.500	2	1	1	0	0	0	0	0	.500	1.000
Sullivan,S	L	.242	153	37	11	2	3	15	19	28	.328	.399
Throws Right	R	.202	253	51	6	1	7	27	28	50	.295	.316
Suppan,Jeff	L	.259	402	104	16	4	17	42	36	53	.320	.445
Throws Right	R	.289	408	118	18	3	11	59	26	50	.333	.429
Suzuki,Makoto	L	.284	222	63	18	0	7	38	34	37	.387	.459
Throws Right	R	.288	212	61	12	1	9	43	30	31	.381	.481
Swindell,Greg	L	.215	93	20	3	0	1	5	5	12	.255	.280
Throws Left	R	.239	142	34	3	3	7	18	16	39	.321	.451
Tam,Jeff	L	.200	15	3	0	0	1	1	3	3	.333	.400
Throws Right	R	.185	27	5	0	0	2	2	1	5	.214	.407
Tapani,Kevin	L	.264	235	62	16	3	7	31	16	28	.307	.447
Throws Right	R	.293	304	89	21	2	5	46	17	45	.334	.424
Tavarez,J	L	.345	84	29	6	0	3	20	9	11	.400	.524
Throws Right	R	.265	136	36	3	0	4	21	16	22	.375	.375
Taylor,Billy	L	.388	98	38	6	1	1	14	15	15	.470	.500
Throws Right	R	.236	127	30	7	1	4	17	8	37	.285	.402
Tejera,M	L	.300	10	3	1	0	0	0	2	2	.417	.400
Throws Left	R	.438	16	7	2	0	1	6	3	5	.526	.750
Telemaco,A	L	.304	69	21	6	0	3	13	14	13	.422	.522
Throws Right	R	.235	132	31	4	1	7	24	12	30	.306	.439
Telford,A	L	.327	171	56	11	0	1	26	19	26	.399	.409
Throws Right	R	.268	209	56	7	0	2	32	19	43	.326	.330
Tessmer,Jay	L	.533	15	8	2	0	1	6	2	1	.588	.867
Throws Right	R	.381	21	8	1	1	0	6	2	2	.458	.524
Thompson,J	L	.268	112	30	9	0	4	21	13	21	.341	.455
Throws Left	R	.275	443	122	16	1	20	56	46	62	.345	.451
Thompson,Ma.	L	.163	43	7	2	0	1	5	7	8	.280	.279
Throws Right	R	.292	65	19	5	1	0	5	10	14	.403	.400
Thomson,John	L	.278	115	32	9	0	6	14	15	13	.366	.513
Throws Right	R	.361	147	53	13	1	5	41	21	21	.435	.565
Thurman,Mike	L	.285	263	75	15	0	6	22	27	39	.355	.411
Throws Right	R	.221	294	65	11	4	11	41	25	46	.291	.398
Timlin,Mike	L	.194	108	21	5	0	4	17	11	21	.275	.352
Throws Right	R	.244	123	30	5	0	5	18	12	29	.329	.407
Tomko,Brett	L	.250	320	80	28	0	12	35	33	73	.320	.450
Throws Right	R	.275	346	95	25	2	19	58	27	59	.330	.523
Trachsel,S	L	.285	355	101	12	3	16	53	37	66	.349	.470
Throws Right	R	.277	452	125	23	3	16	63	27	83	.314	.447
Trombley,Mike	L	.240	146	35	4	2	4	13	21	31	.335	.377
Throws Right	R	.296	196	58	12	1	11	39	7	51	.322	.536
Urbina,Ugueth	L	.198	121	24	3	0	3	19	18	37	.298	.298
Throws Right	R	.215	163	35	6	0	3	20	18	63	.293	.307
Valdes,Ismael	L	.271	336	91	17	3	14	39	27	56	.327	.464
Throws Right	R	.269	454	122	16	2	18	51	31	87	.317	.432
Vazquez,J	L	.234	274	64	13	2	8	40	28	44	.305	.383
Throws Right	R	.272	331	90	24	2	12	43	24	69	.326	.465
Venafro,Mike	L	.193	114	22	0	0	1	14	11	22	.270	.219
Throws Left	R	.299	137	41	6	2	3	26	11	15	.355	.438
Veres,Dave	L	.328	128	42	6	0	6	19	22	24	.425	.516
Throws Right	R	.263	175	46	6	0	8	27	15	47	.325	.434
Villone,Ron	L	.253	87	22	3	1	2	13	8	15	.330	.379
Throws Left	R	.212	433	92	28	2	6	47	65	82	.317	.328
Vizcaino,Luis	L	.286	7	2	0	0	1	2	0	0	.286	.714
Throws Right	R	.167	6	1	0	0	0	0	3	2	.444	.167
Vosberg,Ed	L	.462	26	12	2	0	1	8	1	5	.500	.654
Throws Left	R	.400	25	10	3	1	0	5	2	3	.429	.600
Wagner,Billy	L	.167	48	8	0	0	1	5	6	13	.273	.229
Throws Left	R	.128	211	27	5	0	4	10	17	111	.192	.209
Wagner,Paul	L	.308	13	4	3	0	0	4	3	0	.438	.538
Throws Right	R	.167	6	1	1	0	0	0	0	0	.375	.333
Wainhouse,D	L	.300	50	15	6	0	2	12	4	5	.345	.540
Throws Right	R	.355	62	22	2	1	4	17	12	13	.447	.613
Wakefield,Tim	L	.284	229	65	14	1	7	33	33	37	.369	.445
Throws Right	R	.254	319	81	16	1	12	46	39	67	.340	.423
Wall,Donne	L	.185	108	20	2	0	3	9	10	25	.254	.287
Throws Right	R	.242	157	38	3	0	8	26	13	28	.298	.414
Wallace,Derek	L	.333	9	3	1	0	0	1	3	2	.462	.444
Throws Left	R	.222	18	4	0	0	2	4	2	3	.300	.556
Wallace,Jeff	L	.261	46	12	2	0	1	10	14	12	.426	.370
Throws Left	R	.161	87	14	3	0	1	3	24	29	.342	.230
Ward,Bryan	L	.348	69	24	2	0	6	15	7	18	.408	.638
Throws Left	R	.382	102	39	8	0	4	20	4	17	.402	.578
Wasdin,John	L	.240	121	29	4	1	5	17	6	20	.273	.413
Throws Right	R	.233	159	37	7	0	9	30	12	37	.285	.447
Washburn,J	L	.216	51	11	3	0	1	5	5	13	.298	.333
Throws Left	R	.273	183	50	7	4	5	23	21	26	.345	.437
Watson,Allen	L	.229	96	22	2	1	4	11	8	22	.288	.396
Throws Left	R	.265	189	50	9	0	9	24	27	42	.351	.455
Weathers,Da.	L	.290	124	36	4	0	7	21	19	18	.379	.492
Throws Right	R	.273	242	66	12	4	7	32	19	56	.328	.442
Weaver,Eric	L	.333	12	4	2	0	0	3	4	5	.500	.500
Throws Right	R	.313	32	10	1	0	2	11	4	9	.389	.531
Weaver,Jeff	L	.310	358	111	24	3	20	71	32	57	.378	.561
Throws Right	R	.236	276	65	14	1	7	26	24	57	.314	.370
Wells,Bob	L	.248	121	30	8	0	3	15	14	16	.321	.388
Throws Right	R	.243	202	49	12	1	5	34	14	28	.306	.386
Wells,David	L	.295	156	46	7	1	6	30	10	26	.349	.468
Throws Left	R	.266	751	200	38	4	26	90	52	143	.314	.431
Wells,Kip	L	.267	90	24	6	0	1	12	11	21	.346	.367
Throws Right	R	.209	43	9	2	0	1	3	4	8	.306	.326
Wendell,Turk	L	.268	127	34	3	1	2	11	15	17	.343	.354
Throws Right	R	.230	200	46	8	2	7	23	22	60	.313	.395
Wengert,Don	L	.439	57	25	3	0	3	14	3	4	.459	.649
Throws Right	R	.308	52	16	2	1	3	14	2	6	.327	.558

Pitchers vs. Lefthanded and Righthanded Batters

Pitcher	vs	Avg	AB	H	2B	3B	HR	BI	BB	SO	OBP	SLG
Wetteland,J	L	.265	136	36	8	1	4	16	13	30	.325	.426
Throws Right	R	.258	120	31	6	1	5	14	6	30	.287	.450
Wheeler,Dan	L	.302	63	19	0	1	6	15	10	10	.397	.619
Throws Right	R	.271	59	16	3	0	1	3	3	22	.306	.373
Whisenant,M	L	.220	82	18	1	0	2	14	14	17	.347	.305
Throws Left	R	.271	118	32	7	1	2	20	22	20	.407	.398
White,Gabe	L	.365	74	27	5	1	2	14	6	18	.420	.541
Throws Left	R	.244	168	41	6	0	11	27	8	43	.281	.476
White,Rick	L	.309	188	58	15	0	4	29	12	38	.348	.452
Throws Right	R	.301	246	74	14	0	4	40	26	43	.365	.407
Whiteside,M	L	.438	16	7	2	0	1	6	2	5	.500	.750
Throws Right	R	.375	32	12	5	0	0	8	3	4	.417	.531
Wickman,Bob	L	.197	127	25	5	0	2	13	26	26	.335	.283
Throws Right	R	.314	159	50	7	1	4	19	12	34	.364	.447
Wilkins,Marc	L	.211	71	15	6	0	1	5	8	16	.288	.338
Throws Right	R	.283	120	34	7	0	2	20	18	28	.392	.392
Williams,B	L	.324	111	36	12	1	1	21	19	22	.421	.477
Throws Right	R	.231	143	33	8	1	3	24	16	31	.321	.364
Williams,Jeff	L	.118	17	2	0	0	1	2	3	4	.250	.294
Throws Left	R	.217	46	10	3	0	1	7	6	3	.308	.348
Williams,Mike	L	.253	79	20	7	0	3	11	25	28	.438	.456
Throws Right	R	.289	149	43	5	0	6	30	12	48	.340	.443
Williams,Todd	L	.400	10	4	1	0	1	4	2	1	.500	.800
Throws Right	R	.250	28	7	1	0	0	3	5	6	.382	.286
Williams,W	L	.258	356	92	19	4	10	41	28	62	.309	.419
Throws Right	R	.276	438	121	25	2	23	60	45	75	.343	.500
Williamson,S	L	.171	146	25	6	0	5	12	25	53	.292	.315
Throws Right	R	.172	169	29	6	1	3	17	18	54	.253	.272
Winkelsas,Joe	L	1.000	1	1	0	0	0	0	1	0	1.000	1.000
Throws Right	R	1.000	3	3	0	0	0	2	0	0	1.000	1.000
Witasick,Jay	L	.322	307	99	18	1	11	45	54	50	.422	.495
Throws Right	R	.286	322	92	9	0	12	47	29	52	.352	.425
Witt,Bobby	L	.292	363	106	29	2	12	56	68	62	.404	.482
Throws Right	R	.317	338	107	18	0	11	54	28	61	.366	.467
Wohlers,Mark	L	1.000	1	1	1	0	0	1	3	0	1.000	2.000
Throws Right	R	.000	2	0	0	0	0	0	3	0	.600	.000
Wolcott,Bob	L	.231	13	3	1	0	0	2	1	0	.286	.308
Throws Right	R	.455	11	5	1	0	1	4	2	2	.533	.818
Wolf,Randy	L	.209	86	18	5	1	4	11	12	31	.306	.430
Throws Left	R	.278	388	108	24	2	16	62	55	85	.374	.474
Woodall,Brad	L	.278	18	5	1	0	1	2	3	4	.381	.500
Throws Left	R	.267	45	12	2	0	4	7	3	3	.320	.578
Woodard,St.	L	.279	330	92	25	2	9	39	16	44	.314	.448
Throws Right	R	.305	416	127	26	1	14	53	20	75	.342	.474
Worrell,Tim	L	.285	130	37	11	0	2	31	16	26	.365	.415
Throws Right	R	.229	140	32	6	1	4	17	18	36	.325	.371
Wright,Jamey	L	.329	152	50	12	1	3	20	29	15	.440	.480
Throws Right	R	.293	205	60	14	1	7	29	25	34	.370	.473
Wright,Jaret	L	.294	255	75	12	3	10	44	43	42	.400	.482
Throws Right	R	.261	264	69	12	0	8	37	34	49	.353	.398

Pitcher	vs	Avg	AB	H	2B	3B	HR	BI	BB	SO	OBP	SLG
Yan,Esteban	L	.310	116	36	7	0	4	18	16	21	.393	.474
Throws Right	R	.342	120	41	4	0	4	21	16	25	.448	.475
Yarnall,Ed	L	.190	21	4	1	0	0	1	4	6	.320	.238
Throws Left	R	.283	46	13	3	0	1	7	6	7	.365	.413
Yoshii,Masato	L	.271	292	79	25	3	11	31	36	35	.349	.490
Throws Right	R	.251	354	89	19	4	14	49	22	70	.302	.446
Zimmerman,J	L	.158	146	23	4	0	6	13	11	39	.222	.308
Throws Right	R	.173	156	27	7	0	3	19	12	28	.229	.276
Zimmerman,J	L	.474	19	9	1	0	0	9	4	2	.583	.526
Throws Left	R	.294	17	5	3	0	0	2	0	1	.294	.471
AL	L	.275	—	—	—	—	—	—	—	—	.356	.440
	R	.276	—	—	—	—	—	—	—	—	.342	.440
NL	L	.276	—	—	—	—	—	—	—	—	.354	.440
	R	.262	—	—	—	—	—	—	—	—	.333	.421
MLB	L	.276	—	—	—	—	—	—	—	—	.355	.440
	R	.268	—	—	—	—	—	—	—	—	.337	.430

Runs Created/
Component Earned Run Average

Two years ago, STATS produced two books which we feel set the standard for encyclopedic information. Ask any question about baseball, and the chances are good you'll find the answer in either our *All-Time Major League Handbook* or *All-Time Baseball Sourcebook*.

Among the mountain of statistics available in each book, it's likely that two of them—Runs Created per 27 Outs (RC/27) and Component ERA (ERC)—are the ones which are most compelling. For a definition of each stat, please consult the Glossary. But since the two historical volumes are complete through the 1997 season, the following section provides a complementary update for active players through the year just completed. If you need any more evidence confirming the greatness of Mark McGwire or Pedro Martinez, this is the section to consult.

Runs Created

Player, Team	1999 RC	RC/27	LRC/27	Career RC	RC/27	LRC27
Abbott, Jeff, CWS	0	0.00	5.18	40	3.92	5.04
Abbott, Jim, Mil	0	0.00	5.00	0	0.00	5.00
Abbott, Kurt, Col	48	5.95	5.00	243	4.47	4.72
Abreu, Bobby, Phi	127	8.79	5.00	265	7.79	4.77
Acevedo, Juan, StL	0	0.00	5.00	1	0.43	4.74
Adams, Terry, ChC	0	0.00	5.00	0	0.00	4.72
Agbayani, Benny, NYM	45	5.71	5.00	45	5.31	4.97
Aguilera, Rick, ChC	0	0.00	5.00	10	2.12	4.23
Aldred, Scott, TB/Phi	0	0.00	5.00	0	0.00	5.00
Alexander, Manny, ChC	20	4.08	5.00	96	3.19	4.84
Alfonseca, Antonio, Fla	0	0.00	5.00	0	0.00	4.69
Alfonzo, Edgardo, NYM	117	6.80	5.00	391	5.81	4.72
Alicea, Luis, Tex	14	2.67	5.18	381	4.55	4.63
Allen, Chad, Min	58	4.21	5.18	58	4.21	5.18
Allensworth, Jer., NYM	9	3.91	5.00	138	4.52	4.68
Almanza, Armando, Fla	0	0.00	5.00	0	0.00	5.00
Almanzar, Carlos, SD	0	0.00	5.00	0	0.00	5.00
Alomar, Roberto, Cle	142	8.92	5.18	1143	6.13	4.66
Alomar Jr., Sandy, Cle	23	6.14	5.18	374	4.21	4.85
Alvarez, Gabe, Det	4	2.54	5.18	28	3.72	5.05
Alvarez, Wilson, TB	0	0.00	5.18	0	0.00	4.70
Amaral, Rich, Bal	14	3.43	5.18	214	4.23	5.18
Anderson, Brady, Bal	113	7.09	5.18	923	5.77	4.83
Anderson, Brian, Ari	0	0.00	5.00	0	0.00	4.74
Anderson, Garret, Ana	86	5.03	5.18	384	4.83	5.12
Anderson, Jimmy, Pit	2	8.97	5.00	2	8.97	5.00
Anderson, Marlon, Phi	54	4.13	5.00	63	4.44	4.97
Andrews, S., Mon/ChC	34	3.09	5.00	169	3.72	4.72
Ankiel, Rick, StL	0	0.00	5.00	0	0.00	5.00
Appier, Kevin, KC/Oak	0	0.00	5.18	0	0.00	4.99
Arias, Alex, Phi	51	5.30	5.00	175	4.16	4.64
Arias, George, SD	16	3.31	5.00	42	2.93	5.15
Armas Jr., Tony, Mon	0	0.00	5.00	0	0.00	5.00
Arnold, Jamie, LA	0	0.00	5.00	0	0.00	5.00
Arrojo, Rolando, TB	0	—		0	0.00	5.01
Ashby, Andy, SD	2	0.87	5.00	7	0.46	4.63
Assenmacher, Paul, Cle	0	—		2	1.32	4.14
Astacio, Pedro, Col	8	2.95	5.00	8	0.51	4.63
Aurilia, Rich, SF	79	4.97	5.00	180	4.45	4.78
Ausmus, Brad, Det	70	5.25	5.18	301	4.11	4.78
Aven, Bruce, Fla	70	6.66	5.00	71	6.39	5.00
Avery, Steve, Cin	0	0.00	5.00	16	1.05	4.38
Ayala, Bobby, Mon/ChC	0	0.00	5.00	0	0.00	4.32
Aybar, Manny, StL	0	0.00	5.00	2	1.04	4.69
Baerga, Carlos, SD/Cle	11	2.61	5.08	649	4.79	4.74
Bagwell, Jeff, Hou	157	9.90	5.00	1059	8.01	4.50
Baines, Harold, Bal/Cle	89	7.52	5.18	1534	5.75	4.64
Bako, Paul, Hou	20	3.15	5.00	47	3.14	5.01
Baldwin, James, CWS	1	26.71	5.18	1	3.82	4.99
Banks, Brian, Mil	23	3.56	5.00	39	4.18	4.96
Barajas, Rod, Ari	3	6.21	5.00	3	6.21	5.00
Barber, Brian, KC	0	0.00	5.18	0	0.00	4.70
Barker, Glen, Hou	14	5.98	5.00	14	5.98	5.00
Barker, Kevin, Mil	21	6.65	5.00	21	6.65	5.00
Barrett, Michael, Mon	59	4.86	5.00	63	4.94	4.98
Barry, Jeff, Col	23	4.62	5.00	23	3.52	4.91
Bartee, Kimera, Det	3	1.14	5.18	34	2.63	5.25
Batista, Miguel, Mon	4	3.36	5.00	3	1.09	4.77
Batista, Tony, Ari/Tor	87	5.87	5.13	190	5.32	5.02
Battle, Howard, Atl	4	8.97	5.00	6	5.56	4.97
Bautista, Danny, Fla	21	3.72	5.00	88	3.04	4.94
Beck, Rod, ChC/Bos	0	—		1	1.80	4.50
Becker, Rich, Mil/Oak	40	5.16	5.09	269	4.71	5.10
Belcher, Tim, Ana	0	0.00	5.18	3	0.21	4.10
Belinda, Stan, Cin	0	0.00	5.00	2	2.17	4.32
Bell, David, Sea	84	4.90	5.18	163	3.83	4.96
Bell, Derek, Hou	48	3.08	5.00	519	4.70	4.65
Bell, Jay, Ari	121	7.32	5.00	906	4.94	4.47
Belle, Albert, Bal	125	7.34	5.18	1057	7.08	4.88
Belliard, Ron, Mil	73	5.57	5.00	73	5.50	5.00
Bellinger, Clay, NYY	2	1.44	5.18	2	1.44	5.18
Beltran, Carlos, KC	111	5.88	5.18	122	5.94	5.17
Beltran, Rigo, NYM/Col	0	0.00	5.00	0	0.00	4.72
Beltre, Adrian, LA	79	5.19	5.00	102	4.82	4.89
Benard, Marvin, SF	92	5.90	5.00	213	5.07	4.78
Benes, Alan, StL	0	—		2	0.49	4.65
Benes, Andy, Ari	1	0.45	5.00	20	0.85	4.45
Benitez, Armando, NYM	0	0.00	5.00	0	0.00	5.00
Benjamin, Mike, Pit	42	3.83	5.00	149	3.08	4.71
Bennett, Gary, Phi	12	4.42	5.00	15	3.67	4.88

Player, Team	1999 RC	RC/27	LRC/27	Career RC	RC/27	LRC27
Bennett, Joel, Phi	0	0.00	5.00	0	0.00	5.00
Bennett, Shayne, Mon	0	0.00	5.00	0	0.00	4.68
Benson, Kris, Pit	1	0.43	5.00	1	0.43	5.00
Bere, Jason, Cin/Mil	2	3.17	5.00	2	1.68	4.81
Berg, Dave, Fla	37	4.35	5.00	73	5.43	4.85
Bergeron, Peter, Mon	4	3.08	5.00	4	3.08	5.00
Bergman, Sean, Hou/Atl	0	0.00	5.00	1	0.21	4.70
Berkman, Lance, Hou	10	3.59	5.00	10	3.59	5.00
Berroa, Geronimo, Tor	5	2.43	5.18	380	5.38	5.05
Berry, Sean, Mil	17	2.22	5.00	341	5.05	4.63
Bichette, Dante, Col	110	6.62	5.00	882	5.85	4.59
Biggio, Craig, Hou	119	6.66	5.00	1136	6.39	4.49
Blair, Willie, Det	0	0.00	5.18	0	0.00	4.51
Blake, Casey, Tor	1	0.89	5.18	1	0.89	5.18
Blanco, Henry, Col	29	3.68	5.00	31	3.88	5.00
Blauser, Jeff, ChC	28	4.77	5.00	676	5.16	4.61
Blowers, Mike, Sea	6	4.33	5.18	327	4.81	4.86
Blum, Geoff, Mon	18	4.53	5.00	18	4.53	5.00
Bochtler, Doug, LA	0	—		0	0.00	4.63
Boehringer, Brian, SD	0	0.00	5.00	0	0.00	4.89
Bogar, Tim, Hou	29	3.09	5.00	116	3.19	4.70
Boggs, Wade, TB	38	4.57	5.18	1648	6.75	4.66
Bohanon, Brian, Col	3	1.26	5.00	10	2.07	4.80
Bonds, Barry, SF	82	8.08	5.00	1626	8.31	4.36
Bones, Ricky, Bal	0	—		0	0.00	4.20
Bonilla, Bobby, NYM	6	1.51	5.00	1130	5.87	4.42
Boone, Aaron, Cin	70	5.20	5.00	99	4.94	4.87
Boone, Bret, Atl	77	4.26	5.00	417	4.07	4.69
Borbon, Pedro, LA	0	0.00	5.00	1	6.75	4.91
Borders, Pat, Cle/Tor	6	6.16	5.18	280	3.13	4.66
Bordick, Mike, Bal	76	4.04	5.18	461	3.61	4.95
Borkowski, Dave, Det	0	0.00	5.18	0	0.00	5.18
Bottalico, Ricky, StL	0	0.00	5.00	1	2.08	4.75
Bottenfield, Kent, StL	2	0.90	5.00	5	0.87	4.70
Bournigal, Rafael, Sea	14	4.67	5.18	88	3.08	5.03
Bowie, Micah, Atl/ChC	1	2.45	5.00	1	2.45	5.00
Boyd, Jason, Pit	0	0.00	5.00	0	0.00	5.18
Bragg, Darren, StL	41	5.21	5.00	247	4.71	5.08
Brantley, Jeff, Phi	0	—		1	0.37	4.26
Branyan, Russ, Cle	6	5.34	5.18	6	4.71	5.16
Brewer, Billy, Phi	0	—		0	0.00	4.60
Brocail, Doug, Det	0	—		3	1.14	4.52
Brock, Chris, SF	3	2.52	5.00	3	1.79	4.89
Brogna, Rico, Phi	84	4.76	5.00	365	5.01	4.71
Brosius, Scott, NYY	62	4.32	5.18	414	4.71	5.05
Brown, Adrian, Pit	27	4.04	5.00	50	3.17	4.77
Brown, Brant, Pit	46	4.52	5.00	125	4.88	4.77
Brown, Dee, KC	0	0.00	5.18	0	0.00	5.16
Brown, Emil, Pit	0	0.00	5.00	7	1.56	4.64
Brown, Kevin, LA	-2	-0.62	5.00	6	0.54	4.74
Brown, Kevin L., Tor	2	10.68	5.18	17	4.47	5.04
Brown, Roosevelt, ChC	7	3.36	5.00	7	3.36	5.00
Brownson, Mark, Col	0	0.00	5.00	0	0.00	4.87
Brumfield, Jacob, LA/Tor	22	3.87	5.16	210	4.52	4.84
Buford, Damon, Bos	30	3.40	5.18	155	4.01	5.01
Buhner, Jay, Sea	48	5.94	5.18	813	6.03	4.82
Bullinger, Kirk, Bos	0	—		0	0.00	4.50
Burba, Dave, Cle	1	13.36	5.18	9	1.44	4.57
Burkett, John, Tex	0	0.00	5.18	-4	-0.24	4.37
Burks, Ellis, SF	97	8.70	5.00	974	6.11	4.58
Burnett, A.J., Fla	0	0.00	5.00	0	0.00	5.00
Burnitz, Jeromy, Mil	95	7.08	5.00	373	5.94	4.82
Busby, Mike, StL	0	—		1	4.49	4.61
Bush, Homer, Tor	72	5.37	5.18	86	5.54	5.15
Butler, Rich, TB	1	1.57	5.18	25	3.28	5.02
Butler, Rob, Tor	1	4.45	5.18	23	3.44	4.89
Byrd, Paul, Phi	2	0.88	5.00	5	1.56	4.89
Byrdak, Tim, KC	1	26.71	5.18	1	26.71	5.18
Cabrera, Jolbert, Cle	1	0.86	5.18	1	0.81	5.17
Cabrera, Jose, Hou	0	—		0	0.00	4.60
Cabrera, Orlando, Mon	42	3.77	5.00	72	3.73	4.83
Cairo, Miguel, TB	54	4.01	5.18	113	3.73	5.08
Callaway, Mickey, TB	1	26.71	5.18	1	26.71	5.18
Cameron, Mike, Cin	87	5.48	5.00	195	4.75	4.99
Caminiti, Ken, Hou	46	5.87	5.00	871	5.34	4.38
Cancel, Robinson, Mil	1	0.73	5.00	1	0.73	5.00
Candiotti, Tom, Cle	0	—		0	0.00	4.45
Cangelosi, John, Col	0	0.00	5.00	281	4.66	4.48
Canizaro, Jay, SF	8	21.53	5.00	14	3.28	4.71
Canseco, Jose, TB	77	6.21	5.18	1171	6.21	4.76

338

Player, Team	1999 RC	RC/27	LRC/27	Career RC	RC/27	LRC27
Carlson, Dan, Ari	0	—	—	0	0.00	4.62
Carlyle, Buddy, SD	2	6.73	5.00	2	6.73	5.00
Carpenter, Chris, Tor	0	0.00	5.18	0	0.00	5.09
Carrasco, Hector, Min	0	—	—	0	0.00	4.64
Caruso, Mike, CWS	36	2.24	5.18	105	3.45	5.10
Casey, Sean, Cin	116	7.45	5.00	168	6.84	4.86
Castilla, Vinny, Col	87	4.99	5.00	575	5.87	4.68
Castillo, Alberto, StL	27	3.58	5.00	40	2.95	4.83
Castillo, Carlos, CWS	0	—	—	1	0.00	5.01
Castillo, Luis, Fla	72	5.25	5.00	124	3.99	4.79
Castro, Juan, LA	0	0.00	5.00	25	1.79	4.63
Castro, Ramon, Fla	3	1.42	5.00	3	1.42	5.00
Catalanotto, Frank, Det	38	4.59	5.18	73	4.85	5.10
Cather, Mike, Atl	0	—	—	0	0.00	4.60
Cedeno, Do., Sea/Phi	11	3.10	5.07	128	3.52	5.10
Cedeno, Roger, NYM	77	6.06	5.00	165	5.08	4.77
Charlton, Norm, TB	0	—	—	2	0.61	4.07
Chavez, Eric, Oak	51	4.94	5.18	60	5.19	5.16
Checo, Robinson, LA	0	0.00	5.00	0	0.00	5.00
Chen, Bruce, Atl	0	0.00	5.00	0	0.00	4.84
Cho, Jin Ho, Bos	0	0.00	5.18	0	0.00	5.18
Chouinard, Bobby, Ari	0	0.00	5.00	0	0.00	4.83
Christensen, McKay, CWS	2	1.16	5.18	2	1.16	5.18
Christensen, Ryan, Oak	27	3.07	5.18	74	3.74	5.09
Christiansen, Jason, Pit	0	0.00	5.00	1	2.70	4.68
Cirillo, Jeff, Mil	100	6.15	5.00	471	6.06	5.00
Clapinski, Chris, Fla	6	3.67	5.00	6	3.67	5.00
Clark, Mark, Tex	0	0.00	5.18	-3	-0.31	4.51
Clark, Tony, Det	101	6.68	5.18	379	6.09	5.10
Clark, Will, Bal	44	6.35	5.18	1293	7.05	4.50
Clayton, Royce, Tex	69	5.19	5.18	412	3.59	4.62
Clemens, Roger, NYY	0	0.00	5.18	1	2.45	5.08
Clement, Matt, SD	-1	-0.49	5.00	-1	-0.46	4.97
Clemente, Edgard, Col	19	4.03	5.00	22	4.29	4.97
Clontz, Brad, Pit	0	0.00	5.00	0	0.00	4.74
Cloude, Ken, Sea	0	0.00	5.18	0	0.00	5.03
Clyburn, Danny, TB	3	1.14	5.18	4	1.18	5.14
Colangelo, Mike, Ana	1	26.71	5.18	1	26.71	5.18
Colbrunn, Greg, Ari	26	7.21	5.00	281	4.77	4.62
Coleman, Michael, Bos	1	6.68	5.18	1	1.07	4.97
Collier, Lou, Mil	17	4.28	5.00	54	3.55	4.70
Colon, Bartolo, Cle	0	0.00	5.18	0	0.00	5.13
Cone, David, NYY	0	0.00	5.18	9	0.63	4.07
Conine, Jeff, Bal	67	5.29	5.18	516	5.43	4.71
Cook, Dennis, NYM	0	0.00	5.00	11	3.27	4.12
Cookson, Brent, LA	0	0.00	5.00	1	0.77	5.06
Coomer, Ron, Min	56	4.11	5.18	238	4.48	5.08
Coppinger, Rocky, Bal/Mil	1	13.50	5.06	1	13.50	5.06
Coquillette, Trace, Mon	6	4.04	5.00	6	4.04	5.00
Cora, Alex, LA	0	0.00	5.00	1	0.47	4.78
Corbin, Archie, Fla	0	0.00	5.00	0	0.00	5.00
Cordero, Wil, Cle	31	5.71	5.18	388	4.85	4.77
Cordova, Francisco, Pit	0	0.00	5.00	0	0.00	4.70
Cordova, Marty, Min	70	5.56	5.18	357	5.30	5.13
Cormier, Rheal, Bos	0	—	—	8	1.21	4.29
Cornelius, Reid, Fla	1	5.38	5.00	1	1.17	4.71
Corsi, Jim, Bos	0	—	—	0	0.00	4.56
Counsell, Craig, Fla/LA	11	2.04	5.00	91	4.58	4.71
Cox, Darron, Mon	2	2.83	5.00	2	2.83	5.00
Cox, Steve, TB	0	0.00	5.18	0	0.00	5.18
Crabtree, Tim, Tex	0	—	—	0	0.00	5.01
Creek, Doug, ChC	0	—	—	0	0.00	4.63
Cromer, Tripp, LA	3	1.76	5.00	38	2.41	4.66
Croushore, Rich, StL	0	0.00	5.00	0	0.00	4.80
Cruz, Deivi, Det	60	3.97	5.18	138	3.29	5.05
Cruz, Ivan, Pit	0	0.00	5.00	2	2.56	4.95
Cruz, Jacob, Cle	13	5.18	5.18	22	3.71	4.88
Cruz, Jose, Tor	57	5.52	5.18	173	5.41	5.04
Cummings, Midre, Min	7	6.45	5.18	100	4.17	4.70
Cunnane, Will, SD	0	0.00	5.00	4	8.28	4.70
Curtis, Chad, NYY	27	4.56	5.18	492	4.59	4.95
D'Amico, Jeff, Mil	0	—	—	0	0.00	4.93
Daal, Omar, Ari	2	0.88	5.00	3	0.65	4.80
Dalesandro, Mark, Tor	0	0.00	5.18	13	3.30	5.10
Damon, Johnny, KC	110	6.83	5.18	362	5.33	5.12
Daneker, Pat, CWS	0	0.00	5.18	0	0.00	5.18
Darensbourg, Vic, Fla	0	—	—	0	0.00	4.60
Darr, Mike, SD	6	4.36	5.00	6	4.36	5.00
Daubach, Brian, Bos	77	7.48	5.18	79	7.35	5.15
DaVanon, Jeff, Ana	2	3.14	5.18	2	3.14	5.18
Davidson, Cleatus, Min	1	1.16	5.18	1	1.16	5.18
Davis, Ben, SD	23	2.91	5.00	23	2.89	5.00
Davis, Chili, NYY	78	5.72	5.18	1413	5.66	4.52
Davis, Eric, StL	31	5.64	5.00	908	6.46	4.36
Davis, Russ, Sea	52	3.96	5.18	213	4.44	5.08
Davis, Tommy, Bal	0	0.00	5.18	0	0.00	5.18
Dawkins, Travis, Cin	0	0.00	5.00	0	0.00	5.00
Decker, Steve, Ana	8	3.96	5.18	63	2.97	4.43
DeHart, Rick, Mon	0	—	—	0	0.00	4.60
DeJean, Mike, Col	0	0.00	5.00	1	2.45	4.67
Delgado, Carlos, Tor	112	6.86	5.18	428	6.43	5.13
Delgado, Wilson, SF	6	2.88	5.00	10	3.10	4.87
Dellaero, Jason, CWS	0	0.00	5.18	0	0.00	5.18
Dellucci, David, Ari	23	8.97	5.00	82	5.37	4.68
del Toro, Miguel, SF	0	0.00	5.00	0	0.00	5.00
DeLucia, Rich, Cle	0	—	—	1	2.08	4.64
Dempster, Ryan, Fla	0	0.00	5.00	0	0.00	4.90
DeRosa, Mark, Atl	0	0.00	5.00	0	0.00	4.92
DeShields, Delino, Bal	41	4.18	5.18	663	4.80	4.46
Diaz, Alex, Hou	2	1.31	5.00	63	2.49	5.04
Diaz, Edwin, Ari	2	17.94	5.00	2	5.38	4.72
Diaz, Einar, Cle	48	4.23	5.18	55	4.18	5.16
DiFelice, Mike, TB	30	6.36	5.18	76	3.67	4.89
Dipoto, Jerry, Col	0	0.00	5.00	0	0.00	4.72
DiSarcina, Gary, Ana	24	2.80	5.18	345	3.09	4.94
Doster, David, Phi	8	2.59	5.00	18	3.00	4.85
Dotel, Octavio, NYM	1	1.22	5.00	1	1.22	5.00
Dougherty, Jim, Pit	0	—	—	0	0.00	4.63
Dransfeldt, Kelly, Tex	2	1.16	5.18	2	1.16	5.18
Dreifort, Darren, LA	7	3.43	5.00	11	2.74	4.81
Drew, J.D., StL	60	5.53	5.00	72	6.10	4.97
Ducey, Rob, Phi	37	7.01	5.00	133	4.32	4.76
Dunston, Sha., StL/NYM	41	6.06	5.00	646	4.18	4.33
Dunwoody, Todd, Fla	15	2.67	5.00	67	3.45	4.71
Durazo, Erubiel, Ari	41	10.12	5.00	41	10.12	5.00
Durham, Ray, CWS	96	5.62	5.18	424	5.09	5.11
Durrington, Trent, Ana	4	0.98	5.18	4	0.98	5.18
Duvall, Mike, TB	0	—	—	0	—	—
Dye, Jermaine, KC	101	5.93	5.18	170	4.26	5.00
Easley, Damion, Det	69	4.30	5.18	380	4.52	5.01
Ebert, Derrin, Atl	0	0.00	5.00	0	0.00	5.00
Echevarria, Angel, Col	31	5.60	5.00	42	5.57	4.90
Edmonds, Jim, Ana	28	4.65	5.18	439	6.00	5.10
Edmondson, Brian, Fla	3	11.54	5.00	3	4.04	4.74
Eiland, Dave, TB	0	0.00	5.18	1	1.09	4.32
Elarton, Scott, Hou	1	0.96	5.00	1	0.71	4.90
Eldred, Cal, Mil	1	1.04	5.00	1	0.41	4.78
Embree, Alan, SF	0	—	—	0	0.00	4.60
Encarnacion, Juan, Det	66	4.31	5.18	96	4.62	5.13
Erdos, Todd, NYY	0	—	—	0	0.00	4.60
Erickson, Scott, Bal	0	0.00	5.18	1	1.92	5.07
Erstad, Darin, Ana	63	3.62	5.18	284	5.38	5.09
Escobar, Kelvim, Tor	0	0.00	5.18	0	0.00	5.18
Estalella, Bobby, Phi	1	1.68	5.00	23	3.28	4.64
Estes, Shawn, SF	2	0.87	5.00	4	0.54	4.74
Estrada, Horacio, Mil	0	0.00	5.00	0	0.00	5.00
Eusebio, Tony, Hou	36	3.97	5.00	177	4.54	4.71
Everett, Carl, Hou	108	8.68	5.00	307	5.58	4.70
Eyre, Scott, CWS	0	—	—	0	0.00	4.99
Fabregas, Jorge, Fla/Atl	19	2.52	5.00	124	2.95	5.02
Falteisek, Steve, Mil	0	0.00	5.00	0	0.00	4.70
Farnsworth, Kyle, ChC	0	0.00	5.00	0	0.00	5.00
Fasano, Sal, KC	16	8.72	5.18	63	4.51	5.15
Fassero, Jeff, Sea/Tex	0	0.00	5.18	0	0.00	4.62
Febles, Carlos, KC	67	4.81	5.18	74	5.10	5.17
Fernandez, Alex, Fla	3	2.18	5.00	5	1.32	4.75
Fernandez, Jose, Mon	0	0.00	5.00	0	0.00	5.00
Fernandez, Tony, Tor	99	7.62	5.18	1106	4.99	4.55
Fick, Robert, Det	8	6.29	5.18	15	8.20	5.13
Figga, Mike, NYY/Bal	2	0.73	5.18	2	0.67	5.16
Finley, Chuck, Ana	0	0.00	5.18	0	0.00	5.04
Finley, Steve, Ari	102	6.11	5.00	813	4.89	4.48
Flaherty, John, TB	53	4.06	5.18	209	3.35	4.94
Fletcher, Darrin, Tor	66	5.65	5.18	370	4.34	4.65
Florie, Bryce, Det/Bos	0	0.00	5.00	0	0.00	4.84
Floyd, Cliff, Fla	46	6.48	5.00	252	5.36	4.68
Fonville, Chad, Bos	1	13.36	5.18	54	3.34	4.66
Fordyce, Brook, CWS	55	6.02	5.18	80	4.87	4.92
Fossas, Tony, NYY	0	—	—	0	0.00	4.68
Foulke, Keith, CWS	0	0.00	5.18	0	0.00	4.68
Fox, Andy, Ari	36	4.55	5.00	132	4.56	4.89
Fox, Chad, Mil	0	0.00	5.00	0	0.00	4.68
Franco, John, NYM	0	—	—	1	0.82	4.22
Franco, Julio, TB	0	0.00	5.18	1107	5.41	4.62

339

Player, Team	1999 RC	RC/27	LRC/27	Career RC	RC/27	LRC27
Franco, Matt, NYM	18	4.36	5.00	62	4.18	4.72
Frascatore, John, Ari/Tor	0	—	—	0	0.00	4.61
Frias, Hanley, Ari	23	5.38	5.00	25	4.26	4.94
Frye, Jeff, Bos	15	4.55	5.18	232	4.90	5.04
Fryman, Travis, Cle	43	4.49	5.18	785	5.29	4.87
Fullmer, Brad, Mon	43	4.27	5.00	133	5.23	4.76
Gaetti, Gary, ChC	28	3.22	5.00	1167	4.43	4.59
Gagne, Eric, LA	0	0.00	5.00	0	0.00	5.00
Gant, Ron, Phi	88	6.01	5.00	859	5.46	4.36
Garces, Rich, Bos	0	—	—	0	0.00	4.63
Garcia, Amaury, Fla	3	4.49	5.00	3	4.49	5.00
Garcia, Carlos, SD	0	0.00	5.00	233	3.68	4.64
Garcia, Freddy, Pit/Atl	12	3.08	5.00	39	3.24	4.73
Garcia, Freddy, Sea	1	5.34	5.18	1	5.34	5.18
Garcia, Guillermo, Fla	0	0.00	5.00	3	2.38	4.63
Garcia, Jesse, Bal	1	0.99	5.18	1	0.99	5.18
Garcia, Karim, Det	32	3.78	5.18	68	3.32	4.84
Garcia, Luis, Det	0	0.00	5.18	0	0.00	5.18
Garciaparra, Nomar, Bos	122	9.05	5.18	371	7.25	5.04
Gardner, Mark, SF	0	0.00	5.00	3	0.18	4.46
Gates, Brent, Min	31	3.35	5.18	268	3.87	5.03
Giambi, Jason, Oak	136	8.77	5.18	458	6.96	5.12
Giambi, Jeremy, KC	41	5.02	5.18	46	4.59	5.15
Gibson, Derrick, Col	5	5.38	5.00	10	7.28	4.87
Giles, Brian S., Pit	129	9.11	5.18	294	7.58	5.02
Gilkey, Bernard, Ari	39	6.60	5.00	601	5.48	4.51
Giovanola, Ed, SD	4	2.15	5.00	26	2.73	4.70
Gipson, Charles, Sea	6	2.29	5.18	11	2.65	5.12
Girardi, Joe, NYY	20	2.87	5.18	364	3.75	4.66
Glanville, Doug, Phi	109	6.59	5.00	259	5.04	4.73
Glaus, Troy, Ana	88	5.44	5.18	108	5.10	5.14
Glavine, Tom, Atl	3	1.28	5.00	52	1.77	4.39
Glynn, Ryan, Tex	0	0.00	5.18	0	0.00	5.18
Gomes, Wayne, Phi	0	0.00	5.00	0	0.00	4.68
Gomez, Chris, SD	25	3.62	5.00	279	3.72	4.85
Gonzalez, Alex, Tor	22	5.11	5.18	217	3.40	5.12
Gonzalez, Alex, Fla	69	4.35	5.00	72	3.85	4.94
Gonzalez, Juan, Tex	119	7.87	5.18	911	6.78	4.88
Gonzalez, Luis, Ari	126	7.85	5.00	688	5.36	4.58
Gonzalez, Wiki, SD	4	1.61	5.18	4	1.61	5.00
Gooden, Dwight, Cle	2	53.42	5.18	40	1.55	4.15
Goodwin, Curtis, ChC/Tor	13	2.45	5.01	92	2.92	4.81
Goodwin, Tom, Tex	46	3.75	5.00	317	4.09	5.07
Grace, Mark, ChC	111	6.82	5.00	1140	6.30	4.38
Grace, Mike, Phi	0	0.00	5.00	0	0.00	4.68
Graffanino, Tony, TB	28	7.96	5.18	77	3.93	4.71
Grahe, Joe, Phi	0	0.00	5.00	4	5.70	4.75
Graves, Danny, Cin	0	0.00	5.00	0	0.00	4.80
Grebeck, Craig, TB	20	6.85	5.18	214	4.19	4.74
Green, Scarborough, Tex	1	2.67	5.18	1	0.70	4.75
Green, Shawn, Tor	121	7.20	5.18	407	5.82	5.11
Greene, Charlie, Mil	1	0.75	5.00	1	0.46	5.00
Greene, Rick, Cin	0	0.00	5.00	0	0.00	5.00
Greene, Todd, Ana	32	3.33	5.18	63	3.62	5.14
Greene, Willie, Tor	23	3.30	5.18	230	4.89	4.67
Greer, Rusty, Tex	117	7.57	5.18	576	7.08	5.12
Grieve, Ben, Oak	84	5.98	5.18	210	6.42	5.08
Griffey Jr., Ken, Sea	140	8.31	5.18	1203	7.49	4.80
Grimsley, Jason, NYY	0	—	—	1	0.69	4.11
Grissom, Marquis, Mil	78	4.48	5.00	763	4.77	4.52
Gross, Kip, Bos	0	—	—	1	1.13	4.09
Grudzielanek, Mark, LA	67	5.11	5.00	306	4.10	4.69
Gubanich, Creighton, Bos	9	6.50	5.18	9	6.50	5.18
Guerrero, Vladimir, Mon	134	8.12	5.00	307	7.12	4.75
Guerrero, Wilton, Mon	46	5.10	5.00	129	4.20	4.72
Guevara, Giomar, Sea	1	2.97	5.18	2	2.23	5.06
Guillen, Carlos, Sea	2	2.97	5.18	12	7.32	5.08
Guillen, Jose, Pit/TB	28	3.21	5.11	149	3.80	4.71
Guillen, Ozzie, Atl	21	2.94	5.00	653	3.34	4.71
Gunderson, Eric, Tex	0	—	—	0	0.00	4.20
Guthrie, Mark, Bos/ChC	0	—	—	0	0.00	4.63
Gutierrez, Ricky, Hou	29	3.61	5.00	218	3.44	4.64
Guzman, Cristian, Min	27	2.07	5.18	27	2.07	5.18
Guzman, Edwards, SF	0	0.00	5.00	0	0.00	5.00
Guzman, Juan, Bal/Cin	2	1.73	5.03	2	1.63	5.03
Gwynn, Tony, SD	82	7.53	5.00	1578	6.57	4.30
Haad, Yamid, Pit	0	0.00	5.00	0	0.00	5.00
Hackman, Luther, Col	0	0.00	5.00	0	0.00	5.00
Hairston Jr., Jerry, Bal	22	4.26	5.18	22	4.05	5.17
Halama, John, Sea	1	6.68	5.18	1	1.78	4.75
Halladay, Roy, Tor	0	0.00	5.18	0	0.00	5.18
Halter, Shane, NYM	0	—	—	22	2.17	4.98

Player, Team	1999 RC	RC/27	LRC/27	Career RC	RC/27	LRC27
Hamilton, Darryl, Col/NYM	74	5.43	5.00	641	5.22	4.78
Hamilton, Joey, Tor	0	0.00	5.18	3	0.27	4.63
Hammonds, Jeffrey, Cin	38	5.06	5.00	244	4.99	5.05
Hampton, Mike, Hou	11	5.02	5.00	27	2.66	4.70
Haney, Chris, 0	—	·		1	0.73	4.05
Hansell, Greg, Pit	0	0.00	5.00	0	0.00	5.00
Hansen, Dave, LA	17	5.51	5.00	141	4.53	4.38
Hansen, Jed, KC	7	2.71	5.00	24	4.47	5.05
Harnisch, Pete, Cin	3	1.24	5.00	5	0.29	4.49
Harris, Lenny, Col/Ari	27	5.27	5.00	346	3.86	4.34
Harris, Reggie, Mil	0	0.00	5.00	0	0.00	5.00
Haselman, Bill, Det	13	3.22	5.18	126	3.86	5.06
Hatteberg, Scott, Bos	16	7.01	5.18	109	4.75	5.00
Hawkins, LaTroy, Min	0	0.00	5.18	0	0.00	5.07
Hayes, Charlie, SF	30	3.64	5.00	576	4.10	4.49
Haynes, Jimmy, Oak	0	0.00	5.18	0	0.00	5.08
Heiserman, Rick, StL	0	0.00	5.00	0	0.00	5.00
Helling, Rick, Tex	0	0.00	5.18	0	0.00	4.77
Helton, Todd, Col	121	7.81	5.00	237	7.31	4.79
Hemphill, Bret, Ana	1	1.27	5.18	1	1.27	5.18
Henderson, Rickey, NYM	80	6.69	5.00	1978	6.97	4.59
Henry, Butch, Sea	0	—	—	7	1.25	4.35
Henry, Doug, Hou	0	0.00	5.00	1	1.50	4.68
Hentgen, Pat, Tor	0	0.00	5.18	0	0.00	5.03
Heredia, Felix, ChC	1	13.46	5.00	1	3.85	4.71
Heredia, Gil, Oak	0	0.00	5.18	7	2.42	4.54
Herges, Matt, LA	0	0.00	5.00	0	0.00	5.00
Hermansen, Chad, Pit	5	2.75	5.00	5	2.75	5.00
Hermanson, Dustin, Mon	-2	-0.78	5.00	0	0.00	4.77
Hernandez, Carlos E., Hou	0	0.00	5.00	0	0.00	5.00
Hernandez, Jose, ChC/Atl	74	5.12	5.00	245	4.14	4.71
Hernandez, Livan, Fla/SF	7	3.36	5.00	10	1.75	4.51
Hernandez, Orlando, NYY	0	0.00	5.18	0	0.00	5.04
Hernandez, Ramon, Oak	26	6.55	5.18	26	6.55	5.18
Hernandez, Roberto, TB	0	—	—	0	0.00	4.60
Hershiser, Orel, NYM	0	0.00	5.00	40	1.43	4.26
Hidalgo, Richard, Hou	52	4.50	5.00	91	4.78	4.84
Higginson, Bob, Det	58	5.22	5.18	422	6.24	5.10
Hill, Glenallen, ChC	42	6.01	5.00	486	5.07	4.61
Hill, Ken, Ana	0	0.00	5.18	11	0.85	4.26
Hinch, A.J., Oak	19	2.87	5.18	53	3.08	5.08
Hitchcock, Sterling, SD	-1	-0.42	5.00	-1	-0.16	4.75
Hocking, Denny, Min	50	4.31	5.18	104	3.21	5.10
Hoffman, Trevor, SD	1	13.46	5.00	3	3.00	4.64
Holbert, Ray, KC	8	2.46	5.18	13	1.98	4.90
Hollandsworth, Todd, LA	36	5.05	5.00	185	4.99	4.71
Hollins, Dave, Tor	4	1.35	5.18	519	5.42	4.67
Holmes, Darren, Ari	0	0.00	5.00	0	0.00	4.64
Holt, Chris, Hou	0	0.00	5.00	-1	-0.22	4.77
Holtz, Mike, Ana	0	—	—	0	0.00	4.93
Houston, Tyler, ChC/Cle	28	3.36	5.02	108	4.29	4.75
Howard, David, StL	7	2.77	5.00	145	2.94	4.92
Howard, Thomas, StL	29	5.46	5.00	276	4.06	4.54
Howell, Jack, Hou	4	3.99	5.00	358	4.60	4.54
Hubbard, Trenidad, LA	20	6.81	5.00	75	5.24	4.71
Hudek, John, Cin/Atl	0	0.00	5.00	1	5.40	4.68
Hudson, Tim, Oak	1	8.90	5.18	1	8.90	5.18
Hughes, Bobby, Mil	7	2.42	5.00	28	2.98	4.72
Hundley, Todd, LA	42	3.68	5.00	405	4.68	4.54
Hunter, Brian, Atl	32	5.74	5.00	179	4.19	4.54
Hunter, Brian L., Det/Sea	49	2.97	5.18	299	3.84	4.92
Hunter, Torii, Min	40	3.48	5.18	42	3.49	5.17
Huskey, Butch, Sea/Bos	64	5.89	5.18	226	4.37	4.74
Huson, Jeff, Ana	19	2.82	5.18	158	2.92	4.58
Hyers, Tim, Fla	8	3.31	5.00	20	2.88	4.86
Ibanez, Raul, Sea	27	4.48	5.18	38	3.84	5.11
Irabu, Hideki, NYY	0	0.00	5.18	0	0.00	5.10
Isringhausen, Jason, NYM	0	0.00	5.00	9	2.74	4.70
Jackson, Damian, SD	48	4.09	5.00	62	4.37	4.95
Jackson, Darrin, CWS	15	3.45	5.18	293	3.81	4.40
Jackson, Mike, Cle	0	—	—	2	2.08	4.49
Jackson, Ryan, Sea	6	2.67	5.18	35	3.60	4.73
Jaha, John, Oak	108	8.29	5.18	478	6.31	4.64
Jarvis, Kevin, Oak	0	—	—	1	0.42	4.66
Javier, Stan, SF/Hou	49	4.30	5.00	571	4.43	4.62
Jefferies, Gregg, Det	12	1.78	5.18	753	4.98	4.43
Jefferson, Reggie, Bos	20	3.38	5.18	315	5.39	4.98
Jenkins, Geoff, Mil	87	7.27	5.00	103	5.18	4.84
Jennings, Robin, ChC	0	0.00	5.00	8	3.27	4.68
Jensen, Marcus, StL	4	3.71	5.00	13	2.90	4.73
Jeter, Derek, NYY	146	8.92	5.18	434	6.28	5.12
Jimenez, D'Angelo, NYY	5	11.13	5.18	5	11.13	5.18

	1999			Career		
Player, Team	RC	RC/27	LRC/27	RC	RC/27	LRC27
Jimenez, Jose, StL	0	0.00	5.00	0	0.00	4.95
Johns, Doug, Bal	0	0.00	5.18	1	27.00	5.18
Johnson, Brian, Cin	14	4.05	5.00	128	3.35	4.69
Johnson, Charles, Bal	58	4.57	5.18	242	3.98	4.74
Johnson, Jason, Bal	0	0.00	5.18	0	0.00	5.00
Johnson, Lance, ChC	37	3.80	5.00	713	4.73	4.65
Johnson, Mark L., CWS	22	3.54	5.18	22	3.14	5.16
Johnson, Mike, Mon	0	0.00	5.00	1	1.42	4.67
Johnson, Randy, Ari	1	0.29	5.00	1	0.18	4.79
Johnson, Russ, Hou	25	5.38	5.00	35	5.18	4.88
Johnstone, John, SF	0	—	—	0	0.00	4.60
Jones, Andruw, Atl	101	5.97	5.00	257	5.25	4.74
Jones, Bobby, NYM	0	0.00	5.00	4	0.34	4.63
Jones, Bobby M., Col	2	1.92	5.00	3	1.06	4.75
Jones, Chipper, Atl	144	9.34	5.00	581	7.28	4.70
Jones, Doug, Oak	0	—	—	1	4.50	4.12
Jones, Jacque, Min	48	5.25	5.18	48	5.25	5.18
Jones, Terry, Mon	6	3.36	5.00	24	2.66	4.68
Jones, Todd, Det	0	—	—	1	3.37	4.63
Jordan, Brian, Atl	99	6.07	5.00	466	5.78	4.64
Jordan, Kevin, Phi	43	4.40	5.00	101	3.70	4.76
Joyner, Wally, SD	43	4.54	5.00	1115	5.88	4.63
Judd, Mike, LA	0	0.00	5.00	0	0.00	4.92
Juden, Jeff, NYY	0	—	—	3	0.68	4.59
Justice, David, Cle	85	6.92	5.18	845	7.00	4.56
Kamieniecki, Scott, Bal	0	—	—	0	0.00	4.93
Kapler, Gabe, Det	56	4.48	5.18	57	4.30	5.17
Karl, Scott, Mil	4	1.74	5.00	4	0.84	4.80
Karros, Eric, LA	103	6.43	5.00	642	5.04	4.56
Kelly, Mike, Col	1	26.92	5.00	78	3.81	4.79
Kelly, Pat, Tor	18	5.28	5.18	205	3.37	4.78
Kelly, Roberto, Tex	41	5.19	5.18	671	4.96	4.61
Kendall, Jason, Pit	52	6.93	5.00	303	6.51	4.69
Kennedy, Adam, StL	12	3.99	5.00	12	3.99	5.00
Kent, Jeff, SF	95	6.57	5.00	594	5.56	4.64
Kile, Darryl, Col	0	0.00	5.00	10	0.54	4.56
Kim, Byung-Hyun, Ari	0	0.00	5.00	0	0.00	5.00
King, Curtis, StL	0	—	—	0	0.00	4.60
King, Jeff, KC	10	4.69	5.18	588	4.68	4.53
King, Ray, ChC	0	0.00	5.00	0	0.00	5.00
Kingsale, Gene, Bal	6	2.20	5.18	6	2.14	5.17
Kinkade, Mike, NYM	3	2.12	5.00	3	2.02	4.98
Klassen, Danny, Ari	1	Inf.	5.00	5	1.45	4.60
Klesko, Ryan, Atl	82	7.38	5.00	442	6.48	4.68
Kline, Steve, Mon	0	0.00	5.00	0	0.00	4.70
Knoblauch, Chuck, NYY	113	6.69	5.18	912	6.34	4.91
Knorr, Randy, Hou	0	0.00	5.00	55	3.28	4.90
Koch, Billy, Tor	0	0.00	5.18	0	0.00	5.18
Konerko, Paul, CWS	83	5.76	5.00	98	4.55	4.99
Koskie, Corey, Min	66	7.02	5.18	68	6.58	5.16
Kotsay, Mark, Fla	49	3.39	5.00	124	3.79	4.78
Kreuter, Chad, KC	27	2.66	5.18	218	3.61	4.86
Kubenka, Jeff, LA	1	Inf.	5.00	1	Inf.	5.00
Laker, Tim, Pit	0	0.00	5.00	24	2.38	4.52
Lamb, David, TB	10	2.64	5.18	10	2.64	5.18
Lampkin, Tom, Sea	32	5.55	5.18	149	4.11	4.67
Langston, Mark, Cle	0	0.00	5.18	2	0.65	4.17
Lankford, Ray, StL	72	6.35	5.00	810	6.25	4.47
Lansing, Mike, Col	19	4.87	5.00	442	4.67	4.62
Larkin, Barry, Cin	100	6.10	5.00	1101	6.33	4.39
LaRue, Jason, Cin	10	3.54	5.00	10	3.54	5.00
Latham, Chris, Min	0	0.00	5.18	6	1.32	5.03
Lawton, Matt, Min	57	4.71	5.18	288	5.74	5.09
Ledee, Ricky, NYY	43	6.11	5.18	54	5.75	5.14
Ledesma, Aaron, TB	26	2.99	5.18	83	4.11	5.06
Lee, Carlos, CWS	67	4.85	5.18	67	4.85	5.18
Lee, David, Col	0	0.00	5.00	0	0.00	5.00
Lee, Derrek, Fla	17	2.57	5.00	84	3.88	4.72
Lee, Travis, Ari	47	4.19	5.00	124	4.59	4.76
Leiter, Al, NYM	0	0.00	5.00	0	0.00	4.73
Leiter, Mark, Sea	0	—	—	3	0.42	4.64
Leius, Scott, KC	4	1.70	5.18	159	3.44	4.83
Lennon, Patrick, Tor	3	3.48	5.18	26	4.89	5.02
Leskanic, Curt, Col	2	26.92	5.18	5	3.85	4.60
Levis, Jesse, Cle	0	0.00	5.18	69	3.75	5.04
Lewis, Darren, Bos	41	2.81	5.18	417	3.84	4.72
Lewis, Mark, Cin	27	5.15	5.00	304	4.02	4.75
Leyritz, Jim, SD/NYY	24	4.01	5.06	365	5.21	4.87
Lidle, Cory, TB	0	—	—	0	0.00	4.60
Lieber, Jon, ChC	1	0.45	5.00	6	0.62	4.71
Lieberthal, Mike, Phi	89	6.29	5.00	220	4.85	4.74
Liefer, Jeff, CWS	13	3.90	5.18	13	3.90	5.18

	1999			Career		
Player, Team	RC	RC/27	LRC/27	RC	RC/27	LRC27
Lilly, Ted, Mon	0	0.00	5.00	0	0.00	5.00
Lima, Jose, Hou	-2	-0.63	5.00	-2	-0.32	4.80
Lincoln, Mike, Min	0	0.00	5.18	0	0.00	5.18
Liniak, Cole, ChC	0	0.00	5.00	0	0.00	5.00
Linton, Doug, Bal	0	—	—	0	0.00	4.62
Loaiza, Esteban, Tex	0	—	—	4	0.69	4.62
Lockhart, Keith, Atl	18	3.88	5.00	190	4.68	4.97
LoDuca, Paul, LA	11	3.66	5.00	12	3.55	4.96
Loewer, Carlton, Phi	1	1.42	5.00	1	0.47	4.73
Lofton, Kenny, Cle	77	5.93	5.18	771	6.38	4.92
Loiselle, Rich, Pit	0	0.00	5.00	1	2.70	4.70
Lomasney, Steve, Bos	0	0.00	5.18	0	0.00	5.18
Lombard, George, Atl	1	6.73	5.00	3	10.11	4.80
Long, Terrence, NYM	0	0.00	5.00	0	0.00	5.00
Lopez, Albie, TB	0	—	—	0	0.00	4.97
Lopez, Javy, Atl	44	6.69	5.00	351	5.44	4.66
Lopez, Luis, NYM	13	4.07	5.00	92	3.16	4.66
Lopez, Mendy, KC	5	11.13	5.18	25	3.69	5.02
Loretta, Mark, Mil	80	4.82	5.00	223	4.74	4.92
Lorraine, Andrew, ChC	0	0.00	5.00	0	0.00	5.00
Lovullo, Torey, Phi	3	2.60	5.00	69	3.03	4.78
Lowe, Derek, Bos	0	—	—	0	0.00	4.98
Lowe, Sean, CWS	0	—	—	0	0.00	4.60
Lowell, Mike, Fla	42	4.65	5.00	42	4.45	5.00
Lowery, Terrell, TB	22	4.17	5.18	26	4.27	5.10
Ludwick, Eric, Tor	0	—	—	0	0.00	4.67
Luebbers, Larry, StL	0	0.00	5.00	2	1.59	4.72
Luke, Matt, Ana	5	5.81	5.18	30	3.79	4.66
Mabry, John, Sea	27	3.47	5.18	242	4.33	4.71
Macfarlane, Mike, Oak	20	2.90	5.18	469	4.44	4.78
Machado, Robert, Mon	1	1.50	5.00	13	2.73	5.01
Macias, Jose, Det	1	8.90	5.18	1	8.90	5.18
Maddux, Greg, Atl	2	0.82	5.00	22	0.64	4.36
Maddux, Mike, Mon/LA	0	—	—	0	0.00	4.09
Magadan, Dave, SD	27	3.63	5.00	618	5.68	4.39
Magee, Wendell, Phi	5	13.46	5.00	31	2.90	4.65
Magnante, Mike, Ana	0	—	—	1	9.00	4.60
Mahay, Ron, Oak	0	—	—	1	1.68	5.06
Mahomes, Pat, NYM	2	4.89	5.00	2	4.89	5.00
Mantei, Matt, Fla/Ari	0	0.00	5.00	0	0.00	4.72
Manto, Jeff, Cle/NYY	4	3.82	5.18	92	4.30	4.90
Manwaring, Kirt, Col	21	5.60	5.00	277	3.11	4.42
Manzanillo, Josias, NYM	1	Inf.	5.00	1	3.86	4.65
Marrero, Eli, StL	16	1.54	5.00	47	2.45	4.82
Martin, Al, Pit	90	6.00	5.00	489	5.36	4.67
Martin, Norberto, Tor	2	2.32	5.18	94	3.67	5.09
Martin, Tom, Cle	0	—	—	0	0.00	4.60
Martinez, Dave, TB	81	5.48	5.18	680	4.67	4.55
Martinez, Edgar, Sea	113	8.62	5.18	1018	7.76	4.83
Martinez, Felix, KC	0	0.00	5.18	6	1.43	5.00
Martinez, Manny, Mon	32	3.19	5.00	57	3.33	4.86
Martinez, Pedro, Bos	0	0.00	5.18	-1	-0.10	4.64
Martinez, Ramon, Bos	0	—	—	11	0.52	4.37
Martinez, Ramon E., SF	20	4.60	5.00	22	4.52	4.96
Martinez, Sandy, ChC	0	0.00	5.00	48	3.04	5.12
Martinez, Tino, NYY	91	5.33	5.18	692	5.73	4.96
Masaoka, Onan, LA	0	0.00	5.00	0	0.00	5.00
Mateo, Ruben, Tex	16	4.50	5.18	16	4.50	5.18
Matheny, Mike, Tor	15	2.99	5.18	125	3.07	5.02
Mathews, T.J., Oak	0	—	—	0	0.00	4.66
Mathews, Terry, KC	0	0.00	5.18	4	6.76	4.68
Matos, Pascual, Atl	0	0.00	5.00	0	0.00	5.00
Matthews Jr., Gary, SD	6	5.57	5.00	6	5.57	5.00
May, Derrick, Bal	8	5.48	5.18	278	4.43	4.50
Mayne, Brent, SF	48	5.23	5.00	241	3.95	4.78
Mays, Joe, Min	0	0.00	5.18	0	0.00	5.18
McCracken, Quinton, TB	17	3.63	5.18	192	4.79	4.87
McCurry, Jeff, Hou	0	—	—	0	0.00	4.62
McDonald, Jason, Oak	16	2.70	5.18	73	4.02	5.04
McDonald, John, Cle	1	1.57	5.18	1	1.57	5.18
McElroy, Chuck, Col/NYM	0	0.00	5.00	5	4.10	4.45
McEwing, Joe, StL	64	4.38	5.00	65	4.26	4.98
McGee, Willie, StL	23	2.89	5.00	996	4.69	4.27
McGlinchy, Kevin, Atl	0	0.00	5.00	0	0.00	5.00
McGriff, Fred, TB	118	8.27	5.18	1267	6.69	4.53
McGuire, Ryan, Mon	18	3.97	5.00	53	3.08	4.71
McGwire, Mark, StL	145	9.93	5.00	1310	8.07	4.67
McLemore, Mark, Tex	77	4.65	5.18	555	4.18	4.92
McMichael, Greg, NYM	0	—	—	1	1.92	4.58
McNichol, Brian, ChC	0	0.00	5.00	0	0.00	5.00
McRae, Bri., NYM/Col/Tor	44	3.55	5.04	672	4.50	4.66
Meadows, Brian, Fla	1	0.54	5.00	1	0.26	4.80

341

	1999			Career		
Player, Team	RC	RC/27	LRC/27	RC	RC/27	LRC27
Meares, Pat, Pit	12	4.89	5.00	288	3.82	5.06
Mecir, Jim, TB	0	—	—	0	0.00	5.01
Medina, Rafael, Fla	0	—	—	0	0.00	4.60
Meluskey, Mitch, Hou	2	1.99	5.00	3	2.38	4.92
Mendoza, Ramiro, NYY	0	—	—	0	0.00	5.01
Menechino, Frank, Oak	0	0.00	5.18	0	0.00	5.18
Merced, Orlando, Mon	28	5.06	5.00	535	5.62	4.54
Mercker, Kent, StL	2	1.99	5.00	5	0.56	4.61
Merloni, Lou, Bos	15	3.85	5.18	33	5.05	5.11
Mesa, Jose, Sea	0	—	—	0		—
Meyers, Chad, ChC	10	2.28	5.00	10	2.28	5.00
Miceli, Dan, SD	0	0.00	5.00	1	1.42	4.68
Mientkiewicz, Doug, Min	31	3.06	5.18	33	3.02	5.17
Mieske, Matt, Sea/Hou	23	5.56	5.04	193	4.52	5.11
Millar, Kevin, Fla	63	6.35	5.00	64	6.43	5.00
Miller, Damian, Ari	39	4.67	5.00	71	4.76	4.87
Miller, Kurt, ChC	0	—	—	0	0.00	4.65
Miller, Trever, Hou	0	0.00	5.00	1	3.85	4.89
Miller, Wade, Hou	0	0.00	5.00	0	0.00	5.00
Mills, Alan, LA	0	0.00	5.00	0	0.00	5.00
Millwood, Kevin, Atl	1	0.36	5.00	1	0.19	4.81
Milton, Eric, Min	0		5.18	3	11.51	5.06
Minor, Ryan, Bal	9	2.36	5.18	12	2.92	5.17
Mintz, Steve, Ana	0	—	—	0	0.00	4.63
Mirabelli, Doug, SF	11	4.42	5.00	19	5.12	4.88
Mlicki, Dave, LA/Det	1	4.49	5.12	5	0.83	4.63
Moehler, Brian, Det	0	0.00	5.18	0	0.00	5.00
Mohler, Mike, StL	0	0.00	5.00	0	0.00	5.00
Molina, Ben, Ana	10	3.30	5.18	10	3.26	5.18
Molina, Jose, ChC	1	1.92	5.00	1	1.92	5.00
Monahan, Shane, Sea	0	0.00	5.00	19	2.85	5.02
Mondesi, Raul, LA	105	6.06	5.00	564	5.84	4.69
Montgomery, Jeff, KC	0	—	—	0	0.00	4.52
Montgomery, Steve, Phi	1	Inf.	5.00	1	Inf.	4.54
Mora, Melvin, NYM	1	0.90	5.00	1	0.90	5.00
Morandini, Mickey, ChC	49	3.54	5.00	533	4.45	4.53
Mordecai, Mike, Mon	25	3.70	5.00	61	3.27	4.76
Morgan, Mike, Tex	0	0.00	5.18	-3	-0.16	4.31
Morman, Alvin, KC	0	—	—	0	0.00	4.93
Morris, Hal, Cin	17	6.18	5.00	538	5.10	4.49
Morris, Warren, Pit	77	5.29	5.00	77	5.29	5.00
Mota, Guillermo, Mon	2	Inf.	5.00	2	Inf.	5.00
Mouton, James, Mon	14	3.85	5.00	134	3.48	4.67
Mouton, Lyle, Mil	1	1.92	5.00	95	4.88	5.11
Moyer, Jamie, Sea	1	13.36	5.18	6	1.02	4.20
Mueller, Bill, SF	60	5.09	5.00	234	5.46	4.72
Mulholland, Terry, ChC/Atl	0	0.00	5.00	-4	-0.19	4.34
Munoz, Mike, Tex	0	—	—	1	3.87	4.56
Murray, Calvin, SF	4	7.69	5.00	4	7.69	5.00
Murray, Heath, SD	0	0.00	5.00	0	0.00	4.87
Mussina, Mike, Bal	2	6.68	5.18	2	4.11	5.10
Myers, Greg, SD/Atl	23	4.02	5.00	231	3.46	4.81
Myers, Mike, Mil	0	0.00	5.00	0	0.00	5.00
Myers, Rodney, ChC	3	20.19	5.00	3	8.07	4.80
Nagy, Charles, Cle	0	0.00	5.18	0	0.00	5.06
Nathan, Joe, SF	1	0.96	5.00	1	0.96	5.00
Navarro, Jaime, CWS	0	0.00	5.18	3	0.56	4.68
Neagle, Denny, Cin	2	1.50	5.00	15	1.06	4.63
Nelson, Jeff, NYY	0	—	—	0	0.00	5.01
Nen, Robb, SF	0	—	—	0	0.00	4.58
Nevin, Phil, SD	79	7.26	5.00	171	5.09	5.01
Newhan, David, SD	3	2.12	5.00	3	2.12	5.00
Nieves, Jose, ChC	18	3.25	5.00	18	3.21	5.00
Nilsson, Dave, Mil	68	7.26	5.00	444	5.67	4.96
Nitkowski, C.J., Det	0	0.00	5.18	1	1.93	4.66
Nixon, Otis, Atl	14	2.90	5.00	627	4.14	4.64
Nixon, Trot, Bos	56	5.05	5.18	58	4.87	5.17
Nomo, Hideo, Mil	3	1.58	5.00	6	0.53	4.70
Norton, Greg, CWS	57	4.44	5.00	94	3.98	5.11
Nunez, Abraham, Pit	20	2.47	5.00	31	2.79	4.89
Nunez, Vladimir, Ari/Fla	1	1.04	5.00	1	1.04	5.00
Nunnally, Jon, Bos	0	0.00	5.18	136	5.72	4.88
O'Brien, Charlie, Ana	0	0.00	5.18	239	3.47	4.63
O'Leary, Troy, Bos	95	5.55	5.18	406	5.30	5.11
O'Neill, Paul, NYY	86	4.89	5.18	1059	5.99	4.63
Ochoa, Alex, Mil	51	6.73	5.00	138	4.49	4.82
Offerman, Jose, Bos	99	5.93	5.18	594	4.96	4.74
Ogea, Chad, Phi	0	0.00	5.00	0	0.00	5.00
Ojala, Kirt, Fla	0	—	—	2	1.63	4.60
Olerud, John, NYM	118	7.28	5.00	902	6.86	4.76
Olivares, Omar, Ana/Oak	1	5.34	5.18	21	3.17	4.23
Oliver, Darren, StL	6	2.60	5.00	8	2.42	4.91
Oliver, Joe, Pit	13	3.10	5.00	354	3.80	4.46
Olson, Gregg, Ari	0	—	—	1	8.99	4.64
Oquist, Mike, Oak	0	0.00	5.18	0	0.00	5.01
Ordaz, Luis, StL	1	2.99	5.00	14	2.45	4.62
Ordonez, Magglio, CWS	102	5.78	5.18	184	5.25	5.09
Ordonez, Rey, NYM	52	3.30	5.00	152	2.65	4.73
Orie, Kevin, Fla	33	4.70	5.00	122	4.18	4.70
Orosco, Jesse, Bal	0	—	—	4	1.84	4.17
Ortiz, David, Min	0	0.00	5.18	59	5.89	5.01
Ortiz, Russ, SF	5	2.07	5.00	8	2.45	4.90
Osborne, Donovan, StL	0	0.00	5.00	12	1.33	4.46
Osik, Keith, Pit	5	0.92	5.00	47	3.04	4.76
Osuna, Antonio, LA	0	—	—	0	0.00	4.63
Otanez, Willis, Bal/Tor	20	3.22	5.18	20	3.14	5.17
Owens, Eric, SD	62	4.82	5.00	84	3.75	4.85
Painter, Lance, StL	0	0.00	5.00	5	2.08	4.66
Palmeiro, Orlando, Ana	42	4.54	5.18	91	4.32	5.11
Palmeiro, Rafael, Tex	147	9.62	5.18	1319	6.55	4.71
Palmer, Dean, Det	91	5.63	5.18	602	5.09	4.92
Paniagua, Jose, Sea	0	—	—	0	0.00	4.66
Paquette, Craig, StL	27	6.01	5.00	166	3.47	5.03
Park, Chan Ho, LA	3	1.39	5.00	7	0.96	4.73
Parque, Jim, CWS	1	6.68	5.18	1	3.82	5.11
Parris, Steve, Cin	1	0.73	5.00	6	1.72	4.77
Patrick, Bronswell, SF	0	0.00	5.00	2	3.85	4.63
Patterson, Danny, Tex	0	0.00	5.18	0	0.00	5.18
Paul, Josh, CWS	0	0.00	5.18	0	0.00	5.18
Pavano, Carl, Mon	0	0.00	5.00	2	0.73	4.79
Payton, Jay, NYM	0	0.00	5.00	1	1.17	4.74
Pena, Angel, LA	14	3.59	5.00	14	3.28	4.97
Percival, Troy, Ana	0	—	—	0	0.00	5.39
Perez, Carlos, LA	5	6.12	5.00	11	1.51	4.65
Perez, Eddie, Atl	31	3.35	5.00	91	3.79	4.77
Perez, Eduardo, StL	8	10.25	5.00	119	4.35	4.77
Perez, Neifi, Col	84	4.36	5.00	195	4.01	4.76
Perez, Odalis, Atl	0	0.00	5.00	0	0.00	5.00
Perez, Yorkis, Phi	0	0.00	5.00	0	0.00	4.70
Perisho, Matt, Tex	0	—	—	0	0.00	4.93
Perkins, Dan, Min	0	0.00	5.18	0	0.00	5.18
Perry, Herbert, TB	26	4.01	5.18	52	4.39	5.14
Person, Robert, Phi	0	0.00	5.00	1	0.39	4.89
Peters, Chris, Pit	2	2.99	5.00	5	1.90	4.72
Petersen, Chris, Col	2	4.89	5.00	2	4.89	5.00
Peterson, Kyle, Mil	0	0.00	5.00	0	0.00	5.00
Petkovsek, Mark, Ana	0	—	—	5	1.69	4.63
Petrick, Ben, Col	14	8.76	5.00	14	8.76	5.00
Pettitte, Andy, NYY	0	0.00	5.18	0	0.00	5.08
Phillips, J.R., Col	4	3.59	5.00	44	2.84	4.66
Phillips, Tony, Oak	68	5.69	5.18	1206	5.44	4.71
Piazza, Mike, NYM	95	6.27	5.00	742	7.68	4.65
Pickering, Calvin, Bal	5	3.71	5.18	7	3.47	5.12
Pierzynski, A.J., Min	3	5.01	5.18	6	6.70	5.12
Pisciotta, Marc, KC	0	—	—	0	0.00	4.60
Pittsley, Jim, Mil	0	0.00	5.00	1	5.38	4.99
Plesac, Dan, Tor/Ari	0	0.00	5.00	0	0.00	4.66
Plunk, Eric, Mil	0	—	—	0	0.00	4.76
Polanco, Placido, StL	21	3.25	5.00	32	3.29	4.87
Politte, Cliff, Phi	0	—	—	0	0.00	4.60
Polonia, Luis, Det	60	6.68	5.18	612	4.76	4.67
Ponson, Sidney, Bal	0	0.00	5.18	1	4.48	5.12
Poole, Jim, Phi	0	0.00	5.00	1	2.70	4.70
Porter, Bo, ChC	0	0.00	5.00	0	0.00	5.00
Portugal, Mark, Bos	0	0.00	5.18	25	1.57	4.39
Posada, Jorge, NYY	51	4.59	5.18	139	5.04	5.07
Pose, Scott, KC	18	4.58	5.18	26	3.31	4.98
Powell, Dante, Ari	1	1.17	5.00	10	4.99	4.77
Powell, Jay, Hou	0	—	—	1	2.69	4.65
Powell, Jeremy, Mon	0	0.00	5.00	0	0.00	4.93
Pratt, Todd, NYM	20	5.28	5.00	82	4.70	4.63
Prince, Tom, Phi	0	0.00	5.00	66	2.94	4.37
Pritchett, Chris, Ana	0	0.00	5.18	7	1.68	5.11
Pulsipher, Bill, Mil	0	0.00	5.00	2	0.64	4.74
Quantrill, Paul, Tor	0	—	—	-1	-0.43	4.64
Quinn, Mark, KC	14	9.12	5.18	14	9.12	5.18
Radinsky, Scott, StL	0	—	—	0	0.00	4.62
Radke, Brad, Min	0	0.00	5.18	0	0.00	5.06
Raines, Tim, Oak	12	2.79	5.18	1568	6.50	4.39
Ramirez, Alex, Cle	15	5.64	5.18	15	5.14	5.16
Ramirez, Aramis, Pit	5	2.80	5.00	27	2.96	4.68
Ramirez, Hector, Mil	0	0.00	5.00	0	0.00	5.00
Ramirez, Julio, Fla	0	0.00	5.00	0	0.00	5.00
Ramirez, Manny, Cle	150	10.74	5.18	652	7.76	5.12

Player, Team	1999			Career		
	RC	RC/27	LRC/27	RC	RC/27	LRC27
Ramirez, Roberto, Col	0	0.00	5.00	0	0.00	5.00
Randa, Joe, KC	101	5.89	5.18	284	5.19	5.04
Rapp, Pat, Bos	0	0.00	5.18	0	0.00	4.62
Reboulet, Jeff, Bal	11	2.21	5.18	170	3.65	5.00
Redmond, Mike, Fla	37	5.47	5.00	52	5.17	4.87
Reed, Jeff, Col/ChC	35	4.69	5.00	337	3.99	4.42
Reed, Rick, NYM	3	1.88	5.00	13	1.76	4.60
Reed, Steve, Cle	0	—	—	1	1.35	4.55
Reese, Pokey, Cin	76	4.61	5.00	124	3.82	4.81
Reichert, Dan, KC	0	0.00	5.18	0	0.00	5.18
Rekar, Bryan, TB	0	0.00	5.18	1	0.53	4.69
Relaford, Desi, Phi	24	3.71	5.00	73	3.06	4.71
Remlinger, Mike, Atl	0	0.00	5.00	-1	-0.24	4.57
Renteria, Edgar, StL	77	4.50	5.00	262	4.16	4.72
Reyes, Al, Mil	0	0.00	5.00	0	0.00	4.73
Reyes, Carlos, SD	0	0.00	5.00	0	0.00	4.80
Reyes, Dennys, Cin	0	0.00	5.00	0	0.00	4.65
Reynolds, Shane, Hou	6	2.18	5.00	10	0.69	4.69
Reynoso, Armando, Ari	0	0.00	5.00	5	0.51	4.65
Rhodes, Arthur, Bal	0	—	—	0	0.00	4.97
Rigby, Brad, Oak	0	—	—	0	0.00	4.93
Rincon, Ricky, Cle	0	—	—	0	0.00	4.60
Rios, Armando, SF	31	7.59	5.00	36	8.58	4.99
Ripken Jr., Cal, Bal	63	7.01	5.18	1618	5.27	4.68
Ritchie, Todd, Pit	0	0.00	5.00	0	0.00	5.00
Rivera, Ruben, SD	40	3.07	5.00	83	3.87	4.94
Roberts, David, Cle	15	3.45	5.18	15	3.45	5.18
Robinson, Kerry, Cin	0	0.00	5.00	0	0.00	5.01
Rodriguez, Alex, Sea	97	6.70	5.18	491	6.93	5.12
Rodriguez, Felix, SF	1	5.38	5.00	1	2.99	4.82
Rodriguez, Frank, Sea	1	13.36	5.18	1	8.90	5.10
Rodriguez, Henry, ChC	88	7.29	5.00	412	5.48	4.64
Rodriguez, Ivan, Tex	100	5.95	5.18	638	5.14	4.96
Rodriguez, Liu, CWS	14	4.73	5.18	14	4.73	5.18
Rodriguez, Rich, SF	1	26.92	5.00	3	2.61	4.26
Rogers, Kenny, Oak/NYM	0	0.00	5.02	0	0.00	5.01
Rojas, Mel, LA/Mon	0	—	—	1	0.47	4.34
Rolen, Scott, Phi	72	5.98	5.00	318	6.59	4.71
Roque, Rafael, Mil	0	0.00	5.00	0	0.00	4.81
Rosado, Jose, KC	0	0.00	5.18	0	0.00	5.09
Rose, Brian, Bos	0	0.00	5.18	0	0.00	5.18
Roskos, John, Fla	1	2.69	5.00	1	1.42	4.81
Rueter, Kirk, SF	2	0.88	5.00	7	0.62	4.68
Rupe, Ryan, TB	0	0.00	5.18	0	0.00	5.18
Rusch, Glendon, NYM	0	—	—	0	0.00	4.97
Ryan, Ken, Phi	0	—	—	0	0.00	4.67
Ryan, Rob, Ari	4	4.89	5.00	4	4.89	5.00
Sabel, Erik, Ari	0	0.00	5.00	0	0.00	5.00
Saberhagen, Bret, Bos	0	0.00	5.18	1	0.14	4.51
Sadler, Donnie, Bos	11	3.58	5.18	27	3.91	5.09
Saenz, Olmedo, Oak	37	5.07	5.18	37	4.73	5.18
Salmon, Tim, Ana	72	7.04	5.18	718	7.45	5.04
Sampson, Benj, Min	0	0.00	5.18	0	0.00	5.18
Sanchez, Jesus, Fla	0	0.00	5.00	0	0.00	4.68
Sanchez, Rey, KC	59	4.26	5.18	279	3.45	4.65
Sanders, Anthony, Tor	1	4.45	5.18	1	4.45	5.18
Sanders, Reggie, SD	91	6.69	5.00	565	5.83	4.57
Sanders, Scott, ChC	3	5.38	5.00	7	1.52	4.67
Sanford, Chance, LA	0	0.00	5.00	0	0.00	4.67
Santana, Julio, TB	1	Inf.	5.18	1	5.40	5.00
Santangelo, F.P., SF	47	6.33	5.00	220	5.02	4.69
Santiago, Benito, ChC	40	3.87	5.00	594	3.96	4.37
Sauerbeck, Scott, Pit	0	0.00	5.00	0	0.00	5.00
Saunders, Tony, TB	0	—	—	1	0.00	4.60
Scarsone, Steve, KC	6	2.86	5.18	86	3.44	4.66
Schilling, Curt, Phi	2	1.00	5.00	3	0.17	4.55
Schmidt, Jason, Pit	0	0.00	5.00	0	0.00	4.73
Schourek, Pete, Pit	0	0.00	5.00	10	1.01	4.49
Schrenk, Steve, Phi	0	0.00	5.00	0	0.00	5.00
Seanez, Rudy, Atl	0	0.00	5.00	0	0.00	4.71
Sefcik, Kevin, Phi	26	4.32	5.00	76	4.26	4.75
Segui, David, Sea/Tor	62	5.08	5.18	504	4.95	4.72
Seguignol, Fernando, Mon	13	4.32	5.00	16	3.78	4.88
Sele, Aaron, Tex	0	0.00	5.18	1	2.69	5.08
Serafini, Dan, ChC	0	0.00	5.00	0	0.00	5.00
Servais, Scott, SF	22	3.85	5.00	255	3.59	4.57
Service, Scott, KC	0	—	—	1	1.80	4.52
Sexson, Richie, Cle	67	4.62	5.18	97	4.98	5.13
Sexton, Chris, Col	8	4.39	5.00	8	4.39	5.00
Shave, Jon, Tex	12	5.83	5.18	21	4.43	4.99
Shaw, Jeff, LA	0	—	—	0	0.00	4.58
Sheets, Andy, Ana	14	1.74	5.18	61	3.04	5.01

Player, Team	1999			Career		
	RC	RC/27	LRC/27	RC	RC/27	LRC27
Sheffield, Gary, LA	113	7.45	5.00	913	6.94	4.50
Sheldon, Scott, Tex	0	0.00	5.18	5	3.84	4.97
Shuey, Paul, Cle	0	—	—	0	0.00	4.97
Shumaker, Anthony, Phi	0	0.00	5.00	0	0.00	5.00
Shumpert, Terry, Col	57	8.43	5.00	143	4.14	4.71
Silva, Jose, Pit	0	0.00	5.00	0	0.00	4.73
Silvestri, Dave, Ana	0	0.00	5.18	38	3.54	4.76
Simmons, Brian, CWS	15	4.01	5.18	22	5.21	5.16
Simms, Mike, Tex	0	0.00	5.18	100	5.15	4.65
Simon, Randall, Atl	25	4.15	5.00	30	4.37	4.95
Singleton, Chris, CWS	81	5.82	5.18	81	5.82	5.18
Sirotka, Mike, CWS	0	0.00	5.18	0	0.00	5.10
Slocumb, Heathcliff, StL	0	—	—	1	2.45	4.29
Smart, J.D., Mon	0	0.00	5.00	0	0.00	5.00
Smith, Bobby, TB	13	1.95	5.18	62	3.58	5.08
Smith, Dan, Mon	1	1.04	5.00	1	1.04	5.00
Smoltz, John, Atl	11	6.04	5.00	46	1.77	4.39
Snow, J.T., SF	86	5.25	5.00	489	5.07	4.94
Sodowsky, Clint, StL	0	0.00	5.00	0	0.00	4.63
Sojo, Luis, NYY	10	2.64	5.18	217	3.32	4.85
Soriano, Alfonso, NYY	0	0.00	5.18	0	0.00	5.18
Sorrento, Paul, TB	44	5.09	5.18	497	5.02	4.92
Sosa, Juan, Col	1	3.85	5.00	1	3.85	5.00
Sosa, Sammy, ChC	131	7.41	5.00	849	5.52	4.56
Sparks, Steve, Ana	2	26.71	5.18	2	13.36	5.09
Spehr, Tim, KC	23	4.76	5.18	65	3.71	4.77
Speier, Justin, Atl	0	0.00	5.00	0	0.00	5.00
Spencer, Shane, NYY	19	3.11	5.18	43	5.57	5.14
Spencer, Stan, SD	0	0.00	5.00	0	0.00	4.79
Spiers, Bill, Hou	54	4.86	5.00	412	4.63	4.62
Spiezio, Scott, Oak	33	4.50	5.18	152	4.20	5.02
Spoljaric, Paul, Phi/Tor	0	0.00	5.00	0	0.00	4.99
Spradlin, Jerry, SF	0	0.00	5.00	1	6.75	4.65
Sprague, Ed, Pit	86	6.03	5.00	455	4.12	5.01
Springer, Dennis, Fla	0	0.00	5.00	0	0.00	4.95
Springer, Russ, Atl	0	—	—	0	0.00	4.67
Stairs, Matt, Oak	101	6.58	5.18	316	6.69	5.06
Stanley, Mike, Bos	77	6.45	5.18	686	6.06	4.88
Stanton, Mike, NYY	0	0.00	5.18	3	10.13	4.45
Stein, Blake, Oak	0	—	—	0	0.00	5.01
Steinbach, Terry, Min	53	5.53	5.18	716	4.61	4.78
Stephenson, Garrett, StL	0	0.00	5.00	0	0.00	4.77
Stevens, Dave, Cle	0	—	—	0	0.00	4.60
Stevens, Lee, Tex	74	4.94	5.18	276	4.76	4.83
Stewart, Shannon, Tor	100	5.86	5.00	224	5.82	5.08
Stinnett, Kelly, Ari	32	3.79	5.00	119	4.19	4.76
Stocker, Kevin, TB	37	5.12	5.18	271	3.79	4.73
Stottlemyre, Todd, Ari	0	0.00	5.00	14	2.02	4.70
Stowers, Chris, Mon	0	0.00	5.00	0	0.00	5.00
Strawberry, Darryl, NYY	13	10.52	5.18	1004	6.42	4.25
Stull, Everett, Atl	0	—	—	0	0.00	4.60
Sturtze, Tanyon, CWS	0	—	—	0	0.00	4.68
Stynes, Chris, Cin	13	3.72	5.00	94	4.20	4.78
Sullivan, Scott, Cin	0	0.00	5.00	0	0.00	4.77
Suppan, Jeff, KC	1	6.68	5.18	3	3.51	4.73
Surhoff, B.J., Bal	100	5.44	5.18	864	4.83	4.76
Sutton, Larry, KC	15	4.66	5.18	69	4.78	5.04
Sveum, Dale, Pit	8	3.71	5.00	282	3.70	4.57
Sweeney, Mark, Cin	8	9.79	5.00	91	4.88	4.64
Sweeney, Mike, KC	109	7.00	5.18	192	5.32	5.12
Swindell, Greg, Ari	0	0.00	5.00	8	0.92	4.36
Tam, Jeff, NYM	0	—	—	0	0.00	4.60
Tapani, Kevin, ChC	0	0.00	5.00	6	1.02	4.70
Tarasco, Tony, NYY	2	1.91	5.18	119	4.42	4.77
Tatis, Fernando, StL	112	7.52	5.00	194	5.28	4.93
Taubensee, Eddie, Cin	70	6.04	5.00	365	5.20	4.57
Tavarez, Julian, SF	0	0.00	5.00	0	0.00	4.71
Tejada, Miguel, Oak	88	4.94	5.18	137	4.27	5.10
Telemaco, Amaury, Ari/Phi	0	—	—	1	0.37	4.63
Telford, Anthony, Mon	0	0.00	5.00	1	1.35	4.68
Thomas, Frank, CWS	87	6.38	5.18	1184	8.90	4.88
Thome, Jim, Cle	123	8.95	5.00	656	7.66	5.05
Thompson, Justin, Det	0	0.00	5.18	0	0.00	5.06
Thompson, Mark, StL	0	0.00	5.00	2	0.56	4.69
Thompson, Ryan, Hou	4	6.33	5.00	118	3.76	4.53
Thomson, John, Col	1	1.79	5.00	3	0.70	4.65
Thurman, Mike, Mon	-1	-0.63	5.00	-1	-0.38	4.85
Timmons, Ozzie, Sea	3	2.00	5.18	44	4.03	4.73
Toca, Jorge, NYM	0	0.00	5.00	0	0.00	5.00
Tomko, Brett, Cin	3	1.79	5.00	4	0.73	4.72
Trachsel, Steve, ChC	0	0.00	5.00	14	1.09	4.69
Trammell, Bubba, TB	49	6.20	5.18	94	5.47	5.07

Player, Team	1999			Career		
	RC	RC/27	LRC/27	RC	RC/27	LRC27
Tremie, Chris, Pit	1	2.07	5.00	2	1.49	5.04
Trombley, Mike, Min	0	—	—	0	0.00	4.93
Tucker, Michael, Cin	44	5.06	5.00	247	4.96	4.88
Turner, Chris, Cle	0	0.00	5.18	36	4.17	5.06
Unroe, Tim, Ana	7	4.56	5.18	12	4.59	5.17
Urbina, Ugueth, Mon	0	0.00	5.00	1	0.55	4.69
Valdes, Ismael, LA	0	0.00	5.00	1	0.09	4.71
Valentin, Javier, Min	21	3.26	5.18	28	2.36	5.10
Valentin, John, Bos	60	4.49	5.18	598	5.78	5.02
Valentin, Jose, Mil	42	5.38	5.00	352	4.91	5.03
Vander Wal, John, SD	39	5.58	5.00	195	5.12	4.53
Varitek, Jason, Bos	66	4.63	5.18	94	4.47	5.12
Vaughn, Greg, Cin	113	7.06	5.00	822	5.74	4.73
Vaughn, Mo, Ana	105	7.17	5.18	880	7.39	4.97
Vazquez, Javier, Mon	6	4.14	5.00	9	2.69	4.77
Velandia, Jorge, Oak	3	2.05	5.18	3	1.18	4.95
Velarde, Randy, Ana/Oak	112	6.48	5.18	479	5.06	4.88
Ventura, Robin, NYM	116	7.23	5.00	853	5.82	4.82
Veras, Quilvio, SD	66	4.81	5.00	308	4.72	4.70
Veras, Wilton, Bos	8	2.30	5.18	8	2.30	5.18
Veres, Dave, Col	0	0.00	5.00	2	3.38	4.67
Vidro, Jose, Mon	71	5.25	5.00	108	4.33	4.82
Villone, Ron, Cin	-1	-0.60	5.00	-1	-0.57	4.99
Vina, Fernando, Mil	20	4.45	5.00	297	4.89	4.95
Vitiello, Joe, KC	1	0.72	5.18	67	3.96	5.19
Vizcaino, Jose, LA	27	3.30	5.00	406	3.88	4.58
Vizquel, Omar, Cle	107	6.74	5.18	636	4.14	4.84
Vosberg, Ed, SD/Ari	0	—	—	0	0.00	4.18
Wagner, Billy, Hou	0	—	—	0	0.00	4.65
Wagner, Paul, Cle	0	—	—	5	0.84	4.59
Wainhouse, Dave, Col	0	0.00	5.00	0	0.00	4.70
Wakefield, Tim, Bos	0	0.00	5.18	2	0.69	4.31
Walbeck, Matt, Ana	22	2.47	5.18	167	3.19	5.13
Walker, Larry, Col	129	11.81	5.00	928	7.44	4.45
Walker, Todd, Min	63	4.10	5.18	173	4.68	5.10
Wall, Donne, SD	0	0.00	5.00	1	0.40	4.66
Wallace, Jeff, Pit	0	—	—	0	—	—
Ward, Bryan, CWS	0	—	—	0	—	—
Ward, Daryle, Hou	20	4.72	5.00	21	4.87	5.00
Ward, Turner, Pit/Ari	15	4.21	5.00	211	4.77	4.86
Wasdin, John, Bos	0	—	—	0	—	—
Washburn, Jarrod, Ana	0	—	—	0	0.00	5.01
Watkins, Pat, Col	0	0.00	5.00	15	2.45	4.65
Watson, Allen, NYM	0	0.00	5.00	17	3.04	4.65
Weathers, Dave, Mil	0	0.00	5.00	1	0.21	4.63
Weaver, Eric, Sea	0	—	—	0	0.00	4.60
Weaver, Jeff, Det	1	8.90	5.18	1	8.90	5.18
Webster, Lenny, Bal/Bos	3	1.78	5.18	149	3.70	4.77
Wehner, John, Pit	2	0.94	5.00	51	2.44	4.46
Weiss, Walt, Atl	34	3.98	5.00	539	4.07	4.53
Wells, Bob, Min	0	—	—	0	—	—
Wells, David, Tor	0	0.00	5.18	0	0.00	4.77
Wells, Vernon, Tor	9	3.34	5.18	9	3.34	5.18
Wendell, Turk, NYM	0	0.00	5.00	1	0.85	4.67
Wengert, Don, KC	0	—	—	0	0.00	4.60
Wetteland, John, Tex	0	—	—	3	1.84	4.10
White, Devon, LA	63	4.66	5.00	923	4.69	4.63
White, Gabe, Cin	0	—	—	1	0.96	4.61
White, Rick, TB	0	—	—	0	0.00	4.66
White, Rondell, Mon	83	5.59	5.00	356	5.13	4.70
Whiten, Mark, Cle	2	2.43	5.18	424	4.69	4.63
Whiteside, Matt, SD	0	—	—	0	0.00	4.60
Wickman, Bob, Mil	0	0.00	5.00	0	0.00	4.80
Widger, Chris, Mon	44	4.06	5.00	128	3.87	4.76
Wilkins, Marc, Pit	0	0.00	5.00	1	2.08	4.68
Wilkins, Rick, LA	0	0.00	5.00	265	4.35	4.48
Williams, Bernie, NYY	129	8.30	5.18	783	6.60	4.97
Williams, Brian, Hou	1	13.46	5.00	6	1.88	4.31
Williams, Gerald, Atl	66	5.37	5.00	242	4.22	4.99
Williams, Jeff, LA	0	0.00	5.00	0	0.00	5.00
Williams, Matt, Ari	118	6.87	5.00	890	5.30	4.45
Williams, Mike, Pit	0	0.00	5.00	5	1.19	4.59
Williams, Reggie, Ana	7	3.40	5.18	18	4.24	4.93
Williams, Todd, Sea	0	—	—	0	0.00	4.61
Williams, Woody, SD	3	1.22	5.00	4	1.52	5.00
Williamson, Scott, Cin	0	0.00	5.00	0	0.00	5.00
Wilson, Craig, CWS	30	3.91	5.18	46	5.28	5.16
Wilson, Dan, Sea	47	3.85	5.18	319	4.28	5.10
Wilson, Enrique, Cle	30	2.96	5.18	45	3.45	5.14
Wilson, Preston, Fla	71	5.14	5.00	74	4.77	4.96
Winn, Randy, TB	30	3.38	5.18	66	3.49	5.09
Witasick, Jay, KC	0	0.00	5.18	0	0.00	5.18

Player, Team	1999			Career		
	RC	RC/27	LRC/27	RC	RC/27	LRC27
Witt, Bobby, TB	0	0.00	5.18	4	2.07	4.68
Witt, Kevin, Tor	2	1.91	5.18	2	1.57	5.15
Wohlers, Mark, Atl	0	—	—	1	2.25	4.47
Wolcott, Bob, Bos	0	—	—	0	0.00	4.64
Wolf, Randy, Phi	2	1.79	5.00	2	1.79	5.00
Womack, Tony, Ari	80	4.51	5.00	266	4.77	4.73
Wood, Jason, Det	3	2.11	5.18	6	2.92	5.13
Woodall, Brad, ChC	1	26.92	5.00	5	3.38	4.62
Woodard, Steve, Mil	0	0.00	5.00	0	0.00	4.82
Woodward, Chris, Tor	2	2.43	5.18	2	2.43	5.18
Worrell, Tim, Oak	0	—	—	4	1.54	4.58
Wright, Jamey, Col	0	0.00	5.00	5	0.83	4.69
Wright, Jaret, Cle	0	0.00	5.18	2	5.37	4.99
Yoshii, Masato, NYM	-1	-0.48	5.00	-1	-0.25	4.80
Young, Dmitri, Cin	55	5.34	5.00	182	5.11	4.72
Young, Eric, LA	66	4.78	5.00	510	5.31	4.63
Young, Ernie, Ari	0	0.00	5.00	79	3.27	5.22
Young, Kevin, Pit	117	7.21	5.00	346	4.94	4.72
Zaun, Gregg, Tex	13	4.63	5.18	95	4.06	4.84
Zeile, Todd, Tex	96	5.75	5.18	764	4.93	4.53
Zosky, Eddie, Mil	0	0.00	5.00	0	0.00	4.55

Component Earned Run Average

Pitcher, Team	1999 OAvg	1999 OOB	1999 ERC	1999 LERA	Career OAvg	Career OOB	Career ERC	Career LERA
Abbott, Jim, Mil	.317	.393	7.16	4.56	.276	.340	4.35	4.31
Abbott, Paul, Sea	.193	.278	2.65	4.86	.236	.339	4.08	4.41
Acevedo, Juan, StL	.291	.369	5.78	4.56	.279	.350	4.91	4.32
Adams, Terry, ChC	.245	.319	4.00	4.56	.260	.346	4.24	4.28
Aguilera, Rick, Min/ChC	.219	.259	2.39	4.65	.251	.302	3.38	4.16
Aldred, Scott, TB/Phi	.276	.359	4.31	4.69	.296	.371	5.83	4.56
Alfonseca, Antonio, Fla	.274	.348	3.96	4.56	.285	.359	4.71	4.37
Almanza, Armando, Fla	.154	.286	2.09	4.56	.154	.286	2.09	4.56
Almanzar, Carlos, SD	.316	.386	6.54	4.56	.294	.357	5.54	4.60
Almonte, Hector, Fla	.339	.394	5.73	4.56	.339	.394	5.73	4.56
Alvarez, Juan, Ana	.111	.385	3.04	4.86	.111	.385	3.04	4.86
Alvarez, Wilson, TB	.260	.349	4.87	4.86	.247	.337	4.17	4.60
Anderson, Brian, Ari	.279	.317	4.23	4.56	.284	.321	4.52	4.55
Anderson, Jimmy, Pit	.234	.336	3.62	4.56	.234	.336	3.62	4.56
Anderson, Matt, Det	.232	.383	6.34	4.86	.241	.380	5.27	4.75
Ankiel, Rick, StL	.215	.301	2.89	4.56	.215	.301	2.89	4.56
Appier, Kevin, KC/Oak	.279	.349	4.99	4.86	.243	.309	3.31	4.46
Armas Jr., Tony, Mon	.320	.357	4.53	4.56	.320	.357	4.53	4.56
Arnold, Jamie, LA	.300	.390	5.81	4.56	.300	.390	5.81	4.56
Arrojo, Rolando, TB	.296	.378	6.09	4.86	.273	.350	4.84	4.73
Ashby, Andy, SD	.258	.311	3.78	4.56	.264	.320	3.89	4.21
Assenmacher, Paul, Cle	.347	.415	8.18	4.86	.252	.320	3.53	4.01
Astacio, Pedro, Col	.285	.343	5.08	4.56	.266	.327	4.16	4.20
Avery, Steve, Cin	.222	.364	4.69	4.56	.259	.324	3.85	4.06
Ayala, Bobby, Mon/ChC	.228	.322	3.90	4.56	.263	.340	4.49	4.52
Aybar, Manny, StL	.272	.338	4.68	4.56	.273	.349	4.72	4.35
Baldwin, James, CWS	.278	.348	5.33	4.86	.273	.342	4.86	4.76
Bale, John, Tor	.250	.400	9.87	4.86	.250	.400	9.87	4.86
Barber, Brian, KC	.383	.457	11.42	4.86	.303	.377	6.23	4.53
Barker, Richie, ChC	.300	.400	5.47	4.56	.300	.400	5.47	4.56
Batista, Miguel, Mon	.280	.353	4.62	4.56	.275	.359	4.72	4.36
Beck, Rod, ChC/Bos	.289	.356	4.99	4.66	.244	.288	3.08	4.06
Belcher, Tim, Ana	.315	.369	6.44	4.86	.259	.322	3.94	4.20
Belinda, Stan, Cin	.258	.333	5.20	4.56	.228	.311	3.40	4.17
Beltran, Rigo, NYM/Col	.291	.365	5.78	4.56	.259	.325	3.92	4.35
Benes, Alan, StL	.286	.286	2.31	4.56	.250	.330	4.03	4.21
Benes, Andy, Ari	.273	.343	5.18	4.56	.247	.311	3.56	4.05
Benitez, Armando, NYM	.148	.260	1.69	4.56	.184	.303	2.98	4.64
Bennett, Joel, Phi	.351	.407	11.52	4.56	.341	.413	11.18	4.57
Bennett, Shayne, Mon	.444	.475	14.07	4.56	.290	.365	5.23	4.25
Benson, Kris, Pit	.249	.327	3.78	4.56	.249	.327	3.78	4.56
Bere, Jason, Cin/Mil	.302	.415	7.00	4.56	.255	.365	5.18	4.59
Bergman, Sean, Hou/Atl	.325	.370	5.40	4.56	.295	.354	5.10	4.39
Billingsley, Brent, Fla	.379	.548	16.37	4.56	.379	.548	16.37	4.56
Blair, Willie, Det	.308	.361	6.35	4.86	.283	.341	4.80	4.25
Bochtler, Doug, LA	.224	.316	4.38	4.56	.236	.347	4.42	4.34
Boehringer, Brian, SD	.267	.330	4.12	4.56	.260	.354	4.78	4.55
Boggs, Wade, TB	.429	.429	9.13	4.86	.300	.364	4.93	4.73
Bohanon, Brian, Col	.305	.387	6.27	4.56	.280	.357	5.05	4.38
Bones, Ricky, Bal	.322	.390	6.99	4.86	.281	.343	4.90	4.52
Borbon, Pedro, LA	.209	.314	3.45	4.56	.220	.310	3.06	4.34
Borkowski, Dave, Det	.283	.371	5.75	4.86	.283	.371	5.75	4.86
Bottalico, Ricky, StL	.284	.392	6.16	4.56	.235	.333	3.93	4.28
Bottenfield, Kent, StL	.270	.350	4.68	4.56	.269	.345	4.49	4.24
Bowie, Micah, Atl/ChC	.363	.447	9.69	4.56	.363	.447	9.69	4.56
Boyd, Jason, Pit	.250	.333	3.53	4.56	.250	.333	3.53	4.56
Bradford, Chad, CWS	.474	.583	21.34	4.86	.263	.322	3.61	4.67
Brantley, Jeff, Phi	.161	.325	2.84	4.56	.231	.313	3.44	3.89
Brewer, Billy, Phi	.294	.376	6.05	4.56	.255	.345	4.73	4.57
Brocail, Doug, Det	.206	.276	2.43	4.86	.260	.325	3.96	4.36
Brock, Chris, SF	.291	.357	5.59	4.56	.289	.355	5.25	4.44
Brower, Jim, Cle	.270	.339	5.96	4.86	.270	.339	5.96	4.86
Brown, Kevin, LA	.222	.273	2.51	4.56	.251	.308	3.24	4.25
Brownson, Mark, Col	.333	.378	7.40	4.56	.322	.365	6.61	4.46
Brunson, Will, Det	.367	.421	8.82	4.86	.338	.405	7.23	4.74
Buddie, Mike, NYY	.333	.333	8.13	4.86	.288	.348	4.95	4.66
Bullinger, Kirk, Bos	.286	.444	6.15	4.86	.381	.409	8.21	4.37
Bunch, Mel, Sea	.426	.491	14.28	4.86	.298	.361	6.89	4.74
Burba, Dave, Cle	.254	.336	4.45	4.86	.254	.334	4.23	4.34
Burkett, John, Tex	.307	.358	5.44	4.86	.278	.325	4.05	4.17
Burnett, A.J., Fla	.242	.343	4.00	4.56	.242	.343	4.00	4.56
Busby, Mike, StL	.304	.435	7.62	4.56	.302	.383	6.15	4.30
Byrd, Paul, Phi	.265	.337	4.87	4.56	.251	.326	4.24	4.40
Byrdak, Tim, KC	.308	.424	8.29	4.86	.327	.433	9.08	4.84
Cabrera, Jose, Hou	.196	.252	2.12	4.56	.197	.256	2.03	4.42
Callaway, Mickey, TB	.357	.444	8.89	4.86	.357	.444	8.89	4.86
Candiotti, Tom, Oak/Cle	.300	.367	6.29	4.86	.256	.317	3.70	4.12
Carlson, Dan, Ari	.278	.278	2.93	4.56	.323	.382	7.12	4.40
Carlyle, Buddy, SD	.257	.342	4.95	4.56	.257	.342	4.95	4.56
Carmona, Rafael, Sea	.409	.491	11.44	4.86	.285	.387	6.13	4.88
Carpenter, Chris, Tor	.294	.346	4.90	4.86	.289	.349	4.84	4.71
Carrasco, Hector, Min	.261	.328	3.76	4.86	.248	.338	3.89	4.37
Carter, Lance, KC	.167	.286	4.22	4.86	.167	.286	4.22	4.86
Castillo, Carlos, CWS	.274	.331	5.40	4.86	.258	.327	4.61	4.66
Cather, Mike, Atl	.417	.462	16.62	4.56	.226	.307	3.32	4.23
Charlton, Norm, TB	.257	.372	5.03	4.86	.240	.328	3.64	4.05
Checo, Robinson, LA	.333	.435	10.88	4.56	.309	.393	7.47	4.58
Chen, Bruce, Atl	.208	.315	4.07	4.56	.232	.330	4.48	4.47
Cho, Jin Ho, Bos	.287	.324	4.81	4.86	.305	.339	5.52	4.79
Chouinard, Bobby, Ari	.220	.274	2.27	4.56	.280	.345	4.69	4.64
Christiansen, Jason, Pit	.197	.318	2.85	4.56	.246	.337	3.81	4.26
Clark, Mark, Tex	.329	.392	7.75	4.86	.276	.326	4.26	4.30
Clemens, Roger, NYY	.261	.350	4.59	4.86	.227	.293	2.83	4.33
Clement, Matt, SD	.273	.358	4.89	4.56	.274	.359	4.84	4.54
Clontz, Brad, Pit	.254	.344	4.52	4.56	.261	.336	4.15	4.27
Cloude, Ken, Sea	.346	.435	8.54	4.86	.297	.383	6.51	4.69
Colon, Bartolo, Cle	.242	.314	3.68	4.86	.258	.330	4.09	4.72
Cone, David, NYY	.229	.322	3.76	4.86	.225	.301	3.07	4.16
Cook, Dennis, NYM	.216	.299	3.60	4.56	.249	.319	3.85	4.11
Cooper, Brian, Ana	.228	.363	4.79	4.86	.228	.363	4.79	4.86
Coppinger, R., Bal/Mil	.267	.379	6.50	4.67	.264	.357	5.63	4.84
Corbin, Archie, Fla	.291	.398	6.50	4.56	.256	.382	5.43	4.77
Cordero, Francisco, Det	.284	.416	6.19	4.86	.284	.416	6.19	4.86
Cordova, Francisco, Pit	.273	.339	4.26	4.56	.258	.315	3.65	4.30
Cormier, Rheal, Bos	.246	.307	3.33	4.86	.274	.316	3.86	4.09
Cornelius, Reid, Fla	.229	.280	2.03	4.56	.276	.348	4.68	4.27
Corsi, Jim, Bos/Bal	.288	.383	5.74	4.86	.254	.328	3.54	4.38
Cortes, David, Atl	.214	.389	4.78	4.56	.214	.389	4.78	4.56
Crabtree, Tim, Tex	.280	.328	3.93	4.86	.274	.338	4.16	4.77
Creek, Doug, ChC	.261	.438	8.01	4.56	.233	.366	5.43	4.24
Croushore, Rich, StL	.247	.354	4.73	4.56	.232	.339	4.27	4.42
Cruz, Nelson, Det	.281	.341	5.09	4.86	.279	.338	5.13	4.77
Cunnane, Will, SD	.293	.359	5.87	4.56	.302	.384	6.35	4.29
D'Amico, Jeff, Mil	.250	.250	1.95	4.56	.265	.327	4.84	4.73
Daal, Omar, Ari	.236	.308	3.39	4.56	.256	.327	3.86	4.35
Dale, Carl, Mil	.400	.556	21.62	4.56	.400	.556	21.62	4.56
Daneker, Pat, CWS	.255	.323	3.46	4.86	.255	.323	3.46	4.86
Darensbourg, Vic, Fla	.340	.434	7.90	4.56	.256	.344	4.08	4.34
Davenport, Joe, CWS	.200	.429	4.62	4.86	.200	.429	4.62	4.86
Davey, Tom, Tor/Sea	.250	.367	4.87	4.86	.250	.367	4.87	4.86
Davis, Doug, Tex	.600	.600	41.42	4.86	.600	.600	41.42	4.86
DeHart, Rick, Mon	.545	.643	43.55	4.56	.303	.376	6.46	4.22
DeJean, Mike, Col	.335	.411	7.77	4.56	.299	.365	5.13	4.32
de los Santos, Val., Mil	.343	.465	9.65	4.56	.213	.280	3.09	4.32
del Toro, Miguel, SF	.264	.343	5.34	4.56	.264	.343	5.34	4.56
DeLucia, Rich, Cle	.317	.440	11.41	4.86	.251	.337	4.46	4.21
Dempster, Ryan, Fla	.262	.370	5.49	4.56	.282	.391	6.19	4.47
DePaula, Sean, Cle	.200	.256	1.50	4.86	.200	.256	1.50	4.86
Dipoto, Jerry, Col	.279	.365	5.12	4.56	.279	.356	4.45	4.30
Dotel, Octavio, NYM	.226	.340	4.30	4.56	.226	.340	4.30	4.56
Dougherty, Jim, Pit	.333	.500	10.76	4.56	.298	.380	5.76	4.25
Dreifort, Darren, LA	.260	.340	4.39	4.56	.258	.336	3.96	4.35
Durbin, Chad, KC	.125	.222	1.08	4.86	.125	.222	1.08	4.86
Duvall, Mike, TB	.293	.401	6.56	4.86	.291	.397	6.30	4.84
Ebert, Derrin, Atl	.300	.400	7.17	4.56	.300	.400	7.17	4.56
Edmondson, Brian, Fla	.290	.370	5.39	4.56	.280	.362	5.10	4.41
Eiland, Dave, TB	.294	.349	5.08	4.86	.299	.352	5.24	4.21
Elarton, Scott, Hou	.238	.306	3.16	4.56	.225	.295	2.90	4.46
Eldred, Cal, Mil	.297	.379	7.13	4.56	.256	.332	4.34	4.47
Embree, Alan, SF	.200	.295	2.86	4.56	.240	.330	4.05	4.44
Erdos, Todd, NYY	.192	.290	4.18	4.86	.287	.358	5.57	4.44
Erickson, Scott, Bal	.280	.358	4.97	4.86	.277	.340	4.37	4.51
Escobar, Kelvim, Tor	.293	.371	5.62	4.86	.272	.352	4.75	4.77
Estes, Shawn, SF	.268	.362	4.96	4.56	.251	.347	4.18	4.32
Estrada, Horacio, Mil	.313	.389	10.50	4.56	.313	.389	10.50	4.56
Eyre, Scott, CWS	.339	.419	9.23	4.86	.280	.371	6.37	4.65
Falkenborg, Brian, Bal	.200	.333	2.79	4.86	.200	.333	2.79	4.86
Falteisek, Steve, Mil	.375	.404	8.26	4.56	.342	.384	6.40	4.42
Farnsworth, Kyle, ChC	.271	.340	5.39	4.56	.271	.340	5.39	4.56
Fassero, Jeff, Sea/Tex	.318	.394	7.69	4.86	.255	.317	3.77	4.32
Fernandez, Alex, Fla	.252	.307	3.33	4.56	.252	.311	3.63	4.43
Fetters, Mike, Bal	.278	.393	6.66	4.86	.264	.347	4.22	4.44
Finley, Chuck, Ana	.246	.330	4.03	4.86	.253	.330	3.97	4.39
Florie, Bryce, Det/Bos	.288	.359	5.05	4.86	.260	.350	4.46	4.56
Fossas, Tony, NYY	.667	.700	57.05	4.86	.269	.344	4.33	4.18
Foulke, Keith, CWS	.188	.235	1.80	4.86	.230	.287	3.15	4.65
Fox, Chad, Mil	.355	.444	9.96	4.56	.260	.339	4.30	4.25
Franco, John, NYM	.255	.341	3.77	4.56	.247	.318	3.25	3.86
Franco, Matt, NYM	.429	.600	29.71	4.56	.429	.600	29.71	4.56
Franklin, Ryan, Sea	.238	.373	5.52	4.86	.238	.373	5.52	4.86

	1999				Career			
Pitcher, Team	OAvg	OOB	ERC	LERA	OAvg	OOB	ERC	LERA
Frascatore, J., Ari/Tor	.275	.330	4.29	4.72	.266	.337	4.31	4.34
Fussell, Chris, KC	.329	.428	7.92	4.86	.325	.429	7.79	4.83
Fyhrie, Mike, Ana	.286	.349	5.45	4.86	.290	.357	5.70	4.83
Gaetti, Gary, ChC	.400	.500	23.01	4.56	.417	.500	17.08	4.37
Gagne, Eric, LA	.175	.280	2.42	4.56	.175	.280	2.42	4.56
Gaillard, Eddie, TB	.324	.405	7.10	4.86	.229	.313	3.96	4.65
Garces, Rich, Bos	.171	.262	1.75	4.86	.224	.328	3.70	4.68
Garcia, Freddy, Sea	.263	.345	4.46	4.86	.263	.345	4.46	4.86
Garcia, Mike, Pit	.091	.200	1.23	4.56	.091	.200	1.23	4.56
Gardner, Mark, SF	.267	.341	5.12	4.56	.260	.328	4.24	4.05
Giovanola, Ed, SD	.200	.429	5.91	4.56	.200	.429	5.91	4.56
Glavine, Tom, Atl	.287	.346	4.31	4.56	.252	.314	3.36	3.97
Glover, Gary, Tor	.000	.333	1.26	4.86	.000	.333	1.26	4.86
Glynn, Ryan, Tex	.316	.408	7.77	4.86	.316	.408	7.77	4.86
Gomes, Wayne, Phi	.255	.381	5.00	4.56	.260	.356	4.58	4.34
Gooden, Dwight, Cle	.282	.382	6.21	4.86	.242	.307	3.23	3.91
Gordon, Tom, Bos	.246	.366	5.04	4.86	.244	.331	3.88	4.40
Grace, Mike, Phi	.346	.430	7.90	4.56	.285	.348	4.71	4.29
Grahe, Joe, Phi	.308	.392	5.74	4.56	.287	.366	4.99	4.20
Graterol, Beiker, Det	.250	.400	11.57	4.86	.250	.400	11.57	4.86
Graves, Danny, Cin	.227	.314	3.25	4.56	.255	.332	3.84	4.48
Greene, Rick, Cin	.292	.320	6.18	4.56	.292	.320	6.18	4.56
Grimsley, Jason, NYY	.231	.330	3.87	4.86	.267	.372	5.12	4.51
Groom, Buddy, Oak	.274	.345	3.71	4.86	.296	.365	5.26	4.63
Gross, Kip, Bos	.300	.419	7.85	4.86	.284	.359	4.81	3.80
Guardado, Eddie, Min	.222	.328	3.63	4.86	.273	.345	4.83	4.67
Gunderson, Eric, Tex	.417	.431	9.50	4.86	.293	.354	5.16	4.48
Guthrie, Mark, Bos/ChC	.256	.329	4.45	4.79	.272	.335	4.20	4.20
Guzman, Domingo, SD	.464	.516	14.73	4.56	.464	.516	14.73	4.56
Guzman, Juan, Bal/Cin	.255	.332	4.35	4.74	.242	.324	3.85	4.53
Hackman, Luther, Col	.371	.463	11.65	4.56	.371	.463	11.65	4.56
Halama, John, Sea	.282	.338	4.47	4.86	.284	.342	4.45	4.76
Halladay, Roy, Tor	.270	.359	5.19	4.86	.262	.348	4.84	4.84
Hamilton, Joey, Tor	.298	.364	5.69	4.86	.262	.333	4.05	4.27
Hampton, Mike, Hou	.241	.322	3.25	4.56	.263	.330	3.88	4.29
Haney, Chris, Cle	.270	.348	4.57	4.86	.285	.344	4.80	4.52
Hansell, Greg, Pit	.280	.339	4.42	4.56	.293	.358	5.63	4.74
Harikkala, Tim, Bos	.306	.393	4.72	4.86	.317	.398	6.07	4.86
Harnisch, Pete, Cin	.252	.307	3.65	4.56	.243	.311	3.57	4.03
Harris, Reggie, Mil	.186	.321	3.39	4.56	.238	.361	4.56	4.16
Harville, Chad, Oak	.310	.406	7.09	4.86	.310	.406	7.09	4.86
Hasegawa, Shig., Ana	.276	.352	5.25	4.86	.262	.331	4.31	4.67
Hawkins, LaTroy, Min	.323	.373	6.55	4.86	.317	.372	6.35	4.72
Haynes, Jimmy, Oak	.282	.370	5.79	4.86	.289	.373	5.74	4.75
Heiserman, Rick, StL	.400	.500	16.12	4.56	.400	.500	16.12	4.56
Helling, Rick, Tex	.272	.340	5.03	4.86	.257	.329	4.48	4.66
Henry, Butch, Sea	.303	.375	5.20	4.86	.280	.322	3.98	4.07
Henry, Doug, Hou	.281	.385	6.64	4.56	.247	.333	4.06	4.24
Hentgen, Pat, Tor	.286	.338	5.04	4.86	.264	.329	4.28	4.67
Heredia, Felix, ChC	.272	.347	5.01	4.56	.261	.355	4.59	4.31
Heredia, Gil, Oak	.283	.318	4.13	4.86	.282	.320	4.02	4.43
Herges, Matt, LA	.255	.320	4.61	4.56	.255	.320	4.61	4.56
Hermanson, Dus., Mon	.271	.330	4.03	4.56	.253	.319	3.76	4.34
Hernandez, Liv., Fla/SF	.286	.347	4.88	4.56	.277	.347	4.81	4.35
Hernandez, Or., NYY	.233	.311	3.60	4.86	.229	.306	3.34	4.77
Hernandez, Rob., TB	.245	.330	3.40	4.86	.226	.308	3.13	4.57
Hershiser, Orel, NYM	.260	.342	4.17	4.56	.247	.310	3.31	3.99
Hiljus, Erik, Det	.241	.343	4.96	4.86	.241	.343	4.96	4.86
Hill, Ken, Ana	.270	.369	5.17	4.86	.256	.332	3.87	4.19
Hinchliffe, Brett, Sea	.323	.434	10.10	4.86	.323	.434	10.10	4.86
Hitchcock, Sterling, SD	.254	.320	4.14	4.56	.270	.335	4.60	4.55
Hoffman, Trevor, SD	.197	.240	1.78	4.56	.198	.263	2.19	4.23
Holmes, Darren, Ari	.262	.350	4.14	4.56	.267	.336	4.13	4.21
Holt, Chris, Hou	.303	.363	4.96	4.56	.280	.339	4.24	4.36
Holtz, Mike, Ana	.295	.410	6.85	4.86	.258	.353	4.47	4.74
Howry, Bob, CWS	.229	.336	4.11	4.86	.214	.308	3.37	4.76
Hudek, J., Cin/Atl/Tor	.351	.438	9.25	4.61	.236	.347	4.60	4.25
Hudson, Tim, Oak	.237	.323	3.50	4.86	.237	.323	3.50	4.86
Irabu, Hideki, NYY	.267	.317	4.38	4.86	.259	.326	4.59	4.73
Isringhausen, NYM/Oak	.258	.353	4.94	4.68	.276	.354	4.67	4.29
Jackson, Mike, Cle	.232	.304	3.76	4.86	.217	.301	3.02	4.18
Jarvis, Kevin, Oak	.418	.467	14.40	4.86	.315	.373	6.59	4.30
Jimenez, Jose, StL	.275	.356	4.81	4.56	.273	.352	4.63	4.52
Johns, Doug, Bal	.248	.311	3.62	4.86	.282	.354	4.94	4.84
Johnson, Jason, Bal	.267	.348	4.99	4.86	.285	.361	5.56	4.77
Johnson, Jonathan, Tex	.529	.571	19.55	4.86	.424	.512	12.07	4.73
Johnson, Mike, Mon	.324	.432	9.54	4.56	.309	.375	7.02	4.37
Johnson, Randy, Ari	.208	.266	2.49	4.56	.212	.305	3.12	4.34
Johnstone, John, SF	.203	.267	2.40	4.56	.240	.322	3.77	4.32
Jones, Bobby, NYM	.295	.328	3.95	4.56	.267	.320	3.88	4.22
Jones, Bobby M., Col	.292	.399	7.41	4.56	.294	.385	6.16	4.36
Jones, Doug, Oak	.267	.311	3.62	4.86	.262	.305	3.32	4.22

	1999				Career			
Pitcher, Team	OAvg	OOB	ERC	LERA	OAvg	OOB	ERC	LERA
Jones, Todd, Det	.259	.352	4.55	4.86	.239	.331	3.68	4.40
Judd, Mike, LA	.280	.358	5.26	4.56	.314	.396	7.08	4.45
Juden, Jeff, NYY	.200	.310	4.50	4.86	.253	.341	4.57	4.25
Kamieniecki, Scott, Bal	.250	.348	4.11	4.86	.269	.348	4.58	4.44
Karchner, Matt, ChC	.235	.342	4.73	4.56	.260	.354	4.68	4.67
Karl, Scott, Mil	.312	.370	5.54	4.56	.288	.349	4.90	4.61
Karsay, Steve, Cle	.247	.320	3.45	4.86	.280	.342	4.64	4.63
Kida, Masao, Det	.289	.368	5.23	4.86	.289	.368	5.23	4.86
Kile, Darryl, Col	.298	.387	6.55	4.56	.262	.349	4.45	4.13
Kim, Byung-Hyun, Ari	.211	.375	4.35	4.56	.211	.375	4.35	4.56
King, Curtis, StL	.500	.500	14.52	4.56	.290	.356	4.52	4.22
King, Ray, ChC	.289	.449	8.10	4.56	.289	.449	8.10	4.56
Kline, Steve, Mon	.218	.313	3.40	4.56	.256	.346	4.47	4.39
Koch, Billy, Tor	.235	.328	3.53	4.86	.235	.328	3.53	4.86
Kolb, Danny, Tex	.268	.353	4.63	4.86	.268	.353	4.63	4.86
Kubenka, Jeff, LA	.371	.425	8.56	4.56	.266	.372	4.71	4.38
Kubinski, Tim, Oak	.280	.351	6.04	4.86	.268	.345	5.33	4.71
Langston, Mark, Cle	.288	.362	5.28	4.86	.246	.325	3.89	4.20
Laxton, Brett, Oak	.316	.420	7.39	4.86	.316	.420	7.39	4.86
Lee, Corey, Tex	.400	.500	23.01	4.86	.400	.500	23.01	4.86
Lee, David, Col	.247	.364	4.43	4.56	.247	.364	4.43	4.56
Leiter, Al, NYM	.262	.342	4.17	4.56	.238	.339	3.88	4.38
Leiter, Mark, Sea	.333	.333	4.47	4.86	.266	.336	4.45	4.22
Leskanic, Curt, Col	.272	.374	5.00	4.56	.263	.345	4.53	4.25
Levine, Al, Ana	.247	.311	3.81	4.86	.276	.338	4.60	4.76
Lidle, Cory, TB	.364	.417	6.98	4.86	.280	.326	3.92	4.24
Lieber, Jon, ChC	.279	.315	4.19	4.56	.278	.318	4.15	4.29
Lilly, Ted, Mon	.309	.382	7.76	4.56	.309	.382	7.76	4.56
Lima, Jose, Hou	.265	.296	3.58	4.56	.269	.307	3.90	4.48
Lincoln, Mike, Min	.321	.368	6.16	4.86	.321	.368	6.16	4.86
Linton, Doug, Bal	.296	.369	6.42	4.86	.296	.365	5.83	4.64
Lira, Felipe, Det	.389	.450	16.24	4.86	.279	.348	5.14	4.79
Lloyd, Graeme, Tor	.250	.317	4.00	4.86	.258	.314	3.63	4.70
Loaiza, Esteban, Tex	.275	.329	4.03	4.86	.290	.343	4.77	4.36
Loewer, Carlton, Phi	.287	.332	4.31	4.56	.302	.348	5.10	4.37
Loiselle, Rich, Pit	.281	.397	5.82	4.56	.267	.350	4.41	4.25
Looper, Braden, Fla	.293	.351	4.65	4.56	.295	.352	4.78	4.55
Lopez, Albie, TB	.263	.325	4.27	4.86	.279	.354	5.18	4.69
Lorraine, Andrew, ChC	.293	.350	5.03	4.56	.310	.377	6.13	4.61
Lowe, Derek, Bos	.208	.260	2.14	4.86	.249	.308	3.33	4.70
Lowe, Sean, CWS	.262	.347	4.38	4.86	.289	.373	5.36	4.73
Ludwick, Eric, Tor	.500	.625	24.59	4.86	.334	.417	8.78	4.34
Luebbers, Larry, StL	.261	.333	4.69	4.56	.261	.340	4.38	4.23
Lundquist, David, CWS	.315	.394	6.70	4.86	.315	.394	6.70	4.86
Maddux, Greg, Atl	.294	.323	3.95	4.56	.241	.287	2.63	3.95
Maddux, Mike, Mon/LA	.275	.349	4.61	4.56	.264	.325	3.73	4.03
Magnante, Mike, Ana	.262	.334	3.63	4.86	.278	.345	4.26	4.43
Mahay, Ron, Oak	.123	.162	0.88	4.86	.206	.288	2.86	4.68
Mahomes, Pat, NYM	.198	.316	3.22	4.56	.273	.362	5.57	4.59
Mantei, Matt, Fla/Ari	.189	.329	3.42	4.56	.200	.337	3.46	4.37
Manzanillo, Jo., NYM	.264	.316	4.90	4.56	.250	.340	4.37	4.35
Marte, Damaso, Sea	.390	.468	13.32	4.86	.390	.468	13.32	4.86
Martin, Tom, Cle	.325	.364	6.64	4.86	.297	.372	5.27	4.36
Martinez, Pedro, Bos	.205	.248	1.79	4.86	.212	.278	2.52	4.36
Martinez, Ramon, Bos	.192	.286	2.69	4.86	.235	.314	3.40	3.96
Masaoka, Onan, LA	.222	.348	4.44	4.56	.222	.348	4.44	4.56
Mathews, T.J., Oak	.215	.287	3.02	4.86	.231	.306	3.27	4.46
Mathews, Terry, KC	.289	.360	5.17	4.86	.269	.343	4.45	4.33
Mays, Joe, Min	.270	.336	4.62	4.86	.270	.336	4.62	4.86
McCurry, Jeff, Hou	.478	.520	17.98	4.56	.329	.407	7.41	4.23
McDowell, Jack, Ana	.369	.413	8.79	4.86	.257	.317	3.71	4.35
McElroy, C., Col/NYM	.286	.388	6.36	4.56	.256	.337	3.93	4.11
McGlinchy, Kevin, Atl	.255	.330	3.68	4.56	.255	.330	3.68	4.56
McMichael, NYM/Oak	.276	.377	5.74	4.69	.247	.316	3.34	4.21
McNichol, Brian, ChC	.333	.426	10.58	4.56	.333	.426	10.58	4.56
Meadows, Brian, Fla	.302	.354	5.51	4.56	.308	.356	5.40	4.40
Meche, Gil, Sea	.237	.357	4.47	4.86	.237	.357	4.47	4.86
Mecir, Jim, TB	.205	.333	3.05	4.86	.246	.329	3.76	4.73
Medina, Rafael, Fla	.227	.376	5.23	4.56	.274	.399	6.23	4.32
Mendoza, Ramiro, NYY	.284	.323	4.19	4.86	.289	.330	4.31	4.72
Mercker, Kent, StL/Bos	.290	.370	5.54	4.62	.259	.338	4.24	4.19
Mesa, Jose, Sea	.305	.396	6.83	4.86	.274	.345	4.46	4.40
Miceli, Dan, SD	.266	.360	4.57	4.56	.264	.346	4.65	4.34
Miller, Kurt, ChC	.462	.563	16.63	4.56	.320	.416	7.20	4.23
Miller, Travis, Min	.284	.335	4.01	4.86	.314	.373	5.89	4.75
Miller, Trever, Hou	.299	.400	6.48	4.56	.297	.379	5.88	4.47
Miller, Wade, Hou	.362	.423	11.07	4.56	.362	.423	11.07	4.56
Mills, Alan, LA	.261	.367	5.17	4.56	.239	.349	4.36	4.42
Millwood, Kevin, Atl	.202	.258	2.26	4.56	.234	.292	3.03	4.39
Milton, Eric, Min	.243	.299	3.56	4.86	.261	.322	4.29	4.76
Mintz, Steve, Ana	.381	.435	9.22	4.86	.340	.427	8.37	4.32
Mlicki, Dave, LA/Det	.278	.344	4.91	4.85	.266	.335	4.44	4.35

	1999				Career			
Pitcher, Team	OAvg	OOB	ERC	LERA	OAvg	OOB	ERC	LERA
Moehler, Brian, Det	.294	.347	4.85	4.86	.278	.332	4.49	4.70
Mohler, Mike, StL	.255	.340	3.87	4.56	.269	.363	4.82	4.64
Molina, Gabe, Bal	.256	.373	5.67	4.86	.256	.373	5.67	4.86
Montgomery, Jeff, KC	.343	.404	7.08	4.86	.241	.308	3.33	4.31
Montgomery, Steve, Phi	.229	.318	3.87	4.56	.256	.359	5.47	4.63
Moreno, Orber, KC	.143	.294	2.84	4.86	.143	.294	2.84	4.86
Morgan, Mike, Tex	.323	.380	6.64	4.86	.274	.335	4.21	4.05
Morman, Alvin, KC	.307	.378	6.04	4.86	.285	.371	5.74	4.57
Morris, Jim, TB	.167	.286	3.56	4.86	.167	.286	3.56	4.86
Mota, Guillermo, Mon	.257	.338	4.10	4.56	.257	.338	4.10	4.56
Moyer, Jamie, Sea	.267	.311	3.71	4.86	.271	.325	4.16	4.37
Mulholland, T., ChC/Atl	.297	.340	4.73	4.56	.273	.319	3.91	4.03
Munoz, Mike, Tex	.263	.323	3.82	4.86	.283	.360	4.86	4.24
Munro, Peter, Tor	.318	.382	6.04	4.86	.318	.382	6.04	4.86
Murray, Dan, NYM/KC	.302	.392	9.08	4.80	.302	.392	9.08	4.80
Murray, Heath, SD	.297	.377	5.93	4.56	.328	.415	7.06	4.42
Mussina, Mike, Bal	.268	.312	3.54	4.86	.248	.293	3.19	4.58
Myers, Mike, Mil	.291	.356	5.24	4.56	.274	.361	5.18	4.61
Myers, Rodney, ChC	.289	.354	5.22	4.56	.279	.360	5.16	4.36
Myette, Aaron, CWS	.266	.413	7.09	4.86	.266	.413	7.09	4.86
Nagy, Charles, Cle	.293	.344	4.97	4.86	.278	.332	4.31	4.53
Nathan, Joe, SF	.243	.333	4.78	4.56	.243	.333	4.78	4.56
Naulty, Dan, NYY	.225	.322	4.04	4.86	.231	.321	4.00	4.82
Navarro, Jaime, CWS	.313	.387	6.96	4.86	.283	.340	4.58	4.28
Neagle, Denny, Cin	.229	.300	3.88	4.56	.255	.309	3.64	4.18
Nelson, Jeff, NYY	.245	.380	4.76	4.86	.237	.340	3.71	4.56
Nen, Robb, SF	.275	.337	4.44	4.56	.238	.310	3.30	4.25
Newman, Alan, TB	.333	.421	7.92	4.86	.333	.421	7.92	4.86
Nitkowski, C.J., Det	.213	.319	3.73	4.86	.271	.369	5.39	4.63
Nomo, Hideo, Mil	.256	.333	4.57	4.56	.225	.310	3.46	4.27
Nunez, Vladimir, Ari/Fla	.242	.336	3.88	4.56	.246	.337	3.92	4.55
Ogea, Chad, Phi	.288	.349	5.68	4.56	.272	.333	4.64	4.70
Ohka, Tomokazu, Bos	.362	.415	8.56	4.86	.362	.415	8.56	4.86
Ojala, Kirt, Fla	.438	.482	11.34	4.56	.277	.362	5.12	4.25
Olivares, O., Ana/Oak	.276	.348	4.59	4.86	.272	.349	4.57	4.31
Oliver, Darren, StL	.265	.339	4.11	4.56	.275	.355	4.92	4.66
Olson, Gregg, Ari	.238	.316	3.94	4.56	.236	.325	3.40	4.24
Oquist, Mike, Oak	.283	.358	5.24	4.86	.284	.358	5.28	4.69
Orosco, Jesse, Bal	.239	.352	4.73	4.86	.219	.305	3.02	4.00
Ortiz, Ramon, Ana	.265	.353	5.23	4.86	.265	.353	5.23	4.86
Ortiz, Russ, SF	.244	.351	4.56	4.56	.252	.354	4.70	4.46
Osborne, Donovan, StL	.298	.362	5.35	4.56	.263	.314	3.81	4.04
Osik, Keith, Pit	.400	.625	21.46	4.56	.400	.625	21.46	4.56
Osuna, Antonio, LA	.222	.364	4.14	4.56	.219	.301	2.97	4.22
Padilla, Vicente, Ari	.467	.556	20.65	4.56	.467	.556	20.65	4.56
Painter, Lance, StL	.265	.336	4.12	4.56	.284	.351	5.06	4.26
Paniagua, Jose, Sea	.264	.387	5.06	4.86	.275	.383	5.44	4.57
Park, Chan Ho, LA	.276	.369	5.68	4.56	.239	.332	4.03	4.31
Parque, Jim, CWS	.299	.374	5.98	4.86	.299	.375	5.94	4.77
Parris, Steve, Cin	.260	.338	4.29	4.56	.264	.338	4.39	4.34
Patrick, Bronswell, SF	.375	.429	9.69	4.56	.286	.346	4.75	4.25
Patterson, Danny, Tex	.304	.353	5.11	4.86	.280	.334	4.29	4.70
Pavano, Carl, Mon	.285	.345	4.51	4.56	.266	.328	4.20	4.37
Pena, Jesus, CWS	.259	.429	7.22	4.86	.259	.429	7.22	4.86
Pena, Juan, Bos	.196	.245	1.49	4.86	.196	.245	1.49	4.86
Percival, Troy, Ana	.186	.274	2.83	4.86	.172	.267	2.26	4.76
Perez, Carlos, LA	.317	.389	7.54	4.56	.269	.318	4.02	4.25
Perez, Odalis, Atl	.275	.366	5.42	4.56	.272	.361	5.22	4.53
Perez, Yorkis, Phi	.244	.326	3.96	4.56	.236	.327	3.74	4.25
Perisho, Matt, Tex	.211	.250	1.55	4.86	.328	.424	7.89	4.62
Perkins, Dan, Min	.326	.401	7.40	4.86	.326	.401	7.40	4.86
Person, Robert, Tor/Phi	.250	.353	5.04	4.58	.252	.338	4.77	4.49
Peters, Chris, Pit	.322	.381	7.47	4.56	.279	.348	4.98	4.30
Peterson, Kyle, Mil	.285	.344	4.20	4.56	.285	.344	4.20	4.56
Petkovsek, Mark, Ana	.269	.314	3.51	4.86	.284	.342	4.55	4.29
Pettitte, Andy, NYY	.289	.364	5.22	4.86	.272	.335	4.13	4.75
Phillips, Jason, Pit	.393	.486	11.24	4.56	.393	.486	11.24	4.56
Pisciotta, Marc, KC	.281	.452	8.28	4.86	.242	.367	4.68	4.28
Pittsley, Jim, KC/Mil	.310	.400	6.86	4.73	.300	.382	6.38	4.62
Plesac, Dan, Tor/Ari	.284	.345	5.03	4.71	.247	.311	3.46	4.19
Plunk, Eric, Mil	.251	.357	5.33	4.56	.236	.339	4.11	4.32
Politte, Cliff, Phi	.275	.405	6.47	4.56	.295	.389	6.35	4.34
Ponson, Sidney, Bal	.282	.345	5.08	4.86	.286	.345	5.08	4.78
Poole, Jim, Phi/Cle	.333	.413	6.94	4.57	.265	.341	4.25	4.41
Portugal, Mark, Bos	.292	.337	5.33	4.86	.261	.321	3.95	4.06
Porzio, Mike, Col	.328	.419	9.91	4.56	.328	.419	9.91	4.56
Pote, Lou, Ana	.219	.299	2.56	4.86	.219	.299	2.56	4.86
Powell, Jay, Hou	.282	.372	4.75	4.56	.252	.343	3.91	4.30
Powell, Jeremy, Mon	.302	.385	6.03	4.56	.300	.384	6.08	4.49
Pulsipher, Bill, Mil	.287	.353	5.81	4.56	.278	.346	4.82	4.31
Quantrill, Paul, Tor	.282	.351	4.77	4.86	.295	.345	4.71	4.49
Radinsky, Scott, StL	.270	.371	4.67	4.56	.253	.329	3.65	4.20

	1999				Career			
Pitcher, Team	OAvg	OOB	ERC	LERA	OAvg	OOB	ERC	LERA
Radke, Brad, Min	.280	.314	4.07	4.86	.270	.310	4.01	4.76
Radlosky, Rob, Min	.375	.444	16.36	4.86	.375	.444	16.36	4.86
Rain, Steve, ChC	.418	.474	10.12	4.56	.418	.474	10.12	4.56
Rakers, Jason, Cle	.250	.333	7.30	4.86	.200	.400	7.74	4.79
Ramirez, Hector, Mil	.247	.341	3.63	4.56	.247	.341	3.63	4.56
Ramirez, Roberto, Col	.368	.435	9.69	4.56	.331	.413	8.54	4.47
Ramsay, Rob, Sea	.324	.395	6.71	4.86	.324	.395	6.71	4.86
Rapp, Pat, Bos	.263	.351	4.56	4.86	.277	.366	4.93	4.35
Rath, Gary, Min	.300	.440	9.58	4.86	.281	.410	7.93	4.60
Ray, Ken, KC	.460	.526	13.86	4.86	.460	.526	13.86	4.86
Redman, Mark, Min	.298	.385	7.86	4.86	.298	.385	7.86	4.86
Reed, Rick, NYM	.281	.334	4.71	4.56	.265	.304	3.66	4.17
Reed, Steve, Cle	.285	.341	4.91	4.86	.242	.310	3.66	4.26
Reichert, Dan, KC	.327	.451	7.91	4.86	.327	.451	7.91	4.86
Rekar, Bryan, TB	.313	.385	6.49	4.86	.303	.361	5.83	4.50
Remlinger, Mike, Atl	.215	.297	3.03	4.56	.247	.343	4.38	4.24
Reyes, Al, Mil/Bal	.215	.343	4.19	4.70	.233	.338	4.27	4.55
Reyes, Carlos, SD	.254	.307	3.76	4.56	.269	.341	4.71	4.72
Reyes, Dennys, Cin	.232	.348	4.16	4.56	.254	.358	4.30	4.34
Reynolds, Shane, Hou	.275	.303	3.58	4.56	.269	.307	3.58	4.26
Reynoso, Armando, Ari	.276	.347	4.71	4.56	.284	.351	4.87	4.22
Rhodes, Arthur, Bal	.221	.364	5.07	4.86	.247	.336	4.29	4.52
Rigby, Brad, Oak/KC	.303	.368	5.68	4.86	.302	.357	5.53	4.72
Riley, Matt, Bal	.378	.508	14.43	4.86	.378	.508	14.43	4.86
Rincon, Ricky, Cle	.248	.346	4.38	4.86	.226	.312	3.33	4.38
Riske, David, Cle	.333	.388	6.96	4.86	.333	.388	6.96	4.86
Ritchie, Todd, Pit	.259	.319	3.77	4.56	.271	.331	4.30	4.57
Rivera, Mariano, NYY	.176	.239	1.47	4.86	.215	.278	2.44	4.78
Rivera, Roberto, SD	.240	.310	3.62	4.56	.304	.365	5.71	4.40
Rizzo, Todd, CWS	.500	.636	21.44	4.86	.410	.510	12.01	4.68
Roberts, Willis, Det	.500	.500	12.64	4.86	.500	.500	12.64	4.86
Rocker, John, Atl	.180	.284	2.38	4.56	.177	.292	2.50	4.45
Rodriguez, Felix, SF	.262	.338	4.25	4.56	.264	.360	4.82	4.35
Rodriguez, Frank, Sea	.314	.383	6.48	4.86	.282	.355	5.02	4.78
Rodriguez, Nerio, Tor	.250	.400	14.27	4.86	.278	.356	5.21	4.71
Rodriguez, Rich, SF	.274	.356	4.98	4.56	.256	.328	3.80	3.99
Rogers, K., Oak/NYM	.275	.344	4.38	4.74	.259	.329	4.05	4.53
Rojas, Mel, LA/Det/Mon	.349	.456	13.07	4.70	.237	.315	3.50	4.03
Romano, Mike, Tor	.364	.464	10.55	4.86	.364	.464	10.55	4.86
Romero, J.C., Min	.333	.333	3.95	4.86	.333	.333	3.95	4.86
Roque, Rafael, Mil	.286	.369	6.17	4.56	.269	.356	5.55	4.44
Rosado, Jose, KC	.248	.314	3.76	4.86	.256	.316	3.94	4.74
Rose, Brian, Bos	.280	.332	5.13	4.86	.283	.340	5.45	4.79
Rueter, Kirk, SF	.297	.346	5.19	4.56	.274	.322	4.08	4.27
Runyan, Sean, Det	.237	.295	3.49	4.86	.252	.340	4.46	4.68
Rupe, Ryan, TB	.253	.334	4.32	4.86	.253	.334	4.32	4.86
Rusch, Glen., KC/NYM	.364	.462	10.75	4.80	.303	.357	5.66	4.61
Ryan, B.J., Cin/Bal	.191	.317	2.42	4.83	.191	.317	2.42	4.83
Ryan, Jason, Min	.286	.363	6.23	4.86	.286	.363	6.23	4.86
Ryan, Ken, Phi	.267	.380	5.51	4.56	.250	.352	4.15	4.40
Sabel, Erik, Ari	.300	.417	6.89	4.56	.300	.417	6.89	4.56
Saberhagen, Bret, Bos	.265	.284	3.07	4.86	.252	.288	3.00	4.16
Sampson, Benj, Min	.351	.410	8.68	4.86	.322	.384	7.00	4.82
Sanchez, Jesus, Fla	.291	.411	7.28	4.56	.278	.378	5.61	4.33
Sanders, Scott, ChC	.277	.358	5.41	4.56	.257	.327	4.25	4.33
Santana, Julio, TB	.300	.404	7.29	4.86	.295	.374	5.97	4.66
Santana, Marino, Bos	.444	.500	19.63	4.86	.362	.483	12.41	4.72
Santiago, Jose, KC	.251	.307	3.87	4.86	.268	.323	4.26	4.82
Sauerbeck, Scott, Pit	.220	.336	3.60	4.56	.220	.336	3.60	4.56
Saunders, Tony, TB	.315	.424	7.78	4.86	.265	.367	4.96	4.53
Scheffer, Aaron, Sea	.353	.417	6.63	4.86	.353	.417	6.63	4.86
Schilling, Curt, Phi	.237	.287	3.20	4.56	.235	.288	2.90	4.09
Schmidt, Jason, Pit	.262	.330	4.30	4.56	.271	.342	4.51	4.31
Schoeneweis, S., Ana	.294	.349	4.99	4.86	.294	.349	4.99	4.86
Schourek, Pete, Pit	.287	.358	5.66	4.56	.269	.334	4.35	4.10
Schrenk, Steve, Phi	.223	.301	3.15	4.56	.223	.301	3.15	4.56
Seanez, Rudy, Atl	.234	.307	3.12	4.56	.248	.342	4.19	4.25
Sele, Aaron, Tex	.293	.355	5.17	4.86	.279	.353	4.83	4.71
Serafini, Dan, ChC	.333	.405	7.11	4.56	.315	.380	6.10	4.61
Service, Scott, KC	.294	.379	6.14	4.86	.266	.350	4.69	4.44
Shaw, Jeff, LA	.242	.283	2.96	4.56	.257	.310	3.55	4.19
Shuey, Paul, Cle	.223	.314	3.36	4.86	.243	.339	4.12	4.78
Shumaker, Anthony, Phi	.261	.369	5.39	4.56	.261	.369	5.39	4.56
Silva, Jose, Pit	.281	.349	4.84	4.56	.289	.348	4.71	4.37
Simas, Bill, CWS	.263	.347	4.33	4.86	.252	.339	4.29	4.79
Sinclair, Steve, Tor/Sea	.278	.400	7.75	4.86	.259	.359	5.27	4.77
Sirotka, Mike, CWS	.283	.327	4.41	4.86	.293	.336	4.74	4.75
Slocumb, H., Bal/StL	.267	.375	4.98	4.60	.263	.360	4.42	4.36
Slusarski, Joe, Hou	.083	.267	1.10	4.56	.285	.366	5.67	4.10
Smart, J.D., Mon	.276	.330	4.08	4.56	.276	.330	4.08	4.56
Smith, Dan, Mon	.293	.368	5.59	4.56	.293	.368	5.59	4.56
Smoltz, John, Atl	.245	.288	2.81	4.56	.233	.295	2.96	3.97

Pitcher, Team	1999				Career			
	OAvg	OOB	ERC	LERA	OAvg	OOB	ERC	LERA
Snyder, John, CWS	.311	.371	6.71	4.86	.301	.356	5.91	4.77
Sodowsky, Clint, StL	.455	.538	16.70	4.56	.291	.395	6.27	4.39
Sparks, Jeff, TB	.171	.396	4.98	4.86	.171	.396	4.98	4.86
Sparks, Steve, Ana	.281	.373	5.94	4.86	.277	.360	5.25	4.78
Speier, Justin, Atl	.248	.323	5.27	4.56	.281	.362	6.73	4.42
Spencer, Sean, Sea	.556	.667	25.59	4.86	.556	.667	25.59	4.86
Spencer, Stan, SD	.335	.380	7.78	4.86	.297	.337	5.64	4.41
Spoljaric, Paul, Phi/Tor	.289	.374	5.83	4.81	.259	.359	5.10	4.72
Spradlin, Jerry, Cle/SF	.267	.375	5.23	4.58	.255	.318	3.72	4.26
Springer, Dennis, Fla	.303	.358	5.14	4.56	.276	.350	5.20	4.63
Springer, Russ, Atl	.185	.284	2.63	4.56	.263	.346	4.79	4.37
Stanton, Mike, NYY	.289	.337	4.23	4.86	.251	.322	3.69	4.30
Stark, Dennis, Sea	.370	.452	8.05	4.86	.370	.452	8.05	4.86
Stein, Blake, Oak/KC	.241	.366	5.23	4.86	.250	.362	5.49	4.73
Stephenson, Garr., StL	.275	.339	4.58	4.56	.270	.340	4.45	4.36
Stevens, Dave, Cle	.286	.409	6.61	4.86	.296	.377	6.36	4.69
Stottlemyre, Todd, Ari	.268	.343	4.67	4.86	.261	.330	4.15	4.24
Strickland, Scott, Mon	.231	.342	4.48	4.56	.231	.342	4.48	4.56
Stull, Everett, Atl	.500	.571	25.31	4.56	.450	.556	18.55	4.26
Sturtze, Tanyon, CWS	.200	.273	1.73	4.86	.324	.392	7.22	4.51
Sullivan, Scott, Cin	.217	.308	3.08	4.56	.231	.312	3.45	4.34
Suppan, Jeff, KC	.274	.326	4.33	4.86	.289	.341	4.89	4.68
Suzuki, Ma., Sea/KC	.286	.384	6.19	4.86	.290	.386	6.28	4.82
Swindell, Greg, Ari	.230	.296	3.15	4.56	.269	.309	3.75	4.09
Tam, Jeff, Cle/NYM	.190	.261	2.97	4.57	.219	.292	3.47	4.38
Tapani, Kevin, ChC	.280	.322	4.02	4.56	.272	.316	3.90	4.35
Tavarez, Julian, SF	.295	.384	6.10	4.56	.290	.354	4.78	4.51
Taylor, Billy, Oak/NYM	.302	.369	5.09	4.79	.254	.330	3.76	4.74
Tejera, Michael, Fla	.385	.484	10.73	4.56	.385	.484	10.73	4.56
Telemaco, A., Ari/Phi	.259	.348	5.01	4.56	.272	.331	4.60	4.27
Telford, Anthony, Mon	.295	.359	4.58	4.56	.267	.337	4.24	4.27
Tessmer, Jay, NYY	.444	.512	14.65	4.86	.313	.392	6.60	4.74
Thompson, Justin, Det	.274	.344	5.14	4.86	.257	.322	3.93	4.70
Thompson, Mark, StL	.241	.354	3.85	4.56	.307	.388	6.53	4.24
Thomson, John, Col	.324	.405	7.60	4.56	.296	.354	5.08	4.27
Thurman, Mike, Mon	.251	.321	3.89	4.56	.244	.316	3.78	4.44
Timlin, Mike, Bal	.221	.304	3.46	4.86	.250	.321	3.54	4.52
Tomko, Brett, Cin	.263	.325	4.51	4.86	.249	.313	3.78	4.33
Trachsel, Steve, ChC	.280	.330	4.69	4.56	.264	.327	4.37	4.27
Trombley, Mike, Min	.272	.328	4.49	4.56	.265	.333	4.49	4.61
Urbina, Ugueth, Mon	.208	.295	2.85	4.56	.214	.298	3.20	4.29
Valdes, Ismael, LA	.270	.321	4.38	4.56	.247	.299	3.29	4.28
Vazquez, Javier, Mon	.255	.316	4.02	4.56	.274	.342	4.92	4.39
Venafro, Mike, Tex	.251	.317	3.30	4.86	.251	.317	3.30	4.86
Veres, Dave, Col	.290	.369	5.84	4.56	.261	.329	3.99	4.27
Villone, Ron, Cin	.219	.319	3.20	4.56	.239	.352	4.44	4.56
Vizcaino, Luis, Oak	.231	.375	7.01	4.86	.231	.375	7.01	4.86
Vosberg, Ed, SD/Ari	.431	.466	10.42	4.56	.288	.362	4.86	4.53
Wagner, Billy, Hou	.135	.208	1.20	4.56	.178	.271	2.21	4.32
Wagner, Paul, Cle	.263	.417	6.70	4.86	.277	.352	4.74	4.15
Wainhouse, Dave, Col	.330	.405	7.69	4.56	.308	.400	6.74	4.30
Wakefield, Tim, Bos	.266	.352	5.12	4.86	.259	.339	4.53	4.58
Wall, Donne, SD	.219	.280	3.12	4.56	.264	.321	4.13	4.28
Wallace, Derek, KC	.259	.364	5.35	4.86	.283	.374	5.43	4.38
Wallace, Jeff, Pit	.195	.372	4.03	4.56	.197	.362	3.66	4.48
Ward, Bryan, CWS	.368	.404	8.73	4.86	.333	.371	6.87	4.77
Wasdin, John, Bos	.236	.280	3.41	4.86	.265	.319	4.34	4.76
Washburn, Jarrod, Ana	.261	.335	4.20	4.86	.254	.325	4.15	4.74
Watson, NYM/Sea/NYY	.253	.331	4.45	4.70	.281	.349	5.10	4.36
Weathers, Dave, Mil	.279	.346	5.04	4.56	.300	.376	5.50	4.28
Weaver, Eric, Sea	.318	.423	9.41	4.86	.264	.384	5.88	4.54
Weaver, Jeff, Det	.278	.350	5.21	4.86	.278	.350	5.21	4.86
Wells, Bob, Min	.245	.312	3.37	4.86	.275	.339	4.92	4.79
Wells, David, Tor	.271	.320	4.26	4.86	.260	.306	3.66	4.45
Wells, Kip, CWS	.248	.333	3.80	4.86	.248	.333	3.80	4.86
Wendell, Turk, NYM	.245	.324	3.80	4.86	.246	.336	4.04	4.27
Wengert, Don, KC	.376	.397	8.72	4.86	.312	.370	6.18	4.71
Wetteland, John, Tex	.262	.307	3.90	4.86	.212	.278	2.55	4.22
Wheeler, Dan, TB	.287	.356	5.96	4.86	.287	.356	5.96	4.86
Whisenant, M., KC/SD	.250	.383	5.03	4.78	.256	.375	4.75	4.68
White, Gabe, Cin	.281	.324	4.95	4.86	.253	.305	4.04	4.30
White, Rick, TB	.304	.358	4.96	4.86	.286	.341	4.45	4.53
Whiteside, Matt, SD	.396	.444	8.89	4.86	.288	.348	4.77	4.55
Wickman, Bob, Mil	.262	.351	4.38	4.56	.263	.345	4.22	4.53
Wilkins, Marc, Pit	.257	.354	4.25	4.56	.253	.348	4.13	4.29
Williams, Brian, Hou	.272	.366	4.64	4.56	.282	.374	5.35	4.28
Williams, Jeff, LA	.190	.292	2.86	4.56	.190	.292	2.86	4.56
Williams, Mike, Pit	.276	.378	5.80	4.56	.270	.340	4.50	4.20
Williams, Todd, Sea	.289	.413	6.67	4.86	.292	.375	5.73	4.36
Williams, Woody, SD	.268	.328	4.46	4.56	.256	.326	4.30	4.63
Williamson, Scott, Cin	.171	.271	2.05	4.56	.171	.271	2.05	4.56
Winkelsas, Joe, Atl	1.000	1.000	99.97	4.56	1.000	1.000	99.97	4.56

Pitcher, Team	1999				Career			
	OAvg	OOB	ERC	LERA	OAvg	OOB	ERC	LERA
Witasick, Jay, KC	.304	.387	6.45	4.86	.301	.383	6.69	4.82
Witt, Bobby, TB	.304	.386	6.11	4.86	.265	.357	4.83	4.34
Wohlers, Mark, Atl	.333	.778	41.75	4.56	.232	.328	3.38	4.09
Wolcott, Bob, Bos	.333	.414	7.05	4.86	.299	.359	5.89	4.75
Wolf, Randy, Phi	.266	.362	5.54	4.56	.266	.362	5.54	4.56
Woodall, Brad, ChC	.270	.338	6.12	4.56	.280	.343	5.24	4.25
Woodard, Steve, Mil	.294	.330	4.52	4.56	.279	.318	4.13	4.42
Worrell, Tim, Oak	.256	.344	4.42	4.86	.259	.329	4.17	4.35
Wright, Jamey, Col	.308	.401	6.19	4.56	.307	.389	6.04	4.28
Wright, Jaret, Cle	.277	.376	5.77	4.86	.269	.355	4.96	4.70
Yan, Esteban, TB	.326	.421	7.13	4.86	.287	.378	5.88	4.74
Yarnall, Ed, NYY	.254	.351	4.46	4.86	.254	.351	4.46	4.86
Yoshii, Masato, NYM	.260	.324	4.14	4.56	.258	.320	3.98	4.40
Zimmerman, Jeff, Tex	.166	.225	1.57	4.86	.166	.225	1.57	4.86
Zimmerman, Jor., Sea	.389	.463	9.05	4.86	.389	.463	9.05	4.86

1999 Leader Boards

Our extensive leader boards always generate some interesting table talk. Here are a few choice nuggets from the 1999 season:

In a year in which Mark McGwire and Sammy Sosa broke the 60-homer barrier again and 13 players surpassed 40 home runs, Pedro Martinez and Randy Johnson turned in remarkable seasons. They easily led their respective leagues in strikeouts per nine innings pitched. Martinez topped the majors with a record 13.20 mark while Johnson, whose 364 strikeouts were the highest total since Nolan Ryan's 367 in 1974, ranked first in the National League with 12.06 strikeouts per nine innings. The third-best average in all of baseball was 8.49 by San Diego's Sterling Hitchcock.

Martinez was dominant on all pitching fronts, also easily leading the majors in strikeout-to-walk ratio. His 8.46 ratio far exceeded the 5.32 mark of Shane Reynolds, who ranked first in the National League. In batting average against, Martinez again was the man in the American League by holding hitters to a .205 average. The leader in the majors, though, was a 24-year-old hurler who has won 35 games over the last two seasons. Atlanta's Kevin Millwood stymied major league hitters at a .202 clip.

On the hitting side, the home-run race between McGwire and Sosa didn't generate as much interest as a year ago. Still, no one could touch them in home-run frequency. McGwire led the majors with a homer every 8.0 at-bats and Sosa closed at 9.9. The next best frequency was Larry Walker at 11.8.

Two MVP candidates were among the most dangerous hitters when the game was on the line in 1999. The American League leader in batting in late and close situations was Rafael Palmeiro, who hit .413, while Chipper Jones led the National League with a .417 average. No other hitter topped .400 in late-and-close situations.

With the bases loaded, it shouldn't be a surprise that Fernando Tatis led the majors with a .692 average. He was 9-for-13 with the sacks full, and three of those nine hits were grand slams. Two of them were hit against the Dodgers on April 23, when Tatis became the first major leaguer ever to stroke two slams in the same inning.

There's plenty more where these stats came from. Check out the leader boards that follow.

1999 American League Batting Leaders

Batting Average
minimum 502 PA

Player, Team	AB	H	AVG
N Garciaparra, Bos	532	190	.357
D Jeter, NYY	627	219	.349
B Williams, NYY	591	202	.342
E Martinez, Sea	502	169	.337
M Ramirez, Cle	522	174	.333
O Vizquel, Cle	574	191	.333
I Rodriguez, Tex	600	199	.332
T Fernandez, Tor	485	159	.328
J Gonzalez, Tex	562	183	.326
R Palmeiro, Tex	565	183	.324

On-Base Percentage
minimum 502 PA

Player, Team	PA*	OB	OBP
E Martinez, Sea	608	272	.447
M Ramirez, Cle	640	283	.442
D Jeter, NYY	736	322	.438
B Williams, NYY	697	303	.435
T Fernandez, Tor	576	246	.427
J Thome, Cle	629	268	.426
R Alomar, Cle	682	288	.422
J Giambi, Oak	695	293	.422
R Palmeiro, Tex	674	283	.420
N Garciaparra, Bos	595	249	.418

* AB, BB, HBP, SF

Slugging Percentage
minimum 502 PA

Player, Team	AB	TB	SLG
M Ramirez, Cle	522	346	.663
R Palmeiro, Tex	565	356	.630
N Garciaparra, Bos	532	321	.603
J Gonzalez, Tex	562	338	.601
S Green, Tor	614	361	.588
A Rodriguez, Sea	502	294	.586
K Griffey Jr., Sea	606	349	.576
C Delgado, Tor	573	327	.571
J Canseco, TB	430	242	.563
I Rodriguez, Tex	600	335	.558

Games

B Surhoff, Bal	162
A Belle, Bal	161
M Bordick, Bal	160
K Griffey Jr., Sea	160
3 players tied with	159

Plate Appearances

D Jeter, NYY	739
B Surhoff, Bal	727
C Beltran, KC	723
A Belle, Bal	722
C Knoblauch, NYY	715

At Bats

B Surhoff, Bal	673
C Beltran, KC	663
M Bordick, Bal	631
R Velarde, Ana-Oak	631
J Randa, KC	628

Hits

D Jeter, NYY	219
B Surhoff, Bal	207
B Williams, NYY	202
R Velarde, Ana-Oak	200
I Rodriguez, Tex	199

Singles

R Velarde, Ana-Oak	152
D Jeter, NYY	149
O Vizquel, Cle	146
S Stewart, Tor	144
B Williams, NYY	143

Doubles

S Green, Tor	45
J Dye, KC	44
M Sweeney, KC	44
N Garciaparra, Bos	42
3 players tied with	41

Triples

J Offerman, Bos	11
J Damon, KC	9
C Febles, KC	9
D Jeter, NYY	9
4 players tied with	8

Home Runs

K Griffey Jr., Sea	48
R Palmeiro, Tex	47
C Delgado, Tor	44
M Ramirez, Cle	44
2 players tied with	42

Total Bases

S Green, Tor	361
R Palmeiro, Tex	356
K Griffey Jr., Sea	349
D Jeter, NYY	346
M Ramirez, Cle	346

Runs Scored

R Alomar, Cle	138
S Green, Tor	134
D Jeter, NYY	134
M Ramirez, Cle	131
K Griffey Jr., Sea	123

Runs Batted In

M Ramirez, Cle	165
R Palmeiro, Tex	148
C Delgado, Tor	134
K Griffey Jr., Sea	134
J Gonzalez, Tex	128

Ground Double Play

I Rodriguez, Tex	32
M Bordick, Bal	25
P O'Neill, NYY	24
M Ordonez, CWS	24
M Cordova, Min	22

Sacrifice Hits

O Vizquel, Cle	17
D Cruz, Det	14
D Lewis, Bos	14
R Alomar, Cle	12
C Febles, KC	12

Sacrifice Flies

R Alomar, Cle	13
J Gonzalez, Tex	12
4 players tied with	10

Stolen Bases

B Hunter, Det-Sea	44
O Vizquel, Cle	42
T Goodwin, Tex	39
R Alomar, Cle	37
S Stewart, Tor	37

Caught Stealing

M Caruso, CWS	14
S Stewart, Tor	14
J Encarnacion, Det	12
J Offerman, KC	12
I Rodriguez, Tex	12

Walks

J Thome, Cle	127
J Giambi, Oak	105
A Belle, Bal	101
J Jaha, Oak	101
B Williams, NYY	100

Intentional Walks

K Griffey Jr., Sea	17
B Williams, NYY	17
A Belle, Bal	15
R Palmeiro, Tex	14
2 players tied with	13

Hit by Pitch

B Anderson, Bal	24
C Knoblauch, NYY	21
D Easley, Det	19
C Delgado, Tor	15
O Saenz, Oak	15

Strikeouts

J Thome, Cle	171
D Palmer, Det	153
T Glaus, Ana	143
C Delgado, Tor	141
J Canseco, TB	135

1999 National League Batting Leaders

Batting Average
minimum 502 PA

Player, Team	AB	H	AVG
L Walker, Col	**438**	**166**	**.379**
L Gonzalez, Ari	614	206	.336
B Abreu, Phi	546	183	.335
S Casey, Cin	594	197	.332
J Cirillo, Mil	607	198	.326
M Grudzielanek, LA	488	159	.326
C Everett, Hou	464	151	.325
D Glanville, Phi	628	204	.325
T Helton, Col	578	185	.320
C Jones, Atl	567	181	.319

On-Base Percentage
minimum 502 PA

Player, Team	PA*	OB	OBP
L Walker, Col	**513**	**235**	**.458**
J Bagwell, Hou	729	331	.454
B Abreu, Phi	662	295	.446
C Jones, Atl	701	309	.441
J Olerud, NYM	723	309	.427
M McGwire, StL	661	280	.424
R Henderson, NYM	525	222	.423
B Giles, Pit	627	262	.418
G Sheffield, LA	663	270	.407
F Tatis, StL	639	258	.404

* AB, BB, HBP, SF

Slugging Percentage
minimum 502 PA

Player, Team	AB	TB	SLG
L Walker, Col	**438**	**311**	**.710**
M McGwire, StL	521	363	.697
S Sosa, ChC	625	397	.635
C Jones, Atl	567	359	.633
B Giles, Pit	521	320	.614
V Guerrero, Mon	610	366	.600
J Bagwell, Hou	562	332	.591
T Helton, Col	578	339	.587
M Piazza, NYM	534	307	.575
C Everett, Hou	464	265	.571

Games

J Bagwell, Hou	**162**
A Jones, Atl	**162**
J Olerud, NYM	**162**
S Sosa, ChC	**162**
4 players tied with	161

Plate Appearances

C Biggio, Hou	**749**
N Perez, Col	732
J Bagwell, Hou	729
E Alfonzo, NYM	726
J Olerud, NYM	723

At Bats

N Perez, Col	**690**
C Biggio, Hou	639
E Alfonzo, NYM	628
D Glanville, Phi	628
M Williams, Ari	627

Hits

L Gonzalez, Ari	**206**
D Glanville, Phi	204
J Cirillo, Mil	198
S Casey, Cin	197
2 players tied with	193

Singles

D Glanville, Phi	**149**
J Cirillo, Mil	147
N Perez, Col	143
L Gonzalez, Ari	131
T Womack, Ari	131

Doubles

C Biggio, Hou	**56**
L Gonzalez, Ari	45
J Vidro, Mon	45
M Grace, ChC	44
G Jenkins, Mil	43

Triples

B Abreu, Phi	**11**
N Perez, Col	**11**
S Finley, Ari	10
T Womack, Ari	10
2 players tied with	9

Home Runs

M McGwire, StL	**65**
S Sosa, ChC	63
C Jones, Atl	45
G Vaughn, Cin	45
2 players tied with	42

Total Bases

S Sosa, ChC	**397**
V Guerrero, Mon	366
M McGwire, StL	363
C Jones, Atl	359
T Helton, Col	339

Runs Scored

J Bagwell, Hou	**143**
J Bell, Ari	132
E Alfonzo, NYM	123
C Biggio, Hou	123
2 players tied with	118

Runs Batted In

M McGwire, StL	**147**
M Williams, Ari	142
S Sosa, ChC	141
D Bichette, Col	133
V Guerrero, Mon	131

Ground Double Play

M Piazza, NYM	**27**
J Olerud, NYM	22
D Bell, Hou	20
C Jones, Atl	20
5 players tied with	18

Sacrifice Hits

S Reynolds, Hou	**17**
K Brown, LA	13
J Lima, Hou	13
G Maddux, Atl	13
A Nunez, Pit	13

Sacrifice Flies

D Bichette, Col	**10**
M Grace, ChC	**10**
5 players tied with	9

Stolen Bases

T Womack, Ari	**72**
R Cedeno, NYM	66
E Young, LA	51
L Castillo, Fla	50
2 players tied with	38

Caught Stealing

E Young, LA	**22**
L Castillo, Fla	17
R Cedeno, NYM	17
Q Veras, SD	17
3 players tied with	14

Walks

J Bagwell, Hou	**149**
M McGwire, StL	133
C Jones, Atl	126
J Olerud, NYM	125
B Abreu, Phi	109

Intentional Walks

M McGwire, StL	**21**
C Jones, Atl	18
J Bagwell, Hou	16
V Guerrero, Mon	14
S Casey, Cin	13

Hit by Pitch

E Sprague, Pit	**17**
J Burnitz, Mil	16
F Tatis, StL	16
4 players tied with	12

Strikeouts

S Sosa, ChC	**171**
P Wilson, Fla	156
M Cameron, Cin	145
J Hernandez, Atl	145
R Rivera, SD	143

1999 American League Pitching Leaders

Earned Run Average
minimum 162 IP

Pitcher, Team	IP	ER	ERA
P Martinez, Bos	**213.1**	**49**	**2.07**
D Cone, NYY	193.1	74	3.44
M Mussina, Bal	203.1	79	3.50
B Radke, Min	218.2	91	3.75
J Rosado, KC	208.0	89	3.85
J Moyer, Sea	228.0	98	3.87
B Colon, Cle	205.0	90	3.95
M Sirotka, CWS	209.0	93	4.00
F Garcia, Sea	201.1	91	4.07
O Hernandez, NYY	214.1	98	4.12

Won-Lost Percentage
minimum 13 decisions

Pitcher, Team	W	L	Pct
P Martinez, Bos	**23**	**4**	**.852**
B Colon, Cle	18	5	.783
M Mussina, Bal	18	7	.720
F Garcia, Sea	17	8	.680
A Sele, Tex	18	9	.667
O Hernandez, NYY	17	9	.654
D Wells, Tor	17	10	.630
J Moyer, Sea	14	8	.636
D Burba, Cle	15	9	.625
B Saberhagen, Bos	10	6	.625

Opposition AVG
minimum 162 IP

Pitcher, Team	AB	H	AVG
P Martinez, Bos	**780**	**160**	**.205**
D Cone, NYY	715	164	.229
O Hernandez, NYY	801	187	.233
B Colon, Cle	766	185	.242
E Milton, Min	783	190	.243
C Finley, Ana	801	197	.246
J Rosado, KC	793	197	.248
D Burba, Cle	831	211	.254
R Clemens, NYY	708	185	.261
F Garcia, Sea	779	205	.263

Games

B Groom, Oak	**76**
B Wells, Min	**76**
M Trombley, Min	75
G Lloyd, Tor	74
D Lowe, Bos	74

Games Started

R Helling, Tex	**35**
6 pitchers tied with	34

Complete Games

D Wells, Tor	**7**
S Erickson, Bal	6
S Ponson, Bal	6
P Martinez, Bos	5
J Rosado, KC	5

Games Finished

R Hernandez, TB	**66**
M Jackson, Cle	65
M Rivera, NYY	63
T Jones, Det	62
J Mesa, Sea	60

Wins

P Martinez, Bos	**23**
B Colon, Cle	18
M Mussina, Bal	18
A Sele, Tex	18
4 pitchers tied with	17

Losses

B Moehler, Det	**16**
J Parque, CWS	15
B Witt, TB	15
5 pitchers tied with	14

Saves

M Rivera, NYY	**45**
R Hernandez, TB	43
J Wetteland, Tex	43
M Jackson, Cle	39
J Mesa, Sea	33

Shutouts

S Erickson, Bal	**3**
E Milton, Min	2
B Moehler, Det	2
A Sele, Tex	2
B Witt, TB	2

Hits Allowed

D Wells, Tor	**246**
S Erickson, Bal	244
A Sele, Tex	244
B Radke, Min	239
2 pitchers tied with	238

Doubles Allowed

A Sele, Tex	**56**
K Escobar, Tor	52
G Heredia, Oak	52
K Appier, KC-Oak	50
4 pitchers tied with	49

Triples Allowed

S Erickson, Bal	**8**
R Helling, Tex	**8**
4 pitchers tied with	7

Home Runs Allowed

R Helling, Tex	**41**
J Fassero, Sea-Tex	35
S Ponson, Bal	35
J Baldwin, CWS	34
2 pitchers tied with	32

Batters Faced

S Erickson, Bal	**995**
D Wells, Tor	987
J Moyer, Sea	945
R Helling, Tex	943
D Burba, Cle	940

Innings Pitched

D Wells, Tor	**231.2**
S Erickson, Bal	230.1
J Moyer, Sea	228.0
D Burba, Cle	220.0
R Helling, Tex	219.1

Runs Allowed

L Hawkins, Min	**136**
J Fassero, Sea-Tex	135
D Wells, Tor	132
K Appier, KC-Oak	131
B Witt, TB	130

Strikeouts

P Martinez, Bos	**313**
C Finley, Ana	200
A Sele, Tex	186
D Cone, NYY	177
D Burba, Cle	174

Walks Allowed

S Erickson, Bal	**99**
D Burba, Cle	96
B Witt, TB	96
C Finley, Ana	94
3 pitchers tied with	90

Hit Batsmen

J Weaver, Det	**17**
R Arrojo, TB	14
D Mlicki, Det	12
R Rupe, TB	12
A Sele, Tex	12

Wild Pitches

C Finley, Ana	**15**
D Burba, Cle	13
T Candiotti, Cle	13
F Garcia, Sea	12
3 pitchers tied with	11

Balks

F Garcia, Sea	**3**
C Nitkowski, Det	**3**
10 pitchers tied with	2

1999 National League Pitching Leaders

Earned Run Average
minimum 162 IP

Pitcher, Team	IP	ER	ERA
R Johnson, Ari	**271.2**	**75**	**2.48**
K Millwood, Atl	228.0	68	2.68
M Hampton, Hou	239.0	77	2.90
K Brown, LA	252.1	84	3.00
J Smoltz, Atl	186.1	66	3.19
T Ritchie, Pit	172.2	67	3.49
C Schilling, Phi	180.1	71	3.54
G Maddux, Atl	219.1	87	3.57
J Lima, Hou	246.1	98	3.58
O Daal, Ari	214.2	87	3.65

Won-Lost Percentage
minimum 13 decisions

Pitcher, Team	W	L	Pct
M Hampton, Hou	**22**	**4**	**.846**
S Parris, Cin	11	4	.733
K Bottenfield, StL	18	7	.720
K Millwood, Atl	18	7	.720
C Schilling, Phi	15	6	.714
R Reed, NYM	11	5	.688
J Lima, Hou	21	10	.677
G Maddux, Atl	19	9	.679
K Brown, LA	18	9	.667
R Ortiz, SF	18	9	.667

Opposition AVG
minimum 162 IP

Pitcher, Team	AB	H	AVG
K Millwood, Atl	**831**	**168**	**.202**
R Johnson, Ari	993	207	.208
K Brown, LA	944	210	.222
O Daal, Ari	798	188	.236
C Schilling, Phi	672	159	.237
M Hampton, Hou	854	206	.241
R Ortiz, SF	774	189	.244
J Smoltz, Atl	687	168	.245
K Benson, Pit	738	184	.249
P Harnisch, Cin	754	190	.252

Games

S Kline, Mon	**82**
T Wendell, NYM	80
S Sullivan, Cin	79
A Telford, Mon	79
A Benitez, NYM	77

Games Started

K Brown, LA	**35**
T Glavine, Atl	**35**
R Johnson, Ari	**35**
J Lima, Hou	**35**
S Reynolds, Hou	**35**

Complete Games

R Johnson, Ari	**12**
C Schilling, Phi	8
P Astacio, Col	7
K Brown, LA	5
4 pitchers tied with	4

Games Finished

R Nen, SF	**64**
D Veres, Col	63
B Wickman, Mil	63
U Urbina, Mon	62
J Rocker, Atl	61

Wins

M Hampton, Hou	**22**
J Lima, Hou	21
G Maddux, Atl	19
4 pitchers tied with	18

Losses

S Trachsel, ChC	**18**
D Springer, Fla	16
B Meadows, Fla	15
6 pitchers tied with	14

Saves

U Urbina, Mon	**41**
T Hoffman, SD	40
B Wagner, Hou	39
J Rocker, Atl	38
2 pitchers tied with	37

Shutouts

A Ashby, SD	**3**
6 pitchers tied with	2

Hits Allowed

T Glavine, Atl	**259**
P Astacio, Col	258
G Maddux, Atl	258
J Lima, Hou	256
S Reynolds, Hou	250

Doubles Allowed

D Hermanson, Mon	**54**
B Tomko, Cin	53
B Bohanon, Col	52
C Ogea, Phi	52
S Woodard, Mil	51

Triples Allowed

J Schmidt, Pit	**15**
D Kile, Col	11
O Hershiser, NYM	9
3 pitchers tied with	8

Home Runs Allowed

P Astacio, Col	**38**
C Ogea, Phi	36
A Benes, Ari	34
P Byrd, Phi	34
2 pitchers tied with	33

Batters Faced

R Johnson, Ari	**1079**
J Lima, Hou	1024
T Glavine, Atl	1023
K Brown, LA	1018
P Astacio, Col	1008

Innings Pitched

R Johnson, Ari	**271.2**
K Brown, LA	252.1
J Lima, Hou	246.1
M Hampton, Hou	239.0
T Glavine, Atl	234.0

Runs Allowed

D Kile, Col	**150**
B Bohanon, Col	146
P Astacio, Col	140
S Trachsel, ChC	133
3 pitchers tied with	121

Strikeouts

R Johnson, Ari	**364**
K Brown, LA	221
P Astacio, Col	210
K Millwood, Atl	205
S Reynolds, Hou	197

Walks Allowed

R Ortiz, SF	**125**
S Estes, SF	112
D Kile, Col	109
M Hampton, Hou	101
C Park, LA	100

Hit Batsmen

P Byrd, Phi	**17**
B Bohanon, Col	14
C Park, LA	14
4 pitchers tied with	11

Wild Pitches

S Estes, SF	**15**
S Hitchcock, SD	**15**
D Kile, Col	13
R Ortiz, SF	13
S Williamson, Cin	13

Balks

D Dreifort, LA	**4**
J Schmidt, Pit	**4**
7 pitchers tied with	3

1999 American League Special Batting Leaders

Scoring Position AVG
minimum 100 PA

Player, Team	AB	H	AVG
T Fernandez, Tor	**138**	**55**	**.399**
R Alomar, Cle	176	69	.392
M Ramirez, Cle	189	73	.386
H Baines, Bal-Cle	122	45	.369
D Jeter, NYY	155	56	.361
R Palmeiro, Tex	162	58	.358
D Hocking, Min	85	30	.353
N Garciaparra, Bos	148	52	.351
S Stewart, Tor	123	43	.350
C Koskie, Min	106	37	.349

Leadoff Hitters OBP
minimum 150 PA

Player, Team	PA*	OB	OBP
B Anderson, Bal	**674**	**275**	**.408**
J Offerman, Bos	641	260	.406
K Lofton, Cle	554	224	.404
C Knoblauch, NYY	703	276	.393
S Stewart, Tor	658	248	.377
R Durham, CWS	608	229	.377
J Damon, KC	272	101	.371
T Walker, Min	171	63	.368
O Palmeiro, Ana	177	65	.367
T Phillips, Oak	480	175	.365

* AB, BB, HBP, SF

Cleanup Hitters SLG
minimum 150 PA

Player, Team	AB	TB	SLG
M Ramirez, Cle	**517**	**345**	**.667**
A Rodriguez, Sea	220	135	.614
N Garciaparra, Bos	395	240	.608
J Gonzalez, Tex	562	338	.601
C Delgado, Tor	501	289	.577
J Jaha, Oak	375	211	.563
F McGriff, TB	520	288	.554
M Sweeney, KC	394	215	.546
A Belle, Bal	610	330	.541
D Palmer, Det	346	187	.540

AVG vs. LHP
minimum 125 PA

M Bordick, Bal	**.402**
N Garciaparra, Bos	.400
M Ramirez, Cle	.383
A Belle, Bal	.367
E Martinez, Sea	.358

AVG vs. RHP
minimum 377 PA

D Jeter, NYY	**.366**
B Williams, NYY	.359
N Garciaparra, Bos	.346
R Palmeiro, Tex	.341
F McGriff, TB	.339

AVG at Home
minimum 251 PA

N Garciaparra, Bos	**.378**
E Martinez, Sea	.360
O Vizquel, Cle	.359
I Rodriguez, Tex	.357
J Giambi, Oak	.353

AVG on the Road
minimum 251 PA

D Jeter, NYY	**.369**
M Ramirez, Cle	.354
B Williams, NYY	.346
S Green, Tor	.332
N Garciaparra, Bos	.331

OBP vs LHP
minimum 125 PA

A Belle, Bal	**.508**
M Ramirez, Cle	.493
E Martinez, Sea	.478
N Garciaparra, Bos	.476
M Bordick, Bal	.472

OBP vs RHP
minimum 377 PA

D Jeter, NYY	**.455**
B Williams, NYY	.451
J Thome, Cle	.448
T Fernandez, Tor	.447
R Palmeiro, Tex	.444

AVG Late & Close
minimum 50 PA

R Palmeiro, Tex	**.413**
O Vizquel, Cle	.397
N Garciaparra, Bos	.385
T Clark, Det	.384
K Griffey Jr., Sea	.379

AVG Bases Loaded
minimum 10 PA

B Williams, NYY	**.583**
T Zeile, Tex	.542
B Anderson, Bal	.526
M Ramirez, Cle	.500
R Palmeiro, Tex	.500

SLG vs LHP
minimum 125 PA

A Belle, Bal	**.776**
N Garciaparra, Bos	.764
E Martinez, Sea	.725
M Ramirez, Cle	.687
J Jaha, Oak	.643

SLG vs RHP
minimum 377 PA

R Palmeiro, Tex	**.656**
M Ramirez, Cle	.656
K Griffey Jr., Sea	.640
S Green, Tor	.618
A Rodriguez, Sea	.610

AB per HR
minimum 502 PA

M Ramirez, Cle	**11.9**
A Rodriguez, Sea	12.0
R Palmeiro, Tex	12.0
K Griffey Jr., Sea	12.6
J Canseco, TB	12.6

Times on Base

D Jeter, NYY	**322**
B Williams, NYY	303
J Giambi, Oak	293
A Belle, Bal	289
R Alomar, Cle	288

Pitches Seen

R Alomar, Cle	**2946**
R Durham, CWS	2827
J Giambi, Oak	2818
D Jeter, NYY	2784
C Knoblauch, NYY	2784

Pitches per PA
minimum 502 PA

J Jaha, Oak	**4.38**
E Martinez, Sea	4.30
J Thome, Cle	4.29
R Alomar, Cle	4.24
M Stairs, Oak	4.24

Extra-Base Hits

S Green, Tor	**87**
C Delgado, Tor	83
M Ramirez, Cle	81
J Dye, KC	79
R Palmeiro, Tex	78

Ground/Fly Ratio
minimum 502 PA

C Febles, KC	**2.54**
R Sanchez, KC	2.34
H Bush, Tor	2.19
M Caruso, CWS	2.12
R Clayton, Tex	2.03

GDP/GDP Opp
minimum 50 PA

B Higginson, Det	**0.02**
R Ledee, NYY	0.03
K Garcia, Det	0.04
J Thome, Cle	0.04
P Sorrento, TB	0.05

SB Success %
minimum 20 SB attempts

M Lawton, Min	**86.7**
R Alomar, Cle	86.0
J Damon, KC	85.7
A Belle, Bal	85.0
B Hunter, Det-Sea	84.6

Multihit Games

D Jeter, NYY	**67**
B Surhoff, Bal	62
O Vizquel, Cle	62
S Stewart, Tor	58
B Williams, NYY	58

% CS by Catchers
minimum 70 SB attempts

I Rodriguez, Tex	**52.8**
J Flaherty, TB	38.6
C Johnson, Bal	36.7
B Ausmus, Det	35.2
E Diaz, Cle	34.5

1999 National League Special Batting Leaders

Scoring Position AVG
minimum 100 PA

Player, Team	AB	H	AVG
L Walker, Col	112	47	.420
T Gwynn, SD	97	40	.412
E Burks, SF	98	37	.378
V Guerrero, Mon	167	63	.377
K Millar, Fla	109	40	.367
M McGwire, StL	135	48	.356
C Everett, Hou	138	48	.348
G Jenkins, Mil	124	43	.347
B Abreu, Phi	136	47	.346
A Arias, Phi	102	35	.343

Leadoff Hitters OBP
minimum 150 PA

Player, Team	PA*	OB	OBP
R Henderson, NYM	516	215	.417
M Loretta, Mil	342	134	.392
C Biggio, Hou	743	287	.386
L Castillo, Fla	553	213	.385
E Young, LA	490	187	.382
Q Veras, SD	531	200	.377
D Glanville, Phi	684	257	.376
R Cedeno, NYM	213	79	.371
R White, Mon	224	83	.371
D Hamilton, Col-NYM	286	105	.367

* AB, BB, HBP, SF

Cleanup Hitters SLG
minimum 150 PA

Player, Team	AB	TB	SLG
S Sosa, ChC	298	207	.695
V Guerrero, Mon	577	342	.593
C Everett, Hou	218	128	.587
M Piazza, NYM	530	306	.577
S Rolen, Phi	209	119	.569
J Burnitz, Mil	416	235	.565
P Nevin, SD	268	151	.563
E Karros, LA	344	191	.555
M Grace, ChC	292	160	.548
F Tatis, StL	152	83	.546

AVG vs. LHP
minimum 125 PA

M Grudzielanek, LA	.389
M Lieberthal, Phi	.377
R White, Mon	.374
J Bagwell, Hou	.354
C Jones, Atl	.352

AVG vs. RHP
minimum 377 PA

S Casey, Cin	.356
T Helton, Col	.349
B Abreu, Phi	.348
D Glanville, Phi	.346
L Gonzalez, Ari	.339

AVG at Home
minimum 251 PA

L Walker, Col	.461
T Helton, Col	.385
C Jones, Atl	.366
D Hamilton, Col-NYM	.362
J Cirillo, Mil	.354

AVG on the Road
minimum 251 PA

D Glanville, Phi	.361
R Henderson, NYM	.353
L Gonzalez, Ari	.352
R Cedeno, NYM	.348
S Casey, Cin	.341

OBP vs LHP
minimum 125 PA

R Henderson, NYM	.481
J Bell, Ari	.479
J Bagwell, Hou	.476
E Burks, SF	.465
M Grudzielanek, LA	.451

OBP vs RHP
minimum 377 PA

B Abreu, Phi	.453
J Bagwell, Hou	.448
J Olerud, NYM	.447
C Jones, Atl	.438
B Giles, Pit	.430

AVG Late & Close
minimum 50 PA

C Jones, Atl	.417
T Shumpert, Col	.395
L Gonzalez, Ari	.384
M Barrett, Mon	.375
R Belliard, Mil	.368

AVG Bases Loaded
minimum 10 PA

F Tatis, StL	.692
E Burks, SF	.625
P Nevin, SD	.600
M Williams, Ari	.588
J Bell, Ari	.583

SLG vs LHP
minimum 125 PA

C Jones, Atl	.739
S Sosa, ChC	.712
M McGwire, StL	.705
M Lieberthal, Phi	.697
J Bell, Ari	.661

SLG vs RHP
minimum 377 PA

M McGwire, StL	.694
T Helton, Col	.670
B Giles, Pit	.663
B Abreu, Phi	.612
S Sosa, ChC	.608

AB per HR
minimum 502 PA

M McGwire, StL	8.0
S Sosa, ChC	9.9
L Walker, Col	11.8
G Vaughn, Cin	12.2
C Jones, Atl	12.6

Times on Base

J Bagwell, Hou	331
J Olerud, NYM	309
C Jones, Atl	309
B Abreu, Phi	295
C Biggio, Hou	287

Pitches Seen

J Bell, Ari	3023
J Bagwell, Hou	2962
E Alfonzo, NYM	2951
S Sosa, ChC	2857
B Abreu, Phi	2854

Pitches per PA
minimum 502 PA

J Bell, Ari	4.39
B Abreu, Phi	4.31
R Henderson, NYM	4.27
J Burnitz, Mil	4.26
F Tatis, StL	4.10

Extra-Base Hits

S Sosa, ChC	89
C Jones, Atl	87
M McGwire, StL	87
V Guerrero, Mon	84
T Helton, Col	79

Ground/Fly Ratio
minimum 502 PA

L Castillo, Fla	4.88
R Cedeno, NYM	2.23
Q Veras, SD	2.05
D Bell, Hou	1.83
R Ordonez, NYM	1.78

GDP/GDP Opp
minimum 50 PA

W Weiss, Atl	0.02
R Mondesi, LA	0.02
D Jackson, SD	0.02
N Perez, Col	0.03
S Finley, Ari	0.03

SB Success %
minimum 20 SB attempts

D Glanville, Phi	94.4
C Jones, Atl	89.3
J Kendall, Pit	88.0
A Martin, Pit	87.0
J Drew, StL	86.4

Multihit Games

S Casey, Cin	66
J Cirillo, Mil	64
D Glanville, Phi	62
L Gonzalez, Ari	61
N Perez, Col	60

% CS by Catchers
minimum 70 SB attempts

H Blanco, Col	38.5
M Redmond, Fla	35.2
D Miller, Ari	30.2
M Lieberthal, Phi	29.0
E Perez, Atl	28.8

1999 American League Special Pitching Leaders

Baserunners per 9 IP
minimum 162 IP

Player, Team	IP	BR	BR/9
P Martinez, Bos	**213.1**	**206**	**8.69**
E Milton, Min	206.1	256	11.17
M Mussina, Bal	203.1	260	11.51
J Moyer, Sea	228.0	292	11.53
B Radke, Min	218.2	284	11.69
B Colon, Cle	205.0	268	11.77
O Hernandez, NYY	214.1	282	11.84
J Rosado, KC	208.0	274	11.86
G Heredia, Oak	200.1	270	12.13
D Wells, Tor	231.2	314	12.20

Strikeouts per 9 IP
minimum 162 IP

Player, Team	IP	SO	SO/9
P Martinez, Bos	**213.1**	**313**	**13.20**
C Finley, Ana	213.1	200	8.44
D Cone, NYY	193.1	177	8.24
A Sele, Tex	205.0	186	8.17
R Clemens, NYY	187.2	163	7.82
M Mussina, Bal	203.1	172	7.61
F Garcia, Sea	201.1	170	7.60
D Burba, Cle	220.0	174	7.12
E Milton, Min	206.1	163	7.11
H Irabu, NYY	169.1	133	7.07

Run Support per 9 IP
minimum 162 IP

Player, Team	IP	R	R/9
H Irabu, NYY	**169.1**	**154**	**8.19**
B Colon, Cle	205.0	171	7.51
A Sele, Tex	205.0	170	7.46
C Nagy, Cle	202.0	157	7.00
K Escobar, Tor	174.0	132	6.83
M Mussina, Bal	203.1	154	6.82
A Pettitte, NYY	191.2	141	6.62
F Garcia, Sea	201.1	142	6.35
D Wells, Tor	231.2	161	6.25
G Heredia, Oak	200.1	139	6.24

Opposition OBP
minimum 162 IP

P Martinez, Bos	**.248**
E Milton, Min	.299
J Moyer, Sea	.311
O Hernandez, NYY	.311
M Mussina, Bal	.312

Opposition SLG
minimum 162 IP

P Martinez, Bos	**.288**
D Cone, NYY	.375
C Finley, Ana	.386
J Rosado, KC	.390
O Hernandez, NYY	.392

Hits per 9 IP
minimum 162 IP

P Martinez, Bos	**6.75**
D Cone, NYY	7.63
O Hernandez, NYY	7.85
B Colon, Cle	8.12
E Milton, Min	8.29

Home Runs per 9 IP
minimum 162 IP

P Martinez, Bos	**0.38**
M Mussina, Bal	0.71
F Garcia, Sea	0.80
O Olivares, Oak	0.83
J Moyer, Sea	0.91

AVG vs. LHB
minimum 125 PA

M Rivera, NYY	**.143**
J Zimmerman, Tex	.158
P Abbott, Sea	.159
J Grimsley, NYY	.167
K Foulke, CWS	.183

Avg vs. RHB
minimum 225 PA

P Martinez, Bos	**.186**
O Hernandez, NYY	.187
D Lowe, Bos	.188
D Cone, NYY	.214
C Nitkowski, Det	.215

AVG Allowed ScPos
minimum 125 PA

T Hudson, Oak	**.181**
B Wells, Min	.198
D Cone, NYY	.199
J Thompson, Det	.200
F Garcia, Sea	.202

OBP Lead Off Inning
minimum 150 PA

P Martinez, Bos	**.241**
E Milton, Min	.264
D Cone, NYY	.275
S Sparks, Ana	.275
R Rupe, TB	.290

K/BB Ratio
minimum 162 IP

P Martinez, Bos	**8.46**
G Heredia, Oak	3.44
M Mussina, Bal	3.31
H Irabu, NYY	2.89
J Moyer, Sea	2.85

Grd/Fly Ratio Off
minimum 162 IP

S Erickson, Bal	**2.80**
A Pettitte, NYY	2.08
A Sele, Tex	1.86
C Nagy, Cle	1.77
G Heredia, Oak	1.60

Pitches per Start
minimum 30 games started

R Clemens, NYY	**110.9**
C Finley, Ana	109.5
S Erickson, Bal	109.3
R Helling, Tex	109.0
J Moyer, Sea	108.8

Pitches per Batter
minimum 162 IP

G Heredia, Oak	**3.40**
C Nagy, Cle	3.49
B Radke, Min	3.53
D Wells, Tor	3.55
O Olivares, Oak	3.55

Steals Allowed

D Wells, Tor	**37**
T Wakefield, Bos	35
D Gooden, Cle	27
P Rapp, Bos	27
F Garcia, Sea	26

Caught Stealing Off

R Helling, Tex	**14**
S Ponson, Bal	**14**
C Finley, Ana	13
D Burba, Cle	12
3 pitchers tied with	11

SB% Allowed
minimum 162 IP

J Rosado, KC	**44.4**
M Mussina, Bal	44.4
S Ponson, Bal	46.2
R Helling, Tex	48.1
E Milton, Min	50.0

Pickoffs

S Lowe, CWS	**6**
5 pitchers tied with	5

PkOf Throw/Runner
minimum 162 IP

A Pettitte, NYY	**1.33**
J Parque, CWS	1.13
D Cone, NYY	1.07
B Witt, TB	1.05
O Hernandez, NYY	1.03

GDPs Induced

S Erickson, Bal	**41**
O Olivares, Oak	31
A Pettitte, NYY	28
B Witt, TB	27
J Suppan, KC	26

GDP per 9 IP
minimum 162 IP

S Erickson, Bal	**1.6**
O Olivares, Oak	1.4
B Witt, TB	1.3
A Pettitte, NYY	1.3
J Halama, Sea	1.3

Quality Starts

P Martinez, Bos	**24**
O Hernandez, NYY	23
J Moyer, Sea	21
6 pitchers tied with	19

1999 National League Special Pitching Leaders

Baserunners per 9 IP
minimum 162 IP

Player, Team	IP	BR	BR/9
K Millwood, Atl	228.0	231	9.12
R Johnson, Ari	271.2	286	9.47
K Brown, LA	252.1	276	9.84
J Smoltz, Atl	186.1	212	10.24
C Schilling, Phi	180.1	208	10.38
J Lima, Hou	246.1	302	11.03
S Reynolds, Hou	231.2	288	11.19
P Harnisch, Cin	198.1	252	11.44
O Daal, Ari	214.2	274	11.49
A Ashby, SD	206.0	265	11.58

Strikeouts per 9 IP
minimum 162 IP

Player, Team	IP	SO	SO/9
R Johnson, Ari	271.2	364	12.06
S Hitchcock, SD	205.2	194	8.49
J Lieber, ChC	203.1	186	8.23
H Nomo, Mil	176.1	161	8.22
P Astacio, Col	232.0	210	8.15
K Millwood, Atl	228.0	205	8.09
C Park, LA	194.1	174	8.06
K Brown, LA	252.1	221	7.88
S Reynolds, Hou	231.2	197	7.65
C Schilling, Phi	180.1	152	7.59

Run Support per 9 IP
minimum 162 IP

Player, Team	IP	R	R/9
P Byrd, Phi	199.2	157	7.08
M Hampton, Hou	239.0	180	6.78
K Rueter, SF	184.2	136	6.63
P Astacio, Col	232.0	167	6.48
A Reynoso, Ari	167.0	118	6.36
G Maddux, Atl	219.1	154	6.32
A Benes, Ari	198.1	139	6.31
D Dreifort, LA	178.2	125	6.30
S Estes, SF	203.0	142	6.30
H Nomo, Mil	176.1	123	6.28

Opposition OBP
minimum 162 IP

K Millwood, Atl	.258
R Johnson, Ari	.266
K Brown, LA	.273
C Schilling, Phi	.287
J Smoltz, Atl	.288

Opposition SLG
minimum 162 IP

M Hampton, Hou	.324
R Johnson, Ari	.335
K Brown, LA	.336
K Millwood, Atl	.337
K Benson, Pit	.367

Hits per 9 IP
minimum 162 IP

K Millwood, Atl	6.63
R Johnson, Ari	6.86
K Brown, LA	7.49
M Hampton, Hou	7.76
O Daal, Ari	7.88

Home Runs per 9 IP
minimum 162 IP

M Hampton, Hou	0.45
G Maddux, Atl	0.66
C Holt, Hou	0.66
J Smoltz, Atl	0.68
K Brown, LA	0.68

AVG vs. LHB
minimum 125 PA

M Hampton, Hou	.149
M Mantei, Fla-Ari	.159
S Williamson, Cin	.171
A Benitez, NYM	.177
B Wickman, Mil	.197

AVG vs. RHB
minimum 225 PA

B Wagner, Hou	.128
K Millwood, Atl	.175
K Brown, LA	.189
J Rocker, Atl	.191
S Sullivan, Cin	.202

AVG Allowed ScPos
minimum 125 PA

D Graves, Cin	.162
E Plunk, Mil	.189
R Johnson, Ari	.193
A Fernandez, Fla	.197
J Schmidt, Pit	.199

OBP Lead Off Inning
minimum 150 PA

K Millwood, Atl	.244
R Johnson, Ari	.262
K Brown, LA	.267
T Ritchie, Pit	.269
R Reed, NYM	.275

K/BB Ratio
minimum 162 IP

S Reynolds, Hou	5.32
R Johnson, Ari	5.20
J Lima, Hou	4.25
J Lieber, ChC	4.04
J Smoltz, Atl	3.90

Grd/Fly Ratio Off
minimum 162 IP

M Hampton, Hou	2.56
J Jimenez, StL	2.50
G Maddux, Atl	2.22
K Brown, LA	2.20
C Holt, Hou	2.02

Pitches per Start
minimum 30 games started

R Johnson, Ari	120.2
R Ortiz, SF	112.8
L Hernandez, SF	112.8
A Leiter, NYM	112.1
S Estes, SF	109.4

Pitches per Batter
minimum 162 IP

G Maddux, Atl	3.24
S Woodard, Mil	3.24
T Mulholland, Atl	3.38
O Hershiser, NYM	3.42
B Meadows, Fla	3.43

Steals Allowed

R Johnson, Ari	42
H Nomo, Mil	41
A Leiter, NYM	26
I Valdes, LA	26
3 pitchers tied with	25

Caught Stealing Off

R Johnson, Ari	17
D Springer, Fla	17
P Astacio, Col	14
C Park, LA	14
D Oliver, StL	11

SB% Allowed
minimum 162 IP

T Mulholland, Atl	20.0
K Rueter, SF	33.3
W Williams, SD	37.5
O Daal, Ari	41.2
J Jimenez, StL	41.2

Pickoffs

C Park, LA	7
T Ritchie, Pit	7
4 pitchers tied with	6

PkOf Throw/Runner
minimum 162 IP

A Reynoso, Ari	1.45
I Valdes, LA	1.32
B Tomko, Cin	1.28
K Benson, Pit	1.14
O Daal, Ari	1.12

GDPs Induced

M Hampton, Hou	38
M Clement, SD	28
D Kile, Col	28
S Karl, Mil	26
S Reynolds, Hou	26

GDP per 9 IP
minimum 162 IP

M Hampton, Hou	1.4
M Clement, SD	1.4
D Kile, Col	1.3
T Ritchie, Pit	1.3
T Mulholland, Atl	1.3

Quality Starts

R Johnson, Ari	29
M Hampton, Hou	27
K Brown, LA	25
J Lima, Hou	25
K Millwood, Atl	25

1999 American League Relief Pitching Leaders

Saves

Player, Team	Saves
M Rivera, NYY	45
R Hernandez, TB	43
J Wetteland, Tex	43
M Jackson, Cle	39
J Mesa, Sea	33
B Koch, Tor	31
T Percival, Ana	31
T Jones, Det	30
B Howry, CWS	28
M Timlin, Bal	27

Save Percentage
minimum 20 SvOp

Player, Team	Sv	Op	Pct
M Rivera, NYY	45	49	91.8
R Hernandez, TB	43	47	91.5
M Jackson, Cle	39	43	90.7
B Koch, Tor	31	35	88.6
J Mesa, Sea	33	38	86.8
J Wetteland, Tex	43	50	86.0
T Jones, Det	30	35	85.7
B Howry, CWS	28	34	82.4
M Trombley, Min	24	30	80.0
T Percival, Ana	31	39	79.5

Relief ERA
minimum 50 relief IP

Player, Team	IP	ER	ERA
M Rivera, NYY	69.0	14	1.83
K Foulke, CWS	105.1	26	2.22
J Zimmerman, Tex	87.2	23	2.36
D Brocail, Det	82.0	23	2.52
D Lowe, Bos	109.1	32	2.63
S Karsay, Cle	65.2	20	2.74
R Hernandez, TB	73.1	25	3.07
P Spoljaric, Tor	52.0	19	3.29
M Venafro, Tex	68.1	25	3.29
M Magnante, Ana	69.1	26	3.38

Relief Wins

M Petkovsek, Ana	10
T Mathews, Oak	9
J Zimmerman, Tex	9
4 pitchers tied with	8

Relief Losses

J Paniagua, Sea	11
M Timlin, Bal	9
M Trombley, Min	8
4 pitchers tied with	6

Holds

B Groom, Oak	27
J Zimmerman, Tex	24
D Brocail, Det	23
3 pitchers tied with	22

Blown Saves

J Paniagua, Sea	9
M Timlin, Bal	9
T Percival, Ana	8
4 pitchers tied with	7

Relief Games

B Groom, Oak	76
B Wells, Min	76
M Trombley, Min	75
G Lloyd, Tor	74
D Lowe, Bos	74

Games Finished

R Hernandez, TB	66
M Jackson, Cle	65
M Rivera, NYY	63
T Jones, Det	62
J Mesa, Sea	60

Relief Innings

D Lowe, Bos	109.1
R White, TB	105.2
K Foulke, CWS	105.1
D Jones, Oak	104.0
S Lowe, CWS	95.2

% Inherited Scored
minimum 30 inherited runnrs

R Rincon, Cle	11.9
T Miller, Min	17.5
M Kida, Det	18.9
S Hasegawa, Ana	19.2
E Guardado, Min	20.4

Opposition AVG
minimum 50 relief IP

J Zimmerman, Tex	.166
M Rivera, NYY	.176
T Percival, Ana	.186
K Foulke, CWS	.188
D Brocail, Det	.206

Opposition OBP
minimum 50 relief IP

J Zimmerman, Tex	.225
K Foulke, CWS	.235
M Rivera, NYY	.239
D Lowe, Bos	.260
T Percival, Ana	.274

Opposition SLG
minimum 50 relief IP

M Rivera, NYY	.237
J Zimmerman, Tex	.291
R Hernandez, TB	.295
D Brocail, Det	.309
D Lowe, Bos	.312

1st Batter AVG
minimum 40 first BFP

M Rivera, NYY	.048
B Howry, CWS	.121
A Rhodes, Bal	.132
J Zimmerman, Tex	.143
A Lopez, TB	.146

AVG vs. LHB
minimum 50 relief IP

M Rivera, NYY	.143
J Zimmerman, Tex	.158
J Grimsley, NYY	.167
D Johns, Bal	.179
K Foulke, CWS	.183

AVG vs. RHB
minimum 50 relief IP

T Percival, Ana	.152
J Zimmerman, Tex	.173
D Lowe, Bos	.188
K Foulke, CWS	.192
D Brocail, Det	.200

AVG Runners On
minimum 50 relief IP

D Brocail, Det	.178
J Zimmerman, Tex	.186
D Lowe, Bos	.190
K Foulke, CWS	.192
M Rivera, NYY	.198

AVG Allowed ScPos
minimum 50 relief IP

K Foulke, CWS	.160
B Howry, CWS	.172
M Jackson, Cle	.177
W Blair, Det	.180
J Zimmerman, Tex	.181

Easy Saves

M Rivera, NYY	26
M Jackson, Cle	25
J Wetteland, Tex	25
R Hernandez, TB	22
T Jones, Det	21

Regular Saves

R Hernandez, TB	19
B Koch, Tor	19
M Rivera, NYY	16
M Jackson, Cle	14
T Percival, Ana	14

Tough Saves

J Wetteland, Tex	5
M Trombley, Min	4
M Rivera, NYY	3
T Wakefield, Bos	3
3 pitchers tied with	2

Pitches per Batter
minimum 50 relief IP

B Howry, CWS	4.36
A Rhodes, Bal	4.26
T Jones, Det	4.23
T Percival, Ana	4.11
P Spoljaric, Tor	4.11

1999 National League Relief Pitching Leaders

Saves

Player, Team	Saves
U Urbina, Mon	**41**
T Hoffman, SD	40
B Wagner, Hou	39
J Rocker, Atl	38
R Nen, SF	37
B Wickman, Mil	37
J Shaw, LA	34
M Mantei, Fla-Ari	32
D Veres, Col	31
D Graves, Cin	27

Save Percentage
minimum 20 SvOp

Player, Team	Sv	Op	Pct
T Hoffman, SD	**40**	**43**	**93.0**
B Wagner, Hou	39	42	92.9
J Franco, NYM	19	21	90.5
J Shaw, LA	34	39	87.2
M Mantei, Fla-Ari	32	37	86.5
J Rocker, Atl	38	45	84.4
A Alfonseca, Fla	21	25	84.0
B Wickman, Mil	37	45	82.2
M Williams, Pit	23	28	82.1
U Urbina, Mon	41	50	82.0

Relief ERA
minimum 50 relief IP

Player, Team	IP	ER	ERA
B Wagner, Hou	**74.2**	**13**	**1.57**
A Benitez, NYM	78.0	16	1.85
S Sauerbeck, Pit	67.2	15	2.00
T Hoffman, SD	67.1	16	2.14
H Slocumb, Bal-StL	53.1	14	2.36
M Remlinger, Atl	83.2	22	2.37
S Williamson, Cin	93.1	25	2.41
J Rocker, Atl	72.1	20	2.49
G Swindell, Ari	64.2	18	2.51
J Johnstone, SF	65.2	19	2.60

Relief Wins

S Williamson, Cin	12
D Cook, NYM	10
M Remlinger, Atl	10
G Olson, Ari	9
2 pitchers tied with	8

Relief Losses

B Edmondson, Fla	8
R Nen, SF	8
D Veres, Col	8
B Wickman, Mil	8
5 pitchers tied with	7

Holds

J Johnstone, SF	28
A Embree, SF	22
M Remlinger, Atl	21
T Wendell, NYM	21
2 pitchers tied with	19

Blown Saves

D Graves, Cin	9
R Nen, SF	9
G Olson, Ari	9
U Urbina, Mon	9
3 pitchers tied with	8

Relief Games

S Kline, Mon	82
T Wendell, NYM	80
S Sullivan, Cin	79
A Telford, Mon	79
A Benitez, NYM	77

Games Finished

R Nen, SF	64
D Veres, Col	63
B Wickman, Mil	63
U Urbina, Mon	62
J Rocker, Atl	61

Relief Innings

S Sullivan, Cin	113.2
D Graves, Cin	111.0
A Telford, Mon	96.0
B Edmondson, Fla	94.0
2 pitchers tied with	93.1

% Inherited Scored
minimum 30 inherited runnrs

J Dipoto, Col	12.5
M Myers, Mil	15.4
W Gomes, Phi	16.7
S Kline, Mon	16.9
L Painter, StL	17.5

Opposition AVG
minimum 50 relief IP

B Wagner, Hou	.135
A Benitez, NYM	.148
S Williamson, Cin	.171
J Rocker, Atl	.180
M Mantei, Fla-Ari	.189

Opposition OBP
minimum 50 relief IP

B Wagner, Hou	.208
T Hoffman, SD	.240
A Benitez, NYM	.260
J Johnstone, SF	.267
S Williamson, Cin	.271

Opposition SLG
minimum 50 relief IP

B Wagner, Hou	.212
A Benitez, NYM	.236
J Rocker, Atl	.268
S Williamson, Cin	.292
U Urbina, Mon	.303

1st Batter AVG
minimum 40 first BFP

S Sullivan, Cin	.136
L Painter, StL	.140
J Rocker, Atl	.145
B Wagner, Hou	.145
A Benitez, NYM	.148

AVG vs. LHB
minimum 50 relief IP

J Rocker, Atl	.140
P Borbon, LA	.156
M Mantei, Fla-Ari	.159
S Sauerbeck, Pit	.167
B Wagner, Hou	.167

AVG vs. RHB
minimum 50 relief IP

A Benitez, NYM	.127
B Wagner, Hou	.128
S Williamson, Cin	.172
T Hoffman, SD	.182
P Mahomes, NYM	.189

AVG Runners On
minimum 50 relief IP

J Johnstone, SF	.141
B Wagner, Hou	.151
A Benitez, NYM	.156
M Remlinger, Atl	.156
M Mantei, Fla-Ari	.175

AVG Allowed ScPos
minimum 50 relief IP

D Cook, NYM	.121
J Johnstone, SF	.131
A Benitez, NYM	.141
B Wagner, Hou	.148
S Williamson, Cin	.156

Easy Saves

U Urbina, Mon	27
R Nen, SF	26
J Rocker, Atl	24
T Hoffman, SD	23
3 pitchers tied with	21

Regular Saves

B Wagner, Hou	15
T Hoffman, SD	14
B Wickman, Mil	14
R Bottalico, StL	13
J Rocker, Atl	13

Tough Saves

U Urbina, Mon	6
B Wagner, Hou	5
5 pitchers tied with	3

Pitches per Batter
minimum 50 relief IP

M Mantei, Fla-Ari	4.52
B Wagner, Hou	4.34
A Benitez, NYM	4.17
D Cook, NYM	4.12
P Mahomes, NYM	4.11

1999 American League Bill James Leaders

Top Game Scores of the Year

Pitcher, Team	Date	Opp	IP	H	R	ER	BB	K	SC
P Martinez, Bos	9/10	NYY	9.0	1	1	1	0	17	98
E Milton, Min	9/11	Ana	9.0	0	0	0	2	13	98
D Cone, NYY	7/18	Mon	9.0	0	0	0	0	10	97
R Rupe, TB	5/23	Ana	9.0	1	0	0	0	8	93
P Martinez, Bos	6/4	Atl	9.0	3	1	1	2	16	91
P Martinez, Bos	9/21	Tor	9.0	3	0	0	2	12	91
P Martinez, Bos	9/4	Sea	8.0	2	0	0	3	15	90
D Wells, Tor	7/11	Mon	9.0	2	0	0	1	7	89
E Milton, Min	7/31	Ana	9.0	3	0	0	1	7	87
B Witt, TB	6/27	Tor	9.0	3	0	0	3	8	86

Worst Game Scores of the Year

Pitcher, Team	Date	Opp	IP	H	R	ER	BB	K	SC
R Halladay, Tor	4/29	Ana	2.1	9	11	11	3	1	-7
J Burkett, Tex	5/17	TB	4.0	8	12	12	5	2	-5
A Sele, Tex	5/16	Bal	2.1	11	9	9	4	1	-4
M Mussina, Bal	4/21	TB	3.2	11	10	10	2	3	0
J Navarro, CWS	5/17	Cle	1.1	8	9	9	3	1	0
J McDowell, Ana	8/2	KC	3.0	10	9	9	2	0	1
L Hawkins, Min	8/13	NYY	3.1	12	9	9	1	2	1
B Rose, Bos	7/3	CWS	4.0	12	9	9	2	2	2
J Witasick, KC	6/6	Cin	2.0	10	8	8	1	1	4
J Johnson, Bal	8/9	TB	4.0	12	9	9	0	2	4

Runs Created

M Ramirez, Cle	**150**
R Palmeiro, Tex	147
D Jeter, NYY	146
R Alomar, Cle	142
K Griffey Jr., Sea	140
J Giambi, Oak	136
B Williams, NYY	129
A Belle, Bal	125
J Thome, Cle	123
N Garciaparra, Bos	122

Runs Created per 27 Outs
minimum 502 PA

M Ramirez, Cle	**10.7**
R Palmeiro, Tex	9.6
N Garciaparra, Bos	9.1
J Thome, Cle	9.0
R Alomar, Cle	8.9
D Jeter, NYY	8.9
J Giambi, Oak	8.8
E Martinez, Sea	8.6
K Griffey Jr., Sea	8.3
B Williams, NYY	8.3

Offensive Win Pct
minimum 502 PA

M Ramirez, Cle	**.812**
R Palmeiro, Tex	.776
N Garciaparra, Bos	.754
J Thome, Cle	.749
R Alomar, Cle	.748
D Jeter, NYY	.748
J Giambi, Oak	.742
E Martinez, Sea	.735
K Griffey Jr., Sea	.720
B Williams, NYY	.720

Secondary Average
minimum 502 PA

J Thome, Cle	**.520**
M Ramirez, Cle	.510
J Jaha, Oak	.505
R Palmeiro, Tex	.474
K Griffey Jr., Sea	.469
C Delgado, Tor	.449
R Alomar, Cle	.440
A Rodriguez, Sea	.440
M Stairs, Oak	.433
A Belle, Bal	.433

Isolated Power (Power Pct)
minimum 502 PA

M Ramirez, Cle	**.329**
R Palmeiro, Tex	.306
A Rodriguez, Sea	.301
C Delgado, Tor	.298
K Griffey Jr., Sea	.290
J Canseco, TB	.284
J Jaha, Oak	.280
S Green, Tor	.278
J Gonzalez, Tex	.276
M Stairs, Oak	.275

Power/Speed Number

K Griffey Jr., Sea	**32.0**
R Alomar, Cle	29.1
I Rodriguez, Tex	29.2
B Anderson, Bal	28.8
A Rodriguez, Sea	28.0
S Green, Tor	27.1
C Beltran, KC	24.2
J Encarnacion, Det	24.1
A Belle, Bal	23.3
C Knoblauch, NYY	21.9

Speed Scores
minimum 800 AB over two years

B Hunter, Det-Sea	**8.03**
T Goodwin, Tex	7.97
K Lofton, Cle	7.83
J Damon, KC	7.59
R Durham, CWS	7.58
J Offerman, Bos	7.25
S Stewart, Tor	7.04
B Anderson, Bal	7.01
S Green, Tor	6.98
D Lewis, Bos	6.97

Cheap Wins

B Colon, Cle	**6**
C Nagy, Cle	**6**
K Appier, KC-Oak	5
F Garcia, Sea	5
11 pitchers tied with	4

Tough Losses

E Milton, Min	**7**
J Rosado, KC	6
R Arrojo, TB	4
D Cone, NYY	4
P Martinez, Bos	4
M Mussina, Bal	4
M Portugal, Bos	4
M Sirotka, CWS	4
D Wells, Tor	4
9 pitchers tied with	3

1999 National League Bill James Leaders

Top Game Scores of the Year

Pitcher, Team	Date	Opp	IP	H	R	ER	BB	K	SC
K Millwood, Atl	8/28	StL	10.0	2	0	0	1	9	96
J Vazquez, Mon	9/14	LA	9.0	1	0	0	1	10	94
J Jimenez, StL	6/25	Ari	9.0	0	0	0	2	8	93
R Reed, NYM	10/2	Pit	9.0	3	0	0	0	12	93
J Jimenez, StL	7/5	Ari	9.0	2	0	0	1	9	91
P Harnisch, Cin	8/19	Pit	8.0	1	0	0	2	12	90
K Brown, LA	9/4	ChC	9.0	2	0	0	1	8	90
J Smoltz, Atl	4/30	Cin	9.0	1	0	0	1	5	89
P Astacio, Col	8/10	Mil	9.0	2	1	0	1	9	89
D Oliver, StL	8/3	SD	9.0	4	0	0	2	11	88

Worst Game Scores of the Year

Pitcher, Team	Date	Opp	IP	H	R	ER	BB	K	SC
W Williams, SD	7/3	Col	3.1	13	11	10	2	4	-6
S Bennett, Mon	8/15	Col	4.0	12	10	10	1	1	-2
T Glavine, Atl	5/24	Mil	2.2	11	9	9	3	2	-1
C Pavano, Mon	5/15	Pit	2.0	10	9	9	0	2	2
S Woodard, Mil	5/29	SD	3.0	11	8	8	3	1	3
C Brock, SF	6/15	Col	3.1	10	9	8	3	0	3
S Trachsel, ChC	7/1	Mil	3.2	9	10	9	2	1	4
J Lima, Hou	9/17	StL	3.2	11	9	9	1	3	5
C Park, LA	4/23	StL	2.2	8	11	6	3	2	7
C Eldred, Mil	5/28	SD	3.2	9	8	8	4	0	7

Runs Created

J Bagwell, Hou	157
M McGwire, StL	145
C Jones, Atl	144
V Guerrero, Mon	134
S Sosa, ChC	131
B Giles, Pit	129
L Walker, Col	129
B Abreu, Phi	127
L Gonzalez, Ari	126
T Helton, Col	121

Runs Created per 27 Outs
minimum 502 PA

L Walker, Col	11.8
M McGwire, StL	9.9
J Bagwell, Hou	9.9
C Jones, Atl	9.3
B Giles, Pit	9.1
B Abreu, Phi	8.8
C Everett, Hou	8.7
V Guerrero, Mon	8.1
L Gonzalez, Ari	7.9
T Helton, Col	7.8

Offensive Win Pct
minimum 502 PA

L Walker, Col	.848
M McGwire, StL	.797
J Bagwell, Hou	.796
C Jones, Atl	.777
B Giles, Pit	.768
B Abreu, Phi	.755
C Everett, Hou	.750
V Guerrero, Mon	.725
L Gonzalez, Ari	.711
T Helton, Col	.709

Secondary Average
minimum 502 PA

M McGwire, StL	.674
J Bagwell, Hou	.585
C Jones, Atl	.575
J Burnitz, Mil	.495
B Giles, Pit	.489
L Walker, Col	.477
S Sosa, ChC	.470
G Vaughn, Cin	.467
B Abreu, Phi	.447
F Tatis, StL	.430

Isolated Power (Power Pct)
minimum 502 PA

M McGwire, StL	.418
S Sosa, ChC	.347
L Walker, Col	.331
C Jones, Atl	.314
B Giles, Pit	.299
J Burnitz, Mil	.291
G Vaughn, Cin	.289
J Bagwell, Hou	.286
V Guerrero, Mon	.284
M Piazza, NYM	.272

Power/Speed Number

J Bagwell, Hou	35.0
R Mondesi, LA	34.4
C Jones, Atl	32.1
R Sanders, SD	30.2
M Cameron, Cin	27.0
C Everett, Hou	26.0
F Tatis, StL	26.0
A Jones, Atl	25.0
K Young, Pit	23.8
B Abreu, Phi	23.0

Speed Scores
minimum 800 AB over two years

T Womack, Ari	8.74
D Glanville, Phi	7.63
C Biggio, Hou	7.42
S Finley, Ari	7.29
A Jones, Atl	7.23
E Young, LA	7.22
R Sanders, SD	7.07
R Lankford, StL	6.96
A Martin, Pit	6.88
R Mondesi, LA	6.86

Cheap Wins

B Bohanon, Col	6
K Bottenfield, StL	6
S Karl, Mil	6
A Benes, Ari	5
G Maddux, Atl	5
C Park, LA	5
R Reed, NYM	5
A Reynoso, Ari	5
K Rueter, SF	5
6 pitchers tied with	4

Tough Losses

I Valdes, LA	7
S Hitchcock, SD	6
R Johnson, Ari	6
K Brown, LA	5
C Park, LA	5
S Trachsel, ChC	5
10 pitchers tied with	4

1999 Active Career Batting Leaders

Batting Average
minimum 1000 AB

Player	AB	H	AVG
1 Tony Gwynn	9059	3067	.339
2 Mike Piazza	3653	1200	.328
3 Wade Boggs	9180	3010	.328
4 Nomar Garciaparra	1907	615	.322
5 Frank Thomas	4892	1564	.320
6 Edgar Martinez	4876	1558	.320
7 Derek Jeter	2537	807	.318
8 Todd Helton	1201	378	.315
9 Vladimir Guerrero	1585	498	.314
10 Jason Kendall	1715	535	.312
11 Larry Walker	4592	1431	.312
12 Bobby Abreu	1253	390	.311
13 Mark Grace	6646	2058	.310
14 Kenny Lofton	4379	1356	.310
15 Rusty Greer	2991	923	.309
16 Alex Rodriguez	2572	791	.308
17 Manny Ramirez	3031	932	.307
18 Jeff Cirillo	2811	864	.307
19 Hal Morris	3829	1169	.305
20 Jeff Bagwell	4759	1447	.304
21 Bernie Williams	4269	1298	.304
22 Roberto Alomar	6611	2007	.304
23 Will Clark	6746	2040	.302
24 Mo Vaughn	4352	1312	.301
25 Chipper Jones	2890	871	.301

On-Base Percentage
minimum 1000 AB

Player	PA	OB	OBP
1 Frank Thomas	6091	2681	.440
2 Edgar Martinez	5857	2495	.426
3 Jeff Bagwell	5797	2414	.416
4 Wade Boggs	10711	4445	.415
5 Jim Thome	3781	1558	.412
6 Bobby Abreu	1481	610	.412
7 Barry Bonds	8530	3493	.409
8 John Olerud	5701	2314	.406
9 Rickey Henderson	12029	4874	.405
10 Brian S. Giles	1656	664	.401
11 Manny Ramirez	3561	1421	.399
12 Jason Kendall	1998	797	.399
13 Mark McGwire	6972	2748	.394
14 Chipper Jones	3383	1333	.394
15 Rusty Greer	3464	1363	.393
16 Tim Salmon	4139	1625	.393
17 Gary Sheffield	5539	2174	.392
18 Dave Magadan	4631	1814	.392
19 Mike Piazza	4075	1594	.391
20 Mo Vaughn	5044	1967	.390
21 Derek Jeter	2866	1116	.389
22 Larry Walker	5250	2043	.389
23 Tony Gwynn	9935	3861	.389
24 Bernie Williams	4916	1910	.389
25 Chuck Knoblauch	5980	2318	.388

Slugging Percentage
minimum 1000 AB

Player	AB	TB	SLG
1 Mark McGwire	5652	3316	.587
2 Manny Ramirez	3031	1747	.576
3 Mike Piazza	3653	2101	.575
4 Albert Belle	5294	3035	.573
5 Frank Thomas	4892	2804	.573
6 Juan Gonzalez	4831	2761	.572
7 Ken Griffey Jr.	5832	3316	.569
8 Larry Walker	4592	2603	.567
9 Vladimir Guerrero	1585	898	.567
10 Nomar Garciaparra	1907	1080	.566
11 Barry Bonds	6976	3898	.559
12 Todd Helton	1201	665	.554
13 Alex Rodriguez	2572	1417	.551
14 Jim Thome	3077	1684	.547
15 Jeff Bagwell	4759	2592	.545
16 Mo Vaughn	4352	2340	.538
17 Brian S. Giles	1378	736	.534
18 Carlos Delgado	2332	1238	.531
19 Chipper Jones	2890	1530	.529
20 Vinny Castilla	3516	1858	.528
21 Ryan Klesko	2431	1277	.525
22 Matt Stairs	1669	876	.525
23 Tim Salmon	3483	1826	.524
24 Edgar Martinez	4876	2552	.523
25 Jose Canseco	6472	3363	.520

Hits

Tony Gwynn	3067
Wade Boggs	3010
Cal Ripken Jr.	2991
Rickey Henderson	2816
Harold Baines	2783
Tim Raines	2561
Chili Davis	2380
Gary Gaetti	2280
Willie McGee	2254
Tony Fernandez	2240
Julio Franco	2177
Rafael Palmeiro	2158
Mark Grace	2058
Will Clark	2040
Tony Phillips	2023
Barry Bonds	2010
Roberto Alomar	2007
Wally Joyner	1961
Fred McGriff	1946
Bobby Bonilla	1912

Home Runs

Mark McGwire	522
Barry Bonds	445
Jose Canseco	431
Cal Ripken Jr.	402
Ken Griffey Jr.	398
Fred McGriff	390
Harold Baines	373
Rafael Palmeiro	361
Gary Gaetti	360
Albert Belle	358
Chili Davis	350
Juan Gonzalez	340
Sammy Sosa	336
Darryl Strawberry	335
Matt Williams	334
Frank Thomas	301
Greg Vaughn	292
Jay Buhner	282
Rickey Henderson	278
Bobby Bonilla	277

Runs Batted In

Harold Baines	1583
Cal Ripken Jr.	1571
Chili Davis	1372
Gary Gaetti	1340
Jose Canseco	1309
Barry Bonds	1299
Mark McGwire	1277
Rafael Palmeiro	1227
Fred McGriff	1192
Ken Griffey Jr.	1152
Albert Belle	1136
Will Clark	1135
Bobby Bonilla	1124
Tony Gwynn	1104
Paul O'Neill	1099
Juan Gonzalez	1075
Wally Joyner	1060
Matt Williams	1050
Frank Thomas	1040
Rickey Henderson	1020

Stolen Bases

Rickey Henderson	1334
Tim Raines	807
Otis Nixon	620
Barry Bonds	460
Kenny Lofton	433
Delino DeShields	393
Marquis Grissom	382
Roberto Alomar	377
Willie McGee	352
Eric Davis	347
Craig Biggio	346
Barry Larkin	345
Chuck Knoblauch	335
Lance Johnson	325
Devon White	325
Tony Gwynn	318
Luis Polonia	309
Eric Young	292
Brady Anderson	283
Julio Franco	260

Doubles		Games		At Bats		Runs Scored	
Wade Boggs	578	Cal Ripken Jr.	2790	Cal Ripken Jr.	10765	Rickey Henderson	2103
Cal Ripken Jr.	571	Rickey Henderson	2733	Rickey Henderson	9911	Cal Ripken Jr.	1561
Tony Gwynn	522	Harold Baines	2702	Harold Baines	9541	Tim Raines	1548
Harold Baines	474	Gary Gaetti	2502	Wade Boggs	9180	Wade Boggs	1513
Rickey Henderson	472	Wade Boggs	2440	Tony Gwynn	9059	Barry Bonds	1455
Gary Gaetti	443	Chili Davis	2436	Gary Gaetti	8941	Tony Gwynn	1361
Rafael Palmeiro	426	Tim Raines	2353	Tim Raines	8694	Tony Phillips	1300
Chili Davis	424	Tony Gwynn	2333	Chili Davis	8673	Harold Baines	1270
Barry Bonds	423	Willie McGee	2201	Tony Fernandez	7788	Chili Davis	1240
Tim Raines	419	Tony Phillips	2161	Willie McGee	7649	Rafael Palmeiro	1157

Doubles		Triples		AB per HR		AB per RBI	
				minimum 1000 AB		minimum 1000 AB	
Wade Boggs	578	Lance Johnson	117	Mark McGwire	10.8	Mark McGwire	4.4
Cal Ripken Jr.	571	Tim Raines	112	Juan Gonzalez	14.2	Manny Ramirez	4.4
Tony Gwynn	522	Willie McGee	94	Ken Griffey Jr.	14.7	Juan Gonzalez	4.5
Harold Baines	474	Tony Fernandez	92	Albert Belle	14.8	Albert Belle	4.7
Rickey Henderson	472	Steve Finley	85	Jose Canseco	15.0	Frank Thomas	4.7
Gary Gaetti	443	Tony Gwynn	84	Mike Piazza	15.2	Mike Piazza	4.8
Rafael Palmeiro	426	Ozzie Guillen	69	Manny Ramirez	15.3	Jose Canseco	4.9
Chili Davis	424	Devon White	68	Carlos Delgado	15.7	Jeff Bagwell	5.0
Barry Bonds	423	3 players tied with	65	Barry Bonds	15.7	Carlos Delgado	5.0
Tim Raines	419			Jim Thome	15.7	Mo Vaughn	5.1

Total Bases		Walks		Intentional Walks		Hit by Pitch	
Cal Ripken Jr.	4856	Rickey Henderson	1972	Barry Bonds	298	Craig Biggio	153
Harold Baines	4474	Barry Bonds	1430	Tony Gwynn	200	Brady Anderson	136
Rickey Henderson	4242	Wade Boggs	1412	Chili Davis	188	Chuck Knoblauch	113
Tony Gwynn	4156	Tony Phillips	1319	Harold Baines	180	Mike Macfarlane	97
Wade Boggs	4064	Tim Raines	1290	Wade Boggs	180	Gary Gaetti	96
Chili Davis	3914	Chili Davis	1194	Ken Griffey Jr.	170	Jeff Blauser	91
Barry Bonds	3898	Mark McGwire	1185	Will Clark	152	Jason Kendall	89
Gary Gaetti	3881	Cal Ripken Jr.	1080	Tim Raines	144	Ed Sprague	87
Rafael Palmeiro	3733	Frank Thomas	1076	Fred McGriff	136	Rickey Henderson	86
Tim Raines	3708	Fred McGriff	1045	Mark McGwire	135	2 players tied with	82

Strikeouts		K/BB Ratio		Sacrifice Hits		Sacrifice Flies	
		minimum 1000 AB					
Jose Canseco	1765	Wade Boggs	.528	Jay Bell	144	Cal Ripken Jr.	114
Chili Davis	1698	Tony Gwynn	.546	Ozzie Guillen	140	Gary Gaetti	103
Gary Gaetti	1599	Eric Young	.622	Omar Vizquel	131	Will Clark	97
Tony Phillips	1499	Mark Grace	.626	Roberto Alomar	107	Harold Baines	96
Rickey Henderson	1472	Frank Thomas	.689	Darren Lewis	86	Wade Boggs	96
Fred McGriff	1472	Gary Sheffield	.727	Walt Weiss	86	Bobby Bonilla	96
Devon White	1401	Tim Raines	.727	Mike Bordick	85	Chili Davis	94
Mark McGwire	1400	Gregg Jefferies	.741	Mark McLemore	85	B.J. Surhoff	88
Harold Baines	1375	Dave Magadan	.746	Jose Vizcaino	76	Wally Joyner	87
Sammy Sosa	1369	Rickey Henderson	.746	Gary DiSarcina	75	2 players tied with	82

SB Success %		Caught Stealing		Ground Double Play		AB per GDP	
minimum 100 SB attempts						minimum 1000 AB	
Tony Womack	87.4	Rickey Henderson	315	Cal Ripken Jr.	325	Jose Valentin	150.6
Tim Raines	84.7	Otis Nixon	186	Harold Baines	290	Roger Cedeno	142.5
Eric Davis	84.4	Tim Raines	146	Julio Franco	255	Tony Womack	141.1
Barry Larkin	84.1	Luis Polonia	138	Tony Gwynn	255	Jer. Allensworth	114.6
Stan Javier	83.1	Tony Fernandez	135	Wade Boggs	236	F.P. Santangelo	113.7
Chipper Jones	81.4	Delino DeShields	134	Gary Gaetti	236	Jose Cruz	109.6
Roger Cedeno	80.9	Barry Bonds	132	Chili Davis	232	Luis Castillo	106.7
Rickey Henderson	80.9	Tony Gwynn	124	Paul O'Neill	184	Brady Anderson	103.5
Kenny Lofton	80.2	Willie McGee	121	Terry Steinbach	177	Neifi Perez	99.7
Marquis Grissom	80.1	Tony Phillips	114	2 players tied with	176	Tom Goodwin	96.4

1999 Active Career Pitching Leaders

Wins

Roger Clemens	247
Greg Maddux	221
Orel Hershiser	203
Dwight Gooden	188
Tom Glavine	187
David Cone	180
Mark Langston	179
Bret Saberhagen	166
Chuck Finley	165
Randy Johnson	160

Losses

Mike Morgan	180
Tom Candiotti	164
Mark Langston	158
Bobby Witt	155
Orel Hershiser	145
Chuck Finley	140
Tim Belcher	135
Roger Clemens	134
Greg Maddux	126
Jaime Navarro	120

Winning Percentage
minimum 100 decisions

Pedro Martinez	.682
Mike Mussina	.673
Roger Clemens	.648
Randy Johnson	.645
Kirk Rueter	.642
David Cone	.638
Andy Pettitte	.638
Dwight Gooden	.637
Greg Maddux	.637
Mike Hampton	.619

ERA
minimum 750 IP

John Franco	2.64
Greg Maddux	2.81
Pedro Martinez	2.83
Jesse Orosco	3.03
Roger Clemens	3.04
Jeff Brantley	3.17
David Cone	3.19
Randy Johnson	3.26
Doug Jones	3.26
Mike Jackson	3.26

Games

Jesse Orosco	1090
Paul Assenmacher	884
John Franco	878
Mike Jackson	835
Dan Plesac	822
Doug Jones	792
Eric Plunk	714
Jeff Montgomery	700
Rick Aguilera	678
Mike Stanton	611

Games Started

Roger Clemens	479
Orel Hershiser	460
Greg Maddux	432
Mark Langston	428
Tom Candiotti	410
Mike Morgan	406
Tom Glavine	399
Dwight Gooden	396
Bobby Witt	388
Chuck Finley	379

Innings Pitched

Roger Clemens	3462.1
Orel Hershiser	3105.2
Greg Maddux	3068.2
Mark Langston	2962.2
Tom Candiotti	2725.0
Dwight Gooden	2695.2
Chuck Finley	2675.0
Tom Glavine	2659.2
Mike Morgan	2598.2
David Cone	2590.0

Batters Faced

Roger Clemens	14211
Orel Hershiser	13014
Mark Langston	12562
Greg Maddux	12457
Tom Candiotti	11568
Chuck Finley	11398
Dwight Gooden	11238
Tom Glavine	11173
Mike Morgan	11100
David Cone	10752

Complete Games

Roger Clemens	115
Greg Maddux	93
Mark Langston	81
Bret Saberhagen	76
Tom Candiotti	68
Dwight Gooden	68
Orel Hershiser	68
Randy Johnson	68
Kevin Brown	66
Jack McDowell	62

Complete Game %
minimum 100 GS

Curt Schilling	0.27
Roger Clemens	0.24
Jack McDowell	0.23
Greg Maddux	0.22
Randy Johnson	0.21
Bret Saberhagen	0.21
Kevin Brown	0.19
Mark Langston	0.19
Dwight Gooden	0.17
Tom Candiotti	0.17

Shutouts

Roger Clemens	45
Greg Maddux	28
Orel Hershiser	25
Randy Johnson	25
Dwight Gooden	24
David Cone	22
Ramon Martinez	20
Tim Belcher	18
Tom Glavine	18
Mark Langston	18

Quality Start %
since 1987

Greg Maddux	70.0
Pedro Martinez	68.1
Roger Clemens	67.6
Kevin Brown	67.3
Randy Johnson	67.1
Curt Schilling	67.0
David Cone	65.9
Ismael Valdes	65.3
Tom Glavine	64.2
Mike Mussina	63.8

Strikeouts

Roger Clemens	3316
Randy Johnson	2693
Mark Langston	2464
David Cone	2420
Dwight Gooden	2238
Greg Maddux	2160
Chuck Finley	2151
John Smoltz	2098
Orel Hershiser	2001
Bobby Witt	1918

Walks Allowed

Bobby Witt	1344
Mark Langston	1289
Chuck Finley	1118
Roger Clemens	1102
Randy Johnson	1013
Orel Hershiser	993
David Cone	985
Dwight Gooden	910
Tom Glavine	900
Tom Candiotti	883

Strikeouts/9 IP
minimum 750 IP

Randy Johnson	10.77
Pedro Martinez	10.16
Hideo Nomo	9.66
Roger Clemens	8.62
Paul Assenmacher	8.49
Eric Plunk	8.45
David Cone	8.41
Curt Schilling	8.36
Dan Plesac	8.34
Jesse Orosco	8.16

Walks per 9 Innings
minimum 750 IP

Bret Saberhagen	1.66
Rick Reed	1.78
Shane Reynolds	1.83
Rheal Cormier	1.92
Doug Jones	1.95
Brad Radke	1.98
Greg Maddux	2.03
Greg Swindell	2.03
Jon Lieber	2.07
Mike Mussina	2.14

K/BB Ratio
minimum 750 IP

Shane Reynolds	4.25
Pedro Martinez	3.74
Doug Jones	3.73
Bret Saberhagen	3.62
Curt Schilling	3.46
Jon Lieber	3.40
Mike Mussina	3.15
Greg Maddux	3.13
Rick Reed	3.12
Greg Swindell	3.02

Hits/9 IP
minimum 750 IP

Randy Johnson	6.92
Pedro Martinez	6.95
Mike Jackson	7.08
Jesse Orosco	7.18
David Cone	7.45
Hideo Nomo	7.49
Roger Clemens	7.58
Jeff Brantley	7.63
John Smoltz	7.80
Ramon Martinez	7.87

Baserunners/9 IP
minimum 750 IP

Pedro Martinez	10.03
Greg Maddux	10.36
Bret Saberhagen	10.46
Curt Schilling	10.47
Mike Mussina	10.66
Roger Clemens	10.74
John Smoltz	10.83
Ismael Valdes	11.10
Mike Jackson	11.16
David Cone	11.18

Home Runs/9 IP
minimum 750 IP

Greg Maddux	0.46
John Franco	0.48
Kevin Brown	0.52
Tom Glavine	0.60
Roger Clemens	0.61
Dwight Gooden	0.62
Al Leiter	0.65
Mike Maddux	0.66
Orel Hershiser	0.67
Mike Hampton	0.67

Opposition AVG*
minimum 750 IP

Randy Johnson	.212
Pedro Martinez	.212
Mike Jackson	.217
Jesse Orosco	.219
David Cone	.225
Hideo Nomo	.225
Roger Clemens	.227
Jeff Brantley	.231
John Smoltz	.233
Ramon Martinez	.235

*since 1987

Opposition OBP*
minimum 750 IP

Pedro Martinez	.278
Greg Maddux	.286
Curt Schilling	.288
Bret Saberhagen	.290
Mike Mussina	.293
Roger Clemens	.295
John Smoltz	.295
Ismael Valdes	.299
Rick Aguilera	.299
David Cone	.300

*since 1987

Opposition SLG*
minimum 750 IP

Troy Percival	.302
Mariano Rivera	.305
Armando Benitez	.311
Roberto Hernandez	.317
Mark Wohlers	.325
Trevor Hoffman	.326
Pedro Martinez	.328
Greg Maddux	.328
Gregg Olson	.330
Randy Johnson	.332

*since 1987

Home Runs Allowed

Mark Langston	311
Tim Belcher	256
Chuck Finley	254
Mike Morgan	251
Tom Candiotti	250
David Wells	250
Bobby Witt	242
Roger Clemens	234
Greg Swindell	234
Orel Hershiser	230

Hit Batsmen

Roger Clemens	114
Kevin Brown	108
Orel Hershiser	106
Randy Johnson	101
David Cone	87
Tom Candiotti	85
Darryl Kile	85
Scott Erickson	83
Todd Stottlemyre	81
Greg Maddux	80

Wild Pitches

David Cone	129
Bobby Witt	124
Tom Candiotti	120
Orel Hershiser	119
John Smoltz	119
Chuck Finley	117
Juan Guzman	105
Mike Morgan	100
Tom Gordon	91
Jaime Navarro	91

GDPs Induced*

Scott Erickson	265
Greg Maddux	261
Kevin Brown	254
Chuck Finley	251
Tom Glavine	249
Orel Hershiser	249
Mike Morgan	239
Bobby Witt	207
Roger Clemens	204
2 pitchers tied with	199

*since 1987

GDP/9 IP
minimum 750 IP

Jamey Wright	1.23
Bob Wickman	1.20
Scott Erickson	1.18
Mike Hampton	1.15
Andy Pettitte	1.14
Mark Petkovsek	1.11
LaTroy Hawkins	1.10
Pat Rapp	1.10
Omar Olivares	1.09
Jim Abbott	1.07

Saves

John Franco	416
Jeff Montgomery	304
Doug Jones	301
John Wetteland	296
Rick Aguilera	289
Rod Beck	260
Roberto Hernandez	234
Trevor Hoffman	228
Gregg Olson	217
Robb Nen	185

Save %
minimum 50 SvOp

Trevor Hoffman	88.0
Mariano Rivera	85.4
Troy Percival	85.3
Jose Mesa	85.1
Billy Wagner	84.9
Rod Beck	84.7
John Wetteland	84.6
Robb Nen	84.5
Ugueth Urbina	84.3
Mark Wohlers	84.2

Games Finished

John Franco	711
Doug Jones	618
Jeff Montgomery	549
Rick Aguilera	513
Jesse Orosco	473
John Wetteland	466
Rod Beck	443
Roberto Hernandez	430
Gregg Olson	428
Dan Plesac	386

SB % Allowed*
minimum 750 IP

Terry Mulholland	37.1
Kirk Rueter	38.7
Omar Daal	40.0
Kenny Rogers	40.7
Rich DeLucia	45.5
Chan Ho Park	49.3
Wilson Alvarez	50.3
Greg Swindell	51.5
Rick Helling	51.8
Donovan Osborne	52.0

*since 1987

Player Profiles

There are plenty of guys who had dream seasons in 1999, including Rafael Palmeiro, Derek Jeter, Kevin Millwood, Ivan Rodriguez, Billy Wagner, Luis Gonzalez and Nomar Garciaparra. While all of them deserve a closer look at their numbers, we have space to focus on just three: Mark McGwire, Sammy Sosa and Pedro Martinez. These three profiles provide a wealth of information.

Once again, Sosa defies the free-swinger tag he earned earlier in his career. For a third straight season he saw *more* pitches per plate appearance than the ever-patient McGwire. Still, McGwire drew 55 more walks than Sosa in 51 fewer plate appearances.

Some of the difference in their pitches per plate appearance can be attributed to McGwire's success in hitting the first pitch he sees in an at-bat. McGwire hit 16 of his 65 homers on the first pitch, and those 16 longballs came in just 79 at-bats for a staggering slugging percentage of 1.051 in those situations. Remarkably, both McGwire (.405) and Sosa (.404) hit better than .400 when they put the first pitch in play.

A couple other oddities involving Sosa and McGwire are worth mentioning. Playing on artificial surfaces supposedly benefits hitters, as balls tend to move through turf infields faster. Yet Sosa batted just .229 in 105 at-bats on turf last season. Meanwhile, McGwire was a monster with runners in scoring position. In those 135 at-bats, he hit .356 and slugged at an .815 clip.

We might not have seen this kind of power production from Sosa and McGwire if more guys pitched like Martinez. Two points stand out about the 5-foot-11, 170-pound fireballer. One is that he gets stronger as time rolls on. It was true in most games, as Martinez allowed just a .163 batting average after the sixth inning and a .140 average after his 105th pitch in a game. He also showed incredible stamina as the season wore on, going 4-0 with a 0.86 ERA in his final six appearances in September and October. Second, he is tough when he's in less than comfortable situations. His ERA away from home was 1.88, and he allowed just a .134 batting average in close-and-late scenarios. He didn't allow a single homer with runners in scoring position or in close-and-late situations. All nine homers he allowed were solo shots.

The *Major League Handbook's* companion volume, *STATS Player Profiles 2000*, contains breakdowns like these for every major league player.

Pedro Martinez — Red Sox

	ERA	W	L	Sv	G	GS	IP	BB	SO	Avg	H	2B	3B	HR	RBI	OBP	SLG	CG	ShO	Sup	QS	#P/S	SB	CS	GB	FB	G/F
1999 Season	2.07	23	4	0	31	29	213.1	37	313	.205	160	38	0	9	51	.248	.288	5	1	6.03	24	112	21	10	204	157	1.30
Last Five Years	2.78	86	39	0	158	156	1099.2	307	1265	.212	853	160	18	91	343	.274	.329	27	10	4.90	109	110	93	37	1144	996	1.15

1999 Season

	ERA	W	L	Sv	G	GS	IP	H	HR	BB	SO		Avg	AB	H	2B	3B	HR	RBI	BB	SO	OBP	SLG
Home	2.22	13	2	0	17	16	117.2	96	6	17	167	vs. Left	.222	414	92	24	0	4	27	21	146	.266	.309
Away	1.88	10	2	0	14	13	95.2	64	3	20	146	vs. Right	.186	366	68	14	0	5	24	16	167	.227	.265
Day	2.58	10	0	0	11	10	69.2	60	3	14	90	Inning 1-6	.215	627	135	29	0	8	46	32	242	.258	.300
Night	1.82	13	4	0	20	19	143.2	100	6	23	223	Inning 7+	.163	153	25	9	0	1	5	5	71	.205	.242
Grass	1.90	21	2	0	27	25	184.1	136	9	31	265	None on	.203	487	99	26	0	9	9	27	201	.255	.312
Turf	3.10	2	2	0	4	4	29.0	24	0	6	48	Runners on	.208	293	61	12	0	0	42	10	112	.235	.249
April	2.21	4	1	0	5	5	36.2	29	1	7	48	Scoring Posn	.204	167	34	6	0	0	41	8	72	.236	.240
May	1.84	6	0	0	6	6	44.0	38	1	9	69	Close & Late	.134	67	9	3	0	0	3	3	31	.183	.179
June	2.25	4	1	0	5	5	36.0	23	2	6	48	None on/out	.200	205	41	19	0	0	0	6	82	.241	.293
July	5.03	1	1	0	3	3	19.2	26	1	2	22	vs. 1st Batr (relief)	.000	1	0	0	0	0	0	0	0	.500	.000
August	1.80	4	0	0	6	5	35.0	24	3	7	55	1st Inning Pitched	.193	109	21	4	0	2	7	5	37	.244	.284
Sept/Oct	0.86	4	0	0	6	5	42.0	20	1	6	71	First 75 Pitches	.213	507	108	26	0	6	31	26	196	.260	.300
Starter	2.07	22	4	0	29	29	208.1	157	8	36	306	Pitch 76-90	.193	88	17	4	0	1	7	6	31	.240	.273
Reliever	1.80	1	0	0	2	0	5.0	3	1	1	7	Pitch 91-105	.239	92	22	4	0	2	9	2	41	.253	.340
0-3 Days Rest (Start)	0.00	0	0	0	0	0	0.0	0	0	0	0	Pitch 106+	.140	93	13	4	0	0	4	3	45	.184	.183
4 Days Rest	2.21	9	4	0	14	14	101.2	78	2	20	154	First Pitch	.274	84	23	5	0	1	5	1	0	.284	.369
5+ Days Rest	1.94	13	0	0	15	15	106.2	79	6	16	152	Ahead in Count	.162	456	74	18	0	3	29	0	255	.171	.221
vs. AL	1.71	22	3	0	28	26	194.2	139	8	33	284	Behind in Count	.344	90	31	10	0	2	8	16	0	.450	.522
vs. NL	5.79	1	1	0	3	3	18.2	21	1	4	29	Two Strikes	.141	503	71	16	0	3	20	20	313	.180	.191
Pre-All Star	2.10	15	3	0	18	18	132.2	104	5	24	184	Pre-All Star	.213	489	104	24	0	5	31	24	184	.254	.292
Post-All Star	2.01	8	1	0	13	11	80.2	56	4	13	129	Post-All Star	.192	291	56	14	0	4	20	13	129	.237	.282

Last Five Years

	ERA	W	L	Sv	G	GS	IP	H	HR	BB	SO		Avg	AB	H	2B	3B	HR	RBI	BB	SO	OBP	SLG
Home	2.71	45	20	0	80	79	568.2	447	43	157	651	vs. Left	.219	2115	464	95	11	38	165	177	584	.284	.329
Away	2.86	41	19	0	78	77	531.0	406	48	150	614	vs. Right	.205	1900	389	65	7	53	178	130	681	.262	.330
Day	2.56	37	12	0	57	56	397.1	297	35	112	425	Inning 1-6	.211	3269	689	120	13	77	289	261	1032	.274	.326
Night	2.91	49	27	0	101	100	702.1	556	56	195	840	Inning 7+	.220	746	164	40	5	14	54	46	233	.270	.343
Grass	2.76	50	18	0	84	82	581.0	454	58	148	705	None on	.207	2543	526	110	12	67	67	182	792	.268	.339
Turf	2.81	36	21	0	74	74	518.2	399	33	159	560	Runners on	.222	1472	327	50	6	24	276	125	473	.284	.313
March/April	2.28	12	2	0	20	20	138.0	101	9	36	165	Scoring Posn	.212	803	170	23	0	16	245	88	288	.289	.324
May	2.43	20	3	0	30	30	214.2	170	14	57	240	Close & Late	.214	383	82	20	2	6	35	29	122	.272	.324
June	3.13	14	9	0	28	28	195.2	151	20	54	233	None on/out	.208	1064	221	56	6	23	23	78	316	.271	.336
July	3.42	12	9	0	24	24	168.1	139	18	46	163	vs. 1st Batr (relief)	.000	1	0	0	0	0	0	0	0	.500	.500
August	2.59	18	8	0	30	29	205.0	151	18	61	231	1st Inning Pitched	.191	550	105	23	2	14	40	38	173	.253	.316
Sept/Oct	2.83	10	8	0	26	25	178.0	141	12	53	233	First 75 Pitches	.205	2591	530	102	9	57	207	204	856	.269	.317
Starter	2.79	85	39	0	156	156	1094.2	850	90	306	1258	Pitch 76-90	.236	525	124	15	5	16	56	36	112	.289	.345
Reliever	1.80	1	0	0	2	0	5.0	3	1	1	7	Pitch 91-105	.219	452	99	17	2	12	44	34	152	.273	.345
0-3 Days Rest (Start)	2.25	0	1	0	1	1	8.0	5	0	2	7	Pitch 106+	.224	447	100	26	2	6	36	33	145	.284	.331
4 Days Rest	2.84	46	23	0	88	88	620.2	488	54	188	731	First Pitch	.279	505	141	28	7	7	44	13	0	.302	.404
5+ Days Rest	2.72	39	15	0	67	67	466.0	357	36	116	520	Ahead in Count	.152	2193	333	61	4	29	136	0	1070	.159	.223
vs. AL	2.13	41	9	0	60	58	430.2	314	27	100	546	Behind in Count	.351	575	202	44	2	33	89	133	0	.475	.607
vs. NL	3.20	45	30	0	98	98	669.0	539	64	207	719	Two Strikes	.138	2305	319	56	6	29	132	161	1265	.199	.206
Pre-All Star	2.65	49	17	0	85	85	598.2	459	48	160	688	Pre-All Star	.211	2179	459	94	8	48	176	160	688	.270	.327
Post-All Star	2.95	37	22	0	73	71	501.0	394	43	147	577	Post-All Star	.215	1836	394	66	10	43	167	147	577	.279	.332

Pitcher vs. Batter (career)

Pitches Best Vs.	Avg	AB	H	2B	3B	HR	RBI	BB	SO	OBP	SLG	Pitches Worst Vs.	Avg	AB	H	2B	3B	HR	RBI	BB	SO	OBP	SLG
Midre Cummings	.000	13	0	0	0	0	0	1	3	.071	.000	Carlos Baerga	.667	12	8	2	1	1	5	0	2	.667	1.250
Ken Griffey Jr.	.000	12	0	0	0	0	0	2	6	.133	.000	Marquis Grissom	.571	21	12	3	1	1	2	2	2	.609	.952
Albert Belle	.000	12	0	0	0	0	1	2	6	.133	.000	Mike Piazza	.412	17	7	1	0	3	5	0	3	.444	1.000
Vinny Castilla	.000	11	0	0	0	0	0	0	5	.000	.000	Luis Lopez	.400	10	4	0	0	2	4	1	3	.455	1.000
Marvin Benard	.077	13	1	0	0	0	0	0	4	.077	.077	Charles Johnson	.385	13	5	0	1	2	4	0	4	.385	1.000

	Avg	G	AB	R	H	2B	3B	HR	RBI	BB	SO	HBP	GDP	SB	CS	OBP	SLG	IBB	SH	SF	#Pit	#P/PA	GB	FB	G/F
1999 Season	.278	153	521	118	145	21	1	65	147	133	141	2	12	0	0	.424	.697	21	0	5	2451	3.71	113	202	0.56
Last Five Years	.287	698	2310	513	664	103	1	284	620	600	644	36	52	5	1	.438	.702	86	0	23	11366	3.83	444	894	0.50

1999 Season

	Avg	AB	H	2B	3B	HR	RBI	BB	SO	OBP	SLG		Avg	AB	H	2B	3B	HR	RBI	BB	SO	OBP	SLG
vs. Left	.254	122	31	7	0	16	30	36	32	.425	.705	First Pitch	.405	79	32	3	0	16	39	17	0	.505	1.051
vs. Right	.286	399	114	14	1	49	117	97	109	.423	.694	Ahead in Count	.321	131	42	8	1	17	43	65	0	.543	.786
Groundball	.314	175	55	8	0	28	62	34	38	.425	.840	Behind in Count	.194	227	44	6	0	16	36	0	110	.196	.432
Flyball	.239	88	21	1	1	11	24	16	26	.355	.648	Two Strikes	.144	229	33	6	0	16	36	51	141	.298	.380
Home	.285	260	74	12	1	37	89	70	64	.436	.765	Batting #3	.279	520	145	21	1	65	147	132	140	.423	.698
Away	.272	261	71	9	0	28	58	63	77	.411	.628	Batting #7	.000	0	0	0	0	0	0	1	0	1.000	.000
Day	.263	171	45	5	0	23	46	44	52	.412	.696	Other	.000	1	0	0	0	0	0	0	0	.000	.000
Night	.286	350	100	16	1	42	101	89	89	.429	.697	April	.239	67	16	4	0	5	10	18	19	.407	.522
Grass	.278	436	121	18	1	58	132	114	116	.425	.722	May	.272	92	25	4	0	10	27	22	24	.409	.641
Turf	.282	85	24	3	0	7	15	19	25	.413	.565	June	.258	93	24	5	0	8	23	26	23	.417	.570
Pre-All Star	.266	289	77	14	0	28	72	78	78	.422	.864	July	.295	88	26	2	0	16	30	22	21	.436	.864
Post-All Star	.293	232	68	7	1	37	75	55	63	.426	.810	August	.333	93	31	4	1	12	29	21	27	.453	.785
Scoring Posn	.356	135	48	5	0	19	87	47	33	.511	.815	Sept/Oct	.261	88	23	2	0	14	28	24	27	.416	.761
Close & Late	.235	81	19	1	0	5	14	33	29	.452	.432	vs. NL	.279	473	132	20	1	59	133	124	131	.427	.700
None on/out	.217	83	18	2	1	11	11	18	30	.363	.663												

1999 By Position

Position	Avg	AB	H	2B	3B	HR	RBI	BB	SO	OBP	SLG	G	GS	Innings	PO	A	E	DP	Fld Pct	Rng Fctr	In Zone	Outs	Zone Rtg	MLB Zone
As 1b	.279	520	145	21	1	65	147	132	140	.423	.698	151	150	1257.2	1181	80	13	119	.990	—	238	203	.853	.884

Last Five Years

	Avg	AB	H	2B	3B	HR	RBI	BB	SO	OBP	SLG		Avg	AB	H	2B	3B	HR	RBI	BB	SO	OBP	SLG
vs. Left	.285	550	157	27	0	69	138	174	149	.459	.711	First Pitch	.395	372	147	25	0	59	139	65	0	.491	.938
vs. Right	.288	1760	507	76	1	215	482	426	495	.431	.699	Ahead in Count	.389	488	190	29	1	93	199	271	0	.607	1.025
Groundball	.312	606	189	30	0	80	177	156	149	.458	.757	Behind in Count	.204	996	203	28	0	77	168	0	483	.212	.464
Flyball	.253	411	104	12	1	49	102	89	112	.397	.645	Two Strikes	.151	1082	163	20	0	71	158	264	644	.319	.366
Home	.298	1129	337	56	1	144	323	312	306	.455	.733	Batting #3	.286	1156	331	44	1	154	326	331	342	.446	.726
Away	.277	1181	327	47	0	140	297	288	338	.421	.672	Batting #4	.285	1126	321	57	0	126	286	259	295	.425	.671
Day	.293	817	239	41	0	104	216	231	231	.454	.725	Other	.429	28	12	2	0	4	8	10	7	.575	.929
Night	.285	1493	425	62	1	180	404	369	413	.429	.689	March/April	.287	275	79	20	0	30	81	80	75	.448	.687
Grass	.292	1981	578	91	1	247	545	527	555	.444	.713	May	.301	449	135	21	0	53	126	106	104	.435	.702
Turf	.261	329	86	12	0	37	75	73	89	.400	.635	June	.287	442	127	22	0	53	110	111	114	.436	.697
Pre-All Star	.292	1279	374	68	0	148	349	338	329	.443	.693	July	.273	363	99	13	0	44	86	95	97	.428	.672
Post-All Star	.281	1031	290	35	1	136	271	262	315	.431	.713	August	.291	368	107	15	1	42	94	101	125	.445	.679
Scoring Posn	.303	564	171	32	0	73	335	227	159	.496	.748	Sept/Oct	.283	413	117	12	0	62	123	107	129	.435	.763
Close & Late	.274	351	96	8	0	37	87	128	118	.470	.613	vs. AL	.286	1110	318	50	0	130	286	262	289	.428	.683
None on/out	.279	524	146	23	1	68	68	106	150	.407	.716	vs. NL	.288	1200	346	53	1	154	334	338	355	.446	.719

Batter vs. Pitcher (career)

Hits Best Against	Avg	AB	H	2B	3B	HR	RBI	BB	SO	OBP	SLG	Hits Worst Against	Avg	AB	H	2B	3B	HR	RBI	BB	SO	OBP	SLG
Brian Bohanon	.615	13	8	1	0	5	11	2	2	.688	1.846	Denny Neagle	.000	13	0	0	0	0	0	0	7	.000	.000
Andy Ashby	.474	19	9	3	0	5	10	1	4	.500	1.421	Ismael Valdes	.000	13	0	0	0	0	1	2	4	.125	.000
Livan Hernandez	.455	11	5	1	0	3	5	2	2	.538	1.364	Darryl Kile	.083	12	1	0	0	0	1	1	4	.154	.083
Mark Gardner	.444	9	4	2	0	2	4	3	2	.583	1.333	Rich DeLucia	.105	19	2	1	0	0	0	1	4	.150	.158
Rick Reed	.417	12	5	1	0	3	6	3	1	.533	1.250	Eric Plunk	.105	19	2	0	0	0	3	4	9	.261	.105

Sammy Sosa — Cubs

Age 31 – Bats Right

	Avg	G	AB	R	H	2B	3B	HR	RBI	BB	SO	HBP	GDP	SB	CS	OBP	SLG	IBB	SH	SF	#Pit	#P/PA	GB	FB	G/F
1999 Season	.288	162	625	114	180	24	2	63	141	78	171	3	17	7	8	.367	.635	8	0	6	2857	4.01	173	192	0.90
Last Five Years	.278	751	2972	511	826	113	11	241	637	288	784	16	75	99	41	.343	.567	48	0	22	12876	3.90	891	870	1.02

1999 Season

	Avg	AB	H	2B	3B	HR	RBI	BB	SO	OBP	SLG		Avg	AB	H	2B	3B	HR	RBI	BB	SO	OBP	SLG
vs. Left	.313	163	51	9	1	18	37	23	46	.396	.712	First Pitch	.404	52	21	4	0	9	17	7	0	.467	1.000
vs. Right	.279	462	129	15	1	45	104	55	125	.356	.608	Ahead in Count	.338	157	53	7	1	20	48	31	0	.453	.777
Groundball	.282	202	57	8	1	14	38	14	55	.332	.540	Behind in Count	.250	280	70	10	1	19	46	0	135	.248	.496
Flyball	.336	113	38	3	0	13	24	17	30	.423	.708	Two Strikes	.201	313	63	9	1	18	49	40	171	.290	.409
Home	.325	308	100	15	1	33	71	44	76	.406	.701	Batting #3	.257	327	84	11	1	31	64	39	95	.340	.581
Away	.252	317	80	9	1	30	70	34	95	.328	.571	Batting #4	.322	298	96	13	1	32	77	39	76	.396	.695
Day	.311	351	109	15	1	39	88	48	92	.392	.692	Other	.000	0	0	0	0	0	0	0	0	.000	.000
Night	.259	274	71	9	1	24	53	30	79	.333	.562	April	.253	79	20	6	0	4	11	9	27	.330	.481
Grass	.300	520	156	19	2	57	125	64	138	.376	.673	May	.321	109	35	4	0	13	27	14	22	.398	.716
Turf	.229	105	24	5	0	6	16	14	33	.322	.448	June	.288	104	30	2	1	13	28	10	27	.353	.702
Pre-All Star	.286	336	96	14	1	32	74	35	88	.353	.619	July	.349	106	37	8	1	10	27	8	26	.388	.726
Post-All Star	.291	289	84	10	1	31	67	43	83	.382	.654	August	.284	109	31	2	0	15	28	20	36	.400	.716
Scoring Posn	.299	154	46	5	1	16	81	24	36	.380	.656	Sept/Oct	.229	118	27	2	0	8	20	17	33	.324	.449
Close & Late	.297	91	27	3	0	7	25	14	25	.387	.560	vs. AL	.328	61	20	5	0	2	10	4	15	.358	.508
None on/out	.347	124	43	7	1	10	10	15	28	.417	.661	vs. NL	.284	564	160	19	2	61	131	74	156	.367	.649

1999 By Position

Position	Avg	AB	H	2B	3B	HR	RBI	BB	SO	OBP	SLG	G	GS	Innings	PO	A	E	DP	Fld Pct	Rng Fctr	In Zone	In Outs	Zone Rtg	MLB Zone
As cf	.326	86	28	2	1	12	23	13	19	.410	.791	25	23	194.2	77	3	1	0	.988	3.70	93	73	.785	.815
As rf	.282	539	152	22	1	51	118	65	152	.359	.610				322	5	8	3	.976	2.41	371	307	.827	.810

Last Five Years

	Avg	AB	H	2B	3B	HR	RBI	BB	SO	OBP	SLG		Avg	AB	H	2B	3B	HR	RBI	BB	SO	OBP	SLG
vs. Left	.277	729	202	34	2	59	152	106	196	.368	.572	First Pitch	.357	333	119		3	32	88	39	0	.424	.709
vs. Right	.278	2243	624	79	9	182	485	182	588	.334	.565	Ahead in Count	.382	633	242	38	2	85	223	100	0	.465	.852
Groundball	.306	837	256	40	4	56	171	67	193	.361	.564	Behind in Count	.215	1383	298	40	5	74	199	0	621	.218	.412
Flyball	.284	510	145	14	0	45	111	45	160	.341	.576	Two Strikes	.184	1507	277	33	3	68	188	148	784	.258	.345
Home	.290	1472	427	52	6	138	356	154	363	.356	.615	Batting #3	.272	1088	296	33	2	94	226	103	288	.337	.565
Away	.266	1500	399	61	5	103	281	134	421	.329	.519	Batting #4	.282	1882	530	80	9	147	410	185	494	.346	.568
Day	.289	1660	479	63	8	145	375	178	419	.357	.598	Other	.000	2	0	0	0	0	1	0	2	.000	.000
Night	.264	1312	347	50	3	96	262	110	365	.324	.527	March/April	.267	415	111	18	2	21	63	37	111	.328	.472
Grass	.287	2435	698	95	11	216	558	246	625	.353	.601	May	.309	527	163	25	2	48	120	54	135	.374	.638
Turf	.238	537	128	18	0	25	79	42	159	.296	.412	June	.271	558	151	21	2	50	126	33	133	.310	.584
Pre-All Star	.279	1649	460	72	6	124	334	138	421	.335	.555	July	.292	530	155	27	1	38	121	54	131	.362	.562
Post-All Star	.277	1323	366	41	5	117	303	150	363	.352	.580	August	.268	519	139	13	3	53	125	58	155	.342	.611
Scoring Posn	.289	793	229	29	6	65	384	114	207	.372	.586	Sept/Oct	.253	423	107	9	1	31	82	52	119	.333	.499
Close & Late	.277	469	130	17	1	35	107	52	127	.347	.542	vs. AL	.329	164	54	13	0	11	34	13	40	.374	.610
None on/out	.277	620	172	24	2	45	45	53	141	.336	.540	vs. NL	.275	2808	772	100	11	230	603	275	744	.341	.564

Batter vs. Pitcher (career)

Hits Best Against	Avg	AB	H	2B	3B	HR	RBI	BB	SO	OBP	SLG	Hits Worst Against	Avg	AB	H	2B	3B	HR	RBI	BB	SO	OBP	SLG
Ken Hill	.500	12	6	1	0	2	2	3	1	.600	1.083	Doug Henry	.000	12	0	0	0	0	0	1	4	.077	.000
Mark Petkovsek	.462	13	6	1	0	3	8	1	1	.500	1.231	Mike Jackson	.000	12	0	0	0	0	0	2	6	.143	.000
Cal Eldred	.444	9	4	0	0	3	5	1	3	.455	1.444	Juan Acevedo	.091	11	1	0	0	0	0	0	3	.091	.091
Julian Tavarez	.429	7	3	2	0	1	3	3	1	.636	1.143	Ugueth Urbina	.091	11	1	0	0	0	1	0	5	.091	.091
Rheal Cormier	.417	12	5	1	0	4	8	1	1	.462	1.500	Brian Bohanon	.091	11	1	0	0	0	1	1	2	.167	.091

Manager Tendencies

One of the things about baseball which appeals to many of us is the game's endless opportunity for analysis. . . and few things are analyzed more than managerial decisions. Major league skippers may not have batting averages and slugging percentages to point to at the end of the season, but when it comes time to judge their performance and production, there's no reason we can't take a look at their statistics.

Which manager posted the best stolen-base success rate?

Which skippers were constantly tinkering with their lineups?

Which managers wore out a path to the pitching mound?

It's questions like these that get our second-guessing juices going, and it's questions like these that inspired the following pages, which look at managerial tendencies in a number of situations. Once again, the skippers are compared based on offense, defense, lineups, and pitching use. We don't rank the managers; there is plenty of room for argument on whether certain moves are good or bad. We are simply providing fodder for the discussion.

Offensively, managers have control over bunting, stealing and the timing of hit-and-runs. The *Handbook* looks at the quantity, timing and success of these moves.

Defensively, the *Handbook* looks at the success of pitchouts, the frequency of intentional walks, and the pattern of defensive substitutions.

Most managers spend large amounts of their time devising lineups. The *Handbook* shows the number of lineups used, as well as the platoon percentage. The use of pinch-hitters and pinch-runners is also explored.

Finally, how does the manager use pitchers? For starters, the *Handbook* shows slow and quick hooks, along with the number of times a starter was allowed to throw more than 120 and 140 pitches. For relievers, we look at the number of relief appearances, mid-inning changes and how often a pitcher gets a save going more than one inning (a rare occurrence these days). The categories include:

Stolen Base Success Percentage: Stolen bases divided by attempts.

Pitchout Runners Moving: The number of times the opposition is running when a manager calls a pitchout.

Double Steals: The number of double steals attempted in 1999.

Out Percentage: The proportion of stolen bases with that number of outs.

Sacrifice Bunt Attempts: A bunt is considered a sac attempt if no runner is on third, there are no outs, or the pitcher attempts a bunt.

Sacrifice Bunt Success%: A bunt that results in a sacrifice or a hit, divided by the number of attempts.

Favorite Inning: The most common inning in which an event occurred.

Hit-and-Run Success: The hit-and-run results in baserunner advancement with no double play.

Intentional Walk Situation: Runners on base, first base open, and anyone but the pitcher up. The teams must be within two runs of each other, or the tying run must be on base, at bat or on deck.

Defensive Substitutions: Straight defensive substitutions, with the team leading by four runs or less.

Number of Lineups: Based on batting order, 1-8 for National Leaguers, 1-9 for American Leaguers.

Percent LHB vs. RHSP and RHB vs. LHSP: A measure of platooning. A batter is considered to always have the platoon advantage if he is a switch-hitter.

Percent PH platoon: Frequency the manager gets his pinch-hitter the platoon advantage. Switch-hitters always have the advantage.

Score Diff: The most common score differential on which an intentional walk is called for.

Slow and Quick Hooks: See the glossary for complete information. This measures how often a pitcher is left in longer than is standard practice, or pulled earlier than normal.

Mid-Inning Change: The number of times a manager changed pitchers in the middle of an inning.

1-Batter Appearances: The number of times a pitcher was brought in to face only one batter. Called the "Tony La Russa special" because of his penchant for trying to orchestrate specific matchups for specific situations.

3 Pitchers (2 runs or less): The club gives up two runs or less in a game, but uses at least three pitchers.

Offense

	G	Att	SB%	Ptchout Rn Mvg	2nd SB-CS	3rd SB-CS	Home SB-CS	Double Steals	--Out Percentage-- 0	1	2	Sacrifice Bunts Att	Suc. %	Fav. Inning	Sqz	Hit & Run Att	Suc. %
AL Managers																	
Collins, Terry, Ana	133	93	61.3	2	53-34	4-2	0-0	1	19.4	32.3	48.4	39	79.5	3	1	76	40.8
Fregosi, Jim, Tor	162	167	71.3	7	109-46	10-2	0-0	1	19.2	36.5	44.3	41	87.8	7	0	61	31.1
Hargrove, Mike, Cle	162	197	74.6	3	119-42	28-5	0-3	9	21.8	34.5	43.7	82	87.8	1	0	59	37.3
Howe, Art, Oak	162	107	65.4	7	61-32	9-3	0-2	3	12.1	46.7	41.1	53	88.7	2	0	55	49.1
Kelly, Tom, Min	161	178	66.3	2	109-54	8-3	1-3	6	11.8	38.8	49.4	46	80.4	8	5	108	25.9
Maddon, Joe, Ana	29	23	60.9	1	14-9	0-0	0-0	0	8.7	47.8	43.5	12	83.3	7	0	18	27.8
Manuel, Jerry, CWS	162	160	68.8	2	104-45	7-5	0-0	2	20.6	36.3	43.1	69	76.8	3	1	90	32.2
Miller, Ray, Bal	162	153	69.9	6	95-40	11-5	1-1	3	23.5	26.1	50.3	58	79.3	7	3	75	40.0
Muser, Tony, KC	161	166	76.5	3	122-36	4-2	1-1	3	22.3	33.1	44.6	69	78.3	5	1	101	34.7
Oates, Johnny, Tex	162	165	67.3	2	97-47	14-5	0-2	2	22.4	41.8	35.8	41	92.7	7	2	73	31.5
Parrish, Larry, Det	161	178	60.7	3	100-62	8-5	0-3	2	23.0	32.0	44.9	47	87.2	3	6	101	33.7
Piniella, Lou, Sea	162	175	74.3	4	110-40	18-3	2-2	8	18.3	36.6	45.1	49	85.7	8	4	95	30.5
Rothschild, Larry, TB	162	122	59.8	0	67-41	6-7	0-1	1	26.2	39.3	34.4	45	80.0	8	2	86	37.2
Torre, Joe, NYY	126	129	64.3	1	71-39	11-6	1-1	2	25.6	31.0	43.4	31	83.9	3	1	71	36.6
Williams, Jimy, Bos	162	106	63.2	2	64-35	1-4	2-0	1	32.1	26.4	41.5	47	83.0	8	2	58	48.3
Zimmer, Don, NYY	36	32	65.6	1	20-8	1-3	0-0	1	28.1	37.5	34.4	3	66.7	1	0	22	36.4
NL Managers																	
Alou, Felipe, Mon	162	121	57.9	5	61-47	9-2	0-2	2	15.7	39.7	44.6	84	85.7	8	6	81	30.9
Baker, Dusty, SF	162	165	66.1	4	99-50	10-6	0-0	1	23.0	38.8	38.2	113	78.8	4	5	83	27.7
Bochy, Bruce, SD	162	241	72.2	6	141-56	28-9	5-2	15	23.7	41.5	34.9	60	68.3	3	2	92	39.1
Boles, John, Fla	162	138	66.7	2	88-42	4-1	0-3	1	31.2	29.7	39.1	67	76.1	3	2	95	27.4
Cox, Bobby, Atl	162	214	69.2	6	125-56	22-5	1-5	4	20.6	34.1	45.3	89	82.0	3	6	94	42.6
Dierker, Larry, Hou	162	241	68.9	4	133-63	32-10	1-2	11	15.8	34.9	49.4	106	81.1	6	5	93	35.5
Francona, Terry, Phi	162	160	78.1	0	113-32	12-2	0-1	2	13.8	31.9	54.4	81	86.4	3	7	67	34.3
Garner, Phil, Mil	112	75	70.7	1	42-18	11-4	0-0	3	14.7	36.0	49.3	85	80.0	3	9	46	28.3
Johnson, Davey, LA	162	235	71.1	7	128-56	37-10	2-2	18	19.6	42.6	37.9	89	87.6	5	7	103	35.9
La Russa, Tony, StL	161	182	73.6	1	113-37	20-8	1-3	9	17.6	42.3	40.1	103	78.6	8	4	117	39.3
Lamont, Gene, Pit	161	156	71.8	3	103-39	8-5	1-0	6	19.2	31.4	49.4	107	83.2	3	14	80	26.3
Lefebvre, Jim, Mil	49	39	71.8	0	23-10	5-1	0-0	4	20.5	28.2	51.3	26	88.5	3	3	11	27.3
Leyland, Jim, Col	162	113	61.9	1	58-34	12-7	0-2	5	21.2	41.6	37.2	88	67.0	3	3	66	28.8
McKeon, Jack, Cin	163	218	75.2	5	136-44	28-8	0-2	8	20.2	29.8	50.0	88	81.8	5	0	77	28.6
Riggleman, Jim, ChC	162	104	57.7	2	55-39	5-4	0-1	2	24.0	29.8	46.2	94	72.3	5	9	78	34.6
Showalter, Buck, Ari	162	176	77.8	4	119-35	16-3	2-1	3	34.1	21.0	44.9	75	86.7	3	9	80	33.8
Valentine, Bobby, NYM	163	211	71.1	15	124-49	26-10	0-2	6	28.9	32.7	38.4	72	94.4	5	8	119	37.0

Defense

	G	Pitchout Total	Runners Moving	CS%	Non-PO CS%	IBB	Pct. of Situations	Favorite Score Diff.	Defensive Subs Total	Favorite Inning	Pos. 1	Pos. 2	Pos. 3
AL Managers													
Collins, Terry, Ana	133	7	1	100.0	35.8	10	1.9	-1	16	7	c-4	lf-4	rf-4
Fregosi, Jim, Tor	162	4	2	100.0	29.1	19	2.8	-2	6	8	cf-3	3b-2	2b-1
Hargrove, Mike, Cle	162	28	5	60.0	27.0	36	5.4	-1	22	9	3b-5	c-4	2b-4
Howe, Art, Oak	162	43	11	45.5	30.7	32	4.6	0	56	8	2b-17	lf-16	cf-13
Kelly, Tom, Min	161	13	1	100.0	33.0	10	1.7	-2	30	8	2b-13	cf-5	ss-4
Maddon, Joe, Ana	29	7	0	—	44.4	3	2.7	-2	1	8	2b-1	ph-0	ph-0
Manuel, Jerry, CWS	162	22	8	25.0	31.4	22	3.6	-2	39	9	lf-19	3b-13	cf-6
Miller, Ray, Bal	162	24	3	0.0	35.7	21	3.4	0	18	9	3b-9	rf-3	c-2
Muser, Tony, KC	161	20	3	33.3	30.6	28	4.7	0	12	9	1b-6	ss-2	rf-2
Oates, Johnny, Tex	162	14	3	100.0	51.0	16	2.7	-2	7	4	1b-2	cf-2	rf-2
Parrish, Larry, Det	161	24	4	0.0	36.4	13	2.3	-2	19	7	cf-6	ss-3	lf-3
Piniella, Lou, Sea	162	31	10	80.0	28.6	27	4.3	0	30	8	rf-11	lf-8	1b-7
Rothschild, Larry, TB	162	15	3	33.3	40.7	11	1.7	-1	37	8	3b-11	lf-8	cf-8
Torre, Joe, NYY	126	12	2	100.0	27.8	15	2.8	-2	10	8	lf-4	1b-3	3b-2
Williams, Jimy, Bos	162	75	22	59.1	23.1	15	2.2	-2	9	8	c-4	3b-2	ss-2
Zimmer, Don, NYY	36	5	1	0.0	20.9	4	2.8	-2	0	0	—	—	—
NL Managers													
Alou, Felipe, Mon	162	26	8	37.5	22.4	28	4.0	-2	55	8	cf-14	2b-13	1b-7
Baker, Dusty, SF	162	40	5	20.0	29.4	28	4.3	-1	16	9	rf-4	2b-3	lf-3
Bochy, Bruce, SD	162	29	7	42.9	27.6	39	6.1	-2	21	8	cf-7	1b-4	3b-4
Boles, John, Fla	162	32	8	37.5	41.8	39	5.9	-2	14	8	lf-4	1b-3	2b-3
Cox, Bobby, Atl	162	54	13	69.2	25.7	37	6.4	0	34	8	1b-15	lf-8	ss-6
Dierker, Larry, Hou	162	10	3	66.7	30.6	10	1.7	0	22	7	cf-12	ss-3	3b-2
Francona, Terry, Phi	162	27	9	55.6	25.0	17	3.0	-2	31	8	2b-25	lf-3	ss-2
Garner, Phil, Mil	112	57	16	43.8	18.8	19	4.2	1	5	9	c-2	ss-2	1b-1
Johnson, Davey, LA	162	28	8	25.0	26.5	18	2.6	-1	9	9	2b-4	lf-3	c-1
La Russa, Tony, StL	161	30	9	44.4	46.4	31	4.3	-2	28	7	lf-6	2b-5	rf-5
Lamont, Gene, Pit	161	28	3	66.7	32.9	40	5.8	-1	24	8	rf-15	2b-2	ss-2
Lefebvre, Jim, Mil	49	1	0	—	16.7	15	5.6	-2	10	9	c-6	ss-3	lf-1
Leyland, Jim, Col	162	11	1	0.0	28.0	29	4.3	-2	12	8	lf-4	rf-3	1b-2
McKeon, Jack, Cin	163	14	0	—	21.5	43	5.9	-2	38	8	rf-19	lf-12	2b-3
Riggleman, Jim, ChC	162	20	4	50.0	29.5	35	5.7	-1	30	8	lf-12	cf-12	c-2
Showalter, Buck, Ari	162	15	6	66.7	31.3	34	5.2	0	17	8	ss-8	1b-6	rf-2
Valentine, Bobby, NYM	163	51	8	50.0	23.5	36	5.7	-2	26	8	lf-13	rf-8	cf-2

Lineups

		Starting Lineup			Substitutions					
	G	Lineups Used	%LHB vs. RHSP	%RHB vs. LHSP	#PH	Percent PH Platoon	PH BA	PH HR	#PR	PR SB-CS
AL Managers										
Collins, Terry, Ana	133	113	53.1	66.3	93	77.4	.260	1	26	1-1
Fregosi, Jim, Tor	162	109	55.2	76.2	96	80.2	.238	4	26	1-1
Hargrove, Mike, Cle	162	123	62.7	76.3	99	68.7	.271	1	25	3-0
Howe, Art, Oak	162	129	58.2	75.3	144	75.0	.270	0	62	3-1
Kelly, Tom, Min	161	152	63.4	82.3	165	84.8	.250	2	21	2-1
Maddon, Joe, Ana	29	19	57.1	61.1	29	82.8	.238	1	4	0-0
Manuel, Jerry, CWS	162	109	51.6	86.9	79	79.7	.250	0	35	3-0
Miller, Ray, Bal	162	116	43.6	74.9	145	66.2	.276	4	42	2-2
Muser, Tony, KC	161	110	37.8	86.5	118	77.1	.156	0	31	0-0
Oates, Johnny, Tex	162	71	52.8	71.9	57	82.5	.244	1	28	0-0
Parrish, Larry, Det	161	124	38.6	87.7	102	94.1	.194	2	20	1-2
Piniella, Lou, Sea	162	130	34.9	86.3	122	79.5	.180	2	38	3-3
Rothschild, Larry, TB	162	138	47.8	81.4	67	71.6	.143	0	32	1-1
Torre, Joe, NYY	126	76	57.2	86.2	103	84.5	.235	1	57	3-0
Williams, Jimy, Bos	162	111	54.7	87.6	123	75.6	.287	4	35	1-1
Zimmer, Don, NYY	36	27	55.2	79.2	10	80.0	.222	0	6	1-0
NL Managers										
Alou, Felipe, Mon	162	143	34.1	96.3	247	82.2	.254	3	33	5-4
Baker, Dusty, SF	162	120	56.8	76.3	233	73.4	.216	4	16	0-0
Bochy, Bruce, SD	162	137	50.1	84.6	298	78.5	.203	7	51	6-2
Boles, John, Fla	162	121	36.2	90.6	255	58.4	.205	8	24	0-2
Cox, Bobby, Atl	162	76	45.3	90.7	272	80.9	.208	3	51	11-1
Dierker, Larry, Hou	162	114	36.2	99.0	248	69.0	.234	5	38	13-5
Francona, Terry, Phi	162	85	42.1	75.9	239	54.0	.255	5	13	0-0
Garner, Phil, Mil	112	69	51.5	69.4	182	67.6	.271	3	15	0-1
Johnson, Davey, LA	162	108	31.5	95.5	236	82.2	.271	4	22	2-1
La Russa, Tony, StL	161	138	33.1	82.9	264	71.6	.208	3	32	2-0
Lamont, Gene, Pit	161	108	51.0	79.9	241	75.5	.229	6	12	0-0
Lefebvre, Jim, Mil	49	34	50.5	84.0	106	51.9	.152	1	2	0-0
Leyland, Jim, Col	162	124	48.3	77.6	294	68.7	.278	9	11	0-0
McKeon, Jack, Cin	163	95	37.7	85.1	251	78.1	.257	6	30	1-2
Riggleman, Jim, ChC	162	122	54.3	70.9	312	56.7	.211	8	25	0-1
Showalter, Buck, Ari	162	97	60.5	67.8	220	69.1	.319	5	20	1-0
Valentine, Bobby, NYM	163	76	48.8	75.3	323	75.5	.198	2	43	2-2

Pitching

		Starters					Relievers				
	G	Slow Hooks	Quick Hooks	> 120 Pitches	> 140 Pitches	3 Days Rest	Relief App	Mid-Inning Change	Save > 1 IP	1st Batter Platoon Pct	1-Batter App	3 Pitchers (<=2 runs)
AL Managers											
Collins, Terry, Ana	133	16	10	10	0	3	315	163	2	65.1	23	10
Fregosi, Jim, Tor	162	23	14	7	0	1	377	181	10	59.4	23	21
Hargrove, Mike, Cle	162	21	17	15	0	1	466	187	3	66.3	47	23
Howe, Art, Oak	162	18	12	5	0	0	406	234	19	62.8	44	30
Kelly, Tom, Min	161	13	20	6	0	3	418	220	13	62.8	41	15
Maddon, Joe, Ana	29	0	6	4	0	0	85	47	0	71.8	9	3
Manuel, Jerry, CWS	162	26	21	9	0	2	409	161	8	64.5	31	21
Miller, Ray, Bal	162	19	17	21	0	2	393	188	4	66.4	40	17
Muser, Tony, KC	161	12	16	21	0	2	416	201	10	64.4	26	11
Oates, Johnny, Tex	162	14	18	17	0	4	439	221	6	67.4	37	24
Parrish, Larry, Det	161	26	12	9	0	0	421	186	2	62.9	29	26
Piniella, Lou, Sea	162	20	22	21	1	2	346	165	10	61.7	24	17
Rothschild, Larry, TB	162	20	22	20	1	1	453	213	8	62.0	38	20
Torre, Joe, NYY	126	6	10	26	0	0	276	130	11	63.4	24	13
Williams, Jimy, Bos	162	8	32	13	0	2	412	186	17	60.9	25	33
Zimmer, Don, NYY	36	6	2	2	0	0	83	41	1	56.6	11	4
NL Managers											
Alou, Felipe, Mon	162	15	20	5	0	1	432	172	10	55.1	35	24
Baker, Dusty, SF	162	18	11	27	2	1	450	175	0	69.6	47	25
Bochy, Bruce, SD	162	12	19	4	0	0	403	144	5	63.3	18	23
Boles, John, Fla	162	13	22	16	1	1	453	194	6	61.3	45	25
Cox, Bobby, Atl	162	14	10	13	0	5	394	97	6	49.0	28	33
Dierker, Larry, Hou	162	12	5	10	0	5	339	98	13	49.3	9	23
Francona, Terry, Phi	162	20	18	16	1	1	441	157	7	63.5	27	22
Garner, Phil, Mil	112	16	13	4	0	4	294	124	5	66.0	25	11
Johnson, Davey, LA	162	16	16	8	0	2	399	149	4	66.4	32	19
La Russa, Tony, StL	161	14	26	13	1	2	454	199	14	64.8	38	19
Lamont, Gene, Pit	161	13	19	16	0	0	426	158	7	60.0	30	17
Lefebvre, Jim, Mil	49	1	5	2	0	0	159	69	0	68.6	21	6
Leyland, Jim, Col	162	29	11	19	2	20	421	148	5	66.2	35	17
McKeon, Jack, Cin	163	9	25	9	0	0	381	154	28	64.8	26	19
Riggleman, Jim, ChC	162	19	16	8	0	5	441	176	4	68.1	33	13
Showalter, Buck, Ari	162	12	9	25	2	0	382	149	3	65.4	34	22
Valentine, Bobby, NYM	163	12	16	13	0	3	439	141	8	55.8	25	35

2000 Batter Projections

STATS has been publishing player projections in the *Major League Handbook* since our first edition in 1990, and they've proven their worth over the years. Using Bill James' similarity scores to compare actual player performances to our projections, our average score last year was 897 on a scale of 1 to 1,000. That's quite good (according to Bill, two players with a similarity score of 900 would be considered "truly similar") and consistent with previous year performances. For eight years in a row, the average similarity score for our projections has been right around 900 each year.

Here's a more detailed report card on our 1999 projections, using similarity scores:

Sim Score	# of Players
950+	82
900-949	152
850-899	101
800-849	44
750-799	27
700-749	4
>700	26

Bill says that two players with similarity scores of 950 or greater are "unusually similar," so to have 82 players with scores that high seems pretty darned good.

Our most accurate projections last year were for two reserve catchers:

Bill Haselman	Avg	G	AB	R	H	2B	3B	HR	RBI	BB	SO	SB	CS	SimScr
Actual 1999	.273	48	143	13	39	8	0	4	14	10	26	2	0	
Projected 1999	.257	55	140	17	36	8	0	5	20	9	25	1	1	986
Greg Myers	Avg	G	AB	R	H	2B	3B	HR	RBI	BB	SO	SB	CS	SimScr
Actual 1999	.265	84	200	19	53	6	0	5	24	26	30	0	0	
Projected 1999	.243	80	210	23	51	11	1	5	26	17	38	0	0	986

Our worst projections were for two first basemen we thought would play regularly in the majors, but who wound up playing only briefly:

David Ortiz	Avg	G	AB	R	H	2B	3B	HR	RBI	BB	SO	SB	CS	SimScr
Actual 1999	.000	10	20	1	0	0	0	0	0	5	12	0	0	
Projected 1999	.294	135	435	68	128	32	1	17	74	41	119	3	4	622
Calvin Pickering	Avg	G	AB	R	H	2B	3B	HR	RBI	BB	SO	SB	CS	SimScr
Actual 1999	.125	23	40	4	5	1	0	1	5	11	16	0	0	
Projected 1999	.278	138	417	67	116	20	1	23	80	58	113	3	5	639

Guess we'll have to get to work on projecting guys to hit .000.

Among players who had at least 400 plate appearances last year, our best projections were for Scott Brosius and Troy Glaus:

Scott Brosius	Avg	G	AB	R	H	2B	3B	HR	RBI	BB	SO	SB	CS	SimScr
Actual 1999	.247	133	473	64	117	26	1	17	71	39	74	9	3	
Projected 1999	.263	135	486	72	128	23	1	16	62	50	96	8	4	978
Troy Glaus	Avg	G	AB	R	H	2B	3B	HR	RBI	BB	SO	SB	CS	SimScr
Actual 1999	.240	154	551	85	132	29	0	29	79	71	143	5	1	
Projected 1999	.253	146	538	77	136	29	1	25	88	52	150	5	4	977

We think we can pat ourselves on the back for those two: we correctly predicted that Brosius would fall back to earth after hitting .300 in 1998, and we were also right on about Glaus, a talented young player who's still learning to hit major league pitching.

We're also pretty proud about our 1999 projection for Albert Belle. Remember all the guys who were saying Belle would threaten Mark McGwire's record after moving to Camden Yards? Our projection system forecast more modest production for Albert, and turned out to be right on the money:

Albert Belle	Avg	G	AB	R	H	2B	3B	HR	RBI	BB	SO	SB	CS	SimScr
Actual 1999	.297	161	610	108	181	36	1	37	117	101	82	17	3	
Projected 1999	.300	156	597	106	179	41	2	41	128	77	89	6	3	953

We're not this good *all* the time, of course. Like a lot of other people, we got carried away with J.D. Drew fever:

J.D. Drew	Avg	G	AB	R	H	2B	3B	HR	RBI	BB	SO	SB	CS	SimScr
Actual 1999	.242	104	368	72	89	16	6	13	39	50	77	19	3	
Projected 1999	.305	152	561	109	171	34	3	29	103	96	141	3	13	765

We also underestimated what McGwire and Sammy Sosa would do for an encore:

Mark McGwire	Avg	G	AB	R	H	2B	3B	HR	RBI	BB	SO	SB	CS	SimScr
Actual 1999	.278	153	521	118	145	21	1	65	147	133	141	0	0	
Projected 1999	.264	147	526	103	139	22	0	54	117	138	158	1	1	913
Sammy Sosa	Avg	G	AB	R	H	2B	3B	HR	RBI	BB	SO	SB	CS	SimScr
Actual 1999	.288	162	625	114	180	24	2	63	141	78	171	7	8	
Projected 1999	.266	161	643	105	171	24	4	48	130	58	173	25	9	898

So we're not perfect, but we'd venture to say we're pretty good. In the meantime, we're trying to make our projection system even better. Read on.

—Don Zminda

Updating the Batter Projection System

Ten years ago, in preparation for the debut of the 1990 *Major League Handbook*, Bill James and I developed a system to project batting statistics for major league hitters to be published in the book. The product was successful in two different ways: it produced good projections and it was very well received by the public. Since that time, there has only been one significant enhancement to the system. A few years ago the home run projection technique was modified by Bill James. The new home run technique represented a huge improvement to this aspect of the system.

In the last 10 years, much has changed. The most important aspect that has changed is the ability to look at our historical database. Ten years ago we didn't have this data, but we do now. Not only do we have more data, we have more tools with which to analyze the data. Spreadsheets now have multiple regression formulae built right in, allowing for extensive analysis and testing.

We've been overdue for a review of the system. The time is now.

Summary of Changes

Without going into great detail on the specifics of the changes we have made and are contemplating making in the future, here are the major highlights:

1. This is Phase I of a multi-phase project to improve on an already outstanding system.

2. The improvements in this phase are clear-cut, but not substantial.

3. All statistical categories were reviewed. There was only one statistic, runs scored, where a change to the basis of calculation was beneficial.

4. In the current system, some individual statistics are projected based on three-year rates. Others are based on career rates. Still others are based on combining historical data in a variety of ways. Every statistic was analyzed to determine how career, five-year, three-year and one-year historical performance compare as a basis for projections. Based upon this analysis, it was determined that the current basis for each statistic is good, but might be improved in future analyses. This is the starting point for Phase II of this project.

5. The biggest changes in the new system involve age modifiers. Revised age modifiers were developed for every statistic.

6. The biggest change in age modifiers was done for hits. In the old system a technique was utilized wherein a player's current age relative to his career age created an age modifier designed to lower expected hits, depending on how far a player was from the center of his career. This system was set aside. The technique utilized for most of the other statistics wherein age modifiers are related to specific ages was substituted for projecting hits. The new system resulted in improved results.

7. Age modifiers for home runs were added. Previously there were no age modifiers for home runs.

The Final Results

In order to assess the performance of the new system, we compared recalculated projections based on the new system and compared them to projections on the old system. Each statistic of each projection was reviewed to determine whether or not the new projection for that statistic was better or worse than the old system when compared to the actual batting statistics for that year. In order to eliminate the playing-time factor, the playing time (games and at-bats) were forced to be equal to actual performance in both the old and new projection systems. Table 1 below summarizes the results. As you can see, the table also presents data by various age groupings. In the section comparing all players regardless of age, every statistic category improved under the new method. When broken down by age groupings, the vast majority of elements showed improvement.

The age grouping information was used to review and change the age modifiers as we went through several iterations of running projections using the new formulae. For example, in going from the first round to the second round of running the new projection system, we changed all the age modifiers for runs scored and home runs, while changing just a few modifiers for doubles, walks and strikeouts. This improved the results. We then made some further modifications in the third round as well. We actually ran more that three rounds of testing, but only counted and documented the three rounds I've mentioned.

Table 1

Comparison of Projections for the period from 1991-1993, 1995-1999

All Players Breakdown

	R	H	2B	3B	HR	RBI	SB	CS	BB	K	Avg	Slg
Better	1041	1009	726	219	582	1283	955	694	259	568	1016	1309
Worse	971	830	656	160	458	1089	598	357	217	541	836	1075

25 and under Breakdown

Dir	R	H	2B	3B	HR	RBI	SB	CS	BB	K	Avg	Slg
Better	197	45	102	20	149	216	96	146	35	33	45	191
Worse	215	64	97	10	107	222	70	54	52	43	64	166

26 to 29 Breakdown

Dir	R	H	2B	3B	HR	RBI	SB	CS	BB	K	Avg	Slg
Better	383	359	334	88	298	506	365	333	1	155	362	510
Worse	366	284	326	62	233	421	251	168	0	173	285	401

30 to 34 Breakdown

Dir	R	H	2B	3B	HR	RBI	SB	CS	BB	K	Avg	Slg
Better	361	468	245	92	122	448	407	182	107	262	471	491
Worse	293	387	205	85	102	363	207	113	88	229	390	393

35 and over Breakdown

Dir	R	H	2B	3B	HR	RBI	SB	CS	BB	K	Avg	Slg
Better	100	137	45	19	13	113	87	33	116	118	138	117
Worse	97	95	28	3	16	83	70	22	77	96	97	115

Another way that we reviewed the new projection system was to use similarity scores. Table 2 below shows a comparison of similarity scores under the old and new systems. Once again, all playing time was equalized for comparison purposes. Though the improvements are more subtle in this table, they are definitely there. For example, in 1999 there are four more 950+ projections while there are four fewer of the worst projections.

Table 2
Comparison of Similarity Scores

Old Projection System

	1991	1992	1993	1995	1996	1997	1998	1999
950+	215	228	188	183	208	237	238	231
900-949	107	93	121	124	103	116	133	126
850-899	13	11	25	26	23	16	17	34
800-849	0	2	3	5	3	3	2	4
750-799	0	0	0	0	4	0	0	0
700-749	0	0	0	0	0	0	0	0
<700	0	0	0	0	0	0	0	0
= 0	0	0	0	0	0	0	0	0
Average	954	955	948	945	947	952	951	948

New Projection System

	1991	1992	1993	1995	1996	1997	1998	1999
950+	221	225	198	190	213	235	241	235
900-949	102	92	113	124	102	120	130	126
850-899	12	15	24	21	20	14	17	33
800-849	0	2	2	3	4	3	2	1
750-799	0	0	0	0	2	0	0	0
700-749	0	0	0	0	0	0	0	0
<700	0	0	0	0	0	0	0	0
= 0	0	0	0	0	0	0	0	0
Average	954	954	949	947	949	952	951	949

Finally, in order to get some comfort that the new system wasn't doing something wacky, we ran the projections (still controlling the playing time) and took a look at individual players, comparing the old system, the new system and actual results. I'll run a few players here:

Table 3
Test Projections and Actuals for 1999

Brad Ausmus	Avg	G	AB	R	H	2B	3B	HR	RBI	BB	SO	SB	CS	SimScr
Old Projection	.251	127	458	58	115	19	2	6	45	52	79	14	7	936
New Projection	.258	127	458	58	118	20	2	6	46	50	80	11	7	944
Actual	.275	127	458	62	126	25	6	9	54	51	71	12	9	1000
Carlos Baerga	Avg	G	AB	R	H	2B	3B	HR	RBI	BB	SO	SB	CS	SimScr
Old Projection	.285	55	137	16	39	7	0	3	17	6	13	1	1	942
New Projection	.292	55	137	16	40	7	0	3	18	6	13	1	1	938
Actual	.241	55	137	10	33	1	0	3	10	10	24	2	1	1000
Jeff Bagwell	Avg	G	AB	R	H	2B	3B	HR	RBI	BB	SO	SB	CS	SimScr
Old Projection	.290	162	562	112	163	37	2	35	118	127	109	23	9	939
New Projection	.299	162	562	117	168	38	2	36	123	127	111	19	8	953
Actual	.304	162	562	143	171	35	0	42	126	149	127	30	11	1000
Harold Baines	Avg	G	AB	R	H	2B	3B	HR	RBI	BB	SO	SB	CS	SimScr
Old Projection	.270	135	430	53	116	19	1	15	65	57	62	1	1	897
New Projection	.284	135	430	55	122	20	1	15	67	55	59	1	1	909
Actual	.312	135	430	62	134	18	1	25	103	54	48	1	2	1000

As you can see, the changes for individual players are fairly minimal. But in the big picture, the overall results of the projection system have been improved. Thus we have implemented these revisions to the projection system for the *2000 Major League Handbook*. As stated earlier, this is only Phase I of a multi-phase project to improve our batter projections. We will continue to analyze our projection system in future years in an effort to produce the best, most accurate projections possible.

—John Dewan

Projections for 2000 Batters

Batter	Age	Avg	G	AB	R	H	2B	3B	HR	RBI	BB	SO	SB	CS	OBP	SLG
Abbott,Jeff, CWS	27	.288	98	250	36	72	15	0	8	33	15	28	3	3	.328	.444
Abbott,Kurt, Col	31	.266	105	278	37	74	18	3	7	33	17	74	2	2	.308	.428
Abreu,Bobby, Phi	26	.303	154	551	92	167	28	9	17	81	93	132	21	10	.404	.479
Agbayani,Benny, NYM	28	.259	94	290	41	75	14	2	9	39	35	64	9	5	.338	.414
Alexander,Manny, ChC	29	.248	113	266	34	66	11	2	3	25	18	56	7	3	.296	.338
Alfonzo,Edgardo, NYM	26	.298	156	614	111	183	33	3	22	96	81	76	9	4	.380	.469
Alicea,Luis, Tex	34	.243	63	148	25	36	8	1	3	16	25	26	4	2	.353	.372
Allen,Chad, Min	25	.264	119	420	58	111	24	3	8	52	32	69	11	5	.316	.393
Alomar,Roberto, Cle	32	.297	155	575	106	171	32	4	19	84	74	78	17	6	.378	.466
Alomar Jr.,Sandy, Cle	34	.272	96	313	39	85	17	0	9	43	14	37	1	1	.303	.412
Alou,Moises, Hou	33	.288	119	437	71	126	26	2	22	86	54	67	7	3	.367	.508
Amaral,Rich, Bal	38	.266	75	128	21	34	5	0	0	10	10	23	6	3	.319	.305
Anderson,Brady, Bal	36	.255	139	518	85	132	26	4	20	64	80	95	18	8	.355	.436
Anderson,Garret, Ana	28	.303	158	631	81	191	38	3	17	86	33	77	7	5	.337	.453
Anderson,Marlon, Phi	26	.268	130	489	65	131	24	5	8	55	25	65	16	7	.304	.387
Andrews,Shane, ChC	28	.222	125	392	45	87	18	1	20	59	50	113	2	2	.310	.426
Arias,Alex, Phi	32	.278	99	216	27	60	10	1	2	26	23	23	1	1	.347	.361
Arias,George, SD	28	.250	58	172	24	43	9	1	8	27	13	41	1	0	.303	.453
Aurilia,Rich, SF	28	.274	149	547	71	150	27	1	18	72	45	75	4	3	.329	.426
Ausmus,Brad, Det	31	.266	134	447	59	119	20	2	7	49	50	73	10	7	.340	.367
Aven,Bruce, Fla	28	.282	109	323	51	91	20	1	11	50	37	69	6	3	.356	.452
Baerga,Carlos, Cle	31	.283	78	198	22	56	10	0	3	23	9	22	1	1	.314	.379
Bagwell,Jeff, Hou	32	.293	159	553	123	162	36	2	41	130	130	115	21	9	.428	.588
Baines,Harold, Cle	41	.291	118	361	43	105	19	1	13	63	43	48	1	1	.366	.457
Bako,Paul, Hou	28	.254	50	122	10	31	6	0	1	12	10	30	0	0	.311	.328
Banks,Brian, Mil	29	.254	69	185	24	47	12	1	5	25	20	46	3	2	.327	.411
Barker,Glen, Hou	29	.239	80	109	17	26	4	0	1	10	10	30	6	4	.303	.303
Barker,Kevin, Mil	24	.257	116	378	50	97	20	3	14	65	30	74	2	2	.311	.437
Barrett,Michael, Mon	23	.300	146	507	70	152	38	2	14	74	32	47	4	3	.341	.465
Barry,Jeff, Col	31	.265	72	200	25	53	11	1	7	26	17	33	2	2	.323	.435
Batista,Tony, Tor	26	.272	143	526	86	143	31	2	28	86	41	90	5	3	.325	.498
Baughman,Justin, Ana	25	.267	119	469	64	125	18	7	0	26	22	64	40	15	.299	.335
Bautista,Danny, Fla	28	.258	96	229	31	59	11	1	6	28	12	38	2	1	.295	.393
Becker,Rich, Oak	28	.246	137	321	51	79	18	2	8	36	60	99	10	3	.365	.389
Bell,David, Sea	27	.251	129	490	61	123	26	2	14	57	40	75	3	3	.308	.398
Bell,Derek, Hou	31	.275	119	461	67	127	23	1	14	73	40	99	14	5	.333	.421
Bell,Jay, Ari	34	.259	147	548	89	142	29	3	24	84	76	121	5	4	.349	.454
Belle,Albert, Bal	33	.301	155	592	101	178	40	2	39	128	77	89	7	3	.381	.573
Belliard,Ron, Mil	25	.274	141	497	77	136	31	4	7	57	61	72	15	8	.353	.394
Beltran,Carlos, KC	23	.306	150	615	117	188	31	9	24	106	46	103	23	7	.354	.502
Beltre,Adrian, LA	22	.271	153	558	84	151	29	3	19	78	60	96	20	9	.341	.435
Benard,Marvin, SF	30	.284	145	497	86	141	26	3	10	52	55	86	19	11	.355	.408
Benjamin,Mike, Pit	34	.229	106	301	30	69	14	1	2	26	15	71	4	2	.266	.302
Berg,Dave, Fla	29	.281	115	327	43	92	21	2	4	37	36	60	6	4	.353	.394
Bergeron,Peter, Mon	22	.280	120	371	60	104	20	4	5	36	39	66	18	10	.349	.396
Berkman,Lance, Hou	24	.277	122	375	59	104	28	0	14	64	52	83	6	3	.365	.464
Berroa,Geronimo, Tor	35	.261	53	138	20	36	5	0	5	19	19	32	1	1	.350	.406
Berry,Sean, Mil	34	.268	72	183	22	49	12	1	5	29	16	34	2	2	.327	.426
Bichette,Dante, Col	36	.303	145	568	86	172	33	2	25	115	35	81	10	6	.343	.500
Biggio,Craig, Hou	34	.283	158	623	117	176	44	3	17	73	79	111	29	10	.363	.445

Projections for 2000 Batters

Batter	Age	Avg	G	AB	R	H	2B	3B	HR	RBI	BB	SO	SB	CS	OBP	SLG
Blanco,Henry, Col	28	.238	85	240	26	57	12	1	5	28	25	43	2	2	.309	.358
Blauser,Jeff, ChC	34	.249	122	345	56	86	19	2	10	39	51	82	3	1	.346	.403
Blum,Geoff, Mon	27	.240	63	196	27	47	11	1	5	21	22	32	3	2	.317	.383
Bogar,Tim, Hou	33	.224	107	255	33	57	10	1	3	23	26	48	3	3	.295	.306
Boggs,Wade, TB	42	.299	79	201	27	60	11	1	2	19	24	22	1	0	.373	.393
Bonds,Barry, SF	35	.278	151	515	111	143	31	3	41	119	123	91	24	8	.417	.588
Bonilla,Bobby, NYM	37	.270	58	126	17	34	6	1	4	21	16	22	1	1	.352	.429
Boone,Aaron, Cin	27	.264	125	421	53	111	27	3	11	56	30	77	11	4	.313	.420
Boone,Bret, Atl	31	.255	149	542	73	138	32	2	17	73	48	106	6	5	.315	.415
Bordick,Mike, Bal	34	.246	153	561	64	138	23	2	9	58	45	85	5	4	.302	.342
Bragg,Darren, StL	30	.262	119	325	45	85	20	1	6	37	41	74	5	3	.344	.385
Brogna,Rico, Phi	30	.269	157	592	78	159	35	2	22	98	48	129	7	5	.323	.446
Brosius,Scott, NYY	33	.251	137	487	66	122	24	1	16	67	42	92	7	4	.310	.402
Brown,Adrian, Pit	26	.263	132	399	57	105	14	3	3	28	37	51	19	8	.326	.336
Brown,Brant, Pit	29	.255	128	365	52	93	22	3	15	51	29	98	5	5	.310	.455
Brumfield,Jacob, Tor	35	.220	51	100	13	22	7	1	2	12	10	21	2	1	.291	.370
Buford,Damon, Bos	30	.242	102	293	42	71	14	1	8	37	25	67	10	6	.302	.379
Buhner,Jay, Sea	35	.227	112	362	58	82	17	1	22	68	77	126	0	0	.362	.461
Burks,Ellis, SF	35	.274	128	435	78	119	25	3	25	79	57	94	10	4	.358	.517
Burnitz,Jeromy, Mil	31	.264	148	523	89	138	29	3	32	103	80	132	10	6	.362	.514
Burrell,Pat, Phi	23	.298	140	480	80	143	30	4	25	86	66	132	2	2	.383	.533
Bush,Homer, Tor	27	.288	131	493	69	142	21	2	5	46	25	92	22	11	.322	.369
Cabrera,Orlando, Mon	25	.257	134	479	69	123	27	6	7	50	32	49	13	7	.303	.382
Cairo,Miguel, TB	26	.268	138	507	63	136	23	3	4	43	23	47	22	9	.300	.349
Cameron,Mike, Cin	27	.250	151	553	98	138	28	6	21	71	75	145	33	12	.339	.436
Caminiti,Ken, Hou	37	.251	117	399	65	100	22	1	20	69	64	96	6	3	.354	.461
Canseco,Jose, TB	35	.247	125	466	72	115	22	1	33	91	57	145	8	5	.329	.511
Caruso,Mike, CWS	23	.282	131	507	70	143	14	5	3	48	17	32	17	10	.305	.347
Casey,Sean, Cin	25	.330	147	582	96	192	40	2	22	109	65	78	1	1	.397	.519
Castilla,Vinny, Col	32	.297	155	607	91	180	28	2	38	114	45	90	4	4	.345	.537
Castillo,Alberto, StL	30	.217	97	221	18	48	8	0	3	22	27	42	1	1	.302	.294
Castillo,Luis, Fla	24	.274	139	497	78	136	16	4	0	29	69	91	42	16	.362	.322
Castro,Ramon, Fla	24	.222	108	329	34	73	15	0	11	40	22	64	0	0	.271	.368
Catalanotto,Frank, Det	26	.262	113	336	46	88	20	2	10	41	25	59	5	6	.313	.423
Cedeno,Roger, NYM	25	.275	152	505	83	139	23	4	5	43	67	106	36	13	.360	.366
Chavez,Eric, Oak	22	.287	141	478	76	137	36	2	21	86	47	75	6	5	.350	.502
Christenson,Ryan, Oak	26	.271	122	377	71	102	21	2	5	41	50	83	9	7	.356	.377
Cirillo,Jeff, Mil	30	.306	158	605	93	185	39	2	13	81	74	84	6	5	.381	.441
Clark,Tony, Det	28	.281	151	565	89	159	28	1	34	105	76	132	2	2	.367	.515
Clark,Will, Bal	36	.295	116	404	62	119	24	2	14	61	53	70	1	1	.376	.468
Clayton,Royce, Tex	30	.260	143	523	74	136	25	4	10	51	43	98	20	10	.316	.380
Clemente,Edgard, Col	24	.284	108	359	49	102	21	4	19	52	22	84	3	2	.325	.524
Colbrunn,Greg, Ari	30	.282	97	209	23	59	15	1	5	29	12	39	2	2	.321	.435
Collier,Lou, Mil	26	.272	105	290	38	79	17	2	2	31	26	48	7	4	.332	.366
Conine,Jeff, Bal	34	.279	129	387	46	108	24	1	13	62	38	69	1	1	.344	.447
Coomer,Ron, Min	33	.273	120	444	49	121	21	1	13	64	21	70	2	1	.305	.412
Cordero,Wil, Cle	28	.276	92	337	53	93	22	1	12	51	23	67	2	1	.322	.454
Cordova,Marty, Min	30	.267	102	371	51	99	23	2	11	59	39	87	5	4	.337	.429
Counsell,Craig, LA	29	.279	87	258	36	72	16	2	2	29	30	28	3	1	.354	.380
Cruz,Deivi, Det	24	.268	152	527	60	141	33	1	9	59	16	58	4	4	.289	.385

Projections for 2000 Batters

Batter	Age	Avg	G	AB	R	H	2B	3B	HR	RBI	BB	SO	SB	CS	OBP	SLG
Cruz,Jacob, Cle	27	.289	75	242	36	70	14	1	8	39	24	40	4	3	.353	.455
Cruz,Jose, Tor	26	.248	120	412	72	102	22	2	17	61	70	107	11	4	.357	.434
Curtis,Chad, NYY	31	.259	128	351	61	91	21	2	10	45	57	62	12	6	.363	.416
Damon,Johnny, KC	26	.291	153	574	95	167	27	9	14	68	59	67	27	10	.357	.443
Darr,Mike, SD	24	.266	120	349	49	93	24	1	6	44	30	75	10	4	.325	.393
Daubach,Brian, Bos	28	.257	119	401	57	103	27	1	17	66	46	106	3	4	.333	.456
Davis,Ben, SD	23	.254	139	456	52	116	27	1	10	61	35	86	3	2	.308	.384
Davis,Chili, NYY	40	.263	107	342	41	90	17	1	14	54	55	72	2	1	.365	.442
Davis,Eric, StL	38	.266	76	244	36	65	10	1	11	38	27	65	6	3	.339	.451
Davis,Russ, Sea	30	.257	138	483	65	124	27	1	22	71	34	124	4	3	.306	.453
Delgado,Carlos, Tor	28	.276	152	562	99	155	37	1	40	118	81	141	1	1	.367	.559
DeShields,Delino, Bal	31	.284	129	462	74	131	18	5	8	44	53	67	31	12	.357	.396
Diaz,Einar, Cle	27	.270	104	330	39	89	19	1	4	34	17	29	3	3	.305	.370
DiFelice,Mike, TB	31	.254	75	213	17	54	10	1	4	25	13	39	1	1	.296	.366
DiSarcina,Gary, Ana	32	.255	138	471	52	120	23	2	3	43	18	40	5	4	.282	.331
Doster,David, Phi	29	.252	82	119	14	30	8	0	3	15	9	19	2	1	.305	.395
Drew,J.D., StL	24	.277	149	530	105	147	29	6	22	76	78	108	20	8	.370	.479
Ducey,Rob, Phi	35	.246	101	195	27	48	13	1	5	22	23	54	2	2	.326	.400
Dunston,Shawon, NYM	37	.265	114	211	26	56	10	1	5	22	4	33	7	3	.279	.393
Dunwoody,Todd, Fla	25	.244	81	270	35	66	14	4	7	32	17	74	7	4	.289	.404
Durazo,Erubiel, Ari	26	.321	148	521	97	167	27	4	31	99	68	109	2	2	.399	.566
Durham,Ray, CWS	28	.281	157	631	110	177	34	6	15	66	73	102	32	11	.355	.425
Durrington,Trent, Ana	24	.223	53	157	25	35	6	0	0	11	14	30	12	5	.287	.261
Dye,Jermaine, KC	26	.272	148	596	84	162	30	3	26	90	49	113	5	4	.327	.463
Easley,Damion, Det	30	.257	154	565	85	145	30	2	22	77	55	116	15	7	.323	.434
Echevarria,Angel, Col	29	.307	96	261	37	80	18	0	13	47	17	41	1	1	.349	.525
Edmonds,Jim, Ana	30	.295	133	501	85	148	31	2	22	74	57	93	6	4	.367	.497
Encarnacion,Juan, Det	24	.281	140	516	74	145	28	5	20	73	26	105	25	9	.315	.471
Erstad,Darin, Ana	26	.285	140	554	94	158	32	4	16	72	49	85	16	8	.343	.444
Estalella,Bobby, Phi	25	.225	58	173	23	39	9	0	8	35	24	45	1	1	.320	.416
Eusebio,Tony, Hou	33	.270	94	259	23	70	12	1	2	35	30	50	0	0	.346	.347
Everett,Carl, Hou	30	.287	135	464	73	133	27	2	20	80	43	102	16	9	.347	.483
Fasano,Sal, KC	28	.232	122	353	50	82	15	0	18	50	30	90	1	1	.292	.428
Febles,Carlos, KC	24	.287	140	509	97	146	28	11	13	61	62	88	31	11	.364	.462
Fernandez,Tony, Tor	38	.276	128	435	55	120	24	3	6	53	45	53	6	5	.344	.386
Fick,Robert, Det	26	.286	134	458	76	131	32	3	18	83	48	74	5	3	.354	.487
Finley,Steve, Ari	35	.255	146	561	91	143	25	5	23	77	47	97	11	4	.313	.440
Flaherty,John, TB	32	.251	121	419	38	105	19	0	10	51	26	63	2	3	.294	.368
Fletcher,Darrin, Tor	33	.266	119	394	40	105	21	1	14	60	24	43	0	0	.309	.431
Floyd,Cliff, Fla	27	.280	146	492	72	138	32	3	20	78	50	99	16	9	.347	.480
Fordyce,Brook, CWS	30	.263	107	297	27	78	19	1	7	38	20	42	1	1	.309	.404
Fox,Andy, Ari	29	.254	125	386	57	98	13	3	7	36	45	81	13	6	.332	.358
Franco,Matt, NYM	30	.259	118	162	21	42	14	1	3	21	22	24	1	0	.348	.414
Frias,Hanley, Ari	26	.258	79	236	32	61	10	3	1	20	25	37	8	5	.330	.339
Fryman,Travis, Cle	31	.277	144	542	78	150	31	3	22	94	43	111	7	4	.330	.467
Fullmer,Brad, Mon	25	.283	139	480	62	136	39	1	17	74	32	49	4	4	.328	.475
Galarraga,Andres, Atl	39	.271	114	435	70	118	21	1	28	86	39	118	9	4	.331	.517
Gant,Ron, Phi	35	.234	132	458	70	107	22	2	19	68	63	126	9	3	.326	.415
Garcia,Freddy, Atl	27	.239	56	163	21	39	9	1	9	24	9	40	0	0	.279	.472
Garcia,Karim, Det	24	.246	112	342	49	84	14	5	16	53	25	84	5	4	.297	.456

Projections for 2000 Batters

Batter	Age	Avg	G	AB	R	H	2B	3B	HR	RBI	BB	SO	SB	CS	OBP	SLG
Garciaparra,Nom., Bos	26	.319	144	605	113	193	39	7	33	111	42	62	15	6	.363	.570
Gates,Brent, Min	30	.263	114	319	37	84	20	2	3	42	35	49	2	2	.336	.367
Giambi,Jason, Oak	29	.298	148	497	85	148	35	1	25	92	76	89	1	1	.391	.523
Giambi,Jeremy, KC	25	.313	135	432	68	135	22	1	17	69	65	82	3	3	.402	.486
Giles,Brian S., Pit	29	.285	146	541	101	154	30	4	32	103	104	89	9	4	.400	.532
Gilkey,Bernard, Ari	33	.254	103	224	32	57	13	1	7	33	30	49	4	3	.343	.415
Girardi,Joe, NYY	35	.264	91	292	32	77	13	1	2	33	17	42	4	3	.304	.336
Glanville,Doug, Phi	29	.294	155	637	99	187	32	4	8	58	43	78	23	8	.338	.394
Glaus,Troy, Ana	23	.256	153	559	91	143	31	0	31	92	66	136	5	3	.334	.478
Gomez,Chris, SD	29	.252	115	365	40	92	19	1	3	34	41	76	2	3	.328	.334
Gonzalez,Alex, Tor	27	.249	99	345	42	86	20	2	9	36	25	70	11	4	.300	.397
Gonzalez,Alex, Fla	23	.253	138	561	79	142	23	7	15	62	25	109	4	6	.285	.399
Gonzalez,Juan, Tex	30	.297	151	595	98	177	35	2	41	137	46	119	2	1	.348	.570
Gonzalez,Luis, Ari	32	.282	148	588	92	166	37	4	21	89	68	67	9	6	.357	.466
Goodwin,Tom, Tex	31	.271	112	413	70	112	14	3	2	29	44	67	35	15	.341	.334
Grace,Mark, ChC	36	.302	155	570	90	172	35	2	14	79	85	49	3	3	.392	.444
Graffanino,Tony, TB	28	.253	69	186	26	47	10	1	4	19	18	36	4	3	.319	.382
Grebeck,Craig, Tor	35	.262	70	168	18	44	9	0	1	13	19	21	1	1	.337	.333
Green,Shawn, Tor	27	.288	157	626	112	180	43	4	37	104	60	131	19	7	.350	.546
Greene,Todd, Ana	29	.272	118	386	51	105	23	0	20	64	21	63	2	2	.310	.487
Greene,Willie, Tor	28	.246	91	272	39	67	11	1	14	47	42	62	2	1	.347	.449
Greer,Rusty, Tex	31	.310	152	581	106	180	37	3	20	101	87	83	5	3	.400	.487
Grieve,Ben, Oak	24	.292	153	541	102	158	34	1	27	105	79	112	3	2	.382	.508
Griffey Jr.,Ken, Sea	30	.291	161	621	125	181	35	3	53	146	83	119	16	5	.375	.614
Grissom,Marquis, Mil	33	.264	144	557	73	147	27	3	15	64	39	93	16	8	.312	.404
Grudzielanek,Mark, LA	30	.287	141	557	72	160	31	2	7	50	26	70	16	7	.319	.388
Gubanich,Creigh., Bos	28	.261	57	119	14	31	6	0	5	19	8	33	0	0	.307	.437
Guerrero,Vladimir, Mon	24	.321	160	610	108	196	40	6	39	115	48	74	12	9	.371	.598
Guerrero,Wilton, Mon	25	.292	136	414	54	121	15	7	3	36	15	54	12	6	.317	.384
Guillen,Carlos, Sea	24	.244	120	475	59	116	18	2	8	46	32	95	5	5	.292	.341
Guillen,Jose, TB	24	.275	119	418	53	115	24	2	10	60	20	69	2	2	.308	.414
Guillen,Ozzie, Atl	36	.258	83	209	26	54	8	1	1	19	13	15	2	2	.302	.321
Gutierrez,Ricky, Hou	30	.262	118	378	43	99	14	3	2	35	40	65	7	5	.333	.331
Guzman,Cristian, Min	22	.251	136	474	53	119	21	3	1	35	19	94	13	7	.280	.314
Gwynn,Tony, SD	40	.332	122	455	65	151	26	2	11	68	33	19	6	3	.377	.470
Hairston Jr.,Jerry, Bal	24	.278	134	464	73	129	26	3	9	56	31	56	17	11	.323	.405
Hamilton,Darryl, NYM	35	.285	137	494	78	141	21	3	6	42	64	59	9	7	.367	.377
Hammonds,Jeffrey, Cin	29	.265	124	339	62	90	22	2	16	51	38	72	7	4	.340	.484
Hansen,Dave, LA	31	.258	88	132	16	34	5	0	2	15	30	27	1	1	.395	.341
Harris,Lenny, Ari	35	.273	98	176	18	48	7	0	2	17	10	12	4	2	.312	.347
Haselman,Bill, Det	34	.258	59	151	16	39	8	0	5	19	9	25	1	1	.300	.411
Hatteberg,Scott, Bos	30	.274	75	212	28	58	13	0	6	27	27	35	0	0	.356	.420
Hayes,Charlie, SF	35	.249	80	229	26	57	13	1	6	39	26	43	2	1	.325	.393
Helton,Todd, Col	26	.329	158	563	101	185	41	3	30	107	66	72	4	4	.399	.572
Henderson,Rick., NYM	41	.246	122	422	77	104	19	1	9	36	90	89	30	10	.379	.360
Hermansen,Chad, Pit	22	.247	130	442	64	109	25	2	20	60	36	125	13	7	.303	.448
Hernandez,Carlos, SD	33	.255	69	192	14	49	7	0	4	21	7	35	2	2	.281	.354
Hernandez,Jose, Atl	30	.254	151	426	67	108	17	4	17	57	39	119	5	4	.316	.432
Hernandez,Ram., Oak	24	.255	122	412	57	105	17	1	12	67	36	49	2	2	.315	.388
Hidalgo,Richard, Hou	24	.253	113	380	49	96	26	2	12	52	35	59	6	6	.316	.426

Projections for 2000 Batters

Batter	Age	Avg	G	AB	R	H	2B	3B	HR	RBI	BB	SO	SB	CS	OBP	SLG
Higginson,Bob, Det	29	.281	131	488	75	137	27	2	21	75	66	80	6	4	.366	.473
Hill,Glenallen, ChC	35	.266	100	290	39	77	15	1	14	46	19	66	3	2	.311	.469
Hinch,A.J., Oak	26	.265	109	306	40	81	10	0	10	38	26	60	4	2	.322	.395
Hocking,Denny, Min	30	.240	136	312	39	75	17	2	5	32	21	56	5	4	.288	.356
Holbert,Ray, KC	29	.249	60	177	21	44	6	1	2	14	15	45	6	4	.307	.328
Hollandsworth,Todd, LA	27	.279	100	287	40	80	15	3	7	36	20	56	7	4	.326	.425
Houston,Tyler, Cle	29	.251	115	295	31	74	11	1	9	40	22	60	2	1	.303	.386
Howard,Thomas, StL	35	.261	97	203	24	53	12	1	4	22	18	37	2	2	.321	.389
Hubbard,Trenidad, LA	34	.279	54	111	17	31	7	1	3	13	13	22	4	2	.355	.441
Hughes,Bobby, Mil	29	.249	120	349	40	87	20	1	11	42	23	69	1	1	.296	.407
Hundley,Todd, LA	31	.221	113	335	47	74	16	1	20	57	55	105	1	1	.331	.454
Hunter,Brian, Atl	32	.235	67	162	19	38	9	0	5	22	14	31	1	1	.295	.383
Hunter,Brian L., Sea	29	.260	141	530	79	138	23	4	4	37	43	91	42	11	.316	.342
Hunter,Torii, Min	24	.251	133	434	54	109	25	2	8	45	27	83	9	9	.295	.373
Huskey,Butch, Bos	28	.272	103	334	43	91	15	1	16	56	24	58	4	3	.321	.467
Huson,Jeff, Ana	35	.236	77	140	13	33	6	1	0	12	8	18	3	1	.277	.293
Ibanez,Raul, Sea	28	.259	93	228	33	59	11	1	8	32	18	41	3	2	.313	.421
Jackson,Damian, SD	26	.239	121	393	62	94	20	2	6	34	48	93	20	7	.322	.346
Jackson,Darrin, CWS	36	.256	67	129	15	33	7	1	3	16	4	22	2	1	.278	.395
Jaha,John, Oak	34	.244	133	405	72	99	18	0	24	80	87	119	2	1	.378	.467
Javier,Stan, Hou	36	.266	117	350	51	93	14	2	3	32	44	57	14	4	.348	.343
Jefferies,Gregg, Det	32	.281	68	224	31	63	13	1	5	26	17	13	5	3	.332	.415
Jefferson,Reggie, Bos	31	.296	92	277	37	82	18	1	9	38	20	59	0	0	.343	.466
Jenkins,Geoff, Mil	25	.274	152	515	74	141	35	4	20	83	39	104	3	2	.325	.474
Jeter,Derek, NYY	26	.318	157	641	133	204	32	7	19	91	78	118	22	9	.392	.479
Johnson,Brian, Cin	32	.250	53	136	13	34	7	1	5	18	10	24	0	0	.301	.426
Johnson,Charles, Bal	28	.236	141	466	50	110	22	1	19	60	60	122	1	1	.323	.410
Johnson,Lance, ChC	36	.281	97	335	50	94	11	5	2	26	33	24	15	6	.345	.361
Johnson,Mark L., CWS	24	.250	106	296	46	74	13	2	6	35	60	64	2	1	.376	.368
Johnson,Russ, Hou	27	.255	84	247	36	63	12	1	3	26	33	46	3	4	.343	.348
Jones,Andruw, Atl	23	.271	161	580	97	157	32	4	30	95	67	120	28	11	.346	.495
Jones,Chipper, Atl	28	.306	159	592	118	181	36	3	36	112	105	91	17	4	.410	.559
Jones,Jacque, Min	25	.289	136	471	69	136	35	2	14	66	24	105	11	8	.323	.461
Jordan,Brian, Atl	33	.291	144	515	85	150	27	4	19	91	41	69	13	6	.344	.470
Jordan,Kevin, Phi	30	.279	129	315	32	88	20	1	4	41	14	34	1	1	.310	.387
Joyner,Wally, SD	38	.279	108	315	37	88	17	1	7	48	41	40	1	1	.362	.406
Justice,David, Cle	34	.280	138	479	77	134	23	1	22	83	83	91	4	3	.386	.470
Kapler,Gabe, Det	24	.273	145	509	83	139	35	5	24	88	49	86	8	5	.337	.503
Karros,Eric, LA	32	.274	149	562	70	154	29	1	30	103	54	110	8	4	.338	.489
Kelly,Roberto, Tex	35	.284	91	299	41	85	14	1	10	42	16	58	4	2	.321	.438
Kendall,Jason, Pit	26	.311	129	444	78	138	30	3	10	57	49	45	18	5	.379	.459
Kennedy,Adam, StL	24	.287	125	449	64	129	30	4	9	61	21	47	14	6	.319	.432
Kent,Jeff, SF	32	.268	144	538	85	144	32	2	25	103	53	120	9	5	.333	.474
Kingsale,Gene, Bal	23	.252	68	127	18	32	4	1	0	10	10	21	6	4	.307	.299
Klesko,Ryan, Atl	29	.279	139	444	68	124	26	3	23	79	56	91	4	3	.360	.507
Knoblauch,Chuck, NYY	31	.292	151	602	122	176	32	5	16	66	82	71	35	12	.377	.442
Konerko,Paul, CWS	24	.280	153	557	77	156	29	1	27	96	53	77	1	2	.343	.481
Koskie,Corey, Min	27	.283	142	516	76	146	31	3	21	84	60	113	8	6	.358	.477
Kotsay,Mark, Fla	24	.277	152	545	80	151	27	6	12	69	45	60	12	6	.332	.415
Kreuter,Chad, KC	35	.230	108	291	29	67	13	1	4	33	33	66	1	1	.309	.323

Projections for 2000 Batters

Batter	Age	Avg	G	AB	R	H	2B	3B	HR	RBI	BB	SO	SB	CS	OBP	SLG
Lamb,David, TB	25	.279	56	172	23	48	8	0	1	18	15	23	1	1	.337	.343
Lampkin,Tom, Sea	36	.237	82	177	21	42	7	1	6	23	17	27	2	2	.304	.390
Lankford,Ray, StL	33	.271	137	472	82	128	31	3	21	79	78	132	18	7	.375	.483
Lansing,Mike, Col	32	.270	108	411	57	111	26	1	10	41	29	65	8	4	.318	.411
Larkin,Barry, Cin	36	.289	146	523	88	151	27	4	14	64	84	61	24	7	.387	.436
LaRue,Jason, Cin	26	.281	72	203	28	57	15	1	6	29	14	39	2	1	.327	.453
Lawton,Matt, Min	28	.265	138	472	74	125	26	3	13	65	76	61	13	6	.367	.415
Ledee,Ricky, NYY	26	.271	95	292	51	79	17	2	12	44	33	83	4	3	.345	.466
Ledesma,Aaron, TB	29	.290	107	331	39	96	20	1	1	35	22	48	4	3	.334	.366
Lee,Carlos, CWS	24	.297	144	553	75	164	34	1	19	97	25	65	7	4	.327	.465
Lee,Derrek, Fla	24	.255	76	243	35	62	15	1	9	36	23	68	4	2	.320	.436
Lee,Travis, Ari	25	.266	127	447	65	119	20	2	17	64	60	78	9	3	.353	.434
Lewis,Darren, Bos	32	.244	116	344	50	84	12	3	3	37	38	51	15	7	.319	.323
Lewis,Mark, Cin	30	.261	92	176	21	46	9	1	4	20	14	34	1	1	.316	.392
Leyritz,Jim, NYY	36	.258	76	186	23	48	9	0	6	29	28	48	0	0	.355	.403
Lieberthal,Mike, Phi	28	.264	136	497	70	131	31	1	23	83	43	79	2	1	.322	.469
Liefer,Jeff, CWS	25	.261	63	211	31	55	13	2	6	33	17	50	1	1	.316	.427
Liniak,Cole, ChC	23	.252	120	404	50	102	29	0	11	44	32	63	2	2	.307	.406
Lockhart,Keith, Atl	35	.266	88	173	22	46	12	1	3	23	16	20	2	1	.328	.399
LoDuca,Paul, LA	28	.269	72	193	23	52	10	0	3	21	17	15	5	3	.329	.368
Lofton,Kenny, Cle	33	.298	134	523	101	156	26	6	8	50	79	85	36	13	.390	.417
Long,Terrence, Oak	24	.275	110	342	41	94	15	4	7	41	28	66	12	7	.330	.404
Lopez,Javy, Atl	29	.290	126	449	60	130	22	2	26	79	37	81	2	3	.344	.521
Lopez,Luis, NYM	29	.250	97	152	17	38	8	0	2	15	11	34	1	2	.301	.342
Loretta,Mark, Mil	28	.289	152	575	80	166	26	3	6	65	59	66	7	4	.355	.376
Lowell,Mike, Fla	26	.277	136	462	63	128	25	0	20	72	39	75	2	1	.333	.461
Lowery,Terrell, TB	29	.272	80	239	35	65	14	1	8	33	29	59	4	4	.351	.439
Mabry,John, Sea	29	.264	112	326	38	86	19	0	8	40	30	68	1	1	.326	.396
Macfarlane,Mike, Oak	36	.242	92	248	29	60	16	1	7	33	17	50	1	1	.291	.399
Magadan,Dave, SD	37	.275	100	211	23	58	14	0	2	23	36	31	1	1	.381	.370
Manwaring,Kirt, Col	34	.229	83	223	18	51	8	1	2	18	23	45	1	1	.301	.300
Marrero,Eli, StL	26	.235	122	375	47	88	19	2	12	48	27	58	8	5	.286	.392
Martin,Al, Pit	32	.273	132	479	75	131	26	4	17	57	44	101	20	7	.335	.451
Martinez,Dave, TB	35	.271	127	439	62	119	16	3	6	44	49	68	9	6	.344	.362
Martinez,Edgar, Sea	37	.303	141	498	85	151	36	1	22	86	99	91	2	2	.419	.512
Martinez,Manny, Mon	29	.259	115	324	44	84	18	3	5	31	18	66	10	6	.298	.380
Martinez,Ramon E., SF	27	.270	76	233	32	63	12	1	5	29	21	31	2	1	.331	.395
Martinez,Tino, NYY	32	.276	151	561	87	155	30	1	30	117	68	81	2	2	.355	.494
Mateo,Ruben, Tex	22	.301	138	505	91	152	34	2	25	93	26	72	12	6	.335	.525
Matheny,Mike, Tor	29	.234	86	231	21	54	11	1	4	25	12	48	1	1	.272	.342
Matthews Jr.,Gary, SD	25	.236	122	351	46	83	14	1	6	41	42	86	8	4	.318	.333
Mayne,Brent, SF	32	.265	111	309	31	82	16	0	3	29	36	54	1	1	.342	.346
McCracken,Quint., TB	29	.285	138	414	67	118	22	5	5	49	39	73	19	9	.347	.399
McDonald,Jason, Oak	28	.241	108	294	53	71	11	2	5	26	52	66	17	8	.355	.344
McEwing,Joe, StL	27	.273	119	384	52	105	22	3	7	43	26	54	5	6	.320	.401
McGriff,Fred, TB	36	.284	142	522	68	148	26	1	22	87	73	111	3	2	.371	.464
McGuire,Ryan, Mon	28	.245	88	188	23	46	13	1	3	20	29	39	2	1	.346	.372
McGwire,Mark, StL	36	.263	151	520	104	137	21	0	58	127	130	157	1	0	.411	.638
McLemore,Mark, Tex	35	.254	122	461	72	117	16	2	4	38	70	69	12	6	.352	.323
McRae,Brian, Tor	32	.253	136	407	63	103	21	4	12	46	55	71	13	7	.342	.413

Projections for 2000 Batters

Batter	Age	Avg	G	AB	R	H	2B	3B	HR	RBI	BB	SO	SB	CS	OBP	SLG
Meares,Pat, Pit	31	.267	120	472	59	126	23	3	7	59	23	85	6	4	.301	.373
Meluskey,Mitch, Hou	26	.293	101	307	46	90	24	0	8	43	40	57	1	1	.375	.450
Merced,Orlando, Mon	33	.279	105	287	37	80	19	2	9	45	35	46	3	2	.357	.453
Merloni,Lou, Bos	29	.280	72	218	32	61	12	0	5	28	20	33	1	1	.340	.404
Meyers,Chad, ChC	24	.275	124	426	78	117	27	1	1	38	51	64	31	14	.352	.350
Mientkiewicz,Doug, Min	26	.264	71	220	33	58	16	1	5	28	33	29	4	2	.360	.414
Mieske,Matt, Hou	32	.256	89	180	25	46	11	1	7	26	14	38	1	1	.309	.444
Millar,Kevin, Fla	28	.296	94	318	47	94	19	1	12	59	33	41	2	2	.362	.475
Miller,Damian, Ari	30	.273	98	311	36	85	21	1	8	45	21	67	1	1	.319	.424
Minor,Ryan, Bal	26	.240	61	200	27	48	9	0	8	27	13	60	1	1	.286	.405
Mirabelli,Doug, SF	29	.245	67	147	20	36	9	0	4	20	21	33	1	0	.339	.388
Molina,Ben, Ana	25	.260	57	181	17	47	9	0	3	23	8	11	0	1	.291	.359
Mondesi,Raul, LA	29	.284	157	605	98	172	34	5	33	95	51	118	22	10	.340	.521
Mora,Melvin, NYM	28	.239	78	159	21	38	7	0	2	14	17	29	3	4	.313	.321
Morandini,Mickey, ChC	34	.268	134	470	66	126	22	4	4	36	55	73	11	5	.345	.357
Mordecai,Mike, Mon	32	.235	89	162	20	38	7	1	3	14	13	23	1	1	.291	.346
Morris,Hal, Cin	35	.301	93	133	15	40	8	0	1	15	9	18	1	1	.345	.383
Morris,Warren, Pit	26	.306	154	558	78	171	26	4	18	89	60	93	8	7	.374	.464
Mouton,James, Mon	31	.250	61	92	12	23	7	0	1	11	9	18	4	2	.317	.359
Mueller,Bill, SF	29	.289	135	460	72	133	26	2	5	47	69	70	3	3	.382	.387
Myers,Greg, Atl	34	.245	92	208	22	51	13	1	4	27	23	38	0	0	.320	.375
Nevin,Phil, SD	29	.243	144	419	56	102	22	1	22	67	46	106	1	1	.318	.458
Nieves,Jose, ChC	25	.260	136	466	53	121	30	3	10	54	21	73	10	10	.292	.401
Nilsson,Dave, Mil	30	.281	124	395	57	111	24	1	17	66	50	65	2	2	.362	.476
Nixon,Otis, Atl	41	.258	76	132	19	34	3	0	0	7	15	17	10	3	.333	.280
Nixon,Trot, Bos	26	.257	142	475	73	122	21	3	16	59	59	86	9	5	.339	.415
Norton,Greg, CWS	27	.247	133	417	62	103	25	2	16	56	54	99	4	5	.333	.432
Nunez,Abraham, Pit	24	.239	81	255	28	61	8	1	1	19	24	47	8	4	.305	.290
Nunnally,Jon, Bos	28	.249	78	237	38	59	12	2	10	34	35	59	5	4	.346	.443
O'Leary,Troy, Bos	30	.283	158	587	84	166	35	5	23	95	46	93	2	2	.335	.477
O'Neill,Paul, NYY	37	.285	142	544	72	155	30	1	18	92	61	92	6	4	.357	.443
Ochoa,Alex, Mil	28	.270	124	285	42	77	20	2	5	35	29	41	5	5	.338	.407
Offerman,Jose, Bos	31	.288	141	549	87	158	24	6	6	51	78	82	21	11	.376	.386
Olerud,John, NYM	31	.306	156	575	96	176	40	1	21	98	108	72	1	1	.416	.489
Oliver,Joe, Pit	34	.231	47	121	9	28	7	0	3	16	7	26	0	0	.273	.364
Ordonez,Magglio, CWS	26	.296	155	622	90	184	38	2	24	100	39	66	11	10	.337	.479
Ordonez,Rey, NYM	27	.239	156	524	51	125	19	3	1	46	36	58	6	5	.288	.292
Orie,Kevin, Fla	27	.266	107	342	44	91	24	1	10	47	35	49	1	1	.334	.430
Ortiz,David, Min	24	.285	120	382	58	109	27	1	18	68	43	99	2	2	.358	.503
Otanez,Willis, Tor	27	.251	74	243	33	61	12	0	11	37	19	52	1	1	.305	.436
Owens,Eric, SD	29	.264	125	390	51	103	17	2	7	42	36	52	20	6	.326	.372
Palmeiro,Orlando, Ana	31	.277	88	202	29	56	11	2	0	21	24	17	3	3	.354	.351
Palmeiro,Rafael, Tex	35	.280	157	564	87	158	32	2	37	119	75	89	5	3	.365	.541
Palmer,Dean, Det	31	.262	149	558	82	146	27	1	33	100	50	142	3	2	.322	.491
Paquette,Craig, StL	31	.249	61	189	22	47	10	1	8	30	6	43	1	1	.272	.439
Pena,Angel, LA	25	.271	58	181	23	49	10	0	5	29	12	32	2	2	.316	.409
Perez,Eddie, Atl	32	.260	97	250	27	65	14	0	7	30	17	36	1	1	.307	.400
Perez,Eduardo, StL	30	.254	75	189	26	48	10	1	7	29	20	47	2	1	.325	.429
Perez,Neifi, Col	25	.295	160	661	95	195	35	10	12	70	36	63	10	8	.331	.433
Perry,Herbert, TB	30	.273	74	231	30	63	15	0	7	34	15	43	1	1	.317	.429

Projections for 2000 Batters

Batter	Age	Avg	G	AB	R	H	2B	3B	HR	RBI	BB	SO	SB	CS	OBP	SLG
Petrick,Ben, Col	23	.282	133	479	83	135	30	5	24	82	65	96	10	8	.368	.516
Phillips,Tony, Oak	41	.237	104	379	61	90	16	1	8	36	72	89	6	4	.359	.348
Piazza,Mike, NYM	31	.335	148	550	94	184	28	0	38	119	61	76	2	1	.401	.593
Polanco,Placido, StL	24	.270	93	296	36	80	12	2	1	27	15	26	6	3	.305	.334
Polonia,Luis, Det	35	.314	82	223	28	70	12	4	6	22	11	28	12	6	.346	.484
Posada,Jorge, NYY	28	.251	124	402	62	101	25	2	15	62	59	93	2	1	.347	.435
Pratt,Todd, NYM	33	.273	62	132	17	36	7	1	3	22	13	30	1	0	.338	.409
Quinn,Mark, KC	26	.312	144	504	86	157	34	3	25	95	35	76	4	4	.356	.540
Ramirez,Alex, Cle	25	.283	79	258	37	73	12	3	10	37	10	54	4	3	.310	.469
Ramirez,Aramis, Pit	22	.266	128	447	54	119	26	1	13	52	48	76	2	2	.337	.416
Ramirez,Manny, Cle	28	.311	152	559	112	174	38	1	41	130	89	123	4	3	.406	.603
Randa,Joe, KC	30	.288	153	556	72	160	29	4	12	70	49	79	8	5	.345	.419
Redmond,Mike, Fla	29	.267	92	262	24	70	13	0	2	26	18	31	1	1	.314	.340
Reed,Jeff, ChC	37	.238	108	260	30	62	12	1	6	29	39	60	1	1	.338	.362
Reese,Pokey, Cin	27	.250	148	573	75	143	26	2	8	51	44	96	26	8	.303	.344
Relaford,Desi, Phi	26	.242	109	376	43	91	18	2	4	36	29	62	12	6	.296	.332
Renteria,Edgar, StL	24	.285	151	586	93	167	25	3	7	53	53	88	35	14	.344	.374
Rios,Armando, SF	28	.275	80	236	42	65	14	1	10	40	28	44	6	4	.352	.470
Ripken Jr.,Cal, Bal	39	.268	128	481	58	129	24	1	15	63	37	56	1	1	.320	.416
Rivera,Ruben, SD	26	.207	136	334	56	69	18	3	16	46	43	116	11	6	.297	.422
Roberts,David, Cle	28	.277	55	195	33	54	9	2	2	20	19	30	12	5	.341	.374
Rodriguez,Alex, Sea	24	.312	145	596	128	186	36	3	42	118	51	106	27	8	.366	.594
Rodriguez,Henry, ChC	32	.251	134	455	61	114	25	1	26	80	53	130	2	2	.329	.481
Rodriguez,Ivan, Tex	28	.303	149	600	103	182	35	2	26	91	33	81	10	4	.340	.498
Rodriguez,Liu, CWS	23	.263	66	137	18	36	5	1	1	18	12	20	1	1	.322	.336
Rolen,Scott, Phi	25	.285	137	502	93	143	37	2	26	90	79	120	11	6	.382	.522
Sadler,Donnie, Bos	25	.230	80	244	33	56	11	3	3	20	22	53	8	3	.293	.336
Saenz,Olmedo, Oak	29	.279	89	272	45	76	17	0	12	44	23	34	1	1	.336	.474
Salmon,Tim, Ana	31	.293	135	481	81	141	28	2	26	101	87	112	4	4	.401	.522
Sanchez,Rey, KC	32	.267	131	449	53	120	19	2	2	39	22	57	6	4	.301	.332
Sanders,Reggie, SD	32	.267	125	442	76	118	23	4	20	62	55	120	22	10	.348	.473
Santangelo,F.P., SF	32	.235	128	340	50	80	18	2	4	32	51	71	7	4	.335	.335
Santiago,Benito, ChC	35	.240	90	279	25	67	13	1	8	35	19	63	1	0	.289	.380
Sefcik,Kevin, Phi	29	.282	122	241	32	68	16	3	2	21	27	30	6	3	.354	.398
Sequi,David, Tor	33	.282	132	478	67	135	24	1	16	63	50	71	2	2	.350	.437
Seguignol,Fern., Mon	25	.271	62	192	30	52	12	0	12	35	17	58	2	1	.330	.521
Servais,Scott, SF	33	.246	92	264	25	65	14	0	5	32	18	41	0	0	.294	.356
Sexson,Richie, Cle	25	.268	132	471	73	126	25	3	29	93	36	103	2	2	.320	.518
Sheets,Andy, Ana	28	.241	85	237	33	57	13	1	6	29	22	65	3	2	.305	.380
Sheffield,Gary, LA	31	.285	142	484	89	138	27	1	27	91	109	65	12	7	.417	.512
Shumpert,Terry, Col	33	.298	97	282	42	84	16	2	11	31	23	46	6	4	.351	.486
Simmons,Brian, CWS	26	.254	54	177	31	45	8	2	5	23	19	38	4	3	.327	.407
Simms,Mike, Tex	33	.263	100	262	36	69	14	1	14	55	33	63	1	1	.346	.485
Simon,Randall, Atl	25	.264	88	208	22	55	12	0	4	28	9	29	1	2	.295	.380
Singleton,Chris, CWS	27	.277	139	484	71	134	27	6	11	64	22	63	16	6	.308	.426
Smith,Bobby, TB	26	.242	119	364	44	88	16	2	10	47	35	110	8	6	.308	.379
Snow,J.T., SF	32	.256	150	503	74	129	24	1	20	81	80	110	2	3	.358	.427
Sorrento,Paul, TB	34	.232	94	284	34	66	14	0	12	42	38	86	1	1	.323	.408
Sosa,Sammy, ChC	31	.268	158	624	107	167	24	3	53	133	65	170	14	8	.337	.571
Spehr,Tim, KC	33	.190	53	147	19	28	7	0	6	20	18	41	1	0	.279	.361

Projections for 2000 Batters

Batter	Age	Avg	G	AB	R	H	2B	3B	HR	RBI	BB	SO	SB	CS	OBP	SLG
Spencer,Shane, NYY	28	.256	71	227	33	58	14	0	11	37	25	46	1	1	.329	.463
Spiers,Bill, Hou	34	.267	129	356	52	95	16	2	4	38	52	52	9	4	.360	.357
Spiezio,Scott, Oak	27	.255	114	381	53	97	23	2	12	56	40	53	3	2	.325	.420
Sprague,Ed, Pit	32	.241	138	493	65	119	27	1	21	68	44	98	1	2	.304	.428
Stairs,Matt, Oak	32	.274	143	521	88	143	31	1	32	102	75	105	4	3	.366	.522
Stanley,Mike, Bos	37	.257	131	404	59	104	19	0	19	63	65	97	1	1	.360	.446
Steinbach,Terry, Min	38	.246	116	394	43	97	19	1	10	50	36	84	1	1	.309	.376
Stevens,Lee, Tex	32	.271	137	435	58	118	27	2	21	69	36	106	1	1	.327	.487
Stewart,Shannon, Tor	26	.292	148	602	106	176	34	5	12	68	74	82	41	17	.370	.425
Stinnett,Kelly, Ari	30	.250	108	304	43	76	16	1	13	43	36	83	1	1	.329	.438
Stocker,Kevin, TB	30	.255	108	341	39	87	16	3	4	31	32	67	6	4	.319	.355
Strawberry,Darryl, NYY	38	.233	72	215	31	50	9	1	13	37	35	65	4	3	.340	.465
Stynes,Chris, Cin	27	.270	69	122	17	33	5	0	2	13	8	10	3	1	.315	.361
Surhoff,B.J., Bal	35	.270	156	629	83	170	32	2	22	93	49	82	3	2	.323	.432
Sutton,Larry, KC	30	.257	63	179	22	46	10	0	4	23	21	28	1	0	.335	.380
Sweeney,Mark, Cin	30	.280	75	132	19	37	7	0	3	17	19	23	1	1	.371	.402
Sweeney,Mike, KC	26	.282	151	564	85	159	34	1	21	89	52	61	4	3	.343	.457
Tatis,Fernando, StL	25	.295	153	555	96	164	34	2	28	90	58	112	16	8	.362	.515
Taubensee,Eddie, Cin	31	.278	129	417	54	116	24	1	15	69	40	86	1	1	.341	.448
Tejada,Miguel, Oak	24	.251	150	581	90	146	28	3	21	85	47	104	10	9	.307	.418
Thomas,Frank, CWS	32	.314	146	529	96	166	34	1	26	108	103	77	2	1	.426	.529
Thome,Jim, Cle	29	.276	151	551	115	152	31	2	39	111	136	176	1	1	.419	.552
Trammell,Bubba, TB	28	.267	109	375	54	100	23	0	19	57	42	84	3	2	.341	.480
Tucker,Michael, Cin	29	.261	130	318	50	83	17	3	11	42	36	81	7	4	.336	.437
Valentin,Javier, Min	24	.233	93	283	28	66	14	1	6	33	22	48	1	1	.289	.353
Valentin,John, Bos	33	.275	135	528	85	145	37	2	17	70	58	73	4	4	.346	.449
Valentin,Jose, Mil	30	.245	123	380	57	93	22	2	15	54	50	86	9	5	.333	.432
Vander Wal,John, SD	34	.246	114	179	22	44	10	1	4	26	25	50	1	1	.338	.380
Varitek,Jason, Bos	28	.250	134	420	58	105	26	1	15	59	41	84	2	2	.317	.424
Vaughn,Greg, Cin	34	.237	148	519	91	123	24	1	38	104	78	134	8	3	.337	.507
Vaughn,Mo, Ana	32	.296	145	551	85	163	27	1	34	106	68	144	1	0	.373	.534
Velarde,Randy, Oak	37	.277	135	505	73	140	24	2	11	53	62	91	11	6	.356	.398
Ventura,Robin, NYM	32	.268	156	579	83	155	29	1	25	100	80	103	1	1	.357	.451
Veras,Quilvio, SD	29	.268	141	518	83	139	24	3	6	44	78	85	24	12	.364	.361
Veras,Wilton, Bos	22	.278	117	407	51	113	22	2	9	53	13	51	4	3	.300	.408
Vidro,Jose, Mon	25	.274	154	493	62	135	36	2	10	65	39	60	3	2	.327	.416
Vina,Fernando, Mil	31	.288	128	489	71	141	22	5	5	39	36	33	13	9	.337	.384
Vizcaino,Jose, LA	32	.269	109	361	46	97	13	3	3	34	29	50	6	4	.323	.346
Vizquel,Omar, Cle	33	.275	146	559	87	154	22	2	4	50	61	58	31	10	.347	.343
Walbeck,Matt, Ana	30	.240	115	333	36	80	14	1	4	34	29	61	3	2	.301	.324
Walker,Larry, Col	33	.348	137	485	110	169	33	3	34	102	67	70	17	6	.428	.639
Walker,Todd, Min	27	.296	148	531	72	157	37	3	11	63	52	79	14	8	.358	.439
Ward,Daryle, Hou	25	.292	124	397	57	116	22	0	21	74	30	71	1	1	.342	.506
Weiss,Walt, Atl	36	.249	107	321	46	80	13	1	2	26	50	51	5	2	.350	.315
Wells,Vernon, Tor	21	.285	124	421	51	120	23	1	8	51	26	77	12	5	.327	.401
White,Devon, LA	37	.257	119	428	56	110	22	2	13	59	37	87	14	6	.316	.409
White,Rondell, Mon	28	.292	139	537	77	157	32	4	23	76	35	90	15	8	.336	.495
Widger,Chris, Mon	29	.247	134	421	43	104	23	1	14	56	32	90	3	2	.300	.406
Williams,Bernie, NYY	31	.311	151	569	108	177	33	4	24	104	89	92	12	8	.404	.510
Williams,Gerald, Atl	33	.264	120	352	53	93	22	2	11	43	20	59	11	7	.304	.432

Projections for 2000 Batters

Batter	Age	Avg	G	AB	R	H	2B	3B	HR	RBI	BB	SO	SB	CS	OBP	SLG
Williams,Matt, Ari	34	.270	143	560	79	151	24	2	30	108	39	102	4	2	.317	.480
Wilson,Craig, CWS	29	.263	77	232	31	61	10	0	4	25	20	21	1	1	.321	.358
Wilson,Dan, Sea	31	.264	129	436	48	115	23	1	11	58	33	74	3	2	.316	.397
Wilson,Enrique, Cle	24	.284	101	331	47	94	17	1	4	30	25	32	8	6	.334	.378
Wilson,Preston, Fla	25	.267	150	550	81	147	26	2	30	86	44	170	12	7	.322	.485
Winn,Randy, TB	26	.282	75	298	45	84	13	4	2	26	23	58	16	9	.333	.372
Womack,Tony, Ari	30	.270	152	633	89	171	23	6	4	47	45	91	50	12	.319	.344
Young,Dmitri, Cin	26	.291	140	454	70	132	32	3	14	63	45	81	6	4	.355	.467
Young,Eric, LA	33	.282	133	515	88	145	21	4	6	51	61	39	39	16	.358	.373
Young,Kevin, Pit	31	.275	155	564	87	155	37	3	25	104	51	128	14	7	.335	.484
Zaun,Gregg, Tex	29	.243	38	107	13	26	5	0	2	12	15	14	1	1	.336	.346
Zeile,Todd, Tex	34	.259	151	552	72	143	29	1	21	85	68	98	3	3	.340	.429

These Guys Can Play Too and Might Get A Shot

It's difficult to predict which players will end up getting significant playing time in the major leagues next year. That said, we can say with confidence that if the following players land major league jobs, their final numbers should be consistent with the stats listed below. These players generally fit into one of two categories: they either have a decent chance to play in the majors in 2000, or we think they deserve that chance. What you'll find below are the players' Major League Equivalencies (or MLEs) for their 1999 seasons. An MLE is not a projection for what a player will do in the future; it is an interpretation of what he did in the minors last year. The MLE method adjusts the player's minor league stats and re-expresses them in major league terms. In short, an MLE shows you what a player would have hit if he'd been playing in the majors. It has just as much predictive value as a major leaguer's 1999 stats, but no more. Ages as of June 30, 2000.

Batter	Age	Avg	G	AB	R	H	2B	3B	HR	RBI	BB	SO	SB	CS	OBP	SLG
Alvarez,Gabe	26	.256	110	394	55	101	20	0	18	52	45	84	0	3	.333	.444
Barajas,Rod	24	.278	127	482	55	134	34	1	10	68	14	78	1	0	.298	.415
Bradley,Milton	22	.301	87	332	50	100	21	4	8	40	22	65	10	9	.345	.461
Branyan,Russ	24	.191	109	387	42	74	10	0	25	56	43	196	6	3	.272	.411
Brown,Dee	22	.318	65	223	44	71	11	2	9	42	22	41	6	7	.380	.507
Brown,Roosevelt	24	.310	108	377	49	117	32	1	19	72	24	87	6	4	.352	.552
Cardona,Javier	24	.270	108	396	61	107	25	0	21	67	28	73	2	2	.318	.492
Chiaramonte,Giuseppe	24	.230	114	392	50	90	18	1	17	69	32	96	3	2	.288	.411
Christensen,McKay	24	.265	76	287	45	76	7	4	2	24	22	48	13	6	.317	.338
Coleman,Michael	24	.245	115	453	74	111	28	1	23	57	39	134	9	5	.305	.464
Cox,Steve	25	.297	134	501	73	149	41	2	18	87	45	77	1	2	.355	.495
Crede,Joe	22	.232	74	284	32	66	12	0	3	36	16	49	1	6	.273	.306
DaVanon,Jeff	26	.293	134	474	86	139	29	9	11	55	44	98	18	14	.353	.462
Dellaero,Jason	23	.246	81	264	34	65	11	2	7	38	10	80	4	8	.274	.383
Eckstein,David	25	.294	131	470	90	138	21	3	4	42	62	51	20	8	.376	.377
Gibson,Derrick	25	.273	110	384	52	105	18	5	17	51	23	80	8	6	.314	.479
Hacker,Steve	25	.271	126	465	59	126	34	0	22	82	30	119	0	3	.315	.486
Huff,Aubrey	23	.267	133	468	62	125	34	2	17	57	39	82	1	2	.323	.457
Jimenez,D'Angelo	22	.291	126	499	73	145	26	3	11	66	43	77	18	7	.347	.421
Johnson,Nick	21	.319	132	404	95	129	29	3	11	72	86	93	5	6	.439	.488
Lamb,Mike	24	.312	139	536	88	167	48	4	20	90	40	68	2	2	.359	.528
Lopez,Mendy	25	.282	61	213	32	60	6	0	9	31	14	40	1	1	.326	.437
Lugo,Julio	24	.285	116	424	60	121	22	3	7	32	28	59	17	7	.330	.401
Paul,Josh	25	.258	93	310	40	80	17	2	3	36	21	72	4	6	.305	.355
Pellow,Kit	26	.260	131	458	69	119	24	3	27	78	15	116	4	4	.283	.502
iatt,Adam	24	.291	135	460	88	134	39	2	25	95	58	108	4	3	.371	.548
Porter,Bo	27	.266	111	399	67	106	20	1	23	50	51	127	10	17	.349	.494
Raabe,Brian	32	.289	130	467	70	135	29	3	8	58	35	19	3	7	.339	.415
Roskos,John	25	.274	134	474	60	130	35	0	16	63	37	117	1	1	.327	.449
Soriano,Alfonso	22	.255	109	427	53	109	21	2	13	64	25	89	17	7	.296	.405
Sosa,Juan	24	.293	131	526	65	154	22	5	9	41	24	64	28	11	.324	.405
Toca,Jorge	25	.281	124	431	66	121	22	0	17	74	25	70	3	8	.320	.450
Vitiello,Joe	30	.287	122	428	55	123	28	0	22	77	51	83	2	3	.363	.507
Williams,Jason	26	.303	127	466	70	141	39	2	6	47	40	68	4	3	.358	.433
Wilson,Craig	23	.239	111	348	42	83	19	2	14	51	25	111	0	2	.290	.425
Witt,Kevin	24	.259	114	410	63	106	23	2	20	62	56	114	0	0	.348	.471

2000 Pitcher Projections

Making statistical projections for major league pitchers is a very inexact science, as there are so many elements to a pitcher's season that come into play. He might begin spring training after a solid year and throw with the slightest, unconscious change in his mechanics, making it difficult to duplicate his previous success. Mechanical flaws can lead to a drop in velocity, a breaking pitch that isn't as effective, lost command or an injury. Improved mechanics also can produce an unexpected surge in a pitcher's success. Just as unpredictable is a pitcher's health, which can derail a season, and his role might change as well.

Despite these vagaries of pitching, we take a stab at pitching projections. STATS CEO John Dewan and interactive manager Mike Canter devised a formula that we have used to predict pitching performances for 2000. All pitchers who have 150 games or 500 innings in the majors are covered.

Examples of success at this difficult task include Pat Hentgen and Woody Williams:

Pat Hentgen	W	L	ERA	G	IP	H	BB	SO	BR/9
Actual 1999	11	12	4.79	34	199.0	225	65	118	13.1
Projected 1999	12	12	4.50	31	206.0	214	80	119	12.8

Woody Williams	W	L	ERA	G	IP	H	BB	SO	BR/9
Actual 1999	12	12	4.41	33	208.1	213	73	137	12.4
Projected 1999	12	12	4.57	32	205.0	200	79	139	12.2

As a reminder that projecting pitchers isn't easy, we bring you a couple of cases where we predicted better results for hurlers. Even guys like Roger Clemens don't always meet expectations. And the wheels came off for Carlos Perez:

Roger Clemens	W	L	ERA	G	IP	H	BB	SO	BR/9
Actual 1999	14	10	4.60	30	187.2	185	90	163	13.2
Projected 1999	19	8	2.84	33	244.0	194	92	276	10.5

Carlos Perez	W	L	ERA	G	IP	H	BB	SO	BR/9
Actual 1999	2	10	7.43	17	89.2	116	39	40	15.6
Projected 1999	13	13	3.83	34	230.0	231	60	122	11.4

There is no such thing as infallible pitching projections, but we'll stand behind ours. Enjoy.

—Thom Henninger

Projections for 2000 Pitchers

Pitcher	Age	ERA	W	L	Sv	G	GS	IP	H	HR	BB	SO	BR/9
Adams,Terry, ChC	27	4.10	4	4	15	56	0	68	66	5	35	62	13.4
Aguilera,Rick, ChC	38	3.21	5	3	20	63	0	70	63	8	13	50	9.8
Aldred,Scott, Phi	32	5.44	3	4	2	60	0	48	56	8	20	28	14.3
Alvarez,Wilson, TB	30	4.38	9	10	0	27	27	154	144	17	76	120	12.9
Anderson,Brian, Ari	28	4.61	9	11	0	28	28	160	175	27	34	80	11.8
Appier,Kevin, Oak	32	4.26	12	10	0	31	31	188	184	20	76	118	12.4
Ashby,Andy, SD	32	3.80	12	13	0	32	32	213	212	23	56	139	11.3
Assenmacher,Paul, Cle	39	5.92	3	3	0	60	0	38	49	5	17	34	15.6
Astacio,Pedro, Col	30	5.02	14	12	0	34	34	224	249	36	73	193	12.9
Avery,Steve, Cin	30	6.17	5	9	0	24	20	105	112	12	85	52	16.9
Ayala,Bobby, ChC	30	4.50	4	5	0	65	0	80	81	11	33	75	12.8
Baldwin,James, CWS	28	4.84	10	12	0	36	30	186	196	24	76	120	13.2
Beck,Rod, Bos	31	3.86	4	3	5	56	0	56	57	7	13	46	11.3
Belcher,Tim, Ana	38	5.31	8	12	0	27	27	166	188	29	58	83	13.3
Belinda,Stan, Cin	33	3.78	5	4	5	55	0	81	71	11	31	84	11.3
Benes,Andy, Ari	32	4.26	12	12	0	33	33	209	200	24	87	149	12.4
Benitez,Armando, NYM	27	2.76	3	3	35	75	0	75	46	7	42	110	10.6
Bere,Jason, Mil	29	6.31	3	8	0	20	17	87	95	12	65	59	16.6
Bergman,Sean, Atl	30	4.64	7	8	0	27	20	128	147	14	35	66	12.8
Blair,Willie, Det	34	4.68	8	8	0	37	19	148	161	23	46	81	12.6
Bochtler,Doug, LA	29	4.65	2	2	0	25	0	31	27	4	22	22	14.2
Bohanon,Brian, Col	31	5.54	11	10	0	35	28	182	207	28	85	121	14.4
Bones,Ricky, Bal	31	5.55	2	3	0	31	1	47	58	7	19	26	14.7
Borbon,Pedro, LA	32	3.18	5	3	2	70	0	51	38	4	29	33	11.8
Bottalico,Ricky, StL	30	4.57	2	4	27	58	0	63	61	7	38	60	14.1
Bottenfield,Kent, StL	31	4.55	11	12	0	31	31	184	183	20	86	126	13.2
Brocail,Doug, Det	33	3.32	6	3	0	67	0	76	66	7	27	65	11.0
Brown,Kevin, LA	35	2.66	20	9	0	35	35	254	221	13	59	238	9.9
Burba,Dave, Cle	33	4.52	13	12	0	33	33	215	209	28	94	155	12.7
Burkett,John, Tex	35	5.13	9	10	0	31	27	163	201	17	51	108	13.9
Candiotti,Tom, Cle	42	5.43	3	4	0	12	10	58	66	9	24	30	14.0
Carrasco,Hector, Min	30	3.91	3	3	0	47	0	53	51	4	24	42	12.7
Charlton,Norm, TB	37	5.04	2	3	0	44	0	50	51	5	35	46	15.5
Christiansen,Jason, Pit	30	3.83	3	3	10	46	0	47	44	3	23	49	12.8
Clark,Mark, Tex	32	5.06	7	8	0	21	21	121	132	14	55	86	13.9
Clemens,Roger, NYY	37	3.59	15	9	0	31	31	203	170	15	98	209	11.9
Clontz,Brad, Pit	29	4.17	3	3	2	44	0	41	40	5	18	33	12.7
Colon,Bartolo, Cle	25	4.13	14	10	0	32	32	205	202	21	76	160	12.2
Cone,David, NYY	37	3.91	14	9	0	31	31	198	173	20	92	191	12.0
Cook,Dennis, NYM	37	3.60	5	4	0	72	0	65	54	8	27	73	11.2
Cordova,Francisco, Pit	28	4.03	11	11	0	29	29	181	178	17	66	121	12.1
Cormier,Rheal, Bos	33	3.86	4	3	0	60	0	63	65	6	19	38	12.0
Corsi,Jim, Bal	38	4.02	3	3	0	44	0	47	44	5	20	32	12.3
Crabtree,Tim, Tex	30	4.13	5	4	0	67	0	72	78	5	26	53	13.0
Daal,Omar, Ari	28	3.86	13	11	0	32	32	210	197	20	77	156	11.7
DeJean,Mike, Col	29	4.85	4	4	0	57	0	65	76	7	26	31	14.1
DeLucia,Rich, Cle	35	4.50	2	2	0	24	0	30	25	5	20	30	13.5
Dipoto,Jerry, Col	32	4.28	5	4	0	65	0	82	86	7	33	62	13.1
Dreifort,Darren, LA	28	3.92	11	10	0	31	28	179	167	15	76	154	12.2
Eldred,Cal, Mil	32	5.64	4	8	0	21	18	99	108	14	56	67	14.9

Projections for 2000 Pitchers

Pitcher	Age	ERA	W	L	Sv	G	GS	IP	H	HR	BB	SO	BR/9
Embree,Alan, SF	30	3.79	4	3	0	64	0	57	49	7	25	51	11.7
Erickson,Scott, Bal	32	4.75	13	15	0	35	35	237	258	22	102	144	13.7
Estes,Shawn, SF	27	4.38	11	11	0	30	30	185	173	15	102	155	13.4
Fassero,Jeff, Tex	37	5.98	9	13	0	35	29	179	203	32	95	136	15.0
Fernandez,Alex, Fla	30	3.64	9	8	0	24	24	141	131	16	41	91	11.0
Fetters,Mike, Bal	35	4.28	3	2	0	38	0	40	40	4	20	32	13.5
Finley,Chuck, Ana	37	4.11	13	12	0	33	33	217	202	21	95	204	12.3
Florie,Bryce, Bos	30	4.36	4	4	0	41	9	99	103	9	46	73	13.5
Franco,John, NYM	39	3.86	3	3	12	51	0	49	49	2	22	47	13.0
Frascatore,John, Tor	30	3.99	5	4	2	62	0	79	78	9	29	46	12.2
Gardner,Mark, SF	38	4.69	9	10	0	30	25	163	161	26	67	110	12.6
Glavine,Tom, Atl	34	3.57	16	11	0	34	34	232	218	16	82	148	11.6
Gomes,Wayne, Phi	27	4.28	2	5	25	72	0	80	80	7	44	64	13.9
Gooden,Dwight, Cle	35	5.43	7	8	0	25	22	121	129	15	71	83	14.9
Gordon,Tom, Bos	32	3.76	2	3	25	62	0	67	64	6	28	63	12.4
Grahe,Joe, Phi	32	4.91	1	1	0	13	5	33	40	1	17	16	15.5
Graves,Danny, Cin	26	3.83	3	5	23	71	0	101	96	8	45	57	12.6
Grimsley,Jason, NYY	32	4.68	4	4	0	55	0	75	79	8	40	49	14.3
Groom,Buddy, Oak	34	4.32	4	4	0	76	0	50	55	4	18	33	13.1
Guardado,Eddie, Min	29	4.17	4	4	0	68	0	54	48	8	24	53	12.0
Guthrie,Mark, ChC	34	4.11	3	4	0	56	0	57	56	6	24	41	12.6
Guzman,Juan, Cin	33	4.15	13	12	0	33	33	204	183	26	88	160	12.0
Hamilton,Joey, Tor	29	4.37	9	8	0	26	23	138	142	13	55	89	12.8
Hampton,Mike, Hou	27	4.07	14	12	0	33	33	230	227	16	97	160	12.7
Haney,Chris, Cle	31	5.02	2	2	0	21	7	61	72	8	21	34	13.7
Harnisch,Pete, Cin	33	3.92	13	11	0	33	33	202	192	27	58	137	11.1
Hasegawa,Shig., Ana	31	4.29	5	4	4	63	1	84	82	12	32	58	12.2
Hawkins,LaTroy, Min	27	6.05	7	15	0	33	33	180	233	30	62	102	14.8
Haynes,Jimmy, Oak	27	5.94	8	12	0	31	28	159	186	21	90	108	15.6
Helling,Rick, Tex	29	4.42	14	12	0	34	34	218	207	33	85	148	12.1
Henry,Doug, Hou	36	4.41	3	3	2	43	0	51	48	6	28	46	13.4
Hentgen,Pat, Tor	31	4.31	12	11	0	32	32	192	196	24	63	108	12.1
Heredia,Felix, ChC	24	4.33	4	4	0	70	1	54	55	4	30	51	14.2
Heredia,Gil, Oak	34	4.29	11	9	0	28	28	170	195	20	29	101	11.9
Hermanson,Dust., Mon	27	3.74	13	11	0	33	33	207	194	21	66	153	11.3
Hernandez,Livan, SF	25	4.78	11	13	0	31	31	211	228	26	80	149	13.1
Hernandez,Roberto, TB	35	3.33	3	4	39	70	0	73	61	4	36	66	12.0
Hershiser,Orel, NYM	41	4.28	11	11	0	33	33	187	184	18	80	105	12.7
Hill,Ken, Ana	34	5.03	6	8	0	24	21	120	124	10	71	69	14.6
Hitchcock,Sterling, SD	29	4.87	9	14	0	35	31	196	209	29	72	181	12.9
Hoffman,Trevor, SD	32	1.83	3	2	43	65	0	69	44	5	19	84	8.2
Holmes,Darren, Ari	34	4.50	3	3	0	41	0	50	55	5	20	36	13.5
Hudek,John, Tor	33	5.25	2	2	0	33	0	36	33	5	27	35	15.0
Jackson,Mike, Cle	35	2.69	3	2	38	71	0	67	52	6	22	59	9.9
Johnson,Randy, Ari	36	2.67	20	9	0	35	35	263	201	26	68	353	9.2
Johnstone,John, SF	31	3.33	5	3	0	65	0	73	61	8	29	66	11.1
Jones,Bobby, NYM	30	3.74	9	7	0	22	22	137	140	16	25	79	10.8
Jones,Doug, Oak	43	4.22	6	5	10	70	0	98	106	14	21	69	11.7
Jones,Todd, Det	32	4.02	2	4	26	65	0	65	61	6	35	62	13.3
Juden,Jeff, NYY	29	4.38	2	1	0	12	2	37	36	5	17	31	12.9

Projections for 2000 Pitchers

Pitcher	Age	ERA	W	L	Sv	G	GS	IP	H	HR	BB	SO	BR/9
Kamieniecki,Scott, Bal	36	4.34	3	3	0	33	6	56	57	6	23	33	12.9
Karchner,Matt, ChC	33	4.50	2	2	0	31	0	34	33	4	17	23	13.2
Karl,Scott, Mil	28	4.91	10	14	0	33	33	196	222	23	68	88	13.3
Kile,Darryl, Col	31	5.69	12	13	0	33	33	204	230	24	117	133	15.3
Kline,Steve, Mon	27	4.37	4	5	0	81	0	70	69	8	35	66	13.4
Langston,Mark, Cle	39	5.69	2	3	0	24	9	68	84	10	33	47	15.5
Leiter,Al, NYM	34	3.41	14	9	0	31	31	206	173	14	90	171	11.5
Leiter,Mark, Sea	37	3.30	2	1	0	24	0	30	23	3	16	29	11.7
Leskanic,Curt, Col	32	4.72	5	4	0	64	0	82	85	10	42	69	13.9
Lieber,Jon, ChC	30	4.29	11	12	0	30	30	193	207	25	44	167	11.7
Lima,Jose, Hou	27	3.98	15	13	0	34	34	242	251	33	43	180	10.9
Lloyd,Graeme, Tor	33	3.84	5	3	0	66	0	61	59	7	19	35	11.5
Loaiza,Esteban, Tex	28	4.53	8	7	0	32	19	137	154	17	42	86	12.9
Lopez,Albie, TB	28	5.09	3	5	0	52	0	69	78	10	30	51	14.1
Lowe,Derek, Bos	27	3.32	7	4	15	70	3	114	107	9	34	79	11.1
Maddux,Greg, Atl	34	2.74	18	8	0	33	33	230	214	12	39	166	9.9
Maddux,Mike, LA	38	3.57	4	3	0	52	0	58	57	5	19	39	11.8
Magnante,Mike, Ana	35	3.43	4	3	0	51	0	63	61	2	25	47	12.3
Mahomes,Pat, NYM	29	5.20	3	4	0	39	0	64	64	11	41	48	14.8
Martinez,Pedro, Bos	28	2.21	19	5	0	32	30	220	169	17	38	278	8.5
Martinez,Ramon, Bos	32	3.44	11	7	0	24	24	144	124	12	56	125	11.3
Mathews,T.J., Oak	30	3.52	5	3	0	55	0	64	56	7	24	51	11.3
Mathews,Terry, KC	35	5.18	2	2	0	22	1	33	36	5	16	18	14.2
McElroy,Chuck, NYM	32	3.97	4	4	0	63	0	59	59	5	24	50	12.7
McMichael,Greg, Oak	33	4.00	3	2	0	45	0	45	45	4	20	37	13.0
Mercker,Kent, Bos	32	5.27	7	10	0	30	25	140	157	16	69	74	14.5
Mesa,Jose, Sea	34	4.50	2	4	33	71	0	74	79	8	33	55	13.6
Miceli,Dan, SD	29	4.37	4	5	0	66	0	70	69	9	32	65	13.0
Mills,Alan, LA	33	4.38	4	5	0	69	0	74	63	10	50	54	13.7
Mlicki,Dave, Det	32	4.52	12	11	0	32	31	193	202	23	70	120	12.7
Moehler,Brian, Det	28	4.57	12	12	0	32	32	205	223	25	62	112	12.5
Mohler,Mike, StL	31	4.58	3	3	0	51	0	53	57	5	26	35	14.1
Morgan,Mike, Tex	40	5.83	5	7	0	28	16	105	130	19	36	49	14.2
Morman,Alvin, KC	31	5.40	2	3	2	46	0	45	51	7	23	30	14.8
Moyer,Jamie, Sea	37	3.68	16	10	0	33	33	230	233	23	48	147	11.0
Mulholland,Terry, Atl	37	4.11	8	8	0	51	18	151	161	15	40	83	12.0
Munoz,Mike, Tex	34	4.41	3	3	0	51	0	49	56	4	16	27	13.2
Mussina,Mike, Bal	31	3.75	14	10	0	30	30	204	200	22	52	173	11.1
Myers,Mike, Mil	31	4.70	3	4	0	71	0	44	46	6	18	38	13.1
Nagy,Charles, Cle	33	4.65	13	11	0	33	32	205	228	26	60	122	12.6
Navarro,Jaime, CWS	32	5.71	8	12	0	34	27	164	198	22	73	72	14.9
Neagle,Denny, Cin	31	3.93	11	9	0	27	27	174	162	21	62	130	11.6
Nelson,Jeff, NYY	33	3.71	3	2	0	41	0	34	30	2	18	34	12.7
Nen,Robb, SF	30	3.23	3	3	36	74	0	78	68	5	30	89	11.3
Nomo,Hideo, Mil	31	4.02	10	10	0	28	28	170	149	20	75	167	11.9
Ogea,Chad, Phi	29	5.07	7	9	0	30	22	135	147	21	49	68	13.1
Olivares,Omar, Oak	32	4.50	12	11	0	34	30	198	209	20	78	100	13.0
Oliver,Darren, StL	29	4.79	10	12	0	30	30	184	203	21	69	106	13.3
Olson,Gregg, Ari	33	4.00	4	4	0	62	0	63	61	6	28	47	12.7
Oquist,Mike, Oak	32	5.39	8	10	0	29	26	152	171	21	69	97	14.2

398

Projections for 2000 Pitchers

Pitcher	Age	ERA	W	L	Sv	G	GS	IP	H	HR	BB	SO	BR/9
Orosco,Jesse, Bal	43	3.83	4	3	3	66	0	40	34	5	22	39	12.6
Osborne,Donovan, StL	31	4.21	3	3	0	9	9	47	48	6	16	34	12.3
Painter,Lance, StL	32	4.50	4	4	2	59	0	58	57	8	28	48	13.2
Park,Chan Ho, LA	27	4.26	12	12	0	33	33	203	181	22	105	179	12.7
Patterson,Danny, Tex	29	4.20	4	3	0	54	0	60	67	6	19	46	12.9
Percival,Troy, Ana	30	2.70	3	2	32	62	0	60	39	7	28	74	10.1
Perez,Carlos, LA	29	4.82	7	9	0	23	22	140	148	17	61	71	13.4
Perez,Yorkis, Phi	32	3.92	3	2	0	42	0	39	37	3	18	31	12.7
Petkovsek,Mark, Ana	34	4.25	5	4	0	59	3	91	99	9	28	47	12.6
Pettitte,Andy, NYY	28	4.55	13	11	0	32	31	200	208	16	93	131	13.5
Plesac,Dan, Ari	38	3.91	4	3	0	69	0	46	45	5	16	53	11.9
Plunk,Eric, Mil	36	4.86	4	5	0	66	0	74	73	13	38	71	13.5
Poole,Jim, Cle	34	5.35	3	3	0	49	0	37	46	4	16	22	15.1
Portugal,Mark, Bos	37	5.13	8	11	0	29	27	156	179	27	42	90	12.8
Powell,Jay, Hou	28	3.70	5	4	5	65	0	73	70	4	35	67	12.9
Quantrill,Paul, Tor	31	4.73	3	4	0	55	0	59	70	7	15	39	13.0
Radinsky,Scott, StL	32	3.46	3	2	0	49	0	39	37	2	15	27	12.0
Radke,Brad, Min	27	4.06	13	12	0	33	33	217	227	29	44	134	11.2
Rapp,Pat, Bos	32	5.01	9	11	0	35	28	160	175	16	76	106	14.1
Reed,Rick, NYM	34	4.08	11	10	0	28	28	170	166	22	54	121	11.6
Reed,Steve, Cle	34	3.57	5	3	0	65	0	68	58	9	25	53	11.0
Remlinger,Mike, Atl	34	3.97	6	5	2	60	9	111	98	13	54	110	12.3
Reyes,Al, Bal	29	4.43	4	4	0	52	0	63	58	9	33	63	13.0
Reyes,Carlos, Phi	31	4.74	4	5	0	59	0	74	83	11	23	48	12.9
Reynolds,Shane, Hou	32	3.61	16	11	0	35	35	232	242	23	37	203	10.8
Reynoso,Armando, Ari	34	4.77	7	9	0	24	22	134	144	16	54	68	13.3
Rhodes,Arthur, Bal	30	3.54	4	3	0	44	0	61	51	7	28	66	11.7
Rincon,Ricky, Cle	30	3.53	4	2	0	59	0	51	43	5	23	50	11.6
Rivera,Mariano, NYY	30	2.05	3	1	47	62	0	66	49	2	18	51	9.1
Rodriguez,Frank, Sea	27	4.75	3	3	4	25	7	72	80	8	30	44	13.8
Rodriguez,Rich, SF	37	4.50	4	4	0	64	0	60	63	7	23	43	12.9
Rogers,Kenny, NYM	35	4.07	13	12	0	32	32	210	211	19	74	128	12.2
Rosado,Jose, KC	25	4.20	12	10	0	35	30	197	195	23	68	142	12.0
Rueter,Kirk, SF	29	4.50	11	12	0	33	33	186	200	23	55	98	12.3
Saberhagen,Bret, Bos	36	3.52	10	7	0	25	25	138	143	16	13	85	10.2
Sanders,Scott, ChC	31	4.66	3	5	0	53	5	83	85	13	37	70	13.2
Schilling,Curt, Phi	33	3.00	15	8	0	28	28	210	178	21	51	211	9.8
Schmidt,Jason, Pit	27	4.56	11	14	0	33	33	213	224	22	85	153	13.1
Schourek,Pete, Pit	31	5.15	5	8	0	28	19	117	124	19	51	93	13.5
Seanez,Rudy, Atl	31	2.81	4	2	0	49	0	48	38	3	20	48	10.9
Sele,Aaron, Tex	30	4.80	12	12	0	33	33	208	240	20	71	175	13.5
Service,Scott, KC	33	4.62	5	5	17	70	0	78	81	10	35	80	13.4
Shaw,Jeff, LA	33	2.92	3	3	34	67	0	74	66	6	14	51	9.7
Shuey,Paul, Cle	29	4.06	5	3	5	62	0	71	65	8	37	83	12.9
Simas,Bill, CWS	28	4.13	5	4	0	67	0	72	69	8	30	53	12.4
Sirotka,Mike, CWS	29	4.84	11	13	0	32	32	210	246	27	57	126	13.0
Slocumb,Heathcliff, StL	34	4.50	4	4	0	52	0	64	64	4	41	55	14.8
Smoltz,John, Atl	33	2.75	15	6	0	28	28	180	156	13	39	167	9.8
Sparks,Steve, Ana	34	5.68	7	11	0	26	24	141	154	21	78	83	14.8
Spoljaric,Paul, Tor	29	4.68	4	4	0	46	5	77	75	10	44	78	13.9

Projections for 2000 Pitchers

Pitcher	Age	ERA	W	L	Sv	G	GS	IP	H	HR	BB	SO	BR/9
Spradlin,Jerry, SF	33	3.71	5	4	0	65	0	68	65	7	24	60	11.8
Springer,Dennis, Fla	35	4.85	8	12	0	35	25	169	184	25	55	70	12.7
Springer,Russ, Atl	31	4.04	3	3	0	49	0	49	46	5	25	57	13.0
Stanton,Mike, NYY	33	3.84	5	3	0	71	1	68	64	8	25	65	11.8
Stottlemyre,Todd, Ari	35	4.02	9	8	0	22	22	141	133	15	56	122	12.1
Sullivan,Scott, Cin	29	3.35	7	4	4	75	0	110	93	12	40	91	10.9
Swindell,Greg, Ari	35	3.58	5	4	0	69	0	73	67	9	21	51	10.8
Tapani,Kevin, ChC	36	4.17	9	10	0	27	27	164	176	18	40	96	11.9
Tavarez,Julian, SF	27	4.71	3	4	0	51	0	65	74	6	27	35	14.0
Taylor,Billy, NYM	38	4.21	4	4	0	64	0	62	67	6	22	53	12.9
Telford,Anthony, Mon	34	3.83	6	5	3	78	0	94	93	8	36	64	12.4
Thompson,Justin, Det	27	4.26	11	9	0	27	27	169	164	19	70	108	12.5
Timlin,Mike, Bal	34	3.18	3	3	31	65	0	68	62	7	19	49	10.7
Tomko,Brett, Cin	27	4.09	11	10	0	33	29	185	174	24	64	142	11.6
Trachsel,Steve, ChC	29	4.46	11	14	0	34	34	206	210	30	64	149	12.0
Trombley,Mike, Min	33	4.00	3	5	33	76	0	90	86	11	34	83	12.0
Urbina,Ugueth, Mon	26	3.28	3	3	48	69	0	74	57	8	35	98	11.2
Valdes,Ismael, LA	26	3.76	12	10	0	30	30	194	187	21	55	136	11.2
Veres,Dave, Col	33	4.56	2	4	35	70	0	77	81	9	32	68	13.2
Villone,Ron, Cin	30	3.84	9	8	0	28	23	143	123	11	73	94	12.3
Wagner,Billy, Hou	28	2.19	3	2	39	63	0	70	44	6	27	114	9.1
Wakefield,Tim, Bos	33	4.61	10	10	2	31	26	166	170	24	71	119	13.1
Wasdin,John, Bos	27	4.39	4	4	0	46	3	82	85	13	23	55	11.9
Watson,Allen, NYY	29	4.94	3	3	0	35	7	82	89	13	32	60	13.3
Weathers,Dave, Mil	30	4.91	4	6	0	57	3	99	118	10	41	80	14.5
Wells,Bob, Min	33	4.68	4	5	0	61	0	75	81	13	23	45	12.5
Wells,David, Tor	37	4.06	14	12	0	33	33	226	223	31	60	168	11.3
Wendell,Turk, NYM	33	3.58	6	4	0	75	0	83	70	7	43	69	12.3
Wetteland,John, Tex	33	3.05	3	2	44	62	0	65	53	7	18	65	9.8
Whisenant,Matt, SD	29	4.02	4	4	0	68	0	56	54	3	36	42	14.5
White,Gabe, Cin	28	4.14	4	4	0	56	1	74	71	13	18	62	10.8
White,Rick, TB	31	4.36	4	5	0	55	2	95	106	9	33	64	13.2
Wickman,Bob, Mil	31	4.09	2	5	35	71	0	77	77	6	36	64	13.2
Wilkins,Marc, Pit	29	3.69	2	2	0	36	0	39	36	3	19	30	12.7
Williams,Brian, Hou	31	5.10	3	4	0	50	0	67	74	8	39	49	15.2
Williams,Mike, Pit	31	4.82	1	4	20	51	0	56	60	7	28	66	14.1
Williams,Woody, SD	33	4.61	10	15	0	33	33	209	210	34	73	144	12.2
Witt,Bobby, TB	36	6.14	6	13	0	27	27	154	185	23	82	94	15.6
Worrell,Tim, Oak	32	4.22	4	4	0	50	3	81	81	9	33	65	12.7
Wright,Jamey, Col	25	5.93	7	9	0	22	22	132	158	15	75	59	15.9

Career Assessments

Hi, this is Bill James. For years, I have written an annual introduction to the Player Projections. That's gotten to be kind of boring, and how much space do I really need to brag about the fact that we had projected Carlos Beltran to hit .298 with 20 homers? So we decided this year to do something a little bit different. This year I'm going to write an intro to the Career Assessments.

The Career Standards Assessment System is a simple way of estimating a player's chances of achieving some very difficult goal, such as reaching 3,000 career hits, hitting 600 career homers, or breaking the all-time record for career RBI. To take the 3,000-hit standard as an example, the system asks essentially three questions:

1) How fast is he moving,

2) How far does he have to go, and

3) How much time does he have?

"How fast is he moving?" means "How many hits per season has he been piling up?" Take Craig Biggio, for example. . . Craig Biggio, incidentally, is the best player in baseball, but that's another argument. Biggio had 191 hits in 1997, 210 hits in 1998, and 188 hits in 1999, so he is moving at a rate of about 196 hits per season. 195.83 is the actual figure that we use, and if you're wondering what the formula is, you're missing the point.

How far does he have to go? Well, Biggio now has 1,868 career hits. He needs another 1,132 hits. He needs to keep going for about another six years.

How much time does he have? Nobody knows, of course; Biggio turns 34 in December. We figure that a 33-year-old player has about four-and-a-half years left in his career, but this is just an estimate. If he is moving at a rate of 195.8 hits per season and he has four-and-a-half years left, then we would expect him to get about 881 more hits in the rest of his career.

This would mean that Biggio would fall short of 3,000 hits—but not very far short. He *might* get 3,000 career hits; the odds are against him, but not prohibitively. It is certainly *possible* that he'll get 3,000 hits. We estimate that his chances of getting 3,000 career hits are 28%.

The 1999 season was an interesting one in the 3,000-hit marketplace, a turning of the page, if you will, appropriate to the world's odometer turning over. Two things happened in 1999 which made this a notable season in the 3,000-hit race:

1) The players who have been the best 3,000-hit candidates for the past several seasons, Boggs, Gwynn and Ripken, reached or virtually reached the finish line, closing that chapter, and turning our attention to the next generation of candidates who are shaping up: Roberto Alomar, Ken Griffey, Rafael Palmeiro, Craig Biggio, and others.

2) A couple of old guys suddenly came back to life as 3,000-hit candidates.

In the system that we use to estimate these things, a player's chances of reaching are fairly stable in mid-career. We never project that a very young player will get 3,000 hits; rather, we project that he has some chance to reach the goal. Carlos Beltran starts out at 2%.

As long as he plays well, that number builds up slowly, from 2% to 8, from 8% to 12, from 40% to 50, from 50% to 60. It is a system of small increases as the players keep plugging along—and sudden, sharp decreases when players get injured or cease to play well.

But as a player gets near the finish line, funny things can happen; then a player's chance of getting 3,000 hits *can* explode. Let's take a 35-year-old player who has 2,200 hits. Suppose he gets 180 hits at age 36, 150 at age 37, 120 at age 38, 80 hits at age 39. Is he going to make it? Probably not; he's now 40 years old, limping along, and still 270 hits from his goal.

Suppose, however, that that player suddenly gets 180 hits the next season, at age 40. All of a sudden, he's half a season away from 3,000, and he's got a full head of steam. His chances of getting 3,000 hits can go from 2% to 80% in one year.

In theory, such things can happen, but they rarely do—but last year they did. Rickey Henderson a year ago was coming off of three straight seasons of hitting .248 or less. He turned 40 last Christmas, and he was still 322 hits away from 3,000, and just creeping toward it. He was still stealing bases, but we figured that if that .236 batting average took one more step downward, his career was over.

We estimated a year ago that Henderson's chance of getting 3,000 career hits was only 4%. Now, maybe that wasn't a good estimate, but nobody said anything at the time. Nobody wrote to say that Rickey Henderson was a viable 3,000-hit candidate, and our 4% estimate was too low.

But Rickey had a great year, and now, twelve months later, he is back in the chase. And he wasn't the only one; Harold Baines, a year ago, had dropped completely off the list of 3,000-hit candidates. He was 40 years old, too, he was 351 hits away, and he had only 88 hits in 1998. Do the math: 40 years old, 350 hits away, moving at 88 hits per season.

But Baines drove in 100 runs for the first time since the Cold War. So those two guys take their place near the top of the list of 3,000-hit candidates.

Rickey Henderson is nowhere near a career .300 hitter. He's been hurt a lot, and he's drawn nearly 2,000 career walks; because of injuries and walks, he has had only two seasons in his career in which he has batted more than 554 times. Henderson had 138 hits in 1999; only once in the previous nine seasons had he had more, and then he had 139. So here's a guy for whom 140 hits would be a good season—and yet, he is now a very serious candidate for 3,000 career hits. Remarkable, isn't it?

Of course, what was always most remarkable about Rickey was not the base knocks, but the other bases he picks up, the secondary bases. Walks, power, stolen bases. Rickey went into the 1999 season with 4,547 secondary bases in his career, and added 185 more. By so doing, he moved past a couple of guys named Hank and Willie, and into second place all time, behind a fellow named George Herman:

1.	Ruth	5099
2.	Henderson	4732
3.	Aaron	4727
4.	Mays	4584
5.	T Williams	4273

Of course, no one tracks career secondary bases—even us—but I think it's kind of interesting to look at. There are now 23 players who have 3,000 career hits, counting Cap Anson, who probably had "only" 2,995 in the National League, but had been playing regularly for five years before the National Association evolved into the National League.

Most of those 23 players who had 3,000 hits—16 of them—also had 3,000 secondary bases. A lot of guys have about as many of one as the other, like Cal Ripken, who opens the new millenium with 2,991 hits—and 2,981 secondary bases. He will be the 24th player to get 3,000 hits, and the 34th player to get 3,000 other bases. George Brett had 3,154 hits, 3.187 secondary bases. But what about the guys who *didn't* have 3,000 hits, but *did* have 3,000 secondary bases?

Well, that list would include Babe Ruth (2,873 hits, 5,099 secondary bases), Ted Williams (2,654 hits, 4,273 secondary bases), Frank Robinson (2,943 hits, 4,054 secondary bases), Joe Morgan (2,517 hits, 3,999 secondary bases), Mickey Mantle (2,415 hits, 3,982 secondary bases). It would also include Mel Ott, Lou Gehrig, Reggie Jackson, Mike Schmidt, Barry Bonds—and Rickey Henderson. So which is more impressive, when you think about it. Would you rather have those guys—Ruth, Williams, Gehrig—or would you rather have the guys who had 3,000 hits, but didn't have 3,000 secondary—Rod Carew, Lou Brock, Cap Anson, Nap Lajoie. It's up to you; you choose.

We're another year down the road on the Henry Aaron deathwatch. A year ago the chance that some active player would hit 756 career home runs or more was 78%; now it is 87%. It is not yet inevitable that someone will break this record—but we're getting there.

A year ago, the chance that some active player would break the all-time RBI record (2,297) was about 63%. Now that chance is about 66%.

The ratio between the typical league-leading figure in a category and the all-time record tends to settle, over time, at about 18 to 1. The normal league-leading home run total now is about 55. Thus, given enough time—30 to 50 years—the record for career home runs would settle in the range of 1,000. Of course, it may be unlikely that, over the years, players will continue to hit 55 homers as a normal league-leading figure; this may be just a brief era in baseball history in which these figures were typical, and we may return at any moment to more modest totals. But if players continue to hit 50-65 homers a season, in time, somebody will hit 1,000 homers.

—Bill James

Player	Age	Current H	HR	RBI	Home Runs 500	600	700	756	800	Hits 3000	4000	4257	RBI 2000	2298
Mark McGwire	35	1498	522	1277	NA	96%	79%	48%	32%	—	—	—	19%	—
Barry Bonds	34	2010	445	1299	95%	43%	6%	—	—	2%	—	—	6%	—
Ken Griffey Jr.	29	1742	398	1152	94%	89%	62%	44%	34%	42%	1%	—	57%	30%
Jose Canseco	34	1728	431	1309	94%	36%	4%	—	—	—	—	—	5%	—
Sammy Sosa	30	1413	336	941	92%	85%	48%	35%	27%	19%	—	—	31%	13%
Albert Belle	32	1569	358	1136	90%	32%	8%	—	—	15%	—	—	24%	5%
Juan Gonzalez	29	1421	340	1075	89%	54%	25%	15%	9%	25%	—	—	47%	23%
Rafael Palmeiro	34	2158	361	1227	77%	24%	2%	—	—	35%	—	—	19%	—
Alex Rodriguez	23	791	148	463	55%	32%	17%	11%	7%	24%	1%	—	19%	7%
Manny Ramirez	27	932	198	682	53%	27%	12%	6%	1%	13%	—	—	33%	18%
Jeff Bagwell	31	1447	263	961	42%	14%	—	—	—	9%	—	—	15%	—
Greg Vaughn	33	1197	292	882	41%	12%	—	—	—	—	—	—	—	—
Carlos Delgado	27	622	149	467	35%	16%	4%	—	—	—	—	—	9%	—
Vladimir Guerrero	23	498	92	281	33%	16%	5%	1%	—	18%	—	—	10%	1%
Mo Vaughn	31	1312	263	860	33%	8%	—	—	—	5%	—	—	2%	—
Fred McGriff	35	1946	390	1192	33%	—	—	—	—	4%	—	—	—	—
Chipper Jones	27	871	153	524	31%	13%	1%	—	—	14%	—	—	5%	—
Matt Williams	33	1575	334	1050	30%	—	—	—	—	3%	—	—	3%	—
Dean Palmer	30	1035	235	701	27%	6%	—	—	—	—	—	—	—	—
Jim Thome	28	883	196	579	26%	7%	—	—	—	—	—	—	—	—
Shawn Green	26	718	119	376	24%	9%	—	—	—	11%	—	—	1%	—
Larry Walker	32	1431	262	855	22%	1%	—	—	—	5%	—	—	—	—
Vinny Castilla	31	1049	203	611	21%	3%	—	—	—	2%	—	—	—	—
Tony Clark	27	603	127	402	15%	1%	—	—	—	—	—	—	—	—
Raul Mondesi	28	1004	163	518	15%	—	—	—	—	7%	—	—	—	—
Frank Thomas	31	1564	301	1040	14%	—	—	—	—	10%	—	—	5%	—
Nomar Garciaparra	25	615	96	340	13%	1%	—	—	—	19%	—	—	6%	—
Andruw Jones	22	436	80	257	13%	1%	—	—	—	8%	—	—	—	—
Gary Sheffield	30	1345	236	807	13%	—	—	—	—	3%	—	—	—	—
Mike Piazza	30	1200	240	768	10%	—	—	—	—	—	—	—	—	—
Tino Martinez	31	1156	213	798	9%	—	—	—	—	—	—	—	4%	—
Scott Rolen	24	479	82	297	8%	—	—	—	—	—	—	—	—	—
Eric Karros	31	1217	211	734	7%	—	—	—	—	1%	—	—	—	—
Jeromy Burnitz	30	580	123	406	4%	—	—	—	—	—	—	—	—	—
Todd Helton	25	378	65	221	2%	—	—	—	—	—	—	—	—	—
Jason Giambi	28	700	106	418	1%	—	—	—	—	2%	—	—	—	—
Fernando Tatis	24	364	53	194	1%	—	—	—	—	—	—	—	—	—
Cal Ripken Jr.	38	2991	402	1571	—	—	—	—	—	100%	—	—	—	—
Rickey Henderson	40	2816	278	1020	—	—	—	—	—	55%	—	—	—	—
Roberto Alomar	31	2007	151	829	—	—	—	—	—	44%	—	—	—	—
Harold Baines	40	2783	373	1583	—	—	—	—	—	32%	—	—	—	—
Derek Jeter	25	807	63	341	—	—	—	—	—	31%	6%	1%	—	—
Craig Biggio	33	1868	152	706	—	—	—	—	—	28%	—	—	—	—
Chuck Knoblauch	30	1533	78	523	—	—	—	—	—	20%	—	—	—	—
Mark Grace	35	2058	137	922	—	—	—	—	—	18%	—	—	—	—
John Olerud	30	1434	172	762	—	—	—	—	—	18%	—	—	—	—
Bernie Williams	30	1298	151	681	—	—	—	—	—	15%	—	—	—	—
Garret Anderson	27	858	72	393	—	—	—	—	—	15%	—	—	—	—
Edgardo Alfonzo	25	698	62	339	—	—	—	—	—	14%	—	—	—	—
Edgar Renteria	23	611	23	177	—	—	—	—	—	13%	—	—	—	—
Johnny Damon	25	680	49	264	—	—	—	—	—	12%	—	—	—	—
Ivan Rodriguez	27	1333	144	621	—	—	—	—	—	11%	—	—	—	—
Ray Durham	27	808	60	296	—	—	—	—	—	11%	—	—	—	—
Neifi Perez	24	468	26	163	—	—	—	—	—	11%	—	—	—	—
B.J. Surhoff	34	1738	146	893	—	—	—	—	—	8%	—	—	—	—
Jeff Cirillo	29	864	66	372	—	—	—	—	—	8%	—	—	—	—
Omar Vizquel	32	1429	34	449	—	—	—	—	—	6%	—	—	—	—
Jose Offerman	30	1162	30	381	—	—	—	—	—	6%	—	—	—	—
Luis Gonzalez	31	1242	133	661	—	—	—	—	—	5%	—	—	—	—
Jay Bell	33	1677	162	732	—	—	—	—	—	4%	—	—	—	—
Doug Glanville	28	555	24	167	—	—	—	—	—	4%	—	—	—	—
Marquis Grissom	32	1550	131	601	—	—	—	—	—	3%	—	—	—	—
Darin Erstad	25	527	52	232	—	—	—	—	—	3%	—	—	—	—
Robin Ventura	31	1421	203	861	—	—	—	—	—	2%	—	—	—	—
Carlos Beltran	22	210	22	115	—	—	—	—	—	2%	—	—	—	—
Rusty Greer	30	923	103	503	—	—	—	—	—	1%	—	—	—	—

404

Glossary

% Inherited Scored

A Relief Pitching statistic indicating the percentage of runners on base at the time a relief pitcher enters a game that he allows to score.

% Pitches Taken

The number of pitches a batter does not swing at divided by the total number of pitches he sees.

1st Batter Average

The batting average allowed by a relief pitcher to the first batter he faces in a game.

1st Batter OBP

The On-Base Percentage allowed by a relief pitcher to the first batter he faces in a game.

Active Career Batting Leaders

Minimum of 1,000 At-Bats required for Batting Average, On-Base Percentage, Slugging Percentage, At-Bats Per HR, At-Bats Per GDP, At-Bats Per RBI, and Strikeout-to-Walk Ratio. One hundred (100) Stolen Base Attempts required for Stolen Base Success %. Any player who appeared in 1999 is eligible for inclusion provided he meets the category's minimum requirements.

Active Career Pitching Leaders

Minimum of 750 Innings Pitched required for Earned Run Average, Opponent Batting Average, all of the "Per 9 Innings" categories, and Strikeout-to-Walk Ratio. Two hundred fifty (250) Games Started required for Complete Game Frequency. One hundred (100) decisions required for Win-Loss Percentage. Any player who appeared in 1999 is eligible for inclusion provided he meets the category's minimum requirements.

AVG Allowed ScPos

Batting Average Allowed with Runners in Scoring Position.

AVG Bases Loaded

Batting Average with the Bases Loaded.

Batting Average

Hits divided by At-Bats.

Blown Save

Entering a game in a Save Situation (see Save Situation in Glossary) and allowing the tying or go-ahead run to score.

Career Assessments

Once known as the Favorite Toy, this method is used to estimate a player's chance of achieving a specific goal. In the following example, we'll say 3,000 hits. Four things are considered:

1. Need Hits, the number of hits needed to reach the goal. (Of course, this also could be Need Home Runs, Need Doubles, etc.)

2. Years Remaining. The number of years remaining to meet the goal is estimated by (42 minus Age) divided by two. This formula assigns a 20-year-old player 11.0 remaining seasons, a 25-year-old player 8.5 remaining seasons, a 30-year-old player 6.0 remaining seasons, and a 35-year-old player 3.5 remaining seasons. Any active player is assumed to have at least half a season remaining, regardless of his age. Additionally, if a player is coming off a year with at least 100 hits *and* an offensive winning percentage of at least .500, he's assumed to have at least 1.5 remaining seasons. And if a player is coming off a year with at least 100 hits *or* an offensive winning percentage of at least .500, he's assumed to have at least 1.0 remaining seasons.

3. Established Hit Level. For 1999, the established hit level would be found by adding 1996 Hits, (1997 Hits multiplied by two) and (1998 Hits multiplied by three), then dividing by six. A player can't have an established performance level that is less than 80 percent of his most recent performance. In other words, a player who had 200 hits in 1998 can't have an established hit level less than 160.

4. Projected Remaining Hits. This is found by multiplying Years Remaining by the Established Hit Level.

Once you get the projected remaining hits, the chance of getting to the goal is figured by dividing Projected Remaining Hits by Need Hits, then subtracting .5. Thus if Need Hits and Projected Remaining Hits are the same, the chance of reaching the goal is 50 percent. A player's chance of continuing to progress toward a goal can't be more than .97 raised to the power of Years Remaining. This prevents a player from figuring to have a 148 percent chance of reaching a goal.

Catcher's ERA

The Earned Run Average of a club's pitchers with a particular catcher behind the plate. To figure this for a catcher, multiply the Earned Runs Allowed by pitchers while he was catching times nine and divide that by his number of Innings Caught.

Cleanup Slugging%

The Slugging Percentage of a player when batting fourth in the batting order.

Complete Game Frequency

Complete Games divided by Games Started.

Component ERA (ERC)

A statistic that estimates what a pitcher's ERA should have been, based on his pitching performance. The steps in calculating an ERC are:

1. Subtract the pitcher's Home Runs Allowed from his Hits Allowed.

2. Multiply Step 1 by 1.255.

3. Multiply his Home Runs allowed by four.

4. Add Steps 2 and 3 together.

5. Multiply Step 4 by .89.

6. Add his Walks and Hit Batsmen.

7. Multiply Step 6 by .475.

8. Add Steps 5 and 7 together.

This yields the pitcher's total base esitmate (PTB), which is:

$$(((H-HR) * 1.255) + (HR * 4)) * .89 + ((BB + HB) * .475)$$

For those pitchers for whom there is intentional walk data, use this formula instead:

$$(((H-HR) * 1.255) + (HR * 4)) * .89 + ((BB + HB - IBB) * .56)$$

9. Add Hits and Walks and Hit Batsmen.

10. Multiply Step 9 by PTB.

11. Divide Step 10 by Batters Facing Pitcher. If BFP data is unavailable, approximate it by multiplying Innings Pitched by 2.9, then adding Step 9.

12. Multiply Step 11 by 9.

13. Divide Step 12 by Innings Pitched.

14. Subtract .56 from Step 13.

This is the pitcher's ERC, which is:

$$(((((H + BB + HB) * PTB) / BFP) * 9) / IP) - .56$$

If the result after Step 13 is less than 2.24, adjust the formula as follows:

$$(((((H + BB + HB) * PTB) / BFP) * 9) / IP) * .75$$

Earned Run Average

(Earned Runs * 9) divided by Innings Pitched.

406

Easy/Regular/Tough Saves

These distinctions are made to gauge the difficulty of a save. An Easy Save occurs when the first batter faced doesn't represent the tying run and the reliever pitches one inning or less. A Tough Save occurs if the reliever enters with the tying run anywhere on base. A Regular Save is one that doesn't fall into the Easy or Tough category.

Fielding Percentage

(Putouts plus Assists) divided by (Putouts plus Assists plus Errors).

Games Finished

The last relief pitcher for either team in any given game is credited with a Game Finished.

Game Scores/Cheap Wins/Tough Losses

First determine the starting pitcher's Game Score as follows: (1) Start with 50. (2) Add 1 point for each out recorded by the starting pitcher. (3) Add 2 points for each inning the pitcher completes after the fourth inning. (4) Add 1 point for each strikeout. (5) Subtract 2 points for each hit allowed. (6) Subtract 4 points for each earned run allowed. (7) Subtract 2 points for an unearned run. (8) Subtract 1 point for each walk.

If the starting pitcher scores over 50 and loses, it's a Tough Loss. If he wins with a game score under 50, it's a Cheap Win. The top Game Scores of 1999 are listed in the Leader Board section.

GDP

Ground into Double Play.

GDP Opportunity

Any situation with a runner on first and less than two out.

Ground/Fly Ratio (Grd/Fly)

For batters, groundballs hit divided by flyballs hit. For pitchers, groundballs allowed divided by flyballs allowed. All batted balls except line drives and bunts are included.

Hold

A hold is credited any time a relief pitcher enters a game in a Save Situation (see definition), records at least one out and leaves the game never having relinquished the lead. Note: a pitcher cannot finish the game and receive credit for a hold, nor can he earn a hold and a save in the same game.

Inherited Runners

Any runner on base when a reliever enters a game is considered inherited by that pitcher.

Isolated Power

Slugging Percentage minus Batting Average.

K/BB Ratio

Strikeouts divided by Walks.

Late & Close

A Late & Close situation meets the following requirements: (1) the game is in the seventh inning or later, and (2) the batting team is either leading by one run, tied, or has the potential tying run on base, at bat, or on deck. Note: this situation is very similar to the characteristics of a Save Situation.

Leadoff On Base%

The On-Base Percentage of a player when batting first in the batting order.

LHS

Lefthanded Starting Pitcher.

Major League Equivalency (MLE)

A translation of a Double-A or Triple-A hitter's statistics into a big league equivalent. The formula considers the player's level of competition, league, home ballpark and parent club's ballpark.

Offensive Winning Percentage

A player's offensive winning percentage equals the percentage of games a team would win with nine of that player in its lineup, given average pitching and defense. The formula is the square of Runs Created per 27 Outs, divided by the sum of the square of Runs Created per 27 Outs and the square of the league average of runs per game.

On-Base Percentage

(Hits plus Walks plus Hit by Pitcher) divided by (At-Bats plus Walks plus Hit by Pitcher plus Sacrifice Flies).

Opponent Batting Average

Hits Allowed divided by (Batters Faced minus Walks minus Hit Batsmen minus Sacrifice Hits minus Sacrifice Flies minus Catcher's Interference).

PA*

The divisor for On-Base Percentage: At-Bats plus walks plus Hit By Pitcher plus Sacrifice Flies; or Plate Appearances minus Sacrifice Hits and Times Reached Base on Defensive Interference.

Park Index

A method of measuring the extent to which a given ballpark influences a given statistic. Using home runs as an example, here's how the index is calculated:

1. Add Home Runs and Opponent Home Runs in home games.

2. Add At-Bats and Opponent At-Bats in home games. (If At-Bats are unavailable, use home games.)

3. Divide Step 1 by Step 2.

4. Add Home Runs and Opponent Home Runs in road games.

5. Add At-Bats and Opponent At-Bats in road games. (If At-Bats are unavailable, use road games.)

6. Divide Step 4 by Step 5.

7. Divide Step 3 by Step 6.

8. Multiply Step 7 by 100.

An index of 100 means the park is completely neutral. A park index of 118 for home runs indicates that games played in the park feature 18 percent more home runs than the average park.

PCS (Pitchers Caught Stealing)

The number of runners retired when the pitcher, not the catcher, throws to a base to keep the runner close and the runner breaks to the next base before he is tagged out. Note: such plays are often referred to as pickoffs, but appear in official records as Caught Stealing. The most common scoring for a Pitcher Caught Stealing is a 1-3-6 play. The runner is officially charged with a Caught Stealing because he broke for the next base. A pickoff (with a fielding play of 1-3 being the most common) is not an official statistic.

Pitches per PA

For a hitter, the total number of pitches seen divided by total number of At-Bats.

PkOf Throw/Runner

The number of Pickoff Throws made by a pitcher divided by the number of runners on first base.

Plate Appearances

At-Bats plus Total Walks plus Hit By Pitcher plus Sacrifice Hits plus Sacrifice Flies plus Times Reached on Defensive Interference.

Power/Speed Number

A way to look at power and speed in one number. A player must score high in both areas to earn a high Power/Speed Number. The formula: (HR * SB * 2) divided by (HR + SB).

PPO (Pitcher Pickoff)

The number of runners retired when the pitcher throws to a base to keep the runner close and the runner is out trying to return to that base. A Pitcher Pickoff is not an official stat and does not count as a Caught Stealing.

Quality Start

A Quality Start is an outing in which a starting pitcher works at least six innings and allows three earned runs or less.

Quality Start Percentage

Quality Starts divided by Games Started.

Quick Hooks and Slow Hooks

A quick Hook is the removal of a pitcher who has pitched less than six innings and given up three runs or less. A Slow Hook occurs when a pitcher pitches more than nine innings, or allows seven or more runs, or whose combined innings pitched and runs allowed totals 13 or more.

Range Factor

The number of Successful Chances (Putouts plus Assists) times nine divided by the number of Defensive Innings Played. The average for a player at each position in 1999:

Second Base:	5.09	Left Field:	2.04
Third Base:	2.63	Center Field:	2.67
Shortstop:	4.57	Right Field:	2.14

RHS

Righthanded Starting Pitcher.

Run Support Per 9 IP

The number of runs scored by a pitcher's team while he was still in the game times nine divided by his Innings Pitched.

Runs Created

Bill James has devised 24 different Runs Created formulas, depending on the statistics available in a given year. The current method is as follows:

1. Add hits plus walks plus hit by pitcher.

2. Subtract caught stealings and grounded into double plays from Step 1. This is the A Factor.

3. Add unintentional walks plus hit by pitcher.

4. Multiply Step 3 by .24.

5. Multiply stolen bases by .62.

6. Add sacrifice hits plus sacrifice flies.

7. Multiply Step 6 by .5.

8. Add total bases plus Step 4 plus Step 5 plus Step 7.

9. Multiply strikeouts by .03.

10. Subtract Step 9 from Step 8. This is the B Factor.

11. Add at-bats plus walks plus hit by pitcher plus sacrifice hits plus sacrifice flies. This is the C Factor.

To summarize:

$$A = H + BB + HBP - CS - GDP$$

$$B = ((BB - IBB + HBP) * .24) + (SB * .62) + ((SH + SF) * .5) + TB - (SO * .03)$$

$$C = AB + BB + HBP + SH + SF$$

Each player's runs created is determined as if he were operating in a context of eight other players of average skill. The final steps are:

12. Multiply C by 2.4.

13. Add A plus Step 12.

14. Multiply C by 3.

15. Add B plus Step 14.

16. Multiply Step 13 by Step 15.

17. Multiply C by 9.

18. Divide Step 16 by Step 17.

19. Multiply C by .9.

20. Subtract Step 19 from Step 18.

Expressed as an equation, that's:

$$((((C * 2.4) + A) * ((C * 3) + B)) / (C * 9)) - (C * .9)$$

Where home runs with men on base and batting average with runners in scoring position are available, we make further adjustments. First, figure out the player's home run percentage by dividing his home runs by his at-bats. Then multiply that number by his at-bats with men on base to find his expected home runs in that situation. Subtract the expected total from the real total, and add the result to his runs created. For example, a player with 20 homers in 600 overall at-bats who hit 10 homers in 150 at-bats with men on base would get an extra five runs created because he would have been expected to hit five. If he hit three homers in 150 at-bats with men on base, he would lose two runs created.

The runners-in-scoring-position adjustment works in similar fashion. Multiply a player's batting average by his at-bats with runners in scoring position to determine his expected hits in that situation. Subtract the expected number from the real number, and again add the result to his runs created. A .300 hitter who batted .350 in 200 at-bats with runners in scoring position would get 10 extra runs created (70 hits minus 60 expected hits). If he batted .280 in that situation, he would lose four runs created (56 hits minus 60 expected hits).

The second-to-last step is to round a player's runs created to the nearest integer. Finally, once all of a team's individual players' runs created have been calculated, compare their total to the team's runs scored and reconcile the difference proportionally. For instance, if a team's players created 700 runs and the club scored 728 runs, increase each player's runs created by 4 percent (728 / 700 = 1.04) and round each off to the nearest integer once again. Repeat if necessary until the two are equal.

Runs Created per 27 Outs (RC/27)

This statistic estimates how many runs per game a team made up of nine of the same player would score. The name is actually a misnomer, however, because Bill James has based his revised formula on the number of league outs per team game rather than 27. The calculation is runs created multiplied by league outs per team game, divided by outs made (the sum of a player's at-bats plus sacrifice hits plus sacrifice flies plus caught stealings plus grounded into double plays, less his hits), or:

$$((RC * ((3 * LgIP) / (2 * LgG))) / (AB - H + SH + SF + CS + GDP)$$

Save Percentage

Saves (SV) divided by Save Opportunities (OP).

Save Situation

Credit a pitcher with a save when he meets all three of the following conditions:

1. He is the finishing pitcher in a game won by his club.

2. He is not the winning pitcher.

3. He qualifies under one of the following conditions:

a. He enters the game with a lead of no more than three runs and pitches for at least one inning.

b. He enters the game, regardless of the count, with the potential tying run either on base, or at-bat, or on deck (that is, the potential tying run is either already on base or is one of the first two batsmen he faces).

c. He pitches effectively for at least three innings.

No more than one save may be credited in each game.

SB Success%

Stolen Bases divided by (Stolen Bases plus Caught Stealing).

Secondary Average

A way to look at a player's extra bases gained, independent of Batting Average. The formula:

$$(TB - H + BB + SB - CS) / AB$$

410

Similarity Score

A method of measuring the degree of similarity of two statistical lines for a player or a team. Two identical stat lines would generate a score of 1,000.

Slugging Percentage

Total Bases divided by At-Bats.

Speed Score

To figure speed scores, start with the player's record over the last two seasons combined. With that record, you figure six elements of the speed score:

1. The stolen base percentage. Figure the score here as ((SB + 3) / (SB + CS + 7) - .4) * 20.

2. The frequency of stolen base attempts. Figure the score here as (SB + CS) / (Singles + BB + HBP). Take the square root of that, and divide that by .07. If a player attempts to steal one-tenth of the time when he is on first base, you take the square root of .10 (.316) and divide that by .07, yielding a speed score of 4.52.

3. Triples. Figure the player's triples as a percentage of balls in play (3B) / (AB - HR - SO). From this assign an integer from 0 to 10, based on the following chart:

Less than .001	0
.001-.0023	1
.0023-.0039	2
.0039-.0058	3
.0058-.0080	4
.0080-.0105	5
.0105-.013	6
.013-.0158	7
.0158-.0189	8
.0189-.0223	9
.0223 or higher	10

4. The number of runs scored as a percentage of times on base. Figure first the percentage as (R - HR) / (H + HBP + BB - HR). From this subtract .1, and then divide by .04. Thus, if a player has 150 hits, five hit by pitcher and 95 walks, hits 30 home runs and scores 100 runs, you would figure (100 - 30) / (150 + 5 + 95 - 30), or $70/220$, which is .318. Subtract .1, and you have .218. Divide by .04, and his speed score on this point would be 5.45.

5. The frequency of grounding into double play. The formula here is ((.055 - (GDP / (AB - HR - SO)) / .005).

6. Range factor. If the player is a catcher, his speed score on this point is 1; if a first baseman, 2; if a designated hitter, 1.5. If he plays second base, then his speed score element six is 1.25 times his range factor; if third base, 1.51 times his range factor; if shortstop, 1.52 times his range factor; if the outfield, 3 times his range factor. Remember to figure range factors over a two-year period.

If any speed score is over 10.00, then move it down to 10; if it is less than zero, move it up to zero. No element can be outside the 0 to 10 range. When you have the six elements of the speed score, throw out the lowest one. The player's speed score is the average of the other five.

Times on Base

Hits plus Bases on Balls plus times Hit by Pitches.

Total Bases

Hits plus Doubles plus (2 * Triples) plus (3 * Home Runs).

Win-Loss Percentage or Winning Percentage

Wins divided by (Wins plus Losses).

About STATS, Inc.

STATS, Inc. is the nation's leading independent sports information and statistical analysis company, providing detailed sports services for a wide array of commercial clients.

As one of the fastest growing companies in sports, STATS provides the most up-to-the-minute sports information to professional teams, print and broadcast media, software developers and interactive service providers around the country. STATS was recently recognized as "One of Chicago's 100 most influential technology players" by *Crain's Chicago Business* and a two-time finalist for KPMG/Peat Marwick's Illinois High Tech Award. Some of our major clients are ESPN, the Associated Press, America Online, *The Sporting News*, Fox Sports, Yahoo!, CNNSI, Electronic Arts, MSNBC, SONY and Topps. Much of the information we provide is available to the public via our site on AOL (keyword: STATS) and our web site: www.stats.com. With a computer and a modem, you can follow action in the four major professional sports, as well as NCAA football and basketball and other professional and college sports. . . as it happens!

STATS Publishing, a division of STATS, Inc., produces 12 annual books, including the *Major League Handbook*, *The Scouting Notebook*, the *Pro Football Handbook*, the *Pro Basketball Handbook* and the *Hockey Handbook*. In 1998, we introduced two baseball encyclopedias, *The All-Time Major League Handbook* and *The All-Time Baseball Sourcebook*. Together they combine for more than 5,000 pages of baseball history. We also published *Ballpark Sourcebook: Diamond Diagrams*, an authoritative look at major and minor league ballparks of today and yesterday. Also available is *From Abba Dabba to Zorro: The World of Baseball Nicknames*, a wacky look at monikers and their origins. A new football title was launched in 1999, the *Pro Football Scoreboard*. These publications deliver STATS' expertise to fans, scouts, general managers and media around the country.

In addition, STATS offers the most innovative—and fun—fantasy sports games around, from Bill James Fantasy Baseball and Bill James Classic Baseball to STATS Fantasy Football and our newest game, Diamond Legends Internet Baseball. Check out our immensely popular Fantasy Portfolios and our great new web-based product, STATS Fantasy Advantage.

Information technology has grown by leaps and bounds in the last decade, and STATS will continue to be at the forefront as a provider of the most up-to-date, in-depth sports information available.

For more information on our products, or on joining our reporter network, contact us on:

America Online — (Keyword: STATS)

Internet — www.stats.com

Toll Free in the USA at 1-800-63-STATS (1-800-637-8287)

Outside the USA at 1-847-470-8798

Or write to:

STATS, Inc.
8130 Lehigh Ave.
Morton Grove, IL 60053

Notes

Major League Coverage of the Minor Leagues

STATS Minor League Scouting Notebook 2000

- Evaluation of every organization's top prospects
- Essays, stat lines and grades for more than 1,200 prospects
- Author John Sickels' exclusive list of baseball's top 50 prospects
- Recap of the 1999 amateur draft

"*STATS Minor League Scouting Notebook* is a valuable tool that serves as an excellent complement to our scouting reports."
Greg Smith, Director of Scouting, Detroit Tigers

Item #MN00, $19.95, Available February 2000!

STATS Minor League Handbook 2000

- Career data for all Double-A and Triple-A players
- Bill James' exclusive Major League Equivalencies
- Complete 1999 Class-A and Rookie League statistics

"The place to check for info on up-and-coming players."
Bill Koenig, *Baseball Weekly*

Item #MH00, $19.95, Available Now!
Comb-bound #MC00, $24.95, Available Now!

Order From STATS Today!
1-800-63-STATS   847-470-8798   www.stats.com

Free First-Class Shipping for Books Over $10
Order form in back of this book

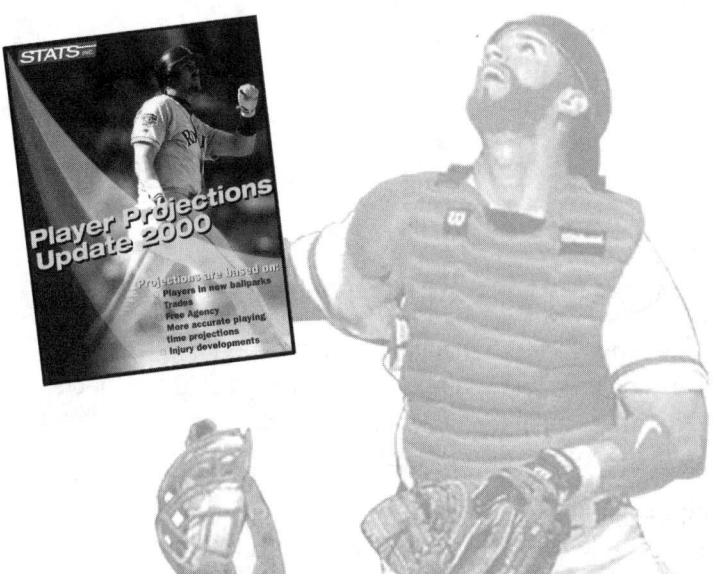

Hard-Hitting Action!

Looking for the leader in NFL statistics? Turn to the *STATS Pro Football Handbook 1999* for all your statistical analysis. Hitting the numbers hard, the *Pro Football Handbook* tackles everything from the passing yards earned by Steve Young to the sacks allowed by Tony Boselli. In fact, STATS provides you with the in-depth coverage you want for each and every NFL player who competed in the 1998 season. That's more than 1,300 players! This sensational book is guaranteed to make your favorite players come alive with the most complete statistical accounts anywhere!

STATS Pro Football Handbook 1999

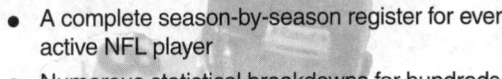

- A complete season-by-season register for every active NFL player
- Numerous statistical breakdowns for hundreds of NFL players
- Leader boards in both innovative and traditional categories
- Exclusive evaluations of offensive linemen
- Kicking, punting and defensive breakdowns

"*STATS Pro Football Handbook* is informative and easy to use."
-Will McDonough, *Boston Globe*

Item #FH99, $19.95, Available Now!
Comb-bound #FC99, $24.95, Available Now!
★ 2000 edition available April 2000 ★

STATS Pro Football Scoreboard 1999

New from STATS, the *Pro Football Scoreboard* follows the lead of the popular *Baseball Scoreboard* while taking an insightful look into the NFL. Like the baseball edition, the *Pro Football Scoreboard* features creative articles and essays about every team that provide fans a greater understanding of all their favorite teams and players. General questions about the game and the league are asked and answered as well.

Topics include:
- Is Dan Marino the best player never to win a title?
- Which defenses say "No Way" to the big play?
- Was Randy Moss' rookie season the best ever?

This unique book is a must-have for all football fans!
Item #SF99, $19.95, Available Now!
★ 2000 edition available July 2000 ★

Order From STATS INC. Today!

1-800-63-STATS   847-470-8798   www.stats.com

Free First-Class Shipping for Books Over $10
Order form in back of this book

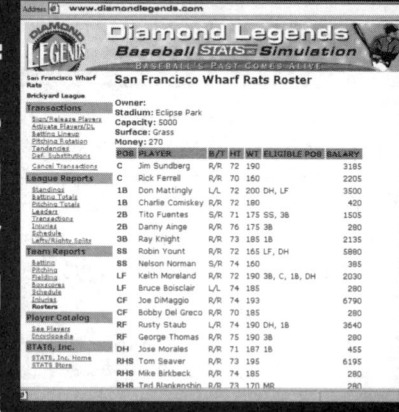

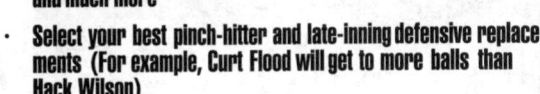

SPORTS TEAM ANALYSIS & TRACKING SYSTEMS

Phone:
1-800-63-STATS
(847) 677-3322

Fax:
(847) 470-9140

Mail:
STATS, Inc.
8130 Lehigh Avenue
Morton Grove, IL 60053

Bill To:
Company_____
Name_____
Address_____
City_____State_____Zip_____
Phone (   )_____Ext.____Fax (   )_____
E-mail Address_____

Ship To: *(Fill in this section if shipping address differs from billing address)*
Company_____
Name_____
Address_____
City_____State_____Zip_____
Phone (   )_____Ext.____Fax (   )_____
E-mail Address_____

Method of payment:
All prices stated
in U.S. Dollars

❏ Charge to my *(circle one)*
   Visa
   MasterCard
   American Express
   Discover

❏ Check or Money Order
   (U.S. funds only)

Please include credit card number
and expiration date with charge orders!

Exp. Date ⬜ / ⬜
    Month Year

X_____
  Signature *(as shown on credit card)*

Totals for STATS Products:	
Books	⬜
Books Under $10 *	⬜
Prior Book Editions *	⬜
order 2 or more books/subtract: **$1.00/book** *(Does not include prior editions)*	⬜
Illinois residents add 8.5% sales tax	⬜
Sub Total	⬜

Shipping Costs		
Canada	Add $3.50/book	⬜
* All books under $10	Add $2.00/book	⬜
Fantasy Games		⬜
	Grand Total	⬜

(No other discounts apply)

(Orders subject to availability)

Free First-Class Shipping for Books Over $10

Books (Free first-class shipping for books over $10)

Qty	Product Name	Item Number	Price	Total
	STATS Major League Handbook 2000	HB00	$19.95	
	STATS Major League Handbook 2000 (Comb-bound)	HC00	$24.95	
	The Scouting Notebook 2000	SN00	$19.95	
	The Scouting Notebook 2000 (Comb-bound)	SC00	$24.95	
	STATS Minor League Handbook 2000	MH00	$19.95	
	STATS Minor League Handbook 2000 (Comb-bound)	MC00	$24.95	
	STATS Player Profiles 2000	PP00	$19.95	
	STATS Player Profiles 2000 (Comb-bound)	PC00	$24.95	
	STATS Minor League Scouting Notebook 2000	MN00	$19.95	
	STATS Batter Vs. Pitcher Match-Ups! 2000	BP00	$24.95	
	STATS Ballpark Sourcebook: Diamond Diagrams	BSDD	$24.95	
	STATS Baseball Scoreboard 2000	SB00	$19.95	
	STATS Diamond Chronicles 2000	CH00	$19.95	
	STATS Pro Football Handbook 1999	FH99	$19.95	
	STATS Pro Football Handbook 1999 (Comb-bound)	FC99	$24.95	
	STATS Pro Football Scoreboard 1999	SF99	$19.95	
	STATS Hockey Handbook 1999-2000	HH00	$19.95	
	STATS Pro Basketball Handbook 1999-2000	BH00	$19.95	
	STATS All-Time Major League Handbook, 2nd Edition	ATHB	$79.95	
			Total	

Books Under $10 *(Please include $2.00 S&H for each book)*

	From Abba-Dabba to Zorro: The World of Baseball Nicknames	ABBA	$ 9.95	
	STATS Baseball's Terrific 20	KID1	$ 9.95	
	STATS Player Projections Update 2000	PJUP	$ 9.95	
			Total	

Previous Editions *(Please circle appropriate years and include $2.00 S&H for each book)*

	STATS Major League Handbook	'91 '92 '93 '94 '95 '96 '97 '98 '99	$ 9.95	
	The Scouting Notebook/Report	'94 '95 '96 '97 '98 '99	$ 9.95	
	STATS Player Profiles	'93 '94 '95 '96 '97 '98 '99	$ 9.95	
	STATS Minor League Handbook	'92 '93 '94 '95 '96 '97 '98 '99	$ 9.95	
	STATS Minor League Scouting Notebook	'95 '96 '97 '98 '99	$ 9.95	
	STATS Batter Vs. Pitcher Match-Ups!	'94 '95 '96 '97 '98 '99	$ 9.95	
	STATS Diamond Chronicles	'97 '98 '99	$ 9.95	
	STATS Baseball Scoreboard	'92 '93 '94 '95 '96 '97 '98 '99	$ 9.95	
	Pro Football Revealed: The 100-Yard War	'94 '95 '96 '97 '98	$ 9.95	
	STATS Pro Football Handbook	'95 '96 '97 '98	$ 9.95	
	STATS Hockey Handbook	'96-97 '97-98 '98-99	$ 9.95	
	STATS Pro Basketball Handbook	'93-94 '94-95 '95-96 '96-97 '97-98 '98-99	$ 9.95	
			Total	

Fantasy Games

	Bill James Classic Baseball	BJCB	$129.95	
	Bill James Fantasy Baseball	PJUP	$ 89.95	
	STATS Fantasy Football	SFF	$ 49.95	
			Total	

1st Fantasy Team Name (ex. Colt 45's): _____
    Which Fantasy Game is the team for? _____

2nd Fantasy Team Name (ex. Colt 45's): _____
    Which Fantasy Game is the team for? _____

Note: $1.00/player is charged for all roster moves and transactions.